the ENCYCLOPEDIA of the MUSICAL THEATRE

SECOND EDITION

The ENCYCLOPEDIA of the MUSICAL THEATRE

SECOND EDITION

1

A–Gi

Kurt Gänzl

Schirmer Books

an imprint of the Gale Group

New York • Detroit • San Francisco • London • Boston • Woodbridge, CT

First edition published 1994 by Schirmer Books and in Great Britain by Blackwell Publishers

Schirmer Books
1633 Broadway
New York, NY 10019

Gale Group
27500 Drake Road
Farmington Hills, MI 48331

Library of Congress Cataloging-in-Publication Data

Gänzl, Kurt.
The encyclopedia of the musical theatre / Kurt Gänzl. — 2nd ed.
p. cm.
Includes bibliographical references and discographies.
ISBN 0-02-864970-2 (set)
1. Musicals—Encyclopedias. I. Title.

ML 102.M88 G3 2001
782.1'4'03—dc21 2001018361

Printed in the United States of America

Printing number
1 2 3 4 5 6 7 8 9 10

This book is printed on acid-free paper

FRONT COVER, CLOCKWISE: Pia Douwes as Velma in the Dutch production of *Chicago* (photography by Marco Klompalberts), *Miss Amerika* sheet music cover, *Sunny* sheet music cover, *La Geisha* sheet music cover, *The Gay Grisette* poster.

GÄNZL, Kurt Friedrich (b Wellington, 15 February 1946).

New-Zealand born, of Viennese stock, Kurt Gänzl studied law and classics at Canterbury University (MA [Hons] 1967) whilst at the same time building a career as a radio and concert vocalist. At the age of 21 he joined the New Zealand Opera Company as a basso soloist and, when that company curled up, moved to London where he soon swapped the operatic world for a life in the musical theatre. Over the next 20 years, he worked in almost every area of the musical theatre, at first as a performer, then as a talent agent and finally as a casting director both for musicals and plays in London's West End and for musical and operatic productions in Europe, America and Australia.

In 1986 his first book on the musical theatre, the two-volume history of *The British Musical Theatre,* was published. Greeted as "one of the great works of cultural reference," it was awarded the Roger Machell Prize for the year's best performing-arts book and the British Library Association's McColvin Medal for the outstanding reference work (any subject) of its season. In the four succeeding years, he followed this with *Gänzl's Book of the Musical Theatre,* commissioned as a companion volume to Kobbé's famous opera guide, with the story of the making of Andrew Lloyd Webber's musical in *The Complete "Aspects of Love,"* and with a survey of recorded musicals, *The Blackwell Guide to the Musical Theatre on Record,* before retiring from the office-bound part of his double life to devote himself full-time to the compilation of *The Encyclopedia of the Musical Theatre*. This work was published in 1994, was a Dartmouth Medal honoree in 1995 and was awarded Outstanding Reference Source in 1997 by the American Library Association.

He has subsequently authored *Gänzl's Book of the Broadway Musical* (1995), a pictorial history of the musical theatre under the title of *Song and Dance* (1995), a history of the international musical stage, *The Musical: A Concise History* (1997), and a 26-hour radio series based on that work which he hosted for Radio New Zealand in the same year, before returning to the *Encyclopedia* to prepare its new and improved edition.

Contents

Volume 1

Preface to the Second Edition	ix
Preface to the First Edition	xiii
Organization of the Encyclopedia	xix
Abbreviations	xxiii
THE ENCYCLOPEDIA OF THE MUSICAL THEATRE, A–GI	1

Volume 2

Organization of the Encyclopedia	vii
Abbreviations	xi
THE ENCYCLOPEDIA OF THE MUSICAL THEATRE, GL–N	777

Volume 3

Organization of the Encyclopedia	vii
Abbreviations	xi
THE ENCYCLOPEDIA OF THE MUSICAL THEATRE, O–Z	1507
Illustration Acknowledgments	2273

Preface to the Second Edition

It's always nice to be given a second chance.

When I sent off those forty Amstrad disks (is anyone still alive who remembers dear old Amstrad?) to Oxford what seems like a half a lifetime ago, I was fairly convinced that I had done everything that I could possibly have done towards putting together a work that contained every fact and figure, every relevant bit of information that I could dig up concerning the 3,000 or so shows and people dealt with in the pages of my encyclopaedia.

I'd worked at it, heaven knows, long enough. I'd tramped and flown and shipped enough thousands of kilometres in search of even the tiniest bit of information. Surely, I thought, I couldn't have missed much.

Of course, as I said at the time, I knew that some of the carrier swallows I'd launched in search of facts and figures, of tunes and photos, would come home to roost when it was too late to squeeze anything further into the past–proof stage printed pages, and that indeed proved to be the case. But they were surprisingly few, those tardy swallows. But those bits of information that did come in I carefully noted down in their proper place in a proof copy of the first edition's pages, alongside the small list of newly come or newly prominent shows and their creators whom I considered I would include next time round if, that is, there was a next time round. Because I'd actually promised myself, after last time, that never again—never again—would I . . .

Well, as you can see my promises to myself didn't get kept. There was a next time. And here it is. Already. Only half a dozen years down the track from the first edition. So soon? Well, yes. What happened was that the first edition was pretty swiftly exhausted, pretty swiftly reprinted, and within a few years nigh on exhausted yet again. Did we, Richard Carlin, my editor at Schirmer Books, asked me one day, reprint again? I suppose I must have mumbled something about how, if we did, I'd like to get in all the little extra bits I'd collected since 1994. Anyway, somehow the words "second edition" arrived in the conversation with the speed of an Apple Macintosh, and before you could say "three more years of my life" I'd committed myself—already!—to putting that much time into preparing a new version of *The Encyclopedia of the Musical Theatre*.

As you can see, it's grown a bit since the first time round, from two volumes to the three it had always threatened to be. But it had to, because once I put on my researching hat once again, once I started delving into history once again, things started to happen.

Since I was being given a second chance, I decided to attack, in particular, three areas where I felt I could perhaps have done better, given more time, more know-how, and less never-stop-running circumstances, in the original edition. I now had the time, and certainly—having between times turned out several more books and researched and written another, as yet unpublished, which taught me more about "how-to-find" than all the rest put together—I had much more know-how. As for the circumstances, well, they were up to me.

My first action in this connection was to purchase myself a microfilm machine and install it in my study. It is sitting in front of me now. Allen Micro Products in Dorset sent me, under my specific instruction, the model with the least moveable parts, thus, theoretically, the least prone to accidents. Its "advance-rewind" handle has broken off with overuse and been replaced by a 6cm nail but, battered as it may now be, it has done its job marvellously.

To go with the machine I purchased a bank of archive films. *The Era* from England, and *The Clipper* and *New York Dramatic Mirror* from America. Why? Because one of the areas I felt needed much more thorough research than I'd been able to give it last time was Britain's provincial theatre and—above all—the American stage outside New York. I had myself chronicled much of the history of the British non–West End stage in my first book, *The British Musical Theatre,* more than 20 years ago now, but the non–New York stage has never been properly dealt with. Even Gerry Bordman's great classic *American Musical Theatre* belies its name a little bit by dealing largely but with Broadway. So, it hadn't been done and, by gum, I would do it.

Well, I have done my darnedest. But unfortunately, I

have to say that the shelves full of microfilms, for which I paid several arms and most of my legs, are not all that I could have wished. Too many of those purchased from the New York Public Library are so poorly filmed as often to be wholly illegible, and I could not in spite of endless efforts persuade the Library of the necessity of replacing them with legible ones. So what can one do? No money-back-guarantees there. I just had to struggle on. And I did. I now wear spectacles. Three pairs.

The struggle was worth it, however; I have now read my way through (most of) 192 reels of microfilm, covering seventy years of American, British and occasionally rest-of-the-world theatre, and I have culled therefrom not only vast amounts of fact, and lashings of gossip and colour, but also a tremendous picture of the theatre—and specifically the musical theatre—in its 19th and early 20th centuries heyday. My historical American articles (and to a lesser degree those concerning other countries) have, I hope, gained a good deal from that long but interesting bit of work.

Another of my determinations was to fill in some of those annoying gaps in the birth and death information at the head of the personal articles. There were far too many "birth [or death] unknown"s disfiguring the pages of the book, far too many "???"s, and I wanted to get rid of them. After all, that's what a history book is for: to give you the facts, and it's pretty much of a cop-out when you have to admit that the facts are "unknown" to you.

I began this exercise (assisted, as ever, by the tireless Andrew Lamb) by going to the British General Register Office, and there armed with pen, paper and patience I started out in search of my missing "bodies and babies." I don't know what led me to start double-checking the dates I thought I already had, but I did, and that led to some very surprising discoveries. I now know not to believe any actor's history as given in *Who's Who in the Theatre* or, indeed, in many other and even more august publications. All I can say is, you will find here dozens, nay hundreds, of alterations to the birth dates and identities given in the first edition. You will also, happily, find quite a few of the "unknown" style of gaps have been filled with real, live fact.

Having got such results from my British diggings, I decided to launch an attack on my French "mysteries" and I duly sent out dozens and dozens of letters to the vital records departments of mairies from one end of France to another. Well, I met some marvellously helpful officials and I met some hopelessly unhelpful ones (the story of this search, if you are interested, can be read on my website, www.ganzl.com), but once again the results were thoroughly worthwhile. More phoney artists' "cv"s hit the dust, more "unknown"s became "known"s.

So I moved on to America. Much more difficult. The records are less well kept, and frustratingly more difficult to access. Freedom of information, it seems, does not reign happy and glorious in the U S of A. Still, helped by the SSDI on-line, by some friendly genealogists in different corners of the country (hi, Deb in Chicago!), and by webfriends who responded to my "Mysteries of the Musical Theatre" and "Whose Baby Were You" pages on the Internet, some headway was made, and when Jessica Carlin in New York put in a concentrated effort at killing off my American "wants" list, the results were—in some states at least (bravo, California!)—satisfying.

Of course, all this information, all these results, inevitably led me on to other things, to other areas of research and other discoveries, and the two and a bit years which I had thought would be ridiculously long a time for the task I'd set myself turned out (of course) to be nothing of the kind.

But now it's done. Now I must stop. Or I'll end up with late-flying swallows coming to roost again, when the book has gone to print. And then I'll end up having to go into a third edition, whisking my long white beard (in spite of widespread opinion, I do not have one yet) off the keyboard to tap with tremulous fingers.

But maybe only then will I finally get to fill those gaps that still remain. For I never did find out what happened to Marie Halton. Or "The Only Leon." Or several dozen other once famous musical-theatre folk. But I'll keep the webpage, with its list of "Help!"s, going, and maybe somebody, someday, tapping in their great-grandmother's name on google.com will find their way to my "Mysteries of the Musical Theatre" and get in touch. I'm not giving up.

Finally, and on a different note, this is the place where I must thoroughly thank everyone who has helped me in this long and often twisty search for the facts and figures of the musical theatre and its history. I'm not even going to try and say individual thank-yous, one way and another so many folk—the faithful old friends who helped me first time round at their head—have lent me a hand for a moment or for a month, or even for more time than that, and I say most sincerely thank you everyone. Thank you, too, to all the folk who have visited and contacted me through the "mysteries" webpage, opening up some ways and places for research of which I would never have thought, and leading me to some unexpected "victories."

I'm going to allow myself just two individual thank-yous.

To Paul Newman of Suffolk, the godfather of the website so frequently referred to above, who hasn't yet taught me a fraction of what he knows about setting up and running such an institution, and to Mike Miller of Los Angeles, who has put my text through a veritable microscope, scanning every line of every article for the infelicities and dicky-finger-errors that are all too easy to make. I blush to think of how many he found. Thanks to him, this edition should—I say should—be blooper free.

If it isn't, blame me, not Mike. But please do write or e-mail and tell me.

And what do I do now? Well, it's drying out time again. So, yes, I'll be off again in a minute or two to the peaceful pastures of New Zealand. Not so peaceful, actually. Part of the drying out process—described again, on the Gänzl webpage—is a new hobby. I have got into harness racing and am in training under masters of the art to become New Zealand's most overaged novice trotting driver. Wish me luck.

But, above all, enjoy this book. I hope you'll find in its pages some things you didn't know before. Some fascinating people. And, well, what else is there left to say but . . .

Merry musical-theatregoing.

[KURT GÄNZL]

Preface to the First Edition

When I was in the long-drawn-out process of compiling my first musical-theatre book, *The British Musical Theatre,* in the 1980s, I became an habitué of second-hand bookstores, ephemera fairs and flea-markets, buying up anything and everything that might yield information on, and/or insight into, all those shows and people I was writing about but had never seen. When that book was published in 1986 I found myself with a huge amount of musical-theatre scores, sheet music, libretti, lyric-books, photos, programmes and other material on my hands. I was caught. It didn't go quietly into the basement, it got shelves built for it and became a "collection." It was (and is) actually quite a remarkable collection of material on the British musical stage (1865–1985), but unfortunately—or fortunately, depending on how you look at it—it did what collections are inclined to do. It expanded round the edges. I unearthed a splendid set of 19th-century American musical-comedy scores in a damp hotel in New York, and suddenly I was a no-holds-barred collector of prewar American material. I was unable to resist a carton of French programmes and 200 libretti in what looked as if it was nothing but a niçoise newsagent's shop, the heaps of operettic playbills and photos to be found in Vienna's much-regretted Kunst und Kultur Markt on the banks of the Donau canal, and all that marvellous Hungarian sheet-music that used to sell for next to nothing in Budapest. I ended up with the collector's equivalent of omnivorousness, and my interests expanded every time the "collection" did.

I had a splendid time playing and singing my way through all this international cornucopia of theatre music, reading the sometimes hilarious, sometimes teeth-curling texts—old, very old and new—arranging the programmes in rows of folders like colourful stamps in a philatelist's album and scouring them for rising and/or repeated names or unexpected credits. And all the time my curiosity was being aroused—I wanted to know as much about these non-British shows and all these writers whose work I was gradually discovering as I'd found out about the people and plays of Britain over the course of my previous ten years of study.

It wasn't, at this stage, a case of putting anything in print. I'd done my "big book" and its equally "big" backlog of preparatory work, and I wasn't counting on getting involved in another. A man has only so many decades in his life. This time I wanted my information straight, complete and nicely assembled and tabulated by someone else, thank you. Only it wasn't that easy. Although there had been a number of more or less detailed surveys of musical-theatre activity in one particular period and/or city (Bruyas on Paris, Bordman on New York, Bauer on Vienna, and others more anecdote- than fact-oriented), as well as a number of sometimes more, sometimes less reliable lexicons and theatrical *Who's Whoses* from various nations, containing little or lots of biographical details on writers and players, there wasn't one hold-all volume of international musical-theatre data to which I could go for full-scale lists of names, dates, places, figures, facts and explanations. Worse. Even when you put together all the material from all the best published books—and that's supposing you could actually get hold of them all—there were still some notable and sizeable gaps. I grumbled about all this to Gerald Bordman, the Boswell of Broadway; I grumbled to Stanley Green, who had started out to do exactly that kind of book in his own *Encyclopaedia of the Musical* but had been forced by a sad chauvinism on the part of the powers-that-publish to limit himself to 20th-century New York in scope; I grumbled suggestively to operetta expert Andrew Lamb who, I knew, had done a great deal of original work gathering together all sorts of information on, in particular, Continental musicians, and to several other stars of the international fraternity of theatre scholars, and not one of them said enthusiastically, "What a good idea, I'll do that." They, without exception, said "What a good idea. I'm doing such and such this year, and such and such next year . . . why don't you do it?" Perhaps, by that time, the memory of the efforts involved in compiling *The British Musical Theatre* had faded a touch. But I took a deep breath, took it on, and, over the past six years—with time off for a few such-and-suches of my own (*Gänzl's Book of the Musical Theatre, The Complete "Aspects of Love,"*

The Blackwell Guide to the Musical Theatre on Record)—most of my time has been spent getting these two volumes together.

What you will find in these pages is my best throw at putting together the sort of work that I missed: a compilation of such material on two or three thousand of the most important (and even some of the less important) and interesting people and plays of the musical stage as I have been able to gather whilst digging and diving my way around the world's libraries, archives and flea-markets over the past few years. I'd like to think that in many or even most cases I've been able to put together something like a complete musical-theatre worklist for the writers and composers involved. And I'm pretty sure I've turned out a reasonably thorough picture of the musical-theatre careers of the performers listed (I soon found that any attempt to include every job of every player was impossible, especially in countries with a repertoire system) and of the principal shows of the 19th- and 20th-century musical stage. But I know that these things are neverending. There is always more information out there, in Nuremberg, in Lyon or in Atlantic City, forgotton shows and probably discreditable credits that will have got through my net. I know, because I found so much of this kind of material on my travels, and because fresh information kept and keeps on coming in, steadily, week upon week. However, the flow eventually came down to a steady but definite trickle, so—after some two final, concentrated years of get-it-all-together work on this project—I thought the time had come to stop fiddling with the 40 disks worth of articles and lists covering my desk, shelves and floors before they and their tiniest details became a real obsession, sandpaper them up and put the result between covers.

The main reason that the job has taken me so long is that I decided early on, with what turned out to be a painful bravado, that whenever possible I wouldn't take anyone else's word for anything. I was going to go back to primary sources for my information: to the programmes, newspapers and magazines of the countries and the eras with which I was dealing. The British end of things was easily managed, thanks to that huge collection of material which I'd put together in the 1980s, but, as far as was humanly and financially possible, the rest of the world needed to be covered in the same way. So off I set.

I sailed across the Atlantic on a cargo ship and spent more than three American months blinking through microfilm files of *The New York Dramatic Mirror, The New York Times* and *Variety,* delving about at length in the vast private collection of American music and scripts gathered by Gerry Bordman whilst he was writing his *American Musical Theatre* and *Companion to the American Theatre,* in the magnificent music archive that is the Rokahr Family Library in Los Angeles, and dipping into material—with all sorts of surprising results—in libraries, museums and newspaper offices from Millersville to Baltimore to Philadelphia. I took a train to Austria and stayed five weeks under the kindly eye of Frau Széles in Vienna's quaint Pension Quisisana in the Windmühlgasse, only a few hundred metres from the house where my father was born, spending my days going—one by one—through the remarkable collection of playbills and programmes in the archives of the Oesterreichisches Theater Museum. Every opening hour (and some that weren't) was spent frantically pounding the information I gleaned onto my trusty Toshiba T1200, all the time trying head-achingly to make sure that, in the sixth or seventh hour of a working day, a slip of tired finger didn't make a 19 into a 29, or cause a letter or a figure to drop out of its proper place. Next, I paddled down the river to Budapest, where Frau Széles had arranged for me to be looked after by her friend Frau Erdéi, and the Magyar Színházi Intézet and its fine archive of theatre material was awaiting me. My studies there were cut a little short when a transport strike threatened to turn into something graver, and I (carrying more than 20 kilos of elderly Hungarian sheet music on my back) slogged 3 kilometers through Budapest's deserted—apart from the odd soldier—streets to the station, to get what looked like being the last train out of town for the duration. It took me 32 hours, clutching the Toshiba and the music, to get back to Nice . . . just to miss the last bus that would take me the final 20 kilometres to my apartment in St. Paul de Vence. My neighbour, Carolanne, drove drown in her pyjamas to rescue a verging-on-the-snuffling voyager.

Not long after recovering from this heroic cavalcade, I headed on to Australia and, there, five weeks glued to more microfilm machines in the State Library and a swift visit to the theatre archives in Canberra allowed me—simply by once more going day by day through contemporary newspapers—to compile a list of all the musical productions played in Melbourne and Sydney since theatre began down under. Sydney was the scene of one of my most memorable moments spent in the search of a missing piece of information: zooming round the 17 hectares of the beautiful cliffside Waverly cemetery in the car of a helpful workman who—out of the thousands of graves—was, with no map, able to pinpoint the last resting place of Johnnie Sheridan. Somehow, it didn't really matter that, when we found it, the stone didn't actually give me the date I was after.

And each time, when the work was done, I hurried back to my hungry computers in St. Paul to copy out and consolidate.

Needless to say, once I really began to try to put order into the mass of information gobbled up in my peregrinations, I soon found that there was an almost unending list of things I'd failed to note down on the way round. Bertrand the St-Paulois postman is now quite used to the parade of parcels with foreign stamps he delivers to "le ouf néo-zelandais" who appears in town for a few months of light-through-the-night working sessions before disappearing off once more to other parts of the world and other, doubtless equally unspeakable, occupations. Those foreign stamps are quite varied, for my network of scholarly pals and friendly library professionals from Budapest and Buar to Croydon and Sydney have done wonders in answering my all-too-frequent howls for help.

In London, Andrew Lamb has spent months of lunchtimes in the national archives tracing birth, death and marriage certificates for dozens and dozens of actors and writers who have "sheltered" their real name, their age and just about everything else you can imagine, in a remarkable bit of detective work. He's found all sorts of those little jigsaw-pieces of information that go to make up a well-wrapped dossier: the whatever-happenend-to of Edward Jakobowski, the once-famous composer of *Erminie,* which the combined efforts of Bordman, Green, Gänzl and the American libraries system had failed, in spite of a long search, ever to discover; the facts on the star whose autobiography neglects to mention that her parents were indeed married, but only eight years after the date she doesn't admit was that of her birth; and many and many another birth date which is one (why?), three, five or eight years further back in time than those admitted by their subjects. In New York, Richard Norton has scoured the libraries and delved into his own mighty musical-theatre collection for answers to the faxes-full of queries on shows from Davidson, Milwaukee or Albany, NY (and even New York, NY) that have zoomed regularly across the Atlantic; in Budapest, Dr György Székely has spent hours putting the accents right on my misspelt Hungarian and digging up information on ancient (and modern) first performances in city which must, then as now, be the most musical-theatre-minded centre in the world, and Támas Gajdó has taken time off from editing his own Hungarian theatre lexicon to dig through the theatre museum's files, filleting out the musical-theatre stories of which the strike deprived me and translating them into French (our language of communication). Vienna's Gerti Fischer has kept me endlessly supplied with packages of Austrian answers, Jacques Derouet in Poitiers has led my French helpers in turning up bits and pieces on early French productions, Rudolf Maeder in Switzerland has taken chunks out of my "Help! List, Germany," Louise Grant in London has turned up regularly with theatre programmes which I would have thought were unfindable, and Hollywood's Hank Moonjean and London's Kevin Gough-Yates have kept an eye on my film-associated references. And, all the time, the phone calls and the envelopes of photocopies have just kept and still keep coming from all corners of the globe ("Kurt? Rida Johnson Young graduated from high school in 1882—I have her graduation list. Her given birth date would mean she was 13. Not possible. She's lied by at least three years. By the way, her name then was just Ida. . . ." "Kurt, I have a score by Jean Gilbert for you, it's called *Der Gauklerkönig* . . . but it isn't on your worklist. . . .").

Finally, on 12 December 1992, the deadline fell. A deputation from Blackwell descended on St Paul, and the print-out of those 40 full-to-meltdown-point disks was packed up into a bevy of suitcases and knapsacks and plastic bags, and carried off to Oxford to be put through the first stages of being made into a book. Or two books. These two books. Along with the text went some 300 photographs that I'd gathered up to accompany the written part of the book. Rather than choose all of them from the shows' first stagings, photos of which have been reproduced regularly over the years, I've purposely picked some that I hope will be new to you, pictures taken from regional theatres and international productions. This at least partly on the principle that the musical theatre's real powerbases are not in London's West End, in Vienna, Paris or on Broadway, but in the thousands of theatres around the world that play the shows after they've been created in the main centres and that are very largely responsible for their continued life. As in the case of the text, you get what I've got, been got or given (for which very much thanks to all the long list of collections, collectors, theatres and theatrical photographers concerned, and especially to Peter Joslin who organized the whole photographic side of the book). I hope you'll find them interesting, and a touch refreshing.

Well, that's the "why" and the "how" of this work. Now for the "what." Way back in 1986, when, having decided to go for it, I sat down to set up the parameters for the (one-volume) *Encyclopedia of the Musical Theatre,* I decided that in spite of its title it had, for practical reasons, to be limited to a coverage of the plays and the people involved in the mainstream of Western musical theatre and, more specifically, to those parts of that musical-theatre tradition which were internationally played and popular. Thus, for example, there is only occasional reference to the Spanish and Italian musical stages, even though both countries have produced fine, durable and popular works for their own home audiences. The Russian musical theatre and that of the other former Eastern bloc countries, similarly, have an almost negligible place. And there are, alas for my chauvinism, only three New Zealand entries.

I selected as my principal areas of concentration that handful of countries and traditions which have been the most productive of original musical plays for the world's stages in the last 150 years: France, Austria, Britain, the

United States of America and Hungary. To these, I added Australia, which, having virtually no home product of its own, has, during those 150 years, sat on the other side of the world from the main production centres, picking and choosing a fascinating microcosm (and not as micro- as all that) of musical theatre for its stages, and Germany, which if it had only a brief hour of glory as a supplier to international stages, has both supplemented the Austrian tradition in a manner impossible to ignore and is showing interesting signs of producing more new works—if as yet mostly copycat ones—than any other area in the 1990s.

Having established my geographical area, I then had to set up that almost-impossibly-fuzzy-edged parameter of what "musical theatre" was to mean for the purposes of this work. As I did in *The British Musical Theatre,* I have chosen to stick with the area I know about. I deal only with the book musical. That is to say, I cover the original musical play in all its shapes, forms and sizes—any original piece with a continuous libretto, lyrics and music, whether it be a sung-through five-act romantic operetta, a Germanic Posse with a half-dozen numbers, or a little farcical piece illustrated by some tap-dancing high-jinks and a tiny bookful of squeaked-out excuses for songs. I draw my line around that area, and in doing so I regretfully—but necessarily—exclude from my survey all such contiguous and/or related forms of musico-theatre entertainment as opera, pantomime (in both the original and the Anglo-Christmas senses of the word), revue, compilation shows, paste-up musicals (mostly), dance shows, concerts, music hall/variety/vaudeville and so forth, as well as musical film and television. This doesn't mean that there is no mention of these areas in the book. They just aren't the subject of the book. Many of the people who worked/work in what I call the musical theatre also operated/operate in these associated areas of the entertainment business and their contributions there are, naturally, noted. But they are noted in the wings of the main stage of the work.

Selecting my headwords—the people and the plays to whom and which I was going to devote space—was the same thought-provoking job that it always is. Every time you put together a work which is not all embracing, which involves a selection of subject matter, almost anyone and everyone who comes near it manages to find something that you have decided not to include that they think—for a variety of reasons and with varying degrees of indignation—should have been put in. All I can say is, I have put in the pieces and people that this longtime lover of the worldwide musical stage thinks should be there. Folks are welcome to disagree and they can put their favourite "missing" ones in their encyclopedias.

I have set out to deal with, first and foremost, the most successful, most prolific and most extensively heard writers and composers for the musical stages of the countries under survey and, in parallel, the most successful, interesting and—the three things are not always compatible—the most widely travelled shows. I have added to this backbone of the work details on those artists who led/have led the fullest and most interesting lives on the musical stage, as well as on a limited number of producers and a very small representative group of creative personnel—directors, choreographers and designers. The ultimate accent, however, is on those two areas that originally prompted me to put the book together—the writers and their shows.

Two of my main and original criteria in picking the headwords were, firstly, that writers, shows and performers who were seen and heard in more than one of my countries should have preference and place here over those which were of interest only in a single centre, and that—for all the folk concerned—a full career in the musical theatre was of more relevance than just one or two appearances, no matter how starry, on the musical stage. Where performers are concerned, I have also leaned heavily towards those players who created roles in new musicals, which means that there is a distinct bias towards those artists who were active in each centre in the period of its creative pre-eminence. By the same token, you won't find in these pages entries on Favourite Flops, no matter how well-known their authors or stars. Although it is undoubtedly important to a detailing of a writer's career to note his unsuccessful work along with his hits, the description and dissection of failed shows in themselves is a job that's been splendidly done—with the kind of gusto that suits this "special taste"—by others.

Of course, it goes without saying that all the criteria with which I started out got bent a little here and there on the way through the compilation, as criteria always do, but since this was a one-man book, rather than one made up of an editor and contributors, I was able just to let it happen. I didn't bother arguing with myself. If a score or a script, a personality or an author appealed to me particularly, I didn't stop myself from popping in a few words about it or him. If I was fascinated, perhaps other folk might be too. As a result, the "final" headword list with which I'd started out got intermittent additions as work progressed. But it also got a certain number of deletions. There were some people and shows I would have liked to have included but on whom/which I was unable to find out the necessary. In spite of all my best efforts, and those of my "network," there were scores and libretti which defied the finding. And although most of the dead people supplied the information I asked for splendidly, a disappointing handful of live ones (and live ones with agents) proved to be less forthcoming. So, the final list that you see here developed by a kind of natural selection.

At the end of the day, I have ended up with this—nearly 3,000 articles in two volumes—smugly accepted by a publisher who had always said that I'd never limit myself to one, but who did smile a little stiffly when I at one stage mumbled "three"—which I hope cover the people and plays of the international musical theatre of the last few generations as fully and as accurately as can be done in two volumes.

Here is perhaps the place to say that when I have not been able to find a piece of information—a date or place of birth or death, a date or place of a production—I have simply left the gap. I have not, as I (dare I say it?) suspect one recent book of reference of doing, taken flying guesses in order to fill in a hole. When in doubt, I have left out (either the fact, or even the article) or used that most useful of devices—the question mark.

Of course, even now when the text has gone out of my hands, and I am under threat of having my PCW cut off if I start sticking any more extra bits of material into the thing when it's trying to be page proofs, the parcels will keep on coming. Having started so many folk chasing so many facts and doing so many flea-markets all around the world, even the past isn't going to stop—as I am supposed to have—on 12 December 1992. Whilst the present rolls inevitably on. But I wouldn't want them to stop. Published or not, the more information I can gather, the happier I'll be. So I'd be delighted to hear (via e-mail, ganzl@bigfoot.com) from all and any specialists on the area that I have covered, and from all and any musical-theatre fans who have extra material (primary sources only, please!) to add to what I've been able to put together. Perhaps someone in America knows what happened to Mizzi Hajós, to Evelyn Herbert and Robert Halliday, to Emmy Wehlen or to that fabulous creature called "The Only Leon"? Perhaps there is a real, live list of the hundred opérettes Vincent Scotto is said to have written (but of which no one, when pressed, is able to give me the titles) hidden in the archive of a Marseille music publisher, or records of a bundle of other quick-flop tryouts like *Page Mr Cupid, The Love School* or *Cocktail* to be found in the newspaper and programme files at Wilkes-Barre, Pa. Perhaps there are other descendants of the famous folk of the past—like the Mrs Nash I met in Millersville, Pa, who turned out to have been Miss Ascher, daughter of Leo—who have music, texts, pictures and memories to share. And there must be mines of information in centres such as San Francisco, Chicago, Prague, Stettin, Hamburg, Lyon and Marseille, none of which I've yet been able to visit, and whose busy musical-theatre history has not, to my knowledge, ever been detailed between covers. A jigsaw-puzzle never gives its full effect until it is completed—and I'd love to complete each and every one of the jigsaws that go to make up this book (and the ones which had to be omitted) before they carry me away. All and any help in this respect would be very gratefully received.

For the moment, however, I'm putting it all aside, and I'm going off to be musical-theatrically "dried out." I've this little farm in the outish-backs in New Zealand which doesn't have a fax, or a computer, or a piano, or a record player (CD? what's that?), or mains water. Or even a bookshelf. So even if someone's discovered whatever happened to Marie Halton, it'll have to keep till the spring. . . .

[KURT GÄNZL]

Organization of the Encyclopedia

Alphabetization

Entries are arranged in a single alphabetical sequence, using a letter-by-letter system, as follows:

MANNEQUINS
DER MANN MIT DEN DREI FRAUEN
MANNSCHAFT AN BORD
MANNSTADT, William
MAN OF LA MANCHA

For alphabetization purposes, the following conventions have been followed:

- the definite and indefinite articles A, The, L', Le, La, Les, Das, Der, Die, etc, are ignored where they appear at the beginning of show headwords;
- the Scots or Irish prefixes "Mac," "Mc" and "M'" are alphabetized letter-by-letter rather than treated as if they were spelt out "Mac";
- and all accented letters are treated as English unaccented letters.

Cross references appear as follows:

MAYTIME *see* WIE EINST IM MAI

with the capital letter indicating the letter under which the entry may be found.

Introductory and supplementary sections to people entries

The articles are written and ordered under the name in which their subject was active in the theatre. When that name is simply an easily shortened version of the subject's real full name, the rest of that real name is given in square brackets.

BROWN, Jon[athan Frederick]

When the bold headword is not simply a shortened form of the real full name or when the nom de théâtre/nom de plume is not that with which the subject was born, the real full name (where known) is given separately, again in square brackets.

BROWN, John [BROWN, Jonathan Frederick]

BROWN, John [BRAUNSTEIN, Johann Friedrich]

The name is followed by the places and dates of birth and death, where known, in parentheses. If the date of death (or birth) is not known it is simply not included.

(b London, 6 February 1933)

On a number of occasions, a birth year is included but is marked with a query. This is generally where a death certificate or obituary has given the subject's age at death, but a birth certificate and/or date has not been found to confirm that information.

(b Paris, ?1946; d Nice, 10 August 1980).

The bibliographies given at the end of entries include a representative selection of biographies, autobiographies or other significant literature devoted to the subject. I have not attempted to list every published work—not least because many of the people who have the most works written about them are those whose principal activity was not the musical theatre.

Introductory and supplementary sections to show entries

The introductory sections to show entries give the title (and subtitle where relevant) under which the show was normally played, followed by any considerably used alternative title, then the credits as given on the playbill, and the date and place of the first production. As in the worklists that appear at the end of people articles (see below), this information refers to the first metropolitan performance. In the case of modern works, the date of the official "first night," rather than that of the first preview performance, is given. Out-of-town tryout dates are shown only when there is an appreciable gap between the initial out-of-town production and any later metropolitan production, or when the show failed to find its way to town at all.

NO, NO, NANETTE Musical comedy in 3 acts by Frank Mandel, Otto Harbach and Irving Caesar based on *My Lady Friends* by Mandel and Emil Nyitray (and *Oh, James!* by May Edgington). Music by Vincent Youmans. Garrick Theater, Detroit, 23 April 1923; Harris Theater, Chicago, 7 May 1923; Globe Theater, New York, 16 September 1925.

The supplementary sections at the end of the show entries consist of a record of the dates and places of the first productions of the show in what, for the purposes of this book, are treated as the "main centers" (Berlin, Budapest, London, Melbourne, New York, Paris, Sydney, Vienna) other than that in which it was first performed. When the show was, on these occasions, given in France, Austria, Britain, America, Australia, Hungary or Germany under a title other than its original, the altered or translated title is given, along with the date and place of the production.

Austria: Theater in der Josefstadt 15 May 1952; France: Theatre Marigny *Feu d'artifice* 1952; UK: Bristol Old Vic *Oh, My Papa!* 2 April, Garrick Theatre, London 17 July 1957

Recordings: selection (Ariola-Eurodisc), selection in English (Parlophone EP)

Mention is also made of films and recordings of, and books on, individual shows. I have made no attempt to give details of recordings, as labels and serial numbers of recordings vary from country to country and a complete list of all the show recordings in question would fill a vast volume. I have merely tried to indicate which of the shows dealt with can be found on record, at least some of the labels that have been responsible for those recordings, and whether "original cast" or foreign-language recordings are included amongst them. Similarly, I have mentioned books only in the rare instances where a book is wholly, or very largely, devoted to the show in question.

Authors' and composers' worklists

The worklists attached to the articles on librettists, lyricists and composers are intended to include all of each writer's credited works for the book musical theatre.

Works for which a writer was not credited on the playbills are not included, and neither are works written for such adjacent musical and theatrical areas as opera, ballet, pantomime and revue.

The original works in the list are given in chronological order of their first production.

When a show has been played under more than one title, the title in bold type is the title under which its main metropolitan run was given, with alternative titles in italic type in parentheses. Titles discarded in tryout are noted as "ex-."

1988 **Ain't Broadway Grand** (ex- *Mike*)

Post-metropolitan changes of title are indicated by the prefix "later-." Where the title change was part of a significant rewrite, the rewrite will have a separate entry as "revised version of [original title]."

The year and title of the piece are followed by the names of the writer's credited collaborators on the show in question, in the order: composer(s)/lyricist(s)/librettist(s). Writers who collaborated with the writer in his or her area are shown by a "w" indicating "with." Thus (Smith/w Brown/w Green) would mean that the person who is the subject of the article worked on the show's lyrics with Brown and its book with Green, and the music was by Smith. The names of the subject's collaborators are given in full on their first mention in a worklist, and thereafter by surname only except where a duplicated surname could lead to confusion, such as in the case of contemporaneous text-writers H B Smith, R B Smith and E Smith. Any variants occurring in a show's author/composer credits are included in square brackets. Major revisions of a show are credited separately in the worklist.

In the case of short works only, the names of the authors are followed by an indication such as "1 act" or "3 scenes." Otherwise all works are "full-length" pieces (in the loosest possible meaning of the term when some works from the 19th-century days of very long evenings are in question) in a minimum of two acts.

Each original work entry on the worklist ends with the place and date of the first metropolitan performance. In the case of modern works, the date of the official "first night" rather than that of the first preview performance is used. Out-of-town tryout dates are shown only when there is an appreciable gap between the initial out-of-town production and any later metropolitan production, or when the show failed to find its way to town at all. In the case of shows initially staged in other cities and subsequently remounted in what, for the purposes of this book, are accounted the "main centers" (Berlin, Budapest, London, Melbourne, New York, Paris, Sydney, Vienna), both dates are given. When the theatre in which the show's premiere is given is not based in the city that may be regarded as being/having been the writer's base, the name of the city is included alongside the theatre. So, for example, a Vienna-centered author will be credited with works at the Carltheater, the Theater an der Wien or the Raimundtheater without further elaboration, but for productions at the Theater am Gärtnerplatz, Munich, the Népszínház, Budapest, or the Thalia-Theater, Berlin, the cities would be specified.

1890 **Erminy** (*Erminie*) German version w Heinrich von Waldberg (Carltheater)

1890 **Der bleiche Gast** (Josef Hellmesberger, Zamara/w von Waldberg) Carl-Schultze Theater, Hamburg 6 September

Shows which are not the original work of the writer in question, but simply adaptations of a musical originally written and produced by other writers in another language, are listed under the year of their production in the version by the subject of the worklist. The year is followed by the title given to the piece in the subject's adaptation, followed in parentheses by the title of the original piece in its original language, a description of the nature of the adaptation (where applicable) and the theatre where the adaptation was first staged.

1889 **Capitän Wilson** (*The Yeomen of the Guard*) German version w Carl Lindau (Carltheater)

On the occasions where I have been unable to trace or to confirm that a show credited to a writer was in fact produced, rather than just being announced for production, I have listed the title at the end of the worklist under the heading "Other titles attributed." Conversely, shows which were definitely produced, but for which my details are incomplete, are included in the worklist, with their details as complete as I have been able to make them. Any dubious dates, places or credits are indicated with a question mark, thus, ?1849.

Occasionally circumstances arose which could not be adequately dealt with by the arrangements described above. In these cases, it has been my main care simply to make whatever the situation and credits might be as clear as possible without clinging too unbendingly to a "standard" layout.

Abbreviations

(X) ad (Y)	the work of (X) adapted by (Y), adapter
add	additional
aka	also known as
(X) arr (Y)	the work of (X) arranged by (Y), arranger
b	born
ch	choreographed by, choreographer
d	died
dir	directed by, director
Eng	English/England
fr	from
Fr	French/France
Frln	Fraulein
Ger	German/Germany
Hun	Hungarian/Hungary
ka	known as
jr	junior
Lat	Latin
lib	libretto
ly	lyric(s)
md	musical director
mus	music
nd	no date known
np	no place known
posth	posthumous
rev	revival
scr	screenplay
Sp	Spanish/Spain
sq/sqq	and that/those following
sr	senior
t/o	takeover (of a role)
UK	United Kingdom
u/s	understudy
USA	United States of America

A

AARONS, Alex[ander] A (b Philadelphia, 15 May 1891; d Beverly Hills, Calif, 14 March 1943).

Although he spread himself around the world of show business rather less flamboyantly than his father, the irrepressible Alfred Aarons, and did not, like him, attempt to double in musical composition, Alex Aarons had a considerably more significant career as a producer of musical theatre than his parent.

He used his entrepreneurial talents at first in the garment trade, holding a controlling interest in the 5th Avenue menswear store Croydons Ltd by his mid-twenties, but he took an early interest in show business through an association with the playwright Frederick Jackson. He made his entry on to Broadway as a producer of musical comedy (with ''considerable aid'' from his father) in 1919 with *La La Lucille* (ex- *Your Money or Your Wife*), a show written by Jackson and sporting the young George Gershwin's first attempt at a theatre score. Although his early years in the theatre brought several failures—including the small-scale *Oui Madame* (1920), one of only a very few Victor Herbert musicals never to make it into New York, and Vincent Youmans's unfortunate rewrite of the British musical comedy hit *A Night Out* (1925 w Edward Laurillard)—Jackson's Fred and Adele Astaire show *For Goodness' Sake* (1922), which the younger Aarons presented both in America and, as *Stop Flirting,* in Britain (w George Grossmith, Pat Malone and Alfred Butt), soon gave him a first taste of international success.

Aarons's most notable productions were mounted in a decade-long partnership with Vinton Freedley, who had earlier been an actor in his musical comedy companies. During the late 1920s and the early 1930s they produced Gershwin's *Lady, Be Good!* (1924), *Tip-Toes* (1925), *Oh, Kay!* (1926), *Funny Face* (1927), *Treasure Girl* (1928), *Girl Crazy* (1930) and *Pardon My English* (1933); De Sylva, Brown and Henderson's highly successful boxing musical *Hold Everything!* (1928), which, in spite of its ephemeral nature, gave the partnership their most substantial Broadway run of all on its original production; Rodgers and Hart's *Spring Is Here* (1929) and *Heads Up!* (1929); and *Here's Howe* (1928). The partners, however, cannily renounced the less-than-successful melodrama with music *Singin' the Blues* (1931) soon after its opening, and it finished its short life being run as a cooperative by its cast.

Most of the partnership's later productions were staged at the Alvin Theater, which Aarons and Freedley had built in 1927, at the peak of their success (and christened with the combined first syllables of their Christian names), and in which, after years headquartered at the New Amsterdam Theater, they made their Broadway base. However, several losing productions and the onset of the depression found them obliged to sell their theatre and, after their staging of the unsuccessful *Pardon My English* at the Majestic Theater, the partnership split up, and Aarons withdrew definitively from the production arena.

His name surfaced occasionally thereafter, attached to abortive Broadway projects, but what show-business activity he maintained in his later years was centered largely on film. He worked at Metro and RKO, and with the A & S Lyons agency in California, and his last involvement with the musical world was when he was taken on by Warner Brothers in an assistant capacity on the Gershwin biopic *Rhapsody in Blue,* a film which was ultimately brought out, after his death, in 1945.

AARONS, Alfred E (b Philadelphia, 16 November 1865; d New York, 16 November 1936).

Alfred Aarons began his career in the theatre in Philadelphia, working first as a callboy and then, at the age of 15, in the box office at William J Gilmore's variety house, the Central Theater. At 16 he set up as a dramatic and vaudeville agent, with an office in that city's Walnut Street, but in 1890 he left Philadelphia and established himself in New York and opened an agency office on Broadway. He subsequently moved on to become, successively, house manager of J M Hill's Standard Theater, business manager for Oscar Hammerstein and his Olympia Music Hall (during which period he secured the highly successful *La Poupée* for his principal) and then, for two years (1897–99), manager of Koster & Bial's Music Hall, which he operated with much-publicized and widely traveling flair, but left in a terminally red-ledgered state. During these managing years, the young man also began to write songs, and he had an early composing success with a ragtime piece called ''Rag Time Liz,'' played in Koster and Bial's entertainment *In Gotham* (1898). He also supplied a number for the successful soubrette Josephine Hall (a Mrs Aarons) to sing in Charles Frohman's production of *The Girl from Maxim's* (1899, w Richard Carle, ''Honi Soit Qui Mal y Pense'').

Aarons made his first venture as a musical-theatre producer when he picked up Louise Beaudet's opéra-bouffe company and its production of *The Dragoon's Daughter* (which had been dropped by F C Whitney in rehearsals) in 1895. The production died on the road a few weeks later. He made his first New York venture when he took Herrmann's Theater to stage a season of vaudeville, and then, in 1900, he launched out both as a composer and as a producer with a piece called *Mam'selle 'Awkins,* written by an old Koster and Bial's pal, comedian Richard Carle. In its Boston tryout *Mam'selle 'Awkins* sported an entire score by Herman Perlet, but by the time it reached New York its musical part was less Perlet and more Aarons. The show's 35 Broadway performances were a prelude to a touring life of four seasons in other hands and in ever-changing musical shape. This first try was sufficiently successful to encourage the striving producer to persevere. In partnership with David Henderson, he took a lease on George Krause's new Schley Music Hall on 34th Street, rechristened it the Savoy Theater, and produced a second home-made musical, *The Military Maid,* with a libretto by proven dramatist George V Hobart (though said to be ''from the French'').

The Military Maid had just a handful of Broadway performances, but Aarons's confidence was such that he soon bought Henderson out of his share in their theatre's lease, only to be quickly booted out of the place and into the courts for not paying the rent. Within a year he had gone bankrupt to the tune of $27,000 after attempting to jump on the then fast-rolling British bandwagon, by producing Ivan Caryll's *The Ladies' Paradise* at no less a venue than the Metropolitan Opera House. This made-for-the-English-provinces piece, starring Miss Hall and Carle, over-produced and underfunded, folded after 14 performances with its chorus and cast (even Carle) and a good few suppliers entirely or partly unpaid. This setback, however, did not stop Aarons producing, nor did it stop him writing. *My Antoinette* (a touring rewrite of *The Ladies' Paradise,* tarted up with four Aarons songs, which stranded in mid-Massachusetts) and *The Knickerbocker Girl* (played by Miss Hall for two Broadway weeks) did nothing, however, to restore his color and he did little better when F C Whitney produced his *A China Doll* (1904), an oddly old-fashioned piece about an automaton, which fared fairly on the road, but was exposed as very weak stuff when it was brought into New York.

His next musical, *The Pink Hussars* (1905), was docketed as a collaboration with the respected composer Julian Edwards, but by the time it got to town Aarons was billed as producer only (Whitney had originally sent the piece out) and Edwards was given full credit for the score of what was now called *His Honor the Mayor* (1906). With this piece, however, Aarons finally found success, and *His Honor the Mayor,* with its variety-based combination of girls, songs and fun, proved a good touring proposition, pleased summer theatregoers in New York for 104 performances and—with popular star Blanche Ring at its head, and an ever-changing set of songs—it played two return engagements there over the following seasons, as part of its vigorous touring existence. His *The Girl from Yama* (1907)—probably the first musical to include a drug addict amongst its characters—also served, if a little less winningly, for several seasons on the road. Edwards's *The Gay Musician* (1908, w John P Slocum) had a respectable career as well, but another producing essay with Edwards's *Molly May* (1909), starring the glamorous soprano Grace La Rue, was less forthcoming.

Aarons subsequently spent a considerable period on the staff of Abe Erlanger's more substantial production outfit, where he is credited with having contributed largely to the development of that office's very efficacious touring booking system. From time to time he resigned from that job to take further turns as an independent manager with such efforts as his last own show to play Broadway, a musequel to *His Honor the Mayor* called *The Deacon and the Lady* (w Louis Werba) concocted for the earlier piece's star, Harry Kelly, or Harry Archer's maiden *The Pearl Maiden* (w Rube Welch). In 1925 he resigned for the last time, apparently after a quarrel with Erlanger, and announced that he would produce the American version of Lehár's *Frasquita* with opera diva Geraldine Farrar starring. Although he did not bring this project to fruition (and it was a disaster for those who did), he had occasional success in these latter years, during which he produced several rather more up-market musicals than before, including George Gershwin's *Tell Me More!* (1925) and Sigmund Romberg's *My Princess* (1927), in between stints working as manager of the Broadhurst Theater and at the New Amsterdam Theater.

1899 **Sir Andy de Bootjack** (Richard Carle) Koster and Bial's Music Hall 17 October

1899 **Children of the Ghetto** (Carle) burlesque in *Round New York in 80 Minutes* Koster and Bial's Music Hall 6 November

- 1900 **Mam'selle 'Awkins** (w Herman Perlet/Carle) Victoria Theater 26 February
- 1900 **The Military Maid** (George V Hobart) Savoy Theater 8 October
- 1901 **The Liberty Belles** (w Aimé Lachaume, A Baldwin Sloane, Clifton Crawford, et al/Harry B Smith) Madison Square Theater 30 September
- 1902 **My Antoinette** (*The Ladies' Paradise*) revised version with additional music by Aarons (w Carle, M E Rourke, Edward Abeles, George Totten Smith) Columbia Theater, Boston 15 January
- 1903 **The Knickerbocker Girl** (Totten Smith) Columbia Theater, Boston 3 March; Herald Square Theater 15 June
- 1904 **A China Doll** (H B Smith, Robert B Smith) Majestic Theater 19 November
- 1905 **The Pink Hussars** (later *His Honor the Mayor*) (w Julian Edwards/Charles J Campbell, Ralph McGay Skinner) Opera House, Chicago 23 October; New York Theater, New York 28 May 1906
- 1907 **[The Girl from] Yama** (R B Smith/Totten Smith) Walnut Street Theater, Philadelphia 4 November
- 1908 **The Hotel Clerk** (R B Smith) Walnut Street Theater, Philadelphia 27 April
- 1910 **The Deacon and the Lady** (ex- *Deacon Flood and the Lady*) (Totten Smith) Ford's Theater, Baltimore 13 September; New York Theater 4 October

ABARBANELL, Lina (b Berlin, 3 February 1879; d New York, 6 January 1963).

The daughter of a theatre conductor, the young Lina Abarbanell made her first stage appearances in 1895, playing in both opera and Operette at Berlin's Residenztheater. She subsequently fulfilled engagements at Posen, Königsberg, Berlin's Neues Königliches Opernhaus—where she scored a personal success in the title role of the German version of the Gaiety musical *A Runaway Girl* (1900, Daisy) and Buntes-Theater (1902), before being contracted by Karczag to play leading parts at Vienna's Theater an der Wien. She appeared there as Sáffi in *Der Zigeunerbaron* and as Adele in *Die Fledermaus,* and created the roles of Lucy Handsome in Gustav Wanda's *Die Dame aus Trouville* (1902), Clara in Lehár's maiden work, *Wiener Frauen* (1902), the prima donna, Bianca Testa, in Ziehrer's *Der Fremdenführer* (1902), Lili in Alfred Grünfeld's *Der Lebemann* (1903) and the leading feminine part, opposite Girardi, of the wild little Oculi in Eysler's highly successful *Bruder Straubinger* (1903). In 1904 she played at the Thalia Theater alongside Guido Thielscher in the burlesque musical comedy *Die grosse Stern* and in *Der Weiberkönig*. She also appeared, in parallel, at the Überbrettl cabaret theatre performing character songs.

In October 1905, Frln Abarbanell went to America, under contract to Hans Conried, and, after appearing in his German-language musical productions at the Irving Place Theater (Hanni in *Frühlingsluft,* Lieutenant von Vogel in *Jung Heidelberg,* Denise in *Mam'zelle Nitouche*) and in his light opera season at the Metropolitan Opera House (Gretel in *Hansel and Gretel*), she made her first appearance in the English-language theatre when she was seen on Broadway as the Princess Ilsa in Reginald De Koven's comic opera, *The Student King* (1906).

She subsequently took the title role in the first American touring production of *The Merry Widow* and succeeded to the role on Broadway (1908), starred on the road in the small-scale British musical *The White Chrysanthemum* (1907, Sybil) and in Henry Savage's production of Eysler's *The Love Cure* (*Künstlerblut* 1909, t/o Nellie Vaughan), and scored what would be her biggest single success on the Broadway stage in the title role of Harbach and Hoschna's remusicked version of the Continental hit *Madame Sherry* (1910, Yvonne). She appeared in the title role of the unsuccessful *Miss Princess* (1912, Princess Polonio) and in the unfortunate Harold Orlob musical *The Red Canary* (1913–14, Jane), took the soubrette role of Molly Seamore in a revival of *The Geisha* (1913) and starred in Chicago's *Molly and I* (1915, Molly), but her only other successful starring role in a Broadway musical was that of the Princess Manja in the American production of Cuvillier's *Flora Bella* (1916).

She then moved on to playing character roles in straight and, occasionally, musical theatre. In 1926 she replaced Madeleine Baxter as Elsie Dayly in a weak musical called *Happy Go Lucky* in time for its Broadway opening, won what notices the piece got, and was promptly herself replaced, but she returned again as the devious Princess von Auen in the short-lived *The Silver Swan* (1929) and, one last time, as Frau Schlitzl in *The Well of Romance* (1930), alongside Norma Terris and Howard Marsh.

Following her retirement from the stage she continued an involvement in the musical theatre as a member of producer Dwight Deere Wiman's staff, acting as a casting director, talent scout and an adviser on musical productions, notably those with a Continental background.

ABBACADABRA Musical fantasy in 2 acts by Alain and Daniel Boublil. Music from the works of Björn Ulvaeus, Benny Andersson and Stig Anderson. Lyric Theatre, Hammersmith, London, 8 December 1983.

A fairy-tale musical for children of the television generation. Snow White, Pinocchio, Cinderella, Bluebeard, Aladdin, Alice and the Little Prince are released from their pages by three tots to do battle with the fairy Carabosse—who, in this version, is the hostess of a TV cooking program—to the accompaniment of the relyrick-

Plate 1. **George Abbott.** *Broadway's longtime doyen.*

ed melodies of such Abba hit songs as "Money, Money, Money" (which became Pinocchio's "Mon nez, Mon nez"), "Dancing Queen" ("The Carabosse Super-Show") and "Thank You for the Music." Originally issued as a concept recording featuring Fabienne Thibeault, Daniel Balavoine, Plastic Bertrand and *Les Misérables* originals Maurice Barrier and Marie-France Roussel in its cast, the show was later adapted to the English stage by David Wood and Don Black (add material by Ulvaeus and Mike Batt) and mounted by Cameron Mackintosh as a 1983 London Christmas entertainment. The cast included Elaine Paige as the Witch, Michael Praed, B A Robertson and Finola Hughes. It was revived for a second season the following year.

Recordings: original concept recording (WEA), Dutch version (DIL), English cast recordings (Epic, 45rpm)

ABBOTT, George [Francis] (b Forestville, NY, 25 June 1887; d Miami Beach, Fla, 31 January 1995).

For many years the doyen of the Broadway stage, George Abbott had an outstanding and unparalleled long career in the theatre, not least in the musical theatre.

Originally an actor, he made what seems to have been his first venture into the musical theatre as the author of a musical farce called *Over the Back Fence* presented in 1912 on a variety bill at the Bijou in Boston, where he was a member of the stock company. He followed up in 1913 both as a playwright (*Head of the Family, Man in the Manhole*), and as an actor (*The Misleading Lady*), but concentrated over the following years largely on a performing career, making an isolated Broadway musical appearance when he appeared as the Second Yeoman in *The Yeomen of the Guard* at the 48th Street Theater in 1915.

Abbott rejoined the ranks of the playwrights when he collaborated with James Gleason on the authorship of the comedy *The Fall Guy* (Eltinge Theatre, 1925), and over the next decade he compounded that success almost annually with a regular stream of new plays, written usually in collaboration. His two major credits from this period were *Broadway* (Broadhurst Theater, 1926), a gangster play illustrated with popular period songs which Abbott, making his Broadway debut as a director, doctored into an international success, and the racing comedy *Three Men on a Horse* (w John Cecil Holm, Playhouse, 1935) which later became regarded as a classic example of its kind and its period. *Three Men on a Horse* was subsequently made twice into a musical, first as *Banjo Eyes* (Vernon Duke/John Latouche/Joe Quillan, Izzy Elinson, Hollywood Theater 25 December 1941) with Eddie Cantor in the starring role, and again as *Let It Ride!* (Jay Livingstone, Ray Evans/Abram S Ginnes, Eugene O'Neill Theater 12 October 1961), but in neither case with equivalent success.

Abbott's first significant venture into the musical theatre was as a director, a function which he had fulfilled with considerable success since the production of *Broadway,* notably with Hecht and MacArthur's famous show-business comedy *Twentieth Century* (1932), a show on which he also made his first venture as a producer. That directorial debut was, however, not on what might have been thought of as a normal first musical for a director of plays: it was a mammoth spectacular, Billy Rose's production of Rodgers and Hart's oversized circus musical *Jumbo* (1935). Abbott continued his association with Rodgers and Hart the following year when he not only directed but collaborated with them on the authorship of the dance musical *On Your Toes.* The three teamed up again on *The Boys from Syracuse* (1938, also producer), for which Abbott took a solo credit for the libretto, adapted from Shakespeare's *The Comedy of Errors,* and he subsequently produced and directed the next two Rodgers and Hart shows, *Too Many Girls* (1939) and *Pal Joey* (1940), without on these occasions being ostensibly involved in the construction of the libretti.

During this period, Abbott had also had further play successes, both as an author and as a director, but from this time on he concentrated, in both of these departments, very largely on the musical stage. As in the case of his plays, his libretti were almost always written either in a collaboration or as adaptations of an existing play or novel. *Where's Charley?* (1948), curiously compounded from Brandon Thomas's comedy *Charley's Aunt* for Frank Loesser, and two musicalized novels, *The Pajama*

Game (1954) and *Damn Yankees* (1955), with songs by the short-lived team of Adler and Ross, gave him his most significant international successes, although *Fiorello!* (1959), a partisan musical comedy based on the life of New York's Mayor La Guardia, also found success on home ground. *A Tree Grows in Brooklyn,* based on Betty Smith's novel, had a quieter but happy life and *New Girl in Town,* a musical version of Eugene O'Neill's *Anna Christie,* also found a good Broadway run.

From the 1960s, however, his writing was less blessed with success and, following the indifferent *Tenderloin* (1960) and 87 performances of *Flora, the Red Menace* (1965), musical versions of *Anastasia* (*Anya,* 1965) and Shakespeare's *Twelfth Night* (*Music Is,* 1976) counted their runs in days. In 1989 he was credited with the libretto and co-direction (w Donald Saddler) of a musical version of Mary Shelley's *Frankenstein* tale mounted at off-Broadway's York Theater in what must be the only example of a musical written by a centenarian.

Abbott directed all his own musicals, but also staged a number of others, including several major hits of the 1940s and 1950s. These included *Best Foot Forward* (1941, which he also produced and on which he seems to have had an uncredited share in the libretto, written by *Three Men on a Horse*'s John Cecil Holm), *Beat the Band* (1942, also producer), the memorable revusical *On the Town* (1944), *Billion Dollar Baby* (1945), *Beggar's Holiday* (1946), *Barefoot Boy with Cheek* (1947, also producer), *High Button Shoes* (1947), *Look Ma, I'm Dancin'* (1948, also producer), the highly successful Ethel Merman vehicle *Call Me Madam* (1950), the comical New-Yorkish *Wonderful Town* (1953), Rodgers and Hammerstein's *Me and Juliet* (1953) and the burlesque fairy tale *Once Upon a Mattress* (1959). The most successful of these were, however, not those staged under his own management and a brief revival of *On Your Toes* in 1954 virtually marked the end of his career as a musical-comedy producer.

In 1962–63 he directed the Broadway and London productions of the enormously successful *A Funny Thing Happened on the Way to the Forum,* and subsequently staged *Fade Out—Fade In* (1964), *How Now, Dow Jones* (1967), *The Education of H*Y*M*A*N K*A*P*L*A*N* (1968) and *The Fig Leaves Are Falling* (1969) for Broadway. He was already in his eighties when he staged a short-lived revival of *The Pajama Game* at the Lunt-Fontanne Theater in 1973, but he made his last Broadway appearance very much more successfully when he directed and co-produced a second revival of *On Your Toes* (Virginia Theater, 1983 and Palace Theatre, London, 1984).

Abbott entered films as early as the 1920s both as an author (notably with *Broadway*) and as a director. He directed the film version of *Too Many Girls* (1940) and acted as producer on Hollywood's versions of *The Pajama Game* (1957) and *Damn Yankees* (1958).

1912 **Over the Back Fence** (Carl Wilmore) Bijou Theater, Boston 15 November

1936 **On Your Toes** (Richard Rodgers/Lorenz Hart/w Rodgers, Hart) Imperial Theater 11 April

1938 **The Boys from Syracuse** (Rodgers/Hart) Alvin Theater 23 November

1948 **Where's Charley?** (Frank Loesser) St James Theater 11 October

1951 **A Tree Grows in Brooklyn** (Arthur Schwartz/Dorothy Fields/w Betty Smith) Alvin Theater 19 April

1954 **The Pajama Game** (Richard Adler, Jerry Ross/w Richard Bissell) St James Theater 13 May

1955 **Damn Yankees** (Adler, Ross/w Douglass Wallop) 46th Street Theater 5 May

1957 **New Girl in Town** (Bob Merrill) 46th Street Theater 14 May

1959 **Fiorello!** (Jerry Bock/Sheldon Harnick/w Jerome Weidman) Broadhurst Theater 23 November

1960 **Tenderloin** (Bock/Harnick/w Weidman) 46th Street Theater 17 October

1965 **Flora, the Red Menace** (John Kander/Fred Ebb/w Robert Russell) Alvin Theater 11 May

1965 **Anya** (Robert Wright, George Forrest/w Guy Bolton) Ziegfeld Theater 29 November

1976 **Music Is** (Adler/Will Holt) St James Theater 20 December

1986 **Tropicana** (Robert Nassif/Peter Napolitano) Musical Theater Works 29 May

1989 **Frankie** (Joseph Turrin/Gloria Nissenson) York Theater 6 October

Autobiography: *Mister Abbott* (Random House, New York, 1963)

ÁBRAHÁM, Pál [Paul] (b Apatin, Hungary, 2 November 1892; d Hamburg, 6 May 1960). The most internationally successful of the Continental composers who attempted to blend traditional European and modern transatlantic styles in the musical theatre of the pre-Hitler years.

After first following studies in the serious musical field, an area in which he also made his earliest attempts as a composer, Ábrahám turned his attention progressively towards lighter music and particularly towards the works of Broadway's songwriters and the style of music that was then called jazz. In 1927 he became conductor and house composer at Budapest's principal musical house, the Fővárosi Operettszínház, and there he contributed songs and incidental music to several musical shows of varying kinds, notably an up-to-date score—featuring some original, some borrowed (the credits included the names of Gus Kahn, Harry Akst, de Sylva, Brown and Henderson, Benny Davis and Sidney Holden) and some arranged tunes—for the entertainment *Zenebona. Zenebona* won him his first good notices (''a young composer who will make his mark'') and the show won a transfer to Vienna under the title *Spektakel* (ad Hans Adler, Paul Frank, Johann Strauss-Theater 3 October 1928).

Ábrahám confirmed this success with a 1928 *Jazz-Kabaré* and, most effectively, with the 1928 operett *Az utolsó Verebély lány,* a musicalization of the Gábor Drégely comedy hit *Kisasszony férje* (1915) which would, in other hands, also become a Broadway musical as *Little Miss Bluebeard* (1923). *Az utolsó Verebély lány* won considerable hometown success and later earned several revivals and a production in Leipzig (ad Rudolf Lothar, Artur Rebner) as *Der Gatte des Fräuleins* (Altes Theater 24 September 1930).

Ábrahám subsequently provided the score for a musical version of the French farce *La Fille et le garçon,* produced at the Magyar Színház in 1929, but the following year he left Budapest and moved to Germany. It was there that he composed the score for what would be his most internationally successful work, *Viktória.* This colorful Hungarian-Japanese piece which combined a dark romanticism and some lightly jazzy dance music in its very of-the-moment score, was produced in Budapest later in the same year and subsequently went on to productions in Leipzig, Berlin and Vienna (1930), in London (1931), Paris (1933), Australia and many other overseas cities. It has remained a regularly produced favorite in the European musical theatre repertoire and is one of the few pieces of its period and place to win revivals more than half a century on.

The following year, Ábrahám's *Die Blume von Hawaii,* an even more exotic piece which put an Al Jolson–style blackface entertainer alongside its operettic South Pacific lovers, confirmed this initial success, and *Ball im Savoy,* produced in Berlin in 1932, gave him a third consecutive hit. Like *Viktória,* both these pieces won international productions, recordings and, in Germany, films, and both have continued to find further productions up to the present day. *Die Blume von Hawaii*'s imitation American cabaret number, ''My Golden Baby,'' even became a song success in America itself, as recorded by Donald Peers.

Obliged to leave Hitler's Germany at the height of his newly acquired fame, Ábrahám settled in Vienna where, over the next few years, he had three further new Operetten produced without, however, finding the success he had won with his earlier pieces. *Märchen im Grand-Hotel,* a musical version of Alfred Savoir's *La Grande-Duchesse et le garçon d'étage* (Théâtre de l'Avenue, Paris 15 May 1924) and later to be the basis for Hollywood's *Here Is My Heart*), was seen 65 times at the Theater an der Wien, the oriental *Dschainah* played 57 times at the same house, and the sporting musical *Roxy und ihr Wunderteam* just twice more.

Ábrahám then moved back to Budapest, which he had continued to supply with music for such pieces as the comedy with songs *Viki* and the musical comedy *Történnek még csodák* during his absences. A major revival of *Az utolsó Verebély lány* and László Szűcs's local production of *Mese a Grand-Hotelben* (aka *A nagyhercegnő es a pincér*) at the Kamara Színház, with Hungarian film favorite Irén Ágay as the grand-duchess of the title, prefaced the production of several new and successful Ábráham operetts. *3:1 a szerelem javára* featuring Rózsi Bársony and Oszkár Dénes, the comic pairing who had made international successes in *Ball im Savoy,* was played for a splendid 73 performances at the Royal Színház in its initial run, and it was still to be seen on Hungarian stages right up to the end of the century. *3:1 a szerelem javára* was followed by *Júlia,* with top diva Hanna Honthy as the lady in question and, finally, *Fehér hattyú,* a First-World-War tale of a ballerina's affair with the Grand Duke Constantin, in which another major local star, Sári Fedák, appeared as the ''white swan'' of the title.

Politics now once more caught up with the composer, however, and soon he moved on again, leaving Hungary and fleeing to France, where a version of his Vienna piece *Roxy und ihr Wunderteam,* done over by French hands to the extent of including the latest British hit song ''The Lambeth Walk'' in the score, was produced at the Théâtre Mogador as *Billy et son équipe.* But, as he continued on to Cuba and, finally, to America, the composer's output faltered and soon ceased altogether. During his years in America the man who had not long since been hailed as one of the coming composers of the European musical theatre, eked out an insecure living as a pianist, and an attempt at putting together a musical play for Broadway, *Tambourin,* written with fellow exile Alfred Grünwald and ''William J Blake,'' failed to make it to the stage. In the mid-1950s a movement was mounted in Germany to secure recognition for Ábrahám and his work. This ultimately resulted in the composer returning to Europe where, after several ill and unhappy years, he died in 1960.

The best of Ábrahám's work was produced in a period of some three years between 1930 and 1932 when his three enduring Operetten and the most successful of his film musical scores, *Die Privatsekretärin* (1931) in which Renate Müller memorably performed his ''Ich bin ja heut' so glucklich'' / ''Today I Am So Happy,'' all appeared for the first time. If unlikely to appeal to conservatives, his music was nevertheless highly regarded in its time and, looked at alongside the heavily romantic later works of Lehár, his happily showy mixture of Operettic elements and fashionable jazzy and South American rhythms shows up as both theatrically colorful and musically effective.

An Operette in 14 scenes entitled *Wintermelodie,* with a score credited to Ábrahám and libretto by Ladislaus Fodor, was produced at the Landestheater, Salzburg 12 February 1978.

1928 **Zenebona** (László Lakatos, István Bródy) Fővárosi Operettszínház 2 March

1928 **Az utolsó Verebély lány** (Gábor Drégely, Imre Harmath) Fővárosi Operettszínház 13 October

1929 **Szeretem a feleségem** (André Birabeau, Georges Dolley ad Adorján Stella) Magyar Színház 15 June

1930 **Viktória** (aka *Viktoria und ihr Husar*) (Imre Földes, Harmath) Király Színház 21 February

1931 **Die Blume von Hawaii** (Földes ad Alfred Grünwald, Fritz Löhner-Beda) Neues Theater, Leipzig 24 July

1932 **Ball im Savoy** (Grünwald, Löhner-Beda) Grosses Schauspielhaus, Berlin 23 December

1934 **Märchen im Grand-Hotel** (Grünwald, Löhner-Beda) Theater an der Wien, Vienna 29 March

1935 **Viki** (Harmath/Adorján Bónyi) Magyar Színház 26 January

1935 **Történnek még csodák** (Imre Halász, István Békeffy) Magyar Színház 20 April

1935 **Dschainah, das Mädchen aus dem Tanzhaus** (Grünwald, Löhner-Beda) Theater an der Wien, Vienna 20 December

1936 **3:1 a szerelem javára** (Harmath/László Szilágyi, Dezső Kellér) Royal Színház 18 December

1937 **Roxy und ihr Wunderteam** (Grünwald, Hans Weigl) Theater an der Wien, Vienna 25 March

1937 **Júlia** (Harmath/Földes) Városi Színház 23 December

1938 **Fehér hattyú** (Harmath/Földes) Városi Színház 23 December

Biography (fictionalized): Sebestyén, G: *Paul Ábrahám: aus dem Leben eines Operettenkomponisten* (Verlag der Österreichischen Staatsdruckerei, Vienna, 1987)

ABSCHIEDSWALZER Operette in 2 acts by Hubert Marischka and Rudolf Österreicher. Music by Ludwig Schmidseder. Wiener Bürgertheater, Vienna, 8 September 1949.

Viennese diplomat Ferry Kornegg (Walter Müller) has been engaged for three years to the singer Anita (Friedl Loor), daughter of the celebrated painter Georg Ferdinand Waldmüller (Hubert Marischka). However, the two have an argument, he sends her a letter breaking off their engagement, and soon ends up down the river in Hungary celebrating a new engagement with pretty little Thussy von Szómary (Waltraut Haas). Papa Waldmüller, who has begun a painting of the wedding of Anita and Ferry, to be called "Hochzeit in Petersdorf," zips back and forth between Vienna and Hungary, and manages affairs so that the pair are finally reunited. Thussy gets personable compensation in the form of Ferry's cousin Laczi (Franz Marischka) and a dowry, and the piece finishes with a staged representation of the completed painting "Hochzeit in Petersdorf."

Marischka, now in his "elder character" period, supplied himself with an effective role, and songwriter Schmidseder's attractive if traditional score, which featured the farewell waltz of the title, "Tanz mit mir einen Walzer," alongside a number of other waltzes and foxtrots, was an effective illustration to both the Viennese and the Hungarian scenes. The show had a successful first run at the Bürgertheater before going on to other productions in both Austria and Germany.

Germany: Städtische Bühnen, Augsburg 15 March 1953

ACE OF CLUBS Musical play in 2 acts by Noël Coward. Cambridge Theatre, London, 7 July 1950.

An uncharacteristic Coward musical, in which the author dipped into the then-fashionable sleazy venues and petty gangster milieux of contemporary London for his characters and action, *Ace of Clubs* mixed the romance of a club singer (Pat Kirkwood) and a sailor (Graham Payn) with a tale about some stolen jewels. The score of the show was a movable one and much of it had, in fact, been originally attached to a rather different libretto which as, variously, *Over the Garden Wall, Hoi Polloi* and *Come Out to Play,* had failed to find a producer at a period when Coward's fortunes were at less than their peak.

If, hoist on the petard of its author's own reputation, the show did not make a genuine success in its London production (211 performances), it nevertheless turned up its quota of durable revue-style songs: the satirical "Three Juvenile Delinquents," mocking the weakness of contemporary "liberal" courts and judges, Miss Kirkwood's cabaret songs "Josephine" and "Chase Me, Charlie," Payn's lilting "Sail Away," which would later turn up again in the show of the same title, and the brittle, pasted-in "I Like America" which subsequently served its writer well in his cabaret act. Miss Kirkwood's pretty "I'd Never, Never Know" proved the most successful of the lyric music, as soprano Sylvia Cecil, who provided the genuine vocal values in the show in the co-starring role of the club owner, was left short of appreciable material.

The show was brought out of retirement for a showing at suburban London's Wimbledon studio in 1999.

Recording: original cast (part record *Noël Coward: The Great Shows*) (EMI)

ACHARD, Marcel (b Sainte-Foy-lès-Lyon, 5 July 1899; d Paris, 4 September 1974).

A successful playwright of comedies (*Jean de la lune, Patate,* etc) and a member of the Académie française, Achard dipped on several occasions into the musical theatre, providing the libretto to *La P'tite Lili,* in which Edith Piaf made a venture into the musical theatre, and authoring an adaptation of the famous screenplay *Some Like It Hot,* played at the Théâtre du Châtelet as *La Polka des lampions* with considerable success. He also wrote a less happy piece for the same house which, based on the life of author Eugène Sue, was entitled *Eugène le Mystérieux* on the excuse that Sue had written *Mystères de Paris.* The show's run of 116 performances placed it well behind another musicalization of that same work made a century earlier, Serafino de Ferrari's Venetian opera buffa *Pipele* (Teatro San Benedetto 25 November 1855).

Achard scripted the film *Valse de Paris,* doing to Offenbach's life what *Das Dreimäderlhaus* had done to Schubert's, and Hollywood to that of many another writer and composer, with the usual minuscule amount of care for things factual. Pierre Fresnay portrayed the composer in memorable style through Achard's invented love affair between Offenbach and Hortense Schneider (Yvonne Printemps). He was also adapter and director of the Hollywood French versions of *Die lustige Witwe* (1934) and *Folies-Bergère* (1935).

Achard's play *Voulez-vous jouez avec moi?* (1923) was musicalized in America as *Come Play with Me* (Dana Suesse/ad Tamara Geva, Halla Stoddard), and produced at the York Playhouse 30 April 1959 with Liliane Montevecchi in the principal role.

1951 **La P'tite Lili** (Marguerite Monnot) Théâtre de l'ABC 3 March

1961 **La Polka des lampions** (Gérard Calvi) Théâtre du Châtelet 15 December

1964 **Eugène le Mysterieux** (Jean-Michel Damase) Théâtre du Châtelet 7 February

Biography: Lorcey, J: *Marcel Achard* (Éditions France Empire, Paris, 1977)

ACKLAND, Joss [ACKLAND, Sidney E Jocelyn] (b London, 29 February 1928). After an early career spent largely in repertory theatre, followed by a period in South Africa variously as a tea-planter and an actor, Ackland joined Britain's Old Vic company in 1958. His first musical-theatre appearance in London came when, as associate director of the Mermaid Theatre, he took the part of Sotmore in their 1962 revival of *Lock Up Your Daughters.* In 1966 he was top-billed in the title role of *Jorrocks* at the New Theatre, scoring a notable personal success as the singing version of the most famous hunting man of English literature.

His next musical role—in a career largely devoted to straight theatre, film and television—was as Fredrik Egermann in the London production of *A Little Night Music* (1975), but his most memorable singing part came in 1978 when he created the role of Juan Peron to the Eva of Elaine Paige in *Evita* at the Prince Edward Theatre. In 1983 he appeared as Romain Gary in the unfortunate National Theatre biomusical of *Jean Seberg,* and in 1985 played a lip-smacking musical Captain Hook to the *Peter Pan* of Bonnie Langford in the first London performances of the American musical-comedy version of Barrie's play.

Autobiography: *I Must Be in There Somewhere* (Hodder & Stoughton, London, 1989)

L'ACQUA CHETA Operetta in 3 acts by Augusto Novelli based on his play of the same title. Lyrics by Angelo Nessi. Music by Giuseppe Pietri. Teatro Nazionale, Rome, 27 November 1920.

One of the most successful Italian operettas of its period, *L'acqua cheta* was adapted by Novelli from his successful 1908 play of the same title. The "still waters" of that title refer to little Florentine Ida (Jole Pacifici) who, in comparison with her sister, Anita (Mimy Aylmer), is a picture of quiet modesty. However, still waters really do run deep in this case, and Ida has a lover called Alfredo with whom, in the course of the evening, she tries to elope. The elopement is discovered by the comical stablelad, Stinchi (Enrico Dezan), and the carpenter, Cecco (Vannutelli), but, when all is sung and done, the marriage still takes place.

Written in a warmly rustic vein, *L'acqua cheta* was illustrated by a delightfully melodic and suitably Italianate score, which ranged from the Mascagani-like tones of its prelude and the beautiful "Trio di ricamo" (Embroidery trio) to the blatantly catchy sound of the popular canzone. The lively, swinging ensemble "O com'è bello guidare i cavalli" for Stinchi and Cecco proved the most popular single number.

Recordings: complete (Cetra), selections (Cetra, EDM)

THE ACT (ex- *Shine It On*) Musical in 2 acts by George Furth. Lyrics by Fred Ebb. Music by John Kander. Majestic Theater, New York, 29 October 1977.

The Act was mounted as a vehicle for singing and cinema star Liza Minnelli, cast in the role of Michelle Craig, a faded film star on the comeback trail as a nightclub singer at Las Vegas's Miramar Hotel. The role gave her the chance to perform a series of Kander/Ebb songs made to her measure. Pieces such as "Shine It On," "The Money Tree" and "City Lights" allowed the star to open up in her audience's favorite, stinging style, "Arthur in the Afternoon" provided a comical moment, and the evening as a whole fulfilled its purpose as a singing, dancing, barnstorming showcase. It also brought its fair share of controversy, notably when it was revealed that the star was leaning even more than had become generally accepted on the use of pre-recorded playback tapes, and then when she took to not playing at all. The Shubert/Feuer and Martin production played for 233 Broadway performances.

Recording: original cast (DRG)

ADAM, Adolphe [Charles] (b Paris, 24 July 1803; d Paris, 3 May 1856). Influential producer and composer at the dawning of the modern musical theatre age.

Along with his compatriots Daniel Auber and Adrien Boïeldieu, Adolphe Adam was one of the most successful musicians of the opéra-comique genre, the most sophisticated of the forms of light musical theatre which held the world's stages in the decades prior to the coming of the opéra-bouffe and a more frankly high-spirited style of popular lyric theatre.

Adam's one-act *Pierre et Catherine* was produced at the Opéra-Comique in 1829 and, of the 52 other opéras-comiques, large and small, which followed, pieces such as the one-act *Le Châlet* (1834, and widely performed in the English language as *The Swiss Cottage*), *Le Postillon de Longjumeau* (1836), *Le Brasseur de Preston* (1838), *Le Roi d'Yvetot* (1842), *Giralda, ou la nouvelle Psyche* (1850) and *Si j'étais roi* (1852) become internationally played favorites. Several of his shorter works, notably *Les Pantins de Violette* (1856) and *La Poupée de Nuremberg* (1852), were near enough in temperament to the later opérette genre to remain around and share bills and repertoires with the early Offenbach and Hervé works both in France and abroad, whilst the humorous libretto to *Giralda* proved its viability in a later age, subsequently reset as a late 19th-century comic opera by Britain's Bucalossi under the title *Manteaux Noirs* (1882) and by Hungary's Jenő Sztojanovits as *A kis molnárné* (1892).

Adam unsuccessfully founded a Théâtre Lyrique in Paris in 1847, but a second attempt in the same vein in 1851 was a splendid success. With Adam himself as manager, and later under the direction of Carvalho, it provided in the 17 years of its existence a production base for such not-so-desperately-grand operas as *Faust, Mireille, Roméo et Juliette, Les Pêcheurs de perles* and *La Jolie Fille de Perth* by the younger French composers, such almost-opérettes as Aimé Maillart's *Les Dragons de Villars* (1856), and a host of one-act opéras-comiques of which a number were headed in style and subject matter towards the less formal opérettic manners of the coming age.

Today Adam is principally remembered for his ballet music, *Giselle,* but he holds an important place in theatre history as one of the principal precursors of the modern era of musical theatre.

Memoirs: *Souvenirs d'un musicien* (Michel Lévy, Paris, 1857), *Derniers souvenirs d'un musicien* (Michel Lévy, Paris, 1859); Biography: Pougin, A: *Adolphe Adam: sa vie, sa carrière, ses mémoires artistiques* (Charpentier, Paris, 1876)

ADAM ET ÈVE Opérette fantastique in 4 acts by Raoul Toché and Ernest Blum. Music by Gaston Serpette. Théâtre des Nouveautés, Paris, 6 October 1886.

The Parisian extravaganza *Adam et Ève* opened in the Garden of Eden, where Satan (Jules Brasseur) outwits the good spirit Adramalec (Berthelier) and gets Ève (Louise Théo) and Adam (Albert Brasseur) to taste the apple. The culpable Adramalec is condemned to celibacy until his fault is expiated and Adam and Ève have been brought back together. The remaining three acts took in episodes in Ancient Rome (Adamis and Eva), in brigand-land Spain (Adamos, the brigand trying to carry off a Spanish Eva) and finally in contemporary France, where the modern artist Saint-Adam finally whisks his Ève away from the clutches of old Baron Sataniel and, thus, releases Adramalec from his painful situation. Marie Lantelme (who would later be mysteriously drowned in the Rhine), Mlle Decrozat and Marguerite Deval were amongst the other ladies of the various eras of Adaming-and-Eveing.

The appearance of Théo as the original Ève, opening the show in the "nude" (with strategically placed ivy), a lively and well-reviewed Serpette score, and a spectacular production contributed towards a first run of 63 consecutive Paris performances. However, the more panting Parisians were disappointed for, it was reported, "Le 'nu' de Théo est d'ailleurs des plus respectables et des guirlandes de fleurs la dissimulent complètement à la vive déception des nombreux spectateurs venus aux Nouveautés dans l'espoir d'en apercevoir davantage." The show was later produced in Budapest (ad Emil Makai, Dezső Bálint) for a successful run of 31 performances with Gabi Bardi as Eve.

Adam and Eve have been the subject of, or the excuse for, a number of other stage works since the days of the mystery plays. An operatic *Adam und Eva* (Theile/C Richter) opened Hamburg's first opera house in 1678, a Posse mit Gesang, *Adam und Eva,* composed by Carl Binder appeared at the Carltheater in 1859 (25 September), a Schwank mit Gesang by Wilhelm Jacoby and L André played under the same title at Mainz in 1884 (14 December), and an Operette by Hugo Wittmann and Julius Bauer, composed by Carl Weinberger, was produced at the Carltheater, 5 January 1899. Like the French work, this *Adam und Eva (Die Seelenwanderung),* with Alexander Girardi as its Adam and American soubrette Marie Halton as Eva, made its way through the ages, beginning in an Indian paradise and parading its stars through impersonations of Joseph and Mme Potiphar, Sokrates and Xanthippe, and Don Quixote and Dulcinea, under the eye of an ever-disguised, comical Mercury (Siegmund Natzler), before finishing with a present-day backstage episode. It played 52 performances.

Amongst the other musical stage pieces to depict the primal couple have been Cuvillier's one-act opérette *Avant-hier matin* (1905), the opening episode of the three-part Broadway musical *The Apple Tree* (1966), the 1990 London *Children of Eden* which, in deference to then-current sensibilities, presented a white Adam (Martin Smith) paired with a black Eve (Shezwae Powell), and the Hungarian rock opera *Az elsõ sírásó* (1995, János Marno/Gyula Papp) which managed to get Catullus, Robespierre, de Sade and an eskimo into the action as well. Paris's *Pom-Pom* (Théâtre de la Potinière, 1928) also visited the Garden of Eden.

Hungary: Népszínház *Ádám és Éva* 10 January 1902

AN ADAMLESS EDEN Comic operetta in 1 act by Savile Clark. Music by Walter Slaughter. Opera Comique, London, 13 December 1882.

An operetta written by men for the all-women troupe of musicians, singers and dancers run by conductor/composer Lila Clay, *An Adamless Eden* necessarily told of the failure of such a society. The women who have got together and sworn to avoid the "tyranny of men" soon begin to cheat, and their Eden is foresworn.

Played for a successful London season as part of the program of Miss Clay's company, in tandem with a concert entitled "Something New," with such established performers as *Pirates of Penzance* contralto Emily Cross, star dancer Emma D'Auban and Gaiety burlesquer Miss Amalia amongst the foolish ladies and original *Trial by Jury* cast-member Linda Verner as one of the triumphant men, the piece was subsequently taken out for several tours, and was soon picked up for production in America. The first such production was seen in Boston, in 1884, where the piece (ad Benjamin E Woolf, John J Braham) was produced in a house supplied with female ticket-sellers, female ushers, female musicians (a canny journalist spotted three men in blonde wigs) and a female musical director and one man, W S Daboll, amongst the otherwise female cast, led by Mrs Daboll. The concert of the first part of the program was replaced by an adaptation of *Lischen et Fritzchen.* It was noticed that the audience was largely . . . female, too.

The piece turned up at Broadway's Comedy Theater later the same year, played by M B Leavitt's company with Marie Sanger, Pauline Hall, Topsy Venn and Venie Burroughs amongst the cast. In the hands of America's most infamous producer of gaudy legshows, Miss Clay's ladylike drawing-room operetta production had now become something else altogether, and this time it was noticed that the audience was mainly . . . male. A repeat Broadway season was played at the 3rd Avenue Theater in 1885 (1 June), and what passed for versions of the show were played by all-female companies in vaudeville programs and theatres throughout the country for several years. However, more and more, the show's slightly suggestive title was used simply as an umbrella for what were, under the management of the louche Leavitt and then of Sam T Jack and of others such, little more than crude burleycue shows featuring "semi-naked" women and low-brow variety acts, entertainments with little relation to the original little show. The burleycue displays and the title lasted longer than the original operetta had.

USA: Oakland Garden, Boston 7 July 1884, Comedy Theater 24 November 1884

ADAMS, Frank R[amsey] (b Morrison, Ill, 7 July 1883; d White Lake, Mich, 8 October 1963). Chicago-based Adams led an eclectic writing career, finding success as a journalist (*Tribune, Examiner, Daily News,* etc), an author and novelist, a film scenarist and, for a number of years in his twenties, as a busy librettist and lyricist for the musical theatre.

As a 20-year-old student at the University of Chicago, he combined with fellow student Will M Hough on the book and lyrics to a musical, *His Highness the Bey.* Set to music by the already established Joe Howard, and produced at the local La Salle Theater, the show found a considerable success and, over the following years, the trio's bright, easygoing and, not infrequently, interestingly original musical shows built up some mighty Chicago runs, a long and lively following on the road, and a premiere place in musical stock company repertoires for many years to come. *The Umpire* (1905), *The Time, the Place and the Girl* (1906), *The Girl Question* (1907), and *A Stubborn Cinderella* (1908), all mounted in the small-sized auditorium of Chicago's La Salle Theatre, proved the most widely appreciated of the set, but—although the team's best work was as good as, maybe better than, and certainly more inventive than most of the current east coast product—not even these, in spite of their years and years of outstanding success around the country, were able to establish themselves in New York where any made-in-Chicago musical was looked upon with some disdain.

The team's producer, Mort Singer, was encouraged by these successes and the apparent development of Chicago as a strong production center to build a second theatre, the Princess, to permit the staging of additional productions. The new theatre was opened successfully with *A Stubborn Cinderella* in 1908, but the second Howard/Adams/Hough show to play the Princess, *The Prince of To-night* (1909), was the first of the team's nine collaborations to date to win only a lukewarm reception, in spite of the fact that it contained the only song from any of these shows to become a standard. "I Wonder Who's Kissing Her Now," although presented and published as the work of Adams, Hough and Joe Howard, was later proved to have been composed by the young Harold Orlob.

Orlob joined the team officially for the 1909 *The Flirting Princess,* without producing a second hit song, and the team went further with interpolations in their 1910 *Miss Nobody from Starland* before Howard split from the group. It was, in any case, becoming clear that the vein which had proved so fruitful over the past half-dozen years had begun to run dry.

While his erstwhile partners went their separate ways within the musical theatre, Adams abandoned the field and spent the remainder of his writing career elsewhere. He provided more than 30 screenplays for early Hollywood films, including such ventures as the *Tarzan* films and *The Ten Commandments,* and also authored a long list of novels. He returned to the theatre rarely, winning one further musical credit when the La Salle Theater management decided to get him to turn his play *Molly and I* into a musical for star soprano Lina Abarbanell before its opening night and making a last appearance on a musical playbill when a story of his was adapted by William Cary Duncan and Lewis Allen Browne as the libretto for the flop *Princess April* in 1924 (Ambassador Theater 1 December).

1904 **His Highness the Bey** (Joe Howard/w Will M Hough) La Salle Theater, Chicago 21 November

1905 **The Isle of Bong-Bong** (Howard/w Hough) La Salle Theater, Chicago 14 March

1905 **The Land of Nod** (Howard/w Hough) Opera House, Chicago 17 June; New York Theater, New York 1 April 1907

1905 **The Umpire** (Howard/w Hough) La Salle Theater, Chicago 2 December

1906 **The Time, the Place and the Girl** (Howard/w Hough) La Salle Theater, Chicago 20 August; Wallack's Theater, New York 5 August 1907

1907 **The Girl Question** (Howard/w Hough) La Salle Theater, Chicago 24 August; Wallack's Theater, New York 3 August 1908

1908 **The Honeymoon Trail** (Howard/w Hough) La Salle Theater, Chicago 23 March

1908 **A Stubborn Cinderella** (Howard/w Hough) Princess Theater, Chicago 31 May; Broadway Theater, New York 25 January 1909

1909 **The Prince of To-night** (Howard/w Hough) Princess Theater, Chicago 9 March

1909 **The Golden Girl** (Howard/w Hough) La Salle Theater, Chicago 16 March

1909 **The Goddess of Liberty** (Howard/w Hough) Princess Theater, Chicago 15 August; Weber's Theater, New York 22 December 1909

1909 **The Flirting Princess** (Harold Orlob, Howard/w Hough) Princess Theater, Chicago 1 November

1910 **Miss Nobody from Starland** (Howard/w Hough) Princess Theater, Chicago 31 January

1911 **The Heartbreakers** (Orlob, Melville Gideon/w Hough) Princess Theater, Chicago 30 May

1915 **Molly and I** (Louis Hirsch) La Salle Theater, Chicago 31 August

ADAMS, Lee [Richard] (b Mansfield, Ohio, 14 August 1924). Lyricist for a pair of Broadway hits.

Whilst continuing early work in newspaper, magazine, TV and radio journalism, the young Lee Adams began a songwriting collaboration with composer Charles Strouse which led to a series of published songs, special material for television and nightclub performers of the early 1950s and, from 1954, contributions to theatrical revue. From writing stage material for a summer resort in the Adirondacks, they progressed to the New York theatre, where they placed pieces in Ben Bagley's *The Littlest Revue* (1956) and *Shoestring '57, The Ziegfeld Follies of 1956* and *Catch a Star* before joining a third habitué of the off-Broadway revue, librettist Michael Stewart, to write a full-scale musical.

Bye Bye Birdie (1960), which kidded the newish rock and roll craze, won its authors a Tony Award, racked up a 607-performance Broadway run, and proved a sizeable international success ("Kids," "Put on a Happy Face," "A Lot of Livin' to Do"). The Adams-Strouse team followed up with the scores for seven further musicals over the next two decades or so. Of these, *Applause,* a musicalization of the screenplay *All About Eve* and its source novel, which starred Lauren Bacall in a first-rate Broadway-grande-dame role, proved the most generally successful (Tony Award), whilst New York and London also welcomed a musical version of the play *Golden Boy* with Sammy Davis jr featured as a black singing version of Clifford Odets's ill-fated boxer.

All American (1962), with a libretto by Mel Brooks and a cast headed by Ray Bolger, and a musical version of the *Superman* comic strips (predating the widely publicized films of the same subject) both found some adherents but insufficient audiences, but an effort to bring a singing, dancing Queen Victoria to the London stage in *I and Albert* foundered nastily. Two later shows, the second an attempt to mount a sequel to *Bye Bye Birdie,* were first-week failures. Adams's more recent collaborations with Albert Hague and Mitch Leigh produced an adaptation of an O Henry story entitled *Flim Flam,* produced as a staged reading at Long Beach in 1987, and a musical biography of Mike Todd mounted in Philadelphia in 1988, and remounted (as *Ain't Broadway Grand*) in New Fairfield, Connecticut, in 1992, prior to a brief Broadway run.

Non-theatre work has included film and television material, including a television musical with Strouse

(*Alice in Wonderland or What's a Nice Kid Like You Doing in a Place Like This?* ABC 30 March 1966) and the theme song to the television series *All in the Family.*

1960 **Bye Bye Birdie** (Charles Strouse/Michael Stewart) Martin Beck Theater 14 April

1962 **All American** (Strouse/Mel Brooks) Winter Garden Theater 19 March

1964 **Golden Boy** (Strouse/Clifford Odets, William Gibson) Majestic Theater 20 October

1966 **It's a Bird . . . It's a Plane . . . It's Superman** (Strouse/David Newman, Robert Benton) Alvin Theater 29 March

1970 **Applause** (Strouse/Adolph Green, Betty Comden) Palace Theater 30 March

1972 **I and Albert** (Strouse/Jay Presson Allen) Piccadilly Theatre, London 6 November

1978 **A Broadway Musical** (Strouse/William F Brown) Lunt-Fontanne Theater 21 December

1981 **Bring Back Birdie** (Strouse/Stewart) Martin Beck Theater 5 March

1988 **Ain't Broadway Grand** (ex- *Mike*) (Mitch Leigh/Thomas Meehan) Walnut Street Theater, Philadelphia 26 March; Lunt-Fontanne Theater, New York 18 April 1993

ADDIO GIOVINEZZA Operetta in 3 acts by Camasio and Oxilia. Lyrics by Alessandro de Stefani. Music by Giuseppe Pietri. Politeama Goldoni, Livorno, 20 January 1915; Teatro Diana, Rome, 20 April 1915.

Pietri's earliest operetta success, and one of the most attractive and enduring pieces to come out of the happiest years of the Italian musical theatre, *Addio giovinezza* was written in the warmly folky manner of the zarzuela rather than the glitzy revusical style which was currently invading the musical theatre. Its characters, too, came from the everyday world which zarzuela writers favored. The little modista, Dorina, falls in love with the student, Mario, who is a lodger in her home, but the young lad, discovering life, seems to be more likely to appreciate the charms of the worldly Elena. Eventually, of course, Mario graduates and says ''addio'' to his youthful flings, and Dorina says goodbye, too, both to ''giovinezza'' and to ''amor.''

Pietri's attractively simple music illustrated the tale aptly in a score which opened and closed with a quote from ''Gaudeamus,'' and which mixed almost light-operatic moments with jaunty student songs and dancing melodies. It was the lyric part of the score which produced the favorite pieces: a wistful solo for Dorina, with a gentle echo of *Cavalleria rusticana* to it (''Non vedo, non senti''), and the unhurriedly waltzing duo for Mario and Dorina (''Tu m'ami, è già qualcosa''). A second waltz duo, with Elena (''Ma lei non è curioso''), in a less romantic vein, a jaunty quintet with imitation trumpets, a duo for Dorina and the soubret-comic, Leone, and marches and choruses in the student style provided the contrasting moments.

Recording: selection (EDM)

ADE, George (b Kentland, Ind, 9 February 1866; d Brook, Ind, 16 May 1944).

A highly regarded comic writer who worked as a journalist on the *Chicago Record* between 1890 and 1900 (''Artie,'' ''Doc Horne,'' ''Pink Marsh'') before moving into the theatre, Ade evinced a particular interest in popular slang, a subject on which he wrote analytically whilst also making active use of its jauntier phrases in his successful ''Fables in Slang'' (subsequently filmed as a series of shorts by Essanay), in a series of vaudeville sketches (''his fable about Xoroaster and Zendavesta the song-and-dance team was one of the funniest vaudeville skits ever written'') and, later, in his books, plays and libretti.

Ade made his theatrical debut, somewhat diffidently, with the farce-comedy *The Night of the Fourth* written as a vehicle for comedy team Mathews and Bulger and introduced by them as part of Dunne and Ryley's ''company of comedians'' season in San Francisco in the summer of 1900 before being taken on the road. His contract stipulated that he was not to be identified as the author, but although his name did not appear on the bills the truth leaked out before the tour had even started. Ade was, however, sure enough of himself in his new function as playwright and librettist that, when Henry Savage subsequently commissioned him to write a musical for the Chicago stage, in tandem with the young English composer Alfred Wathall, his name was this time billed in big letters. The piece the pair produced was the colorful and successful *The Sultan of Sulu* and, and finding that this theatrical work was both lucrative (''I don't care who writes the plays of the nation as long as I collect the royalties'') and appealing, Ade began to devote more conscientious energies to the musical stage, at first in Chicago and then further East.

Of his three initial pieces for Chicago, *The Sultan of Sulu* and *The Sho-Gun* both cashed in on the standard English musical-comedy formula. Tales of dashing hometown boys and girls, plonked down in exotic and scenery-worthy locations, amid curious foreigners and, in particular, comico-threatening orientalish potentates, they were illustrated by bright music and low comedy and proved highly successful. *The Sultan of Sulu* was clearly recognized as amongst the best of the American musical comedies of the period, whilst *The Sho-Gun* was played as far afield as Hungary (where, curiously, its libretto was attributed to cast member Clyde McKinley) and both pieces survived for many years on the American touring circuits. The third piece, *Peggy from Paris,* yielded little to either, clocking up 16 weeks in Chicago and 15 in Boston before a fair (for a ''Chicago musical'') New York run during which one critic opined that, although uneven, its best bits were the best musical comedy yet to have come out of the native American popular lyric theatre.

Ade established himself, simultaneously, as an author of straight plays, scoring particular successes with *The County Chairman* (1903) and *The College Widow* (1904), but he subsequently found most of his best results with musical pieces: two vehicles for popular impersonator-cum-soubrette Elsie Janis—*The Fair Co-Ed,* a piece originally written for the students of Purdue University and set in the same college precincts as *The College Widow,* and *The Slim Princess,* based on one of his own stories and dramatized by three amateur ladies in Indianapolis—and one for the top comedy team of Montgomery and Stone (*The Old Town*). He also authored a "comedy with musical interpolations," *Just Out of College* (1905, "The Magazine Girl") for the touring circuits, a musical version of his comedy *Artie,* entitled *The City Chap* (1910), with a score by his nephew, George Ade Davis and Benjamin Hapgood Burt, which was scheduled for a Cohan and Harris tour but was instead played by the Harlequin Club of Purdue University, and a musical comedy, *The Hermits on Main Street* (23 May 1921, mus: Milton Lusk) played at the Hermit's Club Frolic at Cleveland's Opera House. He also wrote a series of sketches for the variety houses (*The Mayor and the Manicurist,* 1908, etc). He eventually renounced the stage, and retired to spend his winters in Florida and summers on his Indiana farm.

George Ade Davis went on to become manager of Chicago's Studebaker Theater.

The College Widow was later used as the source for the successful musical *Leave It to Jane* (Longacre Theater 28 August 1917, Jerome Kern/P G Wodehouse, Guy Bolton), while *The Slim Princess* made its way to the silent screen (Essanay, May 1915) as a four-part movie starring Ruth Stonehouse, Francis X Bushman and Wallace Beery.

1900 **The Night of the Fourth** (Max Hoffman/J Sherrie Mathews) California Theater, San Francisco 5 August; Victoria Theater, New York 21 January 1901

1902 **The Sultan of Sulu** (Alfred G Wathall) Studebaker Theater, Chicago 11 March; Wallack's Theater, New York 29 December

1903 **Peggy from Paris** (William Lorraine) Studebaker Theater, Chicago 30 January; Wallack's Theater, New York 10 September

1904 **The Sho-Gun** (Gustav Luders) Studebaker Theater, Chicago 4 April; Wallack's Theater, New York 10 October

1905 **Just Out of College** (Frank Callahan/Stanley Murphy) New Haven September 25, West End Theater 23 March 1908

1908 **The Fair Co-Ed** (Luders) Studebaker Theater, Boston 23 November; Knickerbocker Theater 1 February 1909

1909 **The Old Town** (Luders) Studebaker Theater, Chicago 23 September; Globe Theater 10 January 1910

1910 **The Slim Princess** (Leslie Stuart/w Henry Blossom) Star Theater, Buffalo 5 September; Globe Theater, New York 2 January 1911

Biography: Kelly, F C: *George Ade, Warmhearted Satirist* (Bobbs-Merrill, Indianapolis, 1947)

ADLER, Richard (b New York, 3 August 1921). Songwriter for a pair of major hits of the Broadway 1950s.

The son of a musician, Adler had no regular musical training himself but, in the years following a wartime navy stint, he turned his hand to writing songs. In 1950 he teamed up with singer-songwriter Jerry Ross, who had had little more success than Adler in getting his work placed anywhere that it might be significantly heard. Together the two wrote words and music for the radio programs *Broadway Scrapbook* and *Stop the Music* as well as some special material for various artists, and as a result they came to the notice of Frank Loesser. Promoted by Loesser, Adler and Ross had their first song hit with "From Rags to Riches," sung by Tony Bennett and nearly 20 years later repopularized by Elvis Presley, and they then moved into the theatre to provide the songs, first, for the revue *John Murray Anderson's Almanac* (1953), and then for two highly successful Broadway musicals. *The Pajama Game* (1954) and *Damn Yankees* (1955) were both played internationally after long Broadway runs; each produced a pair of hit songs ("Hey There," "Hernando's Hideaway," "Heart," "Whatever Lola Wants"), both became Hollywood films and both found their way to latter-day revivals.

After Ross's premature death in 1955, Adler worked principally in television (*The Gift of the Magi* 9 December 1958, *Little Women, Olympus 7-0000* 28 September 1966) and in commercials, returning to the theatre (after a mooted musical version of Somerset Maugham's *Of Human Bondage* failed to eventuate) only for the short-lived *Kwamina* (1961), *A Mother's Kisses* (1968), which folded prior to Broadway, and *Music Is* (1976), a quick-failure musical version of *Twelfth Night.* He subsequently turned to orchestral and instrumental writing (*Memory of Childhood, Retrospective, Yellowstone, Wilderness Suite, The Lady Remembers*).

Adler, who had ventured early into production, co-produced a 1973 remounting of *The Pajama Game, Music Is* (1976) and the Richard Rodgers musical *Rex* (1976) without success.

He was married for a period to vocalist Sally Ann Howes, and his son from an earlier marriage, **Christopher ADLER** (b New York, 17 January 1954; d New York, 30 November 1984), wrote for the variety show *Shirley Maclaine on Broadway* (1984, w Marvin Hamlisch), for the one-man show *Herman van Veen: All of Him,* and was the lyricist for the unsuccessful musical

Jean Seberg (Hamlisch/Julian Barry, National Theatre, London, 1983, ''based on an original idea by Christopher Adler'').

1954 **The Pajama Game** (w Jerry Ross/George Abbott, Richard Bissell) St James Theater 13 May
1955 **Damn Yankees** (w Ross/Abbott, Douglass Wallop) 46th Street Theater 5 May
1961 **Kwamina** (Robert Alan Arthur) 54th Street Theater 23 October
1968 **A Mother's Kisses** (Bruce Jay Friedman) Shubert Theater, New Haven 23 September
1976 **Music Is** (Will Holt, Abbott) St James Theater 20 December
1994 **Off Key** (Bill C Davis) George Street Playhouse, New Brunswick, NJ 1 April

Autobiography: *You Gotta Have Heart* (Donald I Fine, New York, 1990)

ADONIS Burlesque [a disrespectful perversion of common sense] [or, Ye Statue, Ye Miller, Ye Maiden and Ye Lordly Villain] in 2 acts by Edward E Rice and William Gill (later credited to Gill and Henry E Dixey). Original music by E E Rice. Selected music ''cheerfully contributed by Beethoven, Audran, Suppé, Planquette, Offenbach, Strauss, Mozart, Haydn, Dave Braham, John Eller, Henry Sator and many others too numerous to individualize.'' Hooley's Theater, Chicago, 6 July 1884; Bijou Theater, New York, 4 September 1884.

The most successful pasticcio burlesque/extravaganza produced in the American musical theatre in the last quarter of the 19th century, this ''disrespectful perversion of common sense'' (a jibe at Gilbert's description of his recent *Princess Ida*) took the familiar subject matter so effectively used, in particular, in the libretto to the Viennese Operette *Die schöne Galathée* and gave it the kind of everything-lightly-clad-including-the-kitchen-sink burlesque treatment favored in the 1870s and early 1880s. In this version, the statue which comes to life is not a beautiful maiden, but Adonis (Henry E Dixey), a delectable lad with nude knees. Like Galathée, he is lusted after by everyone who comes in his path, beginning with his sculptress, Talamea (Vernona Jarbeau/Lillie Grubb), and her patroness, the Duchess of Area (Jennie Reiffarth), but his own fancies settle on the extremely simple, excessively broad-beamed Rosetta Turke (Amelia Summerville). Adonis gambols through a variety of disguises in his flight from the lusty ladies of the cast, from the villainous Marquis de Baccarat (Herbert Gresham, also director), and in pursuit of Rosetta, but it all finally gets too much for him, and like Galathée, Niobe and all his other theatrical predecessors in the stone-to-flesh stakes, he turns back into a statue to get a bit of peace and quiet.

The principal raison d'être of *Adonis* was to allow Dixey the opportunity to indulge in a series of songs, dances, disguises and impersonations—including a lengthy impression of everybody's favorite impersonee, Henry Irving—and his initial success in Chicago, followed by an even greater one when the show was taken to New York, earned him the right to expand and elasticize his role at will. Which he did. The most effective musical part of this expansion was the comic song ''It's English, You Know'' (ly: Henry S Hewitt), one of several composed by producer Rice (''I'm O'Donohue from Nowhere,'' ''The Wall Street Broker'') to be added to the original score of pasticcio songs (voted ''weak'' in Chicago) in which Dixey introduced himself, to the strains of Arthur Sullivan's *Iolanthe* music, as ''A Most Susceptible Statue[tte].'' Rice's new song became a hit of the time, its title a popular catchphrase, and the number was promptly lifted by other artists to be interpolated into other pasticcio shows.

The season spent by *Adonis* in Chicago meant that, in contrast to most pieces of the time, the show arrived in New York in a thoroughly worked-in condition. There, the slick and funny entertainment, Dixey's handsome face, wavy forelock and (apparently) naked thighs—all put to good use in a star part made to order—and an otherwise largely feminine and equally underclad cast (four little feminine Robinson Crusoes caused gasps by sporting no trunks over their tights) which, the press noted, contained ''very few back numbers,'' helped *Adonis* to both an immense popularity and a very long run. Like its predecessor in Broadway's gape-at-the-groins stakes, *The Black Crook,* it pulled 'em in vigorously and when Dixey started sporting $5,000 worth of diamonds that outshone those of any burlesque queen in town, the gape-quotient of the show rocketed even higher. *Adonis* became a grade-one hit. The show was given a major musical revamp 2 November 1885, when eight new numbers (including a chunk of *The Mikado* remade as ''Eight Little Japanese Kids'') were introduced and it scored a famous Broadway first when its 500th New York performance was reached on 7 January 1886, and another when the record-breaking last was seen on 17 April (603 performances) before the cast—still headed by Dixey, Gresham and Misses Summerville and Grubb, and with Annie Alliston now playing the Duchess of Area—set off for England and a summer season at the Gaiety Theatre.

London, however, had no need nor wish for an umpteenth old-fashioned burlesque (Gaiety supremo Hollingshead called *Adonis* simply ''a variety show''), especially at a theatre which had just hosted the red-hot ''new burlesque'' *Little Jack Sheppard,* nor indeed for yet another imitation of Henry Irving (people had been ''doing'' him in London eternally). *Adonis* got slated by the press, not least as being ''a very long way ahead of anything previously seen on the London stage in the matter of indecent dressing'' but—while theatrically unenlightened patriots and pressmen back home hurled accusations of ''anti-Americanism'' at London's unappreciated and underwhelmed playgoers—Dixey (whose own notices and reception were fine) stuck it out at the Gaiety. He played, albeit to disappointing houses, through his pre-booked four-month, 105 performance season, before handing over the Gaiety's stage to its new manager, George Edwardes. Edwardes replaced the ''variety show'' with an old-fashioned ''comedy opera'' called *Dorothy.* And *Dorothy* went on to outscore even the long-run record compiled by Dixey on Broadway and to set up a West-End long-run record.

However, Dixey and his show (for which he was now billed as part-author, with Rice now credited simply as ''composer'') still had plenty of life in them. If London didn't want them, America did. Dixey reprised *Adonis* off and on for two decades, round and around the country, returning for brief visits to Broadway in 1886 (5th Avenue Theater 20 September), 1887 (Bijou Theater 2 May) 1888 (Star Theater 12 November), 1892 (Casino Theater 18 April), 1894 (Palmer's Theater 7 May) billed as ''more or less up-to-date,'' and 1899 (Bijou Theater 9 May), usually as a flying part of his endless touring schedule. And the famous first run remained a statistical achievement ever after.

In Australia, what seem to have been the only performances of what was clearly a much personalized version of *Adonis* were played by the supreme female impersonator Francis Leon, appearing for once in something other than a skirt for half of a programme which was completed by his well-known interpretation of the predatory widow in *His Grace the Duke.*

At the height of its fame, *Adonis* suffered that fate of only the most famous of burlesques—it was itself burlesqued, by Koster & Bial's company, by the incessantly touring ''Night Owls'' variety combination as *A-Donis* (Fred Solomon/H M Pitts,) and, in minstrelized form, as a burnt-cork extravaganza called *Black Adonis.*

Australia: Nugget Theatre, Melbourne 26 December 1885; UK: Gaiety Theatre 31 May 1886

Plate 2. **Adonis.** *Henry E Dixey as the delectable statue of Willie Gill's musical.*

AFGAR, ou Les Loisirs andalous Opérette in 2 acts by André Barde and Michel Carré fils. Music by Charles Cuvillier. Théâtre des Capucines, Paris, 2 April 1909.

Barde and Carré's libretto left little doubt as to what the Andalous did with their ''loisirs.'' In their story, the Moorish sultan Afgar (Armand Berthez), unable, after years of over-exertion and political worry, to fulfill his haremic duties, appoints a particularly handsome captive, Oporto (Maxime Capoul) to deputize and, at peril of impaling, to repopulate the land with little Afgars. However, during their years of marital deprivation, the ladies of the harem, headed by Zaydée (Marguerite Deval), have made themselves alternative arrangements. The young Oporto finds himself first balked in his duties and then—when Zaydée turns amorous at the same time that his own fiancée Isilda turns up (apparently as the newest addition to the harem, but in reality to help him escape)—in an altogether nicer but nevertheless decidedly pronged dilemma. For Isilda, hearing what his duties are supposed to be, immediately supposes him faithless, and sets her cap at old Afgar. His problems are solved only when Afgar regains his virility and his interest in his wives, leaving Oporto and his Isilda (with a little interested help from Zaydée) to escape from Afgar-land to less hectic climes.

This Moorish-Parisian tale was set to a Cuvillier score which was often curiously un-French in tone. It was neither in the style of the turn-of-the-century French opérette, nor of the songwriters' musical comedy which would soon take over the Paris stage, but hovered somewhere in between. Several of the numbers—solos and ensembles—had a seeming tinge of the English to them: at moments Cuvillier's often pretty but rarely adventurous melodies held echoes of Daly's theatre. At Daly's, however, the music was never set to lyrics as wickedly witty as those of André Barde.

Played on a bill with two little curtain-raisers (*Petite Tache* and Barde's *Changement de Main*), *Afgar* proved highly successful entertainment at Berthez's little Théâtre des Capucines, from where it moved liberally into French and Belgian provincial theatres and, eventually, into overseas productions. Ten years on, following Cuvillier's London triumph with *The Lilac Domino,* C B Cochran produced *Afgar* (ad Fred Thompson, Worton David) in Britain with Alice Delysia starred as Zaydée in a version which had, not unexpectedly, undergone some severe textual whitewashing. The songs (ly: Douglas Furber) were mostly by Cuvillier—some old, some new, some *Afgar*—but also included Irving Berlin's "You'd Be Surprised" and Fred Fisher's "Dardanella" performed by Mlle Delysia for the three hundred performances for which *Afgar* stayed in town. Baritone Harry Welchman (Don Juan jr, ex- Oporto), John Humphries (Afgar), newcomer Marie Burke (Isilda) and Lupino Lane (Coucourli) completed the star team of a show in which all that was left for the Lord Chamberlain to object to was the dress worn by the dancer Mona Païva.

Morris Gest, who had recently run uncomfortably into officialdom over his highly sexed American production of the Pierre Loüys-based extravaganza *Aphrodite,* took up Cochran's production at the end of its London run and exported it, Delysia, Lane and comedian W H Rawlins (Afgar) to America. There, with its now less-recognizable score heavily added to by Harry Tierney and Joseph McCarthy ("Why Don't You?," etc), and with local cast-members Irving Beebe (Don Juan jr) and Frances Cameron (Isilda) in support, *Afgar* achieved another good run (171 performances).

The show returned to Paris, in 1919 at the Théâtre Antoine, and in 1947 it was brought back again at the little Théâtre Monceau under the management of Gil Roland and Pierre Jourdan, in a new version by Jean de Letraz, with the two managers featuring themselves alongside Catherine Gay (Zaydée), Andrée Grandjean (Isilda), a speciality belly dancer and a piano accompaniment.

UK: London Pavilion 17 September 1919; USA: Central Theater 8 November 1920

L'AFRICAINE, or The Queen of the Cannibal Islands Operatic burlesque in 5 scenes by F C Burnand. Music by Frank Musgrave. Strand Theatre, London, 18 November 1865.

The second of Burnand and Musgrave's original British opéras-bouffes, *L'Africaine*—burlesquing Meyerbeer's opera of the same title which had premiered at Covent Garden just months previously—was a little more substantial than the first, *Windsor Castle,* but it was built and written on the same extravagant lines. Thomas Thorne played the heroine, Selika, in nigger minstrel blackface, the comedians J D Stoyle and David James were Vasco da Gama and Nelusko, and the theatre's principal boy, Miss Raynham, was Don Pedro, in a piece which Burnand evolved in such a way as to include each of the artists' special turns alongside a score which ranged from the burlesque operatic to the bones.

L'Africaine proved a great success for the Swanborough family's Strand Theatre (88 performances), leading to the hope that a British school of original musical burlesques in the vein of Offenbach's greatest triumphs might develop there. However, having been innovative, the Swanboroughs found that their public apparently preferred familiar music as the accompaniment to their burlesque songs, and they returned to the old habit of decorating their entertainments with popular tunes. Although they later revived *L'Africaine* (Strand Theatre 15 April 1876), there were but few further original musical pieces produced under their regime.

A *L'Africaine* burlesque was produced at the Euclid Avenue Opera House, Cleveland, 24 February 1876, by amateurs "for the benefit of the Centennial Committee." It was probably not Burnand's one. Another was mounted at Marseille's Théâtre du Gymnase in January 1867.

DIE AFRIKAREISE Operette in 3 acts by Richard Genée and Moritz West. Music by Franz von Suppé. Theater an der Wien, Vienna, 17 March 1883.

The initial production of *Die Afrikareise* followed not only hard behind Suppé's own greatest successes (*Boccaccio, Gasparone, Donna Juanita*), but also on the heels of the Theater an der Wien's overwhelming triumph with the first run of Millöcker's *Der Bettelstudent* and, although it was unable to come up to the level of success of these enduring shows, it nevertheless had a respectable first run of a month in Vienna and won itself a large number of further productions on both sides of the Atlantic.

Genée and West's story dealt with a dubious adventurer called Miradillo (Alexander Girardi) who, stranded penniless in Cairo, is paid to pose as the husband of Titania Fanfani (Karoline Finaly) when that lady needs to produce a husband in order to claim an inheritance of two million local crowns. However, her uncle, Fanfani Pasha (Karl Blasel), the trustee who is supposed to deliver said crowns, has squandered the money and, as part of his attempts to hide the fact, whisks the couple away to his desert villa. Miradillo's sweetheart Tessa (Marie-Theresia Massa) and her mother Buccametta (Therese Schäfer) turn up, Titania falls in love with a Bedouin chief, Antarsid (Josef Joseffy), and all sorts of amorous and kidnapping complications ensue before the right couples are finally paired up. The naughty Pasha suffers the traditional operettic fate of his kind and gets lumbered for life with the garrulous Buccametta.

Following its original Vienna run, the piece was produced in Germany—playing in Nuremberg, Lübeck, Teplitz and Stettin before finding a spot in the repertoire at the Friedrich-Wilhelmstädtisches Theater in Berlin—and in Hungary (ad Lajos Evva, Jenő Rákosi). It was particularly well received in America, at first in a German-language production mounted at the Thalia-Theater with no less a star than Marie Geistinger playing Titania alongside Alexander Klein (Miradillo), Ernst Schütz (Antarsid), Emma Seebold (Tessa) and Thaller (Fanfani), and then in an English-language production (ad Emil Schwab) at the Bijou Theater, Boston. Vienna's Georgine von Januchowsky (Titania) starred alongside W H Fessenden (Miradillo), Harry Brown (Fanfani) and George W Traverner (Antarsid), "the electric light was used to represent the rising of the River Nile," the show was acclaimed as "a fine successor to *Iolanthe* and *The Beggar Student* on the Bijou boards," and it did so well that its initially intended season was extended.

A Trip to Africa was soon to be seen featured in comic opera seasons and repertoires all around America—played in both German and in English and everywhere with success—and the English-language version was produced twice on Broadway. John and James Duff brought the show in during the November following Boston's hit, with Marie Conron (Titania), Charles Stanley (Fanfani), A L King (Antarsid) and Mae St John (Tessa) playing alongside Klein (repeating his role in English) for just under three months of a season enlivened by the English-language debut of Emma Seebold who, having played Tessa at the Thalia, apparently now took turns at playing both Titania and Antarsid. In 1887 (11 April) the show was revived at the Standard, when Lillian Russell starred as Titania in a high-powered cast including J H Ryley (Fanfani), Eugène Oudin (Antarsid), C W Dungan (Miradillo) and Zelda Seguin (Buccametta) for a five-week season, and it reappeared yet again in 1889 at the German-language Terrace Garten, and once more as late as 1898 when the Castle Square Opera Company included it in their New York repertoire season. In this production the young Raymond Hitchcock appeared as Fanfani Pasha, with the unrisen Frank Moulan in the tiny role of the peddler Nakid, first played at the Standard by D'Oyly Carte veteran Fred Clifton.

Die Afrikareise was revived in Vienna in a revised version, with a new libretto by Fritz Lunzer, at the Wiener Bürgertheater (14 June 1924) with Grete Holm (Titania), Fritz Imhoff (Miradillo), Robert Nästlberger (Antarsid) and Bruno Wiesner (Fanfani) and another remade version was produced at Berlin's Theater des Volkes in 1936 (ad Arthur Bauckner, Andreas Zeltner) under the title *Abenteuer in Afrika* (17 October), but ultimately the piece, in spite of its early success, survived less well on European stages than *Der Bettelstudent, Boccaccio* or even *Gasparone.*

Plate 3. **After the Ball.** *Peter Graves and Vanessa Lee as the musical Lord and Lady Windermere.*

Germany: Saison Theater, Nuremberg 10 June 1883, Friedrich-Wilhelmstädtisches Theater, Berlin 30 January 1884; Hungary: Népszínház *Afrikautazó* 25 September 1883; USA: Thalia-Theater (Ger) 27 December 1883, Bijou Theater, Boston *A Trip to Africa* 21 February 1884, Standard Theater *A Trip to Africa* 23 November 1884

AFTER THE BALL Musical play (opérette) in 3 (later 2) acts by Noël Coward, based on Oscar Wilde's *Lady Windermere's Fan.* Globe Theatre, London, 10 June 1954.

Coward's musical adaptation of Wilde's popular play suffered badly from the remolding that was made due to its casting: Mary Ellis, cast as the pivotal Mrs Erlynne, proved over-parted vocally, leading to her role being musically cut on the run in to London, while what had been, in the play, the peripheral role of Mr Hopper (Graham Payn) was unsuitably enlarged, and Seamus

Locke, the dashing Irish tenor, proved no actor in what should have been the important role of Darlington. Many squalls and alterations after its out-of-town opening, the show reached London to a lukewarm reception and an indifferent run of 188 performances. Like Coward's other less-than-successful stage works, the show nevertheless had its takeaway gems: the comical "A Little Something on a Tray" and "Why Is It [Always] the Woman Who Pays?," Payn's tongue-in-cheek Australian chanty, and the melodious "I Knew That You Would Be My Love" sung by Lord and Lady Windermere (Peter Graves, Vanessa Lee), but the piece as a whole proved to have only a little appeal.

A severely butchered version of the show (ad Barry Day), which nevertheless restored much of Mrs Erlynne's cut material, was presented in 1999 at London's Covent Garden Festival.

USA: Lambertville, NJ 2 August 1955
Recording: original cast (Philips)

AFTER THE GIRL Revusical comedy in 2 acts by Paul Rubens. Lyrics by Percy Greenbank and Paul Rubens. Music by Paul Rubens. Gaiety Theatre, London, 7 February 1914.

The last of the "Girl" musicals at the Gaiety Theatre, this semi-plotless entertainment showed the rising influence of the newly fashionable variety-revue shows both in its shape and its subtitle. With George Edwardes ill and dying, his stage director Pat Malone took over the effective production of this Paul Rubens musical which was, in essence, little more than a series of song, dance and comedy scenes strung together around the character of Miss Doris Pitt (Isobel Elsom) as she was—for various reasons, or none at all—chased by much of the rest of the cast (Lew Hearn and Bonita, Mabel Sealby, Mlle Caumont, Guy Le Feuvre, Willie Stephens) through various picturesque Continental towns. In spite of plenty of lavish production detail and some competent work in Rubens's script and songs, *After the Girl*—with none of the old Gaiety's big names in its bill—failed to catch on with London audiences and closed after 105 performances, ending an era at the Gaiety Theatre.

The show did, however, win itself subsequent productions in areas where Gaiety shows had become popular fare, including a mounting in Australia where Thelma Raye was featured as Doris and her pursuers included veteran Maggie Moore as Mrs Pitt.

Australia: His Majesty's Theatre, Sydney 7 August 1915

AGES AGO Musical legend in 1 act by W S Gilbert. Music by Frederic Clay. Gallery of Illustration, London, 22 November 1869.

A short comic piece written by Gilbert and Clay for the German Reed family entertainment at the Gallery of Illustration, *Ages Ago* featured a scene in which the ancestral paintings of Castle Cockaleekie came to life to point out to penniless Columbus Hebblethwaite (Arthur Cecil) where he might find the proof of his ownership of the castle. Gilbert later reused the conceit in his full-length *Ruddigore.* Reed himself played Sir Ebenezer Tare, Fanny Holland his daughter and Hebblethwaite's beloved, Rose, Mrs Reed was the housekeeper Mistress Maggie McMotherly and Edward L Connell the servant, Angus McTavish, all four doubling as the paintings in the central scene.

Set with a delightful comic operetta score, *Ages Ago* proved to be one of the German Reeds' greatest successes and it was played for several seasons as part of their entertainment (Gallery of Illustration [abridged] 11 July 1870, St George's Hall 20 April 1874, 21 November 1882) whilst also getting theatre showings in America, where (after being first produced by amateurs in a heavily botched version) it shared a Broadway bill with the Reeds' *Charity Begins at Home* (60 performances) before going round the country, and in Australia, where it was played, as in London, as part of a drawing room entertainment in a double bill with *Cox and Box.*

The most recent London performance was given by Morley Opera at King's College 4 and 6 June 1988.

USA: Bijou Theater 31 March 1880; Australia: Victoria Hall, Sydney 3 February 1882

AGGIUNGI UN POSTO A TAVOLA Musical comedy in 2 acts by Pietro Garinei, Sandro Giovannini and Iaia Fiastri based on *After Me the Deluge* by "David Forrest." Music by Armando Trovaioli. Teatro Sistina, Rome, 8 December 1974.

The most widely successful of the many musical plays produced by Italy's Garinei and Giovannini, *Aggiungi un posto a tavola* (bring up a chair to the table) was based on an English novel following the religious and amorous predicaments of a pretty priest (Johnny Dorelli) summoned by the ringing off-stage voice of God (Renato Turi) to be the Noah of the 20th century. In spite of the mocking of unbelievers, headed by the local low-comedy mayor (Paolo Panelli) and distracting temptations of the flesh as represented by ingenue Clementina (Daniela Goggi), our hero builds his ark and ultimately manages to save the world from a second inundation.

The show's Italian production broke every local record with a run of 630 performances, and Spain (*El Diluvio que viene* ad Giorgi, Damasco), Mexico and South America (Chile, Argentine, Venezuela, Brazil) took with a vigorous will to the show's priestly comedy and catchy melodies, its on-stage construction of a vast ark, and the new-worldly appearance of a dove loosed from the gallery. The show went down less well in less Latin countries, particularly in Britain (ad ''David Forrest,'' Leslie Bricusse), where the celibacy of the priesthood, as represented again by Dorelli until a street accident had him replaced by Australian Andrew Sharp and then by Germany's Freddy Quinn, was hardly the burning topic it was in Catholic countries and—witness the famous *Pfarrer von Kirchfeld* of Anzengruber— in earlier times, and where some of its other comedy, its staging and its translation seemed too unsophisticated.

Vienna's Theater an der Wien took a change from its run of British and American musicals to mount *Evviva amico* (ad Peter Turrini, Olympia Gineri, Peter Orthofer) and Quinn starred in a production in Germany (where Garinei and Giovannini's works found regular productions), which was entitled *Himmel Arche und Wolkenbruch* (ad Orthofer, Karl Vibach). The show was revived in Italy in 1990.

Austria: Theater an der Wien *Evviva amico* 19 November 1976; Germany: Bühnen der Hansestadt, Lübeck *Himmel Arche und Wolkenbruch* 9 June 1977; UK: Adelphi Theatre *Beyond the Rainbow* 9 November 1978

Recordings: original cast (CGD, 2 records), London cast (MCA), Spanish cast (EMI/Regal, 2 records), Mexican cast (EMI, 2 records), Italian revival cast (CGD, 2 records)

AHLERS, Anny (b Hamburg, 21 December 1907; d London, 26 March 1933).

Born into a circus family, Anny Ahlers first went on the stage at the age of four. After juvenile appearances in Hamburg and, following the war, in Vienna, she worked as a chorus dancer and then a singer, graduated to small roles, and made her earliest notable adult appearances in Hamburg as an 18-year-old Venus in *Orpheus in der Unterwelt* and in Krefeld in the title role of *Gräfin Mariza.*

The red-haired, blue-eyed singer then progressed to Breslau where she made a considerable success as Amy in the original production of Künneke's *Lady Hamilton,* and she was subsequently introduced to Vienna as a leading lady in the title role of a revival of Fall's *Madame Pompadour* and to Berlin as Barberina in Erik Charell's spectacular Strauss pasticcio *Casanova* (1928). She played in Vienna in 1929–30 in revivals of *Die Bajadere* (Odette) and *Der lustige Krieg* (Violetta), and the productions of *Das Veilchen vom Montmartre* (Ninon) and *Hotel Stadt-Lemberg* (Anna), then at Berlin's Metropoltheater in the title role of *Viktória und ihr Husar,* in *Der Zarewitsch,* as the original Princess Laya in Ábrahám's *Die Blume von Hawaii,* in *Der Vogelhändler,* and opposite Richard Tauber as the heroine of the Johann Strauss pasticcio *Das Lied der Liebe.* She also appeared on the musical screen as *Die Marquise von Pompadour* (1931) and in *Die Faschingsfee* (1931).

In 1932 she went to London to play Jeanne, the title role of the revised version of Millöcker's *Gräfin Dubarry* (*Die Dubarry*) created in Berlin by Gitta Alpár. She scored a great personal success, but 11 months into the show's long run, the 25-year-old star committed suicide by throwing herself from the window of her Duchess Street lodgings.

AHRENS, Lynn (b New York, 1 October 1948).

Librettist and lyricist for a group of the more successful American turn-of-the-21st-century musicals, Ahrens worked in advertising and in children's television before combining with Stephen Flaherty in the early 1980s to write musicals. Their first produced piece was *Lucky Stiff* (1988), a comedy musical based on the how-to-get-rid-of-the-body novel *The Man Who Broke the Bank at Monte Carlo,* which caught the eye, and several awards, when it was produced for a brief season at Playwrights Horizons in 1988.

Their second work together, the West Indian musical *Once on This Island,* based on Rosa Guy's romantic novel *My Love, My Love,* was nurtured in the same fruitful surroundings, and this one progressed to Broadway where it provided some unpretentious entertainment for 487 performances before going on to be seen to less effect in Britain (145 performances).

A musicalization of the screenplay *My Favorite Year* was a quick failure, but Ahrens had a more profitable hand the following year in the Madison Square Garden Christmas spectacular based on Dickens's *A Christmas Carol,* before the partners went on to score their most substantial success to date, providing the music and lyrics to Terrence McNally's dulcified adaptation of the E L Doctorow novel *Ragtime.*

In the wake of their subsequent success, the little *Lucky Stiff* was seen both in London (Bridewell Theatre 27 August 1998) and in Germany (Saarländisches Staatstheater, Saarbrücken 6 March 1998, Staatstheater Cottbus 8 May 1999).

Ahrens and Flaherty also provided the songs for the animated film *Anastasia* (1998).

1988 **Lucky Stiff** (Stephen Flaherty) Playwrights Horizons 25 April

1990 **Once on This Island** (Flaherty) Playwrights Horizons, New York 6 May; Booth Theater 18 October

1993 **My Favorite Year** (Flaherty/Joseph Dougherty) Lincoln Center 10 December

1994 **A Christmas Carol** (Alan Mencken/w Mike Ockrent) Madison Square Garden Theatre 1 December

1996 **Ragtime** (Flaherty/Terrence McNally) Ford Center, Toronto 8 December; Ford Center, New York 18 January 1998

2000 **Seussical** (Flaherty) Richard Rodgers Theater 30 November

AIMÉE, Marie [TRONCHON, Célestine Marie Aimée] (b Lyon, 1846; d Auteuil, 2 October 1887).

Plate 4. **Marie Aimée.** *America's queen of the opéra-bouffe stage.*

French actress and singer who became America's foremost star of opéra-bouffe.

The illegitimate daughter of a certain Mlle Tronchon (who gave out, in later years, that her child had been born in Algeria), the Lyonnaise "Mlle Aimée" is said to have made her first theatrical appearance in Rio de Janeiro at the age of 14, and she was still admitting to being no more than a teenager when she began starring in opéra-bouffe at the capitol of opéra-bouffe itself, Paris's Théâtre des Variétés. She created the lead ingenue roles of Princess Girandole in Delibes's *La Cour du Roi Pétaud* (1869) and of Fiorella in Offenbach's *Les Brigands* (1869), appeared in Hortense Schneider's famous role of *La Belle Hélène* on the very stage where Schneider had triumphed just a few years earlier (1869, "she does not please so well as . . ."), starred opposite José Dupuis as Loïse in *Le Beau Dunois* (1870) and replaced the temperamental Schneider during rehearsals in the title role of Margot in the first production of Offenbach's only semi-successful *La Boulangère a des écus.* She also became amorously linked with Variétés manager, Eugène Bertrand, leading Schneider to the famous pun against the manager who had sacked her: "beaucoup lui sera pardonné parce qu'il a . . . Aimée."

Aimée toured through Europe and then, carried on the crest of the internationally rising opéra-bouffe wave and sped on her way by the Franco-Prussian war and the siege of Paris, she took an engagement to play opéra-bouffe in America. She set foot in America on 15 December 1870 and made her debut at New York's Grand Opera House six days later, under the management of Messrs Grau and Chizzola, as Boulotte in *Barbe-Bleue.* The new French star was greeted with delighted acclaim by American audiences and thereafter she toured the country widely and continuously, through the 1870s, at the head of her own company, with a large and ever-up-to-dated repertoire of opéras-bouffes and opéras-comiques. The company made regular visits to New York to perform the latest pieces and a quick-changing bill of former favorites and wandered to the limits of the continent ("Mlle Aimée's receipts during eight weeks in Havana [1873] amounted to 107,000 dollars, and in Mexico, in seven weeks, to 59,000 dollars in gold . . .") as Aimée established herself, by her regular presence and her superior comic abilities, as the country's foremost star of the opéra-bouffe genre. During his 1876 visit to America, Offenbach conducted her company is a number of his works in New York, Philadelphia, Chicago, etc.

Aimée made several return visits to France and, when she lost some of the fortune she had amassed in America in trying to run theatres in Brussels and in Rouen, she swiftly crossed the Atlantic once more to recoup her losses. Finally, after having for more than a decade performed to her American audiences only in French, she got up one English song, "Pretty as a Picture," to add some by now necessary novelty to her performance. Then, when the opéra-bouffe fashion (and her voice) had fairly thoroughly died, she ventured out in a slightly musical comedy called *Mam'selle* (Kingston, NY 11 September 1884, Toinette) specially constructed to her needs by G H Jessop and Willie Gill. She was able to use what should have been the springboard to a second career for only a short while, for she developed an ovarian tumor and returned to France for surgery. In 1886 she agreed to return to America to play, in English, the title role in the local adaptation of Millöcker's *Die Jungfrau von Belleville,* but she went out instead in her old vehicle, *Mam'selle, Divorçons* and in the title role of a piece called *Marita,* manufactured for her on the bones of a Sardou play. She added a song-studded version of the Parisian farce *Si jamais je te pince* (*Caught in the Act* ad Newton Calspell, mus: Arthur Selden, et al) to her repertoire at Christmas 1886. Soon after, however, performing proved beyond her strength and, after two years of struggle against cancer, she died at her home in Paris's Rue Chanez. Her death certificate reveals that she was not 35, as all had been led to suppose, but 41 years old.

Tending to the then fashionably well-rounded, Aimée combined a useful singing voice with a light and breezy comedy style which led Odell to describe her as "the most arch, the most piquant, the most attractive of all the artists in [the opéra-bouffe] line seen on the American stage." Another contemporary declared that "one of the most consummate and artistic bits of comedy acting ever witnessed in this country was Aimée's singing of the drinking song in *La Périchole,*" whilst Allston Brown simply commented "as a satiric artist her equal has never trod the American stage." In France, however, unlike Paola Marié or Anna Judic, with whom she competed successfully abroad, Marie Aimée was never considered a star of the first rank, and the failure of the first production of *La Boulangère* was charged largely to her lack of personality and presence at its center.

Aimée's American repertoire included, at various periods, Offenbach's *La Grande-Duchesse de Gérolstein, Barbe-Bleue, Les Brigands, La Périchole, La Boulangère a des écus, La Belle Hélène, La Jolie Parfumeuse, Madame Favart, La Vie parisienne, Lischen et Fritzchen, Le Pont des soupirs, Geneviève de Brabant, La Princesse de Trébizonde* and *Les Géorgiennes,* Lecocq's *Fleur de thé, Les Cent Vierges, Giroflé-Girofla, La Marjolaine, La Petite Mariée, Le Petit Duc, La Princesse des Canaries* and *La Fille de Madame Angot,* Hervé's *Le Petit Faust, L'Oeil crevé* and *La Belle Poule,* Planquette's *Les Cloches de Corneville,* Maillart's *Les Dragons de Villars,* Johann Strauss's frenchified *La Reine Indigo,* Suppé's *Boccaccio,* Balfe's *The Bohemian Girl* and Vasseur's *La Timbale d'Argent,* a good number of which she introduced to American audiences. She also introduced Bizet's "Habañera" to America, before *Carmen* as a whole had been played on the left-hand side of the Atlantic.

ALADDIN

The dramatic story of Aladdin and his Wonderful Lamp originated in the collection of oriental tales known as the *Arabian Nights' Entertainment* and the boy with the genie seems to have been first introduced to the musical stage in Denmark. However, his initial appearance in the English-language theatre was, to all evidence, in a pantomime at Covent Garden, on Boxing Day of 1788, in a version of the story dramatized by John O'Keefe with music by William Shield. The tale was thereafter used as the basis for a number of British theatre pieces including an unsuccessful "fairy opera in three acts" with a score by Henry Bishop (Drury Lane 29 April 1826). Continental authors and composers also took to the subject around the same time, and amongst the musical Aladdins which appeared in the early part of the 19th century were Nicolas Isouard's opera *Aladin, ou La Lampe merveilleuse* (Opéra, Paris 6 February 1822), Wenzel Müller's spectacular four-act magical comic opera *Die Wunderlampe* (Prague, 1810), Adalbert Gyrowetz's one-act Vienna Singspiel *Aladin, oder Die Wunderlampe* (Hoftheater 7 February 1819), an opera by Luigi Ricci (*L'abbate Taccarella, ovvero Aladino*) produced in Naples in 1825, and yet another by Gustave Rader mounted in 1855 at Dresden (*Aladin, oder Die Wunderlampe* 4 March).

As the age of burlesque got under way, the spectacular fairy stories of the Arabian Nights fell into the hands of the specialists of that genre and were developed by them into adventures which were much more humorous than dreadful and magical. Gilbert a' Beckett's *Aladdin, or The Wonderful Lamp in a New Light* (Princess's Theatre 4 July 1844) and James Kenney and Albert Smith's *Aladdin* for the Lyceum Theatre (5 August 1844) were the earliest efforts of the kind, but H J Byron's Strand Theatre burlesque *Aladdin, or The Wonderful Scamp* (1 April 1861), which introduced the characters of Widow Twankay and Prince Pekoe into the original fairy tale for the first time as part of a version which made great play with the terms of the tea trade, largely surpassed all previous *Aladdins* in popularity. From that time onwards, Byron's version of the tale became the standard *Aladdin,* and his burlesque was widely used in the latter decades of the 19th century as a first part for Christmas pantomimes. The tale was, nevertheless, also used as the subject for other British burlesques, notably Frank Green's 1874 piece (Charing Cross Theatre 23 December), Robert Reece's Gaiety Theatre *Aladdin* (24 December 1881) and the pasticcii which Lydia Thompson and her blondes and their imitators toured through America in the 1870s, as well as for such American novelties as the Chicago spectacular *Aladdin, or the Wonderful Lamp,* penned by Alfred Thompson (Opera House 4 June 1887) and subsequently played on Broadway as *The Arabian Nights,* and the 1895 *Aladdin Jr* (W H Batchelor, Jesse Greer, W F Glover/J Cheever Goodwin, Broadway Theater 6 April).

In France, Hostein produced a spectacular féerie by Adolphe d'Ennery and Hector Crémieux under the title *Aladin, ou La Lampe merveilleuse* (mus: A de Groot, 3 October 1863, 102 performances) at the newly opened Théâtre du Châtelet, and this piece of machinery-and-scenery theatre was taken up and rewrought for Broadway as a spectacle called *Baba* (Niblo's Gardens, Max Maretzek/Arnold, Sherwood, 18 September 1876). It was so spectacular that it sent the theatre bankrupt. A Danish "adventure-opera" composed by Christian Horneman was mounted in Copenhagen in 1888 (18 November), but by far the most substantial light musical-theatre *Aladdin* of the second half of the 19th century was Alfred Thompson's opéra-bouffe *Aladdin II* composed by Hervé and produced at London's Gaiety Theatre (23 December 1870) and subsequently at Paris's Théâtre des Folies-Dramatiques (*Le Nouvel Aladin*).

The 20th century brought several other musicals using the elements of the tale of the magic lamp, including John Philip Sousa's *Chris and the Wonderful Lamp* (Victoria Theater, New York 1 January 1900), the Gaiety Theatre extravaganza *The New Aladdin* (29 September 1906) with a score by Ivan Caryll and Lionel Monckton, Caryll's highly successful *Chin-Chin,* produced at New York's Globe Theater (20 October 1914) with Montgomery and Stone starred, Rip's Parisian art-nouveau ''opérette féerie'' with music by Willy Redstone and decors by Bakst (Théâtre Marigny 21 May 1919), Cole Porter's television musical (NBC 21 February 1958) subsequently staged at the London Coliseum (17 December 1959), Sandy Wilson's *Aladdin* for the Lyric, Hammersmith (21 December 1979), and the Italian musical show *Accendiamo la Lampada* (30 December 1979), while in 1995 a new Danish version (Sebastian [Knud Christiansen]/ Pierre Westerdahl, Flemming Enevold)—more than two centuries after the one that had started the whole thing going—was mounted at the Gladsaxe Theater (19 February). However, in spite of this proliferation of genie-in-the-lamp pieces it is as a British pantomime subject that *Aladdin* has principally survived its two centuries on the stage.

In 1992 a Disney animated film version with songs by Alan Menken, Howard Ashman and Tim Rice was released.

Recordings: TV (Porter version), London cast (Porter version), original cast (Wilson version), *Accendiamo la lampada* (Cam)

ALADDIN II, or An Old Lamp in a New Light Operatic extravaganza in 5 scenes by Alfred Thompson. Music by Hervé. Gaiety Theatre, London, 23 December 1870.

Aladdin II was John Hollingshead's first venture with an original musical at the Gaiety Theatre, where he had hitherto relied—through the two years of the house's existence—on pasticcio entertainments and French shows. It was written by Alfred Thompson, the theatre's ''resident'' playwright, who had contributed to the very first Gaiety bill in 1868, and composed by the French musician Hervé, whose *Chilpéric* and *Le Petit Faust* had been among the first and biggest opéra-bouffe hits in London. A cleverly plotted burlesque version of the favorite tale, it featured star comedians Johnnie Toole and Nellie Farren in its principal roles of the nasty shopkeeper-magician, Ko-kil-ko, and the umpteenth lad called Aladdin whom he has taken on as shopboy, hoping to find a descendant of the original boy who might lead him to the famous lamp of old. Toole's catchphrase ''Still I am not happy'' became the saw of the town and the show scored sufficient success for it to be taken on tour in Toole's repertoire and later re-presented for a second run at the Gaiety (24 February 1872). Elsewhere, the piece had no luck. A Paris production (ad Hervé) folded prematurely through the fault of an amateurish management, and an American production, announced for Broadway's Bijou Theatre as late as 1884, did not eventuate.

Thompson was later credited as the author of a *The Arabian Nights* mounted at the Chicago Opera House (4 June 1887) and again at New York's Standard Theater (12 September 1887) which was, in fact, a version of *Aladdin.* Hervé had no credit, and the cast list ran very differently from the Gaiety one, so evidently the piece was not—in its primaries at least—taken from *Aladdin II.*

The villain's name, Ko-kil-ko, a borrowing from the French stage where it had been heard just months previously in L'Eveillé's opérette *Le Fils à Ko-kli-ko* (Folies-Marigny, 10 September 1869) was probably a forerunner of W S Gilbert's ultimately more famous Ko-ko (*The Mikado*).

France: Folies-Nouvelles *Le Nouvel Aladin* 16 December 1871

À LA JAMAÏQUE Opérette in 2 acts by Raymond Vincy. Music by Francis Lopez. Théâtre de la Porte-Saint-Martin, Paris, 24 January 1954.

Another success from the Vincy/Lopez mill, *À la Jamaïque* was a vehicle for the comedienne Jane Sourza who starred as one Annie Krushen, a sometime charcutière from Saint-Antoine who has become the happy heiress to a chain of American snack bars. Annie's only remaining problem in life is to find a man—for, in spite of 18 engagements, she hasn't yet got one to the altar. This is because none of the 18, in the run-up to matrimony, has proven to have the qualities Annie so appreciates in the heroes of the romantic novels of Maxime de Saint-Maxient (Jacques Moret), and she's sent each one away, unwed, with a snack bar as a consolation prize. This chain-weakening largesse worries Annie's business manager, Siméon Legrand (Pasquali), who finally decides he will wed Annie himself and enlists the help of the novelist with the promise of a share in the spoils. Annie, of course, ends up wedding not her manager but her author, but not before a sexy Jamaican called Manoël Martinez (Jacques de Mersan) has played red herring and dragged everyone off to his island for a splash of traditional second-act scenery, some Caribbean-flavored dances and songs, and a few quiproquos involving Manoel's lady friend Olivia (chief soprano Maria Candido), a private detective called Peter Noster (Rogers), his Rita-Hayworthy assistant Gilda (Gisèle Robert) and a selection of other colorful folk.

Lopez decorated *À la Jamaïque*'s jolly tale with a predictable set of numbers, the Porte-Saint-Martin stage held the ''grand spectacle'' of the piece well, and the result was a run of nearly a year and a half, after which Mlle Sourza went off to put a version of the show on celluloid. Mlle Robert repeated her stage role on the screen, and the other principal roles were taken by Luis Mariano (Manoël), Darry Cowl (Peter Noster), Fernand Sardou (Legrand) and Orbal (Saint-Maxient).

The show retained a place in the list of Lopez revivables, and it was subsequently given a fresh showing in Paris in a revival at the Théâtre de la Renaissance as well as continuing to turn up in intermittent provincial productions with some regularity for something like half a century.

Film: André Berthomieu 1958

Recording: film cast star (EP) (HMV)

ALBERY, Donald [Rolleston] (Sir) (b London, 19 June 1914; d Monte Carlo, 14 September 1988). British producer and theatre-owner whose list of hits included a number of musicals.

Donald Albery was a descendant of a famous theatrical family, headed by the author **James Albery** (b Southwark, 4 May 1838; d London, 15 August 1889) and his wife Mary Moore (1862–1931). It was she, Mrs/Lady Charles Wyndham [Culverwell] en secondes noces, who, by carrying on the operation of the significant theatrical holdings originally run by Wyndham (London's Criterion, Wyndham's and New Theatres), consolidated what was to be the firm subsequently run by her son, Bronson Albery, and then by his son, Donald.

Although the Criterion, Wyndham's and the New were conceived and operated as playhouses, each was occasionally sublet to house less-than-large-sized musical pieces under the Wyndham regime—*Bilberry of Tilbury, All Abroad, The White Chrysanthemum* (Criterion), *The Girl Behind the Counter* (Wyndham's), *Amasis, The Laughing Husband* (New)—and, similarly, in a family which was known generally for its considerable activities on the 19th-century straight stage, some contribution to the musical stage was to be found.

James Albery himself, best known as the author of such pieces as the highly popular *Two Roses* and the English version of *Pink Dominos,* was also responsible for a not-very-successful musical "romantic legend" in rhyming couplets called *Oriana* (Globe Theatre, 1873, mus: Frederic Clay) and the "fairy spectacular extravaganza" *The Will of Wise King Kino,* played at the Princess's Theatre later the same year, as well as a short operetta *The Spectre Knight* (1878, mus: Alfred Cellier) which the young D'Oyly Carte produced to supplement the original productions of *The Sorcerer* and *HMS Pinafore* at the Opera Comique. He also adapted the vaudeville *La Femme à papa* for an English production under the title *The Mulberry Bush.* Mary Moore's elder sister, Haidée Crofton, who was to have a good second-string career as a performer in the musical theatre, succeeded to the role of Hebe in the same *HMS Pinafore.*

Under the management of Bronson Albery, the theatre group continued to house principally plays, but they chalked up the longest single run in their history when Wyndham's Theatre took in the small-scale musical *The Boy Friend* (1954) for what turned out to be a memorable run of 2,084 performances.

Donald himself began in the theatre at a young age, acting as wartime manager of the Sadler's Wells ballet between 1941 and 1945, but it was 1953 before he began a career as a producer. His ventures were eclectic, often unusual, often adventurous, and included such pieces as Graham Greene's *The Living Room* (1953) and Beckett's *Waiting for Godot* (1955) as well as Anouilh's *The Waltz of the Toreadors* and the play *Gigi* (1956). He produced his first musical (w Neil Crawford) when he transferred *Grab Me a Gondola* (1956) from Windsor's Theatre Royal to the West End, and followed up with an unfortunate musical version of Max Beerbohm's *Zuleika Dobson* (*Zuleika,* 1957) before striking a major hit with the English version of *Irma la Douce* (London, 1958, and New York, 1960).

A close working connection with the Theatre Royal, Stratford East, where Joan Littlewood had established her Theatre Workshop, resulted in his making the transfer of a number of notable plays from that venue (*A Taste of Honey* 1959, *The Hostage* 1959) as well as two successful and widely differing musicals: the excellent *Make Me an Offer,* and the lively, amateurish *Fings Ain't Wot They Used t'Be.* His major success, however, came with a musical originally destined for Stratford, which outgrew that intention: Lionel Bart's piece of musical Dickens, *Oliver!* (1960), which ran for six years at the New Theatre prior to being performed around the world.

In 1962 Albery took over from his father at the head of the theatre group, adding a fourth house to their holdings with the purchase of the Piccadilly Theatre, the only freehold property of the set. He had another fine success with the revue *Beyond the Fringe,* but subsequent musical ventures were less profitable: the oversized *Blitz!* (1962) held up for 16 months, but a production of the American musical *Fiorello!* (1962) failed at the Piccadilly, *The Perils of Scobie Prilt* (1963) closed out of town and a tacky rip-off of *La Cagnotte* called *Instant Marriage* (1964) stayed on for a run simply to occupy the Piccadilly Theatre, where *Man of La Mancha* (1968, 1969) proved much better if less long-lived fare.

Whilst the play successes continued (*Entertaining Mr Sloane* 1964, *The Prime of Miss Jean Brodie* 1966, etc), two further musicals by *Make Me an Offer*'s David Heneker, *Jorrocks* (1966) and *Popkiss* (1972), brought more pleasure than profit, and a transfer of the ragged *Mandrake* (1970) from the Bristol Old Vic brought neither, ending Albery's musical theatre career on an atypically downbeat but typically intuitive production.

He retired in 1978, selling his firm to Associated Newspapers Ltd with his son Ian (b 1939) left in charge, and with the New Theatre now rechristened, in honor of his father, the Albery Theatre. Subsequent financial dealings saw the firm, the theatres and Ian Albery change hands again in the 1980s.

Biography: (family) Trewin, W: *All on Stage: Charles Wyndham and the Alberys* (Harrap, London, 1980)

ALBINI, Felix [ALBINI, Srećko] (b Zupanje, 20 December 1869; d Agram [Zagreb], 18 April 1933).

The Croatian composer Albini trained in Vienna and in Graz, where he also fulfilled his earliest engagement as a conductor, and he made his first attempt at stage writing in the field of opera (*Marion* w Milan Smrekar, Kroatisches Theater, Zagreb, 1901). However, he found more significant success when he turned to the lighter musical field. His first Operette, *Der Nabob,* was played for 18 performances at Vienna's Carltheater in 1905 with Ferdinand Pagin and Therese Loewe in the featured roles, and was also subsequently staged in Budapest (*Az indiai nábob* Budai Színkör 2 July 1910, ad Emil Tabori), whilst his *Madame Troubadour* (1907), a version of the French comedy *La Petite Marquise,* first produced in Zagreb, was later seen in Germany (Stadttheater, Leipzig 27 November 1908) and in an English-language production sponsored by the Shuberts in America (Lyric Theatre, Philadelphia 7 April 1910, Lyric Theater, New York 10 October 1910, ad Joseph W Herbert, aka *The Little Parisienne*). America was a touch taken aback at a musical with "no chorus and no solos" (all the musical numbers being duos, trios and ensembles), but the piece toured staunchly in areas where chorus girls were not a sine qua non of the musical stage, and as a result the Shuberts ventured a bootless production of Albini's last work *The Barefoot Dancer* (ad Howard Jacot, Easton, Pa 27 June 1911).

Albini also composed the score for a musical version of Dickens's *A Christmas Carol* (*Ein Weihnachtsabend*) produced in Vienna in 1906, but his greatest success came with the 1908 Leipzig piece, *Baron Trenck [der Pandur],* which went on from its German premiere to productions in Austria, Hungary, Britain and America.

He subsequently became director of the Opera at Zagreb and, although he continued to write ballet and choral music and songs, from that time he closed down his career as a composer of Operette.

1905 **Der Nabob** (Leopold Krenn) Carltheater 23 September

1906 **Die kühle Blonde** 1 act Apollotheater 31 March

1906 **Ein Weihnachtsabend** (Max Foges) Wiener Colosseum 21 December

1907 **Madame Troubadour** (Bela Jenbach, Richard Pohl) National-Theater, Agram 7 April

1908 **Baron Trenck [der Pandur]** (A M Willner, Robert Bodanzky) Stadttheater, Leipzig 15 February; Stadttheater, Vienna 29 October 1909

1909 **Die kleine Baronesse** (Bodanzky) 1 act Apollotheater 31 March

1909 **Die Barfusstänzerin** (Jenbach) Altes Theater, Leipzig 28 August

ALDREDGE, Theoni V[achlioti] [VACHLIOTI, Theoni Athanasiou] (b Salonika, Greece, 22 August 1932). Greek-born artist who became one of Broadway's most successful costume designers in the 1960s and 1970s.

Trained at the Goodman Memorial Theater, Chicago, Mrs Aldredge participated in her first production there in 1950 and subsequently designed clothes for a number of regional play productions before moving to New York in 1957. One of her earliest Broadway assignments was on Geraldine Page's costumes for *Sweet Bird of Youth* (1959). She has since designed some 150 Broadway shows, moving into the musical theatre for the first time with *The Nervous Set* (1959), *I Can Get It for You Wholesale* (1962), *Mr President* (1962), *Anyone Can Whistle* (1964), *Hot September* (1965) and *Skyscraper* (1965), and clothed several notable successes, including *A Chorus Line* (1975), as part of a long association with Joseph Papp and the New York Shakespeare Festival.

Amongst the other musicals she has costumed are *A Time for Singing* (1966), *Illya Darling* (1967), *Billy* (1969), *Two Gentlemen of Verona* (1971), *Music! Music!* (1974), *The Threepenny Opera* (1976 revival), *Annie* (1977, Tony Award), *Ballroom* (1978), *The Grand Tour* (1979), *I Remember Mama* (1979), *Barnum* (1980, Tony Award), *42nd Street* (1980), *Onward Victoria* (1980), *Woman of the Year* (1981), *La Cage aux Folles* (1983), *Merlin* (1983), *Chess* (London, 1986), *Teddy and Alice* (1987), *Ziegfeld* (London, 1988), *Gypsy* (1989 revival), *Oh, Kay!* (1990 revival), *Annie 2* (1989), *Nick and Nora* (1991), *The Secret Garden* (1991), *The High Rollers Social and Pleasure Club* (1992), *Putting It Together* (1992), *Annie Warbucks* (1992), *Teddy and Alice* revival (1996), and *Annie* revival (1997).

She has also designed for film (*The Great Gatsby,* Academy Award), television, opera and ballet.

ALEXANDRA Operett in 3 acts by Ferenc Martos. Music by Albert Szirmai. Király Színház, Budapest, 25 November 1925.

Alexandra can probably be considered the most internationally successful of Szirmai's operetts, given the amount of traveling that the various versions of the show did. However, the alterations made during the piece's travels beyond Hungary and around the world were considerable, and most of the foreign versions of the show owed only a small debt to the original composer.

The Russian Grand-Duchess Alexandra (Erzsi Péchy) is to be married to the King of Illyria (Dezső Kertész). However, on the day that the ship comes to collect her, Russian revolution breaks out and Alexandra is forced into a hurried wedding with the captain of the ship, Torelli (Jenő Nádor), so that, as an Illyrian citizen, she may safely depart her native shores. It is a marriage which, two acts and much royal comedy later, stands good. Árpád Latábar (Count Szuvarov), Márton Rátkai (Prince Károly) and Nusi Somogyi supplied the humorous moments as supporting Illyrian aristocrats.

Szirmai's music was of his best, the romantic leads being particularly well supplied with the two waltz-refrained duos "Rözsák közt" and "Túl az üveghegyek kék ködén" which were the heart of the score. They were pieces with excitingly unobvious verses, and refrains which became only a little less inventive largely because tied to the familiar 3/4 pattern. A splendid guards' march for solo and chorus, which rattled exhilaratingly along at a rate more like a step dance than a parade-ground tune, the usual dance-based Hungarian-style soubret pieces ("Csókolj meg szép babám") and the hero's almost crooning praises of his "Kicsi feleség" (little wife) went to make up the highlights of a score of conventional proportions, but of well-above-average quality.

Clayton and Waller's London production of *Princess Charming* was the first foreign version of *Alexandra* to hit the boards. Anything as realistic as Russia and its revolution was unthinkable on the London musical stage, so Russia went out of the window and Ruritania stepped in. Winnie Melville (later Evelyn Laye) was Princess Elaine of Novia, John Clarke was Torelli, and adaptors Arthur Wimperis and Lauri Wylie worked in the role of Albert Chuff, an insurance man, for chief comic W H Berry. George Grossmith played Christian II of Sylvania and Alice Delysia was one sexy Wanda Navaro. Additional numbers were credited to Russell Bennett and producer Jack Waller (two apiece), but by the time Kalmar and Ruby's "Babyin' You" and Phil Charig's "Why Do You Roll those Eyes?" (both Delysia/Berry), Stransky's "Kisses" (Laye/Clarke), Hirsch's "Learn to Smile" (Laye) and Weston and Lee's comedy songs "Ninepence a Week" and "Not Old Enough to be Old" (Berry) had been inserted, little beyond Szirmai's concerted music was left, for all that he had sole musical billing. The resultant patchwork of a show, however, ran for 362 performances before going to the country.

Soon after the London opening, a rather less adulterated *Alexandra* (ad Paul Frank, Peter Herz) was mounted by Erich Müller at the Johann Strauss-Theater in Vienna. Emmi Kosáry starred as Alexandra alongside Gisa Kolbe (Krackowianskaja), Robert Nästlberger (Cäsar, ex- Torelli), Fritz Imhoff (Prince Karl Maria), Max Brod (Suwarov) and Manfred Kempel (King) through a fair run of 77 performances.

Italy saw its version of the show as *Mascherine russe* (which means they must have at least avoided Ruritania) but Australia's J C Williamson Ltd preferred to take up London's version of *Princess Charming* for its season in Sydney in 1928 with Cecil Kellaway (Chuff), Kathryn Reece (Elaine), Reginald Dandy (Torelli), Peter Gawthorne and Olive Sloane featured, and again, in Melbourne, nearly a decade later (Her Majesty's Theatre, February 1937) with Albert Frith, Romola Hansen and Herbert Browne in the lead roles. Broadway went one step further and remade the British remake (ad Jack Donahue, ballets by Albertina Rasch, add mus Arthur Schwartz, add ly Arthur Swanstrom, interpolated numbers Robert Dolan and Walter O'Keefe). Director Bobby Connolly and Swanstrom's production featured a cast including Evelyn Herbert and Robert Halliday in the romantic leads, and Grossmith, Victor Moore (now called Irving Huff) and Jeanne Aubert in comic support. A show which was very little of *Alexandra* if rather more of *Princess Charming* flopped in 56 performances.

Alexandra was, however, no longer Szirmai's even in a tiny part when the film version of *Princess Charming,* made in Britain by Gainsborough Films, with Miss Laye, Grossmith, Yvonne Arnaud and Max Miller starring, appeared in 1934. This time, all his music had gone, and only Ruritania and Albert Chuff—as impersonated by Miller—remained.

UK: Palace Theatre *Princess Charming* 21 October 1926; Austria: Johann Strauss-Theater 5 November 1926; Australia: Her Majesty's Theatre, Sydney *Princess Charming* 12 May 1928; USA: Imperial Theater *Princess Charming* 13 October 1930

Film: Gainsborough Films *Princess Charming* 1934

Recording: selection (part record) (Qualiton)

ALGERIA Musical play in 2 acts by Glen MacDonough. Music by Victor Herbert. Broadway Theater, New York, 31 August 1908.

Many years before *The Desert Song* was a twinkle in anyone's eye, Broadway librettist Glen MacDonough wandered into the operettic north African desert with the tale of *Algeria.* Zoradie (Ida Brooks Hunt), the Sultana of the Barakeesh, a powerful desert tribe, develops a passion for the pseudonymous author of the poem "Rose of the World" and determines to seek him out. When the comedians (Harry Tighe, Toby Lyons, Randall Davey), cast as a trio of French army deserters, have been disposed of as candidates, the right man turns out to be the

French Captain de Lome (George Leon Moore), commander of the Oasis of Sidi Ahmoud and nephew of the Governor General (William Pruette). The romantic tale was perforated with comedy from the deserters, and from Mr and Mrs Billings F Cooings from Paterson, New Jersey (Florence Nash, Eugene P Arnold), and with soubrettery from Millicent Madison MD (Harriet Burt), "an American girl practising medicine in the Middle East" (!).

Herbert decorated this book with a score that included two numbers as good as anything he had written: the soaring melody of Zoradie's "Rose of the World," brought back with pounding meaningfulness in the dramatic first-act finale, and her Eastern-rhythmic "Twilight in Barakeesh." The hero lilted out the much-used conceit that "Love Is Like a Cigarette," the soubrette hinted that you should "Ask Her While the Band Is Playing" and Pruette's star status meant that there were two basso numbers in the dozen that made up the score.

However, in spite of the charms of the score, Frank McKee's production of *Algeria* was not particularly well liked in New York, and after 49 performances it was closed and sent on the road with Helen Noldi now singing the part of the sultana. It was well received by the critics in Chicago but, if the stalls overflowed, the gallery and balcony stayed resolutely sparse and *Algeria* ended up in the red. Lew Fields, however, realized that there was something there worth saving. He took up the piece, had the libretto rewritten a little, and revived the show as *The Rose of Algeria* at the Herald Square Theater the following season (20 September 1909). Since the original stars, Miss Brooks Hunt and Pruette, were by then triumphing in the leading roles of Broadway's *The Chocolate Soldier,* he replaced them with Lillian Herlein and the other famous bass of the comic opera circuits, Eugene Cowles. Frank Pollock was the poetic hero, and the score little altered. The alterations were insufficient to allow more than 40 performances before touring time became imperative, and some fine music went to waste.

ALIAS, Charles [Georges] (b Paris, c1852; d London, 11 May 1921). The most famous name in British theatrical costumery in the second half of the 19th century.

The son of a French doctor, the young Alias fought alongside his father in the Franco-Prussian war where he is said to have lost the sight in one eye. Shortly after the war, he visited London's Philharmonic Theatre as a dresser with the French comic dance quartet, Les Clodoches, and there he met and married the costumier, Sarah Ann Price. Although Alias had no previous experience in the theatre, he joined his wife in setting up the freelance firm of M et Mme Alias & Co, sometimes designing and manufacturing, or more often just making up from the designs of such artists as Wilhelm or Faustin, the costumes for an ever-extending series of musical shows.

The Aliases made their mark in the West End when they provided the costumes for the original London production of *La Fille de Madame Angot* (1873) at the Philharmonic, and thereafter they costumed, either wholly or partly, many of London's most important musical productions, including the burlesques at the Gaiety Theatre (*The Bohemian G'yurl, Little Dr Faust, Gulliver, Il Sonnambulo, Pretty Esmeralda,* etc), the Royalty (*Madcap, Pluto,* etc), and the Strand (*The Lying Dutchman, L'Africaine, Nemesis, Loo, Antarctic, Champagne, The Baby, Intimidad,* etc), Gilbert's early *Tospyturveydom* and *Princess Toto,* Gilbert and Sullivan premieres at the Opera Comique (*The Pirates of Penzance*) and the Savoy (*Iolanthe*), the vast spectaculars at the Alhambra (*La Poule aux oeufs d'or,* etc) and, most noticeably, the long string of French opéras-bouffes and opéras-comiques which were produced in Britain in the 1870s and 1880s. These included the record-breaking *Les Cloches de Corneville* (for which the costume bill amounted to an unheard-of £300), *Les Noces d'Olivette, La Famille Trouillat* (*La Belle Normande*), *Le Jour et la nuit* (*Manola*), *La Timbale d'argent* (*The Duke's Daughter*), *La Marjolaine, Les Prés St Gervais* and most of the long string of adaptations from the French made by Alias's close friend Henry Farnie, and produced by Alexander Henderson.

Alias maintained a close connection with his homeland. His home in Soho Square became well known as a first stopping place for Frenchmen new to London and a congenial gathering place for theatricals, and he as a useful and friendly intermediary in various theatrical dealings between London and Paris. Hervé, Planquette, Chassaigne, Audran and Lecocq were all guests at Soho Square and the little costumier was said to have been instrumental in the brothers Mansell bringing Hervé and his *Chilpéric* (1870) to London, and thus helping set off the craze for opéra-bouffe which dominated the 1870s musical theatre in England. He also encouraged Planquette to work with H B Farnie on an original musical for Britain—the result of which was the enduring *Rip van Winkle.*

Alias & Co prospered in the 1880s, having a major success with their new costumes for the transferred version of the amazing *Dorothy,* and on into the 1890s by which stage they had become largely costume-makers rather than designers. Alias himself had by this time become one of the "characters" of the London theatre, always anxiously floating around the theatre asking "What time de repetition generale?" as an opening approached, but always punctually ready with the show's costumes on dress-rehearsal night.

When Mme Alias died (Brighton, 11 April 1897), Charles remarried and continued the business with his new wife, Mme Marie Wallet Floret, from the Paris Opéra wardrobe, up to his death.

ALI BABA [and the Forty Thieves]

One of the 19th-century favorites amongst the tales transferred to the stage from the *Arabian Nights' Entertainment, Ali Baba* became popular, most particularly in Britain, as an extravaganza and pantomime subject. It was, however, at first played as a genuine melodrama, and was seen at Drury Lane (Michael Kelly/R B Sheridan, Ward) as early as 1806 (8 April), and in New York in 1809 (20 March ad George Colman) before, like other such tales of cavalier gore, it turned from being drama to becoming a favorite topic for pantomime and burlesque.

Gilbert a' Beckett ventured an early extravaganza *Open Sesame, or a Night with the Forty Thieves* for the Lyceum (8 April 1844 w Mark Lemon), whilst Planché, H J Byron and the brothers Brough were among the collaborators on a memorable version of *The Forty Thieves* for the Brough Memorial Fund at the same house in 1860. Byron's highly successful Strand Theatre burlesque *Ali Baba and the Thirty Nine Thieves (in accordance with the Author's habit of ''taking one off'')* produced in 1863 was, like its definitive *Aladdin* counterpart, much used as a pantomime first part in the decades that followed. Lydia Thompson's company played an H B Farnie *Forty Thieves* subtitled *''Striking Oil in Family Jars''* and featuring an army of leggy thieves (Niblo's Garden 1 February 1869) all around America in the years that followed, and other *Ali Baba* burlesques included Robert Reece's *Ali Baba à la mode* (Gaiety Theatre, 1872) and *The Forty Thieves* (Gaiety Theatre, 1880) in Britain, as well as a heap of touring variants of Farnie's piece long played by bundles of burlesque blondes in the American regions.

Cherubini (Paris Opéra, 1833 to a libretto by no less authors than Scribe and Mélèsville), Bottesini (Lyceum 1871) and Max Brauer (*Morgiane,* Karlsruhe, 1899) each produced operatic *Ali Baba*s. In the musical theatre, France hosted a Cogniard brothers spectacular *Ali Baba, ou Les Quarante Voleurs* at the Cirque-Nationale (24 October 1853) at the same time that Ernest Dubreuil's drama of the same title was playing at the Théâtre Beaumarchais, and later an 1872 opérette by Adolphe Nibelle, *Les Quatre-Cents Femmes d'Ali Baba;* Berlin had an *Almazinde, oder der Höhle Sesam* as early as 1814; Britain the 1901 Terry's Theatre musical *The Thirty Thieves* (clearly hit by rising costs); and America a Harry B Smith *Ali Baba jr, or Morgiana and the Forty Thieves* (w Franklyn W Lee, John Gilbert, mus: W H Batchelor, et al) and Cheever Goodwin's Chicago burlesque-spectacular *Ali Baba,* retitled *An Arabian Girl and the Forty Thieves* (1899) for its seasons on Broadway. Each of these diverged somewhat from the original tale, as did Johann Strauss's setting of a version of the tale as *Indigo und die vierzig Räuber.*

Lecocq's 1887 opérette à grand spectacle, *Ali-Baba,* played first in Brussels (Théâtre de l'Alhambra 11 November 1887) and later, in a revised version, in Paris (Théâtre de l'Eden, November 1889, Théâtre de la Gaîte-Lyrique, February 1927), and in Munich (Theater am Gärtnerplatz 10 November 1888), actually spared the robbers from their traditional fate in the jars of oil, but that clemency was not extended to the male chorus of the most successful of all *Ali Baba*s, the famous British wartime musical *Chu Chin Chow.*

On this occasion, author-producer-star Oscar Asche embroidered the character of the glamorous spy Zahrat al-Kulub onto the traditional story in order to make a role for his non-singing wife, Lily Brayton, introduced increased romantic and spectacular elements, and redistributed some of the other well-known features of the original tale with as easy a hand as had some of the burlesque writers, while still retaining all the main parts of the original tale.

In recent times, *Ali Baba* has lost its place as a British pantomime subject, perhaps partly because of its explicit demand for a chorus of 40 thieves, unthinkable under modern salary conditions. However, the latest round of pop-opérettes à (very) grand spectacle to hit the French stage has seen a *Les Mille et une vies d'Ali Baba*—numbering a genie amongst its characters and not worrying much about the 40 thieves—make its way from Toulon to Paris (Zénith 23 September 2000).

ALIBERT, Henri [ALLIBERT, Henri] (b Carpentras, 3 December 1889; d Marseille, 23 January 1951). French singer turned librettist who made himself a star with a series of jolly musical comedies in the 1930s.

The dark, sharp-faced little southerner, son of a Carpentras baker, began his working life apprenticed to a pastry-cook. He had a slow beginning to his career as a performer, but after several years performing in the provinces, subsisting largely on imitations of the famous, he ultimately took the first steps towards success as a comic actor and singer in Paris, when he was engaged in 1919 at the Eldorado. His first appearance there was in the role of a cabaret singer in *Le Crime du Bouif.* He subsequently appeared at the Alhambra and the Empire, in an act which often included the songs of Vincent Scotto, the father of his second wife, Juliette.

The success of the marseillais plays of Marcel Pagnol and of the southern-flavored revue, *La Revue marseillaise,* in which Alibert and other marseillais singing stars appeared at the little 200-seater Moulin de la

Chanson in 1932 (26 April), persuaded Alibert (libretto) and the revue's songwriters René Sarvil (lyrics) and Scotto (music) to venture a musical comedy in the same *midi* style. Their first attempt with what they called an "opérette-revue," *Au pays du soleil,* was produced at the Moulin de la Chanson after the closure of the revue, with Alibert playing the central role of a callow and comical marseillais. This lighthearted, unpretentious fare with its jolly, simple story, catchy music-hall songs and sunshiny midi accents proved a perfect contrast and complement to the lush, romantic opérettes à grand spectacle currently becoming popular in Paris. The show was a hit, and Alibert was lifted into the major star category.

The same formula was followed successfully during the 1930s in *Trois de la marine, Zou! le midi bouge, Un de la Canebière, Les Gangsters du Château d'If* and *Le Roi des galéjeurs,* most of which were also filmed, before Alibert went on to appear in his now hugely popular marseillais persona in revue (*Paris-Marseille, C'est tout le Midi,* etc), in several musical shows composed by his habitual conductor, Georges Sellers (*Ma belle Marseillaise, Le Port du soleil*), and in such films as *Titin de Martigues* (Scotto/Sarvil), *Un Soir à Marseille* (Sellers/Sarvil) and *L'Affaire du grand hôtel* (Scotto/Vincy). In parallel, he became a favorite recording star for the Pathé label, notably with the songs from his shows and films ("Sur le plancher des vaches," "Adieu, Venise provençale," "Le Plus Beau Tango du monde," "Les Pescadous," etc).

Alibert was director of Paris's Théâtre des Deux-Ânes from 1931 to the time of his death, and also, for a time, of the Théâtre des Variétés, where he played a repertoire featuring marseillais opérette and Pagnol's plays.

Several of his marseillais opérettes-revues, notably *Un de la Canebière,* which contains the most popular collection of songs in the series, are still performed in France more than half a century after their first appearances.

1932 **Au pays du soleil** (Vincent Scotto/René Sarvil) Moulin de la Chanson 22 October

1933 **Trois de la marine** (Scotto/Sarvil) Nouvel-Ambigu 20 December

1934 **Zou! le midi bouge** (aka *Arènes Joyeuses*) (Scotto/Sarvil) Alcazar 8 December

1935 **Un de la Canebière** (Scotto/Raymond Vincy, Sarvil) Théâtre des Célestins, Lyon 3 October; Théâtre des Variétés, Paris 3 April 1936

1936 **Les Gangsters du Château d'If** (Scotto/Sarvil) Théâtre des Célestins, Lyon 10 November; Théâtre des Variétés, Paris 19 January 1937

1937 **Ceux de la Légion** (Scotto/Sarvil) Théâtre Antoine 15 June

1938 **Le Roi des galéjeurs** (Scotto/Sarvil) Théâtre des Célestins, Lyon 16 April; Théâtre des Variétés, Paris 12 September

1945 **Les Gauchos de Marseille** (Scotto/Sarvil) Théâtre des Célestins 18 May; Théâtre des Variétés, Paris September

ALICE IN WONDERLAND

Lewis Carroll's Alice books, *Alice in Wonderland* (1865) and *Through the Looking Glass* (1872), have been the subject of a large number of adaptations of all kinds for the musical stage. Alice got on to the stage for what seems to have been the first time as early as 1876 when "the transformation scene, never before surpassed," designed by Henry Emden and entitled "Alice in Wonderland or, the End of the Rainbow" was tacked into the pantomime *Twinkle, Twinkle Little Star* at London's Royal Aquarium. More genuine musical *Alice*s were, however, to follow. Far and away the most successful of these was the earliest, a version written by H Savile Clarke—and including "most of the incidents from both books"—with a musical score by Walter Slaughter and produced as a Christmas entertainment at London's Prince of Wales Theatre in 1886 (23 December). Lewis Carroll himself had a hand in the casting of little Phoebe Carlo as the first stage Alice, and designer Lucien Besche reproduced Tenniel's famous illustrations in his stage designs. This *Alice in Wonderland* was revived for 18 further Christmas seasons in the West End, most notably in 1900 when Ellaline Terriss appeared as a not terribly juvenile Alice with Seymour Hicks in the principal comedy role as the Mad Hatter.

Subsequent English-language *Alice*s have been consistently less successful. A 1903 *Through the Looking Glass* at London's New Theatre found little favor, and Eva Le Gallienne's *Alice in Wonderland* (Civic Repertory Theater, New York 12 December 1932 w Florida Frebus, mus: Richard Addinsell), revived in 1947 by the American Repertory Theater (International Theater, New York 28 May, 100 performances), a fresh Clemence Dane/Richard Addinsell adaptation (Scala 1943), a France Pole/John Sacco piece which came out at the same time as the Walt Disney animated film of *Alice in Wonderland,* a Felicity Douglas/Dave King *Alice Through the Looking Glass* (Prince's Theatre, 1954) and a string of lesser attempts all failed to come up to the first version.

Sweden's Stefan Roos produced a version of the tale in 1968, and in 1978 a French *Alice* appeared when the Opéra Royal de Wallonie produced a two act opérette-féerie by Paul Francy at the Théâtre de Liège (19 October), but the most substantial modern *Alice,* originally produced by Vinnette Carroll and New York's Urban Arts Theater, on the wave of hope engendered by the success of *The Wiz,* was also the most substantial flop. It closed out of town at Philadelphia's Forrest Theater in 1978 (31 May, mus: Micki Grant) and failed again, under the title *Never Jam Today* (mus: Bert Keyes and Bob Larimer) at the Longacre Theater in 1979 (31 July). A modernized *Alice* at Britain's Leeds Playhouse and a German *Nachtkind* (1982) and *Alice* (Thalia-Theater,

Hamburg 19 December 1992, and ad Robert Wilson at Brooklyn Academy of Music 6 October 1995) used Carroll's story and characters in a free fashion, but regional and suburban theatres in Britain and elsewhere continue to produce fresh musical versions of the tale in a more or less traditional fashion (*The Adventures of Alice,* Farnham 1985, a John Wells/Colin Davis *Alice in Wonderland* at the Lyric, Hammersmith, 1986, etc), in spite of the piece's apparent unsuitability for the stage.

In 1905 Glen MacDonough and Victor Herbert tried to combine the character of Alice with the story of the Dancing Princesses in a piece mounted in Chicago as—what else?—*Alice and the Eight Dancing Princesses.* However, soon after opening night Alice got cut out of the proceedings and the only trace of her ever having been there that remained by the time the show got to Broadway was in the title. Although the show was now just about the Princesses, it was called *Wonderland.*

Alice has also appeared, rather more happily, on musical film, both in the famous Walt Disney animated version of 1951 and, with human actors, in a 1972 British version which featured the young Fiona Fullerton as Alice, and on television. An American NBC *Alice Through the Looking Glass* of 1966 (6 November), with songs by Moose Charlap and Elsie Simmons, featured Judi Rolin as Alice alongside Robert Coote, Nanette Fabray, Agnes Moorehead, Roy Castle, Jimmy Durante and Jack Palance, and another TV *Alice* of the same year *(Alice in Wonderland, or What's a Nice Kid Like You Doing in a Place Like This)* (Charles Strouse/Lee Adams) was broadcast by ABC on 30 March 1966 with Sammy Davis jr, Hedda Hopper, Zsa Zsa Gabor and Mel Blanc amongst the voices. Davis featured again, as the Caterpillar, in a 1985 CBS *Alice* (songs: Steve Allen).

Recording: TV cast (RCA Victor)

ALIX, Victor (b 1890; d 1968).

Victor Alix was the composer of several successful featherweight Parisian musical comedies of the 1920s and early 1930s, including the oriental tale of *You-You,* and a musical version of Romain Coolus's comedy *Les Bleus de l'amour* mounted at the Théâtre de l'Avenue with Paul Ville and Henri Defreyn featured. The little ten-handed *Mon amant* was produced by Max Danset with the same stars—Ville turning Machiavellian to stop Defreyn having an affair with his wife (Marguerite Deval)—and, later the same year, a second piece written with Coolus, *Boby chéri,* did well enough in its original season at the Scala to warrant a revival in 1934.

In the spirit of the times, Alix indulged in the foxtrot, the shimmy, and even the beguine, alongside the traditional waltz rhythms and couplets in which he was apparently more at home.

Plate 5. **Alice in Wonderland.** *The White Queen (Florence Lloyd) and the White King (Julian Cross) in London's perennial Victorian version of the Alice tale.*

- 1921 **Princesse Lily** (Jean-Claude Vaumousse) Théâtre des Variétés 12 June
- 1922 **You-You** (Jane Ardot, Jacques Sirrah) Théâtre de l'Apollo 25 February
- 1922 **Lulu** (Alain Monjardin) Caen 29 December
- 1923 **Pincette** (Ardot, Paidlon) La Fauvette-Concert 21 September
- 1926 **Les Bleus de l'amour** (Blanche Alix, Henry Jacques/Romain Coolus) Théâtre de l'Avenue April
- 1932 **Mon amant** (Ardot/Henry Darcourt, Maurice Lupin) Théâtre de la Potinière 1 April
- 1932 **Boby chéri** (Ardot/Coolus) Théâtre de la Scala 13 December

ALLEGRO Musical play in 2 acts by Oscar Hammerstein II. Music by Richard Rodgers. Majestic Theater, New York, 10 October 1947.

In *Allegro,* Hammerstein abandoned the highly colored American operetta style of story he had used so effectively in *Oklahoma!* and *Carousel* for a different kind of small-town, small-people tale—one which came to its climax not, like the other two shows, in a murder, but in a bit of common or garden-variety infidelity.

Joe (William Ching) and Marjorie (Annamary Dickie) Taylor give birth to baby Joe. Joe grows up (John Battles), goes to college, becomes a doctor, marries Jenny, the girl back home (Roberta Jonay), moves on to a better if less genuine job in the city and to a higher kind of life. Then, when his socially ambitious wife turns out to be a two-timer, he chucks in the big city and heads back to where he started to take up real doctoring again.

The various events of the life of Dr Joe Taylor, played out in front of a simple set of drops, were linked in the telling by a narrating ensemble who welcomed the baby (''Joseph Taylor Jr''), saw him through his first steps (''One Foot, Other Foot'') and his marriage (''To Have and to Hold''/''Wish Them Well'') to the final call of his mother to ''Come Home.'' In between, Rodgers and Hammerstein's principal songs were sung largely by supporting characters. Lisa Kirk as Dr Joe's loving nurse concluded that ''The Gentleman Is a Dope'' for not seeing what his wife is up to, Gloria Wills as his college flirt sang ''So Far,'' mother and father Taylor suggested conventionally, and not only of their son, that ''A Fellow Needs a Girl,'' whilst Joe jr serenaded the girl back home in ''You Are Never Away'' and waxed moral in the show's title song.

Several of the songs won some popularity, but *Allegro* proved too long on sanctimoniousness and too short on fun and color to succeed in the same way that the two previous Rodgers and Hammerstein shows had done. The Theatre Guild's production ran through 315 Broadway performances—more than many contemporary shows, but insufficient to get it into the black—before going on the road. It was not picked up by overseas producers, and it remains one of the few comparatively forgotten parts of the Rodgers and Hammerstein opus, although the famous names attached to it have won it several ''novelty'' outings over the years, notably in a production at the Goodspeed Opera House, in a ''revised version'' in 1968 (22 July).

Recording: original cast (RCA)

ALL THE KING'S HORSES Romantic musical comedy in 2 acts by Frederick Herendeen based on the play by Lawrence Clarke. Music by Edward Horan. Shubert Theater, New York, 30 January 1934.

All the King's Horses was a *Prisoner of Zenda*-esque piece which had Guy Robertson starred as a movie star called Donald McArthur who deputizes for his lookalike, King Rudolf of Langenstein, long enough for the King to go off for a jolly time in Paris and for MacArthur to have a nice affair with Queen Erna (Nancy McCord).

Following its 120 performances on Broadway, *All the King's Horses* was shipped to Hollywood where it was filmed, with Mary Ellis and Carl Brisson, and, by the time it got to the screen, also with an altered story and different songs. It was then taken up for London by Joe Sacks who had it again rewritten, by Archie Menzies, with a ''happy'' ending and a new title, *Royal Exchange.* This time the rollicking King was knocked off, allowing his stand-in to happily wed his Queen. In London, Carlos Gavalia (as he was now called) was played by a real live movie star in the person of Ramon Novarro, who starred alongside D'Oyly Carte veteran Charles Walenn, Eddie Foy and Doris Kenyon. Novarro got devastatingly bad notices, and the show closed in one week.

UK: His Majesty's Theatre *Royal Exchange* 6 December 1935

ALMA, WO WOHNST DU? Vaudeville in 3 acts ''adapted by Adolf Philipp from the play by Paul Hervé.'' Music by ''Jean Briquet'' and Adolf Philipp. Wintergarten ''Zum schwarzen Adler,'' New York, 25 October 1909; Weber's Theater, New York, 26 August 1910.

Quite what the successful musical *Alma, wo wohnst du?* really was was a ''mystery'' veiled behind a mass of phony credits. For ''Jean Briquet'' never existed and ''Paul Hervé'' didn't either. Both names were simply used to cover the fact that Adolf Philipp, the guiding genius and factotum of the turn-of-the-century New York German-language theatre, was both author and composer of the spankingly bright and lively little musical comedy which he mounted on the fringes of Broadway in 1909 with his Deutsch-Amerikanische Ensemble. And his modest little trick worked. Three generations of theatre writers (and not the least among them) have referred to *Alma* as ''French operetta'' and commented on its French characteristics. In fact, Philipp not only singlehandedly wrote and composed *Alma,* he also directed the show's original production and starred in it alongside Hedwig von Ostermann in the role of the Alma of whom the title asked the address.

Philipp's plot was—even if ''original''—far from new. Alma was an apparently irresistible young lady who was dangled in front of poor, susceptible Pierre Le Peach by interested parties to tempt him to break the conditions of a musical-comedy will. She was also saucy enough to help win the show a great success amongst the German-speaking gentlemen of New York, a further welcome from Teutonic gents in other centers (Chicago Opera House 17 April 1910, and until she was banned by the city authorities as too saucy for Cincinnati at that city's Grand Theatre 9 May 1910) and, the season following her Wintergarten triumph, she was even given a translation into English by George V Hobart for production in a regular Broadway house, under the management of Joe Weber as *Alma, Where Do You Live?* The English version of the musical was subtitled ''a lyrical comedy,'' the fake credits were still in place, and Kitty Gordon starred as Alma, with John McCloskey as Pierre, and Charles A Bigelow as chief comic.

The press consensus was that Hobart had done a splendid job in cleaning up the naughty French original, which of course wasn't French or original in the sense they were meaning at all, and that Philipp's score, featuring a ''Hush the Bogie'' number about ''The Boogie Boo,'' a Tom-Cat song encouraging the girls in his life to come out and ''Love Me'' and some more conventional pieces for the two stars recalling ''Childhood Days,'' exploring ''The Land of the Beautiful Dream'' and waltzing with *Merry Widow* abandon to ''Kiss Me, My Love,'' fitted it perfectly. As in Cincinnati, however, the consensus on the ''cleaning up'' was not shared by quite all of the show's public. One viewer laid a complaint against the show's morals, obliging Mayor Gaynor to an enquiry which came out with the usual ''in the ear of the beholder'' kind of answer and which, of course, did absolutely no harm to the show's box office.

Alma, Where Do You Live? was one of the biggest hits of the vintage 1910–11 Broadway season, outrunning *Naughty Marietta* comprehensively, equalling the record of the loudly praised *Madame Sherry* and giving best only to the hugely successful *The Pink Lady.* But *Alma* was different from each of those three shows—whereas *Naughty Marietta, Madame Sherry* and *The Pink Lady* were large shows equipped with much scenery, many costumes, large choruses and so forth—*Alma* was a small show. A veritable musical comedy, with a comedy book thoroughly in the French vaudeville or German Posse tradition and with songs which were an accessory to that book. Coming, as it did, in the same season as *Madame Sherry* and *The Pink Lady,* two other staunchly (French) book-based hits, it marked the rise to the top of the real and quality musical comedy on the American stage. But whereas its two fellow French shows hedged their ''musical comedy'' bets behind the traditional production values and girlie lineups, *Alma* didn't. She was a small show, produced in a small house, with few frocks, little scenery and no vast girlie quotient. Unless you counted Alma herself, who—especially as impersonated by the beautiful Miss Gordon—did enough damage for a few dozen. *Alma* could fairly be counted a landmark.

Alma in English ran up no less than 232 Broadway performances for Weber before going out on the road for what would be years of touring, with Miss Gordon in her famous role succeeded by Truly Shattuck and a whole series of other devastating young ladies. Philipp remounted the original German-language version at his new 57th Street Theater in the 1912–13 season (17 April 1913) and simultaneously launched himself upon a whole flush of further shows, in German and then in English, all made in the same style, establishing himself in the process as the King of the intimate musical on (and off-) Broadway and provoking imitators and followers amongst local writers and producers.

When she had done touring the country at length, the now spicily celebrated Miss Gordon had a small-scale sequel written to measure, and went on the vaudeville stage playing *Alma's Return* (1914).

The credits for the show got even more tangled than they were in America when the original German version of *Alma* (''a Parisian vaudeville in 3 acts'') was taken up for production back in Berlin. When the piece appeared on the stage of the Luisen-Theater (17 October 1911), still credited to Paul Hervé as adapted by Herr Philipp, the ''Boogie Boo'' and its fellows had been dumped and the show had been equipped with a fresh score by Walter Kollo with lyrics by Louis Taufstein. It was that score which was later heard in Vienna (Lustspieltheater 17 November 1911) when Annie Dirkens appeared as luscious Alma alongside Gustav Maran (Theobald Simonet), Gisela Werbezirk (Louise Parfait) and Louis Holzer (Pierre Roussant) in Josef Jarno's Austrian production of a show which wasn't quite the *Alma, wo wohnst du?* that had begun its life in New York and which, in spite of a hugely successful life, still hadn't been seen—and wouldn't be seen—in its professed city of origin.

ALONSO, Francisco (b Granada, 9 May 1887; d Madrid, 19 May 1948).

Alonso abandoned thoughts of a medical career in favor of one in music, and by the age of 20 he had had his first zarzuela *La niña de los cantares* (1907) produced at the local Teatro Cervantes. He moved to Madrid in 1911, and made his living writing songs for fashionable salons, but theatrical success eluded him until the production of *Música, luz y alegría* in 1914 (20 May). He had his first significant success with *La linda tapada* in 1924 (Teatro Cómico 19 April), followed by another with *La bejarana* (Teatro Apolo 31 May 1924) both of which were taken up in Paris and Latin America.

Alonso subsequently composed a series of further full-length zarzuelas, of which *La Calesera* (12 December 1925, Paris 1926), *La Parranda* (26 April 1928), *La Picarona* (6 February 1930) and *Me llaman la Presumida* (4 December 1935) all found considerable success. He also composed the music for a number of shorter, revusical pieces including the sainete-revista *Las Leandras* (1931) with its widely popular pasacalle ''Por la calle de Alcalá.'' His other works include *El bueno de Guzmán* (1913), *De Madrid al Infierno* (1918), *Los Corsarias*

(1919), *Curro, el de Loro* (1925), *La mejor del puerto* (1928), *La morería* (1928 w Millan), *Rosa la Pantalonera* (1939), *Manuelita Rosas* (1941) and *La zapaterita* (1941).

After the civil war Alonso's career went into eclipse. He tried to adapt his style to the fashionable models of the time, but without ever again attaining the success he had known in the 1920s and the 1930s.

Biography: Alonso, J M: *Francisco Alonso* (Espasa-Calpe, Madrid, 1987)

ALPÁR, Gitta (b Budapest, 5 February 1900; d Los Angeles, 17 February 1991).

The Hungarian coloratura soprano, daughter of a Budapest cantor, made early appearances in her home town both in opera—notably as Gilda (*Rigoletto*) at the Budapest Operaház (1923)—and in Operette, starring at the Király Színház as the heroine of *Három a kislány* (*Das Dreimäderlhaus*). She sang thereafter for some years only in grand opera—including periods at Munich (1925–27) and at Berlin's Staatsoper (1927–30), winning particular praise for her Violetta in *La Traviata,* and guesting at Covent Garden in 1929 as Sophie in *Der Rosenkavalier*—in a useful career, but one which brought her none of the adulation she would later find when she returned to the musical theatre.

It was in 1930 that she made that return, to create the role of Viktória in *Viktória* at Budapest's Fővárosi Operettszínház and again, in German, in Leipzig. As a result of her huge personal success as the Hungarian heroine of Pal Ábrahám's highly successful piece, she was swiftly cast in the stellar part of the Princess Elisabeth, alongside Richard Tauber, in the premiere of Lehár's *Schön ist die Welt* (Metropoltheater, Berlin, 1930) and repeated that initial success. She subsequently appeared in Berlin as Violette in *Das Veilchen vom Montmartre,* and in *Der Bettelstudent,* before taking on her most famous operettic role as Jeanne Dubarry in the reworked version of Millöcker's *Gräfin Dubarry* staged at the Admiralspalast as *Die Dubarry* (1931). She repeated that role in the show's Hungarian production but, after starring as Catherine the Great in *Kaiserin Katharina* and in Ábrahám's subsequent *Ball im Savoy* (1932, Madeleine) and her first musical films *Die—oder keine* and *Gitta endeckt ihr Herz* (1932) in Berlin, the prima donna who had become accepted as the natural successor to Fritzi Massary in the hearts of the German critics and public was forced to flee the country by the early strains of anti-Semitism.

In a career which skipped from one country to another, she appeared in Vienna as the star of Miklós Brodszky's *Die verliebte Königin* (1934), filmed an Hungarian version of *Ball im Savoy* (1935), paired with Owen Nares in a film version of *Die Dubarry, I Give My Heart* (1935) and in the British film *Guilty Melody* (1936), and returned to Budapest as *A szerelmes királynő* (*Die verliebte Königin*) and again as Marie-Antoinette in Károly Komjáti's attempt to repeat the *Dubarry* recipe in *Antoinette* (1938). In 1936 she was announced to appear in London in a Brodszky musical with a text by James Bridie and A P Herbert, but ultimately London audiences saw her instead in Brodszky and Herbert's Coronation revue *Home and Beauty* (1937) alongside Binnie Hale and Nelson Keys.

Alpár thereafter based herself in America where she appeared in several other films (*The Flame of New Orleans,* etc), and was seen in 1941 in a John Murray Anderson revue, but the operettic career which had promised so stunningly in pre–Nazi Germany never again took off in the same way.

ALTON, Robert [HART, Robert Alton] (b Bennington, Vt, 28 January 1897; d Hollywood, Calif, 12 June 1957).

After a first career as a chorus dancer, Alton became a dance assistant and subsequently a choreographer in his own right, beginning his list of Broadway credits with the dances for the 1933 Winter Garden show *Hold Your Horses.* Amongst the musicals for which he subsequently created the dances were *Anything Goes* (1934), *Hooray for What!* (1937), *Between the Devil* (1937), *Leave It To Me!* (1938), *Dubarry Was a Lady* (1939), *Too Many Girls* (1939), *Panama Hattie* (1940), *Higher and Higher* (1940), *Pal Joey* (1940), *Sons o' Fun* (1941), *By Jupiter* (1942), *Count Me In* (1942), the 1952 revival of *Pal Joey* (also "production supervisor"), *Hazel Flagg* (1953) and *Me and Juliet* (1953), as well as several editions of the *Ziegfeld Follies* and a considerable number of other revues. For the Fats Waller musical *Early to Bed* (1943), and the Carol Channing vehicle *The Vamp* (1955) he acted as both director and choreographer.

Alton went to Hollywood for the first time in 1935 to direct the Goldwyn Girls sequences in *Strike Me Pink,* and he later spent a considerable period at MGM (1944–53), and choreographed musical sequences for film versions of *Good News* (1947), *Annie Get Your Gun* (1950), *Show Boat* (1951) and *Call Me Madam* (1953) as well as such films as *The Harvey Girls, The Ziegfeld Follies, Till the Clouds Roll By, The Pirate, Easter Parade, The Barkleys of Broadway, The Belle of New York, White Christmas* and *There's No Business Like Show Business.* He also directed the movies *Merton of the Movies* (1947) and *Pagan Love Song* (1950).

ALT-WIEN Operette in 3 acts by Gustav Kadelburg and Julius Wilhelm. Music taken from the works of Josef Lanner, arranged by Emil Stern. Carltheater, Vienna, 23 December 1911.

Pretty Lini (Mizzi Zwerenz) lives a happy life at the Vienna beerhouse run by her stepfather, Andreas Johann Nepomuk Stöckl (Karl Schöpfer). She entertains the customers with her songs, and she has her beloved Franz (Josef König), and some good, jolly friends like Alois Nussberger, the inn's chucker-out (Richard Waldemar) for company. But one day the police officer Prohaska (Karl Wallner) comes by, bringing with him the Graf Leopold von Tutzing-Garatshausen (Karl Blasel), his sister Philomene (Therese Löwe), his niece Felizitas (Dora Keplinger), and the news that Lini is the nobleman's daughter, the long-lost Countess Hortense. Transported to the Tutzing mansion, Lini finds herself ill at ease in her new home, and when she invites all her friends in for a party in the style she is used to, her new family are aghast. She runs away back to her papa Stöckl and, when the wet nurse finally admits that she lied in order to cover the fact that the noble baby had died, Lini is able to go back to being just the little queen of the ''Zum braunen Hirschen.''

The music of the Strauss family had been arranged and re-rearranged into scores for pasticcio Operetten for many years (*Frühlingsluft, Das Schwaberl aus dem Wienerwald, Das Teufelsmädel, Die weisse Fahne,* etc), and it was only a matter of time before someone got around to moving on to the melodies of Josef Lanner, the other great Viennese dance composer of the same period, as the raw material for a major Operette score. Emil Stern, musical director of the Carltheater, put together 16 pieces of remade Lanner which largely featured the above-the-title Frln Zwerenz and, to a lesser extent, Frln Keplinger (the manager's wife). Lini took part in each of the five numbers of the first act (Couplets with Stöckl, duos with the Baron Seespitz, with Franz, a waltz ensemble with Nussberger and a finale) and had her big solo moment with the Alt-Wienermarsch ''Ich bin nun Komtesse'' in Act II where she also shared a Zepperlpolka with her lofty relations, and a Busserlwalzer with Franz. In the final act, a Gespenster-Quartett (w Nussberger, Stöckl, Franz) led up to the final Couplets, led by Lini and Franz. Felizitas featured a solo to open the second act (''Junges Lieben'') and two duos with Seespitz.

Alt-Wien proved a real success for the Carltheater, running for 159 performances in its first series and remaining in their repertoire for more than a decade thereafter. In 1913 the Carltheater company, which had already guested *Alt-Wien* at Ronacher in Vienna, introduced the original version to Budapest when they played it in a season at the Király Színház, hard on the heels of an Hungarian version (ad Adolf Mérei) which switched the action to Budapest and changed the title to *A régi Pest.* The show was also a considerable success on German stages, but it was not played further afield. In 1944 a revised and modernized version of the piece (ad Alexander Steinbrecher) was produced at Vienna's Raimundtheater (21 April) as typical ''good old days'' entertainment for the last days of the war.

And nobody ever mused in print as to whether Messrs Kadelburg and Wilhelm had ever seen Pinero's famous play *Trelawney of the Wells.* For the libretto to *Alt-Wien* was its Austrian twin sister.

Another musical piece of the same title, written by Eduard Wagner, was produced at the Graz Stadttheater in 1910.

Germany: ?1912; Hungary: Budapesti Színház *A régi Pest* 28 September 1912, Király Színház (Ger) May 1913

AMADI, Madame (Annie TREMAINE) [CRILMAN, Anne] (b Woolwich, 27 January 1848, d unknown). Gaiety Theatre soubrette who became one of London's favorite musical character ladies.

The daughter of a Royal Artillery sergeant, ''Annie Tremaine'' led a career as a vocalist in the music halls from her youngest teens purveying everything from *Lucia di Lammermoor* to sentimental ballads to the habitués of Weston's and other London houses with considerable success, whilst at the same time taking part in classical concerts as ''Miss Crealman.'' She left the music-hall world, never to return, in 1868 when John Hollingshead hired the 20-year-old soprano as a member of his original Gaiety Theatre company. She appeared on the first night at the Gaiety as Albert in W S Gilbert's burlesque *Robert the Devil* and thereafter, continuously, for four years, in the personality soprano and mezzo-soprano roles in such of the house's burlesques and comic operas as *Columbus* (1869, Sennatina), *Wat Tyler MP* (1869, Lucy Straw), *The Quaker* (1869, Cicely), *The Happy Village* (1870, Georgette), *Aladdin II* (1870, Karamel), *The Beggar's Opera* (1870, Lucy), *The Waterman* (1870, Wilhelmina), *Donna Diana* (1871, Fenesa), *Le Mariage aux lanternes* (1871, Catherine), *Thespis* (1871, Daphne), *Cinderella the Younger* (1871, Pamela), *The Forty Thieves* (1871, Hassarac), and the English versions of *La Princesse de Trébizonde* (1870, Zanetta), *Barbe-bleue* (1870, Clémentine), *Fra Diavolo* (1870, Lady Allcash), *Zar und Zimmermann* (1870, Widow Brown) and *La Belle Hélène* (1871, Orestes), as well as in straight comedy. She also toured with the Gaiety's opéra-bouffe company, in 1871 in supporting roles, and in 1872–73 in the prima donna roles of *La Grande-Duchesse, La Belle Hélène, Barbe-bleue, Les Brigands, La Périchole,* etc.

In 1873 she quit the Gaiety and under the name of ''Ada Beaumont'' skipped to America as a member of Lydia Thompson's famous burlesque company. Her ''brilliant singing and dashing demeanour'' in the role of Proserpine in *Méphisto* at Broadway's Olympic Theatre took aback those who had come to regard Lydia's companies as showing more leg than talent, and she caused a small sensation. She also played with the Thompson company in *Sinbad* ("a well deserved encore for her admirable singing of 'Within a Mile of Edinburgh Town'"), *Robin Hood, Aladdin* and *Bluebeard.* From burlesque, however, "Ada Beaumont" went on to grand opera. She became a principal member of Clara Louise Kellogg's Opera Company and later of other American troupes, touring the country (1874–76, Lazarillo in *Maritana,* Frederick then Mignon in *Mignon,* Siebel then Marguerite in *Faust,* Berengaria in *The Talisman,* Anne Chute in *The Lily of Killarney,* Donna Elvira to the Anna of Titjiens in *Don Giovanni,* Adalgisa to the *Norma* of Titjiens, *The Marriage of Figaro* with Jenny van Zandt, etc) to delighted reviews. In 1877 she married George Beaumont Loveday, the British operatic impresario and she continued her operatic career, under the name of Mrs Loveday, in the British provinces (Leonora in *Il Trovatore,* Zerlina in *Fra Diavolo,* etc) until the birth of her two sons, when she retired from the scene.

However, Annie was soon to be back, now sporting a fifth name. In the 1880s and the 1890s, as "Madame Amadi," she returned to the musical theatre and—after first appearing under her new name as Cerisette in a second attempt to launch Genée's *Seekadett* in London—went on to become one of the foremost British players of musical "heavy" character roles, appearing in London in a whole string of comic operas, amongst which two pieces—the title role of *La Boulangere a des écus* (Margot) and *La Belle Normande* (ie, *La Famille Trouillat,* Margot)—played in Paris by Thérésa. Amongst her roles in this metamorphosis were character parts in *The Merry War* (Artemisia), *Our Diva* (Madame Jacob), *Mynheer Jan* (Donna Tralara), *Marjorie* (Lady Alicia), *Captain Thérèse* (La Chanoinesse), *The Golden Web* (Mistress Pamela Patch), *Cigarette* (Comtesse de Montrouget), *The Queen of Brilliants* (Mme Englestein), and *The Taboo* (Wattatauka). In 1893–94 she returned to opera and appeared with the Carl Rosa company as Céléstine in a version of *François les bas-bleus,* Martha in *Faust,* Lady Allcash in *Fra Diavolo,* etc. Her farewell to the stage seems to have been made at the Theatre Royal, Drury Lane as Mrs Cregan in *The Lily of Killarney* in 1895.

LES AMANTS DE VENISE Opérette à grand spectacle in 2 acts by Henri Varna, Marc-Cab and René Richard based on the books *Le Pont des soupirs* and *Les Amants de Venise* by Michel Zevaco. Music by Vincent Scotto. Théâtre Mogador, Paris, 5 December 1953.

One of the most successful of Henri Varna's Théâtre Mogador series of romantic musical spectacles, *Les Amants de Venise* took 17 scenes of Venetian splendor to follow the 16th-century captain and Doge's son, Roland Candiano (Marcel Merkès), through the various stages of his confrontation with a malefic Council of Ten, led by the horrid Altieri (Jacques Harden), who wants to stop him wedding the unaristocratic Léonore Dandolo (Paulette Merval). However, a villainous police-chief (Raymond Danjou), a venal courtesan (Lola Maddalena), a hired assassin (Alexandre Rignault) and a flock of pigeons can, even among them, do nothing to stop our hero conquering all opposition by the strength of his sword and his ringing baritone voice. Jacky Piervil and Jacqueline Mille provided the soubret element, the Ballets de France and Oleg Koby the dance, and the late Vincent Scotto the suitably romantic large-house score, completed shortly before his death.

The piece ran for two full seasons at the Mogador, went to the country, and reappeared in Paris, with Merkès and Merval again heading the cast, for a second run in 1966 (26 November). The baddies were this time headed by Jean-Jacques Steen, Pierre Plessis and Catherine Bréa; Huguette Duval and Michel Dunand were the soubrets, and Varna himself appeared in the role of the Cardinal, as *Les Amants de Venise* added almost another year of performances to its Parisian total before making its way into the repertoire of the provincial houses.

Recordings: selection with original stars (Odéon, CBS)

AMASIS, an Egyptian Princess Comic opera in 2 acts by Frederick Fenn. Music by Philip Michael Faraday. New Theatre, London, 9 August 1906.

This veritable comic opera, an hilarious piece of Ancient Egyptian nonsense about a Prince who accidentally kills a yowling but definitely sacred cat, appeared, from a combination of writers with no West End credits, in the hands of a neophyte management (Louis Calvert) which did not know how to handle such a potential success. Surprised and delighted reviews hailed the piece as a worthy follower of the Gilbert and Sullivan tradition, but the authors and manager got themselves embroiled in theatre trouble, plagiarism suits and internal wranglings and, in the end, the show was closed down after two hundred performances with its creators deep in both financial and personal problems.

The soprano song "Little Princess, Look Up," as introduced by Ruth Vincent in the piece's title role, became a favorite with recording and concert artists, but, although visions of the now very stout Rutland Barrington in a preposterous Pharaonic wig and of Lauri de Frece, as the keeper of the royal crocodiles, cuddling his charges in the same way he would make merry with a lobster a decade later in *The Maid of the Mountains,* remained long in people's memories, the show did not establish itself as it might have following its exciting start. Only the Orient saw it, when the indefatigable Maurice Bandmann snatched up this piece of superior, ill-managed writing for his ravenous Asian and Pacific repertoire company.

AMBIENT, Mark [HARLEY, Harold] (b Rastrick, 20 June 1860; d Hove, 9 August 1937). Theatrical wanna-be, who (with some help) set up the best musical play of the Edwardian age.

Cambridge-educated Ambient tried his hand at both acting (at the Princess's with Wilson Barrett) and songwriting ("The Old Soldiers," "Chorus, Gentlemen," "Love's Return," "Golden Lilies") without finding any notable success, but he did a little better as a writer for the stage. A song "Comme ça," with music by Edward Solomon, made some effect in the Gaiety burlesque *Don Juan* (1893), whilst his "Boots" (mus: Meyer Lutz) as performed by Letty Lind and several numbers written for Harry Monkhouse's touring show *Pat* also proved mildly popular. He had a hand in several plays presented on the London stage, including *Oh Susannah!* (1897), with Louie Freear starred, and *A Little Ray of Sunshine* (1899) with W S Penley, and was responsible for a botched version of Audran's musical comedy *L'Oncle Célestin,* staged with indifferent results in 1895 at the Trafalgar Square Theatre under the title *Baron Golosh.* He also worked with Francis Money-Coutts, a wealthy amateur writer who hired himself co-authors and composers (including Albéniz, introduced to him by Ambient) in order to get his works on the stage, and together they turned out an unproduced musical (mus: Edward Solomon) called *A.D. 3000,* and another piece, *The Shepherd Lord* (w Albéniz), which was allegedly produced in Barcelona. He also joined Coutts and his money as part of the syndicate which, for several years, ran the Lyric Theatre before stumbling into receivership.

Ambient frequented, in particular, the important theatrical group which lived and drank in Brighton and its Ship Inn, and his connection there with Robert Courtneidge led him to suggest to the producer an idea for an original musical. Courtneidge accepted the outline, but since Ambient—not the most stable of characters—proved unable to come up with a script, he paired him with his house writer, Alexander M Thompson, who was ultimately responsible for much of the libretto of the show which was to become *The Arcadians,* the classic musical comedy of its era. Courtneidge duly included Ambient in his writing team for the subsequent *The Light Blues* (1915–16), a disastrous flop which all but put the producer out of business and which ended the would-be author's connection with the musical theatre.

1892 **Pat** (John Crook, Alfred Lee, et al/w Frederick Wood/George Roberts, Harry Monkhouse) Aquarium, Yarmouth 1 August 1892

1895 **Baron Golosh** (*L'Oncle Célestin*) English version w Meyer Lutz, Leslie Stuart, et al (Trafalgar Square Theatre)

1909 **The Arcadians** (Howard Talbot, Lionel Monckton/Arthur Wimperis/w Alexander M Thompson) Shaftesbury Theatre 28 April

1915 **The Light Blues** (Talbot, Herman Finck/Adrian Ross/w Jack Hulbert) Prince of Wales Theatre, Birmingham 13 September/Shaftesbury Theatre 14 September 1916

AMECHE, Don [AMICI, Dominic Felix] (b Kenosha, Wis, 31 May 1908; d Scottsdale, Ariz, 6 December 1993).

Best known as the leading man of a run of 1930s and 1940s films (including an appearance as a singing D'Artagnan in *The Three Musketeers* in 1939), the dapper Ameche appeared, later in his career, in major roles in several stage musicals. He was the leading man of *Silk Stockings* (1955, Steve Canfield), in which he romanced the sternly Russian Hildegarde Neff to the strains of "Paris Loves Lovers," and insisted on "All of You," he co-starred with Elaine Stritch as madcap movie mogul, Max Grady, in the cinema burlesque *Goldilocks* (1958), and passed briefly by as the Chinese father of *Thirteen Daughters* (1961) and as the titular Henry Orient of the 1967 *Henry, Sweet Henry.*

Outside New York, he was seen in *I Married an Angel* (1964) and as Jimmy Smith in *No, No, Nanette* (1972), and in a long and varied career on television (*Don's Musical Playhouse,* 1951, etc), in a TV version of *High Button Shoes* (NBC, 1956) and in the small-screen musical based on Sally Benson's *Junior Miss* (1957).

In 1940 he appeared on film in *Lillian Russell,* in the role of composer Edward Solomon, the performer's sort-of-husband.

AMERICA'S SWEETHEART Musical comedy in 2 acts by Herbert Fields. Lyrics by Lorenz Hart. Music by Richard Rodgers. Broadhurst Theater, New York, 10 February 1931.

America's Sweetheart was a filmland musical written by Fields, Rodgers and Hart and flavored by their own recent experiences in newly talking and singing Hollywood. Geraldine (Harriette Lake, ie, Ann Sothern) and Michael (Jack Whiting) go west to become silent movie stars. She succeeds, he gets left in her wake, and then sound comes and their positions are reversed. The show's songs did not include any which would become part of the Rodgers and Hart songbook, but a depression-time marriage proposal to music, "I've Got Five Dollars," won some popularity. However, even without hit songs, Laurence Schwab and Frank Mandel's production of *America's Sweetheart* proved popular enough to run for 135 performances on Broadway.

In 1995 the show was given a concert performance at New York's Theatre Off Park (10 December) with Darcie Roberts and Jarrod Emick featured.

Another musical with the same title centered on a very different kind of sweetheart. Alfred Uhry and John Weidman's *America's Sweetheart* (mus: Robert Waldman, Hartford Stage, Hartford, Conn 5 March 1985) was the story of criminal Al Capone.

L'AMOUR MASQUÉ Comédie musicale in 3 acts by Sacha Guitry. Music by André Messager. Théâtre Édouard VII, Paris, 15 February 1923.

A small-cast (seven principals and a chorus of ten), free verse play in Guitry's most urbanely humorous style, *L'Amour masqué* was designed as a vehicle for, and decorated with a set songs of songs mostly for, the then Mme Guitry (Yvonne Printemps). Those songs were composed to Guitry's deliciously sophisticated and poetic lyrics by the doyen of elegant, old-style musical theatre composers, 70-year-old André Messager.

Elle (Mlle Printemps), although suitably ''protected'' by not one but two gentlemen, the Baron (Urban) and the Maharadjah (Pierre Darmant), has fallen in love, with all the rapture of her 20 years, with a photograph of an unknown young man which she has passionately stolen from her photographer's studio. When a dashing, greying gentleman (Guitry, playing 15 years older than his veritable age), who resembles the portrait unmistakably, comes to investigate, she makes him promise to bring his son to a masked ball that evening. At the dance, her two disguised servants (Marthe Ferrare, Marie Dubas) efficaciously distract the two official lovers, whilst she wins herself the willing original of the photograph. In the hectic events of the morning after, she realizes that her new, true lover is nobody's son but her previous day's visitor himself, 24 elegant years after his photograph session.

Messager's score was a perfect complement to this witty and often satirical little romantic idyll of the belles années and the beau monde, and it produced one of his most enduring single songs in the heroine's first-act ''J'ai deux amants.'' Saying goodbye to her teens, she laughingly describes her financially satisfying arrangements with the Baron and the Maharadjah, wondering mockingly over the stupidity of men to the celebrated refrain ''Mais, mon Dieu, que c'est bête, un homme. . . .'' Amongst her other songs, the celebration of her ''Vingt ans!'' and her uncomplicated summing up of her own appeal, ''Elle est charmante,'' stood out. The more flagrantly comic songs were the province of the two lovers. The Baron described with horror and in tango time his wife's adventure with a young dancing partner (''Valentine a perdu la tête''), and cockily assured the disguised maid that ''J' n'aime pas les bonnes,'' whilst the Maharadjah's gobbledegook lovemaking (not translated, for once, by his omnipresent interpreter), was a highlight of the entertainment. The role of Lui also had some musical sections, which Guitry spoke through the small accompanying orchestra.

L'Amour masqué scored a fine Parisian success before Guitry and Mlle Printemps moved on to other successes, leaving it behind, but it returned to Paris, at the Palais-Royal, in 1970 with Jean Marais (Lui), Arlette Didier (Elle) and Jean Parèdes featured, and an orchestra conducted by the composer Georges van Parys. A German-language version (ad Robert Blum) was produced by its adaptor as a late-night entertainment at Vienna's Modernes Theater in 1924 with Lea Seidl and Otto Storm featured in the Guitrys' roles, but no one seems yet to have been game to adapt Guitry's exquisite lines into English. First find your Yvonne Printemps. . . .

Austria: Modernes Theater 2 February 1924

Recordings: complete (Gaité-Lyrique), 1970 revival cast (Decca), original star excerpts on *Les Triomphes d'Yvonne Printemps* (EMI)

L'AMOUR MOUILLÉ Opéra-comique in 3 acts by Jules Prével and Armand Liorat. Music by Louis Varney. Théâtre des Nouveautés, Paris, 25 January 1887.

Allegedly based, at least in part, on an ode by Anacreon, Liorat and Prével's libretto for *L'Amour mouillé* was nevertheless set in the 16th century, in a city on the shores of the Ionian sea. A statue of Cupid, left by the Greeks during one of their occupations of Tarento, arouses the curiosity of the local teenage girls. None of them, including the Princess Lauretta (Mlle Darcelle), who is about to be married off to the foolish Ascanio (Guy), knows what ''love'' is, and when they read that this, his representative, shoots kindly people with his arrows, they decide to throw the statue in the sea. They are aghast when a man arises from the waves. They think he is the God of Love, but he is in fact the shipwrecked Prince Carlo of Syracuse (Maria Nixau) and, after two acts of quiproquos it is he who will marry Lauretta. The comical content of the piece was supplied by the politically and nuptially machinating Pampinelli (Jules Brasseur) and his rosy wife, Catarina (Marie Desclauzas), who rediscovers the love of her earlier life in the person of the prince's secretary, Cascarino (Albert Brasseur).

With the role of the Prince being played by a soprano en travesti, the bulk of Varney's attractive score was written for female voices. Carlo's serenade ''Prisonnier dans sa cage'' and its connected waltz duo ''P'tit fi! petit mignon!'' (w Lauretta) proved one of the lyric highlights of the evening, alongside the heroine's pretty barcarolle (''Il pleuvait et le vent soufflait''), her legend of ''L'Amour mouillé,'' and the comical song of Catarina who, in order to help Cascarino escape trouble, hides him in a barrow and pretends to go back to her old career as ''La marchande d'oranges.'' Cascarino had two comedy numbers and shared a duet, but otherwise the 19 numbers (excluding finales) of the score were devoted to the ladies.

With two celebrated comedians such as Brasseur and Mme Desclauzas at the head of the bill, *L'Amour mouillé* was, predictably, a great success on its production at the Nouveautés. It passed its 100th night on 6 June and was ultimately played a splendid 140 times en suite for its first run. It was subsequently reprised at the Athénée-Comique. It was, oddly, only exported a decade later, but its foreign productions, though numerous, had little success, whether in the German language (ad Heinrich Bolten-Bäckers) or in the English version, produced by Tom B Davis at London's Lyric Theatre. Intended there as the producer's successor to his highly successful first venture with *Little Miss Nobody,* the show was produced with much splendor, a cast including Evie Greene (Carlo), Kate Cutler (Catarina), John Le Hay (Pampinelli) and Jessie Huddlestone (Lauretta), and some interpolated songs by Paul and Walter Rubens. In spite of cuts, changes, the importation of some French dancers and a title change to the theoretically more accessible *Cupid and the Princess,* what appeared an essentially old-fashioned piece failed to take in London and closed after less than three forced months.

In Vienna, Alexandrine von Schönerer's staging of *Der verregnete Amor,* with Frln Frey (Carlo), Marie Ottmann (Lauretta) and Karl Blasel (Pampinelli) was taken off after three performances, whilst Lajos Máko and Emil Makai's Hungarian version did little better.

L'Amour mouillé was revived in Paris in 1898 (22 April), at the Athénée-Comique. Jane Pernyn (Carlo), Augustine Leriche (Catarina), Kerny (Pampinelli) and Jeanne Petit (Lauretta) headed the cast.

An earlier musical, a one-act piece also entitled *L'Amour mouillé* and apparently based on an 1850 play of the same title, was produced at the Paris Fantaisies-Parisiennes in 1868 (30 May). Jules Barbier and Arthur de Beauplan were the librettists and the score was composed by E de Hartog.

Austria: Theater an der Wien *Der verregnete Amor* 18 November 1897; Germany: Leipzig *Der Liebesgott* 29 January 1898; UK: Lyric Theatre aka *Cupid and the Princess* 5 April 1899; Hungary: Budai Színkör *Megázott ámor* 16 June 1899

LES AMOURS DE DON JUAN Opérette à grand spectacle in 2 acts by Henri Varna, Marc-Cab and René Richard. Music by Juan Morata. Additional music by Pauline Zevaco. Théâtre Mogador, Paris, 23 December 1955.

Henri Varna's Théâtre Mogador successor to the lush *Les Amants de Venise, Les Amours de Don Juan* brought the stars of the previous show, Marcel Merkès and Paulette Merval, back in another richly spectacular large-stage production. He played a descendant of the famous rake, thrown out of Spain for his sins, and gallivanting round the world in search of sex (Mlle Merval as Antonia) and scenery. A score by Spanish composer Juan Morata began in ''Le Soleil Catalan'' where ''Un Appel de castagnettes'' gave local color and, after he and his hero had said ''Adieu, mon Espagne,'' opened up into a series of romantic numbers (''Mon premier amour,'' ''Viens, mon coeur est a toi,'' ''Ne dites pas 'je t'aime,''' etc) and the occasional bit of local colour. The star team headed the production through most of its 18 months' run with the support of soubrets Eddy Rasimi and Frédérique.

Recording: original cast (Odéon)

ANATEVKA *see* FIDDLER ON THE ROOF

ANDALOUSIE Opérette à grand spectacle in 2 acts by Albert Willemetz and Raymond Vincy. Music by Francis Lopez. Théâtre de la Gaîté-Lyrique, Paris, 25 October 1947.

One of the most successful of the series of postwar musicals authored by Vincy (and, in this case, Willemetz) and Lopez, *Andalousie* adhered closely to the classic formula which had been so successful in their first big hit, *La Belle de Cadix.* There was a big, central tenor role made to feature the earlier show's star, Luis Mariano, who was again paired with a soprano sweetheart and supported by a contrasting soubret pair, a rival-in-love baritone, and some minor comedy characters, all embroiled in a story where romance, comedy and a touch of drama were mixed with a mise-en-scène which, whilst allowing plenty of color, did not rely on its grand spectacle as its principal attraction, as would too many Parisian musical shows a few years later.

The poor Andalusian pot-seller Juanito (Mariano) makes himself a name as a bullfighter and, promising to return, rich and famous, to his beloved Dolores (Marina Hotine), he sets sail to take up a contract in Caracas. To the annoyance of the dashing rebel Rodriguez Valiente (Pierre Faure), he attracts the attentions of the Viennese soprano, Fanny Miller (Sophia Botény), who intercepts his letters home, leaving the disappointed Dolores to give up waiting and take a job as a saucy singer. When Juanito arrives home, triumphant, with Fanny following in his wake, he is horrified to find what has happened, and Valiente venges himself for Frln Miller's indifference by taking up with the Spanish girl. Things come to a peak when the desperate Juanito almost lets himself be gored in the ring. Fanny admits her deception and returns with Valiente (now—thanks to a little revolution—promoted President) to Venezuela, leaving the lovers to a happy ending.

The parallel comic tale concerned little Pépé (Maurice Bacquet), who spends the evening gathering together all the impossible items needed to brew the gipsy love potion which will win him Pilar (Gise Mey), a señorita who is determined to wed only the man predicted to her by a local fortune-teller. Pépé follows Juanito to Venezuela, as does a curious little fellow called Baedecker (O'Brady) who has this crazy idea of writing travel guide books. They get mixed up with a large South American with a larger knife (Metairie) and suffer many a vagary before their happy ending is reached.

Lopez's score was a blatantly tuneful one. The tenor ran the gamut, entering as "Le Marchand d'alcarazas," swearing his love for Dolores ("Je veux t'aimer d'un amour merveilleux") and his country ("Andalucia mia") in throbbing tones, challenging the bull ("Ole Torero"), arriving home rhythmically to "C'est la fête à Seville" and pouring out his troubled heart to "Santa Maria" in a pre-fight prayer, whilst the soprano had one of Lopez's prettiest waltz tunes in the tipsy "Ça fait tourner la tête," sung by Dolores as she nervously sips an unaccustomed sherry whilst awaiting her staged rendezvous with Valiente. The baritone song ("Seul, je vais par tous les chemins") and the soubret pieces were a touch less effective than their *Belle de Cadix* equivalents, but the sum total was a score which was as good as anything of its time and place.

Andalousie confirmed the success of *La Belle de Cadix* with a 12-month run at the Gaîté-Lyrique before heading for the provinces and other French-speaking parts of the world. A pair of film versions were produced, with Mariano and Carmen Sevilla teamed with Baquet and Pirrette Souplex in French and with a Spanish cast for a Spanish-language repeat (*El sueño Andalucia)* and the show returned to Paris in 1954 for a season (Gaîté-Lyrique, August) with Rudi Hirigoyen, Baquet and Mlles Mey (Dolores), Arta Verlen and Doris Marnier featured. Since that date, *Andalousie* has been regularly reprised in French provincial theatres.

Film: Robert Vernay 1950, Luis Lucia 1951

Recordings: original cast recordings compiled (EMI-Pathé), selections (Odéon, Philips, CBS), etc

ANDERSEN, Hans Christian (b Odense, 2 April 1805; d nr Copenhagen, 4 August 1875).

Storyteller Hans Andersen made several attempts as an operatic librettist, adapting Scott's *The Bride of Lammermoor* for Ivar Bredal (before the appearance of Donizetti's opera), Gozzi's *Il Corvo* for J P E Hartmann (1832), and Manzoni's *I promessi sposi* for Franz Glaser (1849) as well as supplying the original text for the successful one-act *Liden Kristin* (mus: Hartmann, 1846) and several plays with music. It is, however, not those pieces but the fairy tales which made him famous which have won him his place in the theatre, providing the subject matter for numerous entertainments of all kinds, all around the world.

There have been Danish operatic versions of his stories of *The Match Girl* (*Pigen med svovlstikkerne*), *The Princess and the Pea* (*Prinsessen paa aerten*), *The Emperor's Nightingale* (*Nattergallen*) and *The Emperor's New Clothes* (*Kejserens nye klaeder*), the Hungarian composer Ede Poldini composed a one-act *A csavargo es kiralylany* on *The Swineherd and the Princess* (1903) and Igor Stravinsky produced, with his *Rossignol* (1914), what is probably the most substantial piece of musical Andersen. In the English-language theatre, Charles Villiers Stanford composed an operatic *The Travelling Companion* whilst Ernst Toch set a *Die Prinzessin auf der Erbse,* later played as *The Princess and the Pea* in New York (1936).

On the light musical stage, *Ib and Little Christina,* originally presented in London as a play by Martin Harvey, was adapted as a musical by Basil Hood, given a score by Franco Leoni, and played at the Savoy Theatre (14 November 1901 Carl St Amory/Avalon Collard, Alfred England), whilst a version of *The Swineherd and the Princess* (Royalty Theatre 19 December 1901) was given a seasonal production the same year. A piece called *Little Hans Andersen* (Adelphi Theatre, London, 1903, Walter Slaughter/Basil Hood) tried out four years earlier at Terry's Theatre as *Hans Andersen's Fairytales* introduced *The Emperor's New Clothes, Ole-Luk-Oie, The Red Shoes, The Princess and the Swineherd, The Tinder Box* and *The Little Mermaid* in the course of its action.

An operettic version of *The Emperor's New Clothes* was composed by the Swedish Charles Kjerulf and produced in Stockholm in November 1889, and *The Princess and the Pea* was apparently put to contribution for an unlikely sounding Czech piece, *König Blaubart und die Prinzessin auf der Erbse,* written and composed by Maria Günther and staged in Prague in 1896. Vienna's Theater an der Wien presented a *Die wilden Schwäne* (ad Feld), with a score by Adolf Müller (8 October 1871) which was billed as a "féerie nachdem gleichnamigen Märchen Andersens," whilst *The Travelling Companion* became *Wanderhansel* (mus: Max Clarus) in Braunschweig in 1914 (Hoftheater 5 December). A piece called *Tausend Küsse,* "based on Andersen" (Lena Stein-Schneider/Walter Mendelssohn) was produced at the Gotha Landestheater in 1928 (9 September).

Vienna's Ronacher and Carltheater presented a piece by L Novak, J Kwapil and Emil Kläger, with a score by Oskar Nedbal, under the title *Andersen* (1914), in which Karl Hübner appeared as Andersen through seven scenes of his tales, but the major stage depiction of Andersen as a character came in a 1974 musical, *Hans Andersen,* based on Frank Loesser's score to the hugely successful

Danny Kaye film, *Hans Christian Andersen,* and with a libretto built round a fictionalized life of the writer. Produced at the London Palladium (Loesser/Tommy Steele, Beverly Cross), it was subsequently revived there and played widely through the British provinces. Another *Hans Andersen,* written by Irene Mann and adapted by Kurt Huemer and Sepp Tatzel, was produced at Vienna's Raimundtheater in 1986 (8 February) and yet another, by Knud Christiansen, at Copenhagen's Gladsaxe Theater in 1996.

Amongst the postwar musicals based on Andersen's works, the most widely successful has been the witty American *Once Upon a Mattress,* like Norbert Schulz and Dolly Hardt's *Die Prinzessin auf der Erbse* (Berlin 28 November 1954), another version of *The Princess and the Pea.* Versions of *The Emperor's Nightingale* have come from Poland (Ernst Bryll/Piotr Hertel), Germany (Hans Schanzara/Herbert Hennies, Cologne 31 December 1947) and America and Britain (Charles Strouse, New York 1982, Buxton Festival 1982), whilst David Wood authored a children's musical version of *The Tinderbox* (Worcester 26 December 1967), a piece which was also the basis of the German musical *Der Soldat und das Feuerzeug* (Thomas Bürkholz/Heinz-Martin Benecke). *The Little Match Girl* was seen at London's Orange Tree Theatre as *Scraps* (27 December 1977) and subsequently televised and revived (Orange Tree 28 November 1991) as *The Little Match Girl,* and *The Emperor's New Clothes* was once more set to music by America's Elizabeth Swados (La Mama 9 May 1996). A version of *The Ugly Duckling* (George Stiles/Anthony Drewe) was produced at England's Watermill Theatre, Newbury in December 1993, and subsequently under the title *Honk!* at the National Theatre (Olivier Theatre 19 December 1999).

Autobiography: *Mit Livs Eventyr (The [True] Story of My Life)* (1855); Biography: Bain, R N: *Hans Christian Andersen, a Biography* (1895)

ANDERSON, Arthur [A] (d 1942). Songwriter and adapter, prominent before and during the war in the London theatre.

After having made his first venture into the musical theatre with the "very neatly turned" lyrics to a flop musical version of *The Lady of Lyons,* Anderson moved on to success when he wrote lyrics and part-libretti for two Frank Curzon productions, *The White Chrysanthemum* and *The Girl Behind the Counter,* and the lyrics to *Butterflies,* an attractive musical version of W J Locke's whimsical play *The Palace of Puck.*

He subsequently adapted and/or relyricked a good number of Continental musical plays for the English stage, but otherwise concentrated largely on non-theatre songwriting, for a while as part of a group which also included James Tate, Clifford Harris, Valentine, Ord Hamilton and Donovan Parsons. He scored a song success with "Somewhere in France with You" (w Tate, Valentine, 1918), and lyricked interpolated numbers in such pieces as *A Night Out, Jenny, His Girl, The Last Waltz* ("Nur eine Nacht" ad as "Just For a While"), and a revival of *The Maid of the Mountains.*

In 1916 he had one further original success with a vaudevillesque piece called *Toto* which toured for several seasons after its original West End run, and was seen as far afield fron London town as Budapest.

1901 **Melnotte, or The Gardener's Bride** (Frank E Tours/Herbert Shelley) Coronet Theatre 30 September

1905 **The White Chrysanthemum** (Howard Talbot/w Leedham Bantock) Criterion Theatre 31 August

1906 **The Girl Behind the Counter** (Talbot/w Bantock) Wyndham's Theatre 21 April

1908 **An Amateur Raffles** (Ralph Nairn/Herbert Clayton) sketch London Pavilion 2 March

1908 **Butterflies** (J H Robertson/w T H Read/W J Locke) Apollo Theatre 12 May

1910 **Two Merry Monarchs** (Orlando Morgan/w Hartley Carrick/w George Levy) Savoy Theatre 10 March

1910 **The Billposter** (Herman Finck/w Herbert Sergent) sketch, Palace Theatre 31 October

1911 **Nightbirds** (*Die Fledermaus*) English lyrics (Lyric Theatre) and as *The Merry Countess* (New York, 1912)

1912 **Darby and Joan** (*Brüderlein fein*) English version (London Coliseum)

1912 **The Daring of Diane** (*Die süssen Grisetten*) English version (Tivoli)

1912 **Two Little Brides** (*Schneeglöckchen*) American version w Harold Atteridge, J T Powers (Casino Theater, New York)

1912 **The Grass Widows** revised version of *Two Little Brides* w Hartley Carrick (Apollo Theatre)

1912 **The H'arum Lily** (*Abenteuer in Harem*) English version w Carrick (London Pavilion)

1913 **The Marriage Market** (*Leányvásár*) English version w Adrian Ross, Gladys Unger (Daly's Theatre)

1914 **The Joy-Ride Lady** (*Autoliebchen*) English version w Carrick (New Theatre)

1916 **Toto** (Archibald Joyce, Merlin Morgan/Gladys Unger) Duke of York's Theatre 19 April

1917 **The Beauty Spot** (James Tate/Clifford Harris, Valentine/w P-L Flers) Gaiety Theatre 22 December

1924 **Springtime** (*Frühling*) 1 act English version (Empire Theatre)

ANDERSON, [James] Maxwell (b Atlantic, Pa, 15 December 1888; d Stamford, Conn, 28 February 1959).

A highly regarded and successful American playwright (*What Price Glory?* w Laurence Stallings, *Winter-*

set, High Tor, Key Largo, Anne of the Thousand Days, etc), Anderson collaborated on two Broadway musicals with a purposefully left-wing political bias with composer Kurt Weill. In *Knickerbocker Holiday,* the first and more successful of the pair, he notably composed the lyric to the show's take-out tune "September Song." The second, *Lost in the Stars,* was a musical theatre adaptation of the South African novel *Cry, the Beloved Country.* Both reached the cinema screen in their musical versions, *Knickerbocker Holiday* in 1944 and *Lost in the Stars* in 1974.

The 1980 off-Broadway musical *Elizabeth and Essex* (York Theater, Doug Katsaros/Richard Engquist/ Michael Stewart, Mark Bramble, 16 performances) was based on Anderson's play *Elizabeth the Queen* (1920), his *High Tor* was adapted as a television film musical, with a score by Arthur Schwartz (CBS 10 March 1956) and his *The Bad Seed* was used as the basis for a burlesque musical (Marvin Laird/Joel Paley) produced off-Broadway under the title *Ruthless!* (Players Theater 6 May 1992).

Anderson also provided the words to Bernard Hermann's music for the short television opera *A Child is Born* (CBS 25 December 1955).

1938 **Knickerbocker Holiday** (Kurt Weill) Barrymore Theater 19 October

1949 **Lost in the Stars** (Weill) Music Box Theater 30 October

Biographies: Clark, B: *Maxwell Anderson: The Man and His Plays* (Samuel French, New York, 1933), Bailey, M D: *Maxwell Anderson: The Playwright as a Prophet* (Abelard-Schuman, New York, 1957), Shivers, A S: *The Life of Maxwell Anderson* (Stein & Day, New York, 1983)

ANDERSON, Percy (b Willesden, 22 March 1851; d Brixton, 30 October 1928). One of Britain's most effective costume designers for the Victorian and Edwardian stage.

Artist Percy Anderson made his debut as a designer for the theatre with the bulk of the costumes for the comic opera *The Lady of the Locket* (1885), the first full-scale stage work composed by his young partner William Fullerton, and produced with much splendor at the new Empire Theatre under the management of actor John Shine and John Hollingshead. These costumes were designed and made with a lavishness and individuality uncommon in the theatre of the time (in a large cast, each chorister's clothes were separately designed) and Anderson won extended critical approval for his "rich and gorgeous dresses," his array of variously shaded crimson Venetian costumes earning him acclaim as the first theatrical designer to use other than those forceful primary colors which had been de rigueur for stage dresses in the age of gas lighting.

Anderson quickly became one of the foremost costume designers in the British musical theatre, being engaged by George Edwardes to supply the costumes for the internationally successful series of Gaiety Theatre new burlesques from *Monte Cristo Jr* in 1886 to *Carmen-Up-to-Data* in 1890, by D'Oyly Carte for the original *The Gondoliers, The Yeomen of the Guard, The Nautch Girl* and the latter day Savoy Theatre comic operas, and for Edwardes's four greatest products from Daly's Theatre, *The Geisha* (1896), *A Greek Slave* (1898), *San Toy* (1899) and *A Country Girl* (1902). He also, during the same period, designed a number of American productions (*The Merry Monarch* 1890, *The Robber of the Rhine* 1892, Lillian Russell's *Giroflé-Girofla* 1892, *The Rainmaker of Syria* 1893, *The Chieftain* 1895, *His Excellency* 1895, *The Geisha* 1896, *Half a King* 1896, *Erminie* revival 1898, *The Little Corporal* 1898, Francis Wilson's *Cyrano de Bergerac* 1899).

During the first years of the 20th century, whilst venturing into all areas of theatre, including the designs for a complete *Ring of the Nibelungs* in Germany, Anderson designed regularly for Edwardes and for other musical managements in Britain and in America, including amongst his work Edward German's *Merrie England* and *A Princess of Kensington,* Ivan Caryll's Napoléonic *The Duchess of Dantzic,* the Gaiety musicals *The Girls of Gottenberg* and *Havana,* the Daly's Theatre *The Cingalee* and the daffodil-drenched *The Belle of Brittany.* However, in 1907 he lost his sizeable weekly retainer as house designer to Edwardes and found himself for some years boycotted by most important London musical-theatre managements after he expressed his opinions of Edwardes and his inner circle of musical-play creators (Pat Malone and James Tanner) in too extravagantly bitchy—and insufficiently private—a fashion during the course of an abusive court case brought against Edwardes by one of his friends.

Anderson went underground for a while, designed the clothes for Henry Savage's Broadway production of *The Merry Widow* (1908), Charles Dillingham's mounting of *The Slim Princess* (1912) and A H Woods's *Tantalizing Tommy* and attempted a comeback on the British scene by hiding his identity behind the name of another designing firm, but to little avail. Eventually, however, he resurfaced for what was, after this period in the wilderness, virtually a second career, a career highlighted by his costuming of Tree's spectacular 1916 production of *Chu Chin Chow* at His Majesty's Theatre, and thereafter of such pieces as *A Southern Maid* at Daly's, the beautifully staged *Monsieur Beaucaire* with Maggie Teyte as its star, the vast Comstock and Gest New York spectacular *Aphrodite,* and Oscar Asche's dazzling pageant *Mecca/ Cairo.* In his 75th year he designed Künneke's *Riki-Tiki* for the Gaiety Theatre.

ANDERSSON, Benny (b Stockholm, 16 December 1946).

A member of the highly popular singing group Abba, Andersson collaborated with fellow member Björn Ulvaeus on the composition of the songs which the group took to the top of the charts (''Dancing Queen,'' ''Knowing Me Knowing You,'' ''The Name of the Game,'' ''Take a Chance on Me,'' ''The Winner Takes It All,'' etc). Their music formed the basis of three juvenile pasticcio made-for-records shows compiled in France, one of which was staged in Britain, before they collaborated with librettist/lyricist Tim Rice on the musical *Chess* (''I Know Him So Well,'' ''Heaven Help My Heart,'' ''One Night in Bangkok''). In spite of the success gained by their score, it was another decade before the partners supplied another to the musical theatre. This time, the subject was one rather nearer to home, Vilhelm Moberg's story of Swedish immigrants in America, *Kristina fran Duvemala.* Produced in Sweden, it proved highly popular and its favorite song ''Guldet Blev Till Sand'' topped the local hit parades.

In 1999, on the crest of the nostalgic revival of interest in Abba's music fuelled by such films as *Priscilla, the Queen of the Desert,* and of the sing-the-score-coming-into-the-theatre show, the popular songs of their heyday were melded into the score of a slightly tongue-in-cheek piece called *Mamma mia!* which at the time of writing seems likely to outscore all their previous stage works in the public favor.

1983 **Abbacadabra** (w Ulvaeus/Alain Boublil, Daniel Boublil ad Don Black, David Wood) Lyric Theatre, Hammersmith, London 8 December)

1986 **Chess** (w Ulvaeus/Tim Rice) Prince Edward Theatre, London 14 May

1995 **Kristina fran Duvemala** (w Ulvaeus/Carl-Johan Seth) Storan Malmö Music Theater 7 October; Cirkus Teater, Stockholm 14 February 1998

1999 **Mamma mia!** (w Ulvaeus/Catherine Johnson) Prince Edward Theatre 6 April

Literature: Oldham, Calder & Irwin: *Abba: The Name of the Game* (Sidgwick & Jackson, London, 1975)

ANDREWS, Julie [WELLS, Julia Elizabeth] (b Walton-on-Thames, 1 October 1935). Coolly attractive actress of stage and screen with a clear, effortless soprano tied to utterly undistorted sung English.

A child soprano in variety and pantomime, Julie Andrews appeared in the 1947 revue *Starlight Roof* singing Ambroise Thomas's coloratura aria ''Je suis Titania.'' She was seen as principal girl in the London Palladium pantomime of 1953 and was subsequently cast in the ingenue role of Polly Browne in the American reproduction of the London success, *The Boy Friend* (1954).

She created the role of Eliza Doolittle in *My Fair Lady* (1956) on Broadway, introducing ''I Could Have Danced All Night,'' ''Show Me,'' ''Wouldn't It Be Loverly'' and ''Just You Wait, Henry Higgins,'' and repeated her triumphant American success opposite Rex Harrison and Stanley Holloway in London's production of the show (1958), before going on to star in Lerner and Loewe's subsequent *Camelot* (1960), playing Queen Guenevere (''Take Me to the Fair,'' ''The Simple Joys of Maidenhood,'' etc) to the King Arthur of Richard Burton. Her success in musical theatre was mirrored in musical film where she appeared in the title roles of *Mary Poppins* (Academy Award, 1964), *Thoroughly Modern Millie* (1967) and, most notably, as Maria von Trapp in the blockbusting film version of *The Sound of Music* (1965, ''I Have Confidence,'' ''Something Good''). She also impersonated Gertrude Lawrence in a filmland biography entitled *Star!* (1968) and appeared in television musical versions of *High Tor* (1956) and *Cinderella* (1957) before quitting the musical scene to to spend nearly 30 years as a film and television actress. She returned to the singing stage to take part in a compilation show *Putting It Together* at the Manhattan Theater Club in 1993, before profiting from a culture which doesn't mind how less than juvenile its great ''juvenile'' stars become—as long as they've been truly great while they were truly juvenile—by taking on the ingenue title role in *Victor-Victoria,* a part which she had (much) earlier played successfully on the screen, in a 1995 Broadway stage musical drawn from that film. Her recorded voice was subsequently heard in the London musical *Doctor Doolittle* (1998) as that of the puppet Polynesia the Parrot.

Plate 6. **Julie Andrews.** *A prisoner of the gutter, Eliza Doolittle meets Henry Higgins (Rex Harrison).*

Biographies: Cottrell, J: *Julie Andrews: The Story of a Star* (Barker, London, 1968), Windeler, R: *Julie Andrews* (Putnam, New York, 1970), etc

AND SO TO BED Comedy in 3 acts by James Bernard Fagan with music and lyrics by Vivian Ellis. New Theatre, London, 17 October 1951.

A musical version of Fagan's highly successful play (Queen's Theatre 6 September 1926) on the fictional flirtations of the historical Samuel Pepys and King Charles II, planned around comic Leslie Henson in the latter days of his career, *And So to Bed* allowed the star to show off a different side of his comic persona from the energetically frog-faced efforts which had made him a favorite. Cast as the unfortunately amorous diarist, caught up in an embarrassing situation with Mistress Knight (Jessie Royce Landis, the almost original Marianne of *New Moon* a quarter of a century earlier), the mistress of the King (Keith Michell), Henson had a comic role of fine farcical potential which required, and got, none of the ad lib gagging usually inserted by musical comedians of that period into their roles.

Ellis's accompanying music was written in an elegant period style, ranging from madrigal to rigadon and jig, and had the air of being more an extended score of incidental songs and music, of a ballad opera nature, than the musical part of a modern musical play.

In spite of the fact that Henson's traditional audience had problems accepting him in such a different style of role, Jack de Leon's production of *And So to Bed* had a fine West End run of 323 performances. The show was subsequently revised and made into more of a regular musical comedy to be taken on tour with Henson supported by the popular singing team of Anne Ziegler and Webster Booth as Mistress Knight and the King.

A British television musical version of Fagan's play, with a score by Cyril Ornadel, was produced by ITV in the 1980s under the title *Pepys.*

Recording: original cast recordings compiled on WRC

ANGEL FACE Musical farce in 3 acts by Harry B Smith based on the play *Some Baby* by Zellah Covington and Jules Simonson. Lyrics by Robert B Smith. Music by Victor Herbert. Colonial Theater, Chicago, 8 June 1919; Knickerbocker Theater, New York, 29 December 1919.

George Lederer's production of Victor Herbert's *Angel Face* did not have a smooth life. A musicalization of the play *Some Baby* (1915), originally played at the Fulton Theater with Francine Larrimore, Frank Lalor and Emma Janvier featured in its cast, it had a plot based on a rejuvenating elixir into which a certain number of singing-dancing young couples were eased. Marguerite Zender was Betty, the ingenuous-looking lass of the musical's title, anxious to entrap the sculptor Arthur Griffin (Tyler Brooke), who is, at the outset, engaged to her older sister, Vera (Minerva Grey). On the comical side George Schiller played a Professor Barlow, who thinks his elixir has turned the comical Tessie (Emilie Lea) into a baby. John E Young was a would-be musical comedy writer, and vaudeville's Jack Donahue topped up the principal cast as a correspondence-school detective called Slooch. The cast was equipped with a Victor Herbert score which included a medley of his old hits, and one new one: ''I Might Be Your Once-In-A-While,'' introduced by Young and Miss Lea.

The show opened in Chicago where it was well received, but it was stopped in its tracks by an actors' strike. It was rerouted to Philadelphia and Boston and, having twice changed comedienne en route (Ada Meade giving way to first Adele Rowland and then Emilie Lea), it landed on Broadway six months after its premiere only to be shunted out after a 57-performance season because the theatre was otherwise booked. It went profitably touring, but attracted further complications when one of the original play's producers sued the other two, claiming they had unilaterally sold off the musical rights and he hadn't been paid.

Angel Face had its worst time, however, when Norman J Norman produced it in London with Winifred Barnes in the title role, alongside Brooke, Mabel Sealby, Eric Blore and George Gregory. It won what were reported as being ''the most adverse press criticisms for some time'' and came off after 13 performances.

UK: Strand Theatre 11 October 1922

ANIMAL CRACKERS Musical comedy in 2 acts by George S Kaufman and Morrie Ryskind. Music and lyrics by Bert Kalmar and Harry Ruby. 44th Street Theater, New York, 23 October 1928.

A third stage vehicle for the Marx Brothers, following their successes with *I'll Say She Is* and *The Cocoanuts, Animal Crackers* had the four comedians performing their special brand of comedy in and around a little plot about a painting stolen from the Long Island home of richly endowed Mrs Rittenhouse (Margaret Dumont). Groucho Marx played the part of a celebrated explorer, the solar-topeed Captain Spalding, who sets out to track down the thief and recover the picture, yet the authors still managed to get him into an elaborate period costume to impersonate King Louis in an encounter with Madame Dubarry. Chico was the suitably Italianate musico Emanuel Ravelli, Zeppo was one Jamison, and Harpo sported knickers and top hat as The Professor, bumbling around in the dark and a simultaneous thunderstorm to remove the not-so-very-crucial picture from its place. Alice Wood completed the principal lineup as ingenue Miss Arabella Rittenhouse.

The short musical score which crept in amongst the clowning included ''Watching the Clouds Roll By,'' ''The Long Island Low Down'' and ''Who's Been Listening to My Heart?,'' but the song success of the piece was Groucho Marx's entrance number, ''Hooray for Captain Spalding'' (and his reply ''Hello, I Must Be Going'').

Animal Crackers proved a good vehicle for the team. Hailed as an ''uproarious slapstick comedy[,] . . . a new fury of puns and gibes'' for what were undoubtedly ''the maddest troupe of comedians of the day. . . [,] nihilists [who combine] vulgar mountebankery [with] bewildering, passing, stinging thrusts at everything in general, including themselves,'' it played a Broadway run of 191 performances, following which the brothers put their performances down on film.

It was barely a musical film, as one new song, ''Why Am I So Romantic?'' replaced almost all of the rest of the stage score—except, of course, ''Hooray for Captain Spalding.'' It was, as the stage show was, a zany comedy show equipped with musical parts which filled a very secondary place. Being so wholly made-to-measure for the Marxes, *Animal Crackers* had little life beyond its original production, but it was given a showing, in a version stiffened with further (mostly) Kalmar/Ruby songs at Washington's Arena Stage in 1982 (8 May), again in Boston (1988), and another at Connecticut's Goodspeed Opera House in 1992 (23 September). It also got a first British showing at Manchester's Royal Exchange in 1998 in a production which was later seen at the Barbican Pit (28 June) and for two months at Shaftesbury Avenue's Lyric Theatre. Bean Keaton, Joseph Alessi and Toby Sedgwick imitated the Marx Brothers.

UK: Royal Exchange, Manchester 12 March 1998

Film: Paramount 1930

ANKLES AWEIGH Musical comedy in 2 acts by Guy Bolton and Eddie Davis. Lyrics by Dan Shapiro. Music by Sammy Fain. Mark Hellinger Theater, New York, 18 April 1955.

Following on behind, and in the same style as the same authors' successful *Follow the Girls, Ankles Aweigh* was a ''musical comedy'' which, in an era where the romantic musical play had become the fashion, thoroughly deserved that description. Jane Kean played a Hollywood starlet called Wynne and Mark Dawson her navy-airman newlywed husband, who spent the evening attempting—in the face of many an empêchement—to consummate their marriage on what was supposed to be a nice, peaceful honeymoon. The smidgin of plot, decorated by lashings of mostly cheerfully low comedy, skated from one picturesque Mediterranean location to another in what was described as ''a story about a movie company on location in Italy, some American sailors, intrigue, misunderstandings, strumpets in Morocco, a stolen code, an interrupted honeymoon, etc.'' The leading lady's sister, Betty Kean (they shared the top billing) paired with Lew Parker in support as Elsey and Dinky.

The four featured players largely cornered the music of the show, which ranged from the enthusiastic ''Kiss Me and Kill Me with Love'' to the heroine's assertion that ''Nothing Can Replace a Man'' and the strange wish to ''Walk Like a Sailor.'' The number-three lady, Betty George, as Lucia indulged in the ''Headin' for the Bottom Blues.''

The show's cheerful ingenuousness provoked such comments from the serious-minded as ''imagine that nothing interesting has developed in the field of musical comedy for the last ten or fifteen years . . . [;] it leaves off where modern musical comedy began, [with] the worn-out staples of show business that presumably were laid away in the store-house a long time ago.'' However, there were sufficient folk about who just liked a good, low, fun time for Anthony Brady Farrell's production to run through 176 Broadway performances without managing to repeat the success won by *Follow the Girls* at home and abroad.

A revival of a revised version (ad Charles Busch) was mounted at the Goodspeed Opera House, Connecticut, 13 July 1988.

Recording: original cast (Decca, AEI)

ANNE OF GREEN GABLES Musical in 2 acts by Donald Harron based on the novel by Lucy Maud Montgomery. Lyrics by Donald Harron and Norman Campbell (later also Mavor Moore, Elaine Campbell). Music by Norman Campbell. Confederation Centre Theatre, Charlottetown, Canada, August 1965.

L M Montgomery's 1908 Canadian novel, *Anne of Green Gables,* a popular favorite with young lady readers through the years, was twice translated to the large screen (silently in 1919 with Mary Miles Minter, 1934 with Anne Shirley) before Donald Harron and Norman Campbell wrote a television musical version which was produced in Canada in 1956. Nearly a decade later, that version was readapted and extended into a full-length stage musical, and produced at Charlottetown, in the area where the events of the novel take place.

Anne is sent from an orphanage to live with Mathew and Marilla Cuthbert, who had intended to adopt a boy to help on their farm. Used to sticking up for herself, she has run-ins with the local busybody and with some chaffing fellow students, but wins friends both in school and at home as she works her way towards the top of the class, at the expense of rival Gilbert Blythe. By the final curtain all hearts, on stage and off, are Anne's.

Three seasons at Charlottetown prefaced showings around Canada for the show, and in 1969 Canadian producer Bill Freedman mounted the show in London. Polly James played Anne, with Hiram Sherman and Barbara Hamilton as her adoptive "parents," through a run of 319 West End performances. *Anne of Green Gables* was subsequently seen for 16 performances at New York's City Center, and has continued to win hardy annual productions in Canada.

UK: New Theatre 16 April 1969; USA: City Center 21 December 1971

Recordings: London cast (CBS), Charlottetown revival 1984 (Ready)

ANNIE Musical in 2 acts by Thomas Meehan based on the cartoon strip *Little Orphan Annie* by Harold Gray. Lyrics by Martin Charnin. Music by Charles Strouse. Goodspeed Opera House, East Haddam, Conn, 10 August 1976; Alvin Theater, New York, 21 April 1977.

Beloved, since 1924, by readers of *The Chicago Tribune* and by other newspaper comic-strip devotees around the world, mop-headed, pinafore-frocked Little Orphan Annie made her way on to the musical stage for the first time, half a century on, at Connecticut's Goodspeed Opera House, around that time the breeding ground for several successful new musicals.

Annie (Kristin Vigard) is an outspoken little orphan who unsuccessfully runs away from the home presided over by the grotesque Miss Hannigan (Maggie Task) into the big, wide world that is New York City. Her second escape is luckier. She succeeds in getting herself chosen to be the unowned child whom exorbitantly rich and powerful Daddy Warbucks (Reid Shelton) will conscience-salvingly treat to a moneyed Christmas. But over the festive season Warbucks falls under the insistent charm of the little girl, and he promises to help her find the parents who, she is sure, would come back for her if they could. He even gets not only the President of the United States but the National Broadcasting Corporation in on the act. Alas, the only candidates who pass the test turn out to be Miss Hannigan's rascally brother and his moll in greedy disguise. Little Orphan Annie really is an orphan, but by the final curtain she has found herself a fine replacement father in Daddy Warbucks.

Strouse and Charnin's songs helped bring the cartoon characters off the page without ever making the mistake of making them too three-dimensional. Little Annie dreamed of her missing family ("Maybe"), joined her orphan friends asserting "It's the Hard-Knock Life," stormed out her optimistic hopes for "Tomorrow" in one of the show's most take-awayable tunes and joined in the jolly hymn in praise of "NYC," whilst the personnel of the radio's Hour of Smiles gave forth with a catchy pastiche of old radioland in "You're Never Fully Dressed Without a Smile." Two of the piece's most effective songs, however, were late arrivals in the score: Miss Hannigan's venomously frightened description of what "Little Girls" do to her nervous equilibrium, and the greasy song-and-dance trio in which she joins her accomplices in dreaming of "Easy Street."

Mike Nichols's Broadway production followed eight months behind the original provincial staging. Shelton repeated his portrayal of bald-headed Daddy Warbucks—a role which was to go on to force many an actor to have his head shaven to chime with the original cartoon—alongside Dorothy Loudon as Miss Hannigan and Andrea McArdle, promoted from minor orphanhood at Goodspeed to the title role, tricked out in the curly red wig and white-collared and-cuffed red dress which would be the uniform of countless Annies. Sandy Faison played Warbucks's secretary, Grace Farrell, Robert Fitch and Barbara Erwin were the phony parents, and there was of course, Sandy, the dog, a familiar character from the original cartoon strip, to provide the "animal" to go with the "child."

The show hit the spot precisely, and was quickly established as a hit of the first degree, with an appeal which went well beyond the family groups which might have seemed at first to be its natural audience. Nichols's production stayed for 2,377 performances on Broadway as *Annie* moved on to multiple productions and translations around the world, even in countries where the *Chicago Tribune* and Little Orphan Annie had never been heard of.

Michael White's London mounting—a reproduction of the Broadway version, staged by lyricist Charnin—imported Miss McArdle to recreate her Annie alongside Stratford Johns (Daddy Warbucks) and Sheila Hancock (Miss Hannigan), and once again the piece scored a major success, remaining more than three and a half years (1,485 performances) at the West End's Victoria Palace before moving on to the road, and to widespread productions in provincial houses. It returned to London for a Christmas season in 1982–83 (20 December, Adelphi Theatre, 66 performances), but took little heed of the season elsewhere. Most of Britain's producing regional theatres have staged *Annie* at one time or another, and the optimistic moppet even made a second return to the West End in 1998 (Victoria Palace 30 September).

Australia carried on the run of successful English-language *Annie*s with J C Williamson Ltd's production, starring top Australian names Hayes Gordon (Warbucks), Jill Perryman (Miss Hannigan) and Nancye Hayes (Lily) alongside the Annie of Sally-Anne Bourne, with New Zealand, Ireland and South Africa following suit, whilst the show was translated for productions in Mexico and

Spain (Teatro Principe, Madrid 25 September 1981), in Denmark (Aalborg Theatre 10 December 1981), Japan and Germany at the head of a very long list of foreign versions.

A film version produced by Columbia in 1982, with Albert Finney (Warbucks), Carol Burnett (Miss Hannigan), Tim Curry (Rooster), Anne Reinking (Grace), Bernadette Peters (Lily) and Aileen Quinn as an Annie chosen after a much-publicized international search, put in five alternative songs—losing ''NYC'' amongst others—and proved much less popular than the stage show.

In an age where successful films breed sequels like guinea pigs, this most successful of theatre shows attempted the same trick. *Annie 2,* subtitled ''Miss Hannigan's Revenge,'' proved a lemming. It featured Dorothy Loudon, repeating her original part in the sub-title role with Danielle Finlay as Annie, as it followed the harridan's attempts to win Daddy Warbucks's (Harve Presnell) contest for a wife and mother to his new daughter. Written by the same team as the original, it was mounted at the Kennedy Center, Washington, DC (4 January 1990), but did not make the announced move to its 1 March 1990 opening at Broadway's Marquis Theater. However, there was to be an *Annie 2a.* A rewritten musequel entitled *Annie Warbucks* was produced at Chicago's Marriot Lincolnshire Theater on 9 February 1992 and proceeded from there towards a Broadway opening at the Neil Simon Theater. The tale was once again that of the search by Warbucks (Presnell) for a mother for his child, but Miss Hannigan was no longer in on the action. Once again it blew out prior to reaching New York. However, in 1993 (9 August) the show did make it to town, off- rather than on-Broadway. Presnell and Kathryn Zaremba were Daddy and his Annie, and the show ran for two hundred performances at the Variety Arts Theater. The original *Annie* returned to Broadway in 1997 (Martin Beck Theater 26 March) with Nell Carter (Miss Hannigan), Brittny Kissinger (Annie) and Conrad John Schuck (Warbucks) featured, but exited after 240 performances. However, London followed (30 September 1998) with Kevin Colson and Lesley Joseph (succeeded by female impersonator Lily Savage) featured and Budapest too brought the urchin back for more as little orphan Annie confirmed her place as as great a stage favorite as she had been a cartoon-strip one.

The show was given a second screen showing when a television version was mounted in 1999 with Victor Garber and Kathy Bates featured.

Annie succeeded *Li'l Abner* and Bruce Bairnsfather's *The Better 'Ole* as the most successful musical theatre piece written around a newspaper cartoon. They had had many predecessors on the American musical stage over almost a century, of which a handful, such as Victor Herbert's *Little Nemo* (taken from Winsor McKay's *New York Herald* ''Little Nemo in Slumberland,'' 115 performances) and a stage musical of another *Herald* cartoon *Buster Brown* (Harmanus Bleeker Hall, Albany, NY 25 December 1903, Majestic Theater, 1905, 95 performances) had some New York success, but by and large cartoon-to-musical results had not been encouraging. Not in the larger metropolitan areas, anyhow. There were, however, a goodly number of ''cartoon musicals'' which cleaned up in no uncertain way in the less sophisticated dates of the American outlands.

The folk of *Hogan's Alley* were amongst the earliest to make the trip to the singing stage, showing up as musical comedy characters on the touring circuits in the mid 1890s (People's Theater 12 October 1896) alongside the equally out-of-town *McFadden's Row of Flats* (Ivan L Davis/E W Townsend, 6 September 1897, People's Theater 27 September 1897), based on R F Outcault's drawings, a piece which was toured under producer Gus Hill's aegis in multiple productions through the smaller dates of the American countryside for a number of years. In the early years of the 20th century Hill's stage musical of *Alphonse and Gaston* (Metropolis Theater 20 December 1902) and others of Rudolf Dirks's *The Katzenjammer Kids* (Edward Blondell, Park Theater, Philadelphia 16 October 1900, 3rd Avenue Theater 26 November 1900), Carl Schultze's New *York Herald* strip *Foxy Grandpa* (Joseph Hart/R Melville Baker Asbury Park, NJ 2 August 1901) and *Looping the Loop* (Music Hall, Webster, Mass 25 August 1902), *The Happy Hooligan* (Nicholas Brown/Frank Dumont Metropolis Theater 10 March 1902), *Mickey Finn* (3rd Avenue 4 May 1903) and, more substantially, of *The New York Herald*'s *Fluffy Ruffles* (W T Francis/Wallace Irwin/J J McNally, Criterion Theater 7 September 1908) proved short-lived in town but long-runners around the one-to-three-night stands.

George McManus's *The Newlyweds and Their Baby* (John W Bratton, Nat Ayer/Paul West, Seymour Brown/Aaron Hoffman, West, Majestic Theater 22 March 1909) proved a multiple-company winner away from the bigger cities, as did the same author's *Panhandle Pete* (Samuel Lehman/Edward Laska, David Kemp/Willard Holcomb, Metropolis Theater 10 September 1906) and *Let George Do It* (Nat Ayer/Paul West, Aaron Hoffamn, West End Theatre 22 April 1912) while his more famous *Bringing Up Father* was used for a series of touring shows—including *Bringing up Father in Ireland* (Seymour Furth/Nat Leroy Lyric Theater 30 March 1925) and *Bringing up Father [at the Seashore]* (Lyric Theater 6 April 1925 Seymour Furth/R F Carroll/Edward Hutchinson, Leroy)—in America as well as for *Patsy from Paris* (Maidstone 1927, Louis Jerome/George Arthurs) in England. Another comic strip series of shows which, similarly, spent most of their life in the boondocks was a Gus Hill set based on the *Mutt and Jeff* characters. *The Dingbat Family* (John Bratton/Mark Swan, Paterson, NJ 28 October 1912) and *Keeping Up* (Crescent, Brooklyn, 1925) based on the ''Pop, Mom and . . .'' cartoons in the *Globe* were other cartoon musicals which did not hit the great metropolites. The Shubert production of *My Boy Friend* (Parsons' Theater, Hartford, Conn 1 December 1924) based on Jack Lait's ''Gus the Bus'' cartoon was, similarly, seen in Boston but not on Broadway.

In more recent times, the world-famous *Superman* was brought to the stage in *It's a Bird . . . It's a Plane . . . It's Superman* (29 March 1966), a piece composed, like *Annie,* by Charles Strouse. The Charles M Schulz ''Peanuts'' strip served as the basis for two musicals—the generally successful *You're a Good Man, Charlie Brown* (Clark Gesner/John Gordon Theater 80 St Marks 7 March 1967) and *Snoopy* (Larry Grossman/Hal Hackady Little Fox Theater, San Francisco 9 December 1975)—whilst Britain turned out stage versions of the Scots *Oor Wullie* (Overground Theatre 20 December 1978), and the *Daily Mail*'s *Andy Capp* (Aldwych Theatre 28 September 1982, 99 performances), with Tom Courtenay as its slobbish hero. Osbert Lancaster's devastating Maudie Littlehampton was given stage life by David Wood in *Maudie* (Thorndike Theatre, Leatherhead 12 November 1974).

In more recent years the animated cartoon film has taken over from the newspaper strip as a source of two-dimensional-character musicals.

Another musical entitled *Annie,* this one dealing with a lady from the Moral Rearmament Group, was produced at that group's Westminster Theatre, London, in 1967 (William Reed/Alan Thornhill 27 July, 398 performances).

UK: Victoria Palace 3 May 1978; Australia: Her Majesty's Theatre, Melbourne 25 October 1978; Germany: Landestheater, Detmold 20 December 1980; Hungary: Thália Színház 7 April 1998

Films: Columbia Pictures 1982, TV film 1999

Recordings: original cast (Columbia), London cast (CBS), Australian cast (Festival), Spanish cast (Bocaccio), Danish cast (Polydor), Norwegian cast, film soundtrack (Columbia), French soundtrack (Rastar), etc, *Annie Warbucks* original cast

Dogography: Betloni, W, Thomas, A: *Sandy, the Autobiography of a Star* (Simon & Schuster, New York, 1978)

ANNIE DEAR Musical comedy in 3 acts by Clare Kummer based on her play *Good Gracious Annabelle.* Music by Sigmund Romberg and Clare Kummer. Times Square Theater, New York, 4 November 1924.

Mrs Kummer's *Good Gracious Annabelle* (Republic Theater 31 October 1916) was originally written as a hopeful libretto, but it ended up being produced by Arthur Hopkins as a straight play (although the authoress-songwriter did manage to sneak in one song, ''Other Eyes,'' for her heroine) with considerable Broadway success (111 performances). Only eight years later was the now highly rated playwright's first hit turned into the musical it had been intended as, under the aegis of Florenz Ziegfeld, as a vehicle for Billie Burke, in Lola Fisher's role of Annabelle.

A sort of a modern variation on the Prince-and-Princess-in-disguise theme decorated with snazzy chat and a bundle of complexities about mining shares, mistaken identities and masquerades, it had for its heroine a dizzy lass called Annie (Miss Burke) who, having fled from her rough country husband immediately after a curious teenage marriage, runs daffily through her allowance, gets mixed up in a divorce and hides as a billionaire's cook to avoid both sets of consequences. On the way she falls in love with mine-owner John Ralston (Marion Green), rival of her ever-intoxicated employer (Ernest Truex), who turns out to be . . . none other than the man she married. He'd got educated, rich and shaved his beard off, so she didn't recognize him.

Romberg and Miss Kummer (six numbers) supplied a lightweight score, suited to the rather more-sophisticated-than-usual dialogue of the play-turned-libretto, and Ziegfeld interpolated some outrageous extravagances into the drawing-room-comedy-sized piece, which brought him to words with the shocked author. *Annie Dear* (which had been called simply *Annie* on its way into town) was received very warmly and played on Broadway for 103 performances.

ANNIE GET YOUR GUN Musical comedy in 2 acts by Herbert and Dorothy Fields. Music and lyrics by Irving Berlin. Imperial Theater, New York, 16 May 1946.

The idea of a musical comedy based on the career of semi-legendary sharpshooter Annie Oakley was first mooted by Herbert and Dorothy Fields, as a potential vehicle for singing star Ethel Merman. The Fields took the project to Rodgers and Hammerstein, at that time riding very high with *Oklahoma!* and *Carousel* as writers, but also active as producers of other people's works. This one—and the star envisaged—didn't fit into the romantic musical-play mode in which the pair were then writing, but the combination of librettists, subject and star appealed mightily to their producing instincts. They took the venture on, and added to the team the most outstanding composer they could come up with: Jerome Kern. However, before *Annie Oakley* got off the ground, Kern died. Irving Berlin, who had wandered away from the world of the book musical, was persuaded by the producers to take his place.

Outback lassie Annie Oakley (Miss Merman) is as naïve as they come, but she can put two bullets through

Plate 7. **Annie Get Your Gun.** *Suzi Quatro's apple-cheeked Annie goes Indian for the benefit of Chief Sitting Bull (Berwick Kaler).*

a bird on the wing without blinking. It is a talent which wins her a job in the Wild West show toured by Buffalo Bill Cody (William O'Neal), but which offends the masculinity of the show's handsome shooting star, Frank Butler (Ray Middleton), and dampens the prospect of a romance between the pair. Unable to handle the situation, Frank finally quits the Wild West show and goes to the opposition, but that way neither of them is happy and neither show prospers. A merger is proposed, but that old pride gets in the way again, and it is only when wise old Sitting Bull (Harry Bellaver) gently shows the unthinking Annie that she can win herself a stubborn man by losing a shooting match, that the happy ending finally arrives.

Berlin's score proved to be full of winning numbers. Annie's singing role was huge. She chortled through the music-hally tale of the folks back home who are used to ''Doin' what Comes Natur'lly,'' bewailed the fact that ''You Can't Get a Man With a Gun,'' belted her little brother and sisters to sleep with ''A Moonshine Lullaby,'' hailed the simple life in ''Sun in the Morning,'' and whooped through her induction into Sitting Bull's tribe in ''I'm an Indian Too.'' Romance touched her hopefully for ''They Say That Falling in Love Is Wonderful'' and ''I Got Lost in His Arms,'' but business won out as she faced up to challenge Frank with a gun declaring ''Anything You Can Do (I can do better)'' at the end of an evening where one hit number had followed another with barely a breath-space. Frank, too, had his hits, both in the duets with Annie, and also with the rueful ballad ''My Defenses Are Down'' and his tuneful serenade to the sugary ideal of ''The Girl That I Marry,'' whilst the supporting characters got a peep-in in a pair of light-footed duets (''Who Do You Love, I Hope?,'' ''I'll Share It All With You'') for the soubret pair (Anne Nyman, Kenny Bowers) and with a rousing affirmation that ''There's No Business Like Show Business'' as Buffalo Bill and his advance manager, Charlie Davenport (Marty May) pointed out the joys of barnstorming to the inexperienced Annie.

Annie Get Your Gun was a huge success. Rodgers and Hammerstein's Broadway production ran for 1,147 performances and, while it ran, the show began to make its way round the world. Emile Littler's London production, featuring Dolores Gray (Annie), Bill Johnson (Frank), Wendy Toye (Winnie) and Irving Davies (Tommy), arrived in town within weeks of two other major hits, *Oklahoma!* and *Bless the Bride,* giving the West End one of the liveliest injections of entertainment it had had in years as London theatre-folk lined up argumentatively to support one new show or another. C B Cochran himself sabotaged *Bless the Bride*'s run, and, if *Oklahoma!* lasted a little longer than *Annie Get Your Gun,* the latter show, housed in the vastness of the London Coliseum, undoubtedly welcomed the larger number of customers in the course of its 1,304 West End performances.

As in London, Australia's *Annie Get Your Gun* didn't cast a star, it made one. Variety performer Evie Hayes was J C Williamson Ltd's choice for Annie Oakley, teamed with Webb Tilton as Frank and with former Savoy star Claude Flemming as Buffalo Bill. When the piece opened in Melbourne, just a few weeks after London's premiere, she and the show scored the kind of sensational long-running hit that Australia was at that time unused to seeing. Ten months in Melbourne were followed by 12 more (425 performances) at Sydney's Theatre Royal (27 August 1948), with June Clyde spelling Miss Hayes, prior to a New Zealand tour, a second round in Australia in 1952 and regular reappearances thereafter.

Earl Covert who took a stint as leading man in this production was also Frank Butler to the Annie of Mary Martin in the first American touring company, which set out on the road soon after the British and Australian premieres and ran through more than 18 months. The London run was also followed by an extensive tour, whilst 1950 saw the production of a film version (originally begun with Judy Garland, but ultimately starring Betty Hutton opposite Howard Keel as Frank) and a French production, mounted by Maurice Lehmann at the huge Théâtre du Châtelet (ad André Mouëzy-Éon, Albert Willemetz). The first Broadway musical to have been produced in Paris since the French capital's love affair with the works of Romberg, *Annie du Far-West* featured Lily Fayol, Marcel Merkès, Pierjac (Cossard, ie, Charlie), Jane Montange (Dolly) and Jack Claret (Tommy) through a 316-performance run which was, however, considered a little disappointing.

The show was one of the first modern American musicals to break into the German-language theatre, following close behind the ground-breaking *Kiss Me, Kate* when it was produced at Vienna's Volksoper (ad Marcel Prawy) in 1957. Berlin followed this lead some years later when Heidi Brühl and Robert Trehy starred in a Theater des Westens production (ad Robert Gilbert), and Scandinavia and most other areas where the light musical theatre was popular, as well as one or two where it wasn't, also saw versions of the show.

Annie Get Your Gun became an often-played favorite in the American musical comedy repertoire, as Billie Worth, Martha Raye, Betty Jane Watson, Ginger Rogers, Debbie Reynolds and other musical stars all took their turns as sometimes not-so-young Annies, but the first major revival in New York did not come until 20 years after the original production. Miss Merman starred once more, alongside the Frank Butler of Bruce Yarnell, Benay Venuta (the screen Dolly) and Bellaver repeating his Sitting Bull in a Music Theatre of Lincoln Center production (31 May 1966) which was also seen on the road and briefly at the Broadway Theater (21 December 1966). For this production, the piece was reorganized and the roles of Annie and Frank made even more prominent by the suppression of the soubrets and their two numbers. Berlin provided an additional number for the two stars, "An Old-Fashioned Wedding." Further reorganizations came in 1999 when an *Annie Get Your Gun* following the sad contemporary American trend for censorship in classic musicals was produced. This ethnically cleansed version (ad Peter Stone, produced at the Marquis Theater 20 February 1999) with Bernadette Peters and Tom Wopat featured, played havoc with the Indian parts of the show and won universal condemnation for its trendiness (one commentator described the adaptation as "a frontal lobotomy"), but the show's name and fame still won it a run.

London waited 40 years for its revival, and it too got the revised version when a scaled-down Chichester Festival Theatre production starring Suzi Quatro and Eric Flynn and with Edmund Hockridge featured in the role of Buffalo Bill was brought to the Aldwych Theatre (29 July 1986). Just half a dozen years later the West End got a short second helping of the show when a Plymouth Theatre Royal production, featuring Kim Criswell, John Diedrich, Meg Johnson and Leon Greene, was taken briefly in to the Prince of Wales Theatre (25 November 1992).

The real-life Annie Oakley herself took to the stage in 1902 as the heroine of Loudon McCormick's *The Western Girl* (Elizabeth, NJ 3 November).

UK: London Coliseum 7 June 1947; Australia: Her Majesty's Theatre, Melbourne 20 July 1947; France: Théâtre du Châtelet *Annie du Far-West* 19 February 1950; Austria: Volksoper 27 February 1957; Germany: Theater des Westens *Annie, schiess los!* 5 September 1963

Film: MGM 1950

Recordings: original cast (Decca), New York 1966 revival cast (RCA), German cast (Philips), London cast 1986 (First Night), Swedish cast (Sonet), Japanese cast (HMI), New York revival cast 1998 (Angel), complete (EMI), studio casts (EMI, TER, etc), film soundtrack (MGM), TV cast 1957 (Capitol), etc

ANTIGNY, Blanche d' [ANTIGNY, Marie Ernestine] (b Martizay, Indre, 9 May 1840; d Paris, 28 June 1874).

The decidedly tall, fairly blonde and very shapely Mlle d'Antigny (''cette grande, bonne et belle fille blonde, respirant la force et la sante, jetant la gaiete a pleines mains'' [Arsene Houssaye]), the daughter of a provincial carpenter, was 14 years old and a Parisian shopgirl when she found her first ''protector.'' He carried her off to Bucharest before she abandoned him, gallivanted about a while with gypsies, and then found another gentleman with whom she returned to Paris. She worked at the Cirque d'Hiver and the Bal Mabille as a dancer and a model, and appeared at the Porte-Saint-Martin as a non-speaking Helen of Troy in d'Ennery's *Faust* before she attracted the amorous attention of the Russian tsarist police chief, Mesentzov. Whisked off to live in luxury in Wiesbaden and St Petersburg, she discovered a further ambition and took a bet that she could, if she would, dethrone Hortense Schneider as the reigning queen of the Paris opéra-bouffe stage and of all the off-stage activity that went with that crown.

Her policeman let her go and try, and thus lost her for, after a few singing and acting lessons and a handful of roles at the Palais-Royal (Lolotte in *Danaé et sa bonne,* Vicomtesse de la Farandole in *Le Château à Toto,* succeeding Schneider in *Les Mémoires de Mimi Bamboche,* 1868), she was cast hastily in the star role of the tempestuous Frédégonde in Hervé's *Chilpéric* (1868) when the originally slated Julia Baron fell ill. She triumphed along with the show, and her bet was, to all intents and purposes, won. She confirmed her success as Marguerite in the same composer's *Le Petit Faust,* played in his *L'Oeil crevé* (where an unkind journalist remarked, apparently without real justification, that ''ses diamants jouaient mieux qu'elle'') and became the delight of the Parisian gentlemen of her day to whom, at the dawn of the 1870s, she was the reigning beauty of the French stage and of its adjacent demimonde.

She subsequently played again at the Palais-Royal and became prima donna at the Folies-Dramatiques (*Le Tour du chien vert* 1871, *L'Oeil crevé, Le Petit Faust, Chilpéric,* a super-risqué operettic *Mazeppa,* in which it was reported ''her third act dress was of such limited proportions as to excite murmurs of indignation'' 1872). Hamburg saw her as Offenbach's Métella (*La Vie parisienne*) and London had its opportunity to gaze at (and listen to) her when the Folies-Dramatiques company visited the old Globe Theatre in 1872 to perform *L'Oeil crevé* (Fleur de Noblesse) and *Chilpéric* (Frédégonde). Later in 1872 she appeared at the Menus-Plaisirs in the spectacular burlesque *La Cocotte aux oeufs d'or* and as Zélie in the vaudeville *La Mariée de la rue St-Denis* (1873), but when the preferred, if not necessarily richest, of her lofty series of lovers foundered financially and vanished, she hurried out of town, and ended up in Cairo. She appeared on the local stage in opéra-bouffe and soon attracted the attentions of the Khedive himself.

Blanche was only 34 years of age when she died in Paris in 1874, but there was little doubt that she had well and truly lived. And in one way she lived on: for Blanche d'Antigny was Zola's model for his infamous ''Nana.''

Biography: Vauzat, G: *Blanche d'Antigny* (Charles Bosse, Paris, 1933)

ANTONY, F[riedrich] [NIKOLOWSKY, Anton] (b Vienna, 7 April 1855; d Vienna, 17 January 1916).

Viennese playwright and sometime house author at the Theater in der Josefstadt, whose 25 years of writing for the stage brought forth a sizeable body of work including a large number of Possen, both musical and music-less. A fruitful collaboration with Carl Lindau produced a number of original pieces for the musical stage and also ''Viennese versions'' of a number of others, from Adolf Philipp's New York–German *Across the Big Pond* (aka *From Across the Pond, New York in Wort und Bild*) to a parody of *Die lustige Witwe.*

One of his own works was adapted by Rudolf Lothar as the libretto to the Eugen d'Albert comic opera *Die verschenkte Frau* (Troppau 3 February 1912).

1886 **Der Aprilnarr** (Karl Kleiber/w Carl Lindau) Theater in der Josefstadt 13 April

1886 **Der Stabstrompeter** Viennese version w Lindau and music by Hanns Krenn (Theater in der Josefstadt)

1887 **Wien bleibt Wien** (Hanns Krenn/ad w Lindau) Theater in der Josefstadt 1 October

1888 **Nigerls Reise nach Paris** (Krenn) Theater in der Josefstadt October

1889 **Der dumme Augustin** (Julius Stern/w Anton Maurer) Theater in der Josefstadt 23 October

1890 **Ein alter Hallodri** (Kleiber/w Heinrich Thalboth) Theater in der Josefstadt 4 October

1890 **Die flotten Weiber von Wien** (Kleiber/w Leon Treptow) Theater in der Josefstadt 5 December

1891 **Wien im XX Jahrhundert** (Ernst Reiterer) Carltheater 5 September

1892 **Unser Volk unter Waffen** (Kleiber/w Lindau, Thalboth) Theater in der Josefstadt 17 September

1893 **Die Arbeit hoch** (Alexander Krakauer/w W Fresking) Raimundtheater 4 December

1894 **Die Deutschmeister sind da** (Karl Bergen) Theater in der Josefstadt 31 March

1894 **Der Herr Bigelhofer** (aka *Ein Wiener in Amerika*) (Reiterer/w E Prudens) Carltheater 8 October

1895 **Wiener Touristen** (Karl Kappeller/w Lindau) Theater in der Josefstadt 2 March

1896 **Die Liebe auf ersten Blick** (Leopold Kuhn) Theater an der Wien 9 May

1896 **Der Hungerleider** Viennese version w music by Roth (Theater an der Wien)

1896 **Flotte Geister** (Max von Weinzierl) Raimundtheater 25 January

?1897 **Der Zauberlehrling** (Josef Bayer/w Max Kalbeck, Eugen Negue)

1900 **Die bessere Hälfte** (Paul Mestrozzi) Kaiser-Jubiläums Theater 10 October

1903 **Herz ist Adutt** (Mestrozzi) Kaiser-Jubiläums Theater 18 January

1903 **Gaudeamus Igitur** (Mestrozzi) Kaiser-Jubiläums Theater 24 January

1903 **Der Bräutigam vom Himmel** (Georg Klammer) Jantschtheater 21 October

1904 **Café Pascha** (Mestrozzi/w Emil Norini) Kaiser-Jubiläums Theater 30 January

1904 **Das goldene Handwerk** (Mestrozzi/w Fresking) Kaiser-Jubiläums Theater 12 November

1905 **Das Schwalbennest** (Henri Hirschmann/Maurice Ordonneau ad Maurice Rappaport) Viennese version Venedig in Wien

1905 **Ausser Rand und Band** (Paul Lincke/w Lindau) 1 act Danzers Orpheum 4 November

1905 **Auf's in Orpheum** (Viktor Hollander/Julius Freund) Viennese version w Lindau (Danzers Orpheum)

1906 **Die drei Engel** (Hellmesberger/w Lindau) Venedig in Wien 4 May

1906 **Das Scheckbuch des Teufels** (*Le Carnet du Diable*) German version w Lindau and add mus Maximilian Steiner (Danzers Orpheum)

1906 **Einer, der sich zu helfen weiss** (Richard Fronz) Bürgertheater 2 September

1906 **Über'm grossen Teich** (*Across the Big Pond*) Viennese version w Lindau and mus Ziegler (Theater an der Wien)

1907 **Der lustiger Witwer** (Julius Freund) Viennese version w Lindau and mus M Steiner (Danzers Orpheum)

1907 **Monte Carlo** (Ludwig Roman Ehmel/w Lindau) Neues Operetten-Theater, Leipzig 7 April

1907 **Die kleine Prinzessin** (Bela von Ujj/w Lindau) Venedig in Wien 5 May

1907 **Eine Sensation** (von Ujj/w Lindau) 3 scenes Danzers Orpheum 20 December

1908 **Unser Franz** (Ludwig Gothov-Grüneke) Raimundtheater 31 October

1908 **Der Prinz von Marokko** (Ehmel) 1 act Munich

1909 **Drei Stunden Leben** (von Ujj/w Lindau) 1 act Apollotheater 1 November

1909 **Am Gänselhäusel** (Franz Ziegler) Raimundtheater 14 November

1910 **Wann der Auerhahn balzt** (Ziegler/w Ziegler) Raimundtheater 3 April

1910 **Die verhexte Wienerstadt** (*The New Aladdin*) German version w Lindau (Venedig in Wien)

1913 **Das haben die Mädchen so gerne** (Ernst Wolf, et al/Friedrich Alfred Löbl, et al/w K Elberg) Wiener Bürgertheater 22 March

ANYONE CAN WHISTLE Musical in 2 acts by Arthur Laurents. Lyrics and music by Stephen Sondheim. Majestic Theater, New York, 4 April 1964.

Having worked together on *West Side Story* and *Gypsy,* librettist Arthur Laurents and lyricist Stephen Sondheim, who had recently made his composing mark as the songwriter of the highly successful *A Funny Thing Happened on the Way to the Forum,* came together again on *Anyone Can Whistle.* Angela Lansbury starred as Cora Hoover Hooper, hereditary boss of a bankrupted town, who, with the help of Police Chief Magruder (James Frawley), Comptroller Schub (Gabriel Dell) and Treasurer Cooley (Arnold Soboloff), sets up a phony therapeutic fountain to attract dumb money. When a group of mentally handicapped, under the care of Nurse Fay Apple (Lee Remick), come to partake, troubles begin. Energetic Dr Hapgood (Harry Guardino) arrives to move along events and to pair off with Nurse Apple in the midst of a confusing saga of sanity and insanity.

The score provided a title number, sung by Miss Remick, which proved both extractable and popular, but Kermit Bloomgarden's and Diana Krasny's production of a show which, willfully meaningful, also came across too often as distasteful and/or tasteless, survived only nine performances. It nevertheless won a number of college and other non-commercial productions in America and, with the swelling of Sondheim's status in later years, was finally given a British provincial production in 1986 with Pip Hinton (Cora), Michael Jayes (Hapgood) and Marilyn Cutts (Fay) heading the cast.

UK: Everyman Theatre, Cheltenham 21 August 1986

Recordings: original cast (Columbia), concert version 1995

ANYTHING GOES Musical in 2 acts by Guy Bolton and P G Wodehouse. Revised version by Howard Lindsay and Russel Crouse. Music and lyrics by Cole Porter. Alvin Theater, New York, 21 November 1934.

Along with the more operettic *Kiss Me, Kate, Anything Goes* remains the most popular and most often performed of the list of musical comedies for which Cole Porter supplied the songs, proving yet again (if it needed proving) that a show rebuilt hastily, considerably, and late can often do as well or better than one carefully and respectfully lifted from the original page to the stage.

Producer Vinton Freedley—previously co-producer of *Girl Crazy*—had planned *Bon Voyage* (book by Bolton and Wodehouse, songs by Porter, starring *Girl Crazy*'s

Plate 8. **Anything Goes.** *William Gaxton (Billy) and Benay Venuta (Reno) were the first to take Cole Porter's merry musical comedy to the American touring circuits.*

Ethel Merman, William Gaxton, Victor Moore and Bettina Hall, and directed by Howard Lindsay) for the 1934–35 Broadway season. But the Bolton/Wodehouse libretto, the final act of which set its group of seafaring bon-voyagers afloat in a disastrous and comical shipwreck, did not meet with the producer's approval. The real-life sinking of the *S.S. Morro Castle* gave Freedley the excuse needed to dump it (and win some publicity), and Lindsay was seconded to get another book made, built around the already hired and hierarched stars, and around Porter's songs.

In the short weeks before rehearsals were due to begin, the new script was written by Lindsay and then Theatre Guild publicity man, Russel Crouse. Miss Merman was cast as an evangelist-turned-nightclub-singer (unlikely, perhaps, but there was a song called "Blow, Gabriel, Blow" to cope with) with a yen for a smart young man (Gaxton) who is, in turn, all of a fluster about a lovely daughter of biggish business (Miss Hall), destined for a dynastical marriage not with a Prince, but with a more flourishing business. Moore was given a splendidly suitable role as an aspiring but low-rated "public enemy" without the ability to rise to Number One, who spent much of the evening disguised as a reverend, and the shipboard scenery of the original script was accommodated by having almost the whole of the action take place during an Atlantic crossing.

In his pursuit of the lovely Hope Hampton, Billy Crocker stows away on the ship bearing her to Britain and a marriage with Sir Evelyn Oakleigh (Leslie Barrie). Whilst trying to change his fair lady's mind about her hand, he goes through any number of disguises and tricks to avoid detection, not only as himself, but as the criminal whose ticket he has been loaned by a subordinate criminal, who is himself traveling disguised as a minister. Chanteuse Reno Sweeney helps him out, even though she fancies Billy for herself, and is ultimately rewarded with the leftover Lord when the business situation changes, and Billy's persistence wins him the hand of Hope.

The songs of what was ultimately called *Anything Goes* included gems for each of the stars. Miss Merman had the lioness's share, topped by the catalog song "I Get a Kick Out of You" (a number left over from an aborted piece written for E Ray Goetz and called *Stardust*) and the powerful "Blow, Gabriel, Blow" as well as two more typical and topical Porter pieces, a second catalog, "You're the Top" (with Gaxton), and the newly written title song "Anything Goes." Gaxton and Miss Hall had the mellow "All Through the Night," she slunk through the admission of "The Gypsy in Me," and Moore twittered out his advice to "Be Like the Bluebird." There was even fine material left behind: Gaxton's "Easy to Love" went before opening, and a sizzling piece advising "Buddie, Beware," originally sung by Miss Merman, survived only a short while after opening, being cut to make way for yet more topicalities in an extra reprise of "I Get a Kick Out of You." The old title song, "Bon Voyage" survived, countermelodied, for the ensemble.

Although there were changes, additions and rewrites on the road to town, *Anything Goes* was never in trouble, and once it opened it was always going to be a success. It was still on the way to the end of its first run of 420 Broadway performances when C B Cochran—who, far from seeking the kind of pre-production plays for his score that modern musicals do, had actually injuncted Carroll Gibbons's Orpheans from playing Porter's *Anything Goes* songs at the Savoy Hotel—mounted his edition at London's Palace Theatre. Although the press had originally reported that Leslie Howard was to play Billy and Leslie Henson was to take Moore's role, alongside French cabaret and theatre star Jeanne Aubert, the lady, sumptuously dressed as Reno (now nationalistically called Lagrange instead of Sweeney), was teamed with Jack Whiting as Crocker, Adele Dixon as Hope, Sydney Howard as the despairingly criminal Moon-Face Mooney, and Peter Haddon in his well-known noodle performance as Sir Evelyn. In the style of the time, a harmony group, the Four Admirals, was engaged to perform the fine shanty "There'll Always Be a Lady Fair." Once again, the producer must have been glad to have lost that *Bon Voyage* shipwreck, for Ivor Novello's sinking ship in Drury Lane's *Glamorous Night* had been the scenic sensation of the season. *Anything Goes* didn't do quite as well as the Novello piece, but it played a smart 261 performances in London before going on the road.

Australia's version, featuring Harry Langdon, Lillian Pertka, Charles Norman and Robert Coote did not, however, do well at all. It proved something of a disappointment as it ran its course in six Sydney and seven Melbourne (Her Majesty's Theatre 11 April 1936) weeks.

The show did not, apparently, attract any takers outside the English-speaking theatre but after the songwriter's death the growing fashion for Porter's works provoked revivals both in America and Britain. A revised version of the show was mounted at off-Broadway's Orpheum Theater in 1962 (15 May, 239 performances), featuring Hal Linden (Billy), Eileen Rodgers (Reno) and Mickey Deems (Moon-Face) and, initiating a sad trend, with a number of extraneous Porter numbers from other sources bundled into the score. Britain saw the show when the extremely young Cameron Mackintosh sponsored a 1969 staging with James Kenney as Billy, Marian Montgomery as Reno (Saville Theater 18 November) and an even larger helping of Porter pops. This version failed in 27 performances.

The most important revival, however, came in 1987. Timothy Crouse (son of Russel) and John Weidman reorganized the libretto sufficiently to retain "It's D'Lovely" and "Friendship" from the last round's tackings-in, to bring back some of the show's outcuts (whilst keeping most of the original score), and to add some other Porter spare parts. Howard McGillin (Billy), Patti LuPone (Reno), Bill McCutcheon (Moon-Face) and Kathleen Mahoney-Bennett (Hope) featured and the resultant show was launched at New York's Vivian Beaumont Theater (19 October 1987). It was a fine success there, going on to a run of nearly two years and 804 performances and setting in motion a round of productions of this particular version of the show. A touring company, with Mitzi Gaynor at its head, went out on the American road in 1989 and, in the same year, *Anything Goes* was mounted both in London (Prince Edward Theatre 4 July 1989) with McGillin, Elaine Paige and comedian Bernard Cribbins starred, and in Australia, where local star Geraldine Turner blew Gabriel right out through the flies and encouraged Australians to be much more receptive than they had to the show's first-round production.

Rather different from this official new *Anything Goes* was another American production of the same period which cast the role of Reno Sweeney as a man, and had Billy rejecting an invitation to the gay life for the caresses of Hope. This version drew the disapproval of the establishment, but the ease with which the part changed sex with no harm (and even some advantage) to the show's story and songs was such as to point up the androgynous nature and appeal of this popular kind of role. As in the original text, the male Reno ended the night on the arm of the English lord.

A German version of *Anything Goes* (ad Rolf Merz, Gerhard Hagen) was first produced at Kaiserslautern in 1981, and the 1987 remake was also given a German showing, notably in a production at Berlin's Theater des Westens (29 January 1993) featuring Hartwig Rudolz, Helen Schneider and Ralf Wolter.

A film version, which used only four numbers from the original show alongside four new ones, was produced in 1936. Bing Crosby played Billy alongside Miss Merman, in her original role, with Charles Ruggles at the head of the comedy, a dubbed Ida Lupino as juvenile girl and Margaret Dumont and Richard Carle in support. Another film, under the same title, but bearing little resemblance to the stage show beyond its use of five of its songs, appeared in 1956 with Crosby teamed up with Zizi Jeanmaire, Donald O'Connor and Mitzi Gaynor. A potted version, with Miss Merman, Frank Sinatra and Bert Lahr, was produced by NBC-TV in 1954.

UK: Palace Theatre 14 June 1935; Australia: Theatre Royal, Sydney 8 February 1936; Germany: Pfalztheater, Kaiserslautern *Anything Goes—Alles OK* 10 February 1981

Film: Paramount 1936 (aka *Tops Is the Limit*)

Recordings: original Broadway and London casts assembled (Smithsonian), London cast included on *Cole Porter in London* (WRC), New York 1962 revival (Epic), New York cast 1987 (RCA), London cast 1989 (First Night), Australian cast (EMC), complete (EMI), film soundtrack 1956 (Decca), etc

APACHEN Operette in 3 acts by Ignaz M Welleminsky and Ralph Benatzky. Music by Ralph Benatzky. Apollotheater, Vienna, 20 December 1920.

A piece evolved around the then-fashionable scenes of deliciously "canaille" Parisian low life, *Die Apachen,* like the famous sadomasochistic apache dance, and like other pieces set in such marginal areas, sugared the milieu and its characters up to make of them nothing but a pretty entertainment, with an "apache" hero who was little more than a jolly scamp.

Like all the best operettic heros, Romain Tièrce (Louis Treumann) is not really a true-born Paris streetthief, but an aristocrat fallen on hard times, who has turned to banditry to restore the family fortunes. His victim is a self-made but unattractive bourgeois who makes sausages and who has a highly attractive wife who, in her turn, has jewels. Tièrce poses as a Duke in order to relieve the wife of the jewels and the sausage-maker of his wife, only to have the real Duke turn up. Our hero dupes the gendarmerie and, in the third act, leads everyone off to the Pyrenées for some scenery and a happy ending.

Josef König, Betty Myra, Olga Bartos-Trau and Rudolf Kumpa supported the evening's overwhelming star, and *Die Apachen,* equipped, of course, with a centrepiece Apache Dance at the heart of its light, Viennesey and (for the time) unsyncopated score, did well enough in its Vienna season to attract attentions from Britain and from America. An American staging apparently foundered on its way to Broadway, but London's Wylie-Tate organization brought *The Apache* (ad Dion Titheradge) to the London Palladium, with dancer and ex-sportsman Carl Brisson starred as Romain Tièrce, Shaun Glenville as merchant Redingote, Adrienne Brune as his wife Marian and Dorothy Ward as Lallage. The dances—including "a sensational new apache dance by Carl Brisson and his sister Tilly"—were arranged by Edward Dolly (brother of the more famous sisters), the costumes were by Dolly Tree, there were the odd song by Kollo ("Is Love Worthwhile") and Leslie Sarony ("Cuckoo"), by Wottitz ("Parlez-vous français?") and Reesen ("Let Me Hold Your Hand, Dear") inserted into the musical part, and the combination pleased London for a run of 166 performances.

UK: London Palladium *The Apache* 15 February 1927

APAJUNE, DER WASSERMANN Operette in 3 acts by F Zell and Richard Genée. Music by Carl Millöcker. Theater an der Wien, Vienna, 18 December 1880.

When pretty Romanian Natalitza (Karoline Finaly) and her Marcu (Alexander Girardi) have celebrated their wedding, the steward Alexandri (Carl Adolf Friese) insists that she go to the castle to ''pay her respects'' to their overlord, Graf Alamir Prutschesko (Felix Schweighofer). Marcu knows what that means, and, accompanied by his friends Manolle Ritschano (Ernst Schütz) and Joza (Ausim), all three disguised as girls, he also heads for the castle. Whilst Ritschano makes rendezvous with Prutschesko's stepdaughter, Jlinka (Frln Rafael), Natalitza holds the itchy-fingered Count at bay with the old tale of Apajune, the watersprite, who watches over the well-being of newlywed girls. Prutschesko dresses up as Apajune to pursue his droit-de-seigneurial way but, instead of coming back to Natalitza, he runs into the befrocked Marcu who promptly throws him in his own river. When the Gräfin Heloise (Therese Schäfer), who can hardly stay deaf to all this activity, starts asking questions, her husband is obliged not only to let Natalitza and Marcu go their way unmolested, but also Ritschano and Jlinka. Apajune has looked after his own.

The third of Millöcker's out-and-out Operetten, following the successful *Das verwunschene Schloss* and the less fortunate *Gräfin Dubarry, Apajune* gave the composer another signal success. The piece stood up very favorably alongside the Theater an der Wien's other major production of the year, Johann Strauss's *Das Spitzentuch der Königin,* and was played for a more-than-respectable month over Christmas and the New Year period, remaining in the theatre's repertoire for the two following seasons for a total of 45 performances. It was quickly exported, being played in the months following its premiere both in Germany and in Budapest (ad Lajos Evva, Jenő Rákosi) where it was the first of Millöcker's Operetten to be seen. A year later it was successfully mounted at New York's German-language Thalia Theater with Jenny Stubel (Natalitza), Adolf Link (Prutschesko) and Alexander Klein (Marcu), and, after a certain amount of jiggery-pokery over the sale of the English-language rights (Augustin Daly insisted he had prior claim, vendor Leo Goldmark just wanted a quick production), the first English version (ad Sydney Rosenfeld) was too hurriedly produced at Broadway's Bijou Opera House by Emilie Melville's up-to-then touring company. The manageress starred as Natalitza alongside the Prutschesko of William Gilbert and the Marcu of Tom Casselli; the show (adaptor uncredited) was noted as ''poorly interpreted and extremely dull'' and remained on the bill just three weeks. However, after a second German-language showing, starring Marie Geistinger, in 1884, *Apajune* got a second chance on Broadway in the more professional hands of John McCaull's troupe (Casino Theater 16 January 1885), with Mathilde Cottrelly (Heloise) and Francis Wilson (Prutschesko) featured. Although it did not prove a genuine hit through five weeks in New York, Boston and the rest of the country welcomed it enthusiastically, and *Apajune* was established for some years as a musical-theatre regular.

Apajune also had a good number of subsequent productions in Germany and it was played in Prague, Zagreb and in other middle-European centers in the first years following its initial production.

In 1903 the piece was given a major revival at the Carltheater (24 September) with Louis Treumann (Prutschesko) and Mizzi Günther (Natalitza), soon after to become famous as the originators of *Die lustige Witwe,* and Carl Streitmann (Marcu) heading the cast. It was played as a supporting piece in the repertoire during some six months, but this revival re-established the show on mid-European stages, and the star pair brought it back again in 1910 at the Johann Strauss-Theater (30 April), where it ran for a straight month.

Germany: Pressburg 21 February 1881, Friedrich-Wilhelmstädtisches Theater, Berlin 10 December 1881; Hungary: Népszínház *Apajune a vízitündér* 4 March 1881; USA: Thalia Theater 13 January 1882; Bijou Opera House *Apajune, or the Water Sprite* 25 February 1882

APPLAUSE Musical in 2 acts by Adolph Green and Betty Comden based on the screenplay *All About Eve* by Joseph L Mankiewicz and the story *The Wisdom of Eve* by Mary Orr. Lyrics by Lee Adams. Music by Charles Strouse. Palace Theater, New York, 30 March 1970.

Applause was an adaptation for the musical stage of the story of the the cult film *All About Eve* (1950), in which the covertly ambitious Anne Baxter pulled stardom from under the feet of the established actress played by Bette Davis. The musical version presented Penny Fuller as Eve Harrington, the harmless-looking fan who becomes the inseparable Girl Friday of theatre favorite Margo Channing (Lauren Bacall), and then gradually works, plots and sleeps her way from backstage to center-stage and, ultimately, into the new starring role that Margo knows was to have been hers. It is some consolation to the older woman that she can see in this disgustingly determined creature something of herself, 20 years earlier, and that, forced from the limelight, she can take a more measured view of her career and of her life with Bill (Len Cariou), whom Eve failed to seduce on her stairway to the stars.

Star-billed Miss Bacall got the lioness's share of the musical score (''But Alive,'' ''Welcome to the Theater,'' ''Hurry Back,'' ''Something Greater,'' etc, plus a share in a piece which used the film's most famous line ''Fasten Your Seatbelts [it's going to be a bumpy night]'' as an opening line), but, since the show represented in the story of *Applause* was not a musical but a play, the plot line moved outside the main story for its production numbers. It found them in the café frequented by those members of Broadway choruses who foregather in each others' company after work, late into the night. It was one of these numbers, the title song describing the unparalleled jolt an artist gets from ''Applause,'' which, as performed by Bonnie Franklin and the show's dancers, became the musical highlight of the evening. A similarly titled song expressing much the same sentiment and written by Burton Lane and Ira Gershwin had previously been heard in the film *Give a Girl a Break* (1953), performed by Gower Champion and Debbie Reynolds, but this one took on better.

Joe Kipness and Lawrence Kasha (w Nederlander Productions and George Steinbrenner III) produced *Applause* on Broadway in a staging by choreographer Ron Field, here taking the director's chair for the first time (Tony Award), and scored a fine success with a run of 896 performances at the Palace Theater. Some imaginative recasting saw the star succeeded during the run by Anne Baxter, who had been the film Eve, and then by redheaded celluloid seductress Arlene Dahl. Miss Bacall headed the subsequent touring company before leaving the road to Eleanor Parker, Patrice Munsel and Eva Gabor and moving to London to star in Bernard Delfont's and Alexander H Cohen's West End version. Angela Richards was Eve and Sheila O'Neill did the show-stealing in ''Applause'' through 382 performances.

Applause went on to be played in Europe in German (ad Julie Kaufmann) and Spanish versions and it was also televised by CBS (15 March 1973) with Miss Bacall and Miss Fuller repeating their original roles and Larry Hagman as Bill, but a 1996 attempt to bring it back to Broadway (Tampa Bay 22 October), with Stefanie Powers starred as Margo Channing, humbled to a halt in Baltimore.

UK: Her Majesty's Theatre 16 November 1972; Germany: Bühnen der Hansestadt, Lübeck 2 May 1975, Theater des Westens, Berlin 6 January 1980

Recording: original cast (ABC)

APPLE BLOSSOMS Musical play in a prologue and 2 acts by William Le Baron based on *Un Mariage sous Louis XV* by Alexandre Dumas. Music by Fritz Kreisler and Viktor Jacobi. Globe Theater, New York, 7 October 1919.

One of the most successful shows of the 1919–20 Broadway season, *Apple Blossoms* followed the way successfully signalled by the German *Maytime* in the romantic Continental operetta style and won itself, if not as outstanding a result as that show, both a run of 256 New York performances and a good touring afterlife. Its libretto was announced as being based on Alexandre Dumas's *Un Mariage sous Louis XV,* but there was little more than the theme of arranged marriage and its consequences that was recognizably Dumas in William Le Baron's non-period, thoroughly romantic and wholly unsuggestive libretto. John Charles Thomas and Wilda Bennett starred as Philip Campbell and Nancy Dodge, a young pair who get wed to please their relatives, but agree that they will carry on their respective love affairs all the same. Philip contrives to let Nancy see the good-for-little Dickie Stewart (Percival Knight) whilst he continues to sigh after pretty widow Anne Merton (Florence Shirley). However, by the time the final curtain has been reached the married couple have decided to be a proper husband and wife.

The show was equipped with a score made up of half a dozen pieces by Hungarian expatriate Viktor Jacobi, and slightly more from violinist-composer Fritz Kreisler. Not unexpectedly, Kreisler got the publicity whilst the composer of *Szibill* and *Leányvásár* supplied the best songs: the leading pair's duo ''You Are Free'' and Philip's ''Little Girls, Goodbye'' (a title dangerously near to the ''Goodbye, Girls, I'm Through'' of a few seasons earlier). There were two dance numbers—one from each composer—for the young Fred and Adele Astaire in supporting roles as ''Molly'' and ''Johnny,'' whilst Kreisler's most successful contribution turned out to be the waltz-song ''Who Can Tell?'' subsequently recycled into the popular ''Stars In Your Eyes,'' and given a second theatrical showing in the violinist's later Operette *Sissy* (''Ich wär' so gern einmal verliebt'').

THE APPLE TREE Musical in 3 acts by Sheldon Harnick, Jerry Bock and Jerome Coopersmith based on stories by Mark Twain, Frank Stockton and Jules Feiffer. Lyrics by Sheldon Harnick. Music by Jerry Bock. Shubert Theater, New York, 18 October 1966.

Three one-act musical plays of very diverse styles and subjects, with a tenuous linking theme of temptation, *The Diary of Adam and Eve, The Lady or the Tiger?* and *Passionella* made up an evening's entertainment, under the umbrella title *The Apple Tree,* which was about as different from its authors' then still-running *Fiddler on the Roof* as could be.

The Diary of Adam and Eve, based on a Mark Twain novella, introduced a very human Adam (Alan Alda) and Eve (Barbara Harris) who become ordinary, everyday folk after the Fall and the birth of the first baby. Larry Blyden played the snake, lubriciously tempting the outgoing Eve to ''Forbidden Fruit'' and the jiggery Alda puzzled endearingly over his child, deciding for want of better references that ''It's a Fish.''

In *The Lady or the Tiger?,* a musicalization of the Frank Stockton tale famous for its cliff-hanger ending,

Miss Harris played the Princess Barbara, caught in compromising position with a Captain of the Guard (Alda) who is, as a result, condemned to the arena. But it is Barbara who is in the no-win situation. She has to indicate which of two doors he must open—one releases a man-eating tiger, the other a beautiful lady. Unlike Sydney Rosenfeld's 1888 full-scale musical adaptation of the same tale, this one maintained the famous lack of an ending. You never find out what is behind the door the lady chooses. (Rosenfeld's lady, by the way, chose the tiger—but when the door was opened it had been poisoned, so . . .)

The humanity of the first play and the classic comedy of the second were replaced by campy extravagance in the Jules Feiffer Cinderella tale which ended the evening. Miss Harris played a little drab who dreams of being a dyed-blonde Hollywood dolly called *Passionella,* paired off with the equally plastic, black-leathered rocker, Flip (Alda). Then she wakes up. Blyden topped the piece, gushing over the lady that "You Are Not Real."

The Apple Tree played 463 Broadway performances and, helped by its unextravagant size, has since received a number of further productions both as a whole piece or, occasionally, of just one of its three rather unequal portions, in America, Canada and in Europe. The German version (ad Max Colpet) underlined the evening's soi-disant theme a little more obviously by calling itself *Die Versuchung* (temptation).

A further musical version of *The Lady or the Tiger?* was brought from London's fringe Orange Tree Theatre to the West End's Fortune Theatre in 1976. The neighboring Overground Theatre Company later produced *The Apple Tree* with Ken Caswell, Jonathan Rowe and Lesley Duff in its cast.

Germany: *Die Versuchung* 6 February 1969; UK: Overground Theatre, London March 1980

Recording: original cast (Columbia), etc

THE ARABIAN NIGHTS

The collection of tales known as the *Arabian Nights Entertainment* or *The Thousand and One Nights,* introduced to European readers in Antoine Gallard's French version in the early years of the 18th century and in a full English version by Edward William Lane in 1839, proved a long and highly fruitful source of subjects for extravaganzas, pantomimes and all other forms of musical theatre. The most popular tales were those of *Aladdin* and *Ali Baba,* both of which were the bases for many major musical productions, but a number of the other tales were also widely used.

Abu Hasan, or The Sleeper Awakened, successfully taken as a subject for an opera by Weber in 1811, was burlesqued by Francis Talfourd (*Abon Hassan or the hunt After Happiness* St James's Theatre, 1854), by an uncredited author as *Abon Hassan or Dead and Alive* (Marylebone Theatre, April 1860), by Arthur O'Neil (*Abon Hasasan, or an Arabian Knight's Entertainment* Charing Cross Theatre, 1869), by J T Douglass (*The Cockney Caliph* Standard Theatre, 1866), and by Joseph Tabrar as *Abou or the Sleeper Awakened* (Coventry, 1885) in England and as *Abou Hassan, the Wag or the Sleeper Awakened* (Holliday St Theater, Baltimore 3 May 1869) in local musician George B Miles's "original American comic opera." It was also taken as comic opera material both for Luscombe Searelle's *Bobadil* (Sydney, 1884) and, most memorably, for Basil Hood and Arthur Sullivan's Savoy show *The Rose of Persia* (1899). The French opérette *La Dormeuse éveillée* (1883) also professed to have had its roots in the tale.

The tale of *Prince Camaralzaman* and his Princess Badoura, highly popular in the mid-19th century, served as the basis for the Broughs' *Camaralzaman and Badoura* (Haymarket Theatre, 1848), the Broadway burlesque *The Tycoon, or Young America in Japan* played by Mrs John Wood and Jefferson in 1860 (Laura Keene's Theater), Bellingham and Best's 1865 *Prince Camaralzaman* at the Olympic, and further burlesques by Byron (Vaudeville Theatre, 1871) and Burnand (Gaiety Theatre, 1884), whilst *Ganem, Slave of Love* was used as the topic of a long popular Francis Talfourd extravaganza, first mounted at the Olympic Theatre in 1852 and subsequently seen throughout the English-speaking theatre world.

Sindbad the Sailor was long popular as a pantomime hero in Britain, and also led a number of extravaganzas, notably H B Farnie's piece for Lydia Thompson, played in both Britain and America, and two further American pieces: Harry B Smith's spectacular and long-running version with music by W H Bachelor (Garden Theater 27 June 1892), and, most notably, the Al Jolson vehicle, a not very *Arabian Nights* piece with a basic score by Romberg and a whole swatch of popular songs as incidental numbers, produced at the Winter Garden Theater 14 February 1918.

The brothers Brough also authored a burlesque which was eventually simply called *The Arabian Nights* (Haymarket Theatre, 1850) in which Priscilla Horton, James Bland and J B Buckstone, in "an entirely new translation taken an immense way from the original Arabic," told of—in the words of its original title—"the second Calendar who was turned into an ape and the Queen of Beauty who had to fight with a genie," and the evocative title of *The Arabian Nights* and its derivatives have been used since for such pieces as Alfred Thompson's 1888 Chicago *Arabian Nights* (which was really an *Aladdin*), the Viennese Johann Strauss pasticcio *Tausend und eine Nacht* (1906), and the American extravaganza *Arabian Nights* (Carmen Lombardo, John Jacob Loeb/ George Marion jr), a piece borrowing elements from *Sindbad* and *Aladdin* and mounted as a spectacular for several seasons at the Jones Beach marine theatre in the 1950s. This last named piece seems to have been a descendant of the Parisian spectacular *Les Mille et une nuits* (Théâtre du Châtelet 12 December 1881) in which Zulma Bouffar featured as Aladdin, Sinbad, Abou Hassan, et al.

Recording: Jones Beach cast (Decca)

ARANYVIRÁG Operett in 3 acts by Ferenc Martos. Music by Jenő Huszka. Király Színház, Budapest, 6 November 1903.

Jenő Huszka followed up his great success with *Bob herceg* with a new vehicle for that show's star, Sári Fedák, in the title role of *Aranyvirág* (gold-flower), the work selected to open Budapest's new musical theatre, the Király Színház, in 1903.

Elza Szamosi and Károly Ferenczy were Ellen Stone and Harry Gould, a pair of American (multi)-millionaires (the adjective and the noun were, at this time, operettically inseparable) out for a slummy, sexy time in turn-of-the-century Naples. Ellen decides to do the thing in style. She changes clothes and places with the street-dancer known as ''Aranyvirág'' and sets her sights on the girl's sailor lover, Beppo (Géza Vécsei), whilst Harry swans around town with the dressed-up dancer on his arm. Beppo and the lazzarone of Naples aren't fooled. In fact, they take the whole thing pretty poorly and no one gets much joy out of the charade. Finally the Americans get bored with their fruitless fun and head off back to the land of the dollar.

Izsó Gyögyi played the Count Daniló Potyoviev, and the locals were headed by Zsofi Csatay as Tina, Zsigmond Torma (Silvio) and Arthur Csiszér (Carlo). The show proved a fine success and, if it endured less well ultimately than several of Huszka's other pieces, it was nevertheless revived for a second run at the Király Színház in 1907 (8 May).

L'ARBRE DE NOËL Féerie nouvelle in 3 acts by Arnold Mortier, Albert Vanloo and Eugène Leterrier. Music by Charles Lecocq. Théâtre de la Porte-Saint-Martin, Paris, 6 October 1880.

L'Arbre de Noël was a vast, spectacular fairy-tale piece in 30 scenes, the stage-cloths painted by no less an artist than Jules Chéret, which followed such performers as Zulma Bouffar (Bagatelle), Ange Milher (Oscar de Pulna), Alexandre (Eucalyptus), Gobin (Popoff) and Alice Reine (Fridolin) and a corps of 180 dancers on their four-hour journey to the Land of Christmas. Going ever for the best, it was musically decorated by melodies taken from the works of Lecocq which included all the traditional accoutrements of the féerie, from a 40-strong children's chorus singing christmas carols to ballets and parades and to genuine prima donna solos, as an accompaniment to the display of scenic art and mass dancing which was the key to the entertainment. The score—far, it seems, from being all new or all Lecocq—also included a French version of the popular old song ''The Two Obadiahs.''

A grand success on its Parisian production (100th performance 28 December 1880), the piece was taken up for further productions elsewhere in Europe, beginning in Brussels where it was mounted (March 1881), with due splendor and the scenery and costumes from Paris, at the Eden-Théâtre, with Mme Tassilly from the Porte-Saint-Martin supported by Marthe Lys (Bagatelle), Merville (Oscar) and Jeanne Achard (Fridolin). It was subsequently produced in Vienna (ad uncredited) where a rather reduced 15-scene *Der Weihnachtsbaum, oder der Schatzgräber* was given a new score by Louis Roth and played a fine season of 70 performances, and in Berlin where *Der Schatzgräber*'s original score was ''adapted'' rather than replaced by Gustav Lehnhardt. An Hungarian version (ad Béla J Fái) was later played in Budapest.

Austria: Theater an der Wien *Der Weihnachtsbaum* 6 May 1881; Germany: Berlin *Der Schatzgräber* 1881; Hungary: Népszínház *A karácsonyfa* 16 October 1881

THE ARCADIANS Fantastic musical play in 3 acts by Mark Ambient and Alexander M Thompson. Lyrics by Arthur Wimperis. Music by Lionel Monckton and Howard Talbot. Shaftesbury Theatre, London, 28 April 1909.

Perhaps the most complete of all the British Edwardian musical comedies, *The Arcadians* mixed the light romantic and the broadly comic, the picturesque and the spectacular, the musically literate and the music hall, in doses which caught not only the fancy of its time, but also the imagination of decades. The idea for the show was initiated by the odd little man-about-town and strivingly occasional writer, Mark Ambient, who, finding himself incapable of developing it, took his outline to producer Robert Courtneidge. Courtneidge put his crony and in-house writer Alex Thompson to fleshing out Ambient's tale, and handed the musical part to lyricist Arthur Wimperis, who had worked effectively on an earlier hit, *The Dairymaids,* for him, and to two of the most successful theatre composers of the age, Lionel Monckton and Howard Talbot.

The libretto had errant aviator James Smith (Dan Rolyat), a second-rate London hotelier, bailing out of his aeroplane over Arcadia, an idyllic area somewhere near the North Pole, where truth is beautiful and the lie unknown. When the noble savages who inhabit the place

Plate 9. **The Arcadians.** *"The Deuce" wins the race, saves the situation and brings Simplicitas (Dan Rolyat) on-stage for the show's second-act curtain.*

catch Smith in an untruth they are horrified. They dip him in the Well of Truth, changing him into "Simplicitas, an Arcadian," and decide to accompany him back to the dreadful city of London to spread their message of truth and beauty amongst the English. Amongst a bevy of philanderings and colorful events at Askwood racetrack and at Smith's Arcadian Restaurant, built to capitalize on the craze started by his newfound friends and his own popularity in his new guise, the lovers of truth and beauty are defeated in their purpose and return to Arcadia, leaving London to its wicked old ways.

It was a story which gave the opportunity for plenty of the gentle social satire popular in musical plays of the time, and also for a flock of songs and dances. Phyllis Dare, in the role of an incidental Irish lassie, described herself enduringly as "The Girl with the Brogue" and joined with juvenile hero Harry Welchman in chatting obliquely about the "Charming Weather" and in deciding to meet at "Half Past Two." Alfred Lester, in the comedy role of the lugubrious jockey, Doody, made a hit with a glum number about "My Motter" which was, impossibly, "always merry and bright"; Dan Rolyat as Simplicitas sang saucily about the ladies chasing him "All Down Piccadilly"; and the dark-eyed and pixie-faced Florence Smithson in the role of the most vocal Arcadian, Sombra, used her dazzling light coloratura soprano to introduce "The Pipes of Pan" and "Arcady is Always Young." There was also some particularly attractive and well-written ensemble music in a score that included a half-dozen pieces which would become musical-comedy standards. During the course of the show's initial run a number of new songs were tried (and Lester took to singing a verse of his "Motter" song in French), but only a couple—Miss Smithson's "The Call of Arcady" and a topical dance piece called "The Two-Step," added for Maud Thornton and Harry Ray to boost the show's dance content—were retained for any time.

Gloriously staged under Courtneidge's own direction, *The Arcadians* was an instant success, and it settled in at the Shaftesbury Theatre for a run of more than two years (809 performances). By the time it closed, it had already been seen in a highly successful Broadway production, and in cities as far apart as Melbourne, Bombay and Vienna. America's *Arcadians,* mounted by Charles Frohman at the Liberty Theater and subsequently transferred to the Knickerbocker, starred Frank Moulan (Simplicitas), Ethel Cadman (Sombra), Julia Sanderson (Eileen), Alan Mudie (Jack) and comedienne Connie Ediss in an enlarged version of the role of the "abandoned" Mrs Smith and ran for 193 performances before moving on to cover the rest of the country. Clarke and Meynell's Australian production, with Maie Sydney (Sombra), William Cromwell (Simplicitas), Essie Perrin (Eileen) and Tom Walls (Doody) proved equally successful, being brought back the following season with Winnie O'Connor starred and establishing the show as firmly in the southern hemisphere as it already was in the northern.

Vienna's version (ad Oskar Friedmann, Fritz Lunzer) of *Die Arkadier,* with Olga Barco-Franck (Sombra), Josef Joseffy (Simplicitas) and Annie Dirkens (Ella, ex-Eileen) which boasted mendaciously "1,000 performances in London!" in its advertising, was played at the large music hall Ronacher, bookended between a flamenco act and an English song-and-dance turn, and took a pause after the first act to allow the audience to have supper. Germany, however, decided on its own *Arcadians.* Julius Freund "adapted" the libretto, Rudolf Nelson composed a new score and the resultant piece was mounted at the Berlin Metropoltheater (27 April 1912) under the title *Schwindelmeier & cie.*

In 1913 *Les Arcadiens* (ad Charles Quinel, Max Dearly) accomplished the rare feat for an anglophone musical of being played in Paris, with Dearly starring as Simplicitas in another music-hall venue, the Olympia, and, only two years later, it returned for a second London season (Shaftesbury Theatre 20 May 1915). The show became a feature of the British touring circuits thereafter, appearing regularly in the provinces for over 30 years, whilst overseas productions continued, and in 1927 its story line and its spectacular scenes (including a second-act finale which brought Simplicitas on stage on the back of a live horse) proved strong enough to warrant it being made into a silent film. In 1984 it was given a major regional revival in Britain under the aegis of Stewart Trotter at the Northcott Theatre, Exeter, and in 1998 it was mounted at the Ohio Light Opera, proving in each case to have lost none of its attractions with the passing of the years.

USA: Liberty Theater 17 January 1910; Australia: Theatre Royal, Melbourne 26 March 1910; Austria: Ronacher *Die Arkadier* 24 February 1911; France: L'Olympia *Les Arcadiens* 3 April 1913

Film: Gaumont British 1927 (silent)

Recordings: complete (Newport Classic), selections (Columbia, MFP)

ARC DE TRIOMPHE Play with music in 3 acts by Ivor Novello. Lyrics by Christopher Hassall and Ivor Novello. Music by Ivor Novello. Phoenix Theatre, London, 9 November 1943.

A lesser Novello work, built to showcase the star of *The Dancing Years,* Mary Ellis, *Arc de Triomphe* traced

Plate 10. **Harry Archer's** *Little Jessie James song went round the world—even becoming (allowing for a touch of hype) "le plus formidable succes actuel" in France.*

the professional and amorous career of a French opera singer through the theatre and the war in much the same way that *The Lisbon Story* was doing simultaneously, on a larger scale and with more success, at the London Hippodrome. The music for *Arc de Triomphe* had an unusual first public playing when it was tried out by orchestra leader Geraldo during a Middle East tour of British army posts, but the score contained little of Novello's better work and only "Dark Music," sung in the show by Elisabeth Welch in a very incidental role, proved to have any lasting value. Enemy action and Novello's conviction on rationing charges hastened the show's closure after a six-months' run (222 peformances).

Recording: original cast (part record *Ivor Novello*) (EMI)

ARCHER, Harry E [AURACHER, Harry] (b Creston, Iowa, 21 February 1888; d New York, 23 April 1960).

Auracher, as he was at first known, was educated at Michigan Military Academy before going on to study music at Princeton University and at Knox, and he was 23 years old (and paragraphed simply as "a Chicago pianist") when, after having placed the odd number in such pieces as Richard Carle's *Jumping Jupiter* (1911), his first all-own musical comedy, *The Pearl Maiden,* was produced by Harry Frazee and George Lederer at Broadway's New York Theater. His music was set to an old-fashioned comic opera libretto "containing every imaginable character from cannibals, pirates, dancing dolls to lovesick girl." Dealing with jiggery-pokery on a South Seas island and proffering more than a whiff of *Florodora,* it was delivered by a cast headed by long-qualified stars Jefferson de Angelis (with 100 percent billing) and Flora Zabelle. The "plentiful and exceeedingly catchy" numbers ("If One Little Girl Loves Me," etc) got better notices than the "spineless plot," and the whole backward-looking affair lasted just 24 performances in New York before hurrying off to Boston and to less demanding dates further afield.

Archer worked as a musician in the years that followed, leading his own jazz band and playing as a member of others, including that of Paul Whiteman, while continuing at the same time to compose intermittently for the theatre. He turned out the scores to a Kitty Gordon vehicle *Love for Sale,* which was seen in some of Pennsylvania's discreeter dates before sinking terminally, to the revue which started out as *Frivolities of 1919* and had become *Frivolities of 1920* (w William B Friedlander, Tom Johnstone) by the time it reached the 44th Street Theater, and to the Clark and McCullough revue *Peek-a-boo* (1921). Then, more than a decade after his first ephemeral Broadway musical comedy, he returned with the songs for the brightly farcical and highly successful musical play *Little Jessie James.* Following its fine Broadway run, versions of *Little Jessie James* were produced in Britain, Germany and Hungary and its hit song "I Love You" (made into a Paris hit by Pierre Lamy and reused in the film *The Sun Also Rises*) gave Archer the biggest single song success of his career.

The 1922 *Paradise Alley,* a more conventional, old-fashioned musical comedy, was brought to town in 1924, after *Little Jessie James*'s success, and played 64 performances there prior to an Australian season, but there was much more future in Archer's continued collaboration with his hit show's librettist, Harlan Thompson, on a series of further small-scale musical farces. Although Lyle Andrews's production of their *My Girl* was considered too undersized—it had, after all, only one set—for the New York papers to send their first-string critics to its opening, it won both fine notices from those who did go and a 291-performance run at the little Vanderbilt Theater. Andrews followed it with *Merry, Merry* ("Little Girl," "I Was Blue," "It Must Be Love"), another piece built on similarly economic and comically play-orientated lines, which confirmed the writers' success with both critics and public (176 performances).

By the time of Louis Werba's mounting of their *Twinkle, Twinkle* (add scenes and numbers by Harry Ruby and Bert Kalmar), a 167-performance success with Joe E Brown in its starring role, one journal was able to announce that although the piece was "a little less intimate than when their works were staged at the Vanderbilt . . . in certain circles the honors, mantles and emoluments of the Princess Theater team of Bolton, Wodehouse and Kern have more or less definitely been assigned [to Thompson and Archer]."

The mantle did not stay on their shoulders even as long as it had on those of their predecessors. Phil Morris and H C Greene's production of the 1928 *Just a Minute* (80 performances) saw the end of the four-show run of success, and the end of Archer's career on Broadway. Although he contributed the odd song thereafter to such pieces as *Sweet and Low* (1930) and wrote music for the revue *Shoot the Works* and the short-lived Provincetown Playhouse revue *Entre Nous* (w Richard Lewine/W B Johnstone, 30 December 1945), he provided no more scores to the musical comedy stage. Many years later, he attempted to bring back a new and revised version of *Little Jessie James,* but the attempt foundered without getting near to the bright lights.

A composer of catchy, lightly jazzy music which was an ideal accompaniment to the modern, farcical tales supplied by his librettist, Archer never succeeded in becoming fashionable and, in spite of a run of success which at least challenged that of the still much-talked-of little shows at the Princess Theater a few years earlier, he is now virtually forgotten.

1912 **The Pearl Maiden** (Earle C Anthony, Arthur F Kales) New York Theater 22 January

1919 **Love for Sale** (w Tom Johnstone, Will B Johnstone, Jack Wilson) Harrisburg, Pa 7 October

1922 **Paradise Alley** (w Carle Carlton, Adorjan Őtvős/Howard Johnson/Charles W Bell, Edward Clark) Providence, RI 18 September; Casino Theater, New York 31 March 1924

1923 **Little Jessie James** (Harlan Thompson) Longacre Theater 15 August

1924 **My Girl** (Thompson) Vanderbilt Theater 24 November

1925 **Merry, Merry** (Thompson) Vanderbilt Theater 24 September

1926 **Twinkle, Twinkle** (Thompson) Liberty Theater 16 November

1928 **Just a Minute** (Walter O'Keefe/H C Greene) Ambassador Theater 8 October

ARIZONA LADY Operette in 2 acts by Alfred Grünwald and Gustav Beer. Music by Emmerich Kálmán. Stadttheater, Berne, 14 February 1954.

Independent, no-nonsense rancher Lona Farrell takes an unwilling fancy to the new cowboy, Roy Dexter, who has tamed her brilliant horse "Arizona Lady." However, thanks to a rash bet, she has no choice but to marry the sheriff, Harry Sullivan, when the horse is beaten in a race because of a girth sabotaged by a rich racing rival who is actually head of a bandit gang. In spite of kidnapping, gangstering and the arrival in mid-plot of a sexy dancer, ''Arizona Lady'' wins the Kentucky Derby and the Sheriff renounces his claims on Lona in favour of Roy at the final curtain. The traditional comedy was supplied by Nelly, a traveling peddler, and the comical and kidnapped cowboy, Chester.

The basic plot of the piece was one that had been well used in turn-of-the-century racing musical comedies, touched up this time with bits of *La Fanciulla del West* and plonked down in *Oklahoma!* country, and Kálmán's score had equally little to do with the 1950s, being laid out in traditional Viennese Operette fashion with its tenor and soprano leads and its supporting soubrets who, amongst them, performed virtually the entire solo music. The heroine's attractive opening song ''War's nicht schön'' was a rangy piece with Hungarian tones, the soubrette's ''Wer führt mich heut' zum Tanzen aus?'' with its dancing rhythms and above-the-stave finish was a far cry from ''I Cain't Say No'' and, if the hero's kleine Cowboylied with its exhortation ''Singender Cowboy reite'' and celebrating ''mein Song, mein Pferd und ich'' had something of the Hollywood cowboy song in its lazy triplets, it was in the minority. There were, however, some moments—such as the first-act finale in which the hero tunefully serenaded Arizona (''Hier ist alles Okay'' was really just too much of an *Oklahoma!* pinch to be true)—which showed more obvious, if not simply ''borrowed,'' transatlantic musical theatre influences.

Arizona Lady, completed by the composer's son Charles, was Kálmán's last staged work, produced in Berne the year after his death and subsequently seen in Germany.

Germany: Städtische Bühnen, Augsburg 26 October 1954

ARKELL, Reginald [''Billy''] (b Lechlade, Glos, 14 October 1882; d Cricklade, 1 May 1959).

A prolific author of magazine articles, light verse, novels and plays, the first of which, *Columbine,* was produced in 1913, Billy Arkell began to write lyrics and, later, libretti for the musical theatre and revue after the war. His first contribution, in 1921, was to the touring musical comedy *Kiki,* but he subsequently collaborated on the libretti and/or lyrics for the English versions of *Der letzte Walzer, Frasquita, Toi c'est moi, Mädi* and *Paganini,* supplied the English libretto for Kurt Weill's unfortunate *Der Kuhhandel* (*A Kingdom for a Cow*), and was involved in four shows for singing star José Collins in her post-Daly's Theater period.

Amongst his revue material (*Jumble Sale, Life, London's Potinière Revue, Savoy Follies*) the highly successful British schoolboy's retelling of history, *1066 and All That* (mus: Alfred Reynolds), was a particular and long-running success.

1921 **Kiki** (Herman Finck/Martin Henry) Ramsgate 7 March

1921 **Now and Then** (Philip Braham/J Hastings Turner, George Graves) Vaudeville Theatre 17 September

1922 **The Last Waltz** (*Der letzte Walzer*) English version w Robert Evett (Gaiety Theatre)

1923 **Catherine** (*Die Siegerin*) English version w Fred de Grésac (Gaiety Theatre)

1924 **Our Nell** (H Fraser-Simson/Harry Graham/w Louis N Parker) Gaiety Theatre 16 April

1925 **Frasquita** English version w de Grésac (Prince's Theatre)

1927 **The Blue Train** (*Mädi*) English version w Dion Titheradge (Prince of Wales Theatre)

1935 **The Gay Deceivers** (*Toi c'est moi*) English version (Gaiety Theatre)

1935 **A Kingdom for a Cow** (*Der Kuhhandel*) English version w Desmond Carter (Savoy Theatre)

1935 **Paganini** English version w A P Herbert (Lyceum)

1937 **The Laughing Cavalier** (Wainwright Morgan/w Stafford Byrne) Adelphi Theatre 19 October

ARLEN, Harold [ARLUCK, Hyman] (b Buffalo, NY, 15 February 1905; d New York, 23 April 1986). Screen and stage songwriter whose numbers have survived better than the shows which housed them.

Arlen started his life in the music world as a sometime jazz player and singer and as a revue and musical theatre rehearsal pianist. During this period, whilst working on the Vincent Youmans musical *Great Day!,* he even appeared briefly on the pre-Broadway stage. Before long he turned his hand to song-writing and scored an initial success with the number ''Get Happy'' (w Ted Koehler), introduced by Ruth Etting in The *9:15 Revue* (1930). Arlen and Koehler continued their partnership through a series of scores and songs for Harlem's Cotton Club shows—''Between the Devil and the Deep Blue Sea'' (1931), ''I've Got the World on a String'' (1932), ''Stormy Weather'' (1933)—and for Broadway revues (*Earl Carroll Vanities, Americana, Life Begins at 8:40* w E Y Harburg, Ira Gershwin) before the composer moved on to Hollywood, where he had already been represented by the inclusion of his ''It's Only a Paper Moon'' (w Harburg, Billy Rose) in the film of the musical *Take a Chance* (1933).

From 1934 Arlen provided songs for 24 feature films through more than two decades. These included *Let's Fall in Love* (1934, ''Let's Fall in Love'' w Koehler), *The Wizard of Oz* (1939, ''Over the Rainbow'' [Academy Award], ''Follow the Yellow Brick Road,'' etc, w Harburg), *Blues in the Night* (1941, ''Blues in the Night'' w Johnny Mercer), *Star-Spangled Rhythm* (1942, ''That

Old Black Magic'' w Mercer), *The Sky's the Limit* (1943, ''One for my Baby'' w Mercer), *Cabin in the Sky* (1943, additional numbers), *Here Come the Waves* (1944, ''Accent-tchu-ate the Positive''), *Four Jills in a Jeep* (1944, ''How Blue the Night'' w Jimmy McHugh), *Up in Arms* (1944, ''Now I Know'' w Koehler), *Casbah* (1948, ''Hooray for Love'' w Leo Robin), *A Star Is Born* (1954, ''The Man That Got Away'' w Ira Gershwin) and *I Could Go On Singing* (1963).

Arlen's first ventures in the field of the book musical—one with Jack Yellen in the cutesy college musical *You Said It* and another with librettists Lindsay and Crouse and lyricist E Y (''Yip'') Harburg in a hotchpotch vehicle for comedian Ed Wynn called *Hooray For What!*—won little attention. However, he had considerably more success and a long Broadway run with the *Oklahoma!*-clone period piece *Bloomer Girl,* and created his best—if not most theatrically successful—theatre score in 1946 with the splendid Cotton Club-sounding *St Louis Woman* (''Any Place I Hang My Hat Is Home,'' ''Come Rain or Come Shine,'' ''Legalize My Name''). The 1950s brought two further black-cast musicals in the short-lived but still-liked *House of Flowers,* with Pearl Bailey, Juanita Hall and Dionne Warwick, and the custom-made and rather plastic *Jamaica,* starring Lena Horne. He made his last contribution to the Broadway stage with the songs for an unsuccessful adaptation of Edna Ferber's period epic *Saratoga.*

Arlen has also been represented on the stage by various theatrical versions of *The Wizard of Oz* using the film score; these have been played at venues as disparate as Britain's Royal Shakespeare Theatre and New York's Radio City Music Hall. His list of favorite songs has been plundered on many occasions for compilation shows.

1931 **You Said It** (Jack Yellen/Sid Silvers, Yellen) 46th Street Theater 19 January

1937 **Hooray for What!** (E Y Harburg/Howard Lindsay, Russel Crouse) Winter Garden Theater 1 December

1942 **The Wizard of Oz** (with score from film and original stage versions) Municipal Opera, St Louis

1944 **Bloomer Girl** (Harburg/Sig Herzig, Fred Saidy) Shubert Theater 5 October

1946 **St Louis Woman** (Johnny Mercer/Countee Cullen, Arna Bontemps) Martin Beck Theater 30 March

1954 **House of Flowers** (Truman Capote) Alvin Theater 30 December

1957 **Jamaica** (Harburg/Saidy) Imperial Theater 31 October

1959 **Saratoga** (Mercer/Morton da Costa) Winter Garden Theater 7 December

Biography: Jablonski, E: *Harold Arlen: Happy with the Blues* (Doubleday, New York, 1961)

ARLETTE Opérette in 3 acts by Claude Roland and L Bouvet. Music by Jane Vieu. Galeries Saint-Hubert, Brussels, 28 October 1904.

First produced in Belgium, Mme Vieu's opérette told of a playboy Prince who is duty bound to marry money for sake of his country. In the end, he does nothing of the sort. He abdicates and marries his unrich sweetheart, whilst the rich girl who had been designated to be queen weds his ambitious and now crown-worthy cousin instead.

The Belgian production, although it lasted but ''a short run,'' was followed by a provincial French one—but the show did not move to Paris. It was, however, somewhat surprisingly, picked up more than a decade later by London's Grossmith/Laurillard combine and, heavily adapted for British consumption, produced in London in 1917. A half-dozen British writers, including director Austen Hurgon, ensured that the *Arlette* staged in London finally bore little resemblance to its original. Of the 19 musical pieces in the new score, only two owed their music to Mme Vieu, the rest being written to order by Ivor Novello and Guy Le Feuvre. The Novello/Clifford Grey song ''On the Staff'' provided a comical hit for the rising comedian Stanley Lupino who, alongside the nominal stars, Winifred Barnes and Merry Widow hero Joseph Coyne, assured a 255-performance run for the little Ruritanian piece.

Novello clearly nurtured fond memories of *Arlette,* for many years later he supplied a complete score for a piece called *How Do, Princess?* (Manchester 16 March 1936), credited to George Arthurs, ''based on an adaptation by José H Levy,'' directed by Christopher Fry and with additional numbers by Maurice Dixon. *How Do, Princess?* was the libretto of *Arlette,* retranslated, readapted and rescored. There was no sign of Mme Vieu.

France: Grand Théâtre, Angers 15 February 1906; UK: Shaftesbury Theatre 6 September 1917

DER ARME JONATHAN Operette in 3 acts by Hugo Wittmann and Julius Bauer based on *Les Deux Anglais* by P-F Merville. Music by Carl Millöcker. Theater an der Wien, Vienna, 4 January 1890.

The most successful Operette of the latter part of Carl Millöcker's career, *Der arme Jonathan* was based by librettists Wittmann and Bauer on the French comedy *Les Deux Anglais* (Odéon, Paris 3 July 1817), an item in the Odéon repertoire for well over half a century. It supplied an outstanding role for Alexander Girardi, the star of the Theater an der Wien (and the rest of Vienna)—that of Jonathan, the comical little cook to eccentric Boston millionaire Vandergold (Rudolf del Zopp).

The world-weary Vandergold decides to give away all his possessions and shoot himself, and at the same time the penniless and homeless little cook, whom he has sacked, embarks, for the very opposite reasons, on the same deadly plan. But, instead, the two come to an agreement. Vandergold ignores all his fawning friends and hangers-on and, making Jonathan the recipient of all his goods and chattels, he disappears. The two have effectively changed places, but they have a pact that should things not work out they will get together again, with their revolvers, and finish what they almost started. They agree on a musical signal for the eventuality. Jonathan and his Molly (Therese Biedermann) go off to lead the high life in Monte Carlo and there they meet Harriet (Ottilie Collin), the little medical student whom Vandergold cherished, now a famous singer under the management of the perky Tobias Quickly (Sebastian Stelzer). Harriet is not really happy, any more than Jonathan and Molly are, whilst Vandergold, who stayed alive only in the hope of winning Harriet, now thinks she has fallen for Jonathan and, utterly miserable, decides to call in his plan. Fortunately, he cannot remember the piece of music, for in the end he gets both his Harriet and his fortune back, Jonathan being only too happy to get rid of the responsibilities of wealth and become a cook once more.

Millöcker's score was unfailingly tuneful in both solo and in ensemble, its hits coming with the jaunty and plot-worthy "Willst du mein Liebster sein?," introduced by Harriet in the first act and repeated at the end of the third, and even more notably with Girardi's obligatory waltz, "Ich bin der arme Jonathan," sung by the star as his entrance in the first act and again as a closer. Harriet, the prima donna, skittered through pages of coloratura on the top lines of the ensembles and finales, but the score of *Der arme Jonathan* was based firmly on the comical. The second act gave the soubrette her chance in a lively song ("Wir reisen im ganzen Italien") and in a showy duet, featuring orchestral imitations, with Jonathan ("Der Mann in allen guten Ehen"). The comedian playing Tobias had two numbers, and the tenor Vandergold, returning from his heartbroken wanderings in the last act, had a jolly, marked sailor song.

Der arme Jonathan was an unequivocal success. It was played 54 times consecutively under Alexandrine von Schönerer's management at the Theater an der Wien, and it was repeated, over the next year or so, more than 50 further times. It passed its 100th performance 2 April 1891 with Girardi now paired with Ilka Pálmay (Molly), and remained in the theatre's repertoire until 1896. Within a fortnight of its premiere the piece was on stage in Berlin, and within two months Budapest's Népszínház opened its enormously successful version (ad Béla J Fái, Ferenc Rajna), featuring Pál Vidor (Jonathan), Aranka Hegyi (Harriet) and the queen of the Budapest stage, Lujza Blaha, as Molly. *Der arme Jonathan* was played throughout central Europe (Zagreb, Prague, Basel, Bucharest, etc), in Scandinavia and Russia (28 March 1890) all within months of the first performance, and America saw its first *Poor Jonathan* (ad by John P Jackson, Ralph A Weil) in October the same year. Produced by Rudolf Aronson and John McCaull at the Casino Theater, with Jeff de Angelis (Jonathan), Fanny Rice (Molly), Harry MacDonough (Rubygold), Edwin Stevens (Tobias) and Lillian Russell (Harriet) starring, it proved the biggest success that theatre had had in a number of years, playing seven months and 208 performances on Broadway before heading for the road. In the meanwhile, the original German version had also come on display at New York's Amberg Theater with Josef Brakl (Jonathan), Paula Loewe (Molly), Adolf Philipp (Vandergold) and Emma Seebold (Harriet) starred, and it too proved a favorite. The German version was repeated at the Irving Place Theater in 1909 (21 October) with Hans Dobers as Jonathan and Hedwig Richard as Molly and an interpolated German coon song sung in blackface.

Australia saw *Poor Jonathan* the following year, when Clara Merivale's company introduced it in Melbourne with the manageress playing Harriet to the Jonathan of Jack Leumane, the Vandergold of W H Woodfield and the Molly of Ida Osborne. Britain, however, ignored the piece until well after the American success and, when Horace Sedger staged a version at the Prince of Wales Theatre in 1893, he had a new libretto written (ad C H E Brookfield, Harry Greenbank) which situated the piece in Britain, busied itself mainly with topical jokes, and cut some of Millöcker's music, replacing it with extra numbers by a young composer currently trying to break in to the West End musical scene, Isaac Albéniz. Harry Monkhouse, Annie Schuberth and the Savoy's Jessie Bond starred in this botched version which was a palpable and salutory failure.

Der arme Jonathan had its first significant Vienna revival at the Johann Strauss-Theater in September 1910, with Louis Treumann as Jonathan and Mizzi Freihardt as Molly (35 performances); it was given a purposeful Nazi working-over by Heinz Hentschke and Günther Schwenn for a 1939 revival at Berlin's Admiralspalast (add mus Josef Rixner), and was played both in the repertoire at the Volksoper in 1952 and, in yet another reworking, at Munich's Theater am Gärtnerplatz in 1959. Latterly, however, with the comedy musical falling out of fashion in favor of the romantic and the spectacular, it has slipped from the schedules.

A film version was produced by UFA Films with Lizzi Waldmüller and Rudi Godden featured.

Germany: Friedrich-Wilhelmstädtisches Theater 16 January 1890; Hungary: Népszínház *Szegény Jonathan* 14 March 1890; US: Casino Theater *Poor Jonathan* 14 October 1890, Amberg Theater (Ger) 2 January 1891; Australia: Opera House, Melbourne *Poor Jonathan* 4 June 1891; UK: Prince of Wales Theatre *Poor Jonathan* 15 June 1893

Film: UFA

Recording: selection (part record) (Vienna Disc)

ARMONT, Paul [PETROCOCCHINO, Dimitri] (b Rostov, Russia, 1874; d Paris, 2 March 1943).

The author of many successful vaudevilles and comedies (and the occasional drama) for the French stage, Armont was known as the playwright who had never written a word of any of his plays. Solely an ''ideas'' man, a brilliant constructor of comedy plots and scenes, he left the actual writing of the dialogue of his works to his collaborators, most often Nicolas Nancey or Marcel Gerbidon. Armont ventured only once into the world of the musical comedy when he co-authored the 1932 hit *Un soir de reveillon,* but his plays proved fertile material for librettists and he was represented across the world by musicalized versions of his biggest hits.

In America his *Jeunes Filles de palaces* (w Marcel Gerbidon, Théâtre de la Madeleine 5 May 1925) was turned into *The French Doll* for Irene Bordoni (Lyceum Theater 20 February 1922), *Souris d'hôtel* (w Gerbidon, Fémina 13 October 1919) was made into Ivan Caryll's *The Hotel Mouse* (aka *Little Miss Raffles*) and Anita Loos transformed *L'École des cocottes* into the 1964 *Go-Go Loves You.* In Britain *Théodore et cie* (w Nicolas Nancey, Paul Gavault, Théâtre des Nouveautés 29 September 1909) became the hit Gaiety musical *Theodore and Co.* (Ivor Novello, Jerome Kern/Adrian Ross, Clifford Grey/H M Harwood, George Grossmith, 19 September 1916), *Le Truc du Brésilien* (w Nancey) was made up into a second hit for the same management in *Yes, Uncle!* (Prince of Wales Theatre 29 December 1917) and *Le Zèbre* (w Nancey, Théâtre des Nouveautés 3 December 1910), a major success as *The Glad Eye* on English stages, was turned into both the touring *Kiki* (Herman Finck/Reginald Arkell, Martin Henry Palace, Ramsgate 7 March 1921) and the metropolitan *Up with the Lark* (Adelphi Theatre 25 August 1927).

No specific sources were given for Ralph Benatzky's Armont and Gerbidon-based musical *Pariserinnin* (Theater in der Josefstadt 7 May 1937) nor for the Hungarian musicals *Papucs* (1933, w Gerbidon, ad Sándor Lestayán, mus: Michael Krazsnay Krausz), produced at the Pesti Színház 18 November, and *Szabo a kastelyban* (w Léopold Marchand, ad Zsolt Harsányi, mus: Alexander Steinbrecher) mounted at the Vígszínház in 1937 (7 October). However, the latter piece reached a wider audience when—attached to a different score—it became the Hollywood musical *Tell Me Tonight.*

1932 **Un soir de reveillon** (Raoul Moretti/Jean Boyer/w Marcel Gerbidon) Théâtre des Bouffes-Parisiens 17 December

ARMS AND THE GIRL Musical comedy in 2 acts by Herbert and Dorothy Fields and Rouben Mamoulian based on the play *The Pursuit of Happiness* by Lawrence Langner and Armina Marshall. Music by Morton Gould. 46th Street Theater, New York, 2 February 1950.

A Theatre Guild production of a musical based on a play by its own executives, *Arms and the Girl* featured Nanette Fabray as the girl who takes up arms in an American Revolution tale of spying and romance. The romance was represented by the French star of *Bless the Bride,* Georges Guétary, who sang of his ideals in a Germanic ''A Cow and a Plow and a Frau,'' whilst Pearl Bailey featured as a black servant with a pair of songs which dropped almost every final consonant in sight (''There Must Be Somethin' Better Than Love,'' ''Nothin' for Nothin'''). The show was a 134-performance failure.

The same title was used earlier, in Britain, for a comic opérette in two scenes, written by Austen Hurgon with music by Richard Fall (London Hippodrome 29 April 1912). Hippodrome manager Albert de Courville attemped to build up the variety programs at his theatre by introducing substantial small musicals which he commissioned or adapted from composers such as Leoncavallo, Heinrich Reinhardt and Leo and Richard Fall. With favorite comic G P Huntley, American soprano May de Sousa and the Gaiety's Jean Aylwin top-billed, backed by a chorus of 65 and an orchestra of 42, *Arms and the Girl* proved to have insufficient pull and de Courville soon changed his policy.

Recordings: original cast, US musical (Decca, Columbia)

ARNAUD, Yvonne [ARNAUD, Germaine] (b Bordeaux, 20 December 1890; d London, 20 September 1958).

Trained principally as a pianist, Mlle Arnaud made an early success as an actress and vocalist when she appeared alongside Gertie Millar in the role of the French Princess Mathilde, originally played by Elsie Spain, in *The Quaker Girl* at London's Adelphi Theatre at the age of 19. The following year, at the Lyric Theatre, she starred as Suzanne in the London version of Jean Gilbert's *Die keusche Susanne* (*The Girl in the Taxi*), a role which she repeated several times over in ensuing years. In 1915 she followed up as Zara in Oscar Straus's *Love and Laughter* and in the lead roles of the British versions of Eysler's *Der lachende Ehemann* (*The Girl Who Didn't,* Etelka von Basewitz) and Gilbert's *Fräulein Tralala* (*Mlle Tralala, Oh! Be Careful,* Noisette).

She subsequently appeared in French roles in two successful postwar musicals, *Kissing Time* (1919, Georgette St Pol) and *The Naughty Princess* (*La Reine s'amuse,* 1920, Chiquette), before abandoning the musical stage for a distinguished career in the straight theatre.

Biography: ''Malet, O'': *Marraine: A Portrait of My Godmother* (Heinemann, London, 1961)

ARNE, Thomas [Augustine] (b London, 28 May 1710; d London, 5 March 1778). One of the most important figures of the English-language musical theatre in the latter years of the 18th century.

Intended by his father for a more worldly career, the young Arne studied music secretly and made his first contributions to the musical theatre with songs for the opera Rosamond, composed to a text by Joseph Addison and produced at Lincoln's Inn Fields (7 March 1733), and with music for a version of Henry Fielding's famous burlesque *Tom Thumb the Great* (originally produced in 1730) and other works from musical farce to pantomime. Over the next decade he supplied much incidental music for such masques as Thomas Bridges's *Dido and Aeneas* (1733), Milton's *Comus* (1738), Congreve's *The Judgement of Paris* (1740), Alfred Mallet's *Britannia* (1743) and the royal production of *Alfred* (1740, ''Rule Britannia''), and for revivals of classic plays, notably the Drury Lane productions of Shakespeare (''Blow, blow, thou winter wind,'' ''When Daisies Pied,'' etc), and also composed a short opera *The Blind Beggar of Bethnal Green* (lib: Robert Dodsley, Theatre Royal, Drury Lane 3 April 1741).

In the mid-1740s, whilst working as musical director at the Theatre Royal, Drury Lane, he made further forays in the lighter genre with the score to Colley Cibber's comic opera *The Temple of Dulness* and Shirley's burlesque *King Pepin's Campaign,* and composed the version of Shakespeare's ''Where the Bee Sucks'' which has survived 250 years as a standard as part of an incidental score to *The Tempest.* However, his most fruitful period came in the 1760s when, now the musical head of the Covent Garden Theatre, he produced not only the most successful English opera of the time, *Artaxerxes* (2 February 1762 Drury Lane, Metastasio ad), but also his two most enduring light works, the comic operas *Thomas and Sally* and *Love in a Village.* The latter piece, whose 43 musical portions included 19 original numbers by Arne, has been noted as the landmark musical show in which the ballad-opera format of a score made up of borrowed rather than specially composed music was first significantly broken away from.

During the 1770s he wrote further works in all fields from different levels of opera (*Olimpiade, Achilles in Petticoats*) and oratorio to incidental music (*Caractacus*), comic opera (*The Rose*), burletta (*The Golden Pippin*) and musical farce (*May Day*), without again finding the very large success of his three principal works.

Arne was given an honorary Doctorate of Music by Oxford University in 1759.

His sister, Susannah Maria (1714–1766, Mrs Theophilus Cibber) was a successful actress and vocalist, and his son Michael Arne (?1741–1786), best known for his melody to the song ''The Lass With the Delicate Air,'' also composed for the theatre.

1733 **Tom Thumb the Great** (aka *The Opera of Operas*) (Henry Fielding) Haymarket Theatre 31 May

1736 **The Fall of Phaeton** (Prichard) Theatre Royal, Drury Lane 28 February

1739 **A Hospital for Fools** (James Miller) Theatre Royal, Drury Lane 15 November

1745 **The Temple of Dulness** (Colley Cibber) Theatre Royal, Drury Lane 17 January

1745 **King Pepin's Campaign** (William Shirley) Theatre Royal, Drury Lane 15 April

1760 **Thomas and Sally, or The Sailor's Return** (Isaac Bickerstaff) Covent Garden Theatre 28 November

1762 **Love in a Village** (Bickerstaff) Covent Garden Theatre 8 December

1764 **The Guardian Outwitted** (Arne) Covent Garden Theatre 12 December

1769 **Tom Jones** (w Joseph Reed) Covent Garden Theatre 14 January

1772 **The Sot** (aka *Squire Badger*) (Henry Fielding ad Arne) His Majesty's Theatre 16 March

1772 **The Cooper** (*Le Tonnelier*) (ad Arne) His Majesty's Theatre 10 June

1772 **The Rose** (Arne) Theatre Royal, Drury Lane 2 December

1773 **The Golden Pippin** (pasticcio arr/Kane O'Hara) Covent Garden Theatre 6 February

1775 **May Day, or The Little Gipsy** (David Garrick) Theatre Royal, Drury Lane 28 October

1776 **Phoebe at Court** (Arne) King's Theatre 22 February

Biographies: Langley, H: *Doctor Arne* (CUP, Cambridge, 1938), Parkinson, J A: *An Index to the Vocal Works of Thomas Arne and Michael Arne* (Detroit Studies in Music Bibliography, Detroit: Information Coordinators, 1972)

ARNOLD, Charles *see* HANS THE BOATMAN

ARNOLD, Franz [HIRSCH, Franz] (b Znim bei Bromberg, 28 April 1878; d London, 29 September 1960) Berlin actor, playwright, librettist and sometime producer.

Although a Franz Arnold is credited with the text on Waldemar Wendland's 1904 flop Operette *Der Negerlein,* produced at the Centraltheater on Christmas night, and again with the Posse *Ach, die Kerls* in 1910, this ''Arnold'' is said (by himself) to have made his debut as a dramatist only with the successful play *Die spanische Fliege* in 1912. He supplied—or seems to have supplied—one musical comedy text to successful composer Jean Gilbert (again, confusingly, the ''Arnold'' author of Gilbert's *Das Fräulein vom Amt* is apparently not our man, as sometimes credited, but actor-playwright Ernst Arnold), before beginning a writing collaboration with fellow performer-writer and director Ernst Bach. It was this collaboration that would produce a long series of successful works for both the musical and non-musical stage.

The pair supplied texts to Walter Kollo (*Die Königin der Nacht*), Gilbert (*Die Fahrt ins Glück,* 235 performances), Hugo Hirsch (the highly successful *Der Fürst von Pappenheim* and *Dolly*) and a number of the other principal songwriters of the wartime and postwartime Berlin theatre up until Bach's death in 1929. Even thereafter, their work got international exposure, notably in Britain where their farce *Hurra! ein Junge* became a major London comedy hit under the title *It's a Boy,* and was later used as the basis for the long-running musical comedy *Blue for a Boy* and the Robert Gilbert musical comedy *Strammer June angekommen* (1953).

Although their worryingly German names and the titles of their worryingly German plays appeared but rarely on a playbill, Arnold and Bach were strongly represented on the British musical stage over a period of some 30 years. One of their pieces—apparently the Hugo Hirsch musical *Der Fürst von Pappenheim*—was made over as a vehicle for Jack Buchanan under the title *Toni* in 1924, and a series of adaptations to the English musical stage followed. It seems that whatever Bach-Arnold comedy it was that became *Strandszerelem* in Hungary was the same one that was musicalized for Leslie Henson as *Nice Goings On* (1933), whilst the piece (again unspecified) that had been successfully adapted to the comic stage as *The Whole Town's Talking,* after being the subject of an abortive Arthur Freed musical, *A Pair o' Fools,* in America (25 January 1926), was turned into the musical comedy *Oh! You Letty* (Palace Theatre 8 December 1937) for London. The partners also had a credit on the flop *The Girl from Cooks* (Gaiety Theatre 1 November 1927), a piece with a tortuous pedigree and a half-Jean Gilbert score which may—or may not—have had something to do with their musical *Die Fahrt ins Glück.*

Hungary was no more precise than Britain in billing its Bach-Arnold musical comedy sources, and several unspecified plays by the pair were also adapted to the musical stage in Budapest. The pair's names appeared on the 1914 *Az ezüstpille* (ad Andor Gábor, mus: Albert Szirmai) produced at the Vígszínház 9 May 1914, the Magyar Színház's *Jó firma* (ad Jenő Molnár, mus arr Mihály Nádor 5 June 1930) and *Strandszerelem* (ad Harmath) played at the Fővárosi Nyári Operettszínház 10 July 1929.

After Bach's death Arnold collaborated on a number of pieces with Emil Golz (*Hulda Pessl in Venedig, Epsteins Witwe, Frau Pick in Audienz,* etc), before quitting Germany to settle in London where he became a naturalized British citizen. There, his Operette *Jack of Hearts,* unproduced in its original German, was mounted unsuccessfully at Drury Lane as *Rise and Shine* and on the road as *Darling You.* In 1955 his name appeared on the libretto of a musical produced in Holland (27 May), with lyrics by Fred Tysh and music by Erik Jaksch.

1910 **Ach, die Kerls** (Julius Einödshofer/w Heinz Saltenburg) Theater Sanssouci 29 October

1913 **Tsching Bum!** (Rudolf Hartmann) Ernst-Drucker-Theater April

1914 **Woran wir denken** (Jean Gilbert/w Walter Turszinksy) Metropoltheater 25 December

1916 **Die Fahrt ins Glück** (Gilbert/w Ernst Bach) Theater des Westens 2 September

1917 **Neptun auf Reisen** (Rudolf Nelson/w Bach) Apollotheater January

1919 **Fräulein Puck** (Walter Kollo/w Bach) Volkstheater, Munich 25 June

1921 **Die Königin der Nacht** (Kollo/w Bach) Neues Operetten-Theater 2 September

1923 **Der Fürst von Pappenheim** (Hugo Hirsch/Alfred Berg, Willi Kollo/w Bach) Deutsches Künstlertheater 16 February

1923 **Dolly** (Hirsch/Rudolf Bernauer/w Bach) Deutsches Künstlertheater 16 October

1924 **Die vertagte Nacht** (Walter Kollo/Robert Gilbert/w Bach) Stadttheater, Mainz 11 November

1924 **Die vertauschte Frau** (Kollo/Willi Kollo/w Bach) Neues Operettenhaus 22 December

1925 **Olly Polly** (Kollo/Willi Kollo/w Bach) Neues Theater am Zoo 3 September

1928 **Arme Ritter** (Kollo/ Günther Bibo, Kurt Schwabach/w Bach) Volkstheater, Munich 22 September

1931 **Frauen haben das gerne** (Kollo/w Bach) Komische Oper 4 June

1933 **Lieber, reich—aber glücklich** (Kollo/w Bach) Komödienhaus 3 November

1936 **Rise and Shine** (aka *Darling You*) (*Jack of Hearts*) (Robert Stolz, et al/Robert Gilbert/ad Desmond Carter, Harry Graham) Theatre Royal, Drury Lane, London 7 May

1942 **Ich bin in meine Frau verliebt** (Kollo, Willi Kollo/w Bach) revised *Olly Polly* Raimundtheater December

ARNOLD, Tom [ARNOLD, Thomas Charles] (b Richmond, Yorks, 19 August 1893; d London, 2 February 1969). Prolific British producer of musicals for both London and the touring circuits over more than 20 years.

Arnold spent his earliest working years as a clerk in the de Frece music-hall organization and in a variety agency office before he began operating as a producer of touring revues, pantomimes and the occasional made-for-touring musical comedy (*Love and Laughter* 1924, *Oh Patsy* 1926, etc) in the early and mid-1920s. In the 1930s he took out full-scale post-London tours of more significant musicals such as *Waltzes from Vienna, The Merry Widow, Anything Goes, The Crest of the Wave, Give Us a Ring* with Flanagan and Allen, *Balalaika, Operette, Wild Oats, Me and My Girl* and *The Fleet's Lit Up,* as well as a heavy complement of revues, pantomimes and ice shows, gaining in the process a reputation as a lavish producer of large-scale musical shows.

His first significant West End success came with the production of Novello's *The Dancing Years* in 1939, a production which his acumen and knowledge of provincial theatre salvaged and turned into a hit when the war closed down the Theatre Royal, Drury Lane, and evicted the new musical a short way into its run. After a triumphant and well-organized wartime tour, *The Dancing Years* returned to London for the long run it had previously been denied.

Arnold produced all of Novello's subsequent musicals (*Arc de Triomphe, Perchance to Dream, King's Rhapsody, Gay's the Word*), as well as the successful series of Cicely Courtneidge vehicles (*Full Swing, Something in the Air, Under the Counter, Gay's the Word*), Noel Gay's wartime *Present Arms* (1940), *The Land of Smiles* with Tauber (1942), Cole Porter's *Let's Face It* (1941), *Panama Hattie* (1943) and Coward's *Ace of Clubs* (1950)—occasionally in partnership with Jack Wallar, Lee Ephraim and/or Emile Littler. He also kept up a continuing presence in the provinces with a wide range of musical shows, produced either alone or with Bernard Delfont, which included revivals of the classics *Monsieur Beaucaire* (1943) and *The Duchess of Dantzic* (1943), *Hit the Deck* (1944), Zeller's *The Birdseller* (*Der Vogelhändler*) (1947) and a new Swedish musical, *Serenade* (1948), unwisely advertised as Scandinavia's answer to *Oklahoma!*

After a limited activity on the musical front in the 1950s, he returned, in partnership with Delfont, to produce three new musicals in the 1960s—*Pickwick* (1963), *Our Man Crichton* (1964) and *Maggie May* (1964)—as well as the London representation of Broadway's *Little Me* (1964).

Following his death, his production office maintained a limited and intermittent action and was involved with such productions as the children's musical *The Water Babies* (1973) and a revival of *The King and I* (1980) at the London Palladium.

ARONSON, Rudolf (b New York, 8 April 1856; d New York, 4 February 1919). New York's principal producer of the all-consuming European comic opera in the 1880s.

At first prominent in the musical and theatrical world as a rising young composer (at 21 he had a march played in a Strauss concert in Berlin) and as the very young musical director of the Metropolitan Concert Hall in New York (to 1880), Aronson was still but in his mid-twenties when he capitalized and built the oriental-looking Casino Theater on New York's Broadway and 39th Street and set himself up as its first manager. The theatre opened with a production of Johann Strauss's *The Queen's Lace Handkerchief* in 1882 and quickly became established as the city's leading house for quality musical theatre. At first, Aronson ran the house—on the behalf of the gentleman investors of the ''New York Concert Company''—

Plate 11. **Rudolf Aronson.** *The man who made the Casino Theater into Broadway's home of classy musical theatre.*

in collaboration with John McCaull, whose classy comic opera company provided much of the product staged there (*Prince Methusalem, La Princesse de Trébizonde, Der Bettelstudent, The Merry War, Falka, Le Petit Duc*), but the two managers soon fell out over McCaull's insistence on artistic control, and he departed leaving Aronson to run the house alone.

In his first decade of operation Aronson mounted or housed an impressive list of exclusively imported musical plays including *Polly, Billee Taylor, Nanon, Die Fledermaus, Amorita* (*Pfingsten in Florenz*), *The Gipsy Baron* (*Der Zigeunerbaron*), *Erminie, The Commodore* (*La Créole*), *The Marquis* (*Jeanne, Jeannette et Jeanneton*), *Madelon* (*La Petite Mademoiselle*), *Nadgy* (*Les Noces improvisées*), *The Yeomen of the Guard, The Brigands, The Drum Major* (*La Fille du tambour-major*), *La Grande-Duchesse de Gérolstein,* Francis Chassaigne's made-to-measure *The Brazilian, La Fille de Madame Angot, Poor Jonathan* (*Der arme Jonathan*), *Apollo* (*Das Orakel*), *Indigo* (*Indigo und die vierzig Räuber*), *The Tyrolean* (*Der Vogelhändler*), *Cavalleria Rusticana, Uncle Célestin* (*L'Oncle Célestin*), *The Child of Fortune* (*Das Sonntagskind*) and *The Vice Admiral* (*Der Vizeadmiral*). Of these, by far the most successful single production was the English show, *Erminie,* which proved to be unchallengeably the longest-running comic opera of the 19th-century Broadway stage and which was revived at the Casino several times in later years. Aronson also opened the first roof-garden theatre in New York, atop Casino Theater roof (1883), a feature that was subsequently copied by a number of other houses, looking to catch the kind of trade that was seeking some light (and often late) entertainment as an adjunct to food and drink.

In 1893 his term at the Casino came to an end. Some of the company's stockholders called in the receivers and Aronson, who had been precariously balancing the theatre's affairs in a way all too common in the theatre world, found his financial jugglings exposed (far from having led the Casino to profitable success with his productions he had resorted to a $75,000 loan just to keep afloat) and himself dispossessed. The theatre he had created was passed over to Thomas E Canary and George Lederer at a rent of $38,000 per annum. Aronson fought back, and was temporarily restored to "his" theatre, but not for long.

Later he became involved with the management of the Bijou Theater where he mounted a version of the British hit *Gentleman Joe* (1896) and a revival of *Erminie* (1897), became a booker in Europe for American theatres, was rumored to be involved in land speculation in Puerto Rico, and announced the building of a Casino Theater in Los Angeles, a project which came to nothing. He also set himself up as the figurehead of a $25,000 company, and tried to continue to mount Operette productions on Broadway—he was responsible for the unsuccessful 1901 version of *Wiener Blut* (*Vienna Life*)—but to all intents and purposes from the time of his eviction from the Casino his career as a producer of quality musical theatre was done.

Alongside his managerial activities, Aronson was also a prolific composer of, mainly, orchestral music, but he also ventured into comic opera and produced one of his own works, *The Rainmaker of Syria* at the Casino in 1893. It failed, but librettist Sydney Rosenfeld had it tarted up with a new score by musical director Ludwig Englander and sent on the road as *The Woman King, or the Royal Prize* (Miner's Theater, Newark, NJ 20 November 1893). Aronson is also credited with a *Sweet Sixteen* (1883) and a *Captain Kidd* (1883) which, if they ever made it to the stage, seemingly did not get a showing in professional circumstances.

Aronson worked at the Casino in collaboration with two of his brothers, Edward Aronson (d New York, 1889) and then Albert Aronson (b Germany, 1848, d New York, 4 December 1896), who subsequently became manager of the Bijou.

1893 **The Rainmaker of Syria** (aka The Woman King) (Sydney Rosenfeld) Casino Theater 25 September

Autobiography: *Theatrical and Musical Memoirs* (McBride, Nast, New York, 1912)

ARRIETA [y Corera], [Pascual Juan] Emilio (b Puente la Reina, 21 October 1821; d Madrid, 11 February 1894).

Musically trained at the Conservatoire in Milan, Arrieta at first tried his hand at writing operas. His *Ildegonda* was played in Milan in 1845, and later in Madrid and Lisbon, and *La conquista de Granada* (also known as *Isabella la catolica*) was produced in Madrid in 1850 and again in 1855 before the composer moved on to composing lighter pieces.

Under the influence of his Italian training, both in so far as form and style were concerned, Arrieta wrote a considerable number of full-length pieces at a time when many Spanish composers were concentrating on the genero chico, or short zarzuela, and his most successful single work was *Marina,* a two-act piece to a text by Francisco Camprodón, first produced in 1855 (Teatro del Circo 21 September) and later extended by its composer and the librettist Miguel Ramos Carrión into a three-act opera (Teatro Real 16 March 1871). *Llamada y tropa* (lib: Antonio Garcia Guttierez, Teatro del Circo 8 March 1861), *La guerra santa* (lib: de Larra, Enrico Perez Eserich, Teatro Zarzuela 4 March 1879) and the short *El Grumete* (lib: Guttierez, Teatro del Circo 17 June 1853) were amongst others of his successful pieces from a list which also included *Al Amanecer* (1851), *El Domino Azul* (1853), *La estrella de Madrid* (1853), *La Carceria real* (1854), *La dama del rey* (1855) *Guerra a muerte* (1855), *El guerrillero* (1855 w Caballero, Ruperto Chapí), *La hija de la providence* (1856), *El sonambulo* (1856), *El planeta Venus* (1858), *Azon Visconti* (1858), *Quien manda manda* (1859), *Los circasianos* (1860), *Un ayo para el niño* (1861), *Dos coronas* (1861), *Al agente de matrimonios* (1862), *La tabernesa de Londres* (1862), *Un trono y un desengano* (1862), *La vuelta del corsario* (1863), *De tal palo tal astilla* (1864) *Cadenas de oro* (1864), *El toque de animas* (1864), *La insula Barataria* (1864), *El capitan negrero* (1865), *El conjuro* (1866), *Un sarao y una soirée* (1866), *La suegra del diabolo* (1867), *Los enemigos-domestico* (1867), *Los novios de Teruel* (1867), *El figle enamorado* (1867) *A la humanidad doliente* (1868), *Los misterios del Parnaso* (1868), *Los progresos del amor* (1868), *Las fuentes del Prado* (1870), *De Madrid a Biarritz* (1870), *El potosi submarino* (1870), *El molin contra equilache* (1871), *La sota de espadas* (1871), *La manzanas de oro* (1873), *Un viaje a Cochinchina* (1875), *Entre el alcade e el rey* (1875), *Heliodoro, o el amor enamorado* (1880), *San Franco di Sena* (1883), etc.

Biography: Cortizo, M E: *Emilio Arrieta. De la pera a la zarzuela* (ICCMU, Madrid, 1998)

ARTHUR, Beatrice [FRANKEL, Bernice] (b New York, 13 May 1926).

A deep-voiced American character actress widely familiar through her television appearances in *Maude* and *The Golden Girls,* Miss Arthur appeared as Lucy Brown in the 1954 off-Broadway *The Threepenny Opera,* and played in the *Shoestring Revues,* in *Seventh Heaven* (1955, Mme Suze) and in the 1960 reprise of *Gay Divorce* (Hortense). The most memorable part of her musical theatre career came, however, in the 1960s when she created the roles of Yente, the matchmaker, in *Fiddler on the Roof* (1964) and best friend Vera Charles (''Bosom Buddies'') in *Mame* (1966, Tony Award). A 1968 show, *A Mother's Kisses* (Meg), in which she was top-billed, folded on the road.

She was at one stage married to director Gene Saks (b New York, 8 November 1921), whose musical theatre credits include *Half a Sixpence* (1965), *Mame* (1966), *A Mother's Kisses* (1966), *The Prince of Grand Street* (1978), *Home Again* (1979) and *Rags* (1986).

ARTHURS, George (b Manchester, 13 April 1875; d Harrow, 14 March 1944). Songwriter whose work ranged from the music hall to the musical comedy.

George Arthurs found his first musical and theatrical success as a lyricist to music-hall songs while making his living as an accountant in his native Manchester. His most enduring efforts in the popular song field included ''I Want to Sing in Opera,'' written in collaboration with Worton David for Wilkie Bard, the wailing serenade to ''Josh-u-a'' (w Bert Lee) as originally performed by Clarice Mayne, Whit Cunliffe's ''A Different Girl Again,'' and ''A Little of What You Fancy [Does You Good]'' (w Fred W Leigh), connected forever to the name of Marie Lloyd. He also wrote sketches for the halls and, intermittently for the theatre, to which he also contributed, often in collaboration, lyrics and libretti for musicals and songs and sketches for revues (*Hullo, Tango,* etc).

Arthurs's first venture into the London musical theatre was with some ''additional lyrics'' for *The Belle of Mayfair* (''And the Weeping Willow Wept'') and *Havana* (the show's hit ''Hello, People,'' ''Would You Like to Motor with Mater?'') both composed by fellow Mancunian Leslie Stuart. He subsequently supplied texts and/or songwords for a number of the Hippodrome and Pavilion revues, for some of the one-act operettas then played in the bigger revue houses, and also for such other revues as *Honeymoon Express* at the Oxford (1914), *The Whirl of the Town* at the London Palladium (1915), *We're All In It* (1916) and *Seeing Life* (1917). He contributed to the words of the rewritten–re-adapted German musical comedy *Oh! Be Careful* (ex- *Mlle Tralala,* 1915), but his most substantial contribution to the book musical came between 1917 and 1919 when he co-wrote libretti and lyrics for four West End shows, the most successful of which were the long-running Leslie Henson vehicle *Yes, Uncle!,* fabricated from the French comedy *Le Truc du Brésilien,* and his adaptation of the famous comedy *La Petite Chocolatière* as *The Girl for the Boy,* a showcase for Gina Palerme. Both *Yes, Uncle!* (Theatre Royal, Melbourne 12 June 1920) and *The Girl for the Boy* (Tivoli, Melbourne 18 September 1920) got showings on both sides of the world.

Arthurs also placed songs in the American productions of several book shows, notably *The Echo* (''I'm Waiting for Kate'' w David), what remained of Winterberg's *Die Dame in Rot* (''Cupid Never Wrote the Alphabet'' w David), *The Girl Behind the Counter* (''Anytime You're Passing By'' w C W Murphy), *Our Miss Gibbs* ('' I Love Mackintosh,'' ''Will You Sing This Glee With Me'') and Leo Fall's *The Dollar Princess* (''I Can Say Truly Rural'' w David, sung by Will West) and *Die Sirene* (''I Want to Sing in Opera'').

His later musical comedy work, in the 1920s and 1930s, was confined to touring shows, of which the easy-going *Archie,* toured liberally in Britain, also made it to productions in Australia (Princess Theatre, Melbourne 7 November 1925, St James Theatre, Sydney 5 November 1927).

1904 **A Chinese Idyll** (E C Brierley/w J Gar Kiddie/Fred Danvers) Grand Theatre, Stalybridge 18 July

1904 **The Belle of the Orient** (Paul Knox, James W Tate/w Clifford Harris, Joe B Peterman) 3 scenes Islington Empire 18 July

1909 **The Roll Call** (Tate) monologue Oxford Music Hall 25 October

1910 **The Maid of Polaria** (Jullien Wilson, R Penso/w Worton David) 1 act Shoreditch Empire 7 March

1910 **The White Knight** (Wilson) 1 act Hippodrome, Crouch End 6 September

1912 **Maison Décolleté** (*Décolleté et cie*) 1 act English version (London Pavilion)

1913 **An Arabian Night** (Wilson) 1 act 18 August

1914 **Dora's Doze** (Louis Hirsch) 1 act London Palladium 6 July

1915 **The Magic Touch** (Leon Bassett/w Charles Danvers) 1 act Walthamstow Palace 18 January

1915 **Go to Jericho** (w Hirsch, Fred Godfrey) 1 act Oxford Theatre 22 February

1915 **The Million Dollar Girl** (Louis Jerome) 1 act Victoria Palace 16 May

1917 **Suzette** (Max Darewski/w Austen Hurgon) Globe Theatre 29 March

1917 **Sugar** (Jerome/Lauri Wylie, Alfred Parker) 1 act Oxford Theatre 16 July

1917 **Sugar Baby** (Grace Vernon/Harry M Vernon) 1 act Victoria Palace

1917 **Arlette** English version w Ivor Novello, Guy LeFeuvre, Adrian Ross, Clifford Grey and Hurgon (Shaftesbury Theatre)

1917 **Yes, Uncle!** (Nat D Ayer/Grey/w Hurgon) Prince of Wales Theatre 29 December

1919 **The Girl for the Boy** (Howard Carr, Bernard Rolt/w Percy Greenbank/w Hurgon, et al) Duke of York's Theatre 23 September

1921 **Peri, the Slave of Love** (William Neale) Grand Theatre, Wolverhampton 21 February

1923 **Biffy** (Gil Roy/Vera Beringer, William Ray) tour

1924 **Archie** (Haydn Wood, Jack Waller/w Worton David) Grand Theatre, Hull 28 July

1927 **Patsy from Paris** (L Jerome) Palace, Maidstone 14 March

1928 **Tipperary Tim** (Joseph Tunbridge/w Arthur Field) Alhambra Theatre, Bradford 6 August

1930 **Wild Rose** (Kennedy Russell/David Fairweather/w Worton David) tour

1936 **How Do, Princess** revised *Arlette* (Novello) Manchester 16 March

AN ARTIST'S MODEL Comedy with music in 2 acts by Owen Hall. Lyrics by Harry Greenbank. Music by Sidney Jones. Daly's Theatre, London, 2 February 1895.

Following the great success of *A Gaiety Girl,* which had been transferred from its production venue at the Prince of Wales Theatre into Daly's Theatre during its run, George Edwardes commissioned from its authors and composer another show in the same new line of modern-dress musical comedy as a follow-up. *A Naughty Girl* was intended to feature Lottie Venne in a role similar to that in which she had scored in *A Gaiety Girl,* and (following the ups and downs the producer had experienced with the American soubrette Marie Halton) Letty Lind, the town's favorite dancing and sort-of-singing ingenue, was tabbed to take the title role in a farcical piece centered around the high jinks of this stock ''romp-of-the-school'' character through the fleshpots of Paris. The whole piece was, of course, to be written in the frothy, smart and satirical manner which had helped make such a hit of the earlier show.

Plans for the show were turned on their head, however, when the hugely popular Marie Tempest returned to London from a triumphant stay in America, and Edwardes signed her for the new show. There was no question of ousting Lottie Venne from the cast, so librettist Jimmy Davis (''Owen Hall'') was simply given instructions to write in a large co-starring role for Miss Tempest. His intelligent answer to this problem was to invent a whole second plot: the tale of a former artist's model, now a rich widow, and her former lover, a poor Parisian artist (a role allotted to Miss Tempest's *Dorothy* and *Red Hussar* co-star Hayden Coffin) chary, under the circumstances, of attempting to renew their youthful romance. This romantic plot was interwoven with the jaunts and japes of madcap Daisy Vane and the cavalcade of her guardian and other susceptible Britons through Paris.

The enforced rewrite turned out to be the best thing that could have happened to the show. The new portion (which annexed the show's title, now *An Artist's Model*) turned out to be the heart of the entertainment, the old portion the decoration and the light relief, in a musical which provided a fine variety of humor and romance in its book, and of lyrical solos and ensembles and character songs in Sidney Jones's score. Lottie Venne scored with a knowing point number ''The Lady Wasn't Going That Way,'' but the most notable public favorites amongst the songs proved to be a dainty song-and-dance piece for Letty Lind telling the fable of ''The Gay Tom Tit,'' and ''The Laughing Song'' as put over by the dashingly darkish Maurice Farkoa, as an incidental artist, and subsequently recorded many times by him as the most successful of all early 78rpm show song recordings.

An Artist's Model set the pattern for one of the most successful series of musicals in theatre history. The two-headed arrangement, with Coffin and Miss Tempest featured in a strong singing romantic partnership, and Miss Lind and, later, other comedy performers heading the equally important soubret and comic portion of the piece, remained standard at Daly's Theatre where, with Edwardes at the helm, Owen Hall, Harry Greenbank and Sidney Jones provided, during the next decade, several of the most enduring and internationally successful shows of the period: *The Geisha, A Greek Slave* and *San Toy.* After its 392 performances at Daly's and in an enforced transfer to the Lyric Theatre, *An Artist's Model* went on the road, at first with Maud Boyd and Leonard Russell starred in Edwardes's Number One Company, and then in many subsequent, and later lesser, companies.

Al Hayman and Charles Frohman mounted a Broadway version of *An Artist's Model* with Australian star Nellie Stewart in Miss Tempest's role and an otherwise largely London cast including Marie Studholme (Daisy), Farkoa, and John Coates (Rudolph) through 56 New York performances and a tour, but the show did not go further afield. It took the next of the Daly's shows, *The Geisha,* to wake the world up to what was going on at Edwardes's theatre.

USA: Broadway Theater 23 December 1895

ASCHE, Oscar [ASCHE, Thomas Stange Heise Oscar] (b Geelong, Australia, 26 January 1871; d Marlow, Bucks, 23 March 1936).

Born in Australia, of Norwegian parentage, the big, barrel-chested Asche made his stage career in Britain, establishing himself as an actor in mostly Shakespearean

Plate 12. **Oscar Asche.** *The man-sized author-director-star followed up his* Chu-Chin-Chow *hit with a similar self-made role in* Cairo.

roles under the management of F R Benson and of Herbert Beerbohm Tree at London's His Majesty's Theatre. It was also with Tree that he had his first experience as a director, for Stephen Phillips's popular drama *Ulysses.* Asche subsequently played several seasons under his own management, taking some of the principal heroic roles in the standard repertoire as well as those in which his physique rendered him particularly effective, from Falstaff and Attila the Hun to Hajj the Beggar in Edward Knoblock's eastern tale, *Kismet.* He also made several forays into the field of authorship, and collaborated with F Norreys Connell on the play *Count Hannibal* (1910).

Asche appeared on the music-hall stage as Hajj in a musical scena written for him by Knoblock, but he made his full-scale entry into the musical theatre in 1916 when he wrote, directed and starred in the rather *Kismet*-like spectacular musical piece *Chu Chin Chow* (''Anytime's Kissing Time,'' ''The Cobbler's Song''), produced by his old master, Tree, and his wife and co-star, Lily Brayton, at His Majesty's Theatre. This version of the Arabian Nights tale of Ali Baba and the 40 thieves, remodeled to give Asche and Miss Brayton starring roles of the kind best suited to them as the robber chieftain and his vengeful slave girl, was directed by Asche in a lavishly dramatic and picturesque fashion, and it became one of the favorite entertainments of the First World War, running on at its London base for an unprecedented 2,235 performances over five years. It made a huge profit for all concerned and notably for Asche who, although his chronic inability to manage money had made him unable to invest in the show as a producer, had won a large share in its running profits by taking as his director's fee a percentage on the show's box office.

The greatest rival to *Chu Chin Chow* during its five years' run was another musical in which Asche also had a hand, although this time as director only: *The Maid of the Mountains* at Daly's Theatre. The spectacular aspect of *Chu Chin Chow* had played a very large part in its success and *The Maid of the Mountains'* striking and expansive production, designed and staged by Asche, proved once again to be an important element of a romantic and exotic stage piece which turned out to be extraordinarily popular with wartime audiences. Asche had a sure touch with the theatrically highly colored, both visually and dramatically, and these two great successes were followed by other similarly lavish productions (*A Southern Maid, Frasquita, Cleopatra, The Swordsman*) which in a few years made him a reputation as the foremost director of the large-scale musical-spectacular play of his time.

There was, however, little further success for him as an author. *Chu Chin Chow* was succeeded by another Eastern extravaganza called *Mecca* (a title subsequently censored into *Cairo*) in which an original story of some ingenuity was evolved to give Asche and Miss Brayton a second chance to appear in the same kind of roles they had played so effectively in *Chu Chin Chow. Cairo* had some success as a dance and scenery piece on Broadway and in London, and was played for a season in Australia, without anywhere rivaling its predecessor, but an attempt to produce a grandiose piece in the Olde English vein, *The Good Old Days,* was a disastrous failure.

Beset by financial troubles which were only partly alleviated by his wife's secure management of her affairs, Asche found success more and more difficult to achieve in his later days and his last work as both a director and performer was in some of the more pretentiously amateurish musical would-be spectaculars of his time (*The White Camellia, El Dorado, Kong*).

Asche also appeared on the musical screen, being seen in the British film of *Two Hearts in Waltz Time* (1934) shortly before his death.

1916 **Chu Chin Chow** (Frederic Norton) His Majesty's Theatre 31 August

1919 **Eastward Ho!** (Grace Torrens, John Ansell/w Dornford Yates) Alhambra Theatre 9 September

1920 **Mecca** (aka *Cairo*) (Percy Fletcher) Century Theater, New York 4 October

1925 **The Good Old Days** (Fletcher) Gaiety Theatre 27 October

Autobiography: *Oscar Asche: His Life, by Himself* (Hurst & Blackett Ltd, London, 1929)

ASCHER, Leo (b Vienna, 17 August 1880; d New York, 25 February 1942). Composer of a long list of musical plays for the Austrian and German stages, whose career was ended by the rise of Nazism.

Educated for a career in the legal world, Leo Ascher qualified as a Doctor of Law, but he carried on his musical studies to such effect that, at the age of 26, he had his first Operette, *Vergeltsgott,* a comical piece written to a text by Victor Léon, produced at no less a venue than the Theater an der Wien. It won some success in this first production, and went on to be seen in Germany (*Der Bettelgraf*) and in Hungary (*A koldusgróf*), confirming the young composer in the career he would follow. In the years that followed, Ascher turned out numerous songs and scores for the little Operetten played at Gabor Steiner's Danzers Orpheum and Venedig in Wien summer theater, and at the Kabarett Fledermaus, where he became, for a time, musical director. The locally colored *Vindobona, du herrliche Stadt* proved the most popular, and several others of these little one-acters were given subsequent productions in Hungarian versions (*A Palatinus lány* 3 September 1910, *Ostrómallapot* 30 January 1912, *Rampsenit,* October 1912).

The more substantial *Die arme Lori,* produced at the Raimundtheater in 1909 with Carl Streitmann, Vera Schwarz and Gerda Walde heading the cast, was given only a few *en suite* performances before going into the repertoire, but two years later the same house mounted the composer's most successful piece to date. The charming *Hoheit tanzt Walzer,* with Betty Fischer in its title role, had a magnificent first run of 230 performances and, in all, played more than 350 performances at the Raimundtheater between 1912 and 1914 before going on to productions further afield, establishing Ascher as a known value in the musical theatre.

His next full-length show, *Was tut man nicht alles aus Liebe,* confirmed his new position, topping 50 nights at Ronachers (50th performance 27 January 1915) before, similarly, going on to other productions, including a botched-into-unrecognizableness one on Broadway (*Follow Me*). *Botschafterin Leni,* mounted at the Theater in der Josefstadt, also progressed to further productions (57 performances at the Berlin Thalia-Theater in 1920–21, *Kotnyeles naccsága* in Hungary) after its initial season of 41 nights, before, in the latter years of the war, the composer turned out the scores for what would be his other biggest musical-theatre successes.

In 1916 Ascher combined with Berlin's favorite Posse authors, Jean Kren and Bernhard Buchbinder, on the pretty little operetta *Der Soldat der Marie,* which Kren used to open his newly acquired Neues Operettenhaus. It scored an enormous success, and the team followed up with the ''musikalischer Schwank'' *Egon und seine Frauen* (1917), another lively musical piece with a score made up of marches, waltzes and polkas, not to mention a Rhinelander and a ländler which proved good for a seven months' Berlin run. In Vienna, in the same year, Ascher scored again with *Bruder Leichtsinn,* which followed the 112 performances of the local production of *Der Soldat der Marie* into the Wiener Bürgertheater. It was played for 176 performances, with a cast headed by longtime stars Streitmann and Joseffy, before going on to make a major success in Hungary under the title *Hejahuja báró.*

By the end of the war, Ascher was established on German, Austrian and Hungarian fronts as one of the most fruitful composers of the musical stage. In the postwar years, however, his new pieces, without ever demeriting, did not quite find the same storming success. *Was Mädchen träumen* had a fine run of over one hundred performances at the Raimundtheater, outpointing the five and a half weeks of *Zwölf Uhr Nachts! Der Künstlerpreis* followed its season at the Apollotheater by going on to be seen in Germany (Horst-Theater am Sophienblatt 11 January 1920) and in Hungary (*Uldöz a pénz* Budapesti Színház 15 May 1923), whilst *Prinzessin Friedl* had three months' run in Berlin and *Baronesschen Sarah,* a musical adaptation of the comedy *Im Klubsessel,* slightly less.

Another Thalia-Theater piece, *Ein Jahr ohne Liebe,* followed a three-and-a-half-month run in Berlin with a production at the Wiener Stadttheater later the same year, the Viennese *Sonja* played 55 performances at the Carltheater, *Das Amorettenhaus,* originally produced in Hamburg, was later seen at Baden-bei-Wien (7 March 1926), and *Ich hab' dich Lieb..!* had a first run of 62 performances at the Raimundtheater.

Fair runs with *Ninon am Scheideweg* in Berlin, the Singspiel *Frühling im Wienerwald* in Vienna and *Bravo, Peggy!,* produced in Leipzig before being mounted at Volksoper, as well as two film scores (*Purpur und Waschblau* 1931, *Mein Leopold* 1932) led to Ascher's final work, *Um ein bisschen Liebe,* for a European stage on which he had been featured for some 30 years, before he joined the Jewish exodus which would drain central Europe of almost all its operettic talent in the 1930s. He settled in America, and was working there on an English version of *Um ein bisschen Liebe* when he died in 1942.

In spite of his popularity in Austria, Germany and Hungary, Ascher's works were little heard in the rest of the world. A Carlo Lombardo pasticcio of his works was mounted in Italy as *La regina della fonografo,* whilst what purported to be a version of *Was tut man nicht alles aus Liebe* was played on Broadway as *Follow Me* (Casino Theater 29 November 1916), with numbers by Sigmund Romberg, Harry Tierney and Robert B Smith comprising most of the score, and Anna Held singing "Stop Tickling Me." *Hoheit tanzt Walzer* was played at New York's Irving Place Theater in German before, transmogrifed into *Princess Tralala,* it was toured around America by Andreas Dippel in 1916.

1905 **Vergeltsgott** (aka *Der Bettlerklub*) (Victor Léon) Theater an der Wien 14 October

1907 **Es gibt nur a Kaiserstadt** (Leopold Krenn) 3 scenes Danzers Orpheum 27 September

1908 **Die grüne Redoute** (Julius Brammer, Alfred Grünwald) 1 act Danzers Orpheum 26 March

1908 **Die kleine Manicure** (Brammer, Grünwald) 1 act Parisiana

1909 **Die arme Lori** (Krenn) Raimundtheater 12 March

1909 **Hut ab!** (Edmund Skurawy, S B Tellheim) 1 act Venedig in Wien 28 May

1909 **Ein Belagerungszustand** (August Neidhart) 1 act Kabarett Fledermaus 1 November

1910 **Die keusche Susanne** (Fritz Löhner-Beda) 1 act Kabarett Fledermaus 1 February

1910 **Die Klubbrüder** (Wilhelm Frieser) 1 act Wiener Colosseum 1 April

1910 **Vindobona, du herrliche Stadt** (Brammer, Grünwald) Venedig in Wien 22 July

1910 **Der fromme Silvanus** (Löhner-Beda) 1 act Kabarett Fledermaus 1 November

Plate 13. **Leo Ascher's** *long list of Austrian hits was boosted further by a run of successful musicals, including* Egon und seine Frauen, *for the Berlin stage of the 1910s.*

1911 **Rampsenit** (Löhner-Beda) 1 act Kabarett Fledermaus 1 January

1911 **Das goldene Strumpfband** (Brammer, Grünwald) 1 act Ronacher 1 May

1911 **Eine fidele Nacht** (Löhner-Beda) 1 act Wiener Colosseum 1 September

1912 **Der Lockvogel** (Alexander Engel, Julius Horst) Walhalla Theater, Wiesbaden 11 January

1912 **Hoheit tanzt Walzer** (later *Hochzeitswalzer*) (Brammer, Grünwald) Raimundtheater 24 February

1913 **Die goldene Hanna** (Löhner-Beda) 1 act Apollotheater 4 January

1914 **Was tut man nicht alles aus Liebe** (Felix Dörmann) Ronacher 17 December

1915 **Botschafterin Leni** (Bernhard Buchbinder) Theater in der Josefstadt 19 February

1916 **Die schone Komödiantin** (Eugen Burg, Louis Taufstein) 1 act Wintergarten, Berlin 13 January

1916 **Der Soldat der Marie** (Buchbinder, Jean Kren, Alfred Schönfeld) Neues Operetten-Theater, Berlin 2 September

1917 **Egon und seine Frauen** (Buchbinder, Kren) Thalia-Theater, Berlin 25 August

1917 **Bruder Leichtsinn** (Brammer, Grünwald) Wiener Bürgertheater 28 December

1919 **Der Künstlerpreis** (Rudolf Österreicher, Horst) Apollotheater 1 October

1919 **Was Mädchen träumen** (Leopold Jacobson, Robert Bodanzky) Raimundtheater 6 December

1919 **Wo Schwalben nisten**

1920 **Prinzessin Friedl** (Buchbinder, Kren) Neues Operetten Theater, Berlin 14 May

1920 **Zwölf Uhr Nachts!** (Dörmann, Hans Kottow) Raimundtheater 12 November

1920 **Baronesschen Sarah** (Neidhart) Komische Oper, Berlin 5 December

1923 **Ein Jahr ohne Liebe** (Ludwig Hirschfeld, Alfred Deutsch-German) Thalia-Theater, Berlin 12 January

1925 **Sonja** (Rudolf Presber, Leo Walther Stein) Carltheater 6 March

1926 **Das Amorettenhaus** (Heinrich von Waldberg, Max Steiner-Kaiser, Bruno Hardt-Warden) Carl-Schultze Theater, Hamburg January

1926 **Ich hab' dich Lieb..!** (Willy Sterk) Raimundtheater 16 April

1926 **Ninon am Scheideweg** (Neidhart) Theater am Zoo, Berlin 27 December

1928 **La Barberina Hamburg**

1930 **Frühling im Wienerwald** (Löhner-Beda, Lunzer) Stadttheater 17 April

1931 **Bei der Wirtin Rosenrot** (Paul Knepler, Löhner-Beda) Theater des Westens, Berlin 14 March

1932 **Bravo Peggy!** (Wilhelm Lichtenberg, Armin Robinson, Harry Waldau) Operetten-Theater, Leipzig 27 March

1936 **Um ein bisschen Liebe** (Rudolf Lothar, Peter Herz) Stadttheater 5 June

ASHLEY, H[enry] J[effries] (b Pimlico, London, 1832; d Lambeth, London, 18 November 1890).

A late arrival in the theatre, after nearly a decade spent working in the engineering office of Maudesley, son and Fields, ''Mr Ashley'' played for several years as a comic actor at Glasgow and through the British provinces before making his London debut at the St James's Theatre in 1860. During his engagement there he appeared in several burlesques (Buonocuore in *Prince Amabel* 1862, Faust in *Faust and Marguerite* 1864, etc). He spent a number of years playing in comedy, drama, burlesque (Achilles in the Adelphi perversion of *La Belle Hélène* 1866, Red Murdoch in *Mountain Dhu* 1867, etc) and musical drama (Conte Luigi Orlando in *Garibaldi in Sicily* 1867, etc) as a member of the company at the Adelphi. He toured with Toole (Ozokerit in *Aladdin II* 1872, etc) and created several good comedy roles in West End comedies with Wyndham at the Criterion but, in spite of limited singing ability, he ultimately found his niche and his greatest success in the musical theatre where he was, for the last decade of his career and his life, one of the most prominent character men in British comic opera. He appeared in leading comedy roles in an almost unbroken run of London productions between 1879 and 1890 including *Madame Favart* (1879, Pontsablé), *Olivette* (1880, Duc des Ifs), *Manola* (1882, Brasiero), *Manteaux Noirs* (Don José), *La Mascotte* revival (Laurent), *Falka* (1883, Tancred), *The Merry Duchess* (1883, Brabazon Sikes), *Pocahontas* (1884, Percival Punsheon Potts), *La Cosaque* (1884, Jules Primitif), *François les bas-bleus* (1885, Pontcornet), *Dr D* (1885, Doctor von Dosemoffen), *Indiana* (1886, Mulberry Mullitt, then Matt o' the Mint on tour), *Robinson Crusoe* (1886, Vavasseur), *Paul Jones* (1889, Bicoquet), *Marjorie* (1889, Simon Striveling) and *Capitaine Thérèse* (1890, Colonel Sombrero). He died of the typhoid during the run of this last piece.

ASHMAN, Howard [GERSHMAN, Howard Elliott] (b Baltimore, Md, 17 May 1951; d New York, 14 March 1991).

Author, lyricist and director, Ashman began his career off-off-Broadway where he had two musicals produced in the late 1970s: *Dreamstuff,* a version of *The Tempest* mounted at the Workshop of the Players Art where he was at the time co-director, and a musicalization of Kurt Vonnegut's novel *God Bless You, Mr Rosewater,* which subsequently moved up from the WPA to off-Broadway's Entermedia Theater (49 performances). Although he had one play, *The Confirmation,* taken from its original small production to an abortive attempt at Broadway, he made most of his writing career on the musical side of the theatre. He authored a rewrite on the libretto of *The Vagabond King* (1977), contributed to the Manhattan Theatre Club's cabaret production *Real Life Funnies* (w Alan Menken) in the 1980–81 season, then scored an international hit with his spoof of the C-grade period horror movie, *Little Shop of Horrors,* which moved from its beginnings at the WPA (24 performances), where Ashman was sole director between 1977 and 1982, to a long run off-Broadway, productions around the world, and a would-be A-grade film version.

He contributed to the 1984 revue *Diamonds* and, in 1986, a musical based on the 1975 film satire of beauty contests, *Smile,* was produced on Broadway. Ashman supplied book and lyrics and also directed this, his one venture on Broadway, which was a 48-performance failure.

He and his *Little Shop of Horrors* partner, Alan Menken, subsequently wrote the songs for the Walt Disney film *The Little Mermaid* (1989) on which he also acted as co-producer (w John Musker), and for its successor, *Beauty and the Beast,* (1991). He had partly written the lyrics for a third cartoon, *Aladdin,* before his premature death, aged not quite 40. His film score for *Beauty and the Beast* was used posthumously as the basis for the score of the stage musical made from the animated film.

"Under the Sea" from *The Little Mermaid* was awarded the Academy Award for Best Song in 1989.

A show entitled *Hundreds of Hats* made up from Ashman's stage and screen writing was produced posthumously at the WPA.

1976 **Dreamstuff** (Marsha Malamet/Dennis Green) WPA Theater 2 April

1979 **God Bless You, Mr Rosewater** (Alan Menken/w Green) WPA Theater 17 May; Entermedia Theater 14 October

1982 **Little Shop of Horrors** (Menken) WPA Theater 6 May; Orpheum Theater 27 July

1986 **Smile** (Marvin Hamlisch) Lunt-Fontanne Theater 24 November

1994 **Beauty and the Beast** (Menken/w Tim Rice/Linda Woolverton) Palace Theater 18 April

ASKEY, Arthur [Bowden] (b Liverpool, 6 June 1900; d London, 16 November 1982).

"Big-hearted Arthur" Askey made his first theatrical appearances in concert party and pantomime before becoming popular as a radio comedian. He starred in the musical comedy *The Love Racket* (1943, Tony Merrick, Tivoli, Melbourne 23 December 1949), which followed in the footsteps of Lupino Lane's cheerful series of musical shows at the Victoria Palace in 1943, and in the decade following this introduction to the musical stage, he top-billed in London in *Follow the Girls* (1945, Goofy Gale), *The Kid from Stratford* (1948, Arthur Prince) and *Bet Your Life* (1952, Arthur Golightly), playing the kind of free-wheeling star comedy roles which had been the backbone of the dance-and-laughter musical comedies of the 1930s. With the passing of such shows, Askey's stage performances became largely limited to pantomime where he remained for many years one of Britain's outstanding exponents of the classic style of pantomime playing.

Autobiography: *Before Your Very Eyes* (Woburn Press, London, 1975)

Plate 14. *"Big-hearted"* **Arthur Askey** *was the star of London's* Bet Your Life.

ASPECTS OF LOVE Musical in 2 acts by Charles Hart and Don Black based on the novel of the same name by David Garnett. Music by Andrew Lloyd Webber. Prince of Wales Theatre, London, 17 April 1989.

Kept on the back burner as a potential subject for a musical play by composer Lloyd Webber and director Trevor Nunn for many years, David Garnett's *Aspects of Love* was developed as a medium-sized musical play in the wake of the composer's success with the extremely elaborate *The Phantom of the Opéra.* Charles Hart, the lyricist of *Phantom of the Opéra,* and Don Black, the composer's collaborator on his most intimate work to date, the song cycle "Tell Me on a Sunday," supplied the text.

The very young Alex Dillingham (Michael Ball), entranced by the touring actress Rose Vibart (Anne Crumb), invites her to spend her weeks out at his wealthy uncle's unoccupied mansion in Pau. Uncle George (Kevin Colson) leaves his own little Parisian idyll with sculptress Giulietta (Kathleen Rowe McAllen) and descends on the intrusive couple with considerable charm. The tale moves on, and when Alex returns from the army, he finds that Rose has moved in with George. Dramatic recrimination gives way to a more comfortable situation as Rose weds George, becomes successful and brings a daughter, Jenny, into the family and the house at Pau. The growing Jenny falls in love with Alex, and the jealousy in the family shifts sides, but when George suffers a heart attack whilst spying on the young people and the widowed Rose pleads with Alex to stay by her, the young man realizes that he will be better off moving on with the uncomplicated Giulietta than remaining behind to be torn between Rose and Jenny.

Like all of the composer's works, *Aspects of Love* was composed through, and again like them, it held some individual numbers within that sung-through construction. The opening number, the tenor "Love Changes Everything," which set the tone and theme of the show, proved to be the most popular piece. Launched as a single before the production of the show, it climbed to second place on the British hit parades, the most successful

Lloyd Webber show song in hit-parade terms since *Evita*'s ''Don't Cry for Me, Argentina.'' In the show, however, it was Rose's funeral evening cry of despair, ''Anything But Lonely,'' which proved the musical highlight, alongside Giulietta's drivingly sung and danced eulogy ''Give Me the Wine and the Dice,'' the broad duetting between Rose and Alex of ''Seeing Is Believing'' and the gentler strains of ''The Last Man You Remember'' and the plangent ''Song of Childhood.''

By the time that *Aspects of Love* made it to the stage, at London's Prince of Wales Theatre, it had lost a little of its initially intended intimacy. If the orchestral accompaniment was still smaller than in the town's vaster musicals, the cast had been increased in size, and the scenic concept used to cover the many shifts of locale included in the text was both mechanically complex and visually lavish. Nevertheless, the show maintained much of the more personal feeling of its small story and it became a particular favorite with those looking for relief from the current fashion for heavily spectacular or glitzy musical shows.

Twelve months after the Really Useful Company's London production had opened, the show was mounted on Broadway with Colson, Ball and Misses Crumb and McAllen repeating their original assignments. It was on a hiding to nothing. Resentment against Lloyd Webber's domination of the musical theatre, and an influential critic, with allegiances elsewhere, who had announced, well before opening, his dislike of the piece, helped ensure some gloatingly negative reviews, and the lack of spectacle and glitter discouraged word-of-mouth reports that might have reversed that decision. Some papers leapt hopefully into print insinuating early closure, but New York was able to find an audience for some 11 months (377 performances), as the show continued its London run through three years (1,325 performances) before taking to the road.

In 1991 a version more in keeping with the originally planned ''chamber'' scale of the piece and played on one set was mounted in Canada with Keith Michell (George), Linda Balgord (Rose) and Ron Bohmer (Alex). This version was subsequently played in America and a similarly reduced-size production was staged in Australia, with Colson in his original role alongside Delia Hannah (Rose) and Peter Couzens (Alex), for a 16-week season in Sydney and a national tour. *Aspects of Love* went on to be seen in Japan (ad Keita Asari Aoyama Theatre 10 January 1992), Denmark (Aarhus Theatre 14 September 1992), Budapest (ad Ferenc Bárány) and other venues, including a brief return to the West End (Prince of Wales Theatre 20 December 1993, 30 performances), finding plenty of friends on the way, but never anywhere threatening to become the kind of blockbusting hit that its composer's earlier and more lavish works had. The show had its German premiere at Dresden in 1997, with Felix Martin (Alex), Jolanta Teresa Kuznik (Rose) and Michael Flöth (George) featured.

USA: Broadhurst Theater 8 April 1990; Australia: Theatre Royal, Sydney 18 November 1992; Hungary: Madách Színház *A szerelem arcai* 26 July 1996; Germany: Staatsoperette, Dresden 16 May 1997

Recordings: original cast (Polydor), Japanese cast (Polydor)

Literature: Gänzl, K: *The Complete ''Aspects of Love''* (Aurum, London, 1990)

ASTAIRE, Fred [AUSTERLITZ, Frederick] (b Omaha, Neb, 10 May 1899; d Los Angeles, 22 June 1987). Dancing star who moved from fame in the theatre to immortality on the screen.

Astaire and his sister, Adele (b Omaha, Neb, 10 September 1896; d Phoenix, 25 January 1981), worked as a dance team in vaudeville from 1906, before making their first appearances in the musical theatre as an item in the 1917 *Over the Top* and in the 1918 version of *The Passing Show.* They performed dance routines in supporting roles in *Apple Blossoms* (1919) and *The Love Letter* (1921) with sufficient éclat to allow them to be effectively promoted to the top of the bill (although the romantic team garnered the plot) in *For Goodness' Sake* (1922); later the same year, in *The Bunch and Judy,* they were even given the principal places in the plot. The following year they repeated *For Goodness' Sake* in London, under the title *Stop Flirting,* with the same personal success they had won at home.

This success was thoroughly confirmed in *Lady, Be Good!* (New York, 1924 and London, 1926), *Funny Face* (New York, 1927 and London, 1928) and the revue *The Band Wagon* (1931), but the musical comedy *Smiles,* in which they appeared in 1930, was a failure. After *The Band Wagon,* Adele retired to become the wife of Lord Charles Cavendish, and Fred continued his career alone. He starred opposite Claire Luce in *Gay Divorce* in New York (1932) in what would be his last Broadway appearance, and in London (1933), before entering the film world. There he became one of the greatest stars of the heyday of the Hollywood musical in a series of films from *Dancing Lady* and *Flying Down to Rio* in 1933, through *The Gay Divorcée, Roberta, Top Hat, Follow the Fleet, Swing Time, Shall We Dance?, A Damsel in Distress, Carefree, The Story of Vernon and Irene Castle, Broadway Melody, You'll Never Get Rich, Holiday Inn, You Were Never Lovelier, Ziegfeld Follies, Blue Skies, Easter Parade* and *The Barkleys of Broadway* in the 1930s and 1940s, and such pieces as *The Band Wagon, Funny Face, Silk Stockings* in the 1950s up to his last musical film appearance in *Finian's Rainbow* (1968). He subsequently appeared in a number of non-musical films, and was nominated for an Academy Award for his character role in *The Towering Inferno* (1984).

As a partnership, Adele and Fred showed an irresistible and apparently off-hand grace and stylishness in dance, which combined with attractive personalities and an understanding of comic timing to produce a performance whose technical difficulties were made to seem exceptional by being made to seem almost casually natural. Both possessed light, accurate singing voices and, above all, the ability to put across a song. In their days together, it was Adele who attracted most of the attention, being particularly praised for her comic gifts, the extent and nature of which can be seen by looking at the variety and style of her role of Susie in the post-production libretto of *Lady, Be Good!* Fred was to come into his own in films, but there is no reason to suppose that he was any more effaced in the stage partnership with his sister than he was by his celluloid dance partners.

Astaire also ventured into songwriting, and one of his numbers ''I'm Building Up to an Awful Letdown'' was heard in the London flop musical *Rise and Shine* and its touring derivative, *Darling You.*

Autobiography: *Steps in Time* (Harper, New York, 1959); Biographies: Green, S & Goldblatt, B: *Starring Fred Astaire* (Dodd Mead, New York, 1973), Croce, A: *The Fred Astaire and Ginger Rogers Book* (Outerbridge & Lazard, New York, 1972), Thompson, H: *Fred Astaire* (Falcon, New York, 1970), Thomas, B: *Astaire, the Man, the Dancer* (St Martin's Press, New York, 1984), Green, B: *Fred Astaire* (Baxter Books, New York, 1979), Mueller, J: *Astaire Dancing: The Musical Films* (Hamish Hamilton, London, 1986), Adler, B: *Fred Astaire: A Wonderful Life* (Carroll & Graf, New York, 1987), etc

AS THE GIRLS GO Musical comedy in 2 acts by William Roos. Lyrics by Harold Adamson. Music by Jimmy McHugh. Winter Garden Theater, New York, 13 November 1948.

A spectacular Mike Todd production of a colorful extravaganza which looked four years into the future and fantasized on the election of a lady president of the United States of America. Lucille Thompson Wellington (Irene Rich) was the lady in question, which made her husband Waldo (Bobby Clark) the consort. Most of the consorting that he did was with a line of blossoming chorines. Clark's comedy, more redolent of the low, adlibbing comic antics of turn-of-the-century musical theatre comedians than of the more orderly postwar years, was supported by a romantic threadlet of plot featuring presidential son Kenny (Bill Callahan) and his Kathy (Betty Jane Watson). The show's numbers were topped by the juvenile man's attractive ''[I Got] Lucky in the Rain'' and ''You Say the Nicest Things, Baby'' and by some cheery pieces of comedy material for Clark, ''It Takes a Woman to Take a Man'' and ''Father's Day.''

As the Girls Go stayed 420 performances on Broadway without turning itself into a financial success.

ATHERTON, Alice [HOGAN, Mary Alice] (b Cincinnati, 25 August 1854; d New York, 4 February 1899). A versatile singing comedienne of the Victorian stage.

Although she was equally capable of taking dramatic and legitimate comedy parts and, indeed, was seen on Broadway in 1871 as Gavroche in the drama *Les Misérables,* Alice Atherton made the bulk of her career in burlesque, extravaganza and musical farce. She began her career as a child actress in Cincinnati and Louisville, moved on to play four seasons as soubrette with the Histrionic Club at Mobile and, still before she was out of her teens, appeared in burlesque with Lydia Thompson (1869) and with Pauline Markham (Glowworm in *Chow Chow, Luna,* Mercury in *Ixion*), in comedy drama with Baker and Farron, and was a member of several burlesque troupes, spending some time at Wood's Museum (1871, Liveretto in *Lucrezia Borgia,* etc) before rejoining Lydia Thompson's troupe. She played with Lydia both in America and in Britain, appearing, amongst others, as Twigletto in *Pippin,* Orion in *Paris,* Arcobrand in *The Forty Thieves,* O'Shacabac in *Bluebeard,* Hermance in *Oxygen,* Queen Ylang-Ylang in *Robinson Crusoe,* Queen Folichonne in *Piff-Paff* and Camille in *Mephisto.* In 1874 she appeared in Boston in the extravaganza *Aladdin.*

She subsequently (1878–79) worked with the two most substantial of the incessantly touring American extravaganza companies—the Samuel Colville Folly Company, which picked up Miss Thompson's repertoire and players when the star returned to England, and E E Rice's Surprise Party (Conrad in *The Corsair,* Lady Macassar, then The Bad Man in *The Babes in the Wood,* Mrs Lo, then Hiawatha in *Hiawatha* 1878, Bon Ton George jr in *Revels,* Crusoe in *Robinson Crusoe,* etc)—and in 1880 led out the similar outfit launched by her husband and known as ''Willie Edouin's Sparks'' (*Revels,* Prince Achmet in *Horrors,* Ruby Chillington in *Dreams,* Molly Maybud in *Ripples*).

She played opposite Edouin in Hoyt's *A Bunch of Keys* (1883, Teddie Keys) in America, and in London the pair won their biggest success together as the rambunctious twins in the burlesque *The Babes, or Whines from the Wood* (1884, Tessie). Although Miss Atherton later starred in the English version of the French comédie-vaudeville *Les 28 Jours de Clairette* (1892, Clairette), and as Mrs Guyer in the London edition of *A Trip to Chinatown* (1894), she was always most at home in the broad comedy of burlesque (Carrie in *Oliver Grumble* 1886, Jane in *Jaunty Jane Shore,* title roles of *Vanderdecken* and *Airey-Annie*), in the loose-limbed Victorian musical-comedy ''comedy dramas'' (Lyza in *The Japs* 1885,

Plate 15. *The versatile* **Alice Atherton** *in two of her ''disguises'' in* The Babes.

Charlie Cott in *Blackberries* 1886, Ruby in *Binks the Downy Photographer* 1893, Maggie Welland in *On the March* 1894) and such American farce musicals as *Hans the Boatman* (1891, Jeffie) and *The Marquis of Michigan* (1898), in which she starred in the last year of her career, playing opposite Sam Bernard in the role of a professional strongwoman called Etna Vesuvius. In such pieces, and playing mostly with or for Edouin, she built herself a fine following on both sides of the Atlantic. Her last stage appearances were in *Rice's Summer Nights* on the Casino Roof Garden (1898) and in the American touring company of *Hotel Topsy Turvey* (1899), starring opposite Henry Dixey.

She carried with her for 30 years two songs, ''The Laughing Song'' and Meyer Lutz's ''Two Eyes of Blue,'' which she interpolated into a number of her musical-theatre performances as well as into her variety act, *A Singing Watermelon* (1898, arr E E Rice), and which became her ''trademark.''

Miss Atherton was the mother of May Edouin and of Daisy Atherton, both of whom made careers as musical-theatre and variety performers.

ATTERIDGE, Harold R[ichard] (b Lake Forest, Ill, 9 July 1886; d Lynbrook, NY, 15 January 1938). Long-serving wordsmith for Broadway's Shubert production house.

A product of Chicago University at around the same time as the successful local musical-comedy-writing team of Adams and Hough, the young Atteridge worked on several musicals in Chicago (*Happy Youngsters, A Winning Miss,* the William Norris vehicle *My Cinderella Girl* which was turned from a farce to a musical whilst in mid-Chicago-run, *The Girl in the Kimono,* etc) and interpolated the occasional song into Broadway shows (''The Dublin Rag'' w Phil Schwartz in *Madame Sherry,* etc) before he became, in the 1910s and 1920s, a regular house writer for the Shubert brothers. In that post, he turned out skeletons and sketches for their revues, and libretti—which could be freely embroidered upon by their stars—for such half-revue/half-musical shows as the made-over remnants of Edmund Eysler's Operette *Vera Violetta* (1911) or the homemade *The Whirl of Society* (1912), *From Broadway to Paris* (1912), *The Honeymoon Express* (1913) or *Dancing Around* (1914).

Amongst the revues and quasi-revues for which Atteridge supplied material over the years were included *The Passing Show* series, *The Whirl of the World* (1914), *Maid in America, A World of Pleasure* (1915), *Doing Our Bit,* (1917), *The Midnight Rounders* (1920), *The Mimic World of 1921, Make It Snappy* (1922), *Hitchy Koo of 1922, Topics of 1923,* the Mistinguett revue *Innocent Eyes* (1924), *Gay Paree* (1925), *The Great Temptations* (1926), *A Night in Spain* (1927), *Greenwich Village Follies of 1928,* and *Pleasure Bound* (1929). He also scored the occasional individual song success, as with the lyrics for ''By the Beautiful Sea'' (w Harry Carroll).

For the musical comedy stage, he adapted Clyde Fitch's English version of the Horst and Engel comedy *Der blaue Maus* as *The Little Blue Devil* for Joe Weber, Harry Leon Wilson's famous *Ruggles of Red Gap* with a Sigmund Romberg score and Ralph Herz starring, Frances Goodrich and Albert Hackett's comedy success *Up Pops the Devil* as *Everybody's Welcome,* Mrs Gertrude Ranken Drew's *Billy* as *Listen, Dearie* (w Gertrude Purcell) and, in tandem with Rida Johnson Young, did over Beulah Marie Dix's and E G Sutherland's *The Road to Yesterday* as a libretto for Victor Herbert (*The Dream Girl*). He also adapted, often heavily, a number of Continental musicals for the American stage. His principal success, however, came with the loose-limbed stage musical vehicles he invented for Al Jolson, the star of the Winter Garden shows, whom he supplied with the bases for his series of Broadway appearances under the Shubert management.

1908 **A Winning Miss** (William Frederick Peters/revised Aaron Hoffman) Garden Theater, Chicago 23 November

1910 **My Cinderella Girl** (Peters/Richard Walton Tully, Robert M Baker) Whitney Theater, Chicago 2 May

1910 **The Girl in the Kimono** (Phil Schwartz/Helen Bagg) Ziegfeld Theater, Chicago 25 June

1911 **Vera Violetta** (*Vera Violetta*) reconstructed American version w Leonard Liebling (Winter Garden Theater)

1912 **Two Little Brides** (*Schneeglöckchen*) American version w James T Powers, Arthur Anderson (Casino Theater)

1913 **The Honeymoon Express** (Jean Schwartz/w Joseph W Herbert) Winter Garden Theater 6 February

1913 **The Man with Three Wives** (*Der Mann mit den drei Frauen*) American version w Paul Potter, Agnes Morgan (Weber & Fields, Music Hall)

1913 **The Little Parisienne** revised *Madame Troubadour* w Herbert (tour)

1914 **The Belle of Bond Street** revised version of *The Girl from Kays* Shubert Theater 30 March

1915 **Ruggles of Red Gap** (Romberg) Fulton Theater 24 December

1915 **The Peasant Girl** (*Polenblut*) American lyrics w Herbert Reynolds (44th Street Theater)

1916 **Robinson Crusoe Jr** (Romberg, et al/w Edgar Smith) Winter Garden Theater 17 February

1918 **Sinbad** (Romberg, et al) Winter Garden Theater 14 February

1919 **Monte Cristo Jr** (Romberg, J Schwartz, et al) Winter Garden Theater 12 February

1919 **The Little Blue Devil** (Harry Carroll) Central Theater 3 November

1920 **Cinderella on Broadway** (Bert Grant, Al Goodman) Winter Garden Theater 24 June

1921 **Bombo** (Romberg, et al) Jolson Theater 6 October

1921 **The Last Waltz** (*Der letzte Walzer*) American version w Edward Delaney Dunn (Century Theater)

1922 **The Rose of Stamboul** (*Die Rose von Stambul*) American version (Century Theater)

1923 **The Dancing Girl** (Romberg) Winter Garden 24 January

1923 **The Courtesan** (J Schwartz, Romberg/w Harry Wagstaffe Gribble) Parsons' Theater, Hartford, Conn 17 October

1924 **Marjorie** (Romberg, Stothart, Philip Culkin, Stephen Jones/Clifford Grey, Fred Thompson) ''additional dialogue'' Shubert Theater 11 August

1924 **The Dream Girl** (Victor Herbert/w Rida Johnson Young) Ambassador Theater 20 August

1925 **Sky High** (*Der Tanz ins Glück*) American version adapted from British version (Shubert Theater)

1925 **Big Boy** (James F Hanley, Joseph Meyer/B G de Sylva) Winter Garden Theater 7 January

1927 **Listen, Dearie** (Charles Gilpin/w Gertrude Purcell) Chestnut Street Opera House, Philadelphia 18 April

1929 **Well, Well, Well** (later *Pleasure Bound,* revue) (Maurie Rubens, Muriel Pollock, Phil Baker, Arthur Schwartz/Max Lief, Nathaniel Lief/w Montague Glass, Jules Eckert Goodman) Chestnut Street Opera House, Philadelphia 7 January

1931 **Everybody's Welcome** (Sammy Fain) Shubert Theater 13 October

1934 **Thumbs Up!** (ex- *The Fatal Blonde*) (Hanley, Henry Sullivan, et al/Ballard McDonald/w H I Phillips, Alan Baxter) St James Theater 27 December

Other titles credited: *Happy Youngsters* (William F Peters, 1908), *The Manicure Girl* (Peters, 1909)

AUBER, Daniel François Esprit (b Caen, 29 January 1782; d Paris, 12 May 1871).

One of the most prominent composers of the French opéra-comique of the first half of the 19th century, Auber was also one of the principal forebears of the various kinds of French opérette of the second part of that same century, and his works were often played alongside the early examples of modern comic opera and opéra-bouffe in the repertoires of the lighter (and sometimes not so light) operatic companies of the crossover period in the 1860s and 1870s.

Although he had an outstanding international success with the serious grand opera *La Muette de Portici* (1828), many of Auber's most popular works were written in the opéra-comique spirit, mixing flagrantly comical scenes with more romantic ones, and even with the dramatic strains of opera. His musical illustration of the lively *Fra Diavolo* (1830), with its Eugène Scribe tale of wicked banditry and disguised lovemaking, stands at the head of his output, but such pieces as *Le Cheval de bronze* (1835), *Le Domino noir* (1837) and *Les Diamants de la couronne* (1841) all reached out towards the style of the romantic comic operas of the later years of the century. In fact, several libretti originally set by Auber later became, with little alteration, the texts for Operetten. The most notable of these was *La Circassienne,* which subsequently became the book for von Suppé's *Fatinitza,* but the text for *Carlo Broschi* went into the making of Hermann Zumpe's successful Operette *Farinelli* and there were doubtless others hidden under the then nebulous and ubiquitous credit which, at that period, admitted that a libretto was pilfered "from the French." The libretto used for his 1833 *Gustave III,* on the other hand, went on to be the basis for Verdi's *Un Ballo in maschera.*

Because of their great popularity on the English stage, a number of Auber's works also took the brunt of the burlesque tradition in Britain, where *La Muette de Portici* (known in its English version as *Masaniello*) became *Masaniello, or The Fish'oman of Naples* in Robert Brough's travesty (Olympic Theatre, 1857) and *Masse-en-yell-oh* as parodied by Harry Paulton and Mostyn Tedde (Comedy Theatre, 1886), *Fra Diavolo* was given a superior treatment by H J Byron as *Fra Diavolo, or the Beauty and the Brigands* (Strand Theatre 5 April 1858) and later as *Young Fra Diavolo, the Terror of Terracina* (Gaiety Theatre 18 November 1878), and the Gaiety (1875) and Imperial (1880) Theatres hosted Robert Reece's burlesque tale of *The Half-Crown Diamonds.*

L'AUBERGE DU TOHU-BOHU Opérette in 3 acts by Maurice Ordonneau. Music by Victor Roger. Théâtre des Folies-Dramatiques, Paris, 10 February 1897.

A farcical musical dealing with what happens when an inn's sign is shifted from its place and put over the door of a private home. The author of this prank is one Saturnin (Burguet) and his reasons are friendly but complex. His pal, Paul Blanchard (Jean Périer), is in love with Cécile Drémer (Mary Bréan), whose father (Bartel) is determined she shall wed the aristocratic Count Zarifouli (Landrin). Cécile and the said Count are to meet for the first time at the Auberge du cheval blanc, outside Paris. Saturnin's relations (Vavasseur, Virginie Rolland) have a house just opposite this inn, and they are away on holiday, so the boys decide to set up their own "Auberge du cheval blanc." Hence the shifted sign. The staff are played by Saturnin's friends—his circus girlfriend, Flora (Jane Pierny) and her troupe—and whilst one Bel Oeil (Simon-Max) disgustingly impersonates Zarifouli to papa Drémer, the troupe's strongman, Le Rougeaud (Gardel), and Flora impersonate the Drémers to the real Zarifouli. Then the owners of the house come home.

The never-still plot and action was decorated with a considerable score of light and bright music, of which Mlle Pierny and Périer won the largest share.

L'Auberge du Tohu-bohu gave the Folies-Dramatiques a long-running hit, totalling 231 performances over two seasons, and it was revived at the Théâtre de la Gaîté in 1901, by which time it had been played in virtually all the other main musical theatre centers.

Arthur Sturgess's London version of *The Topsy Turvy Hotel* had a score largely topped up with songs by Lionel Monckton (several), Harry Fragson and A Stanislas (one popular one, "Toujours les blondes") and Napoleon Lambelet (one) and starred Maurice Farkoa (Paul Blanchard), Florence Collingbourne (Cécile), Violet Lloyd (Flora) and John Le Hay (Lebeau), but even the addition of extra matinées and the young George Grossmith to the cast could not balance the books of William Greet's production beyond two months. For Broadway, Sturgess's libretto was given a local touch by Edgar Smith, and Aubrey Boucicault (Paul), Ethel Jackson (Cécile), Marie Dressler (Flora) and Edwin Foy (Lebeau) headed the cast of Charles Frohman's production. Miss Dressler and Foy let themselves loose on a kind of low comedy which was not precisely French vaudeville, she stuck in a song about "The Gingerbread Doll," he one of his own, "I Happened to Be There," and Miss Jackson departed after three weeks, leaving them to run up a total of 96 Broadway performances on their own. This version proved to be a popular touring vehicle for Foy who toured it thereafter for two seasons. In 1899 the show was played at New Orleans in the original version by a touring French company whose other offerings were *La Reine de Saba* and *La Favorita.*

Juliette Méaly's company touring in Austria, Germany and Hungary presented *L'Auberge du Tohu-bohu* in those countries in 1901, with the star in the role of Flora. However, both Berlin and Vienna had already seen the piece, in a German version, prior to Mlle Méaly's visit. Berlin's Thalia-Theater welcomed *Tohu-Bohu,* hard on the heels of the original Paris production, in 1897, whilst Vienna's Theater in der Josefstadt mounted its version (ad Victor Léon) with Adele Moraw (Florette), Karl Pfann (Blanchard), Ida Sachs (Cécile) and Gustav Maran (Graf Zarifuli) in 1899. Hungary, too, had witnessed a vernacular production under the title *Az Össze-vissza fogadó* (ad Gyula Komor), but like its German counterparts it did not achieve the same success as the original piece had won in Paris.

Germany: Thalia-Theater *Tohu-bohu* 16 October 1897, Friedrich-Wilhemstädtisches Theater (Fr) 15 May 1901; Hungary: Budai Színkör *Az Össze-vissza fogadó* 16 July 1898, Magyar Színház (Fr) 20 April 1901; UK: Comedy Theatre *The Topsy Turvy Hotel* 21 September 1898; USA: Herald Square Theater *Hotel Topsy Turvy* 3 October 1898; Austria: Theater in der Josefstadt *Tohu-Bohu* 28 April 1899, Theater an der Wien (Fr) 23 April 1901

AUDRAN, [Achille] Edmond (b Lyon, 12 April 1840; d Tierceville, Seine-et-Oise, 17 August 1901). One of the most successful composers of the international musical stage during the 19th-century heyday of the French opérette.

Edmond Audran was born into a musical family, the son of the Opéra-Comique tenor, [Pierre] Marius Audran, and with a brother who was, similarly, to become a professional tenor in Parisian opérette. He was given an early musical education, studying at the École Niedermeyer where one of his professors was the opérette composer Jules Duprato and, when his family moved to Marseille in 1861, he became maître de chapelle of the church of Saint-Joseph in that city.

During his early years in Marseille he composed some religious music, including a mass which was performed at Saint-Joseph and an oratorio, *La Sulamite,* as well as a number of short opérettes, based on well-known texts which were produced at the local Grand Theatre and Théâtre du Gymnase in the early 1860s. It was 15 years, however, after the first of these was seen on the stage before Audran saw a substantial stage composition of his mounted in the theatre. The celebrated librettist Henri Chivot, a friend of the family, offered him the book to *Le Grand Mogol* and the resultant piece, with Chivot's name splendidly attached to it alongside that of the neophyte ''local'' composer, was produced at the Théâtre du Gymnase with the young Jane Hading in the starring role. It created considerable interest and, although it was not taken immediately to Paris, it won the young composer both further and foreign productions (Milan, New York, etc) and a commission for a new opérette from Louis Cantin, manager of the Théâtre des Bouffes-Parisiens.

Cantin's commission proved a good move. It brought forth the delightful *Les Noces d'Olivette,* a comic opera which turned out to be a splendid success for the adventurous manager in Paris and an international hit for the rapidly rising composer. However, the following year Audran and his librettists, Chivot and Duru, supplied Cantin with the even more successful *La Mascotte,* a piece which would establish itself as one of the classic opérettes of the period, and the vast and immediate success of the new composer was confirmed with a third consecutive hit, *Gillette de Narbonne,* as he launched forth on what was to be a stream of some 30 musical stage shows over a 20-year period.

More than a few of this perhaps rather overfull list of works proved less successful than the first fine trio of worldwide successes, but there were a good number which, if they did not reach quite the immense and widespread popularity of *La Mascotte,* did equal the record of the other two initial shows. A revised and enlarged version of *Le Grand Mogol* (1884) produced at Paris's Théâtre de la Gaîté established that piece in the general repertoire and won it a wide-ranging series of overseas productions, whilst the popularity of Audran's early works in Britain led the composer to follow the example set by Planquette and set an original English H B Farnie libretto, *Indiana,* specifically for British audiences. Like Audran's 1886 piece, *Serment d'amour, Indiana* was also played in America.

The charming tale of *La Cigale et la fourmi* (1886) gave the Audran/Chivot/Duru team another substantial international success, and the sweetly risqué *Miss Helyett* (1890) proved an immense hit in Paris prior to a career, in variously bleached versions, around the world, but whilst such other Audran pieces such as *L'Oncle Célestin* and *L'Enlèvement de la Toledad* did well in several countries, it was the 1896 opérette *La Poupée* which proved the most successful of Audran's later works. It scored outstanding successes in Britain and, most particularly, in Germany where it became the most widely played French opérette of all time. It also earned the composer a lawsuit when Henri Blondeau and Hector Monréal, authors of the text for Audran's unsuccessful *Les Pommes d'or,* sued him for plundering ''their'' opérette for melodies to reuse in *Miss Helyett* and *La Poupée.*

With 10 of his works played in Britain, 12 in America (if you count the Boston Ideal Company's remade *La Dormeuse éveillé* [*Suzette*], which didn't use his music, and the versions of the less-successful *La Petite Fronde,* Americanized and heavily botched as *The Wedding Day,* and *Pervenche,* similarly treated as *Fleur de lis*), nine in Germany (including the otherwise only moderately popular *Madame Suzette* and *Sainte-Freya*) and a full dozen in Hungary—ranging from the most popular, *Az üdvöske* (*La Mascotte*), to versions of *La Duchesse de Ferrare* (*A Ferrarai hercegnő*), *Madame Suzette* (*Menyeckse kisasszony*), *La Dormeuse éveillée* (*Az ébren álmodó*), *Le Puits qui parle* (*A beszélő kut*), *Les Soeurs Gaudichard* (*Az ikrek*) and *La Fiancée des verts-poteaux* (*A kölcsöncért vőlegény*)—Audran in his lifetime won an international prominence and coverage equalled only by Offenbach and Lecocq amongst 19th-century French composers.

1862 **L'Ours et le pacha** (Eugène Scribe, J X B Saintine) 1 act Grand Theatre, Marseille

1864 **La Chercheuse d'esprit** (Charles Favart) 1 act Théâtre du

Gymnase, Marseille April; Théâtre des Bouffes-Parisiens 26 March 1882

1866 **La Nivernaise** 1 act Théâtre du Gymnase, Marseille December

1868 **Le Petit Poucet** Marseille April

1877 **Le Grand Mogol** (Henri Chivot) Théâtre du Gymnase, Marseille 24 February

1878 **La Saint-Valentin** (Chivot, Alfred Duru) 1 act Cercle Saint-Arnaud

1879 **Les Noces d'Olivette** (Chivot, Duru) Théâtre des Bouffes-Parisiens 13 November

1880 **La Mascotte** (Chivot, Duru) Théâtre des Bouffes-Parisiens 29 December

1882 **Gillette de Narbonne** (Chivot, Duru) Théâtre des Bouffes-Parisiens 11 November

1883 **Les Pommes d'or** revised version (Chivot, Duru, Hector Monréal, Henri Blondeau) Théâtre des Menus-Plaisirs 12 February

1883 **La Dormeuse éveillée** (Chivot, Duru) Théâtre des Bouffes-Parisiens 27 December

1884 **Le Grand Mogol** revised version (Chivot, Duru) Théâtre de la Gaîté 19 September

1885 **Pervenche** (Chivot, Duru) Théâtre des Bouffes-Parisiens 31 March

1886 **Serment d'amour** (Maurice Ordonneau) Théâtre des Nouveautés 19 February

1886 **Indiana** (H B Farnie) Avenue Theatre, London 11 October

1886 **La Cigale et la fourmi** (Chivot, Duru) Théâtre de la Gaîté 30 October

1887 **Le Paradis de Mahomet** Alhambra, Brussels

1887 **La Fiancée des verts-poteaux** (Ordonneau) Théâtre des Menus-Plaisirs 8 November

1888 **Le Puits qui parle** (Paul Burani, Alexandre Beaumont) Théâtre des Nouveautés 15 March

1888 **Miette** (Ordonneau) Théâtre de la Renaissance 24 September

1888 **La Petite Fronde** (Chivot, Duru) Théâtre des Folies-Dramatiques 16 November

1889 **La Fille à Cacolet** (Chivot, Duru) Théâtre des Variétés 10 July

1890 **L'Oeuf rouge** (William Busnach, Alfred Vanloo) Théâtre des Folies-Dramatiques 14 March

1890 **Miss Helyett** (Maxime Boucheron) Théâtre des Bouffes-Parisiens 12 November

1891 **L'Oncle Célestin** (Ordonneau, Henri Keroul) Théâtre des Menus-Plaisirs 24 March

1892 **Article de Paris** (Boucheron) Théâtre des Menus-Plaisirs 17 March

1892 **Sainte-Freya** (Boucheron) Théâtre des Bouffes-Parisiens 4 November

1893 **Madame Suzette** (Ordonneau, André Sylvane) Théâtre des Bouffes-Parisiens 29 March

1893 **Mon Prince!** (Charles Clairville, Sylvane) Théâtre des Nouveautés 18 November

1894 **L'Enlèvement de la Toledad** (Fabrice Carré) Théâtre des Bouffes-Parisiens 17 October

1895 **La Duchesse de Ferrare** (Boucheron) Théâtre des Bouffes-Parisiens 25 January

1896 **Photis** (Louis Gallet) Geneva February

1896 **La Reine des reines** (P-L Flers) Eldorado 14 October

1896 **La Poupée** (Maurice Ordonneau) Théâtre de la Gaîté 21 October

1896 **Monsieur Lohengrin** (F Carré) Théâtre des Bouffes-Parisiens 30 November

1897 **Les Petites Femmes** (Sylvane) Théâtre des Bouffes-Parisiens 11 October

1899 **Les Soeurs Gaudichard** (Ordonneau) Théâtre de la Gaîté 21 April

1901 **Le Curé Vincent** (Ordonneau) Théâtre de la Gaîté 25 October

AUF BEFEHL DER HERZOGIN (aka *Auf Befehl der Kaiserin*) Operetten-idyll aus alten, gemütlichen Tagen in 3 acts by Leopold Jacobson and Robert Bodanzky. Music by Bruno Granichstaedten. Theater an der Wien, Vienna, 20 March 1915.

Bodanzky and Jacobson made no pretence as to what they were trying to provide with their text for *Auf Befehl der Herzogin* (At the Countess's Orders) when they subtitled it ''an Operette-idyll from the good, old days.'' But if the libretto to the piece rested on the good, old combination of love affairs and misunderstandings with a nice dash of period royalty thrown in, it gained more than a little individuality from a particularly well-drawn and sympathetic central character.

The Herzogin (Paula Zulka) discovers that her husband is being unfaithful to her and, hearing that Lintschi (Anny Rainer), the daughter of the old Spannbergerin (Mitzi Schütz), is being courted by a royal officer, hastily assumes that she has found her rival. When Lintschi is warned by the Morality Commissioner (Karl Tuschl) that the Herzogin has her eye on her visitor, she assumes that her Konrad (Hubert Marischka) is out of bounds to her and sadly agrees to the marriage set up by her mother with unhappy Toni (Ernst Tautenhayn), the son of mama's old sweetheart, the sausage-maker Weisskappel (Franz Glawatsch). The Herzogin orders this marriage to take place immediately but, when the Commissioner discovers his mistake, she leaves the palace and hastens in person to the inn with a wedding gift for the girl whom she has wronged. The gift is Konrad, who happily takes the delighted Toni's place as bridegroom.

Bruno Granichstaedten's score followed its tale in good-old-Wienerische-days style, using none of the gently jazzy effects which were the composer's trademark. The first act ran through a selection of Vienna-accented (in speech and music) pieces including numbers for Lintschi, Konrad and Weisskappel, two duos for the lovers and a jolly one for the girl and Toni (''Süsses Fräulein

Karolin'') before the titular Herzogin put in her appearance at the top of the second act with the big number of the evening, ''Wann die Musik spielt.'' Konrad and Lintschi's principal duo, ''Reich mir die Hand und sag' ade,'' and a jolly Viennese trio intervened before the Herzogin closed her appearance with a reprise which showed her determination to follow her husband's carefree footsteps (''Komm' die Herzogin will tanzen . . .''). The final act was Toni's and he brought the show to its musical end with a marriage song and a final jolly duo with the girl who will not, after all, be his bride (''Das hab' ich von meinen Papa'').

Produced by Wilhelm Karczag at the Theater an der Wien, *Auf Befehl der Herzogin* followed behind the patriotic wartime Operette *Gold gab ich für Eisen* and proved (as was proved in other war-busy countries) that escapism goes down better than rousing sentiments in time of trouble. It was an immediate and sizeable success, the largest at the theatre for several years, and Karczag took the unusual step of running it on straight through the summer months when the theatre usually closed its doors. The show played at the Theater an der Wien until the end of October when, after seven months and 177 performances, it moved over to pass its 200th performance (12 November) in the repertoire at the Raimundtheater. In 1926 it posted up its 400th performance during a season at the Bürgertheater (16 January) with Franz Glawatsch and Selma Granichstaedten in the leading roles.

A performance during the original run at the Theater der Wien was given over to the Hungarian war effort, and Hungary itself produced the piece before the year was out (ad Andor Gábor). In Berlin the Herzogin of the title was, not unreasonably, changed to a Kaiserin and the leading lady whose commands were so faithfully obeyed, although still not actually named as anything but ''Die Kaiserin'' in the program, was portrayed as the Austro-Hungarian empress, in a production which gave Granichstaedten by far his greatest success in Germany. Given the war conditions, it was perhaps not surprising that *Auf Befehl der Herzogin* was not seen outside central Europe, but there it had a success that would undoubtedly, in other times, have traveled further.

Hungary; Király Színház *A Czaszarnő* 18 December 1915; Germany: *Auf Befehl der Kaiserin* ?1915

AUGARDE, Amy (Florence) (b London, 7 July 1868; d Reigate, 1 April 1959).

Amy Augarde's career spanned the development of the musical theatre from the comic opera and burlesque of Victorian times through Gaiety musical comedy and the Viennese, French and Broadway musicals of the 1920s, to revue and the song-and-laughter shows of the 1930s in nearly half a century of active stage work which made up one of the most remarkable musical theatre lives of modern times.

A member of a well-known family of musicians, the young Amy started work as a singer whilst in her teens. She played in the chorus of Richard Barker's *Manteaux Noirs* company at 14 or so, toured in the early Gilbert and Sullivan companies of Richard D'Oyly Carte, in Britain and America, and made her West End debut deputizing for Jessie Bond as Mad Margaret in *Ruddigore* (1887) at the Savoy. She appeared as Lydia Hawthorne in *Dorothy* (t/o 1888), created the part of Lady Anne Jerningham in *Doris* (1889) and her fine, full figure and fruity mezzo won her lead roles in touring new burlesque (Marguerite then Faust in *Faust Up-to-Date,* Escamillo then Carmen in *Carmen Up-to-Data,* etc) and musical plays (Katrine in *Rip van Winkle,* Kitty Hetherton in *In Town,* etc), before she graduated ultimately to the Gaiety Theatre itself (Thames Darrell in *Little Jack Sheppard* 1894, t/o Lady Dodo in *The Shop Girl* 1895). She appeared as Mlle Lange in a revival of *La Fille de Madame Angot* (1893), created the title role in the enormously successful touring musical *The New Barmaid* (1895, Ethel Joy) and, in her thirties, mixed leading roles on tour (Dolores in *Florodora,* t/o Celeste in *Campano,* Ethel Joy in *The New Barmaid*) with the occasional West End appearance, playing Simoona in the West End season of Victor Herbert's *The Wizard of the Nile* (1897), The Duchess of Adstock in *Bilberry of Tilbury* (1898) and scoring a particular success as Madame Michu in George Edwardes's production of *Les P'tites Michu* (1905) at Daly's Theatre.

This success was the forerunner of the second part of her career, as a singing character actress of great popularity. In her forties she became the ubiquitous choice as the older and usually comic lady in London musicals, and between 1908 and 1926 she appeared in London in an almost end-to-end string of musical shows, playing Friederike in *A Waltz Dream,* Madame Popoff in The *Chocolate Soldier,* Delphine in *The Girl in the Taxi,* Queen of Magoria in *Love and Laughter,* Lucinda in *The Girl Who Didn't,* Madame Richard in *Mam'selle Tralala,* Ermerance in *Véronique,* Lady Upright in *Cash on Delivery,* Princess Fruzelda in *Violette,* Mrs Bunting in *Nobody's Boy,* Bertha in *The Red Mill,* Countess Kittisch in *The Naughty Princess,* Madame St Martin in *the Little Girl in Red,* Veronika in *Love's Awakening,* Countess Alexandrowna in *The Last Waltz,* Sonya in *Catherine,* Prudence Mardyke in *Our Nell,* Luisa in *Frasquita,* Pani Alvara in *Nicolette* and Chika in *Riki Tiki.*

She went on tour in *Just a Kiss* (1928, Miss Trask) and *Hit the Deck* (1929, the black maid Magnolia, unblacked) and came off the road with *The Damask Rose* (1930, Countess Maria Orzesco) for an unfortunate season at the Savoy. She went back to the provinces in *Lav-*

Plate 16. **Amy Augarde** *was the most ubiquitous British musical character lady of her era; here she is as Bertha in* The Red Mill *alongside Ivy Tresmand, Little Tich and Ray Kay.*

ender (1930, Countess of Harebell), featured as Kathi in London's *White Horse Inn* (1931), toured as the Baroness Villiers in *The Lilac Domino* (1932), and made what seems to have been her last musical-theatre appearances as Dancing Sunbeam in the 1935 revival of *The Rose of Persia* and as Miss Pink in *Please, Teacher* (1936), in which role she went touring when not far short of her 70th birthday.

Her niece **Adrienne [Adele] AUGARDE** (b London, 12 May 1882; d Chicago, 17 March 1913), a deliciously pretty young performer, had a prominent career as a musical comedy ingenue, beginning by touring for Tom Davis as Maggie in *Little Miss Nobody* (1899) and as Angela to her aunt's Dolores in *Florodora* (1900), coming to town as a takeover for Dora in *The Toreador* (1902, she was succeeded by the rising Gertie Millar) and going on to appear in starring roles in *The School Girl* (1903, t/o Mamie), *The Duchess of Dantzic* (1903, Renée de Saint-Mézarde), *Les P'tites Michu* (1905, Blanche-Marie), *Lady Madcap* (1905, Lady Betty Claridge), *See See* (1906, Lee) and *The New Aladdin* (1906, the Princess) in London, and on Broadway in *The Duchess of Dantzic* (1905, Renée), *Peggy Machree* (1908, Lady Margaret McDonnell), *The Dollar Princess* (1909, Daisy) and *The Rose Maid* (1912, Daphne), before turning to vaudeville. She died, reportedly from appendicitis, when just out of her twenties.

AU PAYS DU SOLEIL Opérette-revue (opérette marseillaise) by Henri Alibert. Lyrics by René Sarvil. Music by Vincent Scotto. Moulin de la Chanson, Paris, 22 October 1932.

Au pays du soleil was the first of the series of merry, Marseille-flavored musical plays with which Alibert (as author and performer), Sarvil and Scotto paralleled the success of Marcel Pagnol's famous Marseille plays in the 1930s. It told the story of an out-of-work marseillais lad called Titin (Alibert) whose would-be father-in-law won't let him marry his sweetheart, Miette (Jenny Hélia), and who then finds himself accused of a murder which has really been committed by a local smuggler. Proven innocence and married happiness await at the final curtain.

The show's songs, catchily written in the simple, dancing and heavily accented style of their time and place, included several which became favorites, most particularly in the hands of the author-star: the waltzing "À petits pas" (La Valse marseillaise), the fox-trotting duo "Miette" for hero and heroine, the romantic slow-fox "J'ai rêvé d'une fleur," the one-stepping "Une rose (c'est bien peu de chose)" and the comical "Un fondu, un momo (un jobastre, un fada)."

The original production at Paris's Moulin de la Chanson was a great success and, while its successors in the same style and from (mostly) the same hands prospered in Paris, *Au pays du soleil* went on to tread its way through the provinces of France until it was again seen in Paris, at the Théâtre de la Porte-Saint-Martin (25 May 1951) with Rellys, the inheritor of the mantle of Alibert, and Mireille Ponsard taking the parts of Titin and his girl. In the same year Corsican tenor and film star Tino Rossi portrayed Titin on the screen in a version of *Au pays du soleil* co-written by Sarvil who also appeared in the film alongside Véra Norman, Jacqueline Pierreux, Milly Mathis and Berval. The hits of the original show were supplemented by favorite numbers from the subsequent *Arènes joyeuses* and *Un de la Canebière* and from the Scotto/Sarvil songbook ("Zou! un peu d'aioli," "Adieu, Venise provençale," "Le Plus Beau Tango du monde," "Marseille mon pays").

In 1959 *Au pays du soleil* returned again to the Paris stage, when it was remounted at the Théâtre de l'Européen with Rellys, Sarvil and Mlle Ponsard still at the head of affairs and, although it seems to have been replaced as the favorite representative of its genre in the 1990s by *Un de la Canebière* and *Trois de la marine,* it still appears occasionally on French stages 60 years on.

Film: 1951

Recordings: Sarvil Company (Véga), selection (TLP, Readers Digest), etc

AU SOLEIL DU MEXIQUE Opérette à grand spectacle in 2 acts by Albert Willemetz and André Mouëzy-Éon. Music by Maurice Yvain. Théâtre du Châtelet, Paris, 18 December 1935.

Having killed a man in a brawl, the bullfighter Nino Chicuelo (André Baugé) flees Mexico with the apparent help of his old patron, Felipe Tampico, a two-faced fellow who is really only after getting his hands on the boy's beloved Juanita (Fanély Revoil). Returning secretly from his exile to see Juanita, Nino cannot resist showing off his tauromachic skills at fiesta and he is only saved from arrest by the opportune arrival of wealthy, glamorous American Jessie Thompson (Danielle Brégis), who whisks him amorously off to Waikiki on her yacht. Juanita heads for Guadaloupe and the safety of a convent, but all comes right in the final reel with a little bit of help from a convenient revolution.

With 16 sets, ranging from the bullring to Waikiki, from La Maison de Danse to the Chapelle des Toréadors and the Caribbean convent; events including an eruption, an earthquake and a deluge; and a selection of dances including a Grand Ballet espagnol, a Rumba Fluorescente and a Snake-Dance, Mouëzy-Éon's script for *Au soleil du Mexique* provided all the opportunities for a fine display of traditional Châtelet spectacle. Illustrated by a suitable Yvain-Willemetz score and performed by a particularly strong cast, in which the star vocalists were supplemented by a good dose of comedy from favorite comedian Bach as Jérome Frascator, Jessie's film-star admirer, this exemplary Opérette à grand spectacle made up into a fine success. It ran for 307 performances at the Châtelet and subsequently appeared on provincial stages for several decades.

Yvain's most open-stage piece to date, following his great successes with intimate musicals, *Au soleil du Mexique* prefigured not only his own ultimately even more popular *Chanson gitane,* but also the successful postwar *Belle de Cadix* type of opérette whose highly tuppence-colored tales of love and revenge in sunny places were in a direct line of descent from Mouëzy-Éon's libretto to *Au soleil du Mexique.*

AU TEMPS DES MERVEILLEUSES Opérette à grand spectacle in 2 acts by Albert Willemetz and André Mouëzy-Éon. Music by Henri Christiné and Tiarko Richepin. Théâtre du Châtelet, Paris, 25 December 1934.

Star baritone André Baugé topped the bill in Maurice Lehmann's spectacular production of *Au temps des merveilleuses* playing Roland des Essarts, an émigré plotting from distant Scotland against the French directoire government. Leaving behind his beloved Scottish Lilian (Marcelle Denya) to go and sow trouble in France, Roland is pursued by a comical agent of the government, Pigeonneau (Bach), and then persuaded patriotically to fight for France in the Napoléonic wars. He passes heroically through Egypt, the ruins of Thebes and the tent of Bonaparte on his way to a happy ending and, of course, Lilian. The first act also arranged to allow the performers to visit a fête des tulipes, the old windmills of Holland and the Rivoli as well as the highlands of Scotland, and the second to display a panorama of the Palais-Royal which stretched right to the back of the theatre's vast stage area, and a charge of live horses galloping against a travelator in the show's climax.

The extremely picturesque element of the show was complemented by a strong cast and a score (in which numbers were not individually credited to the two composers) which provided Baugé with the ringing "Partir, c'est mourir un peu" and the romantic "Dis-toi que je t'aime," Gilbert Moryn as a Scottish laird with a fine bass-baritone call for revenge, and the heroine who, with her soubrette (Monique Bert) and her father managed somehow to get into most of the second-act scenes, with

Plate 17. **Autoliebchen.** *The hit song of Jean Gilbert's internationally successful musical comedy, "Das haben die Mädchen so gerne."*

a pair of love songs, "Vers toi mon amour s'envole" and "On dit que l'amour est roi." Although neither Christiné nor Willemetz were as appreciably at home in the profitable world of the opérette à grand spectacle as in their winning and witty musical comedies, it was nevertheless a score which served its purpose for nearly a year's run at the Châtelet (342 performances) and the goodly afterlife which *Au temps des merveilleuses* later lived out in the spectacle-loving theatres of the French provinces.

AUTOLIEBCHEN Posse in 3 acts by Jean Kren based on *Dix minutes d'auto* by Georges Berr and Pierre Decourcelle. Lyrics by Alfred Schönfeld. Music by Jean Gilbert. Thalia-Theater, Berlin, 16 March 1912.

Autoliebchen was the first of the series of hit musical comedies written by Jean Kren and composed by Jean Gilbert specifically for Berlin's Thalia-Theater, following the house's success with the composer's brought-in *Polnische Wirtschaft,* and it was, alone of all the series, not written to an original script by the prolific playwright and producer. The text of *Autoliebchen* was a version of the 1908 Paris comedy *Dix minutes d'auto* by Berr and Decourcelle (Théâtre des Nouveautés 13 November)—the same Georges Berr whose work was simultaneously being plundered with great success for Broadway musical comedy texts (*The Pink Lady, Oh! Oh! Delphine*).

George Triebler (Paul Bechert) is a traveling salesman for the Lindenschmidt wine firm, and to ease the strains of this occupation he has lined up a little female comfort for those evenings far from home in distant Budapest. She is called Prisca von Erdödy (Eugenie della Donna). But now, just when Triebler is all ready to settle down and get married to his hometown Fifi (Rosl Loibner), Prisca turns up, with her do-right-by-my-girl uncle Maurus Somossy (Emil Sondermann) close behind. Since George has cannily called himself "Lindenschmidt" whilst downriver on his boss's business, it is that boss's son—who also happens to be called George and who is himself happily affianced—who collects the accusations. But Triebler has other problems on hand as well. A year earlier, after a jolly carnival ball, dressed in a costume as the Trompeter von Säkkingen, he drove home a pretty masked lady and what happened between them . . . Suffice it to say that when this story comes out, at just the wrong moment, George starts more and more to look like a veritable satyr. However, after an actful of farcical comings and goings in the congenial atmosphere of the Zum kleinen Twostep ballroom, all comes to a comfortable ending. The mysterious lady in the car was none other than Fifi, Lindenschmidt finds a new love in her sister Rely, Prisca gets the handsome Böttchermeister Max Rönnekamp, and Uncle Maurus the girls' mother, Aurelie Werkenthin (Johanna Junker-Schatz), with whom he has shared some of the evening's most comical moments.

The musical hit of the show was the duet "Das haben die Mädchen so gerne," a jaunty march which became one of the most popular numbers of its era, but the evening was full of catchy dance-based numbers—most of them variations on the two-step—from which two other duos, "Fräulein, könn'n Sie links 'rum tanzen" and the song of the "Mädchen im Stübchen und im Salon," also became favorites.

Autoliebchen ran at the Thalia-Theater for a splendid nine months before being replaced by the next of the series, *Puppchen,* and it promptly moved on to Vienna where it was played at the Apollotheater, billed as a "vaudeville in one act," and adapted by Carl Lindau into "the dance-hall 'Klein Paris' on carnival night." Max Nekut was George and Irma Jarkowska played Fifi, with Relly Witzani (Prisca), Rosl Schlager (Rely), Alois Resni (Lindenschmidt), Eugen Günther as Lebrecht Döppchen (ex- Maurus) and Anna Selhofer as Irene (ex- Aurelie).

Budapest saw *Autotündér* (ad Gyula Komor) the following year, and London also snapped up the show in the wake of the success there of Gilbert's *The Girl in the Taxi* (*Die keusche Susanne*). Arthur Anderson and Hartley Carrick redid the book quite considerably, and Rutland

Barrington, Thelma Raye and Bertram Wallis featured. *The Joy-Ride Lady* didn't come up to her predecessor in popularity, but still managed a fair run of 105 performances, broken by a shift to the Garrick Theatre, before things German became undesirable in London's West End.

Austria: Apollotheater 1 December 1912; Hungary: Fővárosi Nyari Színház *Az autotündér* 13 June 1913; UK: New Theatre *Joy-Ride Lady* 21 February 1914

LES AVENTURES DU ROI PAUSOLE Opérette in 3 acts by Albert Willemetz based on the book by Pierre Louÿs. Music by Arthur Honegger. Théâtre des Bouffes-Parisiens, Paris, 12 December 1930.

The first and most successful of the rare ventures of the composer Honegger into the light musical theatre, *Les Aventures du roi Pausole* was adapted by Willemetz from the magazine-serial-become-novel (1901) of Pierre Louÿs as a slightly outrageous opéra-bouffe, and was produced by its librettist at the Théâtre des Bouffes-Parisiens of which he was, at the time, the director.

The folk of the Kingdom ruled by King Pausole (Dorville) live by amorality—both sexual and social. The King has an extensive harem, one wife for each night of the year, but his daughter Blanche Aline (Jacqueline Francell) has been brought up chastely, until the day she runs away with Mirabelle (Meg Lemonnier), the leading dancer of a troupe brought in to entertain the royal family. The King sets out unenthusiastically after the two girls (for, yes, Mirabelle is actually a girl), accompanied by his chief Eunuch (René Koval) and the page, Giglio (Pasquali), and pursued by the Queen of the day, Diane à la Houppe (Germaine Duclos), who is determined not to let events make her miss out on her annual turn at a royal romp. Giglio, however, is the male triumphant. He disguises himself as a girl to join in the lovemaking of Mirabelle and Blanche Aline, then deputizes for the indisposed King so that Diane won't miss her long-awaited night, and ultimately ends up winning the hand of the Princess, granted by an exasperated monarch who will even go to the extent of declaring a republic just to be left in peace.

Honegger's score mixed some characteristic modern tones with elements of traditional opérette and opéra-bouffe in a score which produced some particularly creative ensembles, and a series of set piece solos and duos which did not, however, always follow the text into the zaniness of opéra-bouffe.

Les Aventures du roi Pausole was nothing if not risqué, even osé, with a kind of riskiness very different from that which the happy creatures of the Jazz Age musical comedies—many invented by Willemetz—had been naughtily parading across the Paris stage for a decade. It dangled deliciously on the verge of decadence, though once again a different kind of decadence to that expressed in Louÿs's *La Femme et le pantin,* which had itself been metamorphosed into Operetten of a very different flavor (*Frasquita,* etc). But this flavor, this decadence proved a fine attraction to the audiences who frequented the Bouffes-Parisiens of 1930, and the show had a superb run of some four hundred performances.

It was later produced in Switzerland in the original French (Geneva, 1932), and reprised in Paris in 1937 (Bouffes-Parisiens) and again in 1947 at the tiny Théâtre des Capucines, before getting its first German-language production in Zürich (Stadttheater 1953 ad Hans Zimmermann). Following this it won productions in Hamburg and Munich, remaining thereafter on the fringe of the repertoire in both its French and German versions. It was most recently revived at the Theatre Municipal, Lausanne in 1990, and looks set for further showings in the 21st century, particularly given the fashion of the period for producing light musical theatre pieces by name composers in opera houses.

Germany: Staatsoper, Hamburg *Die Abenteuer des Königs Pausole* 1955

Recording: complete (MGB)

AXEL AN DER HIMMELSTÜR Musical comedy in 3 acts (6 scenes) by Paul Morgan and Adolf Schütz. Lyrics by Hans Weigel. Music by Ralph Benatzky. Theater an der Wien, Vienna, 1 September 1936.

Artur Hellmer's first production after taking over the management at the Theater an der Wien in 1936, *Axel an der Himmelstür* was a piece set in that most favored of contemporary Ruritanias, deepest Hollywood. It hinted that it was à clef and that its heroine was based on Greta Garbo, it suggested that it was a parody of all that went on in Hollywood but, like others of its kind, it simply used the extravagant personalities of Celluloid City as the raw material for a colorful musical comedy. This one used some of the oldest bits of libretto in the book, from disguises to stolen jewels.

Zarah Leander played Gloria Mills, film star, and Max Hansen was Axel Swift, a reporter anxious to get near enough to interview her. He disguises himself as an elderly extra, gets invited to supper in her hotel room, comforts her when it turns out her fiancé, "the Prince," is a confidence trickster, and then pretends to be an intruder when an English lady's jewels are stolen, so as not to compromise her by his presence. He ends up in prison and in court, before his friends clear up the fact that the old and young men are both he. Gloria (whose chauffeur stole the jewels, of course) has stopped being sorry about the "Prince" by the final curtain. No one else apart from the two stars got much of a look in, but the other cast members included co-author Paul Morgan as producer Cecil McScott, Herbert Berghof as director Stuart Williams, Erich Dörner as hairdresser Theodor Herlinger, Heidemarie Hatheyer as Gloria's maid Dinah, and Lisl Kinast as Jessie Leyland.

Benatzky's score mixed the topical and the special material with straighter dance numbers of which the slow fox-trot "Gebundene Hände" proved popular, alongside the tango song "Mein schönes Fräulein, gute Nacht!" and the English waltz "Eine Frau von heut." The topical element was topped by an "In Holly-Holly-Holly-Holly-Hollywood" which crammed Douglas Fairbanks, Charlie Chaplin, Adolphe Menjou, Maurice Chevalier, Mickey Mouse, King Kong, Tarzan and Carl Laemmle into its lyrics, whilst "Die allergrösste Zukunft hat die Liebe!" allowed the star to indulge in imitations of Jan Kiepura, Richard Tauber and Erna Sack. Miss Klaast and Dörner got a share (with Hansen) in a Tabu-fox-trot.

The two stars lit up the evening's entertainment splendidly and *Axel an der Himmelstür* went on to give the theatre its first decent run in four years with an unbroken 190 performances before contracts for real films intervened and dragged first Leander (replaced by Lili Hatvany) and then Hansen away.

The book of the show was later used as the basis for the screenplay of the film *Liebespremiere* (1943), attached to a different score composed by Franz Grothe.

Recording: selection (ORF)

AYER, Nat[haniel] D[avis] (b Boston, 30 September 1887; d Bath, England, 19 September 1952).

American-born pianist and vocalist, and for some years a half of the vaudeville act and songwriting team of Ayer and (A Seymour) Brown, ("Oh! You Beautiful Doll," "Ragtime Suffragette," "King Chanticler," "You're My Baby," "At the Foxtrot Ball," etc), Ayer began his theatre career by contributing songs to such Broadway shows as *Miss Innocence* (1908, "I'm Not That Kind of a Girl"), *The Ziegfeld Follies of 1909* ("Moving Day in Jungle Town"), *The Echo* (1910, "Heigh Ho," "You're Just the Girlie That I Adore"), *A Winsome Widow* (1912, "You're a Regular Girl" w Brown) and *The Wall Street Girl* (1912, "I Should Have Been Born a Boy," "The Indian Rag," "You're Some Girl"). He was credited in 1908 as co-composer of the musical farce *The Newlyweds and Their Baby,* a cartoon-based piece in which the critter in question was kidnapped and replaced by a dwarf for 42 Broadway performances and several long tours around the least sophisticated American touring circuits ("a strong bill in the dollar houses"). A second Leffler-Bratton Company musical based on George McManus's comic strips, *Let George Do It,* followed in its tracks a few years later.

It was in Britain, however, where he was one of the first American song-and-dance writers to arrive as the new craze for American dances and dance music was beginning, that Ayer made the most prominent part of his career. There, after scoring a memorable early success with the songs for the London adaptation of the French revue *Les Fils Touffe sont à Paris* under the title *The Bing Boys Are Here* (1916, "If You were the Only Girl in the World," "Another Little Drink"), he became a regular contributor to revue (*The Bing Boys on Broadway, The Bing Girls Are There, Pell Mell, Look Who's Here, Cartoons*) and to musical comedy, writing a handful of London theatre scores of which the Leslie Henson vehicle *Yes, Uncle!* and *Baby Bunting,* in which American comedian Walter Catlett scored a striking West End success, were highly successful both at home and abroad.

Ayer also performed on the variety stage, scoring a personal success at the London Empire in 1915, in musical comedy, appearing opposite Gertie Millar in his own *Houp-La!* and in revue.

1908 **The Newlyweds and Their Baby** (w John W Bratton/Paul West, A Seymour Brown/West, Aaron Hoffman) Lyceum Theater, Rochester, NY 7 December; Majestic Theater, New York 22 March 1909

1911 **Let George Do It** (West/Hoffman) Lyceum, Scranton, Pa 4 October; West End Theater, New York 22 April 1912

1916 **Houp-La!** (Fred Thompson, Hugh E Wright, Percy Greenbank) St Martin's Theatre 23 November

1916 **Oh, Caesar!** (w Arthur Wood/Adrian Ross/A M Thompson, Max Pemberton) Royal Lyceum Theatre, Edinburgh 23 December

1917 **The Hula Girl** (w Phil Braham, Alfred Haines/George Reynolds, R Guy Keene) 1 act London Hippodrome 18 December

1917 **Yes, Uncle!** (Austen Hurgon, George Arthurs, Clifford Grey) Prince of Wales Theatre 29 December

1919 **Baby Bunting** (Worton David, Grey/F Thompson) Shaftesbury Theatre 25 September

1922 **The Smith Family** (Grey, Stanley Logan, Philip Page) Empire Theatre 6 September

B

BABES IN ARMS Musical in 2 acts by Richard Rodgers and Lorenz Hart. Lyrics by Lorenz Hart. Music by Richard Rodgers. Shubert Theater, New York, 14 April 1937.

The ultimate in what has become fondly known as the ''hey, let's put on a show'' type of musical—the 'tween-wars equivalent of the old variety musical with its plotted first act, and a veritable concert for the final one—*Babes in Arms* was made up of a featherweight book, of which the backbone was the efforts of a group of teenagers who, to prove their self-sufficiency and avoid being sent off to a work farm, try to make themselves into a successful revue troupe, stiffened by some George Balanchine dances (''Johnny One Note,'' ''Peter's Journey'') and a score which contained more enduring songs per squarish page of music than any other of its time.

Amongst the young and mostly up-and-coming cast, Mitzi Green (already seen as a juvenile in movies) lit into ''The Lady Is a Tramp,'' sighed extravagantly over a boy called Valentine in ''My Funny Valentine'' and joined with Ray Heatherton in trying to remember ''Where or When''; 16-year-old neophyte Wynn Murray introduced the tale of ''Johnny One Note'' and dove into the comical plaint of ''Way Out West''; Rolly Pickert and Grace McDonald sparkled through ''I Wish I Were in Love Again''; and the whole company, cast in roles which were made to their measure, joined together to celebrate being ''Babes in Arms.'' The most to-be-familiar names amongst the cast, however, were the for the moment less-featured Alfred Drake, Dan Dailey, the Nicholas brothers and Robert Rounseville.

After a sticky start, Dwight Deere Wiman's Broadway production—at one stage the only musical playing on Broadway in an underpar season—became a splendid success, running 289 performances and largely recouping its costs. However, the show was not mounted outside America, possibly at least partly because of the success of Busby Berkeley's 1939 film version in which the young Judy Garland and Mickey Rooney headed a team of youngsters in memorably capturing the innocence of what little of the original piece beyond its basic premise remained. Of the show score, only the title song and ''Where or When'' were sung in the film, alongside a series of old favorites which were used to make up the show-within-the-show. The songs of *Babes in Arms* found their screen afterlife elsewhere: ''The Lady Is a Tramp'' made it to the movies in *Words and Music* (as did ''I Wish I Were in Love'' and ''Johnny One Note'') and in *Pal Joey* (sung by Jo Ann Greer), whilst ''My Funny Valentine,'' which also appeared in *Pal Joey* (sung by Trudy Ewen), was again heard in *Gentlemen Marry Brunettes.*

A revised version of *Babes in Arms* was mounted at the Goodspeed Opera House in 1979 (10 April, with two songs culled from *Too Many Girls* added to its score) and the popularity of both the favorite songs and of the film version, regularly reseen via television, was responsible for three further attempts (two of which made it to the stage) to mount rewritten versions in Britain in the 1980s. The piece was seen again in New York when presented at the Tarrytown Music Hall (ad George Oppenheimer) in 1985 (26 June) without moving closer in, and yet another adaptation saw the light of stage at Minneapolis (Tyrone Guthrie Theater 15 February 1996, ''new book by Ken La Zebnik''), some 60 years after the original production, as the apparently hopeless task of fitting an acceptable libretto to the set of favorite songs went doggedly on.

UK: Theatre Royal, Plymouth 26 February 1985, Open Air Theatre, Regent's Park, London 3 August 1988

Recordings: complete (New World Records), selection (Columbia)

BABES IN TOYLAND Musical extravaganza in a prologue and 3 acts by Glen MacDonough. Music by Victor Herbert. Grand Opera House, Chicago, 17 June 1903; Majestic Theater, New York, 13 October 1903.

Commissioned by producers Julian Mitchell and Fred Hamlin to follow up their 1902 success with the fairy-tale spectacular *The Wizard of Oz, Babes in Toyland* was purposefully constructed on similar lines to the earlier show. Glen MacDonough's libretto followed little Jane (Mabel Barrison) and Alan (top-billed William Norris) through the colorful realms of Toyland as they struggled, with the help of the familiar characters of children's storybooks, to outwit wicked, miserly Uncle Barnaby (George W Denham) and his allies, the Master Toymaker (Mark Smith) and Contrary Mary (Amy Ricard), and win their way to a happy ending. The production, like its predecessor, was staged with lavish scenic effects, from the prologue's shipwreck (paralleling *The Wizard of Oz*'s tornado) through all kinds of picturesque fairy-tale venues including a country fête in Contrary Mary's Garden, the Spider's Forest, the Floral Palace of the Moth Queen, Toyland's Christmas Tree Grove and the Master Toymaker's workshop and castle, to the final Palace of Toyland and its Court of Justice.

Alongside its spectacle, the other principal attraction of *Babes in Toyland* was its music. Herbert provided a score which was very much in advance of the one which the producers had cobbled together for *The Wizard of Oz*. It had plenty of very fine large-scale and orchestral numbers—notably the enduring ''March of the Toys'' and its succeeding ''The Military Ball''—but also some charming and delicate musical moments ranging from the lovely trio ''Go to Sleep, Slumber Deep'' (Alan, Jane, and a soprano fairy w chorus) and the sweet ''Never Mind, Bo Peep (we will find your sheep)'' sung by Tom Tom (Bessie Wynn) and the widow Piper's other children to the culpable little shepherdess (Nella Webb), to the chirpily childish ''I Can't Do That Sum,'' added to the score after opening for Miss Barrison, and Tom Tom's dreamy hymn to ''Toyland.'' There were occasional more obvious spots—if nothing quite as tacked-in as Lotta Faust singing ''Sammy'' in *The Wizard of Oz*—notably when Contrary Mary sang fairly irrelevantly about ''Barney O'Flynn,'' but on the whole Herbert's score hit the medium line between cultured fairy play and pantomime jollity to perfection.

Babes in Toyland had a highly successful Chicago season of 117 performances (13 weeks) and played through 192 performances at New York's Majestic Theater before going on the road, establishing itself as an enduring favorite of its kind throughout America—sufficient of a favorite, indeed, that it became the subject of a Broadway lawsuit. This one, however, was settled with full logic. In the face of defence testimony from Mitchell, the Hamlin brothers, Ben Teal, MacDonough and others, one loopy Mrs Riley who had claimed that she was the show's real author got short legal shrift.

Babes in Toyland returned briefly to the Majestic in 1905 (2 January, 25 performances) and in 1929 (Jolson Theater 23 December) the Shubert brothers brought the show back to Broadway for a Christmas season, and although it has not had a career outside America, versions of *Babes in Toyland* (sometimes textually quite remote from the original, but always staged with ''grand spectacle'') have been played regularly throughout the country since the first production. It has also been filmed twice, once with a cast including Laurel and Hardy (1934) and once by Walt Disney (1961) in widely variant versions, and was also televised in variously unfaithful forms in 1950, 1954, 1960, 1968 and in a 1986 NBC version in which only ''Toyland'' and ''The March of the Toys'' of Herbert's score survived.

UK: Victoria Hall (copyright performance) 15 June 1903

Films: MGM 1934, Buena Vista 1961

Recordings: selections (Decca, Reader's Digest, AEI), 1961 film soundtrack (Buena Vista)

BABIL AND BIJOU, or The Lost Regalia Fantastic music drama in 18 scenes by Dion Boucicault. Lyrics by J R Planché. Music by Hervé, Frederic Clay, Jules Rivière, et al. Theatre Royal, Covent Garden, London, 29 August 1872.

A hugely extravagant grand opéra-bouffe féerie, created by the well-known playwright Dion Boucicault in imitation of the then-popular French models, *Babil and Bijou* was produced at Covent Garden under the patronage of the wealthy Lord Londesborough. Boucicault announced that his piece would be the means of restoring the Covent Garden theatre to its place as Britain's national theatre, and gathered together such respected talents as Planché, the most celebrated author of English extravaganza poetry, and the French composer Hervé, to contribute to the creation of the piece. However, his show turned out to be a vastly over-written piece of conservatively satirical pseudo-mythology whose principal attractions lay in its production values. What popularity it gained was due to its spectacular scenery and costumes, to the presence in its cast of such favorite performers as comedian/director Lionel Brough, tenor Joseph Maas (Babil), Mrs Howard Paul, Mrs Billington and rising soprano Annie Sinclair as Bijou, and, above all, to one enormous hit song, the juvenile boys' chorus ''Spring Gentle Spring,'' composed by Jules Rivière.

The show was kept on the stage for its announced and pre-planned season of 160 performances but, in spite of building attendances through the run as the entertainment was popularized with cuts, alterations and the addition of stand-up acts, *Babil and Bijou* lost Londesborough his entire £30,000 capitalization and ranked as one of the greatest financial disasters of all theatrical time.

A substantially different show (ad Frank Green) under the same title was staged at the Alhambra Theatre, 8 April 1882. It was of a much more practical size and proved rather more successful.

A piece was produced under the same title at the Boston variety house the Howard Athenaeum (31 March 1873), with Adah Richmond as Bijou and James Vincent as Babil but with no other recognizable character names in its cast list, with the great prima ballerina of London's Alhambra, Jeanne Pitteri, leading the ballets, and a changeable selection of variety acts and a concluding pantomime, but it seems to have shared nothing with Boucicault's piece but that title.

BABIOLE Opérette villageoise in 3 acts by Clairville and Octave Gastineau. Music by Laurent de Rillé. Théâtre des Bouffes-Parisiens, Paris, 16 January 1878.

The most successful of Laurent de Rillé's mostly small opérettes, the pretty, rustic *Babiole* served for two seasons at the Théâtre des Bouffes-Parisiens under Charles Comte's management, before winning a series of overseas productions both in French (Maurice Grau's production with the show's original stars, Paola Marié and Mary Albert, in America) and in English. Maria Liston put out the English-language version of the show (ad Robert Reece) in the British provinces in 1879 with Pattie Laverne starred alongside Henry Hallam (Alain), W G Bedford (Hannibal) and Edmund Rosenthal (Périgueux). When the producer died during rehearsals, the star took over the management, but she didn't manage to get her show to town. Oddly enough, however, it did make it to Australia where Gracie Plaisted plyed Babiole to the Hanibal of Edward Kelly without leaving the most indelible of marks.

The lively if exasperating heroine of the piece (''la plus folle des jeunesses de ces pays'') is the country lass Babiole (Paola Marié), who has decided that she is in love with fellow peasant Alain (Jeannin). She is not to be put off by the fact that Alain is already in love with the Bailli's daughter, Arabelle (Blanche Miroir) who is, in any case, promised to Carcassol (Minart) from the big city of Paris who has, in his turn, had a ding-dong in the past with the loose local miller's wife, Madeleine (Mary Albert), who was once Cascarinette of the Bal de Paphos. In order to win her lad, Babiole resorts to trickery, pseudo-sorcery and not a small touch of blackmail. She threatens to reveal the guilty secrets—and apparently there are plenty, even if they are not all that serious—of half the village, not forgetting the Bailli himself (Daubray), who has been apparently doing something reprehensible in the almond grove.

Laurent de Rillé's score was composed in a prettily old-fashioned style, with the ring of traditional country airs to its most attractive parts, of which Alain's longing for ''un p'tit ferme, un p'tit jardinet'' proved the happiest. The heroine ranged through a leading lady's variety of numbers including a Rondeau de la sorcellerie and some Couplets de charme, whilst Madeleine joined her old lover in repeating the naughty Parisian dance of their premarital days together.

UK: Prince's Theatre, Manchester 10 March 1879; USA: Standard Theater (Fr) 21 October 1880; Australia: Bijou Theatre, Melbourne *Babiole, or the Village Madcap* 22 July 1887

BABOLIN Opérette in 3 acts by Paul Ferrier and Jules Prével. Music by Louis Varney. Théâtre des Nouveautés, Paris, 19 March 1884.

The singer Lorenzo (Louis Morlet), still dressed in his stage costume as the devil, gets embroiled in a country wedding whilst escaping from the angry Karamatoff (Berthelier), husband of his paramour, the lady-in-waiting Bagatella (Mily-Meyer). Lorenzo persuades the bridegroom, Mélissen (Albert Brasseur), to quit his pretty Elverine (Mlle Vaillant-Couturier) and exchange places with him. However, he then discovers to his chagrin that his ''double'' is on the receiving end of the attentions of Bagatella's mistress, the beautiful princess, Mirane (Juliette Darcourt), a royal who goes all weak at the sound of a fine singing voice. All was sorted out to a scoreful of waltzing melodies in Varney's happiest style for a good Parisian season of more than two months at the Théâtre des Nouveautés and a further 37 performances, after the summer break, at the Folies-Dramatiques.

Surprisingly, *Babolin*'s only production beyond France was in America where Francis Wilson starred as the little bridegroom in a version called *The Devil's Deputy* (Abbey's Theater 10 September 1894). For some reason—and it seems to have been financial—Wilson threw out Varney's score, and for reasons confirmedly financial he also threw out J P Sousa, the originally slated replacement composer. Edward Jakobowski ultimately supplied the music for a show which, fortified by a cast including Lulu Glaser, Adele Ritchie, Wilson, Rhys Thomas and J C Miron, ran up a 72-performance Broadway record before going on the road. Cheever Goodwin's translation (which failed to credit the original authors, or even the fact that it was an adaptation at all) included nothing as eyebrow-raising as the French lyric in which the Princess confides ''tu perds ton charme en perdant ton organe'' to her voiceless beloved.

BABY Musical in 2 acts by Sybille Pearson based on a story developed with Susan Yankowitz. Lyrics by Richard Maltby jr. Music by David Shire. Ethel Barrymore Theater, New York, 4 December 1983.

Baby looks at three couples and the effect that having, or in one case not having, a child has on them. It moves on from a dauntingly biological opening (with a lyric that rhymes ''spermatazoa'' and slides depicting the mechanics of producing a child) through some warm and intimate scenes and songs as the rather too-young Lizzie (Liz Callaway) and Danny (Todd Graff), and the perhaps too-old Arlene (Beth Fowler) and Alan (James Congdon) head towards giving birth to their children and, at the same time, to a different kind of life and relationship for themselves. Pam (Catherine Cox) and Nick (Martin Vidnovic) have the disappointment of finding that physical problems make it unlikely they will ever conceive. They put themselves through all kinds of undignified, clinical efforts, but are strong and sane enough to come out at the end of it as close as ever.

The songs mixed the unashamedly sentimental (''Two People in Love,'' ''At Night She Comes Home to Me'') with such friendly, comical moments as a display of the gruesome experience of a first-time-pregnant woman at the hands of those who have already had the experience of giving birth and who love to talk about it in gory detail (''The Ladies Singing Their Song'') and the perspicacious observation of the older father that children are ''Easier to Love'' than an adult partner.

Baby achieved a run of 241 performances on Broadway and was subsequently played at Britain's provincial Manchester Library Theatre, with Susie Blake, Dilys Watling and Tim Flavin amongst its cast, at Sydney's small Q Theatre and at Germany's equally intimate Giessen Kellertheater, while going on to establish itself in playhouses and colleges around the world as an interesting and viable small-scale musical.

Australia: Q Theatre, Sydney 20 November 1987; UK: Forum Theater, Wythenshaw, Manchester 27 September 1990; Germany: Kellertheater, Giessen (Eng) May 1993, Imperialtheater, Hamburg 26 September 1995

Recording: original cast (TER)

BABY BUNTING Musical play in 2 acts by Fred Thompson and Worton David founded on the play *Jane* by Harry Nicholls and William Lestocq. Lyrics by Clifford Grey. Music by Nat D Ayer. Shaftesbury Theatre, London, 25 September 1919.

This lively musical version of the highly successful 1890 farce *Jane* (an uncredited more-or-less-adaptation of Maurice Desvallières' *Prête-moi ta femme,* Comedy Theatre 18 December, 196 performances) top-lined the American comedian Walter Catlett as the stock figure of the hero's haplessly ''helpful'' best friend. Bookkeeper William Pye (Catlett) tries to help his bachelor employer, Bunny Bunting (Ronald Squire), find a temporary wife to convince Samuel Giggleswick (Davy Burnaby), the visiting trustee of a wealthy Uncle, that the injections of cash he is giving to the Bunting ''family'' till are justified. Unfortunately, the role of wife gets double cast (Dorothy Brunton, Daisy Elliston) and confusion reigns for the entire second act.

The score included some attractive lightweight numbers to amusing lyrics—''One Cannot Play Cricket in November,'' ''Married, But Haven't Got a Husband,'' ''What's the Matter With Fifty-Nine (if you feel like twenty-three)''—which illustrated the farcical action of the play happily. One of the biggest attractions of Grossmith and Laurillard's production, however, turned out to be comedian Catlett, whose unfamiliar, laid-back American style of fun scored well with a London public saturated with the repetitive antics of local low comedians. He materially helped the show to a good London run of 213 performances.

A touring production followed, and a version of the show was later mounted by J C Williamson Ltd in Australia, billed as ''Dorothy Brunton's Great London Success'' with Miss Brunton repeating her original role to the Pye of Alfred Frith. She slipped such relevant ditties as ''The Japanese Sandman'' into the remnants of the show's original score through seasons in Sydney and Melbourne (Her Majesty's Theatre 26 February 1921).

Australia: Criterion Theatre, Sydney 24 December 1920

BACALL, Lauren [PERSKE, Betty Joan] (b New York, 16 September 1924).

Famed for her more than 30 years of Hollywood films and her partnership with Humphrey Bogart, sandy-voiced Miss Bacall made her entry into the musical theatre in middle age to top-bill as the sabotaged star Margo Channing in the musical *Applause* (1970, Tony Award) in both New York and in London. She subsequently toured as Ruth Sherwood in *Wonderful Town* (1977) and made a second above-the-title Broadway appearance in another musicalized screenplay as a second strong woman, Tess Harding of *Woman of the Year,* in 1981 (Tony Award).

Autobiographies: *By Myself* (Knopf, New York, 1978), *Now* (Knopf, New York, 1994)

BACH, Ernst (b Eger, Bohemia, 10 May 1876; d Munich, 1 November 1929).

An actor at the Vienna Volkstheater from 1899, and later at Berlin's Residenztheater and Lustspielhaus, Bach subsequently became director of Munich's Volkstheater (1917), a position he held up to his death in 1929.

Parallel to his performing and administrative work, he also led a highly successful career as a playwright and librettist, pairing with Franz Arnold on many popular pieces, both plays (*Der kühne Schwimmer, Der keusche Lebemann, Die Spanische Fliege,* etc) and musical comedies, during the years of the First World War and through the 1920s. Kollo's *Die Königin der Nacht* and Hirsch's *Der Fürst von Pappenheim* and *Dolly,* all widely played in central Europe, were their most successful ventures on to the musical stage.

Plate 18. **Baby Bunting.** *American comedian Walter Catlett (right) scored a lively hit in his one London appearance.*

Several of their comedies were subsequently used as the basis for musicals. *Hurra! ein Junge,* after having already been a major West End success for Leslie Henson under the title *It's a Boy!,* was used as the starting point for the highly successful British musical comedy *Blue for a Boy,* and it was musicalized in a German version in 1953 by Robert Gilbert under the title *Strammer Junge angekommen* (Theater am Besenbinderhof, Hamburg 1 May) with Heinz Erhardt as star. Another Leslie Henson piece, the musical *Nice Goings On,* was also advertised as being based on one of their plays, Jack Buchanan's *Toni* was a semi-remusicked version of their libretto to *Der Fürst von Pappenheim,* and a further unidentified Bach/Arnold piece was gven as the basis for the British musical comedy *Oh, Letty.* In Hungary *Ezüstpille* (ad Andor Gábor, mus: Albert Szirmai, Vígszínház 9 May 1914), *Jó firma* (ad Jenő Molnár, arr Mihály Nádor Magyar Színház 5 June 1930) and *Strandszerelem* (ad Imre Harmath, Fővárosi Nyári Operettszínház 10 July 1929) all arose from (unspecified) Bach and Arnold originals.

1916 **Die Fahrt ins Glück** (Jean Gilbert/w Franz Arnold) Theater des Westens 2 September

1917 **Neptune auf Reisen** (Rudolf Nelson/w Arnold) Apollotheater January

1919 **Fräulein Puck** (Walter Kollo/w Arnold) Volkstheater, Munich 25 June

1921 **Die Königin der Nacht** (Kollo/w Arnold) Neues Operetten-Theater 2 September

1923 **Der Fürst von Pappenheim** (Hugo Hirsch/Alfred Berg, Willi Kollo/w Arnold) Deutsches Künstlertheater 16 February

1923 **Dolly** (Hirsch/Rudolf Bernauer/w Arnold) Deutsches Künstlertheater 16 October

1924 **Die vertagte Nacht** (Walter Kollo/Robert Gilbert/w Arnold) Stadttheater, Mainz 11 November

1924 **Die vertauschte Frau** (Kollo/Willi Kollo/w Arnold) Neues Operettenhaus 22 December

1925 **Olly Polly** (Kollo/Willi Kollo/w Arnold) Neues Theater am Zoo 3 September

1928 **Arme Ritter** (Kollo/ Günther Bibo, Kurt Schwabach/w Arnold) Volkstheater, Munich 22 September

1931 **Frauen haben das gerne** (Kollo/w Arnold) Komische Oper 4 June

1933 **Lieber, reich—aber Glücklich** (Kollo/w Arnold) Komödienhaus 3 November

1942 **Ich bin in meine Frau verliebt** (Kollo, Willi Kollo/w Arnold) revised *Olly Polly* Raimundtheater, Vienna December

BAILEY, Pearl [Mae] (b Newport News, Va, 29 March 1918; d Philadelphia, 17 August 1990).

Originally a successful performer in vaudeville and in cabaret, Pearl Bailey made her first appearance in a Broadway musical in 1946 in the role of the barmaid, Butterfly, in Harold Arlen's *St Louis Woman,* introducing ''Legalize My Name'' and ''It's a Woman's Prerogative (to change her mind).'' In the 1950s she appeared in the musical *Arms and the Girl* (Connecticut, ''There Must Be Somethin' Better Than Love''), in the revue *Bless You All* (1950) and as Madame Fleur in the Caribbean whorehouse tale *House of Flowers* (1954), whilst also featuring in a number of musical films, including those of the stage shows *Carmen Jones* (as Frankie, performing ''Beat Out Dat Rhythm on a Drum'') and *Porgy and Bess* (Maria, 1959), *Variety Girl* (1947), *Isn't It Romantic* and *St Louis Blues* (1958).

In the late 1960s she returned to the musical stage and played the role of Sally Adams in *Call Me Madam* in California and that of Dolly Levi in *Hello, Dolly!* both on Broadway (special Tony Award 1968) and around the country. She reprised this last role through America in 1975–76, making a second and final Broadway appearance as Mrs Levi at the Minskoff Theater, 6 November 1975 (42 performances).

Autobiographies: *The Raw Pearl* (Harcourt Brace & World, New York, 1968), *Talking to Myself* (Harcourt Brace Jovanovich, New York, 1971)

DIE BAJADERE Operette in 3 acts by Julius Brammer and Alfred Grünwald. Music by Emmerich Kálmán. Carltheater, Vienna, 23 December 1921.

Following on behind his wartime successes with *Die Csárdásfürstin* and *Die Faschingsfee* and the postwar *Das Hollandweibchen,* Kálmán scored yet another Vienna triumph with *Die Bajadere,* a romantic backstage Operette which contains some of the most beautiful of all his theatre music.

Brammer and Grünwald's libretto follows the efforts of the eastern Prince Radjami (Louis Treumann) to win the heart and hand of Odette Darimonde (Christl Mardayn), the prima donna of the Operette *La Bayadère.* This romance is counterpointed by the comical amours of the soubrette, Marietta (Luise Kartousch), and her two husbands, Napoléon (Ernst Tautenhayn) and Louis-Philippe (Eugen Strehn), each of whom she fancies only when she is not married to him. Radjami, obliged by his country's laws to take a wife in short time, has to hasten his wooing of the obdurate prima donna and he puts his faith in the power of a bunch of ''love roses.'' Under the spell of the flowers, Odette finds herself accepting his invitation to a hurriedly arranged party, but when he attempts to top the evening with a wedding ceremony she awakens from her trance. It is three months and a further act of quiproquos before the two can bring down the curtain together.

Forgoing the more explicit, driving Hungarian rhythms and tones of *Die Csárdásfürstin* and the later *Gräfin Mariza,* Kálmán instead served the stars with some lush, heavily romantic melodies of which the tenor-baritone leading man's ''O Bajadere,'' in particular, rates as one of the composer's most memorable. He served the comedians equally well, with some sparky, vigorous modern dance tunes (''Fräulein, bitte woll'n sie Shimmy tanzen?,'' ''Schatzi, ich möchte einen Zobel von dir,'' ''Die kleine Bar dort am Boulevard'') in a classically proportioned score in which romance and fun had equal and equally outstanding moments.

Die Bajadere was hugely successful in Vienna. Otto Storm and Raoul Aslan took over as Radjami, and Else Kochhann and Lya Beyer took turns as Odette, as its first run at the Carltheater stretched beyond 12 months and finally ended after 353 performances. It was brought back after *Die Brasilianerin* and *Madame Pompadour* had run their runs, and given a second season, passing its 400th performance, with Mardayn and Eric Deutsch-Haupt in the lead roles, on 8 October 1923 and closing after its 406th. Berlin's Metropoltheater production, which ran concurrently with the Vienna one, starred Mizzi Günther as Odette. If it did not equal its Vienna counterpart in success, it nevertheless swept past its 100th (29 May) and 150th (19 August) nights before closing after 176 performances and giving over the stage to a revue.

In Budapest, Ernő Kulinyi's adaptation of *A bajadér* was, again, a major hit. Produced at the Király Színház, it boasted two of the town's favorite feminine stars at its billhead: Sári Fedák as Odette and the young Hanna Honthy as Marietta, and with Marton Rátkai—the Louis Treumann of Budapest—as the Prince, and Jenő Nador (Napoléon) and Árpád Latabár (Louis-Philippe) in comical support, the show ran straight through its 100th performance (17 February 1923) and on to the beginning of May.

Die Bajadere soon appeared in Madrid (15 November 1923), but France was a little slower to take up the piece which was not seen until Charles Montcharmont's combination of agency and theatre management got the French version of Bertal and Maubon, already seen in Brussels, to the stage in Lyon in 1925. Maguy Warna and Berlin's Herr Leonard headed the romance, Gabrielle Ristori, Urban and Robert Hasti the fun, and Montcharmont found a willing taker for the piece in the brothers Isola, who chose to open their management of the Théâtre Mogador with his production. Maria Kousnetzoff and Leonard (replaced by Mlle Warna and Edmond Tirmont in a recasting which gave increasingly stronger vocal values to Radjami's role), and Urban and Mlle Ristori played through a run of just under three months.

Die Bajadere, curiously, largely missed the English-speaking areas of the world. London, where *The Gipsy Princess* had disappointed, failed to take it up and, by the time it was produced in America, under the management of Abe Erlanger, it had been thoroughly transformed by William Le Baron and Buddy De Sylva into a piece which insisted that its heroine was *The Yankee Princess.* Vivienne Segal starred as the lady in question through 80 Broadway performances. *Die Bajadere* later appeared in New York in another disguise when it was given in a Yiddish version, as *Parisian Love* (Schulman-Goldberg Theater). In 1998 the Ohio Light Opera produced a rather more faithful English version (ad James Stuart).

Plate 19. **Die Bajadere.** *John Pickle (Radjami) and Julie Wright (Odette) in the Ohio Light Opera's 1998 production.*

Die Bajadere reappeared in Vienna in 1929 (28 November) for a four-week season at the Johann Strauss-Theater with Anny Ahlers, Walter Jankuhn, Tilly Maganja and with Tautenhayn in his original role but, in spite of its enormous initial success, a score of Kálmán's finest, and a comical plot line superior to almost any other in the Viennese musical theatre of its time, the piece has slipped behind the other principal Kálmán Operetten in the repertoire during the latter years of the century. The rather dangling third act of the romantic half of the plot seems to be the only possible explanation, apart from fashion or misfortune.

The title *Die Bajadere* was earlier used for an Operette by Fritz Bernhard, produced at the Neues Theater, Mainz, 15 January 1911.

Germany: Metropoltheater 18 February 1922; USA: Knickerbocker Theater *The Yankee Princess* 2 October 1922; Hungary: Király

Plate 20. **Sherlock Holmes, the Musical.** *Ron Moody impersonated the famous detective in London's musical version of his adventures.*

Színház *A bajadèr* 10 November 1922; France: Théâtre des Célestins, Lyon *La Bayadère* 4 March 1925, Théâtre Mogador, Paris 30 January 1926

Recordings: complete in Russian (Melodiya), complete in English (Newport Classics), selection in Hungarian (Qualiton), selection in Italian (Fonit-Cetra), selection in Estonian (Melodiya), selection in Italian (EDM)

BAKER STREET Musical in 2 acts by Jerome Coopersmith based on the *Sherlock Holmes* stories of Arthur Conan Doyle. Music and lyrics by Marian Grudeff and Raymond Jessel. Broadway Theater, New York, 16 February 1965.

Following the success of *Oliver!,* English classic literature—and especially anything containing children—was ripe for the musicalizing and Arthur Conan Doyle's all-deducing Sherlock Holmes, already theatrically triumphant in the hands of American author-actor William Gillette at the turn of the century, soon fell into the basket. The Americo-Canadian musical *Baker Street* used pieces of three Conan Doyle tales to manufacture a libretto in which Holmes (Fritz Weaver) and Watson (Peter Sallis) pursued a Moriarty (Martin Gabel) who is out to steal Queen Victoria's Diamond Jubilee presents. It also managed to involve the traditionally misogynistic detective with a beautiful American actress (Inga Swenson). The juvenile element was represented by the Baker Street Irregulars, a band of Holmes-supportive urchins led by one Wiggins (Teddy Green). The detective and his sidekick pursued Moriarty through Oliver Smith's depictions of London's underworld, docklands and streets, via a representation of the Diamond Jubilee Parade done by the Bill Baird Marionettes, to a boat moored on the Thames, before disposing of the Professor over the white cliffs of Dover (the Reichenbach Falls were a little far from W1) and returning to London to an ending which withheld itself (just?) from pairing Holmes off with the actress. If several of the numbers were reminiscent of earlier shows, the score threw up one piece, the actress's "Letters," which pleased.

Lavishly mounted, expertly publicized (street signs around Broadway pointed to "Baker Street"), and strongly patronized in the early part of its run, Alexander H Cohen's production of *Baker Street* transferred to the Martin Beck Theatre (3 November 1965) and ended its run there after 313 performances.

The show did not play London, but London witnessed its own *Sherlock Holmes* (Cambridge Theatre 24 April 1989 Leslie Bricusse) a quarter of a century later. Holmes (Ron Moody) again chased Moriarty round the sights of London, again got conventionally entangled with a feminine protagonist (Liz Robertson), and the Baker Street Irregulars again did cockney-kiddie song and dance, and, whilst a non-musical Holmes piece with neither children nor women in it prospered tidily just down the road, it foundered quickly.

A successful German Sherlock Holmes musical, entitled *Ein Fall für Sherlock Holmes* (Gerd Natschinski/ Jürgen Degenhardt) and produced at the Städtische Bühnen, Erfurt, 10 April 1982, left Moriarty, children and amorous ladies aside and instead based itself on *The Hound of the Baskervilles,* but Germany had apparently already solved the problem of getting feminine interest into Doyle's tales: in 1907 the Munich Volkstheater produced a piece written by the young Julius Brammer and "A G Wald" (Alfred Grünwald), music by one Georges Criketown, entitled *Fräulein Sherlock Holmes* (31 August).

Recordings: *Baker Street* original cast (MGM), *Ein Fall für Sherlock Holmes* (Amiga), *Sherlock Holmes* original cast (RCA)

BAKONYI, Károly (b Nagyvárad, 29 July 1873; d Budapest, 25 October 1926). Librettist to several of Hungary's all-time musical-theatre hits.

Trained in the law, Bakonyi worked as an adviser at the Ministry of Agriculture and came to the forefront as an operettic librettist when he collaborated with Ferenc Martos on the text for Jenő Huszka's highly successful *Bob herceg,* an operett which treated the British royal family to much the same kind of romantic high jinks that Western European shows imposed on the monarchs of central European states. He had a second and even greater success when he authored the libretto for the exquisite fairy-tale piece *János vitéz,* which, as set with songs by Kacsoh and Heltai, would become the most beloved work of the Hungarian musical theatre.

Kacsoh's subsequent *Rákóczi* was another, if less enduring, success, but Bakonyi found fame beyond the confines of Hungary when he collaborated with another neophyte stage composer, Imre (later Emmerich) Kálmán, on the military operett *Tatárjárás* (*Ein Herbstmanöver, Autumn Manouevres, The Gay Hussars*) and again on a second piece with a military turn, *Az obsitos* (*Soldier Boy, Gold gab ich für Eisen,* etc).

In a remarkable run of quality pieces, he paired with Buttykay on a version of the Cinderella tale, with Kálmán on *A kis király* (*Der kleine König*), once more with Huszka on the successful *Nemtudomka* (*Die Patronesse vom Nachtcafé* Theater in der Josefstadt 15 May 1915), and, finally, with one further rising composer, Albert Szirmai, with whom he turned out the highly successful *Mágnás Miska* (*Der Pusztakavalier*) and *Gróf Rinaldo* (*Rinaldo*).

In a limited (for the time) and remarkable career in which he helped launch some of the period's most successful local composers, and during which he never suffered a single flop, Bakonyi was responsible for a wide diversity of works—from the fantastical to the military vaudeville and the low comical—amongst which were the libretti to many of the most important Hungarian musicals of his era.

1902 **Bob herceg** (Jenő Huszka/Ferenc Martos) Népszínház 20 December

1904 **János vitéz** (Pongrác Kacsoh/Jenő Heltai) Király Színház 18 November

1906 **Rákóczi** (Kacsoh/Sándor Endrődi, Árpád Pásztor) Király Színház 20 November

1908 **Tatárjárás** (Imre Kálmán/Andor Gábor) Vígszínház 22 February

1910 **Az obsitos** (Kálmán) Vígszínház 16 March

1912 **Hamupipőke** (Ákos Buttykay/Imre Farkas, Gábor) Magyar Királyi Operaház 26 October

1914 **Nemtudomka** (Huszka/Zsolt Harsányi) Király Színház 14 January

1914 **A kis Király** (Kálmán/w Martos) Népopera 17 January

1916 **Mágnás Miska** (Albert Szirmai/w Gábor) Király Színház 12 February

1918 **Gróf Rinaldo** (Szirmai) Király Színház 7 November

BALALAIKA Musical play in 3 acts by Eric Maschwitz, a revised version of *The Gay Hussar.* Music by George Posford and Bernard Grün. Adelphi Theatre, London, 22 December 1936.

The show which was to become *Balalaika* was originally produced by Julian Wylie for Moss' Empires and Howard & Wyndham's Tours as part of their drive to supply product to fill their chain of provincial theatres. *The Gay Hussar* (2 October 1933, Manchester) was the work of the BBC's Eric Maschwitz and George Posford who had combined in 1931 on the radio musical *Good Night, Vienna,* and there were distinct similarities in the plot outlines of the two pieces, both of which dealt with European aristocrats reduced by war or revolution, yet finding true love triumphant through misfortune. The principal protagonists here were the Tsarist Count Peter

Karagin and the ballerina Lydia Marakova, daughter of a prominent revolutionary who attempts to murder Karagin's princely father in his box during the ballet. When the revolution succeeds, Peter flees to Paris where, working as a waiter in the cafe "The Gay Hussar," he is ultimately reunited with Lydia when the murderous Marakov is sent to Paris as Ambassador under the new regime.

The Gay Hussar was sent out on the road playing a then very unusual schedule of multiple weeks in a venue, as the huge revolve which was the basis of the show's principal scenic effect, a ballet within a show, had to travel by road and the extensive get-in time meant Monday openings were out. As a result, the production proved not to be viable and *The Gay Hussar* was not persevered with. Following the huge success of Ivor Novello's Drury Lane musical, *Glamorous Night,* Maschwitz rewrote his piece on similar lines, took in new numbers both from Posford (most notably the show's hit, "At the Balalaika") and from German expatriate Bernard Grün, and had it staged as *Balalaika* at the Adelphi Theatre by Novello's director, Leontine Sagan, and choreographer, Joan Davis, with costumes by René Hubert who had, likewise, done the costumes for Novello's most recent piece. Muriel Angelus starred as the ballerina opposite Novello-esque French actor Roger Tréville, and Clifford Mollison and Betty Warren were the soubrets alongside Jerrold Robertshaw (Prince Karagin) and Eric Marshall (Colonel Balakirev).

The spectacular and successful production was soon transferred to His Majesty's Theatre and it fulfilled the bulk of its 570 performances there, returning to the Adelphi for the last months of its run as a twice-nightly show in a version somewhat shortened from its original three and a half hours. It was subsequently produced in Australia, with Robert Halliday, Margaret Adams and Marjorie Gordon starred for a fine three months at Melbourne's Her Majesty's Theatre and almost as long at Sydney's Theatre Royal (18 December 1937), and in Paris in a vast production by Maurice Lehmann at the Théâtre Mogador. There the show's musical content was increased by four additional numbers (two fox-trots, a valse russe and a valse viennoise) by Robert Stolz and Henri Wernert, a top-up which brought the original short and rather fragmentary score, lacking in obvious "numbers," up to proportions regarded as more conventional opérette à grand spectacle ones by Continental audiences. Réda Caire and Jacqueline Francell starred and the celebrated Jean Périer was the Prince, but the lavishly mounted piece held up for only a few months. However, whilst Britain has forgotten *Balalaika,* an even further adapted version (add mus: Jack Ledru) has remained firmly, if marginally, in the French repertoire up to the present day.

The score again came under the hands of the "improvers" when Hollywood took up *Balalaika*—the first British musical to become the object of a Hollywood film—and produced it in 1939 with a cast headed by Nelson Eddy, Ilona Massey and Walter Woolf King. This time it was Sigmund Romberg and others whose work was added, although "At the Balalaika" remained the show's musical feature. The film was in all probability the spur to an American production at the St Louis Muny in 1941, with Nancy McCord and Arthur Kent starred, a revival in 1943 with Marthe Errolle and Bob Lawrence, and another production, with Irene Manning starred, at the Pittsburgh Light Opera in 1947.

Australia: Her Majesty's Theatre, Melbourne 4 September 1937; France: Théâtre Mogador 24 September 1938; USA: Municipal Opera, St Louis 25 August 1941

Film: 1939

Recordings: selection WRC (Australia), film soundtrack (Caliban), selections in French (TLP, Polydor)

BALANCHINE, George [BALANCHIVADZE, Gyorgi Melitonovitch] (b St Petersburg, Russia, 9 January 1904; d New York, 30 April 1983).

Originally a choreographer with the Diaghilev ballet companies, Balanchine made his entry into the lighter forms of theatre when he designed the dances for two London revues (*Wake Up and Dream* 1929, and *Cochran's 1930 Revue*) produced by C B Cochran, and the Divertissement Pastorale, Divertissement des Songes et des Heures, Grand Ballet des Nymphes, Divertissement des Mouches, and Bacchanale for the Isola brothers' starry revival of *Orphée aux enfers* at the Théâtre Mogador (1931), before returning to the ballet world to create works for Colonel de Basil's company. In 1934 he moved to America, where he founded the American Ballet School and the New York Ballet Company and, in 1936, made his first appearance as a choregrapher on Broadway when he contributed the dances to that year's edition of the revived *Ziegfeld Follies.*

Balanchine entered the musical comedy world later the same year when he devised the dances for the heavily choreographic Rodgers and Hart musical *On Your Toes* ("Slaughter on Tenth Avenue," "Princess Zenobia," "On Your Toes"), and then went on to choreograph a series of mostly more conventional Broadway shows from *Babes in Arms* (1937) through the dance-angled *I Married an Angel, The Boys from Syracuse* (1938), *Keep off the Grass, Louisiana Purchase, Cabin in the Sky* (1940), *The Lady Comes Across, Rosalinda* (1942), Lerner and Loewe's *What's Up?* (1943), *Dream with Music, Song of Norway* (1944), *Mr Strauss Goes to Boston* (1945), a revival of *The Chocolate Soldier* (1947) and *Where's Charley?* (1948) to his final *Courtin' Time* (1951).

His work was also seen in the screen version of *On Your Toes* as well as in such less story-lined movies as

The Goldwyn Follies (1938) and *Star Spangled Rhythm* (1942).

Biographies: Taper, B: *Balanchine* (Harper and Row, New York, 1963, 1974), Kirstein, L: *Portrait of Mr Balanchine* (Viking Press, New York, 1984), Caras, S: *Balanchine: A Photo Album and Memoir* (Rizzioli, New York, 1985), Haggin, B H: *Discovering Balanchine* (Horizon Press, New York, 1981)

BALFE, Michael [William] (b Dublin, 15 May 1808; d Romney Abbey, Hants, 20 October 1870).

One of the most popular composers of what was, at the time, called English opera, Balfe began his musical career as a violinist, playing in public from the age of seven. At the age of 9, he composed music for T H Bayley's song "The Lover's Mistake," by 16 he was conducting the orchestra at the Theatre Royal, Drury Lane, and at 19 he appeared on the Paris stage (as Sgr Balfi) in the role of Rossini's Figaro.

Balfe's earliest operas were written in imitation of Italian models and staged in Italy, during his stay there between 1829–31, but he subsequently returned to Britain, where the rest of his works found a ready public, establishing him at the forefront of British theatrical composers. He had early successes with such pieces as *The Siege of Rochelle* and *The Maid of Artois,* set Scribe and de Leuven's text for *Le Puits d'amour* (UK: *Geraldine*) for production at Paris's Opéra-Comique in 1843, and later the same year had his most memorable success with the romantic opera *The Bohemian Girl* ("I Dreamt I Dwelt in Marble Halls").

The Enchantress (1845), *The Rose of Castille* (1857) and *Satanella* (1858) were others of his works which, with *The Bohemian Girl* and with such pieces as Wallace's *Maritana* and Benedict's *The Lily of Killarney,* formed a solid part of the baggage of the touring English operatic companies of the middle-to-later years of the 19th century, traveling to English-language houses across the world in repertoires with translations of the most popular works of Bellini, Rossini and their Continental fellows and, sometimes, a leavening of burlesques.

Sentimental, romantic dramas in their text, the majority of these pieces were set with music which was rarely as demanding as that of either the Italian classic operas, nor the more verismo pieces which would follow, and most of them would certainly have attracted the label "light opera" in later days. It was a quality which undoubtedly added to their popularity, and only in the absence of an obvious comic element did these pieces differ from the light operatic pieces of the second half of the century.

In post–Hervé and Offenbach days, with the light musical theatre well established in fashion, pieces such as *The Bohemian Girl, The Rose of Castille* and the made-over *Letty, the Basketmaker* still remained in the repertoire alongside the newer style of musical play.

Biography: Barrett, W A: *Balfe: His Life and Works* (Remington & Co, London, 1882)

BALKANLIEBE (aka *Die Gräfin von Durazzo*) Operette in 2 acts by E Kahr and Bruno Hardt-Warden. Music by Rudolf Kattnigg. Neues Operetten-Theater, Leipzig, 22 December 1937.

Deposed Prince Marko Franjopan gallivants from the Illyrian countryside to the Hotel Excelsior in Venice, an evening on the Grand Canal and a winter sports venue in the Austrian alps on his way to regaining his throne from the Countess of Durazzo. On the way, he falls in love with her, but it turns out that the "Countess" who has enraptured him is not the Countess at all but his affianced Zlata (Trude Collin), daughter of the helpful bandit Branko Juranitsch, who has captured the monarch and taken her place.

First mounted in Leipzig under the title *Die Gräfin von Durazzo,* this flashy, latter-day piece of Ruritanian romance, set with a lively if conventional score, was one of the few German-language musicals since the 1930s to have gained much attention on home stages and to have won the honors of a commercial recording.

Recording: selection (Ariola-Eurodisc)

THE BALKAN PRINCESS Musical play in 3 acts by Frederick Lonsdale and Frank Curzon. Lyrics by Paul Rubens and Arthur Wimperis. Music by Paul Rubens. Prince of Wales Theatre, London, 19 February 1910.

Following his trend-setting *King of Cadonia,* Freddie Lonsdale's second musical for producer Frank Curzon took the Ruritanian themes of love and royal duty so fruitfully exploited in the earlier piece and this time reversed the sexes to allow producer's wife Isabel Jay to take the royal title role. Her *King of Cadonia* co-star, Bertram Wallis, was the politically unstable Grand Duke whom she converts and weds. Princess Stephanie, refusing five potential husbands proposed by her ministers, goes out among her people in disguise and catches the sixth and only other possible one, Sergius, spreading revolution. She has him arrested, abdicates rather than be forced into marriage with any of the five, but is restored to the throne when the impressed Sergius abandons his anti-royalist stance to stand by her side. A comic subplot had two *Erminie*-type thieves (Lauri de Frece, Charles Brown) masquerading as an eligible nobleman and his servant, and the former becoming entangled with the "widowed" palace charwoman (Mabel Sealby), whose husband (James Blakeley) is actually working at the restaurant where Sergius foments his revolution.

Paul Rubens's score was much less substantial than the Sidney Jones music for the earlier piece, giving the new musical a lighter flavor than *King of Cadonia,* and

Plate 21. **The Balkan Princess.** *''Arrest that Man'' Isabel Jay as the Princess Stephanie gets tough with Bertram Wallis. But not for long.*

the comical characters' numbers came out better than some rather weak attempts at Daly's Theatre–style baritone and soprano material. However, *The Balkan Princess* proved distinctly popular, running for six months in London (176 performances) in the shadow of *The Arcadians, The Dollar Princess* and *Our Miss Gibbs,* before going on to an 111-performance run on Broadway, under the management of the Shubert brothers. Robert Warwick and Louise Gunning were the royal couple in New York, Percy Ames, Teddy Webb and May Boley headed the fun, and the piece was well-enough thought of to win a burlesque at Joe Weber's house as the ''canned comedy'' *The Balky Princess* (by Charles Brown, 17 April 1911), a piece which borrowed Rubens's tunes as its musical part.

Although it was scarcely an outstanding piece, something about *The Balkan Princess* pleased producers and the show proved remarkably tenacious. It was successfully produced in Australia, under the J C Williamson banner, with Florence Young and Frank Greene in the romantic roles and Bert Gilbert, Lottie Sargent and W S Percy in charge of the comedy (and ''I Wonder Who's Kissing Her Now'' squeezed into the score). It appeared in South Africa and on the Oriental circuits, in Puerto Rico and Havana, and it even surfaced at Budapest's Király Színház (ad Andor Gábor) just weeks after the end of the London run. And to top it all, *The Balkan Princess* had an amazingly hardy touring life in Britain, a life which saw it still on the circuits 25 years after its first production, long after the last sighting of *King of Cadonia.*

Hungary: Király Színház *A balkani hercegnő* 23 September 1910; USA: Herald Square Theater 9 February 1911; Australia: Theatre Royal, Sydney 10 June 1911

BALL, Lucille [Desirée] (b Celoron, NY, 6 August 1911; d Los Angeles, 26 April 1989).

The redheaded comedienne and star of TV's long-popular *I Love Lucy* appeared only once on the musical stage when she took the star role in the 1960 musical *Wildcat* (''Hey, Look Me Over''). However, in her more natural habitat, on film, after early appearances in chorus, bit parts and increasing roles in the early 1930s (*Roberta, Top Hat, Follow the Fleet*), Ball starred in the filmed versions of the stage musicals *Too Many Girls* (1940, Consuelo Casey), *Dubarry Was a Lady* (1943, May Daly, singing dubbed by Martha Mears), *Best Foot Forward* (1943, herself) and *Mame* (1970, Mame).

Miss Ball's daughter **Lucie [Desirée] ARNAZ** (b Los Angeles, 17 July 1951) starred on Broadway in *They're Playing Our Song* (1979, Sonia Walsk) and in London in *The Witches of Eastwick* (2000, Alexandra).

Biographies: Gregory, J: *The Lucille Ball Story* (New American Library, New York, 1974), Sanders, C S, Gilbert, T: *Desilu* (W H Morrow, New York, 1993)

BALL, Michael (b Stratford-upon-Avon, 27 July 1962).

After initial work in provincial theatres (*Sweet Charity, Godspell*), the strapping young tenor won the role of Frederic in a Manchester production of *The Pirates of Penzance,* and from there he moved swiftly to London to create the role of Marius in the English version of *Les Misérables* (''Empty Chairs and Empty Tables'').

He went on to succeed to the role of Raoul in London's *The Phantom of the Opéra* and subsequently created the part of Alex in *Aspects of Love,* introducing the song ''Love Changes Everything'' which, in his version, reached number two on the British charts. He followed the London production by repeating his role on Broadway (1990).

In 1992 he represented Britain in the Eurovision Song contest in a career increasingly angled towards pop music and recording, but returned impressively to the musical theatre in 1996 to top-bill in the role of Giorgio in the London production of *Passion.*

THE BALLET GIRL Musical comedy in 2 acts by James T Tanner. Lyrics by Adrian Ross. Music by Carl Kiefert. Additional songs by Leslie Stuart and B Luard Selby. Grand Theatre, Wolverhampton, 15 March 1897.

This British musical, with its words prepared by the practiced Gaiety Theatre team of Tanner and Ross and music by the West End's favorite orchestrator, Carl Kiefert, had the unusual distinction of being shown on Broadway without having been given a West End run. It moved on swiftly from its New York date, but had a successful touring career both in Britain and America. The British production introduced three songs by Leslie Stuart to leaven Kiefert's conventional score. The American score introduced several numbers by the show's producer, Edward E Rice.

The title *The Ballet Girl* was later prematurely used for the Broadway version of *Polenblut,* ultimately played on Broadway as *The Peasant Girl.*

USA: Manhattan Theater 21 December 1897

BALL IM SAVOY Operette in a Vorspiel and 3 acts by Alfred Grünwald and Fritz Löhner-Beda. Music by Pál Ábrahám. Grosses Schauspielhaus, Berlin, 23 December 1932.

The third of Ábrahám's successive trio of major hits, *Ball im Savoy* followed the example set by *Die Blume von Hawaii* by being first presented in Germany.

After the Japanese, Russian and South Pacific venues of the two earlier shows, the new piece went for its colorful location to the slightly more operettically conventional Venice, Nice and Paris, and its action and its characters were correspondingly less extravagant. The ball of the title took place at the Savoy Hotel in Nice, where the Argentinian dancer Tangolita (Trude Berliner) sets out to rendezvous with her former lover, the Marquis Aristide de Faublas (Arthur Schröder) in spite of the fact he is on his honeymoon. With the help of the Turkish attaché, Mustapha Bey (Oszkár Dénes), Aristide sets himself up for a titillating night on the dance floor, but Madelaine (Gitta Alpár), the Marquis's new wife, sees through the men's tricks and she turns up at the Savoy herself, setting the ball alight with scandal as she flirts outrageously with the young Célestin Formant (Victor de Kowa), leading her despairing husband to horrified thoughts of divorce. They are safely in Paris by the time he finds out that it was all a put-up job.

Like the locales and tale, the score for the piece was a little less exotic than before, but the mixture of traditional and modern which had made such an appeal in the earlier shows was the same. On the traditional side, Gitta Alpár triumphed with her soprano ''Toujours l'amour,'' whilst the modern side proved equally winning. Rózsi Bársony, cast in the role of Daisy Parker, a jazz composer, was glued into the proceedings rather as the Jim Boy of *Die Blume von Hawaii* had been, to allow for some of the lightly Eurojazzy numbers in which Ábrahám specialized. Dénes delivered a ''Wenn wir Türken küssen,'' there was a tango in praise of ''La Belle Tangolita'' and the piece's strivings towards an international flavor brought forth a paso doble about ''Sevilla'' and a slowfox entitled ''O Mister Brown!''

A vast success in Berlin, the show hung on when 1933 struck, in spite of its composer's and its star's unwanted Jewishness, and at the same time it quickly moved out towards other productions. London, which had enjoyed *Viktória* but had not taken up *Die Blume von Hawaii,* was the first to mount its version. *Ball at the Savoy* (ad Oscar Hammerstein II) featured Dénes and Bársony in their original roles alongside Maurice Evans and Natalie Hall as the spouses of the piece, Hammerstein directed, and the piece followed a successfully imported and luxuriantly staged version of *Wenn die kleinen Veilchen blühen* (*Wild Violets*) into the Theatre Royal, Drury Lane. In spite of the two clever Hungarians, it ran just half as long as the Stolz piece, folding in 148 performances as Drury Lane plunged into the tenuous position from which only Ivor Novello would eventually rescue it.

Hungary not unsurprisingly gave the piece (ad Jenő Heltai) a better reception. Hilda Harmath and Jenő Törzs appeared as the principals of the action, with Mária Lázár as the naughty dancer, but once again it was the subordinate roles with their jazzy melodies which drew the greatest applause: Gyula Kabos as Mustapha, and the ebullient Marika Rökk as Daisy. In Vienna, this prized pair of roles were taken by Irén von Ziláhy and Curt Bois in Rudolf Beer's production at the old Johann Strauss-Theater, which was now called the Scala Theater. Egon von Jordan and Mary Losseff played the nominal leads and Hans Thimig was the young decoy. Rózsi Bársony arrived during the run to guest as Daisy, but the show's slightly disappointing run of under three months did not solve the failing theatre's problems.

If Vienna got Bársony, Australia got the other half of the family and the partnership when J C Williamson Ltd took husband Dénes to Sydney to play his original role alongside Mabel Gibson/Marie Bremner (Madelaine), Nellie Barnes (Daisy), Robert Coote (Célestin), James Raglan/Sydney Burchall (Aristide) and Cecil Kellaway through four weeks in Sydney and a bare month in Melbourne (5 October 1935).

Although *Ball im Savoy* disappointed in its English version, it nevertheless remained a favorite in central Europe. It was revived at Budapest's Fővárosi Operettszínház, 16 January 1948 and 23 April 1965, and in 1962 Marika Rökk once again took up the part she had played in the Hungarian premiere, 30 years earlier, in a revival at Vienna's Raimundtheater. The show had been made over by Hugo Wiener into two acts (still with the Venetian prologue), and the star was supported in the plotworthier roles by Margit Bollmann, Spiro Makri and Franco Steinberg. Rökk was seen as Daisy as late as 1983 (''eine jazz-komponistin'' can, after all, be any age) in a (thankfully) rare example of an artist appearing in one and the same role half a century on. The piece has been played in Hungary in recent years at Pécs (15 October 1993), at the Fővárosi Operettszínház (23 June 1994), Szeged (26 May 1995), Veszprém (8 December 1995) and Nyíregyháza (7 December 1996).

An Hungarian film version which captured the performances of cast members Alpár and Bársony was made in 1935, whilst a 1936 German film featured Conrad Nagel and Marta Labarr, and a second, in 1954, featured Rudolf Prack and Eva Ingeborg Scholz in the leads, Bibi Johns as Daisy, Rudolf Platte as Mustapha and Nadja Tiller as Tangolita. It allowed a certain Herren Gietz and Gaze loose on the music, and director Paul Martin and Franz Tassié souped up a book which got Daisy rather more into the action than originally, as well as into an apropos-of-nothing ''Musik-Show'' which also featured Caterina Valente, John Bubbles and the Three Peiheros.

UK: Theatre Royal, Drury Lane *Ball at the Savoy* 8 September 1933; Hungary: Magyar Színház *Bál a Savoyban* 23 December 1933; Austria: Scala Theater 25 December 1933; Australia: Theatre Royal, Sydney *Ball at the Savoy* 6 July 1935

Films: István Szekeley (Hun) 1935, (Ger) 1936, Central-Europa Film 1954

Recording: selection in Polish (Muza)

EINE BALLNACHT Operette in 3 acts by Leopold Jacobson and Robert Bodanzky. Music by Oscar Straus. Johann Strauss-Theater, Vienna, 11 October 1918.

There was little that was new in Jacobson and Bodanzky's libretto for Oscar Straus's 1918 Operette *Eine Ballnacht.* The ingenue was Countess Edith, niece to the old Graf Klemens Ortendorff, and destined in marriage for Count Harry, son of the equally aristocratic Fürst Gregor Gerolsheim, a young man whom she has never seen. The soubrette was the little shopgirl Riki Schöngruber who, although engaged to the commis Willi Höfer, goes to the ball of the title in Edith's place, and the usual ensuing complications and comicalities filled the remainder of the evening before everyone ended up happily in the arms of their predestined ones at the third-act curtain.

Straus provided a pretty score made up of a vertebral number of waltzes, varied by polka, galop and other bouncy dance rhythms. Riki and Harry drew the prettiest waltz tune with their ''Wie nett wär's, könnten Sie vergessen,'' but of the 3/4 melodies it was Willi's first act opener ''Ach! Was haben wir Frau'n für Sorgen'' which was plugged most diligently through the evening. Riki had the most prominent moments of the score, sharing a dance duo with Clemens and a march duo and another waltz with Willi, whilst the ingenue role had its best moment in another dancing number (w Harry), ''Ich möchte mit Ihnen allein sein.''

The show won through by its tunes and by the manner of its telling rather than by any interesting elements in its tired tale, and it ran through a healthy season at Vienna's Johann Strauss-Theater. It did even better in Berlin, however. During the 1919–20 season it was played for more than 250 performances under Heinz Saltenberg's management at the Wallner-Theater and the Komische Oper, with Käthe Dorsch starred as Riki, before going on to join *Ein Walzertraum* and *Der letzte Walzer* at the head of the list of Straus's most played works in Germany. In Hungary (ad Imre Harmath), the role of Riki fell to another outstanding young artist, the rising soubrette Hanna Honthy, in a satisfactory production at the Revü Színház. Undoubtedly handicapped by its origins, at a time when German works were unwelcome outside Europe, *Eine Ballnacht* did not, however, go further and did not succeed in establishing itself in the revived repertoire.

Germany: Wallner-Theater 1919; Hungary: Revü Színház *A bálkirálynő* 29 January 1921

BANDITENSTREICHE Comic opera in 1 act by B Boutonnier. Music by Franz von Suppé. Carltheater, Vienna, 27 April 1867.

Suppé's short comic opera *Banditenstreiche,* produced at the Carltheater in 1867, was a disappointment. Its little tale of a swashbuckling bandit who helps a pair of young lovers to outwit the girl's ambitious father was illustrated by some fine Suppé music, but the piece did not win anything like the success of his *Das Pensionat, Die schöne Galathee, Flotte Bursche, Leichte Cavallerie* or *Zehn Mädchen und kein Mann.* After its initial production, it was put on the shelf whilst the Carltheater continued to play the older Suppé pieces or such favorites as *Mannschaft am Bord, Des Löwen Erwachen* or *Der Meisterschuss von Pottenstein.* In 1874, after Offenbach's *Die Banditen* (*Les Brigands*) had been seen in Vienna, an attempt was made to revive it, in a revised version (2 August), but the exercise lasted just three performances.

Two attempts have been subsequently made to build full-sized Suppé pasticcios around the *Banditenstreiche* text and score. The first, by that determined adaptor Gustave Quedtenfeldt and Otto Urak, was introduced at Nuremberg (25 February 1940) and the second by Ludwig Bender and Peter Waldenmaier 15 years later at Trier (28 April 1955).

BANÈS, Antoine [Anatole] (b Paris, 8 June 1856; d Paris, 10 January 1924).

Conservatoire-trained Banès made a career as a composer of light music whilst holding posts as an archivist at, and later deputy administrator of, the Paris Opéra library (1911 sq) and also working as a music critic for the *Nation* and, after the war, the *Figaro.* The most successful of his stage works—largely written in the earlier part of his career—was the internationally popular *Toto* (1892). Bilhaud and Barré's double-travesty musical comedy with its highly grateful star role ran an excellent 129 performances on its first Paris production and was subsequently played in Germany and Austria (*Tata-Toto*), Hungary (*Toto és Tata*), Britain, and at New York's Irving Place Theatre in its German translation, as well as in a vernacular version on the regular Broadway stage.

Banès's subsequent works, although often written with proven authors, were reckoned by some to have owed a large part of their relative failure to unattractive libretti, but he scored a small success with the production of *Léda* at the Monte-Carlo Opera House, under the management of Pierre Comte-Offenbach, and saw his *Le Roi frelon* win foreign productions at Budapest's Fővárosi Nyári Színház as *Korhelykirály* (20 September 1901 ad Emil Makai, Ferenc Molnár) and as *Pick und Pocket* in German (ad Hans Brennert, Erich Urban, add mus Bogumil Zepler) at the Belle Alliance Theater, Berlin (21 March 1903). By this stage it featured a cakewalk. His *Le Nouveau Régiment* was staged at Vienna's Theater in der Josefstadt (*Das neue Regiment* ad Heinrich Bolten-Bäckers, 12 October 1898) following its original Paris season and his *Le Bonhomme de neige* was dressed up as a Christmas pantomime for London audiences as *The Snowman* (Lyceum 21 December 1899 add mus: Walter Slaughter).

His other works included two short pieces given at the Opéra-Comique; an "operatorio," *L'Arche de Noë,* staged at Marseille in 1911; a number of ballets and pantomimes for Parisian and provincial stages; and a one-act play *La Lyre brisée,* produced at Le Havre in 1878 (6 October).

1882 **Un do malade** (Pittaud de Forges, "Laurençin") 1 act Eldorado 9 September

1883 **La Cadiguette** (Louis Péricaud, Lemoine) 1 act Eldorado 3 November

1884 **L'Escargot** (Paul Adély, Albert Barré) 1 act Eldorado 19 April

1884 **La Jarretière** (Adély, Barré) 1 act Eldorado 27 September

1885 **Au coq huppé** (Germain Villemer, Lucien Delormel) Eldorado 21 March

1887 **Les Délégués** (Émile Blavet, Fabrice Carré) Théâtre des Nouveautés 30 November

1892 **Toto** (Paul Bilhaud, Barré) Théâtre des Menus-Plaisirs 10 June

1893 **Madame Rose** (Bilhaud, Barré) 1 act Opéra-Comique 25 September

1894 **Le Bonhomme de neige** (Henri Chivot, Alfred Vanloo) Théâtre des Bouffes-Parisiens 19 April

1895 **Le Roi frelon** (Barré) Théâtre des Folies-Dramatiques 11 April

1896 **Une nuit d'amour** (Maxime Boucheron, Barré) Théâtre des Bouffes-Parisiens 11 May

1897 **Le Nouveau Regiment** (aka *Mademoiselle Portez-Arme*) (Barré, E Martin, Henri Bernard) L'Olympia 12 March

1899 **La Pomme d'Adam** (Lucien Augé de Lassus) 1 act Casino, Trouville 25 August

1901 **La Soeur de Jocrisse** (Vanloo) 1 act Opéra-Comique 9 July

1909 **Léda** (Pierre Veber, Augé de Lassus) Théâtre de Monte-Carlo 17 April

1911 **Les Gabelous** (Barré) Théâtre des Variétés, Marseille 4 November

BANTOCK, [Ernest] Leedham [Sutherland] (b London, 18 May 1870; d Richmond, Surrey, 15 October 1928).

A doctor's son, who worked initially for the Eastern Telegraph Company, Leedham Bantock quit his job in his early twenties when the company wanted to transfer him from Land's End to West Africa, and turned from the amateur to the professional stage. He became a useful character man in George Edwardes's companies, appearing through some 20 years in secondary roles in such London pieces as *A Gaiety Girl* (1893, Harry Fitzwarren, t/o Bobbie Rivers), *An Artist's Model* (1895, t/o James Cripps), *The Geisha* (1896, Arthur Cuddy), *San Toy* (1899, t/o The Emperor), *The School Girl* (1903, t/o Tubby Bedford), *A Country Girl* (1902, Douglas Verity), *The Cingalee* (1904, t/o Boobhamba) and *Lady Madcap* (1904, Colonel Layton), as well as in America and Australia (Hopkins in *In Town,* Bertie Boyd in *The Shop Girl,* Dawson in *Gentleman Joe,* Sir Lewis in *A Gaiety Girl*). Bantock also worked as both a director—notably for Marie Lloyd's only venture into the musical theatre, *The ABC* (1898)—and as an author, collaborating on the libretti for several successful musical comedies composed by Howard Talbot, the most fruitful of which was George Edwardes's production of *The Girl Behind the Counter.* He also won an international hearing with the mini-musical *The White Chrysanthemum,* produced by Frank Curzon, and with *The Belle of Brittany,* mounted by Tom B Davis, both of which, like *The Girl Behind the Counter,* won good runs in town and country in Britain and several overseas productions. Bantock also ventured as a producer, touring a musical comedy drama *Sweet Briar* with himself and his brother, Claude, featured in 1898.

Bantock's elder brother, **Granville [Ransome] BANTOCK** (b London, 7 August 1868; d London, 16 October 1946), celebrated, and knighted in later life, was a composer and conductor of serious music and an arts administrator, who also worked in the light musical theatre in the early part of his career. He composed interpolated numbers for several West End shows (*Monte Carlo* "Who'll Give a Penny to the Monkey," etc), wrote the bulk of the score for Marie Lloyd's touring vehicle *The ABC or Flossie the Frivolous* (w others/"Richard Henry" Grand Theatre, Wolverhampton 21 March 1898), and was musical director of George Edwardes's musical comedy company, touring America and Australia in 1894–95 with *A Gaiety Girl, The Shop Girl, In Town* and *Gentleman Joe.* He also coauthored a book describing this tour which remains an enjoyable record of life in the Victorian musical theatre (*Around the World with "A Gaiety Girl"* w F Aflalo, John Macqueen, 1896).

A second brother, **Claude [Ronald] Bantock** (b Kensington, 1875), also worked as an actor in the musical theatre, notably in Australia.

1905 **The White Chrysanthemum** (Howard Talbot/w Arthur Anderson) Criterion Theatre 31 August

1906 **The Girl Behind the Counter** (Talbot/w Anderson) Wyndham's Theatre 21 April

1907 **The Three Kisses** (Talbot/w Percy Greenbank) Apollo Theatre 21 August

1908 **The Belle of Brittany** (Talbot/w P J Barrow) Queen's Theatre 24 October

1909 **A Persian Princess** (Sidney Jones/Greenbank/w Barrow) Queen's Theatre 27 April

1912 **Santa Claus** (Theodore Holland/w Alfred de Manby, Harold Simpson) Scala Theatre 26 December

1917 **Physical Culture** (w Harold Simpson) 1 act Metropolitan Music Hall 30 April

Biographies: Bantock, M: *Granville Bantock: A Personal Portrait* (Dent, London, 1972), Anderton, H O: *Granville Bantock* (John Lane, London, 1915)

BARBE-BLEUE Opéra-bouffe in 3 acts by Henri Meilhac and Ludovic Halévy. Music by Jacques Offenbach. Théâtre des Variétés, Paris, 5 February 1866.

After their enormous success with *La Belle Hélène* at the Théâtre des Variétés, the Meilhac-Halévy-Offenbach team followed up with a burlesque of another favorite old tale, that of the gruesomely oversexed and apparently necrophiliac Chevalier Raoul, commonly known as Bluebeard, and his string of murdered wives. By the time Meilhac and Halévy had finished having their fun with Perrault's version of this bloody, revengeful tale, it had rather a different ring to it.

Bluebeard's last and avenging wife, the ladylike Fatima of the legend, became, in the opéra-bouffe version, a bubbling country wench of burstingly obvious charms and indifferent morals called Boulotte (Hortense Schneider). Boulotte attracts the attentions of the many-wived local overlord, the Sire de Barbe-bleue (José Dupuis), when, against all natural justice, she wins the raffle for the virginal post of rosière and, unaware of the fate of her predecessors in the post of Mme Barbe-bleue, she is delighted to have found herself such an advantageous match. Boulotte, however, has to share Meilhac and Halévy's plot line both with the area's obsessively jealous over-overlord, King Bobèche (Kopp), a monarch who has the habit of executing courtiers who look too appreciatively at his Queen, Clémentine (Aline Duval), and with the complex family affairs of this curious royal family. The helpful courtier Count Oscar (Grenier) rediscovers Princess Hermia (Mlle Vernet)—the baby daughter Bobèche and Clémentine exposed when they thought they had a son—living disguised as a florist in Boulotte's village, and takes her back to court. Hermia's favorite shepherd, Saphir (Paul Hittemans), turns out, in the best operettic tradition, to be the prince she is scheduled to marry. All would now be well at the court of Bobèche, did not the newly wed Bluebeard now decide that he prefers Hermia to Boulotte. He arranges with his alchemist, Popolani (Henri Couder), to dispose of Boulotte in the same way as he disposed of his previous wives, and sets off to besiege the defenceless Bobèche (who has melted down all his guns to make statues of himself) into giving him Hermia. But Nemesis is nigh. Popolani hasn't actually killed any of Bluebeard's wives, but has instead kept them all stashed secretly away, alive, for his own entertainment. And softhearted Oscar hasn't executed Clementine's admirers either. They are all hidden in the royal basement. And so, Boulotte comes "back to life," leads the undead in the exposure of the nasty habits of the two potentates, and drags Bluebeard home by the ear to live unhappily ever after.

Offenbach's score to the deliciously comical text of his collaborators was as sparkling as its predecessor. Barbe-bleue stalked the countryside declaring in the quickly famous Légende de Barbe-bleue: "Je suis Barbe-bleue, ô gué, jamais veuf ne fut plus gai . . . ," gaily condemned Boulotte to her death ("Le voilà donc, le tombeau/Vous avez vu ce monument") and threatened Bobèche with his cannons ("J'ai pas bien loin dans la montagne") in gay tenorial tones, but it was the prima donna who had the showiest role. She began as a saucy country lass ("Y'a des bergers dans le village") elected May Queen, got to play both a maiden under threat of murder ("Pierre, un beau jour, parvint") and a death scene ("Holà! Holà! ça me prend là!") in the second act, and invaded Bobèche's court disguised as a gypsy in the third ("Nous possédons"). The ingenue florist turned Princess was equipped with two numbers, her mother with one, and the piece also included a goodly amount of bristling choruses—notably a decidedly pointed one of fawning courtiers—to make up a score which bubbled with burlesque gaiety.

Barbe-bleue thoroughly confirmed the success of *La Belle Hélène* and ran through five solid months up to the summer recess. The week that it closed, the first of what were to be countless international productions throughout the next decade opened, at London's Olympic Theatre (ad H Bellingham) under the management and direction of Horace Wigan. Presented as an English-style burlesque, squashed up into a four-scene jollification of comedy under the title *Bluebeard Re-paired* and subtitled "a worn out story done up a-new" it announced its score as "music composed by Offenbach, selected and arranged by J H Tully." Its only concession to opéra-bouffe was that the text was written in prose dialogue rather than in the, up to then, inevitable rhyming couplets of English burlesque. Irish tenor William Mulready Terrott in a Hibernian version of the title role and Susan Galton as Mopsa (ex- Boulotte) led the company, with two future stars in Miss Everard (Queen Greymare, ie, Clémentine) and Nellie Farren (Robert, ie, Oscar) in supporting roles, through the month and a bit to the end of the season, playing the potted and played-about-with *Bluebeard* as an afterpiece to *The Lady of Lyons.*

Friedrich Strampfer and Vienna's Theater an der Wien followed with a rather less hacked-about *Blaubart*

Plate 22. **Barbe-Bleue.** *A beautiful Broadway Boulotte from the 19th century . . . oh! Who is she?*

(ad Julius Hopp) a few months later, using many of the team that had won such a triumph with *Die schöne Helena* at the same theatre the previous year. Marie Geistinger and Albin Swoboda swapped the roles of Helen and Paris for those of Boulotte and Bluebeard in the same way that Schneider and Dupuis had done in Paris, Karl Blasel went from Menelaos to Bobèche, Carl Adolf Friese from Agamemnon to Oscar and Matthias Rott from Calchas to Popolani. The newly discovered singing voice of actor Jani Szika was put to use as Saphir. The success of the earlier piece was at least partly repeated and, although *Blaubart* did not and never would equal the outstanding record of *Die schöne Helena* in the German language, the show was played in repertoire through the 1870s and was brought back at the Carltheater in 1887 with Geistinger starred alongside Alexander Guttmann (Bobèche), Adolf Brackl (Barbe-bleue) and Antonie Link (Hermia), again in 1897–98 and yet again in 1902. Hopp's German version was readapted by Emil Pohl for Berlin's Friedrich-

Wilhelmstädtisches Theater, which welcomed Josefine Gallmeyer as its original Boulotte.

Hungary, although a little slow off the mark, also reserved a fine welcome for *Kékszakállú herceg* when Endre Latabár's version was produced first at Kassa and then in Budapest—where the German version had already been seen—with Ilka Medgyaszay and Halmi (another pair who had introduced *La Belle Hélène* locally) starred. In 1873 a major new production was mounted in Budapest, with Lujza Blaha (Boulotte) and János Kápolnai (Barbe-bleue) in the lead roles, and this star pair later played the piece at the Népszínház as it settled comfortably into the Hungarian Offenbach repertoire.

New York got its first *Barbe-bleue* in French, with Mlle Irma appearing as Boulotte to the *Barbe-bleue* of Aujac, and Marie Aimée made Boulotte a regular character in her repertoire during her years of touring America with French opéra-bouffe, but several English-language productions of the piece also put in an appearance soon after, albeit, as far as New York was concerned, in decidedly hacked-about shape. The Worrell sisters appeared on Broadway in December of 1868 in a version which was "adapted by J P Ware, with all the original music arranged by Mr Tissington." Sophie played Barbe-bleue, Jennie sang Boulotte and Irene was Hermia. However, if this production sported a female hero, there was another which sported a male Boulotte. It was the Kelly and Leon Minstrels' lavishly staged five-scene *Barber Blu* (Brooklyn 24 August, Kelly and Leon's Theater 31 August 1868) with "the only Leon" in his usual post as prima donna as Bullyette ("a capital imitation of Irma, and not a burlesque") to the Barber of Edwin Kelly, and with "the favourite airs of the opera carefully retained." It was not so much burlesqued, but potted. The San Francisco Minstrels followed up with a *Barber Brown, or the Pacific Sloper.* The West Coast did rather better by Offenbach and his librettists. On October 12 *Barbe-bleue* was brought to the boards of the San Francisco Alhambra in the hands of a family rather better equipped to play it than the Worrells: for the Howson family of Australia boasted both girls—sisters Emma as Boulotte and Clelia as Hermia—and men—brother John was Popolani—amongst their numbers and their version, with the splendid Swedish operatic tenor Henry Nordblom starred as Barbe-bleue and Jeff de Angelis as Bobèche came much nearer to the ideal of opéra-bouffe than its very low-burlesquey fellows on the East Coast.

In 1875 Alexander Henderson and Samuel Colville brought another botched *Barbe-bleue* to Broadway (Wallacks' Theater 19 August) when they starred Britain's Julia Mathews in what they called *Boulotte* alongside Alfred Brennir, G H McDermott and Haydn Corri. This version not only chopped around Offenbach's score, it even popped some bits of Strauss's *Indigo und die vierzig Räuber* into the proceedings. It was played for a fortnight on Broadway in repertoire with the more popular *Grande-Duchesse* and *Giroflé-Girofla.*

Australia did not get its first *Barbe-bleue* until 1872, when the Lyster & Cagli company introduced the piece in their Melbourne and Sydney seasons. Alice May (Boulotte), Richard Stewart (Bobèche), Armes Beaumont (Barbe-bleue) and T H Rainford (Popolani) featured amongst the cast of a production which was followed, in years to come, by many another as *Barbe-bleue* became, as it had elsewhere, a standard part of the revivable opéra-bouffe repertoire in Australia.

In Paris, *Barbe-bleue* was brought back in 1872 with Dupuis and Schneider—who had in between times given London their original characterizations in a visit to the St James's Theatre (28 June 1869)—repeating their now famous roles, whilst an 1888 revival gave Jeanne Granier the opportunity to play Boulotte on the same stage and opposite the same leading man as her illustrious predecessor; she was followed in 1904 by Anna Tariol-Baugé. The most recent Parisian production, in 1971 at the Théâtre de Paris, was of a foolishly revised version souped up to create a starring role where none was before, but *Barbe-bleue* has subsequently been seen in its original form outside Paris.

Apart from its home city, it was London, which actually gave the piece more hearings than either *Orphée aux enfers* or *La Belle Hélène,* which proved the most interested in *Barbe-bleue* in the decades after its production. After Schneider and Dupuis's visit in 1869, a new and more faithful English version of the show (ad Charles Lamb Kenney) was mounted at the Standard Theatre with Emily Soldene as a bosomy, mezzo-soprano Boulotte and Wilford Morgan as Bluebeard, and that version was taken up by John Hollingshead at the Gaiety, the following year, with Julia Mathews and E D Beverley starred. Miss Soldene, who had deputized for composer Hervé in the title role of *Chilpéric* in his show's London production, later renounced the role of Boulotte and gave Australian audiences her interpretation of the very masculine part of Barbe-bleue. The show was given again at the Alhambra in 1871, and in the 1880s the popular couple Florence St John and Claude Marius (Bobèche) found in the piece a vehicle for their highly effective talents. They appeared in *Bluebeard,* with Henry Bracy as their tenor, at both the Avenue Theatre (16 June 1883) and the Comedy (16 January 1885) before the piece was put into suspended animation for three-quarters of a century. It was brought out in 1966 when the Sadler's Wells Opera Company continued its memorable series of Geoffrey Dunn translations, in a staging by Gillian Lynne, which remained several seasons in the repertoire.

Germany has similarly shown an enduring fancy for *Blaubart* (aka *Ritter Blaubart*). A 1929 Metropoltheater production by Fritz Friedmann-Friedrich with Leo Slezak starred as the randy Ritter alongside the Boulotte of Kathe Dörsch was taken to Vienna in 1930 with Slezak, Grete Finkler, Fritz Imhoff (Bobèche) and Hanns Wilhelm (Popolani) featured, and in 1963 the Berlin Komische Oper mounted a highly successful production of a revised version (*Ritter Blaubart*), with Anny Schlemm as a bubbling Boulotte. This has led to regular further German stagings of an opéra-bouffe which, in spite of all its extravagant charms, remains today firmly in the shadow of *Orphée aux enfers* and *La Belle Hélène*.

The originally gory tale of an oriental wife-killer whose last spouse survives and proves his undoing is found in many cultures, but it has come down to the modern Western world through Perrault's *Histoires et contes du temps passé* (otherwise *Contes de ma mére l'Oye*) as originally translated into English by Robert Samber. It has found its way on to the stage in many different versions, from spectacular melodrama to musical extravaganza, of which Offenbach's has survived as by far the most memorable, but of which several others found success in their time. André Grétry's 1789 "heroic comic-opera" *[Raoul] Barbe-bleue* (lib: Jean-Michel Sedaine), played in German as *Raoul der Blaubart,* was an early success and it was followed by the first English-language stage musical versions: a 1791 pantomime at Covent Garden written by George Colman, and a 1798 Drury Lane "musical dramatic romance" with music by Michael Kelly. Paris welcomed a 16-scene féerie *Barbe-bleue* by Alphonse Kellér at the Funambules in 1851 (23 August), and a verse piece, *Sept Femmes de Barbe-bleue,* in 1852, whilst another féerie of that same title by Anicet-Bourgeois and Masson was produced, at the Théâtre Beaumarchais, two seasons later (23 April 1854).

Bluebeard remained a favorite British pantomime topic for a century, whilst also coming regularly into the hands of the burlesque makers. Planché provided a *Bluebeard, or Female Curiosity* for Vestris in 1839 (Olympic Theatre 1 January), and later efforts included *Hints to the Curious, or Bluebeard according to Act of Parliament* at the Strand Theatre (27 June 1853); H J Byron's *Bluebeard from a new point of hue* (Adelphi Theatre 26 December 1860); a Crystal Palace piece by H T Arnold (29 March 1869) with Lionel Brough featured; *The Latest Edition of Bluebeard* (Alexandra Theatre, May 1870); H B Farnie's celebrated burlesque *Bluebeard, or The Mormon, the Maiden and The Little Militaire,* written for Lydia Thompson and played by her throughout Britain (Globe Theatre 1 March 1875) and America; a *Bluebeard Retrimmed* (Royal Park Theatre, May 1877); F C Burnand's Gaiety piece *Bluebeard, or the hazard of the dye* (12 March 1883); and J Pitt Hardacre's touring *Bluebeard-up-to-Date* (1893). In America, where the subject was long a favorite as a mid-19th-century circus production, Fred Eustis, Richard Maddern and Clay M Greene brought out a *Bluebeard Jr* in Chicago (11 June 1889) and at New York's Niblo's Garden in the following year (13 January 1890).

The 20th century has seen the man with the overly replaceable wives go rather out of fashion both as a tale and as a stage character, but in 1918 Béla Bártok turned out the most famous of operatic *Bluebeards* with *A kékszakállú herceg vára* (*Bluebeard's Castle*), a one-act opera composed to a text by Béla Balázs and produced at Budapest's Opera House (24 May) prior to productions around the world. Another, full-length, operatic *Bluebeard* was composed by Emil Reznicek (*Ritter Blaubart* Darmstadt 29 January 1920).

UK: Olympic Theatre *Bluebeard Re-paired* 2 June 1866; Austria: Theater an der Wien *Blaubart* 21 September 1866; Germany: Friedrich-Wilhelmstädtisches Theater *Blaubart* 13 March 1867; Hungary: Kassa *A kékszakállú herceg* 7 November 1868, Budai Színkör *Blaubart* 15 June 1869, *Kékszakállú herceg* 29 May 1870; USA: Niblo's Garden (Fr) 13 July 1868, National Theater, Washington (Eng) *Bluebeard* 9 December 1868, Worrell Sisters Theater *Bluebeard* 19 December 1868; Australia: Princess Theatre, Melbourne 22 April 1872

Recordings: complete (Bourg), selection (UORC)

Video: Classic Video Dreamlife (Berlin Komische Oper) 1973

EL BARBERILLO DE LAVAPIÉS Zarzuela in 3 acts by Luis Mariano de Larra. Music by Francisco Asenjo Barbieri. Teatro de la Zarzuela, Madrid, 18 December 1874.

One of the most successful zarzuelas of its period, *El barberillo de Lavapiés* had for its central character Lamparilla (Miguel Tormo), the little Madrid barber of the title, a medical and general factotum related to the more famous Figaro or the Benjamin Partridge of German's *Tom Jones.* This little barber, however, gets mixed up in meaningful political doings: a plot against the Italianizing Prime Minister in favor of the more Spanish Count de Floridablanca. The Infanta herself supports the latter, and it is her lady-in-waiting, the Marquesita Estrella (Cecilia Delgado), who has to cross Madrid, through many a danger, as part of the plotting. Lamparilla's girlfriend, Paloma (Dolores Franco de Salas), volunteers him as escort. Jealousies, plots, disguises and another two acts of music intervene before the coup d'état is successfully accomplished.

El barberillo de Lavapiés was one of the few zarzuelas to be played outside Spanish-language territories and in any language but its own. It was seen in Germany under the title of *Lamparilla,* and heard in broadcast (ad Geoffrey Dunn, BBC, 1954) and played by amateurs in

Britain, and it remains a popular item in the repertoire in Spain up to the present day (Teatro de la Zarzuela, April 1998).

Recordings: complete (EMI, Alhambra/Columbia, Montilla/Zafiro, Auvidis Valois)

TV film: Teatro Lirico Español (1968); Video: Teatro Calderon production (Pierson Metrovideo 1996)

BARBIERI, Francisco [de Asís Esteban] Asenjo (b Madrid, 3 August 1823; d Madrid, 17 February 1894).

Barbieri trained at Madrid Conservatoire from the age of 14 and worked at first as an orchestral and band clarinetist, an incidental pianist, occasionally as a vocalist, and in a variety of other musical and musical-theatre jobs before he succeeded in getting his first one-act zarzuela *Gloria y peluca* produced (9 March 1850), at the age of 26. He had a considerable success with his first full-length piece, *Jugar con fuego* (6 October 1851), the following year, and thereafter turned out a steady stream of theatre pieces, establishing himself as one of the favorite zarzuela composers of his time. His most popular pieces included the 1854 *Los diamantes de la corona* (Teatro Circo 15 September), *Pan y toros* (Teatro de la Zarzuela 22 December 1864), *Robinson Crusoe* (Teatro Circo 18 March 1870), *El hombre es débil* (14 October 1871), *Chorizos y Polacos* (Teatro Principe Alfonso 24 May 1876) and one of the most memorable of all Spanish musical theatre pieces, *El barberillo de Lavapiés* (Teatro de la Zarzuela 18 December 1874).

His other titles include *Tramoya* (1850), *Escenas de Chamberí* (1850), *Por seguir a una mujer* (1851, w others), *La hechicera* (1852), *Gracias a dios que está puesta la mesa* (1852), *El Marqués de Caravaca* (1853), *Galanteos en Venecia* (1853), *Don Simplicio Bobadilla* (1853, w J Inzenga, R Hernando), *La cisterna encantada* (1853), *La cotorra* (1853), *Aventura de un cantande* (1854), *El sargento Federico* (1855), *Mis dos mujeres* (1855), *Los dos ciegos* (1855), *El vizconde* (1855), *El Diablo en el poder* (1856), *Entre mi mujer y el negro* (1859), *Compromisos del nover* (1859), *Un tesoro escondido* (1861), *El secreto de una dama* (1862), *De tejas arriba* (1866), *El pavo de navidad* (1866), *El pan de la boda* (1868), *Los holgazanes* (1871), *El tributo de las cien doncellas* (1872), *Sueños de oro* (1872), *El proceso del can-can* (1873), *Los Comediantes de antaño* (1874), *Domador de pieras* (1874), *Artistas para la habana* (1877), *El Diablo cojuelo* (1878), *La guerra santa* (1879), *De getafe al paraíso* (1883), *El señor Luis el tumbón* (1891), *¡Hoy sale, hoy!* (1884 w Chueca), *Un dia de reinado, Gibraltar* and *El testamento azul.*

Outside his composing work, Barbieri also promoted concerts, did considerable work as a musical historian and, in later life, became a teacher at his local conservatory.

Barbieri's music was heard on Broadway in 1881 when Niblo's Garden mounted a spectacular piece called *Castles in Spain* (which seems as if it may have been a version of *El diablo cojuelo*) in which most of the score was of his composition.

Biographies: Martinez Olmedilla, A: *El maestro Barbieri y su tiempo* (Imp. Saez, Madrid, 1950), Casares, E: *Francisco Asenjo Barbieri* (ICCMU, Madrid, 1994)

BARDE, André [BOURDONNEAU, André] (b Meudon, 17 July 1874; d Paris, 18 October 1945).

The determinedly bohemian Barde, described by Yvain as "un des derniers poètes decadents de Montmartre," made his name first as a writer and performer of "verses of his own composition [giving] a pessimist's view of the silly young men and women of our day, lashing the vain and stupid follies of this end of century," and later, in the years before the war, as an author of a series of witty small-house revues, most particularly, in collaboration with Michel Carré, for such venues as La Cigale (*Pourquoi pas?, Midi a 14 heures,* etc), the Théâtre des Capucines (*La Double Revue, Paris-Sport,* etc), the Théâtre Marigny (*Le Tour de Babel*) or the Scala. It was at the Capucines that he first entered the area of musical comedy when he provided the sexy, word-comical texts for Charles Cuvillier's highly successful *Son p'tit frère* and *Afgar, ou Les Loisirs andalous.* Although Barde continued to devote most of his theatre time to revue material, he and Cuvillier turned out not only further small-scale pieces but also a pair of successful larger opérettes: *La Reine s'amuse,* which made its way from Marseille to Paris before going on, like their earliest collaborations, to overseas productions, and *Flora Bella,* initially staged in a German version in Munich and later played both in a botched version on Broadway and in the original French in Lyon.

Whilst Cuvillier wandered the world along with his musical plays, Barde retrenched into revue. He had some success with a *Carmen* burlesque, *Carminetta,* which went from Paris to a production by C B Cochran in London, but although he collaborated on another pair of pieces with Cuvillier, amongst which was yet another ancient-world burlesque in the medieval *Nonnette,* the brightest successes of his days as a witty young fellow seemed as if they were now a year or two behind him.

However, nearly 20 years after his first sparkling introduction to the musical theatre with *Son p'tit frère,* Barde's librettic career suddenly took off. Producer Gustave Quinson, looking for another Albert Willemetz to turn out texts for the new style of Jazz Age musical comedy with which he was profitably filling his theatres, put Barde together with composer Maurice Yvain, recently triumphant with his first musical comedy, *Ta bouche.* The result was a second triumph, *Pas sur la bouche,* and Barde, whom the new style of musical comedy (which, give or take a dash of period burlesque, was pretty much an up-to-date version of his old style) fitted perfectly, was launched on a series of successes which lasted as long as the fashion for the combination of witty, slightly spicy texts and lively, dancing music held sway in the French theatre. His collaboration with Yvain continued through a decade with *Bouche à bouche, Un bon garçon, Elle est à vous, Kadubec, Pépé, Encore cinquante centimes* (w Christiné), *Oh! Papa . . .* and *Vacances* in an almost unbroken run of success, as Barde simultaneously turned out hit shows with others of the top bracket of current French composers: *Comte Obligado* with Raoul Moretti, *Arthur* with Henri Christiné and—in what might have been a kind of a theatrical thank-you to an Hungarian stage which gobbled up his works gratefully—a remake of Lajos Lajtai's Hungarian hit *Őfelsége frakkja* (1931) as *Katinka.*

He occasionally ventured into the city's more commodious theatres, but by and large his work prospered in the kind and size of houses where the words could be heard, and where they actually mattered.

Along with Willemetz, Barde led the French musical theatre through one of its brightest periods, carrying on the tradition for superior comic libretti which had illuminated the French musical theatre in the days of Nuitter, Tréfeu, Vanloo, Leterrier, Chivot, Duru, Meilhac and Halévy and their most talented contemporaries. The sexual emphasis of many of his libretti, however, meant that few of his works were exported undamaged. Nevertheless, not only Hungary, but also London, New York, Munich and Melbourne got a glimpse of the author's likeably louche humor and sophisticated style in close (Hungary) or distant (anything in the English language) adaptations of his works.

1907 **Son p'tit frère** (Charles Cuvillier) Théâtre des Capucines 10 April

1909 **Afgar, ou Les Loisirs andalous** (Cuvillier/w Michel Carré fils) Théâtre des Capucines 2 April

1910 **Les Muscadines** (Cuvillier) Théâtre des Capucines 28 April

1911 **L'Astronome et l'étoile** (Cuvillier/w Bertrand de St-Rémy) Buenos Aires July

1912 **Sappho** (Cuvillier/w Carré) Théâtre des Capucines 26 February

1912 **La Reine s'amuse** (Cuvillier) Théâtre des Variétés, Marseille 31 December

1913 **Flora Bella** (Cuvillier/ad Felix Dörmann) Theater am Gärtnerplatz, Munich 5 September

1917 **Carminetta** (Émile Lassailly/w Charles Charpentier) Théâtre Michel 16 March

1917 **La République des vierges** revised *Sappho* Théâtre Édouard VII 6 September

1917 **Judith Courtisane** (Cuvillier/w Régis Gignoux) Théâtre Michel 22 December

1918 **La Reine joyeuse** revised *La Reine s'amuse* Théâtre Apollo 1 November

1922 **Nonnette** (Cuvillier) Théâtre des Capucines 28 March

1923 **Benjamin** (René Mercier/w Benjamin Rabier, Paul Murio) Ba-ta-clan 11 April

1924 **Bob et moi** (Cuvillier/w Lucien Meyrargue) Théâtre Michel 6 April

1925 **Pas sur la bouche** (Maurice Yvain) Théâtre des Nouveautés 17 February

1925 **Bouche à bouche** (Yvain) Théâtre de l'Apollo 8 October

1926 **Un bon garçon** (Yvain) Théâtre des Nouveautés 13 November

1927 **Comte Obligado** (Raoul Moretti) Théâtre des Nouveautés 16 December

1928 **Déshabillez-vous** (Rene Mercier) Théâtre des Bouffes-Parisiens 22 December

1929 **Elle est à vous** (Yvain) Théâtre des Nouveautés 22 January

1929 **Arthur** (Christine) Théâtre Daunou 4 September

1929 **Kadubec** (Yvain) Théâtre des Nouveautés 12 December

1930 **Rosy** (Moretti) Théâtre des Folies-Wagram 1 March

1930 **Pépé** (Yvain) Théâtre Daunou 25 October

1930 **La Femme de minuit** (Moretti) Théâtre des Nouveautés 11 December

1930 **Laïs, ou la courtisane amoureuse** revised *Son p'tit frère* (tour)

1931 **Encore cinquante centimes** (Christiné, Yvain) Théâtre des Nouveautés 17 September

1931 **La Scarabée bleu** (Jean Nouguès) Théâtre de la Gaîté-Lyrique 30 October

1933 **Le Garçon de chez Prunier** (Joseph Szulc/w Carré) Théâtre des Capucines 19 January

1933 **Oh! Papa . . .** (Yvain) Théâtre des Nouveautés 2 February

1933 **Katinka** (*Őfelsége frakkja*) French version w Pierre Varenne, Robert Delamare (Théâtre de l'Empire)

1933 **La Madone du promenoir** (Christiné) Concert-Mayol 3 November

1934 **Les Soeurs Hortensia** (Moretti) Théâtre des Nouveautés 11 April

1934 **Vacances** (Yvain/w Henri Duvernois) Théâtre des Nouveautés 20 December

1935 **Tonton** (Lajos Lajtai) Théâtre des Nouveautés 19 March

1935 **L'Auberge du Chat Coiffé** (Szulc/Alfred Lavauzelle) Théâtre Pigalle 18 December

1935 **Le Train de 8h47** (Cuvillier/Georges Courteline ad w Léo Marchis) Palais-Royal 22 December

1936 **La Poule** (Christiné, Lajtai/w Duvernois) Théâtre des Nouveautés 9 January

BARKER, Richard [WARTER, Henry de Grey] (b Bath, ?1834; d London, 1 August 1903).

Grandson and son of Pontesbury, Shropshire, landed proprietors (his father was christened, less aristocratically, plain ''Henry Diggory Warter'') and for a number of years an amateur actor and director with the West of England Histrionic Club, Barker made his way into the professional theatre after his marriage in 1865 to Maria Cruise, a popular and long-serving member of J B Chute's famous Bath and Bristol stock company. Over the next three years, the pair played at Bath, Bristol, Newcastle, Torquay, Exeter and other such venues, he as ''first low comedian and burlesque'' and she as ''singing chambermaids and burlesque boys.'' At the same time, he continued a parallel career as a now professional stage director, a career which received a great boost when, during their time at Exeter, he mounted (and played Nat Gosling in) the premier of Boucicault's soon to be highly successful *The Flying Scud* (April 1868). Later the same year, the couple were engaged by John Hollingshead for his initial Gaiety Theatre company, and Barker appeared on that theatre's opening night in the low comedy role of Bertram in W S Gilbert's burlesque *Robert the Devil.* In the summer of 1869 he also appeared alongside Maria at the opening of the Charing Cross Theatre in Gilbert's subsequent burlesque *The Pretty Druidess* (Oroveso).

In 1872 he appeared at the Opera Comique as The Sentry in *L'Oeil crevé* and as one of Offenbach's *The Blind Beggars* as well as directing the two pieces, and he subsequently took a tiny role in the same theatre's *The Bohemians* (*Le roman comique,* 1873). The following year his name appeared on the bill of the Criterion Theatre as having directed Gilbert's one-act piece *Topsyturveydom* and as an actor in *Normandy Pippins* (The Notary), and also on that of the Opera Comique as the stager of Amy Sheridan's ''scandalously unclothed'' *Ixion Rewheeled.*

Around this period in time, Maria seems to have drifted out of the theatre and of Barker's life, but the striving director found an even more useful connection . . . the W S Gilbert one. He was stage director at the Opera Comique when Richard D'Oyly Carte and his Comedy Opera Company produced the earliest Gilbert and Sullivan operas at that house and he subsequently became a combination of company manager, stage director and confidante to Carte in the early days of the producer's London career. He played a large part in getting Carte his freedom from his backers after the success of *HMS Pinafore.* He was even billed as lessee of the Opera Comique on the producer's behalf during the battle between Carte and the Comedy Opera Company. Over the years, thereafter, he worked both as a company manager and as a stage director for Carte, and he even turned briefly and unsuccessfully to management himself when he joined Hollingshead at the head of the Opera Comique following Carte's departure to the Savoy.

In the 1880s and 1890s he had a busy career as a director, at first in Britain and later, increasingly, in America. He mounted John Hollingshead's revival of *Princess Toto* (1881) and his successful production of the comic opera *Dick,* Kate Santley's *The Merry Duchess* in both Britain and America, Ivan Caryll's maiden *The Lily of Leoville* (1886), the spectacular *The Lady of the Locket,* and the original London production of *Ruddigore.* Some eyebrows were raised triangular when he was paid a vast £300 to stage the burlesque *Joan of Arc* in 1891—it was an unprecedented amount to pay a man for the utilitarian task of arranging the actors on the stage.

Barker's American assignments included many reproductions of Continental (*Nadjy, The Oolah, The Merry Monarch, La Cigale, The Lion Tamer,* Lillian Russell's *Giroflé-Girofla* revival, *The Voyage of Suxette, The Little Trooper, The Queen of Brilliants,* etc) and British comic operas (*The Yeomen of the Guard, Erminie* revival, *The Chieftain,* etc) and musical comedy (*Gentleman Joe*), as well as local pieces from both ends of the musical theatre scale—comic operas such as *The Wedding Day, The Jolly Musketeer, The Mandarin, Fleur de lis, The Robbers of the Rhine, The Devil's Deputy, The Little Corporal, The Daughter of the Revolution,* the Philadelphia *Princess Bonnie, Half a King,* musical comedy as in Annie Pixley's *Polly Middles,* middlebrow extravaganzas like the Chicago *Aladdin Jr* and *Sinbad,* Philadelphia's *King Cole II* or the Broadway *The Twentieth Century Girl* and the lower brow burlesques of the *Pippins* brand and farce-comedies such as *A Stag Party* and *The Caliph.*

At the turn of the century he returned to Britain, notably to the Savoy Theatre, where, with Gilbert no longer in charge of directing his own works, he staged the post-Gilbertian *The Lucky Star, The Rose of Persia, The Emerald Isle* and *The Willow Pattern.* He is also sometimes given credit for the direction of the hugely successful Daly's Theatre musical *San Toy,* elsewhere credited to Pat Malone.

Barker, along with such colleagues as Charles Harris and Gilbert himself, was instrumental in raising the function of the stage director a little above that of a man who merely grouped the largely static chorus of singers, platooned the chorus dancers around the stage and moved principal players from left to right when they agreed to move. The latitude given to stars, particularly comedians, and the amount of gagging and ad-libbing permitted and even encouraged in most comic operas and musical comedies, still meant at this stage that even the physical staging of a show was very far from controlled by a director, but a balance between organization and untrammelled performance was—thanks to Barker, Harris and their kind—now nearer to being established than at any time before.

Barker's first wife, **Maria CRUISE** (b Dublin, 1831; d Bristol, 28 August 1887), a petite niece of the composer Balfe and related to many a well-known musician and performer of the era, spent some 10 years performing with the Bristol and Bath company. She appeared in *The Pretty Druidess* (1869, Flaxius) in London, and toured as Wanda in Britain's earliest production of *La Grande-Duchesse* in 1870 before retiring from the stage.

BARNA, Izsó (b Budapest, 4 September 1859; d Budapest, 1940).

At first a conductor at Szeged and later at other provincial Hungarian houses, Barna subsequently became musical director at Budapest's Városligeti Színház. He simultaneously led a busy career as a theatre composer, providing the incidental music for many plays, both Hungarian and adapted (Kotzebue's *Doktor Pipitér és szolgája Retipip,* Rónaszéki's *A Betörők,* Kövessy's *A Vigécek* and *A kaméliás férfi,* Mathias Feld's *Az északsarki utazók* and *A demokratos,* Georges Ohnet's Sarah grófnő, Soma Guthi's *A mádi zsidó, Az éjjeli ügyész* and *A mozgópostásné,* Paul Ferrier's *Az anyós,* the Jules Dornay/Xavier Montépin *Kintornás leány,* Jenő Faragó's *A lőcsei fehér asszony,* the Gavault/Ordonneau *Kis városi botrány,* Ferenc Herczeg's *Avató játék,* etc), and turning out scores for a long line of Possen, Singspiele and Operetten, as well as one short opera (*A szerzetes*), a number of spectaculars and revues. None of these works succeeded in winning productions beyond Hungary, but several, notably his version of the *Casanova* story, and Guthi's musical play *Smolen Toni* proved popular on home ground. His 1913 operett *A csodavászon* was notable for its use of the new Edison kinetophone.

1885 **A szoknyás hadnagy** (*A Franciák Oroszorsáagban*) (Géza Kyss) Gyor; Budai Színkör 8 June 1888

1886 **Oh! Oszkár** (Béla Ujvári) Sopron November

1890 **Florinda kisasszony** (Albert Kövessy) Budai Színkör 2 August

1893 **A paradicsom** (Géza Gárdonyi) 1 act Szeged 7 February; Budai Színkör 18 September 1894

1894 **Huszárosan** (Gusztáv Rónaszéki) Budai Színkör 31 August

1895 **A Méltóságos csizmadia** (Rónaszéki) Budai Színkör 22 June

1896 **Vasárnap délutan** (Rónaszéki) Budai Színkör 12 April

1899 **Midász Király** (Ujvári) Népszínház 20 January

1899 **Singer-gyár** (Kövessy) Budai Színkör 21 July

1900 **Asszonyháború** (Károly Gerő) Népszínház 21 November

1901 **Mézeshetek** (Jenő Faragó/Ede Sas) Népszínház 13 April

1901 **Budapest szépe** (Faragó, Géza Márkus) Budai Színkör 20 July

1902 **Egy görbe nap** (Bors Csicseri, Adolf Ágai, Tihamér Almási Balogh) Népszínház 8 February

1902 **Kin-Fu, vagy egy kínai ember Kalandjai** (Faragó, Márkus) Népszínház 31 May

1902 **Casanova** (Faragó) Népszínház 11 October

1903 **Senki** (Antal Nyárai, Miklos Balla) Népszínház 14 November

1904 **Rézi** (Alexander Engel, Julius Horst ad Árpád Abonyi, Faragó) Népszínház 16 September

1904 **A löcsei fehér asszony** (Faragó) Népszínház 27 October

1905 **Smolen Toni** (Soma Guthi) Fővárosi Nyári Színház 21 July

1906 **Vigyázz a csókra** Télikert 31 August

1907 **Berger Zsiga** (Ferenc Révész) Városligeti Nyári Színkör 29 May

1907 **A századik menasszony** (Géza Vágó, Adolf Mérei) Budai Színkör 7 June

1907 **A bús özvegy** (Faragó, Feld) Városligeti Nyári Színház 18 June

1910 **Világ vége** Városligeti Népszínház 16 April

1912 **A papa csataba megy** (Faragó) Ferenczy kabaré 30 October

1913 **A csodavászon** (Faragó) Népopera 12 December

1915 **Kávéházi Konrád** (Faragó/Soma Guthi) Budai Színkör 30 July

1916 **Négy a kislány** (Géza Vágó, Emil Tábori) Budai Színkör 11 August

1917 **Lavotta szereleme** (arr/Vágó) Városligeti Nyári Színház 13 April

1917 **Márványmenyasszony olajban** Kristálypalota 1 May

1918 **Jogot a nőknek** (Kövessy) Budapesti Színház 27 July

1923 **Mintha álom volna . . .** (Mihály Erdélyi, Ernő Kulinyi) Budai Színkör 1 September

1926 **Blahané** (Ede Sas) Budapesti Színház 25 June

BARNABEE, Henry Clay (b Portsmouth, NH, 4 November 1833; d Jamaica Plains, Mass, 16 December 1917). The original and only principal comedian of the famous Boston Ideal Comic Opera Company.

At first a "lyceum platform entertainer" ("The Cork Leg," "Watkins' Evening Party," "Darius Green and his Flying Machine") and the proprietor of a Boston-based concert party, The Barnabees, Henry Barnabee appeared as Sir Joseph Porter in the Bostonians' first and acclaimed production of *HMS Pinafore* and, remaining with the company throughout its existence, made his career playing equivalent roles in a whole range of comic operas, both imported and original, in a comic style which was rather better-mannered than that of some of his contemporaries, without being in any way less effective.

His most important creation was the all-consuming central comedy role of the Sheriff of Nottingham in De Koven's *Robin Hood* (1891), a role which became the keystone of a career which also included new roles in such pieces as De Koven's *Don Quixote* (1889, Quixote), *The Knickerbockers* (1893, Governor William the Testy),

Prince Ananias (1894, La Fontaine), *The Maid of Plymouth* (1894, The Elder), *The Ogalallas* (1894, General Theophilus Andover), *A Wartime Wedding* aka *In Mexico* (1896, Ezra Stebbins), *The Serenade* (1896, Duke of Santa Cruz), *Rip van Winkle* (1897, Rip), *Ulysses* (1898, Oudeis), *The Smugglers of Bayadez* (1898, Don Brandieu), *The Viceroy* (1900, Viceroy of Sicily), *Maid Marian* (1901, Sheriff of Nottingham) and *The Queen of Laughter* (1903, King Lachryma).

He was also seen in the wide repertoire of the Bostonians' company as the Mayor of Perth (*Rob Roy*), Major General Stanley (*Pirates of Penzance*), Lorenzo (*La Mascotte*), Abbé Bridaine (*Les Mousquetaires au couvent*), Bailie (*Les Cloches de Corneville*), John Wellington Wells (*The Sorcerer*), Lambertuccio (*Boccaccio*), Duc des Ifs (*Les Noces d'Olivette*), Bunthorne (*Patience*), Palsambleu (*François les bas-bleus*), Lord Allcash (*Fra Diavolo*), Izzet Pascha (*Fatinitza*), Lurcher (*Dorothy*), Chrysos (*Pygmalion and Galatea*), Don Japhet (*Giralda*), Bobèche (*Barbe-bleue*), Marcassou (*Les Braconniers*) and others such, as well as in a number of other comic lightish-operatic roles.

Barnabee, ultimately the leading light in and part owner of the company, was over 70 when the Bostonians folded in 1905 and, although he appeared at South Framingham later that year as the Hon Jefferson Jackson Clover in the comic opera *Cloverdell,* he then put a virtual end to his career.

In 1880 the house where Barnabee was born, in Portsmouth, was pulled down, and on its site was erected the city's first theatre, the Franklin Theatre. On 14 October Barnabee presided over its opening.

Autobiography: *My Wanderings* (Chapple Publishing Co, Boston, 1913)

BARNETT, Alice (b London, 17 May 1846; d London, 14 April 1901).

A granddaughter of Henry Kemble, a grandniece of Sarah Siddons, and related by blood or marriage to many well-known theatrical personalities, including Sir Charles Santley, the exceedingly tall and imposing Alice Barnett trained with Natalia Macfarren—wife of the composer—and appeared from 1871 on the concert stage. She made her first foray into the musical theatre when D'Oyly Carte cast her as Little Buttercup in the 1879 tour of *HMS Pinafore,* and she made her mark thereafter as a heavy lady with Carte's companies, appearing as Little Buttercup in New York and Ruth (1879, *Pirates of Penzance*) in London, before creating the roles of Lady Jane in *Patience* (1881, "Silvered is the Raven Hair") and, most famously, the towering Fairy Queen in *Iolanthe* (1882), introducing "O Foolish Fay" and powering out her operatic contralto rage at being "bearded by these puny mortals" in the first-act finale.

In a career interrupted by illness, which (helped by the fact that Gilbert wrote no role for her in *Princess Ida*) led her to give up her position at the Savoy Theatre in favor of Rosina Brandram, she appeared at London's Empire Theatre in *Pocahontas* (1884, Widow Thompson), spent a convalescent period with Teddy Solomon and Lillian Russell in America (Buttercup, Lady McCassar in *Polly,* Arabella in *Billee Taylor*) and played for some three years with J C Williamson's Royal Comic Opera Company in Australia, where she was seen in the principal contralto roles of the British comic opera repertoire and also appeared as Martha in the company's production of *Faust.*

From 1889 she appeared in Britain again, playing not only in comic opera—though she returned twice to Carte to play the Duchess of Plaza Toro (*The Gondoliers*) and created the roles of Mistress Shelton in Cellier's *Doris* and of Dame Hecla Courtlandt in *His Excellency*—but also in opera (Ugly Sister in Rossini's *Cinderella* with the Burns-Crotty company), in burlesque (Martha in *Faust Up-to-Date,* Micaëla in *Carmen Up-to-Data*) and in musical comedy. She toured in *In Town* (1893, Duchess of Duffshire) and several times in *The Telephone Girl* (1897, Miss Berry McNab), briefly succeeded Lillie Belmore (one of her relations by marriage) as Ada Smith in *The Shop Girl* at the Gaiety Theatre, appeared grotesquely opposite the very small Little Tich in *Billy* (1898, Becky Blissett) and toured as Melanopis in *A Greek Slave* (1899). She also visited America on two further occasions, first with *His Excellency* (1895) and finally being, as usual, a very tall, contralto heavy lady in *The Mandarin* (1896, Sing Lo).

BARNUM Musical in 2 acts by Mark Bramble. Lyrics by Michael Stewart. Music by Cy Coleman. St James Theater, New York, 30 April 1980.

A biomusical with a bit of a difference, this romanticized version of some events in the life of showman Phineas Taylor Barnum was told by a handful of principal performers and a relatively small team of singing-dancing-circus-feat-performing actors in a part-stylized, part-naturalistic production which gave the impression of playing out its tale in a circus ring.

P T Barnum (Jim Dale) has a great belief in the version of the old adage that you can fool almost all the people almost all the time. Therefore he is happier trying to make a career in show business than in the more conventional kind of job his schoolmistress wife, Chairy (Glenn Close), would have him take. Barnum moves from promoting freak shows to promoting better freak shows and, in spite of setbacks, rises up the success ladder. When he moves into classier areas and brings the soprano Jenny Lind (Marianne Tatum) to America, he finds himself caught up in an affair. But he breaks it off, returns repentant to Chairy and attempts to give up showmanship and lead a regular life. It proves impossible. When he is gypped of the political ambitions his wife has bred in him, and then widowed, he goes back into the show world, and Barnum and Bailey's circus is born.

The score for the show was highlighted by some of the most rousing march music to come out of the musical theatre in many years as the company demanded that everyone "Come Follow the Band" and "Join the Circus," alongside a series of songs for the central character which ranged from a pattering list of attractions in his Museum Song to a frenetic claim to be "The Prince of Humbug" and a gentler duet with his wife on "The Colors of My Life." Amongst the supporting characters, Jenny Lind featured a set piece "Love Makes Such Fools of Us All," Tom Thumb (Leonard John Crofoot) danced to a bouncy assertion that "Bigger Isn't Better," and Joice Heth (Terri White), who Barnum would have us believe is the "oldest woman in the world," decided, looking at the modern state of things, "Thank God I'm Old."

The production featured a ringmaster (William Witter) on a tall unicycle, rope-slides, stilt-walking, funambulism, plate-spinning, baton-twirling and all sorts of juggling and acrobatics, all slipped into and around the action of the piece in a whirl of movement which took the story on from one scene to the next. One of the show's most successful numbers featured Miss White and the company describing the life in "Black and White" which suits the hero so ill, in a performance half a minstrel show and half a blues recital.

A fine success on its original production, Barnum racked up 854 performances on Broadway, but it failed to take in the country with Stacy Keach in its central role. In London, however, it more than confirmed its New York success. Harold Fielding's production starred Michael Crawford as Barnum, supported by Deborah Grant (Chairy), Broadway's Witter repeating his one-wheeled Ringmaster, Sarah Payne (Jenny) and Jennie McGusty (Joice/Blues Singer) and, with the original Joe Layton staging enlivened with a few more circus tricks for the well-trained and dazzlingly febrile star, it ran at the London Palladium for 655 performances. After a lay off for star recovery, the piece was mounted again, in Manchester, and returned for a second London run (14 March 1985, 383 performances) with Crawford now teamed with Eileen Battye, Michael Heath, Christina Collier and Sally Lavelle. In the latter stages of the rerun, the Tom Thumb spot was reorganized, with the balletic dance created for Crofoot being replaced by a highly acrobatic tumbling routine, and this production of the show was filmed for the BBC. An amateurish attempt to mount a third London season folded in disaster, but a 1991 British touring production, with Paul Nicholas in its central role and a much reduced star circus content, ventured into the West End for a Christmas season in 1992–93 (Dominion Theatre 17 December), giving the piece a remarkable third West End showing in a decade.

Barnum spread itself to more parts of the globe than almost any other Broadway musical of the 1980s. France's Charles Level and Jacques Collard made the mistake of blowing the piece up and playing it in the Paris Cirque d'Hiver where, with Jean-Luc Moreau starred, it became an undersized circus rather than a multi-skilled small-cast musical (65 performances), but in Germany a former circus man become very popular vocalist, Freddy Quinn, found the role of Barnum an ideal vehicle for his talents (62 performances). Italy's Massimo Ranieri, Spain's Emilio Aragon and Australia's Reg Livermore (without most of the tricks) headed productions in their respective countries, Broadway takeover Mike Burstyn was Barnum in the Netherlands, whilst South Africa boasted the most athletic star of all in the person of British actor and popular vocalist Mark Wynter. Wynter later appeared in perhaps the most perilous version of the show, wire-walking his way to his wife in a *Barnum* played on the *SS Norway,* cruising in the Caribbean. A second French production, mounted at Lyon's Théâtre des Céléstins (30 November 1993) returned to the show's original dimensions, and a revival there the following year proceeded to Paris (Grand Théâtre de la Mutualité 27 October) for a short run.

Phineas Taylor Barnum was earlier portrayed on the musical stage in a number of other musicals, often ephemerally, but more substantially by Thomas A Wise in the Jenny Lind biomusical *The Nightingale* (1927). An earlier musical based on his life was mounted in his former home town of Bridgeport, Connecticut, in 1962 (*Nobody but Barnum* Klein Memorial Theater 30 November Albert Dickson, William Puva, Edward Marfiak, Steve Martin, Harry Ahlers). During his lifetime he was burlesqued as "Mr Blarneyem" in *She's Come! Jenny's Come!,* an Extravaganza in one act, with several startling situations, grand processions, romantic songs and other curiosities, produced by and starring William Burton (Burton's Theater 2 September 1850) on the occasion of Jenny Lind's visit to America.

France: Cirque d'Hiver 21 March 1981; UK: London Palladium 11 June 1981; Australia: Adelaide Festival Theatre 11 January 1982; Germany: Theater des Westens 27 March 1983

Recordings: original cast (CBS), London cast (Chrysalis), French cast (JMB), Australian cast (RCA), Italian cast (RGM), Spanish cast (Bat), Dutch cast (private), etc

BARON, [Louis] [BOUCHENÉ, Louis] (b Alençon, 20 September 1837; d Asnières, 2 March 1920).

The son of an Alençon limonadier, Baron spent his teenage years as a shopboy in Paris, before—at first calling himself "Cléophas"—he made his debut on the stage, in 1857, at the Théâtre de la Tour d'Auvergne. He worked subsequently at Limoges, Troyes, Toulouse and Rouen before making his first important Parisian appearances. He played early on in *Le Petit Poucet* at the Gaîté, and then joined the company at the Théâtre des Variétés, making his debut there in *Le Photographe* in 1866. Although he briefly left the company to run the Théâtre de la Tour d'Auvergne after the Franco-Prussian war, he soon returned and he made the bulk of his very considerable career as a comic actor at the one and the same theatre. Over half a century, he created roles in plays, vaudevilles, revues and opérettes in standard 19th-century buffo-comic fashion ("the success of M Baron is principally based upon his gestures, that are often grotesque, and upon his scared look, as well as his walk, and finally his costumes, the exaggeration of which often goes beyond the range of comedy and borders on burlesque"). He became enormously popular in Paris and was, it is said, in his time the most highly paid comedian in the French theatre. When he joined Eugène Bertrand in the direction of the Variétés in 1886, it was reported that he was paid 6,000 francs a month and a percentage in the profits—nearly 20 percent more than even José Dupuis—and when Debruyère tried to lure him to quit the Variétés for the Gaîté he had to offer him 9,000 francs and 1 percent of the gross.

At the Variétés, Baron created roles in a number of Offenbach pieces, notably as the chief of the Carabiniers in *Les Brigands* (1869)—in which the composer was forced to alter the accompaniment to the famous march of the Carabiniers so that the not very musical comedian could get and hold his notes—and as Baron Grog in *La Grande-Duchesse de Gérolstein* (1867). In spite of his terror of singing, he appeared in *Les Braconniers* (1873, Camagnasse), *La Vie parisienne* (1873 revival, Urbain, 1883 revival Bobinet), the second version of *La Périchole* (1874, Panatellas), *La Boulangère a des écus* (1875, Coquebert), *La Belle Hélène* (1876 revival, Calchas), *Le Docteur Ox* (1877, Niklausse), *La Permission de dix heures* revival (Lanternick), in Hervé's *Le Trône d'Ecosse* (1871, Baron des Trente-Six Tourelles) and Coste's little *Les Charbonniers* (1877, Bidard), as well as starring alongside Anna Judic in the hit series of Théâtre des Variétés vaudeville-opérettes in which she featured in the 1870s and 1880s: *Le Grand Casimir* (Grand Duc), *Niniche* (Le Comte Corniski), *Lili* (Vicomte de Saint-Hypothèse), *La Roussotte* (Dubois-Toupet), *La Femme à Papa* (Baudin-Bridet), and, creating his most memorable role of all, as Célestin, the double-living composer of *Mam'zelle Nitouche.* He later played in such musical pieces as *Mam'selle Gavroche* (1885, Baron de Boistêtu), *La Petit Poucer* (1885, Truffentruffe), *La Noce à Nini* (1887, Montflammard), now as Puck instead of Grog in *La Grand-Duchesse* (1887), *Nos bons jurés* (1887, La-Terreur-de-Grenelle), *La Fille à Cacolet* (1889, Baron Cordesco), *Madame Satan* (1893, Satan), *Le Carnet du diable* (1895, Prince Belphegor) and *Le Carillon* (1896, Margotin), amongst the comedies which were the main part of his activity, before resigning from the Variétés, after a quarter of a century, rather than play the part allotted him in *Le Pompier de service* (1897).

He appeared from time to time away from the Variétés, being seen at the Gaîté, the Folies-Dramatiques, the Palais-Royal and in the grandiose *La Poudre de Perlinpinpin* at the Châtelet, and spent each summer, while the Variétés was closed, touring his own company lucratively round the provinces, but he returned ever to his favorite theatre—*Mademoiselle George* (1900, Marquis de Rochencourt), reprise of *Niniche* (1901), Bobèche (1904)—right up until his retirement.

His son, Louis BOUCHENÉ (b Paris, 27 December 1870), who worked as **BARON fils**, played for many years in both musical and non-musical roles in the Paris theatre, making early appearances in *Fleur de vertu* at the Bouffes-Parisiens (1894), at the Folies-Dramatiques in *La Falote, Nicol-Nick* (1895, Pont Cadet), *La Perle du Cantal* (1895, Moulinet) and *François les bas-bleus* (1895–96) and at the Athenée as Katana in *La Geisha* and Ascanio in *L'Amour mouillée* (1898 revival), in *Le Cabinet Piperlin* and *Madame Putiphar* (1897–98), and later, after a career spent largely in comedy at the Vaudeville, in such modern musical comedies as *Dédé* (1921, Leroydet), *J'adore ça* (1925, Monseigneur Spaghetto) and *Le Temps de s'aimer* (1926).

BARON TRENCK, der Pandur Operette in 3 acts by A M Willner and Robert Bodanzky. Music by Felix Albini. Stadttheater, Leipzig, 15 February 1908.

The libretto to Croatian composer Albini's most successful Operette, *Baron Trenck,* was written around a romanticized characterization of the scapegrace irregular army leader Franz von der Trenck (1711–1749) whose tale had—minus its less agreeable items of brutality, thievery and corruption—been famously metamorphosed into a lively romance by Hungarian author, Mór Jókai, and into pieces for the dramatic stage by many an other (S J Arnold's 1830 drama for London's Surrey Theatre, etc).

Baron Trenck, commander of the royal Pandur troops, and rather too famous for his fire in battle and his amiability with the ladies, rescues the royal lady-in-waiting, Countess Lydia von Schwalbenau, from bandits. He gets little in the way of gratitude. The fascinating Lydia rides off on his horse, bearing with her a little rustic bride, on whom, before the interruption, he had been preparing to exercise his droit de seigneur. The two meet again, soon after, at Maria Theresia's little Favorita pleasure palace. The Empress has arranged for Lydia to wed the aged French ambassador, the Marquis de Bouillabaisse, and dutifully she will not respond to the lovestruck Trenck's urging to run away with him. The maddened Baron lets himself be put up as the prize in a royally organized lottery. Lydia takes a ticket, wins, and declares her love for Trenck in front of the scandalized court, only to be repudiated by the proud Pandur chief for as long as it takes to get from Act II to the brief Act III in which the natural operettic ending is tied.

The score of Albini's show was that of a big-sing Operette for the two leading players, whose two principal long and large duets—the waltzing description of their amorous tastes in the first act (''Sei, wie er will, nur kein Kalfakter'') and their second-act encounter (''Engel! Ich seh' dich endlich, endlich wieder'')—provided the themes for thundering reprises in the big finales of the piece. The hero's marching entry-song (''So ist der Trenck!''), the heroine's introductory waltz (''Das ist zwar schrecklich'') and a sextet Croatian March were the other principal numbers of a score which also included some soubret work for the little bride and her mate, and a comical number for Lydia's aging maiden aunt and the royal major-domo.

First produced in Leipzig, *Baron Trenck* quickly found popularity and went on to make its way around the world. Vienna saw it in Rainer Simons's production at the Volksoper, with Buers (Trenck), Frln Ritzinger (Lydia), Markowsky (Bouillabaisse), Fr von Kellersberg (Kornelia) and Fischer (Trautenbach); Budapest (ad Frigyes Hervéy) saw it at the Városligeti Színkör and then, two years later, at the Budai Színkör, and it was translated into Croatian by Milan Smrekar for the enjoyment of Albini's countrymen.

The English-language rights were taken up by F C Whitney, who mounted the piece in London in a version (ad Frederick Franklin Schrader, dramatic editor of the *Washington Post*) altered into two acts and equipped with some of the worst lyrics the London stage had heard in recent years. Walter Hyde and Caroline Hatchard did the big singing, Rutland Barrington, Marie George and Walter Passmore headed the lighter moments, and the piece was hailed as ''a great and undeniable success'' by a critic who was pleased to find it ''more grandly operatic than is usual in a work of this class . . . by no means all gaiety and jingle.'' When it didn't go, Passmore was set to work up his role, new numbers for Barrington and Miss Hatchard were squeezed in, and the third act ''reconstructed,'' but to no avail. The show closed after playing 43 performances in the theatre Whitney had named after himself.

Whitney took his show to New York, and produced it at the Casino Theater. The book had been redone by Henry Blossom, and Albini's score had been further chopped up, pushed around and infiltrated by a trio, a chorus of ''Bold, Bad Bandits,'' and a waltz song for the heroine, all composed by Alfred Robyn. Fritz Sturmfels (Trenck), Blanche Duffield (Lydia), John Slavin (Nikola), Pacie Ripple and Joseph Herbert starred through 40 performances on Broadway.

Another Operette of the same title written by Franz Salemhofer and Otto Emmerich Groh was produced at the Vienna Bürgertheater 26 April 1935.

Austria: Volksoper (Kaiserjubiläums Stadttheater) 29 October 1909; Hungary: Városligeti Színkör *Trenk Baró* 1909; UK: Strand Theatre 22 April 1911; USA: Casino Theater 11 March 1912

BARRÉ, Albert (b Paris, 29 December 1854; d Paris, 31 May 1910).

The author of a goodly number of comedies and libretti for the French stage, Barré had his most considerable successes with the libretto for Antoine Banès's musical comedy *Toto* and with the 1904 vaudeville *Une nuit de noces* (w Kéroul). This latter piece was subsequently musicalized in Britain as *Telling the Tale* (Ambassador's Theatre, 1918, Philip Braham/Sydney Blow, Douglas Hoare) and in America under the title of *Oh! I Say* (Casino Theater, 1913, mus: Jerome Kern). His *Le Portrait de ma tante* (w Kéroul) became the musical comedy *Léni néni* in Hungary (Zsigmond Vincze/Jenő Heltai, Magyar Színház 2 May 1914), and both the Berlin musical *Ihr sechs-Uhr Onkel* (Paul Lincke/Alfred Schönfeld/Jean Kren, Thalia Theater 15 August 1907) and Italy's *Supermoglie* (Checcacci, 1920) were credited as being based on unidentified Kéroul and Barré works.

1884 **L'Escargot** (Antoine Banès/w Paul Adély) 1 act Eldorado 19 April

1884 **La Jarretière** (Banès/w Adély) 1 act Eldorado 27 September

1892 **Toto** (Banès/w Paul Bilhaud) Théâtre des Menus-Plaisirs 10 June

1893 **Madame Rose** (Banès/w Bilhaud) 1 act Opéra-Comique 25 September

1895 **Le Roi frelon** (Banès) Théâtre des Folies-Dramatiques 11 April

1896 **Une nuit d'amour** (Banès/w Maxime Boucheron) Théâtre des Bouffes-Parisiens 11 May Port

1897 **Le Nouveau Regiment** (aka *Mademoiselle Portez-Arme*) (Banès/w E Martin, Henri Bernard) L'Olympia 12 March

1907 **La Princesse Sans-Gêne** (Marius Baggers/w Henri Kéroul) Théâtre du Châtelet 16 November

1910 **La Vie joyeuse** (Henri Hirschmann/w Antony Mars) Théâtre Molière, Brussels 10 March

1911 **Les Gabelous** (Banès) Théâtre des Variétés, Marseille 4 November

1916 **Les Maris de Ginette** (Felix Fourdrain/w Kéroul) Théâtre Apollo 18 November

BARRIE, J[ames] M[atthew] (Sir) (b Kirriemuir, 9 May 1860; d London, 19 June 1937).

Although his theatrical fame is due wholly to his plays, the author of *Peter Pan* and *The Admirable Crichton* also made several sallies into the musical theatre. In 1893 he collaborated with Arthur Conan Doyle on an arch little musical comedy, *Jane Annie,* for the Savoy Theatre and, 22 years later, misled by his admiration for the French revue performer Gaby Deslys, he compiled the revusical *Rosy Rapture, the Pride of the Beauty Chorus,* with lyrics by E V Lucas and music by Jerome Kern and Herman Darewski, as a vehicle for her. He also ventured a ''revue in 3 scenes of yesterday, today and tomorrow'' called *Josephine* (1906), played as part of a triple bill at the Comedy Theatre, with Dion Boucicault in the title role, and a couple of skits of his writing were interpolated into Broadway musical comedies of the 1910s: *A Slice of Life,* a skit on the problem play with Richard Carle and Hattie Williams playing Mr and Mrs Hyphen-Brown, was popped into the middle of *The Girl from Montmartre* (1912) and *The Censor and the Dramatists* (October 1913) was interpolated into the second act of the local version of *Das Püppenmädel* (*The Doll Girl*) after having been previously seen in London's revue *Hello, Ragtime.*

Both his musical book shows were quick failures, and Barrie has fared little better with the many musical versions made of his plays by other hands. *Peter Pan* has been given various degrees of music since John Crook's charming and long-used original score for the play itself, the most substantial being a 1950 Broadway remake of the play with a Leonard Bernstein/Trude Rittman score of five songs and incidental music (Imperial Theater 24 April) and an American musical comedy version (Moose Charlap, Jule Styne/Comden, Green Winter Garden 20 October 1954), tricked out with comical dancing Indians and peluche animals, and with a roughly filleted book made up from some portions of Barrie's text and some other material. *What Every Woman Knows* was made over twice under the title of *Maggie* (National Theater, New York 18 February 1953, William Roy/Hugh Thomas; Shaftesbury Theatre, London 12 October 1977, Michael Wild); *The Little Minister* became *Wild Grows the Heather* (London Hippodrome 3 May 1956, Jack Waller, Joseph Tunbridge); *The Admirable Crichton*—already in 1934 manhandled into a Crosby-Lombard musical film as *We're Not Dressing*—was once again brutally reorganized as an *Our Man Crichton* (Shaftesbury Theatre 22 December 1964) where the star was the soubrette; *A Kiss for Cinderella* became *The Penny Friend* off-Broadway in 1966 (William Roy again); and *Walker, London,* which Barrie had specifically refused to allow to be musicalized in 1925, was given songs after his death in 1962 (Birmingham, 29 May).

The most successful musicalization of Barrie was practiced on the most likely candidate, *Quality Street,* which was prettily remade as *Our Miss Phoebe* in London (Phoenix Theatre 13 October 1950), and in Germany as the hugely successful *Drei alte Schachteln* (Walter Kollo/Hermann Haller, Rideamus Theater am Nollendorfplatz 6 October 1917). This latter became, less successfully, *Miss Phoebe of Quality Street* in New York. The show was again and more discreetly adapted to music as *Phoebe* at the Pennsylvania's Buck's County Playhouse (23 August 1965).

A musical version of Barrie's other most probably adaptable piece, *Dear Brutus,* written by Julian Slade is, at time of writing, unproduced.

1893 **Jane Annie** (Ernest Ford/w Arthur Conan Doyle) Savoy Theatre 13 May

1915 **Rosy Rapture, the Pride of the Beauty Chorus** (Jerome Kern, Herman Darewski/E V Lucas) Duke of York's Theatre 22 March

Biographies: Walbrook, H: *J M Barrie and the Theatre* (F V White, London, 1922), Hammerton, J A: *Barrie: The Story of a Genius* (Sampson Low, London, 1929), Darlington, W A: *J M Barrie* (Blackie, London, 1938), Mackail, D: *The Story of J M B* (Peter Davies, London, 1941), Dunbar, J: *J M Barrie: The Man Behind the Image* (Houghton Mifflin, Boston, 1970), Birkin, A: *J M Barrie and the Lost Boys* (Constable, London, 1979), etc

BARRINGTON, Rutland [FLEET, George Rutland] (b Penge, 15 January 1853; d London, 31 May 1922). Musical comedian who made his first fame in the Savoy operas and his second in an equally long series of George Edwardes shows.

The young Barrington worked as a clerk in the city before securing his first engagement as an actor with Henry Neville at the Olympic Theatre (Lafleur in *The Two Orphans* 1874, Mr Porcelain in *Family Jars* 1875, etc). He subsequently joined Mrs Howard Paul's entertainment and remained with her, on the road, until she disbanded her company to take up the role of Lady Sangazure in *The Sorcerer* (1877). As the only star of D'Oyly Carte's cast, Mrs Paul was able to suggest that he hire her 24-year-old colleague as well, and Barrington thus successfully created the role of the curate, Dr Daly, in Gilbert and Sullivan's piece (''Time Was When Love and I Were Well Acquainted''). He remained with Carte to become the first Captain Corcoran in *HMS Pinafore* (1878, ''I Am the Captain of the Pinafore,'' ''Fair Moon, to Thee I Sing,'' ''Never Mind the Why and Wherefore'') and, when it seemed that there would be no role for him in *The Pirates of Penzance,* he himself suggested that he be given the comparatively small part of the Police Sergeant (1880, ''When a Felon's Not Engaged in His Employment''), originally intended for Fred Clifton, who had played Bill Bobstay in *HMS Pinafore.*

Barrington continued as a backbone member of the D'Oyly Carte Company for more than a decade, creating Bunthorne (*Patience*), Lord Mountararat (*Iolanthe,* "When Britain Really Ruled the Waves"), King Hildebrand (*Princess Ida*), Pooh Bah (*The Mikado*), Sir Despard (*Ruddigore*) and Giuseppe (*The Gondoliers*), before leaving the company to set up in management on his own account. When this venture bankrupted him, he ended up on the road with the operatic company run by one Mme Ilma Norina (otherwise Josephine Muntz, and Mrs Samuel Genese) performing a second-rate piece called *The Rose of Windsor,* and he was pleased to return to the Savoy where he appeared in such latter-day D'Oyly Carte productions as *The Nautch Girl* (1891, Punka, the Rajah), *The Vicar of Bray* (1892, Rev William Barlow), *Haddon Hall* (1892, Rupert Vernon), *Jane Annie* (1893, Proctor), *Utopia Ltd* (1893, King Paramount) and, in his last return, *The Grand Duke* (1896, Ludwig).

In 1894 he again left the Savoy, this time to join George Edwardes's company at Daly's Theatre, replacing Harry Monkhouse in the senior comic role in *A Gaiety Girl.* He thus began another fruitful run of roles, a run which saw the now stout and jowly Barrington introducing for Edwardes the character/comedy roles of the Prince Regent/Nils Egilson in *His Excellency* (1895), Marcus Pomponius in *A Greek Slave* (1898, "I Want to Be Popular"), the Mandarin, Yen How in *San Toy* (1899, "Six Little Wives"), Quinton Raikes in *A Country Girl* (1902) and Boobhamba in *The Cingalee* (1904), as well as succeeding Monkhouse as Marquis Imari in *The Geisha.*

In his fifties Barrington continued his series of large comic creations in such pieces as *The White Chrysanthemum* (1905, Admiral Sir Horatio Armitage KCB) and as a ridiculous Pharoah in *Amasis* (1906, Amasis IX) and, between appearances on the music halls (*The Tramp, The Silent Way, The Moody Mariner*) and in the non-musical theatre, repeated his Gilbert and Sullivan roles in revival and took several comedy roles in the new wave of Continental musicals—Lucas van Tromp in *The Girl in the Train* (*Die geschiedene Frau,* 1910), the Major Domo in *Baron Trenck* (1911) and Max Somossy in *The Joy-Ride Lady* (1914, *Autoliebchen*). He was forced into retirement by a stroke in 1919.

Barrington wrote the texts for several small operettas, including *Quid Pro Quo,* played as a forepiece to *Princess Toto* at the Opera Comique, and *A Knight Errant* (1894) played as a curtain-raiser to Gilbert's *His Excellency.* He also authored the childrens' musicals *The Water Babies* (1902) and *Little Black Sambo and Little White Barbara* (1904), played as Christmas entertainments at the Garrick Theatre.

1881 **Quid Pro Quo** (Wilfred Bendall/w Cunningham Bridgman) 1 act Opera Comique 17 October

Plate 23. **Rutland Barrington.** *The famous Savoy comic had a second career as the star of several George Edwardes shows. Here he is seen as Marcus Pomponius, the dying-to-be-popular Roman potentate of* A Greek Slave.

1890 **A Swarry Dansong** (Edward Solomon) 1 act Criterion Theatre 5 June

1891 **Incompatibility of Temper** (Solomon) 1 act privately

1894 **A Knight Errant** (Alfred J Caldicott) 1 act Lyric Theatre 14 November

1895 **The Professor** (Solomon) 1 act St George's Hall 15 July

1902 **The Water Babies** (Frederick Rosse) Garrick Theatre 18 December

1904 **Little Black Sambo and Little White Barbara** (Bendall, Rosse) Garrick Theatre 21 December

1905 **Fritz** (Walter Slaughter) sketch London Coliseum 3 July

1907 **His Escape** (H M Higgs) 1 act Coronet Theatre 15 July

Memoirs: *Rutland Barrington: A Record of 34 Years' Experience* (Grant Richards, London, 1908), *More Rutland Barrington* (Grant Richards, London, 1911)

BARRON, Muriel[le] (b Glasgow, 12 April 1902; d Northwood, 16 May 1996).

Soprano Muriel Barron joined the D'Oyly Carte Opera Company at the age of 22, and played minor roles (Plaintiff, Giulia, Isabel, etc) with them for several years. She covered the part of Shirley Sheridan in *The Cat and the Fiddle* in London (1932) before playing it on tour, toured as *The Dubarry* in 1934, and then joined the cast of *Glamorous Night* at Drury Lane (1935, Dulcie Glassborough/Phyllis), covering Mary Ellis and subsequently taking over her role after the London run. She appeared in the West End in Coward's *Operette* (1938, Elsie Jewell), and returned to Novello to once again succeed Mary Ellis, this time in the star role of *The Dancing Years* (1939), when the piece was forced out of London by the war. When it returned to the West End for its principal run at the Adelphi Theatre in 1942, she retained the role of Maria Ziegler, and then continued on into the principal soprano role of Novello's next show, *Perchance to Dream,* in which she introduced "Love Is My Reason for Living." She subsequently succeeded Phyllis Dare as Marta Karillos in *King's Rhapsody* (1950).

BÁRSONY, Rózsi (b Budapest, March 1909; d Vienna, March 1977).

A child actress, the blonde and beautiful Bársony joined the chorus at Budapest's Király Színház at the age of 16 and soon rose to principal parts as a soubrette in revue and operett. She made her first mark in the musicals *Éva grófnő* (1928) and *Eltörött a hegedüm* (Bözsi), starred with Ilona Titkos as the *Sisters* (1930, Rózsi) of Szirmai's successful operett, and made a hit in the soubrette role in *Viktória* (1930, O Lia San, introducing "Mausi"). She played in Eisemann's *Alvinci huszárok* (1930), in *Az okos Mama* (Zizi), appeared as an American flapper in *Amerikai lányok* (1931)—a curious piece claiming to be American which credited Eliot and J C Nugent's *The Poor Nut* as its libretto and its songs to Messrs Cowan, C I May and Albert Gumble—and took the soubrette roles in Szirmai's *A balerina* (1931) and the Leipzig premiere of Ábrahám's *Die Blume von Hawaii* (1931, Bessy).

She formed a partnership, both on-stage and off, with comedian Oszkár Dénes, and the two appeared together in the Viennese production of Ábrahám's *Die Blume von Hawaii* (1932) before winning their biggest success of all when they created the soubret parts in the same composer's *Ball im Savoy* (1932) in Berlin. Bársony played Daisy Parker, "eine jazz-komponistin." The pair repeated these roles in the London production of the show, and Bársony also took over her original role in Vienna.

She subsequently appeared in Budapest in such pieces as *Én és a kisöcsém* (1934) and *3:1 a szerelem javára* (1936, "Nagysád jónapot"), in Vienna in *Märchen im Grand-Hotel* (1934, Mary-Lou), *Dschainah* (1935) and *Roxy und ihr Wunderteam* (1937) at the Theater an der Wien and in film (*Ball im Savoy, 3:1 a szerelem javára, Viki, A harapos férj,* Ilonka in *Walzerkrieg,* etc). She settled in Vienna after the war, and finished her career there, being seen at the Raimundtheater as Dodo in a revival of *Hochzeitsnacht im Paradies* as late as 1957.

BART, Lionel [BEGLEITER, Lionel] (b London, 1 August 1930; d Hammersmith, London, 3 April 1999). Songwriter who scored several sizeable successes on the British stage of the late 1950s and early 1960s.

Bart made his name in the mid-1950s as the writer of some of the earliest British rock-and-roll songs, notably for (and sometimes with) Tommy Steele ("Rock With the Caveman," "Butterfingers," "A Handful of Songs," "Little White Bull"), Cliff Richard ("Living Doll") and, later, Anthony Newley ("Do You Mind").

His first experience of theatre work was in revue at the politically committed Unity Theatre where the musical *Wally Pone,* a Soho gangster perversion of *Volpone* for which he contributed book, lyrics and music, was briefly staged in 1958, but the following year he found substantial success both with his lyrics for the Bernard Miles/Laurie Johnson musical *Lock Up Your Daughters* ("When Does the Ravishing Begin?," "On a Sunny Sunday Morning," "I'll Be There") and with the songs for the East End musical *Fings Ain't Wot They Used t'Be* ("Fings Ain't Wot They Used t'Be"). He topped these successes with an international one with his 1960 musical adaptation of Dickens's *Oliver Twist, Oliver!,* which turned the evil Fagin of the novel into a loveable rogue to the accompaniment of a score of equally loveable songs ("Where Is Love?," "Oom Pah Pah," "It's a Fine Life," "Food, Glorious, Food," "You Got to Pick a Pocket or Two," "Consider Yourself," "I'd Do Anything"), yet which produced the most remarkable torch song of at least the decade in the powerful "As Long as He Needs Me." *Oliver!* established a long-run record for a musical in the West End (2,618 performances), and ran up a continuing and regular series of overseas productions and revivals, establishing itself as one of the great family musicals of the postwar era.

The spectacular *Blitz!* (1962), a wartime saga of Cohens and Kellys in an East End setting, and the splendidly gritty Liverpudlian saga of *Maggie May* (1964, "It's Yourself I Want"), written to a libretto by Alun Owen, gave Bart further London successes, but a feeble burlesque of the Robin Hood legend, *Twang!!* (1965), was a violent failure. Bart ploughed his own fortune into keeping this sinking production alive and ended by ruining himself. In the period of financial and personal problems which followed, Bart's career foundered. A musical version of the celebrated film *La Strada* (1969) failed in one performance on Broadway, an NBC musical version of *Dr Jekyll and Mr Hyde* (7 March 1973) to which he contributed some songs came and went, and other projects were floated over the following 20 and more years, including an oft-announced musical on *The Hunchback of Notre Dame,* a new version of Offenbach's *La Vie parisienne,* and a heavily publicized contribution to a musical on the life of Winston Churchill which did not come to fruition.

Outside the theatre, Bart's most enduring composition was the theme song for the James Bond film *From Russia With Love* (1963).

A musical compilation show based on his life was staged, under the title *Lionel,* at the New London Theatre in 1977.

1958 **Wally Pone** Unity Theatre 18 July

1959 **Fings Ain't Wot They Used t'Be** (Frank Norman) Theatre Royal, Stratford East 17 February; Garrick Theatre 11 February 1960

1959 **Lock Up Your Daughters** (Laurie Johnson/Bernard Miles) Mermaid Theatre 28 May

1960 **Oliver!** New Theatre 30 June

1962 **Blitz!** Adelphi Theatre 8 May

1964 **Maggie May** (Alun Owen) Adelphi Theatre 19 August

1965 **Twang!!** (w Harvey Orkin) Shaftesbury Theatre 20 December

1969 **La Strada** Lunt-Fontanne Theater, New York 14 December

1972 **The Londoners** (Stephen Lewis) Theatre Royal, Stratford East 27 March

1972 **Costapacket** (w Norman, Alan Klein) Theatre Royal, Stratford East 5 October

Biography: Roper, D: *Bart!* (Pavilion, London, 1994)

BARTHOLOMAE, Philip H[enry] (b Chicago, 3 July 1880; d Winnetka, Ill, 5 January 1947). Playwright, librettist and producer who scored a handful of hits with musical versions of his plays in the 1910s and 1920s.

Son of a well-off family, and educated in Chicago and in his father's hometown of Heidelberg, Bartholomae originally worked in his father's business before venturing fully into the theatre. He tried his hand at writing both plays and libretti from an early age, but made his first connection in the professional entertainment world as a manager, promoting the vaudeville violinist, Saranoff. He placed his artist on a bill with Sarah Bernhardt, and the actress subsequently performed a sketch Bartholomae had written. He had, however, to pay for his regular debut as a dramatist. Unable to place the play *Over Night,* written whilst he was still an undergraduate at the van Renselaer Polytechnic in Winnetka, he put up the finance for the production himself. *Over Night* was picked up from its ''vanity'' production, taken to Broadway, and brought him a first and firm success as a writer (Hackett Theater 2 January 1911, 162 performances), a success which was soon followed by a second even greater with another winning farce, *Little Miss Brown.* His first attempts at musical comedy, a series of shows with music by Silvio Hein, brought him mixed fortune. The young writer produced his own first musical venture, *When Dreams Come True,* with Joseph Santley starred and his violinist protégé Saranoff featured. It started its metropolitan life in Chicago and, after a successful season there, made its way east. It managed just a fair eight weeks at Broadway's Lyric Theater, but it proved thoroughly to the taste of the touring circuits where, with its determined author's backing, it held a place, often in duplicate (one company headed by Joseph Santley, the other by his brother Frederic), for several seasons.

Another musical launched in the same season did less well. His *Kiss Me Quick* started off as a straight filmland farce but when, after a promising season in Boston, the comedy proved a flop on Broadway (24 August 1913), producer Bartholomae decided to turn author Bartholomae's farce into a musical, and by the time *Kiss Me Quick* reached Chicago's Cort Theater it had acquired songs, chorus girls, dances and a new title—*Glorianna* And Bartholomae was loudly giving his opinions to the press as to the value of New York critics and New York first-nighters. Chicago's critics proved no more to his taste, not *Glorianna* to theirs.

His next attempt, the pretty *Miss Daisy,* in spite of being tried in three different versions, did even less well. It folded in 29 performances in New York, and subsequent efforts to revise it proved fruitless, and a variety house musical playlet, *One of the Boys,* featured on the Palace bill by Florenz Tempest and Donald McDonald was voted ''callow'' and ''feeble'' and lasted no time at all.

Bartholomae came back to something like the level of his early successes, however, when he collaborated on a musical adaptation of *Over Night,* under the title *Very Good Eddie,* for Ray Comstock and Bessie Marbury, but when Miss Marbury subsequently joined with the Shuberts to produce his next attempt at an original music, *Girl o' Mine,* the results were rather less positive (48 performances and a bootless remake). However, two further partly self-made adaptations of his plays brought him two further successes. *Tangerine,* based on an apparently unproduced non-musical collaboration between Bartholomae and Lawrence Langner, was a long-running hit of the 1921–22 season, and *Kitty's Kisses,* a musical version of his 1912 play *Little Miss Brown,* followed its Broadway run by being recycled for use as the book to the highly successful show which was, in Britain, called *The Girl Friend.* A musical version of the successful comedy *Barnum Was Right,* by the same team of Conrad, Kahn and Bartholomae, which was announced at the same time as *Kitty's Kisses* did not apparently eventuate.

Bartholomae also contributed material to the Shubert revue *Over the Top* (1918) and to *The Greenwich Village Follies.*

He subsequently abandoned the theatre, moving to the West Coast where he spent 15 years writing for the films before retiring in his early sixties.

1913 **When Dreams Come True** (Hein) Garrick Theater, Chicago 7 April; Lyric Theater, New York 18 August
1913 **Glorianna** (Silvio Hein/George V Hobart) Cort Theater, Chicago 12 October
1914 **The Model Maid** (Hein) Opera House, Providence 17 August, Majestic Theater, Boston 24 August
1914 **Miss Daisy** (revised *The Model Maid*) (Hein) Shubert Theater 9 September
1914 **At the Ball** (Hein/w Alice Emery Gerstenberg) (revised *Miss Daisy*) Van Curler Opera House, Schenectady 12 December; American Music Hall, Chicago 25 December
1915 **One of the Boys** (Hein) Palace Theater 24 May
1915 **Very Good Eddie** (Jerome Kern/Schuyler Greene/w Guy Bolton) Princess Theater 23 December
1918 **Girl o' Mine** (aka *Oh Mama!*) (Frank Tours, Augustus Barrett) Bijou Theater 28 January
1918 **The Victory Girl** (revised *Girl o' Mine*) (ad Alex Sullivan, Lynn Cowan) Syracuse, NY 16 November
1921 **Tangerine** (Monte Carlo, Alma Sanders/Howard Johnson/w Bolton) Casino Theater 9 August
1926 **Kitty's Kisses** (Con Conrad, Gus Kahn/w Otto Harbach) Playhouse Theater 6 May

LA BASOCHE Opéra-comique in 3 acts by Albert Carré. Music by André Messager. Opéra-Comique, Paris, 30 May 1890.

''La Basoche'' is a guild of law students, two centuries old by the time this piece takes place, which has a legal ''King'' and various other dignitaries at its head, and which has wide jurisdiction over the students. In the story, 17-year-old Princess Mary of England (Lise Landouzy), wed by proxy to the King of France and on her way to meet her royal husband, takes a night out at a Paris inn. She sees student king Clement Marot (Gabriel Soulacroix) in his ''royal'' garb and assumes him to be her husband. The other half of the misunderstanding comes when Marot's wife, Colette (Mme Molé-Truffier), is taken to the real King of France as ''the Queen'' and stoutly denies him in such a way that he suspects that his proxy, the Duc de Longueville (Lucien Fugère), has been carrying proxy too far. Mary finally makes it to court, and, not without a touch of regret, exchanges her teenaged ''King'' for the real one.

Messager's score was an Opéra-Comique score par excellence, with some of its songs based on the words of the historical poet, Marot, and with its lyrical music contrasted with a comical highlight in Lucien Fugère's self-contented ''Elle m'aime!'' when the King's misunderstandings and accusations lead him to believe that Princess Mary prefers her ageing proxy to a royal husband.

Produced at the Opéra-Comique with considerable success, *La Basoche* was subsequently revived there in 1900 with Jean Périer as Marot (16 November), and again in 1919 (20 December), in 1931 and 1939, with Fugère hanging on long to his original role. It was also played at the Théâtre de la Gaîté in 1908 (30 May) with André Baugé and Edmée Favart featured, reprised at that house in 1927 with Ponzio and Louise Dhamarys, and again at the Théâtre de la Porte-Saint-Martin in 1934 under the management of Maurice Lehmann with Baugé paired this time with Yvonne Brothier. The show has subsequently remained more well-considered than performed, but in 1991 it was produced at the Théâtre Graslin, Nantes, with Piero Calissano and Sophie Fournier at the head of the cast and Vincent Le Texier in the role of the Duc, identified forever with Fugère.

Two different German versions of the show were produced, one in Hamburg and one in Berlin, and London and New York, similarly, mounted two different English-language versions. In Britain, Sir Augustus Harris and Eugene Oudin provided the text for D'Oyly Carte's production at his new Royal English Opera House (soon to be the Palace Theatre) with Ben Davies starred as a tenor Marot alongside Esther Palliser (Mary), Lucile Hill (Colette), David Bispham (Longueville) and W H Burgon (King), but a splendid critical reception was not followed by public interest and Carte announced that he would play *La Basoche* in rotation with Sullivan's *Ivanhoe* and with Bemberg's *Elaine* before the whole scheme collapsed.

America's version was made by Madeleine Lucette Ryley and produced by the Duff Opera Company at Chicago's Auditorium (2 January 1893) and at the Casino Theater with her husband, the popular comic opera comedian, J H Ryley, as the Duke and Helen Bertram (Mary), Lilly Post/Juliette Corden (Colette) and Charles Bassett (Marot) in the other leading roles. It lasted just two weeks on Broadway before the company switched to *The Gondoliers.*

Germany: Stadttheater, Hamburg *Die zwei Könige* 19 October 1891, Friedrich-Wilhelmstädtisches Theater *Die Basoche* 29 October 1891; UK: Royal English Opera House 3 November 1891; USA: Casino Theater 27 February 1893

Recordings: complete (Gaîté-Lyrique), selection (EMI-Pathé)

BA-TA-CLAN Chinoiserie musicale in 1 act by Ludovic Halévy. Music by Jacques Offenbach. Théâtre des Bouffes-Parisiens, Paris, 29 December 1855.

One of the zaniest of Offenbach's short opérettes-bouffes, *Ba-ta-clan* has also remained steadily one of the most appreciated, with regular performances both in French and in translation being given since the time of its first production up to the present day.

There is a lot of conspiratorial behaviour going on in Ché-i-no-or, the exceptionally curious oriental kingdom ruled over by Fé-ni-han (Pradeau). Ko-ko-ri-ko (Guyot) the captain of the guard, is secretly plotting to usurp the ruler's job, and two courtiers, who have been masquerading under impossible Eastern names, but whose real, French names are Virginie (Marie Dalmont) and Alfred (Berthelier), are also plotting—but only to escape and get back to their homes in faraway France. In fact, unbeknown to all, Fé-ni-han himself is also a Frenchman, a shipwrecked sailor who has spent eight miserable years (mis)ruling this country without knowing a word of the local lingo. He means to force Alfred to take his place so that he can go home. Foiled escapes, dreadful threats, and ghastly tortures loom, but all is solved when Ko-ko-ri-ko who, as his name implies, is also actually a Frenchman, sends a letter (the rules of the contemporary stage meant he couldn't speak, three actors was the limit) to say he will happily have the throne and they can all three go back to Europe.

The little score of *Ba-ta-clan* echoed the rebounding craziness of the story, with the voices and the orchestra soaring eccentrically as flights of gibberish Chinese mix with plumbingly deep Italian and sprays of occasionally illogical French in a merry burlesque of grand opera. There were also some more straightforward pieces for the three principals: Virginie's tale of her earlier life (''J'étais aimable, élégante''), her duo of reminiscences of Paris with Albert (''Te souviens-tu de la maison dorée,'' La Ronde de Florette) and the monarch's ultimate revelation of his own history (''Je suis français'').

The piece was introduced on the opening program at Offenbach's ''winter'' Bouffes-Parisiens, and it helped to set the new theatre off on very firm feet. In 1863 an enlarged version was mounted at the same theatre, but by that time *Ba-ta-clan* had begun its voyage to all corners of the world. Britain first heard the show in French, during a visit by the Bouffes-Parisiens company in 1857, but it was eight years before an English-language version by William Brough and Thomas German Reed was produced as *Ching-Chow-Hi, or A Cracked Piece of China* at the little Gallery of Illustration. Augusta Thomson, J A Shaw, R Wilkinson and Thomas Whiffen were the cast, and the piece did well enough for Reed to revive it two seasons later. The same English version was later played at Broadway's Theatre Comique and around America by Susan Galton's troupe (''[she] intoduced a new song 'Beautiful Snowdrops' by J R Thomas''), with her sister, Blanche (later to be famous as Mrs Whiffen), playing the male lead in breeches. Paul Juignet's Theatre Français had given the original at Niblo's Saloon in 1864. A personalized version was also played by the Kelly and Leon Minstrels, who later gave the piece its earliest Australian

Plate 24. **Ba-ta-clan.** *Jennifer McGregor (Fe-an-nich-ton) and Paul Ferris (Ke-ki-ka-ko) in the Australian Opera Company's production of 1984.*

performances. In their edition of course, the disguised Frenchfolk became disguised Americans, and space was made for a burlesque of the currently topical acrobatics of Risley's Japs.

Vienna's Carl Treumann quickly had *Ba-ta-clan* adapted—the characters were, in his version, all Viennese rather than French—and played as *Tschin-Tschin* at Johann Nestroy's Carltheater. Nestroy appeared as Tschin-Tschin, with Röhring, Swoboda and Frln Rudini in support. Treumann took the piece with him when he moved to his own little Theater am Franz-Josefs-Kai, where it was played with Wilhelm Knaack as Tschin-Tschin and Treumann himself as ''Peter Gix, steersman of a European frigate'' (ie, Alfred), Therese Schäfer as a Virginie who was now an odalisque and Grois as the ambitious ''ober-Bonze'' in a cast which, unhampered by Parisian restrictions, now numbered no fewer than 11. Treumann's version was played in Budapest in 1862, but no Hungarian version seems to have resulted.

In more recent years, *Ba-ta-clan* has appeared at Paris's Théâtre Déjazet (23 December 1987), whilst other productions have included one in 1982 by the Australian Opera Company (4 March, Sydney Opera House), where Offenbach's happy oddity shared a program with Walton's *The Bear,* and another in 1983 by the Hamburg Staatsoper.

The opérette also gave its name to one of Paris's most celebrated cafés-concerts.

UK: St James's Theatre (Fr) 20 May 1857, Gallery of Illustration *Ching-Chow-Hi* 14 August 1865; Austria: Carltheater *Tschin-Tschin* 13 October 1860; Hungary: Budai Színkör *Tschin-Tschin* 11 April 1862; USA: Theatre Français (Fr) 25 February 1864, Theatre Comique *Ching-Chow-Hi* 16 November 1868; Australia: Opera House, Sydney *Ching-Chow-Hi* 10 January 1880

Recordings: (Érato, Milan, Pluriel)

BATES, [Thomas] Thorpe (b London, 11 February 1883; d London, 23 May 1958).

Initially successful as a concert singer, Bates made his first theatre appearance starring opposite José Collins in *The Happy Day* (1916) at Daly's Theatre, where his dashing if slightly stiff demeanour and fine baritone won him an enthusiastic following. His popularity increased when he was again paired with Miss Collins to create the principal male singing role of Beppo in *The Maid of the Mountains* (''A Bachelor Gay Am I''). He switched to musical comedy to appear at the Gaiety in the 1920 revival of *The Shop Girl* (Bobbie Blake), but quickly returned to operetta for heroic roles in *The Rebel Maid* (1921, Derek Lanscombe), in which he introduced the staunchly patriotic ''The Fishermen of England,'' *The Golden Moth* (1921, Captain Paul d'Artois), Broadway's version of *Die Bajadere* (*The Yankee Princess,* 1922, Radjami), and the less than successful London productions of Lehár's *The Three Graces* (1925, Duke of Nancy) and *Frasquita* (1925, Armand), in which he was reunited with Miss Collins. For several seasons he took the role of Schober in productions of *Lilac Time* and it was in this part that he made his last West End appearance in 1930.

BATTLE, Hinton (b Neubracke, Germany, 29 November 1956).

A member of the Dance Theater of Harlem, Battle made his Broadway debut with a notable performance as a teenaged dancing Scarecrow in *The Wiz* (1975). He subsequently played in the dance show *Dancin',* on Broadway and on the road, and in the Broadway production of the Duke Ellington dance revue *Sophisticated Ladies* (1981, Tony Award, Featured Actor in a Musical). He succeeded to the role of James Thunder Early in *Dreamgirls* (1984) and created the part of Uncle Dipsey in *The Tap Dance Kid* (1984, Tony Award, Featured Actor in a Musical).

Battle subsequently played in *Ain't Misbehavin'* in Las Vegas and in the out-of-town tryout of *Stardust,* and took a third Tony Award for his performance as John in the Broadway edition of *Miss Saigon* (1991). In 1998 he succeeded to the role of Billy Flynn in Broadway's revival of *Chicago.*

BATTLING BUTLER Musical farce in 3 acts by Stanley Brightman and Austin Melford. Lyrics by Douglas Furber. Music by Philip Braham. Additional numbers by Donovan Parsons and Melville Gideon, and F W Thomas. New Oxford Theatre, London, 8 December 1922.

A musical seemingly inspired by F C Burnand's play *The Benicia Boy* if, in fact, it was not the French comedy *Le Contrôleur des wagons-lits, Battling Butler* was used by Jack Buchanan to star himself as an errant husband who ends up having to take to the boxing-ring when his ''away weekend'' excuse of being a boxer in training is rumbled by his forceful wife (Sydney Fairbrother). Fred Groves played the ''Battling'' Butler of the title, the pugilist whom Alfred Butler has been pretending to be; Sylvia Leslie was the ''other'' Mrs Butler (complications guaranteed here); and Peggy Kurton was Alfred's ingenue ward who accidentally gives the plot away, but still gets herself a Hugh (Fred Leslie) in the final wind-up.

Phil Braham's lighthearted and up-to-date score, including the pretty and popular ''Dancing Honeymoon'' and the lovey-dovey ''Apples, Bananas and You,'' as well as a humorously plotful solo sung by poor Alfred as he prepares to face his doom in the boxing ring (''It's a Far, Far Better Thing''), aided a good comic script to a fine London success on its production at the Oxford Theatre. The show was still running strongly when C B Cochran wanted his theatre back, so Buchanan transferred *Battling Butler* to the Adelphi Theatre where it ran out the last part of its 238-performance London life.

A revamped, relocated (to New England) version (ad Ballard MacDonald), mounted by small-time touring producer George Choos under the title *Mr Battling Buttler* (''a musical knockout in three rounds''), did even better on Broadway. Braham's score was heavily invested with local songs, mostly written by Walter Rosemont, Choos's habitual supplier of numbers for his very small-town tours, and Charles Ruggles, Walter Kent and Frances Halliday starred for a fine 312 performances before the show went out on the road with its title changed to that of its most popular song, *The Dancing Honeymoon.* America's version of the show also won a production in Australia where Dorothy Brunton and Charles Heslop top-billed alongside something called ''Millie the Mullet'' through two and a half months in Melbourne and a month at Sydney's Grand Opera House (28 February 1925).

An MGM silent film of the piece was made in 1926 with Buster Keaton starred as Butler alongside heroine Sally O'Neil and Snitz Edwards.

USA: (aka *The Dancing Honeymoon*) Detroit 19 August 1923, Selwyn Theater *Mr Battling Buttler* 8 October 1923; Australia: New Princess Theatre, Melbourne *Mr Battling Butler* 31 May 1924

Film: MGM 1926

BAUER, Julius (b Raab Sziget, 15 October 1853; d Vienna, 11 June 1941).

A journalist on the *Wiener Extrablatter,* an author and librettist, and later a theatre director, Bauer made a fine start to his career as an operettic librettist when he collaborated with Hugo Wittmann on the book and lyrics for the younger Adolf Müller's successful Operette, *Der Hofnarr.* The pair subsequently provided Carl Millöcker with four libretti, including those for the memorable *Der arme Jonathan* and the internationally played *Das Sonntagskind* and *Die sieben Schwaben,* wrote the text for *Fürstin Ninetta* for Johann Strauss and evolved the revusical *Adam und Eva,* set by Weinberger and played by Girardi and Marie Halton at the Carltheater.

Bauer subsequently wrote the texts for both *Die Juxheirat* and *Der Mann mit den drei Frauen* for Lehár with limited success, and *Heimliche Liebe* and *Der arme Millionär* for Paul Ottenheimer—and star Alexander Girardi—with considerably more, without a collaborator, but he rejoined Wittmann for a 1918 stage version of *Der Kongress tanzt.* His last musical theatre work was a Schubert pasticcio, arranged by Julius Bittner, a dozen years in the wake of *Das Dreimäderlhaus.*

1886 **Der Hofnarr** (Adolf Müller jr/w Hugo Wittmann) Theater an der Wien 20 November

1887 **Die sieben Schwaben** (Carl Millöcker/w Wittmann) Theater an der Wien 29 October

1890 **Der arme Jonathan** (Millöcker/w Wittmann) Theater an der Wien 4 January

1892 **Das Sonntagskind** (Millöcker/w Wittmann) Theater an der Wien 16 January

1893 **Fürstin Ninetta** (Johann Strauss/w Wittmann) Theater an der Wien 10 January

1894 **Der Probekuss** (Millöcker/w Wittmann) Theater an der Wien 22 December

1899 **Adam und Eva** (*Die Seelenwanderung*) (Carl Weinberger/w Wittmann) Carltheater 5 January

1904 **Die Juxheirat** (Franz Lehár) Theater an der Wien 22 December

1908 **Der Mann mit den drei Frauen** (Lehár) Theater an der Wien 21 January

1911 **Heimliche Liebe** (Paul Ottenheimer) Johann Strauss-Theater 13 October

1913 **Der arme Millionär** (Ottenheimer) Johann Strauss-Theater 17 October

1918 **Der Kongress tanzt** (Karl Lafite/w Wittmann) Wiener Stadttheater 9 November

1928 **Der unsterbliche Franz** (Franz Schubert arr Julius Bittner/w Ernst Decsey, Bittner) Volksoper 24 April

BAUGÉ, André (b Toulouse, 4 January 1893; d Paris, 25 May 1966). The son of opérette prima donna Anna Tariol-Baugé, André Baugé became one of the most popular baritones of the French musical theatre in a career on stage, film and record reaching over 40 years.

After half a dozen years singing in the French provinces (initially as ''André Grillaud''), Baugé made his Paris debut in 1918, at the Théâtre des Variétés, in the role of Lord Barsons in *La Dame de Monte-Carlo.* In the 1920s he spent a period at the Opéra-Comique where he was seen, amongst others, in the lead role of Messager's *La Basoche,* as Clavaroche in *Fortunio,* Jean in *Les Noces de Jeannette* and Florestan in *Véronique,* as well as appearing as Escamillo, Alfio, Pelléas, Figaro and Lescaut. He left the Opéra-Comique temporarily to play in revivals of *Véronique* and *La Fille de Madame Angot* (1920) alongside Marguerite Carré, then definitively to create the leading role in the French version of *Monsieur Beaucaire* (1925, Beaucaire). He subsequently appeared in Tiarko Richepin's spectacular *Venise* (1927, Gianetto), in which he played alongside his mother, in France's baritonic version of Lehár's *Paganini* (1928, Paganini), and of Granichstaedten's *Der Orlow* (1928, Alex), in *Vouvray* (1929) and as Robert Misson in *Robert le Pirate* (*New Moon,* 1929).

In the 1930s he starred in Goublier's less than successful *Billy-Bill,* in *Le Clown amoureux* (1931, Jim), the French productions of *Nina Rosa* (Jack) and *Valses de Vienne* (Strauss jr), in the title role of Pierné's much-admired *Fragonard* (1934), in the Châtelet's spectacular *Au temps des merveilleuses* (1934, Marquis Roland des Essarts), *Au soleil du Mexique* (1935, Nino) and Romberg's *Le Chant du Tzigane* (1937, *Forbidden Melody,* Gregor). He also took the title role in the opérette *Beaumarchais,* for which he had himself written the libretto to a pasticcio Rossini score, as well as performing regularly the roles of the classic repertoire, notably the title role of Planquette's *Rip* and the Marquis in *Les Cloches de Corneville.* Although he retired in the mid-1940s he returned to the stage as late as 1958 when he appeared at the Théâtre du Châtelet as the elder Strauss in *Valses de Vienne.*

Baugé was, for a period, director of the Trianon-Lyrique, a well-meaning house producing a determined diet of opérette, and also played regularly in film (*La Fille de Madame Angot,* 1935, etc).

1931 **Beaumarchais** (Gioachino Rossini arr Eugene Cools) Théâtre des Variétés, Marseille; Théâtre de la Porte-Saint-Martin 19 May 1932

LES BAVARDS Opérette in 1 act (later 2 acts) by Charles Nuitter based on the intermezzo *Los Habladores* attributed to Cervantes. Music by Jacques Offenbach.

First produced as *Bavard et Bavarde* Théâtre du Kursaal, Bad Ems, 11 June 1862. Expanded version, Théâtre des Bouffes-Parisiens, Paris, 20 February 1863.

The original one-act version of *Bavard et Bavarde,* a little rustic opérette based on the tiny 17th-century Spanish piece *Los Habladores* (1624), was produced at the spa-town of Bad Ems in the summer of 1862, and it had sufficient success there not only to be brought into Paris and the Théâtre des Bouffes-Parisiens, but also to undergo an expansion into a more substantial, two-act work on the way.

Spendthrift, chatterbox Roland is in love with Inès, the niece of Sarmiento, but when he tries to insinuate himself into their household he does so on a windstorm of words. Poor Sarmiento, already afflicted with a wife, Béatrix, who is a nonstop talker, suddenly has an idea. He sets Roland on to his wife, and the young man's verbosity quells even her. Roland's prize is a purse of money and the hand of Inès. Sarmiento's prize is a much quieter life in the future.

The score to *Les Bavards* is full of the humor of its characters, peaking in the second act in the tea-table scene which leads up to Roland's bravura gabble-victory over Béatrix, and a marvelous three-soprano trio for Béatrix, Inès and Roland (the ''boy'' role is played en travesti).

The two-act *Les Bavards* was actually seen in Vienna before its first Parisian performance. In November 1862 a version written by Carl Treumann, under the title *Die Schwätzerin von Saragossa,* was mounted at his Theater am Franz-Josefs-Kai with Treumann playing a male Roland to the Béatrix of Anna Grobecker, the Sarmiento of Matthias Rott and the Inès of Anna Marek. Grois and Knaack supported as the Alcade and his scribe, and were supplied with a comical duet. Paris saw the show three months later, at the Bouffes-Parisiens with Delphine Ugalde (Roland), Lucille Tostée (Béatrix), Désiré (Cristoval), Augusta Thomson (Inès), Pradeau (Sarmiento) and Édouard Georges (Torribio) featured. It scored a splendid success, staying on the bill till it had passed its 100th night (29 February 1864), before giving way to the new *Les Géorgiennes.* It was revived in 1866 (2 May), in April 1870 with Anna van Ghell featured and again in 1871; it returned to Paris at the Menus-Plaisirs in 1890, and was played at the Opéra-Comique in 1924 (3 May) with Germaine Gallois as Roland and Nini Roussel as Inès.

The rest of Europe also took to *Die Schwätzerin von Saragossa,* as Treumann's remake continued to be called in Austria and Germany, or to *A fecsegök* or *A Saragossai fecsegök,* as Pál Tarnay's Hungarian version of that German version was variously called, and to their Russian, Swedish, Croatian, Spanish, Italian and Norwegian equivalents. The show was seen again in Vienna when it was played on a double bill with *La Chanson de Fortunio* for four performances at the Carltheater in 1896 with Sarolta von Rettich-Birk a memorable Beatrice and Julius Spielmann (Roland) and Betty Stojan as the lovers, and Berlin had another viewing in 1895 (Theater Unter den Linden 1 August) and again in 1919 when the piece was played at the opera house (4 June). Apparently the only major European center which somehow missed a vernacular *Les Bavards* was London. A brief French-language season from the visiting Brussels Fantaisies-Parisennnes company at the Gaiety Theatre in 1871 with Paola Marié (Inez), Mlle Clary (Roland), Mlle Chain (Béatrix) and Edouard Georges (Torribio) featured, seems to have been the city's only sighting of the show.

America first saw *Les Bavards* as *Der Schwätzer von Saragossa* with Hedwig L'Arronge in breeches in the now title role of Roland, then in French from H L Bateman's company, with Lucille Tostée of the original Paris cast out-talking Mlle Duclos (Béatrix), Aline Lambèle as Inès and Duchesne as Sarmiento. Tostée played the show in repertoire for two seasons at Pike's Opera House and at the Fifth Avenue Theater before returning to France. The show was later played around America in as English version (with both Béatrix and Inès played by low comics in frocks!) as part of the repertoire of Alice Oates's touring comic opera company (ad H J Byron). Mrs Oates, who played Roland, was still playing it as late as 1880. Subsequently, an American comic opera, *Castles in the Air,* which was based on *Les Bavards* (although professedly on its source) but which swapped Offenbach's score for the music of Gustave Kerker (Broadway Theater 5 May 1890), was produced by the De Wolf Hopper Opera Company.

Vienna: Theater am Franz-Josefs-Kai *Die Schwätzerin von Saragossa* 20 November 1862; Germany: Frankfurt 30 September 1863, Friedrich-Wilhemstädtisches Theater, Berlin 9 November 1863; Hungary: Budai Népszínház *A fecsegök* 24 October 1863, Budai Színkör *A saragossai fecsegök* 3 May 1867; USA: Stadttheater *Der Schwätzer von Saragossa* 28 October 1867, Pike's Opera House (Fr) 9 October 1868, De Bar's Opera House, St Louis *The Chatterers* 21 November 1872, Park Theater, New York 10 March 1873; UK: Gaiety Theatre (Fr) 1 July 1871

Recording: complete (Érato)

BAYARD, Jean-François (b Charolles, Seine-et-Loire, 20 March 1796; d Paris, 19 February 1853). An enormously prolific and successful French playwright who wrote, generally in collaboration, some two hundred colorful, popular-dramatic, romantic and comic plays which found repeated productions throughout Europe and beyond in the 19th century.

Bayard's style of play proved ideal fodder for the libretto-makers of the comic operas of later years, the example well set to them by no less a composer than Donizetti, who made an enormous success of an opéra-comique written to Bayard and Jules Vernoy de Saint-George's *La Fille du régiment* (Opéra-Comique 11 February 1840). In an age where the authors of, in particular, German- and English-language libretti plagiarized freely from the French stage, and gave no credit (or at best a furry sort of "taken from the French" one), many writers were gypped of their due. Some of Bayard's works were internationally too well-known not to be given the credit they were owed, but undoubtedly many Operetten of the age, beyond those which acknowledged him as their source, owed something of their story or their construction to one or another of his plays.

The popular *Le Vicomte de Letorrières* (1841 w Philippe Dumanoir), a play adapted from a novel by Eugène Sue, underwent a whole series of European musicalizations, becoming *Der galante Vicomte* (aka *Der galante Abenteuer*) with music by Adolf Müller, at Vienna's Theater an der Wien (30 November 1877) with Frln Heisler starred as the Vicomte, and later making up with considerable success into *Az eleven ördög* (mus: József Konti, Népszínház 16 December 1885) in Hungary, and *Der Vielgeliebte* (Eduard Künneke/Rideamus, Herman Haller Theater am Nollendorfplatz, Berlin, 1919) in Germany. An Hungarian musical comedy version appeared as *A primadonna* (Aladár Tombor/Albert Kövessy, Budai Színkör 1 July 1893), and one German comic opera *Der Vicomte de Letorrières* by Bogumil Zepler and Emil Taubert, was played at the Hamburg Stadttheater (4 February 1899) and later at Berlin's Neues Deutsches Theater (16 January 1903) and another (mus: Gustav Hohmann) was premiered in April 1887. A vaudeville version, made by Carl Marg and decorated with a pasticcio score taken from Auber, Tolbecque, Caraffe, Labarre and Adolf Müller, was played at Vienna's Theater an der Wien, just two seasons after the play's original production, as *Die Gabe für sich einzunehmen, oder Arthur de Montpensier* (25 April 1843). A Spanish musical adaptation, *El Vizconde de Letorieres* (Manuel Fernández Caballero/Garcia), was produced at Madrid's Teatro del Circo in 1858.

Of Bayard's other collaborations with Dumanoir, *La Vicomtesse Lolotte* became the successful Hungarian *A titkos csók* (Szidor Bátor, Béla Hegyi Népszínház 7 December 1888); *Les Premières Armes de Richelieu* was made into *Az ötödik pont* (Dezső Megyeri Népszínház 16 December 1893) and into the British "play with music" *The Dashing Little Duke,* written by Seymour Hicks, with songs by Frank Tours and Adrian Ross, and featuring Ellaline Terriss and Hicks, in turn, in its title role (Hicks Theatre 17 February 1909); and *Le Capitaine Charlotte* was turned with international success into Richard Genée's Operette *Der Seekadett* as well as an Italian comic opera, *Il Capitano Carlotta,* composed by Raffaele Mazzoni (Città delle Pieve 22 April 1891).

In Hungary there was further success for musical Bayard when his *Le Gamin de Paris* (w Émile-Louis Vanderburch) was made into *A suhanc* for *Az eleven ördög*'s composer József Konti (Népszínház 12 January 1888), whilst in Britain the musical version of the 1852 comédie-vaudeville *Un Fils de famille* (w de Biéville), produced as *The Dandy Fifth* (Clarence Corri/George R Sims, Duke of York's Theatre, London 16 August 1898), proved a long-lived favorite which toured Britain for many years. In America, the same piece was decorated with a small handful of songs under the title *The Lancers,* whilst Spain got a musicalization as *El hijo de familia* (Gaztambide, Oudrid/Luis Olcona, Teatro del Circo, Madrid 24 December 1853) just a year and a bit after the play's first appearance on the French stage.

A musical version of the play *La Frontière de Savoie* (w Eugène Scribe, to whose niece Bayard was married) was mounted in Austria and Germany as *Der Cognac-König* (Franz Wagner/Victor Léon, Ludwig Held 20 February 1897), whilst *Le Mari à la campagne* (w Jules de Vailly), originally written as a comédie à couplets, was more fully musicalized in Berlin in 1893 as *Der Leutnant zur See* (Louis Roth/E Schlack, L Herrmann Friedrich-Wilhelmstädtisches Theater 21 December). The most powerful of Bayard's musical theatre credits was, however, a rather nebulous one. The text of Suppé's *Boccaccio* was intermittently said to be adapted from a piece by Bayard, Adolphe de Leuven and Arthur de Beauplan, without any further precision being given.

Bayard's name was also attached as librettist (along with that of Scribe) to Hérold's 1832 one-act opéra-comique *Le Medecin sans medicine,* to the full-length *Le Remplaçant* (1837), Boulanger's one-act *Le Diable à l'école* (1842) and Gastinel's one-act *Le Miroir* (Opéra-Comique 19 January 1853), as well as to other operas-comiques in Boulanger's *Une Voix* and Montfort's *L'Ombre d'Argentine* (w de Biéville), and to two pieces designated opera: Jakob Rosenhain's *Le Demon de la nuit* (w E Arago Paris Opera 17 March 1851) and Thys's *Alda* (1835).

LA BÉARNAISE Opérette in 3 acts by Eugène Leterrier and Albert Vanloo. Music by André Messager. Théâtre des Bouffes-Parisiens, Paris, 12 December 1885.

Produced by Delphine Ugalde as her initial production as manager at the Bouffes-Parisiens, *La Béarnaise* got off to a sticky start when the performer cast by Mme Ugalde for the show's large title role proved unable to cope with Messager's music and had to be dropped during rehearsal. The young Messager was encouraged to play and sing his score over to the fearsome diva Jeanne

Granier, and he got only part way through the first act before Mlle Granier stopped him and accepted the role. She learned it and rehearsed it in a week and scored a splendid success.

Young Captain Perpignac (Vauthier) has made himself rather unpopular at the French court with his good looks and flirtatious behaviour, and when he finally goes too far he finds himself royally transferred—to the out-of-the-way court of the Duke of Parma—with an obligation to get himself swiftly and thoroughly married. To give the man she loves a chance to redeem himself, Jacquette (Mlle Granier) gets into masculine garb and takes Perpignac's place at the Italian court, carrying the pretence so far as to go through a marriage ceremony with the Countess Bianca (Mily-Meyer), before honor is restored and a more conventional marriage can take place. The principal comic roles were those of the nosy Girafo (Gerpré), intent on tripping up the young soldier and, ultimately, comically confounded, and the elderly, and thus also inevitably confounded, Chevalier Pomponio (Édouard Maugé).

The show's score went, in its largest part, to the star who had no less than six solos during the course of the evening: couplets as both Jacquette (''Eh, la! Papa tu me fais rire'') and as Jacquet (''Pour mes tours et pour mes malices''), a drinking song and an attractive lullaby in the second act, as well as a chanson villageoise in the finale and half of a military duo sung with Perpignac. Bianca opened proceedings enjoying her widowhood to the strains of ''C'est si charmant le veuvage'' and, later, after her marriage to Jacquet, puzzled through the comical couplets ''Pour un detail,'' wondering why her pretty new husband is so backward on fulfilling his marital obligations. Perpignac took his main musical moment in a madrigal.

La Béarnaise ran just under two months (64 performances) at the Bouffes-Parisiens, before beginning its foreign travels. The German-language theatre seems to have ignored it, but Budapest's ravenous Népszínház mounted a version (ad Béla J Fái, Lajos Evva) with Ilka Pálmay, Pál Vidor, Árpád Szathmari and Béla Szilágyi (15 performances), and both London and New York also took the show up. In Britain (ad Alfred Murray), Florence St John starred as Jacquette with the young Marie Tempest as her bride, and G H Snazelle (Perpignac) and Edwin Lonnen heading the comedy, and the show played for a little over two months (75 performances). America's version (ad Cheever Goodwin), mounted by John McCaull as *Jacquette,* with Mathilde Cottrelly in the title role, Jefferson de Angelis as Girafo, Hubert Wilke (Perpignac) and Marion Manola (Bianca), played three Broadway weeks before going out on the road in the McCaull company repertoire.

Hungary: Népszínház *A bearni leány* 26 February 1886; UK: Prince of Wales Theatre 4 October 1886; USA: Wallack's Theater *Jacquette* 13 June 1887

LE BEAU DUNOIS Opérette in 1 act by Henri Chivot and Alfred Duru. Music by Charles Lecocq. Théâtre des Variétés, Paris, 13 April 1870.

An opérette which verged merrily on the opéra-bouffe, *Le Beau Dunois* was set in the medieval times which the French burlesque writers had so successfully invested so many times before. In this episode, the gallant La Hire (Kopp) swears not to consummate his recent marriage to the lovely Loyse (Marie Aimée) until the English have been beaten back from Montargis. He gallops off to battle, leaving his new wife under the eye of the handsome young Dunois (José Dupuis), and the inevitable happens. When La Hire comes glumly back, having lost his battle, he is not unhappy to lose his wife as well. Léonce (Caprican) and Lucy Abel (Odette) supported the more plot-worthy folk.

The little score included a lilting laughing song, ''Avoir l'air de me dire en face,'' for Loyse, a mock-innocent waltz duo pastorale with the refrain ''O mon Lubin,'' a little drinking song for Dunois (''La vie à jeun est bien morose'') and a basso-baritone scene for La Hire, handing over his wife, which led into a trio and chorale with a ''la faridondaine, la faridondon'' refrain.

An agreeable success in Paris, the piece was subsequently played both in a German version in Vienna (ad Richard Genée) and in an Hungarian one (ad Endre Latabár) in Budapest, whilst London was given the piece in French by a visiting company headed by Grenier, Luce and Mlle LeGrand. The visit caused a small sensation, for whilst *Le Beau Dunois* and other such ''dirty'' shows were being given at the Lyceum, the British censor saw fit to prevent the visiting Comédie française from giving certain ''too-blue'' classics from their repertoire just round the corner at the Opera Comique.

Austria: Theater an der Wien *Der schöne Ritter Dunois* 17 September 1870; Hungary: Budai Színkör *A szép Dunois lovag* 21 April 1871; UK: Lyceum (Fr) June 1871

BEAUMARCHAIS Opérette in 3 acts by André Baugé. Music taken from the works of Rossini arranged by Eugène Cools. Théâtre des Variétés, Marseille, 1931. Théâtre de la Porte-Saint-Martin, Paris, 19 May 1932.

Written by the popular baritone Baugé as a vehicle for himself, Beaumarchais allowed its star to perform the largest part of a score in which familiar melodies from *Il barbiere di Siviglia, Guglielmo Tell, Comte Ory* and *L'italiana in Algieri* were turned into such numbers as ''La beauté, chacun le sait bien,'' ''Les trois Colombes,'' ''Pour Madame de Pompadour'' and ''Pleure, mon coeur.'' *Beaumarchais* played a respectable Paris season, at the end of which Baugé returned to playing classic opérette with a revival of *Rip!*

Adaptations of the works of the real-life Pierre Augustin Caron de Beaumarchais (1732–1799), most particularly his *Le Barbier de Seville* (1775) and *Le Mariage de Figaro* (1784), seem to have been limited to the operatic (if comic operatic) stage, from Paisiello's first introduction of Figaro to the opera stage in 1782 through the celebrated works of Rossini and Mozart, to the comic hero's most recent appearance in William Hoffman and John Corigliano's Metropolitan Opera *The Ghosts of Versailles* (1991).

BEAUMONT, Alexandre [BEAUME, Louis Alexandre] (b Paris, 1 August 1827; d Paris, 11 March 1909).

The collaborator of Charles Nuitter in the adaptation of a number of popular operas—including Weber's *Abu Hassan, Preciosa* and *Oberon,* Mozart's *Die Zauberflöte,* Verdi's *Macbeth,* Pedrotti's *Tutti in Maschera* and Ricci's *Il Marito e l'Amante* and *Crispino e la Comare* (*Le Docteur Crispin*)—to the French stage, and also on several original operatic texts (Joncières' *Le Dernier Jour de Pompeii,* etc), and a series of cantatas, Beaumont found one major success in the lighter musical theatre when, teamed again with Nuitter, he was responsible for the text to Lecocq's intricately plotted opérette *Le Coeur et la main.*

1855 **Une Nuit à Seville** (Frédéric Barbier/w Charles Nuitter) 1 act Théâtre Lyrique 14 September

1855 **Rose et Narcisse** (Barbier/w Nuitter) 1 act Théâtre Lyrique 21 November

1858 **Le Peau de l'ours** (Samuel David) 1 act Folies-Nouvelles 28 March

1863 **Un Othello** (Isidore Legouix/w Nuitter) 1 act Théâtre des Champs-Élysées 20 June

1864 **Le Lion de Saint-Marc** (Legouix/w Nuitter) 1 act Theatre Saint-Germain 24 November

1867 **Cardillac** (Lucien Dautresme/w Nuitter) Théâtre Lyrique 11 December

1868 **Le Vengeur** (Legouix/w Nuitter) Théâtre de l'Athénée 20 November

1874 **Les Dernières Grisettes** (Legouix/w Nuitter) Fantaisies-Parisiennes, Brussels 12 December

1875 **Amphytrion** (Paul Lacome/w Nuitter) 1 act Salle Taitbout 5 April

1882 **Le Coeur et la main** (Charles Lecocq/w Nuitter) Théâtre des Nouveautés 19 October

1888 **La Volière** (Lecocq/w Nuitter) Théâtre des Nouveautés 11 February

1888 **Le Puits qui parle** (Edmond Audran/w Paul Burani) Théâtre des Nouveautés 15 March

1888 **La Demoiselle de Belleville** (*Die Jungfrau von Belleville*) French version w Nuitter (Théâtre des Folies-Dramatiques)

Plate 25. **Roma Beaumont** *played the child, Grete, to the Rudi of Ivor Novello in the Theatre Royal, Drury Lane production of* The Dancing Years.

1890 **L'Égyptienne** (Lecocq/w Nuitter, Henri Chivot) Théâtre des Folies-Dramatiques 8 November

1898 **Le Soleil à minuit** (Albert Renaud/w Nuitter) Théâtre des Bouffes-Parisiens 14 October

Other titles attributed: *Le Clef d'argent* (Legouix), *Marion* (Boulanger)

BEAUMONT, Roma [Minnie Cecilia] (b Kennington, London, 31 July 1913).

A child performer, then a chorister and supporting player (*Stand Up and Sing* 1931, Winnie in *Mr Whittington* 1933) in London musicals, Miss Beaumont rose to principal roles as the ingenue of touring productions of *For the Love of Mike, Tell Her the Truth* and *The Crest of the Wave.* This last engagement earned the very pretty and young-looking 24-year-old the important role of the child, Grete, in Novello's *The Dancing Years* (1939) at the Theatre Royal, Drury Lane (''Primrose''). She remained with this show through its very long-running success in London and the provinces, and then moved on to create the tripartite star role of Melinda/Melanie/Melody built to her measure in Novello's next musical, *Perchance to Dream* (1945, ''The Night That I Curtsied to the King''). She subsequently appeared as Alice in Wonderland and Cinderella in London seasons, before retiring from the stage as the wife of producer Alfred Black.

BEAUTY AND THE BEAST Musical in 2 acts by Linda Woolverton based on the film of the same title. Music by Alan Menken. Lyrics by Howard Ashman and Tim Rice. Palace Theater, New York, 18 April 1994.

The on-the-verge-of-the-21st-century equivalent of America's early-20th-century fairy-tale spectaculars (*The Wizard of Oz, Babes in Toyland,* etc), *Beauty and the Beast* was brought to the stage, following its successful career in the animated cinema, by its screenmakers, filmland's longtime kings of the (usually) classy cartoon, Walt Disney Productions.

This rewriting of Madame de Beaumont's classic 18th-century French fairy tale had a ''Beauty'' called Belle who still sported the Cindy-doll traits of a classic Disney heroine, and still piped the sweet soprano of a classic Disney heroine, but who showed intermittent (though only intermittent) signs of having been dipped in attitude, and who came out from time to time with some hilariously p.c. pouts. The Beast of the occasion (still called ''Beast''), a shumbling puss of an animal, roared a little tantrum occasionally but he was depicted in this version as more of a would-be endearing buffoon than a frightening animal. However, if hero and heroine suffered in this retelling from a bit of brain or personality softening, they were shored up through the story and the show by some altogether stauncher folk, headed by a six-foot square-chinned villain called Gaston with a yen for himself and also for the heroine, three squealing-sighing maids unitedly lusting after the said Gaston, the jolly half-humanized inhabitants of the booby Beast's forest castle—from a candlestick to a teapot with its kiddie teacup, to a wardrobe and a pendulum clock—and a slavering bunch of wolves which were altogether more fearsome than the nominal scarer of the fable.

The discreet set of songs that accompanied the show's tale (the 1991 screen score being here expanded with additional numbers by Menken and by Tim Rice, replacing the late Howard Ashman), included a rhythmic paean to the charms of ''Gaston'' and a lullabyish title number (Academy Award), but sported nothing of the enduring genre of such rollicking Disney superclassics as ''Never Smile at a Crocodile'' or ''Bibbity-Bobbity-Boo.''

Like its forebears in the genre, however, the stage *Beauty and the Beast* existed not to show off either text or music, but as a monument to the stage designer's and technicians' art, and the highpoint of the theatre evening, as of the film, came in a big, whirling routine in which a seemingly endless parade of enchanted household goods insisted (seemingly endlessly) ''Be Our Guest,'' as they filled the stage with colorful, costumed, choreographic action. An atmospheric deep dark forest with the aforesaid wolves, and a prettily drooping rose with a meaning were amongst the other winning visuals.

Beauty and the Beast was brought to the Broadway stage at the Palace Theater with Burke Moses (Gaston), Terrence V Mann (Beast) and Susan Egan (Belle) featured and Tom Bosley, acclaimed more than thirty years earlier as the star of *Fiorello,* playing the part of Belle's Gepetto-ish father. Thoroughly thumbs-downed by the award-givers, even on its visual and technical side (only the costumes were Tonyied in a very un-costume-y year) the show, however, thoroughly outlasted the other four musicals of its season, running on for five and a half years (2,250 performances) before being moved out (after a mooted shut-down had been vetoed) to end its run in a reduced-size version at the Lunt-Fontanne Theater (12 November 1999).

Whilst the Broadway run continued, the show made its way to London, where Alasdair Harvey and Julie Alanah Brighten were cast in the title roles of what turned out a two-and-a-half-year run, to Australia, where 13 months in Melbourne were followed by 10 in Sydney (Her Majesty's Theatre 19 October 1996), to Japan, South America and to the European Continent. Germany, fast threatening to become the new champion of the copycat show, turned out a preemptive *Die Schöne und die Biest* at Cologne (Sartory Theater 22 September 1994) which, in true copycat style, didn't get within a whiff of challenging the real thing, which was introduced to Continental Europe the following year at Vienna's Raimundtheater with Ethan Freeman and Caroline Vasicek in its title roles. Germany's production of the real thing, mounted at Stuttgart seven months later, was introduced by Uwe Kröger and Leah Delos Santos.

Britain, too, uncharacteristically jumped on the copcat wagon, with a *Beauty and the Beast* musicked by favorite singer David Essex (Albert Hall 18 August 1995); Jerôme Savary resuscitated *La Belle et la bête* at Paris's Magic Circus, and in Italy a *La Bella e la Bestia* put in an appearance as part of a perfect rush of versions of an otherwise largely forgotten tale whose sudden rise back to the heights of popularity was blatantly fuelled by Disney's film and show.

Grétry's 1771 successful opéra-comique *Zémire et Azor* (allegedly based on a 1742 play *Amour par amour*) seems to owe its story to Mme Villeneuve's earlier version of *La Belle et la bête,* but the French theatre was apparently not inspired to opérettic action by this tale in the way it was by so many others among the aristocratic fairystories of the times. A pantomime-ballet produced at the Théâtre de la Renaissance in 1873 seems to have been the only major *Belle et la bête* of its period. Britain, however, took to the tale enthusiastically. After melodramatic versions of the piece had been played at the Surrey (1812) and the Adelphi (1819), Planché turned out a *Beauty and the Beast* extravaganza which was produced at the Theatre Royal, Covent Garden (12 April 1841) with Eliza Vestris playing Beauty to the Beast of operatic tenor William Harrison, on the wings of which the tale became a regular topic for pantomime productions, up to and beyond the turn of the century.

America, which for many years played localized versions of Planché and other English *Beauty and the Beast* extravaganzas, got what seems to have been a first original *Beauty and the Beast* at San Francisco's Tivoli in 1892 (7 August). It was written by a Salt Lake City dentist, J P Wilson, and composed by the Tivoli's conductor, Adolf Bauer. Another, the work of one George Foster Platt, produced at Milwaukee in 1901 (Academy of Music 28 October), managed to get a bad fairy, the Queen of the Land of Happy Dreams and the Guardian of the Nightmare Shades into a tale where the nominal principals seem to have got a bit lost amongst scenery, specialities and stage effects. In 1901 Klaw and Erlanger reproduced a version (ad Fred Solomon, J Cheever Goodwin, J J McNally) of the previous year's Drury Lane pantomime on Broadway under the title of *The Sleeping Beauty and the Beast* (Broadway Theater 4 November). None of these got within miles of the 1990s version either in spectacle or in popularity, but the last named harbored a hit song, Jerome and Schwartz's ''Rip van Winkle Was a Lucky Man.''

Australia: Princess Theatre, Melbourne 8 July 1995; Austria: Raimundtheater *Die Schöne und das Biest* 28 September 1995; UK: Dominion Theatre 13 May 1997; Germany: SI-Centrum, Stuttgart *Die Schöne und das Biest* 5 December 1997.

Recordings: original film score (Disney), original cast (Disney), London cast (Disney), German cast (Polydor), Japanese cast, Australian cast

Literature: Frantz, D: *Disney's Beauty and the Beast* (Disney, 1995)

THE BEAUTY OF BATH Musical play in 2 acts by Seymour Hicks and Cosmo Hamilton. Lyrics by Charles H Taylor. Music by Herbert E Haines. Additional music by Frederic Norton and Jerome D Kern. Aldwych Theatre, London, 19 March 1906.

A successful musical play from the continuously successful Charles Frohman/Seymour Hicks producing and writing team, *The Beauty of Bath* was based on the key scene from the favorite play *David Garrick* in which the hero attempts to disgust the heroine with his own bad behavior so that, for her own good, she may be dissuaded from marrying him. The twist in this version of the tale was that the antics were intended to put the lass off the hero's double. Hicks and his wife, Ellaline Terriss, played the principal roles—she as a nice young lady with a passion for an actor, he as the actor's double, who has fallen in love with her photograph and who takes on the task of disillusioning her—and the piece happily confirmed the team's success with *The Catch of the Season.* The physical likeness of the naval officer hero and the famous actor was achieved by the casting of Hicks's brother, Stanley Brett, in the look-alike role.

A strong book was supported by a colorful staging, in which a group of showgirls, playing the daughters of Sir Timothy Bun (''the Bath Buns''), provided a special attraction, and an enjoyable score in which the show's nominal composer, Herbert Haines, provided both the prettiest number—the title waltz—and the most amusing—an operatic burlesque duo for Sydney Fairbrother as a lugubriously lovelorn char and the juvenile Albert Valchera as her similarly smitten son. A liberal dose of interpolated numbers included the first songs written specifically for the London stage by 21-year-old Jerome D Kern, ''Mr Chamberlain'' with a lyric by the equally new Pelham G Wodehouse, and ''The Frolic of a Breeze,'' as well as Frederic Norton's music-hally ''George's Little Love Affairs'' and the initial stage success of 22-year-old Herman Darewski, ''My Little Hyacinth,'' which Miss Terriss made into the show's most popular number. It remained so in spite of the second act ball-scene of what had begun as a remarkably coherent musical play before being filled up with extraneous songs, dances, impersonations and other items during the show's run.

Produced at the Aldwych Theatre, the show was transferred to Frohman's newly built Hicks Theatre in Shaftesbury Avenue as its opening attraction, and there it ran out its 10-month, 287-performance London run, prior to heading for the provinces. During the London run, a parallel version of the show played completely by children (including the show's star juvenile, Valchera, the young Ivy Sawyer and—in the chorus—future leading lady Winifred Barnes) was mounted (11 February 1907) for a series of matinées.

THE BEAUTY PRIZE Musical comedy in 3 acts by George Grossmith and P G Wodehouse. Music by Jerome Kern. Winter Garden Theatre, London, 5 September 1923.

A mid-Atlantic collaboration between English producer/author Grossmith and the American-based Wodehouse and Kern, attempting to reproduce their Winter Garden Theatre success with *The Cabaret Girl, The Beauty Prize* was constructed round the stars of the earlier show: ingenue Dorothy Dickson, principal comedian Leslie Henson, Grossmith himself as dude comic, and Heather Thatcher, representing low comedy with glamor. The plot had Miss Dickson winning a newspaper beauty contest, for which the prize is the hand of Henson in marriage. Since she has the dashing Jack Hobbs already lined up, the exchange is rather improbable. By the end, Henson is more suitably paired off with Miss Thatcher, and Miss Dickson reconciled with her former fiancé.

The incidentals included a shipboard setting, a ballet based on the new craze for Mah Jong, a number in the jargon of Sinclair Lewis's fashionable book *Babbit* (''Meet Me Down on Main Street'') performed by Henson and Grossmith, a song bemoaning the fact that ''You Can't Make Love By Wireless'' and another for Henson about the ''Non-Stop Dancing'' craze, but *The Beauty Prize* proved nowhere near as attractive as its predecessor and owed its six-month and 213-performance life largely to the reputations won over previous shows by its cast and theatre.

THE BEAUTY SPOT Musical comedy in 3 acts by Joseph W Herbert. Music by Reginald De Koven. Herald Square Theater, New York, 10 April 1909.

Joseph Herbert's libretto to *The Beauty Spot* had already done duty as a play in South Africa and again, with music by Edward Jones attached, as a flop musical as produced in London by South Africa's Frank Wheeler (also director, choreographer, comic lead) and theatre-owner George H Broadhurst (also additional numbers) under the title *The Prince of Borneo* (Strand Theatre 5 October 1899, 31 performances), before it was wedded in its third, American life to a standard Reginald De Koven score.

Popular comedian Jefferson de Angelis starred in the now leading role of General Samovar, with Viola Gillette as his ex-actress wife, a lady who once modeled, rather unclad, for the painting entitled ''The Beauty Spot'' which she is now anxious to disown. The spot in question is, however, damning evidence. Alongside this saucy tale, the General's daughter, Nadine (Marguerite Clark), made her way to marrying the painting's artist Jacques (George MacFarlane), rather than the cousin (Alfred de Ball) to whom she has been engaged since birth and who has, in any case, wed a Bornean lady (Isabel de Armond) in the meanwhile. The show ended with the offending painting being propped on an easel before the audience whilst the artist solved all problems by deftly covering the lady's nakedness with some lightning draperies, and turning the identifying mole into a little mouse.

New York did not object to the indelicacies of the birthmark plot as London had done with its standard sanctimonious vigor and, although De Koven's score (which retained a song called ''The Prince of Borneo'') was no more notable than Jones's had been, the show did very much better in its Broadway incarnation and totted up a fine 137 summer season performances before moving on to a cheerful and extended life on the road.

The same title was later used for a musical play in two acts by Arthur Anderson, adapted from the French of P-L Flers, with lyrics by Anderson, Clifford Harris and ''Valentine'' and music by James W Tate, which was produced at London's Gaiety Theatre, 22 December 1917. This ''beauty spot'' was not a birthmark, but a landmark, and the plot of the show dealt with how naughty Napoléon Bramble (Arthur Whitby) enriched himself on the publication of a book of traveler's tales really written by a dead friend. The show was, however, orientated by Parisian revueist P-L Flers much more towards the picturesque than the coherent, and the production was largely sculpted to feature the talents of the ill-fated French danseuse Régine Flory and her Polish dancing partner Jan Oyra. Their principal set piece ''Kadouja and the Spirit of Haschisch'' depicted Flory as a victim of the drug as portrayed by her partner. (The idea was modish rather than innovative, 50 years earlier the German Reeds had played a whole ''hasheesh'' operetta at their Gallery of Illustration). Some light pieces by the show's nominal songwriters were supplemented by a couple of established American song hits: ''Poor Butterfly,'' taken from the previous year's New York Hippodrome *Big Show,* and Harry Tierney's spelling song ''M.I.S.S.I.S.S.I.P.P.I.''

Producer Alfred Butt tried, with *The Beauty Spot,* to establish himself in power at the Gaiety Theatre, from where he had ousted the successful Grossmith and Laurillard management, but the public preferred to follow the old team to the Prince of Wales Theatre and Butt's attempt to make himself the new George Edwardes got off to a poor start when the show lasted only an unprofitable 152 performances. Mlle Flory salvaged the ''haschisch'' routine and took it back to Paris where she introduced it into the Casino de Paris reuve *Pa-ri-ki-ri* (1918).

THE BEAUTY STONE Romantic musical drama in 3 acts by Arthur Pinero and Joseph Comyns Carr. Music by Arthur Sullivan. Savoy Theatre, London, 28 May 1898.

Following the definitive termination of the Gilbert and Sullivan collaboration, Carte teamed his composer on a musical play with a celebrated pair of writers in Pinero and Comyns Carr. In perhaps trying too hard to write in a style that was not comparable to that of Gilbert, and mindful of Sullivan's wish to try more serious subjects, the librettists supplied their composer with a sentimental medieval romance which was ill-fitted to the sort of musical treatment which the traditions of the Savoy Theatre encouraged.

Ruth Vincent played the cripple, Laine, who is given a beautifying talisman by the devil (Walter Passmore), which wins her the heart of the Flemish Lord, Philip of

Mirlemont (George Devoll). When Mirlemont goes to war, his former mistress, Saïda (Pauline Joran), gets hold of the stone, and Laine returns to her former, twisted state, but Philip returns home blinded and, as the stone returns to the devil, to the arms of the woman whom he had known so beautiful. Henry Lytton and Rosina Brandram played Laine's parents—he, for a while, the rejuvenated holder of the stone and pursued by Saïda—Emmie Owen was given a role as ''crazy Jacqueline'' which got her into boy's clothes and allowed her to nurture a passion for the devil, and a tiny role as an entrant in Philip's bride-seeking beauty contest was taken by chorister Ethel Jackson, the future *Merry Widow* of Broadway.

Sullivan's score included moments both gently appealing (Laine's prayer ''Dear Mother Mary'') and showily dramatic (Saïda's powerful ''Mine, Mine At Last!''), but, with lyrics which insisted on ''ye''-ing and ''thou''-ing throughout, *The Beauty Stone* could be little more than an awkwardly sub-operatic piece whose pieces fitted badly together. It was shunted out of the Savoy after 50 performances.

Recording: complete (Pearl)

BEER, Gustav (b Vienna, 16 June 1888; d Nyack, NJ, 26 July 1983).

The son of composer Josef Beer (1851–1908), Gustav Beer was a regular purveyor of texts to the Viennese stage in the 1920s and early 1930s, collaborating with several of the most popular composers of the time—Eysler, Straus, Künneke, Reinhardt, Gilbert, Stolz—and with several successful librettists and lyricists, but without turning out any one major success. His first full-length piece *Die Millionengretl* had a 50-performance run at the Raimundtheater with Franz Glawatsch starred, but the subsequent *Die blonde Sphinx,* starring Rita Georg, played only three weeks at the Burgertheater. Of his other productions at the main musical houses, *Prinzessin Ti-Ti-Pa* lasted 53 performances with Josef König and Steffi Walidt featured in the lead roles and with the ageing Mizzi Zwerenz as character lady, *Der Bauerngeneral* played just under two months, and *Die Dame mit dem Regenbogen* 74 performances. The most successful of this group of his works was the Suppé pasticcio *Die grosse Unbekannte* (Johann Strauss-Theater, 101 performances). He also contributed screenplays to Berlin's active UFA studios.

Beer joined the artistic exodus from Germany and Austria after 1933 and settled in America where, under the occasional nom de plume of Gustave W Wheatley, he was active in musical affairs and became president of the American League of Authors and Composers from Austria (ALACA). He did not write for the American theatre but, with another expatriate, Alfred Grünwald, supplied the texts for Kálmán's posthumous *Arizona Lady,* mounted in Berne in 1954, and for the Operette *Fiesta,* produced in Munich in 1955. An unspecified Beer play (w Hans Kottow) was musicalized for the Hungarian stage under the title *Krizantém* (Mihály Nador/Ernő Kulinyi Városi Színház 19 December 1924).

1911 **Der Minenkönig** (Robert Stolz/w Ernst Marischka) 1 act Apollotheater 3 October

1914 **Eine verschenkte Nacht** (Béla Laszky/w Fritz Lunzer) 1 act Deutsches Künstlertheater 1 February

1914 **Das Narrenhaus** (Hans Albert Cesek, Tivadar Pallós/w E Marischka) 1 act Hölle 1 February

1915 **Die Millionengretl** (Franz Schönbaumsfeld/w Alfred Deutsch-German) Raimundtheater 26 November

1920 **Rund um die Bühne** (Edmund Eysler/w Armin Friedmann) Apollotheater 1 March

1920 **Der König heiratet** (Eysler/w E Marischka) Künstlerbühne April

1922 **Der Glückstrompeter** (Heinrich Reinhardt/w Friedmann) Komödienhaus 7 December

1923 **Der Hampelmann** (Stolz/w Lunzer) Komödienhaus 9 November

1924 **Alles per Radio** (Fritz Lehner/w Karl Farkas) Ronacher 21 March

1924 **Puszipajtások** (Pallós/w E Marischka ad Zsolt Harsányi) Lujza Blaha Színház, Budapest 9 October

1925 **Die blonde Sphinx** (Max Niederberger/ad Imre Földes) German version Wiener Bürgertheater 27 March

1925 **Die grosse Unbekannte** (Franz von Suppé arr Karl Pauspertl/w Julius Wilhelm) Johann Strauss-Theater 8 April

1928 **Prinzessin Ti-Ti-Pa** (Stolz/w Lunzer) Carltheater 15 May

1928 **Die singende Venus** (Eduard Künneke/w Lunzer) Schauspielhaus, Breslau 9 June

1930 **Durchlaucht Mizzi** (Eysler/w Lunzer) Neues Wiener Schauspielhaus 23 December

1931 **Der Bauerngeneral** (Straus/w Julius Brammer) Theater an der Wien 28 March

1933 **Die Dame mit dem Regenbogen** (Jean Gilbert/w Brammer) Theater an der Wien 25 August

1934 **Das ist der erste Liebe** (Eysler/w Hans Kottow) Volksoper 23 December

1954 **Arizona Lady** (Emmerich Kálmán/w Alfred Grünwald) Stadttheater, Berne 14 February

1955 **Fiesta** (Juan Cardona/w Grünwald) Theater am Gärtnerplatz, Munich 11 February

Other title attributed: *Das einzige Mittel*

THE BEGGAR'S OPERA Comic opera in 3 acts by John Gay. Music selected and arranged by Johann Christoph Pepusch. Lincoln's Inn Fields Theatre, London, 29 January 1728.

The most successful ballad opera of the 18th century, *The Beggar's Opera* has survived as virtually the only representative of its class and period still to win regular productions on the 20th-century stage.

Plate 26. **The Beggar's Opera.** *The Peachum family—papa (H Peters), mama (Sofie Lis) and daughter Polly (Sheila Wolk)—in the Hessisches Staatstheater, Wiesbaden, production of 1985.*

Gay, an intermittent author and poet, disappointed in his expectations for royal patronage after many years spent being agreeable to those headed for power and position, is said to have taken his revenge in a piece in which the words and sentiments of "fine gentlemen and ladies, satirists and philosophers" were put into the mouths of a crowd of Newgate-bait characters in a piece in which "the scenes, characters and incidents are, in themselves, of the lowest and most disgusting kind." In fact, whatever satire there was in Gay's work initially, the piece soon became simply a comical musical play about lust and greed amongst the picturesquely low-life folk of London, and it was as that rather than as a piece of any purposefully satirical character that it has succeeded through the centuries.

Refused by Colley Cibber at the Theatre Royal, Drury Lane, the show was taken up by Rich at the Lincoln's Inn Fields Theatre and set with a musical part, in an avowed burlesque of the Italian opera, compounded by the theatre's musical director, Dr Pepusch. Pepusch's 69 musical items were manufactured from a wide variety of popular melodies—from Ferrabosco and Rizzio to Handel's *Rinaldo*—and topped off by an original overture.

Mr Peachum (Mr Hippesley) is a thief-master and fence in London town, with an influence and connections which make him a powerful man. He and his wife (Mrs Martin) are horrified when their daughter Polly (Lavinia Fenton) gets secretly wed to the sexy thief-leader, Macheath (Tom Walker), and they devote themselves to getting their new son-in-law arrested and, if possible, hung. Thanks to their efforts, Macheath is betrayed to the law by the jealous whore, Jenny Diver (Mrs Clarke), and held under lock and key by Peachum's old pal, the jailor Lockit (Jack Hall), but he contrives to escape with the help of another of his feminine conquests, Lockit's daughter, Lucy (Mrs Eagleton). Recaptured, he seems bound for the gallows, but a last-minute pardon returns him to the arms of Polly, the only one of his apparently numerous "wives" who had the acumen actually to get him before a clergyman.

The largest part of the original lyrics was the work of Gay, but it was said that other folk including Swift ("When You Censure the Age"), Sir Charles Williams ("Virgins Are Like the Fair Flow'r"), Lord Chesterfield ("The Modes of the Town") and the Master of the Rolls, Fortescue ("Gamesters and Lawyers Are Jugglers Alike") also made contributions. The highlight of an evening in which all the principal characters were liberally supplied with vocal pieces was, however, Polly's little solo "Oh, Ponder Well! Be Not Severe." The score, however, underwent constant change as 18th-century artists and managements swapped it around and interpolated into it at will.

The Beggar's Opera proved just the thing to appeal to those folk whom Gay intended to satirize, and it attracted enough fulminating from the righteous to boost its prospects even further. It became a huge hit, was played on the bill for 63 nights in its first season, returned in the fall, was played in 1729 with a cast of midgets, and brought back very frequently in the seasons that followed, entering the Theatre Royal, Haymarket, in 1728, and both the Theatre Royal, Drury Lane, and the Theatre Royal, Covent Garden, with Stoppelaer as Macheath, in 1732. In the same year, the famous Irish actress Peg Woffington, who had appeared as Macheath at the age of 10 in a children's company, apparently succeeded in trebling the roles of Macheath, Mrs Peachum and Diana Trapes, but the majority of leading men in the show were male and Charles Hulst, O'Keefe and Incledon were amongst the favored Macheaths of the 18th-century stage. New York got its first sight of the piece in 1750 when it was given at the Nassau Street Theater for a couple of performances.

The piece was played on English-speaking stages around the world throughout the 18th and 19th centuries, with Charles Santley, Sims Reeves and Mrs Howard Paul amongst the more memorable Macheaths of the 1800s, but William Harrison felt obliged to make a bowdlerized version of the show for his production in 1854. In 1840 a burlesque of what was itself in a large part a burlesque, *The Beggar's Opera Burlesqued,* was produced at the Adelphi Theatre (16 November) with Mrs Keeley as Macheath and Paul Bedford as Polly; in 1870 another parody, *The Beggar's Uproar (not quite Gay but much more lively)* by Hubert J Morice, was played at London's Surrey Theatre (7 May) and Gay's text was subsequently adapted into a whole series of "revised versions." The most successful of these was a 1920 revision, with a score arranged by vocalist "Frederic Austin" [né Frederick Woellhaf], which was produced at London's Lyric Theatre, Hammersmith (5 June), with Frederick Ranalow starred as Macheath, Austin as Peachum and Sylvia Nelis as Polly. This production ran up a remarkable total of 1,463 performances, and reestablished the show throughout the world, even though it lasted only 37 performances when transferred to New York's Greenwich Village Theater (27 December 1920), with Percy Heming, Charles Magrath and Miss Nelis in its chief roles. The new wave of interest also won it a showing—in English—in France, when Wilfred Easton and Taylor Platt's company, headed by Andrew Shanks (Macheath) and Dorothy Gill (Lucy) went to play the piece at Paris's Théâtre Caumartin for a fortnight's season, and in other European venues.

Regularly produced in London's commercial theatre through the decades since, *The Beggar's Opera* was played in the West End in 1935, 1940 (w Michael Redgrave), 1941, 1948 (w Peter Pears), 1954, 1963 and 1968, at the National Theatre in 1982 and the Royal Shakespeare Company in 1992–93. In New York it was repeated in 1928, 1957 and at the Billy Rose Theater in 1982 with Kevin Kline as Macheath. A film version was produced in 1952 with Laurence Olivier as Macheath, Dorothy Tutin and Adele Leigh respectively acting and singing the role of Polly and Stanley Holloway as Lockit, and it has been televised on several occasions.

Foreign-language versions of *The Beggar's Opera* have, by and large, preferred to build new scores and/or shows on to Gay's story rather than to present the piece as written. Although the regular *Beggar's Opera* was not seen in Vienna until 1949, the Carltheater mounted a German version after the Lyric, Hammersmith triumph, under the title *Der Liebling von London,* with text adapted by Felix Dörmann and the musical score arranged by Hans Ewald Heller (19 April 1924). It ran exactly a month, but it prompted another German-language adaptation, the much more successful Elisabeth Hauptmann, Bertolt Brecht/Kurt Weill *Der Dreigroschenoper.* Amongst later German versions there have been *Der Bettleropers* by Hans Magnus Enzensberger, music by Wolfgang Fortner and Volkmar Fritsche (Städtische Bühnen, Heidelberg 19 June 1966) and by Arim Tacke, music by Hans Hoffmann (Oldenberg 1988). Another adaptation of the story, this one in English, was made by John Latouche, as the American musical comedy *The Beggar's Holiday* (26 December 1946), set with music by Duke Ellington, and Vaclav Havel turned out a Czech version in 1972. The latest remakes have been *Blood Red Roses* (Marc Berry/Michael Korth, Stadttheater, Aachen 8 August 1998), which set the tale in the clichéd Chicago gangsterlands of the 1920s, and a British National Theatre production, *The Villain's Opera* (Stephen Warbeck/ Nick Dear), which boasted in its advertisements "this production contains strong language." Gay hadn't needed that kind of advertisement.

Gay's musequel to *The Beggar's Opera,* a piece entitled *Polly,* was originally banned, apparently for being personally and offensively satirical, but when it was ultimately produced, 50 years on (Haymarket Theatre 19 June 1777), it proved to be neither one nor the other, merely dull. It was a quick failure, as its predecessor continued to prosper. *Polly* was, nevertheless, revived several times in London, notably following the success of the Lyric, Hammersmith version of *The Beggar's Opera,* with one production, at the Kingsway Theatre (30 December 1922 ad Clifford Bax) running for 327 performances, at the height of the briefly reborn fashion for ballad opera.

USA: New York 3 December 1750; Australia: Albert Theatre, Hobart 30 March 1842; France: Théâtre Caumartin 22 November 1921; Austria: Johann Strauss-Theater 4 December 1949

Films: British Lion 1952, TV film (Chelsea Theater Centre) 1973; BBC-TV film: Polygram video 1983

Recordings: complete versions (HMV, Argo, Desto, Decca, etc), cast recordings (EMI, CBS, London, etc)

Literature: Kidson, F: *The Beggar's Opera, its Predecessors and Successors* (Macmillan, New York, 1922), Schultz, W E: *The Beggar's Opera, Its Content, History and Influence* (Yale University Press, 1923), Lewis, P: *John Gay: The Beggar's Opera* (Barnes & Noble, New York, 1973)

THE BEGUM Comic opera in 3 acts by Harry B Smith. Music by Reginald De Koven. Fifth Avenue Theater, New York, 21 November 1887.

The first work of both its soon-to-be-ubiquitous librettist/lyricist and of the composer of *Robin Hood* to be played in New York, *The Begum* was produced by John McCaull with Mathilde Cottrelly starred in the title role of the man-eating Begum of Oude and De Wolf Hopper as her husband, Howja-Dhu. Having tired of him, as she has of all her previous spouses, the Begum promotes Howja-Dhu to the head of the army, declares war, and sits back to select her next consort whilst he gets himself killed. Since Hopper was the top-billed star of the show, it went without saying that Howja-Dhu survived this Machiavellic bit of queen-spidering and returned to claim his own.

The piece mixed elements of extravaganza and opéra-bouffe (notably loud echoes of *La Grande-Duchesse*) with the kind of grotesque low comedy which would become a favorite feature of early American comic operas and, contrastingly, a rather well-mannered score. It was cast up to the hilt (''probably the greatest cast ever seen in comic opera in America''), with its other Offenbachishly named characters being played by Hubert Wilke (Klahm-Chowdee), Digby Bell (Myhnt-Jhuleep), Edwin Hoff (Pooteh-Wehl), Jefferson de Angelis (Jhust-Naut), Harry MacDonough (Asch-Kart), Laura Joyce Bell (Namouna) and Marion Manola (Aminah). However, following its Philadelphia tryout (Chestnut Street Opera House 7 November) it was played for only three weeks on Broadway before McCaull moved his ever-traveling repertoire company on to other more profitable cities, notably for a packed engagement in the authors' hometown of Chicago (Chicago Opera House 25 December 1887), where ''society went to see [it] in such droves that nearly every night manager Henderson had to close the doors.''

Advised press opinion concurred ''the success of the piece is due in a large measure to the cast. There is a great deal in the libretto that in less competent hands would fall flat, and the music too could be improved upon, but taken altogether there is every reason to believe that *The Begum* will be a go.'' Except in Chicago. There it was voted simply tremendous, even by the critics. *The Begum* and its cast proved enough of a ''go'' to hold their place alongside *Bellman* and *Falka* in McCaull's touring repertoire throughout the season. One season.

LES BEIGNETS DU ROI Opérette in 3 acts by Albert Carré based on a vaudeville by Benjamin Antier. Music by Firmin Bernicat. Alcazar, Brussels, 10 February 1882. Revised version by Paul Ferrier with additional music by André Messager as *Les Premières Armes de Louis XV* Théâtre des Menus-Plaisirs, Paris, 16 February 1888.

Hurriedly written and then rewritten by its highly strung composer prior to its production in Belgium, *Les Beignets du Roi* scored a big success on its first appearance in Brussels. The tale of the piece centered on the very young King Louis XV (Hélène Chevrier) and the complications ensuing on the awakening of his libido. Soubrette Antoinette (Mme Nadau) wins his favor by cooking his favorite beignets for him, and he then discovers that he would like more than a bit of puff pastry from her. However, the clever maid outwits him in the end, and gets him to decree that she may marry her Gaston de Norcy (Bréhy) rather than the lofty Duc de Meillan (Mercier) decreed to her by her ambitious aunt (Mme Bouland). A more romantic romance, between Antoinette's school chum Atalante de Narbonne (Mme Désir) and Don Rodriguez (Lary), ran parallel to the lighter tale.

Antoinette's solo ''Le Roi m'a dit'' was the saucily ingenuous hit of the score, whilst the King sang of how ''J'adore la crême au chocolat'' and demanded ''Savez-vous faire une omelette?'' before getting on to less culinary affairs, and there was a comic musical moment in the Trio des pendus in which Norcy, Rodriguez and the King all got ready to commit simultaneous suicide over unresolved love.

After the success of Bernicat's posthumous *François les bas-bleus,* the earlier piece was given a Paris staging with its finales revamped and several songs added by the young Messager (who had completed *François les bas-bleus*). The resultant piece played a barely satisfactory 44 times at the Menus-Plaisirs.

BEI KERZENLICHT Musical comedy by Siegfried Geyer and Karl Farkas. Music by Robert Katscher.

Siegfried Geyer's seven-handed comedy *Bei Kerzenlicht,* a dainty enough example of the most conventional master-and-man, mistress-and-maid identity swapping plot, had a fine international success, and it was produced both in London in Harry Graham's English version as *By Candlelight* (Prince of Wales Theatre 18 September 1928) for a splendid run of 477 performances, and on Broadway in P G Wodehouse's version (30 September 1929, 128 performances) before Geyer adapted his play as a musical comedy, equipped with songs by Robert Katscher.

The resulting small-scale musical play was—lacking all and any evidence to the contrary—seemingly first produced, not in Germany as would have perhaps been most likely, but in Hungary (ad Armand Szantó, Mihály Szécsen) before being taken up by the Shuberts for Broadway. The little piece was then regularly Shubertized, in line with the principle that bigger was better. Katscher's songs were thrown out, and the recently accidented Cole Porter hired to replace them. Rowland Leigh souped up the intimate play to conventional (over)size, ladled glitzy chorines and additional settings into the action, and *You Never Know* (with a credit for ''additional numbers'' given to Edwin Gilbert and Alex Fogerty . . . and Robert Katscher) was produced at the Shubert Theater, New Haven on 3 March 1938. By the time it reached New York's Winter Garden Theater (21 September 1938), with Clifton Webb, Lupe Velez, Rex O'Malley and Libby Holman heading affairs, it was in a condition to play 78 performances. The Porter connection has, however, given *You Never Know* an afterlife and it has been exhumed in various forms in American houses since his death and canonization.

Vienna went back to the original Katscher version when the musical *Bei Kerzenlicht* was produced at the Wiener Künstlertheater in 1946 and again in 1956 when a production at the Theater in der Josefstadt (16 March) rang up an outstanding 143 consecutive nights on the boards of a theatre which rarely saw such runs. Szantó's Hungarian version of the show has been seen in Budapest as recently as 1994 (Klapka Sztárszínház 15 October).

A British attempt, some two decades on, to stage another remade version of *Bei Kerzenlicht,* written by Eric Maschwitz, also brought the piece back to more manageable size with eight principals, headed by Jacques Pills, Sally Ann Howes, Patricia Burke and Roger Dann, and a chorus of four. *Romance in Candlelight* (Piccadilly Theatre 15 September 1955) replaced Katscher's music with songs by Sam Coslow and closed in 53 performances.

Hungary: Royal Színház *Gyertyafénynél* 1 October 1937; Austria: Wiener Künstlertheater 22 May 1946

Recording: *Romance in Candlelight* selection (Columbia, EP)

BÉKEFFY, István (b Szeged, 31 August 1901; d Budapest, 9 June 1977).

A hugely prolific author of comedies, often written in collaboration with László Vadnai or Adorján Stella, of musical plays and adaptations, of novels, screenplays and lyrics, Békeffy wrote texts and/or lyrics for many musical plays, including a long series, many highly successful, in collaboration with Lajos Lajtai.

A number of his musical pieces were seen beyond Hungary in the 1930s, several in German versions—*A régi nyár* as *Sommer von einst, Sisters, Éjféli tangó* as *Tango am Mitternacht, Esö után köpönyeg* as *Verzeih, das ich dich liebe*—whilst his *Őfelsége frakkja,* as adapted by André Barde, successfully became *Katinka* in France. Békeffy was still writing in his seventies, and his musical comedy *A Kutya* was played in German as *Der Hund, der Herr Bozzi hiess* (ad Géza Engel, Henriette Engel, Meiningen 29 September 1978) after his death.

1926 **Hol jártál az az éjszaka?** (w László Vadnai) Sziget Színpad 26 March

1927 **Mesék az irógépről** (Lajos Lajtai/w István Szomahazy) Városi Színház 8 October

1928 **A régi nyár** (Lajtai) Budai Színkör 15 June

1928 **Párizsi divat** (Lajtai) Városi Színház 22 December

1929 **Ez hát a szerelem** (*So This Is Love*) Hungarian version (Fővárosi Operettszínház)

1930 **Sisters** (Lajtai) Király Színház 10 January

1930 **Lila test, sárga sapka** (Lajtai/w László Békeffy) Nyári Operettszínház 7 June

1930 **Az okos mama** (Lajtai) Király Színház 26 November

1931 **Egy kis csókor** (Dezső Losonczy) Andrássy uti Színház 3 January

1931 **Őfelsége frakkja** (Lajtai) Király Színház 19 September

1932 **Éjféli tangó** (Károly Komjáthy/w Vadnai) Király Színház 27 February

1932 **Régi orfeum** (Lajtai/w Jenő Faragó) Fővárosi Operettszínház 12 March

1932 **Amikor a kis lányból nagy lány lesz** (Lajtai) Budai Színkör 10 June

1932 **Egy asszony, aki tudja, mit akar** (*Eine Frau, die weiss, was sie will*) Hungarian lyrics w Tamás Emőd (Vígszínház)

1932 **A Rotschildok** (Lajtai/Ferenc Martos) Fővárosi Operettszínház 25 November

1932 **Bridge-Szalon** Andrássy uti Színház 27 November

1932 **Ecet és olaj** (*Essig und Öl*) Hungarian lyrics (Andrássy uti Színház)

1932 **Kadétszerelem** (Pál Gyöngy/w László Szilágyi) Fővárosi Operettszínház 23 December

1933 **Egy csók és más semmi** (Mihály Eisemann/Imre Halász) Magyar Színház 12 May

1934 **Őméltósága sofőrje** (Gyöngy) Király Színház 24 February

1934 **A cirkusz csillaga** (Eisemann, Komjáthy/László Bús Fekete) Vígszínház 22 June

1934 **Nápolyi kaland** (Lajtai/w Vadnai) Fővárosi Operettszínház 10 November

1935 **Törtennek még csodák** (Pal Ábrahám/Halász) Magyar Színház 20 April

1936 **Esö után köpönyeg** (Michael Krasznay-Krausz/Mihály Szécsen) Andrássy uti Színház 6 November

1938 **A hölgy hozzám tartozik** (Eisemann/Pierre Veber ad w Adorján Stella) Andrássy Színház 21 January

1938 **Dinasztia** (Miklós Brodszky/w Imre Harmath/Pál Vaái) Magyar Színház 16 April

1939 **Az Angol bank nem fizet** (Tamás Bródy/w Adorján Stella) Pesti Színház 18 March

1939 **Pusztai szerenád** (Szabolcs Fényes/w Szilágyi) Fővárosi Operettszínház 29 September

1945 **Csárdáskirálynő** (*Die Csárdásfürstin*) new Hungarian adaptation (Fővárosi Operettszínház)

1946 **Florentin kalap** (*Un chapeau de paille d'Italie*) musical version w Tibor Polgár Fővárosi Operettszínház 19 April

1946 **Csicsónénak három lánya** (Komjáthy/w Dezső Keller) Fővárosi Operettszínház 5 October

1947 **Rigó Jancsi** (Fényes/Sándor Lestyán ad) Fővárosi Operettszínház 9 May

1947 **Nincsenek véletlenek** (Bródy) Belvárosi Színház 25 July

1949 **VIII osztály** (Bródy) Fővárosi Operettszínház 4 February

1949 **Rip van Winkle** new Hungarian adaptation w Bródy, Fényes (Fővárosi Operettszínház)

1951 **Palotaszállo** (Bródy, János Kerekes/w Kellér, Tibor Mérei) Fővárosi Operettszínház 23 February

1952 **Luxemburg grófja** (*Der Graf von Luxemburg*) new Hungarian adaptation w Kellér (Fővárosi Operettszínház)

1954 **Szombat délutan** (Fényes) Fővárosi Vígszínház 19 February

1955 **Szerencsés flótás** (Fényes) Fővárosi kis Színpad 23 March

1971 **Mit vesztett el kisasszony?** (Fényes/w Iván Szenes) Fővárosi Operettszínház 26 February

1976 **A Kutya, akit Bozzi urnak hivnak** (Fényes/w György G Dénes) Fővárosi Operettszínház 27 February

BELL, Digby V[alentine] [BELL, William Digby] (b Milwaukee, Wis, 8 November 1849; d New York, 20 June 1917). Tenor turned comedian who had a fine career on American musical stages.

The son of a New York banker and nephew of the collector of customs for Detroit, ''Kid'' Bell dumped a career as a passenger agent for the White Star line to go to Naples to study to become a singer. He made his first professional stage appearances in Malta (where in those days a debut could be more easily bought for ready money than in Italy) as the Count in *La Sonnambula* and as Ashton in *Lucia di Lammermoor.* Returning to America in 1876, he performed first in concert at the Chickering Hall and then made his debut on the musical stage with the Martinez English Opera Company in Montreal, playing Beppo in *Fra Diavolo* (1877). He quickly found himself cast in comic rather than romantic roles and, in a subsequent career of more than 30 years, he established himself as one of the most popular properly singing comedians in the American musical theatre.

His first appearance in musical comedy came at the height of the *Pinafore* craze when he toured with one of the many *Pinafore* companies (The Saville Engish Opera Company) that filled the country's stages in 1879 playing Sir Joseph Porter and John Wellington Wells (*The Sorcerer*). His wife, Lilian Brooks Bell, played Josephine and the company briefly visited Broadway's Madison Square Theater in June of the year. His earliest full New York engagement was playing the British German Reed repertoire under the management of John McCaull at the Bijou Theater (1880) where, in spite of his young age, he appeared as Ebenezer Tare in *Ages Ago,* Joe Bumpus in *Charity Begins at Home* and Otho in *The Spectre Knight.* During the early 1880s, he also appeared on Broadway with the Comley-Barton troupe as Alfred Puddifoot in *Lawn Tennis* (1880, subtitled ''an English comic opera''); as Coquelicot in America's first production of the megahit musical *Les Noces d'Olivette* (1880); as Charles Favart in *Madame Favart* and as Don Pizzaro in *Manola* (1882, *Le Jour et la nuit);* and spent two years in Augustin Daly's company, where his musical assignments included the German *Nisida* (1881, *Zanina* as Booma Poota) and the homemade *Cinderella at School* (t/o Jack Polo), which he missed out on creating after being knocked down by a horse cab on his way to the theatre and breaking his leg.

He appeared thereafter at the Bijou Theater as Grosvenor (1882, *Patience*), Dr Daly (1882, *The Sorcerer*), as Samuel Nubbles in Edward Solomon's *Virginia* (1883), as Don Gaetan in *Hand and Heart* (1883, *Le Coeur et la main*) and in *Orphée aux enfers* (1884, Jupiter), and at the Casino Theatre in *La Princesse de Trébizonde* (1883, Trémolini), but spent much of the remainder of the decade as a star member of McCaull's top-rank traveling musical-theatre companies, with whom he appeared in New York and round the country as Grosvenor to the Bunthorne of J H Ryley, and in American versions of the Operetten *Der Feldprediger* (*The Black Hussar,* Piffkow), *Der Bettelstudent* (Ollendorf), *Boccaccio* (Lotteringhi), as King Charles in Planquette's *Nell Gwynne* (1884), Ko-Ko in *The Mikado* (1885), *Don Cesar* (1886, Onofrio), *The Crowing Hen* (1886, Gavadeau), in Audran's *Indiana* (1887, Matt o' the Mill), Czibulka's *Der Glücksritter* (1889, *The May Queen,* Toby), *Fatinitza* (1889, Izzet Pasha), etc. In 1887 he was seen at the Fifth Avenue Theater as chief comic Myhnt-Julep in McCaull's production of the home-brewed Harry B Smith and Reginald De Koven musical *The Begum,* and in the summer of 1889 he appeared in Boston as Sir Joseph Porter, to his wife's Buttercup, in *HMS Pinafore* and toured in *Paola* playing Sapolo to Laura's Margarine.

In the early 1890s he mixed classic roles (Koko, Major General Stanley, Baron Puck, Don Boléro d'Alcarazas) with native works, appearing with top billing in two productions written for him by Harry B Smith and mounted by McCaull's successor, Harry Askin—*The Tar and the Tartar* (1891, Muley Hassan) and, under the banner of the ''Digby Bell Opera Company,'' *Jupiter* (1892, Jupiter)—and opposite Lillian Russell in both *Princess Nicotine* (1893, Don Pedro) and the Austro-British *The Queen of Brilliants* (1894, Della Fontana). In 1894 he appeared in summer season at Philadelphia's Grand Opera House (Sir Joseph Porter, etc), in 1895 he revived *The Tar and the Tartar* and toured as Gabe Swift in an underpar piece called *Nancy Lee,* which folded in Terre-Haute, Ind and in 1896–97 he and his wife toured as Deacon Tidd and Lizzie Grout in a production of Hoyt's *The Midnight Bell.* In his later years in the theatre he appeared largely in comedy and rural drama, starring mostly alongside his wife in warm and sympathetic roles with a touching skill that surprised some, but, between the plays and vaudeville engagements, he was also seen guesting with the Castle Square company in *The Mikado* (1901), as Adam Hogg in *The Chaperons* (1902), and as Sam Weller to DeWolf Hopper's Pickwick in the 1903 musical *Mr Pickwick,* and he appeared in Gilbert and Sullivan revivals (Ko-Ko in *The Mikado* 1910, Dr Daly to the Wells of Hopper in *The Sorcerer* 1915, etc) well into his sixties.

Bell was married (second time for both of them) in 1883 to the singing character-lady **Laura Joyce BELL** (née MASKELL) (b Newport, Mont, 6 May 1854; d New York, 29 May 1904), daughter of theatrical agent James Henry [''Dauncey''] Maskell and his wife, Maria (née Dauncey) a well known reciter. She had had a brief British career as a teenaged drawing room entertainer and as a supporting member of Mrs Howard Paul's entertainment, plus a first experience on the boards at the Manchester Theatre Royal (Oberon in *The Children in the Wood*), when she was hired, aged 18, to go to Niblo's Garden where she appeared in the spectacles *Leo and Lotos* (1872, Babette) and *Azrael* (1873, Lisette). Months later, she married a wealthy Bostonian and retired to motherhood. However, she soon got rid of the Bostonian and returned to the theatre in a revival of the not-yet-famous burlesque *Evangeline* in Boston (1875). She followed up by creating the role of Minniehaha in the burlesque *Hiawatha* (1878) at the same theatre. Having worked in stock in Baltimore and Washington, DC (it was reported that ''she paralysed Joseph Jefferson with her Lydia Languish''), she returned to the musical stage in Tracy Titus's company playing Germaine to the Serpolette of Catherine Lewis in *Les Cloches de Corneville* (1879), in J Crossey's Philadelphia North Broad Street company (Vladimir in *Fatinitza,* Lady Allcash in *Fra Diavolo,* Emily Gooding in *The First Life Guards in Brighton,* Lange in *La Fille de Madame Angot*) and as a youngish Little Buttercup to the Josephine of Annis Montague at Broadway's Haverley's Theater (1879). She then appeared as Ruth in an early *Pirates of Penzance* company (1880), before joining Augustin Daly's company in New York in 1881 (Zanina in *Zanina,* Merope Mallow in *Cinderella at School*), and swiftly establishing herself as one of the best singing heavy ladies of her era. She appeared thereafter, often alongside her husband, in a long series of comic operas on Broadway and round the country, including *Patience* (1882, t/o Lady Jane), *The Sorcerer* (1882, Lady Sangazure), *Virginia* (1883, Sally Cowslip), *Hand and Heart* (1883, Donna Scholastica), *Orphée aux enfers* (1884, Diana), *La Princesse de Trébizonde* (1883, Paola), *Nell Gwynne* (1884, Lady Clare), *The Black Hussar* (1885, Barbara), *The Mikado* (1885, Katisha), *Don Cesar* (1886), *The Crowing Hen* (1886), *Bellman* (1887, Tronda), *The Begum* (1887, Namouna), *Indiana* (1887, Lady Prue), *Der Bettelstudent* (Palmatica), *Boccaccio* (1888, Peronella), *The May Queen* (1889, Roxana), *The Tar and the Tartar* (1891, Alpaca), *Jupiter* (1892, Pandora), *The Mikado* (Katisha), and in later years in such pieces as Philadelphia's *Princess Bonnie* (1894), Boston's *The Sphinx* (1895, Pteecha), The *Walking Delegate* (1897, Columbia Hale), *The Regatta Girl* (1900, Lady Paynton), *The Burgomaster* (1901) and *Mr Pickwick* (1903, Mrs Bardell), in a career which—in spite of the fact that she was but 50 at her death—marked her out as the most successful contralto character lady of her era on the Broadway stage.

BELL, Rose [BERDALLE de LAPOMMERAYE, Anne Célina] (b Rouen, 23 November 1834; d Nice, April 1886).

One of the foremost players of opéra-bouffe in Britain at the height of the craze for such productions, Rose Bell (a sister of the celebrated Parisian critic and teacher, Henri de Lapommeraye) first came to notice in America when, already into her thirties, she toured—anglophone name and all—with Jacob Grau's direct-from-Paris company, sharing the leading roles with no less a star-to-be than Marie Desclauzas. She won the *New York Times*'s commendation as having ''the best French voice we have ever had in New York,'' a comment dimmed just a little by the subsequent ''she sings skillfully and with spirit, but she is not in the slightest degree funny.'' *The Clipper* voted her ''tall, handsome and possessing a clear, sweet, highly-cultivated voice, acting with a great deal of spirit and animation''; she had, it claimed, ''a splendid voice, now high and thrilling, anon low, soft and voluptuous.'' But it still didn't say anything about ''funny.'' She appeared in New York and round America as the Duchess (*La Grande-Duchesse*), Drogan (*Geneviève de Brabant*), Dindonette (*L'Oeil crevé*), Césarine (*Fleur de thé*), Gabrielle (*La Vie parisienne*) and Frédégonde (*Chilpéric*) between 1868 and 1869. She next surfaced in Britain, two seasons later, when she appeared at the Opera Comique, succeeding Julia Mathews as Fleur de Noblesse in *L'Oeil crevé* (1872), and teaming with Pattie Laverne as the heroes of *The Bohemians* (1873, *Le Roman comique,* Enguerrand des Moranges) and *The Wonderful Duck* (1873, *Le Canard à trois becs,* Spaniello). It was noted that although she showed ''real ability'' her ''imperfect knowledge of English is a hindrance.'' Yet she would make virtually her whole career in the English-singing theatre.

Later the same year, she moved to the Alhambra, where she played in a series of French and British musical productions, again often in travesty roles. At the height of her popularity, in the mid-1870s, she was paired in three pieces with Kate Santley—as a soprano Paris (*La Belle Hélène*), as Clorinde in *La Jolie Parfumeuse* and in the title role of *Don Juan*—and the two rival actresses developed fanatical followings which led to pitched fights, pages of publicity, and the law courts.

She also played lead roles in the Alhambra's productions of *The Demon's Bride* (1874, Algar), *Le Roi Carotte* (1874, Robin Wildfire) and *Le Voyage dans la lune* (1876, Prince Caprice), starred in *La Fille de Madame Angot* (Lange to the Clairette of Catherine Lewis) and *Les Géorgiennes* (Lady Feroza) at the Philharmonic, and toured as Trainette in *Pom,* as Lange, and as the page in

John de Paris, returning, after appearances in the music halls (in an act of ''Bacchanalian chansonettes'' featuring ''a novel costume which combined masculine and feminine elements'') and pantomime, for her last West End appearance to play Siebel in the 1880 Alhambra revival of *Mefistofele II* (*Le Petit Faust*). She then apparently married (again—she had previously been the wife of Gambogi, the chorus master of the Grau troupe), and retired from the stage to motherhood.

BELLE, or The Ballad of Doctor Crippen Music-hall musical in 2 acts by Wolf Mankowitz from a play by Beverley Cross. Lyrics and music by Monty Norman. Strand Theatre, London, 4 May 1961.

A lively, small-scale piece which told the story of poisoner Dr Crippen as performed by the members of the company of the Bedford Music Hall under the compering of their chairman, Lasher (Jerry Desmonde). The title character of Belle was the over-plumed, under-voiced music-hall singer (Rose Hill) to whom the meek Crippen (George Benson) had the misfortune to be married. He discovers love with his nurse, Ethel (Virginia Vernon), and events move on to their celebrated and deadly climax via a set of songs which either parodied or imitated turn-of-the-century styles. The most successful number was the ''Dit-Dit'' song, in which the land-to-sea telegraph, which facilitated Crippen's and Ethel's high-seas capture, was sung of with much more amorous connotations. Other pieces, such as the heroine's tongue-in-cheek admission that ''I Can't Stop Singing'' and her medical love duet with Crippen, gave enjoyable moments alongside some cornier numbers for the music-hall folk.

Belle chose its time poorly. The critical fashion was all for the low-life, Soho-style musical, and ''realism-in-musicals'' was briefly as much the rage as ''politics-in-musicals'' would become in the 1990s. And yet this piece encountered some opposition due to its ''tasteless'' subject matter. That, added to the fact that out-of-town problems meant that *Belle* was still patchy on arrival, scuppered it in six weeks. A revival of a reconstruction of *Belle* by the Tavistock Repertory Company proved, 20 years later, that the show had deserved a better fate.

The real-life Mrs Crippen was a competent music-hall singer who was also forcefully active in the affairs of the Women's Music Hall Guild.

Recording: original cast (Decca)

LA BELLE ARABELLE Opérette in 2 acts by Marc-Cab and Francis Blanche. Music by Guy Lafarge and Pierre Philippe. Théâtre de la Porte-Saint-Martin, Paris, 4 October 1956.

A made-to-order vehicle for the popular singing quartet Les Frères Jacques, *La Belle Arabelle* (the title was the name of the houseboat on which the four lived) featured the men as Arsène, André, Arthur and Alfred, four young fellows who go up and down the canals of France, earning their living by running a fair-booth. When they save a pretty amnesiac girl (Lucie Dolène) from drowning, potentially amorous complexities ensue, but it turns out she is a princess, her memory comes back, and she marries her Henri (Robert Piquet), whilst the boys go back to their barge and their ''guardian angel,'' Domino (Jeannette Batti). The show's score featured its quartet in ''La Colle au pinceau,'' ''J'emmène les gendarmes,'' ''Les Boît's à musique,'' ''Les Barons de Ballencourt'' and a title song in characteristic style.

La Belle Arabelle ran for nine months at the large Théâtre de la Porte-Saint-Martin, and the show was later toured—without its stars—in a version which reduced the family to three brothers. It was later revived by the Opéra Royal de Wallonie in 1983 (Verviers 11 November) with the harmony group Les Poivre et Sel featured as its jolly bargees.

Recording: original cast (Philips 45rpm)

LA BELLE BOURBONNAISE opéra-comique in 3 acts by Ernest Dubreuil and Henri Chabrillat. Music by Auguste Coedès. Théâtre des Folies-Dramatiques, Paris 11 April 1874.

La Belle Bourbonnaise (named after a popular old song) had the difficult task of taking over the bills of the Folies-Dramatiques at the end of the record-breaking run of *La Fille de Madame Angot,* and although it didn't have a shout of coming out on a level with that famous piece, it nevertheless came through with some credit.

The central figure in the piece was countryfied Manon, ''la belle bourbonnaise,'' as played by Marie Desclauzas, whose astonishing likeness to Madame Dubarry (also played by Desclauzas) makes her a pawn in the game of the Abbé Camerlet (Raoult), who is trying to oust the royal mistress from favor. The pawn, however, gets together with the Dubarry (how did they manage that?) and it is the royal mistress who goes to the rendezvous with the King arranged by his enemy, whilst the country girl stays at the palace. Milher had the evening's best comic role as the Dubarry's secret agent, Grison, alongside Luco as Manon's preferred country swain, Mlle Tassilly as her unprepossessing cousin, and the veteran Opéra-Comique star Sainte-Foy as another plotter, the Baron de Cotignac.

Desclauzas's tour de force in the double role, a pretty score by Coedès, and a fine production meant that *La Belle Bourbonnaise* held its place well until it was time to bring back the inevitable *La Fille de Madame Angot.* Rather squeezed from the Folies-Dramatiques programs by its famous predecessor, *La Belle Boubonnaise* nevertheless got an occasional extra showing thereafter.

The piece was played later the same year in Brussels, with no less a star than Judic featured as Manon, and in Vienna (add mus Josef Brandl), where Antonie Link took the star role alongside Franz Eppich (Camerlet), Karl Blasel (Cotignac), Wilhelm Knaack (Grison), Herminie Meyerhoff (Billette), and Therese Schäfer and Josef Matras among the other members of the country family in Paris. It seems also to have been subsequently played in Berlin.

Austria: Carltheater *Die schöne Bourbonnaise* 16 October 1874; Berlin: Friedrich-Wilhelmstädtisches Theater *Die schöne Bourbonnaise* ?1874

LA BELLE DE CADIX Opérette in 3 acts by Raymond Vincy and Marc-Cab. Lyrics by Maurice Vandair. Music by Francis Lopez. Casino-Montparnasse, Paris, 24 December 1945.

As much as one show can, *La Belle de Cadix* marked the same kind of a turning in the musical theatre in France as, around the same time, the production of *Oklahoma!* encouraged in America. It led the fashion definitively away from the light-footed and -hearted comedy musicals which had triumphed during the 1920s, but had now rather lost their zing, back to an up-to-date version of the colorful, romantic musical play with its standard operettic construction and cast.

The hero of the tale was celluloid star Carlos Médina (Luis Mariano) who goes to the Spanish hills to film scenes for his *La Belle de Cadix.* Local girl Maria-Luisa (France Aubert) is chosen to play his gypsy bride, but over-helpful Pépa (Jacquie Flynt) supplies a real gypsy king for the part of the screenic gypsy king and, thus, the two are married for real. Since Carlos is engaged to an American tobacco heiress (Simone Chobillon) and Maria-Luisa to a jealous and macho gypsy (Fabrézy), there is an actful of problems to be surmounted before they choose to stay married. Alongside the romantic tale ran the comical one of the little production assistant, Manillon (Roger Lacoste), who pretends to be the film's director in order to attract the girls, and who gets more than he bargained for in Pépa.

Vincy's well-proportioned book was illustrated by a set of songs which, first and foremost, gave the leading tenor an opportunity to shine. Mariano made himself a star with his performance of the tenor's long list of numbers and at the same time turned the show's title song into an enormous hit. ''La Belle de Cadix'' was followed up with his praises of ''Maria-Luisa,'' memories of ''Le Clocher du village,'' the celebration of ''La Fiesta bohémienne,'' a dejected farewell to Spain (''Une nuit à Grenade'') and a duetting ''Rendez-vous sur la lune'' which seemed to owe just a little to Rudolf Friml's ''Indian Love Call,'' all of which still left place for the heroine

Plate 27. **La Belle de Cadix.** *Luis Mariano in his first famous role, paired here with Lina Dachary as his Maria-Luisa.*

to wander through ''Les Sentiers de la montagne,'' Ramirès the gypsy to make another hit out of his scornful baritone piece on ''Le Coeur des femmes,'' and Manillon and Pépa to bounce through several happy soubret numbers.

Produced with all the color that its settings (designed by Mariano, a former art student) allowed, *La Belle de Cadix*—which had been originally commissioned by Laurallier of the Casino Montparnasse for a 50-performance season over the Christmas period to replace a cancelled Edith Piaf show—emerged as a major hit. It celebrated the end of the war by playing two full seasons in Paris, and just two years later it was revived, in an enlarged version, by Maurice Lehmann at the Théâtre de l'Empire (17 December 1949) with Mariano paired with top soprano Lina Dachary. Thereafter *La Belle de Cadix* barely quitted the stages of France. It returned to Paris again in 1958 (Gaîté-Lyrique 20 November) with Antonio Rossano starred, in 1977 (Théâtre Mogador 5 February, 85 performances) with Miguel Cortez, in 1979 (Théâtre de la Renaissance) with José Villamor, who had played Ramirès in the previous production, and again in 1991 (Théâtre de la Renaissance 17 February) with Cortez and Carlo di Angelo alternating in Mariano's role. A film version was made in 1953 with Mariano starred alongside Carmen Sevilla, Jean Tissier, Pierjac, Claude Nicot and Claire Maurier.

Like the rest of the French musical plays of its time, *La Belle de Cadix* has, in spite of its continuing home popularity, been rarely seen outside France, although

Plate 28. **La Belle Hélène.** *Whilst the heavy stuff is going on back at the palace, a burlesque Orestes just has a good time (Sadler's Wells Theatre, 1967).*

Lopez related in his rather braggy autobiography that a contract for a Broadway production that was to have been signed between his publisher, Salabert, and the Shubert organization was abandoned when Salabert was killed in a plane crash on his way to America. Maybe. Maybe not.

Film: 1953

Recordings: original cast (EMI-Pathé), selections (Odéon, CBS), etc

LA BELLE HÉLÈNE Opéra-bouffe in 3 acts by Henri Meilhac and Ludovic Halévy. Music by Jacques Offenbach. Théâtre des Variétés, Paris, 17 December 1864.

The fourth of Offenbach's great opéras-bouffes burlesqueing ancient historical legend or mythology (after *Orphée aux enfers, Geneviève de Brabant* and *Le Pont des soupirs*), *La Belle Hélène* was also his first written with the authorial team of Henri Meilhac and Ludovic Halévy, who would go on to supply him with the texts for many of his most famous works. It was also the first written expressly for its leading lady, Hortense Schneider, who would become the darling of pre-(Prussian-) war Paris in a series of similar roles in Offenbach opéras-bouffes.

Being the most beautiful woman in the world can be a real burden. Especially when goddesses go round promising you to some exceptionally handsome shepherd (José Dupuis) as a prize in a contest, without stopping to think that you are already married to Ménélas, the King of Sparta (Kopp). There really isn't much the beautiful Helen (Mlle Schneider) can do, when fate, Venus and the augur Calchas (Grenier) conspire to send her husband off to Crete, and then send her this ''dream'' of the handsome shepherd, who is actually Prince Paris of Troy in disguise and . . . a very tangible dream. When the wretched husband objects noisily to being divinely cuckolded, Venus revengefully sends a plague of immorality upon Greece, and poor hard-done-by Ménélas gets the blame. He sends for the grand priest of Cythera, who prescribes a pilgrimage to Venus's shrine for the almost-lapsed Queen, but all is not what it seems: when Helen is safely aboard the island-bound ship the priest throws off his disguise—it is Paris, he's got Helen in his hands for the length of a whole sea voyage, and the Trojan War can now take place.

Offenbach's score was one of his gayest and most memorable. Paris's sweetly tenorizing tale of his Judgement (''Au mont Ida trois déesses''), Helen's celebration of ''Amours divins!,'' her invocation of the interfering Venus (''Dis-moi, Vénus''), and Paris and Helen's waltzing attempts to convince themselves that their lovemaking is all a dream (''Oui! C'est un rêve'') were the lyrical highlights of the evening. Then, in contrast, came the swingeing march (''Voici les rois de Grèce'') which introduced individually the famous Kings of Greece from a burlesque Agamemnon (Couder) to a boiling Achilles (Guyon) and the twin Ajaxes (Hamburger, Andof), the bouncing Patriotic Trio for Calchas, Agamemnon and Ménélas (''Lorsque la Grèce est un champ de carnage''), and a jolly lad-about-town number (''Au Cabaret du labyrinthe'') for a monocled, travesty Orestes (Léa Silly), as well as such extravagant follies as the dazzling tyrolienne (in ancient Greece!) of the last act finale, sung by a yodelling Paris in his disguise as the Grand Priest.

Cogniard's production of *La Belle Hélène* hit several sticky patches. A feud between the star and the second lady, Mlle Silly, was temporarily pasted over, but when the Judgement of Paris number, the tenor's best spot, went for nothing at dress rehearsal, Offenbach decided drastically to rewrite the number. Overnight, he composed three different settings of the verses. He summoned Dupuis the next morning, ordered him to choose the one he liked best, then set to orchestrate it whilst the tenor learned his new melody. As in so many other cases, the last-minute song proved one of the great gems of the score.

The reviews of the show were mixed, but it got some splendid publicity from the indignant antics of the more rabid critics. One, who had reviled the authors for defiling the sacred works of classical antiquity with their burlesque, was taken down a peg by the revelation that he was unable to read a word of Greek. After a slow start, the show became first popular and then both enormously popular and enormously fashionable. It ran right through the more than six months to the summer recess, and returned later in 1865 for further performances whilst the authors worked on its successor. The first burlesque, a glance at *La Belle Hélène dans son ménage* (G Rose/Merenville), appeared at the Nouveautés (11 July 1867). In Belgium, Messrs Booch and Hivry churned out a musequel which they called *Siège de Troie.* And at the same time *La Belle Hélène* began its dissemination through the world's theatres.

Friedrich Strampfer was first off the mark with his production (ad F Zell, Julius Hopp) at Vienna's Theater an der Wien, and he scored an unmitigated triumph. The young Marie Geistinger caused a sensation as the lightly clad and distinctly schöne Helena, and, with Albin Swoboda as her Paris, Karl Blasel as Ménélas, and Carl Adolf Friese (Agamemnon), Matthias Rott (Calchas) and Frln Beyer (Orestes) in support, the Theater an der Wien company played the piece a splendid 65 times during its first nine months in the repertoire, in spite again of some organized opposition amongst the ''high-art'' pundits and journalists who railed against the burlesquing of antiquity and against the brilliant gaiety of the piece. Disinformation was sprayed through the international press (''the educated classes show the cold shoulder[;] [it] would have been withdrawn after a few nights' performance had not vast expense been incurred''), but Vienna clearly had sufficient uneducated and un-press-believing classes to make *Die schöne Helena* a severe hit. Geistinger clocked up the show's 200th performance (to the Menelaus of Girardi) on 30 December 1875.

The show was seen in Prague and in Berlin in German, with Geistinger repeating her Vienna role, but apparently in a different adaptation, written by Ernst Dohm, which inexplicably (to me) omitted the patriotic trio. Once again the star and the show were greeted with some vilifying comments from the press, the *Preussische Zeitung* railing hectically against ''this Jewish speculation on the spirit of modern society—a speculation which, in the most refined manner and with the aid of music, scoffs at, ridicules and caricatures whatever is regarded as high and sacred in domestic life.'' As ever, this tantrumming didn't hurt business.

If the German production caused a ''moral'' scandal, the Belgian one raised fuss of a different kind. The Galeries Saint-Hubert produced *La Belle Hélène* (3 June 1865) with Dupuis as Paris without asking Offenbach and his authors. And when the composer took manager Delvil to court, he lost. The court decided that the copyright laws at the time meant that any Belgian theatre could play any French piece, without asking, as long as the due royalties were paid. The *La Belle Hélène* case became a precedent, and Stockholm's Sodra Theatre (11 June 1865) was quick off the mark with its ''free'' vernacular production (ad E A Wallmark) of the new hit opéra-bouffe.

The first English-language version was heard in London, when F C Burnand's much tampered-with *Helen, or Taken from the Greek* was mounted at the Adelphi Theatre with Theresa Furtado as its Helen, Mrs Alfred Mellon playing Paris in travesty, and the comedians Paul Bedford (Calchas) and Johnnie Toole (Agamemnon) in support, for some two hundred nights, but, after London had seen Schneider's performance of the original French show (St James's Theatre 13 July 1868), a more faithful version was made for British consumption by Charles Lamb Kenney. This one was produced at the Gaiety Theatre by John Hollingshead (18 July 1871) with Australia's Julia Mathews as its Helen and Constance Loseby another travesty Paris. With Annie Tremaine also playing in travesty as Orestes, the cross-dressing traditions of British burlesque were well maintained. Burnand had a second and more dignified try when he redid *La Belle Hélène* for the vast stage of the Alhambra and its star team of Kate Santley (Helen), Rose Bell (Paris) and Harry Paulton (Menelaos). The production ran an excellent 109 consecutive performances.

New York, curiously, had its first taste of *La Belle Hélène* in German when Hedwig L'Arronge-Sury appeared as die schöne Helena in a repertoire production at the Stadttheater. The city's German theatres reproduced the piece regularly in the years that followed even though, just a few months after that premiere, Lucille Tostée and her company had given New York a taste of the original piece in all its French glory. Without creating the sensation that her *Grande-Duchesse* had done, Tostée's *La Belle Hélène* ran for a full month of consecutive performances, and both she and the tirelessly touring American queen of opéra-bouffe, Marie Aimée, played Helen liberally round the country during their American seasons for as long as opéra-bouffe was alive. The first American English version (ad Molyneux St John) was seemingly done by the enterprising if approximate Worrell sisters—Sophie was Helen, Irene was Paris and Jennie was Orestes—in 1868 (I can find no confirmation of a supposed performance in Chicago in 1867), followed up in 1869 (28 April) by something apparently equally approximate called *Paris, or the Judgement* (ad C Rattray from Burnand's version!), produced at the Waverley theatre by the Elise Holt burlesque troupe with its manager as Orestes, and in 1870 by Kelly and Leon's inevitable and superior parody *La Belle L-N* (July 1870), with Leon as Helen and Kelly as Paris. A more substantial English-language version appeared in 1899 (ad Louis Harrison) when a version of the show was mounted at the Casino Theater with Offenbach's score improved by Ludwig Englander and Lillian Russell starred as a well-rounded Helen for 52 performances.

The Scandinavian countries were amongst the first to stage their versions of *La Belle Hélène,* Italian and Spanish adaptations were swiftly mounted and, as always, Hungary was amongst the quickest to have a vernacular version of the show on the stage. Strangely, that version (ad Endre Latabár) was first mounted in Kassa, and *Szép Helena* was seen in Szeged (w Antónia Hetényi), Arad, Koloszvár, Miskolc, Nagyvárad and Debrecen (both these last two with the young Lujza Blaha as Helen) before playing Budapest for the first time, four years after the Zell/Hopp German version had already been seen there. Ilka Medgyaszay (Helen), Ferenc Halmi (Paris) and Ferenc Erczi (Ménélas) led the initial Várszínház production, which was overshadowed a dozen years later (7 October 1882) when the Népszínház took the show into its repertoire and mounted it with a big-gun cast: Ilka Pálmay (Helen), János Kápolnai (Paris), Vidor Kassai (Menelaos) and Elek Solymossy (Calchas).

Australia, rather than importing the show, manufactured its own version. W M Akhurst's *Paris the Prince and Helen the Fair or the Giant Horse and the Siege of Troy* (Theatre Royal, Melbourne 11 April 1868) used some of Offenbach's music, but mixed it with chunks of *Un Ballo in maschera, Les Huguenots* and some music-hall melodies. Marion Dunn (Paris) and Miss Chester (Helen) featured, but the stars of the evening were manager H M Harwood as a deeply depressed Cassandra and Richard Stewart as a comical Patroclus with a yen for Helen—characters which Meilhac and Halévy had not included in their version. The colony got its first genuine *La Belle Hélène* in 1876, when Emilie Melville, Armes Beaumont (Paris), Jeannie Winston (Orestes), Henry Bracy (Ménélas) and George Leopold (Calchas) appeared at Sydney's Royal Victoria Theatre in an uncredited version. Soon after, Australians were able to see Emily Soldene's more Rubensesque Helen, as Miss Melville moved on to take her version of the piece to India and round the Pacific and adjacent oceans in her repertoire of opéras-bouffes and -comiques.

In France, *La Belle Hélène* established itself as one of the staples of the Offenbach repertoire. The Variétés remounted it in 1876 with Anna Judic as Helen and Dupuis in his original role, and again 10 years later with the same pair still featured. Judic gave her last Parisian Helen in 1889 and was succeeded by Jeanne Granier (1890) and then by Juliette Simon-Girard (1899). The Opéra-Comique's Marguerite Carré appeared as Helen to the Paris of Fernand Francell and the Calchas of Max Dearly in 1919 (Gaîté-Lyrique 5 October), Géori Boué starred in a 1960 revival (Théâtre Mogador 25 February) and an undersized revival was mounted at the Bouffes-Parisiens in 1976 (24 September). Since then, more substantial revivals have played at the Opéra-Comique (25 April 1983, 21 September 1985) and at the Théâtre de Paris (13 November 1986) with multiple casts, and in 1999 a sadly tawdry and gimmicky "director's" mounting, showing no comprehension of the opéra-bouffe idiom, was seen at the Festival d'Aix.

In 1926 a sort of sequel, written by Fernand Nozire and set to music by Fernand Raphael, was mounted at Paris's Théâtre Daunou under the title of *Hélène.*

Elsewhere, the piece has also kept its popularity if, occasionally, lost its identity. Vienna was amongst the first to butcher the show when Gábor Steiner produced his own "burlesque opérette from the French," *Die schöne Helena von heute* (w Leopold Krenn, mus arr Ludwig Gothov-Gruneke), with Helene Ballot playing her namesake, as part of the 1911 and 1912 seasons at Ronacher. Max Reinhardt's typically spectacular version of a grossly rewritten version of the show—produced at Berlin's Theater am Kurfürstendamm, in 1931, with opera star Jarmila Novotna starred as a Helen with a very much larger voice than Mlle Schneider would ever have dreamed of possessing (or Offenbach of hearing), and with Egon Fridell (Paris), Hans Moser, Theo Lingen, Friedl Schuster, Otto Wallburg and Max Pallenberg as Ménélas—favored the visual side rather than the textual, and a subsequent remake of this version for London, ''adapted'' by A P Herbert and (musically) by E W Korngold to the extent of inventing a wholly new third act, won gasps of approval for Oliver Messel's extravagant settings and the two-thousand-ship beauty of its Helen (Evelyn Laye) as George Robey turned his hand to the comicalities of Ménélas. The ''authors'' of this thoroughly raped Helen collected Offenbach's, Meilhac's and Halévy's royalties through 193 performances, and producer C B Cochran lost a small fortune.

Vienna proved particularly partial to the show. When memories of Geistinger's Helen (seen at the Carltheater again in 1887) had barely faded, Ilka Pálmay brought her Spartan sexpot to the Theater an der Wien (1891) and was followed the next year by Minna Baviera and, as the show resurfaced regularly in the repertoire through the 1890s, by Julie Kopácsi-Karczag, Frln Frey, Annie Dirkens and others. During the prewar years of the new century, both the principal Viennese houses played the show in repertoire with Kopácsi-Karczag, Dirkens and Pálmay being joined by Betty Stojan, Frau Saville, Flora Siding, Dora Keplinger and Phila Wolff as the latest Helenas until a major revival was launched in 1911 (12 October) with Mizzi Günther playing Helen to the Ménélas of Louis Treumann and the Paris of Ludwig Herold. Later the same year (31 December) the show was seen at the Volksoper with Maria Jeritza in the starring role as another very vocal Greek queen. The show reappeared in Vienna regularly both during the war (Carltheater, Bürgertheater w Ida Russka) and after, proving itself the most enduring of Offenbach's pieces on the Viennese stage. It was most recently played in Vienna in 1990 at the Wiener Kammeroper with English soprano Gaynor Miles starred as a particularly glamorous and lightly clad Helena. In Budapest, István Zágon's adaptation was still to be seen at the Fővárosi Operettszínház with Zsuzsa Kalocsai as its Helen in 1994 (11 March).

If, in Germany, the butchering begun by Reinhardt and his allies was followed up by more butchering, in London the wrongs of A P Herbert were righted, 30 years later, when the Sadler's Wells Opera Company produced a fine, funny and faithful new translation (ad Geoffrey Dunn 31 May 1963) with Joyce Blackham starred as a luscious mezzo-soprano Helen. The same company (English National Opera) revived that version in 1975, and the show was given a later staging by the ill-fated New Sadler's Wells company.

New York also went through a version of the souped-up Reinhardt/Korngold version under the title *Helen Goes to Troy* (24 April 1944), with Novotna repeating her heavy-weight Helen 14 years on, and a program which actually boasted ''Korngold . . . has not only rearranged and reorchestrated the original Offenbach score, but also interpolated 14 newly adapted numbers, substituting [these] for some wilted music pieces of the original score.'' Herr Korngold's Offenbach hash lasted 96 performances. *La Belle Hélène* survived this and other tasteless attacks (a *La Belle* perpetrated by one William Roy curled up before getting to Broadway) and it has made its way, as elsewhere, into American opera houses. It was played in 1976 at the New York City Opera with Karan Armstrong as Helen. Fortunately with all the bits Herr Korngold considered wilted safely back in their brilliant and beautiful place.

The tale of the Iliad and the siege of Troy was a fertile source for musical theatre writers. Achilles and Aeneas, Dido and Oenone, Cassandra, Hector and the rest of them were favorite subjects with 18th-century operatic composers. The rape of Helen was operaticized by Freschi as early as 1677. Of more recent operatic Trojans, Berlioz's double-header, *Les Troyens à Carthage* and *La Prise de Troie,* and Michael Tippett's *King Priam* remain amongst the better known. In the musical theatre, the story of Paris and his ''judgement'' (or lack of it) featured in such pieces as Burnand's burlesque *Paris, or Vive Lemprière,* Terrasse's successful latter day opéra-bouffe *Paris ou le bon Juge* and the American even more latter-day opéra-bouffe *The Golden Apple;* the siege of Troy was made into an Astley's Theatre entertainment by O'Keeffe (*The Siege of Troy* 21 July 1795) and burlesqued by Robert Brough (Theatre Royal, Lyceum 27 December 1858), Australia's W M Akhurst and by Belgium's MM Booch and Hivry; and the post-sacking story of Dido and Aeneas, famously set as an opera by Purcell, was more amusingly treated in F C Burnand's successful burlesque of *Dido* and in the Parisian opéra-bouffe *Didon* (Blangini/Adolphe Belot, Léon Journault), produced at the Bouffes-Parisiens in 1866 (5 April).

Austria: Theater an der Wien *Die schöne Helena* 17 March 1865; Germany: Friedrich-Wilhelmstädtisches Theater *Die schöne Helena* 13 May 1865; UK: Adelphi Theatre *Helen, or Taken from the Greek* 30 June 1866; Hungary: Kassa *Szép Helena* 7 March 1866, Budai Színkör (Ger) 6 May 1866, Várszínház *Szép Helena* 30 April 1870; USA: Stadttheater, New York *Die schöne Helena* 3 December 1867, National Theatre, Cincinnati (Fr) 6 April 1868, Théâtre Français (Fr) 26 March 1868, New York Theater *Paris and Helen, or the Greek Elopement* 13 April 1868; Australia: Royal Victoria Theatre, Sydney 31 May 1876

TV film: Unitel (Ger) 1974

Recordings: complete (Musidisc Festival, EMI-Pathé, EMI, Accord), cast recordings (Vega, Barclay), selections (EMI-Pathé, Philips etc), complete in Russian (Melodiya), complete in German (Philips), selection in English (HMV), selection in Polish (Muza), selection in Czech (Supraphon), etc

BELLE LURETTE Opéra-comique in 3 acts by Raoul Toché, Édouard Blau and Ernest Blum. Music by Jacques Offenbach. Théâtre de la Renaissance, Paris, 30 October 1880.

The last full-length opérette of Jacques Offenbach, its orchestration completed after the composer's death by Leo Delibes, *Belle Lurette* was produced posthumously at the Théâtre de la Renaissance in 1880, and had a respectable life, without establishing itself as part of the composer's revivable repertoire.

Belle Lurette (Jane Hading) is a little laundress, working in the establishment run by Marcelline (Mily-Meyer), courted by the jolly fellows of the area (Vauthier, Jannin, Alexandre), and putting her faith in the tarot cards which predict her a fine future. That future arrives in the person of Malicorne (Alfred Jolly), who picks the pretty laundress to be the bride of the Duke of Marly (Henri Cooper). When it turns out that she is to be a wife in name only to cover her husband's current affair, but yet ensure him his inheritance, Lurette raises the roof. By the end of the evening she has won him properly, and Marcelline has pinned down Malicorne who turns out to be the fellow who helped himself to her virtue years before and then disappeared.

In a score which was heavily angled towards the heroine, the best-liked pieces were her countrified Ronde de Colette, a rhythmic Chanson du Jabot with which Alexandre, in the role of Belhomme, opened the evening's proceedings, and a parody of Strauss's ''Blue Danube'' performed by Mily-Meyer and Jolly. An ensemble, ''Nous sommes les amoureux,'' and two further pieces for the heroine, the rondeau ''Chez la baronne'' and a first-act romance (''Faut-il ainsi nous maudire''), were voted amongst the other most attractive musical moments.

The posthumous show opened ''with a kind of gloom hanging over it'' and in spite of much applauded performances from Mily-Meyer and Mlle Hading, *Belle Lurette* lasted only a fair 82 performances in Paris. However, it traveled fairly vigorously. It was on the stage at Brussels's Galéries Saint-Hubert days after its Paris opening, with Lucy Abel as Lurette and Mesmacker as Malicorne, it was played by the Renaissance company in London, in its original French, with no little success, and was later given in an English version (ad Frank Desprez, Alfred Murray, Henry S Leigh) for a respectable 83-performance run at the Avenue Theatre with Florence St John (Lurette), Lottie Venne (Marcelline), Claude Marius (Malicorne) and Henry Bracy (Marly) heading a strong cast. In America, although briskly announced by Emily Soldene, the Comley-Barton Troupe and others, it finally got seen only at Boston's Gaiety Theatre, under the management of J W Norcross, where two members of Soldene's by-then-disbanded company, Rose Stella (Lurette) and Maggie Duggan (Dragonette) featured alongside Henri Laurent (Hildebert) and Norcross (Eustache de Toledo) in a different English adaptation, done by the manager. It lasted just two nights.

Belle Lurette was reprised in Paris in 1883 with Jeanne Granier in the title role (''augmented by several morceaux culled from the composer's earlier scores''), appeared a couple of decades on in Austria (ad F Heidrich, F Maierfeld) with one Frln Kramm playing the title role in the ''1 Auffuhrung in deutscher Sprache'' under August Lischke's direction at the Jantschtheater, and was subsequently played both in Hungary (ad Sándor Hevesi) and in Russia.

UK: Gaiety Theatre (Fr) 6 July 1881, Avenue Theatre *Lurette* 24 March 1883; USA: Gaiety Theater, Boston 25 October 1881; Austria: Jantschtheater *Die schöne Lurette* 3 May 1900; Hungary: Király Színház *Szép Mosónő* 3 September 1904

Recording: selection in German (Amiga)

THE BELLE OF BOHEMIA Musical farce in 2 acts by Harry B Smith. Music by Ludwig Englander. Additional music by Harry T MacConnell. Casino Theater, New York, 24 September 1900.

A musical with a two Dromios libretto and a serviceable score, *The Belle of Bohemia* was played at the Casino Theatre with star comic Sam Bernard and his brother Dick in the roles of the swappable Adolf Klotz (''a wandering photographer'') and Rudolph Dinkelhauser (''a brewer'') and a supporting cast including Trixie Friganza (Chloe), Virginia Earle (Katie), Irene Bentley (Geraldine McDuffy), English comedienne Marie Dainton (Paquita) and the two comedian brothers of British composer Teddy Solomon, Fred (Yellowplush) and Sol ('Arris).

Sam Bernard featured ''He Was a Married Man,'' Dick hailed ''Beer, Glorious Beer!,'' Miss Earle described ''What Eve Said to Adam'' and Miss Dainton advised ''Be Clever'' and delivered ''The Champagne Waltz.'' The musical proceedings came to their peak with the hailing of ''The Belle of Bohemia'' in a carbon copy of *The Belle of New York*'s welcome to its heroine.

Although *The Belle of Bohemia* lasted only 55 performances at the Casino Theater, it was shipped off to Britain by producer Lederer, in the wake of the success there of his *The Belle of New York,* with Richard Carle (Algy Cuffs) at the head of its cast supported by Miss Friganza, Marie George and Marie Dainton. It did not have the novelty attraction for Londoners that the earlier piece had had and, after a little over two months at the Apollo Theatre, Carle, Marie Dainton, and the Casino company moved on to play *The Belle of New York* and *The Casino Girl,* but not *The Belle of Bohemia,* in Budapest, Berlin and Vienna.

UK: Apollo Theatre 21 February 1901

THE BELLE OF BRITTANY Musical play in 2 acts by Leedham Bantock and P J Barrow. Lyrics by Percy Greenbank. Music by Howard Talbot. Additional numbers by Marie Horne. Queen's Theatre, London, 24 October 1908.

A charming light musical show, written by the Bantock/Talbot team which had been responsible for the winning mini-musical *The White Chrysanthemum, The Belle of Brittany* mixed the style and storytelling of the old-fashioned opéra-comique, its marquises and country maidens, with some of the more contemporary traditions of turn-of-the-century musical comedy.

The story dealt with the hurdles that moneyless Marquis's son Raymond (Lawrence Rea) and miller's daughter Babette (Ruth Vincent) need to negotiate on the way to marriage. His father (George Graves) needs cash for his mortgage and wants his son to marry rich Denise (Lily Iris), her father (M R Morand) holds the mortgage but wants his daughter to marry the famous chef Baptiste Boubillion (Walter Passmore). The deus ex machina is old Jacques, the clarionet player (E W Royce), who gets hold of the important papers in the affair and ensures a happy ending.

Talbot's score was more than a mite conventional with its songs celebrating "Daffodil Time in Brittany," "The Kingdom of a Woman's Heart," "A Little Café" and "Little Country Mice," but it had its fine moments, as in Passmore's jolly description of himself as "The King of the Kitchen" and in some pretty soprano numbers for Miss Vincent. A certain delicacy in the show's writing and production meant that its success, though certain, was more limited than that of some more obvious pieces of the time, but Graves soon ensured that delicacy went out the window as he began to pad his part with the kind of stand-up low comedy he had recently used in *The Merry Widow.* Miss Vincent and soubrette Maudi Darrell ("A Bit of the Very Best Brittany") were given extra numbers in some kind of compensation.

Tom Davis's production had a respectable run in London (147 performances) before Graves took it into the provinces, and the following year the Shuberts produced a version on Broadway. Although Fritzi Scheff was originally announced for the starring role, Christine Nielson and Frank Daniels starred as Babette and the Marquis, some Harold Atteridge/Harry Carroll numbers were inserted into Howard Talbot's score, and the piece ran through 72 performances in New York before Daniels took it to the country with considerable success.

The Belle of Brittany was also seen in Australia, where Winifred O'Connor (Babette), Tom Walls (Marquis), Percy Clifton (Poquelin), Gertrude Gilliam (Toinette) and Charlie Stone (Baptiste) took time out from the success of *The Arcadians* to play a satisfactory season of the lesser piece.

USA: Daly's Theater 8 November 1909; Australia: Criterion Theatre, Sydney 25 February 1911

THE BELLE OF MAYFAIR Musical comedy in 2 acts by Basil Hood and Charles H E Brookfield (later billed as by Cosmo Hamilton and Brookfield). Music by Leslie Stuart. Vaudeville Theatre, London, 11 April 1906; new version, 8 February 1907.

The Belle of Mayfair was originally conceived and carefully constructed by librettist Basil Hood as a modern high-society version of Shakespeare's *Romeo and Juliet* but, in the hands of producer Charles Frohman, it ultimately dissolved into an attractive but hardly unconventional Edwardian musical comedy of pretty girls, pretty dresses and very pretty songs tacked together with some light society chit-chat and various kinds of comedy, and Hood insisted that his name be withdrawn from the book credit.

Since the pretty girls involved were headed by Edna May, the darling of London since her success in *The Belle of New York,* and by the latest transatlantic sensation, beauty-contest winner Camille Clifford, whose figure and walk had won a crazed following in *The Prince of Pilsen* and *The Catch of the Season,* and since Leslie Stuart's score threw up such winning songs as "Come to St George's," Miss May's Red Indian coon song [*sic*] "In Montezuma" and several delightful ballads to what remained of Basil Hood's lyrics, any serious intent in the show's construction was not missed and *The Belle of Mayfair* became composer Stuart's biggest success after *Florodora.*

Miss May was Julia Chaldicott, daughter of nouveau-riche Sir John (Arthur Williams), and her Romeo was Raymond Finchley (Joe Farren Soutar), the son of the lofty Earl of Mount Highgate (Sam Walsh). There were more-or-less equivalents of some of the other characters of Shakespeare's play: Paris became the Comte de Perrier (Charles Angelo), Friar Lawrence was Dr Marmaduke Lawrence, the Nurse became a cockney maid (Lillian Digges) and Mercutio was turned into Hugh Meredith, as played by Courtice Pounds, equipped with one of the evening's most attractive numbers, "What the World Will Say." The plot, however, had Raymond disguised as the leader of a Bashi-Bouzouk band, working his way into the second-act ball to elope with Julia and, since this was musical comedy, to the final consent of their parents rather than a lot of messy deaths. Louie

Pounds, as an incidental fairy-godmotherish person who didn't seem to have any parallel in Shakespeare, scored a particular success with Hood's pretty "Said I To Myself" and a piece about how "The Weeping Willow Wept."

After its troubled life prior to opening, and a premiere where all the cheers went to the talented Poundses rather than to the nominal star, *The Belle of Mayfair* continued to have a career that, if decidedly healthy (416 performances), was not unspotted with incidents. The most remarkable occurred several months into the run when the overshadowed Edna May walked out of the show. Irked by the amount of publicity accorded to Camille Clifford, she threw in the towel when that lady announced her engagement to the heir to Lord Aberdare and thus became the chief attraction of the evening to much of a curious public. There was further publicity when May's understudy, Ethel Newman, hopelessly sued the producers when she was not given the takeover, and more when 15-year-old Phyllis Dare was whisked from her convent school to be brought in as leading lady.

There were court proceedings in America too, when the Shuberts attempted to hijack the hit of the show "Come to St George's" by including it, under a different title, in one of their new shows before *Florodora* producer Thomas Ryley, who had purchased the Broadway rights to the new Stuart show, could get *The Belle of Mayfair* on to the stage. Ryley won his point and also success when *The Belle of Mayfair* proved that it did not need an Edna May or a Camille Clifford to ensure its popularity by sensational means and, with Christie MacDonald in its title role, turned out one of the hits of the 1906/7 Broadway season. Van Rensslaer Wheeler was Raymond-Romeo, Irene Bentley took Louie Pounds's role, and the beauteous Valeska Suratt performed Miss Clifford's walk through a fine 140 performances.

USA: Daly's Theater 3 December 1906; Australia: Theatre Royal, Melbourne 20 June 1908

THE BELLE OF NEW YORK Musical comedy in 2 acts by "Hugh Morton" (C M S McLellan). Music by Gustave Kerker. Casino Theater, New York, 28 September 1897.

George Lederer's Casino Theater production of *The Belle of New York* featured pale, pretty Edna May as a Salvation Army lassie called Violet Gray and Harry Davenport as the debauched young man whose inheritance she threatens, in what was largely a ragbag of comedy scenes and characters from the stockpot of the 19th-century American musical theatre, all illustrated by some bright if undistinguished songs by the prolific Gustave Kerker.

Harry Bronson (Davenport) is living the high life in New York on the contents of his wealthy, strictly moral father's wallet, and he finds its difficult to clean up his act when father Ichabod (Dan Daly) suddenly decides to come to town. Harry's intended bride, the gold-digging "queen of comic opera," Cora Angélique (Ada Dare), the music hall's Kissy Fitzgarter (Marie George), who also has claims on him, and his chef's daughter, Fifi (Phyllis Rankin), don't help matters, but the most worries come from the polite but insane Karl von Pumpernick (J E Sullivan). Pumpernick is literally mad about Cora and he is pursuing this Mr Bronson who is threatening to wed her with a knife and harmful intent. Needless to say, he lights on the wrong Mr Bronson. It is papa who gets stalked.

In spite of the fact that Ichabod turns out to be anything but overly strict, he disinherits worthless Harry in favor of Violet, his old business partner's daughter, and, while she devotes herself to good works, Harry has to go to work as a soda jerk. After a lively finale day out at Narragansett, when other incidental characters including Mamie Clancy (Paula Edwardes) and her boxer boyfriend, Blinky Bill (William Cameron), get to do a number or a speciality in the best tradition of the variety musical, the final curtain happily sees the two young people getting together, just as papa had planned all along.

A 56-performance failure on its New York production, *The Belle of New York* was almost closed after its second week when the authors sued producer Lederer for not paying them their royalties. Lederer retorted with a typical Broadway countersuit saying that (for reasons ungiven) the authors owed him $30,000, and kept going. But if *The Belle of New York* had a sticky beginning, things looked up soon after. Its post-Broadway Boston engagement was a distinct success and Lederer, Kerker and McLellan (apparently back on good terms again) set off for London "with the avowed pupose of making arrangements to present some of the Casino extravaganzas in London." Many of the Casino extravaganzas being rip-offs of British and/or French works, threats of lawsuits soon hung over the intrepid trio, but *The Belle of New York* had the advantage over these of being as original as it was necessary to be, and it was thus *The Belle of New York* for which the trio, within days of setting foot in London, found themselves a buyer. That buyer was Australian producer George Musgrove, down on his uppers and desperate to find a successful novelty for his ailing Shaftesbury Theatre. To him Lederer and his writers sold not only their show, but their production, and *The Belle of New York* was shipped bodily from America to Britain. When it opened in London, the show took the public fancy by storm by its freshness and its newness. If the lively Yankee characters and Kerker's tunes for the show were old hat on Broadway they were, if anything, refreshing to a London accustomed to a beloved but fairly unvarying diet at the Gaiety and Daly's theatres. Gentle, cotton-wool-voiced Edna May became a star overnight, J E Sullivan's portrait of the ''polite lunatic'' was copied everywhere, and the other comedians of the company, headed by Dan Daly and Frank Lawton (Bill), found themselves lionized as they had never been at home. The buxom, busy American chorus line which flung itself energetically into its choreography instead of parading elegantly and dancing trippingly like a British chorus, also made a huge hit.

The Belle of New York was the overwhelming novelty of the 1898 London season and much of the 1899 one as well, remaining at the Shaftesbury for 697 perfomances, a record for an American musical in Britain that would stand for several decades. By the time it closed, its tunes, the best and/or best-liked of which were a lilting title waltz, Violet's ''They All Follow Me'' and the attractive if unoriginal ''Teach Me How to Kiss'' sung by Harry and Fifi, and its title had become sufficiently ingrained in the public consciousness to ensure it an extensive afterlife. *The Belle of New York* became a perennial touring show on the British and colonial circuits and returned for West End seasons in 1901, 1914, 1916, 1919 (additional songs by Herman Darewski), 1931, 1933, 1934 and in 1942 (ad Emile Littler) with Evelyn Laye as Violet, in ever changing textual and musical shape.

Plate 29. **The Belle of New York.** *In the person of Edna May.*

Musgrove, who had come to verbal blows with his partner J C Williamson over his productions at the Shaftesbury, made up and mounted the piece with Williamson in Australia with an imported company headed by Louise Hepner as Violet, former D'Oyly Carte man, Charles Kenningham, as Harry, Oscar Girard as Ichabod and Louise Royce (Cora). It proved a disappointment in a little more than a month in both Melbourne and Sydney (Her Majesty's Theatre 6 May 1899), but Williamson—who blamed the flop on Musgrove for sending him doggy chorines from Britain—had the costumes and scenery on his hands, so it was brought out for further performances in 1902, 1903 and 1904 and eventually established itself as a familiar favorite.

The recent Continental successes won by the Gaiety and Daly's shows, and in their wake by other British musicals, encouraged European houses to pick up this latest London hit and *The Belle of New York* appeared throughout Europe around the turn of the century. The anglophile Gábor Steiner took up the piece for Vienna and produced a German version (ad Leopold Krenn, Carl Lindau) at his summer theatre, Venedig in Wien, with Frln Milton as Violet and director Karl Tuschl as Habakuk (ie, Ichabod). The Narragansett entertainment became a ''grosses Casino-Fest'' featuring a Festmarsch of 40 marchers, a valse d'ensemble by the ballet, a pas de deux by a gentleman billed as being from La Scala, Milan, and the ballerina étoile, an idyll waltz with song, and a ''can-can amusant'' before the finale, which was composed, like the rest of this material, by Steiner's musical director Karl Kappeller, was reached. The piece had such success that Steiner played some performances at his winter house, Danzers Orpheum (18 November), and then brought it back to the Prater for a second summer season (31 May 1901). This time the role of Cora Angélique was played by one Frln Massari, later to be better known as Fritzi Massary. Simultaneously, *The Belle of New York* was given in English for a week at the Carltheater by the Casino Theater company which, with Richard Carle, Marie Dainton, Trixie Friganza and Lawton at its head, was touring Europe after the London failure of *The Belle of Bohemia.* Steiner's company finally played their hit show at the Theater an der Wien itself (15 March 1902).

Another German version (ad Benno Jacobson) was mounted at Berlin's Centraltheater, with Mia Werber as Violet, and in Hungary Emil Makai and Ernő Salgó's *New-York Szépe* was produced at the Magyar Színház (1900), where it passed its 100th performance 11 January 1902, with London's Madge Perry playing in English alongside a castful of Hungarians, and at the Budai Színkör (2 May 1903). The Casino Theater's touring English version was seen at the Vígszínház (21 May 1901), and the show returned to Budapest as late as 1934 in a revival at the Király Színház (24 October).

Paris's P-L Flers, seeing the huge success that his Viennese counterpart, Steiner, was enjoying with his American musical in Vienna, mounted the show (ad Paul Gavault) at the Moulin-Rouge, hitherto devoted to music hall, with considerable extravagance. Gavault did some cheerful ravaging of the book—the role of Pumpernickle, the "polite lunatic," which had been one of the play's favorite features was entirely cut out—but with Marie Marville and Ellen Baxone at the head of a music-hally line of glamor girls, the show scored an enormous popular success, was taken up to Brussels's Scala Théâtre (January 1904) for a season, with Jane Dyt featured, and was both revived at the Moulin-Rouge (2 August 1911 with Frank Lawton in the cast and "two hundred costumes") and then restaged in Paris, first at the Théâtre des Variétés in 1915 with Jane Marnac, then at the Ba-ta-clan in 1918 and, again, in a rewritten version as *La Belle de mon coeur* (ad Henri Varna, Marc-Cab, René Richard) in 1953. Brussels subsequently saw the young Yvonne Printemps in Edna May's role, and the show was brought back to the Scala in 1909.

In 1916 the down but not quite out George Lederer announced a major revival of the piece, but having failed to lure Miss May out of "retirement" (she went off and played another Salvation girl in the movie *Salvation Joan* for Vitagraph instead) or to secure his other two wished-for stars, Ina Claire or Mary Pickford, he abandoned the project. Broadway did later get a revised version of *The Belle of New York,* restaged as *The Whirl of New York* (additional material by Al Goodman and Lew Pollack, Winter Garden Theater 13 June 1921), and once again showed limited interest. However, the potency of the show's title was demonstrated when it was attached to a Vera-Ellen/Fred Astaire film which had nothing to do with the stage piece.

The Belle of New York undoubtedly owed its survival to Musgrove's apparently irrational act in importing the whole Casino company to London, but its wide and enduring popularity since has demonstrated that it must have had more attractions to it than just a sexy chorus line, a couple of catchy songs, a bundle of interchangeable variety acts and some very low comedy.

UK: Shaftesbury Theatre 12 April 1898; Australia: Princess Theatre, Melbourne 1 April 1899; Hungary: Magyar Színház *New-York Szépe* 30 January 1900, Vígszínház *The Belle of New York* 21 May 1901; Austria: Venedig in Wien *Die schöne von New-York* 18 July 1900, Carltheater (Eng) 30 May 1901; Germany: Central-Theater *Die schöne von New-York* 22 December 1900; France: Théâtre du Moulin-Rouge 29 May 1903, revised version as *La Belle de mon coeur* Théâtre Mogador 28 February 1953

Recording: selection (EMI, 45EP)

LA BELLE POULE Opérette in 3 acts by Hector Crémieux and Albert de Saint-Albin. Music by Hervé. Théâtre des Folies-Dramatiques, Paris, 29 December 1875.

When Hortense Schneider—the greatest star of the Parisian musical stage—decided to leave the Théâtre des Variétés, she was courted by each and every management with a musical bent. After listening to the score of *La Belle Poule,* she chose to go to the Folies-Dramatiques.

La Belle Poule followed the love story of lusty village Poulette (Schneider) and her gentle Poulet (Simon-Max) through the usual kinds of operettic ups and downs. Poulet goes off to Paris to earn money so that he can wed his sweetheart the sooner, is temporarily supposed to be the illegitimate son of the Baron de Champignol (Ange Milher), and gets entangled with the sexy Foedora (Mlle Prelly) who, in her turn, temporarily abandons the wealthy Baron for his sake. Poulette turns out (also temporarily) to be the long-lost Mlle Diane de Montfrison and is thus scheduled to be wed to the suitably lofty Chevalier d'Aigrefille (Eugène Didier). A cocky village rival, Jean Marcou (Luco) with an impersonation of an eccentric Scotsman, and a motherly Marquise (Mlle Toudouze) provided the comic diversions of the evening which, of course, ended up with all the right folk being paired with the right folk.

Hervé's score included a large number of winning opportunities for his star: a Chanson Bordelaise ("Au cun d'un bo"), a military Chanson du dragon with a trumpeting refrain, a Péricholish letter song in which Poulette read out Poulet's farewell note, and some pretty couplets in which she pleaded with her rival "C'est un joujou pour vous, madame, ne l'cassez pas, rendez-le moi." The young Simon-Max, making his opérette debut, had his finest moment in a gently comical tyrolienne ("Je souis un Prince de Tolède"), Foedora scored in a waltz song ("Dans votre empire"), whilst the Marquise de Montfrison went into musical raptures over her newly rediscovered role as a mother.

La Belle Poule was not a hit, and Schneider, flagrantly too old at 43 to be playing juvenile leads, was not a hit in it. The piece played for just over a month before the diva and her producer called it a day. Nevertheless, *La Belle Poule* went on to be seen elsewhere. Marie Aimée played Poulette to the Poulet of Raoult around America, as part of her touring repertoire, but it was the widely traveling Emily Soldene (only a few years Schneider's junior) who proved to be the show's champion. She introduced her English version of *Poulet et Poulette* in New Orleans, appearing as Poulette to the Poulet of Charles J Campbell, and supported by a cast including Rose Stella (Foedora), Cissie Durrant (Marchioness), Edward Marshall (Baron) and John Wallace (Marcou), and went on to play it in repertoire first in other American cities, then in New Zealand and in Australia. Down under, it was greeted as "a very agreeable compilation [with] the advantage over many opéras-bouffes of being coherent from first to last in its plotting and counter-plotting," but it remained a supporting item on Soldene's programs, and although she tested it, on her return to Britain, in a pair of matinée performances at the Gaiety Theatre, she did not finally take it round England.

In 1895 I W Norcross jr readapted the libretto of *La Belle Poule* as *The Dragoon's Daughter* (I wonder how a dragoon got into the story?), Hervé's music was replaced with a score by local ditty-maker Herman Perlet, and the resultant piece (Castle Square Theater, Boston 7 January 1895) set off round the American tour circuits under the banner of the Louise Beaudet opéra-bouffe company. It didn't get far before it collapsed.

USA: Bidwell's Academy of Music, New Orleans *Poulet et Poulette* 8 February 1877, Eagle Theater, New York (Fr) 27 March 1877; Australia: Theatre Royal, Sydney *Poulet and Poulette* 6 October 1877; UK: Gaiety Theatre *Poulet et Poulette* 29 March 1878

BELLMAN Operette in 3 acts by Moritz West and Ludwig Held. Music by Franz von Suppé. Theater an der Wien, Vienna, 26 February 1887.

The script for Suppé's *Bellman* was written around the character of the historical Swedish poet Karl Michael Bellman (1740–1795), as portrayed in the show's original production by Josef Joseffy. His lady was the Gräfin Ulla (Regina Stein), mistress to the King Gustav III, and the comedy of the piece came from the antics of the herring-seller Niels Elvegaard (Siegmund Stelzer) and a pair of gunpowder-makers, Axel Junk and Claasen Steen (Franz Eppich, Carl Lindau). The ins and outs of the tale—which focused on the battle between the "hat" (nationalist) and "cap" (pro-Russian) parties in Swedish politics—held nothing as dramatic as that other Gustavan tale *Un Ballo in maschera,* but it nevertheless provoked Suppé to some slightly more operatic music than was his wont.

Mounted at the Theater an der Wien by Camillo Walzel, *Bellman* proved a disappointment, and was played only 19 times. Nevertheless, its composer's reputation ensured it further showings, and John McCaull's American production (ad J Cheever Goodwin, William von Sachs), which featured Hubert Wilke in the title role alongside De Wolf Hopper (Elvegaard), Jefferson de Angelis (Claasen), Laura Joyce Bell (Tronda) and Marion Manola (Ulla), was played at Broadway's Wallack's Theater from late August 1887 to the end of the season on 8 October, before going on to a fine reception and full houses in Philadelphia, and further success around America. A Budapest production (ad György Verő) confirmed Vienna's verdict (4 performances).

USA: Wallack's Theater 22 August 1887; Hungary: Népszínház 7 September 1887; Germany: ?1887

BELLS ARE RINGING Musical comedy in 2 acts by Adolph Green and Betty Comden. Music by Jule Styne. Shubert Theater, New York, 29 November 1956.

Memories of the heroines of those half-century-old musical comedies *Ein Blitzmädel* and *La Demoiselle du téléphone,* as well as the more recent *The Five o'Clock Girl,* resurfaced in 1956 when Comden and Green turned out a new telephone-girl musical which was equipped with the latest up-to-date refinement: the answering service.

Ella Peterson (Judy Holliday) works at Susanswerphone, the answering service office run by Sue Summers (Jean Stapleton), but she doesn't have the same brisk, efficient style as her boss. Ella gets interested in her clients. She gets so interested that she develops a more-than-motherly feeling for Plaza 04433, otherwise playwright Jeffrey Moss (Sydney Chaplin). When things get troublesome for Jeff, she leaves her telephone and goes out into the world to help him. On her way through some of the more and less picturesque sights of New York (the underground railway provided the opportunity for one routine), she makes a few other "helpful" calls to clients who might be useful to other clients. As a result of her interference, life takes a happy turn for them all and, needless to say, for Ella and Jeff. A subplot involved Sue with a little crook (Eddie Lawrence) using Susanswerphone as a cover for illegal betting, and a comical policeman (Frank Aletter) and his underling (Jack Weston) added to the fun as they tracked Ella through New York, convinced that her newfangled firm is up to no good, only accidentally to catch the gambling gangsters at the final curtain.

The Comden/Green/Styne songs for the show included two which would become recital and recording standards: Ella's joyful thoughts of how she found Jeff "Just in Time" and her gentle, dejected realization that she does not fit in with his brittle, campy friends or with the "good fairy" image he has built up for her ("The Party's Over"). More tied to the script were two other enjoyable numbers for the heroine, "It's a Perfect Relationship," in which she described the mother-and-son telephone relationship between herself and her client, and her lively, if temporary, farewell to her telephone when she realizes she cannot keep her sentiments out of her work ("I'm Goin' Back"). There were further comical moments for Sándor the bookie and Sue, and a revusical piece of special-material party chatter ("Drop That Name") in a score where the fun was never long away.

The Theatre Guild's Broadway production of *Bells Are Ringing* was a first-class hit. Miss Holliday—

formerly a member of the nightclub group in which Comden and Green had performed—scored a personal success as the heroine of the evening and the show gamboled up a run of 924 performances on Broadway before taking to the road in 1959. By this time, London's Sándor Gorlinsky had taken up *Bells Are Ringing* and reproduced it in the vastness of the London Coliseum with Janet Blair (Ella), George Gaynes (Jeff), Eddie Molloy (Sándor) and Jean St Clair (Sue) featured. A run of 270 performances left it rather short of those built up in smaller houses by such contemporary pieces as *Free as Air, Where's Charley?, Grab Me a Gondola* and *Expresso Bongo,* but the show found many takers.

There were further takers in Berlin, where the show was produced at the Titaniapalast (ad Ralf Wolter) in 1960, but not so many in Australia, where a Garnet Carroll production featuring Shani Wallis and Bruce Trent ran just over two unprofitable months in Melbourne. *Bells Are Ringing* has continued to win occasional productions in regional houses and in the years that followed and in the 1980s it was seen in both American and British out-of-town productions before, at last, a return to Broadway was mooted. At the time of writing, a revival with Faith Price as star is scheduled for the Broadway Theater in April 2001.

A film version, with Miss Holliday starred opposite Dean Martin, and Miss Stapleton repeating her original performance alongside Eddie Foy jr, retained almost half of the score, including ''Better Than a Dream'' which had been added during the Broadway run, and added one additional number.

UK: London Coliseum 14 November 1957; Australia: Princess Theatre, Melbourne 5 April 1958; Germany: Titaniapalast *Ein Engel in der Leitung* 5 December 1960

Film: MGM 1960

Recordings: original cast (Columbia), film soundtrack (Capitol)

BELMORE, Bertha [née COUSINS] (b Manchester, 20 December 1882; d Barcelona, 14 December 1953). Britain's top musical character lady of the 1930s and 1940s.

After an early career as a song-and-dance girl in variety and a principal boy in pantomime, Bertha Belmore switched first to straight theatre, appearing with Ben Greet's company (1911) in Shakespeare and, in later days, to the musical theatre and films, where she became the outstanding British ''dragon'' lady of her time. She shared the first part of this career between Britain, where she played in *Irene* (1920, Mrs Cheston), and America, where she appeared in the *Ziegfeld Follies* and succeeded Edna May Oliver as Parthy Ann in *Show Boat.* She repeated her *Show Boat* role and played Mrs Medway in *Turned Up* in 1929 in Australia and, from 1933, she was for some years almost continuously present in London's West End playing comic heavies in such musicals as *Give Me a Ring* (1933, Mrs Trellis), *Yes, Madam?* (1935, Miss Peabody), *Please, Teacher!* (1936, Miss Pink), *Big Business* (1937, Emmeline Ray), *Virginia* (Minnie Fortescue), *Oh! You Letty* (1937, Mrs Summers) and *Bobby Get Your Gun* (1938, Prunella Lockwood).

She returned to Broadway in Rodgers and Hart's *By Jupiter* (1942)—playing Pomposia, mother of the King of Pontus, and performing the song and dance duo ''Life With Father'' with Ray Bolger—and again in *Rhapsody* (1944, Tina), and to the West End in *Blue for a Boy* (1950, Emily Bompard). Formidable of face (''she wasn't born, she was quarried'') and of tone, she also appeared in characteristic roles in several musical films, notably the filmed versions of *Over She Goes, Yes, Madam?* and *Please, Teacher.*

Miss Belmore was married in 1903 to actor Herbert Belmore [Herbert Norman Belmore GARSTIN], and thus a member by marriage of a famous theatrical family which included Lillie Belmore (1871–1901), the original Ada Smith of *The Shop Girl.*

BENATZKY, Ralph [BENATZKY, Rudolph Josef František] (b Mährisch-Budwitz, 5 June 1884; d Zürich, 16 October 1957). Versatile composer of grand spectacle music and intimate musical comedies, remembered almost entirely outside Germany for his songs for *Im weissen Rössl.*

Born in Moravia, the young Benatzky moved to Vienna to join the army as a 15-year-old officer cadet after being summarily dismissed from his Leitmaritz school for insubordination. His military career was ended in similar fashion to his school one, when he was dishonorably discharged from the corps, allegedly for fighting a duel, but apparently for more medical reasons. He was subsequently educated in Vienna, Prague and Munich, achieving a PhD degree in philology at the same time as he pursued his musical studies. Benatzky was in his midtwenties before he opted seriously for a career in music, making his mark at first as a songwriter, in a highly successful team with his first wife, chanteuse Josma Selim, and, from 1910, in the theatre. He began this latter life as a conductor at the Kleines Theater in Munich.

As he moved on from this first engagement, through musical-direction posts in several cabaret-theatres, he supplemented his songwriting (''Ich muss wieder einmal in Grinzing sein,'' ''Draussen im Schönbrunner Parke,'' ''Ich weiss auf der Wieden ein kleines Hotel'') with the composition of the scores, and often the texts as well, for a number of short cabaret musicals and Operetten, several of which (*Laridon, Kokettchens Mission, Das blonde Abenteuer*) were produced both in Germany and in Vienna, where Benatzky ultimately became musical director at the Kabarett Rideamus. The little vaudeville *Prinzchens Frühlingserwachen* was played by Fritzi Massary and Max Pallenberg at Vienna's Apollotheater, and one of his little pieces was also adapted to the British variety stage as *The Frolics of Gabrielle* (Tivoli 25 March 1912, ad A Grey-Venne) following the success there of Reinhardt's similarly small-sized *Die süssen Grisetten.*

An early full-length Operette, *Der lachende Dreibund,* was staged at Berlin's Theater am Nollendorfplatz in 1913, but Benatzky had his first significant success with the Operette *Liebe im Schnee,* produced by Oscar Straus and staged by Miksa Preger at Vienna's Établissment Ronacher in 1916, with Mizzi Günther starred, before going on to other productions in other countries. *Liebe im Schnee* was followed by several other successes: *Yuschi tanzt,* which played a 109-performance run and a fortnight's revival at Vienna's Bürgertheater before productions in Germany and Hungary; *Apachen* (1920), first produced at the Apollotheater with Louis Treumann starred, which ended up in another celebrated variety theatre, the London Palladium; *Pipsi* (1921) which confirmed *Yuschi*'s run with 104 performances in its first run at the Wiener Bürgertheater before moving on to Budapest; and the 1922 *Ein Märchen aus Florenz* which played a hundred nights at Vienna's Johann Strauss-Theater (14 September 1923) and a run at Berlin's Deutsches Opernhaus with Richard Tauber as star.

Following this profitable run of Viennese productions, Benatzky moved to Berlin, and there became attached to the staff at the Grosses Schauspielhaus, providing music for their revues (*An alle, Für Dich*) and—after one further Viennese success with *Adieu Mimi,* which played a fine first run of 159 performances at the Johann Strauss-Theater in 1926—for a series of the extravagantly staged musical plays for which the Schauspielhaus became famous. His Johann Strauss pasticcio *Casanova* (1928) with its famous "Nuns' Chorus" went on from Berlin to successes on other stages, but both it and a vast version of *Die drei Musketiere* (1929), for which he composed and arranged the score, were thoroughly eclipsed by his and the theatre's most famous work, *Im weissen Rössl* (1930). A hit as oversized as its staging, *Im weissen Rössl*—for which Benatzky's basic score ("Es muss was Wunderbares sein," "Im weissen Rössl am Wolfgangsee," "Im Salzkammergut," etc) became encrusted with a whole variety of interpolations as time went on—moved on from its initial triumph at the Grosses Schauspielhaus to an international career as *White Horse Inn, L'Auberge du cheval blanc, Fehér ló, Al cavallino bianco* and so forth, a career which would make it one of the most popular musical plays the world had ever seen.

Parallel to his activities in the world of the opérette à grand spectacle, Benatzky kept his hand in the world of the small-sized musical comedy which had been his earliest area of work, and 1930 gave him a second international hit when he adapted the French comedy *Ma soeur et moi* (1928) to the musical stage as *Meine Schwester und ich.* Another little musical comedy, *Cocktail,* also did well in Berlin and was tried out without a tomorrow by the Shuberts in America, whilst *Zirkus Aimée* followed its German production with a Vienna one, as Benatzky continued a prolific output of Operette, revue (*Wien lacht wieder, Alles aus Liebe,* etc), musical comedy and film scores from which the 1933 *Bezauberndes Fräulein,* a German musicalization of Paul Gavault's oft-adapted little comedy *La Petite Chocolatière,* proved the most individually successful in the theatre.

The composer won good notices for the "taste and delicacy" with which his scores underlined the action and the mood of these light, comic pieces ("a rare combination of tickling comedy selvaged by a most personal fabric of melody and rhythm. . . I am at a loss whether to hand the palm to Benatzky the scribe or Benatzky the composer") and one of the foremost critics of the time asserted that "[he is] one of the small group of composers who have the stuff to step into the shoes of the old guard." But at the height of his success came the rise of the Nazi party and Benatzky joined the general exodus of musical theatre talent from Germany, moving his center of operations successively to Vienna, Paris and, with the dawning of war, to America and Hollywood.

Vienna's Theater an der Wien mounted his Hollywood tale of *Axel an der Himmelstür* with Zarah Leander and Max Hansen starred and with some considerable success whilst, in a Paris still dazzled by the Théâtre Mogador's all-conquering production of *Im weissen Rössl,* he provided the music for another opérette à grand spectacle, *Deux sous de fleurs,* a period Scots piece produced by Léon Brigon at the Théâtre de l'Empire. Rita Georg, the prima donna of the Empire's previous success, *Katinka,* starred opposite tenor Charles Friant of the Opéra-Comique and the highly popular comedian Dranem, supported by 60 Max Rivers Girls, Dorothea Bachelor and the 12 Highland Queens, Major Simpson and his four bagpipers and Noni Prager, "the marvellous skating dancer." A probable success was aborted when the notorious Stavisky affair broke, for it was said that the fraudulent Russian had financed both of the Empire's shows.

Benatzky continued, as before, simultaneously to work on smaller-scale pieces, and, in the wake of *Meine Schwester und ich* and *Bezauberndes Fräulein,* he adapted a number of further French comedies as the kind of genuine musical comedy for which—rather than his large-stage work—he was known and appreciated: Tristan Bernard's *Le Petit Café* became *Das kleine Café*, de Flers and de Caillavet's *Le Roi* was turned into *Majestät-privat* and one of Armont and Gerbidon's comedies became Benatzky's *Pariserinnin* in Vienna and *Párizsi nők* at Budapest's Belvárosi Színház. Following his departure for America, *Der Silberhof*, a musical adaptation of Charlotte Birch-Pfeiffer's celebrated play *Grille*, for which he wrote both text and music, was produced in Mainz.

Benatzky returned to Europe after the war, and spent his later years in Switzerland, continuing to write, rewrite and compose up to the last years of his life.

In the course of his highly active and varied career, Benatzky also wrote the libretti for Karl Kaskel's opera *Die Schmieden von Kent* (Dresden, 1916) and for Max Ast's one-act *Die Blinde* (Volksoper, Vienna 12 March 1927 aka *Aria Appassionata*), and adapted *Porgy and Bess* into German.

In the cinematic world, he composed a part-replacement score for a film of Eysler's Operette *Der unsterbliche Lump*, as well as musically illustrating such other films of the early 1930s as *Die letzte Kompagnie*, *Arm wie eine Kirchenmaus*, *Chauffeur Antoinette* and *Ihre Durchlaucht, die Verkäuferin*. He adapted *Im weissen Rössl* for its 1935 film, readapted *La Petite Chocolatière* as a film under the title *Wer wagt gewinnt!* (w Siegfried Schulz) and worked on both the script and the musical portion of the musical films *Die Puppenfee* (''Ich bin gut aufgelegt'') and *Mädchenpensionnat*, and the scores of *Zu neuern Ufern* (''Yes, Sir!,'' ''Ich steh' im Regen'') and *Der ganz grossen Torheiten*. He was also briefly at one stage contracted to MGM, but found their ways untenable and swiftly returned to Europe. His own *Meine Schwester und ich* (ad Friedrich Schröder) and *Bezauberndes Fräulein* (ad Georg Häntzschel) were both adapted to the screen by other hands in the 1950s.

1910 **Die Walzerkomtesse** (Ludwig Bruckner, Julius Friedrich) 1 act Kabarett Fledermaus, Vienna 1 October

1910 **Der Walzer von heute Nacht** (Adolf Klein) Walhalla-Theater, Wiesbaden 16 October

1911 **Laridon** 1 act Intimes-Theater, Hamburg 21 February; Kabarett Fledermaus, Vienna 1 March 1912

1911 **Cherchez la Femme** 1 act Künstlertheater, Munich 28 July

1911 **Kokettchens Mission** 1 act Künstlertheater, Munich; Kabarett Fledermaus, Vienna February 1912

1911 **Das blonde Abenteuer** 1 act Künstlertheater, Munich; Kabarett Fledermaus, Vienna February 1912

1913 **Der lachende Dreibund** (Leopold Jacobson) Theater am Nollendorfplatz, Berlin 31 October

1914 **Prinzchens Frühlingserwachen** 1 act Apollotheater, Berlin 16 March

1914 **Anno 14, drei Bildern aus unsern Tagen** (w Fritz Grünbaum) 1 act Kabarett Rideamus, Berlin 22 September

1914 **Das Scheckbuch des Teufels** 1 act Kabarett Rideamus, Berlin 18 November

1914 **General Wutzikoff** (Grünbaum) 1 act Budapester Orpheum 1 December

1915 **Fräulein Don Juan** (Paracelsus) 1 act Gartenbau 1 February

1916 **Du, goldige Frau** 1 act Budapester Orpheum 1 September

1916 **Liebe im Schnee** (w Willy Prager) Ronacher 2 December

1918 **Die tanzende Maske** (w Alexander Engel) Apollotheater 1 December

1919 **Die Verliebten** (Julius Wilhelm) Raimundtheater 29 March

1919 **Liebesreigen** (w Karl Zimmer) Theater am Lietzenfee, Berlin 30 August

1920 **Graf Cheveraux** (Fanfaron, ie, Armin Friedmann) 1 act Rolandbühne 1 March

1920 **Yuschi tanzt** (Jacobson, Robert Bodanzky) Wiener Bürgertheater 3 April

1920 **Bluffodont** 1 act Apollotheater 31 July

1920 **Apachen** (w Ignaz M Welleminsky) Apollotheater 20 December

1921 **Pipsi** (Julius Horst, Engel) Wiener Bürgertheater 30 December

1922 **Ein Märchen aus Florenz** (w Oscar Friedmann, Toni Schwanau) Johann Strauss-Theater 14 September 1923

1926 **Adieu Mimi** (Engel, Horst) Johann Strauss-Theater 9 June

1926 **Die Nacht von San Sebastian** (Hans Bachwitz) Operettenhaus am Dittrichring, Leipzig 23 December

1927 **Alles auf Liebe** (Ernst Marischka, Karl Karkas) Stadttheater 30 September

1928 **Casanova** (Johann Strauss arr/Ernst Welisch, Rudolf Schanzer) Grosses Schauspielhaus, Berlin 1 September

1929 **Die drei Musketiere** (Schanzer, Welisch) Grosses Schauspielhaus, Berlin 28 September

1929 **Mit dir allein auf einer einsamen Insel** (w Arthur Rebner) Residenztheater, Dresden 31 December; Metropoltheater, Berlin August 1930

1930 **Meine Schwester und ich** (Robert Blum) Komödienhaus, Berlin 29 March

1930 **Im weissen Rössl** (w others/Robert Gilbert/Hans Müller) Grosses Schauspielhaus, Berlin 8 November

1930 **Cocktail** (Karl Vollmöller) Komödienhaus, Berlin 15 December

1931 **Zur gold'nen Liebe** (w Max Wolff, Martin Zickel) Komische Oper, Berlin 16 October

1931 **Morgen geht's uns gut** (Buchbinder ad Hans Müller) Lessingtheater, Berlin 31 December

1932 **Zirkus Aimée** (w Kurt Götz) Stadttheater, Basle 5 March

1932 **Flirt in Nizza** (w Robert Blum)

1933 **Bezauberndes Fräulein** Deutsches Volkstheater, Vienna 24 May

1933 **Deux sous de fleurs** (Saint-Granier/Paul Nivoix) Théâtre de l'Empire, Paris 6 October (?)

1934 **Büxl** (Arno Holz ad) Deutsches Volkstheater, Vienna 15 March

1934 **Das kleine Cafe** Deutsches Volkstheater, Vienna 20 April

1934 **Die Prinzessin auf der Leiter** revised *Meine Schwester und ich* Theater in der Josefstadt 3 August

1935 **Der König mit dem Regenschirm** Theater in der Josefstadt 18 April

1935 **The Flying Trapeze** (pasticcio w Mabel Wayne/Douglas Furber, Desmond Carter, Frank Eyton/H Müller ad Furber) Alhambra, London 4 May

1936 **Der reichste Mann der Welt** (H Müller) Deutsches Volkstheater, Vienna 3 April

1936 **Axel an der Himmelstür** (Paul Morgan, Adolf Schütz, Hans Weigel) Theater an der Wien 1 September

1936 **Egy lány, aki mindenkié** (*Wer gewinnt, Colette?*) (ad Tamás Emőd) Müvész Színház, Budapest 19 December

1937 **Pariserinnin** Theater in der Josefstadt 7 May, revised version Lucerne 22 December 1964

1937 **Herzen im Schnee** (Robert Gilbert/w H Gilbert, Armin Robinson) Volksoper 8 September

1937 **Majestät-privat** (ad w Karl von Hellmer) Theater an der Wien 18 December

1939 **Landrinette** Stadttheater, Berne 17 December

1940 **Angielina** (*Domeinica*) Basle 17 February

1941 **Der Silberhof** Stadttheater, Mainz 4 November

1947 **Kleinstadtzauber** (Nikolai Gogol ad) Zürich 7 September

1950 **Liebesschule** (aka *Don Juans Wiederkehr*) Deutsches Theater, Göttingen 1 October

1951 **Mon Ami René** revised *Büxl* Karlsruhe 9 September

Biography: Hennenberg, F: *Es muß was Wunderbares sein: Ralph Benatzky: Zwischen ''Weißen Rößl'' und Hollywood* (Paul Zsolnay Verlag, Vienna, 1998)

BENEŠ, Jára (b Prague, 5 June 1897; d Vienna, 10 April 1949).

Czech conductor and composer of popular dance music and songs who wrote more than 50 film scores (*Kein Wort von Liebe, Adresse unbekannte,* etc) and also more than a dozen stage pieces. The most successful of these latter was the 1936 *Auf der grünen Wiese,* produced at Vienna's Volksoper and subsequently filmed. Beneš left Czechoslovakia when the Communist régime took over and his music was, in retaliation, banned there.

1935 **Der gütige Antonius** (Fritz Löhner-Beda, Hugo Wiener) Volksoper 23 December

1936 **Auf der grünen Wiese** (Löhner-Beda, Wiener) Volksoper 9 October

1938 **Gruss und Kuss aus der Wachau** (Löhner-Beda, Wiener, Kurt Breuer) Volksoper 17 February

1947 **Endstation** (Béla Szenes, Josef Petrak) Wiener Bürgertheater 20 May

1948 **Der gestohlene Walzer** (Fritz Eckhardt) Wiener Künstlertheater 5 March

1948 **Pfui Pepi** Wiener Künstlertheater

1949 **Sebastian, der Seitenspringer** (Peter Schwarz, Neumann) Theater ''Auges-Gottes'' 16 January

1949 **Die kleine Schwindlerin** (A M Willner) Theater ''Auges-Gottes'' 1 March

BENNETT, Michael [DI FIGLIA, Michael] (b Buffalo, 8 April 1943; d Tucson, 2 July 1987). Choreographer and director who developed and staged the record-breaking *A Chorus Line.*

After a short career as a chorus dancer on Broadway (*Subways Are for Sleeping, Here's Love, Bajour*), Bennett moved swiftly on to work as a choreographer and, having done the dances for two short-lived shows (*A Joyful Noise, Henry Sweet Henry*), had his first connection with success when he choreographed the musical play *Promises, Promises* (1968) with its lively office party scene, ''Turkey Lurkey Time.'' The following year, he choreographed the more extravagant but less interesting *Coco,* before teaming with director Harold Prince on the highly successful production of *Company* (''Tick Tock'') and then, with co-directorial billing, on *Follies* (''Mirror, Mirror,'' Tony Award). Brought in to doctor the musical *Seesaw* on the road—a function which he fulfilled on a number of shows without credit—he supervised revision to such an extent that he was ultimately billed as author of the piece's libretto as well as its director, and also as part of a complicated four-person choreography credit. The Tony Award for that choreography, however, was awarded to Bennett.

In the mid-1970s, Bennett was midwife to the creation of *A Chorus Line,* a musical built up on the tales of the professional and personal experiences of a group of dancers, and he subsequently directed (Tony Award) and choreographed (Tony Award w Bob Avian) the show which was to become not only one of the outstanding pieces of musical theatre of its era, but also one of the most successful and long-running. Although the Tony Awards for libretto and score which the show won went to its billed authors, Bennett was included in the citation when the piece was nominated as Pulitzer Prize winner of the 1975–76 season. To follow *A Chorus Line* was difficult, and the gentler tale of middle-aged romance in a *Ballroom* (1979, Tony Award w Avian, choreography) was not successful, but Bennett had a second major Broadway success with his staging of another show-business musical, *Dreamgirls,* in 1981. Signed to direct *Chess* for its London opening in 1986, Bennett cast the show, but was prevented by his final illness from fulfilling the contract.

He was for a period married to dancer **Donna McKECHNIE** (b Detroit, November 1944), who was his principal dancer in *Promises, Promises* and *Company* and who created the role of Cassie in *A Chorus Line* (Tony Award). Miss McKechnie continued in the musical theatre in London's revival of *Can-Can* (1988, Môme Pistache) and *No Way to Treat a Lady* (1998, multiple role), on Broadway in *Annie Warbucks* (1993, Mrs Sheila Kelly) and *State Fair* (1996, Emily Arden), and regionally in America as Sally in *Follies* (1998), etc.

Biographies: Mandelbaum, K: *A Chorus Line and the Musicals of Michael Bennett* (St Martin's Press, New York, 1989), Kelly, K: *One Singular Sensation* (Doubleday, New York, 1990), etc

BENNETT, Robert Russell (b Kansas City, 15 June 1894; d New York, 18 August 1981).

Bennett began his musical life as an orchestral and dance band musician and subsequently worked for the publishing firm of Schirmer as a copyist and arranger. His earliest work as a musical-theatre arranger was on the songs for Herbert Stothart and Oscar Hammerstein II's 1922 musical comedy *Daffy Dill,* and other early assignments included full or part-orchestrations for Vincent Youmans and Stothart's *Mary Jane McKane* and *Wildflower* and *Rose Marie* and Jerome Kern's *Sitting Pretty, Sunny, Show Boat* and *Sweet Adeline.* Later credits, in a schedule in which he turned out four or five or six musical comedies, romantic musicals and revues per season, included George Gershwin's *Funny Face, Girl Crazy, Of Thee I Sing* (w Gershwin, William Daly), *Pardon My English,* Cole Porter's *Gay Divorce* and *Anything Goes* (w Spialek), *Jubilee, Red, Hot and Blue* and *Kiss Me, Kate,* Kern's *The Cat and the* Fiddle, *Music in the Air, Roberta,* Rodgers and Hart's *America's Sweetheart,* the Broadway version of *The Great Waltz* and Irving Berlin's *Annie Get Your Gun* (w Lang, Royal) as Bennett established himself as the most important and successful orchestrator in the American musical theatre of his time.

Bennett was responsible for the orchestration of the music for *Oklahoma!,* which won him an Academy Award when the show was transferred to the screen, and subsequently for *Allegro, South Pacific, The King and I, Pipe Dream, Flower Drum Song* and *The Sound of Music,* thus creating the "Rodgers and Hammerstein sound" which became the standard Broadway musical sound of the 1950s and 1960s. He collaborated with Phil Lang on the orchestration of *My Fair Lady* and *Camelot,* and, over a period of some 50 years worked on the music of more than two hundred American musical plays. Amongst his other postwar credits were numbered such shows as *Carmen Jones, Finian's Rainbow, By the Beautiful Sea, Bells Are Ringing, Redhead* and *New Girl in Town.*

Outside his theatre work, Bennett was also a composer of orchestral and chamber music and, in spite of his domination of and contribution to the Broadway orchestration scene, he was quoted as having more musical ambition in those fields than time or taste for the light musical theatre.

1933 **Hold Your Horses** (w others/Corey Ford, Russel Crouse) Winter Garden Theater 25 September

1944 **Rhapsody** (Fritz Kreisler arr/w John Latouche, Leonard Levison, Arnold Sundgaard) Century Theater 22 November

BENNETT, Wilda (b Asbury Park, NJ, 19 December 1894; d Winnemucca, Nev, 20 December 1967).

Through a decade, the young Wilda Bennett appeared on Broadway as a leading lady in Continental and American operettas, beginning with Victor Herbert's *The Only Girl* (Ruth Wilson) in 1914 and continuing through *The Riviera Girl* (*Die Csárdásfürstin,* 1917, Sylva Varescu), Ivan Caryll's *The Girl Behind the Gun* (1918, Lucienne), and Victor Jacobi and Fritz Kreisler's *Apple Blossoms* (1919, Nancy). She took over the star role of Jean Gilbert's *The Lady in Ermine* (*Die Frau im Hermelin,* 1922, Mariana) when Eleanor Painter walked out during rehearsals, and inherited the title role of Fall's *Madame Pompadour* (1924), following the even noisier pre-Broadway sacking of Hope Hampton. In 1927 she made a final appearance on the metropolitan musical stage when she replaced Edna Leedom in the show which became *Lovely Lady* by the time it reached Broadway.

BERÉNY, Henrik [aka BERÉNY, Henri] (b Kassa, Hungary, 1 January 1871; d Budapest, 22 March 1932).

The young Berény orientated his music studies towards the violin and composition, taking lessons from, amongst others, Liszt in Hungary and the violinist Leonard in Paris. He composed his first stage work, the opera *Talmah* (1894), at the age of 23, and saw it played at the court theatre of Mannheim, at Baden and in Scandinavia. He subsequently made something of a speciality of writing scenarios and music for pantomimes (dance mime dramas), and won considerable success with such pieces as *Premier Carnaval, L'Homme aux poupées* and, most particularly, the melodramatic *La Main*—performed to the best effect by his wife, Charlotte Wiehe. These pieces won multiple productions in Hamburg, Paris, Copenhagen, Stockholm, Berlin (Opera House), Budapest, New York (Vaudeville Theater, Savoy Theater, Garden Theater), Boston and London (St George's Hall), and established the name of the young composer, who obligingly made up his wife's programs with a few violin solos on short-program nights. He had a similar success when he switched his activity to the rather more profitable and visible world of the regular musical theatre, winning widespread productions with the best of the small group of Operetten to which he composed the scores in the years before the Great War.

His first such piece, *Miss Chipp,* described as a romantic musical play, was produced in Paris in 1903 with Mdlle Wiehe starred as the chief of a pickpocketing gang in a role which required her not only to act and mime but also to (with rather less success) sing, and the piece was sufficiently well-liked to be played subsequently in his native Hungary (ad Géza Goda, Frigyes Hervay Vígszínház 11 May 1905). If his next piece, *Der kleine Korsar,* apparently went no further than its initial production in Stuttgart, his next two important works, premiered in Vienna and Berlin respectively, both won a degree of international success. *Lord Piccolo,* written to a libretto by Lindau and Schanzer, followed its run at the Johann Strauss-Theater with productions in Germany and Hungary and, most successfully, in a version by the Smith brothers, under the title *Little Boy Blue,* in America, whilst the vaudeville *Das Mädel von Montmartre,* adapted from the French comedy *La Dame de chez Maxim,* was played on Broadway and round America by Richard Carle as *The Girl from Montmartre.* Another Operette, *Mein Mäderl,* was given 50 performances at the Raimundtheater with Betty Fischer, Anton Matscheg and Franz Glawatsch featured.

After the war, however, Berény worked again largely in the field in which he had begun, turning out the scores to such pieces as the "musical legend" *A pupos Boldizsár* and the dance melodrama *Hasis* (Baden-Baden 8 September 1923), and his last appearance in the musical theatre seems to have been with the score for the Parisian musical *Chou-Chou* in 1925.

1903 **Miss Chipp** (André de Lorde, Michel Carré) Théâtre des Bouffes-Parisiens, Paris 31 March

1904 **Der kleine Korsar** Stuttgart

1908 **Fastnacht in Nizza** (Mardi Gras) Hansa Theater, Hamburg 1 February

1910 **Lord Piccolo** (Carl Lindau, Rudolf Schanzer) Johann Strauss-Theater, Vienna 1 September

1911 **Das Mädel von Montmartre** (Schanzer) Neues Theater, Berlin 26 October

1913 **Mein Mäderl** (Eugen Burg, Lindau, Schanzer) Raimundtheater 21 January

1913 **Tubicam** Kisfaludy Színház, Győr 28 November

1922 **A pupos Boldizsár** (Mihály Timar) Magyar Színház, Budapest 15 September

1925 **Chou-Chou** (Raoul Praxy, Max Eddy) Théâtre Ba-ta-clan, Paris 28 February

BERKELEY, Busby [ENOS, William Berkeley] (b Los Angeles, 29 November 1895; d Palm Springs, Calif, 14 March 1976). Celebrated cinema choreographer who also worked for the stage.

After an early career as a performer, which included an appearance in the role of Madame Lucy on the initial national tour of *Irene,* Berkeley devoted himself to working as a choreographer. His first Broadway assignment, in 1925, was on the indifferent German musical *Holka Polka* (*Frühling im Herbst* aka *Spring in Autumn* and *Nobody's Girl*) with operatic tenor Orville Harrold, the original star of *Naughty Marietta,* and his soubrette daughter, Patti, a takeover as *Irene,* in the lead roles, but Berkeley had much more success with the choreography for the Chicago musical *Castles in the Air* (1925), the biggest hit the town had bred in its history. The following year he directed the dances for Friml's *The Wild Rose,* followed up by *Lady Do,* the Rodgers and Hart *A Connecticut Yankee* and Friml's musicalization of *The Squaw Man, The White Eagle.*

He returned to the stage briefly in Rodgers and Hart's *Present Arms,* performing "You Took Advantage of Me," then provided the dances for a considerable series of musicals (*Good Boy, Rainbow, Hallo Daddy, Pleasure Bound,* Kálmán's *The Duchess of Chicago, A Night in Venice, Nina Rosa*) in the space of just two seasons whilst also setting himself up as a producer/director with a musical called *The Street Singer.* The all-round results were, at best, indifferent and Berkeley was represented on Broadway thereafter only by a handful of revues before he moved to Hollywood to make himself famous as the best marshaller of massed pretty girls in cinema history.

His cinema credits included film versions of the stage shows *Whoopee* (1930), *Flying High* (1931), *Wonder Bar* (1934), *Babes in Arms* (1939), *Strike Up the Band* (1940), *Lady, Be Good!* (1941), *Cabin in the Sky* (1943), *Girl Crazy* (1943), *Rose-Marie* (1954) and *Jumbo* (1962), as well as the classics *42nd Street,* the *Gold Diggers* films, *Dames, Babes on Broadway* and many others, some of which he also directed.

He made an inauspicious attempt at a return to the theatre with the Jule Styne musical *Glad To See You* (1944) which closed on the road, but he came back to Broadway in 1971 to direct the revival of *No, No, Nanette* for which, after many vagaries, he was eventually credited as "supervisor."

Literature: Pike, B, Martin, D: *The Genius of Busby Berkeley* (Sherbourne Press, Los Angeles, 1974), Thomas, T, Terry, J: *The Busby Berkeley Book* (Graphic Society, New York, 1973), Rubin, M: *Showstoppers: Busby Berkeley and the Tradition of Spectacle* (Columbia University Press, New York, 1993)

BERLIN, Irving [BALINE, Israel] (b Mogilev, Belorussia, 11 May 1888; d New York, 22 September 1989). Celebrated Russian-born American songwriter who wrote intermittently for the musical theatre and revue, but abandoned more musicals than he got staged.

Irving Berlin began the theatrical part of his career interpolating songs into Broadway musicals (*The Boys and Betty, The Girl and the Wizard, The Jolly Bachelors, He Came from Milwaukee*), revues and vaudeville sketches (Jesse Lasky's *Society Buds,* 1910 w R H Bowers/William Le Baron, etc), before gaining worldwide fame with the song "Alexander's Ragtime Band" in 1911. The result of that fame was a first commission for a musical play, *The Pet of the Petticoats,* for which Berlin collaborated on the score with Ted Snyder and E Ray Goetz. This was completed and in rehearsal—under the

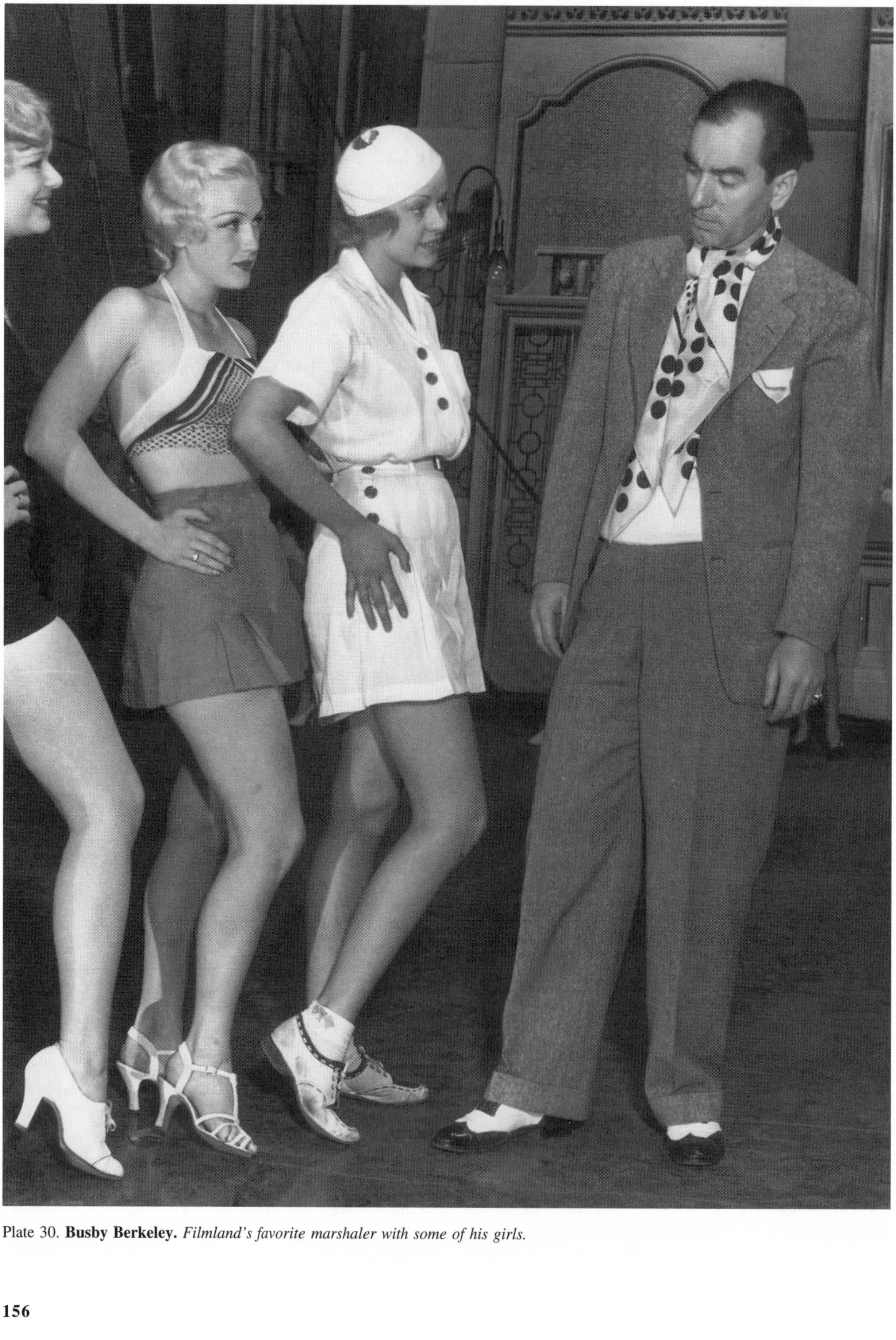

Plate 30. **Busby Berkeley.** *Filmland's favorite marshaler with some of his girls.*

management of A H Woods and with Eddie Foy as star—for an Asbury Park opening 25 August 1911, when (or so it was said) producer and performer fell out and the piece was abandoned.

He supplied further individual numbers to such pieces as Richard Carle's *Jumping Jupiter, The Never Homes, The Fascinating Widow, Gaby, My Best Girl, The Queen of the Movies,* and various Weber and Fields shows before—after another aborted attempt at a stage musical with *From Soup to Nuts* (w Hauerbach, 1914 for Arthur Hammerstein)—he turned out his first full Broadway score, for the Charles Dillingham revue *Watch Your Step* (1914). Subtitled "a syncopated musical show," this very lightly plotted entertainment featured the ragtime rhythms Berlin had been instrumental in giving a wider popularity in the 15 years and more since pieces like the Matthews and Bulger "ragtime opera" *By the Sad Sea Waves* and Belle Davis and her pals at Koster and Bial's Roof Garden (*A Ragtime Opera*) had purveyed ragtime more discreetly on the musical stage or songwriters like Alfred Aarons and Ned Wayburn had delivered ragtime songs on Broadway without raising too many ears. "If I live long enough," Berlin told an interviewer in that same year of 1914, "I shall write an opera completely in ragtime." Well, he certainly lived long enough, but, like many of his theatre projects down through the years, the opera in question never materialized.

Berlin subsequently provided the songs for another piece with a vestige of musical comedy libretto, the Gaby Delys show *Stop! Look! Listen!* (1915, "the music becomes indistiguishable after the first scene"), and for a series of large-scale revues including several editions of *The Ziegfeld Follies* and *The Music Box Revue,* staged at his own Music Box Theater, the highly successful *As Thousands Cheer,* and the army show *This Is the Army.* Many of these shows produced extractable songs which became long-term favorites, including "Oh, How I Hate To Get up in the Morning," "A Pretty Girl Is Like a Melody," "What'll I Do?," "All Alone," "Easter Parade" and "You'd Be Surprised."

Berlin contributed further interpolated numbers to the scores of *Step This Way, Jack o'Lantern, Rambler Rose* and *The Royal Vagabond,* placed one song, and then a second, in Ivan Caryll's score for *The Canary* (1917), and co-wrote a piece called *Dance and Grow Thin* (w Blanche Merrill) produced at the Coconut Grove (18 January 1917), but his first solo attempt at a book musical to make it to the stage was an unusual one. Abandoning the more straightforward task of composing a piece which was to be called *Ring Around Rosie* and to feature soubrette Queenie Smith, he opted instead to illustrate a low comedy vehicle for the Marx Brothers. *The Cocoanuts* (1925), as might have been expected, owed its success to the extravagant antics of its stars, and the 14 numbers which made up the musical part of the show ("The Monkey Doodle-Doo," etc) took a decidedly secondary place to the comedy. But the show was a fine success. His next announced project, a musical with Frederick Lonsdale intended for London's Theatre Royal, Drury Lane, was said to have been abandoned when half-written on the excuse that the house was too big, and over the next two decades, Berlin provided songs for just two book musicals, both of which followed the fashion for anti-anyone-elected political musicals. *Face the Music* (1932), on which the songwriter also shared the book credit with Moss Hart, introduced "Let's Have Another Cup of Coffee" and "Soft Lights and Sweet Music" in the course of a story which decked up some anti-police maunderings with revusical glitter for 165 performances, and *Louisiana Purchase* (1940), which mixed tarty ladies, young love and naughty politicians in a more traditional way, produced "It's a Lovely Day Tomorrow" and "Fools Fall in Love," and did more than twice as well (444 performances). Both shows served to emphasize Berlin's talents as a writer of individual songs rather than of show scores.

It was not until his 58th year that Berlin achieved an international hit with a book musical, when he replaced the late Jerome Kern as the composer of the Herbert and Dorothy Fields sharpshooting musical *Annie Get Your Gun. Annie Get Your Gun* proved not only to be a major theatre hit throughout the world, but also turned out a scoreful of songs, including "There's No Business Like Show Business," "Anything You Can Do (I can do better)," "The Girl That I Marry," "My Defenses Are Down" and several more which each and all became individually and widely popular. A second piece for *Annie Get Your Gun* star, Ethel Merman, written with Howard Lindsay and Russel Crouse, turned out a small masterpiece of vehicle writing in *Call Me Madam* ("You're Just in Love," "It's a Lovely Day Today"), and won a second widespread success, but *Miss Liberty* (1949, "Let's Take an Old-Fashioned Walk") and yet another political musical, *Mr President* (1962), were both failures.

Film versions of *The Cocoanuts, Annie Get Your Gun* and *Call Me Madam* were made, but Berlin also provided the scores or songs for numerous other movies from *Top Hat* ("Cheek to Cheek," "Isn't It a Lovely Day?," etc), *Follow the Fleet* and *Alexander's Ragtime Band* to *Holiday Inn* ("White Christmas"), *Easter Parade, This Is the Army* and *White Christmas,* introducing or reintroducing handfuls of popular songs on each occasion.

Berlin's chief fame remains as one of America's most productive and successful writers of all styles of popular songs from "God Bless America" to "Blue

Skies'' over nearly half a century of active writing, but his work for *Annie Get Your Gun, Call Me Madam* and the revue in its palmiest days also earned him a superior place in the history of the musical theatre.

1925 **The Cocoanuts** (George S Kaufman) Lyric Theater 8 December

1932 **Face the Music** (Moss Hart) New Amsterdam Theater 17 February

1940 **Louisiana Purchase** (Morrie Ryskind) Imperial Theater 28 May

1946 **Annie Get Your Gun** (Herbert Fields, Dorothy Fields) Imperial Theater 16 May

1949 **Miss Liberty** (Robert E Sherwood) Imperial Theater 15 July

1950 **Call Me Madam** (Howard Lindsay, Russel Crouse) Imperial Theater 12 October

1962 **Mr President** (Lindsay, Crouse) St James Theater 20 October

Biographies: Ewen, D: *The Story of Irving Berlin* (Holt, Rinehart & Winston, New York, 1950), Woolcott, A: *The Story of Irving Berlin* (Stein & Day, New York, 1974), Freedland, M: *Irving Berlin* (W H Allen, London, 1974), Whitcomb, I: *Irving Berlin and Ragtime America* (Century Hutchinson, London, 1987), Bergreen, L: *As Thousands Cheer* (Viking, New York, 1990), Barrett, M E: *Irving Berlin: A Daughter's Memoir* (Simon & Schuster, New York, 1994), Hamm, C: *Irving Berlin: Songs from the Melting Pot—The Formative Years 1907–1914* (OUP, New York, 1997), etc

Literature: Suskin, S: *Berlin, Kern, Rodgers, Hart, and Hammerstein: A Complete Song Catalogue* (McFarland, Jefferson, North Carolina, 1990)

BERNARD, Sam [BARNETT, Samuel] (b Birmingham, England, 3 June 1863; d at sea, 18 May 1927). Dialect comedian who won durable fame in Broadway musicals.

Sam Bernard began his career in show business appearing at Henderson's Music Hall in Coney Island in a double act with his brother, **Dick BERNARD** [né Reuben BARNETT] (b Birmingham, 21 December 1866; d USA, 25 December 1925), but went single before returning to his native Britain to play briefly in music halls there. After a number of years spent playing in vaudeville, comedy (*The Corner Grocer, Lost in London,* etc) and burlesque (*Night Owls Co,* 1888–91 also stage manager, French Folly Co in *Rip van Winkle, Adam and Eve's Daughter* 1891, also acting mgr); in farce comedy (*He, She, Him and Her*), where his speciality was a version of the heavily accented ''Dutch'' low comedy character popular at the time; and, under his real name, a first more regular musical appearance as Captain Dietrich in a revival of *Evangeline* (1896) Bernard was taken on by Weber and Fields. He appeared at their theatre in burlesques of current theatrical hits such as *The Heart of Maryland* (*The Art of Maryland,* Sergeant Grunt), *The Geisha* (*The Geezer,* Two Hi), *The Red Robe* (*Under the Red Globe,* Captain Payroll ''The Lovelorn Lobster''), *Secret Service* (*The Glad Hand,* Harold Meyer/Corporal Matson), *La Poupée/The First Born/The Little Minister* (*Pousse Cafe,* Herr Weilshaben, Chane Gang, Neal Dow), *The Highwayman* (*The Way-high-man,* Captain Kidney) and *The Conquerors* (*The Con-Curers,* Lt Payrent), and in *Mr New York* (1897, Benzine). His success there was such that he was able to move on and up to star billing as Hermann Engel in his own production of *The Marquis of Michigan* (1898) at the beginning of a series of comedy-centered musicals which established him as a Broadway favorite: *A Dangerous Maid* (an adaptation of the protean German Posse *Heisses Blut* 1898, Schmalz), the revusical *The Man in the Moon* (1899, Conan Doyle), *The Casino Girl (* 1900, Khedive) and *The Belle of Bohemia* (1900, Adolf Klotz).

He returned for a while to burlesque (Louis Quince in *De Hurry,* 1902, etc), but was quickly back on the musical stage and going from one success to another. The leading comedy role of Leslie Stuart's London musical *The Silver Slipper* (Samuel Twanks) was remodeled to suit Bernard's dialect-comedy character for its Broadway production and won a long run, but it was another British piece, *The Girl from Kays* (1903), which gave him his biggest success when he introduced to American audiences the likeably ghastly nouveau riche Yankee ''Piggy'' Hoggenheimer (''I'm not rude, I'm rich''), so memorably created in London by Willie Edouin. During his career, Bernard returned three further times to the character of Hoggenheimer, commissioning a new musical built around *The Rich Mr Hoggenheimer* in 1906, revising the original piece as *The Belle of Bond Street* (1914) with more success in America than in an abortive London season and, finally, a few months before his death, performing a new version of his musequel under the title *Piggy* at Broadway's Royale Theater.

In between Hoggenheimers, the little, balding comedian expertly continued to turn out German and Jewish low-comedy characters in musicals such as a remake of *A Dangerous Maid* as *The Rollicking Girl* (1905, Schmalz), *Nearly a Hero* (1908, Ludwig Knödler), *The Girl and the Wizard* (1909, Herman Scholz), *He Came from Milwaukee* (1910, Herman von Schellenvein) and *All for the Ladies / The Modiste Shop* (1912–13, Leo von Labenheimer). He also appeared as Ko-ko in the Casino Theater's all-star *Mikado* (1910) and spread his comic talents into the field of revue in the Americo-Anglo-originally-French *As You Were* (''Who Ate Napoléons With Josephine When Bonaparte Was Away?'') and *The Music Box Revues* in the years following the war.

Sam Bernard was married to (amongst others) performer Lizzie B Raymond (née Reardon), and brother

Reuben-Dick married her sister, Marguerite. Dick appeared at Koster and Bial's in prominent comic roles in *In Gotham* (1899, Mr Winkle), *Sir Andy de Bootjack* (Andy), *Round New York in 80 Minutes* (1899, Otto Snitzel), *Sharp Becky* (Rawdon Crawley), etc; on Broadway in *The Belle of Bohemia* (1900, Rudolph Dinkelhauser) and *Hip! Hip! Hooray* (1907, t/o Michael Schulz); and in 1910 went out starring as Henry Schniff in *The Girl Behind the Counter* in a useful career as a musical comedian.

BERNARD, Tristan [BERNARD, Paul] (b Besançon, 7 September 1866; d Paris, 7 December 1947).

Prolific and popular French playwright (*Triplepatte, Le Costaud des Épinettes, Le Petit Café, Le Sexe fort,* etc) who ventured occasionally into the musical theatre, providing the text for Terrasse's successful opéra-bouffe *La Petite Femme de Loth* and the Garden of Eden tale which was the basis of Cuvillier's early *Avant-hier matin.*

His 1911 play *Le Petit Café* was musicalized by Ralph Benatzky in Germany, Ivan Caryll and C M S McLellan in America, and also on home ground, his *La Soeur* became, on the Broadway stage, the 1907 musical *The Hoyden* (Paul Rubens, et al/Henry Blossom, John Golden, Cosmo Hamilton, 19 October) and another of his plays (unidentified) was the source for Budapest's *Finom familia* (Béla Zerkovitz/Adolf Mérei, Royal Orfeum 31 January 1913).

1900 **La Petite Femme de Loth** (Claude Terrasse) Théâtre des Mathurins 10 October

1905 **Avant-hier matin** (Charles Cuvillier) 1 act Théâtre des Capucines 20 October

1912 **Miss Alice des PTT** (Terrasse/Maurice Vaucaire) La Cigale 14 December

1938 **Le Flirt ambulant** (Henri Christiné/w Albert Willemetz) Théâtre Michel 13 January

Biography: Bernard, J J: *Mon père, Tristan Bernard* (1955)

BERNAUER, Rudolf (b Budapest, 20 January 1880; d London, 27 November 1953). Berlin producer and librettist of a number of successful Operetten and Possen for the Austrian and German stages.

Hungarian-born Bernauer studied in Berlin and he began his theatrical career there, at the age of 20, as an actor at the Deutsches Theater. The following year, together with Carl Meinhard, he initiated the satirical Bösen-Büben-Bälle. He subsequently abandoned acting to become Régisseur at the Deutsches Theater (1906) and then, again in tandem with Meinhard, moved into theatre management on his own account. The pair began by promoting various small tours and sponsoring limited seasons in metropolitan houses, but they finally became full-scale lessees when they took on the Berliner Theater in 1908 (16 September). They operated the Berliner for 16 mostly successful years, nourishing it largely on a diet of old Possen and then, increasingly, of new musicals. They also expanded their management activities to take on, at various times, the Theater in der Königgratzer-Strasse (1911), the Komödienhaus (1913) and the Theater am Nollendorfplatz.

During his days at the the Deutsches Theater, Bernauer also began a career as a playwright, supplying, amongst his earliest efforts, the libretto which was to be blamed for the failure of Leo Fall's first major work, *Der Rebell.* However, he found his first, and one of his most considerable successes as a librettist soon after his move to the Berliner Theater when he collaborated with Leopold Jacobson on the adaptation of G B Shaw's *Arms and the Man* into the libretto to *Der tapfere Soldat* for Oscar Straus. Another adaptation, of Sardou's *Divorçons* as *Frau Lebedame* for the theatre at Prague, proved less successful, but a second piece for the same house, the olde-Englishe *Die keusche Barbara* (w Rudolf Schanzer), gave him another fair success and set in motion the career of its young composer, Oskar Nedbal.

The large part of Bernauer's writing was, however, done for his own theatre, where the team made up of himself, Schanzer, composer Walter Kollo and musical director/composer Willi Bredschneider turned out a series of hits in the years before and during the Great War. *Filmzauber* (1912), which capitalized on the new fashion for moving pictures, was exported to Britain and America as *The Girl on the Film,* whilst Bernauer and Schanzer's text of the highly successful *Wie einst im Mai,* attached to a new score by Sigmund Romberg, became a major success in America under the title *Maytime.* The war effectively put a stop to further exports, but the Berliner Theater throve on such Bernauer pieces as *Die tolle Komtess* (350 performances), *Blitzblaues Blut* (nearly 300), a revival of the team's 1910 *Bummelstudenten, Sterne, die wieder leuchten* (seven months and an American production) and *Prinzessin Olala* (142 performances and revivals) and hits from other hands such as *Madame Pompadour* (1922) and *Mädi* (1923).

Hit by the rise of inflation and by some oversized gambling debts, Bernauer and Meinhard closed down their operation in 1925, and Bernauer thereafter had only a minor part to play in the Berlin musical theatre where he had so long been a dominant force. He turned to the cinema (*Ihre Majestät der Liebe, Der Frechdachs,* etc), but, banned from working on stage or screen in 1933, he joined the general artistic exodus from Germany, and ended his days in England. His credits there included work on, and an appearance in, the screen version of *The Lilac Domino* (1937).

1903 **Schlumpeline Schlumebumbum** (Bogumil Zepler) Neues Kindertheater, Berlin 21 November

1905 **Der Rebell** (Leo Fall/w Ernst Welisch) Theater an der Wien 29 November

1906 **Der Fuss** (Fall) 1 act Centraltheater, Chemnitz 18 September

1907 **Frau Lebedame** (Anselm Götzel/w Alexander Pordes-Milo) Deutsches Theater, Prague 31 December

1908 **Der tapfere Soldat** (Oscar Straus/w Leopold Jacobson) Theater an der Wien 14 November

1910 **Die keusche Barbara** (Oskar Nedbal/w Jacobson) Theater Weinberge, Prague 14 September; Raimundtheater, Vienna 7 October 1911

1910 **Bummelstudenten** (Zepler, Willi Bredschneider, et al/ad w Rudolf Schanzer) Berliner Theater 31 December

1911 **Grosse Rosinen** (Leon Jessel, Zepler, Bredschneider, et al/w Schanzer) Berliner Theater 31 December

1912 **Der liebe Augustin** revised *Der Rebell* (Leo Fall/w Welisch) Neues Theater 3 February

1912 **Filmzauber** (Kollo, Bredschneider/w Schanzer) Berliner Theater 19 October

1913 **Wie einst im Mai** (Kollo, Bredschneider/w Schanzer) Berliner Theater 4 October

1914 **Jung England** (Leo Fall/w Welisch) Montis Operettentheater 14 February

1915 **Wenn zwei Hochzeit machen** (Kollo, Bredschneider/w Schanzer) Berliner Theater 23 October

1916 **Auf Flügeln des Gesanges** (Kollo, Bredschneider/w Schanzer) Berliner Theater 9 September

1917 **Die tolle Komtess** (Kollo/w Schanzer) Berliner Theater 21 February

1918 **Blitzblaues Blut** (Kollo/w Schanzer) Berliner Theater 9 February

1918 **Sterne, die wieder leuchten** (Kollo/w Schanzer) Berliner Theater 6 November

1920 **Frau Ministerpräsident** (Fall/w Welisch) Residenztheater, Dresden 3 February

1921 **Prinzessin Olala** (Jean Gilbert/w Schanzer) Berliner Theater 17 September

1923 **Dolly** (Hugo Hirsch/Ernst Bach, Franz Arnold) Deutsches Künstlertheater 16 October

1924 **Geliebte seiner Hoheit** (Gilbert/w Rudolf Österreicher) Theater am Nollendorfplatz 24 September

1927 **Der Mikado** revised text w Österreicher (Grosses Schauspielhaus)

1927 **The Birdseller** (*Der Vogelhändler*) English version w Harry S Pepper, Austin Melford (Palace Theatre, London)

1945 **Gay Rosalinda** (*Die Fledermaus*) English version w Melford, Sam Heppner (Palace Theatre, London)

Autobiography: *Das Theater meines Lebens* (Lothar Blanvalet, Berlin, 1955)

BERNICAT, Firmin (b Lyon, ?1843; d Chatou, 4 March 1883).

Highly regarded throughout his career as a musician, Bernicat nevertheless for many years found only journeyman work as an orchestrator and arranger in Parisian musical and theatrical circles. He had some success with songs for the cafés-concerts (''La Ronde du Garde-Champêtre,'' etc) and apparently had an important hand in the orchestrations of some of Planquette's—and maybe other folks'—greatest successes, but although he supplied the music for a number of one-act opérettes played at such venues as the Café Tertulia, the Folies-Bergère and the Eldorado (where his little *La Cornette* scored a decided hit), he had to wait for his own confirmation as a composer in the regular theatre until 1882 when his full-length opérette *Les Beignets du Roi* was produced at Brussels's Alcazar with considerable success.

Bernicat was in the middle of a second major work, *François les bas-bleus,* when he died. Completed by Messager, *François les bas-bleus* was a great success at the Folies-Dramatiques, won foreign productions and regular revivals for over 50 years, and led to Messager moderately successfully revising *Les Beignets du Roi* for Paris under the title *Les Premières Armes de Louis XV* (1888, 45 performances). In Britain, a posthumous Bernicat pasticcio, with a libretto by actress-manageress Kate Santley, toured as *Vetah* for several seasons, and several of his short pieces were revived at the Moulin Rouge (*La Cornette* 27 March 1895, *On demande un Arlequin* 5 April 1896) and in other venues, ultimately giving the late composer more success in the years following his death than he had ever had in some dozen years of attempts during his lifetime.

1870 **Ali pot de rhum** (Gedhé [ie, G Delafontaine]) 1 act Alcazar 17 December

1872 **Monsieur et Madame Véronique** (Léon Quentin, Gedhé) 1 act Alcazar 15 July

1872 **Deux à deux** (Quentin) 1 act Café Tertulia 14 October

1873 **La Queue du Diable** (Quentin, Gedhé) 1 act Café Tertulia 15 February

1874 **Ah c't' Indien** (Gedhé) 1 act Folies-Bergère

1874 **Par la fenêtre** 1 act Folies-Bergère

1875 **Les Trois Grands Prix** (Alfred Delilia, Charles Le Senné) 1 act Salle Taitbout 28 March

1875 **Cabinet numéro six** (Th Massine) Théâtre des Bouffes-Parisiens 10 December

1876 **Les Deux Omar** (Gedhé, William Busnach) 1 act Fantaisies Oller 4 April

1876 **Le Voyage du petit marquis** (Louis Péricaud, Germain Villemer) 1 act Fantaisies Oller 5 October

1877 **La Jeunesse de Béranger** (Péricaud, Villemer) 1 act Eldorado 20 January

1877 **Le Pâté empoisonné** (Élie Frebault) 1 act Alcazar 22 September

1877 **Fou-yo-po** (Émile Max) 1 act Alcazar 10 October

1877 **La Cornette** (Péricaud, Villemer, Lucien Delormel) 1 act Eldorado

1878 **Le Moulin des amours** (Péricaud, Villemer) 1 act Eldorado 25 January

1878 **Une aventure de la clairon** (Péricaud, Villemer) 1 act Eldorado 23 November

1878 **Les Cadets de Gascoyne** (Georges Dorfeuil, Charles Mey) 1 act Alcazar 25 November

1878 **Les Barbières de village** (Charles Blondelet, Félix Baumaine) 1 act Alcazar 28 November

1878 **L'Agence Raburdin** (Dorfeuil) Eldorado 17 December

1878 **Une poule mouillée** (Auguste Jouhaud, Péricaud, Villemer) Concert du 19ème 21 December

1878 **Les Triomphes d'Arlequin** (Alexandre Guyon) 1 act Eldorado

1878 **On demande un Arlequin** (Péricaud, Delormel) 1 act Eldorado

1879 **Les Tziganes de Longjumeau** (Dorfeuil) Alcazar, 12 April

1882 **Les Beignets du Roi** (Albert Carré) Alcazar, Brussels 10 February

1882 **Le Forban** (Dorfeuil, Mey) 1 act Gaîté-Montparnasse 23 April

1882 **Les Premières Armes de Parny** (Péricaud, Delormel) Eldorado 20 June

1883 **François les bas-bleus** (w André Messager/Ernest Dubreuil, Eugène Humbert, Paul Burani) Théâtre des Folies-Dramatiques 8 November

1886 **Vetah** (arr and add music Georges Jacobi, Frederick Bowyer/Kate Santley) Theatre Royal, Portsmouth 30 August

1888 **Les Premières Armes de Louis XV** revised *Les Beignets du roi* ad Messager Théâtre des Menus-Plaisirs 16 February

Other titles attributed: *Le Petit jeune homme, Un mari à l'essai, Deux coups de marteau*

BERNSTEIN, Leonard [BERNSTEIN, Louis] (b Lawrence, Mass, 25 August 1918; d New York, 14 October 1990). Internationally celebrated conductor and musician who supplied Broadway with several superior musical scores and at least one of its most outstanding shows of all time.

The young Leonard Bernstein had won recognition as a symphonic conductor before he entered the theatre as a composer in 1944 with the score for *Fancy Free* (18 April), a ballet choreographed by Jerome Robbins. The pair subsequently developed the theme of the ballet into the musical *On the Town* (1944, "On the Town," "Carried Away," "New York, New York," etc), a light romantic comedy song-and-dance piece written in collaboration with Betty Comden and Adolph Green which had a fine success on Broadway, won several overseas productions, and was later metamorphosed into a merry film.

Bernstein provided incidental music, including a handful of songs, for a 1950 production of J M Barrie's fairy play *Peter Pan* (Imperial Theater 321 performances) and composed the songs and dance music for another highly successful musical comedy—the musicalized version of the hit play *My Sister Eileen* as *Wonderful Town* ("Ohio," "A Little Bit in Love," etc)—in the standard Broadway format of the time, before he produced a much more ambitious score for a short-lived first musical version of Voltaire's *Candide* (1956).

Plate 31. **Leonard Bernstein.** *Puffing away at the keyboards, in rehearsal, c1949.*

With the music for his next stage musical, *West Side Story* (1957), he took yet another path, combining the substance of the *Candide* score and the dance-orientation of *On the Town* with a driving and exciting contemporary quality to illustrate a modern New York version of the *Romeo and Juliet* story set amongst juvenile immigrant gangs. The worldwide success of *West Side Story* ("Tonight," "Maria," "A Boy Like That," "America," etc) both on stage and screen established it as one of all-time greats of the musical theatre, but Bernstein preferred thereafter to concentrate on the other areas of his internationally successful musical life and wrote only one further stage musical, the unsuccessful *1600 Pennsylvania Avenue* (1976).

In 1973 a rewritten and more humorous version of *Candide* was produced. It moved on to Broadway success and the piece has, in a variety of different versions, been subsequently played in opera houses in America and Britain.

Apparently able to provide music to suit any style of text, Bernstein displayed his outstanding ability as a composer of class light theatre music most clearly in his two most enduring scores, *West Side Story* and *Candide,* whilst also providing for his shows orchestral and dance music which was of a substance and quality which has rarely been found in any area of the theatre.

Bernstein's other works for the theatre included the libretto and music for the one-act opera *Trouble in Tahiti* (19 April 1955), the incidental music for the play *The Lark* (1955) and the vocal music for *The Firstborn* (Coronet Theater 29 April 1958). He also composed the score for the film *On the Waterfront* and authored books on music, notably *The Joy of Music* (1959).

1944 **On the Town** (Adolph Green, Betty Comden) Adelphi Theater 28 December

1953 **Wonderful Town** (Comden, Green/Joseph Fields, Jerome Chodorov) Winter Garden Theater 25 February

1956 **Candide** (Richard Wilbur, John Latouche, Dorothy Parker/ Lillian Hellman) Martin Beck Theater 1 December

1957 **West Side Story** (Stephen Sondheim/Arthur Laurents) Winter Garden Theater 26 September

1973 **Candide** (revised version w Hugh Wheeler, Sondheim) Chelsea Theater Center 18 December

1976 **1600 Pennsylvania Avenue** (Alan Jay Lerner) Mark Hellinger Theater 4 May

Biographies: Ewen, D: *Leonard Bernstein* (Chilton, New York, 1960), Briggs, J: *Leonard Bernstein* (World, New York, 1961), Gruen, J: *The Private World of Leonard Bernstein* (Viking, New York, 1968), Freedland, M: *Leonard Bernstein* (Harrap, London, 1987), Gradenwitz, P: *Leonard Bernstein: The Infinite Variety of a Musician* (Berg, New York, 1987), Peyser, J: *Leonard Bernstein* (William Morrow/Beech Tree Books, New York, 1987), Burton, H: *Leonard Bernstein* (Faber, London, 1994), Secrest, M: *Leonard Bernstein, a Life* (Knopf, New York, 1994)

BERR, Georges (b Paris, 30 July 1867; d Paris, 25 July 1942).

A member of the company at the Comédie-Française from the age of 19, and later a sociétaire and administrator, a professor at the Paris Conservatoire, and a theatrical director, Berr was also, over a period of more than 30 years, and in spite of being semi-blind and unable either to read or write from his early forties onwards, a highly successful author of comic plays for the Paris stage. He began his writing career with a plethora of little comedies and one-acters, monologues and even songs, but also turned out some substantial plays (*Fiacre à l'heure, Plaisir d'amour* signed by the pseudonym ''Georges Colias''), several pieces for the Grand-Guignol and even a ballet *Phebe* for the Opéra-Comique before going on to establish himself as one of the city's most prominent comic playwrights. He made only a brief skirmish into the musical theatre, in 1902, when he collaborated on the text for the successful Louis Varney opérette *La Princesse Bébé* and on the book for the Châtelet spectacular *Les Aventures du Capitaine Corcoran.*

In the second decade of the 20th century, however, when the fashion for musical plays based on strong comedic libretti, usually taken from the French, became the prevailing style on the English-language stage, Berr's plays served as the bases for a whole series of extremely successful musical comedies. The composer Ivan Caryll, the instigator of the series, made two major hits from Berr's works—the internationally successful *The Pink Lady* was based on *Le Satyre* (1907 w Marcel Guillemaud) and its successor *Oh! Oh! Delphine* on *La Grimpette* (1905 w Guillemaud)—whilst *Un Coup de téléphone* (1912 w Paul Gavault) became, in the same musician's hands but with more modest results, London's *The Kiss Call* (Gaiety Theatre 8 October 1919).

In Germany, *Dix minutes d'auto* (Théâtre des Nouveautés 13 November 1908 w Pierre Decourcelle) was turned into the Thalia-Theater's highly successful *Autoliebchen* (1912), whilst a number of years later his 1928 piece *Ma soeur et moi* (w Louis Verneuil) was made into Ralph Benatzky's international hit musical comedy *Meine Schwester und ich* (1930). In Italy, Berr maintained a credit on the Carlo Lombardo operetticization of *Changez la Dame,* and, back on the home front, his name appeared alongside that of Verneuil as the author of the Châtelet musical *Le Coffre-fort vivant* (1938), a version of the Frederic Mauzens novel of the same title which Verneuil had earlier musicalized for Broadway as *The Canary* (mus: Caryll).

1902 **La Princesse Bébé** (Louis Varney/w Pierre Decourcelle) Théâtre des Nouveautés 18 April

1902 **Les Aventures du Capitaine Corcoran** (Adrien Vély/w Paul Gavault) Théâtre du Châtelet 30 October

1926 **Qui êtes vous?** (Charles Cuvillier/w H Genty, Jouvault) Monte-Carlo 13 November

1938 **Le Coffre-fort vivant** (Maurice Yvain ps ''Jean Sautreuil,'' Joseph Szulc/Henri Wernert/w Verneuil) Théâtre du Châtelet 17 December

BERRY, W[illiam] H[enry] (b London, 23 March 1870; d London, 2 May 1951). Star comedian of 20 years of West End musicals.

''Bill'' Berry paired a career in the city with amateur performances as a comic and concert entertainer for twelve years (''Mr and Mrs W H Berry in song and musical sketch,'' Effingham Ramsgate 1903, Lawn Gardens, Broadstairs 1901–5, etc), before George Edwardes was inspired to put him and his wife, **Kitty HANSON**, under contract. His first appearance under Edwardes's management was at the Empire, in 1905, playing MacSherry in an excerpt from *Madame Sherry* but thereafter he appeared at the Prince of Wales, the Gaiety and Daly's in a series of increasingly important comedy roles from *The Little Cherub* (1906, Shingle) through See See (1906, Cheoo), *Les Merveilleuses* (1906, St Amour/Tournesol), *The Merry Widow* (1907, Nitsch), *Havana* (1908, Reggie), *The Dollar Princess* (1909, Bulger), *A Waltz Dream* (1911, Lothar), *The Count of Luxembourg* (1911, Brissard), *Gipsy Love* (1912, Dragotin), *The Marriage Market* (1913, Blinker), *A Country Girl* (1914, Barry), and *Betty* (1915, Achille Jotte) before moving to a semi-permanent berth at the Adelphi Theatre. There for more than eight years and through several managements he remained installed as the theatre's accepted star and as a potent public draw to the musical comedy *Tina* (1915, van Damm), the from-the-French American hit *High Jinks* (1916, Dr Thorne), the long-running Pinero musicals *The Boy* (1917, Meebles) and *Who's Hooper?* (1919, Valentine Hooper), *The Naughty Princess* (*La Reine s'amuse* 1920, King Michael), Novello's comic opera *The Golden Moth* (1921, Dipper Tigg), *The Island King* (1922, Hopkins) and *Head Over Heels* (1923, Alfred Wigg).

He continued as a great audience favorite through the 1920s, playing similar comedy roles, most successfully as father Veidt in *Lilac Time* and Albert Chuff in *Princess Charming,* but less profitably in Lehár's *The Three Graces* (1924, Bouquet) and the American musical comedies *Poppy* (1924, Eustace McGargle, the role invented for W C Fields), *The Blue Kitten* (1925, Christopher Popp) and *The Girl from Cook's* (1927, Higgins), in Szirmai's *The Bamboula* (1925, Prince Robert) and the Anglo-American *Blue Eyes* (1928, Pilbeam) and in *Merry, Merry* (1929, Jimmie Diggs). In the 1930s Berry appeared as Calchas in C B Cochran's all-star perversion of *La Belle Hélène* (*Helen!*) and repeated his earlier successes as Lothar and Veidt before abandoning the stage for film (*Mr Cinders, Funny Face,* etc) and radio.

At his peak, during and after the Great War, the endearingly boggle-eyed and moon-faced Berry was the town's most popular musical comedian, but a sad lack of suitable roles and strong shows in later years gave him little chance to maintain the position built on the splendid series of Edwardes productions in prewar years, and in his best starring roles at the Adelphi.

Autobiography: *Forty Years in the Limelight* (Hutchinson, London, 1939)

BERTÉ, Heinrich (b Galgócz, Hungary, 8 May 1857; d Voeslau nr Vienna, 24 August 1924). Austro-Hungarian composer who ultimately made his name as an arranger.

Berté and his brother Emil moved from Hungary to Vienna as children, and "Harry" was given a serious musical education both there and in Paris, where he studied under Delibes. Although the late-arriving composer's first staged work was an Operette, *Bureau Malicorne,* produced at the open-roofed Sommer Theater at Baden bei Wien, most of his earliest attempts at stage music were in the realm of ballet (*Die goldene Märchenwelt* Vienna Hofoper 2 April 1893, *Karnaval in Venedig* Munich 1901, *Automatenzauber* Orpheum 1901). His one-act comic opera *Die Schneeflocke* was produced in Prague in 1896, and subsequently both at Berlin's Neues Königliches Opernhaus and in Budapest (*Hophély* Magyar Királyi Operaház 4 March 1899), but his first major opportunity in the musical theatre did not come until 1904 when he had a full-length Operette, *Der neue Burgermeister,* accepted for production the Theater an der Wien.

Der neue Burgermeister played only seven performances, in spite of boasting the hugely popular Viennese star Alexander Girardi at the head of its cast but, in the following half-dozen years, Berté turned out a regular flow of such pieces, mostly for German regional theatres, with a respectable degree of success. Two, *Die Millionenbraut* and *Der schöne Gardist,* were brought to the Theater an der Wien for 26 and 32 performances respectively, the latter being also produced at Budapest's Budai Színkör (*A Szép gardista*), whilst his 1910 Hamburg piece, *Kreolenblut,* was played briefly on Broadway under the title *The Rose of Panama,* in Hungary as *Kreolvér* (1911) and in the French provinces as *Coeur de Créole* (1913). *Der Glücksnarr,* premiered at Vienna's Carltheater with Mizzi Zwerenz, Karl Blasel and Josef König featured, was less well-received and flopped in 20 performances.

A significant hit eluded Berté and, after this series of, at best, half-successes, further commissions did not eventuate. Deeply depressed, Berté turned to Emil, now an influential music publisher, for assistance, and it was the elder Berté who put forward his brother's name to his colleague Karczag at the Raimundtheater as a potential arranger/composer for the so-called Singspiel which was to become *Das Dreimäderlhaus.* This Schubert pasticcio became one of the most successful Viennese shows of all time, securing Berté financially as it was transformed into *Lilac Time, Blossom Time, Chanson d'amour, Három a kislány* and so forth in various parts of the world and everywhere with huge success. Berté, however, never considered the piece as "his" and, although he completed a second Schubert musical, he turned down the opportunity to work on the *Dreimäderlhaus* musequel, *Hannerl,* preferring to attempt once more to make the world appreciate his original writings.

Although one of his two subsequent shows, *Die drei Kavaliere,* was played in Hungary (*Három a gavaller*

Várszínház 25 April 1922) and published in France following its first showing in Hamburg, neither made any notable impact and, to his despair, *Das Dreimäderlhaus* remained his one claim to fame.

1887 **Bureau Malicorne** (F W Schmiedell) Sommer Theater, Baden bei Wien 22 February

1896 **Die Schneeflocke** (A M Willner) 1 act Prague 4 October

1904 **Der neue Burgermeister** (Ernst Gettke, Robert Pohl) Theater an der Wien 8 January

1904 **Die Millionenbraut** (Willner, E Limé) Theater am Gärtnerplatz, Munich 3 April; National-Theater, Berlin 2 December

1905 **Der Stadtregent** (Gettke, Pohl) Theater am Gärtnerplatz, Munich 1 April

1907 **Der schöne Gardist** (Alexander Landesberg, Willner) Neues Operetten-Theater, Breslau 12 October; Theater an der Wien 4 April 1908

1907 **Der kleine Chevalier** (Willner) 1 act Central-Theater, Dresden 30 November

1908 **Die Wunderquelle** (Wilhelm Sterk, Emmerich von Gatti) 1 act Hölle 1 November

1908 **Der Glücksnarr** (E Limé ad Landesberg, Willner) Carltheater 7 November

1909 **Der erste Kuss** Neues Operetten-Theater, Hamburg 14 November

1910 **Kreolenblut** (Ignaz Schnitzer, von Gatti) Neues Operetten-Theater, Hamburg 25 December

1914 **Der Märchenprinz** (Willner, Sterk) Schauburg, Hanover 28 February

1916 **Das Dreimäderlhaus** (Franz Schubert arr/Willner, Reichert) Raimundtheater 15 January

1917 **Tavasz es szerelem** (*Lenz und Liebe*) (Schubert arr/Bruno Hardt-Warden, Ignaz Welleminsky ad Jenő Heltai) Városi Színház, Budapest 15 September; Neues Operetten-Theater, Hamburg February 1918

1919 **Die drei Kavaliere** (Lothar Sachs, von Gatti) Neues Operetten-Theater, Hamburg 5 November

1920 **Kulissengeheimnisse** (Henri Cain, Édouard Adenis ad) Neues Operetten-Theater, Hamburg 28 January

Berte's nephew, the younger **Emil BERTÉ** (b Vienna, 6 December 1898; d Vienna, 17 January 1968), supplied the music for a handful of Operetten/Singspiele including yet another arrangement of Schubert, *Der Musikus von Lichtenthal,* and, most notably, the successful *Musik in Mai* produced at the Raimundtheater with Ernst Tautenhayn starred and subsequently played on Broadway as *Music in May* (ad Fanny Todd Mitchell, J Kiern Brennan, add mus Maurice Rubens, Casino Theater 1 April 1929).

1927 **Musik in Mai** (Heinz Merley, Kurt Breuer) Raimundtheater 13 May

1928 **Der Musikus von Lichtenthal** (Schubert arr/Breuer) Neue Wiener Bühne 30 March

1929 **Steppenkinder** (Hans Borutzky, Alfred Steinberg-Frank) Stadttheater, Augsburg 15 December

1930 **Das Kaiserliebchen** (Ernst Decsey, Steinberg-Frank, Max Blau) Wiener Stadttheater 4 January

1955 **Melodie aus Wien** Landestheater, Linz 22 October

BERTHELIER, [Jean-François Philbert] (b Panissières, Loire, 14 December 1828; d Paris, 29 September 1888). Comic actor and singer who was one of the major stars of the 19th-century French musical theatre.

The young Berthelier worked as a bookshop assistant in Lyon and as a commercial traveler in paintings before making his first stage appearances as a tenor in the theatre at Poitiers in 1849. A couple of years later, he made his way to Paris and there made himself a small name as an actor and, in particular, as a singer in cafés-concerts. It was at one of these latter, in Rue Madame, that Offenbach heard the young man singing Étienne Tréfeu's popular song ''Vive la France'' and engaged him to be a member of his initial company at the Bouffes-Parisiens. Berthelier's fame was made overnight when he introduced the role of Giraffier in *Les Deux Aveugles* (1855). He created roles in *Une nuit blanche* (1855, Hercule), *Le Rêve d'un nuit d'été* (1855, John Bull), *Le Violoneux* (1855, Pierre), *Paimpol et Périnette* (1855, Paimpol) and *Ba-ta-clan* (1855, Ke-ki-ka-ko) during the Bouffes' first months, before going on to stints at the Palais-Royal and at the Opéra-Comique (1856–62), taking part during the latter engagement in the premieres of Gevaert's *Château Trompette* and of Offenbach's *Barkouf* (Xailoun). At the same time he continued a highly successful career as a chansonnier, now provided with songs especially made to his measure by such popular songwriters of the time as Gustave Nadaud, Edmond Lhuillier and Tréfeu (''Le Baptême du p'tit Énéniste,'' ''L'Invalide à la tête de bois,'' etc).

He subsequently created further and mostly more substantial Offenbach roles in the triple part of Myriame/Colin/Nicot in *Les Bergers* (1865), King Cacatois in *L'Île de Tulipatan* (1868), Casimir in *La Princesse de Trébizonde* (1869), Le Caporal in *Boule de Neige* (1871), Lastécouères in *Les Braconniers* (1873), the cretinous pupil in *Le Leçon de Chant* (1873, Jean Matois), and Flammèche in *La Boulangère a des écus* (1875), played Paris in *La Belle Hélène* in Brussels (1866), and introduced roles in Lecocq's *Le Testament de M Crac* (1871, Isolin de Castafiol), Hervé's *La Veuve du Malabar* (1873, Le Nabab Kéri-Kalé) and Serpette's *Le Manoir du Pictordu* (1875, Comte Saturnin de Pictordu), as well as such less memorable and more fugitive opérettes as *Le Docteur Rose* (1872) and *Le Roi dort* (1876).

When the fashion and the wheel of success turned from Offenbach to Lecocq, Berthelier was on hand, as a member of the Théâtre de la Renaissance company, to partake of further major successes, starring in some of his best comedy roles in Lecocq's *La Marjolaine* (1877, Palamède van der Boom), *Kosiki* (1876, Xicoco), *Le Petit Duc* (1878, Frimousse), *La Petite Mademoiselle* (1879, Taboureau) and *La Camargo* (1878, Pont-Calé), and later, at the Nouveautés, in the two most important works of the second part of the composer's career, *Le Jour et la nuit* (1881, Don Brasiero de Tras os Montes) and *Le Coeur et la main* (1882, King of Aragon). He also appeared as Zappoli in the French Johann Strauss concoction *La Tzigane* (1877) at the Renaissance, and at the Nouveautés in *Le Voyage en Amérique* (1880, Girandol), and *La Cantinière* (1880, Rastagnac), going on to a long, long list of further comic creations at that house, few of which, however, came up to the roles with which he had been favoured at the height of Lecocq's success.

Amongst the shows in which he initiated parts in his later years were included *Le Droit d'aînesse* (1883, Tancrède), *Premier Baiser* (1883, Zug), *Le Roi de Carreau* (1883, Tirechappe), *L'Oiseau bleu* (1884, Bricoli), *Babolin* (1884, Karamatoff), *La Nuit aux soufflets* (1884, Hercule III), *Le Château de Tire-Larigot* (1884, Marquis de Valpointu), *La Vie mondaine* (1885, Chiquito), *Serment d'amour* (1886, Gavaudan), *Adam et Ève* (1886, Adramalec), *Princesse Colombine* (1886, Sénéschal), *Ninon* (1887, Benoït), *Dix Jours aux Pyrénées* (1887, Chaudillac), *Le Bossu* (1888, Cocardasse) and, at the Gaîté, *Le Dragon de la reine* (1888, Cornensac). The by this time grossly overweight comedian died during the run of the last-named show.

Considered by some to be more of a vocalist than an actor—and his way with a comic song was apparently second to none—it was, nevertheless, in important comical roles that he secured and kept, over more than 30 years, his prominent place in the Paris musical theatre.

Berthelier, the lover of the young Hortense Schneider in her early Paris days, was responsible for her introduction to Offenbach and the Bouffes-Parisiens and, as such, was depicted on film in the Offenbach-loves-Hortense movie, *Valse de Paris.*

BERTRAND, Eugène (b Paris, 15 January 1834; d Paris, 30 December 1899). The manager of Paris's Théâtre des Variétés from 1869 until 1891.

Bertrand began his life in the theatre as an actor, going from the Conservatoire to join the company at the Odéon after which he worked briefly in America, at the Parc Théâtre in Brussels, and at the Grand Théâtre in Lille. It was in Lille, at the Grand, that he became a manager for the first time, and from there he moved on to Paris to take over the theatre which had been the birthplace in recent years of *La Belle Hélène, Barbe-bleue, La Grande-Duchesse de Gérolstein* and *La Périchole* from their now extremely wealthy producer, Hippolyte Cogniard. He carried on where his illustrious predecessor had left off, mounting Offenbach's *Les Brigands* (1869) and, after the end of the war, continued with productions of such new works as Hervé's *Le Trône d'Ecosse,* Offenbach's *Les Braconniers,* the expanded *La Périchole* with Schneider starred, Lecocq's *Les Prés Saint-Gervais* (1874), Serpette's *Le Manoir du Pic-Tordu,* Offenbach's *La Boulangère a des écus* (1875), Costé's *Le Dada* (1876), Offenbach's *Le Docteur Ox* and the winning little *Les Charbonniers* (1877), mixed with revivals of opéra-bouffe and vaudevilles, spectacles-coupés, comedies and revues.

In 1878 Bertrand began the triumphant series of vaudeville-opérettes, with Anna Judic starred, which would be the highlight of his management: *Niniche* (1878), *Le Grand Casimir* (1879), *La Femme à Papa* (1879), *La Roussotte* (1881), *Lili* (1882), *Mam'zelle Nitouche* (1883) and *La Cosaque* (1884). When the vogue for this type of entertainment faded, the aging Hervé, who had composed much of the music for the series, contributed a score to *Mam'selle Gavroche* (1885) in which Jeanne Granier attempted to take up where Judic had left off, before, in 1886, Bertrand took the actor Louis Baron into partnership.

Plays, and revivals of musical pieces from *La Belle Hélène* and *Les Brigands* up to the recent Judic favorites, did rather better for the partners than their productions of new musicals, but the old formula proved it was run thoroughly dry when a vaudeville from the Millaud, de Najac and Hervé team, *La Noce à Nini,* flopped in 1887. Pieces such as *La Japonaise* (1888) and *La Fille à Cacolet* (1889) did no better, and Bertrand's last days at the Variétés did not again bring the success he had known so richly in his Judic days. In 1892 he moved on to become director of the Paris Opéra.

Bertrand was also involved in the management of the Théâtre de l'Eden, in partnership with Plunkett and Louis Cantin, in the mid-1880s.

BEST FOOT FORWARD Musical comedy in 2 acts by John Cecil Holm. Music and lyrics by Hugh Martin and Ralph Blane. Ethel Barrymore Theater, New York, 1 October 1941.

Another in the Broadway parade of college musicals, the wartime *Best Foot Forward,* with its young cast of under-draftable-age actors, joined *Good News* and *Leave It to Jane* on the successful list when its original production played 326 Broadway performances and put the phrase ''Buckle down, Winsocki'' into the current parlance.

The college which welcomed the action of the piece was Pennsylvania's Winsocki, and this time, for a change, there wasn't a football game in sight. It was prom time. Bud Hooper (Gil Stratton jr) is going steady with Helen Schlesinger (Maureen Cannon) but, as a josh, invites Hollywood starlet Gale Joy (Rosemary Lane) to be his date for the college prom. To his astonishment, she accepts, as her PR man (Marty May) thinks he can get press-inches out of the event. There turns out to be more event than he had suspected, for Helen launches a ripping revenge and Gale's dress suffers embarrassingly. The status quo is reestablished when the starlet goes back to her Hollywood heaven. June Allyson (Minerva Brooks) and Jack Jordan jr (Dutch Miller) were number two couple whilst Nancy Walker was Winsocki's eternal and eternally hopeful Blind Date. Choreography was by the young Gene Kelly.

Producers George Abbott and Richard Rodgers auditioned for songwriters to supply the songs for the show and chose the untried Hugh Martin and Ralph Blane, whose score hit the collegiate tone to a nicety and, with "Buckle Down, Winsocki," produced a lively cheerleading hit which was well supported by a second favorite in the comedienne's "Just a Little Joint with a Jukebox."

Best Foot Forward's style and subject matter probably accounted for the fact that it won no attention outside America, but at home it proved repeatedy popular. Hollywood took it up for a 1943 film in which Jordan and Misses Allyson and Walker and five of the show's songs repeated their Broadway assignment alongside Tommy Dix, Gloria deHaven and Lucille Ball (playing the film starlet as herself) and five new numbers. It was broadcast on the Railroad Hour in 1949, and televised in 1954 with a cast headed by Jeannie Carson, Marilyn Maxwell, Robert Cummings and Jimmy Komack, in each case with a reduced score (and in each case without the little joint and its jukebox). A New York revival was mounted in 1963 (Stage 73 Theater 2 April) with Glenn Walken (Bud), Karin Wolfe (Helen), Paula Wayne (Gale), Grant Walden (Jack) and the young Liza Minnelli performing "You Are for Loving," one of three further additional numbers added for the occasion to three from the film and rather more than half the original songs. The revival played for 224 performances.

Film: MGM 1943

Recording: 1963 revival (Cadence)

THE BEST LITTLE WHOREHOUSE IN TEXAS

Musical in 2 acts by Larry L King and Peter Masterson. Music and lyrics by Carol Hall. Actors' Studio, New York, 20 October 1977; Entermedia Theater, 17 April 1978; 46th Street Theater, 19 June 1978.

The story to the musical *The Best Little Whorehouse in Texas* sprang from an article about the real-life "chicken ranch" brothel, written by journalist Larry L King, in *Playboy* magazine. Adapted into a stage show by King and Texan Peter Masterson, with a score by singer-songwriter Carol Hall, it was first produced at a workshop at the Actors Studio in November 1977 with Henderson Forsythe and Liz Kemp in the principal roles. It was subsequently mounted at off-Broadway's Entermedia Theater the following year for a season of 50 performances before, with the backing of Universal Pictures, moving on to a long and successful career on Broadway.

Miss Mona (Carlin Glynn) runs a tidy little whorehouse—"a l'il ole bitty pissant country place"—in the town of Gilbert, Texas, until the day that Melvin P Thorpe (Clinton Allmon), broadcaster, personality and power-crazed poseur, hones in on the "Chicken Ranch" as the newest target upon which to display the extent of his influence and importance. When he shows up in Gilbert with his cameras, the primping intruder gets a dusty mouthful of a goodbye from sheriff Ed Earl Dodd (Henderson Forsythe), which is all relayed to the moral folk of Texas by the wonderful power of TV. Thorpe then sets up a trap, and invades the Chicken Ranch with his crew on the night the Aggie football team and their sponsoring senator are celebrating their big game win in traditional fashion. Waving his evidence, he then proceeds to corner the Governor of Texas (Jay Garner), putting him in a position where, to save face, he has to voice shocked disapproval. It all gets far too big and high-up for little Gilbert and for Ed Earl. When orders come from as far above as the state government, the Chicken Ranch has to close. The girls and Miss Mona leave their home to look for another as Melvin P Thorpe struts towards a civic honor under the arc-lights of glorious self-satisfaction and television.

King and Masterson's libretto crackled with hilariously unbelievable (to a non-Texan) technicolored Texan oaths and adjectives, which were reflected in the songs. The accompanying band opened proceedings with a country-and-folksy description of "Twenty Fans," turning to keep everyone in the brothel cool; Miss Mona gave gentle encouragement to a shy new recruit ("Girl You're a Woman") and, at the end of the affair, glanced back at her own early days ("The Bus from Amarillo") as she set out to start over again; whilst Ed Earl mused over the "Good Ol' Girl" who was almost his lover. A plain little waitress longed to be more daring in her dress and doings ("Doatsey Mae"), the Governor of Texas did his best to dance "The Side Step" in double-talk and soft-shoe around the insistent Thorpe, and the footballers leaped into action in a virile Tommy Tune dance routine to the strains of "The Aggie Song."

The production was a splendid success on Broadway, running for 1,584 performances and returning swiftly for a repeat season at the Eugene O'Neill Theater in 1982 (31 May). Elsewhere, however, things went less well. In London, in spite of urgings that the show should go into the friendly, middle-sized Prince of Wales Theatre, Universal chose to mount *The Best Little Whorehouse* in the vastness of the Theatre Royal, Drury Lane. Miss Glynn and Forsythe were joined by Fred Evans (Governor), Sheila Brand (Doatsey Mae) and Nigel Pegram (Thorpe) in a version which was never comfortably at home through 204 performances. In Australia television soap star Lorraine Bayly starred as Miss Mona alongside expatriate American Alfred Sandor, and once again the piece failed to catch in seasons in Sydney and Melbourne (Her Majesty's Theatre 7 February 1981). Hungary staged a belated premiere (ad György Kéth) in 1996, with Éva Vári and Lajos Németh featured.

In 1982 Universal turned out the film version. Dolly Parton was a swimmingly voluptuous Miss Mona who supplied a couple of additional numbers of her own to add to the remnants of the score, whilst Burt Reynolds played a matinée idol, Ed Earl. It was all a long way from Texas, except in that it went thoroughly south.

An attempt at a sequel, *The Best Little Whorehouse Goes Public,* by the same writers (Lunt-Fontanne Theater 10 May 1994), featuring Dee Hoty as a back-from-retirement Miss Mona setting up shop in Las Vegas, went the way of virtually all musequels in just 15 performances.

Australia: Her Majesty's Theatre, Sydney 13 September 1980; UK: Theatre Royal, Drury Lane 26 February 1981; Germany: Landestheater, Altenburg *Die beste kleines Hurenhaus in Texas* 17 April 1994; Hungary: Józsefvárosi Színház *Volt egyszer egy kupleráj . . . (Texasban!)* 28 September 1996

Film: Universal 1982

Recordings: original cast (MCA), film soundtrack (MCA), *Best Little Whorehouse Goes Public* (Varese Sarabande)

Literature: King, L: *The Whorehouse Papers* (Viking, New York, 1982)

DER BETTELSTUDENT Operette in 4 acts by F Zell and Richard Genée based on *Fernande* by Victorien Sardou and *The Lady of Lyons* by Edward Bulwer-Lytton. Music by Carl Millöcker. Theater an der Wien, Vienna, 6 December 1882.

Millöcker's most successful Operette and, indeed, one of the very few 19th-century Viennese pieces which do not have the fashionable name of "Strauss" attached to them which have survived on to the modern stage, *Der Bettelstudent* was one of the triumphs of the European musical theatre of its era, and was played regularly throughout the Continent for many years. Part of the show's attraction was that it was based on a particularly strong main plot line, one which borrowed elements from both Sardou's *Fernande* and Edward Bulwer-Lytton's celebrated *The Lady of Lyons* in its construction—and also had airs of Scribe and Halévy's 1841 opera *La Guitarréro*—but which has lasted longer than either of its nevertheless celebrated and once hugely popular models.

Colonel Ollendorf (Felix Schweighofer) of the ruling Saxon army has been rebuffed. He kissed the Polish Countess Laura Nowalska (Karoline Finaly) on the shoulder at last night's ball, and was slapped in the face for his pains. Now he is out for revenge. He has a handsome pair of beggar-students, Symon Rymanowicz (Alexander Girardi) and Jan Janicki (Josef Joseffy), released from jail, disguises them as the Count Wybicki and his secretary and lets them loose on the proud but poor Laura. She is soon captivated, and agrees to wed the apparently rich and powerful nobleman. Symon, too, has fallen genuinely in love and wants to expose the trickery rather than wed under false pretences, but Jan, who is an important official in the exiled Polish court's designs, begs him not to undo their incognitos until he has had time to bring his plots to fruition. Eventually, Laura goes to the altar unknowing, and Ollendorf has his revenge when he looses the inmates of the prison at the couple's wedding as the bridegroom's friends. Symon, however, has another role to play. Ollendorf, now aware that the rebel Poles are hiding the King's son somewhere, has bribed Jan to deliver him up. Jan encourages Symon to pretend to be the royal fugitive, and Symon's impersonation holds up events long enough for the rebels to storm Ollendorf's fortress and win the day. Symon and Laura are reunited, whilst Jan finds happiness with Laura's soubrette sister, Bronislawa (Frln Jona).

The hit of the score, unusually, turned out to be neither in the soprano nor the tenor numbers, nor in the soubrette's supply of lively moments. It came from the role of Ollendorf, lugubriously describing to an unforgettable waltz melody the story of the fateful kiss ("Ach ich hab' sie ja nur auf die Schulter geküsst"). There were plenty of other outstanding moments for the other lead players, however—Symon's light tenor praise of Polish women ("Ich knüpfte manche zarte Bande") and his patriotic "Ich hab' kein Geld, bin vogelfrei," the jolly masquerade of the two men ("Das ist der Fürst Wybicki mit seinem Sekretär") and two superb trios for Laura, Bronislawa and their mother, the exuberantly and indomitably aristocratic Countess Palmatica (Therese Schäfer, in one of the best older character roles of the repertoire), out shopping ("Einkäufe machen") or gluttonously preparing for the wedding ("Einen Mann hat sie gefunden").

Der Bettelstudent was produced by Franz Steiner at the Theater an der Wien and proved an immense success. By the time the 100th performance was passed on 3 September 1883, the company had visited the Carltheater to play their hit show, and the Theater an der Wien had host-

Plate 32. **Der Bettelstudent.** *The Countess Palmatica (Anny Schlemm) faces up to the inimical Colonel Ollendorf in the Vienna Volksoper's production of 1989.*

ed a performance by the Hungarian company from the Népszínház of their version of *A koldusdiák.* The 150th performance (5 September 1884) boasted a ''new overture'' and by 1887 Siegmund Stelzer had taken possession of the role of Ollendorf alongside Ottilie Collin (Laura), Therese Biedermann (Bronislawa), Carl Streitmann (a rather more heroic Symon than the original) and Joseffy, as the piece continued as a fixed part of the theatre's repertoire through its 200th (March 1895) performance.

In Berlin, the Friedrich-Wilhelmstädtisches Theater's production proved a sensation, racing past its 200th performance in seven months (13 August 1883), and in Hungary (ad Lajos Evva, Béla J Fái) the reception won by *A koldusdiák* was equally as violent. The Népszínház's number one star, Lujza Blaha, was a travesty Symon with Aranka Hegyi as her Laura, János Kápolnai and Ilka Pálmay were the second pair, and Elek Solymossy (Ollendorf) and Anna Jenei (Palmatica) completed a star lineup with the biggest names Hungary had to offer. The production was played 93 times in repertoire, putting itself into the top 10 musical pieces up to then played in the history of Budapest's most important musical theatre.

America heard its first *Bettelstudent* in German, but also with its star tenor role played in travesty. That star was one no less important than Hungary's Marie Geistinger herself, playing alongside the Ollendorf of Carl Adolf Friese and the Laura of Emma Seebold. Ten days later, the first English version (ad Emil Schwab) opened in direct competition. W T Carleton was a male Symon to the Laura of Bertha Ricci and the Ollendorf of the English comic Fred Leslie, with ex-German soubrette Mathilde Cottrelly as Bronislawa and Rose Leighton as Palmatica. The competition did no harm, for the English version racked up 110 performances whilst the original-language one popped in and out of the German houses' repertoires. *The Beggar Student* returned later in the year (6 October 1884) with Mark Smith (Symon), Digby Bell (Ollendorf), Lilly Post (Laura) and Cottrelly for a second season and it came back to Broadway again in 1913 (Casino Theater 22 March) in a Shubert-Brady production with De Wolf Hopper playing Ollendorf, and yet again in 1930 (Heckscher Theater 17 November). A new version by James Stuart was mounted at the Ohio Light Opera in 1996, and the piece still gets occasional mountings in the English language.

London's *The Beggar Student* (ad W Beatty-Kingston) was mounted on the splendid stage of the Alhambra with a grand military ballet by Jacobi and a pastorale by Boccherini added to up the spectacle quotient but also with not the very best London cast. Fannie Leslie was a principal-boy style Symon, Savoy star Marion Hood was Laura, a capable comic in the person of Fred Mervin played Ollendorf, and Violet Melnotte, soon to be celebrated as a producer, took the small but featured role of Ensign von Richthofen. Fred Leslie took over his Broadway role during the show's run. In 1884 the piece was given in the repertoire of the Carl Rosa Opera Company, with Ben Davies and Georgina Burns starred, and in 1886 it turned up back in London again for a nine weeks' season at the Comedy Theatre (13 December). This time Henry Bracy was a more suitable Symon, with Mervin repeating his Ollendorf and Ada Lincoln as Laura. *The Beggar Student* was seen in London again in 1895 (Royalty Theatre 12 January), was played by a German company with Emil Katzorke as Ollendorf and most recently reappeared in 1990 played by the semiprofessional John Lewis group.

Although Brussels soon had the show on its stages (ad Albin Valabrègue, Alfred Hennequin), and that same French-language version was allegedly given soon after at Lille, Paris, which had not welcomed much Viennese musical theatre with any enthusiasm, did not deign to a production until 1889 (ad E Hermil [ie, Ange Milher], A J Numès), when Bartel as the burlesquily renamed Puffendorff, Gellio (Simon), Marcellin (Jan), Clara Lardinois (Laure) and Mlle Duroche (La Comtesse) featured in an undercast production at the little Menus-Plaisirs. Paris, happy in the wisdom that it was producing much of the best musical theatre the world had to offer at the time, sniffed at Millöcker's work as a potpourri of dance music and closed the show in 22 performances.

In central Europe, after the first very fine flush, *Der Bettelstudent* held its place at the forefront of the repertoire and when the Theater an der Wien finally let the show loose from its repertoire after some 13 years, it soon began to appear in other Viennese houses. It was played at the Raimundtheater (8 May 1901), where it was reprised by Karczag in 1908 with Franz Glawatsch as Ollendorf, Marthe Winternitz-Dorda (Laura) and the evergreen Streitmann (Symon) featured, again in 1916, in 1920 and in 1938 (ad Carl Hagemann) with Mizzi Günther as Palmatica, Fritz Imhoff (Ollendorf) and Hans Heinz Bollmann as Symon. It was introduced to the Jantschtheater in 1902 (17 October), the Johann Strauss-Theater in 1911, the Bürgertheater in 1917, and the Kaiser-Jubiläums Stadttheater (Volksoper) in 1909.

If there were one libretto of the Viennese Operette stage which ought—apart from a travesty or so—to have remained safe from the "improvers" of later ages, it would have seemed to be *Der Bettelstudent.* However, the lure for a publisher of a renewed copyright, the lure for a rewriter of royalties on the back of an out-of-copyright work, inevitably prove too much in central Europe and, in consequence, in 1949 Herr Eugen Otto had a go at putting an old-fashioned Operette cliché or two into *Der Bettelstudent*'s text. In his tidily conventionalized version, amongst other alterations, Jan Janicki turns out to be—wait for it—the very Duke Adam Casimir that he has asked Symon to impersonate. Like so many similarly unfortunate (and similarly "recopyrighted") remakes, it is this truly feeble one that holds the stage to this day in such venues as the Vienna Volksoper, who last remounted the work in 1983.

The original production of *Der Bettelstudent* was successful enough to provoke a number of spin-offs. On 25 March 1884 a humorous prologue to the piece, written by Wilhelm Henzen, illustrating the incident of the famous *Der Kuss auf die Schulter,* was mounted in Leipzig, whilst at Lübeck Franz Odemar's *Der Komponists Traum* (6 December) also used *Der Bettelstudent* as its subject matter.

Der Bettelstudent made its way to the (silent) screen for the first time in 1922, and further versions came with a 1927 film starring a still silent Harry Liedtke, and one in 1931 with the very unsilent Hans Heinz Bollmann, Jarmila Novotna and Hans Jaray. In 1936 Georg Jacoby put out a version featuring Johannes Heesters, Marika Rökk and Fritz Kampers and the highlights of Millöcker's score complemented by two pastiches of his music done by Alois Melichar set to words by Franz Baumann. When it was rereleased, the music of this version was credited to Peter Kreuder. Another film, dating from 1956, credited its text to Fritz Böttger and its musical reorganization to Bruno Uher. Gerhard Riedmann (Symon), Waltraut Haas (Laura) and Gustav Knuth (Ollendorf) featured and the Kessler twins somehow got into the film, if not the plot, as a pair of wandering dancers. An English-language film was brought out in 1932 with Lance Fairfax and Shirley Dale featured alongside comics Jerry Verno and Mark Daly, Frederick Lloyd and Jill Hands, and a 1957 East German *Mazurka der Liebe* also credited

Zell and Genée's text as its source. The most recent *Bettelstudent* to come to the screen did so in Hungary in 1977. Local operetta star Marika Németh played Palmatica.

Several other musical pieces had been produced under the title *Der Bettelstudent* prior to this Operette, notably a 1781 Munich comic opera by Winter, and another by Buchweiser, mounted for the first time in 1793.

Germany: Friedrich-Wilhelmstädtisches Theater 24 January 1883; Hungary: Népszínház *A koldusdiák* 23 February 1883; USA: Thalia Theater (Ger) 19 October 1883, Casino Theater *The Beggar Student* 29 October 1883; UK: Alhambra Theatre *The Beggar Student* 12 April 1884; France: (?) Lille September 1883, Théâtre des Menus-Plaisirs *L'Étudiant Pauvre* 18 January 1889; Australia: Opera House, Sydney 3 June 1889

Films: Hans Steinhoff 1922, J & L Fleck 1927, Viktor Janson 1931, British Dominion Films (Eng) 1932, Georg Jacoby 1936, Werner Jacobs, Hans Müller *Mazurka der Liebe* 1957, Lazslo Seregei (Hun) 1977

Recordings: complete (Amadeo, Eurodisc, EMI), complete in Russian (Melodiya), selections (Telefunken, Eurodisc, etc), selection in Hungarian (Qualiton), selection in Swedish (Telestar), selection in Czech (Supraphon)

THE BETTER 'OLE Fragment from France in 2 explosions, 7 splinters and a gas attack by Bruce Bairnsfather and Arthur Eliot. Lyrics by James Hurd. Music by Herman Darewski. Oxford Theatre, London, 4 August 1917.

During the later part of the First World War, London's musical theatre featured a third huge popular hit alongside the romantic spectaculars *Chu Chin Chow* and *The Maid of the Mountains. The Better 'Ole* had neither the staging splendors nor the musical values of this pair, but, from the sandbags decorating the theatre foyer to the positive picture, on stage, of the British at war, it was a piece and a production which had a huge appeal to returning servicemen and to their families.

The Better 'Ole (the title came from a cartoon of two soldiers sheltering from enemy fire in a shell crater: "If you know a better 'ole, go to it!") was in essence little more than a series of sketches, detailing the wartime adventures of "Old Bill," the favorite cartoon character created by artist Bruce Bairnsfather (1888–1959) and celebrated in his *Fragments from France* (1916). It painted a lighthearted but feeling portrait of the common man at war in confusing foreign parts as Old Bill (Arthur Bourchier) and his two pals Alf (Sinclair Cotter) and Bert (Tom Wootwell) gamboled through an evening of comedy and popular song, accidentally heroic adventures, and girls, in a way which won the hearts of all. They gamboled for no less than 15 months, running up 811 performances on a heavy performance schedule, and the main run was followed by a quick revival.

Herman Darewski's catchy numbers "My Word, Ain't We Carrying On?," "From Someone in France to Someone in Somerset" and "We Wish We Were in Blighty" were supplemented by the American hit "What Do You Want to Make Those Eyes at Me For?" in a show which changed its elements freely. The most substantial alteration was not, however, a musical one. It came when producer C B Cochran temporarily popped the whole one-act dramatic scena *Les Gosses dans les ruines* by Francisque Poulhot, in which the young Sybil Thorndike made an appearance, into the running-order of the show.

Following its London run, *The Better 'Ole* went on tour with enormous success, playing at one point in three simultaneous companies in the English provinces and provoking copycat shows both in the theatre and the music halls. In 1918 a (silent) film version was made with Charles Rock starred as Old Bill, whilst a second film, starring Syd Chaplin, made in 1927 by Vitaphone, was equipped with a synchronized musical score.

In spite of the show's London success there was some considerable difficulty in setting up an American production. However, when the show was staged as a co-operative venture in Greenwich Village, with Charles Coburn starring as Old Bill, it quickly proved popular enough to warrant a transfer to the uptown Cort Theater, and subsequently to the Booth Theater for a fine run of 353 performances. Coburn was succeeded as Old Bill by De Wolf Hopper, and whilst Hopper took the show on to major tour dates, and companies covered America, he organized a condensed version of the show which he toured in American variety theatres. These tours met the same problem as was encountered by an Australian production, featuring Arnold Bell as Bill, Percy Cahill (Bert) and David Hallam (Alf). They arrived after the first film version and the Australian producers were obliged to advertise that "this is the play, NOT the motion picture" through seasons at Melbourne's Tivoli and Sydney's newly reopened Tivoli (24 May 1919) for six weeks apiece.

USA: Greenwich Village Theater 19 October 1918, Cort Theater 18 November 1918; Australia: Tivoli Theatre, Melbourne 8 March 1919

Films: Welsh-Pearson 1918, Vitaphone 1927

Literature: Holt, T & V: *In Search of the Better 'Ole* (Milestone Publications, Portsmouth, England, 1985)

BETTY Musical play in 3 acts by Frederick Lonsdale and Gladys Unger. Lyrics by Adrian Ross and Paul Rubens. Music by Paul Rubens. Additional numbers by Ernst Steffan and Merlin Morgan. Daly's Theatre, London, 24 April 1915.

Although the name of Paul Lincke was murmured in some quarters, the libretto of *Betty* was almost certainly intended by George Edwardes to be musically set by Victor Jacobi whose *Leányvásár* (*The Marriage Market*) had been such a success for him at Daly's Theatre. However, the intervention of the war forced Edwardes to change his plans and, in the place of a ''German'' composer, Paul Rubens was ultimately given the assignment. When a rumor-mongering journalist hinted that Rubens had merely put his name to a score written by Jacobi, the composer took him to court, but withdrew his case after a recantation. The journalist in question had clearly not listened to the music, for the score of *Betty* was simply the best and brightest of Rubens and nothing at all like the altogether more substantial work of Jacobi.

The story of *Betty* had a reprobate young aristocrat wedding Betty, the kitchen maid, to spite his reprimanding father, but finding himself tricked when the father then settles the young man's allowance on the wife. Purse-strung, he is finally charmed into a happy ending by his wife of convenience. A new leading lady, 20-year-old soprano Winifred Barnes, was Betty (''Can it be Love,'' ''The Duchess of Dreams''), Donald Calthrop played her reticent lover (''It's a Beautiful Day Today''), and G P Huntley as an aristocratic Lord Playne and Bill Berry as a comic couturier, Achille Jotte (''Opposite the Ducks''), with a bevy of models to hand, shared the show's comedy. The most popular number of the evening was a trio, ''We Ought to Combine.'' *Betty* proved a solid success at Daly's Theatre (391 performances) and subsequently made itself a remarkable touring life through more than a decade in the British provinces.

A New York production under the management of Charles Dillingham, with Joseph Santley and Ivy Sawyer as the couple, Raymond Hitchcock and Peter Page as the comedy, and veteran Joseph W Herbert as the hero's father, did not take on in the same way and managed only 63 performances before going to the rest of the country. This comparative failure may have discouraged an immediate Australian production, but Sydney and then Melbourne (Her Majesty's Theatre 7 February 1925) did finally see the show a decade on, with Edith Drayson and Maud Fane (who slipped Lehár's ''Gigolette'' into the score) featured in the title role in turn, alongside Harold Pearce (Beverly), Alfred Frith (Playne) and Cecil Kellaway (Jotte).

USA: Globe Theater 3 October 1916; Australia: Her Majesty's Theatre, Sydney 22 November 1924

BETTY IN MAYFAIR Musical play in 3 acts by J Hastings Turner adapted from his play *The Lilies of the Field.* Lyrics by Harry Graham. Music by Harold Fraser-Simson. Adelphi Theatre, London, 11 November 1925.

A light musical play of some charm which starred Evelyn Laye as a modern miss who, having won her man (Arthur Margetson) whilst dressed in demure Victorian garb, keeps up the pretence of being an old-fashioned lass until honesty wins out and she confesses. Only then does she find he prefers her as a modern miss. Mary Leigh was the heroine's brighter sister, paired with Jack Hobbs in the livelier songs of Harold Fraser-Simson's pretty score (''The Days of Old,'' ''I Love You''), a score which was very largely made up of duets and other ensembles.

In a London season dominated by the advent of *No, No, Nanette* and *Rose Marie,* the comparatively quiet and old-fashioned *Betty in Mayfair* nevertheless found itself an appreciative audience and ran its way sweetly through six West End months (193 performances) before going out for a year of touring. An American production, announced by Lee Ephraim with Edna Best for star, did not eventuate.

BET YOUR LIFE Musical comedy in 2 acts by Alan Melville. Music by Kenneth Leslie-Smith and Charles Zwar. London Hippodrome, 18 February 1952.

Bet Your Life was a farcical comedy with songs, featuring favorite comic Arthur Askey as a jockey who is married to the daughter (Julie Wilson) of an anti-gambling crusader, and who dreams winning racing tips on his Corsican honeymoon. It was a libretto and a show which belonged to an earlier era, with its comedy tale reminiscent of the old Stanley Lupino and Lupino Lane shows, and a finale which brought the little hero on as the winner of the big race at Ascot, astride a real horse, much in the vein of *The Arcadians.*

The songs were a mixture of aggressive ''American'' material for the American vocalist, Miss Wilson (''I Want a Great Big Hunk of a Man''), and more ''English'' traditional pieces for Sally Ann Howes as the juvenile love interest, paired here with Brian Reece (radio's famous PC 49) in the role of a racing journalist, as well as a little dash of the comic, and of the gypsyish, which the Corsican setting permitted.

Jack Hylton's production survived notices which found the show unpleasingly old-fashioned and unsophisticated, and secured an audience for four months at the Hippodrome, after which the piece was slimmed down, Miss Wilson replaced by Noele Gordon, and the schedule switched to a twice-nightly one which enabled *Bet Your Life* to run up a slightly flattering 362-performance total.

Recording: selection (Blue Pear)

BEZAUBERNDES FRÄULEIN Musical comedy (Lustspiel mit Musik) in 4 scenes, based on Paul Gavault's *La Petite Chocolatière,* by Ralph Benatzky. Music by Ralph Benatzky. Deutsches Volkstheater, Vienna, 24 May 1933.

Benatzky followed his adaptation of the French comedy *Ma Soeur et moi* as the highly successful *Meine*

Schwester und ich with another musicalization of a Parisian piece, Paul Gavault's hit comedy *La Petite Chocolatière* (1909). It was not exactly an original choice, for the play had already been turned into a musical in America as *Tantalizing Tommy* (Hugo Felix/Adrian Ross, Michael Morton, Criterion Theater 1 October 1912), in Britain as *The Girl for the Boy* (Howard Carr, Bernard Rolt/Percy Greenbank/Austen Hurgon, George Arthurs, Duke of York's Theatre 23 September 1919) and in Italy as *La piccola cioccolataia* (Schinelli). However, Benatzky's version, a 12-handed, chorusless musical comedy, made in the manner of the best Parisian pieces of the 1920s, proved more successful than any of these.

Paul (Max Hansen), Felix (Hans Olden) and Felix's girlfriend, Rosette (Ingeborg Grahn), are spending the weekend at Paul's place in the country when a young woman turns up, victim of a motoring accident. Felix notices Paul's attraction to her, and sees here the chance of prying his friend free from the dreary idea of marrying Luise (Gusi Witt), the daughter of his employer (Alexander Fischer-Marich). His designs are confirmed when it turns out that Annette (Lizzi Waldmüller) is "la petite chocolatière," the heiress to a cocoa fortune. Felix arranges things so that she is forced to stay the night and when, first, Luise and her papa and, then, Annette's father and fiancé (Otto Schmöle) turn up the next day, things get decidedly sticky. Back in town, Paul tries to patch things up with his boss, whilst Felix continues with his matchmaking tricks. When Paul, his future apparently in ruins, has got as far as thinking of jumping in the river, Annette appears on the scene, dressed in Salvation Army costume and, apparently, having renounced all worldly goods. Except Paul.

The score, slanted heavily in the direction of humor and of lively dance melodies, ranged from rumba to waltz, with Paul's "Ach, Luise, kein Mädchen ist diese!" and Felix's "Hokuspokus fidibus" topping the list in musical popularity.

Bezauberndes Fräulein followed its Vienna season with another in Berlin, with Max Hansen and Lizzi Waldmüller repeating their Vienna roles, later in 1933, and it was played in Italy the following year as *La Ragazza indiavolata* (Teatro Quirino, Rome 5 November 1934). It returned to Vienna in 1946 (Rex-Theater) and, amongst its other, intermittent but continuing productions, was recorded by German television in 1971.

Benatzky also wrote the screenplay for a filmed version of the same play, *Wer wagt gewinnt!* (1935), and *Bezauberndes Fräulein* was itself filmed in 1953 with his score adapted by Georg Hatzschel.

Germany: Deutsches Künstlertheater 1933

Film: 1953

LA BICHE AU BOIS

The fairy tale *La Biche au bois* written by the Countess d'Aulnoy (1649–1705) in the early 18th century and published as part of her *Fées à la mode,* became a favorite subject with producers of spectacular and fantastical pieces in the 19th century. The most celebrated of such shows was the Parisian vaudeville-féerie written by the brothers Cogniard, Hippolyte and Théodore, first produced at the Théâtre de la Porte-Saint-Martin (29 March 1845), with the accompaniment of a pasticcio score by Pilati, and subsequently staged in various versions, mostly with similarly made-up musical scores, throughout the 19th century.

The Cogniard version had the Princess Désirée, daughter of the King of the Island of Bells, transformed into a hind (biche) when a spell cast on her by the wicked fairy who wasn't invited to her christening is triggered off by her looking for the first time on the forbidden light of day. The Moorish Princess Aïka, jealous of the efforts of Prince Domino to free the enchanted Désirée from her feral shape, is the principal enemy of the pair as they struggle through the Kingdom of Fish, the Kingdom of Vegetables, the Siren Sea, the Depths of the Earth and other picturesque locations and ballet scenas, until good triumphs over evil in a blaze of stage effects. The loosely episodic fabric of this style of show provided the opportunity for the addition and substitution of scenes, songs and ballets as required to keep the piece both up-to-date and interesting to umpteenth-time visitors.

La Biche au bois was given a significant revival in 1867 (15 June) when it was restaged at the Théâtre de la Porte-Saint-Martin with the young Hervé cast in the role of Prince Souci. For *La [Nouvelle] Biche au bois,* Hervé, Jean-Jacques de Billemont and Artus provided fresh music and arrangements and the producers supplied five live lions, which became six when a female gave birth during a performance. The piece was a great success, but closed down in November when the entire scenery and properties were bought for export to America. In 1896, the Théâtre du Châtelet, which became the principal home of *La Biche au bois* in the last decades of the century, was able to announce that 16 fresh scenes, from the hands of patented playwrights Ernest Blum and Raoul Toché, had been added to the original 14 for its fresh edition of the show. The most appreciated of these turned out to be one slipped into the Kingdom of the Vegetables portion of the plot, and representing "the amusing wedding scene of the dill-pickle and the tomato."

English-language versions of *La Biche au bois* included *The Princess Changed into a Deer* produced by Alfred Bunn at the Theatre Royal, Drury Lane, in 1845, removed after one performance, but nevertheless played subsequently on Broadway (*The Magic Deer* National

Theater 8 March 1852), Planché's successful extravaganza *The Prince of Happy Land, or The Fawn in the Forest* (Lyceum Theatre 26 December 1851) and F C Burnand's *The White Fawn,* illustrated with a mixture of music from the Offenbach and Hervé canon and music-hall songs, and produced at Liverpool for Christmas 1867 and the following year at Holborn. In 1872 a grand opéra-bouffe féerie version, modelled on the Cogniards' piece, with a score of original music commissioned from Georges Jacobi and Frederic Clay, was mounted at London's Alhambra Theatre (23 December) under the title—borrowed from the successful American leg opera—of *[The] Black Crook,* and it scored a considerable success.

Black Crook was the wicked fairy (Cornélie d'Anka) but it was the comical Dandelion (Harry Paulton) and soubrette Gabrielle (Kate Santley), the princess's helpmate, who had the best roles (the princess, of course, being an animal for half the show). The much-photographed Branscombe sisters, a lightning caricaturist and all the famous forces of the Alhambra ballets also featured prominently through a fine run of 204 performances. A slightly slimmed version of the piece was revived at the same theatre in 1881 (3 December).

In America, *La Biche au bois* (which had nothing to do with the show presented as *The Black Crook*) was given as a spectacular *The White Fawn* in a version credited to James Mortimer—but seeming to owe a lot to both the Cogniards and to Burnand, and using that scenery which had been shortly before whisked out from under the Parisian actors' feet—at Niblo's Garden, 17 January 1868 for 150 performances. Mark Smith (King Dingdong), Lizzie Wilmore (Finetta), Mena Montague (Aïka) and Lucy Egerton (Prince Leander) shared the center of attention with a grand ballet of fireflies, a danse de poissons, a grand ballet of bells and a transformation scene which required 80 stagehands and 20 gasmen to operate it. The show progressed from Broadway to a superior 11 weeks in Boston and was a great spectacular success wherever it went thereafter.

Friedrich Strampfer at Vienna's Theater an der Wien also had a splendid success with the ''grosse Spektakel-Féerie mit Gesang, Tanz und Evolutionen in 4 akten und einem Vorspiel, in 13 Bildern'' entitled *Prinzessin Hirschkuh* (11 June 1866). Matthias Rott (King Klingerlinging LXXVII), Carl Adolf Friese (Pelikan, ie, Dandelion), Frln Lamberti (Aïka), Fr Berg (Furibunda), Carl Swoboda (Prince) and Frln Meyr (Giroflée, ie, Gabrielle) led a cast who—doubtless not without reason—were billed much smaller than the suppliers of costumes, scenery, props and the machinists, notably the gentleman who provided the ''Wasserwerke und elektrische Licht-Batterien'' (already!). The largest type on the bill, however, was reserved for the BALLETS: the ballet of the fishes, the ballet of the vegetables, relating the tale of the love of a turnip for a carrot, the five-part grosses Tanz-Divertissement ''Les Amazones,'' and the dance of the sirens. *Prinzessin Hirschkuh* was played in Vienna 174 times in the 1860s and early 1870s.

BICKERSTAFF, Isaac [John] (b Dublin, 26 September 1733; d ?1812). One of the most successful and undoubtedly the best librettist for the 18th-century British musical stage.

Originally an officer in the army and then in the marines, Bickerstaff was, so it is said, drummed out of the service for persistent sodomy and shifted his activities instead to the theatre. There, he became one of the top stage writers of his time, writing and/or rewriting the texts for several plays (*The Plain-Dealer, The Absent Man, The Hypocrite, 'Tis Well It's No Worse,* etc) and, most particularly, for a series of musical comedies which include most of those from that period which are still considered for occasional production in the 20th century.

The comic opera *Thomas and Sally,* the semi-pasticcio musical play *Love in a Village* (''The Miller of Dee'') and *The Maid of the Mill,* a ballad opera based on Richardson's novel *Pamela,* were all considerable successes not only in Britain but throughout the English-speaking stages of the world, but it was *The Padlock,* a comic opera based on Cervantes' *El celoso extremeño,* which proved the most widely popular of Bickerstaff's pieces. It was played, with considerable success, all around the English-speaking world and even beyond, appearing, amongst other venues, in translation in Vienna (*Das Vorhängeschloss* with a fresh musical score by Carl Binder), and in Budapest (*A lakat*). It was most recently seen in London at the Old Vic in 1979.

Thomas and Sally was seen in London's West End as late as 1941 (New Theatre 1 July) and at New York's Little Theater in 1938 (4 January), and versions of *Love in a Village* were reprised in London at the Everyman Theatre in 1923 and, in 1928, at the Lyric, Hammersmith (mus arr Arthur Reynolds), where a revamped *Lionel and Clarissa,* also musically made over by Reynolds, had been previously seen in 1925 (28 October).

It has been suggested that the libretto to Mozart's *Die Entführung aus dem Serail* was descended from Bickerstaff's 1769 pasticcio comic opera *The Captive* (itself borrowed from Dryden), but the author, conversely, himself borrowed the text of Pergolesi's *La serva padrona* to make up the libretto for his *The Maid the Mistress / He Would If He Could,* and, in the style of the period, made use of such classic and Continental models as he pleased without always crediting his sources.

At the height of his success Bickerstaff's recurring habit got him into trouble again and this time the 39-year-old author was obliged to flee the country. In 1782 the *Biographica Dramatica* reported "He is said to be still living abroad, to which a deed without a name has banished him, and where he exists poor and despised by all orders of people." Unlike Oscar Wilde, a century later, he apparently lived some 30 years more, whether poor and despised is not known, but like Wilde he contributed no more to the British stage, which was much the poorer for his loss.

1760 **Thomas and Sally, or the Sailors Return** (Thomas Arne) Theatre Royal, Covent Garden 28 November

1762 **Love in a Village** (comp and arr Thomas Arne) Theatre Royal, Covent Garden 8 December

1765 **The Maid of the Mill** (Samuel Arnold, et al) Theatre Royal, Covent Garden 31 January

1765 **Daphne and Amyntor** (various) Theatre Royal, Drury Lane 8 October

1767 **Love in the City** (Charles Dibdin, et al) Theatre Royal, Covent Garden 21 February

1768 **Lionel and Clarissa** (C Dibdin) Theatre Royal, Covent Garden 25 February

1768 **The Padlock** (C Dibdin) Theatre Royal, Drury Lane 3 October

1768 **A Royal Garland** (Arnold) 1 act Theatre Royal, Covent Garden 10 October

1769 **The Ephesian Matron** (C Dibdin) 1 act Ranelagh House 12 May

1769 **The Captive** (C Dibdin) Theatre Royal, Haymarket 21 June

1770 **The Maid the Mistress** (C Dibdin) Ranelagh House 28 May

1770 **A School for Fathers** revised *Lionel and Clarissa* Theatre Royal, Drury Lane 8 February

1770 **The Recruiting Sergeant** (C Dibdin) 1 act Ranelagh House 20 July

1770 **The Brick-dust Man and the Milk-Maid** (C Dibdin) Sadler's Wells Theatre 25 July

1771 **He Would If He Could, or An Old Fool Worse Than Any** (C Dibdin) revised *The Maid the Mistress* Theatre Royal, Drury Lane 12 April

1774 **The Romp** (pasticcio ad Bickerstaff, C Dibdin) revised *Love in the City* Crow Street Theatre, Dublin 23 March

1775 **The Sultan, or A Peep in the Seraglio** (various) Theatre Royal, Drury Lane 12 December

Biography: Tasch, P: *The Dramatic Cobbler* (Bucknell University Press, Lewisburg, Pa, 1971)

THE BICYCLE GIRL

The popularization of bicycling as a fashionable pastime in Victorian times resulted in musical-comedy heroines being put in the saddle by various devices. The "Girl" of W A Wolf and Louis Harrison's American *The Bicycle Girl* (Red Bank, NJ 21 August 1895), portrayed by Nellie McHenry, had her marital destiny decided by a cycle race, whilst her British counterpart ("a musical bicycle comedy" by Charles Osborne and E M Stuart; music by Orlando Powell; Nottingham 29 March 1897), as impersonated by Billie Barlow, got into gear herself and headed off the villain of the piece by the strength of her pretty leg-muscles. A second British piece, *The Lady Cyclist, or a Bicycle Belle* (which had lost a court contest for the more obvious title) had its heroine swapping clothes with her lover on a cycling tour prefatory to some low comedy. All were opportunist pieces of little quality and faded away quickly, leaving the song "Daisy Bell" as the most successful outcome of the bicycling craze. Many years later, Broadway's *The Girl Friend* went again to the bicycle—this time the seven-day cycle-racing world—for its subject matter, but the libretto was not liked and the British production of the show junked the cycling tale and replaced it with the libretto of another show.

BIEDERMANN, Therese (b Vienna, 24 April 1863; d Vienna, 9 June 1942). Long-popular soubrette of the Viennese musical stage.

Therese Biedermann was on the stage from an early age, working as a child at the Theater in der Josefstadt, and then from 1882 in adult roles in Operette at Mädling, at Vienna's Strampfertheater, at Brünn and from 1885 at the Landestheater in Graz. She had been at Graz only one season when she was signed to join the company at the Theater an der Wien, thus beginning a career of nearly 20 years as one of the favorite soubrettes of the Vienna theatre.

She made her debut at the Theater an der Wien as Ciboletta in the Viennese production of *Eine Nacht in Venedig,* appeared as Isabella in *Boccaccio* (1886), Leni in *Drei Paar Schuhe* and Bronislawa in *Der Bettelstudent* and went on to create and/or play, amongst other roles, Lutte in Suppé's *Bellman* (1887), Hannele in *Die sieben Schwaben* (1887), Pitti-Sing in *Der Mikado* (1888), Christine in *Pagenstreiche* (1888), Scrollina in *Capitän Fracassa* (1889), Lerina in *Das Orakel* (1889), a splendidly lively Molly to the Jonathan of Girardi in the highly successful *Der arme Jonathan* (1890), Orestes in *Die schöne Helena* (1891), Friquette in Lacome's *Madame Bonbon* (ie, *Madame Boniface*), Justine in *Fanchon's Leyer* (1892, *La Fille de Fanchon la vielleuse*), Paquerita in *Der Bajazzo* (1892), Anastasia Knapp in Strauss's *Fürstin Ninetta* (1893), Manotte Chicard in *Der Schwiegerpapa* (1893), another fine part as Nelly in *Der Obersteiger* (1894), Susanne in *Husarenblut* (1894), Nitouche to Girardi's Célestin (*Mam'zelle Nitouche*) and Regerl to his Andredl (*Das verwunschene Schloss*), Annita in Strauss's *Jabuka* (1894) and Lisbeth in his revised *Simplicius,* Ludmilla Boroshazyi in *Kneisl & Co* (1894),

Vreneli in Millöcker's *Der Probekuss* (1894), Ninetta in Dellinger's *Die Chansonette* (1895), Wan-Li in *Der goldene Kamerad* (1895), Jeanne in Strauss's *Waldmeister* (1895), Follette in *General Gogo* (1896), Polly in *Mister Menelaus* (1896), the travesty role of the boy, Beppo in *Der Schmetterling* (1896), Tilli in *Die Schwalben* (1897), Fritella in *Der verregnete Amor* (1897, *L'amour mouillé*), Susette in Strauss's *Die Göttin der Vernunft* (1897), Kitty Tortle in *Die Blumen-Mary* (1897), the dancer Feodora in *Der Opernball* (1898), Graf Nicki Sternfeld in the Hungarian operett *Die Küchen-Komtesse* alongside Ilka Pálmay (1898), Serpolette in a revival of *Die Glöcken von Corneville,* in *Die Gräfin Kuni* (1898), Madelon in *Der Blondin von Namur* (1898), Marianka Wondraschek in *Fräulein Hexe* (1898), Cascarette in *Katze und Maus* by Johann Strauss III (1898), Iris in *Die grieschisches Sklave* (London's *A Greek Slave*), Madame Sillery in *Ihre Excellenz* (1899), the comical Pampeluna (ex- Carmenita) in *Ein durchgeganges Mädel* (1899, *A Runaway Girl*), the boy Heinrich in *Die Puppe* (1899, *La Poupée*), Yvette in *Fräulein Präsident* (1899) and Friquet in *La Chanson de Fortunio* before moving, at the turn of the century, to the opposition Carltheater.

The Carltheater served her up with the same mixture of repertoire roles, new flops and also some rather more grateful new roles for, as well as appearing as Fritz in *Die Diva* (1900), Aurore in *Die Primadonna,* Käthe in *Die drei Wunsche,* Marion in the Viennese version of *Les Saltimbanques* (*Circus Malicorne*), Sylvia in *Die Debutantin,* Molly Seamore in *Die Geisha* (1901), and giving a repeat of her Regerl, this time to the Andredl of Franz Glawatsch (1901), she introduced first the comical role of Dudley in the Viennese version of *San Toy* (1900) and then another showy role as the soubrette Fritzi in *Das süsse Mädel* (1901). She followed up as Régina in a revival of Offenbach's *La Princesse de Trébizonde* (1902), the gymnastic Jerry Bergauer in Reinhardt's *Der liebe Schatz* (1902) and, in her best Carltheater role to date, as Mizzi in the first production of *Der Rastelbinder* (1902). She continued as Catherine in *Madame Sherry* (1903), Roustanne in *Der Mameluck* (1903), Gusti Weinstein in *Das Marktkind* (1903), Charis in *Der Göttergatte* (1904), Franzi in *Das Veilchenmädel* (1904), Emma in *'s Zuckersgoscherl* (1904), Lona in *Der Schätzmeister* (1904), Rosette in the Hungarian operett *Der Schnurrbart* (1905), Sári in *Kaisermanöver* (1905) and Gilda in *Der Polizeichef* (1905) before moving on to a few performances on the variety stage and then, finally, putting an end to an enormously busy 20 years in the Viennese theatre in favor of spending more time as Frau von Singer.

BIG BEN Light opera in 2 acts by A P Herbert. Music by Vivian Ellis. Adelphi Theatre, London, 17 July 1946.

Big Ben was an earnestly preachy piece in which MP Herbert let his politics get the better of his theatricality, and which was only lifted into some semblance of an entertainment by Vivian Ellis's delightful light music. In the same vein as Hugh McLellan's *Nelly Neil,* more than three decades before, Herbert presented a singing socialist heroine (Carole Lynne) and—what even the earlier show had balked at—had her straight-facedly voted into Parliament, asserting in the show's most plugged number that "I Want to See the People Happy." Needless to say, like Nellie, she paired off with a nice, rich and right-wing hero (Eric Palmer) at the final curtain, after having spent most of the act struggling in the house to beat an anti-drunkenness law which she judged unfair to the "working" classes and getting sent to the Tower of London, in a moment of light relief, for contempt of parliament.

Herbert's libretto, which had actually been offered first to William Walton before Ellis applied for and got the job of writing the music, had solely the merit of reuniting the men who would, soon after, in collaboration with the show's producer, C B Cochran, follow up *Big Ben*'s indifferent 172 performances with *Bless the Bride.*

Recording: original cast recordings on *Three by Vivian Ellis* (WRC)

BIG BOY

1. Musical comedy in 2 acts by Harold Atteridge based on *In Old Kentucky* by Charles T Dazey. Lyrics by B G De Sylva. Music by James F Hanley and Joseph Meyer. Winter Garden Theater, New York, 7 January 1925.

The Shuberts' Winter Garden extravaganza of 1925 starred Al Jolson, well into his second decade as a Broadway favorite, in a show where what plot there was had him as stable boy Gus, plotting against the plotters who are trying to stop him riding for the Bedford family (Maude Turner Gordon, Patti Harrold, Frank Beaston) in the Derby. Real horses galloped across the stage, and Gus, of course, won the race. In the meanwhile, however, he had got down to the real business of the evening and sung "California, Here I Come," "Keep Smiling at Trouble" and, briefly, "If You Knew Susie." The last named number didn't go for him, so he cut it out and left it for Eddie Cantor to turn into a hit.

Big Boy, however, didn't go as well as its predecessors and after less than two months it closed down when it was announced that the star was unwell. That common euphemism was given some credence when the show was reopened the following season and ran through 120 further performances before being taken out to clean up on the road.

2. Musical comedy in 2 acts by Douglas Furber, Fred Emney and Max Kester. Lyrics by Douglas Furber. Additional lyrics by Emney. Music by Carroll Gibbons. Saville Theatre, London, 12 September 1945.

Plate 33. **Big River.** *John Bell, Cameron Daddo (Huckleberry Finn) and Drew Forsythe are the travelers on the Mississippi in Australia's version of the show.*

A comedy musical designed to exploit the talents of hefty comedian Fred Emney (in the title role of Sir Frederick Bolsover) and his former Gaiety Theatre colleague, the acrobatic Richard Hearne (as his good friend Pastry), Britain's *Big Boy* was put together by Douglas Furber who had supplied much of the successful material performed by the pair with Leslie Henson at the Gaiety. It included the inevitable jewel thieves, the making of a movie, a singing shopgirl (Carole Raye) who becomes a film star, and a handful of self-effacing songs (''Where Do You Go When You Dream?''), but mostly comic set pieces for the benefit of its two stars, which they played through 174 performances in London before touring. The show's principal legacy was the soubriquet ''Mr Pastry'' which Hearne carried with him the rest of his career.

BIG RIVER, the Adventures of Huckleberry Finn Musical in 2 acts adapted from the novel by Mark Twain by William Hauptman. Music and lyrics by Roger Miller. Eugene O'Neill Theater, New York, 25 April 1985.

After many years of mostly unimpressive attempts at musicalizing the works of Mark Twain, *Big River* finally got the author's Mississippi characters and one of their tales successfully on to the musical stage where, under the management of a consortium of producers, it won itself a Tony Award as the best musical of 1985 and a run of 1,005 performances through two and a half years on Broadway.

Huckleberry Finn (Daniel Jenkins) runs away from his drunken father (John Goodman) and sets off down the Mississippi River on a raft in the company of the runaway slave Jim (Ron Richardson). On the way the pair are joined by two confidence tricksters (Bob Gunton, René Auberjonois) in whose company Huck takes part in a phony booth show, and in an attempt to blarney the recently bereaved Wilkes family out of their inheritance.

When one of the family turns out to be a pretty girl (Patti Cohenour), Huck makes sure she gets the money back, but in the meantime his fine finagling friends have cashed in by selling Jim as a slave. With the help of a real friend, Tom Sawyer (John Short), Jim gets stolen back, and as the show ends both he and Huck set off into the future.

The songs for *Big River,* the initial work of popular country singer-songwriter Roger Miller (''King of the Road,'' ''Little Green Apples,'' etc) for the musical theatre, caught the warmly unshowy nature of the tale and its people in such pieces as the attractive Huck-Jim duos ''Muddy Waters'' and ''River in the Rain,'' the country comicalities of Tom's ''Hand for the Hog'' and Papa Finn's bilious ''Guv'ment,'' and the Dixieland song of the treacherous showmen (''When the Sun Goes Down in the South''). The feminine element was given its moments in two goodbye songs for pretty Miss Wilkes, one bidding her father's corpse farewell (''You Oughta Be Here With Me'') and the other saying goodbye to helpful Huck (''Leavin's Not the Only Way to Go''), and in a solo featured in the slave-sung ''The Crossing.''

Brought to Broadway after tryouts at the La Jolla Playhouse and the American Repertory Theatre, Cambridge, Mass, (17 February 1984, 28 performances) in an attractively unpretentious production, and with a minimum of ballyhoo (right behind a much ballyhooed and vastly glitz-ridden show which flopped smartly), *Big River* turned out, in a very soft season, to be a pleasant family-entertaining sleeper. From its fine run on Broadway it went on the road in America, and in 1989 was mounted by John Frost and Essington Entertainments in Australia. Cameron Daddo (Huck), Drew Forsythe (King), John Bell (Duke) and Karen Knowles (Mary Jane) featured in a long and highly successful nationwide run.

Australia: Her Majesty's Theatre, Sydney 7 January 1989

Recordings: original cast (MCA), Australian cast (BRR)

BILLEE TAYLOR Nautical comic opera in 2 acts by Henry Pottinger Stephens. Music by Edward Solomon. Imperial Theatre, London, 30 October 1880.

Billee Taylor was a genuine comic opera in a nautical vein which followed closely (in time) in the traces of *HMS Pinafore* without in any way imitating it. Stephens's book used as its inspiration the old ballad tale of *Billee Taylor,* which had already been used as the subject of a number of earlier stage musical shows—including a burlesque at the Adelphi Theatre (*Billy Taylor, or The Gay Young Fellow* J B Buckstone 9 November 1829, which incorporated a famous burlesque of the Wolf's Glen scene from *Der Freischütz*), another in 1856 (12 May), Mowbray's *Soho Billy Taylor, or The Gay Young Fellow* (1 April 1861) and F C Burnand's *Military Billee Taylor, or The War in the Cariboo* (22 April 1869)—in telling of the press-ganged sailor followed to sea by his lady love in man's attire.

Plate 34. **Billee Taylor.** *''We Stick to Our Letters''—the Charity Girls's chorus was one of the highlights of this long favorite nautical opera-bouffe.*

In ''Pot'' Stephens's version, however, the story was treated in a gently tongue-in-cheek fashion which took a different tone both from standard burlesque and from the witty and wordful style of W S Gilbert. Billee, ''a virtuous gardener'' (Frederic Rivers), is a vain beauty of a boy who has attracted the attentions of Arabella Lane (Emma Chambers), the daughter of nouveau-riche Sir Mincing Lane (Arthur Williams). Arabella leaves pints of ale in the garden shed to attempt to attract the object of her affections. Billee, however, plights himself to the poor but plucky charity girl Phoebe (Kathleen Corri) and, to prevent this marriage, aching Arabella allies herself with Crab (J A Arnold), a schoolmaster with a longing to be a genuine villain, and short-staffed Captain Flapper (Fleming Norton) of the *HMS Thunderball,* to get Billee press-ganged and carried off to sea. Phoebe and her chorus of charity-girlfriends promptly get into uniform and go after them, but Billee's apparent virtues have won him quick promotion and, in his new position, he rather feels that a well-off wife would be an asset. Faithful Phoebe is rejected in favor of persistent Arabella. The hero's come-uppance is at hand, however, when it is revealed that the exploits for which he won his promotion were phony. He is reduced to the ranks and his lieutenancy given instead to another fine sailor—Phoebe! Virtue is triumphant and the prig and the plotters get their desserts.

The score, the first full-scale work of 25-year-old Edward Solomon, musical director at the Globe Theatre, was in the happiest comic opera vein. He provided some very attractive ballads, but the show's most successful musical moments came in the comic pieces, notably the rollicking "All on Account of Eliza" in which the show's low comedian, Ben Barnacle (J D Stoyle), told of how he became a press-gang man because his sweetheart played him false. Another of the show's song successes was the Charity Girls' chorus "We Stick to Our Letters," a success which owed not a little to the fact that the chorus in question had been cast with some exceedingly pretty girls, demure in their little grey dresses and brisk white mobcaps and aprons.

Following six months behind the London production of *The Pirates of Penzance,* and obliged to bear comparison with Gilbert and Sullivan's piece both in the press and with the public, *Billee Taylor* shared the honors evenly, winning some fine notices. D'Oyly Carte was quick to show an interest in what was clearly a piece of genuine competition for his show, but his interest was one of the elements which proved *Billee Taylor*'s undoing. The inexperienced management, which was already having problems coping with a potential hit show, quarrelled with the authors and, in the end, *Billee Taylor* was taken off after only three months at the Imperial Theatre. Carte—who had snapped up the American rights—promptly shipped director Charlie Harris off to New York and, three weeks after the London closure, his production of *Billee Taylor* opened on Broadway where, with J H Ryley (Flapper), William Hamilton (Crab), Alice Burville (Arabella) and A W F McCollin (Ben) featured, it fulfilled a splendid season of three and a half months at the Standard Theatre and turned itself into the nationwide hit of the moment. *Billee Taylor* companies and productions sprung up like mushrooms in all quarters of the country—many off them extremely approximate in their book, but all helping themselves to the non-copyrighted Solomon score—and within months of the Broadway opening dozens of musical companies of all kinds—including such outfits as the Emilie Melville and Emily Soldene troupes—were traipsing America playing what were more or sometimes very less versions of Stephens and Solomon's show. In Boston, for example, Fred Stinson's "version" featured Richard Golden as Captain the Hon Tholepin Flatbottom, RN and the young Henry Dixey as "Sir Muslin Delaine" and the parallel with *HMS Pinafore* was emphasized by making Phoebe into . . . Hebe (Dora Wiley). Burlesque *Billee Taylor*s too, each and every one using, of course, much of Solomon's now hugely popular music, also flourished. Tony Pastor, the San Francisco Minstrels (*Billy the Tailor*), the low-brow Rentz-Santley Company (*Billy the Tailor, or The Lass Who Stuck to the Sailor* with Mabel Santley as Captain Flip-Flapper and John Henshaw as Mincemeat Laner), and a whole heap of other variety houses, large and small, all came out with their versions of the latest megahit. For, as Carte had suspected, *Billee Taylor* was the biggest original musical comedy success to have arrived on the American stage since *Pinafore.*

Other English-language stages soon snapped up this red-hot piece, and Australia saw its first *Billee Taylor* the next year. Top local tenor Armes Beaumont was Billie and Nellie Stewart played Phoebe, with Edwin Kelly as Sir Mincing Lane, H M Harwood as Ben and Emma Wangenheim as Arabella. The critic of the Melbourne *Argus* took violently against the show, which didn't help its prospects, but he was no longer around when it was revived by Williamson, Garner and Musgrove at the same house four years later with Julia Sidney playing Phoebe and the D'Oyly Carte's Alice Barnett as Eliza, and again in Sydney in 1886, each time with positive results.

Billee Taylor stuck around for a good long time and it was revived in both London (Gaiety 1882 twice, 1883, 1885, Crystal Palace 1886, Toole's Theatre 1886) and in New York (Niblo's Garden 1881, Booth's 1882, Bijou 1882, Fifth Avenue 1882, Casino 1885, American Theater 1898) in years to come. It never amassed a long metropolitan run, but it was played long and wide in the American country and in the British colonies, and was also seen in several European countries, notably in a tour organized by the composer and his paramour, soprano Lillian Russell ("manager: J H Thorp") in 1884. Originally scheduled to play in France, Belgium, Netherlands and Italy before seasons in Vienna, Berlin and Paris, it got to Brussels's Galeries Saint-Hubert and to Le Havre, but stranded soon after, after the star jumped ship.

The show, and its hot song, became ingrained in theatrical and popular memory in America so strongly that as late as 1900 Leo Ditrichstein put out a comedy with the title *All On Account of Eliza* (Park City Theater, Bridgeport, Conn 23 August). And an American performer took the stage name of Billee Taylor.

USA: Standard Theater 19 February 1881; Australia: Princess Theatre, Melbourne 26 August 1882; France: Le Havre 21 February 1884

BILLY Musical in 2 acts by Ian La Fresnais and Dick Clement adapted from *Billy Liar* by Keith Waterhouse and Willis Hall. Lyrics by Don Black. Music by John Barry. Theatre Royal, Drury Lane, London, 1 May 1974.

''Billy Liar,'' the north country lad with the wishful imagination which he equates too closely with fact for the comfort of anyone around him, became a classic figure of English literature as Keith Waterhouse's original novel was translated first to the stage (1960 w Willis Hall), then to the screen with Tom Courtenay as *Billy Liar* (1963), and finally in 1974 to the musical stage.

Billy Fisher (Michael Crawford) daydreams his way through life in Stradhoughton, Yorks, and lies his way out of each of the uncomfortable positions that real life puts in front of him. Current problems, apart from facing life in general, are that he has more or less proposed to both the primly devoted Barbara (Gay Soper) and rough-as-guts Rita (Elaine Paige), and that he has filched the stamp money from the firm of undertakers where he works. Both situations have come to a point when good friend Liz (Diana Quick) appears from the outside world, persuading him to come to London and do something instead of just talking about it. Billy gets as far as the train station, but in the end he turns back to the safety of Stradhoughton where his daydreams can stay alive.

Billy's fantasies provided some colorful scenas amongst the daily grind of his little life of sad Yorkshire mishaps. He descended by parachute to review the all-girl army of his private country of Ambrosia, returned from the outside world as a Jack Buchanan top-hat and tails song-and-dance man to the acclaim of all Yorkshire, and pounded out a pop-star song as Billy Fisher, hitmaker (''The Lady from LA''), declaring with simple self-delusion ''Some of Us Belong to the Stars'' until it was time to admit ''I Missed the Last Rainbow.''

The show's other musical moments included a duo for Barbara and Rita, both waiting with rather different attitudes for Billy to turn up for a double-date (''Any Minute Now''), a gently reminiscing number for Billy's old employer remembering that ''It Were All Green Hills (when I were a lad)'' and a merrily gruesome piece of family table-talk (''And'') from which Billy escapes into dreamland.

Billy was a major hit, with Crawford's performance in the title role, in his stage musical debut, winning him a special place amongst the superlatives. H M Tennent Ltd and Peter Witt's production of the show played 904 performances to the large auditorium of the Theatre Royal, Drury Lane, with Roy Castle replacing Crawford in the last part of the run. In 1976 a German-language version (ad Werner Schneyder) was mounted at Vienna's Theater an der Wien, but a 1991 revival of *Billy* scheduled for London and an announced 1995 tour with Jason Donovan as star both folded in the preparatory stages.

The title, *Billy,* was earlier used in Britain for a musical comedy by George Cooper and Adrian Ross, lyrics by Ross and music by F Osmond Carr (Tyne Theatre and Opera House, Newcastle 11 April 1898), conceived as a touring vehicle for the diminutive music-hall comic Little Tich who appeared as an impecunious wee nobleman battling against a horrid big businessman. With a cast featuring the young Evie Greene, exceedingly tall Alice Barnett and Joe Farren Soutar, it toured eight months.

In America, the same title was used for a musical by Stephen Glassman suggested by Herman Melville's *Billy Budd* (music and lyrics by Ron Dante and Gene Allen, Billy Rose Theater 22 March 1969).

Austria: Theater an der Wien 19 February 1976

Recording: original cast (CBS)

THE BIOGRAPH GIRL Musical comedy in 2 acts by Warner Brown. Lyrics by David Heneker and Warner Brown. Music by David Heneker. Phoenix Theatre, London, 19 November 1980.

A small-scale, revusical piece constructed around the myths and legends of the silent-movie days of Hollywood, *The Biograph Girl* featured a scoreful of deftly made songs and some comical and charming scenes in which the actors appeared as D W Griffith (Bruce Barry), Adolf Zukor (Ron Berglas), Mack Sennett (Guy Siner), Lillian Gish (Kate Revill), Mary Pickford (Sheila White) and other historical and semi-historical characters. Griffith apostrophized a world ''Beyond Babel'' in rousing bass-baritone tones and scowled over the accolades which would come too late (''He Was One of the Pioneers''), Mary simpered to the press ''I Like To Be the Way I Am (in my own front parlour)'' and joined with Lillian and Mack to wonder what would become of their work in the future (''Put It in the Tissue Paper'').

In the giant shadow of *Evita, The Biograph Girl* had a short London career, but was subsequently played in New Zealand and Japan with great success as well as, in a much expanded version, in the British provinces.

Recording: original cast (TER)

BISSON, Alexandre [Charles Auguste] (b Briouze, Orne, 9 April 1848; d Paris, 27 January 1912).

The highly successful French playwright, author of such widely produced pieces as *115 Rue Pigalle, Le Deputé de Bombignac, Les Surprises du divorce* (w Antony Mars), *La Souricière* (w Albert Carré), *M. le Directeur* (UK: *The Chili Widow*), *Le Contrôleur de wagons-lits, Le Coup de fouet, Un Mariage d'étoile, Feu Toupinel* and *La Femme X,* provided the libretti for several musical pieces, of which the musical comedy *Un Lycée de jeunes filles* (played in Hungary as *Színitanoda* and in Germany

Plate 35. **The Biograph Girl.** *"I Like to Be the Way I Am in My Own Front Parlour . . .": Mary Pickford (Sheila White) puts on an act for the press (Philip Griffith, Ron Berglas).*

as *Mädchenschule*) proved the most widely successful. Toulmouche's *La Veillée de noces,* produced in England as *The Wedding Eve,* and *Captain Thérèse,* written for the Carl Rosa Light Opera Company expressly to feature their contralto star, Agnes Huntington, also found some degree of success.

A number of Bisson's plays were used as the source for later musical comedies. On Broadway, *Le Péril jaune* (w Albert St Albin) became the Louis Hirsch/Channing Pollock and Rennold Wolf musical *The Grass Widows* (1917) and *Les Surprises du divorce* was musicalized by Ephraim Zimbalist and Joseph Herbert as *Honeydew* (1920), whilst the Jerome Kern musical *The Night Boat* was based, without precise credit, on *Le Contrôlleur de wagons-lits.* The same play was musicalized in Italy in 1924 with a score by Romolo Alegiani as *Il Controllore dei Vagoni letto.* Off-Broadway's Martinique Theatre hosted a version of *Le Véglione* (w Albert Carré) under the title *For the Love of Suzanne* (Deed Meyer/Bill Galarno) in October 1974, whilst in Czechoslovakia, Bisson's *Madame Durosel* (1890) was made into *Mama vom Ballett* (Bernard Grün/Rudolf Stadler, Ernst Stadler Deutsches Theater studio 20 February 1926).

Bisson also authored a two-volume *Petite Encyclopédie musicale* in collaboration with composer Théodore Lajarte.

1881 **Un Lycée de jeunes filles** (Louis Gregh) Théâtre Cluny 27 December

1882 **Ninetta** (Raoul Pugno/w Alfred Hennequin) Théâtre de la Renaissance 26 December

1885 **Le Moutier de Saint-Guignolet** (Frederic Toulmouche/E Bureau, F Jattiot) Galeries Saint-Hubert, Brussels 5 May

1888 **La Veillée de noces** revised *Le Moutier de Saint-Guignolet* Théâtre des Menus-Plaisirs 27 November

1889 **Mam'zelle Pioupiou** (William Chaumet/w André Sylvane) Théâtre de la Porte-Saint-Martin 31 May

1890 **Captain Thérèse** (Robert Planquette/ad F C Burnand, Gilbert a' Beckett) Prince of Wales Theatre, London 25 August

Plate 36. **Bitter-Sweet.** *Carl Linden (Georges Metaxa) fights the lecherous Captain Lutte (Austin Trevor) for the sake of his wife (Peggy Wood).*

1903 **La Petite Maison** (Chaumet/w Georges Docquois) Opéra-Comique 5 June

1909 **Chez la sonnambule** (Toulmouche) Théâtre Grévin 24 March

BITTER-SWEET Operette in 3 acts by Noël Coward. His Majesty's Theatre, London, 12 July 1929.

The most wholly successful stage musical written by the author of *Private Lives, Hay Fever* and so many brittle and witty revue songs and sketches was, perhaps surprisingly, an almost entirely sentimental operetta. Avowedly written under the influence of *Die Fledermaus,* it nevertheless replaced that piece's bubbling light comedy with a tale of romantic drama. Sarah Millick (Peggy Wood), a young English girl engaged to be married to man of her own class and milieu, runs away to Vienna with her romantic music teacher, Carl Linden (Georges Metaxa), only to discover there that woman cannot live on love alone. She ends up working in the second-rate café where Carl conducts the band, as a dancing partner, but she soon finds that more than just dancing is expected of her. She refuses, and Carl is killed defending her honor against an amorous officer (Austin Trevor). Sari, as she is now called, goes on to become a successful singer and settles for a loveless but comfortable life as the wife of a kindly nobleman (Alan Napier).

Two scenes of English society life frame the sentimental and dramatic events of the lovers' life in Vienna which forms the centerpiece of the story in an effectively shaped libretto, accompanied by a rich operetta score which includes much of Coward's best stage music. The numbers range from the piece's key love song ''I'll See You Again,'' introduced in the opening act by the two lovers, to a beautiful harmonized sextet for six aging society ladies (''Alas the Time Is Past''), to the understated fun of a handful of Viennese ''Ladies of the Town'' or a group of would-be aesthetes sporting their ''Green Carnation.'' The show's third important role, that of the cabaret vocalist Manon, who enlivens the Viennese scenes with her jealousies and with a sparkling stand-up act, had the show's other most enduring number, the rueful ''If Love Were All.''

Evelyn Laye was originally offered the starring role of Sarah in the premiere production of *Bitter-Sweet,* but refused it because she felt Coward had been less than supportive during the time that Jessie Matthews was busy lifting her husband from her. Thus, it was the American actress Peggy Wood who ultimately created the role alongside Romanian Georges Metaxa, who had been playing in one of producer C B Cochran's London revues whilst a Europe-wide search for a romantic Continental hero had been pursued. Tiny revue artist and composer Ivy St Helier made the triumph of her career as Manon in a performance which was caught on film in the first and less wayward of two film versions.

Miss Laye subsequently played Sarah on Broadway and in London but, although the piece was produced in such diverse countries as Australia, with London vocalist Marjorie Hicklin as Sarah, Herbert Browne as Carl and Saffo Arnay as Manon, in France (where Jane Marnac produced and starred in ''The Time of Waltzes'') and in Hungary (where its title translated as ''Long Ago and Now''), it was, curiously, not taken into the international light opera repertoire and the first major revival (in an unfortunately cut version), with opera star Valerie Masterson as Sarah, was mounted only in 1988 (Sadler's Wells Theatre 23 February).

The first filmed version (ad Monckton Hoffe) starred Anna Neagle and Fernand Graavey and concentrated on the romantic action to the detriment—Miss St Helier's scene apart—of the score, but nevertheless created some fine, atmospheric moments. The second, with Jeanette MacDonald and Nelson Eddy, not surprisingly squeezed Manon right out, ignored all but the central Viennese episode, cut all the bitter out of the bitter-sweet and invented several new songs to put alongside some of the real ones. They were sung, inevitably, by the two stars.

USA: Ziegfeld Theater 21 October 1929; Hungary: Király Színház *Régen és most* 6 December 1929; France: Théâtre Apollo *Au Temps des valses* 2 April 1930; Australia: Theatre Royal, Melbourne 26 March 1932

Films: British & Dominion 1933, MGM 1940

Recordings: complete (TER), selections (WRC, HMV, Columbia, etc)

BLACK, Don [BLACKSTONE, Gerald] (b London, 21 June 1936). British lyricist who has scored major successes in theatre, film and popular song.

A member of the staff at *New Musical Express,* a sometime stand-up comedian, and a music business agent, Black was knocking 30 when he authored the first of a series of lyrics to popular songs, beginning with the English version of Udo Jürgens's Eurovision song ''Warum nur, warum?'' as ''Walk Away'' (1964). Numbers such as film themes ''Thunderball'' (1965), ''Born Free'' (1966 w John Barry, Academy Award) and ''To Sir with Love'' followed, before he made his first venture into the musical theatre with the songs for a post-*Hair* musical about impotence called *Maybe That's Your Problem.* He had more success with the composer of that show, Walter Scharf, when they won an Academy award nomination for their song ''Ben'' in 1972, and further film-song successes with numbers for *Diamonds Are Forever* (w Barry, 1972), *The Man with the Golden Gun, The Pink Panther Strikes Again* and *True Grit* followed.

A second musical play, *Billy* (''Some of Us Belong to the Stars,'' ''I Missed the Last Rainbow,'' ''Any Minute Now'') brought him a major stage success, but several other theatrical essays in the following decade, both in London and on Broadway, were less forthcoming. However, the song-cycle *Tell Me on a Sunday,* written with Andrew Lloyd Webber, produced first a hit song and, later, when the cycle was revised, extended and staged as one half of the entertainment *Song and Dance,* an international theatre success. The Broadway magic show *Merlin,* for which he supplied the songwords, also played through six months in New York.

In association with Laurence Myers he produced his second television-to-musical piece (after the unfortunate *Bar Mitzvah Boy* a decade earlier), a stage musical based on the Adam Faith series *Budgie* which folded quickly, but a second collaboration with Lloyd Webber (w Charles Hart) on *Aspects of Love* (''Anything But Lonely'') gave him both another chart song (''Love Changes Everything'') and another long-running West End success. He subsequently provided the lyrics to Lloyd Webber's music for the stage musical adaptation of the screenplay *Sunset Boulevard* (Tony Award) which was seen in productions around the world.

In 2000 a compilation show based on his work was staged in Bromley under the title *Black Goes With Everything* (Churchill Theatre 24 March).

Black served for some time as the chairman of the British Academy of Songwriters, Composers and Authors (BASCA).

1970 **Maybe That's Your Problem** (Walter Scharf/Lionel Chetwynd) Roundhouse 16 June

1974 **Billy** (John Barry/Ian La Fresnais, Dick Clement) Theatre Royal, Drury Lane 1 May

1978 **Bar Mitzvah Boy** (Jule Styne/Jack Rosenthal) Her Majesty's Theatre 31 September

1980 **Tell Me on a Sunday** (Andrew Lloyd Webber) 1 act Royalty Theatre January

1982 **The Little Prince and the Aviator** (John Barry/Hugh Wheeler) Alvin Theater, New York 1 January

Plate 37. **The Black Crook.** *Kate Santley scored the hit of London's edition with her ''Nobody Knows As I Know,'' and Harry Paulton joined her to take the comic honors.*

1982 **Song and Dance** (including a revised version of *Tell Me on a Sunday*) (Palace Theatre)

1983 **Merlin** (Elmer Bernstein/Richard Levinson, William Link) Mark Hellinger Theater, New York 13 February

1983 **Dear Anyone** (Geoff Stephens/Jack Rosenthal) Cambridge Theatre 9 September

1983 **Abbacadabra** English version w David Wood (Lyric Thetre, Hammersmith)

1988 **Budgie** (Mort Shuman/Keith Waterhouse, Willis Hall) Cambridge Theatre 18 October

1989 **Aspects of Love** (Lloyd Webber/w Charles Hart) Prince of Wales Theatre 17 April

1993 **Sunset Boulevard** (Lloyd Webber/w Christopher Hampton) Adelphi Theatre 12 July

1997 **The Goodbye Girl** lyrics for revised version (Albery Theatre)

THE BLACK CROOK

1. Extravaganza by Charles M Barras. Music by Thomas Baker and others. Niblo's Garden, New York, 12 September 1866.

Often, in earlier times, quoted as the first landmark in the history of the American musical theatre, this production, a spectacular put together on the lines of the French grand opéra-bouffe féerie and/or its German equivalent, was long alleged to have been created by the last-minute insertion into a fairy tale piece destined for Niblo's Garden of the personnel and some of the repertoire of a stranded French ballet troupe, whose theatre had burned down. This myth (which put itself in place soon after the events, and was subsequently repeated in variously ''improved'' versions in the obituaries of those concerned in the making of the show) has now been itself relegated to the fairy tale books, and contemporary sources tell a less circumstantial tale (in which the bones of the myth can nevertheless be discerned) about the genesis of the show and of the burning of the New York Academy of Music, where Grau's Italian Opera company were playing on that fatal 22 May 1866. A full three months before Niblo's even put *The Black Crook* into rehearsals.

It seems what really happened was this: Actor Charles Barras wrote *The Black Crook* as a spectacular touring vehicle for himself and his wife, dancer Sallie St Clair, and in order to equip his show with the required imprimatur of ''a New York success'' prior to touring, he negotiated with William Wheatley, manager of Niblo's Garden, for one hundred performances at his theatre. For Wheatley to agree to this remarkably long run, success or failure, Barras must have come up with some stinging inducement. It appears that this inducement was some kind of a sharing terms arrangement, but it is fairly obvious that Mr Barras was in effect paying for his piece to go on to establish its title for the future. The deal in place, the author set to preparing the scenery and properties for his production at the Academy of Music in his summer hometown of Buffalo, NY. At this stage, Messrs Henry Jarrett and Henry Palmer came into the picture. Having recently formed a producing partnership, they'd been over in Europe ''looking for novelties'' to import to America. Amongst what they'd seen were a production of *La Biche au bois* in Paris, and the pantomime at Astley's Theatre in London, and they had decided that they would put on a show back home which utilized some of the more original spectacularities they'd seen in those two pieces. They'd talked to some of the lead dancers from the Paris show, they'd negotiated the purchase of the big transformation scene from the London panto and they had had the thought their as yet unwritten show might go well (and not too expensively) at the Academy of Music. But then the Academy burned down, and so the would-be-producers made their way instead to the other home of New York spectaculars, Niblo's. But Niblo's wasn't available. Mr Barras had booked it for his one hundred performances. Quite whose idea it was to mix and match, and to slip the bit of British panto Jarrett and Palmer had already paid out their money for into *The Black Crook* isn't recorded. But the result of the negotiations that ensued among Wheatley, Jarrett, Palmer and Barras was that Barras was relieved of his potentially onerous ''sharing'' terms and paid instead a small flat sum as a royalty, and Jarret and Palmer effectively took over as producers of the New York mounting of his play. And the first thing Jarrett did was to set off overseas again to start gathering up the ideas, decorations and personnel which they wanted to change the show from a spectacular melodrama into something more like Paris's *La Biche au bois.* A veritable potpourri of scenery, mechanics, costume and girls. Barras's scenic and costume designs, of course, went completely by the board. His half-made sets and clothes stayed behind in Buffalo, whilst the new producers ordered new ones more in line with the Parisian-Londonish spectacle they intended to produce. In the end, Jarrett arrived back in New York only the day before rehearsals began, bringing with him 45 dancers and actors to add to the local contingent hired by Wheatley (''wanted: 60 ballet girls for *Black Crook* at Niblo's''), and many a crate of European props.

By the time they opened, the extravaganza (''written expressly for Mr Wheatley'') ran for a full five hours. And that in spite of the fact that great chunks of Barras's text, including his big final climax, which had got in the road of the panto transformation, had simply and blatantly been cut out. But if there wasn't too much construction left, the show now included a full score of songs and choruses by various writers, some new and some borrowed, selected and arranged by house musical director Baker, a great deal of ooh-aah mechanical scenery and a vast dose of the legshow ballets and parades typical of the more grandiose French productions, all of it mixed in with Barras's scenes of fairy tale drama and romance to make up a highly attractive if reasonably incoherent and lengthy opéra-bouffe féerie entertainment. The show's priorities were visible from its advertising: the splendid ''Tableaux, Costumes, Marches, Scenery'' (''operated by 71 stage-hands'') and the ''premium transformation'' (''purchased entire from Astley's Theatre, London'') were splashed large across announcements which did not even mention the text or the music, and the ''Grand Parisienne Ballet Troupe'' (62 girls, 39 American and 23 British, but nevertheless advertised as being fashionably French) and the ''Garde Imperiale'' of marching girls were prominently billed, whereas the names of the principal actors and singers were nowhere in sight.

Barras's tale was rather more Germanic than French, telling of the plots concocted by the vile Hertzog (C H Morton), under the spell of the diabolic Zamiel (E B Holmes), to deliver up a monthly ration of human souls to the powers below. Hertzog selects the artist, Rudolf (G C Boniface), whom he frees from the clutches of Count Wolfenstein (J W Blaisdell), as his victim of the night but, as he leads him to his fate, the young man saves the life of a benighted dove. The dove is the disguised fairy, Stalacta (Scottish opera soprano Annie Kemp Bowler), and in the course of the evening she outwits Hertzog and steers Rudolf to a happy ending with the fair Amina (Rose Morton). The comedy was provided by the dramatic folks' servants, with J G Burnett as von Puffengruntz producing the lowest of it, and the musical hit of the show was a soubrette number ''You Naughty, Naughty Men'' as introduced by Millie Cavendish (who died four months into the run) in an incidental role.

The Black Crook provided New York with its most effective piece of grosse Spektakel-Feerie to date, and—perhaps even more attention-pullingly—its most uninhibited mass view of apparently little-clad female limbs to date, and those legs and the displays of scenic machinery roused an unparalleled interest as, with an ever fluid program of components, the show ran on on Broadway for fifteen and a half months, closing 4 January 1868 after 475 performances. With his title more established than he could ever have dreamed, Barras quickly got his rather less grandiose production (''without the imported nudities'') off the mark at Buffalo, and the show was repeated thereafter, in often largely varying versions, all around the country, to the great profit of its author who had, as planned from the start, reserved to himself all outside-New York production rights. Thus, for the few years of his life that remained, he collected largely as *Black Crook* productions—many bearing little resemblance to his play, and merely using the title as a come-on signalling ''legshow with scenery''—sprung up. The show also made intermittent return visits to the New York stage over a number of years (Niblo's Garden 1870, 123 performances; 1871, 87 performances; 1873, 130 performances, etc) and in latter days it was toured long around America by the country's most determined spectacle merchants, the Kiralfy brothers.

A sad coda to the tale. Wheatley, Jarrett and Palmer all made fortunes from the Niblo's run of *The Black Crook*. The bought-out Barras had to wait till a little later to make his money. He certainly did—John McDonough snapped up the rights for a dozen major cities, John Meech of Buffalo for 16 lesser ones, and Maeder, Davey and Curran for the minor towns of 15 states—but he had little joy of it. Sallie, for whom the piece had been written, died (Buffalo, NY, 9 April 1867) even before the New York run had ended and, soon after, a depressed Barras sold his mansion at Cos Cob to Edwin Booth. Finally, on 30 March 1874, he threw himself from a moving train.

The Black Crook became, during its months as a Broadway phenomenon, the butt of burlesque in virtually every minstrel and burlesque troupe in town. Christy's Minstrels, the San Francisco Minstrels, and Kelly and Leon (*The Great Black Crook Burlesque*) all featured parodies of the show; Tony Pastor offered John F Poole's *The White Crook* and visiting British actor Edward Warden penned a *Black Cook* which went round the country.

A silent film based on the *Black Crook* story was produced in 1916 (11 January), with Australian ex-tenor Henry Hallam as Wolfenstein, E P Sullivan as Hertzog and Mae Thompson as Stalacta.

The favored mytho-story of the creation of *The Black Crook* was used as the background for the show *The Girl in Pink Tights* (Sigmund Romberg/Joseph Fields, Jerome Chodorov Mark Hellinger Theater 5 March 1954).

2. Grand opéra-bouffe féerie in 4 acts by Harry and Joseph Paulton founded on *La Biche au bois*. Music by Georges Jacobi and Frederic Clay. Alhambra Theatre, London, 23 December 1872.

An early effort to reproduce in Britain the same kind of vast and spectacular grand opéra-bouffe féerie which was then popular in France, this version of the *La Biche au bois* legend owed nothing to its American homonym except its title. Lovely opéra-bouffe star Cornélie d'Anka starred as the vicious witch of the title out to thwart the enchanted Princess Désirée and her Prince, but the largest part of the evening's entertainment was, as in the American show, given over to its physical production, its ballets and the low comic element as personified by author Harry Paulton as a comic vizier and Kate Santley (who had appeared for a while as Stalacta in the American *Black Crook*) as the heroine's maid, in which role she delivered the show's stand-out song ''Nobody Knows As I Know'' in the overtly roguish style she favored. The production, staged for Christmas, played until the following August.

A simplified version with revised text and music was successfully produced at the same theatre in 1881.

Film: (silent) US version Kalem 1916

[THE LATEST EDITION OF] BLACK-EYED SUSAN, or The Little Bill That Was Taken Up Nautical burlesque in 5 scenes by F C Burnand. Music arranged by Theodore Hermann. Royalty Theatre, London, 29 November 1866.

Douglas Jerrold's famous melodrama *Black-Eyed Susan, or All in the Downs* (Surrey Theatre 8 June 1829) told the story of honest tar William, long at sea and now ready to quit the navy and return to his wife, the Susan of the title. But William's commander, Captain Crosstree, takes a fancy to Susan and, when he tries to lay hands on her, William knocks him down. For striking a superior officer, William is brought to court martial and, although everyone is on his side, the letter of the law condemns him to death. But then the repentant Crosstree brings out William's discharge papers—on the fatal day, William was no longer a serviceman and thus falls not under service jurisidiction. He is free. The other characters included the villainous Uncle Doggrass, the owner of the cottage which houses long-alone Susan and William's old mother, Dame Hatley; his fellow smugglers, Hatchett and Raker; and good little Gnatbrain and his sweetheart Dolly Mayflower.

It became the habit down through the years to introduce the occasional nautical song or dance into the action of Jerrold's drama—the St James's Theatre, for example, inserted the song ''All in the Downs'' for Cecilia Ranoe in the minor role of Blue Peter, and a double hornpipe for Lydia Thompson (Dolly) and Charles Young (William)—but a number of genuine musical versions of the play also followed. Thomas H Reynoldson and John Tully's ballad opera *William and Susan, or All in the Downs,* produced at Drury Lane, 28 February 1858, with

Catherine Lucette (Susan), Henry Haigh (William), Edmund Rosenthal (Captain Cameron) and Fanny Huddart (Bella Primrose) in the lead roles, found some success, but Meyer Lutz's light opera remake, done in tandem with the playwright's son as *All in the Downs* (Gaiety Theatre 5 November 1881), had less of a future. A goodly list of *Black-Eyed Susan* burlesques found their way to the stage, beginning with the quickly-to-the-stage *Black-eyed Sukey, or All in the Dumps* of Frederick Fox Cooper (Olympic Theatre December 1829), with George Wild as the hero and Miss Stuart as Susan, and including *William That Married Susan, or A Squall in the Downs* (Britannia Theatre 21 March 1859); *Black-Eyed Susan, or The Ups and Downs of Deal* (Marylebone Theatre 10 June 1867), in which Augusta Thompson starred as Crosstree; Oscar Barrett and Horace Lennard's *Too Lovely Black-Eyed Susan* (Crystal Palace 2 April 1888); and *Blue-Eyed Susan* (F Osmond Carr/Henry Pettitt, George R Sims Prince of Wales Theatre 6 February 1892). The most notable amongst these was, however, the 1866 burlesque written by F C Burnand, a piece which proved to be one of the outstanding works of the British burlesque tradition.

Burnand's piece was produced by Pattie Oliver at the Royalty Theatre, with Frederic Dewar as Captain Crosstree (''who would have had a very long part if he hadn't been cut down in the 3rd scene''), Nellie Bromley, the future creator of the Plaintiff in *Trial by Jury,* as Dolly Mayflower, Miss Oliver herself as Black-Eyed Susan (''who has accepted a Bill, which she hopes the public will endorse''), Rosina Ranoe and later Annie Collinson as William (''the Bill of the play''), John Russell as Doggrass and the acrobatic Edwin Danvers in a famous comical creation as William's mother. Charles Wyndham, later Sir Charles and a celebrated London manager, played the part of the smuggler, Hatchett. Needless to say, in the burlesque version, William's appearance before the court martial of a dazzling selection of colorful admirals for having murdered (in this version) Crosstree was aborted by the sudden revival of his supposed victim and all ended happily. Amongst his ''selected and arranged'' score, which ranged from bits of Balfe to selections from street minstrelsy, musical director Hermann included one number, the quintet ''Pretty See-usan, Don't Say No,'' which became a Victorian standard.

The burlesque ran for over four hundred performances at the Royalty, creating what was at the time an all-time record for a West End musical, and causing a local wit to refer to the long-serving cast as ''Black-eyed Susannah and the elders.'' It was subsequently played throughout the English-speaking theatre world, surfacing in Australia in 1867 and appearing on Broadway later the same year with Kate Ranoe (William), Mark Smith (Crosstree) and Mary Gannon (Susan) featured, and J C Williamson in the small role of Shaun O'Ploughshare. After the first night, most of the songs were cut because the performers couldn't sing them, and Lester Wallack removed the burlesque after just two weeks. However, Broadway saw the piece again in 1869 in an ''americanized version'' as *Black-Eyed Susing, or The Leetle Bill Which Was Taken Up* (Fifth Avenue Theater 21 June), with Stuart Robson starring as Crosstree to the Susan of Mary Cary, again in 1870 with Robson and Lina Edwin, and in 1876 with Nat Goodwin and Minnie Palmer.

In London, it was revived first at the Royalty, in 1870, as *Black-Eyed Susan (Encored),* and later in an expanded shape and a spectacular production, with the favorite songs supplemented by new ones by Alfred Lee, the composer of ''Champagne Charlie,'' at the Alhambra under the management of William Holland (2 August 1884).

Australia: Haymarket Theatre, Melbourne 9 September 1867; USA: Wallack's Theater *The Latest Edition of Black-Eyed Susan* 25 September 1867

THE BLACK PRINCE Opéra-bouffe in 3 acts by H B Farnie. Music taken from the works of Charles Lecocq and others. St James's Theatre, London, 24 October 1874.

Lecocq protested in print when this show was announced: ''This is the only information I have ever received of having composed a work under that title.'' In fact, in a period when Lecocq's name was a sure draw and his output limited, the London publishers J B Cramer and their in-house writer H B Farnie had taken it on themselves to compile this piece from a libretto carpentered together from three uncredited French plays (one of which was apparently Labiche and Delacour's *Le Voyage en Chine*) and music taken from some of the composer's one-act opérettes, topped up with pieces by Olivier Métra, Léon Roques and others. The program admitted discreetly that ''the comedy is founded on a piece by MM Labiche and Delacour and the music has been selected from works of Lecocq unrepresented in England.''

Following similar depredations practiced by London managers on Hervé's *Les Chevaliers de la table ronde* and Offenbach's *Vert-Vert, The Black Prince,* in spite of a short run, focused attention on the unsatisfactory position in existence regarding authors' rights and copyright. In spite of a cast headed by Selina Dolaro, John Rouse and Nellie Bromley, and a featured spot for Mr E W Latham, ''the champion skater'' in a Skaters' Fête scene in the Isle of Wight, *The Black Prince* was a salutory flop.

THE BLACK RIDER, the Casting of the Magic Bullets By William S[eward] Burroughs based on *Der*

Freischütz by Friedrich Laun and Johann August Apel. Music and lyrics by Tom Waits. Thalia Theater, Hamburg, 31 March 1990.

In the last years of his life, American writer William Burroughs (1914–1997) shelved the attention-grabbing themes of drugs, sadism and homosexuality which had made his name known (*Junkie, The Naked Lunch,* etc) many years before to produce a slightly off-center musical-stage version of the old German legend of *Der Freischütz*. The story of the marksman to whom the devil gave seven bullets, six of which would hit their target infallibly, the seventh to go where the devil decreed, had been famously brought to the musical stage in Kind and Weber's important and enduring opera of 1821, but *The Black Rider,* which ''framed'' the tale in a kind of *Cabinet of Dr Caligari* setting of darkness and insanity, aspired to be a *Freischütz* for the 1970s or 1980s. In this version, which swapped the original happy ending for a ''modern'' deadly one, the central character was the diabolical creature of the title, manipulating the people of the story to his whim. Here, when the young Wilhelm barters his soul to the ''black rider'' in exchange for the magic bullets which will allow him to win the shooting contest and the hand of his Käthchen, the devil turns his final bullet on Käthchen. She dies and Wilhelm ends his days in a madhouse.

American rock 'n' roll musican Tom Waits (previously the composer of a Chicago musical, *Frank's Wild Years)* provided a discreetly rattly score of a dozen numbers, full of reminiscences of that period, from cowboy tunes to cabaret numbers to bits of Broadway and back, as accompaniment.

The original production (ad Wilhelm Wiens), mounted at Hamburg's Thalia-Theater by Robert Wilson, featured Annette Paulmann (Käthchen), Dominique Horwitz (Pegleg/Stelzfuss, ie, the black rider), Stefan Kurt (Wilhelm) and Susi Eisenkolb (Bridesmaid) amongst its cast. Its director/designer's habitual O'Horganesque trendiness in staging proved effective as allied to the material, and the musical—of which little had been expected, in spite of the showy names attached to it—turned out a surprise triumph. Following its first run, *The Black Rider* went on to be seen in the Vienna Festival, and in a guest week in Paris (with French surtitles), and it subsequently returned to Hamburg for several further seasons before going on to be seen, often in gimmicky productions with gimmicky points to make, in regional theatres all around Germany. The Thalia company later took their production of the show to other venues including Hong Kong (16 Feb 1998), and *The Black Rider* had its first production outside Germany in Denmark in 1999 (Betty Nansen Theater 16 December).

Austria: Messepalast 12 June 1990; France: Théâtre du Châtelet (Ger) 8 October 1990

Recording: composer (Island)

A BLACK SHEEP, and How It Came out in the Wash Musical comedy in 3 acts by Charles Hoyt. Music by Richard Stahl, Hoyt, William Devere, Otis Harlan, Harry Conor, Kelly and others. [Music selected and arranged by Percy Gaunt.] Academy of Music, Buffalo, NY, 10 September 1894; Hoyt's Theater, New York, 6 January 1896.

One of Hoyt's successful comedies with songs strewn about here and there, this one allowed its broadly comic story about likeable drunken layabout, ''Hot Stuff'' Mudd (Otis Harlan), and an eccentric inheritance to run on to its predictable happy ending, whilst most of the musical numbers were provided by the members of a variety troupe providentially visiting the scene of the second-act action. These ranged from Felix McGlennon's *Shop Girl* hit, ''Her Golden Hair Was Hanging Down Her Back'' and *Robin Hood*'s Armourer's Song to a quadrille arranged on the melodies from *Ruddigore.* Comedian William Devere and vocalist Belle Black headed the support cast.

Its lively, unselfconscious mixture of fun and music kept the young Julian Mitchell's staging on the road for a number of years, including a stay on Broadway of a decidedly good 144 performances.

A silent film version featured Harlan in its central role.

Film: (silent) Selig 1915

BLAHA, Lujza [née Reindl-Várai, aka KÖLESI, Lujza, SOLDOSNÉ, Lujza] (b Rimaszombat (Gömör), 8 September 1850; d Budapest, 18 January 1926). The outstanding leading lady of the Hungarian stage during her lifetime, Blaha became, in a career of nearly half a century, a sufficiently great figure in Hungary to have one of the principal squares of Budapest named in her honor, and her 50th birthday made a national holiday.

Natural daughter of an actor and an actress, and herself a performer from her childhood, Blaha—at the time the wife of conductor János Blaha—made starring appearances as a teenager in comedy and opéra-bouffe in the Hungarian provinces, appearing at Nagyvárad as Offenbach's Helene at the age of 18 and at Debrecen in the same role at 19. Widowed in 1870, she joined the staff of the Nemzeti Színház in Pest in 1871, making her debut there in the musical comedy *Tündérlak Magyarországon* (Marcsa) and playing, during her four years with the company, in comedy and in a range of musical pieces including Auber's *Le Domino noir* (Angelo) and as Boulotte in *Barbe-bleue* (12 April 1873).

In 1875 she began both a four-year period as the wife of landowner Sándor Soldos (she was billed during this time as Soldosné), and a much longer association—some 26 years—with the newly built Népszínház, the theatre which would quickly become the most important musical house in Budapest. Amongst the early musical pieces in which she played there were *Le Voyage de MM Dunanan* (Pamela), *La Rose de Saint-Flour, La Fille de Madame Angot* (Clairette), the celebrated Hungarian play *A falu rossza,* in which she appeared as the singing Rózsi Finum, *La Boulangère* (Margot), *Le Canard à trois becs* (Margit), *Die schöne Galathée* and *La Princesse de Trébizonde.* She made a fine success as Fanchette in Genée's *Der Seekadett;* starred in another breeches role in Lecocq's *Kosiki,* once more as Boulotte; took the title role of *La Marjolaine* and then, having made an enormous hit in the play *A sárga csikó,* scored another when she succeeded to the role of Serpolette in *Les Cloches de Corneville.* She notched up a further pair of major successes when she appeared as Lecocq's *Le Petit Duc* and as Zsófi Tőrők in the famous play *A piros bugyelláris* in successive productions. In 1879 she played the title roles of Lecocq's *La Camargo* and Offenbach's *Madame Favart,* and (now divorced, and once again Blaháné) of the local version of Suppé's *Boccaccio,* a role which gave her one of the biggest musical successes of her career.

In 1880 she played in an early Hungarian operett success, Ferenc Puks's *Titilla hadnagy* (Lieutenant Petittrouvaille) but, with other members of the company taking more and more of the operettic roles, the theatre's star now picked and chose her parts, many of which were in the non-musical area of the Népszínház repertoire. As she became, in real life, the Baroness Ödön Splényi (without changing her stage name), she now went only for the best and most suitable musical parts, such as Bettina in *La Mascotte* (1881), a travesty Symon in *Der Bettelstudent* (1883), Hanka in the Hungarian play with music *A tot leány* and Molly in *Der arme Jonathan* (1890), whilst the theatre's newer musical stars, Aranka Hegyi and Ilka Pálmay, assured the casting of many of the other pieces. In 1883 the Népszínház company visited Vienna and Theater an der Wien audiences saw Blaha's versions of Serpolette, Symon and Bettina.

If her musical appearances were now less numerous, she did, however, take part in a number of the rising Hungarian-written and -composed operetts mounted at the Népszínház, starring as the Vicomte de Letorrières in József Konti's *Az eleven ördög* (1885), in *Királyfogás* (1886, Fjóra), as the titular "gamin de Paris" in *A suhanc* (1888), in Sztojanovits's Turandot musical *Peking rózsája* (1888), Erkel's *A kassai dáak* (1890), Szabados's Labiche musical *Az előo és a második* (1892) and *Talmi hercegnő* (1898) among a wide-ranging straight and musical repertoire. In her later career, she appeared only occasionally on the musical stage but, at the age of 58, she memorably created the title role of Raoul Mader's musical version of Csiky's play *Nagymama* (Countess Szerémy), a role which she later repeated on film.

In 1921 Budapest's 11-year-old Revü-Színhaz was renamed the Lujza Blaha Színhaz and was opened with a Lujza Blaha overture composed for the occasion by Izsó Barna. Barna subsequently wrote the score for a 1926 musical based on her life (lib: Ede Sas), produced at the Budapesti Színház (25 June). A second Budapest theatre bearing her name operated between 1954 and 1960.

Literature: Verő, G: *Lujza Blaha és a Népszínház* (Franklin-Társulat kiádas, Budapest, 1926), *Blaha Lujza naplója [The Diary of Lujza Blaha]* (Gondolat, Budapest, 1987)

BLANCHE, Ada [ADAMS, Ada Cecilia Blanche] (b Brixton, London, 16 July 1863; d London, 1 January 1953).

The daughter of music-hall manager Sam Adams (b Cannon Park, Herts, 25 October 1837; d London, 1 June 1893) and his well-known singer-actress wife "Cicely Nott" (née Sarah Ann Harris, b Gosport, ?1832; d Nunhead, 3 January 1900), Miss Blanche first went on the stage at the Adelphi, under Chatterton, as a young teenager in a children's pantomime (Demon Envy in *Little Goody Two-Shoes,* 1876). She played juvenile roles in plays, graduated to young adult parts, mostly in plays and in pantomimes, and made her first important musical-theatre appearance touring as Fiametta to the Peronella of her mother, in Emily Soldene's production of *Boccaccio* (1882). She toured with Lila Clay's all-women company (Sophie Syntax in *Adamless Eden,* May Filbert in *Posterity,* etc), with the Holmes British Burlesque Company in America and, from 1886, worked at the Gaiety Theatre as a supporting player and understudy to Nellie Farren in burlesque (Boatswain in *Monte Cristo Jr* 1886, Ernest in *Miss Esmeralda* 1887, etc). She subsequently played Farren's roles in these pieces on tour. In the years that followed, she found her most significant success as an outstanding and long-serving pantomime principal boy at the Theatre Royal, Drury Lane, on the road in the title role of the long-touring English version of Serpette's *La Demoiselle du téléphone* (1897–1900) and, latterly, in character roles in musical comedy. In her forties and fifties she created the heavy-lady comedy roles of Mrs Smith in *The Arcadians* (1909), Mitsu in *The Mousme* (1911), Mrs Baxter Browne in *The Pearl Girl* (1913) and Lady Elizabeth Weston in *The Rebel Maid* (1921), all under the management of her brother-in-law, Robert Courtneidge.

Of her three actress sisters, **Addie BLANCHE** [Adelaide Emily ADAMS] (b Kennington Park, 21 July 1870; d Ryde, Isle of Wight, 30 November 1945) also appeared successfully in Gaiety burlesque. She was the wife of William Peacock, sometime managing director of the Harrogate Opera House, and the mother of **Marie BLANCHE** [Marie Adelaide PEACOCK] (b Scarborough, 5 November 1891), who appeared prominently in the West-End musicals *Princess Caprice* (1912, Anna), *The Joy Ride Lady* (1914, Fifi), *High Jinks* (1916, Mrs Thorne), *Carminetta* (1917, Lady Susan), *Telling the Tale* (1918, Sidonie de Matisse), *His Little Widows* (1919, Blanche) and *Cherry* (1920, Cherry Burleigh). Another sister, **Rosie NOTT** [Rosaline May ADAMS] (b Islington, 25 July 1868; d Marylebone, August 1914), who played in her young years as Rosaline Blanche, was the first wife of Robert Courtneidge and the mother of Cicely Courtneidge. The fourth sister, **Edith BLANCHE** [Edith Maude ADAMS] (b Islington, 19 April 1865; d Harrogate, 17 January 1929), was seen in pantomime, drama and intermittently in the musical theatre (Lena in *The Gay Grisette,* etc).

The sole brother of the family, **Bert ADAMS** [Albert George Downs ADAMS] (b Islington, 11 December 1866; d Liverpool, 17 April 1904) worked as a theatrical manager in Manchester and Liverpool.

LA BLANCHISSEUSE DE BERG-OP-ZOOM Opérette in 3 acts by Henri Chivot and Alfred Duru. Music by Léon Vasseur. Théâtre des Folies-Dramatiques, Paris, 27 January 1875.

Following his great success with *La Timbale d'argent* and a less happy experience with *La Famille Trouillat,* Vasseur submitted the pretty *La Blanchisseuse de Berg-op-Zoom* at the Folies-Dramatiques. Chivot and Duru's tale told of the marriage of Albert van der Graff, the brewer, and Guillemine, the laundress, imposed on them by her fisherman father, Peterboom, when he catches the lad climbing up to her bedroom window after dark. The marriage, however, has unexpected consequences. Once upon a time young van der Graff seduced the pretty wife of an old innkeeper, van der Pruth and now that the lad is married his victim is out for revenge. Since there is little hope of his luring away the new wife in person, he calls in the aid of the very personable young Jockel. But the trick backfires. The resulting jealousy is all that is needed to make the brewer see the advantages of his enforced wife, and the final result is that the newlyweds realize that their marriage is a good idea after all.

With Anna van Ghell in its title role, supported by Luco, Ange Milher as the Machiavellian innkeeper, Mario Widmer, Mlle Tassily and Vavasseur, the piece was given some 50 performances in Paris, and it was picked up for production at Vienna's Theater an der Wien (ad and add mus Julius Hopp) later the same year. Lori Stubel played the Wäschermädchen of the title in a cast which included Jani Szika (Albert) and top comics Alexander Girardi (Jockel) and Felix Schweighofer (van der Pruth) through 17 performances. This was apparently sufficient for it to be tried in Germany the following year with reasonably good results.

Plate 38. **Karl Blasel.** *Still near the beginning of his famously long career on the Viennese musical stage, Blasel appeared as King Bobèche in Offenbach's* Blaubart.

Austria: Theater an der Wien *Die Perle der Wäscherinnin* 14 November 1875; Germany: Woltersdorff-Theater *La Perle des blanchisseuses* February 1876

BLASEL, Karl (b Vienna, 16 October 1831; d Vienna, 16 June 1922).

Karl Blasel lived what was probably the most remarkable career in the history of the musical theatre. He created more than a hundred musical theatre roles, and the Viennese versions of an uncountable number more, over a period of 80 years on the stage and some 60 spent at the two most important houses of the German-speaking musical theatre which, for a part of that time, also meant of the world.

Blasel began his career as a child, appearing at the Hofoper as one of the animals in *Die Zauberflöte,* and at the age of 18 he joined the chorus at the Laibacher Theater. By 1863, established as a comedian, he joined the company at the Theater an der Wien and there began a career that would eventually make him into the "grand

and great old man of Viennese comics.'' He appeared early on as Menelaos, Bobèche and Le Menu (1866, *Die Schäfer*), teamed with Matthias Rott as the gens d'armes of *Genoveva von Brabant* (1868) and played Urban (*Das Donauweibchen*), Pagatl (1866, *Prinzessin Hirschkuh*) and many other such roles in local pieces before he left the Theater an der Wien, in 1869, for the Carltheater.

There, in the 1870s and 1880s, he created the Viennese versions of more of Offenbach's principal comic roles (Prince Paul, Cornarino, Ficus in *Tulipatan,* the dance-master Baladon in *Kakadu,* Cabriolo, Kaschmyr in *Schneeball,* Jolicoeur in *Fleurette,* Vertpanné in *Trombal-ca-zar,* Persiflage in *Schönröschen,* Delicat to the Flammèche of Matras in *Margot die Millionbäckerin,* etc) and appeared in reprises of others of the composer's works (Bobinet, Fortunio, Jupiter, Mosthaber in *Hanni weint,* in travesty as Madame Madou in *Die Damen der Halle,* Popelinot in *Der Regimentszauberer,* etc) as well as in a long list of other French opérettes (Cucurbitus in *Der Flötenspieler von Rom,* Alexibus XXIV in Delibes' *Confusius IX,* Anatol in *Hundert Jungfrauen,* Boléro in *Giroflé-Girofla,* Trénitz in *Madame Angots Tochter,* Baron de Cotignac in Coedès's *Die schöne Bourbonnaise,* Montefiasco in *Graziella,* Bidard in *Der Kohlenhändler von Paris,* Briolet in *Jeanne, Jeannette, Jeanneton,* Beaupersil in *Niniche,* Job in *Papas Frau,* Picasso in *Der grosse Casimir,* Palamède in *La Marjolaine,* Merimac in *Olivette,* etc). He also played Passepartout in the Carltheater's long-running adaptation of Verne and d'Ennery's *Reise um die Erde in 80 Tagen.*

Simultaneously, he created and/or played the lead comedy roles of a number of the earliest Viennese works of the modern tradition, including *Wein, Weib, Gesang* (Mehlthau), Suppé's short-lived *Isabella* (1869, Don Marullo Cariazzo de los Crocodilos), *Der Herr von Papillon* (von Trommetron), Suppé's *Die Jungfrau von Dragant* (1870, Ritter Mordigall) and Brandl's extremely popular *Des Löwen Erwachen* (1872, Placide) and *Cassis Pascha* (1874), Zaytz's *Mannschaft am Bord* (Jean), Conradin's *Flodoardo Wuprahall* (Schmafukerle), and Suppé's *Die Frau Meisterin* (1874, Longinus), *Leichte Kavallerie* (Bums) and *Zehn Mädchen und kein Mann* (Agamemnon). He also created the principal comedy roles in Suppé's major Operetten—war-correspondent-by-accident Julian von Golz in *Fatinitza* (1876), Muzerelli in *Der Teufel auf Erden,* the goofy Lambertuccio in *Boccaccio* (1879), Don Pomponio di San Sebastian in *Donna Juanita* (1880), Baron Rompinelle, Governor of Martinique, in *Der Gaskogner* (1881) and Fanfani Pasha in *Die Afrikareise* (1883)—as well as in such other full-sized Viennese pieces as Strauss's *Prinz Methusalem* (Mandelbaum), *Die Mormonen* (the police chief), Zeller's *Die Carbonari* (1880, Conte Seneca da Ruffoli), *Der Kukuk* (Rastagnol) and Genée's *Nisida* (1880, Don Leonida Palestro) and *Rosina* (1881, Gaspard).

In 1883 Blasel returned to the Theater an der Wien company where, over the next two years, he was seen as Fanfani Pasha in *Die Afrikareise,* as Don Pomponio, Cabriolo, as the Chevalier des Martines in *Der Marquis von Rivoli,* Baron Foret de Lorges in *Der schöne Nikolaus,* Heidekrug, Sparacani in Czibulka's *Pfingsten in Florenz,* Ben-Selim in *Zwillinge* and Griffardin in *Gillette de Narbonne* before, in 1886, he moved on again, this time to take up the position of director of the Theater in der Josefstadt. Three years later, he took over control of the Carltheater where, during six years in command, he continued to perform in his old roles (Bobinet in *Pariser Leben,* Cabriolo, Jupiter, Lambertuccio, Menelaos, etc) whilst adding a whole list of new ones—Bob (otherwise Cadeau) in *Erminy,* Syfar in *Die Uhlanen,* Jérome Pasquille in *Die Kätzchen,* Pontarcy in *Das Fräulein von Telephone,* Cyprian Boxtel in *Lachende Erben,* Kilian in *Edelweiss,* Prosper Giraud in *Le Pays d'or,* Wassermann in Jakobowski's *Die Brilliantenkönigin,* Porfirio Karka in *Die Königin von Gamara,* Marchese Tortoloni in *Lady Charlatan,* Birnhuber in *Coeur d'ange,* Toulouse in *Les Forains* (*Olympia*), Pan Gabriel Ostrogski in *Die Lachtaube,* Pinsonnet in *Le Voyage de Suzette,* Hadji-Chlasa Pascha in *Die Lieder des Mirza Schaffys,* etc—in a program of productions in which musical pieces were heavily featured.

Blasel gave up the management of the Carltheater to Franz Jauner in 1895, but he stayed on briefly at the Carltheater as a performer (Tomasso Stirio in *Das Modell, Eine tolle Nacht,* Biseaux in *Der kleine Duckmauser,* etc) before returning once more to the Theater an der Wien for a further long series of new roles beginning with that of Baptiste in Verő's *Der Löwenjäger* (October 1896) and including the detective Niki in Millöcker's *Nordlicht,* Louis Brebillant in Weinberger's *Der Schmetterling,* Graf Wenzel von Dubrowa in *Die Schwalben* (1897), Pampinelli in *L'Amour mouillé* (*Das verregnete Amor*), Bonhomme in Strauss's *Die Göttin der Vernunft,* John James Pickleton, New Orleans umbrella merchant, in *Die Blumen-Mary* and Mats the Syndic in the German version of Gilbert's *His Excellency* (*Der Herr Gouverneur,* 1897). He had one of his best new roles for some time as Beaubuisson in Heuberger's version of the farcical *Pink Dominos* tale, *Der Opernball* (1898), and introduced roles in *Die Küchen-Komtesse* (Peter Knapp), *Der Dreibund* (Holger), *Der Blondin von Namur* (Duke of Melphi), *Fräulein Hexe* (Gottlieb Berger), Johann Strauss III's shortlived *Katze und Maus* (Gustav), *Ihre Excellenz* (Dupiton), *Gräfin Kuni,* the local adaptation of *A Runaway Girl* (Jaromir Spindel) and *Fräulein Präsident* (Graf Chapuzot). On his seventieth birthday, he appeared as Menelaos to the schöne Helena of Julie Kopácsi-Karczag.

Another switch then took him back to the Carltheater once again to create—at what would have been a very late stage in anyone else's career—some of his most splendid roles. He was cast as Graf Balduin in the Reinhardt hit *Das süsse Mädel* (1901) and Glöppler in Lehár's triumphant *Der Rastelbinder* (1902), introduced Vienna to old MacSherry in *Madame Sherry* (1903), and created the parts of Hagen in Oscar Straus's burlesque of Wagner, *Die lustigen Nibelungen* (1904), Daszewski in *Die Schützenliesel* (1906) and Tobias Blank in *Künstlerblut* (1906), both of the last two alongside Girardi, as well as the comical King Joachim XIII in *Ein Walzertraum* (1907), the bemused papa, Pieter te Bakkenskijl, in *Die geschiedene Frau* (1908) and the old landowner Dragotin in *Zigeunerliebe* (1910). He was Pomarel, the husband of the lady who is supposed to be *Die keusche Susanne* (1911), and took the cameo part of lay brother Mattheus who unravels the plot of *Der liebe Augustin* (1912), whilst also repeating his Beaubuisson, Sindulfo (*Gasparone*), Izzet Pascha (*Fatinitza*), Don Pomponio and Lambertuccio and creating further roles in *Das gewisse Etwas* (Philidore Taponet), *Das Baby* (Christian Schwabach), *Der liebe Schatz* (Tom Blackmayer), *Der Glücklichste* (Derim Khan), *Das Marktkind* (Sebastian Siebert), *Der Mameluck* (Kanno), *Der Göttergatte* (Maenandros), the highly successful *Das Veilchenmädel* (Graf Willy Sickendorff), *'s Zuckersgoscherl* (Kreuzschnabel), *Der Schätzmeister* (Clearing), *Der Schnurrbart* (Bela von Kozary), *Kaisermanöver* (Li-hu-Schwappl), *Der Polizeichef* (Spadillo), *Die Bonbonniere* (Max Wohlmann), *Krieg im Frieden* (Henkel), *Der Elektriker* (Count Lamonde), *Hugdietrichs Brautfahrt* (King Ladislas), *Mutzi* (Dr Stroh), *Der selige Vincenz* (Kajak), *Der Rosenjungling, Der schwarze Tenor* (Leslo), *Johann der zweite* (Prosper), *Der Glücksnarr* (King Balduin), Oscar Straus's *Didi* (Belivon), *Das Puppenmädel* (Buffon), *Majestät Mimi* (Aladrio), *Alt-Wien* (Graf Leopold) and the Viennese version of *A kis Gróf* (*Susi,* Dr Theophrastus Haring). In a special performance given to mark his 60 years in the business, he appeared as Choufleuri and as Fancourt Babberley in *Charley's Aunt* (1909) at the age of 78.

In 1913 he ceased to be a member of the Carltheater company, but he returned there as a guest to play in *Der erste Küss* (King Erwin XXX), Hopp's *Zwei Mann von Hess* and Ziehrer's *Fürst Casimir* (George Washington Didfeller). On 28 June 1920 he took part in the 500th performance of *Der Rastelbinder* and, shortly before his death, at the age of 90, he appeared in *Salon Pitzelberger* and in his roles—which he had never relinquished—in *Der Rastelbinder* and *Die Schützenliesel.*

His wife **Johanna Blasel** (1840–1910) played small roles in plays and step-outs in musicals at the Carltheater from 1870, during her husband's time there, being occasionally featured (Javotte in *Angot,* Iwan in *Fatinitza,* Toinon in *Prinz Conti*), whilst their son **Leopold Blasel** (1866–1931) worked with his father in the management of his two theatres.

DIE BLAUE MAZUR Operette in 2 acts (3 scenes) by Leo Stein and Bela Jenbach. Music by Franz Lehár. Theater an der Wien, Vienna, 28 May 1920.

One of Lehár's last ventures into the light and sprightly comical musical play before setting off into the romantic unhappy-end pieces of his later years, *Die blaue Mazur* was written to a featherweight libretto. It told of how the heroine Blanka von Lossin (Betty Fischer), having wed the playboy aristocrat, Count Juljan Olinski (Hubert Marischka), has still to be convinced that he has left and will continue to leave his gallivanting past behind him. An unfortunate overheard comment about "lost liberty" at the wedding reception leads to Olinski finding himself alone on his wedding night as Blanka flees to the home of old Baron von Reiger (Emil Guttmann) and his inseparable and aged bachelor friends (Josef Hauschultz, Karl Tuschl) until peace is made. The Theater an der Wien's leading romantic players were backed by their regular light comic partners, Ernst Tautenhayn as Adolar von Sprintz, a model young man with a double life, and Luise Kartousch as Gretl Aigner of the ballet, who belongs to the half of that life that Adolar's uncle von Reiger knows nothing about.

Die blaue Mazur began as it went on, with one attractively dancing Lehár melody following another from the polonaise of the opening, through the mazurka and waltz rhythms of the principal pair's first duet ("Komm' ich sag' dir was ins Ohr"), the march septet which introduced the soubrets, Juljan's waltz-song ("Ich darf nur Eine lieben") and Blanka's leap back into mazurka strains for the first act finale. The second act opened with a gavotte trio, moved on to a madrigal quintet and wound up with Blanka in full waltz-time ("Lockend erwartet mich das Leben"), whilst the final scene began with two waltz duos and a third waltz for the soubrette before the two most popular pieces of the score, Blanka and Julian's title mazurka ("Tanzt der Pole die Mazur") and the polka duo for Adolar and Grete ("Mäderl, mein süsses Grederl"), led up to the last finale with its all-round reassurances of Julian's intent to settle down.

Die blaue Mazur was a first-rate hit in Vienna. It zoomed past its 200th consecutive performance on 11 January 1921 and held the boards right through until 28 April. By the time it had played out a ration of matinées and odd performances in the Lehár season that ended 1922, it had totted up 333 performances at the Theater an der Wien. Elsewhere, however, it proved rather less of a

Plate 39. **Bless the Bride.** *''I Was Never Kissed Before . . .'': Jan Hartley-Morris (Lucy Willow) and Philip Creasy (Pierre) are overspied by the jealous Michelle Todd (Suzanne) (Northcott Theatre, Exeter).*

favorite. Having been given in Berlin with Vera Schwarz starred in 1921, it went down as one of the less popular of Lehár's works in the German regions, and the Budapest production of *Kék mazur* (ad István Zágon) at the Király Színház went no further towards evoking the kind of enthusiasm that the Vienna one had. The show took its time to get to Britain, where a 1927 production by James White at Daly's Theatre (ad Monckton Hoffe, Harry Graham, add songs Herman Darewski), starring Gladys Moncrieff, lasted only 140 performances, and longer still to arrive in France (ad Marcel Dunan) where, with Pépa Bonafé as Blanche de Raisme and the rest of the cast and action similarly Gallicized, it had an unmemorable season under the management of Jean Casanova at the Ba-ta-clan two years later.

Germany: Metropoltheater 27 March 1921; Hungary: Király Színház *Kék mazur* 13 May 1921; UK: Daly's Theatre *The Blue Mazurka* 19 February 1927; France: Théâtre Ba-ta-clan *La Mazourka bleue* 8 February 1929

Recording: selection in Italian (EDM)

BLESS THE BRIDE Musical show in 2 acts by A P Herbert. Music by Vivian Ellis. Adelphi Theatre, London, 26 April 1947.

Following the failure of *Big Ben,* C B Cochran mounted a second and much more successful piece by the same team of Ellis and Herbert. Eschewing, this time, the political and the purposeful, *Bless the Bride* followed instead the tradition of the romantic comic opera in its period tale of Lucy Willow (Lizbeth Webb) who runs away with a romantic Frenchman (Georges Guétary) on her wedding day, loses him to the wars, and then finds him again just when she is about to marry her original unfortunate Englishman (Brian Reece). The heart of Herbert's charmingly unpretentious book came in the second-act antics of the bride's family, pursuing their improper daughter through devastatingly un-English France, while Ellis's score, in the happiest comic opera vein, ranged through all three acts with equal felicity, from the delicious waltzing melody of the first act trio, ''I Was Never Kissed Before,'' via the hero's ringing set piece ''Ma Belle Marguerite'' and his rhapsodic ''A Table for Two,'' to the jilted groom's touching if comic ''My Big Moment'' and the humorous family ensemble ''The Englishman.'' The most memorable moment of the score, however, came in the idyllic duo ''This is my Lovely Day'' delivered by the beautiful young soprano and the darkly handsome Egypto-Frenchman, each of whom made themselves a name in these roles.

Bless the Bride opened in London in the same week that the much-publicized *Oklahoma!* bowed at the Theatre Royal, Drury Lane, and the two, which shared a certain old-fashioned style and sentimentality but otherwise formed a lively contrast, remained, with *Annie Get Your Gun,* at the top of the town's musical entertainments for the next two years. However, after 886 performances Cochran decided to close *Bless the Bride* in order to free the Adelphi Theatre for his next Herbert/Ellis musical, *Tough at the Top.* It was a decision which proved a singular error of judgment, as there had been months or even years of life still in the earlier production and the new show failed.

Bless the Bride proved a great favorite on the provincial circuits for many years, and a top-class revival at Exeter's Northcott Theatre in 1985 with Jan Hartley-Morris in the role of Lucy prompted a London revival at Sadler's Wells Theatre in 1987 (11 August). Miss Hartley starred again, alongside Frenchman Bernard Alane, but the otherwise ill-cast and unfortunately cut version was not a success and a West End transfer did not eventuate. *Bless the Bride* surfaced once again in London (June 1999), at the same King's Head Theatre Club which had done such magnificent service to Ellis's works over the years, but here again it was played in an ''improved'' version (ad Martin Charnin). Tiffany Edwards and Guillaume Tobo featured for a short season.

Recordings: original cast (WRC, Columbia, AEI), selection (MFP), etc

BLITZ! Musical play in 2 acts by Lionel Bart. Adelphi Theatre, London, 8 May 1962.

A panoramic spectacular of wartime London, Lionel Bart's successor to *Oliver!* lacked much of the heart of its famous predecessor, but had many more opportunities for stage display. A Cohens-and-Kellys tale of racial and family rivalry played out under Hitler's bombs on a huge and magnificent physical production, it nevertheless produced some attractive musical numbers ranging from the lively wartime pastiche "Who's That Geezer Hitler?" to a pair of thoughtfully characterized pieces for the Jewish mother of the tale (Amelia Bayntun) ("Be What You Want To Be," "So Tell Me") and a diffident little love song called "I Want To Whisper Something" for the young man of the piece. The show's visual values accounted for much of the 16-month (568 performances) run which Donald Albery's production achieved.

A 1990 production by the National Youth Theatre, seen at the West End's Playhouse Theatre, prompted a further production by Theatre North which was subsequently toured through Britain in 1991.

Recording: original cast (HMV)

EIN BLITZMÄDEL Posse mit Gesang in 4 acts by Karl Costa. Music by Carl Millöcker. Theater an der Wien, Vienna, 4 February 1877.

One of the most successful of the musical comedies written by the team of Costa and Millöcker—the following year *Ihr Korporal* would bring them another long-lived success—*Ein Blitzmädel* existed around its star part, a veritable role à tiroirs which, surprisingly enough, was introduced not by a Gallmeyer or a Geistinger but by Frln C Bendel as her debut role at the Theater an der Wien.

The star played Caroline, a telegraph operator who, in the course of her daily work, is required to send out a dispatch by which she discovers that beastly Baron István Inhass (Heinrich Thalboth) is plotting to get his protégé a job that she wants her lawyer boyfriend, Rudolf Kern (Herr Eichheim), to have. To expose this nepotism, and to win her point, the job and the resultant setting of her wedding date, Caroline goes out into the world in a whole series of disguises—a French marquise, a nun, a Spanish dancer, an anarchist—accompanied by her friend, the tenor singer Brüller (Felix Schweighofer, variously as an old marquis, a toreador, a student, etc), gamboling through four acts of impersonations, antics, songs and dances from "Im Telegrafenbureau" to "Für den guten Zweck," "Der Balletmeister und seine Nichte" and "Bruder Studio" until they have visited and enlightened all the functionaries who stand to lose by the Baron's plan. The result is, of course, a happy ending. Millöcker provided a happily waltzing score for the piece which was, nevertheless, largely secondary to the comical antics of the show's plot and action.

Produced in Vienna under the management of Maximilian Steiner, the show was played 45 times in two seasons, was quickly taken up on other German-language stages, and was seen again in Vienna for no fewer than 39 successive nights at the Theater in der Josefstadt in 1882–83 (9 December). The year after its Vienna opening, it was already on the program of New York's Germania Theater with Julie Catenhausen in the principal female role, and that city got repeated revivals thereafter, notably at the Thalia Theater in 1885, the Amberg Theater (27 September 1890) with Paula Loewe starred, and again in the repertoire of the famous Viennese star Felix Schweighofer who played his original role of Brüller to the Caroline of Anna Leonardi in the 1899–1900 season. In 1909 the Irving Place Theater played it yet again (5 October), as *The Lightning Girl,* with Hedwig Richard starred.

An Hungarian version (ad Antal Bánfalvy) was first produced in 1884 and the original version reappeared yet again in Vienna at the Carltheater in May 1892 and, in 1916, at the Wiener Bürgertheater.

USA: Germania Theater 20 April 1878; Hungary: Budai Színkör *A tüzröl pattant leány* 3 July 1884

BLITZSTEIN, Marc (b Philadelphia, 5 March 1905; d Fort-de-France, Martinique, 22 January 1964). Striving composer who finally made his mark on the musical theatre with his one attempt at translation.

Blitzstein studied music in New York and Berlin and began his career as a composer writing contemporary music. He placed a short operetta, *Triple Sec,* in *The Garrick Gaieties* but, having failed to break through in either serious or light music, he decided to make his music an adjunct to left-wing political propaganda. The musical play *The Cradle Will Rock,* for which he wrote book, lyrics and music, won more attention for the politically based fuss which surrounded it than for its merits, and a 1937 radio musical *I've Got the Tune,* and a five-performance tryout *No for an Answer* followed in the same vein with conspicuous lack of success.

After the war, he composed the music for a "socially conscious" ballet *The Guests,* and for a musical stage adaptation of Lillian Hellman's play *The Little Foxes,* called *Regina,* which played 56 performances on Broadway. The latter piece subsequently found itself an occasional home in variously hacked-about versions in opera houses. However, Blitzstein ultimately earned himself recognition in the theatre not as a composer but as an adapter, when he provided a new English-language libretto for *Die Dreigroschenoper* (Brandeis University Music Festival, Waltham, Mass 14 June 1952). During a long subsequent off-Broadway run, this version was ultimately responsible for arousing interest in Hauptmann, Brecht and Weill's piece in America.

Further attempts at a Broadway musical with *Reuben, Reuben,* which closed without reaching New York, and an adaptation of Sean O'Casey's *Juno and the Paycock,* under the title *Juno,* which folded in 16 performances, proved to have no more appeal than his earlier pieces. His final contribution to the New York stage was in the form of incidental songs to Hellman's play *Toys in the Attic* (Hudson Theater 25 February 1960).

Blitzstein was murdered in Martinique in 1964. A compilation show of his work was staged at the Provincetown Playhouse under the title *Blitzstein!* in 1966 (30 November, 7 performances).

1930 **Triple Sec** (Ronald Jeans) 1 act (in *Garrick Gaieties*) Guild Theater 4 June

1938 **The Cradle Will Rock** Windsor Theater 3 January

1941 **No for an Answer** Mecca Temple 5 January

1949 **Regina** 46th Street Theater 31 October

1952 **The Threepenny Opera** (*Die Dreigroschenoper*) new English version (Brandeis University Music Festival)

1955 **Reuben, Reuben** Shubert Theater, Boston 10 October

1959 **Juno** (Joseph Stein) Winter Garden Theater 9 March

Biography: Gordon, E: *Mark the Music: The Life and Work of Marc Blitzstein* (St Martin's Press, New York, 1975)

BLONDEL Musical in 2 acts by Tim Rice. Music by Stephen Oliver. Old Vic, London, 9 November 1983; Aldwych Theatre, 20 January 1984.

Originally conceived by its author as a small-scale piece on the lines of *Joseph and the Amazing Technicolor Dreamcoat,* in the early days of his collaboration with Andrew Lloyd Webber, *Blondel* was finally written nearly a decade later, in collaboration with operatic composer Stephen Oliver, and found itself, following Rice's spectacular run of West End success, mounted as a full-scale adult musical.

Blondel (Paul Nicholas) is a fairly hopeless pop-bard with dreams of stardom. When King Richard (Stephen Tate) gets imprisoned, however, he follows the history books and hurries off to Europe with his backing group, the Blondettes, to set royalty right as to what his horrible understudy of a brother is doing to England. On his way, he is tracked by an assassin (Chris Langham) hired by Prince John (David Burt) to stop him. But Blondel gets to Richard, gets him out and home, and even gets his singing stardom thanks to a jolly opportunist number claiming "I'm a Monarchist."

Some of the most enjoyable parts of the score were the narratives that linked the set-piece numbers, sung in cathedral harmonies by the harmony group Cantabile as they swung a Benedictus and hurried the tale along, whilst one lyric actually took the form of an acrostic on the name of Prime Minister Margaret Thatcher. Richard, in prison, bewailed his "Saladin Days" as John, on the other edge of the Continent hissed ambitiously "I Want To Be King," the hit man admitted "I'm an A double S,A,S,I,N" and an intrusive creature called Fiona (Sharon Lee Hill), a loud-mouthed serf and Blondel's girlfriend, popped irritatingly in and out of the mostly male show and sang a piece about "Running Back for More."

Blondel transferred from the Old Vic to the West End's Aldwych Theatre, but Cameron Mackintosh's production's run of 365 performances was a forced one and the show proved to have a limited future. *Blondel* did, however, resurface a dozen years later at Amstetten, Austria when Andreas Bieber appeared as Rice and Oliver's merry minstrel in the German language.

Blondel and/or King Richard have provided the substance for a number of other musical stage pieces, including an 18th-century comic opera *Richard Coeur de Lion* by Jean-Michel Sedaine and André Gretry (Théâtre Italien, Paris 21 October 1784), which was one of the outstanding successes of its time and is still occasionally played today. The Brough brothers brought out a *Richard Coeur de Lion, and The Knight of the Couchant Leopard*—a travesty of Sir Walter Scott's *The Talisman*—at the Theatre Royal, Drury Lane, in 1853 (mus arr T German Reed, 28 March), with Mr Yarnold playing Blondel as "the original minstrel boy" and singing "Gaily the Troubadour" in "lugubrious tones"; H J Byron launched his career as a writer of burlesque with a *King Richard of the Lionheart* at London's Strand Theatre in 1857 (23 November); John S Strachan's burlesque *Coeur de Lion (Revised and his enemies corrected),* with music selected and arranged by John Fitzgerald, was played at the Strand in 1870 (22 December); and a Germano-Hungarian operetta, *Királyszöktetés* (*König und Spielmann*) (József Kerner/Hugo Stein ad Mór Fenyéri), about the King and his minstrel, was mounted at Budapest's Budai Színkör on 11 August 1891. The pair also got into the action in Lydia Thompson's burlesque *Robin Hood, or The Maid That Was Arch and the Youth That Was Archer.* The King was played by the usually aggressively under-dressed Amy Sheridan, whilst Louise Beverley, another stage beauty but one with rather more of a voice, was Blondel.

The King has also—from Victorian days—become an habitual part of the British pantomime of *The Babes in the Wood,* arriving as an end-of-the-evening deus ex machina to pardon Robin Hood, who has also got himself tacked into the traditional version of the tale of the *Children in the Wood.* Blondel only occasionally gets in as well. But I notice him in the pantomime *King Pumpkin* at London's roaring Surrey Theatre, played by (very) low

Plate 40. **Blood Brothers.** *Andrew Wadsworth (center) and George Costigan (right) as the parted twins of the title in the musical play's original Liverpool production.*

comedian Edmund Edmunds, in 1864. What he was doing in this burlesque of Offenbach's *Roi Carrotte* I cannot imagine. But this minstrel has got around.

Austria: Johann Pölz Halle, Amstetten 24 July 1996

Recording: original cast (MCA)

BLOOD BROTHERS Musical in 2 acts by Willy Russell. Liverpool Playhouse, 8 January 1983; Lyric Theatre, London, 11 April 1983.

A modern version of the *Corsican Brothers* story, set in Liverpool, *Blood Brothers* follows the tale of twin brothers separated at birth. One is brought up by a well-off family, the other by his impoverished mother. Without knowing their relationship, the two boys become friends, but when their different backgrounds and abilities lead them to civil position and prison respectively, in adult life, the tale ends in the tragedy that has been foretold.

Both funny and moving in its scenes of the childhood of Eddie (Andrew Wadsworth) and Mickey (George Costigan), the show focused principally on their mother, Mrs Johnstone, originally played by popular vocalist Barbara Dickson, to whose abilities most of the folk-strained songs of the show were tailored. The songs, however, were secondary to the story in this musical and, apart from Eddie's gentle love song ''I'm Not Saying a Word'' and his mother's final ''Tell Me It's Not True,'' were largely incidental. The play itself was a sinewy piece, most effective when concentrating on its people rather than on social generalizing, but in spite of outstanding performances from, in particular, the two ''boys,'' it failed to take on in London for more than an eight-month run. With the notice posted, however, the show suddenly became popular. It was too late to continue the run, but a second production, with boxing champion John Conteh clumsily cast as its narrator, was soon after sent on the road by Robert Fox with the avowed intent of bringing the show back to town.

This revival closed before reaching London but, after a wide range of provincial productions, as well as mountings in Germany (ad Jürgen Flügge, Hans Jorg Betschart) and in America, producer Bill Kenwright, who had been the making of *Joseph and the Technicolor Dreamcoat* after a similarly unpromising start, took his touring production starring popular singer Kiki Dee from the provincial circuits into London's Albery Theatre in 1988 (28 July). This time, the show achieved take off and a vast metropolitan run, with Angela Richards, Stephanie Lawrence, Miss Dickson, Clodagh Rogers and Lyn Paul succeeding to the role of Mrs Johnstone as *Blood Brothers* continues, at the time of writing, into its twelfth year, now at the Phoenix Theatre (December 1991). In 1993 Miss Lawrence led the cast of a company playing this production to America, and she was succeeded there by Petula Clark (who subsequently led out a two-year American touring company), Carole King and Helen Reddy during the two years (839 performances) that the show stayed on Broadway. In Britain, *Blood Brothers* also took to the road, playing for a continuing four years around Britain whilst the West End production ran on.

A film version of the show was at one stage announced but, in spite of author Russell's cinema success with *Educating Rita* and *Shirley Valentine,* and the continuing high profiles of the stage show, it has never appeared.

Following a Munich production of an altered version, the English *Blood Brothers* was played in Germany in 1991 (English Theatre, Frankfurt 22 November 1991), followed in turn by a vernacular *Blutsbrüder* (Stadttheater, Heilbronn 11 April 1992) which followed more closely the original piece. Budapest's Kamaraszínház followed up with an Hungarian version (ad Pál Békés) and further translated versions have appeared in several other countries as the piece established itself widely in a manner which seemed impossible at the closing night of the original production.

Germany: Schauburg Theater, Munich 7 April 1987; USA: Downtown Cabaret, Bridgeport, Conn 22 January 1988, Music Box Theater, New York 25 April 1993; Hungary: Budapesti Kamaraszínház *Vértestvérek* 25 February 1994; Austria: Landestheater, Linz *Blutsbrüder* 13 October 1995, Theater Akzent, Vienna *Blutsbrüder* October 1998

Recordings: original cast (Legacy), 1988 revival cast (First Night), new recording revival cast (First Night), Japanese cast (Polydor), Dutch cast (Red Bullet), New Zealand cast (First Night), Catalan cast *Germans de sang* (Dindi), Israeli cast (Helicon), ''international'' recording (First Night)

BLOOMER GIRL Musical in 2 acts by Sig Herzig and Fred Saidy based on a play by Lilith and Dan James. Lyrics by E Y Harburg. Music by Harold Arlen. Shubert Theater, New York, 5 October 1944.

Bloomer Girl arrived on Broadway hard in the wake of *Oklahoma!* and proved not only one of the quickest to attempt to imitate the successful formula of Rodgers and Hammerstein's show but also, with its period American tale, its Agnes de Mille ballets and even two of the same featured players, one of the most closely imitative. It was also one of the longer-running.

Evelina (Celeste Holm) is a niece and disciple of ''Dolly'' Bloomer (Margaret Douglass), a liberated lady who is into feminine suffrage and is also the popularizer of the ''liberating'' knickerbocker dress. Unfortunately for family harmony, Evelina's father, Horatio Applegate (Matt Briggs) manufactures hoopskirts and has unilaterally chosen his daughter's bridegroom, southerner Jeff Calhoun (David Brooks). The ''bloomer girl'' chooses dramatically to disparage her father's wares in public but she is, on the other hand, attracted by her chosen swain, whom she on principle refuses to wed. Dolly and Evelina get into trouble for helping runaway slaves, then the Civil War happens and Jeff is on the other side, but there are happy endings all round when Applegate and Dolly turn his factory to a touch of war-profiteering, making army uniforms (and bloomers), and when Jeff gets converted to the Union cause.

Arlen's score was not out of his top drawer, although Jeff's tuneful reactions to ''Evelina'' and a pair of the negro-style pieces in which the composer specialized—''The Eagle and Me'' and ''I Got a Song''—assigned to the black slave characters of the cast, emerged from the score, and a duo for hero and heroine, ''Right as the Rain,'' also won some popularity. The principal ballet section was a Civil War Ballet, and there was also a staged production of *Uncle Tom's Cabin* to the music of ''Liza Crossing the Ice.'' *Oklahoma!*'s Joan McCracken featured as principal dancer.

John C Wilson's production of *Bloomer Girl* played an excellent 654 performances on Broadway, but there the parallels with *Oklahoma!* ended for, although it was subsequently televised in 1956, with Barbara Cook and Keith Andes featured, and revived at the Goodspeed Opera House in 1981 (16 September), the show did not follow its predecessor into the theatres of other countries.

Recording: original cast (Decca)

BLOSSOM, Henry M[artyn jr] (b St Louis, Mo, 10 May 1866; d New York, 23 March 1919). Well-considered librettist and lyricist to the early 20th-century American stage.

The young Henry Blossom originally worked in his father's insurance firm but, after having had success in placing an early effort at a short story, he turned his ambitions and talents to the writing of a full-scale book. One of the works that followed was *Checkers,* a horse-racing novel which he subsequently dramatized and which was produced with some success in its theatrical form by Kirk La Shelle at Chatterton's Opera House, Springfield, Ill (12 March 1903).

At this stage of his career, Blossom turned his hand to anything and everything in the way of writing, and his name turned up on a Broadway theatre bill, for what seems to be the first time, when a song, "Dearie, my Sweet," which he had written with George A Spink, found its way into the score for George Edwardes's London musical *Three Little Maids*. It was a pointer and a beginning, and his next venture took him thoroughly in the way which he would follow, when he supplied the book and lyrics for the American musical comedy *The Yankee Consul*. The show had a splendid Chicago success, leading to the announcement that Blossom and composer Alfred Robyn had been signed to a five-year, five-show contract by producer Henry Savage, and it went on to garner fine New York reviews for having "no horseplay, no local jibes, Rialtoisms or Tenderloin slang," to a grand run on Broadway, and to a long touring life. The five shows with Robyn did not, however, eventuate. Blossom's next partner was no less a musician than Victor Herbert, and the first two texts with which he supplied the composer brought him two of his biggest successes: the Continental-style comic operetta *Mlle Modiste* (1905) and the low-comedy star-vehicle *The Red Mill* (1906) for Montgomery and Stone. Now at the top of his profession, and considered by many as the most literate and playwrightly of American librettists of his time, Blossom did not, however, wholly confirm his three big initial successes.

Of two vehicles for Elsie Janis, *The Slim Princess* proved superior to an adaptation of Tristan Bernard's *La Soeur* as *The Hoyden* without either being a success of the calibre of *The Yankee Consul* or *The Red Mill*, an adaptation of Maurice Ordonneau's *Un Voyage Cooks* as *The Man from Cook's* got drowned in variety acts on its way to the Broadway stage, and his one reunion with Robyn, another piece taken from the French (Hennequin and Mitchell's *Aimé des femmes*) and produced as *All for the Ladies*, not by Savage but by the Shuberts, had only a fair run in spite of top comic Sam Bernard at the peak of the bill. It was later chopped down to make a touring turn for the comedian.

Blossom's repeats with Herbert were more successful, for if *The Prima Donna* failed to come up to hopes, an adaptation of Frank Mandel's *Our Wives* as the libretto for *The Only Girl* gave him one more hit, and there was more than a little praise for both *The Princess Pat* and *Eileen* with their rather different Irish heroines. He was less lucky with two rewrites of Charles Hoyt's *A Texas Steer*, first as *A Trip to Washington* and then as *We Should Worry*, whilst, in another two-time try, his version of Frederick Jackson's *A Full House*, produced under the Klaw and Erlanger management as *She Took a Chance*, was withdrawn before Broadway and reset with a score by Victor Herbert as *The Velvet Lady*. Neither version, apparently, appealed to the mercurial Jackson who made his own unsuccessful musical version of his play for Britain as *The Purple Lady*. Blossom's last musical-theatre work, an adaptation of Walter Hackett and Roi Cooper Megrue's *It Pays to Advertise*, produced posthumously by the Selwyns, did not move on from its Boston tryout.

Amongst Blossom's other assignments, he provided "additional lyrics" to the 1909 musical *The Candy Shop* and what book there was to Ziegfeld's *The Century Girl* revue (1916), but he left it to other hands to musicalize his own successful stage play. *The Honey Girl* (aka *What's the Odds?*, Cohan and Harris Theater 3 May 1920, 142 performances), based on *Checkers*, with songs by Albert von Tilzer, had a libretto credited at various times to Edgar Allen Woolf and to Edward Clark.

1903 **The Yankee Consul** (Alfred G Robyn) Tremont Theater, Boston 21 September; Broadway Theater 22 February 1904

1905 **Mlle Modiste** (Victor Herbert) Knickerbocker Theater 25 December

1906 **The Red Mill** (Herbert) Knickerbocker Theater 24 September

1907 **The Hoyden** (Paul Rubens, John Golden, Robert Hood Bowers, et al/w Cosmo Hamilton, et al) Knickerbocker Theater 19 October

1908 **The Prima Donna** (Herbert) Knickerbocker Theater 30 November

1910 **The Slim Princess** (Leslie Stuart/w George Ade) Star Theater, Buffalo 5 September; Globe Theater, New York 2 January 1911

1912 **Baron Trenck** American version of Frederick Schraeder's English version (Casino Theater)

1912 **The Man from Cook's** (Raymond Hubbell) New Amsterdam Theater 25 March

1912 **All for the Ladies** (Robyn) Lyric Theater 30 December

1913 **A Trip to Washington** (Ben Jerome) La Salle Theater, Chicago 24 August

1913 **A Glimpse of the Great White Way** (rewritten *All For the Ladies*) 44th Street Theater 27 October

1914 **The Only Girl** (Herbert) 39th Street Theater 2 November

1915 **The Princess Pat** (Herbert) Cort Theater 29 September

1917 **Eileen** (ex- *Hearts of Erin*) (Herbert) Shubert Theater 19 March

1917 **We Should Worry** (A Baldwin Sloane) Apollo Theater, Atlantic City 25 October

1918 **Follow the Girl** (Zoel Parenteau) 44th Street Theater 2 March

1918 **She Took a Chance** (ex- *The Bubble Girl*) (Oza Waldrop) Tremont Theater, Boston 22 October

1919 **The Velvet Lady** (revised *She Took a Chance* w music by Victor Herbert) New Amsterdam Theater 3 February

1919 **Among the Girls** (Hubbell/w Glen MacDonough/w Roi Cooper Megrue) Shubert Theater, New Haven 9 May; Park Square Theater, Boston 19 May

BLOSSOM TIME Musical in 3 acts by Dorothy Donnelly based on *Das Dreimäderlhaus* by A M Willner and Heinz Reichert. Music taken from Franz Schubert's works arranged by Sigmund Romberg. Ambassador Theater, New York, 29 September 1921.

Following the enormous Continental success of *Das Dreimäderlhaus,* the Shuberts produced their own version of the Franz Schubert biomusical. It followed the Viennese piece in many ways, but used new lyrics by Donnelly and some different musical arrangements of the Schubert raw material made by Romberg. For all that it was less artistically done than the Heinrich Berté version, it proved a huge Broadway success over 592 performances and toured apparently endlessly through America thereafter. The British version, *Lilac Time,* once again reorganized and rearranged, and once again less effective than Berté's effort, was another major hit which cornered the remaining English-language markets whilst *Blossom Time* satisfied its copyright owners by cleaning up long and large in America.

Another, English *Blossom Time,* written by Rodney Ackland with lyrics credited to Harry Purcell, John Drinkwater and G H Clutsam and a pasticcio Schubert score arranged by Clutsam, was produced at the Lyric Theatre, London, 17 March 1942. Yet another version of the *Dreimäderlhaus* story and score, it was arranged to permit Richard Tauber to appear as the composer for 96 performances.

Recordings: US versions, selections (RCA Victor, Readers Digest)

BLUEBELL IN FAIRYLAND Musical dream play in 2 acts by Seymour Hicks. Lyrics by Aubrey Hopwood and Charles H Taylor. Music by Walter Slaughter. Vaudeville Theatre, London, 18 December 1901.

One of the most successful of all Victorian and Edwardian children's fairy or fantasy plays, *Bluebell* had its little heroine transported to Fairyland to restore a good monarch to his throne. Its author, Hicks, in the dual role of the little crossing-sweeper Dicky (pre-Fairyland) and the Sleeping King (in the fairy scenes), starred with his wife, Ellaline Terriss, in the show's title role, and their personal popularity helped to stretch the appeal of *Bluebell* well beyond the children for whom it was nominally intended. In his habitual style, Hicks larded Slaughter's pretty score with popular music-hall style songs, mostly borrowed from the American repertoire, and Miss Terriss scored a notable success with William H Penn's "The Honeysuckle and the Bee."

Bluebell became a perennial British Christmas entertainment and returned to London both in 1905 (Aldwych Theatre 23 December) in a version announced as "elaborated" and in 1916 in a major revival (106 performances) with its original stars and with some new songs by Herman Darewski. Regular London showings continued till 1937.

In 1910 Hicks and Slaughter rearranged a part of their show as a music-hall playlet, and it was produced at the Croydon Hippodrome, 17 October, and then at the London Hippodrome, 31 October.

Australia: Theatre Royal, Sydney 14 December 1907

BLUE EYES Musical play in 2 acts by Guy Bolton and Graham John. Music by Jerome Kern. Additional numbers by Frank Tours. Piccadilly Theatre, London, 27 April 1928.

In the midst of the fun-and-dance shows of the late 1920s, *Blue Eyes,* a romantic costume musical about Bonnie Prince Charlie, sat oddly in London's West End. Guy Bolton and Graham John's very old-fashioned book had Evelyn Laye in the role of actress Nancy Ann Bellamy disguising herself as a boy to help her brother (George Vollaire) escape the clutches of the "Butcher of Culloden" (Bertram Wallis). Bill Berry was the comic relief as a helpful actor who provided the reverse of the travesty coin by getting into disguise as a woman, as well as a humorous Scotsman, a French dancing master, and a flea-circus proprietor. The stiffly antique book, which nevertheless gave the opportunity for lots of colorful military costumes and allowed Miss Laye to fight a dashing duel, was illustrated by an up-to-date Jerome Kern score in which the lilting "Back to the Heather," sung by Vollaire and his partner (Sylvia Leslie) caught the ear. After Lee Ephraim's production of *Blue Eyes* had played out its life in 276 performances at the brand new Piccadilly Theatre and then at Daly's (playing simultaneously with the composer's *Show Boat* at the Theatre Royal, Drury Lane), one gently swinging number called "Do I Do Wrong?," sung by baritone George Gwyther in the role of Nancy's noble lover, was rescued by Kern to be relyricked as "You're Devastating" in *Roberta.*

Another musical under the same title had previously been produced on Broadway (Casino Theater 21 February 1921). Written by Leroy Clemens, Leon Gordon, Z Myers and Isidore Benjamin Kornblum, it was no period piece but an adaptation of a play called *Let Tommy Do It* starring comedian Lew Fields and with Mollie King in the title role of a tiny tale of love and lies. It played 56 performances.

BLUE FOR A BOY, or What Shall We Do with the Body? Musical romp in 2 acts by Austin Melford adapted from *Hurra! ein Junge* by Franz Arnold and Ernst Bach. Lyrics by Harold Purcell. Music by Harry Parr Davies. His Majesty's Theatre, London, 30 November 1950.

This farce musical, built around the comic talents of Fred Emney, Richard Hearne and author Austin Melford, used the remnants of Bach and Arnold's comedy (Lustspielhaus, Berlin 22 December 1926), as previously made into the successful comedy *It's a Boy!* (Strand Theatre, 1930, 366 performances), to supply as many opportunities for disguises, impersonations, and what were essentially variety turns, as it could be devised to hold. The vast Emney, with his cigar and monocle, bounced about in kiddie rompers pretending to be a baby, Bertha Belmore did an impression of a booming, over-dressed lady authoress, and Hearne impersonated the same lady who, when she finally turned up for real, was soubrette Eve Lister. It was Miss Lister who had the principal singing moments of the evening, sharing the title song with Hermene French, and performing "Lying Awake and Dreaming" and "At Last It's Happened" alone.

Ultimately a series of sketches interspersed with songs, this jolly, unsophisticated combination of entertainments caught on where other such pieces had failed and Emile Littler's production remained for a year and a half (664 performances) at His Majesty's Theatre before going on the road.

A German musical comedy, *Strammer Junge angekommen* (Robert Gilbert) produced at the Hamburg Theater am Besenbinderhof in 1953 (1 May) was also based on *Hurra! ein Junge.*

THE BLUE KITTEN Musical comedy in 2 acts by Otto Harbach and William Cary Duncan based on *Le Chasseur de Chez Maxim* by Yves Mirande (and Gustave Quinson). Music by Rudolf Friml. Selwyn Theater, New York, 13 January 1922.

Mirande (and nominally, at least, Quinson)'s highly successful 1920 Palais-Royal comedy underwent certain modifications in the hands of Otto Harbach and William Cary Duncan before it was mounted on Broadway with the aging Joseph Cawthorn starred as a former waiter called Theodore Vanderpop. Vanderpop has come into money, quit his job at Maxim's, and is now suffering the familiar torture of the nouveau riche—his former customers may recognize him. The torture gets excruciating when one of his daughter's suitors turns out to be a gay young blade who frequented the restaurant in his waitering days.

Friml decorated this formerly French (but now Dutch-accented) tale with a determinedly up-to-date American score, topped by such sprightly numbers as "Cutie" and "The Blue Kitten Blues," but Arthur Hammerstein's production, which featured former Ziegfeld star Lillian Lorraine alongside Cawthorn at the top of the bill, played through 140 Broadway performances without making itself into a genuine success. When Hammerstein put it on the road with Richard Carle at its bill-head it turned out a quick flop.

Three years later, however, the show turned up at London's Gaiety Theatre. It had been adapted by Dion Titheradge, given extra lyrics by Greatrex Newman and extra songs by Howard Carr, Ivy St Helier and others, and Bill Berry starred as Christopher Popp alongside Ethel Levey, Roy Royston, Dorothy Brown and Bobby Howes, under the direction of Broadway's R H Burnside. Once again, the show ran precisely 140 performances.

UK: Gaiety Theatre 23 December 1925

Recording: selection on *Rudolf Friml in London* (WRC)

BLUE MONDAY Folk opera in 1 act by B G De Sylva. Music by George Gershwin. Globe Theater, New York, 28 August 1922.

Gershwin's short, melodramatic folk opera ("Blue Monday Blues," "Has Anyone Seen My Joe?," "I'm Gonna See My Mother") was originally played as part of *George White's Scandals of 1922,* but it proved to be too startling and downbeat for the tone of the revue and it was withdrawn after the first night. De Sylva's text was a little tale of jealousy in which Vi, egged on by the villainous Tom, shoots her boyfriend Joe whom she suspects of being unfaithful. The "other woman" turns out, as in *Iolanthe,* to be, if not a fairy, at least his mother.

The show survived this single performance. It was reorganized and produced at Provincetown (2 June 1932), and again, under the title *135th Street,* at New York's Lincoln Center (20 May 1968) whilst continuing to be a source of fascination to lovers of Gershwin's music.

Germany: Opernstudio, Opernhaus Cologne 16 May 1985

Recordings: (Turnabout, Penzance)

THE BLUE MOON Musical play in 3 acts by Harold Ellis. Lyrics by Percy Greenbank and Paul Rubens. Music by Howard Talbot and Paul Rubens. Northampton, 29 February 1904; Lyric Theatre, London, 28 August 1905.

A piece in the tradition of *The Geisha,* with a well-used story featuring an oriental singing girl (Florence Smithson), a British naval gentleman (Vernon Davidson) and much comedy (E Statham Staples, Alfred Clarke, Frank Couch), *The Blue Moon* was an early production effort by Gaiety stage-manager Pat Malone and ex-actor turned theatre manager, Robert Courtneidge. An attractive score and a standout performance by petite, dark, stratospherically soprano Miss Smithson in the heroine's role made the show a fine success on the road and Courtneidge brought it to town the following year.

Librettist Ellis having died meanwhile, Courtneidge had the show rewritten by his crony Alexander Thompson into something more in the popular musical comedy vein than the original light operatic one, and he cast star comics Willie Edouin (Moolraj the idolmaker, juggler and marriage-broker), Walter Passmore (low-comedy soldier) and Courtice Pounds (oversized and tenorious army Major) at the head of the bill. Miss Smithson was recalled at the last moment to replace a further star name, Ida Rene, and her singing of ''The Poplar and the Rainbow'' and ''Little Blue Moon'' did much to help the show to success. Elsewhere the comedy was rife, lurching from the topical (''A Good Time in Mars'') to the burlesque (''Entertainments''), whilst soubrette Carrie Moore and ingenue Billie Burke were both featured in light numbers.

The Blue Moon did well in London (182 performances) and was duly sent on the road, with Miss Smithson still starring, in 1906, in three companies in 1907 and into 1908, as well as being taken up for America by the Shubert brothers. With the comic role of the private soldier, Charlie Taylor, hugely expanded for the benefit of James T Powers, Ethel Jackson featured in Miss Smithson's role, and Arthur Donaldson serenading ''Chandra-Nil, my lotus lily'' (by G A Spink) in one of the local additions to the score, it played 76 performances on Broadway before going round America.

The Blue Moon won considerable favor in Australia, where it was produced in 1907 by J C Williamson Ltd at Melbourne's Princess Theatre and Sydney's His Majesty's Theatre with Amy Murphy starred as Chandra Nil and Victor Gouriet and Edward Noble heading the English version of the comedy. The show also toured South Africa in 1908 under the management of Frank Wheeler, and was played in India and the East by the Fred Ellis Opera Company, but it remains significant largely in that it brought together the producer, star and two of the writers who, four years later, would collaborate on the very much more memorable *The Arcadians.*

USA: Casino Theater 3 November 1906; Australia: Princess Theatre, Melbourne 25 June 1907

THE BLUE PARADISE *see* EIN TAG IM PARADIES

BLUE ROSES Musical play in 2 acts by Desmond Carter and Caswell Garth. Lyrics by Desmond Carter. Music by Vivian Ellis. Gaiety Theatre, London, 20 January 1931.

Producer Laddie Cliff's attempt to emulate the system initiated at the Gaiety Theatre by Hollingshead and Edwardes, and to create an alternative star team to hold the fort while he took his hit dance-and-laughter musicals on tour, included the production of two shows starring monocled provincial dude comic George Clarke. *Blue Roses,* which reached back in time for a plot which was a little too like the Gaiety's famous old *The Orchid,* boasted a pretty (if short) score, topped by the charming duo ''If I Had Three Wishes,'' originally performed by Vera Bryer and Roy Royston.

The enterprise proved to be a rather underpowered one and *Blue Roses* failed in 54 performances. However, it was later played successfully in Australia by Cliff's number-one team juvenile dance stars Madge Elliott and Cyril Ritchard in whose hands the piece might have done better in London. The Gaiety ''B'' team was soon abandoned.

Australia: Her Majesty's Theatre, Sydney 13 February 1932

THE BLUE TRAIN *see* MÄDI

BLUM, Ernest (b Paris, 15 August 1836; d Paris, 18 September 1907).

Following his debut as a dramatist at the Théâtre des Variétés at the age of 18, Ernest Blum was for many years a supplier of all kinds of theatrical pieces—comedies, dramas, vaudevilles, spectacular féeries, revues and little and large opérettes—to the Paris stage, and a well-known figure in Paris theatre-café society. Albert Vanloo described him as ''un boulevardier impénitent'' who, having eaten his supper, would pop into the Théâtre des Variétés for a look at the curtain-raiser. But he did not stay for the main piece, as it was his invariable rule to be in bed by 9 PM.

Amongst a plethora of revues and vaudevilles, often written in collaboration with Alexandre Flan, Paul Siraudin and/or Clairville, Blum's earliest attempts in the musical theatre were in the shape of small opérettes and féeries (*L'Escarcelle d'or, Cendrillon, Le Voyage de Gulliver*), and his first significant success in the field came when he was already in his late thirties with his first full-sized musical comedy, Offenbach's *La Jolie Parfumeuse.* He quickly followed it with an equally successful drama, *Rose Michel.* Blum collaborated on two further pieces with Offenbach (*Bagatelle, Belle Lurette*), had a hand in the making of the enormously successful vaudeville-opérette *Lili* (and also, apparently, without credit, of *Mam'zelle Nitouche* and a number of other shows) but, by this stage, he had already begun the partnership with Raoul Toché which was to lead them to a series of comedy successes including *Madame Mongodin* and *Monsieur Coulisset* (both hits at the Théâtre du Vaudeville and then on the international stage), the Palais-Royal hits *Le Parfum* and *La Maison Tamponin,* and the enormously popular *Le Voyage en Suisse,* the opérette-pantomime played by the Hanlon-Lees acrobatic company in every corner of the globe in the later years of the 19th century.

The partnership provided the large-scale *Madame l'Amiral* and *Les Aventures de Monsieur de Crac* (1886,

Plate 41. **Blue Roses.** *George Clarke and the Gaiety chorus line up for a team photo.*

157 performances) to the Théâtre du Châtelet, but in general they did a little less well in the musical theatre. They nevertheless found success with the spectacular fantasy *Le Château de Tire-Larigot* and the tale of *Adam et Ève,* both written with the musical collaboration of Gaston Serpette.

After Toché's suicide, Blum worked mostly with Paul Ferrier and/or Pierre Decourcelle, turning out further Châtelet spectaculars, including *Le Petit Chaperon Rouge, Robinson Crusoe,* and, most notably, two colorful and successful hodgepodges, *Le Carnet du Diable* and *Le Royaume des femmes,* described as "neither fairy play nor opérette, nor a spectacle nor vaudeville[, but] . . . a popular, half-witty nothing full of fun, naughtiness, deviltry and go[;] . . . joyous, objectionable."

Along with *La Jolie Parfumeuse* and *Lili,* these two latter-day pieces proved internationally the most successful of Blum's musical theatre output. *Le Carnet du Diable* became *Cupido & Co* in Berlin and *Das Scheckbuch des Teufels* at Vienna's Danzers Orpheum, whilst remusicked versions of his text for *Le Royaume des femmes* were produced as *Das Paradies der Frauen* and *Die verkehrte Welt* in Germany, as *Die verkehrte Welt* at Vienna's Venedig in Wien and as *Felfordult Világ* in Hungary.

Several of Blum's most successful comic works later became the bases for musical plays. *La Maison Tamponin* (w Toché) became first *Prima Ballerina* (mus: Carl Weinberger, Carltheater 23 November 1895, Thalia-Theater, Berlin 24 October 1896) and then *Auch so Eine!* (Theater in der Josefstadt 18 October 1901); *Madame Mongodin* (*Mrs Ponderbury's Past* in its English-language version) was the source for Richard Carle's American musical comedy *Mary's Lamb* (1908); whilst *Le Parfum* was succesfully made into *Im Pavillon* (Karl Kappeller/ad Ludwig Fischl, Alexander Landesberg) and played for 52 consecutive performances at Vienna's Theater in der Josefstadt (6 March 1896).

Alongside his theatrical career, Blum led a parallel career as a journalist (*Charivari, Rappel, Le Gaulois*), writing on topics from the comical to the stock market, and he also turned out a number of comic and biographical books.

1855 **Latrouillat et Truffaldini** (Hervé/w J Petit) 1 act Folies-Nouvelles 10 May

1862 **Le Hussard persecuté** (Hervé) 1 act Délassements-Comiques 30 May

1862 **La Fanfare de Saint-Cloud** (Hervé/w Paul Siraudin)1 act Délassements-Comiques 30 May

1864 **La Revue pour rire** including **Roland à Rongeveaux** (Hervé/w Clairville, Siraudin) Théâtre des Bouffes-Parisiens 27 December

1866 **Cendrillon, ou la pantoufle merveilleuse** (Victor Chéri/w Clairville, A Monnier) Théâtre du Châtelet 4 June

1866 **Le Royaume des femmes** new version Théâtre des Variétés 1 September

1869 **L'Astronome du Pont-Neuf** (Émil Durand/w Jules Prével, Alexandre Flan) 1 act Théâtre des Variétés 18 February

1872 **L'Égyptienne réaliste** (Victor Chéri/w Clairville) 1 act Café Tertulia 20 January

1873 **La Jolie Parfumeuse** (Offenbach/w Hector Crémieux) Théâtre de la Renaissance 29 November

1874 **Les Parisiennes** (Léon Vasseur/w Jules Moinaux, Victor Koning) Théâtre des Bouffes-Parisiens 31 March

1874 **Bagatelle** (Offenbach/w Crémieux) 1 act Théâtre des Bouffes-Parisiens 21 May

1874 **La Famille Trouillat** (Léon Vasseur/w Crémieux) Théâtre de la Renaissance 10 September

1877 **La Foire Saint-Laurent** (Offenbach/uncredited w Crémieux, Saint-Albin) Théâtre des Folies-Dramatiques 10 February

1878 **Le Chat botté** (de Bourdet, Gaston Serpette, Coedès/w Etienne Tréfeu) Théâtre de la Gaïté 18 May

1879 **Le Voyage en Suisse** (uncredited/w Raoul Toché) Théâtre des Variétés 30 August

1880 **Belle Lurette** (Offenbach/w Édouard Blau, Raoul Toché) Théâtre de la Renaissance 30 October

1882 **Lili** (Hervé/w Albert Millaud, Maurice Hennequin) Théâtre des Variétés 10 January

1884 **Le Château de Tire-Larigot** (Gaston Serpette/w Toché) Théâtre des Nouveautés 30 October

1884 **Le Diable au corps** (Romuald Marenco/w Toché) Théâtre des Bouffes-Parisiens 19 December

1885 **Mam'zelle Gavroche** (Hervé/w Edmond Gondinet, Albert de Saint-Albin) Théâtre des Variétés 24 January

1885 **Le Petit Chaperon Rouge** (Serpette/w Toché) Théâtre des Nouveautés 10 October

1886 **Les Aventures de M Crac** (uncredited/w Toché) Théâtre du Châtelet 19 April

1886 **Adam et Ève** (Serpette/w Toché) Théâtre des Nouveautés 6 October

1889 **Le Royaume des femmes** (pasticcio/Cogniard ad w Toché) Théâtre des Nouveautés 28 February

1892 **Madame l'Amiral** (uncredited/wToché) Théâtre du Châtelet 17 September

1895 **Le Carnet du Diable** (Serpette/w Paul Ferrier) Théâtre des Variétés 23 October

1896 **Le Royaume des femmes** new version (Serpette/ad w Ferrier) Eldorado 24 February

1896 **Le Carillon** (Serpette/w Ferrier) Théâtre des Variétés 7 November

1900 **Le Petit Chaperon Rouge** (Marius Baggers/w Ferrier, Pierre Decourcelle) Théâtre du Châtelet 22 December

DIE BLUME VON HAWAII Operette in 3 acts by Imre Földes adapted by Alfred Grünwald and Fritz Löhner-Beda. Music by Pal Ábrahám. Neues Theater, Leipzig, 24 July 1931; Metropoltheater, Berlin, 29 August 1931.

Ábrahám's follow-up to his successful *Viktória (und ihr Husar)* swapped that show's exotic Japanese, Russian and Hungarian settings for an equally colorful Hawaiian venue and a final act in a cabaret in Monte Carlo. The principal pair of plot lines centered on the unsuccessful efforts of a local leader to bring the Princess Laya back to the Pacific seas to reclaim her hereditary Hawaiian crown and thus thwart American efforts to annex the island, and on the love story between the Princess and her princely cousin, Lilo-Taro.

The show's deliciously eclectic score ranged from the Prince's full-blooded tenor serenades to ''Ein Paradies am Meeresstrand'' and to his ''Blume von Hawaii'' and the Princess's showy ''Traumschöne Perle der Südsee'' to some up-to-date 1930s dance rhythms in the soubret pair's ''Ich hab' ein Diwanpüppchen'' and ''My Little Boy'' and a series of jazzy numbers given to a tacked-in Jolsonesque cabaret vocalist called Jim-Boy, which sported suitably mid-Atlantic titles to go with their catchy tunes—''My Golden Baby,'' ''Bin nur ein Jonny,'' ''Wir singen zur Jazzband im Folies-Bergère.'' ''My Golden Baby'' proved a sufficiently good imitation of its American models to become a song success in its English-language version.

Alhtough written originally in Hungarian, the show was first produced in a German version, in Leipzig, before being moved briskly to Berlin where it opened at the Metropoltheater with Annie Ahlers starring as Princess Laya, Alfred Jerger as the tenor prince and Harald Paulsen, Serge Abranovic, Fritz Steiner and Claire Rommer in support. It quickly won success, with most of the loudest plaudits going to the musical score, and was soon reproduced in all the main Continental venues. In Hungary, with Juci Lábass (Laya), Jenő Nador (Lilo-Taro) and Márton Rátkai wearing the blackface of Jim-Boy, it scored a similar success, while the Theater an der Wien's Vienna production was played 150 times with Rita Georg

Plate 42. **Die Blume von Hawaii.** *A little advertising shelters Bessie (Marianne Lang) and Buffy (Hans-Jörg Bock) from the tropical sun, but not from the lassie's papa (Theater Hof, 1986).*

and Otto Maran starring, and the Hungarian pair Oszkár Dénes and Rózsi Bársony featured as the jazzy Jim-Boy and the soubrette, Bessy.

A French production (ad Georges Delance) took place as part of a venture to start a new cheap-price musical theatre in Paris. Aimée Mortimer and Régine Marelli shared the role of Laya and tenors Max Moutia and Cyprien Delcros did the serenading as part of a project which never really got off the ground. When it sank it took *La Fleur d'Hawaï* with it.

Unlike Ábrahám's other two principal works, *Die Blume von Hawaii* did not travel to English-speaking climes, but it has remained highly popular on the Continent and it remains to this day a regularly played part of the repertoire in Operette houses. Two film versions have been produced under the title, the first by Richard Oswald (1933) starring Márta Eggerth as the Hawaiian princess and the second by Géza von Cziffra (1953) with Maria Litto as a hopeful actress who stows away on a Hawaii-bound vessel in search of a role in a production of *Die Blume von Hawaii* and wins both tenor and triumph.

Hungary: Király Színház *Hawaii Rózsája* 28 January 1932; Austria: Theater an der Wien 19 August 1932; France: L'Alhambra *La Fleur d'Hawaï* 1933

Films: Richard Oswald 1933, EOS-Films 1953

Recordings: selection (Philips, EMI Odéon, Eurodisc, Telefunken, Polydor, etc), selection in Italian (EDM)

THE BLUSHING BRIDE Musical in 2 acts by Cyrus Wood based on a libretto by Edward Clark and the play *The Chaperon* by Jocelyn Brandon and Frederick Arthur as adapted by Mark Swan (*The Third Party*). Lyrics by Cyrus Wood. Music by Sigmund Romberg. Astor Theater, New York, 6 February 1922.

A love story set in a cabaret venue provided the opportunity for a musical comedy consisting of little more than a series of comical sketches, songs and speciality acts, pasted together around the talents of favorite touring musical-comedy stars Cecil Lean and Cleo Mayfield. He played Coley Collins, a professional gooseberry who dines with couples who should not be dining together alone, who habitually chaperones his clients to the nightclub where the little Quaker girl Lulu Love (Miss Mayfield) looks after the hats-and-coats department. Comic Tom Lewis appeared as a plump little fellow taking a girl out to dinner and inevitably having his wife turn up. The Swanson sisters, Beatrice and Marcelle, put in an appearance and the vaudeville act, the Glorias, did their well-known routine of ice-skating without any ice. The basic score of the show was topped by "Love's Highway," "A Regular Girl" and a quartet about "Springtime."

Lee and J J Shubert's production started its life under the title of the original play *The Third Party* (Shubert Theater 3 August 1914). It was next called *Lulu* and equipped with songs by perpetual loser and publicists' darling Gitz Rice (who never went anywhere without his wartime "Lieutenant" glued to his name) before finally it came to the stage at Atlantic City (20 September 1920), still with Rice's songs, under the title *The Girl in the Private Room,* with the Swansons teamed with comic Fred Hillebrand and Queenie Smith featured in a toe dance. Title, score and most of the cast all went under the axe before, 17 months later, the piece reached New York equipped with its new stars, fresh accoutrements and enough appeal to last a more than respectable 144 nights on Broadway.

BOBADIL Comic opera in 2 acts by Walter Parke (also given as by L Travelli). Music by Luscombe Searelle. New Opera House, Sydney, 22 November 1884.

The expansive New Zealand-bred Searelle promised and got many international productions for his light operatic variant on the Abu Hassan legend following its initial production, in the repertoire seasons of the Majeroni-Wilson Opera Company, in Sydney and Melbourne. Charles Harding (Bobadil), Gracie Plaisted (Princess Zorayda) and Frances Saville (Lulu) headed the original cast, the composer conducted, and, beginning with an eight-weeks run in Sydney, the piece went on to a fine success in Adelaide, in Melbourne (Bijou Theatre 9 May 1885) and throughout Australia.

Bobadil was duly produced by its composer in New Zealand and South Africa, again with some success, but although its American production, with Isabelle Underwood, W S Rising, J K Murray and Clara Lane featured, won fair notices on its debut in Boston in spite of the fact that the scenery had allegedly not arrived on opening night, the show had a truncated tour, stopping short of New York. It got just one copyright performance in Britain. A century later, however, it remains the only musical show to have come out of Australia and/or New Zealand to have been given metropolitan productions—no matter how brief—on four continents.

USA: Columbia Theater, Boston 5 January 1903; UK: Bijou Theatre, Teddington 4 January 1903

BOB HERCEG Operett (daljáték) in three acts by Károly Bakonyi and Ferenc Martos. Music by Jenő Huszka. Népszínház, Budapest, 20 December 1902.

Jenő Huszka's *Bob herceg,* the most successful Hungarian musical play up to its time, is credited with marking the beginning of what would prove to be the richest period in the Hungarian musical theatre. It was equipped with a libretto by the two best and most successful of Hungary's contemporary musical theatre writers, who chose to set their piece in Great Britain, treating that

Plate 43. **Bob herceg.** *Sári Fedák as Prince Bob of England and Gizella Ledofsky as his commoner beloved. They don't seem much more Victorian-Britain than the pretty folk pictured on the fairy-tale-ish music cover.*

country in the same sort of way that Western authors did when making operettas out of the things that they imagined might happen in Balkan and central European kingdoms.

The action takes place in London. George (Sári Fedák), the son of the Queen of England (Sarolta Krecsányi), has the habit of going out into the city, disguised, under the name of ''Bob,'' as a poor, wandering student. On his ramblings, he meets and falls in love with a girl of the people, the baker's daughter Annie (Gisella Ledofszky). Annie's suitor, the barber Plumpudding (Antal Nyárai), is decidedly put out but, like the rest of the townsfolk, he is also fall-to-your-knees stunned when Bob's real identity comes out one day, in the middle of Bowie-Street [*sic*]. His Queen of a mother, who is intent that George-Bob should marry the Countess Victoria of Clarence (Margit Dóri), finds that her son is willing to give up his crown and the sword of Saint-George to marry as he will. When the Countess Victoria is discovered to be dallying elsewhere, and it becomes evident that she is clearly only after the crown and not the heart of Prince ''Bob,'' the tale is one more step on the road to a happy ending. For everyone except poor Plumpudding. Géza Rásko played Lord Lancaster, the Captain of the Guard, Mihály Kovács was the Prince's faithful steward, Sir Pomponius, and the landlord of the pub was called Simson Pickwick.

Huszka's score featured some touches of ''Englishness,'' notably a very lively Guards March chorusing about ''Szép Albion'' (fair Albion), in a piece whose score was severely devoted to its leading ''man,'' the heir to the throne of England, as played in travesty by megastar Fedák. She indulged, during the evening, in a drinking song (''Borba fojtom örömem''), a serenade (''Pöngeti, veri, billegeti a lantot ujjam''), a piece about Herkules and Omphale (Dal az Aranyszöke hajszálról, ie, the song of the golden-blonde), an aubade (Hajnali dal), the lecke-kuplé (chastizing song) and the Dal az első csókról (Song of the first kiss).

The Népszínház's production of *Bob herceg* was a huge hit. It ran quickly to its 100th performance (8 April) and ended up playing a first run of 134 nights, outstripping in durability every Operette, foreign or home-made, since *Rip,* 20 years earlier. It was quickly brought into the repertoire at the new Király Színház (12 May 1905), and won regular productions in Hungary thereafter (Városi Színház 20 November 1926, etc). It also visited Vienna, when a German-language version (ad Max Neal, Konrad Dreher) was mounted by Karczag and Wallner at the Theater an der Wien. Gerda Walde played the travesty

Prince, with Sarolta von Rettich-Birk as his mother, Ida Lorenz as Annie and Annie Wünsch as Countess Victoria, whilst the house's two actor-librettists, Bodanzky and Brammer, supported as Lord Southwell, royal master of Ceremonies, and Marshall Lord Bevis. *Prinz Bob* was, however, played only ten times. Henry Savage purchased the piece for America, but does not seem ever to have got it to the stage, and *Bob herceg* has remained a favorite only in its home country.

Austria: Theater an der Wien *Prinz Bob* (*Der Gassenkönig*) 23 September 1905

Recording: selection (Qualiton)

BOB'S YOUR UNCLE Musical farce in 2 acts by Austin Melford. Lyrics by Frank Eyton. Music by Noel Gay. Saville Theatre, London, 5 May 1948.

Leslie Henson and Vera Pearce headed the romping through this latter-day musical farce which was one of the most successful examples of its kind in 1940s London. He played Uncle Bob Popejoy, she was the overaged and oversexed Mrs Edgoose, and both were tangled up in the wedding of Hector (Gordon Humphris) and June (Valerie Tandy), which June's old flame Dick (Hamish Menzies) is trying to stop—until he meets Sheila (Sheila Douglas-Pennant) in time for the final curtain.

The score provided some humorous numbers, notably Miss Pearce's ludicrously imaginative ''He Loves Me'' and her duet with Henson ''Like Me a Little Bit More'' as the show careered through a 10-month run (363 performances) and commensurate touring which marked one of the last successes for its comical kind of show before the onset of the new wave of romantic musicals.

BOCCACCIO Operette in 3 acts by F Zell and Richard Genée. Music by Franz von Suppé. Carltheater, Vienna, 1 February 1879.

Franz von Suppé followed up his first great success with a full-length Operette, *Fatinitza,* with a second, three years later. *Boccaccio's* neatly constructed text was allegedly borrowed from an unspecified theatre piece by Bayard, de Leuwen and de Beauplan, but, whether it was or not, it certainly helped itself to some plot motifs from one of the chapters of the real Boccaccio's famous work, the collection of often ribald tales known as *The Decameron.* It had, otherwise, little enough to do with the historical Italian author, Giovanni Boccaccio (1313–1375), for whom it was named—a trend which would long persist in the musical theatre—but at least his name supplied a nicely recognizable and slightly suggestive title.

Giovanni Boccaccio (Antonie Link) is a poet and novelist who takes the plots for his tales of duped husbands and faithless women from life and from his experience of it. This excuse of ''research'' is, of course, an excellent one for making off with any available 14th-century Florentine wives (other people's) he can. The latest of these is Beatrice (Frln Bisca), wife of Scalza (Hildebrandt), the barber. However, Beatrice is put in the shade and Boccaccio all swept away when he sees the unmarried Fiametta (Rosa Streitmann), the foster-daughter of the grocer Lambertuccio (Karl Blasel) and his wife, Peronella (Therese Schäfer). What he does not know is that Fiametta is no grocery miss, but the farmed-out daughter of the Duke of Tuscany. Pietro, Prince of Palermo (Franz Tewele), a royal with an itch to be an author on Boccaccio's lines and principles, comes to Florence incognito in search of some ''real life,'' and the writer and his friends take him on a jaunt with Isabella (Regine Klein), the wife of the cooper, Lotteringhi (Franz Eppich), which ends up with the Prince hidden in a barrel to escape the jealous husband. Boccaccio himself, caught kissing Fiametta, persuades the foolish grocer that his olive tree has hallucinatory powers. Finally Fiametta is summoned home, to marry a royal husband. Fortunately, the royal in question is none other than Pietro, who is willing and able to hand her over to her slightly reformed Boccaccio. The final act, set in the Tuscan court, justified the poet's presence by positing that he had been hired to write and stage an entertainment for the royal betrothal. That entertainment, when given, took the form of a moral commedia dell'arte piece in which the principal comedians took part: Blasel as Pantalone, Eppich as Brighella, Hildebrandt as Narcissino, with the young Carl Streitmann as Arlecchino and Frln Pöth as Colombina.

Suppé's score was a worthy successor to that for *Fatinitza,* featuring such winning romantic numbers as Boccaccio and Fiametta's waltzing third-act ''Florenz hat schöne Frauen''; their second-act duo ''Nur ein Wort'' and the serenade ''Ein Stern zu sein,'' alongside a tunefully winsome yet amusing trio (''Wonnevolle Kunde, neu belebend'') in which Fiametta, Isabella and Peronella read the love/sex-notes wrapped around stones and hurled at their feet by Boccaccio, Pietro and Leonetto; the march septet (''Ihr Toren, ihr wollt hassen mich'') leading up to the conclusion of the show; and some substantial and substantially written finales. The comical highlight of the piece was the song of the cooper, banging away at his barrel-making to drown out his wife's nagging (''Tagtäglich zankt mein Weib''), whilst the other cuckolded husbands also had their moments of fun, as in the opening act when Scalza and his friends serenade his wife to the plunking of his umbrella (''Holde Schöne''). The quality of the score for the second and, particularly, the third act—an act often used in Operette simply to briefly tie up the ends—helped to give *Boccaccio* an additional shapely strength.

Boccaccio was a splendid success at the Carltheater. It was played 32 times en suite before Antonie Link went

Plate 44. **Boccaccio.** *Whilst Boccaccio (Manfred Kusch) woos his Fiametta (Anne-Hagan Rentz), the comical action of the night pursues its merry way in a pretty production at the Landestheater, Schleswig-Holstein.*

into retirement and left her role to Regine Klein, and no fewer than 80 times by the end of the year. The 115th performance was played on 3 October 1881, by which time *Boccaccio* had become established as an international hit of some scope, but the Carltheater then curiously let the piece drop from its repertoire and thereafter it appeared there only intermittently (matinées in 1906 and 1922, 16 October 1923 w Erika Wagner and Christl Mardayn). The other Viennese theatres, however, snapped the show up and *Boccaccio* was mounted at the Theater an der Wien in 1882 (16 September) with Karoline Finaly in the title role, Alexander Girardi as Pietro, Carl Adolf Friese (Scalza), Josef Joseffy (Lotteringhi), Felix Schweighofer (Lambertuccio), Marie-Therese Massa (Beatrice) and with Fr Schäfer and Frln Streitmann in their original roles. A new production was staged there in 1885, Julie Kronthal was Boccaccio in 1891 and the piece reappeared in 1901 and 1907. It also appeared at the Venedig in Wien summer theatre in 1899 (5 July), entered the Volksoper in 1908 (10 November), played at the Johann Strauss-Theater in 1911, and Paula Zulka starred as Boccaccio at the Raimundtheater in 1915 (2 January).

Subsequent to this merry run of performances, *Boccaccio* began to suffer under the hands of the ''improvers'' and, for a show which won such success on its initial productions and has ever since been quoted as one of the classic comic operas of its period, it has since been chopped up, deconstructed and musically maltreated more often that would have been expected. A version which aimed to operaticize a show which was very far from being an opera, replacing dialogue with recitative and tacking in extraneous bits of Suppé music, was done by Artur Bodanzky and, after being seen at New York's Metropolitan Opera House in 1931, was staged at the Vienna Staatsoper, in each case with Maria Jeritza as Boccaccio. Another heavily remade version (ad Adolf Rott, Friedrich Shreyvogel, mus ad Anton Paulik, Rudolf Kattnigg) also gained currency and royalties for its remakers and publishers for a while, and the trend has continued in Vienna to the present day, where the most recent Volksoper production, whilst eschewing recitative, turned what remained of the piece (ad Torsten Fischer) from a comic opera into shapeless black-and-scowling melodrama, simply altering or cutting any portion of text or score which did not fit into the unimaginative 1960s-style ''concept'' imposed by its director/adapter. Amongst the other unnecessary (although not unprecedented) alterations made, Boje Skovhus, who played the mangled role of Boccaccio, was not a mezzo-soprano.

Boccaccio followed up its original success in Vienna with another in Germany and a huge one in Budapest (ad

Lajos Evva). Produced at the Népszínház with Lujza Blaha in the title role, and Elek Solymossy (Pietro), Mariska Komáromi (Fiametta), János Kápolnai (Lotteringhi), Zsófi Csatay (Isabella) and Emilia Sziklai (Beatrice) amongst the cast, it raced to its 50th performance (30 October 1880), was revived in 1882 (11 October), 1883 (11 September), 1887 (14 January) and 1889 (2 May w Aranka Hegyi), passed its 100th performance on 9 May 1890, and was reprised again on 1 October 1904, running up a record which only *Les Cloches de Corneville, Der Zigeunerbaron* and *Rip van Winkle* amongst early musical plays equaled in the Hungarian capital. It found its way also into other houses, and in 1922 Juci Lábass starred in a revival at the Városi Színház.

Following its first German production, in Frankfurt, the original version was quickly seen in Prague (23 March 1880), Nuremberg (4 April 1880), Berlin and at New York's Thalia Theater where Mathilde Cottrelly donned the poet's breeches. The first English version, which had premiered in Philadelpha in early April of 1880, arrived on Broadway only weeks after this, when Jeannie Winston appeared as Boccaccio at the Union Square Theater with Mahn's English Opera Company. W A Morgan (Pietro), A H Bell (Lambertuccio), Marie Somerville (Isabella), Hattie Richardson (Beatrice) and Fred Dixon (Lotteringhi) supported. This staunchly touring company brought the show back to New York the following year (Niblo's Garden 17 November 1881), by which time the Boston Ideal Company had another version, entitled *The Prince of Palermo, or The Students of Florence* (ad William Dexter Smith, Boston Theatre 10 May 1880), prominently displayed in their repertoire; Emilie Melville had appeared with great success at San Francisco's Bush Theater (7 June 1880) and on the road in an Oscar Weil/G Heinrichs adaptation; and *Boccaccio* had become a nationwide favorite. In 1888 (Wallack's Theater 11 March), the piece got a high-class revival from the De Wolf Hopper company with the star as Lambertuccio to the Boccaccio of Marion Manola, the Scalza of Jeff de Angelis, the Lotteringhi of Digby Bell and the Peronella of Laura Joyce Bell. Broadway saw *Boccaccio* again (ad H B Smith) when Fritzi Scheff took on the role at the Broadway Theatre in 1905 (27 February) before Bodanzky and the Metropolitan Opera brought their operaticky version to the New York stage. Another heavily rewritten *Boccaccio* was seen in 1932 with film star-to-be Allan Jones featured in the title role.

It was 1882 before London saw its first *Boccaccio* (ad H B Farnie, Robert Reece) at the Comedy Theatre with Violet Cameron starred in the title role alongside Alice Burville (Fiametta), James G Taylor (Pietro), Lionel Brough (Lambertuccio), Will S Rising (Leonetto), Louis Kelleher (Lotteringhi), Kate Munroe (Isabella) and Rosa Carlingford (Peronella). It had, of course, been previously pillaged by the pasticcio-makers of London, and the Alhambra production of *Babil and Bijou,* which was running concurrently with Alexander Henderson's *Boccaccio,* was using no less than five numbers lifted from Suppé's score. This preview didn't seem to harm the show's prospects, for the Comedy Theatre production ran for an excellent 129 straight performances before the theatre was shut for repairs, and it returned thereafter to carry on for nearly another month until the new *Rip van Winkle* was ready. It was brought back to the same house in 1885 (30 May) when Miss Cameron repeated her role opposite the young Marie Tempest (Fiametta) and Arthur Roberts (Lambertuccio) for a brief season.

Australia welcomed Emilie Melville and her version "as sung more than 300 times by her in America" with Armes Beaumont (Pietro), Annie Leaf (Fiametta) and Mrs J H Fox (Isabella) in support, and this was followed into town by the Reece and Farnie version, played by Alfred Dunning's London Comic Opera Company with Kate Chard, and advertised as being "in no way similar" to the American *Boccaccio!* Australia thereafter saw the piece regularly for a number of years, played in various comic opera companies' repertoires.

As was so often the case, *Boccace* (ad Henri Chivot, Alfred Duru) reached Brussels in its French version (Galeries Saint-Hubert 3 February 1882) before moving into Paris. In the Folies-Dramatiques production Mlle Montbazon starred in the title role to the Orlando (ex-Pietro) of Désiré, with Luco, Lepers and Maugé in the other male roles and Berthe Thibault as Béatrice (ex- Fiametta) as the show added one more success to its international list. It was revived in Paris in 1896 with Anna Tariol-Baugé, at the Théâtre de la Gaîté-Lyrique in 1914 with Jane Alstein and again in 1921 with Marthe Chenal starred.

Boccaccio has continued to win revivals, if all too frequently in botched versions, in both opera and operetta houses in Europe, as well as being the subject of a justifiable quota of recordings. A film version which was produced in 1936 with Willi Fritsch playing Boccaccio seems, on the evidence of that casting, as if it probably didn't stick very close to the original. A 1940 Italian one junked the book but used some of the music and at least had a female lead.

The title was reused for an American musical (Richard Peaslee/Kenneth Cavander) based on tales from *The Decameron* and played for seven performances at the Edison Theater in 1975 (24 November), whilst a number of other musical shows have been announced over the years as being "based on a tale by Boccaccio." At some periods, such an announcement would seem to have been nothing but a way of adding the respectability of a dead, foreign, classic author to a libretto which got closer to other parts of the body than to the knuckle. Others merely used a pale and proper outline of Boccaccio's tales. The poet is credited, amongst others, as source on the highly successful French comic opera *Le Coeur et la main* (Lecocq/Charles Nuitter, Alexandre Beaumont, Théâtre des Nouveautés 19 October 1882); Lecocq's little *Gandolfo;* in tandem with Shakespeare as the bases of the libretto to Audran's *Gillette de Narbonne;* on a *Malbruck,* written by Angelo Nessi and composed by Ruggiero Leoncavallo (Teatro Nazionale, Rome 19 January 1910); and Harry and Robert Smith's flop musical *The Masked Model* (National Theatre, Washington, DC 7 February 1916), which was later revamped as *Molly O* (Cort Theater 20 May 1916).

In France, a fictional opéra-bouffe called *Le Roi Candaule* founded on Boccaccio's tale of the same name, was used as the subject matter for Meilhac and Halévy's comedy *Le Roi Candaule,* which dealt with the high-jinks that go on in a theatre when husbands take each other's wives out to see a naughty show and, of course, end up in the same box.

Germany: Viktoria Theater, Frankfurt 13 March 1879, Friedrich-Wilhelmstädtisches Theater 20 September 1879; Hungary: Népszínház 1 October 1879; USA: Thalia Theater 23 April 1880, Chestnut Street Theater, Philadelphia (Eng) 5 April 1880, Union Square Theater (Eng) 15 May 1880; France: Théâtre des Folies-Dramatiques 29 March 1882; UK: Comedy Theatre 22 April 1882; Australia: Opera House, Melbourne 2 September 1882

Films: Herbert Maisch 1936, (It) 1940

Recordings: complete (EMI), selections (Philips, Eurodisc, etc), selection in Hungarian (Qualiton, part record)

BOCK, Jerry [BOCK, Jerrold Lewis] (b New Haven, Conn, 23 November 1928). Composer of one of Broadway's greatest hits who closed up shop in his mid-forties.

Following music studies at the University of Wisconsin, Bock began his career as a composer writing material for college and camp shows, for radio, television and revue, making his first appearance on the Broadway stage when three numbers written in collaboration with Larry Holofcener were used in the revue *Catch a Star* in 1955. He subsequently contributed to the resuscitated *Ziegfeld Follies* (1957), but in between times had provided the score for his first Broadway musical, the Sammy Davis jr vehicle, *Mr Wonderful. Mr Wonderful* provided not only a certain Broadway success (383 performances) but also gave its songwriters two numbers—''Too Close for Comfort'' and the show's title song—which proved hits both in the hands of the original artists and as recorded by Miss Peggy Lee.

Bock subsequently began a working partnership with lyricist Sheldon Harnick, from which the first musical theatre score to emerge was that for the short-lived prizefighting musical *The Body Beautiful* (60 performances), but their second collaboration, on *Fiorello!* (''Little Tin Box''), a biomusical of New York's former Mayor La Guardia, brought them a considerable hit with a run of nearly 800 Broadway performances. A more conventional politics-and-prostitutes musical, *Tenderloin* (1960), from the same writing team, did a little less well, but the pair compounded their success with the smaller-scale *She Loves Me* (1963), an adaptation of an Hungarian play already played in English both on the stage and screen.

The year after *She Loves Me,* however, Bock and Harnick topped all their previous successes when they combined on the score for *Fiddler on the Roof* (''Matchmaker,'' ''Sunrise, Sunset,'' ''If I Were a Rich Man,'' etc). A record-breaking hit on Broadway, *Fiddler on the Roof* this time gave the composer a show success beyond America, as it established itself throughout the world as a classic of the modern musical theatre and a solid part of the basic repertoire wherever the musical theatre is performed.

Two further stage works, the three one-act plays of *The Apple Tree* (1966) and another Jewish saga of adversity, *The Rothschilds* (1970), both won good Broadway runs and further productions within America but, oddly, in view of the vast success of *Fiddler on the Roof* in other areas, they—like Bock's pre–*Fiddler on the Roof* shows—did not find the same acceptance elsewhere.

Amongst Bock's other works have been included the short film score *Wonders of Manhattan* (1956), the puppet musical *Man in the Moon* (1963) for Bill and Cora Baird's marionettes, incidental music for *Generation* (1965) and a television musical version of *The Canterville Ghost* (ABC 2 November 1966 w Harnick).

1956 **Mr Wonderful** (w Larry Holofcener, George Weiss/Joseph Stein, Will Glickman) Broadway Theater 22 March

1958 **The Body Beautiful** (Sheldon Harnick/Stein, Glickman) Broadway Theater 23 January

1959 **Fiorello!** (Harnick/Jerome Weidman, George Abbott) Broadhurst Theater 23 November

1960 **Tenderloin** (Harnick/Abbott, Weidman) 46th Street Theater 17 October

1963 **She Loves Me** (Harnick/Joe Masteroff) Eugene O'Neill Theater 23 April

1964 **Fiddler on the Roof** (Harnick/Stein) Imperial Theater 22 September

1966 **The Apple Tree** (Harnick/w Harnick, Jerome Coopersmith) Shubert Theater 16 October

1970 **The Rothschilds** (Harnick/Sherman Yellen) Lunt-Fontanne Theater 19 October

BODANZKY, Robert (b Vienna, 20 March 1879; d Berlin, 2 November 1923). One of the most successful librettists of the 20th-century Viennese stage.

At first an actor, Bodanzky was, like fellow librettist Julius Brammer, for a while a bit-part player at the Theater an der Wien where he appeared in 1904–5 in *Das Garnisonsmädel* (von Czapszynski), *Pufferl* (A Frenchman), *Prinz Bob* (Lord Southwell), *Vergeltsgott* (Police Commissioner), *Der Rebell* (Ein Chauffeur), *Die Fledermaus* (Marquis Carriconi), *Die Geisha* (Bronville), *Wiener Blut* (Graf Bitowsky) and the original production of *Die lustige Witwe* (Pritschitsch). It was at that same house that his first stage pieces were mounted: the little *Phryne*—later seen at Frankfurt's Intimes-Theater—in the studio theatre, Hölle, and the children's piece *Peter und Paul reisen ins Schlaraffenland* as a Christmas entertainment for three successive years in the main house.

Pieces such as the jokey little one-acter *Mitislaw der moderne,* the internationally played Felix Albini Operette *Baron Trenck* with its Croatian military-romantic libretto, and Ziehrer's *Liebeswalzer,* which was played more than a hundred times at the Raimundtheater before, like *Baron Trenck,* going on to be seen on Broadway, established him within a couple of years as a top-flight librettist, and the vast success of his German-language adaptation of Kálmán's *Tatárjárás* (*Ein Herbstmanöver*) at the Theater an der Wien put the seal on his status. Thereafter, Bodanzky contributed to many of the most successful Operetten of his time, turning the libretto for the failed *Die Göttin der Vernunft* into the much more felicitous text to Lehár's *Der Graf von Luxemburg* and inventing the tempestuous *Zigeunerliebe, Eva* and *Endlich allein* for that same composer, the almost-féerique *Die schöne Risette* for Leo Fall, the long-running *Rund um die Liebe, Eine Ballnacht* and *Dorfmusikanten* for Oscar Straus, *Hanni geht tanzen, Wenn zwei sich lieben* (*Julicka* in Italy, *Lieutenant Gus* in America) and many others for Edmund Eysler, *Auf Befehl der Herzogin* for Bruno Granichstaedten, *Marietta* for Walter Kollo and *Der Tanz ins Glück* and *Die Tanzgräfin* for Robert Stolz, as well as many other pieces which, if not the national and international hits that these were, did well enough in one or several productions: Reinhardt's *Prinzess Gretl* (156 performances at the Theater an der Wien), Benatzky's *Yuschi tanzt* (109 performances), Acher's *Was Mädchen träumen* (more than 100 Vienna performances), Straus's *Nachtfalter* (99 performances), *Die Liebe geht um!* (92 performances at the Raimundtheater and the Bürgertheater), Kálmán's *Der kleine König* (70 performances) and Eysler's *Das Zirkuskind* (77 performances), not to mention his German versions of the Hungarian hits *Szbill, Az ezüst sirály, Offenbach* and *Mágnás Miska.*

Bodanzky died at the age of 44, having contributed a remarkable amount—including a certain amount of originality in an era when that quality was not always present in Operettic libretti—to the Viennese musical stage. However, of his many successful shows, only those with the name of Lehár attached to them—principally *Der Graf von Luxemburg* and *Zigeunerliebe*—have survived into the standard repertoire.

The libretto to the 1931 ''Wiener Operette'' *Mädel aus Wien* (Heinrich Strecker/Jo Gribitz, Fritz Gerold, Bürgertheater) was noted as being ''nach Bodanzky,'' and his name also appeared in a similar capacity on the bill for Stolz's *Hallo! Das ist die Liebe* (w Bruno Hardt-Warden ad Hugo Wiener), a remake of *Der Tanz ins Glück* produced at the Raimundtheater (4 January 1958).

1906 **Phryne** (Edmund Eysler/w Fritz Grünbaum) 1 act Hölle 6 October

1906 **Peter und Paul reisen ins Schlaraffenland** (Franz Lehár/w Grünbaum) Theater an der Wien 1 December

1907 **Ein Rendezvous** (Béla Laszky) 1 act Hölle 1 October

1907 **Mitislaw der Moderne** (Lehár/w Grünbaum) 1 act Hölle 5 January

1907 **Amor in Panoptikon** (Laszky) 1 act (puppet-musical) Hölle 1 November

1908 **Loreley** (Laszky) 1 act Hölle 31 January

1908 **Liebeswalzer** (Carl Michael Ziehrer/w Grünbaum) Raimundtheater 24 October

1908 **Baron Trenck [der Pandur]** (Felix Albini/w A M Willner) Stadttheater, Leipzig 15 February; Kaiser-Jubilaums Stadttheater 29 October 1909

1909 **Ein Herbstmanöver** (*Tatárjárás*) German version (Theater an der Wien)

1909 **Die kleine Baroness** (Albini) 1 act Apollotheater 31 March

1909 **Der Graf von Luxemburg** (Franz Lehár/w Willner) Theater an der Wien 12 November

1910 **Zigeunerliebe** (Lehár/w Willner) Carltheater 8 January

1910 **Das Glücksmädel** (Robert Stolz/w Friedrich Thelen) Raimundtheater 28 October

1910 **Die schöne Risette** (Leo Fall/w Willner) Theater an der Wien 19 November

1911 **Das Zirkuskind** (Eysler/w Thelen) Raimundtheater 18 February

1911 **Eva (das Fabriksmädel)** (Lehár/w Willner) Theater an der Wien 24 November

1911 **Casimirs Himmelfahrt** (Bruno Granichstaedten/w Willner) Raimundtheater 25 December

1912 **Der kleine König** (*A kis király*) (Emmerich Kálmán/Károly Bakonyi, Ferenc Martos ad) Theater an der Wien 27 November

1913 **Prinzess Gretl** (Heinrich Reinhardt/w Willner) Theater an der Wien 31 January

1913 **Leute vom Stand** (Fall/w Grünbaum) 1 act Hölle 1 March

1914 **Endlich allein** (Lehár/w Willner) Theater an der Wien 30 January

1914 **Rund um die Liebe** (Oscar Straus/w Thelen) Johann Strauss-Theater 9 November

1915 **Auf Befehl der Herzogin** (Granichstaedten/w Leopold Jacobson) Theater an der Wien 20 March

1915 **Wenn zwei sich lieben** (Eysler/w Willner) Theater an der Wien 29 October

1916 **Warum geht's denn jetzt?** (Eysler/w Jacobson) Bundestheater 5 July

1916 **Hanni geht tanzen** (Eysler) Apollotheater 7 November

1916 **Der Pusztakavalier** (*Mágnás Miska*) German version (Komische Oper, Berlin)

1917 **Nachtfalter** (Straus/w Jacobson) Ronacher 13 March

1918 **Walzerliebe** (Granichstaedten/w Granichstaedten) Apollotheater 16 February

1918 **Die Modebaronin** (Richard Goldberger/w Hans Sassmann) Konzerthaus 1 March

1918 **Eine Ballnacht** (Straus/w Jacobson) Johann Strauss-Theater 11 October

1919 **Sybill** (*Szibill*) German version (Stadttheater)

1919 **Der Liebesteufel** (Julius Bistron/w Jacobson) Komödienhaus 17 October

1919 **Dorfmusikanten** (Straus/w Jacobson) Theater an der Wien 29 November

1919 **Was Mädchen träumen** (Leo Ascher/w Jacobson) Raimundtheater 6 December

1920 **Yuschi tanzt** (Ralph Benatzky/w Jacobson) Wiener Bürgertheater 3 April

1920 **Liebesrausch** (*Az ezüst sirály*) German version (Carltheater)

1920 **Der Tanz ins Glück** (Robert Stolz/w Bruno Hardt-Warden) Raimundtheater 23 December

1921 **Die Tanzgräfin** (Stolz/w Jacobson) Wallner-Theater, Berlin 18 February

1921 **Indische Nachte** (Granichstaedten/w Hardt-Warden) Apollotheater 25 November

1921 **Eine Sommernacht** (Stolz/w Hardt-Warden) Johann Strauss-Theater 23 December

1922 **Die Liebe geht um!** (Stolz/w Hardt-Warden) Raimundtheater 22 June

1922 **Offenbach** (aka *Der Meister von Montmartre*) German version w Hardt-Warden (Neues Wiener Stadttheater)

1923 **Marietta** (Walter Kollo/w Hardt-Warden, Willi Kollo) Metropoltheater, Berlin 22 December

THE BOHEMIAN GIRL Opera in 4 acts by Alfred Bunn. Music by Michael Balfe. Theatre Royal, Drury Lane, London, 27 November 1843.

The most popular of the many so-called operatic works of the composer Balfe, *The Bohemian Girl* was part of a small group of English-language musical-theatre works of the mid-19th century which became exhaustingly frequently played favorites wherever English-language musical theatre was played. This group formed the backbone of the repertoires of the touring English opera companies which provided the basic musical theatre entertainment of British provincial and colonial towns through many years in the mid-19th century until the introduction of opéra-bouffe brought an alternative style of musical theatre. Along with such pieces as *Maritana* and *The Lily of Killarney, The Bohemian Girl* was one of the most important pieces in a tradition which would provide the bases for the romantic and sentimental portions of those comic operas (not always as comic, at least in part, as their description might hint) which were the principal fodder of the musical theatre of the third quarter of the 19th century.

The Bohemian Girl was a romantic tale of a mysterious girl called Arline, rescued from a stag by a noble Polish exile, Thaddeus, and carried off by his gypsy friends. Restored many years later to her family, she finally weds her rescuer in spite of the machinations of the amorous gypsy queen. Balfe's attractive score, more in what would now be considered a light operatic vein, included the soprano ''I Dreamt I Dwelt in Marble Halls,'' the most popular English show song of its time, as well as several other song hits, notably the lovely ''The Heart Bowed Down'' and ''When Other Lips.''

The tens of thousands of performances given *The Bohemian Girl* around the world, in a multiplicity of languages (but mostly in the original English), ensured that it would come into the hands of the burlesque writers. The best-known amongst such efforts included the brothers Brough's *Arline, or The Fortunes and Vicissitudes of a Bohemian Girl* (Haymarket Theatre 21 April 1851) with Priscilla Horton as Thaddeus; William Best and Henry Bellingham's *Arline, the Lost Child, or The Pole, the Policeman and the Polar Bear* (Sadler's Wells 23 July 1864); W S Gilbert's *The Merry Zingara, or The Tipsy Gipsy and the Pipsy-wipsy* (Royalty Theatre 21 March 1868) in which Pattie Oliver featured as a burlesque Arline; H J Byron's *The Bohemian G'yurl and the Unapproachable Pole* (Opera Comique 31 January 1877) in England; and New York's highly successful *The Bohea Man's Girl* (Olympic Theater 11 March 1845). Emma Taylor and Mary Taylor were duplicate Arlines and Charles Walcot played Floorstain in a version which made great play with the terms of the tea trade.

In 1934 an updated version of the show, reset in America, was staged briefly at Broadway's Lyric Theater under the title *Gypsy Blonde* (F Gabrielson/K Jones 25 June).

Several films using bits of the book have appeared over the years, notably a silent of 1922 in which Ivor Novello plays Thaddeus to the Arline of Gladys Cooper and the Devilshoof of C Aubrey Smith. A 1936 Hollywood *Bohemian Girl* managed to get Laurel and Hardy into the action, but retained ''I Dreamt I Dwelt in Marble Halls.''

USA: Park Theater 25 November 1844; Australia: Royal Victoria Theatre, Sydney 13 July 1846; Austria: Theater an der Wien *Die Zigeunerin* 22 July 1846; Germany: Hamburg *Die Zigeunerin* 17 December 1846; France: Rouen *La Bohémienne* 23 April 1862

Recordings: complete (Argo), selection (part record) (HMV), etc

BOHEMIOS Zarzuela in 1 act by Guillermo Perrín and Miguel Palacios. Music by Amadeo Vives. Teatro de la Zarzuela, 24 March 1904.

An un-Spanish kind of zarzuela, with a libretto set in period Paris, *Bohemios* nevertheless found itself a fine degree of popularity in its own country. Perrín and Palacios turned out one of those familiar tales of genius starving in a Montmartre garret of which the principals were the composer Roberto and his poet pal Victor, who are together writing The Great Opera, and the old singer Marcelo coaching his soprano daughter, Cossette, for fame. A nice chap called Girard helps out, and when Cossette does her audition at the Opéra-Comique, accompanied by Roberto and singing his music, the garret goes out the window and wedding bells, fame and fortune fly in.

The piece has been filmed in Spain for both cinema (1937) and television (1968).

Films: Cinematografica Mexicana 1934, Francisco Elias 1937, Spanish TV 1968

Recordings: cast recording c1930 (Blue Moon), complete (Hispavox, Audivis Valois, etc)

BOHRMANN, Heinrich (b Saarbrücken, 28 May 1838; d Vienna, 8 October 1908).

Playwright and librettist, Bohrmann wrote several comedies and Operetten for the Viennese stage in collaboration with "J Riegen," otherwise Julius Nigri von Saint-Albino (1849–1895), whilst working variously as a theatre director at the Komische Oper in Pressburg, as the editor of Vienna's *Wiener Almanach* (1893–99) and subsequently of the fashion magazine *Im Boudoir* (1900–1907).

The pair's two works for the Viennese theatre brought them one fine success—with a little help from a more professional rewriter in Richard Genée—with Strauss's *Das Spitzentuch der Königin,* and a more moderate result with Josef Bayer's *Der Chevalier von San Marco,* played first at the Carltheater and subsequently at New York's Thalia Theater (30 January 1882). The following year, the Thalia also mounted another Bohrmann-Riegen piece, set to music by the house's musical director, Ludwig Englander. *Der Prinz Gemahl* did well enough to be seen later outside New York, and at Broadway's Wallack's Theater in an English translation, but did not get seen in its land of origin. Bohrmann also authored an adaptation of Wilson Barrett's *The Sign of the Cross* as "an historical tableau of the time of the Emperor Nero in 5 acts and 9 scenes" with songs and music by William Rose, and the text for Hugo Kobler's opera *Grüne Ostern* (Brünn 22 April 1899).

Riegen collaborated intermittently with other authors, including Richard Genée with whom he wrote the libretti for Czibulka's successful *Pfingsten in Florenz* and for Tomaschek's opera *Die Teufelsbrucke* (Pilsen, 1892), and Bohrmann also ventured some other pieces without his habitual partner. None, however, came up to the notoriety of their first musical piece as a team.

1880 **Das Spitzentuch der Königin** (Johann Strauss/w Riegen, Richard Genée) Theater an der Wien 1 October

1882 **Der Chevalier von San Marco** (Josef Bayer/w Riegen) Carltheater 7 November

1883 **Der Prinz Gemahl** (*The Prince Consort*) (Ludwig Engländer/w Julius Hopp, Riegen) Thalia Theater, New York 11 April

1886 **Der schöne Kurfürst** (Josef Hellmesberger/w Riegen) Theater am Gärtnerplatz, Munich 15 May

1891 **Der Gouverneur von Tours** (Carl Reinecke) Schwerin 20 November

1895 **Figaro bei Hof** (Alfred Müller-Norden/w Riegen) Centraltheater, Berlin 4 May

1897 **Ein Traum** (Max von Weinzierl/w Marko Bombelles) Raimundtheater 4 March

1901 **Djellah** (Rodolphe Weys) Lübeck April

BOLGER, Ray[mond Wallace] (b Dorchester, Mass, 10 January 1904; d Los Angeles, 15 January 1987).

A warmly funny dancing comedian, Bolger appeared on Broadway in *The Merry World* (1926), in a supporting role in the musical comedy *Heads Up!* (1929, Georgie) and in the revues *George White's Scandals* (1931) and *Life Begins at 8:40* (1934), before making a memorable success in the role of Phil Dolan III, the composer and teacher of popular music who gets mixed up with the ballet world in Rodgers and Hart's musical *On Your Toes* ("There's a Small Hotel," "On Your Toes") in 1936.

Bolger subsequently appeared in further revues (*Keep Off the Grass, Three to Make Ready*) and introduced two further large leading roles in musical comedies: as the henpecked Sapiens in Rodgers and Hart's *By Jupiter* (1942), and as the character called Charley Wykeham (who was actually a combination of the original Charley and the disguisable Lord Fancourt-Babberley) in the musical remake of *Charley's Aunt* called *Where's Charley?* (1948, "Once in Love With Amy," Tony Award). He repeated his role in this last piece on film, having previously, in a dozen years in films, played in such pieces as *The Great Ziegfeld* (1936 as himself), *Rosalie* (1937) and *Sweethearts* (1938), appeared most memorably as the scarecrow in *The Wizard of Oz* (1939), and performed in *Sunny* (1941 as Bunny Billings), *The Harvey Girls* (1946) and *Look for the Silver Lining* (1949 as Jack Donahue).

He later appeared as Uncle Barnaby in the 1960 film version of *Babes in Toyland* and returned to the stage in two further musicals, *All American* (1962, Professor Fodroski) and *Come Summer* (1969, Phineas Sharp), in the later days of a career which frittered into nightclubs, concert and some television appearances and left the impression of having deserved more and, generally, better musical theatre roles.

BOLTEN-BÄCKERS, Heinrich (''Heinz'') [BOLTEN, Heinrich Eduard Hermann] (b Chemnitz, 10 April 1871; d Dresden, 30 January 1938). Author of the Berlin Apollotheater's series of turn-of-the-century Revue-Operetten.

Born in Chemnitz but brought up in Dresden, Bolten became dramaturge at the Ostend Theater in his early twenties and it was there that his first pieces, *Berlin unter Wasser* and *Ein alter Spielmann,* were staged. He mixed theatrical occupations through the 1890s, adapting French operas (*L'Attaque du moulin, La Vivandière*), opérettes and vaudevilles for various German and Austrian theatres, writing German libretti for the operas of Urich (*Das Glockenspiel* 1895, *Der Lootse* Hamburg 26 September 1895), directing a touring theatre company, and working for a while at the Scala Theater in Cologne, before combining with his old colleague, Paul Lincke, formerly an orchestral player at the Ostend Theater and now reaching out as a composer, to write the short revue-Operette *Venus auf Erden* for the program of Berlin's variety-based Apollotheater. Although he continued adaptation work in the straight theatre, providing German versions of the works of Pinero and other important foreign writers, his musical theatre output thereafter was almost entirely devoted to supplying texts for Lincke, with whom he scored considerable successes with a series of further short spectaculars for the Apollotheater: *Frau Luna, Lysistrata* (Glühwürmchen Idyll) and *Im Reiche des Indra.* His little musical comedy *Am Hochzeitsabend,* after showings in Germany and Austria, was produced in England as *In a Mirror* (Palace Theatre 3 May 1909).

Bolten otherwise devoted himself to theatre management in Berlin, to high-profile activity in the German Authors and Composers' Association, and to ventures into early film production.

1895 **Die kleinen Schäfen** (*Les Petites Brebis*) German version (Theater in der Josefstadt)

1896 **Cousin-Cousine** German version (Thalia-Theater)

1897 **Der verregnete Amor** (aka *Der Liebesgott*) (*L'Amour mouillé*) German version (Theater an der Wien)

1897 **Venus auf Erden** (Paul Lincke) Apollotheater, Berlin 6 June

1898 **Das neue Regiment** (*Le Nouveau Régiment*) German version (Theater in der Josefstadt)

1898 **Die kleinen Michus** (*Les P'tites Michu*) German version w Julius Freund (Metropoltheater, Berlin)

1899 **Brigitte** (*Véronique*) German version (Neues Königliches Operntheater, Berlin)

Plate 45. **Ray Bolger.** *Spring-heeled Ray achieves take-off.*

1899 **Die weisse Henne** (*La Poule blanche*) German version (Lustspieltheater)

1899 **Le Cabinet Piperlin** German version (Lustspieltheater)

1899 **Frau Luna** (Lincke) 1 act Apollotheater, Berlin 1 May

1899 **Im Reiche des Indra** (Lincke/w Leopold Ely) Apollotheater, Berlin 18 December

1900 **Fräulein Loreley** (Lincke) 1 act Apollotheater, Berlin 15 October

1902 **Lysistrata** (Lincke) Apollotheater, Berlin 1 April

1902 **Nakiris Hochzeit** (Lincke) Apollotheater, Berlin 6 November

1903 **Am Hochzeitsabend** (Lincke) 1 act Danzers Orpheum, Vienna 31 March

1905 **Prinzess[in] Rosine** (Lincke/w Friedendorf) Apollotheater, Berlin 18 November

1906 **Das blaue Bild** (Lincke) Apollotheater, Berlin 18 May

1906 **Kadettenstreiche** (Viktor Holländer) Eden-Theater, Aachen 19 July

1907 **Die schöne Vestalin** (*La Plus Belle*) German version (Apollotheater, Vienna)

1911 **Gri-gri** (Lincke/Jules Chancel, Henriot [ie, Henri Maigrot] ad) Metropoltheater, Cologne 25 March

1913 **Rackerchen** (Theodore Blumer) Neues Luisen-Theater, Königsberg February

BOLTON, Guy [Reginald] (b Broxbourne, Herts, 23 November 1882; d Henley, 6 September 1979). Librettist to half a century of musical comedies on both sides of the Atlantic.

Born in Britain, of American parents, Bolton spent his earliest years working towards a career in architecture but, after the production of his first play in 1911, he orientated himself towards the theatre in preference. In a career that lasted 50 years, he worked, particularly in the earliest years, at an enormously high speed, turning out a number of plays and libretti every year. In the three years surrounding his first contributions to the musical stage, he saw the plays *The Rule of Three* (Harris Theater 16 February 1914), *The Fallen Idol* (Comedy Theater 23 January 1915), a version of Jack London's *The Sea Wolf* (Hartford, Conn 12 March 1915) and the "social problem play" *Her Game* (Buffalo 21 June 1915) mounted; he "suggested" (w George Middleton) *Hit-the-Trail Holliday* (Astor Theater 13 September 1915) to George M Cohan, who was listed as author; wrote the playlet *Children* (w Tom Carlton) for the Washington Square Players (20 March 1916) and also *Happy Thought* (w Middleton, Cleveland 26 June 1916); and authored his first musical comedy script and adapted three others.

If the original piece, *Ninety in the Shade,* a vehicle for comedy stars Marie Cahill and Richard Carle, set by Jerome Kern with dance melodies of the day, was a failure, the adaptations were, all three, successes. *Nobody Home,* a remake of the delightful and successful little London musical *Mr Popple of Ippleton,* with a replacement score by Kern, had a fair run of 135 performances at the intimate Princess Theater and the larger Maxine Elliott before touring. *Very Good Eddie,* a musical adaptation of the hit play *Over Night* done with its author, Philip Bartholomae, and Kern, followed in the same style of farcical comedy with song-and-dance and scored a splendid success (341 performances), whilst an adaptation of the richly dancing Hungarian musical play *Zsuzsi kisasszony* (*Miss Susie*) as *Miss Springtime* for Klaw and Erlanger welcomed even more customers in 224 performances at the rather larger New Amsterdam Theater.

After this felicitous beginning, Bolton carried on in both strains, collaborating with Kern on further farcical comedies with dancing songs, written somewhat in the style of the French vaudeville (if usually without some of that genre's more comic complexities) and also adapting existing works for the American musical stage, in an amazingly prolific schedule which ranged from further shows for the tiny Princess Theater to such splashy pieces as the Charles Dillingham revue *Miss 1917* (Kern, Victor Herbert/w P G Wodehouse Century Theater), not to mention a parallel if less substantial schedule of non-musical plays.

The Kern musicals proved, mostly, to be extremely successful. If *Have a Heart,* which followed the basics of a French comedy plot but reset the action in America, survived only 76 performances, *Oh, Boy!,* the next show in what was becoming regarded as a series at the Princess Theater, was a triumph. Like *Have a Heart,* it acknowledged no source for its libretto, but the elements of its plot were familiar ones of the Paris vaudeville and its British derivatives, bound together here in a briskly farcical piece which was one of Bolton's smartest achievements. *Oh, Lady! Lady!!,* written in a similar if less bristling style, was only a fair-to-middling success (219 performances), but an adaptation of George Ade's hit farce *The College Widow* as *Leave it to Jane* (an unrepresentative 176 performances) confirmed both the success of *Oh, Boy!* and the fact that there was plenty of subject and plot matter suitable to real comic musical plays closer at hand than Paris. Finally, five years and seven shows after the beginning of their collaboration, Bolton and Kern moved away from the vaudeville style of vigorously comic musical plays and into a romantic dance-and-song musical built on more operettic libretto lines and triumphed all over again with the pretty, if textually loose, *Sally.*

In the meanwhile, Bolton had found mixed success elsewhere. Transplanting the very central European action and music of *Die Csárdásfürstin* into *The Riviera Girl* did not work (78 performances) and an attempt to Americanize Josef Szulc's musical comedy *Loute* under one of the theoretically catchy but meaningless titles of the age, *See You Later,* foundered twice on the road. However, a collaboration with the man who had been more influential than any other in bringing the French musical-comedy style to Broadway, *The Pink Lady*'s Ivan Caryll, gave him a fine success with the Klaw and Erlanger production *The Girl Behind the Gun* (160 performances). Transported to London as *Kissing Time,* this musical adaptation of the French vaudeville *Madame et son filleul* gave its author his first real West End hit (430 performances), following the disappointing London runs of *Very Good Eddie* and *Oh, Joy,* and would remain one of the internationally most successful works of his career.

A second collaboration with Caryll on another ex-French piece, Armont and Gerbidon's *Souris d'hôtel,* was interrupted by the composer's death and the resultant *Little Miss Raffles / The Hotel Mouse* failed (88 performances), but a musical version of another play written by and with *Very Good Eddie*'s Philip Bartholomae produced another hit in the colorfully comical *Tangerine* (337 performances), a piece whose plot's trip to the Southern Seas happily brought back memories of turn-of-the-century native comic opera.

In 1924 George Grossmith, the London producer of *Kissing Time,* teamed Bolton with the young composer George Gershwin on a show for his Winter Garden Theatre. What value *Primrose* had was more in its performances and some of its songs than in its undoubtedly well-tailored libretto, but the collaboration thus cemented with Gershwin would soon bring forth riper fruit. Back on American stages, Bolton joined with Fred Thompson, another Grossmith man, to provide the libretti for Gershwin's dance-and-comedy shows *Lady, Be Good!* and *Tip-Toes* and with his longtime collaborator, P G Wodehouse, on probably his most successful single text, *Oh, Kay!,* which, although announced as a version of the Paris hit *La Présidente,* showed little signs of that ''source'' by the time it reached its final form.

Trips into the field of the romantic biomusical with a Jenny Lind show called *The Nightingale*—written to feature his then wife Marguerite Namara (number 2 of 5) as the famous singer, but ultimately and unsuccessfully played without her—and into farce comedy with the Clark and McCullough vehicle *The Ramblers* and opérette à grand spectacle with the swashbuckling South American tale of *Rio Rita,* were mixed with more vaudevillesque musical comedies, including the successful *The Five o'Clock Girl* (280 performances) and a share in the 1928 *She's My Baby* (the former sporting plot-line flavors of *La Demoiselle du telephone* and the latter of London's *Baby Bunting,* Germany's *Madame Sherry* and others), and another vehicle for *Sally*'s dance star, Marilyn[n] Miller, this time Ruritanianized as Princess *Rosalie.* He also took time to musicalize Belasco's *Polly with a Past,* an exercise which gave him a rare and real flop in just two Broadway weeks.

The Broadway successes kept on coming: Ed Wynn's fairy-tale vehicle *Simple Simon,* another piece with Gershwin, *Girl Crazy,* and a first collaboration with Cole Porter on the famous libretto for *Anything Goes* which had to be rewritten by Lindsay and Crouse when current events were alleged to have rendered it distasteful. It was not rewritten by Bolton, because he had now shifted his headquarters to Britain where, during the 1930s, he turned out a series of musical shows which were amongst the most successful of their time. Britain was going through a fashion for the star-vehicle, comedy-based musical show and, for that reason, few pieces of the period survived beyond their original purposes and the people for whom they were designed, but the series of musical comedies which Bolton and his associates provided for the Gaiety Theatre company headed by Leslie Henson (*Seeing Stars, Swing Along, Going Greek, Running Riot*), the Flanagan and Allen *Give Me a Ring,* Jack Buchanan and Elsie Randolph's *This'll Make You Whistle* and Cicely Courtneidge and Bobby Howes's *Hide and Seek* were all fine of-the-moment successes which more than compensated for such occasional misfires as the attempts to doctor the Australian musical presented as *At the Silver Swan* and Eric Maschwitz's embarrassing *Magyar Melody.*

Throughout the years, Bolton had followed the fashions in musical theatre with alacrity and efficiency, always a collaborator prized and much-liked for his inevitably swift and to-the-point work and his agreeable and ''English-gentleman'' personality. From his wartime return to America, however, the writer—now in his mid-sixties—began to loose touch a little with the trends. His only subsequent musical successes were the lively and old-fashioned comedy musical *Follow the Girls* and its less long-lived successor *Ankles Aweigh.* Such other pieces as the weak Offenbach pasticcio biomusical *Music at Midnight* and the spectacle *Rainbow Square* were unfortunate episodes. His final work to make it to the stage in his 80th year was a share in the musicalization of his highly successful English version of Marcelle Maurette's French play *Anastasia.* Subsequent pieces, including a musical version of the Jeeves stories (*Come On, Jeeves*), a rewrite of *Anastasia* as *I Live Again* for the Marre/Diener team and a further piece for San Francisco failed to get a production.

One of Bolton's other non-musical plays, *Who's Who?* (1934 w Wodehouse) was made into *Who's Who, Baby?* (Johnny Brandon/Gerald Frank, Players Theater 20 January 1968).

Bolton also wrote a number of film screenplays and novels including a piece detailing, with admitted fictional details and ''improvements'' to the truth, his musical comedy life, under the title *Bring on the Girls: The Improbable Story of Our Life in Musical Comedy, with Pictures to Prove It* (Simon & Schuster, 1953).

1915 **Ninety in the Shade** (Jerome Kern/Harry B Smith, Clare Kummer) Knickerbocker Theater 25 January

1915 **Nobody Home** (*Mr Popple of Ippleton*) American adaptation w new music by Jerome Kern (Princess Theater)

1915 **Very Good Eddie** (Kern/Schuyler Greene/w Philip Bartholomae) Princess Theater 23 December

1916 **Miss Springtime** (*Zsuzsi kisasszony*) English version (New Amsterdam Theater)

1917 **Have a Heart** (Kern/w P G Wodehouse) Liberty Theater 11 January

1917 **Oh, Boy!** (UK: *Oh, Joy!*) (Kern/w Wodehouse) Princess Theater 20 February

1917 **Leave It to Jane** (Kern/w Wodehouse) Longacre Theater 28 August

1917 **The Riviera Girl** (*Die Csárdásfürstin*) American version w Wodehouse (New Amsterdam Theater)

1918 **See You Later** (*Loute*) English version w additional music by Jean Schwartz/P G Wodehouse (Academy of Music, Baltimore)

1918 **Oh, Lady! Lady!!** (Kern/w Wodehouse) Princess Theater 1 February

1918 **The Girl Behind the Gun** (aka *Kissing Time*) (Ivan Caryll/w Wodehouse) New Amsterdam Theater 16 September

1918 **Oh, My Dear!** (ex- *Ask Dad*) (Louis Hirsch/w Wodehouse) Princess Theater 26 November

1919 **The Rose of China** (Armand Vecsey/Wodehouse) Lyric Theater 25 November

1920 **Sally** (ex- *Sally of our Alley*) (Kern/Clifford Grey) New Amsterdam Theater 21 December

1921 **Tangerine** (Monte Carlo, Alma Sanders/w Bartholomae) Casino Theater 9 August

1921 **Little Miss Raffles** (Caryll/Grey) Stamford, Conn 1 December

1922 **The Hotel Mouse** (revised *Little Miss Raffles* w add mus by Vecsey) Shubert Theater 13 March

1922 **Daffy Dill** (Herbert Stothart/Oscar Hammerstein II/w Hammerstein) Apollo Theater 22 August

1924 **Sitting Pretty** (Kern/w Wodehouse) Fulton Theater 8 April

1924 **Primrose** (George Gershwin/Desmond Carter, Ira Gershwin/w George Grossmith) Winter Garden Theatre, London 11 September

1924 **Lady, Be Good!** (G Gershwin/I Gershwin/w Fred Thompson) Liberty Theater 1 December

1925 **Tip-Toes** (G Gershwin/I Gershwin/w Thompson) Liberty Theater 28 December

1925 **The Bamboula** (Albert Szirmai, Harry Rosenthal/Irving Caesar, Douglas Furber/w Harry M Vernon) His Majesty's Theatre, London 24 March

1926 **The Ramblers** (ex- *The Fly-By-Nights*) (Bert Kalmar, Harry Ruby/w Kalmar, Ruby) Lyric Theater 30 September

1926 **Oh, Kay!** (ex- *Cheerio!*) (G Gershwin/I Gershwin, Howard Dietz/w Wodehouse) Imperial Theater 8 November

1927 **The Nightingale** (Vecsey/w Wodehouse) Jolson Theater 3 January

1927 **She's My Baby** (Richard Rodgers/Lorenz Hart, Kalmar, Ruby/w Kalmar, Ruby) Globe Theater 3 January

1927 **Rio Rita** (Harry Tierney/Joseph McCarthy/w Thompson) Ziegfeld Theater 2 February

1927 **The Five o'Clock Girl** (Kalmar, Ruby/w Thompson) 44th Street Theater 10 October

1928 **Rosalie** (Gershwin, Sigmund Romberg/w William Anthony McGuire) New Amsterdam Theater 10 January

1928 **Blue Eyes** (Kern) Piccadilly Theatre, London 27 April

1929 **Polly** (Phil Charig, Stothart/Irving Caesar/w George Middleton, Isabel Leighton) Lyric Theater 8 January

1929 **Top Speed** (Kalmar, Ruby) 46th Street Theater 25 December

1930 **Simple Simon** (Rodgers/Hart/w Ed Wynn) Ziegfeld Theater 18 February

1930 **Girl Crazy** (G Gershwin/I Gershwin/w Jack McGowan) Alvin Theater 14 October

1931 **The Song of the Drum** (Vivan Ellis, Herman Finck/Desmond Carter/w Thompson) Theatre Royal, Drury Lane, London 9 January

1933 **Give Me a Ring** (Martin Broones) London Hippodrome 22 June

1934 **Anything Goes** (Cole Porter/w Wodehouse ad Russel Crouse, Howard Lindsay) Alvin Theater 21 November

1935 **Seeing Stars** (Broones/Graham John/w Thompson) Gaiety Theatre, London 31 October

1936 **At the Silver Swan** (Edmond Samuels, Percival Mackey/Grey) Palace Theatre, London 19 February

1936 **Swing Along** (Broones/John/w Thompson, Douglas Furber) Gaiety Theatre, London 2 September

1936 **This'll Make You Whistle** (Maurice Sigler, Al Goodhart, Al Hoffman/w Thompson) Palace Theatre, London 14 September

1936 **Going Places** (Ellis/w Thompson) Savoy Theatre, London 8 October

1937 **Going Greek** (Sam Lerner, Goodhart, Hoffman) Gaiety Theatre, London 16 September

1937 **Hide and Seek** (Ellis, Lerner, Goodhart, Hoffman/w Thompson, Furber) London Hippodrome 14 October

1938 **The Fleet's Lit Up** (Ellis/w Thompson, Bert Lee) London Hippodrome 17 August

1938 **Running Riot** (Ellis/w Firth Shephard, Furber) Gaiety Theatre, London 31 August

1938 **Bobby Get Your Gun** (Jack Waller, Joe Tunbridge/Grey, Lee, Carter/w Lee, Thompson) Adelphi Theatre, London 7 October

1939 **Magyar Melody** revised *Paprika* (George Posford, Bernard Grun/Harold Purcell, Eric Maschwitz/w Thompson, Maschwitz) His Majesty's Theatre, London 20 January

1940 **Walk with Music** (ex- *Three after Three*) (Hoagy Carmichael/Johnny Mercer/w Parke Levy, Alan Lipscott) Ethel Barrymore Theater 4 June

1940 **Hold on to Your Hats** (Burton Lane/E Y Harburg/w Matt Brooks, Eddie Davis) Shubert Theater 11 September

1944 **Jackpot** (Vernon Duke, Howard Dietz) Alvin Theater 13 January

1944 **Follow the Girls** (Phil Charig/Milton Pascal, Dan Shapiro/w Davis, Thompson) Century Theater 8 April

1947 **The Chocolate Soldier** (*Der tapfere soldat*) revised American version w Bernard Hanighen (Century Theater)

1950 **Music at Midnight** (Offenbach arr Hans May/Purcell) His Majesty's Theatre, London 10 November

1951 **Rainbow Square** (Robert Stolz/w Purcell) Stoll Theatre, London 21 September

1955 **Ankles Aweigh** (Sammy Fain/Dan Shapiro/w Davis) Mark Hellinger Theater 18 April

1965 **Anya** (Rachmaninov arr /George Forrest, Robert Wright/w George Abbott) Ziegfeld Theater 29 November

Literature: Davis, L: *Bolton and Wodehouse and Kern: The Men Who Made Musical Comedy* (James H. Heineman, Inc, New York, 1993)

BOMBASTES FURIOSO Burlesque in 1 act by William Barnes Rhodes. Haymarket Theatre, London, 7 August 1810.

One of the most famous of pre-Victorian burlesques, this extravagant and grotesque mockery of the bombast of the dramatic stage, its writers and its performers, was a short play into which a half dozen musical pieces, set to the tunes of ''Tekeli,'' ''Hope Told a Flatt'ring Tale,'' ''Paddy's Wedding,'' ''O Lady Fair,'' ''My Lodging is on the Cold Ground'' and ''Tural Lural Laddi,'' were inserted. It proved a popular part of playbills throughout Britain, remained on British-influenced stages for many decades and survived into occasional performances long after the fashions in burlesque had changed.

USA: Park Theater 15 October 1816; Australia: Emu Plains Theatre 16 May 1825

BOMBO Extravaganza in 2 acts by Harold Atteridge. Music by Sigmund Romberg. Jolson Theater, New York, 6 October 1921.

Built as a vehicle for Al Jolson at the peak of his pulling-power, *Bombo* justified its star's appearance in blackface by casting him as the negro servant to no less a gentleman than Christopher Columbus. Any pretence that the show was a musical play was fairly soon dissipated, and the words ''extravaganza'' and ''revue'' were subsequently used to describe an entertainment which was, in fact, little more than a dressed-up concert for its star. Jolson took over the proceedings in the second act and simply delivered one number after another in his inimitable style. Amongst those numbers appeared, at various times, Buddy De Sylva and Louis Silvers's ''April Showers,'' the Gus Kahn/Dan Russo, Ernie Erdman ''Toot-toot-Tootsie'' and, during the post-Broadway touring, Joseph Meyer and De Sylva's ''California, Here I Come.'' Lost in this recital of minstrelsy were 20 pieces by Sigmund Romberg, several by Con Conrad and others by Cliff Friend.

Bombo served Broadway for 218 performances before Jolson took it on the road for two seasons.

BOND, Jessie [Charlotte] (b London, 11 January 1853; d Worthing, 17 June 1942).

Mythology relates—thanks to agent-producer Richard D'Oyly Carte's practiced manufactuary of phony curricula vitae—that 25-year-old Jessie Bond was heard by Carte singing at a Royal Academy of Music concert and was hired in extremis to replace the ailing Mrs Howard Paul in the role of Hebe in the original production of *HMS Pinafore.* In fact, Miss Bond was a longtime client of Carte's musical agency who had been performing in concert since the age of 18, had sung the contralto part in *Messiah* at Liverpool at 20, and had appeared alongside Mrs Paul in her entertainment on numerous occasions. What she had apparently not done before, however, was spoken lines in a stage play and when the young singer proved unable to cope with Hebe's dialogue, what had been written as a principal comic-cum-contralto role in the vein of Mrs Paul's Lady Sangazure in *The Sorcerer* was cut to virtually nothing. However, Miss Bond made sufficient of her negligible remaining opportunities to be taken to America to repeat her role and to be engaged for the next Carte production, *The Pirates of Penzance* (1880). She remained a member of the D'Oyly Carte company through nine of the Gilbert and Sullivan comic operas, creating the roles of Kate (*The Pirates of Penzance*), Lady Angela (*Patience*), Iolanthe, Pitti Sing (*Mikado*), Melissa (*Princess Ida*), Mad Margaret (*Ruddigore*), Phoebe (*The Yeomen of the Guard,* a role written by Gilbert to allow her simply to be ''her own sweet self'') and Tessa (*The Gondoliers*), as well as the more extravagantly comical Chinna Loofah in George Dance and Edward Solomon's *The Nautch Girl* (1891).

She left the Savoy company to attempt to cash in on her fame by touring a Drawing Room Entertainment, but the enterprise was not a success, and she quickly returned to the theatre. She subsequently appeared successfully in Continental and British comic opera—as Martha in Lacome's *Ma mie Rosette* (1892), as Molly opposite Harry Monkhouse in *Der arme Jonathan* and as the comical Susan Sinnett in *Wapping Old Stairs,* as well as, less happily, in the fiasco *Miami*—and as the fashion in entertainments changed, moved into the rising field of musical comedy to appear as the heroine of the Osmond Carr/Adrian Ross *Go Bang* (1894). She found herself quite eclipsed by dancing soubrette Letty Lind, and returned to Gilbert, declaring that ''never again will I appear as a lady in modern dress,'' to play the equivalent of her old Savoy roles as Nanna in *His Excellency* (1894) before retiring from the stage.

Her younger sister, [Miriam] **Neva BOND** (b 1854), also worked in the musical theatre, creating the role of Isobel in London's *The Pirates of Penzance* (1880).

MacGeorge, E: *Life and Reminiscences of Jessie Bond, the Old Savoyard* (John Lane, London, 1930)

UN BON GARÇON Opérette (comédie musicale) in 3 acts by André Barde. Music by Maurice Yvain. Théâtre des Nouveautés, Paris, 13 November 1926.

One of the succession of lively Jazz Age musical comedies for which Barde turned out his usual spirited comic libretto and for which Yvain supplied another up-to-date and dancing score (''Je t'emmène à la campagne,'' ''Ce n'était pourtant pas bien difficile,'' ''Pour danser le Charleston,'' ''La Musique grisante''). The show's cast was headed by the comic Milton in the role of interfering Achille, who sets out to persuade an old lady friend of his called Madame Bouillon-Falloux (Mary Hett) that her daughter, Camille (Davia), should not, as Madame would have it, marry Lucien de Gravère (Robert Ancelin), who is already devoted to pretty Arlette Méryl (Pierrette Madd). Urban (Pontavès), Gildès (Abbé

Colignac) and Germain Champell (M de Gravère) completed the principal cast, under the direction of Régina Camier, and Benoît-Léon Deutsch's production of this sparky example of Jazz Age musical comedy had a run of over a year in Paris before going on the French road and overseas.

Hungary produced *Un bon garçon* in a version by István Zágon which altered the title to *Csattan a csók* (literally "Stunning Lips") in order to include the "bouche" element of Yvain's earlier show titles, whilst an American version (ad Gertrude Purcell, Max and Nathaniel Lief) changed the sex of the title role (*Luckee Girl*) but also squeezed in so many interpolated songs by Maurie Rubens and others that there was little room left for the Paris score. Broadway audiences were adjudged more likely to prefer Werner Janssen and Mann Holiner's "Come On and Let's Make Whoopee" to Yvain's classy dance melodies. Irene Dunne (Arlette), in her first Broadway lead role, had to give second best to the voluminous variety comic Billy House (Hercules), but this pair, Irving Fisher (Lucien), Frank Lalor (Pontavès), Doris Vinton (Camille) and the Four Diplomats got only 81 New York performances out of the resultant mishmash. French-speaking theatergoers in New York had a chance to see the original *Un bon garçon* as played by a touring French musical comedy company with Hans Servatius and Jane de Poumeyrac featured during 1929.

Hungary: Magyar Színház *Csattan a csók* 7 October 1927; USA: Casino Theater *Luckee Girl* 15 September 1928, Jolson Theater (Fr) 18 March 1929

BONHEUR, Alice (b Paris, 10 February 1874).

Charming soprano whose long and truly international career mixed musical comedy engagements with appearances in variety and music hall in France, America and throughout Europe.

Pretty, vivacious Alice Bonheur—who had started her working days as a modiste's apprentice—began her life in the theatre playing at the Bodinière and at the Menus-Plaisirs (*Mariage galant* 1892, *Le Docteur blanc,* Molda in *Timbale d'argent* revival). She went on to create soubrette roles in a half-dozen-year series of opérettes, mostly at the Bouffes-Parisiens, a series amongst which the outstanding success was Messager's *Les P'tites Michu* (1897, Marie-Blanche), and which included *La Duchesse de Ferrare* (1895, Jeanne), *La Saint-Valentin* (1895, Germaine), *La Dot de Brigitte* (1895, Nicole), *Ninette* (1896, Diane), *Une nuit d'amour* (1896), *La Reine des Reines* (Eldorado, 1896), *Les Petites Femmes* (1897, Bengaline), *La Dame de trèfle* (1898, Lucy), *La Petite Tache* (1898, Marguerite), *Le Soleil à minuit* (1898, Savine) and *Le Roi Dagobert* (1898).

She made a singular success in Paris and London in the little Théâtre des Capucines opérette *Chonchette* (1902), toured South America, and appeared in the leading role of Henri Christiné's early *Service d'amour* at the Scala, in the title role of the French version of Lionel Monckton's *A Country Girl* at L'Olympia (1903), and at the Boîte à Fursy in *Minne* (1905). She returned to the Capucines to play in Cuvillier's *Avant-hier matin* and to create the role of Glycère in Terrasse's whimsical *Paris, ou le bon juge* (1906), then swapped that tiny stage for the vastness of the Châtelet where she was seen in *La Boîte à malices* (1907) and *La Princesse Sans-Gêne* (1907). She found her way back to the Capucines for *Le Coq de l'Inde* (1908), was seen at Vienna's Apollotheater in variety in 1909, created the French version of Franzi in the Parisian premiere of *Ein Walzertraum* (1910), and then took another trip to the Argentine.

Back in Paris, she played in *Berlingot* at the Concert Mayol, in *La Fille de Madame Angot* and *La Fille du tambour-major* at the Gaîté, then toured to Egypt and through France before moving into a series of wartime revues in Paris. In 1918 she appeared at the Palais-Royal as Jacinthe in Cuvillier's *Mademoiselle "Nom d'une pipe"* and in 1919 she played the more senior and less soubrette (if still semi-nude) role of Mme Phidias in the Brussels production of *Phi-Phi.* She subsequently took over this role in the long-running Paris production, playing it for over two years at the Bouffes-Parisiens. She later graduated to older character and comic roles, appearing on the Parisian musical stage as late as *Vacances* (1934) and *L'Auberge du Chat Coiffé* (1935).

BONITA Comic opera in a prologue and 2 acts by Wadham Peacock. Music by Harold Fraser-Simson. Queen's Theatre, London, 22 September 1911.

An ephemeral piece of South American romance-cum-adventure hokum which won notice in retrospect as the first composing venture of Fraser-Simson (his next would be *The Maid of the Mountains*) and as the one venture of the distinguished Shavian (etc) director, Granville Barker, on the musical stage. Barker's presence encouraged the critics to some nonsensically deep analyses of the work and its staging, but the director's attempts to teach motivation to the ladies and gentlemen of the *Bonita* chorus were not a success and the piece folded in 42 performances.

Bonita was also the primitive title of a Sigmund Romberg musical, an adaptation of Augutus Thomas's successful play *Arizona,* which went through a couple of other titles (*Love Song, My Golden West*) before it finally reached Broadway as *The Love Call* (Majestic Theater 24 October 1927).

LA BONNE D'ENFANT[S] Opérette-bouffe in 1 act by Eugène Bercioux. Music by Jacques Offenbach. Théâtre des Bouffes-Parisiens, Paris, 14 October 1856.

The ''bonne d'enfants'' of the title is Dorothée (Mlle Garnier), and the action of the piece is a not unfamiliar one, more than a little reminiscent of the famous old farce *The Area Belle.* Dorothée receives visits from two followers in one evening: the chimneyman, Gargaillou (Michel), and the sapeur, Mitouflard (Dubouchet). Gargaillou disguises himself in feminine garb when Mitouflard arrives and the comical situations fly until Dorothée gets rid of them both and goes off with the trumpeter, Brin d'Amour. In the meanwhile, the cast have tripped through half a dozen pretty burlesque numbers, including a jolly duet for Dorothée and her first-come pretender (''Je rôtis, je brûle''), another for the two fellows, drooling over the ''Superbe créature,'' and a strong representation of the military, as in Mitouflard's number about ''La Garnison de Charenton'' and the Couplets ''De la trompette, j'entends les accents'' with their ta-ra-ra refrain.

First seen on the bill at the Bouffes-Parisiens, *La Bonne d'enfant(s)* was introduced to London during Offenbach's 1857 season at the St James's Theatre, and to Vienna by the Bouffes-Parisiens company, with Lucille Tostée as Dorothée, in their summer season of 1862. It was subsequently seen in Vienna in its successful Hungarian version (ad Pál Tarnay) and in two different German adaptations, played in Germany as *Dorothea* (revived at the Theater Unter den Linden as late as 1895), and an English remake was introduced at the Crystal Palace in 1874 under the title *Rouge et Noir.* As recently as 1991 the piece was played in a program at Metz (22 March) and subsequently seen, in the repertoire of the little Opéra de Guyenne, in the French provinces.

UK: St James's Theatre 26 May 1857, Crystal Palace Opera Theatre (Eng) *Rouge et Noir, or One Too Many* 22 September 1874; Austria: Theater am Franz-Josefs-Kai (Fr) 1 June 1862, Harmonietheater *A Dajka* (Hun) 27 May 1866 and *Die Kindsmädchen* 2 November 1867, Fürsttheater *Die Kindergartnerin* 31 May 1884; Hungary: Budai Népszínház *A Dajka* 28 February 1863; Germany: as *Dorothea*

BOOTH, Shirley [FORD, Thelma Booth] (b New York, 30 August 1898; d Chatham, Mass, 16 October 1992).

A warm, versatile actress who made a name as a quality player of both comedy and drama in the theatre (*Three Men on a Horse, The Philadelphia Story, My Sister Eileen, Goodbye, My Fancy, Come Back, Little Sheba, The Time of the Cuckoo,* etc) and on the screen large (*Come Back, Little Sheba,* Academy Award) and small (on the world's television sets as the loveable *Hazel*), Miss Booth made occasional ventures into the musical theatre, the earliest of which as the archetypal gossip columnist Louhedda Hopsons in the *HMS Pinafore* burlesque *Hollywood Pinafore* (1945).

In the 1950s she starred in three musicals, beginning with Arthur Schwartz's musical version of *A Tree Grows in Brooklyn* in which she played dear Aunt Cissy, dreaming of her long-lost love (''He Had Refinement'') until disillusion sets in, and continuing in a similar character as loveable Lottie Gibson in the same composer's *By the Beautiful Sea* (1954). In 1959 she took the title role in *Juno,* an attempt at musicalizing Sean O'Casey's classic drama *Juno and the Paycock* in which, in the classic dramatic role made famous by Sara Allgood, she introduced the ''Song of the Ma,'' ''Old Sayin's'' and ''Where?'' for 16 performances. She made a final musical appearance in 1970 as Mother Maria, the church-building Superior of the only marginally less short-lived *Look to the Lilies.*

BORDMAN, Gerald [Martin] (b Philadelphia, 18 September 1931).

After university studies in medieval English (Ph D) and a number of years running the family chemical business, Bordman retired and began what would be a series of definitive theatre reference works with the publication of *American Musical Theatre: A Chronicle* in 1978. The first and only systematic coverage of the history of the Broadway musical stage, it was particularly successful in that it avoided the overly ''patriotic'' and/or proselytizing attitudes of some earlier works, and described the productions, imported and home-made, of the American musical stage in a popular academic style and from a factual ''eye-of-god'' viewpoint.

He has subsequently authored the biographies of Jerome Kern (*Jerome Kern: His Life and Music,* 1980) and Vincent Youmans (*Days to Be Happy, Years to Be Sad,* 1982), monographs on *American Operetta* (1981), *American Musical Comedy* (1982) and *American Musical Revue* (1985), and the *Oxford Companion to American Theatre* (1984 and revisions), as well a three-volume survey of *American Theatre* and several updated versions of *American Musical Theatre.*

BORDONI, Irene (b Corsica, ?16 January 1895; d New York, 19 March 1953). Broadway's French vedette of the 1920s.

The apparently Corsican Mlle Bordoni is said to have begun her stage career in France at the age of 13, playing at the Théâtre des Variétés, the Moulin-Rouge (*Par dessus le moulin,* 1908), the Capucines (Maggy in the revue *V'la la comète,* 1910), the Scala and La Cigale before crossing the Atlantic. By these temporal calculations, she was just 17 years of age when she first appeared on musical Broadway performing a ''prehistoric'' pantomime dance sketch *The First Affair* (the title spoke for itself) with Émile Agoust in the revue *The Passing Show of 1912* and in its successor at the Winter Garden, *Broadway to Paris.* The engagemenet ended, she returned to

Plate 46. **Irene Bordoni.** *Broadway's Corsican-born epitome of Parisian-ness who had a fine hit introducing ''Let's Do It'' in the show called, simply,* Paris.

France where she appeared again in revue at the Capucines (1913) and La Cigale (1913), impersonating Mistinguett; in the comedy *La Tontine* at the Théâtre Antoine (1914); and in Rip's famous revue *1915* (''La Chanson du militaire'') before recrossing the Atlantic.

Back in America Mlle Bordoni appeared as a tiny and extremely (sometimes excessively) French soubrette in a the 47 performances of the Elsie Janis show *Miss Information* (1915, Elaine); played at Fysher's cabaret mondaine and at the French theatre in a war drama, *Son homme;* featured in two editions of Raymond Hitchcock's *Hitchy-Koo;* and took a turn on the vaudeville stage before making her mark in the multiple feminine lead in the Broadway version of the London version (where the role was taken by Alice Delysia) of Rip's Parisian revue *Plus ça change,* anglicized under the title *As You Were.*

She remained tiny and extremely French as, in the same manner as Anna Held before her and like Delysia in London, she made herself a subsequent career as the epitome of Broadway Frenchness, starring, under the management of her then husband E Ray Goetz, in a series of Americanized Continental vehicles. These began with a version of the Armont/Gerbidon play *Jeunes Filles de palaces,* adapted as a song-studded *The French Doll* (1922, Georgine Mazulier), and included a version of Gábor Dregely's *A kisasszony férje* or *Der Gatte des Fräuleins* produced as *Little Miss Bluebeard* (1924, Colette), which she also played in London; a version of the French opérette *Pouche,* described as a romantic song-farce and entitled *A Naughty Cinderella* (1925, Germaine Leverrier), which allowed her to sing Paul Ruben's ''I Love the Moon,'' Henri Christiné's ''Do I Love You?,'' ''Mia luna'' and ''That Means Nothing to Me'' in place of the original score; the title role in Sacha Guitry's *Mozart* (just before Yvonne Printemps arrived to give Broadway her version of her original role); and the 1928 *Paris* (Vivienne Rolland) in which she performed several made-to-measure Cole Porter songs (''Let's Do It,'' ''The Heaven Hop,'' etc), plus Walter Kollo's ''The Land of Going to Be'' (Goetz) and Harry Warren's ''Wob-a-ly Walk.'' She filmed a version of this last show in 1930.

The last of her vehicles, *One More Night* (Herman Hupfeld/Russel Medcraft), an Americanization of a Louis Verneuil piece (which would seem to have been *Ma Cousine de Varsovie*) in which she appeared as the Princess de Gouremnitza-Guvgulli (aka Colette) equipped with seven numbers which admitted only to being ''arranged by Russell Bennett,'' was produced by Galen Bogue in 1931. It did not make it to New York, but she returned to the Broadway musical stage in 1938 in *Great Lady* (Madame Colette) and, with rather more success, as Madame Bordelaise in *Louisiana Purchase* (1940). She later appeared in the Tchaikovsky pasticcio musical *The Lady from Paris* (1950) and in 1951 played for a while as Bloody Mary in the national tour of *South Pacific* in what is undoubtedly one of the rare times that the role has been played, physically (give or take a complexion), nearly as described in the text.

In 1953 she took part in the tryout of *Maggie* but was dropped before Broadway and replaced by Odette Myrtil. It was her last stage appearance: two months later she was dead.

THE BOSTONIANS (The Boston Ideal Comic Opera Company).

Originally formed by theatrical and vocal agent M H [''Effie''] Ober in 1879, at the height of the *Pinafore* craze, to give an ''ideal'' production of that show (Boston Theater 14 April 1879), the Ideal Comic Opera Company, which its manager always insisted be vocally impeccable, won an enormous success with its initial production and, as a result, soon developed into a light opera repertoire company touring America from its Boston base. The company, familiarly known as ''The Bostonians,'' quickly added such pieces as *The Sorcerer, The Pirates of Penzance,* a version of *Boccaccio* (*The Prince of Palermo*), *Les Cloches de Corneville, Les Noces d'Olivette, Fatinitza, The Bohemian Girl, La Mascotte, Zar und Zimmermann* and *Les Mousquetaires au couvent* to their repertoire, followed later by *Giroflé-Girofla, La Girouette, Barbe-bleue, Fanchonette* (apparently Serpette's *Fanfreluche,* Academy of Music, Rochester 19 November 1884) and *François les bas-bleus* as well as the opéras-comiques *The Marriage of Figaro,* America's alledgedly first vernacular *Giralda* (ad Oscar Weil, Bunnell's Museum, New Haven 26 March 1885), *Fra Diavolo, L'Elisir d'Amore* (as *Adina*), *Les Mousquetaires de la reine* (as *The Maid of Honour,* American premiere Rand's Opera House, Troy 22 February 1886), *La Reine Topaze* and *Martha.*

Miss Ober withdrew from the management in 1885, and in 1887 the company's finances curled up and it collapsed. However, it was reconstituted as ''The Bostonians'' and, with several of its most famous members—comic Henry Clay Barnabee, tenor Tom Karl, baritone W H MacDonald—at the helm, began a second lease of life. If such old favorites as *Fatinitza, The Bohemian Girl* and *Fra Diavolo* held their place in the repertoire, the new management also added a number of fresh pieces, ranging from *Mignon* to Offenbach's *Les Braconniers,* Cellier's *Dorothy* and a piece called *Pygmalion and Galatea* (Academy of Music, Buffalo 24 November 1888), made up by Oscar Weil from Gilbert's play along with music allegedly ''from the French of Ambroise Thomas.'' They also began a new policy of mounting original native works, and it was there that the group found their biggest hit since *HMS Pinafore.* Reginald De Koven and Harry B Smith supplied them first with a short-lived *Don Quixote* (Boston Theater 18 November 1889) and then with *Robin Hood* (Opera House, Chicago 9 June 1890), the show which would become the classic American comic opera of its period. Later, having given an early opportunity to Victor Herbert with *Prince Ananias* (Broadway Theater, New York 20 November) the company mothered another long popular piece in his *The Serenade* (Knickerbocker Theater, New York 16 March 1897).

Amongst the other original works mounted by the company were *The Lion of Peru* (Leonard Wales/E A Wood Grand Opera House, Pittsburgh 9 May 1889), with Zélie de Lussan as the star of what seems to have been a paid-for production by a pair of Pittsburghers; Oscar Weil and Louis Latour's remusicalization of Audran's *La Dormeuse éveillée* as *Suzette* (Baldwin's Theater, San Francisco 31 May 1889), with Marie Stone in the title role; Weil's original but ''worthless'' *In Mexico* (aka *A Wartime Wedding* Columbia Theater, San Francisco 4 November 1895, lib C T Dazey, Murray Hill Theater 19 October 1896); Henry Waller and Young E Ellison's *The Ogalallas* (Columbia Theater, Chicago 16 February 1892); De Koven's *The Knickerbockers* (Tremont Theatre, Boston 5 January 1893) and *Maid Marian* (Chestnut Street Opera House, Philadelphia 4 November 1901); Thomas Pearsall Thorne's *The Maid of Plymouth* (Columbia Theater, Chicago 27 November 1893); Jules Jordan's *Rip van Winkle* (Opera House, Providence, RI 24 May 1897); the short-lived *Ulysses* (W H Neidlinger/ Roland E Phillip, Euclid Avenue Opera House, Cleveland 1 December 1898) and *The Smugglers of Bayadez* (Giacomo Minkowsky/Frederick Ranken, Waterford, Conn 19 October 1899); Herbert's *The Viceroy* (lib: H B Smith, Columbia Theater, San Francisco 12 February 1900); and *The Queen of Laughter* (William Brady/ Ysobel Kaplin, Spokane, Wash 13 February 1904).

The company suffered badly when their leading soprano, Alice Nielsen, walked out to set up her own company and took several important members of the troupe with her, and within a half-dozen years both companies were gone. The Bostonians closed down in 1905, leaving behind a reputation and many memories of a first-class light opera company which had been responsible for producing two of the most popular American-bred musical shows of the turn of the century years.

BOUBLIL, Alain (b Tunis, 5 March 1941).

Originally an employee of Europe 1 radio, Boublil subsequently became a songwriter and music publisher and, under the influence of *Jesus Christ Superstar,* made an attempt at writing a piece of recorded musical theatre based on a similarly ''large'' topic: *La Revolution française* (mus: Claude-Michel Schönberg, Raymond Jeannot). The recording, labeled ''rock opera,'' had a notable success, and the piece followed *Jesus Christ Superstar*'s example by being brought to the stage, at Paris's Palais des Sports.

Boublil's next venture followed the first in taking a vast subject as its bases. *La Revolution française* was succeeded by a recorded musical based on Victor Hugo's *Les Misérables.* Like the first show, this one moved from record to a stage presentation: a spectacular mounting by Robert Hossein at the Paris Palais des Sports.

A further record-to-stage venture followed, with the children's musical *Abbacadabra,* a fairy-tale piece which used the music of the pop group Abba as its score. Boublil subsequently worked on two further pieces in the same vein which remained records only (*La Fusée de Noë, Les Chevaliers des étoiles* w Jean-Pierre Bourtayre).

The great step in Boublil's career came, however, when Cameron Mackintosh, the London producer of *Abbacadabra,* then took up *Les Misérables.* Produced in London in a revised version, it established itself as one of the most outstanding and successful musicals of its era. Whilst *Les Misérables* ran on, in productions all around the world, Mackintosh produced a further Boublil/ Schönberg musical, this time made to measure for the British and American commercial theatre rather than for disc. *Miss Saigon,* an updated version of the *Madame Butterfly* tale set in the context of the Vietnam war, showed the altered position and aims of its author too clearly. But its clumsily shaped libretto and cold lyrics found partisans amongst those who admired its choice of the now fashionably expiatory Vietnam as a topic and, with all the power of the most successful and important producing house in the world behind it, the show went on to runs in London, New York and Tokyo, in the shadows of its overwhelmingly successful forebear.

A third musical, *Martin Guerre,* brought out by the same authors and the same production house in 1996 showed its creators back in the form of their earlier works, but the writers had to battle to find a definitive form for their piece and, in spite of its attractions—and in spite of a hefty remake (ad Herbert Kretzmer) during its run at the Prince Edward Theatre, it failed to take. A revised version launched at Leeds's West Yorkshire Playhouse in 1998 ultimately made its way to America, but failed to reach Broadway.

1973 **La Révolution française** (Claude-Michel Schönberg, Raymond Jeannot/w Jean-Max Rivière) Palais des Sports

1980 **Les Misérables** (Schönberg/w Jean-Marc Natel) Palais des Sports 17 September

1983 **Abbacadabra** (Björn Ulvaeus, Benny Andersson/w Daniel

Boublil ad David Wood) Lyric Theatre, Hammersmith, London 8 December

1985 **Les Misérables** revised English version ad Herbert Kretzmer Barbican Theatre, London 8 October

1989 **Miss Saigon** (Schönberg/w Richard Maltby jr) Theatre Royal, Drury Lane, London 20 September

1996 **Martin Guerre** (Schönberg/Edward Hardy, Stephen Clark) Prince Edward Theatre, 10 July

1998 **Martin Guerre** revised version West Yorkshire Playhouse, Leeds 8 December

BOUCHE À BOUCHE Comédie musicale in 2 acts by André Barde. Music by Maurice Yvain. Théâtre de l'Apollo, Paris, 8 October 1925.

The series of Maurice Yvain "bouche" musicals, launched so successfully with *Ta bouche,* was continued, on a rather larger stage, in 1925 with *Bouche à bouche.* Thérèse Dorny played the demi-mondaine Natacha who mistakes the shy Bernard (Henri Defreyn) for a film star and sets her cap at him. Her miffed gentleman protector (Félix Oudart) doesn't tell her she's made a mistake. When all the comical situations are danced and done, Bernard is more suitably paired off with the old gentleman's ingenue daughter, Jenny (Maguy Warna). Milton headed the comedy as Boris, and Gabrielle Ristori supported in the role of Micheline.

Defreyn had the best musical moments of the piece in "J'étais trop ému," "Ça ne colle pas" and the waltzing title duet, shared with Mlle Warna, whilst Oudart delivered "Où, quand et comment" and joined with Milton and Mlle Dorny in a set of comical couplets in praise of the petrol shares which were an essential part of the plot, "Royal Dutch," in which Standard Oil and Shell were amongst those that got a plug. The comic highlight of the evening was the burlesque of an American film production which closed the second act.

Whilst not in the same enduring class as *Ta bouche* and *Pas sur la bouche, Bouche à bouche* produced plenty of attractive material and lasted several months in its rather less-than-intimate house.

BOUCHERON, Maxime [BOUCHERON, René Maximilian] (b Paris, 9 March 1846; d Paris, 9 November 1896). Librettist to 30 years of Parisian shows.

Originally a functionary at the Préfecture de la Seine, and later a journalist and theatrical columnist (*Le Triboulet, Le Figaro*), Boucheron made a notable entry into the musical theatre when he teamed with Paul Burani and composer Léon Vasseur on the eminently saucy 1878 opérette *Le Droit du seigneur* (229 performances and a revival in1884). The same team reassembled for a second success with *Le Billet de logement* at the same theatre the following year, but a third volley, with *Le Petit Parisien* (70 performances) did less well. After some years away from the musical stage, Boucheron returned with another winsomely below-the-waistline libretto for *Miss Helyett* which, as musically illustrated by Audran, won him the biggest success of his writing career. Several other pieces written with Audran and, most particularly, the circus musical *Les Forains,* musically set by Louis Varney, had respectable careers before Boucheron's career ended with his premature death in 1896.

The Viennese Posse mit Gesang *Wolf und Lampel* (Julius Stern/Hoffmann/F Zell, Theater an der Wien 13 October 1888) was based on his successful vaudeville *Cocard et Bicoquet* (w Hippolyte Raymond, Théâtre de la Renaissance 22 February 1888).

1878 **Le Droit du seigneur** (Léon Vasseur/w Paul Burani) Théâtre des Fantaisies-Parisiennes 13 December

1879 **Le Billet de logement** (Vasseur/w Burani) Théâtre des Fantaisies-Parisiennes 15 November

1880 **Le Voyage en Amerique** (Hervé/w Hippolyte Raymond) Théâtre des Nouveautés 16 September

1882 **Le Petit Parisien** (Vasseur/w Burani) Théâtre des Folies-Dramatiques 16 January

1883 **Le Bouquet de violets** (André Martinet/w Georges Grisier) 1 act Casino d'Aulus 10 August

1883 **L'Ami d'Oscar** (Martinet) 1 act Casino d'Aulus 14 August

1888 **La Légende du Magyar** (A Godard) Galeries Saint-Hubert, Brussels 11 March

1890 **L'Entracte** (Martinet) 1 act Théâtre des Menus-Plaisirs 14 February

1890 **Miss Helyett** (Edmond Audran) Théâtre des Bouffes-Parisiens 12 November

1891 **Le Mitron** (Martinet/w Antony Mars) Théâtre des Folies Dramatiques 24 September

1892 **Article de Paris** (Audran) Théâtre des Menus-Plaisirs 17 March

1892 **Sainte-Freya** (Audran) Théâtre des Bouffes-Parisiens 4 November

1892 **Mariage galant** (Edmond Missa, Piétrapertosa/w François Oswald) Théâtre des Menus-Plaisirs 3 December

1894 **Les Forains** (Varney/w Mars) Théâtre des Bouffes-Parisiens 9 February

1895 **La Duchesse de Ferrare** (Audran) Théâtre des Bouffes-Parisiens 25 January

1896 **Une nuit d'amour** (Antoine Banès/w Albert Barre) Théâtre des Bouffes-Parisiens 11 May

1896 **Tante Agnès** (Frédéric Toulmouche) Olympia 27 October

1904 **Pitchounette** Opéra-Bouffe ?October

1909 **Mam'zelle Gogo** (Émile Pessard/w Léon Xanrof) Théâtre Molière, Brussels 27 February

BOUCICAULT, Dion [BOURSIQUOT, Dionysius Lardner] (b Dublin, 26 December 1820; d New York, 18 September 1890).

Although he authored a handful of small operettas and, on one occasion, a pantomime, the celebrated playwright and actor Boucicault impinged rarely on the musical theatre. However, he transferred his theatrical belief that "sensation" and spectacle was what the public wanted to the musical stage when he wrote and produced the vast, scenic féerie *Babil and Bijou* at London's Covent Garden Theatre in 1872. The public enjoyed the elaborate, fantastical show for what it was and Lord Londesborough, who had backed it, lost a fortune unheard of up to that time in a theatrical venture.

Boucicault remade (w John Oxenford) his hit play *The Colleen Bawn* as the libretto for Julius Benedict's famous opera *The Lily of Killarney* ("The Moon Has Raised His Lamp Above," "Eily Mavourneen") but, of his highly colored plays, seemingly natural fodder for the musical stage, only *The Streets of New York* seems to have been thus adapted. A version by Edward Eliscu and Sol Kaplan was produced as *The Banker's Daughter* at off-Broadway's Jan Hus House in 1962 (21 January) and a second, by Barry Alan Grael with music by Richard B Chodosh, the following year at the Maidman Playhouse (29 October), whilst the British version of the same play was also adapted as a musical, *The Streets of London* (Gary Carpenter, Ian Barnett), produced at the Theatre Royal, Stratford East (18 March 1980) and subsequently played for three months at the West End's Her Majesty's Theatre (21 October 1980).

Boucicault's plays were obvious meat for the burlesquers of his time, but once again he seems to have been, with one exception, strangely spared. *The Colleen Bawn* was the exception. On its production, it was greeted by a positive rash of parody extravaganzas—H J Byron's *Miss Eily O'Connor* (Drury Lane 25 November 1861/Strand Theatre 6 August 1862, mus: James Tully), the Soho Theatre's *A Rale Collin Born,* the Surrey's *The Cooleen Drawn (from a Novel Source), or The Great Sensation Diving Belle* (Martin Dutwell, J B Johnstone, 14 October 1861) and William Brough and Andrew Halliday's *Colleen Bawn, Settled at Last* at the Lyceum (5 July 1862).

The Shaughraun was burlesqued at New York's Olympic Theater when John L Poole mounted a *The Shock-raun,* and at San Francisco's Bella Union Theatre (July 1875), and his English version of *Les Frères corses (The Corsican Brothers)* also provoked a large number of burlesques of Dumas's tale.

His son, actor **Aubrey [Robertson] BOUCICAULT** (b London, 23 June 1869; d New York, 10 July 1913), appeared in Chicago in *The Birth of Venus* (1895), on the Boston and New York musical stage in the comic opera *Kismet* (1895, Dan de Lyon), in a leading role in Julian Edwards's comic opera *Madeleine* (1895, Baron Grimm), in the flop *Leonardo* (1895, Angelo), as Major Murgatroyd to the *Patience* of Lillian Russell (1896), alongside Eddie Foy in the Broadway version of *L'Auberge du Tohu-bohu* (1898, also add songs), alongside Elsie Janis in *The Vanderbilt Cup* (1902) and with Weber and Fields in *Higgledy-Piggledy* in a career largely devoted to non-musical theatre, whilst an elder son, **Dion G BOUCICAULT** (b New York, 23 May 1859; d Hurley, Bucks, 25 June 1929) produced a number of musical shows during a largely play-producing partnership with Robert Brough between 1886 and 1896 in Australia, and later directed several London musicals (*Rosy Rapture, The Beloved Vagabond*).

Daughter Nina Boucicault (1867–1950) created the title role of J M Barrie's *Peter Pan* (1904).

1844 **The Fox and the Goose, or the Widow's Husband** (Ambroise Thomas/w Benjamin Webster) 1 act Adelphi Theatre 2 October

1846 **The Wonderful Water Cure** (w Webster) Haymarket Theatre 15 July

1853 **The Sentinel** (Robert Stoepel) Strand Theatre 10 January

1854 **Apollo in New York** (arr John Cooke) 1 act Burton's Theater, New York 11 December

1872 **Babil and Bijou, or The Lost Regalia** (Hervé, Frederic Clay, Jules Rivière, et al/J R Planché) Theatre Royal, Covent Garden 29 August

Autobiography (w Kenney, C L): *The Life and Career of Dion Boucicault* (New York, 1883); Biographies: Walsh, T: *The Career of Dion Boucicault* (Dunlap Society, New York, 1915), Hogan, R: *Dion Boucicault* (Rayne, New York, 1969), Fawkes, R: *Dion Boucicault* (Quartet, London, 1979)

BOUFFAR, Zulma [BOUFFLAR, Zulma Madeleine] (b Nérac, 24 May 1841; d Pont-aux-Dames, 20 January 1909). One of the star prima donnas of the Offenbach age.

Zulma Bouffar made her first appearance on the stage at the age of six, at Marseille in *La Fille bien gardée,* and went on to appear as a juvenile vocalist at Lyon with some success. Owing to the French laws limiting child performers, her father then took her abroad, and the girl gave performances as a singer in a variety of venues in Belgium, Germany, Holland, Sweden and Denmark. After her father's death, the 13-year-old Zulma continued the life of a peripatetic entertainer, including in her repertoire songs from some of the new opérettes and opérettes-bouffes which were than becoming popular, among them pieces from the Bouffes-Parisiens repertoire.

She was seen by Offenbach in a performance in Liège or Homburg (reports differ), and the composer promptly brought her to his favorite watering place of Bad Ems where she made her theatre debut in his opérette *Lischen et Fritzchen* (Lischen). She repeated the piece that season at the Bouffes-Parisiens with great success. At the same time, so it is said, she became the composer's mistress.

Over the next years Mlle Bouffar created a series of leading roles on the Paris stage, the largest number in Offenbach opéras-bouffes where the music was made to measure for her highly agile soprano: the trousers role of Nani in *Les Géorgiennes* (1864), a double role in *Les Bergers* (1865, L'Intendant/Jeannet), Gabrielle in *La Vie parisienne* (when at Offenbach's insistence she was added to the slightly singing original cast at the Palais-Royal), and a run of travesty roles in *Geneviève de Brabant* (1867, Drogan), *Le Château à Toto* (1868, Toto de la Roche), Delibes's *La Cour du Roi Petaud* (1869, Prince Léo), *Les Brigands* (1869, Fragoletto) and *Le Roi Carotte* (1872, Robin Luron). She left the cast of this last-named piece to fulfill a lucrative engagement in South America. She donned skirts for *Les Braconniers* (1873, Ginetta) and *Il Signor Fagotto* (Moschetta), but returned to breeches for her last Offenbach creation as Prince Caprice in *Le Voyage dans la lune* (1875). In the shorter *Jeanne qui pleure et Jean qui rit* (Jean/Jeanne) she played both male and female roles.

Mlle Bouffar appeared in star roles in Johann Strauss's *La Reine Indigo* (1875, Fantasca) and as the sexually mixed-up Kosiki in Lecocq's *Kosiki* (1876) and, at this time, so it is told, she was seriously considered by Bizet as a possible creator for the title role of *Carmen,* but instead she rounded off the principal part of an outstanding career as a diva playing Princesse Arabelle in a Johann Strauss piece, which included some of the music from *Die Fledermaus,* entitled *La Tsigane,* in a revival of *Le Voyage dans la lune* at the Châtelet (1877), and as the legendary danseuse *La Camargo* in Lecocq's opérette of the same name (1878).

Between her Paris engagements, she played throughout Europe, appearing notably in Belgium and in Russia, but she was still to be seen in the French capital in the 1880s, appearing in the 1880 production of *L'Arbre de Noël* at the Porte-Saint-Martin ("a little tired, a little heavier, a little older"), in *Mille et une nuits* at the Châtelet (1881, Sinbad, Aladdin, etc) and in several other spectaculars where the demands were lesser than in less scenic works and where her looks, never dazzling and now quite simply ugly, were less important than her ever attractive personality. In 1883 she appeared in her old role of Gabrielle in *La Vie parisienne* at the Variétés. In 1887 she was seen at the Ambigu as Rigolette in *Les Mystères de Paris* ("a somewhat mature grisette"), equipped with a Serpette ballad written for her for the occasion.

In later years, she attempted for a short and unsuccessful period the management of the Théâtre Ambigu (1891–93) which ended in bankruptcy. She announced her retirement in 1902.

LA BOULANGÈRE A DES ÉCUS Opérette in 3 acts by Henri Meilhac and Ludovic Halévy. Music by Jacques Offenbach. Théâtre des Variétés, Paris, 19 October 1875.

La Boulangère a des écus brought the team of Meilhac, Halévy and Offenbach back together for the first time since *Les Brigands,* six years and a war earlier. More than that, the show was mounted by Eugène Bertrand at the Théâtre des Variétés, the site of the trio's earlier and greatest successes, and the titular role of the baker, Margot, was made to order for the star of those shows, Hortense Schneider, with fine parts also included for the other stars of the very starry Variétés company: Dupuis, Baron, Léonce, Pradeau, Berthelier and Paola Marié.

The handsome hairdresser Bernadille (Dupuis) has, through excess of gallantry, got himself mixed up in an abortive aristocratic conspiracy to murder the Regent and he is on the run, pursued by a droll pair of constables, Flammèche (Berthelier) and Délicat (Léonce). He runs to his sweetheart, the barkeeper, Toinon (Mlle Marié), but, with his bloodhounding pursuers heading straight to this obvious hideout as well, Bernadille ends up being hidden instead by Toinon's friend Margot, a baker who has become hugely rich by dabbling in stocks and shares. Coquebert (Baron), who has lost all his fortune on the same stockmarket, and has now become Margot's adoring Switzer, muddies the pursuit by swapping places with the fugitive, but the Commissaire of police (Pradeau) is soon on the track. Complications ensue when Margot takes a shine to her friend's fellow, but in the end it is she who manufactures the happy ending. She uses her money to bribe her way into the Regent's presence and charm him into pardoning Bernadille. The hairdresser and his Toinon head for the happily ever after, and Margot, equipped now with a purchased title, makes do with a particle and the devotion of Coquebert.

Even though the characters of the policemen and the foolish Switzer were supremely comical creations, *La Boulangère* had little of the bouffonnerie of its authors' early days and plays about it, and it leaned heavily towards the style of *La Fille de Madame Angot,* in particular, in some of its parts. It was, however, a fine and clever libretto which Offenbach decorated with some lively and attractive melodies ranging from the star's entrance number ("Lorsque j'étais fill' de boutique") to the jolly duo for Berthelier and Léonce, switching their disguises from charcoal-burners to flour-merchants ("Tout noir . . . tout blanc"), to Toinon's pretty admission of love ("J'ai que je suis amoureuse"), her jealous scene with Bernadille when he puts in an appearance after a week away conspiring, and Bernadille's reflections on undeserving love.

All the plans for *La Boulangère* came to fruition, excepting one. Mlle Schneider, edging on the decline, compensated by throwing tantrums in rehearsal and finally got so impossible that Bertrand sacked her. She sued for 50,000 francs for breach of contract, and got 5,000. Her replacement was Bertrand's girlfriend, Marie Aimée, the pretty Fiorella of *Les Brigands*. A delightful artist, Aimée simply did not have the booming star presence the role of Margot had been written to provide for, and, when *La Boulangère* was produced, it proved to have a soft center. It played just 47 times.

However, the following year Bertrand came up with an idea that nearly worked dazzlingly. He cast the celebrated star of the cafés-concerts, Mlle Thérésa, in a revival of *La Boulangère* (27 April), and that lady brought all the star presence needed to the role, successfully erasing the obvious fact that it had been written to the measure of Schneider. Offenbach did some considerable rewrites on, in particular, the second act, and brought it to a show-stopping climax with a finale in which Thérésa (''avec une verve, une vigeur, une furia dont il est impossible de se faire une idée'') and Paola Marié joined in a patriotic ''marseillaise'' (''Nous sommes ici trois cents femelles'') which brought down the house. The third act, too, was improved and *La Boulangère* Mark 2 ran up to the summer break, and returned thereafter. Arnold Mortier reported ''Dupuis was encored, Berthelier and Léonce were encored, Thérésa was encored in the famous finale of 300 women. Too many encores. You end up having the show twice in one evening. In a word, a hit. The *Boulangère* will carry on taking money. ''It did, for a handy season of 61 nights, but too late to allow the piece to become established as it deserved.

In spite of its delayed and/or semi-success, the show was promptly picked up around the world. In Budapest (ad Jenő Rákosi), where Lujza Blaha played Margot and Emilia Sziklai was Toinon, *A talléros pékné* went down a treat and was given a fine season of 28 performances. In Vienna the title became a little more explicit—the heroine was *Margot, the millionaire baker of Paris* as portrayed by Antonie Link and she was supported by Karoline Finaly (Toinon), Franz Eppich (Bernadille) and by Blasel, Matras and Ausim as the comical cops. In spite of her limited success in the role in Paris, Aimée put *La Boulangère* into her repertoire (and her rendition of ''La Paloma'' into *La Boulangère*) when she returned, shortly afterwards, to America. She played Margot to the Toinon of Mlle Duparc and the Bernadille of Raoult, and she played it round the country for several seasons, without persuading anyone to essay an English version. However, an English version did emerge, eventually, in London when Alexander Henderson produced H B Farnie's adaptation of *La Boulangère* with the characterful Madame Amadi (Margot), Tilly Wadman (Toinon), Frank Celli (Bernadille), Harry Paulton, Charles Ashford and George Temple as the policemen and the young Richard Mansfield as Coquebert. In typical Farnie fashion (or was this part of the French ''revisions''?), the principal page became the juvenile King of France in disguise, thus allowing a less spicy but boringly old-fashioned ending. The English *La Boulangère* ran only 40 London nights, but it prompted an American mounting at the enterprising Winter Gardens in San Francisco, as part of its quickly turning-over repertoire of sometimes unusual musical shows. Louise Lester was the (brief) American Margot.

The title *La Boulangère a des écus* was previously used for a two-act vaudeville by Théaulon and a three-act piece of the same genre by Armand de Jallais, Henri Thiéry and Alphonse Vulpian (Délassements-Comiques 8 November 1856), as well as for Prémaray's five-act drama played at the Théâtre de la Porte-Saint-Martin in 1855.

Hungary: Népszínház *A talléros pékné* 22 February 1876; Austria: Carltheater *Margot, die Millionbäckerin von Paris* (*Margot, die reiche Backerin*) 17 February 1877; USA: Eagle Theater (Fr) 26 February 1877, Winter Gardens, San Francisco *The Bakeress Who Has Money* 21 November 1881; UK: Globe Theatre *La Boulangère* 16 April 1881

Recording: complete (Golden Age of Opera)

BOULE DE NEIGE Opérette in 3 acts by Charles Nuitter and Étienne Tréfeu. Music by Jacques Offenbach. Théâtre des Bouffes-Parisiens, Paris, 14 December 1871.

The ''boule de neige'' or ''snowball'' of Nuitter and Tréfeu's libretto was a bear, and their tale told of how he was set up as the ruler over a revolting populace. The boyfriend of the bear's trainer, Olga, fleeing from one of the bear's sillier laws, takes refuge in a bearskin and by the time the evening is out he has deposed the animal. Equipped with a score which was largely secondhand—much of it being taken from Offenbach's failed *Barkouf* (Eugène Scribe, Henry Boisseaux Opéra-Comique 24 December 1860)—the show played only a fair run with Marie Peschard (Olga), Berthelier (Le Caporal) and Desiré (Balabrelock) in its featured roles. It was subsequently taken up for a production in Vienna (ad Julius Hopp) where, after a premiere conducted by Offenbach himself, it played for a respectable 16 straight performances at the Carltheater with Frln Roeder (Olga), Josef Matras (Caporal) and Wilhelm Knaack (Balabrelock) starred, then 5 more in repertoire, before being brought back the following year four times more.

Austria: Carltheater *Schneeball* 3 February 1872

BOULLARD, Marius (b Ghent, 27 December 1842; d Paris, 22 October 1891).

As musical director at the Théâtre des Variétés, Boullard supplied the usual amount of ''composed and arranged'' material to the Paris stage of the 1860s and

1870s. It was, however, only after he had left his post at the Variétés to Adolphe Lindheim that he found his principal successes. After supplying manager Bertrand with the score for the flop féerie *Le Roi dort,* he was again called upon, as a last minute replacement, to provide the score—composed and arranged—for the vaudeville-opérette *Niniche.* The huge international success of that show did not always carry his score with it, but Boullard's tactful arrangement of the show's music, to the measure of star Anna Judic, had done its share in launching *Niniche's* original production. He later supplied part of the music for *La Roussotte,* another in the Variétés series of Judic vaudevilles, but Bertrand chose to go to the likes of Lecocq and Hervé for the rest of his shows, and the utilitarian Boullard rested on his rather unlikely laurels, as the composer of the oft-revived *Niniche.*

Boullard visited America in 1876 as second conductor to Offenbach in his transatlantic tour, and conducted performances by the Aimée company of *La Vie parisienne* at Booth's Theatre.

1863 **Nedel** (Mme Lionel de Chabrillan) 1 act Théâtre des Champs-Élysées 23 May

1863 **Militairement** (Mme de Chabrillan) 1 act Théâtre des Champs-Élysées 28 October

1866 **L'Île des Sirènes** (Xavier de Montépin, Jules Dornay) Théâtre des Nouveautés 27 November

1867 **Le Grillon** (Hector Girard) 1 act Théâtre des Nouveautés 9 March

1876 **Le Roi dort** (Eugène Labiche, Alfred Delacour) Théâtre des Variétés 30 March

1878 **Niniche** (Albert Millaud, Alfred Hennequin) Théâtre des Variétés 15 February

1881 **La Roussotte** (w Lecocq, Hervé/Meilhac, Halévy, Millaud) Théâtre des Variétés 28 January

1887 **Nos bons jurés** (Paul Ferrier, Fabrice Carré) Théâtre des Variétés 5 December

BOURVIL [RAIMBOURG, André Robert] (b Prétôt-Vicquemare, 27 July 1917; d Paris, 23 September 1970). Star comedian of the postwar French stage and screen.

After early work as a comedian in cabaret and on radio, where he established a fine reputation playing and singing more often than not in a dumb peasant character, Bourvil moved out, after the war, into films and into the theatre. He made his first appearances in the musical theatre at the Alhambra in *La Bonne Hôtesse* (1946) and, promoted to top of the bill, in *Le Maharadjah* (1947) and then moved on to the Théâtre de l'Étoile for *M'sieur Nanar* (1950). On the insistence of Georges Guétary, who was searching for a comedian with whom to establish a Crosby-Hope style of partnership, the slightly floundering actor was then offered the comedy lead in the musical comedy *La Route fleurie* (1952) and it was his performance, alongside Guétary and another newcomer, Annie Cordy, in this long-running show which hoisted him to major stardom.

At intervals during a busy career in films, both comic and dramatic as well as musical (*Le Chanteur de Mexico, Sérénade au Texas,* etc), he returned several times to the theatre, appearing again with Guétary in the highly successful *Pacifico* (1958, "C'est du nanan," "C'est pas si mal que ça chez nous," "Bonne année"), in *La Bonne Planque* (1963) with Pierette Bruno, and with Annie Cordy in the opérette à grand spectacle, *Ouah! Ouah!* (1965, "Les Abeilles," "Les Goths," "Notre Jour J"), at the Alhambra.

A comedian of great drollery and warmth, his voice contained an irresistible laughter which survives on the handful of musical comedy discs he made for Pathé-Marconi, including definitive performances of such classic opérettes as *Phi-Phi* (Phi-Phi) and *L'Auberge du Cheval Blanc* (Léopold).

Biographies: Lorcey, J: *Bourvil* (Pac, Paris, 1981), Berruer, P: *Bourvil du rire aux larmes* (Presses de la Cîté, Paris), Claude, C: *Un certain Bourvil* (Messidor, Paris, 1990)

THE BOY Musical comedy in 2 acts by Fred Thompson based on Arthur Pinero's play *The Magistrate.* Lyrics by Adrian Ross and Percy Greenbank. Music by Lionel Monckton and Howard Talbot. Adelphi Theatre, London, 14 September 1917.

The Boy (a title chosen for the musical by Pinero himself) was an expert adaptation of the playwright's famous play *The Magistrate,* telling of the legal gentleman who, after a jolly night on the town with his young stepson (whose mother has docked his real age to keep her own as minimal as possible, if not probable), ends up in court sentencing his own wife, who had been out protecting her guilty secret, for being nabbed in the very shady hotel he and the boy had themselves been visiting.

Aided materially by a lively score from Monckton and Talbot and a star performance of the first degree from Bill Berry as the guilty magistrate, Meebles, *The Boy* established itself as a major hit in London in the last part of the war. The song favorite of the piece was a lugubrious little ballad, "I Want to Go to Bye-Bye," sung by the exhausted magistrate the morning after, and a pretty Make-Up duet for the equally ravaged Mrs Meebles (Maisie Gay) and her sister (Nellie Taylor) and a bristling "A Game That Ends with a Kiss" for the soubrette (Billie Carleton, soon to be dead of a drug overdose) were other highlights. As the show ran on, the score was slimmed and the comedy increased but, as cast changes intervened, fresh songs (including Jerome Kern's "Have a Heart") were introduced and by the time *The Boy* went on the road after a West End run of 801 performances it was musically as plump as ever.

The Messrs Shubert's American production of the retitled *Good Morning Judge* (ex- *Kiss Me*) supplemented the score as well, notably with numbers by the young George Gershwin and Irving Caesar (''There's More to a Kiss Than the XXX,'' ''I Was So Young and You Were So Beautiful'' w Alfred Bryan) and Buddy De Sylva/Louis Silvers (''I'm the Boy [and I'm the girl]''). With George Hassell starring as the Judge of the title, but bereft of virtually all singing duties including ''I Want to Go to Bye-Bye,'' it did well both on Broadway (140 performances) and on the road. Australia's production of the English version, with Arthur Stigant (Meebles), Ethel Morrison (Mrs Meebles), Maud Fane (Joy), Lance Lister (Hughie) and Gladys Moncrieff (Diana) hopped successfully through four theatres in Melbourne and Sydney.

The Austrian musical *Das Baby* (Richard Heuberger/A M Willner, Heinrich von Waldberg, Carltheater 3 October 1902) was also based on *The Magistrate,* as apparently was (without credit) an American piece written by Junie Macree under the title *Mama's Baby Boy.*

USA: Shubert Theater *Good Morning Judge* 6 February 1919; Australia: Theatre Royal, Melbourne 23 October 1920

THE BOY FRIEND Musical comedy in 2 acts (originally 1 act) by Sandy Wilson. Players' Theatre, London, 14 April 1953; Wyndham's Theatre, 14 January 1954.

Originally commissioned as a short piece to make up one of the three halves [*sic*] of the program at London's Players' club theatre, *The Boy Friend* was author-composer Wilson's first solo venture into the area of the musical play after successful work as a revue writer for the same kind of intimate theatre. Conceived and written as a small-scale ''new 1920s musical,'' *The Boy Friend* affectionately combined some of the favorite plot and style elements of the 1920s musical stage, whilst providing roles for some of the principal members of the club.

Heiress Polly Browne (Anne Rogers) is the only girl at the Riviera finishing school run by Mme Dubonnet (Joan Sterndale Bennett) who doesn't have that sine qua non, a boy friend. Every prospective beau is suspected of being only after her attractive fortune until, with the Carnival Ball looming, she meets messenger boy Tony (Anthony Hayes). He thinks she's only a secretary and romance blossoms but, alas, before the big night, he vanishes, suspected of theft, and Polly's heart is cruelly chipped. But the truth comes out under the fairylights of the Ball: Tony is no messenger boy but a wealthy lordling in search of true love. And like Polly, he has found it. Maria Charles (Dulcie) and Ann Wakefield (Maisie) featured as the heroine's friends; Larry Drew was Bobby, the rich American won by Maisie; Fred Stone played Polly's father, Percival; whilst John Rutland was the hero's paternal English Lord and Violetta doubled as his wife and the French maid required to open the evening.

The show's score captured the feeling of the tale and the times prettily as the young pair dreamed of loving poverty in ''A Room in Bloomsbury'' or promised that ''I Could Be Happy with You (if you could be happy with me).'' Maisie bounced out her theory that there is ''Safety in Numbers'' where men are concerned and swung into daytime dance with her Bobby in anticipation of the evening in ''Won't You Charleston with Me?'' Dulcie encouraged the sparkle in the eye of ageing Lord Brockhurst in ''It's Never Too Late to Fall in Love,'' whilst Madame Dubonnet swooned accusingly into ''Fancy Forgetting,'' suffered the ''You-Don't-Want-to-Play-with-Me Blues'' as she tried to rekindle a wartime romance with Percival Browne, and consoled the heroine to the tale of ''Poor Little Pierrette.''

The Boy Friend's lovingly humorous re-creation of its period, avoiding all burlesque and forced extravagance, won it fine reviews and a fond public and the Players' Theatre remounted their show, tactfully lengthened into a full evening's entertainment, for a second season the following year, before taking it to the suburban Embassy Theatre for a Christmas season and, ultimately, to the West End's Wyndham's Theatre, with largely the same cast which had played the show from its beginning. *The Boy Friend* proved one of the phenomena of its period, playing for five years and 2,084 performances in London whilst overseas productions followed in procession.

Feuer and Martin's Broadway production, featuring the young Julie Andrews as Polly alongside John Hewer (Tony), Ann Wakefield (Maisie) and Dilys Laye (Dulcie), swapped the affectionate atmosphere of the original for a more burlesque style and larger production values all round, but still played 485 performances. New York got a chance to see a more sincere *Boy Friend* shortly afterwards when a revival mounted at off-Broadway's Cherry Lane Theater (25 January 1958) had a 763-performance run, and a Broadway reprise was given in 1970 (Ambassador Theater 14 April, 119 performances).

Australia's *Boy Friend* began its career at the Elizabethan Theatre in Sydney for a five-week season with John Parker (Tony), Marie Tysoe (Polly) and Laurel Mather (Mme Dubonnet) featured. It soon moved on to the Comedy Theatre and to Melbourne (Her Majesty's Theatre 31 March 1956), as the show established itself around Australia in the same way that it had in the rest of the English-speaking world.

The Boy Friend was subsequently produced in Germany (ad Karl Vibach, Marianne Schubart) and Scandinavia, a Paris production was mounted by Simone Berriau with Valérie Sarne (Polly), James Sparrow (Tony), Jean Moussy (Bobby) and Suzy Delair (Mme Dubonnet) featured, and the show kept up an almost permanent presence in the British provinces for many years, returning to London for a fresh run in 1967 (Comedy Theatre 29 November, 365 performances) with Cheryl Kennedy, Tony Adams and Marion Grimaldi, and again in 1984 (Albery Theatre 20 September, 156 performances) in a version gussied up with additional dance, and with Jane Wellman, Simon Green and Anna Quayle in the leading roles. Another revival was mounted in 1994, back where it had all started, at the Players' Theatre (April 1994).

A film version, which used most of the score, and which featured Twiggy, Christopher Gable, Moyra Fraser and Tommy Tune, guyed some remnants of the piece—which were put into a framework which allowed the director to indulge in the extravagant spectacle the piece specifically denied—and was not successful.

USA: Royale Theater 30 September 1954; Australia: Elizabethan Theatre, Sydney 30 January 1956; Germany: Nordmark Landestheater, Schleswig 29 January 1960, Theater in der Leopoldstrasse, Munich 20 August 1969; France: Théâtre Antoine 18 September 1965

Film: 1972 MGM

Recordings: original cast (HMV), American cast (RCA), American 1970 cast (Decca), Australian revival cast (Ace of Clubs), London 1968 cast (Par), London 1984 cast (TER), German cast (Symbiotic Systems), etc

Plate 47. **The Boy Friend.** *''We're perfect young ladies . . .'': The girls of the original Players' Theatre company.*

THE BOY FROM OZ A musical in 2 acts by Nick Enright. Music from the works of Peter Allen. Her Majesty's Theatre, Sydney, 5 March 1998.

A biomusical of the Australian singer-songwriter Peter Allen, illustrated with a selection of his songs, the 1998 *The Boy from Oz* has been the most successful homegrown musical show to come from a country which has, surprisingly, through the years, consistently failed in its sporadic attempts to initiate an exportable original book musical. This one, which was compiled in that style of the 1990s which uses secondhand songs to make up pasticcio scores in the time-dishonored manner of the mid-19th-century musical, was at least partly original. It was also extremely successful.

Todd McKenney played Allen, patented Australian musical-comedy star Jill Perryman was his mother, Angela Toohey impersonated the Liza Minnelli whom he briefly married, Murray Bartlett was his boyfriend, and Chrissie Amphlett took the part of her mother.

The piece played 41 weeks in Sydney, 14 weeks in Brisbane and a seven months season in Melbourne (14 May 1999) before heading on to other cities but not, to date, to the countries further afield announced in the first flush of success.

Recordings: pre-production disc, original cast (EMI)

THE BOYS AND BETTY Musical comedy in 2 acts by George V Hobart based on *Le Papillon* by Robert Daunceny and René Peter. Music by Silvio Hein. Wallack's Theater, New York, 2 November 1908.

Betty was Betty Barbeau (Marie Cahill) and the boys were the students and boulevardiers of Paris who flock around to see her in George Hobart's tale of a runaway American wife who makes good as a florist in the French capital and then has to fight off the money-sticky fingers of her estranged husband (John Kellerd). Fortunately for her, he has compromised himself sufficiently with a dumb lady from the Folies-Bergère for her to win her freedom and the most handsome of her boys (Edgar Aitchison-Ely). The famous operettic basso, Eugene Cowles, featured in the role of a bluegrass Major.

Miss Cahill scored a fine success with ''Marie Cahill's Arab Love Song'' (''Oh, wait for me in your home by the Pyramids, Love me all you can, I'll be your King and you'll be Queen of my caravan'') in a score which took in such frenchified pieces as ''The Folies-Bergère,'' ''I Want to Go to Paris'' and ''Girls, Girls, Girls,'' topped up with contributions from a bundle of the sort of composers who contributed single numbers to such shows. Will Marion Cook provided ''Whoop 'er Up with a Whoop-la-la!'' and London's Frederic Norton inserted ''A Little Farther'' and ''Laura Lee,'' whilst a piece called ''She Was a Dear Little Girl'' gave the young Irving Berlin his first single song credit in a Broadway show.

The Boys and Betty played 104 times on Broadway before Miss Cahill took husband Dan V Arthur's production around America.

THE BOYS FROM SYRACUSE Musical comedy in 2 acts by George Abbott based on Shakespeare's *The Comedy of Errors.* Lyrics by Lorenz Hart. Music by Richard Rodgers. Alvin Theater, New York, 23 November 1938.

Richard Rodgers claimed on a number of occasions that he was particularly delighted with his idea of making a musical from a Shakespeare play because no one had ever done so before. Maybe nobody ever told him that he was wrong a good number of times over, and that in fact *The Comedy of Errors* itself had been musical-comedied almost exactly half a century earlier, by Charles F Pidgin, starring Harry Crandall and Grace Huntington, under the title *Miss Fitz* (Theater, Lynn, Mass 5 November 1888) in a version reset in Philadelphia. Nevertheless his claim has been duly repeated as gospel down the years. The turning of *The Comedy of Errors* into a Rodgers and Hart musical (whoever's idea it was) resulted very much from the fact that Hart's actor brother, Teddy, bore a strong resemblance to another comedian, Jimmy Savo, and Larry Hart had the idea that the two of them would make a fine pair of musical comedy Dromios. The songwriters brought their *On Your Toes* collaborator George Abbott in on the project and, although it had been intended that all three would collaborate on the libretto, Abbott apparently finished it so speedily that it ended up being a solo effort. He also volunteered to be not only the show's director, but also its producer.

If there were, thus, rather fewer people involved on the making of this musical play than was usual, there were correspondingly fewer problems too, and *The Boys from Syracuse* made its way to Broadway and a happy reception quite uneventfully. Rodgers and Hart supplied a very uneven score, but one of which the best parts were headed straight for the standards list. Adriana (Muriel Angelus) introduced the lovely, dancing "Falling in Love with Love," Luciana (Marcy Wescott) and Antipholus of Syracuse (Eddie Albert) amazed "This Can't Be Love (because I feel so well)" and romanced through "You Have Cast Your Shadow on the Sea," whilst the two girls teamed with Wynn Murray, in the comic role of Luce, in the trio "Sing for Your Supper."

The Boys from Syracuse ran for 235 performances on its initial run, but it was not picked up by overseas producers. It did, however, win a film version and in 1940 Universal Pictures issued a movie which starred Allan Jones, Joe Penner, Martha Raye and Rosemary Lane and which used a handful of numbers from the stage show plus two new and additional pieces ("The Greeks Have No Word for It," "Who Are You?").

But that was not the end of the show's life. Unexpectedly, a small-scale revival, produced more than 20 years later at the off-Broadway Theater Four under the management of Richard York (15 April 1963) and featuring Stuart Damon, Ellen Hanley, Karen Morrow, Danny Carroll and Julienne Marie in its cast, caught on. It ran for 502 performances in its little theatre and, as a result, the piece finally ended up crossing the Atlantic. With the sort of perversity that can come only from dollar-blinded eyes, it was produced by Prince Littler in no less a venue than the huge Theatre Royal, Drury Lane. Bob Monkhouse, Denis Quilley, Lynn Kennington, Ronnie Corbett and Maggie Fitzgibbon headed the cast. The show survived this overblown treatment for less than three months, but it was nevertheless mounted at the Theatre Royal in Sydney, Australia, little more than a year later with a cast including Hazel Phillips, James Kenney, Lynne Cantlon, Alton Harvey and Nancye Hayes. It played 10 weeks there but was not persevered with thereafter.

Nearly 30 years later, however, London got a second and slimmer glimpse of the show when it was mounted for a summer season at the Open Air Theatre, Regent's Park (July 1991).

UK: Theatre Royal, Drury Lane 7 November 1963; Australia: Theatre Royal, Sydney 5 February 1966; Germany: Pforzheim 19 November 1972

Film: Universal 1940

Recordings: New York 1963 cast (Capitol), London cast (Decca), concert 1997 (DRG), selection (Columbia)

LES BRACONNIERS Opérette in 3 acts by Henri Chivot and Alfred Duru. Music by Jacques Offenbach. Théâtre des Variétés, Paris, 29 January 1873.

Chivot and Duru's libretto for Offenbach's opérette *Les Braconniers* was a perfect skein of comic opera disguises and mistaken identities, with things being not what they seemed more often than even W S Gilbert could have wished. The poachers of the title, who are stripping the estates of horrid Count Lastécouères de Campistrous (Berthelier), are led by one Bibletto (Marie Heilbronn), who is actually not a Bibletto at all but a Bibletta. She is the child of one de Birague who, thanks to the result of a lawsuit which intervenes half way through Act II, is proved to be the real heir to the Campistrous estates. However, before the jolly poacheress can rise to woman's estate and the hand of the usurper's nice son, Eléonore (Grenier), there are many subplotting comicalities to go through, the chief of which involve the rustic Marcassou (José Dupuis). On the night of his wedding to Ginetta

(Zulma Bouffar, replacing Céline Chaumont in extremis) the poor muletier is mistaken for the poacher chief, the next day he finds his wife denying him because she is sheltering Bibletta as her "husband," and eventually he is even suspected of being the missing heiress. Léonce had an ubiquitous role as the helpful Bibès, turning up in a variety of disguises to urge the plot along, and Baron played Ginetta's barber uncle.

Offenbach's score was highlighted by Les Couplets du Bouton de rose, a serenade, and a Galop de la mule, but *Les Braconniers,* although starting its career by breaking the house record at the Variétés with a one-night take of 6,075 francs, and going on to an honorable career in Paris, did not make the same effect as the great opéras-bouffes that its composer had put out in the preceding years. The reputation and worldwide success of those earlier pieces, however, ensured that it got a viewing beyond France. Eugène Humbert mounted the piece with his Brussels Fantaisies-Parisiennes company, and that company introduced the show to London, just months after the Paris opening, alongside their memorable *La Fille de Madame Angot, Les Cent Vierges* and *La Belle Hélène* in a season at the St James's Theatre. Pauline Luigini (Ginetta), Alfred Jolly (Campistrous), Mario Widmer (Marcassou) and Mlle Fonti (Bibletto) featured, the "scanty inspiration of the composer" was remarked on, and *Les Braconniers* was snuffed out by Lecocq's hugely admired piece.

Marie Geistinger and Maximilian Steiner mounted the piece in Vienna with the manageress preferring the soubrette role of Ginetta to that of Bibletto. That fell to Irma Nittinger, alongside Jani Szika (Marcassou), Martinelli (Lastécouères), Schreiber (Eléonore) and Carl Adolf Friese (Bibès), for the 22 times that *Die Wilderer* (ad Zell, Richard Genée) was played. An English version (ad Oscar Weil) was produced in America at the San Francisco Tivoli in 1885 as *The Pretty Poacher,* and what seems to have been a readaptation of the piece (also credited to Weil) was given a mounting under the title *The Poachers* by the recently reconstituted light opera company The Bostonians. Barnabee was Marcassou, Juliette Corden Ginetta and Marie Stone Bibletto. It proved a lesser favorite amongst their repertoire and was not played in any of their Broadway seasons.

UK: St James's Theatre (Fr) 26 July 1873; Austria: Theater an der Wien *Die Wilderer* 22 November 1873; USA: Tivoli Theater, San Francisco *The Pretty Poacber* 25 May 1885, Worcester Theater, Worcester, Mass *The Poachers* 3 October 1887

BRACY, Henry F [DUNN, Samuel Thomas] (b Cwindu, Maesteg, Wales, 8 January 1846; d Sydney, Australia, 31 January 1917).

During the late 1870s and the 1880s, Henry Bracy was one of the best and most successful comic opera tenors on the English-singing stage. He created leading roles in the English versions of *Les Mousquetaires au couvent* (Gontran), *La Mascotte* (Fritellini), *The Grand Mogol* (Mignapour), *Belle Lurette* (Marly) and *Babette* (Duc de la Roche Galante), as well as introducing the role of Hilarion in Gilbert and Sullivan's *Princess Ida* and the tenor parts in two of the most successful English musicals of the time, Bucalossi's *Manteaux Noirs* (Don Luis) and *Erminie* (Eugene Marcel). He also appeared in the West End in *The Lady of the Locket,* as the Chevlier de Lauvenay in *The Lily of Léoville* (1886) as Grénicheux (*Les Cloches de Corneville*), Hector (*Madame Favart*), Valentin (*Olivette*), Simon (*Der Bettelstudent*), Don Florio (*The Naval Cadets*), Offenbach's *Barbe-bleue* and as Peter in Cellier's *The Sultan of Mocha,* whilst simultaneously working as a stage director, latterly at the Avenue Theatre.

Plate 48. **Henry Bracy.** *Top tenor of the 19th-century stage on both sides of the world.*

Son of an accountant in the Welsh iron-fields, Bracy escaped from having to follow, as intended, in his father's footsteps thanks to the early discovery of a tenor voice and a taste for comedy. After fulfilling some concert engagements in the Midlands, he got his first job in opéra-bouffe when he faked a knowledge of French to win a place in the chorus for Hortense Schneider's season at the St James Theatre. He went through acting-with-songs engagements at Plymouth, and with Captain Disney Roebuck's touring company, but then moved firmly and finally into the musical theatre when he joined Henry Leslie's company to play Trémolini in what became a long-touring version of *La Princesse de Trébizonde.* When the company extended its repertoire, he played Falsacappa in *Les Brigands,* Fritz in *La Grand-Duchesse* and Cocorico in *Geneviève de Brabant.* And he went from there to make his first significant appearance in the West End in the Opera Comique production of *The Wonderful Duck.*

In 1873 he acquired a wife, Clara (née Hodges and known as Thompson), and soon after he and his wife acquired a contract to play leading roles in Australia. In the years that followed, much of their time would be spent in the southern hemisphere and, although they made several substantial trips "home" (during which time Bracy amassed the top-line credits listed above) and others to America, Australia ultimately became Bracy's home. He began his Australian career playing in *Lischen and Fritzchen* and in singing roles in several plays (*Guy Mannering, The Merchant of Venice, The Wedding March*) before being engaged by operatic producer W S Lyster. With Lyster he performed in some of the first Offenbach and Lecocq performances in Australia (Menelaos in *La Belle Hélène,* Defendant in *Trial by Jury,* Piquillo in *La Périchole,* Boléro in *Giroflé-Girofla,* Ange Pitou in *La Fille de Madame Angot,* etc) and appeared as Bras-de-Fer in the producer's famous operatic pantomime *Fortunatus.* He also appeared in Australia in *La Jolie Parfumeuse* (1876), as Eisenstein in *Die Fledermaus* (1877) with Fanny Simonsen, as Giletti to the *Madame l'Archiduc* of Catherine Lewis (1877), in *La Petite Mariée* (San Carlo) and *La Princesse de Trébizonde* and, in 1878, launched his own Bracy-Leopold company with former colleague George Leopold, producing, directing and touring such pieces as *The Bohemian Girl, La Fille de Madame Angot,* the pantomime *Egbert the Great,* and introducing *Les Cloches de Corneville* (Grénicheux) to Australia for the first time.

At the end of this first five-year stay, the Bracys returned to Britain, but after a decade working largely in the British theatre they went back to the colony, in 1889, to settle in St Kilda. Bracy formed his own English and Comic Opera Company, directing and starring in *The Old Guard, The Sultan of Mocha, The Beggar Student, Nemesis,* Lecocq's *Pepita* (*La Princesse des Canaries*), *The Bohemian Girl, Charity Begins at Home,* etc. The venture ended, however in a resounding bankruptcy and, renouncing the cares of management, Bracy settled in, first as principal tenor in the flagship Williamson & Garner Royal Comic Opera Company (*Dorothy, La Cigale,* Wilfred in *Marjorie, Iolanthe, The Mikado, Trial by Jury, The Vicar of Bray, The Mountebanks,* etc) and then as house director for the same company. In this capacity, over perhaps the most prosperous decade of J C Williamson's musical comedy activities, he was responsible for staging the Australian productions of such pieces as *The Geisha, Florodora,* Sullivan's *The Rose of Persia, The Mountebanks, Mam'zelle Nitouche, Dorothy, La Poupée* and regular revivals of the Gilbert and Sullivan repertoire, whilst still appearing on stage in such roles as Gaston in *La Belle Thérèse* (1895), Marmaduke in *Miss Decima* (1896), Simon in *The Beggar Student* (1897), Calino in *Nemesis* (1897), Peter in *The Sultan of Mocha,* Thaddeus in *The Bohemian Girl,* etc. In 1903 he was briefly made General Manager of J C Williamson's production company and he continued a close association with Williamson and his organization up until his death.

His wife, **Clara THOMPSON** [Clara Rose HODGES] (b London, 1 January 1848; d Los Angeles, 22 February 1941), daughter of the licensee of Islington's Canonbury Tavern and a half-sister to the more famous Lydia Thompson, also had a long and substantial career in comic opera and musical comedy, from 1862 when she rode to bit parts in pantomime and later in plays at Drury Lane behind her famous sibling. She made a brief trip to Broadway with Lydia's troupe of blondes (a trick bicycle speciality then Amber in *The Forty Thieves,* The Fairy Hope in *Sinbad the Sailor,* etc), appeared in London in burlesque and comedy with Pattie Oliver (Lady Anne in *The Rise and Fall of Richard III,* Charles Stuart in *Claude Du-val, or A Highwayman for the Ladies* 1869, etc), on the road in Leslie's *La Princesse de Trébizonde* (Zanetta), *La Grande-Duchesse* (Wanda) and *Geneviève de Brabant* (Brigitte), in pantomime and alongside Julia Mathews in the Gaiety Theatre's touring opéra-bouffe company before her marriage and the subsequent visit to Australia.

In the early 1870s she introduced Clairette (*La Fille de Madame Angot*), the twin title role of *Giroflé-Girofla* (1875), *La Périchole* (1875) and other star opéra-bouffe roles to Australia, appeared with Emilie Melville in *Fortunatus* (Little King Pippin), and starred around the country as Rose Michon in *La Jolie Parfumeuse* (1876), Graziella in *La Petite Mariée,* Serpolette in *Les Cloches de Corneville,* Regina in *La Princess de Trébizonde, La Belle Hélène,* Fiorella in *Les Brigands, Maritana,* Prince Conti in *Les Prés Saint Gervais,* etc. She was less prominent than her husband when they returned to Britain, although she took over as Serpolette in London's *Les Cloches de Corneville,* but she found a second career when, on their return to Australia, she moved to more characterful roles such as Mme Moutonnet (*La Belle Thérèse,* 1895), Mrs Merton (*The Vicar of Bray*), Mrs Bumpus (*Charity Begins at Home*), La Señora (*Miss De-*

cima, 1896), Duchess (*In Town,* 1896), Palmatica (*The Beggar Student,* 1897), Aunt Turlurette (*Nemesis,* 1897), Dame Durden (*Robin Hood,* 1899), Lady Constance (*The Geisha,* 1899) and the Gilbert and Sullivan heavy ladies. She was subsequently seen at the Lincoln Square Theatre in 1907 in the opera *Matilda,* made a very fine career as a character actress in America (*Camille, Magda, Hedda Gabler, The Old Lady Shows Her Medals, Belinda* with Ethel Barrymore, *Humpty Dumpty* with Otis Skinner), and took part in early films for Kinemacolor and Biograph and in later, talking ones through to her middle eighties.

Two of their three sons appeared in supporting roles on the musical comedy stage in Britain, America and Australia. **Philip H BRACY** [DUNN, Philip Henry] (b St Kilda, Melbourne, 6 December 1874) was seen as Grant in *The Medal and the Maid,* Regnier in *The Duchess of Dantzic* [UK and US] and So-Long in *See See.* **Sidney BRACY** [DUNN, Sidney Alfred N] (b Melbourne, 18 December 1877; d Hollywood, Calif, 5 August 1942) played Moreno in the original Gaiety production of *The Toreador,* Lupin in *Amorelle* (1810) and Mustapha in *A Persian Princess* in London, Yussuf in Broadway's *Rose of Persia* (1900), the title role in *The Woggle Bug* (1905), Rudolph Schiller in the American production *of A Polish Wedding* (*Polnische Wirtschaft*), in *Baron Trenck* (1912, t/o Marquis), as Guy of Gisborne in a 1912 revival of *Robin Hood* and Sandy MacSherry in *Rob Roy* (revival 1913). He subsequently went on to a solid career as a screen actor in Hollywood, beginning with Robin Hood (1913, the Baron) and the silent serial *The Million Dollar Mystery* (1914) and carrying on into hundreds of roles in the talking age.

BRADFIELD, W[alter] Louis (b Hornsey, London, 13 June 1866; d Brighton, 12 August 1919). All-purpose Victorian musical leading man with an unusual ability to take either romantic or comic roles.

Louis Bradfield began his career as a musical comedy star playing the Fred Leslie and Arthur Roberts low-comedy new burlesque roles in the touring companies of Auguste van Biene (Don Caesar, Servant, Captain Crosstree, etc). He appeared in London for the first time when he succeeded Roberts in the star role of Captain Coddington in George Edwardes's production of *In Town* and he created his first metropolitan role, also for Edwardes, as Bobbie Rivers in *A Gaiety Girl* (1893). He played this part with the Gaiety company in Australia (where he also appeared in the title role of *Gentleman Joe*) and in America, and his versatility as a performer proved extremely useful during the tour when he was able to deputize not only for the lead comic but also, thanks to a handsome figure and a good baritone voice, for the principal singing hero as well.

This combination of talents won him a career-long run of roles under Edwardes's management, as one of the few actors whom the producer could move back and forth between leading and featured roles at Daly's Theatre and the Gaiety and the different styles of musical plays they housed in the heyday of his management (*An Artist's Model, My Girl, The Geisha, The Circus Girl, A Runaway Girl, San Toy, The Girl from Kays, The Cingalee, Les P'tites Michu, The Little Cherub, Les Merveilleuses, The Girls of Gottenberg*). He succeeded to the juvenile baritone role of Donegal in *Florodora* (1900) and the following year created the equivalent role of Berkeley Shallamar in *The Silver Slipper,* starred in the British production of *Madame Sherry* (1903) and scored a fine success as the fey, puckish Widgery Blake in *Butterflies* (1908). Latterly, he played for Edwardes and other managers in the provinces, appearing in the leading roles of such pieces as *The Merry Widow* and *The Quaker Girl.* Only months before his death, he was touring in the musical *Gay Trouville* alongside another aging Daly's star, Hayden Coffin.

BRADLEY, Buddy [EPPS, Clarence Bradley] (b Alabama, 24 July 1905; d New York, 17 July 1972). American choreographer and teacher who made most of his career purveying American dance techniques in Britain.

The young Bradley appeared on the revue stage as a dancer with Florence Mills but, while still in his early twenties, he largely abandoned performing in favor of choreography and teaching, providing tap and jazz dance routines for some of the era's favorite dance stars—Ruby Keeler, Eleanor Powell, Adele Astaire—under the management of producers George White, Earl Carroll and Florenz Ziegfeld before crossing to Britain in 1930 to do the dances for C B Cochran's production of the Rodgers and Hart revue *Evergreen.* He stayed in Britain thereafter, choreographing many pieces for the British stage during the period when dancing principals were the fashion, including *Hold My Hand* (1931) with Jessie Matthews, *The Cat and the Fiddle* (1932), *Mr Whittington* (1933, co-), *Nice Goings On* (1933), *Lucky Break* (1934, co-), *Mother of Pearl* (1933), *Happy Week-End* (1934), London's *Anything Goes* (1935), *This'll Make You Whistle* (1935) with Jack Buchanan and Elsie Randolph, Émile Littler's ill-fated *Aloma and Nutane* (1938) and Jessie Matthews' equally short-lived *I Can Take It* (1939), *Full Swing* (1943, co-), the Buchanan/Randolph *It's Time to Dance, Something in the Air* (1943) and *La-di-da-di-da* (1943, co-), as well as numerous revues.

He also occasionally took to the stage as a performer (*Cochran's 1931 Revue, It's Time to Dance*), and appeared in several films (*Evergreen, Gangway,* etc).

He for many years ran the Buddy Bradley Studios of Dance in London, before ultimately returning to America in 1967.

Bradley varied his birthdate from 1908 to 1913, his place of birth from Alabama to Harrisburg, Pa, and his real name from Robert Bradley to Epps. The American Social Security records have him listed as Bradley Epps, and reveal that he was born in 1905.

BRAHAM, David H [ABRAHAM, David] (b London, ?1838; d New York, 11 April 1905).

Braham moved from London to America whilst in his teens and worked first as a violinist in Pony Moore's Minstrel company. He played in various pit orchestras, at one stage in Robinson's Military Band, and composed music-hall songs and theatre music, before becoming first an orchestral member and then musical director at, successively, Fox and Curran's Canterbury Concert (Music) Hall (1860), the American Theater, Wood's Minstrel Hall, the "New Idea," R W Butler's 444 Broadway and at the Mechanics' Hall. He was musical director at the Theatre Comique from July 1864, with Josh Hart and later with Horace Lingard as director, making a first theatrical hit as a composer with his replacement score for the English burlesque *Pluto.* He accompanied the early opéra-bouffe performances of the Galton sisters in America, and in turn headed the orchestras at the 8th Avenue Opera House, the Olympic, the Eagle and at the newly opened Union Square Theater (1871) before in 1873 he joined Harrigan and Hart in a similar position as musical director. As part of his job, over the years that followed, he provided original music for Edward Harrigan's vast output of songs and slightly musical (often just one song) sketches.

When the pair began to extend their comical sketches-with-songs into musical farces, Braham's job of composing such music as was required, to Harrigan's lyrics, found him in effect writing musical comedy scores. He held his position with Harrigan and Hart, and, following Hart's departure, with Harrigan alone, through the entire length of their famous careers as theatrical entertainers and during that period he composed a number of enduring songs which first saw the light of stage in their shows, including "Whist! the Bogey Man!," "The Mulligan Guards," "The Babies on our Block," "The Skids Are Out Tonight," "Sallie Waters," "The Little Widow Dunn," "Paddy Duffy's Cart," "Widow Nolan's Goat," "Ebb and Flow," "Maggie Murphy's Home," "My Dad's Dinner Pail," "No Wealth without Labor," etc.

During his years with Harrigan and Hart, Braham also occasionally provided music for other projects including Annie Pixley's 1882 *Zara,* the vaudeville act of Mealey and Mackey, and Maggie Mitchell's 1888 vehicle *Maggie the Midget.* After Harrigan's days were done Braham worked out his career at the Grand Opera House, and finally at Wallack's Theater where he was engaged up to his final illness.

The son of one Joseph Braham and his wife Elizabeth née Haley, Braham was related (in some way unspecified) to the celebrated English singer and songwriter **John BRAHAM** [né ABRAHAM] (b London, 20 March 1777; d London, 17 February 1856) and thus to his singing sons **Augustus BRAHAM** (d St Leonards on Sea, 31 May 1889), **[John] Hamilton BRAHAM** (d Rochester, 22 December 1862), Ward Braham and **Charles [Bampfield] BRAHAM** (d London, 11 June 1884). A brother **Joseph BRAHAM** (b London, ?1827; d New York, 1 July 1877), also a musician, was the father of four further musicians and conductors: **John J BRAHAM** longtime Boston musical director and composer, who conducted America's first *HMS Pinafore,* **Harry BRAHAM** (who was the first Mr Lillian Russell), Albert and William. David himself was married to a sister of the celebrated pantomimist and dancer Marietta Ravel, and their sons, David jr and George F, worked respectively as an actor-songwriter and conductor-composer (Harrigan's *Under Cover,* etc). A third son, Edward J Braham, who played in *Reilley and the 400* at the Theatre Comique died at the age of 14 (d 1 April 1894). One of their daughters, Annie, became Mrs Edward Harrigan, and another, Rose, also worked on the musical stage (*The Telephone Girl,* etc).

1869 **Pluto, or The Young Lady Who Charmed the Rocks** replacement score for H J Byron's burlesque *Orpheus and Eurydice* ad H B Farnie, Theatre Comique 1 February

1872 **Aladdin the Second** Byron's *Aladdin* revised by H S Murdoch Olympic Theater 11 November

1873 **Gabriel Grub, or The Story of the Goblins Who Stole the Sexton** (Fred Lyster) Olympic Theater 22 December

1877 **Old Lavender** (Harrigan) Theatre Comique 3 September (revised version 22 April 1878)

1877 **The Rising Star** (Harrigan) Theatre Comique 22 October

1877 **The Pilsbury Muddle** (Harrigan) sketch Theatre Comique 17 December

1877 **Sullivan's Christmas** (Harrigan) Theatre Comique 24 December

1878 **A Celebrated Hard Case** (Harrigan) Theatre Comique 18 March

1878 **The Mulligan Guards' Picnic** (Harrigan) Theatre Comique 23 September

1878 **The Lorgaire** (Harrigan) Theatre Comique 25 November

1879 **The Mulligan Guards' Ball** (Harrigan) Theatre Comique 13 January

1879 **The Mulligan Guards' Chowder** (Harrigan) Theatre Comique 11 August

1879 **The Mulligan Guards' Christmas** (Harrigan) Theatre Comique 17 November

1880 **The Mulligan Guards' Surprise** (Harrigan) Theatre Comique 16 February

1880 **The Mulligan Guards' Nominee** (Harrigan) Theatre Comique 22 November

1881 **The Mulligan Silver Wedding** (Harrigan) Theatre Comique 21 February

1881 **The Major** (Harrigan) Theatre Comique 29 August

1882 **Squatter Sovereignty** (Harrigan) Theatre Comique 9 January

1882 **Zara** (Marsden) Comstock's Theater, Columbus, Ohio 28 August

1882 **The Blackbird** (Harrigan) Theatre Comique 26 August

1882 **Mordecai Lyons** (Harrigan) Theatre Comique 26 October

1882 **McSorley's Inflation** (Harrigan) Theatre Comique 27 November

1883 **The Muddy Day** (Harrigan) Theatre Comique 2 April

1883 **Cordelia's Aspirations** (Harrigan) Theatre Comique 5 November

1884 **Dan's Tribulations** (Harrigan) Theatre Comique 7 April

1884 **Investigation** (Harrigan) Theatre Comique 1 September

1885 **McAllister's Legacy** (Harrigan) Park Theater 5 January

1885 **The Grip** (Harrigan) Park Theater 30 November

1886 **The Leather Patch** (Harrigan) Park Theater 15 February

1886 **The O'Reagans** (Harrigan) Park Theater 11 October

1887 **McNooney's Visit** (Harrigan) Park Theater 31 January

1887 **Pete** (Harrigan) Park Theater 22 November

1888 **Waddy Googan** (Harrigan) Park Theater 3 September

1889 **4-11-44** (revised *McNooney's Visit*) (Harrigan) Park Theater 21 March

1889 **McKenna's Flirtation** (Edgar Selden) (Harrigan) Park Theater 2 September

1890 **Reilly and the Four Hundred** (Harrigan) Harrigans Theater 29 December

1891 **The Last of the Hogans** (Harrigan) Harrigans Theater 21 December

1893 **The Woolen Stocking** (Harrigan) Harrigans Theater 9 October

1894 **Notoriety** (Harrigan) Harrigans Theater 10 December

1895 **My Son Dan** (Braham) Opera House, Paterson, NJ 21 October

1896 **Marty Malone** (Harrigan) Bijou Theater 31 August

1898 **The Finish of Mr Fresh** (Thomas H Davis, William T Keogh) Star Theater 7 November

See under HARRIGAN, EDWARD *for early sketches*

BRAHAM, Leonora [ABRAHAM, Leonora] (b London, 3 February 1853; d London, 23 November 1931). Savoy Opera star soprano through much of Gilbert & Sullivan's best period.

At the age of 21, Leonora Braham joined Mr and Mrs German Reed's company at the St George's Hall, appearing there continuously in the juvenile soprano roles of their highly popular four- or five-handed musical playlets for more than four years. Her first ventures into the regular theatre were in America where she starred in the New York productions of the British comic operas *Princess Toto* (1879) and *Billee Taylor* (1880) and, on returning to Britain, she was hired by D'Oyly Carte to create the title role in *Patience,* a part which had been rejected as too soubrette-y by his current prima donna, at the Opera Comique ("I Cannot Tell What This Love May Be"). For the next six years Miss Braham held the position of leading lady at the Savoy Theatre, through the creations of *Iolanthe* (Phyllis), *Princess Ida* (Ida, following Carte's quarrel with Lillian Russell), *The Mikado* (Yum-Yum, introducing "The Sun Whose Rays" and "Three Little Maids") and *Ruddigore* (Rose Maybud) and the first revival of *The Sorcerer* (Aline).

In 1887–88 she and her then husband, tenor J Duncan Young, spent a season with Williamson, Garner and Musgrove's Royal Comic Opera Company in Australia (*Dorothy, Erminie, The Mikado,* etc) but, on her return, she did not, in spite of her old position in the world of comic opera, succeed in finding appreciable work. She appeared in London only as a replacement in *Carina* (1888, t/o Zara) and in the short-lived *Gretna Green* (1889–90, Ruth Ferris), and on tour in the title role of *Nanon,* in Edward Jakobowski's *Paola* (1889, Paola) and the burlesque *Miss Esmeralda.* She went to South America with Edwin Cleary's comic opera company in 1890, then produced and starred in a tour of a small comic opera, *The Duke's Diversion,* on her own account in 1892 before again leaving Britain to spend two years touring British comic opera in South Africa. During this tour she also made a venture into heavier waters, and appeared as Santuzza in *Cavalleria Rusticana.*

Her only subsequent West End appearance of note was in the comedy role of Lady Barbara Cripps in George Edwardes's musical comedy *An Artist's Model* in 1895, although she continued to make provincial appearances around Britain (Julia Jellicoe in *The Grand Duke* and the Carte repertoire, Nora in *Shamus O'Brien,* Bathilde in *Olivette,* Madame Michu in *Les P'tites Michu,* Widow Melnotte in *Melnotte*), and on Broadway (Donna Adelina Gonzales in *Because She Loved Him So,* 1899) until after the turn of the century.

BRAHAM, Philip [Edward] (b London, 18 June 1881; d London, 2 May 1934). British songwriter who was quick to catch the new dancing style in theatre music in the postwar years.

Educated at Charterhouse and Cambridge, Braham began a career in show business as a member of the March Hares concert party, for whom he also composed

Plate 49. **Phil Braham's** *"Dancing Honeymoon" proved a hit in both Britain and America as displayed in Battling Butler. France took the song but not the show.*

an amount of performance material. He supplied some additional material for the Gaiety fairy play *Two Naughty Boys* as early as 1906, but his first own regular theatre composition was the music-hall sketch *Alice Up-to-Date,* written with no less a librettist than Fred Thompson and actor-cum-writer Eric Blore and played at the London Pavilion. In the early part of the war years he provided similar sketches and revues (*Sugar and Spice, Nurses, Brides,* etc) for several London variety houses. His first work on a major show was in supplying some songs for the musical comedy *Mr Manhattan,* of which Howard Talbot was the principal composer, and then on additional numbers for the revue *The Bing Boys Are Here.*

In the next decade he composed or contributed to a huge number of West End revues, proving, for some while, the most successful of local composers in the face of the fashion for transatlantic songs (*Bubbly, Tails Up, Back to Blighty, See-Saw, Pot Luck, The Latest Craze, Jumble Sale, Rats, London Calling* w Noël Coward, *The Co-Optimists, Charlot's Revue, On with the Dance* w Coward, *Still Dancing, Charlot's Revue of 1928,* etc). He also contributed botching material for imported shows (two songs in *Dédé,* etc), and provided the scores for a number of the song-and-dance musicals of the day. The farcical *The Officers' Mess* (200 performances) and the Jack Buchanan vehicle *Battling Butler* ("The Dancing Honeymoon"), subsequently played on Broadway with a largely different score, were his most successful book musicals in a career largely devoted to revue, before, in his last years, he became a musical director on early British sound films.

"Limehouse Blues" (w Douglas Furber) seen in *A to Z* and *Charlot's Revue* and used in the films of *The Ziegfeld Follies* and *Star,* remains Braham's most famous single number.

1913 **Alice Up-to-Date** (Eric Blore, Fred Thompson) 1 act London Pavilion 29 December

1914 **Violet and Pink** (Thompson) East Ham Palace 4 May, London Pavilion 11 May

1914 **Beauties** (Sydney Blow, Douglas Hoare) 1 act Victoria Palace 14 December

1915 **Sugar and Spice** sketch Plymouth 5 April

1916 **Mr Manhattan** (w Howard Talbot, Frank E Tours/C H Bovill, Fred Thompson) Prince of Wales Theatre 30 March

1916 **Back to Blighty** (w George H Clutsam, Herbert Haines/Blow, Hoare) Oxford Theatre September

1917 **The Hula Girl** (w Nat D Ayer, Alfred Haines/George Reynolds, R Guy Keene) 1 act Hippodrome 18 December

1918 **Telling the Tale** (Blow, Hoare) Ambassadors Theatre 31 August

1918 **The Officers' Mess** (Blow, Hoare) St Martins Theatre 7 November

1919 **Hustle** (Ronald Jeans) Finsbury Park Empire

1921 **Yes, Papa** (Eric Blore, Austin Melford) Coliseum, Cheltenham 21 February

1921 **Now and Then** (Reginald Arkell/J Hastings Turner) Vaudeville Theatre 17 September

1922 **Battling Butler** (Douglas Furber/Stanley Brightman, Austin Melford) New Oxford Theatre 8 December

1924 **Boodle** (w Max Darewski/Furber/Blow, Hoare) Prince of Wales Theatre, Birmingham 26 December; Empire Theatre 10 March 1925

1927 **Up with the Lark** (Furber/Furber, Hartley Carrick) Adelphi Theatre 25 August

BRAMBLE, Mark (b Maryland, 7 December 1950).

Originally an employee in David Merrick's office, Bramble wrote one off-off-Broadway piece and collaborated with Michael Stewart on two musical adaptations—Werfel's *Jacobowsky und der Oberst* as *The Grand Tour,* and Maxwell Anderson's play *Elizabeth the Queen* as the off-Broadway *Elizabeth and Essex*—before finding international success with two consecutive stage musicals launched within four months of each other in 1980: the circus musical *Barnum* and the stage version of the famous musical film *42nd Street.*

A subsequent rewrite of the Rudolf Friml operetta *The Three Musketeers,* directed by its adapter as a swashbuckling action show, had less success (nine performances on Broadway), and the largest amount of the now London-based Bramble's work in the years that followed was as a director, notably of productions of *42nd Street* in Britain, Europe and Australia. He adapted and directed a British production of the French children's musical *Fat Pig* in 1987 and, in 1991, mounted the tryout of a new musical play based on Victor Hugo's *Notre Dame de Paris.*

1977 **T*ts D*amond** (Lee Pockriss/Steve Brown) The Loft January

1978 **Pal Joey** revised libretto w Jerome Chodorov (Ahmanson Theater, Los Angeles)

1979 **The Grand Tour** (Jerry Herman/w Michael Stewart) Palace Theater 11 January

1980 **Elizabeth and Essex** (Doug Katsaros/Richard Engquist/w Stewart) South Street Theater 24 February

1980 **Barnum** (Cy Coleman/Michael Stewart) St James Theater 30 April

1980 **42nd Street** (pasticcio/w Stewart) Winter Garden Theater 25 August

1983 **The Three Musketeers** revised libretto Hartman Theater, Stamford, Conn, 18 March, Broadway Theater, New York, 11 November 1984

1987 **Fat Pig** (*Le Cochon qui voulait maigrir*) English version (Henry Krieger/w Jenny Hawkesworth) Haymarket Theatre, Leicester 20 November

1991 **Notre Dame** (Callum McLeod/Paul Leigh) Old Fire Station, Oxford 25 June

BRAMMER, Julius (b Schraditz Mähren, Czechoslovakia, 9 March 1877; d Juan-les-Pins, 18 April 1943). Top librettist of the heyday of the 20th-century Viennese stage.

For more than a decade a bit-part actor/singer at the Theater an der Wien, Brammer appeared fairly insignificantly in such roles as an Innkeeper (*Die Dame aus Trouville*), Quendel (*Der Vogelhändler*), Probitt (*Der Toreador*), Ein Kellner (*Der Fremdenführer*), Schneider (*Wiener Frauen*), The Man with the monocle (*Der Lebemann*), Major Abatutta (*Bruder Straubinger*), Tabourin (*Die beiden Don Juans*), Heuven (*Der neue Burgermeister*), Baron Grenzenstein (*Der Generalkonsul*), Graf Montgrigny (*Befehl des Kaisers*), Dr Runkel (*Der Herr Professor*), The Director of the New York Hotel Bristol (*Die Millionenbraut*), Lord Percy (*Wiener Blut*), von Abstorff (*Das Garnisonsmädel*), an Englishman (*Pufferl*), Lord Bevis (*Prinz Bob*), Third Rat (*Der Rebell*), Kraps (*Peter und Paul*), Nowak (*Ein Herbstmanöver*), Cyprian Vollrath (*Der Mann mit den drei Frauen*), Hans (*Der schöne Gardist*), the dancemaster, Monsieur Deschamps (*Schneeglöckchen*), Graf Arrois (*Die schöne Risette*) and Lieutenant Rincke (*Ihr Adjutant*) between 1902 and 1911.

From 1907, in collaboration with Alfred Grünwald, he began writing libretti and lyrics for the musical theatre and, although a number of these works found their way to the stage in Germany and Austria, he did not give up his job as a performer until after Robert Winterberg's *Die Dame in Rot* had assured the pair of their future as stage writers. Thereafter, Brammer and Grünwald became the most accomplished and successful team writing for the Austrian stage. In the years before the war, they had major Viennese hits with Ascher's *Hoheit tanzt Walzer* and Eysler's *Der lachende Ehemann,* and they scored one of the biggest successes of the war years with the outstanding *Die Rose von Stambul* as well as authoring the scripts for such other successes as *Die schöne Schwedin, Bruder Leichtsinn* and Leo Fall's *Fürstenliebe* (*Die Kaiserin*) and preparing the replacement libretto for Lehár's *Der Göttergatte* score as *Die ideale Gattin* (which they would later re-rewrite as *Die Tangokönigin*).

During the 1920s, the pair had virtual end-to-end hits with such internationally successful Operetten as *Der letzte Walzer, Die Bajadere,* the rather less popular *Die Perlen der Cleopatra, Gräfin Mariza, Die Zirkusprinzessin* and *Die gold'ne Meisterin.* Their final piece together, *Das Veilchen vom Montmartre,* gave them a further success, but Brammer's last Viennese collaborations with other partners, during those few years before the activities of the 1930s drove him out of Austria and out of the musical theatre, proved less fruitful.

1907 **Fräulein Sherlock Holmes** (Georges Criketown/w ''A G Wald'' [ie, Alfred Grünwald]) Volkstheater, Munich 31 August

1908 **Die grüne Redoute** (Leo Ascher/w Grünwald) 1 act Danzers Orpheum 26 March

1908 **Die lustigen Weiber von Wien** (Robert Stolz/w Grünwald) 1 act Colosseum 16 November

1908 **Die kleine Manicure** (Ascher /w Grünwald) 1 act Parisiana

1909 **Elektra** (Béla Laszky/w Grünwald) 1 act Kabarett Fledermaus 1 December

1910 **Georgette** (Laszky/w Grünwald) 1 act Kabarett Fledermaus 16 March

1910 **Vindobona, du herrliche Stadt** (Ascher/w Grünwald) Venedig in Wien 22 July

1911 **Das goldene Strumpfband** (Ascher/w Grünwald) 1 act Ronacher 1 May

1911 **Die Dame in Rot** (Robert Winterberg/w Grünwald) Theater des Westens, Berlin 16 September

1911 **Das Damenparadies** (Richard Fall/w Grünwald) 1 act Wiener Colosseum 1 November

1912 **Hoheit tanzt Walzer** (Ascher/w Grünwald) Raimundtheater 24 February

1912 **Eine vom Ballet** (Oscar Straus/w Grünwald) London Coliseum 2 June

1913 **Der lachende Ehemann** (Edmund Eysler/w Grünwald) Wiener Bürgertheater 19 March

1913 **Die ideale Gattin** (Franz Lehár/w Grünwald) Theater an der Wien 11 October

1915 **Die schöne Schwedin** (Winterberg/w Grünwald) Theater an der Wien 30 January

1915 **Die Kaiserin** (aka *Fürstenliebe*) (Fall/w Grünwald) Metropoltheater, Berlin 16 October

1916 **Fürstenliebe** revised *Die Kaiserin* Carltheater 1 February

1916 **Die Rose von Stambul** (Fall/w Grünwald) Theater an der Wien 2 December

1917 **Bruder Leichtsinn** (Ascher/w Grünwald) Wiener Bürgertheater 28 December

1919 **Dichterliebe** (Felix Mendelssohn arr Emil Stern/w Grünwald) Komische Oper, Berlin 20 December

1920 **Der letzte Walzer** (Straus/w Grünwald) Berliner Theater, Berlin 12 February

1921 **Die Tangokönigin** revised *Die ideale Gattin* w Grünwald Apollotheater 9 September

1921 **Die Bajadere** (Emmerich Kálmán/w Grünwald) Carltheater 23 December

1923 **Die Perlen der Cleopatra** (Straus/w Grünwald) Theater an der Wien 17 November

1924 **Gräfin Mariza** (Kálmán/w Grünwald) Theater an der Wien 28 February

1926 **Die Zirkusprinzessin** (Kálmán/w Grünwald) Theater an der Wien 26 March

1927 **Die gold'ne Meisterin** (Eysler/w Grünwald) Theater an der Wien 13 September

1928 **Die Herzogin von Chicago** (Kálmán/w Grünwald) Theater an der Wien 5 April

1930 **Das Veilchen vom Montmartre** (Kálmán/w Grünwald) Johann Strauss-Theater 21 March

1931 **Der Bauerngeneral** (Straus/w Gustav Beer) Theater an der Wien 28 March

1932 **Donauliebchen** (Eysler/w Emil Marboth) Wiener Bürgertheater 25 December

1933 **Die Dame mit dem Regenbogen** (Jean Gilbert/w Beer) Theater an der Wien 25 August

1952 **Bozena** (Straus/w Grünwald) Theater am Gärtnerplatz, Munich 16 May

BRANDL, Johann (b Kirchenbirk, Bohemia, 30 October 1835; d Vienna, 9 June 1913).

Conductor in several Viennese suburban theatres, from 1865 to 1866 at the Theater in der Josefstadt, and a member of the music staff of the Carltheater between 1866 and 1882, Brandl composed a long list of musical accompaniments for the Possen and other forms of more or less musical comedies played during his various tenures. These assignments included replacement scores for the German-language versions of the enormously successful French vaudevilles introduced by Anna Judic at the Paris Théâtre des Variétés (*Niniche, Papas Frau, Die Kosakin*), and for a range of other French vaudevilles and musical comedies (*Der Kukuk, Coco, Kleine Anzeigen,* etc) as well as for shoals of local pieces by such prolific comic authors as O F Berg, Anton Langer and Julius Rosen.

Brandl botched to order for the Carltheater, interpolating more or less numbers into the French imports of the day (Costé's *Les Charbonniers,* Lecocq's *La Marjolaine* and *Hundert Jungfrauen,* Coedès's *La Belle Bourbonnaise,* Offenbach's *La Jolie Parfumeuse,* etc) when he was not replacing entire scores, but he also ventured as an author, writing or collaborating on the texts for several of his own pieces.

The Carltheater also produced Brandl's rather shorter list of original Operetten, including the highly successful and long-lived *Des Löwen Erwachen* (1872), a one-act piece which was regularly revived during the 19th century and played in 1893 at the Hofoper, the popular little *Cassis Pacha,* and two of his full-length pieces, *Die Mormonen* (1879, eight performances)—a piece which had Brigham Young as its principal character—and *Die drei Langhalse* (1880). The four-act Posse *Der Walzerkönig* (1885) was another success for which he was credited as composer, and his *Der liebe Augustin* was produced by Camillo Walzel at the Theater an der Wien in 1887 for 27 performances.

1862 **Der Fremde** (Georg Szechenyi) Baden-bei-Wien July

186? **Die Freiwilligen in Mexico** (Julius Stern)

1865 **Tiktak** 1 act Pressburg August

1865 **Österreichs Rheinfahrt** (Carl Elmar) Theater in der Josefstadt 31 October

1865 **Die Universalerben** (Theodor Flamm) Theater in der Josefstadt 25 November

1865 **Diesseits und jenseits** (O F Berg) 1 act Theater in der Josefstadt 2 December

1865 **Ambo Solo** (Julius Rosen) Theater in der Josefstadt 9 December

1865 **Die Wiener auf der Alm** (Karl Bayer) 1 act Theater in der Josefstadt 16 December

1865 **Unterm Christbaum** (Elmar) 1 act Theater in der Josefstadt 16 December

1865 **Das alte und das neue Jahr** (Carl F Stix) 1 act Theater in der Josefstadt 31 December

1866 **20,000 Taler Reugeld** (Josef Doppler) 1 act Theater in der Josefstadt 8 January

1866 **Der erste Rausch** (Bayer) 1 act Theater in der Josefstadt 9 January

1866 **Ein Bauernball** (Elmar) 1 act Theater in der Josefstadt 27 January

1866 **Ein Narrenball** (Stix) 1 act Theater in der Josefstadt 27 January

1866 **Der Schuster-Michel** (Julius Findeisen) Theater in der Josefstadt 1 March

1866 **Alte Schulden** (Friedrich Kaiser) Theater in der Josefstadt 14 April

1866 **Eine Wiener Burgertochter** (J Seitz, Friedrich Schuster) Theater in der Josefstadt 28 April

1866 **Das Kreuz in der Klamm** (Kaiser) Thalia-Theater 12 August

1866 **Eine Promesse von Sothen** (Adolph L'Arronge) Carltheater 27 December

1866 **Meine Memoiren** (Berg) 1 act Carltheater 16 May

1867 **Die Schäferin** 1 act Harmonietheater 1 May

1867 **Eine Weinprobe** (Wilhelm Fellechner, Carl Heimerding) 1 act Carltheater 9 May

1867 **Eine neue Einrichtung** (Berg) 1 act Carltheater 16 May

1867 **Dreizehn** (Anton Langer) 1 act Carltheater 7 September

1867 **Füchsl auf der Pariser Ausstellung** Carltheater 23 October

1867 **Der kleine Beamte** (Berg) Theater in der Josefstadt 2 November

1867 **Der Direktor von Langenlois** (Berg) 1 act Carltheater 30 November

1867 **Landsturm und Zivilehe** (Langer, Julius Rosen) Carltheater 31 December

1868 **Die Pfarrerköchin** (Berg) Carltheater 20 April

1868 **Vom Schützentage** (Langer) 1 act Carltheater 21 July

1868 **Strizow in Wien** (Berg) 1 act Carltheater 15 September

1868 **Der Herr Landesgerichtsrat** (Berg) Carltheater 26 November

1868 **Wer ist tot?** 1 act Carltheater 12 December

1869 **Wort und Tat** (Rosen) Carltheater 5 January

1869 **Antikenschwindel** (Heinrich Wilcken) Carltheater 20 February

1869 **Der Hanswurst** (Rosen) 1 act Carltheater 20 February

1869 **Nur gemütlich** (Langer) 1 act Carltheater 16 December

1870 **Das Vergissmeinnicht** (Brandl) 1 act Carltheater 21 May

1870 **Brididi** (Henri de Rochefort) 1 act Carltheater 21 May

1870 **Im Redaktionsbureau** (Langer) 1 act Carltheater 21 May

1870 **Eine ländliche Verlobung** (Arthur Müller) 1 act Carltheater 24 September

1870 **Das Hasenschrecker** (Louis Grois) 1 act Carltheater 24 September

1870 **Zu Dreien** (Karl Grün) 1 act Carltheater 7 December

1871 **Zahnschmerzen** (Emil Pohl, Stix) 1 act Carltheater

1871 **Eine Vereinsschwester** (Langer) 1 act Carltheater 17 October

1871 **Pelikan der Zweite** (Labiche, Delacour ad) 1 act Carltheater 2 December

1872 **Raten und Renten** (Robert Jonas) 1 act Carltheater 6 April

1872 **Des Löwen Erwachen** (Julius Rosen) 1 act Carltheater 26 April

1872 **Sein Salonstiefel** 1 act Carltheater 14 June

1872 **Vater Gorilla** (L'Arronge, Gustav von Moser) 1 act Carltheater 14 December

1873 **Der polnische Jude** (Erckmann-Chatrian ad) Carltheater August

1873 **Einst und jetzt** (Langer) 1 act Carltheater 2 December

1874 **Cassis Pascha** (*Un Turc pris dans une porte*) (Édouard Brisebarre, Eugène Riou ad) 1 act Carltheater 28 February

1874 **Die Bartolomäusnacht** (Aimé Wouwermans) 1 act Carltheater 29 April

1875 **Die Probirmamsell** (w Müller/Berg) Carltheater 6 November

1876 **Die Weiber, wie sie nicht sein sollen** (Berg) Carltheater 29 April

1876 **Vindobona** (Berg) Carltheater 7 October

1877 **O diese Weiber!** (Rosen) Carltheater 17 March

1877 **Ein vorsichtiger Mann** (Gustav Moser, E Jacobson) Carltheater 1 April

1877 **Die alte Jungfer** (Berg) Carltheater 14 April

1877 **Gevatter Neid** (Berg) Carltheater 14 November

1878 **S'Jungferngift** (Ludwig Anzengruber) Carltheater 21 April

1878 **Die verfallene Mauer** (Wilhelm Hess) 1 act Carltheater 21 September

1878 **Niniche** German version (replacement score) w Richard Genée (Carltheater)

1879 **Coco** German version with added music (Carltheater)

1879 **Der grosse Casimir** (*Le Grand Casimir*) German version (new part-score) Carltheater 15 April

1879 **Wildröschen** (Wilhelm Mannstadt, "A Weller" [ie, J A Müller]) Carltheater 4 July

1879 **Die Mormonen** (w Albert Klischnegg) Carltheater 22 November

1880 **Wiener Karrikaturen** (Berg) Carltheater 3 January

1880 **Papas Frau** (*La Femme à Papa*) German version (replacement score) w Genée (Carltheater)

1880 **Die Theatergredl** (Berg) Carltheater 9 April

1880 **Der Kukuk** (*Le Coucou*) (Hippolyte Raymond, Alphonse Dumas ad) Carltheater 22 April

1880 **Kleine Anzeigen** (*Les Petites Correspondances*) German version with songs Carltheater 25 September

1880 **Die drei Langhälse** (Emil Pohl, Richard Genée) Carltheater 11 December

1881 **Die Statuten der Ehe** (Karl Morré) Carltheater 17 December

1882 **Die Tochter des Dionysus** (J S Müller) 1 act Carltheater 20 January

1882 **Hopfenraths Erben** (Wilcken ad Franz von Radler) Carltheater 11 February

1882 **Die Unzufriedenen** (Otto Weiss, Fedor Marmoth) Carltheater 18 March

1882 **Alois Blumauer** (Radler) Carltheater 30 December

1885 **Der Walzerkönig** (Mannstadt, Costa, Bruno Zappert) Carltheater 9 October

1887 **Der liebe Augustin** (Hugo Klein) Theater an der Wien 15 January

1891 **Die Kosakin** (*La Cosaque*) German version (replacement score) w Moritz West (Theater an der Wien)

1901 **Der Kellermeister** completed Zeller's score (Raimundtheater)

BRANDRAM, Rosina [MOULT, Rosina] (b London, 2 July 1845; d Southend-on-Sea, 28 February 1907). Long-serving Savoy Theatre heavy lady.

Encouraged on to the stage—or so her Carte-manufactured biography insisted—following some family financial problems, Miss Brandram, who had reportedly had a young gentlewoman's singing lessons with Sgr Nava in Italy in her early teens but had, since the age of 19, been a safely married lady, joined the chorus of Richard D'Oyly Carte's Comedy Opera Company during its initial production of *The Sorcerer,* at the Opera Comique (1877). In fact, Miss Brandram was the daughter of a south London cabbie and had doubtless never been near Italy in her life. She covered and played for Mrs Howard Paul as Lady Sangazure in *The Sorcerer,* took over the role for the show's first tour (1878), and thereafter remained in the employ of Carte and his successors for almost her entire career. She played the part of Little Buttercup in *HMS Pinafore* in loco Harriet Everard and created that of Kate in the American premiere of *The Pirates of Penzance* (1879), before succeeding Alice Barnett as Ruth in the same production and, later, at the Savoy, as Lady Jane in *Patience.* She appeared with the other principal understudies in several of the D'Oyly Carte one-act curtain raisers, and also deputized for Jessie Bond in the role of Iolanthe before creating her first of Gilbert's "dragon" ladies—roles previously barred to her by her youth and by the presence of Misses Everard and Barnett in the company—as Lady Blanche in *Princess Ida.*

Thereafter, Miss Brandram created all of the Savoy heavy ladies: Katisha (*Mikado,* "Hearts Do Not Break," "There Is Beauty in the Bellow of the Blast"), Dame Hannah (*Ruddigore*), Dame Carruthers (*The Yeomen of the Guard,* "When Our Gallant Norman Foes"), the Duchess of Plaza Toro (*The Gondoliers,* "On the Day That I Was Wedded"), Widow Jackson (*Captain Billy*), Mrs Merton (*The Vicar of Bray*), Lady Vernon (*Haddon Hall*), Miss Sims (*Jane Annie*), Lady Sophie (*Utopia Ltd*), the Marquise (*Mirette*), Inez de Roxas (*The Chieftain*), Baroness von Krakenfeld (*The Grand Duke*), Joan (*The Beauty Stone*), Dancing Sunbeam (*The Rose of Persia*), Wee Ping (*The Willow Plate*), the Countess of Newtown (*Emerald Isle*), Queen Elizabeth (*Merrie England* "O Peaceful England") and Nell Reddish (*A Princess of Kensington*), taking time away from her base in the Strand only to appear for Gilbert as Dame Hecla Courtlandt in *His Excellency.*

When the comic opera company left the Savoy, Miss Brandram went with it and appeared with William Greet on tour in *Merrie England* and at the Savoy in the Christmas show *Little Hans Andersen* (1903), but when Greet moved into musical comedy there was no place nor part for her and, in the last performances of her career, she appeared instead as Ermerance in George Edwardes's very successful version of *Véronique.*

BRASSEUR, Jules [DUMONT, Jules Victor Alexandre] (b Paris, 26 January 1828; d Paris, 6 October 1890).

After youthful years working as an assistant in a glove shop, the comic actor Jules Brasseur made his debut at the Théâtre de Belleville in 1847. He moved from there first to the Folies-Dramatiques and then, in 1852, to the Palais-Royal and, during twenty-five vastly popular and profitable years as a member of the company at that theatre created, amongst many others, the triple role of the Brazilian/Prosper/Frick in Offenbach's *La Vie parisienne* ("Je suis Brésilien"), Schnitzberg in Lecocq's *Le Myosotis* (1866), and Pitou in *Le Château á Toto* (1868). He later appeared with considerable success in a large number of the musical pieces which he produced during his period at the head of the Théâtre des Nouveautés (1878–1890), the house which he set up in replacement of the old Fantaisies-Parisiennes and which, under his management, was the site of the productions of such pieces as Coedès's *Fleur d'oranger* and *Les Deux Nababs,* Hervé's *Le Voyage en Amérique* (Barbazan), Lecocq's splendid *Le Jour et la Nuit* (Calabazas) and *Le Coeur et la main,* Chassaigne's *Le Droit d'aînesse,* de Lajarte's *Le Roi de Carreau* (La Roche Trumeau), Serpette's *Le Château de Tire-Larigot* (Chevalier de St-Roquet), *Adam et Ève* (Satan) and *La Lycéenne,* Planquette's *La Cantinière* (Babylas), Audran's *Serment d'amour* and *Les Puits qui parle* (Anastasius), Varney's *L'Amour mouillé* (Pampinelli) and *La Vénus d'Arles* (Le Baron), Jonas's *Premier Baiser,* Lacome's *Les Saturnales* (1887, Barbinus), *Les Délégués* (1887, Filochet), *La Volière* (1888, Mortadello), the latest version of *Le Royaume des femmes* (1889, Le Père Prudent) and *La Vocation de Marius* (1890, Latarède).

In 1884 he also took over for a time a share of the direction of the Théâtre des Folies-Dramatiques which he reopened with the French premiere of Planquette's memorable *Rip.*

His son **Albert [Jules] BRASSEUR** (b Paris, 12 February 1862; d Maisons-Lafitte, 13 May 1932) made his first stage appearance alongside his father in *Fleur d'oranger* and subsequently—with a short pause for military service—created light comic singing roles in many musical works at the Nouveautés (Pepinet in *La Cantinière,* Arthur in *Le Droit d'aînesse,* Mistigris in *Le Roi de Carreau, Le Petit Chaperon rouge,* Beppo in *L'Oiseau bleu,* Mélissen in *Babolin,* Adrien Bézuchard in *Le Château de Tire-Larigot,* Grivolin in *Serment d'amour,* Adam in *Adam et Ève,* Apollon Bouvard in *La Lycéenne,* Cascarino in *L'Amour mouillé,* Christian in *Ninon,* Eymeric de la Grande-Dèche in *La Vie mondaine,* Camusot in *La Vénus d'Arles,* Eusèbe in *Le Puits qui parle,* Samsonnet in *Samsonnet,* Antonin in *Les Délégués,* Bomilcar in *Les Saturnales,* Sosthène IV in *La Volière,* Alcindor in *Le Royaume des femmes,* Marius in *La Vocation de Marius,* etc). After his father's death, he moved to the Théâtre des Variétés (1890) where, over some 20 years, he played with great success in both musical and non-musical pieces, appearing in his father's role in *La Vie parisienne,* and in other classic comic roles such as the title role of *Chilpéric* (Variétés 1895 revival), Ménélas, the caissier in *Les Brigands,* Aristée/Pluton and later Styx, Frimousse, the Duke d'Enface of *L'Oeil crevé,* James (*Miss Helyett*), Grabuge the gendarme in *Geneviève de Brabant* and Valentin in *Le Petit Faust* as well as creating the roles of Célestion in *Madame Satan* (1893), Arsène Majavel in *La Carnet du* diable (1895), Auguste in *Le Pompier de service* (1897), Robert Garnier in *Les Petites Barnett* (1898), Fassinet in *Mademoiselle George* (1900), Follentin in *L'Age d'or* (1905), Coucy in *Le Sire de Vergy* and the title role of *Monsieur de la Palisse.* He played at the Ambigu during the First World War in revivals of *Lili, La Roussotte* and *Mam'selle Nitouche,* and in *La Ceinture de Vénus* (1919) at the Apollo with Odette Myrtil, but in the 1920s he appeared most frequently in comedy.

Brasseur also collaborated on the libretto of Planquette's unsuccessful *La Cremaillère,* and was associated with his father in the last years of his management of the Théâtre des Nouveautés.

Plate 50. **Albert Brasseur**

BRATTON, John W (b Wilmington, Del, 21 January 1867; d Brooklyn, NY, 7 February 1947).

At first a performer, then a conductor in the musical theatre, Bratton later moved into the production of ''dollar circuit'' touring plays and musical comedies (*The Dingbat Family, The Newlyweds and Their Baby, Let George Do It,* etc), in partnership with Johnny Leffler, whilst also composing more than a decadeful of songs, which were used both as decoration for his own productions and, interpolated into musical comedies on both sides of the Atlantic, in those of others. On several occasions he provided the whole, or a large part of a musical comedy score, mostly for shows of a fairly loose musical construction.

Bratton had song successes with such numbers as ''Henrietta, Have You Met Her?'' (w Walter Ford, *The Belle of Cairo*); the hugely popular ''In a Cosy Corner'' (later developed as ''My Cosy Corner Girl,'' w Chas Noel Douglas) sung in London in *The Earl and the Girl,* in New York in *The School Girl,* around America by Nellie McHenry in *M'liss,* in Paris in the 1904 Moulin-Rouge revue and in Australia tacked into the musical comedy *The Rose of the Riviera;* ''He Was a Sailor'' (*The Earl and the Girl*); ''My Little Hong Kong Baby'' (w Paul West), sung by Adele Ritchie in Broadway's *A Chinese Honeymoon* and Ellaline Terriss in London's *The Cherry Girl;* ''A Picture No Artist Can Paint'' (*Hodge, Podge & Co*); ''In Black and White'' (*The School Girl*); ''Sue, Sue, I Love You,'' ''I'll Be Your Honey,'' ''Gladys O'Flynn,'' ''Resolved'' (w West, *Buster Brown*); ''I'm On the Water Wagon Now'' (w West, the hit of *The Office Boy*); ''Mender of Broken Dreams'' (*Charlot's Revue*); ''The Sunshine of Paradise Alley'' (w Ford), ''The Same Old Way,'' the children's classic ''The Teddy Bear's Picnic'' (w Jimmy Kennedy) and ''Sweetheart, Let's Grow Old Together'' (w Leo Edwardes).

Amongst the numerous other shows in which his songs were heard were *Sergeant Brue* (w West, ''Skating,'' ''Line of Duty,'' ''Sergeant Brue''), *Fad and Folly* (''She Reads the New York Papers Every Day''), *Mrs Black Is Back* (''Can't You Guess?'' w West), *The Rollicking Girl* (''The Girl I Left in Boston Town'' w Douglas, Ernest Ball, ''Tricks'' w West) and *The Gay White Way* (''Somebody's Been Around Here Since I've Been Gone'' w West). His other titles included such pieces as ''The Amorous Esquimaux,'' ''There Are 57 Ways to Catch a Man'' (*The Man from China*), ''I Want to Play Hamlet,'' ''He Ought to Have a Tablet in the Hall of

Fame" "Isabelle (a Girl who is One of the Boys)" and "O'Dwyer Caught Cold."

Although he moved out of the musical theatre after the first war, Bratton remained active as a lyricist until the last years of his life.

1900 **Hodge, Podge & Co** (Walter Ford/ad George Hobart) Madison Square Theater 23 October

1900 **Star and Garter** (Ford/J J McNally) Victoria Theater 26 November

1901 **The Liberty Belles** (w Aimé Lachaume, A Baldwin Sloane, Clifton Crawford, Alfred Aarons, et al/Harry B Smith) Madison Square Theater 30 September

1904 **Buster Brown** (West/Charles Newman, George Totten Smith) Harmanus Bleeker Hall, Albany, NY 25 December; Auditorium, Philadelphia 4 January; Majestic Theater 24 January 1905

1904 **The Man from China** (Paul West) Majestic Theater 2 May

1905 **The Pearl and the Pumpkin** (West/West, W W Denslow) Broadway Theater 21 August

1908 **The Newlyweds and Their Baby** (w Nat Ayer/Paul West, Seymour Brown/West, Aaron Hoffman) Lyceum Theater, Rochester, NY 7 December; Majestic Theater, New York 22 March 1909

1912 **The Dingbat Family** (Mark Swan) Lyceum, Paterson, NJ 28 October

BRECHT, [Eugen] Bertolt [Friedrich] (b Augsburg, 10 February 1898; d East Berlin, 14 August 1956).

Better known for his non-musical plays (*Mutter Courage und ihr Kinder, Der gute Mensch von Setzuan, Der aufthaltsame Aufstieg des Arturo Ui,* etc) and for his clamorous left-wing political stance, to the service of which his theatre works were often subjugated, Brecht also collaborated with composer Kurt Weill on several musical pieces, over a period of some three years, at the end of the 1920s. *Die Dreigroschenoper,* his jolly adaptation of Elisabeth Hauptmann's German version of John Gay's *The Beggar's Opera,* proved an enduring entertainment, but the two authors' second piece for the musical theatre, the flung-together *Happy End,* was a quick failure. Weill and Brecht also collaborated on the operas *Aufstieg und Fall der Stadt Mahagonny* (1929) and *Der Jasager* (1930).

1928 **Die Dreigroschenoper** (Kurt Weill/w Elisabeth Hauptmann) Theater am Schiffbauerdamm 31 August

1929 **Happy End** (Weill/w Hauptmann) Theater am Schiffbauerdamm 2 September

BREDSCHNEIDER, Willi (b Arndorf, 31 January 1889; d Berlin, 16 January 1937).

Musical director at the Berliner Theater from the age of 20 (1909–16), Bredschneider wrote songs and stage music for a number of the theatre's productions, contributing to the extremely successful new version of the old Posse *Auf eigenen Füssen* which was played there as *Bummelstudenten* (1910), to its equally popular successor, *Grosse Rosinen,* and to two major international successes in *Wie einst im Mai* and *Filmzauber* amongst the successful run of musical comedies mounted at the Berliner Theater before and during the Great War.

He later worked as musical director at the Wallner-Theater and, as a composer, had success in both Germany and the Netherlands with one of the few musical shows for which he supplied the entire score, *Die beiden Nachtigallen.*

1910 **Bummelstudenten** (w Bogumil Zepler, et al/ad Rudolf Bernauer, Rudolph Schanzer) Berliner Theater 31 December

1911 **Die grüne Neune** (Toni Impekoven) Lustspielhaus 22 March

1911 **Grosse Rosinen** (w Leon Jessel, Zepler, et al/Bernauer, Schanzer) Berliner Theater 31 December

1912 **Filmzauber** (w Walter Kollo/Bernauer, Schanzer) Berliner Theater 19 October

1913 **Hochherrschaftliche Wohnungen** (Impekoven) Komödienhaus 5 April

1913 **Wie einst im Mai** (w Kollo/Bernauer, Schanzer) Berliner Theater 4 October

1914 **Extrablätter** (w Kollo/Schanzer, Heinz Gordon) Berliner Theater 24 October

1915 **Wenn zwei Hochzeit machen** (w Kollo/Bernauer, Schanzer) Berliner Theater 23 October

1916 **Auf Flügeln des Gesanges** (w Kollo/Bernauer, Schanzer) Berliner Theater 9 September

1917 **Hampelmanns Geburtstag** (Impekoven) Schauspielhaus, Frankfurt-am-Main 17 March

1921 **Die beiden Nachtigallen** (Leo Walther Stein) Stadttheater, Halle am Saale 26 December

1927 **Mops der Spitzbube** (Karl Müller-Hoyer) Thalia Theater, Dresden 3 September

1929 **Das Wunderkind** (L W Stein, Rudolf Presber) Brussels

Other title attributed: *Ein Mädel mit Tempo*

BRETÓN [y Hernandez], Tomás (b Salamanca, 29 December 1850; d Madrid, 2 December 1923).

One of the principal composers of the zarzuela in the three decades of its greatest prosperity, Tomás Bretón also worked, in parallel, as an operatic composer, going further than most of his compatriots towards establishing an exportable school of Spanish opera. His earliest operas, the one-act *Guzmán el bueno* (25 November 1875) and *El campañero de Begoña* (1878) made little mark, but the 1889 *Los amantes de Teruel* (1889) was a success which was played in Vienna and Prague as well as in Spain and Argentina, and there was also some recognition for the Italian *Garín, l'eremita de Montserrat* (1892). *La Dolores* (Teatro Zarzuela 16 March 1895) was the most successful of his operatic works, being internationally staged and regularly revived for many years, but of his latter works—*Raquel* (1900), *Farinelli* (1902), *El certamen de Cremona* (1906, one act), *Don Gil* (1914) and *Salamanca* (1916)—only the grandiose *Tabaré* had anything like a success.

His most significant success in the zarzuela field also came, after 20 years of liberally supplying the lighter musical theatre with both full-length and short musical plays, in the early 1890s, with the one-act *La verbena de la paloma,* which has remained a staple in the zarzuela repertoire ever since. His other titles for the zarzuela stage include *El alma en un hilo* (1874), *Los dos caminos* (1874), *El viaje a Europa* (1874) *El 93* (1875) *El inválido* (1875) *María* (1875), *Un chaparrón de maridos* (1876) *Vista y sentencia* (1876), *Cuidado con los estudiantes* (1877), *Los dos leones* (1877) *Huyendo de Elfas* (1877), *El bautizo de Pepin* (1878), *Bonito pais* (1878), *El barberillo de Orán* (1879) *Corona contra corona* (1879), *Los amores de un principe* (1881), *Las señoritas de conil* (1881), *El grito en el cielo* (1886), *El domingo de ramos* (1895), *Las nieves* (1895), *Botin de guerra* (1896), *El guardia de corps* (1897), *El puente del Diablo* (1898), *El reloj de cuco* (1898), *El clavel rojo* (1899), *Ya se van los quintos madre* (1899), *La Cariñosa* (1899), *Covadonga* (1901), *El caballo del señorita* (1901), *La bien planta* (1902), *La generosa* (1909), *Piel de oso* (1909), *Al alcance de la mano* (1911), *Las percheleras* (1911), *Los husares del Czar* (1914), and *Las cortes de amor* (1916).

Biographies: Sanchez Salcedo, A: *Tomás Bretón: su vida y sua obra* (Imp. Clasica Espanola, Madrid, 1924), de Montillana, J: *Bretón* (Salamanca, 1952)

BRIAN, Donald [?O'BRIEN, Donald] (b St Johns, Newfoundland, 17 February 1877; d Great Neck, NY, 22 December 1948). Bright-eyed and boyish star of more than 20 years of Broadway musicals.

Brian made his earliest professional singing appearances as a member of a glee club, but played for a while in the straight theatre before taking on his first musical roles in touring productions of *Three Little Lambs* and *The Chaperons* (1901, Tom Schuyler, still as ''D Brine''). He made his first Broadway musical appearance at the Winter Garden Theater, on the roof of the New York Theater, in a couple of slapdash pieces called *The Supper Club* (1901, Castor Beane) and *The Belle of Broadway* (1902, Tom Finch), as well as taking over as Captain Donegal in *Florodora* when it played the same theatre, a performance which led to his succeeding Cyril Scott in the same role in the principal tour company. He followed up in Scott's role of Berkeley Shallamar in *The Silver Slipper,* and played on the road alongside Chauncey Olcott in *Myles Aroon,* before coming to his first major Broadway creations: the juvenile lead roles of Henry Hapgood in George M Cohan's *Little Johnny Jones* (1904) and of Tom Bennett in his *Forty-Five Minutes from Broadway* (1906).

Brian appeared again for Cohan in *Fifty Miles from Boston,* but then shot to the upper fame level in 1907 when he was cast as America's Danilo alongside Ethel Jackson in Henry Savage's production of *The Merry Widow.* Thereafter, for more than a decade, his remained a bankable top-of-the-bill name, and he appeared in the leading roles of a run of imported musicals with unbroken success: as self-made Freddy who is out to win *The Dollar Princess* (1909), the spy-master Marquis de Ravaillac in *The Siren* (1911), Jack Fleetwood, the backwoods hero of *The Marriage Market* (1913), Sandy Blair who sets out to rescue *The Girl from Utah* from the polygamous Mormons (1914) and the Grand Duke who finds himself with a delightful if phony wife in his arms in *Sybil* (1916). In each of these last four shows he co-starred with the beautiful Julia Sanderson. In between the last two, he took time out to make a debut as a film actor in the ''crook play'' *The Voice in the Fog.*

He found less joy in Victor Herbert's *Her Regiment* (1917, André de Courcy), but two other wartime musicals, *The Girl Behind the Gun* (1918, Robert Lambrissac), with its French comedy and Ivan Caryll music, and the sentimentally winning *Buddies* (1919, Sonny) gave him further Broadway successes. After a long and successful tour with *Buddies,* Brian reappeared on Broadway as Bumerli in a revival of *The Chocolate Soldier* (1921), but he walked out of the starring (and vocally demanding) role of Achmed Bey in *The Rose of Stambul* (1922) prior to the Broadway opening and, instead of appearing as the romantic poet of Fall's Operette, came back briefly to New York as the sweetly prosaic Albert Bennett of the Tierney/McCarthy *Up She Goes.* Alternating plays and musicals, he appeared on the road opposite Alice Delysia in *The Courtesan* (1923, The Vicomte), as Billy Early in *No, No, Nanette* (1925) and opposite his wife, **Virginia O'Brien**, as takeovers in the Chicago hit *Castles in the Air* (1926). He also started out playing opposite Edna Leedom in *Ain't Love Grand* (1927, Prince Paul de Morlaix) but he was replaced by Guy Robertson before the troubled show reached Broadway as *Lovely Lady.*

In a career which thereafter mostly embraced light comedy plays he was seen on Broadway as a takeover in *Yes, Yes, Yvette,* as a rather older Danilo on the road (1930) and at Broadway's Erlanger Theater (1931 and 1932), as Bumerli (1934) again, as a replacement Bruno Mahler in *Music in the Air* and, finally, in his sixties, in *Very Warm for May* (1939, William Graham).

An occasional songwriter, Brian interpolated his ''Mendocino Stroll'' in *The Marriage Market.*

BRIAN BORU Romantic opera in 3 acts by Stanislaus Stange. Music by Julian Edwards. Broadway Theater, New York, 19 December 1896.

A rare late 19th-century attempt to serve up some heroic/romantic Irish material instead of the cheerful Mulliganneries usually seen and heard in contemporary American theatres, accompanied by a score from the most strivingly substantial of the period's light musical theatre composers, *Brian Boru* (ex- *The Maid of Erin*) was mounted by F C Whitney with a measure of success, which included 88 performances on Broadway.

Max Eugene featured as Ireland's champion, equipped with a bass-baritone "For Ireland" and "Sheathe the Sword" and faced with the attempts of the English Princess, Elfrida (Amanda Fabris), to woo him from his duty with repeated high Cs ("The Earth's Richest Dower"). The best of the soprano music, however, fell to Grace Golden, in the role of Boru's sister, Erina, alongside some stirring basso stuff for Bruce Paget as a Standard Bearer ("The Irish Patriot") and a selection of the regulation comic opera style of Irishisms as delivered by comedian Richard O'Carroll ("Paddy's Legs," "Paddy and His Pig") and Amelia Summerville as "Baby Malone, the Child of a Giant" (trio: "The Irish Cuckoo"). The English got little of a look-in with either fun or music in ex-Liverpudlian Stange's libretto and ended up confounded and defeated, a plot turn which, alone, sent *Brian Boru*'s audiences home in a happy frame of mind.

Ireland itself occasionally celebrated its ex-King theatrically as well. In 1871 Dublin's Monster Saloon, Crampton Court, mounted a determinedly local pantomime which gloried in the title *King Brian Boru and Harlequin Ireland, or The Beautiful Fairy Maid of Morrogh's Well and the Genii of the Giant Causeway.*

BRICUSSE, Leslie (b London, 29 January 1931). Songwriter who had early successes on the stage and the hit parades and later ones in films before becoming a ubiquitous adapter of classic literature to the fin de siècle musical stage.

Bricusse first came to the fore as a writer with his Cambridge University shows, the revue *Out of the Blue* and the musical comedy *Lady at the Wheel* (1953 w Frederick Raphael), which was subsequently given a professional production (1958) with Maggie Fitzgibbon starred as a Monte Carlo rallyeuse who wins a nice Englishman (Peter Gilmore) rather than a beastly foreigner (Bernard Cribbins) ("Siesta," "Pete Y'Know"). By this time, Bricusse had already appeared in London as a performer in *An Evening with Beatrice Lillie,* and as a replacement director on a money-no-object vanity production called *Jubilee Girl* (1956), whilst also making a name in films and as a songwriter ("Out of Town" w Robin Beaumont for Max Bygraves in *Charley Moon* 1956, "Summer is a-comin' In" as sung by Kathie Kay 1958, etc).

He won an international stage and song success when he collaborated with Anthony Newley on *Stop the World—I Want to Get Off* ("What Kind of Fool Am I?," "Once in a Lifetime," "Typically English," etc), and scored further song hits when he supplied the lyrics to the musical *Pickwick* ("If I Ruled the World") and collaborated again with Newley on *The Roar of the Greasepaint . . . the Smell of the Crowd* ("Who Can I Turn To?," "Nothing Can Stop Me Now," "On a Wonderful Day Like Today"), but thereafter his success came in the film world rather than in the theatre as he turned out the theme songs for *Goldfinger* (w Newley, John Barry) and *You Only Live Twice* (w Barry), and the scores for the musical films *Doctor Doolittle* (1967 "Talk to the Animals" Academy Award), *Goodbye, Mr Chips* (1969), *Scrooge* (1970) and *Willie Wonka and the Chocolate Factory* (1971).

A third show with Newley, *The Good Old, Bad Old Days* did not come up to the first, a show about King Henry VIII (*Kings and Clowns*) was a surprisingly unprofessionally written and produced London flop, and *The Travelling Music Show,* a pasticcio show set up around television personality Bruce Forsythe, was another quick failure. Musical versions of the play *Harvey* and of the British mystery classics of Conan Doyle (*Sherlock Holmes*) and Robert Louis Stevenson (*Jekyll and Hyde*), and expanded stage versions of the filmed *Goodbye, Mr Chips* and *Scrooge* were subsequent projects which were seen briefly on the stage in Britain and America, whilst Bricusse carried on with such assignments as *The Return of the Pink Panther* (1975), *Superman* (1978) and *Victor/Victoria* (1982) in the cinema, and the score for a 1976 ATV *Peter Pan* (w Newley) and a botched version of Victor Herbert's *Babes in Toyland* (NBC 19 December 1986) for television.

Latterly a stage version of *Victor/Victoria* and a resuscitated *Jekyll and Hyde* were both played for considerable runs on Broadway, and a stage *Doctor Doolittle,* for which the writer took credits on book, lyrics and music, was presented in London, offering evidence that if Bricusse's writing talent seemed to have run dramatically down since the days of *Stop the World,* his ability to find producers for his shows certainly had not.

- 1958 **Lady at the Wheel** (Robin Beaumont/Frederick Raphael, Lucienne Hill) Lyric Theatre, Hammersmith 23 January
- 1961 **Stop the World—I Want to Get Off** (Anthony Newley) Queen's Theatre 20 July
- 1963 **Pickwick** (Cyril Ornadel/Wolf Mankowitz) Saville Theatre 4 July
- 1964 **The Roar of the Greasepaint . . . the Smell of the Crowd** (Newley) Theatre Royal, Nottingham 3 August

1972 **The Good Old, Bad Old Days** (Newley) Prince of Wales Theatre 20 December

1978 **Kings and Clowns** Phoenix Theatre 1 March

1978 **The Travelling Music Show** (Newley) Her Majesty's Theatre 28 March

1978 **Beyond the Rainbow** (*Aggiungi un posto a tavola*) English lyrics (Adelphi Theatre)

1981 **Say Hello to Harvey** Royal Alexandra Theatre, Toronto 14 September

1982 **Goodbye, Mr Chips** (Roland Starke) Chichester Festival Theatre 11 August

1989 **Sherlock Holmes, the Musical** Cambridge Theatre 24 April

1990 **Jekyll and Hyde** (Frank Wildhorn) Alley Theater, Houston 25 May; Plymouth Theater, New York 28 April 1997

1992 **Scrooge** Alexandra Theatre, Birmingham 10 November, Domion Theatre 12 November 1996

1995 **Victor/Victoria** (Henry Mancini, Wildhorn/w Blake Edwards) Marquis Theater, New York 25 October

1998 **Doctor Doolittle** Apollo Labatt's, Hammersmith 14 July

BRIGADOON Musical play in 2 acts by Alan Jay Lerner. Music by Frederick Loewe. Ziegfeld Theater, New York, 13 March 1947.

The enduring hit of the 1947–48 Broadway season, *Brigadoon* launched the three-show-old partnership of Alan Jay Lerner and Frederick Loewe on what would be one of the remarkable musical theatre careers of the following decade and more. The most thoroughly romantic of the new swell of romantic Broadway musicals, *Brigadoon* dipped into the sweet waters of the well of the fantastical and the fairy for its subject matter and came out with a tale that succeeded in being wholly charming and not a whit saccharine. Nevertheless, the authors thought it best to pull that oft-used and theoretically disarming trick of pretending that their story was based on an old Continental legend.

Americans Tommy Albright (David Brooks) and Jeff Douglass (George Keane) are on a hunting trip in Scotland when they stumble on a little village that is not on the map. It is Brigadoon and, when the hunters arrive, the folk are preparing for the wedding of Jeannie MacLaren (Virginia Bosler) and Charlie Dalrymple (Lee Sullivan). Tommy is enchanted by Jeannie's sister Fiona (Marion Bell) whilst Charlie is pursued by the forward Meg Brockie (Pamela Britton), but they soon discover that Brigadoon is not what it seems. The town is under a spell, by which it appears on earth only one day in a century and, at the end of the day it will vanish into sleep for another hundred years. Disaster threatens when Jeannie's rejected suitor Harry (James Mitchell) tries to leave Brigadoon and send the town for ever into the darkness, but he is accidentally killed in his flight. The men leave before Brigadoon's day is done but, back in the loud shallows of New York, Tommy finds he cannot forget Fiona. He returns to Scotland and, in another miracle, Brigadoon awakes from its sleep, allowing Tommy to go to join the girl he loves.

Plate 51. **Brigadoon.** *A feller never knows what he'll find in the gloaming. Robin Nedwell (Jeff) found Leslie Mackie (Meg Brockie) in London's 1988 revival.*

The tale was illustrated with one of the most attractive sets of songs of its era, ranging from the charmingly tartan-tinted "The Heather on the Hill," "Waitin' for My Dearie" and the tenor's "I'll Go Home with Bonnie Jean" and "Come to Me, Bend to Me," to the romantic "It's Almost Like Being in Love" and "There, But for You, Go I" and the sparkling, but never brash, moments of man-hunting Meg Brockie's "The Love of My Life" and "My Mother's Wedding Day," supported by some fine ensembles and lashings of dance music to serve the large dance routines which were the fashion of the post-*Oklahoma!* period. The most effective of these was Agnes de Mille's depiction of the dusk-time chase of the villagers, through the rocks and trees, to prevent Harry's escape from Brigadoon, whilst the wedding of Jeannie and Charlie gave the opportunity for plenty of lively Scottish steps.

Brigadoon's dance-heavy layout, as well as the death of its "baddie" and the man-hunts of Meg, prompted some comparisons with *Oklahoma!* and its Judd Fry and Ado Annie, but only on the first ground did this seem justified. After all, baddies had been dying in the musical theatre for many decades, and most opérette soubrettes had sex on the brain. In fact, *Brigadoon*'s fantasy-flavor, spiced with just a dash of the brashly modern in its New York scene, was very different from the tone of the Rodgers and Hammerstein show. What the two pieces did have in common was simply success and, as the show's songs worked their way swiftly into the standards list, Cheryl Crawford's production of *Brigadoon* ran on through a 581-performance stay on Broadway.

A reproduction under the management of Prince Littler at London's His Majesty's Theatre proved equally successful. Philip Hanna (Tommy), Patricia Hughes (Fiona), Hiram Sherman (Jeff) and Noele Gordon (Meg) headed a cast of characters of whom many, curiously, had their surnames altered, through a run of 685 performances. In Australia, Gwen Overton, Ken Cantril, Peter Turgeon and Olive Lucius were featured for nearly six months in Melbourne and something over four at Sydney's Theatre Royal (15 December 1951), confirming the appeal of the show for English-language audiences at both ends of the world.

A 1954 film version, which featured Gene Kelly and Cyd Charisse (sung by Carole Richards) as the principal lovers and Van Johnson as Jeff, cut the role of Meg down to almost nothing and eliminated her two comical songs, successfully remaking the piece as a virtually wholly romantic musical film which, nevertheless, retained a very large part of the rest of the show's score.

Brigadoon was slow to find itself major metropolitan revivals, although it was televised in 1968 with Sally Ann Howes and Robert Goulet featured, and reprised regularly at New York's City Center over the years. It returned to Broadway only in 1980 (Majestic Theater 16 October) with Martin Vidnovic, Meg Bussert, Elaine Hausman and Mark Zimmerman in the lead roles, and with Olympic ice-skating star John Curry briefly seen as Harry, for 133 performances and was played again, in 1986, by the New York City Opera. In Britain, after several abortive announcements of a revival from Scotland over the years, a touring production sponsored by Ronnie Lee and with Robert Meadmore, Jacintha Mulcahy, Robin Nedwell and Leslie Mackie at the top of the bill was brought to the West End and played for 327 performances at the Victoria Palace in 1988–89 (25 October 1988).

Given the success of *My Fair Lady* in central Europe, it was a little surprising that *Brigadoon* did not find itself a German-language production until 1980, but that production (ad Robert Gilbert), at Karlsruhe, did not prove sufficient to encourage others and the show's career has been largely in the English-speaking theatre.

UK: His Majesty's Theatre 14 April 1949; Australia: Her Majesty's Theatre, Melbourne 17 March 1951; Germany: Badische Staatstheater, Karlsruhe 10 May 1980

Film: MGM 1954

Recordings: original cast (RCA), London revival cast (First Night), studio cast (Showtime, TER, EMI), complete (Angel), selection (Columbia)

LES BRIGANDS Opéra-bouffe in 3 acts by Henri Meilhac and Ludovic Halévy. Music by Jacques Offenbach. Théâtre des Variétés, Paris, 10 December 1869.

The fifth and last of the famous group of 1860s opéras-bouffes written by the team of Meilhac, Halévy and Offenbach for the Théâtre des Variétés, now under the management of Eugène Bertrand, *Les Brigands* rendered nothing to its famous four predecessors (*La Belle Hélène, Barbe-bleue, La Grande-Duchesse de Gérolstein, La Périchole*) in burlesque gaiety and dazzling comic music. It did, however, have two distinct differences from them. The first was that it was not constructed with a starring feminine role for the overwhelming leading lady of the other four shows, Hortense Schneider. The second was that its Parisian career was impeded by the onset of the Franco-Prussian war, so that it did not succeed in establishing itself in quite the same way that its predecessors had.

The leading lady of *Les Brigands* was, in fact, a boy. Zulma Bouffar appeared in a role which can surely never have been intended, as has been suggested, for la Schneider, as Fragoletto, a young farmer who has turned brigand for the love of Fiorella (Marie Aimée), the daughter of the bandit chief Falsacappa (José Dupuis). All three become part of a conspiracy to trick three millions of money out of the Duchy of Mantua. The money is to be paid over to the representative of the government of Granada when that country's Princess arrives in Mantua to wed the Duke. The bandits waylay the Granadan embassy, Fiorella takes the place of the Princess (Mlle Lucciani) with her father impersonating the lofty Gloria-Cassis (Gourdon) and Fragoletto as the Princess's pet page (Cooper), and they present themselves to Mantua (Lanjallay) and his treasury only to find that there is no money. The Duke's unprepossessing cashier (Léonce) has spent his country's funds on wining and dining pretty ladies. Charles Blondelet played Campotasso, the Duke's first minister, and Kopp was the brigand Pietro, but the choice comical role went to Baron, cast as the chief of the local carabiniers, endlessly pursuing the brigand band and always, but always arriving on the scene just too late to effect a capture.

It was Baron and his clumsy band whose plodding chorus "Nous sommes les carabiniers" became the catch-phrase from Offenbach's score, but there were many and more melodious moments as well: Fragoletto's helter-skelter saltarello description of how he has passed his initiation to the brigand band by robbing the Granadan envoy of ''Le Courrier du cabinet,'' Fiorella's lively bolero introduction as ''la fille du bandit'' and her directions to the benighted Duke, lost in the mountains (''Après avoir pris à droite''), Falsacappa's ringing description of his qualifications in banditry (''Quel est celui qui par les plaines?'') and the last act solos of the Duke, preparing to give up women for marriage (''Jadis régnait un prince''), and of the guilty cashier (''Ô mes amours, ô mes maîtresses'') were features of a score which also gave place to much more concerted music than had been the case in the earlier pieces. If that pleased the connoisseurs mightily, the theatregoing public were equally as happy with the comical carabiniers and the bristling burlesque bandits and their music.

Les Brigands ran through its first series of performances in December and January and returned to the Variétés stage for a second run in August. Almost immediately after this, war was declared and soon the Variétés was closed down. By the time *Les Brigands* returned to their theatre 12 months later (September 1871), in a slightly revised version, it had already been seen throughout the world.

Marie Geistinger and Maximilian Steiner mounted the piece (ad Richard Genée) at Vienna's Theater an der Wien where Jani Szika (Falsacappa), Karoline Finaly (Fragoletto) and Carl Adolf Friese (Antonio, the cashier) were, at various times, amongst the cast, and it was reprised over the next three seasons for a total of 72 performances without winning the same enormous fame as *Die Grossherzogin von Gerolstein* and *Die schöne Helena.* In Berlin a different adaptation, by Ernst Dohm, was used at the Friedrich-Wilhelmstädtisches Theater. The usually prompt Budapest, which saw *Die Banditen* soon after the German premiere, does not seem, however, to have got its Hungarian version (ad Ferenc Toldy) until 1871, and America, which was quickly introduced to *Les Brigands* in French by James Fisk's company in a in splendid five-and-a-half-weeks' straight run at the Grand Opera House (Elise Persini as Fragoletto, Constant Gausins as Falsacappa and Céline Montaland as Fiorella), and later by original star Marie Aimée and by Paola Marié, apparently did not get a vernacular production until as late as 1886. On the wings of the Grand Opera House success, however, New York did earn a burlesque by the San Francisco Minstrels who—burlesquing a burlesque—had Rollin Howard apearing as Fiorella Montaland de Silly in a piece which was as much a parody of opéra-bouffe in general as of *Les Brigands* (19 December 1870), and Dan Bryant later (1875) had a go at burlesquing Aimée in the same role in a minstrel parody called *Les Brigands noir* [*sic*]. Kelly and Leon gave a more substantial, three-act burlesque version to San Francisco (Alhambra 18 August 1873) with Jennie Reiffarth playing Fragoletto to Leon's Fiorello and the tenorious Falsacappa of Kelly. Around the same time, down in Baltimore, Lydia Thompson added *The Brigand* to her repertoire (it was, however, not Offenbach's piece but an old pasticcio burlesque on the Massaroni story which allowed the star to do her famous ''Rifle Dance''). The Worrell girls dragged up an old piece called *The Italian Brigands* and Philadelphia's Fox's American put out a grand ballet entitled *The Brigands,* but no one at this time attempted to put the real thing into English. Unless, that is, the incessantly number-3-date one-night-stand-touring Wallace sisters really meant it when they advertised the show in their 1871 ''repertoire'' alongside most of the rest of Offenbach's works. The first English *Les Brigands* seems to have been the one produced at the San Francisco Tivoli under the title *The Robbers* (18 October 1886), but the piece got regular showings in American comic opera seasons in the 1890s.

In Britain, however, an English *Falsacappa* (ad Henry S Leigh) was produced in 1871 at the Globe Theatre with Alfred St Albyn (Falsacappa), Marguerite Debreux (Fragoletto), Annetta Scasi (Fiorella) and Cornelie d'Anka in travesty as the Prince of Boboli (ie, the Duke), before the piece was played in French at the St James's Theatre in 1873 (30 June). It was later given a second English-language run, this time as *The Brigands* (13 September 1875) for two and a half months back at the Globe Theatre, with Ada Ward, Camille Dubois, Nellie Bromley, William Worboys and Lin Rayne featured. One version which did not appear on the stage at this time was one commissioned by the publishers, Boosey and Co, from the young W S Gilbert. However, once the author had become famous, this version was remembered by some astute person and, in 1889, Broadway welcomed *The Brigands* by W S Gilbert and Jacques Offenbach (Casino Theater 9 May). Unfortunately ''Mr (Gus) Kerker has been trying to improve on the one and Mr (Max) Freeman on the other'' a critic remarked sourly. Fannie Rice (Fragoletto), Lillian Russell (Fiorella) and Edwin Stevens (Falsacappa) featured and, in spite of Messrs Kerker (six numbers including a topical ditty and a kissing duet) and Freeman, the show proved a hit, passing its 100th performance on 31 August, taking a break from 14 September and returning in the new year to run again from 6 January to 23 February. When the ever-opportunistic Horace Lingard mounted a touring production of this version in Britain and then brought it to London, ''freshened'' with a few textual alterations of his own, not to mention such odd bits of extra music as conductor van Biene's own ''Come Back to Me,'' the furious Gilbert sued. Lingard moved quickly out of town. New York got another sighting when the show was revived at off-Broadway's Terrace Garden as part of a summer season in 1903.

Australia saw its first *The Brigands* in 1877, in a version which admitted that it had been "translated and partly rewritten by Fred Lyster." Local star tenor Armes Beaumont was Falsacappa, with the British performers Henry Bracy (a tenor Fragoletto) and his wife, Clara Thompson (Fiorella), playing the lovers.

If the initial record won by *Les Brigands* in Paris was, due to circumstances, rather disappointing, the show nevertheless succeeded in holding itself a place in the repertoire. The Variétés reprised it in 1872 with Dupuis cast alongside Mlle Bertal as Fragoletto and Anna van Ghell as Fiorella, but the fact that the temper of times had changed was shown when objections were made about the burlesquing of the French army and its uniforms in what had been the comic highlight of the original production, the "always arriving too late" carabiniers and their chief. Around the same time, a new piece *Le Dompteur,* which featured a comical gendarme amongst its characters was refused production by the same censor. But, then, war often has the effect of ridding those who watch it (as opposed to those who take part) of their sense of self-humor.

Les Brigands was revived again in 1874, 1875, 1885, 1887 with Dupuis and Baron still there and Jeanne Thibault as Fragoletto and in 1900 with Juliette Méaly as Fragoletto, Anna Tariol-Baugé as Fiorella, Brasseur as Antonio, Amélie Diéterle as the Duke, Guy as the brigand chief and Baron still in his famous role of the chief carabinier. In 1878 a M Weinschenk, following Offenbach's example in "expanding" his earlier pieces, produced a spectacular four-act version, with the little band of comical bandits now a hundred strong, and the whole decorated with "Spanish ballets, military displays, cortèges, triumphal entries, and the arrival of the Duke of Mantua staged in imitation of Makart's celebrated painting *Entry of Charles V* into Antwerp." Christian, Léonce, Blondelet, Grivot, Mme Grivot and Marie Peschard struggled through the scenery. In 1921 the show was revived at the Gaîté-Lyrique with Jean Périer as the brigand chief, and in 1931 it was taken into the repertoire at the Opéra-Comique (13 June) where Louis Musy (Falsacappa), Marcelle Denya (Fragoletto) and Emma Luart (Fiorella) were joined by musical comedy star Dranem as Antonio. The show was televised in 1970, and new productions mounted in Geneva in 1986 and in Lyon in 1988 (the production subsequently shown on television), before the piece made it back to Paris, to be played at the Opéra Bastille (3 December 1993).

Outside France, too, the show has made regular reappearances, if not always in pristine condition. Budapest saw Zsolt Harsányi's new Hungarian translation in 1933 (1 April) whilst the Fővárosi Operettszínház played *A Banditák* (ad Károly Kristóf) 2 March 1962, and several German adaptations of varying honesty have appeared over recent decades, one of which, by Karl-Dietrich Gräwe and Caspar Richter, was produced at the Berlin Opera in 1978 (4 February). The Gilbert *Brigands* was mounted at the Edinburgh Festival in 1982, and the Amsterdam Opera produced a version in 1991. However, in spite of its persistence in the repertoire, *Les Brigands* remains in many ways the forgotten member of the famous five prewar opéras-bouffes of the Variétés repertoire.

Austria: Theater an der Wien *Die Banditen* 12 March 1870; Germany: Friedrich-Wilhelmstädtisches Theater *Die Banditen* 24 September 1870; Hungary: (Ger) 13 October 1870, Budai Színkör *A rablok* 24 June 1871; USA: Grand Opera House (Fr) 14 November 1870, Casino Theater 9 May 1889; UK: Globe Theatre *Falsacappa* 22 April 1871; Australia: Opera House, Melbourne 7 August 1877

Recordings: complete (EMI, Lyon version), complete in German (RCA, Golden Age of Opera), selections (Milan, Decca), etc

Video: French TV 1970

BRIGHTMAN, Sarah (b London, 14 August 1960).

As a member of the dance group Pan's People, Sarah Brightman had an early success when she fronted the group in the song "I Fell in Love with a Starship Trooper" (November 1978) which made its way into the British hit parades.

She appeared on the London musical stage for the first time in the original cast of *Cats* (Jemima) and moved from there to succeed Bonnie Langford in the role of Kate in the Theatre Royal, Drury Lane, revival of *The Pirates of Penzance.* She withdrew from the cast on her marriage to composer Andrew Lloyd Webber.

She was subsequently seen as Tara Treetops in the musical version of the puzzle-book *Masquerade* at the Young Vic and in the title role of the Charles Strouse light opera *The Nightingale* at the Lyric Theatre, Hammersmith, before creating the role of Christine Daäé, the pursued and pre-Raphaelite heroine of *The Phantom of the Opéra,* a part composed for her by Lloyd Webber ("All I Ask of You"). She repeated her role in *The Phantom of the Opéra* in New York and Los Angeles and subsequently succeeded to the part of Rose in Broadway's production of her, by then, ex-husband's *Aspects of Love,* a role which she later also took over in the London production. Thereafter, however, although appearing briefly on the non-musical stage, Miss Brightman deviated her attentions to the concert and recording stages, having a notable success with the duet "Time to Say Goodbye" with tenor Andrea Boccelli.

During her marriage to Lloyd Webber, Miss Brightman also created the written-to-measure soprano role in the composer's *Requiem,* taking the duet "Pie Jesu" into the top ten, and recorded his song cycle "Tell Me on a Sunday" for BBC television. She also appeared in series of concerts entitled "The Music of Andrew Lloyd Webber" in America and Britain.

BROADHURST, George H[owells] (b Walsall, 3 June 1866; d Santa Barbara, Calif, 31 January 1952).

Born in Britain, Broadhurst emigrated to America at the age of 20 and worked at first as a theatre manager in Milwaukee, Baltimore and at San Francisco's Bush Theater. He made his debut as a playwright-producer (w his brother, Thomas W Broadhurst [b Old Wedensfield; d New York 1 May 1936]) with *The Speculator* (1896) starring Thomas Q Seabrooke, then followed up with the successful comedies *The Wrong Mr Wright* (1897), *What Happened to Jones* (1898) and *Why Smith Left Home* (1899, with songs), pieces which scored particularly well in Britain. In 1899 the Broadhurst brothers took over London's Strand Theatre, and amongst their productions there was the Americo–South African–British musical *The Prince of Borneo* (1899) for which Broadhurst wrote a number of songs.

Amongst a continuing list of stage pieces through the following years Broadhurst authored several farce comedies (at first under the pseudonym "Charles Newman"), and he subsequently adapted his first two hit comedies as musical plays—*The Wrong Mr Wright* as *The Lady from Lane's* and *What Happened to Jones* as *The Girl and the Drummer.* As a manager, he also produced (w Currie) a number of musical farce comedies and variety musicals (*Mr Jolly of Joliet, Buster Brown, A Lucky Dog, The Son of Rest,* etc).

In 1906 Broadhurst had a sizeable success with the play *The Man of the Hour* (1906) and he subsequently turned away from the musical stage.

Broadway's Broadhurst Theater was named for him, and he was for a time its manager.

A musical version of *The Wrong Mr Wright* was played on the American tour circuits in 1915 by Dillon and King, and another was produced in Hungary under the title *A kedves bácsi* (1905, Magyar Színház, ad Jenő Heltai).

1901 **Rudolph and Adolph** [as Charles Newman] Academy of Music, Richmond, Va 28 August

1902 **Mr Jolly of Joliet** [as Chas Newman] (various) Port Jervis NY 27 August; Lyceum, Cleveland 1 September

1903 **Nancy Brown** (Henry Hadley/w Frederick Ranken) Hyperion Theater, New Haven 11 February; Bijou Theater 16 February

1903 **Buster Brown** (John W Bratton/West/[as Charles Newman] w George Totten Smith) Harmanus Bleeker Hall, Albany, NY 25 December; Auditorium, Philadelphia 4 January 1904; Majestic Theater 24 January 1905

1905 **The Duke of Duluth** (Max S Witt) McVickers Theater, Chicago 14 August; Majestic Theater 11 September

1907 **Lady from Lane's** (Kerker) Lyric Theater 19 August

1910 **The Girl and the Drummer** (Augustus Barratt) Long Branch, NJ 8 August; Grand Opera House, Chicago 4 September

1918 **He Didn't Want to Do It** (Silvio Hein) Broadhurst Theater 20 August

BRODSZKY, Miklos [aka Nikolaus or Nicholas BRODSZKY] (b Odessa, Ukraine, 20 April 1905; d Hollywood, Calif, 24 December 1958). Composer of several musicals for the Hungarian and Austrian stage who made his name further afield as the supplier of screen songs to Mario Lanza.

Ukraine-born, but Hungarian-raised, Brodszky studied music in Budapest and Rome and, at the age of 24, had a great success with his first Operette, *Szökik az asszony* (a runaway girl). Initially mounted at the Budai Színkör, the show moved on to the Városi Színház where, with Hanna Honthy starred, it ran up more than 150 performances by the end of its first year, before going on to be played in Berlin and in Innsbruck (30 January 1932) under the title *Die Flucht in die Ehe* and in Vienna, as *Die entführte Frau,* by a company from Olmütz (1930).

Brodszky confirmed that early success with his second piece, *Az első tavasz* (the first spring), again starring the very popular Hanna Honthy, whilst a third successful piece, *Die verliebte Königin,* introduced by Gitta Alpár for a two-month run in Vienna and later successfully played as *A szerelmes királynő* in Budapest (ad Harmath, Városi Színház 10 October 1936), encouraged London impresario C B Cochran to take the composer to Britain to write a new musical play for Alpár to a text by James Bridie. This show never eventuated, but Brodszky did supply music for the 1937 Cochran revue *Home and Beauty* (Adelphi Theatre 128 performances) and later contributed to another London revue, *Big Top.*

Brodszky wrote liberally for the musical film—notably, in his early days, for such artists as Alpár, Franziska Gaal and for Richard Tauber—as well as for radio and recording, and if his years in Britain brought forth no stage scores, he continued to supply music to the screen. In 1949 he moved on to America where he provided, amongst others, songs for the films *The Toast of New Orleans* (1950, "Be My Love"), *Because You're Mine* (1952, "Because You're Mine") and *Serenade* for Mario Lanza, for *The Flame and the Flesh* ("No One But You"), *Rich, Young and Pretty* ("Wonder Why"), *Love Me and Leave Me* ("I'll Never Stop Loving You") and *Meet Me in Las Vegas,* as well as additional material for the film version of *The Student Prince,* without again returning to the theatre.

In his early days in Budapest Brodszky was also credited with an opera, *Az igéret földje* (ad Rudolf von Gottschall) produced at the Városi Színház in 1929 (8 November).

1929 **Szökik az asszony** (Imre Harmath, Andor Kardos) Budai Színkör 14 June

1930 **Az első tavasz** (Harmath/Ernő Andai) Budai Színkör 16 June

1932 **Ezer jó** Royal Orfeum 12 June

1933 **A kék lámpás** (Harmath, László Szilágyi) Király Színház 3 March

1934 **Die verliebte Königin** (*A szerelmes királynő*) (Alfred Grünwald, Fritz Löhner-Beda) Scala Theater, Vienna 21 December

1935 **Mariora** (Harmath/László Bús Fekete)

1938 **Dinasztia** (Harmath, István Békeffy) Magyar Színház 16 April

BRÓDY, István (b Nagykároly 1 May 1882; d Budapest, 4 January 1941). Theatre manager, director and playwright, Bródy authored musical comedy texts for Lajtai, Renyi, and Ábrahám, as well as for his brother, **Miklos BRÓDY** (b 30 March 1877; d Kolozsvár, 17 December 1949). His musical play *Zenebona* was played in Vienna under the title *Spektakel.*

1903 **Bob Király** (Jenő Virányi/w Dezső Urai) Uj Színház 16 May

1903 **A.B.C.** (Miklós Bródy/w Ferenc Révész) Pest 26 November

1915 **Tiszavirág** (Aladár Renyi/w László Vajda) Király Színház 27 March

1916 **Csókvásár** (Pál Leitner) Revü Színház 1 June

1920 **Pünkösdi rózsa** (Imre Farkas) Revü Színház 3 January

1921 **Férjhez megy a feleségem** (Alfred Márkus, M Bródy) Esküitéri Színház 16 April

1923 **Az asszonyok bolondja** (Lajos Lajtai) Budai Színkör 9 May

1925 **Leányálom** (Sándor Szlatinai/w Vajda) Városi Színház 14 November

1925 **Miámi** (Viktor Jacobi arr/w Vajda) Fővárosi Operettszínház 27 November

1928 **Zenebona** (Pál Ábrahám/Imre Harmath/w László Lakatos) Fővárosi Operettszínház 2 March

1929 **Kikelet-utca 3** (Egon Kemény/Imre Harmath/w Imre Harmath) Fővárosi Operettszínház 27 April

1936 **Zöld béka** (Pál Gyöngy/Dezső Késller) Kamara Színház 9 May

BRÓDY, Miksa (b Nagyvárad, 1875; d Budapest, 4 May 1924).

Journalist, theatre critic, playwright and librettist, Bródy provided the libretti for four of the most successful Hungarian operetts of the early 1910s: Vincze's *Tilos a csók* (*Das verbotene Kuss*), Jacobi's two international hits *Leányvásár* (*The Marriage Market*) and *Szibill* and Kálmán's *Zsuzsi kisasszony* (*Miss Springtime*) in his only four ventures as a musical theatre author during that period. He also adapted Louis Ganne's French opérette *Hans le joueur de flûte* for the Hungarian stage with an efficacity which resulted in its becoming more popular in Hungary than in other areas beyond France. He subsequently adapted two Robert Stolz Operetten with considerable success, and authored one further original work, the text to the Buttykay operett *Olivia hercegnő,* which opened the Fővárosi Operettszínház in 1922.

1909 **Tilos a csók** (Zsigmond Vincze/w József Pásztor) Király Színház 8 October

1911 **Leányvásár** (Viktor Jacobi/w Ferenc Martos) Király Színház 14 November

1912 **Furulyás Jancsi** (*Hans le joueur de flûte*) Hungarian version (Népopera)

1913 **Szökik a nagysaga** (?/w Martos) Budapesti Színház 22 March

1914 **Szibill** (Jacobi/w Martos) Király Színház 27 February

1915 **Zsuzsi kisasszony** (Imre Kálmán/w Martos) Vígszínház 27 February

1921 **Szerencsetánc** (*Der Tanz ins Glück*) Hungarian version (Városi Színház)

1921 **A kis grizett** (*Die Tanzgräfin*) Hungarian version (Vígszínház)

1922 **Olivia hercegnő** (Ákos Buttykay/w Imre Földes) Fővárosi Operettszínház 23 December

BROMME, Walter (b Berlin, 2 April 1884; d Berlin, 30 March 1943).

The son of a coal merchant, Bromme began his professional life working in his father's business before moving into the theatre in the dual capacity of theatre manager and composer of musical plays. In 1916 he joined Carl Wessel in the management of the former Deutsch-Amerikanisches Theater, now renamed the National-Theater, and mounted several musical comedies to which he had provided the cheerfully straightforward and often catchy songs, winning himself several popular successes. He occasionally provided his own lyrics, under the pseudonym of ''Walter Berg.''

He moved on to the Berliner Theater for the summer of 1919 and mounted his more ambitious *Die Dame im Frack,* with Kathe Dörsch in the starring role, for a run of two months, and continued thereafter to lease various Berlin houses for such pieces as *Eine Nacht im Paradies* (four months) and the most successful of his shows, *Mascottchen,* which had an eight-month run in Berlin and a season of 38 performances in Vienna (Carltheater 26 September 1924).

Schäm' dich, Lotte played 121 Berlin performances, and *Donnerwetter—ganz famos* provoked one of the best critics of the time to comment of the ''workmanlike'' composer ''he knows his business and sooner or later will write a show of real international calibre.'' But he didn't.

1916 **Heiratsfieber** (''Walter Berg'') Viktoria-Theater, Breslau 1 December

1917 **Studentenliebchen** (Theo Halton) National-Theater 15 January

1917 **Was junge Mädchen träumen** (Rudi Schwarz/Max Herbert) National-Theater

1917 **Das ist die Liebe** (Hugo Döblin) National-Theater 1 September

1918 **Die ist richtig . . . !** (Will Steinberg/Arthur Lippschitz) National-Theater 16 January

1918 **Prinzenliebe** (Steinberg/Gerhard Schätzler-Perasini) National-Theater 7 September

1919 **Die Kinopuppe** (Leonhard Haskel) National-Theater 28 February

1919 **Die Dame im Frack** (Steinberg/Alexander Pordes-Milo) Berliner Theater 2 August

1920 **Eine Nacht im Paradies** (Steinberg/Georg Okonkowski) Theater am Nollendorfplatz 30 April

1921 **Mascottchen** (Steinberg/Okonkowski) Thalia-Theater 15 January

1921 **Schäm' dich, Lotte** (Steinberg/Okonkowski) Thalia-Theater 2 September

1922 **Madame Flirt** (Steinberg/Okonkowski) Berliner Theater 15 April

1923 **Schönste der Frauen** (Steinberg/Okonkowski) Metropoltheater May

1925 **Tausend süsse Beinchen** (Steinberg/Okonkowski) Metropoltheater 28 March

1925 **Messalinette** (Richard Bars, Pordes-Milo) Berliner Theater 23 December

1926 **Donnerwetter—ganz famos** (Steinberg, Richard Kessler) Berliner Theater 1 May

1926 **Miss Amerika** (Kurt Schwabach/Okonkowski, Steinberg) Berliner Theater 20 August

1927 **Heute Nacht . . . eventuell** (Fritz Friedmann-Friedrich) Neues Theater am Zoo 25 December

1931 **Die Damenfriseur** (Robert Blum) Thalia-Theater 18 September

1933 **Marie-Louise** (H H Hermann) Metropoltheater 7 October

1934 **Spiel nicht mit der Liebe** (Richard Kessler) Komische Oper 4 October

1936 **Ball am Bord** (Kessler) Städtische Bühnen, Chemnitz 26 January

BRONHILL, June [GOUGH, June Mary] (b Broken Hill, Australia, 26 June 1929).

As a member of the Sadler's Wells Opera Company during the 1950s and 1960s, soprano June Bronhill (the name, like that of her compatriot Melba, was based on her home town) appeared in the light soprano repertoire, most notably as Eurydice in the company's celebrated production of *Orpheus in the Underworld.*

She made her first appearance on the London musical stage in the role of Elizabeth Barrett Browning in *Robert and Elizabeth,* a role written to the measure of her

Plate 52. *Poster for* **Walter Bromme's** Studentenliebchen.

uniquely fluid, high and staunch soprano with the type of demanding tessitura rarely seen in the musical theatre (''Woman and Man,'' ''I Know Now,'' Soliloquy, etc). She repeated that part in Australia where she was also seen as Maria in *The Sound of Music.* She later toured Britain as *The Merry Widow,* but returned only once to the West End, in later years, to play the Mother Superior in the 1981 revival of *The Sound of Music.*

In Australia, however, where she returned latterly to live, she continued to appear both in concert and on the stage appearing as the Merry Widow as late as 1983 and, no longer the tiny svelte performer of earlier days, in pieces and parts ranging from *Women Behind Bars* (in the role created by female impersonator Divine) to Little Miss Splendid in the *Mr Men* children's musical to *A Little Night Music* (1978), Mrs Pearce in *My Fair Lady* (1988), Katisha in *The Mikado,* Ruth in *The Pirates of Penzance* (1984) and Miss Jones in *How to Succeed in Business* (1993).

During the 1960s she recorded a series of light operas and musicals which remain the standard English recordings of such pieces as *Tom Jones, Merrie England, The Arcadians, The Merry Widow, The Count of Luxembourg, Lilac Time, The King and I,* et al.

Autobiography: *The Merry Bronhill* (Methuen, London, 1987)

BROONES, Martin (b New York, 10 June 1892; d Beverly Hills, Calif, 10 August 1971).

After almost a decade contributing music to revues (*Park Theater Revue, Hassard Short's Ritz Revue,* etc) and plays, Broones provided the full score for the 1927 revue *Rufus Le Maire's Affairs,* featuring his wife Charlotte Greenwood (''I Can't Get Over a Girl Like You [loving a boy like me]'') on Broadway, and later toured widely with Sophie Tucker. He subsequently became musical supervisor at MGM in the earliest years of sound cinema and worked in Hollywood for four years. In 1933 he returned to the musical theatre and provided the scores for four successful London musical comedy shows, the Flanagan and Allen vehicle *Give Me a Ring,* a remusicked version of the French hit *Toi c'est moi* featuring Miss Greenwood in the starring role, and two pieces for producer Firth Shephard which set in motion the Leslie Henson series of comedy shows at the Gaiety Theatre.

1933 **Give Me a Ring** (R P Weston, Bert Lee, Guy Bolton) London Hippodrome 22 June

1935 **The Gay Deceivers** (*Toi c'est moi*) new score for English version (Gaiety Theatre)

1935 **Seeing Stars** (Graham John/Bolton, Fred Thompson) Gaiety Theatre 31 October

1936 **Swing Along** (John, Douglas Furber/Bolton, Thompson) Gaiety Theatre 2 September

BROUGH, Lionel (b Pontypool, 10 March 1836; d Lambeth, London, 8 November 1909). Much-loved comedian of the musical and straight stages of Victorian London.

The son of Barnabas Brough, at one time a writer for the stage under the pseudonym of ''Barnard de Burgh,'' and the brother of top burlesque and extravaganza writers William Brough and Robert Brough, the young Lionel (fondly known as ''Lal'') began his working life in a lowly job in the offices of the *Illustrated London News.* He subsequently rose to an assistant publisher's position on the *Daily Telegraph* and was responsible there for organizing the first street papersellers, a troupe of 240 boys.

During this time he confined his theatrical ambitions and stage appearances largely to the amateur theatre, but he appeared with Vestris and Charles Mathews at the Lyceum in 1854 in his brother William's burlesque *Prince Prettypet and the Butterfly* and a comedy, ventured again in 1858 under the nom de theatre ''Lionel Porter'' in a drama by Edmund Falconer, and yet again with an entertainment called *The Photographic Studio* which he toured in partnership with his brother, John. When the experiment was done, he returned to the newspaper world as a subeditor on the *Morning Star,* but in 1864 he threw in journalism and joined Alexander Henderson's company at the Prince of Wales' Theatre, Liverpool.

Brough made himself a fine name as a comic actor in Liverpool and, after three years, moved on to London and an engagement at the Queen's Theatre. He quickly became very prominent in the West End, playing in comedy and burlesque, and appearing, amongst many other burlesques, in the title role of the Crystal Palace *Bluebeard* to the Sister Ann of Edward Terry; in Reece's *The Stranger Stranger Than Ever,* W S Gilbert's *La Vivandiere* (Count Roberto) and Burnand's *Fowl Play* (Joseph Wylie) at the Queen's; as John Smith to the Pocohantas of Mrs John Wood in *La Belle Sauvage,* as Black Brandon to her Poll in *My Poll and Partner Joe* (1871) and as Bunn to her Jenny Leatherlungs in *Jenny Lind at Last* at the St James's; as Patent Leatherby in the Gaiety's *Guy Fawkes;* and in the title role of another *Blue Beard,* as Jim Cocks in *Robinson Crusoe,* King Gramerci XXXVII in *Piff Paff* and Don José in *Carmen, or Sold for a Song,* all with Lydia Thompson's company.

He starred in and directed the vast stage musical *Babil and Bijou* (1872) for Dion Boucicault at the Theatre Royal, Covent Garden, and played in comedy and burlesque at the Gaiety Theatre (Mumphs in *Our Own Antony and Cleopatra,* 1873, etc). The coming of opéra-bouffe and -comique saw him extend his talents to such roles as Baron Gondremarck in *La Vie parisienne,* Baron Palamède in *La Marjolaine,* Menelaus in *La Belle Hélene,* Valentin in *Le Petit Faust,* Laurent XVII in *La Mascotte,* Lambertuccio in *Boccaccio,* The Beadle in *Nell Gwynne* and Nick Vedder in *Rip van Winkle,* occasionally staging the shows as well as performing, and winning himself a place as one of the town's favorite musical comedians.

During the 1870s and 1880s he mixed appearances on the musical stage (Valentine in *Mefistofele* II 1880, etc) with classic comedy (Tony Lumpkin being one of his notable successes) and Shakespeare, played with Willie Edouin's troupe (Bill Booty in *The Babes, The Japs,* etc), visited America with Violet Cameron's company (1885, title role in *The Commodore,* Sir Richard Varney in *Kenilworth*) and toured comedy in South Africa (1889). In the 1890s he was still appearing in fine West End roles, playing Matt in *La Cigale,* creating Pietro in *The Mountebanks* and Mr McGuire in *Haste to the Wedding* for W S Gilbert and, in his early sixties, starring with Kate Cutler as Dominie Crockett in *Little Miss Nobody.*

Regarded as one of the great all-round comedy performers of his era, Brough was beloved by actors, critics and audiences. When he appeared in a miserable piece called *Mignonette* which had the audience hooting at its ineptitudes, he was spared, and a voice from the gods said it all: ''we're sorry for you, Lal Brough!''

BROUGH, Robert [BROUGH, Lionel Barnabas] (b South Lambeth, London, 13 July 1855; d Sydney, Australia, 20 April 1906). The son of burlesque writer Robert Brough and his wife, the well-known vocalist Elizabeth Romer, the younger Robert made an early start as an actor, performing comic roles in the British provinces before succeeding to the role of Dick Deadeye in D'Oyly Carte's second touring company of *HMS Pinafore* (1879). He appeared in 1881–82 as Zapeter in *Princess Toto,* Vulcan in the burlesque *Vulcan* and in the operettas *Lovers' Knots* and *Quid Pro Quo* at the Opera Comique, in 1882 as King John in the burlesque *Little Robin Hood* at the Gaiety, in 1883 in the principal comedy role of the Doge in *Estrella* (Manchester/Gaiety) and in 1884 took over as the Emperor of Morocco in Jakobowski's *Dick* and appeared as Corporal O'Flanagan in the short run of Solomon's *Pocahontas* (Empire), a piece which he also co-directed.

In 1885 he and his wife, the contralto **Florence TREVALLYAN** [Florence MAJOR b Covent Garden, London, 4 November 1856; d Sydney, 7 January 1932]—who had played with Kate Santley as Juno in *Orpheus in the Underworld,* in *Princess Toto* and *La Fille de Madame Angot* on the road (1877) and *La Marjolaine* (1877, Karl) and *Gillette* (1883, Suzanne) in town, toured for D'Oyly Carte as Little Buttercup and Mrs Partlett (1878–79) and with Alfred Heming in burlesque (Zuniga in *Cruel Carmen,* etc) and comedy, as well as appearing in London in the comic operas *Manteaux Noirs* (1882, Clorinda) and *Estrella* (1883, Brigetta)—went to Australia to join the Williamson, Garner and Musgrove's company. They appeared together in *Iolanthe* (Lord Chancellor, Fairy Queen) and *Falka* (Tancred, Alexina) and Brough repeated his Zapeter in Australia's *Princess Toto,* but they soon seceded from the company and Brough went into a management partnership with Dion Boucicault jr.

Amongst their early productions were *Young Fra Diavolo* (with Brough as Beppo), *Little Jack Sheppard* (Jonathan Wild), *Dick* (director, Alderman Fitzwarren) and *The Forty Thieves* (Ali Baba) but, under the influence of the determined Florence, who now pronounced a distaste for and an unease in musical theatre, the firm then abandoned musicals in favor of straight theatre. Brough and Boucicault managed the Criterion, Sydney and the Bijou, Melbourne, operating successfully together for a decade and when Boucicault returned to Britain, Brough continued alone until 1902, producing what were regarded as the best quality theatrical entertainments in Australia, until shortly before his death when he gave up management and returned to performing for other firms.

After his death Florence remarried and, her Australian popularity having faded, returned to Britain.

Florence's sister, **Bessie MAJOR**, who made her career largely in the non-musical theatre, created the small role of Zanim in *Chu Chin Chow* and played it throughout the show's entire record-breaking run.

Plate 53. **Lionel Brough** *in a low comic role in W S Gilbert's burlesque* La Vivandière.

BROUGH, William (b London, 28 April 1826; d Haverstock Hill, 15 March 1870). The son of Barnabas Brough and the elder brother of actor Lionel, William Brough paired with his other brother, **Robert B[arnabas] BROUGH** (b London, 10 April 1828; d Manchester, 26 June 1860), to establish a great reputation as one of the most successful purveyors of fine and fanciful extravaganza and burlesque to the English-speaking stages of the 1850s.

The "Brothers Brough" were brought up in Wales, but they moved to Manchester in 1843 and there began to supply their classy comic writings liberally to papers and magazines of all kinds. They made their first appearance on a playbill when their burlesque of Shakespeare's *The Tempest, The Enchanted Isle,* was produced at the Empire Theatre in Liverpool in early 1848, under the management of W R Copeland. The production was seen by Benjamin Webster, manager of London's Adelphi Theatre, and in consequence *The Enchanted Isle* was given a Christmas season in London the same year. It proved an enormous success, and was revived the following year at Webster's Haymarket Theatre with Priscilla Horton as Ariel and Buckstone as Caliban, in 1850, and again in 1860. The Haymarket, too, had a Brough Brothers extravaganza for the Christmas season of 1848–49, and this version of the *Prince Camaralzaman* tale from *The Arabian Nights* proved even more successful than their first piece, going on to be played throughout the country and becoming a regular basis for pantomime performances in the years that followed. Buckstone and Miss Horton starred again in the 1850 *The Arabian Nights* alongside the vocalist Annie Romer who, the following year, became Mrs William Brough.

The partnership between William and Robert lasted for over five years, during which time the brothers regularly supplied the Easter and Christmas extravaganzas for Webster's two theatres. When the pair decided to write individually, William spread his talents wide, writing comedies, burlesques for the Lyceum Theatre, musical and non-musical playlets and sketches for the earliest entertainments for Mr and Mrs German Reed (the former Miss Horton) at what was to become their famous Gallery of Illustration (*A Visit to Holly Lodge After the Ball, The Enraged Musician* [both w R Brough], *A Month from Home, My Unfinished Opera, Our Home Circuit, Seaside Studies, An Illustration on Discords, The Rival Composers, The Bard and His Birthday, A Peculiar Family*) and even turned his hand to the writing of burlesque material for the Christy Minstrels (*La Sonnambula,* etc).

In the burlesque field, he had a particular success with his parody of Byron's *The Corsair* as *Conrad and Medora* (USA: *Conrad the Corsair*) and, an even greater one with the burlesque of Shakespeare's *A Winter's Tale* as *Perdita, or The Royal Milkmaid,* produced by Charles Dillon at the Lyceum with Marie Wilton, Miss Woolgar and the young J L Toole amongst the cast, and with the author himself making a first and rare stage appearance as Polixenes. In the fashion of the day, these pieces were equipped with pasticcio scores of a wide range in musical styles. His burlesque of *Ernani,* for example, used tunes from "Pop Goes the Weasel" to "Suoni la tromba" as the melodies for the author's comic lyrics. Amongst his later works, the fairy extravaganza *Prince Amabel* and the historical burlesque *The Field of the Cloth of Gold,* both regularly reprised after their initial productions, became long-lived favorites, the latter eventually proving the most internationally popular of all Brough's works. Within months of its first staging, whilst it continued its remarkable Easter-to-Easter run in London, it had gone round the English-speaking theatre world. In February of 1869 whilst it played at the Strand in London and at Wood's Museum in New York, it was to be seen in two rival productions at Chicago's Crosby's Opera House and McVicker's Theatre, opening at both houses in the same week that Melbourne's Duke of Edinburgh's Theatre put up Australia's first production.

Brough also had success in the area of imported opéra-bouffe, for his adaptation of Offenbach's *Ba-ta-clan* as *Ching-Chow-Hi* became the standard English version of the piece throughout the English-speaking theatre, and it would undoubtedly have been prelude to many more versions of French pieces, had not his death intervened in his early forties.

His 1864 farce *The Area Belle* (w Andrew Halliday) was made into the operetta *Penelope* by George P Hawtrey with music by Edward Solomon (Comedy Theatre 9 May 1889).

Robert Brough also turned out several years' worth of further burlesque pieces, including *Mephistophiles, or An Ambassador from Below* (w Henry Sutherland Edwards, Haymarket Theatre 14 May 1852), *The Overland Journey to Constantinople as Undertaken by Lord Bateman, with Interesting Particulars of the Fair Sophia* (Adelphi Theatre 17 April 1854), *Medea, or The Best of Mothers with a Brute of a Husband, or A Libel on a Lady of Colchis* (Olympic Theatre 14 July 1856), *Masaniello, or the Fish'oman of Naples* (Olympic Theatre 2 July 1857), *The Doge of Duralto* (Olympic Theatre 26 December 1867), *The Siege of Troy* (Theatre Royal, Lyceum 27 December 1858), and *Alfred the Great, or The Minstrel King* (Olympic Theatre 26 December 1859 mus arr J Barnard), before his death at the age of 32.

1848 **The Enchanted Isle, or Raising the Wind on the Most Approved Principles** (pasticcio/w Robert Brough) Liverpool Amphitheatre; Adelphi Theatre, London 20 November

1848 **Camaralzaman and Badoura, or The Peri Who Loved a Prince** (pasticcio/w R Brough) Haymarket Theatre 26 December

1849 **The Sphinx** (pasticcio/w R Brough) Haymarket Theatre 9 April

1849 **Frankenstein, or The Model Man** (pasticcio/w R Brough) Adelphi Theatre 26 December

1849 **The Ninth Statue, or The Jewels and the Gem** (pasticcio/w R Brough) Haymarket Theatre 26 December

1850 **The Last Edition of Ivanhoe, with all the newest improvements** (pasticcio/w R Brough) Haymarket Theatre, 1 April

1850 **The Second Calendar, or The Queen of Beauty Who Had the Fight with the Genie** (aka *The Arabian Nights*) (pasticcio/w R Brough) Haymarket Theatre 26 December

1851 **Arline, or The Fortunes and Vicissitudes of a Bohemian Girl** (Michael Balfe arr/w R Brough) Haymarket Theatre 21 April

1851 **The Princess Radiant, or The Story of Mayflower** (pasticcio/w R Brough) Haymarket Theatre 26 December

1851 **Little Red Riding Hood** (pasticcio/w R Brough) Adelphi Theatre 26 December

1852 **O Gemini, or Brothers of Course** (pasticcio/w R Brough) Adelphi Theatre 12 April

1853 **Richard Coeur de Lion, and The Knight of the Couchant Leopard** (pasticcio arr T German Reed/w R Brough) Theatre Royal, Drury Lane 28 March

1854 **Prince Prettypet and the Butterfly** (pasticcio) Theatre Royal, Lyceum 26 December

1856 **Perdita, or The Royal Milkmaid** (pasticcio arr W H Montgomery) Theatre Royal, Lyceum 15 September

1856 **Conrad and Medora** (pasticcio) Theatre Royal, Lyceum 26 December

1857 **Lallah Rookh and the Peri, the Princess and the Troubadour** (pasticcio) Theatre Royal, Lyceum 24 December

1858 **The Caliph of Baghdad** (pasticcio) Adelphi Theatre 5 April

1859 **Dinorah Under Difficulties, or The Rehearsal of an Opera** (pasticcio) Adelphi Theatre 7 November

1860 **The Forty Thieves** (pasticcio arr J Barnard/with others) Theatre Royal, Lyceum 7 March

1860 **The Sylphide** (pasticcio arr Montgomery) Royal Princess's Theatre 9 April

1860 **Endymion, or The Naughty Boy Who Cried for the Moon** (pasticcio) St James's Theatre 26 December

1861 **The Nigger's Opera, or The Darkie That Walked in His Sleep** (pasticcio) 1 act, St James's Hall (Christy Minstrels) 18 March

1861 **Perseus and Andromeda, or The Maid and the Monster** (pasticcio) St James's Theatre 26 December

1862 **Prince Amabel, or The Fairy Roses** (aka *Turko the Terrible*) (pasticcio) St James's Theatre 5 May

1862 **A Shilling Day at the Great Exhibition** (pasticcio/w Andrew Halliday) Adelphi Theatre 9 June

1862 **The Colleen Bawn Settled at Last** (pasticcio/w Andrew Halliday) Lyceum Theatre 5 July

1862 **Rasselas, Prince of Abyssinia, or The Happy Valley** (pasticcio) Haymarket Theatre 26 December

1863 **The Great Sensation Trial, or Circumstantial Effie-Deans** (pasticcio) St James's Theatre 6 April

1863 **King Arthur, or The Days and Knights of the Round Table** (pasticcio arr Dan Spillane) Haymarket Theatre 26 December

1864 **Hercules and Omphale, or The Power of Love** (pasticcio arr Ferdinand Wallerstein) St James's Theatre 26 December

1865 **A Peculiar Family** (pasticcio arr Thomas German Reed) entertainment Gallery of Illustration 15 March

1865 **Ching-Chow-Hi, or A Cracked Piece of China** (*Ba-ta-clan*) English version w Thomas German Reed (Gallery of Illustration)

1865 **Ernani, or The Horn of a Dilemma** (pasticcio arr Barnard Isaacson) Alexandra Theatre 20 May

1865 **Papillionetta, or The Prince, the Butterfly and the Beetle** (pasticcio) Prince of Wales Theatre, Liverpool 26 December, Sadler's Wells Theatre 2 June 1866

1867 **Pygmalion, or The Statue Fair** (pasticcio arr Frank Musgrave) Strand Theatre 22 April

1868 **The Field of the Cloth of Gold** (pasticcio arr Musgrave) Strand Theatre 11 April

1868 **The Gnome King, or The Fairy of the Silver Mine** (pasticcio) Queen's Theatre 26 December

1869 **Joan of Arc** (pasticcio arr Musgrave) Strand Theatre 29 March

1869 **The Flying Dutchman, or The Demon Seaman and the Lass that Loved a Sailor** (pasticcio arr Theodore Hermann) Royalty Theatre 2 December

1869 **Cinderella, or The Royal Game of Hunt the Slipper** (pasticcio arr Musgrave) Alexandra Opera House, Sheffield 21 December

BROUGHTON, Phyllis [WRIGHT, Phyllis Harriet] (b Lambeth, London, 17 March 1860; d London, 21 July 1926).

Daughter of a Norfolk architect's clerk and his theatrical wife, Phyllis Broughton made her first stage appearance at the age of 14 as a principal dancer at the Canterbury Music Hall (*Ceres* 1876, *The Reign of Love* 1877, etc), and she and her sister Emma were subsequently hired by John Hollingshead for the Gaiety Theatre. They played there principally in the house's burlesque productions and Phyllis graduated from featured dancing parts to leading roles through Ben Zoualle ("with a schottische") in *The Forty Thieves* (1880), Prince Chiboko in *Whittington and His Cat* (1881), Ho-Fi in *Aladdin* (1881), Sir Ralph Mont-Faucon in *Little Robin Hood* (1882), Henry in *Valentine and Orson* (1882), Joliquet in *Bluebeard or the Hazard of the Dye* (1883), Ferdinand in *Ariel* (1883), Mary Kenyon in *Called There and Back* (1883), Leucippe in *Galatea, or Pygmalion Re-versed* (1883), Maimoune in *Camaralzaman* (1884), *Little Don Caesar de Bazan* (1884), Orestes in *Our Helen* (1884), Ophelia in *Very Little Hamlet* (1884) and Olinska in *Mazeppa* (1885), before leaving the Gaiety to join the burlesque and comic opera company at the Avenue Theatre, under the direction of Claude Marius (Sir Walter Raleigh in *Kenilworth,* Onduletta in *Lurline,* Polly Hopkins in *Robinson Crusoe,* Lady Prue in *Indiana* 1886, Suzanne in *Madame Favart* 1887, Follow-the-Drum in *The Old Guard* 1887).

She created and played a series of soubrette roles with the Carl Rosa Light Opera Company at the Prince of Wales (Chopinette in *Paul Jones* 1889, Cicely in *Marjorie* 1890, Marcelline in *Captain Thérèse* 1891), appeared as Virginia Squeeze in the pantomime *The Swiss Express* (1891) in the musical playlet *A Pantomime Rehearsal* (t/o Lily Eaton-Belgrave) and in burlesque (Catherine of Rochelle in *Joan of Arc,* t/o Dolly in *Blue-Eyed Susan,* 1892) before moving into the latest style of entertainments in the very first of George Edwardes's modern-dress musical comedies.

She was cast in the travesty role of the teenaged Lord Clanside in *In Town* (1892) and after appearing in the

Gaiety's revival of *La Mascotte* (1893, Fiametta) and the unfortunate *All My Eye-van-hoe* (1894, Rebecca Hothouse-Peach), she succeeded Lottie Venne as Lady Virginia Forrest in *A Gaiety Girl,* the first of a series of roles as smart middle-aged ladies which was pursued with Arthur Roberts in *Gentleman Joe* (1895, t/o Mrs Ralli Carr), Biarritz (1896, Tessie Carew) *Dandy Dan, the Lifeguardsman* (1897, t/o Lady Catherine Wheeler) and *HMS Irresponsible* (1901, t/o Victoria Chaffers). She also replaced Cissy Fitzgerald in the central role of *The Prince of Borneo* (1899) and appeared as the Princess in the seasonal musical *The Swineherd and the Princess* (1901). Appearing less frequently in her forties and fifties, she was seen in *The Earl and the Girl* (1903 and 1914, Virginia Bliss) and *The Dairymaids* (1906, 1908, Lady Brudenell) as well as in a small number of non-musical plays. In 1905–6 she appeared on the music halls in the musical comedietta *The Chief Cook* (Nancy Dene).

An attractive and spirited performer, Broughton was notably popular with both public and professionals through some 20 years of regular London performances. She was on several occasions called in to replace an insufficient or ailing leading lady and was a favorite (ie, supportive and uncomplaining) partner of the notoriously unreliable Roberts. She also spent a certain amount of time at the center of some nice publicity-worthy scandal, and won £2,500 and costs from Lord Dangan in 1889 in a breach of promise suit. When the said Lord Dangan grew up, and had a son, he ended up on the other end of the stick, for his son ran away from home, found himself disinherited, and ended up as a Gaiety Theatre chorister (1911) on 45s a week.

Miss Broughton was the daughter of Emily Charlotte Jecks, and thus the niece of another top-class musical actress, **Harriet [Martha] COVENEY** (b London, 1 November 1827; d Ramsgate, 24 February 1892) and cousin to her daughter, Clara Jecks. Phyllis's sister, **Emma [Marion] BROUGHTON** (b Lambeth, 1863; d Paddington, 28 February 1926), who had a less colorful career as a performer (*Mynheer Jan,* Wagner in *Faust Up-to-Date,* etc), later became the wife of the prominent music-hall proprietor Edwin [Adam] Villiers.

BROWN, Georgia [KLOT, Lilian C] (b London, 21 October 1933; d London, 6 June 1992).

Georgia Brown first came to notice on the musical stage when she appeared at London's Royal Court Theatre in the role of Lucy Lockit in *The Threepenny Opera* (1955), a part she repeated in the rather more successful off-Broadway production in New York. She returned to the Royal Court in the short-lived *The Lily-White Boys* (1960) and then, later the same year, created her most memorable role as Nancy in *Oliver!* (1960), introducing ''As Long as He Needs Me,'' ''Oom Pah Pah'' and ''It's a Fine Life.'' She again visited America to repeat her Nancy in the 1962 Broadway production.

London saw her once more when she succeeded to the title role of Bart's later musical *Maggie May,* but her career as a vocalist brought her back to the theatre only intermittently thereafter. She took over in the compilation show *Side by Side by Sondheim,* played the title role in *Carmelina* (1979), Broadway's musical version of *Buona Sera, Mrs Campbell,* appeared as the slightly ageing star, Dorothy Brock, in London's edition of *42nd Street* and starred in the short-lived Gilbert Bécaud musical play, *Roza* (1987) in America, without finding another new vehicle of the importance of *Oliver!*

BROWN, Lew [BROUNSTEIN, Louis] (b Odessa, Ukraine, 10 December 1893; d New York, 5 February 1958). One unit of the songwriting trio of De Sylva, Brown and Henderson.

Moving to America when Louis was still a child, the Brounstein family continued from their original stop in New Haven to settle in New York where the young Louis attended high school. After a variety of post-school jobs, he tried his hand at writing song lyrics and took his first serious steps in the music business when in 1912 he began a working relationship with Albert von Tilzer, the established composer of numbers like ''Take Me Out to the Ball Game'' and ''Put Your Arms Around Me, Honey.'' Together, the pair had some fine song successes over a period of eight years—''I'm the Lonesomest Gal in Town'' (1912), ''Give Me the Moonlight, Give Me the Girl'' (*Hullo, America,* UK 1917), ''I May Be Gone for a Long, Long Time'' (*Hitchy Koo of 1917*), ''Oh, By Jingo, Oh By Gee!'' (*Linger Longer Letty,* 1919), ''Chili Bean'' (*Pot Luck,* UK), ''My Gee-Gee from the Fiji Isles,'' ''I Used to Love You,'' ''Dapper Dan'' (*A to Z,* UK)—before Brown was introduced to musician Ray Henderson.

The first Brown/Henderson effort was a song called ''Georgette,'' sung with success in the 1922 *Greenwich Village Follies,* and the two continued a non-exclusive collaboration (''Why Did I Kiss That Girl?,'' ''Don't Bring Lulu'' w Billy Rose, ''If You Hadn't Gone Away'' w Rose) whilst Brown continued to turn out songs with a variety of other composers: ''Red Moon'' (w Travers, Max Kortlander, de Martini), ''Last Night on the Back Porch'' (w Carl Schraubstader), ''When It's Night Time in Italy, It's Wednesday Over Here'' (w James Kendis), ''Shine'' (w Cecil Mack, Ford Dabney), ''Where The Lazy Daisies Grow'' and ''Then I'll Be Happy'' (w Cliff Friend), ''Collegiate'' (w Moe Jaffe, Nathan J Bonx), ''I'd Climb the Highest Mountain'' (w Sidney Clare).

The songwriting team that was to become famous to a generation as ''De Sylva-Brown-n-Henderson'' came together for the first time on Broadway with a contribution to Al Jolson's *Big Boy* (1925), and success came with their score for the 1926 edition of the revue *George White's Scandals.* The lasting hit of the 1925 *Scandals,* for which they had also written the main score, had been Irving Berlin's interpolated "All Alone," but in the 1926 show the hits were their own. A Blues section which included several famous old blues numbers, Gershwin's "Rhapsody in Blue" and bits of Schubert and Schumann, was topped off by De Sylva, Brown and Henderson's new "The Birth of the Blues," whilst Ann Pennington danced frenetically to the rhythms of their Charlestonny new dance, "The Black Bottom."

Brown's first full Broadway musical comedy score was written not with these partners, but with his early songwriting associate, Cliff Friend. *Piggy* was comedian Sam Bernard's third variation on the antics of his favorite character, Mr Hoggenheimer of Park Lane, as originally played by him in the British musical *The Girl from Kays,* and it was lively enough to last out 11 weeks. Major success came, however, with the trio's first book musical score, their set of songs for the college musical *Good News* ("The Best Things in Life Are Free," "The Varsity Drag") and, over the next four years, whilst continuing to supply *George White's Scandals* with annual material, they turned out four further pieces in the same vein. They were four pieces of variable value, but each one was popular through a good Broadway run and most were exported (with uneven results) to London and to Australia and even, on one occasion, to France. *Manhattan Mary,* a vehicle for Ed Wynn, was short on song hits but long on personality; *Hold Everything!* invaded the world of boxing, introduced "You're the Cream in My Coffee," and made a star of Bert Lahr; *Follow Thru* turned to golf and produced "Button Up Your Overcoat"; and *Flying High* gave Lahr the opportunity to take to the skies, if without any staying-powerful songs.

The hottest songwriting team on contemporary Broadway was, naturally, courted by Hollywood, and they had some outstanding film success with songs for pieces such as *The Singing Fool* (1928, "Sonny Boy") and *Sunny Side Up* (1929, "If I Had a Talking Picture of You," "Sunny Side Up"), but the combination broke up when De Sylva moved on to an executive position in the film industry, and Brown and Henderson returned to Broadway. They turned out a score for the *Scandals of 1931* in which "Life Is Just a Bowl of Cherries" was the take-away tune, but they did not succeed in producing anything of the same kind of lasting value for either of the two subsequent revusical shows to which they contributed the songs. *Hot-Cha!,* even with Bert Lahr, was a 15-week semi-flop, and *Strike me Pink,* which the pair produced themselves, had Jimmy Durante and a lot of limp material.

Brown teamed with Harry Akst on an unimpressive 1935 revue, *Calling All Stars,* before going back to Hollywood to become a director, producer and sometime writer in films, returning to the theatre just once more as producer-director-librettist-lyricist-part composer of a curiously flimsy piece called *Yokel Boy.* It had a six-months' run and added "Comes Love" and a version of the interpolated "Beer Barrel Polka" (Wladimir Timm, Jaromir Vejvoda) to Brown's list of successful song credits, a list which was occasionally added to in the following years by such pieces as the 1943 song "Madame, I Like Your Crêpes Suzette" (w Burton Lane, Ralph Freed), written for De Sylva's film version of *Dubarry Was a Lady.*

Brown was portrayed by Ernest Borgnine in a De Sylva-Brown-n-Henderson film biomusical called *The Best Things in Life Are Free.*

1927 **Good News** (Ray Henderson/w B G De Sylva/Laurence Schwab, De Sylva) 46th Street Theater 6 September

1927 **Manhattan Mary** (Henderson/w De Sylva) Apollo Theater 26 September

1927 **Piggy** (Cliff Friend/Daniel Kusell, Alfred Jackson) Royale Theater 22 October

1928 **Hold Everything!** (Henderson/w De Sylva/Jack McGowan, De Sylva) Broadhurst Theater 10 October

1929 **Follow Thru** (Henderson/w De Sylva/Schwab, De Sylva) 46th Street Theater 9 Janaury

1930 **Flying High** (Henderson/w De Sylva/McGowan) Apollo Theater 3 March

1932 **Hot-Cha!** (Henderson/w H S Kraft, Mark Hellinger) Ziegfeld Theater 8 March

1933 **Strike Me Pink** (Henderson/Mc Gowan, Mack Gordon) Majestic Theater 4 March

1939 **Yokel Boy** (Sam H Stept/Charles Tobias) Majestic Theater 6 July

BROWN[E], Louise (b Madison, Wis).

A durable dancing ingenue of indeterminate age who was promoted as "the spinning top" because of her pirouetting propensities, Louise Brown(e) first came to notice in her native America when after succeeding to the role of Sally in the musical *Sally, Irene and Mary* (1925), she was cast in the starring role of Suzanne Trentoni created on the straight stage by Ethel Barrymore in the musical *Captain Jinks.* This plum part had been announced as a vehicle for Marilyn[n] Miller, several years earlier, but the show had not materialized and, when it finally did—with different writers and sponsors attached—Miss Browne got the job instead. It won her a two-year contract with Miss Miller's chief sponsor, Florenz Ziegfeld, who featured her in his revue *No Foolin'* the following year.

Louise Browne visited Britain in 1927 to star as Kitty Brown in *The Girl Friend* (US: *Kitty's Kisses*), appeared on Broadway as the heroine of a trio of non-hits—*Rainbow* (1928, Virginia Brown), *Lady Fingers* (1929, Hope Quayle) and *Woof Woof* (1929, Susie Yates)—and then returned to London to star in *Heads Up* (1930, Mary Trumbell), and in Adele Astaire's role of Pat in *The One Girl* (1932). Thereafter she made her career in Britain, playing in the revues *Yours Sincerely* and *After Dark,* briefly in the Hungarian musical *Happy Weekend* (*Zackbamackska* 1934, Polly Petworthy), touring in *Gay Divorce* (1934) and creating the role of April in *Jill Darling,* in which she introduced ''I'm on a See-Saw'' (w John Mills) to London audiences.

She then renewed a partnership with light comedian-dancer Roy Royston, pairing in a series of dancing-ingenue leads, constructed on the Cyril Ritchard-Madge Elliott plan, in a run of successful comic musicals at the Gaiety Theatre: *Seeing Stars* (1935, Princess Valerie), *Swing Along* (1936, Lili Breval), *Going Greek* (1937, Iris Carew) and *Running Riot* (1938, Betty Browne). When the war intervened, Miss Browne and her ubiquitous stage mother vanished from the London theatre scene and, apparently, all others. Although I cannot get information from Scandinavian parts, it appears that she ended in Norway where, as ''Madame Louise Browne,'' she was instrumental in founding today's Norwegian Ballet Company.

BRUDER LEICHTSINN Operette in a Vorspiel and 2 acts by Julius Brammer and Alfred Grünwald. Music by Leo Ascher. Wiener Bürgertheater, Vienna, 28 December 1917.

Bruder Leichtsinn (Otto Storm) is not a person but a personification. He is irresponsibility, negligence, thoughtlessness and, like all virtues and vices, he has his favorites amongst human beings. One of these was the well-known singer, Adèle Garnier (Ida Russka), who gave up the love of a good man for a carnival night fling with Graf Fabrice Dunoir (Karl Streitmann), of which was born their daughter, Musotte (Frln Russka again). Leichtsinn watches over ''his'' child, as she leads a lively, heedless life with her friends in a private school in Brussels, and falls in love with an anonymous person who writes her the most charming letters. Dunoir comes to Brussels to adopt her, but it is again carnival night and Leichtsinn takes everyone on the town. Whilst Musotte's schoolfriend, Nelly (Mimi Kott), nets her lawyer (Carlo Böhm), and papa Karl Pampfinger (Josef Joseffy) is caught by his wife (Viktoria Pohl-Meiser) flirting with the apparently respectable school-headmistress (Emmy Stein), Musotte's father allows her, as he had promised her mother, to make her free choice of husband. She chooses the anonymous letter-writer. Leichtsinn looks after his own: the writer is the mulatto engineer Jimmy Wells (Ludwig Herold), who wrote to the girl because he speaks so poorly . . . but he loves her.

Ascher's score featured several winning waltzes: the duet between Leichtsinn and Adele in the Vorspiel (''Wer den Leichtsinn liebt''), Musotte's letter song, ''Mein reizendes Fräulein,'' the carnival night duet between Leichtsinn and Dunoir (''Das Küssen und Kosen und Lieben'') and a waltz-ensemble (''Lockend klingt mein Walzermärchen''), set alongside a group of marches and a dance duo for Pampfinger and the schoolmistress which started out in tango time (''Den Tango den tanz' ich so fesch'').

The show ran for a fine 176 performances in wartime Vienna, was subsequently seen in Germany, and scored a particularly strong success in Hungary under the title of *Hejehuja báró* (ad Imre Harmath, Adorján Ötvös), totting up an exceptional initial run of over a hundred performances.

Germany: ?1918; Hungary: Margitszigeti Színkör *Hejehuja báró* 15 June 1918

BRUDER STRAUBINGER Operette in 3 acts by Moritz West and Ignaz Schnitzer. Music by Edmund Eysler. Theater an der Wien, Vienna, 20 February 1903.

At a time when the Viennese musical theatre was desperately in need of new, and preferably modern, musical blood to replace the departed composing stars of the 19th century, the chief sources of hope seemed to come from Carl Michael Ziehrer's *Die Landstreicher,* Heinrich Reinhardt's *Das süsse Mädel* and the young Franz Lehár's *Der Rastelbinder,* until Karczag and Wallner of the Theater an der Wien mounted the old-Austria piece *Bruder Straubinger,* the maiden full-length work of another young composer, Edmund Eysler.

West and Schnitzer had put together their libretto around a splendid role for the theatre's star, Alexander Girardi, as ''brother'' Straubinger who, when his identity papers are stolen by Bonifaz, an army deserter (Arthur Strasser), is obliged to make do with those of his grandfather—which make him 114 years old. Disguised as an army veteran, he gets a 1,000 gulden-a-month pension out of the Landgraf Philipp (Karl Meister), but sees his sweetheart, Marie (Lina Abarbanell), who works for the showman Schwudler (Siegmund Natzler) as a wild-woman exhibit called Oculi, first pursued by the Landgraf and then, when the Landgräfin Lola (Mary Hagen) spots it, about to be forcibly engaged to the phony Straubinger. The young pair convince the Landgräfin that the ''old'' husband is a preferable match and, in the end, the papers are restored, the ''old'' man can become young again, and the naughty Landgraf returns, chastened, to his wife.

Eysler's score, partly manufactured from pieces left over from his first attempt to write a show to Schnitzer's

Strauss-rejected *Der Schelm von Bergen* libretto (as *Der Hexenspiegel*), was full of waltzing and marching melody, and it was topped by what was to be one of the biggest show-song hits in years: Girardi's "Küssen ist keine Sünd," a catchy waltz-song in which the elderly veteran expounds on the virtues of kissing. The star also had a lively entrance number, the bouncing, waltzing "Gott grüss' dir, Bruder Straubinger," as did both the Landgraf (the more lyrical waltz "Es kommt mit leisem Kosen"), and Oculi with her wildly jaunty 3/4 showpiece (up to D in alt), "Ja, so singt sie." She later joined Straubinger happily in a winning march-time Trommel-Duett ("Er ist ganz in mich verschossen"). There were also two comical numbers for Schwudler, a delicious swinging waltz for Lola ("Bald ist die Wilddieb hier"), a drinking song for the aristocratic pair and ensembles, ranging from the softly surging trio "Vierblättriger Klee" to a brisk march quartet in the final act. A large part of the score became popular without any other single number equalling the phenomenal and enduring favor given to "Küssen ist keine Sünd."

The show was a singular hit, but Karczag was obliged by treaty to mount Planquette's *Mam'zelle Quat' Sous* (*Die beiden Don Juans*) during the season and so, after little more than a month, *Bruder Straubinger* was replaced. After two weeks, however, with the contractual obligation out of the way, the French piece was whisked off, and Girardi got back into his veteran's outfit until the end of the season (65 performances). When the theatre reopened after the summer break, *Bruder Straubinger* reopened with it, and it played on to its 109th performance. It passed its 125th in repertoire on 2 February 1905 before going on to be seen at the Raimundtheater between 1909 and 1911 in Girardi's seasons there (200th performance 14 February 1911), and at the Johann Strauss-Theater in 1913 (11 April). A new production was mounted at the Wiener Bürgertheater in 1929, and the show returned to the Theater an der Wien in 1934 for special performances to mark Eysler's 60th birthday. On this occasion, Hubert Marischka played the Girardi role, with Mimi Shorp as Oculi and Fritz Steiner as Schwudler. On 8 March of that year it notched up its 300th performance.

Although the show was apparently "translated into 16 languages," its greatest popularity was very largely centered in middle Europe. It became the most popular of all of Eysler's popular works in Germany, after its initial production at the Centraltheater with Carl Schulz (Straubinger), Mia Werber (Oculi) and Ander (Schwudler) featured, and played a good initial 36 performances (ad Jenő Faragó) at Budapest's Népszínház in its initial production there. However, in a period where Viennese Operette had not yet begun to export in the way that it would do in a couple of years' time, post–*Die lustige Witwe,* it did not appear on the vernacular stages of London, Paris or New York. Australia got just a fragment, the hit song, when soubrette Carrie Moore interpolated "Kissing Is No Sin" into a musical farcical comedy called *Much Married* which was played at Melbourne's Bijou Theatre in 1913 (5 July).

A film version was produced in 1950 under the title of the show's still famous song.

Germany: Centraltheater 26 September 1903; Hungary: Népszínház *Vandorlegeny* 30 October 1903

Film: *Küssen ist keine Sünd* 1950

BRÜDERLEIN FEIN Altwiener Singspiel in 1 act by Julius Wilhelm. Music by Leo Fall. Bernhard Rose-Theater, Berlin, 31 December 1908.

A little three-handed, one-act piece, containing seven musical numbers, *Brüderlein fein* followed the old musician Josef Drechsler and his wife, Tony, on a sentimental journey of remembrances on the occasion of their 40th wedding anniversary. A musical clock rings out with the little melody "Brüderlein fein" and Drechsler remembers the time when he composed the tune, for a production of Raimund's *Der Jugend,* and the day of their wedding. The third character of the piece was the old housekeeper, Gertrud, who also played the hero of *Der Jugend* in the dream sequence. The principal numbers of the score were the waltz duo "Nicht zu schnell und nicht zu langsam" for Drechsler and Tony, their pseudo-waltz "Unter dem blühenden Lindenbaum" and Gertrud's Lied der Jugend.

First played at Berlin's Rose-Theater and subsequently at the Theater an der Wien's studio theatre, Hölle, *Brüderlein fein* won all hearts, and proved to be one of the best-liked and most often reprised of smaller works in a period where such shows were much less seen than they had been in earlier years. It was reprised in Vienna, at the Johann Strauss-Theater in 1913 as a forepiece in a "Girardi Zyklus," and again in 1920 in a spectacle-coupe with Reinhardt's *Die süssen Grisetten,* and at the Theater an der Wien in 1919, whilst winning performances in similar situations in Germany and Hungary.

In London, during the short-lived fashion for playing one-act Operetten in variety houses, *Darby and Joan* (ad Arthur Anderson) was played on the bill at the London Coliseum with Ivy St Helier featured, whilst America heard the little piece in its original German as purveyed by Mady Christians at the Irving Place Theater, and later in an English version by Arthur Gillespie and Ballard MacDonald taken round the vaudeville houses by Chapine.

Austria: Hölle 1 December 1909; Hungary: Urania Színház Édes öregem 24 November 1910; UK: London Coliseum *Darby and Joan* 11 December 1911; USA: Irving Place Theater

BRUMMELL Opérette in a prologue and 3 acts by Rip and Robert Dieudonné. Lyrics by Rip. Music by Reynaldo Hahn. Théâtre des Folies-Wagram, Paris, 17 January 1931.

Although the real ''Beau Brummell''—George Bryan Brummell (1778–1840)—was a close friend of George IV of England and a man whose career knew some dramatic highs and (mostly) lows, his name has become synonomous in modern times simply with the idea of the rarefied dandy. Rip's opérette presented Pizani as the Beau, an elegant gentleman in prey to a passion for his little washerwoman and childhood friend Peggy (Sim-Viva). He rusticates himself in private misery, only to be followed to his retreat by half of fashionable Bath, headed by the amorous Lady Eversharp (Marguerite Deval) and the Prince of Wales (Henri Jullien), all, following the maker of their fashions, dressed in peasant garb. Ultimately Brummell lets Peggy go to a more suitable lover and puts on again the motley of his courtly calling. Producer/director Edmond Roze appeared himself in the supporting role of Helliot.

Reynaldo Hahn's score contained some typically pretty pieces, including Peggy's solo ''Entre les deux mon coeur balance'' and the hero's Chanson pastorale. There was a song in praise of ''le knock-out'' from boxing-mad Jim, who also headed the search for Brummell, declaring that the best method to find him was simply ''Cherchez la femme,'' whilst rustic Dick longed in song to be one of ''les Dandys de Brummell . . . aussi pauvres que des cigales, mais riches de l'or d'Israël.'' The best part of the score, however, fell to Mlle Deval, whether joining in a hunting chorus and delivering her Couplets de l'equitation (''À dada''), heading some aristocratic ''Bergers Watteau,'' consoling Brummell in her Air Galant or, in a paroxysm of Rip lyrics redolent of the unforgettable Lady Parvula of *Valmouth,* musing on the attractions of a rough man: ''lorsque cet éffronté a soudain éructé une phrase méchante . . . il m'enchante, lorsque ce parvenu pose sur un sein nu son oeil de cannibale . . . il m'emballe, quand cet ex-épicier, après un mot grossier, parle de savoir-vivre . . . il m'enivre, quand ce vil clabaudeur raconte sans pudeur ses amours qu'il méprise, il me grise.''

Brummell did not find the same kind of prosperity as its partner-in-pastels, *Ciboulette,* and won only a fair run. This French opérette, however, presented Brummell altogether more successfully than did two British musicals of the 1930s—*Beau Brummell* (Saville Theatre, 1933) with Harry Welchman as Brummell and *By Appointment* (New Theatre, 1934), in which the dandy was played by Gavin Gordon—both of which were quick flops. An American musical *Beau Brummell,* written by Gladys Unger, lyrics by Edward Eliscu and Raymond Egan, and with music by Harry Tierney, was tried out at St Louis's Municipal [Light] Opera in 1933 (7 August) with Leonard Ceeley playing the Beau and Nancy McCord (Marianne), Allan Jones (Reginald), Doris Patston (Kathleen) and George Hassell (Prince of Wales) in the other principal roles, the whole ''under the personal direction of J J Shubert.'' It failed to go further.

Recording: selection (Musidisc)

BRUNTON, Dorothy (b Melbourne, Australia, 14 October 1893; d Sydney, 5 June 1977).

Dorothy Brunton was the daughter of one of Australia's foremost scenic artists, the English-born John Brunton (d Sydney, 21 October 1909), sometime of the Theatre Royal, Plymouth, and latterly of Liverpool's Royal Alexandra Theatre, who had been brought south by Arthur Garner in 1886, and who spent the remainder of his career working in Australia, latterly for 15 years with Bland Holt.

''Dot'' made her first appearance on the musical stage under Williamson's banner in a small role in *The Balkan Princess* (1911) and subsequently covered lead roles in *The Girl in the Taxi* and several other musicals, before playing five years of soubrette and, later, lead roles for the Williamson organization in such pieces as *Nightbirds, The Cingalee* (Peggy), *The Merry Widow* (Fifi), *Autumn Manoeuvres* (June), *Gipsy Love* (Jolan), *The Girl in the Taxi* (Jacqueline), *The Girl on the Film* (Freddy), *Dorothy* (Phyllis), *Princess Caprice* (Clementine), *The Belle of New York* (Fifi/Violet), *High Jinks* (Sylvia), *So Long, Letty* (Letty), *Tonight's the Night* (June), *A Waltz Dream* (Franzi), *Canary Cottage* (Trixie) and *Three Twins* (Kate). In the process, she became one of Australia's favorite musical comedy performers of the wartime years.

A venture to Britain saw her playing good roles in Isidore Witmark's *Shanghai* at the Theatre Royal, Drury Lane (1918), *Soldier Boy* (1919) and, more successfully, with Walter Catlett in *Baby Bunting* (1919, Janet Chester) before she returned to Australia for a further run of lead roles in the Australian productions of such pieces as *Yes, Uncle!* (Mabel), *Baby Bunting, Going Up, Oh, Lady! Lady!!, Battling Butler* (Mrs Butler), *The Rise of Rosie O'Reilly* (Rosie), the Australian musical version of *Tons of Money* (Louise Allington) and *Little Jessie James* (Jessie), whilst repeating her most successful roles of earlier years, notably the hardy musical comedy roles of *High Jinks* and *So Long, Letty.*

A second London venture brought only the Harry Welchman turkey *The White Camellia* (1928, Fleurette Chamier), and she returned definitively to Australia where she starred in *Dearest Enemy* (Betsy), *Florodora* (Dolores), *The Merry Widow* (Hanna) and *The Duchess of Dantzic* (Catherine) in the later part of a prominent career before retiring to marriage.

BRUYAS, Florian (d 1974).

A former member of the French senate and administrator of the Conservatoire of Music at Lyon, Bruyas was the author of the only systematic and detailed chronicle of the history of the musical theatre in France (*Histoire de l'opérette en France 1855–1965* Emmanuel Vitte, Lyon, 1974). He died shortly after the publication of his work, before he was able to introduce the additions, revisions and corrections he had subsequently gathered, but his book remains, in spite of this, one of the principal vertebrae in the backbone of scholarly world musical theatre literature.

BRYAN, Dora [BROADBENT, Dora M] (b Parbold, Lancs, 7 February 1923).

Singing comedienne Dora Bryan appeared in several successful London revues (*The Lyric Revue, The Globe Revue, At the Lyric,* etc) and in a number of non-musical films (*The Fallen Idol, The Cure for Love, The Blue Lamp,* etc) before making a personal hit in her first appearance in a book musical as the heart-of-gold Lily in *The Water Gipsies* (1955, "Why Did They Call Me Lily?," "It Would Cramp My Style"). In a career mixing comedy and film (*A Taste of Honey*) with occasional musical appearances, she subsequently took the role of Lorelei Lee in the London production of *Gentlemen Prefer Blondes* (1962) and succeeded Mary Martin as Dolly Levi in *Hello, Dolly!* with considerable success, taking the piece on tour after her London run was over. After many years away from the musical stage, she returned in 1986 to play alongside Cyd Charisse in a revival of *Charlie Girl* (Kay Connor), reprised her *Hello, Dolly!* on the road, and top-billed in a very personalized and revusical production of *70 Girls 70* (Ida) at the Chichester Festival in 1990, in the West End the following year, and subsequently on tour around Britain. In the 1990s she was to be seen only in non-musical pieces, as she established herself as one of Britain's most admired older character actresses.

Autobiography: *According to Dora* (Aurum Press, London, 1986)

BRYNNER, Yul [KHANO, Taidje] (b Sakhalin, 11 July 1911; d New York, 10 October 1985).

Born in Russia, and brought up in China and France, Brynner began his career as an actor in America where, in 1945, he made his Broadway musical debut alongside Mary Martin in the Chinese-set musical *Lute Song* (1946, Tsai-Yong), a role he subsequently repeated in the show's London production (1948). In 1951 he starred opposite Gertrude Lawrence as the King of Siam in *The King and I* ("A Puzzlement," "Shall We Dance?"), a role which he repeated opposite Deborah Kerr on film, and with which he became thoroughly identified through repeated reappearances on stage in America and in Britain. Brynner was seen on Broadway as the King more than 30 years after his creation of the role, shortly before his final illness. He appeared in only one further musical role, as Odysseus in the short-lived *Home Sweet Homer* (1975).

Biography: Brynner, R: *The Man Who Would Be King* (Simon & Schuster, New York, 1989)

Plate 54. **Yul Brynner.** *"Long live the king . . .": Brynner in his one, unforgettable role.*

BUB ODER MÄDEL? Operette in 2 acts by Felix Dörmann and Adolf Altmann. Music by Bruno Granichstaedten. Johann Strauss-Theater, Vienna, 13 November 1908.

Fürst Fritz Ragan (Louis Treumann) has lived a wild-oat-flinging life on the expectation of inheriting the fortune of his childless uncle, Fürst Johann Georg Ragan (Karl Mauth), and he has even lined himself up a sweetheart without a gulden to her name (Mizzi Freihardt).

Uncle Johann thinks it time to bring to boy to heel, and he announces that his own wife is about to give birth to an heir. Fritz has to take a pull in his high living and is obliged to go looking for a rich wife in Lady Brighton's "Amerikanischen-Millionmädchen-Heiratschule." Of course, in the end there is no baby and the chastened Fritz is able to marry where his heart is.

If the story was barely new, it was told in a lively style and tricked out with up-to-date references, comical debt-collectors and picturesque rich Americans—including the pretty pensionnaires of the millionaire-girls' Marriage-School—and it was illustrated by Granichstaedten with a score in his novel, catchy, bordering-on-the-jazzy style.

Leopold Müller's production at the Johann Strauss-Theater ran for 86 straight performances, followed by a further handful in repertoire which brought its total to 101 nights by 26 March 1909, but, although the show went on to productions in Germany and in Hungary (ad Adolf Mérei), its most considerable success came in America.

Louis Werba and Mark A Luescher's Broadway production (ad H B Smith, Raymond W Peck, R B Smith) featured J Humbird Duffey as the extravagant Duke of Barchester and Adrienne Augarde as his housekeeper's daughter, Daphne, whilst a comical quartet of the Duke's creditors brought together the comedians Ed Gallagher (Dennis) and Al Shean (Schmuke) for the first time. Adaptors Harry and Robert Bache Smith were advertised as the "authors of *The Spring Maid,*" the producers' biggest and recent hit, and "The Rose Waltz" and "The Moon Song" were billed as "the whistling successes of the Continent." Well mounted and managed, almost unbotched (a couple of minor bits by Robert Hood Bowers), the show proved a worthy successor to the earlier hit, playing for 176 performances on Broadway and touring vigorously through America.

Germany: ?1909; Hungary: Várszínház *Fiu vagy leány* 20 October 1910; USA: Globe Theater *The Rose Maid* 22 April 1912

BUCALOSSI, Procida [Joseph Henry Edwards] (b London, ?1838; d Godstone, Surrey, 10 May 1918).

The composer of a number of comic operas for the British stage, London-born Bucalossi scored an international hit with his *(Les) Manteaux Noirs,* a version of Scribe's *Giralda,* set previously as an opéra-comique by Adolphe Adam, and rewritten by Harry Paulton for the English stage. None of his other works found anything like the same success, but Bucalossi was well enough considered as a musician in Victorian London to be invited to submit the music for one act of the vast Alhambra spectacle *Rothomago* along with Teddy Solomon, Georges Jacobi and Gaston Serpette.

A regular contributor of songs and dance music to the West-End musical theatre (*La Poule aux oeufs d'or,* the Drury Lane pantomime *Beauty and the Beast,* etc), Bucalossi also worked as a conductor at several London theatres, including a period at the Theatre Royal, Drury Lane, but he made his principal mark as a writer of ballads (originally as "Charles Valentine") and as a prolific and extremely popular arranger and composer of dance music.

His sons **[Procida] Ernest [Luigi] BUCALOSSI** (b London, 27 May 1863; d Ottershaw, Surrey, 15 April 1933) and **Brigata [Procida Leonardo] BUCALOSSI** (b London, 17 June 1862; d London, 21 December, 1924) were both active in the musical theatre. Ernest worked at first as a performer with D'Oyly Carte's companies (under the name Ernest Elton) and later as a musical director and composer (*A Shower of Blacks* 1887, *Cinderella the Second* 1893, *Binks, the Downy Photographer* 1893, *En Route* 1896, *The Maid and the Motor Man, Robin Hood* burlesque 1907, *A Wife for a Song* [sketch] 1910, *The Jead of the House* [sketch] 1910, etc), whilst Brigata worked as a performer, a not very successful producer, sometime composer (*A Capital Joke* 1889, *The Prancing Girl* 1891) and, most particularly, a conductor, a position which, like his father, he held for a period at the Theatre Royal, Drury Lane.

1862 **Catching a Husband** 1 act Royalty Theatre 21 April

1865 **Love Wins the Way** (Finlay Finlayson) 1 act Gallery of Illustration 24 October

1876 **Pom** (Bucalossi) Royalty Theatre 25 March

1876 **Coming Events** (Bucalossi) 1 act Royalty Theatre 22 April

1879 **Rothomago** (w Edward Solomon, Gaston Serpette, Frederic Clay/H B Farnie) Alhambra Theatre 22 December

1881 **The Stores** (Edward Rose, Augustus Harris) 1 act Theatre Royal, Drury Lane 14 March

1882 **(Les) Manteaux Noirs** (Harry Paulton, Walter Parke) Avenue Theatre 3 June

1884 **Lallah Rookh** (Horace Lennard) Novelty Theatre 1 May

1889 **Delia** (Frank Desprez) Prince's Theatre, Bristol 11 March

1892 **Brother George** (Desprez) Theatre Royal, Portsmouth 16 May

1894 **Massaroni** (F Leslie Moreton, Arthur Rousbey) Leinster Hall, Dublin 23 January

1896 **En Route** (ex- *Bombay to Henley*) (w Ernest Bucalossi/Parke, Cecil Maxwell) Parkhurst Theatre 21 September

Other titles attributed: *Dolly's Wedding, The Market Girl, The Great Grand Duke*

THE BUCCANEER Musical play in 2 acts by Sandy Wilson. New Watergate Theatre, London, 8 September 1953; Lyric Theatre, Hammersmith, 8 September 1955.

Wilson's successor to *The Boy Friend,* and deliberately written in a different though equally light vein, *The Buccaneer* told the tiny tale of the attempt to save a comic

paper embodying the virtues of old Britain. At first mounted, like *The Boy Friend,* in a club venue, it was later given a more substantial production by H M Tennent Ltd in which Kenneth Williams repeated his singular performance as a precocious child, with some success.
Recordings: London cast (HMV, AEI), etc

BUCHANAN, Jack [BUCHANAN, Walter John] (b Helensburgh, Scotland, 2 April 1891; d London, 20 October 1957). Dance and comedy star of the London theatre between the wars.

Buchanan made his first London appearance as a slim, dapper, dancing juvenile man at the age of 21, in the small role of the dancing-master Deschamps in the Austro-American musical *The Grass Widows* (1912), and he subsequently mixed revue engagements—notably a personal success in Charlot's *Bubbly* in 1917—with a tour in George Grossmith's role of Dudley Mitten in *Tonight's the Night* and short periods in London's *Wild Geese* (1920, Bill Malcolm) and *Faust on Toast* (1921, Faust). His first book musical success came when he starred as the titular Mr Alfred Butler in the six-month run of his own production, *Battling Butler* (1922), and he followed this by appearing as the eponymous *Toni* in Grossmith and Malone's touring adaptation of the Berlin musical *Der Fürst von Pappenheim,* leaving the show on the road to go to America for André Charlot.

After scoring a fine Broadway success in *Charlot's Revue* (1924), he returned to Britain to take up the part of Toni for a London season and he followed this with 20 further years of starring roles in musical comedy, interspersed with both musical and light comedy films. He began his stage series with his own production of the circus musical *Boodle* (1925, Algernon Kenilworth) and followed up with a good run as the hero of *Sunny* (1926, Jim Deming) before, in 1928, beginning his celebrated top-of-the-bill partnership with dancing comedienne Elsie Randolph.

Miss Randolph, who had been seen in minor roles in *Battling Butler* and *Toni* and better ones in *Boodle,* where she still gave second best to June, and *Sunny* became a wisecracking foil to Buchanan's suave light comedy and a superb dancing partner in a stage relationship which, like that of the Astaires, was a humorous one rather than a romantic one. In *That's a Good Girl* (1928, Bill Barrow)—produced, directed and choreographed (w Anton Dolin) by Buchanan—they blended the lightest of comedy, dance and song to a nicety and to the taste of the age for 363 London performances, a tour and a film. As producer, Buchanan did better here than with *Lady Mary* (w Lee Ephraim), which he mounted in the same year, but in which he did not appear. Thereafter, his producing ventures were limited to shows in which his own attractive name topped the bill.

Plate 55. **Jack Buchanan** *and* **Elsie Randolph.** *Britain's favorite pair of dance-and-laughter merchants.*

Buchanan filmed *Paris* (1930) in Hollywood, then returned to Britain for a new stage show, *Stand Up and Sing* (1931, Rockingham Smith), in which he added a coauthor's credit to his previous multiple functions. This piece happily repeated the West End success of the previous musical, as did the delightful *Mr Whittington* (1933–34, Dick Whittington) in which the favorite pair appeared for Moss' Empires through a tour and nearly three-hundred London performances. After a mistaken venture into the Erik Charell flop *The Flying Trapeze* (1935, René), a spectacular circus piece based on a potpourri of music by Ralph Benatzky, he returned to Miss Randolph, his accepted matinée idol style and to the way of success in his own production of *This'll Make You Whistle* (1935–36, Bill Hopping) and its subsequent film. The pair appeared happily together one last time, after a collaboration of more than 15 years, in *It's Time to Dance* (1943, Willmot Brown).

In between, Buchanan had made one of his periodic trips to New York, this time for his first Broadway book musical, *Between the Devil* (1937, Peter Anthony), filmed *The Gang's All Here* (1939) and produced and directed an unfortunate Chopin potpourri called *Waltz without End* (Cambridge Theatre, 1942), but thereafter his theatrical activities became more sporadic. In 1947 he produced *Good Night Vienna,* which he had filmed so successfully more than a decade previously, as a tour with Bernard Delfont, he appeared in the revue *Fine Feathers* and, at 60 years of age, took over the suave, young lead role of *King's Rhapsody* following Ivor Novello's death. The Hollywood film of *The Bandwagon* (1953) showed that he was no longer either young or suave and, although he still evinced producing interest in the 1950s, that side of his career ended, similarly, on a gentle fade.

Biography: Marshall, M: *Top Hat and Tails* (Elm Tree, London, 1978)

BUCHBINDER, Bernhard [KLINGER, Gustav] (b Pest, 7 July ?1854; d Vienna, ?24 June 1922).

At first a journalist on the *Neues Pester Journal* in his native Budapest, Klinger-Buchbinder (whose date of birth is given variously as anything between 1849 and 1854, and on the 6th, 7th or 8th of July) first found success as the author of backstairs novels, and it was not until, already well into his thirties, he quit Hungary for Austria and fiction for a career in the theatre, that he entered the most successful phase of his writing life.

His first substantial attempts in the musical theatre were in a collaboration with conductor/composer Rudolf Raimann on a piece played at Munich and with the Operette *Colombine* ''based on an idea by Julius Riegen'' and set to music by Hans von Zois. Produced at Graz, this latter was sufficiently successful to be subsequently taken up by Fritz Steiner for the Carltheater (15 March 1889), where it was directed by Carl Adolf Friese and played by a cast including Wilhelm Knaack and Emma Seebold. However, Buchbinder had, by then, already broken into the metropolitan theatre with his adaptation of Scribe's *Ne touchez pas à la reine* as the text to Alfred Zamara's *Der Sänger von Palermo,* produced at the same theatre with the same director and stars the previous year, but neither piece stayed long in the repertoire, and the author turned to operatic ventures with Raoul Mader's Spieloper *Die Flüchtlinge,* produced at the Hofoper (19 February 1891), and Robert Fuchs' *Die Teufelsglocke,* played at Leipzig in 1893, and to plays, both adapted from the Hungarian and original, before finally venturing into the world of the musical comedy.

A collaboration with top-flight Operette writer A M Willner produced three libretti, including that of *Die Göttin der Vernunft* for Johann Strauss, of which *Der Schmetterling* (57 performances) was the most successful, but real success finally came when he returned to collaborate with his earliest partner, Rudolf Raimann, now musical director at the Theater in der Josefstadt. Together, the two men produced the highly successful Posse *Er und seine Schwester* (80 performances), in which the wife of the theatre's manager, Josef Jarno, the star soubrette Hansi Niese, starred alongside Alexander Girardi. Vienna's original version of *Er und seine Schwester* was repeated regularly in seasons to follow and became a major hit in Budapest as *A postás fíu és a huga* and they followed up with a series of like collaborations, notably *Das Wäschermädl* as a vehicle for Niese (38 performances, *A szoknyashos* 15 June 1906 in Hungary) and *Der Schusterbub* (53 performances) which again paired Niese and Girardi. However, Buchbinder's most enduring success came with yet another vehicle for Niese, a romantic musical comedy written in collaboration with composer Georg Jarno, the star's brother-in-law. The countrified tale of *Die Förster-Christl* and her attractions for the Austrian emperor was one of the most popular pieces of its era—an era which was under the sway of the very differently spiced *Die lustige Witwe,* produced a couple of years earlier—and, after a fine first run, it remained in the repertoire for many decades thereafter.

Buchbinder collaborated with Jarno (*Das Musikantenmädel, Die Marinen-Gustl*), Zerkovitz (*Die Wundermühle*) and Leo Ascher (*Botschafterin Leni*) on further pieces for the Josefstädter Theater and Niese, most of which were subsequently played in Germany and in Hungary (*A Muzikusleány* 4 April 1911, *Tengerész Kató* 21 September 1912, *Kotnyeles naccsága* 4 April 1915), and some of which made it to the German-language theatres of America (*Das Musikantenmädel, Frau Gretl,* Irving Place Theatre 25 December 1991 w Mathilde Cottrelly, etc), before moving on to center his activity on Berlin, where Girardi had had a considerable success with his Posse *Immer oben auf* in the years before and during the First World War. There, he had the second of his most important musical comedy successes when he collaborated with the tried producer/author team of Jean Kren and Alfred Schönfeld on the book and lyrics for Ascher's *Der Soldat der Marie.* This was the first of six mostly successful musical plays written for the Berlin theatre over the next few years, to scores variously by Jean Gilbert, Robert Winterberg and Ascher. Gilbert's *Das Vagabundenmädel* ran for nearly 200 performances at the Thalia-Theater and was played in Hungary as *Csavargolány* (Budapesti Színház 22 November 1918), Ascher's *Egon und seine Frauen* played seven months at the Thalia and *Jungfer Sonnenschein* was seen 140 times at the same house following a season at the Carltheater in Vienna. At the Neues Operettenhaus, *Die Dame vom Zirkus* passed the 200-performance mark in its first run and was revived soon after and *Prinzessin Friedl* held the stage for three months, whilst *Graf Habenichts* was played successfully at the Wallner-Theater.

Buchbinder died in 1922 (on a date almost as ill agreed-upon as that of his birth), after a career of nearly

20 successful years in the theatre during which his pieces had been widely and successfully played in Austria, Germany and Hungary. Posthumously, his *Nachtfalter* (1926) was produced in Bozen, his version of the Hans Müller Posse mit Gesang *Morgen geht's uns gut,* with music by Ralph Benatzky, was produced at the Raimundtheater (31 August 1929), and his name appeared as the author of the screenplay to the musical film *Versuchen sie meine Schwester?*

His libretto (w Willner) for *Die Göttin der Vernunft* was later made over to become the text for the rather more successful *Der Graf von Luxemburg.*

1887 **Studenten am Rhein** (Josef Goldstein) 1 act Pest 8 January

1887 **Das Ellishorn** (Rudolf Raimann/w Philippi) Theater am Gärtnerplatz, Munich 7 May

1887 **Colombine** (Hans von Zois) Graz 12 November; Carltheater, Vienna 15 March 1889

1888 **Der Sänger von Palermo** (Alfred Zamara/Scribe ad) Carltheater 14 February

1890 **Held Marko** (*Der Mameluck Napoléons*) (Emil Rosé) St Petersburg December

1891 **Die Flüchtlinge** (Raoul Mader) Hofoper 19 February

1893 **Das Wiener Volkslied** (Karl Kleiber) Theater in der Josefstadt 21 October

1894 **Heirat auf Probe** (Leopold Kuhn/C Görss/Karl Gerő ad w Ferenc Rajna) Theater an der Wien 7 April

1895 **Der Heirathsschwindler** (Max von Weinzierl) Raimundtheater 5 October

1896 **Der Schmetterling** (Carl Weinberger/w A M Willner) Theater an der Wien 7 November

1896 **Ein kecker Schnabel** (Leopold Natzler) Raimundtheater 14 November

1897 **Die Göttin der Vernunft** (Johann Strauss/w Willner) Theater an der Wien 13 March

1897 **Verlogenes Volk** (von Weinzierl) Raimundtheater 18 November

1898 **Die Küchenkomtesse** (*A kuktakisasszony*) German version w add music by Raimann (Theater an der Wien)

1898 **Fräulein Hexe** (Josef Bayer/w Willner) Theater an der Wien 19 November

1900 **Die Diva** (Weinberger/w Josef Wattke) Carltheater 12 October

1901 **Die dritte Eskadron** Theater an der Wien 2 November

1902 **Der Spatz** (Weinberger) Deutsches Volkstheater 14 January

1902 **Er und seine Schwester** (Raimann) Theater in der Josefstadt 11 April

1903 **Der Musikant und sein Weib** (Raimann) Theater an der Wien 12 April

1903 **Der Glücklichste** (Hans Cesek) Carltheater 25 April

1903 **48 Stunden Urlaub** (Ludwig Gothov-Grüneke) Raimundtheater 7 November

1903 **Der Mameluck** revised *Held Marko* (Ludwig Schytte/w Mór Jókai) Carltheater 22 December

1905 **Das Wäschermädl** (Raimann) Theater in der Josefstadt 31 March

1906 **Der Schusterbub** (Raimann) Theater in der Josefstadt 16 January

1907 **Sie und ihr Mann** (Raimann) Raimundtheater 5 April

1907 **Der Eintagskönig** (Raimann/w Hans Liebstockl) Lustspieltheater 15 May

1907 **Die Förster-Christl** (Jarno) Theater in der Josefstadt 17 December

1908 **Immer oben auf** (Paul Lincke/Alfred Schönfeld/w Jean Kren) Thalia-Theater, Berlin 22 January

1909 **Paula macht alles** (Raimann) Theater in der Josefstadt 23 March

1909 **Der Weiberfeind** (Alfred Rieger) Bellevue Theater, Stettin 10 December

1910 **Das Musikantenmädel** (Jarno) Theater in der Josefstadt 18 February

1911 **Die Frau Gretl** (Raimann) Theater in der Josefstadt 7 April

1911 **Das neue Mädchen** (Richard Fronz) Bürgertheater 2 September

1912 **Die Marinen-Gustl** (Jarno) Theater in der Josefstadt 22 March

1912 **Unser Stammhalter** (Raimann) Lustspieltheater 15 November

1914 **Die Wundermühle** (Béla Zerkovitz) Theater in der Josefstadt 24 March

1915 **Botschafterin Leni** (Leo Ascher) Theater in der Josefstadt 19 February

1916 **Der Soldat der Marie** (Ascher/Schönfeld/w Kren) Neues Operettentheater, Berlin 2 September

1916 **Das Vagabundenmädel** (Jean Gilbert/Schönfeld/w Kren) Thalia-Theater, Berlin 2 December

1917 **Egon und seine Frauen** (Ascher/w Kren) Thalia-Theater, Berlin 25 August

1918 **Jungfer Sonnenschein** (Jarno) Volksoper, Hamburg 16 February; Carltheater 18 May

1918 **Graf Habenichts** (Robert Winterberg/w Kren) Wallner-Theater, Berlin 4 September

1919 **Die Dame vom Zirkus** (Winterberg/w Kren) Neues Operettentheater, Berlin 31 May

1920 **Prinzessin Friedl** (Ascher/w Kren) Neues Operettentheater, Berlin 14 May

1926 **Ein Nachtmanöver** (*Der Nachtfalter*) (Weinberger/w Mathilde Schurz) Bozen March

BUCKLEY, Betty [Lynn] (b Big Springs, Tex, 3 July 1947).

After early performances in her native Texas, Betty Buckley was first seen on Broadway when she created the role of Martha Jefferson in *1776* (1969), introducing "He Plays the Violin." She followed this up by appearing as Fran Kubelik in London's production of *Promises, Promises* later the same year, and was next seen in New York in the short-lived off-Broadway piece *The Ballad of Johnny Pot* (1971). She later succeeded to the role of Catherine in *Pippin* in a career which moved on to embrace film (*Carrie, Tender Mercies*) and television (*Eight is Enough*) as well as musical theatre (*I'm Getting My Act Together and Taking It on the Road*) and cabaret, and returned to Broadway to appear as Grizabella in the American production of *Cats* (1982).

She subsequently created the role of Drood in the musicalization of *The Mystery of Edwin Drood* (1986), replaced Bernadette Peters in Broadway's version of *Song and Dance,* took the role of Carrie's mother, Margaret White, created in Britain by Barbara Cook, in the Broadway version of the musical based on the film, *Carrie,* appeared in Washington top-billed in a compilation musical called *Stardust* (1990), succeeded with notable success to the role of Norma Desmond in *Sunset Boulevard* both in London and on Broadway (1996), and appeared in the musical version of Marivaux's *Triumph of Love* (1997, Hesione). In 1998 she appeared regionally as Rose in *Gypsy.*

BUDAY, Dénes (b Budapest, 8 October 1890; d Budapest, 19 October 1963).

Composer and conductor Buday won his early success as a writer of vocal music, and made his first venture on to the musical stage in Vienna with a one-act opera, *Loreley,* before finding his way into the lighter musical theatre. He had his first big success with the operett *Csárdás,* produced at the Budai Színkör with Hanna Honthy starred, and subsequently had a second hit with the same star in the 1941 *Fityfiritty.* His preferred musical mixture of native Hungarian operett elements and modern dance rhythms was also employed in film in Hungary and in Germany.

1916 **Fogadjunk!** (Imre Harmath) Budai Színkör 21 July

1921 **Matyas Király** (w Frigyes Fridl/Andor Zsoldos) Magyar Királyi Operaház 18 September

1923 **A kék póstakocsi** (Szilágyi) Várszínház 22 December

1926 **Ki a Tisza vizét issza** (Harmath) Kisfaludy Színház 3 September

1927 **Diákszerelem** (Ernő Andai/Ernő Innocent Vincze) Kisfaludy Színház May

1929 **Erdélyi diákok** (Andai/Innocent Vincze) Budai Színkör 31 August

1936 **Csárdás** (László Szilágyi) Budai Színkör 16 June

1936 **Szakitani nehéz dolog** (Mihály Szécsen/Kálmán Csántho) Magyar Színház 12 December

1940 **Három huszár** (Szilágyi, Gyula Halász) Fővárosi Operettszínház 12 April

1941 **Fityfiritty** (Rudolf Halász) Fővárosi Operettszínház 8 March

1941 **Csodatükör** (József Babay) Fővárosi Operettszínház 7 October

1943 **Egy boldog pesti nyár** (w Mihály Eisemann, Szabolcs Fényes/Szilágyi, Attila Orbok) Fővárosi Operettszínház 14 April

1943 **A tábornokné** (Miklós Toth, Kálmán Vandor) Magyar Színház 24 April

1956 **Három szegény szabólegény** (Babay) Petőfi Színház 20 January

BUDDIES Comedy of quaint Brittany in 2 acts and an epilogue by George V Hobart. Music and lyrics by B C Hilliam. Selwyn Theater, New York, 27 October 1919.

The postwartime *Buddies* set a familiar little love story in the battered fields of Brittany to the accompaniment of a ration of love songs, a few numbers colored with the kind of common-man-at-war sentiments which had so successfully been used in the recent *The Better 'Ole,* and some unashamedly sentimental recreations of the kind of moments in wartime France that the returned soldiers were happy to remember.

When Babe (Roland Young), Sonny (Donald Brian) and their American army pals are billeted in the French farmhouse of Madame Benoît (Camille Dalberg), Babe takes the opportunity to fall in love with young Julie Benoît (Peggy Wood). But he is too shy to express his feelings and Julie, hoping to make him speak, flirts instead with Sonny. It is an old trick, but it works. The score by B C Hilliam (subsequently Mr Flotsam of the British variety act "Flotsam and Jetsam") featured such longing titles as "Hello, Home," "My Buddies," "The Homes They Hold So Dear" and "To Be Together Is the Thing," as well as the good old-fashioned "Fairy Tales" (known as The Cinderella Song), the half-hesitant "Darling, I . . ." and the praises of "My Indispensable Girl." The interpolations included a Cole Porter/Melville Gideon piece called "I Never Realized." The evening's top musical moment came, however, in the piece known as The Italie Marching Song: "Oh! Tell Me Where My Buddie [*sic*] Is."

Arch Selwyn's production of *Buddies*—originally subtitled "a comedy of quaint Brittany," but later just "a merry musical play"—had a grand success and a 265-performance run on Broadway before going on the road. It provoked a follow-up from author Hobart in the sentimental melodrama *Sonny* (Cort Theater 16 August 1921, 80 performances), which was not, in fact, about the character of the previous piece, but simply another wartime tale musicked this time by Raymond Hubbell. It also encouraged Hilliam to a second musical, *Princess Virtue* (Central Theater 4 May 1921), which did not repeat the success of *Buddies.* It flopped in two weeks. A later musical show, featuring Bill "Bojangles" Robinson and Adelaide Hall in another World War I jaunt, called itself *Brown Buddies* (Liberty Theater 7 October 1930) through 111 performances.

A BUNCH OF KEYS, or The Hotel Musical comedy in 3 acts by Charles Hoyt [and Willie Edouin]. Music selected and arranged by Watty Hydes. Park Theater, Newark, NJ, 13 December 1882; San Francisco Minstrels' Opera House, New York, 26 March 1883.

An ''original operatic absurdity,'' otherwise a farce comedy, combining the most obvious of low comedy mixed with broad songs and dances, *A Bunch of Keys* was commissioned from the then theatrically unknown Charles H Hoyt by actor-manager Willie Edouin as a vehicle for himself, his wife Alice Atherton, and his troupe, Willie Edouin's Sparks. Hoyt turned out the umpteenth piece of recent decades which used a musical comedy will as its centerpiece, but managed to imbue the tale with enough differences and, above all, enough exuberantly popular humor to make it a long-touring favorite.

Edouin played Littleton Snaggs, a lawyer, who is responsible for disposing of an unprofitable hotel which has been left to whichever of the three Keys sisters (Alice Atherton, Anna Günther, Anna Brevoort) is adjudged the plainest. Although their gentleman friends are willing to accept the stigma for what they think will be the profit, the girls are not. Before a happy ending was reached, with faces literally saved all round, Miss Atherton in particular (''Arthur and Martha,'' ''I Won't Play with You Any More'') and the rest of the company in their turn had entertained with a two-act barrage of movable song and dance numbers, gathered from hither and yon, and an album of character impersonations. The young James T Powers played the hotel's bellboy, Grimes, in a flurry of acrobatics and physical comedy, and director-of-the-future Julian Mitchell was Gilly Spooner ''devoted to Rose.''

In the wake of the success of *Fun on the Bristol* and of *My Sweetheart,* similar loose-limbed pieces crowded into the British provinces in the 1880s, but Edouin ventured a version of *A Bunch of Keys* (ad George Lash Gordon) in the sophisticated purlieus of London. There, in spite of a cast including himself and his wife, Powers, and worthy locals Hetty Chapman and Irene Verona (both future ''heavies'') as the other two sisters, it was greeted as ''pitiful trash'' and bundled quickly out of town. Australia got a glimpse of the piece in 1897 when Harry Rickards toured it in secondary and variety-orientated houses. The show was still to be seen on the American road in the early years of the 20th century.

Like others of Hoyt's widely popular works, *A Bunch of Keys* served as the source for an early silent film. John Slavin and June Keith featured.

UK: Avenue Theatre 25 August 1883; Australia: Opera House, Brisbane 18 September 1897

Film: (silent) Essanay 1915

BUONA NOTTE, BETTINA Musical comedy in 2 acts by Pietro Garinei and Sandro Giovannini. Music by Gorni Kramer. Teatro Lirico, Milan, 14 November 1956.

An Italian musical play avowedly suggested by Françoise Sagan's success with her novel, *Bonjour tristesse, Buona Notte, Bettina* featured Walter Chiari and Delia Scala in a tale of what happens when a demure young lady writes a risqué novel. Following its success on home ground, the piece was seen in several Eastern European countries (Poland, Eastern Germany, Hungary, Czechoslovakia), in Spain as *Buenas nochas Bettina* (Teatro de la Commedia 31 December 1958), Portugal, South America and in Britain (ad Ted Willis, Ken Ferrey, Eric Shaw, Sonny Miller) where Jack Hylton mounted the show as *When in Rome . . .* with Dickie Henderson and June Laverick in the leading roles (298 performances).

UK: Adelphi Theatre *When in Rome . . .* 26 December 1959; Germany: Rostock *Gute Nacht Bettina* 13 February 1966; Hungary: Fővárosi Operettszínház *Tigris a garázsban* 21 October 1966

Recordings: original cast (Carisch), *When in Rome* (Oriole) 45 rpm

BURANI, Paul [ROUCOUX, Urbain] (b Paris, 26 March 1845; d Paris, 9 October 1901). Prolific, all-purpose Parisian author whose successes included several in the musical theatre.

At first a clerk in the public service, then a part-time actor, Burani made himself a name as a popular singer-songwriter, performing his own compositions in the cafés-concerts (''Les Pompiers de Nanterre,'' ''Le Sire de Fish-Tong-Kang,'' ''Pour vingt-cinq francs,'' etc) whilst continuing to hold down his day job in a government office. He wrote lavishly for both magazines and newspapers (*Gil Blas, L'Evènement, L'Estaffette,* etc), authored tales (*Contes de la Chambrée*), authored novels, and at one stage founded his own satirical journal which in its short life earned him three months in prison for ''intemperance of language.'' He was also prominent in the Parisian theatre for a period of 20 years as the eclectic author of everything from revues (with composers of the quality of Varney, Vasseur and Hervé) to melodramas (*Le Metropolitain de Londres,* etc), and from vaudevilles to libretti and lyrics for opérette—ultimately making it to the Opéra-Comique with the text to Chabrier's *Le Roi malgré lui* (w Émile de Najac, 18 May 1887)—as well as a barrage of military, fairy and modern spectaculars (*Coco Fêlé, Orient-Express,* etc).

Amongst his early works, Burani had long-running opérette successes with two pieces written with Maxime Boucheron and composed by Léon Vasseur (*Le Droit du seigneur, Le Billet de logement*), provided the text for *La Cantinière* to Planquette and scored a considerable hit with Bernicat's internationally played *François les bas-*

bleus (*Victor the Bluestocking, Fanchon, Die Strassensängerin, Kék Feri, Fantine,* etc). He subsequently wrote two further pieces with the young composer who had finished the uncompleted score for Bernicat's posthumous piece, André Messager, in *La Fauvette du Temple* and *Le Bourgeois de Calais.* He also adapted Dumas's *Le Mariage au tambour* (*Die Marktenderin, Esketés dobszóval*) to the spectacular musical stage, provided Audran with the text for his *Le Puits qui parle* (*A beszélő kut* in Hungary) and had a further success with the text to Planquette's *Le Talisman* (*The Talisman, A varázgyűrű*).

The most celebrated of his vaudevilles, *Le Cabinet Piperlin* (w Hippolyte Raymond), originally written to be played as a musical comedy but ultimately presented without music, was later played as a musical both in France (*Le Cabinet Piperlin*) and in England (*The Antelope,* Waldorf Theatre 28 November 1908). He was also credited, with Maurice Ordonneau, as the author of the original of Ordonneau's subsequent text for the highly successful *Madame Sherry.*

1873 **Pomponne et Fridolin** (w Carlo Wansinck, Émile Clerc) Théâtre des Batignolles 2 August; Ba-ta-clan 3 September

1875 **Le Neveu du Colonel** (Léopold Wenzel/w Wansinck) 1 act Alcazar 30 September

1875 **Absalon** (Campésiano/w Alfred Pouillon) 1 act Folies-Bergère 13 November; Alcazar 25 May 1876

1876 **Les Oeufs de Pâques** (J Müller) 1 act Scala 10 April

1877 **La Goguette** (Antonin Louis/w Hippolyte Raymond) Théâtre de l'Athenée 13 April

1878 **Le Droit du seigneur** (Léon Vasseur/w Maxime Boucheron) Fantaisies-Parisiennes 13 December

1879 **Mon gendre, tout est rompu** (Auguste Coedès/w William Busnach) 1 act Casino de Dieppe 22 August

1879 **Le Billet de logement** (Vasseur/w Boucheron) Théâtre des Fantaisies-Parisiennes 15 November

1880 **Madame Grégoire** (Édouard Okolowicz, et al/w Maurice Ordonneau) Théâtre des Arts 20 May

1880 **La Cantinière** (Robert Planquette/w Félix Ribeyre) Théâtre des Nouveautés 26 October

1881 **La Reine des Halles** (Louis Varney/w Alfred Delacour, Victor Bernard) Comédie Parisienne 4 April

1882 **Le Petit Parisien** (Vasseur/w Boucheron) Théâtre des Folies-Dramatiques 16 January

1882 **Mimi-Pinson** (Gustave Michiels/uncredited w Ordonneau, Arthur Verneuil) Théâtre Cluny 14 March

1882 **Un carnaval** (Campésiano/w Pouillon) 1 act St Germain-en-Laye 6 May

1882 **La Barbière improvisée** (Joseph O'Kelly/w Jules Montini) 1 act Salle Herz 10 December; Théâtre des Bouffes-Parisiens 1 May 1884

1882 **La 1002ème Nuit** (Lucien Poujade/w P Richard) Reims 27 December; Théâtre du Château d'Eau 8 July 1885

1883 **François les bas-bleus** (Firmin Bernicat, André Messager/w Ernest Dubreuil, Eugène Humbert) Théâtre des Folies-Dramatiques 8 November

1883 **Fanfreluche** (revised *La Nuit de Saint-Germain*) (Gaston Serpette/Gaston Hirsch, Raoul de Saint-Arroman ad) Théâtre de la Renaissance 16 December

1885 **Le Mariage au tambour** (Vasseur) Théâtre du Châtelet 4 April

1885 **Coco-fêlé** (uncredited/w Paul Ferrier, E Floury fils) Théâtre du Châtelet 26 September

1885 **La Fauvette du Temple** (Messager/w Humbert) Théâtre des Folies-Dramatiques 17 November

1885 **La Cremaillère** (Planquette/w Albert Brasseur) Théâtre des Nouveautés 28 November

1887 **Ninon** (Vasseur/w Émile Blavet, Emil AndréThéâtre des Nouveautés 23 March

1887 **Le Bourgeois de Calais** (Messager/w Dubreuil) Théâtre des Folies-Dramatiques 6 April

1887 **Le Roi malgré lui** (Emmanuel Chabrier/w Emile de Najac) Opéra-Comique 18 May

1888 **Le Puits qui parle** (Edmond Audran/w Alexandre Beaumont) Théâtre des Nouveautés 15 March

1888 **La Belle Sophie** (Edmond Missa/w Eugène Adenis) Théâtre des Menus-Plaisirs 11 April

1889 **Le Prince Soleil** (Vasseur/w Hippolyte Raymond) Théâtre du Châtelet 11 July

1890 **Orient-Express** (Goudesone) Théâtre du Châtelet 12 July

1891 **Compère Guilleri** (Henri Perry/w Jean Cavalier) Théâtre des Menus-Plaisirs 18 September

1892 **Le Commandant Laripète** (Vasseur/w Armand Silvestre, Albin Valabrègue) Palais-Royal 3 March

1893 **Le Talisman** (Planquette/w Adolphe d'Ennery) Théâtre de la Gaîté 20 January

1893 **Jean Raisin** (Marius Carman) Théâtre des Folies-Dramatiques 30 March

1894 **L'Élève de Conservatoire** (Wenzel/w Henri Kéroul) Théâtre des Menus-Plaisirs 29 November

1895 **Les Vingt-huit jours de Champignolette** (Planquette) Théâtre de la République 17 September

1896 **Rivoli** (André Wormser/w Michel Carré) Théâtre des Folies-Dramatiques 30 October

1897 **Le Cabinet Piperlin** (Hervé/w Raymond) Théâtre de l'Athénée Comique 17 September

1902 **La Bouquetière du Château d'Eau** (Constantin Lubomirski) Théâtre du Château d'Eau 10 January

1902 **Madame Sherry** (Hugo Felix/w M Ordonneau ad Benno Jacobson) Centraltheater, Berlin 1 November

BURKE, Billie [BURKE, Mary William Ethelbert Appleton] (b Washington, DC, 7 August 1884; d Los Angeles, 14 May 1970).

The daughter of entertainer William E Burke (b Waterford, Ohio, 1843; d Huddersfield, England, 5 October 1906) of the team of Burke, Andrus and Frisco, ''Billie'' Burke played in British pantomime and variety before she made her first musical comedy appearance, at the age of 17, playing an American girl in George Edwardes and

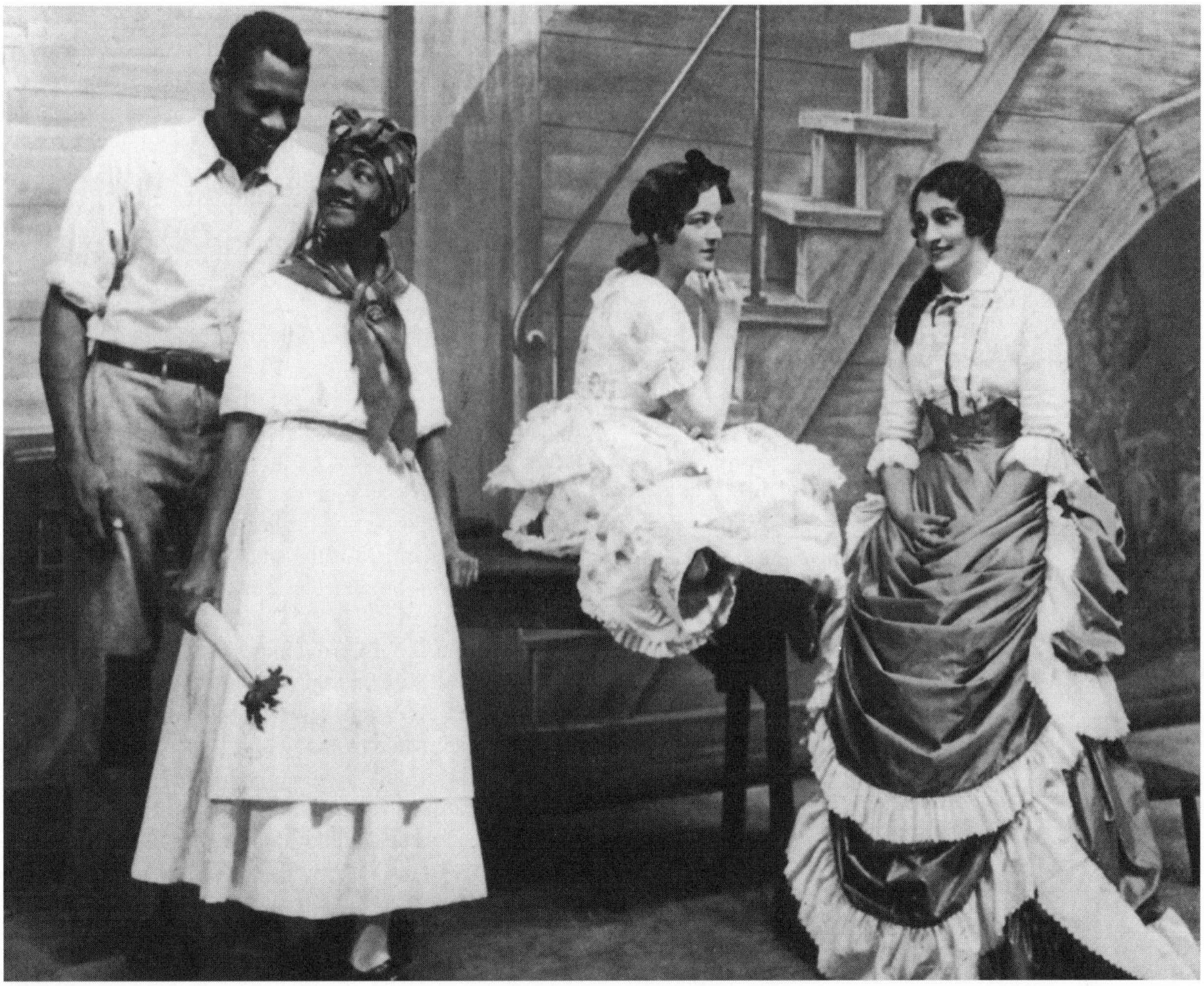

Plate 56. **Marie Burke** *as Julie in London's* Show Boat, *alongside Paul Robeson (Joe), Alberta Hunter (Queenie) and Edith Day (Magnolia).*

Charles Frohman's London production of *The School Girl,* and performing Leslie Stuart's ''My Little Canoe.'' She took over the soubrette role in Edwardes's *The Duchess of Dantzic* (1903) and toured in the juvenile part of the same piece, played a supporting role in Robert Courtneidge's London production of *The Blue Moon* and appeared in both revue and variety before succeeding to the much squabbled-over lead role of *The Belle of Mayfair* for its last performances.

She made the largest part of her subsequent career in non-musical theatre and film and in the real-life role of Mrs Florenz Ziegfeld jr, but she returned to the musical stage just once in the title role of Annabelle Leigh (whom she had portrayed in the 1919 film of the play *Good Gracious Annabelle,* on which the show was based) in Ziegfeld's musical *Annie Dear* (1924). On film, during a long and successful career as an often feather-headed character lady, she memorably devoted the remnants of her pretty voice to the role of the good witch, Glinda, in *The Wizard of Oz* (1939). She also appeared in the 1940 film of *Irene* as Mrs Vincent, in *The Barkleys of Broadway* (1949, Millie Belney), and was herself portrayed on film, in her lifetime, by Myrna Loy in *The Great Ziegfeld* (1936).

Memoirs: *With a Feather on My Nose* (Appleton-Century-Crofts, New York, 1949), *With Powder on My Nose* (Coward, McCann, New York, 1959)

BURKE, Marie [ALT, Marie Rosa] (b London, 18 October 1894; d London, 21 March 1988).

Trained as a vocalist in Italy, Marie Burke (the ''Burke'' came from her early but brief marriage to a fellow student, operatic tenor Tom Burke) began her career in opera, appearing as Musetta at Verona and as Nedda and Micaëla in a small Milan theatre. She gave several concerts in Italy before returning to Britain in 1917 and made her first stage appearance there in London as Isilda in C B Cochran's production of *Afgar* (1919). She subsequently played in *Make It Snappy* and *The Lady in Ermine* (Sophie Lavalle, then Mariana) in America before touring in a concert party in Britain and then going first to South Africa, and then to Australia, as a vocalist in a variety combination with Arthur Klein. During her stay in Australia, the Williamson & Tait organization hired her for their musical comedy company, and she spent the next three and a half years in Australia appearing in starring roles in the highly successful local productions of *Wildflower* (Nina) and *Katja the Dancer* (Katja), in *The Cousin from Nowhere* (Julia, replacement) and in *Frasquita* (Frasquita).

On returning to London, she was cast in the part of Julie in London's *Show Boat* and she followed up as a series of titled and often exotic ladies in the appalling *Open Your Eyes* (Countess Zanini), the unsuccessful *The Student Prince* (Margaret), Drury Lane's *The Song of the Drum* (Countess Olga von Haultstein) and the long-running London version of *Walzer aus Wien* (another Countess Olga). She then joined Bobby Howes at the Saville Theatre as the vamp of *He Wanted Adventure* (1933, Ziska) before, the following year, repeating her *Walzer aus Wien* role in New York.

She subsequently appeared largely in non-musical theatre, whilst continuing to sing in variety and concert and as a popular principal boy in pantomime, making late musical theatre appearances in her sixties in *King's Rhapsody* and *Happy Holiday* (1954, Hon Fiona McLeod).

Her sometime husband, **Tom BURKE** [Thomas Aspinall BURKE] (b Leigh, Lancs, 2 March 1890; d Sutton, 13 September 1969), after a dazzling opera debut alongside Melba at Covent Garden in 1919, soon found himself ''relegated'' to musical comedy, variety, revue, concert and concert party work. He was seen in the musical theatre in Broadway's *The Dancing Girl* (1923, Rudolpho, introducing George Gershwin's 'Why Am I Sad?''), *The Mikado* (1925, Nanki-Poo), *HMS Pinafore* (1926, Ralph) and the 15-performance *The Lace Petticoat* (1927, Paul Joscelyn) and in London in *Dear Love* (1929, Pierre) and the flop *The Gay Masqueraders* (1935, Carol).

Their daughter **Patricia BURKE** (b Milan, 23 April 1917), after an early career in straight theatre (and one musical appearance in *Nymph Errant,* aged 16), worked through supporting roles in the foolish *Take It Easy* (1937, Ruth Marsden), the Cicely Courtneidge/Bobby Howes *Hide and Seek* (1937, Rene), *Sitting Pretty* (1939, Mary Pugh) and several revues, and became a musical leading lady in the stage and film versions of the topical wartime musical *The Lisbon Story* (1943, Gabrielle). Thereafter she returned largely to the straight theatre, appearing on the musical stage only briefly in *Romance in Candlelight* (1955), *Belle* (1961) and in succession to Hy Hazell in *Charlie Girl.*

BURKHARD, Paul (b Zürich, 21 December 1911; d Zell-im-Tösstal, 6 September 1977). Modest Swiss composer who notched up a show and song hit when one of his little pieces was glitzed up into a revusical entertainment.

Burkhard studied at the Zürich Conservatoire and subsequently worked as a repetiteur and then conductor at the Berne Stadttheater (1932–35) and at the Zürich Schauspielhaus (1939–45) before becoming the musical director of the Beromünster radio orchestra (1945–57). After a local success with his first piece, *Hopsa* (text and music), a Swiss Operette with a trendy American setting, he composed two further theatre scores before he turned out the songs for the small-scale Lokalstuck *Der schwarze Hecht,* produced at Zürich's Schauspielhaus in 1939. A decade later, Erik Charell partly rewrote, and gave a very much larger and thoroughly extravagant staging to the little piece in a production in Munich, and this Revue-opérette version, under the title *Feuerwerk,* gave Burkhard and the song ''O, mein Papa'' an international success. As a result, *Hopsa* was given the same Revue-opérette treatment (ad Armin Robinson, Robert Gilbert, Paul Baudisch) but without the same kind of results.

Burkhard subsequently had a number of further musical plays produced in Switzerland, including the locally flavored *Die kleine Niederdorf-Oper* and an adaptation of Oscar Wilde's *The Importance of Being Ernest* (*Bunbury*). He also provided incidental music for Friedrich Dürrenmatt's *Frank V, Oper einer Privatbank* (Munich 1960), and created the scores for a number of children's pieces, notably the Christmas opera *Ein Stern geht auf aus Jakob* (Hamburg 6 December 1970).

1935 **Hopsa** Stadttheater, Zürich 30 November

1936 **Dreimal Georges** (Rudolph Schanzer, Ernst Welisch) Stadttheater, Zürich 3 October

1938 **Die Frauen von Coraya** (aka *Das Paradies der Frauen*) (Eduard Rogati) Stadttheater, Stettin 19 February

1939 **Der schwarze Hecht** (Jürg Amstein) Schauspielhaus, Zürich 1 April

1942 **Casanova in der Schweiz** (Richard Schweizer) Stadttheater, Zürich

1947 **Tic-Tac** (Guy de Pourtalès ad Fridolin Tschudi, Fritz Schulz)

1948 **Weh, dem, der liebt** (Labiche ad Albert Pulmann, K Nachmann)

1949 **Das kleinen Märchentheater** (Tschudi)

1950 **[Das] Feuerwerk** revised *Der schwarze Hecht* (Amstein, Robert Gilbert/Erik Charell, Amstein) Bayerisches Staatsoperette, Munich 16 May

1951 **Die kleine Niederdorf-Oper** (Walter Lesch) Schauspielhaus, Zürich 31 December

1956 **Spiegel, das Kätzchen** (G Keller) Theater am Gärtnerplatz, Munich 20 November

1957 **Hopsa** (revised version ad Armin Robinson, Paul Baudisch, Robert Gilbert) Wiesbaden 12 October

1957 **Die Pariserin** (Henri Becque ad N O Scarpi, Tschudi) Schauspielhaus, Zürich 31 December

195? **Das Kaffeehaus** (Hans Weigel/Carlo Goldoni ad Lola Lorme, Leoard Steckel) Schauspielhaus, Zürich

1960 **Hex? Zitterbein möcht' ich Königin sein** (Margit Brägger) Stadttheater, Berne 4 December

1961 **Barbasuk**

1962 **Die Dame mit der Brille** (Karl Suter, Robert Gilbert) Schauspielhaus, Zürich 31 December

1964 **Die Schneekönigin** Zürich

1965 **Bunbury** (Weigel) Stadttheater, Basel 7 October 1965

1966 **Noah** (w Cl Martin)

1973 **Freu dich mit uns, Jona** (Michael Longard)

1977 **Regenbogen** (Longard) Stadttheater, Basel 30 November

Biography: Flury, P, Kaufman, P: *''O Mein Papa,'' Paul Burkhard: Leben und Werk* (Orell Füssli Verlag, Zürich, 1979)

BURNABY, G[eorge] Davy (b Buckland, Herts, 7 April 1881; d Angmering, 17 April 1949). Big Davy Burnaby led a long career as a comedian in plays, concert parties, revue and, most particularly, as a regular comic presence in the postwar West End musical theatre.

During his early career, he toured in George Grossmith's role in *The Orchid,* and he first played on the West End musical stage when he succeeded to the part of Viscount Gushington in *The Girl Behind the Counter* and appeared in the light comedy role of the Comte de Casserole in *The Belle of Britanny* (1908). He took part in George Grossmith's revue, *Hullo . . . London!* at the Empire Theatre in 1910 but it was from 1914, when he appeared in both America and in Britain in a comedy role in the same Grossmith's *Tonight's the Night* (Robin Carraway), that he began the series of musical roles which would make him a West End favorite: *The Only Girl* (John Ayre), *Theodore & Co* (Duke of Shetland), *Yes, Uncle!* (Brabazon Hollybone), *Baby Bunting* (Samuel Gigglewick), *The Little Whopper* (Butts), *Oh! Julie* (General Zonzo) and *A Night Out* (Matthieu). From 1921 he spent nearly a decade as a basic member of *The Co-Optimists* concert party, before returning bulkily to the musical stage in *Waltzes from Vienna* (Ebeseder). In 1942 he made a last stage musical appearance as General Malona in the revival of *The Maid of the Mountains.*

Burnaby also appeared in many comedy films including *Three Men in a Boat* (1933), *Are You a Mason?* (1934) and *Feather Your Nest* (1937) as well as the filmed *The Co-Optimists* (1929).

The author of numerous song lyrics, including the wartime hit ''Lords of the Air'' (w Michael North), he also wrote the libretto and some of the lyrics for the successful touring comic opera *The Maid of the East* (1919).

1919 **The Maid of the East** (William Neale/w Edward Lauri) Tyne Theatre, Newcastle 10 February

BURNAND, F[rancis] C[owley] (Sir) (b London, 29 November 1836; d Ramsgate, 21 April 1917). Bulwark of the Victorian burlesque tradition.

Educated at Eton and at Cambridge, Burnand was instrumental in the founding of the Cambridge University Dramatic Society (ADC), where some of his earliest efforts as a dramatist were played. Three of these, the burlesques *Villikins and His Dinah* (1854), *Lord Lovel* (1856) and *Alonzo the Brave* (1857), were subsequently played in the British provinces and *Villikins* even appeared in India before the young writer succeeded in placing his first piece on the West End stage. The burlesque *Dido* (1860) was mounted by Chatterton at the St James's Theatre with Charles Young playing the travestied Queen of Carthage, and it proved a great success, running for some 60 nights in London and being swiftly seen throughout the colonies, with Young appearing in his original role (Theatre Royal, Melbourne 2 September 1861).

In the years that followed, Burnand began writing material for the popular comic papers of the time, notably *Fun* and *Punch,* while supplying Easter and Christmas burlesques and plays to a remarkable number of London theatres. In 1863 he achieved one of the most outstanding burlesque successes of the period with the classical extravaganza *Ixion, or the Man at the Wheel,* first produced by Mrs Charles Selby for the Pelham sisters at the Royalty Theatre and played regularly in English-speaking theatres for more than a decade thereafter.

In 1865, when French opéra-bouffe, headed by the works of Offenbach, held sway as the most advanced form of musical theatre, Burnand combined with composer Frank Musgrave, musical director at the Strand Theatre, to produce the first British efforts in that field with the original operatic burlesques *Windsor Castle* and *L'Africaine,* both successfully produced under the management of the Swanborough family. Arguably the first British opéras-bouffes—with original book, lyrics and music—they gave credibility to Burnand's later claim to have been the originator of the contemporary British musical.

The following year he was responsible for the fairly rough first English adaptation of Offenbach's *La Belle Hélène* as *Helen, or Taken from the Greek,* and also for the most successful burlesque of the age, the famous travesty of Douglas Jerrold's nautical drama *Black-Eyed Susan* which played for the unprecedented total of four hundred nights in its first run. Equally successful was another adaptation, a one-act operetta version of Maddison Morton's famous farce *Box and Cox,* set to music by Ar-

Plate 57. **F C Burnand** *and* **H J Byron.** *Victorian Britain's barons of burlesque.*

thur Sullivan to be played by an amateur group of which Burnand's friend Quintin Twiss was a leading light. Staged professionally at the German Reed's Gallery of Illustration, *Cox and Box* gave that establishment the biggest success of its long and admired career and it has remained one of the few short Victorian operettas—and the only example of Burnand's work—to have survived into the modern repertoire.

Burnand ventured in all directions. He was credited as the composer of one of the songs (''Little Wilhelmina'') used in the score arranged by W C Levey for his little Drury Lane piece, *The Girls of the Period,* and he went against the accepted tradition when he produced what was another comparative novelty in the musical theatre: a burlesque written not in rhyming couplets, but in prose. *The Military Bill Taylor* was sniffed at as ''a most eccentric piece . . . a farcical extravaganza in prose, interspersed with songs and music after the fashion of burlesque, and aiming at nothing higher than the creation of a passing laugh out of the most incongruous materials.'' Originality paid, on this occasion, as *Bill Taylor* ran more than a hundred nights at the Royalty (100th performance 17 August) without yet encouraging the burlesque in general to forsake its couplets and take up rhymeless dialogue.

A further collaboration with Sullivan produced the full-length musical *The Contrabandista,* but when Sullivan turned to W S Gilbert as a permanent partner, Burnand took the ''desertion'' badly and he missed no opportunity thereafter to snipe bitterly at Gilbert and his work, principally through the pages of *Punch* where he became increasingly important and influential, ultimately taking up the post of editor in 1880 and maintaining it for 25 years.

His considerable dramatic output continued, alongside a great bulk of other writing, until the mid-1890s. It consisted principally of pasticcio burlesques, notably a series for the Gaiety Theatre, as well as some further short pieces for the German Reeds, but his most important single success came with the play *The Colonel,* a piece loosely adapted from the French comedy *Le Mari de campagne,* and twitting the aesthetic craze. It is said that Burnand hurried his play to the stage to try to deflate the effect of Gilbert's forthcoming *Patience* after an unguarded conversation with Freddie Clay had enlightened him to his ''rival's'' new theme.

Burnand was also responsible for English adaptations of a number of Continental musicals, including Strauss's *Indigo und die vierzig Räuber, La Vie parisienne, La Cigale et la fourmi, Miss Helyett, Le Coeur et la main* and the vaudeville *La Demoiselle du téléphone,* but in later years he contributed only the burlesque *Tra-la-la-Tosca* and the comic opera *His Majesty,* with a score by Sir Alexander MacKenzie, to the original musical theatre.

In company with Henry Byron and Robert Reece, Burnand dominated a whole era and area of light musical theatre in Britain. These three writers and their less prolific and/or successful fellows took the burlesque and extravaganza tradition which had been crystallized by Planché and continued by the Broughs, the a' Becketts and Talfourd, and broadened it into a much more vigorous type of entertainment. The emphasis on punning and other forms of wordplay became much heavier and sometimes excessive, the stories eventually less and less related to the topic which they nominally burlesqued, and the music less often from opera, opéra-bouffe or the traditional song but rather from the music hall or the street organ. Burnand's facility enabled him to turn out a great number of such works and his credit lies in the fact that, while burlesque was beginning to droop from its most literary and literate state, he produced, in *Ixion* and *Black-Eyed Susan,* two of the most popular and long-lasting examples of the genre.

In collaboration with William Brough, Burnand authored *Beeton's Book of Burlesques* (London, 1865).

1854 **Villikins and His Dinah** (pasticcio)

1856 **Lord Lovel** (pasticcio)

1857 **Alonzo the Brave, or Faust and the Fair Imogene** (pasticcio)

1860 **Dido** (pasticcio arr Hayward) St James's Theatre 23 March

1860 **Light and Shade** (various) drawing-room entertainment Hanover Square Rooms 21 December

1861 **The King of the Merrows, or The Prince and the Piper** (pasticcio) Olympic Theatre 26 December

1862 **Fair Rosamond, or The Maze, the Maid and the Monarch** (pasticcio) Olympic Theatre 21 April

1862 **Robin Hood, or The Forester's Fate** (pasticcio arr James H Tully) Olympic Theatre 26 December

1863 **Acis and Galatea, or The Nimble Nymph and the Terrible Troglodyte** (pasticcio arr Tully) Olympic Theatre 6 April

1863 **Ixion, or The Man at the Wheel** (pasticcio arr Theodore Herman) Royalty Theatre 28 September

1863 **Patient Penelope, or The Return of Ulysses** (pasticcio) Strand Theatre 25 November

1864 **Venus and Adonis, a Story of the Two Rivals and a Small Boar** (pasticcio arr Dan Spillane) Haymarket Theatre 29 March

1864 **Rumpelstiltskin, or The Woman at the Wheel** (pasticcio arr Herman) Royalty Theatre 30 March

1864 **Faust and Marguerite** (pasticcio arr Ferdinand Wallerstein) St James's Theatre 9 July

1864 **Snowdrop, or The Seven Mannikins and the Magic Mirror** (or *The Seven Elves, the Magic Mirror and the Fatal Sewing Machine*) (pasticcio) Royalty Theatre 21 November

1864 **Cupid and Psyche, or As Beautiful as a Butterfly** (pasticcio) Olympic Theatre 26 December

1865 **Pirithous, the Son of Ixion** (pasticcio) Royalty Theatre 13 April

1865 **Ulysses, or The Iron Clad Warrior and the Little Tug of War** (pasticcio) St James's Theatre 17 April

1865 **Windsor Castle** (Frank Musgrave) Strand Theatre 5 June

1865 **The Widow Dido in a New Dress** (revised *Dido*) (pasticcio) Royalty Theatre 8 November

1865 **L'Africaine** (Musgrave) Strand Theatre 18 November

1866 **Paris, or Vive Lemprière** (pasticcio arr Musgrave) Strand Theatre 2 April

1866 **Bobadil el chico, or The Moor the Merrier** (pasticcio arr Tully) Astley's Theatre 2 April

1866 **A Yachting Cruise** 1 act Gallery of Illustration 2 April

1866 **Sappho, or Look Before You Leap** (pasticcio) Standard Theatre 11 June

1866 **Helen, or Taken from the Greek** (*La Belle Hélène*) English version (Adelphi Theatre)

1866 **Der Freischutz, or A Good Cast for a Piece** (pasticcio arr Musgrave) Strand Theatre 8 October

1866 **Anthony and Cleopatra, or His-tory and Her-story in a Modern Nilo-metre** (pasticcio) Haymarket Theatre 21 November

1866 **The Latest Edition of Black-Eyed Susan, or The Little Bill That Was Taken Up** (pasticcio arr Hermann) Royalty Theatre 29 November

1866 **Guy Fawkes, or The Ugly Mug and the Couple of Spoons** (pasticcio) Strand Theatre 26 December

1867 **Cox and Box, or The Long Lost Brothers** (Arthur Sullivan) 1 act Adelphi Theatre 11 May

1867 **Mary Turner, or The Wicious Willain and Wictorious Wirtue** (pasticcio arr George Richardson) Holborn Theatre 26 October

1867 **The Contrabandista, or The Law of the Ladrones** (Sullivan) St George's Opera House 18 December

1867 **The White Fawn** (pasticcio arr Charles Hall) Prince of Wales Theatre, Liverpool 26 December; Holborn Theatre 13 April 1868

1868 **Hit and Miss, or All My Eye and Betty Martin** (*L'Oeil crevé*) English version (Olympic Theatre)

1868 **Fowl Play, or A Story of Chikkin Hazzard** (pasticcio arr W H Montgomery) Queen's Theatre 20 June

1868 **Enquire Within** (Thomas German Reed) 1 act Gallery of Illustration 2 August

1868 **The Rise and Fall of Richard III, or A New Front to an Old Dicky** (USA: *Bad Dickey*) (pasticcio arr Theodore Hermann) Royalty Theatre 24 September

1868 **The Frightful Hair** (pasticcio) Haymarket Theatre 26 December

1869 **Claude Duval, or The Highwayman for the Ladies** (pasticcio arr Hermann) Royalty Theatre 23 January

1869 **The Girls of the Period** (pasticcio arr William C Levey) Theatre Royal, Drury Lane 25 February

1869 **The Military Bill[y] Taylor, or The War in the Cariboo** (pasticcio arr Hermann) Royalty Theatre 22 April

1869 **Very Little Faust and More Mephistopheles** (pasticcio) Charing Cross Theatre 18 August

1869 **The Beast and the Beauty, or No Rose without a Thorn** (pasticcio arr Hermann) Royalty Theatre 4 October

1870 **Beggar My Neighbour (A Blind Man's Bouffe)** (*Les Deux Aveugles*) English version (Gallery of Illustration)

1870 **Sir George and a Dragon, or We Are Seven** (pasticcio arr John Fitzgerald) Strand Theatre 31 March

1870 **F M Julius Caesar, or The Irregular Rum-Un** (pasticcio) Royalty Theatre 7 September

1870 **E-liz-a-beth, or The Don, the Duck, the Drake and the Invisible Armarda** (pasticcio) Vaudeville Theatre 17 November

1870 **The White Cat, or Prince Lardi Dardi and the Radiant Rosetta** (pasticcio) Globe Theatre 26 December

1871 **My Poll and Partner Joe** (pasticcio) St James's Theatre 6 May

1871 **All About the Battle of Dorking** (pasticcio/w Arthur Sketchley) Alhambra Theatre 7 August

1871 **Arion, or the Story of a Lyre** (pasticcio) Strand Theatre 20 December

1872 **La Vie parisienne** English version (Holborn Theatre)

1872 **King Kokatoo** (*L'Île de Tulipatan*) English version (Theatre Royal, Leeds)

1872 **My Aunt's Secret** (James L Molloy) 1 act Gallery of Illustration 13 March

1872 **Very Catching** (Molloy) 1 act Gallery of Illustration 18 November

1873 **Little Chang, or A Storm in a Teacup** (Offenbach arr) Tyne Theater, Newcastle-upon-Tyne 6 May

1873 **Mildred's Well** (Thomas German Reed) 1 act Gallery of Illustration 6 May

1873 **Kissi-Kissi** revised *King Kokatoo* (Opera Comique)

1873 **Our Own Anthony and Cleopatra** (pasticcio) Gaiety Theatre 8 September

1873 **La Belle Hélène** new English version (Alhambra Theatre)

1873 **Little Tom Tug, or The Fresh-Waterman** (pasticcio arr Frederic Stanislaus) Opera Comique 12 November

1874 **The Great Metropolis** (*Le Voyage de MM Dunanan père et fils*) English version with pasticcio score (Gaiety Theatre)

1874 **He's Coming (via Slumborough, Snoozleton and Snoreham)** (German Reed) 1 act St Georges Hall 12 May

1874 **Here's Another Guy Mannering** (pasticcio) Vaudeville Theatre 23 May

1874 **Too Many By One** (Frederic H Cowen) 1 act St George's Hall 26 June

1874 **Ixion Rewheeled** (revised *Ixion,* pasticcio arr W C Levey) Opera Comique 21 November

1875 **A Tale of Old China** (Molloy) 1 act St George's Hall 19 April

1876 **On the Rink, or The Girl He Left Behind Him** (T Gough, et al) Duke's Theatre 26 February

1876 **Matched and Mated** (German Reed) 1 act St George's Hall 6 November

1877 **Our Babes in the Wood, or The Orphans Released** (pasticcio) Gaiety Theatre 2 April

1877 **Number 204** (German Reed) 1 act St George's Hall 7 May

1877 **King Indigo** (*Indigo und die vierzig Räuber*) English version (Alhambra Theatre)

1877 **The Red Rover, or I Believe You, My Buoy** (pasticcio arr Fitzgerald) Strand Theatre 26 December

1878 **Answer Paid** (Walter Austin) 1 act St George's Hall 4 February

1878 **Dora and Diplunacy, or A Woman of Uncommon Scents** (pasticcio arr Fitzgerald) Strand Theatre 14 February

1878 **A Tremendous Mystery** (King Hall) 1 act St George's Hall 5 November

1878 **Overproof, or What Was Found in a Celebrated Case** (pasticcio arr W F Glover) Royalty Theatre 6 November

1879 **The Hunchback Back Again, or Peculiar Julia** (pasticcio arr Karl Meyder) Olympic Theatre 23 December

1879 **Robbing Roy, or Scotched and Kilt** (pasticcio arr Lutz/w Henry Pottinger Stephens) Gaiety Theatre 11 November

1879 **Balloonacy** (pasticcio arr Edward Solomon/w Stephens) Royalty Theatre 1 December

1880 **The Corsican Brothers and Co Ltd** (pasticcio/w Stephens) Gaiety Theatre 25 October

1880 **Sandford and Merton's Christmas Party** (A Scott Gatty) 1 act St George's Hall 27 December

1881 **Whittington and His Cat** (pasticcio) Gaiety Theatre 15 October

1883 **Bluebeard, or The Hazard of the Dye** (pasticcio) Gaiety Theatre 12 March

1883 **Ariel** (pasticcio) Gaiety Theatre 8 October

1884 **Camaralzaman** (pasticcio) Gaiety Theatre 31 January

1884 **Paw Claudian** (pasticcio) Toole's Theatre 14 February

1885 **The O'Dora, or A Wrong Accent** (pasticcio arr John Fitzgerald) Toole's Theatre 13 July

1885 **Mazeppa, or Bound—to Win** (pasticcio arr Lutz) Gaiety Theatre 12 March

1886 **Faust and Loose, or Brocken Vows** (pasticcio arr Fitzgerald) Toole's Theatre 4 February

1888 **Airey Annie** (pasticcio) Strand Theatre 4 April

1889 **Pickwick** (Solomon) 1 act Comedy Theatre 7 February

1889 **The Tiger** (Burnand) 1 act Old Stagers, Canterbury August; St James's Theatre 3 May 1890

1890 **Tra-la-la Tosca** (Florian Pascal) Royalty Theatre 9 January

1890 **Domestic Economy** (Solomon) 1 act Comedy Theatre 7 April

1890 **Captain Thérèse** English version Prince of Wales Theatre 25 August

1890 **La Cigale** (*La Cigale et la fourmi*) English version (Lyric Theatre)

1891 **Miss Decima** (*Miss Helyett*) English version (Criterion Theatre)

1892 **Incognita** (*Le Coeur et la main*) English version (Lyric Theatre)

1893 **Sandford and Merton** (Solomon) 1 act Vaudeville Theatre 20 December

1894 **The Chieftain** (revised *The Contrabandista*) Savoy Theatre 12 December

1896 **The Telephone Girl** (*La Demoiselle du téléphone*) English version w Augustus Harris, Arthur Sturgess (Grand Theatre, Wolverhampton)

1897 **His Majesty** (Alexander MacKenzie/R C Lehmann) Savoy Theatre 20 February

Autobiography: *Records and Reminiscences* (Methuen, London, 1904) (2 vols)

BURNETT, Carol [Creighton] (b San Antonio, Tex, 26 April 1933).

A ratchet-voiced comedienne who first made her name performing in nightclubs and on television, Miss Burnett won herself the public ear when she performed "I Made a Fool of Myself over John Foster Dulles" on television's *Jack Parr Show*. In consequence, she made her musical comedy debut in a starring role, as the lusty Princess Winnifred (she of the pea) in the fairy tale burlesque *Once Upon a Mattress* (1959), which moved from off-Broadway to on-Broadway and won both itself and her a fine success.

After several years of further and ever increasing television success (including TV versions of *Once Upon a Mattress* and *Calamity Jane*), a memorable appearance with Julie Andrews in concert at Carnegie Hall (1962), and a detour to the film world for *Who's Been Sleeping in My Bed?* (1963), she returned to the musical stage as Hope Springfield, the accidental movie star of *Fade Out—Fade In* (1964). This show had a bumpy time on Broadway (a number of the bumps raised by the star herself, who was unhappy with her material) and in spite of being withdrawn, revamped and restaged, it failed to gel.

From 1967 to 1978 she starred in *The Carol Burnett Show* on CBS-TV but, although she performed in any number of specials and concerts and several films, her theatre appearances were few. She repeated her teaming with Julie Andrews at the Lincoln Center (1971) and paired with Rock Hudson in a regional *I Do! I Do!*, but latterly her nearest approaches to a return to the musical theatre were in the film of *Annie* (1982, Miss Hannigan), the concert version of *Follies* (1985, Carlotta Campion), Long Beach appearances in the one-act musicals *From the Top* and *Company* (1993), and a season in the compilation show *Putting It Together* in Los Angeles in 1998.

Autobiography: *One More Time* (Random House, New York, 1986)

BURNS, David (b New York, 22 June 1902; d Philadelphia, 12 March 1971).

A plumpish, pugnacious comedian, much in demand in his early days as a gangster-type, Burns made his first Broadway musical appearance in Irving Berlin's *Face the Music* (1932, Louie), but spent much of the next six years in London where he appeared as Constantine in Cole Porter's *Nymph Errant* (1933) and as various gangsters in the British musical comedies *Big Business* (1937, Spike Morgan), *Hide and Seek* (1937, Bennie) and *Bobby Get Your Gun* (1938, Flash Tomkins).

Back home, he succeeded to the part of Ludlow Lowell in *Pal Joey* (1941) and later to that of Ali Hakim in *Oklahoma!* (1946), and appeared in character roles in *My Dear Public* (1943, Walters), as another gangster in *Billion Dollar Baby* (1945, Dapper Welch), in *Heaven on Earth* (1948, H H Hutton) and *Out of This World* (1950, Niki Skolianos). His greatest successes, however, came in his fifties and sixties when, apart from playing his last musical hoodlum role in *Do Re Mi* (1960, Brains Berman), he created a trio of top-class crusty senior roles as Mayor Shinn in *The Music Man* (1957), Senex in *A Funny Thing Happened on the Way to the Forum* (1962, Tony Award) and Horace Vandergelder in *Hello, Dolly!* (1964). His final musical role on Broadway was as the foolish old Colonel Purdy in the brief run of a musicalized version of *Teahouse of the August Moon* as *Lovely Ladies, Kind Gentleman* (1970), as he died after collapsing onstage at Philadelphia's Forrest Theater, during the road tryout of *70 Girls 70,* the following year.

BURNSIDE, R[obert] H[ubberthorne] (b Blythswood, Glasgow, Scotland, 13 August 1873; d Metuchen, NJ, 14 September 1952). Stage director and librettist for a series of Broadway extravaganzas and musical comedies.

Burnside was born to the theatre. Son of an actress, grandson of a sometime manager of Glasgow's Gaiety Theatre, he worked from an early age in various backstage capacities in the London theatre, including a period at the Savoy, where he ultimately became an assistant to director Richard Barker, another as resident stage manager at the suburban Parkhurst Theatre (1893), and as an occasional performer. He moved to America in 1894 and there, from the burlesque *Thrilby* (1895) through nearly half a century of productions, he made an extensive career as a director of musicals and, most notably, of the grandiose spectacles staged on one of the world's largest stages at the New York Hippodrome. Amongst the book musicals which he staged were included, in the wake of his Savoy experience, the American productions of the Savoy company's *The Emerald Isle* for "the Jefferson de Angelis Opera Company under the management of R H Burnside" (1902) and *The Earl and the Girl;* the successful early American musical *Fantana* (1905); the series of musicals produced at the Globe Theater for the Montgomery and Stone comedy team and, after Montgomery's death, for Stone alone (*The Lady of the Slipper, Chin-Chin, Jack o'Lantern, Tip Top, Stepping Stones, Three Cheers*); and, among the less book-orientated, a whole variety of revues, including the ''syncopated musical show'' *Watch Your Step* (1914), pageants, dance spectacles and scenery shows.

His Broadway directorial credits during this period included additionally *The Wedding Day* (1898), *A Royal Rogue* (1900), *The Mocking Bird* (1902), *Winsome Winnie, The Girl from Dixie* (1903), *Sergeant Kitty, Lady Teazle* (1904), *Happyland, The Press Agent, The Babes and the Baron* (1905), *Mexicana, The Social Whirl, The Tourists, My Lady's Maid* (*Lady Madcap*) (1906), *The Belle of London Town, Fascinating Flora* (also co-prod) (1907), *The Pied Piper* (1908), *The Red Rose, When Sweet Sixteen, The Three Romeos* (1911), *Over the River, The Dove of Peace* (1912), *The Beauty Shop, The Dancing Duchess* (1914). A typical review (for *Three Romeos*) criticised ''unworthy material'' but commented ''the most delightful moments were due to R H Burnside whose ingenious hand was evident in all the specialities of the evening. The piano turned into a millinery counter, the chorus into a bank of roses, their hats into moons, and all sorts of other clever transformations [occurred].''

In the 1920s he directed Broadway's version of *Madame Pompadour,* Jerome Kern's *The City Chap* and *Criss-Cross* and Youmans's *Great Day!* and visited London to stage Friml's *The Blue Kitten* and his own short-lived paste-up piece, *The Girl from Cook's,* at the Gaiety Theatre—a production which ended in fiasco with cast and landlords fighting over the costumes to replace monies owed.

In 1903 Burnside began a parallel career as a librettist and lyricist and, alone or in collaboration, he turned out regular texts for musical comedies as well as the structures and such words and/or lyrics as were needed for the Hippodrome extravaganzas (*Hip Hip Hooray, Happy Days, Good Times, Better Times*), over a period of some 25 years. A number of his early pieces were written with composer Gustave Kerker, but his most successful musical plays were the pieces to which he and Anne Caldwell wrote the libretti (and Ivan Caryll the music) for Montgomery and/or Stone.

In his seventies he was still active as a director, mounting a cowboy spectacular for the World's Fair in New York and staging productions of the Gilbert and Sullivan canon. In 1944 he directed the revival of De Koven's *Robin Hood* at Broadway's Adelphi Theater.

1903 **Sergeant Kitty** (A Baldwin Sloane) Montauk Theater, Brooklyn 16 November; Daly's Theater 18 January 1904

1904 **Burning to Sing, or Singing to Burn** (aka *Very Grand Opera*) (Gustave Kerker) 1 act Lyric Theater 10 May (Lambs' Club Gambol)

1906 **The Girl from Vienna** (Kerker) Casino Theater 16 February

1906 **The Tourists** (Kerker) New Lyric Theatre, Philadelphia 21 May; Daly's Theater 25 August

1906 **My Lady's Maid** (*Lady Madcap*) American version (Casino Theater)

1907 **Fascinating Flora** (Kerker/w Joseph W Herbert) Casino Theater 20 May

1908 **The Pied Piper** (ex- *What Happened Then*) (Manuel Klein/w Austen Strong) His Majesty's Theater, Montreal 14 September; Majestic Theater 3 December

1910 **The International Cup** (Klein) New York Hippodrome 3 September

1911 **The Girl I Love** (John S Zamecnik, H L Sandford/w Clarence Vincent Kerr) La Salle Theater, Chicago 5 February

1911 **The Three Romeos** (Raymond Hubbell) National Theater, Washington, DC 2 October; Globe Theater 13 November

1914 **The Dancing Duchess** (Milton Lusk/w Kerr) Casino Theater 19 August

1914 **Chin-Chin** (Ivan Caryll/w Anne Caldwell) Globe Theater 20 October

1917 **Jack o'Lantern** (Caryll/w Caldwell) Globe Theater 16 October

1919 **Miss Millions** (Hubbell) Punch & Judy Theater 9 December

1920 **Tip Top** (Caryll/w Caldwell) Globe Theater 5 October

1923 **Stepping Stones** (Kern/w Caldwell) Globe Theater 6 November

1927 **The Girl From Cook's** (Hubbell, Jean Gilbert/ad w Greatrex Newman) Gaiety Theatre, London 1 November

1928 **Three Cheers** (Hubbell, et al/w Caldwell) Globe Theater 15 October

BURROWS, Abe [BOROWITZ, Abram Solman] (b New York, 18 December 1910; d New York, 17 May 1985).

Originally an accountant, later a commercial broker, and also a performer, Burrows supplied his earliest writings to radio and from 1939, from a Hollywood base, to film, whilst establishing himself in the late 1940s as a chat-show personality with his own shows on CBS. He entered the musical theatre when he was brought in to collaborate on the until then unsatisfactory adaptation of Damon Runyon's stories as the libretto for *Guys and Dolls* (Tony Award), and thereafter worked on a number of further musical plays, both as author and/or director, and also on a several occasions (without credit) as a play doctor.

Burrows took an unadvertised hand in the turning of Molnár's *A jó tündér* into a conventional musical play as *Make a Wish* (102 performances) and joined Charles O'Neal to adapt his book *Three Wishes for Jamie* to the musical stage (94 performances, also director), but he had much more success with the original libretto to *Can-Can* (also director) and the adaptation of the screenplay *Ninotchka* as the basis for another Cole Porter musical, *Silk Stockings.* He collaborated with *Pajama Game* author

Richard Bissell and his wife on a musical about the making of that musical which, as *Say, Darling* (also directed), gave him a further success, but found that musicalizing Jane Austen's *Pride and Prejudice* as *First Impressions* was a less profitable and pointful exercise (84 performances, also director).

A reunion with Frank Loesser, a decade after *Guys and Dolls,* on an adaptation of the book *How to Succeed in Business without Really Trying* (also directed) gave the pair a second major hit, and a second Tony Award, but it was to be Burrows's last. He worked (as did several other writers, in turn) on the continuing but fruitless attempts to make a musical play out of *Breakfast at Tiffany's,* contributed to the 1976 efforts to revive the *Hellzapoppin* formula, without the results being seen on Broadway, and directed a brief revival of *Can-Can* in 1981 as his final efforts in the musical theatre.

His other directing assignments included *Two on the Aisle, Happy Hunting* and *What Makes Sammy Run.*

1950 **Guys and Dolls** (Frank Loesser/w Jo Swerling) 46th Street Theater 24 November

1951 **Make a Wish** (Hugh Martin/w Preston Sturges) Winter Garden Theater 18 April

1952 **Three Wishes for Jamie** (Ralph Blane/w Charles O'Neal) Mark Hellinger Theater 21 March

1953 **Can-Can** (Cole Porter) Shubert Theater 7 May

1955 **Silk Stockings** (Porter/w George S Kaufman, Leueen McGrath) Imperial Theater 24 February

1958 **Say, Darling** (Jule Styne/Adolph Green, Betty Comden/w Richard & Marian Bissell) ANTA Theater 3 April

1959 **First Impressions** (Robert Goldman, Glenn Paxton, George Weiss) Alvin Theater 19 March

1961 **How to Succeed in Business without Really Trying** (Loesser/w Jack Weinstock, Willie Gilbert) 46th Street Theater 14 October

1966 **Breakfast at Tiffany's** (Bob Merrill/w others) Majestic Theater 14 December

Autobiography: *Honest, Abe (is there really no business like show-business?)* (Little, Brown, Boston, 1980)

BURVILLE, Alice [Julia] (b Mile End Old Town, Stepney, 11 July 1856; d Littlehampton, 4 July 1944).

The daughter of a London photographer, pretty young Alice Burville took to the stage at a very early age and went on to become a favorite "principal girl" soprano of the 1870s and early 1880s British and American stage. She began her West End career in the tiny role of a Maid of Honour in *La Branche cassée* (1874), and continued through roles in *Ten of 'em* (*Zehn Mädchen und kein Mann*) and the 1874 pantomime (Kohinoor in *Aladdin*) at the Theatre Royal, Drury Lane, and burlesque (Meenie in *Young Rip van Winkle* 1876 opposite Nellie Farren), to take the leading ingenue roles in London presentations of *Dagobert* (1875, Princess Fleur d'amour), *Fleur de thé* (1875, Fleur de thé), *The Duke's Daughter* (*La Timbale d'argent,* 1876, Malvina), *La Chanson de Fortunio* (1876, Laurette) and *Le Petit Duc* (1878, la Duchesse). She also took over as Rosalinde in London's first *Die Fledermaus* (1877) and as Josephine in the original production *of HMS Pinafore* and played the title role in a major revival of *Geneviève de Brabant.*

In 1877 she visted America as a member of Lydia Thompson's troupe playing Polly Hopkins in *Robinson Crusoe,* Suzel in *Oxygen,* Joconde *in Piff-Paff,* Fatima in *Bluebeard,* etc, and she subsequently went round the United States with Nat Goodwin's Froliques (Minnie Clover/Constance in *Hobbies,* 1880) being adjudged by the local press "an excellent specimen of an English burlesque actress, fair and buxom and a capital songstress." She also appeared on Broadway as Arabella in *Billee Taylor* (1881) and Lady Angela in *Patience* (1881–82). She returned home, amongst scandalous rumors of a paid-off marriage to the actress-chasing son of a hugely wealthy stockbroker, to appear as Fiametta in the British production of *Boccaccio* (1882), but this was her last major London role, her work thereafter being largely in the provinces where she appeared in the title role of *Merry Mignon,* composed by her newly acquired (1883) husband, John Crook, and took the lead in the provincial musical *The Bachelors* (1885). She was last stage-sighted playing in pantomime at the suburban Standard Theatre in 1887 and at Leicester at Christmas 1893 when she played Drogan in *Geneviève de Brabant* alongside a couple of other veterans of that famous show's earlier productions.

Prior to her marriage to Crook, and to the stockbroker scandal, Miss Burville was briefly married (1876) to the actor and singer W H Denny.

BUSNACH, [Bertrand] William (b Paris, 7 March 1832; d Paris 21 January 1907).

The descendant of an Algerian Jewish family (original name Abou-Djenach), the eccentric Busnach made himself a small fortune in Paris as an exchange agent before turning his attentions to the theatre. In the years that followed, he became a prodigiously prolific author of theatrical pieces, from vaudevilles and comedies to sketches and opérettes, from the heaviest of dramas to the most spectacular of spectaculars. Always writing, always with pieces of some kind playing in several theatres, always with 10 others in preparation with a variety of collaborators, he lived in a perpetual personal muddle, but always with his fingers on everybody's doings, and at the middle of a spider's-web of connections.

His earliest contribution to the musical stage was in the way of a veritable shower of the little one-act opérettes which were liberally used and used up in spectacles-coupés, as forepieces or as occasional pieces in the French theatre of the 1860s. None of these pieces proved particularly durable, and Busnach made a more important contribution to the Parisian musical stage when he turned manager and, during some two years of struggle at the head of what he and his financially supportive colleague Léon Sari called the Théâtre de l'Athénée (but which others called "Les Folies Busnach"), gave the first significant opportunities to the young Charles Lecocq by producing his *L'Amour et son carquois* and *Fleur de thé.*

As an author, he got very rarely near the standard of those pieces, but he did supply Offenbach—with whom he had been associated as early as 1855 as co-scenarist on the pantomime *Polichinelle dans le monde*—with the text of his charming little *Pomme d'api,* and collaborated on the texts for Litolff's outraging *Heloïse et Abélard* and Lecocq's *Kosiki* and *Ali Baba.* With one or two of his other hats on, he also adapted Zola's *Nana, L'Assommoir, Germinal* and *Pot-Bouille* to the stage, as well as co-authoring *Le Remplaçant* with Georges Duval, and teaming with Clairville on the Châtelet féerie *La Belle au bois dormant.*

Busnach's output also included a number of unsuccessful novels and a newspaper, *La Gazette des Parisiennes,* which appeared in 1866 for one issue. He died at the age of 74 shortly after a surprise marriage to a young woman in her twenties.

1861 **Les Brioches du Doge** (F Demarquette/w Hector Crémieux) 1 act Théâtre des Bouffes-Parisiens 19 August

1864 **Les Virtuoses du pavé** (Auguste L'Éveillé/w Édouard Cadol) Théâtre des Folies-Marigny 19 April

1864 **Les Petits du premier** (Émile Albert/w Brunswick) 1 act Théâtre Saint-Germain 3 December

1865 **Les Gammes d'Oscar** (Georges Douay) Théâtre des Folies-Marigny 20 May

1866 **Robinson Crusoë** (Jules Pillevesse) 1 act Fantaisies-Parisiennes 21 February

1866 **Le Myosotis** (Charles Lecocq/w Cham) 1 act Palais-Royal 2 May

1866 **Le Don Juan des Fantaisies** (w Alexandre Flan) 1 act Fantaisies-Parisiennes 19 June

1866 **Quai Malaquais** (A de Roubin/w Élie Frébault) 1 act Folies-Marigny 6 July

1866 **La Vipérine** (Jean-Jacques de Billemont/w Jules Prével) 1 act Théâtre des Folies-Marigny 19 October

1867 **L'Écaillère africaine** (Georges Douay/w Marquet) 1 act Folies Saint-Germain 18 April

1867 **Marlborough s' en va-t-en guerre** (Georges Bizet, Émile Jonas, Isidore Legouix, Léo Delibes/w Paul Siraudin) Théâtre de l'Athénée 15 December

1868 **L'amour et son carquois** (Lecocq/as "A J R Delbès" w Marquet) Théâtre de la Athénée 30 January

1868 **Un merlan frit** (Douay/w Marquet) 1 act Folies-Marigny 9 April

1868 **La Pénitente** (Comtesse de Grandval/w Henri Meilhac) 1 act Opéra-Comique 13 May

1868 **Les Jumeaux de Bergame** (Lecocq) 1 act Théâtre de l'Athénée 20 November

1869 **Ce bon roi Dagobert** (Douay/w Marquet) 1 act Folies-Marigny 12 March

1869 **L'Ours et l'amateur de jardins** (Legouix/w Marquet) 1 act Théâtre des Bouffes-Parisiens 1 September

1871 **Bichetta Papa** (Douay/w Marquet) 1 act Folies-Marigny 9 March

1871 **Le Phoque à ventre blanc** (Douay) 1 act Alcazar 17 July

1872 **Les Visitandines** 1 act Folies-Bergère 5 March

1872 **Héloïse et Abélard** (Henri Litolff/w Clairville) Théâtre des Folies-Dramatiques 19 October

1872 **Sol-si-ré-pif-pan** (Henri Vincent) 1 act Théâtre du Château d'Eau 16 November

1873 **Blanche et Blanchette** (A de Groot/w Victor de Saint-Hilaire) Théâtre de la Renaissance 12 May

1873 **Mariée depuis midi** (Georges Jacobi/w Armand Liorat) 1 act Théâtre du Gymnase, Marseille 20 August; Théâtre des Bouffes-Parisiens 6 March 1874

1873 **Pomme d'api** (Jacques Offenbach/w Ludovic Halévy) 1 act Théâtre de la Renaissance 4 September

1873 **La Liqueur d'or** (Laurent de Rillé/w Armand Liorat) Théâtre des Menus-Plaisirs 11 December

1874 **La Belle au bois dormant** (Litolff/w Clairville) Théâtre du Châtelet 4 April

1874 **Charbonnier est maître chez lui** (Édouard Clairville fils/w Clairville) 1 act Théâtre du Château d'Eau 29 November

1876 **Les Deux Omar** (Firmin Bernicat/w Gedhé [G Delafontaine]) 1 act Fantaisies Oller 4 April

1876 **Kosiki** (Lecocq/w Liorat) Théâtre de la Renaissance 18 October

1877 **L'Oppoponax** (Léon Vasseur/w Charles Nuitter) 1 act Théâtre des Bouffes-Parisiens 2 May

1879 **Mon gendre, tout est rompu** (Auguste Coèdes/w Paul Burani) Casino de Dieppe 22 August

1880 **La Princesse Marmotte** (de Rillé/w Clairville, Octave Gastineau) Galeries Saint-Hubert, Brussels 24 January

1882 **La Petite Reinette** (Louis Varney/w Clairville) Galeries Saint-Hubert, Brussels 11 October

1886 **Madame Cartouche** (Vasseur/w Pierre Decourcelle) Théâtre des Folies-Dramatiques 19 October

1886 **Le Signal** (Paul Puget/w Ernest Dubreuil) 1 act Opéra-Comique 17 November

1887 **Le Chevalier timide** (Edmond Missa) 1 act Théâtre des Menus-Plaisirs 1 September

1887 **Ali Baba** (Lecocq/w Albert Vanloo) Alhambra, Brussels 11 November

1890 **L'Oeuf rouge** (Edmond Audran/w Vanloo) Théâtre des Folies-Dramatiques 14 March

1891 **La Fille de Fanchon la vielleuse** (Varney/w Liorat, Albert Fonteny) Théâtre des Folies-Dramatiques 3 November

1893 **Cliquette** (Varney) Théâtre des Folies-Dramatiques 11 July

1896 **Le Lézard** (Frédéric Toulmouche/w Liorat) 1 act Scala 29 August

1906 **Le Rat** (Raidich/Clairville ad) 1 act Théâtre Grévin 14 January

BUTT, Alfred [Sir] (b London, 20 March 1878; d Newmarket, 8 December 1962). Theatrical businessman and politican who juggled several London theatres to varying degrees of profit.

Having begun his working life as a clerk in the accounts office at Harrod's department store, Butt moved on to become secretary to Charles Morton at the Palace Theatre (1898) and eventually rose through the positions of assistant manager and manager to become managing director and chairman of the theatre. At various times thereafter he also gathered under his aegis the management of the Empire Theatre (1914–28), the Theatre Royal, Drury Lane (1925–31) and, after squeezing out the successors of George Edwardes from the Gaiety board, for a while took over the management of both the Gaiety and the Adelphi Theatres (1916–19). He was also responsible for the construction and management of the Victoria Palace (1911–30) and Paris's Théâtre Mogador (1919), the latter built allegedly out of admiration for the singer Régine Flory but disposed of after the opening show failed. He also controlled the Dominion Theatre, the Queen's, the Globe and a number of provincial houses for longer or shorter periods.

Under Butt's management, the Palace and Victoria Palace were largely given up to variety and revue, the former hosting only Seymour Hicks's *Cash on Delivery,* Lily Elsie's indifferent return to the stage in *Pamela* (1917) and the very brief British production of *Very Good Eddie* until Jack Waller took the house to produce *No, No, Nanette.* The Adelphi Theatre, however, prospered as a musical house with its series of Pinero musicals starring Bill Berry (*The Boy, Who's Hooper?,* etc), and the Theatre Royal, Drury Lane, did splendidly with its run of large-scale American operettas (*Rose Marie, The Desert Song, Show Boat, The New Moon, The Three Musketeers,* etc). Butt failed, however, to find the measure of the smaller Gaiety Theatre, with its special traditions in the world of the musical comedy, and his ventures there (*The Beauty Spot, The Kiss Call*) foundered so badly that he had to dispose of his interests in both the Gaiety and the Adelphi after less than three years in control.

Amongst the other imported shows produced wholly or partly under his managements were the three Adele and Fred Astaire vehicles *Stop Flirting* (w Aarons, Malone and Grossmith) (1923), *Lady, Be Good!* (1926) and *Funny Face* (1928), the De Sylva, Schwab and Gensler *Queen High* (1926), Ábrahám's *Viktória* (1931) and the less successful *The Red Mill,* produced at the Empire in 1919. After almost two decades of holding the strings of much of London's theatreland, Butt sold out his theatrical holdings to Stoll Moss in 1930 and resigned from Drury Lane the following year, his final production there being the musical spectacular *The Song of the Drum.*

An expert manipulator of companies and shareholdings, Butt was a theatrical landlord to whom shows were product, and he had most of his principal successes with proven, imported material or with established formulae like the Berry series of musicals, and showed little or none of the ability of some of his less expansive contemporaries, the producers, for introducing and/or creating new shows.

Butt was knighted for his wartime services in connection with food rationing in 1918, became a Unionist member of Parliament in 1922, and was created a baronet in 1929, but he was subsequently disgraced and left public life.

BUTTERFLIES Musical play in 3 acts founded on *The Palace of Puck* by William J Locke. Lyrics by T H Read and Arthur Anderson. Music by J A Robertson. Apollo Theatre, London, 12 May 1908.

Butterflies was created as a for-the-provinces vehicle for actress-manager Ada Reeve, cast here as Rhodanthe, a warm and wise woman of the world, mixed up in a series of events which resembled an earlier and much politer version of *The Rocky Horror Show.* The characters of the piece included two former Daly's Theatre favorites, Hayden Coffin as the star's dashing love interest and W Louis Bradfield as the whimsical Puck, in whose home the events of the piece take place. Under his influence, the collection of folk who have apparently wandered into "the palace of Puck" have their eyes opened, their uneasy souls calmed, and are sent forth in the morning—knowing themselves a little better than before—to find their own road to happiness.

Some pretty songs ("Morals," "Three Blind Mice," "The Girl with the Clocks") by Australian musical director J A Robertson, some of which featured lyrics by Percy French, plus Coffin's inevitable interpolations, provided a pleasant musical side to the entertainment, but it was the show's solid basis in its original play which won it a shift to a London theatre and an unexpected 217-performance London run. Following the London season, Miss Reeve took *Butterflies* to Glasgow for Christmas, publicizing her show with papier-mâché butterflies stuck to a burr with which Scotland's children obliged by sticking them on everyone in sight. It later went on the road for which it had originally been intended.

Butterflies gave a first opportunity to dancer Phyllis Monkman, taken from the chorus to be featured in "La Naissance du papillon" when the incumbent of the role refused to wear the scanty dress provided.

BUTTERWORTH, Clara (b Manchester, 18 July 1888; d Chobham, Surrey, 30 October 1996).

The concert vocalist Clara Butterworth made her first West End appearances as the Indian Princess in the 1914 revival of *The Country Girl* and as the heroine of *Young England* (1916, Betty Sydenham) at Daly's Theatre. She found celebrity when she starred in the leading role of Georgine in the long run of *The Lilac Domino* (1919) and confirmed her status as a musical-theatre prima donna when she created the role of Lady Mary Trefusis in the light opera *The Rebel Maid* (1921) composed by her husband, **Montague [Fawcett] PHILLIPS**, and appeared as Lilli Veidt in a second long-running hit, the London production of *Lilac Time*. She was also seen in one quick flop, London's version of The Dutch musical *Medorah* (1920, t/o Medorah).

If Miss Butterworth broke no records in the theatre, she can however fairly lay claim to being the longest lived musical comedy personality of all time. When she died in 1996 she had reached the age of 108.

BUTTYKAY, Ákos [GÁLSZÉCSY ÉS BUTYKAI, Ákos] (b Halmi, 22 July 1871; d Debrecen, 26 October 1935). Composer of several superior operetts for European stages.

Buttykay studied both law and music in Budapest, before going to Weimar for a year to further his studies in piano and composition. He continued studying at the Budapest Zeneakadémia whilst making his first attempts both as a theatre composer, with the ballet *A bűbájos malom,* and in the orchestral field. His first symphony, a piece of serious intent, was played with some success before, to general surprise, he produced an operett, *A bolygó görög* (the wandering Greek). A piece written in a light operatic vein, it was produced at the Király Színház in 1905 with considerable success, leading to a revival as early as 1909.

He had further theatre successes with his music to the Singspiel *A harang* (w Kacsoh) and with *Csibészkirály*—a piece which would turn up, curiously, nearly a decade later in America under the title *Pom-Pom,* stripped of Buttykay's score (Hugo Felix/Anne Caldwell Cohan Theater 28 February 1916)—and composed the incidental music for Imre Madách's drama *Az ember tragédiája* (1918), before turning out his one genuine international triumph in the musical theatre: *Az ezüst sirály* (the silver seagull), an operett in which his wife, singing star Emmi Kosáry, and Ernő Király played the leading roles first in Budapest and then for a run of over two-hundred performances at Vienna's Carltheater (*Liebesrausch* ad Robert Bodanzky) in 1920–21. The show had a similar success in Germany and was apparently given a performance in German in New York (2 October 1923).

In 1922 his *Olivia hercegnő,* with Kosáry and Király again starred, was selected to open the new Fővárosi Operettszínház, and in the same year he ended a career of 15 years as a piano professor at the Zeneakadémia. Thereafter, although he turned out several more stage pieces, including a revised version of his old collaborator Kacsoh's famous *János vitéz* in 1931, he devoted his writing largely to orchestral and concert works (''Magyar rapszódia''), and to chamber and piano music.

1905 **A bolygó görög** (Árpád Pásztor) Király Színház 19 October

1907 **A harang** (w Pongrác Kacsoh/Pásztor) Király Színház 1 February

1907 **A csibészkirály** (Lajos Széll) Király Színház 21 February

1912 **Hamupipőke** (Károly Bakonyi, Imre Farkas, Andor Gábor) Magyar Királyi Operaház 26 October

1920 **Az ezüst sirály** (Imre Földes) Városi Színház 6 February

1922 **Olivia hercegnő** (Földes, Miksa Bródy) Fővárosi Operettszínház 23 December

1925 **A császárnö apródja** (Jenő Faragó, Imre Harmath) Király Színház 24 March

BYE BYE BIRDIE Musical in 2 acts by Michael Stewart. Lyrics by Lee Adams. Music by Charles Strouse. Martin Beck Theater, New York, 14 April 1960.

With ''college'' musicals a thing of the past, *Bye Bye Birdie*—the first American musical comedy to take the new trends in ''pop'' music for its subject—brought their 1960s equivalent to Broadway in the same welter of innocent good humor and catchy songs heretofore provided by such pieces as *Leave It to Jane* or *Good News.*

Conrad Birdie (Dick Gautier) has hit pop-star success, and the bank account of his manager, Albert Peterson (Dick van Dyke), should be just about to start heading happily for the black, but nothing is going right. Albert's faithful secretary-and-girlfriend, Rosie (Chita Rivera), is resigning until he gets a proper job, and Conrad is about to be drafted. Albert lines up one last promotion: Conrad will kiss goodbye to lucky 15-year-old fan Kim MacAfee (Susan Watson), to the accompaniment of a special new song, on national TV. Disaster strikes in every possible form. Kim's steady, Hugo (Michael J Pollard), knocks Conrad out in front of NBC's cameras, the star runs off into what passes for nightlife in Sweet Apple, Ohio, and gets arrested for consorting threateningly with an underaged girl, and on top of all that, Albert's mother (Kay Medford) gets in on the act as only a Broadway musical mother can. At the end of it all, Albert is happy to throw in the pop-music business and head quietly off with Rosie to a small-town teaching job.

The songs of the show included a package of winners: Albert's bright advice to ''Put on a Happy Face'' to the teeny-fans who are losing their idol to the army, their chorused insistence that ''We Love You, Conrad,'' the pop-singer's frantic realization that he's got ''A Lot of Livin' to Do'' before getting incarcerated in the army, his plastic confession to his public that all you need to do in life to be him is to be ''Honestly Sincere,'' the plaint of the parents of Sweet Apple over the problems with modern ''Kids,'' and those kids tying up the town's telephone system with their delightfully-staged ''Telephone Hour.'' There were two dance routines inserted, in the manner of the time, featuring Rosie, the first as she furiously goes through a list of ways ''How to Kill a Man'' who lets his mother tell him what to do, the other an incidental irruption into a Shriners' meeting during her night on the town after the disaster.

Edward Padula's production of the show was a 607-performance hit on Broadway, and *Bye Bye Birdie* headed out into the country and across the Atlantic where H M Tennent Ltd mounted a reproduced London version with Peter Marshall (Albert), Marty Wilde (Conrad), Sylvia Tysick (Kim) and Angela Baddeley (Mrs Peterson) featured alongside Miss Rivera. London had already had its first musical about the pop world in the very differently and more darkly colored *Expresso Bongo* and it did not reserve the same welcome for *Bye Bye Birdie* that Broadway had. The run was stretched to 268 performances, but the show did not establish itself in the revivable repertoire in Britain in the same way that it did in America. An Australian production, with Frank Buxton and Patricia Finlay featured, played four months in Melbourne and was subsequently seen at Sydney's Her Majesty's Theatre (21 October 1961).

A film version, produced in 1963, retained van Dyke and much of the score (although reallocating numbers), added a zingy title song and featured Ann-Margret (Kim), Janet Leigh (Rosie), Maureen Stapleton (Mrs Peterson), Jesse Pearson (Conrad) and pop vocalist Bobby Rydell as a pumped-up Hugo.

An attempt to *Bring Back Birdie,* written by the same authors and produced at the Martin Beck Theater (5 March 1981) with Donald O'Connor, Maria Karnilova, Maurice Hines and Miss Rivera played just four performances, but the original show, 30 years on become as delightful a period piece as the shows of the *Good News* era, continued its healthy life, going on the road in a major revival in 1991 with Tommy Tune and Anne Reinking in the leading roles. Two additional songs by Adams and Strouse (''A Giant Step,'' ''He's Mine'') were added to the score for this production which ran seven months on the road but stopped short of Broadway.

In the 1990s it was the subject of an unloved TV production with Jason Alexander and Vanessa Williams featured.

UK: Her Majesty's Theatre 15 June 1961; Australia: Her Majesty's Theatre, Melbourne 4 March 1961

Film: Columbia 1963

Recordings: original cast (Columbia), London cast (Philips), film soundtrack (RCA Victor), TV cast (RCA), *Bring Back Birdie* (original cast), etc

BY JEEVES Musical in 2 acts by Alan Ayckbourn based on the Jeeves stories of P G Wodehouse. Music by Andrew Lloyd Webber. A revised version of the musical *Jeeves* by the same authors. Stephen Joseph Theatre, Scarborough, 24 April 1996; Duke of York's Theatre, London, 2 July 1996.

Much dramatized since their first appearance on the printed page, the stories of the merry Bertie Wooster—everybody's favorite silly-ass Englishman—and his infallible and impassive factotum, Jeeves, made their first appearance on the musical stage in 1975 when Alan Ayckbourn, the English stage's most successful comic playwright, and Andrew Lloyd Webber, riding high as the composer of the triumphant *Jesus Christ Superstar,* combined on a *Jeeves* produced by Robert Stigwood and Michael White at London's Her Majesty's Theatre (22 April). David Hemmings featured as Wooster and Michael Aldridge as Jeeves in a piece which was ''like a dream of all the Wodehouse novels combined into the ultimate ghastly weekend,'' decorated with some lightweight period-flavored songs, and which went under, unloved, in 38 performances.

Twenty years on, the two writers—both of whom had gone on to even mightier success in the meanwhile—came back together to have a second go at a rather smaller-scaled *Jeeves.* The framework of the original—in which Bertie related his escapades during a holdup in a banjo concert—was retained along with all the favorite characters, whilst five of the original songs (the lilting ''Travel Hopefully,'' ''Banjo Boy,'' ''Half a Moment'') were topped up with some new material in a similar vein (notably a chaotically funny comic ensemble ''It's a Pig''), and the new version, retitled *By Jeeves,* was mounted at Ayckbourn's theatre in Scarborough. Stephen Pacey played Wooster and Malcolm Sinclair was Jeeves. It subsequently transferred to London, to play first at Wyndham's Theatre and then at the Lyric. However, in the age of the spectacular musical play there was little call for a small, friendly piece with an engaging air of village-hall dramatics about it, and *By Jeeves* never looked likely to challenge the success of its composer's large romantic works. It ran for eight months.

By Jeeves was given a showing at America's Goodspeed Opera House while the London version ran on. John Scherer (Bertie) and Richard Kline (Jeeves) headed the cast.

An earlier Jeeves musical, *Come on Jeeves,* put together by Wodehouse and Guy Bolton in the late 1960s, failed to make it to the stage.

USA: Goodspeed Opera House (Norma Terris Theater) 17 October 1996

Recordings: *Jeeves* (MCA), *By Jeeves* (RUG), *By Jeeves* American edition (RUG)

BY JUPITER Musical in 2 acts by Richard Rodgers and Lorenz Hart based on *The Warrior's Husband* by Julian Thompson. Lyrics by Lorenz Hart. Music by Richard Rodgers. Shubert Theater, New York, 3 June 1942.

The Warrior's Husband (1932), originally produced on Broadway with Katharine Hepburn in its starring role as the warrior queen, Hippolyta, was musicalized by Rodgers and Hart very largely in a clinic where Hart was drying out after one of his more excessive bouts with alcohol. Its theme of the subjugation of a powerful woman by an inferior man by his use of the appendages of his sex was a well-worn one on the musical stage, but it was stated here with rather more aplomb than usual and prettily dressed up in the usually infallible garb of Ancient Greece.

Hippolyta (Benay Venuta), Queen of the Amazons, and her army of female warriors rule and protect their country whilst the Consort, Sapiens (Ray Bolger), and the other husbands stay at home. This situation is not, you understand, because the women are in any way meritorious, but because Hippolyta has this magic girdle which ensures her superiority. The Greeks, led by Theseus (Ronald Graham) and Hercules (Ralph Dumke), apparently find this arrangement some kind of a challenge and they invade Pontus to steal the girdle and ensure masculine superiority. They get beaten in the field, but their irresistible anatomy wins the day. The feeble Sapiens becomes King and, since Hippolyta has a husband in this version, Theseus is unhistorically paired off with her sister, Antiope (Constance Moore).

The score of *By Jupiter* did not produce any Rodgers and Hart standards, but several of the pieces worked well in the theatre: the comical ''Ev'rything I've Got'' for Hippolyta and Sapiens, the pretty ballad ''Nobody's Heart,'' Bolger's comical turn ''Now That I've Got My Strength'' and, most particularly, his dance routine to the otherwise not first-class ''Life with Father'' with boot-faced character actress Bertha Belmore, cast (as she had been in the 1932 play) as the King's mother, Pomposia.

By Jupiter, produced by Rodgers himself and Dwight Deere Wiman, ran for 427 performances on Broadway, closing when Bolger withdrew to go and do some troop entertaining and it was not considered practical to replace him. It was picked up for Britain by Jack Waller and produced at Manchester with Bobby Howes top-billed as Sapiens alongside Marjorie Brooks (Hippolyta), Adele Dixon (Antiope), Chic Elliott (Pomposia) and Bruce Trent (Theseus), with one Hyacinth Hazell in the role of Penelope. It closed on the road to London.

In New York, however, the piece was brought back to the Theatre Four in 1967, following the successful revival there of *The Boys from Syracuse* (1963), with a cast headed by Bob Dishy (Sapiens), Jackie Alloway (Hippolyta), Robert R Kaye (Theseus), Sheila Sullivan (Antiope) and Irene Byatt (Pomposia). It did not do as well as its predecessor and closed after 118 performances.

UK: Prince's Theatre, Manchester 25 July 1944

Recordings: off-Broadway revival cast (RCA), etc

BYNG, George W[ilford Bulkeley] [BULK[E]LEY, George Wilford] (b Whitehaven, 21 January 1861; d Winterbourne, nr Bristol, 29 June 1932). Longtime conductor and journeyman composer for the British stage.

A descendant of several well-known British theatrical families of the 18th century—the Bulkleys, the Wilfords and the John Richs—and the son of a Dublin actor and solicitor, David Bulkley Byng (1811–1881), George Byng became a member of the orchestra at the local Theatre Royal at the age of 11, working latterly under the baton of Frederic Stanislaus with whom he was subsequently engaged at Manchester. He worked as an orchestral player and then a conductor in a whole series of London theatres, being first violin at London's Gaiety Theatre, sub-conductor at the Empire, musical director at the new Shaftesbury Theatre (1888), conductor for the tour of *Girouette* (1889) and at the Royalty with comedian Arthur Roberts in 1889–90 (*The New Corsican Brothers, Tra-la-la Tosca*) and subsequently on tour with Roberts in *Guy Fawkes Esq* (for which he also provided the score) and *In Town.* He accompanied the Gaiety burlesque company which played *Faust Up-to-Date* and *Carmen Up-to-Data* around the European capitals, and he returned to London to conduct Willie Edouin's season at the Strand (1893), to act initially as second conductor then as principal at the Empire, and to take the baton for *On the March* and Roberts's *The White Silk Dress* at the Prince of Wales (1896–97). He then spent a long period as musical director in succession to Georges Jacobi at the Alhambra (1897–1910).

Byng turned out scenic music as required over the years and, for the Alhambra, the large amount of dance music featured on their programs, including the ballets *Jack Ashore, The Gay City, The Red Shoes, A Day Off, Napoli, The Handy Man* (with many sung numbers), *Inspiration, Gretna Green* (with songs and choruses), *On the Sands, Cupid Wins* and Mlle Leonora's burlesque dance of the seven veils in *Sal, Oh My!,* but he also scored all or part of several musical comedies, including Roberts's highly successful touring vehicle *HMS Irresponsible.* He revised Audran's *La Poupée* (originally intended to be a Roberts vehicle) for Henry Lowenfeld's vastly successful London production and, in contrast, supplied the music for *The Showman's Sweetheart,* a touring vehicle for Minnie Palmer, and 11 numbers for what was virtually a new score for the touring show *A Trip to Chicago*.

1884 **Polly's Birthday** (Charles S Fawcett) 1 act Gaiety Theatre, Manchester 3 March

1890 **Guy Fawkes Esq** (''Doss Chidderdoss'' [Mr Marshall]/ Fred Leslie, Herbert Clark) Theatre Royal, Nottingham 7 April

1894 **The House of Lords** (w Ernest Ford/Harry Greenbank) 1 act Lyric Theatre 6 July

1896 **The White Silk Dress** (w Alick McLean, Reginald Somerville/H J W Dam) Prince of Wales Theatre 3 October

1898 **The Showman's Sweetheart** (Guy Eden, Arthur Law/ Law) Queen's Theatre, Crouch End 29 August

1898 **An Old Muff** (E A Morton) 1 act Alhambra 31 October

1898 **A Trip to Chicago** replacement songs w E Boyd Jones (tour)

1899 **The Mysterious Musician** (Eden) 1 act Terry's Theatre 27 June

1900 **Punch and Judy** revised *The Showman's Sweetheart* (w Arthur Meredyth/Law) Theatre Royal, Croydon 25 June

1900 **HMS Irresponsible** (J F Cornish) Royalty Theatre, Chester 2 August; Royal Strand Theatre 27 May 1901

1902 **The Variety Girl** (Albert E Ellis/Chris Davis) Opera House, Cork 1 September

1904 **The Duchess of Sillie-Crankie** (Herbert Fordwych, Arthur Wimperis/Fordwych) Terry's Theatre April

BYRON, H[enry] J[ames] (b Manchester, 8 January 1835; d Clapham Park, London, 11 April 1884). Victorian man of the theatre whose burlesques were the backbone of the British tradition.

Born in Manchester, the son of the British consul at Port au Prince, Byron worked at first as a doctor's clerk and then studied for the law before turning definitively to the theatre. There he became one of the most notable figures of his time, both as a prolific writer of more than a hundred successful plays (the record-breaking *Our Boys, Uncle Dick's Darling, A Lancashire Lass, Tottles, Wait and Hope, Dearer Than Life,* etc) and musical shows and, most particularly, as the supreme exponent of the punning burlesque and extravaganza. He also operated as a producer, being for a time the partner of Lady Bancroft (Marie Wilton) at the famous Prince of Wales Theatre, and lessee of Liverpool's Royal Alexandra Theatre and Royal Amphitheatre, which sent him bankrupt in 1868. He also worked occasionally as a performer.

Amongst Byron's early works, his burlesque of *La gazza ladra, The Maid and the Magpie,* in which Marie Wilton won outstanding praise as a burlesque boy, and the burlesque version of *Aladdin,* which introduced the character of Widow Twankay into the story for the first time, were the most memorable pieces, but others burlesques such as *Cinderella* (introducing the character of ''Buttons'' which would become a British pantomime favorite), *Fra Diavolo, The Lady of Lyons, The Pilgrim of Love, The Miller and His Men, Mazeppa* and *Miss Eily O'Connor* all won more than one London run as well as long provincial lives and a wide dissemination to the English-speaking stages of America and the colonies.

His Arabian Nights and fairy-tale burlesques became used and reused as some of the most favored pantomime openings (followed by the ever-reducing harlequinade), his *1863* was an early English-language example of the genuine, Parisian-style ''review'' of the year's events before the ''revue'' genre degenerated into a virtual variety show and his adaptation of *La Fille de Madame Angot* for the English stage proved the most faithfully adept of the series of such versions and helped lead the show to triumph on English-language stages, whilst his burlesques for the Gaiety Theatre provided the famous team of players there with the material they required to make and hold their fame. Oddly, however, in spite of his great straight play successes, Byron never authored an original libretto to a legitimate musical play, his only venture in that area being on the Alhambra's romantic spectacular *The Demon's Bride* in which the book was commissioned from France's Leterrier and Vanloo and Byron's job was merely to ''adapt'' it to the Alhambra's purposes.

1857 **King Richard of the Lionheart** (pasticcio) Strand Theatre 23 November

1858 **The Lady of Lyons, or Twopenny Pride and Pennytence** (pasticcio) Strand Theatre 1 February

1858 **Fra Diavolo, or The Beauty and the Brigands** (pasticcio arr W H Montgomery) Strand Theatre 5 April

1858 **The Bride of Abydos, or The Prince, the Pirate and the Pearl** (pasticcio arr Montgomery) Strand Theatre 31 May

1858 **The Maid and the Magpie, or The Fatal Spoon** (pasticcio arr Montgomery) Strand Theatre 11 October

1858 **Mazeppa** (pasticcio arr John Barnard) Olympic Theatre 27 December

1859 **The Very Latest Edition of the Lady of Lyons** (pasticcio) Strand Theatre 11 July

1859 **The Babes in the Wood and the Good Little Fairy Birds** (pasticcio) Adelphi Theatre 18 July

1859 **The Nymph of the Lurleyburg, or The Knight and the Naiads** (pasticcio arr Charles Hall) Adelphi Theatre 26 December

1859 **Jack the Giant Killer, or Harlequin, King Arthur and ye Knights of ye Round Table** (pasticcio) Princess's Theatre 26 December

1860 **The Forty Thieves** (pasticcio arr Barnard/w Planché, W & R Brough, Halliday, Buckingham, Kennedy) Lyceum Theatre 7 March

1860 **The Pilgrim of Love** (pasticcio) Haymarket Theatre 9 April

1860 **The Miller and His Men** (pasticcio/w Francis Talfourd) Strand Theatre 9 April

1860 **Cinderella, or The Prince, the Lackey and the Little Glass Slipper** (pasticcio arr Frank Musgrave) Strand Theatre 26 December

1860 **Bluebeard from a New Point of Hue** (pasticcio arr Charles Hall) Adelphi Theatre 26 December

1861 **Aladdin, or The Wonderful Scamp** (pasticcio arr Musgrave) Strand Theatre 1 April

1861 **Esmeralda, or The Sensation Goat** (pasticcio arr Musgrave) Strand Theatre 28 September

1861 **Miss Eily O'Connor** (pasticcio arr Tully) Theatre Royal, Drury Lane 25 November

1861 **The Rival Othellos** (pasticcio) Strand Theatre 28 November

1861 **Puss in a New Pair of Boots** (pasticcio arr Musgrave) Strand Theatre 26 December

1862 **The Sensation Fork, or The Maiden, the Maniac and the Midnight Murderer** (pasticcio) Her Majesty's Concert Room 19 May

1862 **Goldenhair the Good** (pasticcio) St James's Theatre 26 December

1862 **Ivanhoe According to the Spirit of the Times** (pasticcio arr Musgrave) Strand Theatre 26 December

1863 **Beautiful Haidee, or The Sea Nymphs and the Sallee Rovers** (pasticcio) Princess's Theatre 6 April

1863 **Ali Baba and the Thirty-Nine Thieves** (pasticcio) Strand Theatre 6 April

1863 **Ill-Treated Trovatore** (pasticcio) Adelphi Theatre 21 May

1863 **The Motto 'I Am All There'** (pasticcio) Strand Theatre 16 July

1863 **Lady Belle Belle, or Fortunio and His Seven Magic Men** (pasticcio) Adelphi Theatre 26 December

1863 **1863, or The Sensations of the Past Season (with the shameful revelation of Lady Somerby's Secret)** (pasticcio arr F Wallerstein) St James's Theatre 26 December

1863 **Orpheus and Eurydice, or The Young Gentleman who Charmed the Rocks** (pasticcio arr Musgrave) Strand Theatre 26 December

1864 **Mazourka, or The Stick, the Pole and the Tartar** (aka *Tiddeliwinki*) (pasticcio arr Musgrave) Strand Theatre 27 April

1864 **Princess Springtime, or The Envoy Who Stole the King's Daughter** (pasticcio) Haymarket Theatre 26 December

1864 **The Grin Bushes, or The Mrs Brown of the Missis Sippi** (pasticcio) Strand Theatre 26 December

1865 **Pan, or The Loves of Echo and Narcissus** (pasticcio) Adelphi Theatre 10 April

1865 **La! Sonnambula, or The Supper, the Sleeper and the Merry Swiss Boy** (pasticcio) Prince of Wales Theatre 15 April

1865 **Lucia di Lammermoor, or The Luckless Laird, the Lovely Lady and the Little Lover** (pasticcio) Prince of Wales Theatre 25 September

1865 **Little Don Giovanni, or Leporello and the Stone Statue** (pasticcio) Prince of Wales Theatre 26 December

1866 **Der Freischutz, or The Belle, the Bill and the Bullet** (pasticcio) Prince of Wales's Theatre 10 September

1866 **Pandora's Box, or The Young Spark and the Old Flame** (pasticcio arr J T Haines Princess's Theatre 26 December

1867 **William Tell with a Vengeance, or The Pet, the Patriot and the Pippin** (pasticcio) Royal Alexandra Theatre, Liverpool 4 September; Strand Theatre 5 October

1868 **Lucrezia Borgia M D, or The Grande Doctress** (pasticcio arr Haines) Theatre Royal, Holborn 28 October

1869 **Pluto, or The Young Lady Who Charmed the Rocks** revised *Orpheus and Eurydice* with replacement score by Dave Braham (Tammany, New York)

1869 **The Corsican Bothers, or The Troublesome Twins** (pasticcio arr George Richardson) Globe Theatre 17 May

1869 **Lord Bateman, or The Proud Young Porter and the Fair Sophia** (pasticcio arr Richardson) Globe Theatre 26 December

1870 **Pippin, or The King of the Golden Mines** (pasticcio) burlesque version of 1869 London pantomime *The Yellow Dwarf* Niblo's Theater 4 April

1870 **Robert Macaire, or The Roadside Inn Turned Innside out** (pasticcio) Globe Theatre 16 April

1870 **The Enchanted Wood, or The Three Transformed Princes** (pasticcio) Adelphi Theatre 4 May

1871 **The Orange Tree and the Humble Bee, or The Little Princess who was Lost at Sea** (pasticcio) Vaudeville Theatre 13 May

1871 **Giselle, or The Sirens of the Lotus Lake** (pasticcio arr G Barnard) Olympic Theatre 22 July

1871 **Camaralzaman and the Fair Badoura, or The Bad Djinn and the Good Spirit** (pasticcio) Vaudeville Theatre 22 November

1872 **The Lady of the Lane** (pasticcio arr John Fitzgerald) Strand Theatre 31 October

1873 **La Fille de Madame Angot** English version (Philharmonic Theatre)

1873 **Les Bavards** English version (Alice Oates Company, USA)

1873 **Max, the Merry Swiss Boy** (J K Emmet) Academy of Music, Buffalo 8 September; Broadway Theater 6 October

1873 **Don Juan** (arr Georges Jacobi) Alhambra Theatre 22 December

1874 **Guy Fawkes** (arr Meyer Lutz) Gaiety Theatre 14 January

1874 **Normandy Pippins** (pasticcio arr Frederick Stanislaus) 1 act Criterion Theatre 18 April

1874 **La Jolie Parfumeuse** English version (Alhambra Theatre)

1874 **The Demon's Bride** (Georges Jacobi/Eugene Leterrier, Albert Vanloo ad) Alhambra Theatre 7 September

1875 **Phil, the Foundling** (Emmet) Theatre Royal, Sydney 1 November

1876 **Little Don Caesar de Bazan, or Maritana and the Merry Monarch** (pasticcio arr Meyer Lutz) Gaiety Theatre 26 August

1877 **The Bohemian G'yurl and the Unapproachable Pole** (pasticcio arr Lutz) Opera Comique 31 January

1877 **Little Doctor Faust, the Gaiety not the Goethe Version** (pasticcio arr Lutz) Gaiety Theatre 13 July

1878 **The Forty Thieves** (pasticcio arr Lutz/w Gilbert, Burnand, Reece) Gaiety Theatre 13 February

1878 **Il Sonnambulo, and Lively Little Alessio** (pasticcio arr Lutz) Gaiety Theatre 6 April

1878 **Young Fra Diavolo, the Terror of Terracina** (pasticcio arr Lutz) Gaiety Theatre 17 November
1879 **Pretty Esmeralda, and Captain Phoebus of Ours** (pasticcio arr Lutz) Gaiety Theatre 2 April
1879 **Handsome Hernani, or The Fatal Penny Whistle** (pasticcio arr Lutz) Gaiety Theatre 30 August
1879 **The Magic Slipper** revised *Cinderella* (Haverley's Theater, New York)
1879 **Gulliver** Gaiety Theatre (pasticcio arr Lutz) 26 December
1880 **Il Trovatore, or Larks with a Libretto** (pasticcio arr Lutz) Olympic Theatre 26 April
1881 **Pluto, or Little Orpheus and His Lute** (revised *Orpheus and Eurydice*) (pasticcio arr Michael Connelly) Royalty Theatre 26 December
1882 **Frolique** (w H B Farnie) (pasticcio) Strand Theatre 18 November

Literature: Wise, J (ed): *Plays by H J Byron* (Cambridge University Press, Cambridge, 1984)

BY THE BEAUTIFUL SEA Musical in 2 acts by Herbert and Dorothy Fields. Lyrics by Dorothy Fields. Music by Arthur Schwartz. Majestic Theater, New York, 8 April 1954.

Following the pretty period musical *A Tree Grows in Brooklyn* in 1951, lyricist Dorothy Fields, composer Arthur Schwartz and star Shirley Booth came together a second time on a show with a similarly winning and unextravagant flavor in *By the Beautiful Sea,* built up around the character of real-life performer Lottie Gibson.

Miss Booth played Lottie Gibson, otherwise known as "The Little Magnet," a vaudeville performer who spends her off-season at her boarding house in Coney Island. There she leads to the good her love for the impecunious Shakespearean actor Dennis Emery (Wilbur Evans). The main hurdles which have to be got over are money and Emery's daughter by an earlier marriage, the 17-year-old child actress Betsy Busch (Carol Leigh), who has become jealously possessive of her refound father and resents Lottie's vaudeville connections. She is finally won over when Lottie gets her out of her impersonation of a 13-year-old, into a pretty frock and the arms of a handsome waiter (Richard France). Schwartz and Fields's songs included the heroine's rueful admission that "I'd Rather Wake Up by Myself" than with any man but Dennis, and his quiet thoughts that he has been "Alone Too Long," alongside a lively opening title chorus and a speciality spot in which Lottie performed her act-as-known.

Robert Fryer and Lawrence Carr's production ran through an insufficient 270 performances on Broadway before the show was put away. Thirty years later, Schwartz worked on a fresh version of the text, reset in Blackpool, England, as a vehicle for British stars Dora Bryan and Bonnie Langford, with a score made up of Schwartz standards and some new material, but the project did not come to fruition.

Recording: original cast (Capitol)

C

CAB, Marc *see* MARC-CAB

CABALLERO, Manuel Fernández (b Murcia, 14 March 1835; d Madrid, 26 January 1906).

A musician and conductor in various Madrid theatres during the 1850s and 1860s (Teatro Real, Teatro de Variedades, Teatro Lírico, Teatro Lope de Vega, Teatro Español), Caballero composed and arranged the usual quantity incidental music used in his theatres whilst at the same time turning out original scores for a number of zarzuelas. He subsequently went to South America as conductor to a zarzuela company and, on his return, set himself to composition with such a will that in the next years—although latterly blind and composing with the assistance of Hermoso and of José Serrano by dictation—he turned out a huge number of new works, apparently bringing his total of musical-theatre shows large and small to well over two hundred.

Amongst the most successful of his pieces were *El salto del pasiego* (lib: Luis de Eguilaz, Teatro Zarzuela 17 March 1878), *El duo de la Africana* (lib: Miguel Echegaray, Teatro Apolo 13 May 1893), *La viejecita* (w Hermoso, lib: Miguel Echegaray, 1 act Teatro Zarzuela 4 April 1897), *Gigantes y cabezudos* (lib: Miguel Echegaray, 1 act Teatro Zarzuela 29 November 1898) and *Los sobrinos del Capitan Grant* (lib: Miguel Ramos Carrión, Teatro Circo de Rivas, 1877), a musicalization of Jules Verne's tale. He also composed an *El Vizconde de Letorières* (Teatro del Circo, 1858) on Bayard and Dumanoir's much-musicalized play *Le Vicomte de Letorrières, El prima dia feliz* (Teatro Zarzuela 30 January 1872) using the text of Auber's opera *Le Premier Jour de bonheur* (played in Madrid in 1870), and a version of the *1001 Nights* (*Las mil y una noches,* 1882 w Rubio).

La viejecita was seen in a Spanish-language double-bill on Broadway in 1919 (Cort Theater 14 July).

His other titles include *Tres madres para una hija* (1854), *La vergonzosa en palacio* (1855), *Mentir a tiempo* (1856), *Juan Lanas* (1856), *La jardinera* (1857), *Un cocinero* (1858), *Frasquito* (1859), *Los dos primos* (1860), *La reina topacio* (1861), *El loco de la guardia* (1861), *Equilibrios do amor* (1862, w Cristóbal Oudrid y Segura), *Los dos mellinos* (1862), *Los suicios* (1862), *Luz y sombra* (1867), *El atrevido en la corte* (1872), *La gallina ciega* (1873), *Las hijas de Fulano* (1874), *El velo de encaje* (1874), *Este joven ne conviene* (1875 w Casares), La clave (1875), *Las nuevas de la noche* (1875 w Casares), *Entre el alcade y el rey* (1875 w Emilio Arrieta), *La marsellesa* (1876), *El siglio que viene* (1876), *Las dos princesas* (1878), *El lucero del alba* (1879), *El cepillo de las animas* (1879), *El corpus de sangue* (1879), *Amor que empieya y amor que acaba* (1879), *Las hazanas de Hercules* (1880), *Al polo* (1880 w Joaquín Espin), *El sacristan de San Justo* (1880 w Nieto), *Mantos y capos* (1881 w Nieto), *De Verano* (1881 w Angelo Rubio), *La farsanta* (1881 w Rubio), *El gran Tamerlano di Persia* (1882 w Nieto), *La nina bonita* (1882), *El Capitan Cestellas* (1883 w A Almagro), *Trabajo perdito* (1884), *Los bandos de Villafrita* (1884), *El guerillero* (1885 w Ruperto Chapí, Arrieta), *La mejor receta* (1885), *Una noche en Loreto* (1885), *Locos de amor* (1886), *Cielon XXII* (1886), *Las mujeres que matan* (1887), *Bazar* (1887), *Château Margaux* (1887), *Aguas azotados* (1888), *El golpe de gracia* (1888), *Olé Sevila* (1889), *Los Zangolatinos* (1889), *A ti suspiramos* (1889 w Hermoso), *España* (1890), *La choza del Diablo* (1891), *El fantasma de fuego* (1891), *Los aparecidos* (1892), *La triple alizanza* (1893), *Los dineros del sacristan* (1894), *Campañero e sacristan* (1894 w Hermoso), *Los africanistas* (1894), *El cabo primero* (1895), *El rueda de la fortuna* (1896), *Tortilla al ron* (1896 w Hermosa), *El Saboyano* (1896), *El padrino del nene* (1896), *L'espulsion de los Judios 1493* (1896 w Hermoso), *El Señor Joaquim* (1898), *Aun hay patria, Veremundo!* (1898 w Hermosa), *La magia negra* (1898 w Valverde jr), *La virgen del puerto* (1899 w Mario Caballero), *Citrato? Der ver sera* (1899 w Valverde jr), *El traje de luzes* (1899 w Hermoso), *El rey de los aires* (1900), *Los estudiantes* (1900), *La tribu savage* (1901 w Hermoso), *La barcarola* (1901 w Lapuerta), *La diligencia* (1901), *El favorito del duque* (1902), *La*

Plate 58. **Cabaret.** *Joel Grey repeats his original role as the master of ceremonies at the St Louis Muny.*

trapera (1902 w Hermoso), *La manta zamorana* (1902), *Sena Justa* (1902), *El dios grande* (1903 w Mario Caballero), *La inclusera* (1903 w Valverde jr), *Rusia y Japan* (1905 w Hermoso), *Los huertanos* (1905 w Hermosa), *Aires nacionales* (w Calleja), *La cacharrera* (1906 w Hermoso), etc.

CABARET Musical in 2 acts by Joe Masteroff based on the play *I Am a Camera* by John van Druten and the stories of Christopher Isherwood. Lyrics by Fred Ebb. Music by John Kander. Broadhurst Theater, New York, 20 November 1966.

The libretto of the musical *Cabaret* was based on Christopher Isherwood's lightly autobiographical short stories about life in Berlin in the years under the rule of the Nazi party, and on the play drawn by John van Druten from them and produced, with considerable success, as *I Am a Camera* (Empire Theater, New York 28 November 1951). The musical's action was set up in the ''framework'' manner, so successfully used on *Man of La Mancha* the previous season, with the principal tale of the piece loosely (though not wholly) inset into the entertainment and goings-on in a strivingly decadent Berlin cabaret house, and introduced by a leering, epicene Master of Ceremonies (Joel Grey).

Sally Bowles (Jill Haworth), a little middle-class lass from Chelsea, London, is working as a singer at Berlin's Kit Kat Club and doing her not very good best to live the thrillingly decadent life which the city is supposed to offer. Into her orbit comes Cliff Bradshaw (Bert Convy), a young American writer, and Sally soon moves determinedly in on him, joining him in his room in the boarding house run by Frln Schneider (Lotte Lenya). Their fellow lodgers include the cheerful whore, Frln Kost (Peg Murray), and the gentle, greying fruiterer Herr Schultz (Jack Gilford). As the clouds gather, Sally, now pregnant by Cliff, is still determined to show the world what a good time she is having and she will not or cannot hear the noises of Nazism around her. But the others can.

Schultz courts Frln Schneider with old-world courtesy and they become engaged, but the fruiterer is Jewish and, when some Nazi sympathizers break up their engagement party, the old maid is obliged to let her dream of a marriage go. Cliff finds he has been almost unwittingly couriering Nazi funds for one of his language pupils and he is beaten up when he refuses to continue to do so. It is time to leave Berlin. But poor, self-deluded Sally cannot let the party end. She has her child aborted and, all responsibility gone, she watches Cliff take the train for Paris alone. Back in the cabaret, the emcee introduces the same show as before, but it is harsher, and soon it will be dark.

Ebb and Kander's songs were shared between material for the cabaret scenes and numbers set into the two romances of the text. Amongst the cabaret songs, Sally fluted out a plea ''Don't Tell Mama'' and insisted that life is a ''Cabaret'' where you must live for the day, whilst the Emcee welcomed the audience with a polyglot ''Willkommen,'' tried to make a little jolly troilism suitably decadent in ''Two Ladies,'' danced with a gorilla to explain that ''If You Could See Her Through My Eyes'' she wouldn't look Jewish at all, led a number in praise of cash (''The Money Song'') and, in a different vein, another about the hope of the youthful Hitlerians that ''Tomorrow Belongs to Me.'' The role of Frln Schneider was enriched with her thrill over a gift of a pineapple (''It Couldn't Please Me More'') and of being ''Married,'' and with the pragmatic ''So What?'' and ''What Would You Do?,'' explaining the logic of her decision to let married happiness go in the face of trouble, whilst Cliff wallowed in the surprise of his ''Perfectly Marvelous'' affair with Sally in ''Why Should I Wake Up?''

Harold Prince's production (Tony Award) played 1,166 performances on Broadway, and the show went on to a first national tour, with Signe Hasso (Schneider), Robert Salvio (Emcee), Gene Rupert (Cliff) and Melissa Hart (Sally) featured, followed by further productions throughout America and beyond. In London, Richard Pilbrow joined with Prince to present a reproduction of the show with Lila Kedrova (Schneider), Kevin Colson (Cliff), Peter Sallis (Schultz), Barry Dennen (Emcee) and with Judi Dench (later Elizabeth Seal) as Sally, which played through 336 performances. In Vienna (ad Robert Gilbert), the Theater an der Wien's production effectively cast the role of the Emcee with a woman, Blanche Aubry, alongside Lya Dulizkaya (Schneider), Violetta Ferrari (Sally), Klaus Wildbolz (Cliff) and Harry Füss (Schultz) for a season of 59 performances. But Australia's J C Williamson Ltd, having announced a production for Sydney's Theatre Royal in 1971, then cancelled it. Four weeks of *1776* and the British comedy *Move Over Mrs Markham* were hustled in instead. *Cabaret* got its first Australian performance ''by arrangement with J C Williamson'' in the less upmarket but maybe more suitably atmospheric Doncaster Theatre Restaurant.

The show had had a good and widely enough spread life, if not an outstanding one, and that might pretty well have been it. But a 1972 film version of *Cabaret* gave the show a second and even more popular lease on life. The screenplay kept, though slightly altered, the Cliff/Sally story, but cut the Schneider/Schultz plot and replaced it by another love story, for younger and more beautiful people, culled from elsewhere in Isherwood's tales. The score, deprived of Frln Schneider's characterful numbers, more than compensated with a new solo for Sally in the trumpetingly desperate ''Maybe This Time,'' a raunchier ''Mein Herr'' to replace the nicely nearly naughty ''Don't Tell Mama,'' and a new money number, ''Money, Money, Money,'' which, like the two other added pieces, featured the film's star, Liza Minnelli, in the role of Sally. Grey repeated his stage Emcee, at the head of Bob Fosse's cabaret entertainment, whilst Marisa Berenson and Fritz Wepper were the personable pair with problems of Jewishness and Helmut Griem appeared as a representative of cultured decadence, a beautiful, blue-eyed Baron who has affairs with both Sally and Brian (ex- Cliff).

The enormous success of the film—one of the very few films of a popular musical play to actually outrank its original stage show—led not only to worldwide fame for the piece, and to many further productions in a multiplicity of areas and languages, but also to a considerable alteration in the nature of the show and, in particular, of the role of Sally Bowles. The stinging vocalizing of Miss Minnelli was remembered by future inhabitants of the role rather than the vulnerable character that went with it and, as a result, a typically mounted French production (ad Jerome Savary) which toured Europe from 1986 introduced a brazen-voiced vamp of a Sally (Ute Lemper) who was about as far from the silly, sympathetic and real little creature of the original show as could be. The production was reprised in 1995 (Théâtre Mogador 24 January) with Dee Dee Bridgewater featured. As directors revelled in the show's ''decadence'' in much the same way that the section of Berlin folk portrayed in the piece did in the 1930s, rare was the production—amongst the many annual ones mounted worldwide, in theatres large and small—in the 1980s and 1990s which featured a Sally Bowles rather than a Liza Minnelli-Bowles.

In the second, postfilm life of *Cabaret,* Australia finally got its first-class production, 13 years after the stillborn one, and 25 years later a second ''compressed'' edition produced by John Frost at Sydney's Footbridge Theatre (September 1997) with Angela Toohey as Sally and Geraldine Turner as Frln Schneider. New York witnessed a first revival in 1987 (22 October, Imperial Theater) with Grey repeating his original role alongside Regina Resnik (Schneider), Alyson Reed (Sally), Gregg Edelmann (Cliff) and Werner Klemperer (Schultz) for a run of 254 performances, whilst a London repeat, which inserted the successful new numbers from the film score into the stage script, and featured Vivienne Martin (Schneider), Kelly Hunter (Sally), Wayne Sleep (Emcee), Peter Land (Cliff) and Oscar Quitak (Schultz) was mounted at the Strand Theatre in 1986 (17 July) and ran through 322 performances. A further London repeat, of a version using items culled from film and revised stage versions, was mounted at the Donmar Warehouse (2 December 1993) with Jane Horrocks (getting nearer to the striving-to-shock little girl from Chelsea than had become usual) as Sally featured alongside Sara Kestelmann (Schneider) and Alan Cumming (Emcee), and with the auditorium made—in the manner of a *Wunder-Bar*—to represent a cabaret room. It was well received through 130 performances, shown in a potted form on television, and later reproduced in New York in another intimate venue (Kit Kat Club/Henry Miller Theater 19 March 1998) with Natasha Richardson featured as another less than stingingly-singing Sally, Mary Louise Wilson as Frau Schneider and Cumming repeating his London assignment. Highly successful, the production subsequently transferred to the larger Studio 54 (13 November 1998). The Vienna Sofeinsaal brought the show back in December 1998, with Uwe Kröger as the Emcee, Berlin's Theater am Kurfürstendamm took in a revival on 2 September 1999, and everywhere productions proliferated as, on the edge of the 21st century and more than 30 years on from its initial production, *Cabaret* established itself as more popular than ever before.

UK: Palace Theatre 28 February 1968; Austria: Theater an der Wien 14 November 1970; Australia: Doncaster Theatre Restaurant, ?1972; Germany: Theater des Westens 31 December 1978; France: Théâtre du 8ème, Lyon 13 May 1986

Film: Allied Artists 1972

Recordings: original cast (Columbia), London cast (CBS), Austrian cast (Preiser), Italian cast (Carisch), Dutch cast (Disky), London

Plate 59. **The Cabaret Girl.** *The entertainment catchword of the moment went into the title of this piece, and its heroine's ambitions were a place in the cast of the Midnight Follies instead of the usual Ziegfeld variety.*

Revival cast 1986 (First Night), New York revival cast 1998 (RCA), Israeli cast (Reverso/BMG), Vienna cast 1996 (Reverso/BMG), Vienna cast 1998 (Kroger), studio cast (TER), film soundtrack (ABC), etc

THE CABARET GIRL Musical comedy in 3 acts by George Grossmith and P G Wodehouse. Music by Jerome Kern. Winter Garden Theatre, London, 19 September 1922.

When the box office for the happily successful *Sally* at London's Winter Garden Theatre base finally faded away, almost overnight, the producer-performer George Grossmith decided to order his own musical play from that show's composer, Jerome Kern, as a hurried replacement. Using the in topic of the newly popular style of entertainment called cabaret as a keystone, Grossmith and P G Wodehouse cobbled together a standard the-showgirl-and-the-aristocrat libretto whilst heading across the ocean to America and a meeting with the composer. They spent a week with him lyricking his tunes whilst he composed the melodies to the action numbers and finales supplied from their text, and, less than a fortnight later, the two Englishmen were able to get back on their ship and head home with a rehearsal script for *The Cabaret Girl.*

London's *Sally* star, Dorothy Dickson, was Marilynn Morgan (an open reference to original *Sally* star Marilynn Miller) who, in the course of the evening's little bit of action, gets herself both a job with the fictional equivalent of London's Hotel Metropole late-night cabaret and a handsome young aristocrat (Geoffrey Gwyther)—in pretty much the same way as had all those ''dancing-Cinderella'' Broadway musical heroines who for the past few years had been crowding out the fictional star dressing rooms of the *Ziegfeld Follies* and the homes of the upper four hundred. Grossmith paired with Leslie Henson (who was out ill for much of the run and depped by Norman Griffin) as Messrs Gravvins and Gripps, the producers of the cabaret (and both ''Gr'' for Grossmith), a pair who meddled in everything going, permitting them to comick their way through the largest portion of the entertainment. They were equipped with the number ''Mr Gravvins, Mr Gripps,'' which borrowed happily from the *Ziegfeld Follies'* celebrated Gallagher and Shean song. ''Borrowed'' or not, it proved one of the most popular numbers of the show alongside two solos for Miss Dickson—''Ka-lu-a,'' brought in from Kern's earlier *Good Morning, Dearie,* and ''Shimmy with Me''—and a happy duo for the little star and Grossmith, ''Dancing Time.''

Pretty costumes and songs, the Winter Garden favorites and the theatre's reputation for lively entertainment did more to help *The Cabaret Girl* to a fine run of 361 performances in London than any integral merits. However, set up by that run, it toured into 1925 and was given an Australian production, with Madge Elliott top billing as the now renamed Flick Morgan and Alfred Frith and Cyril Ritchard heading the comedy, through two months in Melbourne (Her Majesty's Theatre 8 March 1924) and a little more in Sydney.

In spite of one of those ''announcements'' of a forthcoming Broadway version made, alongside a host of others, by a hustling Broadway producer of the time, the show was never transported to America.

Australia: Her Majesty's Theatre, Sydney 25 August 1923
Recording: selection on *Jerome Kern in London* (WRC)

LE CABINET PIPERLIN Opérette in 3 acts by Hippolyte Raymond and Paul Burani. Music by Hervé. Théâtre de l'Athénée-Comique, Paris, 17 September 1897.

The agency of the title of *Le Cabinet Piperlin* was one which offered gentlemen insurance against the infidelity of their wives and, in this tale, it is threatened with bankruptcy because of the widely spread-about attractions of one particular young gentleman. The head of the agency has only one solution. He sets out his own very pretty wife, Colombe, to distract the young man in question from his expensive depredations.

Hervé had written a full musical score for the original production of *Le Cabinet Piperlin* at the Théâtre de l'Athénée in 1878, but the theatre's director, alarmed at the size of the musical content provided for what was intended to be a simple vaudeville à couplets, refused to use it in its entirety. In an all-or-nothing gesture, Hervé withdrew the whole music and the piece was ultimately played, with great and international success, as a comedy without music. After the composer's death, his son, the actor and director Gardel, discovered the widowed score amongst his father's effects and the 20-year-old opérette-cum-vaudeville was dusted off, its 22 musical pieces arranged by Hervé jr, and *Le Cabinet Piperlin* presented as a musical by Maurice Charlot at the Athénée-Comique. Guyon fils played Piperlin, with Augustine Leriche as Colombe, and Vallières (Dardinel), Jannin (Vétiver), Baron fils (Roussignac) and Jeanne Petit (Zenaïde) supporting through a run of 70 nights, prior to the show being mounted in both Budapest (ad Viktor Rákosi, Emil Makai) and in Vienna (ad Heinrich Bolten-Bäckers).

The original vaudeville was also used as the basis for the unsuccessful Adrian Ross/Hugo Felix musical *The Antelope* (Waldorf Theatre, London 28 November 1908).

Hungary: Magyar Színház *B.A.L.E.K.* 3 December 1898; Austria: Lustspieltheater 25 December 1899

CABIN IN THE SKY Musical fantasy in 2 acts by Lynn Root. Lyrics by John Latouche. Music Vernon Duke. Martin Beck Theater, New York, 25 October 1940.

God has decided that Little Joe (Dooley Wilson), the no-good husband of the devout Petunia Jackson (Ethel Waters), has had his time on earth, but he listens to Petunia's pleas and allows the fellow six months in which to shape up and earn himself a longer life. The Lord's General (Todd Duncan) is sent down from heaven to help the sinner on the path to repentance and improvement. However, there is competition for the body and soul of Little Joe in the shape of the infernal Lucifer (Rex Ingram) and it is he who wins. The man quarrels with his wife and shoots her dead. But foolishly faithful Petunia has the last word. At the gates of Saint Peter, she persuades the powers that be to find a place in heaven for her errant husband.

The sentimental fantasy of the book was accompanied by a score which was highlighted by Miss Waters's "Taking a Chance on Love," a happy title duo for the Jacksons and "Honey in the Honeycomb" delivered by co-choreographer Katherine Dunham (as the slinky Georgia Brown) through a Broadway run of 156 performances. A film version of the tale made in 1943 with Miss Waters starred alongside Ingram, Eddie "Rochester" Anderson and Lena Horne retained just those three numbers, complementing them with three pieces by Harold Arlen, two by Duke Ellington and one by Cecil Mack, Lew Brown and Ford Dabney.

The show was revived at off-Broadway's Greenwich Mews Theater in 1964 (21 January) with Rosetta LeNoire, Tony Middleton, Bernard Johnson and Ketty Lester featured in a version for which Duke extended his original score (46 performances).

Film: MGM 1943

Recordings: 1964 revival cast (Capitol), film soundtrack (Hollywood soundstage)

CAESAR, Irving [CAESAR, Isidor] (b New York, 4 July 1895; d New York 17 December 1996). *No, No, Nanette* lyricist who never found another book musical hit.

After an early working life including stints as a stenographer and a press representative, Caesar toured as a performer in vaudeville before beginning to write song lyrics. His first major hit came when he wrote the words for George Gershwin's "Swanee" (1918), introduced into the show *Sinbad* by Al Jolson, and he thereafter contributed a few lyrics to Ivan Caryll's *Kissing Time* (1920), more to the disastrous *Lady Kitty Inc* (1920) and to F C Coppicus's short-lived production of the American version of Hugo Hirsch's *Die tolle Lola* (1921, *Lola in Love*), as well as to a number of revues, notably several editions of *The Greenwich Village Follies.*

He came securely into the musical theatre in 1923 when he took an "additional lyrics" credit alongside Otto Harbach, Frank Mandel and Vincent Youmans on the score for *No, No, Nanette.* In spite of that credit, however, Caesar's portion of the words included those for most of the show's highlight songs: "Tea for Two," "I Want to Be Happy," "Too Many Rings Around Rosie," "You Can Dance with Any Girl At All" and the "Where Has My Hubby Gone Blues."

Caesar contributed some additional material to a second international hit in *Mercenary Mary* and worked on the naively appealing *Honeymoon Lane* with and for Eddie Dowling, but none of the other original stage musicals with which he was subsequently involved as lyricist, and occasionally as a librettist, as a rerewriter with or without credit, or even as a composer, brought him anything like the same success. *Yes, Yes, Yvette* (in which he placed his song "I'm a Little Bit Fonder of You") did not live up to its predecessor; Romberg's *Nina Rosa* found its major success when its lyrics were rewritten in French; Caesar's adaptation of Robert Katscher's Continental hit revusical comedy *Die Wunder-Bar,* made into a vehicle for Al Jolson, had a run of over 200 performances at the Savoy in London, but was not a hit in New York; and it was Harry Graham's London translation of *White Horse Inn* (*Im weissen Rössl*) which became the standard English-language one rather than Caesar's edition, written for the vastly spectacular Center Theater production in New York. His final Broadway appearance was as producer, librettist, colyricist and composer of the unsuccessful *My Dear Public* (1943).

Caesar wrote elsewhere for revue and films, and his song successes included several in the ''Swanee'' vein (''My Mammy,'' with music by Walter Donaldson, ''Yankee Doodle Blues,'' ''Is It True What They Say about Dixie?,'' ''Dixie Rose''), ''That Funny Melody,'' Joseph Meyer and Roger Wolfe Kahn's ''Crazy Rhythm'' (*Here's Howe*), and Youmans's ''Sometimes I'm Happy,'' which was interpolated into the show *Hit the Deck.* All of these hits later appeared in various compilation shows.

1920 **Lady Kitty Inc** (Paul Lannin/w Melville Alexander/ Edward A Paulton) Ford's Opera House, Baltimore 16 February

1922 **Lola in Love** (*Die tolle Lola*) English version (Scranton, Pa)

1923 **No, No, Nanette** (Vincent Youmans/w Otto Harbach/Frank Mandel, Harbach) Garrick Theater, Detroit 23 April; Palace Theatre, London 11 March 1925

1924 **In Dutch** (Joseph Meyer, Alfred Newman, William Daly/w William Cary Duncan) Newark, NJ 22 September

1924 **Betty Lee** (Louis Hirsch, Con Conrad/w Harbach/Harbach) 44th Street Theater 25 December

1925 **The Bamboula** (Albert Szirmai/w Douglas Furber/Guy Bolton, Harry Vernon) His Majesty's Theatre, London 24 March

1926 **Sweetheart Time** (Meyer, Walter Donaldson/Harry B Smith) Imperial Theater 19 January

1926 **Honeymoon Lane** (James T Hanley/w Eddie Dowling) Knickerbocker Theater 20 September

1926 **Betsy** (Hart, Rodgers/ w David Freedman) New Amsterdam Theater 28 December

1927 **Talk About Girls** (ex- *Suzanne*) (Stephen Jones, Harold Orlob/J H Booth, William Cary Duncan) Waldorf Theater 14 June

1927 **Yes, Yes, Yvette** (Phil Charig, Ben Jerome) Harris Theater 3 October

1928 **Here's Howe** (Roger Wolfe Kahn, Meyer) Broadhurst Theater 1 May

1929 **Polly** (Charig, Stothart/w Guy Bolton,George Middleton, Isabel Leighton) Lyric Theater 8 January

1930 **Ripples** (Oscar Levant, Szirmai, et al/w Graham John/ William Anthony McGuire) New Amsterdam Theater 11 February

1930 **Nina Rosa** (Romberg/Harbach) Majestic Theater 20 September

1931 **[The] Wonder Bar** (*Die Wunder-Bar*) revised English version w Aben Kandel (Nora Bayes Theater)

1933 **Melody** (Romberg/Edward Childs Carpenter) Casino Theater 14 February

1936 **White Horse Inn** (*Im weissen Rössl*) English lyrics (Center Theatre)

1943 **My Dear Public** (Gerald Marks/w Sam Lerner) 46th Street Theater 9 September

LA CAGE AUX FOLLES Musical in 2 acts by Harvey Fierstein based on the play of the same name by Jean Poiret. Music and lyrics by Jerry Herman. Palace Theater, New York, 21 August 1983.

Jean Poiret's play, first produced at Paris's Palais-Royal in 1973, had a seven-year run there (2,467 performances), prior to being made into an equally successful French film and then, after many and lavishly reported problems, writings and rewritings, into a musical.

Georges (Gene Barry) and Albin (George Hearn) run a night-club, ''La Cage aux Folles,'' at Saint-Tropez, where the feature is a travesty floor show with Albin, otherwise ''Zaza,'' as the glittering star. Albin's tantrums apart, theirs is a loving ménage, and it is even blessed with a son, Jean-Michel (John Weiner), the result of a small aberration of Georges's with a chorus girl a couple of decades previously. However, that son has now got to the age where he wishes to marry. He wishes to marry a girl, and he has to introduce Anne Dindon (Leslie Stevens) and her parents to his parents, about whom he has lied a little. Lying was necessary, as Anne's father (Jay Garner) is a local politician of a staunchly reactionary breed who is not likely to appreciate the fact that his future son-in-law's mother is a man. Albin is to be demoted to Uncle Al for the night of the Dindons' visit but, when Jean-Michel's real mother refuses to appear, he saves the moment and descends on the party as a boundingly impressive tasilo-suited ''maman.'' A series of farcical events leads up to his eventual exposure, Jean-Michel and Anne join Georges in standing by him, and, with the press awaiting gloatingly at the door to record his connection with the kind of people he has always condemned, deputé Dindon can only give in and allow his daughter's marriage.

Herman's songs ranged from a veritable blowtorch song for the ''betrayed'' Albin, ''I Am What I Am,'' a number which soon made its way out of the show and into a hundred club acts (m and f) and cabaret performances, to the gentle, loving strains of Georges's chanson ''Song on the Sand,'' the lilting ''With Anne on my Arm'' for Jean-Michel (and later for Georges and Albin) and a singalong ''The Best of Times,'' headed by Albin and restauranteuse Jacqueline (Elizabeth Parrish), in a colorful score which illustrated its tale happily and effectively.

Allan Carr's Broadway production, directed by Arthur Laurents and choreographed by Scott Salmon, played through a successful 1,761 performances, and the show was subsequently taken up by overseas producers in a way that few Broadway musicals of the 1970s and

1980s had been. However neither a production at London's Palladium, with Dennis Quilley and Hearn featured (301 performances), nor one in Australia, starring Keith Michell and Jon Ewing, turned out to be a success. A German adaptation (ad Erika Gesell, Christian Severin) mounted at the Theater des Westens with Gunter König and Helmut Baumann in the lead roles, was followed by a remarkable small-theatre Austrian premiere at the Sommerfestspiele in Amstetten, with Joachim Kemmer and Wolf-Dietrich Berg playing Albin and Georges in a production which reproduced the atmosphere and choreography of the "Cage aux Folles" much more realtistically and excitingly than the vastness of stages such as the Palladium. This success resulted in the show spreading itself widely through German and Austrian provincial theatres, its prospects not hindered by the odd theatre director who welcomed the opportunity to produce a show that allowed him to pop into skirts in a way become more popular in the 1980s and 1990s than at any time since the Victorian era.

La Cage aux Folles (sometimes literally translated as *Ein Käfig voller Narren*) was taken up from Amstetten to be mounted at the Vienna Volksoper in 1991 with larger means and without equal felicity, but the ever-enterprising Budapest Fővárosi Operettszínház successfully added the piece to its repertoire in 1991 with Sándor Németh (Georges) and Péter Haumann (Albin) initiating the lead roles happily. Rome's Teatro Sistina welcomed an Italian version (9 October 1991) and finally, the full circle completed, the musical version was mounted at Paris's Théâtre Mogador 2 with Patrick Rocca and Bernard Alane starred. *La Cage aux Folles* had by that time established itself as the most popular Broadway musical of its era on central European stages.

The French play and film were subsequently made up into a non-musical American film entitled *The Bird Cage.*

Australia: Her Majesty's Theatre, Sydney, 2 March 1985; Germany: Theater des Westens *Ein Käfig voller Narren* 19 October 1985; UK: London Palladium 7 May 1986; Austria: Theater Amstetten *Ein Käfig voller Narren* 3 August 1989; Hungary: Fővárosi Operettszínház *Őrult nők kektrece* 20 September 1991; France: Théâtre Mogador 29 September 1999

Recordings: original cast (RCA), Australian cast (RCA), German cast (Polydor), Colombian cast (Talete), Italian cast (Carisch), Austrian cast (Volksoper) (Reverso), Mexican cast *La Jaula de las locas* (no label), etc

CAGE ME A PEACOCK Musical in 2 acts by Noel Langley based on his novel of the same name. Additional lyrics by Adam Leslie. Music by Eve Lynd. Strand Theatre, London, 18 June 1948.

A spicily comical little musical based on the South African novelist's saucy retelling of the *Rape of Lucrezia* legend. If the stage version needfully softened down the multiplicity of sexual variations explicitly implicit in the tongue-in-everything-including-the-cheek novel, it still made for an enjoyable evening and won a 10-month run in London's West End. Bill O'Connor was the organizing Mercury, Yolande Donlan the nymphet who becomes Lucrezia, Simon Lack played Tarquinius, and Roy Dean the shyly and bisexually obliging Casso.

With the 337 performances of *Cage Me a Peacock,* Eve Lynd notched herself up a spot as the first woman composer to have a musical staged in the West End since Liza Lehmann, nearly half a century earlier. She supplied a set of songs for the show which included a successful single ("Time Alone Will Tell") and which, half a century on—admittedly against very little competition—still allow her to hold the London long-run record for a musical composed by a woman.

During his time in Hollywood as a highly successful screenwriter (*The Wizard of Oz,* etc), Langley had previously had his piece played in a musicalized version at Los Angeles' Pelican Theater (23 April 1942) with a different score, by Bud McCreery, attached.

CAGLIOSTRO IN WIEN Operette in 3 acts by F Zell and Richard Genée. Music by Johann Strauss. Theater an der Wien, Vienna, 27 February 1875.

Johann Strauss's first Operette after *Die Fledermaus* did not live up to the expectations aroused by the success of its predecessor.

Cagliostro in Wien centered itself, in name at least, on a colorful historical character, the 18th-century Italian adventurer and quack alchemist, Count Alexander Cagliostro (otherwise Giuseppe Balsamo, 1743–95). Librettists Zell and Genée being at the time suspected by theatrical commentators of a wholesale inability to come up with an original text, the local papers posited Goethe's *Gross Kophta* and Dumas's *Josef Balsamo* as apparent sources, whilst overlooking the most likely inspiration: the French comic opera *Cagliostro* (Adolphe Adam/J Vernoy de St Georges, Eugène Scribe Opéra-Comique 10 February 1844). However, the name of Cagliostro had become, by the 19th century, synonomous simply with the archetypical charlatan, and the adventures theatrically attached to his name very often had little or nothing to do with his real life. It seems, however, that Adam's librettists stayed rather closer to history—or at least to the accepted tales—than their Viennese colleagues. In real life, or so it is said, Cagliostro was a master impostor who was involved in the reasonably dramatic affair of Marie-Antoinette's diamond necklace. He died in a Roman prison after falling foul of the Italian police, whilst his assistant and mistress, Lorenza, ended her days immured in a convent. Here the "hero" of the piece and his lady were fictionally transported into a Viennese setting and into a rather less lively adventure.

The first act of Zell and Genée's comic opera was set during a 1783 festival marking Vienna's hundred years of freedom from Turkish oppression, to which the charlatan Alessandro Cagliostro (Carl Adolf Friese), his wife Lorenza Feliciani (Marie Geistinger) and his servant, Blasoni (Alexander Girardi) come to dazzle the profitable people of Vienna with their tricks. During the festivities Lorenza attracts the attentions of the dandy young Hungarian officer, Graf Stefan Fodor (Jani Szika), whilst his friend, the Rittmeister Baron Lieven (Eichheim), romances pretty Emilie (Karoline Finaly), niece of the wealthy widow, Frau Adami (Henriette Wieser). When Cagliostro tries to set up a big coup, Lorenza—her sensitivities awakened by her honest if stupid young admirer—refuses to help. Cagliostro agrees to divorce her, for a consideration, and sets his sights and talents on the winning of the heiress, Emilie. He attempts to drug Lieven to keep him out of the way whilst his marriage ceremony with Emilie goes ahead, but now Blasoni also proves faithless and, his plan in tatters, the alchemist flees from the law, leaving both the young folk, and Fodor and Lorenza, to their happy ending.

The opportunities of Strauss's score were given mainly to the leading lady. Lorenza had two fine numbers in the opening act: a gypsyish Zigeunerkind piece (''Wie glänzt dein Haar''), immediately followed by a Strofenlied (''Ja Cagliostro heisst der Mann''), as well as a healthy share in the big first-act finale, working up her ''Beim Dudeln war'n Weana'' through some high tessitura vocalizing and even a bit of yodelling to the climax of the act. The second-act ''Mag alle Welt auch preisen der Alchimie'' and the third-act waltz ''O süsses Wörtchen'' gave her further opportunities. Cagliostro himself had little in the way of music, finding his best moment in a magic mirror trio with Emilie and her mother who, in her turn, had a second-act romanze (''Bald sind die Künzeln alle Weg'') and got involved in some delightful cod wooing with Blasoni in the waltzing ''Ihnen fliegen durchs Leben an Ihnen Seite.'' Fodor made the most of an entry song on horseback and joined Lorenza in the big duet of the evening, the hard and high ''Belieben sie mich zu anhören.'' However, a soldiers' chorus, a sextet of old women and a pretty Ländler proved better liked by Viennese audiences than the showier numbers.

Cagliostro was played at the Theater an der Wien 35 times in its initial run, to good houses, given 14 more showings during the season, and then dropped from the repertoire. It was played at Berlin's Friedrich-Wilhelmstädtisches Theater the same year, and in its German version in both Budapest and Prague, but it proved one of the least liked of Strauss's stage works and seems to have gone little further. France merely got some bits of its score—mostly Lorenza's biggest and showiest bits—pasted together with some of *Die Fledermaus* and some freshly written bits to make up the music for the Parisian Strauss show *La Tzigane.*

The saleable name of Strauss, however, persuaded people to persist with the piece. In 1881 the Theater an der Wien brought *Cagliostro* back in a new production which was played just seven times before being shelved. The Wiener Bürgertheater mounted a new version (1927)—textually rewritten by Ludwig Herzer, with the music rearranged by Erich Wolfgang Korngold, and featuring Jacob Feldhammer as Cagliostro, Ida Russka as Lorenza Feliciana and Mizzi Zwerenz as ''the rich hostess of the 'Blauen Insel' inn''—which lasted all of 17 performances, and there were other periodic and mostly hacked-about revivals mounted in Germany, including one rewritten by that indefatigable rewriter Gustav Quedtenfeldt (w Karl Tutein) under the title of *Verzaubertes Wien* (Danzig 3 May 1941). However, in spite of the name of Strauss on the billhead, the piece regularly and resolutely refused to go, no more so than when a mannered, poppy version, which was scarcely a version at all, was mounted at Vienna's Ronacher in 1986 (22 May).

Germany: Friedrich-Wilhelmstädtisches Theater 18 September 1875; Hungary: Deutschige Theater in der Wollgasse May 1876

Recording: 1986 selection (Cagliostro)

CAHILL, Marie (b Brooklyn, NY, 7 February 1870; d New York, 23 August 1933). Cheerful comic star of the early 20th-century American stage.

After making her earliest beginnings in the theatre playing in stock, the young Marie Cahill enjoyed a wide-ranging juvenile career which embraced farce-musicals (Patsy in *A Hole in the Ground* 1887, Patsy in *A Tin Soldier* 1888, Mary Ellen Ryan in *McKenna's Flirtation* with Barry and Fay, Patty in *The Fakir* 1890, Mora in the original production of the Hanlons' *Superba*); romantic drama (Maggie McBride in *The Banshee* 1891); French musical comedy (*Miss Helyett* tour 1892); an appearance at the Paris Théâtre de la Gaîté; another as a guest act in the musical comedy *Morocco Bound* at London's Shaftesbury Theatre and at the Trafalgar Theatre (''dainty and graceful dancing''); and touring burlesque around America (Blanche Calvé Santootsie in *Excelsior Jr,* Lyric Theater, New York, 1895)—all before she established herself as a successful musical comedienne and, ultimately, a musical comedy star on Broadway.

She appeared in a comic song-and-dance role in Victor Herbert's *The Gold Bug* (1896, Lady Patty Larceny), toured as Flo Honeydew in *The Lady Slavey* (1897), paired with Sadie Kirby as one of the music-hall Gelatine Sisters in the Broadway staging of the British musical

Monte Carlo (1898), played a baddie alongside Raymond Hitchcock in *Three Little Lambs* (1899, Phyllis Argyle), took to vaudeville burlesque with the Agoust family jugglers in *Star and Garter* (1900, Mme Piquet), appeared as Aramantha Dedincourt in *The Chaperons* (1901) and interpolated much the same kind of friendly comedy and the song ''Nancy Brown'' (with considerable benefit to the show's receipts) into Harry B Smith's rather more structured *The Wild Rose* (1902, Vera von Lahn).

She moved firmly into the star circle in 1902 in the title role of *Sally in Our Alley,* in which she made a particular hit with the song ''Under the Bamboo Tree,'' and she repeated this success the following year in a show named for her earlier hit number, *Nancy Brown* (''Congo Love Song''). However, her penchant for giving her own performance and her own songs in no matter what book-musical context resulted in a showdown with Victor Herbert and her removal from the star comedy role of his *It Happened in Nordland* (1904, Katherine Peepfogle). Thereafter she stuck starrily to such less musically structured shows as *Moonshine* (1905, Molly Moonshine ''of the U.S. secret service,'' ''I'm a' Lookin'''), a musical adaptation of the play *My Wife's Husbands* as *Marrying Mary* (1906, Mary Montgomery, ''I Love the Last One Best of All''), *The Boys and Betty* (1908, Betty Barbeau, Marie Cahill's ''Arab Love Song'') and *Judy Forgot* (1910, Judy Evans), each produced under the management of her husband, Daniel V Arthur, whilst being served as to her songs principally by Silvio Hein, Cole and Johnson, and Benjamin Hapgood Burt.

Miss Cahill appeared as Little Buttercup in a starry New York *HMS Pinafore* (1911) and as Céleste Derémy in an Americanized version of Heuberger's successful Viennese Operette *Der Opernball* (1912), and in 1915 she starred opposite Richard Carle in the maiden Guy Bolton/Jerome Kern musical, *Ninety in the Shade* (Polly Bainbridge, ''Whistling Dan,'' ''My Mindanao Chocolate Soldier''). In 1919 she decorated George Hobart and Herbert Hall Winslow's *Just Around the Corner* with several songs, and in 1930 she and Carle took their last Broadway bows together in *The New Yorkers* (Gloria Wentworth).

A strong, healthy little comedienne of buxom proportions and a very positive personality, she won most of her success by simply playing and singing herself, but she proved equally, in several shows, that she was capable of actually acting a role as well as simply being a star.

CAHN, Sammy [COHEN, Samuel] (b New York, 18 June 1913; d New York, 15 January 1993). Top filmland songwriter whose stage career was less productive.

Originally a violinist, the young Cahn joined Saul Chaplin in organizing a dance band, and he moved into songwriting when the theme song they wrote for themselves, ''Rhythm Is My Business,'' found success above and beyond its original use. Thereafter, Cahn turned out the lyrics for a large number of popular songs (''Three Coins in a Fountain,'' ''Thoroughly Modern Millie,'' ''The Tender Trap,'' ''High Hopes,'' ''Love and Marriage,'' ''My Kind of Town,'' ''It's Been a Long, Long Time,'' ''Five Minutes More,'' ''Call Me Irresponsible,'' ''The Second Time Around,'' ''The Things We Did Last Summer,'' ''All the Way,'' etc), including many for the motion picture world which rewarded him with four Academy Awards. He also made several incursions into the musical theatre, the first and the last of which in person. He was seen deputizing for the show's star comedian in the bootless Philadelphia tryout of his earliest stage musical, *Glad to See You,* and in his elder years appeared performing his own works with a small supporting group variously as *Words and Music* and *Sammy Cahn's Songbook* in New York and London. Only *High Button Shoes* of the book musicals to which he contributed, however, proved a genuine success.

Cahn also combined with James van Heusen on television musical versions of Thornton Wilder's play *Our Town* (lib: David Shaw, NBC 19 September 1955), of *Robin Hood* (NBC 18 February 1968), of *Jack and the Beanstalk* (NBC 26 February 1967) and of *Once Upon a Brothers Grimm* (CBS 23 November 1977).

1944 **Glad to See You** (Jule Styne/Fred Thompson, Eddie Davis) Shubert Theater, Philadelphia 13 November

1947 **High Button Shoes** (Styne/Stephen Longstreet) New Century Theater 9 October

1964 **Les Poupées de Paris** (James van Heusen) puppet-show World's Fair 22 April

1965 **Skyscraper** (van Heusen/Peter Stone) Lunt-Fontanne Theater 13 November

1966 **Walking Happy** (van Heusen/Roger O Hirson, Ketti Frings) Lunt-Fontanne Theater 26 November

1970 **Look to the Lilies** (Styne/Leonard Spigelgass) Lunt-Fontanne Theater 29 March

1980 **An April Song** (Mitch Leigh/Albert Marre) John Drew Theater of Guild Hall 25 August

Autobiography: *I Should Care* (Arbor House, New York, 1974)

CAILLAVET, G[aston] A[rman] de (b Paris, 15 March 1870; d Essendièras, Périgord, 15 January 1915).

The author of a richly successful list of plays and libretti, de Caillavet and the partner de plume of most of his career, Robert de Flers, were regarded as the most cultured and witty of humorists and theatrical authors of their time. The heart of their musical theatre work consists of four much-admired opéras-bouffes, set to music by Claude Terrasse (*Les Travaux d'Hercule, Le Sire de Vergy, M de la Palisse, Paris, ou le bon juge*), in which they tickled Grecian and Gallic antiquity with the same kind of verve that Crémieux, Tréfeu, Meilhac and Halévy had done in Offenbachian days. They also supplied the text for a much-liked little Terrasse opérette, *Chonchette,* and libretti for two pieces for André Messager: a light operatic adaptation of de Musset's *Le Chandelier* entitled *Fortunio,* and a dramatization of a piece by Charles Nodier as the text to the légende lyrique *Béatrice* (Théâtre de Monte Carlo 21 March 1914). Both of these, although distinctly different in tone, were played at the Opéra-Comique. Their last works for the musical stage, before de Caillavet's premature death, were the enormously successful French adaptations of *Die lustige Witwe* and *Der Graf von Luxemburg.*

The plays of de Caillavet and de Flers were subsequently used as the bases for a number of musical comedies: their 1906 comedy *Miquette et sa mère* was the source for Fall's *Das Puppenmädel, Le Roi* (1908), which had already been illustrated with some music by Emmanuel Arène on its original production, was made into a full scale musical comedy by Ralph Benatzky under the title *Majestät-privat* (Theater an der Wien 18 December 1937), and an Italian musical, *Primarosa,* was taken from their *Primerose* (1911), whilst *La Belle Aventure* (1914) became the source for *In der Johannisnacht* (Jean Gilbert/Robert Gilbert, Thalia Theater, Hamburg 1 July 1926).

1901 **Les Travaux d'Hercule** (Claude Terrasse/w Robert de Flers) Théâtre des Bouffes-Parisiens 7 March

1902 **Chonchette** (Terrasse/w de Flers) 1 act Théâtre des Capucines 11 April

1903 **Le Sire de Vergy** (Terrasse/w de Flers) Théâtre des Variétés 16 April

1904 **Monsieur de la Palisse** (Terrasse/w de Flers) Théâtre des Variétés 2 November

1906 **Paris, ou le bon juge** (Terrasse/w de Flers) Théâtre des Capucines 18 March

1907 **Fortunio** (André Messager/w de Flers) Opéra-Comique 5 June

1909 **La Veuve joyeuse** (*Die lustige Witwe*) French version w de Flers (Théâtre Apollo)

1912 **Le Comte de Luxembourg** (*Der Graf von Luxemburg*) French version w de Flers (Théâtre Apollo)

CAIRD, John (b Edmonton, Canada, 22 September 1948).

The associate director of Britain's Royal Shakespeare company, John Caird was the co-director and co-adapter of *Les Misérables* (Tony Award), the director of London's *Song and Dance* (1982) and subsequently adapted and co-directed the National Theatre's successful production of *Candide* (1998 w Trevor Nunn). He also has authored two musicals, *Children of Eden* and *Jane Eyre.*

1991 **Children of Eden** (Stephen Schwartz) Prince Edward Theatre 8 January

1996 **Jane Eyre** (Paul Gordon) Royal Alexandra Theatre, Toronto 12 November 1996; revised version, La Jolla Playhouse, Calif 29 August 1999; Brooks Atkinson Theater 3 December 2000

CAIRO Mosaic in music and mime in 3 acts and 11 scenes by Oscar Asche. Music by Percy Fletcher. Century Theater, New York, as *Mecca,* 4 October 1920.

Oscar Asche's successor to *Chu Chin Chow* did not, as might have been expected, make its first appearance on the stage of Her Majesty's Theatre, London, but that was only because there was no question of closing the lucrative *Chu Chin Chow,* which was running on strongly there, making its way towards its record-breaking total of performances. Instead, it was *Chu Chin Chow*'s American producers, F Ray Comstock and Morris Gest, who mounted it as *Mecca* at Broadway's Century Theater, and it was Lionel Braham, Gladys Hanson and John Doran who introduced the roles that Asche had written for himself, his wife Lily Brayton and *Chu Chin Chow*'s most valuable star, Courtice Pounds. These roles were, not unnaturally, written to be as like to those of the previous hit as was possible in an original tale which, even more than its predecessor, seemed to owe a good deal to Eddie Knoblock's *Kismet.*

Charlatan Ali Shar (Braham), his pretty daughter Zummurud (soprano Hannah Toback) and his clown (Doran) come to Cairo and, when the young Sultan (Orville R Caldwell) falls in love with and weds Zummurud, they find themselves mixed up in the power struggle between the Sultan and the evil Wazir, Nur-al-Din (Herbert Grimwood). The Lily Brayton role, like that in *Chu Chin Chow,* was one of a dramatically vengeful non-singing lady. Miss Hanson played the part of the Princess Sharazad, who seeks out and revenges herself on the murderer of her son, who is, of course, the wicked Wazir. Another wily easterner part, a Chinese spy called Wei San Wei, was provided for *Chu Chin Chow*'s Frank Cochrane (and played on Broadway by Thomas Leary) and paired with a comic-feminine counterpart, Wei Wa Shi, as played by tiny Ida Mülle.

The other parallel between *Mecca* and *Chu Chin Chow* was in its production values. If the earlier show had been spectacular, the new one was super-spectacular. Asche, unable to direct it himself because of his role in *Chu Chin Chow,* handed over the job to his faithful lieutenant E Lyall Swete, who had staged Broadway's *Chu Chin Chow* for him. London's Joseph and Phil Harker were again hired to do the scenery, top British designer Percy Anderson was teamed with Alice O'Neil and Léon Bakst for the costumes, and ballet choreographer Michel Fokine set to create the vast, spectacular dance routines.

Plate 60. **Cairo.** *The famous bacchanale finale of Act II, choreographed by Fokine for America . . . and redone by Espinosa for London.*

The result was visually stunning, and hailed all round as the most vivid piece of spectacular entertainment ever seen on the Broadway stage. Fokine's second-act closer, a balletic bacchanale of semi-naked (for the time) easterners, proving the gasp-worthy highlight of the night.

Mecca played 130 nights on Broadway, and the following year duly followed *Chu Chin Chow* onto the London stage. Asche, Miss Brayton, Pounds and Cochrane all took up "their" parts, Fedora Rozelli was the soprano, Gracie Leigh the comedienne, and the dances were redone by Espinosa. But the title was different. In spite of the fact that the word *Mecca* had been and was being used as a brand name for everything from cafés to constipation cures, someone was able to convince the Lord Chamberlain that it would be indecent to call a musical play by the name of the holy city of Islam. So, in an early example of that linguistic fascism which passes nowadays as "political correctness," *Mecca* became *Cairo.* Which apparently wasn't holy to anyone.

Once again, the show's production won wild reactions, rather masking the fact that Asche's dialogue and lyrics were pretty creaky stuff and that Fletcher had not succeeded in turning out anything to equal the favorite songs of *Chu Chin Chow. Cairo* played 287 times in London, and Asche then sold off his scenery and costumes to Australia's J C Williamson Ltd and set off to the southern hemisphere to play what would be the last performances of his show. He presented *Cairo* for eight weeks in Sydney and then for a further seven weeks in Melbourne (Her Majesty's Theatre 23 December 1922) before switching to *Julius Caesar* and *Chu Chin Chow* for the last five weeks of his down-under engagement.

UK: His Majesty's Theatre 15 October 1921; Australia: Her Majesty's Theatre, Sydney 16 September 1922

CALDWELL, Anne [CALDWELL, Anna Payson] (b Boston, 30 August 1867; d Beverly Hills, Calif, 22 October 1936).

The young Anna P Caldwell began her theatrical career in her early teens, dancing in a Boston production of *Billee Taylor* (1880), before going on to play with the George A Jones and the Braham & Scanlan juvenile comic opera companies, and then going adult touring as Fiametta in *La Mascotte* (1883). Thereafter she worked with the Boston Burlesque Company and with the cut-price P Harris Opera Company (1884), and ultimately made her New York debut, alongside Selina Dolaro, in a production of *The Bridge of Sighs* which folded in just a few nights. The ''little, plump brunette'' continued her career in burlesque (as Idex in *The Naiad Queen* with Mann & Benoit's Co, 1885), and, in the 1890s—after a short matrimonial pause as Mrs William Linder Vinal of Boston—in comic opera, musical comedy (Maud S in *U & I* 1891, *The Tar and the Tartar* 1892, etc), and, later, in farce comedy (Daisy Rosa in *A Sure Cure,* 1898) and in vaudeville as a team with her (second) husband, Charles A Wayne (George M Cohan's sketch *To Boston on Business,* 1899, etc).

She then retired from performing and turned instead to writing for the theatre, making first a brief attempt as a composer (''Young Antelope,'' ''Rosy,'' etc) during which she and her (third) husband, the successful lyricist **James O'DEA** (b Hamilton, Ont, 25 December 1871; d Rockville Center, NY, 12 April 1914; ''Sammy,'' ''The Sweetest Girl in Dixie,'' 'Silver Heels,'' 'Hiawatha,'' ''Send Me Back to Tee-Pee Land'') had songs included in the English import *Sergeant Brue* (1905, ''Every Saturday Afternoon''), *The Babes and the Baron* (1905, ''The Light of the Honeymoon''), the Casino Theater's *The Social Whirl* (1906, ''Old Man Manhattan'') and Sam and Lee Shubert's juvenile show *The Top of the World* (1907). However, she soon switched from the music to the words, and went on to a career as a prolific Broadway librettist and lyricist. Although she was never responsible for the book of an enduring success, or of more than a tiny handful of lyrics for songs which would become standards, Miss Caldwell led a successful career in the musical theatre for some 15 years.

Her first musical comedy venture, following several attempts at playwriting (*A Model Girl, The Nest Egg,* the 1911 *Uncle Sam* starring Thomas A Wise and John Barrymore), was as co-librettist on *The Lady of the Slipper,* a starry Charles Dillingham variation on the Cinderella tale, with a score by Victor Herbert, which featured Elsie Janis and Montgomery and Stone at the head of its bill. It proved a fine success and Caldwell continued the association with Dillingham, Montgomery and Stone by supplying the lyrics and a share of the libretto for their next, and last, show, the Aladdin variant *Chin-Chin* and, after Montgomery's death, all of Stone's subsequent star vehicles (*Jack o' Lantern, Tip Top, Stepping Stones, Criss Cross, Three Cheers*), at first with Ivan Caryll as her musical collaborator (''Wait Till the Cows Come Home''), then with Jerome Kern and, lastly, with Raymond Hubbell.

It was during the production of *Go To It!,* an unfortunate musical adaptation of the old Hoyt comedy *A Milk White Flag,* at the Princess Theatre that Caldwell encountered the composer of that theatre's previous successes, Jerome Kern, and the two subsequently came together as author and composer of Dillingham's production *She's a Good Fellow.* This had a sufficient success for them to continue the collaboration over a series of shows which combined American variations on Continental and British farce plots with the kind of songwriters' scores currently popular and, often, also with a dose of star turns and even palpable variety acts. If the Caldwell/Kern shows are, in consequence, not remembered as the most replayable of the celebrated composer's stage pieces, they nevertheless included several reasonably long-running successes and some songs, to Caldwell's lyrics, which rate comparison with his more famous pieces (''The First Rose of Summer,'' ''Left All Alone Again Blues,'' ''Whose Baby Are You?,'' ''Ka-lu-a,'' ''Once in a Blue Moon'').

In between these two major portions of her career—the Montgomery & Stone part and the Kern part—Caldwell authored a musical, *The Model Maid,* which served to launch Australian swimming star Annette Kellerman as a musical comedy player and collaborated on several shows with composer Hugo Felix, who was staunchly attempting to repeat his early success with *Madame Sherry.* The pair did reasonably well both with a rehashed version of the Lajos Széll/Akos Buttykay Hungarian hit *Csibészkirály,* here called *Pom-Pom,* and a happily touring piece called *The Sweetheart Shop,* without pulling out a real hit. She also combined with Vincent Youmans on the numbers for *Oh, Please!,* amongst which was ''I Know That You Know,'' and had a latter-day success with the musical *Take the Air,* which mixed a female airpilot, some smugglers and the conventional amount of singing and dancing for a run of over two hundred Broadway performances.

A plump and agreeable person with a tidy and efficient pen rather than any inspired touches, Caldwell proved her ability regularly to turn out material suitable to star performers such as Montgomery and Stone, on the one hand, and libretti in the popular light farcical style on the other, as well as composing unfussy, well-measured lyrics which satisfied such major figures as Dillingham, Caryll and Kern into repeated collaborations.

O'Dea provided the bulk of the songs for such touring shows as Ward and Vokes's *A Pair of Pinks* (1903 W Adams), *Busy Izzy* (1903 W Adams) and *The Grafter* (1905 w W C Powell).

1907 **The Top of the World** (Manuel Klein/w James O'Dea/Mark Swan) Majestic Theater 19 October

1907 **The Circus Man** (Harry von Tilzer/Vincent Bryan/w O'Dea) Harmanus Bleeker Hall, Albany 9 December

1912 **The Lady of the Slipper** (Victor Herbert/O'Dea/w Lawrence McCarthy) Globe Theater 28 October

1914 **When Claudia Smiles** (Jean Schwartz) (revised version) 39th Street Theater 2 February

1914 **Chin-Chin** (Ivan Caryll/w R H Burnside) Globe Theater 20 October

- 1915 **The Model Maid** (Raymond Hubbell) Apollo Theater, Atlantic City 26 January
- 1916 **Pom-Pom** (Hugo Felix) Cohan Theater 28 February
- 1916 **Go To It!** (John Golden/w Golden, John Hazzard) Princess Theater 24 October
- 1917 **Jack o' Lantern** (Caryll/w Burnside) Globe Theater 16 October
- 1918 **The Canary** (Caryll/w P G Wodehouse/Louis Verneuil ad H B Smith) Globe Theater 4 November
- 1919 **She's a Good Fellow** (ex- *A New Girl*) (Jerome Kern) Globe Theater 5 May
- 1919 **The Lady in Red** (*Die Dame in Rot*) American version (Lyric Theater)
- 1920 **The Night Boat** (Kern) Liberty Theater 2 February
- 1920 **The Sweetheart Shop** (Felix) Knickerbocker Theater 31 August
- 1920 **Tip Top** (Caryll/w Burnside) Globe Theater 5 October
- 1921 **Good Morning, Dearie** (Kern) Globe Theater 1 November
- 1922 **The Bunch and Judy** (Kern/w Hugh Ford) Globe Theater 28 November
- 1923 **Stepping Stones** (Kern) Globe Theater 6 November
- 1924 **Peg o' My Dreams** (Felix) Jolson Theater 5 May
- 1924 **The Magnolia Lady** (Harold Levey) Shubert Theater 25 November
- 1925 **The City Chap** (Kern/James Montgomery) Liberty Theater 26 October
- 1926 **Criss Cross** (Kern/w Otto Harbach) Globe Theater 12 October
- 1926 **Oh, Please!** (Vincent Youmans/w Harbach) Fulton Theater 17 December
- 1927 **Yours Truly** (Hubbell) Shubert Theater 25 January
- 1927 **Take the Air** (Dave Stamper/Gene Buck) Waldorf Theater 22 November
- 1928 **Three Cheers** (Hubbell/w Burnside) Globe Theater 15 October

CALL ME MADAM Musical comedy in 2 acts by Howard Lindsay and Russel Crouse. Lyrics and music by Irving Berlin. Imperial Theater, New York, 12 October 1950.

Irving Berlin's second vehicle, after the hugely successful *Annie Get Your Gun,* for star vocalist Ethel Merman cast her, in much the fashion that English comedienne Cicely Courtneidge had been cast a few years earlier in the successful *Her Excellency,* as an interfering Ambassadress in foreign parts. Lindsay and Crouse's romantic-comic and wholly unsatirical tale presented the star as Mrs Sally Adams (a character said to be modeled on the real-life Pearl Mesta, rather than Miss Courtneidge), a famed and beloved Washington hostess to the powerful, who is sent as United States representative to the tiny and unprofitable duchy of Lichtenburg. But Sally takes a shine to local politician Cosmo Constantin (Paul Lukas) and she promptly starts to break the laws of diplomacy by using her position and her personal millions to get him the job of Prime Minister. Ambassadressing takes second place to romancing, and Sally's assistant Kenneth (Russell Nype) is not slow to follow his chief's example, taking a reciprocal fancy to the local Princess Maria (Galina Talva). As Prime Minister, Cosmo proudly refuses the millions in aid Sally has organized from America, and she is soon recalled for having trampled over diplomatic rules but, at the curtain fall, it is clear that "madame" will soon be on her way back to Lichtenburg as Mrs Cosmo, the Prime Minister's wife.

Berlin equipped his star with a swingingly joyous set of numbers, which had her declaring herself "The Hostess With the Mostes'," leading the "Washington Square Dance," expansively wooing Cosmo with the offer "Can You Use Any Money Today?" and with the blunt information that "The Best Thing for You Would Be Me," but scoring her best and most memorable moment, in counter-melody, with her prognosis to the off-his-oats Kenneth, "You're Just in Love." The rest of the cast were well-equipped musically, too, with Kenneth and Maria joining sweetly in "It's a Lovely Day Today," Cosmo welcoming everyone to "Lichtenburg" and expressing his determination never to make a money match ("Marrying for Love"), and a comical bunch of visiting American politicians going into a stand-up routine insisting how "They Like Ike."

Leyland Hayward's production of *Call Me Madam* had a fine 644-performance run on Broadway, and sent out its national touring company with Elaine Stritch and Kent Smith at its head early in 1952. Shortly before this, Jack Hylton opened *Call Me Madam* at the London Coliseum where, with Billie Worth and Anton Walbrook at the head of proceedings and Jeff Warren and Shani Wallis as the juvenile pair, it scored another fine success through 485 performances before going on the British road. The following year Australia saw the show, with local *Annie Get Your Gun* star Evie Hayes following Miss Merman's path to the role of Sally alongside René Paul (Cosmo) and Sid Lawson (Kenneth) through four and a half Melbourne months and a similar period at Sydney's Theatre Royal (30 January 1954).

A 1953 film version, pairing Miss Merman with George Sanders and featuring Vera-Ellen and Donald O'Connor as the younger pair, retained much of the original score, but added one song culled from the 1940 *Louisiana Purchase* (which had not been used in its own film version) and, for some reason, replaced "The Washington Square Dance" with an even earlier "International Rag."

Call Me Madam has been intermittently played in the decades since its first productions, and it won a full-scale London revival when a provincial production featuring TV soaps star Noele Gordon was transferred to the Victoria Palace in 1983 (14 March) for 72 performances.

UK: London Coliseum 15 March 1952; Australia: Her Majesty's Theatre, Melbourne 5 September 1953

Film: Twentieth Century Fox 1953

Recordings: original cast star (Decca), members of original cast (RCA), London cast (Columbia), Danish cast (Decca), concert cast 1995 (DRG), film soundtrack (Decca)

LA CAMARGO Opéra-comique in 3 acts by Albert Vanloo and Eugène Leterrier. Music by Charles Lecocq. Théâtre de la Renaissance, Paris, 20 November 1878.

Charles Lecocq and producer Victor Koning followed up their great hit *Le Petit Duc* with another, if less durable, success in an opérette featuring as its heroine La Camargo, otherwise the historical 18th-century Belgian ballet dancer Marie-Anne de Cupis de Camargo (1710–1770). Mlle de Camargo (already the subject of a *La Camargo* by Dupuety and Fontan) underwent the usual kind of operetticization, lending her name to a character and an adventure that doubtless had little to do with her, as authors Vanloo and Leterrier cooked her into a tale with the equally historical, if rather (historically) younger and—apparently deservedly—short-lived, French brigand Louis Mandrin (1724–1755).

Zulma Bouffar played the danseuse and Vauthier the brigand who, having fallen for her charms, wins his way to her side at first backstage at the Opéra, in disguise as a nobleman, then by having her kidnapped and brought to his castle, and finally by getting himself hired as a detective under the orders of her accepted ''protector,'' the police chief Marquis de Pontcalé (Berthelier), with the mission to track himself down. Ultimately, Camargo—herself disguised as a little street singer—outwits Mandrin but, having had her revenge upon him for his deceits, she helps him escape arrest at the final curtain.

Into the tale of Mandrin's pursuit of the dancer and Pontcalé's pursuit of the brigand, the authors wove a set of delicious roles for the principal members of the Théâtre de la Renaissance company. The very rising young soubrette Mily-Meyer, who had shot to the fore as la Petite Duchesse in the previous opérette, played the sparky little Colombe, daughter of Pontcalé's draper (Pacra) and affianced to the draper's son, Saturnin (Lary). Saturnin discovers womanhood in the person of Camargo and wants to postpone his wedding until he has had a chance to experience a worldly love affair, but after a couple of acts fetching and carrying for the star for no return, he is happy to settle down back in Lyon with Colombe. Marie Desclauzas followed up her imperishable performance as *Le Petit Duc*'s Diane de Château-Lansac with a very different creation, the lavish Creole ''Juana, princesse de Rio-Negro, from Santo Domingo, Antillllllles!'' Persuaded that she has been ravished by Mandrin during a robbery, she has made it her mission in life to reform the bandit, and she goes round richly indemnifying all his victims until she finally discovers, disappointedly, that she wasn't ravished at all.

Lecocq's score was a typically tuneful one, with the heroine of the piece getting the most frequent opportunities. The first of these came in an entrance number (''Partout on me fête'') and a rondo in the opening act, followed up by a pretty plea (''Laissez-moi, monsieur le voleur''), a full ballet-pastorale (''Voici d'abord une bergère'') which rippled up to high C, and a duo (''Ce serait une vie heureuse'') and couplets with Mandrin in the second, and a duo with Pontcalé and two pieces in her street-singer disguise (Duetto de Javotte et Margotte, Chanson de la marmotte en vie) in the last. Mily-Meyer had a pair of spunky little numbers, Pontcalé boasted about his talent for detective work in the Couplets de l'oeil and paired with his phony ''assistant'' to sing about ''La police, la justice,'' whilst Juana related her adventure (''Je dormais, tout dans la nature'') in comic song, Saturnin pleaded his ignorance of sex in a sweet romance, and Mandrin and his bandits joined in some lively musical moments, the vocal balance in which was helped by the fact that two of the bandits were played by two of the prettiest young ladies of the company (Léa d'Asco, Mlle Piccolo) in travesty.

La Camargo was pronounced a sure success and it held the stage for three months at the Renaissance. It was later remounted there (14 November 1881) with Hélène Chevrier in the title role alongside Alfred Jolly (Pontcalé), Desclauzas, Vauthier, Mily-Meyer and Jannin (Saturnin). Then, rather curiously, it simply faded from the repertoire.

Outside France, things went little better. The piece was played in the repertoire of Maurice Grau's opéra-bouffe company in America with Paola Marié as the dancer (''with her pet monkey perched on her shoulder'') and Jouard as the bandit alongside Mme Angèle (Juana), Mlle Grégoire (Colombe) and Mézières (Pontcalé), and it was seen just six times in a German version at Austria's Theater an der Wien in 1879, but in Budapest (ad Béla J Fái) it became a genuine success when Lujza Blaha took up the all-singing, all-dancing, all-comedy prima donna role for a season of 25 performances.

Hungary: Népszínház *Kamargo* 28 March 1879; Austria: Theater an der Wien 9 December 1879; USA: Booth's Theatre (Fr) 10 December 1879; Germany: Aachen 19 June 1880

Recording: complete (Rare Recorded Editions)

CAMELOT Musical in 2 acts by Alan Jay Lerner based on *The Once and Future King* by T H White. Music by Frederick Loewe. Majestic Theater, New York, 3 December 1960.

Camelot had the impossibly difficult task of following behind *My Fair Lady* in the opus of Lerner and Loewe, and it emerged from the trial with very considerable credit, in the face of much adversity.

Based on T H White's whimsical retelling of the Arthurian legend, the show presented a boyish and immature Arthur (Richard Burton) and a skittishly innocent Guenevere (Julie Andrews) brought together to grow into their positions as King and Queen, as the patrons of the famous Round Table and the representatives of all that is good and orderly in the world. Arthur's old tutor and protector, the magician Merlyn (David Hurst), is lured away by the spirit Nimue, leaving the young man with only his own resources on which to rely in creating the best of all possible worlds. However, for all his goodness and all his efforts, he sees his queen falling helplessly in love with his best friend, Lancelot du Lac (Robert Goulet), and is eventually undone by the evil Morgan Le Fey (M'el Dowd) and her vicious son, Mordred (Roddy McDowall). Camelot and the ideals for which it stood were too good to last. Robert Coote appeared as a comical knight, Sir Pellinore, passing through the evening's action in his pursuit of the Questing Beast.

The score of the show brought forth several sentimental pieces which became favorites: Lancelot's ringing ''If Ever I Would Leave You,'' Guenevere's gentle ''I Loved You Once in Silence'' and the King's ruminatings on ''How to Handle a Woman'' whose lyric resulted in the axiom that loving is the best method. The romantic portions were contrasted with some more sprightly moments—Guenevere's disappointed prayer to her patron Saint over having never experienced any of the storybook excitements which an Early English princess should go through as part of ''The Simple Joys of Maidenhood,'' or the catalogue of ghastly fates she encourages her followers to propose for the irritatingly virtuous Lancelot in ''Take Me to the Fair''—by some warmly picturesque ones, such as the description of ''Camelot,'' and by some, such as Mordred's attack on ''The Seven Deadly Virtues,'' more hectic.

Staged with spectacular period lavishness, *Camelot* was an indubitable success, winning a little extra glamor from the well-publicized approval of President John Kennedy (who was said, by those who did not favor him, to compare himself and his America with Arthur and Camelot) and ran for 873 performances on Broadway. William Squire and Kathryn Grayson headed out the first American national tour, whilst J C Williamson Ltd mounted an Australian production in 1963 with Paul Daneman and

Plate 61. **Camelot.** *Julie Andrews (Guenevere) and Richard Burton (Arthur) as the British royal family.*

Jacquelyn McKeever starred, which was designed even more luxuriantly than the original by John Truscott. It played at Her Majesty's, Melbourne (22 February 1964) for more than seven months and at Sydney's Her Majesty's thereafter (17 October 1964). As a result of this production's success, Truscott was retained to design Jack Hylton's London production, mounted with truly extravagant spectacle on the stage of the Theatre Royal, Drury Lane. Laurence Harvey and Elizabeth Larner appeared in the starring roles with Barry Kent (Lancelot), Nicky Henson (Mordred) and Miles Malleson (Merlyn) in support through a run of 518 performances.

In 1967 a film version (again designed by Truscott) was made, with Richard Harris and Vanessa Redgrave starred, and a dubbed Franco Nero as Lancelot. Harris later took up the role of King Arthur on the stage, touring it for many years through America, and playing it, in the wake of a revival with Burton and Christine Ebersole starred (New York State Theater 8 July 1980), on Broadway (Winter Garden Theater 15 November 1981) and—in a sadly truncated and dilapidated state—in London (Apollo Victoria Theater 12 November 1982) and Australia (Sydney Entertainment Centre 24 September 1984). In 1992 Goulet—now graduated from Lancelot to Arthur—headed out a further touring company as *Camelot* began to show signs of making up ground even on *My Fair Lady* in the enduring popularity stakes. His production visited Broadway for 56 performances (Gershwin Theater 21 June 1993), during which Goulet played his Arthur to the Guenevere of Patricia Kies and the Lancelot of Steve Blanchard. London got another brief glimpse in 1996 when Paul Nicholas appeared as Arthur.

A German-language version (ad Marcel Valmy) was seen for the first time at Karlsruhe in 1981with Manfred Behm (Arthur), Steve Barton (Lancelot) and Pamela Hamblin (Guenevere) featured.

The Arthurian legend has served regularly as material for the musical theatre down the ages. Dryden and Purcell's opera *King Arthur* (Dorset Gardens, London, 1691) was the most notable amongst the early such works, Garrick launched a *King Arthur* in 1770, and Alfred Bunn produced Isaac Pocock's *King Arthur and the Knights of the Round Table* at Drury Lane at Christmas 1834, with T P Cooke featured as Sir Roland and also credited with the music. The most effective Camelottish musical of the Victorian age was William Brough's *King Arthur, or The Days and Knights of the Round Table* (26 December 1863 mus: D Spillane), produced at the Haymarket Theatre with Louise Keeley as Arthur, Fanny Wright as Guinevere, Henrietta Lindley as Sir Lancelot and Mr Tilbury as Merlin. Although John Clarke played Morgan le Fey in travesty, the piece was not a grotesque burlesque, but an extravaganza which followed the legend of the sword-in-the-stone and its sequels faithfully, give or take the inclusion of rather a lot of fairies and a Guinevere who danced à pas seul. The grotesque got its rein in such pieces as *Lancelot the Lovely, or The Idol of the King* (Avenue Theatre 22 April 1889), concocted for low comic Arthur Roberts as Lancelot to the Guinevere of Annie Halford and the Arthur of Alec Marsh, in W M Akhurst's *King Arthur, or Lancelot the Loose, Gin-ever the Square and the Knights of the Round Table and other Furniture* (Theatre Royal, Melbourne 31 October 1868) and *Merry Mr Merlin, or Good King Arthur* (E H Paterson, Harry Grattan Elephant and Castle 11 February 1895). Operatic composer Karl Goldmark also contributed a *Merlin* (Vienna 19 November 1886), a title which was reprised on Broadway in 1983 for Doug Hemming's magic show.

Hervé's opéra-bouffe *Les Chevaliers de la table ronde* included Merlin and Lancelot as minor characters in a plot which didn't have anything to do with Arthur and Guenevere, and Planché's *Knights of the Round Table* was even less Camelottish, the ''knights'' in question being a gang of Henry II–period con men. But it was a good, catchy title.

Sir Arthur Sullivan supplied a considerable score of mostly choral music (''Chant of the Grail,'' ''Sleep Song,'' etc) to J Comyns Carr's drama *King Arthur* as produced at the Lyceum 12 January 1895 with Henry Irving (Arthur), Ellen Terry (Guinevere), Forbes Robertson (Lancelot) and former opera-singer Genevieve Ward as Morgan Le Fay.

Hungary added its musical mite to the Arthurian heap with a *Megyeri Gyalog Galopp* (Kolibri Színház, Budapest 22 April 1994 ad Mária Révész) in which the credits bore the names of Terry Gilliam and Graham Chapman, and would thus seem to signify that it was a version of *Monty Python and the Quest for the Holy Grail.*

Australia: Her Majesty's Theatre, Adelaide 30 November 1963; UK: Theatre Royal, Drury Lane 19 August 1964; Germany: Badische Staatstheater, Karlsruhe 3 October 1981

Film: 1967 Warner Brothers

Recordings: original cast (Columbia), London cast (HMV), film soundtrack (Warner Bros), London 1982 cast (TER)

CAMERON, Violet [THOMPSON, Violet Lydia] (b London, 7 December 1862; d Worthing, 25 October 1919). Top London musical star of the mid-Victorian era.

Daughter of the singer Mary Ann Brougham, a niece (by a network of second marriages) of Lydia Thompson, and a cousin of the successful musical-comedy performers Violet and Florence Lloyd and of actress Zeffie Tilbury, Miss Cameron made her first appearances on the stage as a child performer, playing in burlesque (*Snae Fell* at the Gaiety), pantomime and plays and, under a three-year contract, in children's roles at Drury Lane. She is said to have sung Siebel in *Faust* at the age of 12 and at 13 she played Perdita in *A Winter's Tale* at Liverpool.

She toured with the musical companies of her uncle-in-law, Alexander Henderson, and appeared as a very young teenager at the Folly Theatre with ''aunt'' Lydia Thompson in *Bluebeard* (Sister Ann), *Piff-Paff* (Joconde), *Robinson Crusoe* (Polly Hopkins) and *Oxygen* (Suzel). She then segued into the French opéras-bouffes which Henderson next staged at the Folly (Pearline in *The Sea Nymph,* Antoinette in *La Créole,* Alexandrivoire in *L'Oeil crevé*) and was subsequently cast, as the company ingenue, in the juvenile role of their following production, the English premiere of *Les Cloches de Corneville* (1878). The huge London success of that production, and her winning performance as Germaine, made the not yet 16-year-old Violet a star, and she moved on from this first triumph to play in the rocket-speed-rising Henderson's Strand Theatre productions in leading ''principal girl'' roles in *Nemesis* (revival), *Madame Favart* (Suzanne), *The Naval Cadet* (Inez Maria Estrella) and *Olivette* (Bathilde), whilst at the same time hitting the scandalous headlines thanks to an alleged affair with the criminal Lefroy.

She made a second major hit when she was starred by Henderson as Bettina in London's edition of *La Mascotte,* a third when she introduced the English version of the title role of his production of *Boccaccio,* and more as the original Gretchen to the *Rip van Winkle* of Fred Leslie and in the title role of *Falka* in a four-year period in the early 1880s which were the remarkable one-hit-after-another peak of her career. She subsequently appeared in comic opera (*The Lady of the Locket*) and burlesque (*The Vicar of Wideawakefield, Kenilworth, Lurline*) without the same success, and was launched on a Broadway season in 1886 with a version of *La Créole* entitled *The Commodore* and the burlesque *Kenilworth.* This season was financed by Hugh Cecil Lowther, Lord Lonsdale, with whom her name was noisily and scandalously linked. Greeted with violent hostility by moral New York, Violet and her Lord cut their seven-month New York booking to seven weeks, and Violet returned home to sue the damagingly "jealous" and otiose husband who had been responsible for breaking the scandal for divorce on grounds of cruelty and slander. And also to give birth to Lonsdale's daughter, modestly christened Lydia Lowther.

Back in London, she starred in Lydia Thompson's production of *The Sultan of Mocha* (1887, Dolly) and, whilst tales of her divorce filled the nothing-more-momentous-to-report papers, succeeded to the role of Fraisette in *The Old Guard* and took over first as Faust in George Edwardes's *Faust Up-to-Date* and then as *Captain Thérèse,* in place of the insufficient Attalie Claire, with the Carl Rosa Company. She remained at the Prince of Wales Theatre to play Prince Giglio in *The Rose and the Ring* and Alan a Dale in the American comic opera *Robin Hood* (1891, retitled *Maid Marian*), and then moved to the Shaftesbury to appear as Adeline Dupret in the short-lived *La Rosière* (1893) and as Ethel Sportington in the musical comedy *Morocco Bound* (1893).

She next starred in the title role of an unfortunate light-operatic version of *The Green Bushes* known as *Miami,* but then took her distance from the musical stage, appearing for a little while in variety and on the music halls before retiring from the stage. She returned thereafter only to appear in revue at the Crystal Palace, as principal boy in the 1900 Drury Lane pantomime and, one last time, in 1903, to play a Mother Superior with a wimple and a specially written song in Leslie Stuart's musical comedy *The School Girl.*

Her son, actor and vocalist **Cecil CAMERON** [Cecil Horace David de BENSAUDE] (b 1885), married May Leslie Stuart, daughter of the composer of her last show, whilst her daughter, Doris Cameron, wed the D'Oyly Carte company's Frederick Hobbs. Quite what happened to Lydia Lowther I cannot discover.

Plate 62. **Violet Cameron.** *One of the most successful stars of London's Victorian musical stage.*

LE CANARD À TROIS BECS Opéra-bouffe in 3 acts by Jules Moinaux. Music by Émile Jonas. Théâtre des Folies-Dramatiques, Paris, 6 February 1869.

The most successful of Jonas's works for the theatre, *Le Canard à trois becs* was a piece written and composed in the extravagantly bouffe style of the 1860s. The three-beaked duck of the title is the mascot of the city of Ostend, and it is said that Flanders will be protected from the marauding armies of Spain as long as it survives. Three randy young Spaniards, Pasmotto (Mendasti), Spaniello (Marcel) and Chutentos (Speck), steal the bird, raising sufficient alarm for the burgomaster (Girardot), the entire city guard and sea captain van Ostebal (Ange Milher), who has never yet been to sea, unwillingly to set off to save their city. The trio's unwarlike objective is thus, theoretically, achieved—for all they wanted was to get van Ostebal out of town so they can chat up, respectively, his daughter Madeleine (Mlle Massue), his wife Marguerite (Mlle Lovato) and his maid, Barbe (Mlle Daroux). But the water-wary van Ostebal doesn't leave town: he decides to chase the crooks on home ground. Unfortunately for him, he gets on the wrong scent, and whilst he stalks the inoffensive secretary (Chaudesaigue) of the burgomaster, whom he has labeled as a dangerous duck-nicking insurgent, and his maiden-lady sister, Sophronie

(Adèle Cuinet), stalks Spaniello with amorous intent, the intended infidelities are all happily arranged. So is the duck, which ends up, drumsticks upwards, on the finale table.

The three sexy fellows, together and separately, had the jolliest time of the musical part of the evening. They launched a martial trio declaring "Les Castiliens sont tous des frères," a tyrolienne trio with Spaniello yodelling happily away on the top line, and a piece describing "la théorie de la sérénade"—"pour composer une sérénade vous prenez le mot manola, vous y joignez celui d'alcade, grille, résille, et puis alza . . ."—and went through a comical ensemble in the final act, trying to hide the wretched pilfered duck ("Le canard l'a bien passée") in the face of determined enquiries. Spaniello also had his romantic moments, waylaying his prey in a first-act waltz duo, wooing her in the waltz Couplets de la fascination, and going solo in his Rondeau de la voyage. Van Ostebal blustered out his claims to fame ("Van Ostebal est un marin, un malin . . .") and made love to his wife in a fashion which compared poorly with what Spaniello had been offering shortly before, Sophronie gave out her Couplets de la rosière, Marguerite her Couplets de la cocotte and the chorus had its moment in a winning Patrol Chorus with a "ra fla rra rra rra" refrain.

Le Canard à trois becs was well received in Paris, became a thorough favorite in the French provinces and, without quite placing itself in the very top row of revivable pieces after its fine first run, was nevertheless brought back at the Folies-Dramatiques in 1872 (August) with Paola Marié as Marguerite, Luce, Vavasseur and Speck as the boys and Vauthier as van Ostebal. It appeared again at the Théâtre de la Renaissance in 1881 (9 May), with a cast headed by Marie Desclauzas, Vauthier, Marie Gélabert, Alfred Jolly and Lary, and once more at the Bouffes-Parisiens in 1888. It was also widely seen throughout other theatrical centers. It was played at Vienna's Carltheater for five performances in the repertoire of Eugène Meynadier's company, with Mme Matz-Ferrare and Christian featured, before, later the same year, a German version was produced at the Strampfertheater. London, too, got its first glimpse of the piece in the original French, sharing a bill of the visiting Folies-Dramatiques company with the second act of *Chilpéric*. Vauthier played van Ostebal, Paola Marié was Marguerite, Mendasti and Speck repeated their original characters, and the piece was hailed as "one of the drollest specimens of the opéra-bouffe we have seen." It was duly mounted in the West End the following year in English (ad Charles Lamb Kenney) with Nita de Castro, Rose Bell, Harriet Coveney, George Honey, Edward Perrini and Edwin J Odell in the cast. The program was filled out with Offenbach's *L'Île de Tulipatan* and the bill ran a good two months. America also saw the show in French, with a cast headed by Coralie Geoffroy (Marguerite), but in spite of a fine reception, did not pursue it into English.

In Hungary, *A háromcsórő kacsa* (ad Endre Latabár, Gábor Beödy Balogh) did exceedingly well. First mounted at the Budai Színkör with Elek Solymossy as van Ostebal, it was subsequently taken up by the Népszínház where, after a first production in 1876 with Lujza Blaha in the role of Margit, it was revived in 1882 (15 September) and again in 1888 (31 May) with Aranka Hegyi (Margit), Izsó Gyöngyi (van Ostebal), Sándor Dardai (Spaniello) and Vidor Kassai (van Bontrouche). The close of the 1880s more or less marked the end of the show's career, but during its two decades—the palmy days of the opéra-bouffe—it had held its place amongst the most popular pieces of its kind.

Austria: Carltheater (Fr) 17 July 1871, Strampfertheater *Die Ente mit den drei Schnabeln* 18 November 1871; UK: Globe Theatre (Fr) 13 July 1872, Opera Comique *The Wonderful Duck* 31 May 1873; Hungary: Budai Színkör *A háromcsórő kacsa* 12 September 1872; USA: Lyceum Theater (Fr) 16 October 1875

THE CANARY *see* LE COFFRE-FORT VIVANT

CAN-CAN Musical in 2 acts by Abe Burrows. Music and lyrics by Cole Porter. Shubert Theater, New York, 7 May 1953.

A jolly piece of Parisian ooh-la-la built around a classic set of comic and romantic characters, and illustrated with a scoreful of American-in-Paris numbers which included a good percentage that would become durable favorites, *Can-Can* gave songwriter Cole Porter his second longest Broadway run without establishing itself internationally in the same way that the top-ranking *Kiss Me, Kate* had done.

The girls who dance the can-can at Montmartre's Bal du Paradis, under the management of la Môme Pistache (Lilo), are regularly arrested on morals charges, then regularly acquitted, until the day a serious-minded new judge, Aristide Forestier (Peter Cookson), decides that the law is being made light of. He goes to Montmartre to see the law-breaking for himself and instead falls for Pistache. When he tries, with the utmost correctitude, to advise her, he gets caught and summarily debarred. Indignant at the injustice, he joins Pistache in the opening of a new venue with the plan that they will be arrested and brought to trial, thus allowing him to have, in open court, the say he has been denied by his peers. After a vicissitude or two, the pair stand up in court together to show the world that obscenity is in the eye of the beholder. The romantic plot was contrasted with a comic one which involved the dancer Claudine (Gwen Verdon) with a penniless bad artist called Boris (Hans Conried) and a randy art critic, Hilaire Jussac (Erik Rhodes).

The songs of *Can-Can* included Pistache's romantic ''I Love Paris'' and ''C'est magnifique,'' the more pointed ''Never Give Anything Away (that you can sell)'' and ''Live and Let Live,'' and a moving little number called ''Allez-vous en,'' whilst Aristide sang passively to a passing poule that ''It's All Right with Me'' and the comical characters played up such pieces as the topico-comical ''Come Along with Me'' and ''Never Be an Artist.'' One of the highlights of the show was the Garden of Eden Ballet, staged as part of the entertainment at the Quat'z arts ball which closed the first act, and which put Gwen Verdon, dancing the central part, into prominence. Miss Verdon's threatening to steal the show resulted in her role being severely cut (at the behest of the nominal star's husband) before opening, but she went ahead and stole it anyhow.

Cy Feuer and Ernest Martin's production of *Can-Can* ran for 892 performances on Broadway, during which time Prince Littler and Rodgers and Hammerstein (as Williamson Music Ltd) reproduced the show on the huge stage of the London Coliseum with Irene Hilda (Pistache), Gillian Lynne (Claudine), Edmund Hockridge (Aristide), Alfred Marks (Boris) and George Gee (Jussac) featured. London's version played 394 performances. Following the Broadway run, the show went on the road in America with Rita Dimitri, Ronnie Cunningham and John Tyers in the leading roles, whilst in Australia Sheila Arnaud (Pistache), William Newman, Eric Reiman and Eleanor Trieber featured in a good run at Melbourne's Her Majesty's Theatre and Sydney's Empire (12 May 1956).

A film, made under the same title, used Frank Sinatra, Shirley Maclaine, Louis Jourdan and Maurice Chevalier and eight of the show's musical pieces (plus three others from other Porter shows) attached to a different and less attractive story, which tried a little too hard to be another *Gigi* and didn't make it.

The huge success of *Kiss Me, Kate* in German-language theatres helped to win *Can-Can* (ad Robert Gilbert) a number of productions in Austria and Germany. The first of these was seen in Stuttgart in 1965, and the show was subsequently played in Rostock (1 June 1968) and at Vienna's Theater an der Wien, where it played a season of 52 performances. Back home, *Can-Can* reappeared in a short-lived 1981 production featuring Zizi Jeanmaire in the role of Pistache (Minskoff Theater 30 April, 5 performances) and in 1988 London hosted a heavily revised version (ad Julian More Strand Theatre 28 October) with an international cast including America's Donna McKechnie (Pistache), France's Bernard Alane (Aristide), Britain's Janie Dee (Claudine) and Ireland's Milo O'Shea (Jussac), and the score expanded with a songbookful of Porter numbers belonging to other shows, through 102 performances. The butchering went even further when the remains of the show were staged at America's Goodspeed Opera House in 1995 (ad Martin Charnin) with Bill Ullman as Aristide and a bundle of songs Porter had judged it better to junk included instead of the ones he had favored.

The tale of the can-can, its banning, and the bringing of its exponents before the law courts had been used nearly a century earlier as the subject of the Hungarian operett *Cancan a törvényszék előtt* (the can-can before the tribunal) written by István Friebeisz Rajkai, composed by Jakab Jakóbi, and produced at the Budai Népszínház 17 April 1864 and later at Vienna's Theater an der Wien (*Der Cancan vor Gericht* 22 June 1865). This piece later became the source for the comic dance piece *Farsangi kaland* (Népszínház 8 March 1878), and it was also reorganized as a Spanish zarzuela by Francisco Asenjo Barbieri (*El proceso del can-can,* 1873).

UK: London Coliseum 14 October 1954; Australia: Her Majesty's Theatre, Melbourne 29 October 1955; Germany: Staatstheater, Stuttgart 28 August 1965; Austria: Theater an der Wien 2 March 1968; Hungary: Győr *Kánkán* 30 September 1995

Film: Twentieth Century Fox 1960

Recordings: original cast (Capitol), London cast (Parlophone), film soundtrack (Capitol), London 1988 version (Virgin), Mexican cast (RCA), German cast (Spectrum), Swedish cast (Amigo), Japanese (Takarazuka) cast (HMI), etc

LA CANCIÓN DEL OLVIDO Zarzuela in 1 act and 4 scenes by Federico Romero and Guillermo Fernández Shaw. Music by José Serrano. Teatro Lírico, Valencia, 17 November 1916.

One of the most popular ''genéro chico'' pieces amongst those zarzuelas which use traditional international operetta plot and character elements rather than the Spanish ''slice-of-life'' as their material. *La canción del olvido* is set in turn-of-the-18th century Naples, and its heroine is a Roman princess, Rosina. Rosina has fallen in love with a swash-unbuckling army captain called Leonello and has followed him to the Neapolitan countryside where she finds that he is busy setting his sights at the courtesan Flora Goldoni. In good operettic style, Rosina gets herself a bundle of disguises and a tenor helpmate, the troubadour Toribio, and by the end of the fourth scene she has won her soldier. The principal pieces of Serrano's score were Leonello's womanizing ''Junto al puente de la Peña'' and the ''song of oblivion'' of the title (''Marinella, Marinella'').

Recordings: Alhambra, Zafiro, Columbia, Hispavox

CANDIDE Comic operetta in 2 acts by Lillian Hellman based on the satire by Voltaire. Lyrics by Richard Wilbur. Additional lyrics by John Latouche and Dorothy Parker.

Music by Leonard Bernstein. Martin Beck Theater 1 December 1956. Revised version by Hugh Wheeler with additional lyrics by Stephen Sondheim, Chelsea Theater Centre, 11 December 1973; Broadway Theater, 8 March 1974.

Voltaire's extravagant, satiric saga, with its mockery of ''the best of all possible worlds'' and the innocent hero who believes in such a thing, was at first made into a comic operetta by playwright Lillian Hellman with lyrics largely by Richard Wilbur set to music by Leonard Bernstein. The resultant piece was produced by Ethel Linder Reiner and Lester Osterman jr at New York's Martin Beck Theater with Robert Rounseville (Candide), Barbara Cook (Cunégonde), Max Adrian (Pangloss) and Irra Petina (Old Lady) featured, but failed in 73 performances. A London version mounted in 1959, under the management of Linnit and Dunfee, with Denis Quilley, Mary Costa, Laurence Naismith and Edith Coates in the principal roles fared even less well and closed after 60 performances.

In 1974 a rewritten version by Hugh Wheeler, which emphasized the comic extravagances of the text and made its black points through humor rather than a less attractive dogmatism, was produced by Harold Prince and the Chelsea Theater Center in Brooklyn, New York. The musical score had been altered along with the text, and additional lyrics supplied by Stephen Sondheim. Prince mounted the now highly colorful show on a set consisting of multiple acting areas, arranged around the audience, and this time the reaction was positive. This production of *Candide* moved to the Broadway Theater, which was suitably reconstructed to allow the same style of presentation, and it remained there for 740 performances, establishing the show and its new version as one of the most interesting and intelligent of its time.

At the Castle Thunder-ten-Tronck, Westphalia, the philosopher Dr Pangloss (Lewis J Stadlen) teaches the baronial family's daughter Cunégonde (Maureen Brennan), son Maximilian (Sam Freed) and bastard nephew Candide (Mark Baker) his optimistic creed that all is for the best in the best of all possible worlds. He teaches rather more physical things to the maidservant Paquette (Deborah St Darr). The world soon begins to test his maxim to the full. First Candide is expelled from the castle for experimenting with his cousin in the garden, then Westphalia is invaded, Cunégonde is raped 98 times and Candide is carried off by Bulgarians, and strolling players and merrily flagellated by the Inquistion, before he meets up with his beloved Cunégonde again. Cunégonde has put her 98 experiences to good use by becoming a fashionable courtesan, but Candide accidentally kills her two protectors and, helped and hindered by an Old Lady (June Gable) with an alarmingly physical history, they head off to find a piece of the world in which they can peaceably appreciate Pangloss's words of wisdom together. From Cadiz to Cartagena, from a monastery to El Dorado, via piratical attacks, repeated ravishment all round and separations and encounters not only with each other but with Maximilian and Paquette (who apparently escaped the massacre at Thunder-ten-Tronck after all) and the Old Lady, they arrive by separate paths—she as an odalisque, he with the gold of El Dorado to buy her release—in Turkestan. There, their optimism and philosophy still intact in spite of all, they find the Wisest Man in the World, who seems to be Pangloss but who has changed his dicta. He is now keen on the work ethic, so Candide and Cunégonde, being of the dutiful kind, settle down blissfully on a little farm with a cow. It promptly drops dead. The world is just as good as it ever was.

The score of *Candide* was one which thoroughly merited the description of comic operetta although, by this stage, opéra-bouffe might have been nearer the point. It included ensemble and orchestral music of a quality and adventurousness rarely seen on the postwar musical stage, as well as some magnificently funny solo set pieces of which Cunégonde's extravagantly coloratura burlesque of the operatic jewel song, ''Glitter and Be Gay,'' proved the take-out tune. Elsewhere, the score ranged from the opening, innocent conviction of the young folk that ''Life Is Happiness Indeed'' and their discovery of sex in ''Oh Happy We'' to a bouncing celebration of the Inquisition's ''Auto da fé'' and the Old Lady's encouraging description of her sliced-off charms in ''I Am Easily Assimilated.'' The nasty Governor of Cartagena (doubled in this version by the actor playing Pangloss) serenaded a befrocked Maximilian (''My Love'') and led a lively ''Bon Voyage'' as he sent Candide and his friends off to sea in a leaky boat, whilst a moment of peaceful contrast amid the hurly-burly and horrors came in a sweet duet for two El Doradian sheep. Several numbers from the original version (Candide's Lament, ''Quiet,'' the waltz ''What's the Use?,'' etc) were omitted or revamped in the revised *Candide,* and three new numbers inserted.

The new *Candide* made its way slowly around the world. It was produced in Vienna in 1976, in a version by Marcel Prawy based closely on the Chelsea Theater Center text, under the direction of Larry Fuller, with Heinz Marecek (Pangloss), Heinz Ehrenfreund (Candide), Melanie Holliday (Cunégonde) and Blanche Aubry (Old Lady), and successfully mounted at Birmingham Repertory Theatre in England in a production which was then played at the Edinburgh Festival of 1981 with Nickolas Grace (Pangloss), Rosemary Ashe (Cunégonde), Mark Wynter (Maximilian), Nichola McAuliffe (Old Lady) and William Relton (Candide), but an Australian production staged at Sydney's Seymour Centre, prior to a Melbourne season at the Comedy Theatre (19 July 1982), confused camp with bouffe in its staging, and failed to take.

In 1982 an attempt was made, at the New York City Opera, to reshape the show yet again, reusing parts of the original score which had been abandoned, but that version was itself abandoned after that production, and yet another remake was practiced on the show (which showed no signs of needing a remake) for a Scottish Opera production, subsequently played at London's Old Vic (6 December 1988 ad John Wells, 34 performances). This one attempted to whiten-out the comical opéra-bouffe aspect of the piece as played so effectively on Broadway and replace it with more of the black moralizing of the first *Candide*. Grace, Marilyn Hill Smith (Cunégonde), Mark Baker (Candide) and Ann Howard/ Patricia Routledge (Old Lady) featured in a *Candide* which proved to have lost more than a little of the cutting edge and wisdom which, as authors such as John Gay and the best librettists of Offenbach have shown, is rarely so effectively displayed as in the bouffe idiom. A Broadway reproduction of 1997 (Gershwin Theater 29 April), again mounted by Prince, returned to a version a bit more like his still-by-far-the-most-successful version of 1973. Jim Dale (Pangloss), Harolyn Blackwell (Cunégonde) and Jason Danieley (Candide) featured through 103 performances. In 1999 the show was presented, in yet one more version, at London's National Theatre (ad John Caird, add ly Wilbur 13 April 1999) with Simon Russell Beale featured as Pangloss, Daniel Evans as Candide and Alex Kelly as Cunégonde. It will doubtless not be the last.

A second German adaptation (ad Johannes Felsenstein) was produced in Germany in 1989, France saw 37 performances of the show (ad Jean-Louis Pichon, Henri-Louis Matter) in eight different cities in 1995, and in the meanwhile, in English-speaking countries, *Candide* made its way resolutely into the repertoire of the opera houses which can afford to give its orchestral textures the values needed, if not always its text the vital burlesque comedy and its sung music the most suitable weight of voices.

An earlier, French opéra-bouffe version of *Candide* ''in the acts and six tableaux'' was prepared by Charles Nuitter, Alexandre Beaumont and composer Albert Renaud in the 1890s, but does not seem to have seen the light of stage.

UK: Saville Theatre 30 April 1959; Austria: Stadthalle, Vienna 5 August 1976; Australia: York Theatre, Seymour Centre, Sydney 20 April 1982; Germany: Wuppertaler Bühne 14 May 1989; France: Esplanade, St Étienne 12 January 1995

Recordings: original cast (Columbia), 1973 revival cast (Columbia), New York City Opera cast (New World), Scottish Opera cast (TER), New York 1997 cast (RCA), National Theatre cast (First Night), studio cast w Bernstein (Deutsche Grammophon), etc

TV film: New York City Opera (1968), concert film (1989, Barbican Centre, London)

CANTERBURY TALES Musical in 2 acts by Martin Starkie and Nevill Coghill. Lyrics by Nevill Coghill. Music by Richard Hill and John Hawkins. Phoenix Theatre, London, 21 March 1968.

The first ''version'' of what would eventually become the musical *Canterbury Tales* was a play put together from Professor Coghill's modern English version of Chaucer's medieval poem by actor and broadcaster Starkie, and performed by the John Ford Society of Exeter College at the Oxford Playhouse (26 October 1964) as part of the College's 650th anniversary celebrations. Separately and simultaneously, composers John Hawkins and Richard Hill produced a concept recording, *Canterbury Pilgrims,* which utilized some of Coghill's translation as its text. When they applied for the requisite permissions, the two projects became one and the musical comedy which was called *Canterbury Tales* resulted.

The piece, like the poem, framed the famous tales in the situation of a pilgrimage to Canterbury and the authors selected four of those tales for inclusion: ''The Miller's Tale,'' ''The Reeve's Tale,'' ''The Merchant's Tale'' and ''The Wife of Bath's Tale.'' The songs were little and, in the main, bouncy, illustrating the simplicity of the tales in an uncomplicated way. The juvenile hero of the ''Miller's Tale'' (Nicky Henson) gave forth with a version of a medieval lyric which crowed ''I Have a Noble Cock,'' the much-married Wife of Bath (Jessie Evans) rousted her way through ''Come Along and Marry Me, Honey'' and the Prioress (Pamela Charles) provided the legitimate soprano moments in the ''April Song'' and in the thanksgiving closer to an evening of unmitigated if harmless sexual entertainment, ''Love Will Conquer All.'' Kenneth J Warren (Miller) and Wilfred Brambell (Reeve) played various foolish and lecherous old men, Billy Boyle (Clerk of Oxenford) became the young Knight of the ''Wife of Bath's Tale,'' whilst Gay Soper was all the ingenues.

Starkie's production of *Canterbury Tales* hit London at just the right moment. The restrictions on things sexual in the theatre were in an advanced state of erosion and the stage censor was soon to be abolished. Also, with the label of ''classic'' hung on it (much in the same way that softish-porn films so often insist they are based on de Maupassant stories), it was both rude and all-right at the same time. Chaucer was on the curriculum, and this was a family show even if it did show one chap getting a red-hot poker up his backside, and included voyeurism, rape, cuckoldry and various other things that could be called ''bawdy,'' because they belonged safely to a literary and long past age, rather than ''censorable.'' It also hit just the right tone and level and, as a result, the show became a singular hit. *Canterbury Tales* played 2,080 West End performances in a run of some five years, briefly attempting the authors' original idea of introducing new tales from time to time with versions of the ''Nunne Priest's Tale'' and the ''Pardoner's Tale,'' before going out to multiple productions in provincial theatres. In the meantime, it had traveled round the world from Scandinavia to South Africa, and from Germany (ad Robert Gilbert) and Hungary (ad Márton Mesterházi) to America and Australia.

The American version, made up of four tales rather than the five which the English one had become with the addition of the ''Nunne Priest's Tale,'' added instead one extra number for Hermione Baddeley as the Wife of Bath. Reid Shelton (Knight), Ed Evanko (Squire), George Rose (Reeve), Martyn Green (Chaucer) and Sandy Duncan (all the ingenues) featured in a production which proved, in America's different moral climate, to have few of the attractions it had had back home and played only 122 performances. In Australia, however, with Johnny Lockwood and Evelyn Page top-billed, the show was a major success. An initial two and a half months at Sydney's Theatre Royal was followed by a Melbourne season (Comedy Theatre 16 August 1969) before the show went round the country twice, returning for two further Sydney months the following year (24 April 1970). As a result, it was Australia that was later chosen to launch a sequel, *More Canterbury Tales* (Her Majesty's Theatre, Melbourne 23 October 1976). It went the way of all musequels and quicker than most.

Revivals in both London (Shaftesbury Theatre 24 April 1979) and New York (Rialto Theater 12 February 1980) suffered the same fate: if *Canterbury Tales* had timed its first entrance exceedingly well, it was clearly seen to be not a piece for the I've-seen-it-*all*-hang-out 1980s.

The era which brought out the show also spawned several other at least partly musical *Canterbury Tales* shows, anxious to capitalize on Chaucer's permissible permissiveness. An American *Get Thee to Canterbury* (Paul Hoffert/Jan Steen, David Secter) followed hot behind the London show (Sheridan Square Playhouse 25 January 1969, 20 performances), and the 1960s lasted long enough (or arrived late enough) in Switzerland for a new *Canterbury Tales* musical to be mounted in St Gallen in 1991 (Roman Rutihauser/Liana Ruckstuhl 31 December).

More modest Chaucerian musicals were put out in earlier years by Charles Villiers Stanford (*The Canterbury Pilgrims* Drury Lane 28 April 1884, lib: Gilbert a'Beckett) and by Reginald de Koven (Metropolitan Opera, New York 8 March 1917, lib: Percy Mackaye).

USA: Eugene O'Neill Theater 3 February 1969; Australia: Theatre Royal, Sydney 17 May 1969; Hungary: József Attila Színház 21 February 1970; Germany: Theater im Goetheplatz, Bremen September 1970

Recordings: original cast (Decca), American cast (Capitol), etc

CANTIN, Louis [ALLARD, Louis Alexandre Didier] (b Avignon, 14 November 1821; d Antibes, 11 April 1893). For 15 years, at the height of the French domination of the world's musical stages, producer Louis Cantin controlled an important part of the Paris musical theatre.

The young Louis Cantin (who operated through his theatrical life under the name of his actual father, rather than that of his mother's husband) started his musical-theatre career as an orchestral viola player, but his career as a musician was ruined when he damaged a finger in a game of toupie hollandaise and he had, ultimately, to have it amputated. For a while he worked as a clerk and then as a stockjobber, but he continued to take an interest in the theatre, and eventually rose to having a financial interest in the Théâtre des Folies-Dramatiques. Then, when the lease of the then unfortunate house came up for sale, he managed to get together enough money to take the building on. If things were difficult at first, and even at periods during his later occupancy, he nevertheless brought to the stage of his theatre the two greatest and most successful opérettes of the era. The first was *La Fille de Madame Angot* (1872), picked up from Brussels's Théâtre des Fantaisies-Parisiennes, and then, after a run of mostly less successful works of which Lacome's *Jeanne, Jeannette et Jeanneton* (1876) was the most durable, he topped even that first triumph with the production of the first full-sized work by the young Robert Planquette, *Les Cloches de Corneville* (1877).

Having lifted the Folies-Dramatiques into an eminent position alongside the Théâtre des Variétés, the Théâtre de la Renaissance and the Théâtre des Bouffes-Parisiens as one of the principal musical houses of the town, Cantin sold out while *Les Cloches de Corneville* was still profitably running and instead, in September 1879, ''in partnership with a horse dealer named Rivière,'' took over the control of the Bouffes-Parisiens from Charles Comte. Before long, he achieved a high rate of success in his new theatre, commissioning and producing, notably, the first metropolitan works of two further young composers destined for stardom: Edmond Audran (*Les Noces d'Olivette,* 1879) and Louis Varney (*Les Mousquetaires au couvent,* 1880). Although works by other composers including Serpette, Hervé and Lacome were presented at the Bouffes, Audran became virtually Cantin's house composer and, as a result, the theatre became the launching pad for his enormously successful *La Mascotte* (1880) and *Gillette de Narbonne* (1882).

Cantin swiftly brought the Bouffes to the undisputed head of the opérette world, but a series of failures in

1883–84, beginning with Audran's first flop *La Dormeuse éveillée,* and proceeding with Leopold Wenzel's *Le Chevalier Mignon* and Raoul Marenco's *Le Diable au corps,* discouraged the manager to such a degree that he decided, in January 1885, to give up the Bouffes and, although he thereafter dabbled in theatrical ventures—notably the construction of the oversized and constitutionally unsuccessful Théâtre de l'Eden—his influential and outstanding days were at an end.

Enormously rich from his theatrical successes (and his canny and timely withdrawals), Cantin lived out his days in splendor between his mansion on the Boulevard Péreire, later the home of Sarah Bernhardt, a country estate at St Mandé and a villa at Cap d'Antibes, declaring that the loss of his finger was, in fact, the origin of his fortune.

LA CANTINIÈRE Opérette (vaudeville) in 3 acts by Paul Burani and Félix Ribeyre. Music by Robert Planquette. Théâtre des Nouveautés, Paris, 26 October 1880.

A vaudevillesque piece in the popular military mode, *La Cantinière* featured Léa Silly, years previously the original Orestes of Offenbach's *La Belle Hélène,* in its title role as Victoire, who along with her husband Babylas (Jules Brasseur), is the happy purveyor of nourishment to the 36th cavalry régiment. Berthelier featured as the vain, womanizing Adjutant Rastagnac, Albert Brasseur as Pépinet, the volunteer son of a provincial merchant family who calls himself the Vicomte de Bellechasse, and Mlle Gilberte as Nichette, a potential rival cantinière, through a series of amorous and professional complications accompanied by a Planquette score which was topped by Berthelier's vigorous Chanson de l'Adjutant: ''Je le coupe en deux, en trois, en quatre.''

La Cantinière played for a little short of two months at the Nouveautés before giving way to the year's Christmas revue, but it was brought back for a second season in 1885 (4 April), and remounted both at the Folies-Dramatiques in 1887 and again at the Théâtre des Menus-Plaisirs in 1897 with Mlle Debriège as Victoire and Dekernel as Rastagnac.

America got a glimpse of the show, too, when an English version was produced at San Francisco's Winter Garden Theater in 1881, and again in the repertoire of the Wilbur Opera Company (Gaiety Theater, Boston 19 January 1882) with Susie Kirwin (Victoire) and Harry Brown (Rastagnac) in the lead roles.

USA: Winter Garden Theater, San Francisco *The Pretty Cantinière* 20 October 1881

CANTOR, Eddie [ITZKOWITZ, Isidore] (b New York, 31 January 1892; d Hollywood, Calif, 10 October 1964). A frenetic, jigging little singing comedian who became a blackface star in the *Ziegfeld Follies.*

After a number of years working a blackface act in vaudeville (including an appearance in the London revue *Not Likely*), and the odd musical comedy engagement (apparently as early as 1905 he joined George Lederer's production of *Smiling Island* in Philadelphia), Cantor made his defintive (re)entry on to the musical comedy stage when he was cast as the ''effeminate negro,'' Sam Beverley Moon, in Oliver Morosco's west-coast production of *Canary Cottage* (1916). He did not go on with the show to New York, where what had been his role became ''Sam Abstestos Hicks'' and was played by Hugh Cameron, for he had already moved on to Ziegfeld and the shows which would make him famous. It was not until after half a dozen years playing in revue (*Midnight Follies,* four editions of the *Ziegfeld Follies, Make It Snappy*), that he made the first of what would be a small handful of starring appearances in book musicals on Broadway. Ziegfeld's production of *Kid Boots* (1923, ''Kid'') featured him as a golf caddy-master and allowed him to sing ''Dinah,'' ''Alabammy Bound'' and ''If You Knew Susie'' alongside the show's regular score, and *Whoopee* (1928, Henry Williams) had him as the hypochondriac ''nervous wreck'' of the original play's title, performing ''Makin' Whoopee'' through a successful Broadway season. Cantor subsequently filmed both shows—*Kid Boots* as a silent film in 1926 and *Whoopee,* with sound, in 1930.

After a long career in Hollywood (*The Kid from Spain, Roman Scandals, Kid Millions, Strike Me Pink,* etc) and on radio, he appeared once more in a Broadway musical, in 1941, as the star of the musical version of *Three Men on a Horse, Banjo Eyes,* singing ''We're Having a Baby'' and a blackface potpourri of his past hits.

Cantor's voice was heard in the film *The Eddie Cantor Story* (1953) in which he was impersonated by Keefe Brasselle.

Autobiographies: *My Life Is in Your Hands* (Harper, New York, 1927), *Take My Life* (Doubleday, New York, 1957), *The Way I See It* (Prentice-Hall, New Jersey, 1959), *As I Remember Them* (Duell, Sloan and Pearce, New York, 1963); Biographies: Koseluk, G: *Eddie Cantor: A Life in Show Business* (McFarland & Company, Inc, Jefferson, North Carolina, 1995), Goldman, H G: *Banjo Eyes* (OUP, New York, 1997)

LE CAPITAINE FRACASSE

Théophile Gautier's 1863 novel of the Baron-turned-actor has, in theory, proved a regular basis for musical theatre pieces over the years. However, *Kapitän Fracassa,* the comic Operette in three acts ''taken from a French original'' by Richard Genée and F Zell, with music by Rudolf Dellinger, and produced at Hamburg (2 March 1889) and subsequently at the Theater an der Wien (21 September 1889, 17 performances), apparently shared little with the original book but its title. The tale of this Ger-

Plate 63. **Eddie Cantor.** *The star poses for a photo in rehearsals. The pianist is Irving Berlin.*

man Operette was a Venetian one of stolen jewels and a conventional Operettic romance between the disguised Count Oberto and the Princess Blanche de Coligny, and Fracasse was a comical and apparently almost plot-incidental character in the affair. He was, however, played in the Viennese version by Alexander Girardi. After his success with Dellinger's earlier *Don César,* producer John McCaull mounted the piece in America in 1889 (Chicago Opera House 30 December ad H B Smith) as a vehicle for De Wolf Hopper (Fracasse) and Jeff de Angelis (Momo), with Marion Manola and Eugene Oudin as the lovers, but to unenthusiastic response. It was subsequently given a showing at San Francisco's Tivoli (May 1897).

A 1909 Italian comic opera in three acts by Guglielmo Emmanuel, O Magici and Mario Costa (Teatro Alfieri, Turin 14 December), which clearly credited the novel as its source, had a more widespread success. After being presented in its country of origin with Emma Vecla (Isabella) and Riccardo Tegani (di Sicognac) starred, it was seen at the Vienna Volksoper (26 January 1911) and was purchased by George Edwardes for Britain, without, however, getting to the stage before the producer's death intervened. An earlier Italian *Captain Fracasse,* written by Luigi Campesi and composed by Giovanni Valente, had been produced before either of the better-known pieces, at Naples's Teatro della Varieta in 1881 (3 January).

A French *Capitaine Fracasse,* with a score by Émile Pessard, was produced in Paris in 1878 (lib: Catulle Mendès, Théâtre Lyrique 2 July) with Melchissdec and Pauline Luigini starred, whilst a ''comédie musicale'' under the same title, by Jean-Marie Lecocq and Louis Dunoyer de Segonzac, was played at the Théâtre de la Renaissance in 1986 (25 June) before being seen around France, and later in Germany.

EL CAPITAN Comic opera in 3 acts by Charles Klein. Lyrics by Thomas Frost. Music by John Philip Sousa. Broadway Theater, New York, 20 April 1896.

One of the earliest successful comic operas to come out of America, *El Capitan* was also the one successful attempt by ''March King'' John Philip Sousa to provide an enduring musical score for the theatre. This success owed no small debt to Charles Klein's libretto which, if it was made in the familiar mold of Continental comic opera texts, and composed of a web of well-used plot elements, was nevertheless a shapely, coherent and funny piece of its kind. It also owed no small debt to the performance of the tall, basso comedian de Wolf Hopper in its starring role.

The Viceroy of Peru, Don Luiz Cazzaro (Thomas S Guise), has been deposed by the Spanish government, and Don Errico Medigua (Hopper) sent out to replace him. Cazzaro has, however, not taken his dismissal lightly and is plotting, with a band of bravos and some of the local populace, to regain his position by force. To this end he has hired the famous Spanish mercenary known as ''el Capitan.'' But Don Medigua has discovered all this plottery whilst still on the high seas to South America and, knowing el Capitan to have been killed in a shipboard, he concocts a wily plot to turn the tables on Cazzaro. On his arrival, he hides himself away from the Peruvian populace, and devotes himself to building the reputation of el Capitan up to a ferocious height. Then—when the moment is ripe—he emerges, himself, in personation of the mercenary and takes command of Cazzaro's forces. The phony el Capitan leads the rebel army round in swashbuckling circles until they are too exhausted to face the Spanish troops, after which Medigua (now as himself) defeats himself (as el Capitan) in battle and, with his viceregal hat now firmly in place and all resistance quashed, he takes up his Peruvian throne in time for the curtain.

Alice Hosmer played Medigua's wife, Princess Marghanza, distraught at being seconded to the wilds of Peru in exile from the social delights of the European metropolis; Bertha Walzinger was his daughter, Isabel, who conducts an incidental romance with one Count Hernando Verrada (Edmund Stanley) in order to provide the opportunity for some sentimental music; Edna Wallace Hopper was the tempestuous Estrelda, daughter to Cazzaro, and determined to hook herself the famous war leader as a husband; whilst librettist Klein himself appeared as the bewildered court Chamberlain, Signor Amabile Pozzo, kidnapped by the enemy in mistake for his employer.

Sousa's comic-operatic score, an amount of it reused from his previous shows, which had not made it to New York, included some fine concerted music, and a regular layout of typical numbers from the romancing of the juveniles (''Sweetheart, I'm Waiting''), to the comical ''A Typical Tune of Zanzibar'' and the marching strains of el Capitan's entrance song, both sung by the disguised Medigua.

After *El Capitan*'s first Broadway run of 112 performances, Hopper took ''his'' show to the country, running it round America for two full seasons (''phenomenal houses ; the chorus is big enough to hide the scenery''), returning for repeat showings in New York both in 1897 (Broadway Theater 22 February, 4 weeks) and 1898 (Fifth Avenue Theater 21 February) before taking the company across to London to play *El Capitan* at the Lyric and Comedy Theatres with Miss Hosmer, Jessie Mackaye, Nella Bergen, Harold Blake and Henry Norman in support of the star. The show was well received in London, and it ran for some five months, after which Hopper produced his and Sousa's subsequent *The Charlatan* (*Mystical Miss*).

Hopper kept *El Capitan* to hand for a number of years, and it now shares with *Robin Hood* the distinction of representing 19th-century American comic opera to end-of-20th-century folk, a fact which has earned it a number of interested revivals, notably one at the Goodspeed Opera House in 1973 (11 June) with John Cullum featured in Hopper's role.

What seems to have been a primitive version of the show, set in Spain and entitled *The Wolf,* was announced for production by Francis Wilson as early as 1889. If so, Klein and Sousa were lucky that they waited for Hopper.

UK: Lyric Theatre 10 July 1899

Recordings: Minnesota Opera Co (3 records), University of Illinois (Zephyr)

LE CAPITOLE Opéra-bouffe in 3 acts by Paul Ferrier and Charles Clairville. Music by Gaston Serpette. Théâtre des Nouveautés, Paris, 5 December 1895.

In between the famous Ancient Greek Parisianisms of *La Belle Hélène* and those of *Son p'tit frère* and *Phi-Phi,* there were plenty of other pieces produced on the musical stage which garbed what were in essence boulevard comedies in the trappings of classical times with less, but by no means negligible, success. One of these was *Le Capitole.*

The central figure of the piece is Métella (Jane Pierny), nubile wife of the pompous and elderly consul, Cornélius Major (Germain), and a descendant of the famously raped Lucretia. Cornélius is careless enough to send his wife the tidings of his victory over the Ligurians by his unnecessarily handsome lieutenant, Narcisse (Abel Tarride), and the action leaps into forward gear. Unlike her ancestress, Métella initially keeps her virtue, but not the semblance of it. Her husband prefers to pretend ignorance as he is expecting to be awarded a Triumph, and cannot risk the ridicule of having been cuckolded. However, before the three acts of the evening are done, ridicule has well and truly arrived along with all the other elements of a bedroom farce which ends in classic style with the old husband thoroughly bamboozled and the young wife making the most of his lieutenant.

Serpette decorated the tale with a score which was rated one of his most lighthearted and melodious, and *Le Capitole* played seasons in Paris in 1895–96 and again later in 1896, before going on to further productions in Germany (ad Wilhelm Mannstädt) and in two different versions in Hungary (ad Gyula Komor, ad Dezső Bálint).

Germany: Theater am Alexanderplatz *Metella* 4 October 1897; Hungary: Budai Színkör *Az erenyes Metella* 26 September 1896, Népszínház *A konzul felesége* 20 May 1904

CAPTAIN THÉRÈSE Comic opera in 3 acts by Alexandre Bisson and F C Burnand. Lyrics by F C Burnand and Gilbert a' Beckett. Music by Robert Planquette. Prince of Wales Theatre, London, 25 August 1890.

The fifth Planquette opérette made, or seriously remade, specifically for the London stage, *Captain Thérèse* was also made specifically as a starring vehicle for the American contralto Agnes Huntington, who had made a great hit in the title role of the Carl Rosa Light Opera Company's Planquette piece *Paul Jones.* Alexandre Bisson evolved a tale which allowed the statuesque Miss Huntington to get into men's clothes again as quickly and as long as possible, and his work was translated by F C Burnand, set by Planquette and handed over to the Carl Rosa Company.

Unfortunately, by that time, Miss Huntington had walked out on Rosa and gone home where she could earn better money than was available in England and where she was soon to marry a millionaire socialite. The role of *Captain Thérèse,* who gets into soldier's uniform for the usual operettic reasons, was instead played by Canadian vocalist Attalie Claire (soon dubbed insufficient and replaced by Violet Cameron), the Vicomte Tancrède de la Touche was Hayden Coffin, singing of "A Soldier's Life," Joseph Tapley played the tenor hero Philip de Bellegarde, Phyllis Broughton the soubrette, and Madame Amadi a nun, in a post–*Paul Jones* line-up which was more than a touch more-of-the-sameish.

London's *Captain Thérèse* was played 40 times, before the show went on to be seen in a series of other productions and countries. It was played in America, with Miss Huntington now taking the role written for her alongside Eric Thorne (Tancred), Clinton Elder (Philip) and Effie Chapuy (Marcelline) pausing briefly on Broadway (11 performances) during its touring career, in Paris with Yvonne Kerlord (Thérèse), Vauthier (Sombrero), Paul Fugère (Duvet) and Lucien Noël (Bellegarde) starred (26 performances), and in Budapest (ad Béla J Fái, Jenő Faragó) for eight performances, without achieving a proper success anywhere.

USA: Opera House, Trenton, NJ 9 October 1891, Union Square Theater 15 February 1892; France: Théâtre de la Gaîté 1 April 1901; Hungary: Népszínház *Teréz kapitány* 15 November 1901

THE CARD Musical in 2 acts by Keith Waterhouse and Willis Hall based on the novel by Arnold Bennett. Music and lyrics by Tony Hatch and Jackie Trent. Queen's Theatre, London, 24 July 1973.

Arnold Bennett's novel of the English provinces was made up into a musical play in the *Half a Sixpence* vein by the authors of *Billy Liar,* Waterhouse and Hall, and the husband and wife songwriting team Tony Hatch and Jackie Trent ("Downtown," "I Couldn't Live without Your Love," "Where Are You Now?," etc).

Denry Machin, the tart little hero of this "how-to-succeed-in-business-politics-and-love-by-trying-exceedingly-hard" tale was played by Jim Dale, one time pop singer and *Carry On* film star turned respectable actor. Millicent Martin (Ruth) and Eleanor Bron (Countess of Chell) were the women he used to help his rise, Joan Hickson was his mother, and John Savident the hated employer whom he was to rise above. When he does get to the top, however, Denry sees clearly enough to turn for love to the faithful Nellie (Marti Webb) who has slogged for him since the beginning. The mostly upbeat score included a lively retailing of the capitalist system in "That's the Way the Money Goes" and a pretty ballad for Nellie, "I Could Be the One," alongside its most popular number, the duet "Opposite Your Smile."

One hundred and thirty performances in the West End, under the management of the young Cameron Mackintosh and Jimmy Wax, did not seem enough to establish *The Card* as a revivable prospect, but the piece did win a production in Germany with the rather literally translated title of *Das As* in 1979, and in 1992, after Mackintosh had risen to be the world's most successful producer of musicals, he sponsored a revival of a rewritten version (add ly Anthony Drewe) of *The Card* at Newbury's Water Mill Theatre followed by a season at the Open Air Theatre, Regent's Park (1 August 1994). Peter Duncan, Hayley Mills, John Turner, Jessica Martin and Jenna Russell featured, and in the cold light of the 1990s *The Card* proved to be a paler-even-than-remembered *Half a Sixpence* clone.

Germany: Staatsoperette, Dresden *Das As* 22 June 1979

Recordings: original cast (Pye), revival recording 1992 (First Night)

CARELESS RAPTURE Musical play in 3 acts by Ivor Novello. Lyrics by Christopher Hassall. Theatre Royal, Drury Lane, London, 11 September 1936.

After the truncated success of *Glamorous Night* at the Theatre Royal, Drury Lane, the board of that theatre turned down Novello's next piece and instead mounted a pantomime and a disastrous failure in a semi-German mish-mash of a musical called *Rise and Shine.* They were quickly back at Novello's door, and *Careless Rapture* ultimately went into the theatre for which it had been designed after all. Its author starred as the sculptural Michael, bastard brother of Sir Rodney Alderney (Ivan Samson) and in love with the same woman, musical comedy star Penelope Lee (Dorothy Dickson). He follows her from a beauty parlour run by Zena Dare, to a singing les-

Plate 64. **Careless Rapture.** *Ivor Novello and Dorothy Dickson climbed every mountain in China in one of the scenic moments of the author's second Drury Lane musical spectacular.*

son with Olive Gilbert, to the theatre, for an extract of the operetta *The Rose Girl,* and then whisks her off to Hampstead Heath for a jolly time amongst a carnival of scenery. When Sir Rodney takes her as far away as China in search of the evening's special effects, Michael follows, and, after time out for a rehearsal by the local operatic society, an earthquake and an attack by Chinese bandits (the chief of whom was also played by Novello) he finally gets the girl in time for the final curtain.

If the tale was fairly preposterous, the settings that it linked together were Drury-Lane gorgeous, the dance opportunities for the dancing Miss Dickson and Walter Crisham legion, the earthquake equally as good a piece of spectacular stagecraft as the shipwreck of the previous show, and Miss Dickson's ''Music in May,'' Miss Gilbert's deeply intoned ''Why Is There Ever Goodbye?'' and the duo ''Love Made the Song,'' sung by the leading lights of the Chinese operatic society, just a notch below the *Glamorous Night* songs, a set which had been written for an altogether more substantial and rangy leading lady's voice.

Novello's popularity and the spectacle helped *Careless Rapture* to 296 performances at Drury Lane, before it was replaced by *Crest of the Wave,* the next in the Novello series of romantic spectaculars, and it subsequently toured through 1937–38, with Barry Sinclair and Ivy Tresmand featured in the roles created by Novello and Miss Dickson.

Recordings: original cast (HMV, EMI), selection (EMI, WRC)

CARIOU, Len [CARIOU, Leonard] (b St Boniface, Manitoba, 30 September 1939). Broadway leading man of the 1970s.

Cariou began his career as a chorus singer in his native Canada, but made his Broadway debut in classic drama, returning to the musical theatre in 1970 to play the love interest to top-billed Lauren Bacall in *Applause* (Bill). He made intermittent essays in musical roles over the next 20 years, creating the role of Fredrik Egermann, the central character of *A Little Night Music* (1973), and the title role of *Sweeney Todd* (1979) as well as appearing briefly as Teddy Roosevelt in Broadway's *Teddy and Alice* and as Florenz Ziegfeld in the London extravaganza loosely based on the famous producer's life (*Ziegfeld*, 1988). In 1997 he was seen on the American road as Cap'n Andy in *Show Boat.*

He repeated his *A Little Night Music* role in the cinema version of the show.

CARLE, Richard E [CARLETON, Charles Nicholas] (b Somerville, Mass, 7 July 1871; d Hollywood, Calif, 28 June 1941). Long-popular comedy star of the American musical theatre.

Carle began his stage career playing supporting comedy roles in mostly musical theatre—the Emerson Comedy company's *Cranks* (1892), the musical farce-comedies *A Mad Bargain* (1892, Worthington) and *A Country Sport* (1893, Washington Strutt), the Boston musical *Davy Jones* (1894), the burlesque *Excelsior Jr* (1895, Tomagnio De Reske Tenorini) and in the British variety musical *The Lady Slavey* (1896, Lord Lavender) as an effete and awkward English Lord—before rising to the top of the bill in the revusical *A Round of Pleasure,* a return season of *The Lady Slavey* (1898, this time in an introduced character as William Endymion Sykes) , *Yankee Doodle Dandy* (1898, Pasquale de Mackerel), on the road alongside Madge Lessing and Cissie Loftus in *A Dangerous Maid* (1899, Schmaltz) and in the star comedy role of the beleaguered soothsayer, Heliodorus, in the Broadway production of Sidney Jones's *A Greek Slave* (1899). In 1900 he took the chief comic part in the musical comedy *Mam'selle 'Awkins* (Rev Jonathan Job Meacham, aka Slippery Jack) for which he had himself written the straightforward and lightly blue libretto.

At the same time, he worked rather less prominently as a librettist and lyricist, supplying song words to such pieces as the play (with a song) *The Girl from Maxim's, The Belle of New York* (''A Cloud Came O'er his Brow'' for Dan Daly), *A Round of Pleasure* (''I Really Don't Know What You Mean''), *The Rogers Brothers in Wall Street* (''Licorice Lize'') and *The Rogers Brothers in Central Park.* He also authored and sometimes played in the little burlesque pieces mounted at the Casino Roof and Koster and Bial's Music Hall (Charley Swivel in *In Gotham,* 1899, Christian Endeavour in his own *Sir Andy de Bootjack* 1899, Lenox Lyceum in *Way Up East,* 1899, Englander Kerker de Koven in *The Maid in the Moon* 1899, etc), and, in addition, turned out vaudeville sketches for a variety of performers (*Mrs Bruno's Burglar* [1898], etc).

In the uninfectious rash of American musical comedies which briefly swept London after the singular success there of *The Belle of New York,* Carle starred in the West End at the head of the New York Casino Theater company in *An American Beauty* (1900, Bayley Bangle), *The Casino Girl* (1900, J Offenbach Gaggs) and *The Belle of Bohemia* (1901, Algy Cuffs). When London proved no real taker for the Casino shows, he went with the company on a tour of the Continent, appearing in Austria, Germany and Hungary as Ichabod Bronson in *The Belle of New York* and in *The Casino Girl.* During his British stay he worked also with the British composer Walter Slaughter on the writing of a musical, *Little Miss Modesty,* which ultimately remained unstaged.

Carle returned to America to star in another British musical, the George Dance/Ivan Caryll *The Ladies' Paradise* (1901), which his *Mam'selle 'Awkins* collaborator, producer Alfred Aarons, staged lavishly and disastrously at no less a venue than the Metropolitan Opera House. Then, with $3,000 alegedly owing to him in unpaid salary, he moved on to Chicago—then flourishing extremely as a source of new musical theatre—to appear in and collaborate on the writing and composing of a number of new works, which featured the kind of put-upon, awkward star-comic characters and out-front, rudish humor in which he specialized.

He toured in the established Chicago favorite *The Burgomaster* (1901, Peter Stuyvesant) and in the city's new *The Explorers* (1902, Bonaparte Hunter) and *The Storks* (1902, Mlzadoc, Bugaloo of Bakteria), and then launched himself on a trio of writing-playing-directing-producing (with partner Charles Marks) successes which confirmed their author-stager-star as a nation-wide favorite. *The Tenderfoot* (1903, Professor Zachary Pettibone LLD BA, also dir), *The Maid and the Mummy* (1904, Washington Stubbs, also dir) and *The Mayor of Tokio* (1905, Marcus Orlando Kidder, also dir) all started out from Chicago and each took in New York seasons only as part of long and lucrative touring lives. During this same period he contributed to what was announced as Chicago's first local, topical revue, the 1905 *All Around Chicago,* mounted by William Brady at McVickers Theater. He topped off this impressive run of acting and writing successes with a small triumph in a written-over version of the London Gaiety Theatre hit *The Spring Chicken.* Equipped with an Americanized (by him) text and with several additional songs of his own making added to remnants of the original score, Carle starred in the little-man role of Girdle, created by Edmund Payne in Britain, under the banner ''Richard Carle presents himself and his songs in George Edwardes' success of two London seasons . . . ,'' and found his biggest success to date. Whilst he toured *The Spring Chicken* (1906 ssq), his latest piece of authorship, *The Hurdy Gurdy Girl* (also dir, co-ch), set out from Boston under the management of Charles Marks without him, and with Annie Yeamans, John W Ransome and John E Hazzard starring. Carle, however, played the piece briefly in Chicago in 1909 (Pericles Pettingill).

His success with *The Spring Chicken,* a piece based firmly on a hit French comedy, prompted him to himself adapt a French comedy, *Madame Mongodin* (better known to English audiences as *Mrs Ponderbury's Past*), to the musical stage. His 1909 show *The Boy and the Girl* (a piece written for the Boston Bank Officers amdrams in 1907, made over and billed as ''Richard Carle's whistling summer show'') flopped quickly, but Carle rebounded by turning an earlier adaptation, *Mary's Lamb* (1907, also dir), originally produced with Harry Conor in the starring role, into a vehicle for himself, which lasted his for two years of highly successful touring in the meek and mild role of ''Leander Lamb, a martyr.''

Back in Chicago, he appeared in Charles Dillingham's production of William Le Baron and Deems Taylor's *The Echo* (1910), but he preferred to go on the road with Lederer and Frazee's production of one of his own creations, *Jumping Jupiter* (1910, Professor Goodwillie, dir), when the earlier piece went towards New York. Both shows failed, but another French farce/ Viennese Operette adaptation, *The Girl from Montmartre* (1912), taken by Harry B Smith from a text based on Feydeau's *La Dame de Chez Maxim,* produced by Charles Frohman and featuring Carle (Dr Petypon) opposite another drawing name in Hattie Williams, did very much better. A second show with the same team, an Americanized version of Leo Fall's charming *Das Puppenmädel*—originally the French comedy *Miquette et sa mère*—peppered with homemade songs and entitled *The Doll Girl* (1913, Marquis de Tourelle) also did well.

The peak of his popular success having now passed, and his producing operation, Carle-Marks, Inc, having gone into bankruptcy (with a name like that, what did he expect?) after *Jumping Jupiter,* Carle limited his activities to performing for hire. In the years that followed he mixed musical stage appearances with revue (*The Cochran Revue of 1916*), vaudeville (*If We Said What We Thought* 1914) and film parts, appearing in tryout of a musicalized version of Schönthan's *Der Schwalbenstreich* called *The Red Fez* (1914), on Broadway in character roles in *Ninety in the Shade* (1915, Willoughby Parker) and *Adrienne* (1923, John Grey), in *Happy Days* (1928), paired with Marie Cahill, in *The New Yorkers* (1930, Windham Wentworth), on the road in *The Blue Kitten* (1922), as Chauncey Cheesboro in Chicago's *Molly Darling* (1922), and in *Some Colonel* (1922).

Late in life, Carle, who had performed in films from the earliest soundless days (*Mary's Lamb* 1915, ''the cleverest comedy of the season,'' *Madame X,* etc), made a fine second career as a cinematic character actor, being seen in, amongst others, such screen pieces as *Anything Goes* (1936, Bishop Dobson), *The Merry Widow* (1934, an attorney), *One Hour with You* (1932, a detective), *San Francisco* (1936) and *One Night in the Tropics.*

1898 **Way Up East** (pasticcio) 1 act Casino Roof Garden 5 September

1899 **The Maid in the Moon** (Fred Solomon) 1 act Casino Roof Garden 31 July

1899 **The Rogers Brother in Wall Street** (Maurice Levi/J J McNally) Victoria Theater 18 September

1899 **Sir Andy de Bootjack** (Alfred Aarons) Koster and Bial's Music Hall 17 October

1899 **Children of the Get-Dough** (Aarons) burlesque in *Round New York in 80 Minutes* Koster and Bial's Music Hall 6 November

1900 **Mam'selle 'Awkins** (Aarons, Herman Perlet) Victoria Theater 26 February

1902 **My Antoinette** (revised *The Ladies' Paradise*) with add mus by Aarons Columbia Theater, Boston 15 January

1902 **The Storks** (Frederic Chapin/w Guy F Steeley) Majestic Theater, Boston 16 February

1903 **The Tenderfoot** (Harry L Heartz) Dearborn Theater, Chicago 12 April; New York Theater, New York 22 February 1904

1904 **The Maid and the Mummy** (Robert Hood Bowers) Garrick Theater, Chicago 30 May; New York Theater, New York 25 July

1905 **The Mayor of Tokio** (William Frederick Peters) Studebaker Theater, Chicago 12 June; New York Theater, New York 4 December

1906 **The Spring Chicken** American adaptation and additional songs (Daly's Theater)

1907 **The Hurdy Gurdy Girl** (Heartz) Tremont Theater, Boston 3 June; Wallack's Theater, New York 23 September

1907 **Mary's Lamb** (Carle) Walnut Street Theater, Philadelphia 28 October; New York Theater 25 May 1908

1909 **The Boy and the Girl** (Heartz/w M E Rourke) Whitney Theater, Chicago 20 March; New Amsterdam Aerial Gardens, New York 31 May

1910 **Jumping Jupiter** (w others/w Sydney Rosenfeld) Cort Theater, Chicago 4 August; Criterion Theater, New York 6 March 1911

1914 **The Red Fez** (Heartz) Cape Theater, Portland, Me 29 June

CARLETON, William T[urnham] *see* CELLI, FRANK

CARMEN JONES Musical play in 2 acts by Oscar Hammerstein II based on Meilhac and Halévy's adaptation of Prosper Merimée's *Carmen.* Music by Georges Bizet. Broadway Theater, New York, 2 December 1943.

An Americanization of the *Carmen* tale and of Bizet's opera, written by Oscar Hammerstein II, *Carmen*

Jones featured a Carmen who works in a parachute factory in the southern United States, a G I Joe (ie, Don José) with a girlfriend called Cindy Lou, and an Escamillo who was no longer a bullfighter, but a boxer called Husky Miller. If the characters' names sounded like something out of a Weber and Fields burlesque, the show nevertheless followed the same tragic lines as the opera and had nothing of the burlesque to it, beyond the fact that many of the lyrics that were fitted to reorchestrated versions of Bizet's melodies were written in a coon-songish ''Dis'' and ''Dat'' and ''Dere'' lingo. The Flower Song became ''Dis Flower,'' the Card Song was ''Dat Ol' Boy,'' the Habanera was ''Dat's Love,'' the smugglers' quintet became ''Whizzin' Away Along de Track'' and, in the high-spot of the evening, the Chanson Bohémienne was turned into ''Beat Out Dat Rhythm on a Drum.''

Billy Rose's original production of *Carmen Jones* had its lead roles double cast, with Muriel Smith and Muriel Rahn alternating as Carmen Jones, Luther Saxon and Napoleon Reed sharing Joe, and Carlotta Franzell and Elton J Warren taking turns at Cindy Lou. Glenn Bryant did Husky Miller every night. The show had a successful 502-performance run on Broadway and was subsequently toured and then filmed with Dorothy Dandridge (sung by Marilyn Horne), Harry Belafonte (sung by LeVern Hutcheson) and Joe Adams (sung by Marvin Hayes) in the principal roles.

It took some time for the piece to travel. *Carmen Jones* was first played in Britain at the Crucible Theatre, Sheffield, in 1986 with Laverne Williams and Lynne Kieran sharing the title role, and it reached London in 1991 (8 April) when it was mounted for what turned out to be a run of nearly two years (740 performances) at the Old Vic, with Sharon Benson and Wilhelminia Fernandez alternating as Carmen, whilst a production by the New York Harlem Ensemble was toured through European one-night stands in 1987.

The story of *Carmen* or, more particularly, the remaking of it as known from Bizet's opéra-comique, has been reused in many ways on the stage since the original piece first appeared at Paris's Opéra-Comique in 1875. In Victorian times, when *Carmen* verged on the repertoire of the light opera companies, it was subjected to many burlesque versions, notably Robert Reece's pasticcio *Carmen, or Sold for a Song,* played with wide success by Lydia Thompson with Lionel Brough as Don José and John Howson as Escamillo; John Wilton Jones's *Cruel Carmen* (pasticcio arr D. Gribben Pavilion, Southport 15 March 1880); the Frank Green/Frank Musgrave *Carmen, or Soldiers and Seville-ians* played by Selina Dolaro on Broadway (Haverley's Theater 13 September 1880); Alfred Murray's *Little Carmen* (Globe Theatre 7 February 1884), which introduced Edward Jakobowski's music to the West End; a Max Freeman operatic burlesque played by the Kimball Operatic Company with little Corinne in its lead (Jacob's Opera House, Paterson, NJ 1 September 1890); a *Carmencitada* brought to Miner's Bowery Theatre (5 January 1891) with topical songsters and trapeze and gymnastic acts popped into the action; and, most successfully of all, the Gaiety Theatre's *Carmen Up-to-Data.* One music-less *Carmen* burlesque was that put on film in 1916. Charlie Chaplin played Darn Hosiery to the Carmen of Edna Purviance in a four-parter informatively titled *Charlie Chaplin's Burlesque on Carmen.*

In 1917 André Barde and Charles Carpentier authored a tongue-in-cheek musequel to the tale told by Merimée, Meilhac and Halévy in a piece called *Carminetta* (mus: Émile Lassailly, Théâtre Michel, Paris 16 March), which later had some success when produced by C B Cochran in Britain.

The most successful of modern *Carmen* variations have been the operatic *La Tragédie de Carmen* as remodeled by Peter Brook for presentations in France and America (ad Sheldon Harnick), and the small-scale Anglo-Viennese musical *Carmen Negra* (arr Callum McLeod/Stewart Trotter) which reset the piece in a South American republic with an Escamillo who is the captain of his country's World Cup football team. The Toreador's Song became ''Santa Maria's Going to Win the Cup.'' Produced at Vienna's Kammeroper in 1988, with Lynne Kieran (Carmen) and Michael Heath (José) starred, the piece caused a sensation and was played for three successive seasons before being recorded for television. It also set off a temporary boom in Carmen variants, and was followed on the European touring circuits—whilst *Carmen Jones* extended its run at London's Old Vic into its second year—by another remake entitled *Rocky Carmen* with a pop star Esca Millo, which, undoubtedly will not be the last perversion of Merimée and/or Bizet to find its way to the world's stages.

An earlier purposefully all-black-cast *Carmen* was produced at the Lexington Opera House, New York, in May 1900 by Theodore Drury and his company. This one was, however, the opéra-comique almost as writ, pure and undefiled in most of its details.

UK: Crucible Theatre, Sheffield 14 March 1986, Old Vic 8 April 1991; France: tour 1987

Film: 1954 Twentieth Century Fox

Recordings: original cast (Decca), soundtrack (RCA), studio cast w Grace Bumbry (Heliodor), British cast (EMI)

CARMEN UP-TO-DATA Burlesque in 2 acts by George Sims and Henry Pettitt. Music by W Meyer Lutz. Gaiety Theatre, London, 4 October 1890.

Sims and Pettitt prepared their burlesque version of *Carmen* to follow the enormous success of their *Faust*

Up-to-Date and, even though their new show did not benefit from the support of the Gaiety's star team of Nellie Farren and Fred Leslie, who had gone touring with the last Gaiety piece, they scored another grand hit.

Florence St John, London's queen of comic opera and an artist quite capable of singing Bizet's original operatic version, was their Carmen, opposite Edwin Lonnen as an Irish masher of a Don José. Escamillo (Jenny Dawson/Alma Stanley) was played as a principal boy in tights and Michaela (Maria Jones) became a bulgingly healthy country wench. The part of Zuniga was made into a principal comic role for Arthur Williams as "The Villain of the Day." Meyer Lutz's score for the show ranged from the genuine romance of "One Who Is Life to Me" to the saucy "Ask Me to Marry" for the star, Escamillo demonstrated "The Swagger" and Jose sang about "The Jolly Boys' Club," whilst Letty Lind as an incidental señorita did farmyard imitations and danced a hornpipe. However, the song hit of the show fell to Lonnen. Since the comedian had made himself famous with his series of Irish songs in previous burlesques, the authors had justified this show's expected interpolation by actually making José Irish, but Lonnen asked instead for a version of the Dave Braham song "Whist! the Bogie Man," then the rage of the minstrel world. Lutz, Sims and Pettitt put together a colorable imitation called "Hush, the Bogie" which, performed in the semidark to a bouche fermée chorus, became the rage of the whole country.

The show underwent many alterations through its 248 London performances, often due to cast changes—at one time Escamillo stopped being a "boy" and was sung by very legit vocalists W H Brockbank and Frank Celli—before heading off to the country where it toured solidly for three years before living out many more years on the minor circuits. George Musgrove took the Gaiety company to Australia in 1892, with Marion Hood starring as Carmen alongside Lonnen and Robert Courtneidge as Zuniga, and two British companies took productions to the Continent. Josephine Findlay and Walter Passmore starred in Berlin, Bremen, Hamburg and Brussels (*Carmen fin de siècle*), whilst Percy Hutchinson's Royal English Burlesque Company with Fanny Wentworth (Carmen), Fred Wright (José), Grace Huntley (Escamillo) and James Stevenson (Zuniga) played *Carmen von heute* in Vienna, Bucharest and Budapest.

Only the title—or versions of it—made it to America. Jennie Kimball rechristened her already well-used *Carmen* burlesque *Carmen Up-to-Data* in order to be up-to-date, and Fred Solomon turned out a burlesque for Koster & Bial which insisted that it was *Carmen Up Too Late*.

Germany: Reichsallen Theater *Carmen fin de siècle* 14 April 1892; Australia: Theatre Royal, Adelaide 16 July 1892; Austria: Carltheater *Carmen von heute* September 1892; Hungary: Városligeti Színkör *Carmen von heute* 19 September 1892

LE CARNET DU DIABLE Opérette fantaisie in 3 acts by Ernest Blum and Paul Ferrier. Music by Gaston Serpette. Théâtre des Variétés, Paris, 23 October 1895.

A féerie à grand spectacle, lavishly staged by Fernand Samuel at the Variétés, *Le Carnet du diable* was hailed as "an impudently smutty piece, . . . a spicy compound into which the authors have thrown an unusual dash of originality and the composer a sprinkling of tuneful grace" as it established itself as one of the best liked of its kind throughout fin de siècle Europe.

Satanella (Mlle Théry) complains to her uncle, the King of the Underworld (Édouard Georges), about the philanderings of her husband Belphegor (Baron) and Satan inflicts upon the errant little devil a punishment of a year's celibacy. He may lust but not assuage that lust: his check book on the bank of love is withdrawn. But Belphegor finds a way out: he makes a deal with the luckless student Arsène Marjavel (Albert Brasseur) by which he will give the boy good luck in exchange for his carnet de banque. Belphegor rushes off to spend, spend, spend his new supply of sex-checks, while Arsène, who has been previously miserably cut out by his cousin Casimir (Schütz) with the gorgeous Peruvian belle Mimosa (Juliette Méaly), now not only wins but weds her. Alas! Come the wedding night, his bargain with the devil catches up with him. He has no carnet and cannot call on his "account" with Baron Cupido's bank. The bride will stay undeflowered. Fortunately Venus (Mlle de Gaby) responds to Mimosa's indignant pleas and a new check book is issued in time for a consummation and a pictorial apotheosis. One of the subplots was a comical romance between Mimosa's impossibly wealthy papa, General Ruy del Rio Secco (A Simon), and a bar wench, Jacqueline, as played by Ève Lavallière.

The scenes ranged from views of Hell and Paris to the comical banking establishment run by the Baron Cupido (Lassouche), there were ballets, tableaux vivants, pantomime and burlesque dance (Lavallière impersonating Cléo de Mérode), and there were also the titillating moments so beloved of the Paris spectacular: the wedding night undressing of the bride, the appearance of Venus in all her heroic nudity, and the usual bevy of scantily clad chorines.

Le Carnet du diable proved a fine success at the Variétés, and it was subsequently tarted up and trotted out for further runs, the first just two seasons on (18 September 1897, 40 performances), the next "enlarged and revised" in 1899, and again in 1900 with Mlle Méaly, Baron and Brasseur still in their original roles. In the meantime, it made the tour of central Europe, being mounted in Berlin under the title of *Cupido & Co* (add material by Maurice Rappaport and Hermann Haller) and in Vienna as the "phantastiche Burleske" *Das Scheck-*

buch des Teufels (ad Carl Lindau and F Antony, add mus Maximilian Steiner). The subject matter proved, predictably, just too much for the English-speaking countries.

Germany: Belle-Alliance Theater *Cupido & Co* 23 December 1902; Austria: Danzers Orpheum *Das Scheckbuch des Teufels* 21 December 1906

CARNEVAL IN ROM Comic opera in 3 acts by Josef Braun based on *Piccolino* by Victorien Sardou. Music by Johann Strauss. Theater an der Wien, Vienna, 1 March 1873.

The second Operette composed by Johann Strauss was founded on a solid piece of French theatre in Victorien Sardou's sentimental comedy *Piccolino* (Gymnase 18 July 1861), a piece which had already served as the basis for an operatic version by Mme de Grandval (Théâtre des Italiens, 5 January 1869) and was to become, three years later, the libretto (w Charles Nuitter) to Ernest Guiraud's three-act opéra-comique *Piccolino,* mounted with success at the Paris Opéra-Comique (11 April 1876). In fact, *Piccolino,* which was subsequently played a number of times in Britain, in Budapest, in Latin America and Scandinavia, ultimately had a much wider success than Strauss's work but, without the saleable name of the waltz king attached to it, it has faded away in the 20th century.

Marie Geistinger starred in *Carneval in Rom* as a little peasant girl, Marie. She has passed an idyllic time in her Swiss mountain village with the visiting painter Arthur Bryk (Albin Swoboda), but now Bryk has gone on to Rome, leaving her with only her portrait and the hope he will return, as he has promised. Instead, two other painters, Benvenuti Rafaeli (Jani Szika) and Robert Hesse (Schreiber), turn up. Rafaeli is a wealthy amateur of no talent, and he buys Bryk's painting of Marie to sell as his own work. She uses the money from the sale to go to Rome in search of Arthur. Bryk is on the brink of an adventure with the coquettish Countess Falconi (Karoline Charles-Hirsch), wife of the elderly Count (Carl Adolf Friese), but Marie—who has made her trip disguised as a boy—gets herself taken into Arthur's house as a pupil and succeeds in spoiling each opportunity for a rendezvous between the Countess and the painter. When Rafaeli turns up with Arthur's painting of Marie, realization blooms in the man's brain and, as Rome celebrates Carnival, he finally comes back together with his little Swiss maid. The final carnival scene gave the producer and choreographer the opportunity to feature a 12-handed Ländler, a pas de trois "Fete du carnaval," a 30-dancer Intermezzo, a ballet of clowns and flowers (with specially credited "living flowers"), and a grand dance finale. The other specially credited item was a so-called Velocipedes-Wagen.

Strauss's score of 16 musical pieces gave the showiest moments, as might have been expected, to Charles-Hirsch, the creator of *Die Fledermaus*'s Adele and a Hofoper Queen of the Night, in the role of the sophisticated soprano Gräfin Falconi. She featured a coloratura aria "Kann er nicht liebenswürd'ger sein" and duos with Bryk ("Was auch immer gesche") and her husband ("Nich länger duld' ich dieses Treiben"). But Marie was the prima donna role, and it was not neglected. If her opportunities were less showy, pieces such as the little love song "Nur in Liebe kan ich leben," the dancing "Wer bleibt auf seinem Platze lang" and her duos with Bryk in the second and third acts assured Geistinger's place at the top of the bill. The Count contributed a waltz song ("So ein arme, arme Ehemann"), Bryk an aria in which, disguised as a "fromme Pilgermann," he auctioned off goods that pretended to come from the holy land ("Dies Paar Pantoffel") and the second act wound up to a jolly choral tarantella as the carnival took over.

Carneval in Rom proved, by and large, a success. It was played 54 times during its first year at the Theater an der Wien, reappeared in 1874, again in 1880 for another 20 performances, and was brought back in a new production in 1894 (28 April) with Carl Streitmann (Bryk), Josef Joseffy (Hesse), Lilli Lejo (Marie) and Karl Wallner (Falconi) for seven performances. Productions were also mounted in the other German-speaking countries and in 1881 Marie Geistinger included the piece in the repertoire for her American season, appearing in a production with Adolfi, Fritsch, Max Lube and Emma Seebold at the German-language Thalia Theater in New York. However, the only English-language production seems to have been one mounted at San Francisco's Bush Street Theater in 1880 (ad Harry McDowell), with Emilie Melville in the role of Marie supported by Alonzo Hatch (Bryk) and Helene Dingeon (Countess). It failed and was withdrawn after one week.

Strauss's fame guaranteed *Carneval in Rom* the occasional revival—it was seen at Berlin's Theater unter den Linden 17 March 1897, at the Carltheater for a handful of performances with Ottilie Collin, Felix and Sigmund Natzler in 1898 (4 October), at the Volksoper, and in the inevitable remakes, first as *Der blaue Held* (lib: Ferdinand Stollberg) in 1912 (Theater an der Wien, 18 October), and subsequently, under its original title, for a production at Dortmund (Eugen Rex/Franz Marszalek, Stadttheater, 30 November 1937).

Germany: Friedrich-Wilhelmstädtisches Theater 25 April 1874; USA: Bush Street Theater, San Francisco *Carnival in Rome* 11 October 1880, Thalia Theater, New York (Ger) 1 April 1881

Recording: 1937 version (RCA)

CARNIVAL Musical in 2 acts by Michael Stewart based on the screenplay *Lili* by Helen Deutsch and the story by Paul Gallico. Music and lyrics by Bob Merrill. Imperial Theater, New York, 13 April 1961.

At first a story by Paul Gallico, *Lili* became a successful Hollywood film in 1953, with Leslie Caron featured in its title role and Mel Ferrer as leading man, before being made up into a musical play. Screenwriter Miss Deutsch and Bronislaw Kaper supplied a hit song, "Hi Lili, Hi Lo," as an accompaniment to the film, but it was another prolific writer of song hits, Bob Merrill, who joined with librettist Michael Stewart to provide the score for *Carnival.*

The orphaned Lili (Anna Maria Alberghetti) finds work in Schlegel's "Grand Imperial Cirque de Paris" but, although she attracts the flamboyant eye of magician Marco the Magnificent (James Mitchell) and the unconfident heart of the crippled ex-dancer Paul Berthalet (Jerry Orbach), it seems that she will not be able to hold a place in the company. Then she meets four little puppets, created by Paul. They can speak to her, as Paul cannot, and she makes a bubbling front-lady in a team with them, a performance which ensures her popularity and her job. She is still dazzled by Marco, however, and it is only when she is contemplating running away with the magician that she realizes that the love the puppets have shown her comes, in reality, from their master.

Merrill produced a number which topped even "Hi Lili, Hi Lo" in the carouseling theme to the show, "Love Makes the World Go Round," at the front of a score which went from lively, circusy pieces ("Direct from Vienna," "The Sword, the Rose and the Cape"), to charming songs for Lili solo ("Yes, My Heart") and with the puppets ("Yum Ticky, Ticky, Tum, Tum"), and the more deeply felt moments of Paul's "I've Got to Find a Reason (for living on this earth)" and "Everybody Likes You." It even touched on zany comedy as the faithless Marco plunged swords into the box containing his assistant and girlfriend, Rosalie (Kaye Ballard), as he assured her that "It Was Always You." Director/choreographer Gower Champion provided one of the memorable moments of the evening in his setting of the opening of the show, depicting the mounting of the circus tents and the gradual winding up of the personnel until they leaped into life as the rather too-grandly named Grand Imperial Cirque de Paris.

David Merrick's Broadway production of *Carnival* ran through 719 performances, but the show was on the road, with Susan Watson and Ed Ames featured, well before the New York run was finished. H M Tennent Ltd mounted a London reproduction in 1963 with Sally Logan, Michael Maurel, Mitchell and Shirley Sands featured, but it proved peculiarly ill-cast and folded in just 34 performances. An Australian production by J C Williamson Ltd with Patricia Moore starred, supported by Kevin Colson and Jill Perryman, was also a failure. In Raymondo de Larrain's French production (ad Jean Cosmos, Paul Misraki) Christine Delaroche played the role of *Mouche* alongside Jean-Claude Drouot and Magali Noël, whilst a German-language adaptation (ad Robert Gilbert) was mounted in 1962 at the Stadttheater, Zürich. In 1993 an off-Broadway revival was staged at St Peter's Church.

Australia: Her Majesty's Theatre, Melbourne 19 October 1962; UK: Lyric Theatre 8 February 1963; France: Théâtre de la Porte-Saint-Martin *Mouche* 7 October 1966

Recordings: original cast (MGM), London cast (HMV), French cast (Barclay EP)

CAROUSEL Musical play in 2 acts by Oscar Hammerstein II based on *Liliom* by Ferenc Molnár. Music by Richard Rodgers. Majestic Theater, New York, 19 April 1945.

Ferenc Molnár's 1909 play, *Liliom, egy csirkefogó élete és halála* (*Liliom, the life and death of a vagrant*), followed its enormous success in Budapest by slowly making its way around the world—to Berlin's Lessing-Theater (1914), to London's Kingsway Theatre (as *The Daisy,* 1920), to Bucharest (1922), Paris (1923), Shanghai (1925) and to Hamburg's Thalia-Theater (1925) where the title role, created by Gyula Hegedűs, was played by Max Pallenberg. Broadway saw it under the aegis of the Theatre Guild in 1921 (ad Benjamin Glazer 20 May) with Joseph Schildkraut and Eva Le Gallienne, and it was that production which was to lead to the play ultimately being made into a musical.

The Theatre Guild had produced the first collaboration between Oscar Hammerstein II and Richard Rodgers, *Oklahoma!,* with outstanding success, and in looking for a follow-up, the Guild's Terry Helburn suggested a musicalized *Liliom.* It seemed a sane idea: like *Oklahoma!* the piece was rural, innocent yet dramatic-with-a-death, and there was no need for it to be set in its original Hungary, nor to maintain the bitter and unhopeful ending in which the deceased *Liliom,* allowed briefly back on earth, succeeds for a second time in messing up the lives of those he loves. Its principal difference from the prosaic *Oklahoma!* was its introduction of the fantastical elements in the show's heavenly scene. Molnár, who was said to have refused Puccini permission to make the piece into an opera, permitted the authors of *Oklahoma!* to make it into a musical.

Carousel was set in New England. The sexy fairground barker Billy Bigelow (John Raitt) is sacked by his jealous employer (Jean Casto) for dallying with mill-girl, Julie Jordan (Jan Clayton). Julie loses her job too, and the pair of them settle down together and go through the problems of making ends meet. When they don't, Billy becomes sullen, rough and withdrawn, and he is finally drawn to easy, dishonest means of supplying for himself, Julie and their unborn child. He takes part in a robbery and is killed. But, 16 years on, he is allowed by the representatives of the powers on high to come down from Heaven to speak with the daughter he never met. He blows it, just as he blew the rest of his life, but as he returns to Heaven the child is led into her growing-up years on a message of sweetness and hope. The fantasy characters of the musical—the guardians of Heaven—were originally written as a church-minister-like gentleman and his wife representing Mr and Mrs God, but in the final version they were replaced by the Starkeeper, a jot further down the heavenly line of command, and a little more conducive to a touch of wryness in his character.

The score of *Carousel,* which began with the whirling tones of the fairground's Carousel Waltz where a potpourri overture would have been more conventional, included a long list of numbers which became favorites: another, and equally as pretty, piece in the oblique ''People Will Say We're in Love'' line of love song which pretended ''If I Loved You,'' the rumbustiously joyful ''June is Bustin' Out All Over,'' the sweet dream of the future of the number two couple, best-friend Carrie Pipperidge (Jean Darling) and her comfy salt, Enoch Snow (Eric Mattson), ''When the Children Are Asleep,'' and Julie's lovely love song ''What's the Use of Wond'rin'?' The most substantial musical piece, which filled out and softened down the inherently unattractive character of swaggering, shallow Billy, was his lengthy baritone Soliloquy on learning of his impending fatherhood—half proud, half worried, and only a little tough. The most durable number, however, eventually turned out to be the hope-filled anthem sung by Nettie Fowler (Christine Johnson), ''You'll Never Walk Alone,'' the first of what would be a series of big, soaring songs for robustly voiced (mezzo-)sopranos in Rodgers and Hammerstein's musicals. For some unknown reason, this piece with its gospel message ''you'll never walk alone while you walk with God'' and its distinctly tricky tessitura, became the hymn of the supporters of British football teams, ensuring itself a roaring (if vocally truncated) performance by a cast of 50,000 all around the United Kingdom most Saturdays of every year.

Apparently Molnár who, having begun his career translating Operetten for the Hungarian stage, was no novice in the musical theatre, approved the sweetened ending and the softened characterizations, and the public soon proved that he was right to do so. The Theatre Guild's production of *Carousel* ran for 890 performances on Broadway, toured for two seasons, and the show was mounted at London's Theatre Royal, Drury Lane, in the footsteps of *Oklahoma!,* which was shunted out to finish its run at the unloved Stoll Theatre in order to let its successor in. Stephen Douglass (Billy), Iva Withers (Julie), Mattson, Margot Moser (Carrie) and Marion Ross (Nettie) featured in the cast of Prince Littler's production and, if its run fell somewhat short of that of the blither *Oklahoma!,* its 566 performances more than confirmed the earlier hit.

However, the darkish-colored *Carousel* did not find general acceptance easy. J C Williamson Ltd in Australia rejected it as gloomy, and even the success of the well-cast and sung, if further softened, film version with Gordon Macrae and Shirley Jones in the leading roles did not help the piece to other stages. Australia finally saw *Carousel* nearly 20 years on when, after the success of *The Sound of Music,* Garnet Carroll followed up by producing the older Rodgers and Hammerstein show. The results were not comparable.

The show was played by an American company at the Brussels Worlds Fair in 1958, it was seen again in New York in a Music Theater of Lincoln Center production in 1965 (10 August) with Raitt starring opposite Eileen Christy, and it was televised in America in 1967 with Robert Goulet as Billy, but it did not, by and large, receive the follow-up attention that the other Rodgers and Hammerstein hits did. In the 1980s, with the rise of director power in the theatre, the show won some regional productions under the aegis of directors who found its source and those very ''serious'' elements which had earlier hampered its wider acceptance, preferable to the ''frivolity'' of other musical shows. It rode into a major ''operatic'' recording and a production at Britain's National Theatre (10 December 1992) on the crest of such sentiments and from there, under the management of Cameron Mackintosh, to London's West End (Shaftesbury Theatre 10 September 1993) and to Broadway.

The London production, featuring Michael Hayden (Billy), Joanna Riding (Julie) and Patricia Routledge as Nettie, played 121 performances on the South Bank before toting up another 294 performances on Shaftesbury Avenue. Hayden featured again at the season at New York's Vivian Beaumont Theater (24 March 1994) alongside Sally Murphy (Julie) and with opera's Shirley Verrett powering out ''You'll Never Walk Alone,'' through a total of 337 performances.

The exercise confirmed thoroughly that, however much *Carousel* may appeal in some highminded quarters, with the theatre-going public it rates down the list as a favorite amongst the musicals of Rodgers and Hammerstein.

A German-language version (ad Robert Gilbert) was seen at the Vienna Volksoper in 1972, and a new German version (ad Frank Thannhäuser) put in an appearance in the wake of the National Theatre production, in 1995.

UK: Theatre Royal, Drury Lane 7 June 1950; Australia: Princess Theatre, Melbourne 6 June 1964; Austria: Volksoper *Karussel* 15 October 1972; Germany: Pfalztheater, Kaiserslautern 4 September 1981

Film: Twentieth Century Fox 1956

Recordings: original cast (Decca), London cast (Columbia), film soundtrack (Capitol), television cast (Columbia), 1965 revival (RCA), London revival 1993 (First Night), New York revival 1994 (Broadway Angel), Japanese cast (Toshiba), etc

TV film: ABC 1967

CARR, F[rank] Osmond (b Hunslet, Yorks, 23 April 1858; d Uxbridge, Mddx, 29 August 1916). Composer for several of the earliest Victorian "musical comedies."

A Mus Doc and MA graduate, Carr made a first pseudonymous step into the musical theatre along with a fellow Cambridge University man, Arthur Ropes, when four matinée performances of their burlesque *Faddimir* were given in London in 1889. *Faddimir*'s quality won both lyricist Ropes (later to be Britain's busiest lyricist as "Adrian Ross") and "Oscar Neville" (Carr) immediate notice from George Edwardes and, within months, the composer had a song being sung by Nellie Farren in *Ruy Blas and the Blase Roué* at the Gaiety Theatre and Edwardes had commissioned Carr and Ross to write the songs for his burlesque of *Joan of Arc.* Soon after, they were allotted the score for *In Town* (1892), the piece with which the producer initiated his famous series of modern-dress musical shows.

The collaborators also provided the songs for the even more successful *Morocco Bound* (1893), a piece which crystallized the half-book/half-music-hall "variety musical" form, and for the musical comedy *Go-Bang,* both for producer Fred Harris, before Edwardes reclaimed Carr to collaborate with W S Gilbert (at that stage divorced from Arthur Sullivan) on the author's clever *His Excellency.* The composer took the stride from the music-hall strains of *Morocco Bound*'s hit "Marguerite of Monte Carlo" to Gilbertian comic opera skillfully and, in spite of the inevitable comparisons with Sullivan, produced a sufficiently successful score to allow the show a good London run and several overseas productions.

When 1896 vehicles for Little Tich (*Lord Tom Noddy*) and *In Town* star Arthur Roberts (*Biarritz,* libretto by Jerome K Jerome) both flopped, and a final London attempt with *The Maid of Athens* (1897), which he was obliged to produce himself, was a total write-off, the composer who for two or three years had been the toast of the town was suddenly done. The half-dozen musicals he wrote in the next decade were played only in the provinces, and his most metropolitan showing came with an "old English ballet," *Sir Roger de Coverley,* written to a text by his original collaborator, Ross, and produced at the Empire in 1907 with Adeline Genée starred, and with material for John Shine's music-hall act *The Actor's Art* (1908).

A more than competent all-round musician, Carr was pushed into perhaps excessive limelight by the two great novelty hits for which he composed the music, but he proved in *His Excellency* that he was capable of writing substantial music on a level just below the top.

1889 **Faddimir, or The Triumph of Orthodoxy** (Adrian Ross) Vaudeville Theatre 29 April

1891 **Joan of Arc** (Ross, John L Shine) Opera Comique 17 January

1892 **Blue-Eyed Susan** (Henry Pettitt, George Sims) Prince of Wales Theatre 6 February

1892 **In Town** (Ross, James Leader [ie, James T Tanner]) Prince of Wales Theatre 15 October

1893 **Morocco Bound** (Ross/Arthur Branscombe) Shaftesbury Theatre 13 April

1894 **Go-Bang** (Ross) Trafalgar Square Theatre 10 March

1894 **His Excellency** (W S Gilbert) Lyric Theatre 27 October

1895 **Bobbo** (Ross, Tanner) 1 act Prince's Theatre, Manchester 12 September

1896 **Thrillby** (W Muskerry) Theatre Royal, Richmond 11 May

1896 **My Girl** (ex- *The Clergyman's Daughter*) (Ross/Tanner) Theatre Royal, Birmingham 13 April; Gaiety Theatre, London 13 July

1896 **Lord Tom Noddy** (George Dance) Theatre Royal, Bradford 6 April; Garrick Theatre 15 September

1896 **Biarritz** (Ross/Jerome K Jerome) Prince of Wales Theatre 11 April

1897 **The Maid of Athens** (Charles Edmund Pearson, H Chance Newton) Opera Comique 3 June

1898 **Billy** (G Cooper, Ross) Tyne Theatre and Opera House, Newcastle 11 April

1898 **The Celestials** (C H Abbott, John D Houghton) Her Majesty's Opera House, Blackpool 1 August

1901 **The Southern Belle** (Hugh Moss, Hugh Carson) Empire Theatre, Southend-on-Sea 7 March

1901 **An Actor's Romance** (Frederick Martell) sketch South London Music Hall 31 July

1903 **The Rose of the Riviera** (Reginald Bacchus, George Sheldon) Eden Theatre, Brighton 25 May

1904 **Miss Mischief** (Bacchus) West London Theatre 30 October

1905 **The Kimona Girl** 1 act Pavilion, Glasgow 2 October

1905 **Little Miss Artful** 1 act Pavilion, Glasgow 16 October

1906 **The Scottish Bluebells** (David James) Grand Theatre, Edinburgh 31 March

CARRÉ, [Hugues Michel] Albert (b Strasbourg, 22 June 1852; d Paris, 12 December 1938).

A nephew of the elder Michel Carré, and cousin to Michel fils, Albert Carré began in the theatre as an actor and occasional librettist before moving on to start what would be his principal theatrical career, as a manager, at Nancy in 1884. He subsequently shifted his activities to Paris, where he spent periods in charge, successively, of the Théâtre du Vaudeville (1885 w Deslandes), the Gymnase (w Porel), in the wake of Leon Carvalho at the Opéra-Comique (1898–1913 and 1918–25), and at the Comédie-Française (1914–18). Under his management, the Opéra-Comique knew some of its finest hours as he produced, amongst other pieces, Reynaldo Hahn's *Île de Rêve,* d'Indy's *Fervaal, La Bohème,* Massenet's *Cendrillon, Grisélidis* and *Le Jongleur de Notre Dame,* Charpentier's *Louise,* Camille Erlanger's *Le Juif polonais, Hansel und Gretel,* Debussy's *Pelléas et Mélisande, Tosca,* Leroux's *La Reine Fiamette,* Dukas's *Ariane et Barbe-Bleue,* Messager's *Fortunio,* Ravel's *L'Heure espagnole, La Lepreuse* and de Falla's *La vida breve.* After a period at the Comédie-Française and another as a Colonel in the army, he returned to the Opéra-Comique for a further seven years. The latter part of his life, however, was less fortunate, and he died in want in 1938.

Over the years, Carré also wrote a number of plays (*La Bosse du vol, Le Docteur Jojo, La Souricière,* etc) and several libretti for the musical theatre, including the book to *Les Beignets du roi,* composed by Firmin Bernicat for Brussels and later produced in a revised version in Paris, the text of Messager's successful light opera, *La Basoche,* which he himself mounted at the Opéra-Comique, and the féerie *La Montagne enchantée* (1897 w Émile Moreau), produced at the Théâtre de la Porte-Saint-Martin, and equipped with incidental music by two of his Opéra-Comique regulars, Messager and Xavier Leroux.

In 1897 a musical piece called *The Kangaroo Girl* (ad Hamilton Aidé), based on *Le Docteur Jojo,* was toured in the British provinces (Pleasure Gardens, Folkestone 12 July mus: Oscar Barrett) and his play *Le Végline* (w Alexandre Bisson) was adapted as *For the Love of Suzanne* at off-Broadway's Martinique Theater in 1974.

His two-time wife, **Marguerite CARRÉ** (née Marguerite Caroline VAILLANT, b Cabourg, 16 August 1880; d Paris, 26 December 1947), was the illegitimate daughter of Louis Giraud, the manager of the theatre at Nantes. She was hired by Carré for the Opéra-Comique in 1902 and, under his nurturing and—it is said—in proportion to the increase in his passion, she rose from small roles to be prima donna at the Salle Favart. There she appeared as Mimi, Butterfly, Snegourotchka, Mélisande and Pamina, and created lead roles in such pieces as Chaumet's *La Petite Maison* (1903, Gabrielle), Messager's *Fortunio* (1907, Jacqueline), Terrasse's *Le Mariage de Télémaque* (1910, Hélène), Leroux's *Le Carillioneur,* Albéniz's *Pepita Jimenez,* Nogues' *Chiquito le joueur de pelote,* Hué's *Titania, La Lepreuse* and *La Fille de Roland.* After the First World War she temporarily left the Opéra-Comique and went to star at the Gaîté-Lyrique, appearing in *La Belle Hélène, Les Travaux d'Hercule, La Petite Femme de Loth,* as Lange in *La Fille de Madame Angot,* as O Mimosa San in *The Geisha* and regularly in a made-to-order minimusical, *Manon en voyage.* She left for a second time in 1924, divorcing Carré at the same time, but she returned both to husband (they were remarried 27 years after the first time) and to the Salle Favart in 1929.

1876 **Les Amants d'Amanda** (Victor Robillard) Théâtre des Ambassadeurs 20 August

1880 **Maître Pierrot** (Félix Pardon) 1 act Contrexéville 9 August

1882 **Les Beignets du roi** (Firmin Bernicat/Benjamin Antier ad) Alcazar, Brussels 10 February

1883 **L'Amour en livrée** (Georges Street/w Paul Meyan) 1 act Eldorado 10 March

1884 **Le Panache blanc** (Philippe Flon/w A Audibert) 1 act Théâtre de la Monnaie, Brussels 15 February

1888 **Les Premières Armes de Louis XV** revised version of *Les Beignets du roi* Théâtre des Menus-Plaisirs 16 February

1890 **La Basoche** (André Messager) Opéra-Comique 30 May

1891 **Deux Reservistes** (Street/w Meyan) 1 act Casino de Paris 22 October

1895 **Le Roi Frelon** (Antoine Banès) Théâtre des Folies-Dramatiques 11 April

1924 **Faust en ménage** (Claude Terrasse, Régine Flory, et al) Théâtre de la Potinière 5 January

1927 **Frétillon** (Terrasse) Théâtre Municipal de Strasbourg 5 March

1932 **Le Roi bossu** (Elsa Barraine) 1 act Opéra-Comique 17 March

Autobiography: *Souvenirs de théâtre* (Plon, Paris, 1950)

CARRÉ, Fabrice [LABROUSSE, Fabrice] (b Paris, 9 July 1856; d Paris, October 1921).

The author of a number of plays, in collaboration with such authors as Bisson, Bilhaud (*Ma Bru*), Paul Ferrier and Émile Blavet, Fabrice Carré nevertheless had his most successful moments in the musical theatre, particularly with the libretti for the joyously comical vaudeville-opérette *Joséphine vendue par ses soeurs* (1886 w Ferrier) and the similarly imaginative and happily flavored *L'Enlèvement de la Toledad* (1894). His *Mam'zelle Carabin,* musically set by Pessard, gave him a third musical theatre success both in France and abroad.

1883 **Mademoiselle Irma** (Victor Roger) 1 act Casino de Trouville 18 August

1886 **Joséphine vendue par ses soeurs** (Roger/w Paul Ferrier) Théâtre des Bouffes-Parisiens 20 March

1887 **Les Délégués** (Antoine Banès/w Émile Blavet) Théâtre de la Renaissance 30 November

1887 **Nos bons jurés** (Marius Boullard/w Paul Ferrier) Théâtre des Variétés 5 December

1889 **Le Retour d'Ulysse** (Raoul Pugno) Théâtre des Bouffes-Parisiens 1 February

1890 **La Vocation de Marius** (Pugno/w Émile Dehelly) Théâtre des Nouveautés 29 March

1892 **La Femme de Narcisse** (Varney) Théâtre de la Renaissance 14 April

1893 **Mam'zelle Carabin** (Émile Pessard) Théâtre des Bouffes-Parisiens 3 November

1894 **L'Enlèvement de la Toledad** (Edmond Audran) Théâtre des Bouffes-Parisiens 17 October

1896 **Monsieur Lohengrin** (Audran) Théâtre des Bouffes-Parisiens 30 November

1898 **La Petite Tache** (Roger) Théâtre des Bouffes-Parisiens 26 March

CARRÉ, Michel [Antoine] (b Paris, 7 February 1865; d Paris, 11 August 1945).

Michel Carré (fils) was the son of **Michel [Antoine Florentin] CARRÉ** (b Besançon, 20 October 1821; d Argenteuil, 27 June, 1872), the celebrated French operatic librettist of *Faust, Le Pardon de Ploërmel, Les Pêcheurs de perles, Mireille, Mignon, Roméo et Juliette, Hamlet, Paul et Virginie,* and *Les Contes d'Hoffmann.* However, although he worked with Gounod, Meyerbeer, Saint-Saëns, Ambroise Thomas, Bizet and Félicien David on serious works, the elder Carré also collaborated in a lighter vein with Massé on his two most successful pieces, *Galathée* (the source for Suppé's *Die schöne Galathee*) and *Les Noces de Jeannette,* with composers such as Aimé Maillart, Jules Duprato, Erlanger and Théophile Semet, with Offenbach on the short and very sweet *Le Mariage aux lanternes* and *La Rose de Saint-Flour,* and, in another different vein, on the great, extravagant Jules Verne spectaculars.

Carré fils, having switched from painting to writing before his 20th birthday, quickly became a prolific playwright, revuist, and librettist for the musical stage. In his later days he also worked as a screenwriter and film director but, in contrast to his father, his operatic work was limited, including only two works composed by the Belgian composer Van den Eeden (*Numance* 1898 and *Rhéna* 1912), three borderline pieces by Missa—the 1894 *Dinah* (w Paul de Choudens, based on Shakespeare's *Cymbeline*), *Muguette* and the one-act drame lyrique, *Maguelone* (1903)—and the 1929 *Le Peau de chagrin* (Charles Levadé/w Pierre Decourcelle).

In the light musical theatre he worked early on with composer Gabriel Pierné on the spectacular *Bouton d'or,* and also on one piece with the ageing Lecocq, but he had his first significant success with the scenario for André Wormser's wordless pantomime *L'Enfant prodigue* (Théâtre des Bouffes-Parisiens, 1890), which pleased Paris, Vienna and London mightily through good runs and revived interest in a once popular genre which had, by then, somewhat faded from favor. The only one of his book musicals which achieved a notable success was the saucy *Afgar, ou les loisirs andalous,* on which he collaborated with his habitual revue-writing partner André Barde and composer Charles Cuvillier, but, in a wide-ranging career stretching over nearly half a century, he had the unusual distinction of working in traditions as wide apart as the opérettes of Lecocq, a soi-disant ''opérette'' for the scandalous Cléo de Mérode (*Le Premier Pas*), and the cinema, where he was responsible for the production of the first full-length French movie with his 1907 screen version of *L'Enfant prodigue.*

1887 **Adèle de Ponthieu** (André Wormser) Aix-les-Bains 10 September

1890 **Friquette et Blaisot** (Alfred Millet/w Charles Narrey) 1 act Casino, Cabourg 13 January; Théâtre des Bouffes-Parisiens 13 January 1890

1890 **Hilda** (Millet/w Narrey) 1 act Opéra-Comique 5 January

1893 **Bouton d'or** (Gabriel Pierné) Nouveau-Théâtre 4 January

1894 **Nos bons chasseurs** (Charles Lecocq/w Paul Bilhaud) Nouveau-Théâtre 10 April

1895 **Le Dragon vert** (Wormser) Nouveau Théâtre 21 February

1895 **Pris au piège** (André Gedalge) 1 act Opéra-Comique 7 June

1896 **Rivoli** (Wormser/w Paul Burani) Théâtre des Folies-Dramatiques 30 October

1899 **Le Quart d'heure de Rabelais** (Petras Martin/w Henri Rémond) Théâtre de l'Application 17 May

1902 **Miss Bouton d'or** (Louis Ganne) Olympia 14 October

1903 **Miss Chipp** (Henri Berény/w André de Lorde) Théâtre des Bouffes-Parisiens 31 March

1903 **Muguette** (Edmond Missa/w Georges Hartmann) Opéra-Comique 18 March

1906 **Miss Fauvette** (Ludo Ratz) Little-Palace 29 January

1906 **La Clé du Paradis** (Rodolphe Berger) Théâtre des Mathurins 3 December

1909 **Afgar, ou Les Loisirs andalous** (w Barde/Cuvillier) Théâtre des Capucines 2 April

1909 **Le Premier Pas** (Georges Menier) 1 act Théâtre Michel May

1911 **Marmaid** (Alexandre Duval) Comédie-Royale 22 March

1912 **Sappho** (Cuvillier/w Barde) Théâtre des Capucines 26 February

1918 **La Fausse Ingénue** (Cuvillier) Théâtre Fémina 17 March

1920 **L'Amour qui rôde** (Vincent Scotto/w Albert Acrémant) Eldorado 30 April

1920 **La Mousmé** (Marius Lambert/w Acrémant) Théâtre Michel 10 July

1921 **Le Coq a chanté** (Jean Rioux) Marseille 4 May, Théâtre de la Gaîté-Lyrique 6 September

1922 **Pan-Pan** (Scotto/w Acrémant) Ba-ta-clan 19 April

1922 **Le Fakir de Bénarès** (Léo Manuel) Théâtre Mogador 21 April

1926 **Les Rendez-vous clandestins** (Léo Pouget/w Yoris d'Hansewick) La Cigale 26 April

1929 **Mariska** (Mario Cazès/w Sibre, Goudard) Trianon-Lyrique 22 December

1931 **Vieux garçons** (Louis Urgel) 1 act Théâtre de la Gaîté-Lyrique 21 February

1932 **Sylvette** (Henri Février, Marc Delmer/Claude Roland/w René Peter) Trianon-Lyrique 12 February

1933 **Le Garçon de Chez Prunier** (Joseph Szulc/w Barde) Théâtre des Capucines 19 January

CARROLL, Earl (b Pittsburgh, Pa, ?21 September 1892; d Mt Carmel, Pa, 17 June 1948).

Carroll worked hopefully in and around the theatre and songwriting worlds from an early age before, in 1912, finding himself a position in a New York music publishing house. He began supplying lyrics (sometimes as ''Carl Earl'') to the popular tunesmiths of the time (''Montezuma'' w Carl Eggert in *Over the River* 1912, ''Honey You Were Made for Me'' w Jack Glogau in *All Aboard* 1913, etc) and, over the next few years, he provided the songwords and even some tunes for a number of musical plays, notably in collaboration with west-coast producer and writer Oliver Morosco. Together they scored a double success in the early war years with *So Long, Letty* and *Canary Cottage,* both of which shows followed up their careers on the west coast, on Broadway, and round America with successful productions in Australia.

Carroll turned to management in 1919, and became celebrated as the guiding spirit behind a series of girlie revues produced over 17 years as the *Earl Carroll Vanities* (13 episodes) and, occasionally, the *Earl Carroll Sketch Book* (2). He ventured barely into the book musical, sponsoring *How's the King* (1925), the publicity musical *The Florida Girl* (1925), which was backed by and vaunted the wares of a property company, the revusical *Murder at the Vanities* (1933) and the society piece *Just Because,* mounted on $75,000 gathered from its writer's wealthy friends. A second vanity production, *Fioretta,* to which he also put his name as a co-writer, lost $350,000 for its wealthy sponsoress and ended with one of the distraught writers committing suicide.

He built the Earl Carroll Theater in New York in 1922, and a second house under the same name in 1931. He was killed in an airplane crash in 1948.

A fictionalized biography concentrates on depicting Carroll as what it hopefully calls ''the most notorious connoisseur of female flesh in show business.''

1914 **Pretty Mrs Smith** (Alfred Robyn, Henry James/Elmer B Harris, Oliver Morosco) Burbank Theater, Los Angeles 25 January; Casino Theater, New York 21 September

1915 **So Long, Letty** (Harris, Morosco) Morosco Theater, Los Angeles 3 July; Shubert Theater, New York 23 October 1916

1916 **Canary Cottage** (Harris, Morosco) Empress Theater, San Diego, 18 March; Morosco Theater, New York 5 February 1917

1917 **The Love Mill** (Alfred Francis) Lyric Theater, Allentown, Pa 5 February; Illinois Theater, Chicago 6 May; 48th Street Theater, New York 7 February 1918

1929 **Fioretta** (George Bagby, ''G Romilli''/w Charlton Andrews) Earl Carroll Theater 5 February

Biography: Murray, K: *The Body Merchant* (Ward Ritchie, Pasadena, 1976)

CARTE, Richard D'Oyly (b London, 3 May 1844; d London, 3 April 1901). Godfather to the Savoy operas.

The son of Richard Carte, a topflight flute-maker, musical agent (w Henry A Rudall) and London musical personality, Richard D'Oyly Carte worked as a young theatrical and concert agent, a tentative composer (''Charing Cross''), and then as business and company manager for several comic opera companies. In 1874 he took the Opera Comique, to present Eugène Humbert's Brussels company in a season of *Giroflé-Girofla* and an English version of Serpette's *La Branche cassée.* He also announced that he had offered Offenbach £3,000 to write him an original opéra-bouffe. The original opéra-bouffe did not eventuate, but Carte would soon have his original show, from a composer destined to be equally as famous as Offenbach, and for rather less than £3,000.

While he was engaged as manager for Selina Dolaro's season at the Royalty Theatre in 1875 the search for a forepiece to share the bill with the diva's version of Offenbach's *La Périchole* led to his being instrumental in bringing composer Arthur Sullivan and librettist W S Gilbert significantly back together. Their one-act cantata *Trial by Jury,* composed specifically to fill the empty spot, not only fitted the bill perfectly but also proved the highlight of the season and ensured its success. In 1876 Carte co-produced (w George Dolby) the Parisian opéra-bouffe *La Timbale d'Argent* (*The Duke's Daughter*) at the Royalty and he subsequently took out two opéra-bouffe tours, playing *La Fille de Madame Angot, La Grande-Duchesse de Gérolstein, The Duke's Daughter, Trial by Jury* and his own short *Happy Hampstead,* before returning to the Royalty in 1877 as manager for Kate Santley and her productions of *Orphée aux enfers* and *La Marjolaine.*

In late 1876 it had been announced that Fred Sullivan, brother of Arthur and already the producer of a provincial season of *The Contrabandista,* was to take the Globe Theatre to produce a new and full-length work by Gilbert and Sullivan. But Fred Sullivan died in January 1877 and, after raising the necessary capital (a part from music publishers, a part from the to-be prima donna and conductor of the new company) and putting together "The Comedy Opera Company," it was Carte who instead opened Gilbert and Sullivan's first full-sized comic opera, *The Sorcerer,* at the Opera Comique in November 1877, as manager for his syndicate. He kept his alternatives open by simultaneously managing the production of *The Little Duke* for Charles Head at the Philharmonic, but *The Sorcerer* won sufficient success for the team to venture a second similar piece at the Opera Comique and, when *HMS Pinafore* turned out to be an enormous hit, Carte declared himself independent of his backers. With Gilbert and Sullivan supporting him, he faced out their clumsy (if, apparently, at least partly justified) counterattacks and won himself the position of producer and rights-holder to *HMS Pinafore.* Thereafter, Carte produced all of the celebrated Gilbert/Sullivan comic operas, at first at the Opera Comique and subsequently at the Savoy Theatre, built (like its contiguous hotel) partly on the profits from *HMS Pinafore* and *The Pirates of Penzance* . . . but also partly on finance supplied by one now forgotten Joseph Pyke, and by Dublin's Gunn brothers.

From *The Pirates of Penzance* in 1880 to *The Gondoliers* in 1889 the team had a run of almost unbroken success, unparallelled in the history of the British musical theatre until that time. Carte ran Gilbert and Sullivan's shows end-to-end at the Savoy, operated multiple repertoire companies playing them around Britain and occasionally on the Continent, and had a hand in most of their principal American productions, leading—on behalf of their shows—an intermittent but forceful fight against the copyright incoherencies and piracies of the time. He also kept a close watch on other potentially winning writers, and was instrumental in staging some of the best of the other British pieces of the time (*Rip van Winkle, Manteaux Noirs, Billee Taylor,* etc) in America and/or on the road.

When Gilbert and Sullivan split, Carte continued to run comic opera at the Savoy, producing Edward Solomon's *The Nautch Girl* and *The Vicar of Bray,* Sullivan's *Haddon Hall,* and the unfortunate *Jane Annie* before his writers came back together to supply him, less happily than before, with *Utopia (Limited)* and *The Grand Duke.*

At this same time, he built and opened the Royal English Opera House in Cambridge Circus, initiating it with Sullivan's *Ivanhoe* and following up with Messager's *La Basoche* and Bemberg's *Elaine* before getting out of what had from the start proven an unprofitable venture. His theatre was sold off for £90,000 to become the Palace Music Hall, and then the Palace Theatre.

With no further new Gilbert and Sullivan musicals to fill the Savoy, Carte instead produced Messager's *Mirette,* a rewrite of Sullivan's early *The Contrabandista* as

Plate 65. **Richard D'Oyly Carte.** *Godfather to the Savoy operas.*

The Chieftain, McKenzie's *His Majesty,* a new version of *La Grande-Duchesse de Gérolstein,* Sullivan's *The Beauty Stone,* a remusicked version of *L'Étoile* as *The Lucky Star* and a series of revivals of Gilbert and Sullivan favorites before finding his most appreciable new piece in several years with the pairing of Sullivan and Basil Hood on *The Rose of Persia.* It was to be his last, for shortly before the production of the first piece by the two writers who seemed as if they might provide him with comic operas for years to come, Carte died.

His wife, Helen (née Black, aka Lenoir) (d London, 5 May 1913) continued to run the operation for some time, but the profitability of comic opera had been severely dampened by the vogue for musical comedy and she soon had to give in. During the run of *The Emerald Isle,* she ceded the Savoy Theatre and its company to William Greet.

The D'Oyly Carte company continued at first with comic opera. Greet produced *Ib and Little Christina, The Willow Pattern, Merrie England* and *A Princess of Kensington* before briefly, and at first not unsuccessfully, switching the company to the more profitable field of musical comedy with *The Earl and the Girl.* Ultimately, however, it was the Gilbert and Sullivan repertoire to which they returned, and the company which bore Carte's name continued to purvey the ''Savoy operas'' to Britain and the rest of the world until financial considerations forced its closure in 1982. However, on the death of Bridget D'Oyly Carte, granddaughter of Richard, a substantial legacy from her personal fortune enabled a new D'Oyly Carte Opera Company to be set up. That company began operations in 1988 with productions of *Iolanthe* and *The Yeomen of the Guard* and ran seasons for several years in London and the British provinces before getting into difficulties and fizzling away into little more than a name.

1868 **Dr Ambrosias, His Secret** (T H Bayley) St George's Hall 8 August

1871 **Marie** (E Spencer Mott) 1 act Opera Comique 26 August

1876 **Happy Hampstead** (Frank Desprez) Alexandra Theatre, Liverpool 3 July; Royalty Theatre, London 13 January 1877

CARTER, [Herbert] Desmond (b Bristol, 15 June 1895; d London, 3 February 1939). Ubiquitous West End lyricist of the 1920s and 1930s.

Carter worked as an insurance clerk before finding his way into the worlds of songwriting and the musical theatre where he would make his name. His earliest theatrical experiences were gained in the provinces, where he contributed his first songwords to a pair of regional children's productions, but he moved swiftly on to another level when he was given his first London break on the George Grossmith production of *Primrose* at the Winter Garden Theatre. His words were set to the music of the young George Gershwin.

Thereafter, Carter quickly became one of the town's busiest lyric-writers, contributing over the 15 years of his career to such revues as *Shake Your Feet, Cochran's Revue of 1930* (''Wind in the Willows''), *The Chelsea Follies, Fanfare, Rhyme and Rhythm, Follow the Sun, Transatlantic Rhythm, And on We Go,* and posthumously *Rise Above It,* supplying additional or alternative lyrics for both imported and new shows (*Merely Molly, So Long, Letty, The Millionaire Kid, A Connecticut Yankee at the Court of King Arthur, Love Laughs, Follow Through,* the revival of *Tonight's the Night, Tell Me More, Lady, Be Good!, Sunny, Funny Face, Lido Lady,* etc), and having a major lyricist's credit on more than 30 shows, including many of the dance-comedy hits of the era (*Lady Luck, That's a Good Girl, So This Is Love, Love Lies, The Love Race, Jill Darling, Sporting Love, Over She Goes*). He also had a hand in the more operettic adaptations of *Walzer aus Wien, Die Dubarry* and *Wenn die kleinen Veilchen blühen* and contributed to such novelties as the dance play *Ballerina.*

1922 **The Rose and the Ring** (Robert Cox/Harris Deane) Liverpool Playhouse December; Wyndham's Theatre, London 19 December

1923 **The Magic Sword** (Cox/Deane) Liverpool Playhouse 22 December

1924 **Primrose** (George Gershwin/w Ira Gershwin/George Grossmith, Guy Bolton) Winter Garden Theatre 11 September

1925 **Dear Little Billie** (H B Hedley, Jack Strachey/Firth Shephard) Shaftesbury Theatre 25 August

1926 **Just a Kiss** (*Pas sur la bouche*) English lyrics w Graham John, Vivian Ellis (Shaftesbury Theatre)

1926 **My Son John** (*Riquette*) revised English lyrics w Harry Graham (Shaftesbury Theatre)

1927 **Lady Luck** (Hedley, Strachey/Shephard) Carlton Theatre 27 April

1927 **Peg o' Mine** (Phil Charig, Vivian Ellis/Fred Jackson) Empire Theatre, Sunderland, England 31 October

1928 **The Yellow Mask** (Vernon Duke/Edgar Wallace) Carlton Theatre 8 February

1928 **So This Is Love** (''Hal Brody''/Stanley Lupino, Arthur Rigby) Winter Garden Theatre 25 April

1928 **That's a Good Girl** (Phil Charig, Joseph Meyer/w Furber, I Gershwin/Furber) London Hippodrome 5 June

1929 **Love Lies** (''Hal Brody''/Lupino, Rigby) Gaiety Theatre 20 March

1930 **Darling, I Love You** (Hedley, Harry Acres/Stanley Brightman, Rigby) Gaiety Theatre 22 January

1930 **Here Comes the Bride** (Arthur Schwartz/w Howard Dietz/R P Weston, Bert Lee) Piccadilly Theatre 20 February

1930 **The Love Race** (Jack Clarke/Lupino) Gaiety Theatre 25 June

1930 **Little Tommy Tucker** (Vivian Ellis) Daly's Theatre 19 November

1931 **The Song of the Drum** (Ellis, Finck/Fred Thompson, Bolton) Theatre Royal, Drury Lane 9 January

1931 **Blue Roses** (Ellis/w Caswell Garth) Gaiety Theatre 20 January

1931 **My Sister and I** (*Meine Schwester und ich*) (aka *Meet my Sister*) English lyrics w Frank Eyton (Shaftesbury Theatre)

1931 **Waltzes from Vienna** (*Walzer aus Wien*) English version w Garth (London Coliseum)

1931 **Hold My Hand** (Noel Gay/Lupino) Gaiety Theatre 23 December

1932 **The Dubarry** (*Die Dubarry*) English version w Rowland Leigh (His Majesty's Theatre)

1932 **Wild Violets** (*Wenn die kleinen Veilchen blühen*) English version w Hassard Short, Reginald Purdell (Theatre Royal, Drury Lane)

1932 **The Compulsory Wife** (Strachey/w Collie Knox, Strachey/C Bailey Hick) tour

1933 **That's a Pretty Thing** (aka *Paste*) (Gay/Lupino) Daly's Theatre 22 November

1933 **Jill Darling** (Ellis/w Marriot Edgar) Alhambra Theatre, Glasgow 23 December; Saville Theatre 19 December 1934

1934 **Sporting Love** (Billy Mayerl/w Eyton/Lupino) Gaiety Theatre 31 March

1935 **The Flying Trapeze** (Ralph Benatzky arr Mabel Wayne/w Douglas Furber, Eyton/Furber) Alhambra Theatre 4 May

1935 **A Kingdom for a Cow** (*Der Kuhhandel*) English lyrics (Savoy Theatre)

1936 **Rise and Shine** (ex- *Jack of Hearts* aka *Darling You*) (Robert Stolz, et al/w Graham, et al/ad w Graham, then Con West, Geoffrey Orme) Theatre Royal, Drury Lane 7 May

1936 **Over She Goes** (Mayerl/w Eyton/Lupino) Saville Theatre 23 September

1937 **Big Business** (Jack Waller, Joseph Tunbridge/w Lee/w Lee, K R G Browne) London Hippodrome 18 February

1937 **Crazy Days** (Mayerl/w Eyton/Lupino) Shaftesbury Theatre 14 September

1938 **Bobby Get Your Gun** (Waller, Tunbridge/w Clifford Grey, Lee/Thompson, Bolton, Lee) Adelphi Theatre 7 October

CARYLL, Ivan [TILKIN, Félix Marie Henri] (b Liège, Belgium, 12 May 1861; d New York, 29 November 1921). Principal composer and conductor for the heyday of the Gaiety musical comedy who encouraged the development of a more book-orientated type of comedy musical in a second career in America.

Born in Belgium, the son of an industrial businessman, and educated at the Paris Conservatoire, Ivan Caryll settled in Britain in the mid-1880s and made the bulk of his career there, becoming, in tandem with Lionel Monckton, the composer for the internationally famous series of musical comedies created at the Gaiety Theatre under the management of George Edwardes in the 1890s and 1900s.

Caryll's earliest days in London were spent largely in musical hackwork and in teaching. However, he got a serious opportunity as a composer in 1886 while he was working at the Comedy Theatre on the extremely successful comic opera, *Erminie.* That show's producer, Violet Melnotte, looking for a follow-up to her hit, decided to produce his opéra-comique *The Lily of Léoville,* a piece written during Caryll's Parisian days in collaboration with an apparently French librettist, Félix Rémo. Although *The Lily of Léoville* was a failure, the music gained some fair notice and a German version was subsequently produced in Hamburg (*Das Andreasnacht,* Carl-Schultze Theater 6 December 1890, ad Friedrich Wilhelm Wulff, W Behre). It was to be several years before Caryll gained a second chance at a full score.

In the meanwhile, however, he made contact with some of the town's other important producers, supplying, amongst other journeyman work, four pieces to be interpolated into the score of George Edwardes's Gaiety burlesque *Monte Cristo Jr* (1886).

It was as a conductor that Caryll made his first noticeable mark. When Henry J Leslie bought the Gaiety theatre production of *Dorothy* from Edwardes and transferred it to the Prince of Wales Theatre, Gaiety musical

Plate 66. **Ivan Caryll.** *The 19th century's most widely successful composer of musical comedies.*

director Meyer Lutz remained at his own theatre, and Caryll was appointed conductor for the revamped show which was to become the musical-theatre hit of the era. He remained Leslie's musical director through the whole four years and three shows of the producer's dramatic career, shifting with him to his new Lyric Theatre on Shaftesbury Avenue where *Dorothy*'s successors, *Doris* and *The Red Hussar* were produced, and remaining there, when Leslie's operation exploded, as musical director for the theatre's new manager, Horace Sedger.

Under Leslie, Caryll fulfilled the musical director's normal function of supplying incidental music as necessary, and he composed several short curtain-raisers to order, but when Sedger's first attraction, Audran's *La Cigale et la fourmi,* was extensively revamped to suit what the producer considered British tastes, that revamping included the cutting of some of Audran's score, and Caryll was called upon to supply alternative numbers. He finally contributed nearly a third of the music, including two principal songs for the leading man and a full-scale finale, to the finished score. His work on this highly successful production brought him commissions similarly to work over Audran's *Miss Helyett* (1891) and Lacome's *Ma mie Rosette* (1892) for their London productions and, following the death of Alfred Cellier, to complete the arrangement of *The Mountebanks* (1892) for production at the Lyric. In 1891 he also composed the whole music to Augustus Moore's 60-minute pantomime *Moonflowers,* produced at a Gaiety matinée on the heels of the success of Wormser's *L'Enfant Prodigue.*

Finally, Sedger entrusted Caryll with the composition of his first full score since *The Lily of Léoville.* The manager had used a sexy little American performer called May Yohé in his production of Albéniz's *The Magic Opal* and he now (convinced by a large cash injection from the lady and her lordly backer) decided to have a piece written specially for her. The result was a latter-day burlesque called *Little Christopher Columbus* for which Caryll, handicapped by a star with a vocal range of about an octave, composed a set of songs which finally put him on the road to success as a theatre writer. From a delightful light score which danced neatly between the comic opera style of *Dorothy* and *La Cigale* and a refined kind of music-hall writing, Miss Yohé's coon song "Oh Honey, My Honey" and the ballad "Lazily, Drowsily" became enormous popular hits, and both the ballads and the comedy numbers showed that the well-educated and versatile Caryll was an ideal composer for that new type of musical theatre, part comic opera and part burlesque, which was now becoming popular.

The ever-watchful George Edwardes was quick to realize this and, at the end of the run of *Little Christopher Columbus,* Caryll made the move from the Lyric to the Gaiety. The success of *Little Christopher* was soon confirmed by Caryll's score for the landmark production of *The Shop Girl* ("Love on the Japanese Plan," "Over the Hills") and the 33-year-old musician settled firmly in as composer-in-residence and musical director at the Gaiety Theatre. He remained there for 15 years, baton in hand, supplying music for all the great hits of that fmaous theatre's most prosperous period from *The Shop Girl* (1894) through to *Our Miss Gibbs* (1909). Under Edwardes's aegis, a writing partnership with Lionel Monckton evolved, beginning with Monckton as a subsidiary "additional songs" partner, but later on more equal terms, with both partners turning out much of the best of the light theatre music on the London stage in its most successful Victorian and Edwardian years.

After his move to the Gaiety, Caryll continued to work for Sedger. An attempted follow-up for May Yohé called *Dandy Dick Whittington* failed under the double handicap of an old pantomime book and the lady's cavalier attitudes to work, but when Sedger brought the touring musical *The Gay Parisienne* to town, and had it equipped with a particularly catchy replacement Caryll score, it proved a mighty success, both at home and overseas. The Caryll version continued to tour Britain for several decades. Amongst other "outside" work, he provided a new score for Vanloo and Leterrier's *L'Étoile* for D'Oyly Carte, composed the music for George Dance's unhappy *The Ladies' Paradise* and provided additional songs for two of the biggest hits of the era, *Florodora* and *A Chinese Honeymoon.* The soon-faded Miss Yohé gave him an additional Broadway showing by introducing his "Down by the River" and "Kiss Me to Sleep" into Broadway's *The Giddy Throng* (1900).

As Edwardes spread his production arm further afield, Caryll was given the opportunity to vary his style from the regular Gaiety formula, and the early years of the new century saw him turn out some of his best work both in the musical comedy manner with the charming *The Girl from Kays* and in the light opera vein with *The Duchess of Dantzic,* a piece begun in his Prince of Wales Theatre days and originally intended as a vehicle for Florence St John. Evie Greene played the titular Madame Sans-Gêne, equipped with a score which echoed the most attractive tones of French opéra-comique. *The Earl and the Girl,* written with Seymour Hicks and staged by William Greet with the remnants of the D'Oyly Carte Opera Company, was another notable Caryll success in this period. At Christmas 1903, Caryll had the until recently unparallelled distinction of having five musicals running at the same time in the West End of London (*The Girl from Kays, The Duchess of Dantzic, The Orchid, The Earl and the Girl, The Cherry Girl*).

In 1910, with *Our Miss Gibbs* still giving him one of the greatest successes of his career, Caryll decided to leave both the Gaiety and Britain and head for New York. Still not 50 years old, he had plenty left to give, but the feeling at the Gaiety was changing and Edwardes, as he had always done, was looking for new ways and new faces to keep the old theatre ahead of the times. Caryll had worked with the American librettist C M S McLellan on a piece called *Nelly Neil* in an ill-judged attempt to provide Edna May with a West-End successor to *The Belle of New York,* and the pair joined forces again in New York with a series of musicals based, like *The Girl from Kays,* on modern French comic plays, a series which attempted, with some success, to rival the current fashion for Viennese operetta. Caryll, whose talent was a chameleon one, made the transition with aplomb and his second Broadway venture, *The Pink Lady,* in particular, proved as great a success as his English shows. While everything that was singable in Vienna was making its way to America, *The Pink Lady* (adapted from the Parisian farce *Le Satyre*) actually made the reverse trip to play London, Paris and Budapest. Its most famous tune, the Pink Lady Waltz ("My Beautiful Lady"), which remains one of Caryll's best known numbers, resurfaced as recently as 1988 in the score of the London Palladium extravaganza, *Ziegfeld.* A musical version of the Paris farce *La Grim-*

pette under the title *Oh! Oh! Delphine* was another delightful and happily exported triumph, and a third piece built on the same strong-booked principle, *The Little Café,* if not quite such a hit as the previous two, nevertheless did well.

Caryll's subsequent Broadway shows included three successful fairy-tale-style musical comedies written to feature comedian Fred Stone, at first with his partner, Dave Montgomery (*Chin-Chin*) and, following Montgomery's death, alone (*Jack o' Lantern,* "Wait Till the Cows Come Home," *Tip Top*). At the same time, George Grossmith picked up Caryll's latest French-based musical comedy, *The Girl Behind the Gun,* and transferred it to London under the title *Kissing Time* to open the new Winter Garden Theatre. It was a huge success, and Caryll returned to London for one last Gaiety musical, a version of the Paris farce *Un coup de téléphone* called *The Kiss Call* (1919).

His final shows did a little less well. Both were musical comedies—one adapted from Adolf Philipp's touring musical *Mimi* as *Kissing Time* (borrowing the title of the London version of *The Girl Behind the Gun*), the other a version of the international comedy hit *Le Souris d'hôtel,* played as *Little Miss Raffles* and then as *The Hotel Mouse*—and both were produced on Broadway, the latter posthumously, with only relative success.

During his whole career in both England and America, Caryll maintained close links with the European, and particularly the Parisian theatre and, indeed, kept a richly appointed home in France to which he repaired regularly with his current wife and children. He continued to write songs and incidental music for Parisian comedies—notably *La Marraine de Charley,* the French version of the English farce *Charley's Aunt* ("La Canotière d'Oxford," "Le Chanson des Houblons" and a version of "Honey, My Honey")—and versions of five of his English-language musicals (*Le Toréador, La Demoiselle de magasin, Les Jolies Filles de Gottenberg, La Dame en Rose, Hello!! Charley* otherwise *The Earl and the Girl*) received Paris productions in a period when the products of the English stage were largely shunned by the French.

Although these imports gained some considerable success, the musical *S.A.R.* (1908), a version of the hit play *Le Prince Consort* written specifically for Paris, was probably the most interesting amongst those of his works seen in France. Caryll also composed one score, for the spectacular *Die Reise nach Cuba,* specifically for Gabor Steiner's Venedig in Wien pleasure-garden theatre in Vienna, another city which had welcomed versions of his British musicals (*Die Ladenmamsell, Das Cirkusmädel, Der Toreador, Ein durchgeganges Mädel, Miss Gibbs, Der Laufbursche, Die verhexte Wien[erstadt]* ad from *The New Aladdin*).

Caryll's career encompassed three eras of musical theatre and he seemed to be equally happy in each of them. If his greatest successes were made in the light musical comedy area, epitomized by the Gaiety Theatre shows in which he made his name, he proved with scores as divergent as the classic operetta *The Duchess of Dantzic* and *S.A.R.* on the one hand and the postwar *The Girl Behind the Gun,* with its modern fox-trot and one-step rhythms, on the other, that he was a theatre composer who, unlike his contemporaries Lionel Monckton and Sidney Jones, could and would move with the times and musical styles. His scores for *The Pink Lady* and *Oh! Oh! Delphine,* a pair of shows which marked a turning towards a more intimate, book-based kind of musical play on the Broadway stage, contain numbers which equal the best that both the Viennese waltz-masters and the new wave of American dance-songwriters were writing in the years around the First World War. A true theatre composer of his time, he was equally as capable of turning out a complicated finale or concerted number as he was a catchy point number or comedy song but, largely because so much of his work was written for a kind of show which was by its nature ephemeral, few of his songs have survived as standards.

Caryll was married for a period to the American vocalist Geraldine Ulmar and later to another performer, dancer Maud Hill (tour *Morocco Bound,* t/o *King Kodak,* Edgeworth Bess in *Little Jack Sheppard* rev, Maud Plantaganet in *The Shop Girl,* etc). His daughter Primrose Caryll was seen as a musical comedy performer on the American stage in a modest career (Fairy Godmother/Renée in *Criss Cross,* etc) which included an appearance in her father's *Kissing Time,* whilst his son Felix Caryll took minor roles in several London musicals (*Mr Whittington,* 1933, etc).

1886 **The Lily of Léoville** (Félix Rémo ad Alfred Murray) Comedy Theatre 10 May

1887 **Jubilation** ("Richard Henry") 1 act Prince of Wales Theatre 14 May

1888 **Warranted Burglar Proof** (w Henry Leslie/B C Stephenson) 1 act Prince of Wales Theatre 31 March

1889 **Love's Trickery** (Cunningham Bridgman) 1 act Lyric Theatre 31 August

1890 **La Cigale** (*La Cigale et la fourmi*) additional music for English version w F C Burnand (Lyric Theatre)

1890 **The Sentry** 1 act (Rémo, T Murray Watson) Lyric Theatre 5 April

1891 **Miss Decima** (*Miss Helyett*) additional music for revised English version w F C Burnand (Criterion Theatre)

1891 **Love and Law** (Frank Latimer) 1 act Lyric Theatre 4 March

1892 **Ma mie Rosette** revised English version w George Dance (Globe Theatre)

1892 **Opposition** ("Richard Henry") 1 act Lyric Theatre 28 June

1893 **Little Christopher Columbus** (USA: *Little Christopher*) (George R Sims) Lyric Theatre 10 October

1894 **The Shop Girl** (w Lionel Monckton/Adrian Ross, H J W Dam/Dam) Gaiety Theatre 24 November

1894 **The Yaller Girl** (Sims) 1 act Moore and Burgess Minstrels 31 December

1895 **Dandy Dick Whittington** (aka *The Circus Boy*) (Sims) Avenue Theatre 2 March

1895 **Uncle Tom's Cabin** (Sims) tableaux vivants Moore & Burgess Minstrels, St James's Hall 7 October

1896 **The Gay Parisienne** (USA: *The Girl from Paris*) (w others/ George Dance) Duke of York's Theatre 4 April

1896 **The Circus Girl** (w Monckton/Harry Greenbank, Ross/ Walter Palings, James T Tanner) Gaiety Theatre 5 December

1897 **La Beigneuse** (Sims) 1 act Palace Theatre

1898 **A Runaway Girl** (w Monckton/H Greenbank, Aubrey Hopwood/Seymour Hicks, Harry Nicholls) Gaiety Theatre 21 May

1899 **The Lucky Star** (*L'Étoile*) new score for English version w Charles H E Brookfield Savoy Theatre 7 January

1900 **The Messenger Boy** (w Monckton/Ross, Percy Greenbank/ Murray, Tanner) Gaiety Theatre 3 February

1901 **Die Reise nach Cuba** (Leopold Krenn, Carl Lindau) Venedig in Wien, Vienna 3 August

1901 **The Ladies' Paradise** (George Dance) Theatre Royal, Hanley 11 March

1901 **The Toreador** (w Monckton/P Greenbank, Ross/Nicholls, Tanner) Gaiety Theatre 17 June

1902 **The Girl from Kays** (w Cecil Cook/Owen Hall) Apollo Theatre 15 November

1903 **The Duchess of Dantzic** (Henry Hamilton) Lyric Theatre 17 October

1903 **The Orchid** (w Monckton/Ross, P Greenbank/Tanner) Gaiety Theatre 28 October

1903 **The Earl and the Girl** (P Greenbank/Hicks) Adelphi Theatre 10 December

1903 **The Cherry Girl** (Hopwood/Hicks) Vaudeville Theatre 21 December

1905 **The Spring Chicken** (Ross, Greenbank/Grossmith) Gaiety Theatre 30 May

1906 **The Little Cherub** (aka *The Girl on the Stage*) (Ross/Owen Hall) Prince of Wales Theatre 13 January

1906 **The New Aladdin** (w Monckton/Ross, Greenbank, et al/ Tanner, W H Risque) Gaiety Theatre 29 September

1907 **Nelly Neil** (C M S McLellan) Aldwych Theatre 10 January

1907 **The Girls of Gottenberg** (Ross, et al/Grossmith, L E Berman) Gaiety Theatre 15 May

1908 **Son Altesse Royale** (*S.A.R.*) (Léon Xanrof, Jules Chancel) Théâtre des Bouffes-Parisiens, Paris 11 November

1909 **Our Miss Gibbs** (Ross, P Greenbank/Tanner, et al) Gaiety Theatre 23 January

1911 **Marriage à la Carte** (McLellan) Casino Theater, New York 2 January

1911 **The Pink Lady** (McLellan) New Amsterdam Theater, New York 13 March

1912 **Oh! Oh! Delphine** (McLellan) Knickerbocker Theater, New York 30 September

1913 **The Little Café** (McLellan) New Amsterdam Theater, New York 10 November

1914 **The Belle of Bond Street** revised *The Girl from Kays* Shubert Theater, New York 30 March

1914 **Chin-Chin** (Anne Caldwell, James O'Dea/Caldwell, R H Burnside) Globe Theater, New York 20 October

1914 **Papa's Darling** (H B Smith) New Amsterdam Theater, New York 2 November

1917 **Jack o' Lantern** (Caldwell, Burnside) Globe Theater, New York 16 October

1918 **The Girl Behind the Gun** (aka *Kissing Time*) (Guy Bolton, P G Wodehouse) New Amsterdam Theater, New York 16 September

1918 **The Canary** (Wodehouse, Caldwell/ Louis Verneuil ad H B Smith) Globe Theater, New York 4 November

1919 **Kissing Time** (revised version of *The Girl Behind the Gun*) Winter Garden Theatre, London 20 May

1919 **The Kiss Call** (P Greenbank, Ross, Clifford Grey/Fred Thompson) Gaiety Theatre 8 October

1920 **Tip-Top** (Caldwell, Burnside) Globe Theater, New York 5 October

1920 **Kissing Time** (Philander Chase Johnson, Grey, Irving Caesar/George Hobart) Lyric Theater, New York 11 October

1921 **Little Miss Raffles** (Grey/Guy Bolton) Stamford, Conn 1 December

1922 **The Hotel Mouse** revised *Little Miss Raffles* w Armand Vecsey Shubert Theater, New York 13 March

CASANOVA, Giovanni Jacopo de Seingalt (b Venice, 1725; d Bohemia, 4 June 1798).

The name of Giovanni Jacopo Casanova has, thanks to a 12-volume set of memoirs that are probably as about as genuine as those of Frank Harris, joined that of Don Juan as synonymous with the notion of the dashing, Mediterranean-macho sex maniac. However, on those allegedly rare occasions when he was not out putting it about, the real Casanova was apparently a highly skilled adventurer and intriguer who made himself a profitable place in Venice, Paris, St Petersburg, Constantinople, Madrid and in various other cities where royalty and public figures were ready to be attracted by his charms and to find useful his spying talents. His name has been attached, over the years, to a whole series of theatrical pieces, some concentrating more on the spying and the royal connections, others on the more trouserless moments, and most getting happily fictional in both directions.

The best-known of the *Casanova* musical shows is undoubtedly the spectacular Operette in seven scenes by Rudolph Schanzer and Ernst Welisch, illustrated with music from the works of Johann Strauss arranged by Ralph Benatzky, and produced at Berlin's Grosses Schauspielhaus in 1928 (1 September). Michael Bohnen played a Casanova who wooed the dancer Barberina (Anny Ahlers) in scene one, the Countess Dohna (Emmy Sturm) in scene two, carried off the virginal Laura (Anni Frind) from her convent in scene three on behalf of his friend Hohenfels, waltzed with the Empress of Austria in scene four, and returned to Venice, his exile rescinded, in scene seven in time for Carnival, which allowed the theatre's designer, Ernst Stern, to go to town with a revolving stage depicting great chunks of the Grand Canal. The vastly extravagant Erik Charell staging and a well-arranged score, which made one piece of reprocessed Strauss (a combination of the the waltz "Aeols-Töne" (op 68) and the main waltz theme of the operetta *Blindekuh*) into a hit as the Nuns' Chorus, helped the show to a fine success and productions on the equally spectacle-filled stage of the London Coliseum (24 May 1932) and of Vienna's Volksoper (10 October 1935).

Another, earlier German *Casanova,* an Operette in 3 acts by Jacques Glück and Wilhelm Steinberger, with music by Paul Lincke, with a text based on just one of its hero's amorous adventures, was first produced in Chemnitz (5 November 1913), and later seen in Budapest (ad Emil Balassa) as *A szerelem királya* ("the king of love" Revü Színház 16 October 1920). By that time Hungary, however, had already had its own, highly successful *Casanova* in the grand operett in 3 acts by Jenő Faragó, music by Izsó Barna, first produced at the Népszínház 11 October 1902 for a splendid run of 56 performances, and revived on a number of occasions thereafter.

A further German *Casanova,* a musical by Helmut Bez and Jürgen Degenhardt, composed by Gerd Natschinksi, which gallivanted through as many traditional Operette settings, from Warsaw to London, and as many ladies as could be fitted in to two acts, was produced in Berlin in 1976 (Metropoltheater 10 September), whilst the 1942 Paul Burkhard comic opera *Casanova in der Schweiz* apparently took the much-librettoed hero to its composer's native Switzerland.

The German fascination with the gentleman also reached into more operatic spheres, when Lortzing composed a successful *Casanova* (Leipzig, 1841) based on a French vaudeville, *Casanova au Fort Saint-André* (the fellow really got around), followed by a 16-scene spectacular by Ernst Ritterfeld, music by Robert Leonard, mounted at the Centraltheater, Hamburg, 25 October 1898, another opera by B Pulvermacher (Liegnitz 21 November 1890) and yet another by Arthur Kusterer (Karlsruhe 22 September 1922). The Polish composer Rózycki followed the example in 1923 (Warsaw 3 May), imitated soon after by Volkmar Andreae whose *Der Abenteuer des Casanova* was produced in Dresden in 1924 (17 June).

The rest of the world has shown less interest than Germany in the gallivanting Giacomo, although it was announced in 1931, in the wake of Benatzky's piece, that Rudolf Friml and Bernard Bercovici were preparing a *Casanova* (which had started out to be a *Don Juan*) for the benefit of Dennis King, just at the same time that another musical on the same subject was also announced. Neither happened, and a British provincial *Casanova* (Norton York/Ivor Burgoyne 11 April 1972) which managed to swish him past Madame de Pompadour, Catherine the Great, David Garrick, the Duke of Bedford and others, folded out of town. France dragged *Casanova, l'aventurier de Séville* out one more time in 1994 (Guy Motta/Philippe Lecoursonnais/Claude Dufresne, Trianon 5 October) and this time he chased after La Camargo. Cagliostro also got in on the act somewhere, too.

Recordings: selection (Asco), Berlin 1976 version

THE CASINO GIRL Musical farce in 3 acts (later 2) by Harry B Smith. Music by Ludwig Englander. Casino Theater, New York, 19 March 1900.

The Casino Girl was one of the most successful examples of turn-of-the-century American musical comedy. Built on the Gaiety Theatre principle, it used that house's standard combination of exotic settings, pretty girls (Mabelle Gilman in the title role, Virginia Earle in breeches, and all the Casino chorus, mostly hired for looks rather than talent), much comedy (principally from Sam Bernard) and some lighthearted and topical songs from a variety of composers (the playbill credited "interpolated numbers by John Philip Sousa, Harry T MacConnell, Reginald De Koven, Arthur Nevin, Will Marion Cook and Fred Solomon"), including such jolly titles as "Isabella's Umbrella," "A Lesson in Acting," "American Heiresses" and "De Voodoo Man," to make up a piece which was designed to be the Casino Theater's copycat answer to the enormously popular products of the London stage—a function it fulfilled more than adequately.

The songs and comedy were set into a story which had Casino chorus girl, Laura Lee (Mabelle Gilman), pursued to Cairo by an amorous English earl called Percy Harold Ethelbert Frederick Cholmondley (Virginia Earle), and the other characters included such standard favorites as the amorous Pilsener Pasha, khedive of Egypt (Bernard) with "Only a Hundred Wives" and a Dutch accent, a soubrette called Dolly Twinkle to sing about "The Automobile Girl," girls rejoicing in the names of Lotta Rocks (Irene Bentley) and Roxy Rocks (Ella Snyder) and a pair of comic thieves, Fromage (Albert Hart) and Potage (Louis Wesley), blatantly borrowed from *Erminie,* the former of whom pretends to be "The Diamond Dude." One of the novelty numbers, in a second act made up largely of speciality acts, and constantly done over during the show's run, was an "Electric ballet," danced on a darkened stage with red and/or white lights variously illuminated in the dancers' cleavage, under their hats or around their hips, and finally lighting up a large butterfly on each hat, so that only the butterflies were seen exiting.

In between the three seasons of the various versions of the show which made up *The Casino Girl*'s Broadway life—91 initial performances plus 40 more in R B Smith's revised version (6 August 1900), then 32 more the following season from 8 April 1901 in its ''anglicized'' version at the Knickerbocker—producer George Lederer took an American cast including Richard Carle (yankee impresario J Offenbach Gaggs), James E Sullivan (Pasha), Miss Gilman (Laura) and Marie George (Dolly) to Britain. There, with the English earl turned into an American dude called Percy Harold Ethelbert van Stuyvesant and no longer played in travesty, it more than confirmed its original success with a fine run of 196 performances at the Shaftesbury Theatre, the only transatlantic musical to find success in London in the wake of *The Belle of New York.* It also became one of the few Broadway shows of its era to travel even further, when, as well as being seen under J C Williamson's management in Australia, where George Lauri (Pilsener), Carrie Moore (Laura), Charles Kenningham (Percy), Hugh J Ward (Gaggs) and Grace Palotta (Roxana) headed the cast, it was also taken to the Continent in the repertoire of the Casino company. Ultimately, it was even made over into an Hungarian version (ad Jenő Heltai), which was briefly played at Budapest's Népszínház in 1902.

The Casino even went as far as to stage its own burlesque of its show. *The Casino Boy* was produced on the theatre's Roof Garden, and was written around a little episode (which had been part of the theatre's faked publicity for its show) concerning some poisoned sweets sent to Miss Earle. Anna Laughlin played ''Ginger Early'' and George Fortescue was the villainess, Nether Saphosole (a parody of Olga Nethersole in *Sapho*).

UK: Shaftesbury Theatre 11 July 1900; Australia: Her Majesty's Theatre, Sydney 6 July 1901; Hungary: *Az aranyos* Népszínház 28 February 1902

CASSIDY, Jack [CASSIDY, John] (b Richmond Hill, NY, 5 March 1927; d Los Angeles, 12 December 1976).

Cassidy first appeared on Broadway in 1943 in *Something for the Boys,* and played in the chorus of the musicals *Sadie Thompson* (1944), *Marinka* (1945), *The Firebrand of Florence* (1945), the road-folding *Spring in Brazil* (1945, Pancho), *The Red Mill* (1945 revival), *Around the World in 80 Days* (1946) and *Music in My Heart* (1947), in the revues *Inside USA, Small Wonder* and *Alive and Kicking,* and regionally as Rocky Barton in *Billion Dollar Baby* (1949), before succeeding to a minor part in Broadway's *South Pacific* (1952 t/o Richard West). He had his first leading role on Broadway when he played the dreamboat Chick Miller in *Wish You Were Here,* introducing the show's title song, and followed up as Johnny O'Sullivan in *Sandhog* before taking *Oklahoma!* (Curly) to Paris and Rome in a State Department sponsored tour in 1955.

He starred opposite Carol Lawrence in the short-lived *Shangri-La* (1956, Charles Mallinson) on Broadway, took *Wonderful Town* overseas, appeared as Macheath in *The Beggar's Opera* at the City Center (1957), and appeared regionally in *Half in Earnest* (1957, Jack), *The Vagabond King* and *Gypsy,* but he was not seen on Broadway again until 1963 when he successfully created the role of the slickly unpleasant Kodaly in *She Loves Me.* He followed up as the film star Byron Prong in *Fade Out—Fade In* but, of his following Broadway shows, *Pleasures and Palaces* (1965, replacing Alfred Marks as Potemkin) folded on the road, and *It's a Bird . . . It's a Plane . . . It's Superman* (1966, Max Mencken) and *Maggie Flynn* (1968, Phineas) were short-lived.

His sometime wife, **Shirley [Mae] JONES** (b Smithton, Pa, 31 March 1934), best known for her memorable film interpretations of Laurey in *Oklahoma!,* Julie Jordan in *Carousel* and Marian the librarian in *The Music Man,* appeared on Broadway opposite Cassidy in *Maggie Flynn* and regionally in *Bitter-Sweet, The King and I* and other musical shows. His sons, **David Cassidy** (b New York, 12 April 1950), **Shaun Cassidy** (b Los Angeles, 27 September 1958), and **Patrick Cassidy** (b New York, 4 January 1962), made a youthful impact in television and/or popular music. David was seen in the musical theatre in *The Fig Leaves Are Falling* (1969, Billy), *Joseph and the Amazing Technicolor Dreamcoat* (1983, t/o Joseph), *Blood Brothers* (1993, Mickey), a copycat *Martin Guerre* (1993) and as replacement for Michael Crawford in the Las Vegas *EFX* (1996); Shaun played on Broadway in *Blood Brothers* (1993, t/o Eddie) and regionally in *Dangerous Music, Romace Romace* and *They're Playing Our Song;* whilst Patrick appeared on Broadway in the role of Frederic in *The Pirates of Penzance* in 1982 and in *Leader of the Pack* (1985, Jeff Barry) and at Playwrights Horizons in *Assassins* (1990, Balladeer).

Autobiographies: (Shirley Jones w Ingels, M, Herschkowitz, M): *Shirley and Marty* (Wm Morrow, New York, 1990), (David Cassidy w Deffas, C): *C'mon Get Happy* (Warner Books, New York, 1994); Biographies: (David Cassidy) Gregory, J: *The David Cassidy Story* (Shaun Cassidy), Schumacher, C: *Shaun Cassidy*

CASTLE, Vernon [BLYTH, Vernon William] (b Norwich, 2 May 1887; d Houston, Tex, 15 February 1918).

The son of a London and Norwich publican, the young singing, dancing English actor played in America, from the age of 19, in a series of shows for producer/

comedian Lew Fields—appearing on Broadway between 1906 and 1911 as A Contractor in the burlesque *The Great Decide,* the Hon Aubrey Battersea/John Blobbs in *The Girl Behind the Counter,* Souseberry Lushmore in *The Midnight Sons,* Hon Algy Clymber in *Old Dutch,* Oxford Tighe in *The Summer Widowers* and Zowie in *The Hen Pecks*—as well as in the revusical *About Town* (1906, Vicomte Martino) and the revue *The Mimic World,* mostly in the kind of dude roles which his relative-by-marriage, George Grossmith, had made so popular, alongside the low comedy of Fields. In 1911 French producer Jacques Charles hired Castle to repeat the comedy barbershop routine which he performed in *The Hen Pecks* at the Paris Olympia and agreed to take his girlfriend, Irene Foote, as a chorine and a possible dance partner for the comic if the pair were able to put together a dancing act.

Before the two arrived in Paris, the now Mrs **Irene CASTLE** (b New Rochelle, NY, 7 April 1893; m New Rochelle 28 May 1911; d Eureka Springs, Ark, 25 January 1969), who had been a dancer in Castle's last shows with Fields, had persuaded Vernon to renounce the inelegance of the low comedy for which he had been hired and to develop the dance act Charles had suggested. Thus, they simply and designedly failed to turn up for the show in which Vernon should have played his barber sketch, and when they did they arrive in Paris, they were put into the bill at the Olympia without attracting notice. Charles subsequently loaned the unprofitable pair to the Café de Paris, whose management was in search of a new attraction, and suddenly and surprisingly they became the rage of the town with their elegant ''foreign'' performance of the fox-trot and the one-step. Breaking their contract with the Olympia, they moved full-time to the Café de Paris where their success continued unabated until they decided to return to America. They had profited from their Paris stay not only financially but also professionally: they had picked up both the tango and the maxixe from South American teachers in Paris and Irene had equipped herself with a wardrobe to make both male and female eyes fall from their sockets. These were the elements which would make their success on their return home.

That return did not begin easily. The couple were first engaged to appear with Montgomery and Stone in *The Lady of the Slipper* (1912, Atzel), but Irene's insistence on wearing a particularly revealing dress from her new wardrobe in what was essentially a family show led to a battle with producer Dillingham. This time, Mrs Castle did not get her own way and she left the cast before opening. Her husband followed her soon after. Broadway's first opportunity to see the Castles together came in the American version of the Gaiety musical *The Sunshine Girl* (1913, Lord Bicester), but once again Irene lost

Plate 67. **Vernon Castle.** *The comedian-dancer takes a 1913 dance-step with partner Irene.*

out, and Vernon introduced the tango with the show's star, Julia Sanderson. *The Sunshine Girl* and its tango put an end to Castle's career in musical comedy. Thereafter, he and Irene continued their career as exhibition dancers, making themselves the best-known purveyors of dances to the ballrooms of the world. They appeared as themselves in the Irving Berlin revue *Watch Your Step* in a final Broadway appearance, and made some short films and one feature, *The Whirl of Life,* for the cinema, but their career came to an untimely end when Castle was killed in a wartime air crash in Texas at the age of 30. Irene subsequently made film appearances as an actress.

In 1939 a romanticized version of the Castles' career was filmed, as *The Story of Vernon and Irene Castle,* with Fred Astaire and Ginger Rogers appearing as the dancing pair. One dance routine, which had been preserved on a Parisian film, was precisely recreated under Mrs Castle's direction to such effect that the Castles' reputation has moved into the future boosted by the talents of Astaire and Rogers. In fact, they were technically much less adept than their film equivalents: an elegant English light comedian and a well-trained American chorus dancer whose combined skills, appearance, and decisive opportunism in creating dance crazes on both sides of the Atlantic in what was a very short career, made them into household names—names given a renewing boost 20 years later by the talents of Astaire and Rogers.

Castle's sister, **Coralie [Maud] BLYTHE** (b Bow, 28 January 1881; d 24 July 1928), was a successful musical comedy soubrette in London, appearing for George Edwardes for a number of years at the Gaiety and Daly's, understudying the Edwardes stars, and creating good supporting roles in a number of London musicals including *The Silver Slipper* (1901, Wrenne), *Mr Popple of Ippleton* (1905, Louise), *The Girl Behind the Counter* (1906, Susie), *The Three Kisses* (1907, Ethel Trevor) and *The Dashing Little Duke* (1909, Césarine). She also toured liberally in leading roles in musical comedy and played briefly in America in *About Town* (1906, Millie Bounder), *The Blue Moon* (1906, Evelyn Ormsby) and the tryout of *The White Chrysanthemum* (t/o Sybil). She was the wife of Lawrence [Randall] Grossmith (1877–1944), younger son of George Grossmith.

Biography: Castle, I: *Castles in the Air* (Doubleday, New York, 1958)

CASTLES IN THE AIR Comic opera (musical comedy) in 3 acts by Raymond W Peck. Music by Percy Wenrich. Olympic Theater, Chicago, 22 November 1925; Selwyn Theater, New York, 6 September 1926.

This sole successful attempt by songwriter Percy Wenrich ("On Moonlight Bay," "When You Wore a Tulip") at a stage musical had a plot which mixed a touch of *She Stoops to Conquer* with a disguised Prince, high society and a trip to Latvia, as well as a light if unexceptional score of songs ("Land of Romance," "The Rainbow of Your Smile," "I Would Like to Fondle You"). Stanley Forde played the central role of Philip Rodman, a comical yankee millionaire who helps the Prince (Irving Beebe) from his disguise as an American student called John Brown back to his throne with pretty Evelyn Devine (Vivienne Segal) at his side.

John Meehan and James W Elliott's production of the piece, which had gone through the titles of *Romance Land* and *The Land of Romance* before settling on the slightly less obvious *Castles in the Air,* opened in Chicago, where it was acclaimed as the biggest musical hit the city had yet seen. London's C B Cochran—doubtless remembering how Jack Waller had not so long ago found *No, No, Nanette* in Chicago—snapped up the English rights, and the show ran on for an amazing 37 weeks before a second company was sent out to tour, the A-team headed for Broadway, and Donald Brian and Virginia O'Brien took over in the continuing run in Chicago. Without finding quite the mode that it had in Chicago, the piece lasted 160 performances on Broadway, with Forde, Miss Segal and J Harold Murray starred, but the happy adventure ended in court when the two producers stopped seeing eye to eye. Elsewhere, happiness didn't get a look in. Cochran's London production with Helen Gilliland and Allen Kearns starred lasted only 28 performances, whilst an Australian J C Williamson Ltd mounting with Roy Russell and Rowena Ronalds in its leading roles did not create enough interest to make the usually automatic move from Sydney to Melbourne worthwhile.

The same title had been previously used on Broadway for a comic opera by Charles A Byrne based on Cervantes's *Los dos habladores* with music by Gustave Kerker (Broadway Theater 5 May 1890). A vehicle for the comedy of the newly risen star De Wolf Hopper, whose role as a jolly judge called Filacoudre didn't have much to do with a plot which was based on the same original as Offenbach's *Les Bavards,* it featured Marion Manola in breeches as the young man who outtalks the garrulous wife (Rose Leighton) of the father (Thomas Q Seabrooke) of his beloved (Della Fox), amongst a host of comic incidentals, for a run of 105 nights. A second piece under the same title (Walter Howe Jones/Harlan E Read) was produced in Jackson, Ill, on 30 October 1902 and stayed there.

London, too, had seen a previous *Castles in the Air,* a version of Bolten-Bäckers and Lincke's Berlin musical *Frau Luna,* played at the Scala Theatre in 1911 in a double bill with a demonstration of Kinemacolour. Neither half drew for long.

Luftschlösser (castles in the air) a Posse by Wilhelm Mannstädt and A Weller was produced in Berlin (Woltersdorff Theater, music Adolf Möhr) in 1875 and at Vienna's Theater an der Wien (11 July 1876) in a version with music by Richard Genée. It was also played in New York by Pepi Gallmeyer.

UK: Shaftesbury Theatre 20 June 1927; Australia: Her Majesty's Theatre, Sydney 15 October 1927

THE CAT AND THE FIDDLE Musical love story in 2 acts by Otto Harbach. Music by Jerome Kern. Globe Theater, New York, 15 October 1931.

When Jerome Kern deliberately turned to writing what he hoped would be a style of musical play more substantial than the flyweight pieces he had favored in the 1910s and 1920s, he did not follow up the American period-operetta line which he had exploited so well in *Show Boat.* Both *The Cat and the Fiddle* and its successor, *Music in the Air,* looked back to the European continent for their settings and subject matter and, in spite of their texts being written by Otto Harbach and Oscar Hammerstein respectively, the result was that he was served up two of the weakest and most hyperconventional libretti of his career. *The Cat and the Fiddle,* which presented the same confrontation as had been seen a dozen years earlier on Broadway in a little French one-acter called *La Musique adoucit les coeurs* (André Mauprey, Théâtre Parisien 15 December 1919), had the advantage over its fellow piece of being the more contemporary in flavor and in involving some lively American-in-Brussels scenes and songs.

The young American musician Shirley Sheridan (Bettina Hall) meets the romantic Roumanian composer Victor Florescu (Georges Metaxa) on the quais of Brussels and romance blossoms. They lose touch when a letter goes astray, and meet again only when Shirley is approached by Clement Daudet (Jose Ruben) to interpolate some of her light, jazzy songs into an overly-romantic musical scena in a revue. *The Passionate Pilgrim* is Victor's seriously conceived and composed unhappy-ending work. Shirley loosens up his conservatoire tones and changes his ending, but although the show is a success, the lies of the jealous Odette (Odette Myrtil) hold off a romantic reconciliation until the final curtain. Doris Carson (Angie) and Eddie Foy jr (Alexander) provided the light comedy as Shirley's dancing brother and sister-in-law, whilst the Metropolitan Opera's George Meader made a special hit as a street singer, Pompineau, and the Albertina Rasch dancers added to the spectacle of this show about the writing of a show.

The song success of *The Cat and the Fiddle* was the jaunty little "She Didn't Say 'Yes,' " presented as a specimen of Shirley's work and sung in the show first by the street singer and later, in meaningful context, by Shirley. Pompineau also delivered the serenade "The Night Was Made for Love" and "I Watch the Love Parade," whilst Victor sang his newly composed songs "The Breeze Kissed Your Hair" and "A New Love Is Old," Shirley delivered a more romantic effort of her own, "Try to Forget," and Odette led the representation of an excerpt from *The Passionate Pilgrim* in a score where a large part of the music was simply tacked into the script as being "numbers" written as such.

Max Gordon's production of *The Cat and the Fiddle* played for a slightly forced 395 performances on Broadway in the early days of the depression, with salary cuts and even a shift in theatre included as Gordon worked to keep the show alive until it was time to take it touring. C B Cochran mounted a London edition at the Palace Theatre with his *Bitter-Sweet* star, Peggy Wood, as Shirley and Francis Lederer as Victor. The old romantic musical comedy star Henri Leoni played Pompineau, and Alice Delysia appeared as what had been Odette but was now Alice. The show ran 226 West End performances, which was not enough to help Cochran out of the financial hole dug for him by *Helen!* in the same season, and had a short tour.

A film version, with a screenplay by Sam and Bella Spewack, dug frantically into the book of operettic conventions and came up with an altered plot which had Shirley (Jeanette MacDonald) going on for the Odette character—now played by a real diva in Vivienne Segal—when she walks out on the show. Joseph Cawthorn supplied the intentional comedy and Ramon Novarro was romance.

An earlier musical with the same title was played on the American touring circuits in 1907. A soi-disant "spectacular musical dramatic fantasy" or "Melodrama-musical-comedy-extravaganza-trick-play" of a kind not meant for Broadway consumption, it nevertheless put in a brief New York appearance at the West End Theater (16 December 1907). Out of town, however, it lasted very much longer than its more willfully upmarket successor, trouping minor dates in multiple companies for a number of years.

London followed its *The Cat and the Fiddle* not with another but with a *Hi Diddle Diddle,* a revue mounted at the Comedy Theatre (3 October 1934) with June and Douglas Byng.

UK: Palace Theatre 4 March 1932

Film: MGM 1934

Recording: selection (part record) (RCA, Fontana)

THE CATCH OF THE SEASON Musical comedy in 2 acts by Seymour Hicks and Cosmo Hamilton. Lyrics by Charles H Taylor. Music by Herbert Haines and Evelyn Baker. Vaudeville Theatre, London, 9 September 1904.

Seymour Hicks's musical, a straightforward, modern version of the Cinderella tale, was written as a vehicle for himself and his wife, Ellaline Terriss. When Mrs Hicks got pregnant, the production looked in danger, but Charles Frohman decided to continue, and brought in the young Zena Dare to create the central role of Angela Crystal opposite Hicks's Duke of St Jermyns. Hicks got his star share of the action by using the Fairy-Godmotherless version of the old tale in which the disguised Prince and Cinderella meet long before the ball. Statuesque Ethel Matthews and Hilda Jacobson featured as the heroine's very un-ugly sisters, whilst Sam Sothern appeared as the Dandini-equivalent Lord Dundreary, doing an impersonation of the famous performance given by his father in *Our American Cousin.* Juvenile Albert Valchera was the page boy, Bucket, sighing comically over the heroine, whilst Shakespearean actress Rosina Filippi played Lady Caterham, the wealthy aunt who turns up in time to replace the fairy element and transform Angela into ''Molly O'Halloran from County Clare'' in time for the ball. A topical element was introduced with the character of little Mr William Gibson (Compton Coutts), with his front line of very tall daughters, the Gibson Girls. Modeled on the famous drawings of Charles Dana Gibson, the ''girls'' had actually been pipped at the post by a pair of American duettists who'd pranced Gibsonesquely across the stage in Princess gowns, picture-hats and parasols the previous week at the Palace Music Hall, but the little duo were non-starters when Frohman's team hit town. His Gibson Girls, decked out in specially created and heavily publicized ''emotionalized costumes' designed by Lady Duff Cooper became an outstanding feature of the show, none more so than Camille Clifford (Sylvia Gibson), swiped from the cast of the American show *The Prince of Pilsen* and added to the line-up to display her allegedly 11-inch waist, blossoming bosom, amazing posture and inexistent singing voice before a gasping public.

Herbert Haines and Evelyn Baker's first West End score accompanied the performance well. Hicks sang briskly of ''The Church Parade,'' Miss Dare got Irish as ''Molly O'Halloran,'' and the Hon Honoria Bedford (Miss Jacobson) sang to her ''Cigarette'' and enumerated the amorous adventures that went with each of the ''Charms on My Chain.'' In Hicks's favorite fashion, however, the score soon became dotted with interpolations, as *The Catch of the Season* ran on and on, making itself into one of the favorite actor's greatest successes. There was time for Mrs Hicks to have her baby, return to take up the role intended for her, and still be succeeded by sister-in-law Maie Ash, Alice Russon, Zena Dare's younger sister, Phyllis, and little Madge Crichton before the show got to its 621st and last London performance. The Gibson Girls turned over as quickly as the song content, and at least one got herself a genuine Earl.

Whilst London's production ran on, Frohman opened the show on Broadway, with Edna May as Angela to the Duke of Joe Farren Soutar, Fred Kaye playing the Dandini role, now no longer an impersonation of anyone and rechristened Lord Baghdad Monteagle, former Gaiety girl Margaret Fraser (Honoria) and Fred Wright jr (Gibson). The inimitable Sylvia Gibson had disappeared (though the song about her hadn't), and in her place was a barrage of new songs from the pens of Jerome D Kern, musical director William T Francis and Luke Forwood (''My Little Buttercup''). The resultant piece ran for 93 performances.

The Catch of the Season continued to tour in Britain until 1908, but it also surfaced at Budapest's Népszínház in 1907 (ad Jenő Heltai), in Australia, where Fanny Dango played Angela to the Duke of Andrew Higginson and her real-life sister, Lydia Flopp, appeared as Sophia, and, several years later, in Vienna (ad Fritz Lunzer, Karl Tuschl) both at the Venedig in Wien summer theatre and later as a Christmas entertainment at the Theater an der Wien. Tuschl himself played Gibson, with Paul Guttmann doing Lord Dundreary and Clara Karry and Max Willenz heading the romance. The score had by now undergone a further facelift, and one Captain Rushpool (Bernhard Bötel) enlivened Act I with musical director Otto Stransky's ''Küss, mein Mädel, mich ein letztes Mal,'' Guttmann led a tango quartet in the second act, and there was a ''grotesque dance trio'' for Tuschl, Guttmann and Karl Matuna, as the heroine's father, which demanded ''Kennen Sie schön den neusten Tanz?''

The Catch of the Season returned to London in a wartime revival (Prince's Theatre 17 February 1917) with Hicks starring alongside Isobel Elsom for a season of 84 performances.

USA: Daly's Theater 28 August 1905; Hungary: Népszínház *A balkirályno* 16 November 1907; Australia: Her Majesty's Theatre, Sydney 18 December 1909; Austria: Venedig in Wien *Die Ballkönigin* 15 July 1913, Theater an der Wien 25 December 1913

CATLETT, Walter H (b San Francisco, 4 February 1889; d Los Angeles, 4 November 1960).

Walter Catlett spent his earliest years in the theatre—he was a brownie in *Brownies in Fairyland* at the San Francisco Alhambra at age 13—playing in stock in California (Tivoli Opera House, Alcazar, in *The Idol's Eye* with Ferris Hartman at Idora Park, Oakland 1908, etc), and he appeared on the New York stage for the first time in the juvenile comedy role of Artie, Earl of Somerset, in a revival of *The Prince of Pilsen* (1910). Half a dozen years of variegated touring—including spells with the Manhattan Opera Company summer season at Elmire, NY, the multicompanied *Madame Sherry* and the cheap-rate touring musical *The Red Rose* (September 1912)—intervened before he returned to Broadway, this time as the comical Harry Miller in the successful west-coast musical *So Long, Letty* (1915), but after a second and less forthcoming west-coast musical, *Look Pleasant,* and a stint in the *Ziegfeld Follies of 1917,* he lined up a series of good musical comedy roles. He was seen in New York in *Follow the Girl* (1918, Buck Sweeney) and *Little Simplicity* (1918, Prof Erasmus Duckworth), made a very successful London debut as the hero's flip, jokey sidekick in *Baby Bunting* (1919, William Pye) and scored his biggest success to date in the role of the wisecracking Otis Hooper (of the Anglo-American Vaudeville Agency, Squantumville, Maine) in *Sally* (1920) at New York's New Amsterdam Theater (''The Church 'Round the Corner,'' ''On with the Dance,'' ''The Lorelei'').

Another Jerome Kern musical, *Dear Sir* (1924, André Bloxom), briefly gave him another brash comedy

Plate 68. **Cats.** *A litter of Japanese cats surround Old Deuteronomy.*

part as a phony millionaire, but his second grand new role came later that same year when he created the part of the slick-pattering lawyer, ''Watty'' Watkins in *Lady, Be Good!,* alongside Adele and Fred Astaire, introducing the show's title number.

The West Coast musical productions of *Patsy* (1926) and *Honey Girl* (1926) and New York's *Lucky* (1927, Charley Simpson) were less forthcoming and *Here's Howe* (1928, t/o Basil Carroway) and *Treasure Girl* (1928, Larry Hopkins) closed out Catlett's Broadway career on a note somewhat lower than the days of *Sally* and *Lady, Be Good!* It closed, however, simply because he moved on towards Hollywood and a three-decade film career as a character performer (*Rain, Mr Deeds Goes to Town, On the Avenue, Bringing up Baby, Yankee Doodle Dandy, Look for the Silver Lining, Here Comes the Groom, Friendly Persuasion,* etc) highlighted for many by his loan of his voice to Mr J Worthington Foulfellow in Walt Disney's cartoon *Pinocchio.*

CATS Musical in 2 acts based on T S Eliot's *Old Possum's Book of Practical Cats.* Music by Andrew Lloyd Webber. New London Theatre, London, 11 May 1981.

The most popularly successful musical of the 1980s and, depending on which way you count your statistics, possibly of all time, *Cats* is, in any case, one of the most remarkable phenomena in the history of the musical theatre.

The show had its origins in the settings of some of T S Eliot's poems from *Old Possum's Book of Practical Cats* (1939) made by composer Lloyd Webber and originally performed privately at his Sydmonton Festival. They were well enough received for the composer to consider taking them further, and it was variously envisaged that they might make up a song cycle, a television program, or even half of a two-part stage show, sharing a program with a staged version of his orchestral piece ''Variations on a Theme of Paganini.'' Ultimately, however, it was resolved to make *Cats* into a full evening's entertainment on its own.

Lloyd Webber and young producer Cameron Mackintosh assembled a team headed by director Trevor Nunn and choreographer Gillian Lynne, who had worked together on two productions with a dance content at the Royal Shakespeare Company, and the selection of songs and personalities that made up *Cats* were arranged on to a slim, meticulously worked-out framework of character and motivation in which the climax of affairs was the Jellicle Ball, and the opportunity given there to one cat to have an additional life. With the cooperation of Valerie

Eliot, the poet's widow, the team was able to make use of a range of various published and unpublished Eliot pieces and it was from these that the character of Grizabella, the glamor cat, who had not made her way into *Old Possum's Book,* was reconstructed, to be literally given a second chance. For at the end of the evening, with its presentation of a bounding gallery of feline characters, it was the tarty, bedraggled Grizabella who became the heroine of the tale as she ascended radiantly from her rubbish-tip on an old car tire, transported towards a rebirth and the Heaviside Layer.

The most unusual element of the show's concept was that it was planned as a dance show, choreographed from beginning to end in a fashion unprecedented in a West End musical, and with all its roles barring two—the venerable Old Deuteronomy and Grizabella—played by skilled dancers. That concept was given extra breadth when it was decided to mount the show in the unloved New London Theatre, Sean Kenny's ''theatre of the future'' which had for seven years floundered along, seeming to have no future. The large revolve built into the three-sided auditorium floor became the playground for *Cats.* However, the unusual show soon hit unusual problems and, given the pressures put on artists rehearsing a dance piece longer than most full-length ballets, injuries were legion. The most devastating was that to Royal Shakespeare Company star Judi Dench and, late in rehearsals, she had to be replaced. The dance element of her role was taken by another company member, her part as Grizabella was taken up by *Evita* star Elaine Paige.

In spite of its special form and a ''plotline'' which was—by the time the show came to the stage—not at all evident, *Cats* was an instant success. Its cavalcade of scrambling, dancing creatures immediately took hold of the audience as they leaped from the giant, revolving rubbish heap that was the setting for the entertainment, around the auditorium and back, to begin the series of items that make up the evening: the plump and comical Gumbie Cat (Myra Sands); the pop-pussy Rum-Tum-Tugger (Paul Nicholas); Bustopher Jones (Brian Blessed), the cat of the gentlemen's clubs, in his white spats; the kitten burglars Mungojerrie (John Thornton) and Rumpleteazer (Bonnie Langford); Gus, the Theatre Cat (Stephen Tate), with his grand tale of the terrible Growltiger (Tate) and his lady Griddlebone (Susan Jane Tanner); Skimbleshanks, the Railway Cat (Kenn Wells); the magical Mister Mistoffelees (Wayne Sleep); and the mysterious Macavity (Thornton), his tale walloped out by a pair of vamp-cats (Geraldine Gardner, Sharon Lee Hill), all danced and sang through their poem-numbers, until the final ball scene when Grizabella (Miss Paige) got her apotheosis.

Although there was an attempt to launch a couple of numbers pre-production, the songs of the show were not the kind to become popular singles, with one exception. Grizabella's despairingly hopeful ''Memory,'' put together from an existing Lloyd Webber melody and a lyric made up by Nunn from fragments and suggestions of Eliot and powered forth achingly by Miss Paige, became a highlight of the show, and a major hit outside it.

There were problems in reproducing the original production of *Cats* in other theatres without tearing auditoria to pieces and, as further productions followed, an alternative version of the London staging adapted to a semi-proscenium or proscenium theatre was evolved. Broadway's version of the show also included some alterations in the score—replacing the original Billy McCaw ballad in the pirate scene with a burlesque Italianate aria, and rearranging Mungojerrie and Rumpleteazer's music—and these were mostly maintained in subsequent productions.

The Broadway production opened little more than a year after London's, with Betty Buckley (Grizabella), Stephen Hanan (Gus), Ken Page (Deuteronomy), Harry Groener (Munkustrap), Bonnie Simmons (Griddlebone) and Terence V Mann (Rum-Tum-Tugger) amongst the cast. The show received much the same reception as in Britain, and found much the same long-lived success. T S Eliot won a posthumous Tony Award for his ''libretto'' to put with the one he had won, living, for *The Cocktail Party,* and the Nobel Prize he had picked up in 1948. At the time of writing, *Cats* is in its 19th year at the New London Theatre, the longest running musical in the history of the West End theatre, and has just recently closed, after 17 years and 7,393 performance, at Broadway's Winter Garden Theater (where on 19 June 1997 it became the longest running show in Broadway history), whilst its kittens, in all sorts of languages (but always in the original production, give or take a permitted variation) have been seen all over the world from Zürich to Mexico City.

A Los Angeles company, an American touring company, reproductions in Canada, Australia, Vienna (ad Michael Kunze), Budapest (ad Jozsef Romhanyi, in repertoire), in a specially built theatre in Tokyo, in Norway and in Finland led the introduction of *Cats* to the rest of the world. Miss Lynne went to Hamburg to stage a German production—which would hold its own with London and New York as far as long life was concerned—and, in 1989, she traveled to Paris to mount the first production of a British musical there since *Jesus Christ Superstar.* In Britain, meanwhile, a first provincial company went out whilst the show still held the stage in London, an unusual exercise in postwar Britain. In London, the *Cats* advertising changed from ''the longer you wait, the longer you'll wait'' to the curiously imprecise ''now and forever.'' Forever is, of course, quite a long time, but *Cats* is getting closer to it than any major-house musical before it.

An animated film version of *Cats* was long rumored, but instead, in 1998, a videofilm version was issued. Elaine Paige and the ageless Susan Jane Tanner repeated their original roles, with Ken Page now upped to the part of Old Deuteronomy, John Mills featured as the theatre cat and Geoffrey Garratt threatened to steal the show as Skimbleshanks.

USA: Winter Garden Theater 7 October 1982; Hungary: Madach Színház *Macskak* 25 March 1983; Austria: Theater an der Wien 24 September 1983; Australia: Theatre Royal, Sydney 27 July 1985; Germany: Operettenhaus, Hamburg 18 April 1986; France: Théâtre de Paris 23 February 1989

Recordings: original cast (Polydor), Broadway cast (Geffen), Hungarian cast (Favorit), Austrian cast (Polydor), Japanese cast (Canyon), Australian cast (EMI), German cast (Polydor), Dutch cast (Mercury), Mexican cast (Polydor), French cast (Polydor), Norwegian cast (Polygram), etc

Video: Polygram 1998

CATTARINA, or Friends at Court Comic opera in 2 acts by Robert Reece. Music by Frederic Clay. Prince's Theatre, Manchester, 17 August 1874; Charing Cross Theatre, London, 15 May 1875.

One of the earliest British musical plays of the modern age, *Cattarina* was commissioned by the performer/producer Kate Santley who played it successfully on tour and for a fine 75 performances in London. A Ruritanian setting and a half-burlesque, half-opéra-comique libretto of peasants, princes, disguises, usurpers and topical jibes held up a charming score from which Miss Santley turned the roguish ''It Is So Like the Men'' into a popular hit. Touted before production as Britain's answer to *La Fille de Madame Angot,* it did not come anywhere near the level of Lecocq's piece, but it nevertheless provided a stone in the path leading to *The Sorcerer* and to *HMS Pinafore,* which did.

CAWTHORN, Joseph (b New York, 29 March 1867; d Beverly Hills, Calif, 21 January 1949). Favorite ''Dutch'' comedian of a quarter-of-a-century of American musicals.

Cawthorn started his stage life as a child in music hall—allegedly aged three in a picanniny entertainment at Robinson Hall—and worked, at first in a team with his elder brother Herbert, as the Cawthorne Children, in both America and Britain (1876–80) in minstrel shows (Haverly's Mastodon Minstrels, etc), pantomime and vaudeville (sketch *Patent Medecine,* etc) before moving into the theatre. He appeared with Herbert (''Comical Little Cawthorne'') in the musico-comical *The Little Nugget* (1889–90) before the brothers went their separate ways, each to become a topliner in his own field. Cawthorn found his niche in musicals, where he made a speciality of the ''Dutch'' dialect comedy roles which were widely and extravagantly popular at the time (with Patti Rosa in *Miss Dixie* 1892, in *A Girl's Way* with Gladys Wallis, as ''Jolly Joe Cawthorn,'' as Schnitz Gyzer in *A Fool for Luck* 1895, etc).

He toured alongside Corinne in *Henrik Hudson* (1896, Kill von Kull) and in *Excelsior Jr* with the equally up-and-coming Marie Cahill, continuing on into ''Dutch'' roles in the spectacle *Nature* (1897, Hans Schultz, with his concertina speciality) and—until it stranded in Seattle—in *Miss Philadelphia* (1897, William Penn jr), in well noticed performances which led in 1898 to his engagement for the comic tenor role of Boris in Alice Nielsen's production of the Victor Herbert comic opera *The Fortune Teller.* He then moved on to the Casino Theater to match the Dutch humor of his Siegfried Gotterdammerung with the Turkish-Irishisms of Thomas Q Seabrooke and the lugubrious comicalities of Dan Daly in *The Rounders* (1899) before returning to Miss Nielsen both for Herbert's *The Singing Girl* (1899, Aufpassen) and for a trip to London for a season of a revised version of *The Fortune Teller* in 1901.

He appeared at the New Amsterdam Theatre in 1903–4 in the title role of an Americanized version of the Drury Lane pantomime *Mother Goose* before returning to the Dutch dialect to recreate the most famous of all dialect characters, J K Emmet's Fritz, in a new Fritz show called *Fritz in Tammany Hall* in 1905 and to play in John Philip Sousa's *The Free Lance* (1906, Siegmund Lump). He was tacked into the plot and cast of the Elsie Janis vehicle, *The Hoyden* (Baron Hugo Weybach), for the show's post-Broadway tour, and carried on in similarly accented roles in the cartoon musical *Little Nemo* (1908, Dr Pill), *Girlies* (1910, Dr Oscar Spiel), and Leslie Stuart's *The Slim Princess* (1911, Louis von Schloppenhauer), again alongside Miss Janis.

In 1913–14 he had a considerable success, playing now opposite Julia Sanderson, in two musicals imported from London's Gaiety Theatre: *The Sunshine Girl,* in which he played a revised version of Teddy Payne's Floot, rechristened Schlump to allow him to indulge his favorite Continental accent, and *The Girl from Utah,* for which Payne's Trimmit became similarly renationalized as Trimpel. He took the comic lead of Otto Spreckles when Miss Sanderson played the title role in Victor Jacobi's Hungarian operett *Sybil* (1916) and teamed with her yet again in Jacobi's Broadway piece *Rambler Rose* (1917, Joseph Guppy) and in Ivan Caryll's French farce musical *The Canary* (1918, Timothy).

Like the last two of these shows, another Jacobi musical, *The Half Moon* (1920), cast Cawthorn in a non-Germanic role as the Hon Hudson Hobson, but he was back to being Otto in *The Bunch and Judy* before a broken kneecap forced him to renounce the role during the

Plate 69. **Joseph Cawthorn** *teamed with Julia Sanderson and Donald Brian in a famous combination for Broadway's* The Girl from Utah.

show's pre-Broadway run. He returned to town star-billed in Rudolf Friml's *The Blue Kitten* (1922, Theodore Vanderpop) and in 1925, after a remarkable career at the top of his profession, made his farewell to Broadway as the loveable and duly accented father of Marilyn Miller in Kern's *Sunny* (Siegfried Peters).

Cawthorn, however, was far from finished. Although he had quit the stage, he then went on to a successful and prolific career as a character actor in films. His celluloid credits ran from *The Taming of the Shrew* and *White Zombie* to musical pieces such as *Street Girl, Good News, Love Me Tonight* (Doctor with a song with Jeanette MacDonald), *Twenty Million Sweethearts, Music in the Air, Sweet Music, Sweet Adeline, Gold Diggers of 1935, Harmony Lane, Go Into Your Dance, Naughty Marietta* (Herr Schumann), *The Great Ziegfeld* (Dr Florenz Ziegfeld sr), *Scatterbrain* and *Lillian Russell.*

Cawthorn also turned his hand to occasional songwriting and provided himself with such numbers as ''My Father's Wooden Leg'' (*The Hoyden* w Harry Dillon), ''That's Why I Never Married'' (*The Hoyden* w John L Golden), ''I Can Dance with Anyone But My Wife'' (*Sybil* w Golden) and ''You Can't Play Every Instrument in the Band'' (*The Sunshine Girl* w Golden) to perform in his stage musical appearances.

Cawthorn was married to musical comedy actress Queenie Vassar.

Herbert CAWTHORN, seen on Broadway as early as 1872 playing *The Old Man's Drunk Again* at Tony Pastor's, worked largely as an Irish comic in vaudeville, but he was also seen from time to time on the musical stage, notably in George Hoey's *A Cork Man* (1894), as Peter Stuyvesant in *The Burgomaster* (1900), *The Prima Donna* (1901, Meyerbeer Supnoodle), *The Sleeping Beauty and the Beast* (1903, Nurse Lena), *Mr Bluebeard* (1903, Irish Patshaw), *The Isle of Spice* (1904, Mickey O'Grady), *The Yankee Tourit* (1907, Griggs) and *Mar-*

celle (1908, Schwindel). He also penned the occasional song, such as May Irwin's "Dat Coon's Got a Soft Spot for Me."

CELLI, Frank H[ubert] [STANDING, Francis] (b Dalston, 8 April 1845; d London, 27 December 1904). A fine-voiced baritone singer, with a superb moustache and a rather stiff neck, who took leading roles in Victorian musicals on both sides of the Atlantic.

The son of a customs office clerk, Celli began his working life in the civil service, and started his singing career as an amateur in Monmouthshire at 18. He went on the stage professionally (at first as "Frank Standing," then as "Frank Crellin") whilst in his earliest twenties, appearing on the London stage for the first time in 1867 in Augusta Thomson's company at the Marylebone Theatre. His roles there included Matt o' the Mint in *The Beggar's Opera,* Osbaldistone in *Rob Roy* and Tom Tug in *The Waterman.* He played with the famous Bristol and Bath company in pieces ranging from *Rob Roy* to *Romeo and Juliet* (Benvolio) and in the pantomime *Aladdin* (Boghee), repeated his *Romeo and Juliet* at London's Princess's Theatre, and then turned to operetta, appearing with Louisa Pyne's little company in the provinces (*Mariage aux lanternes,* etc), in curtain-raisers at the Gaiety (1869, *The Two Harlequins, An Eligible Villa*) and at the St James's Theatre (1869, *Treasure Trove*). He soon moved on to larger roles and larger shows, and was seen in the West End during the 1870s in such roles as Prince Jonquil in *The Black Crook,* Cornarino in *The Bridge of Sighs,* as Fridolin in *Le Roi Carotte* and Belamy in *The Dragoons* (*Les Dragons de Villars*). He also appeared, between musical theatre engagements, in oratorio, concert, concert party and—Italianized now as "F H Celli"—in baritone roles with both the Mapleson (1871) and Carl Rosa (1874 sqq) Opera Companies.

In 1880 he was London's Brissac in *Les Mousquetaires,* and the following year he appeared as the Marquis in *Les Cloches de Corneville,* before going on to appear as Januario in a revival of *The Naval Cadets,* as Armand in *La Belle Normande,* as Bernadille in *La Boulangère* and in the title role of Edward Solomon's *Claude Duval.* In 1884 he took the lead role of John Smith in the same composer's short-lived *Pocahontas,* and in 1885 made his debut on Broadway playing Fra Bombardo in the Casino Theater's production of *Amorita* (*Pfingsten in Florenz*). However, not far into the run he was obliged to return home, following the death of his wife.

He played regularly during the 1880s with the Rosa company, but also with several second-string opera tours (including, at one stage, a rather struggling "Frank Celli Opera Co"), and returned to the musical theatre as the cod-operatic Monotosol in *Our Diva* (1886, *Joséphine vendue par ses soeurs*) and as Ralf of Chestermere in the London tryout of *Marjorie* (1890), only to be succeeded by his former understudy, Hayden Coffin, when the show was mounted in the evening bill. In 1890 he also created the part of Thorgrim in Bennett's opera *Thorgrim* at Drury Lane. In 1891 he went to the Gaiety Theatre to succeed to the role of Escamillo in *Carmen Up-to-Data,* which had originally been played by a girl in travesty. He later appeared singing baritone ballads in the music halls, but was seen in the theatre as a takeover in *Miss Decima* (Paul, 1892), in the short-lived light opera *The Bric-à-Brac Will* (1895, Roberto) and in 1898 took part in Augustin Daly's Broadway revival of *La Poupée* (Brother Maxime) and appeared as Brother Tamarind in his production of *A Runaway Girl.* He subsequently played at the Alhambra, singing "Jack's the Man" in the production *The Handy Man* (1900), and, in his last West End appearance—in a role as far away from opera as could be imagined—he played the comical Spoofah Bey in the variety musical *Morocco Bound.* He was, however, seen on the road as late as 1902, starring with Mlle Mars and Wilfred Shine in the "musical stage society play" *Nana,* and in 1903 he toured musical comedy through South Africa.

Celli twice left the stage for a comfortable retirement, but was obliged to return when he lost his savings on speculations. On the second occasion, he reconverted as a singing teacher, and he was engaged in that capacity at the Guildhall at his death.

He was the author of a number of song lyrics ("Sing a Song of Victory" mus: Finck, etc) and also of a touring musical comedy drama, *Stirring Times,* in which he featured on the British road.

Celli's first wife was **Susan[nah] PYNE** (b London, ?1820; d London, 5 January 1886), a vocalist with many major operatic roles to her credit, and sister to the important manager-prima donna Louisa [Fanny] Pyne of the Pyne-Harrison Opera Company. His brothers were the actor Herbert Standing and the prominent Broadway musical theatre vocalist William T Carleton, whose son, William P Carleton, also performed on the musical stage in America.

W[illiam] T[urnham] CARLETON [William STANDING] (b Peckham, 23 August 1848; d Flushing, NY, 25 September 1922) had a career every bit as fruitful as that of his elder brother, but mostly on the left-hand side of the Atlantic. After early experience in music hall, opera (Florio in *The Rose of Castile,* Herman in *Letty the Basketmaker,* etc) and opéra-bouffe (Popolani in *Barbe-bleue,* Boom in *La Grande-Duchesse,* Agamemnon in *La Belle Hélène,* Pietro in *Les Brigands* with the Gaiety opéra-bouffe company, etc) in Britain, he crossed in 1873 to America. He played there for much of the 1870s in the Clara Kellogg (di Luna, Richard Coeur de Lion in the

American première of *The Talisman,* Danny Mann in *The Lily of Killatrney,* etc) and C D Hess English opera companies (Raoul in *Les Huguenots,* Danny Mann in *The Lily of Killarney,* Dutchman in *The Flying Dutchman,* Escamillo in *Carmen,* Plunkett in *Martha, Maritana, Rigoletto,* Valentin in *Faust, Mignon, Il Trovatore, The Star of the North, Aida,* etc) before returning to Britain and to the comic-opera stage as Robert in London's production of *La Fille du tambour-major* in 1880. He returned to America to play Escamillo to the Carmen of Marie Roze with the Strakosh-Hess Company, but it was as a musicals performer that he made what would be his major mark, beginning when he appeared alongside Selina Dolaro in the hugely successful New York mounting of *Olivette* (1881, Valentine). He quickly became one of Broadway's top musical-theatre baritones, appearing in the first half of the 1880s in *Patience* (Colonel Calverley), *Claude Duval* (Duval), *La Mascotte* (Pippo), *The Merry War* (Umberto), *Manteaux Noirs* (Don Luis), *Rip van Winkle* (Rip), *Iolanthe* (Strephon), *The Queen's Lace Handkerchief* (Cervantes), *The Beggar Student* (Symon) and *Nanon* (D'Aubigné) before, in 1885, leaving the baritone slot in *Amorita* to brother Celli and taking out his own comic opera company. He toured around America for a number of years with a repertoire including *The Merry War, La Mascotte, Fra Diavolo, Nanon, The Mikado, The Queen's Lace Handkerchief, The Brigands,* et al, and produced and starred in *Erminie*'s successor, *Mynheer Jan* (1888, Karl). For a number of years the Carleton company had a fine reputation for quality, but in later years there was something of a falling off, and finally Carleton disbanded his troupe. He subsequently returned to Broadway to play Vincent Knapps to the *La Cigale* of Lillian Russell, Pietro in her *The Mountebanks* and Mourzouk in her *Giroflé-Girofla* (1892), Danny Man in José van den Berg's revival of *The Lily of Killarney* (1895), Grosvenor to the Bunthorne of Dixey in *Patience* (1896), the Marquis in a revival of *Erminie* (1899) and Dakota Dick in *Three Little Lambs* (1899).

In 1898 he took a turn into vaudeville, playing a musical comedietta called *An Opera Rehearsal,* but he soon returned to the theatre and in 1901 he was seen as Cyrus Gilfain during the run of *Florodora.* He followed up as the Lord Lieutenant in *The Emerald Isle* (1902), Lord Belton in *The Medal and the Maid* (1903, without a song) and as Sir Peter Teazle in Lillian Russell's *Lady Teazle* (1904), in a career now often angled towards non-musical roles. However, he was seen on the musical stage in *When Johnny Comes Marching Home* (1905), *The Tourists* (1906, t/o Rajah), as Gilfain again in 1908, opposite Lulu Glaser in *Mlle Mischief* (1908, Lt Berner), in *The Prince of Bohemia* (1910, Ashby Tritton) and *The Balkan Princess* (1911, pre-Broadway & t/o Boethy) and—after a series of dramatic roles—again as late as 1919 when he took over from De Wolf Hopper in *Everything* at the Hippodrome. He also appeared in some 30 silent films between 1914 and 1920, notably as Zamaliel in the spectacle *Fantasma.*

William P CARLETON [William Propert STANDING] (b London, 24 October 1873; d Hollywood, Calif, 6 April 1947) began his career playing with Oscar Hammerstein (La Popilinière in *Le Talisman* 1893) and Francis Wilson (Vicomte de Briassac in *Erminie* 1893) in operetta and with Augustin Daly's company (Auguste in *A Gaiety Girl* 1895), and had a decade in the limelight as a musical comedy juvenile, appearing in *The Cherry Pickers* (1896), *The Belle of New York* (1900 rev, Harry Bronson), *The Cadet Girl* (1900, Lucien), *The Prima Donna* (1901, Abdallah), with the Garden Theater Opera, Cleveland (1901, Viceroy in *La Périchole,* Sulpice in *Daughter of the Regiment,* etc), *Winsome Winnie* (1903, Desmond Poverish), *The Tattooed Man* (1907, Abdalah), *Mam'selle Sallie / A Knight for a Day* (1906–7, Marco Bozzaris), *The Yankee Girl* (1910, Capt John Lawrence), *The Wall Street Girl* (1912, Dexter Barton), and—after a spell as leading man in Boston stock (*The Circus Girl,* etc)—in *Broadway and Buttermilk* (1916, Tom Burrowes), as well as a selection of plays. He later appeared in a long run of films, silent and spoken, notably as Count Arnheim in the 1936 Hollywood version of *The Bohemian Girl.* He was killed in a motoring accident.

Carleton married musical comedy actress **Toby CLAUDE** [Harriette Mary KAVANAGH] (b Dublin, c1877; d Los Angeles, 27 October 1962), "the tiniest creature and the best-shaped that even sang and danced," who appeared in such musical comedies as *The Belle of New York* (1900, Fifi), *The Cadet Girl* (1900, Daisy), *The Prima Donna* (1901, Peggy), *The Supper Club* (1901, Nan), *Florodora* (1902, t/o Angela), *A Chinese Honeymoon* (1902 tour, Fi-Fi), *Baroness Fiddlesticks* (1904, Isabelle) in America, and later performed in Australia (*A Knight for a Day,* 1910, etc). In the 1920s she was seen in character roles in films.

One of Celli and Carleton's sisters, **Ellen STANDING** (b Peckham, 1853; d London, 23 March 1906), also appeared as a character actress in such musicals as *The Shop Girl, Little Miss Nobody* and *A Chinese Honeymoon,* and brother **[James] Herbert STANDING** (b Peckham, 13 November 1846; d Los Angeles, 5 December 1923), a leading actor, also ventured occasionally on to the musical stage, from early days when he starred in the Stanley-finds-Livingstone burlesque *How I Found Crusoe* (1872, Gustavus Adolphus Swagg) at the Olympic, and most notably starring in the West End as Hon Tom Splinterbarre in Farnie's hashed up *La Vie parisienne* (1883), as a takeover in *Nell Gwynne* (1884, Buckingham), in the title role of the revival of *Chilpéric* which opened London's Empire Theatre and in the successful musical comedy *The French Maid* (1897, Paul Lecuire). His son, **[Cecil] Wyndham STANDING** (b 23 August 1880), was seen as the Earl of Bloomsbury in the film version of *Little Johnny Jones* (1923).

Celli's daughter was an actress under the name Faith Celli (1888–1942), whilst his nephew (Sir) **Guy STANDING** (b London, 1 September 1873; d Hollywood, Calif, 24 February 1937)—seen briefly in Broadway's version of *La Falote* in 1897—married the well-known American musical comedy actress **Isabelle URQUHART** (b New York, 9 December 1865; d Rochester, NY, 7 February 1907, originally Belle Urquhart, *Billee Taylor, Claude Duval, Elfins and Mermaids, The Merry Duchess,* Cora Piper in *Madame Piper,* Mars in *Ixion,* Ensign Daffodil in *Polly,* Venus in *Orpheus and Eurydice,* Mae in *The Marquis,* Cerise Marcel in *Ermine,* Pompanon in *Madelon,* Etelka in *Nadjy,* Dame Caruthers in *The Yeomen of the Guard,* Princess of Granada in *The Brigands,* Iza in *La Grande-Duchesse,* Barbara Bellasys in *The Red Hussar,* etc). By a second marriage, he was the father of actress Kay Hammond, whose son returned to the name his great-grand-uncles had shunned and has had a fine stage career as **John STANDING** [John Ronald LEON] (b 16 August 1934). He appeared in the musical theatre as Clive Popkiss in *Popkiss* (1972).

CELLIER, Alfred (b London, 1 December 1844; d London, 28 December 1891). Composer of London's longest-running musical of the 19th century.

The son of Arsène Cellier, an East London schoolteacher of French descent, and a schoolmate of Sullivan at the Chapel Royal, Alfred Cellier began his musical career as a boy chorister. He continued as a church and concert organist and, for a period, as director of the Belfast Philharmonic, but he ended up by following the same path as his more famous contemporary, as a theatre conductor and composer. His first one-act operetta, *Charity Begins at Home* (1872), was very successfully staged by Thomas German Reed, who had produced Sullivan's early works, as part of the entertainment at his Gallery of Illustration. It proved popular enough to be regularly revived in Britain, played for a season on Broadway, and mounted several times in Australia, and established itself alongside *Cox and Box* and *Ages Ago* amongst the most durable items of the German Reeds' repertoire.

After a period as musical director at London's Court Theatre, during which time he illustrated several of their musical pieces, including a'Beckett's burlesque *Christabel* (1872), with scores ''arranged, with original scraps by . . .,'' Cellier took up a similar post under Charles Calvert at the Prince's Theatre in Manchester. There he supplied incidental scores for productions ranging from Calvert's large-scale *Henry IV* to the annual Christmas pantomime. He took out a Frederic Sullivan tour of *The Contrabandista* in 1874 and, later the same year, had his first full-length comic opera *The Sultan of Mocha,* written to a libretto by an anonymous local gentleman, produced at the Prince's. *The Sultan of Mocha* was received with great delight and was played in Manchester for several seasons before being taken to London in 1876, where it proved itself to be one of the most notable British-written works of that new era of musical theatre which had not long since been set in motion by the French composers of opéra-bouffe.

Manchester produced Cellier's next three full-length works, *Tower of London, Nell Gwynne* and *Belladonna,* without comparable success, as well as an *Aladdin the Great* (1875) written to a text by Alfred Thompson and starring Mrs John Wood and Constance Loseby, but in the meanwhile the composer had left the Midlands and returned to London, where he busied himself providing music for a range of theatres, writing genteel operetta for Reed's Gallery of Illustration, pantomime music for Covent Garden (1878), or incidental music for pieces such as George Lash Gordon's *Millions in It* (1877) and Ross Neil's fairy play *Elfinella* (1878), as the commission demanded. In 1877 he succeeded George Allen as the conductor of the Comedy Opera Company's production of Gilbert and Sullivan's comic opera *The Sorcerer* at the Opera Comique, and he subsequently took musical charge of Richard D'Oyly Carte's productions in Britain, America and Australia on a number of occasions. He conducted the original London productions of *HMS Pinafore* and *Ivanhoe,* the New York *Billee Taylor,* and also supplied a series of highly successful and long-running one-act forepieces for the Savoy operas, before his brother, **François [Arsène] CELLIER** (b Hackney, 14 December 1849; d London, 5 January 1914), definitively took over the position of company musical director, a post which he retained until Carte's death in 1901, and beyond (1902 South African tour, etc).

Alfred continued throughout to turn out a steady stream of vocal and theatre music. His connection with Blanche Roosevelt, a one-time Josephine from London's *HMS Pinafore,* led to her ''Blanche Roosevelt English Opera Company''—which had played *The Sultan of Mocha* in America—producing the première of his musical based on Longfellow's *The Masque of Pandora* at Boston. With Ms Roosevelt starring alongside Hugh Talbot, Charlotte Hutchings, Joseph Greenfelder and W S Daboll, it was a two-week failure. Cellier, however, stayed on for a time in America, and conducted for the Comley-Barton Company's more successful production of *Olivette.*

Back in Britain, he provided a full score of incidental music for the Kendals' 1885 production of *As You Like*

It at the St James's Theatre, but his major success as a composer came in 1886 when George Edwardes, to whose burlesque *Little Jack Sheppard* he had contributed several pieces, produced his comedy opera *Dorothy* at the Gaiety Theatre. A musical revision of the Manchester *Nell Gwynne* score attached to a new libretto by *Charity Begins at Home* librettist, Charlie Stephenson, *Dorothy* was produced whilst the delicately constitutioned Cellier was in Australia, getting a change of air, conducting a comic opera season for the management of Williamson, Garner and Musgrove, and winning himself a certain social success.

Dorothy proved to be a phenomenon. It gave Cellier the biggest song hit of the time in the baritone serenade, ''Queen of My Heart,'' and it ultimately became the longest-running musical show of its era in the London theatre. This overwhelming success resulted in a new West End run for *The Sultan of Mocha,* a production for a Stephenson remodel of *Tower of London* as *Doris* (1889) and a pairing with W S Gilbert for *The Mountebanks* (1892), a work which was completed by Ivan Caryll when Cellier died before finishing his score. *Doris,* which turned out a tenor bon-bon in ''I've Sought the Brake and Bracken,'' and *The Mountebanks* both had good London runs and the latter piece, if not quite at the level of the best of Gilbert and Sullivan's collaborations, was exported with some success.

Some time after his death, some of his music was used as additional material in Frederick Rosse's score for the Rutland Barrington children's musical *The Water Babies,* produced at the Garrick Theatre in 1902 (18 December) and revived there again the following Christmas.

Elegant and infallibly musical, Cellier's work has a refinement and a pretty, somewhat dignified melodiousness, not altogether compatible with his voluble, bohemian character, and lacking only the sense of humor and burlesque gaiety of which Sullivan was capable. This fact renders most unlikely his alleged claim, reported in one Australian paper during his stay there, that during his time as musical director with Carte's company he had been the uncredited composer of *The Pirates of Penzance*'s ''Poor Wandering One.''

François Cellier's son, **Frank CELLIER** [né François CELLIER] (b Surbiton, 23 February 1884; d London, 27 September 1948), also appeared on the musical comedy stage (Rochester in *The King's Diamond,* 1904, etc) in the earliest stages of a notable career as an actor and producer. He was the husband of Florence Glossop Harris, daughter of Sir Augustus Harris.

1872 **Charity Begins at Home** (B C Stephenson) 1 act Gallery of Illustration 7 February

1873 **Dora's Dream** (Arthur Cecil) 1 act Gallery of Illustration 3 July

1874 **Topseyturveydom** (W S Gilbert) 1 act Criterion Theatre 21 March

1874 **The Sultan of Mocha** (?Albert Jarret) Prince's Theatre, Manchester 16 November

1875 **Tower of London** (anon) Prince's Theatre, Manchester 4 October

1876 **Nell Gwynne** (H B Farnie) Prince's Theatre, Manchester 17 October

1877 **Two Foster Brothers** (Gilbert a' Beckett) 1 act St George's Hall 12 March

1878 **The Spectre Knight** (James Albery) 1 act Opera Comique 9 February

1878 **Belladonna** (Alfred Thompson) Prince's Theatre, Manchester 27 April

1878 **After All** (Frank Desprez) 1 act Opera Comique 23 December

1880 **In the Sulks** (Desprez) 1 act Opera Comique 21 February

1881 **The Masque of Pandora** (Stephenson) Boston Theater, Boston 10 January

1883 **Too Soon** (Charles Barnard) 1 act Madison Square Theater, New York 18 February

1886 **The Carp** (Desprez) 1 act Savoy Theatre 13 February

1886 **Dorothy** (Stephenson) Gaiety Theatre 25 September

1888 **Mrs Jarramie's Genie** (w François Cellier/Desprez) 1 act Savoy Theatre 14 February

1889 **Doris** (Stephenson) Lyric Theatre 20 April

1892 **The Mountebanks** (Gilbert) completed by Ivan Caryll Lyric Theatre 4 January

François Cellier also composed a number of short musical plays for the Savoy and co-authored a book on the Savoy operas.

1888 **Mrs Jarramie's Genie** (w Alfred Cellier/Frank Desprez) 1 act Savoy Theatre 14 February

1891 **Captain Billy** (Harry Greenbank) 1 act Savoy Theatre 24 September

1897 **Old Sarah** (H Greenbank) 1 act Savoy Theatre 17 June

1900 **Pretty Polly** (Basil Hood) 1 act Savoy Theatre 8 December

1903 **Bob** (Cunningham Bridgman) 1 act His Majesty's Theatre, Walsall 8 April; Adelphi Theatre 8 June

LES CENT VIERGES Opérette in 3 acts by Clairville, Henri Chivot and Alfred Duru. Music by Charles Lecocq. Théâtre des Fantaisies-Parisiennes, Brussels, 16 March 1872; Théâtre des Variétés, Paris, 13 May 1872.

Paris proved slow to give Lecocq another opportunity after his success with *Fleur de thé,* Belgium seemed a propitious place to be during the Franco-Prussian war and the days of the commune, and Brussels boasted one of the most go-ahead producers around at the time in the person of the enthusiastic Eugène Humbert. These circumstances combined to make Humbert's Théâtre des Fantaisies-Parisiennes the launching pad for the composer's second major work, the delightfully ridiculous and thumpingly saucy *Les Cent Vierges.*

An English colony in the south seas, under the governorship of Sir Jonathan Plupersonn (Alfred Jolly), has been established with a wholly male population. To relieve the pressing situation thus provoked, the government is sending out a shipload of a hundred girls ("vierges"). Unfortunately, the ship gets lost, and the deprived colonists are left to their own resources a bit longer whilst a second load of potential brides is recruited. Pretty French honeymooner Gabrielle (Mlle Gentien) and her bosomy pal Eglantine (Mme Delorme), sightseeing at London docks, get uncomprehendingly included in the hundred and end up heading for the Green Islands, with their husbands, Duc Anatole de Quillembois (Mario Widmer) and Poulardot (Charlier), following in horrified pursuit. By the time the bride-ship gets to its destination, however, all but 14 girls have jumped ship, and Plupersonn decides that they (plus the two extras caught prowling about, who are the two husbands in disguise), will have to be distributed by lottery. The drooling governor and his secretary, Brididick (Nardin), draw the two phony virgins, and the situation winds up to a farcical series of events which are only defused when the original "lost" ship arrives with a chorus of girls for all.

The showpiece of Lecocq's score was Gabrielle's second-act waltz song of homesickness, "O Paris, gai sejour," but the prima donna was well supplied with other numbers, from her opening admission "J'ai la tête romanesque" to her final extravagant burlesque of passion as she seduces the jelly-kneed governor in order to give her husband time to lead the revolt of the womanless islanders ("Je t'aime! Je t'aime!"). Anatole, at first romantic, then plotting in quartet with his wife and the Poulardots, had his best moments in his guise as Emeraldine, getting into character with "J'ai pour mari Barbarini" and following up in the comical quartet with his "mother" (Poulardot) and their "husbands," "A table, chassons l'humeur noire," then, finally, trying to delay the end of their dinner, and what must inevitably follow, with a comical song ("Un vieux et riche Céladon").

Les Cent Vierges was a ringing hit in Brussels and, less than two months from opening night, Eugène Bertrand produced a Paris edition for his Théâtre des Variétés. Anna van Ghell (Gabrielle), Gabrielle Gauthier (Eglantine), Berthelier (Anatole), Paul Hittemans (Poulardot), Kopp (Plupersonn) and Léonce (Brididick) headed the top-class cast, and the piece made it past its 100th performance before being taken up by the stages of the world. The original French version was seen in St Petersburg and in New York, where Marie Aimée's company, with the prima donna as Gabrielle alongside Juteau, Duchesne, Lecuyer and Mlle Bonelli, played the first of several seasons of *Les Cent Vierges* in repertoire, whilst the first foreign-language versions were mounted in Berlin and in Madrid.

As was regularly the case at the time, the Spanish only actually borrowed the libretto of the show and reused it with local music. *El Tributo de la cien donzellas,* a three-act zarzuela by Santisteban, with music by Francisco Asenjo Barbieri, was produced at the Teatro Zarzuela on 7 November 1872.

Franz Jauner at the Vienna Carltheater produced *Hundert Jungfrauen* soon after, with Hermine Meyerhoff (Gabrielle), Karl Blasel (Anatole), Josef Matras (Rumpelmeier, ex- Poulardot), Franz Eppich (Plupersonn), Lori Stubel (Eglantine) and Lecocq's score titivated by Johann Brandl with a sailor song and chorus in Act I, a song for Antonie Link in the travesty character of a sea cadet in Act II, and a quartet in Act III. The show played 24 times straight off and another 15 during the season, was brought back four times more the following year and thrice in 1875. It popped up again in the repertoire in 1878–79 with Carl Streitmann as Brididick (28 December, 5 performances) and was revived yet again in 1900 (17 March).

The first English-language performances of the show seem to have been given in Australia, closely followed by Britain, by then anxious for more Lecocq in the wake of the huge success of *La Fille de Madame Angot.* There had been a brief sighting of *Les Cent Vierges* during a London visit by the Brussels company in 1873, with most of the original cast and Pauline Luigini as Gabrielle, but it had suffered "violent attacks on its immorality" and had had to be taken off. However, this did not stop Mrs Sara Lane putting out a version by the Australian writer William M Akhurst, a version already seen in his home country a few months earlier, under the title *To the Green Isles Direct,* at the Britannia Theatre, Holborn. In September a second, "freely adapted" English version was produced by Mr and Mrs A D McNeil at Edinburgh's Royal Princess's Theatre (*Green Isle of the Sea* 21 September). Mrs Liston's company tried another version (ad John Grantham, Theatre Royal, Brighton 19 October 1874), whilst John Hollingshead produced yet another, by Robert Reece, which was staged under the slightly more titillating title of *The Island of Bachelors,* and which apparently got rid of much of what *The Era* described as that "perilous stuff" without altering the basic plot too much. Constance Loseby and Nellie Farren were the girls, Arthur Cecil and J G Taylor their husbands, and Charles Lyall the Governor through two months of performances. In 1881 the plot was pinched by one Henry Llewellyn Williams for a musical farcical piece called *Blighted Bachelors* (Corn Exchange, Derby 29 August 1881), as played by the ever-touring Milton Ray combine. Lecocq's music was replaced by some poppy selected and arranged tunes.

In America, the show had a rather unusual English-language production, with the multiple disguises of the plot getting a confusing fillip when a remade version of Reece's *The Island of Bachelors* was performed by Kelly and Leon's Minstrels. Leon, as ever, took the prima donna role of Gabrielle, so that while the men of the plot were disguised as women, the leading lady was, in fact, played by a man.

In Paris, *Les Cent Vierges* had a major revival at the Folies-Dramatiques in 1875 with Mlle Prelly, Simon-Max, Luco, Milher and Mlle Toudouze featured, and it was reprised again at the Bouffes-Parisiens in 1885 with Charles Lamy, Mlle Edeliny, Édouard Maugé, Mesmaker and Mlle Keller, but when the show was reproduced at the Théâtre Apollo during the Second World War (15 September 1942), all the British content had, by order, to be removed, and in consequence Albert Willemetz and André Mouëzy-Éon were set to rewrite the piece with all reference to beastly Britons wiped. The music remained untouched, but was occasionally resituated in a libretto which kept the bones of the original, but which now set the first part in France and gallicized the Governor as Duflacnard and his assistant as Clopinette. It also introduced a very funny new character called Marcel, pursuing the wedded but unbedded Gabrielle from Paris to the Green Isles in a barrage of disguises and ultimately winning her whilst her rakish and unsuitable husband returns to his life amongst the girls of the Bal Mabille. Germaine Roger (Gabrielle), Duvaleix (Poulardot), Urban (Duflacnard), Milton (Anatole) and René Lenoty (Marcel) headed the cast. This skillful adaptation—which had the rare quality of actually heightening the comedy of its original—was subsequently staged by Mlle Roger during her management of the Gaîté-Lyrique (1946), with Madeleine Vernon, Pasquali, Léo Bardollet, Robert Destain and Jane Montange, and it has become the standard version of the piece still played in France.

Germany: Friedrich-Wilhelmstädtisches Theater *Hundert Jungfrauen* 5 December 1872; USA: Olympic Theater (Fr) 23 December 1872, Kelly and Leon's Music Hall *The Island of Bachelors* 17 July 1876; Austria: Carltheater *Hundert Jungfrauen* 15 March 1873; UK: St James's Theatre (Fr) 20 June 1873, Britannia Theatre *To the Green Isles Direct* 25 May 1874, Gaiety Theatre *The Island of Bachelors* 14 September 1874; Australia: Opera House, Melbourne 27 February 1874; Hungary: Budai Színkör *Szaz Szüz* (*A zöld Sziget*) 1 July 1874

CHABRIER, [Alexis] Emmanuel (b Ambert, 18 January 1841; d Paris, 13 September 1894).

The youthful Chabrier, who had gone through a couple of years of musical training following his general education, made a couple of half-hearted efforts at writing an opérette to words by the poet Rimbaud (*Fisch-ton-Kan* 1863, *Vaucochard et fils 1er* 1864) and also tried his hand at an opera. However, in spite of a life which, away from his day job with the Ministry of the Interior, was led largely in artistic circles, it was a good number of years before he finally composed a piece which was produced on the commercial stage.

It was those artistic contacts which gave him the opportunity. A meeting with librettist Albert Vanloo, already a force in the musical theatre, persuaded the author and his partner, Eugène Leterrier, to entrust their next libretto to Chabrier and, with their name attached to it, the piece was accepted by Charles Comte for the Théâtre des Bouffes-Parisiens. *L'Étoile* had only a short run and the composer, disappointed, turned away from the genre, contributing, for private performance, only one further piece—a one-act opérette, *Une education manquée,* again to a text by Vanloo and Leterrier. In a successful subsequent career as a composer, the theatrical features were the production of two operas, the heavyweight Scandinavian *Gwendoline* (1886, ''he has out-wagnered Wagner'') and the lighter and more enduring comic opera *Le Roi malgré lui* (1887).

In spite of the limited attention paid to his pieces at the time of their production, Chabrier's works and, in particular, *L'Étoile* have become favorites with a group of enthusiasts and they have won a number of recordings and productions in recent years.

1877 **L'Étoile** (Albert Vanloo, Eugène Leterrier) Théâtre des Bouffes-Parisiens 28 November

1879 **Une education manquée** (Vanloo, Leterrier) 1 act Cercle Internationale de la Presse 1 May

1887 **Le Roi malgré lui** (Emile de Najac, Paul Burani) Opéra-Comique 18 May

Biographies: Martineau, Réné: *Emmanuel Chabrier* (Dorban, Paris, 1910), Myers, R: *Emmanuel Chabrier and His Circle* (Dent, London, 1969)

CHAMPION, Gower (b Geneva, Ill, 22 June 1919; d New York, 25 August 1980). Choreographer and director for several sizeable Broadway successes.

Champion began his career as a dancer, appearing (temporarily as ''Christopher Gower'') in the theatre in such pieces as *The Streets of Paris* (1939), *The Lady Comes Across* and *Count Me In* (1942), in television and in films, both solo (*Till the Clouds Roll By*) and in a partnership with his then wife, **Marge CHAMPION** [née BELCHER, Marjorie Celeste, aka Marjorie Bell] (b Los Angeles, 2 September 1921) (*Mr Music, Show Boat, Lovely to Look At, Give a Girl a Break, Jupiter's Darling, Three for the Show*) up to the mid-1950s. By this time he had already begun a career as a choreographer and director with the revues *Small Wonder, Lend an Ear* and *Three for Tonight,* which top-billed the Champions themselves, and had choreographed his first Broadway book musical, the Hugh Martin/Preston Sturges *Make a Wish* (1951) at the Winter Garden Theater.

Champion directed several pieces, including the George M Cohan musical *Forty-Five Minutes from*

Broadway, for television, but significant theatre success first came his way in 1960, when he directed and choreographed the youth-orientated first musical of Michael Stewart, Lee Adams and Charles Strouse, *Bye Bye Birdie.* This bright-eyed tale of kids, parents and pop music had some memorable staging moments ranging from a tangle of teenage telephone calls, to Chita Rivera's irrelevant but exciting performance of a madcap dance routine in a Shriners' meeting (Tony Awards, direction, choreography).

Champion confirmed his *Bye Bye Birdie* success the next year in Stewart's charming adaptation of the film *Lili* into the long-running *Carnival,* and director and author hit the very biggest time with their third effort together, *Hello, Dolly!* (1964, Tony Awards direction, choreography), in which Champion's staging of the show's title number, with its dancing waiters and extended use of the stage, won particular praise. In 1966 he showed that he was capable of ingenuity without mass spectacle or dancing stars when he directed Robert Preston and Mary Martin in the two-handed *I Do! I Do!* for *Hello, Dolly!* producer David Merrick, for whom he also staged *The Happy Time* (1968), *Sugar* (1972) and *A Broadway Musical* (1978). A further piece from this period, *Prettybelle* (1971), closed out of town.

A colorful rewrite of the old hit musical *Irene,* staged with infectious life and period style, had more luck and more staying power than the inherently downbeat Michael Stewart/Jerry Herman successor to *Hello, Dolly!,* the filmland tale of *Mack and Mabel.* However Champion's last work, the direction and choreography for the stage version of the movie musical *42nd Street* (1980), gave him one more international hit. But the Tony Awards which he was given for both his direction and choreography of the show came posthumously for Champion, who died on the day that *42nd Street* opened on Broadway.

CHANCEL, Jules (b Marseille, 1867; d 1944).

Journalist (*Écho de Paris, Le Gaulois, l'Illustration, Figaro, Charivari* and various provincial papers) and intermittent playwright (*Maîtresse femme, Cercle vicieux, L'Erreur, Son professeur,* the Eldorado saynète *Grandeur et servitude, L'Auréole,* etc), Chancel had his biggest success, in tandem with Léon Xanrof, as the author of the play *Le Prince Consort.* The pair later adapted their play as a libretto for Ivan Caryll under the title *S.A.R.* (*Son Altesse Royale*). They were also responsible for the French version of the libretto of *Ein Walzertraum,* a piece which, for all its acknowledgment of a Germanic source, had a principal plotline very close to that of *Le Prince Consort.*

Chancel was also credited (w Henriot) as the author of the unnamed play from which Paul Lincke's successful Operette *Gri-Gri* was taken, and of that piece's French version.

1908 **S.A.R.** (Ivan Caryll/w Léon Xanrof) Théâtre des Bouffes-Parisiens 11 November

1910 **Rêve de Valse** (*Ein Walzertraum*) French version w Xanrof (Théâtre Apollo)

1924 **Gri-Gri** French version w Henriot (Gaîté-Rochechouart)

CHANNING, Carol [Elaine] (b Seattle, Wash, 31 January 1921).

A hugely blonde and pop-eyed musical comedienne, Carol Channing appeared in a minor capacity in *No for an Answer* (1941) and *Let's Face It!* (1942), before coming properly to the fore for the first time when she was featured by Gower Champion in the 1948 revue *Lend Me an Ear* with its musical comedy burlesque "The Gladiola Girl." This performance helped win her the starring role of Lorelei Lee in the stage musical version of *Gentlemen Prefer Blondes* (1949), in which she created "A Little Girl from Little Rock" and "Diamonds Are a Girl's Best Friend" and a decided reputation for herself as a musical comedienne.

Miss Channing subsequently replaced Rosalind Russell as Ruth Sherwood in Broadway's *Wonderful Town,* toured in the same role (1955) and appeared in the title roles of the short-lived musical *The Vamp* (1955, Flora Weems)—which cast her as another husky, wide-eyed girl-on-the-make—and the showcase revue *Show Girl* (1961), before making her greatest success with an acclaimed performance as the eponymous heroine of *Hello, Dolly!* (1964), introducing the celebrated title song, "Goodbye, Dearie" and "Before the Parade Passes By." She played this role for 18 months on Broadway and subsequently on tour in America before being party to an attempt to bring Lorelei Lee back to Broadway, 25 years after her creation, in a version of *Gentlemen Prefer Blondes* retitled *Lorelei* (1974). The exercise had only a limited success. In 1995, more than 30 years on from her triumph as Dolly Levi, and in spite of less-than-triumphant 1978 (Houston, New York) and 1979 (Theatre Royal, Drury Lane, London) revivals of a broadened and coarsened latter-day version of *Hello, Dolly!,* the star revisited Broadway in her most famous role. Diminishing returns continued to diminish, and the show moved out after 118 performances.

Miss Channing also appeared in her own revue (*Carol Channing with Ten Stout-Hearted Men,* 1970) in Canada, America and in Britain; in a tryout of the Jerry Herman compilation show *Jerry's Girls;* as a blonde Trilby in the television musical *Svengali and the Blonde* (NBC 1955); and contributed to the memorable fun of the musical film *Thoroughly Modern Millie* as a daft champagne-blonde with aeronautic tendencies.

LA CHANSON DE FORTUNIO Opéra-comique in 1 act by Hector Crémieux and Ludovic Halévy. Music by Jacques Offenbach. Théâtre des Bouffes-Parisiens, Paris, 5 January 1861.

The little opéra-comique *La Chanson de Fortunio* was a descendant of de Musset's famous four-act comedy *Le Chandelier,* the principle of which was that if a married woman has an obviously sighing would-be lover around her, a jealous husband will be so busy keeping his eye on the foolish fellow that he will miss detecting his wife's real liaison. *Le Chandelier* was played, until censorship struck it, for a number of years at the Comédie-Française and, during that time, the young Offenbach supplied the music for the song in which the amorous lawyer's clerk, Fortunio, expresses his adoration of his master's wife.

Crémieux and Halévy's pocket-sized piece on the same theme took for its central character the same Fortunio (Désiré), older, now himself a laywer, and married to a young wife, Laurette (Mlle Chabert), who is sighed after by the young clerk, Valentin (Julia Pfotzer). The lawyer's clerks dig up the famous song which did the trick for Fortunio and use it to conquer their girlfriends whilst Valentin makes sufficient progress with Laurette, in spite of her husband's suspicions, to leave him some hope at the final curtain. The chief clerk, Friquet, was played by the lanky comic Bache, the others by girls.

The song, a version of Offenbach's old number, was made over by its composer to suit the light-operatic talents of Mlle Pfotzer rather than the barely singing performance of the Comédie-Française's Daubray, and became the centerpiece of the entertainment, as sung by Valentin as the climax of the show. Valentin, equipped with a drinking song—about water—and his admission of love (''Je l'aime''), Friquet (''C'est moi qui suis le petit clerc'') and the other little clerks had the bulk of the show's music, with Laurette having her moment chiding her husband for his jealousy in ''Prenez garde à vous!''

First produced by Offenbach at the Bouffes-Parisiens, *La Chanson de Fortunio* was both highly admired and hugely enjoyed, and it became one of the staples of the Offenbach repertoire of one-act opérettes, regularly revived over the years in spectacles coupés. Offenbach himself revived it at the Bouffes in 1874, on which occasion Mme Peschard played Valentin to the Laurette of Mdlle Fonti and the Fortunio of the same Daubray who had originally essayed Offenbach's song.

The piece also found great popularity outside France, most particularly in the German language. Carl Treumann mounted the piece (ad Ferdinand Gumbert) at his Theater am Franz-Josefs-Kai in 1861, with himself in the role of Fortunio alongside Anna Grobecker (Friquet), Anna Marek (Valentin) and Therese Schäfer (Laurette). This version, which apparently gave the ''adventure'' to Friquet and introduced Babette the cook (Babet, a grisette, in the original French version), played by Elise Zöllner, as the second boy's love interest, was a great success. Not counting the performances of the original piece given at Treumann's theatre by the Bouffes company in 1862, with Désiré and Mlle Pfotzer in their original roles, *Meister Fortunio* was played no less than 75 times in the repertoire of the Kaitheater, the highest total achieved by any work during the little house's existence. When Treumann returned to the Carltheater, *Meister Fortunio* was played there regularly, Schäfer moving on to play Babette, whilst Karl Blasel (Fortunio) and Hermine Meyerhoff (Laurette) played alongside Grobecker in one of her happiest, remade-to-measure trouser roles. The show was revived at regular intervals in later Viennese years.

Berlin followed with another German version (ad Georg Ernst) whilst, a few months after the Bouffes company had introduced the show to Budapest on their 1861 tour, the Nemzeti Színház brought out an Hungarian version (ad Lajos Csepregi) with Kálmán Szerdahelyi, Vilma Bognar and Ilka Markovits featured, which was to have a similarly long and often reprised career. In America, the piece was first played in the German/Treumann adaptation with Klotz as Fortunio, Hedwig l'Arronge as Valentin and Eugenie Schmitz as Friquet, then, in the original French version, by Bateman's opéra-bouffe company with Irma (Valentin), Francis (Fortunio), Aline Lambèle (Laurette) and Leduc (Friquet), on a double-bill with *Les Bavards.* It remained a regular item on the German theatre's bills for a decade, but this did not apparently encourage anyone to try an English version in New York until 1900.

The first English adaptation seems to have been that produced at London's Gaiety Theatre—already the scene of an 1871 performance by the visiting Brussels Fantaisies-Parisiennes company—in 1876 (ad uncredited) as part of Johnnie Toole's season. W H Leigh was Fortunio, Alice Burville played Lauretta and Miss Stembridge, Valentine, but the piece never caught on in the English-language theatre in the same way that it had in German and French. It did, however, reappear in the repertoire of the Welsh National Opera in 1979.

Le Chandelier itself was subsequently adapted as an opéra-comique by Gaston de Caillavet and Robert de Flers, set to music by André Messager, and produced at the Opéra-Comique 5 June 1907 as *Fortunio* with a considerable success which has led to its survival in the occasional repertoire up to the present day.

Austria: Theater am Franz-Josefs-Kai *Meister Fortunio und sein Liebeslied* 25 April 1861; Germany: Friedrich-Wilhelm-städtisches Theater 21 August 1861; Hungary: Nemzeti Színház (Fr) 13 July 1861, Nemzeti Színház *Fortunio (báj)dala* 21 January 1862; USA: Stadttheater *Fortunioslied* 14 September 1867, Pike's Opera House (Fr) 21 December 1868, American Theater *The Magic Melody* 22 January 1900; UK: Gaiety Theatre (Fr) 1 July 1871, *The Song of Fortunio* 3 January 1876

Recordings: (Bourg, Gaité-Lyrique)

CHANSON GITANE Opérette in 2 acts by André Mouëzy-Éon and Louis Potérat. Music by Maurice Yvain. Théâtre de la Gaîté-Lyrique, Paris, 13 December 1946.

Following the immense success of Lopez's *La Belle de Cadix,* Maurice Yvain, whose greatest stage successes had been with the jazzy musical comedies of the 1920s, collaborated musically on a romantic opérette in the style of the new hit. *Chanson gitane,* lavishly produced at the Gaîté-Lyrique, told the familiar story of Count Hubert des Gemmeries (André Dassary) and the gipsy girl, Mitidika (Mag Walter), whom he marries but for whom he cannot find acceptance in society. She goes back to her people, followed by an accusation of the theft of the diamonds of the Duchesse de Berry, but ultimately the pair come together again to live their lives far away from the prejudices of his people and hers.

Yvain's score had a ready-made hit in the gipsy girl's song ''Sur la route qui va,'' already popularized in the cinema, but it also included a number of delightful new pieces ranging from the hero's ardent solos (''L'Amour qu'un jour tu m'as donné'') and some coloratura for the soprano (Rita Mazzoni) cast as the Duchesse de Berry, to the rhythmic ''Au pas du petit poney'' and a splendid danced ''Aragonesa'' for the heroine and soubrette.

A 10-month run at the Gaîté-Lyrique was followed by Parisian revivals in 1950 and 1954, and provincial productions have continued at regular intervals since, as *Chanson gitane* established itself alongside the very different *Ta bouche* and *Pas sur la bouche* as one of the core items of the composer's stage work.

Recording: selection (Pathé-EMI)

LE CHANTEUR DE MEXICO Opérette à grand spectacle in 2 acts by Félix Gandéra and Raymond Vincy. Lyrics by Henri Wernert and Raymond Vincy. Music by Francis Lopez. Théâtre du Châtelet, Paris, 15 December 1951.

Le Chanteur de Mexico followed behind *La Belle de Cadix* and *Andalousie* in the continuing series of Raymond Vincy/Francis Lopez opérettes, as a vehicle, and an ever more lavish one—mounted this time on the stage of the huge Théâtre du Châtelet—for star tenor Luis Mariano.

Mariano played Vincent Etchebar, a striving singer from Saint Jean-de-Luz who, with his pal Bilou (Pierjac) in tow, goes up to Paris to try his luck in the big city. They fall in with pretty Cri-Cri (Lilo), and before long Vincent wins a competition and, without knowing it, the heart of Cri-Cri. The opérette singer Eva (Jacqueline Chambard) needs someone to replace her tenor, Miguelito, who is refusing to go on tour to Mexico, and Vincent gets the job. When he arrives in South America, he gets mixed up with the rebel Zapata (Robert Jysor) and the whip-cracking Tornada (Monique Bert)—both of whom are after the real Miguelito—and events both hair-raising and amorous make up the action of the second act before the happy ending arrives with its ritual pairing-off.

The songs of *Le Chanteur de Mexico* were in the already recognizable Lopez vein, and existed very largely for the benefit of Vincent/Mariano. He yodelled out the praises of ''Mexico'' and ''El Tequila,'' crooned to the ''Rossignol de mes amours'' and his ''Mateïchu,'' got misty over his home-town in ''Il est un coin de France'' whilst nevertheless insisting that ''Je me souviendrai d'Acapulco'' and, from way above the city—in one of the evening's most appreciated stage pictures—commented on what it was like ''Quand on voit Paris d'en haut.'' The other principals got the odd look in, Cri-Cri coming out the best with her ''Ça me fait quelqu'chose,'' Eva waltzingly admitting that she is ''Capricieuse'' and Zapata pounding out the regulation baritone number which had become a feature of the Vincy/Lopez shows since *La Belle de Cadix*'s ''Le Coeur des femmes.''

Le Chanteur de Mexico was all it was designed to be: a first-rate vehicle for Mariano and a splendid stage spectacle, and if it was a little less fresh and attractive than the two preceding vehicles, the public enjoyed it just as much. They filled its vast theatre for a year for Mariano and then a second year for his successor, Rudi Hirigoyen—no taller than Mariano, but equipped with a popular tenor voice which did masculine miracles with the music. By the time the show finished its first Paris run, it had clocked up 905 performances.

In 1956 Mariano teamed with Bourvil (Bilou), Tilda Thamar (Eva) and Annie Cordy (Cri-Cri) to put *Le Chanteur de Mexico* on film in what proved, in spite of some rather lopsided cutting of the original story line, to be one of the most popular French musical films of its time. As for the show, there can scarcely have been a year in the some 50 since its first performances where it has not toured or played at least one provincial French house, remaining one of the most frequently played of all Lopez's popular early works.

Film: Richard Pottier 1956

Recordings: complete (Festival), selections (Odéon, etc)

CHAPÍ [y Llorente] Ruperto (b Villena, Alicante, 27 March 1851; d Madrid, 25 March 1909).

Chapí studied at the Madrid Conservatoire and worked as a musician in theatre orchestras and as a military bandmaster whilst taking his first steps as a composer. He followed further studies in Rome, in his twenties, and made an attempt at operatic composition—several of his operatic pieces being produced in Madrid (*Las naves de Cortés, La hija de Jefté, Roger de Flor, La muerte de Garcélaso*)—but in the 1880s he returned to the light musical theatre where, nearly a decade after the production of his first zarzuela, he found an initial success with *La tempestad* (lib: M Ramos Carrión, Teatro de Jovellanos 2 March 1882), a three-act musical version of Erckmann-Chatrian's *Le Juif polonais.*

Amongst the list of more than 150 full-length and, mostly, short zarzuelas that he subsequently composed, the three-act *La bruja* (lib: Carrión, Vital Aza Teatro de la Zarzuela 10 December 1887), the shorter *Los tentaciones de San Antonio* (lib: A Ruesga, V Prieto, Teatro Felipe 20 August 1890), which was played in Italian in both Italy and Vienna, *El rey que rabío* (lib: Carrión, Vital Aza Teatro de la Zarzuela 20 April 1891), produced in Hungary as *Az unatkozó király* (Népszínház 10 December 1898), and *La revoltosa* (lib: Jose Lopez Silva, Carlos Fernandéz Shaw, Teatro Apolo 25 November 1897) proved some of the most successful at home and, occasionally, abroad.

Chapí also continued to write operatic scores, his three-act opera, *Circe,* being mounted as the opening attraction at Madrid's Teatro Lirico in 1902, followed by a *Don Juan de Austria* and his final work *Margarita la Tornera,* and devoted himself as well to the foundation and running of the Spanish performing rights society.

Chapí's other works included *Abel y Cain* (1873) *La calandria* (1880), *Los dos huérfanas* (1880), *Música clásica* (1880), *La calle de carretas* (1880), *Nada entre dos platos* (1881), *La Flor de lis* (1884), *El milagro de la Virgen* (1884), *El Guerrillero* (1885 w Arrieta, Manuel Fernández Caballero), *El Pais de Abaniro* (1885), *Término medio* (1885), *Los quintos de mi pueblo* (1885), *¡Ya pican!, ¡Ya pican!* (1885), *El domingo gordo* (1886), *El figón de las desdichas* (1887), *Playeras* (1887), *Los lobos marinos* (1887), *El fantasma de los aires* (1887), *Ortografía* (1888), *El Cocodrilo* (1889), *A casarse tocan* (1889), *Las hijas del Zebedeo* (1889), *Nocturno* (1890), *Todo por ella* (1890), *La leyenda del rey monje* (1890), *¡Las doce y media y serena!* (1890), *Los nuestros* (1890), *Los alojados* (1891), *El mismo Demonio* (1891), *Los trabajadores* (1891), *La bala del rifle* (1892), *El organista* (1892), *Las campanadas* (1892), *El reclamo* (1893), *Los gendarmes* (1893), *Via libre* (1893), *El Duque de Gandía* (1894 w A Llanos), *La Czarina* (1894), *El moro muza* (1894), *El tambor de Granaderos* (1894), *El cura del regimiento* (1895), *Mujer y reina* (1895), *El cortejo de la Irene* (1896), *El Señor Corregidor* (1896), *La gitanilla* (1896), *El bajo de arriba* (1896), *Los golfos* (1896), *Las bravías* (1896), *El niño del estanguero* (1897), *El segundo de legeros* (1898), *Pepe Gallardo* (1898), *La chavala* (1898), *Curro Vargas* (1898), *Los hijos del batallón* (1898), *El fonografo ambulante* (1899), *La cara de Dios* (1899), *La seña Frasquita* (1899), *Los buenos mozos* (1899), *La cortijera* (1900), *Maria de los Angeles* (1900), *El gatito negro* (1900), *Mississippi* (1900), *El estreno* (1900), *El barquillero* (1900), *Blasones y talegas* (1901), *¿Quo vadis?* (1901), *El sombrero de plumas* (1902), *El puñao de rosas* (1902), *Plus ultra* (1902), *La venta de Don Quijote* (1902), *El tio Juan* (1902), *El rey mago* (1903), *El equipage del Rey José* (1903), *La chica del maestro* (1903), *La cuna* (1904), *La tragedia de Pierrot* (1904), *La guardia de honor* (1905), *Miss Full* (1905), *El seductor* (1905), *La leyenda dorada* (1905), *El hijo de Doña Uraca* (1905), *El amor en sol-fa* (1905 w J Serrano), *El alma del pueblo* (1905), *La sobresalienta* (1905), *La reina* (1905), *La cortijera* (1906), *La joroba* (1906), *El maldito dinera* (1906), *El Triunfo de Venus* (1906), *La pesadilla* (1906), *El rey del petróleo* (1906), *La fragua de Vulcano* (1906), *La patria chica* (1907), *El pino del norte* (1907), *Ninon* (1907), *Los veteranos* (1907), *El gallo de la pasión* (1907 w J Valverde, J Q Valverde), *La carabina de Ambrosio* (1908), *El merendero de la alegria* (1908), *La Doña roja* (1908), *Las mil maravillas* (1908), *Las Madrileñas* (1908), *Las calderas de Pedro Botero* (1908), *Aquí hace farta un hombre* (1909), *Los majos de plante* (1909), *El diablo con faldas* (1909), *La magia de la vida* (1910), *Entre rocas* (1910), *Los mostenses, Las peluconas, Los guerrilleros,* etc.

Biographies: Salcedo, A S: *Ruperto Chapí, su vida y sus obras* (Cordoba, 1929), Aguilar Gómez, J: *Ruperto Chapí y su obra lirica* (Excma, Alicante, 1973), Sagardía, A: *Ruperto Chapí* (Espasa-Calpé, Madrid, 1979), Iberni, L G: *Ruperto Chapí* (ICCMU, Madrid, 1995)

LES CHARBONNIERS Opérette in 1 act by Philippe Gille. Music by Jules Costé. Théâtre des Variétés, Paris, 4 April 1877.

Les Charbonniers is a little piece about a pair of coal merchants—Thérèse Valbrezègue (Anna Judic) and Pierre Cargouniol (José Dupuis)—with a quarrel. They take their grievances before the local undersecretary to the comissioner of police (Baron) and, by the time they are through putting across their points of view, they have come to have more than a little liking for each other. Léonce rounded out the cast as Tardivel, an interrupting running-joke of a fellow with a need for a passport.

Decorated with a pretty score by Jules Costé, which comprised a trio, a duo, a Chanson du Coucou (''Deux paysans, hors du village''), some Couplets (''Ah! mais, monsieur! Ne me chatouillez pas comme ça!'') for Judic and an air for Dupuis (''Mais regardez-moi ces bras-là!''), *Les Charbonniers,* played initially on a double bill with Edmond Gondinet's vaudeville *Professor pour dames,* gave all concerned a welcome success. So great a hit did the it prove that manager Bertrand—allegedly in gratitude, but with a weather eye to publicity—opened his second gallery free to the coal-merchants of Paris, on the condition that they came, black-faced, from their work. The little piece proved to be remarkably durable, and it was played in several other countries and languages over the 25 years following its first appearance, as well as being revived on several occasions in Paris.

Many cities were introduced to *Les Charbonniers* by the busily traveling Judic, who retained it as a supporting item for a number of years. Vienna saw its first performance during her visit to the Theater an der Wien in 1883, and then another, played in a spectacle coupé with *Le Fiacre 117.* When the star returned to the Carltheater in 1889 (4 May), on the same tour in which she introduced *Les Charbonniers* in London, she played the piece again, and in 1892 she brought it back yet again. The Carltheater had, however, long since introduced a German-language version, with musical interpolations by Brandl, which was mounted immediately following the Paris production with Hermine Meyerhoff, Karl Blasel, Franz Eppich and Hildebrandt in the cast, as a curtain-raiser to the French farce *Bébé.* It was given 30 times over a 12-month period. The German version appeared again as late as 1901 (30 October), when it replaced a version of *Trial By Jury* as a forepiece to a ballet at Danzers Orpheum.

Budapest's Népszínház mounted an Hungarian version (ad Jenő Rákosi) on a double bill with Offenbach's *Ancsi sir, Jancsi nevet* (*Jeanne qui pleure et Jean qui rit*) in 1878 and that version was revived frequently (Vígszínház 5 November 1901, etc).

The show's text was used as the basis for several other pieces, with music by other hands replacing Costé's tunes, amongst them the little London musical *A Shower of Blacks* (ad Walter Parke, Arthur Shirley, mus: Ernest Bucalossi, Terry's Theatre 26 December 1887) and a Lewis Clifton/J W Houghton piece called *Cuckoo.* A later London adaptation of the piece, played as *The Judgement of Paris,* which retained Costé's music, was mounted as a forepiece at the Lyric Theatre in 1897 with Marie Elba, Homer Lind and A S Winckworth in the cast, whilst a fresh Hungarian version, *Szenesek, ha szerelmesek,* was seen at Budapest's Vígszínház as late as 15 June 1940.

Germany: Friedrich-Wilhelmstädtisches Theater September 1877; Hungary: Népszínház *Szenes legény, szenes lány* 18 January 1878; Austria: Carltheater *Der Kohlenhandler von Paris* 1 February 1878; Theater an der Wien (Fr) 18 November 1883; UK: Gaiety Theatre (Fr) 8 June 1889; Lyric Theatre *The Judgement of Paris* 30 October 1897

CHARELL, Erik [LÖWENBERG, Erich Karl] (b Breslau, Germany, 9 April 1895; d Zug, 15 July 1974).

A dancer, turned choreographer, turned director, Charell made his name as a stager of the 1920s entertainments at the Grosses Schauspielhaus, Berlin. The earliest of these were revues (*An Alle* 1924, *Für dich* 1925, etc), highly colored pieces relying on much in the way of spectacular scenery and special effects, many and glittering costumes and much gymnastic and regimented mass dancing, and Charell subsequently carried these revusical techniques over into large-scale productions of musical plays, including the theatre's homemade versions of the grandiose *Casanova* (1928) and *The Three Musketeers* (1929), and the Berlin production of Fall's *Madame Pompadour* with Fritzi Massary and Max Pallenberg starred. He was altogether less happy with his gimmicky productions of such classics as *The Mikado* and *Die lustige Witwe,* both of which were transported out of their era and setting to allow for glitzy scenic display and a mass of extraneous dancing, with texts lazily rewritten when they refused to be forced into his ''concept.'' Both these productions were lambasted by press and public, and the disaster of the jazzed-up *Die lustige Witwe* production led Massary, the queen of the Berlin musical stage, to quit the musical theatre.

In 1930 Charell had his most memorable success when he staged the Grosses Schauspielhaus's world première of *Im weissen Rössl.* Put into the Austrian mountains, miles from the nearest spangle and shimmy-step, he created a genuine piece of coherent large-stage theatrical spectacle around the famous old play and the songs supplied by house composer Benatzky and others, contributing sufficiently to the show's creation as a whole to later be given an intermittent author's credit. He was also billed as author of the Grosses Schauspielhaus's 1926 show *Von Mund zu Mund* (1 September, mus: Herman Darewski). He followed up his biggest stage triumph with a second major success, this time in the film world, when he directed the spectacular movie *Der Kongress tanzt* in 1931.

Charell subsequently directed *White Horse Inn* and *Casanova* in Britain and *L'Auberge du Cheval Blanc* in Paris with equivalent success, but he was shorn of his job in Berlin by the Nazi régime and encouraged to leave Germany. An attempt to create a new Benatzky pasticcio spectacular on a circus theme in London (*The Flying Trapeze* Alhambra Theatre, 1935) was an expensive failure and an attempt at *Swingin' the Dream* (1939) for Broadway was a 13-performance flop, but a decade later, having now returned to peacetime Germany, he put the circus idea to good use when he took the tiny Swiss musical *Der schwarze Hecht* and, giving it a rewrite and a typically whooped-up staging full of tricks and effects, turned it into the highly successful *Feuerwerk* (1950). He also collaborated on turning *Der Kongress tanzt* into a stage musical, first produced at the Théâtre Royal, Liège in 1976.

1950 **[Das] Feuerwerk** revised *Der schwarze Hecht* (Paul Burkhard/Jürg Amstein, Robert Gilbert/w Amstein) Bayerisches Staatsoperette, Munich 16 May

1976 **Le Congress s'amuse** (*Der Kongress tanzt*) (Hermann Thieme/w Alain Melville, Franz Geiger ad Robert Deniau, Tommy Banyai, André Hornez) Théâtre Royal, Liège 17 December

CHARIG, Phil[ip] (b New York, 31 August 1902; d New York, 21 July 1960).

Songwriter Charig showed up on Broadway for the first time in 1926, when his ''Sunny Disposish'' (ly: Ira Gershwin) earned him notice alongside the Gershwin brothers' material in the revue *Americana* at the Belmont Theater. This success set him off on a short-lived flush of theatre composing, beginning with the Chicago revue *Allez-Oop* (1927 w Leo Robin) and two book musicals for Broadway: *Yes, Yes, Yvette* and *Just Fancy* (''You Came Along'' w Joseph Meyer, Robin).

Under the aegis of the publishers Chappell, he was paired with the young British composer Vivian Ellis on the score for a British touring musical based on *Peg o' My Heart;* contributed additional numbers to the score put together by ''Doc'' Szirmai, at that time based in Britain, for the not unsuccessful *Lady Mary* (''You Came Along,'' ''I've Got a Feeling for Somebody''); and was set to work to supply a score for the Jack Buchanan/Elsie Randolph vehicle *That's a Good Girl.* ''Fancy Our Meeting,'' ''The One I'm Looking For,'' ''Sweet So-and-So'' and the rest of that show's songs were all improbably credited to a five-sided combine of musicians and lyricists, but the result was sufficiently accommodating for Buchanan two years later to order from Charig (paired this time with Ellis) a second score for *Stand Up and Sing* (''There's Always Tomorrow,'' ''It's Not You,'' ''Stand Up and Sing'').

Helped by the frenzied fashion for American music and composers in Britain at the time, Charig was also allotted the score for Weston and Lee's *Lucky Girl,* and, in between times, he supplied the American stage with scores for ephemeral musicalizations of Belascos's *Polly with a Past* (*Polly*) and Rudolf Lothar's *The Phantom Ship* (*The Pajama Lady*) but, after some four or five years had passed without another ''Sunny Disposish'' appearing, his services became less in demand. Following a short-lived musical called *Nikki,* which had the peculiarity of starring filmland's Fay Wray and Douglas Montgomery and of featuring the young Archie Leach (later Cary Grant) in its cast, Charig vanished from the Broadway and West End lists for over a decade.

He returned with the score for the lively, loose-limbed wartime show *Follow the Girls,* which gave him a sizeable success in New York and in London—despite including nothing outstanding in the way of music and producing only one number, the suggestive ''I Wanna Get Married,'' that garnered its composer notice. In 1955 his name was attached with those of Sammy Fain, Jerry Bock and Neil Simon to a quickly gone revue, *Catch a Star!,* at Broadway's Plymouth Theater, a piece which marked Charig's exit from the musical theatre, 30 fairly discreet years after his first appearance.

1927 **Yes, Yes, Yvette** (w Ben Jerome/Irving Caesar/James Montgomery) Harris Theater 3 October

1927 **Just Fancy** (w Joseph Meyer/Leo Robin/Joseph Santley, Gertrude Purcell) Casino Theater 11 October

1927 **Peg o' Mine** (w Vivian Ellis/Desmond Carter/Fred Jackson) Empire Theatre, Sunderland, England 31 October

1928 **That's a Good Girl** (w Meyer/Douglas Furber, Carter, Ira Gershwin) London Hippodrome 5 June

1928 **Lucky Girl** (Furber/R P Weston, Bert Lee) Shaftesbury Theatre, London 14 November

1929 **Polly** (w Herbert Stothart/Caesar/Guy Bolton, George Middleton, Isabel Leighton) Lyric Theater 8 January

1930 **The Pajama Lady** (w Richard Myers/R B Smith, John Mercer/H B Smith, George Lederer) National Theater, Washington, DC 6 October

1931 **Stand Up and Sing** (w Ellis/Furber, Jack Buchanan) London Hippodrome 5 March

1931 **Nikki** (James Dyrenforth/John Monk Saunders) Martin Beck Theater 29 September

1944 **Follow the Girls** (Dan Shapiro, Milton Pascal/Guy Bolton, Fred Thompson) Century Theater 8 April

CHARITY BEGINS AT HOME Operetta in 1 act by B C Stephenson. Music by Alfred Cellier. Gallery of Illustration, London, 7 February 1872.

An early collaboration by the authors of *Dorothy,* this little piece—the first from the pen of composer Cellier—was written for the German Reed family's drawing-room entertainment at the Gallery of Illustration. Stephenson's book, supported by a small and sparkling score, dealt with the efforts of a tiny village school, threatened with closure, to come up to the inspector's demands, and allowed the performers—Mrs Reed, Alfred Reed, Corney Grain and Fanny Holland—to disguise themselves as school pupils for some comical scenes and songs with the Inspector (Arthur Cecil). Along with *Cox and Box* and *Ages Ago, Charity Begins at Home* proved to be the most enduringly successful of all the many German Reed productions, was regularly revived over the next 30 years (St George's Hall 1874, 1876–79, 1892, 1902) and became a popular choice as a forepiece and a benefit item in the Victorian theatre.

John McCaull and Charles E Ford programmed *Charity Begins at Home* (with *Ages Ago*) as the opening attraction for Broadway's Bijou Theater and, with a cast including Digby Bell and Carrie Burton, the little piece played for nearly two months on Broadway, before being sent on tour. It was subsequently taken up in other English-speaking theatres around the world, and in the 1890s was played throughout America by W T Carleton's company as a curtain-raiser to *The Lily of Killarney,* under the title *The Charity Girls.* As late as 1902, it turned up at Pittsburgh's Duquesne Garden, played on a double bill with *Cavalleria Rusticana!*

USA: Bijou Theater 31 March 1880; Australia: Princess Theatre, Melbourne 5 February 1887

CHARLIE GIRL Musical comedy in 2 acts by Hugh and Margaret Williams and Ray Cooney. Music and lyrics by David Heneker and John Taylor. Adelphi Theatre, London, 15 December 1965.

An up-to-date version of the Cinderella story, at one stage angled towards being a comedy vehicle for Cicely Courtneidge, *Charlie Girl* was ultimately produced in London under the management of Harold Fielding with the former film star and musical comedy ingenue Anna Neagle top-billed alongside popular singer Joe Brown. She was Lady Hadwell, the impoverished owner of Hadwell Hall and the mother of three daughters—two suitably ladylike, and the third a scruffy tomboy (Christine Holmes). He was the ''Buttons'' of the affair, the estate handyman, Joe, with an easygoing manner and a heart full of love for the youngest daughter, Charlie. Prince Charming arrives on the scene in the person of Jack Connor (Stuart Damon), the dreamboat son of Lady Hadwell's old chorus-line buddy, Kay (Hy Hazell), who married American and very, very rich, but Cinderella and the Prince do not get together in this version. Joe wins the pools, saves the stately home, and ends up with his Charlie, whilst Jack contents himself with the more obvious possibilities of her elder sister. In a flashback to the earliest days of modern musical comedy and the famous role of Roberts in *The Lady Slavey,* Derek Nimmo appeared as a pools man who agrees to stand in as a butler to impress the visitors and thereafter contributes most of the evening's comedy.

The show's score mixed the tones of the modern popular music world in Charlie's ''Like Love'' and ''Bells Will Ring'' with Joe's cockney praises of ''Charlie Girl'' and old-time music hall ''Fish and Chips,'' and with some more gracious material for Miss Neagle who closed the first act, setting off for the ball on the arms of the male chorus, with a smiling admission that ''I Was Young (when this last happened to me).'' Jack admired his perfect profile to ''What's the Magic?' and suffered horrors at an apparent rejection (''That's It?''), the two old girlfriends plotted a marriage between their offspring in ''Let's Do a Deal'' and Kay walloped out her enjoyment of ''The Party of a Lifetime,'' whilst, instead of singing, Nimmo went through a routine in which he displayed his double-jointed toes to the audience at length.

Charlie Girl, almost universally damned by the critics, proved to be a combination of elements which throughly appealed to the public. It ran for five-and-a-half years (2,202 performance) in the West End, with Miss Neagle and Nimmo holding their roles throughout, and put itself into the top league of London long-runs before heading on to Australia. There, with Miss Neagle and Nimmo starring alongside local pop star Johnny Farnham, it proved a surprise hit all over again. Business was so great on the first stop of what was supposed to be a tour, that the entire Australian season was spent in Melbourne, with time only for a quick visit to Auckland, New Zealand, on the way home.

The show was not toured in Britain, but 20 years on Fielding revived it, in a revised version, at London's Victoria Palace (19 June 1986), with Cyd Charisse in a personalised version of Miss Neagle's role alongside Paul Nicholas, Lisa Hull, Dora Bryan, Mark Wynter and Nicholas Parsons. After a 246-performance run in town, the show finally went to the British provinces, with Nicholas and Bonnie Langford paired alongside former ballerina Doreen Wells, in what had now become a dance role, as Lady Hadwell.

Australia: Her Majesty's Theatre, Melbourne 25 September 1971

Recordings: original cast (CBS), Australian cast (HMV), London revival cast (First Night), etc

CHARLOT, André (b Paris, 26 July 1882; d Woodland, Calif, 20 May 1956).

André Charlot was one of the earliest producers to introduce the modern style of variety-based revue to prewar London and subsequently, with C B Cochran, the most successful purveyor of this kind of entertainment in Britain. He first appeared on the London scene with the George Grossmith/Melville Gideon revue *Kill That Fly!* at the Alhambra in 1912, eight months after the earliest important such entertainment, *Everybody's Doing It,* had been produced at the Empire and two before *Hullo, Ragtime* made its appearance at the Hippodrome.

Between the wars he kept up a steady stream of revue productions in London, took both his 1924 and 1925 productions to New York, and, at the same time, intermittently and rarely successfully tried his hand at book musicals. The first of these, *Flora* (1918), lasted two months, in spite of having Gertie Millar in the title role; a London production of Jerome Kern's *Very Good Eddie* (1918) vanished in 46 performances; and the loose-limbed musical farce *The Officers' Mess* (1918) proved the best of the group with a total of 200 performances in two theatres. An unrecognizably ''adapted'' version of Charles Cuvillier's *Son p'tit frère* played 112 performances at the Comedy Theatre under the title *Wild Geese,* but *Now and Then* (1921), virtually a revue, failed in two months and a badly mangled version of Willemetz and Christiné's delicious *Dédé* (1922) survived only 46 performances at the Garrick before being tricked out revusically and sent on the road as *The Talk of the Town* in a vain effort to recoup.

It was 1930 before Charlot looked at a libretto again and that was for a show part musical play and part cabaret, Robert Katscher's novel Revue-Operette *Die Wunder Bar.* Its tidy 200-performance West End run may have been responsible for his venturing to Vienna to produce Miklòs Brodszky's *Die verliebte Königin* at the Johann Strauss-Theater, and his staging of another Continental piece, Hans May's *Dancing City* (*Der tanzende Stadt*) at the London Coliseum in 1935. He shouldn't have. The latter piece, a vast operetta spectacular with Lea Seidl and Franco Foresta starred, proved a total flop and was the last book musical Charlot produced.

CHARNIN, Martin [Jay] (b New York, 24 November 1934).

Charnin originally ran parallel writing and performing careers and, within weeks of his first lyrics being professionally performed in the off-Broadway revue *Kaleidoscope* (1957), he appeared on Broadway in the original cast of *West Side Story* (Big Deal). He wrote material for several more off-Broadway revues—*Fallout* (1959), *Pieces of Eight* (1959), *The Little Revue* (1960), *Seven Come Eleven* (1961)—before working on his first book musical, the short-lived *Hot Spot,* in 1963. His next two musicals failed to make it to Broadway, Lionel Bart's *La Strada,* for which he supplied ''additional material'' with Elliott Lawrence, was a one-performance flop, and it was 1970 before he tasted success, in a collaboration with Richard Rodgers on the Danny Kaye musical *Two by Two.* However, the musicalized cartoon strip *Annie* (1977, ''Tomorrow,'' ''Easy Street,'' ''You're Never Fully Dressed without a Smile'') more than made up for previous disappointments, giving its lyricist his one, but very considerable, international theatre success to date.

Charnin has produced and directed for television (notably several compilation shows related to musical theatre), for the straight theatre and for the nightclub circuits where he has performed his own ''An Evening With Martin Charnin.'' He conceived and mounted the cabaret revue *Upstairs at O'Neals* (1982) and *The No Frills Revue* (1987), and he directed the musical *Starcrossed: The Trial of Galileo* in 1994 at the Goodspeed Opera House, a revival of his *Mata Hari* for the York Theater Company in 1996, various productions of *Annie,* and in 1999 a ''revised'' version of the classic *Bless the Bride* at London's King's Head Theatre Club.

His most successful non-theatre song to date has been ''The Best Thing You've Ever Done,'' introduced by Barbra Streisand.

1963 **Hot Spot** (Mary Rodgers/Jack Weinstock, Willie Gilbert) Majestic Theater 19 April

1963 **Zenda** (Vernon Duke/w Leonard Adelson, Sid Kuller/Everett Freeman) Curran Theater, San Francisco 5 August

1967 **Mata Hari** (Edward Thomas/Jerome Coopersmith) National Theater, Washington, DC 18 November

1968 **Ballad for a Firing Squad** revised *Mata Hari* Theater de Lys 11 December

1970 **Two by Two** (Richard Rodgers/Peter Stone) Imperial Theater 10 November

1977 **Annie** (Charles Strouse/Thomas Meehan) Alvin Theater 21 April

1979 **I Remember Mama** (Richard Rodgers/w Raymond Jessel/Meehan) Majestic Theater 31 May

1981 **The First** (Bob Brush/w Joe Siegel) Martin Beck Theater 17 November

1990 **Annie 2** (Strouse/Meehan) Kennedy Center, Washington, DC 4 January

1992 **Annie Warbucks** revised *Annie II* Marriot's Lincolnshire Theater, Chicago 9 February; Variety Arts Theater, New York 9 August 1993

1995 **Can-Can** revised libretto (Goodspeed Opera House, East Haddam)

1999 **Bless the Bride** revised libretto (King's Head Theatre Club, London)

CHASSAIGNE, Francis (b Belgium, ?1848; d Paris, December 1922). French composer of two major English-language hits.

Chassaigne studied music in Brussels and began his composing life by writing popular songs (Thérésa's ''Jeanne la sabotière,'' ''Les Leçons d'anglais'' w Paul Boisselot as interpolated regularly by Aimée, etc) and a long list of small theatrical pieces for production at the Eldorado and other Parisian cafés-concerts. In 1883 Brasseur gave him his chance to compose a full-length work for the Théâtre des Nouveautés, to a libretto signed by no less experts than Leterrier and Vanloo, but in spite of all the care and casting lavished on it *Le Droit d'aînesse* was only a semi-success in Paris. Elsewhere, however, it was a very different case for, under the title of *Falka,* H B Farnie's English version of *Le Droit d'aînesse* triumphed hugely in Britain, America, Australia and South Africa, toured for decades throughout the English-speaking world, and was even used as the basis for another British comic opera-burlesque, *Brother Pelican.*

A similar, if less extravagant, reaction greeted his only other full-length work for the Paris stage, *Les Noces improvisées* (1886) which, after only a fair run at the Théâtre des Bouffes-Parisiens, once again found markedly more favor on foreign shores, and most notably in America, under the title, in Alfred Murray's English translation, of *Nadgy.* That outstanding New York success was undoubtedly the reason for the production, two seasons later, of a full-length piece called *The Brazilian,* commissioned directly from the composer and *Falka* remaker Farnie for Broadway's Casino Theater by its manager Aronson. However, *The Brazilian* (or *La Mexicana* as Farnie had originally called the piece sketched out before his death), did not succeed in giving the French composer a third English-language success.

1868 **À qui la faute** (Louis de Romain) 1 act Alcazar

1869 **Matou dix-sept** (Romain) 1 act Eldorado 15 November

1872 **Un coq en jupon** (Lucien Delormel, Germain Villemer) 1 act Eldorado 4 July

1872 **La Bergère de Bougival** (Delormel, Villemer) 1 act Eldorado 20 July

1873 **Un double clé** (Jules de Rieux) 1 act Eldorado 1 February

1873 **Les Horreurs de carnaval** (Auguste Jouhaud) 1 act Eldorado 27 February

1873 **Monsieur Auguste** (de Rieux) 1 act Eldorado 3 May

1873 **L'Héritage de Madame Angot** (de Rieux, Villemer) 1 act Eldorado 24 October

1874 **Une nuit de Mardi Gras** (Jouhaud, Villemer) 1 act Eldorado 27 January

1874 **Le Professeur de tyrolienne** (Villemer, Delormel) 1 act 21 March

1874 **Une table de café** (de Rieux, Alexandre Guyon) 1 act Eldorado 25 July

1875 **Les Tyroliens de Pontoise** 1 act Eldorado 17 November

1876 **Deux mauvaises bonnes** (Delormel, Louis Péricaud) 1 act Eldorado 11 November

1877 **À l'américaine** (Alphonse Siégel) 1 act Eldorado 10 November

1877 **Trois têtes dans un bonnet** (Jouhaud, Péricaud, Villemer) 1 act Concert du 19ème 6 March

1877 **Les Enfants de la balle** (Delormel, Péricaud) 1 act Eldorado 24 March

1877 **La Famille de Paméla** (Delormel, Péricaud) 1 act Eldorado 11 August

1878 **La Tache de sang** (Gaston Marot) 1 act Eldorado 12 January

1878 **Actéon et la centaure Chiron** (de Leuven) 1 act Palais-Royal 28 January

1878 **Un vieux rat** (Louis de Gabillaud) 1 act Concert Européen 24 May

1878 **Une servante qui jure** (Charles Blondelet, Félix Beaumaine) 1 act Eldorado

1878 **Les Frères Paléale** (Siégel) 1 act Eldorado 24 September

1879 **Une Demoiselle de compagnie** (Péricaud, Delormel) 1 act Eldorado 20 March

1879 **Claude l'ivrogne** (A A Charles) 1 act Eldorado 22 April

1879 **Un Concièrgicide** (''Hermil'' [ie, Ange Milher], Numès) 1 act Eldorado 23 August

1881 **Zizi** (A Philibert, Siégel) 1 act Eldorado

1883 **Le Droit d'aînesse** (Eugène Leterrier, Albert Vanloo) Théâtre des Nouveautés 27 January

1886 **Les Noces improvisées** (Armand Liorat, Albert Fonteney) Théâtre des Bouffes-Parisiens 13 February

1890 **The Brazilian** (Max Pemberton, William Lestocq ad Edgar Smith) Theatre Royal, Newcastle upon Tyne 19 April; Casino Theater, New York 2 June

Other title attributed: *Tog* (Hermil, Numès)

LE CHÂTEAU DE TIRE-LARIGOT Opérette fantastique in 3 acts by Ernest Blum and Raoul Toché. Music by Gaston Serpette. Théâtre des Nouveautés, Paris, 30 October 1884.

The spirit Alcofribas (Lauret) has been condemned by the Devil to rebuild the Château de Tire-Larigot, but he cannot, for the Château is doomed to stay a ruin until the honor of the Valpointu family has been revenged upon those Saint-Roquets who once upon a time did them unforgiveable wrong. Since there are now no Valpointus left, the portrait of the old Marquis (Berthelier) comes down from his frame, and tries to seduce the new wife (Jeanne Andrée) of the very distant last descendant of his old enemy, Saint-Roquet (Brasseur). But the paiting of Saint-Roquet also turns from paint to flesh, and a three-act battle for the virtue of the lady, involving many a disguise and picturesque location, ensues.

Illustrated with a score by Serpette, who was becoming the most attractive Parisian composer of such fantastical pieces, *Le Château de Tire-Larigot* played for over a hundred performances in its first run, was briefly revived the following year, and found its way onto the program of Budapest's Népszínház (ad Viktor Rákosi) the year after that.

Hungary: Népszínház *As összedült kastély* 23 January 1886

LA CHATTE MÉTAMORPHOSÉE EN FEMME Opérette in 1 act by Eugène Scribe and Mélèsville, based on the vaudeville by the same authors and the fable by La Fontaine. Music by Jacques Offenbach. Théâtre des Bouffes-Parisiens, Paris, 19 April 1858.

A rare venture by the aged Scribe into the modern musical theatre, the remake of his little play of ''the cat changed into a woman'' made up into a distinctly successful short opérette which was played around the world for several decades.

Set (for some reason) in Biberach in Swabia, the piece had for its central character a distressed fellow called Guido (Tayau), a Trieste businessman who has fallen on hard times. To make ends meet, he is obliged to get rid of everything he owns, even his cat which he adores with an almost unnatural passion. The charlatan Dig-Dig (Désiré) comes to his house and offers a little metempsychosis: he will transfer the soul of the cat into the body of a young woman. Suddenly the cat-like Minette (Lise Tautin) is there, and Guido is delighted, to say the least, and then distraught when he finds that his housekeeper Marianne (Marguerite Macé) has already sold "the cat" to the governor's wife. Of course, it is all a trick. Dig-Dig is Guido's wealthy uncle's intendant in disguise and Minette is the cousin whom Guido has always refused to marry. The outcome is satisfactory all round. The governor's wife can have the real cat, and Minette will be Guido's wife.

The score gave Minette some delightful feline moments, including a trilly Air to Brahma and a miaou song, as well as a big love duo and an eating trio; Marianne had a introductory song ("Le Ciel a voulu dans sa sagesse") with which to set things going; and Dig-Dig and Guido joined in a comical invocation to the forces of metempsychosis.

First produced at the Bouffes-Parisiens just months after Hervé's Folies-Nouvelles had mounted its particular little metempsychosis musical, *Bel-Boul, La Chatte métamorphosée en femme* was a fine success. It was maintained in the theatre's repertoire for some time thereafter and it was also played by the Bouffes company during their foreign tours. This led to several local adaptations appearing in its wake, the first of which was that played in Budapest, at the Nemzeti Színház (ad Endre Latabár, Kálmán Szerdahelyi), two seasons after the French company's visit. Carl Treumann included *Die verwandelte Katze* in the repertoire at his little Viennese Kaitheater, and the libretto pleased sufficiently for Julius Hopp to turn out a version (presumably of the original vaudeville) with his own music attached (Theater an der Wien, 1865), and for Theodor Hauptner also to venture an *Die entzauberte Katze* seen both in German and Hungarian versions. An English remake of the original vaudeville produced at the Princess's Theatre in 1859 (ad Robert Keeley 27 October) under the title *Puss, or Metempsychosis* introduced two songs, including one from Offenbach's opérette for leading lady Louise Keeley, but the complete opérette was later produced by the German Reeds at the St George's Hall where it shared the bill with the first production of Sullivan's *The Contrabandista.* Mlle Anna was the cat, Harriet Aynsley Cook the housekeeper and Mr Neilson played Dig-Dig. New York got an English-language version when the Kelly and Leon minstrels produced *The Enchanted Cat* in 1876 with Leon playing Marianne alongside Kelly, Edwin Lester and J H Surridge.

Intermittently played in the 20th century, *La Chatte métamorphosée en femme* was again seen in 1986 on the program of the Carpentras Offenbach Festival.

USA: Theatre Français (Fr) 21 November 1859, Kelly and Leon's Opera House *The Enchanted Cat* 5 February 1877; Hungary: Budai Népszínház 12 July 1861, Nemzeti Színház *Az átváltozott macska* 12 October 1863; Austria: Theater am Franz-Josefs-Kai *Die verwandelte Katze* 25 September 1862; UK: St George's Hall 18 December 1867; Australia: Opera House, Sydney 6 September 1879

CHAUMONT, Céline (b Paris, 1848; d Paris, 4 February 1926).

After a good half-dozen years in the theatre, Mlle Chaumont made a memorable debut on the musical stage, at the age of 21, in the leading feminine role of Régina in Offenbach's *La Princesse de Trébizonde* (1869) at the Théâtre des Bouffes-Parisiens. In spite of limited vocal means, she scored a considerable personal success through her charm, excellent diction and her undoubted ability as an actress with a particular way with a double entendre ("with no more voice than a cat when you squeeze her tail, she contrives by artful singing to put more expression into the music than could be imagined"). She subsequently starred in Hervé's *Le Trone d'Écosse* (1871, Flora), caused a sensation as the undone heroine of the exceedingly near-the-knuckle tale of Vasseur's *La Cruche cassée* (1875, Colette) and created the feminine leading role of Lecocq's *Le Grand Casimir* (1879, Angelina, and revival 1884). She visited London in 1872 to play *La Princesse de Trébizonde* at the St James's Theatre, and again for a fortnight of comedies and songs ('La première feuille,'' 'La noce à Clémence,'' etc) at the Opera Comique in 1876, but the largest part of her subsequent career was spent making a highly successful place for herself in the non-musical theatre where she created, amongst others, the role of Cyprienne in Sardou's famous *Divorçons.*

She later took over the management of the Palais-Royal for a period, and subsequently moved into teaching drama.

CHEIREL, Jeanne [LERICHE, Jeanne] (b Paris, 18 March 1868; d Paris, 26 October 1934).

A niece of the actress and singer Augustine Leriche (thus the anagrammatic stage name), who had appeared in many vaudevilles and opérettes during a long and highly successful theatrical career (*La Femme à papa, Rip, La Fiancée en loterie, La Geisha, L'Amour mouillée, Madame Putiphar,* etc), the young Jeanne began her stage career as an straight actress with Victor Koning at the Gymnase (*Frou-Frou, Sapho, L'Abbé Constantin,* etc). She subsequently moved, in succession, to the Variétés, the Porte-Saint-Martin (*Le Crocodile*) and, in 1890, the Palais-Royal (*Le Paradis, Un fil à la patte, Coralie et Cie,* etc). Although she had in her early days performed as a vocalist at the Scala café-concert, she did not make her first appearance on the musical stage until some time later, when she appeared in the unsuccessful opérette, *Le Commandant Laripète* (1892), at the Palais Royal. She subsequently created the role of the prudish Marquise, Edith de Chatellerault, in the enormously successful *Les Fêtards* (1897) at the same house.

A career of more than 20 years as a "solide et sure" leading actress on the Paris stage prefaced a memorable return to the musical theatre, in her fifties, as the conniving "Countess" in the Jazz Age musical comedy *Ta bouche* (1922, "Des terres et des coupons") and, thereafter, she became the model of the musical middle-aged character lady of charm, using her agreeable light baritone singing voice in specially written roles and numbers in a series of similarly styled musical comedies: Hortense in *Madame* (1923); La Baronne Sakrinkolovitz in *Gosse de riche* (1924, "Combine," "Avez-vous compris?," "Quand on est des gens du monde"); a memorable Mlle Poumaillac in *Pas sur la bouche* (1925, "Quand on n'a pas ce qu'on aime," "O Sam!"), in which she actually got the ingenue's man in the final reel; as Hélène in Reynaldo Hahn's *Le Temps d'aimer* (1926) at the Michodière; and in Marcel Lattès's richly cast *Le Diable à Paris* (1927) alongside Dranem, Raimu, Edmée Favart and Juliette Simon-Girard.

In her later days she also made a fine name on the cinema screen.

Plate 70. **Jeanne Cheirel.** *A juvenile leading lady who became a character lady par excellence in the Parisian Jazz Age theatre.*

LA CHERCHEUSE D'ESPRIT Opéra-comique in 1 act by Charles S Favart. Music taken from various sources. Théâtre de la Foire Saint Germain, Paris, 20 February 1741.

A sweetly rustic piece, in which Madame Justine Favart starred as a simple girl whose mother insists she lacks "esprit," but who nevertheless ends up marrying the young man she likes instead of being stuck—as mama had intended—with his widowed father. Enormously popular, it was played on its initial production for more than two hundred successive nights, a vast run for the period, and was frequently revived both in France (including performances both at the Académie Royale de Musique 1 March 1778, and the Opéra-Comique 22 February 1900 ad Weckerlin) and abroad, proving one of the most successful of such entertainments to come from the French stage.

No one is credited with the compilation of the 70 musical fragments taken from popular melodies ("Tes beaux yeux, ma Nicole," "L'Autre Jour Colin," "Attendez-moi sous l'orme," "Diversité flatte le gout," etc) which made up the show's original musical illustration, but there have been a number of subsequent attempts to rearrange or replace the pasticcio score, notably by Jules François Pillevesse (Théâtre du Vaudeville 2 June 1863) and by the young Edmond Audran (1864 Gymnase, Marseille and later in Paris, Alcazar 1888).

In Offenbach's *Madame Favart,* the actress's offstage performance of *La Chercheuse d'esprit* is the key to the happy ending of the plot.

UK: Little Haymarket Theatre 28 November 1749; Germany: Munich 1749

THE CHERRY GIRL Musical play in 2 acts by Seymour Hicks. Lyrics by Aubrey Hopwood. Music by Ivan Caryll. Vaudeville Theatre, London, 21 December 1903.

Following the success of *Bluebell in Fairyland,* Charles Frohman and Seymour Hicks attempted to repeat the show's pattern with another seasonal fairy-play-cum-musical-comedy. This time Ellaline Terriss played Pansy, a little girl in a London attic, who changes places with the Queen of the Pierrots and gets into all sorts of adventures with a nice white pierrot (Seymour Hicks) and a nasty black one (Stanley Brett). Thanks to an opportunely introduced magic talisman, everyone zoomed off

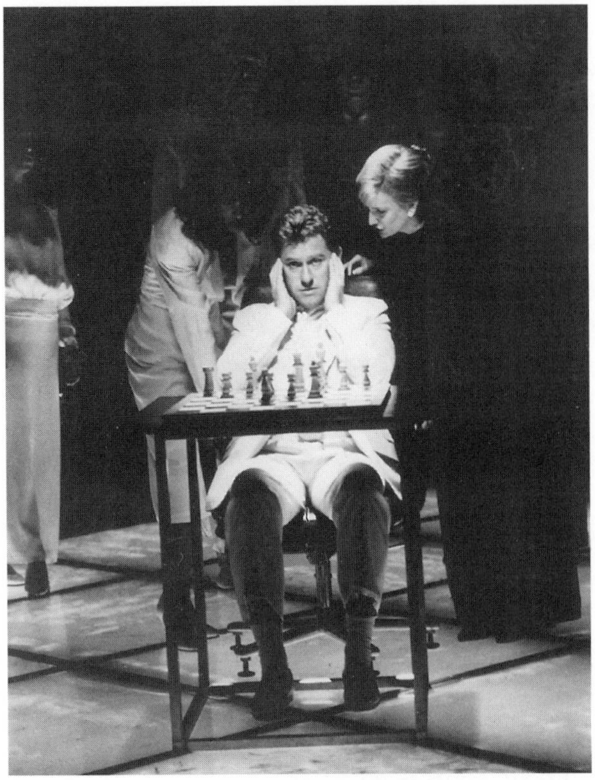

Plate 71. **Chess.** *Anatoly (Tommy Korberg) tries to concentrate on winning the world championship whilst distractions surge in on him from every side.*

to 18th-century England in the second half. The Ivan Caryll score was supplemented by a veritable mass of popular American songs ("Little Yellow Bird," "Rip van Winkle Was a Lucky Man," "My Little Hong Kong Baby," "Dixieland Cakewalk"), in the "borrowing" style Hicks favored, mostly for the benefit of himself and his wife, whilst tenor Courtice Pounds got to serenade "Fascinating Frou-Frou of the Frill" and joined Murray Hill to sing of "When the Stars Are Shining in the Sky." Pounds, however, got into trouble when it was decided that one of his comedy lines insinuated that the makers of the beef extract Bovril used horse meat for their product. Bovril attacked Frohman, and the line had to be tactfully (if transparently) altered.

Staged with the same fairy-tale glamour as *Bluebell,* and largely featuring children and dancing alongside its sing-along songs, *The Cherry Girl* was a distinct success in 215 London performances and a tour, without winning the repeat productions the earlier show had done.

CHESS Musical in 2 acts by Tim Rice. Music by Björn Ulvaeus and Benny Andersson. Prince Edward Theatre, London, 14 May 1986.

A collaboration between British librettist and lyricist Rice and the two male members of the famous Swedish popular singing group Abba, *Chess* was founded on an idea which Rice and Andrew Lloyd Webber had long juggled about as a possible topic for a musical, in the wake of the mediasization of the game of chess in the Bobby Fischer years. Originally written and produced, *Jesus Christ Superstar*–style, as a concept recording, and subsequently performed in concert in Europe in 1984, the sung-through *Chess* was ultimately brought to the stage in London in 1986, under the management of Robert Fox. Its production encountered a major setback when director/choreographer Michael Bennett fell terminally ill after the casting and designing had been done, and Trevor Nunn (director) and Molly Molloy (choreography) were brought in to replace him through an expensively extended rehearsal period, in which they attempted to fit a differently felt production into the already established settings and casting.

The World Chess Championship is being played at the picturebook Tyrolean town of Merano, between the American Frederick Trumper (Murray Head), and the Russian Anatoly Sergeievsky (Tommy Korberg). The temperamental, loud-mouthed Trumper is accompanied by his manager and girlfriend, Hungarian-American Florence Vassy (Elaine Paige), whilst Sergeievsky is surrounded by a vast backup team, headed by the finagling Molokov (John Turner), determined that he shall not lose national prestige by a defeat. The whole event, under the management of a theoretically impartial Arbiter (Tom Jobe), is surrounded by considerations of merchandising, profit-making and national propaganda poorly masked under a domino of sport. A sympathy springs up between the Russian and Florence, the edgy Trumper loses his temper, his confidence and the match, and the previously forbearing Florence walks out on him to join Sergeievsky who celebrates his win by defecting. A year later, he defends his title in Bangkok against a new Molokov-supported Soviet. Molokov plots with American TV-man Walter de Courcey (Kevin Colson) to exchange Florence's long imprisoned father for a chess-table triumph for his man, and Sergeievsky's abandoned wife, Svetlana (Siobhan McCarthy), is brought from Russia in an attempt to destabilize the champion. With unexpected support from Trumper, Sergeievsky keeps his concentration and wins, but then returns to Russia. Perhaps to ensure the liberty of Florence's father—if he is still really alive.

Chess won itself a place in the hit parades before the opening of the show when the mistress/wife duet "I Know Him So Well," as sung by Miss Paige and Barbara Dickson, topped the charts. Murray Head's performance of the atmospheric "One Night in Bangkok" followed suit, becoming a hit throughout Europe, but the stage production threw into relief several other numbers from a score which was as rich in outstanding songs as any other of the past 20 years: the Russian's determined ''Who Needs a Dream?'' and his soaring pop tenor Anthem (''My Land''); the American's flaming tantrum of self-justification ''Pity the Child,'' with its scalding use of the high tenor register; Florence's gentle ''Heaven Help My Heart'' her heated ''Nobody's on Nobody's Side''; and the pair of duets with Sergeievsky: the awkward getting-to-know-each-other of the Mountain Duet and ''You and I.'' A comical moment was provided by two English Embassy officials, prissily processing the defector's papers (Embassy Lament) and another by Molokov and his men (''The Soviet Machine''), whilst the Endgame section of the score, with Sergeievsky striving to win his match as distractions pound at him from all sides, was a fine and theatrically effective moment of concerted music.

The production at the Prince Edward Theatre showed little sign of any of the earlier problems except in the ''One Night in Bangkok'' number, which there had been insufficient time to choreograph into a proper dance routine as originally intended. On a stage dominated by banks of television screens, and a vast floor of chessboard squares from which arose a dazzling mountainside scene, the drama of the piece and its music powered through to enormous effect. *Chess* played for three years (1,209 performances) in London.

Curiously, one person was not happy with *Chess,* and that was director Nunn. He shunned his production throughout its run and, when the time came for the show to be produced on Broadway, he rejected the London staging and devised a different production. In the decades-old tradition of the Shubert producing firm, *Chess* was botched. The piece was reshaped, bits of dialogue tacked in, music cut and other music—at least by the show's original writers and not, as in the old days, from outside songwriters—put in to replace it. The alterations proved ill-judged (the unsympathetic portrait of the show's American character even brought forth risibly touchy mumblings of anti-Americanism!), the new *Chess* (ad Richard Nelson), with David James Carroll, Philip Casnoff and Judy Kuhn in its central roles, was unhappily received, and the production folded in 68 performances.

If the alterations made for this production were largely abandoned thereafter, the show seemed nevertheless fated to be one of those which are eternally fiddled with by foreign hands. Some of the alterations were claimed to be justified by the changed political situation and the fall of the communist world—for events had made *Chess* a period piece rather more swiftly than had seemed likely. Rather more of them were simply the efforts of other directors to produce a *Chess* in line with their own imagination: a rare opportunity in the fin de siècle musical theatre, where breath-for-breath reproductions of major musicals had become the rule. Both on tour and regionally in America—where, in spite of its short Broadway life, *Chess* had won many friends—and on tour in Britain and in Australia, later productions were mounted under the command of directors given an apparently free hand, even to the extent of altering the text and score to fit their concepts. Australia's version, which cast the piece curiously young and set the entire tale and its romance in one brief championship in Bangkok, rather unbalanced affairs by bolstering the part of the Russian wife with an extraneous (ex-Broadway version) number in a lively, colorful production which lost the moody drama of the original and failed to find an audience for more than six months.

In 1992, whilst a production in New Zealand which featured Head and Korberg in their original roles went stirringly through a four-city tour of longer seasons than was normal in that lightly populated land, *Chess* made a discreet return to New York. This time it was played off-Broadway (Master Theater 1 February, 83 performances), with a reduced cast. Later the same year, as English-language productions of varying versions and in varying stagings continued, the piece made its first stage appearances in Europe when an Hungarian version (ad Ágnes Romhányi) was produced at Budapest's Rock Színház (1992), and a German-language version was mounted at St Polten in Austria in early 1993. The Hungarian version was revived for a second season in 1995 (6 October).

USA: Imperial Theater 28 April 1988; Australia: Theatre Royal, Sydney 3 February 1990; Hungary: Rock Színház/Arizona 29 May 1992; Austria: Stadttheater, St Polten 13 March 1993; Germany: Baden-Baden 5 February 2000

Recordings: concept recording (RCA), American cast (RCA), concert version Gothenberg 1994 (Mono)

Literature: Hartson, W: *Chess: The Making of the Musical* (1986)

CHEVALIER, Maurice [Auguste] (b Ménilmontant, 12 September 1888; d Paris, 1 January 1972). Parisian music-hall star who became Hollywood's singing very-Frenchman.

After an early career spent performing in cafés and suburban music halls, Chevalier scored his first significant success at Marseille. Soon after, he made his earliest Paris stage appearances, featuring in a minor capacity in revue at the Folies-Bergère under such stars as Mistinguett and Morton. During the war years he established himself alongside Mistinguett at the head of the Folies bill, and in 1921 made his initial appearance on the musical-comedy stage, starring as Robert Dauvergne, the irresponsible and louche best friend of the hero of *Dédé,* the show with which Albert Willemetz and Henri Christiné followed up their enormous hit, *Phi-Phi.*

Although his role was not the title one, it was made up to give the top-billed star an infinity of chances for applause, and his songs, the gently loping "Dans la vie faut pas s'en faire" and the sexually generous "Je m'donne" became popular hits in a hit show. Announced by Cochran for a London version of the show and by Dillingham for a Broadway one, he did neither, but instead followed up the next year in Paris in another successful Jazz Age musical comedy, Maurice Yvain's *Là-haut,* in which he played the recently deceased Evariste, returning to earth and his lady under the eye of a guardian angel. Again he had songs made to measure ("Si vous n'aimez pas ça n'en degoutez pas les autres," "C'est Paris"), but he also had a co-star in the brilliant comedian Dranem who, as the angel, managed to pretty well wipe him off the stage. Chevalier walked out of the show, and ended his musical theatre career.

Thereafter came the straw hat and the 1930s Hollywood films (*The Love Parade, One Hour with You, Love Me Tonight, Folies-Bergère,* etc), including one or two tenuously based on stage musical shows (*The Smiling Lieutenant, The Merry Widow* w Jeanette MacDonald), until his popularity abruptly faded and he returned to France and the variety stage. A mixture of music hall and movies filled most of the 1950s and 1960s, musically marked by appearances in his seventies in the films *Gigi* (1958, Honorine, "I'm Glad I'm Not Young Any More," "Thank Heaven for Little Girls"), *Can-Can* (1959) and the non-musical digest of *Fanny* (1961).

Memoirs: *C'est l'amour* (Julliard, Paris, 1960) in English as *With Love* (Little, Brown, Boston, 1960), *Môme à cheveux blancs* (Presses de la Cité, Paris, 1969) in English as *I Remember It Well* (Macmillan, New York, 1970), *Maurice Chevalier's Own Story* (Nash & Grayson, London, 1930), *The Man in the Straw Hat* (Cromwell, New York, 1949), etc; Biographies: Rivollet, A: *Maurice Chevalier: De Ménilmontant au Casino de Paris* (Bernard Grasset, Paris, 1927), Willemetz, A: *Maurice Chevalier* (Rene Kistler, Paris, 1954), Harding, J: *Maurice Chevalier* (Secker & Warburg, London, 1982), Boyer, W: *The Romantic Life of Maurice Chevalier* (Hutchinson, London, 1937), Bret, D: *Maurice Chevalier: Up on Top of a Rainbow* (Robson, London, 1992) Behr, E: *The Good Frenchman: The True Story of the Life and Times of Maurice Chevalier* (Villard Books, New York, 1993), etc

LES CHEVALIERS DE LA TABLE RONDE Opéra-bouffe in 3 acts by Henri Chivot and Alfred Duru. Music by Hervé. Théâtre des Bouffes-Parisiens, 17 November 1866.

A burlesque of the heroic age, which was only marginally connected with the Arthurian legend, *Les Chevaliers de la table ronde* was Hervé's first attempt at a full-length opéra-bouffe. The young Chivot and Duru provided him with a libretto perhaps a little less zany than he might have fabricated himself, but the result was, if not a triumph, at least a fair success which boded well for what was to come.

Angélique, daughter of the Duke of Rodomont (Milher) has been brought up by her preceptor, Merlin, in ignorance of the existence of love, but the time comes when this incomprehension is wiped out by a young troubadour called Médor. However, Rodomont has set up a great tournament with his daughter as prize, and thus the young man is obliged to get himself into knightly gear to attempt to win his fair one. Alas, he blows it, and it is the wandering knight, Roland (Hervé), who takes the prize. This infuriates the enchantress, Mélusine (Delphine Ugalde), who desires Roland for her own, and at the victory banquet she slips a mickey finn into his winning wine. Mélusine whisks the "dead" knight off to her enchanted gardens, and Rodomont throws most of the rest of the cast into jail, but his comical Duchess, Merlin and his seneschal escape and find their way to Mélusine's garden disguised as a trio of tumblers. The Duke and his daughter and the little troubadour—in varying disguises—all get in on the act as well, and in the end papa is fooled into letting his daughter and her minstrel pair off, leaving Mélusine to her knight.

The score of the piece was thoroughly in Hervé's "bouffe" manner, including such pieces as a "tragic" solo for the Duke—which burst into a tyrolienne—a "famously catchy, feverish rondo" and caricatures both of the minstrel songs of the middle ages and of the Italian and Meyerbeeresque opera.

The cast included Joseph Kelm, Léonce, Garnier, Jannin, Desmonts, Mlle Castello, Mlle Darrier and Mlle Linden.

Following its goodish Paris run the piece was given at the Brussels Fantaisies-Parisennes, whose company brought it to Britain in the summer of 1871 with Paola Marié as Angélique, Mlle Gentien as Mélusine, Mario Widmer as Médor, Charlier as the Duke, Alfred Jolly as the seneschal and Hervé himself guesting as Roland. Subsequently, the Holborn Amphitheatre set up an English version (ad G M Layton) under the title *Melusine the Enchantress.* The production was, however, seriously underfunded, and since the producer objected to paying hire for Hervé's orchestrations he had his musical director make over the piano score. Rose Lee appeared as Mélusine, with the music-hall comic-dancer Marie Barnum as Angélique and Fred Sullivan as the Duke, in a short-lived season.

Les Chevaliers de la table ronde was revived at the Folies-Dramatiques in 1872 (3 March) "with new music added" and with the company's newest recruit, the soon to be famous Vauthier, in the supporting role of Merlin.

UK: Gaiety Theatre 8 July 1871, Holborn Amphiheatre *Melusine the Enchantress* 17 October 1874

CHICAGO Musical vaudeville in 2 acts by Fred Ebb and Bob Fosse based on the play by Maurine Dallas Watkins. Lyrics by Fred Ebb. Music by John Kander. 46th Street Theater, New York, 3 June 1975.

Miss Watkins's ''satirical comedy'' *Chicago* was a 182-performance success when mounted on Broadway in 1926 (30 December) by Sam H Harris, with Francine Larrimore in the role of the murderess Roxie Hart, freed to spend her life touring as a gape-worthy attraction in vaudeville thanks to the efforts of a three-faced, money-grubbing lawyer and a manipulable press.

The 1975 musical based on the play followed its outlines fairly securely. It played up the show-business side of the story and eliminated some of the newspaper-world portion of the original, cutting one of the play's principal characters, a newspaperman, and building up the role of Velma Kelly, a rival murderess with showbusiness ambitions, from almost nothing to a major part.

When the furniture salesman whom Mrs Roxie Hart (Gwen Verdon) has been screwing on the side decides to call it a day, she shoots him dead and, to her amazement and horror, she is arrested. In the prison run by Mama Morton (Mary McCarty) Roxie soon discovers that the one thing a soon-to-be-tried murderess has to have on her side is lawyer Billy Flynn (Jerry Orbach), a skin-smooth talking machine who has never yet lost a case for a female client. Under his tutelage, a sensational, if fiction-studded, interview with newspaper sob sister Mary Sunshine (M O'Haughey) gets Roxie on the nation's front pages. She's suddenly big news, and she takes to it like a lemming, squeezing out the up-to-then newsworthy Velma Kelly (Chita Rivera) with her tales, and getting herself the prime trial date Velma had counted on. Tutored by Flynn, she gives a fine performance on the big day, only to find, as she is acquitted, that there has been a sensational multiple murder in a nearby court and she is now nothing but yesterday's news. The front-page photos are a thing of the past. There is nothing left in life for Roxie Hart, famous for a few days, a few weeks even, except to hit the lesser vaudeville circuits in a slightly notorious double act with the equally passé Velma Kelly.

The score of *Chicago* included many suitably show-bizzy numbers which became popular both in the show and, particularly with theatre folk, outside it: Velma's slinky introduction to the age of jazz, sex and liquor, ''All That Jazz,'' the mercenary Billy's twinkle-toothed creed ''All I Care About (is love)'' and his belief that ''Razzle Dazzle'' is all you need in life, dumb cluck Amos Hart's identification of himself as ''Mr Cellophane,'' and the sextet of murderesses relating the circumstances of the crimes they didn't commit in the ''Cell Block Tango.'' Velma and Mama Morton duetted sourly about whatever happened to the ''Class'' they so clearly lack, Mary Sunshine—played by a falsetto male—touched on the coloratura as she twittered out her belief that ''There's a Little Bit of Good in Everyone,'' whilst Roxie cooed out the praises of the ''Funny Honey'' husband who she thinks is going to take the rap for her, and finished each half in tandem with Velma, giving out with the realization that ''(I am) My Own Best Friend'' and a vaudevillesque hymn to ''Nowadays.''

The story was played like a succession of vaudeville acts on a black-hole of a stage, with the accompanying jazz band, perched above the action, under the leadership of a conductor who also announced the ''turns.'' This style of presentation gave the opportunity for a number of director/choreographer Bob Fosse's characteristic dance pieces of which Billy's entrance, in a shower of pink feather fans, was the most amusing, and everything danced by Misses Verdon and Rivera was unforgettable.

Chicago played 898 performances on Broadway before going into a series of overseas productions. A German production (ad Erika Gesell, Helmut Baumann) was mounted in Hamburg in 1977, whilst in Britain a slightly shabby production originating at the Crucible Theatre in Sheffield was transferred to London's Cambridge Theatre, with Antonia Ellis, Jenny Logan and Ben Cross featured, for 590 performances. This success sparked a number of further provincial productions in Britain before, in 1981, Australia's Sydney Theatre Company produced *Chicago* with Nancye Hayes, Geraldine Turner and Terence O'Donovan featured. It proved highly successful and the show was brought back for several further Australian seasons.

On the wings of a concert performance staged in the *Encores!* series at City Center in 1996 (2 May), a major revival of *Chicago* was remounted on Broadway (Richard Rodgers Theater 14 November) with the leading players of that concert—Ann Reinking (Roxie), Bebe Neuwirth (Velma), James Naughton (Billy) and Joel Grey, featured as Amos Hart—in a version which went even further towards the staged-concert concept than the original had done. This minimalist production—a black stage, a pair of stools, a glittering orchestra and Reinking's as-stunning-as-remembered recreation of Fosse's dance routines—was a great success, transferring to the Shubert Theater (12 February 1997) and, whilst folk whispered seriously about its ''new relevance'' in the light of the flim-flammy trials of such as President Clinton and O J Simpson, establishing itself there as a long-running hit. A similar reproduction was soon mounted in Britain (Adelphi Theatre 18 November 1997) with Ruthie Henshall, Ute Lemper and Clarke Peters featured and the piece won a better West End reception than it had first time round and settled in for an extended West End run with a swiftly turning-over roll call of well-known perfomers, including Chita Rivera now playing Roxie a quarter of a century on, taking over the leading roles.

On the wings of this new success for the show, Budapest's József Attila Színház (7 February 1998), Vienna's Theater an der Wien (23 September 1998), with Rainhard Fendrich, Friederike Haas and Anna Montanaro featured, and Berlin's Theater des Westens (25 September 1999) took in major revivals. An open-ended run was set up at Las Vegas's Mandalay Bay Hotel (3 March 1999) and the piece was also brought out for its umpteenth Australian revival as *Chicago,* in its second coming, turned itself into an even bigger international hit than it had been first time round.

Germany: Thalia Theater, Hamburg 21 May 1977, Theater des Westens 4 April 1987; UK: Cambridge Theatre 10 April 1979; Austria: Theater an der Wien 28 February 1979; Australia: Sydney Opera House/Drama Theatre 6 June 1981; Hungary: Szegedi Nemzeti Színház 20 May 1994

Recordings: original cast (Arista), Australian cast (Polydor), Broadway revival cast 1996 (RCA), London revival cast (RCA), Austrian revival cast live (RCA)

CHILPÉRIC Opéra-bouffe in 3 acts and 4 tableaux by Hervé. Théâtre des Folies-Dramatiques, Paris, 24 October 1868.

One of the most successful of extravagantly humorous full-length opéras-bouffes written and composed by the playwright/composer Hervé, *Chilpéric* went even further in its almost surreal burlesque humor than Meilhac and Halévy had done with their recent texts for Offenbach's *La Belle Hélène, Barbe-bleue* or *La Grande-Duchesse de Gérolstein.* Hervé went back to the medieval era, so successfully used by Offenbach and Tréfeu in *Geneviève de Brabant,* for his subject matter, and he alighted on the Merovingian King Chilpéric I of Neustria and Soissons, whose lastingest claim to fame (apart from this opéra-bouffe) seems to have been that he was the first monarch to construct a circus in Paris. Chilpéric's life and career were decorated with murderous women. His second wife, Galswinthe, was murdered by Frédégonde, who became his third wife, and who subsequently came to clutches with Galswinthe's sister, Brunehaut. All these dangerous ladies turned up in Hervé's opéra-bouffe.

Frédégonde (Blanche d'Antigny, a late replacement for *Oeil crevé* star Julia Baron) starts the evening as an innocent little shepherdess, but she is spotted during the course of a hunt by the randy king (Hervé) and whisked off to court to be royal laundress, etc. No one else is very pleased, not Frédégonde's peasant swain, Landry, nor Chilpéric's brother Sigebert (Berret), nor, especially, his brother's Spanish wife Brunehaut (Caroline Jullien), who had lined up her sister Galswinthe (Mlle Berthal) as a wife for the King, intending then to assassinate the royal couple and claim the throne herself by kinship. Since this Spanish marriage brings advantages of state, however, it is still on, and when it becomes imminent Chilpéric has to get rid of the slightly used Frédégonde. But Frédégonde has shown remarkable powers of adaptation in her swift transformation from shepherdess to royal plaything, and she doesn't let herself be evicted quietly. She screams, howls, and sings embarrassing top Cs all round the throne room. And now the murdering starts. Brunehaut has seduced Landry and persuaded him to kill Frédégonde, Frédégonde has attracted the court chamberlain, Le Grand Legendaire, and has asked him nicely to strangle Galswinthe on her wedding night, whilst Chilpéric has become deeply suspicious of Brunehaut's machinations and ordered the court doctor (Milher) to slip her something poisonous. Everything comes to a peak in the nuptial chamber on the royal wedding night, when the King has slipped out for a bit to defend his city against an irritatingly untimely attack by a disloyal brother. The three would-be murderers attack, the three women fight back, and in the dark it all gets very confused before someone presses a button which sends the whole lot of them—and the bed—straight down to the dungeons. Chilpéric wins his little battle, pops back home and sorts everyone out in time for a jolly finale with no deaths and only a little bit of stripping and whipping.

Hervé's lively score was as full of fun as his libretto, with Frédégonde being particularly well-provided with an introductory waltz (''Voyez cette figure''), the pyrotechnic musical tantrums on her dismissal from court, and a lament in burlesque of the grand operatic (''Nuit fortunée''), whilst Chilpéric scored with his entrance number, the nonsensical Chanson du jambon, sung perched unhappily on the back of a real, live horse like the ones they use at the Opéra, and with his second-act butterfly song (''Petit papillon, bleu volage''). Galswinthe's boléro (''À la Sierra Morena'') added a touch of the Spanish, whilst a basso druid (Varlet) opened proceedings *Norma*-like, invoking ''Prêtres D'Ésus.''

The Folies-Dramatiques production was a fine success, running for more than a hundred nights, and *Chilpéric* was soon gratified by Christmas-tide burlesques of its burlesque. Hervé's music was borrowed to decorate the Eldorado's *Chilméric* (10 December 1868), whilst the Alcazar made a double shot, combining both the season's big hits in the title of its revue *Chilpéricholle* (31 December 1868). At the same time the show began to be seen in other countries. America was apparently the first, getting a taste of the original French version when Joseph Grau's opéra-bouffe troupe introduced the show with Carrier (Chilpéric), Rose Bell (Frédégonde), Marie Desclauzas (Galswinthe) and Mlle Rizarelli playing Landry in travesty at the head of the cast. The current craze for French opéra-bouffe meant it had much competition and, since Grau held the season's megahit *Geneviève de Brabant* in his repertoire, *Chilpéric* was played only irregu-

Plate 72. **Chilpéric.** *The Spaniards arrive and the big trouble of the evening's entertainment begins.*

larly, though not without its own share of success, as a supporting piece to Offenbach and Tréfeu's hit. An English-language version was seen later, in 1874, when Emily Soldene visited America and took the role of the comical king alongside Agnes Lyndhurst and Lizzie Robson.

Soldene had already appeared as Chilpéric in London, when she had deputized for the composer-star in Richard Mansell's production (ad Mansell, Robert Reece, F A Marshall) at the Lyceum. London's *Chilpéric* was probably the most successful staging of the show anywhere. Hervé repeated his Paris performance alongside soprano Emily Muir (Frédégonde) and the young Selina Dolaro (Galswinthe), and the show caused a real sensation, giving a huge boost to the budding craze for opéra-bouffe in Britain. It ran from 22 January to 9 April, being taken off only to allow the composer's *Le Petit Faust* to be given its share of the season's time. The following year Soldene, who had in between times toured the piece in the British provinces, brought a version back to London (Philharmonic Theatre 9 October), playing her version concurrently with another production mounted by John Elliot Mallandaine at the Royalty Theatre (28 September). In 1872 the Folies-Dramatiques company visited London to play the show in French (Globe Theatre 3 June), with Luce as the King and Mlles d'Antigny and Jullien and Milher all in their original roles, and in 1875 (10 May) the Alhambra gave *Chilpéric* an extravagant new mounting with Charles Lyall (Chilpéric), Lennox Grey (Frédégonde), Kate Munroe (Galswinthe), Adelaide Newton (Landry), Harry Paulton (Dr Ricin) and Emma Chambers (Brunehaut) featured, a production which ran for three months. A fresh English version (ad Henry Hersee, H B Farnie) was produced at the new Empire Theatre in 1884 (17 April) with Herbert Standing, Camille d'Arville and Madge Shirley in the leading roles, capping a British career for *Chilpéric* which was only bested by a handful of opéras-bouffes.

In America, the pieces was given a further brief showing at New York's Robinson Hall (19 July 1875), with ex-Soldene tenor Henri Laurent as the King. Pauline Markham, ex- of Lydia Thompson's blondes, toured what claimed to be a version of *Chilpéric* in her repertoire in the late 1870s, and Broadway saw the piece again briefly in 1879 when a Mlle Ninon Duclos appeared at Tony Pastor's (7 May) in an uncredited, unappreciated and mutilated version of *Chilpéric,* which was quickly withdrawn.

Australia followed quickly where London led—although W S Lyster felt obliged to add a subtitle "the King of the Gauls" to help antipodeans likely to be bemused by the show's unfamiliar name—and mounted a production featuring Henry Bracy as the said King. Local burlesque queen Lydia Howard subsequently toured a highly approximate version decorated with more extraneous music than original Hervé, and Australia and New Zealand got the international article in 1877–78, when Soldene appeared around both countries in what was announced as "her original role."

In 1872 the Folies-Dramatiques remounted *Chilpéric* with Hervé supplying two new songs, a romance for Siegebert and a solo for Alfred, the principal page, and in 1876 Paris saw a further reprise of the show with Hervé again in his original role (Théâtre des Menus-Plaisirs, October). In 1895 the Théâtre des Variétés mounted a new production, the libretto now reorganized into three acts by Paul Ferrier. With a cast headed by Albert Brasseur (Chilpéric), Marguerite Ugalde (Frédégonde) and Marcelle Lender (Galswinthe), and with Baron as the doctor and Vauthier as Siegebert, the quarter-of-a-century old piece found itself a renewed popularity which led it to both a straight run of over a hundred nights and, this time, to a production in the German language. Eduard Jacobson and Wilhelm Mannstädt's *König Chilperich* was seen at Berlin's Theater Unter den Linden later the same year, with Alexander Klein and Frln Fischer in the lead roles, with sufficient success for it to be brought back again in the new year. The Vienna Carltheater staged the same version 11 months later with Julius Spielmann playing Chilpéric, Betty Stojan as Frédégonde and Ernst Tautenhayn as Landry. It was played some 25 times.

The passing out of favor—and of comprehension—of the more extreme style of burlesque in the 20th century has led *Chilpéric* to disappear from the repertoire since.

USA: Theatre Français (Fr) 1 June 1869, Lyceum Theater (Eng) 9 December 1874; UK: Lyceum Theatre 22 January 1870; Australia: Prince of Wales Theatre, Melbourne *Chilpéric, the King of the Gauls* 25 July 1874; Germany: Theater Unter den Linden *König Chilperich* 21 December 1895; Austria: Carltheater *König Chilperich* 28 November 1896

CHIN-CHIN, or A Modern Aladdin Musical fantasy in 3 acts by Anne Caldwell and R H Burnside. Lyrics by Anne Caldwell, et al. Music by Ivan Caryll. Globe Theater, New York, 20 October 1914.

An updated version of the Aladdin story, rewritten to feature the comedians Montgomery and Stone, *Chin-Chin* cast its stars as twin slaves of the lamp, Chin Hop Hi (Stone) and Chin Hop Lo (Montgomery), who managed the evening's affairs rather like a couple of French revue compères. The action zipped from one location to another as the two funny genii tried to stop the nasty Abanazar (Charles T Aldrich) from robbing Aladdin (Douglas Stevenson) of the lamp, or helped the boy win the hand of Violet Bond (Helen Falconer), daughter of the ridiculously rich Cornelius Bond (R E Graham), a gentleman who is himself eager to lay greedy hands on the magic lamp. When he wasn't being a genie, Stone appeared as Paderewski, a ventriloquist, Madame Falloffski and a gendarme, whilst Montgomery impersonated the Widow, a coolie, a clown and a second gendarme.

The stars introduced themselves singing about "A Chinese Honeymoon" (ly: Bryan Williams), and Stone followed the then fashion for all that swung by launching into "Ragtime Temple Bells" (ly: James O'Dea), whilst Aladdin and his Violet shared some romantic moments ("Love Moon," "The Mulberry Tree") and the hero scored a success with his farewell to youthful excesses in "Goodbye Girls, I'm Through" (ly: John Golden). Some lyric soprano pieces were inserted for a creature called the Goddess of the Lamp, as played by Belle Story, who waltzed about "Violet" (the color, not the girl) and the "Grey Dove," and got sentimental in the final "In January, You May Love Mary." A toys' chorus, a piece about "Shopping in the Orient" and a ballet divertissement, "Will o'the Wisp," were amongst the other items on the evening's merry bill.

Chin-Chin was a splendid success, and served its fun-making stars for 295 performances on Broadway before they took it to the country for a long tour. A production announced by Alfred Butt for London's Palace Theatre in 1915 did not in the end take place.

A CHINESE HONEYMOON Musical comedy in 2 acts by George Dance. Music by Howard Talbot. Theatre Royal, Hanley, 16 October 1899; Royal Strand Theatre, London, 5 October 1901.

One of the many landmark musicals which started small, A *Chinese Honeymoon*—thrown together in four weeks by its authors—was first staged at Hanley, in the British potteries country, under the management of touring producer, H Cecil Beryl. It was sent out for an eight-week tour which was scheduled to end in time for the artists to take up their pantomime engagements, but it did well enough in this first little season for Beryl to send it out again, in the new year, to another nine dates. Then, the show having more than served the purpose for which it had been made, he handed it back to author Dance. Dance put it out again himself for 32 weeks more, and announced fresh tours to come. But Frank Curzon now surfaced with a proposal for a London run, so Dance offered his touring scenery, costumes and rights to producer Milton Bode. Bode said ''no, thanks'' and Dance thus retained what would become some of the most valuable touring rights in the prewar theatre. Before taking *A Chinese Honeymoon* to London, Frank Curzon ordered some rewrites, in particular the expansion of the role of the little waitress Fi-fi as a vehicle for tiny comedienne Louie Freear, and some extra songs. The alterations were duly made and the resultant show was produced at the unfashionable Royal Strand Theatre. It stayed there for 1,075 performances, becoming the first musical play in theatre history to top 1,000 consecutive metropolitan performances.

British visitor Tom Hatherton (Stephen Adeson originally/Leslie Stiles in town) falls in love with a little Chinese girl and he stays in China to woo her, spending his other hours in the company of the devoted little waitress Fi-fi (Miss Freear). Unfortunately, Tom's beloved is none other than Soo-Soo (Violet Dene/Beatrice Edwards), daughter of the local Emperor Hang-Chow (W T Thompson/Picton Roxburgh) and thus thoroughly out of his plebeian British reach. Hang Chow is himself looking for a new wife, and has sent Admiral Hi Lung (Herbert Bouchier/Percy Clifton) around the world with a photograph to find him one, without revealing his rank. Hang Chow is no beauty and Hi Lung comes home without an Empress. Now arrive honeymooning Mr Pineapple (Lionel Rignold) and his jealous new little bride (Florence Wilton/Marie Dainton). The two have a honeymooners' tiff and on the rebounce Mr Pineapple goes and kisses the disguised Soo Soo. Since she is royal, the law of the land means he must marry her, so poor Pineapple is carried off to court to be wed all over again, whilst Mrs Pineapple is rounded up as a candidate for the Emperor's hand. Pineapple's life is made even more difficult by the fact that the wifeless Hang Chow has engaged an official mother-in-law from Britain and the imcumbent, Mrs Brown (Marie Daltra/Mary Ann Victor), is none other than Pineapple's old housekeeper, who was furiously slighted at his wedding another. When Soo-Soo, who loves Tom, takes a sleeping drug to feign death and escape from the palace, Pineapple is ordered to commit suttee, and things get very hot indeed for all the English folk before the ultimate deus ex machina, the British Consul, turns up and sets his subjects to rights. Tom and Soo Soo are wed, the Pineapples reunited, Mrs Brown becomes Empress Hang Chow and poor Fi-fi is left to waitress alone.

The show's songs became quickly popular, most especially the three music-hally ones sung by Louie Freear who, herself, became a star overnight. She described her painful musical family in ''Martha Spanks the Grand Pianner,'' insisted hopelessly that ''I Want to Be a Lidy'' and told about her piano teacher's . . . er . . . habits in Ernest Woodville's ''The Twiddley Bits.'' Mrs Pineapple's up-to-date piece about ''The à la Girl,'' Tom and Soo Soo's romancing to the strains of ''Roses Red and White,'' the Pineapples' title sextet with their omnipresent sextet of bridesmaids and a set of topical tunes were mixed with pretty ballads in a score which left plenty of place for what would be a cavalcade of subsequent interpolations.

Whilst the London production ran on and on, Dance kept *A Chinese Honeymoon* on the road, and the overseas productions followed—everywhere with success. George Walton had been the quickest off the mark, opening the show at Cape Town's Theatre Royal on 14 February 1901, before it had even been scheduled for the West End, and he was followed by the young American team, the Shubert brothers, making their debut as Broadway producers in nominal partnership with Messrs Nixon and Zimmerman. Their production featured Thomas Q Seabrooke and Adele Ritchie as the Pineapples, Van Rensselaer Wheeler (Tom), Katie Barry (Fi-fi), Amelia Stone (Soo Soo), William Pruette (Hi Lung), Annie Yeamans (Mrs Brown) and some interpolated numbers by Gustave Kerker, et al through a splendid 356 New York performances, before going out to confirm the way the brothers were about to continue with further success on the road. The tour schedule included a passing season at New York's Academy of Music in 1904 (28 March, 31 performances, with Julia Sanderson, May de Souza and Emma Mabella Baker now featured).

George Musgrove produced *A Chinese Honeymoon* in Australia, with Edward Lauri and Cissie Neil as the Pineapples, former star tenor Henry Hallam as the Emperor, Josephine Stanton as Soo Soo and May Beatty as Fi-fi, and once again the show was a major hit. Its 165-performance run in Melbourne established a long-run record for that city before Musgrove took the show on round Australia and New Zealand. Maurice Bandmann toured *A Chinese Honeymoon* in the Mediterranean countries, Henry Dallas's Company took it to the Orient, playing to English audiences from Hong Kong to Shanghai, and by 1903 there were five companies playing the show in Britain and four more in Canada and America. One of two German versions (ad C M Roehr, Richard Wilde) was produced by Jose Ferenczy in Berlin as *Chinesiche Flitterwochen* with Schulz as August Timpe and Frln

Heinrich as his Marie, whilst Hungary saw *Khinai mézeshetek* (ad Jenő Farágo, Béla J Fái) for 25 performances in repertoire at the Népszínház with Klára Küry starred.

In Britain, provincial tours went out end-to-end for many years and in 1915 *A Chinese Honeymoon* was given a wartime revival in London, in which Arthur Wellesley and Marie George played the Pineapples and Maria Daltra took up her old role of Mrs Brown for a 36-performance season.

It was suggested at one time that Dance had pilfered the libretto for *A Chinese Honeymoon* from the early Lecocq success *Fleur de thé,* but although one plot line indeed followed more or less the same course, the show was no more nor less derivative than most others, and their Eastern setting—not precisely a novelty—was the two shows' most similar element.

USA: Casino Theater 2 June 1902; Australia: Princess Theatre, Melbourne 30 June 1902; Germany: Centralhallen Theater, Hamburg *Ein Honigmond in China* 12 February 1903, Centraltheater, Berlin *Chinesische Flitterwochen* 25 April 1903; Hungary: Népszínház *Khinai mézeshetek* 21 April 1903

CHIVOT, Henri [Charles] (b Paris, 13 November 1830; d Le Vésinet, 18 September 1897). Star librettist of the peak years of French opérette.

A clerk in a lawyer's office at 17, later a pen-pusher in the offices of the PLM, and subsequently, for 30 years, a chef de bureau in the direction générale, Henri Chivot made his earliest excursion into the theatre in 1855, when he placed a play at the Palais-Royal. His first ventures in the field of musical theatre were in opera and opéra-comique, a decade on, when he was responsible for the texts for such pieces as Savary's one-act *Un rêve* (1865), von Flotow's *Zilda* (w J H Vernoy de St-Georges) and Frédéric Barbier's *Le Soldat malgré lui* (1868), but it was as the author of some of the outstanding libretti written for the French light-musical stage, at the height of its 19th-century success, that he found his fame.

Chivot teamed, from early on, with Alfred Duru, and the two continued an almost exclusive writing partnership for nearly a quarter of a century, until Duru's death in 1889. The pair did well with their first major opéra-bouffe text, a burlesque of the Arthurian age which was set by Hervé as *Les Chevaliers de la table ronde.* It had a good Parisian run, followed by a season in a badly botched version in London (*Melusine, the Enchantress* Holborn Amphitheatre ad G M Layton 24 September 1874). They confirmed this debut with their first collaboration with the young Charles Lecocq on the oriental comic opera *Fleur de thé.* The saucy *Fleur de thé* went on to a fine international career and its libretto was, thereafter, borrowed from—sometimes more, sometimes less—for several other musical plays around the world. However, the pair's next collaboration with Lecocq, the vaudevillesque *Le Carnaval d'un merle blanc,* a piece long held in the repertoire in Paris after its original season, was borrowed from even more successfully. Britain's master-thief, H B Farnie, adapted the libretto into English and, attaching it to a pasticcio score of Lecocq, Serpette, Offenbach, Hervé and anything else available, presented the result as *Loo and the Party Who Took Miss* at London's Strand Theatre (28 September 1874). A remarkable first run of 163 performances was prelude to several West End revivals.

The authors had another, and even more considerable, hit in collaboration with Lecocq when they turned out the deliciously comical libretto for his *Les Cent Vierges,* but the composer found different collaborators after his important success with *La Fille de Madame Angot* and the only time that the trio again came together during the next decade was on the Parisian flop (but Hungarian hit), *Le Pompon.* Instead, Chivot and Duru supplied Offenbach, with whom they had already had a considerable success with the comical one-acter *L'Île de Tulipatan* some years previously, with the texts for the two most successful works of the later years of his career: the splendidly constructed libretto to the comic opera *Madame Favart,* and the joyous tale of *La Fille du tambour-major.*

Around the same period, Chivot gave an Oriental libretto, which he had written without Duru's collaboration, to the aspiring composer son of a family friend, Opéra-Comique tenor Marius Audran. Edmond Audran's *Le Grand Mogol* was a hit in Marseille, and set the budding composer off on what was to be an oustanding career in the musical theatre. He was more than a little helped on his way by the series of splendid libretti provided to him by Chivot and Duru: the complex tale of *Les Noces d'Olivette,* the international favorite *La Mascotte,* and the allegedly Shakespearean-based *Gillette de Narbonne.*

A revised version of *Le Grand Mogol* (this time done with Duru) and the cautionary Belgian tale of *La Cigale et la fourmi* brought the pair further international successes with Audran. A reunion with Lecocq brought forth the widely played *La Princesse des Canaries,* and the authors also combined with Robert Planquette on the seafaring tale of *Surcouf,* later to become—with the indefatigable Farnie's aid—a major success in the English-language theatre, as *Paul Jones.* Finally, in what was to be the last of their works together, they teamed up with Léon Vasseur on the spectacular and widely produced *Le Voyage de Suzette.*

After Duru's death, Chivot collaborated in the writing of several other and even more spectacular pieces (*Le Pays de l'or, Le Bonhomme de neige*), but the great success of earlier days did not repeat itself. He did, however, apparently have an uncredited hand in several profitable pieces, including Victor de Cottens and Paul Gavault's four-act ''opérette-vaudeville'' *Le Papa de Francine.*

Even apart from the fruitful depredations of Mr Farnie, a number of Chivot and Duru's libretti were reused—detached from their original scores—outside France, although not always with credit. America's most frequent plagiarist of the same period, J Cheever Goodwin, made the libretto for their Audran opérette *Pervenche* into the text for his American musical *Fleur-de-lis* (mus: William Furst, 1895), whilst their *La Petite Fronde,* in the hands of Stanislaus Stange, became the book for Julian Edwards's *The Wedding Day* (1897). Oscar Weil's *Suzette,* produced by the Bostonians at Herrmann's Theater in 1891 (11 October), was a remusicked version of Chivot and Duru's opérette *La Dormeuse éveilée,* whilst the Broadway musical *The Prima Donna* (Aimé Lachaume/ Harry B Smith, Herald Square Theater 14 April 1901) did not dispose of any French music, but was simply based on Chivot and Duru's 1880 vaudeville *Le Siège de Grenade.*

In Vienna, another of their successful vaudevilles, *Les Noces d'un reserviste,* became *Die Hochzeit des Reservisten* as adapted by Zell, Hofmann and Fuchs and set to music by Julius Stern (Theater an der Wien 26 December 1888), and their vaudeville *L'Oncle Bidochon* (Théâtre Cluny 2 March 1894 w Vanloo, Roussel) became the Berlin Schwank *Frau Lohengrin* (ad Eduard Jacobson, Wilhelm Mannstädt, ly: G Gorss, mus: Gustave Steffens, Adolf-Ernst-Theater 21 December 1895). Berlin also gave a *Kam'rad Lehmann* (Jean Kren, Leopold Ely, mus: Julius Einödshofer, Julius Stern, Belle-Alliance Theater 7 May 1904) which was billed as taken from an unspecified Chivot/Duru work.

1865 **Un rêve** (Edmond Savary/w Alfred Duru) 1 act Théâtre Lyrique 13 October

1866 **Les Chevaliers de la table ronde** (Hervé/w Duru) Théâtre des Bouffes-Parisiens 17 November

1867 **Les Défauts de Jacotte** (Victor Robillard/w Duru) 1 act Fantaisies-Parisiennes 27 April

1868 **Fleur de thé** (Charles Lecocq/w Duru) Théâtre de l'Athenée 11 April

1868 **L'Île de Tulipatan** (Jacques Offenbach/w Duru) 1 act Théâtre des Bouffes-Parisiens 30 September

1868 **Le Soldat malgré lui** (Frédéric Barbier/w Duru) Fantaisies-Parisiennes 17 October

1868 **Le Carnaval d'un merle blanc** (Lecocq/w Duru) Palais-Royal 30 December

1869 **Gandolfo** (Lecocq/w Duru) 1 act Théâtre des Bouffes-Parisiens 16 January

1869 **Le Docteur Purgandi** (Robillard/w Duru) 1 act Folies-Bergère 2 May

1869 **Le Rajah de Mysore** (Lecocq/w Duru) 1 act Théâtre des Bouffes-Parisiens 21 September

1870 **Le Beau Dunois** (Lecocq/w Duru) Théâtre des Variétés 13 April

1872 **Les Cent Vierges** (Lecocq/w Clairville, Duru) Théâtre des Fantaisies-Parisiennes, Brussels 16 March

1873 **Les Braconniers** (Offenbach/w Duru) Théâtre des Variétés 29 January

1873 **Les Pommes d'or** (w Duru, Henri Blondeau, Hector Monréal) Théâtre du Château d'Eau 8 February

1875 **La Blanchisseuse de Berg-op-Zoom** (Léon Vasseur/w Duru) Théâtre des Folies-Dramatiques 27 January

1875 **Le Pompon** (Lecocq/w Duru) Théâtre des Folies-Dramatiques 10 November

1877 **Le Grand Mogol** (Edmond Audran) Théâtre du Gymnase, Marseille 24 February

1878 **La Saint-Valentin** (Audran/w Duru) 1 act Cercle Saint-Arnaud

1878 **Madame Favart** (Offenbach/w Duru) Théâtre des Folies-Dramatiques 28 December

1879 **Les Noces d'Olivette** (Audran/w Duru) Théâtre des Bouffes-Parisiens 13 November

1879 **La Fille du tambour-major** (Offenbach/w Duru) Théâtre des Folies-Dramatiques 13 December

1880 **La Mère des compagnons** (Hervé/w Duru) Théâtre des Folies-Dramatiques 15 December

1880 **La Mascotte** (Audran/w Duru) Théâtre des Bouffes-Parisiens 29 December

1882 **Boccace** (*Boccaccio*) French version w Duru, Gustave Layge (Galeries Saint-Hubert, Brussels; Théâtre des Folies-Dramatiques, Paris)

1882 **Gillette de Narbonne** (Audran/w Duru) Théâtre des Bouffes-Parisiens 11 November

1883 **La Princesse des Canaries** (Lecocq/w Duru) Théâtre des Folies-Dramatiques 9 February

1883 **Les Pommes d'or** revised version with score by Audran Théâtre des Menus-Plaisirs 12 February

1883 **La Dormeuse éveillée** (Audran/w Duru) Théâtre des Bouffes-Parisiens 27 December

1884 **Le Grand Mogol** (revised version w Duru) Théâtre de la Gaîté

1884 **L'Oiseau bleu** (Lecocq/w Duru) Théâtre des Nouveautés 16 January

1885 **Pervenche** (Audran/w Duru) Théâtre des Bouffes-Parisiens 31 March

1886 **La Cigale et la fourmi** (Audran/w Duru) Théâtre de la Gaîté 30 October

1887 **Surcouf** (Robert Planquette/w Duru) Théâtre des Folies-Dramatiques 6 October

1888 **La Petite Fronde** (Audran/w Duru) Théâtre des Folies-Dramatiques 16 November

1889 **La Fille à Cacolet** (Audran/w Duru) Théâtre des Variétés 10 July

1890 **Le Voyage de Suzette** (Léon Vasseur/w Duru) Théâtre de la Gaîté 20 January

1890 **L'Égyptienne** (Lecocq/w Charles Nuitter, Alexandre Beaumont) Théâtre des Folies-Dramatiques 8 November

1892 **Le Pays de l'or** (Vasseur/w Vanloo) Théâtre de la Gaîté 26 January

1893 **Bicyclistes en voyage** (pasticcio ad Marius Carman/w Blondeau) Théâtre de la Gaîté 5 October

1894 **Le Bonhomme de neige** (Antoine Banès/w Vanloo) Théâtre des Bouffes-Parisiens 19 April

1897 **La Souris blanche** (Vasseur, de Thuisy/w Duru) Théâtre Déjazet 9 November

1898 **Le Maréchal Chaudron** (Lacome/w Georges Rolle, "J Gascogne," E Ratoin) Théâtre de la Gaîté 27 April

THE CHOCOLATE SOLDIER *see* DER TAPFERE SOLDAT

CHODOROV, Jerome (b New York, 10 August 1911).

Originally a journalist, Chodorov subsequently worked as a screenwriter in Hollywood before joining Joseph Fields to write for the stage. The pair had a considerable success with the plays *My Sister Eileen* (1940) and *Junior Miss* (1941). Chodorov supplied some sketches to revue in the 1940s, and made his first full-scale venture with a revue called *Pretty Penny* which was produced at the Bucks County Playhouse, with a consort of biggish names involved, in the summer of 1949. It did not go any further, but his first attempt at a book musical, a version of *My Sister Eileen,* moved him promptly on to a different level. Set with a score by Comden, Green and Bernstein, *Wonderful Town* was a major success.

Neither *The Girl in Pink Tights* (115 performances), a piece using a ficticious version of the staging of the 1866 opéra-bouffe féerie *The Black Crook* as its background, nor the comical *I Had a Ball* (199 performances) with Buddy Hackett starred, achieved the same kind of success as *Wonderful Town,* and Chodorov's musical theatre work was subsequently limited largely to revisions and adaptations both credited (*The Great Waltz, The Student Prince, Pal Joey*) and, as a script doctor, uncredited. In 1967 he authored the libretto for a biomusical of Dumas father and son, set to a Saint-Saëns pasticcio and staged on the West Coast, and a television musical *Olympus 7-0000* (ABC 28 September 1966) with a score by Richard Adler.

1953 **Wonderful Town** (Leonard Bernstein/Betty Comden, Adolph Green/w Joseph Fields) Winter Garden Theater 25 February

1954 **The Girl in Pink Tights** (Sigmund Romberg/Leo Robin/w J Fields) Mark Hellinger Theater 5 March

1964 **I Had a Ball** (Jack Lawrence, Stan Freeman) Martin Beck Theater 15 December

1965 **The Great Waltz** (Johann Strauss arr Robert Wright, George Forrest) San Francisco 14 September

1966 **The Student Prince** revised libretto (Los Angeles Civic Light Opera)

1967 **Dumas and Son** (Camille Saint-Saëns arr Wright, Forrest) Dorothy Chandler Pavilion, Los Angeles 1 August

1978 **Pal Joey** revised libretto w Mark Bramble (Ahmanson Theater, Los Angeles)

CHONCHETTE Opérette in 1 act by Robert de Flers and Gaston de Caillavet. Music by Claude Terrasse. Théâtre des Capucines, Paris, 11 April 1902.

The Chonchette (Alice Bonheur) of the title is a pretty laundress who is hesitating between marriage to her Charles (Le Gallo) or venturing on to the stage. Max Dearly played the garrulous old actor, Saint-Guillaume, from whom the heroine has been taking acting lessons, whilst the comical figures of the Baron (Saidreau) and the Vicomte (Rousseau) completed the cast of the five-handed, eight-number little piece which became a hit for manager Mortier at the tiny Théâtre des Capucines. The Capucines company played the show in a bill with Berény's mimodramas *La Main* and *L'homme aux poupées* at London's St George's Hall, and the piece was subsequently played both in a German version in Vienna, with Mimi Marlow as Chonchette, in Canada where it shared a double-bill with *Cavalleria rusticana* (Académie, Montréal 27 December 1909), and for 14 performances at the Théâtre Parisien in New York with Robert Casadesus as Saint-Guillaume and Lucienne Debrennes as Chonchette. For many years after its production, *Chonchette* was fondly remembered and occasionally restaged by those with a taste for the charming and classy in the musical theatre.

UK: St George's Hall 28 June 1902; Austria: Venedig in Wien (Parisiana) 1909; USA: Théâtre Parisien 19 November 1919

CHOPIN, Frédéric [Fryderyk Franciszek] (b Zelazowa Wola, Poland, 22 February 1810; d Paris, 17 October 1849).

The musical-playmakers of the post-*Dreimäderlhaus* era decided that the Polish composer's celebrity-cluttered romantic life was ideal material for the same treatment that had been suffered by Schubert, and the defenseless Chopin became the subject of two musically fabricated Operetten in the 1920s. In Germany, *Chopin,* a Singspiel by Rudolf Presber and Leo Walther Stein, with Chopin's music arranged by Harry Schreyer (Staatstheater Bemberg, 1924), had a discreet life, but an Hungarian musical play made on the same lines by Jenő Farágo (who had already "done" Offenbach with considerable success) and István Bertha and produced at Budapest's Király Színház under the same title (4 December 1926), with Juci Labáss top-billed as Aurora and Jenő Nador as Chopin, proved a considerable success. It was later metamorphosed into a Broadway piece which was eventually called *White Lilacs* (previously *Chopin,* then *The Charmer* 10 September 1928), credited to Harry B Smith and Hungarian musical director Károly Hájos, and produced by the Shuberts, with Guy Robertson starring as the composer and Odette Myrtil as George Sand. In London, G H Clutsam, who had been musically responsible for a couple of Britain's versions of *Dreimäderlhaus* (*Lilac Time and Blossom Time*), combined with fading producer Robert Courtneidge on a Chopin follow-up. Their *The Damask Rose* (Golders Green 17 June 1929, Savoy Theatre 26 March 1930) did not, however, go for a Fred-loves-George libretto, but instead involved Walter Passmore, Amy Augarde, Nancie Lovat and friends in a Russian tale. It was a quick flop.

Another *Chopin,* billed as an opera in four acts with music arranged by Giacomo Orefice to a biomusical text by Angelo Orvieto was produced in Milan in 1901 (Teatro Lirico 25 November), and a German one written by Eduard Rogati and Hans Sichert with the music adapted by Walter Keyl, appeared at the Stadttheater, Fürth, 8 April 1939. Britain's Eric Maschwitz and Bernard Grün jumped on the Chopin-wagon the following year with a London piece called *Waltz without End* (Cambridge Theatre 29 September 1942), and Broadway took a second swing at the composer's music in *Polonaise* (Alvin Theater 6 October 1945, mus ad Bronislaw Kaper/John Latouche/Gottfried Reinhardt, Anthony Veiller) but this time without attaching anything of his life story—genuine or fictional—to it.

Chopin's piano fantaisie-impromptu, made up into the song ''I'm Always Chasing Rainbows'' by Harry Carroll and Joseph McCarthy, appeared in the Broadway musical *Oh, Look!* (Vanderbilt Theater 7 March 1918) and later in the 1973 revival of *Irene,* as well as in the films *The Ziegfeld Girl* and *The Dolly Sisters,* whilst the second melody of the ''Minute Waltz'' was used as the tune to the original *Irene*'s ''Castle of My Dreams.''

A CHORUS LINE Musical by James Kirkwood and Nicholas Dante. Lyrics by Edward Kleban. Music by Marvin Hamlisch. Public (Newman) Theater, New York, 15 April 1975; Shubert Theater, New York, 25 July 1975.

A backstage musical with a singular difference, *A Chorus Line* became the longest-running musical in Broadway's history after playing for some 15 years and 6,137 performances at the Shubert Theater between 1975 and 1990.

A Chorus Line was evolved from the life stories and theatrical experiences of a group of Broadway chorus dancers, and it was put together, through a series of taping sessions and performance workshops, under the aegis of director-choreographer Michael Bennett, who had previously been involved in two other musicals constructed on similar lines, if by more conventional writing methods. The 1970 *Company* and the 1971 *Follies* had both been built on a semi-revusical format, in which a group of people were brought together on stage, in those two previous instances for a party, before the loosely structured entertainment turned aside to look at various members of the group, their personality and/or their problems, in more or less detail, in scene or in song. *A Chorus Line* differed in that its characters were gathered together for a more rigorous purpose—to dance an audition for a job—and had their personalities and problems, as well as their dance talents, put on show for a purpose—to win one of the places available in the chorus line. Unlike its predecessors, too, *A Chorus Line* built to a firm finish, with the selection of the artists chosen for the job resolving the evening's action in a way that neither of the earlier shows did. However, within that more positive framework it still retained what was largely an at least seemingly randomly ordered series of ''spots'' for the artists involved.

The action takes place in an unoccupied theatre, where the final recalls for the small chorus of an unnamed show are taking place. The dancers perform an encapsulated version of the set routines, and a first cut is made. Those 17 performers who have been asked to remain for a further round of auditioning are not, however, asked to dance again. They are asked to talk. The show's choreographer, Zach (Robert LuPone), tries to bring each one out to tell his or her story in front of the others. Their problems, past and present, and their preoccupations pour out in a series of songs and speeches, some accompanied by dance, and the series is only interrupted when one dancer, Paul (Sammy Williams), finds the strains of baring his life story too much, and breaks down. When the dancing is resumed, it is Paul, physically fragile as well, who is again the casualty, and when he has been taken off to be cared for, the dancers resume their work aware, all over again, that it could have been any one of them carried, crippled, from the stage: their livelihood and their careers hang on such tenuous things. At last, the choreographer makes his choice from amongst the auditionees, and the action ends as the dancers are seen performing the routine they earlier rehearsed, dressed in the sparkles and spangles of that kind of showbiz.

The songs which accompanied the action were largely built around one or other of the artists and her or his tale, with only such pieces as the opening audition dance, the show number ''One,'' and the expression of the dancers' feelings about their work headed by Diana Morales (Priscilla Lopez) in ''What I Did for Love'' standing outside the ''revusical'' section. Three girls (Carole Bishop, Kay Cole, Nancy Lane), come to dancing originally as the escape from unlovely homes, entwined their voices to sing of how everything was beautiful ''At the Ballet,'' the lively Mike (Wayne Cilento) tapped himself catatonic describing his start in dance after seeing his sister's ef-

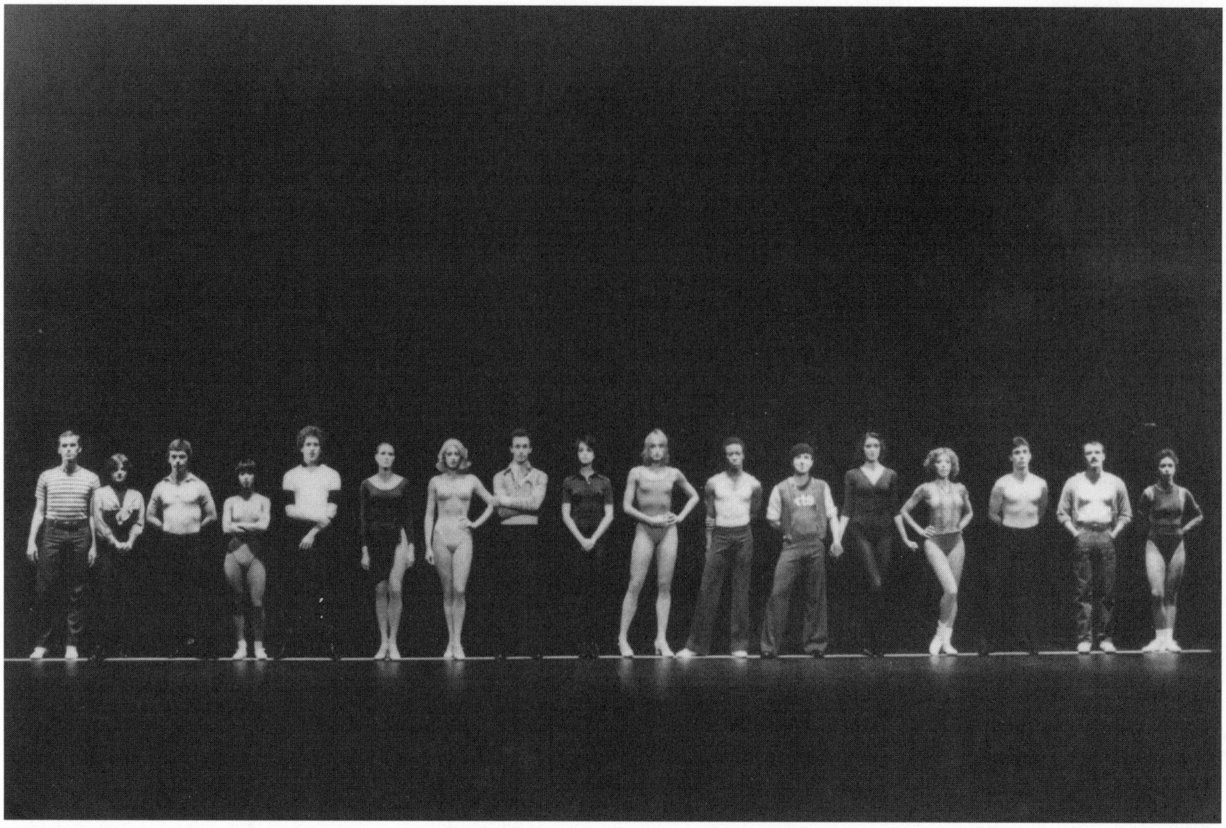

Plate 73. **A Chorus Line** *on parade.*

forts (''I Can Do That''), Kristine (Renée Baughman) with the support of her husband, Al (Don Percassi), verged on hysteria as she pointed out her bête noire—her inability to ''Sing,'' and Diana Morales related the sour tale of an unsympathetic drama teacher who could have put her off theatre for life (''Nothing''). Talented Val (Pam Blair) told of how her looks stopped her getting jobs (''Dance: Ten, Looks: Three'') until she indulged in a touch of plastic surgery to her ''tits and ass,'' the pains and joys of puberty burst forth in the ensemble ''Hello Twelve,'' and Cassie (Donna McKechnie), Zach's ex-mistress and a failed actress now returning to her first and loved métier as a dancer, gave her all to ''The Music and the Mirror.''

A Chorus Line, with a cast including a number of the dancers who had taken part in the taping sessions which had provided much of the raw material for the libretto (though not, necessarily, always playing ''themselves''), was first mounted as part of the season of the New York Shakespeare Festival. The good word flew round theatre circles from the first preview performance, and the show was a packed-out hit in its little house as it was honed into its final form. The most significant ''plot'' alteration at this time concerned the character of Cassie, which had become the most important of the female roles. Originally, this dancer who had gone on from chorus work to featured roles was portrayed, realistically, as unable to restrict herself in her performance style to playing identically to seven other choristers, and she was—undoubtedly logically—not chosen for the final line. But audiences apparently found it unacceptable that the girl, willing and eager to take a job for which she was perhaps over-qualified, just to get back to work, should be rejected. Sentiment and audience-pleasing won out over truth, and Cassie became part of the final selection.

The show moved briskly to Broadway, and met there with both the same kind of triumph it had found in its festival performances and with a bundle of the season's Tony Awards, as its favorite extractable numbers, notably ''What I Did For Love'' and ''One,'' caught on as popular song favorites outside the theatre. Whilst the show passed its 15 memorable years at the Shubert Theater, a series of re-productions followed, the earliest being an American touring company which began its career in San Francisco in May 1976, and a Canadian production which opened in Toronto at the same time. It was this latter company which introduced the show to London. Ever since the show's opening on Broadway, word had been carefully passed round in British theatre circles that it could not and would not be staged in London—

Britain, it was said, lacked dancers with the abilities to take the roles. Thus, the ground was neatly laid for the "Canadian" company (dubbed "international," although it played only London beyond the American continent) to introduce *A Chorus Line* to Britain.

When, after six months, this competent but rather unexciting company was obliged to move on, the show was recast with British performers. If the quality of the performances was in no way technically reduced (a number of the artists would go on to create or play roles in London's *Cats*), the detractors were proved unexpectedly right in one area. Most of the young Britons imitating the very real and wholly American "Broadway gipsies" of the show were unconvincing dramatically. Whereas the chorus artists in the American companies had, more or less, to play themselves, the British—bred in a different theatrical environment—were being required to play roles ultimately foreign to them. Britain's replacement-cast *A Chorus Line* also suffered some distasteful publicity with the dismissal in rehearsal of Tony Award–winning actress and dancer Elizabeth Seal (Cassie) in a dramatic and much-reported case which outdid anything in the show's own action. The episode left a sour taste in British theatre circles, and was responsible for British Equity forcing a revision in casting-and-firing legislation. In some strange, undefinable way, *A Chorus Line* did not ever catch the imagination of the theatregoing public in Britain in the same way it had in America, yet it totaled 903 performances in more than two years at the Theatre Royal, Drury Lane, and was later toured.

Australia's production of *A Chorus Line,* its cast headed by Ross Coleman (Paul), Peta Toppano (Diana), Cheryl Clark (Cassie), Scott Pearson (Zach) and Pamela Gibbons (Sheila), was, conversely, greeted with great enthusiasm, but the show was seen only rarely in translated versions, and when it was introduced to France and other Continental countries, more than a decade after its Broadway debut, it was played by American touring performers and not in a local adaptation. A German-language version (ad Michael Kunze) was produced at Vienna's Raimundtheater in 1987, but proved as much of a disappointment as the tour, and an Italian adaptation (ad Gerolamo Alchieri, Michele Renzullo) was mounted at the Todi Festival in 1990 (5 September) and played for a season in Milan. In 1997 an American tour company, directed by original cast member Baayork Lee, and a British touring company each gave the show another outing.

A film version, produced by Feuer and Martin and directed by Richard Attenborough in 1985, updated the piece, opened it out to go beyond the confines of the audition stage which was the sole set of the stage show, and introduced several new musical pieces, at the expense of some of the original music. Alyson Reed, Michael Douglas, Cameron English, Yamil Borges, Vicki Frederick, Charles McGowan and Audrey Landers were amongst those featured. The film provoked a certain amount of discussion, and won some partisans, but was ultimately not a success.

A Chorus Line was the outstanding phenomenon of the Broadway musical theatre in the 1970s and, if it left fewer reusable parts in the way of extractable numbers than other shows of its period, and if it exported less well than some less special shows of its era, its original New York production remains nevertheless an undying memory to all who saw it in its original form and a landmark in the history of the musical stage.

UK: Theatre Royal, Drury Lane 22 July 1976; Australia: Her Majesty's Theatre, Sydney 21 May 1977; Germany: Theater des Westens 4 October 1980; Austria: Raimundtheater 16 October 1987; France: Théâtre du Châtelet 16 December 1987

Film: Embassy Films 1985

Recordings: original cast (Columbia), Norwegian cast (NorDisc), Austrian cast (Polydor), Italian cast (Carisch), Japanese cast (Pony Canon), film soundtrack (PolyGram), etc

Literature: Mandelbaum, K: *A Chorus Line and the Musicals of Michael Bennett* (St Martin's Press, New York, 1989); Flinn, D M: *What They Did for Love* (Bantam, New York, 1989); Viagas, R, Walsh, T, Lee, B: *On The Line* (Morrow, New York, 1990)

CHRISTINÉ, Henri [Marius] (b Geneva, 27 December 1867; d Nice, 12 November 1941). The first and one of the foremost composers of the postwar age of French musical comedy.

Swiss-born, of French parents, the young Christiné began his working life as a schoolteacher in his native Geneva. His career orientation was changed when he married a café-concert singer and abandoned Switzerland for the southern part of France. The couple made their headquarters in Nice, and there Christiné began to turn out songs, at first for the use of his wife and then, with considerable success, for the established stars of the music halls of the time. From a prodigious output, such pieces as "La Petite Tonkinoise," "La Légende des flots bleus," "Je sais que vous êtes jolie," "Elle est épatante, cette petite femme-là," "Reviens," "Le Long du Missouri" and "La Dame du Métro," for which Christiné supplied words and/or music, numbered amongst a long line of successes which resulted in his setting up his own music publishing company.

He made his earliest entry into the world of the musical theatre with the two-act *Service d'amour,* advertised as a "piece à grand spectacle" and produced at the Scala with Alice Bonheur, Claudius, Sulbac and Girault featured, on a bill with the pantomime *La Chula,* and turns by Jane Thylda and Mayol. Though noticed as "beautifully mounted" with "extravagant costuming and pleasing music" it was also adjudged to be "not wonderful in any way.'' However, it did well enough, and Christiné, over the years that followed, provided the music for several other such pieces, written in collaboration with Charles Esquier of the Comédie française, for the same house, culminating in the 1908 *Cinq minutes d'amour* with Arlette Diorgère and Polin starred, without detracting from his principal career as a songwriter. It was 10 years from the last of these early theatrical ventures, in the last days of the war, that he was asked to supply the score for a little classical burlesque intended for Gustave Quinson's tiny new underground Théâtre de l'Abri. Circumstances led *Phi-Phi* (''Les petits païens,'' ''Ah! tais-toi!,'' ''Ah, cher monsieur, excusez-moi,'' ''Bien chapeautée,'' etc), with its dazzling musical combination of the chanson and up-to-date opérette and dance strains, of sprightly song and splendidly written ensemble-work, to be mounted—just as victory broke out—at the Théâtre des Bouffes-Parisiens instead. It proved both an enormous success and this ''victory musical'' went on to become the impetus and model for a whole era of Jazz Age musical comedies which dominated the French musical stage through the 1920s and into the 1930s.

Christiné held his place at the forefront of the new genre he had been instrumental in propelling to popularity, turning out the scores for a series of successful musicals, headed by the durable *Dédé* (''Je m'donne,'' ''Dans la vie faut pas s'en faire,'' ''Si j'avais su'') and including such pieces as *Madame, J'aime, Arthur* (filmed as *Le Culte de beauté)* and *Encore cinquante centimes,* until the tales and tunes of sophisticated musical comedy began to become repetitive and the vogue for things more spectacular and less witty arrived in the 1930s. When that happened, Christiné switched styles, and he composed some of his last theatre music for the large-scale romantic costume musicals *Au temps des merveilleuses* and *Yana* at the Théâtre du Châtelet.

In 1934 a musicalized version of Francis de Croisset's successful play *Le Bonheur, mesdames!* was produced equipped with a pasticcio score of Christiné music.

If the brightly melodious and modern musical comedies which Christiné and his authors turned out for the delight of postwar Paris won him a place second to none in the French musical theatre of his time, his works—in spite of a quality evidently superior to most of what was being contemporaneously produced in other centers—exported poorly. England did unspeakable things to the libretto of *Phi-Phi* and treated that of *Dédé* little better, using for excuse the same sort of moral compunctions that had led to the French opéras-bouffes being bowdlerized on the insular side of the English Channel half a century earlier, but Britain's producers also ripped the scores to pieces, larded them with sub-standard interpolations, and, not surprisingly, ended up with a pair of flops. America, after an abortive attempt with another botched version of *Phi-Phi* which closed out of town, and Charles Dillingham's failure to come up with his annnounced production of *Dédé,* simply ignored the whole genre and concentrated instead on home-composed musical comedies and imported romantic Operetten.

If the libretti of the French shows were more than the dainty non-Gallic theatres could take, versions of Christiné's songs, nevertheless, proved popular as interpolations into such Broadway shows as *A Naughty Cinderella* (''Do I Love You?,'' ie, ''L'Homme du dancing''), *The Better 'Ole* (''It's Our Wedding Day,'' ie, ''Je sais que tu es gentil''), *The Doll Girl* (''That's Love With a Capital 'L',''' ie, ''Je sais que tu es gentil'' again), *Ninety in the Shade* (''My Mindanao Chocolate Soldier''), *The Echo* (French Fandango) and *The Lady in Red* (''Lulu Lavinia''). And the song ''Valentine'' (ly: Albert Willemetz), as purveyed by Maurice Chevalier in the film *The Innocents of Paris,* became a standard which appeared here, there and everywhere.

Only Hungary, which simultaneously welcomed *Mercenary Mary* with acclaim whilst wholly bypassing the contemporary works of such as Gershwin, Porter and Kern, showed a boundless enthusiasm for the shows of Christiné and of his Parisian contemporaries. *Fi-Fi* (Lujza Blaha Színház 7 December 1921), *Szeretlek* (*J'aime* Király Színház 26 May 1928), *A Csodadoktor* (*Encore cinquante centimes* Magyar Színház 12 May 1934), *Békebeli boldogsag* (*Le Bonheur, mesdames!* Andrássy uti Színház 20 September 1934) and *Leányálom* (*La Madone du promenoir* Andrássy uti Színház 4 January 1935) all got showings in Budapest.

1903 **Service d'amour** (Maurice Dumas) Scala 20 February
1904 **Mam'selle Chichi** (Charles Esquier) Scala 2 July
1907 **Les Vierges du harem** (Esquier) Scala 26 February
1908 **Cinq minutes d'amour** (Esquier) Scala 29 February
1918 **Phi-Phi** (Albert Willemetz, Fabien Sollar) Théâtre des Bouffes-Parisiens 13 November
1921 **Dédé** (Willemetz) Théâtre des Bouffes-Parisiens 10 November
1923 **Madame** (Willemetz) Théâtre Daunou 14 December
1925 **J'adore ça** (Willemetz, Saint-Granier) Théâtre Daunou 14 March
1925 **P.L.M.** (Rip) Théâtre des Bouffes-Parisiens 21 April
1926 **J'aime** (Willemetz, Saint-Granier) Théâtre des Bouffes-Parisiens 22 December
1929 **Arthur** (André Barde) Théâtre Daunou 4 September
1931 **Encore cinquante centimes** (w Maurice Yvain/Barde) Théâtre des Nouveautés 17 September
1933 **La Madone du promenoir** (Barde) Concert-Mayol 3 November
1934 **Le Bonheur, mesdames!** (de Croisset, ad Willemetz, Fred de Grésac) Théâtre des Bouffes-Parisiens 6 January

Plate 74. **Chrysanthemum.** *Chrysanthemum Brown (Pat Kirkwood) comes home with the milk too many years after she went out for it for her father (Raymond Newell) not to have a few questions to ask.*

1934 **Au temps des merveilleuses** (w Tiarko Richepin/Willemetz, André Mouëzy-Éon) Théâtre du Châtelet 25 December

1936 **La Poule** (w Lajos Lajtai/Henri Duvernois/ad Barde) Théâtre des Nouveautés 9 January

1936 **Yana** (w Richepin/Willemetz, Mouëzy-Éon, Henri Wernert) Théâtre du Châtelet 24 December

1938 **Le Flirt ambulant** (Tristan Bernard, Willemetz) Théâtre Michel 13 January

CHRYSANTHEMUM Melodrama in ragtime in 2 acts by Neville Phillips and Robin Chancellor. Music by Robb Stewart. New Lindsay Theatre Club, London, 14 March 1956; Prince of Wales Theatre, 13 November 1958.

Another product of the adventurous club theatres of the British 1950s, *Chrysanthemum* did for the 1910s what *The Boy Friend* did for the 1920s and *Grease* for the 1950s, with just a touch more of the burlesque in its makeup. If it did not have the success in establishing itself that those other two blockbusters did, that seems to have been due as much to bad luck and its authors' naivety as anything else. Moved from its club venue to the West End, with Pat Kirkwood and her then husband, Hubert Gregg, top-billed, Sandor Gorlinsky's production suffered a series of vicissitudes which, after a change of underbooked theatre, resulted in a closure after 148 performances.

Chrysanthemum Brown (Valerie Tandy/Pat Kirkwood), who vanished from her London home whilst going out for the milk, returns home in prosperous state years later, refusing to say where she has been. In fact, she was kidnapped by the horrid Ma Carroty who white-slaved her off to Buenos Aires and a fate not quite as bad as death. Ma Carroty is still at it, even now, and her next victim is the beloved of our heroine's brother Bob (Donald Scott/Roger Gage), ingenue Mary-Ann Blessington-Briggs (Patricia Moore). But the villainess has not counted on Chrysanthemum who, disguised as a Chinese cabaret vocalist, eases her way into Ma Carroty's lair at the gruesome transpontine Skull and Chopsticks, leads the rescue, proves that her virtue survived in Argentina, wins the heart and hand of Mary-Ann's brother, John (Colin Croft/Gregg), and exposes the real identity of the evening's criminal . . . it is . . . !

From a score bristling with gentle parodies and witty lyrics, the pretty waltz song ''Love Is a Game'' proved the favorite. The young lovers gave forth with a version of the prewar weather duet (''Thanks to the Weather'') and the disguised Chrysanthemum pounded out a ''Shanghai Lil,'' but the best material, added to beef up the leading man's part for Gregg when the show transferred to the West End, came in a couple of wordfully witty numbers in which he lectured his little sister on the perils of walking in the park (''Watch Your Step'') and frantically phoned Scotland Yard after her disappearance, only to get a series of wrong numbers. When *Chrysanthemum* was later mounted in America, with Patrice Munsel starred in the title role, some further material was added which gave an extra comic flavor to the already vast role à tiroirs of Chrysanthemum. She avoided her father's queries over her disappearance in a catalog of improbabilities (''Don't Ask Me That'') and, in mid-rescue, took time out to relate at vast length to Mary-Ann, lying trussed up in Ma Carroty's den and wanting only to be set free, the awful tale of her South American adventure.

This American production provoked interest from Gower Champion and also from Hollywood, but any prospects of a film died in 1967 when America's very own version of *Chrysanthemum, Thoroughly Modern Millie,* hit the screens. Protected by the expensive American legal system from three penniless young Britons who had no doubt at all that they had been plagiarized, *Thoroughly Modern Millie* went on to classic status, whilst *Chrysanthemum* was relegated to an occasional production in provincial and amateur theatres.

USA: Royal Ponciana Playhouse, Palm Beach 22 January 1962

Recording: original cast (Nixa, AEI)

CHU CHIN CHOW Musical tale of the east in 3 acts by Oscar Asche. Music by Frederic Norton. His Majesty's Theatre, London, 31 August 1916.

Chu Chin Chow was a version of the Arabian Nights Ali Baba and the 40 thieves tale, put together by actor, director and sometime playwright Asche as a vehicle for himself and his wife, actress Lily Brayton, and produced in wartime London in the theatre which normally housed the respected dramatic productions of Beerbohm Tree. Staged with a sumptuous extravagance, it proved to be one of the phenomena of the British stage of the early part of the century. The show's initial London run of 2,235 performances set a London long-run record for a musical which survived for some 40 years, and *Chu Chin Chow* went on to be an international hit in English-speaking theatres.

The robber chief Abu Hasan (Asche) is preparing to pull a coup in the home of the rich merchant Kasim Baba (Frank Cochrane), and the bandit's beautiful captive, Zahrat al-Kulub (Lily Brayton), has been introduced into the house, in the guise of a slave girl, to spy out the land. Ali Baba (Courtice Pounds), Kasim's poor, layabout brother, accidentally discovers Hasan's lair and the riches hidden there and, when the greedy Kasim goes to steal what he can from the hoard, he is captured and killed. Hasan plans to launch his attack on the late merchant's household on the occasion of the wedding of Ali's son Nur al-Huda (J V Bryant) and the slave girl Marjanah (Violet Essex), but Zahrat foils his plan and wins her revenge, disposing of Hasan's men with the traditional boiling oil before stabbing the robber chief to death. Ali ends the evening in the well-padded arms of his brother's widow, Alcolom (Aileen D'Orme).

Norton provided a score which included two numbers which became standards: Pounds and Miss D'Orme billed and cooed with comical, middle-aged passion to the strains of ''Any Time's Kissing Time,'' whilst the Cobbler (also Frank Cochrane, whose character had by then been killed off!), hired to sew the pieces of Kasim's quartered body back together for burial, sang of his trade in the bass-baritone Cobbler's Song (''I sit and cobble at slippers and shoon . . .''), a number which became a drawing room and concert standard for half a century of low-voiced vocalists. Ali's comical ''When a Pullet is Plump (she's tender),'' Nur al-Huda's serenade ''Corraline,'' the staunch march for the 40 thieves (''We Are the Robbers of the Wood'') and Hasan's disguised declaration ''I Am Chu Chin Chow of China'' were other favorite moments of a score which also included a lot of incidental music to serve the show's many scene changes (originally 15, later several more), parades and dances. Amongst the several songs and scenes which were inserted during the show's run, Miss D'Orme's lovely, plaintive ''I Long for the Sun'' was the most successful.

The well-rounded soprano won her extra number through being one of the hits of the show, alongside Pounds—the keystone and real star of the evening—and the magnificent production values (scenery by Joseph and Phil Harker, costumes by Percy Anderson, director Asche, dances by Espinosa) whilst Asche and Miss Brayton provided the dramatic backbone to the entertainment with strong, melodramatic performances which complemented the comical ones ideally. The show was indeed ''a beauty show—of scene and person, of dress and undress,'' but it also had a fine strong story, familiar and happy characters and characterizations, and attractive songs which helped to ensure its survival after that first lavish production.

Grossmith and Laurillard took the show to the provinces with a cast headed by Bobbie Comber (Ali), Henry Latimer (Hasan) and Madge McIntosh (Zahrat), and *Chu Chin Chow* kept up a provincial presence in Britain for many years until, in 1940 (3 July), it was brought back to London for a second wartime run with the famous melodrama villain Lyn Harding as Hasan, Rosalinde Fuller as Zahrat, Jerry Verno as Ali, Kay Bourne as Alcolom, Dennis Noble as Nur al-Huda and with Sydney Fairbrother repeating her original role as Ali's shrewish and ill-fated wife, Mahbubah. Chased from London by the bombs after 80 performances, it returned, partly recast, the following year for another 158 nights. In 1953 *Chu Chin Chow* was given as an ice-rink production at London's Empire Pool, Wembley.

Elliott, Comstock and Gest produced *Chu Chin Chow* in New York the year after its London opening. Tyrone Power (Hasan), Henry E Dixey (Ali), Florence Reed (Zahrat), Kate Condon (Alcolom) and Tessa Kosta (Marjanah) featured, the London designs were repeated, and Alexis Kosloff aranged new parades and dances for what looked like being another successful production. However, management went awry and, after a transfer—less than three months into the run—to the Century Theater, the expensively staged show closed after 208 performances, still in the red. It was left to a highly successful post-New York tour to recoup and add considerable profits to the producers' outlay. The show returned briefly to the strike-bothered Broadway of 1919 (Century Theater 8 August, 33 performances) with Lionel Braham, Don Ferrandou and Marjorie Wood featured, and Eugene Cowles (Abdallah) and Albert Howson, of the famous Howson family (Kasim) in supporting roles.

Asche himself later took *Chu Chin Chow* to his native Australia, but only after Hugh D Mackintosh had already mounted a version there, with ex-Savoy star C H Workman (Ali), Vera Pearce (a Zahrat who sang better than any other female member of the cast!), Louie Pounds (Alcolom) and Maggie Moore (Mahbubah) amongst the cast and with original cast member Frank Cochrane restaging Asche's direction. Ward's version played nearly three months in Melbourne before moving on to Sydney's Grand Opera House (26 March 1921).

Herbert Wilcox made a silent film version of *Chu Chin Chow* in 1923 but, after the coming of sound, a second version was made with George Robey starred as Ali Baba and Thelma Tuson as a richy funny Alcolom. Anna May Wong played the melodrama of Zahrat with conviction, whilst Fritz Kortner gave a burlesque stage performance as Hasan in what was, otherwise, one of the best

Plate 75. **Chu Chin Chow.** *On its way to its long-run record.*

filmed musicals of its time. Sydney Fairbrother and Frank Cochrane (just the cobbler this time) both put their unequalable original performances on celluloid.

USA: Manhattan Opera House 22 October 1917; Australia: Tivoli, Melbourne 11 December 1920; Belgium: (in French) Casino, Brussels August 1930

Films: Graham-Wilcox Films 1923 (silent), Gainsborough Films 1934

Recordings: selections (MFP, HMV)

CHUECA, Federico (b Madrid, 5 May 1848; d Madrid, 20 June 1908).

Originally set for a career in medicine, Chueca came gradually to music as a player, a conductor and only last as a composer. The final impetus for a change of career was given when a set of waltzes he had composed was included, with great success, in the schedules of the Sociedád de Conciertos. His earliest works for the theatre were composed in collaboration with Joaquín Valverde, who is said to have expanded Chueca's melodies into harmonized and orchestrated numbers as the musical illustration to a series of short zarzuelas which included several—notably *La canción de la Lola* (1880)—that became highly popular in their country of origin. They also provided the music for what became the most internationally successful of all Spanish pieces, *La Gran Via.*

The other Chueca/Valverde pieces include *Las ferias* (1878), *Fiesta nacional* (1882), *Luces y sombras* (1882), *La Plaza de Anton Martin* (1882), *De la noche a la mañana* (1883), *Caramelo* (1884), *Vivitos y coleando* (1884), *Cadiz* (1886), *De Madrid a Barcelona* (1888), *Un año pasado por agua* (1889), *Le magasin de musique* (1889), and *De Madrid à Paris* (1889) whilst the further list of Chueca's other collaborations and single-handed compositions for the stage include *¡Hoy sale, hoy!* (1884 w Francesco Asenjo Barbieri), *El último chulo* (1889), *El chaleco blanco* (1890), *El arca de Noé* (1890, aka *Fotografías animadas*), *La caza del oso* (aka *El tendero de comestibles*) (1891), *Los descamisados* (1893), *El coche correo* (1895), *Las zapatillas* (1895), *Los arrastraos* (1896, aka *El capote de paseo*), *Agua, azucarillos y aguardiente* (1897), *El mantón de Manila* (1898), *La alegría de la huerta* (1900), *Mayas y toreros* (1901), *El bateo* (1901) *La corría de toros* (1902), *La borracha* (1904), *El estudiante* (1907 w L Fontanals), *Las mocitas del barrio* (1913), *Turcos y rusos* and *Locuros madrileñas.*

Biography: Girbal, F H: *Federico Chueca: el Alma de Madrid* (Ediciones Lira, Madrid, 1992)

LA CHULAPONA Zarzuela in 3 acts by Federico Romero and Guillermo Fernández Shaw. Music by Federico Moreno Torroba. Teatro Calderón, Madrid, 31 March 1934.

La Chulapona was amongst the most popular of the latter-day Spanish musical plays, and it has remained in the zarzuela repertoire during the more than a half-century since its initial production, being the subject of a major Madrid revival as recently as 1988.

In the tradition of the classic zarzuela, *La Chulapona* is set in the suburbs of Madrid and deals with the everyday (love) lives of the people who live there. The principals are two laundry-workers, Manuela (Selica Pérez Carpio) and Rosario (Felisia Herrero), and José Maria (Vicente Simón), the boyfriend of the former. The jealous Rosario—the chulapona, or come-hitherish girl of the title—briefly seduces José Maria away from her friend, but the boy soon returns repentant and is reconciled with the girl he really loves. There is, however, no happy ending. Rosario is pregnant, and rather than let the child be born fatherless, Manuela gives up her man and her dream of happiness.

Moreno Torroba's score was full of dancing rhythms, ranging from mazurka and schottische (chotis) to paso doble, a jaunty guajira and habañera, but those apparently lighthearted rhythms never got in the way of the romantic/dramatic nature of the show's main story, and some impressive pieces—both solo and ensemble—were the result. If the Act I duo between José-Maria and Rosario ("Es pañuelito blanco") proved the musical highlight of the evening, the soprano/chorus mazurka of the opening scene ("Yo que con las demas"), the tenor romanza of the second and the soaring final showdown rendered it nothing in effectiveness in a piece which had something of the air of a lilting Spanish *Cavalleria rusticana* to it.

An English-language version of the piece (ad Mary Lynn Whitman) was played in New York in 1959, but elsewhere beyond Spain the show has been seen largely as given by touring Spanish zarzuela companies. Britain's first performance was given at the Edinburgh Festival by a visiting company from the Teatro de la zarzuela.

USA: Greenwich Mews Theatre *Ole!* 18 March 1959; France: Opéra-Comique 19 May 1989; UK: Playhouse Theatre, Edinburgh August 1989

Recording: selection (Columbia/Zacosa/BMG)

CIAO, RUDY Commedia musicale in 2 acts by Luigi Magni, Piero Garinei and Sandro Giovannini. Lyrics by Garinei and Giovannini. Music by Armando Trovaioli. Teatro Sistina, Rome, 7 January 1966.

This Italian biomusical on film star Rudolph Valentino starred Marcello Mastroianni, the star of, amongst others, Fellini's film *8 1/2* (1963), alongside a cast of no fewer than 13 feminine partners including Ilaria Occhini and Olga Villi as his two wives and Raffaela Cara as the dancer Bonita. Mastroianni sang of "Il mio nome" and demanded "Questa si chiama amore?," and joined in an ensemble with the women on "Piaceva alle donne," which more or less summed up the subject of the work.

After a run of a hundred performances at the Teatro Sistina, the show lost its élan when Mastroianni's other prospects resulted in his departure, but *Ciao, Rudy* was subsequently remounted by Leo Wachter in 1972, with Alberto Lionello and nine feminine partners (including Paola Borboni, Guisi Raspani Dandolo and Simona Sorlisi from the original team). The show's principle was later borrowed for a Broadway piece based on the Mastroianni film *8 1/2* and called *Nine.*

Recordings: original cast (RCA), revival cast (RCA)

CIBOULETTE Opérette in 3 acts by Robert de Flers and Francis de Croisset. Music by Reynaldo Hahn. Théâtre des Variétés, Paris, 7 April 1923.

The most successful stage musical work of Reynaldo Hahn, *Ciboulette* was written to a text by two of the most admired French playwrights of its time, de Flers and—in succession to his longtime partner de Caillavet—Francis de Croisset. It was no longer a burlesque text, like the ones de Flers and de Caillavet had written for Terrasse with such success, but a piece of prettily pastel-colored romance, with some gentle humor and a certain charm, which Hahn illustrated with a score written in a similar vein.

Rodolphe Duparquet (Jean Périer), comptroller of the Les Halles markets, watches sadly as the actress Zénobie (Jeanne Perriat) plays fast and loose with the affections of the naive young Vicomte Antonin de Mourmelon (Henri Defreyn) and, finally, he reveals her duplicity to the young man. Antonin has lost a mistress but found a friend, and soon he finds another in the person of Ciboulette (Edmée Favart), a little farm-girl who comes into town to sell her goods at Les Halles. Ciboulette has been told that she will find her destined husband under a cabbage, win him away from a woman who will go white-haired in an instant, and that she will receive notice of his death in a tambourine. When the sleepy Antonin emerges from the back of her vegetable cart, the first condition is fulfilled, when Ciboulette tips a bag of flour over Zénobie's head, the second comes true, and, in the third act, when Ciboulette has gone on to become a famous prima donna, like all the best operettic vegetable-sellers, she gets the letter—which the suicidal Antonin had entrusted to a butler for later delivery—after their reunion has been happily effected.

Hahn equipped his Ciboulette with several sweet and sprightly soprano numbers (''Dans un' charrett',' ' ''Moi, j' m'appelle Ciboulette,'' ''C'est sa banlieue,'' the Chanson de Route), as well as a prima donna number for the last act (''Amour qui meurs, amour qui passes!''), and she joined prettily in the duet ''Comme frère et soeur'' with her new-found friend. The highlight of the show, however, was Duparquet's number ''C'est tout ce qui me reste d'elle.'' When the tearful Ciboulette comes to dampen his shoulder after giving the insufficiently backboned Antonin his marching orders, Duparquet tells her his own sad story of love. His Christian name gives it away—he is the Rodolphe of Murger and of Puccini, and his love story is the tale of his little, lost Mimi. All that he has left is a tiny handkerchief that was hers, which he keeps in his coat pocket, next his heart. Daringly ingenuous and sentimental, Duparquet's scene and song triumphed by the quality of their writing, and they added an extra dimension to an otherwise conventional, if skillfully made, opérette with which Hahn and his librettists had the curious idea to challenge the fashionable musical comedies of the 1920s.

Ciboulette was a decided success in Paris, and it was reprised on several occasions: at the Théâtre Marigny in 1926 (2 October) with Mlle Favart and Defreyn and with André Baugé as Duparquet, again at the Gaîté-Lyrique in 1931 with Nini Roussel starred, and in 1935 (20 January) with Renée Camia, André Noël and Aquistapace. In the same year, a film version was produced by Claude Autant-Lara with Simone Berriau, Dranem and Robert Burnier featured. However, although the piece proved both popular and well-regarded in France, it attracted no buyers elsewhere. Hassard Short announced a production for Broadway which never eventuated, and the other main centers showed no interest. Yet the piece continued to hold its place in the French repertoire, returning to Paris in 1953 (13 March) at no less a venue than the Opéra-Comique with Géori Boué, Raymond Amade and Roger Bourdin featured, and again in 1975 (25 October) with Nicole Broissin, André Battedou and Henri Gui. It has also continued to be played regularly in provincial houses without showing any signs of being considered old or, by modern standards, saccharine.

What seems to have been an American premiere (ad James Stuart) was mounted by the Ohio Light Opera in 1990 with Michael Jones as Duparquet, Dawn Hess as Ciboulette and William Joyner as Antonin.

USA: Ohio Light Opera 3 July 1990

Film: Claude Autant-Lara 1935

Recordings: complete (EMI), original cast selection on *L'Opérette française par ses créateurs* (EPM), selections (EMI, Decca, Ducretet Thomson), etc

LA CIGALE ET LA FOURMI Opérette in 3 acts by Henri Chivot and Alfred Duru. Music by Edmond Audran. Théâtre de la Gaîté, Paris, 30 October 1886.

The almost tragic tale of ''the grasshopper and the ant,'' as retold by Chivot and Duru, provided Edmond Audran with the basics for a highly successful opérette which brought to a peak the (mostly) fine run of successes that had followed the great triumphs of the composer's earliest years in the theatre.

The busily home-proud ant is Charlotte (Mlle Thuillier-Leloir) who lives contentedly in her native village with her country husband, Guillaume (Émile Petit); the grasshopper is her fun-loving and irresponsible foster-sister, Thérèse (Jeanne Granier), who uses her charms on her Uncle Mathias (Scipion) to such effect that he sets her up in a flower stall in a hotel in the big city of Bruges. She soon catches a number of eyes, among them those of the Chevalier Frantz de Bernheim (Mauguière) who, needing a cover for his affair with the married Duchesse de Fayensberg (Mlle Fassy), uses Thérèse as his ''beard,'' before falling in love with her. At the same time, however, the starry-eyed Duc de Fayensberg (Raiter) is promoting her on a career which quickly makes her the reigning prima donna of the town. When Thérèse discovers the truth about Frantz's first approaches to her, she causes a public scandal by singing a song which thinly veils the truth at Fayensberg's society ball, and then flees from the city. She wanders the land, working as a street singer, until she finally comes to the warm small-town home that the industrious Charlotte has built for her family. There she is nursed back to health, and there Franz comes at last to find her.

The prima donna's role was well supplied with songs: the happy, country Chanson de la cigale, the rustic number in which the flower girl's talents are displayed to Fayensberg (''Un jour, Margot''); the popular gavotte ''Ma mère, j'entends le violon,'' which the fashionable diva sings at a fair for the benefit of a beggar; her plea to Frantz for honesty (''Franz, je vous ai donné ma vie''); the fatal fable (''C'est l'histoire d'une cigale''); and the dramatic ''Je suis sans pain et sans asile.'' Charlotte had a contrasting Chanson de la fourmi, and joined happily with Thérèse in memories of childhood Christmases, whilst there was a touch of gentle comedy in the number for Vincent, the lovesick peasant boy who follows Thérèse to Bruges and takes a job as prompter at the theatre where she is starring, just to be near her (''Je souffle! Metier peu folâtre'').

Debruyère's production at the Gaîté was mounted in a style suitable to its large stage, with a ballet of the Judgement of Paris inserted into the second-act ball scene as a spectacular highlight, and it did extremely well, playing for 140 performances before the producer replaced it temporarily with a revival of *Orphée,* bringing the show back after the summer break for a further series of performances. It was later restaged at the Gaîté in 1904 (10 November), with Juliette Simon-Girard starred as ''the cricket'' alongside Dalcourt (Frantz), Mlle Leclerc (Charlotte), Regnard (Duc) and Émil Soums (Vincent), and in October 1905, again in 1915 at the Trianon-Lyrique (26 October), and once more at the Théâtre des Gobélins in 1921 with Rosalia Lambrechts in the central role.

In the meanwhile, however, the piece had had a remarkable career further afield. If the German and the Hungarian theatres, which played many of Audran's lesser works, oddly did not pick up on *La Cigale,* London's Horace Sedger did. He had the piece adapted by old-timers F C Burnand and Gilbert a' Beckett and had Ivan Caryll revamp the score in order to make the huge title role, made thus for the benefit of Granier, less overwhelming, by adding solos for Frantz and replacing a number of other songs. The resultant show—with Geraldine Ulmar as Marton (as the heroine was now called), an American tenor who went to considerable trouble to prove he had the right to call himself the Chevalier Scovel as Frantz, Lionel Brough as Mathias and with Lila Clay and her 15-woman orchestra featured on stage—was a major success (''a more exquisite comic opera . . . has not been seen in London for many years''). *La Cigale* played a remarkable 423 times at the Lyric Theatre before going on the road (although Sedger's dubious management—or creative accounting—meant that at the end of it the books showed the production £2,380 in the red), whilst a Broadway production, starring Lillian Russell (Marton) and Viennese star Carl Streitmann (Frantz) and directed by Richard Barker, was running through its 112 performances at the Casino Theater. Miss Russell took the show on the road the following season with Hayden Coffin as Franz.

Australia saw the show in J C Williamson's production with Charles Ryley (Frantz), Howard Vernon (Duc), Flora Graupner (Charlotte) and America's very young London-takeover star Marie Halton (Marton) the following year. Miss Halton's sudden departure cut what looked like being an exceptional first run, but the piece was remounted for several consecutive Australian seasons, and it continued to tour English-language theatres all around the world for a number of years, making itself one of the few European musicals to have found a wider appreciation outside the old Continent than at home.

UK: Lyric Theatre *La Cigale* 9 October 1890; USA: French Opera House, New Orleans (Fr) 11 January 1891, Casino Theater *La Cigale* 26 October 1891; Australia: Princess Theatre, Melbourne *La Cigale* 12 February 1892

CIN-CI-LÀ Operetta in 3 acts by Carlo Lombardo. Music by Virgilio Ranzato. Teatro dal Verme, Milan, 18 December 1925.

One of the most popular Italian operettas of its period, *Cin-ci-là* was set to a libretto which had an aura of the previous century about it. The tale was set in China, and its principals were a sexually unenlightened Prince and Princess who, having been wed, apparently expect their heir to arrive by the next stork. When Papa's little Parisian lady-friend, Cin-ci-là, arrives in town, with her boyfriend Petit-Gris, the lessons on lovemaking are in good hands.

The score to the piece didn't have much of the previous century about it. It boasted what it called (but which didn't sound much like) a blues number and also a reasonably perfunctory chorus fox-trot, but was at its happiest when relaxing into less determinedly modern rhythms. Cin-ci-là and Petit-Gris came out best with a couple of lighthearted dancey pieces, a ''Boxe d'amore'' which mixed intermittently Chinesey tones with a refrain about ''Picca-dilly-dilly-dilly'' and a hip-cocking little ''Oh, Cin-ci-là,'' and the Parisian lady flaunted herself in ''Rose! Rose!'' to a bouncy music-hally melody which sounded for all the (rest of the) world like ''Margie.'' The little bride and groom had their happiest moments when least strenuous in a loping duo ''La Favola delle tortore.''

Still performed, three-quarters of as century later, in the repertoire of such touring Italian operetta companies as survive, *Cin-ci-là* has also been played in a German version (ad Rolf Sievers, Will Kaufmann, Rudolf Perak)—one of the few operettas of its class to win a production beyond Italy.

Germany: Centraltheater, Dresden *Chinchilla* 3 November 1937

Recordings: selection (Oxford), part-record (EDF, Cetra), etc

CINDERELLA

The tale of Cinderella, otherwise known as Cendrillon, Aschenbrödl or Aschenputtl, Cenerentola, Hamupipőke, Popelka or by may and various other nationally different names, has come down to modern days from the French tales of Perrault. The now standard version of the story of the unloved stepdaughter, whose fairy godmother sent her to the Prince's ball in a magic coach and gown with glass slippers and a time limit, and who was subsequently tracked down by the love-struck royal thanks to having such abnormally tiny feet that no other fitted the shoe she had lost in her midnight flight, has been played on the stage for two centuries. It has gone through all kinds of transformations, modernizations and alterations, it has been played as an opera, an opérette, a burlesque, updated as a musical comedy, and undergone all kinds of rather undignified treatment as a British seasonal pantomime. It has often (away from the pantomime world) seen its magical element and the fairy godmother dispensed with, but always, at the end of the affair, the penniless, ill-treated, smut-faced lass gets the prince.

Quite when this winsome creature first made her stage appearance is not certainly known, but a one-act *Cendrillon* by Jean-Louis Laruette and Louis Anseaume was produced at the Paris Opéra-Comique on 20 February 1759. Britain first saw the lady of the glass slipper at the Theatre Royal, Drury Lane on 14 January 1804, when a piece entitled *Cinderella, or The Glass Slipper,* written by a Mr James and with music composed by Michael Kelly, featured Miss Decamp as its heroine for a fine 51 performances. A highly successful operatic version of the tale composed by Nicolas Isouard was produced at the Opéra-Comique in 1810 (22 February), but it was supplanted just a few years later by Rossini's all-conquering work *La Cenerentola, ossia La bontá in trionfo* (Rome 25 January 1817). Several other operatic Cinderellas followed, and the fact that Rossini had largely cornered the field did not prevent composers of the quality of Massenet (Opéra-Comique 24 May 1899) and Wolf-Ferrari (Venice 22 February 1900) from joining the ranks of Cinderella composers. An English-language opera by John Farmer and Henry S Leigh was premiered at Harrow (or, according to some sources, Oxford) in 1882–83.

In parallel to her operatic career, Cinderella also became—eventually—a favorite as a burlesque and pantomime heroine. Although Rophino Lacy's adaptation of Rossini's opera was produced at Covent Garden as early as 1830, the first significant English Cinderella burlesques seem to have been those produced at the Olympic in 1844 (*Cinderella, or The Great Fairy and the Little Glass Slipper,* by E L Blanchard 8 April) and at the Lyceum in 1845 (12 May, by T P Taylor and Albert Smith). However, it was H J Byron's 1860 piece, *Cinderella, or The Lover, the Lackey and the Little Glass Slipper* (Strand Theatre 26 December)—which introduced the character of Buttons, the amorous pageboy, for the first time—that gave *Cinderella* its shape and its impetus for the future, as it went on to be played over and over again in all corners of the English-speaking world, both as an extravaganza (notably in Willie Gill's American version as *The Magic Slipper*) and as a pantomime opening. The stage days were numbered for such British seasonal pieces as *Cinderella, or Harlequin and the Magic Pumpkin and the Great Fairy of the Little Glass Slipper*—which opened in the Hobgoblins' Hermitage, progressed to the Butterfly Haunt in the Dell of Delight for a Grand Pas de Papillons, and then to the Enchanted Fountain, before getting around to the Baron Pumpolino, and his daughters Clotilda, Thisbe and Cinderella. Byron had, to a large degree, put definitive order into the tale for the English-speaking world.

He and his definitive burlesque did not, however, stem the flow of Cinderella shows. In 1870 Henry Lemon wrote a *Cinderella* for the Crystal Palace Theatre (18 April), Frank Green authored a piece mounted in 1871, and in the latter year Alfred Thompson and Émile Jonas's *Cinderella the Younger,* a full-scale opéra-bouffe with an original score, was produced at the Gaiety Theatre, prior to an international career under the title *Javotte.* In 1883 (8 September) the Gaiety Theatre produced an *Our Cinderella* written by Robert Reece, and the same theatre was the venue for *Cinder-Ellen Up Too Late* (24 December 1891), originally prepared and produced during the Gaiety's Australian tour to star Ellen (Nellie) Farren. The prize for the most inventive title, however, surely belonged to Fawcett Lomax and J O Shepherd's *Donetoa-Cinderella, or The Drudge, the Prince and the Plated Glass Slipper* (Exeter 12 September 1881). The most recent British burlesque came in 1962 (17 December) with the production of Ned Sherrin and Caryl Brahms's part-pasticcio *Cindy-Ella, or I Gotta Shoe.*

In a period where pantomimes gave up pasticcio scores for original music, a number of well-known British composers provided scores to the story. In 1889 John Crook put music to J Hickory Wood's version, in 1908 Alfred and Herbert Haines supplied a new score for the Adelphi Theatre's *Cinderella,* and J M Glover put Drury Lane's 1919 pantomime version to music. In 1966 the

Shadows pop group provided original music for the London Palladium's pantomime production, whilst a television musical score written by Rodgers and Hammerstein (31 March 1957) was brought to the stage by Harold Fielding in 1958 with Tommy Steele starred as Buttons. It was subsequently played at St Louis's ''Muny'' (1961) and, in variously titivated versions, in numerous other houses thereafter. The most recent version (ad Steve Allen, Robert Johansen), boasting—in line with the fashion of the day for pasting in outcuts or extraneous songs when writers are safely out of the way—''three never-before-staged Rodgers and Hammerstein numbers,'' was mounted by the New York City Opera (9 November 1993). A further-yet-fiddled-with version was refilmed by ABC television in 1997 (2 November).

On the Continental stage, in the shadow of Rossini and Massenet, operettic-cum-féerie versions of the tale were composed in France by Victor Chéri (*Cendrillon, ou la pantoufle merveilleuse,* Clairville, Blum, Monnier Théâtre du Châtelet 4 June 1866), de Groot and others, and in Italy by Ottorino Piccini (December 1922, Empoli), whilst Victor Roger and Gaston Serpette supplied the score for a *Cendrillonnette,* written by Paul Ferrier and produced at the Bouffes-Parisiens on 24 January 1890. Another *Cendrillonnette* appeared in Paris on 20 December 1913. Several famous names tackled the subject in Austria: amongst a rash of *Aschenbrödl*s (Fred Langer, Leo Blech, etc), appeared the burlesque *Die Maxen sind Pfutsch, oder Das Aschenbrödel* written by Johann Nestroy with music by Adolf Müller, and a Johann Strauss *Aschenbrödl* ballet preceded by several years another written by Sidney Jones for London.

In Hungary two highly ranked composers, Ákos Buttykay and Ede Poldini, produced versions of *Hamupipőke,* whilst a spectacular by Leo Vécsey and Gyula Selley gave the heroine an ''aranycipő'' or golden slipper, rather than the usual if unlikely glass one. Amongst the many other central European variants and versions of the tale, from the most traditional to the modernized, Czechoslovakia added another up-to-date Cinderella with Lubomir Veteka and Franticek Aacharnik's *Aschenbrödl Cindy* (Janác k Theater, Brno 12 October 1979) and Jos Brink put out a Dutch *Zzinderella,* whilst in Germany the lassie with the little feet went touring as *Pretty Woman* (5 September 1997).

America, which—after mounting such homegrown minstrel parodies as *Shin-de-heel-a, or Who Can Wear Dis Shoe?* (Italian Opera House, 1850)—had welcomed Byron's burlesque, also followed up with several burlesques, extravaganzas and musical shows on the Cinderella theme or with her decorating their titles, including Woolson Morse's burlesque *Cinderella at School* (1881); Alfred Thompson and Harry B Smith's *The Crystal Slipper* (Chicago 26 November 1887); the 1904 Boston piece *Cinderella and the Prince* (R A Barnet/Louis F Gottschalk); Chicago's 1908 *A Stubborn Cinderella,* which wasn't actually about the lady at all; and, most substantially, the 1912 Victor Herbert musical *The Lady of the Slipper,* mounted on Broadway with Elsie Janis as its Cinderella and Montgomery and Stone as its comedy. There were also a revusical *Cinderella on Broadway;* a Jazz Age *Cinders* (Dresden Theatre 3 April 1923); a modernish *If the Shoe Fits* (Century Theatre 5 December 1946); a campy one in the Jules Feiffer *Passionella* which made up one-third of the tripartite entertainment *The Apple Tree;* a 1970s-minded one produced in the 1995–96 season under the tell-tale title of *Ms Cinderella* at Marriott's Lincolnshire Theatre, Chicago (Michael Duff/Cheri Coons/Sean Grenman); *A Tale of Cinderella* (Will Severin/George David Weiss); and another gospelly one, *Sisterella* (Larry Hart Pasadena Playhouse 8 March 1996), also seen briefly in Germany and disastrously in Australia.

Apart from the long list of children's pieces which have descended from the tale of Cinderella, there have also been a rash of musical plays which have used the story as their source. The 1904 hit *The Catch of the Season,* the 1929 *Mr Cinders,* which reversed the sexes of the tale, and the 1965 *Charlie Girl,* all produced in Britain, were all long-running hits, whilst America went through a whole period of ''Cinderella'' heroines in the 1910s and 1920s—musical comedy heroines whose rise from poverty to Princes (or at least rich commoners) mostly had little enough in common with the rest of Perrault's smut-nosed heroine's activities. So popular did these tales become that the period 1921 to 1924, following the hits of *Sally, Irene,* and *Mary,* became known as ''the Cinderella era'' on Broadway.

Of the genuine Cinderellas, it is Rossini's opera (without fairy godmother) which has survived to the present day, rather than any of her lighter sisters, but Byron remains the champion in the burlesque area and Jonas's *Cinderella the Younger* (also without fairy godmother), which had a fine career in its time, remains probably the most solidly amusing and attractive of the non-pantomime pieces.

CINDERELLA THE YOUNGER Opera-burlesque (musical extravaganza) in 3 acts by Alfred Thompson. Music by Émile Jonas. Gaiety Theatre, London, 23 September 1871.

One of the first British musical plays of the modern era, *Cinderella the Younger* was the follow-up to the Gaiety Theatre's first successful burlesque operetta, *Aladdin II,* and, as on that occasion, Hollingshead entrusted the score to a proven composer of French opéra-bouffe, this time Émile Jonas of *Le Canard à trois becs* fame. Alfred Thompson, author, director and costume designer of the previous piece, supplied a happily bouffe version of the famous tale as a libretto.

Javotte (Julia Mathews) lives in the town of Pumpernickel with her two horrible sisters Pamela (Annie Tremaine) and Bellezza (Constance Loseby), her existence made bearable only by the kindness of her godfather, the night watchman Peter (John Furneaux Cook), and by the secret visits of the royal dancing master (Mlle Clary), who has taken a fancy to her. He is, of course, not a dancing master at all, but the local Grand Duke Max out in good traditional disguise. However, before Javotte goes to the ball, etc, etc, etc, and becomes Grand Duchess of Pumpernickel, etc, etc, etc, there are several scenes of howling comedy, featuring two rogues called Dodgerowski (J D Stoyle) and Prigowitz (J G Taylor), to be negotiated. The pair invade the ugly sisters' boudoir dressed as hairdressers, and woo them in order to rob them, and they turn up again at the Duke's ball, this time disguised as policemen, but with larcenous intent.

Jonas's music was decidedly attractive; among its happiest musical moments were the heroine's ''Take Back the Ring You Gave Me'' and ''It Isn't Much Sleep That I Get''; a jolly Policeman's song for John Maclean as von Tickelsbach, the Lord High Everything, one of whose many posts (and he has to remember which he is in) is Chief of Police; a Brindisi for the Duke; and a gendarmes' chorus for the line of travesty chorus girls.

Cinderella the Younger played only 24 performances at the Gaiety, but it was later given in Paris as *Javotte*—with Dephine Ugalde playing Javotte alongside Marius Audran (father of the composer), Aujac, Peters, Solon and Mlle Douan—as well as in Vienna, and in Budapest during the early 1870s. It was revived by Strampfer, in 1882, at the Carltheater (16 September) with Jenny Stubel as Javotte and Karl Drucker and Steinberger as the thieves, and again at Budapest's Várszínház in 1884 (16 December), making it the most traveled and translated of Britain's pre–*HMS Pinafore* modern musical theatre products.

France: Théâtre de l'Athenée *Javotte* 22 December 1871; Austria: Strampfertheater *Javotte, das neue Aschenbrödl* 8 November 1872; Hungary: Budai Színkör *Javotte* 23 August 1873

CINDER-ELLEN UP TOO LATE Burlesque in 3 (later 2) acts by ''A C Torr'' (Fred Leslie) and W T Vincent. Music by Meyer Lutz. Princess Theatre, Melbourne, 22 August 1891; Gaiety Theatre, London, 24 December 1891.

Although *Cinder-Ellen Up Too Late* still—a century on—holds the record as the longest-running West End musical to have been first produced in Australia, the record is a rather phony one. The show did, indeed, see the stage for the first time at Melbourne's Princess Theatre, but—apart from a small musical contribution to the score by locals J A Robertson and Bert Royle, and the fact that the sets and costumes were locally made—the show was an entirely ''away-from-home'' British production.

George Edwardes's Gaiety Theatre company, complete with its biggest stars, Nellie Farren and Fred Leslie, was touring in Australia and, as the tour drew on, they began to prepare the new show which they would open at their home base for Christmas. *Cinder-Ellen,* mostly written by Leslie, featured his co-star as Cinderella (complete with the pun on her real christian name, Ellen), whilst he—to the audience's amazement—was listed simply as a ''Servant.'' But he still had the largest and most comical role in the show.

Cinder-Ellen was not the best of the Gaiety new burlesques, but it was severely handicapped, on its London production, by being deprived of Nellie Farren, ill and effectively at the end of her career. After an indifferent opening, with Leslie paired with Katie James in co-starring replacement, the show was rearranged, remade and recast. The best of the songs—the Australian ''Bright Little Glass,'' borrowed from John Sheridan's *Bridget O'Brien Esq,* debutant Lionel Monckton's ''What Will You Have to Drink?,'' the comical Irish ''Teaching McFadyen to Dance''—were supported with some new ones and, finally and effectively, the show was enlivened by the interpolation into the evening of the music hall's Lottie Collins, performing her adored ''Ta-ra-ra-boom-de-ay.''

It was Miss Collins and her high-kicking dance who and which really turned the tide, and ultimately *Cinder-Ellen* did take off. It ran through six months at the Gaiety, a major tour, and then a return to the Gaiety, with Letty Lind now playing Cinder-Ellen (''I'm in Love With the Man in the Moon'') in a piece which had been so altered since Melbourne as to be barely recognizable. Then Fred Leslie died. Deprived of both its stars, *Cinder-Ellen* closed in 10 days. The days of the ''new burlesque'' were all but over.

THE CINGALEE, or Sunny Ceylon Musical play in 2 acts by James Tanner. Lyrics by Adrian Ross and Percy Greenbank. Music by Lionel Monckton. Additional dialogue, music and lyrics by Paul Rubens. Daly's Theatre, London, 5 March 1904.

By the time of the production of *The Cingalee,* George Edwardes's run of musical plays at the Daly's Theatre was nigh on a decade old. It had produced such classics of the musical theatre as *The Geisha* and *San Toy* in a run of unbroken success, a run that had continued even when the producer had switched to a combination of writers—Monckton and Tanner—which more resembled his ''Gaiety team'' than the Jones/Hall combination of the theatre's greatest days. After the new pair had triumphed with *A Country Girl,* they followed up with *The Cingalee.*

It was not in the same class. Its plot was a very *Florodora*-cum-*Nautch Girl* one, with its little Sinhalese tea-picker, Nanoya (Sybil Arundale), in love with her boss, Harry Vereker (Hayden Coffin), who is not really her boss because she is, in deeply hidden reality, the legal owner of the plantation. Nanoya has gone into hiding, to avoid consummating a marriage contracted in childhood with the potentate Boobhamba (Rutland Barrington). The crooked lawyer Chambuddy Ram (Huntley Wright) is ordered to find her, and also to recover a famous black pearl which has been stolen and which turns up in the possession of comedienne Peggy Sabine (Gracie Leigh). After a few quiproquos, all comes right when Boobhamba decides rather anticlimactically he'd rather wed someone else anyway.

The Cingalee was rather like a pale remake of the earlier Daly's hits, with Coffin yet again a high-collared hero, Wright as yet another wily Easterner, Barrington as yet another Pasha, and a score which was not in any way up to those for *The Geisha* or *Florodora.* There were romantic pieces (''Pearl of Sweet Ceylon,'' ''Sloe Eyes,'' ''My Cinnamon Tree'') for Coffin, Miss Arundale and Isabel Jay as Lady Patricia Vane, and comical ones for Wright and Miss Leigh (''The Wonderful English Pot,'' ''Monkeys,'' ''Gollywogs''), mostly written by Paul Rubens. There were also £14,000 worth of production values, many picturesque dances and, before long, plenty of alterations including the heavy write-up of a best-friend role to allow W Louis Bradfield to add some extra attractions to the show.

Oddly enough, it didn't seem to need it. Underpowered or not, *The Cingalee* ran for 365 performances at Daly's before going out to a considerable life on the road. However, some of the profits went west when one of those unproduced authors who seemed to cling to Edwardes's heels claimed that the libretto had been plagiarized from his unseen masterwork and, in one of the British courts' more ludicrous decisions, won £2,000 damages from a judge with no understanding of things theatrical. The *Cingalee* lawsuit split the Daly's team irrevocably (designer Anderson and star Coffin were boyfriends with the unproduced gentleman) and resulted in Edwardes chucking homemade shows at Daly's in favor of proven imports with proven authors. More than half a century later *The Cingalee* improbably resurfaced in London when Harold Fielding produced a potted version of the show as part of the entertainment at his Fielding's Music Hall.

John C Duff took the show to America and produced it with Melville Stewart (Harry), Genevieve Finlay (Nanoya), Hallen Mostyn (Boobhamba), William Norris (Ram) and complete lack of success (33 performances), whilst J C Williamson introduced it to Australia in 1905, with Margaret Thomas (Nanoya), Alexia Bassian (Peggy), George Lauri (Ram) and Haigh Jackson (Harry). Like Edwardes, Williamson too apparently found some staying power in it, for he played it in his company's repertoire as late as 1912, with Miss Arundale repeating her original role on the other side of the world.

USA: Daly's Theater 24 October 1904; Australia: Her Majesty's Theatre, Sydney 6 May 1905

THE CIRCUS GIRL Musical play in 2 acts by James T Tanner and ''Walter Palings'' (Walter Pallant). Lyrics by Harry Greenbank and Adrian Ross. Music by Ivan Caryll. Additional music by Lionel Monckton. Gaiety Theatre, London, 5 December 1896.

One of the most thoroughly popular of the Gaiety Theatre series of musical comedies, both at home and abroad, *The Circus Girl* was conceived after George Edwardes had seen a Viennese production of the hugely successful Julius Freund/Wilhelm Mannstädt Posse *Eine tolle Nacht,* and been taken with a scene in which the action took place in a circus ring, viewed from backstage. He bought the rights to the piece, then had his house author, James T Tanner, write a musical around that one scene and situation. Walter Pallant, chairman of the Gaiety Theatre's board of directors, also contributed sufficiently in the way of ideas to get a co-author's credit.

The good old plot (if that was not too much of a name for it) placed a bunch of English folk in Paris, mixed them up with the personnel of a touring circus company, and let the obvious happen. Ellaline Terriss was Dora Wemyss, the intended wife of the Hon Reginald Gower (Lionel Mackinder), but deeply taken with Dick Capel (Seymour Hicks) who she thinks is a circus artist. Reggie, in his turn, is (at least initially), keen on the Circus Girl, La Favorita (Ethel Haydon). Harry Monkhouse was Sir Titus, Dora's papa, on the loose in naughty Paris and eventually shot out of the circus cannon; Maurice Farkoa was a philandering Frenchman; Arthur Williams played the circus ringmaster, Drivelli, and Connie Ediss his plumply jealous wife; whilst little Teddy Payne was the bartender, Biggs, who has to fight the circus strongman, Toothick Pasha (Arthur Hope), to win his Lucille (Katie Seymour). Tanner took his characters through the streets of Paris, via the circus ring, to a police commissariat and finally, with all the pairs paired up as intended, to an Artists' Ball.

The songs of the show were in the already established Gaiety mold. Ellaline Terriss scored the hit of the night with the plain little ditty called "A Simple Little String"; Connie Ediss, left stranded at the costume ball, snorted furiously, with many a topical reference, that it wasn't "The Way to Treat a Lady"; Payne and Seymour went through two of their comical dance-and-song duos ("Professions," "Clowns") with pantomime, impersonations and eccentricities; whilst Hicks and Miss Terriss had a routine called "In the Ring" into which they were able similarly to squeeze a display of the variety of their talents. Farkoa did his matinée idol bit, singing of "Wine, Woman and Waltz" with a toss of his blonded forelock, and Payne described his barman's calling and the therapeutic values of various drinks.

The Circus Girl was a great hit at the Gaiety. It ran for 497 performances in London before going out for an extended touring life in the British provinces, to productions in almost every outpost of Empire, and even beyond.

Augustin Daly took up the show for Broadway, and produced it at his own theatre with a cast which featured Virginia Earle (Dora), Herbert Gresham (Titus), former opéra-bouffe star Catherine Lewis as Mme Drivelli and James T Powers as Biggs, alongside a supporting cast made up from members of his much admired repertory company. Once again a fine success, it ran through 172 performances, with a summer break in the middle, and returned the following season for another 40 nights, while the burlesquers accoladed the town's newest hit in the only way they knew how. Weber and Fields mounted their burlesque as *The Circus Horse* and brought on six of them, while Koster and Bial's called theirs *The Museum Lady.* Following this initial success, *The Circus Girl* was played regularly in American musical houses for a number of years, and it became for a while a summer-seasonal regular in Boston. Australia's version of the show, mounted by J C Williamson, included George Lauri (Biggs), Carrie Moore (Dora), Florence Young (La Favorita) and Harold Thorley (Dick) in its cast through a good series of performances in repertoire.

The Circus Girl even made the rare trip from the West End to the Continent in the years following its production. Budapest saw an Hugarian version (ad Jenő Faragó, Béla J Fái) produced in 1901 at the Népszínház for 26 performances, and Vienna followed shortly after with a German-language version (ad Leopold Krenn, Carl Lindau) when Gabor Steiner introduced *Das Cirkusmädel* at his Danzers Orpheum, with Karl Tuschl heading the comedy as Bix of the Café Régence, Frln Grabitz as Dora, the young Frln Massari [*sic*] in the role of La Favorita, and an Artists' Ball full of "Ballet-Evolutionen." It played 50 performances at the Orpheum before Steiner took it across town to play a handful of performances in a summer guest season at the Theater an der Wien.

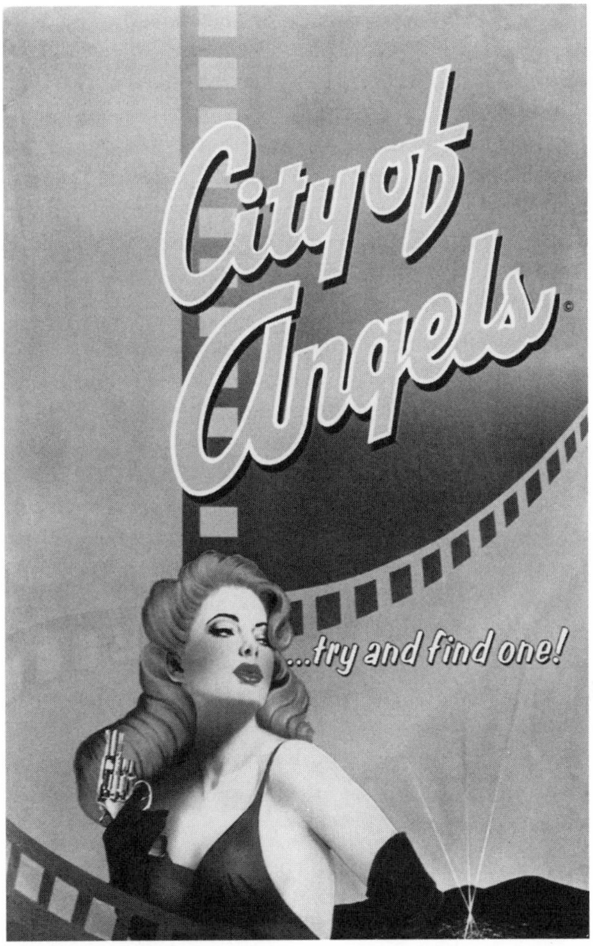

Plate 76. **City of Angels**

Mannstädt and Freund did all right out of Edwardes's fancy for their situation and scene. They got a royalty on every *Circus Girl* performance, all round the world, for years and years, and on one occasion, when an American tour company "forgot" to come up with the cash (as such companies were wont to do), they took them to court. And they won.

USA: Daly's Theater 23 April 1897; Hungary: Népszínház *Czirkusz-élet* 20 March 1901; Austria: Danzers Orpheum *Das Cirkusmädel* 31 January 1902; Australia: Her Majesty's Theatre, Melbourne 19 July 1902

CITY OF ANGELS Musical in 2 acts by Larry Gelbart. Lyrics by David Zippel. Music by Cy Coleman. Virginia Theater, New York, 11 December 1989.

Author Stine (Gregg Edelman) has been hired by Hollywood to turn his detective novel, *City of Angels,* with its mumblingly macho private-eye hero, Stone (James Naughton), into a screenplay. The scenes of the screenplay, shown on the stage in black and white, are interspersed with scenes (in color) showing Stine's comical struggle to keep together what he regards as the "integrity" of his work—in the face of cuts and changes made by his commercially (if at all)-minded producer-director, Buddy Fidler (René Auberjonois)—and his equally unsuccessful attempts to keep his pants on during the absence of his wife (Kay McClelland). Randy Graff played Donna, Buddy's secretary, who messes up his happy home by helping him get off the aforementioned pants, and also played the role of Oolie, secretary to Stone, in the film tale.

That tale put Stone into a complex and murderous high-society mystery which involved the glamorous and (so it eventuates) dangerous Alaura Kingsley (Dee Hoty), her iron-lung-bound, megamillionaire husband (Keith Perry), nymphet stepdaughter Mallory (Rachel York) and stepson, Peter (Doug Tompos), in an airport-paperback saga of bullets and bedrooms. Fidler ensures that any attempts to water down the sex 'n' violence of the script with such dreary nonsense as social significance—as represented by the character of a racist Hispanic cop (Shawn Elliott)—are quickly bundled out, and that the character with whom he identifies (also played by Auberjonois) is given an improved fate. In the end, both Stone and Stine rebel when the screenplay becomes an unrecognizable mess, and when a posey popular vocalist is cast to play the detective in the film.

If Coleman's score did not bring out any numbers in the hit-parade-extractable vein of his early shows, it nevertheless included plenty of enjoyable moments which made their point in context. Stine and Stone assured each other liltingly that "I'm Nothing without You," Donna did herself down craftily as a bad-luck-with-men girl in "You Can Always Count on Me," the irritating Fidler gave his credo in "The Buddy System" and Alaura and Stone swapped Hollywood come-on clichés in "The Tennis Song." Miss McClelland expended one of the most beautiful voices heard on Broadway in many seasons on the rueful, wifely "It Needs Work" and, in her alter ego as Stone's fallen and temporarily lost love in the movie scenes, the cabaret song "With Every Breath I Take."

City of Angels bucked the once upon a time normal out-of-town tryout system, saving its cartel of producers (Nick Vanoff, Roger Berlind, Jujamcyn Theaters, Suntory International Corp, Shubert Organisation) something like a million dollars in production expenses by opening almost cold on Broadway, having run itself only in a series of previews at the Virginia Theater. The risk proved, in the event, not to be one, and the show was frozen at an early date prior to opening to fine reviews and a solid success.

The show, with its wittily written, niftily constructed book, studded with swarms of pithy one-liners and dazzlingly, but unobtrusively, directed by Australian director Michael Blakemore, showed that—in spite of much recent evidence to the contrary—intelligent life still existed in the world of the musical comedy libretto. Coming at the end of the most unproductive Broadway decade for a century, it was doubly welcome. Those virtues were recognized by Tony Awards for best musical, book and score as well as for Naughton and Miss Graff. However, the show's very intelligence and its demands on audiences—who needed to pay attention to the show's lines and sometimes even its lyrics at peril of getting confused in the switches between reality and filmland—meant that, like other, earlier shows which shared its qualities, it found strong favor amongst "practiced playgoers," but rather less amongst that part of the public to whom the word "musical" was and is simply synonymous with revusical glitz.

Edelmann was succeeded by Michael Rupert and Naughton by Tom Wopat as Broadway's production ran on for two years and 878 performances, whilst a touring company, headed by Barry Williams, took the show to other areas of the country. Following the New York closure, *City of Angels* was introduced to London with Roger Allam (Stone), Martin Smith (Stine), Susannah Fellowes (Alaura) and Haydn Gwynne (Donna) featured. It found itself on the end of some of the best reviews won by a new musical in very many years, but found also that practiced playgoers were even thinner on the ground in London than in New York and, in spite of a newspaper writers' revolt in its support, it closed after only 263 performances. In 1995 a German-language version (ad Michael Kunze) was premièred at Heilbronn with Ingo Brosch (Stine) and Thomas Henniger von Wallersbrunn (Stone) featured, and the show was subsequently given a showing in the enterprising Amstetten summer season of 1998 with Victor Gernot and Adi Hirschal featured, but the wider popularity won by "easier" shows—whether more romantic or spectacular or cabarettish—has been denied to *City of Angels,* and it remains a connoisseur's cherished evening rather than a blockbuster.

UK: Prince of Wales Theatre 30 March 1993; Germany: Heilbronner Theater 17 September 1995; Austria: Johann-Pölz-Halle, Amstetten 29 July 1998

Recordings: original cast (Columbia), London cast (First Night)

CLAIRE, Ina [FAGAN, Inez] (b Washington, DC, 15 October 1893; d San Francisco, 21 February 1985).

Ultimately best known as a light comedienne of considerable style, Ina Claire began her career in stock in Washington, DC, and, from 1907, as an impersonator (of Harry Lauder!) in vaudeville before appearing in leading ingenue roles in several musicals, prior to the First World War. Her first such part was alongside comedian Richard

Carle in his own *Jumping Jupiter* (1910, Molly) and she followed this, later in the same year, with an engagement at New York's ill-fated Folies-Bergère and with the title role, created in London by Gertie Millar, in the American production of Lionel Monckton's *The Quaker Girl,* playing opposite Clifton Crawford at Broadway's Park Theater for an extended run.

In 1913 she joined Al Jolson and Gaby Deslys in the cast of *Honeymoon Express* in replacement for Fannie Brice (Marcelle), before traveling to London to create the title role in Sidney Jones's *The Girl from Utah* (Una Trance), under the management of George Edwardes at the Adelphi Theatre. She appeared at the same venue in the ingenue role of Sam Bernard's imported production of *The Belle of Bond Street* before returning to America and another short-lived musical, the variety-based *Lady Luxury* (1914) at the Casino Theater.

Thereafter she appeared in vaudeville, in two editions of the *Ziegfeld Follies,* but also increasingly in straight theatre and, from 1915, in films, where she repeated such of her stage successes as *Polly with a Past* and *The Awful Truth,* without returning to the musical theatre.

CLAIRVILLE [NICOLAÏE, Louis François Marie] (b Lyon, 28 January 1811; d Paris, 7 February 1879).

The celebrated vaudevilliste known simply as Clairville was born into a theatrical family—his father, Alexandre Henri Nicolaïe, also known as Clairville, was an actor and later the prompter at the Bobino—and himself took to the stage at the age of 10. He continued to perform for a number of years, and later worked as a stage director as well but, beginning by turning his hand, as a sideline, to the writing of additional lyrics and bits of dialogue ''as required,'' he soon found his real niche in the theatre, as an author. Clairville is said to have written some four hundred (some reports say six hundred) theatrical pieces: opérettes and musical comedies, comedies, sketches, revues, dramas and, above all, a long series of fairy spectaculars—the French equivalents of the British Victorian pantomime—with their good and bad sprites, their princes and princesses, and their advantageously organized trips through all the delights of the scenic artists', the machinists' and the dance-master's repertoires. Shows such as *Rothomago* (w Adolphe d'Ennery, A Monnier), *Les Sept Châteaux du Diable* (w d'Ennery), *Les Voyages de Gulliver* (w Monnier, Ernest Blum), *La Belle au bois dormant* (w William Busnach), *Les Bibelots du Diable* (w Cogniard brothers), *Le Puits qui chante* (w Eugène Grangé), *La Poule aux oeufs d'or* (w d'Ennery), *Cendrillon* (w Monnier, Ernest Blum), *Peau d'âne* (w Émile Vanderburch, ''Laurençin''), *La Queue de chat* and *La Patte à Coco* (both w Gaston Marot), *Les Contes de ma mère l'oye* (w Jules Cordier), *Pif-Paf* (w Monréal, Blondeau), and Thérésa's vehicles *La Cocotte aux oeufs d'or* and *La Reine Carotte,* the forerunners or bastard-cousins of the grands opéras-bouffes féeries, were—give or take a pasticcio score—virtual musicals, and some of Clairville's later spectaculars, such as *Peau d'âne,* with its full score of original music, crept firmly over the difficult line between the genres.

A number of the Clairville féeries were taken up by overseas producers. *Rothomago,* illustrated with an original score, became a success as a grand opéra-bouffe féerie at London's vast Alhambra Theatre, where a pasticcio version of *La Poule aux oeufs d'or* also got a splendid showing, whilst *Peau d'âne,* Germanized as *Die Eselshaut,* turned up as a musical spectacular in Austria, credited to Therese Megerle and composer Adolf Müller, and *Die Tochter der Teufels,* a ''grand phantastische Zauberposse mit Gesang und Tanze'' adapted by Emmerich von Bukovics, and with music credited to Lecocq and Karl Alexander Raida, was played at Berlin's Viktoria Theater. Like many other such productions throughout central Europe, its program did not credit the French authors from whose original it had been lifted.

Clairville's earliest ventures into genuine opérette and opéra-comique included the libretto to Hervé's first full-length work, the revusical *Les Folies dramatiques* (1853), the text for Adolphe Adam's *Le Muletier de Tolède,* later reused with slightly more success by Michael Balfe as the book of his *The Rose of Castille* (1857), and that for Offenbach's little *Daphnis et Chloë,* but he moved thoroughly into the contemporary musical theatre when he co-authored the text for Lecocq's *Les Cent Vierges* in a team with the young duo of Chivot and Duru.

In the years that followed, his name was attached as co-author (although, in each case, it was apparently he who did the actual writing of both book and lyrics as opposed to merely producing ideas) to the two greatest international hits of the musical theatre of the era: *La Fille de Madame Angot* and *Les Cloches de Corneville.* There were other fine, and notably finely written, successes too—Lacome's *Jeanne, Jeannette et Jeanneton,* Litolff's *Heloïse et Abélard*—and Clairville was still at the peak of his powers when he died at the age of 68, leaving behind him a bundle of work which kept the Paris theatre in Clairville premières for several further years. It was 14 years after his death that the last ''new'' Clairville musical made its debut with Varney's setting of *Cliquette* (1893).

A number of his pieces, again often uncredited, later served as the bases for musical plays by others. *Coco,* a ''grand vaudeville in 5 acts'' (w Eugène Grangé, Alfred Delacour, Théâtre des Nouveautés, June 1878) played at the Budapest Népszínház with its original music by

Coedès and others in May 1879, at the Vienna Carltheater (22 March 1879) with music by Brandl attached, and in Ghent in an adaptation by one Wytink (*Koko*) with music by Franz Herzeele (November 1885), which was one of the most successful, but the earliest seems to have been the one-act opérette *Die kleinen Leiden des menschlichen Lebens* (''nach Clairville''), produced at Vienna's Hoftheater as early as 1846. In London, his libretto to de Billemont's *Le Grand Duc de Matapa* (w Octave Gastineau) served as the bases for Lydia Thompson's 1876 extravaganza *Piff-Paff, or The Magic Armoury* (Criterion Theatre 31 January), a piece which, in its turn, was readapted as the comic opera *Glamour* by William Hutchison (1886).

Clairville's son, Édouard, billed as Clairville fils, composed the scores to several small opérettes, some with texts by his father.

Clairville's output was so prodigious and his level of originality and of success so notable that it was, as in other similar cases, insisted by gossip (and the press) that he could not possibly have written his works alone, and that he had a secret collaborator. The favorite candidate for this post of collaborator was a mysterious clerk called Miotte. But the mythical M Miotte never came forward.

1848 **La Tireuse de cartes** (pasticcio/w ''Jules Cordier'') Théâtre des Variétés 9 January

1849 **Le Moulin joli** (Alphonse Varney) 1 act Théâtre de la Gaîté 18 September

1852 **Les Néréides et les cyclopes** (pasticcio/w Lambert Thiboust) Théâtre du Vaudeville 26 June

1853 **Les Folies dramatiques** (Hervé/ w Philippe Dumanoir) Tuileries 1 March; Palais-Royal 2 March

1853 **L'Amour, qué qu'c'est que ça?** (Julien Nargéot/w Thiboust, Alfred Delacour) 1 act Théâtre des Variétés 6 April

1853 **Les Trois Gamins** (pasticcio/w Louis Vanderburch) Théâtre des Variétés 22 November

1854 **Les Étoiles** (Auguste Pilati) Théâtre Lyrique 6 February

1854 **Le Muletier de Tolède** (Adolphe Adam/w Adolphe d'Ennery) Théâtre Lyrique 16 December

1858 **La Chaise à porteurs** (Victor Massé/w Dumanoir) 1 act Opéra-Comique 28 April

1858 **L'Agneau de Chloë** (Édouard Montaubry) 1 act Théâtre Lyrique 9 June

1860 **La Belle Nini** (Hervé/w Dumanoir) Palais-Royal 28 January

1860 **Daphnis et Chloë** (Jacques Offenbach/w ''Cordier'') 1 act Théâtre des Bouffes-Parisiens 27 March

1860 **La Fille du Diable** (Nargéot/w Paul Siraudin, Thiboust) Théâtre des Variétés 9 June

1861 **Panne-aux-airs** (Frédéric Barbier) Théâtre Déjazet 30 March

1861 **Ya-Mein-Herr** (comp and arr Victor Chéri/w Delacour, Thiboust) Théâtre des Variétés 6 April

1861 **Les Danses nationales de la France** (Chéri/w Delacour, Thiboust) Théâtre des Variétés 19 August

1864 **La Liberté des théâtres** (Hervé) Théâtre des Variétés 10 August

1864 **La Revue pour rire/Roland à Rongeveaux** (Hervé/w Siraudin, Ernest Blum) 1 act Théâtre des Bouffes-Parisiens 27 December

1865 **Les Chevrons de Jeanne** (L Giunti-Bellini) 1 act Folies-Marigny 2 October

1866 **Cendrillon, ou la pantoufle merveilleuse** (Victor Chéri/w Blum, A Monnier) Théâtre du Châtelet 4 June

1868 **Roger Bontemps** (Jean-Jacques de Billemont/w Bernard Lopez) Théâtre des Fantaisies-Parisiennes, Brussels 18 March

1868 **Le Grand Duc de Matapa** (de Billemont/w Octave Gastineau) Théâtre des Menus-Plaisirs 16 November

1870 **Deucalion et Pyrrhe** (Eugène Diache/w Adolphe Guénée) 1 act Théâtre des Variétés 26 March

1872 **Les Coulisses de la scène** (Félix Parent, J-E Cohen/Victor Koning, Victor Bernard) Théâtre des Menus-Plaisirs 13 January

1872 **L'Égyptienne réaliste** (Chéri/w Blum) 1 act Café Tertulia 20 January

1872 **Les Cent Vierges** (Charles Lecocq/w Henri Chivot, Alfred Duru) Théâtre des Fantaisies-Parisiennes, Brussels 16 March

1872 **Les Griffes du Diable** (Hervé, Auguste Coedès/w Charles Gabet) Théâtre des Menus-Plaisirs 18 April

1872 **Heloïse et Abélard** (Henri Litolff/w William Busnach) Théâtre des Folies-Dramatiques 19 October

1872 **La Fille de Madame Angot** (Lecocq/w Koning, Siraudin) Théâtre des Fantaisies-Parisennes, Brussels 4 December; Théâtre des Folies-Dramatiques, Paris 21 February 1873

1872 **La Cocotte aux oeufs d'or** (Coedès/w Grangé, Koning) Théâtre des Menus Plaisirs 31 December

1874 **La Résurrection de la Mère Angot** (Lecocq) 1 act Théâtre des Folies-Dramatique 24 February

1874 **Le Treizième Coup de minuit** (de Billemont/w Gaston Marot) Théâtre du Château d'Eau 1 September

1874 **La Belle au bois dormant** (Litolff/w Busnach) Théâtre du Châtelet 4 April

1874 **Charbonnier est maître chez lui** (Édouard Clairville fils/w Busnach) 1 act Théâtre du Château d'Eau 29 November

1875 **Madame la Baronne** (Clairville fils) 1 act Théâtre du Tivoli 31 July

1876 **Jeanne, Jeannette et Jeanneton** (Paul Lacome/w Delacour) Théâtre des Folies-Dramatiques 27 October

1877 **Les Cloches de Corneville** (Robert Planquette/w Gabet) Théâtre des Folies-Dramatiques 19 April

1878 **Babiole** (Laurent de Rillé/w Gastineau) Théâtre des Bouffes-Parisiens 16 January

1878 **Le Troisième Mari** (Clairville fils) 1 act Théâtre des Folies-Dramatiques 10 April

1878 **Le Cabaret du pot cassé** (Pauline Thys/w Thiboust) Fantaisies-Parisiennes, Brussels 18 October

1879 **Panurge** (Hervé/w Gastineau) Théâtre des Bouffes-Parisiens 10 September

1879 **L'Éducation mutuelle** (Clairville fils) 1 act Théâtre des Bouffes-Parisiens 13 September

1879 **Pâques fleuries** (Lacome/w Delacour) Théâtre des Folies-Dramatiques 21 October

1880 **La Princesse Marmotte** (de Rillé/w Busnach, Gastineau) Galeries Saint-Hubert, Brussels 24 January

1881 **Les Deux Roses** (Hervé/w Bernard, Grangé) Théâtre des Folies-Dramatiques 20 October

1882 **La Petite Reinette** (Varney/w Busnach) Galeries Saint-Hubert, Brussels 11 October

1893 **Cliquette** (Varney/w Busnach) Théâtre des Folies-Dramatiques 11 July

CLAIRVILLE, Charles [Victor Nicolaïe] (b Paris, 27 November 1855; d Paris, 1918).

A nephew of the famous Clairville, Charles worked for much of his life as a civil servant whilst also operating on the side as a journalist and—from 1881, when he (w Ernest Depré) provided the Nouveautés with a burlesque of Zola's *Nana* (*Oh Nana!* 19 February)—authoring a large number of mostly very lightweight comedies, libretti, féeries, revues and monologues for the Paris stage. His very first full-scale opérette, *Madame Boniface,* remained his most substantial and successful, but a number of his other opérettes and vaudeville-opérettes were played beyond France after hometown successes—*Le Fétiche* (*A babona* in Hungary), *Le Brillant Achille* (*Die eiserne Jungfrau* in Austria and Germany), *Patart, Patart et Cie* (*Kneisl & Co* in Vienna), *Le Capitole* (*Az erenyes Metella* in Hungary, *Metella* in Germany), *Ninette*—without his managing ever to find a really first-class musical theatre hit.

1880 **Pierrot jaloux** (Lucien Roulland) 1 act Deauville 1 August

1883 **Madame Boniface** (Paul Lacome/w Ernest Depré) Théâtre des Bouffes-Parisiens 20 October

1884 **Le Chevalier Mignon** (Leopold Wenzel/from Clairville w Depré) Théâtre des Bouffes-Parisiens 23 October

1885 **Le Baron Frick** (various/w Depré) Cercle Artistique et Littéraire December

1888 **Le Valet de coeur** (Raoul Pugno/w Paul Ferrier) Théâtre des Bouffes-Parisiens 19 April

1889 **Riquet à la houppe** (Louis Varney/w Ferrier) Théâtre des Folies-Dramatiques 20 April

1890 **Le Fétiche** (Victor Roger/w Ferrier) Théâtre des Menus-Plaisirs 13 March

1891 **La Famille Vénus** (Léon Vasseur/w R Bénédite, Depré) Théâtre de la Renaissance 2 May

1891 **Mademoiselle Asmodée** (Paul Lacome, Roger/w Ferrier) Théâtre de la Renaissance 23 November

1892 **Le Brillant Achille** (Varney/w Fernand Beissier) Théâtre de la Renaissance 21 October

1892 **Nini Fauvette** (Edmond Missa/w André Sylvane) Théâtre des Nouveautés 16 January

1893 **Patart, Patart et Cie** (Louis Gregh/w Sylvane) Théâtre des Folies-Dramatiques 9 October

1893 **Mon Prince!** (Edmond Audran/w Sylvane) Théâtre des Nouveautés 18 November

1893 **Miss Dollar** (André Messager/w Albert Vallin) Nouveau Théâtre 22 December

1895 **Chiquita** (Gaston Serpette) 1 act Théâtre des Nouveautés 4 February

1895 **Le Capitole** (Serpette/w Ferrier) Théâtre des Nouveautés 5 December

1896 **Ninette** (Lecocq/w Eugène Hubert, Christian de Trogoff) Théâtre des Bouffes-Parisiens 28 February

1898 **La Dame de trèfle** (Émile Pessard/w Maurice Froyez) Théâtre des Bouffes-Parisiens 13 May

1898 **Gueule d'or** (Charles Raiter/w Benjamin Lebreton) Bobino 12 August

1898 **La Geisha** French version w Jacques Lemaire, Antony Mars (Théâtre de l'Athenée)

1899 **Excéllente affaire** (Vasseur, de Thuisy/w Henri Bocage, C Worms) Théâtre des Folies-Dramatiques 18 February

1902 **Le Minotaure** (Paul Marcelles/w Adrien Vély) Galeries Saint-Hubert, Brussels 5 November

1903 **Le Sire de Montgicourd** (Porinelly/w d'Arbois, Mirabaud)

1904 **Voluptata** (Marcelles/w P-L Flers) Moulin Rouge 20 January

1904 **La Môme Phémie** (Le Barré) 1 act La Cigale 31 May

1904 **Frou-frous et culottes rouges** (w Paul Blouet)

1906 **Descends, donc, de ton cadre** (Marcelles/w Gaston Guérin) 1 act Boîte à Fursy 1 March

1906 **Le Rat** (Raidich/w William Busnach) 1 act Théâtre Grévin 14 January

1907 **Eglé, ou L'enfant de la vache** (Claude Terrasse/w Émmanuel-Philippe Moreau, Depré) Moulin Rouge 7 May

1914 **Mam'zelle Caprice** (Albert Chantrier) Nouvelle Cirque 20 March

CLARK, Bobby [CLARK, Robert Edwin] (b Springfield, Ohio, 16 June 1888; d New York, 12 February 1960). A low comedian of the old school, smart-assed but likeable, with "baggy top-coat [and] cigar smoked both ends" Bobby Clark, "recklessly swinging his fatstick" and sporting a pair of spectacles drawn onto his face, was considered by many to be quite simply the funniest man on Broadway, through 30 years of musicals and revues.

The young Clark established a partnership with fellow comedian Paul McCullough (1883–1936) in 1905, and together they built a successful career in minstrelsy, vaudeville and ultimately in revue and the musical theatre. They appeared in London in the revue *Chuckles of 1922* and on Broadway in two editions of the *Music Box Revue* before going into their first book musical, Lyle Andrews's production of a musical, based on an Edward Laska play, which went from being called *We've Got to Have Money* to *The Fly-by-Nights* to *The Ramblers* (1926). When it got to town, with Clark starring as the spiritualistic medium Professor Cunningham, alongside the servant Sparrow, of McCullough, it proved a jolly

Broadway success. *The Ramblers* played for 290 performances, a run for which the two comedians took a large share of the credit. In between variety and film engagements, they subsequently appeared together in *Strike Up the Band* (1930, Man About Town/Colonel Holmes), *Here Goes the Bride* (1931, Hives), the revue *Walk a Little Faster* (1932) and *Thumbs Up* before McCullough's suicide in 1936.

Clark then continued his career alone, playing in the *Ziegfeld Follies of 1936, The Streets of Paris,* and the revusical *Star and Garter,* appearing top-billed as the happily crooked Joe Bascom of *Mexican Hayride,* as the star of a revival of *Sweethearts* (1947), as Waldo Wellington, husband to America's first woman President, in *As the Girls Go* (1948) on Broadway and, in Los Angeles, alongside Mitzi Gaynor in *Jollyanna* (1952), a rewrite of the Broadway failure *Flahooley.*

He later turned his hand to directing, but continued to perform away from Broadway appearing in the television musical *Once Upon an Eastertime* in 1954, and on tour, in 1956, as Applegate in *Damn Yankees* in his final appearance on the musical stage.

Clark was portrayed by Gerry Vichi in the musical *Ain't Broadway Grand* (1993).

CLARK, Petula [OLWEN, Sally] (b Ewell, Surrey, 15 November 1932). Durable British star whose late entry into the musical theatre proved highly successful.

Petula Clark appeared as a vocalist on British radio and a juvenile actress in films (*London Town, The Huggets, The Card,* etc) from a young age, before making a career as a popular singer at first in Britain (''The Little Shoemaker,'' ''Majorca,'' ''Suddenly There's a Valley,'' ''With All My Heart,'' ''Alone,'' etc), then in France (''Ya Ya Twist'') and ultimately on an international scale (''Downtown,'' 1964). She topped the British hit parade with ''Sailor'' in 1961. During the 1960s she placed a series of numbers in the British and American charts (''My Love,'' ''I Couldn't Live without Your Love,'' etc) and scored another UK number one with Charlie Chaplin's ''This is my Song.'' She subsequently appeared in her own television programs on both sides of the Atlantic.

In 1968 she appeared alongside Fred Astaire and Tommy Steele in the American film of *Finian's Rainbow* and the following year opposite Peter O'Toole in a musicalized *Goodbye, Mr Chips,* but it was another decade before she made her stage musical debut when, in what seemed a bit of tardy casting, she was cast as Maria in the first post-Julie Andrews revival of *The Sound of Music* in London (1981). The gamble, however, proved not to be one, and Clark's Maria proved both viable and popular. She subsequently appeared in London as Grizabella in *Cats,* in both London and on Broadway as Mrs Johnstone in *Blood Brothers* (1993, t/o), and also wrote and starred in her own musical *Someone Like You.* Originally produced by the Cambridge Theatre Company, it was subsequently picked up by Harold Fielding (whose office had originally turned it down) and transported to the Strand Theatre where it expired quickly.

She subsequently took over the role of Norma Desmond in the London production of *Sunset Boulevard,* giving the character both the star quality and the vocal values it required but had so rarely had in tandem, and after the show's closing went on tour in America playing Miss Desmond in a de-hydraulicized version of the same show. Some half a century after her first stage appearances, she was clearly good for decades to come.

1989 **Someone Like You** (Dee Shipman/Fay Weldon, Robin Midgley) Cambridge; Strand Theatre 22 March 1990

Biography: Kon, A: *This Is My Song* (Comet, 1983)

CLARY, Mlle

One Mlle Clary (née Poirel-Tardieu), equipped with ''a remarkably graceful figure, easy movements, a nice soprano voice and a very handsome face'' and billed as being ''of Saint-Petersburg,'' went to Britain as a member of Eugène Humbert's Théâtre des Fantaisies-Parisiennes company—which played at the Gaiety Theatre in 1871 (Hélène in *La Belle Hélène,* Roland in *Les Bavards,* etc)—and stayed on, pleading in court, when Humbert tried to force her to return to continue her contract in Belgium, that she suffered too heavily from seasickness to make the crossing. Her court performance must have been convincing, for she remained in Britain where she created the roles of the Grand Duke in Jonas's *Cinderella the Younger* (1871) and Sparkeion in Sullivan and Gilbert's *Thespis,* and played Naphtha in a revival of Hervé's *Aladdin II,* all at the Gaiety, as well appearing as Alexandrivoire in London's *L'Oeil crevé* (1872), Méphisto in *Le Petit Faust* at Holborn, and as La Belle Adrienne in Offenbach's *The Bohemians* (*Le Roman comique,* 1873) at the Opéra-Comique. She then vanished from London and, as far as can be seen, from theatrical annals.

In 1879 another Mlle Clary, this one admitting to the first name of Élise, wholly untrained and 17 years of age, was taken on by Parisian producer Louis Cantin and given the starring ingenue role of Audran's *Les Noces d'Olivette.* She scored a considerable personal success in that considerable success, and she subsequently created two further important roles in French opérettes: the soubrette part of Louise in *Les Mousquetaires au couvent* (''Mon Père, je m'accuse'') and the bright little gardener girl, Josefa, in Lecocq's *Le Coeur et la main.* She was still to be seen in the company at Folies-Dramatiques in

1883 (Hermos in *L'Amour qui passe,* etc) but then she too disappeared.

There was even a third and later Mlle Clary on the Paris musical stage, but she achieved nothing to rate with her homonyms before she, in her turn, did the Clary vanishing act.

One of them . . . I wonder which . . . surfaced in 1887 at the Gaîté in the role of L'Opinion Publique in the year's revival of *Orphée aux enfers.*

CLAY, Frederic [Emes] (b Paris, 3 August 1839; d Marlow, Bucks, 24 November 1889). The first significant composer of the modern era of British musical theatre.

The son of James Taylor Clay (d London, 26 September 1873), cousin to a baronet and MP for Hull over a period of some 20 years, but more celebrated for his skill as a whist player, young Clay studied music in Leipzig but began his working life as a civil servant, in the Treasury Department. He subsequently became secretary to a series of cabinet ministers, including the future Lord Wolverton, and was employed on several occasions to carry out confidential missions on behalf of Mr Gladstone himself.

Freddie Clay's music was heard in London for what seems to have been the first time in 1860, when Florence Lancia included his ballad ''Ninety-Three'' in her drawing room entertainment, and his first efforts to compose for the stage were written for society amateurs (*The Pirate's Isle*) and/or for one-off occasions—*Out of Sight* was given at a matinée by a cast including Erminia Rudersdorff and J G Patey, and *Court and Cottage* for Louisa Pyne's Benefit at Covent Garden. An inheritance of £6,000 allowed him to give up his secretarial duties and to devote himself full-time to a musical career, the first fruits of which were the cantata *The Knights of the Cross* (lib: Robert Reece) produced at King's College Hospital 20 July 1866 with Arthur Sullivan conducting, and revised as *The Red Cross Knight* (St James's Hall 22 November 1871 w Titiens, Trebelli-Bettini, and Sullivan at the organ), and three short operettas written to texts by three highly successful librettists, the celebrated modern playwright Tom Robertson, Charlie Stephenson and W S Gilbert.

The last of these, *Ages Ago,* made an enormous success at the German Reeds' Gallery of Illustration, and Clay subsequently wrote three further works with Gilbert, another one-acter for the Reeds and Gilbert's first two full-length comic operas, *The Gentleman in Black* (arguably the first genuine British musical comedy of the modern era) and *Princess Toto,* each of which found a certain success if not, in either case, a long West End run.

Clay was well-enough established, by 1872, as Britain's foremost light theatre composer, to be teamed with the Continental musicians Hervé, Rivière, de Billemont and Jacobi on the scores for the year's two London grands opéras-bouffes féeries, *Babil and Bijou* (River of Life March, ''Wanda, Pure Spirit of the Waters'') and *The Black Crook.* He more than held his musical own with his European fellow composers, and his ''Nobody Knows as I Know,'' as sung by Kate Santley, was the song hit of the second show.

Plate 77. **Mlle Clary.** *The seasick one.*

Miss Santley then commissioned Clay to write an entire opéra-bouffe for her, and the resultant *Cattarina* was successfully toured (with Clay conducting) and played in London. It did not challenge the best French models of the period either in style or in stamina, but a second venture with Miss Santley produced finer fare. W S Gilbert proved a more effective librettist than Robert Reece, and *Princess Toto* was successful enough to not only be brought to London (where a disagreement between Gilbert and the composer seems to have cut its life short) but to be played in both America and Australia, and to be later revived.

Santley's *Black Crook* co-star and author, Harry Paulton, also called upon Clay and his music again when he wrote himself another Alhambra spectacular, *Don Quixote,* but the most successful of Clay's theatre pieces was undoubtedly a third piece for Miss Santley, his 1883 collaboration with George Sims on the racing musical *The Merry Duchess.* The fair producer starred in the piece in London for 177 performances, before it was sent on tour and played, like *Princess Toto,* in America and Australia, and everywhere with a little more success than the earlier show had achieved.

A second collaboration with Sims produced a fine fairy tale piece, *The Golden Ring,* for the Alhambra but, walking home from the theatre with his colleague one evening soon after the opening, Clay suffered a stroke. Although he gradually recovered, he was unable to write any further music and, shortly after his fiftieth birthday, he died. His brother Cecil, a barrister, husband of Rosina Vokes, and the author of the remarkably successful musical playlet *A Pantomime Rehearsal* (mus: Edward Jones, Terry's Theatre 6 June 1891, Theatre Royal, Sydney 25 July 1903, etc) later used some of Freddie's trunk music as part of the score of a musical version of the Vokes Family's *In Camp* entitled *On the March* (1896).

Apart from his theatre work, which included such items as a song and incidental music for the plays *Shipmates* (1873) and *Monsieur Jacques* (1876, Gaiety Theatre) and for the 1881 production of Pinero's *The Squire,* Clay also composed a number of successful single songs including "The Sands of Dee" (to Charles Kingsley's poem), "She Wandered Down the Mountainside," "'Tis Better Not to Know" and, particularly, "I'll Sing Thee Songs of Araby," introduced by Edward Lloyd as part of a cantata, *Lallah Rookh,* which was first performed at the Brighton Festival in 1877 (Dome, Brighton 13 February). Another cantata *Sardanapalus* was produced at the Leeds Festival of 1882.

Until the advent of Arthur Sullivan, whom he is said to have introduced to Gilbert at the Gallery of Illustration, Clay held pride of place amongst British theatre composers of the mid-19th century but, like all his contemporaries bar Sullivan, nothing of his work has survived into the modern repertoire.

1859 **The Pirate's Isle** (Stephenson) played by amateurs

1861 **Out of Sight** (B Charles Stephenson) 1 act Bijou Theatre 8 July

1862 **Court and Cottage** (Tom Taylor) 1 act Royal English Opera, Covent Garden 22 March

1865 **Constance** (Tom Robertson) 1 act Royal English Opera, Covent Garden 23 January

1868 **The Bold Recruit** (B C Stephenson) 1 act Theatre Royal, Canterbury 4 August; Gallery of Illustration 19 July 1870

1869 **Ages Ago** (W S Gilbert) 1 act Gallery of Illustration 22 November

1870 **The Gentleman in Black** (Gilbert) Charing Cross Theatre 26 May

1871 **In Possession** (Robert Reece) 1 act Gallery of Illustration 20 June

1872 **Happy Arcadia** (Gilbert) 1 act Gallery of Illustration 28 October

1872 **Babil and Bijou** (w Hervé, Jules Rivière, Jean-Jacques de Billemont/J R Planché/Dion Boucicault) Theatre Royal, Covent Garden 29 August

1872 **Ali Baba à la Mode** (w John E Mallandaine, George Richardson, George Grossmith & pasticcio/Robert Reece) Gaiety Theatre 14 September

1872 **[The] Black Crook** (w Georges Jacobi/Harry Paulton, Joseph Paulton) Alhambra Theatre 23 December

1873 **Oriana** (James Albery) Globe Theatre 16 February

1873 **Don Giovanni in Venice** (w Reece, James Molloy, W Meyer Lutz & pasticcio/Reece) Gaiety Theatre 18 February

1874 **Cattarina** (Reece) Prince's Theatre, Manchester 17 August; Charing Cross Theatre 15 May 1875

1876 **Don Quixote** (H Paulton, Alfred Maltby) Alhambra Theatre 25 September

1876 **Princess Toto** (Gilbert) Theatre Royal, Nottingham 26 June; Strand Theatre 2 October

1883 **The Merry Duchess** (George R Sims) Royalty Theatre 23 April

1883 **The Golden Ring** (Sims) Alhambra Theatre 3 December

1896 **On the March** (w Edward Solomon, John Crook/William Yardley, B C Stephenson, Cecil Clay) Prince of Wales Theatre 22 June

CLAY, Lila [HUTTON, Lelia Constance] (b Camden New Town, London, 12 June 1860; d London, 28 July 1899). Musician and guiding light of the all-feminine musical theatre activities which appeared intermittently in Victorian London.

The daughter of a commercial clerk from Camden Town, Miss Clay was a prize pupil at the London Academy of Music. She subsequently worked as a piano demonstrator at a Baker Street music showroom and made appearances as a pianist with van Noorden's Blondinette minstrels until, at just 19 years of age, she launched a £2,000 company (only c500 was subscribed) and got together the personnel to produce her own Ladies' Minstrels Show. Her program included an all-women operetta, *A Dress Rehearsal* (1879), written for her by George Sims and Louis Diehl. Months later the hopelessly insolvent company was wound up. Thereafter "Lila" worked cheerfully in the the theatre as a pianist—and even occasionally on the stage, as someone unbelonging called Lorenza in *La Fille du tambour-major* (1881), in pantomime at Liverpool's Royal Court Theatre, and in a burlesque at the Gaiety (t/o in *Little Jack Sheppard,* 1885)—and, when she could gather some backers, at the head of her Lady Minstrels. She found a marked success when she and the Minstrels—a company including such popular performers as Emily Cross (the original London Ruth in *The Pirates of Penzance*), star dancer Emma D'Auban, contralto Alice Aynsley Cook and the Swiss soprano Edith Vane—appeared at the Opera Comique, with Lila conducting a program consisting of half a minstrel show, under the title *Something New,* and another all-women operetta—at first *On Condition,* then the very successful *An Adamless Eden* (1882). She quarrelled with her American backer, "Colonel" R B Caverley, when he tried to get heavily commercial and started doing things with *An Adamless Eden* of which she did not approve, and she ended up taking her ladies off on tour round Britain with another operetta, *Posterity* (1884), under her own management.

For many years thereafter Lila got some unwanted publicity, winning a kind of fame around America that she could well have done without. When the transatlantic versions of *An Adamless Eden*—now turned from a comic operetta into a vulgar legshow—were sent out around America by such burleycue producers as Mike Leavitt and Sam Jack, they were billed big as being played by "Lilly Clay's company" (accompanied by a picture of a big, busty woman which resembled the trim Lila not a whit). But Leavitt and Jack worked on the principle that a woman's name at the top of the bill was a come-on (Leavitt flogged "Madame Rentz's Minstrels" round the country for years . . . Mme Rentz didn't exist), and Lila—although she protested—could do nothing about their antics. When she finally took a lawsuit, the defendants simply claimed that the name was a phony one that some person had used to front some female minstrels in London, and that was that.

Lila found her way to a second West End success in 1892, when she was hired to lead an on-stage ladies' orchestra in *La Cigale* at the Lyric Theatre (for which she also wrote a little music), and she led her orchestra on occasion at both Covent Garden and Drury Lane, but an attempt to bring back the Lady Minstrels in 1896 in collaboration with Caverley fizzled out expensively.

"Featherbrained always and foolish often," as George Sims described her, yet "to talk with her was always an exhilarating experience," the ever-cheerful Lila drifted happily through her off-and-on musical and theatrical life until her early death.

CLAYTON, Herbert [William] (b Hornsey, 1 December 1874; d London, 16 February 1931). Baritone-turned-producer and librettist, who pulled off one of the more unexpected coups of the 1920s by introducing *No, No, Nanette* to Britain.

For a number of years a member of the Musketeers concert party, along with George Ridgewell and Leslie Stiles (himself later a West End leading man of musicals), the tall, handsome Clayton made what seems to have been his first musical-theatre appearance in 1895 at Richmond, playing Mr Lampton in the burlesque *Good Queen Bess.* The following year he joined the chorus at the Gaiety Theatre for *The Circus Girl* and he subsequently went on tour playing the small role of the Turk in the same show. In 1900 he visited America to play the character role of Abdallah (created at the Savoy by his old colleague Ridgewell) in *The Rose of Persia,* and in 1901 he had his most significant London role under George Edwardes's management as Carajola, the real toreador, in *The Toreador.* After several years of touring in leading baritone roles in Edwardes's companies (*San Toy, A Greek Slave,* Geoffrey Challoner in *A Country Girl, The Duchess of Dantzic, The Count of Luxembourg*), he returned to London to create his most important role as the handsomely rejected Captain Papp in Frank Curzon's production of *Miss Hook of Holland* (1907, "Soldiers of the Netherlands"). The following year he co-starred with *Hook* star, G P Huntley, in an unsuccessful musical, *The Hon'ble Phil* (1908, Captain Jules de Valéry), which the two of them had written together, and the following year visited Australia, where he starred for J C Williamson in *King of Cadonia* (1909, Alexis), *A Country Girl* (1909, Challoner), *The Dollar Princess* (1910, Fredy) and *A Knight for a Day* (1910).

On his return to Britain, Clayton turned first to concert party work, and then switched away from performing to producing, writing and directing, beginning this part of his career with several small-scale revues on the minor British touring circuits. He supplied the text and the direction for a Number 3-houses piece called *Sunshine and Laughter,* produced by first-time producer-cum-composer Jack Waller and, in the wake of this venture, the two went into into partnership, at first writing musical shows which were produced in the music halls by Tom Walls, then, from 1924 onwards, sponsoring similar pieces themselves. In that same year, with the ambition of branching out into top-line musical-theatre production, the pair ventured to America and during their visit they bought up the British rights to several transatlantic musical comedies. The shopping basket they brought home contained *Canary Cottage, The Kiss Burglar, So Long, Letty* and a piece then playing in Chicago called *No, No, Nanette.* Later, when other British managements began chasing the soon enormously successful *Nanette,* they found that its British rights were already the property of two men who had never staged a London show. When Clayton and Waller did produce *No, No, Nanette,* as their first London venture, it launched them straight to the top of the West End world.

They followed up with a further list of imported plays and musicals including the highly successful *Mer-*

cenary Mary (1925), *Hit the Deck* (1927), what passed as *The Girl Friend* (1927), *Good News* (1928), *Merry, Merry* (1929) and *Hold Everything!* (1929), as well as producing a piece of their own, *Virginia,* which, given the temperature of the times, they pretended was not their own, but an American piece until after the notices had come in. *Virginia* gave them a good run and a hit song, ''Roll Away Clouds.'' However, the losses incurred on *Good News* and *Hold Everything!* (and the large percentages required by the writers and producers of transatlantic shows) encouraged them thereafter to renounce imports and instead to construct another major musical of their own. The result was *Dear Love,* a romantic piece starring opera singer Tom Burke, which won fine notices, was snapped up by the Shuberts and which closed after five months. The Shuberts' production was gradually metamorphosed into a revue in which little (if anything) of *Dear Love* remained by the time Broadway was reached.

The partners did better with a spectacular piece called *Silver Wings,* produced at the vast new Dominion Theatre, but Clayton and Waller then dissolved their partnership and went their separate ways. Clayton subsequently combined with touring manager Robert MacDonald on a revival of *The Maid of the Mountains* (1930) and the production of the Vivian Ellis musical *Little Tommy Tucker* at Daly's Theatre (1930) before his premature death in 1931.

1903 **The M.I.s** (Augustus Barratt/w Harry Grattan) sketch Comedy Theatre 24 March

1908 **An Amateur Raffles** (Ralph Nairn/Arthur Anderson) sketch London Pavilion 2 March

1908 **The Hon'ble Phil** (Harold Samuel/Harold Lawson/w G P Huntley) Hicks Theatre 3 October

1923 **Our Liz** (Jack Waller, Pat Thayer/w Con West) Hippodrome, Southampton 13 August

1923 **Suzanne** (Waller, Haydn Wood/w West) Palace Theatre, Plymouth 31 December

1924 **Tilly** (Wood, Waller/Bert Lee, R P Weston/w West) Empire Theatre, Leeds 21 July

1928 **Virginia** (Waller, Joseph A Tunbridge/w Weston, Lee, Douglas Furber) Palace Theatre 24 October

1929 **Dear Love** (Waller, Tunbridge, Wood/w Lauri Wylie, Dion Titheradge) Palace Theatre 14 November

CLÉRICE, Justin (b Buenos Aires, 16 October 1863; d Toulouse, 9 September 1908). A popular French composer who turned out a stream of musical stage pieces, and who saw his works produced in several European countries without achieving any one major success.

Born of a French father, whose profession as a carriage-maker had taken him to the Argentine, the young Clérice followed his pianist sister into musical pastimes and, at 15, wrote and conducted an amateur opérette in Buenos Aires. After his father's death, his mother brought her family back to Paris where the teenaged Justin and his brother, Charles, got their first jobs in the musical world—designing sheet music covers: Charles (later a successful designer) the drawings, Justin the letters. Playing the piano in cabaret to earn a living, he attended the Paris Conservatoire, where he studied with Pessard and Delibes, and soon began writing theatrical pieces. He won his first production at Lisbon, where his *O Moliero d'Alcala* had more than a little success, but, in spite of this, he found that doors were not so easy to open in Paris and he was unable to place any of his writings there until his friend, the actor Volny, persuaded producer/composer Oscar de Lagoanère to give the young composer an opportunity.

Thus, Clérice made his Paris debut at the Bouffes-Parisiens as the composer of a one-act opérette, *Figarella,* which was followed soon after by a second, *Monsieur Huchot,* played as a curtain-raiser to a revival of *La Mascotte,* but, in spite of placing a ballet *Au pays noir* (1891) at the Theatre Royale in Antwerp, his theatrical career did not take off. During this period, however, he made himself a place within a section of elegant Parisian society and turned out several successful songs (''Pour elle,'' ''Deux sous d'amour'') in collaboration with lyricists including Maurice de Féraudy and Miguel Zamacoïs for artists such as Paulette Darty and Lyse Berty.

When Clérice finally achieved a Paris production of a full-length work with the attractive *Le Troisième Hussards,* it was to find disappointment and a run of less than a month, and, although he did altogether better with the score for Fernand Beissier's pantomime *Léda* (1896), produced at the Concert Européen, his next substantial opportunity came in London where Henry Lowenfeld staked the profits he had made on *La Poupée* on staging a new Clérice piece, *La Petite Vénus,* written with Maurice Ordonneau and translated to the English stage as *The Royal Star.* He followed this with an English version of *O Moliero d'Alcala* (*The Coquette* 11 February 1899). The first show ran three months, but the latter folded in five stormy weeks and resulted in the temperance-beer-tycoon producer bowing out of the theatre for good.

In the early years of the 20th century Clérice continued to write in all musical spheres in search of significant success: an épopée militaire called *Vercingetorix;* the ballet *Une fête à Rome* (1900) for the Hippodrome, *Paris-fêtard* for the Olympia, and the long-running spectacular dance piece, *Timbre d'or,* for the Folies-Bergère; incidental music for the Comédie-Française's production of Francis de Croisset's *Chérubin,* small opérettes, of which *Minne* was the best received, a three-act piece called *Au temps jadis* which was christened a ballet-opéra (Monte

Carlo, 1905), and a series of full-length stage pieces each of which achieved some measure of success without winning major acclaim or a place in the repertoire.

In spite of the fact that Clérice's works broke no records in Paris, they were nevertheless welcomed in other countries. Hungary hosted productions of *Les Petites Vestales* (*A vesztaszüzek* Magyar Színház 11 October 1901), *Le Voyage de la mariée* (*A férjhezment kisasszony* Magyar Színház 16 September 1905), *Ordre de l'Empereur* (*Liliom kisasszony* Király Színház 5 October 1905), and *Les Filles Jackson et Cie* (*Cserelányok* Király Színház 28 February 1906), both the last-named piece (*Die Tochter Jackson und Cie*) and *Die kleinen Vestalinnen* (Munich 1902) were played in Germany whilst *Ordre de l'Empereur* was seen at Vienna's Theater an der Wien (*Auf Befehl des Kaisers* 16 April 1904).

Les Filles Jackson et Cie was Clérice's last major work played in Paris, although he contributed to revues at such venues as the Parisiana (*Les Plaques de l'Année, Vive la Parisienne!, Paris s'amuse*) and had the one-act *Oeil de gazelle,* which presented the peculiarity of including the tango in its score, staged in Monaco. His opéra-comique *Les Bohémiens, L'Amour aux castagnettes,* and another military piece written in collaboration with the specialist of the genre, Antony Mars, were all unproduced when he died in 1908 at the age of 44, with the unusual record, for an admittedly second-string composer, of having had his works produced in Portugal, France, Britain, Belgium, Germany, Austria and Hungary.

A one-act opera called *Lorraine* written by one Walter E Grogan with music by Giovanni or "J" Clerici or Clerice was produced at Torquay, England, 10 January 1898, and at St George's Hall, 31 October 1899, on a bill where the composer conducted and played a series of his own piano pieces. Maybe it was him. Maybe it wasn't.

Clérice was married to the vocalist Marguerite [Jeanne Eugénie] Esquilar who played the lead in *Ordre de l'Empereur* and alongside Mariette Sully in *La Bouquetière du Château d'Eau.*

1887 **O Moliero d'Alcala** (Eduardo Garrido, Armand Lafrique) Theatro Trinidade, Lisbon 10 April

1889 **Figarella** (Charles Grandmougin, Jules Méry) 1 act Théâtre des Bouffes-Parisiens 3 June

1889 **Monsieur Huchot** (Jacques Térésand) 1 act Théâtre des Bouffes-Parisiens 3 October

1892 **Pierrot remouleur** 1 act Hotel Continental 30 April

1894 **Le Troisième Hussards** (Antony Mars, Maurice Hennequin) Théâtre de la Gaîté 14 March

1895 **Phrynette** (Fernand Beissier) 1 act Parisiana 29 January

1896 **Hardi les Bleus** (Léon Garnier, A L'Hoste) Ba-ta-clan 24 October

1896 **Pavie** (Garnier, J Joubert) Casino Municipale, Nice; Ba-ta-clan 28 January 1897

1897 **La Vie du soldat** 1 act Parisiana 17 April

Plate 78. **Justin Clérice**

1897 **Oncle Jean** (de Méria) 1 act Dunkirk 4 December

1898 **Le Roi Carnaval** (Lucien Puech, Bannel) 1 act Parisiana 1 February

1898 **The Royal Star** (*La Petite Vénus*) (Maurice Ordonneau ad Francis Richardson) Prince of Wales Theatre, London 16 September

1900 **Les Petites Vestales** (w Frédéric Le Rey/Ernest Depré, Arthur Bernède) Théâtre de la Renaissance 22 November

1902 **L'Agence Léa** (w Rodolphe Berger, Édouard Mathé/ Miguel Zamacoïs) Théâtre des Capucines 31 January

1902 **Ordre de l'Empereur** (Paul Ferrier) Théâtre des Bouffes-Parisiens 4 March

1904 **Le Béguin de Messaline** (Maurice de Féraudy, Jean Kolb) La Cigale 30 January

1904 **Une journée à Paris** (Germain, Paul Moncousin) 1 act Théâtre de la Gaîté 1 December

1904 **Les Robinsonnes** (P Delay) 1 act Eldorado 8 September

1904 **Otéro chez elle** (Germain, Moncousin) 1 act Théâtre des Mathurins 10 October

1904 **Le Voyage de la mariée** (w Edmond Diet/Paul Ferrier, Ordonneau) Galeries Saint-Hubert, Brussels 9 December

1905 **Minne** (Willy) 1 act Boîte à Fursy 6 February

1905 **Paris s'amuse** (Eugène Joullot) Parisiana March

1905 **Au temps jadis** (Maurice Vaucaire) Monte Carlo 16 April

1905 **Les Filles Jackson et Cie** (Ordonneau) Théâtre des Bouffes-Parisiens 29 November

1906 **Paris-fêtard** (Ernest Grenet-Dancourt, Georges Nanteuil) 1 act Olympia 3 February

Plate 79. **Laddie Cliff** *as Albert ''Skinney'' Skinner and Vera Bryer as Jane give choreographic illustration to the lyric ''Dance the Polka Again'' in* The Millionaire Kid.

1907 **Vive la Parisienne!** (w Charles Borel-Clerc, Émile Bonnamy, et al/Maurice Froyez) Parisiana 16 January

1908 **Oeil de Gazelle** (Paul Ferrier) 1 act Monte Carlo February

1909 **Le Baiser de Ninon** (Moncousin) 1 act Saint-Cloud September

CLIFF, Laddie [PERRY, Clifford Albyn] (b Bristol, 3 September 1891; d Montana, Switzerland, 8 December 1937). Bespectacled comedian and dancer who successfully turned producer in the dance-and-laughter era of the British musical theatre.

Laddie Cliff began his performing career under the name of ''Little Cliff,'' making his first appearance at Lerwick in the Shetland Islands in the Calvertos Concert Party at the age of six. He played in concert parties, in music hall (Tivoli, Oxford Music Hall, etc), and in pantomime (Toddlums in *Blue Beard* Crystal Palace, 1901, etc, ''a sand, step and clog dancer of exceptional cleverness'') in his juvenile years before quitting Britain for Australia (1906) and then, at Christmas the following year, for the vaudeville stages of America where eventually, now billed as ''Laddie'' Cliff, he was introduced to the musical theatre playing a burlesque King Manuel of Portugal to the Gaby Deslys of Ethel Levey in the little *Gaby* (1911). He also took part in a production of *To-night's the Night* in Chicago (1915), appearing in the role of Henry originated by Lauri de Frece and played in London by the young Leslie Henson.

He returned to Britain in 1917 and made his West End debut playing in the revue *The Bing Girls Are There* at the Alhambra (1917) before landing his first London musical comedy role in Bernard Hishin's London production of *His Little Widows* (1919, Pete Lloyd), supporting Gene Gerrard and dance-and-duetting ''I Don't Believe You'' with Joan Hay. His dancing talents won him choreographic assignments on Charlot's *The Wild*

Geese and the revue *Pins and Needles,* his comic abilities a place in the cast of the revue *Jigsaw* performing "Swanee," and the combination of all his talents found him a prominent place in the celebrated concert-party The Co-Optimists.

He appeared in revue and also in several musicals over the following years, replacing Joe Coyne in the light comedy lead of *Katinka* (1923, t/o Hopper), succeeding Lupino Lane in the cast of *Brighter London* and taking part in Charlot's *Leap Year* and 1925 revue, as well as choreographing George Grossmith and Pat Malone's production of Gershwin's *Primrose* (1924), before making his first attempt as a producer of musical comedy.

Cliff's first production, in conjunction with Firth Shephard, was the musical comedy *Dear Little Billie* (1925, Sir Frederick Fotheringay), written by Shephard, composed by H B Hedley and Jack Strachey, directed by Cliff and featuring his fellow Co-Optimist and wife, Phyllis Monkman, Robert Michaelis, Vera Robson and Cliff himself in the lead roles. It had a fair tour and 86 performances in London. The following year he took a reef in his producing activities and performed in *Tip-Toes* (1926, Al Kaye) at the Winter Garden, but in 1927 he took a lease on the newly built Carlton Theatre and, in partnership with Edward O'Brien, opened it with another Shephard/Hedley and Strachey musical, a new version of *His Little Widows* called *Lady Luck* (1927, Biff Morton). This time he and Miss Monkman were joined at the head of the cast by Leslie Henson and the Australian song and dance pair, Madge Elliott and Cyril Ritchard; Felix Edwardes and Max Rivers were hired to direct and choreograph, and the result was a run of nearly ten months.

Edgar Wallace's musical comedy drama *The Yellow Mask* (mus: Vernon Duke), which followed *Lady Luck* into the Carlton, found Cliff producing in partnership with provincial panto giant Julian Wylie and had Bobby Howes making his star debut. It provided another success, although one which had to be moved twice owing to theatre problems, and it ended up as a then rare example of a musical played in the variety hallows of the London Palladium.

In 1928 he turned back to the kind of show he had mounted with *Dear Little Billie* and produced *So This Is Love,* a dance-and-laughter musical in which he successfully featured himself (as Hap J Hazzard) and Stanley Lupino alongside Ritchard and Miss Elliott at the Winter Garden. This piece established a comedy-with-choreography formula which was then most successfully followed up in *Love Lies* (1929, Rolly Ryder), *The Love Race* (1930, Bobby Mostyne) and *The Millionaire Kid* (1931, Albert Skinner), with Lupino and Cliff supplying the fun, Ritchard and Elliott the graceful dancing and romance, and Cliff teaming up with a soubrette (such as Vera Bryer) for the more lighthearted dance pieces.

Whilst this run of productions played London and the provinces, Cliff continued with further musical-theatre enterprises. He presented Phyllis Monkman in *So Long, Letty* in the provinces, stepped unconvincingly into unfamiliar territory with the production of Lehár's *Frederica,* starring Joseph Hislop and Lea Seidl, at the Palace, and attempted twice, with limited success, to set up a "B team," headed by the monocled provincial comedian George Clarke, to hold the fort in town while his "A" team toured their London hits. *Darling, I Love You* (1929) and *Blue Roses* (1931) proved much less effective than the "A" shows.

Ritchard and Miss Elliott subsequently moved on to America and Australia, but the Lupino/Cliff partnership continued and, after a short break filled with revue and concert party activities, they came back to the Gaiety Theatre in 1934 for 10 months of *Sporting Love* (Peter Brace). Lupino was absent for the three months of *Love Laughs—* (1935, Gus Burns), but he returned to join Cliff for another big success in *Over She Goes* (1936, Billy Bowler) and for *Crazy Days* (1937, James J Hooker). For this last occasion it was Cliff who was missing from the team. Taken ill during the tryout, he had to be replaced and, a fortnight after the show's failure in London, he died.

In his later years, Cliff appeared in a number of films and, of his productions, *Love Lies, The Love Race, Sporting Love* and *Over She Goes* were all made up into films. In the two earlier pieces Cliff's stage roles were taken by Jack Hobbs, but in the last two he himself appeared to put his partnership with Lupino on celluloid.

CLIFFORD, Camille [OTTERSON, Camilla Antoinetta] (b Antwerp, ?1885; d Churt, Frensham, 28 June 1971). Belgian-born and Danish-bred showgirl and beauty contest winner, who became a short-lived sensation on the British musical stage.

Brought up in Antwerp, Christiana and Nova Scotia, Miss Clifford ran away, so it is said, to Boston at the age of 14, worked as a walk-on and as a cigar and candy girl at the Columbia Theater, and had her first chorus line job in the Boston-born US production of *Morocco Bound* (1901). She made it to town in the chorus of the Herald Square Theater's musical comedy *The Defender* (1902), and rehearsed seven weeks and played just one in another Boston-starter, *Bobadil,* before going on the road as a decorative element of a tour of two rather surer if older shows: *The Mikado* and *HMS Pinafore.* She finally found herself a hit show when she was cast in the front line for *The Prince of Pilsen* (1903) and in 1904 she went to Britain as part of the American company which played that show at London's Shaftesbury Theatre. Her wordless but well-staged appearance as "the Gibson Girl" made her the fashion of the London season, and she stayed in Britain to make the most of the unexpected stardom conferred on her by her reputed 11-inch waist and adjacent measurements.

A role was written into the London hit *The Catch of the Season* for her in which she spoke and voicelessly made her way through a number called ''The Gibson Girl,'' and a spot was then organized for her in which to strut her stuff in a new musical, *The Belle of Mayfair.* She proved so popular that she was again given a song, ''Why Do They Call Me a Gibson Girl?,'' and billing of a size which provoked the walkout of the show's nominal star, Edna May. Miss Clifford was able to enjoy her fame for the rest of the run, after which it was put to rest in a marriage with the Hon Henry Lyndhurst Bruce (1906) and retirement from the stage.

After her husband's death in action at Ypres, she returned briefly to the stage, appearing in 1916 in a music-hall scena, *The Girl of the Future,* before remarrying and once again demurely quitting the boards for a long retirement as the horse-racing Mrs J M J Evans.

CLIVIA Operette in 3 acts by Charles Amberg and F Maregg (ie, Franz Massarek). Music by Nico Dostal. Theater am Nollendorfplatz, Berlin, 23 December 1933.

A local-colorful German Operette which moved into the topical Ruritania of America's filmland for its story, *Clivia* had a heroine (Lillie Claus) who was the 1930s equivalent of an operettic fairy princess—a film star. Sent out to Boliguay, South America, to work on a movie, Clivia Gray gets mixed up with a hugely complex and intermittently political plot featuring one Juan (Walter Jankuhn), who is really the President of Boliguay in disguise; his sister, Jola (Lill Sweet), a kind of Boliguayan Amazon, who heads a troupe of feminine border guards; a comical German tourist called Kasulke (Egon Brosig), who invents things; a comical American reporter called Lelio (Erik Ode), who is destined to pair off with Jola; and a Chicago financier called Potterton, who is using the filming as a front and is really bent on fomenting revolution. When Juan is finally convinced that Clivia is not part of the by-then-failed plot, she can become Mrs President.

Dostal's score illustrated the rather garish combination of jolly improbabilities and screenish romance aptly, featuring several showy numbers for its leading lady, notably the umpteenth ''Ich bin verliebt'' of Operette history, and some romantic baritone work for the President, but the most enjoyable musical moment came in a little tarantella for the lighthearted Lelio, singing of what goes on ''Am Manzanares.''

Clivia did well enough at Jankuhn's Theater am Nollendorfplatz to earn a return season (17 September 1937) with Lillie Claus (Frau Dostal) again featured in the title role. It was subsequently played widely in German houses, introduced in Poland, Luxembourg, Switzerland, Finland and Yugoslavia, filmed for television with Claude Farell and the voice of Anneliese Rothenberger featured, and has held a place on the fringes of the German-language repertoire since. In the 1960s it was seen in Belgium (Liège 13 November 1965) and in France in a French-language version (ad René Rogé, Freddy Ledain, Marcel Désiron).

France: Grand Théâtre, Bordeaux 25 January 1966

TV film: Central-Europa/Prisma 1952

Recordings: selections (RCA), part-record (Eurodisc, EMI Electrola, Telefunken), etc

LES CLOCHES DE CORNEVILLE Opéra-comique in 3 acts by Clairville and Charles Gabet. Music by Robert Planquette. Théâtre des Folies-Dramatiques, Paris, 19 April 1877.

Les Cloches de Corneville was the first full-length opéra-comique to be written by 24-year-old composer Robert Planquette, whose career to that time had been limited largely to the world of the café-concert, where he had, in his teens, made his mark with the march ''Sambre et Meuse'' and with various songs and scenas for Anna Judic and others.

The libretto to *Les Cloches de Corneville,* written very much in the old opéra-comique style with its marquises and maidens and missing heirs, was basically the work of one Charles Gabet, a police inspector with theatrical aspirations and a few mediocre play credits. It was accepted, with some misgivings, by Louis Cantin, the most adventurous and outstanding Parisian impresario of his time, and given to Clairville, the co-author of *La Fille de Madame Angot,* for a remake and fresh lyrics. Cantin originally offered their piece to Hervé for its musical setting, but the inventor of the opéra-bouffe found the text lacking in the kind of comic extravagance in which he specialized and, when he came up with some outrageously crazy suggestions for changes to the script, the athors demurred and Cantin had to look elsewhere for the show's music. It was apparently thanks to the persistent plugging of Pierre Véron, the editor of the journal *Charivari* and Planquette's sometime librettist and permanent champion, that the text of *Les Cloches de Corneville* was ultimately offered to the young composer. Clairville, originally indignant at his text going to an unknown, was soon won by the young man's attractive melodies and good presentation (Planquette had a good baritone voice with which to demonstrate his work) and according to one version of the piece's history (there are several, very contradictory ones about) the first act was completed within three days, the whole thing in ten days, and rehearsals were soon under way at the Folies-Dramatiques. Confidence in the show was, apparently, not high but the music-publisher Bathlot heard a rehearsal and promptly bought the publishing rights for the piece, a gesture which allowed it to make its way to its first night in uncut form.

Another ''version'' of the genesis of the show has the writers and composer hawking the completed piece around for four years during which—nearly a century before *Jesus Christ Superstar* and its pre-production recording—Planquette's music was heard in preview on musical plate stands. Only four years on, so this version goes, did Cantin accept the show for the Folies-Dramatiques. However, since the system in the French theatre of those days was for the manager to accept a libretto and commission a score, the earlier story seems the more likely one.

Miserly old Gaspard (Ange Milher) is the steward of Corneville castle, the lords of which fled the troubled region many years previously along with the Comte de Lucenay who, at the same time, left his young daughter, Germaine (Marie Gélabert) in the trustee's care. Through the years, Gaspard has cared for the castle estates, piling up the revenues, which he has come now to regard as virtually his own, and weaving a myth that the castle is haunted to keep the local peasants away. When a new magistrate (Luco) comes to town and talks of reopening the castle, Gaspard decides to win him over by giving him Germaine as a wife. But Germaine has already promised to wed no one but the layabout Jean Grénicheux (Simon-Max), who saved her from drowning, and Grénicheux, previously promised to Gaspard's maid, Serpolette (Juliette Simon-Girard), is delighted at the thought of such a profitable marriage.

A mysterious young man, who is none other than Henri, the long absent heir to the Marquisate of Corneville (Ernest Voix), turns up in town and hires himself three servants at the hiring fair—they are Grénicheux and Serpolette, who are thus protected from the furious Gaspard, and Germaine, safe, for the period of her hiring, from marriage to the magistrate. Henri announces his identity and the fact that it was he, not his new servant, who saved Germaine from the sea, and the merry band head off to take possession of Henri's ancestral castle. There they discover both Gaspard's hoard and the papers proving that he houses the heiress of Lucenay. The old man comes to the castle to gloat over his gold, and is frightened literally out of his wits when Henri and his friends appear, ghostlike, in the armor of the Marquis's ancestors. In the final act Gaspard recovers his reason and his honesty and all is confessed. Henri will wed Germaine, Serpolette, who for an act supposed herself to be Mlle de Lucenay, takes Grénicheux . . . as her servant, and the old magistrate sagely forgets about the foolishness of taking a young wife.

If the libretto was perhaps not the most original, it did have the great advantage of containing a series of splendid characters and acting roles, and Cantin's casting emphasized this advantage. The comedian Milher, cast as Gaspard, with his two big central comic yet dramatic scenes—his second-act confrontation with the ''ghosts'' and his third-act mad scene and confession—proved adept at both the comedy and the pathos. The young Simon-Max mixed comedy and tenorizing as the cocky Grénicheux in a way which was to characterize an exceptional career, whilst the two girls' roles were cast with fresh-voiced teenagers: Marie Gélabert, straight out of the Conservatoire, who had originally refused the part of Germaine in order to get married but returned at the last moment when Berthe Stuart, the singer cast instead, fell ill, and Juliette Girard (Serpolette). Both were to become enduring stars of the Parisian musical stage.

The trump card of *Les Cloches de Corneville* was, however, its musical score. From end to end, it was a veritable parade of hits, highlighted by Grénicheux's lilting carol to the sea, ''Va, petit mousse'' and his sweetly sung pack of lies ''Je regardais en l'air,'' telling how he saved the drowning girl; Germaine's famous legend of the bells with its ''digue-digue-don'' refrain; Serpolette's vigorous ''Chanson du cidre de Normandie''; Henri's waltz rondeau ''J'ai fait trois fois le tour du monde''; and the soaring, powerful march entrance of his ghostly troupe ''Sous les armures de leur taille,'' which climaxed the first act. There were also some splendid ensembles, topped by the comical trio ''Fermons les yeux.'' The music won some sneeringly snooty comments from the loftier critics. One of them chose to dub it ''musiquette,'' others accused it of being stained with the simplicity of the café-concert, but Planquette's score won an uncompromisingly warm reception from the public.

Les Cloches de Corneville played for two months and then closed whilst other shows necessarily passed across the Folies-Dramatiques stage. But it was only a temporary closure, and six weeks later the show was back, to begin a nonstop run of nearly 18 months—a dazzling record for the times. Perhaps it could have run even longer, but Cantin left the Folies-Dramatiques to take up the management of the Bouffes-Parisiens, and his successor Blandin, his vanity only able to take an inherited triumph for so long, removed *Les Cloches* on Christmas day, after its 580th performance, in order to introduce a triumph of his own: Offenbach's most successful later show, *Madame Favart.* Offenbach's work was, in its turn, removed before its time to allow what was to be the first of many reprises of *Les Cloches de Corneville* at the Folies-Dramatiques, prior to its emigration on to other metropolitan stages. By that time it had largely passed its thousandth Parisian performance. In 1892 the Gaîté presented the show with a particularly fine cast headed again by Mlle Gélabert, by the actor Paulin Menier as Gaspard, the star baritone, Louis Morlet, as Henri and Paul Fugère as a comical Grénicheux, and the piece was repeated frequently there over the next 65 years. Juliette Simon-Girard (she had married her *Cloches* co-star, Simon-Max) repeated her original role at the Théâtre de la Porte-Saint-Martin in 1908, and André Baugé (Théâtre Mogador, 1940) and Michel Dens (Gaîté-Lyrique, 1953, 1958) were both seen as the Marquis in later revivals. The last major Parisian revival was at the Théâtre de la Porte-Saint-Martin in 1968.

France saw one non-Parisian performance of *Les Cloches de Corneville* in 1901 which was rather a special one. It was mounted at the place of the title itself—Corneville-sur-Risle. Corneville's church did not have—and had in fact never had—either a tower or bells and, a quarter of a century after the production of the opérette which had made known worldwide the name of Corneville, the Marquis de Rochethulon headed an appeal to permit the town famous for its (non-existent) bells finally to have some. The bells were duly cast, but there was insufficient money to pay for the building of the belfry, and so a performance of Planquette's opérette was given, and the money raised therefrom.

The career of *Les Cloches de Corneville* outside France was equally spectacular. Whilst the piece was still playing its first months at the Folies-Dramatiques, it appeared in Madrid and in Brussels and, in its first English-language production, it was played at New York's Fifth Avenue Theater by the touring C D Hess Opera Company with Zelda Seguin (Germaine) and Emilie Melville (Serpolette) starring. Within the next few years, New York would hear the French *Cloches* from Mlle Aimée and Paola Marié and English ones from Catherine Lewis and Laura Joyce, from the Boston Ideals and Emma Abbott's Opera Company, as the piece became an obligatory part of the baggage of every touring comic opera company. It appeared on Broadway in repertoire in 1898 with Frank Moulan as the old Bailli, in a potted version at Proctor's Music Hall in the same year, and in 1913 a revival was mounted by the Aborn brothers. It featured elephants in the hiring-fair scene and a swing chorus, and a ditty called "When It's Apple Blossom Time in Normandy" was interpolated into the score! The show, apparently without elephants and "Apple Time," was reproduced by Milton Aborn in New York as late as 1931 (Erlanger's Theater 2 November).

If the repertoire system then in vogue for opéra-bouffe and opéra-comique productions in America did not allow *Les Cloches de Corneville* to set up any kind of a Broadway run, the same was not the case in Britain where such shows played straight seasons and runs. Until the arrival of Planquette's piece, however, none had ever played as long as *Les Cloches de Corneville.* The story is told that publisher Joseph Williams arrived late for his visit to the Paris production, and then walked out straight after the first number he heard. That number was the Legend of the Bells, and he walked out in order to buy the British rights. Those rights he sublet to producer Alexander Henderson who staged the piece (ad H B Farnie, Robert Reece) at the second-rate Folly Theatre with his resident stars American soprano Kate Munroe (Serpolette), very young Violet Cameron (Germaine) and Australian baritone John Howson (Henri), all of whom had recently appeared in his potted version of Offenbach's *La Créole.* Gaspard was played by the Australian-Irish actor Shiel Barry. The show was a sensational success and, come summer, Henderson closed down his production briefly to effect a transfer from the Folly to the rather better Globe Theatre. There *Les Cloches de Corneville* remained past its second anniversary, closing after 704 performances largely to permit the now hugely successful Henderson to produce what promised to be another major hit in Genée's *Der Seekadett.* That piece, however, was quickly gone and, less than three months after closing, *Les Cloches de Corneville* was back in the West End for another four and a half months. Following not-very-successful productions of *La Famille Trouillat* and *La Boulangère,* it returned yet again the next year for three further months, breaking every London long-run record and comprehensively outrunning its famous contemporary, *HMS Pinafore,* housed similarly in an unfashionable theatre. Shiel Barry is said to have played Gaspard for every one of the London performances and thereafter he made a career of the role in the endless tours which swarmed through British theatres for decades. A potted, half-hour *Cloches de Corneville* was played in British variety houses as late as 1905–6 with Hermann Vezin as Gaspard; a ballet version, using the music from the show (ad George Byng) was mounted at the Alhambra in 1907 (7 October); and the show's last London appearance to date was in 1931.

Meanwhile, *Les Cloches de Corneville* had caused an equal sensation in the other main European musical capitals. In Budapest (ad Jenő Rákosi), with young Ilka Pálmay as Serpolette, it proved to be the most successful musical piece in the glorious history of the city's principal musical house, the Népszínház. At Vienna's Theater an der Wien, where Albin Swoboda (Henri), Felix Schweighofer (Gaspard), Hermine Meyerhoff suceeded by Frln Olma (Haiderose, ie, Serpolette), Sophie König (Germaine) and Alexander Girardi (Grénicheux) starred in Maximilian Steiner's production, it outpointed both of the year's two other major production, Millöcker's highly favored *Das verwunschene Schloss* and Strauss's *Blindekuh,* and it was retained in the repertoire until 1883 (100th performance 26 November 1882). It was thereafter given further productions both there (in repertoire 1898–1902 w Therese Biedermann as Serpolette, 1922) and at several other Viennese theatres (Carltheater 30 November 1883; Jantschtheater 30 November 1901; Kaiser-Jubiläums-Stadttheater 29 January 1908; Raimundtheater, 1909 w Gerda Walde as Haiderose, Franz Gross as Gaspard; Bürgertheater, 1917–20 w Grete Holm as Haiderose).

Ernst Dohm's German version was mounted in Berlin, and the show was also played in Czech, Polish, Italian, Swedish, Slovenian, Latvian, Estonian, Norwegian, Finnish, Lithuanian and Croatian, remaining a prominent part of the European repertoire for more than half a century.

The British colonies reacted no differently to the rest of the world. *Les Cloches de Corneville* triumphed on the Pacific and oriental circuits just as it had everywhere else. The first Australian production was staged by Henry Bracy, with himself in the role of Grénicheux and his wife, Clara Thompson, as Serpolette, and the show was repeated by most comic opera combinations which played in the colony thereafter. Pattie Laverne was a popular Serpolette, Emilie Melville played the same role to the Germaine of Nellie Stewart, and Australia and New Zealand also saw performances from the inveterately touring juvenile troupe, Pollard's Lilliputians, as well as Kelly and Leon's Minstrels' production of the show in which Kelly appeared as Gaspard and Leon as Serpolette. Kelly, however, later went on to play the miser alongside more conventional soubrettes when he appeared as Gaspard with the Royal Comic Opera Company and with other companies throughout Australia and New Zealand.

Les Cloches de Corneville shares with Lecocq's *La Fille de Madame Angot* the distinction of being the most internationally successful product of the French post-opéra-bouffe musical theatre. In the last two decades of the 19th century, these two pieces were revived regularly in the main centers and played almost unbrokenly on the touring circuits, even after the advent of the George Edwardesian musical comedy and the decline in interest in the French style of opéra-comique in the last years of the 19th century. In the early part of the 20th century, the show was still almost permanently on display in France. However, whilst a limited selection of the works of the more marketable names in light musical theatre—Offenbach, Strauss and Lehár—have found a way to remain in the repertoire of some modern houses, *Les Cloches de Corneville* has now virtually ceased to be played outside France. In France, however, it continues to hold its place in the repertoire, and it remains one of the outstanding musical theatre classics of the 19th century.

Plate 80. **Cloclo.** *Maria Rolle was Lehár's little heroine—seen here with Gunter Fritzsche as Chablis—in the Dresden Staatsoperette's 1971 production.*

USA: Fifth Avenue Theater *The Chimes of Normandy* 22 October 1877; UK: Folly Theatre 23 February 1878; Hungary: Népszínház *Kornevilli harangok* 23 March 1878; Germany: Friedrich-Wilhelmstädtisches Theater *Die Glocken von Corneville* 27 March 1878; Austria: Theater an der Wien *Die Glocken von Corneville* 28 September 1878; Australia: Academy of Music, Melbourne 23 November 1878

Recordings: complete (EMI, Decca), complete in Russian (Melodiya), selections (EMI-Pathé, Philips, Vega, etc)

CLOCLO Operette in 3 acts by Béla Jenbach taken from the play *Der Schrei nach dem Kind* by Alexander Engel and Julius Horst. Music by Franz Lehár. Wiener Bürgertheater, Vienna, 8 March 1924.

Luise Kartousch starred as Parisian revue star, Cloclo Mustache, whom the evening followed through the ups and downs of her love affairs with her beloved, but distressingly poor, Maxime de la Valle (Robert Nästlberger) and the wealthy and distinctly married Severin Cornichon (Ernst Tautenhayn), Mayor of Perpignan. Maxime, of course, wins in the end but Severin is a good egg and—having stuck by his little friend through some troubles with the law, and even blushed silently as his own wife, Melousine (Gisela Werbezirk), believing Cloclo to be Severin's wild-oat daughter, has taken the girl under her wing—he sticks by her when she becomes a married woman.

Lehár's score, with tinges of modern dance now appearing alongside the basic waltzes and marches, and much third-act champagne, was the last in which he employed his gay, prewar *Die lustige Witwe* style before moving on to the lusher, romantic unhappy-ending mode of his later works. The bulk of the opportunities fell to the heroine. She made her entrance claiming "Ich suche einen Mann," cooed with Maxime "Wenn eine schöne Frau besiehlt" and, having told Severin "Geh schön nach Haus zu deiner Frau," joined with him to dance to the strains of the "Tonga Bay," which she insisted was "erotisch . . . schick und modern." The most enjoyable moment, however, came when provincially correct Melousine sang topically about her intention to throw over respectability and follow the ideas recently popularized in the scandalous novel, "La Garçonne."

Cloclo was not a triumph. It played to 31 May, visited Berlin, where Gisela Werbezirk repeated her show-stealing performance, and was revived at the Johann Strauss-Theater on 4 September 1925 with Gisela Kolbe (Cloclo) and Max Brod (Severin) for a further two-month season during which it passed its 100th Viennese performance (17 September). In the meanwhile, Budapest had seen an Hungarian version (ad Zsolt Harsányi), rebaptized *Apukam!*

A London production (ad Douglas Furber, Harry Graham) with Cicely Debenham (Cloclo), Claude Bailey (Maxime), A W Baskcomb (Severin) and Sidney Fairbrother (Melusine) in the lead roles interpolated four songs by Max Darewksi and one by Harry Rosenthal (the whole third-act music was non-Lehár) and played 95 performances at the Shaftesbury and Adelphi Theatres. What seems to have been a film version appeared in 1935, with Marta Eggerth in its title role, as *Die ganze Welt dreht sich um Liebe* in Europe and *When the World's in Love* in America.

Another Operette with the same title, with a score by Ferdinand Pagin and a text by Leo Stein and Alexander Landesberg, was produced at Danzers Orpheum, Vienna 23 December 1902 with Fritzi Massary as the titular Clotilde (31 performances), and a couple of decades on yet another put in an appearance in Paris (Albert Valsien/ Francis Kams/Jean Guitton, Eldorado 3 September 1920).

UK: Shaftesbury Theatre 3 August 1925; Hungary: Fővárosi Operettszínház *Apukam!* 15 April 1924; Germany: Berliner Theater 8 November 1924

Film: Viktor Tourjanksy 1935

Recording: selection in Italian (EDM)

CLOSE, Glenn (b Greenwich, Conn, 19 March 1947).

Best known for her appearances on the screen (*Fatal Attraction, Dangerous Liaisons,* etc), Glenn Close has nevertheless led a full career in the theatre, both non-musical (*The Real Thing, Death and the Maiden,* etc) and musical. In the early part of her career she played in the Broadway production of the unsuccessful *Rex* (1976) and created the role of Chairy Barnum in *Barnum* (1980 "The Colors of my Life," "One Step at a Time"). Thirteen years later, having in the meantime become a major star name, she returned to the musical theatre to star in the American production of *Sunset Boulevard* (1993, Norma Desmond).

LA COCARDE DE MIMI-PINSON Opérette in 3 acts by Maurice Ordonneau and Francis Gally. Music by Henri Goublier fils. Théâtre de l'Apollo, Paris, 25 November 1915.

A little patriotic musical play, which scored a hit in Paris in the early days of the Great War, *La Cocarde de Mimi-Pinson* was set in the couture house Robichon-Frivolet and its heroine was Marie-Louise (Jenny Syril), the seamstress who sews a little medallion and a cocarde of ribbons inside the jacket of Jean Robichon (Albert Beauval), the son of her employer (Héraut), to keep him from harm at the front. The charm works, and Marie-Louise wins the wounded, but safe, Jean from Mme Frivolet (Valentine Rauly) in the final act. That finale also paired soubrette Zoë Crochu (Mary Richard) and comic La Mazette (Alphonse Massart), and the cook Sophie (Madeleine Guitty) and Jean's batman Bourriche (Carlos Avril), in time for a patriotic chorus and a parade of soldiers headed by a lieutenant bearing a tricolore. Goublier's largely red-white-and-blue score included several pretty numbers for the heroine (Légende des petits rubans, Rondo de la cocarde, etc), some lively pieces for soubrette Zoë, who led a nurses' march in the second act, and a delightfully comical duo for Bourriche and Sophie dreaming of their future together running a little bar ("Un petit comptoir en étain").

The show had a first run of 130 performances, a fine wartime career, and was remounted in Paris, at the Ba-ta-clan in 1920 with Zabeth Capazza featured and, later, at the Gaîté-Lyrique (20 April 1936). On this last occasion, with the topical and patriotic element no longer apt, the piece was shifted three hundred years back, to a more picturesque costume era, whilst leaving intact the score, which had won much popularity in its time. Sylvane Pressac (Marie-Louise), Monette Dinay (Zoë), Jeanne Perriat (Frivolet), Christiane d'Or (Sophie), Robert Allard (Bourriche) and Le Clezio (Jean) headed the cast through a brief run.

La Cocarde de Mimi-Pinson still receives occasional productions in the provinces of France.

Recording: two record set (Decca)

COCÉA, Alice [Sophie] (b Sinaia, Romania, 1897; d Paris, 2 July 1970).

Born in Romania, but brought to France in her early teens, Mlle Cocéa made her first appearances on the professional stage whilst still a student, and she began her Parisian career in 1917 when she took part in a revival of Guitry's *Le Scandale de Monte-Carlo* at the Théâtre des Bouffes-Parisiens. She followed up in *Psyché* and *La Petite Reine* (1917) at the Gymnase and soon after this appeared, singing American ragtime tunes and impersonating Cleopatra in a Shakespearean burlesque, in the opening revue (*Une revue*) at Gustave Quinson's tiny wartime Théâtre de l'Abri. Quinson next cast her in the ingenue role of the little musical comedy intended to follow the revue, but circumstances resulted in *Phi-Phi* being moved to his Théâtre des Bouffes-Parisiens and there both the show and its 19-year-old leading lady made a sensation. As Aspasie, the wide-eyed courtesan of this long-running Greek historiette, she introduced "Bien chapeautée," "Mon cher Monsieur, excusez-moi" and "Je connais toutes les historiettes." She continued on to star in *Phi-Phi*'s successor, *Dédé,* as the amorous shoe-shop vendeuse, Denise. In this role she made a further hit performing "Et voilà comme" and duets with Maurice Chevalier ("Si j'avais su") and Urban ("Tous les chemins menent a l'amour"), and acting out the sprighly comedy of the show's book.

Mlle Cocéa appeared thereafter in starring ingenue roles in several further musical pieces: alongside Henri Defreyn in the one-act *Ne m'épousez pas!* (1922), opposite Dranem in Raoul Moretti's *En chemyse* (1924), in the title role of Yvain's *Gosse de riche* (1924), and with Defreyn and Marguerite Deval in *À Paris tous les deux* (1926), before heading definitively for the non-musical theatre and the cinema and returning to the musical stage only in 1935 to play in *Trente et quarante.* She was seen on the screen as late as 1964 playing an old concierge in *La Ronde.*

En route, she became la Comtesse Stanislas de la Rochefoucauld with, as one French commentator remarked cattily, "grand profit pour sa carrière."

COCHRAN, C[harles] B[lake] (Sir) (b Lindfield, Sussex, 25 September 1872; d London, 31 January 1951).

After early experience as an actor, as a music-hall and theatrical agent (an experience which ended in 1904 with him up in court charged with embezzlement), as the promoter of "The Devil's Wheel," of rolling skating, of the International Horse Show at Olympia and the "Gem" cinema-with-music-hall Great Yarmouth (1908, more court cases), of the spectacle *The Miracle,* a zoo and other such Barnummeries, C B Cochran entered the theatrical-producing field as a highly successful mounter of revue (*Odds and Ends, More, Pell Mell*). Like Britain's other most-publicized revue producer, André Charlot, he subsequently found that book musical successes were harder to come by.

His first attempt at a musical play was *Houp-La!* (1916), with a score by revue composer Nat D Ayer and with Gertie Millar starring, and it was a whole-hearted failure. However, the revusical wartime saga of Bruce Bairnsfather's Old Bill, staged at the Oxford Theatre as *The Better 'Ole* (1917), proved a long-running success and versions of two French pieces, Émile Lassailly's burlesque opérette *Carminetta* (1917) and Charles Cuvillier's colorful *Afgar* (1919), also had good runs. Whilst the revue successes continued, he found less joy in the pageant *Jolly Jack Tar* (1918), the homemade musicals *Pretty Peggy* and *Cherry* (1920) and Marcel Lattès's *Maggie* (1919). He brought a badly mangled version of Christiné's *Phi-Phi* (1922) to the London Pavilion and failure, from America he took George M Cohan's *Little Nellie Kelly* (1923) to the New Oxford for a good run, and he produced a musical version of the old farce *Turned Up* (1926) at the same venue with less, but not negligible, results.

In 1929 Cochran produced the first musical by Noël Coward, with whom he had worked over the years on revues. *Bitter-Sweet* was a splendid success, and Cochran subsequently produced Coward's *Conversation Piece* (1934). Otherwise, however, he preferred to look for patented overseas successes to bring to London and in the 1930s he introduced London to Kern's *The Cat and the Fiddle* (1932) and *Music in the Air* (1933), Porter's *Anything Goes* (1935), Oscar Straus's *Eine Frau, die weiss, was sie will* (*Mother of Pearl*) as a vehicle for Alice Delysia, Lehár's *Paganini* (1937) with Richard Tauber and Evelyn Laye, and a spectacular revival of another tastelessly mangled classic, Offenbach's *La Belle Hélène* (*Helen!*). Porter's piece was the most successful of the group, running over six months, and of the others only *Paganini* was an quick-fold failure, although the very lushly staged *Helen!* lost large amounts of money for its producer. The only musical initiated by Cochran during the 1930s, Porter's *Nymph Errant,* failed to come up to expectations.

After nearly a decade without producing a musical and several years without producing anything, Cochran put an effective coda to his career, in his seventies, by producing three works by Vivian Ellis and A P Herbert. If *Big Ben* (1946) and *Tough at the Top* (1949) were not very impressive stayers, the second of the trio, *Bless the Bride* (1947), in contrast, gave him the longest-running musical theatre success of his busy and colorful career as a showman producer. When the total of his career as a producer of musical plays was summarized, Cochran was able to take the credit for the creation of a quartet of fine and successful musicals: *Bless the Bride, The Better 'Ole, Bitter-Sweet* and *Conversation Piece.* One per decade of his life in the musical theatre.

Memoirs: *Secrets of a Showman* (Heinemann, London, 1925), *I Had Almost Forgotten* (Hutchinson, London, 1932), *Cock-a-Doodle-Doo* (Dent, London, 1941), *A Showman Looks On* (Dent, London, 1945); Biography: Cleugh, J: *Charles Blake Cochran: Lord Bountiful* (Pallas, London, 1946), Graves, C: *The Cochran Story* (W H Allen, London, 1951), Heppner, S: *Cockie* (Frewin, London, 1969), Harding, J: *Cochran* (Methuen, London, 1988)

COCO Musical in 2 acts by Alan Jay Lerner. Music by André Previn. Mark Hellinger Theater, New York, 18 December 1969.

A slightly biomusical on the life of Parisian couturière, Coco Chanel, the famed popularizer of the ''little black dress'' and the godmother of the Chanel No 5 perfume, *Coco* presented the ageing and long-retired Mlle Chanel (Katharine Hepburn) making a return to the scene of her fame. Her lawyer, Greff (George Rose), unconvinced that she can remake herself a place in the modern fashion world, hires the fussy, limp-wristed Sebastian (René Auberjonois), boyfriend of a leading fashion critic, as her assistant. When she sees the gussied-up dresses he is intending to produce under her name, Chanel tears and snips the excrescences from every one, bringing back some of the simplicity that was her trademark. Paris and Sebastian's pal hate what she has done, but the American mass-market chains love it. Orbachs, Bloomingdales, Best and Saks provide a happy ending. A juvenile love story between Noëlle (Gale Dixon) and Georges (David Holliday) was worked into the main plot.

The short score included six numbers for the star, refusing to knuckle under to the fact that ''The World Belongs to the Young'' and ending up ''Always Mademoiselle,'' Noëlle sang of the healing virtues of ''A Brand New Dress'' and Sebastian revelled in the ''Fiasco'' of the dress show. The many gowns for the show were designed by *My Fair Lady* couturier Cecil Beaton.

Freddie Brisson's production of *Coco* owed its 333 Broadway performances principally to the musical comedy debut of Miss Hepburn (replaced for the last performances by Danielle Darrieux), but they were insufficient to balance the books.

The same title was also used, some years earlier, for the internationally successful spectacular musical comedy written by Clairville, Eugène Grangé and Alfred Delacour, and played throughout Europe with a score, variously, by Auguste Coedès and others (Théâtre des Nouveautés, Paris 12 June 1878, Budapest Népszínház 16 May 1879), Karl Alexander Raida (Germany), Johann Brandl (Carltheater, Vienna 22 March 1879) or Franz Herzeele (Ghent November 1885).

Recording: original cast (Paramount)

THE COCOANUTS Musical comedy in 2 acts by George S Kaufman. Music and lyrics by Irving Berlin. Lyric Theater, New York, 8 December 1925.

A comedy-musical vehicle for the famous vaudeville team the Marx Brothers, *The Cocoanuts* had a tiny, hoary main plot about stolen jewels. The jewels belong to rich Mrs Potter (Margaret Dumont), the thieves are Harvey Yates (Henry Whittemore) and Penelope Martyn (Janet Velie), but the suspect is the impecunious Robert Adams (Jack Barker), the beloved of Mrs Potter's niece Polly (Mabel Withee). That plot, however, was an incidental in a show where the antics of the very dubious, octopus-like Henry W Schlemmer, Florida developer and hotelier (Groucho Marx), and his confederates Willie the Wop (Chico Marx), Silent Sam (Harpo Marx) and Jamison (Zeppo Marx)—occasionally mixed up in the plotline, but more often wildly and zanily doing their own thing—were the thing. The ribbing of the Florida developers was undoubtedly an answer to an earlier musical show of the same year, Earl Carroll's *Florida Girl* (aka *Oh, You!*), backed by the Coral Gables Development Company and unashamedly touting its wares via the musical stage. Irving Berlin's songs, also rather incidental to most of the comedy, ranged from the opening desciption of ''Florida by the Sea'' to dances relatively normal (tango, ''They're Blaming the Charleston'') or zoological and abnormal (''The Monkey Doodle-Doo''), from numbers such as ''A Little Bungalow'' and ''Lucky Boy'' to an excerpt from *Carmen* reset as ''The Tale of the Shirt.''

Sam H Harris's production of *The Cocoanuts* served its purpose splendidly, and the Marx Brothers played 377 Broadway performances of an ever-changing show which was accounted ''one of the season's outstanding successes.'' The brothers subsequently put a version of their show on film. Oscar Shaw (Bob), Mary Eaton (Polly) and Kay Francis (Penelope) joined Miss Dumont in a screenplay (ad Morrie Ryskind) which used only three of the show's songs (''Florida by the Sea,'' ''The Monkey Doodle-Doo'' and the travestied *Carmen*), plus one new number (''When My Dreams Come True'').

An attempt to mount *The Cocoanuts* in London, without the Marx Brothers, but with British provincial comic Fred Duprez (Julius Slimmer) and Madeleine Seymour (Mrs Potter) in the featured roles, lasted only 16 performances. In America, similarly, the piece was long considered too attached to the image of its famous creators to be revivable, but Washington's Arena Stage mounted a production on the occasion of Irving Berlin's 100th birthday (11 May 1988) with Stephen Mellor as Schlemmer and Halo Wines as Mrs Potter, and in 1996 the American Jewish Theater followed suit (12 May). This production transferred to off-Broadway's American Place Theater (15 August 1996) where it played 165 performances with Michael McGrath and Celia Tackaberry featured.

UK: Garrick Theatre 20 March 1928

Film: Paramount 1929

Recording: film soundtrack (Soundtrack)

COE, Peter [Leonard] (b London, 18 April 1929; d nr Byfleet, 25 May 1987). Refreshingly unmannered British director whose ventures into the musical theatre turned out both some important new works in the early years of his career, and some fine stagings of imported pieces in his later days.

After early work in provincial repertory theatres, Coe was appointed director at the newly built Mermaid Theatre in 1959. In its first season he directed his first musical piece with the production of Bernard Miles's adaptation of Henry Fielding, *Lock Up Your Daughters.* Owing to the restrictions of the Mermaid stage space, Coe and designer Sean Kenny evolved a multiple-area series of skeletal constructions to represent the various scenes of the action, a technique not then common in the musical theatre. The style was refined and enlarged for Coe's next musical play, the original production of *Oliver!* (1960). Both production and setting were reproduced many times thereafter in Britain, America and elsewhere.

Amongst a subsequent series of mostly play productions, Coe directed *Pickwick,* the inevitable follow-up to *Oliver!,* in Britain (1963) and America; the Dumas burlesque *The Four Musketeers* (1967); *Kiss Me, Kate* for the Sadler's Wells Opera Company (the first modern musical to be played there); his own attempt at a post-censorship show, *Decameron '73* (1973); and, in contrast, the Moral Rearmament musical *Ride, Ride* (1976).

He spent a period in Canada running the Citadel Theater (1978–81) and another in America as Artistic Director of the American Shakespeare Theatre in Stratford, Connecticut (1981–82), but continued between times to work in Britain where he directed Michael Crawford in *Flowers for Algernon* (1979) and staged Harold Fielding's British productions of the Broadway musicals *On the Twentieth Century* (1978) and *Barnum* (1981, 1985). He was killed in a road accident in 1987 at the age of 58.

COEDÈS, Auguste [Charles] (b Paris, 11 December 1840; d Passy, 13 July 1884). A composer of songs and piano music, prompter at the Opera and later chef de chant at the Théâtre Lyrique, who provided scores for a variety of Parisian musicals shows in the 1870s.

After beginning his working life as an employee of the post office, Coedès turned to music as profession and made his living at first as a pianist and as an accompanist with touring productions. One of these engagements was with an opérette company traveling in the Argentine, and it was there that he stayed and worked for the three years that France was involved in the Franco-Prussian war. On his return to France he won the prompter's post at the Opéra and thereafter became a well-known figure in Parisian musical circles, prized as a lively companion and an excellent pianist and vocalist. His early theatrical compositions included ballet music for the Folies-Bergère (*Les Folies amoureuses*) and some pieces for the féerie spectacular *La Cocotte aux oeufs d'or.* In 1874, following the success of his first important opérette, *La Belle Bourbonnaise,* produced by Louis Cantin at the Folies-Dramatiques with Marie Desclauzas in the title role, and later seen at Vienna's Carltheater and Berlin's Friedrich-Wilhelmstädtisches Theater (*Die schöne Bourbonnaise*), he gave up his employment at the Opéra to concentrate on composing for the theatre.

In the half-dozen years following he had little luck with his shows—whether produced under the management of Cantin or with Brasseur at the Nouveautés, where his *Fleur d'oranger* was chosen as the first opérette to play the new theatre—until his last opérette, *La Girouette,* in 1880. After a good Paris run, this work was produced by Augustin Daly in America as *The Weathercock* (1882) and in Britain with the young Robert Courtneidge starred (1889, Portsmouth/Avenue Theatre). His final stage work was the score for the Théâtre des Nouveautés revue *Les Parfums de Paris* (1880), which brilliantly top-lined Hortense Schneider, Brasseur and Berthelier. During the rehearsals of this revue, the composer became convinced that he had become suddenly enormously wealthy and, claiming that he was being stalked by an enemy, started wandering intently round the theatre with a loaded revolver. Eventually and with difficulty he was removed to an insane asylum where he died, a few years later, at the age of 43.

Coedès also supplied some of the music which accompanied the vaudeville *Coco* (w Adolphe Lindheim, et al), first produced in Paris (Théâtre des Nouveautés 12 June 1878), then in Budapest (Népzsinház 16 May 1879) and expanded into a fuller-scale musical comedy, with additional music by Karl Alexander Raida in Germany, by Johann Brandl in Austria (Carltheater 22 March 1879), and by Franz Herzeele in Belgium (Ghent November 1885).

1872 **Les Griffes du Diable** (Clairville, Charles Gabet) Théâtre des Menus-Plaisirs 18 April

1872 **Le Bouquet de Lise** (Ernest Gerny, Eugène Sari) 1 act Folies-Bergère 20 April

1872 **La Cocotte aux oeufs d'or** (w Hervé, G Raspail/Clairville, Eugène Grangé, Victor Koning) Théâtre des Menus-Plaisirs 31 December

1873 **Il y a un trou** (Pagès de Noyez) Fantaisies-Pigalle 15 March

1873 **Une drole de soirée** (Élie Berthet) 1 act Théâtre de l'Odéon 3 April

1874 **La Belle Bourbonnaise** (Ernest Dubreuil, Henri Chabrillat) Théâtre des Folies-Dramatiques 11 April

1875 **Claire de lune** (Dubreuil, Henri Bocage) Théâtre des Folies-Dramatiques 11 March

1876 **Fleur de baiser** (Alexandre) Théâtre des Folies-Dramatiques 24 February

1876 **Les Mirlitons** (Alfred Duru, Chabrillat, Bocage, Ernest Blum) Théâtre des Folies-Dramatiques 19 April

1877 **L'Éducation d'Achille** Cercle Artistique et Littéraire 28 February

1877 **Le Chevalier de Lastignac** (Bias) Casino Théâtre, Dieppe 14 August

1878 **Le Chat botté** (w Gaston Serpette, de Bourdeau/Étienne Tréfeu, Blum) Théâtre de la Gaîté 18 May

1878 **Fleur d'oranger** (Alfred Hennequin, Victor Bernard) Théâtre des Nouveautés 7 December

1879 **Mon gendre, tout est rompu** (Paul Burani, William Busnach) 1 act Casino de Dieppe 22 August

1879 **Les Deux Nababs** (Hippolyte Raymond, Alphonse Dumas) Théâtre des Nouveautés 21 January

1880 **La Girouette** (Bocage, Émile Hémery) Théâtre des Fantaisies-Parisiennes 3 March

LE COEUR ET LA MAIN Opérette in 3 acts by Charles Nuitter and Alexandre Beaumont. Music by Charles Lecocq. Théâtre des Nouveautés, Paris, 19 October 1882.

After his split with Victor Koning of the Théâtre de la Renaissance, Lecocq struck up a new alliance with manager Brasseur at the Théâtre des Nouveautés and, showing in no mean way that he was far from being finished, as Koning had apparently feared, the composer went on to produce two of his finest works for that house. The first was *Le Jour et la nuit,* the second *Le Coeur et la main,* the libretto of which was said to be based on an unspecified tale of Boccaccio.

Princess Micaëla of Aragon (Mlle Vaillant-Couturier) is to be wed, sight unseen, to Prince Gaétan, Duke of Madeira (Vauthier), but, unlike most of her musical theatre sisters, she is happy enough to accept what is a normal enough occurrence in royal families. It is the Prince who balks. He slips his royal guard on the way to Aragon, and climbs over a wall into a garden where he quickly sets himself to chatting up the pretty girl gardener. There is nothing he can do about the marriage—state affairs are, after all, state affairs—but he sulks his way through the, ceremony and won't even look at his bride. The King (Berthelier) and the duenna, Dona Scolastica (Mlle Felcourt), put guards on all the corridors surrounding the nuptial chamber to make sure he doesn't shirk his wedding-night duty, but Gaétan spends the night with the gardener-girl before going off to join the army the very next morning. On manoeuvres, the gardener-girl keeps coming to visit him, in various disguises, and he is very put out when the King congratulates him on his husbandly success: the Princess is pregnant. But Gaétan hasn't been cuckolded, the gardener-girl is, after all, Micaëla who just happened to be down amongst the plants that day when . . . Élise Clary played Josefa, the real gardener-girl, and Montaubry her soldier lover, Morales, who joined her to provide the soubret entertainment and plenty more complexities, whilst Scipion appeared as the comical Don Mosquitos.

The most popular parts of the score of *Le Coeur et la main* were Micaëla's set-piece bolero "Un soir Perez, le capitaine," delivered as an entertainment for Gaétan as they make merry over supper on their wedding night, and Gaétan's Chanson du Casque, also delivered as an item, at the post-wedding ball. The King had his comical moments ("Vlan! j'ai perdu mon gendre"), Morales a lively drinking song ("Au soldat après la parade") and Micaëla a pretty rondeau ("À l'ombre des charmilles"). Josefa and Morales peeped longingly at the empty royal bedroom in "C'est là leur chambre nuptiale" before making use of it, whilst the Prince went into shock at the thought that his unseen wife has been unfaithful ("Quand ça tombe sur un confrère") to good comical effect, in a charming score which joined with a particularly sparkily written text to good effect.

Brasseur's production of *Le Coeur et la main* played a fine 128 performances on its first run and was brought back in the following season (2 May 1883) for another 54 performances. By this time, the first foreign productions had already got under way. In Budapest, where the piece (ad Lajos Evva, Béla J Fái) was, not unreasonably, titled *A kertészleány* (the gardener-girl), Ilka Pálmay scored a great hit as Micaëla to the Gaston [*sic*] of Pál Vidor and the King of Elek Solymossy through a fine run of 40 nights, and the show was revived in 1889 (25 October). The Népszínház company also played *A kertészleány* in Vienna, which seems to have been the only occasion on which that city saw *Le Coeur et la main.*

The first English-language production came in America, where the show was the subject of a race and a subsequent court case over rights between John McCaull and James Duff. McCaull mounted *Heart and*

Hand with John Howson as the King, Marianne Conway (Micaëla) and Laura Joyce (Scolastica), and 11 days later the opposition put out *Micaëla,* with J H Ryley, Marie Conron and Wallace McCreery as Morales. The conflict did no one any particular good and McCaull took his piece off to the touring circuits after his usual three weeks with Duff close behind. A third English-language version was played, nearly a decade later, in Britain. Horace Sedger's production of *Incognita* (ad F C Burnand, Harry Greenbank) was heavily botched by numbers by ''Yvolde,'' Herbert Bunning and Hamilton Clark, and it featured a lady who called herself Sedohr Rhodes (Micaëla), Wallace Brownlow (Gaëtan), Harry Monkhouse as a King who got disguised as a gipsy girl in the third act, Aida Jenoure (Josefa) and John Child (Morales O'Donoghue) in a version in which the carefully constructed bedroom farceries of the original were replaced by elderly burlesque and grotesque comedy. It played a fair 103 performances without *Le Coeur et la main* being given a real chance. It was, perhaps, no coincidence that the only foreign country to make a success of the show was Hungary, where the text had been intelligently treated.

In France, however, the piece was given its due. It was brought back to the Nouveautés in December 1886 with Maria Nixau featured alongside Vauthier, Homerville and Blanche-Marie, and was seen freely around the country for years thereafter.

Hungary: Népszínház *A kertészleány* 16 December 1882; USA: Bijou Theater *Hand and Heart* 15 February 1883, Standard Theater *Micaëla* 26 February 1883; Austria: Theater an der Wien *A kertészleány* 15 June 1883; UK: Lyric Theatre *Incognita* 6 October 1892

Recording: complete (Gaîté-Lyrique)

Plate 81. **Hayden Coffin** *in one of his most enduring roles, as Edward German's singing Tom Jones.*

COFFIN, [Charles] Hayden (b Manchester, 22 April 1862; d London, 8 December 1935). Identikit baritone leading man of the Victorian and Edwardian eras.

English-born of American parents, the baritone Coffin, blessed with a fine masculine face and figure and a strong, ringing singing voice, made his first professional stage appearances with Percy North's operetta and concert party (July 1885), and he made a mark in his very first London engagements, taking over from Frank Celli as John Smith in *Pocahontas* (1885), playing Cosmo, the Venetian hero of *The Lady of the Locket* (1885), Boleslas in *Falka* (1885) and as the hero of Ivan Caryll's first opérette, *The Lily of Léoville* (1886, Coriolon). However, he was moved into star class by his performance of the serenade ''Queen of My Heart'' in the role of Harry Sherwood in Cellier's very long-running *Dorothy* at the Gaiety Theatre in 1886.

He partnered his co-star, Marie Tempest, in the successors to *Dorothy—Doris* (1889) and *The Red Hussar* (1889)—appeared for the Carl Rosa company in *Marjorie* (1890, Ralf) and *Captain Thérèse* (1890, Tancrède de la Touche), sang ''O Promise Me'' in the role of Robin Hood in the British production of De Koven's comic opera (rechristened there *Maid Marian,* 1891), and took over first as Vincent and then the role of Frantz de Bernheim from the insufficient ''Chevalier Scovel'' in the successful London production of *La Cigale* (1891). He starred opposite Decima Moore in the English mounting of *Miss Decima* (*Miss Helyett,* 1891, Peter Paul Rolleston), and confirmed himself through this series of roles as London's preferred baritone hero before making a trip to America to play the romantic lead in Maurice Barrymore's unfortunate *The Robber of the Rhine* (1892, Waldemar).

He subsequently joined Lillian Russell in a 1892–93 New York season of *La Cigale* (Frantz), *The Mountebanks* (Alfredo) and *Giroflé-Girofla* (Marasquin), before returning home to Britain. There and then he found his most famous niche, when he became one of the four resident stars of what would become George Edwardes's Daly's Theatre company, playing staunchly romantic musical comedy heroes alongside Miss Tempest, Letty Lind and comic Huntley Wright. Over the next decade, he created the romantic leads in *A Gaiety Girl* (1893, Charlie Goldfield, "Tommy Atkins," "Sunshine Above") at the Prince of Wales and Daly's, in *An Artist's Model* (1895, Rudolph), *The Geisha* (1896, Reginald Fairfax, "Star of my Soul," "Jack's the Boy"), *A Greek Slave* (1898, Diomed, "Freedom"), *San Toy* (1899, Bobbie Preston, "Love Has Come from Lotus Land"), *A Country Girl* (1902, Geoffrey Challoner, "In the King's Name . . . Stand!") and *The Cingalee* (1903, Harry Vereker) at Daly's, and in *Véronique* (1904, Florestan) before a very public bust-up with Edwardes, caused by his introducing into the Daly's circle a would-be-playwright pal who subsequently sued the producer for plagiarism. Coffin moved on to other managements and further starring roles in such pieces as *The Girl Behind the Counter* (1906), the title role in Edward German's *Tom Jones* (1907), *Butterflies* (1908, Max, until he slung a snit and walked out), *The Dashing Little Duke* (1909, Chevalier de Matignon), and *Two Merry Monarchs* (1910, Prince Charmis) and, with all now apparently forgiven or at least forgotten, worked one more time for Edwardes in what would be (on the eve of his fifties) the most successful role of his later career in *The Quaker Girl* (1910, Captain Charteris).

After the First World War, with dance music taking over musical theatre, Coffin, who had personified the virile musical theatre hero to London audiences for more than a quarter of a century, diversified into straight theatre and films, performing into his seventies but making only occasional musical-theatre appearances, and those in such staunchly old-fashioned pieces as *Young England* (1916, John Oxenham), *Valentine* (1918, Gaston Dulacq), the touring *Gay Trouville* (1919, Raphael Corrèze), *The Rebel Maid* (1921, Lord Milverton), *The Damask Rose,* and alongside another *Gaiety Girl* veteran, Lottie Venne, as Jenkins in the Lyric, Hammersmith, *Lionel and Clarissa* (1925). He was seen on the road playing Lord Lorimer in the short-lived musical *On the* Air as late as 1933. Amongst his other latter day engagements were several seasons in the role of the Mad Hatter in the musical version of *Alice in Wonderland,* touring productions of *Monsieur Beaucaire* and *The School for Scandal,* and a number of film roles.

In 1892 Coffin was cited as co-respondent in the divorce suit of composer Alberto Randegger, and he subsequently married the ex-Mme Randegger (Adeline de Leuw).

Autobiography: *Hayden Coffin's Book* (Alston Rivers, London, 1930)

LE COFFRE-FORT VIVANT Opérette à grand spectacle in 2 acts and 20 scenes by Georges Berr and Louis Verneuil based on the novel by Frederic Mauzens. Lyrics by Henri Wernert. Music by Joseph Szulc and "Jean Sautreuil" (Maurice Yvain). Théâtre du Châtelet, Paris, 17 December 1938.

An opérette à grand spectacle staged with suitable splendour by Maurice Lehmann on the great Châtelet stage, *Le Coffre-fort vivant* (the living safe) followed the fortunes of a jewel of great price—from the lid of the very first and diamond-studded tobacco case—which is accidentally swallowed by shop-boy Mathias (Bach). Pursued by gangsters (Dinan, Robert Allard), the vendor (Jean Coizeau), the would-be buyer (Edmond Castel), a hospital nurse (Monette Dinay) and the piece's singing hero (Robert Burnier), Mathias gallops from Martinique to Mexico to Hollywood, his flight illustrated by La Macouba (grand ballet antillaise), a Hollywood Romantique routine, a parachute scene and a series of tableaux and specialities, as well as a regulation amount of songs, until the diamond reappears in the course of nature.

In fact, this libretto had been around for more than 20 years. The rights had originally been secured by composer Ivan Caryll who had a scenario prepared by Verneuil (in French) written up by Harry B Smith (in English) and got the resultant musical produced on Broadway by Charles Dillingham as *The Canary* (Globe Theater 4 November 1918) with Julia Sanderson (Julie) and Joseph Cawthorn (Timothy) top-billed. The "canary" of the title was the name of the diamond. A 152-performance run in New York was followed by a good American touring life.

Second time around, the musical part to the libretto was composed by Joseph Szulc and "Jean Sautreuil," a pseudonym which for some unfathomable reason covered the identity of Maurice Yvain, who had written the Châtelet's previous show without need of such disguise. Aided by Lehmann's lavish production, the star comedian-and-matinée-idol tandem of Bach and Burnier, and an attractive if not memorable score, *Le Coffre-fort vivant* played six months at the Châtelet before being closed down for the summer months. When the summer of 1939 was over, the theatre remained closed.

COGNIARD, [Charles] Théodore (b Paris, 30 April 1806; d Versailles, 13 May 1872).

COGNIARD, [Jean] Hippolyte (b Paris, 29 November 1807; d Paris, 6 February 1882).

The Cogniard brothers, celebrated Parisian theatre directors and authors in the middle years of the 19th century, were a pair of orphans who studied medicine before directing their intentions towards the theatre. Their first piece as authors, the ''episode de la guerre d'Alger'' *La Cocarde tricolore,* was produced at the Folies-Dramatiques in 1831. It scored a considerable success, running for more than two hundred nights, and the brothers followed it up with a bevy of spectaculars, dramas, vaudevilles and libretti, establishing themselves at the forefront of the brigade of purveyors of large-scale entertainments with such pieces as *Le Royaume des femmes* (1833, by Hippolyte Cogniard and Desnoyers), *La Fille de l'air* (Théâtre des Folies-Dramatiques 3 August 1837), *Le Naufrage de la Méduse* (Théâtre de la Renaissance 31 May 1839, mus: Flotow, Grisar, Pilati, et al), *Pied de mouton* (Théâtre de la Porte-Saint-Martin 8 September 1860 w Hector Crémieux), *Les Mille et une nuits* (Théâtre de la Porte-Saint-Martin 24 January 1843), *La Biche au bois* (Théâtre de la Porte-Saint-Martin 29 March 1845), *La Chatte blanche* (Cirque Nationale 14 August 1852) and *La Poudre de Perlinpinpin* (Cirque Nationale 24 December 1853).

Over the years—either together or singly—they directed a series of Paris theatres, notably the Folies-Dramatiques (together), the Théâtre du Vaudeville (Hippolyte) and, most memorably, the Théâtre des Variétés (Hippolyte), during the period of the production of Offenbach's famous opéras-bouffes: *La Belle Hélène, Barbe-bleue* and *La Grande-Duchesse de Gérolstein.*

A number of their féeries and spectaculars were reprised for decades in Paris's larger houses, and several were in the course of time given a full and fresh score of music, turning them into legitimate opérettes or, more often, grands opéras-bouffes féeries. *La Biche au bois* was remade several times, in several countries, with scores by various hands including those of Hervé, *La Cocarde tricolore* was made into an opérette by Maurice Ordonneau with music by Robert Planquette (1892), whilst *Le Naufrage de la Méduse* was remusicked by Friedrich von Flotow for the German stage under the title of *Die Matrosen* (Hamburg 23 December 1845). *Le Royaume des femmes,* banned at one stage, went through a whole series of remakes in France, being rewritten by Blum and Desnoyers in 1862 (as *La Reine Crinoline*); by Blum and Cogniard for the Variétés (1866); by Blum and Toché for the Nouveautés during the Exhibition of 1889; and again by Blum and Ferrier, to a score by Serpette, in 1896 for the Eldorado; but it also became *Die Fraueninsel* (*Die verkehrte Welt*), with a score by Carl Millöcker, at the Deutsches-Theater, Pest (1868 February) and two different *Die vekehrte Welt*s (adapted from the two last French versions) in Berlin, Vienna and Budapest. *La Fille de l'air,* already Lisbonicized as *A filha de ar* (Joaquim Casimiro, Lisbon Gymnase 17 June 1856) was later remade by Armand Liorat and composer Paul Lacome for a Parisian production. The text for the Louis Varney opérette *Coquelicot* (Théâtre des Bouffes-Parisiens 2 March 1882) was based on the brothers' vaudeville of the same title (Théâtre des Folies-Dramatiques 14 January 1836), by librettist Armand Silvestre, whilst many other pieces, credited and uncredited, and not always oversized, also looked back to the kings of the Paris spectacular theatre for their inspiration.

The Cogniards were not, however, wedded as authors only to the vaster forms of popular entertainment. Their names also appeared on bills at the Opéra-Comique (*Le Souper du mari* mus: Despreaux 14 January 1833 w Desnoyers, etc) and at the Théâtre Lyrique (*La Fée Carabosse* mus: Victor Massé 28 February 1859 w Lockroy, etc) as part of a musical theatre career of the widest and most brilliant kind.

COHAN, George M[ichael] (b Providence, RI, 3 July 1878; d New York, 5 November 1942). The much-loved ''Yankee-doodle-boy'' of the American musical stage, Cohan—as author, performer and producer—was responsible for many of the best examples of a bristling, positive and tuneful brand of genuine musical comedy which took the old farce-comedy style of show into the 20th century.

Born into a family of vaudeville artists, Cohan began his performing life at an early age, appearing as a boy actor, a dancer and, with his parents, Jere (né Jeremiah Joseph Keohane; d 1 August 1917) and Helen Frances Cohan (née Costigan; d 26 August 1928), and his sister, Josephine Cohan, as a member of the highly successful family act known initially as ''The Cohan Merrymakers'' and later ''The Four Cohans'' in stage shows (Lydia Yeamans-Titus's *On the Road,* 1895, etc) and in vaudeville. He also began early a parallel career as a stage writer, turning out a long list of increasingly substantial sketches and songs both for his own, and his family's, use (*Money to Burn* 1895, *The Professor's Wife* 1896 , *Running for Office* 1898, the 50-minute *The Governor's Son* 1900). He wrote as well for some of the many flourishing vaudeville duologue players of the time, amongst which Barnes and Sisson's *A Theatrical Agent* (1897); Filson and Errol's *A Tip on the Derby* (1897); Fred Hallen and Mollie Fuller's *His Wife's Hero* (1898); *To Boston on Business* for Anna Caldwell and Charles Wayne (1899); *A Game of Golf* for Beatrice Moreland and Charles M Seay (1899); a new act for Al Leech and his Three Blossoms (1899); a revision of *Jack's Past* for S Miller Kent (1899); *Hogan of the Hansom* for Walter Leroy and Florence Lacey (1900); *A Romance of New Jersey* for the Russell Brothers (1901); the Ellinore sisters' *Her Daughter's Friend;* and Edmund Hayes and Emily Lytton's highly successful *A Wise Guy.* This last-named half-hour skit was later lengthened into a full-scale three-act farce comedy, with songs and specialities, and toured by its

Plate 82. **George M Cohan** *(right) and father Jere.*

performers for several seasons in theatres and vaudeville houses. Cohan also reworked Johnny and Emma Ray's vehicle *A Hot Old Time* for its 1898 and 1899 tours, and saw it go round the country, alongside *A Wise Guy,* for many more seasons, and as late as 1901 turned out *A Trip to the Vaudevilles* for Tim Cronin. He also supplied individual numbers for interpolation into touring farce comedies (''The Patriotic Coon,'' The Lord Knows Who'' in *A Sure Cure* 1898, ''I Guess I'll Have to Telegraph my Baby'' in *The Finish of Mr Fresh* 1898, etc).

He was still in his earliest twenties when he developed the latest and longest of the sketches from the Cohans' act into a full-length song-and-dance show—a piece on the same broad lines of the popular 19th-century musical farcical comedies—writing the text and composing the songs. In the earliest part of 1901, after bidding a well-publicized farewell to vaudeville from the stage of Hyde and Behman's, Brooklyn, he opened the following week at Hartford under the management of Louis Behman, in the title role of his first musical comedy *The Governor's Son* (1901, Algy Wheelock). The Four Cohans and George's wife, Ethel Levey, all had leading roles in this rather confusing traditional mish-mash of mistaken identity, disguise and detectiving, broadly played and perforated by lively, raw songs which, although it stayed only a few weeks at New York's Savoy Theater, provided the family with an ever-developing vehicle for two full seasons of touring round America. They took just one week out from their new career as theatrical artists, to appear at the Masonic Temple Theatre, Chicago for $3,000—''the largest weekly salary ever paid to any act in the world.'' All manager Murdock got for his money was a repeat of the old sketch *Running for Office,* but the house was packed to its limits.

The success of *The Governor's Son* encouraged Cohan to follow it with another theatre piece on the same lines, a musical comedy developed from that same five-year-old sketch *Running for Office* (1903, Augustus Wright ''Always Leave Them Smiling When You Say Goodbye''), which had already served the Cohans so well in the vaudeville houses, and then with a freshly conceived musical play, *Little Johnny Jones* (1904, Johnny Jones). This one was a zippy, vigorous piece of up-to-date crooks-and-heroes stuff, with Georgie starring—the billing no longer read ''the Four Cohans in'' but ''George M Cohan in''—as its brash, cheeky all-American-boy hero, outwitting the baddies and rescuing his girl (Miss Levey) from the dens of Chinatown, to the accompaniment of such songs as ''The Yankee Doodle Boy,'' ''Give My Regards to Broadway'' and ''Life's a Funny Proposition After All.'' Staged with enormous vigor and ingenuous enthusiasm *Little Johnny Jones* was a fine success and, in spite of a good dose of critical disdain, it paid three profitable visits to New York during its first highly popular year of touring.

From there on, Cohan continued regularly to turn out pieces in the same spirit and style. In 1906 he provided himself and Miss Levey with a new vehicle in *George Washington Jr* (George Belgrave, ''You're a Grand Old Flag,'' ''I Was Born in Virginia'') and penned and, on commission from Abe Erlanger, directed the successful *Forty-Five Minutes from Broadway* in which Donald Brian, the juvenile lead man from *Little Johnny Jones,* was starred with comedienne Fay Templeton and Victor Moore. The score included ''Mary's Grand Old Name,'' ''So Long, Mary'' and a happy, catchy title number to add to Cohan's growing list of popular favorites.

In 1907 Cohan decided to add the duties of producer to his other functions and, in partnership with Sam Harris, the producer of *Little Johnny Jones* and *George Washington Jr,* he began a busy production schedule which, in the years that followed, included all the future Cohan musicals, both those with and those without the author starred, and the parallel list of successful straight plays which he wrote in the same period (*Get-Rich-Quick Wallingford, Broadway Jones,* etc). The partnership also mounted pieces by other writers, including the musicals *The Red Widow* (Chas Gebest/Channing Pollock, Rennold Wolf) and *The Beauty Shop* (Gebest), both starring Raymond Hitchcock, and the extremely successful *Going Up* (Louis Hirsch/James Montgomery), as well as such occasional imports as Jean Gilbert's Berlin hit *Polnische Wirtschaft* (*The Polish Wedding*). In 1910 Cohan and Harris, already proprietors of Broadway's Gaiety Theater, built the 1,000-seater George M Cohan Theater on Broadway and 43rd Street but, when it moved out of their hands and into the control of Abe Erlanger, they instead took command of the Astor and the Grand Opera House.

The series of Cohan musicals continued for a half-dozen years, with Cohan writing, composing, directing and starring in an expanded version of *Running for Office* called *The Honeymooners* (1907, Augutus Wright); *The Yankee Prince* (1908, Percy Springer); *The Little Millionaire* (1911, Robert Spooner), which marked his parents' last appearance as performers; and a new version of *Forty-Five Minutes from Broadway* (1912, Kid Burns); whilst his other pieces were left in the hands of other performers. *The Talk of New York* (1907) reused the character of Kid Burns, created by Victor Moore in *Forty-Five Minutes from Broadway; Fifty Miles from Boston* (1908) introduced the song ''Harrigan'' and had the young Edna Wallace Hopper as its heroine; *The American Idea* (1908) counted Trixie Friganza amongst its cast; and *The Man Who Owns Broadway* (1909), a musical remake of Cohan's play *Popularity,* top-lined Raymond Hitchcock in his first star role for Cohan and Harris. *The Little*

Blonde Lady was a vaudeville-house vehicle constructed around the aggressively untalented Hope Booth.

From 1914 Cohan spent a time in and on revue (*Hello, Broadway!, The Cohan Revue*) before he and Harris produced their last show, Cohan's burlesqued comic opera *The Royal Vagabond,* together in 1919. From then, Cohan went out on his own, producing *Mary* (1920), the latest work of *Going Up* composer Louis Hirsch, with great success, and the same composer's *The O'Brien Girl* (1921) with only a little less, before turning out his first real "Cohan musical" for a number of years in *Little Nellie Kelly* (1922). A jaunty piece well in the tradition of the currently fashionable Cinderella genre best exemplified by *Irene* and *Sally,* with a song hit something like those of earlier shows in "Nellie Kelly I Love You," *Little Nellie Kelly* gave him another splendid success all around America. It also became the first and only Cohan musical to play in Britain when C B Cochran transported it to the New Oxford Theatre for a fine seven-and-a-half-month run.

The Rise of Rosie O'Reilly, the following year, repeated the formula with sufficient success in both America and also in Australia where *Little Nellie Kelly* had similarly prospered. In 1927 Cohan returned to the musical stage to appear for the last time in one of his own works, *The Merry Malones.* Although the piece was well and truly in what had now become the old-fashioned musical comedy format, little more than a sparky remake of everything Cohan had written before in the way of scenes and songs, under the flourishing and different conditions of the 1920s American stage it had a much longer run at the new Erlanger Theatre than had had his earlier, more genuinely and youthfully zippy shows.

Billie, a musicalization of his play *Broadway Jones,* closed out the canon of Cohan musicals and, thereafter, Cohan concentrated on writing, performing and producing for the straight theatre, returning only once to the song-and-dance stage, in 1937, to play the role of Franklin D Roosevelt in Rodgers and Hart's *I'd Rather Be Right* for his old partner, Sam Harris.

Cohan's down-to-earth farcical and sentimental plays, his simple, catchy songs full of obvious and chauvinistic sentiments irresistibly displayed, his colorful, unflaggingly energetic staging, and his brash, breezy star performances all combined to keep alive and give a joyful fillip to the continuing tradition of popular American musical comedy as established by Hoyt and Harrigan.

His life was used as the basis for the musical *George M* (1968) which featured many of his best-known songs as its score, as did a 1942 film, *Yankee Doodle Dandy,* in which James Cagney portrayed Cohan.

Josephine COHAN (Mrs Fred Liedtke Niblo) (b 24 December 1876; d New York, 12 July 1916) played with the family group up till its dissolution in June 1904 (Mrs Dickie Dickinson in *The Governor's Son,* Madeleine Tiger in *Running for Office*), and then moved on the be leading lady to the Rogers Brothers (Marjorie Kelleher in *The Rogers Brothers in Paris* 1904). She returned to work with her brother in *The Yankee Prince* (1908, Evelyn Fielding) before moving back to vaudeville work.

Cohan's daughter, **Georgette COHAN** (b Los Angeles, 26 August 1900), played on the straight and vaudeville stages.

1898 **Running for Office** sketch Poli's Theater, Waterbury, Conn 9 June

1898 **A Hot Old Time** (pasticcio) new version Grand Opera House, Stamford, Conn 2 September

1899 **A Wise Guy** (pasticcio) Grand Opera House, Brooklyn 2 October; Star Theater, NY 8 October 1900

1900 **The Governor's Son** 1 act Empire Theater, Providence 19 February; Proctor's Fifth Avenue Theater 28 May

1901 **The Governor's Son** expanded version Parsons' Theater, Hartford Conn 11 February; Savoy Theater 25 February

1903 **Running for Office** expanded version Majestic Theater, Utica, NY 6 April; 14th Street Theater 27 April

1904 **Little Johnny Jones** Liberty Theater 7 November

1905 **Forty-Five Minutes from Broadway** Great Southern Theater, Columbus, Ohio 25 September; New Amsterdam Theater, New York 1 January 1906

1906 **George Washington Jr** Herald Square Theater 12 February

1907 **Fifty Miles from Boston** Court Square Theater, Springfield, Mass 28 March; Garrick Theater 3 February 1908

1907 **The Honeymooners** (revised *Running for Office*) New Amsterdam Theater 3 June

1907 **The Little Blonde Lady** Shubert Theater, Brooklyn 31 August

1907 **The Talk of New York** Knickerbocker Theater 3 December

1908 **The Yankee Prince** Knickerbocker Theater 20 April

1908 **The Belle of the Barber's Ball** 1 scene in *Cohan and Harris Minstrels* New York Theater 3 August

1908 **The American Idea** New York Theater 5 October

1909 **The Man Who Owns Broadway** New York Theater 11 October

1911 **The Little Millionaire** Cohan Theater 25 September

1914 **Hello, Broadway** Astor Theater 25 December

1918 **The Voice of McConnell** Manhattan Opera House 25 December

1919 **The Royal Vagabond** (ex- *Cherry Blossoms*) revised libretto Cohan and Harris Theater 17 February

1922 **Little Nellie Kelly** Liberty Theater 13 November

1923 **The Rise of Rosie O'Reilly** Liberty Theater 25 December

1927 **The Merry Malones** Erlanger Theater 26 September

1928 **Billie** Erlanger Theater 1 October

Autobiography: *Twenty Years of Broadway, and the Years It Took to Get There* (Harper, New York, 1925); Biographies: McCabe, J: *George M Cohan, the Man Who Owned Broadway* (Doubleday, Garden City, 1973), Morehouse, W: *George M Cohan, Prince of the American Theater* (Lippincott, Philadelphia, 1943)

COLE, Bob [COLE, Robert Allen] (b Athens, Ga, 1 July 1869; d Catskill, 2 August 1911). A slickly elegant song and dance man who doubled as a composer of songs for turn-of-the-century American shows.

Originally a bellboy in at Atlanta hotel, Cole began his career as a musical performer working in a series of different musical acts and touring shows before joining Sam Jack's Creoles and then, in 1894, putting together his own All-Star Stock Company, a touring group of black performers. Following the quick demise of this unprofitable venture, he joined the established Black Patti Troubadours (1896), appearing in the "musical skit" *At Jolly Coon-ey Island,* put together by himself and fellow performer Billy Johnson, in which he appeared as a "little tramp" character called Willy Wayside. However, after a quick quarrel with managers Voelckel and Nolan, he left the Black Pattis and organised another outfit of his own under the management of William Black. The new group presented a Cole and Johnson musical farce-comedy *A Trip to Coontown,* in which Cole once again appeared as Willy Wayside ("Pickin' on a Chicken Bone," "I Can Stand for Your Color, But Your Hair Won't Do") to his partner's Jim Flimflammer. Jesse Shipp's mounting of the piece proved a surprise success in the road season of 1897–98. In the summer the partners returned to vaudeville, playing at Koster and Bial's billed as "the kings of Koondom," but at the start of the new season they returned to the road with *A Trip to Coontown.* It proved good for four seasons around the country. During this time, Cole and Johnson also began to provide numbers to other theatre shows and in the next few years their songs turned up in the scores of such variety musicals as *A Reign of Error* (1899), *The Supper Club* (1901), *Champagne Charlie* (1901), *The Hall of Fame* (1902), *Huck Finn* (1902), *Mugg's Landing* (1904) and *The Awakening of Mr Pipp* (1904, "The Pretty Little Squaw from Utah"), while others of their numbers were, from time to time, borrowed to serve as part of the patchwork scores of the mass of old 'n' new pasticcio shows that filled the touring circuits.

When Johnson's drinking habits turned him into an unreliable partner, Cole broke up the team and, whilst Billy linked himself with a group of Creole Belles to tour solo, Cole—after an interregnum going it alone—formed a fresh partnership with another Johnson: J Rosamund Johnson. The new duo (billed as "the new Cole and Johnson") went successfully into vaudeville as an act, performing much of their own material, but they also supplied numbers not only to the narrow world of specifically black shows and the rather wider one of vaudeville, but also to such mainstream Broadway artists as May Irwin, who made something of a speciality of belting out the kind of made-to-measure negro numbers popularly known as coon songs. Amongst the shows in which Cole and the second of his Johnsons placed numbers were *The Little Duchess* (1900), *The Rogers Brothers in Central Park* (1900), *Sally in Our Alley* (1902, "Under the Bamboo Tree"), *The Sleeping Beauty and the Beast* (1902), *The Girl from Dixie* (1903, six songs), *Mr Bluebeard* (1903), *Whoop-do-doo* (1903, "Flowers of May in Dixieland"), *Nancy Brown* (1903, eight songs), *Mother Goose* (1903), *In Dahomey* (1903, "My Castle on the Nile"), *An English Daisy* (1904, "Big Indian Chief"), *A Little of Everything* (1904, "Fishing," "The Evolution of Ragtime"), *Smiling Island* (1904) and *Moonshine* (1905, "The Conjure Man"). They also wrote much of the music for the musical comedy *The Belle of Bridgeport* (1900), the made-over British pantomime *Humpty Dumpty* (1904, "Sambo and Dinah," "Mexico," "On Lalwanna's Shore") and *In Newport* (1904).

In 1905 the partners performed in Paris (June–July) and at the Palace, London (July–August), in 1906 they went around America in vaudeville houses with their own novelty *He Handed Me a Lemon,* in 1907 they brought their full-length touring musical, *The Shoofly Regiment* (Hunter Wilson, "Won't You Be My Little Brown Bear?," There's Always Something Wrong," etc) to Broadway (15 performances), and two years later they followed up with a second such piece, *The Red Moon* ("Love Me, Baby Mine"), produced by A L Wilbur (32 performances). Both these shows, however, in spite of considerable touring, proved seriously unprofitable under Broadway conditions, and the pair went back to performing in vaudeville. Soon after, however, badly affected by paresis, the incurably ill Cole drowned himself.

1897 **At Jolly Coon-ey Island** (pasticcio w orig songs/Billy Johnson) sketch Pleasure Palace 17 May

1897 **A Trip to Coontown** (B Johnson/w Johnson, Samuel Corker jr) South Amboy, NJ 27 September; Third Avenue Theater 4 April 1898

1899 **7-11-77** (William J Accooe) sketch in *The Octoroons* Third Avenue Theatre 2 October

1900 **The Belle of Bridgeport** (J Rosamund Johnson, et al/w James W Johnson, et al/Glen MacDonough) Bijou Theater 29 October

1904 **Humpty Dumpty** (w Fred Solomon, J R Johnson/Wood, Collins ad J J McNally) New Amsterdam Theater 14 November

1904 **In Newport** (J R Johnson/J W Johnson) Liberty Theater 26 December

1905 **The Shoofly Regiment** (J R Johnson/J W Johnson, et al) Washington, DC 20 August; Grand Opera House, New York 3 June 1907; Bijou Theater 6 August 1907

1908 **The Red Moon** (w J R Johnson) Wilmington, Del 31 August; Majestic Theater 3 May 1909

COLE, Jack (b New Brunswick, NJ, 27 April 1911; d Los Angeles, 16 February 1974). Much admired but un-

Tony-ed Broadway choreographer of the postwar decades with a flair for the exotic.

Originally a dancer, during which career he appeared in several musicals and revues (*Caviar, Thumbs Up!,* Raki in *Venus in Silk, May Wine, Ziegfeld Follies, Alive and Kicking*), Cole made his Broadway debut as a choreographer on *Something for the Boys* in 1942. He subsequently worked on the short-lived *Allah Be Praised!* and *Magdalena* before creating the famous dances for *Kismet* (1953, Dance of the Ababu Princesses), dances which were reproduced both in London and, largely, in the subsequent film version. He choreographed *Jamaica* for Broadway, *Candide* for London, and both directed and choreographed *Donnybrook* (1961) and *Kean* (1961), before staging the dances for two further hits, *A Funny Thing Happened on the Way to the Forum* (1962) and *Man of La Mancha* (1965), as well as the unsuccessful *Foxy, Zenda* (1964), *Royal Flush* (1964, also director), *Chu-Chem* (1966, also Lord Hoo Hah) and *Mata Hari* (1967).

Cole's stage career was paired with an equally effective one in the cinema where he choreographed a number of musical and part-musical films from *Cover Girl* in 1944, through such pieces as *The Jolson Story* (1946), *The Merry Widow* (1952), *Gentlemen Prefer Blondes* (1953) and *Kismet* (1955) up to *Let's Make Love* in 1960.

Wayne Cilento appeared as Cole in a musical piece based on his works.

Biography: Loney, G: *Unsung Genius: The Passion of Jack Cole* (Franklin Watts, New York, 1984)

COLEMAN, Cy [KAUFMAN, Seymour] (b New York, 14 June 1929). The most evidently versatile of Broadway composers working between the 1960s and the 1990s, Coleman turned out a three-decade-plus series of hit shows which included both a number of song standards and some of the most genuinely comic musical stage-writing of the postwar era.

Educated classically, Coleman made a fast start in the musical world, perfoming as a pianist in venues including the Steinway and Carnegie Halls from the age of six. He moved on into the world of jazz and, in his twenties, played with his own trio in New York nightclubs whilst at the same time beginning a career as a songwriter. In the late 1950s he was responsible for several song hits (''Witchcraft'' 1957 w Carolyn Leigh, ''The Best Is Yet to Come'' 1959) and contributions to revues such as *John Murray Anderson's Almanac* (''Tin Pan Alley''), *Ziegfeld Follies of 1956* (''The Lady Is Indisposed'') and *Demi-Dozen* (''You Fascinate Me So''), before he completed his first musical comedy score, *Wildcat* (1960), an unpretentious Broadwayish star vehicle for television star Lucille Ball. *Wildcat* gave him his biggest song hit to date in the star's infectious invitation, ''Hey, Look Me Over.''

A musicalization of Patrick Dennis's *Little Me* (1962) to a libretto by Neil Simon produced a very funny burlesque of the celebrity biography with astutely witty musical illustrations (''The Other Side of the Tracks,'' ''Real Live Girl,'' ''I've Got Your Number'') which demonstrated the composer's rare talent for musical humor and parody, whilst *Sweet Charity* (1966), a brassy Tin-Pan-Alley show with a big-hearted heroine, gave him an international show hit and a parallel song hit. *Seesaw* (1973), another tale of a klutzy girl who scares away a conventional man, brought forward some further fine songs (''Nobody Does It Like Me,'' ''It's Not Where You Start''), whilst *I Love My Wife* (1977), a small-scale and long-running comedy with songs, went on from Broadway to success in several other countries.

On the Twentieth Century (1978), a dazzling operetta burlesque, brought its composer a belated first Tony Award, whilst *Barnum* (1980, ''Come Follow the Band,'' ''The Colors of My Life,'' also co-producer), a surprisingly affecting piece of spectacular razzmatazz based on the character of the famous showman, went on from major success on Broadway and in London to be played in more countries throughout the world than any other Coleman work, and than almost any other Broadway show of its period.

After several false starts during the 1980s, Coleman returned to the top of the heap in 1989 with a third sizzling burlesque in the highly successful parody of the gumshoe cinema, *City of Angels* (Tony Award, ''With Every Breath I Take,'' ''I'm Nothing Without You''), and he followed this in the next season with another ''best musical'' award for a very different type of show in the glittery *The Will Rogers Follies* (''I Never Met a Man I Didn't Like''). His third musical of the nineties, *The Life,* followed the retrograde fashion for the ''lowlife'' in its libretto, but its score of songs found the musician, nearly forty years on from his first Broadway show, still producing live-wire Broadway songs (''I'm Getting Too Old for the Oldest Profession'') in an undiminished fashion that few other show-writers in history have managed.

Coleman has also worked in both television (Shirley Maclaine's *If They Could See Me Now* and *Gypsy in My Soul,* etc), and in film where, beyond the cinematic version of *Sweet Charity,* he supplied scores for such films as *Father Goose, The Art of Love, The Troublemaker, Power, Garbo Talks* and *Family Business.* He has also continued a performing and recording career as a pianist.

1960 **Wildcat** (Carolyn Leigh/N Richard Nash) Alvin Theater 16 December

1962 **Little Me** (Leigh/Neil Simon) Lunt-Fontanne Theater 17 November

1966 **Sweet Charity** (Dorothy Fields/Simon) Palace Theater 29 January

1973 **Seesaw** (Fields/Michael Stewart ad Michael Bennett) Uris Theater 18 March

1977 **I Love My Wife** (Stewart) Ethel Barrymore Theater 17 April

1978 **On the Twentieth Century** (Adolph Green, Betty Comden) St James Theater 19 February

1979 **Home Again, Home Again** (Barbara Fried/Russell Baker) American Shakespeare Theater, Stratford 12 March

1980 **Barnum** (Stewart/Mark Bramble) St James Theater 30 April

1988 **Let 'em Rot** (w A E Hotchner/Hotchner) Coconut Grove Playhouse, Florida 16 February

1989 **Welcome to the Club** (revised *Let 'em Rot*) Music Box Theater 13 April

1989 **City of Angels** (David Zippel/Larry Gelbart) Virginia Theater 11 December

1991 **The Will Rogers Follies** (Green, Comden/Peter Stone) Palace Theater 1 May

1997 **The Life** (Ira Gasman/w Gasman, David Newman) Ethel Barrymore Theater 26 April

1998 **Exactly Like You** (Hotchner) Goodspeed Opera House, East Haddam

COLETTE, [Gabrielle Sidonie Claudine] (b Saint-Sauveur-en-Puisaye, 28 January 1873; d Paris, 3 August 1954).

A music-hall artist of limited talent, "Colette" caused a brief scandal when she appeared at the Moulin-Rouge with the Marquise de Belbeuf in an overtly lesbian pantomime which was quickly withdrawn from the bill. She had considerably more success as a writer, becoming a much admired figure in French arts and letters, and the second woman to be awarded the Légion d'honneur. Several of her celebrated novels and novellas were subsequently adapted to the stage (w Léopold Marchand), occasionally with musical trimmings. A musical based on her *Claudine* tales, with a libretto by Henri Cain and Gustave Adénis and music by Rodolphe Berger, was played at the Moulin-Rouge (13 November 1910) with Polaire, Marise Fairy and Claudius heading the cast, and the much-loved Hollywood film based on her tale of *Gigi* (Frederick Loewe/Alan Jay Lerner) was subsequently adapted, with limited success, as a stage musical.

There have also been several unsuccessful attempts to put the lady herself on the stage. In America, Diana Rigg was featured as *Colette* in a new and Broadway-bound version of a 1970 off-Broadway *Colette* (originally played at the Ellen Stewart Theater 6 May, with Zöe Caldwell as its heroine), with songs by Tom Jones and Harvey Schmidt, which folded on the road (Seattle 9 February 1982). It subsequently became *Colette Collage* (York Players 31 March 1983) in a third metamorphosis. In Britain, Fenella Fielding was seen in the first version of the Schmidt/Jones piece, out of town, and Cleo Laine appeared in the title role of a *Colette* (mus: John Dankworth) brought from the provinces to the Comedy Theatre in 1979 (24 September, 47 performances).

Recordings: *Colette* (MIO), *Colette Collage* (Colosseum), UK version (Sepia)

Biography: Thurman, J: *Secrets of the Flesh: A Life of Colette* (Knopf, New York, 1999)

COLLIN, Ottilie [née MÜLLER] (b Vienna, 19 May 1863; d Vienna, 29 February 1960). Viennese soprano who created important roles in a number of classic 19th-century Operetten.

Ottilie Collin made her stage debut at Graz and appeared at Teplitz, in the title role of Suppé's *Die schöne Galathee,* at 18 years of age. In 1883 she was engaged at Berlin's Friedrich-Wilhelmstädtisches-Theater and, in her two seasons there, she created, amongst others, the principal soprano part of Annina in Johann Strauss's *Eine Nacht in Venedig.* Impressed by her performance, the composer had her taken to Vienna to repeat the role in the revised version of the show staged there, and she remained in Austria to create, with even more sensational success, the role of Sáffi in his *Der Zigeunerbaron* (1885, "Habet acht!," "Wer uns getraut?").

In a period of seven years as a principal soprano at the Theater an der Wien she created the roles of Rita in Czibulka's *Pfingsten in Florenz* (1884), Minna Heidekrug in *Der Feldprediger* (1884), Georgine von Callac in *Zwillinge* (1885), Gilda in *Der Viceadmiral* (1886), Poldi in *Der Botschafter* (1886), Felisa d'Amores in *Der Hofnarr* (1886), Christell Eimen in Brandl's *Der liebe Augustin* (1887), Tilly in Strauss's *Simplicius* (1887), Yum-Yum in the Viennese version of *Der Mikado* (1888), Syuda in *Die indische Witwe* (1889), Lisa in *Der Schlosserkönig* (1889), Pythia in *Das Orakel* (1889), Harriet in *Der arme Jonathan* (1890) and Princess Marie in *Der Vogelhändler* (1891, "Fröhlich Pfalz," "Als geblüht der Kirschenbaum"). She also appeared in such parts as Raphaël (*La Princesse de Trébizonde*), Laura (*Der Bettelstudent*), Fiametta (*Boccaccio*), Adele (*Die Fledermaus*), Kätchen (*Die sieben Schwaben*) and Else (*Der lustige Krieg*), before returning to Berlin and the post of prima donna at both the Theater Unter den Linden (Sáffi, Adele in *Die Fledermaus,* Eurydice in *Orpheus in der Unterwelt, Der Probekuss,* etc) and Friedrich-Wilhelmstädtisches Theater (Jelka in *Jabuka, Ein armes Mädel,* etc).

She remained in Berlin until 1896, after which she limited her activities to intermittent guest appearances, playing in Munich, at the Theater Unter den Linden, as Henri in *Der Opernball* (1898), at the Vienna Carltheater in *Carneval in Rom, Der lustige Krieg* (Violetta) and as

Lili in Ferron's *Das Krokodil* (1898), and returning to the Theater an der Wien as late as 1901 to repeat her Sáffi in the last stages of a famous career.

COLLINS, José [COLLINS, Josephine Charlotte] (b London, 23 May 1887; d London, 6 December 1958). Dark and dashing British vocalist who found fame as the heroine of *The Maid of the Mountains.*

Illegitimate daughter of the music-hall star Lottie Collins, the famous performer of ''Ta-ra-ra-boom-de-ay,'' and of the oboist-theatre-conductor José Van den Berg, José Collins also made her earliest appearances in the music halls. She later toured in Britain in *A Chinese Honeymoon* (1904, Mrs Pineapple) and in *Three Little Maids,* made her West End debut in the short-lived *The Antelope* (1908, Iris Fenton), appeared regularly on the halls and played in several other musicals in the British provinces, before making a firm mark on the musical stage during a period of some five years spent in America.

She appeared on Broadway in local versions of a number of Continental Operetten—Eysler's revusical *Vera Violetta* (1911, Mme von Grunberg), *Die Fledermaus* (*The Merry Countess,* 1912, Rosalinde), *Endlich allein* (*Alone at Last,* 1915, Tilly Dachau) and Rényi's *A kis gróf* (*Suzi,* 1914, Suzi)—played in revue (Angela to the Gus of Jolson in *The Whirl of Society, The Passing Show of 1914*) and appeared both solo and teamed with Maurice Farkoa (and with her father conducting) in vaudeville before returning to Britain, under contract to the struggling post–George Edwardes era Daly's Theatre. She made her first appearance there as Camille Joyeuse in *The Happy Day* (1916), but it was her second show for Daly's, the record-breaking *The Maid of the Mountains* (''Love Will Find a Way,'' ''Farewell,'' ''A Paradise for Two,'' etc), in which she created the role of the gypsyish heroine, Teresa, which launched her as a major star of the British musical theatre.

In five years at Daly's, as she followed Teresa with another gypsyish role in *A Southern Maid* (1920, Dolores) and with the very vocal Hungarian prima donna of Jacobi's *Sybil* (1921), José Collins was instrumental in rebuilding a following for the once famous house, restoring it to its old-time prosperity, but when the Edwardes estate sold the theatre to tycoon Jimmy White, manager Robert Evett and his star decamped and set up their own productions at another once famous Edwardes house, the Gaiety. Miss Collins subsequently starred in English versions of *Die letzte Walzer* (*The Last Waltz,* 1922, Vera Lisaweta) and *Frasquita* (1925, Frasquita) and in the title roles of remade-to-measure vehicles such as *Catherine* (*Die Siegerin,* 1923) and *Our Nell* (1924, ex- *Our Peg*), but without ever recreating the wild euphoria of the Daly's years in which she had been one of the British theatre's brightest stars.

In 1926 she toured for White in the role of Maia in a revival of *A Greek Slave* which closed prior to London, and thereafter she abandoned the musical theatre, appearing only in revue, variety and the occasional straight play in the last years of her career.

Mother, **Lottie COLLINS** [Charlotte Louisa COLLINS] (b London, 16 August 1865; d London, 1 May 1910) was the daughter of a minstrel performer. She worked mostly in the music halls, initially in a sister act with her siblings Marie [Mary Ann COLLINS] and Lizzie [Eliza COLLINS], but appeared on the musical stage at the Gaiety (1886, Mariette in *Monte Cristo Jr* 1891, *Cinder-Ellen Up Too Late*), around America in *Miss Helyett* (1893), as the titular Ethel Joy in the London production of *The New Barmaid* (1896), on tour in Britain in *The White Blackbird* (1898, Nelly Catchpole), *The Dressmaker* (1902) and the music-hall musical comedietta *Bill Bailey in Japan* (1904, Bedelia), and on the American stage in the one-act operetta *The Devilbird* (John S Baker/Frederick Bowyer, Columbia Theater, Boston 24 September 1894). She was married, successively, to agent Stephen Cooney and songwriter James W Tate.

José Collins's elder sister, Lucia, who worked as Lucia Lottie Collins (whilst denying that she was seeking to be compared with or capitalize on the fame of her mother), went out with José in a tiny part in that first *Chinese Honeymoon* tour (1904), and later appeared in variety and music hall.

Autobiography: *The Maid of the Mountains: Her Story* (Hutchinson & Co, London, 1932)

COLLITS' INN Musical romance in 3 acts by T Stuart Gurr. Lyrics by Gurr and Varney Monk. Music by Mrs Monk. Princess Theatre, Melbourne, 23 December 1933.

Collits' Inn was probably the most successful attempt made, during the 1930s, to create a native Australian musical play as a vehicle for the country's biggest ever stay-at-home musical theatre star, Gladys Moncrieff. The historic Collits' Inn is an olden days pub in the Blue Mountains and, in the story set around it, Miss Moncrieff played the owner's daughter, Mary, sought in wedlock by both the bushranger Robert Keane (Claude Flemming) and John Lake (Robert Chisholm), the army officer in charge of the local road-making. Comedian George Wallace decorated the piece with ad libs in Victorian manner as Dandy Dick, the pub's roustabout. Mrs Monk's music included a ''Stay While the Stars Are Shining'' for her soprano star and a military ''The Red Coat'' for her hero, as well as a picturesque aboriginal corroboree which proved the production highlight of the evening.

First produced by amateurs, the show was subsequently mounted professionally by filmmaker Frank Thring (Eftee Attractions), with the idea that, after having established itself in the theatre, it would then make a movie. A fine run of over a hundred performances in Melbourne was followed by a Sydney season at the New Tivoli Theatre (21 June 1934) and a return to Melbourne, and, although the intended film never got past the stage of a few tests, the popularity of *Collits' Inn* prompted Thring to a second attempt at a stage musical. Mrs Monk's *The Cedar Tree* (Princess Theatre, Melbourne 22 December 1934), did not, however, find the same success, and there proved similarly to be limited audiences for his subsequent productions of two London musicals with Australian or New Zealand input, *The Beloved Vagabond* (Princess Theatre 14 April 1934) and *Jolly Roger* (Princess Theatre 3 November 1934). Before a fifth attempt—a version of *Robbery Under Arms* composed by *The Beloved Vagabond*'s Dudley Glass—was completed Thring died, leaving *Collits' Inn* as the most successful of his series.

Recording: selection (RZ)

COLORADO Opérette à grand spectacle in 2 acts by Claude Dufresne. Lyrics by Jacques Larue. Music by Jacques-Henry Rys. Théâtre de la Gaîté-Lyrique, Paris, 16 December 1950.

Where America had *Oklahoma!,* France had *Colorado* (without the exclamation mark), a song-and-scenery show produced by Germaine Roger-Montjoye at the Gaîté-Lyrique. The libretto pitched Jim Bullit (Armand Mestral, bass and dressed in black), the powerful goldfields landowner and boss of its lucrative saloon, against the young, aspiring golddigger Ricardo Diaz (Lou Pizzara, tenor and dressed in white); the beautiful Katharina Sanders (Claude Chenard, soprano), come west in 1877 to lay her hands on some of the land to which her late father had laid claim; and the little saloon pianist, Pancho (Maurice Baquet). A Christmas scenario with a children's ballet, a Fête des Étoiles with a ''Ballet des Nationalités,'' a routine called Gold-Fever, a tap dance *en pointe* and a masked ball with a Ballet des Valses Romantiques were amongst the entertainment's visual attractions, whilst a lively march in praise of ''Colorado'' and Ricardo's hymn to ''Katharina'' were the most popular portions of a score which also included a fox-trot (''Je suis Inca''), a blues (''Crois à ta chance'') and a negro lullaby, all of which owed more to the French opérette à grand spectacle tradition than to Rodgers and Hammerstein.

The show had a considerable success, playing through 11 months, during which time the baritone Michel Dens alternated with Pizzara in the hero's role, and after a solid provincial career, it returned to the Gaîté for a second run in 1959 (12 February) with Mestral and Baquet repeating alongside Bernard Alvi (Ricardo) and Andrée Grandjean (Katharina), prior to further touring and occasional provincial productions right into the 1990s.

COLSON, Kevin [William] (b Sydney, Australia, 28 August 1938). Australian actor and vocalist who has had two careers in the musical theatre.

Tall, rich-voiced Colson had his earliest successes in the musical theatre as a young leading man, taking top roles in the Australian productions of *Irma la Douce* (1961, Nestor), *Carnival* (1962, Paul) and *Sail Away* (1963, John van Mier) before moving on to London where he succeeded Keith Michell in the co-starring role of *Robert and Elizabeth,* and played the parts of Cliff in London's edition of *Cabaret* (1968) and Charles Darnay to the Carton of Edward Woodward in *Two Cities* (1969), both at the Palace Theatre.

He then moved out of the theatre and into the world of business, returning only at the end of this career to once more appear on the musical stage. This second stage-life began when he played the role of Ben in the British premiere of *Follies* (1985) at Manchester, after which he created the role of Walter de Courcey in *Chess,* subsequently playing Molokov in the same production, before going on to introduce the part of George in *Aspects of Love* at the Prince of Wales Theatre. He went on to play the same role in the show's productions in New York and in Australia. He was subsequently seen at Bromley in *Jekyll* (1996), at Chichester as Percival Browne in a revival of *Divorce Me, Darling!* (1997), in London in *Maddie* (1997, Al Turner) and in 1998 as Daddy Warbucks in a revival of *Annie.*

COMDEN, Betty [COHEN, Basya] (b New York, 3 May 1915). A half, to the other-half of Adolph Green, of the most durable lyric and book-writing pairing in musical theatre history.

Having begun in the music business as a performer in a night club act, The Revuers, Miss Comden there established a lyric-writing partnership with fellow performer, Green, which began with their devising cabaret material, both for themselves and for others. The group appeared in and they supplied three songs (''We Had a Show,'' ''Variety,'' ''The Baroness Bazooka'') for the aborted production of *Three after Three* (New Haven 24 November 1939), but Comden and Green blossomed as writers when they supplied both text and lyrics for a first full Broadway musical, the free-wheeling and sparkling *On the Town* (1944). That show's popularity set the partnership into a Broadway orbit in which their lyrics to Leonard Bernstein's music in *Wonderful Town* (1953,

''Ohio''); the book and lyrics of *Bells Are Ringing* (1956, ''Just in Time,'' ''The Party's Over''), a musical written to feature Judy Holliday who had been a member of their act; the adaptation of *All About Eve* as *Applause* (1970, ''Applause''); and the libretto and lyrics to the opéra-bouffe version of *On the Twentieth Century* (1978) have brought them notable successes around the world.

Several other shows to which they contributed more or less of the sung and/or spoken portion—*Do Re Mi* (400 performances, ''Make Someone Happy''), *Say, Darling* (332 performances), *Hallelujah, Baby!* (293 performances) and a musical comedy version of Barrie's *Peter Pan*—also had good Broadway runs and, in the case of the last named, a number of subsequent productions. In 1991, after a rather discreet decade which brought no new Broadway success, the pair returned as the lyricists of the Tony Award-winning *The Will Rogers Follies* in 1991.

Other stage credits have included the sketches and lyrics for the 1951 revue *Two on the Aisle,* material for several other revues and compilation shows, and additional material for the transformation of Jule Styne's *Gentlemen Prefer Blondes* into *Lorelei.*

A considerable period of the pair's early writing career was spent in Hollywood, where they provided scripts and/or songs for many musical films, including *Good News* (1947), *The Barkleys of Broadway* (1949), the screen adaptation of *On the Town* (1949) and *The Band Wagon* (1954), and screenplays for comedies (*Auntie Mame,* etc). Their best-known original film screenplay was that for the movie musical classic *Singin' in the Rain* which they subsequently remade in an unfortunate Broadway stage version. A different adaptation of their tale, written by actor-author Tommy Steele for the British stage, was, however, mounted in several other countries with very much happier results.

Miss Comden has continued to make infrequent stage appearances since featuring in the original cast of *On the Town,* appearing with Green in the revue *A Party with Comden and Green* (1958, 1977) and in concert in *Follies* as well as playing, in extremis, in the comedy role of Letitia Primrose in *On the Twentieth Century.* She has also appeared on the non-musical stage.

1944 **On the Town** (Leonard Bernstein/w Adolph Green) Adelphi Theater 28 December

1945 **Billion Dollar Baby** (Morton Gould/w Green) Alvin Theater 21 December

1947 **Bonanza Bound** (Saul Chaplin/w Green) Shubert Theater, Philadelphia 26 December

1953 **Wonderful Town** (Bernstein/w Green/Jerome Chodorov, Joseph Fields) Winter Garden Theater 25 February

1954 **Peter Pan** (Jule Styne, Mark Charlap/w Green, Carolyn Leigh/J M Barrie ad w Green) Winter Garden Theater 20 October

1956 **Bells Are Ringing** (Styne/w Green) Shubert Theater 29 November

1958 **Say, Darling** (Styne/w Green/Richard Bissell, Marian Bissell) ANTA Theater 3 April

1960 **Do Re Mi** (Styne/w Green/Garson Kanin) St James Theater 26 December

1961 **Subways are for Sleeping** (Styne/w Green) St James Theater 27 December

1964 **Fade Out—Fade In** (Styne/w Green) Mark Hellinger Theater 26 May

1967 **Hallelujah, Baby!** (Styne/w Green) Martin Beck Theater 26 April

1970 **Applause** (Charles Strouse/Lee Adams/w Green) Palace Theater 30 March

1974 **Lorelei** revised *Gentlemen Prefer Blondes* (Palace Theater)

1978 **On the Twentieth Century** (Cy Coleman/w Green) St James Theater 19 February

1982 **A Doll's Life** (Larry Grossman/w Green) Mark Hellinger Theater 23 September

1985 **Singin' in the Rain** (pasticcio/w Green) Gershwin Theater 2 July

1991 **The Will Rogers Follies** (Coleman/w Green/Peter Stone) Palace Theater 1 May

1999 **Die Fledermaus** American version w Green (Metropolitan Opera House)

Autobiography: *Off Stage* (Simon & Schuster, New York, 1995)

COME SPY WITH ME Comedy musical in 2 acts by Bryan Blackburn. Whitehall Theatre, London, 31 May 1966.

A vehicle for travesty artist Danny La Rue which took a few swipes at such glamorous-spy television series of the era as *The Man from Uncle* and *The Avengers* whilst cheerfully accomplishing its principal aim of getting La Rue into as many frocks and fixes as possible in the space of two acts. Agent Danny Rhodes (La Rue) is on the trail of beastly Dr Sigmund Fink (Barrie Gosney), vampish Tamara Flesch (Valerie Walsh), ''Greensleeves'' (Riggs O'Hara) and Momma (Rose Hill), trying to stop them getting their hands on a vital-to-the-nation virility drug. Since Fink knows him of old, Agent Danny gets into a frock—that is to say, several frocks—as an Irish nurse, a diplomatic lady and a cabaret singer, and as each of the other principal ladies. The most up-front of these was the little lift operator, Mavis Apple (Barbara Windsor), the unwitting possessor of the vile phial who, alas, in an unguarded moment accidentally swallows its contents.

It was Mavis who had the best ''number'' of the show, a telephone distress monologue, calling for help from the den of iniquity that is the gang's base, only to butt against wrong numbers and officious operators, but amongst the other musical moments Danny's ally, the smoother than shampoo Agent VO3 (Gary Miller), had some croony bits in bordering-on-burlesque style and the baddies got to sing a number about (shudder!) the welfare state. A mixture of burlesque and British films, directed by Ned Sherrin, with a much-appreciated star performance at its center, Peter Bridge and Brian Rix's production of *Come Spy with Me* spent a jolly 468 performances in the West End.

A French musical, *SO6,* which featured comedian Roger Nicolas in a similar parody of telly-spyland, was mounted in Paris the following year.

Recording: original cast (Decca)

COMPANY Musical in 2 acts by George Furth. Music and lyrics by Stephen Sondheim. Alvin Theater, New York, 26 April 1970.

An unusual piece for its time, the entertainment *Company* did not have a conventional, forward-going plotline, but was made up of a series of revusical character sketches, comical scenes and songs linked together by the character of bachelor Robert (Dean Jones), a friend of all the ''lurrrvly'' New York married couples who made up most of the rest of the cast. Their main aim in life is quickly seen to be that of getting poor Robert as married as they as quickly as possible.

The show opens with everyone gathering to celebrate Robert's birthday, before it sidesteps into a series of flash-around scenes showing him visiting each couple: niggling, bourgeois Sarah (Barbara Barrie) and Harry (Charles Kimbrough); adoring Peter (John Cunningham) and Susan (Merle Louise), who are getting fashionably divorced but not separated; effortfully trendy David (George Coe) and his tactfully conservative Jenny (Teri Ralston); likeable Paul (Steve Elmore) and his temporarily frenetic Amy (Beth Howland), who are finally getting married after years of living together; and patiently adult Larry (Charles Braswell) and the smart, loudmouthed Joanne (Elaine Stritch) he's got himself stuck with. His encounters with this parade of often irritatingly trivial and foolish folk were interspersed with some different kinds of encounters. Air hostess April (Susan Browning), kooky Marta (Pamela Myers) and dancing Kathy (Donna McKechnie) roll in and out of his bed but, in spite of them, and in spite of the efforts of all those friends, Robert emerges at the end of the entertainment 35 years old and still his own man. But, given the pressures, you can't help wondering for how long.

The songs of the show illustrated its characters and its topics wittily and incisively. Harry and Sarah's bickering lies were accompanied by the assertion that ''It's the Little Things You Do Together'' which make a marriage work, Robert tried to make flattering postcoital conversation as one-night April clambered out of bed to catch her plane to ''Barcelona,'' drink-sodden Joanne got waspish about the serious middle class to which she belongs as represented by ''The Ladies Who Lunch,'' whilst the whole brigade patted themselves on the back in harmonized unison at being such good friends to ''Poor Baby'' Robert in ''What Would We Do without You?' and ''Side by Side by Side.''

In a score which rendered up many durable concert and nightclub favorites, probably the most enjoyable pieces were two which did not extract so easily from the show: Amy's gallopingly frantic list of last-minute reasons why she is not ''Getting Married Today,'' counterpointed by the happy premarital crooning of her husband-to-inevitably-be and the dour soprano comments of a church chorister, and the trio for Marta, April and Kathy, boop-be-dooping exasperatedly and in thoroughly up-to-date style through the assertion that ''You Could Drive a Person Crazy'' with marital half-promises. Robert himself got to let loose in the last stages of the show with a piece which was in a different vein to the rest of the evening's crisp, dry and/or slightly satirical material: a striving, sentimental hymn to ''Being Alive'' which quickly found its way into the repertoire of half a hundred male torch singers and was for many years thereafter torn to a tatter 20 times a day in musical comedy auditions.

Harold Prince's Broadway production of *Company* proved a fine success, running through 705 performances whilst, a year into the run, a company took the show on the road with George Chakiris (Robert) at its head. Both were still in action when Prince and Richard Pilbrow mounted a London production at Her Majesty's Theatre. Larry Kert, who had replaced Jones as Robert a few weeks after the show had opened, and several of the original cast (Misses Howland, McKechnie, Ralston, Elmore) took part at the head of an all-American cast, but the show found more acceptance amongst theatre professionals than with the general public in a run of what was considered a disappointing 344 performances. Its appeal to theatre folk (not unconnected with the fact that each actor had a role and a scene), its well-known songs and its economic, chorusless construction all combined, however, to ensure it a steady run of subsequent provincial productions, both in America and in Britain, as well as occasional showings elsewhere.

The 1990s saw the show return both to London and to New York. London's production, originated at the Donmar Warehouse (13 December 1995), saw the show put to the kind of ''adaptation'' that helpless classics (though not normally ones with living authors with living agents) seem to suffer in end-of-20th-century days. Laden with tacked-in 1990s clichés and characterizations, and with character going out the window in favor of attitude, the show ended up with one foot in 1970 and the other in somewhere around 1990, and the distance of two decades was large enough to make that a deeply uncomfortable stance. This sort-of-1990s *Company,* with Adrian Lester as Bobby, transferred to the Albery Theatre (March 1996) for a commercial run.

The show returned to Broadway at Roundabout Theater 5 October 1995 with Boyd Gaines (Robert) at the center of its web of now cravenly politically corrected relationships. It played a set season of 68 performances at Criterion Center Stage Right, but did not follow Roundabout's previous mounting, *Damn Yankees,* into an open-ended run.

A production in Germany followed close on behind the original staging, in 1973, but an Australian professional production did not emerge until 1986 when the piece was mounted for a season with a cast including many of Australia's best musical theatre performers at the Sydney Opera House's Drama Theatre.

UK: Her Majesty's Theatre 8 January 1972; Germany: Düsseldorf 1973, Theater des Westens 22 March 1986; Australia: Drama Theatre (Opera House), Sydney 9 January 1986

Recordings: original cast (Columbia), London cast (CBS), London revival cast (First Night), New York revival (Varese Sarabande)

COMSTOCK, F Ray (b Buffalo, NY, 1880; d Boston, 15 October 1949). A Broadway producer who mounted both small-house musicals and vast spectaculars in a widely varying career, Comstock is largely remembered (when he is remembered) for his productions at the little Princess Theater, in the 1910s.

After beginnings as a theatre usher and box-office manager, notably at Casino Theater, New York, the young Comstock made his debut as a producer of musical comedy in 1904 with a touring production of the Chicago show *The Runaways,* which had been taken to Broadway the previous year by another young producer, Sam Shubert. He toured *The School Girl* in 1905, *Fantana* (w Morris Gest) in 1907, and moved on to Broadway for the first time, in collaboration with director-author R H Burnside, with *Fascinating Flora* (1907), a run-of-the-mill musical comedy which nevertheless rated a useful 113 performances in New York before going on the road. Comstock subsequently became lessee of the Savoy Theater, Atlantic City (1908 w Morris Gest) and as a producer interested himself for a while in the black musical comedies which were threatening to turn profitable in the years prior to the war. He mounted two of the better-liked ones—Williams and Walker's in *Bandana Land* (1908) and Bert Williams's *Mr Lode of Koal* (1909)—just as the thin vein was running unprofitably out. In 1909 he also joined with Gest to mount the Broadway production of Joseph Herbert's much-rewritten *The Beauty Spot* for a good 137 performances in New York and a long life on the road, and produced De Koven and Paulton's *The Yankee Mandarin* ("the Comstock Amusement Co") with Ada Lewis in Boston, without getting it to Broadway. Comstock and Gest later had a "by arrangement" credit on the Shubert production of *The Peasant Girl* (1914–15), and were also involved (w William Brady) in the restaging of the Drury Lane pantomime *Hop o' my Thumb* at the Manhattan Opera House in 1913.

Comstock struck a more productive line when he teamed, variously, with agent Elisabeth Marbury, with Gest and with William Elliott on a series of musical plays mounted in the postwar years at the small Princess Theater. Beginning with an adaptation of the successful London musical comedy *Mr Popple of Ippleton* (*Nobody Home*) in 1915, he co-mounted *Very Good Eddie* (1915), *Go To It* (1916), *Oh, Boy!* (1917), *Oh, Lady! Lady!!* (1918) and *Oh, My Dear!* (1918) in the little house, whilst also staging *Oh! Look* (1918) at the almost-as-small Vanderbilt and *Leave It to Jane*—squeezed out of the Princess by the success of *Oh, Boy!*—and the musical comedy *Kitty Darling* (1917, w Gest, Elliott) in larger houses. The more successful piece among this list provided fine fodder for the tour circuits for a number of years.

From the small-sized Princess Theater–style pieces, Comstock went to the other end of the scale when, in continuing partnership with Morris Gest, he mounted the Broadway productions of the grandiose London hits *Chu Chin Chow* (1917 w Elliott) and *The Maid of the Mountains* (1918 w Elliott), the risqué spectacular *Aphrodite* (1919), C B Cochran's picturesque London version of the equally sexy *Afgar* (1920) and *Chu Chin Chow*'s vast successor, *Mecca* (1920). Amongst a heavy schedule of plays and imported companies they also sponsored such pieces as the Russian revue *Chauve-Souris* and the extravagant *The Miracle.* Comstock also, however, suffered a number of failures, including Kern's *Zip Goes a Million,* an Americanized and botched *Phi-Phi* and Armand Vecsey's *The Rose of China,* and he went from having 11 shows on Broadway and/or announced to appear there, and 9 touring, at the beginning of 1920, to a virtual wipe-out of his musical comedy activities a year later. He retired formally from the theatre in 1929.

COMTE OBLIGADO Opérette in 3 acts by André Barde. Music by Raoul Moretti. Théâtre des Nouveautés, Paris, 16 December 1927.

The "Comte Obligado" is not a real count, he is Antoine (Milton), the little lift-boy (the "boy" has nothing to do with age) in the Paris couture house Maison Amandine, who has inherited a magnificent fortune. Alas, for all his dreamy plans, by the time the government has thievingly helped itself to 90 per cent of his windfall, there is just enough left for him to blow on one wild spree. And so "Comte Obligado" goes out into the world where, taken under the wing of the wealthy and social

Madame de Miranda (Marthe Ferrare) who is under the impression that he is a fabulously rich Algerian, he is made a fuss of by all until the truth comes out. Dropped by his fair-weather leeches, the sad lad flings the last of his disappointing money on a horse. It wins him a second, untaxed fortune. Which goes to show that, in France (and it couldn't possibly be so anywhere else, could it?), the government prefers you to win your money gambling than from the life's work of your family.

Milton, equipped with a delightful role, also had two song hits in Raoul Moretti's score with ''La Caravane'' (otherwise ''La Fille du bédouin'') and ''Les Artichauts,'' whilst the incidental but necessary juvenile couple, played by Davia and Robert Darthez, took the central part of the score with her solo ''Si Maman le veut'' and their duos ''Ça fait passer un moment'' and ''Un petit bout de femme.'' The dandy Urban tangoed to ''Mio padre'' and sang of ''Le Petit Oiseau des Îles,'' and Mlle Ferrare ventured ''Yoo-oo, ma Caroline'' in the other principal parts of a musical accompaniment which helped *Comte Obligado* to a fine success.

The piece which, in the modern musical comedy vein, featured a cast of 13 and no chorus, was played for many years throughout the French provinces and, in 1935, Milton starred in a filmed version. New York also got a quick glimpse of *Comte Obligado* when a touring French musical comedy company, with Servatius in the comic lead, included the show in its season on Broadway in 1929.

USA: Jolson Theater 11 March 1929

Film: Léon Mathot 1935

A CONNECTICUT YANKEE Musical in a prologue and 2 acts by Herbert Fields adapted from Mark Twain's *A Connecticut Yankee in King Arthur's Court.* Lyrics by Lorenz Hart. Music by Richard Rodgers. Vanderbilt Theater, New York, 3 November 1927.

Twain's satirical fantasy novel *A Connecticut Yankee in King Arthur's Court* (1889) was made into a slightly less satirical silent film by Harry Myers in 1920, and a sight of that film encouraged Fields, Rodgers and Hart to option the novel as material for a musical. It was 1927 before the piece finally got written and, when it did, it was both updated and sweetened up with some good old-fashioned anachronism-jokes and situations to make it into a lively, traditional musical comedy book.

The prologue introduced Martin (William Gaxton), on the eve of his wedding, paying more attention to pretty Alice Carter (Constance Carpenter) than to his fiancée, Fay Morgan (Nana Bryant), until the exasperated lass understandably whacks him over the head with a bottle of champagne. Martin goes down . . . and back. When he wakes up, he is in King Arthur's Court. Fay, naturally, is Morgan le Fay, Alice is the delicious Alisande la Carteloise, friend Lawrence Lake (William Roselle) has become Lancelot du Lac, Gerald Lake (Jack Thompson) is Galahad, alongside Merlin (William Norris), Arthur (Paul Everton) and so forth. Rescued from the inexplicably arrived stranger's fate that seems to threaten him by a convenient prediction of an eclipse, Martin then proceeds to modernize Camelot with 20th-century ''improvements'' in precisely the same way that comic-opera comedians of the 19th century regularly ''improved'' foreign lands by introducing English (or American) habits and institutions into their backward way of life. But Morgan le Fay is on the war path . . . and when Martin truly wakes up, he is determined to swap the modern Fay for Alice.

The score of *A Connecticut Yankee* brought forth a pair of hit numbers, one new, one borrowed. The new one was the demi-period duet for Martin and Alisande, ''Thou Swell,'' the borrowed one was ''My Heart Stood Still,'' originally used in Rodgers and Hart's London revue *One Dam Thing After Another* earlier the same year and, according to Rodgers, stuck hastily into this show in order to stop insufficiently voiced comedienne Beatrice Lillie claiming it for another of their shows. As sung by the star pair, it gave them a second winner. Stanley Green has pointed out that the entire chorus lyric of this unstaccato song holds only six bisyllabic words, all the rest are, unusually, monosyllables. Galahad and his Evelyn (June Cochrane) were the number two pair, singing about being ''On a Desert Island with Thee.''

Lew Fields and Lyle Andrews's intimate-house production of *A Connecticut Yankee* had a fine Broadway run of 418 performances, the longest metropolitan life of any of the Rodgers-Hart musicals of that period, and the show was taken up by ''British Amalgamated Theatres Ltd'' to be produced at London's rather larger Daly's Theatre. Miss Carpenter repeated her original role opposite Harry Fox, with Billy Holland and Gladys Cruickshank in support and J G Taylor as Merlin. For Britishers, who were apparently presumed not to know what Connecticut was, the musical was retitled *A Yankee in King Arthur's Court,* and Vivian Ellis and Desmond Carter had two songs interpolated into the score—one, ''I Don't Know How,'' to replace the hit number that England had already heard. The show lasted only 43 performances at a theatre that had given a much warmer welcome to the same songwriters' *Peggy-Ann,* before it was bundled briefly on the road in the new year.

In 1943 Rodgers himself sponsored a Broadway revival (Martin Beck Theater 17 November 1943) in an effort to give the sinking Hart an interest and a job. The text was partly rewritten to put it into a 1943 wartime setting and five pieces of the original score topped up with a half dozen new ones. Vivienne Segal, as Morgan le Fay, reaped the best of what would be Hart's last songs, relating how she had disposed of each of her husbands "To Keep My Love Alive." Dick Foran and Julie Warren played the number one couple, and Vera-Ellen and Chester Stratton the second, through 135 performances. This version of the show was televised in America in 1955 with Eddie Albert and Janet Blair featured and staged at London's Open Air Theatre, Regent's Park in the summer of 1993.

UK: Daly's Theatre 10 October 1929

Recordings: selection from 1943 cast (Decca), TV cast 1955 (AEI)

CONRAD, Con [DOBER, Conrad K] (b New York, 18 June 1891; d Van Nuys, Calif, 28 September 1938). At first a pianist in film houses and a performer in vaudeville, Conrad turned out a bundle of popular songs in the 1920s, and also contributed to a small group of mostly successful musical plays.

A long list of single songs—"Singin' the Blues (till my daddy comes home)," "Palesteena" (both w J Russell Robinson), "Ma! He's Making Eyes at Me" (w Sidney Clare), "Barney Google" (w Billy Rose), "Lonesome and Sorry" (w Benny Davis), "Let's All Go to Mary's House" (w Harry Woods), "Margie" (w Robinson, Davis), "Goodnight" (w Harry Woods, Irving Bibo), "A Prisoner of Love" (w Leo Robin), "Memory Lane" (w B G de Sylva, Larry Spier), "You've Got to See Mamma Every Night (or you can't see mamma at all)"—and, following his move to Hollywood in 1929, of music for such films as Fox Movietone *Follies of 1929* ("The Breakaway," "That's You Baby," "Walking with Susie"), and most notably for *The Gay Divorcee* ("The Continental," winner of the initial Academy Award in 1934, "A Needle in a Haystack" w Herbert Magidson) make up much of Con Conrad's credits, but he also contributed for several years to the Broadway musical theatre. Amongst his stage work were included revue songs (*Greenwich Village Follies of 1923* w Louis Hirsch, *Americana* w others, *Broadway Brevities*); interpolated numbers in such shows as *Bombo* (1921, four, including Jolson's "Morning Will Come"), *Big Boy* (1925) and *Take the Air* (1927); and, most substantially, a handful of musical comedy scores.

Although each of the four Broadway musicals on which Conrad worked between 1924–26 had a good run in America, it was in Britain and in Hungary that *Mercenary Mary* ("Honey, I'm in Love with You") proved a long-running hit, whilst his songs for the comical *Kitty's Kisses* got a longer showing when some of that show's music was amalgamated with some pieces by Rodgers and Hart to make up the score of what London called *The Girl Friend.* His *Betty Lee* followed its American run by being produced by Hugh J Ward in Australia (Princess Theatre, Melbourne 12 June 1926) alongside the local production of *Mercenary Mary.*

Conrad also supplied the handful of numbers which illustrated *My Boy Friend,* the Shuberts' musical play based on Jack Lait's *Gus the Bus* cartoon.

In 1928 he briefly turned producer and mounted the musical *Keep Shufflin'* on Broadway.

1924 **Moonlight** (William B Friedlander/William Le Baron) Longacre Theater 30 January

1924 **My Boy Friend** (aka *Gus the Bus*) (Jack Lait) Parsons' Theater, Hartford, Conn 1 December

1924 **Betty Lee** (w Louis Hirsch/Irving Caesar, Otto Harbach/Paul Armstrong, Rex Beach) 44th Street Theater 25 December

1925 **The Comic Supplement** (w Henry Souvaine/J P McEvoy/McEvoy, Augustin Duncan) National Theater, Washington, DC 20 January

1925 **Mercenary Mary** (w Friedlander/Caesar/Isabel Leighton) Longacre Theater 13 April

1926 **Kitty's Kisses** (Gus Kahn/Harbach, Philip Bartholomae) Playhouse Theater 6 May

THE CONSUL Musical drama in 3 acts by Gian-Carlo Menotti. Barrymore Theater, New York, 15 March 1950.

Although uncompromisingly dramatic and operatic in its content, *The Consul,* like many of Gian-Carlo Menotti's other works, attempted to straddle the line between the commercial theatre and the opera house. The show dealt with the plight of Magda Sorel (Patricia Neway), the wife of a conspirator in an iron curtain country, who tries unavailingly to get through the bureaucratic barriers of a consular office to join her escaped husband (Cornell MacNeil) abroad, and whose frustration and failure ultimately leads to a despairing suicide. The drama's musical centerpiece was Magda's aria "To This We've Come (that men withhold the world from men)." Gloria Lane played the important role of the Consulate secretary and Marie Powers, star of Menotti's *The Medium,* had top billing in the supporting role of Magda's mother.

Produced on Broadway under the management of Chandler Cowles and Efram Zimbalist jr, and directed by an author-composer who was outspokenly critical of the manner in which a director and/or producer could distortionately come between the writer and the audience in commercial theatre, the piece was much admired and succeeded in playing through a run of 269 performances. It was subsequently staged in London both commercially with Misses Neway and Lane (Cambridge Theatre, 1951) and then at Sadler's Wells Opera (11 November 1954) with Amy Shuard as Magda and Anna Pollak as the Secretary; produced in Australia in 1953 with Marie Collier as Magda as part of an operatic season; and televised by American PBS in 1978. Since its initial performances, it has, however, gravitated naturally towards a small niche in the opera house repertoire rather than in that of the commercial stage which, particularly given Menotti's dicta, seemed an unlikely place for it anyway.

UK: Cambridge Theatre 7 February 1951; Germany: Hamburg 1951, Theater des Westens, Berlin 7 September 1951; Austria: 1951; Australia: Melbourne Opera Group 1953

Recordings: original cast (Decca), TV film (Mercury)

TV films: Cleveland Playhouse 1952, Spoleto Festival 1978

THE CONTRABANDISTA, or The Law of the Ladrones Comic opera in 2 acts by F C Burnand. Music by Arthur Sullivan. St George's Opera House, London, 18 December 1867.

F C Burnand's claim to have been at least the co-instigator of the modern English-language musical theatre is confirmed not merely by the fact that he wrote the texts for the first two British opéras-bouffes with original musical scores (*Windsor Castle, L'Africaine*), but also by his authorship of the first genuine comic opera of the era. The libretto of *The Contrabandista,* mounted by Gallery of Illustration manager Thomas German Reed in his first attempt at staging a full-length show in a proper theatre, showed that its author had a good knowledge of the most recent (and not so recent) French musical stage, but the piece was none the worse for being derivative.

Since there has been a dead heat in the voting for the new leader of the Ladrones, it is decreed, by brigand law, that the new chief of the band shall be the first stranger who wanders into their territory. A little British photographer, Peter Adolphus Grigg (J A Shaw), is captured, invested with burlesque pomp, and given in marriage to the fierce chieftainess, Inez de Roxas (Lucy Franklein). But the defeated candidates cheat. Sancho (Mr Neilson) overhears San José (Thomas Aynsley Cook) plotting murderously with Inez to snatch command, and he resolves to turn traitor. Things get sticky for Grigg and Rita (Arabella Smythe), a hostage who sings the soprano line, until the cavalry arrive, headed by Rita's tenorious boyfriend Vasquez (Edward Hargrave).

Grigg had the best role and the best song of the young Arthur Sullivan's score, the bouncy "From Rock to Rock," but there were some fine ensemble pieces as well and Miss Franklein had some splendidly rumbling contralto writing included in her role.

Played on a bill with Offenbach's *Ba-ta-clan* and *La Chatte métamorphosée en femme,* and later with Auber's *L'Ambassadrice,* the show was given an excellent 72 times. It was later played in the English provinces under the management of Sullivan's brother, Frederic (1874, with Alfred Cellier conducting), and on a number of occasions on tour in America, after *HMS Pinafore* had made Sullivan's name saleable. The conductor of one of these tours was John Philip Sousa, who subsequently took the libretto of *The Contrabandista* as the basis for a score of his own called *The Smugglers* (Jersey City 7 December 1879). He was, in fact, not the only one to do so, for a piece produced, and allegedly written, by Horace Lingard under the title *I Ladroni,* billed on its San Francisco premiere as "an entirely new and comic opera," also turned out to be a variation—to put it politely—on *The Contrabandista.* Guiseppe Operti (1830–1886) (he of the "composed and arranged by" of Broadway's *The Black Crook* revival, but also sometime musical director at the Assembly Rooms, Dundee, Scotland) was credited with selection, arrangement and composition of the music, and Lingard starred as Mr Triptollinmoss Figg, performing "From Rock to Rock" in an evening that included several other pieces of recognizable Sullivan and a goodly amount of made-over Burnand. Lingard pulled *I Ladroni* out on several future occasions, in both Australia and New Zealand, and—after the *Pinafore* craze hit Broadway, he announced it on a Bijou Theater bill along with *The Sorcerer* (10 May 1879). Signor Operti was now forgotten, and the piece was largely billed as "Sullivan's *I Ladroni.*" However, when the night came, they played *Pinafore* instead. America ultimately got its first "real" *Contrabandista* in Philadelphia, when the intrepid manager "Fatty" Crossy varied his amazingly long-running (11 weeks) *Pinafore / Trial by Jury* production at the North Broad Street Theater by mounting the older piece as well. Louise Leighton featured as Rita. It was subsequently toured by a group called The London Opera Company (1879) and by other repertoire companies anxious to feature as much of the now hugely fashionable Sullivan's work as possible.

In 1894 Richard D'Oyly Carte, at a loss for a new entertainment, had the authors revise *The Contrabandista* for the Savoy Theatre (12 December). Lengthened, broadened, retitled *The Chieftain* and cast with Walter Passmore (Grigg), Courtice Pounds (Vasquez), Florence St John (Rita), Rosina Brandram (Inez), M R Morand (José), Richard Temple (Sancho) and Florence Perry in the new role of Mrs Dolly Grigg, it was a 97-performance disappointment. A production of *The Chieftain* by A H Canby at New York's Abbey Theater (9 September 1895) with Christie MacDonald as Dolly, Lulu Glaser as Rita and Francis Wilson as Grigg played 54 times, and a German version by Richard Genée was mounted at Munich's Theater am Gärtnerplatz later the same year.

The title *Los Contrabandistas* was earlier used for a one-act Parisian opérette by Émile Thierry and Julien Nargeot, produced at the Théâtre ds Champs-Elysées, 28 May 1861.

USA: North Broad Street Theater, Philadelphia 16 April 1879

Recording: amateur version with rewritten lyrics (Rare Recorded Editions)

CONVERSATION PIECE Romantic comedy with music in 3 acts by Noël Coward. His Majesty's Theatre, London, 16 February 1934.

Written by Coward as a vehicle for the French actress and vocalist Yvonne Printemps, who spoke no English, *Conversation Piece* told the tale of a young French singer, Melanie (Mlle Printemps), who is taken to Brighton and richly set up for the season under the management of the impoverished Paul, Duc de Chaucigny-Varennes (Coward), with the object of winning her a rich husband who will support them both. The girl's charms are sufficient to enchant the young Marquis of Sheere (Louis Hayward) to an offer of marriage, his father, Lord Beneden (Athole Stewart), to a more equivocal offer of ''protection,'' and to win an approach from a representative of the Prince Regent himself, but Melanie does not play the game. She has fallen in love with Paul and when, with the help of his old and amorous friend Lady Julia Charteris (Irene Browne), he sets up a party to help her progress, she ruins all his plans by inviting in the courtesans of Brighton (Heather Thatcher, Moya Nugent, Betty Shale). The furious Paul is about to find financial salvation with the patient Julia when he realizes, in time for the final curtain, where his heart truly lies.

Like the script (which had just a whisper of the plot of the previous year's Parisian hit *Oh! Papa . . .* about it), the score was written to measure for the star, who had the only solos of the evening, the most enduring of which was the lovely waltz ''I'll Follow My Secret Heart.'' The supporting cast got the comical moments with the gentlemen's description of ''Regency Rakes'' and the professional ladies complaining that ''There's Always Something Fishy about the French.''

Coward stepped in, in rehearsals, to replace the actor Romney Brent who had been cast as Paul, and his presence on the bill undoubtedly added to the appeal of a piece which, at moments enchanting, was at others very talky and at others, for the benefit of the star, even lapsed into French. When he withdrew, to be replaced by the rather more apt Pierre Fresnay (Mlle Printemps's longtime partner à la ville), the Parisian star's name proved to be insufficient to support the box office and Coward was obliged to return. C B Cochran's production of *Conversation Piece* ran for a semi-satisfactory 177 performances before Archie Selwyn and Harold Franklin joined the producer in taking it across the Atlantic for a Broadway season. Mlle Printemps and Fresnay scored personal hits at the head of a British cast mostly taken from the originals, but 55 performances was the limit of its run.

Conversation Piece was played for eight performances at the New York Barbizon-Plaza (18 November 1957) with a cast headed by René Paul and Joan Copeland, but has not received a major revival.

USA: 44th Street Theater 23 October 1934

Recordings: complete with dialogue (Columbia), original cast excerpts (HMV)

COOK, Barbara [Nell] (b Atlanta, Ga, 25 October 1927). Classy young Broadway soprano who transformed into a cabaret vocalist and character lady.

Barbara Cook first appeared on Broadway in the juvenile soprano role of Sandy in *Flahooley* (1951) and subsequently played Ado Annie in *Oklahoma!* (1953) and Carrie in *Carousel* (1954) at the City Center and appeared as Jane in the 1954 TV version of *Babes in Toyland.* She created the roles of Hilda Miller in *Plain and Fancy* (1955) and of Cunégonde in the original version of Leonard Bernstein's *Candide* (1956), introducing the vocally taxing burlesque jewel song, ''Glitter and Be Gay,'' starred in revivals of *Carousel* (1957, Julie) and *The King and I* (1960, Anna), and in 1957 created her most memorable role as Marian, the librarian, in *The Music Man* (''Goodnight My Someone,'' ''Till There Was You'').

She subsequently appeared on Broadway as Liesl Brandel in *The Gay Life* (1961), Amalia Balash in *She Loves Me* (1963, ''Ice Cream''), Carol Deems in *Something More!* (1964) and as Dolly Talbo in *The Grass Harp* (1971), played in *Funny Girl, The Boy Friend* and *The Unsinkable Molly Brown* outside New York, and appeared as Evelina in a television *Bloomer Girl.* She then quit the heroine's roles her exceptional soprano and attractive looks had kept her in for so long and orientated herself towards the nightclub and cabaret world.

Her solo theatre-concert performances and a TV/recording portrayal of Sally in *Follies* in the late 1980s won her a strong, particular following and seemed as if it would signal the beginning of a second theatre career as a character performer. That career, however, began less fortunately than the first had done, with the leading role in the tryout of the flop musical *Carrie* at Stratford-on-Avon, and Miss Cook back-pedaled to a high profile career as a solo performer.

COOK, J[ohn] Furneaux (b London, 1839; d London, 19 January 1903). One of the most substantial singing character men of the 19th-century British musical stage.

Young Cook sang in glee clubs as a boy, and appeared as a child actor in *The Tempest* (1857) and *King John* at the Princess's Theatre, but he renounced singing when his voice broke and for a while followed his father's profession as an engraver until his brother-in-law, the composer and conductor Meyer Lutz, directed him towards the lyric stage. He toured for several seasons in

Henri Corri's operatic company, in Stanley Betjeman and Richard Temple's striving company, and in the Charles Durand Opera Company (as "Mr J C Furneaux," King in *Maritana, L'Africaine,* etc) before appearing at the Gaiety Theatre in April 1871 as Corbillon in the Offenbach pasticcio *Malala,* Lord Lyndham in *Peter the Shipwright* (*Zar und Zimmermann*) and in Balfe's *Letty, the Basketmaker.* He had his first original musical role later that year when he created the part of the godfatherly Peter the Watchman in Jonas's *Cinderella the Younger* (1871) and, although he spent another period touring with Durand, the bulk of his long subsequent career was spent playing baritone roles in the musical theatre.

Amongst his early engagements he toured as the Grand Vizier in *Kissi-Kissi* and as the old fiddler in *Breaking the Spell* (1873); created the roles of the Sultan in *The Sultan of Mocha* (1874 and 1881), Baron de Montmorency in *The Tower of London* (1875), Weasel in *Nell Gwynne* (1876) and the Magistrate in Solomon's little *Contempt of Court* (1877); played Larivaudière in *La Fille de Madame Angot* (Alhambra revival); and toured for D'Oyly Carte in the initial tour of *The Sorcerer* (1878, Dr Daly). He also appeared as Prince Casimir in the Alhambra's *La Princesse de Trébizonde* revival and created the parts of Sir Ralph Ashton in *The Lancashire Witches* (1879) in Manchester and of Samuel in *The Pirates of Penzance* (1879) in New York. He later toured as the Sergeant of Police in the last-named piece, took over as Sir Mincing Lane in the original production of *Billee Taylor* (1880), created Sergeant Crowe in *The King's Dragoons* (1880) and toured both with Alice Barth's company (*Widows Bewitched,* etc) and with Carte as Corcoran and Sir Marmaduke (*Sorcerer*).

He appeared in London as Batifol in *La Belle Normande* (1881), the Lord Mayor in *The Grand Mogol* (1881), Gnatbrain in Lutz's *All in the Downs* (1881) and Mr Dunn in his *Knight of the Garter* (1882), as Farmer Bowman in *The Merry Duchess* (1883), and in *Cox and Box* at the Court Theatre (1883) before rejoining D'Oyly Carte's tours yet again (1884–85) to play Pooh Bah, Mountararat, Dick Deadeye and the Sergeant of Police. In 1886 he created the role of the heroine's father, Squire Bantam, in *Dorothy* (singing again some of the music he had performed in its earlier existence as *Nell Gwynne*), and he repeated that part later in the 1892 revival and again at his Gaiety Theatre benefit in 1897.

Cook followed this long-running success with its successor, playing Alderman Shelton in *Doris* (1889), then created the roles of Elvino di Pasto in W S Gilbert and Alfred Cellier's *The Mountebanks* (1892), Bullion in Goring Thomas's *The Golden Web* (1892), the comical heavy, Silas Block in the latter-day burlesque *Little Christopher Columbus* (1893), and Major Penyon in the

Plate 83. **Tom Aynsley Cook,** *"the grumpy basso," caricatured by his fellow singer, Charles Lyall.*

farcical musical comedy *The White Silk Dress* (1896). He toured as John Mayfield in the comic opera *Kitty* and as the Christian and chorus master in Wilson Barrett's famous *The Sign of the Cross,* but around this time his eyesight began to fail, and he was obliged to give up the stage. Totally blind for the last three years of his life, the unmarried singer was cared for in the home of Meyer Lutz (now married to a second of his sisters), until he died at the age of 63.

Thomas Aynsley COOK (b London, July 1831; d Liverpool, 16 February 1894), the elder brother of Furneaux Cook, worked as a boy soprano at the Temple before attending Würzburg Conservatoire and making his first almost adult appearance as a teenage Commendatore in *Don Giovanni.* On his return to Britain, he was seen at the Surrey in Lutz's *The Charmed Harp* (1852) and he subsequently worked for many years touring and in town seasons with English opera companies (Joseph H Tully's company, National English Opera Co, Pyne-Harrison, English Opera Co, Parepa-Rosa Co, Henri Corri's Co, etc) playing basso roles in both Britain and America (Henry Cooper's Co, etc) in the late 1850s and early 1860s. He created character roles in a number of English operas of the period (*Love's Triumph, The Armourer of Nantes,* Sergeant Peterman in *The Desert Flower,* Aesop in *Blanche de Nevers,* etc), yet proved versatile enough to appear on the bill with Bryant's Ministrels (New York 1860) or at the Broadway Musical Hall, where he sang his songs alongside another young performer with a future, Tony Pastor.

At the coming of opéra-bouffe he made an immediate impact when he appeared as Britain's first General Boum in *La Grande-Duchesse,* and thereafter his career included long periods of musical-theatre appearances amongst which were included the roles of the Commandant in Freddie Clay's first professional musical, *Constance* (1865), José in Sullivan's first full-length work *The Contrabandista* (1867), several seasons at the Gaiety Theatre playing in such pieces as Adam's *Dolly* (*La Poupée de Nuremberg*), Popolani in *Barbe-bleue,* as Matt o' the Mint in *The Beggar's Opera,* the title role of *The Quaker,* Donizetti's *Betly,* Daniel in *Zampa,* Giacomo in *Fra Diavolo,* Sackatoo in the Offenbach pasticcio *Malala,* Lunastro in *Letty, the Basketmaker,* Von Bett in *Peter the Shipwright* (*Zar und Zimmermann*), Danny Mann in *The Lily of Killarney* and Don Jose in *Maritana.* He also appeared in burlesque (Lord Tristan in *Martha*) and in such pantomime roles as Baron Sponsorwitz in Covent Garden's *The Sleeping Beauty* (1870) or the Wolf in Manchester's *Little Red Riding Hood* (1874).

An original member of the Parepa-Rosa Opera Company, together with his wife (**Mrs Aynsley COOK**, née Harriet Farrell Payne b Smithfield, Mddx, 26 July 1829; d London, 6 October 1880, a member of the famous pantomime family), he returned regularly to that company whilst still building a list of musical theatre credits to rival that of his brother: Valentine in the London production of *Le Petit Faust,* Morzouk in *Giroflé-Girofla* (1876), General Kantschukoff in London's *Fatinitza* (1878), Cocorico (ex- Sifroy) in *Geneviève de Brabant* (1878 revival), the Viceroy in *La Périchole* with Emily Soldene (1878), King Gros-Minet in *La Poule aux oeufs d'or* (1878) at the Alhambra—performing two duets by Gevaert with Soldene who here played his daughter—Dick Deadeye on tour with Blanche Roosevelt (1879), The Marquis in *The King's Dragoons* (1880), King James in *The Lancashire Witches* (1881), Monthabor in *La Fille du tambour-major* (1881), Sir Temple Griffin in Solomon's *Lord Bateman* (1882), Schnapps in the London edition of *The Beggar Student* (1883), Count Pomposo di Vesuvio in *Estrella* (1883), Arimanes in *The Golden Ring* (1883), Captain Santiago in *La Serenata* (1888) Dr Manacle in Goring Thomas's *The Golden Web* (1893), and Gruyer in *Fanchette* (*François les bas-bleus*) with Carl Rosa. He was taken ill in Liverpool whilst touring with Rosa and died there at the age of 62.

Cook's unflagging career in the theatre was altogether more successful than an attempt to turn publican. He was briefly the licencee of Hampstead's Jack Straw's Castle, and sent himself bankrupt over it.

His daughter, Annie, a contralto with the Carl Rosa opera company, became Mrs Eugene Goossens.

Alice Aynsley COOK [née Alice COOK] (b Stockwell, London, 24 May 1849; d London, 7 April 1938), the Cooks' youngest sister, began her career in burlesque (creating Alfred Lee's *Carrot and Pa-snip,* 1872, Pierre) and touring opera before joing the company at the Gaiety Theatre to play Hassarac in *Ali Baba à la Mode* (1872), Zerlina in *Don Giovanni,* in *Martha,* and in the little operetta *Fleurette* (1873). She went on tour first with the Gaiety opéra-bouffe company (Clementine in *Barbe-bleue,* etc) and later as Mme Lange in Fred Wright's tour of *La Fille de Madame Angot* (1874), but returned to the Gaiety to play Fanny in *The Island of Bachelors* (1874), before going on to create or play a series of mezzo-soprano roles in British musical plays—Meg in *Tower of London* (1875), Lady Clare in *Nell Gwynne* (1876), Frank Musgrave's little *Prisoners at the Bar* (1878), Widow Nutter in *The Lancashire Witches* (1879), the title role of the touring burlesque *Cruel Carmen* with the Walton family (1880), Dorothy in Crook's *The King's Dragoons* revival (1881), Dolly Mayflower in Lutz's *All in the Downs* (1881), Felix in *On Condition* with Lila Clay's all-woman company and Miss Newton in Lutz's *The Knight of the Garter* (1882)—as well as appearing occasionally in the non-musical theatre.

She played as Ruth, Lady Sangazure, Little Buttercup, Lady Jane and Katisha with D'Oyly Carte's touring companies (1884–85); toured with the Vokes family (1884, 1886–88 *In Camp, Fun in a Fog,* etc) and in the title role of the extravaganza *Randolph the Reckless* (1889); visited South America in 1891 for Edwin Cleary with a repertoire including *Billee Taylor, Erminie, Dorothy* and the Gilbert and Sullivan canon; and later visited South Africa for the Edwardes-Wheeler Company in *A Gaiety Girl* (Lady Virginia), *In Town* (Duchess) and *Morocco Bound* (Countess). She was again seen on the British stage, now as a "heavy lady," as Lady Joan Saxmundham in Arthur Roberts's burlesque *Claude Duval* (1894); on tour for Edwardes as Dame Hecla Courtlandt in *His Excellency* and then in *The Telephone Girl;* as Miss Seraphine Plummer in *Regina BA* (1897), Mrs Amelia Rourke in *That Terrible Turk* (1898), Mlle Tournesol in *Milord Sir Smith* (1898), Mrs Miranda Q Strongmynde in *The American Heiress* (1899), Countess Nitsky in *The Prince of Borneo* (1899), Dancing Sun-

LEFT: Plate C-1. Aladdin II. *Nellie Farren as "son of Aladdin" in the Gaiety Theatre's early British musical comedy.*
BELOW: Plate C-2. Alma, wo wohnst du? *A real musical comedy, from Broadway's king of the German-language theatre.*

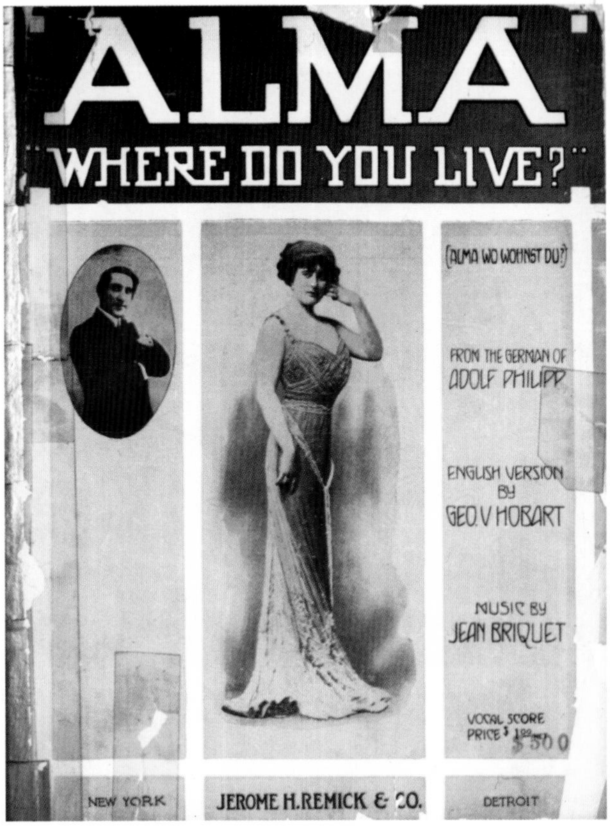

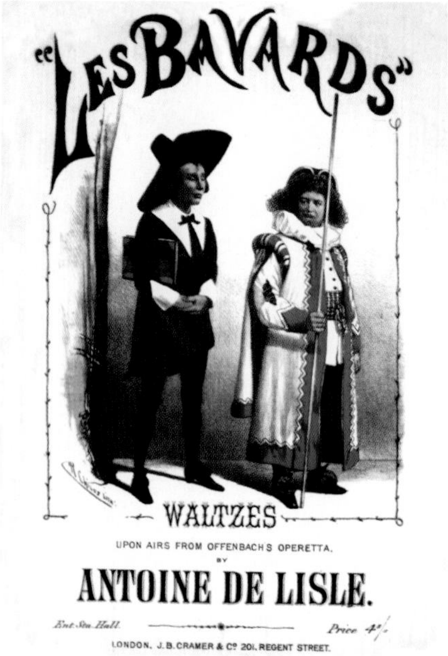

COUNTERCLOCKWISE: Plate C-3. Babil and Bijou. *A sketch artist's impression of two scenes from the bank-breaking Dion Boucicault production at London's Theatre Royal, Covent Garden.* **Plate C-4. Barnum.** *Phineas Taylor Barnum (Mark Wynter) gets his showbiz career going exhibiting Joice Heth, "the oldest woman in the world," in the biomusical's South African production.* **Plate C-5. Les Bavards.**

CLOCKWISE: Plate C-6. The Belle of New York. *Edna May in full color.* **Plate C-7. Billee Taylor.** *These sailor boys are girls!* **Plate C-8. Richard Carle's** *musical version of the French play* Madame Mongodin *proved a fine touring vehicle for comic Harry Conor as the show's hagridden "hero."*

Plate C-9. A Chinese Honeymoon.
The plot in easy stages.

CLOCKWISE: **Plate C-10. Les Cloches de Corneville.** *A jolly knees-up at Corneville fair.* **Plate C-11. José Collins** *made a hit of* The Maid of the Mountains, *and the show made a star of her.* **Plate C-12. Dandy Fifth.** *An original touring poster.* **Plate C-13. Claude Duval.** *Did the horses get on the stage?*

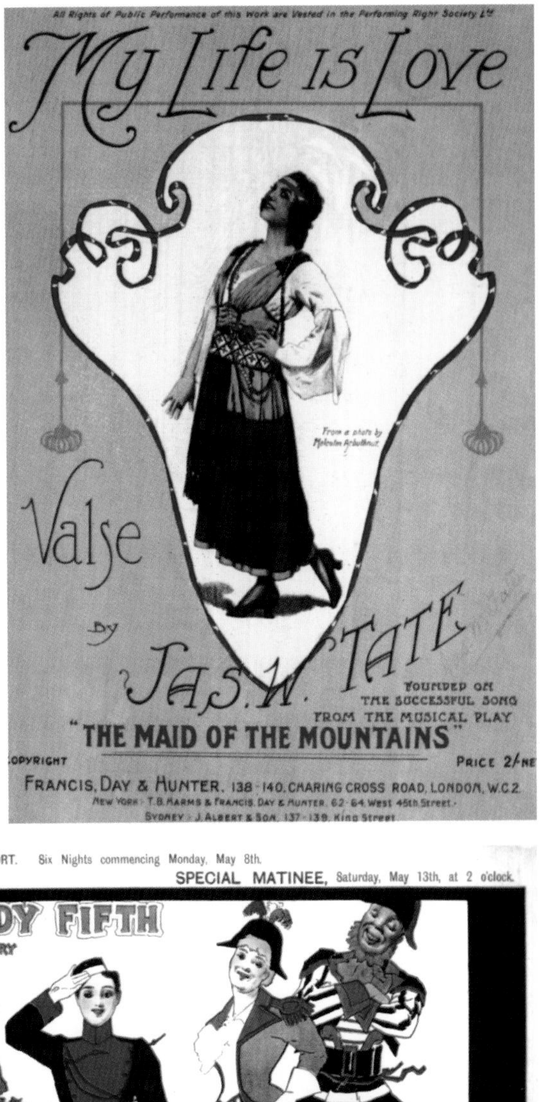

Clockwise: Plate C-14. Elisabeth. *Pia Douwes (Elisabeth) and Viktor Gernot (Franz Josef) as the Kaiser and Kaiserin of Austria.* **Plate C-15. Faust Up-to-Date.** *E J Lonnen was the devil who vowed "I shall 'ave 'em . . . !"* **Plate C-16. La Fille de Madame Angot.** *Under the music of a glorious Lecocq waltz, there is counterrevolution being plotted.* **Plate C-17. Gay's the Word.** *Cicely was gay.*

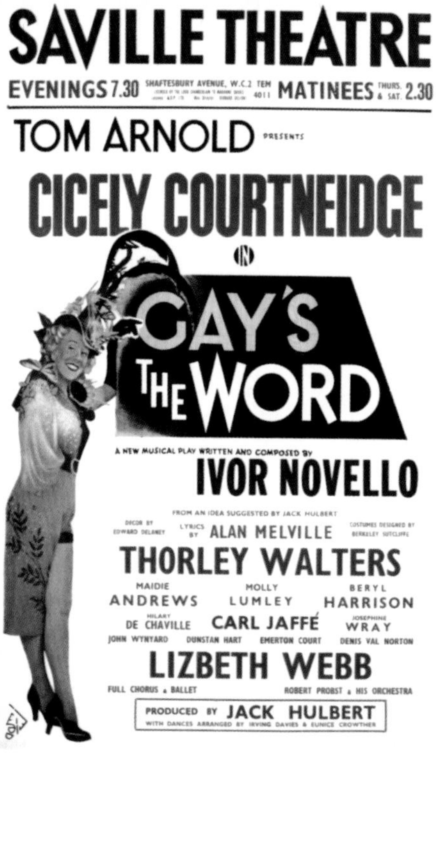

Plate C-18. The Geisha *was one of the most outstanding hits of the 19th-century musical stage—played and played again in Germany, France, Italy, Sweden, Yugoslavia, Hungary and many other countries throughout the world.*

Plate C-19. The Girl Behind the Counter.
Gowns for the girls of the front line.

beam in *The Rose of Persia* (1900), Sarah Slade in *The Gay Cadets* (1901), Countess of Newtown in *The Emerald Isle* tour (1901), Mrs Bumble in *The Golddiggers* (1902), Lady Bingo Barr in *Bill Adams* (1903) and finally, as Mrs Marjorie Buttery in Ada Reeve's *Moll, the Rogue* (1905); towards the end of a career of more than 30 years as a musical-theatre character lady.

COOK, Will Marion (b Washington, DC, 27 January 1869; d New York, 19 July 1944). The composer of much music for black theatre shows and performers in an era when there seemed briefly to be commercial possibilities in such entertainments.

The son of a well-off and well-educated family, Cook studied music at Oberlin College from the age of 13 and, later, in Europe, with the aim of a career as a concert violinist. When that career proved unattainable, he instead began composing black-accented songs—often, but not always, with lyrics littered with ''dis'' and ''dat'' and ''dem''s—for the popular stage. He had a small success with his first full stage piece, the 45-minute *Clorindy, or The Origin of the Cakewalk* (''Who Dat Say Chicken in Dis Crowd?,'' ''Darktown is Out Tonight,'' ''Jump Back, Honey''), which had a good summer run when produced as a post-show entertainment on the stage of the Roof Garden of New York's Casino Theater, but the piece failed when put on the road as a regulation-sized musical. He thereafter placed songs in several Broadway shows (*The Casino Girl, The Wild Rose*) and provided the songs for a little ''operetta'' about a social-climbing negro, *Jes' Lak White Fo'ks* (1901, ''the music is pleasing if reminiscent''), played for one week on the bill at the New York Theater's roof garden, before writing and putting together the basic score—much interpolated into—for the full-length Williams and Walker musical comedy *In Dahomey* (''Brown-Skin Baby Mine,'' ''Molly Green,'' ''Leader of the Colored Aristocracy,'' ''On Emancipation Day''). After an indifferent New York run (53 performances), *In Dahomey* established itself as a favorite in London where its unfamiliar fun, its general novelty and its high spirits took it to a run of 251 performances. The songwriter was behind the baton when the piece went on tour with a replacement cast in 1904.

Broadway success, however, eluded Cook. His co-written and composed *The Southerners,* ''a musical study in black and white,'' which dreamed itself revusically from the old-time south to ''the Island of Ballyhoo'' to the accompaniment of such ditties as ''Mandy Lou,'' ''Mint Julep,'' ''Dandy Dan'' and ''My Little Irish Canary'' won a little notoriety for mixing black and white performers (although this was, in fact, not novel), but George Lederer's ''summer show'' production proved a flop. Two further Williams and Walker pieces, *Abyssinia* (31 performances) and *Bandana Land* (89 performances), had rather longer lives out of town than in New York, and his Broadway career was largely limited to supplying the occasional interpolated number, as in earlier years, to such shows as *The New Yorkers* and *The Boys and Betty* (''Whoop her up with a whoop-la-la!''). He also got a brief showing on the Viennese stage when one of his songs, relyricked by Max Baer as ''Liebesabenteuer,'' was interpolated into the Theater an der Wien's production of the Gaiety Theatre musical *Der Toreador* for Carlo Böhm (1903).

Cook was involved, in one capacity or another, with a number of specifically black musical plays in the 1910s, composing the basic scores for the Negro Players' *The Traitor,* the Black Patti company's *Captain Jasper,* and Miller and Lyles's *Darkydom,* but his career was ever hampered by a bitterly unstable temperament and by an inability to accept the limitations of his life in music after the extravagant hopes and overdone publicity of his early years.

Cook was married for a while to musical-theatre performer **Abbie MITCHELL** (Mandy Lou in *The Southerners,* Mandy Lou in *Bandanna Land,* Minnie Ha Ha in *The Red Moon,* etc).

- 1898 **Clorindy, or the Origin of the Cakewalk** (Paul Laurence Dunbar) sketch Casino Roof Garden 5 July
- 1900 **Jes' Lak White Fo'ks** (Dunbar, et al/Cook) 1 act Cherry Blossom Grove 25 June
- 1902 **In Dahomey** (w others/Alex Rogers, Dunbar/Jesse A Shipp) Grand Opera House, Stamford, Conn 8 September; New York Theater 18 February 1903
- 1904 **The Southerners** (''William Mercer,'' Richard Grant) New York Theater 23 May
- 1906 **Abyssinia** (w Will Vodery, Bert Williams, et al/Earl C Jones/Shipp, Rogers) Majestic Theater 20 February
- 1908 **Bandana Land** (w others/Rogers/Shipp, Rogers) Majestic Theater 3 February
- 1913 **The Traitor** (w others) Lafayette Theater March
- 1913 **Captain Jasper** (w others) Grand Opera House, 12 May
- 1915 **Darkydom** (Henry S Creamer/Henry Troy) Lafayette Theater 23 October

COOPER [VANDERJUICH, Henri] (b Brussels, 1845; d Paris, 7 December 1914). An always young-looking tenor and light comedy actor, long a feature of 19th-century Parisian musical shows.

Cooper (he was always billed just as ''Cooper,'' and when in America averred tactfully that he took the name from admiration of J Fenimore) made his first appearance in Paris at the Théâtre des Bouffes-Parisiens in *La Bonne aux camélias* before joining the company at the Théâtre des Variétés where he remained for the bulk of the next

25 years. His attractive tenor was put to early use there, and he won quick notice when he created the role of the pretty page Adolphe de Valladolid in *Les Brigands* (1869). He subsequently created a number of other Offenbach parts including Frontignac (*La Créole*), Frantz (*Le Docteur Ox*) and le Duc de Marly in *Belle Lurette* (Théâtre de la Renaissance, 1880), but his biggest personal successes came in Hervé's *Mam'zelle Nitouche* (1883) in which he created the romantic-comic tenor role of Champlâtreux opposite Anna Judic, in the comedy *Ma Cousine* and, on a "loan" to the Théâtre de la Gaîté, when he played Prince Mignapour in the first metropolitan production of Audran's *Le Grand Mogol* (1884). He also toured with Judic's company to America in 1885–86 playing in *La Vie parisienne* (Gardefeu), *Mam'zelle Nitouche* (Champlâtreux), *Lili* (Plinchard), *La Femme à papa* (Prince de Chypre), *La Cosaque* (Jules Primitif), *La Mascotte* (Fritellini), *La Grande-Duchesse* (Prince Paul) and the rest of the star's vaudeville and opérette repertoire.

Cooper created many other roles in both plays (notably *Le Crocodile*), vaudevilles (Gontran in *Nos bons jurés,* 1887, etc) and opérettes (Mignard in *Ninon* 1887, Serpin in *Mam'zelle Crénom,* 1888 *Le Valet de Coeur, La Fille à Cacolet,* etc), and also appeared in revivals of the classic opéra-bouffe, opérette and féerie repertoire (Ange Pitou, Gardefeu, San Carlo in *La Petite Mariée,* Blaisient in *Rothamago,* etc), and in such parts as Raoul Duplessis in *Orient-Express* and Lieutenant Richard in *Les Voltigeurs de la 32ème.* He scored one of his biggest successes as Faust in Hervé's *Le Petit Faust* in the big 1882 revival at the Théâtre de la Porte-Saint-Martin, and reappeared in the same role again in 1891 at the Variétés and, long after the end of his contract there in 1893, in 1908 at the Folies-Dramatiques.

In the later part of his career he began performing early 19th-century songs in the cafés-concerts, but in the theatre he inclined more to non-musical comedy, touring Russia with the Théâtre Michel and spending a number of years as a member of the company at the Palais-Royal.

CORDY, Annie [COOREMAN, Léonie] (b Scharebeck, Belgium, 16 June 1928). France's most outstanding musical comedy soubrette for some 40 years, in a career handicapped—in that field at least—by the paucity of new material in postwar France.

Mlle Cordy came to Paris in the early 1950s, soon after beginning a singing career in her native Belgium, and was appearing in variety at the Bobino when she was selected to play the comedy soubrette role in Raymond Vincy and Francis Lopez's small-scale musical *La Route fleurie,* alongside Georges Guétary, Claude Arvelle and another variety performer, Bourvil. The long run of *La Route fleurie* established her as a comedy and singing star and, thereafter, she led a crammed career of stage, film and variety work for some 40 continuous years. Following *La Route fleurie,* she appeared with Luis Mariano in the film of the Vincy/Lopez *Le Chanteur de Mexico* and, on the stage, was starred above the title as *Tête de linotte* (1957) and again opposite Mariano in *Visa pour l'amour* (1961), both for long runs.

She paired with Bourvil for the musical comedy *Ouah! Ouah!,* with comedian Darry Cowl in *Pic et Pioche* (1967) and starred in a third musical comedy, *Indien vaut mieux que tu l'aura,* before taking the title role in the French production of *Hello, Dolly!* (1972). Her latest stage musical appearances have been as the star of *Nini la chance* (1980) and *Envoyez la musique* (1982) in a career now largely devoted to television (sitcom, drama and variety) and some major character roles on film.

Autobiography: *Nini La Chance: Mémoires* (Belfond, Paris, 1998)

THE CORSAIR Burlesque in 2 acts by Edward E Rice. Music by John Braham. Bijou Theater, New York, 18 October 1887.

Byron's celebrated romantic poem *The Corsair* fell under the pens of the burlesquers on several occasions, and the results included William Brough's sizeable London success *Conrad and Medora* (Lyceum 1856), introduced to America by Mrs John Wood as *The Corsair* later the same year, and James A Barnes's American *Chow Chow, or A Tale of Pekin* (Wood's Museum 9 September 1872).

In 1878 Edward Rice, looking for a successor to his successful burlesque of Longfellow's *Evangeline,* hired that piece's librettist, J Cheever Goodwin, to supply him with a new piece. However, when *Le Petit Corsair* was produced 29 September 1878 at the Boston Museum, with the book credited to Goodwin and the music to Rice, and with Eliza Weathersby and Venie Clancy featured as Conrad and his Medora, W H Crane as Birbanto and Nat C Goodwin as Yussef, the reaction was decidedly unenthusiastic. Goodwin, it turned out, had lazily done little more than adapt and localize Brough's well-known text. He excused himself on the grounds of family illness, but *Le Petit Corsair* as it stood had no chance of emulating *Evangeline* and was soon put away. However, nigh on a decade later Rice exhumed the piece, gave it a thorough going-over (the credits now gave Rice for the book, and Boston musical director Braham for the music!), and tried it again. A spectacular staging, the bulging Amelia Summerville in tights as the titular Conrad, and such incidentals as an apparently dancing mule (paralleling the beloved dancing heifer of the earlier show), plus the usual ration of leggy burlesque belles and the fact that Brough's work was now rather less remembered, helped Miles and

Barton's production of *The Corsair* to 180 Broadway performances prior to a long life on the road and even a bit of one across the seas. Rice toured a company to Australia in 1891–92 which included *The Corsair,* with Virginia Earle and local contralto Fanny Liddiard featured, amongst its repertoire. The show was, in fact, so successful in America that it inspired Lew Dockstader's minstrel company to burlesque the burlesque, and they brought out a piece called *The Coarse Hair.*

Byron's work was also the basis for several serious operas: an English one, composed by Charles Deffell, and played at the Crystal Palace (1 April 1873) with Henry Nordblom and Fanny Heywood as Conrad and Medora, and two Italian, Verdi's 1848 *Il corsaro* (Trieste 25 October) and Alessandro Marracino's *Corrado* (Theatro Adriano, Rome 21 May 1900).

Byron's other Turkish verse work, *The Bride of Abydos,* also fell into the hands of the extremes of the musical theatre, making up both into an opera (*La Fiancée d'Abydos,* Adrien Barthe/Jules Adénis, Théâtre Lyrique, Paris 30 December 1865) and, more famously, into another highly successful burlesque, *The Bride of Abydos, or The Prince, the Pirate and the Pearl,* by H J Byron, produced at London's Strand Theatre (31 May 1858) with Pattie Oliver in its title role and Louisa Swanborough as her leading man.

Australia: Opera House, Melbourne 3 October 1891

CORT, John L[insley] (b Newark, NJ, 1859; d Stamford, Conn, 17 November 1929). Theatre-owner and producer of mostly unsuccessful or undistinguished musicals, Cort nevertheless kept up a presence on Broadway for over 20 years.

Originally a performer in vaudeville, manager of several vaudeville houses in the Pacific Northwest—the Stand Theater, Seattle (1888), the Paine Opera House, Walla Walla, Wash (1894), the Academy of Music in Milwaukee, the Imperial Music Hall, Chicago and the New Orpheus Musical Hall in Chicago (1897)—then proprietor of the minor Marie Bell Opera Company (1897) and of something he audaciously called the Metropolitan Opera Company (1899, toured *Les Cloches de Corneville*), Cort switched subsequently to speculating on theatre-building, and built up a successful chain of vaudeville houses before over-stretching himself and losing the lot. He began over again, and soon put together a new set of playhouses, in wide-apart areas of America, beginning with the Cort Theater in Chicago (1908) and including Broadway's Cort Theater (1912, opened memorably with *Peg 'o My Heart*) and similarly named houses in Boston, in Jamaica, Queens, in the Bronx (later the Windsor Theater), Atlantic City and elsewhere. At the same time he launched a heavy schedule of productions, a large number of them musicals, too many of which were distinctly not number-one entertainments, no more frequently so than when from the pen of his son, **Harry L[insley] Cort** (b Seattle, 15 November 1889; d New York, 6 May 1937), who himself attempted for a while a career as a producer in Chicago. Another son, Edward, a theatre manager at North Yakima, Wash, and in Long Island, also occasionally picked up a pen.

Cort allied himself, first, with Klaw and Erlanger's theatrical combine and then, when they seemed to be encroaching on his preserves, with the Shuberts, whom he in turn renounced to return to the Klaw and Erlanger umbrella, successfully keeping himself afloat in a competitive business for some two decades.

Cort's musical theatre ventures included the W G Stewart Opera company (1906, repertoire, *Dorothy, The Two Roses, Babette,* etc); *The Alaskan* (1907), written by the son of a millioniare newspaper owner; the college-y *Commencement Days* (1909); the imported *The Rose of Panama* (*Kreolenblut*); Gustav Luders's *The Gipsy;* Leo Ditrichstein's *Jingaboo* (1911); Frank Mandel's early effort *Miss Princess* (1912); Sousa's *The American Maid* (1913); the Boston *What's Going On* ? (1915); the Chicago hit *A Modern Eve* (a largely remusicked *Die moderne Eva*); Victor Herbert's attractive *The Princess Pat* (1915); Cuvillier's much botched *Flora Bella,* the short-lived *Molly O* (1916); the successful *Flo-Flo* (1917); Friml's *Glorianna; Fiddlers Three* (1918); the flyweight but successful *Listen Lester* (1918) and *Just a Minute* (1919), both co-written by Harry; *Roly Boly Eyes* (1919); Harry's *Jim Jam Jems* (1920); *Go-Go;* Harry's *Sharlee* (1923); *Suzanne;* and Harry's *China Rose* (w Charles Dillingham, Martin Beck 1925). He also took part in the production of *Shuffle Along* (1921) as part of the Nikko Producing Company.

LA COSAQUE Comédie-vaudeville in 3 acts by Henri Meilhac and Albert Millaud. Music by Hervé. Théâtre des Variétés, Paris, 1 February 1884.

La Cosaque was the last of that series of vaudevilles, of which *Niniche, Lili* and *Mam'zelle Nitouche* had been the enduring triumphs, mounted by Eugène Bertrand at the Variétés with Anna Judic as their overwhelming star. Tasting just a little of being one dip too many into the same well, it was—in spite of being "gay and full of droll ideas and amusing bons mots" with "bright and sparkling music"—unable to top its predecessors and it ran for only 70 performances at the Variétés, in comparison with the several hundred nights of even the least popular of the others.

Princess Anna Semionowna Makinskoff (Judic) has come of age, and gone exorbitantly extravagant with the family fortunes, so her family have decided to lock her up until she can be safely married off to her cousin Féodor (Lassouche). Anna swaps clothes with a maidservant, hitchhikes a ride to Paris with the lace salesman, Jules Primitif (José Dupuis), and ends up with a job in the shop where he works. When she is about to be sacked she promptly buys the business, and when she is ordered by the Czar, no less, to wed within 24 hours, she proposes to Jules. He, refusing to wed the multimillionairess simply to spite her family, finally does so for better reasons. Christian (Prince Grégoire) and Roux (Prince Cyrille) played the other Russian aristocrats.

The score was almost entirely for the benefit of Judic who had nine numbers—including La Légende de Marfa (''La Cosaque, la voilà!''), the rondeau ''Je suis une femme accomplie,'' the Couplets de la Patte and the Couplets de l'enlèvement—in the first act, the Couplets des parapluies, and a Chanson des Joncs in the second, and the Couplets du Coiffeur and her final declaration (''Tu ne comprends donc rien'') in the last. She also interpolated into the proceedings topical impersonations of Marie van Zandt playing *Lakmé,* Paulus in his café-concert act and the ''darkie's dance'' from the spectacular ballet *Sieba,* then playing at the Eden-Théâtre. Dupuis had two numbers, but the original Paris of *La Belle Hélène* nowadays ventured no higher than an F natural.

Judic played *La Cosaque* in her repertoire in London after its closure in Paris, and the following year repeated it at Broadway's Star Theater, but London had already seen the piece, little more than two months after its Paris opening, when the irrepressible Kate Santley produced an English version at the Royalty Theatre. Claude Marius (Prince Grégoire), Henry Ashley (Jules), Miss Amalia (Mme Dupontin) and Sidney Harcourt (Prince Féodor) supported the star for 41 performances, tactfully closing the week before Judic arrived in town. Both Santley and Emily Soldene subsequently played *La Cosaque* in the British provinces. In Vienna, the Hervé score was replaced, as had been done in local productions of the other Judic vaudevilles, by one by Johann Brandl when *Die Kosakin* (ad Moritz West) was produced for 27 performances at the Theater an der Wien. Ilka Pálmay was Anna, Girardi played Casimir (ex- Jules) and Carl Lindau (Prince Cyril), Siegmund Stelzer (Prince Gregor) and Herr Stillfried (Prince Feodor) were the aristocrats.

UK: Royalty Theatre 12 April 1884, Gaiety Theatre (Fr) 18 June 1884; USA: Boston Theater, Boston 5 November 1885, Star Theater (Fr) 4 March 1886; Austria: Theater an der Wien *Die Kosakin* 31 October 1891

COSCOLETTO, or Le Lazzarone Opéra-comique in 2 acts by Charles Nuitter and Étienne Tréfeu. Music by Jacques Offenbach. Bad Ems, 24 July 1865.

A tiny tale about a little ''bandit,'' a flowergirl and a married macaroni cook, some amorous entanglements and a touch of food poisoning, all set in Neapolitan banditland, *Coscoletto* was not one of Offenbach's more popular works, but following its initial showing at Bad Ems, where Madame Albrecht appeared in the travesty role of the brigand, it proved of sufficient interest to win several other productions.

It was seen at Vienna's Theater an der Wien (ad Julius Hopp) with no less a star than Marie Geistinger as the brigand of the title, and the famous comics Knaack (Arsenico), Swoboda (Policarpo) and Rott (Frangipani) in support, sharing a bill with Therese Braunecker-Schäfer's imitation of *Die falsche Carlotta Patti* for 28 nights. In Hungary, one Hungarian version was played at the Budai Népszínház with Janós Timar, István Szentgyörgi and Vidor Kassai in 1868, whilst another was mounted three years later at the Budai Színkör.

Coscoletto was not taken up for a Paris production and, unlike most of Offenbach's works, was not purchased for publication either, but it nevertheless put in a reappearance in 1992 in Nuremberg (Opera, July) in what may have been its first German staging—127 years after its birth.

Austria: Theater an der Wien 5 January 1866; Hungary: Budai Népszínház *A Makarónjárus* 1868, Budai Színkör *Coscoletto, a Nápolyi lazzaroni* 7 June 1871

COSTA, Karl [KOSTIA, Karl] (b Vienna, 2 February 1832; d Vienna, 11 October 1907). Prolific and successful author of a long list of musical comedies, and plays with more or less music, for the Viennese stage.

Costa began his professional life as a lottery official and subsequently worked as secretary to the playwright Anton Langer. This proximity encouraged him to write himself, and he became a regular supplier of Volksstücke, Possen, Operette and all kinds of musical comedy texts to the Viennese stage. Of the Operetten, his first, the book for Suppé's *Leichte Kavallerie,* remained his most successful, but his other most significant hits were made in a series of Possen written with Carl Millöcker and including *Ein Kassastück* (1877), *Ein Blitzmädel* (1877) and the long-lived *Ihr Corporal* (1878). He had another fine success with the Posse *Der Walzerkönig,* set to music by Brandl.

Costa was for a while director of the Theater in der Josefstadt. His highly successful Volksstuck *Bruder Martin* was subsequently made into a full-scale musical by Wilhelm Sterk and composer Leon Jessel under the title *Die goldene Mühle* (Volksoper 2 March 1937, Johann Strauss-Theater 21 April 1937).

1866 **Leichte Kavallerie** (Franz von Suppé) Carltheater 21 March

1866 **Die Hexe von Boissy** (Giovanni von Zaytz) Carltheater 24 April

1866 **Die Freigeister** (Suppé) Carltheater 23 October

1866 **Der Hausdoktor** (Karl Kleiber) 1 act Fürsts Singspielhalle 10 November

1868 **Die Frau Meisterin** (aka *Die verwandelten Weiber*) (Suppé) Carltheater 20 January

1868 **Wiener Zugstücke** (Anton Storch) Theater in der Josefstadt 26 April

1868 **Ihr Seliger** (Storch) Theater in der Josefstadt 30 December

1870 **Eine Frau nach der Mode** (Franz Roth) Theater in der Josefstadt 7 September

1870 **Die Jungfrau von Dragant** (Suppé/w Moritz A Grandjean) Carltheater 30 November

1870 **Wir Demokraten** (Franz Roth) Theater in der Josefstadt 25 December

1871 **Der Prinz von der Nadel** (F Roth) Theater in der Josefstadt 6 January

1871 **Der blinde Harfenist** (Kleiber) Theater in der Josefstadt 21 October

1872 **Das Orakel zu Delphi** (Carl Michael Ziehrer) Linz 21 September

1874 **Der Registrator auf Reisen** (Carl Ferdinand Conradin/w Moser, Adolf L'Arronge)

1874 **Stunden der Täuschung** (Conradin) Carltheater 13 June

1875 **Ein Kreuzer** (Kleiber) Theater in der Josefstadt 30 January

1875 **Ein alter Junggeselle** (F Roth) Theater in der Josefstadt 6 March

1876 **Fliegende Blatter** (Richard Genée) 1 act Theater an der Wien 1 August

1876 **Luftschlösser** (Genée/Wilhelm Mannstädt, A Weller [ie Johann Müller] ad) Theater an der Wien 11 July

1876 **Die Hölle im Hause** (pasticcio) Theater an der Wien 29 September

1877 **Ein Blitzmädel** (Carl Millöcker) Theater an der Wien 4 February

1877 **Ein Kassastück** (Millöcker) Theater an der Wien 21 October

1878 **Ihr Corporal** (Millöcker) Theater an der Wien 19 January

1879 **Alexander der Grosse** (Ziehrer) Marburg January

1879 **Himmelschlussel** (Millöcker) Theater an der Wien 15 March

1882 **Der Mann im Monde** (Millöcker/w Jacobson) Theater an der Wien 16 February

1882 **Der Putzgredl** (pasticcio) Theater in der Josefstadt 8 October

1884 **Ein Medium** (Ernst Reiterer) Theater in der Josefstadt 13 April

1884 **Der Erbe des Wucherers** (Eugen Schreiber) Theater in der Josefstadt 27 September

1884 **Abrakadabra, oder Über Land und Meer** (Schreiber) Theater in der Josefstadt 25 December

1885 **Ihr Reservist** (Pohl) Theater in der Josefstadt 22 April

1885 **Der Walzerkönig** (Johann Brandl/w Bruno Zappert/w Wilhelm Mannstädt) Carltheater 9 October

1890 **Die Hochzeit von Leni** (Louis Roth) Carltheater 14 February

1890 **Zur fesche Wienerin** (Kleiber) Theater in der Josefstadt 19 April

1890 **Der Gimpel** Austrian version (Carltheater)

1891 **Haben's kein Türken g'sehn?** (Adolf Gisser) Fürsttheater 15 September

1892 **Der Freiwillige** (F Sonkup/w Genée) Prague 29 June

1894 **Der Komet** (Karl Kratzl) 1 act Ronacher

1894 **Der Bajazzo in der Heimat** (Eduard Kremser, pasticcio/w Benjamin Schier) Theater in der Josefstadt 7 March

1894 **Bruder Martin** (Max von Weinzierl) Raimundtheater 5 December

1896 **Der Schönheitspreis** (von Weinzierl) Raimundtheater 7 March

1896 **Wiener Edelknaben** (F Roth) Deutsches Volkstheater 8 September

1897 **Glücksnarren** (von Weinzierl) Raimundtheater 8 April

1897 **Die Goldtante** (Leo Held) Theater an der Wien 6 November

1898 **Die Fechtbruder** (von Weinzierl) Raimundtheater 29 November

1905 **Onkel Sonders** (F K Holtzer) Raimundtheater December

COSTA, [Pasquale] Mario (b Taranto, 24 July 1858; d Monte Carlo, 27 September 1933).

Originally a writer of Neapolitan songs, Costa came to the theatre for the first time with the score for the 1893 Parisian pantomime *L'Histoire d'un pierrot* (Théâtre Déjazet 14 January 7 performances). He had a notable hometown success with his light operatic version of Théophile Gautier's *Le Capitaine Fracasse,* and another with his 1922 operetta, *Scugnizza* (w Carlo Lombardo), a piece which remained one of the principal items of the Italian operetta repertoire for many years. Lombardo also compiled a pasticcio operetta, *Il re di chez Maxim* (ly: Arturo Franci) based on Costa's music which found a certain success (Teatro Fossati, Milan 10 May 1919).

1909 **Il Capitan Fracassa** (O Magici, Guglielmo Emmanuel) Teatro Alfieri, Turin 14 December

1921 **Posillipo** (Di Giacomo, Murolo, A Campanile) Teatro Eliseo 8 November

1922 **Scugnizza** (w Carlo Lombardo) Teatro Alfieri, Turin 16 December

1925 **Il re delle api** Teatro Lirico, Milan 11 February

1925 **Mimi Pompom** (G Adami) Teatro Lirico, Milan 23 October

COTTENS, Victor de [CRINSOZ de COTTENS, Victor Jean Edgar] (b Eaux-Vives, Switzerland, 21 August 1862; d Vichy, 24 February 1956).

The French-born, Algerian-educated de Cottens worked as a journalist before making his way into the theatre as an author of comedies, vaudevilles, a long list of revues and a regular supply of opérette libretti. He had several successes in the musical theatre with libretti set by Louis Varney, the most important of which was the first, the spectacular vaudeville *Le Papa de Francine,* and the largest, the Châtelet show *Les Cinq Cents Coups du Diable,* which allegedly brought one thousand performers on to the stage. He collaborated on a number of other spectacular pieces for the great Châtelet stage and, latterly, adapted several English-language successes to the French theatre, but in the first decade of the 20th century was above all known as "the king of the Paris revue." He also moved into management, directing successively the Théâtre du Vaudeville, the Folies-Wagram, the Olympia and the Théâtre Marigny before ultimately retiring to Vichy where he set up a casino.

1891 **Mam'zelle Coquelicot** (Monteux-Brissac/w Paul Ginisty) 1 act La Cigale 30 October

1896 **Le Papa de Francine** (Louis Varney/w Paul Gavault) Théâtre Cluny 5 November

1896 **Napoléon malgré lui** (w Gavault) 1 act Le Fourmi 3 April

1897 **Le Pompier de service** (Varney/w Gavault) Théâtre des Variétés 18 February

1898 **Les Demoiselles de Saint-Cyriens** (Varney/w Gavault) Théâtre Cluny 28 January

1899 **Robinson n'a pas cru Zoë** (Harry Fragson, Victor Maurel/w Robert Charvay) Boîte à Fursy 23 December

1900 **Le Fiancé de Thylda** (Varney/w Charvay) Théâtre Cluny 26 January

1900 **Frégolinette** (Varney) 1 act Théâtre des Mathurins 25 April

1900 **Mademoiselle George** (Varney/w Pierre Veber) Théâtre des Variétés 1 December

1902 **Le Voyage avant le noce** (Varney/w Charvay) Trianon-Lyrique 19 December

1904 **A Country Girl** French version w Arnold Fordyce (L'Olympia)

1905 **Les Cinq Cent Coups du Diable** (Marius Baggers/w Victor Darlay [ie, Victor Demonts]) Théâtre du Châtelet 23 December

1906 **Pif-Paf-Pouf! ou un voyage endiablé** (Baggers/w Darlay) Théâtre du Châtelet 6 December

1907 **Le Prince de Pilsen** (*The Prince of Pilsen*) French version (L'Olympia)

1908 **Son Altesse l'amour** (Maurice Jacobi/w P Veber) Moulin-Rouge 25 March

1915 **La Chasse aux Boches** (F Perpignan/Leroux) 1 act Folies-Bergère 9 April

Autobiography: *Paris dont je rêvais* (Vichy, 1948)

COTTRELLY, Mathilde [née MEYER, Mathilde] (b Hamburg, 7 February 1851; d White Plains, NY, 15 January 1933). German actress and theatre administrator who made a prominent career in New York's German and English-language theatres.

The daughter of Wilhelm Meyer, a Hamburg orchestra leader, Mathilde Meyer began working in the theatre as a child ("die kleine Meyer") and appeared in plays and in musical theatre (*Geneviève de Brabant, La Belle Hélène,* etc) around Germany, and for two years in café-chantant in Berlin prior to marrying the English circus equilibrist George Cottrelly and retiring, at the age of 17 to motherhood and to follow her husband to Russia. Widowed at 19, she returned to the stage, playing in drama at the Wallner-Theater and managing her own theatre in Breslau, before moving to America in 1875.

In America, she performed at first only in the German language theatre ("a genuine comic singing actress"), appearing for two years at the Germania Theater in New York in a series of plays and musical comedies (*Lockere Zeisige, Comtesse Hélène, Ziegenlieschen, Das Mädel ohne Geld, Luftschlösser, In Freud' und Leid, Die Reise durch New York in 80 Stunden, Ein vorsichtige Mann, Drei Paar Schuhe, Verfehlter Beruf, Geldfieber*), and also in St Louis, at San Francisco's Stadt-Theater (1877–78) and at the same city's California Theater, where she made her English-speaking debut on 21 October 1878 in America's first performances of *Fatinitza.* However, she returned immediately to the German-speaking stage at New York's Thalia (ex- Bowery Theater), which she opened as a German repertoire house in conjunction with Gustav Amberg and Wilhelm Kramer in 1879. Mme Cottrelly was billed as "directress" and Amberg as "business manager." At the Thalia she appeared in a series of comedies and in the musicals *Die Fledermaus* (Adele), *Die Lachtaube* (Pauline), *Flotte Bursche* (Frincke), *Drei Paar Schuhe* (Irma) and *Orpheus in der Unterwelt* (Eurydice), in the title roles of *Boccaccio, Giroflé-Girofla* and *Nisida,* and made an enormous hit as Fanchette Michel in Genée's *Der Seekadett.* During the 1880–81 season Mme Cottrelly brought Marie Geistinger to America and she repeated her Adele to Geistinger's Rosalinde, and Isabella to the German star's *Boccaccio,* in New York and round the country, before moving thoroughly and definitively into the English-language theatre when she joined John McCaull's top-rank comic opera company in the autumn of 1882.

She appeared with McCaull in English-language versions of a string of international comic operas including *The Queen's Lace Handkerchief* (1882, *Das Spitzentuch der Königin,* Donna Irene), *Prince Methusalem* (Methusalem), *The Merry War* (*Der lustige Krieg,* Else), *Falka* (*Le Droit d'aînesse,* Edwige), Planquette's *Nell Gwynne* (Nell), *Die Fledermaus* (Adele), Millöcker's *The Black Hussar* (*Der Feldprediger,* Barbara), *Chatter* (Lotti, which she also played as *Die Näherin* in German), *The Seven Swabians* (Black Grete), *Apajune the Water-sprite* (Heloise), *Der Bettelstudent* (Bronislawa), Dellinger's *Don Cesar* (Pueblo Escudirro) and *Lorraine* (t/o Ollivier), *The Crowing Hen* (*Serment d'amour,* the Marquise), *Joséphine vendue par ses soeurs* (Benjamine), von Suppé's *Clover* (*Die Jagd nach dem Glück,* Señora Petronella) and Messager's *Jacquette* (*La Béarnaise,* Jacquette), and also created the title role of De Koven's *The Begum* (1887) and that of Polyxena in another American comic opera, Sydney Rosenfeld's version of *The Lady or the Tiger.* Her popularity with audiences was enormous, and no matter what she played—juvenile soubrette or looming character lady (and sometimes it was one one week and the other the next)—she invariably won fine notices in the press.

During her period of some nine years with McCaull she became—following the manager's split with Aronson and the Casino Theater—a partner in his management, dealing with both the financial and artistic sides of their affairs with some skill, athough apparently not sufficient for the organization and her investment in it ultimately to make ends more than just meet. During these years she was also involved, beyond her performing duties, in rehearsing the shows and designing many of the company's costumes.

In 1890 Cottrelly and McCaull sold out their interest in the company to Harry Askin, and soon after the lady announced her retirement from English comic opera. She retreated to her home in New Rochelle, and announced that from then on she would appear only in the German theatre. However, she was seen, thereafter, amongst regular performances in non-singing roles, in both the German (*Die Näherin,* Elizabeth in a *Tannhäuser-Parodie,* Gabrielle in *Pariser Leben, Die Frau Gretl*) and the English musical theatre, touring for Askin as Alpaca in *The Tar and the Tartar* 1892; playing in the short-lived *A Tin Napoleon* 1892 with Gus Bruno; in summer season at St Louis's Schnaider's Garden (1893, Serpolette, Fritellini in *La Mascotte,* Eliza Dabsey in *Billee Taylor,* etc); in a revamped *The City Directory* (1893, Baroness Smith of Coney Island); with Henry Dixey in the latest version of the burlesque *Adonis* (1894, Duchess of Area); alongside Jeff de Angelis as Bulbul in *The Caliph* (1896); in *About Town* (1899) on the road and at the Casino Theater; in *The Robber Baron* in 1901 at the Terrace Garden; and as Mme Phillpard in the Anna Held show *Mam'selle Napoléon* (1903). She also appeared briefly in vaudeville, playing the operetta *A Midnight Promise* with tenor John Perugini (1896), but in her more senior years her stage appearances were largely in character roles in plays. Her always obvious Continental accent led her to be cast frequently in Jewish parts, and among her creations were those of Mrs Isaac Cohen in *Abie's Irish Rose,* Madame Viard in *Trilby,* Emilia Müller in *The Bubble,* the dowager Frau Rothschild in the American version of the play *The Five Frankfurters,* and the character lady of the later *Potash and Perlmutter* plays.

She did not, however, abandon the musical stage. In 1907 she created a role in Richard Carle's musical comedy *The Hurdy Gurdy Girl* at Boston; in 1911 she appeared in *Die Frau Gretl* at the Irving Place Theatre (in German); in 1912 she was featured in the American production of the musical *A Polish Wedding* (*Polnische Wirtschaft,* Gabrielle); and in 1913, while playing in *The Five Frankfurters,* she returned to the Broadway musical stage to play Palmatica for one matinée in a revival of *The Beggar Student,* an appearance which seems to have been her musical last.

An outstanding and versatile performer, ''Madame Cottrelly'' seems never to have had a bad notice in a career during which she made herself one of the most popular performers on the American stage.

A COUNTRY GIRL Musical play in 2 acts by James T Tanner. Lyrics by Adrian Ross. Additional lyrics by Percy Greenbank. Music by Lionel Monckton. Additional songs by Paul Rubens. Daly's Theatre, London, 18 January 1902.

After the vastly successful orientalisms of Sidney Jones's *The Geisha* and *San Toy,* George Edwardes made a purposeful change of policy at his thriving Daly's Theatre. The new show for London's top romantic musical theatre was not written by the old Daly's team of Jones, Hall and the late Harry Greenbank, but by what had been essentially, to that time, part of the producer's Gaiety Theatre team, a team used to producing entertainment of a much more frothy and insubstantial nature. Lionel Monckton and James Tanner, with the Daly's team of stars to serve, wrote a modern-dress piece set wholly in England, but one which featured a tale and a score made well to the measure of the Daly's audiences.

Geoffrey Challoner (Hayden Coffin), the impoverished squire of a Devonshire village, has let his manor to wealthy Sir Joseph Verity (Fred Kaye) and gone off, with his faithful servant Barry (Huntley Wright), to seek his fortune. When he returns, he has with him a Rajah (Rutland Barrington)—who is no Rajah at all but an Englishman who fictitiously fell off an Alp, years ago, to escape an encumbering wife—and the Indian Princess Mehelaneh (Maggie May). The Princess is anxious to give herself and her vast fortune to Geoffrey, and Barry actively promotes the match, but Geoffrey's heart is true to his hometown Marjorie Joy (Lillian Eldée). While he has been away, Marjorie Joy has become a famous singer, but she returns home and puts on her old sunfrock and bonnet and pretends to be still the little village girl. Misunderstandings—notably a chaste kiss between Geoffrey and the village flirt, his old friend Nan (Evie Greene)—intervene before the lovers are reunited, in the midst of a series of comical scenes, at a ball in a London mansion.

Ethel Irving played Barry's sweetheart Sophie, become Madame Sophie and a couturiere, and Beryl Faber was the formidable Mrs Quinton Raikes, past and present wife to the phoney Rajah.

Monckton's score included some pieces in his happiest vein, notably Nan's lilting little song "Try Again, Johnnie" and her cautionary tale of "Molly the Marchioness," the Princess's lovely soprano description of her home "Under the Deodar," and a jolly seafaring piece for Barry, "Yo Ho, Little Girls, Yo Ho!" Paul Rubens, supplying additional numbers in the same way that Monckton had served Sidney Jones in the earlier shows, turned out one of the show's most well-liked numbers in "Two Little Chicks" for Wright and Miss Irving, and the Geoffrey/Marjorie duet "Coo," the exemplary banality of which did nothing to stop it becoming popular. Coffin had his best moment in the virile "In the King's Name—Stand!" and Barrington with a topical patter waltz, no less, called "Peace! Peace!"

The show was a hit of the proportions of its great predecessors at Daly's Theatre. It played there for two years and 729 performances, and was on the road for the first of what would be many years of touring within a matter of months. J C Duff opened his production at the New York Daly's Theater immediately after, with Melville Stewart (Geoffrey), Hallen Mostyn (Rajah), William Norris (Barry), Helen Marvin (Nan), Grace Freeman (Marjorie), Minnie Ashley (Sophie) and Genevieve Finlay (Princess) featured, and he too had a fine success through 115 metropolitan performances, followed by a substantial tour.

During 1903 four companies were playing *The Country Girl* in Britain, variously under the banners of Edwardes, George Dance and Charles Macdona. Edwardes's South African Wheeler-Edwardes company had the show featured in its repertoire, and Australians got their first sight of it in J C Williamson's production with Florence Young (Marjorie), George Lauri (Barry), Harold Thorley (Geoffrey) and Evelyn Scott (Nan) featured. The following year, as no less than five *Country Girl* companies did the rounds on the British circuits, the show was given an unaccustomed production in France. The brothers Isola mounted a French version (ad Victor de Cottens, Arnold Fordyce) at L'Olympia, during their four-show flirtation with foreign musicals there, with a cast headed by Max Dearly (Barry), Alice Bonheur and Mariette Sully. "We are not accustomed to so much rapid fire dancing and rushing about," commented a critic, "but it has pleased, and is drawing."

A Country Girl returned to Broadway in 1911, in a production sponsored by and starring its original Broadway hero, Melville Stewart (Geoffrey), with Misses Freeman and Finlay still, nine years on, in their same roles and John Slavin now playing Barry (Herald Square Theater, 29 May, 32 performances), and the show was seen again in London in 1914 when Edwardes remounted it at Daly's Theatre (28 October) with Robert Michaelis (Geoffrey), Gertie Millar (Nan), W H Berry (Barry) and Nellie Taylor (Marjorie) heading its cast for a fine 173 intended-to-be-just-a-stopgap performances. The indefatigable touring manager J Bannister Howard brought the piece back to London again in 1931 (Daly's Theatre 29 September, 56 performances), as part of his series of seasons of old favorites, with Dorothy Ward featured as Nan.

USA: Daly's Theater 22 September 1902; Australia: Her Majesty's Theatre, Sydney 7 November 1903; France: L'Olympia 24 October 1904

COUPS DE ROULIS Opérette in 3 acts by Albert Willemetz based on the novel of the same title by "Maurice Larrouy" (René Milan). Music by André Messager. Théâtre Marigny, Paris, 29 September 1928.

With the coming of the Jazz Age musical comedy in the years following the First World War, the much-admired composer of *Les P'tites Michu* and *Véronique,* by then well into his sixties, proved himself game to switch genres and attempt to compete with the new wave of musical theatre composers on their own ground. In such pieces as *La Petite Fonctionnaire* (1921) and *Passionnément* (1926) he adapted with increasing success to the light comedy, rhythmic dance melodies and small orchestra and chorus the new style imposed. *Coups de roulis* (a deliciously untranslateable French expression referring to those uncomfortable rocks-and-rolls made by a stirred-up sea), written to a libretto by the new movement's first and most celebrated librettist, Willemetz, was the next and last of his efforts in the style. Its story, in line with its title, took place largely at sea, where a pompous politician, Puy Pradal (Raimu), and his pretty daughter, Béatrice (Marcelle Denya), on a fact-finding mission aboard the warship "Montesquieu," get involved, respectively, with an ambitious Egyptian actress called Sola Myrrhis (Maguy Warna) and with not one but two of the ship's officers, Captain Gerville (Pierre Magnier) and Ensign Kermao (Robert Burnier), as the ship trots back and forth between France and Egypt.

The hit of the show's score was the march "En amour, il n'est pas de grade" with which the favored suitor (Burnier) brought the first-act finale to a climax, but both the Opéra-Comique's Mlle Denya ("Tous les deux me plaisent," "C'est charmant, très parisien," "Coups de roulis," "Les hommes sont tous les mêmes") and Mlle Warna were well equipped, and Burnier's couplets "Ce n'est pas la première fois" again showed Messager's decided facility with the new mode of dance-based light music. The more lyrical moments were accompanied by a brochette of lively comedy numbers for Raimu—describing how one can make a contribution to the country's good ''Avec la danse''—or for Gustave Nelson, as a common sailor, singing about sea-legs.

Messager died during the show's run, but *Coups de roulis* was a splendid success both in Paris, where it was revived in 1934 (Gaîté-Lyrique 30 October), and in the provinces where it still appears from time to time, 70 and more years after its first production.

A 1932 film version had Max Dearly as its star and Roger Bourdin, Edith Manet and Lucienne Herval in support.

Film: Jean de la Cour 1932

Recordings: complete (Gaîté-Lyrique), original cast selection on *L'Opérette française par ses créateurs* (EPM)

LA COUR DU ROI PÉTAUD Opéra-comique in 3 acts by Adolphe Jaime and Philippe Gille. Music by Léo Delibes. Théâtre des Variétés, Paris, 24 April 1869.

La Cour du Roi Pétaud was Delibes' one full-length opérette, written after a goodly number of short pieces, and before he moved on to make his name in the world of opera with *Le Roi l'a dit, Jean de Nivelle* and *Lakmé.* The comical fairy-tale plot turned on the terms made for the marriage of the daughter of the titular King Pétaud and the son of his friendly enemy, the neighbouring Grand Duke of Madopolam. The King and his ministers go to ridiculous lengths to keep their Princess innocent of the meaning of ''love'' through the 16 years until her prince shall come, and then find themselves obliged to put her through a crash course in human biology and sentiment so that she will respond to the young man's advances when he does come. The young man proves to be the best teacher. Marie Aimée (Princess Girandole) and Zulma Bouffar (Prince Léo) were the lovers of the original cast, with Grenier, Léonce and Christian holding up the comedy of a piece, the success of whose score—most particularly a long and lovely duet for hero and heroine—was an undeniable encouragement to its composer to continue to more ambitious works.

The show had a wide international distribution, but without achieving any particularly dazzling results. In H B Farnie's London version Selina Dolaro was the Princess and Emily Soldene her Prince, alongside the comedy of Teddy Marshall, Edward Cheesman and Henry Lewens, to rave reviews but only for a dutiful ten weeks' run at the Philharmonic Theatre; whilst in Austria (ad Julius Hopp), where the piece became *Confusius IX,* Lori Stubel (Leo), Hermine Meyerhoff (Girandole), Josef Matras (Confusius), Karl Blasel (Alexibus) and Wilhelm Knaack (Wetterhahn) headed the cast through 17 performances in the last days of 1872, and four more later in repertoire (1873, 1874). Emil Follinusz's Hungarian version used Hungarianizations of both the French and German titles for its brief productions at the Budai Színkör and the Népszínház (23 February 1877).

Plate 84. **Cicely Courtneidge** *and husband Jack Hulbert.*

Austria: Carltheater *Confusius IX* 11 December 1872; UK: Philharmonic, Islington *Fleur de Lys* 9 April 1873; Hungary: Budai Színkör *Pető király udvara* (*Confucius*) 25 July 1874

COURTNEIDGE, Cicely [Esmeralda] (Dame) (b Sydney, Australia, 1 April 1893; d London, 26 April 1980). Britain's favorite funny, singing auntie of the wartime years.

Born at Sydney's Royal Hotel during her father's tour around Australia with the Gaiety Theatre Company, Cicely Esmeralda was named for one theatrical grandmother (Cicely Nott) and for the show playing that night—the burlesque *Miss Esmeralda.* She made her earliest appearances on the musical stage under her father's management, taking a tiny role in *Tom Jones* (1907, Rosie Pippin) and covering both Phyllis Dare and May Kinder in *The Arcadians* (1909) before taking over briefly, and then being given, the soubrette role in *The*

Mousmé (1911, Miyo ko San) at the age of 18. She had an irrelevant role with a number in Courtneidge's version of *Der liebe Augustin* (Princess Caprice, 1912, Clementine), and in *The Pearl Girl* (1913, Betty Biddulph) she was paired in a light comedy role with the young Jack Hulbert, who was soon to become her husband and long-time professional partner.

She won top billing romancing Harry Welchman as the juvenile of *The Cinema Star* (1914, Phyllis), and played Eileen in a revival of *The Arcadians* (1915), but went down with the disastrous *The Light Blues* (1916, Cynthia Petrie) and her father's poleaxed finances, and ended up touring in his very much less grand *Oh, Caesar!* (1916, Margaret Potts). With Courtneidge Père no longer significantly active, she found work and especially good work harder to come by and, over the next decade, she was seen in the London theatre only in a handful of revues, as she turned from soubrette into comedienne. In fact, her only musical theatre performance in the 20 years following *Oh, Caesar!* was an appearance at the Gaiety in Rodgers and Hart's *Lido Lady* (1926, Peggy Bassett), alongside Phyllis Dare, this time under the management not of her father, but of her husband.

In the later 1920s and the 1930s, Hulbert established himself as a producer and the couple starred themselves not only in *Lido Lady* but in several successful revues (*By the Way, Clowns in Clover, The House That Jack Built, Folly To Be Wise*), before Hulbert's venture collapsed. They then turned to films and, although performing mostly separately in pieces such as *Jack's the Boy* (him) or *Aunt Sally* and *Soldiers of the King* (her), confirmed themselves in the public's mind as a beloved comic couple to bouncing box offices.

Miss Courtneidge returned to the stage to star opposite Bobby Howes in *Hide and Seek* (1937, Sally), and serious success struck next time up, when she and Hulbert paired in the comical spy musical *Under Your Hat* (1938, Kay Porter), which totted up over 500 London performances in a run diced by wartime circumstances. The great success of *Under Your Hat* set in motion a thereafter unbroken series of similar shows which continued with *Full Swing* (1942, Kay Porter again) and *Something in the Air* (1943, Terry Porter) through more than four years in the West End.

With Hulbert concentrating largely on directing, the on-stage partnership was split for *Under the Counter* (1945, Jo Fox), in which Courtneidge scored one of her biggest successes in both Britain and Australia. However, she felt herself criticked out of New York by a kind of general anti-British feeling which was not again to raise its curious head until the late 1980s. She followed up her Australian venture with two further London musicals in which she capitalized on her now-established public character of the zany English grandeish dame with a twinkle in her eye and unending vitality—*Her Excellency* (1949, Lady Frances Maxwell) and *Gay's the Word* (1951, Gay Daventry, "Vitality")—but, after a less than triumphant return to revue in *Over the Moon* (1953) and a musical which didn't make town (*Starmaker* 1956, Susie Green), she played thereafter largely in comedy (*The Bride and the Bachelor, The Bride Comes Back,* etc) and in films (*The L-Shaped Room, Those Magnificent Men in their Flying Machines,* etc).

She missed the chance of one last long West End run when she turned down the star role of *Charlie Girl* to take on that of Madame Arcati in the short-lived London production of *High Spirits* (1964), leaving the run and the money to Anna Neagle, and she only returned to the musical stage thereafter at an advanced age, in tandem with Hulbert, in a compilation show based on their lives (*Once More with Music* Guildford, 1976).

Autobiographies: *Cicely* (Hutchinson, London, 1953), Hulbert, J: *The Little Woman's Always Right* (W H Allen, London, 1975)

COURTNEIDGE, Robert (b Anderston, Glasgow, 29 June 1859; d Brighton, 6 April 1939). Producer for the British stage whose up-and-down career was highlighted by his introduction of *Tom Jones* and *The Arcadians.*

Courtneidge began his theatrical career as an amateur actor in his native Scotland before winning supporting roles at the Prince's Theatre, Manchester, then with the Charles Dillon and Barry Sullivan companies, and—in the musical theatre—in companies touring the Gaiety Theatre burlesques, with Kate Santley in her *Vetah* (1886, Hamet Abdulerim Abensellan), as Pepin in the British production of Coedès's *La Girouette* (1889) and as Major Styx in the Scots musical *Pim Pom.* In 1892 he traveled to Australia, playing comic roles in the Gaiety company's *Carmen Up-to-Data* (Zuniga), *Faust Up-to-Date* (Valentine), *Miss Esmeralda* (Gringoire) and *Joan of Arc* (Jacques), and he stayed on when the company went home to appear (1893–94) with Williamson, Garner and Musgrove in *La Mascotte* (Rocco), *Paul Jones* (Petit-Pierre), *Princess Ida* and opposite Ethel Haydon in pantomime. On his return to Britain in 1894 he worked with Miss Fortescue and toured for George Edwardes in the musical *His Excellency* (1895, Governor Griffenfeld).

In 1896 Courtneidge became manager of the Prince's Theatre (Manchester) and, as such, a prominent member of the Provincial Managers' Association. In 1898, in a quest for material to fill their houses, the PMA ventured into production, with Courtneidge as their executive. The extensive success of the George Dance/Carl Kiefert musical *The Gay Grisette,* which Courtneidge produced and directed for them, led him to a directing assignment for George Edwardes on the original production of Ivan Caryll's *Madame Sans-Gêne* operetta, *The Duchess of Dantzic* (conducted by Kiefert), and then to an extended career as a producer-director. He began, following his resignation from his Manchester post in 1904, with the production (w Arthur Hart and Pat Malone) of *The Blue Moon* at Northampton.

Courtneidge mounted a revised version of this piece, starring the young Florence Smithson, in London the next year and, following a successful season, it was picked up by the Shuberts for New York. He followed up with the farcical and highly successful *The Dairymaids* (1906), Edward German's beautifully crafted *Tom Jones* (1907) and, in 1909, mounted his biggest hit, Lionel Monckton and Howard Talbot's *The Arcadians.*

The Mousmé, the successor to *The Arcadians,* proved a very expensive semi-failure for its producer, so far used to nothing but success, but versions of Fall's *Der liebe Augustin* staged as *Princess Caprice* (1912) and Ivan Caryll's American musical comedy *Oh! Oh! Delphine* (1913) did altogether better. The homemade musical comedy *The Pearl Girl* was something of a disappointment, but just when it seemed that Courtneidge might have another genuine hit on his hands with *The Cinema Star,* the war intervened, and this German musical comedy, a version of Jean Gilbert's *Die Kino-Königin,* was forced to close its London run.

From there on things went badly for Courtneidge. The very appreciable but indifferently cast *My Lady Frayle* failed to take on, a trivial piece called *The Light Blues* (which counted the young Noël Coward in its cast) was a full-scale flop, and the rather stiff-necked patriotic operetta *Young England* went nowhere towards recouping anything lost. The producer turned his attentions, instead, to the provinces and to less expensive productions and put out *Oh, Caesar!* (an early appearance for the young Evelyn Laye) and the music-hally *Petticoat Fair, Fancy Fair* and *Too Many Girls,* extravaganzas which played theatres and variety houses indifferently. As a director he fared better, with his staging of the long-running hit *The Boy* for Alfred Butt at the Adelphi Theatre.

In 1920 Courtneidge again ventured into the West End with a share (w MacDonald and Young) of Cuvillier's short-lived *The Sunshine of the World,* and attempted slightly stiffer stuff with the production of the comic opera *The Rebel Maid,* but monetary considerations soon forced him back into the provinces where the old-fashioned *Gabrielle* (1921) proved a continuous money-spinner for several years and *The Little Duchess* something less of one.

He returned to London several more times with plays, but on only two further occasions with musicals, as director of Lehár's *The Blue Mazurka* (1927) for James White at Daly's and as producer-director of an unimpressive Chopin potpourri called *The Damask Rose* (1930). He made one final provincial venture with the musical *Lavender,* but none of these later efforts proved a hit and he never again reached the heights of his earliest days as a producer, and of the great years of *The Arcadians.*

Courtneidge was regularly credited with co-authoring status on a number of his shows, although it is doubtful whether his input as a writer was much greater than needed to allow him to claim a continuing interest in the copyright and royalties of the pieces in question. His name appears on some material for *The Dairymaids, Tom Jones, The Arcadians, The Mousmé, Too Many Girls, Gabrielle, The Little Duchess, The Damask Rose, Lavender,* and as the sole author of *Petticoat Fair* and *Fancy Fair,* as well as on the libretto of *The Babes and the Baron,* a revamped version of a Princes' Manchester pantomime played for a short run in New York.

A seriously professed socialist, Courtneidge was known for giving opportunities to brothers in conviction—most notably the left-wing journalist turned highly effective librettist, Alexander M Thompson—and he is said to have given a practical turn to his beliefs by becoming the first producer to pay chorus members for rehearsals and to give his casts holidays with pay. However, he showed less consideration for his suppliers and backers: he was bankrupted several times, leaving them to whistle for the money he owed them, whilst he started up operations once again with a clean slate.

Autobiography: *I Was an Actor Once* (Hutchinson, London, 1930)

COUSIN BOBBY Operette in 3 acts by Benno Jacobson and Franz Wagner. Music from the works of Carl Millöcker adapted by L Sänger. Theater des Westens, Berlin, 29 December 1906.

"Cousin" Bobby is nobody's cousin. He is a variety-theatre impresario (Fritz Werner) who, in a tale which seems to contain more mistaken identities than virtually any other similar piece, gets mistaken for one Agamemnon Mogulopulous, the wealthy nephew of penniless Swiss hotel owner Nero Sanstleben, who is looking to his unknown relative for financial help. When the real Agamemnon turns up, he is mistaken for the new barman. The ladies in the piece were Nero's daughter Herta (Frln Döringer), his sister and Agamemnon's mother, Lydia, and the variety singer, Marietta Leona, as well as the four Mogulopulous daughters and Bobby's four little chorus girls who are, en masse, mistaken for each other.

The music of the show was put together from the late Carl Millöcker's trunk, and the resultant show was successful enough in Berlin (56 performances) to be taken up in Hungary (ad Emil Tabori) and to be optioned, prepared and announced for Broadway's 1909–10 season. It got no further, however, than one performance at a private Shubert brothers tryout (ad Mark Swan).

Hungary: Budai Színkör *A komédiások* 28 April 1908

COUSIN-COUSINE Opérette in 3 acts by Maurice Ordonneau and Henri Kéroul. Music by Gaston Serpette. Théâtre des Folies-Dramatiques, Paris, 23 December 1893.

The part of the show which dealt with the cousin-cousine relationship showed two cousins (male and female, as per the show's title), from two non-speaking parts of a family, falling in love. Thérèse Courtalin (Aline Vauthier) pretends to be her schoolfriend, Henriette de Rochefontaine (Mlle de Berio), so that the course of love with Edgard de Pommerol (Perrin) can run smoothly. Meanwhile, Henriette (pretending to be Thérèse) runs a similar course with Gaston Jolivet (Lamy). The other part of the show dealt with the eccentric lawyer, Patenôtre (Guy), whose passion for choral music intrudes into his daily life to such an extent that his office workers, organized into an orphéon, make up a permanent chorus (Greek variety) for the play. Patenôtre is ''visiting'' the housemistress (Louise Balthy) of the girls' school when fire breaks out and he is forced to escape in feminine garb. The two young lovers turn up with fire hoses and encounter their sweethearts, apparently sporting each other's names, and it takes another act of comedy, with regular appearances by Patenôtre's ever-interrupting choristers, before things come to their natural operettic end.

Played for 90 highly successful nights in its first run at the Folies-Dramatiques, *Cousin-Cousine* did not reach the stages of Britain, America or Austria, but it was seen in several other countries and languages. It was mounted in Australia, with Florence Young taking the title role of what had become (for the ungendered English) *La Belle Thérèse* alongside Henry Bracy (Gaston), Courtice Pounds (Louis Pomerol), Clara Thompson (Mme Moutonnet) and Howard Vernon (Bellefontaine), in Germany (ad Heinrich Bolten-Bäckers), and in Hungary (ad Gyula Komor), where the unloved title was changed to the distinctly more commercial ''Fire at a girls' school,'' and also had ''a long and most successful run'' at Brussels's Théâtre Molière.

Australia: Princess Theatre, Melbourne *La Belle Thérèse* 7 December 1895; Germany: Thalia-Theater 18 September 1896; Hungary: Budai Színkör *Tüz a leánygimnaziumban* 15 August 1902

COWARD, Noël [Pierce] (b Teddington, Mddx, 16 December 1899; d Firefly Hill, nr Port Maria, Jamaica, 26 March 1973).

Dramatist, revue-writer, lyricist, performer and personality, Noël Coward made himself a special place in the theatre of his age whilst finding only one genuine success as a composer and author for the book musical stage.

Coward began his connection with the theatre as a child actor in plays and musical comedies (Jack Morrison in *The Happy Family,* 1916), but before long began writing and composing songs—of which ''Forbidden Fruit'' (1915) is the earliest surviving example—and plays, of which *I'll Leave It to You* (1920) was the first to be staged. His earliest contributions to the musical theatre as a writer were in the form of pieces of revue material for André Charlot and for the Co-Optimists concert party, and in 1923 he collaborated with Ronald Jeans on the writing of Charlot's successful revue, *London Calling,* in which he also performed. His career as a playwright began to blossom soon after, and he successfully mixed a run of his own individual kind of brittle, personal comedies and slightly daring dramas with further revues (*On with the Dance, This Year of Grace*) until, according to his own tale, a hearing of *Die Fledermaus* tempted him into trying his hand at a musical play.

The result was *Bitter-Sweet* (1929), a lushly sentimental period piece which he called an ''opérette'' and which, in the midst of the current craze for dance-and-laughter musical shows and revues, seemed an unlikely winner. However, the show, with its hit songs ''I'll See You Again'' and ''If Love Were All,'' proved to be just that, becoming the first British romantic musical to triumph in London since the war, and running for nearly two years before going on to Broadway, to Paris, to Budapest and on to film. Its success encouraged Coward to continue in the same vein and, in the 1930s and 1940s, while he turned out the most famous of his comic plays (*Private Lives, Present Laughter, Blithe Spirit*) and further bright and witty revues (*Words and Music, Set to Music, Sigh No More*), he persisted in following the romantic operetta trail with his musical stage pieces.

Conversation Piece (1934), which he wrote for and played with French actress Yvonne Printemps, and which produced perhaps his most famous lyrical song, ''I'll Follow My Secret Heart,'' won some success, but *Operette* (1938, 133 performances) and *Pacific 1860* (1946, 129 performances) were both failures in spite, in the latter case, of containing some of his best music. An attempt to be more modern, with a *Wunder-Bar*-ish crooks-and-cabaret musical called *Ace of Clubs* (1950) misfired uncomfortably, and he returned to period operetta with a not very successful adaptation of Oscar Wilde's *Lady Windermere's Fan* as *After the Ball* (1954). The 1961 musical *Sail Away* (''Why Do the Wrong People Travel?,'' ''The Customer's Always Right'') had its lead soprano and her love story cut out during pre-Broadway tryouts and thus, almost accidentally, Coward ended up writing the show which, of all his musical stage pieces, was nearest in tone to his revues. It was also the nearest since *Conversation Piece* to being a success. A final musical theatre score, in the wake of *My Fair Lady,* for an adaptation of Terence Rattigan's *The Prince and the Showgirl* as the uncomfortably imitative *The Girl Who Came to Supper* was both uncharacteristic and a quick failure.

Alongside his conventional musicals, Coward also wrote songs which were utilized in several of the plays which made up the various evenings of the collection of one-act pieces called *Tonight at 8.30* (''Has Anybody Seen Our Ship?,'' ''We Were Dancing''), and in the patriotic play *Cavalcade* (''Twentieth Century Blues'').

Coward's many-faceted career as a writer and performer, which included books of autobiography, poetry, short stories and novels as well as stage works, was extended in his later years by a series of very successful cabaret performances of largely his own material in which many songs which might otherwise have gone down with failed shows were given a second life. He turned down the offer to star as the Emperor of China in the London production of Cole Porter's *Aladdin* (1959) and in 1967 he made his nearest approach to a reappearance on the musical stage since *Conversation Piece* when he appeared on television as Caesar in the Richard Rodgers/Peter Stone musical adaptation of *Androcles and the Lion.*

Largely self-taught as a composer, Coward relied on more traditionally educated musicians to notate and fill out his musical lines, but his melodic invention and the immaculate blending of his words and music made his songs extremely effective. He used the traditional elements of the light musical theatre as his bases and succeeded in producing some outstanding lyrical pieces (the waltzes ''I'll See You Again,'' ''I'll Follow My Secret Heart'' and *Pacific 1860*'s ''This Is a Changing World,'' ''This is a Night for Lovers''), such sympathetic words-and-music pieces as ''If Love Were All,'' and a whole series of those brisk and brittle comedy songs, overflowing with genuinely clever and sometimes wicked words, rhymes and ideas (''Green Carnations,'' ''His Excellency Regrets,'' ''Alice Is at It Again,'' ''There's Always Something Fishy About the French,'' ''The Stately Homes of England,'' ''Three Juvenile Delinquents,'' ''The Customer's Always Right,'' ''The Bronxville Darby and Joan,'' ''Josephine''), which became his trademark and which, like his plays, have survived individually more strongly than any of his stage musicals.

Coward's story *Me and the Girls* was posthumously adapted as a stage musical for off-off-Broadway's Village Theater Company (James Merillat, Dick Pasqual, 9 July 1993).

1929 **Bitter-Sweet** His Majesty's Theatre 12 July

1934 **Conversation Piece** His Majesty's Theatre 16 February

1938 **Operette** His Majesty's Theatre 16 March

1946 **Pacific 1860** Theatre Royal, Drury Lane 19 December

1950 **Ace of Clubs** Cambridge Theatre 7 July

1954 **After the Ball** Globe Theatre 10 June

1961 **Sail Away** Broadhurst Theater, New York 3 October

1963 **The Girl Who Came to Supper** (Harry Kurnitz) Broadway Theater, New York 8 December

Autobiographies: Morley, S (ed): *Autobiography (Present Indicative, Future Indefinite, Past Conditional)* (Methuen, London, 1986), Payn, G, Morley, S (eds): *The Coward Diaries* (Macmillan, London, 1982); Biographies: Lesley, C: *The Life of Noël Coward* (Jonathan Cape, London, 1976), Morley, S: *A Talent to Amuse* (Heinemann, London, 1969), Castle, C: *Noël* (Abacus, London, 1972), Mander, R, Mitchenson, J: *Theatrical Companion to Noël Coward* (Rockliff, London, 1957), Fisher, C: *Noël Coward* (Weidenfeld & Nicolson, London, 1992), etc.

COWLES, Eugene [Chase] (b Stanstead, Quebec, Canada, 17 January 1860; d Boston, 22 September 1948). The possessor of an impressive bass voice, Cowles played two decades of priests, fathers and such other akin roles as basses of all ages are traditionally doomed to, on the turn-of-the century Broadway stage.

Originally a clerk in the First National Bank of Stanstead and a local church and concert singer, he joined the Boston Ideal Opera Company (The Bostonians) in 1888. He remained an important member of the group for eight years, creating the role of Will Scarlett in *Robin Hood* as well as often written-to-measure bass parts in such other early American pieces as De Koven's *The Knickerbockers* (1893, Antony von Corlear), Victor Herbert's *Prince Ananias* (1894, George Le Grabbe), *The Maid of Plymouth* (1894, Miles Standish), *The Ogallallas* (1894, Cardenas), *A Wartime Wedding* (1896, Felipe), *The Serenade* (1897, Romero) and *Rip van Winkle* (1897, Rip), and he appeared as Squire Bantam (*Dorothy*) and in other like roles in the company's wide-ranging repertoire.

When Alice Nielsen split from the group to form her own company, Cowles went with her, and he appeared in America and Britain as Sándor in her production of Victor Herbert's *The Fortune Teller,* in which he created the celebrated Gypsy Love Song (''Slumber On, My Little Gypsy Sweetheart''), and then as Duke Rodolph in *The Singing Girl* (1899, ''The Wonderful Magician''). He later toured his own Eugene Cowles Opera and Concert Company, with which he produced a little operetta *Snow Bound* (Albany 7 March 1902), returning to Broadway alongside Fritzi Scheff as Mondragon in Herbert's *Babette* (1903) and with Marie Cahill as Henry Clay Kulpepper in the musical comedy *Marrying Mary* (1906). He subsequently appeared in James Hackett's Chicago production of *The Alcayde* (1906); as a bluegrass army man in *The Boys and Betty* (1908, Major Gordon); as General Petipons in Herbert's *The Rose of Algeria* (1909); in *Sweet Sixteen* (1910, John Hammond); as Bill Bobstay in the ''all-star'' *HMS Pinafore;* and on the road in *The Tik-Tok Man of Oz* (1913, Ruggedo). He played in a number of Gilbert and Sullivan productions (Bill Bobstay, Major

Murgatroyd, Pirate King, Poo Bah) on Broadway in the early 1910s, and, at the age of almost 60, was still to be seen, on the road and briefly on Broadway, playing the small role of Abdallah in *Chu Chin Chow.*

COX AND BOX, or The Long Lost Brothers Musical triumviretta in 1 act adapted from J Maddison Morton's farce *Box and Cox* by F C Burnand. Music by Arthur Sullivan. Adelphi Theatre, London, 11 May 1867.

One of the most successful of the short musical plays written in Britain in the wake of the success of the little works of Offenbach, *Cox and Box* was apparently the result of Sullivan's attempting to produce a little piece on the lines of Offenbach's widely played hit *Les Deux Aveugles.* Burnand adapted the script from Maddison Morton's frequently performed comedietta (itself, allegedly, a version of the French *Une chambre à deux lits*), and the first performances of the little three-handed comedy musical were given in private by the society amateur group, the Moray Minstrels, with George du Maurier as Box, Harold Power as Cox, and John Forster as Bouncer. ''Sullivan played the piano behind a door, where I [Burnand] also prompted.'' The time and place of this first performance is much argued by Gilbert and Sullivan scholars, but Burnand went on record placing it at his own home, 102 Belgrave Rd, and clocking the hour as . . . 11 PM! There is, however, no argument over the fact that *Cox and Box* got its first public performance at a benefit concert at the Adelphi Theatre.

Mr Bouncer (Arthur Cecil) has rented the same room both to the hatter Mr Cox (Quintin Twiss) and the printer Mr Box (George du Maurier), since one works at night and the other in the day. Inevitably, one day, the two coincide and, after the hard words have flown, they find they have a common interest in one Mrs Penelope Ann Wiggins. Their interest is to avoid her and, at first, each tries to force the other to take the lady off his hands until news comes that she has drowned and left her fortune to her intended. Then both are less anxious to disclaim her. But Penelope Ann has not drowned. She is heading for London to find Box and/or Cox with the news that she has married Knox. Cox and Box delightedly discover that they are, by the laws of the dramatic theatre, indubitably long-lost brothers and they decide to share the wretched Bouncer's room. The songs of the piece included a ''Rataplan'' piece for Bouncer, reminiscing interminably over his days in the military, a Lullaby for the snoozy Box, and a serenade, ''The Buttercup,'' to help pass the time.

After its Adelphi Theatre performances, *Cox and Box* was put on the program at the German Reeds' Gallery of Illustration with Reed (Cox), Cecil (Box) and J Seymour (Bouncer) in the cast. It was played on a double bill with W S Gilbert's *No Cards* and, later, with *Ages Ago,* for an entire year. In contrast to these intimate surroundings, it was also played as part of the program at the vast Alhambra Theatre with the composer's brother, Fred, playing Cox, and later on seen on several occasions at the Court Theatre. It was ultimately taken into the repertoire of the D'Oyly Carte companies and played at the Savoy as a forepiece to *The Chieftain,* becoming—in spite of not being written by Gilbert—accepted thereafter as part of the Savoy canon.

The piece won other English-language performances following its London success, being first mounted in Australia as part of a ''Gallery of Illustration'' program given by Alice May with Edward Farley (Cox) and Howard Vernon (Box) featured. Offenbach's *The Rose of the Auvergne* and a local extravaganza *The Belle of Woolloomooloo* made up the program. It is said to have been played for the first time in New York in August 1875 (though I can find no report of this performance), but Broadway's Lyric Hall saw some kind of a performance as part of ''Mr H Galt's Entertainment'' in December of that year, and, in the wake of the success of *HMS Pinafore,* when producers were scrambling to find anything by Gilbert and/or Sullivan to decorate their bills, the Standard Theatre hosted it as a forepiece to *Pinafore* as played by Thomas Whiffen (Box), Hart Conway (Cox) and Charles Makin (Bouncer). Many another touring musical troupe included the show in its repertoire in the last days of the 1870s, but it seems that the first ever performance in America was very probably the one staged by Susie Galton's English operetta troupe in San Francisco in March 1874, with John Howson as Cox, Alfred Kelleher as Box and Miss Galton playing Mrs Bouncer. The operetta shared a program on this occasion with a performance by the California Minstrels.

Both British and other English-speaking stages later hosted *Cox and Box* principally as a forepiece to the shorter full-length works of the Gilbert and Sullivan repertoire.

Australia: Masonic Hall, Sydney 26 December 1872; USA: Opera House, San Francisco 11 March 1874, Lyric Hall, New York 22 December 1875, Standard Theater, New York 14 April 1879

Recordings: complete (Decca), selections (BASF, PRT, etc)

TV films: WPIX (1948), Brent-Walker 1982

COYNE, Joseph [E] (b New York, 27 March 1867; d Virginia Water, Surrey, 17 February 1941). Light comedy actor-who-sings who moved from silly-ass roles in his native America to stardom as Britain's Danilo in *The Merry Widow.*

Coyne first appeared on the New York stage at Niblo's Gardens in the Kiralfy Brothers' Italian dance-and-drama spectacular *Excelsior* at the age of 16, but he spent most of his earliest years touring in vaudeville as half of the act "Coyne and Evans." He played in the variety farce-comedies *Rush City* (1895, Washington Chumley), *The District Attorney* (1895, Corrigan), *The Star-Spangled Dollar* (1897), *The Good Mr Best* (1897, Marmaduke Mush), *A Stranger in New* York (1898, Stranger), *A Dog in the Manger* (1899, A Jackson Bright) and *The Girl in the Barracks* (1899, Paul Roland), and featured as Willett Work in *Star and Garter* (1900), a vaudeville farce constructed for the benefit of the Agoust family of jugglers, and in *The Night of the Fourth* (1901); most of the above passed briefly through New York. On the opening night of the last-named piece, he deputised at the last minute for star J Sherrie Mathews in the leading role of Keenan Swift. He made his first appearance in a regular musical as Bertie Tappertwit (the name of the character speaks for itself) in Charles Frohman's London production of *The Girl from Up There* (1901), a piece basically constructed as a vehicle for *Belle of New York* star Edna May.

Returning to America, he got his Broadway break in the George Grossmith role of Archie in the Gaiety musical *The Toreador* (1902) and he followed up with a range of more or less goofy gentlemen in *The Rogers Brothers in London* (1903, Harold Harvey, "It's Awfully Hard to Shop"), *In Newport* (1904, Percy van Alstyne), *The Rollicking Girl* (1905, Panagl, 'Won't You Be My Lovey Dovey?"), the comedy *Abigail, The Social Whirl* (1906, Artie Endicott, "Love Among the Freaks") and as the American version of *Lady Madcap*'s Trooper Brown (*My Lady's Maid,* "They Handed Me a Lemon"), originated by G P Huntley, before returning to London for Frohman, this time to play leading man to Edna May in a palpable, but weak, attempt to clone *The Belle of New York* called *Nelly Neil.* However, his personal success in the role of the loose-limbed, comic-aristocratic Billy Ricketts sparked something in the mind of rival producer George Edwardes and Coyne found himself offered a role rather different to the upper-class dopes he had been accustomed to playing—the part of Count Danilo Danilowitsch in Edwardes's English-language version of Lehár's *Die lustige Witwe.*

Coyne's success in *The Merry Widow* made him an enormous London star and led him into a whole series of major light comic-romantic leading roles for Edwardes, first opposite his *Merry Widow* co-star Lily Elsie in *The Dollar Princess* (1909, Harry Condor), then with Gertie Millar in *The Quaker Girl* (1910, Tony Chute) and *The Dancing Mistress* (1912, Teddy Cavanaugh), and with Ina Claire in *The Girl from Utah* (1913, Sandy Blair). During the war he appeared in several plays, in London's production of Irving Berlin's revues *Watch Your Step* and *Follow the Crowd,* and in the local revue *The Bing Girls Are There,* but he returned to the musical theatre to play opposite Winifred Barnes in the Grossmith and Laurillard version of the Belgian musical *Arlette* (1917, Prince Paul) and to star, successively, in the Gaiety Theatre's long-running production of the American musical *Going Up* (1918, Robert Street), in Charlot's version of the French musical comedy *Dédé* (1922, André La Huchette), and in the London production of Friml's *Katinka* (1923, Thaddeus T Hopper).

He had another huge success when, knocking sixty, he was cast in the role of Jimmy Smith in Clayton and Waller's triumphant British production of *No, No, Nanette* (1925), followed by the London version of *Queen High* (1926, T Boggs Johns), but his last appearances in a musical—in the disastrous *Open Your Eyes* (1929) and in the unsuccessful London version of Benatzky's *Meine Schwester und ich* (1931, *Meet My Sister,* Filosel)—were less memorable.

Coyne was married (in his first essay at marriage) to **Anna BOYD** (d 5 June 1916), Broadway's original Widow in *A Trip to Chinatown* and long a leading lady, then a character performer, on the American musical stage. She was seen during a full career as Gabriel in *Evangeline* (1887), Flirt/Clarence Lightfoot in *Zig-Zag* (1888–89), in the star role of the tryout of *Overlook* (1890), succeeding Fay Templeton as *Hendrik Hudson* (1890), *The Dazzler,* in the title role of *Aladdin Jr,* as Pearl Dodo in *The Nancy Hanks* (1896, "The Girl from the West"), Mlle Mirabeau in *My Lady Molly* (1904), Letitia Hemingway in *The Tourists* (1906), Donna Isadora in *The Girl and the Governor* (1907), Amelia Parling in *A Skylark* (1910), Mary Ann in *Her Little Highness* (1913), etc.

CRAWFORD, Cheryl (b Akron, Ohio, 24 September 1902; d New York, 7 October 1986).

Cheryl Crawford worked as a secretary with the Theatre Guild, as an actress and as a casting director before being instrumental in the founding of the Group Theatre (1931), where she directed several productions. She moved into management in 1938, and produced her first musical piece in 1942 with a revival of *Porgy and Bess.* In a wide-ranging theatrical career thereafter, during which she collaborated on the establishment of the American Repertory Theater (1946) and the Actors' Studio (1946), she produced, amongst a series of mostly less than successful plays, several distinctly successful Broadway musicals—*One Touch of Venus* (1943), *Brigadoon* (1947) and *Paint Your Wagon* (1951). She also mounted several less successful ones—*Love Life* (1948), *Regina* (1949), *Flahooley* (1951), *Jennie* (1963), *Celebration* (1969), the off-Broadway *Colette* (1970), and *Reuben Reuben* (1955) which died prior to New York—but it was notable that, in spite of her many efforts towards the avant-garde in the theatre, her biggest producing successes came with the most traditional of musical plays.

The Cheryl Crawford Theater at the West Side Arts Center is named for her.

Literature: Grismer, K: *Cheryl Crawford Presents* (UMI, Ann Arbor, Mich, 1993)

Autobiography: *One Naked Individual* (Bobbs-Merrill, Indianapolis, Ind, 1977)

CRAWFORD, Clifton (b Edinburgh, 2 April ?1875; d London, 3 June 1920). A popular light comedy-with-dance player through some 20 years of Broadway musicals.

Son of a Scots theatrical manager, Crawford first appeared on the stage as a juvenile pianist. When his family moved to New Zealand and then to Australia, he tried his luck as a Highland dancer instead, and he subsequently essayed a career on the music halls first in Britain and then in America. Finding no success, he quit the theatre and became a golf coach, settling amid the green fields of Boston to pursue his new calling. But he was heard entertaining his wealthy clients at the Boston Golf Club by R A Barnet of the Boston Cadets amateur musical company and, before long, he had again exchanged his niblick for a stick of grease paint.

Crawford was first seen on Broadway in his mid-twenties when he appeared in such musical shows as A H Chamberlyn's ex-Cadets production of *Milady and the Musketeers* (1901, Arra-Miss), *Foxy Grandpa* (1901–2, Jack Richman), *The Jewel of Asia* (1903, Yussuf Potiphar), *Mother Goose* (1903, Mayor of Chatham) and *Seeing New York* (1906, Sir Montiford Knight). He took himself out on the road as a monologue artist thereafter, but soon slipped back into the theatre and into light-handed leading-man roles, appearing as Tom Stanhope in the successful *Three Twins* (1908), opposite Ina Claire in the role created by Joe Coyne in *The Quaker Girl* (1910, Tony Chute), as the juvenile leading man of his own musical, *My Best Girl* (1912, Richard Vanderfleet), and paired with Emma Trentini in Friml's *The Ballet Girl* (1914), and a version of Nedbal's *Polenblut* which reached Broadway as *The Peasant Girl* (1915, Bronio von Popiel). When the last-named show was burlesqued in *The Passing Show of 1915,* Crawford was ''played'' by . . . Marilyn[n] Miller.

After taking time out from Broadway to visit London, where he starred in the Gaiety Theatre's revusical comedy, *After the Girl* (Freddy Charlston), he appeared in New York in the Winter Garden show *A World of Pleasure* (1915, Tony van Schuyler), in the revamped Hungarian operett *Her Soldier Boy* (1916, Teddy McLane) and, billed above the title alongside Marilyn Miller, in *Fancy Free* (1918, Albert van Wyck).

Crawford also worked, from his golfing days, as a songwriter and he scored a major song hit with the number ''Nancy Brown'' as sung by Marie Cahill in *The Wild Rose.* He interpolated songs into a number of other productions, including several in which he appeared—*Miss Simplicity* (''Don't Mind Me,'' ''The Interrogative Child''), *Mother Goose* (''Rafferty'' and ''Girls will be Girls'' for himself, and ''Social Éclat'' for Joe Cawthorn), *The Peasant Girl* (''Mary Had a Little Lamb''), *The Liberty Belles* (''De Trop,'' ''Starlight''), *Her Soldier Boy* (''Slavery,'' ''History,'' ''Military Stamp''), *The Quaker Girl* (''I Want to Tell You Something,'' ''Get Away, I Am a Married Man''), *Fancy Free* (''Eve''), *The Canary* (''This Is the Time''), *London's My Darling* (''The Shady Side of Bond Street''), *The Passing Show of 1916* (''What's the Matter With You?'') and the original production of the play *My Lady Friends* (''I Want to Spread a Little Sunshine''), which would later be the basis for *No, No, Nanette.* He had less luck with his attempts to compose a Broadway musical. Neither *Captain Careless,* played around the country by B C Whitney for two seasons, nor *I Love a Lassie*—announced by its librettist-lyricist-producer-star for Broadway, but a casualty at Providence, Rhode Island, after a fortnight's life—made it to New York, whilst *My Best Girl,* which did, had only a limited stay (68 performances).

Crawford was killed when he fell from a window in a London hotel at the age of 45.

1901 **The Liberty Belles** (w others/H B Smith) Madison Square Theater 30 September

1906 **Seeing New York** (A Baldwin Sloane/Joseph Hart/w Hart) New York Theater Roof 5 June

1906 **Captain Careless** (w Bob Adams/Robert Melville Baker, Hal Stephens) Princess Theater, Toronto 27 August; Chicago Opera House 13 May 1907

1912 **My Best Girl** (w Augustus Barratt/Rennold Wolf, Channing Pollock) Park Theater 12 September

1919 **I Love a Lassie** (Jerome K Jerome ad Erwin Connelly) Shubert Theater, New Haven 15 May

CRAWFORD, Michael [SMITH, Michael Patrick] (b Salisbury, 19 January 1942). One of Britain's most popular comedy actors, who found a singing voice and international fame in the musical theatre.

First seen on the musical stage as a boy soprano in Benjamin Britten's *Noye's Fludde* and *Let's Make an Opera,* Crawford had early adult successes on the stage in the *Black Comedy / White Lies* double bill of plays and the farce *No Sex, Please, We're British* and in such films as *The Knack* and *The Jokers,* before tackling his first musical roles as Hero in the screen's *A Funny Thing Happened on the Way to the Forum* (1966) and Barnaby in the film version of *Hello, Dolly!* (1969).

He became one of the best known and most loved of all British performers through his television characterization of the gormless, accident-prone Frank Spencer in the long-running series *Some Mothers Do Have 'Em,* and he paralleled his television career by taking four major musical theatre roles over a period of some 15 years with a success which ultimately redirected his career towards the musical stage.

In 1974 he scored a first-class hit when he starred in his first stage musical as the forever fibbing Billy Fisher in *Billy* ("Some of Us Belong to the Stars") at the Theatre Royal, Drury Lane, but his second musical venture, as the mentally retarded hero of *Flowers for Algernon* (1979), was, in spite of undeniable qualities, short-lived. In 1981 he returned to the musical stage to play the title role (with additional tricks) in the London production of the Broadway musical *Barnum,* scoring a second major hit and following the exhausting first run of the show with a return run and a television film of the show in 1985. At the end of that run he joined the cast of *The Phantom of the Opéra,* creating the role of the Phantom ("Music of the Night") in London, New York and Los Angeles in the third outstanding hit of a musical theatre career where the three roles had filled more than ten years of his working life.

More recently, he has appeared throughout the world as the featured performer of the concert "The Music of Andrew Lloyd Webber," and in the Las Vegas spectacle *EFX!*

Autobiography: *Parcel Arrived Safely: Tied with String* (Century, New York, 1999); Biography: Hayward, A: *Michael Crawford: The Phantom Unmasked* (Weidenfeld & Nicolson, London, 1991)

Plate 85. **Michael Crawford**—*before he disappeared behind a mask—as London's P T Barnum.*

CRÉMIEUX, Hector [Jonathan] (b Paris, 10 November 1828; d Paris, 30 September 1892). One of the most brilliant authors of opéra-bouffe texts in the palmiest days of the genre.

The young Crémieux studied law and subsequently entered on a career in the state service where he came under the eye of the theatrically inclined and highly influential Duc de Morny. With Morny's encouragement, he progressed from his earliest attempt, in collaboration with his brother, at writing for the dramatic stage (*Fiesque,* 1850), to a series of féeries (the internationally successful *Pied de mouton, Aladin, ou la lampe merveilleuse,* etc), comedies (*L'Abbé Constantin* w Decourcelle), vaudevilles and short opérettes, making himself a reputation as one of the most outstanding exponents of the witty, cockeyed opéra-bouffe style of the moment. His burlesque talents were demonstrated in his collaborations with Halévy on the libretti for Offenbach's *Orphée aux enfers* and *Le Pont des soupirs* and with Adolphe Jaime on *Le Petit Faust, Les Turcs* and *Le Trône d'Écosse* for the most marvellously cockeyed composer of them all, Hervé, whilst on the smaller scale he also authored or co-authored the texts for some of the most internationally successful short musicals pieces of the 1850s and 1860s, including Offenbach's *Une Demoiselle en loterie, La Chanson de Fortunio* and *Monsieur Choufleuri* and Henri Caspers's *Ma tante dort.*

Crémieux continued to be successful when opéra-bouffe gave way to the more measured opéra-comique style in the postwar era, having his biggest success of this period, once more in collaboration with Offenbach and with Ernest Blum with the vaudevillesque tale of *La Jolie Parfumeuse.*

In 1887 he retired and took up a post as secretary general of the Société des dépots. The society failed, Crémieux got into personal financial difficulties and, already ill himself, suffered the deaths of his wife and his brother in quick succession before putting a bullet through his own head at the age of 63.

1856 **Élodie, ou le forfait nocturne** (Léopold Amat, Jacques Offenbach) 1 act Théâtre des Bouffes-Parisiens 19 January

1856 **Le Financier et le savetier** (Offenbach/w Edmond About) 1 act Théâtre des Bouffes-Parisiens 23 September

1857 **Une Demoiselle en loterie** (Offenbach/w Adolphe Jaime) 1 act Théâtre des Bouffes-Parisiens 27 July

1858 **Orphée aux enfers** (Offenbach/w Ludovic Halévy) Théâtre des Bouffes-Parisiens 21 October

1860 **Ma tante dort** (Henri Caspers/w About) 1 act Théâtre Lyrique 21 January

1861 **La Chanson de Fortunio** (Offenbach/w Halévy) 1 act Théâtre des Bouffes-Parisiens 5 January

1861 **Le Pont des soupirs** (Offenbach/w Halévy) Théâtre des Bouffes-Parisiens 23 March

1861 **Monsieur Choufleuri restera chez lui le . . .** (Offenbach/w "Saint-Rémy," Halévy) Présidence du Corps-legislatif 31 May, Théâtre des Bouffes-Parisiens 14 September

1861 **La Baronne de San Francisco** (Caspers/w Halévy) Théâtre des Bouffes-Parisiens 27 November

1861 **Le Roman comique** (Offenbach/w Halévy) Théâtre des Bouffes-Parisiens 10 December

1861 **Les Deux Buveurs** (Léo Delibes/w Halévy) 1 act Théâtre des Bouffes-Parisiens January

1861 **Les Eaux d'Ems** (Delibes/w Halévy) 1 act Kursaal, Bad Ems; Théâtre des Bouffes-Parisiens 9 April 1863

1862 **Un fin de bail** (Adolphe Varney/w Halévy) 1 act Théâtre des Bouffes-Parisiens 29 January

1862 **Mon ami Pierrot** (Delibes/w Halévy) 1 act Kursaal, Bad Ems July

1862 **Jacquéline** (Offenbach/w Halévy) 1 act Théâtre des Bouffes-Parisiens 14 October

1865 **Les Bergers** (Offenbach/w Philippe Gille) Théâtre des Bouffes-Parisiens 11 December

1867 **Robinson Crusoë** (Offenbach/w Eugène Cormon) Opéra-Comique 23 November

1867 **Geneviève de Brabant** 3-act version w Étienne Tréfeu Théâtre des Menus-Plaisirs 26 December

1869 **Le Petit Faust** (Hervé/w Jaime) Théâtre des Folies-Dramatiques 28 April

1869 **Les Turcs** (Hervé/w Jaime) Théâtre des Folies-Dramatiques 23 December

1871 **Le Trône d'Écosse** (Hervé/w Jaime) Théâtre des Variétés 17 November

1872 **La Tour du cadran** (pasticcio) Théâtre des Variétés 9 September

1873 **La Veuve du Malabar** (Hervé/w Alfred Delacour) Théâtre des Variétés 26 April

1873 **La Jolie Parfumeuse** (Offenbach/w Ernest Blum) Théâtre de la Renaissance 29 November

1874 **Bagatelle** (Offenbach/w Blum) 1 act Théâtre des Bouffes-Parisiens 21 May

1874 **La Famille Trouillat** (Léon Vasseur/w Blum) Théâtre de la Renaissance 10 September

1875 **Geneviève de Brabant** (revised version w Jaime) Théâtre de la Gaîté

1875 **Le Manoir du Pic-Tordu** (Gaston Serpette/w Alfred de Saint-Albin) Théâtre des Variétés 28 May

1875 **La Belle Poule** (Hervé/w Saint-Albin) Théâtre des Folies-Dramatiques 29 December

1877 **La Foire Saint-Laurent** (Offenbach/w Saint-Albin [and Ernest Blum]) Théâtre des Folies-Dramatiques 10 February

1881 **L'Oeil crevé** revised version (Théâtre de la Renaissance)

LA CRÉOLE Opérette in 3 acts by Albert Millaud [and Henri Meilhac]. Music by Jacques Offenbach. Théâtre des Bouffes-Parisiens, Paris, 3 November 1875.

There was very little that was notable about the simplistic plot of *La Créole* except for the color of its prima donna. Having to stain herself each night with réglisse in order to play this show's title role may indeed, as it was suggested, have hastened Anna Judic's departure from the company at the Bouffes in favor of the Variétés.

Commander Feuilles-Mortes (Daubray) wants his ward, Antoinette (Mlle Luce), to marry his nephew, René (Anna van Ghell). This is unfortunate, for Rene's friend Frontignac (Cooper) is in love with Antoinette, whilst René has set his heart on the dusky Guadaloupean Dora (Anna Judic). Dora goes after an important letter so that, with the help of a little bribery, all the right pairings can come about in time for the final curtain.

Judic was given some compensation for having to spend extra time making up by having the first act off. It was baritone Lucien Fugère, in the supporting role of Saint-Chamas, who set affairs moving and, thereafter, soprano Anna van Ghell in the breeches role of René got the largest part of the music, with the Commandant popping in a little Romance by way of musico-comic relief. When Dora did appear, brought back to France aboard the Commander's ship once all the exposition had been done, she more than made up for lost time, delivering a romance of her own ("Il vous souvient de moi, j'espère"), the couplets "Si vous croyez que ça m'amuse," a Chanson créole in the second-act finale ("Oui, c'est René que j'aime") and a lively Chanson des dames de Bordeaux ("C'est dans la ville de Bordeaux") in the final act. The jeune première, Antoinette, had a pretty little villanelle ("Je croyais que tu m'aimais").

La Créole was not particularly successful. It managed only to pass its 60th night at the Bouffes before being withdrawn. However, Offenbach's name on the score guaranteed it productions elsewhere. In London, the piece was produced in a slimmed-down version (ad H B Farnie, Robert Reece) on a bill with two short pieces, Hervé's *Up the River* and Lecocq's *The Sea Nymphs* (*Ondines au champagne*). Kate Munroe starred as the creole with a cast including Nellie Bromley (René), Violet Cameron (Antoinette) and John Howson (Commodore). It held its place in the bill when Lecocq's piece was replaced by a potted version of *L'Oeil crevé,* and closed after a fine season of three months. A decade later, Miss Cameron chose the piece as a vehicle for a season her gentleman friend, Lord Lonsdale, sponsored for her in America. Played as *The Commodore,* it was given one trial performance at the Avenue Theatre before the company set out. The liaison between producer and star was turned into a juicy scandal in New York, and, in the anti-British-aristocracy flurry that ensued, their show lasted only a handful of nights longer than it had in London.

Maximilian Steiner's production of *Die Creolin* at Vienna's Theater an der Wien (ad Julius Hopp) boasted no less a star than Marie Geistinger in the role of Dora, alongside Felix Schweighofer (de Feuillemorte), Jani Szika (Frontignac), Bertha Steinher (Antoinette), Frln Wieser (René) and Alexander Girardi as the ''first notary,'' but it was played just 27 times, and the piece never took on in German-langauge theatres.

It must have seemed a bright idea to dig up *La Créole* when a Parisian musical theatre piece was being organised to star colored American variety star Josephine Baker. Albert Willemetz and Georges Delance did a heavy remake on the libretto and its score—one which allowed a new character called Cartahut (Dréan) to open the evening on its highest note with ''Les Dames de Bordeaux'' and brought Dora on straight afterwards with the Chanson créole. No waiting till the second act in 1934—get the star on. For, after all, she didn't have Judic's problem with making up. The new version of *La Créole* was produced at the Théâtre Marigny (15 December) with René-Charle (René), Rose Carday (Antoinette) and Urban (Commandant) supporting and with Carmen Lahez as a new comical character called Crême-Fouettée, and it turned out to be not such a very bright idea. The lithe Mlle Baker showed up with much less voice even than Mlle Judic (she also wore much less clothing), but the production nevertheless found both a special audience and won a new hearing for Offenbach's music.

Austria: Theater an der Wien *Die Creolin* 8 January 1876; Germany: Wallner Theater *Die Creolin* 4 June 1876; UK: Folly Theatre 15 September 1877, Avenue Theatre *The Commodore* 10 May 1886; USA: Casino Theater *The Commodore* 4 October 1886

Recording: 1934 version, complete (Bourg)

Plate 86. **La Créole.** *Anna Judic blacked up for this role . . . but not very much, by the looks of it.*

CROFT, Annie (b Skirlaugh, Hull, 17 August 1896; d Parkstone, Dorset, 23 March 1959). Vocalist and producer for the London and provincial musical stage.

Annie Croft appeared in London as a young soprano in leading juvenile roles in *The Cinema Star* (1914, t/o Phyllis) and *My Lady Frayle* (1915, Virginia) and, after a long period playing in revue and pantomime, returned to the musical theatre in the title role of Steven Jones's *Poppy* (1924), as Riquette in the pre-London tour of Oscar Straus's *Riquette* (1925) and in its later London incarnation as *My Son John* (1926, Sandy Fayre). In 1928–29 she starred in *The Girl Friend* (Kitty), *Hit the Deck* (Looloo) and *The Five o'Clock Girl* (Patricia) in Australia, and after returning to London took the soprano role in the arioso musical *Dear Love* (1929, Suzanne) and appeared in José Collins's famous role of Teresa in a revival of *The Maid of the Mountains* (1930). She toured in two Continental West-End failures, Benatzky's *Meet My Sister* (*Meine Schwester und Ich,* 1931, Dorine) and Eisemann's *Happy Week-End* (*Zsákbamacska,* 1934, Polly Petworthy), but had more success when she moved into management on her own behalf to star in several tours of *The Chocolate Soldier* and two new musicals, the comedy opera *Prudence* (1932, Prudence) and the colorful *Tulip Time* (1935, Angela), which she brought to London's large Alhambra Theatre for a heavy schedule of profitable performances.

She was married initially to actor **Reginald SHARLAND** (b Southend 19 November 1886; d 21 August 1944), who appeared on the musical stage in *The Gay Gordons* (tour 1912, Angus), *The Pearl Girl* (1913, Lord Matlock), *The Cinema Star* (1914, t/o Billy), *Jenny* (1922, Jack Trender), in touring musical comedy and in revue, and alongside his wife in *Poppy* (1924, William Herbert), *Riquette* (1925, Gaston de Revière), *My Son John* (1926, John Reveir) and her Australian shows. He subsequently moved into films. Their son **David CROFT** [David John SHARLAND] (b Sandbanks, Dorset, 7 September 1922), better known as a television writer and producer, wrote lyrics for the musical plays *Star Maker* (1956), *The Pied Piper* (1958) and *Ann Veronica* (1969), which he also directed. A second son, **Peter CROFT** [Peter Reginald SHARLAND] also appeared on the musical stage.

CROISSET, Francis de [WEINER, Frantz] (b Brussels, 28 January 1877; d Neuilly-sur-Seine, 8 November 1937).

A scion of a Belgian family more used to producing painters and sculptors than writers, de Croisset studied law before turning to the writing of verse, journalism and some light-handed theatrical pieces, tinted occasionally with a saleable coloring of scandalousness. Following the death of Gaston de Caillavet, de Croisset joined his former partner, Robert de Flers, to write a number of plays and also the book and lyrics of *Ciboulette,* a sweetly genteel tale which made up into a popular and often-played opérette. In a career largely devoted to the non-musical theatre, and a life centered on travel—usually to India and the east, where he ultimately converted to Buddhism—he also collaborated on the libretto for Massenet's 1905 opera *Chérubin,* and on the 1934 musical version of his first major play success, *Le Bonheur, mesdames!* Adapted to the musical stage with the addition of a pasticcio score of prewar Christiné songs, it followed its Parisian run by being seen in Hungary under the title *Bekbéli boldogsag.*

His highly successful play, *La Passerelle* (w Fred de Grésac), was subsequently made into the Broadway musical *Orange Blossoms* (1922), whilst his 1907 *Paris-New York* (w Emmanuel Arène), musicalized by Jean Bénédict, was played at the Trianon-Lyrique in 1919.

1923 **Ciboulette** (Reynaldo Hahn/w Robert de Flers) Théâtre des Variétés 7 April

1927 **Le Diable à Paris** (Marcel Lattès/w de Flers) Théâtre Marigny 27 November

1934 **Le Bonheur, mesdames!** (Henri Christiné arr/w Albert Willemetz, Fred de Grésac) Théâtre des Bouffes-Parisiens 6 January

Memoir: *La Vie parisienne au theatre* (Grasset, Paris, 1929)

CROOK, John [Francis] (b Marylebone, London, ?1848; d London, 10 November 1922). Longtime conductor for the London and provincial musical stage who, late in his career, found major success as a songwriter for touring musical comedy.

One of the succession of fine conductor/composers who took musical control of Manchester's Prince's Theatre and Theatre Royal in their heyday in the 1870s and 1880s, Crook was locally known, along with Alfred Cellier and Frederic Stanislaus, as one of the ''Manchester three.'' Originally an organist in Norwich, he subsequently became a viola player-cum-pianist in the orchestra at Astley's Theatre, then conductor with the ''Royal National Opera Company'' (1872), with Henry Leslie *Princesse de Trébizonde* opéra-bouffe company (1872–73), the Gaiety Theatre touring company (1873), the Henri Corri Opera Company, at Liverpool's Amphitheatre (1873–74), with Charles Durand's English Opera Company (1874), and at Edinburgh's Theatre Royal (1876–77), before taking over the baton at Manchester in succession to Stanislaus. Like his two predecessors, he successfully composed a full-scale comic opera for production at Captain Bainbridge's theatres and although, like Stanislaus's *The Lancashire Witches* the previous year, *The King's Dragoons* did not reach London, it found success elsewhere in the British provinces and as far afield as Australia and New Zealand.

From his Manchester base, Crook supplied the songs for two long-lived touring shows, the burlesque comic opera *Merry Mignon* and the musical comedy *Larks,* before he caught the attention of the influential librettist and director H B Farnie. Farnie took Crook to London along with the comic opera *Indiana,* which had been produced under his musical direction at Manchester's Comedy Theatre, to oversee the musical side of his new collaborations with Audran and Planquette.

Crook conducted *Indiana* at the Avenue Theatre, interpolating music of his own into Audran's score in the time-honored fashion, and simultaneously organized the musical side of the remaking of Planquette's *Les Voltigeurs de la 32ème* into The *Old Guard* (1887), one of the most durable touring comic operas of the period, of Chassaigne's *Les Noces improvisées* as *Nadgy* (1888) and of Wenzel's *Le Dragon de la reine* as *The Young Recruit* (1892). Largely uncredited, he also composed such music as was necessary to the rewriting of the pieces. When the French connection faded out, the Avenue Theatre returned to burlesque and Crook composed original scores for the old favorite *The Field of the Cloth of Gold* and the Arthur Roberts vehicle *Lancelot the Lovely,* while maintaining his place in the pit for both shows and also for the Tito Mattei comic opera *La Prima Donna* which followed.

He subsequently moved to the Prince of Wales Theatre to conduct the Carl Rosa Light Opera Company's *Captain Thérèse* and the mime *L'Enfant prodigue,* and worked regularly as a conductor in London thereafter, leading the orchestras at the Theatre Royal, Drury Lane, the Adelphi (1895–98), the Lyceum, the Duke of York's and the Vaudeville (1901) before going to Australia to conduct *The Scarlet Feather* for George Musgrove. He was subsequently musical director for Charles Frohman on *The Admirable Crichton* (London and Paris), etc. Latterly, he doubled as a singing teacher and coach from ''John Crook's Musical Studio'' at 69 Berners Street.

Crook continued throughout as a prolific songwriter both for the theatre and the music hall, supplying songs for many stand-up stars—most famously ''The Coster's Serenade'' for Albert Chevalier—and as interpolated numbers for various musicals. He also composed and compiled the songs for several of the earliest and the most outstanding touring musical comedies of the turn of the century. His score for the Methusalemic variety musical *The Lady Slavey* became encrusted with interpolations over 20 years of constant touring, but the success of the songs which he wrote for *The New Barmaid* was such that the bulk of the score remained as originally written throughout its 20-year run around the British provinces and colonies.

Capable of writing a score in the classic comic opera vein, as he had proven with his very first stage piece, Crook found himself instead one of his era's most sucessful composers of popular burlesque and musical comedy songs of his time, a talent witnessed to by his large contribution to *The Lady Slavey* and *The New Barmaid,* the two most successful variety musicals of all time. When that particular craze had passed, however, he continued his conducting career in Britain and in Australia, and turned his hand to a different kind of theatre music, composing on the one hand the original, and for a long time standard, incidental music for Barrie's *Peter Pan* and, alongside songs by Darewski and Kern, for the same author's musical comedy *Rosy Rapture,* and on the other the accompaniment for Henry Lee's world-touring entertainment *Great Men, Past and Present.*

Crook's second and final legal wife (there was at least one de facto in between) was the opéra-bouffe soprano Alice Burville.

1880 **Sage and Onions** (Alfred Maltby) 1 act Prince's Theatre, Manchester 12 April

1880 **The King's Dragoons** (John Wilton Jones) Theatre Royal, Manchester 1 November

1881 **Young Dick Whittington, or Here's the Cat** (comp & arr/ Jones) Theatre Royal, Leicester 14 March

1882 **Merry Mignon, or The Beauty and the Bard** (Jones) Royal Court Theatre, Liverpool 24 April

1883 **Tit Bits** (George Lash Gordon, Fred Stimson) Winter Gardens, Blackpool 25 May

1883 **Columbus the Younger** (w Barrett, Ross/T F Doyle) Theatre Royal, Bradford 13 August

1886 **Larks** (w Meyer Lutz, Frederic Stanislaus, Barrett, Alfred Lee/Jones) Winter Gardens, Southport 22 February

1886 **Robinson Crusoe** (H B Farnie, Robert Reece) Avenue Theatre 23 December

1888 **Quits** (B T Hughes) 1 act Avenue Theatre 1 October

1889 **Lancelot the Lovely** (''Richard Henry'') Avenue Theatre 22 April

1889 **The Houseboat** (H W Williamson) 1 act Avenue Theatre 6 May

1889 **The Field of the Cloth of Gold** (new score/William Brough) Avenue Theatre 24 December

1890 **Venus** (new score/William Yardley, Edward Rose, Augustus Harris) Prince of Wales Theatre, Liverpool 24 March

1891 **Orpheus and P [Eurydice]** (comp & arr/Rose, A Coe) Aquarium, Great Yarmouth 20 July

1893 **Helen of Troy Up-to-Date, or The Statue Shop** (Jones) 1 act Pier Theatre, Folkestone 23 May

1893 **A Modern Don Quixote** (George Dance) Theatre Royal, Nottingham 17 July; Strand Theatre 25 September

1893 **The Lady Slavey** (Dance) Theatre Royal, Northampton 4 September

1894 **Jaunty Jane Shore** (''Richard Henry'') Strand Theatre 2 April

1894 **King Kodak** (w Walter Slaughter, Edward Solomon, Alfred Plumpton, Milton Wellings, Herman Finck, Lionel Monckton/Arthur Branscombe) Terry's Theatre 30 April

1894 **Claude Du-val** (w Monckton/Frederick Bowyer, Arthur Roberts) Prince's Theatre, Bristol 23 July; Prince of Wales Theatre 25 September

1894 **The County Councillor [on the Hop]** (Harry Graham) Pavilion, Ramsgate 20 August; Parkhurst Theater 19 November

1894 **Giddy Miss Carmen** (w Lutz, Sidney Jones, et al/Sidney Lester) Brighton Aquarium 27 August

1894 **All My Eye-Van-Hoe** (w Howard Talbot, Solomon, et al/ Philip Hayman) Trafalgar Square Theatre, 31 October

1895 **One of the Girls** (w Lutz, Jones/Herbert Darnley, J J Dallas) Grand Theatre, Birmingham 9 March

1895 **Qwong Hi** (Fenton Mackay) 1 act Prince's Theatre, Bristol 1 April

1895 **The New Barmaid** (Frederick Bowyer, W E Sprange) Opera House, Southport 1 July

1895 **Newmarket** (w J M Capel, Plumpton, et al/Mrs Frank Taylor, Ernest Boyd-Jones) Opera Comique 22 August

1896 **On the March** (w Solomon, Frederic Clay/Yardley, B C Stephenson, Cecil Clay) Prince of Wales Theatre 22 June

1896 **The Transferred Ghost** (Neville Lynn) 1 act Garrick Theatre 19 November

1897 **Breaking It Off** (Neville Doone, Horace Newte) 1 act Empire, Southend 21 March

1898 **Black and White** (Mark Melford, W Sapte) Prince of Wales Theatre, Southampton 3 January

1898 **Oh! What a Night** (*Eine tolle Nacht*) new score to English version by William Terriss, Clement Scott (Opera House, Wakefield)

1902 **Nana** (w Herbert Simpson, Henry May/Brian Daly) Grand Theatre, Birmingham 5 May

1903 **His Fatal Beauty** (w Jesse Williams, Henry May/H Chance Newton, Herbert Shelley, Walter Parke/Arthur Shirley) Metropole Theatre, Camberwell 27 April

1911 **A Little Japanese Girl** (Loie Fuller) 1 act London Coliseum

1915 **Rosy Rapture, the Pride of the Beauty Chorus** (w Herman Darewski, Jerome Kern/E V Lucas [as F W Mark]/J M Barrie) Duke of York's Theatre 22 March

CROQUEFER, ou Le Dernier des Paladins Opérette-bouffe in 1 act by Adolphe Jaime and Étienne Tréfeu. Music by Jacques Offenbach. Théâtre des Bouffes-Parisiens, Paris, 12 February 1857.

An extravagant bouffonnerie, in the line of the composer's *Ba-ta-clan, Croquefer* brought to the stage the inherited battle between two curious medieval knights. The crazy Croquefer (Pradeau) and his servant Boutefeu (Léonce) are defending the one remaining tower of Croquefer's castle against the remnants of Mousse-à-Mort (Michel), who has lost not only a leg, an arm and an eye but, since theatrical restrictions allowed at the time only four speaking characters per opérette, also his tongue. Croquefer holds his rival's daughter, Fleur de Soufre (Mlle Maréchal), captive and thinks of marrying her, but (just when the two knights have finally got round to coming together on horseback in combat) the lady discovers some Borgia poison in the wine cellar (which has fortunately not been destroyed) and spikes everyone's drinks long enough for them to sing an operatic-tragic burlesque quintet. Finally the maiden weds Croquefer's physically perfect nephew, Ramasse-ta-tête (Tayau), instead and in timely fashion the feud and the opérette are declared over.

The seven musical pieces of the score included a regretful ballad for Croquefer (''Mon château, qu'il était chic''), a duet for the two young folk (''Comment, c'est vous, un gentilhomme?'') which ended up in typically loony fashion with couplets in praise of the Paris Opéra, and a drinking song (''A vos santés, je bois'') for the poisoned wine.

The Bouffes-Parisiens company took *Croquefer* in its repertoire to Britain and to Austria, and it was later played in German at the Theater an der Wien, and in Hungarian (ad Pál Tarnay) in Budapest. Robert Reece proved himself game to translate its surreal incongruities into English, and Thomas German Reed played *The Last of the Paladins* on the program at his Gallery of Illustration without it finding further takers.

UK: St James's Theatre (Fr) 1 July 1857, Gallery of Illustration *The Last of the Paladins* 23 December 1868; Austria: Theater am Franz-Josefs-Kai (Fr) 1 June 1862, Theater an der Wien *Ritter Eisenfrass, der letzte der Paladine* 1 October 1864; Hungary: Budai Népszínház *A vasgyúró* 25 February 1864

Recording: complete (Bourg, TLP)

CROUSE, Russel [McKinley] (b Findlay, Ohio, 20 February 1893; d New York, 3 April 1966).

After an initial career as a newspaperman, Crouse made his first venture into the musical theatre in collaboration with Morrie Ryskind, Oscar Hammerstein and composer Lewis Gensler on the gangstery musical *The Gang's All Here* in 1931. In spite of this show's quick failure, Crouse then gave up his journalistic job and became instead a publicist for the Theater Guild, with the intention of devoting himself to writing for the stage. After an involvement in a Shubert spectacular called *Hold Your Horses,* he found his first success when he was brought in, in an emergency, to help director Howard Lindsay revamp the libretto for Vinton Freedley's production of the Cole Porter musical, *Anything Goes.*

Following the wide and long success of *Anything Goes,* Crouse wrote a series of both plays and musical libretti in collaboration with Lindsay. The plays included the enormously successful *Life with Father* and *State of the Union,* and the musicals began with an attempt to repeat the success of *Anything Goes* with Porter and the earlier show's star, Ethel Merman, in *Red, Hot and Blue!* Fourteen years on, and after a long interval away from the musical stage, the team—this time with Irving Berlin as songwriter—constructed Miss Merman another swingeing, made-to-measure role, as the Washington matron let loose in Ruritanian politics in *Call Me Madam,* but their greatest success came with the libretto which they provided for another lady star, Mary Martin, as the nun-turned-nanny heroine of the last of the Rodgers and Hammerstein musicals, *The Sound of Music* (1959). This show achieved the kind of enduring success won by few, equalling and even passing its authors' earlier triumph with *Life with Father* in its international longevity.

Alongside their trio of major musical hits, Crouse and Lindsay also teamed with Harold Arlen on the Ed Wynn musical *Hooray for What!,* authored a fourth Merman musical, *Happy Hunting,* and a second Irving Berlin one, *Mr President,* with rather less success. In 1956 a musical version of their play *Strip for Action* folded on the road.

1931 **The Gang's All Here** (Lewis Gensler/w Morrie Ryskind/Oscar Hammerstein II) Imperial Theater 18 February

1933 **Hold Your Horses** (Robert Russell Bennett, et al/w Corey Ford) Winter Garden Theater 25 September

1934 **Anything Goes** (Cole Porter/w Lindsay, Bolton, Wodehouse) Alvin Theater 21 November

1936 **Red, Hot and Blue!** (Porter/w Lindsay) Alvin Theater 29 October

1937 **Hooray for What!** (Harold Arlen/E Y Harburg/w Lindsay) Winter Garden Theater 1 December

1950 **Call Me Madam** (Irving Berlin/w Lindsay) Imperial Theater 12 October

1956 **Strip for Action** (Jimmy McHugh/Harold Adamson/w Lindsay) Shubert Theater, New Haven 17 March

1956 **Happy Hunting** (Matt Dubey, Harold Karr/w Lindsay) Majestic Theater 6 December

1959 **The Sound of Music** (Richard Rodgers/Oscar Hammerstein/w Lindsay) Lunt-Fontanne Theater 16 November

1962 **Mr President** (Berlin/w Lindsay) St James Theater 20 October

Biography: Skinner, C Otis: *Life with Lindsay and Crouse* (Houghton Mifflin Co, Boston, 1976)

CRYER, Gretchen (b Dunreith, Ind, 17 October 1935).

Playwright and performer in both musical (*Little Me, 110 in the Shade, 1776*) and straight theatre, Cryer collaborated with composer Nancy Ford on a series of small-scale musical plays for off-Broadway venues in the 1960s and 1970s.

They had some success with their *Now Is the Time for All Good Men,* a piece about an imprisoned draft dodger who can't get over his past (112 performances, also cast member) in 1967, and with *The Last Sweet Days of Isaac,* a three-handed piece which went on from its New York production to be seen in York and, briefly, in London, but they scored a substantial hit with their tale of a 1970s woman with a band and man problems, *I'm Getting My Act Together and Taking It on the Road,* in which Cryer took the central role in the earliest part of the long run. In 1968 the partners provided a musical based on the life of Eleanor Roosevelt to the Williamstown festival. Cryer subsequently quit the theatre, but in 1998 penned a quasi-industrial show, *The American Doll* for a Chicago doll manufacturer.

Cryer and Ford performed their songs both in concert and on record, and a revue of their songs, *Hang on to the Good Times* (Cryer, Ford w Richard Maltby jr), which included material from *Shelter* and *I'm Getting My Act Together,* was mounted at the Manhattan Theatre Club in 1985.

1965 **Booth Is Back in Town** (Arthur Rubinstein/Austin Pendelton) Forum, Lincoln Center, workshop

1967 **Now Is the Time for All Good Men** (aka *Grass Roots*) (Nancy Ford) Theater de Lys 26 September

1970 **The Last Sweet Days of Isaac** (Ford) Eastside Playhouse 26 January

1971 **The Wedding of Iphigenia / Iphigenia in Concert** (Peter Link/w Doug Dyer, Link) Public Theater 16 December

1973 **Shelter** (Ford) John Golden Theater 6 February

1978 **I'm Getting My Act Together and Taking It on the Road** (Ford) Public Theater 14 June; Circle in the Square 16 December

1986 **Eleanor** (*Don't Frighten the Horses*) (Ford) The Extension, Williamstown, Mass 15 August

DIE CSÁRDÁSFÜRSTIN Operette in 3 acts by Leo Stein and Béla Jenbach. Music by Emmerich Kálmán. Johann Strauss-Theater, Vienna, 17 November 1915.

One of the most successful, and certainly the most widely enduring of Kálmán's Operetten, *Die Csárdásfürstin* was nevertheless composed to a very conventional libretto detailing the umpteenth operettic romance between an aristocrat and a cabaret singer. The singer is the Hungarian Sylva Varescu (Mizzi Günther), the aristocrat is Edwin Ronald (Karl Bachmann), the son of the Viennese Fürst Leopold Maria von und zu Lippert-Weylersheim (Max Brod). He promises to wed her, and goes through a form of betrothal, but his family announces his engagement to their niece, the Countess Stasi (Susanne Bachrich). Sylva turns up at a ball at Edwin's home on the arm of Graf Boni Káncsiánu (Josef König), who has pretended to be her husband for the occasion, and Edwin makes a public stand, refusing the alliance with Stasi as Sylva reveals herself as no countess but a common cabaret singer. Ultimately Edwin's father cannot object to his son's choice, for the aging good-time aristocrat Feri von Kerekes (Antal Nyárai) recognizes in the venerable Fürst's wife a chorus girl with whom he had had a fling many years ago. Boni pairs off with Stasi in the all-round happy ending.

The score of the piece was in Kálmán's happiest Austro-Hungarian vein, with Boni and Feri's little march-time memories of "Die Mädis, die Mädis, die Mädis vom Chantant," the pretty Schwalbenduett ("Machen wir's den Schwalben nach") between Edwin and Stasi, and Boni and Stasi's song and dance "Mädel guck!" contrasting with the more thoroughly lyrical moments of Edwin and Sylva's waltz duets, "Tausend kleine Engel singen," "Mädchen gibt es wunderfeine" and "Weisst du es noch?" Sylva's cabaret showpiece "Heia, heia, in den Bergen ist mein Heimatland" and Boni's laughingly rueful "Doch ganz ohne Weiber geht die Chose nicht" were other successful moments in a score that was almost everywhere successful.

Erich Müller's production of *Die Csárdásfürstin* was a great wartime hit in Vienna, running through the whole of 1916 and, as Cordy Millowitsch and Irene Fidler succeeded Frln Günther in the title role, into 1917, closing in May after a first run of 533 performances. It was kept in the repertoire of the Johann Strauss-Theater for a decade thereafter. In Hungary *Csárdáskirálynő* (ad Andor Gábor) scored a similarly great hit at the Király Színház, with Emmi Kosáry and Ernő Király as its romantic leads and Ida Szentgyörgi and Márton Rátkai as the second pair, running for nearly two hundred performances in its first series, passing the 200th performance on 15 May 1917 and the 300th on 29 January 1918, and being given a major revival at the same house in 1927 (16 April). The show also quickly established itself as the most popular of Kálmán's works in Germany.

The English-language versions of the piece did rather less well. In Klaw and Erlanger's American production (ad Guy Bolton, P G Wodehouse) the Hungarian vocalist of the original became *The Riviera Girl,* a vaudeville singer as played by Wilda Bennett, and the show's score was gratified with the addition of such local lollipops as

Plate 87. *Hans-Joachim Müller gets the kind of attention he is used to from the Mädis vom Chantant in the 1985 Lübeck Bühnen der Hansestadt production of* **Die Csárdásfürstin.**

Juliette Day and Sam Hardy's un-Hungarian suggestion "(Let's Build a Little) Bungalow in Quogue." The show lasted 78 performances on Broadway. London's less tastelessly tinkered-with version made its heroine, a little less improbably, into *The Gipsy Princess* (ad Arthur Miller, Arthur Stanley) and producers Claude B Yearsley and Walter de Groot imported a real Hungarian prima donna, Sári Petráss, to play the starring role alongside Germany's M de Jari (Edwin), Phyllis Titmuss (Stasi), Billy Leonard (Boniface), Mark Lester (Feri) and three speciality dancers. They got 204 performances out of runs at the Prince of Wales and the Strand Theatres before the show went into the provinces where it was played rather more and longer than most other shows that had only managed a choppy 200-odd performance life in town. It was seen again, in a brief wartime revival, at the Saville Theatre (14 June 1944) in a scaled-down "modern version" by Miller, but it was not until 1981, when a new adaptation by Nigel Douglas was played at Sadler's Wells Theatre (1 August), with Douglas himself playing Feri alongside Marilyn Hill Smith (Sylva) and Tudor Davies (Boni), that London finally got to see a faithful and effective English *Csárdásfürstin.*

A late first Australian production appeared in 1936, with Maria Elsner as *The Gipsy Princess,* London's Dunstan Hart as Edwin and Charles Heslop and Cecil Kellaway heading the roués in Sydney, and Gladys Moncrieff teaming with Heslop and Don Nicol in Melbourne (Her Majesty's Theatre 17 October 1936). Like its English counterpart it did only fairly, but the piece was given a fresh showing in the 1980s when the Douglas version of the show—still for some reason insisting that its title-heroine was *The Gipsy Princess*—was played in the repertoire of the Australian Opera Company.

Die Csárdásfürstin was very slow to get to France, and it was not until 1930 that *Princesse Czardas* (ad André Mauprey, René Peter, Henri Falk) was mounted at the Trianon-Lyrique with Louise Balazy, Léon Marcel, Paul Darnois, Charles Darthez and Reine Prévost featured. The production was successful enough for the show to be restaged the following year at the much larger Gaîté-Lyrique (7 August 1931) with Maya Silva, Gilbert Nabos and Lamy, and the show went on to prove the most popular of all Kálmán's shows with French audiences. *Princesse Czardas* was seen again in Paris in 1950, with Marta Eggerth and Jan Kiepura featured in the leading roles and, in France, as in Austria, Germany and Hungary, it has remained part of the standard repertoire, one of the few Viennese Operetten regularly produced in provincial French houses to the present day.

A major revival was seen in Berlin, at the Admiralspalast, in 1931, whilst in the postwar years a largely rewritten script was manufactured in Hungary to make a star role out of the part of Edwin's mother as a vehicle for the country's greatest but now aged operett star, Hanna Honthy. In Vienna, the most recent production has been that played at the Volksoper (23 October 1982), in another altered version by Robert Herzl which includes an interpolated Kálmán song, "Heute Nacht hab' ich getraumt von dir," for the previously songless Edwin. Budapest's latest sightings have been at the Arany János Színház (19 March 1993) the Művész Színház (15 August 1994), and the Fővárosi Operettszínház (12 June 1996).

The show has been regularly filmed, firstly in two silent versions with Ida Russka and then Liane Haid in the title role. In 1934 UFA issued simultaneous German (starring Marta Eggerth) and French (starring Meg Lemonnier)-language versions, and the director of these films, Georg Jacoby, put out a further version 14 years later with Marika Rökk, Johann Heesters and Hubert Marischka (Feri) starred. A 1971 film version starred Anna Moffo and René Kollo, and 1970 saw a TV version.

Germany: Neues Operetten-Theater, Hamburg 16 September 1916; Hungary: Király Színház *Csárdáskirálynő* 3 November 1916; USA: New Amsterdam Theater *The Riviera Girl* 24 September 1917; UK: Prince of Wales Theatre, London *The Gipsy Princess* 20 May 1921; France: Théâtre du Trianon-Lyrique *Princesse Czardas* 12 March 1930; Australia: Theatre Royal, Sydney *The Gipsy Princess* 4 July 1936

Films: Emil Leyde 1919, Hans Schwarz 1927, UFA (Ger and Fr) 1934, Georg Jacoby 1951, Mafilm-Unitel (Hung and Ger) aka *The Csardas Queen* 1971

Recordings: complete (EMI, Eurodisc, Denon), complete in French (Chant du Monde), complete in Hungarian (revised version, Qualiton), complete in Russian (Melodiya), selections (Eurodisc, CBS, Saga etc), selection in Italian (EDM), selection in Czech (no label), selection in Swedish (Stora Teatern), etc

CULLUM, John (b Knoxville, Tenn, 2 March 1930). One of Broadway's finest singing actors of the postwar era.

Cullum first appeared musically on Broadway in the role of Sir Dinadan in *Camelot* (1960) but, apart from a brief spell in the road-closed *We Take the Town* (1962, Johnny Sykes), in a cast which ranged from Robert Preston to Romney Brent and the infant Pia Zadora, straight theatre work, including a Laertes to Richard Burton's *Hamlet,* kept him away from the musical theatre until 1965. In that year he succeeded Louis Jourdan in the role of Dr Mark Bruckner in *On a Clear Day You Can See Forever* during the show's tryout, and created the show's title song and "Come Back To Me" in its Broadway production. He subsequently succeeded Richard Kiley and José Ferrer in the title role of *Man of La Mancha* (1967), appeared as the Captain in the 1967 television musicalization of *Androcles and the Lion,* took over the role of Edward Rutledge, which he later played also in the film version, in *1776* in the New York production (1971), and created the role of Christopher Columbus in Meredith Willson's *1491* at the Los Angeles Civic Light Opera.

He appeared at Jones Beach as the King (*The King and I,* 1972) and Billy Bigelow (*Carousel,* 1973) and in Washington as Don Medigua in a revival of *El Capitan,* and in 1975 he starred as Civil War protester Charlie Anderson in the long-running stage musical version of *Shenandoah* at New York's Alvin Theatre. In 1978 he turned in a virtuoso comedy-and-singing performance as the flamboyantly baritone Oscar Jaffee in the operetta burlesque *On the Twentieth Century* which, like the *Shenandoah* performance, earned him a Tony Award as Best Actor in a Musical. He returned briefly to Broadway in a touring revival of *Shenandoah* in 1989, and subsequently succeeded Kevin Colson in the role of George in *Aspects of Love* (1990) and John McMartin as Cap'n Andy in the revived *Show Boat* (1996).

CURLEY McDIMPLE Musical in 2 acts by Mary Boylan and Robert Dahdah. Music and lyrics by Robert Dahdah. Bert Wheeler Theater, New York, 22 November 1967.

An off-Broadway burlesque of Hollywood tot-stars of the 1930s, with special reference to Shirley Temple. Eight-year-old Bayn Johnson as Curley McDimple headed a cast of seven, including Bernadette Peters (Alice) and Paul Cahill (Jimmy), equipped with a list of songs with titles like "Dancing in the Rain," "Love Is the Loveliest Love Song," "Hi de Hi de hi, hi de hi de ho," "Swing-a-ding-a-ling," "I've Got a Little Secret" and, of course, "Curley McDimple" and lashings of tot-n-tap-dancing, through a fine run of 931 performances. During those performances, a role was interpolated into the proceedings for Butterfly McQueen—the maidservant of the cinema's *Gone with the Wind.*

Recording: 2 songs 45rpm (Capitol)

CURZON, Frank (Sir) [DEELEY, Francis Arthur] (b Wavertree, Liverpool, 17 September 1868; d Newmarket, 2 July 1927).

The young Curzon left his job with his father's oil business to become an actor and, after a couple of tentative tries at management at the Marina Theatre, Lowestoft, and with the play *Tom, Dick and Harry* in London (each of which sent him bankrupt) in the early 1890s, and later with several years of touring productions, he finally found success as a producer, in partnership with Charles Hawtrey, with his presentations of the plays *A Message from Mars* and *Lord and Lady Algy.*

In 1900 he took a lease on the Prince of Wales Theatre and presented Marie Tempest as *English Nell,* and the following year he expanded to take in the Royal Strand Theatre as well. He hit the jackpot when he purchased the London rights to the touring musical comedy *A Chinese Honeymoon* from author George Dance and took it from the provinces to this unfashionably half-West and half-East End theatre. *A Chinese Honeymoon* became the first musical in theatre history to run over a thousand consecutive metropolitan performances, making Curzon's fortune, and allowing him to stretch further afield with his future projects in both the musical and straight theatre. He soon became long-term manager of the Prince of Wales Theatre (1901) and at various other times was installed at, or busy subleasing, London's Avenue, Comedy, Wyndham's and Criterion Theatres, Croydon's Grand Theatre and the Coronet, Camden Town, as well.

As a musical comedy producer, he followed up *A Chinese Honeymoon* at the Strand with the successful *Sergeant Brue* (1904) and the very unsuccessful *Miss Wingrove* (1905), then staged the small-scale *The White Chrysanthemum* (1905, Criterion), *The Girl Behind the Counter* (1906) and *Captain Kidd* (1910, Wyndhams), *The Three Kisses* (1907, Apollo) and, after housing several of George Edwardes's musical comedy successes at the Prince of Wales, ran up a series of new musicals of his own there: the winning *Miss Hook of Holland* (1907), *My Mimosa Maid* (1908), Frederick Lonsdale and Sidney Jones's substantial and successful *King of Cadonia* (1908), *Dear Little Denmark* (1909) and *The Balkan Princess* (1910). Each of these Prince of Wales shows starred his wife, former D'Oyly Carte Opera Company soprano Isabel Jay. After his lease on the Prince of Wales Theatre expired in 1915 he ceased to produce musicals, but he remained in the public eye, taking the honors in the 1927 Derby shortly before his death.

1910 **The Balkan Princess** (Paul Rubens/Rubens, Arthur Wimperis/w Frederick Lonsdale) Prince of Wales Theatre 19 February

CUSHING, Catherine Chisholm (b Mount Perry, Ohio, 15 April 1874; d New York, 19 October 1952).

Sometime editor of *Harper's Bazaar,* Miss Cushing was also the author of a number of successful plays including *Kitty McKay* (1913) and a stage version of *Pollyanna* (1916) as well as vehicles for such stars as May Irwin and Billie Burke. She had a less full life in the musical theatre, but she authored a number of adaptations, including two based on her own works, for the musical stage over a period of a half-dozen years.

Her first original Broadway musical, *Glorianna,* set with a score by Rudolf Friml, was based on her own play *Widow by Proxy* (1913) and her second, the much-praised *Lassie,* with a score by Hugo Felix, on her *Kitty McKay.* The third, *Marjolaine,* was a version of Louis Napoleon Parker's equally romantice-centered piece, *Pomander Walk,* and her fourth a musical version of *Uncle Tom's Cabin,* which was peculiarly constructed to allow the variety performers The Duncan Sisters to play practically the whole famous tale by themselves, in the characters of *Topsy and Eva.*

Glorianna had only a fair Broadway run, but proved a much stronger prospect when played in Chicago and on the road by Fritzi Scheff and it held a place on the touring circuits for an extended period. *Lassie,* which was touted as one of the best musical plays for years after a hugely popular run in to Broadway, proved to be more the critic's choice than the public's and, though the producers Paul Salvain and Gil Boag pushed its run to 149 performances at the Nora Bayes Roof-Garden Theater and then in a transfer in an effort to get New Yorkers to agree with the press and patrons of other towns, the piece did not fulfil the more extravagant hopes it had aroused. *Marjolaine* played 136 performances on Broadway and had a brief London production, but whilst the Duncan sisters imitated *Topsy and Eva* for only 159 New York performances, and a short London season dogged by illness, during which one of the sisters was temporarily replaced by Gracie Fields, their show had an exceptionally long and profitable road life.

The author's only effort at a wholly original musical libretto was the 1922 piece *Bibi of the Boulevards* which, attached to a score by Friml, failed on the road, a rare occurrence in a career which seemed otherwise to have a subscription to at least semi-success.

1918 **Glorianna** (Rudolf Friml) Liberty Theater 28 October

1920 **Lassie** (Hugo Felix) Nora Bayes Theater 6 April

1922 **Marjolaine** (Felix/Brian Hooker) Broadhurst Theater 24 January

1922 **Bibi of the Boulevards** (Friml) Majestic Theater, Providence, RI 12 February

1923 **Topsy and Eva** (Rosetta Duncan, Vivian Duncan) Chicago; Harris Theater, New York 23 December 1924

CUTLER, Kate [Ellen Louisa] (b London, 14 August 1864; d London, 14 May 1955). A, and for many the favorite, ingenue of the early musical comedy days in London.

The daughter of a London outfitter, Kate Cutler made her musical-theatre debut as Inez in the English version of Lecocq's *La Princesse des Canaries* (*Pepita*) at the age of 23, and she subsequently appeared with the Carl Rosa Light Opera Company as Malaguena in *Paul Jones* (1889) and in its curtain-raiser *John Smith* (1889, Eliza Smith) before beginning a steady rise to what would be an outstanding career as a leading lady in musical comedy.

She joined the company of George Edwardes's *In Town* as takeover to the lesser role of Lady Gwendoline, but succeeded Florence St John in the star part, then moved up once again from a smaller part (Edytha Alwyn) to replace Decima Moore as the singing ingenue of *A Gaiety Girl* (Rose Brierly). She succeeded Ada Reeve in the title role of *The Shop Girl* (1894) and Isa Bowman as the juvenile lady of *All Abroad* (1895, Connie), and created her own first musical comedy lead role as the ingenue heroine of the Arthur Roberts show *Gentleman Joe* (1895, Mabel Kavanagh). She appeared as Trilby in *A Model Trilby* (1895), created the juvenile lead of *My Girl* (1896, May Mildreth) out of town (Ellaline Terriss took over for the London run), and then began a run of London lead roles through *Monte Carlo* (1896, Dorothy Travers), the long-running *The French Maid* (1897, Suzette), *Little Miss Nobody* (1898, Elsie Crockett) and *L'Amour mouillé* (1899, Catarina), culminating in the ingenue role of Angela in the original production of *Florodora* (''The Fellow Who Might''), a performance which established her firmly at the head of the ingenue field.

She took on the task of starring opposite Arthur Roberts again in a London season of his *HMS Irresponsible* (1901, Victoria Chaffers), took over the soprano lead in *A Chinese Honeymoon* (1901, Soo Soo) when that piece began to be cast up once success became evident, and created one of her most appealing roles as Nora, the befuddled young bride of *The Girl from Kays* (1902, ''Papa'') opposite Willie Edouin. *The Lovebirds* (1904, Grace Rockingham) gave her a rare experience of failure, quickly remedied by a delightful star role as the Baroness Papouche in Edwardes's Gaiety Theatre musical *The Spring Chicken* (1905), before—now an over-forty ingenue—she abandoned the musical stage to begin a second outstanding career as a straight actress. She did, however, make brief returns to the musical stage as gracious older ladies in *That's a Good Girl* (1928, Helen, also on film), *Dear Love* (1929, Mrs Gerard) and *Command Performance* (1933, Queen of Vassau).

Unfailingly graceful, ladylike and charming (''she always looks as if she has a sprig of lilac under her nose'') and the possessor of a pretty light soprano, Miss Cutler was, as a genuine and durable ingenue, the ideal partner for some of the more rumbustious comedy actors of her time.

Plate 88. **Kate Cutler** *as Suzette in* The French Maid.

She was married to director and choreographer Sidney Ellison, the stager of *Florodora,* during the run of that show.

CUVILLIER, Charles [Louis Paul] (b Paris, 24 April 1877; d Paris, 14 February 1955). French tunesmith whose simple, often rather un-French, music illustrated several successful shows during the interregnum between the old days of the opérette and the arrival of the Jazz Age musical comedy.

After some early efforts composing ballet and incidental music, the Conservatoire-trained Cuvillier made his first entry into the light musical theatre in his late twenties with the opérette *Avant-hier matin,* produced at the little Théâtre des Capucines in 1905. This tiny three-handed piece about Adam and Eve in the Garden of Eden—written by the up-and-coming playwright Tristan

Bernard and played only with piano accompaniment—won its composer a certain success. That success was compounded 18 months later by two rather larger-scale works seen on the same stage: *Son p'tit frère,* a comical piece of sexy classical antiquity, and *Afgar, ou Les Loisirs andalous,* which also delved into exotic places—an eastern harem—for the amorous high-jinks of its subject matter. Both pieces had libretti by André Barde, later to be one of the mainstays of postwar musical comedy in France, and they anticipated the more famous *Phi-Phi* and its successors in that genre both in their intimate comedy style and their light and lively music.

Cuvillier supplied other small-scale pieces to the Paris stage, but also had an opérette produced in Buenos Aires and another piece, a fresh scoring of the old Charles Favart opéra-comique *Les Trois Sultanes,* staged at the Opera in Monaco. Neither of these works progressed to a Paris production, and neither did a third ''foreign'' Cuvillier piece, first seen in Germany. The composer's first full-scale, large-stage opérette and his biggest single theatrical success was never seen in France. The 1912 *Der lila Domino* was produced first in Leipzig and there picked up for America, where its Harry and Robert Smith version was played for three months on Broadway. Joseph L Sacks staged this version at London's Empire Theatre where, further adapted by Adair Fitzgerald and Howard Carr, it won an enormous success as a wartime entertainment.

In the wake of this trans-Channel triumph, Cuvillier became all the rage in London, where Cochran's production of his 10-year-old *Afgar,* starring Alice Delysia, at the London Pavilion confirmed him in public favor. A fairly unrecognizable version of *Son p'tit frère* as *The Wild Geese* and a made-for-England musical, *The Sunshine of the World,* fared less well, but a collaboration with Harry Vernon and Clifford Grey on the revue *Johnny Jones* for George Robey and an adaptation of his *La Reine s'amuse,* produced by Grossmith and Laurillard at the Adelphi Theatre as *The Naughty Princess,* both had excellent runs. *La Reine s'amuse,* produced originally at Marseille, finally gave Cuvillier full-sized success in France as well, and provided him with the biggest song hit of his career in the waltz ''Ah! la troublante volupté.''

Flora Bella, another piece produced first in Germany, and later played in the French provinces, was seen for a reasonable run on Broadway, although in a badly botched form, in 1916. However, in spite of the fact that most of his pieces were staged outside France in large auditoriums like London's Empire Theatre and Broadway's New York Theater, Cuvillier continued during and after the war to work at home on the smaller scale which he had been instrumental in making popular. Allied mostly with Barde, he composed the music for several other agreeable and successful musical comedies both for small, and occasionally larger, Paris stages without—in spite of the fact that, as late as 1926, he was announced in the trade papers as preparing an operetta, *Incognito,* in collaboration with Peter Garland and a musical comedy, *Ça ira,* with American intentions—reaching out again to the international scene.

1905 **Avant-hier matin** (Tristan Bernard) Théâtre des Capucines 20 October

1906 **La Carte forcée** (Hugues Delorme) 1 act Palais-Royal 4 October

1907 **Le Flirt de Colombine** (Jacques Redelsperger) Nice, 30 January, Théâtre des Capucines 3 February

1907 **Son p'tit frère** (André Barde) Théâtre des Capucines 10 April

1908 **Les Rendez-vous strasbourgeois** (Romain Coolus) 1 act Comédie-Royale 12 February

1909 **Afgar, ou Les Loisirs andalous** (Barde, Michel Carré fils) Théâtre des Capucines 2 April

1909 **Mam'selle Main-leste** (Miguel Zamaïcos) Scala 1 December

1910 **Les Muscadines** (Barde) Théâtre des Capucines 28 April

1911 **L'Astronome et l'Étoile** (Barde, Bertrand de St-Rémy) Buenos Aires July

1912 **Les Trois Sultanes** (Charles Favart) Opéra de Monte Carlo, Monaco January

1912 **Der lila Domino** (Emmerich von Gatti, Béla Jenbach) Stadttheater, Leipzig 3 February

1912 **Sappho** (Barde, Carré) Théâtre des Capucines 26 February

1912 **L'Initiatrice** (Robert Dieudonné, Delorme) Concert Mayol 6 November

1912 **La Reine s'amuse** (Barde) Théâtre des Variétés, Marseille 31 December; Olympia, Paris 6 February 1913

1913 **Les Adam** revised *Avant-hier matin* Automobile Club 20 February

1913 **Flora Bella** (Barde ad Felix Dörmann) Theater am Gärtnerplatz, Munich 5 September

1917 **La République des vierges** revised *Sappho* Théâtre Édouard VII 6 September

1917 **Judith Courtisane** (Régis Gignoux, Barde) Théâtre Michel 22 December

1918 **La Fausse Ingénue** revised *Les Muscadines* (Carré) Théâtre Fémina 17 March

1918 **Mademoiselle ''Nom d'une pipe''** (Georges Duval) Palais-Royal 16 July

1918 **La Reine joyeuse** revised *La Reine s'amuse* Théâtre Apollo 1 November

1920 **The Sunshine of the World** (Gladys Unger, James Heard) Empire Theatre, London 18 February

1920 **Phryné** (Redelsperger)

1922 **Nonnette** (Barde) Théâtre des Capucines 28 March

1922 **Par amour** (Maurice Magre) Théâtre Fémina 28 October

1922 **Annabella** (Magre) Théâtre Fémina 8 November

1924 **Bob et moi** (Barde, Lucien Meyrargue) Théâtre Michel 6 April

1926 **Qui êtes-vous?** (H Genty, Jouvault, Georges Berr) Monte-Carlo 13 November

1929 **Boulard et ses filles** (Louis Verneuil, Saint-Granier, Jean le Seyeux) Théâtre Marigny 8 November

1930 **Laïs, ou la courtisane amoureuse** revised *Son p'tit frère* (Barde)

1935 **Le Train de 8h 47** (Georges Courteline ad Léo Marchis, Barde) Palais-Royal 22 December

CYRANO DE BERGERAC

Like several other famous and (all too) obvious subjects which or who have been regularly musicalized over the years, Edmond Rostand's tale of the man with the nose and the dose of self-abnegation, *Cyrano de Bergerac* (1897) has repeatedly proved unattractive as a musical theatre prospect.

In 1899 Victor Herbert set a book by Stuart Reed and lyrics by Harry B Smith as a *Cyrano de Bergerac* which was produced by Francis Wilson at the Knickerbocker Theater (18 September) with himself as Cyrano to the Roxane of Lulu Glaser. Since Wilson was star and producer, this version rather shirked the original ending, leaving at least the possibility at the final curtain that Cyrano will get the girl after all. But no one cared very much. Herbert's musical lasted 28 nights on Broadway and even proved a dog on the touring circuits. Wilson tried playing it as a burlesque of itself, but that too failed and the show was put away.

Walter Damrosch composed an operatic *Cyrano* which was mounted forgettably at the Metropolitan Opera House (27 February 1913) with Pasquale Amato and Frances Alda starred, and in 1932, the Shuberts tried another musical piece on the same subject (Charles O Houston, Samuel D Pockrass), mounted at the St Louis Municipal Light Opera under the title *Roxane*. After taking it no further than this tryout first time around, they dragged it out again seven years later, in a revised version with new music by Vernon Duke as, variously, *The White Plume* and *The Vagabond Hero* (Washington 26 December 1939). It still stayed staunchly away from Broadway. A further variant on the theme, a Wright and Forrest *A Song for Cyrano* with a libretto by its Cyrano, José Ferrer, played a regional summer season in 1972.

In 1973, however, at the half-dozenth time of trying, a *Cyrano* did make it to Broadway (Michael J Lewis/ Anthony Burgess, Broadway Theater 13 May), with Christopher Plummer starred as the gloomed Gascon and Leigh Beery as his Roxane. It ran just 49 performances. However it resurfaced for another showing in another language when it was mounted in Karlsruhe, Germany, in 1986 (25 October).

Music-hall managers and stars Weber and Fields had, perhaps, more success than any of these serious and semi-serious Cyranos when they presented a musical burlesque of the original Rostand play at their celebrated Broadway music hall. Staged as *Cyranose de Bric-a-Brac* (3 November 1898) it featured the low comical Lew Fields as a Dutch-accented Gascon. Koster and Bial's replied with a *Sir Andy de Bootjack.*

Away from America there has been less interest in making music with de Bergerac, but slightly more in the way of positive results. Lecocq's *Ninette,* even though its title might not have suggested the fact, began its pre-production life as a serious variant on the *Cyrano* tale, intended for the Opéra-Comique. Cyrano himself, as portrayed by Albert Piccaluga, was still in the story when *Ninette* appeared at the Bouffes-Parisiennes (28 February 1896) but he had been displaced insofar as the title was concerned by the historical Ninon de l'Enclos. Clairville's libretto had the lady measuring wits with the nasal Gascon and coming out the better, and she did it for 107 Parisian nights. Henri Cain prepared another French text on the subject which, adapted into Italian, was made into an opera, *Cyrano,* composed by Franco Alfano. It went on from Rome's Teatro Reale (22 January 1936) to further performances in Buenos Aires and at Paris's Opéra-Comique. As in America, burlesques of Rostand were also in evidence in Paris. The Eldorado was responsible for a *Cyrau-nez de Blairgérac* (12 February 1898) and in the Variétés revue *La Tour du Bois* a royal cast including Baron, Cooper, Guy, Germaine Gallois and Ève Lavallière performed a *Cyrano* burlesque with music by Serpette.

Central Europe had a go at Rostand too. A *Cyrano de Bergerac* (Paraschkev Hadijev/Banko Banev) was produced in Bulgaria in 1912 and in 1977 a Czech rock opera (*Cyrano aus der Vorstadt,* Marian Varga/Kamil Peteraj, Jan Strasser, Alta Vasova) presented a *Your Own Thing* type of *Cyrano* with the hero as a member of a pop band, Roxane as the vocalist, and Christian the front singer for whom Cyrano writes the songs. The ''Cyrano'' connection was a meagre one, which may have helped the piece to its success in Bratislava.

London has remained without a musical *Cyrano,* but not for lack of trying. Producers' desks have received a number of variations on his theme over the years, but only once has anyone seen almost fit to put one on the stage. Written, composed and co-produced (w Harry Lowe) by American tenor Lyn (Leonard) Ceeley, who starred himself as Cyrano to the Roxane of soprano Lorraine Bridges, it was ultimately entitled not Cyrano, as its original advertisements had billed it, but *Gardenia Lady* (Leeds 11 August 1947) and Mr Ceeley switched to playing René the Lionheart of Bordeaux instead of Cyrano de Bergerac at the last minute. Nell Gwynn and King Charles also got into the evening's action. The owner of the program I have wrote across it in purple ink "It stank!"

Unbelieveably, 1992 saw yet another, Dutch *Cyrano* (Ad van Dijk/Koen van Dijk Stadsschouwburg, Amsterdam 17 September) join the list. Bill van Dijk (Cyrano), Ryan van Akker (Roxane) and Danny de Munk (Christian) featured in a production mounted on a scale in keeping with its international ambitions, and the show (ad Peter Reeves) was subsequently taken with much fanfare to Broadway (Neil Simon Theater 21 November 1993). Van Dijk was again Cyrano, and the losses whirled frighteningly around the 12 million dollar mark after 137 doggedly disastrous performances. It was subsequently given in Germany (ad Curt Werner, 28 July 1999). But in spite of the jinx attached to musical Cyranos, still they came, in 1992 saw Cyrano de Bergerac back yet again on the French musical stage. This time, however, the hero was not romancing a Roxane, but facing up to Molière in a "cyranopéra" (Louis Dunoyer de Segonzac /Jean-Marie Lecocq) based on its hero's *L'autre monde.* The piece, entitled *Les Empires de la lune* was produced first at Amiens, and subsequently seen at Paris's Théâtre Déjazet (3 February 1995). And, not to be left out of the unoriginality, in the sad era of the copycat musical, both Denmark and Australia weighed in with a *Cyrano* as well. The Danish work (Sebastian [Knud Christiansen]/ Pierre Westerdahl, Flemming Enevold) was mounted at Copenhagen's Gladsaxe Theater and subsequently in a German version in Berlin (Theater des Westens 11 September 1994 53 performances), but Hal Shaper and David Reeves' Australian piece limited itself to a 1994 concert tour and a recording.

The most recent *Cyrano de Bergerac* musical seems to be that produced at the Saarbucken Staatstheater (Marc Schubring/Wolfgang Adenberg) in 1995 (October 22). Is it too much to hope that it will be the last?

Recordings: 1973 original cast (AM), 1992 Dutch version (Indisc), Australian version (Prestige), Danish version (Polydor)

CZIBULKA, Alfons (b Szépesváralj [ie, Spisská Nová Ves, Slovakia], 14 May 1842; d Vienna, 27 October 1894). Hungarian-born composer whose earliest theatre works marked him out as one of the hopes of the Viennese Operette.

Czibulka made his earliest mark in the music world as a teenaged concert pianist, but he subsequently worked in Linz, Innsbruck, and Trieste, at Pest's Nemzeti Színház, and—mostly—in Vienna, as a conductor and a military bandmaster. He also composed a considerable amount of dance music, both original and in the form of arrangements of theatre melodies by other composers, amongst which his potpourris of the works of Sullivan proved particularly popular. In the last decade of his life he also turned out the scores for several Operetten produced variously in Germany and at Vienna's Theater an der Wien and Carltheater, where he was for a period musical director. He subsequently became a military bandmaster with an Austro-Hungarian Infantry Regiment.

His two most successful Operetten, the (virtually) initial *Pfingsten in Florenz* and *Der Glücksritter,* produced in Vienna, were both played subsequently in Hungary (*Pünkösd Flórenzben, A szerencselovag*) and in Germany, and were also seen in English-language versions on Broadway, under the titles of *Amorita* and *The May Queen* (1889), respectively. His later works were less successful, and his death in his early fifties intervened before the promise of his first works was thoroughly fulfilled.

1860 **'S Lorle** (*Ein Berliner im Schwarzwalde*) Pressburg 30 July

1884 **Pfingsten in Florenz** (Richard Genée, Julius Riegen) Theater an der Wien 20 December

1885 **Der Jagdjunker [der Kaiserin]** (Genée, F Zell) Walhalla Theater, Berlin 3 December; revised version Carltheater 20 March 1886

1887 **Der Glücksritter** (Genée, Wilhelm Mannstädt, Bruno Zappert) Carltheater 22 December

1888 **Gil Blas von Santillana** (Zell, Moritz West) Carl-Schultze-Theater, Hamburg 23 November

1892 **Der Bajazzo** (Victor Léon, Heinrich von Waldberg) Theater an der Wien 7 December

1893 **Monsieur Hannibal** (Mannstädt, Karl Dreher) Theater im Gärtnerplatz, Munich 5 September

D

THE DAIRYMAIDS Farcical musical play in 2 acts by Alexander M Thompson and Robert Courtneidge. Lyrics by Paul Rubens and Arthur Wimperis. Music by Paul Rubens and Frank Tours. Apollo Theatre, London, 14 April 1906.

Robert Courtneidge's second West-End venture was a largely low comical musical in which a couple of sailors win a couple of upper-class lasses who are playing at being dairymaids on a model farm. In the final act the girls (Carrie Moore, Agnes Fraser) were back at school, which allowed the boys (former Savoy comic Walter Passmore, Horace Land and acrobatic newcomer Dan Rolyat as their servant) to get dressed up as schoolgirls to follow them. Courtneidge's *Blue Moon* singing star Florence Smithson was pasted in to the story as a more demure love interest and was allotted the least flimsy of the songs, whilst longtime favorite Phyllis Broughton played the aristocratic mistress of the farm.

The show proved highly successful, partly due to its fine cast and partly to a novel item in the shape of a gymnasium routine in which Carrie Moore and four little chorines wielded tiny dumbbells to the strains of the show's hit song, "The Sandow Girl." A catty number about ladies' clubs called "Dover Street" for Passmore and the tale of "The Sea Serpent," as comically put over by Rolyat and the girls, proved other popular moments of musical fun. The show ran eight months before coming off to allow the cast to go to fulfill their Christmas pantomime engagements, but it was subsequently toured, with Phyllis Dare featured and equipped with some newly tailored Rubens songs, and also revived ("several new numbers . . . more or less rewritten") in London in 1908 (Queen's Theatre 5 May) with Rolyat and Misses Smithson and Broughton repeating alongside Miss Dare, and again in 1915 (Aldwych Theatre 22 May) in an 18-performance season by touring manager J Bannister Howard.

Charles Frohman mounted *The Dairymaids* on Broadway, with Huntley Wright in the role created by Rolyat and Julia Sanderson heading the Sandow girls for a run of 86 performances, Australia got a J C Williamson production, with London's Fanny Dango wielding the dumbbells, and gave it a fine welcome, and Frank Wheeler took the show around South African cities in his repertoire from 1907 onwards, whilst three companies continued through the British provinces in 1908 until newer shows came along to squeeze this most unoriginal and lightweight, but apparently pleasing, of entertainments out.

USA: Criterion Theater 26 August 1907; Australia: Her Majesty's Theatre, Melbourne 7 September 1907

DALE, Jim [SMITH, James] (b Rothwell, Northants, 15 August 1935).

After early work as a variety comedian, Dale began a stage career in his late twenties. He shot quickly up through six years of theatre and film work, ranging from Shakespearean roles (Autolycus, Bottom, Gobbo, Petruchio) and a notable Scapino (Young Vic, 1970), to play the gormless young men of the *Carry On* film series, before he made his musical theatre debut in the title role of Denry Machin in the musical version of Arnold Bennett's *The Card* (1973).

He later moved to America and there created the athletic title role in the musical *Barnum* (1980, Tony Award, "The Colors of My Life," "The Prince of Humbug"), going on to further musical theatre appearances when he succeeded Robert Lindsay as Bill Snibson in Broadway's *Me and My Girl,* later taking the piece on tour, and playing Dr Pangloss/Voltaire in the 1997 Broadway remounting of *Candide.* He also appeared at the London Palladium in 1997, succeeding for a period to the role of Fagin in *Oliver.*

DALY, [John] Augustin (b Plymouth, NC, 20 July 1838; d Paris, 7 June 1899).

One of the most celebrated drama producers of the American theatre during the last 30 years of the 19th century, Daly—who expected an all-round training and unquestioned versatility from his contract actors—on several occasions staged musical pieces as part of his program at the New York theatre named for him (1879 ssq). Although star specialist musical players were brought in to play especially sung roles in some pieces, the result of this policy was that, in the best tradition of the repertory theatre, a performer such as the rising Ada Rehan appeared in supporting roles in musical shows between her dramatic performances.

In the earlier part of his career Daly was responsible for the too-extravagant-to-make-a-profit New York staging of Offenbach's *Le Roi Carotte,* produced with an outstanding cast headed by John Brougham, Mrs John Wood, Emma Howson and Rose Hersee, but his Daly's Theater productions tended to be proven musical comedies selected from amongst London's and George Edwardes's most surefire hits (*A Gaiety Girl, The Geisha, The Circus Girl, A Runaway Girl*). He did however occasionally mount both homemade burlesque (*Cinderella at School*) and German Operette (the spectacular *Zanina*) at his flagship theatre during his career.

In the early 1890s Daly was involved, in collaboration with Edwardes, in the construction in London's Leicester Square of what was originally to have been the Agnes Huntington Theatre, the original idea being that the house would be shared between Daly's drama performances and Edwardes's musical ones. However, Daly soon gave up his British trips and, in consequence, the theatre, which had ultimately been named after him rather than the hard-to-hold Miss Huntington, became the base for the important and influential series of musical plays, headed by *The Geisha,* which Edwardes produced there. This theatre, with his name always attached (and with he and his estate punctiliously collecting their financial dues from his interest in it), was later the home of many other musical hits, notably the wartime *The Maid of the Mountains,* but it was destroyed in 1937 to allow the building of a particularly unattractive cinema.

A prolific and proud adaptor of mostly Continental plays (the original author's name was inclined to vanish from the bills) for his theatre and company, Daly also had an adaptory hand in the American version of *Le Roi Carotte* and, apparently, of the highly successful *The Royal Middy* (*Der Seekadett*), a text initially credited to Fred Williams.

1872 **Le Roi Carotte** American version (Grand Opera House)

Biographies: Daly, J F: *The Life of Augustin Daly* (Macmillan, New York, 1917), Felheim, M: *The Theater of Augustin Daly* (Harvard University Press, Cambridge, Mass, 1956)

DALY, Dan (b Boston, ?1858; d New York, 26 March 1904). A gangling, deadpan comic who became a star in turn-of-the-century Broadway musicals.

Daly began his career as an acrobat in circuses and variety, but soon switched to the theatre where he made the most famous part of his career. He appeared in 1880—billed as Master Danny Daly—with Corinne's company, playing Dandino in the extravaganza *The Magic Slipper* (brother Bobbie was Baron Balderdash), then moved on to play in the comedy *Mrs Partington* (1881, Ike), and for four years around the country with his brothers, Thomas A, William J and Robert J and Thomas's wife Lizzie Derious Daly in a ''salmagundi of amusing nonsense'' written by Thomas and called *Vacation, or Harvard vs Yale* (Opera House, New Haven 14 December 1883). The ''Daly Brothers'' subsequently played three seasons in *Vacation*'s successor, the farcical, circussy *Upside Down* (Amsterdam, NY 27 October 1887, Will Getthere). He took supporting roles—as Daniel Daly—in the tryout of *Overlook* (1890) with Anna Boyd, in *The City Directory* (1891, John Smith) and *The Tourists* (1891) and larger ones in the variety musicals *A Society Fad* (1892, Wiggins), *The Golden Wedding* (1893, Sir Thomas Topack) and Russell's Comedians's *About Town* (1894, Rube Hayes), the Boston musicals *Davy Jones* (1894, Captain Shay), and *Prince Pro Tem* (1894, Justice), George Lederer's slightly more vertebrate *The Twentieth Century Girl* (1895) and the Casino revue *The Merry World* (1895, De Neipperg) before winning a leading part in a short-lived Broadway version of *Niniche* called *The Merry Countess* (1895, Vicomte de Beaupersil).

He toured as the star of *After the Ball* (1895–96), played the leading comic role of the bailiff-turned-butler, Roberts, in the American rewrite of *The Lady Slavey* (1896, William Endymion Sykes) and Willie Badboy in *The Whirl of the Town* (1897) at the Casino Theater and stayed with the Casino company for his most famous creation—Ichabod Bronson, the two-faced President of the Young Men's Rescue League and Anti-Cigarette Society of Cohoes, in the Casino Theater's *The Belle of New York.* He played this role first in New York, and then in London, where his mixture of lugubrious comedy and acrobatic dancing was found highly original and hugely enjoyable, and where his status as a star comic was thoroughly confirmed.

He followed up playing the goofy Duke of Paty de Clam in another Casino show, *The Rounders* (1899, a version of the Paris hit *Les Fêtards*), and as Baron Chartreuse in another, and less successful, Continental adaptation, *The Cadet Girl* (1900), at the Herald Square Theater and appeared in *The Girl from Up There* (1900, t/o), a calculated but barely successful attempt to create another international success like *The Belle of New York* which featured a number of the earlier show's stars, headed by the Belle of New York, Edna May, herself. He subsequently had top-billing as a penniless American in Paris, Upson Downes, in the Herald Square's *The New Yorkers*

(1901), in *The New Clown* (1902) and in the title role of an attempt to put George Hobart's tale of *John Henry* (1903) on the stage.

This last-named show was, however, his final musical comedy appearance, as he thereafter appeared only in variety, where he could earn the $1,000 per week which a book show could not come up with, before a premature death at a reported age of anywhere between 40 and 45, one week after the passing of his wife.

William J Daly (b Boston, 1856; d Revere, Mass, 4 April 1912) in November 1883 swapped acrobatics for a seat in the Massachussets legislature, and ''Bobbie'' J Daly (b Boston 25 January 1864) withdrew from the *Vacation* troupe at an early age through illness and died at Charlestown, Mass, in 1889 (10 January). Two sisters, Lucy Daly and Margaret Daly Vokes, toured regularly in farce comedy with their husbands, the well-known [Harry] Vokes and [''Happy''] Ward team, and played in the original Broadway production of *A Trip to Chinatown.*

DAM, H[enry] J[ackson] W[ells] (b San Francisco, c1859; d Havana, Cuba, 26 April 1906).

For reasons which are now lost in time, George Edwardes commissioned the libretto of his initial Gaiety Theatre ''musical comedy'' not from one of his usual writers, nor from the men who had just given him such a fine success with *A Gaiety Girl,* but from the little-known journalist and playwright H J W Dam, formerly of San Francisco and New York (*New York Times*) but now based in London where, having been initially London rep for the *New York Herald,* he was now working on the *Star* newspaper. Dam's principal theatre credits to that time had been the plays *The Silver Shell* and *Diamond Deane* and the readaptation of Brandon Thomas's adaptation of the text to Edward Jakobowski's *The Queen of Brilliants* (*Die Brillanten-Königin*) for Abbey and Grau's American production. He had, however, nearly a decade earlier, when ''secretary to Governor Stoneman and a young man of some thirty years,'' committed the libretto to Fred Eustis's music for a disastrous ''satirical opera'' called *Mizpah* (''as silly a thing as ever found its way on to a stage''), produced by ''high-roller'' Colonel Frank A Burr and played in Philadelphia and Chicago (Hooley's Opera House 26 December 1886) before collapsing—but doubtless Edwardes did not know about that.

For *The Shop Girl,* Dam accomplished a fair imitation of the style of Owen Hall's *A Gaiety Girl* book and also provided the lyrics to some of the show's songs, but in spite of the success of the new musical comedy he did not work again at the Gaiety. In a discreet subsequent career, he provided a farcical book for Arthur Roberts's semi-successful *The White Silk Dress* and adapted Clérice's Portugese hit *O Moliero d'Alcala* for Henry Lowenfeld, without confirming his undoubtedly successful entry into the musical theatre with *The Shop Girl.* He finished his life editing a Sunday supplement in New York.

Dam's short story, *The Transmogrification of Dan,* was used as source material for the musical comedy *The Heir to Hoorah,* and Dam sued for royalties. He died before the case came to judgment, but his widow continued the fight and in 1910, in a precedent-setting case (which could surely have been called upon many a time in the 1990s), she won the right to ''the whole profits from the play.''

1886 **Mizpah** (Fred J Eustis) Chestnut Street Theater, Philadelphia 21 December

1894 **The Queen of Brilliants** (*Die Brillanten-Königin*) American adaptation of English version (Abbey's Theater, New York)

1894 **The Shop Girl** (Ivan Caryll/w Adrian Ross) Gaiety Theatre 24 November

1896 **The White Silk Dress** (Alick McLean, Reginald Somerville, George Byng) Prince of Wales Theatre 3 October

1899 **The Coquette** (*O Moliero d'Alcala*) English version (Prince of Wales Theatre)

LA DAME EN DÉCOLLETÉ Opérette in 2 acts by Yves Mirande and Lucien Boyer. Music by Maurice Yvain. Théâtre des Bouffes-Parisiens, Paris, 22 December 1923.

Following his great successes with *Ta bouche, Là-haut,* et al, Yvain attempted, in *La Dame en décolleté,* to compose a score which included a little more romantic and lyric music to put alongside the series of bright, jazzy melodies which had helped make the earlier pieces such great favorites. Edmond Tirmont (Georges du Vélin) and Marthe Davelli (Lucette de Verneuil), both pensionnaires of the Opéra-Comique, took the romantic roles of a couple of fêtards preparing to renounce their naughty ways for true love and marriage, alongside star comedian Dranem, in the role of the clerk, Girodot, who loses the remnants of the bride's inheritance at baccarat and sets in train the events which hold up the wedding until the end of the evening. In spite of some lovely lyrical moments provided by the leading singers, it was Dranem who scored the song hit of the evening with his comical ''Je n'ai pas pu.'' The Paris public soon made it clear that they preferred the mixture as before and Yvain's other musical of the season, the lively and less musically substantial *Gosse de riche,* had a longer life than the two months *La Dame en décolleté* spent in Paris before it set out on a rather more extended provincial life.

DIE DAME IN ROT Operette in 3 acts by Julius Brammer and Alfred Grünwald. Music by Robert Winterberg. Theater des Westens, Berlin, 16 September 1911.

Brammer and Grünwald's libretto for the Operette *Die Dame in Rot* went near to taking on *Bob herceg* for the most amusing (from a British point of view) attempt at a British-Ruritanian tale. The first act took place in the London Royal Academy, the director of which is called Mister Lolipop, Marie Ottman played the lovely Miss Pearly Queensland, cousin to Lord Snobly Middletown, and other characters rejoiced in the names of Lord Wonderfull, Kitty Weed and Lord Fred of Cookstown.

In fact, the tale of the show could have been set anywhere, for it dealt simply with a *Miss Helyett* / *The Beauty Spot* type of a slightly sexy scandal. The artist Felix Werndorff glimpsed the lovely socialite Miss Queensland skinny-dipping and went home and painted the scene. When the painting was exhibited at the Royal Academy the unwitting model was recognized and gossip ran rife. Her betrothal to Lord Snobly was broken off, the picture slashed, and by the final curtain Pearly is, naturally, ready to become not Lady Snobly but Mrs Artist.

Susanne Bachrich (Kitty), Albert Kutzner, Gustav Matzner and Franz Gross (as a Japanese count called Dr Graf Ikamo Hitamaro) supported the star through an encouraging run at the Theater des Westens (78 performances), after which *Die Dame in Rot* went on from Berlin to the German provinces, but apparently not to Vienna. This omission didn't stop it, of course, from finding its way to Budapest in 1915 (ad Zsolt Harsányi) and, with the rage for Continental Operette still burning beyond the Atlantic, to America. It got off to a first start in America in 1915, under the management of E C Herndon and music publisher Louis Dreyfus, and was produced at Atlantic City with Dreyfus's wife, the Anglo-German singer Valli Valli, in the starring role of Sylvia Stafford and Glenn Hall as the artist, in an Anne Caldwell version which swapped the comical and demi-Australian names for staunchly suitable ones. The show was gratified with excellent notices as it ran through Toronto, Philadelphia and Chicago, but the producing partners fell out when their show proved a big Chicago hit, and *The Lady in Red* ended up being taken off in mid-career.

Four years later, however, the orphaned show resurfaced and, after passing through several pairs of hands, was put out again under the management of John P Slocum. Slocum got rid of much of the score, trying to ensure success by pumping up the remnants of the original music with songs from a veritable hit parade of the world's best show composers: Walter Donaldson (China Dragon Blues, "Play Me That Tune"), Henri Christiné ("Lulu Lavinia"), Leo Fall ("Visions of the Fireside"), George Gershwin ("Something about Love"), Jean Gilbert ("Mr Love Will Catch You Yet") and Jerome Kern ("Where is the Girl for Me?"), as well as the more modest English music-hall songwriters George Arthurs and Worton David ("Cupid Never Wrote the Alphabet") and Otto Motzan. Adele Rowland was *The Lady in Red* this time, once again the pre-Broadway reviews were fine, but when the show finally reached New York 48 performances proved to be its metropolitan lot.

USA: Atlantic City *The Lady in Red* 19 April 1915, Lyric Theater, New York *The Lady in Red* 12 May 1919; Hungary: Budai Színkör *A pirosruhás hölgy* 3 July 1915

DAMES AT SEA New '30s musical in 2 acts by Robin Miller and George Haimsohn. Music by Jim Wise. Bouwerie Lane Theater, New York, 20 December 1968.

A very small-scale, six-handed burlesque musical which, with a delightful cheek, took up the challenge of giving its own affectionate version of the movie musicals of the 1930s, with their vast casts and spectacular production values. Little Ruby from Centerville, USA, finds fame, fortune and the juvenile man amongst a bevy of showbiz and Hollywood clichés and a scoreful of tongue-in-cheek songs which range from a one-handed, tap-danced, ticker-tape-draped paean to "Wall Street," a torch song of desperate proportions to "That Mister Man of Mine" and a swoopingly comical do-you-remembering Beguine ("Do you remember . . . Pen-sa-co-o-o-la?"), to the little heroine's breathless longing for "The Sailor of My Dreams" and her superdejected admission that it is "Raining in My Heart."

Originally staged in a one-act version in Greenwich Village's Café Cino through the summer of 1966, subtitled *Golddiggers Afloat,* the piece was subsequently upped to two acts and produced at off-off-Broadway's Bouwerie Lane Theater with Bernadette Peters (Ruby) and David Christmas (Dick) repeating their recreations of the Keeler and Powell–types which the names of their characters indicated. It ran there, and subsequently at the Lucille Lortel Theater, for 575 performances, and then saw out a third summer at Plaza Nine in the Plaza Hotel. From New York, it went forth to be seen in London and Paris with Sheila White featured as Ruby first in English and then in French, and with Joyce Blair and Nicole Croisille as the English and the French Mona, and was seen in a Harry Miller production at the Playbox Theatres in Sydney and Melbourne (11 March 1970) with Nancye Hayes as ingenue.

Thanks to its comical charms and its economical size, *Dames at Sea* has become a perennial favorite with provincial and touring companies with limited resources, playing from São Paolo to Denmark, Finland and Japan, and it has even occasionally reventured near to big-time venues. A production from Sarasota, Florida was brought to New York for a second round in 1985 and played at off-Broadway's Lamb's Theater (12 June) for 278 performances with Donna Kane (Ruby) and George Dvorsky (Dick) in the widest-eyed roles, and London got a second glimpse in 1996 when the show reappeared for a fortnight's season at the Ambassador's Theatre (8 June) as part of the Covent Garden Festival.

Dames at Sea was also televised by NBC in 1971 with Ann-Margret, Ann Miller and Dick Shawn amongst the cast.

UK: Duchess Theatre 27 August 1969; Australia: Playbox Theatre, Sydney 10 September 1969; France: Théâtre des Nouveautés *Les p'tites femmes de Broadway* 1969; Germany: Sandkorn Theater, Karlsruhe *Girls an Bord* 21 October 1994

Recordings: off-Broadway cast (Columbia), London cast (CBS), UK tour cast (TER), TV cast (private label)

DAMN YANKEES Musical in 2 acts by George Abbott and Douglass Wallop based on Wallop's novel *The Year the Yankees Lost the Pennant.* Music and lyrics by Richard Adler and Jerry Ross. 46th Street Theater, New York, 5 May 1955.

The initial success scored by the Adler/Ross team with *The Pajama Game* was followed by a second hit, again shared with author Abbott (this time also director) and choreographer Bob Fosse, in this everyday American version of the Faust legend in which—with more than a reminiscent touch of the Vebers' 1926 French show *L'Homme qui vendit son âme au Diable*—Joe Hardy (Stephen Douglass) sells his soul to the devil (Ray Walston) in order to see his favorite team win baseball's top honors. Metamorphosed from paunchy middle-age into the exciting, home run–hitting ''Shoeless Joe from Hannibal, Mo,'' Joe finds that glory and the pennant are not everything in the face of separation from his wife (Shannon Bolin), a nosily investigative reporter (Rae Allen) determined to question his origins, and the prospect of eternal hellfire.

The show was a splendid mixture of a warm and funny libretto and a fine popular score, from which the baseball players' ingenuous barbershop assertion that all you need to win a game is ''Heart'' (as opposed to talent and training), and ''Whatever Lola Wants,'' the self-confidently sexy tango sung by the devil's mantrap assistant (Gwen Verdon), both became standards. *Damn Yankees* was shot through with an appealingly human (when it wasn't superhuman) quality, which had been much less evident in the team's earlier show, and which helped assure it a grand run of 1,019 performances on Broadway followed by a long touring life.

Walston had a fine role as the plausibly devilish Applegate, thwarted of his rightful prey, but Gwen Verdon as the luscious Lola, who changes sides at the vital moment, was lifted into the star category by her performance, a performance highlighted by her hit song and her performance of Fosse's comedy mambo ''Who's Got the Pain?''

A fine London season starred Ivor Emmanuel, Elizabeth Seal (a quick replacement for Belita) and Bill Kerr for 258 performances at the vast London Coliseum, whilst Australia saw Barbara Newman (Lola), Alton Harvey (Applegate) and Warren Brown (Joe) featured through three and a half months in Melbourne prior to a season at the Sydney's Empire Theatre (17 June 1958).

Damn Yankees was subsequently made into a film in which Miss Verdon and Walston starred alongside Hollywood starlet Tab Hunter as Joe, whilst a television version was broadcast in 1967 with Phil Silvers and Lee Remick in the principal roles.

In the 1970s the show was given a German production, happily localized by Franklin Fanning so that it referred to the football team of the city which produced it instead of the (to non-Americans the world over) utterly incomprehensible game of baseball.

The show was brought back in a major Broadway revival in 1994 (Marquis Theater 3 March) with Jarrod Emmick (Joe), Victor Garber (Applegate) and Bebe Neuwirth (Lola) featured. It was withdrawn after nine months, but reopened 12 March 1995 with old-time screen comedy star Jerry Lewis starring in a personalized version of the role of Applegate. It played a further five months, bringing the revival's tally to 533 performances, before Lewis took the production first on the road and then to London (Adelphi Theatre 4 June 1997). When its pull proved insufficient, a proposed move and recast was abandoned and *Damn Yankees* left the West End after just two months. The show was also given a revival in Berlin with a cast led by Cusch Jung and Helmut Baumann.

UK: London Coliseum 28 March 1957; Australia: Her Majesty's Theatre, Melbourne 1 February 1958; Germany: Oberhausen *Damn Yankees, oder Das Jahr in dem rot-weiss Oberhausen Deutscher Meister wird* 19 May 1979, Theater des Westens *Damn Yankees (Im Stadion ist der Teufel los!)* 10 March 1995

Recordings: original cast (RCA Victor), revival cast 1994 (Mercury), film soundtrack (RCA), etc

DANCE, George (Sir) (b St Mary, Nottingham, 14 October 1857; d London, 22 October 1932). Versatile librettist and lyricist who wrote the texts for several major hits in the Victorian musical theatre before moving on to a highly successful career as a touring manager.

The son of a Nottingham pipe-manufacturer, the teenaged Dance spent the first three years of his working life in his father's office whilst at the same time turning his hand to writing music-hall and drawing-room comedy songs with some considerable success (''Girls Are the

Ruin of Man,'' ''His Lordship Winked at the Counsel,'' ''English as She Is Spoke'' for Charles Coburn, Alice Atherton's ''Laughing Song''). After his father's death, he renounced the pipe business to become a journalist and theatrical correspondent, and he entered the musical theatre as a writer in 1886, when he compiled an unsolicited but made-to-measure burlesque about Oliver Cromwell, equipped with a mixture of old and new music, for the touring company of Willie Edouin and his wife Alice Atherton. Edouin accepted the piece by return mail and *Oliver Grumble* proved a happy enough vehicle for the Edouins in the provinces to be given a short London season, getting bumped from their repertoire only because the Mark Melford comedy *Turned Up,* produced by the company in the same season, proved a major hit.

Dance penned the pantomime for the Theatre Royal, Nottingham in 1886 (*Aladdin, or The Wonderful Lamp,* music Alfred R Watson) and for several years thereafter, and supplied another burlesque, *Columbus,* to the aging Lydia Thompson for her last US tour, but it was five years before he was heard of again in the London musical theatre, and this time under very different circumstances—as the author of a comic opera destined for the Savoy Theatre in the interregnum occasioned by the first breakup between Carte and Gilbert. *The Nautch Girl,* set to music by Edward Solomon, proved an excellent piece, witty and funny and in no way inferior to the Savoy's recent productions. It played for two hundred nights at the Savoy, went on tour and even to the Orient, but the collaboration with Solomon and Carte was not pursued and Dance's next assignments were again in different areas.

He adapted Paul Lacome's *Ma mie Rosette* from five acts into two for the London stage, where it ran longer than the original piece had done in Paris, and composed another burlesque, this time for Arthur Roberts (*A Modern Don Quixote*), which was subsequently judged worthy of not one but two London showings. It was, however, another show designed for the provinces which provided his first really big hit. *The Lady Slavey,* the archetypical example of the vastly popular ''variety musical''—all story in the first act, and frittering away into a series of ''turns'' in the second, with the story returning to have its ends tied up only in the last minutes—had a London run and, indeed, productions on Broadway and in many other venues around the English-speaking world, but it was the touring show par excellence and held a sometimes multiple place on the roads of Britain for some 20 years.

The Gay Parisienne, which came along the following year, was more vertebrate, more successful in the metropolises (US: *The Girl from Paris*) and almost as successful on the road as *The Lady Slavey,* touring ceaselessly for more than a decade. However, a rather tasteless vehicle for the dwarfish variety star Little Tich, *Lord Tom Noddy,* provoked some very off-color reactions and did not catch on.

With *The New Mephisto* and *The Gay Grisette,* Dance proved yet again that he had British provincial tastes taped to a nicety, and both pieces toured almost continuously for many years whilst avoiding the West End, but a third piece tailored similarly for the provinces, *A Chinese Honeymoon,* was taken out of the touring circuits and moved into town by Frank Curzon. Suitably polished up for metropolitan consumption, *A Chinese Honeymoon* proved the biggest hit in musical theatre history. It became the first musical ever to run one thousand consecutive performances in London (or any other theatrical center), was played worldwide, toured incessantly for years and years, and made itself into a landmark of musical-theatre history.

Dance's only two subsequent pieces were not successful, and a last work called *Mlle Paris* never made it to the stage, but his principal activity by this time was management. Again avoiding the West End, and preferring tried and proven popular pieces to new material, he concentrated over many years on sending out long-running touring companies of established West End musical hits, notably the number one and number two companies of the big musical successes produced by George Edwardes at the Gaiety, Daly's and the Adelphi Theatres. He often, during the early years of the 20th century, had more than a dozen companies on the British road at one time. His intelligently managed touring operations and his phenomenal authorial success meant that, in spite of a large amount of practical philanthropy (a £30,000 gift to the Old Vic fund earned him a knighthood in 1923), he has been one of the very few theatrical producers to leave a considerable fortune at his death.

A genuine man of the theatre, Dance was involved in all areas of British theatre life and management. He was for a time the proprietor of the Theatre Royal, Richmond, had an interest in the Hippodrome in his native Nottingham and in the Oldham Palace Hippodrome, and took over briefly as managing director of the Gaiety Theatre after George Edwardes's death, before throwing in his hand in the face of the power politics and property-grabbing going on in the theatre at that time.

1886 **Oliver Grumble** (pasticcio) Prince of Wales Theatre, Liverpool 15 March; Novelty Theatre 25 March

1889 **Columbus** (w Archibald Gordon) Grand Opera House, Los Angeles 11 January

1891 **The Nautch Girl** (Edward Solomon/w Frank Desprez) Savoy Theatre 30 June

1892 **Ma mie Rosette** English adaptation w Ivan Caryll (Globe Theatre)

1893 **A Modern Don Quixote** (Crook) Theatre Royal, Nottingham 17 July; Strand Theatre 25 September

1893 **The Lady Slavey** (John Crook) Theatre Royal, Northampton 4 September; Avenue Theatre, London 20 October 1894

1894 **The Gay Parisienne** (Ernest Vousden, later Caryll, et al) Theatre Royal, Northampton 1 October; Duke of York's Theatre, London 4 April 1896

1895 **Buttercup and Daisy** (Arthur Richards) Nottingham, Theatre Royal, Kilburn 9 September

1896 **Lord Tom Noddy** (F Osmond Carr) Theatre Royal, Bradford 6 April; Garrick Theatre 15 September

1897 **The New Mephisto[pheles]** (Vousden) Grand Theatre, Leeds 29 March

1898 **The Gay Grisette** (Carl Kiefert) Theatre Royal, Bradford 1 August

1899 **A Chinese Honeymoon** (Howard Talbot) Theatre Royal, Hanley 16 October; Royal Strand Theatre, London 5 October 1901

1901 **The Ladies' Paradise** (Caryll) Theatre Royal, Hanley 11 March

1902 **The West End, or The Doings of the Smart Set** (Edward Jones/Ernest Boyd-Jones/w George Arliss) Theatre Royal, Norwich 29 September

1904 **Madame Sherry** revised English libretto (Kennington Theatre)

1908 **The Burglars' Ball** (pasticcio) sketch Richmond Hippodrome 8 February

1908 **The Local Amateurs** (pasticcio) sketch Richmond Hippodrome 24 August

THE DANCING MISTRESS Musical play in 3 acts by James T Tanner. Lyrics by Adrian Ross and Percy Greenbank. Music by Lionel Monckton. Adelphi Theatre, London, 19 October 1912.

George Edwardes reteamed his *Quaker Girl* authors and stars for this follow-up to the earlier hit at the Adelphi Theatre. Gertie Millar appeared as a dance teacher at a ladies' finishing school, Joe Coyne as an aviator, Gracie Leigh as the school's Scottish tuck-shop lady and Mlle Caumont as a vast French mistress, in a plot which took them picturesquely from Brighton to Oberwald and a hotel in London. Other favorite features included a chorus of schoolgirls, some skating and skiing (providing Miss Leigh with the opportunity for a comic routine with her equipment) and a jolly dance to ''The Porcupine Patrol.'' Georges Carvey followed his hit with *The Quaker Girl*'s ''Come to the Ball'' with another charming waltz, ''When You Are in Love,'' and Miss Millar sang happily through ''Dance, Little Snowflake'' for a satisfactory 242-performance run without the piece ever looking like becoming another *Quaker Girl.*

An Australian production featured Maggie Dickinson in the role made for Miss Millar and Leslie Holland as the aviator, supported by soprano Ethel Cadman, the veteran Maggie Moore as the Frenchwoman and Minnie Love as the Scots one, for a fairly brief run in repertoire in Sydney and Melbourne (16 October 1913).

Australia: Criterion Theatre, Sydney 2 August 1913

THE DANCING YEARS Musical play in 3 acts by Ivor Novello. Lyrics by Christopher Hassall. Theatre Royal, Drury Lane, London, 23 March 1939.

The most successful of Ivor Novello's series of spectacular musical plays, *The Dancing Years* was produced at the Theatre Royal, Drury Lane not long before the outbreak of war, and told a story which was actually relevant to and inspired by the conflict. The suppression of the music of Jewish composers in Germany (much on the lines of the suppression of German music in Britain in the First World War) was the spur to a Ruritanian musical with a bitter twist to it.

Rudi Kleber (Novello) is brought from suburban obscurity to fame as a composer of operettic music by the prima donna Maria Ziegler (Mary Ellis) but, although they live happily together, he cannot ask her to marry him because of a promise given to a child friend (Roma Beaumont) in his early days. In the misunderstandings that result, Maria marries her old admirer, Prince Metterling (Anthony Nicholls), and the lovers are foolishly parted forever, but when the war comes the Princess is able to use her social position to save the arrested, Jewish Rudi.

Novello starred in his usual non-singing capacity opposite Mary Ellis, the leading lady of his *Glamorous Night,* who introduced several songs which were to become Novello standards—the showy ''Waltz of My Heart,'' the gentle ''My Dearest Dear'' and the first act's enduring closer ''I Can Give You the Starlight.'' As was Novello's habit, the first two of these were presented as songs written by the composer within the show, as were the soprano/contralto duet ''The Wings of Sleep'' introduced by Miss Ellis and Olive Gilbert, and the long musical section representing Rudi's Operette, *Lorelei,* which included the soaring tenor melody ''My Life Belongs to You.'' Miss Beaumont, as the young Grete, danced and sang a parody of a turn-of-the-century musical comedy song called ''Primrose'' and Freddie Carpenter choreographed the lovely ''Leap Year Waltz'' into one of the highlights of the show.

After opening to a fine reception at the Theatre Royal, Drury Lane, *The Dancing Years* became an early casualty of the war. It was closed down by enemy action and, when it became safe to reopen, it found its theatre unavailable through having been taken over as the headquarters of the troops' entertainment unit, ENSA. Producer Tom Arnold, however, was an old habitué of the road, and he instead remounted *The Dancing Years* in Manchester (16 September 1940), with Muriel Barron replacing Miss Ellis in the prima donna role, and sent it out on a very extended tour. Its success on the road was so great that, in March 1942, he took the continuing produc-

Plate 89. **The Dancing Years.** *Rudi Kleber (Ivor Novello) is taken by the Nazis.*

tion (with most of its original company still intact) back into the West End and there, at the Adelphi Theatre, *The Dancing Years* was able to compile the sort of West End run it had been promised before the interruption (969 further performances). At the end of the run, the company went back on the road and *The Dancing Years* was to be found traveling through Britain almost unbrokenly over the next five years.

The show was staged in Australia (the only one of Novello's shows so to be) by J C Williamson Ltd with Max Oldaker, Tara Barry and Elizabeth Gaye featured, given an American premier in St Louis with Wilma Spence, Eduard Franz and Marjorie Bell in the leading roles, revived in London in 1947 starring Jessica James and Barry Sinclair, and filmed with Gisèle Preville and Dennis Price in 1950, and Arnold brought the show back to London once more in 1954 in an on-ice version. In his will the author-composer left the rights of *The Dancing Years* to Arnold's young son who saw it return to London yet again in 1968 with June Bronhill as Maria (Saville Theatre 6 June) but who has since been less keen to allow it to be produced again in the West End in spite of continuing provincial performances, sometimes in a version which takes the bitter from the bittersweet and renders the show no more than a sentimental operetta by removing the final Nazi episode.

Australia: Her Majesty's Theatre, Melbourne 29 June 1946; USA: Municipal Opera, St Louis 5 June 1947

Films: Associated British 1950, TV Film (ATV) 1979

Recordings: original cast (HMV), 1968 revival cast (RCA), selections (Columbia, Philips, MFP)

DANDY DAN, THE LIFEGUARDSMAN Musical comedy in 2 acts by Basil Hood. Music by Walter Slaughter. Belfast, 23 August 1897; Lyric Theatre, London, 4 December 1897.

Following the grand success of his impersonation of the cabby *Gentleman Joe,* comedian Arthur Roberts commissioned a second vehicle from that show's authors, Basil Hood and Walter Slaughter. The character they created for him this time, a soldier with a "mash" on a pretty nursemaid, provided the irresponsible comedian with all the opportunities for broad comedy and quick-change impressions expected of him by his public, the latitude for unscripted deviations that he required and some bright and brittle-lyricked songs in the same mold as the *Gentleman Joe* ones ("Dandy Dan, the Lifeguardsman," "The Magic of My Eye," "My Little Game"). Phyllis Broughton and Bill Denny headed the support, with little Isa Bowman as the nursemaid and George A Highland, later to be one of Australia's most prominent directors of musicals, in a small role.

Dandy Dan had a run of 166 London performances, latterly in a "second edition," with a burlesque on the current theatrical scene entitled *Much Ado About Something, or Beerbohm Tree-lawney of the Wells* inserted as an extra plaything for the star, before Roberts took it out on a profitable tour.

THE DANDY FIFTH English military comic opera in 3 acts by George R Sims based on *The Queen's Shilling* by G W Godfrey, being an adaptation of *Un Fils de famille* by Jean-François Bayard and de Biéville [ie, E Desnoyers]. Music by Clarence C Corri. Prince of Wales Theatre, Birmingham, 11 April 1898; Duke of York's Theatre, London, 16 August 1898.

A latter-day military comic opera of the kind very popular in Britain 20 and more years earlier (and interminably popular in France), *The Dandy Fifth* was adapted from a half-century-old original, the very popular *Un Fils de famille* (Théâtre du Gymnase, Paris 25 November 1852), played in London as *The Queen's Shilling* in 1879. It was expressly designed by Sims for the provincial audiences he had previously proved he understood so well. The story, which centered on the efforts of an army private, Dick Darville (Arthur Appleby/H Scott Russell), to win Kate (Ruth Davenport), the daughter of his General, in spite of the rivalry of Colonel Slasherton (Leonard Calvert/Cecil Morton York), was filled with plenty of boisterous good fun and simple heroics and illustrated with songs by Clarence Corri, musical director at the Manchester Theatre Royal and a member of a famous musico-theatrical family. Several of these songs, such as the endearing "The Sprig o' Horringe Blossom" and the patriotic "Toast of the Dandy Fifth" were successful both in and out of the show, but the hit of the evening was "Tommy's Tournament" a tambour-thumping piece with its cheerworthy cap line "a little British army goes a long way."

The Dandy Fifth toured in Britain for more than a decade, taking in an eight-week London season, but mostly sticking to the provinces where its unsophisticated good humor and sentiment and easily digestible score made it a long-term favorite.

Un Fils de famille was musicalized as *El hijo de familia* in Spain (Gaztambide, Oudrid/Luis Olcona, Teatro del Circo 24 December 1853) and played in America in a version with songs under the title *The Lancers* (George Spink, Cecilia Loftus, et al/Rida Johnson Young J Hartley Manners Daly's Theater 5 December 1907).

DANIELE, Graciela (b Buenos Aires, 8 December 1939).

Miss Daniele began her career as a dancer in the early 1960s, touring internationally with Josephine Baker, and she made her Broadway debut when she was cast as the Latin bombshell, Rita Rio, in *What Makes*

Sammy Run? (1964). She subsequently appeared in the ensembles of the one performance of *Here's Where I Belong* (1968), *Promises, Promises* (1969) and *Coco* (1969), featured as Vanessa in *Follies* (1971) and worked as dance assistant to Michael Bennett, Alan Johnson and Bob Fosse.

She made her debut as a choreographer with the ephemeral *A History of American Film* (1978) and the slightly longer-lived 1979 revival of *The Most Happy Fella,* but came to notice thoroughly with her energetic dances for the Wilford Leach version of *The Pirates of Penzance* (1980–81). She subsequently choreographed the 1983 revival of *Zorba,* the roller-skating *The Rink* (1984) and *The Mystery of Edwin Drood* (1985), directed and choreographed the off-Broadway *In a Pig's Valise* (1989) and the well-liked *Once on This Island* (1990) and mounted the first combination of *March of the Falsettos* and *Falsettoland* into one entertainment at Hartford Stage (1992) with considerable success. In 1993 she choreographed the Broadway production of *The Goodbye Girl.*

During the 1990s, she conceived, wrote and staged a series of Latinate dance-dramas. The first, *Tango apasionada,* based on the works of Jorge Luis Borges provoked considerable interest but, thanks to copyright problems, did not transfer from its off-Broadway origins. Two subsequent pieces, based on the works of Gabriel García Márquez, *Dangerous Games* (which featured many similarities with *Tango apasionada*) and *Chronicle of a Death Foretold,* were not successful.

Her most recent credits have been the direction of Broadway's politically corrected *Annie Get Your Gun* (1999) and the modern-musicalized *Medea* called *Marie Christine* (1999). She has also choreographed for the Ballet Hispanico, the filmed version of *The Pirates of Penzance* production (1983), and musical sequences for the Woody Allen films *Bullets Over Broadway* (1994), *Mighty Aphrodite* (1995) and *Everyone Says I Love You* (1996).

1987 **Tango apasionada** INTAR Hispanic American Arts Center, Westbeth Theatre Center 28 October

1989 **Dangerous Games** (William Finn/Astor Piazzolla/w Jim Lewis) Nederlander Theater 19 October

1995 **Chronicle of a Death Foretold** (Bob Telson/w Jim Lewis) Plymouth Theater 15 June

DANIELS, Frank [Albert] (b Dayton, Ohio, 15 August 1856; d West Palm Beach, Fla, 12 January 1935). Impish little comic who had a fine career as a top-billed star in the musical theatre.

After an apprenticeship as a wood-engraver in Boston, Daniels began a stage career at 19 playing at Salem in *Stars* (1879, doing an imitation of comedian Gus Williams) and in often not-exactly-youthful roles in comic opera—the Bailie in *Cloches de Corneville,* Judge in *Trial by Jury,* Dick Deadeye. He was also seen briefly as Shovel-off in the "original American opéra-bouffe" *Sancho Pedro* produced in Boston in 1879, before rising—after comparatively little experience—to lead roles. He toured as John Bobble Twilt in a low comic adaptation of *La Poupée de Nuremburg* as *Jollities, or The Electrical Doll* (1880), starred as Johnnie Bull in its successor *The Electric Spark* around America (1882) and in Britain (1883), briefly played the undersized (so he felt) role of the jailor Enterich in a Boston production of *Der Bettelstudent* (1883) and toured in *Peck's Bad Boy* (1884) before finding significant successes in musical farce-comedy, playing broadly comical roles in Charles Hoyt's *A Rag Baby* (1884, Old Sport) and in *Little Puck* (Academy of Music, Buffalo 20 September 1887, Packingham Giltedge) for long periods on the American tour circuits. He caused his first headlineable sensation, however, offstage rather than on. At age 23, he ran off with his employer, Jennie Yeamans, "to be wed," but the pair were dragged back to Galveston and to Jennie's unpaid company of actors by the sherrif, and they never did get wed.

Daniels appeared in the chief comic part of the Philadelphia musical *Princess Bonnie* (Shrimps), but found himself with a genuine musical-comedy star part for the first time when he was cast in the grotesque title role of Kibosh, in Victor Herbert's colorful burlesque-comic opera *The Wizard of the Nile* (1895). Herbert and *Wizard of the Nile* librettist Harry B Smith created a second comic opera, *The Idol's Eye* (1897), to feature the new comedy star, and Kirk La Shelle and Frederick Ranken joined with the composer in fabricating him a third vehicle on the same lines, *The Ameer* (1899, Iffie Khan).

In 1901–2 Daniels starred as "My Man Blossoms" in *Miss Simplicity* on the road and at the Casino Theater, and the following year appeared as the little jockey-in-spite-of-himself in Charles Dillingham's production of *The Office Boy* (*Le Jockey malgré lui,* 1903, Noah Littler) as made over for America by Smith and Ludwig Englander, at the Victoria, providing himself in each case with a vehicle in which to tour for the rest of each of the year in question. In 1905 he took up the rather less broadly out-front role of *Sergeant Brue,* created by Owen Hall for Willie Edouin in London, and successfully played it at the Criterion Theater.

In 1907 Dillingham starred him in *The Tattooed Man,* another Herbert/Smith piece, suggested by the hit song of *The Idol's Eye,* which once again cast him as a broadly painted and played Easterner, here called Omar Khayyam jr, for a successful New York season and a long tour. He stayed on the road thereafter for a good stretch playing G P Huntley's role of the bumbling Mr Hook in *Hook of Holland* (the "Miss" of the original title was removed to allow him to have the title role); the comical Marquis de St Gautier, created by George Graves, in another British import, *The Belle of Brittany;* Frank Lalor's role of the naughty Dondidier in Ivan Caryll's New York hit *The Pink Lady*; and in *The Girl in the Train* (1910, Judge van Tromp). He returned to Broadway for a stint at Weber and Fields's establishment (*Roly Poly, Without the Law*) at the end of 1912 in his last New York engagement before retiring from the stage.

D'ANKA, Cornélie [ANKER, Kornélia] (b Budapest, c1852; d Herne Bay, 13 November 1927). Attractive, blonde and bordering-on-the-buxom star of the opéra-bouffe era in Britain.

Mlle d'Anka made her debut on the London stage—improbably (but I suppose not impossibly) billed as being "of the Imperial Opera, Vienna"—as the Prince of Boboli in *Falsacappa* (April 1871) and created quite a stir. She did not, however, impress the New York *Clipper* which printed a story insisting that the Globe's stage manager had promptly recognized this shapely new opéra-bouffe starlet as one Miss Solomons, daughter of a neighbouring furniture merchant, who had—so it claimed—been three months on the Continent acquiring a voice, an accent and a new name. Cornélie subsequently appeared at the Court Theatre as (an Hungarian-accented) Richard Coeur de Lion in the burlesque *Isaac of York* (1872) and as a comical Catherine of Braganza in *Charles II* (1872), and at the Alhambra in the thoroughly soprano roles of Princess Cunégonde in *Le Roi Carotte* (1872), the title role of *Black Crook* (1872), Offenbach's Eurydice (*Orphée aux enfers,* 1877) and in the title role of *Grande-Duchesse de Gérolstein* (1878). She was seen between times as Cattarina Cornaro in *The Bridge of Sighs* (1875) at Manchester, and on the road as *Madame Favart* but her most celebrated and frequently played role was that of the luscious merveilleuse Mlle Lange in *La Fille de Madame Angot* in which she appeared at the Globe (1874), the Opera Comique (1875), the Alhambra (1878), the Connaught (1879) and at the Theatre Royal, Drury Lane (1880).

In the mid-1880s, married (she filled in her wedding banns in spite of the *Clipper* as "daughter of Ludwig Anker of Pest"), still active, still blonde, and decidedly plumper, she was seen touring less than happily in latter-day opéra-bouffe productions and in the title role of *Estrella,* and appeared briefly as "a rather massive" Zoë in Violet Cameron's 1886 production of *The Commodore* (*La Créole*)—she was sacked and sued (and won)—and at the Strand Theatre as a replacement for Alma Stanley in the burlesque *Atalanta* (1888 t/o Aphrodite). She withdrew from this last production after just a few performances, "ill" and, like so many of her contemporaries, she then simply disappeared from theatrical annals to live out her years on the Kentish coast, with her master-dyer husband.

LA DANSEUSE AUX ÉTOILES Opérette à grand spectacle in 2 acts by Henri Varna and Guy des Cars based on the novel *La Demoiselle de l'Opéra* by des Cars. Music by Vincent Scotto. Théâtre Mogador, Paris, 18 February 1950.

Henri Varna built a spectacular show around Guy des Cars' romantic histoire d'amour between the celebrated ballerina Adeline Piedplus (Marta Labarr) and the handsome Lieutenant Ludovic de Chanalèze (Jean Chesnel). He purposefully reduced the tale from the novel's lifelong timespan to just a few years, to allow the protagonists to remain young and attractive throughout the evening, and set it in a succession of stage pictures of the Paris of the 1870s, ranging from a tableau-vivant of Dégas' "Les danseuses à la barre" through the coulisses of the Paris Opéra, the city's cafés and "le bal de la Closerie des Lilas" to the gardens of the Elysée and the performance of a full-scale ballet, the whole set to the accompaniment of a Vincent Scotto score in which dance music predominated. *La Danseuse aux étoiles* was played through a run of more than a year and a half, with Tessa Beaumont succeeding Mlle Labarr in the starring role.

DAPHNIS ET CHLOË Opérette (musical-parody idyll) in 1 act by Clairville and Jules Cordier. Music by Jacques Offenbach. Théâtre des Bouffes-Parisiens, Paris, 27 March 1860.

A little parody of the pastoral in general, and the pastorale of the same name by Longus in particular, *Daphnis and Chloë* was a version of an 1849 playlet (Théâtre du Vaudeville) supplied to Offenbach by the prolific Clairville and, under the pseudonym of "Cordier," which had served him for occasional writings since 1840, by Monsieur Éléonor Tenaille de Vaulabelle.

The lubricious Pan (Désiré) has his eyes on the innocent nymph, Chloë (Mlle Chabert), and he takes the place of his own statue to fool the girl into giving him a kiss. But Chloë is in love with the beauteous and exceedingly coveted shepherd Daphnis (Juliette Beau) and he—though he understands not what the emotions that stir in him are—returns her feelings. The jealous Calisto (Marie Cico) and her accompanying bacchantes try to make Daphnis forget Chloë by administering him a little Lethe water, whilst Pan takes on the job of instructing the naive hamadryed in the workings of that thing called love. His lessons are helpful enough that, when he is laid low by an accidental draught of Lethe water, Chloë can pass on what she has learned to Daphnis. It is all that is needed to produce a happy ending.

Plate 90. **Daphnis und Chloë.** *Dirk Löhr as Daphnis and Carmen Weber as Chloë in the Dresden Staatsoperette's production of the enlarged version of Offenbach's little operette.*

The tiny tale was accompanied by a score of nine numbers, beginning with a Bacchic ode of embarrassment as each bacchante sees her manoeuvrings to meet Daphnis alone stymied by her sisters, and including a pastorale for Daphnis, and duos for Chloë with both her lover and the lecher.

Following its Paris production, *Daphnis and Chloë* was seen in Berlin and then in Vienna, where, played as one of the earliest productions at Karl Treumann's Theater am Franz-Josefs-Kai during a guest season by Johann Nestroy, it became highly popular. What seems to have been Wilhelm Friedrich's version (it is sometimes attributed to Treumann or to Nestroy, and uncredited on the playbills) turned the little piece into a virtual stand-up vehicle for Nestroy in the role of Pan, a role rewritten in a satirical ''revue-compère'' style to parallel his success as Jupiter in *Orpheus in der Unterwelt.* Anna Grobecker and Anna Marek were the overwhelmed pair of Arcadians, and Anna Müller appeared as Calisto. The original version was played at the Carltheater the following year (6 July) and further adaptations were later played at the Variététheater (1870) and at the Komische Oper (1874). The French original was brought back at the Bouffes-Parisiens in 1866 (October) with Delphine Ugalde (Daphnis), Mlle Milla (Chloë) and Léonce (Pan).

Daphnis und Chloë is still intermittently played in German-language theatres, although the ''versions'' have crept even further from the original, and the score has been puffed up with music taken from other sources to help make the show into a full evening's entertainment.

Two other full-length opérettes by the same title were later staged in Paris, one by Jules and Pierre Barbier with music by Henri Mareschal (Théâtre Lyrique, November 1899) and a second written by André Mouëzy-Éon and Félix Gandéra, composed by Henri Moreau-Febvre, subtitled ''la leçon d'amour'' (Théâtre Édouard VII, Paris, 1918) and starring Marguerite Deval and Henri Defreyn.

Germany: Friedrich-Wilhelmstädtisches Theater 23 December 1860; Austria: Theater am Franz-Josefs-Kai 2 March 1861; Hungary: Budai Színkör (Ger) 22 April 1862, Budai Népszínház 11 June 1862

DARE, Phyllis [DONES, Phyllis Constance Haddie] (b London, 15 August 1890; d Brighton, 27 April 1975). One of the most enduring ingenues of the London musical theatre, occasionally in vocally demanding roles.

Phyllis Dare made her first stage appearances, mostly with her elder sister, Zena, as a child, playing regularly in pantomime, in *Ib and Little Christina* (1900, Christina) and alongside Seymour Hicks and Ellaline Terriss in *Bluebell in Fairyland* (1901, Mab) at the Vaudeville Theatre. She was still only 15 years old when Hicks called on her to take over as the fifth in a succession of leading ladies who played the Cinderella role of Angela in *The Catch of the Season,* a role which had originally been created by her sister. Although she returned to her schooling when her stint at the Vaudeville was over (advised gossip said in fact that she'd gone to ground to have Hicks's child), she was soon back on the stage, in newsworthy circumstances. When Edna May flounced out of Leslie Stuart's *The Belle of Mayfair* (1906), producer Stephano Gatti called on Phyllis to take over the show's very large made-for-May role and, while lawsuits lurched around on all sides, the young star confirmed herself as one of the town's most attractive ingenues.

She subsequently played the star juvenile parts of Robert Courtneidge's long-running successes *The Dairymaids* (1907, Peggy) and *The Arcadians* (1909), introducing "The Girl with the Brogue" in her role as Irish Eileen, and made a notable success of the role of the tempting Gonda van der Loo in the English version of Leo Fall's *Die geschiedene Frau* (*The Girl in the Train,* 1910) for George Edwardes. Edwardes subsequently starred her in *Peggy* (1910, Peggy), in Gertie Millar's role of Prudence in the Paris season of *The Quaker Girl,* in *The Sunshine Girl* (1912, Delia Dale), in succession to Miss Millar in *The Dancing Mistress* (1913, t/o Nancy Joyce) and in tandem with Ina Claire in *The Girl from Utah* (1914, Dora Manners).

She continued to tot up the juvenile star roles for more than another decade, appearing in a revival of *Miss Hook of Holland* (1914, Sally Hook), in the title role of *Tina* (1915, "The Violin Song"), in the musical comedy *Kissing Time* (1919, Lucienne), as Mariana in the English version of Gilbert's *Die Frau im Hermelin* (1922, *The Lady of the Rose*), in what was effectively her own production of *The Street Singer* (1924, Yvette), in *Lido Lady* (1926, Fay Blake, provoking some harsh words from Richard Rodgers about being "landed with" a 40-year-old ingenue) and *The Yellow Mask* (1928, Mary Bannister) before turning to straight theatre.

She subsequently toured in the very vocal role of Frieda in Jerome Kern's *Music in the Air* (1934) and made a late and last return to the musical stage to play the lightly musicked part of Marta Karillos, the King's mistress, opposite Ivor Novello, in his *King's Rhapsody* (1949, "The Mayor of Perpignan").

Her sister, **Zena DARE** [Zena Florence Harriet DONES] (b London, 4 February 1886; d London, 11 March 1975) made an equally early start in musical comedy, starring in Seymour Hicks' touring musical *An English Daisy* (1902, Daisy Maitland) at 15 and creating the juvenile lead of *Sergeant Brue* (Aurora Brue) in London two years later. When Ellaline Terriss was unable through pregnancy to play the star role of the new Hicks musical, *The Catch of the Season,* Zena Dare created this latest and long-running Cinderella part opposite Hicks and played it until Miss Terriss was able to return from giving birth and take over.

Plate 91. *"Bring me a rose . . .": **Phyllis Dare** and Alfred Lester in the racecourse scene from* The Arcadians.

She succeeded Adrienne Augarde in the title role of *Lady Madcap,* under the management of George Edwardes, and appeared for him again in *The Little Cherub* (1906, Lady Isobel Congress) the following year, before returning to Hicks to succeed Miss Terriss in the star role of *The Beauty of Bath* (1906, Betty Silverthorne). In *The Gay Gordons* (1907, Victoria Siddons) she played second lead alongside Miss Terriss, taking over the star part when the show moved out of town. She appeared in several little musical pieces in the music halls (*You and I* w Stanley Brett, *Mitislaw der moderne* w Farkoa, 1909, etc), as the fashion for one-act shows in variety caught on, and subsequently toured in Miss Terriss's breeches role of *The Dashing Little Duke* before retiring to marriage in 1911.

When she returned to the stage, 15 years later, it was to play in often dramatic roles in straight theatre (including a fondly remembered Mrs Darling in *Peter Pan*) until Ivor Novello induced her back to the musical stage with a non-singing role in *Careless Rapture* (1936). She subsequently succeeded Margaret Rutherford as Lady Charlotte Fayre in Novello's *Perchance to Dream* and appeared with her sister, for the first time since their childhood, when cast in the strong acting role of the conniving Queen Elana in *King's Rhapsody* (1949). She was over 70 when she appeared at the Theatre Royal, Drury Lane, as Mrs Higgins in the first London production of *My Fair Lady,* a role which she then retained for seven years in London and on the road.

Autobiographies: *From School to Stage* (Collier and Co, London, 1907), *Phyllis Dare, by Herself* (1921)

DAREWSKI, Herman [Edouard] (b Minsk, Russia, 17 April 1883; d Kennington, London, 2 June 1947). Songwriter and music publisher whose song successes were contrasted with some flamboyant business failures.

Born in Russia, brought up in England, Darewski studied music in Vienna and then returned to Britain where he became a conductor at the spa town of Bridlington, then at Blackpool, a member of the staff of Francis, Day & Hunter music publishers, and an adept writer of popular songs and interpolated numbers for musical comedy. His first song success came with "My Little Hyacinth," interpolated into *The Beauty of Bath* (1906) by Ellaline Terriss, and he had further success with "In the Twi-twi-twilight" (w Charles Wilmot) sung in the American edition of *The Dairymaids* (1907) and "I Used to Sigh for the Silvery Moon" as interpolated into Charles Dillingham's Broadway production of *The Candy Shop* (1909). He also provided the tune to Elsie Janis's lyrics for "For I Love Only You" (*The Slim Princess,* 1911). He subsequently established his own Herman Darewski Music Publishing Company Ltd which, apart from publishing his own works, also put out such popular numbers as "Any Old Iron," "Sussex by the Sea," "Arizona," "I Know Where the Flies Go in Wintertime," "Ours is a Nice House Ours Is" and ensured the British distribution of many American hits.

His first musical theatre scores, mostly put together in collaboration with other writers, were written for revue, beginning with such shows as *Mind Your Backs* (Hackney Empire, 1913), and Austen Hurgon's 1914 Coliseum piece *Happy Days* (1914) and including de Courville's Hippodrome shows *Business As Usual* ("When We've Wound Up the Watch on the Rhine"), *Push and Go* (1915 w Jean Schwartz, et al) and *Joyland* (1915), and the Comedy Theatre *Shell Out* (1915). Alongside the revue songs, and such singles as Jack Norworth's "Sister Susie's Sewing Shirts for Soldiers" (1915), he found time to contribute more or less music to a number of musical plays, of which the first was J M Barrie's vehicle for Gaby Deslys, *Rosy Rapture* (1915), a revusical affair in which his songs (including "Which Switch Is the Switch, Miss, for Ipswich?") supplemented half a score by Jerome Kern.

Darewski contributed numbers to such pieces as Émile Lassailly's *Carminetta* and revivals of *Bluebell in Fairyland* and *The Catch of the Season,* but he scored his biggest success when he supplied the bulk of the songs for the enormously successful C B Cochran wartime musical *The Better 'Ole* (1917). The unfortunate Gertie Millar vehicle *Flora* (1918) gave him only a brief exposure, but his remusicked version of the Rip revue *Plus ça change* for Cochran and Alice Delysia as *As You Were* ("If You Could Care for Me") was another hit, whilst his "The Shimmy Shake" and "Le Petit Nid" ("In That Little Home That's Built for Two") gave him a wider audience when they were heard in the Parisian version of Ivan Caryll's *The Earl and the Girl, Hello!! Charley* (1919).

At this time, often three or four West End revues and/or musicals at one time bore Darewski's name, in a larger or smaller capacity, on their bill. However, with the exception of a Gaiety Theatre revival of *The Shop Girl* (1920) for which the original Ivan Caryll score was topped up with eight new Darewski songs ("The Guards' Brigade"), none of the musical comedies for which he provided the major part of the score (*Jolly Jack Tar, The Eclipse, Oh! Julie*) proved particularly successful and, by the early 1920s, his name was much less frequently seen.

In 1920 Darewski (who had bought up the old music publishers Charles Sheard in 1918) purchased the famous publishing house of Metzler, but in 1922 he encountered financial problems and was obliged to sell his publishing interests in bankruptcy. From the 1920s he operated once more as a musical director at various seaside resorts and at the head of his own band, whilst still providing the odd song to such musicals as *The Blue Mazurka* and *Up with the Lark,* but without ever regaining the profile he had had in the 1910s.

1908 **Teashop Girls** (*The Tea-Shop Strike*) (w Charles Willmott/H Maurice Vernon) sketch Empire, Nottingham 27 April; Hackney Empire 1 June

1914 **The Chorus Girl** (Harry Grattan) 1 act London Palladium 20 July

1914 **Going, Going, Gone** 1 act Chelsea Palace

1915 **Rosy Rapture, the Pride of the Beauty Chorus** (w Jerome

Kern/F W Mark/J M Barrie) Duke of York's Theatre 22 March

1917 **The Better 'Ole** (James Hurd/Bruce Bairnsfather, Arthur Eliot) Oxford Theatre 4 August

1918 **Flora** (w Melville Gideon/Harry Grattan, Heard) Prince of Wales Theatre 12 March

1918 **Jolly Jack Tar** (Heard, Davy Burnaby, J P Harrington/ Seymour Hicks, Arthur Shirley) Prince's Theatre 29 November

1919 **A Good-Looking Lass** (Leon Pollack, Lauri Wylie) 1 act Chelsea Palace 11 August

1919 **The Eclipse** (w Gideon, Cole Porter/Adrian Ross/Fred Thompson, E Phillips Oppenheim) Garrick Theatre 12 November

1920 **Oh! Julie** (w H Sullivan Brooke/Harold Simpson/Firth Shephard, Lee Banson) Shaftesbury Theatre 22 June

1922 **Listening In** (Worton David, Will Hay) Apollo Theatre 31 July

Autobiography: *Musical Memories* (Jarrold, London, 1937)

Darewski's brother, Julius Darewski, was a very prominent London theatrical and musical agent and occasional producer, whilst another (disowned) brother, operating under the name **Ernest C ROLLS** [Josef Adolf DAREWSKI] (b c1888; d London, 20 January 1964), produced musical comedy and revue in both Britain and in Australia with more side than skill. He was sued for theatrical dishonesty before he was 21, bankrupted in 1921 after losing £16,000 on the musical *Oh! Julie* and £12,000 on the revue *Laughing Eyes,* and his mismanagement of Australia's J C Williamson Ltd almost led that famous firm to disaster. After directing some extravagant productions of a series of mostly American musicals on the Australian stage (*Sunny, Good News,* etc), he went into management there on his own behalf, mounting Australia's *Whoopee* (1929) and the flop local *Funny Face* (1931), and, in the wake of Frank Thring's promotion of home-written Australian musical productions, even producing an original piece, *Flame of Desire* (Apollo Theatre, Melbourne 19 October 1935), for which he took a half book-credit with J L Gray (mus: Jack O'Hagan) and imported Ethelind Terry to star. He sacked her, and the show went down the drain anyway. It was then, through engineering a financial takeover of the firm by New Zealand department store magnate John McKenzie who put him in charge, that he won the job at Williamson's. His production of *I Married an Angel* was Williamson's all-time top money-loser and he was quickly given the boot when his second year's contract expired. Rolls's family did not disown him for his failures, nor for his flash manners and flashy productions (all well-established family failings). They disowned him first, in print (well, father and two brothers did, mother stuck by him a little longer), over his arrests for dishonesty, and then all over again when he was convicted of exposing himself in a rather different kind of ''flash.''

A further brother, **Max DAREWSKI** [Marks Maximilian A DAREWSKI] (b Manchester, 3 November 1894; d London, 25 September 1929), also composed for the musical theatre. In his earliest years, Max was celebrated as an infant prodigy at the piano, touring through Europe (under the not always appreciated ''management'' of brother Herman) and appearing before crowned heads in the best prodigy fashion. He also conducted his own and other music, in novelty circumstances, before the age of 10 (Albert Hall, 1904, etc). Amongst a proliferation of piano compositions, he composed music for a number of revues, including *Oh! Molly* (1912) and the *Venus Limited* produced by brother Rolls, at the Pavilion and the Finsbury Park Empire respectively, but without being connected with anything very successful. He also got a tiny Broadway showing when he shared a credit on the title song for the 1916 musical *Go to It.*

He provided the score for Alfred Butt's musical comedy vehicle for Gaby Deslys, *Suzette* (1917), which, with a London run of 255 performances—not really due to its songs—proved his longest-lived piece. His only other full score was for the touring musical *Mam'zelle Kiki* (1924), but he shared credit for the composition of the Gaiety musical *His Girl* (1922) and the Jack Buchanan musical *Boodle* (1925) and had songs interpolated into various other musicals including the London versions of *Der Orlow* (*Hearts and Diamonds*), for which he was also musical director, Lehár's *Cloclo,* and revivals of *Tonight's the Night* and *The Maid of the Mountains.* He also provided a handful of songs for Broadway's *Hammerstein's 9 o'Clock Revue* (1923). Maurice Chevalier made a success of his ''One Hour of Flirt with You'' (1917) under the less curious title of ''J'aime les fleurs'' in the Casino de Paris revue *Pa-ri-ki-ri.* In what seemed to be the family tradition, he was glaringly bankrupted in 1924.

Max Darewski was married to showgirl Ruby Miller, who recounted their lives in the book *Believe Me or Not* (1933).

1917 **Seeing Life** (Arthurs) 1 act Oxford Music Hall 15 January

1917 **Suzette** (Austen Hurgon, George Arthurs) Globe Theatre 29 March

1922 **His Girl** (w Ernest Longstaffe/Austen Hurgon, F W Thomas, Claude E Burton, Arthur Anderson) Gaiety Theatre 1 April

1924 **Mam'zelle Kiki** (Douglas Hoare, Graham John, Sydney Blow) Portsmouth 25 August

1924 **Boodle** (w Phil Braham/Hoare, Blow, Douglas Furber) Prince of Wales Theatre, Birmingham 26 December; Empire Theatre 10 March 1925

D'ARVILLE, Camille [DYKSTRA, Neeltye] (b Overijssel, Netherlands, 21 June 1863; d San Francisco, 10 September 1932). Biggish blonde Dutch soprano who had a long and successful career as a leading lady on both sides of the Atlantic.

Having studied music in Amsterdam and in Vienna, where she made her first stage appearance, the "extremely tall but surprisingly graceful" Mlle D'Arville first went to Britain in 1882 to fulfill an engagement which turned out to be bogus. She remained there, however, and made some appearances in the music halls before landing the title role in Harry Paulton's comic opera, *Cymbia* (1883). She then succeeded to the lead juvenile role of Katrina in *Rip van Winkle* at the Comedy Theatre (1883), played Gabrielle Chevrette in the H B Farnie version of *La Vie parisienne* (1883), Frédégonde in a revival of *Chilpéric* and starred in *Falka* on tour before going back to Holland to appear in the Dutch production of *Rip!* On her return to Britain, she toured with her original "discoverer," Harry Paulton, in *Erminie,* created the leading soprano role in Paulton's next work *Mynheer Jan* (1887, Katrina) and then traveled to America with him to appear there in *The Queen's Mate* (*La Princesse des Canaries,* 1888, Anita). She subsequently took leading roles in the British versions of the French *Babette* (1888, Babette) and *Surcouf* (*Paul Jones,* 1888, Yvonne) and in the British musicals *Carina* (1888, Carina) and *Marjorie* (1890, Marjorie), succeeded Marion Hood as leading lady to Nellie Farren in the Gaiety tour of *Monte Cristo Jr* (1889, Mercedes), and made an appearance on the music-hall stage (Trocadero, 1891) but then returned to America, where she was to spend almost all of the remainder of her career.

After appearances at the Casino Theater as Lange in *La Fille de Madame Angot* and in local versions of *La Grande-Duchesse* and *Der arme Jonathan,* and at Palmer's Theater with Henry Dixey in *La Mascotte* (1892), she joined the Boston Ideal Opera Company and, as their prima donna through two season, played the classic comic opera repertoire—including many performances of *Robin Hood* (Maid Marian), *The Bohemian Girl* (Arline) and *La Mascotte* (Bettina)—as well as creating the roles of Edith in *The Ogallallas* (1892) and Katrina in *The Knickerbockers* (1893). She next appeared in the title role of *Prince Kam* (1894), in Boston in *The Pirates of Penzance* and *Falka* (1894), and in a star role, created especially for her, in Julian Edwards's comic opera *Madeleine, or The Magic Kiss* (1895, Madeleine), going on to star in *A Daughter of the Revolution* (1895, Marion Dunbar), in Oscar Hammerstein's *Santa Maria* (1896) and in the American comic opera *Kismet* (1897, Kismet), before going on the road at the head of her own Camille D'Arville Comic Opera Company as *Peg Woffington* in a specially commissioned Victor Herbert/Harry Smith comic opera. *Peg Woffington* was not a success, and she returned to New York to spell Hilda Clark as Lady Constance in *The Highwayman* (1898) before quitting the theatre and switching instead to the vaudeville stage. She returned to the theatre a few years later and was seen at the San Francisco Tivoli in *The Highwayman* (1903), as Lady Belinda Manners in another Edwards musical, *The Belle of London Town,* 1906–7), and with Jeff de Angelis and Emma Carus in *The Gay White Way* of 1908–9, before taking a more definite farewell of the musical theatre after nearly 30 years as a thoroughly value-for-money leading lady.

THE DASHING LITTLE DUKE Play with music in 3 acts by Seymour Hicks based on the play *A Court Scandal,* itself an adaptation of *Les Premières Armes de Richelieu* by Jean-François Bayard and Philippe Dumanoir. Lyrics by Adrian Ross. Music by Frank Tours. Hicks Theatre, London, 17 February 1909.

The Dashing Little Duke was written by Hicks as a vehicle for his wife, Ellaline Terriss, at a time when travesty playing was, apart from pantomime, largely a thing of the past. As an underaged husband separated from his wife by courtly machinations (unlike the better-known couple of *Le Petit Duc,* this wife is wholly adult), Miss Terriss had the lightest and most musical-comedy part of a score in which supporting performers such as American soprano Elizabeth Firth (Britain's Valencienne in *The Merry Widow*), and top vocalists Courtice Pounds and Hayden Coffin were given the more musically substantial songs. When Miss Terriss, nevertheless, found the role rather heavy, Hicks (who had played the part of the little duke in the source play, *A Court Scandal*) stepped in to play matinées for her in what must be the only example of a husband and wife sharing a star role in a major musical.

The show did not catch on as well as its star's importance might have suggested it would, and Hicks reorganized it, making it into more of a standard musical comedy by working up the incidental soubrette role, with the addition of three Jerome Kern songs, for American musical comedy star Julia Sanderson. His efforts were in vain and *The Dashing Little Duke* closed after 101 performances with a large deficit which was not recouped on a tour where the role of the Duke was taken by Zena Dare.

Another musical, the Hungarian *Az ötödik pont* (the fifth point) by Dezső Megyeri (Népszínház 16 December 1893), was based on the same play.

DASSARY, André [DEYHÉRASSARY, Marie André Camille] (b Biarritz, 10 September 1912; d Biarritz, 7 July 1987). Flowing-voiced tenor who made a highly successful career as a stage performer and as a recording artist with a repertoire ranging from popular songs to light opera.

Having at first worked successfully as a masseur, notably with the French team at the World University

Games of 1937, Dassary began a singing career as vocalist with the orchestra of Ray Ventura. In 1941 he had his first stage success in the leading role of the opérette à grand spectacle *L'Auberge qui chante,* at the Théâtre Mogador. He subsequently starred in *Valses de France* (1942, Victor Capoul) at the Châtelet, in *L'Ingénue de Londres* (1946), and had his biggest stage success when he created the star tenor role of Hubert in Maurice Yvain's long-running romantic opérette *Chanson gitane* (1946) at the Gaîté-Lyrique.

He followed up with the less successful *Symphonie portugaise* (1949), but scored two further successes as the tenor star of Francis Lopez's *La Toison d'or* (1954, Stanislas Monestier) and the Lehár pasticcio *Rose de Noël* (1958, Count Michael Andrássy). Thereafter, he was seen, like opérette in general, largely outside Paris whilst remaining widely heard on radio and television. He also appeared in several musical films (*Feux de joie, Tourbillon de Paris, Paris chante toujours,* etc) and recorded a variety of musical comedy and opérette music ranging from *Le Pays du sourire* and *Frasquita* to French versions of *The Desert Song* and *Rose Marie.*

D'AUBAN, [Frederick] John [DOBBIN, Frederick John] (b ?1841; d London, 15 April 1922).

The son of C J D'Auban (Charles Henry DOBBIN, b ?1799; d London, 29 May 1866), a "well-known professor of dancing, many years connected with the principal theatres and concert halls," and his song-and-dancing wife, Sarah (b ?1819; d London, 28 February 1867), Johnnie D'Auban was, with his sister Mariette, trained into the family act from an early age ("the D'Auban family[:] character songs by Mme D'Auban[,] . . . the fascinating dancing of the children . . . choreographed by their father"). He worked largely in music halls ("the D'Auban children, pantomimic dancers and vocalists"), and seasonally as harlequin to his sister's Columbine in pantomime, but also appeared latterly on the Continental stage. In 1868, Johnnie and John Warde, billed as "a pair of accomplished pantomimists and comic dancers . . . from the Théâtre de la Porte-Saint-Martin," were engaged by Hollingshead (under whom they had been engaged previously at the Alhambra Music Hall) for the first program at the new Gaiety Theatre as "principal grotesque dancers and pantomimists." The pair appeared on the opening program in Gilbert's burlesque *Robert the Devil* as "two mysterious fiddlers."

D'Auban continued to perform for a good number of years, briefly running London's Raglan Music Hall (1870), visiting Brussels and appearing, in duo with Mariette or in a foursome with John and Emma Warde, at the Metropolitan and other of the principal music halls in such pieces of his own devising as the comic ballets

Plate 92. **The Dashing Little Duke.** *Ellaline Terris got into pants for this role. And sometimes her husband got into them too.*

All's Well That Ends Well, The Cripples, The Butterfly Hunt, I'm a Married Man Myself, Life, The Nightmare and *Haunted;* in pantomimes at Drury Lane and elsewhere; in sketches comic and terpischorean; and also in a whole range of productions at the Gaiety where he was, for a period, dance master. However, he made his career increasingly as a choreographer, establishing himself over some 30 years as one of the foremost dance designers in both the music-hall world and also in the musical theatre. He was associated with D'Oyly Carte throughout virtually the impresario's entire career, from *The Sorcerer* to *The Grand Duke* and *The Emerald Isle,* as well as with the Gaiety Theatre's famous series of new burlesques, and each of these areas brought forth one of his two most famous single routines: the comic dance for Emma Howson, George Grossmith and Richard Temple to the trio "Never Mind the Why and Wherefore" in the original production of *HMS Pinafore,* and the celebrated pas-de-quatre (barn-dance) introduced into the Gaiety burlesque *Faust Up-to-Date.*

Amongst the original musical shows which D'Auban choreographed for the British stage (in an era when the dances were not always formally credited on theatre programs) were *Cattarina* (1874), *Princess Toto* (1876), *The Sorcerer* (1877), *HMS Pinafore* (1878), *Gulliver* (1879), *Billee Taylor* (1880, also played Jumbo, the black cook, featured dancer), *The Corsican Brothers & Co Ltd* (1880), *Patience* (1881), *Claude Duval* (1881), *All in the Downs* (1881), *Rip van Winkle* (1882), *Iolanthe* (1882), *Sinbad* burlesque (1882), Lila Clay's *An Adamless Eden* and *On Condition* (1882), *Falka* (1883), *The Mikado* (1885), *Vetah* (1886), *Ruddigore* (1887), *Miss Esmeralda* (1887), *Frankenstein* (1887), *The Yeomen of the Guard* (1888), *Faust Up-to-Date* (1888), *Ruy Blas and the Blasé Roué* (1889), *The Red Hussar* (1889), *Paul Jones* (1889, also USA), *Carmen Up-to-Data* (1890), *The Rose and the Ring* (1890), *The Nautch Girl* (1891), *The Mountebanks* (1892), *Haddon Hall* (1892), *Jane Annie* (1893), *Utopia (Limited)* (1893), *Little Christopher Columbus* (1893), *King Kodak* (1894, "The Ostrich Dance"), *The Queen of Brilliants* (1894), *His Excellency* (1894), *The Chieftain* (1894), *An Artist's Model* (1895), *The New Barmaid* (1896 w Will Bishop), *The Grand Duke* (1896), *Man About Town* (1897), *His Majesty* (1897), *The Yashmak* (1897), *Regina BA* (1897 w John Tiller), *Lost, Strayed and Stolen* (1897), *The Beauty Stone* (1898), *Little Miss Nobody* (1898), *The Gay Pretenders* (1900) and *The Emerald Isle* (1901).

His wife, **Emma D'AUBAN** [née REDBOURNE, ka WARDE] (b c1848; d Staines, 13 October 1910) performed with John, and with the D'Aubans and Wardes team, in music hall, pantomime and musical theatre for 30 years, and took occasional principal dancing roles in musicals, creating the part of the ballet girl, Nellie Bly, in Edward Solomon's *The Vicar of Bray,* playing in Lila Clay's *An Adamless Eden* company, and appearing with John in a featured spot in *The Golden Web* (1893).

Their son, **Ernest [Henry] D'AUBAN** (b London, 28 October 1873; d Tonbridge, 3 February 1941) worked as a director and choreographer, notably for many years at the Theatre Royal, Drury Lane, whose pantomimes he also reproduced on Broadway.

Sister **Mar[r]iette D'AUBAN** [?Eliza Mary DOBBIN] (b London, 22 January ?1844; d London, 3 July 1906), dancer and choreographer, and the partner of John as "the D'Auban children" in their childhood, had a full career as a dancer, and later worked as a choreographer on such shows as *Mignonette* (1889), *Cinder-Ellen Up Too Late* (1891), *In Town* (1892), *Morocco Bound* (1893), *The Lady Slavey* (1894), *Don Juan* (1893 w Warde) and *Go-Bang* (1894). Subsequently, billed as "of Drury Lane and Gaiety Theatres, London, and the principal theatres in Paris and St Petersburg," she ran a school of dancing in London. She was briefly the wife of the pantomimist and Drury Lane harlequin, Tom Stonette (d 1873).

DAVIES, Harry Parr (b Briton Ferry, Wales, 24 May 1914; d Chelsea, London, 14 October 1955). Composer of a range of popular numbers from character songs to ballads in a short career on the British stage and screen.

Accompanist to Gracie Fields from the age of 18, Davies simultaneously supplied the singer with a series of successful numbers, including "The Fairy on the Christmas Tree," "The Sweetest Song in the World" (from the film *We're Going To Be Rich,* 1938), and her famous "Wish Me Luck as You Wave Me Goodbye" (w Phil Park, in the film *Shipyard Sally,* 1939), as well as penning several cinema songs for George Formby ("In My Little Snapshot Album" w Will Haines, Jimmy Harper in *I See Ice,* 1938, the title song of his 1938 film *It's in the Air*).

He made his first appearance in the West End as the composer of George Black's long-running Hippodrome revue *Black Velvet,* and followed that with scores or songs for a series of other revues: *Haw Haw, Come Out to Play, Top of the World, Gangway* ("My Paradise" for Ann Ziegler and Webster Booth), *Happidrome, Big Top, Best Bib and Tucker, Fine Feathers, The Shephard Show* and the Coronation revue *Glorious Days* (1952) at the Palace Theatre.

His first musical comedy score was that for Cicely Courtneidge's successful *Full Swing,* but he scored a major success with the wartime Hippodrome musical play *The Lisbon Story* in which a quartet, incidental to the spy drama, performed his most famous show song, "Pedro the Fisherman," as a scene-change cover and the romantic heroine sang "Never Say Goodbye." There was further success for him in another Cicely Courtneidge vehicle, *Her Excellency,* and in the charming pastel adaptation of J M Barrie's *Quality Street* as *Dear Miss Phoebe* ("I Leave My Heart in an English Garden"), but statistically the longest run of all his pieces was won by the farcical musical *Blue for a Boy* in which Fred Emney starred for over six hundred West End performances. It was also his last, for the young composer died in 1955 at the age of 41.

1942 **Full Swing** (w George Posford/Arthur Macrae, Archie Menzies, Jack Hulbert) Palace Theatre 16 April

1943 **The Lisbon Story** (Harold Purcell) London Hippodrome 17 June

1943 **The Knight Was Bold** (Barbara Gordon, Basil Thomas/ Emile Littler) Piccadilly Theatre 1 July

1944 **Jenny Jones** (Purcell/Ronald Gow) London Hippodrome 2 October

1949 **Her Excellency** (w Manning Sherwin/Purcell, Max Kester/ Purcell, Kester, Menzies) London Hippodrome 22 June

1950 **Dear Miss Phoebe** (Christopher Hassall) Phoenix Theatre 13 October

1950 **Blue for a Boy** (Purcell/Austin Melford) His Majesty's Theatre 30 November

DAVIS, Jessie Bartlett [née BARTLETT] (b nr Morris, Ill, ?17 September 1856; d Chicago, 14 May 1905). Biggish, blondish and beautiful contralto who won fame as a member of the Boston Ideal Comic Opera Company.

Jessie Bartlett began her career, in Chicago, as a concert and church singer, and made an early stage appearance with Caroline Riching's company in 1876 (''a youthful and vivacious member of the troupe''). She went on to appear with Hayden and Davis's Chicago Church Choir *HMS Pinafore* company as Little Buttercup (''Miss Jessie Bartlett, Church of the Messiah'') and the Counsel in *Trial by Jury* (1878), before becoming Mrs Davis (wife of Will J Davis manager of Haverly's Theater, Chicago and sometime half of the team of Hayden and Davis) and assuming the name under which she would become celebrated. She toured several years, under Davis's management, with the Choir company (Lady Angela in *Patience,* 1882, etc) and also in various operatic companies and, on one occasion, sang Siebel to the Marguerite of Adelina Patti. After a brief period studying in Paris, she returned to the American stage and appeared with W T Carleton's company (1884–85) appearing as a travesty Griolet (*La Fille du tambour-major*), Fritellini (*La Mascotte*) and Pygmalion in Massé's *Galathée* and in skirts as Else (*Der lustige Krieg*) and Lady Allcash (*Fra Diavolo*), and subsequently with the over-grandly named and underachieving American Opera Company.

In 1888 she joined the recently reformed Boston Ideal Comic Opera Company as a replacement for the equally statuesque and deeply contralto Agnes Huntington and, over the following years, she appeared with the Bostonians in such repertoire items as *Pygmalion and Galatea* (Cynisca), *Fatinitza* (Wladimir), *The Bohemian Girl* (Gipsy Queen), *Martha* (Nancy), *Il Trovatore* (Azucena), in the title role of *Carmen* and in such new or nearly-new pieces as Oscar Weil's *Suzette* (1889, Marchioness of Tollebrauche), *Don Quixote* (1890, Dorothea), *The Knickerbockers* (1893, Priscilla), in Indian roles in both *The Maid of Plymouth* (1893, Masconoma) and *The Ogallallas* (1894, Minnetoa), in *Prince Ananias* (1894, Idalia), *In Mexico* (1896, Theresa), *The Serenade* (1897, Dolores), *Rip van Winkle* (1897, Katrina/fairy queen), *Ulysses* (1898, Circe), and, most famously, in the breeches role of Alan-a-Dale in *Robin Hood* (1890), in which part she became associated with the celebrated Clement Scott/De Koven solo ''O Promise Me,'' apparently introduced by Hayden Coffin in the show's London version.

She left the company in 1899 to launch the Jessie Bartlett Davis Opera Company, but soon headed instead for the lucrative land of vaudeville. She was, however, seen once more on Broadway, now alarmingly under-voiced, in the brief role of the cadet Delaunay (enlarged by the interpolation of ''O Promise Me'') in the 1903 revival of *Erminie* before a premature death.

Her sister, character actress and vocalist **Josephine BARTLETT** (b Morris, Ill, 1859; d Chicago, 14 October 1910), was also a member of the Church Choir Company and later a popular member of both the Carleton Company (Paolo in *La Mascotte,* Abbess in *La Fille du tambour-major,* etc) and the Bostonians, being particularly noted for her Dame Durden in *Robin Hood.* She started her career with the Chicago Ideals company in 1883 and played with the Casino touring company (Javotte in *Erminie,* 1887) before joining up with the Boston company with whom she created parts in *Pygmalion and Galatea* (1888, Daphne), *The Ogallalas* (1892, Mrs Diana Scarborough), *The Knickerbockers* (1893, Dame), *The Maid of Plymouth* (1893, Dame Prudence), *Prince Ananias* (1894, Felicie), *The Serenade* (1896, Mother Superior), *Ulysses* (1898, Penelope), *The Viceroy* (1900, Ortensia), and *Maid Marian* (1901, Dame Durden). She appeared on tour in *The Mocking Bird,* and subsequently played alongside Fritzi Scheff in a series of shows, creating the roles of Eva in Victor Herbert's *Babette* (1903), Mrs Oldfield in the *She Stoops to Conquer* musical *The Two Roses* (1904), Mme Cécile in *Mlle Modiste* (1905) and Mother Justine in *The Prima Donna* (1908) and playing the contralto roles of *Fatinitza* (Wassildschi), *Boccaccio* (Peronella) and *Giroflé-Girofla* (Aurore). She died at the reported age of 49 after being knocked down by an automobile.

DAVIS, Owen (b Portland, Maine, 29 January 1874; d New York, 14 October 1956).

The Harvard-educated Davis made himself a highly lucrative career as the author and sometime producer of sentimental melodramas (*Nellie, the Beautiful Cloak Model, Tony the Bootblack,* etc)—rousingly lowbrow back-blocks pieces which often included the occasional musical number, to which Davis was happy to provide such lyrics as were required—before the market for such shows was killed by the rise of the movies. He moved on to try his talents in the profitable purlieus of Broadway and there made his mark with a number of successful comedies and later with some more serious pieces, one of which (*Icebound*) won him a Pulitzer Prize (1923).

His few purpose-built musicals did not range as widely in value as his plays. In fact, they were flops. His earliest such piece was a little sketch for Laura Joyce Bell, *The New Prima Donna, or Up Goes the Price of*

Milk, which prompted a critic to sneer of the future Pulitzer winner "Davis obviously knows more about the price of milk than writing plays" and the next a showful of vaudeville acts tacked together with a bit of plot for producer Gus Hill. He then turned to compiling the kind of touring musical farce comedies and melodramas with interpolated songs and specialities played on far from the best circuits. One of these, *Anita the Singing Girl,* "combining the better features of melodrama and comedy-drama with those of musical comedy" and put out by Spencer and Aborn with the intent of bucking the usual cheap melodrama houses which Davis's plays had filled so effectively, and playing nothing less than dollar houses, proved to have several seasons of upwardly striving life in it.

His first attempts at conventional musical comedy fared poorly. The lowbrow *Cupid at Vassar* had a short tour and the the Broadway-bound Shubert production of his *Page Mr Cupid,* with Ernest Truex starred, folded on the pre–New York road. However, he had a major musical theatre success, at one step removed, when his play *The Nervous Wreck* (1922) was used as the source for the hit musical *Whoopee* (New Amsterdam Theater 4 December 1928) with Eddie Cantor in its leading role. As a result of this hit, the next musical theatre months brought two further Davis adaptations. His *Easy Come, Easy Go* (1925) was turned into *Lady Fingers* (Vanderbilt Theater 31 January 1929) for Eddie Buzzell (132 performances) and he adapted his own *Shotgun Wedding* as the text for the Rodgers and Hart musical *Spring Is Here* (104 performances).

A second collaboration with Rodgers and Hart, and with producers Aarons and Freedley, on a piece called *Me for You,* folded up after a fortnight's tryout and was transformed by other hands into *Heads Up!* (1929), whilst a final return to the musical theatre, eight years later, brought another failure with the 60-performance run of *Virginia.*

1897 **The New Prima Donna, or Up Goes the Price of Milk** (uncredited) sketch Pleasure Palace 13 June

1899 **Over the Fence** (various) Derby, Conn 28 September; Milwaukee 3 December (new version)

1901 **Circus Day** (George E Nichols) Majestic Theater, Utica 17 September; Metropolis Theater 30 September

1905 **How Baxter Butted In** (various) Lyceum Theater, Elizabeth, NJ 14 August; Murray Hill Theater 13 November

1907 **Cupid at Vassar** (A Baldwin Sloane/w George Totten Smith) Poli's Theater, Waterbury, Conn 23 August

1907 **Anita, the Singing Girl** (Harold Orlob) Auditorium, Baltimore 26 August

1908 **The Battle of Port Arthur** (Manuel Klein) 2 scenes Hippodrome 13 January

1909 **Back Again** (Karl Hoschna/w Otto Hauerbach) Olympic Park, Newark 7 June

1909 **Sal, the Circus Girl** (various) Brooklyn 7 August

1920 **Page Mr Cupid** (Jean Schwartz/Blanche Merrill) Crescent Theater, Brooklyn 17 May

1929 **Spring Is Here** (Richard Rodgers/Lorenz Hart) Alvin Theater 11 March

1929 **Me for You** (Rodgers/Hart) Shubert Theater, Detroit 15 September

1937 **Virginia** (Arthur Schwartz/Albert Stillman/w Laurence Stallings) Center Theater 2 September

Autobiographies: *I'd Like To Do It Again* (Farrar & Rinehart, New York, 1931), *My First Fifty Years in the Theater* (Walter H Baker, Boston, 1950)

DAVIS, Sammy, jr (b New York, 8 December 1925; d Los Angeles, 16 May 1990). Charismatic little song-and-dance man who made occasional stage musical appearances.

Davis began his career as a juvenile dancer and impressionist in a variety act with his father, Sammy Davis, and his uncle, Will Mastin, before embracing stage and film acting. His first appearance on the musical stage was in *Mr Wonderful* (1956, Charlie Welch) in which he appeared alongside his father and uncle as a rising young nightclub performer who bore more than a passing resemblance to himself. His performance helped both the song "Too Close for Comfort" and *Mr Wonderful* to degrees of success.

In a career mixing nightclub performing, variety, recording, stage and film, Davis appeared as Sportin' Life in the movie version of *Porgy and Bess* (1959), returned to the stage as the hero of a musical version of Clifford Odets's boxing play *Golden Boy* (1964), which he played in both America and Britain, appeared as the Street Singer in the 1963 film of *Die Dreigroschenoper* and as Big Daddy in Hollywood's version of *Sweet Charity* (1968). He also appeared several times on the stage in the very central role of Littlechap in the musical *Stop the World—I Want to Get Off* (State Theater, 1978, etc), the principal work of songwriters Anthony Newley and Leslie Bricusse, whose torchy, self-interrogating ballads were latterly a basic part of his act.

Davis also featured in two television musicals on the *Alice in Wonderland* tale (ABC 1966, CBS 1985).

Autobiographies: w Boyar, J & B: *Yes, I Can* (Farrar, Straus & Giroux, New York, 1966), *Hollywood in a Suitcase* (Morrow, New York, 1980), *Why Me?* (Farrar, Straus & Giroux, New York, 1989)

DAVIS, Thomas B[uffen] (b London, 27 March 1867; d Tunbridge Wells, 14 December 1931).

Tom Davis, a former solicitor who had spent some years finding himself a place in the theatre (Queen's Theatre, Birmingham, behind the scenes in London's *The*

Bric à Brac Will 1895, *The New Barmaid* 1896, *The Little Genius* 1896, etc), made his official bow as a West End manager when he picked up the rights to the musical *Little Miss Nobody,* which the actor Yorke Stephens had staged at the Cheltenham Opera House for one shop-window performance. He brought *Little Miss Nobody* (1898) to London in a season when the town was quite buzzing with outstanding new pieces and, cleverly cast and carefully rehearsed and staged, at a time when it was more usual to fix up a show after it had opened rather than before, he succeeded, against all expectations, in coming out with a hit.

With his hit in hand, Davis secured a long lease on the Lyric Theatre, where *Little Miss Nobody* was playing, and he followed that show first with an English version of Varney's *L'Amour mouillé* and, when that failed to take, with a season by De Wolf Hopper and his American company in *El Capitan,* while he prepared what was to be his big play for success, the first musical by top songwriter Leslie Stuart and librettist-of-the-hour Owen Hall. When *Florodora* was produced, in November 1899, Davis found himself with a bigger hit on his hands than anyone, including himself, could have envisaged. A year and a half's run at the Lyric was only the very beginning of a fabulous national and international career for the show.

Stuart and Hall's follow-up, *The Silver Slipper* (1901), had a good if not outstanding run, but Davis's attempt to take on the reconstructed Adelphi Theatre, renamed the New Century, with an American musical comedy, *The Whirl of the Town,* foundered, and a repairing of Hall and his *Geisha* partner, Sidney Jones, produced an unexpected flop in *The Medal and the Maid* (1903).

This turn of fortune meant that Davis was forced to give up the Lyric Theatre and, when he returned to town the following year with *Mr Popple of Ippleton,* he took a lease on the next-door Apollo Theatre instead. Both *Mr Popple* and the subsequent *The Belle of Brittany* (1908) did well, but an English version of *Le Sire de Vergy* (1905) and Sidney Jones's *A Persian Princess* (1909) were both very short-lived disasters, and another severe failure with the Austro-American musical *The Grass Widows* (1912) ended Davis's series of musical productions on a sadly downward beat.

The Apollo Theatre nevertheless flourished as a musical house under Davis's leasehold, and for an extended period it housed H G Pelissier's *Follies,* a pierrot show-cum-revue which Davis had been instrumental in bringing to London.

After his peak period was past, Tom Davis long retained an interest in the theatre in Birmingham, and was responsible for the construction of the city's Theatre Royal. And in the year of his death he saw *Florodora* make one more return to the West End.

DAWN, Hazel [TOUT, Hazel Dawn] (b Ogden, Utah, 23 March 1890; d New York, 28 August 1988). An extremely attractive girl from Utah who launched her career in musical theatre before going on to further success as an actress.

At the age of 18, Hazel Dawn, who had prepared herself for a musical career by studying voice and violin on the Continent and at London's Royal College of Music, made her musical comedy début in a tiny featured role in Frank Curzon's production of *Dear Little Denmark* (1909) at London's Prince of Wales Theatre. She segued into another bit part in the same management's *The Balkan Princess* (1910) and then into another, in George Edwardes's London production of *The Dollar Princess.* However, she had to return to America to win her big break. In 1911 she was cast in the leading role of the Broadway production of Ivan Caryll's *The Pink Lady,* an enormous success which established her as a star and allowed her to return to Britain in that capacity for a season of *The Pink Lady* at the Globe Theatre, blondely performing the famous *Pink Lady* waltz song, ''My Beautiful Lady,'' and accompanying herself on the violin.

She followed up this hit of a lifetime as another French demi-mondaine, Gaby Gaufrette—Queen of the Night Restaurants, equipped with another winning waltz-song (''Just Because It's You'')—in Caryll's musical version of Tristan Bernard's *The Little Café* (1913), and then, less successfully, as the daughter of an English lord who is *The Débutante* of the title in Victor Herbert and Harry B Smith's 1914 musical. After this production she abandoned the musical theatre for Ziegfeld revue (*The Century Girl*), film (*One of Our Girls,* a detective disguised as a nurse in *The Lone Wolf, Under Cover,* etc) and the straight theatre (*Getting Gertie's Garter, Up in Mabel's Room*) before settling down, in 1931, to more than a half-century of retirement which included a stint as a caster for J Walter Thompson.

Miss Dawn's sister, **Margaret ROMAINE** [Margaret Elizabeth TOUT] (b Ogden, 23 September 1888; d Los Angeles, July 1984), followed the same studies in Europe, was heard briefly at the Paris Opéra-Comique, and returned to America to take a leading role in the Broadway musical *The Midnight Girl* (1914, Hélène) and in *Have a Heart* (1917, t/o Peggy Schoonmaker), while her daughter, who billed herself fatally as Hazel Dawn jr, also had a small and rather unprepossessing career in musicals (Susan van Tuyl in *My Romance,* etc) and 1940s movies.

DAY, Edith [Marie] (b Minneapolis, Minn, 10 April 1896; d Barnes, London, 1 May 1971). Pretty, sweet-

Plate 93. **Edith Day** *and Sydney Arnold as Noël Coward's Mr and Mrs Sweeney, the dear old couple who hate one another, in* Sail Away.

voiced ingenue who starred in some of the biggest musical hits of the American and British stage during the 1910s and 1920s.

Edith Day first appeared on the New York stage in support of Mitzi in the Hungaro-American musical *Pom-Pom* at the Casino Theatre in 1916 (Evelyn, the maid, with half the opening duet, and Gina, a thief, in Act II). She subsequently played a supporting role in the Anna Held vehicle *Follow Me* (1916, Denise, a fortune teller, "Two Happy Tadpoles," "How Would You Like to Bounce a Baby on your Knee?") and toured as the principal ingenue in *His Little Widows* before landing her first Broadway lead role as Grace Douglas in George M Cohan and Sam Harris's highly successful production of *Going Up* at the Liberty Theatre (1917), singing and dancing the show's hit number, "The Tickle Toe." This success was followed by an even greater one, when she created the role of Irene O'Dare in Carle Carleton's production of *Irene,* introducing "Alice Blue Gown," opposite Walter Regan at New York's Vanderbilt Theatre and (having briefly become Mrs Carle Carleton), opposite her next (and equally brief) husband, Pat Somerset, at the Empire Theatre, London. During her days with Carleton, the producer also attempted to launch her as a film actress in Crest Pictures's *The Grain of Dust* (1918), but the success the little dark actress had won on the stage was not repeated on the screen.

An attempt to follow up the memorable hit of *Irene* with a weak British imitation of the show called *Jenny* (1922) at the same London theatre was a flop and Miss Day returned to America where she added to her growing tally of successes when she created the musical version of the famous Kitty of *The Marriage of Kitty* in Victor Herbert's musical of the play, *Orange Blossoms* (1922, "A Kiss in the Dark"). She made yet another musical comedy hit when she starred as Nina Benedetto, the heroine of the Vincent Youmans musical *Wildflower* (1923, ''Bambalina''), before again visiting Britain, this time to play the title role, created in New York by Mary Ellis, in the triumphant London version of *Rose Marie* (1925) at the Theatre Royal, Drury Lane.

She followed up with equal success, at the same theatre, as Margot Bonvalet in *The Desert Song* (1927) and as Magnolia Hawkes in *Show Boat* (1928), establishing herself over a period of some four years as one of London's top singing heroines, but thereafter the success which had followed her so faithfully failed her, and the flops of London's version of *Rio Rita* (1930, Rita), of Friml's *Luana* (1932, Luana), which failed even to reach London, and of *Sunny River* (1934, Lolita) at the Piccadilly Theatre were relieved only by repeat appearances as Rose Marie and Margot before her ingenue career was done.

In 1962 Noël Coward, hearing that she was in money difficulties, persuaded producer Harold Fielding to offer her the role of Mrs Sweeney in *Sail Away.* She paired with Sydney Arnold in one of the show's high points as the dear old couple who hate one another in ''Bronxville Darby and Joan.'' But Mr Fielding had been wasting his sympathies: when Mrs Edith Marie Horne died, nine years later, she left behind a tidy little fortune of £45,000.

A DAY IN HOLLYWOOD, A NIGHT IN THE UKRAINE Musical double feature by Dick Vosburgh. Music by Frank Lazarus. New End Theatre, London, 15 January 1979; May Fair Theatre, 26 March 1979.

The work of American comedy writer Vosburgh and South African musician/performer Lazarus, *A Day in Hollywood, A Night in the Ukraine* was first produced at north London's New End Theatre, a tiny and short-lived fringe-theatre venue transformed from a morgue. Its Hollywood part featured a number of revusical items, old and new, on movie-mag topics (''I Love a Film Cliché,'' ''Movie Fan's Love Song,'' ''All God's Chillun Got Movie Shows,'' ''Goldwyn and Warner and Mayer and Zanuck and Zukor and Cohn'') as performed by a group of six cinema ushers, whilst the second part had the same artists giving a performance of a little musical comedy based on Chekhov's *The Bear,* played in the style of a Marx brothers film. Lazarus gave an uncanny impersonation of Chico, whilst Sheila Steafel, mutely plucking unheard music from the spokes of a bicycle wheel, was an unforgettable Harpo.

Under the management of Helen Montagu, the little show transferred to the larger May Fair Theatre, where it found an audience for 168 performances, but a subsequent Broadway production of a truly colored-up version, mounted by Alexander H Cohen, did very much better. The cheerful end-of-the-pier material of the first half was cut away and replaced by American material old (a Richard Whiting songbook) and new to newish (three Jerry Herman songs including the wonderfully woeful saga of paternal pride ''The Best in the World'') and some glittering choreography by Tommy Tune, and the resultant entertainment garnered a handful of Broadway awards and a long run (588 performances).

An updated version of *A Night in the Ukraine* was produced in Washington, DC, in 1991 (23 October).

Author Vosburgh repeated his attractive trick twenty years later when he authored the comical *A Saint She Ain't* (mus: Denis King), a Hollywoodized version of Molière's *La Malade imaginaire* (King's Head Theatre) in which the characters were played by actors imitating Gene Kelly, W C Fields, Rita Hayworth and others. The songs burlesqued as they imitated the mid-century cinema with their clever and laughable rhymes and tinkly rhythmic tunes, and out-Portered Cole Porter with their catalogs of celebrity names (''A Saint She Ain't,'' ''You're the Only Star in my Heaven'') in a score that fumbled only once, with a cheaply vulgar Mae Western piece (''The Banana for my Pie''). *A Saint She Ain't* progressed from its original venue to a West End (Apollo Theatre 16 September 1999) which hadn't seem too much musical comedy entertainment in recent years. It won a happy reception but a short run.

USA: John Golden Theater 1 May 1980

Recordings: *A Day in Hollywood* US cast (DRG), *A Saint She Ain't* original cast (First Night)

DE ANGELIS, [Thomas] Jefferson (b San Francisco, 30 November 1859; d Orange, NJ, 20 March 1933). For more than 30 years one of the classiest comic actors in the Broadway musical theatre, de Angelis introduced comedy roles in many of the earliest American comic operas and musical comedies of the modern era.

Son of the blackface comic Johnny De Angelis (b Philadelphia, c1815; d San Francisco, 25 December 1877) of ''Hernandez and De Angelis, the rival darkies,'' who had appeared in some of California's and America's earliest English opéra-bouffe productions, ''Jeff'' began in show business as a child working with his father and sister in vaudeville, and made his first Broadway appearance as a 14-year-old member of the Union Square Theatre stock company. He spent a period purveying two-handed ''Dutch'' sketches in vaudeville houses in tandem with La Petite Sally (his sister, Sarah), was seen in the San Francisco extravaganza *Zamiel* (1878) and then, at the age of 21, put together a dramatic company with which he took to the roads not only of America but of Australia and the Orient, for some four years. He began by purveying a Fred Maeder ''protean drama'' *One Word* (1880) in which, teamed again with sister

Sally, he appeared as old Karl Hoffnung, a German musician, as his son Karl, as Max, a stockbroker, and as Schnitzberg, a grocer, giving songs and banjo solos in between the moments of drama and sentiment and costume-change. He later included versions of the Gilbert and Sullivan musicals and several French musical shows amongst his presentations. In 1882, while they were playing Capetown, Sally (now Mrs Sarah Fulton) committed suicide when her attempt to elope to Australia with another member of the company was foiled. After returning home, de Angelis found himself a more practical niche as an actor in musical farce-comedy and extravaganza and he made his first adult Broadway appearances as Hermann Zwugg in *A Bottle of Ink* (1885), as Bacchus in an otherwise almost-all-female version of *Ixion* (1885, also choreography) and as August Glotzheimer in the Mestayers' touring *We, Us & Co* (1886).

He now recognized that low comedy rather than high drama was his forte, and soon found himself a place as a comedy artist in the musical theatre. He took over the role of Lord Dolphin in the Philadelphia musical *The Little Tycoon* in 1886, and then in 1887 joined the McCaull Opera Company, appearing in good comedy roles during the two years that followed at Wallack's Theater, other New York venues and also on the road. Amongst the roles which he played for McCaull were Girafo in *Jacquette* (*La Bearnaise*), Cyprian in *Prinz Methusalem,* D'Effiat in Dellinger's *Lorraine,* Sir Mulberry Mullitt in Audran's *Indiana,* Scalza in *Boccaccio,* Clausen in Suppé's *Bellman* and Don Cristoval d'Olivarez in the same composer's *Clover* (*Die Jagd nach dem Glück*), Giles in Czibulka's *The May Queen* (*Der Glücksritter*) and Momo in the unsuccessful production of Dellinger's *Capitan Fracasse,* as well as comedy parts in *Ruddigore, Falka, Der Bettelstudent, Princess Ida, The Mikado* and in two new native pieces, *The Begum* (1887, Jhustt-Naut) and *The Lady or the Tiger* (1888, Menander).

During 1890 he appeared at the Casino Theater opposite Lillian Russell and Fanny Rice in the title role of Millöcker's *Der arme Jonathan,* and over the next five years he was featured at New York's flagship comic opera theatre in another series of principal comic roles in imported shows: Hellmesberger's *Apollo* (Adrastas), *La Grande-Duchesse* (Puck), *Indigo* (Ali Baba), *The Tyrolean* (*Der Vogelhändler,* Tipple), *Oncle Célestin* (Pontaillac), Millöcker's *The Child of Fortune* (*Das Sonntagskind,* Tristan) and *The Vice Admiral* (Punto) and *The Little Trooper* (*Les 28 Jours de Clairette,* Gibard), before moving on to yet another series of musical shows, this time American-made works.

He supported De Wolf Hopper in *The Lady and the Tiger* (1892, Menander) and Lillian Russell in De Koven's *The Tzigane* (1895, Vasili), got above the title for the first time in William Furst's *Fleur-de-lis* (1895, Comte des Escarbilles) and starred subsequently in Ludwig Englander's *The Caliph* (1896, Hardluck XIII) and in three Julian Edwards musicals, *Brian Boru* (1896, Pat O'Hara), the successful *The Wedding Day* (1897, Polycop) and *The Jolly Musketeer* (1898, Comte de Beauprêt), which provided him with a useful vehicle for two years of touring. *A Royal Rogue* (1900, Baptiste Ballou), which starred him alongside Josephine Hall, was a quick failure, but he was well provided with the role of Professor Bunn in Edward German's *The Emerald Isle* in New York and on the road and followed this up with another English musical, appearing around America as Sammy Gigg in *The Toreador,* under his own management.

His biggest success as a modern musical comedy star came with the Robert Smith/Raymond Hubbell *Fantana* (1905, Hawkins), a success which was not repeated with *The Girl and the Governor* (1906–7, Don Pascal de Mesquita), but he returned more happily in the revue *The Gay White Way* (1907, George Dane), in a vaudeville musical sketch called *The Rehearsal* (1908), and in *The Beauty Spot* (1909) playing a comedy character called General Samovar, dreamed up by his fellow comedian-cum-writer Joseph Herbert and set to music by De Koven. *The Beauty Spot* company also produced his own musical comedy *The Jolly Tar* with Frank Doane in its leading role. In 1910 he appeared as Ko-Ko in the starry *Mikado* at the Casino and in the Viennese travesty of Rostand's *Chantecler* called *A Barnyard Romeo* (1910), and the following year toured for H H Frazee and George Lederer in his own musical *The Ladies' Lion,* and took a star turn in *The Little Trooper* at St Louis's Delmar Gardens, but the best moments of his career had now passed, and, although he had been many years a much-loved star, passed without him having really found one outstanding role with which he could be identified.

Over the next dozen years he continued to work in the musical theatre, playing New York and/or the road in such pieces as *The Pearl Maiden* (1912, Pinkerton Kerr), *Rob Roy* (rev 1913, Dugald MacWheeble), *Madame Moselle* (1914, Gabriel Smudge), the short-lived Fritzi Scheff vehicle *Husbands Guaranteed* (1916), revivals of De Koven's *Rob Roy* (1913, Mayor of Perth) and *The Highwayman* (1917, Foxy Quiller) and of the veteran farce-comedy *A Trip to Chinatown* (Welland Strong); in revue (*Marie Dressler's All Star Gambol, The Passing Show of 1917*); in vaudeville (playing his own sketch *All at Sea* 1912); and alongside Gertrude Lawrence in the unsuccessful *Rock-a-Bye Baby* (1919). He even appeared as Bumerli in *The Chocolate Soldier* when over 60 years of age. His final appearances in the Broadway musical theatre were as Nitsch in a revival of *The Merry Widow* (1921/2) and as a brief Don Bolero in a revival of *Giroflé-Girofla* in 1927 (also director).

In 1915 de Angelis also made a new attempt at being a manager when he set up a summer stock company to play comic opera at Lancaster, Pennyslvania. When the local sponsor failed to come up with the first week's wages, he was obliged to produce $1,000 from his own pocket to pay what was owed before shutting down the company.

Sally de Angelis's daughter, Natalie Fulton, also took to the stage as Natalie de Angelis.

1910 **A Jolly Tar** (William T Francis) Alvin Theater, Pittsburgh, Pa 1 April

1911 **The Ladies' Lion** (Francis) Illinois Theater, Chicago 23 September

1912 **All at Sea** sketch Proctor's Theater 26 August

Autobiography (w Harlow, A): *Vagabond Trouper* (Harcourt, Brace, New York, 1931)

DEAREST ENEMY American musical comedy in 2 acts by Herbert Fields. Lyrics by Lorenz Hart. Music by Richard Rodgers. Knickerbocker Theater, New York, 18 September 1925.

After Broadway's "discovery" of Rodgers and Hart's work in *The Garrick Gaieties,* the writers were able at last to get a production for the musical play which they had been auditioning around town for the past year. *Dearest Enemy,* set in the American revolution, had its heroine Betsy Burke (Helen Ford) and her female friends waylaying the British, and notably the gallant Captain Sir John Copeland (Charles Purcell), with their charms long enough to allow a cornered detachment of American troops to make their escape and assemble for battle. Betsy and Sir John fall in love, but the girl nevertheless carries out her part in the plan which results in an American victory in which John is taken captive. General Washington is the deus ex machina who brings the happy ending in the last scene.

The highlight of the show's score was Purcell and Miss Ford's performance of the love duet which climaxed the first act, "Here in My Arms." Flavia Arcaro as Mrs Murray led the girls of the piece in both lamenting ("Heigh-ho, lackaday") and appreciating ("War Is War") the state of war, and performed two pieces in the variety-musical style entertainment designed to keep the British soldiers from thoughts of leaving her house ("The Hermits," "Full Blown Roses," "Where the Hudson River Flows"). The two lovers joined in two further duets, "Bye and Bye" and "Here's a Kiss," (both of which were picked by the out-of-town critics as hit material above "Here in My Arms"), alongside Betsy's admission of her love, "I'd Like to Hide It." Mrs Murray's daughter Jane (Helen Spring) and her officer, Captain Harry Tryon (John Seymour) provided the traditional soubret moments ("I Beg Your Pardon," "Sweet Peter").

In spite of the concurrence of *The Vagabond King, Sunny* and *No, No, Nanette,* all of which opened in New York at around the same time as *Dearest Enemy,* and in spite of predictions that the piece would prove too serious in its subject matter for popular consumption, George Ford's production had a fine 36-week, 286-performance run at the Knickerbocker Theater, setting the Broadway foundation stone for the long and memorable career of the Rodgers and Hart partnership. It subsequently went on the road in America, but found its only taker outside its homeland in a J C Williamson Ltd Australian production. Dot Brunton (Betsy), Maidie Hope (Mrs Murray) and Sydney Burchall (John) starred in a version peppered with interpolated songs for a disappointing month and a half in Melbourne (Theatre Royal 12 September 1931) and less than a month in Sydney.

A proposed 1931 Broadway revival, under Ford's management, was called off before making it to the stage, but the show was seen again when it was revived at the Goodspeed Opera House in 1976.

Australia: Her Majesty's Theatre, Sydney 7 March 1931

Recordings: studio cast (Beginners Records), selection (AEI)

DEARLY, Max [ROLLAND-MAX-[DEARLY], Lucien Paul Marie Joseph] (b Paris, 22 November 1874; d Neuilly-sur-Seine, 2 June 1943). Longtime star of the French musical, comic and variety stages, who also worked as a director and a writer.

After 10 years performing in the French provinces, Dearly made it to Paris and a job at the Scala café-concert where, between 1898 and 1900, he performed a series of comic songs of his own writing which won him considerable popularity. In 1901 he joined the company at Fernand Samuel's Théâtre des Variétés, and he soon established himself there as a Parisian favorite in comedy and musical-comedy roles. In his first years at the Variétés he appeared as Mercury in *Orphée aux enfers,* in the premiere of Terrasse's *Le Sire de Vergy* in which he later graduated to the title role, as St Guillaume in *Chonchette,* as Tourillon in the first regular performance of a French version of *Die Fledermaus,* in such classics as *La Vie parisienne, Le Petit Duc* and *L'Oeil crevé,* in the French version of *The Country Girl,* and as Radaboum in the premiere of *Le Paradis de Mahomet* (1906), the last and posthumous work of Planquette.

In the years that followed, he appeared in a rich list of plays and musical pieces both at the Variétés and—after quitting that house for what seemed like a lucrative engagement at the Châtelet (it wasn't, because he got taken to court and lost heavily)—at other Parisian theatres, as well as playing regularly in the music halls where he was responsible notably for writing and creating "La Danse apache," the treat-'em-rough athletic dance routine performed to Offenbach's *Papillon* music which became for a while the sort-of-sadistic sensation of Paris (Moulin-Rouge, 1908) and later the rest of the world. With few original native pieces of distinction giving him the kind of opportunities he might capitalize on (*La Reine s'amuse, Boulard et ses filles,* etc), Dearly appeared largely in the classic musical repertoire—as Golo in *Geneviève de Brabant,* Bobinet then Gondremarck in *La Vie parisienne,* Trénitz in *La Fille de Madame Angot,* Calchas in *La Belle Hélène*—as well as in French versions of foreign works—Imari in *The Geisha,* Simplicitas in *The Arcadians,* Baron des Aubrais in *La Chaste Suzanne* (*Die keusche Susanne*)—and, working in an individual style which mixed a relaxed kind of comedy with a sufficient singing voice, established himself as one of the great performers of the French musical theatre of his era.

First seen in Britain in a visit to the St George's Hall with the Théâtre des Capucines company and *Chonchette* early in his career, he later worked there in variety and in 1915 appeared for a time at the Winter Garden Theatre under the management of Grossmith and Laurillard in the role of Pedro, created by Maurice Farkoa, in the London production of *Tonight's the Night.*

Dearly had a hand in the adaptation of *The Arcadians* for its French performance and in the libretto for the 1931 musical *Billy-Bill* (Scala, 1931), and also worked in later years as a director, staging the first French production of Messager's *Monsieur Beaucaire* at the Théâtre Marigny, a lavish *La Vie parisienne* (1931, also played Gondremarck) and the vast and starry *Orphée aux enfers* (1931, also played Jupiter) at the Mogador. He also provided material for revue (*Paris-Singerie* Olympia, 1909, etc).

DEAR MISS PHOEBE Musical play in 2 acts by Christopher Hassall, adapted from J M Barrie's play *Quality Street.* Music by Harry Parr Davies. Phoenix Theatre, London, 13 October 1950.

A tasteful musical adaptation of Barrie's hit play of 1902 in which the dowdied Phoebe Throssel (Carol Raye) poses as her own bright, young niece to win back the love of Valentine Brown (Peter Graves) whom she lost to the Napoléonic wars. A chastely English score ("Whisper While You Waltz," "Living a Dream," "Spring Will Sing a Song for You") turned up one enduring number in the all-but-patriotic duet "I Leave My Heart in an English Garden." Eight months in London prefaced a tidy tour.

An earlier *Quality Street* musical, *Drei alte Schachteln* (Walter Kollo/Rideamus/Herman Haller) was a considerable success in Germany, but a brisk Broadway flop (*Phoebe of Quality Street* Shubert Theater 9 May 1921).

DEAR WORLD Musical in 2 acts by Jerome Lawrence and Robert E Lee based on *The Madwoman of Chaillot* by Jean Giraudoux. Music and lyrics by Jerry Herman. Mark Hellinger Theater, New York, 6 February 1969.

Following the success of *Mame,* authors Lawrence and Lee, composer Jerry Herman and star Angela Lansbury came together in a second musical which allowed the star to portray a flamboyantly eccentric woman of a certain age. The role of Giraudoux's Countess Aurelia—the Madwoman of Chaillot who pits herself against the horrid Developers to save her "Dear World" from pollution and destruction—gave the star at least as many splendid opportunities as its predecessor, if in a very different style. However, *Dear World*'s more sophisticated tone and delightful, though less obvious, score (including a loopy tea party scene which remains one of Herman's finest pieces of writing) did not have the same general appeal as the earlier show and Alexander H Cohen's Broadway production won only a disappointing 132-performance run.

In an era where the show's subject of the "development" of the earth's resources for private profit has become a major international issue, *Dear World* has been mooted several times for revival, and at the time of writing is scheduled to be seen in new productions (one "remade," one faithful) on the two coasts of America.

Recording: original cast (Columbia)

DÉDÉ Opérette in 3 acts by Albert Willemetz. Music by Henri Christiné. Théâtre des Bouffes-Parisiens, Paris, 10 November 1921.

After Willemetz and Christiné had sent the new Jazz Age comédie musicale into orbit with the incomparable *Phi-Phi,* it remained to be seen with what they would follow their hit of an era. In fact, they followed it with another hit, one which stuck to the smallish-scale musical comedy lines they had established (only smallish, there were now six chorus girls and even some chorus men, which there had not been in the previous piece), but which, otherwise, was completely different in its text and style.

Dédé (which traded on the connection with *Phi-Phi* in its title, at least) was an up-to-date story of Jazz Age naughtiness, set in a modern shoe shop, where the owner, Dédé de la Huchette (Urban), is trying to set up an affair with Odette (Maguy Warna), an apparently married woman he has met at a tango-tea. Dédé is adored by his head assistant, Denise (Alice Cocéa), who is, in turn, sighed after demonstratively by her last employer, the lawyer Leroydet (Baron fils), and everybody, at some stage during the proceedings, gets a cheerfully useless helping hand from Dédé's irritating, penniless, self-confident old chum, Robert (Maurice Chevalier). The

Plate 94. **Dédé.** *James Sparrow (Dédé) and the vendeuses of his Parisian love-nest shoe-shop . . . a staff borrowed from a nightclub chorus!*

comedy, full of extremely funny and almost inevitably sex-based situations, zipped along cheerfully in the hands of such experienced performers as Urban, *Phi-Phi* star Mlle Cocéa, and of the music hall's Chevalier, making his musical theatre debut as the blandly laid-back Robert.

Christiné's score was full of catchy, lilting songs. Chevalier had all the cream, expressing his shrugful philosophy in ''Dans la vie faut pas s'en faire,'' singing cheerfully about his sexual laissez-aller in ''Je m'donne'' and joining Mlle Cocéa for the lazily bouncing ''Si j'avais su.'' All three songs became hits. There were, however, plenty of good things for all in the score of *Dédé,* not only in the way of solos but also in some highly comical ensembles, such as the second-act finale in which Dédé and Robert invent a play within a play to create an opportunity for the compromised Odette to escape unseen from her shoe-shop rendezvous (''Une femme de monde trompait son mari'').

Dédé had a highly successful first run of seven months, returning, after the summer had been filled with a *Phi-Phi* revival, in the autumn for the second half of its run through nearly six months more. It was revived in Paris in 1927, filmed in 1934 with a cast headed by Albert Préjean, Danielle Darrieux, Mireille Perrey, Baron fils and Claude Dauphin, played regularly throughout France in tours and provincial productions, revived again in 1973 (Théâtre des Nouveautés) with the popular singer Antoine in Chevalier's role and the English actor James Sparrow as Dédé, and brought back to the Paris stage yet again in 1981 (Théâtre de la Renaissance), whilst keeping up a regular presence in the French provinces culminating in a major revival at Lyon's Théâtre des Célestins with Sparrow and Jean-Paul Lucet in 1992 (27 November).

The Paris success encouraged both Charles Cochran in London and Charles Dillingham on Broadway to go after the show and its star, and negotiations got far enough for each of them to announce a forthcoming production with Chevalier in the cast, but neither happened. America did not see *Dédé* at all, whilst London got a damaged version (ad Ronald Jeans) produced by André Charlot and Paul Murray, starring Guy Le Feuvre (Robert), Joe Coyne (Dédé) and the young Gertrude Lawrence (Denise). Coyne was top-billed, and thus got ''Si j'avais su'' and ''Dans la vie faut pas s'en faire'' (''Trouble Never Troubles Me'') as well as a couple of Phil Braham extras (''There's a Proper Time,'' ''Collecting Girls'') added to his part. This *Dédé* survived only 46 performances, before it was closed down, frilled up with extraneous revusical material and sent unrecognizably on the road under the title *The Talk of the Town.*

UK: Garrick Theatre 17 October 1922; Hungary: Lujza Blaha Színház 1 February 1923

Film: René Guissart 1934

Recordings: complete with dialogue (Decca), 1973 revival cast (RCA), original cast selection on *L'Opérette française par ses créateurs* (EPM)

DE FRECE, Lauri [DE FRECE, Lawrence Abraham] (b Barbican, London, 3 March 1881; d Trouville, 25 August 1921). Favorite British musical theatre comedian of the early part of the 20th century, whose career was cut short by a premature death.

Son of a London jeweller and a scion of a busy theatrical family, owners of Liverpool theatres and music halls and "the oldest provincial theatrical agency in Britain, 1 Murray St and Williamson Sq, Liverpool," little Lauri de Frece began a career as a musical comedian in his early twenties. He toured for a considerable time with George Dance's traveling versions of George Edwardes's musicals, notably as Chambuddy Ram in *The Cingalee,* and in the South African musical comedy company of Sass & Nelson, before making his first London success as Sebak, the comical keeper of the crocodiles, in the comic opera *Amasis* (1906). He followed this with further personal successes as the chauffeur, Yarker, in Ada Reeve's production of *Butterflies* (1908) and as Blatz in Frank Curzon's production of *The Balkan Princess* (1910). He joined George Edwardes's organization to tour as Van Eyck in *The Girl in the Train,* then moved to town and to Daly's Theatre to replace W H Berry in *The Count of Luxembourg* (1911, Brissard) at Daly's Theatre and followed up there as Kajetan in Edwardes's production of *Gipsy Love* (1912).

He played older roles in the tour of *Gipsy Love* (Dragotin) and in Robert Courtneidge's productions of *The Pearl Girl* (1913, Jecks) and *The Cinema Star* (1914, Josiah Clutterbuck), then joined Grossmith and Laurillard for their American production of *Tonight's the Night* (1914, Henry). He subsequently took part in the short-lived tryout of *Hands Up* with Fannie Brice and Lew Fields at New Haven. The rising Leslie Henson took the role of Henry for London, and de Frece moved back to Daly's to succeed Berry again, this time in *Betty* (Achille Jotte), before, the following Christmas, he finally found his best own part since *Amasis* when he created the comedy role of little wife-fleeing Antonio in *The Maid of the Mountains* (1917), pairing memorably with Mabel Sealby in "Husbands and Wives" and holding a comical conversation with a lobster in the same manner that he had chatted to *Amasis*'s crocodile a decade earlier. He played this role for the three and a half years of the show's run, but was stricken with peritonitis whilst sailing on Solly Joel's yacht, 18 months later, and died not long after his fortieth birthday.

His wife, **Fay COMPTON** [Virginia Lilian Emmeline Compton MacKENZIE] (b London, 18 September 1894; d Hove, 12 December 1978) (formerly the wife of *Follies* impresario, Henri G Pelissier, and later of two others) also appeared in *The Pearl Girl* (t/o Iris), *The Cinema Star, Tonight's the Night* (USA, Victoria) and the flop tryout of *Hands Up* (1915), and played in the London version of Victor Herbert's *The Only Girl* before beginning a career in the straight theatre which made her a major star in pieces ranging from *Hamlet* (Ophelia to Gielgud's Hamlet) and *Blithe Spirit* (Ruth) to *The Little Foxes* (Regina) and *Autumn Crocus* (Fanny Grey). She also, however, appeared regularly as a pantomime principal boy, and in 1943 she returned briefly to the musical stage to play Ivan Caryll's *The Duchess of Dantzic* on tour for Bernard Delfont.

A brother, **[Sir] [Abraham] Walter De Frece** (b Liverpool, 7 October 1870; d Monte Carlo, 7 January 1935), continued the family interest in theatre property, controlling a wide circuit of Hippodromes throughout the country and running the De Frece Circuit of vaudeville entertainments whilst also acting as a Member of Parliament. He was married to the music-hall vocalist and male impersonator **Vesta TILLEY** [Matilda Alice POWLES] (b Worcester, 13 May 1864; d Monte Carlo, 16 September 1952), one of the numerous daughters of the comic vocalist known as Harry Ball, who made occasional appearances on the musical stage, notably as *Randolph the Reckless* in Victor Stephens's touring extravaganza (1891), in the burlesque *Cartouche & Co* (1892), in Chicago's *Aladdin Jr* (1895) and, briefly and unsuitably, on Broadway in the title role of the comedy opera *My Lady Molly* (1904).

Memoir: Compton, F: *Rosemary* (Alston Rivers, London, 1926)

DEFREYN, Henri (b Brussels). Charming, light comedy leading man, with more of a tenorish baritone singing voice than most such, who found his most famous role as France's first Danilo in *La Veuve joyeuse.*

Defreyn made his first appearance on the stage in his native Brussels, in the premiere of the aged Lecocq's opérette *Yetta* (1903), but he moved swiftly thereafter to Paris where his elegant stage presence and pleasant light baritone quickly won him roles at the Bouffes-Parisiens (*La Fille de la mère Michel,* 1903, Gontran), at the Boîte à Fursy (*Le Chien d'Alcibiade, Le Retour du quincaillaire* 1905) and at the Théâtre des Variétés, where in 1906 he took the juvenile leading role of the Prince in Planquette's last work, *Le Paradis de Mahomet,* playing opposite Juliette Méaly and alongside Max Dearly, Baron and Amélie Diéterle.

The following year, he was the hero of Cuvillier's *Son p'tit frère* (Agathos) at the Capucines, playing for the first time opposite Marguerite Deval, with whom he paired effectively for a second time in Ivan Caryll's French musical *S.A.R.* (1908) and, again, as the sexually overworked hero of Cuvillier's *Afgar* (1909). He also appeared in a further Cuvillier work, *Les Rendez-vous strasbourgeois* (1908, Müller) with Anna Tariol-Baugé at the Comédie-Royale and introduced Belgium to the distinctly successful not-very-ancient-Greek fun of *Son p'tit frère.*

His most important opportunity to date came when he created the role of Danilo in the French version of *Die lustige Witwe* (*La Veuve joyeuse*) at the Apollo in 1909 and, in the some five years which followed, he remained at that theatre playing a mixture of Viennese imports and largely new French works, peppered with repeated repeat seasons of *La Veuve joyeuse.* Amongst the translated roles which he created for the French stage at this time were romantic leads in *Rêve de valse* (*Ein Walzertraum,* Niki), *La Divorcée* (*Die geschiedene Frau,* Karl von Lysseveghe), *Le Comte de Luxembourg* (René), *Le Soldat de Chocolat* (*Der tapfere Soldat,* Bumerli) and *La Chaste Suzanne* (*Die keusche Susanne,* Hubert), whilst his mostly less impressive list of home-grown roles during the same period included Baron Placide in the 1913 revival of Terrasse's *Monsieur de la Palisse,* de Tièrce in the same composer's *Les Transatlantiques* (1911), Hirchmann's *Les Petites Étoiles* (1911), Lattès' *La Jeunesse dorée* (1913, Lord Sweet), Ganne's *Cocorico* (1913, Chamaillac) and the first Paris performances of his *Hans, le joueur de flûte* (1910, Yoris) and of Xavier Leroux's *La Fille de Figaro* (1914, Sanchez). The occasional classic revival at the Apollo gave him the opportunity to be seen in such a role as Pippo in *La Mascotte.*

Defreyn visited London to play in the tryout of *Véronique* at the Adelphi Theatre (1915) and, back at home, appeared in revivals of *La Fauvette du Temple* (Gaîté, 1914, Joseph) and *Son p'tit frère* and in such new pieces as *Le Poilu* (1916, Robert Valdier) at the Palais-Royal opposite the young Yvonne Printemps, *La Petite Dactylo* and Cuvillier's *La Fausse ingénue* (1918, Clerambault), mixing musical comedy with revue and comedy appearances before joining the company at the Théâtre Édouard VII for a period of four years (*Daphnis et Chloë, Rapatipatoum,* etc). At the end of this engagement he moved on to star in further musicals—the Franco-British *Nelly* (1921, Roger d'Herblay), the Franco-American *La Dame en rose* (1921, Garidel), Messager's *La Petite Fonctionnaire* (1921, Le Vicomte), as well as repeats of his Apollo triumphs—before, with his voice now having strengthened notably from the light, pleasant instrument of his earlier days, he at last created an enduring role in a native work when he introduced the role of Antonin, the lightly comical hero of Reynaldo Hahn's *Ciboulette,* alongside Edmée Favart, in that piece's initial production (1923).

Defreyn switched eras with ease, comfortably leaving behind the old style of opérette to star in a number of postwar French Jazz Age musical comedies including Szulc's *Flup..!* (1922, Duc Raymond de Florigny), Yvain's *Gosse de riche* (1924, André Sartène), *Les Amants légitimes* (1924) alongside Yvette Guilbert, *Bouche à bouche* (1925, Anatole), *Pouche* (1925, Bridier) and the Elys/Ménier *À Paris tous les deux* (1926), but he appeared still, periodically, and always with considerable success as Danilo, 15 years after his original performances.

In the late 1920s and the 1930s he was still elegantly in evidence in the French musical theatre, appearing in a whole variety of pieces ranging from Reynaldo Hahn's *Le Temps d'aimer* (1926, François Bucaille), a version of Puss in Boots called *Carabas et Cie,* and a pair of successful little Victor Alix musical comedies (Gaspard de Phalines in *Les Bleus de l'amour,* Julien de Château-Fronsac in *Mon amant!*) to the dashing central characters of the musical comedy *Le Groom s'en chargera* (Jules Audincourt) produced in 1934 at the Variétés, where he had first starred nearly 30 years earlier, and of George van Parys's *Ma petite amie* (1937), mounted at the Bouffes-Parisiens where he had made his first Paris appearance even longer ago.

DE GRÉSAC, Fréd[érique Rosine] (b France, 1866; d Los Angeles, 19 February 1943).

An enterprising journalist, author, playwright and social personality in turn-of-the-century Paris, Mme de Grésac won herself a certain notoriety during the Dreyfus case. Journalists having been forbidden to cover the case, the authorities were unable to discover how news was getting from the purposely out-of-town venue of the trial back to the *Figaro.* No one suspected the handsome, well-dressed society woman who made her way, each evening, back to the capital with all the news a paper could want.

In less exciting times and circumstances, Mme de Grésac was also the author of a number of plays, ranging from drawing room comedy to melodrama, and she had her biggest stage success, in collaboration with Francis de Croisset, with the play *La Passerelle* (*The Marriage of Kitty*), first produced in Paris in 1902. Another play, *La Troisième Lune* (1904 w Paul Ferrier) also found success and introduced its authoress to the musical theatre when it was adapted as a musical by Charles Brookfield,

Plate 95. **Frédérique de Grésac**—*better known as Fred—the author of libretti for the Paris and Broadway stages.*

with music by Sidney Jones, and produced at London's Prince of Wales Theatre under the management of George Edwardes as *See See* (20 June 1906).

She subsequently moved, with her husband, the celebrated operatic baritone Victor Maurel, to the United States and there she wrote the libretti for several musicals, teamed with such seasoned practicioners as Victor Herbert and Harry B Smith, the most successful of which were Kitty Gordon's vehicle, *The Enchantress* ("I Want to Be a Primadonna," "The Land of My Own Romance"), and the cute if textually confused bit of Ruritanian nonsense that was *Sweethearts.* She had a "sleeper" success with the Silvio Hein musical *Flo-Flo,* provided the text for a "scandalous" little vaudeville-circuits show called *The Bride Shop,* whose scandal came largely from its inclusion of a fashion parade of feminine underwear, and in 1922 had her second Parisian play musicalized. *Orange Blossoms* (1922), produced by Edward Royce for a Broadway run of 95 performances, was a musical version of *La Passerelle.*

Her work was seen once more on the London stage when she was commissioned by José Collins and Robert Evett at London's Gaiety Theatre to provide a vehicle for the singer, based on the Continental hit *Die Siegerin,* in the character of Catherine the Great. As *Catherine* the piece ran 217 performances. And a decade further on she had one further Parisian credit, on the libretto of a pasticcio musicalization of her old collaborator de Croisset's hit play *Le Bonheur, mesdames!*

Mme de Grésac later moved to Hollywood where she became a successful author of film scenarios for such performers as Rudolph Valentino, Douglas Fairbanks and Lilian Gish. She died in Hollywood at the reported age of 75.

1911 **The Enchantress** (Victor Herbert/w Harry B Smith) New York Theater 19 October

1911 **The Wedding Trip** (Reginald De Koven/w H B Smith) Knickerbocker Theater 25 December

1913 **The Purple Road** (*Napoleon und die Frauen*) English version w William Cary Duncan (Liberty Theater)

1913 **Sweethearts** (Herbert/Robert B Smith/w Harry B Smith) Academy of Music, Baltimore 24 March; New Amsterdam Theater 8 September

1917 **Flo-Flo** (Silvio Hein/Edward A Paulton) Cort Theater 20 December

1918 **The Bride Shop** (Hein, Walter Rosemont/Darl McBoyle)

1922 **Orange Blossoms** (Herbert/B G De Sylva) Fulton Theater 19 September

1923 **Catherine** (*Die Siegerin*) English version w Reginald Arkell, Louis N Parker (Gaiety Theatre, London)

1934 **Le Bonheur, mesdames!** (Henri Christiné arr/w Francis de Croisset, Albert Willemetz) Théâtre des Bouffes-Parisiens 6 January

DE KOVEN, [Henry Louis] Reginald (b Middletown, Conn, 3 April 1861 [1859?]; d Chicago, 15 January

1920). A prolific composer of comic opera for the American musical stage of the 1890s and 1900s, De Koven scored one enduring hit with his *Robin Hood* amongst a long series of often tidily attractive, if inherently old-fashioned, theatre scores.

At the age of 13, De Koven was taken by his clergyman father to England, where he was educated at St John's, Oxford, before moving on to further studies in Stuttgart, Frankfurt and Florence. He went into business on his return to America in 1882, but, having made an advantageous marriage, soon retired from the desk allotted to him in his father-in-law's firm to devote himself to composing music.

His first attempt at a comic opera, *Cupid, Hymen and Co,* failed to make its opening night when the producer went broke even before rehearsals were over, and so it was *The Begum,* written in conjunction with another neophyte, librettist Harry B Smith, and produced by John McCaull at New York's Fifth Avenue Theater with a fine cast including De Wolf Hopper, Mathilde Cottrelly, Jeff de Angelis and Hubert Wilke which marked De Koven's advent into the American musical theatre. *The Begum* played only three New York weeks before being sent out of town, but in Chicago, where the De Kovens were socially important, it did decidedly well, and it held its end up in the McCaull repertoire through the season. *The Begum* was followed by a version of the *Don Quixote* tale, mounted by the enterprising light opera company, the Bostonians, with Henry Clay Barnabee as the Don. It was played fairly discreetly in their repertoire for only one season, but the company nevertheless put their faith in De Koven and Smith a second time and the pair came up very much more happily with a piece based on another famous character of literature and stage, *Robin Hood. Robin Hood,* with its neat, four-square comic-opera score (''Brown October Ale,'' ''O Promise Me,'' Armourer's Song) and a traditional emphasis on low comedy in its book, was a major hit, proving one of the most successful homemade pieces to yet be played on the American musical stage and providing the cornerstone to its composer's career.

The writers of *Robin Hood* easily found takers for a run of further pieces in a similar style, but the results were uneven. *The Fencing Master* was produced, with Marie Tempest and Hubert Wilke starred, at the Casino Theater and won a fine run of more than three months, whilst the Bostonians brought out *The Knickerbockers,* a ''real New York operetta'' with Camille D'Arville, Edwin Hoff, Barnabee and Jessie Bartlett Davis featured, and drew a quick blank. Miss Tempest joined the composer again for *The Algerian,* and won another good run, but Harry Smith hit the target most effectively when he brought to the American musical stage his comic opera version of the

Plate 96. **Reginald De Koven.** *The man who set Robin Hood to music.*

tale another British folk hero, Rob Roy. William Pruette starred in the title role of a piece which was in no way inferior—and in some ways superior—to *Robin Hood,* boasted some splendid songs (''In Darkness Deep,'' ''The Merry Miller'') in the same mode as its successful predecessor, and won a first run of 168 performances, quickly brought up to the excellent total of some 200 Broadway nights by a return engagement.

Rob Roy was to remain De Koven's longest-running Broadway show, just as *Robin Hood* would remain his most popular and long-lived. Thereafter, his rather backward-looking light opera scores, often little in tune with a public taste which was running more towards dance music and simple-rhythmed modern songs as its theatrical diet, began too frequently to sound too much alike. But they nevertheless decorated many a comic opera which filled many a theatre round America for many years.

In the seasons following the Broadway success of *Rob Roy,* his new pieces *The Tzigane* (36 performances), with Lillian Russell, Wilke and De Angelis as potent attractions, and *The Mandarin* (40 performances), with Bertha Waltzinger and George Honey featured, could muster only a little more than a month in New York, whilst *The Paris Doll* did not even make it to town. *The Highwayman,* produced by Andrew A McCormick, with Jerome Sykes in the chief comic role of Foxy Quiller, did altogether better, running up 126 Broadway performances and touring vigorously, but when Sykes headed the production of *The Three Dragoons* the following season the result was mediocre (48 performances).

De Koven contributed to the music for a multiple-authored spectacular, *The Man in the Moon* (192 performances), and was called in by Florenz Ziegfeld to ''improve'' the scores for Broadway versions of the Anna Judic shows *La Femme à Papa* (combined with bits of *Mam'zelle Nitouche*) and *Niniche* as vehicles for Anna Held, whilst Klaw and Erlanger, in their turn, commissioned the music for a sequel to *The Highwayman* for Sykes. *Foxy Quiller* lasted a respectable 50 Broadway performances before going to the country, a total which was marginally less than another attempt at a musequel: a *Robin Hood* follow-up produced by the Bostonians under the title of *Maid Marian.*

The Jersey Lily played just 24 performances in New York, in spite of Blanche Ring's performance of the interpolated up-to-date song ''Bedelia,'' and Ziegfeld's production of the Ruritanian bandit piece *The Red Feather* with Grace van Studdiford starred played 60 New York nights in the brand new Lyric Theater, where De Koven had announced the foundation of his American School of Opera. The School lasted longer in Manhattan than *The Red Feather,* but not very much longer, and the operetta had a vigorous afterlife on the road. In the meanwhile, the Lyric had housed the composer's successful venture into the whimsical fairy-tale world of *Happyland* with De Wolf Hopper (82 performances). Another Ruritanian piece, *The Student King,* with Lina Abarbanell starred, was done with in 40 Broadway performances, whilst *The Golden Butterfly,* a piece about a ''stolen'' Hungarian opera, written with a preponderance of brilliant soprano numbers for its producer-star Grace van Studdiford, did little better (48 performances), and the success obtained by the low-comical *The Beauty Spot* (137 performances) could not, in all fairness, have been said to owe much to its score. All three pieces, however, proved solid propositions on the road, with the vaguely ''naughty'' *The Beauty Spot* going on to an extended touring life.

Booked for the music of Sam Bernard's *Nearly a Hero,* De Koven failed to come up with a score, and ''anything handy'' was hurriedly substituted. *Nearly a Hero* with its last minute melodies went on to a fine success. It was a success de Koven could have done with latterly. He switched styles in *The Yankee Mandarin* (1909) and attempted to turn out a ''catchy and popular'' score in the modern manner, but the piece failed to make it to Broadway and two further quick flops put an end to a career of a quarter of a century composing for the Broadway theatre. His final attempt at a light musical piece, a semi-period piece called *Yesterday,* which transported its contemporary hero back to 1867 Paris to impersonate a Grand Duke, rehearsed 10 weeks and died in 2 when the Shuberts canceled its scheduled opening at Broadway's Broadhurst Theater and folded it away in Washington, DC. De Koven retired to journalism, writing music criticism for the *New York Herald,* and then moved to Chicago and, in his last years, turned out—rather than musical plays—the scores for two light operas, *The Canterbury Pilgrims* (8 March 1917) and a *Rip van Winkle* (Chicago 2 January 1920), the latter produced just a few days before his death.

De Koven's career in the musical theatre was one which was regarded in very different ways by different of his contemporaries. To those critics, in particular, who had little time for the freer rhythms and looser, less academic harmonies of musical comedy, his traditional comic operas represented a step in the right direction, and he often won fine notices as a result. To others, he and his music were fossilized and dull, and his successes were attributed more to the antics of the comedians than to the show's scores. There is also probably something in his own claim that his social and financial position, not to speak of his Oxfordized manner and monocle eyeglass, won him if not enemies at least happy detractors amongst those in and, more especially, those around the theatre. Looking back at his music, a century on, it is true that there is much in it that is academic and somewhat lifeless, but there are also a number of pages which are comic-operatic writing of a very attractive kind.

1887 **The Begum** (H B Smith) Fifth Avenue Theater 21 November

1889 **Don Quixote** (H B Smith) Boston Theater 18 November

1890 **Robin Hood** (H B Smith) Opera House, Chicago 9 June; Standard Theater, New York 28 September 1891

1892 **The Fencing Master** (H B Smith) Star Theater, Buffalo 26 September; Casino Theater, New York 14 November

1893 **The Knickerbockers** (H B Smith) Tremont Theatre, Boston 5 January; Garden Theater, New York 29 May

1893 **The Algerian** (H B Smith) Garden Theater 26 October

1894 **Rob Roy** (H B Smith) Herald Square Theater 29 October

1895 **The Tzigane** (H B Smith) Abbey's Theater 16 May

1896 **The Mandarin** (H B Smith) Herald Square Theater 2 November

1897 **The Paris Doll** (H B Smith) Parsons' Theater, Hartford, Conn 14 September

1897 **The Highwayman** (H B Smith) Hyperion Theater, New Haven, Conn 28 October; Broadway Theater 13 December

1899 **The Three Dragoons** (H B Smith) Broadway Theater 30 January

1899 **The Man in the Moon** (w Ludwig Englander, Gustave Kerker/Louis Harrison, Stanislaus Stange) New York Theater 24 April

1899 **Papa's Wife** (*La Femme à Papa*) new score (Manhattan Theater)

1900 **Broadway to Tokio** (w A Baldwin Sloan/George Hobart, Harrison) New York Theater 23 January

1900 **Foxy Quiller** (H B Smith) Broadway Theater 5 November

1901 **The Little Duchess** (*Niniche*) new score (Casino Theater)

1901 **Maid Marian** (H B Smith) Chestnut Street Opera House, Philadelphia 4 November; Garden Theater, New York 27 January 1902

1903 **The Jersey Lily** (George Hobart) Victoria Theater 14 September

1903 **The Red Feather** (Charles Emerson Cook/Charles Klein) Lyric Theater 9 November

1905 **Happyland** (ex- *Elysia*) (Frederick Ranken) Lyric Theater 2 October

1906 **The Student King** (Stange, Ranken) Lyceum Theater, Rochester, NY 17 May; Studebaker Theater, Chicago 21 May; Garden Theater 25 December

1907 **The Snowman** (Stange) Majestic Theater, Boston 18 March

1907 **The Girls of Holland** (revised *The Snowman*) (Stange) Lyric Theater 18 November

1908 **The Golden Butterfly** (H B Smith) Broadway Theater 12 October

1908 **The Magic Bottle** (Stange) 1 act American Theater, St Louis 23 November

1909 **The Beauty Spot** (Joseph W Herbert) Herald Square Theater 10 April

1909 **The Yankee Mandarin** (Edward A Paulton) Opera House, Providence 11 June; Majestic, Boston 14 June

1911 **The Wedding Trip** (H B Smith, Fred de Grésac) Knickerbocker Theater 25 December

1913 **Her Little Highness** (ex- *Queen Anna*) (Channing Pollock, Rennold Wolf) Liberty Theater 13 October

1919 **Yesterday** (Glen MacDonough) Playhouse, Wilmington 10 March

Biography: De Koven, Anna: *A Musician and His Wife* (Harper, New York, 1926)

DELACOUR, Alfred [LARTIGUE, Pierre Alfred] (b Bordeaux, 3 September 1817; d Paris, 31 March 1883).

Originally a doctor, a pharmacist (as had been his father) and a medical author, Alfred Lartigue switched careers in 1847 and, although he continued to manufacture a pill which he had patented which apparently had saleable effects on gout and rheumatism, he became instead, under his mother's maiden name, the author of a long list of some 130 dramas and comedies, many written in association with such top-flight authors as Eugène Labiche, Clairville, Eugène Grangé, Marc-Michel and Maurice Hennequin. The most widely successful of these were, on the humorous hand, the famous farces *Les Dominos roses* (w Alfred Hennequin) and *La Cagnotte* (w Labiche), and, on the dramatic, the equally famous *Le Courrier de Lyon* (w Paul Siraudin, Eugène Moreau). Delacour also collaborated on the texts of a wide-ranging set of musical theatre pieces including Offenbach's successful one-act opérette *Un mari à la porte,* a burlesque of Wagner's opera *Tannhäuser,* the internationally successful opéra-comique *Le Voyage en Chine,* and Paul Lacome's most enduring opérette, the delightful and cleverly constructed *Jeanne, Jeannette et Jeanneton.*

In 1877 he joined with Victor Wilder to create two pieces with music by Johann Strauss but neither proved to be an enduring success. The pair fabricated a new libretto to some of the score of Strauss's *Die Fledermaus* for Paris (the original French basis to the Viennese work had been used without authority and could not be played in France) and supplied Vienna with the libretto to *Prinz Methusalem.* Written in French by Delacour and Wilder, and adapted into German before being set by the composer, the show lasted longer than *La Tzigane* but nevertheless won only limited success.

Les Dominos roses was adapted into a musical in Britain and America as *Tonight's the Night,* in Hungary as *Három légyott* (Népszínház 22 October 1897) and, most successfully, in Austria as *Der Opernball. La Cagnotte* became the Posse mit Gesang *Vergnügungszügfer* (Karl Stix/C F Stenzl), produced at the Carltheater in 1870 and *Die Sparbüchse* (Ludwig Kusche/Charles Regnier, Saarbrücken Stadttheater 31 December 1953) and in France it kept its original title and was produced at Lille in 1983 (Jack Ledru/Guy Lafarge). It was also apparently plundered, without credit, for a shabby British musical called *Instant Marriage.*

1851 **Le Coup de pied retrospectif** (w Adolphe Guenée) 1 act Délassements-Comiques 24 December

1852 **Paris qui dort** (Julien Nargéot/w Lambert Thiboust) Théâtre des Variétés 21 February

1853 **L'Amour, qué qu'c'est que ça?** (Nargéot/w Thiboust, Clairville) 1 act Théâtre des Variétés 6 April

1859 **Un mari à la porte** (Jacques Offenbach/Léon Morand) 1 act Théâtre des Bouffes-Parisiens 22 June

1861 **Ya-Mein-Herr** (Victor Chéri, et al/w Clairville, Thiboust) Théâtre des Variétés 6 April

1861 **Les Danses nationales de la France** (Chéri/w Clairville, Thiboust) Théâtre des Variétés 19 August

1865 **Le Voyage en Chine** (François Bazin/w Eugène Labiche) Opéra-Comique 9 December

1867 **Le Fils du brigadier, ou Le Cheval de l'adjoint** (Victor Massé/w Labiche) Opéra-Comique 25 February

1868 **Le Corricolo** (Fernand Poïse/w Labiche) Opéra-Comique 27 November

1873 **La Veuve du Malabar** (Hervé/w Hector Crémieux) Théâtre des Variétés 26 April

1876 **Le Roi dort** (Marius Boullard/w Labiche) Théâtre des Variétés 31 March

1876 **Jeanne, Jeannette et Jeanneton** (Paul Lacome/w Clairville) Théâtre des Folies-Dramatiques 27 October

1877 **Prinz Methusalem** (Johann Strauss/w Wilder tr Karl Treumann) Carltheater, Vienna 3 January

1877 **La Tzigane** (*Die Fledermaus,* etc) new libretto w Victor Wilder, Théâtre de la Renaissance 30 October

1878 **Coco** (Auguste Coedès/w Clairville, Eugène Grangé) Théâtre des Nouveautés 12 June

1879 **Pâques fleuries** (Lacome/w Clairville) Théâtre des Folies-Dramatiques 21 October

1879 **Fatinitza** French version w Wilder (Théâtre des Nouveautés)

1881 **La Reine des Halles** (Louis Varney/w Victor Bernard, Paul Burani) Comédie-Parisienne 4 April

1882 **La Nuit de Saint-Jean** (Lacome/Erckmann-Chatrian ad w J de Lau-Lusignan) 1 act Opéra-Comique 13 November

DELFONT, Bernard (Lord Delfont of Stepney) [WINOGRADSKY, Boris] (b Tokmak, Russia, 5 September 1909; d Anmering, 28 July 1994).

At first a dancer, with his brother Louis—later Lord Lew Grade (d London, 13 December 1998)—and then a theatrical agent, Delfont began as a producer touring plays and mounting revivals of such musicals as *The Duchess of Dantzic* (1943 w Tom Arnold) and *The Count of Luxembourg* (1943 w Joseph Fenstone) on the road, and of *Rose Marie* (Stoll Theatre, 1942) and *The Student Prince* (Stoll Theatre, 1944) in London. His first original production was the Richard Tauber comic opera *Old Chelsea,* his first West End importation the Broadway musical *Something for the Boys* (1944), and he subsequently mounted the Fred Emney vehicle, *Big Boy* (1945), Cicely Courtneidge's *Under the Counter* (w Arnold, Lee Ephraim), a souped-up version of *Die Fledermaus* retitled *Gay Rosalinda,* the Viennese *The Birdseller* (*Der Vogelhändler* w Arnold, Littler), with Tauber as conductor, Britain's first stage production of *The Wizard of Oz* (1946), the long-running musical comedy *Bob's Your Uncle* (1948) and the decidedly short-lived *Hat in the Air* (*Roundabout*) in London, whilst touring such pieces as *Good Night, Vienna* (w Jack Buchanan), *Bless the Bride* and the interminable *The Chocolate Soldier.*

After a period during which he was principally involved with the staging of a series of "French" revues at the London Hippodrome and the Prince of Wales Theatre, he ventured back into the musical theatre, and over two decades racked up a good percentage of successes as he produced, or had an interest in the production of, such pieces as the Cicely Courtneidge musical *Starmaker* (1955), the London production of *Where's Charley?* (1957), *Stop the World—I Want to Get Off* (1961), *Pickwick* (1963 w Arnold), *Maggie May* (1964), Little Me (1964), *Our Man Crichton* (1964 w Arnold, Arthur Lewis), *The Roar of the Greasepaint . . . the Smell of the Crowd* (1964), *Twang!!* (1965 w John Bryan), *When You're Young* (aka *Smilin Through* 1966), *The Matchgirls* (1966 w Geoffrey Russell), *Funny Girl* (1966), *Joey, Joey* (1966), *Queenie* (1967), *Sweet Charity* (1967 w Harold Fielding), *The Four Musketeers* (1967), *Golden Boy* (1968), *You're a Good Man, Charlie Brown* (1969 w Fielding), *Mame* (1969 w Fielding), *Your Own Thing* (1969), *Promises, Promises* (1969 w David Merrick, H M Tennent), *The Great Waltz* (1970 w Fielding), *Applause* (1972), *The Good Old Bad Old Days* (1972), *The Threepenny Opera* (1972 w Michael White), *The Good Companions* (1974 w Richard Mills, Richard Pilbrow), *A Little Night Music* (1975 w Pilbrow), *Mardi Gras* (1976), *The Best Little Whorehouse in Texas* (1981), *Underneath the Arches* (1982) and the *Little Me* revival of 1984.

Alongside his musical theatre activities, Delfont continued a parallel production schedule of plays, revues and, most particularly, of summer season variety shows throughout Britain. He was knighted in 1974 and made a peer in 1976 for his contribution to entertainment and to charity, and continued into the 1990s as President of the First Leisure Corporation and as a member of the board of Delfont Mackintosh Theatres controlling London's Prince of Wales and Prince Edward Theatres.

Delfont was married to musical-comedy actress **Carole LYNNE** [Helen Violet Carolyn HAYMEN] (b Rochester, 16 September 1918) who appeared in several London revues of the later 1930s, as well as in the musicals *Paprika* (1938, Susan Townsend), *Old Chelsea* (1943, Mary Fenton), *The Student Prince* (Kathie, tour), *Jill, Darling* (1943, Jill), *Jenny Jones* (1944, Dilys) and *Big Ben* (1946, Grace Green).

Autobiography: *East End, West End* (Macmillan, London, 1990)

DELIBES, [Clément Philibert] Léo (b St Germain du Val, 21 February 1836; d Paris, 16 January 1891).

Before going on to write the works which ensured his international fame—the ballets *Coppélia* (1870), *La Source* (1866 w Minkus) and *Sylvia,* and the opéras-comiques *Lakmé, Le Roi l'a dit* (1873) and *Jean de Nivelle*—the young Léo Delibes contributed scores through more than a decade to the musical theatres of Paris, producing a series of one-act opéras-bouffes and opérettes in the manner of, and for the use of, the composer/theatre-managers Hervé and Offenbach and others.

It was Hervé who gave the teenaged composer his first opportunity, when he mounted and played in Delibes's little burlesque *Deux sous de charbon* at his Folies-Nouvelles, but his second piece, the low comic *Les Deux Vieilles Gardes,* produced by Offenbach, was much more successful and, like the subsequent bouffonnerie *L'Omelette à la Follembûche,* it was included in the Bouffes-Parisiens international touring repertoire in the early 1860s. *Six Demoiselles à marier,* which also found its way into theatres beyond France (Drury Lane 13 March 1867, etc), was seen at Vienna's Theater an der Wien (13 October 1860) in a version musically adapted by Adolf Müller, with sufficient impact for its libretto to be later reused to make up the text for Suppé's more celebrated *Zehn Mädchen und kein Mann. Le Serpent à plumes* and, in particular, his last short work, the delightful five-handed *L'Écossais de Chatou* also found success, the latter being played in Austria as *Ein Schotte* (Theater an der Wien 20 November 1880) and in Hungary as *A chatoui skótok* (ad Ferenc Reiner). In 1869 Delibes produced the score to his one full-length opera-bouffe, the successful *La Cour du Roi Pétaud,* before moving on into loftier spheres.

One of Delibes opérettes was produced at Koster and Bial's Music Hall, New York, in 1893 (6 January) under the title *The Miller's Daughter.* Contemporary sources don't permit a guess as to which one it was.

1856 **Deux sous de charbon** (Jules Moinaux) 1 act Folies-Nouvelles 9 February

1856 **Les Deux Vieilles Gardes** (Villeneuve, H Lemonnier)1 act Théâtre des Bouffes-Parisiens 8 August

1856 **Six Demoiselles à marier** (Adolphe Choler, Adolphe Jaime) 1 act Théâtre des Bouffes-Parisiens 12 November

1857 **Maître Griffard** (Eugène Mestépès, [Jaime]) 1 act Théâtre Lyrique 3 October

1859 **L'Omelette à la Follembûche** (Eugène Labiche, Marc-Michel) 1 act Théâtre des Bouffes-Parisiens 8 June

1860 **Monsieur de Bonne-Étoile** (Philippe Gille, [Jaime]) 1 act Théâtre des Bouffes-Parisiens 4 February

1861 **Les Musiciens de l'orchestre** (w Aristide Hignard, Erlanger/Bourdois) Théâtre des Bouffes-Parisiens 25 January

1861 **Les Deux Buveurs** (Hector Crémieux, Ludovic Halévy) 1 act Théâtre des Bouffes-Parisiens January

1861 **Les Eaux d'Ems** (Crémieux, Halévy) 1 act Kursaal, Bad Ems; Théâtre des Bouffes-Parisiens 9 April 1863

1862 **L'Homme entre deux âges** (w H Cartier/Émile Abraham) 1 act Théâtre des Bouffes-Parisiens 6 May

1862 **Mon ami Pierrot** (Crémieux, Halévy) 1 act Kursaal, Bad Ems July

1863 **Le Jardinier et son seigneur** (Théodore Barrière, Michel Carré) 1 act Théâtre Lyrique 1 May

1864 **La Tradition** (Henri d'Erville) 1 act Théâtre des Bouffes-Parisiens 5 January

1864 **Le Serpent à plumes** (Gille, Cham) 1 act Théâtre des Bouffes-Parisiens 16 December

1865 **Le Boeuf Apis** (Gille, Eugène Furpille) Théâtre des Bouffes-Parisiens 15 April

1867 **Marlborough s'en va-t-en guerre** (w Georges Bizet, Émile Jonas, Isidore Legouix/William Busnach, Paul Siraudin) Théâtre de l'Athenée 15 December

1869 **L'Écossais de Chatou** (Jaime, Gille) 1 act Théâtre des Bouffes-Parisiens 16 January

1869 **La Cour du Roi Pétaud** (Jaime, Gille) Théâtre des Variétés 24 April

Literature: Studwell, W: *Adolphe Adam and Léo Delibes: A Guide to Research* (Garland Publishing, Inc, New York, 1987)

Biographies: de Curzon, H: *Léo Delibes, sa vie et ses oeuvres* (Legouix, Paris, 1926), Coquis, A: *Léo Delibes: Sa Vie et Son Oeuvre* (Richard-Masse, Paris, 1957)

DELLINGER, Rudolf (b Kraslice, 8 July 1857; d nr Dresden, 24 September 1910). Composer of Germany's first real Operette hit and of several other pieces popular in that country in their time.

The son of a musical instrument-maker, Dellinger was trained at the Prague Conservatorium, and became first an orchestral clarinetist and subsequently a conductor at the Stadttheater in Brno. He moved on from there to similar posts at the Carl-Schultze Theater in Hamburg and, ultimately, at the Residenztheater, Dresden. His first Operette, *Don Cesar,* a piece based on the same French original as the eternally successful English *Maritana,* was produced at Hamburg during his tenancy there and it met with enormous success. It was subsequently produced at Budapest's Népszínház, the Vienna Carltheater and Berlin's Walhalla-Theater later in the same year, and by John McCaull in New York the following year, with sufficient success for the American management to option Dellinger's next work sight unseen. Thus *Lorraine,* another period French piece, although a comparative failure in Hamburg and Leipzig, nevertheless won a brief production at New York's Star Theater (ad William J Henderson) with a cast including De Wolf Hopper, Emily Soldene and John Perugini.

Dellinger had two further works produced at Hamburg during his 10-year period at the theatre's musical helm: a musicalization of Dumas's *Les Demoiselles de Saint-Cyr* and a *Capitän Fracassa,* a further French-based piece, with a text by Zell and Genée, which found sufficient success to warrant a production at Vienna's Theater an der Wien (17 performances) and another by McCaull in America (Chicago Opera House 30 December 1889) with De Wolf Hopper starred as Fracasse. Then, in 1893, he shifted to Dresden. Of his three final works, all produced at Dresden, *Die Chansonette*—in which he finally abandoned his period French settings for a modern Italian one—was subsequently seen for an appreciable 43 performances at the Theater an der Wien (16 February 1895), at Berlin's Theater Unter den Linden, and had a highly healthy career in the German provinces, whilst the 1901 *Jadwiga* also found some success, without braving the metropolites. None, however, came up to the level of popularity he had won with his first and most successful piece, which continued to be revived in both town and country for many years.

1885 **Don Cesar** (Oskar Walther) Carl-Schultze Theater, Hamburg 28 March

1886 **Lorraine** (Walther) Carl-Schultze Theater, Hamburg 2 October

1889 **Capitän Fracassa** (Richard Genée, F Zell) Carl-Schultze Theater, Hamburg 2 March

1891 **[Das Fräulein von] Saint-Cyr** (Walther) Carl-Schultze Theater, Hamburg 10 January

1894 **Die Chansonette** (Victor Léon, Heinrich von Waldberg) Residenztheater, Dresden 16 September; Theater Unter den Linden, Berlin 22 August 1895

1901 **Jadwiga** (Paul Hirschberger, Robert Pohl) Residenztheater, Dresden 5 October

1910 **Der letzte Jonas** (Wilhelm Ascher, Pohl) Residenztheater, Dresden 2 April

DELYSIA, Alice [LAPIZE, Alice] (b Paris, 3 March 1889; d Brighton, 9 February 1979). Parisian showgirl-turned-diseuse who made herself a French niche on the British stage.

Delysia made her first appearances on stage in the chorus of the Paris production of *The Belle of New York,* in revue at the Théâtre des Variétés, in opérette at the Gaîté-Lyrique, and (billed as Elise Delisia) as one of the eight French lovelies chosen to go to New York to appear in the Broadway production of *The Catch of the Season* in 1905. She got her first opportunity to show off her ample charms in a principal role as the jealous actress, Diane, in the French production of Lionel Monckton's *The Quaker Girl* at the Olympia (1912), and subsequently appeared prominently both in revue, and as Séraphine in Cuvillier's opérette *La Reine s'amuse* (1913), before she visited London to play in the comedy *L'Ingénue.* She remained in Britain to appear with great success in several revues for C B Cochran (*Odds and Ends, More, Pell-Mell*) and then in the leading roles of his London productions of the French musicals *Carminetta* (1917, Carminetta) and *Afgar, ou les loisirs andalous* (1919, Zaidée) and of Rip's revue *Plus ça change* (*As You Were*).

She visited America to repeat her "slightly scandalous" *Afgar* role in 1920, and again to tour with Donald Brian in a musical play called *The Courtesan* (1923, Marie Pélissier), and on returning to London, starred in a solid series of West End revues, musicals and plays which included—on the musical side—*Princess Charming* (1926, Wanda Navaro), *The Cat and the Fiddle* (1932, Alice ex- Odette), and, in perhaps her most successful performance of all, as Josephine Pavani, singing "Every Woman Thinks She Wants to Wander" in Oscar Straus's *Mother of Pearl* (*Eine Frau, die weiss, was sie will,* London 1933, Australia 1934). She also appeared briefly in London in the semi-Australian musical *At the Silver Swan* (1936, Alice Brevanne), but her subsequent career was devoted to straight theatre, and to music hall and concert appearances.

DE MILLE, Agnes [George] (b New York, 18 September 1905; d New York 6 October 1993). Choreographer whose balletic scenas in *Oklahoma!* led to a rash of similar dance pieces on the postwar Broadway stage.

A member of a well-known American theatre family, dancer and choreographer Agnes de Mille worked as a character dancer and ran her own troupe from an early age. She made her first significant foray into the musical theatre under the aegis of C B Cochran, in London, when she arranged the original set of dances for his production of the Cole Porter musical *Nymph Errant* (1933) and devised the ballet *Three Virgins and a Devil* for the revue *Why Not Tonight?* (1934). Returning to America, she choreographed a ballet scena for the Ed Wynn musical *Hooray for What!* (1937) and also worked on the short-lived *Swingin' the Dream.* Whilst continuing to perform herself, she worked extensively with New York's Ballet Theater (*Black Ritual, Drums Sound in Hackensack*) and choreographed *Rodeo* for de Basil's Ballet Russe de Monte Carlo, before returning to the musical theatre to stage the dances for the new musical *Oklahoma!* (1943). The show itself proved a sensational success, and Miss de Mille's contribution, notably the dream sequence ballet "Laurey Makes Up Her Mind," conceived with a balletic artistry and performed by a body of dancers of high technical skills, won strong admiration amongst the general admiration for the show as a whole.

Oklahoma! made its choreographer the dance director of the moment, and Miss de Mille and her ballet scenas (not to mention imitations of them by other folk) appeared in many major musicals over the following seasons. She worked on two subsequent Rodgers and Hammerstein musicals, *Carousel* (Carousel Waltz) and *Allegro* (also director), on *One Touch of Venus* ("Venus in Ozone Heights," "Forty Minutes for Lunch"), the patent attempt to photocopy *Oklahoma!* which was *Bloomer Girl* (Civil War Ballet), and with particular success on *Brigadoon* with its choreographed chase episode, its Scottish wedding scena and (very) lengthy funeral dance sequence. She also choreographed a second Loewe and Lerner musical in the virile *Paint Your Wagon* (1951).

Whilst continuing her work in the fields of ballet and American dance, Miss de Mille also lined up musical-theatre choreographic credits on such pieces as *Gentlemen Prefer Blondes* (1949), *The Girl in Pink Tights* (1954), *Goldilocks* (1958), *Juno* (1959), *Kwamina* (1961)

and *110 in the Shade* (1963), and directorial credits on *Out of This World* (1950) and *Come Summer* (1969).

Although ballet, of varying degrees of expertise, had been widely used in the musical theatre since its earliest days, and the so-called integration of dance into the story fabric of a show had been both intermittently deemed desirable and practiced on numberless occasions during the previous centuries, the acclaim won by Miss de Mille's ballets for *Oklahoma!* precipitated a new fashion for balletic dancing in musical comedy, as opposed to the drills, chorus unison dance, speciality solos and/or ballroom dance, all of which had been popular in the preceding decades of often dance-heavy productions. For a number of years after *Oklahoma!* no musical play of any pretension was deemed complete without its ballet or dance drama scena, and the trend had an undoubted effect on the formation of American musical theatre dance and dancers of those most productive Broadway decades which followed.

Miss de Mille's father, William C de Mille, and her uncle, Cecil B de Mille, whose name became a byword in the movie world as the purveyor of extravagant filmed spectacle, both authored musical comedies in the early part of their careers (Andrew Mack's *Sergeant Devil May Care, The Spring Girl, The Antique Girl, At the Barracks, The Military Girl, The Genius*).

Autobiographies: *Dance to the Piper* (Little, Brown, Boston, 1952), *And Promenade Home* (Little, Brown, Boston, 1958), *Speak to Me, Dance with Me* (Little, Brown, Boston, 1973), *Reprieve: A Memoir* (Doubleday, Garden City, 1981); Biography: Easton, C: *No Intermissions* (Little, Brown, Boston 1996)

LA DEMOISELLE DU TÉLÉPHONE Vaudeville-opérette in 3 acts by Maurice Desvallières and Antony Mars [and André Sylvane, uncredited]. Music by Gaston Serpette. Théâtre des Nouveautés, Paris, 2 May 1891.

Agathe Liseron (Mily-Meyer), the heroine of Desvallières and Mars's highly successful vaudeville, is a telephone operator who is able, thanks to her professional occupation, to keep an ear on her chap and on his conversations when he seems to be dallying with a lady of the stage called Olympia (Jane Pierney). The complications develop in lively style as Agathe sets out to discredit her rival, with a boxful of disguises close to hand, and a song ever at the ready even if one isn't always really necessary. Colombey (Pontarcy), Germain (Pichard), Guy (Sigismond) and Abel Tarride (Blackson) headed the male team of Paris's Théâtre des Nouveautés company through what looked rather like a close cousin to Vienna's hit musical comedy of 14 years earlier, *Ein Blitzmädel.*

A first Parisian run of 116 performances set this full-of-comedy musical off round the world. German versions were played in Berlin and at Vienna's Carltheater (ad Hermann Herschl, add song by E Kornau, J Löti), where Karl Blasel (Pontarcy), Wilhelm Knaack (Richard), Paula Delma (Agathe) and Frln Andrée (Olympia) appeared for six performances, and *The Young Lady of the Telephone* got a highly successful showing in Dutch at Amsterdam's Frascati Theatre (1892). In England, adapted by Sir Augustus Harris, F C Burnand, Arthur Sturgess and (musically) by James Glover, *The Telephone Girl* was a big success all round the country, touring provincial and suburban theatres, with Ada Blanche starring as Lottie (ex- Agathe), for several years without tackling the West End.

Broadway's Casino Theater version threw out the Serpette score and, as was the habit at this house at that time, replaced it with some Gustave Kerker material for Clara Lipman, Louis Mann and Eleanor Elton. It also added some lower comedy than the original authors had planned, and the resultant show, also called *The Telephone Girl,* racked up 104 performances in New York, before setting off for a life of many, many years on the American touring circuits where, when all was totted up and tallied, it ultimately saw its greatest number of productions and performances of all.

Germany: Wallner Theater *Telephone-Amt* 7 8 October 1891; Austria: Carltheater *Das Fräulein vom Telephon* 28 February 1892; UK: Grand Theatre, Wolverhampton *The Telephone Girl* 25 May 1896; USA: Casino Theater *The Telephone Girl* 27 September 1897

UNE DEMOISELLE EN LOTERIE Opérette-bouffe in 1 act by Adolphe Jaime and Hector Crémieux. Music by Jacques Offenbach. Théâtre des Bouffes-Parisiens, Paris, 27 July 1857.

One of the number of little Offenbach works of the 1850s which found more favor in its German-language versions than its original. The demoiselle who puts herself up for lottery is the footloose Aspasie (Lise Tautin), who counts on this game to collect a neat dowry to take to the winner. The lottery attracts the cousin, Agénor Pigéonneau (Désiré), who has helped himself to what should have been Aspasie's inheritance, and in the end, after some jolly and often vocally extravagant opéra-bouffe music, the clever girl ties him up as a comfortable husband.

After the piece's Paris premiere, the Bouffes-Parisiens company, headed by Mlle Tautin, introduced it first to Vienna's Theater am Franz-Josefs-Kai and then to Budapest's Budai Népszínház, and it was subsequently played both at the Theater an der Wien and at Budapest's Budai Színkör in a German version by F Zell. An English-language version was mounted in Liverpool by the little company set up by Norman Kirby in the early 1870s specifically to produce Offenbach's small works, and featured Kirby himself alongside Edith Percy (Mrs Kirby) and Albert Brennir.

Austria: Theater am Franz-Josefs-Kai (Fr) 10 June 1861, Theater an der Wien *Die Kunstreiterin* (*Eine weibliche Haupttreffer*) 15 February 1864; Hungary: Budai Népszínház (Fr) 13 July 1861, Budai Színkör *Eine Kunstreiterin* 28 April 1864; UK: Theatre Royal & Opera House, Liverpool *Nothing Venture, Nothing Have* 2 September 1872

DENNY, W[illiam] H[enry] [DUGMORE, William Henry] (b Balsall Heath, Birmingham, 22 October 1853; d London, 31 August 1915).

The son of actor Henry Leigh [Henry Thomas DUGMORE] (b Dublin, c1818; d London 7 June 1881) and his wife, the very well-known singing character actress Mrs Leigh, 11-year stalwarts of the Birmingham Theatre Royal company, Denny worked in the theatre (initially as ''W H Leigh'') from the age of six. After a first job as an assistant master in a Brighton college, he began in the adult theatre at 17 and appeared in London for the first time with Phelps's company playing small roles in Shakespeare and in classic plays. He was seen at the Gaiety in comedy, operetta (*Chanson de Fortunio,* 1876) and burlesque (Nick Vedder in *Young Rip van Winkle* 1876, Marquis in *Little Don Caesar de Bazan* 1876), and toured with Richard D'Oyly Carte (1876, Trénitz in *La Fille de Madame Angot,* Barthel in *The Duke's Daughter,* Tarapote in *La Périchole,* etc) whilst in his twenties. He then played in drama, comedy and in burlesque (*The Miller and His Men* 1883, Aurungzebe in *Lallah Rookh* 1884, Dr Chanery in *Scalded Back,* Captain Crosstree in *Black-Eyed See-usan* 1885, as Denny) around London; toured America (1886, again as ''Leigh'') with Lydia Thompson (Generalissimo in *Piff Paff,* etc); and appeared at several New York and London theatres in both drama and comedy before, in 1888, he joined D'Oyly Carte's company at the Savoy Theatre. At the Savoy, he replaced Rutland Barrington, who had gone into management on his own account, and thus created the role of the lugubrious jailer Shadbolt in *The Yeomen of the Guard.* When the chastened and poorer Barrington returned to Carte, Denny remained with the company to create further Savoy Theatre comic roles in *The Gondoliers* (Grand Inquisitor, ''I Stole the Prince''), *The Nautch Girl* (Bumbo, the idol), *Haddon Hall* (The McCrankie) and *Utopia (Limited)* (Scaphio).

He moved on from the Savoy after some four years in residence to feature in the London edition of *Poor Jonathan* (1893, Herr Steinbach), and to work with Arthur Roberts, playing General Jenkinson in *A Modern Don Quixote* (1893) and succeeding Eric Thorne as Sir Philip Saxmundham in the burlesque *Claude Du-val* (1894), and subsequently appeared with Lillian Russell in Jakobowski's Broadway-bound comic opera *The Queen of Brilliants* at the Lyceum (1894, Lucca Rabbiato) and toured for Morell and Mouillot in *Don Juan* (Rodrigo). He rejoined Roberts to play the fine role of the comical nouveau riche Pilkington Jones in *Gentleman Joe* (1895), to appear as the star's policeman rival-in-love in *Dandy Dan, the Lifeguardsman* (1897, t/o) and to play Bob Chaffers in the loose-limbed *HMS Irresponsible* (1900–1901), in between which engagements he took the chief senior comic role of Major Fossdyke in the West End run of *The Gay Parisienne* (1897, ''The Battersea Butterfly Hunters''), and featured briefly as the Court Clown in the fairly unsuccessful extravaganza *Her Royal Highness* (1898).

In 1902 he appeared in the British touring musical *The Gay Cadets* before working out the latter end of his multi-colored career in Shakespeare in Australia (Malvolio, Bottom), drama (*Madame X,* 1909, etc) and musical comedy in America (Mr Hazell in *The Earl and the Girl* 1906, Loofah in *The Tourists* 1906, Baron Lecocq in *The Beauty Spot* 1909, Herr Starke in *The Gay Hussars* 1909, etc), and latterly on the music halls in Britain.

His mother, Elizabeth DUGMORE, née Brown (b ?1825; d London, 20 November 1915) but billed inevitably as just ''**Mrs [H] LEIGH**,'' became a member of the Gaiety Theatre company in 1869, soon after its opening, and remained there for 12 years as the house's stock ''old woman'' in both plays and musicals. She created the part of Diana in Gilbert and Sullivan's *Thespis,* appeared as Amaranthe in Emily Soldene's *La Fille de Madame Angot* and made a particular feature, for many years, of the role of Mrs Bundle in *The Waterman.*

His sister, **''Georgie'' LEIGH** [Georgiana DUGMORE] (b Birmingham, 6 June 1855; d Sunderland, August 1884) also had a good career in provincial and colonial musical theatre up to a sudden death while still in her twenties, whilst his son, **Reginald DENNY** [Reginald Leigh DUGMORE] (b Richmond, 20 November 1891; d Los Angeles, 16 June 1967), after early appearances in touring productions of *The Merry Widow* and *The Quaker Girl,* and with the Newark Brownell stock company in America as Gaston in *Alma, Where Do You Live?* (1916), became a well-known stage and screen actor (Algy Longworth in the *Bulldog Drummond* series, etc). He was seen in the 1927 film of *On Your Toes* (Elliott Beresford).

DENS, Michel [MARCEL, Maurice] (b Roubaix, 22 June 1912; d Aulnay-sur-Bois, 19 December 2000).

After an early career in the French provinces, where he mixed operatic and opérette roles in several of the larger theatres, Dens played for the first time at the Opéra-Comique in 1947, beginning his tenancy there as Albert in *Werther.* He appeared in the same year at the Paris Opéra in the title role of Rigoletto. In the 1950s he was seen in a long series of opérettes at the Théâtre de la Gaîté-Lyrique, playing both the classic baritone roles (Marquis de Corneville, Brissac, etc) and several generally accepted tenor roles, notably Sou Chong in *Le Pays du sourire,* and taking part in several more recent French works (Ricardo in *Colorado, Romance au Portugal,* Karl in *Le Moulin sans souci*). At this period he also recorded for Pathé-Marconi the leading baritone (and some tenor) roles in the majority of the famous series of classic opérette recordings which have remained standard reference in the genre ever since. He continued to perform through into his late seventies, appearing in 1988 as Ménélas (*La Belle Hélène*) and in Jean Périer's high-baritone title role in *Hans, le joueur de flûte* in the provinces.

DESCLAUZAS, Marie [ARMAND, Malvina Caroline Ernestine] (b Paris, 13 July 1841; d Nogent-sur-Marne, 25 March 1912). Buxom and eventually hefty star of the opérette stage who became the most admired musical character comedienne of her era.

Marie Desclauzas began her stage career as a child, touring and—in her mid-teens—appearing in Paris at the Ambigu, the Cirque and the Châtelet under Hostein in dramas and in féeries where her attractively rounded figure earned her a series of leggy travesty roles. She then turned to the world of opéra-bouffe and there made herself a solid career as leading lady. This seems to have been initiated by a co-starring season (with the young Rose Bell) under the management of Jacob Grau and James Fisk in 1868–69 in America, where she appeared alternatively as Geneviève and Drogan in *Geneviève de Brabant,* as Boulotte, Fleur de Noblesse (*L'Oeil crevé*), Piquillo (*La Périchole*), Césarine (*Fleur de thé*), Galswinthe (*Chilpéric*) and in *La Vie parisienne.* She followed up with seasons in Nantes, Marseille, Bordeaux, Toulouse and Alexandria before being appointed prima donna of the fine company at the Brussels' Théâtre des Fantaisies-Parisiennes.

When that theatre's director, Eugène Humbert, produced the latest opéra-comique by the young Charles Lecocq, whose *Les Cent Vierges* had done so well for them earlier in the year, 32-year-old Desclauzas was duly given the leading role. She made such a success as Madame Lange, the luscious, plotting merveilleuse of *La Fille de Madame Angot* that, when the piece was taken to Paris and scheduled to be recast with metropolitan performers, Lecocq himself insisted that the Belgian creatrice of Lange be retained. Humbert released his star to the management of the Folies-Dramatiques and Desclauzas triumphed all over again in the capital. After a long stretch playing Lange, she appeared as Manon in Auguste Coedès's *La Belle Bourbonnaise,* as La Belle Cousine in Hervé's *Alice de Nevers,* and as Heloïse in a

Plate 97. **Marie Desclauzas.** *The greatest character lady of the opéra-comique stage, pictured here as Coedès's* La Belle Bourbonnaise.

revival of Litolff's *Heloïse et Abélard* (1874), but her now rather considerable bulk, especially when not hidden under the useful lines of *Angot*'s empire gowns, barred her from most leading roles and she tactfully changed direction, at 35, to make a speciality of character roles which required a strong singing voice and a powerful personality rather than a shapely leg.

In the 20 years that followed, Desclauzas created roles of this kind in a whole line of opérettes and plays, many at the Théâtre de la Renaissance and for Lecocq, and many written especially to suit her now thoroughly uncovered comic talents. These included the spectacle *La Mère Gigogne* at the Château d'Eau (1875, ''she is given an opportunity for a repetition of nearly every favourite air in her repertoire''); the Parisian production of *Le Roi d'Yvetôt* (1876), which she had created in Brussels three years earlier; *Le Petit Duc* (1878, Diane de Lansac, Directrice of the Académie pour Demoiselles Nobles); *La Camargo* (1878, Donna Juana de Rio-Negra); *La Petite*

Mademoiselle (1879, Madelon); *La Jolie Persane* (1879, Babouche); *Les Voltigeurs de la 32ème* (1880, Dorothée), which she played along with *Le Petit Duc, La Petite Mariée* (Lucrézia) and *Giroflé-Girofla* (Aurore) in London in 1881; *Janot* (1881, Alexina); *Mademoiselle Moucheron* (1881, Mme Boulinard); the disastrous *Le Sais* (1881); *Madame la Diable* (1882, Baronne Paméla); *La Bonne Aventure* (1882, Beppa); *Ninette* (1882, Countess Kouci-Kouca); *Les Trois Devins* (1884, Christine); *Les Petits Mousquetaires* (1885, Armide de Tréville); *Il était une fois* (1886, La Reine Virginie); *L'Amour mouillé* (1887, Catarina); *Le Petit Moujik* (1896, Mme Picou); *Les Fêtards* (1896, Madame Maréchale) and *La Petite Tache* (1898). She also appeared in such repertoire roles as the Marquise d'Enface of *L'Oeil crevé,* Aurore (*Giroflé-Girofla*), Lucrézia (*La Petite Mariée*), Marcelline (*Belle Lurette*), Marguerite (*Le Canard à trois becs*) and Fanfreluche (*La Poule aux oeufs d'or*), in Bisson's military *Mam'selle Piou-Piou* (1889, Madame Papillon) at the Porte-Saint-Martin, and took time off to appear, with equal success, in comedy for Koning at the Gymnase (Mme Baudoin in *Les Amants légitimes,* Déborah in *L'Homme à l'oreille cassée,* Comtesse Gypsy in *Autour du mariage,* etc), at the Porte-Saint-Martin in the fantastical *La Montagne enchantée* (1897, Fatima) and elsewhere. She officially retired from the stage in 1910, just two years before her death at the age of 71.

Her most famous creations were the irresistibly comical role of the Directrice in *Le Petit Duc,* a part to which she returned again and again over a period of 20 years, and the vast, blowsy wardrobe mistress of the farcical *Les Fêtards,* with her memories of her days as a tight-waisted circus rider and her royal romance, but such was the artist's hold over this kind of role in her time that, for decades thereafter, such character parts, in old and new opérettes, were known in France as ''les roles de Desclauzas.''

THE DESERT SONG Musical play in 3 acts by Otto Harbach, Oscar Hammerstein II and Frank Mandel. Lyrics by Otto Harbach and Oscar Hammerstein II. Music by Sigmund Romberg. Casino Theater, New York, 30 November 1926.

The most internationally successful and the most enduring of Sigmund Romberg's long line of romantic musical plays, *The Desert Song* was—so it was seriously said—based on the doings of a genuine Berber chieftain (it was later that Arab's chief qualification for a *New York Times* obituary), but its tale of romance and disguise, deftly mixed with the standard amount of parallel comic action, as put together by Hammerstein, Harbach and Mandel ran smoothly in the regulation comic opera groove and, if anything, seemed to owe much more of its color and its incidents to the recent Hollywood success *The Sheik* (1922) than to Morocco's publicity-hungry desert murderers.

The anti-French Arab guerillas of the North African deserts who have been raiding and pressuring the colonial government, as represented by army chief Captain Paul Fontaine (Glen Dale) and the new Governor, General Birabeau (Edmund Elton), are led to damaging effect by a mysterious person known as the Red Shadow. In fact, the Red Shadow is none other than the Governor's native-loving son, Pierre (Robert Halliday), who pretends to be a weak-witted fool at home whilst secretly sneaking out to put on Arab garb and lead the locals' attacks on his father's forces. His gormless act means that he has little chance of winning the lovely Margot Bonvalet (Vivienne Segal) from Fontaine, so to pursue his suit he gets into his sheikish costume and carries her romantically off into the desert. When General Birabeau comes to free her, Pierre is unable to draw his sword against his father and thus forfeits his leadership of the Arab band. But later, when Fontaine has set forth to take the Red Shadow, dead or alive, the jealous Arab dancing girl, Azuri (Pearl Regay), reveals to the General that he has put a price on the head of his own son. But the ending is happier than *Il Trovatore*: Pierre produces the Red Shadow's costume and announces that he has killed the rebel. Only his father and maybe—just maybe—Margot, need know the truth. The comic element was provided by Bennie Kidd (Eddie Buzzell), a society columnist deputizing uncomfortably as a war correspondent, and his desperately devoted secretary, Susan (Nellie Breen).

Romberg's score contained several songs which were to become romantic standards—the hero's waltzing invitation to Valentino-style desert bliss in ''The Desert Song'' (''Blue heaven, and you and I . . .''), Margot's soprano dreams of Elinor-Glynnish ''Romance,'' the driving chorus of ''The Riff Song'' and the Red Shadow's ballad, ''One Alone,'' which was one part of an impressive ''Eastern and Western Love'' section which also included the lovely ''Let Love Go'' and the counter-tenor ''One Flower Grows Alone in Your Garden.'' A pretty ''Why Did We Marry Soldiers?'' and French Marching Song for the ladies' chorus, a lightly humorous demonstration of tough seduction techniques (''I Want a Kiss''), and the heroine's showpiece Sabre Song were amongst other highspots of a score in which the straight comedy numbers—Bennie's musings over the feminine quality known as ''It,'' his fears, under pressure from a saucy Spaniard (Margaret Irving), that he will soon be ''One Good Man Gone Wrong,'' and Susan's ''I'll Be a Buoyant Girl''—were slightly submerged.

The libretto of *The Desert Song* was, give or take a sag in the last stages of the second act, very much better made than those for most contemporary musical romances, and the show's emphasis on the sentimental and seductive side of its content, richly illustrated musically, proved to be well in the line of current taste. Schwab and Mandel's production of *The Desert Song* (prematurely entitled *Lady Fair* on its initial showing at Poli's Theater in Washington, DC) was a great Broadway hit through a run of 471 performances, as the preface to a very long career.

London's Theatre Royal, Drury Lane production with Harry Welchman (Pierre) and Edith Day (Margot) starred, Maria Minetti as Clementine and Clarice Hardwicke as Susan, echoed the popularity of the Broadway edition with a splendid run of 432 performances, and the show was soon on the road for what would be the first of a seemingly interminable number of tours in both countries. In Australia, too, where Lance Fairfax introduced the exploits of the Red Shadow alongside Virginia Perry (Margot), Herbert Mundin (Benny), Peter Gawthorne (Birabeau) and Stephanie d'Este (Azuri) in J C Williamson Ltd's production, the piece was a huge hit. It ran some 220 performances in its initial season in Melbourne, and, with Marie Bremner succeeding to the role of Margot, some five months in Sydney (Her Majesty's Theatre 30 March 1929), becoming a perennial and oft-reproduced favorite with which its star (and his entrance on horseback) was identified ever after.

Whilst, in America, *The Desert Song* returned only once, and briefly, to Broadway (Uris Theater 5 September 1973) as well as to the repertoire of the New York City Opera, in Britain a number of further metropolitan appearances followed the first. Alec Fraser and Sylvia Welling starred in a 1931 reprise (Alhambra Theatre 8 June), the original stars returned to the London Coliseum in 1936 (24 September), and Bruce Carfax and Doris Francis featured in a 1939 revival at the Garrick Theatre (29 June). Welchman made a third London appearance as the Red Shadow, this time paired with Eleanor Fayre, at the Palace Theatre in 1943 (16 January) and in 1967 provincial favorite John Hanson braved London, paired with soprano Patricia Michael, for a 383-performance run at the Palace Theatre.

Unlike its near contemporary *Rose Marie, The Desert Song* did not make major inroads into Europe, with one exception: France. After the serious success of *Rose-Marie,* the Isola Brothers had followed up with *Hallelujah!* (ie, *Hit the Deck*) with much less satisfactory results. They hastened to mount another American romantic piece and *Le Chant du désert* (ad Roger Ferréol, Saint-Granier), produced as an ''Opérette à grand spectacle en 2 parties et huit tableaux,'' served their purpose well. Robert Couzinou (Pierre) played l'Ombre Rouge, Marcelle Denya was Jenny (ex- Margot) singing ''Rêver,''

Plate 98. **The Desert Song.** *Valentino meets Elinor Glyn under the blue heaven where the sand kisses a moonlight sky.*

whilst the comic Dorville was Onésime (ex- Bennie) in his quest for ''Ça!'' The production had a seven-month career, and though it did not come near challenging the remarkable success of Friml's piece in France, it survived well enough to be seen in revival at Lille's Théâtre Sebastapol as recently as 1994 (24 April).

The Desert Song made its way briskly on to film, with John Boles appearing in ''the first all-singing-and-talking operetta'' as the Red Shadow to the Margot of Carlotta King and with Myrna Loy (Azuri), Edward Martindel (Birabeau), Louise Fazenda (Susan) and Johnnie Arthur (Bennie) featured, in the first (1929) of three Warner Brothers films. Dennis Morgan and Irene Manning paired for a second version in 1943, and a third, a decade later, featured Gordon MacRae and Kathryn Grayson. Warners also issued a 20-minute potted version in 1932. An NBC television broadcast of 1955 gave Nelson Eddy an airing as the Red Shadow.

Three-quarters of a century on, *The Desert Song* remains in the repertoire in English-speaking countries and, beyond American shores, it shares with *Rose Marie* and with the increasingly fashionable *Show Boat* the representation of its era of American romantic musicals.

UK: Theatre Royal, Drury Lane 7 April 1927; Australia: Her Majesty's Theatre, Melbourne 15 September 1928; France: Théâtre Mogador *Le Chant du désert* June 1930

Films: Warner Brothers 1929, 1943 and 1953

Recordings: selections (HMV, Capitol, RCA, Columbia, Decca, etc), selection in French (TLP)

DÉSHABILLEZ-VOUS Comédie musicale in 3 acts by André Barde. Music by René Mercier. Théâtre des Bouffes-Parisiens, Paris, 22 December 1928.

Titles had got a good deal saucier in Jazz Age musical comedy since the relatively harmless *Ta bouche.* With Mireille Perrey going on about "Nuits d'Argentine," Jacqueline Francell insisting "L'Amour ça n'a l'air de rien," Edmond Roze juxtaposing "Trop petit, trop grand" and Jeanne Perriat and Robert Ancelin detailing what happens "Dans un chemin de fer," this one more or less earned its titular command to "get 'em off" in a four-month run, without succeeding in going very much further.

DÉSIRÉ [COURTECUISSE, Désiré] (b Lille, 29 September 1823; d Asnières, September 1873).

In 1847 the young comedian known as Désiré asked Hervé for a two-handed musical sketch to play at his benefit. Since Désiré was short and plump and Hervé tall and gangling, the author selected the subject of Don Quixote, wrote a zany burlesque of Cervantes' tale for the two of them to play together and illustrated it with original music rather than the borrowed tunes usual in such pieces. The two performers made a great success of their saynète and it was subsequently taken up by Adolphe Adam and played at his Théâtre Lyrique in 1848. *Don Quichotte et Sancho Pança* is quoted in most histories which like to try to put a finger on the first this and the first that as being the first opérette of the modern era.

Désiré subsequently became a star comedian in opéra-bouffe at Hervé's Folies-Nouvelles and Offenbach's Bouffes-Parisiens and he created comic roles in many of Offenbach's works, large and small, decorating them with the improvisations which were his trademark. Amongst the roles he introduced were Dig-Dig in *La Chatte métamorphosée en femme,* Pan in *Daphnis et Chloë,* Fortunio in *La Chanson de Fortunio,* M Choufleuri in *M Choufleuri restera chez lui le . . . ,* Cristoval in *Les Bavards,* Bertolucci in *Il Signor Fagotto,* Cabochon in *Jeanne qui pleure et Jean qui rit,* Fritzchen in *Lischen et Fritzchen,* the title role in *Vent du soir,* Pigeonneau in *Une Demoiselle en loterie,* Mardi Gras in *Le Carnaval des revues,* Madame Madou in *Mesdames de la Halle,* Signor Gorja in *Les Vivandières de la grande armée,* Ragotin in *Le Roman comique,* Villebriquin in *L'Amour chanteur,* Robin in *Le Soldat magicien,* Jol-Hiddin in *Les Géorgiennes,* Dunanan père in *Le Voyage de MM Dunanan,* Veautendon in *Les Bergers,* Raphaël in *La Diva,* Balabrelock in *Boule de neige* and, above all, the original Jupiter of *Orphée aux enfers* (1858), the Golo of *Geneviève de Brabant* (1859), the Cornarino Cornarini of *Le Pont des soupirs* (1861) and the Cabriolo of *La Princesse de Trébizonde* (1869).

Amongst the roles which he created in works by other writers were the Marquis de Criquebouef in Delibes's *L'Omelette à la Follembûche* and Ducornet in his *L'Écossais de Chatou* and, having moved on in turn to the Variétés, the Palais-Royal and the short-lived Athenée, the role of the tubby mandarin Tien-Tien (paired with the skinny Léonce as Ka-o-lin) in Lecocq's first major work, *Fleur de thé* (1868). He also played in Lecocq's *L'Amour et son carquois,* created Madopolam in his *Le Rajah de Mysore,* and Chicorat in his *Le Testament de M Crac* (1871), and introduced the principal comic role of the judge, Raab, in Vasseur's hugely successful *La Timbale d'argent.* In 1872 he appeared at the Bouffes-Parisiens in *Le Docteur Rose* (Dr Capsulo) and in 1873 alongside Judic in Vasseur's *La Petite Reine* (Pastello) in one of his last new roles before his death later that same year.

The same name was later assumed by another French musical comedy actor, who appeared from the 1880s in such pieces as *Boccace* (1882, Orlando), *Jeanne, Jeannette et Jeanneton, Ali Baba* (1889, Zizi), *Miss Helyett, Le Cadeau de noces, Le Roi Dagobert, La Fille de Madame Angot* (Larivaudière in the Opéra-Comique performance), *La Divorcée, Les Transatlantiques, Les Cloches de Corneville* (Bailli), *Les 28 Jours de Clairette* (Capitaine), *Madame Boniface* (Jacquot), *Mam'zelle Nitouche* (Château-Gibus), *Rip* (Nick Vedder), etc.

DESLYS, Gaby [CAIRE, Marie Élise Gabrielle] (b Marseille, 4 November 1881; d Paris, 11 February 1920). Little, blonde, extravagantly-half-dressed Marseillaise dancer who made herself a reputation in variety and theatre around the world.

Mlle Deslys made her first Parisian appearances in revue at the Théâtre des Mathurins, and quickly became a fashionable beauty of the early years of the new century, famous for her fabulous dresses and headdresses and also for her determinedly publicized liaison with Manoël, King of Portugal. A professional liaison with dancer Harry Pilcer was more durable and almost as famous, whilst the adoration of author J M Barrie resulted in her appearing on the London stage, with decidedly fractured English, as the star of a curious Barrie concoction called *Rosy Rapture, the Pride of the Beauty Chorus* (1915).

Although Mlle Deslys's career was made largely and extremely successfully in the music halls (*La Journée d'une parisienne, The Magic Toy,* etc) and in revue, she was seen in several theoretically more vertebrate pieces. In 1906 George Edwardes interpolated her into *The New*

Aladdin at the Gaiety Theatre with a couple of songs and some success, and in 1910, after her scandal value had rocketed thanks to Manoël's dethroning (his mania for her was blamed for the revolution!), she appeared at Vienna's Apollotheater in the three-scene vaudeville *Susettes Launen* (Albert Chantrier/Gabriel Timmony). In 1911 she visited America and featured first in the "two-scene comedietta" *Les Débuts de Chichine* in the Shuberts' Winter Garden *Revue of Revues,* and then in what had started out at the same Vienna Apollotheater as Eysler's short Operette *Vera Violetta,* in its Broadway metamorphosis into a virtual variety program. She was cast as Mme Adèle de la Cloche and performed Louis Hirsch's "Gaby Glide" with Pilcer as her partner. In 1912 she returned to Vienna with Pilcer to play the sketches *Eine Woche in Trouville* and *Mam'selle Chic* and she repeated at London's Palace with *Mam'selle Chic, or A Day in Trouville* (26 August) before quitting Britain in disgust, so she confided spicily, at "having been censored," and returning to America to give *Vera Violetta* to the touring circuits.

In 1913 she played the London Palace in the musical comedietta *À la carte,* visited Chicago with an act called *La Petite Parisienne* and featured in Broadway's "spectacular farce with music" *The Honeymoon Express* (Yvonne Dubonnet). She was seen again on the London stage (presumably uncensored) in the brief 1914 *The Belle of Bond Street* and finally, in 1917, in the musical comedy *Suzette* in which she performed a kind of apache dance-scena called "The Cat and the Canary," with Pilcer, and a murder mime called *La Fourchette,* whilst her final Broadway appearance was in another piece more revue than book musical, Irving Berlin's *Stop! Look! Listen!* in 1915–16. Australia, unable, apparently, to afford Gaby, decided to make do with what it clearly considered the important part of her act: Harry Rickards advertised "the Gaby Deslys costume" and the "Gaby Deslys Parade" as part of his 1914 show at Melbourne's Tivoli.

Mlle Deslys also appeared on film, playing in such pieces as *Infatuation* in which the public was warned that she displayed "the wiles, the charm, the gowns of the woman who causes the overthrow of a monarchy" and *The God of Luck.* Soon, however, she burnt herself out and she died of a "respiratory ailment" following "a sore throat and a bout of 'flu," at the age of 38.

An Operette entitled *Gaby Deslys,* with a score by Bernhard Grün was produced in central Europe in 1935, and it was also rumored that the Ruggiero Leoncavallo operetta, *La Reginetta delle rose,* produced in Rome in 1912, was an à clef piece based on the affair between Portugal and Mlle Deslys. There was, however, nothing demurely à clef about the "satirical revuette" called *Gaby* produced by Henry B Harris and Jesse Lasky on Broadway in 1911 (Folies-Bergère 27 April). It was full frontal. Ethel Levey was Gaby (singing Irving Berlin's "I Beg Your Pardon, Broadway") and the young English dancer

Plate 99. **Gaby Deslys** *was famous for her millinery and famed in song. Louis Hirsch's "Gaby Glide" was one of the many numbers which crowded out Eysler's score in the Shuberts' Winter Garden production of the short Operett* Vera Violetta.

Laddie Cliff was ''King Manny,'' insisting ''Don't Stop, Mr Jenkinson'' and joining his inamorata in singing about ''Down the Strand.'' The evening came to a climax with a March of the Beauties of the Nations, of which Gaby was, of course, a feature.

Biographies: Gardner, J: *Gaby Deslys: A Fatal Attraction* (Sidgwick & Jackson, London, 1986), Sirkis, J-J: *Les Années Deslys* (Jeanne Laffitte, Paris, 1990)

DESPREZ, Frank (b Bristol, 10 February 1853; d Barnet, 22 November 1916).

After having spent some youthful time, far from his native Bristol, as a cowboy in Texas, Desprez returned to Britain in 1875. After working initially as a riding master, he began his career as a theatrical writer unpromisingly, supplying prima donna Selina Dolaro with mutilated versions of *La Périchole* and of a *La Fille de Madame Angot* which all but eliminated the co-starring role of Clairette and expanded that of Mlle Lange (who doesn't normally appear till Act II) for his employer. When this last piece went on the road, he also authored a little forepiece for it. *Happy Hampstead* was set to music by Dolaro's manager, Richard D'Oyly Carte.

Desprez subsquently became one of Carte's closest friends and worked with him for many years as secretary whilst, at the same time, writing the texts for the little operettas which preceded the Gilbert and Sullivan shows on the bills at the Opera Comique and the Savoy. Virtually all of these had very long runs, in tandem with and sometimes beyond the runs of the principal pieces, and they were played throughout the country as forepieces and short-program items, much as the short works of Offenbach and his contemporaries had been in France a decade and more earlier. Working with composers such as Cellier and Solomon, Desprez established himself as the best-displayed practitioner of the one-act form in Britain.

Perhaps his most played work, however, was the two-act (but still short) musical comedy *Tita in Thibet,* written for Kate Santley. It later became a staple in the touring baggage of the Majilton company by whom it was played more than a thousand times in the provinces. Undoubtedly his best work was his lyrical contribution to the Savoy Theatre's *The Nautch Girl,* the show which deputized more than adequately for the Gilbert and Sullivan series during the quarrel between the two famous writers.

In 1884 Desprez began writing for *The Era,* London's foremost theatre paper, and he became its editor in 1893, a position he held until illness forced him to retire in 1913.

His stage works have not proved enduring, but Desprez's name is still known today as the author of ''Lasca,'' a poem describing an Englishman's memories of his time in Texas and of the girl, Lasca, whom he met there. A truncated version of the poem (''the best cowboy poem ever'') was long recited in schools throughout cowboy country, and can be found on the Internet in the 21st century.

1875 **La Périchole** English version (Royalty Theatre)

1875 **La Fille de Madame Angot** English version (Royalty Theatre)

1876 **Happy Hampstead** (Richard D'Oyly Carte) 1 act Alexandra Theatre, Liverpool 3 July

1878 **After All** (Alfred Cellier) 1 act Opera Comique 23 December

1879 **Tita in Thibet** (aka *Brum, a Birmingham Merchant*) Royalty Theatre 1 January

1880 **In the Sulks** (A Cellier) 1 act Opera Comique 21 February

1881 **Quite an Adventure** (Edward Solomon) 1 act Olympic Theatre 7 September

1881 **Mock Turtles** (Eaton Fanning) 1 act Savoy Theatre 15 October

1883 **Lurette** (*Belle Lurette*) English version w Alfred Murray, H S Leigh (Avenue Theatre)

1883 **A Private Wire** (Percy Reeve/w Arnold Felix) 1 act Savoy Theatre 31 March

1885 **Round and Square** (Solomon) 1 act Theatre Royal, Manchester 6 April

1886 **The Carp** (A Cellier) 1 act Savoy Theatre 13 February

1888 **Mrs Jarramie's Genie** (A Cellier, François Cellier) 1 act Savoy Theatre 14 February

1889 **Delia** (Procida Bucalossi) Prince's Theatre, Bristol 11 March (as ''F Soulbieu'')

1891 **The Nautch Girl** (Solomon/w George Dance/Dance) Savoy Theatre 30 June

1892 **Brother George** (Bucalossi) Theatre Royal, Portsmouth 16 May

DESTRY RIDES AGAIN Musical in 2 acts by Leonard Gershe based on the story by Max Brand. Music and lyrics by Harold Rome. Imperial Theater, New York, 23 April 1959.

A musical theatre version of the story which had previously been made successfully into a film several times over, most memorably in 1939 with James Stewart and Marlene Dietrich and Friedrich Holländer's well remembered song ''See What the Boys in the Back Room will Have,'' but also with such western heroes as Tom Mix and Audie Murphy.

This time Andy Griffith was Tom Destry, son of a famous lawman, summoned to be deputy sheriff of outback Bottleneck by Wash (Jack Prince), the theoretically innocuous town drunk promoted to puppet sheriff by the real boss of the town, gambler Kent (Scott Brady). Destry sets to his job without the use of a gun, escapes the wiles of Kent's moll, the dance-hall girl, Frenchy (Dolores Gray), set on him by the gambler, and arrests Kent's crony, Gyp Watson (Marc Breaux), the killer of the last sheriff. Things get rough when Kent's gang set out to break Watson from jail, and finally the peace-loving sheriff is forced to put on his guns. A virtuoso display of gunfire ensures him victory and the love of a reformed Frenchy. The spare and straight dramatic-comic story of the original was here musical-comedied-up by the addition of a conventional set of stage prostitutes and their madam.

Rome supplied some nicely gentle comic moments for his hero, realizing that he will remember "Tomorrow Morning" all sorts of clever things with which he could have defended himself against his tormentors today; enumerating the consistently ghastly fate of the famous gunmen of history ("Ballad of the Gun"); or explaining opaquely "Only Time Will Tell," to hide the fact that he has been to fetch a Federal judge to head the murderer's trial and put it out of Kent's crooked reach. Frenchy had her best moment heading the mock-trial "Are You Ready, Gyp Watson?," topped off by a fine and funny male chorale tipping the verdict of "Not Guilty," whilst the dried-out deputy sheriff of Bottleneck leaped about to a lively "Hoop-de-Dingle." Breaux joined with Swen Swenson and George Reeder in the show's dance highlight, a dazzling Michael Kidd number danced with bullwhips, which proved to be the most remembered moment of the production.

Hampered by trade union demands, David Merrick's production had an insufficient 472-performance run on Broadway, and *Destry Rides Again* did not progress further afield until 1982 when director Robert Walker produced a slimmed-down version of the show on the London fringe. A cast of 17 actor-musicians, headed by Alfred Molina (Destry) and Jill Gascoine (Frenchy), played, sang and acted their way with acrobatic vigour through a *Destry* from which the prostitutes and their numbers had been salutorially cut, in which the famous fight between Frenchy and Mrs Callahan, played on screen by Dietrich and Una Merkel, was brought up, and which no longer in any way resembled a conventional musical comedy. The production won the show many London friends and fans without progressing to a West End house or, it seems, to further productions on the same sparely healthy lines.

UK: Donmar Warehouse 30 September 1982

Recordings: original cast (Decca), London version (TER)

DESVALLIÈRES, [Georges Ernest] Maurice (b Paris, 3 October 1857; d Paris, 23 March 1926).

The grandson of author and playwright Ernest [Wilfred] Legouvé (b Paris, 14 February 1807; d Paris, 14 March 1903, *Adrienne Lecouvreur, La Bataille de dames, La Cigale, Les Doigts de fée,* etc), and himself the author of a long list of vaudevilles and comedies, Desvallières had his most important successes with the comedies *L'Hôtel du libre échange* (Eng: *Hotel Paradiso* or *A Night Out,* w Georges Feydeau), *Fils à papa* (w Antony Mars) and *Champignol malgré lui* (*The Other Fellow,* w Feydeau). He also contributed to six original musical pieces, of which *La Demoiselle du téléphone* (played in Britain, America and Australia as *The Telephone Girl,* in Austria as *Das Fräulein vom Telephon,* in Germany as *Telephone-Amt*), *Mam'zelle Quat' Sous* (produced in Austria as *Die beiden Don Juans* with Girardi, and in Hungary as *A garasos kisasszony*) and the highly comical Mormon tale of *Les Douze Femmes de Japhet* (*Japhet und seine zwölf Frauen, Jafet 12 feleség*) were the most successful. His most enduring musical theatre work, however, came in two adaptations from the German musical stage, *Die Dollarprinzessin* and *Die keusche Susanne,* this latter a musicalization of his own *Fils à papa,* both of which won long and continuing lives in their French versions.

L'Hôtel du libre échange has been made into a musical comedy as the highly successful *A Night Out* (Winter Garden, London 19 September 1920) and with much less success as *Hotel Passionato* (Philip Springer/Joan Javits/Jerome J Schwartz, East 74th Street Theater, 1965), whilst Leoncavallo's *Prestami tua moglie* (lib: Edmondo Corradi, Casino, Montecatini 2 September 1916), London's *Baby Bunting* (Nat Ayer/Clifford Grey/Fred Thompson, Worton David Shaftesbury Theatre 25 September 1919) and the Hungarian musical play *A kölcsönkért feleség* (Fővárosi Nyári Színház 27 July 1921), adapted by Géza Vágo and musically set by Andor Szoldos to lyrics by Mihály Szántó, were all based—more, or in the second case a little less—on Desvallières's very first Parisian play *Prête-moi ta femme* (Palais-Royal 10 September 1883).

1890 **Mademoiselle Nounou** (w Georges Feydeau) 1 act Brussels 25 April

1890 **Les Douze Femmes de Japhet** (Victor Roger/w Antony Mars) Théâtre de la Renaissance 16 December

1891 **La Demoiselle du téléphone** (Gaston Serpette/w Mars) Théâtre des Nouveautés 2 May

1897 **Mam'zelle Quat' Sous** (Robert Planquette/w Mars) Théâtre de la Gaîté 5 November

1905 **L'Âge d'or** (Louis Varney/w Feydeau) Théâtre des Variétés 1 May

1908 **Mam'zelle Trompette** (Hirlemann/w Paul Moncousin) Théâtre des Folies-Dramatiques 15 September

1911 **La Princesse Dollar** (*Die Dollarprinzessin*) French version w Mars (Théâtre de la Scala)

1913 **La Chaste Suzanne** (*Die keusche Susanne*) French version w Mars (Théâtre des Célestins, Lyon)

1920 **La Princesse Carnaval** (Henri Hirschmann/w Moncousin) Théâtre Apollo 24 January

DE SYLVA, B G [DE SYLVA, George Gard] (''Buddy'') (b New York, 27 January 1895; d Los Angeles, 11 July 1950). Lyricist whose greatest success on the musical stage came as one head of the songwriting team De Sylva, Brown and Henderson.

The son of a vaudeville artist, De Sylva began writing song lyrics while at college getting the kind of education which would mean he wouldn't have to go into show business. Al Jolson took kindly to his work and used several of his lyrics, resulting in the young writer's first hits when ''I'll Say She Does'' (mus: Gus Kahn) and ''Chloe'' (mus credited to Jolson) emerged from the half-dozen of his numbers used at various times in Jolson's Winter Garden show *Sinbad* (1918). ''I'll Say She Does'' later became the title of one of De Sylva's first musical comedy ventures, when he supplied the songs for a musical version of Avery Hopwood's *Our Little Wife* which was initially produced under that fashionably meaningless title-phrase. After a tryout in stock it was revamped and remounted by producer A H Woods as *Dodo,* but it still failed to find its way to Broadway.

De Sylva had, by this stage, moved to New York and taken a job with the music publishers Remick, as a result of which he was allotted the writing of part of the lyrics for George Gershwin's 1919 musical comedy début, *La La Lucille.* He also supplied the words to the songs for Jerome Kern's *Zip Goes a Million* and although that show, like *Dodo,* folded pre-Broadway, one song from its score later found itself a home in the score of Kern's *Sally.* ''Look for the Silver Lining'' turned out to be De Sylva's biggest hit to date, along with two more numbers written for Jolson and used by him in *Bombo* (1921). The star plugged both ''April Showers'' (mus: Louis Silvers) and ''California, Here I Come'' (mus: Joseph Meyer) happily into the standards class.

Subsequent theatre assignments included a collaboration with Victor Herbert on *Orange Blossoms,* the adaptation of Kalman's European hit *Die Bajadere* as *The Yankee Princess,* two further book shows and three editions of *George White's Scandals* with Gershwin (''Stairway to Paradise,'' ''Somebody Loves Me'') and one with Joseph Meyer, which included yet another song hit, ''If You Knew Susie,'' for Al Jolson. Two successful Broadway collaborations with composer Lewis Gensler (*Captain Jinks, Queen High*) kept him to the musical comedy forefront thereafter, but at the same time an even more fruitful collaboration was being born in the revue world. For the 1925 and 1926 editions of *George White's Scandals,* De Sylva joined up with lyricist Lew Brown and composer Ray Henderson, each, like himself, the writer of recognized song hits, and after having produced ''The Birth of the Blues,'' ''The Girl Is You and the Boy Is Me,'' ''Lucky Day'' and the ''Black Bottom'' for the 1926 show, the trio continued on into the musical theatre together, scoring a major hit with their first effort as a team, the ultimate college musical, *Good News* (1927).

They followed up this winner with an Ed Wynn vehicle for George White, *Manhattan Mary;* the boxing musical *Hold Everything!* (''You're the Cream in My Coffee''), which hoisted Bert Lahr to stardom; *Follow Thru,* which dealt with golf and contained ''Button Up Your Overcoat''; and (after boxing and golf) an aeronautics musical, *Flying High*—whilst at the same time putting a first foot into the cinematic world. Their first screen ventures included the scores for Al Jolson's *The Singing Fool* (''Sonny Boy'') and for *Sunny Side Up* which, apart from its title song, also produced ''If I Had a Talking Picture of You'' to add to their list of hits.

De Sylva broke up the team to move on to a further career as a producer of films and, subsequently, of Broadway shows. He teamed with Laurence Schwab, the producer of *Good News* and *Follow Thru,* with whom he had also earlier worked as a co-librettist, to stage *Take a Chance* (''Eadie Was a Lady'') with Ethel Merman and Jack Haley topping the bill, then doubled book writing and producing on another and more successful show which also starred Miss Merman when he presented the Cole Porter musical *Dubarry Was a Lady* (1939). He was also involved as co-producer on two other successful musicals in the following year—Irving Berlin's *Louisiana Purchase* and Porter's *Panama Hattie.*

After the split with Brown and Henderson and *Take a Chance,* De Sylva did little more in the way of songwriting, confining his later writing to libretti.

A 1956 Hollywood biopic on the team, *The Best Things in Life Are Free,* had De Sylva portrayed by the robust singing actor Gordon MacRae.

1919 **La La Lucille** (George Gershwin/w Arthur Jackson/ Frederick Jackson) Henry Miller Theater 26 May

1919 **I'll Say She Does** (Avery Hopwood) Garrick Theater, Washington, DC 10 August

1919 **Zip Goes a Million** (Jerome Kern/Guy Bolton) Worcester Theater, Worcester, Mass 8 December

1920 **Dodo** revised *I'll Say She Does* Poli's Theater, Washington, DC 25 April

1922 **The Yankee Princess** (*Die Bajadere*) American version w William Le Baron (Knickerbocker Theater)

1922 **Blue Monday** (Gershwin) 1 act (in *George White's Scandals of 1922*) Globe Theater 28 August

1922 **Orange Blossoms** (Victor Herbert/Fred de Grésac) Fulton Theater 19 September

1924 **Sweet Little Devil** (ex- *A Perfect Lady*) (Gershwin/Frank Mandel, Laurence Schwab) Astor Theater 21 January

1925 **Big Boy** (Joseph Meyer, James Hanley/Harold Atteridge) Winter Garden Theater 7 January

1925 **Tell Me More!** (Gershwin/w Ira Gershwin/Fred Thompson, William K Wells) Gaiety Theater 13 April

1925 **Captain Jinks** (Lewis E Gensler, Stephen Jones/Mandel, Schwab) Martin Beck Theater 8 September
1926 **Queen High** (Gensler/w Schwab) Ambassador Theater 8 September
1927 **Good News** (Henderson/w Brown/w Schwab) 46th Street Theater 6 September
1927 **Manhattan Mary** (Henderson/w Brown/w George White) Apollo Theater 26 September
1928 **Hold Everything!** (Henderson/w Brown/w Jack McGowan) Broadhurst Theater 10 October
1929 **Follow Thru** (Henderson/w Brown/w Schwab) 46th Street Theater 9 January
1930 **Flying High** (Henderson/w Brown/McGowan) Apollo Theater 3 March
1932 **Humpty Dumpty** (Nacio Herb Brown, Richard Whiting/ Schwab) Pittsburgh, Pa 12 September
1932 **Take a Chance** revised *Humpty Dumpty* (Brown, Whiting, Vincent Youmans/Schwab) Apollo Theater 26 November
1939 **Dubarry Was a Lady** (Porter/w Herbert Fields) 46th Street Theater 6 December
1940 **Panama Hattie** (Porter/w Herbert Fields) 46th Street Theater 30 October

LES DEUX ARLEQUINS Opérette in 1 act by Eugène Mestépès. Music by Émile Jonas. Fantaisies-Parisiennes, Paris, 29 December 1865.

A little saynète for two, in which Harlequin (Bonnet), wishing to test his Colombine's fidelity after a long absence from home, brings news of his own death. She (Ghislaine Fontanel) sees through the trick, tells the ''stranger'' that she has found another harlequin, and then—to his discomfort—impersonates the ''rival.''

One of the most successful of Jonas's short pieces, it was played throughout Europe following its Paris premiere, being seen most notably on the opening program at the London Gaiety Theatre (ad Gilbert a' Beckett) when the two harlequins were played by Charles Lyall and Constance Loseby.

Austria: Theater an der Wien *Die beiden Harlekine* 26 January 1867; UK: Gaiety Theatre *The Two Harlequins* 21 December

LES DEUX AVEUGLES Bouffonnerie musicale in 1 act by Jules Moinaux. Music by Jacques Offenbach. Théâtre des Bouffes-Parisiens, Paris, 5 July 1855.

A two-handed comic sketch in which two phony blind beggars squabble for the best begging-patch, indulging first in a musical battle in which Giraffier (Berthelier) accompanies himself on a mandolin and Patachon (Pradeau) blasts away on a trombone, and then in a game of cards which shows up the pretense of their blindness.

Produced as the opening attraction at Offenbach's summer Théâtre des Bouffes-Parisiens, Moinaux's little comedy became the theatrical must of the season and its success helped materially to launch Offenbach both as a composer and as a theatre manager. It was played frequently thereafter, throughout France, reaching the Opéra-Comique in 1858, and also helped to set in motion the passion, soon to become overwhelming, for Offenbach's works in the other parts of the world. It was the first Offenbach piece played in Berlin, in Vienna (initially by Paris's Pierre Levassor, in French, later in a German-language version) and in Antwerp and it was featured in London, first by Levassor and his partner Jules Lefort in their concert bouffe and later in the repertoire of the Bouffes-Parisiens company. Thereafter English translations, in particular, proliferated (*Going Blind, Beggar My Neighbour, A Mere Blind, The Blind Beggars, Two Blinds, Blind Imposters,* etc) as the piece was played over and over again as a favourite part of 19th-century multiple-part bills and even, as in Australia's first performances by the Harry Rickards company, as an item on a virtual variety bill.

Germany: Krolls Theater 10 March 1856; Austria: Carltheater (Fr) 19 April 1856, Theater am Franz-Josefs-Kai *Zwei arme Blinde* 26 May 1863; UK: Hanover Square Rooms (Fr) 27 June 1856, Gallery of Illustration *Beggar My Neighbour* 29 March 1870, etc; USA: Metropolitan Music Hall (Fr) 31 August 1857, Wallack's Theater *Going It Blind* 31 October 1858; Hungary: Budai Színkör *Die beiden Blinde* 15 June 1865; Australia: School of Arts, Sydney *The Blind Beggars* 9 September 1873

Recording: complete (Bourg)

DEVAL, Marguerite [BRULFER DE VALCOURT, Marguerite] (b Strasbourg, 19 September 1868; d Paris, 18 December 1955). Extremely popular and long-admired soubrette turned comedienne, with a career of more than 60 successful years on the Paris stage.

Marguerite Deval began her Parisian career in 1884 as a little round-faced, curly-headed soubrette in the very short runs of Wenzel's *Le Chevalier Mignon* (Louise, ''the debutante made quite a hit and is destined to be one of the bright and shining lights of the opéra-bouffe stage'') and Marenco's *Le Diable à corps* (Bertha) at the Bouffes-Parisiens, and she moved on, through a lively career as a leading actress, to the role of an aged concièrge in a post-(second)-war musical comedy. In spite of being involved in the creation of few musical shows which have remained in even the marginal repertoire, she nevertheless introduced several pieces which were highly successful in their time, running the gamut of styles from 1880s opéra-comique and opérette in her young days, through starring roles in many a Parisian revue, to the often intimate song-and-dance musical comedies of the years between the wars, in which she found herself particularly at home. She scored most of her biggest successes in the smaller theatres, where finesse rather than flash paid.

In the earliest category were included, apart from the classic juvenile roles, creations in Serpette's *Adam et Ève*

Plate 100. **Marguerite Deval.** *One of Paris's favorite musical comediennes and meneuses de revue for several decades.*

(1886, Suzanne), Lacome's *La Fille de l'air* (1890, Lucette) and three Audran opérettes, *Article de Paris* (1892, Rose), *Mon Prince!* (1893, soubrette Rita with three numbers) and *Monsieur Lohengrin* (Une Dame), plus pieces in the rather different styles of Terrasse, for whom she created the leading roles of *La Petite Femme de Loth* (1900) and *Peché véniel;* of Ivan Caryll, whose *S.A.R.* (1908) gave her a magnificent role as the plotful Queen Mother, Xénofa; of Rodolphe Berger and P-L Flers for whom she created the title role of *Messalinette, ou le tour du demi-monde en 80 nuits* (1902); and, most particularly, of Cuvillier, in whose *Son p'tit frère* (1907, Laïs) and *Afgar* (1909, Zaydée) she created the starring roles, pairing in both pieces with the actor/singer Henri Defreyn, with whom she would form a winning duo on many occasions.

She had another outstanding success in Rip's celebrated revue *1915,* and passed from further opérettes—(*La Folle Nuit* 1917, *La Petite Femme de Loth* revival 1918, *Daphnis et Chloë* 1918, etc) to postwar musical comedy in *Mon Vieux, Ri-Ri,* Willemetz and Richepin's *Rapatipatoum,* in a pairing with Dranem at the head of the comedy of Christiné's *P.L.M., À Paris tous les deux, Le Renard chez les poules,* Georges Auric's *Sans façon, Zou* (1930, as the meddling mother, Léa de Bourges), *Rosy* (1930), *Brummel* (1931, Lady Eversharp) and Victor Alix's *Mon Amant!* . . . (1932, Baronne de Mazelles), in which she played yet again in tandem with Defreyn. She was 77 years of age when she appeared at the Théâtre des Capucines, which had seen some of her best musical moments prior to the first war, as the old concièrge of Joseph Szulc's *Pantoufle* in 1945.

THE DEVIL TO PAY, or The Wives Metamorphos'd Ballad farce in 3 acts (later 6 scenes) by Charles Coffey, based on the farce *The Devil of a Wife, or A Comical Transformation* by Thomas Jevon. Music uncredited. Produced at the Theatre Royal, Drury Lane, 17 August 1731.

One of the most successful and influential pieces of the English-language musical stage of the 18th century, *The Devil to Pay* was described by its Irish author as a ''ballad farce'' in a willful play on the term ''ballad opera'' as applied to the pasticcio-scored *The Beggar's Opera,* which had come out with such extraordinary success three years earlier. An adaptation of an even earlier comedy, produced in 1686 at the Theatre, Dorset Gardens, which itself was said by the learned of the time to have been drawn from a story, *Mopsa,* from Sir Philip Sidney's *Arcadia,* it did not seek, as Gay's work had professedly done, to make any kind of burlesque point, but simply joined farcical comedy and songs in pure musical-comedy style and with enormous success.

The story told of two unhappy couples, one humble and one aristocratic: the uncouth and boozy cobbler Jobson and his maltreated wife, Nell, and the kindly and generous Sir John Loverule and his haughty, termagent wife. One day Lady Loverule drives a benighted Doctor from her door, and the man finds shelter instead with soft-hearted Nell. But this Doctor is no ordinary Doctor, and he delivers his thanks and takes his despite in the form of a little sorcery. Nell and Lady Loverule find they have changed places: Nell now benefits from the grace and warmth of Sir John and the richness of his home, whilst the haughty Lady, finding herself bruised and beaten by the cobbler and made to lie in a lowly cot, bites back with a vixenish will. And no one except the two women is aware of the switch. The world in general sees just two amazing character changes. When the magic is finally undone, and the two women return home, both Jobson and Lady Loverule have been thoroughly chastened by their experiences.

The 16 (later 11) musical pieces that decorated the tale ranged from a too-much-drinking song for the Cobbler (who took the great share of the music) to a little Sorcerer's number for the good Doctor, and a couple of gentle melodies for Nell.

After its first season at Drury Lane, *The Devil to Pay* went round Britain, and then—in a whole bevy of slightly or heavily remade versions—on to the rest of the world. In Germany, after being first given in an adaptation by Standfuss (1752) it was made into *Der Teufel ist los,* text by Christian Weisse and original music by Johann Hiller, and produced in Leipzig, 6 October 1754. This German version proved to be even more successful than the English one, and *Der Teufel ist los* is quoted, to this day, as the foundation stone of the German Singspiel tradition. The play was later readapted for Vienna by Ferdinand Paër under the title *Poche ma buone* (Hoftheater 18 December 1800) and again by top playwright Karl Costa and Franz von Suppé, under the title of *Die Frau Meisterin* (Carltheater 20 January 1868), but neither version, nor a remake of the Suppé one, 30 years on, as *Die Pariserin* (Carltheater 26 January 1898) displaced the original German version.

In France the piece was remade as *Le Diable à quatre, ou la double metamorphose* (Opéra-Comique 19 August 1756) with a text by Sedaine (his first venture as a stage writer) and a score arranged by Philidor, and the remake was remade for the same house in 1806 (*Le Diable à quatre ou la femme acoriâtre,* Solié, Adam/Creuzé de Lesser 30 November) and, thereafter, regularly in all sorts of shapes (including a ballet version with a score by Adolphe Adam) up till 1872 when a spectacular opéra-bouffe féerie entitled *Les Griffes du diable* (ad Clairville, Gabet) was produced at the Menus-Plaisirs (18 April) with Léa Silly starring in the role of Margot and new music by Hervé and Coedès.

The show had a number of descendants in the English language as well, the most notable direct one being a setting (on the heels of several ballet adaptations) by Balfe of a revised text by Alfred Bunn. Originally produced at the Surrey Theatre under the title *The Devil's In It* (26 July 1852) with William Travers (Count of Wallenburg), Elizabeth Poole (Countess), Emma Romer (Letty), Henri Corri (Herman) and Borrani (Lunastro) creating the lead roles, it was subsequently produced in America under the title *The Basket-maker's Wife* (New York 17 December 1852) with Anna Thillon and Clara Fisher Maeder featured, played through the British provinces, and revived at the Strand in 1856 and again by Hollingshead at the Gaiety (14 June 1871) as *Letty the Basket-maker.* Julia Mathews (Letty), Connie Loseby (Countess), Francis Gayner (Count), Charles Lyall (Herman) and Tom Aynsley Cook (Lunastro) featured in this major revival, which the Gaiety company subsequently took round the country.

Amongst the indirect descendants of Jevon and Coffey's plays may be noted the early works of W S Gilbert (*Creatures of Impulse, The Gentleman in Black,* etc) with their metempsychotic themes.

A burlesque based on Coffey and Jevon's tale was produced in 1864 under the title *Mazourka, or The Stick, the Pole and the Tartar* (aka *Tiddeliwinki*) (pasticcio arr Musgrave/H J Byron Strand Theatre 27 April), and in 1877 (24 December) a spectacular remake was mounted as *Wildfire* on the vast stage of the Alhambra. Patty Laverne starred as the Baroness Hey Derry Down.

Coffey subsequently wrote a musequel *The Merry Cobbler, or The Second Part of The Devil to Pay* (Drury Lane 17 May 1735) which went the way of all musequels.

USA: Dock Street Theater, Charleston 16 March 1736, Nassau Street Theater, New York 7 January 1751; Germany: Berlin 24 January 1743

DIBDIN, Charles (b Southhampton, 4 March 1745; d London, 25 July 1814).

One of the most important writers for the English-language musical theatre of the 18th century, Charles Dibdin made a career not only as a composer and author but also as an actor and singer. He worked as a vocalist at the Covent Garden Theatre from the age of 15, and later as a principal in productions both there and at Drury Lane, and also performed many of his own songs, both in and out of a musical-play context. He found quick success as a theatrical songwriter when he allied himself with the cleverest musical stage author of the age, Isaac Bickerstaff, winning a major success with his songs for the 1768 piece *Lionel and Clarissa* and with the triumphant *The Padlock,* in the second of which he also appeared (after the sacking of the original actor in rehearsal) in the prime comic role of the black servant, Mungo.

From an early age Dibdin also worked steadily as a dramatic author, at first mostly adapting and/or adding original songs to versions of other, largely foreign, works such as *La serva padrona* (as *The Maid and the Mistress*), Duni's *La Fée Urgèle* (*A Christmas Tale*), Philidor's *Blaise le Savetier* (*The Cobbler*) and *Le Déserteur* and Grétry's *Les Deux Avares,* and then, more effectively, moving into a field of original ballad opera where his contribution was highlighted by such enduring works as *The Waterman* and *The Quaker.* In later days, he worked as a solo recitalist, managed a small theatre, and ultimately retired from the theatrical scene at the age of 60.

The author or adapter of over a hundred stage works, he was one of the few composers of 18th-century popular light theatre music whose shows survived beyond the coming of the opéra-bouffe and the profound change in musical theatre which operated in Britain in the 1860s, and some of his pieces such as *The Padlock* and *Lionel and Clarissa* even survived into productions in the 20th century, alongside his most successful single song "Tom Bowling."

Dibdin's illegitimate sons, Charles [Isaac Mungo] Dibdin (1768–1833) and Thomas [John] Dibdin (1771–1841), also had careers in the theatre.

1764 **The Shepherd's Artifice** (Dibdin) Theatre Royal, Covent Garden 21 May

1767 **Love in the City** (w pasticcio/Isaac Bickerstaff) Theatre Royal, Covent Garden 21 February

1768 **Lionel and Clarissa** (Bickerstaff) Theatre Royal, Covent Garden 28 February

1768 **The Padlock** (Bickerstaff) Theatre Royal, Drury Lane 3 October

1769 **Damon and Phillida** (Colley Cibber ad Dibdin) Theatre Royal, Drury Lane 21 February

1769 **The Ephesian Matron** (Bickerstaff) 1 act Ranelagh House 12 May

1769 **The Captive** (Bickerstaff) Theatre Royal, Haymarket 21 June

1769 **Amphytrion** (Hawksworth) Theatre Royal, Drury Lane 23 November

1770 **The Maid the Mistress** (*La serva padrona*) new music for English version by Bickerstaff Ranelagh House 28 May

1770 **The Recruiting Sergeant** (Bickerstaff) Ranelagh House 20 July

1770 **The Brick-Dust Man and the Milk-Maid** (Bickerstaff) 1 act Sadler's Wells Theatre 25 July

1771 **He Would If He Could** revised *The Maid the Mistress* 1 act Theatre Royal, Drury Lane 12 April

1773 **The Wedding Ring** (*Il filosofo di campagno*) (Dibdin) Theatre Royal, Drury Lane 1 February

1773 **The Deserter** (*Le Déserteur*) English version w additional new songs Theatre Royal, Drury Lane 2 November

1773 **A Christmas Tale** (*La Fée Urgèle*) new English version w new songs Theatre Royal, Drury Lane 27 December

1774 **The Romp** revised *Love in the City* Crow Street Theatre, Dublin 23 March; Theatre Royal, Covent Garden, London 18 March 1778

1774 **The Waterman, or The First of August** (Dibdin) His Majesty's Theatre 8 August

1774 **The Cobbler, or A Wife of Ten Thousand** (*Blaise le Savetier*) English version w new music Theatre Royal, Drury Lane 9 December

1775 **The Two Misers** (*Les Deux Avares*) (w pasticcio/Kane O'Hara) Theatre Royal, Covent Garden 21 January

1775 **The Quaker** (Dibdin) Theatre Royal, Drury Lane 3 May

1775 **The Sultan, or A Peep into the Seraglio** (Bickerstaff) Theatre Royal, Drury Lane 12 December

1776 **The Blackamoor wash'd white** (Henry Bate Dudley) Theatre Royal, Drury Lane 26 June

1776 **The Metamorphosis** (Dibdin) Haymarket Theatre 26 August

1776 **The Seraglio** (w Edward Thompson) Theatre Royal, Covent Garden 14 November

1777 **All Is Not Gold That Glitters** (Dibdin) Theatre Royal, Covent Garden

1778 **Poor Vulcan** (w Arne, Arnold/Dibdin) Theatre Royal, Covent Garden 4 February

1778 **The Gipsies** (Arnold) His Majesty's Theatre 3 August

1778 **The Wives Revenged** (Sedaine ad Dibdin) 1 act Theatre Royal, Covent Garden 18 September

1778 **Rose and Collin** (*Rose et Colas*) (Sedaine ad Dibdin) 1 act Theatre Royal, Covent Garden 18 September

1778 **Annette and Lubin** English version Theatre Royal, Covent Garden 2 October

1779 **The Touchstone** (w Hannah Cowley) Theatre Royal, Covent Garden 4 January

1779 **The Chelsea Pensioner** (Dibdin) Theatre Royal, Covent Garden 6 May

1780 **The Shepherdess of the Alps** (*La Bergère des alpes*) Theatre Royal, Covent Garden 18 January

1780 **The Islanders** (Saint-Foix ad) Theatre Royal, Covent Garden 25 November

1781 **The Marriage Act** revised *The Islanders* Theatre Royal, Covent Garden 17 September

1781 **Jupiter and Alcmena** Theatre Royal, Covent Garden 27 October

1782 **None Are So Blind As Those Who Won't See** (Arnold) Theatre Royal, Haymarket 2 July

1785 **Liberty Hall, or The Test of Good Behaviour** (Dibdin) Theatre Royal, Drury Lane 8 February

1785 **A Match for a Widow** (Joseph Atkinson) Theatre Royal, Dublin

1787 **Harvest Home** (Dibdin) Theatre Royal, Haymarket 16 May

1789 **The Fortune Hunters, or You May Say That** Sadler's Wells Theatre 13 April

1798 **Hannah Hewitt, or The Female Crusoe** 1 act Theatre Royal, Drury Lane 7 May

1806 **The Broken Gold** Theatre Royal, Covent Garden 8 February

Other titles credited: *The Widow of Abingdon, The Razor-Grinder, An Old Woman of Eighty, She's Mad for a Husband* (1778), *The Mad Doctor, The Impostor,* etc

Autobiographies: *The Musical Tour of Mr Dibdin* (Sheffield, 1788), *The Professional Life of Mr Dibdin* (London, 1803); Biographies: Kitchener, W: *A Brief Memoir of Charles Dibdin* (London, 1884), Thorn, H: *Charles Dibdin* (London, 1888), Fahrner, R: *The Theater Career of Charles Dibdin the Elder* (Peter Lang, New York, 1989), etc

DICK Comic opera in 2 acts by Alfred Murray. Music by Edward Jakobowski. Globe Theatre, London, 17 April 1884.

A comic-opera variation on the familiar *Dick Whittington* story, this piece had Dick outwitting the Emperor of Morocco to win the hand of Alice Fitzwarren in a plot in which the key cat-eats-rats part of the tale was almost incidentally popped into the final act to round off what was basically a good deal of topical and Oriental high jinks. A commission from the Gaiety Theatre's John Hollingshead to the up-and-coming author and composer, it was played at three London theatres (Globe, Gaiety, Empire) for a total of over a hundred performances with Camille Dubois (later Fannie Leslie) and soprano Ethel Pierson as hero and heroine and co-producer and comic John Shine as Fitzwarren. It was also subsequently played both in Australia, by the Brough and Boucicault management with Fanny Robina featured as Dick, and on the Eastern circuits.

Other stage musical variants of the Dick Whittington tale have included the London opéras-bouffes *Whittington* (Jacques Offenbach/H B Farnie, Alhambra 26 December 1874) and *Dandy Dick Whittington* (Ivan Caryll/George Sims, Avenue Theatre 2 March 1895), and the 19th-century burlesques *Whittington Junior and His Sensation Cat* (Robert Reece, Royalty, 1870), *Young Dick Whittington or Here's the Cat* (J Wilton Jones, Leicester, 1881) and *Whittington and His Cat* (F C Burnand, Gaiety Theatre, 1881), as well, in more recent days, as a long run of pantomimes, in which form the tale has found its most enduring exposition.

A 1909 Shubert "musical comedy extravaganza," adapted from a British pantomime script, which got to Boston's Majestic Theater (3 January 1910) with Louise Dresser, Alexander Clark and Kate Elinore featured doesn't seem to have gone much further.

A 1930s Jack Buchanan-Elsie Randolph show, *Mr Whittington,* showed even less care for the old tale than *Dick* had done, and limited itself to the basic "turn again" theme. It didn't even have a cat in the cast.

Australia: Melbourne Opera House 6 August 1887

DICKENS, Charles [John Huffham] (b Portsea, 7 February 1812; d Gadshill, 9 June 1870).

The popular novelist Charles Dickens made one venture into the musical theatre in his lifetime, when he combined with the composer John Hullah on an operetta, *The Village Coquettes,* produced at the St James's Theatre 6 December 1836. However, he won a much wider theatrical representation after his death, when many of his works were adapted for the stage, both straight and musical.

The composer Karl Goldmark made a highly successful opera, *Das Heimchen am Herd* (Hofoperntheater, Vienna 21 March 1896), from the novel *The Cricket on the Hearth,* a work which was also set to music by Zandonai (Turin 28 November 1908) and by Alexander Mackenzie (London 6 June 1914), whilst Albert Coates made a three-act opera, *Pickwick,* from *The Pickwick Papers,* but the majority of Dickens adaptations were in a lighter musical vein.

The Pickwick tales were used again in the 19th century as the bases for Edward Solomon's one-act London operetta *Pickwick,* and for Charles and Manuel Klein's full-length *Mr Pickwick,* produced at Broadway's Herald Square Theater in 1903 with De Wolf Hopper starred as Pickwick, and *The Cricket on the Hearth* was burlesqued by E L Blanchard (Olympic Theatre 15 January 1846) as *The Cricket on Our Own Hearth,* whilst the other most-used Dickens piece of earlier years, *Barnaby Rudge,* was put to use (mixed with other elements) in making up the American comic opera *Dolly Varden* (Princess Theater, Toronto 23 September 1901, Herald Square Theater 27 January 1902). A British piece on the same bases, *Dolly Varden, or the Riots of '80* (Brighton Aquarium, E Cympson) was produced in 1889 and a third *Dolly Varden* made regular appearances in the repertoire of British juvenile operetta companies. *A Christmas Carol* was the source for an early Broadway pantomine, *Santa Claus, or Harlequin Bob Cratchit and Ding Dong Dell* (Eagle Theater 1 January 1877), whilst in Hungary Iszó Barna wrote a musical score for a version entitled *Karácsony* (Népszínház 13 December 1901), which was not strictly a musical but a seasonal spectacular. In 1904 *The Marchioness,* a little piece based on the character from *The Old Curiosity Shop* (Edward Jones /ad Bert W Findon), was given a showing at London's His Majesty's Theatre (23 June), but more than 30 years earlier New York's San Francisco Minstrels had offered a rare Dickensian burlesque, *The Dickens to Pay, or Little Nell* (February 1868), on the same subject.

It was the production of the enormously successful British musical comedy version of *Oliver Twist* as *Oliver!* (1960) which opened the floodgates for singing-and-dancing Dickens adaptations, most of them for the English-language stage. In *Oliver!*'s wake, *The Pickwick Papers* was given another musicalization as a long-running vehicle for then substantial Welsh star Harry Secombe (*Pickwick* Saville Theatre 4 July 1963), and yet another, as *Herr Pickwick,* in Prague (Petr Zdenk/Ivo Fischer 1970). *David Copperfield* became, more snappily (but without an exclamation point), *Copperfield* (Joel Hirschorn/Al Kasha Anta Theater 16 April 1981) for 13 performances on Broadway, and *A Tale of Two Cities,* with its title similarly circumcised to just *Two Cities* (Jeff Wayne/Jerry Wayne/Constance Cox Palace Theatre 27 February 1969), played 44 uncomfortable nights on the London stage with Edward Woodward pounding out "it is a far better thing . . ." nightly to a deeply banal melody and unfortunate audience giggles. *A Christmas Carol* got a number of goings-over as a festive entertainment, including two American remakes, *Comin' Uptown* (Garry Sherman/Peter Udell/Philip Rose, Udell Winter Garden Theater 20 December 1979) and *Penny for Penny* (Michel Legrand/Sheldon Harnick) with Richard Kiley as

Ebenezer Scrooge, and a British one as *Scrooge* (Leslie Bricusse, 1992). Three attempts at versions of *Great Expectations* (*My Gentleman Pip* Harrogate 3 December 1968; *Great Expectations* Guildford 24 December 1975 with John Mills as Joe Gargery; *Great Expectations* Thear Clwyd, Mold 6 December 1993) and a *Hard Times* (Coventry 6 November 1973) have been seen in the British provinces.

If *Nicholas Nickleby* escaped being made holus bolus into *Nicholas!,* its most eligible characters, the theatrical Crummles family, were plucked out and used for a range of musical shows including William Mitchell's 19th-century American burlesque *The Savage and the Maiden* and two small-scale modern English pieces, *Step into the Limelight* (Bristol 15 January 1962) and *Nickleby and Me* (Ron Grainer/Caryl Brahms, Ned Sherrin Stratford East 16 December 1975). The same period also brought forward several singing-Dickens films, including musical versions of *A Christmas Carol* and *The Old Curiosity Shop* (Quilp), and a television musical of *The Cricket on the Hearth* (Maury Laws/Jules Bass/ Romeo Muller, Arthur Rankin 18 December 1967).

The most recent musicalized dollops of Dickens to deck the Broadway and London stage have included the music-hally retelling, with alternative endings, of the melodramatic incidents of his uncompleted *The Mystery of Edwin Drood* (Imperial Theater 2 December 1985) and a new version of the 1973 Coventry piece based on the ''sullen, socialistic'' *Hard Times* (and worryingly billed as ''an hilarous new musical'') produced for a brief run at London's Haymarket Theatre (22 May 2000), but the Dickens piece that has endured the most as the meat for musical-makers (or, at least, spectacle-makers with music) is undoubtedly *A Christmas Carol.* New York's Radio City Music Hall produced a large-scale version (featuring Santa's Toy Fantasy, a host of decidedly un-Dickensian elves and a pasticcio score of Christmassy numbers) as its 1993 and 1994 ''Christmas spectacular''; the also vast Madison Square Garden bit back for the '94 festive season with a rather more Disney-Dickensy megaversion (Alan Menken/Mike Ockrent, Lynne Ahrens, 1 December) which has been repeated annually since; *Scrooge* was dragged back to the stage in Britain; Hungary got an *Isten pénze* (Peter Müller/László Tolcsvay, Madach Színház 23 December 1995); and New Zealand's Canterbury Opera Company produced a comic opera *Christmas Carol* with a text and score by Philip Norman, 27 November 1995.

DICKSON, Barbara (b Dunfermline, Scotland, 27 September 1947). Folksinger who found success in two major West End musical roles and with two major West End songs.

Originally a vocalist in her native Scotland (''Answer Me,'' etc), Barbara Dickson made her first mark on the musical-theatre scene playing in Willy Russell's musical play *John, Paul, George, Ringo . . . and Bert* (1974). In 1977 she created the Mistress's Song ''Another Suitcase in Another Hall'' on the pre-production recording of *Evita,* a number which in her hands went to number 18 on the British hit parades.

She returned to the musical stage in another Russell piece, *Blood Brothers,* creating the central role of Mrs Johnstone in the show's Liverpool season (''Easy Terms,'' etc) and subsequently playing it in the West End during its initial run, but thereafter went back to the popular music world. Her next musical-theatre entry was another into the charts: this time sharing with Elaine Paige the pre-production recording of the *Chess* duet ''I Know Him So Well.'' This one went right to number one.

In 1993 she repeated her performances as Mrs Johnstone in the long-running London revival of *Blood Brothers,* and in 1999 added to her charmed if intermittent career in the musical theatre in introducing her first new role for 20 years, as Viv Nicholson in the London production of *Spend, Spend, Spend.*

DICKSON, Dorothy (b Kansas City, 26 July 1893; d London, 25 September 1995). American dancing ingenue of the 1920s who scored several successes in such roles on the London stage before becoming Ivor Novello's leading lady for two shows.

Dorothy Dickson began her performing career in a ballroom dance team with her husband, **Carl HYSON** [né Heisen], and was moved into the theatre when Ray Comstock spotted them performing in a Kansas City hotel. She made her first stage appearances paired with Hyson as a featured dance duo in the original production of *Oh, Boy!* and in the *Ziegfeld Follies* of 1917, played the Coconut Grove and then moved up to play the ingenue role in Frank Tours's musical *Girl o'Mine* (1918, Betty) at the Bijou Theater. A few weeks after that show's quick passing, she was popped hurriedly into a featured dancing role in Jerome Kern's *Rock-a-Bye Baby* (Dorothy Manners) and when that show, too, vanished swiftly, she moved on to a third Broadway engagement within six months, back in the *Ziegfeld Follies.* In 1919 she took a dancing role in George M Cohan's parody comic opera *The Royal Vagabond* (Carlotta) and the following year appeared with Hyson in a spot in *Lassie* at the Nora Bayes Theater (Lady Gwendolyn Spencer-Hill).

In 1921 the pair were seen in London in C B Cochran's revue *London, Paris and New York* and, as a result, Miss Dickson was offered the title role in George Grossmith and Pat Malone's London production of *Sally.* The success of *Sally* established her as a West End star

Plate 101. **Dorothy Dickson** *takes a singing lesson from Olive Gilbert in* Careless Rapture.

and, settling in Britain, she appeared in the years that followed in ''Marilynn Miller''–style roles in two other Jerome Kern musicals, *The Cabaret Girl* (1922, Marilynn Morgan) and *The Beauty Prize* (1923, Carol Stuart), as well as in the title role of the British musical *Patricia;* in Charlot's revue; as *Peter Pan* in a revival of Barrie's play; and in local versions of three made-for-Broadway pieces, *Tip-Toes* (1926, Tip-Toes Kaye), *Peggy-Ann* (1927, Peggy-Ann) and, in succession to Mamie Watts, in *Hold Everything!* (1929, t/o Sue O'Keefe).

After playing in the London productions of the Continental musicals *The Wonder Bar* (1930, Liane) and *Casanova* (1932, Princess Potomska), she appeared for a while in revue and in straight theatre, but she returned to the musical stage in 1936 to play opposite Ivor Novello in his grandiose *Careless Rapture* (Penelope Lee) and *The Crest of the Wave* (1937, Honey Wortle) at the Theatre Royal, Drury Lane. Her later work was limited to revue, plays and variety.

Her daughter **Dorothy HYSON** [Dorothy Wardell HEISEN] (b Chicago, 24 December 1914; d London, 23 May 1996) also appeared on the musical stage (Liberty in *Who's Taking Liberty,* 1939). She was also seen in the film version of *That's a Good Girl.*

DIETZ, Howard (b New York, 8 September 1896; d New York, 30 July 1983). The lyricist of many enduring songs and popular revues, who did not ever approach finding a real success in the field of the book musical.

Dietz began writing light verse at college, where he numbered Hammerstein and Lorenz Hart amongst his contemporaries and, after working in both journalism and advertising, had an early song success with ''Alibi Baby'' (mus: Stephen Jones) in the musical comedy *Poppy* (1923). He was thrown in at the deep end when asked by Jerome Kern to write the lyrics for the musical comedy *Dear Sir,* but the show failed and, in the years that followed, whilst Dietz concentrated on the first part of his 30-year Hollywood stint as head of publicity at MGM, his theatre-lyrical output was largely angled towards revue.

One of these revues was *The Little Show,* in which he paired with composer Arthur Schwartz, and that pairing turned out to be a durable one. In the decade 1927–37, Broadway welcomed a wave of Dietz/Schwartz revues and a long list of popular songs (''I Guess I'll Have to Change My Plan,'' ''Something to Remember You By,'' ''Dancing in the Dark,'' ''A Shine on Your Shoes,'' etc), but the only musical comedy scores which the team produced were a tacked-together affair made up for the British show *Here Comes the Bride* and Broadway's *Revenge with Music* and *Between the Devil.* The first of the three was produced by Julian Wylie at the Blackpool Opera House in 1929, played at the Piccadilly and Lyceum Theatres in London for 175 performances in early 1930 and produced one memorable song, ''High and Low.'' The second, a piece based on the Spanish ''Three-cornered Hat'' tale, which Dietz also directed, had a shorter life but left a richer legacy (''You and the Night and the Music,'' ''If There is Someone Lovelier Than You,'' 158 performances), as did the farcical *Between the Devil* (''I See Your Face Before Me,'' ''By Myself,'' 93 performances).

It was 1944 before, after a false start with the quickly closing *Dancing in the Streets,* Dietz returned to Broadway with two further shows written in collaboration with composer Vernon Duke. Neither proved successful, and it was 15 years more before he and Schwartz made their only further attempts together at a book musical for Broadway, first with the old-fashioned *The Gay Life* (1961, 113 performances) and then with an unfortunate period vehicle for Mary Martin, *Jennie* (1963, 82 performances).

He also combined with Schwartz on the television musical *A Bell for Adano* (CBS 2 June 1965).

Dietz was married to designer **Lucinda BALLARD** (b Boston, 3 April 1906; d New York, 19 August 1993) (*Annie Get Your Gun, Silk Stockings, The Sound of Music,* etc).

1924 **Dear Sir** (Jerome Kern/Edgar Selwyn) Times Square Theater 23 September

1929 **Here Comes the Bride** (Arthur Schwartz/w Desmond Carter/R P Weston, Bert Lee) Blackpool Opera House 7 October; Piccadilly Theatre, London 20 February 1930

1934 **Revenge with Music** (Schwartz) New Amsterdam Theater 28 November

1937 **Between the Devil** (Schwartz) Imperial Theater 22 December

1943 **Dancing in the Streets** (Vernon Duke/w John Cecil Holm) Boston 23 March

1944 **Jackpot** (Duke/Guy Bolton, Sidney Sheldon, Ben Roberts) Alvin Theater 13 January

1944 **Sadie Thompson** (Duke/w Rouben Mamoulian) Alvin Theater 16 November

1950 **Die Fledermaus** lyrics to new English version (Metropolitan Opera House)

1961 **The Gay Life** (Schwartz/Fay and Michael Kanin) Shubert Theater 18 November

1963 **Jennie** (Schwartz/Arnold Schulman) Majestic Theater 17 October

Autobiography: *Dancing in the Dark* (Quadrangle, New York, 1974)

DILLINGHAM, Charles [Bancroft] (b Hartford, Conn, 30 May 1868; d New York, 30 August 1934). Top-flight Broadway producer of the first decades of the 20th century.

Apart from a teenage escapade as a cattle-herder in Wyoming, and a brief connection with the world of minstrelsy, Dillingham spent the bulk of his early working life in the newspaper world, at first in Chicago and latterly as a dramatic critic and an editor at the *New York Evening Sun.* However, in 1898 he wrote and produced a play of his own and, although it was a failure, he soon found himself a live-in part of the American theatre world. He took a job for a while on the staff of producer Charles Frohman, but within two years he had set himself firmly on the way to a secure career as a producer with a regular and often ambitious program of plays.

He produced his first musical, an adaptation of the French opérette *Le Jockey malgré lui,* with its score torn out and replaced by some Ludwig Englander music, in 1903, under the title *The Office Boy.* Frank Daniels was its star and Louise Gunning and Eva Tanguay sang most of its songs through two Broadway months before taking it round the country with sufficient success. Thereafter, for some 30 years, Dillingham staged a regular list of musicals, largely homemade, turning only very occasionally, and usually with fine taste, to European stages for proven material which (with one notable exception) he treated better than he had *Le Jockey malgré lui*—the jolly *Sergeant Brue* for Daniels (1905), the international hit *The Girl in the Train* (1910, *Die geschiedene Frau*), London's *Betty* (1916), the unfortunate *One Kiss* (the notable exception—a sad, sanitized version of the French *Ta bouche,* 1923) and Leo Fall's splendid *Madame Pompadour* (1924).

His earliest efforts as a producer included a series of Victor Herbert musicals, beginning with the underfortunate Fritzi Scheff vehicle *Babette* (1903), continuing with *Miss Dolly Dollars* (1905) and, with very much more success, a second piece for Miss Scheff, *Mlle Modiste* (1905), the Montgomery and Stone comedy musical *The Red Mill* (1906) and another Daniels vehicle, *The Tattooed Man* (1907). The association between Herbert and

Dillingham continued through the years, sometimes with more and sometimes with less success. *The Prima Donna* (1908), for Scheff, was not a winner, but *The Lady of the Slipper* (1912), for Montgomery and Stone, very definitely was, and the association ended only after 14 years of collaboration with the revues *The Century Girl* (1916) and *Miss 1917,* both co-productions between Dillingham and spectacle specialist Florenz Ziegfeld.

The association with Montgomery and Stone, however, continued even beyond that, and with considerable success. *The Red Mill, The Old Town* (1910) and *The Lady of the Slipper* were followed by *Chin-Chin* (1914) and, after Montgomery's death, Dillingham produced for Stone, alone, *Jack o'Lantern* (1917), *Tip Top* (1920), *Stepping Stones* (1923), *Criss Cross* (1926) and *Ripples* (1930), this last being Dillingham's final musical comedy production.

Two Ludwig Englander musicals—the olde Englishe *A Madcap Princess* (1904) and the musicalization, for Miss Scheff, of *She Stoops to Conquer* as *The Two Roses* (1904)—plus a concoction made over from Tristan Bernard's *La Soeur* by many hands into something called *The Hoyden* and Gustave Luders's *The Fair Co-Ed,* both constructed to feature the young impressionist Elsie Janis, were also amongst the other productions of Dillingham's earlier years—at the end of which he had done sufficiently well to sponsor the building of the new Globe Theater on Broadway and 46th Street.

The Old Town was the opening attraction at the new theatre, and Dillingham continued there with *The Echo* with Bessie McCoy as billed star (a quick failure) and *The Girl in the Train,* which also surprisingly failed to run. Leslie Stuart's made-for-Broadway musical *The Slim Princess* (1911) with Elsie Janis in the title role did a little better, but it wasn't until Eddie Foy arrived at the beginning of 1912 with *Over the River* that Dillingham (in association again here with Ziegfeld) had something that looked like a success back in his theatre.

There was no doubt, however, about the success of the Irving Berlin revue *Watch Your Step* which, with *Chin-Chin,* made 1914 a bonanza year for their producer, and thereafter Dillingham turned much of his attention to revue productions. The following year he took over the management of the vast New York Hippodrome from the Shuberts and, beginning with *Hip! Hip! Hooray!* (1915), produced, over the next seven years, a series of extravagant and generally successful supersized spectacles.

On the musical comedy front, Dillingham continued to place his faith in the attractions of the multi-talented Elsie Janis (*Miss Information,* 1915) and the music of Ivan Caryll, who had served him so well with his scores for the Fred Stone shows (*The Canary,* 1918), but he also produced a series of musical comedies with scores by Jerome Kern, beginning with *Miss Information* and continuing through the *Miss 1917* revue (w Herbert), *She's a Good Fellow* (1919), *The Night Boat* (1920), *Good Morning, Dearie* (1921), *The Bunch and Judy* (1922), *The City Chap* (1925) and *Lucky* (1927), with varying results, until a lucrative success was reached with *Sunny* in 1925.

The operetta *Apple Blossoms* (1919), with a score by Victor Jacobi and Fritz Kreisler, was a splendid success at the Globe, but *The Girl from Home* (1920), a musical version of *The Dictator* brought in from Chicago, gave him the quickest failure of his career when squabbles amongst author, star and producer forced him to close after just three weeks on Broadway. It was left to Fred Stone and *Tip Top* to keep the Dillingham production schedule bubbling along profitably in 1920. When Jacobi supplied Dillingham with a second score, for *The Half Moon* (1920), and a third, *The Love Letter* (1921), fortune failed to smile as it had the first time.

Dillingham shared billing with John Cort and Martin Beck to produce one last work by the composer A Baldwin Sloane, who had been one of the earliest American writers to point his nose in musical comedy three decades previously, but *China Rose* did less well than Dillingham's solo productions of the inevitable Elsie Janis revue, *Puzzles of 1925,* and of *Sunny* which brought 1925 to a successful finish for him. The failure of Vincent Youmans's *Oh Please!* (1926) and of Rodgers and Hart's *She's My Baby* (1928) were unpleasant surprises, and the variety musical *Sidewalks of New York* (1927) and *Three Cheers* (1928), intended for Fred Stone who had to drop out in favor of Will Rogers, did a little to even the balance.

Whatever balance there might have been, however, went wholly awry when the depression struck. Dillingham was ruined, and although his name appeared as producer of the revue *New Faces* in 1934, it was only as a mark of esteem to a hugely liked man from the fellow producers who backed the show and pinned his name to the masthead. Shortly after, Charles Dillingham died.

An endlessly enthusiastic and gentlemanly producer with a lavish yet tasteful production style, his long list of musical productions glittered with the great names of the period, but all too often with the wrong shows. He produced nine musicals with scores by Jerome Kern, yet amongst all the flops and semi-successes he got only *Sunny* and, to a lesser degree, *The Night Boat* and *Good Morning, Dearie* of the real money-makers. He produced no less than nine Victor Herbert pieces and, though he got *The Red Mill* and *Mlle Modiste,* he missed *Naughty Marietta* and *Sweethearts.* After *Watch Your Step* and *Stop! Look! Listen!* (1915) he got nothing else from Berlin, and the Youmans, Rodgers and Hart and Leslie Stuart pieces he produced were nowhere near their best. Similarly, having secured the American rights to such internationally successful foreign shows as *Die geschiedene Frau* and *Ta bouche,* he found them drawing a blank on Broadway. Yet he was not only a successful theatrical businessman, but one of the most respected, trusted and liked men on Broadway.

In his pre-producing days, Dillingham was briefly married to actress and vocalist Jennie Yeamans (1862–1906).

DIRKENS, Annie [DREWS, Marie Therese Agnes] (b Berlin, 25 September 1869; d Vienna, 11 November 1942). Star soubrette of the Viennese stage for 20 years up to the First World War.

The German-born daughter of a railway official of British origin, Annie Dirkens trained for the stage in Berlin and Dresden and appeared at Berlin's Viktoria-Theater at 19 years of age as a soubrette. She subsequently played at the Adolf-Ernst Theater, at Hamburg's Carl-Schultze Theater and at the Leipzig Stadttheater before being engaged, in 1895, at the Theater an der Wien. There, after making her début as Zeller's Brief-Christl, she created a two-year series of Operette roles, including Catherine Molton (*Der goldene Kamerad*), Pauline (Johann Strauss's *Waldmeister,* 1895), Tessa (*Mister Menelaus*), the title role of the marvellous ''boy'' violinist Paola/Paolo in von Taund's *Der Wunderknabe,* the trouser-role of Gaston Dulac in the German-language version of Verő's *Der Löwenjäger* (1896) and Comtesse Mathilde Nevers in Strauss's *Die Göttin der Vernunft* (1897). During the same period she visited London with the Saxe-Coburg company and appeared briefly in the British version of *Der Wunderknabe* (*The Little Genius*).

Mixing straight and musical shows, she played for a period at the Theater in der Josefstadt, scoring a major hit in the German version of *Les Fêtards* (*Wie man Männer fesselt*) in both Vienna and Berlin, and made her début at the Carltheater, star-billed, as Adrienne in Weinberger's *Die Diva* (1900). She appeared there again the following year in the title role of *Die Primadonna* (Nina Traquet), starred at the Berliner Theater in *Der jungste Leutnant* (1904), *Mam'zelle Nitouche, Lili,* etc and took the title role in the French spectacular *Die Ringstrassen-Prinzessin* (*Messalinette,* 1905) at Danzers Orphenn, before, in 1906, traveling to America where she repeated her *Fêtards* role at the Irving Place Theater.

Subsequent Viennese musical appearances included Minna in *Miss Hook of Holland* (1907), her most memorable creation as the free-loving actress Gonda van der Loo in *Die geschiedene Frau* (1908), a season at the Établissement Ronacher in Ziehrer's *In fünfzig Jahren,* then as Ella (ex- Eileen) in *Die Arkadier* (1911), and the title role of the irresistible Alma in *Alma, wo wohnst du?* at the Lustspiel-theater (1911).

A field sister in the ambulance corps during the First World War, she had the misfortune to have her own husband, the Baron von Hammerstein, brought, dying, into her care. When she returned to the theatre after the war, she found that her best days were past. She appeared at the Bürgertheater in Hugo Hirsch's *Die Scheidungsreise* (1921), but otherwise played largely in non-musical theatre before her career faded out. In her elder days she ran a tobacco kiosk near the Vienna Burgtheater.

LA DIVA Opéra-bouffe in 3 acts by Henri Meilhac and Ludovic Halévy. Music by Jacques Offenbach. Théâtre des Bouffes-Parisiens, Paris, 22 March 1869.

A piece written and composed specially for the great opéra-bouffe star, Hortense Schneider, which, for all that there were apparently striking similarities with an earlier work, *Adelaïde, ou Dix ans de la vie d'une artiste,* was touted as being all but an autobiomusical. Schneider played a Parisian shopgirl who, when her intended turns up late for her wedding, chucks him and her shopworking life and goes off to become a star. She shoots to the top, and soon has marquises and dukes chasing after her in all too predictable a fashion. Désiré headed the male cast in the role of Raphaël.

In spite of an attractive score, in which the simple duo ''Tu la connais, ma douce maîtresse, la blonde Lischen'' proved both the most reminiscent and the most popular, and in spite of Schneider at the head of affairs, the piece was apparently found to be in less than the best taste, and it was a round flop. However, such failure in Paris did not stop even this least successful of Offenbach works from being given further showings, albeit in a heavily worked-over state. The piece produced at the Theater an der Wien by Marie Geistinger and Maximilian Steiner, under the title *Die Theaterprinzessin* (ad F Zell, Richard Genée), was advertised as a ''musikalische Burleske'' which made ''partial use'' of the plot of *La Diva* (but apparently rather more than ''part'' of its score). In it, Geistinger starred as housemaid Susi Apfelwein who, five years later, is seen in a new metamorphosis as the Viennese Operette prima donna Adèle Cliquot. Geistinger played Susi-Adèle for just 23 performances. The following year this version was played in Hungary, and the show was subsequently seen in Germany, but without establishing itself in any of these areas as a repeatable part of the Offenbach canon.

The show's slightly self-congratulatory title seems to be unlucky. It was also used for a German Operette, Weinberger's *Die Diva,* produced at Vienna's Carltheater with Annie Dirkens starred, which did no better than Offenbach's work, and pieces called *The Prima Donna* have found a similar fate in both Britain and America.

Plate 102. **Divorce Me, Darling!** *Anna Sharkey (left) and Patricia Michael (center) forget themselves momentarily to look amazed-horrified at the goings-on between Fred Stone and Joan Heal.*

Austria: Theater an der Wien *Die Theaterprinzessin* 21 December 1872; Hungary: *Adel, vagy színpad a színpadon* 1873; Germany: Wallnertheater *Die Theaterprinzessin* 1875

DIVORCE ME, DARLING! Musical comedy of the 1930s in 2 acts by Sandy Wilson. Players' Theatre, London, 15 December 1964; Globe Theatre, 1 February 1965.

A sequel to Wilson's blockbusting *The Boy Friend, Divorce Me, Darling!* followed the characters of the first show beyond marriage and towards some tiny threatenings of divorce. Polly (Patricia Michael) flirts a little with Bobby (Cy Young), whose sister (Irlin Hall) turns up equipped with a stout pair of lungs and a song called ''Here Am I, But Where's the Guy?'' Mme Dubonnet (Joan Sterndale Bennett) has become a cabaret artiste (''Blondes for Danger'') and an even older Lord Brockhurst is still ''On the Loose'' chasing nubile girlies. Several Boy Friend artists played ''themselves'' again (Maria Charles, Geoffrey Hibbert, Violetta) in a charming not-so-small piece whose 87 performances in the West End did not reflect the extent of its attractions. The show was revived at the Chichester Festival of 1997 (10 July) richly cast with Kevin Colson (Percival Browne), Tim Flavin (Bobby), Linzi Hately (Hortense), Ruthie Henshall (Polly), Marti Webb (Hannah), Liliane Montevecchi (Mme Dubonnet) and old-time concert party stars Jack Tripp and Joan Savage as the Brockhursts.

A production at the Texas Theatre Under the Stars in 1984 paired *Divorce Me, Darling!* in an evening's entertainment with the original short version of *The Boy Friend.*

USA: Theatre Under the Stars, Houston, Texas 14 July 1984

Recordings: original cast (Decca), Chichester cast (TER)

DIXEY, Henry E [DIXON, Henry] (b Boston, 6 January 1859; d Atlantic City, 25 February 1943). Musical burlesque and comedy star, who won enduring fame in the long-running *Adonis.*

Dixey began his career as a boy actor at Howard's Athenaeum in Boston and made what he always counted as his adult début as half-the-dancing-heifer in E E Rice's 1875 Boston revival of *Evangeline.* He subsequently played a variety of supporting roles in the touring company of *Evangeline,* in the burlesques *Le Petit Corsair* (Syng Smaul, Yussuf, and Mlle Henriette Dixette with a "grand pas de pâté de foie gras"), *Robinson Crusoe* (Whatdoyousay) and *Hiawatha* (Romulus Smith), and in the entertainments *Revels* (1879, Sir Ramsgate Bramblewig, Professor Inkijab) and *Horrors* (1879, The Jester, Rajah Zog) played by Rice's Surprise Party company of musical farce-comedians, and made early Broadway appearance with the company in *The Babes in the Wood,* (Doctor, Tommy) and in *Horrors* at the Union Square in 1879. He toured (1880) with Fred Stinson's Co in *Evangeline, Babes in the Wood* and other extravaganzas; appeared on Broadway with the Boston English Opera Company as the harem-keeper, Mustapha, in *Fatinitza* at Booth's Theatre (1880); and in Boston as Major General Stanley (*Pirates of Penzance*), Sir Muslin Delaine in a pirate version of *Billee Taylor* (1881), Sir Joseph Dublin Porter in a *Reconstructed Pinafore* (1881), Dr Syntax in *Cinderella at School* and as William Crank in the original Boston musical *Pounce & Co* (April 1883). His first major Broadway engagements came in 1883 when he was seen at the Fifth Avenue Theatre playing J H Ryley's role of the Lord Chancellor opposite the original American Iolanthe, Marie Jansen, and, paired with the same lady star, as the comical monarch, Laurent XVII, in *La Mascotte.*

He appeared thereafter in further leading musicocomic roles as Sir Joseph Porter, Sir Mincing Lane in *Billee Taylor,* Peter Papyrus in *The New Evangeline,* partnering Louise Lester as the comical horse-dopers of the English musical *The Merry Duchess,* as Frippaponne (with Henry Irving impersonation) in Rice's *Captain Hélène of the Guards* and as John Wellington Wells in *The Sorcerer,* and in 1884 his longtime employer, Edward Rice, provided him with the plum part needed to turn a lead comedy actor into a popular star when he produced the burlesque *Adonis* at the Bijou Theatre with Dixey in the leggy title role.

Adonis, a sort of *Die schöne Galathee* with the sexes reversed and liberally decorated with a movable set of songs ("It's English, You Know," "I'm Nobody from Nowhere," "The Wall Street Broker") and burlesque scenes, had a record-breaking 19-month run on Broadway, returned there from its road travels regularly over the next decade, and was also played for a summer season at London's Gaiety Theatre, in each case with Dixey—tight white-tighted and dripping with diamonds—in the very large central role which had made him famous. His appearances thereafter ranged from classic comedy to a variety of star vehicles, most of which were musical, including a revusical piece called *The Seven Ages* (1889), a spectacular burlesque *Rip van Winkle* which didn't get out of Chicago (1890), a modernized *Adonis* (1893), revivals of *Patience, Iolanthe, La Mascotte* and *The Sorcerer,* under his own management, and all-star Gilbert and Sullivan at the Herald Square Theatre in 1896 in which he was seen as Sir Joseph Porter and Bunthorne.

In 1897 Dixey was presented on Broadway by Edward Bloom in a different guise—he appeared at the Garden Theatre as "Dixey the Magician" performing an illusion act—and in that same year he also took for a while to the music halls, purveying a quick-change act (*The Mystery of the Mortgage*), but musical theatre still provided him with most of his employment. He appeared in *In Gayest Manhattan* (1897) at Koster & Bial's and in the revusical *Mr New York Esq.* (1897) at Weber and Fields's and in this second he was put once more into the famous *Adonis* white tights, allowing it to be observed by the press and public that his pins were, if still nimble, not as shapely as before. Neither was he now sporting the famous "Adonis diamonds" which had been such a crowd-pulling item 16 years earlier. They had long been pawned to producer John Stetson, and the following year they would be newsworthily stolen. Dixey toured in 1898 with *Hotel Topsy Turvey* (Lebeau), paired with Francis Wilson as Ravannes in a revival of *Erminie,* the show which (depending how you count) had deprived *Adonis* of its long-run records, and in 1900 (having just gone round once more with *Adonis*) he had his first modern musical comedy role when he took a turn as Peter Stuyvesant in Luders and Pixley's long-touring *The Burgomaster.*

He visited London in 1901 and appeared at the Adelphi Theatre in a version of the New York revue *The Whirl of the Town,* but on his return to America appeared almost entirely in plays (including Barrie's *Little Mary*), in sketches, musical (*Castle Romance,* 1914, etc) and non-musical, and in vaudeville, returning to the musical stage only in 1917 to play Courtice Pounds's role of Ali Baba in the spectacular Broadway production of *Chu Chin Chow.* He later played alongside Fay Marbe and Vivienne Segal in the out-of-town tryout of Ivan Caryll's *Little Miss Raffles* (1921) and made his final appearance on the musical stage in 1928 when he replaced George M Cohan in Cohan's own *The Merry Malones.*

Dixey produced a number of pieces, mostly revivals, usually in alliance with Rice or with the firm of R E J Miles and Barton (*The Corsair*), and made sufficient contribution to the eternal remaking of the text of *Adonis* to be sometimes credited as its co-author.

He died after being knocked down by a bus in Atlantic City at the age of 84.

LE DOCTEUR OX Opérette in 3 acts by Philippe Gille and Arnold Mortier, adapted from the novel by Jules Verne. Music by Jacques Offenbach. Théâtre des Variétés, Paris, 26 January 1877.

Mortier and Gille's musical version of Verne's story followed the career of Doctor Ox (José Dupuis) and his attempts to rouse the very underpaced village of Quiquendonne to vigor and intellectual excellence by spraying its inhabitants with oxygen. It did not follow the original novel, however, when it introduced a couple of opéra-bouffe love stories for the benefit of the Théâtre des Variétés' leading ladies. Anna Judic played an amorous gipsy princess, Prascovia, who is rebuffed by the scientific doctor and thereafter determines to wreck his plans, whilst Mlle Beaumaine played Suzel, the daughter of the burgomaster van Tricasse (Pradeau), who awakens peculiar feelings of friendship in Ox. Léonce appeared as Ygène, the Doctor's familiar (Ox + Ygène = oxygène), Baron was burgomaster Niklausse van Tricasse, Guyon was the local fire-commissioner and Cooper appeared as his son, Franz.

The show was decorated with a typical Offenbach score in which Judic's couplets "Tout s'éveille dans la nature" with its roucouling runs, her marche bohémienne ("Pour l'enfant de Bohème"), her Légende de la Guzla (apparently a musical instrument) and her dialect Duo flamand with the Doctor ("Changeons de langue") proved the star highlights, alongside an entrance number for Dupuis and some last-act couplets for the number two couple, Cooper and Mlle Beaumaine.

Le Docteur Ox was produced with all the lavishness and the starry casting the Variétés had at its disposal at the time but, in spite of a warm initial reception, it failed to draw for long. It managed only a disappointing 42 performances in Paris, but even that was more than Franz's Steiner's Vienna production (ad uncredited) featuring Hubert Wilke as Ox, Karoline Finaly as Prascovia, Girardi as Ygène and Wilhelm Knaack as the Burgomaster. It failed wholly to take and was played just 10 times.

Docteur Ox itself may have had a limited career, but it spawned an exceedingly long-lived British burlesque, *Oxygen* (arr John Fitzergald/Robert Reece, H B Farnie 31 March 1877), based on a mixture of Verne's story and Offenbach's opérette, which was played by Lydia Thompson and her company in both Britain and America, and by Lydia wanna-bes in every English-speaking corner of the world thereafter.

A revised version of the original work was produced in Cologne in 1978 (19 September).

Austria: Theater an der Wien *Doktor Ox* 29 April 1882

THE DOCTOR OF ALCANTARA Opéra-bouffe in 2 acts by Benjamin E Woolf. Music by Julius Eichberg. Boston Museum, Boston, 7 April 1862; Theatre Français, New York, 28 May 1866.

The first American musical play to make a success both in America and abroad, *The Doctor of Alcantara,* although both derivative and imitative in text and music, is a much more substantial and significant piece than *The Black Crook* (produced four years later) which used once upon a time to serve as a starting point for histories of America's musical stage. A text written by British-born, American-bred Benjamin Woolf, "literary man to the Boston Museum" (who wrote texts for a long series of musicals and plays staged mostly in Boston), was compiled mainly from familiar scenes and situations plucked from British and Continental comic operas—most notably those of Damiant's popular French *La Guerre ouverte, ou ruse contre ruse*—and paired with a score by German-Bostonian Julius Eichberg, musical director at the Boston Museum, the whole making up into an agreeable and much appreciated little light opera.

The plot followed the student, Carlos, in his attempts to woo Isabella, daughter of the Doctor Paracelsus, against the wishes of her vain and ambitious mother. When Carlos, in his attempt to get past his sweetheart's guardian, is delivered to the house in a basket, it is dumped in the river, when he is offered wine it turns out to be a sleeping draught and the Doctor thinks he has committed murder, but, at the end of everything, the boy turns out to be—of course—the very unknown young man whom Isabella's parents had earmarked for her.

The dozen items of the first act included a pretty tenor/soprano duo "I Love, I Love," a serenade ("Wake, lady, wake") and cavatina for the tenor (Carlos), a ballad ("The Knight of Alcantara") and a romance for the soprani, and an arietta ("When a Lover is Poor") for the contralto, as well as a basso piece declaring "I'm Don Hypolito Lopez Pomposo" for the Alguazil, whose presence topped up the buffo element of the piece, and some ensemble and choral work. The shorter second act included only a trio, a quartet and a finale.

After having been successfully played in its native Boston, with Emily Mestayer in the role of Donna Lucretia, *The Doctor of Alcantara* was toured by the American Parlor Opera Troupe (1863) and it was eventually produced in New York, with Caroline Richings at the head of a cast featuring Edward Seguin, William Castle, S C Campbell and Zelda Harrison. It proved a great success ("it draws like a poor man's plaster") for several weeks until the management attempted to capitalize on their hit by upping the prices and killed their audience. The season collapsed. A few months later another production claiming to be "the genuine version" and directed by Eichberg himself was mounted at the New York Theater (3 October 1866), with Mark Smith (Paracelsus), Maria Norton (Isabella), Maria Gomersal (Inez), William Gomersal (Balthazar) and John Farley (Carlos) featured, and the piece again won appreciative audiences for a fortnight. Indeed, it was reckoned successful enough that the Kelly and Leon Minstrels made it the subject of one of their operatic burlesques. Eichberg promptly followed up with another of his pieces, *A Night in Rome* (17 October), but back-pedaled to his successful show after just two nights before collapsing in his turn. Caroline Richings's company toured the piece back to Boston in 1868 and gave fine coverage to Eichberg's works thereafter.

The Doctor of Alcantara became a popular item with American operatic companies across the country. It was produced in Washington in 1873 by T Harry Donehue's "Colored Opera Troupe" "the first and only organisation of its kind," and included in the otherwise wholly English and French repertoire of Susie Galton's company (1873) and of the stalwart Holman troupe from Canada, and it reappeared in New York as late as 1882 when Fred Zimmerman's company played it as part of their program at the Metropolitan Alcazar (5 July). It also—thanks to its parti-colored roles and undemanding music—became a regular choice with American amateur companies through many, many years.

In Britain, the show was taken into the repertoire of the newly fledged Carl Rosa Opera Company, in a version advertised as having been made "exceedingly racy and sparkling" by Andrew B Baildon, and produced with Aynsley Cook, the young Catherine Lewis and Rose Hersee at the head of its cast. Eichberg's music was judged "without pretension and if not quite original at least of a character likely to become popular[;] . . . the orchestration is somewhat danc-y and Offenbachish." *The Village Doctor* failed to hold a place in the Rosa repertoire, but the piece was later given a London showing at Holborn, under the management of J W Currans, with Blanche Ellerman, W H Woodfield, Lia Rohan, George Bassett and J A Arnold heading the cast. This set of performances gave the comic opera the distinction of being the first American musical to be played in London's commercial theatre. A few weeks later it won the same distinction in Australia when the Kelly and Leon minstrel company produced their version of *The Doctor of Alcantara* at their theatre on the corner of Sydney's King and York Streets. Kelly appeared as Dr Paracelsus, with his son, Edwin Lester, as Balthazar, Leon in travesty as Inez and Emma Wangenheim as Isabel. It was well enough received to be brought back for further performances later in the minstrel company's season.

UK: Royal Alexandra Theatre, Liverpool *The Village Doctor* 21 October 1873, Connaught Theatre, London *Alcantara* 1 November 1879; Australia: Kelly and Leon's Opera House, Sydney 26 December 1879

DO I HEAR A WALTZ? Musical in 2 acts by Arthur Laurents, based on his play *The Time of the Cuckoo.* Lyrics by Stephen Sondheim. Music by Richard Rodgers. 46th Street Theater, New York, 18 March 1965.

Do I Hear a Waltz? brought Arthur Laurents and Stephen Sondheim, who had already collaborated on book and lyrics for *West Side Story, Gypsy* and *Anyone Can Whistle,* together with veteran composer Richard Rodgers, whose sole Broadway show in the six years since *The Sound of Music* and the death of Oscar Hammerstein had been the 1962 *No Strings.*

Do I Hear a Waltz? was based on Laurents's play *The Time of the Cuckoo,* a Broadway success with Shirley Booth starred and already metamorphosed into a film, *Summertime,* with Katharine Hepburn in the central role. It followed a middle-aging New York secretary, Leona (Elizabeth Allen), on a trip to Venice. There she at last encounters romance, in the person of the older, married and illusionless Di Rossi (Sergio Franchi). It is a kind of romance which does not fit in with her preconceptions and which, in spite of the fact that she will probably never have another such chance, she finally rejects.

With all three writers contributing of their very finest, the show boasted a feeling libretto and a memorable score ranging from the soaring tenor solos "Stay," "Someone Like You" and "Take the Moment" to the crisply comic "What Do We Do? We Fly!" and "We're Gonna Be All Right" allotted to supporting characters, the heroine's excited "Someone Woke Up" and "Do I Hear a Waltz?," and a lovely trio in which three women look at the "Moon in My Window" and think about their respective men.

In spite of all its plusses, the show was not a popular success. Its "musical play" nature frightened both Rodgers and director John Dexter, and some more traditional Broadway elements (including dancers and dancing) were shoveled into the production on the road, leaving it to reach Broadway in a dishevelled state for a run of 220 performances. And so *Do I Hear a Waltz?* remains a very superior piece of musical-theatre writing waiting around for an aging Pavarotti or Domingo, in search of a musical-comedy star role, to justify a second chance for its original untampered-with version.

Recording: original cast (Columbia)

DOLARO, Selina [SIMMONDS, Selina] (b London, 20 August 1849; d New York, 23 January 1889).

The daughter of the London theatrical musical director Ben J Simmonds (d Pimlico, 3 November 1910), "Dolly" Dolaro was trained at the Paris Conservatoire and made her official stage debut at the Lyceum, in the role of the burlesque Spanish Princess Galswinthe, in the milestone London production of *Chilpéric* (1870). Her dashing Jewish looks and fine soprano voice swept her straight away to nearly-stardom. She followed up by appearing in *Breaking the Spell* at the same theatre, in the pantomime *Harlequin Blackbird* at Manchester, and in *Magic Toys* (Urgandula), *Malala* (Oronooka), *No Song, No Supper,* and W S Gilbert's *Robert le Diable* burlesque with the Gaiety Theatre company (1871). At the opening of the Philharmonic Theatre in October 1871 she featured alongside Emily Soldene in the potted opéra-bouffe that was the house's main attraction (Frédégonde in *Chilpéric*), and when the Phil switched to full scale productions scored her greatest success to date in the title role of the megahit *Geneviève de Brabant.* She was obliged to quit the cast to bear the last of her four children, but, after ventures to Holborn (Marguerite in *Le Petit Faust*), the Royal Court (Camilla in *Zampa or the Buckaneer and the Little Dear*) and Liverpool (*Petit Faust,* Diana in *Endymion*) she returned to her part in *Geneviève de Brabant* and to take the principal girl role in the Phil's English version of *La Cour du Roi Pétaud* (Princess Girandole to the Prince of Soldene).

She went back to the Gaiety to star opposite Nellie Farren as Cleopatra in a flop *Anthony and Cleopatra* burlesque (1873), but tied up to success again, back at the Phil, as the original Clairette of the first and triumphant English-language *La Fille de Madame Angot.* She subsequently took her own company on the road playing the piece of the moment. "Dolly" returned to town to star in the unfortunate Lecocq pasticcio, *The Black Prince* (1874, Sybil) at the St James's and, the following year, presented herself as *La Périchole* and now as Mlle Lange in a much altered star-vehicle version of *Madame Angot,* completing her program with the first-ever performances of *Trial by Jury,* in which she herself did not, however, appear.

In 1876 she took over in *The Duke's Daughter* (the English version of *La Timbale d'argent,* 1876, Malvina) and then went on the road with an opéra-bouffe company run by the young Richard D'Oyly Carte. However, in typical fashion, she walked out on at least one occasion and had the orchestra sacked on another. She played at the Alhambra during 1877–78 in Strauss's *King Indigo* (Fantasca) and the inevitable *La Fille de Madame Angot,* and then in 1878 she commissioned her own original opéra-bouffe vehicle, *Belladonna,* from Alfred Cellier. It failed to reach London. However, "Dolly" came back to town instead in a much more remarkable role: she was cast by opera impresario J H Mapleson in his 1879 season as the first English-language Carmen in Bizet's opera.

After this intermediary, she continued as producer-star, presenting herself in the lead roles in *Les Dragons de Villars* (Rose Friquet), *La Périchole,* the burlesque *Another Drink* and *Madame Favart* in London and around the country, and then crossed to America to repeat her Carmen at New York's Academy of Music (27 October 1879). In Mapleson's next season, in spite of the presence of the original British Carmen, Minnie Hauk, in the company, she again played Carmen and added Frederic in *Mignon* to her operatic bow, but her opera career ended there, and she returned to Alexander Henderson's high-flying management to star in the London production of Genée's *Der Seekadett* (Cerisette).

Plate 103. **Selina Dolaro.** *"Dolly," a prima donna par excellence and the darling of 19th-century London nightlifers.*

The Naval Cadets was not a success, and Dolaro accepted a fresh offer from America. She again played Carmen, but this time in the burlesque *Carmen, or Soldiers and Seville-ians,* winning fine notices both for her singing and her much better than usual acting, and she followed this up by starring in *La Fille du tambour-major* (1880, Stella) for the same management. Unfortunately for her that management was Mr M B Leavitt, a well-known purveyor of louche girlie shows, and the two soon fell out. Dolly swiftly walked. She remained in America, however, and scored a further first-class success as the heroine of Audran's hit show *[Les Noces d'] Olivette* (1881, Olivette), followed by further starring engagements in *La Mascotte* (1881, Bettina), and, in breeches, as Mignapour in his *Le Grand Mogol* (*The Snake Charm-*

er, 1881) under the management of Fred Zimmerman, and then in the Broadway versions of the British musicals *Manteaux Noirs* (1882, Girola), *Rip van Winkle* (1882, Katrina) and *The Merry Duchess* (1883, Duchess of Epsom Downs). She also appeared in the straight theatre, notably as Polly Eccles in *Caste.*

Now, however, both her health and her fortunes began to flag. She was seen in New Orleans in the summer of 1884 in an embarrassing approximation of *La Périchole* and at the Grand Opera House in a rough-and-ready production of *Le Pont des soupirs* (April 1885) which went quickly broke on the road. She adapted and starred in Sardou's *Justine* at the Park (''she is the weak feature her failure was regretted by all''), played a summer season of *La Fille de Madame Angot* and *La Périchole* at Atlantic City—alongside lead tenor Charley J Campbell (whom she had employed as a beginner in her London starring days)—was dropped on the road from the cast of the play *Moral Crime,* and was seen briefly in the role of a comic opera star in the play *In Spite of All* (1885), before, in March 1886, a pulmonary hemorrhage laid her low and she disappeared from the stage.

She worked for a while as a play-reader at Wallack's Theater, tried her hand at journalism, poetry, novel- and playwriting, and The Lambs Club raised $4,000 at a benefit to support the lady who had been a popular ''queen of Bohemia'' to late-night gentlemen on both sides of the Atlantic, but—refusing ever to leave the bright lights of the city for a healthier atmosphere—she died shortly after at the age of 39.

The daughter, Genevieve, born during the run of *Geneviève de Brabant* later went on the stage in a minor way.

DIE DOLLARPRINZESSIN Operette in 3 acts by A M Willner and Fritz Grünbaum, based on a comedy by Gatti-Trotha. Music by Leo Fall. Theater an der Wien, Vienna, 2 November 1907.

One of the most generally popular of Leo Fall's works, *Die Dollarprinzessin* was a Ruramerican piece, written very much in the format of the British musical comedies which had been sweeping the world for the past decade and more, and almost certainly constructed with an eye to the lucrative English-language market. It had a heroine who is the daughter and deputy of a millionaire New York coal businessman (millionaires, at this period, were obligatorily American—if the rich were Continental, they were noblemen) and who describes herself as an ''echtes Selfmademädel.'' Her feminist attitudes lead Fredy, the desirable young German she has perversely made her secretary, proudly to refuse her as a wife until he has left her employ and, in good Operettic fashion, spent the interval between Acts II and III becoming a wealthy coalman in his own right.

The roles of Alice and Fredy were created by the original stars of *Die lustige Witwe,* Mizzi Günther and Louis Treumann, immediately following their long run together in the earlier piece. The untried but soon-to-be-famous Luise Kartousch (Daisy) as a teenaged American and Karl Meister (Hans) as a penniless German aristocrat provided the soubret parallel. The latter pair's jaunty song and dance to ''Wir tanzen Ringelreih'n'' was the jolliest and most popular musical moment of the entertainment, but Fall's score included several other delightful numbers: the title quartet in waltz time, a chorus of up-to-date typists accompanied by the clacking of their machines, and a nicely vulgar ''Olga von der Wolga'' for the cabaret artist, Olga Lapinska (Mizzi Wirth), who temporarily snares Alice's father (Franz Glawatsch, also director).

Karczag and Wallner's production was taken off after two and a half months to permit the newest Lehár work, *Der Mann mit den drei Frauen,* to be staged, and the show was little played in Vienna thereafter. However, *Die Dollarprinzessin*—no little thanks to the personal triumph scored by Frln Kartousch—was accounted a definite success. The show quickly appeared in Germany, where it proved an enormous hit, passing its 500th performance on 9 October 1909, and in Hungary (ad Jenő Faragó), but the all-important (for the writers' finances) British production was slow in coming. George Edwardes, who had immediately taken up the rights to the show, had Daly's Theatre filled with the long-running *The Merry Widow.* In consequence, his version held fire and a different English *Dollar Princess,* written by George Grossmith and directed by Edwardes's stage manager Pat Malone, opened on Broadway shortly before the Basil Hood/Adrian Ross adaptation Edwardes had ordered reached London. Both were, however, considerable successes.

Broadway's *The Dollar Princess* ran to 288 performances, even though Charles Frohman's production decorated Fall's score with a wave of interpolated numbers by Jerome Kern (''A Boat Sails on Wednesday,'' ''Red, White and Blue,'' ''Not Here, Not Here''), Frank Tours, W T Francis and even Fall's brother Richard, for a cast headed by the Broadway Danilo, Donald Brian and English performers Valli Valli, Adrienne Augarde, Louie Pounds and F Pope Stamper. During the run ''four new numbers by Leo Fall'' were added. *Die Dollarprinzessin* was eventually seen in New York in its unbotched form 1 November 1911, as given by a Viennese company featuring Vilma Conti as *Die Dollarprinzessin,* and again in 1926 when Hans Golle's company presented it in German at the Irving Place Theater (19 February).

Like Vienna, London also used its *Merry Widow* stars, Lily Elsie and Joe Coyne, for the leading roles (played by Hilda Moody and Richard Golden pre-London) of *The Dollar Princess,* but it cast the latter as the heroine's brother (here, doubtless in deference to Coyne's dashing new image, replacing the role of father from the original text) and gave the romantic role to the more legitimately voiced Robert Michaelis, who had succeeded Coyne to the role of Danilo. It also revamped the subplot concerning Daisy (Gabrielle Ray), added a new role for comedy star Bill Berry, and fresh songs by both Fall and his brother Richard (some cut following the Manchester tryout). The alterations clearly did not harm the show's appeal, for London appreciated it enormously and watched *The Dollar Princess* 428 times. Australia's *Dollar Princess* opened while London's ran on. Grace Edinsell (Alice), Herbert Clayton (Freddy), Lottie Sargent (Daisy) and J Roland Hogue (Dick) followed a Melbourne season with a good six weeks at Sydney's His Majesty's Theatre (28 May 1910).

France did not take up *Die Dollarprinzessin* at all until the Olympia-Casino at Nice enterprisingly mounted a version done by ''Willy'' (Henri Gauthier-Villars, the husband of Colette), which actually remained fairly close to the original, in 1911, with sufficient success for it to be picked up for Paris. The Théâtre de la Scala, however, ordered yet another version, from Antony Mars and Maurice Desvallières, for its production with ex-*Veuve joyeuse* Alice O'Brien starred opposite Dutilloy, and the young Edmée Favart as Daisy paired with the tenor Edmond Tirmont in the lighter roles.

Die Dollarprinzessin held a place in the Continental repertoire for some time after its first series of productions but, like the majority of Fall's works, it has largely slipped from the repertoire in recent decades, even on the home front. It was filmed in 1927, with Liane Haid, Hans Albers and Georg Alexander, and potted for a German telefilm, featuring Tatnia Iwanow and Horst Niendorf, in 1971.

Hungary: Király Színház *A Dollárkirálynő* 21 March 1908; Germany: Neues Schauspielhaus 6 June 1908; USA: Knickerbocker Theater *The Dollar Princess* 6 September 1909; UK: Prince's Theatre, Manchester 24 December 1908, Daly's Theatre *The Dollar Princess* 25 September 1909; Australia: His Majesty's Theatre, Melbourne *The Dollar Princess* 9 April 1910; France: Olympia-Casino, Nice *La Princesse Dollar* 11 March 1911, Théâtre de la Scala, Paris 6 December 1911

Films: Felix Basch *Die Dollarprinzessin und ihre sechs Freier* 1927, TV 1971

Recordings: selections (part-records Philips, EMI, Polydor, etc), selection in Italian (part-record Fonit-Cetra), selection in Spanish (Blue Moon), selection in Danish (Polydor)

DOLLY VARDEN Comic opera in 2 acts by Stanislaus Stange. Music by Julian Edwards. Princess's Theater, Toronto, 23 September 1901; Herald Square Theater, New York, 27 January 1902.

Allegedly based on the character from Dickens's *Barnaby Rudge,* Stanislaus Stange's *Dolly Varden* was, in its plot, rather more a mishmash of Garrick's *The Country Girl* and its original, *The Country Wife.* Written in a comic-opera style, with no low comedian (a Broadway sine qua non of the day) featured, and Lulu Glaser starring as Dolly opposite Van Rensslaer Wheeler, it won fine initial notices from those critics who preferred the older styles in music to up-to-date dance tunes (''a prodigious and unqualified hit,'' ''real comic opera''), and it had a 154-performance run in New York before producer Sam Shubert took it to the country and also to Britain. In London, with two numbers from Edwardes's *When Johnny Comes Marching Home* bolstering the score (''Katie, My Southern Rose'' became ''Dolly, My English Rose''), it was politely received for three months. Not sufficiently politely, however, for Shubert who made a furious press statement accusing British ''managers and upper-class playgoers'' of being anti-American and left the embarrassed, Manchester-born librettist to explain on behalf of himself and his Liverpudlian composer-collaborator that the outburst was nothing personal: Shubert was like that with everyone.

A 1993 attempt to musicalize *The Country Wife* under the title *Lust* (Heather brothers, Haymarket Theatre 19 July 1993), with Denis Lawson featured as Horner, proved laughable only in its embarrassingly jejeune attempts to live up to its come-on title. It embarrassed all over again in Philadelphia (Walnut Street Theater 3 May 1995) and at New York's way-off-Broadway John Houseman Theater (13 July 1995), each time with Lawson in the central role.

UK: Avenue Theatre 1 October 1903

DOÑA FRANCISQUITA Zarzuela in 3 acts by Federico Romero and Guillermo Fernández Shaw based on Lope de Vega's *La discreta enamorada.* Music by Amadeo Vives. Teatro Apolo, Madrid, 17 October 1923.

One of the most popular zarzuelas of the género grande, *Doña Francisquita* has been widely played on Spanish-language stages since its first production in 1923. The tale, an updated (to 19th-century Madrid) version of a Lope de Vega work, is in the classic vein of would-be-matrimonial comedy, and the Francisquita (Mary Isaura) of the title is the piece's ingenue. It is she who is the ''discreta enamorada'' of the original title, and the object of her affections is the student Fernando (Juan de Casaneve). When his widowed father, Don Matías, comes instead to offer for her hand—an offer, in time-honored fashion, mistakenly taken to herself by the heroine's widow mother; Doña Francesca (Felisa Lázaro)—Francisquita resorts to a useful fib and tells the gentleman that his son has been writing her love letters. Misunderstandings, misdirected love-notes and the amorous frivolities of a spitfiring soubrette called Aurora la Beltrana (Cora Raga), from the local theatre, are all mixed up with incidental song and dance and the festivities of carnival week before youth wins its way, Matías gives up his "bride," and the actress goes back to her bullfighting boyfriend of yore.

The favorite pieces from Vives's score included Fernando's tenor romanza "Por el humo se sabe donde está el fuego" and a night-time street chorus of necking lovers ("Coro de románticos").

A version of *Doña Francisquita* was produced in Monaco (ad A de Badet, R Bergeret) in January 1934, and the piece was subsequently played in this French translation in Brussels and in the French provinces. In 1998 it was given an American performance, under the aegis of Placido Domingo, at Washington's National Opera.

It has also been filmed on three separate occasions in its original language.

USA: National Opera, Washington, DC 1998

Films: 1934, 1952, 1988 (TV)

Recordings: complete (Columbia, Edigsa, Hispavox, Auvidis Valois, Sony, etc), selections (Zafiro, Columbia, Blue Moon, etc)

DONAHUE, Jack [DONAHUE, John Joseph] (b Charlestown, Mass, 29 December 1888; d New York, 1 October 1930). Dancing leading man who starred in several Broadway shows before an early death.

Donahue began his career as a boy, playing in a medicine show and subsequently appeared in burlesque and vaudeville, making himself a place in the latter field as a speciality dancer, part of the act Donahue and Stewart. He made his entry into the musical theatre as a dancer in *The Woman Haters* as early as 1912, but had his first substantial part as Slooch in the long tour and less substantial Broadway season of *Angel Face* in 1919. He subsequently played on Broadway in *The Ziegfeld Follies* (1920), *Molly Darling* (1922, Chic Jiggs) and *Be Yourself* (1924, Matt McLean), before pairing successfully with Marilyn Miller in *Sunny* (1925, Jim Denning) and again in *Rosalie* (1928, Bill Delroy).

For some years a writer for magazines and also, occasionally, for the stage, he extended his interests when he not only starred in, but also co-wrote the 1929 success *Sons o'Guns* (1929, Jimmy Canfield) and he subsequently adapted the London version of Szirmai's *Alexandra* (*Princess Charming*) for the Broadway stage before his death from nephritis at the age of 41.

1929 **Sons o'Guns** (J Fred Coots, Benny Davis, Arthur Swanstrom/w Fred Thompson, Bobby Connolly) Imperial Theater 26 November

1930 **Princess Charming** (*Alexandra*) American version of English text (Imperial Theater)

Memoir: *Letters of a Hoofer to His Ma* (Cosmopolitan Books, New York, 1911)

DONALDSON, Walter (b New York, 15 February 1893; d Santa Monica, Calif, 15 July 1947). Highly successful resident of Tin Pan Alley who ventured only twice with a full-scale Broadway score, but hit pay dirt there as well.

The son of a musical family, Donaldson made a brief start on a career in a brokerage firm, but he soon switched to music and took a position as a pianist in a musical publishing house. He began a serious career as a songwriter at 18 and found immediate success with such pieces as "Back Home in Tennessee" and "I've Got the Sweetest Girl in Maryland." During the First World War he worked in the same entertainment division of the army as Irving Berlin and in 1919 he joined Berlin's music publishing company from where, for the next nine years, he turned out the tunes for a regular string of popular songs including "How Ya Gonna Keep 'Em Down on the Farm?," "My Mammy," "My Sweet Hortense" (all w Sam Lewis, Joe Young), "Carolina in the Morning," "My Buddy," "Beside a Babbling Brook," "Yes, Sir, That's My Baby," "That Certain Party," "I Wonder Where My Baby Is Tonight," "Let's Talk About My Sweetie," "There Ain't No Maybe in My Baby's Eyes," "My Ohio Home" (all w Gus Kahn), "My Sweet Indiana Home," "Roamin' to Wyomin," "Chili Bom Bom" and "Let It Rain Let It Pour" (both w Cliff Friend), "After I Say I'm Sorry," "Where'd You Get Those Eyes," "Sam, the Old Accordion Man," "At Sundown," "Just Like a Melody out of the Sky," and "My Blue Heaven" (w George Whiting).

In 1926 he collaborated with another songsmith, Joseph Meyer, on the score of the short-lived musical *Sweetheart Time,* but another, solo try at a Broadway score brought very different results. *Whoopee,* built as a vehicle for Eddie Cantor and produced by Florenz Ziegfeld, was a major stage hit, not a little thanks to such Donaldson numbers as "Makin' Whoopee," "I'm Bringing a Red, Red Rose" and "Love Me or Leave Me." It was subsequently made into a film, by Sam Goldwyn, with Cantor starred, and without the last two named songs in 1930.

By this time Donaldson had split from the Berlin organization, founded his own publishing company and moved to Hollywood where he subsequently wrote songs for many films and planted his old successes in many more (*Kid Millions, The Great Ziegfeld,* etc).

1926 **Sweetheart Time** (w Joseph Meyer/Irving Caesar, Ballard McDonald/H B Smith) Imperial Theater 19 January

1928 **Whoopee** (Gus Kahn/William A McGuire) New Amsterdam Theater 4 December

DON CESAR Comic Operette in 3 acts by Oskar Walther based on the play *Don César de Bazan* by Philippe Dumanoir and Adolphe d'Ennery. Music by Rudolf Dellinger. Carl-Schultze Theater, Hamburg, 28 March 1885; Walhalla Theater, Berlin, 23 September 1885.

An operettic version of the much-retold *Don César de Bazan* story—the most famous of all the many blindfold marriage tales of the 19th-century stage—with more than a little flavor of *La Périchole* added, Dellinger's *Don Cesar* was extremely well received on its production in Germany. After making its way from its original Hamburg production to Berlin's Walhalla Theater (22 September 1885), it went on to multiple regional productions, becoming, alongside the now-classic works of the repertoire, one of the most widely played pieces of its time, and certainly the most successful of all German 19th-century Operetten.

The disguised King of Spain, taken by the charms of the gypsy singer Maritana, finds that she will not let him have his way with her unless she is first wed to him. Since the King already has a Queen, he arranges for Don Cesar, arrested after a duel, to go through the marriage ceremony in his place. After the wedding, Cesar's friend Pueblo helps him escape, and ultimately the King is balked in his designs as Maritana and her legal husband settle down to happily ever after. The comic element was supplied by the King's Ministers, Don Onofrio and Don Fernando, and the former's wife, Doña Uraca.

The show's straightforwardly merry score was at its best when galloping frankly into the bolero rhythms which Dellinger used for such pieces as the entrances of both his heroine (''Ach, ach, ach, du erster Liebestraum'') and his hero (''Von altem Stamm der letzte Zweig''), spreading a Spanish flavor amongst a bundle of more conventional waltz measures. Cesar's piece and, in particular, his second-act dream-serenade (''Komm herab, o Madonna Theresa'') became popular with tenors outside the show.

Don Cesar was produced in Zürich, St Petersburg, Strasbourg, Prague, Sofia, Zagreb, Stockholm and many other European centers, whilst in Vienna, following its first successful run at Carl Tatartzy's Carltheater with Adolf Brakl (Cesar), Endtreffer (King), Felix Schweighofer (Onofrio) and Gabriele Mrak (Maritana) (30 performances in 1885, and more in 1886 and 1887), it was given a new production in 1888 with Brakl, Max Monti (King), Carl Adolf Friese (Onofrio) and Frln Tischler (Maritana), and later revived at the Lustspieltheater (5 October 1902) and at the Raimundtheater (9 September 1911) with Bernard Bötel (King), Ida Russka (Maritana) and Otto Storm (Cesar).

In Budapest, the show was seen first in German, then in Ferenc Rajna's Hungarian adaptation, and it was given

Plate 104. **Don Cesar.** *The most successful musical play to come out of Germany in the 19th century.*

a major revival as late as 1906 at the Király Színház (10 April) in which Sári Fedák played a travesty Don Cesar. Perhaps because of the enormous popularity of Vincent Wallace's English opera, *Maritana,* and of Gilbert and Sullivan's 1888 *The Yeomen of the Guard,* both of which used more or less the same story, *Don Cesar* was not staged in Britain, but when John McCaull introduced it to America (ad William von Sachs) with John Perugini (Cesar), Louise Lablache/Bertha Ricci (Maritana) and Edwin Hoff (King) in the central roles and De Wolf Hopper (Onofrio) and Mathilde Cottrelly (Pueblo Escudiro) starring, it served him (in spite of only a brief Broadway showing) as a highly popular item in his touring repertoire for several seasons. New York German-speaking theatregoers were able to see the piece in German at the Amberg Theater in 1891.

Berlin saw a revival in 1904 (10 December) when the piece was produced at the Theater des Westens with Turmfeld (Don Cesar), Frln Linda (Maritana), Mary

Hagen, Gaston and Below in the cast, and another in 1914 (14 November).

The *Don César* story, as well as being the subject of a number of burlesques—most of which were connected rather to *Maritana* (*Mary Turner, Little Don Caesar de Bazan*) rather than to the play—was also used as the basis for an opera by Massenet (Opéra-Comique 30 November 1872).

Hungary: Stadt Theater (Ger) 21 September 1885, Budai Színkör *Don Cézár* 7 May 1887; Austria: Carltheater 20 November 1885; USA: McCaull's Opera House, Philadelphia 29 March 1886, Wallack's Theater 3 May 1886

DON GIOVANNI, or A Spectre on Horseback Burlesque in 2 acts by Thomas Dibdin. Royal Circus and Surrey Theatre, London, 12 May 1817.

Described as a "comic, heroic, operatic, tragic, pantomimic burlesque burletta spectacular parody," this piece was one of the earliest hits among the musical pasticcio-burlesques, in the rhyming couplet style, which were to become so very popular with English-language playgoers during the middle years of the 19th century. The burlesque was pinned to Mozart and Da Ponte's 1787 opera (which author Dibdin had seen a few days before penning his piece) and to Lord Byron's poem, rather than to the other main stage versions of the story of the Sevillian rake related by Tirso, Molière and Goldoni, or the musical versions by Glück, Abertini, Gazzaniga and Carnicer. Its score was made up of melodies taken from a list of British composing royalty: Arne, Blow, Purcell, William Reeve, Stephen Storace, William Shield, Parry, Händel and the lesser known Etheridge, Zerbini, Davy and Sanderson, supplemented by imported melodies from the works of such as Nicolai, Glück, Kreutzer and Querini, and topped off by Mozart's overture to Da Ponte's operatic version. The piece was produced at the Surrey Theatre and there it achieved a momentous run for its time, being played for one hundred straight nights.

Contrary to later burlesque fashion, there was little travesty playing. Mr Short appeared as Giovanni, with Fitzwilliam as Leporello and Mrs Brooks as Donna Anna, and the only cross-sexual casting was that of Mr Yarnold as the low-comedy mother of the bride (ex- Zerlina). The playbill advised that the Marble Horse of the statue was to be played by "a real poney" and that the "views are intended to represent several places in and near the city of Seville with (by way of a Pictorial Episode) a fine scene of Blackfriars Bridge."

Another successful early pasticcio version of the Don Giovanni tale was William T Moncrieff's *Giovanni in London, or The Libertine Reclaimed* (Olympic Theatre 26 December 1817), an operatic extravaganza in two acts in which Giovanni ended up wedding the heroine, and the music of which included "The Bluebells of Scotland," "Wapping Old Stairs," "Robin Adair," *The Beggar's Opera*'s "Cease your funning," "Scots What Hae" and a melody borrowed from Boieldieu's *John of Paris*. Produced by Elliston, it was later revived by him at Drury Lane (1820) and helped launch the young Eliza Vestris to celebrity. Moncrieff followed this piece up with a *Giovanni in Ireland* (Theatre Royal, Drury Lane 22 December 1821) four years later, and the Olympic with a ballet entitled *Giovanni in Botany, or The Libertine Transported* (12 March 1822) which whisked the reprobate roisterer off to Australia. *Don Giovanni in London* was revived at the Victoria Theatre as late as 1879.

Other English burlesque and extravaganza adaptations of the Don Juan story (and of Mozart's opera thereupon) have included Henry J Byron's 1865 *Little Don Giovanni* produced at the Prince of Wales Theatre with Marie Wilton as the Don, a male Zerlina and a female Masetto; the Alhambra *Don Juan* spectacular of 1873 (Frederick Clay, Georges Jacobi, et al/H J Byron); two Gaiety burlesques—*Don Giovanni in Venice* (Robert Reece, February 1873) with Johnnie Toole as Giovanni and Nellie Farren as Leporello, James Tanner's Gaietyed Byron *Don Juan* (28 October 1893)—and the Brothers Prendergast's *Don Juan Junior* (Royalty 3 November 1880).

In France, Henri Varna and the Théâtre Mogador staged a piece under the title *Les Amours de Don Juan* (Juan Morata/Varna, Marc-Cab, René Richard) which professed to be "d'après Lord Byron" and which had its Don Juan (Marcel Merkès) galloping round the world (Istanbul, Russia, Scotland, etc) in a display of picturesque scenery and multinational ladies, accompanied and finally subdued by a soubrette called Antonia (Paulette Merval).

A Galt MacDermot/Derek Walcott musical on the same theme, originally commissioned by Britain's Royal Shakespeare Company, was played in Trinidad as *The Joker of Seville* (1974).

DON JUAN Burlesque in 3 acts on Lord Byron's *Don Juan* by James T Tanner. Lyrics by Adrian Ross. Music by Meyer Lutz. Gaiety Theatre, London, 28 October 1893.

Conceived by the Gaiety's star comic, Fred Leslie, as a vehicle for himself and his co-star Nellie Farren, this burlesque of Byron's *Don Juan* was put aside when Leslie's death and Farren's illness ended the famous partnership. It was taken up later, when burlesque had largely given way to the new modern-dress musical comedy, and was staged at the Gaiety with Arthur Roberts, perhaps the most popular burlesque comic to follow Leslie (although in a rather different and decidedly lower style), as Pedrillo and Millie Hylton, one of the five famous Rudge sisters and a music-hall star, as the Don. Miss Hylton successfully introduced the interpolated song "Linger Longer Loo," which had started Sidney Jones' career and Teddy Solomon's "Comme ça," whilst Roberts repeated his own very particular version of "After the Ball." Cissie (later Cecilia) Loftus, as the not-at-all-Byronic heroine, did her speciality: impersonations. The show created a diplomatic incident when the Turkish Ambassador objected to the indignities suffered by a character named "the Sultan of Turkey" and George Edwardes diplomatically altered the offending personage's title to "Jabez Pasha."

One of the less effective of the great series of Gaiety new burlesques, *Don Juan* still had a nine-months' run, but Edwardes did not repeat the experience, concentrating thereafter on his new musical comedies and leaving the faded tradition of burlesque behind.

DONNA JUANITA Comic opera in 3 acts by F Zell and Richard Genée. Music by Franz von Suppé. Carltheater, Vienna, 21 February 1880.

As in Suppé's earlier hit comic opera, *Fatinitza,* the lady of this show's title does not exist—she is a young man in disguise. In the context of the Spanish revolution, the army cadet René Dufour dresses up as (amongst other things) the seductive Donna Juanita, to charm and to spy on the buffoonish English governor of San Sebastian, Sir Andrew Douglas, and the Alcade, Don Pomponio, who is making himself troublesome to René's brother's fiancée. By the final curtain both the political and the amorous missions have been satisfyingly completed. The role of René, designed like Wladimir-Fatinitza as a breeches role for a mezzo-soprano, was created in Vienna by the soubrette Rosa Streitmann, with Gross and Karl Blasel as the two comic dignitaries and Therese Schäfer featured as the Alcade's libidinous wife.

Donna Juanita, with its lively score bristling with marches, polkas and waltzes, won amazed reviews ("his best yet") and a splendid success in Vienna and, following its first run, it was brought back to the Theater an der Wien in 1884 with Streitmann, Blasel, Schäfer, Guttmann, and Girardi as Riego Manrique, and produced and revived thereafter in many versions throughout Europe, notably in Spain where it put up a long first run before nestling into the revivable repertoire, and in Russia, where it has remained more popular than Suppé's elsewhere more famous works. Budapest's Népszínház played *Donna Juanita* (ad Antal Radó) in both 1880 and 1884 (17 September) and, eight years after Leterrier and Vanloo's French version—a version which had rather altered the plot so that the French in the piece didn't come out so badly—had been heard at Brussels's Galeries Saint-Hubert (*Juanita* 22 October 1883), Marguerite Ugalde starred as René Belamour, alongside Louis Morlet (Riego) and Maurice Lamy (Gil Polo), in a tardy Paris edition. In 1894 the piece was revived at the Théâtre Parisien (19 July) with Eugénie Gauthier as René.

London did not venture a production of the show, but in New York Marie Geistinger scored a considerable success with her rendition of the original piece at the German-language Thalia Theater, several months after H B Mahn had introduced the piece to Broadway in an English version with Jeannie Winston starred as René/Juanita alongside Ellis Ryse (Pomponio), Arthur H Bell (Douglas) and Rose Leighton (Olympia). The show was again seen on Broadway the following season as played by the Boston English Opera Company (Tony Pastor's Theater 25 September 1882) with Rose Beaudet as René, and was played liberally throughout America.

A rewritten version was played at Berlin's Friedrich-Wilhelmstädtisches Theater under the title *Der pfiffige Kadett* in 1915 (30 December); a second remake, by Julius Wilhelm and Gustav Beer, with a libretto reset in Paris, with a hairdresser and an actress as its leading ladies, and with Suppé's music rearranged by Karl Pauspertl, was produced by Erich Müller at the Johann Strauss-Theater 8 April 1925 as *Die grosse Unbekannte* (101 performances) and later played at Berlin's Theater des Westens (12 June 1926, 31 performances); whilst a third rearrangement (ad Artur Bodanzky, A Mattulath) was produced at New York's Metropolitan Opera House (2 January 1932) and yet another appeared in Koblenz (6 November 1937 ad A Treumann-Mette).

Germany: Carl-Schultze Theater, Hamburg 11 September 1880, Friedrich-Wilhelmstädtisches Theater 2 October 1880; Hungary: Népszínház 25 December 1880; Canada: Theatre Royal, Montreal 23 April 1881; USA: Opera House, Providence, RI 29 April 1881, Fifth Avenue Theater 16 May 1881, Thalia Theater (Ger) 27 September 1881; France: Théâtre des Folies-Dramatiques *Juanita* 4 April 1891

DONNELLY, Dorothy [Agnes] (b New York, 28 January 1880; d New York, 3 January 1928). Broadway librettist and lyricist who found her greatest successes in the field of romantic operetta.

The daughter of the manager of New York's Grand Opera House, Miss Donnelly had, at first, a considerable career as an actress, playing in New York in the title roles of Yeats's *Kathleen-ni-Houlihan* and Shaw's *Candida,* in *Soldiers of Fortune, Man of Destiny,* Ibsen's *When the Dead Awaken, Daughters of Men,* and, most famously, in the title role of the hit French play, *Madame X* (1910).

Concurrently with her performing career, she began to write libretti for the musical theatre, collaborating on the English book for Charles Cuvillier's Franco-German *Flora Bella* (1916) and then concocting the libretto for the Shuberts' production of the Marilyn Miller vehicle *Fancy Free* (1918). When the time came to readapt the existing adaptations of the hugely successful *Das Dreimäderlhaus* for the Shuberts' American audiences, Miss Donnelly was put to work on both the libretto and the lyrics and, in collaboration with Sigmund Romberg, she turned out a highly romantic variant of the Franz Schubert life-and-songs show which, as *Blossom Time,* won as enduring a success throughout America as *Das Dreimäderlhaus* had done in its original form in Europe.

This success encouraged her to put an end to her acting career and to concentrate thereafter on writing. Her first collaboration thereafter was with composer Stephen Jones on the musical comedy *Poppy* (1923), a season-long success of 344 performances on Broadway with W C Fields starring, which also managed five months at London's Gaiety Theatre (1925) in the wake of the success of the not dissimilar *Sally.* It was, however, her next effort which gave her her greatest success when she came together with Romberg a second time to adapt the old German play *Alt Heidelberg* as the libretto and lyrics for *The Student Prince.* This work proved to be one of the most successful of all the Broadway operettas of the 1920s and put a whole bundle of its author's songs into the standards list (''Deep in My Heart, Dear,'' The Drinking Song, Serenade, ''Golden Days,'' etc).

Miss Donnelly subsequently wrote two further shows with Romberg, the modified Barbara Frietchie tale *My Maryland,* which broke every record in Philadelphia but didn't even dent those of New York, and the unsuccessful *My Princess,* as well as the unfortunate *Hello, Lola,* a piece based on Booth Tarkington's successful *Seventeen,* before her death early in 1928, during the run of *My Maryland.*

1916 **Flora Bella** English version w Cosmo Hamilton (Casino Theater)
1918 **Fancy Free** (Augustus Barratt) Astor Theater 11 April
1921 **Blossom Time** (Schubert arr Romberg) Ambassador Theater 29 September
1923 **Poppy** (Stephen Jones, Arthur Samuels) Apollo Theater 3 September
1924 **The Student Prince** (Romberg) Jolson Theater 2 December
1926 **Hello, Lola** (William B Kernell) Eltinge Theater 12 January
1927 **My Maryland** (Romberg) Jolson Theater 12 September
1927 **My Princess** (Romberg) Shubert Theater 6 October

Biography: McLean, L: *Dorothy Donnelly: A Life in the Theatre* (McFarland, New York, 1999)

DONOHUE, Jack [DONOHUE, John Francis] (b New York, 3 November 1908; d Marina del Rey, Calif, 27 March 1984).

Originally a dancer (*Ziegfeld Follies of 1927, Good News, Follow Thru, America's Sweetheart, Shoot the Works, Free for All,* as a speciality act in *Shady Lady*), Donohue began a career as a Broadway choreographer with the 1932 Fred and Dorothy Stone extravaganza *Smiling Faces,* the Queenie Smith show *The Little Racketeer* (1932, ''under the supervision of Albertina Rasch''), the nightclub dances featured in *Shady Lady,* and Jerome Kern's Amerikaner-strudel operetta *Music in the Air,* before spending a number of years working largely in Britain, where he made a double career as a performer of light comic roles and a dance director.

His choreographic credits there included the Drury Lane staging of Ábrahám's *Ball im Savoy* (1933), with its celebrated soubret dances, the revue *Please,* some of the numbers for Jack Buchanan and Elsie Randolph's dance and comedy show *Mr Whittington* (1934, w Buchanan, Buddy Bradley), the original touring production of *Jill, Darling* (Jack and Jill), the George Robey musical *Here's How!,* the Gaiety Theatre's *Going Greek* (1937), in which Louise Browne performed her sylvan ballet, its successor *Running Riot* (1938) and Firth Shephard's *Wild Oats* and *Sitting Pretty.* His stage appearances included *Here's How!* (Tim Regan), *On Your Toes* (1937, Morrosine), *Wild Oats* (1938, Val) and *Sitting Pretty* (1939, Jimmy Gay).

The war occasioned Donohue's return to America, where he worked in stock and regional theatres, notably as Denikov in the St Louis premiere of *Balalaika* (1941, also choreography) and returned to Broadway as a performer in *Panama Hattie* (1940, Mike), as a choreographer in the revue *The Seven Lively Arts* and *Are You with It?* (1945) and then, in a directing début, with the Phil Silvers musical *Top Banana* (1951). He subsequently directed Bobby Clark in the revised version of *Flahooley* called *Jollyanna* (1952) in Los Angeles, Sammy Davis jr's Broadway début in *Mr Wonderful* (1956, also choreography) and *Rumple* (1957).

Outside his theatre assignments, Donohue also worked widely in film and television. Beginning with *Curly Top* (1935), he choreographed many of the Shirley Temple films, as well as the film versions of *Music in the Air* (1934), *Louisiana Purchase* (1941), *The Fleet's In* (1942), *Girl Crazy* (1943), *Best Foot Forward* (1943), *Calamity Jane* (1953) and *Babes in Toyland* (1961), and many television variety shows and specials.

DON QUIXOTE

Cervantes' 1605 tale of the chivalric Don Quixote and his faithful Sancho Panza, of the windmill which represents a giant, and the girl whom the idiosyncratic hero dreams to be his fair Dulcinea, has been translated to the stage on numberless occasions, including many in the musical theatre. Amongst the earliest were included a 1680 Venetian operatic version, *Don Chisciotte della*

Mancia (Carlo Sajon/Marco Morosini), another mounted in Hamburg in 1690, a sizeable three-part affair with music by Henry Purcell put out in 1694, and a Parisian opera of 1712.

Amongst the tidal wave of 18th-century examples were numbered Philidor's one-act *Sancho Pança [dans son île]* (Comédie-Italienne, Paris 8 July 1762), Conti's *Don Chisciotte in Sierra Morena* (Vienna 2 February 1719), Caldara's pair of burlesque operas *Don Chisciotte in corte della duchessa* (Vienna 6 February 1727) and *Sancho Panca, governatore dell'isola Barataria* (Vienna 27 January 1733), Piccini's comic Singspiel *Il Don Cuiscotte* (1770), which apparently did better than a like piece by Paisiello, and the *Don Quixote und Sancho Panza* of Gerl and Giesecke (Wiedner Theater, Vienna 17 April 1790). Henry Fielding assumed a *Don Quixote in England* (New Haymarket Theatre, 1734), whilst Karl Ditters von Dittersdorf's *Don Quixote der zweite* (Oels 4 February 1795) and Champein's Parisian *Le nouveau Don Quichotte* (25 May 1789) went in for second-generation Dons.

The most famous, retrospectively at least, of the 19th-century works was the little *Don Quichotte et Sancho Pança* written, composed and performed by Hervé in the earliest stages of the opéra-bouffe years, but musical *Don Quixote*s continued worldwide through the 19th century, in equally as great numbers and in as many different languages as in the preceding era. There were a number of not very successful ones in the English language: Frederic Clay composed a *Don Quixote* comic opera to a text by Harry Paulton and Alfred Maltby for London's Alhambra Theatre in 1876 (25 September), conductor/producer Adolf Neuendorff of the New York Germania Theater composed a version to a text by someone called Italianer in 1882 (9 January), and Reginald De Koven and Harry B Smith ventured a *Don Quixote* for the Bostonians company in 1889 in which celebrated comic Henry Clay Barnabee was featured as the Don alongside the Sancho of George Frothingham, which was seen in Boston (18 November) but which did not get a showing on Broadway.

In Europe, Louis Roth and Max von Weinzierl composed the score for a 1879 comic operetta (Komische Oper 15 February) and Émile Pessard supplied a one-act *Don Quixote* to Paris's Salle Érard (lib: Deschamps, 13 February 1874) and Théâtre des Menus-Plaisirs (4 July 1889), Émile Vuillermoz gave his musical *Don Quixote* also in Paris, whilst Wilhelm Kienzl's operatic *Don Quixote* was produced at the Berlin Opera in 1898 (18 November) with Herr Bulss as the Don and with more success than George Macfarren's 1846 *The Adventures of Don Quixote* (Drury Lane 3 February) or Jacques-Dalcroze's Swiss opera *Sancho Panza* (Geneva 13 December 1897). Luigi Ricci gave an 1881 *Don Chisciotte* in Venice (4 February 1881), Manuel Garcia turned out one which was later played in New York, and Felix Mendelssohn's first effort at an opera, *Die Hochzeit des Gamacho,* also concentrated on one of the additional episodes in Cervantes's work. What might have been the most famous of *Don Quichotte*s, however, failed to eventuate. In 1875–76 Messrs Sardou and Offenbach were engaged by Albert Vizentini of the Théâtre de la Gaîté to provide him with a *Don Quichotte* in which there would be a role for . . . Thérésa. One wonders if the stocky, salacious chanteuse might have tried her hand at Sancho Panza. However, Offenbach never finished his score and Sardou's text (adapted from his 1863 *Don Quichotte* w Nuitter) only made it to the stage in 1895 (Théâtre du Châtelet 9 February) with an incidental score composed by Albert Renaud, with Barral as the Don, Dailly as Sancho and no Thérésa.

The early years of the 20th century brought forth several more new versions of the famous tale, in all shapes and sizes, on the musical stage. New Zealand's Alfred Hill composed a *Don Quixote de la Mancha* to a text by W H Beattie (1904), Nagyvárad premiered a *Don Quijote* by Karoly Liptai with music by Béla Garami (31 January 1909) later played at Budapest's Fővárosi Nyári Színház (19 August 1909), whilst Richard Heuberger's *Don Quichotte,* an Operette in two acts to a text by Reichert and Grünbaum, was produced at the studio theatre Hölle in Vienna in 1910—the same year that Massenet premiered his fine and durable operatic version (Monte Carlo 19 February)—and de Falla turned out a one-act *El retablo de maese Pedro,* another piece based on an episode from Cervantes, in Seville, 23 March 1923.

In later years, far and away the most successful Quixote was the American musical play *Man of la Mancha* (22 November 1965, ANTA Washington Square), but its appearance and its international success did not wholly stop the flow of musicals on the subject and a more recent Russian musical, later played in East Germany (14 January 1977) as *Dulcinea von Toboso* (Gennadji Gladkov/Alexander Wolodin), followed the trend of the modern stage by giving the title to the lady of the piece.

DO RE MI Musical in 2 acts by Garson Kanin. Lyrics by Betty Comden and Adolph Green. Music by Jule Styne. St James Theater, New York, 26 December 1960.

Favorite TV comedian Phil Silvers starred in *Do Re Mi* as Hubie Cram, an all-time loser with an infinite supply of crazy get-rich projects, who attempts to wade his way into the recording and jukebox market with the help of some superannuated gangsters. For once, one of his schemes works. He accidentally turns a waitress, Tilda Mullen (Nancy Dussault), into a singing star, and the money rolls in. But Tilda ends up falling in love with the competition, dreamboat vocalist John Henry Wheeler (John Reardon) and, with one thing and another, it is not long before Hubie ends up back where he started.

Silvers and Nancy Walker, as his loving if long-suffering wife, Kay, headed the comedy which was the show's backbone and Reardon performed the best-liked number, ''Make Someone Happy,'' through 400 performances for producer David Merrick without *Do Re Mi* ever getting into the black. A London version, mounted by H M Tennent Ltd and Leslie A MacDonnell, with Max Bygraves (Hubie), Maggie Fitzgibbon (Kay), Jan Waters (Tilda) and Steve Arlen (Wheeler), ran for 169 performances.

UK: Prince of Wales Theatre 12 October 1961

Recordings: original cast (RCA), London cast (Decca), concert cast (DRG), etc

DORFMUSIKANTEN Operette in 3 acts by Leopold Jacobson and Robert Bodanzky. Music by Oscar Straus. Theater an der Wien, Vienna, 29 November 1919.

The village musician of the title is Friedl Pausinger (Hubert Marischka), who makes and plays his violins with such skill that he wins a one hundred–Thaler prize. Alas his skill and fortune threaten—for the space of a couple of acts—to come between him and his little Luisl (Luise Kartousch), the foster daughter of the villager Peterl (Ernst Tautenhayn). Alongside their tale of love and talent (with its requisite happy ending), the light-hearted Baron Heini von Solingen (Fritz Neumann) courted Adelheid (Betty Fischer), daughter of the violin-maker Tobias Brendl (Josef Hauschultz).

The famous team of Tautenhayn and Kartousch had their by now traditional dance duo (''Sie war siebzehn, ich war zwanzig''), whilst Friedl's prize song (''Weisst du noch? weisst du noch?'') headed a busy musical evening for the show's leading man in which he partook of a whole series of duos and trios. Adelheid and Heini headed a supper waltz in the second-act entertainment at the Baron's castle, where Friedl and Luisl joined together to give their principal waltz duo (''Einen Mann, den muss man halten'').

Dorfmusikanten had a solid run of five months and 166 performances at the Theater an der Wien, as well as being played at the Raimundtheater by the Theater an der Wien company, headed by Karl Melzer and Lotte Ferry and with Tautenhayn still as old Peterl (2 May 1920), for a short season.

DAS DORF OHNE GLOCKE Singspiel in 3 acts based on the musical play *A harang* by Árpád Pásztor. Music by Eduard Künneke. Friedrich-Wilhelmstädtisches Theater, Berlin, 5 April 1919.

Eduard Künneke's first musical theatre work was a remusicked version of the Hungarian piece *A harang,* the successful three-act ''legend'' set to music by Pongrác Kacsoh and Ákos Buttykay and produced at Budapest's Király Színház in 1907 (1 February) with Lujza Blaha in the leading feminine role.

The old priest, Father Benedikt (Josef Joseffy), is given five hundred gulden by his parishioners which is to go towards giving the village the church bells it has lacked so many years. But Benedikt gives the money to the desperately needy blacksmith, Peter (Kurt Schönert), and his wife Eva (Katarina Garden), and trouble stirs in the village until the Baron Erwin von Lertingen (Sven Holm) comes to the rescue. When the bells he has had installed during the night ring out the next day, the villagers are reconciled to their priest.

Künneke's score was one which fitted the ''Singspiel'' description of the show. The songs were not numerous, although each of the three acts—particularly the second—was endowed with a considerable concerted finale. The supporting characters had much of the music, with the soubrette, Resi (Alice von der Linden), leading several pieces and the housekeeper, Sophie (Otti Dietze), and Der Schmied (Rudolf Hilberg) pairing in two duets. The last act featured an unaccompanied Agnus Dei and Gloria.

The piece was well received through some two months of performances in Berlin and was subsequently mounted at Vienna's Volksoper.

Austria: Volksoper 2 December 1925

DORIAN GRAY Rock opera in 2 acts based on *The Picture of Dorian Gray* by Oscar Wilde by Gunar Braunke and János Acs. Music by Mátyás Várkonyi. Vígszínház, Budapest, 16 June 1990.

The great success in Hungary of the modern style of so-called rock musical, from *Jesus Christ Superstar* to *Evita* and *Les Misérables,* resulted both in the foundation of a theatre in Budapest specifically devoted to ''rock'' musicals, and in a continuing series of local efforts at writing in the same vein. Many of these have followed their models by taking religious or historical (*István, a király*) subjects. One of the most successful of the theatre's original productions, however, followed another central European preoccupation: the musicalizing of the works of Oscar Wilde.

The Picture of Dorian Gray was adapted by German librettist Braunke and put into Hungarian by director Ács for its first production at Budapest's Rock Színház. The score was composed by Várkonyi, director of the Rock Színház and the composer of an earlier show for that theatre, the ancient Roman *Sztárcsinálók* (1981, lib: Tibor Miklós). It was produced in 1990, on the 100th anniversary of the original magazine publication of the novel.

Attila Csengeri played Dorian Gray, the beautiful Englishman who stays young through the 18 years of the tale, whilst his portrait, painted by the adoring Basil Hallward (Sándor Sásvári), ages in his stead. Led on by the high-living Lord Henry Wotton (János Tóth), Gray embarks agelessly on a hedonistic career amid the pleasures and vices Victorian London has to offer, and tragedy follows him. The young actress Sibyl Vane (Andrea Malek) whom he momentarily loves kills herself, and Gray himself murders Hallward rather than have the secret of the portrait revealed. When, however, he turns his knife on the painting the spell breaks: it it the raddled, vice-ridden Dorian Gray who falls dead whilst the picture is once again young.

A score written in the light rock/theatre style popularized by Andrew Lloyd Webber featured two modern tenor voices as Gray (''Ewiger Schönheit,'' ''Dorian Gray'') and Hallward. The main feminine moment of the predominantly male score came in Sibyl's despairing Farewell (Bucsu).

Played initially at Budapest's Vigszínház, *Dorian Gray* was subsequently seen at the rock theatre's own Arizona Színház (1991) and broadcast complete on Hungarian television (22 January 1992) during its initial run. A German version (ad Michael Kunze) was mounted at the Stadttheater, Heilbronn in 1992 for a season of 32 performances with Felix Martin as Gray, and in 1995 the company from the Budapest Rock Színház, with Csengeri, Sásvári and Hal Fowler featured, gave six showcase performances of an altered version of the show (ad Miklós-Gábor Kerényi, ly: Duncan Shiels) at London's Bloomsbury Theatre. In 1996 this revised version was seen in Germany, Switzerland (Theater am Staatgarten 21 September 1996), Austria, Holland (Nederlands Congresgebouwand, Den Haag 28 September 1996) and Luxembourg (Stadttheater, Esch-sur-Alzette 28 March 1998) with Karl M Sibelius and Zsolt Hommonay successively as Gray.

In the manner of the 1990s, a copycat production was mounted at off-Broadway's Judith Anderson Theater 17 September 1996 (Allan Resier/Gary Levinson/Don Price).

Germany: Stadttheater, Heilbronn 26 September 1992; UK: Bloomsbury Theatre, London 3 May 1995; Austria: Stadtsaal, Vöcklabruck 17 March 1998

Recording: compilation of cast recordings (Braunke)

DORIS Comedy opera in 3 acts by B C Stephenson. Music by Alfred Cellier. Lyric Theatre, London, 20 April 1889.

This Stephenson/Cellier successor to the record-breaking *Dorothy* was another musical put together from second-hand pieces. Some of the story and more of the music was taken from Cellier's 1875 *Tower of London,* a semi-success in Manchester but unproduced after that, to make up a costume drama tale which—just six months after the productiion of *The Yeomen of the Guard*—had Doris (Annette Albu from the Carl Rosa Opera), her lover, Martin (Ben Davies), and the Lady Anne Jerningham (Amy Augarde) trying to save Sir Philip Carey (Hayden Coffin) from the Tower and execution. In spite of the fact that the comic depredations of Arthur Williams in *Dorothy* had made a large part of its success, Stephenson refused to take the popular musical-low/topical-comedy route in his new show and Williams' role, as the foolish and bucolic Dinniver, was a less appreciable one, written in the staunchly old-style comic opera flavor the librettist favored.

Cellier's score was at least as good as that for the earlier piece. The tenor ballad ''I've Sought the Brake and Bracken'' became enormously popular, and a recording artist's favorite under the title ''So Fare Thee Well,'' Williams's hilarious post-drinking song ''What Has Become of the Door?'' was a comic opera joy and Coffin scored with a virile ''Honour Bids Me Speed Away.''

With a cast, apart from its leading lady, made up entirely from *Dorothy* veterans (Alice Barnett, Harriet Coveney, John Le Hay and John Furneaux Cook all took supporting roles), Henry J Leslie's production of *Doris* ran 202 performances in London prefatory to a six-month touring career, but the show never threatened to repeat the monumental success of *Dorothy.*

DÖRMANN, Felix [BIEDERMANN, Felix] (b Vienna, 29 May 1870; d Vienna, 26 October 1928). Librettist and lyricist for several internationally successful Viennese Operetten of the early 20th century.

The author of a ballet scenario (w Otto Theime) for Josef Bayer at the age of 22 and later of a number of plays (*Ledige Leute,* etc) before moving into the musical theatre, Dörmann had an enormous success, first up, when he collaborated on the libretto for Oscar Straus's 1907 hit *Ein Walzertraum.* He followed up with two further fine successes in *Bub oder Mädel?* (w Adolf Altmann) for Bruno Granichstaedten and the ''Altwiener Stück'' *Der unsterbliche Lump,* written without a collaborator, for composer Edmund Eysler and, if Count Lubomirski's *Die liebe Unschuld* was a fortnight-long failure at the Raimundtheater, both *Majestät Mimi* at the Carltheater and *Was tut man nicht alles aus Liebe* at Ronacher had good runs at home and won export orders.

During the war, Dörmann supplied a couple of little pieces to the Apollotheater programs, but after the hostilities had ended he did not again find the success of his earlier years in the musical theatre. A version of *The Beggar's Opera* (*Der Liebling von London*) played a month at the Carltheater and inspired the authors of *Die Dreigroschenoper* to their adaptation, *Hoheit Franzl* lasted only three weeks at the same theatre, and *Die verbotene Frau,* with a Vienna run of 62 performances, proved the not-very-good best of the bunch. He also provided the text for a one-act opera *Hagith* (Karol Szymanowski) produced in Warsaw in 1922 and, in his last work before his death, made the famous adventures of the Baron Munchhausen into the text for a musical show mounted, with Erik Wirl starred, in Berlin.

A version of his text for *Der unsterbliche Lump,* musically reset by Benatzky, was made into a film in 1953.

1907 **Ein Walzertraum** (Oscar Straus/W Leopold Jacobson) Carltheater 2 March

1908 **Bub oder Mädel?** (Bruno Granichstaedten/w Adolf Altmann) Johann Strauss-Theater 13 November

1910 **Der unsterbliche Lump** (Edmund Eysler) Wiener Bürgertheater 15 October

1911 **Majestät Mimi** (Granichstaedten/w Roda-Roda) Carltheater 17 February

1912 **Die liebe Unschuld** (''W Lirski'' [Count Lubomirski]) Raimundtheater 27 April

1914 **Was tut man nicht alles aus Liebe** (Leo Ascher) Ronacher 17 December

1915 **Das Finanzgenie** (Béla Zerkowitz/w Hans Kottow) Apollotheater 1 November

1916 **Arizonda** (Jean Gilbert) Apollotheater 1 February

1918 **Die Lilli vom Chor** (*Korista lány*) German version (Bundestheater)

1918 **Eriwan** (Oskar Nedbal) Wiener Komödienhaus 29 November

1919 **Die galante Markgräfin** revised version of *Das Tal der Liebe* (Straus/Rudolf Lothar) Volksoper 24 January

1920 **Zwölf Uhr Nachts** (Ascher/w Kottow) Raimundtheater 12 November

1924 **Der Liebling von London** (arr Hans Ewald Heller) Carltheater 19 April

1924 **Hoheit Franzl** (Ernst Steffan) Carltheater 7 November

1926 **Die verbotene Frau** (Max Wallner/w Karl Gerold) Carltheater 5 March

1927 **Munchhausens letzte Liebe** (Steffan/w Isenbach) Theater des Westens, Berlin 23 December

DOROTHY Comedy opera in 3 acts by B C Stephenson. Music by Alfred Cellier. Gaiety Theatre, London, 25 September 1886.

Following the indifferent reception of the Alfred Cellier/H B Farnie musical *Nell Gwynne* at Manchester in 1876, Farnie withdrew his libretto and he subsequently had it reset by Planquette into a more widely played *Nell Gwynne.* Cellier was handed back his music and he, too, decided to put it to reuse. Charlie Stephenson, the librettist for his early and successful *Charity Begins at Home,* was set to write a new libretto into which the *Nell Gwynne* music might be fitted, and the resultant work was entitled *Dorothy,* that being the name of the heroine of the piece before, disguised in country clothes, she becomes Dorcas and, in time-honored fashion, charms the naughty cousin who is refusing to marry her.

Geoffrey Wilder (Redfern Hollins) has been spreading his wild oats a little too liberally, and when he asks his uncle, Squire Bantam (John Furneaux Cook), to bail him out, the price of the rescue is that he come and live quietly in the country and marry his cousin, Dorothy. On their way to Chantecleer Hall, Geoffrey and his friend Harry Sherwood (Hayden Coffin) stop off at an inn, and there they become bewitched by two local damsels, to such an extent that Geoffrey's doubts about wedding the probably very plain Dorothy Bantam are solidified into a refusal. Of course, the two girls are Dorothy (Marion Hood) and her friend Lydia (Florence Dysart) out having a little fun as pretend milkmaids, and, back in their fine gowns and powdered wigs, the girls take the opportunity, that night, to win each other's rings from their gallants of the afternoon. By staging a fake robbery, the boys win enough money from the grateful Squire to pay off the comic bailiff, Lurcher (Arthur Williams), who has pursued them from town, but their getaway—in search of ''Dorcas'' and ''Abigail''—is held up by a duel, a betrayal and more disguises until it is time for a happy final curtain.

In a pretty comic opera score, Wilder sang in praise of Dorcas (''With Such a Dainty Dame''), the girls warned a little country fiancée not to get tied up to a representative of the species, man (''Be Wise in Time''), and Lurcher described himself in comical couplets (''I Am the Sheriff's Faithful Man'') alongside some well-written ensembles and finales.

The authors had difficulty finding a producer for their show and, although it was at first announced to be produced by and with Kate Santley, it was finally staged at the Gaiety by George Edwardes, in a gap in the schedule between his newly successful burlesques and the theatre's annual French play season. Although the music was appreciated by the critics, the show was indifferently received, with Stephenson's rather deliberately old-fashioned text, with its improbable comic opera disguises and incongruities, coming heavily under fire. Edwardes ordered alterations. Cuts were made to both book and music, Arthur Williams was given carte blanche to jolly up his role in an up-to-date way that made Stephenson blench, and a new song, fabricated from an old Cellier melody and some swiftly written lyrics, was introduced for the richly baritonic Coffin who, improbably, had no solo. The rewrites helped enormously. The increased comedy—notably Lurcher's amorous antics with the so-

Plate 105a. **Dorothy.** *Two country wenches (Constance Drever, Louie Pounds) attract two young blades (John Bardesley, Hayden Coffin) under the eye of innkeeper John Tuppitt (Fred Vigay).*

ciety widow, Mrs Privett (Harriet Coveney)—helped the book and the new song, "Queen of My Heart," quite simply became the biggest song hit the West End had ever known. But Edwardes had more faith in his burlesque company than in the lasting power of this "comedy opera" and, when the burlesque team was ready to return to the Gaiety, he decided to close *Dorothy.*

However, the theatre's accountant, Henry Leslie, purchased the production from the Gaiety company, and he transferred the show to the Prince of Wales Theatre. He replaced the two original stars, bringing in the rising young Marie Tempest and the Carl Rosa Opera's sweetly tenor Ben Davies to play Dorothy and Geoffrey. Miss Tempest's arch and comic soubrette performance—replacing the coolly lovely interpretation of Miss Hood—changed the whole temper of the show and *Dorothy* took off at the box office. By the time it closed, after 931 performances, it had broken every London long-run record, outstripping all the Gilbert and Sullivan shows and even *Les Cloches de Corneville,* and Leslie had built Shaftesbury Avenue's Lyric Theatre on the profits.

The show toured for decades in Britain, in four or five separate and simultaneous companies during the earlier years, and for many years with Lucy Carr-Shaw, sister of George Bernard, in the role of Dorothy. Miss Carr-Shaw was just one of several performers who made almost a whole career out of playing *Dorothy* around the provincial towns of England, Scotland, Ireland and Wales in the later years of the 19th century. The piece was revived in London in 1892 (Trafalgar Square Theatre 26 November) with Miss Dysart in her original role alongside Decima Moore (Dorothy), Joseph Tapley (Geoffrey), Leonard Russell (Harry) and William Elton (Lurcher), and again in 1908 (New Theatre, then Waldorf Theatre 21 December) with Coffin and Williams from the original cast alongside Constance Drever (Dorothy), Louie Pounds (Lydia) and John Bardesley (Geoffrey). Both revivals were, however, quick failures (15 performances and 49 performances respectively).

The show was produced on Broadway by J C Duff, with a fine cast headed by Lillian Russell (Dorothy) and Harry Paulton (Lurcher), but it proved to have limited appeal for New York and was played for just 48 performances. However, when Duff's production moved on to Boston's Hollis Theater (30 January 1888) the reaction was just the opposite, and *Dorothy* soon established itself as a repertoire item in summer seasons and comic opera repertoires around America. W T Carleton's superior

Plate 105b. *But how should the flirty boys recognize "Abigail" and "Dorcas," bewigged and powdered, as the ladies of Chantecleer Hall?*

touring company also included the show in its repertoire and, played alongside *The Mikado* and *Erminie,* his version of *Dorothy* proved a well-liked item in San Francisco and cities beyond. In 1895 (August 15) New York City got a second glimpse of the show when a production from Lake George, with Dorothy Morton in the title role, visited the Standard Theater.

In Australia, too, the show had an indifferent start as first mounted by Williamson, Garner and Musgrove with Savoy Theatre prima donna Leonora Braham as Dorothy, supported by a top-rank London cast—W H Woodfield (Geoffrey), Fred Federici (Harry), William Elton (Lurcher), Alice Barnett (Mrs Privett), former star tenor Albert Brennir (Bantam)—and local Aggie Kelton as Lydia. However, the Williamson company, never one to waste costumes and scenery, brought the show back in 1888, 1889 and 1892, with Nellie Stewart and then the globe-trotting American soubrette, Marie Halton, taking on the title role and, as in London, the show grew into a favorite, returning regularly over a period of 20 years for further runs. *Dorothy* also surfaced in South Africa, Canada, on the Oriental circuits and almost everywhere else where English-language theatre was played, and it even made its way to Hungary (ad Bertalan Gunszt, Antal Radó) where what seems to have been its only foreign-language version was played at the Budapest Népszínház in 1888.

Although *Dorothy* was never advertised as "based on" any other work, rival dramatist E L Blanchard went into print soon after the show's premiere accusing Stephenson of having taken his text from the 1715 comedy *Country Lasses, or The Custom of the Manor* by Charles Johnson. He also traced the lineage of that play back through works by Aphra Behn (*The City Heiress*), Fletcher (*The Custom of the Country*) and Middelton (*A Mad World, My Masters*), and down through pieces by Kenrick (*The Lady of the Manor*), and Kemble (*The Country Lasses, The Farm Houses*). And all that well before *Dorothy* became a hit. When it did, the fruits of Blanchard's super-long memory were quite forgotten.

Australia: Princess Theatre, Melbourne 20 August 1887; USA: Standard Theater 5 November 1887; Hungary: Népszínház *Dorottya* 9 May 1888

DORSCH, Käthe (b Nuremberg, 29 December 1890; d Vienna, 25 December 1957). Singing actress who became a favourite star in the German musical theatre before going on to a substantial career on the straight stage.

Käthe Dorsch began her career as a teenage chorus singer in her native Nuremberg, and spent several years in the ensembles at the Stadttheater in Mainz and at Rotterdam before making her first appearances in Berlin under the management of Max Monti. In 1913 she was seen as the Princess in the premiere of Jessel's *Die beiden Husaren* at the Theater des Westens and in 1916 she created the role of Marie in Leo Ascher's *Der Soldat von Marie* for Jean Kren, and she went on to star in such pieces as Walter Bromme's *Die Dame im Frack* (1919), *Das süsse Mädel,* as Suppé's *Boccaccio,* Winterberg's *Die Dame vom Zirkus* (1919) and in Straus's *Eine Ballnacht* (1919, Riki), before making her first substantial attempts at non-musical theatre. The experiment proved a success, and thereafter she mixed the musical and non-musical theatres, scoring her most important musical successes as the original star (opposite the Goethe of Richard Tauber) of Lehár's *Friederike* ("although not gifted as a singer [she] acts and sings with such intense reality [and] the fragrance of naïveté"), as Boulotte to the *Blaubart* of Leo Slezak in the Metropoltheater's 1929 production of Offenbach's piece, as the heroine of Oscar Straus's *Mariette* and that of the rewritten version of Künneke's *Liselott* (1932).

In later years she wholly abandoned the musical stage for the straight theatre in Germany and, from 1938, in Vienna, becoming a highly appreciable leading lady in both the classic and modern repertoire, and ending her career in the company at the Vienna Burgtheater where she remained up to her death. She also appeared in a number of German-language films, both straight and musical, pairing on occasion, as on the stage, with leading men with the strongest of voices (*Die Landwirtin vom Rhein* w Hans-Heinz Bollmann, etc).

Biographies: Weltmann, L: *Käthe Dorsch* (1929), Ihiering, H: *Käthe Dorsch* (Zinnen Verlag, Munich, 1944)

DOSTAL, Nico[laus Josef Michaël] (b Korneuberg, 27 November 1895; d Vienna, 27 October 1981).

Nico Dostal was the nephew of Hermann Dostal (1874–1930), a composer who had had some considerable sucess with Operette scores to works such as *Nimm mich mit!,* produced at the Theater an der Wien in 1919, *Das geborgte Schloss* (Leipzig 15 May 1911), *Urschula* (Apollotheater 1 September 1916, and in Hungary as *Milliomos Kati* 30 June 1917) and the little *Eine göttliche Nacht* (Hölle 1 March 1910, *Isteni éj* in Hungary) and *Der fliegende Rittmeister* (Apollotheater 5 October 1912). This last was seen on the American variety stage as *The Knight of the Air* (Palace, Chicago, September 1913).

The young Dostal had his first Mass played at the Linzer Dom at the age of 18, before going on to follow studies in both law and music. After serving in the army for four years, he returned to begin a career in the musical theatre, first at the Innsbruck Stadttheater and then in conducting posts at St Pölten near Vienna, in Roumania and at Salzburg. In 1924 he moved to Berlin, where he began by arranging and orchestrating other people's Operetten for the stage, while at the same time turning out songs for theatre and film, and ended by composing his own first musical comedy score. The colorful movies-and-politics-in-South-American-places piece, *Clivia,* was produced at Berlin's Theater am Nollendorfplatz, where he had been a conductor since 1927, in 1933. It had a fine success and Dostal followed up with another successful piece in *Die Vielgeliebte* (1935). Like *Clivia, Die Vielgeliebte* starred the Viennese prima donna Lillie Claus, later to become the second Frau Dostal.

Of the regular series of mostly successful musicals which followed over the next seven years the most appreciated were *Monika* (1937), *Die ungarische Hochzeit* (1939) and *Manina* (1942). At the same time, Dostal continued to write for the cinema where his scores included a revision of the one for *Monika* under the title *Heimatland.* In 1943 he left Berlin for the less bomb-prone Austria and Bad Aussee and his theatre activities all but ceased. In 1947 *Manina* was staged at Vienna's Raimundtheater and in 1949 his first new work for seven years, a little musical comedy called *Süsse kleine Freundin,* was staged in Wuppertal.

The following year, *Zirkusblut,* written with his old *Monika* partner, Hermecke, and *Der Kurier der Königin,* staged almost simultaneously at Leipzig and Hamburg respectively, set things in motion again and over the next dozen years Dostal produced, alongside revue and film music (this latter including a musical reworking of Strauss's *Eine Nacht in Venedig*), scores for a further five musicals of which *Doktor Eisenbart* (1952) was the most successful.

In 1955 his *Liebesbriefe* was given its first performance at the Vienna Raimundtheater, the only one of his works to have been premiered in Austria, and, living into his late eighties, he was around long enough to see his *Die ungarische Hochzeit* brought to the stage of the Volksoper in 1981 in a sign of recognition of his position as the last surviving representative of the tradition of German-language operetta.

1933 **Clivia** (Karl Amberg, "F Maregg") Theater am Nollendorfplatz 23 December

1935 **Die Vielgeliebte** (Maregg, Rudolf Köller) Schillertheater 5 March

1936 **Prinzessin Nofretete** (Maregg, Köller) Opernhaus, Cologne 12 September

1937 **Extrablätter** (Gustav Quedtenfeld) Staatstheater, Bremen 17 February; Grosses Schauspielhaus, Berlin 30 April

1937 **Monika** (Hermann Hermecke) Staatstheater, Stuttgart 3 October

1939 **Die ungarische Hochzeit** (Hermecke) Staatstheater, Stuttgart 4 February
1940 **Die Flucht ins Glück** (Hermecke) Staatstheater, Stuttgart 22 December
1942 **Die grosse Tänzerin** (Hans Schachner) Opernhaus, Chemnitz 15 February
1942 **Eva im Abendkleid** (Fritz Maria Gribitz) Opernhaus, Chemnitz 21 November
1942 **Manina** (Hans Adler/Alexander Lix) Admiralspalast 28 November
1949 **Süsse kleine Freundin** (Gribitz) Kammerspiele, Wuppertal 31 December
1950 **Der Kurier der Königin** (Max Wallner, Kurt Feltz) Theater am Besenbinderhof, Hamburg 2 March
1950 **Zirkusblut** (Hermecke) Volksbühne, Leipzig 3 March
1952 **Doktor Eisenbart** (Hermecke) Opernhaus, Nuremberg 29 March
1954 **Der dritte Wunsch** (Hans Adler) Opernhaus, Nuremberg 20 February
1955 **Liebesbriefe** (Hubert Marischka, Rudolf Österreicher) Raimundtheater, Vienna 23 November
1961 **So macht man Karriere** (Peter Herz, Willy Fuchs) Opernhaus, Nuremberg 29 April
1963 **Rhapsodie der Liebe** (Paul Knepler) Städtische Bühnen, Nuremberg 9 November

Autobiography: *Ans Ende deiner Traume kommst du nie* (Pinguin Verlag, Innsbruck, 1982)

LA DOT DE BRIGITTE Operetta in 3 acts by Paul Ferrier and Antony Mars. Music by Gaston Serpette and Victor Roger. Théâtre des Bouffes-Parisiens, 6 May 1895.

The ''dowry of Brigitte'' (Juliette Simon-Girard) is in fact non-existent, which is why Lieutenant Brétigny (Théry) is, by the rules of the French services, not supposed to marry her. Another impediment is the fact that the girl's Auvergnat schoolmaster father (Barral) is opposed to soldiers on principle. So Brétigny courts and weds Brigitte as an often-away-from-home commercial traveler. But then his regiment is ordered to the Auvergne, the lieutenant's superior officer (Félix Huguenet) makes a play for Brigitte and the farcical complications begin to wind up. There is, of course, a happy ending.

''An abundance of military airs and several very pretty songs'' sung by a fine cast including Charles Lamy (Mulot), Alice Bonheur (Nicole) and Germaine Gallois as the Colonel's wife decorated the farce, and *La Dot de Brigitte* proved a fine success through 73 nights at the Bouffes-Parisiens.

La Dot de Brigitte was played in Vienna as *Frau Lieutenant* (ad Léon, Waldberg 14 performances) with Julius Sachs (Marquis), Elsa Felsen (Brigitte) and Karl Pfann (Brétigny), in Germany under the same title (ad Hermann Hirschel) and in Hungary as *Brigitta* (ad Emil Makai, 22 performances).

Hungary: Népszínház *Brigitta* 19 October 1895; Germany: Thalia-Theater *Frau Lieutenant* 12 January 1898; Austria: Theater in der Josefstadt *Frau Lieutenant* 13 January 1900

DOUWES, Pia (b Amsterdam, 5 August 1964). Striking singing-dancing star of the European musical theatre of the turn-of-this-century years.

Pia Douwes studied in Austria, Germany and Britain and made an early appearance on the musical stage as Chrystal in the Viennese *Little Shop of Horrors* (1986), before being cast in the original Dutch production of *Cats* (1987). During the course of the show's run she appeared in several different roles (Spikkelpikkelmies, Antimakassa, Gillebeen, Grisabella) before going on to play in the show's Viennese production, and on its tour through Europe (Gumbie Cat, Jellylorum/Griddlebone, Grizabella). She subsequently toured as Maria in *West Side Story* (1990), introduced the role of Fantine in the Dutch version of *Les Misérables* (1991) and in 1992 created the role of Elisabeth, empress of Austria, in the Viennese hit musical *Elisabeth* at the Theater an der Wien (1992, ''Ich gehör nur mir'').

Mixing plays (*Jane Eyre, Savannah Bay,* etc) and musicals thereafter, she was seen in Prague, in Austria in *West Side Story* (1994, Maria) and in the Raimundtheater production of *Grease* (1994, Rizzo), in Germany in *Cabaret* (1995, 1996, Sally Bowles) and *The Rocky Horror Show* (1997, Janet) and in Holland in *Evita* (1995, Evita), the latest revival of *Chicago* (1999, Velma) and in the Dutch production of her most celebrated show, *Elisabeth* (1999).

She has also appeared in revue (*It Takes Two, [Still] In Love with the Musical,* etc), on musical television (duetting ''All I Ask of You'' w José Carreras, etc) and supplied the voice for the Dutch version of Disney's *Pocohantas* (1995).

LES DOUZE FEMMES DE JAPHET, Vaudeville-opérette in 3 acts by Antony Mars and Maurice Desvallières. Music by Victor Roger. Théâtre de la Renaissance, Paris, 16 December 1890.

Easily the best of the many musical plays written in the decades surrounding the turn of the century which used the Mormon way of life as the basis for their comedy, *Les Douze Femmes de Japhet* was a vaudevillesque piece which had now the crazy air of a *Ba-ta-clan,* now the farcical air of a *Madame Sherry* or at times the high comedy of *La Vie parisienne* about it.

Japhet Paterson (Regnard) of Salt Lake City (he of the 12 wives) is not really a Paterson. He is the once footloose Beaujolais from Paris, who married the American widow Paterson (Irma Aubrys) and her late husband's thriving preserves factory, and profited by the local customs to then wed 10 other wives, chosen by the local pastor, plus a little opérette singer from home called Arabella (Alice Berthier). However, Beaujolais's rich uncle, the commissaire de police Baliveau (Bellot), having been cuckolded late in life by a young wife, has forbidden his nephew to wed on the pain of disinheritance. So each year Beaujolais goes to Paris, for a fortnight's rest from his heavy conjugal duties, and is a dutiful celibate in front of his uncle, whose chief delight in life is now uncovering other folks' marital infidelities. It is Arabella, however, who is the loose stone in this comfortable edifice. She turns out to have been the miscreant wife not only of Baliveau, but also of a singer-turned-marital agent called Cassoulet de Casabianca (Victorin) who now enjoys making mismatches which will end in disaster. Worse, she was also almost the bride of Beaujolais's old friend des Toupettes (Gildès). It is des Toupettes who, hoping to get her back, pretends to the women that Japhet has gone to Paris to visit an old girlfriend, and all the wives indignantly head after him on the next steamer. After two acts of intricately ingenious comical situations, Japhet, like W S Gilbert's Bunthorne, is left the only single man at the final curtain.

The musical part of the show was light, including, alongside several ensembles for the wives, a set of finales, a rondeau for Arabella (''Je viens d'ach'ter *la Vie parisienne*''), some regretful couplets for the aged Deborah Paterson (''Jadis je vous trouvais plus tendre''), and a further song for Arabella in the third act (''Là, vrai! Ce n'est pas amusant'') which proved the musical highlight of the evening.

The Théâtre de la Renaissance production of *Les Douze Femmes de Japhet* played an initial season of 41 performances before the show went on to be seen in Germany, in a version adapted by Julius Freund with new music by Victor Holländer, in Vienna (ad Otto Eisenschitz), and in Budapest (ad Emil Makai) where, after a first run of 26 performances in 1898, it was revived for a second run in 1901 (Népszínház 14 September). Paris got a second helping of the show in 1897 when it was revived at the El Dorado with Regnard and Bellot repeating their original roles, Maurice Lamy as des Toupettes and Victorine Augier as Deborah.

Austria: Theater in der Josefstadt *Japhet und seine zwölf Frauen* 13 October 1897; Hungary: Népszínház *Jafet 12 felesege* 27 May 1898; Germany: Metropoltheater *Die Zwölf Frauen des Japhet* 29 November 1902

LE DRAGON DE LA REINE Opérette in 3 acts by Pierre Decourcelle and Frantz Beauvallet. Music by Leopold Wenzel. Théâtre de l'Alhambra, Brussels, 25 March 1888.

Wenzel's most widely seen piece, *Le Dragon de la reine* was premiered in Belgium before winning productions first in Paris and then throughout Europe.

Plate 106. **Pia Douwes** *as Velma in the Dutch production of* Chicago.

A young stonemason called Sedaine has attracted the attentions of a lofty lady, the Comtesse de la Belle-Ardoise, but—while others pursue this rich widow avidly—the boy has eyes only for his village lassie. During the course of the evening's action, he goes from being a manual laborer to a soldier—in which guise he goes through a series of disguises and all sorts of jiggery-pokery with a lost despatch—and ends up at one stage as a member of a troupe of strolling players. At the end of the evening, of course, he gets his sweetheart whilst the amorous Countess is paired off with his superior (elderly) officer.

Debruyère mounted *Le Dragon de la reine* at the Paris Gaîté just two months after its Brussels opening, with Juliette Simon-Girard starred in the rôle à tiroirs of Sedaine, which she had created in Belgium, and equipped with the best of the show's music (''Colin et Colinette,'' drinking song) as well as the bulk of its opportunities. Marie Gélabert (Rose), Simon-Max (Pamphile), Jane Evans (the Countess) and Berthelier (Cornensac) topped the rest of the cast. It was the great Berthelier's last role, for he died during the 36-performance run.

In spite of this discouraging record, the piece was promptly picked up to be played in Germany (ad Karl Alexander Raida), and in Britain (ad B C Stephenson, Augustus Harris, lyrics by Harry Nicholls, Harry Greenbank and Adrian Ross, additional and alternative music by John Crook). It was put on the British road by Augustus Harris as ''a burlesque opera'' with American singer Tillie Wadman starred as Joe Adams alongside John Shine (Captain de Bang) and Nicholls (Sir Hercules Pettifer) and provoked one critic to comment that he thought there must be ''very little of the original left.'' It did not make town. However, it did make it, some time later, to Budapest's main musical house (ad Lajos Evva, Viktor Rákosi) where it was given 12 performances in the repertoire. In the end, only the Belgians really liked it, but everyone else had had their chance.

France: Théâtre de la Gaîté 31 May 1888; Germany: Viktoriatheater *Die Dragoner der Königin* 7 October 1888; UK: Tyne Theatre, Newcastle *The Young Recruit* 14 March 1892; Hungary: Népszínház *A királyné dragonyosa* 4 May 1895

LES DRAGONS DE VILLARS Opéra-comique in 3 acts by Lockroy [Joseph Simon] and Eugène Cormon. Music by Aimé Maillart. Théâtre Lyrique, Paris, 19 September 1856.

Les Dragons de Villars was one of the few opéras-comiques of the pre-opéra-bouffe era which held its own in the repertoires of the world's musical theatre companies once the rage for the works of Offenbach and Hervé and their opéra-bouffe successors had struck.

A unit of dragoons arrives in a little Provençal mountain village in search of renegade Protestants. The goat girl, Rose Friquet (Juliette Borghèse), sets the soldiers loose in the best wine cellar in the village, and helps the persecuted folk to attempt escape by an unfamiliar mountain path. In the meanwhile, the Sergeant Belamy (Grillon) makes free with Georgette (Caroline Girard), the not unwilling wife of the farmer Thibault (Girardot), who is only recalled to connubial duty by the ringing of the bell of the hermitage which, legend says, peals when a married woman is about to fall from grace. In spite of Thibault's rumor-mongering and Belamy's threats, Rose succeeds in her *Sound of Music*-type mission and as a bonus wins the pretty farm boy Sylvain (Scott).

Maillart's attractive, grateful music gave the principals every opportunity. Rose made her entrance with the farmer's mules she has rescued in the mountains (''Maître Thibault, vos mules sont charmantes''), and followed up with a Ronde Militaire, a disarming duo with her farm lad (''Moi! Jolie?'') and an explosion of joy at the thought of being loved (''Il m'aime! Espoir charmant''), whilst Georgette featured a Chanson Provençale and the legend of the hermits' bells with its ''din, din, din, din'' refrain. Sylvain begged Rose's help (''Ne parle pas, Rose, je t'en supplie'') and opened the second act with a pretty Vilanelle, whilst Belamy led the Dragoons in a song in praise of their horses and courted Georgette musically, alongside a series of ensemble pieces which made up a particularly strong score.

A grand success at the Théâtre Lyrique, the piece was quickly produced in other French-language venues before going on to establish itself at the Opéra-Comique (6 June 1868) where Galli-Marié played Rose in the first of the 377 performances played there over the next 50 years. A German version by Ernst was mounted in Berlin and Vienna, and revived frequently thereafter, under the title of *Das Glöckchen des Eremiten* (the Hermit's bell), and it was that version that was first heard in America in 1868 introduced by Hedwig L'Arronge-Sury (Rose), Frln Haffner (Georgette), Wilhelm Formes (Belamy) and Theodore Habelmann (Sylvain). Shortly after, the libretto was ripped off by Charles Gayler for a drama, *The Mountain Bell,* produced at Brooklyn's Park Theatre, and in 1869 New York was given the piece in French by Adolph Birgefeld's company, with Irma Marié as Rose, in a repertoire otherwise mainly opéra-bouffe. The piece was regularly played around America thereafter in Marie Aimée's seasons, but it was not until 1878 that an English version was seen on Broadway, played by the C D Hess Company. The show was done by Emilie Melville's company under the title *Friquet* (1880), and later under the title *Fadette* (Binghampton, NY 12 October 1892).

Selina Dolaro introduced *The Dragoons* (ad Henry Hersee) in London in 1879, with herself as Rose Friquet to the Belamy of Frank Celli, the Thibaut of Fred Leslie and the Georgette of Alma Stanley, but it, like the American version, had apparently been preceded by an earlier English-language version, *The Hermit's Bell* (ad uncredited), first played in Melbourne in 1877 and later in Sydney (13 June 1881 Gaiety Theatre), Australia, by the Simonsen company. The English versions of the show did not have quite the same success that the long-lasting French and German ones did, but the show was translated into a bevy of other tongues, including a Hungarian version by Lajos Evva and Jenő Rákosi, which was played at the Népszínház as late as 1881 with Aranka Hegyi starred as Rose Friquet.

Germany: Friedrich-Wilhelmstädtisches Theater *Das Glöckchen des Eremiten* 29 November 1860; Austria: Hofoperntheater 14 September 1861; USA: Stadttheater (Ger) 22 April 1868, Fifth Avenue Theater (Fr) 10 May 1869, Union Square Theater (Eng) 6 June 1878; UK: Gaiety Theatre (Fr) 24 June 1875, Folly Theatre *The Dragoons* 14 April 1879; Australia: St George's Hall, Melbourne *The Hermit's Bell* 9 June 1877; Hungary: Népszínház *A Dragonyosok (A remete csengetyüje)* 14 January 1881

Recording: complete (Decca)

DRAKE, Alfred [CAPURRO, Alfredo] (b New York, 7 October 1914; d New York, 25 July 1992). Compelling, rich-voiced actor and baritone vocalist who introduced several major Broadway lead roles in the 1940s and 1950s.

Drake made his earliest stage appearances as a chorus singer, covered the role of Leopold in *White Horse Inn,* played supporting roles in *Babes in Arms* (1937, Marshall Blackstone) and the Victorian pasticcio *The Two Bouquets* (1938, Albert Porter), and took part in several revues, including *Two for the Show* in which he introduced ''How High the Moon,'' before his combination of dark good looks and a warm, easy baritone won him his first lead role as Curly in the original production of *Oklahoma!* (''The Surrey with the Fringe on Top,'' ''Oh What a Beautiful Mornin',' ' ''People Will Say We're in Love''). He played this role for more than a year before moving on to other musical leads in *Sing Out Sweet Land* (1944, Barnaby Goodchild), the remake of *The Beggar's Opera* as *The Beggar's Holiday* (1946, Macheath) and a revival of *The Cradle Will Rock* (1947, Larry Foreman), and a single musical film role, top-billed with Janet Blair, in *Tars and Spars* (1946).

His second major musical creation came in 1948, when he appeared as Fred Graham/Petruchio in Cole Porter's *Kiss Me, Kate,* introducing a further clutch of soon-to-be-standard songs—''So in Love,'' ''Wunderbar,'' ''I've Come to Wive it Wealthily in Padua''—and his third in 1953 with his memorable playing of the wily baritonic beggar, Hajj, in Wright and Forrest's musical version of *Kismet* (''The Olive Tree,'' ''Gesticulate,'' ''And This is My Beloved''), a role which he repeated in the show's London production. In between he succeeded Yul Brynner in the role of the King in *The King and I,* wrote and directed the short-lived Goldoni musical *The Liar,* and directed the charming but unsuccessful *Courtin' Time* (1951).

In his visits to the musical stage during a subsequent career spent largely in straight theatre and as a director, he did not again find as effective vehicles as his three major hits, in spite of appearing as the hero of a Wright and Forrest musical remake of *Kean* (1961), and in the role of Honoré (otherwise Maurice Chevalier) in a stage version of *Gigi* (1973). Other short-lived assignments included *Zenda* (1963, Richard Rassendyl/King Rudolf V), *After You, Mr Hyde* (1968) and *Gambler's Paradise* (1975).

He appeared on television in *The Adventures of Marco Polo* (1956, Marco Polo), *Naughty Marietta* (1955, Dick Warrington), *The Yeomen of the Guard* (Jack Point) and *Kiss Me, Kate* (1958) and recorded selections from a number of classic musical comedies.

As a writer, he also provided the English surtitles for the Broadway performances of the Italian musical *Rugantino* (1964), and as a director mounted the American production of *Lock Up Your Daughters* (1960).

Plate 107. **Dranem.** *The star comic of two decades of Paris musicals.*

1950 **The Liar** (John Mundy/w Edward Eager) Broadhurst Theater 18 May

DRANEM [MÉNARD, Armand] (b Paris, 23 May 1869; d Paris, 13 October 1935). Star of the French music hall who transferred to the musical theatre and there became one of the biggest comic stars of his generation.

After spending his earliest working years in a jewelry workshop, Dranem began his performing career at the age of 25 as a comic singer in the cafés-concerts, appearing at the Concert du Champ-de-Mars in 1894, at the Concert de l'Époque, the Concert Parisien (1895), the Divan Japonais (1896), the Alcazar and, from September 1899, at the Eldorado where he became, in the early years of the 20th century, one of the field's most appreciated stars in revues, playlets and comic songs (''Les p'tits pois,'' ''L'Enfant du cordonnier,'' ''Aglaë,'' ''Tu sens le menthe,'' ''La Boîte à clous,'' ''Avec mon ocarina,'' ''Chasseurs, sachez chassez,'' ''Le Beau Môme,'' ''Allumeur-Marche,'' etc).

In 1912 he made an unaccustomed appearance in the theatre when Antoine cast him in Molière's *Le Medecin malgré lui* in a matinée at the Odéon and he later guested in the small role of Buteau in the gala performance of *La Fille de Madame Angot* at the Opéra-Comique, but, from the early 1920s, he began to appear regularly in musical comedy. Among his early appearances were the title role of the Paris production of *Flup..!* (1920) and leading parts in *Pétoche* at the Concert Mayol, a revival of *Mam'zelle Nitouche* (Célestin) and *Les 28 Jours de Clairette* at the Trianon-Lyrique (1921). He returned to the Mayol to play in *L'Hôtel des deux amours* then made such an enormous success, opposite Maurice Chevalier, in the comical role of the guardian angel who brings a dead man back to earth to settle his affairs in Yvain's *Là-haut* (1923, Frisotin), that Chevalier, the top-billed star of the show, ended by walking petulantly out of his role.

Over the next 12 years, through his fifties and sixties and right up to his death, Dranem doubled a continuing flow of hit songs with an almost constant presence on the Parisian musical stage, providing the comic backbone to one new musical after another as he made starring appearances in *La Dame en décolleté* (1923, Girodo, "Les Bains de mer," "Je n'ai pas pu," "Si l'on refléchissait"), *En chemyse* (1924, Lahirette, "La Girl et le homard," "Lahirette!"), *Troublez-moi!* (1924, Picotte, "J'ai eu tort de me mettre en toréador," "Cordon, s'il vous plaît," "Le Petit revenez-y"), *P.L.M.* (1925, Le Controleur, "Mon coeur est un compartiment," "On s'y fait," "Trop nerveux," "Paris-Lyon-Mediterranée"), *Trois jeunes filles . . . nues!* (1925, Hégésippe, "Est-ce que je te demande?"), as Mephistophélès in *Le Diable à Paris* (1926), in the title role of *Louis XIV* (1929), in *Six filles à marier* (1930, "Un million," Chanson sinueuse, "T'as bonne mine"), *Bégonia* (1930, "Chanson de petits bateaux," "L'Argent," "L'Oeil en vrille"), *Encore cinquante centimes* (1931, Hercule Boulot, "Avec les femmes," "Je reviendrai demain matin," "Essayez donc"), *Un soir de reveillon* (1932, Honoré, "Quand on perd la tête"), the Scottish spectacular *Deux sous de fleurs* (1933, Archibald), *Les Soeurs Hortensia* (1934) and *Tonton* (1935), clipping out a regular series of popular songs from their scores and contributing largely, with his adored, individual comicalities, to the successs of those which succeeded.

He also appeared occasionally in the classic repertoire, with marked success, playing the role of Antonio, the corrupted treasurer, in a major revival of *Les Brigands* at the Opéra-Comique, Frimousse in *Le Petit Duc* at the Châtelet, and Valentin in *Le Petit Faust* at the Porte-Saint-Martin.

He appeared in a number of musical films including the cinematic versions of *Un soir de réveillon* (1933, Honoré), *Ciboulette* (1935) and *La Mascotte* (1935).

DREAMGIRLS Musical in 2 acts by Tom Eyen. Music by Henry Krieger. Imperial Theater, New York, 20 December 1981.

A gotta-make-it-good-in-showbiz tale which seemed, to knowing commentators, to be based on the careers of the girls who made up the popular 1960s and early 1970s singing group, the Supremes. The *Dreamgirls* group was called the Dreams, and they, too, were operational in the decade 1962–72. Plump and powerful Effie White (Jennifer Holliday), glamorous Deena Jones (Sheryl Lee Ralph) and svelte Lorrell Robinson (Loretta Devine) are the three members of the "Dreamettes" who work their way from Chicago and a talent contest win onto the books of the hustling agent Curtis Taylor jr (Ben Harney), and a place as a support act to the singer James Thunder Early (Cleavant Derricks). On their way up, Curtis shifts his affections from Effie to Deena, and shifts Deena into the lead vocal spot of the group. Then underattractive Effie is right out, replaced by a third slim and glamorous girl (Deborah Burrell). The newly constituted group makes it to the top and, when Curtis sees Effie making a comeback as a solo act, he tries to stymie her by covering her successful single with a version by the Dreams. He fails, she conquers, and she is on her way to stardom as the Dreams disband to allow each of the other girls to go on to the putative next stage of their careers.

The showpiece number of a score, which mostly recreated the sounds of the popular music of the period in which it was set, was the first-act curtain number for Effie, "And I'm Telling You I'm Not Going," a piece of ripping, howling agony in which the rejected girl fought against the whole world in a wide-ranging piece of music which wrought great demands on the pop-soul voice of its performer. A number of the other pieces in the show were presented as pop songs, the repertoire of the characters in the show, notably the successful "One Night Only" (Effie's comeback song) and the bouncy hymn to the "Cadillac Car."

Directed and co-choreographed by co-producer Michael Bennett in spectacular high-tech style, *Dreamgirls* had an outstanding 1,522-performance run on Broadway, but its only sightings in main centers outside America have been through performances given by American touring companies which have played several European cities—though, in spite of announcements, not London. One of these companies took the show back to Broadway for a season (28 June 1987, 168 performances) with Lillias White featured in the lead role, but several subsequent attempts at bringing the show back to Broadway—both in a newly staged version, and in a reproduction of Bennett's original staging have run out of steam before reaching New York.

France: Palais des Congrès (Eng) 5 May 1987; Germany: Theater des Westens (Eng) 14 February 1998

Recording: original cast (Geffen)

Plate 108. **Dreamgirls**

DREI ALTE SCHACHTELN, oder Was nützt denn dem Mädchen die Liebe Operette in a Vorspiel and 3 acts by Hermann Haller. Lyrics by Rideamus. Music by Walter Kollo. Theater am Nollendorfplatz, Berlin, 6 October 1917.

The "three old maids" of the title of *Drei alte Schachteln* are Ursula Krüger (Elli Neuback), her young sister Lotte (Grete Freund), and their cook, Auguste (Claire Waldoff), and the plot is basically that of J M Barrie's *Quality Street,* with some considerable low comedy (for the cook) added. The three women's men all go off to the wars and, when Lotte's Klaus returns, years later, he finds her apparently turned into a spinsterish schoolmarm. But Lotte doffs her work clothes and her sober manner and, pretending to be her own "niece," Dörte, enchants all of Klaus's fellow soldiers on the night of their regimental ball. Klaus falls in love with the mysterious Dörte, but when he goes to meet her again at the sisters' home, Lotte is obliged to be her schoolmarmy "self." Auguste impersonates the "niece" and does so so poorly that the pretence is soon made obvious. Klaus and Lotte are united for the final curtain, and the cook has a happy ending too, with her safely returned man, Klaus's batman Cornelius Hasenpfeffer.

The action was accompanied by a lively Kollo score, from which the cook's number, "Ach Jott, wat sind die Männer dumm," proved the most popular piece, alongside a trio for the three ladies, "Drei alte Schachteln, die geh'n zum Ball," Lotte's "Ein Märchenglück, ein Sommentraum," Klaus's "Ihr goldnen Locken, ihr blauen Sterne" and the ensemble "Was nützt denn dem Mädchen die Liebe." That score helped Haller's low-comedy version of Barrie to become hugely popular, running for over 450 performances in its first run at the Theater am Nollendorfplatz and being widely played for many years thereafter in Germany. The show did not, however, find many takers further afield. It was produced in Vienna at the end of the First World War with Elly Bach (Ursula), Ida Russka (Lotte), Steffi Walidt (Auguste), Karl Bachmann (Klaus) and Max Brod (Cornelius) featured and, a couple of years further on, on Broadway, in an adaptation by Edward Delaney Dunn under the title of *Phoebe of Quality Street* which moved back a little closer to the original play. British husband-and-wife team Dorothy Ward (Phoebe) and Shaun Glenville (Sergeant Terence O'Toole) starred alongside Warren Proctor (Valentine) and Gertrude Mudge (Patty, the cook) for 16 performances.

Quality Street also served as the basis for the successful British musical *Dear Miss Phoebe* (13 October 1950 Phoenix Theatre) and for a *Phoebe* (Philip Springer/Joan Javits/John Ott 23 August 1965) played for 16 performances at Pennsylvania's Bucks County Playhouse.

Austria: Johann Strauss-Theater 1919; Hungary: Budapesti Színház *Három a vénlány* 5 June 1920; USA: Shubert Theater *Phoebe of Quality Street* 9 May 1921

Recording: complete (Eurodisc)

DREI ARME TEUFEL Operette in 3 acts by Rudolf Österreicher and Heinz Reichert. Music by Karl Weinberger. Theater am Gärtnerplatz, Munich, 11 March 1916.

When violinist Nelly Wolfgang wins both an American contract to the value of $60,000 and a marriage proposal from Graf Alfred Harpen on the same day, she tries to propitiate fate by giving her meagre savings to the first poor folk she sees—the composer, Eduard Krüger, the modiste, Poldi Berndl, and the serving-man, Obermaier. When Obermaier, with his talking dog, gets the American vaudeville contract she thought she had secured and Poldi proves to have a prior claim on her would-be-fiancé, Nelly is further back than she started, but fate and the "three poor devils" set things aright in the final act—Nelly is offered the job of musical director to the dog, and Poldi prefers her Kruger to the faithless aristocrat.

One of Weinberger's most successful Operetten in Germany, *Drei arme Teufel* was also given, under the management of Oscar Fronz, at Vienna's Bürgertheater with Grete Holm (Nelly), Paul Kronegg (Alfred), Ernst Wurmser (Obermaier) and Ellie Kreith (Poldi) featured, and the interpolation of the Schrammelquartett "Die Finken" from the Établissement Bratwurstglöckerl into the second act. It played 51 times.

Austria: Wiener Bürgertheater 15 June 1923

DIE DREIGROSCHENOPER Piece with music in a prelude and 8 scenes, adapted from John Gay's *The Beggar's Opera* by Elisabeth Hauptmann and Bertolt Brecht. Music by Kurt Weill. Additional lyrics from the works of Rudyard Kipling and François Villon. Theater am Schiffbauerdamm, Berlin, 31 August 1928.

The hugely successful 1920 London revival of John Gay's *The Beggar's Opera* at the Lyric Theatre, Hammersmith, set the once-popular piece off on both a new round of productions and a series of fresh adaptations, amongst which were Felix Dörmann's *Der Liebling von London,* with music arranged by Hans Ewald Heller, produced at Vienna's Carltheater in 1924 (19 April), and a second German-language version, resulting from this one, but with a rather different flavor, made up from an adaptation of the English show prepared by Elisabeth Hauptmann done over and added to by Bertolt Brecht, and mounted at Berlin's Theater am Schiffbauerdamm by Josef Aufricht in 1928. Where *The Beggar's Opera* had taken a poignard to its subjects, *Die Dreigroschenoper* took a cleaver. The unaffectedly ribald and smilingly satirical tone of the original piece was replaced by a much more direct style, scornful and scathing, in a text replete with loathing, whilst the daintily incisive and often incidental musical numbers of the original gave place to a set of darkly colored Kurt Weill pieces which were equally incisive, sometimes equally incidental, but far from dainty.

Beggar-king Jonathan Jeremiah Peachum (Erich Ponto) and his wife (Rosa Valetti) are appalled when they discover that their daughter, Polly (Roma Bahn), has married the notorious thief and womanizer Macheath (Harald Paulsen) and Peachum determines to use his influence to get the man hanged, in spite of the highwayman's friendship with the London police chief, Tiger Brown (Kurt Gerron). Sex leads to Macheath's downfall. Mrs Peachum bribes the whore, Jenny (Lotte Lenya), to betray her customer to the law, and the thief ends up in jail, uncomfortably near to another "wife," Brown's daughter Lucy (Kate Kühl). When she thinks Macheath prefers her to Polly, Lucy helps him escape, but another sizeable dose of corruption gets him rearrested, condemned and led to the gallows before he is, at the last, reprieved in an amnesty on the occasion of a Coronation and, indeed, raised to the peerage.

The songs of the piece included several which would ultimately become great favorites, notably the opening Moritat ("Und der Haifisch, der hat Zähne"), in which an unnamed street-singer introduces the deeds of the anti-hero of the tale, and the vindictive pub song "Die Seeräuber-Jenny" ("Meine Herrn heut sehn Sie mich Gläser aufwaschen"). Polly's (or Lucy's, depending on which source you believe) Barbarasong, the Salomonsong, in which Jenny reflects on the downfall of great men, the wedding-night duet for Polly and Macheath, "Siehst du den Mond über Soho," and a jealousy duet for Polly and Lucy ("Komm heraus, du Schönheit von Soho") were amongst the other principal numbers of the score.

A curious mixture of a piece, with its sad conviction of and concentration on the rottenness and corruption of the entire world, and with its almost voyeuristic reveling in the representing on stage of whores and other things sexual—not with the happy enjoyment of a French comedy, but with a kind of energetic disgust—as the other motor (apart from greed) of man's deeds, and yet topped off by a fantasy or burlesque ending reeking of old-fashioned opéra-bouffe, it proved, nevertheless, to hit a spot. A success in its original Berlin production, it subsequently won further productions through Germany and

Europe. It was produced at the Vienna Raimundtheater, under the management of Rudolf Beer, with Paulsen repeating his original role alongside Kurt Lessen (Peachum), Pepi Glöckner (Mrs Peachum), Luli Hohenberg (Polly), Walter Brandt (Brown) and Elisabeth Markus (Lucy), accompanied by the Wiener Jazz-Symphonie Orchester, for a run of just over three months, at Budapest's Vígszínház (ad Jenő Heltai) for a brief 13 performances, and then in Paris (ad André Mauprey).

In English it initially did not do well. In Britain, where the Lyric Hammersmith *The Beggar's Opera* made regular reappearances, no need was felt for the more hammer-handed *Die Dreigroschenoper,* whilst an American version (ad Clifford Cochran, Jerrold Krimsky), with Robert Chisholm (Macheath), Steffi Duna (Polly) and Rex Weber (Peachum) featured, folded in a dozen performances at Broadway's Empire Theater.

The heavily politicized Brecht, apparently embarrassed by being associated—even as just co-author/adapter—with a success which made no propaganda point, later revised his text in an attempt to make it more political and insisted, in spite of Weill's distaste for revisions which made the piece lumpenly didactic, that only the new version be permitted. However, it was not Brecht's rewrite which resulted in the show having a longer life, but a version made in English.

American musician and writer Marc Blitzstein, encouraged by the composer, wrote an adaptation which was eventually produced twice at off-Broadway's Theater de Lys (10 March 1954, 30 September 1955) with Scott Merrill (Macheath), Leon Lishner (Peachum), Jo Sullivan (Polly) and with Lotte Lenya, the composer's wife and the original Jenny, repeating her role of nearly 30 years earlier. The venue, the timing of the production in an era when anti-establishment feeling and the belief in wholesale corruption were high, and the skillful adaptation combined to make *The Threepenny Opera* a long-running success (2,611 performances) and ''Mack the Knife'' (Moritat) a hit-parade number.

Thus relaunched, the show was given its first London production, in 1956, with a cast headed by Bill Owen (Macheath), Daphne Anderson (Polly) and Eric Pohlmann (Peachum). London did not give it more than 140 performances and, although the piece has since received regular British performances, including a starry revival in 1972 (Prince of Wales Theatre 10 January) and even a production at the National Theatre (13 March 1986), that country has never given it the welcome that it has given on several occasions to the original *The Beggar's Opera.* In America, the Blitzstein adaptation was put aside in 1976 when the New York Shakespeare Festival mounted a new adaptation by Ralph Mannheim and John Willett. Raul Julia played Macheath through 30 performances (Vivian Beaumont Theater 1 May).

Australia's semi-professional Union Theatre Company gave the piece its first Australian English-language production in 1959 (ad Richard Samuel), and it has received intermittent Australian revivals since, including one by the Old Tote company at the Sydney Opera House's Drama Theatre in 1972. The piece also returned to Paris when Aufricht staged a version there in 1937, for which occasion Weill composed two additional songs to add to the role of Mrs Peachum, played for the occasion by the famous chanteuse Yvette Guilbert, and again in 1979.

Die Dreigroschenoper's determinedly aggressive sentiments and style fitted well into the grand-guignolesque production styles of Western theatre in the 1970s and 1980s, and the show found itself a multitude of productions during those decades, often played (in spite of Weill's stated wish for ''real'' voices) by actors-who-sort-of-sing in a strange spit 'n' snarl style at odds with both the moments of the piece which seek reality and those which ring of fanciful burlesque. With this oddly unsophisticated style stuck to it (and with Ms Hauptmann's name now vanished from the credits), however, it has been seen again and again, including productions at Paris's Théâtre du Châtelet in 1986 (ad Giorgio Strehler, Myriam Tannant), at Berlin's Theater des Westens in 1987 (23 May), briefly on Broadway in 1989 (Lunt-Fontanne Theater 5 November ad Michael Feingold) with popular singer Sting as Macheath and Alvin Epstein, Georgia Brown and Maureen McGovern as the Peachum family, and at Budapest's Kamaraszínház (8 May 1993 ad László Márton), at Paris Théâtre du Chaillot for four weeks in 1995 (7 November) and at Budapest's Művész Színház (15 October 1993 ad Tamás Blum), Ódry Színpad (27 March 1997) and Új Színház (31 January 1998 ad István Vas).

Die Dreigroschenoper made a quick move from the stage to the cinema screen when G W Pabst made a double film version, in German (ad László Vajda, Leo Lania, Béla Balász) with Rudolf Forster as Macheath and Carola Neher, who had left the original cast in rehearsals, as Polly, and in French (ad Solange Bussi) with Albert Préjean and Florelle. In 1962 Kurt Ulrich filmed another version with a cast headed by Curt Jurgens (Macheath) and June Ritchie (Polly), which was put out both in German and—with Sammy Davis jr performing the Moritat—in English, and in 1989 Menachem Golem issued a version under the title *Mack the Knife,* with Raul Julia repeating his previous stage performance as Macheath.

Austria: Raimundtheater 9 March 1929; Hungary: Vígszínház *A koldus operája* 6 September 1930; France: Theatre Montparnasse *L'Opéra de quatre sous* 13 October 1930: USA: Empire Theater *The Threepenny Opera* 12 April 1933; UK: Royal Court Theatre *The Threepenny Opera* 9 February 1956; Australia: Union Theatre, Melbourne *The Threepenny Opera* 8 January 1959

Plate 109. **Das Dreimäderlhaus.** *The three little sisters of the original Vienna production: Anni Fischer (Hannerl), Else Lord (Haiderl) and Vally Ernst (Hederl).*

Films: Nero Films (Ger/Fr) 1930, Kurt Ulrich Film (Ger/Eng) 1962, 21st Century Film Corp (Eng) 1989

Recordings: complete versions (Vanguard, CBS, Polydor, Fontana, London/Decca, etc), complete in French (Jacques Canetti), selections (Neue Welt, Telefunken, Capriccio, etc), off-Broadway revival 1954 (MGM), Broadway revival 1976 (CBS), London revival 1997 (Jay), film soundtrack (London), etc

Literature: Hinton, S: *Kurt Weill: The Threepenny Opera* (Cambridge, 1990), Wöhrle, D: *Bertolt Brecht: Die Dreigroschenoper* (Diesterweg, Frankfurt 1996), etc

DAS DREIMÄDERLHAUS Singspiel in 3 acts by A M Willner and Heinz Reichert adapted from the novel *Schwammerl* by Rudolf H Bartsch. Music from the works of Franz Schubert selected and arranged by Heinrich Berté. Raimundtheater, Vienna, 15 January 1916.

The most widely successful, and also one of the most enduring, of all pasticcio musical plays, from *The Beggar's Opera* to *Kismet, Das Dreimäderlhaus* was put together, around a sentimentalized version of the love life of composer Franz Schubert, invented by the German author Bartsch in 1912, under the aegis of producer Wilhelm Karczag of the Raimundtheater. According to one version of the story, Karczag heeded the suggestion of publisher Emil Berté that his out-of-luck composer brother, Harry, be given the opportunity to write the score to the libretto Willner and Reichert had drawn from the novel. That story goes on to tell that Karczag rejected the first score which Berté provided, as the composer had included too much of his own original music and insufficient bits of real Schubert, but the final result, even if it and its success perversely hurt the touchy composer's pride, proved a masterly transformation of gold into gold.

Poor composer Franz Schubert (Fritz Schrödter) meets Hannerl Tschöll (Anny Rainer) when she comes to chaperone her two sisters, Haiderl (Else Lord) and Hederl (Vally Ernst), to a rendezvous with their boyfriends, Bruneder (Louis Gross) and Binder (Alexander Nessl), under his Viennese window. She becomes his singing pupil, and he falls in love with her but, hampered by shyness, he cannot bring himself to declare his love. Hannerl, too, has warm feelings for the composer but, when the actress, Demoiselle Grisi (Therese Tautenhayn), the jealous mistress of Schubert's poet friend Franz Schober (Victor Flemming), warns the girl against the womanizing "Franz," Hannerl mistakes her meaning and her man. Schubert writes a song to express his love for Hannerl and the easy-going Schober sings it to her, but the girl, believing that the feelings expressed are Schober's, responds by agreeing to marry him. Schubert is left at the final curtain with only his music for consolation.

The song used for the key point in the plot was Schubert's Serenade ("Ich schnitt' es gern in alle Rinden ein"), and the other musical highlights of the evening included the introduction of the three little sisters of the title to the strains of the composer's Air de ballet from *Rosamunde* as they declared themselves as "Haiderl und Hederl und Hannerl Tschöll," Schubert's version of Shakespeare's "Hark, Hark, the Lark" sung by the quartet of Schubert's friends, and his A-major waltz, here made into Schubert and Hannerl's duo "Was Schön'res könnt's sein als ein Wiener Lied." The show's most endearing musical moment fell to father Tschöll (Franz Glawatsch), comforting his wife over the imminent marriage of their daughters in the warmly felt "Geh, Alte, schau."

Produced in the best tradition of the good-old-days Operette, a genre which has always proven so successful in time of war or trouble, *Das Dreimäderlhaus,* with its picturesque recreation of the Biedermeier era, scored an enormous hit at the Raimundtheater. The piece ran quickly to its 100th performance (19 April) as Artur Preuss and Karl Streitmann each took a turn at the role of Schubert, crossed town for a Gastspiel at the Theater an der Wien, and returned home to hit 200 nights (7 September 1916), 300 nights (13 December 1916) and, with Julius Spielmann now as Schubert, its 400th night on 8 March 1917.

Hans Golle and Fritz Neumann both appeared as Schubert as the show ran on to its 600th performance (13 December 1917), ultimately closing 7 February 1918 to leave the Raimundtheater stage to a soi-disant sequel, *Hannerl,* in which Glawatsch once again appeared as Tschöll and Anny Rainer as Hannerl—the daughter of her original character. But *Das Dreimäderlhaus* remained in the repertoire after *Hannerl* had been and gone and it passed its 1,100th performance at the Raimundtheater on 9 April 1927, with Preuss still appearing, more than a decade on, in the role of Schubert.

The huge Viennese success of the show was repeated in Berlin. Produced at the Friedrich-Wilhelmstädtisches Theater in 1916, *Das Dreimäderlhaus* ran there until 11 September 1918, eventually giving way to *Hannerl* as the evening entertainment but running on in matinées to pass its 1,000th Berlin performance on 12 November 1918. Budapest, too, gave the piece a delighted welcome. *Három a kislány* (ad Zsolt Harsányi), with the operatic tenor Béla Környei (Schubert), Emmi Kosáry (Medi, ex-Hannerl, with Erzsi Gerő and Hanna Honthy as her sisters), Gyula Csortos (Schober) and Ferenc Vendrey (Tschöll) featuring in the principal roles, ran at the Vígszínház for 151 performances, before the piece moved on to a production at the Városi Színház (6 November 1919) with Környei and Kosáry again starred, returning to the Vígszínház as soon as 1922 (8 October), as it established itself as firmly in the repertoire in Hungary as in German-language theatres. It has been seen in Budapest as recently as 1997 (Erkel Színház 22 March 1997).

It was probably wartime conditions which slowed the progress of this enormous hit to the rest of the world but, when it did get to the other main theatrical centers, it thoroughly confirmed its central-European success. *Chanson d'amour* (ad Hugues Delorme, Léon Abric), mounted at Paris's Théâtre Marigny by Constance Maille, with Henri Fabert starred as Schubert alongside Marcelle Ragon (Annette Mühl, ex- Hannerl Tschöll), Louis Marie (Schober) and Max Mario (Mühl), shifted quickly to the Théâtre Apollo (1 July 1921), where it ran out a fine season. It was revived in Paris in 1928, with Gilbert Moryn as Schubert, again in 1931 (Gaîté-Lyrique), and in 1933 was later played at the Théâtre de la Porte-Saint-Martin in the original German with Richard Tauber and Irene Eisinger featured. Roger Bourdin played Schubert in a revival at the Théâtre de la Porte-Saint-Martin in 1934. In France, as elsewhere, the piece has remained in the repertoire ever since.

The Shubert brothers took up *Das Dreimäderlhaus* for America but, in their normal fashion, having paid for it, they had both book and score thoroughly remade. Dorothy Donnelly's melodramatic version of the libretto, which rather oddly had Schubert dying broken-heartedly (to the sound of full-blooded angelic strains) at the final curtain, like a Viennese Jack Point, was accompanied by some semi-fresh Schubert arrangements made by Sigmund Romberg. The Unfinished Symphony provided the material for the most popular song, "Song of Love." Less well made than its original, *Blossom Time* was, nevertheless, no less successful. With Bertram Peacock as Schubert, Howard Marsh as Schober and Olga Cook as Mitzi Kranz (once Hannerl Tschöll), the show ran a splendid 592 performances at the Ambassador Theater before beginning a very, very long series of tours and revivals. It returned to Broadway at the Jolson Theater in 1924 (19 May) and 1926 (8 March) in Shubert seasons, was revived at its original home in 1931, again in 1943 (4 September) and once more at the 46th Street Theater in 1938 (26 December). Latterly, as in the case of *The Student Prince,* its reputation suffered somewhat, simply from the number of *Blossom Time* productions and companies—often not of a very high standard—which wore a groove around the country and, eventually, it dropped exhaustedly out of the repertoire.

Britain's *Lilac Time* (ad Adrian Ross) also had the Schu-Berté score revamped, by the well-educated Australian composer George Howard Clutsam, but his version stayed a little closer to Berté's original, and the Viennese adapter was given a co-credit. In a masterly piece of casting, the (not-too-) aging Courtice Pounds, years earlier the original hero of *The Gondoliers,* was cast as Schubert alongside opera star Percy Heming (Schober) and the fine soprano Clara Butterworth (Lili Veit, a very long while back Hannerl Tschöll). Music publishers Chappell & Co produced the piece at the Lyric Theatre for a first run of 626 performances, and *Lilac Time* began a touring career almost as full as that of its American equivalent. London had return seasons in 1927 and 1928 (Daly's Theatre) with Frederick Blamey, Heming and Evelyn Laye starred, in 1930 with Blamey, Gertrude Wolfle and Thorpe Bates and in 1932 with Maurice d'Oisly as Schubert. In 1933 Richard Tauber appeared in his own personalized version of the piece, followed just weeks later by another season with d'Oisly and Helen Gilliland (Alhambra Theatre), who paired again three years later in a season at the London Coliseum (29 July 1936). A wartime revival at the Stoll Theatre (13 October 1942) starred Frank Titterton, Irene Eisinger and Derek Oldham, and a final West End sighting occurred in 1949 (His Majesty's Theatre 24 February) with John Lewis, Celia Lipton and Bruce Trent featured before, as in America, the show slid away, suffering from under-quality over-exposure.

Australia waited until 1924 before seeing *Lilac Time* (the British version was preferred to the Donnelly/ Romberg one). First time round, John Ralston (Shubert),

Claude Flemming (Schober), Eve Lynn (Lili) and Arthur Stigant (Veit) had to be shunted out of their theatre in favor of a Toti dal Monte opera season and thus managed only an initial seven weeks in Sydney, but a year and a bit later Melbourne (Theatre Royal 9 January 1926) welcomed Ralston, Flemming and American soprano Harriet Bennet much more enthusiastically, and their 126-performance season established the show for a number of later returns.

The first screen version of *Das Dreimäderlhaus* came out soon after its opening when Richard Oswald produced a 1917 silent film based on the piece. An English film version was made in 1934, as *Blossom Time,* with Richard Tauber starred, and E W Emo turned out a German sound film in 1936. Paul Hörbiger played Schubert. France's Schubert biomusical, *La Belle Meunière,* was not strictly a version of *Das Dreimäderlhaus,* but rather a piece constructed in the same way for the benefit of star tenor Tino Rossi, but in 1958 Ernst Marischka wrote and helmed one further German-language film, which featured Karlheinz Böhm as Schubert, Johanna Matz as Hannerl and Rudolf Schock as Schober and was, musically, a touch more straight Schubert than Berté's version.

A biomusical on the fictionalized life of a composer, illustrated by arrangements of his own music, was no new idea and even Schubert himself had already been thus served on several occasions, notably by a distinctly successful Viennese Singspiel by Hanns Max, with a score arranged by Franz von Suppé, produced at the Carltheater in 1864 (10 September), but the triumph of *Das Dreimäderlhaus* was responsible for a worldwide flood of such pieces, as composers including Offenbach, Chopin, Mendelssohn, Grieg, Tchaikovsky and Schumann found their putative love lives transferred to the musical stage, several of them with no little success. None, however, managed to approach the overwhelming international fame won by *Das Dreimäderlhaus* and its various national variants.

Hungary: Vígszínház *Három a kislány* 23 April 1916; Germany: Friedrich-Wilhelmstädtisches Theater 1916; France: Théâtre Marigny *Chanson d'amour* 7 May 1921; USA: Ambassador Theater *Blossom Time* 29 September 1921; UK: Lyric Theatre *Lilac Time* 22 December 1922; Australia: Her Majesty's Theatre, Sydney *Lilac Time* 24 May 1924

Films: Richard Oswald (1917) (silent), *Blossom Time* BIP (1934), *Drei Mäderl am Schubert* Emo (1936), Ernst Marischka (1958)

Recordings: complete in French (Decca), selections (EMI, Ariola Eurodisc, Amadeo, etc), selection in English (*Lilac Time*) (EMI, etc), (*Blossom Time*) (RCA), selection in Italian (Fonit-Cetra), selection in Hungarian (Qualiton), selection in Danish (polyphon), etc

DREI PAAR SCHUHE Lebensbild in 3 acts and a Vorspiel by Karl Görlitz adapted by Alois Berla. Music by Carl Millöcker. Theater an der Wien, Vienna, 5 January 1871.

The German play *Drei Paar Schuhe,* as adapted to the Viennese musical stage by playwright Berla and composer Millöcker, was a major success when it was first produced at the Theater an der Wien with Marie Geistinger starred in the heavily local-accented central role of Leni, the wife of shoemaker Lorenz Flink (Jani Szika). Romantically minded Leni goes out to deliver the three pairs of shoes of the title—one pair each to the homes of the wealthy Stangelmeier family (Herr Romini, Frln Singer), of the opera singer Laura Eder (Frln Stauber) and of the variety performer Irma (Karoline Finaly)—getting mixed up in the world of wealth and of the theatre for the space of three acts as she arrives, like a good fairy, just in time to clear up the problems of each household.

The musical part of the show was mostly for the benefit of the star, who had an opening song (''O Himmelkreuzmordelement'') and a lullaby (''Schlaf ein, mein Kind'') in the prologue and, following the musicless first act, the hugely successful yodeling song ''I und mein Bua'' in the second, and a drinking song (''Brausender Schaum'') in the third, as well as a part in some extensive concerted music. There was also a song each for Laura (''Von Mozart umsäuselt, von Verdi gequält''), for Irma (''Cancan tanzt sie'') and, in particular, for Carl Adolf Friese as the roué Nachtfalter—who appears in two of the three episodes—declaring in the show's second big hit number ''Bei Tag, da bin ich hektisch, bei Nacht wird ich elektrisch.''

Drei Paar Schuhe was played for a whole month at the Theater an der Wien before the production of Strauss's *Indigo* forced it aside, but it was brought back again and again over the next 30 years, both at the Theater an der Wien, where it totaled 169 repertoire performances during that time, and also at other Viennese houses, at first in the original and subsequently in the inevitable ''adapted'' versions. It was played in Germany and in the German theatres of America, both by local companies and by Geistinger herself on her various tours, and it was also given a successful production in Hungarian (ad Ferenc Nándori Toldy).

A second musical version of the original play, with a score by Conradi, was also produced in Vienna, whilst a third, an adaptation by Jean Kren with lyrics by Alfred Schönfeld and music by Jean Gilbert, was produced at the Berlin Thalia-Theater in 1915.

A version of the show (ad F A Harris) was toured in America by Katie Putnam in 1878, and another American remake, entitled *At the French Ball* (rather than the originally mooted *A Frau's Frolic*) was toured with considerable success by Fannie Rice and her company from 1895 (Omaha, Neb 5 December) and played briefly at Broadway's Bijou Theater in 1897. Fannie played a Leni who was now called Nancy and played her all round the country for three seasons.

Hungary: Budai Színkör *Három pár cipő* 31 July 1872; USA: Germania Theater 19 May 1873

DREI WALZER Operette in 3 acts and 12 scenes by Paul Knepler and Armin Robinson. Music written and arranged by Oscar Straus with the use of music from the works of Johann Strauss I and Johann Strauss II. Stadttheater, Zürich, 5 October 1935.

The most skillful and attractive of the endless list of pasticcio works to have been made up from strippings of Strauss music, *Drei Walzer* was laid out in three eras, on the lines of the successful *Wie einst im Mai,* and its score was compiled in function of this. Act I, set in 1865 Vienna, utilized the melodies of Johann Strauss père; Act II, which moved on to 1900, was musically illustrated by the music of Johann Strauss fils; whilst the musical part of the third act, played in the present day (ie, 1935), was composed of new music from the pen of Oscar Straus.

The first act followed the ill-starred love story of dancer Fanny Pichler and Count Rudi Schwarzenegg. Realizing, with a little help from his kindly but imperturbably aristocratic aunt, that marrying her would force Rudi to give up his career in the Imperial army and his social position, Fanny quietly leaves Vienna. In the second act Rudi's son, Count Otto, seeks out Fanny's daughter, Charlotte, an Operette star, and they fall in love, but Otto's jealous former mistress comes between them and for a second generation the lovers are parted. The final act is set in a modern film studio where a film about Rudi and Fanny is being made. Film star Franzi, Charlotte's daughter, is portraying her grandmother. When the actor playing Rudi drops out, the present day Count Schwarzenegg, who has come to complain about the making of the film, is co-opted to play the role. By the end of the act, the third generation are well on their way to the happy ending the first two missed. The agent, Johann Brünner, young in Fanny's day and vastly aged by Franzi's, linked all three stories in much the same way that the Methusalem of *Wie einst im Mai* had done.

Drei Walzer did not have a large career in its German-language original, but a conversation between the divette Yvonne Printemps and composer Straus resulted in its becoming a major success in France. The show and the triple-headed roles of the lovers were adapted by Léopold Marchand and Albert Willemetz to suit the needs of Mlle Printemps and her on- and off-stage partner Pierre Fresnay. The musical part of his role was pruned away (Fresnay couldn't sing), whilst hers was beefed up with much of what had once been his, plus a little extra; the second act was given a different ending; and the episodes of the piece, which was now set in France, were linked to the years of the great Paris Exhibitions (1867, 1900, 1937). Profiting remarkably from its skillful remake, and from the performances given to the central roles by its two memorable stars in Willemetz's production at the Théâtre des Bouffes-Parisiens (1937), *Trois valses* turned out a major hit.

The highlights of a score which was built up with consummate skill and varied period color, were the numbers given to Mlle Printemps, in the roles of Fanny, Yvette and Irène Grandpré: the first-act ''C'est la saison d'amour'' and ''Te souvient-il?,'' both taken from Strauss père waltzes, the dazzling ''Je t'aime'' and the sprightly ''Oui, je t'aime ô Paris'' of the second act, and the modern, jaunty ''Je ne suis pas ce que l'on pense'' (the ''little extra'' added at the last minute) and ''Mais c'est le destin peut-être' of the final part. The aged Brünner (René Dary) of the last act had the best song outside the prima donna role, with a reminiscing ''Comme autrefois,'' and the score elsewhere included some small comical pieces and several ensembles, of which the antimarriage meeting of the lofty de Chalency (ex-Schwarzenegg) family in Act I was one of the most enjoyable.

After the original season of *Trois valses,* the star pair filmed the show (ad Marchand, Hans Müller), under the direction of Ludwig Berger. Henri Guisol was Brünner, and such celebrated artists as Jean Périer and Boucot appeared in supporting roles in a movie which remains one of the most attractive of its era and type. Printemps and Fresnay subsequently played a return season of *Trois valses* at the Théâtre de la Michodière in 1939 (31 January), and, whilst provincial productions flowed freely through the country, the show was brought back to Paris again in 1952 and in 1959, under the actor-management of Germaine Roger of the Théâtre de la Gaîté-Lyrique. It remains a regularly performed piece in France to the present day.

The Paris success provoked productions in both New York and London. Kitty Carlisle starred alongside Michael Bartlett in Broadway's *Three Waltzes* (ad Rowland Leigh, Clare Kummer), whilst in London Evelyn Laye and Esmond Knight were ideally cast at the head of another English version (ad Diana Morgan, Robert MacDermott). Neither production, however, proved as successful as the French version, the Broadway piece making 122 performances, and London's running to 189 without, in either case, establishing the show in the revivable repertoire.

France: Théâtre des Bouffes-Parisiens *Trois valses* 22 April 1937; USA: Majestic Theater *Three Waltzes* 25 December 1937; UK: Prince's Theatre *Three Waltzes* 1 March 1945, Germany: Statische Bühnen, Nuremberg 12 November 1950.

Film: Ludwig Berger (1939)

Recordings: original cast recordings (EMI), complete in French (Decca), selections in French (EMI-Pathé, Decca, etc)

DRESSLER, Marie [VAN KOERBER, Leila Marie] (b Cobourg, Canada, 9 November 1869; d Santa Barbara, Calif, 28 July 1934). Hefty, plug-ugly singing comedienne, who led a career in burlesque and musical theatre prior to her incarnation as a classic movie heavy.

Because of her concrete-block physique and deep voice, Miss Dressler began playing heavies from a young age, appearing as a teenaged Katisha and as Ruth (1889), in senior character roles on tour with Moulton and Bennett and with George A Baker (Peronella, Barbara in *The Black Hussar,* Princesse de Gramponneur, *Les Cloches de Corneville*), in the title role of *La Grande-Duchesse* and in *La Mascotte* (1892) before making her first Broadway appearance in Lillian Russell's company in a character role in *The Robber of the Rhine* (1892, Cunigonde). She was seen in *Princess Nicotine* (1893, Duchess), took over as the Queen of Spain (a role created by a female impersonator) in Edward Rice's extravaganza *1492,* played the extravagantly comical "heavy" mother of marriageable twins in a revival of *Giroflé-Girofla* (1894, Aurore), performed in *Madeleine* (1895, Mary Douclée), Chicago's *Little Robinson Crusoe,* (1895, Ophelia Crusoe) and *A Stag Party* (1895, Georgia West), and in 1896 she appeared at the Casino Theater as the flashy music-hall artist Flo Honeydew (who doesn't get the man) in the American version of the British variety musical *The Lady Slavey.*

She appeared on the road in May Irwin's role in *Courted into Court* (1897, Dottie Dimple) until it blew a gasket in Kansas City, then alongside Eddie Foy in the Broadway version of the French *L'Auberge du Tohu-bohu* (1898, Flora), and over the next decade played substantial roles in a series of homemade musical and revusical pieces in theatres and in music halls on Broadway, burlesquing Henrietta Crosman's Kitty Bellairs in *Sweet Kitty Swellairs* and Viola Alum in *The Man in the Moon,* appearing in *Miss Printt, The King's Carnival* and *The Hall of Fame,* as ex-Queen Tarantula in *King Highball,* in the revusical *Higgledy Piggledy* and *Twiddle Twaddle* and in the musical comedy *The Boy and the Girl* (1909, "I'm Just a Respectable Working Girl"). In 1909 she presented herself in London in a double bill of *Philpoena* (an excerpt from *Higgledy Piggledy*) and *The Collegettes.* When she won poor notices and poorer audiences she decamped stormily back to America ("Shylock must have been an Englishman how you English hate Americans"), leaving £5,000 in unpaid debts, and her cast and her employees to whistle for their wages. Whilst the papers reported that she was "looking after her mining interests" in America, she filed for bankruptcy for the second convenient time in eight years.

Justice clearly slept, for the first role which the welshing producer took up on her return home was the one which was to give her the star status London had denied her. As the dreaming slavey of *Tillie's Nightmare* (1910, Tillie Blobbs) she delivered "Heaven Will Protect the Working Girl" and scored what would be her biggest Broadway success as a performer. However, when she took the show out on the post-Broadway road under her own management, it ended up with more unpaid artists and another collapse. It would not be the last time. Dressler was hauled into court soon after for not paying a sacked act, and she walked out on her cast at the end of the season without paying their wages, obliging them to run to their union and to the law to recoup their due. However she was soon back on the road again with the farce comedy (with songs) *In a Mix-Up,* this time under the management of the Shuberts.

With her portrayal of George Hobart's Tillie, however, Dressler had created a character which was soon transferred—with its creator—to film. It was a switch of medium which came in good time, for she had by now made herself pretty unemployable, and even unbookable in the theatre (a West Coast manager actually locked her out of his theatre in 1914 as "trouble") and it started her on a second career of some 20 years as the classic boot-faced harridan of MGM's films of the 1920s and 1930s. She appeared thereafter in a couple more stage musicals, being last seen in 1923 as Gloria Seabright in a semi-book show called *The Dancing Girl,* but most of her latter-day theatre appearances—and they were, in any case, much less frequent than her screen ones—were in revue and vaudeville.

Autobiographies: *The Life Story of an Ugly Duckling* (Mc Bride, New York, 1924), *My Own Story* (Little, Brown, Boston, 1934); Biographies: Lee, B: *Marie Dressler: The Unlikeliest Star* (University Press of Kentucky, 1997), Kennedy, M: *Marie Dressler* (McFarland, Jefferson, NC, 1999)

DREVER, Constance (b Conoor, Neilgherry Hills, Madras, c1880; d England, 21 September 1948).

Miss Drever, who had studied voice on the Continent, made a dramatic first appearance on the musical stage when she was promoted at the very last minute, from a minor role, to the star part of Kenna for the opening night of Edward German's *A Princess of Kensington* (1903), in place of ailing prima donna Agnes Fraser. She subsequently worked for a period on the concert stage, returning to the theatre to tour in the comic opera *Amasis* (1907), and then to first take over the role of Natalie (ie, Valencienne) from Elizabeth Firth and later move into the star role of Sonia (ex- Hanna) in George Edwardes's production of *The Merry Widow* at Daly's Theatre. After an appearance at the New Theatre in the title role of a revival of *Dorothy,* she went to Paris and there created the part of Missia (ex- Sonia, ex- Hanna, ex- *Die lustige Witwe*), otherwise France's *La Veuve joyeuse,* with enormous success. Her performance left such a mark on the piece and the role that for many years the star role of *La Veuve joyeuse* was—decidedly curiously, given the plot—obligatorily played in France with a strong English accent.

Back in Britain, she introduced ''My Hero'' to Londoners in the role of Nadina in the English version of *The Chocolate Soldier* (1910) and she then moved on to star as Rosalinde in a remake of *Die Fledermaus* called *Nightbirds* (1911), as Lizzi Flora in Straus's short-lived *The Dancing Viennese* (*Eine vom Ballet,* 1912) at the Coliseum, as Tatjana in Kerker's *Grass Widows* (1912) and, in succession to Gertie Millar, as Lady Babby in the rewritten *Zigeunerliebe* (*Gipsy Love,* 1912).

After making her music-hall debut at the Coliseum, she thereafter spent much of her time singing on similar programs and she played out the last decade of her career as an actress and vocalist on the variety stage.

Miss Drever was the first wife of tenor-turned-musical agent Frank Boor (Isidor Notador in *Poor Jonathan* 1893, Dramaleigh in Broadway's *Utopia (Ltd)* 1894, t/o Katana in *The Geisha* 1896, t/o Lollius in *A Greek Slave* 1898, etc).

LE DROIT D'AÎNESSE Opérette in 3 acts by Eugène Leterrier and Albert Vanloo. Music by Francis Chassaigne. Théâtre des Nouveautés, Paris, 27 January 1883.

Le Droit d'aînesse had a curious career. Produced at the Paris Théâtre des Nouveautés in 1883 with a top-flight cast headed by Marguerite Ugalde (Falka), Juliette Darcourt (Edwige), Berthelier (Tancrède), Vauthier (Boléslas), Albert Brasseur (Arthur) and Scipion (Pelican), it met—in spite of a score voted ''bright, gay, without any pretentiousness and pleasant to listen to''—with little better than indifference and was removed after 49 performances, never to be seen on the Paris stage again. However, in spite of this, it was taken up for a British production and, nine months later, an H B Farnie adaptation, rechristened *Falka,* was produced by Alexander Henderson at London's Comedy Theatre. This time there was no indifference: *Falka* was an instant and very sizeable hit.

Folbach (Harry Paulton), the military governor of Mongratz, is the uncle of Tancred (Henry Ashley) and of Falka (Violet Cameron) and, proposing to bestow on his nephew all his wordly goods, thus disinheriting the girl child, he summons the boy to him. But on the way Tancred is made captive by the brigand, Boléslas (William H Hamilton) who accuses him of seducing his pretty robber-maid sister Edwige (Tilly Wadman) and insists on a marriage. Edwige helps him to escape, however, and he ends up—as we move into the story's complexities—running around the country, just ahead of the brigand and his knife, disguised as a waiter. The frisky Falka, on the other hand, runs away from her convent school with her boyfriend, Arthur (Louis Kelleher) and, to avoid the unwelcome attentions of Uncle Folbach, she ends up disguising herself as Tancred, with Arthur disguised as . . . her! In the tangling and untangling of the situations that led up to the final and expected satisfactory pairing up, W S Penley, in the character of the lay brother Pelican supplied much of the comedy.

Falka played for 157 performances at the Comedy Theatre, and returned to London as soon as 1885 (Avenue Theatre 19 September) whilst the first of the many touring companies which would be seen on the road in the next decade or so set off round the country.

Farnie's version of the show was taken up for America and, initially mounted by the Casino Theater's touring company in Philadelphia, it opened on Broadway, at the Casino Theater, with Bertha Ricci (Falka, replacing Philadelphia's Cécile Fernandez), J H Ryley (Folbach, replacing the tour company's Francis Wilson), Hubert Wilke (Boléslas), Frank Tannehill jr (Tancred), Mathilde Cottrelly (Edwige, supplanting the tour's Jeannie Winston) and Alfred Klein (Pelican) featured, and it once again scored a hit, compiling a run of 103 nights while the road company made its way to the other main centers. Continuing its triumphal way around the world's English-speaking theatres, the show also proved a popular success in Australia. First introduced there by Annette Ivanova (Falka), Edwin Kelly (Pelican), Florence Trevallyan (Edwige) and Robert Brough (Tancred), it was given an additional boost when the area's favorite opéra-bouffe prima donna, Emilie Melville, returned from touring India and took over as Falka.

For many years a popular item in the repertoire of touring comic opera companies on both sides of the Atlantic, *Falka* (which had long forgotten it had ever, briefly, existed as *Le Droit d'aînesse*) had a particularly long life in Britain where it was for many years taken round and round the country by Horace Lingard's provincial company which, at one stage, presented its own burlesque version of the show under the title *Brother Pelican.*

UK: Comedy Theatre *Falka* 29 October 1883; USA: Haverley's Theater, Philadelphia 4 March 1884, Casino Theater *Falka* 4 April 1884; Australia: Opera House, Melbourne *Falka* 24 April 1886

LE DROIT DU SEIGNEUR Opérette in 3 acts by Paul Burani and Maxime Boucheron. Music by Léon Vasseur. Théâtre des Fantaisies-Parisiennes, Paris, 13 December 1878.

When the young director Debruyère took over the old Théâtre Beaumarchais and turned it into a lyric theatre, one of his first ventures was the production of Vasseur's saucy opérette, *Le Droit du seigneur.*

The show's story lived up to its title, with Denizot featured as a busy Baron who tries on behalf of the local Duc (Sujol) to reestablish the old custom of the overlord's right to deflower every young bride in his fief. The villagers, to get round this situation, simply decide to do without the marriage ceremony. However, Lucinette (A Humberta) and her Bibolais (Cyriali) do get wed, and they then spend half the evening trying to keep out of the way of the Baron. Bibolais is imprisoned and threatened with the gallows for not handing over his wife and, when he is suddenly freed, he, not unreasonably, suspects his wife of having given in. But by the time the Baron and the Duc catch up with the pair they've already connubed and, since the Duc can't now be the plucker of the flower, his droit de seigneur is invalid. Adèle Cuinet played the Baron's wife, a former paramour of the Duc, and the mother of his long-lost child, the solving of whose identity provided another complication to the plot.

Amongst the musical moments, Lucinette's gently suggestive Couplets du coquelicot with its cuckoldy refrain (''coquelicot, coquelicot''), and the Duc's song reasoning that, since all the other first fruits are reserved by vassals for their overlord, it follows that he should have the maidenhead of their wives, were both popular, as were Bibolais's romance, ''Adieu bois touffus, vert ombrages'' and Lucinette's little solo (''Avec ma plus belle révérence''), sweetly thumbing her nose at the Duc after the deed is irreparably done. Means was also found to introduce a lively hunters' chorus into the proceedings.

The show was a considerable hit, running for 229 performances and 10 further in 1880, and when Debruyère took over the Théâtre de la Gaîté in 1884 he revived it again. It reappeared in 1889 at the Bouffes-Parisiens with Louise Théo starred, and yet again for 38 performances in 1893 at the Théâtre des Menus-Plaisirs (31 October) with Mlle Léonetti as Lucinette.

Whilst the original Paris production ran, an English version (ad Arthur Matthison) was produced in London by the gentlemen of the Comedy Opera Company, determined to make a hit following their noisy split with D'Oyly Carte over *HMS Pinafore.* Lizzie Mulholland (Marigold), George Mudie (Duc de Noces-Defendues) and Arthur Rousbey (Ferdinand) featured in *Marigold* for a season of five weeks which put an end to the Comedy Opera Company. Whether because of this or because of the impossibility of bleaching the sexual content from the libretto, the other main centers passed on the show, but the British provinces got the chance to hear at least a part of Vasseur's score when it was lifted to illustrate a touring burlesque called *Cruel Carmen.*

UK: Olympic Theatre *Marigold* 29 October 1879

DRUCKER, Karl (b Brünn, 3 August 1855; d Brünn, 11 January 1888).

After successes in smaller Austrian theatres and particularly in his home town of Brünn, the tenor Drucker was engaged at the Carltheater in 1879. He spent several years there in leading roles, creating such parts as Gaston Dufaure in Suppé's *Donna Juanita,* Polyphem von Croustillac in *Der Gaskogner* (1881), the tenor role of *Das Herzblättchen* (1882), Flagerlot in Genée's *Rosina* (1881), and Don Montiel de Carragui in his *Nisida* (1880), and appearing as Valentin in *Olivette* (1881), Tom in Émile Jonas's *Javotte* (1882), Don Luis de Rosamonte in *Drei Schwarzmäntel* (1882), Fitzo in *Kosiki* (1882) and Don Januario in *Der Seekadett* (1882).

In 1883 he quit the Carltheater and, with his companion, the soubrette Jenny Stubel, went prospecting for lucrative engagements in other Austrian and German theatres. Then, suddenly, he disappeared from view. His stage nerve had cracked. He was finally rediscovered back in Brünn, where he died soon after at the age of 32.

DIE DUBARRY Operette in 9 scenes by Paul Knepler and Ignaz M Welleminsky. Music by Carl Millöcker adapted by Theo Mackeben. Admiralspalast, Berlin, 14 August 1931.

The little milliner Marie-Jeanne Beçu (Gitta Alpár) goes out one day to meet her painter boyfriend, René Lavallery (Robert Nästlberger), in the park and there catches the eye of the Comte Dubarry. He follows her to René's studio, causing a breach between the young pair by his attentions, and finally, after putting her through a marriage with his brother so that she can be officially the Comtesse Dubarry, he takes her to court as a candidate for the important and influential post of mistress to the King. Obliged to choose between her painter and the royal bed, Jeanne, unlike most of her operettic predecessors, pragmatically chooses the King, and History can now begin. Jeanne's actress friend, Margot (Edith Schollwer), and her boyfriend, Brissac (Igor Gutmann), made up the soubret part of the entertainment.

An amount of the music used in this version of the semi-fictional life and loves of Madame du Barry was adapted from the score to Millöcker's earlier piece on the same subject, the indifferently successful 1879 Operette *Gräfin Dubarry* (Theater an der Wien 31 October 1879, Brünn 15 January 1879, Friedrich-Wilhelmstädtisches Theater 20 January 1879, Fifth Avenue Theater, New York (Ger) 12 February 1883, etc). The leading lady's role was supplied with a fine barrage of soprano numbers, beginning in the first scene with the happy ''Heut' hab' ich Glück,'' continuing through her declaration of fidelity (''Ich schenk mein Herz''), her apprehensive first steps at court (''Ob man gefällt oder nicht gefällt'') and rising

Plate 110. **The Dubarry.** *Grace Moore and the glamour chorus in Broadway's production of the Mackeben-Millöcker paste-up Operette.*

to its peak in the final scene with the glittering, jaunty "Ja, so ist sie, die Dubarry." René supplied the tenor music, both solo and in duet with Jeanne.

Die Dubarry scored a fine success in its Berlin premiere, with Gitta Alpár winning a memorable triumph in the role of Jeanne ("the best [prima donna] central Europe has to offer'). Further productions soon followed in its wake, with London the first of the major centers to take the show up (ad Rowland Leigh, Desmond Carter). Stanley Scott's production confirmed the Berlin success, and once again the show's prima donna, German vocalist Anny Ahlers, won enthusiastic praise, but tragedy struck when the unstable star committed suicide during the run. With Sylvia Welling replacing, opposite the René of Heddle Nash, and such names as Farren Soutar (Chamard), Margaret Yarde (Sauterelle) and Helen Haye (Maréchale) in support, the piece ran to its 397th performance before going on the road. It was revived in the West End in 1947 (Prince's Theatre 8 October) with Irene Manning as Jeanne, John Hendrik (René) and a supporting cast including Ada Reeve (Sauterelle), Jerry Verno (de la Marche) and John Le Mesurier (Lamond).

Singing star Grace Moore was Broadway's Dubarry, in Tillie Leblang and Morris Green's production, alongside William Hain (René), Pert Kelton (Margot) and Marion Green (King Louis) for a disappointing 87 performances, whilst Alpár repeated her celebrated portrayal in her native Hungary (ad László Lakatos, Andor Szenes) alongside Dezső Kertész, Miklos Hajmássy, Ella Kertész, Klári Tabódy and László Bánát. Miss Welling repeated her London performance, paired with John Dudley (René), in an Australian production at Sydney's Theatre Royal and Melbourne's King's Theatre (31 March 1934), and Paris saw Fanély Revoil as the Dubarry in André Mouëzy-Éon and Albert Willemetz's French version through a good run. Oddly enough, the show took its time to get to Vienna, but the Theater an der Wien finally mounted an 11-scene version, under the management of Hans Knappl, in 1935 with Mary Lossef starred alongside Wladimir Antscharoff (René), Olly Gebauer (Margot), Willy Stettner (Brissac) and Alfred Gerasch (Louis) for 35 performances.

Having thoroughly done the rounds of the world's stages, *Die Dubarry* returned to the Admiralspalast in 1938, and the piece remained popular in Germany, Britain and Australia for some time. In 1935 an English-language film version was produced, under the title *I Give My Heart,* with Miss Alpár repeating her portrayal of the Dubarry opposite Owen Nares, whilst in 1951 a German film, using the Operette simply as its background but calling itself *Die Dubarry,* was produced by Georg Wildhagen with a cast headed by Sári Bárabás, Albert Lievin and Willy Fritsch.

The rearranged Operette was itself several times subsequently rearranged, notably in a weak version by Hans Martin Cremer (Städtische Bühnen, Breslau 1938) which added a few more wearily conventional turns to the plot—on her way from millinery to mistressing, his Jeanne takes a turn as a cabaret singer!—and another new version of *Gräfin Dubarry,* made by Wilhelm Neef, was produced in Rostock in 1959 (24 March).

Madame Dubarry made two other notable appearances on the musical stage, in the delightful Parisian piece *La Belle Bourbonnaise* (1874) where Marie Desclauzas got to play both the grand lady and her peasant double, and in the American musical comedy *Dubarry Was a Lady* (1939), where she was dreamed up by Bert Lahr in the form of Ethel Merman. She was also the subject of an ''opera seria'' by Enrico Golisciani and G Antona-Traversi.

UK: His Majesty's Theatre 14 April 1932; USA: George M Cohan Theater 22 November 1932; Hungary: Fővárosi Operettszínház 5 September 1933; France: Théâtre de la Porte-Saint-Martin 21 October 1933; Australia: Theatre Royal, Sydney 20 January 1934; Austria: Theater an der Wien 30 August 1935

Films: Marcel Varnay *I Give My Heart* (aka *The Loves of Madame Dubarry*) 1935, International Film *Die Dubarry* 1951 (Ger)

Recordings: UK cast recordings (Pearl), selections (Eurodisc, Philips, HMV), selection in Hungarian (Qualiton), etc

DUBARRY WAS A LADY Musical comedy in 2 acts by Herbert Fields and B G De Sylva. Music and lyrics by Cole Porter. 46th Street Theater, New York, 6 December 1939.

A costume comedy musical, *Dubarry Was a Lady* used the favorite old dream-sequence trick of Victorian days to whisk its comedian back in time to the court of King Louis XV of France. Bert Lahr played little Louis Blore, a lavatory attendant in a New York nightclub, who has a passion for the place's star vocalist, May Daley (Ethel Merman). Needless to say, May has slightly loftier aims—she has her eye on the newspaperman, Alex Barton (Ronald Graham), even though he has a wife already. Encouraged to action after a big win on the sweepstakes, Louis determines to stake his claim. He spikes his rival's drink, but then mistakenly takes the mickey finn himself and finds himself dreaming that he is King Louis and that May is his Madame du Barry. He pursues his royal suit with comic gusto but, just as he is about to conquer his fair French lady, he wakes up. Realizing that he is never going to win May, he spends his winnings (after tax) on helping her boyfriend get his divorce, and goes back to his old job.

Cole Porter's score for the show was far from his most memorable, but it nevertheless brought forth a couple of enduring pieces. The topical duo ''Well, Did You Evah?,'' performed in the show, in a supporting role, by the young Betty Grable and by Charles Walters, was later made a favorite by its interpolation into the film *High Society,* whilst a ditty for Lahr and Miss Merman about ''Friendship'' resurfaced in several of the Porter paste-up shows of subsequent years, and now seems to have found a displaced home in the 1990s version of *Anything Goes.* Miss Merman also told of how ''Katie Went to Haiti'' in an elaborate nightclub number, shared the tasty but censored ''But in the Morning, No'' with Lahr and, in a last-minute addition to the score, advised with surprisingly little lyrical subtlety, ''Give Him the Ooh-La-La.''

Buddy De Sylva's production of what Miss Merman described as ''a tired businessmen's show'' had a fine Broadway run of 408 performances, and the show was subsequently produced by Tom Arnold and Harry Foster in London with Arthur Riscoe and Frances Day starred as Louis and his lady and Bruce Trent purveying the ballads as Alex/Alexandre. In spite of a less than enthusiastic reception, the production ran a pretty good five months and 178 performances at His Majesty's and the Phoenix Theatres before taking a turn around the provinces.

In 1943 *Dubarry Was a Lady,* which had actually been conceived by its authors in the first instance as a possible film project, was adapted for the screen. Lucille Ball—with the assistance of dubbing vocalist Martha Mears—and Red Skelton starred in a version in which only ''Katie Went to Haiti,'' ''Friendship'' and the ballad ''Do I Love You?'' survived from the original score, alongside a set of new numbers in which Burton Lane, Ralph Freed, Lew Brown, Roger Edens and E Y Harburg had a hand and amongst which were included ''Madame, I Like Your Crêpes Suzette'' and ''Salomé.''

UK: His Majesty's Theatre 22 October 1942

Film: MGM 1943

Recording: selection (Decca)

THE DUCHESS OF DANTZIC Romantic light opera in 3 acts by Henry Hamilton. Music by Ivan Caryll. Lyric Theatre, London, 17 October 1903.

Written some 8 or 10 years before its production, and announced in between times as a vehicle for London's ''queen of comic opera,'' Florence St John, and as a Charles Frohman production with Alice Nielsen, Ivan Caryll's Napoléonic musical *The Duchess of Dantzic* leaned musically towards his earliest works, in the French style, rather than in the direction of the Gaiety musical comedies which he had since made his speciality. Hamilton's version of Victorien Sardou and Émile Moreau's

Madame Sans-Gêne story made the role of the outspoken washerwoman Catherine Upscher (Evie Greene) into an even a huger leading part than it had been in the original play, for she cornered virtually all the show's lyric music, the principal male role of Napoléon Bonaparte (Holbrook Blinn) being written as a virtually non-singing one.

Catherine is a Paris washerwoman, wed to a soldier, and the foster mother of an aristocratic child orphaned in the revolution. One of her clients is a poor Corsican lieutenant who cannot pay his bill. Over the years, Lefèbvre, Catherine's husband, rises to a high post in the army and in court, and ultimately the Emperor Napoléon orders him to divorce his untutored, rough-spoken wife and wed the imperial ward, Renée de St Mézarde (Adrienne Augarde). Lefèbvre refuses, and so does Renée, who is in love with Catherine's foster son, Adhémar (Lawrence Rea). Finally, Catherine forces her way into the imperial presence and, his old, unpaid laundry bills in her hand, reminds the Emperor of his early days and his youthful idealism, shaming Napoléon into being less high-handed. Catherine ends up being created a rough-tongued Duchess of Dantzic, and the young couple are allowed to wed as they wish.

Such of the show's music not devoted to the star fell to the juveniles, to the staunch-voiced Denis O'Sullivan as Lefèbvre, and to the comic relief—Courtice Pounds as a parvenu milliner and Napoléon's bitchy sisters as played by Kitty Gordon and Violet Elliot. The style of the show meant that it was not written for ''hit numbers'' as such, but a beautiful sobbing trio ''A Real Good Cry,'' Catherine's ''Mirror Song'' and the vigorous baritone ''Noblesse Oblige'' all demonstrated Caryll's real ability with a comic opera style he had largely forsaken in favor of popular song.

Evie Greene made an enormous success in George Edwardes's London production (236 performances) as the washerwoman who becomes a duchess through frankness. She made, indeed, such a hit that, although Fritzi Scheff had originally been announced for the part, she was subsequently taken to New York to repeat the role at the head of a British cast for an American season. The company returned home after their fixed total of 93 Broadway performances, promising to come back for a second season after the summer, but in the event they didn't. Evie Greene went on instead to play Catherine in the British provinces where *The Duchess of Dantzic* was to be seen touring for several years.

French- and German-language theatres did not pick the show up, but Budapest's Király Színház staged *A Danzigi hercegnő* in 1905 in an Hungarian version written by Adolf Merei and Jenő Heltai. Otherwise, the show's success was all in its original language. In Australia the local star Florence Young scored strongly in the grateful title role alongside the Napoléon of Wybert Stamford, and Anna Hickish and Julius Royston introduced the show to South African audiences in 1906. Dorothy Ward was Catherine when Bannister Howard revived the piece at London's Daly's Theatre in 1932 and Fay Compton starred in a major British touring revival in 1943, whilst Australia's J C Williamson Ltd, also recognizing the potency of the play and of its fine leading role, mounted a revival for one of that country's favorite musical artists, Dot Brunton, in 1931.

Another musical version of *Madame San-Gêne* written by Hans Weigel and composed by Bernard Grün was produced at the Theater an der Wien in 1937 (1 September) and yet another was mounted at Aachen in 1997 under the title *Catharine* (Klaas van Dijk/Seth Gaaikema, Stadttheater 14 June).

USA: Daly's Theater 14 January 1905; Hungary: Király Színház *A Danzigi hercegnő* 15 April 1905; Australia: Her Majesty's Theatre, Sydney, 2 January 1909

THE DUENNA, or The Double Elopement Comic opera in 3 acts by Richard Brinsley Sheridan. Music composed and arranged by Thomas Linley sr and Thomas Linley jr. Covent Garden Theatre, London, 21 November 1775.

One of the most successful British comic operas of the 18th century, *The Duenna* was played for more than 70 nights at the Covent Garden Theatre in the 1775–76 season. It was continually revived on English-language stages around the world in the following decades, survived strongly into the 19th century, and was also mounted in several sizeable productions in Britain in the 20th century.

The duenna of the piece (Jane Green) is the guardian of Louisa (Isabella Mattocks), daughter of Don Jerome. However, instead of keeping Louisa away from her young Antonio (Charles Du Bellamy), and ready for her marriage to a rich, Portuguese Jew called Isaac Mendoza (John Quick), she actually connives at the young people's meetings. When the duenna is caught, dismissed and ordered from the house, Louisa takes her place and, disguised in the dark gown of the governess's calling, flees from her father's home to Antonio's side. Isaac is tricked into wedding the duenna instead. The other half of the ''double elopement'' concerns Jerome's son, Ferdinand (George Mattocks), and Clara d'Almanza (Miss Brown), daughter to the wealthy Don Guzman.

The 26 musical numbers which illustrated the score were part pasticcio and partly the work of the Linleys, father and son.

The show seems to have been introduced to the American stage by Lewis Hallam, who played it originally in Jamaica, and it was seen in Charleston, Philadelphia and the other principal American theatrical centers before what looks like its first New York showing at a benefit in 1787 (unless the piece played by Hallam's company previously as *The Elopement,* the title used in Charleston, was also *The Duenna*). After this introduction, it became a regularly played part of the American comic opera repertoire.

The principal modern productions of *The Duenna* have been at London's Lyric Theatre, Hammersmith, where the show was produced in a version with the score adapted by Alfred Reynolds in 1924 (23 October), in the wake of their success with *The Beggar's Opera,* and again in 1931 (22 April), and at the Bristol Old Vic, whose production with music by Julian Slade was subsequently brought to London's Westminster Theatre (28 July 1954). This version was later played on a number of occasions in the British provinces.

USA: Charleston *The Elopement* 28 September 1786

DUFF, James C[hristopher] (b New York, 16 March 1855; d New York, 31 August 1928).

The son of **John C[hristopher] Duff** (b Scotland, 10 March 1820; d New York, 31 March 1889), sometime restauranteur and later operator of, in turn, the Olympic, Broadway and Standard Theaters, James Duff worked first as a manager for his father. He took over the Broadway Theater (the former Wood's Museum) in 1877 and began producing comic opera, on his own behalf, whilst still in his twenties. His J C Duff Comic Opera Company introduced many of the classics of opéra-bouffe and opéra-comique from France, Britain and Austria to American-speaking audiences in New York in the late 1870s, the 1880s and the 1890s. He produced the first New York version of *HMS Pinafore* in 1879, but when Carte began staging his own New York productions Duff tried to challenge him and the two came to blows over Broadway's versions of *The Mikado.* Duff did not win. He had another misfortune when, having secured the rights to the London musical, *Erminie,* he let them lapse and missed the biggest Broadway hit of the era.

Duff remained active for 30 years, importing such pieces as *Le Petit Duc, Les Noces d'Olivette, Le Coeur et la main* (*Hand and Heart*), *Eine Nacht in Venedig* (*A Night in Venice*), *Dorothy, Paola, A Country Girl, The Cingalee* and *Les P'tites Michus* to the Broadway stage, and nearly half a century after his first Broadway productions he brought London's freshly revised hit version of *The Beggar's Opera* to New York.

Duff's sister, Mary, was the wife of producer and play-adaptor Augustin Daly.

DUHAMEL, Biana (b ?1870; d Paris, 26 October 1910). Palely pretty ingénue who scored one huge Parisian musical theatre success as Audran's *Miss Helyett.*

The 15-year-old Biana Duhamel (looking "no more than 12 or 13") made her first recorded appearance as Petit Poucet (Tom Thumb) in the féerie of the same name at the Paris Gaîté in 1885, but she made herself into a star five years later when she appeared at the Bouffes-Parisiens in two new pieces, firstly as Phrynette in André Wormser's pantomime *L'Enfant prodigue* and then, in another adolescent role, as the heroine of Audran's vastly successful *Miss Helyett.*

She took leading roles in the Bouffes-Parisiens' following productions—Audran's next and slightly more musically demanding work, *Sainte-Freya* (1892, Freya), Paul Lacome's *Le Cadeau de noces* (1893, Geneviève), and yet another Audran work, *Madame Suzette* (1893, Suzette)—without finding another role like Miss Helyett in which her youthful charm and limited vocal talents could shine. Her Miss Helyett, repeated as late as 1900 at the Théâtre de la Porte-Saint-Martin, remained a performance of choice spoken of with special warmth by old theatregoers for many years, yet the little ingenue who had enchanted le tout Paris was soon forgotten: she died destitute at the age of just 40.

DUKE, Vernon [DUKELSKY, Vladimir] (b Parafianovo, Russia, 10 October 1903; d Santa Monica, Calif, 16 January 1969). Russian-born composer, mostly for the American stage, whose few successes were undershadowed by what seems to be a record percentage of full-blooded flops.

Dukelsky underwent a classical music education in Russia and apparently worked as a dancer with the Diaghilev ballets but, having fled Russia's civil war, at first to America and then to Britain, he submerged his classical ambitions in writing for the lucrative London musical theatre of the mid-1920s. He supplied sufficient additional music (nine and a half numbers including the one-step "It's Nicer to Be Naughty") to a version of Jean Gilbert's *Uschi,* produced at the Palace Theatre by George Edwardes as *Yvonne,* to win a co-composer's credit, and he wrote his first full stage score for *The Yellow Mask,* a Desmond Carter-Edgar Wallace Oriental mystery musical in which the up-and-coming young comic Bobby Howes was paired with Phyllis Dare under the management of Laddie Cliff. In spite of two enforced changes of theatre, the spectacular mixture of romance and comedy and suspense had a reasonable career but when it was made into a film the fairly functional songs were omitted.

Duke next collaborated with Carroll Gibbons on the score for the disastrous *Open Your Eyes* which stranded its company in Scotland in the third week of its tour. It somehow made it to town the following year for an anguished 24 performances, but by this time Duke had already left Britain to try his luck once again in America.

There he interpolated individual songs into several Broadway shows and collaborated on several revue scores, one of which, *Walk a Little Faster,* produced one of his most remembered songs, ''April in Paris.'' It was 1940 before his first full Broadway theatre score, *Cabin in the Sky,* was heard, by which time he had moved far enough away from the Russian ballet to supply a boogie-woogie as part of the musical illustration of Lynn Root's morality tale of the negro southlands. ''Taking a Chance on Love'' was the show's take-away tune, one of three songs and two bits of the stage score which survived into a subsequent film version.

Duke's subsequent musicals did not find the same degree of success. Of his two further collaborations with lyricist John Latouche, *Banjo Eyes* turned *Three Men on a Horse* into a musical for Eddie Cantor and 128 performances, which was 125 more than their *The Lady Comes Across* managed. Three pieces with Howard Dietz, for whose *Keep Off the Grass* (1940) he had earlier provided some dance music, proved little happier, and the 1946 *Sweet Bye and Bye,* written with a royal roster of funny men, failed to get past its tryout. A revue, *Two's Company,* was played on Broadway in 1952, two songs and incidental music were used for a production of Anouilh's play *Time Remembered* (1957), and a 1963 musical *Zenda* was played in California without progressing further.

In 1952 Duke supplied the score to a short television musical, *Autumn in New York* (lib: Arnold Schulman, CBC 16 May 1952).

In spite of his very limited success rate in the theatre and a relatively small number of standard songs from a large output, Duke and his material have remained favorites with fossickers, and that éminence rose of the almost forgotten show song, Ben Bagley, showed particular favor to Duke's work in his recordings.

1926 **Yvonne** (*Uschi*) additional music for English version w Percy Greenbank (Daly's Theatre)

1928 **The Yellow Mask** (Edgar Wallace/Desmond Carter) Carlton Theatre, London 8 February

1930 **Open Your Eyes** (w Carroll Gibbons/Frederick Jackson) Piccadilly Theatre, London 8 September

1939 **The White Plume** (aka *The Vagabond Hero*) (Charles O Houston, Samuel D Pockrass) revised *Roxane* Washington 26 December

1940 **Cabin in the Sky** (John Latouche/Lynn Root) Martin Beck Theater 25 October

1941 **Banjo Eyes** (Latouche, Harold Adamson/Joe Quillan, Izzy Ellinson) Hollywood Theater 25 December

1942 **The Lady Comes Across** (Latouche/Fred Thompson, Dawn Powell) 44th Street Theater 9 January

1943 **Dancing in the Streets** (Howard Dietz/Dietz, John Cecil Holm, Matt Taylor) Boston 23 March

1944 **Jackpot** (Dietz/Guy Bolton, Sidney Sheldon, Ben Roberts) Alvin Theater 13 January

1944 **Sadie Thompson** (Dietz/Rouben Mamoulian) Alvin Theater 16 November

1946 **Sweet Bye-and-Bye** (Ogden Nash/S J Perelman, Al Hirschfield) Shubert Theater, New Haven 10 October

1959 **The Pink Jungle** (Leslie Stevens) Alcazar Theater, San Francisco 14 October

1963 **Zenda** (Everett Freeman/Martin Charnin, et al) Curran Theater, San Francisco 5 August

Autobiography: *Passport to Paris* (Little, Brown, Boston, 1955)

DUMANOIR, Philippe [PINEL DUMANOIR, Philippe François] (b Guadeloupe, 25 July 1806; d Pau, 13 November 1865).

A prolific playwright and vaudevillist, Dumanoir had a long list of straight theatre successes, most notably with a sizeable series of pieces written in collaboration with Jean-François Bayard, but also in tandem with Adolphe d'Ennery (*Don César de Bazan,* 1844) and with many others of the principal writers of his period. He ventured only occasionally into the musical theatre with the texts for such pieces as Louis Clapisson's one act opéra-comique *La Perruche* and, later, Hervé's *Les Folies dramatiques,* the Massé opera *La Mule de Pedro* (Opéra 4 March 1863) and opérette *La Chaise à porteurs* and the féerie *La Chatte merveilleuse* (1862).

His straight works, however, provided the bases for many libretti by other hands. His most celebrated work, *Don César de Bazan,* provided the starting-point for Wallace's *Maritana* (1845), Massenet's opera *Don César de Bazan* (Opéra-Comique, 1872) and Dellinger's operetta *Don Cesar* (Hamburg, 1885), as well as, eventually, W S Gilbert's *The Yeomen of the Guard* and a long series of burlesques. Of his collaborations with Bayard, *Les Premières Armes de Richelieu* became *The Dashing Little Duke* in London and *Az ötödik pont* in Hungary (Dezső Megyeri, Népszínház, 1893), *La Vicomtesse Lolotte* became Hungary's *A titkos csók* (Béla Hegyi, Szidor Bátor, Népszínház, 1888), the hugely popular *Le Vicomte de Letorrières* became *Az eleven ördög* in Hungary (József Konti, Budai Színkör, 1884), *Der Vielgeliebte* in Germany (Eduard Künneke/Rideamus, Herman Haller Theater am Nollendorfplatz, Berlin 17 October 1919), *Der Vicomte de Letorrières* in Czechoslovakia (Bogumil Zepler/E E Taubert Neues Deutsches Theater, Prague 16 January 1903) and *El vizconde de Letorières* in Spain, and, perhaps most successfully of all on the international stage, *Le Capitaine Charlotte* became Genée's widely played *Der Seekadett* and the Italian *Il Capitano Carlotta.*

His play *La Savonette impériale* (Palais-Royal 23 November 1835 w Auguste Anicet-Bourgeois) was operetticized on home ground as the successful *Ordre de l'empereur,* with a score by Justin Clérice (Théâtre des

Bouffes-Parisiens 4 March 1902), and his *La Nuit aux soufflets* (1842 w d'Ennery) was musicalized under the same title with a score by Hervé (ad Ferrier, d'Ennery, Théâtre des Nouveautés 18 September 1884).

1840 **La Perruche** (Louis Clapisson/w Henri Dupin) 1 act Opéra-Comique 18 April

1852 **Roméo et Mariette** (Hervé) 1 act Palais-Royal

1853 **Les Folies dramatiques** (Hervé/w Clairville) Palais-Royal 2 March

1858 **La Chaise à porteurs** (Victor Masse/w Clairville) 1 act Opéra-Comique 28 April

1862 **La Chatte merveilleuse** (Albert Grisar/w Adolphe d'Ennery) Théâtre Lyrique 18 March

DUMAS, Alexandre [DAVY DE LA PAILLETERIE, Alexandre] (b Villers-Cotterets, 24 July 1802; d Puys, nr Dieppe, 5 December 1870).

The works of the famous French novelist and playwright have provided the material for many musical plays, from the severely operatic to the bulgingly burlesque. On the operatic side, Donizetti set to music a version of Dumas's *Charles VII chez ses grands vassaux* as *Gemma di Vergy* (1834) and Cui reused the same work as the source of his *The Saracen;* Saint-Saëns's *Ascanio* (1890) was based on his play of the same title; Humperdinck set *Les Demoiselles de Saint-Cyr* for Berlin as *Die Heirat wider willen* (1905); and Isidore de Lara made an operatic version of *Les Trois Mousquetaires* (1921). Samara's *Mademoiselle de Belle-Isle* (1905) and Enna's *Gloria Arsena* (1917) were also based on Dumas works.

Les Trois Mousquetaires (1844) went through a variety of adaptations, both swashbuckling and burlesque, of which Rudolf Friml's Broadway musical and the spectacular German piece, musically set by Ralph Benatzky, proved the most notable, whilst *Le Comte de Monte Cristo* (1844) was made into a range of musical pieces from the Operette *Der Graf von Monte Christo* (C Pleninger/Beyer, Residenztheater, Dresden January 1883) and the musical play *Monte Cristo* (Jean-Claude Auvray, Michel Legrand/Jean Cosmos, Eddie Marnay, Théâtre de la Monnaie, Brussels 18 September 1975) to the highly successful British burlesque *Monte Cristo Jr* with its "principal boy" Edmond Dantès in tights.

Dumas's play *Kean* (1836) became a musical both on Broadway, as *Kean* (Robert Wright, George Forrest/Peter Stone, Broadway Theatre 2 November 1961), and in Romania, where it was played as *Soarele Londrei* ("The Sun of London") in a version by Florian Comisel and Nicosur Constantinescu.

Les Demoiselles de Saint-Cyr was given a comic opera treatment by Rudolf Dellinger and Oskar Walther as *Saint-Cyr* (Hamburg, 1891) and the French musical *Le Mariage au Tambour* by Paul Burani and Léon Vasseur was also based on a Dumas work (w Adolphe de Leuven, Brunswick). The Broadway musical *Apple Blossoms* quoted *Un Mariage sous Louis XV* as its source, *La Tulipe noire* (1850) became an opérette à grand spectacle in the hands of André Mouëzy-Éon, Albert Willemetz and Tiarko Richepin (Gaîté-Lyrique 19 March 1932), and Messager's unsuccessful comic opera *Le Chevalier d'Harmenthal* was based on Dumas's 1849 piece (w Auguste Maquet) of the same title, a piece which had earlier provoked Le Prevost and Beauvallet's burlesque *La Chevalière du chignon rouge* (Théâtre Déjazet 19 November 1869).

Dumas's novel *Les Frères corses,* later adapted to the stage by Eugène Grangé and Xavier de Montépin (1850) and, in English, with huge popularity by Dion Boucicault, was clearly not the material for a musical comedy, but it became the subject of several English-language burlesques, beginning as early as 1852 with *O Gemini!, or The Brothers of Co(u)rse* by Mark Lemon and Gilbert a' Beckett (Haymarket Theatre 12 April) and followed by an Irish *The Corkonian Brothers* (Strand Theatre 27 February 1853) for Irish comedian George Hodson, *The Corsican Bothers* (Globe Theatre, 1869), *The Corsican Brothers & Co* (Gaiety Theatre, 1880), George Sims's *The Of Course-Akin Brothers, Babes in the Wood* (Theatre Royal, Hull 19 March 1881) and *The New Corsican Brothers* (Royalty Theatre, 1889).

Dumas actually made a small personal contribution to the lyric stage, providing the libretti for such pieces as the opéra-comique *Piquillo* (w Gérard de Nerval) set by Hippolyte Monpou and played at the Opéra-Comique in 1837 (31 October), the two-act *La Bacchante* (Eugène Gautier/w de Leuven, de Beauplan, Opéra-Comique 4 November 1858) and Ambroise Thomas's *Le Roman d'Elvire* (w de Leuven, Opéra-Comique 4 February 1860).

His illegitimate son, **Alexandre DUMAS** (b Paris, 28 July 1824; d Paris, 27 November 1895), known as Dumas fils, was the author of the celebrated *La Dame aux camélias* (Théâtre du Vaudeville, Paris 2 February 1852). Originally produced as a "piece en cinq acts, mêlée de chant," with music by Montaubry accompanying the couple of musical numbers involved, it was later operaticized as *La Traviata* (1853) and burlesqued by Leicester Buckingham as *La Traviata, or The Lady Camelon* (Strand Theatre 7 September 1857). In the 1990s *La Traviata* was again burlesqued (*La Traviata, die Binde war ihr Schicksal,* lib: Walter Bockmayer) at Cologne's Kaiserhof (1 October 1998), and a Danish *Kamiliendame* was produced at Aarhus (3 September 1999). The "drame lyrique" *La Femme de Claude* (Louis Gallet/Albert Cahen, Opéra-Comique 1896) was also based on his original 1873 play of the same title.

In 1967 father and son themselves became the subject of a musical when the San Francisco and Los Angeles Light Opera produced a *Dumas and Son* (Dorothy Chandler Pavilion 1 August), written by Jerome Chodorov, and with a score by Wright and Forrest arranged from the music of Camille Saint-Saëns.

Biography: Gribble, F: *Dumas Father and Son* (Knopf, New York, 1930)

DUNAIEVSKY [DUNAJEVSZKIJ], Isaak Osipovitch (b Lokhvitza, Ukraine, 30 January 1900; d Moscow, 25 July 1955).

Dunaievsky studied music at the Kharkov conservatory (piano and violin) and made his earliest composition attempts in his late teens in the light music field, composing incidental music for a number of plays at the Kharkov Theatre from the age of 19. He wrote incidental theatre music, Operette scores and a considerable amount of film music, largely in a traditional style, whilst holding several state music posts—notably between 1936 and 1948 as musical director of the Moscow Railways' Central Cultural Establishment Song and Dance Ensemble. The texts which he illustrated were often politico-didactic in intent, but he nevertheless produced several songs which became popular and which helped his shows to be appreciated in a number of iron curtain countries. The most successful, *Vol'nyj veter* (Moscow 29 August 1949), was played in East Germany as *Freier Wind* (Volkstheater, Rostock 23 April 1953) and in Hungary as *Szabad szél* (Fővárosi Operettszínház 6 May 1950).

Biographies: Danilevitch, L: *Isaak Dunaievsky* (Moscow, 1947), Tchernov, A: *Isaak Dunaievsky* (Moscow, 1961)

DUNCAN, [Robert] Todd (b Danville, Ky, 12 February 1903, d Washington, DC, 28 February 1998).

Duncan made his first major theatrical appearance in his thirties, in *Cavalleria Rusticana,* and soon after created the leading role in the folk opera *Porgy and Bess* (1935), introducing "Bess, You Is My Woman Now" and "I Got Plenty o' Nuttin'." He subsequently appeared in the London spectacular *The Sun Never Sets* (1938) at the Theatre Royal, Drury Lane, singing "River God" and "Drums," and on Broadway as the Lawd's General in *Cabin in the Sky* (1940). He later worked in opera and in films, and repeated his performance as Porgy on many occasions, but devoted himself more to the concert stage and returned only once to the Broadway musical theatre, to play Stephen Kumalo in *Lost in the Stars* (1949). He subsequently retired to teaching.

DUNCAN, William Cary (b North Brookfield, Mass, 6 February 1874; d North Brookfield, Mass, 21 November 1945). A regular contributor to the American musical stage for 17 years, Duncan, in spite of working with some top-drawer collaborators, never succeeded in getting his name on a truly top-drawer show.

An English teacher at Brooklyn Polytechnic preparatory school for the first 20 years of his working life, Duncan first surfaced in the musical theatre as the author of Joseph Gaites's touring musical *Katie Did* when already in his mid-thirties. He subsequently wrote lyrics for the same producer's remusicked version of the Hungarian musical play *A Gyurkovicslányok,* unsuccessfully produced for Fritzi Scheff as *The Love Wager* (1912), and co-adapted the Vienna musical *Napoleon und die Frauen* for the American stage, under the title *The Purple Road.* He found sufficient success with his book to the Mormon musical *His Little Widows* (later filched to act as the text for a British piece, *Lady Luck*) to encourage him to give up English teaching, but his first success, two years later, came when George M Cohan burlesqued his seriously intended Ruritanian comic opera *The Royal Vagabond* into a Broadway run.

Duncan subsequently adapted the French farce *Le Chasseur de Chez Maxims* as the libretto to *The Blue Kitten* for Friml, revised Otto Harbach's libretto for *Molly Darling,* worked with Hammerstein and Youmans on *Mary Jane McKane,* provided Gallagher and Sheen with the text for *In Dutch,* adapted Hennequin and Veber's *Le Monsieur de cinq heures* as *Sunny Days* for producer/director Hassard Short, and collaborated on *Yes, Yes, Yvette,* a version of the hit play *Nothing But the Truth* which didn't succeed in giving *No, No, Nanette* producer H H Frazee a follow-up success. He also adapted John Hunter Booth's *Rolling Home* as a libretto for Harold Orlob, and teamed with Youmans again on the romantic old-America piece *Great Day,* in the wake of the success of *Show Boat.* In spite of some fair runs, however, none of these projects scored him a genuine hit, and he ended his busy career without having produced anything enduring.

1910 **Katie Did** (Karl Hoschna/w Frank Smithson) Colonial Theater, Chicago 18 February

1912 **The Love Wager** (Charles Hambitzer/Edith Ellis) Ford's Theater, Baltimore 16 September

1913 **The Purple Road** (*Napolon und die Frauen*) English version w Fred de Grésac (Liberty Theater)

1913 **When Love Is Young** (William Schroeder/Rida Johnson Young) Cort Theater, Chicago 28 October

1916 **A Regular Girl** (Winthrop Cortelyou, Hambitzer/w F Otis Drayton) Rochester, NY 18 September

1917 **Captain Cupid** (Schroeder/w Young) Shubert Theater, Minneapolis 15 April

1917 **His Little Widows** (aka *Some Little Girl*) (Schroeder/w Young) Astor Theater 30 April

1918 **Fiddlers Three** (Alexander Johnstone) Cort Theater 3 September

1919 **The Royal Vagabond** (Anselm Götzl/w Stephen Ivor Szinnyey) Cohan and Harris Theater 17 February

1919 **Sunshine** (A Johnstone) Trent Theater, Trenton 11 April

1920 **Three Showers** (Creamer and Layton) Harris Theater 5 April

1921 **The Rose Girl** (Götzl) Ambassador Theater 11 February

1922 **The Blue Kitten** (Rudolf Friml/w Harbach) Selwyn Theater 13 January

1922 **Molly Darling** (Tom Johnstone, Phil Cook/Clifford Grey, Joseph Herbert, et al/Otto Harbach ad) Liberty Theater 1 September

1923 **Just Apples** (Fred J Coots) Academy of Music, Brooklyn 9 March

1923 **Mary Jane McKane** (Vincent Youmans, Herbert Stothart/w Oscar Hammerstein II) Imperial Theater 25 December

1924 **In Dutch** (Joseph Meyer, William Daly, Alfred Newman/w Irving Caesar) Newark, NJ 22 September

1924 **Princess April** (Monte Carlo, Alma Sanders/w Lewis Allen Browne) Ambassador Theater 1 December

1925 **Suzanne** (Harold Orlob/w John Hunter Booth) Worcester, Mass, 28 September

1927 **Talk About Girls** (revised *Suzanne*) (Orlob, Stephen Jones/Caesar/w Daniel Kusell) Waldorf Theater 14 June

1927 **Yes, Yes, Yvette** (Phil Charig, Ben Jerome, Caesar/w James Montgomery) Harris Theater 3 October

1928 **Sunny Days** (Jean Schwartz/Clifford Grey) Imperial Theater 8 February

1929 **Moon Madness** (Sol Cohen/w Alice Barney) Figueroa Playhouse, Los Angeles 30 September

1929 **Great Day** (Youmans/w John Wells) Cosmopolitan Theater 17 October

DUNNE, Irene [Marie] (b Louisville, Ky, 20 December 1898; d Los Angeles, 4 September 1990). Charming singing ingenue who topped her half-dozen years of stage leads by a famous career in films.

At 22, Miss Dunne toured in the title role of *Irene,* and she subsequently played a succession of musical ingenue roles on Broadway in *The Clinging Vine* (1922, Tessie), *Lollipop* (1924, Virginia), *The City Chap* (1925, Grace Bartlett), *Sweetheart Time* (1926, Violet), *Yours Truly* (1927, Diana), *She's My Baby* (1928, Polly) and *Luckee Girl* (1928, Arlette) without finding a hit until she went on the road as Magnolia Hawks in the first national tour of *Show Boat* (1929).

There were hits a-plenty when she moved to movies and starred, most notably, in the celluloid versions of *Show Boat* (Magnolia), *Roberta* (Princess Stephanie) and *Sweet Adeline* (Addie), in *High, Wide and Handsome* and *The Joy of Living,* as well as in many important nonmusical roles.

DUPUIS, José [DUPUIS, Lambert Joseph Jacques Édouard] (b Liège, Belgium, 18 March 1833; d Nogent-sur-Marne, 9 May 1900). ''The greatest of the great . . . the most all-round actor I have ever known'' (Yvette Guilbert). Comedian and tenor who created lead roles in many of Offenbach's greatest works in the early years of a long career as a Parisian musical and comedy star.

The son of a drawing master, the 18-year-old Dupuis got his first chance to perform on the stage when a rich Liégois built a private theatre and he was given a spot there as an amateur singer. He did sufficiently well with his performances of light and comic songs to progress to professional engagements and, in 1854, he made the move to Paris. His had his first job there at the Bobino but, by the end of 1855, he had been given a contract at Hervé's Folies-Nouvelles where he made his first appearance in the one-acter *Jean et Jeanne* (1855) and found himself appreciated more for his talents as a light comedian than for his petite tenor singing voice. He was subsequently cast alongside Joseph Kelm in such little musical pieces as *Les Trois Troubadours, La Demoiselle de la Roche-Trombelon* and de Rille's *Le Jugement de Paris.*

He moved from the Folies-Nouvelles to the Théâtre Déjazet in 1859, playing there in such pieces as *Les Premières Armes de Figaro* and *Monsieur Garat,* and then, in 1861, joined the company at the Théâtre des Variétés. He soon became one of the theatre's principal comic players, performing in a range of pieces both with and without music (*Le Sylphe, Les Mille et une songes, L'Infortunée Caroline,* etc). His still light, but now much more secure and rangy, singing voice meant that he was able to take leading roles in substantial musical works and thus, in 1864, he created Hervé's *Le Joueur de Flûte* (Dyachilium) alongside the débutante Léa Silly, before being starred, the following year, in the role which would seal his fame: opposite Hortense Schneider as Paris in *La Belle Hélène* (''Au Mont Ida trois déesses'').

The triumph which Dupuis made in *La Belle Hélène* was confirmed in a run of outstanding creations at the Variétés over the next four years, as he introduced some of Offenbach's most famous comic-tenor characters in the opéras-bouffes *Barbe-bleue* (Barbe-bleue, ''Je suis Barbe-bleue, ô gué''), *La Grande-Duchesse de Gérolstein* (Fritz) and *La Périchole* (Piquillo), all as leading man to Mlle Schneider, and as the burlesque brigand-chief, Falsacappa, in *Les Brigands* alongside Zulma Bouffar. After a short detour into a Hervé piece (Robert Mouton in *Le Trône d'Écosse*) he continued in a further series of Offenbach creations—Marcassou in *Les Braconniers,* Bernadille in *La Boulangère à des écus,* Docteur Ox in *Le Docteur Ox*—of other new musicals—Dunois in *Le Beau Dunois* (1870), Pierre Cargounioul in *Les Charbonniers,* Boulboum in Hervé's *La Veuve du Malabar* (1873)—and repertoire and revival productions, including notable repeats of his own celebrated roles, but also the part of Baron Gondremarck in the first Variétés production of *La Vie parisienne.*

Dupuis subsequently starred alongside Anna Judic in the famous series of Théâtre des Variétés vaudeville-opérettes, playing the disappearing circus-owner, Casimir, and in Lecocq's *Le Grand Casimir,* in the dual role of de la Boucanière father and son in Hervé's *La Femme à Papa,* as Grégoire in *Niniche,* the three ages of Plinchard in *Lili,* Médard in *La Roussotte* and Jules Primitif in *La Cosaque,* but further reprises as Paris, Fritz and Falsacappa in the mid-1880s proved that his singing voice was no longer sufficient to the task. From this time on, he had to rely on his comic abilities and the public's memories to pull him through in the musical shows which were mixed with the Variétés' regular schedule of plays (Saint-Galmier in *Mam'zelle Gavroche,* 1885, etc).

In the late '80s he tactfully abandoned the comic jeune premier roles he had held so long, and moved across to the character tenor parts, making a particular success as the fussy pedant, Frimousse, in revivals of *Le Petit Duc,* but he retained the roles of Gondremarck and Falsacappa until his last performances, still at the Variétés, in his sixties.

DURANTE, Jimmy [DURANTE, James Francis] (b New York City, 10 February 1893; d Santa Monica, Calif, 29 January 1980).

After an early career in vaudeville, as part of the quickly successful act Clayton, Jackson and Durante, the comedian with the famous nose—familiarly known as his "schnozzola"—appeared on Broadway with his partners in the 1929 *Show Girl* (Snozzle) and the 1930 *The New Yorkers* (Jimmie Deegan).

The team was disbanded in 1931 and, in a subsequent career which switched back and forth among theatre, film and variety performances, Durante, who had always been the featured member of the group, went on to star in the revue *Strike it Pink* (1933), as the finagling pressman Claudius Bowers in Billy Rose's circus spectacular, *Jumbo* (1935), opposite Ethel Merman as the convict, Policy Pinkle, in *Red, Hot and Blue!* (1936), in the unfortunate movieland piece *Stars in Your Eyes* (1939, Bill) and, in a last Broadway appearance, in the Shubert flop revue *Keep Off the Grass* (1940).

Durante also appeared in a number of musical films, including the movie versions of *Sally, Irene and Mary* (1938, Jefferson Twitchell) and *Jumbo* (1962, Pop Wonder), and occasionally turned his hand to songwriting, contributing several numbers to the score of *Show Girl.*

Durante, a musical based on his "life and times," written by Frank Peppiate and John Aylesworth to a pasticcio score, was produced at the St Lawrence Center, Toronto, 12 August 1989, with Lonny Price as Durante. It folded on the road.

Biographies: Fowler, G: *Schnozzola, the Story of Jimmy Durante* (Viking, New York, 1951), Robbins, J: *Inka Dinka Doo* (Paragon House, New York, 1991)

DURU, [Henri] Alfred (b Paris, ?1 June 1828; d Paris, 30 December 1889). The partner of Henri Chivot in what became one of the most outstanding and fruitful libretto and lyric-writing partnerships of the French opérette and comic stages.

The pair worked only occasionally with other writers (*La Fille du clown,* the burlesque of the benefit system called *Les Mirlitons,* the successful comedies *Doit-on le dire?* w Labiche and *La Boïte à Bibi* w St Agnan Choler 1877, etc), and their partnership endured for over 30 years, until Duru's death, during an influenza epidemic and the rehearsals for their *Le Voyage de Suzette,* at the age of 60.

Duru wrote several pieces alone, amongst which was the successful vaudeville *Les Deux Noces de M Boisjoli,* metamorphized by H B Farnie into a major London hit with a pasticcio score under the title of *Nemesis* and into *Zwei Hochzeiten und ein Bräutigam* at Vienna's Carltheater (1873), where the score was provided by Conradin.

1865 **Un Rêve** (Edmond Savary/w Henri Chivot) 1 act Théâtre Lyrique 13 October

1866 **Les Chevaliers de la table ronde** (Hervé/w Chivot) Théâtre des Bouffes-Parisiens 17 November

1867 **Les Défauts de Jacotte** (Victor Robillard/w Chivot) Fantaisies-Parisiennes 27 April

1868 **Fleur de thé** (Charles Lecocq/w Chivot) Théâtre de l'Athenée 11 April

1868 **L'Île de Tulipatan** (Jacques Offenbach/w Chivot) 1 act Théâtre des Bouffes-Parisiens 30 September

1868 **Le Soldat malgré lui** (Frédéric Barbier/w Chivot) Fantaisies-Parisiennes 17 October

1868 **Le Carnaval d'un merle blanc** (Lecocq/w Chivot) Palais-Royal 30 December

1869 **Gandolfo** (Lecocq/w Chivot) 1 act Théâtre des Bouffes-Parisiens 16 January

1869 **Le Docteur Purgandi** (Robillard/w Chivot) 1 act Folies-Bergeres 2 May

1869 **Le Rajah de Mysore** (Lecocq/w Chivot) 1 act Théâtre des Bouffes-Parisiens 21 September

1870 **Le Beau Dunois** (Lecocq/w Chivot) Théâtre des Variétés 13 April

1872 **Les Cent Vierges** (Lecocq/w Clairville, Chivot) Théâtre des Fantaisies-Parisiennes, Brussels 16 March

1873 **Les Braconniers** (Offenbach/w Chivot) Théâtre des Variétés 29 January

1873 **Les Pommes d'or** (w Chivot, Henri Blondeau, Hector Monréal) Théâtre du Château d'Eau 8 February

1875 **La Blanchisseuse de Berg-op-Zoom** (Léon Vasseur/w Chivot) Théâtre des Folies-Dramatiques 27 January

1875 **Le Pompon** (Lecocq/w Chivot) Théâtre des Folies-Dramatiques 10 November

1876 **Les Mirlitons** (Auguste Coedès/w Henri Chabrillat, Henri Bocage, Ernest Blum) Théâtre des Folies-Dramatiques 19 April

1878 **La Saint-Valentin** (Edmond Audran/w Chivot) 1 act Cercle Saint-Arnaud

1878 **Madame Favart** (Offenbach/w Chivot) Théâtre des Folies-Dramatiques 28 December

1879 **Les Noces d'Olivette** (Edmond Audran/w Chivot) Théâtre des Bouffes-Parisiens 13 November

1879 **La Fille du tambour-major** (Offenbach/w Chivot) Théâtre des Folies-Dramatiques 13 December

1880 **La Mère des compagnons** (Hervé/w Chivot) Théâtre des Folies-Dramatiques 15 December

1880 **La Mascotte** (Audran/w Chivot) Théâtre des Bouffes-Parisiens 29 December

1882 **Boccace** French version w Chivot, Gustave Layge (Galeries Saint-Hubert, Brussels, Théâtre des Folies-Dramatiques, Paris)

1882 **Gillette de Narbonne** (Audran/w Chivot) Théâtre des Bouffes-Parisiens 11 November

1883 **La Princesse des Canaries** (Lecocq/w Chivot) Théâtre des Folies-Dramatiques 9 February

1883 **Les Pommes d'or** revised version with score by Audran Théâtre des Menus-Plaisirs 12 February

1883 **La Dormeuse éveillée** (Audran/w Chivot) Théâtre des Bouffes-Parisiens 27 December

1884 **Le Grand Mogol** revised version w Chivot (Théâtre de la Gaîté)

1884 **L'Oiseau bleu** (Lecocq/w Chivot) Théâtre des Nouveautés 16 January

1885 **Pervenche** (Audran/w Chivot) Théâtre des Bouffes-Parisiens 31 March

1886 **La Cigale et la fourmi** (Audran/w Chivot) Théâtre de la Gaîté 30 October

1887 **Surcouf** (Robert Planquette/w Chivot) Théâtre des Folies-Dramatiques 6 October

1888 **La Petite Fronde** (Audran/w Chivot) Théâtre des Folies-Dramatiques 16 November

1889 **La Fille à Cacolet** (Audran/w Chivot) Théâtre des Variétés 10 July

1890 **Le Voyage de Suzette** (Léon Vasseur/w Chivot) Théâtre de la Gaîté 20 January

DUVAL, Georges [RIEUX, Claude] (b Paris, 2 February 1847; d Paris, 28 September 1919).

Journalist (*L'Evènement,* etc), the author of many plays and novels, the translator of the complete works of Shakespeare into French, of Bulwer-Lytton and of Sheridan, and a writer on the subject of both the French and British classic stage, Duval also authored a number of opérette libretti with an unusually high percentage rate of success.

His first work, Planquette's military opérette *Les Voltigeurs de la 32ème,* won a firm success in France and an outstanding one in Britain (*The Old Guard*), the lively, vaudevillesque *Mam'zelle Crénom* lasted out the hundred metropolitan performances which in those days marked out a hit, and the texts for *Les P'tites Michu* and *Véronique* were admirable pieces of late classic opérette writing which, attached to Messager's sparkling scores, gave their authors worldwide success.

His highly successful play *Coquin de printemps* (w Adolphe Jaime) formed the basis for the Josef Strauss pasticcio *Frühlingsluft* (ad Karl Lindau, Julius Wilhelm, Ernst Reiterer), and for London's Gaiety Theatre musical *The Spring Chicken,* though apparently not for the equally successful French musical play of the same title.

1880 **Les Voltigeurs de la 32ème** (Robert Planquette/w Edmond Gondinet) Théâtre de la Renaissance 7 January

1881 **Faublas** (François Luigini/w Édouard Cadol) Théâtre Cluny 25 October

1883 **L'Éducation d'Achille** (Pauline Thys) 1 act Grand Théâtre, Nantes March

1884 **La Bagasse** (Jean Brus/w Édouard Cadol, Édouard Philippe) Théâtre des Menus-Plaisirs 18 October

1888 **Mam'zelle Crénom** (Léon Vasseur/w Adolphe Jaime) Théâtre des Bouffes-Parisiens 19 January

1888 **Le Mariage avant la lettre** (Olivier Métra/w Jaime) Théâtre des Bouffes-Parisiens 5 December

1891 **Tout Paris** (Louis Ganne) Théâtre du Châtelet 16 June

1896 **Mignonette** (Georges Street) Théâtre des Nouveautés 3 October

1897 **Les P'tites Michu** (André Messager/w Albert Vanloo) Théâtre des Bouffes-Parisiens 16 November

1898 **Véronique** (Messager/w Vanloo) Théâtre des Bouffes-Parisiens 10 December

1900 **La Belle au bois dormant** (Charles Lecocq/w Vanloo) Théâtre des Bouffes-Parisiens 19 February

1905 **Les Dragons de l'Imperatrice** (Messager/w Vanloo) Théâtre des Variétés 13 February

1913 **Cocorico** (Ganne/w Maurice Soulié, P Jailly) Théâtre Apollo 29 November

1918 **Mademoiselle "Nom d'une pipe"** (Charles Cuvillier) Palais-Royal 16 July

E

THE EARL AND THE GIRL Musical comedy in 2 acts by Seymour Hicks. Lyrics by Percy Greenbank. Music by Ivan Caryll. Adelphi Theatre, London, 10 December 1903.

Having taken over the late Richard D'Oyly Carte's interests at the Savoy Theatre, William Greet attempted to continue to produce comic opera there in the traditional manner. However, in spite of such succès d'estime as *Merrie England,* he found himself obliged first to tour the Savoy company and then to bend to the all-consuming fashion for modern musical comedy. Thus the Savoy stars, long nurtured on Gilbert, Sullivan, Hood and German, were pitched into an up-to-date Seymour Hicks show, with Henry Lytton expected to play the Hicks role, principal tenor Robert Evett a straight modern juvenile called the Hon Crewe Boodle, Savoy prima donna Agnes Fraser cast to be another Ellaline Terriss, and her husband, Walter Passmore, a longtime Ko-Ko and Jack Point, to play musical-comedy comedy. The cast was completed with more regular musical comedy players in soubrette Florence Lloyd and character lady Phyllis Broughton, an American comedian, John C Dixon, and a heavy lady (Helen Kinnaird), and the show directed by Hicks, but with Savoy musical director Hamish MacCunn conducting.

Fortunately for all concerned, the vehicle provided for the company was an excellent, if fairly unoriginal, one of its kind. Passmore played a little circus dog trainer, Jim Cheese, who earns some necessary money by agreeing to impersonate an earl called Dick Wargrave (Lytton), who needs an incognito to allow him to elope discreetly with his beloved Elphin Haye (Miss Fraser). The action took place to the accompaniment of a collection of examples of most of the regular kinds of musical comedy numbers, ranging from the patriotic song (''The Grenadiers'') to the drawing-room ballad (''Thou Art My Rose'') and something that sounded not unlike the currently ubiquitous ''Tell Me, Pretty Maiden.''

The success of *The Earl and the Girl* was helped by two elements for both of which Hicks was responsible: it came to its first night much more slickly directed and rehearsed than was normal at the time, and Caryll's score was stuffed full of bristling interpolated numbers, many from America. One of these, the naive ''My Cosy Corner Girl'' (John Bratton/Charles Noel Douglas), became a major hit for Lytton and Miss Fraser, whilst two other already proven transatlantic hits, Blanche Ring's ''Sammy,'' now sung by Louie Pounds, and ''In Zanzibar'' also did well.

The show ran for over a year in London (371 performances)—during which time a number of new songs were introduced—and a string of overseas productions followed. The Shuberts mounted their American production in Chicago with Alexander Clarke featured as Jim Cheese in place of Eddie Foy (who'd walked out over money), alongside Georgia Caine (Elphin) and Savoy veteran W H Denny, in an Americanized version in which Jerome Kern's ''How'd You Like to Spoon with Me,'' performed by Victor Morley and Miss Caine and featuring a distracting row of chorines swinging out over the audience on floral swings, ''If It's Good Enough for Vanderbilt It's Good Enough for Me'' and ''Nicolini'' were favorites amongst the numbers which replaced the already too-well-Broadway-exposed interpolations used in London. Slated for the burned-out Casino Theater, the show had to be sidetracked to Philadelphia's Lyric Theater when the Casino's rebuilding schedule got behind time, but it scored well on its five-months-later-than-intended arrival on Broadway, with Foy by now starring largely in the place originally intended for him. It remained in New York for a run of 147 performances before going back to the country for a long touring life.

In Australia, the travesty comedian John Sheridan got into male attire to star as Jim Cheese alongside Maud Amber (Elphin) and Winfield Blake (Dick), but the production's singular success was ended by its star's premature death. Further afield, Sass and Nelson included *The Earl and the Girl* in their Edwardes-related companies' repertoires in South America and South Africa, and Greet himself toured the piece around the British provinces for several years whilst letting the secondary town rights to J Bannister Howard.

The Earl and the Girl reappeared in London in 1914 (Aldwych Theatre 4 November) and proved the most successful of the bundle of past favorites which were played in the early days of the war (107 performances). It also got a late first translation when *Hello!! Charley* (ad P-L Flers) was produced in Paris, after the end of the hostilities, under the management of Léon Volterra, in a version featuring Henri Vilbert, Aimé Simon-Girard, Félix Oudart, Rose Amy, Yvonne Yma and Thérèse Dornay, and in which the second act ended with everyone doing Herman Darewski and Arthur Wimperis's ''The Shimmy Shake'' (which they hadn't done before).

USA: Garrick Theater, Chicago 18 March 1905, Casino Theater 4 November 1905; Australia: Criterion Theatre, Sydney 22 July 1905; France: Théâtre Apollo *Hello!! Charley* 3 April 1919

EARLE, Virginia [née EARL] (b Cincinnati, Ohio, 6 August 1873; d Englewood, NJ, 21 September 1937). Turn-of-the-century star soubrette of Broadway's musical theatre.

The child of actor Nathaniel Wheeler Earl and his Irish actress wife, Sarah, Virginia Earle made her first stage appearances in juvenile theatre, before beginning her barely adult career touring with the Pike Opera Company. She subsequently moved on into musical theatre, touring as a teenager through America with Hallen and Hart (Susie Caps in *Later On,* 1889) and Rice's Surprise Party (Priscilla in *The World's Fair,* 1890, etc) and visiting Australia in the burlesques *Evangeline* (Evangeline) and *The Corsair* (Medora) with another of the same manager's companies. She stayed behind to appear in Melbourne's 1891 Christmas attraction as Bandini in Byron's *Cinderella* before returning home. Although it was dramatically reported that she was likely to have a hand amputated, following a misadventure with an exploding soda bottle in Sydney, she emerged in one well-publicized piece and instead joined De Wolf Hopper's company, making her first Broadway appearance, in 1894, in revue at the Casino Theater.

She created her first sizeable role in T Pearsall Thorne's romantic comic opera *Leonardo,* supporting George Devoll and Marguerite Lemon in a flop show which unhistorically married da Vinci off to a duke's daughter, before returning to the Casino for more revue and for the first of the roles which would establish her as one of the town's favorite soubrettes—the delightful Phyllis of the Casino's botched version of *The Lady Slavey* and Miss Lotta Bonds in the short-lived *The Gold Bug* (1896).

From 1896 she appeared in a series of plays and imported musicals for Augustin Daly at his New York theatre, starring in *The Geisha* (succeding Violet Lloyd as Molly), *The Circus Girl* (Dora), *La Poupée* (Alésia) and *A Runaway Girl* (Winifred) as well as playing Flora to the *Meg Merrilees* of Ada Rehan in a new musical version of *Guy Mannering* and Ariel in Daly's production of *The Tempest,* before returning to the Casino. There she featured in several of the now free-flowing home-bred musicals—*The Casino Girl* (1900, in breeches as juvenile lead Earl Cholmondley), *The Belle of Bohemia* (1900, Katie), *The Girl from Up There* (1901, Phrynette)—visiting Britain with the company of this last-named show, in its attempt to repeat the success of *The Belle of New York.*

In 1902 she played Lady Holyrood in a revival of *Florodora,* the following year succeeded Blanche Ring in *The Jewel of Asia,* and in 1903 she was given star billing for the first time in George White's production of the Baldwin Sloane comic opera *Sergeant Kitty* (Kitty La Tour), a billing she had to relinquish when she followed up by appearing with Fay Templeton in the less successful *In Newport* (1904, Viola Cartwright). She played in the revusical *Lifting the Lid* (1905, Bessie Otis Adams) and Nanki-Poo in the accompanying Gilbert and Sullivan revue at the New Amsterdam's Aerial Roof Gardens in 1905, but thereafter she turned to vaudeville, touring in a musical sketch *A Midnight Mistake* (1907), and was little seen in the musical theatre, until—coming back from a 1910 nervous breakdown—she repeated her *The Geisha* role at the age of 38 in a last recorded musical comedy appearance.

L'EAU À LA BOUCHE Opérette in 3 acts by Serge Veber. Music by Georges van Parys and Philippe Parès. Théâtre Daunou, Paris, 5 September 1928.

Following the success of their *Lulu,* the rising team of Parès and van Parys were given a second production at the Théâtre Daunou and won a second success with their lively, up-to-date, made-for-dancing songs. Fernand Graavey scored with a spicy, self-deprecating piece declaring ''il triche au jeu, il boit mais qu'importe . . . il a une belle auto, Toto,'' and joined Loulou Hégoburu, star of *No, No, Nanette,* in the fox-trot ''Oh! Dis! Claudie''; she glided through the bluesy ''Ce n'est qu'un mannequin'' whilst Germaine Auger put across ''Donne-moi-z'en un bout'' for a run of five months.

EBB, Fred (b New York, 8 April 1932). Highly successful Broadway lyricist whose most successful material has been for a selection of female stars.

A graduate of New York and Columbia universities, lyricist Ebb did his earliest songwriting with composer Paul Klein in a collaboration which produced a novelty hit number ''Close the Door (they're coming in the window)'' (1955), contributions to the revues *Put It in Writing, From A to Z* (1960) and *Vintage 60* (1960, ''Dublin Town''), and one short-lived ''play with music,'' *Morning Sun.* Ebb both adapted the libretto from a story by Mary Deasy and composed the lyrics for this piece which, with Patricia Neway and Bert Convy starring, folded in nine performances off-Broadway.

In the early 1960s Ebb teamed up with composer John Kander, and the pair had an early success with the songs ''My Coloring Book'' and ''I Don't Care Much,'' recorded by Barbra Streisand. Their first stage musical venture together, *Flora, the Red Menace,* survived only 87 performances on Broadway, but they hit the jackpot with their second try. *Cabaret* (''Willkommen,'' ''Two Ladies,'' ''Don't Tell Mama,'' ''Cabaret,'' ''If You Could See Her'') earned its writers a fine run, a Tony Award and an international career. When they topped up their score for the show's film version with some more numbers for the top-cast Liza Minnelli (''Mein Herr,'' ''Maybe This Time,'' ''Money, Money, Money''), numbers which, while perhaps less suitable to the play and the character, proved enormously popular both in and out of it, they added an Academy Award to their show's score of trophies.

Whilst *Cabaret* went on to became a major international favorite in the wake of the film's vast success, the pair moved from its acrid prewar Berlin setting to a much gentler French-Canadian one as the locale for their follow-up, the warmly colored *The Happy Time.* David Merrick's production of this work ran only a fair 286 Broadway performances, but the same year brought the songwriters another important hit when they ventured into another colorful European setting with a musical version of the tale of *Zorba the Greek. Zorba,* which did not have the stage-within-a-stage from which *Cabaret* had profited to introduce stand-up material, naturally produced less in the way of popular songs than its famous predecessor, but it proved a highly successful and effective musical play with some lively, and some very affecting, song moments (''Happy Birthday''). It has won numerous overseas productions, become particularly popular in central Europe, and survived healthily in the American repertoire.

A musical version of the English comedy *Breath of Spring* under the confusing title of *70, Girls, 70* (''Coffee in a Cardboard Cup'') was a failure, but the satirical black-and-tinsel *Chicago,* a vaudevillesque retelling of a showbizzy Jazz Age murder, found Ebb and Kander back in the stand-up songs area which they had so effectively inhabited in *Cabaret* and, like *Cabaret, Chicago* produced some outstanding song success, (''Razzle Dazzle,'' ''All That Jazz,'' ''Mr Cellophane,'' ''All I Need is Love''). The musical itself also proved a long-running and enduring hit, not only in America but, notably, in both England and Australia.

A vehicle for Liza Minnelli, staged on Broadway as *The Act,* followed the act-within-a-show formula further but less successfully, but *Woman of the Year,* another show with a large and forceful central female star role, played first by Lauren Bacall and then by Raquel Welch and Debbie Reynolds, held the Broadway stage longer, and hosted a much-liked duet called ''The Grass Is Always Greener'' and an extractable ''(I'm one of the girls who's just) One of the Boys.''

An emotional, double-headed female star piece, *The Rink,* with Miss Minnelli and Chita Rivera in the roles of an eventually reconciled daughter and mother, played for 204 performances on Broadway and was later seen briefly in Britain and on several occasions on the Continent without establishing itself in the same way as the team's major hits, after which—give or take a revival—Ebb and his partner disappeared from the world's major stages for a surprisingly long time. However, they returned at the beginning of the 1990s with a musical version of the successful novel, play and film *Kiss of the Spiderwoman,* written to allow the inclusion of the glittery show-numbers which had become its songwriters' speciality within its grim prison framework. This piece side-stepped Broadway and its then critic and, after a Westchester tryout, instead opted for a London opening, with Miss Rivera starring, two years later. The piece subsequently moved on to Broadway for a respectable run.

In 1997, after another disappointingly long break, Kander and Ebb returned one more time with the score for a depression-era piece called *Steel Pier* which centered on the marathon dancing contests of those days. Whilst a highly popular revival of *Chicago* ran on, and productions of *Cabaret* flourished worldwide, this one went under in 76 performances.

Beyond the three stage musicals and the film rewrite of *Cabaret,* Ebb and his partner have written considerable further special material for Liza Minnelli, notably her television specials *Liza* and *Liza with a Z,* the program *Sam Found Out* (1988) with its one-act musical, her pairing with Goldie Hawn in *Goldie and Liza Together,* a nightclub act, and the musical portion of the film *Lucky Lady.* They also wrote and produced Chita Rivera's nightclub act, *Chita Plus Two,* and have supplied material both for further films (notably for Barbra Streisand in *Funny Lady,* and the extremely hit title song for *New York, New York*) and other television star vehicles (Frank Sinatra's *Ole Blue Eyes Is Back, Baryshnikov on Broadway,* Shirley Maclaine's *The Gypsy in My Soul*) as well as the TV musical *Three for the Girls* (CBS 5 November 1973).

Several compilation shows of Ebb and Kander material have been produced over the years (*2X5, City Lights,* etc), the most successful being the off-Broadway production *And the World Goes 'Round* (Westside Theater 18 March 1991).

1963 **Morning Sun** (Paul Klein) Phoenix Theater 6 October

1965 **Flora, the Red Menace** (Kander/George Abbott, Robert Russell) Alvin Theater 11 May

1966 **Cabaret** (Kander/Joe Masteroff) Broadhurst Theater 20 November

1968 **The Happy Time** (Kander/N Richard Nash) Broadway Theater 18 January

1968 **Zorba** (Kander/Joseph Stein) Imperial Theater 17 November

1971 **70, Girls, 70** (Kander/Masteroff) Broadhurst Theater 15 April

1975 **Chicago** (Kander/w Bob Fosse) 46th Street Theater 3 June

1977 **The Act** (aka *Shine It On*) (Kander/George Furth) Majestic Theater 29 October

1981 **Woman of the Year** (Kander/Peter Stone) Palace Theater 29 March

1984 **The Rink** (Kander/Terrence McNally) Martin Beck Theater 9 February

1990 **Kiss of the Spiderwoman** (Kander/McNally) Westchester 1 May; Shaftesbury Theatre, London 20 October 1992

1997 **Steel Pier** (Kander/David Thompson) Richard Rodgers Theater 24 April

1999 **Over and Over** (Kander/Stein) Signature Theater, Washington, DC 9 January

EDDY, Nelson (b Providence, RI, 29 June 1901; d Miami Beach, Fla, 6 March 1967). Hollywood's all-time favorite operetta leading man, with a limited stage exposure.

Eddy at first led a career "in commerce" and studied singing with the baritone David Bispham who had, himself, performed with notable success in both opera and light opera in Britain and America. He made his earliest appearances on the stage, from 1922 onwards, in both operatic and light operatic roles, including the Gilbert and Sullivan repertoire, before—aided by a smooth profile and a tidy figure with which to complement his suave high baritone voice—he began a film career in 1931.

During the 1930s and early 1940s Eddy starred for MGM in the film versions of a number of stage musicals, including *Rose-Marie, Naughty Marietta, Rosalie, Sweethearts, Maytime, Balalaika, The New Moon, Bitter-Sweet, The Chocolate Soldier, I Married an Angel* and *Knickerbocker Holiday* (many of which bore only a small resemblance to their stage counterparts), mostly in partnership with soprano Jeanette MacDonald. The pair became the biggest singing film-stars of their time and Eddy's performances of such roles as Jim Kenyon in *Rose-Marie* ("Indian Love Call"), Captain Dick in *Naughty Marietta* ("Tramp, Tramp, Tramp," "Ah! Sweet Mystery of Life," "I'm Falling in Love with Someone") and the hero of the severely rewritten *The New Moon* ("Stout Hearted Men") became the models for the large cinema audience who saw them and, thus, for future stage productions.

Eddy was commemorated in the song "Nelson" in the American edition of the musical show *A Day in Hollywood, a Night in the Ukraine.*

Biographies: Kiner L F: *Nelson Eddy: A Bio-Bibliography* (Scarecrow Press, Metuchen, NJ, 1992), Lulay, G: *Nelson Eddy: America's Favorite Baritone* (Goldfleet Publishing, Wheeling, Ill, 1990)

EDISS, Connie [COATES, Ada Harriet] (b Brighton, 11 August 1870; d Brighton, 18 April 1934). The most successful musical comedienne of the Gaiety Theatre age of British musical comedy.

A performer of comic songs on the halls from the age of 12 (initially as "Connie Coutts"), and in pantomime (Hon Halliwell Lane in *Jack & Jill,* Manchester 1894, as Connie Ediss), plump and pleasing Connie was spotted by George Edwardes who in 1895 sent her to America to play the role of the phony orphan millionairess in his Broadway production of *The Shop Girl.* She returned to play the role at the Gaiety Theatre for the last months of the show's London run and there she remained, almost unbrokenly, for the next decade, building herself a huge following as the town's favorite musical comedienne.

Her first creation was the role of the Lady Mayoress in *My Girl* (1896) in which she performed a relyricked version of May Irwin's Bully Song as "When My Husband Is Sir Tom," and she followed this decided success with long-running roles as the jealous Ringmaster's wife in *The Circus Girl* (1896, "The Way to Treat a Lady"), the Hackney Spaniard Carmenita in *A Runaway Girl* ("Society") and Mrs Bang, the washerwoman mother of *The Messenger Boy* ("Comme çi, Comme ça"). She was lured away by Tom B Davis's *Florodora* finances to appear in that show's successor, *The Silver Slipper* (1901, Bella Gimper), at the Lyric, but she returned to the Gaiety as soon as *The Silver Slipper* closed to replace the sacked Claire Romaine as Mrs Malton Hoppings in *The Toreador* (1901) and to appear as Caroline Twining in *The Orchid* (1903, "Fancy Dress"), as the suspicious Mrs Girdle in *The Spring Chicken* (1905, equipped with one of her best songs in "I Don't Know But I Guess") and as an overweight genie in *The New Aladdin* (1906, "I Want to be Mortal"). In between times she appeared with Henry Lytton on the music-hall stage in George Rollit's musical comedy sketch *United Service* (London Pavilion 12 August 1906).

When Connie left Edwardes's theatre, in 1907, to go to South Africa for a healthful break, an era ended at the

Gaiety, where the endearingly chubby and chirpy performer had become the personification of the modern musical as purveyed by George Edwardes and his imitators, and where her pairings with the little comedian Teddy Payne had created some of the most marvellous moments in London musical comedy.

She continued from Africa to America and was soon snapped up to play more of the weighty-lady comic roles of which she had become the Edwardian archetype. She starred with Lew Fields in *The Girl Behind the Counter* (1907, Mrs Schniff), toured unprofitably in the Shuberts' *The Girl From the States/The Golden Widow* (1909, Madame Wowski) and returned to Broadway to play an expanded (for her benefit) version of the role of Mrs Smith, created by Ada Blanche, in *The Arcadians.* She later went on the road with the show round America. Back in London, she appeared again for Edwardes in the less robustly comic role of Martje in *The Girl in the Train* (1910, *Die geschiedene Frau*), toured the music halls with the Herbert Clayton sketch *Laura Kicks* (1911), returned to the Gaiety for *Peggy* (1911, Lady Snoop) and *The Sunshine Girl* (1912, Brenda Blacker), and then appeared in both London and New York as Euphemia Knox in *The Girl on the Film* (1913) and in New York alone in the American production of Renyi's *A kis gróf* (*Suzi,* 1914, Lina Balzer).

In 1915–18 she visited Australia and New Zealand to play in a series of musicals (Grace in *So Long, Letty,* Mrs Dick Winters in *Three Twins,* Penelope in *Oh, Boy!,* Mrs Payton in *You're in Love,* Victoria in *Tonight's the Night, The Girl in the Taxi, The Carnival Girl,* Fifi in *A Waltz Dream,* Blanche Moss in *Canary Cottage,* etc), then, after another brief American interlude (*Oh, Uncle!* 1919), returned to Britain. But now, after a quarter of a century, her musical career was all but done. Instead she developed a highly successful career in straight comedy, appearing on the musical stage only in the revusical *The Smith Family* at London's Empire Theatre in 1922 during the last dozen years of her working life.

EDOUIN, Willie [BRYER, William Frederick] (b Brighton, 1 January 1846; d London, 14 April 1908). Star comedian of nearly 40 years and several generations of musical theatre in Britain and America.

The son of a dancing master, John Edwin Bryer, Willie Edouin first appeared on the stage with his brothers and sisters **[Edwin] Charles BRYER** ka **EDOUIN** (b Brighton, 1833; d Etawate, nr Agra, India, 9 May 1869), **John [William] BRYER** ka **EDOUIN** (b Brighton, 16 September 1840; d Bombay, India, 17 December 1875), **Eliza [Sarah] BRYER** ka **EDOUIN** (b Brighton, 18 April 1842; d Forest Creek, Australia, 3 October 1857), **Julia [Lucy] BRYER** ka **EDOUIN** (b Brighton, 10 December 1847; d Philadelphia, 3 March 1891) and "the infant Grimaldi," **Rose BRYER** ka **EDOUIN** (b Brighton, 29 January 1844; d Harrogate, 24 August 1925). They were seen, billed as "The Edouin Family," at London's Strand Theatre in the "petite pantomime" *Harlequin and Gulliver* at Christmas 1852 and played the following summer in their home town of Brighton as "Mr Bunn's Living Marionettes," whilst Willie subsequently appeared in children's roles in pantomime at Drury Lane, at Sadler's Wells and the Surrey Theatre, and in both burlesque (*Belphegor*) and pantomime (*Taffy Was a Welshman,* 1854, etc) at the Strand.

In 1856 the Edouin family abandoned Britain for Australia. Billed as "The Edouin Juvenile Vaudeville and Ballet Company," they played an introductory week of their entertainment *Frolics in France* and the seriocomic ballet *Hob in the Well* with Gustavus V Brooke at Melbourne's Theatre Royal and then toured the gold rush camps, traveling in a wagon built to carry their wardrobe and props in its belly, with seats at either end for the family. "It was drawn by three horses and painted on the side in red and white letters was 'the celebrated Edouin family in farce, comedy and burlesque.' We would get to a new 'rush' and give a performance in the dining-tent or even on the grass—in fact anywhere we could get." The family finally settled in Melbourne where they played at the Cremorne Gardens and appeared in pantomime ("I played clown and made the shoes for the whole family and manufactured my own properties and tricks as well as my clown's costume every Christmas"). They later traveled the Asian circuit from China, Japan and India (where two of Willie's brothers died) to the West Coast of America.

In 1866 the by now adult and gone-solo Willie based himself in America. He worked at first on the West Coast, where he was for a time a member of the original and memorable stock company at San Francisco's California Theater (January 1868), and then in New York, performing as a comedian and actor in variety and ministrel sketches (Narcissus Fritzfrizzle in *The Dancing Barber,* Murphy in *Handy Andy* with Bryant's Minstrels, etc) and featuring such burlesque turns as a ballet-skirted imitation of the dancer Bonfanti. In mid-1870 he joined up with Lydia Thompson's famous "British Blondes" company, performing featured comic roles with the troupe in both America—where brother John and his wife Tilly Earl also made up part of the country—and, during Miss Thompson's visits to Britain, between 1874 and 1876, at the Charing Cross, Globe and Criterion Theatres in London. Amongst the pieces in which he appeared with this famous burlesque company were *Ixion* (Cupid), *Sinbad* (Hadji), *The Forty Thieves* (Ali Baba), *St George and the Dragon* (Sultan), *The Brigand, Bluebeard, or the Mor-*

Plate 111. **Willie Edouin** *had two careers: as a youngish 19th-century farce-comedy player (left) and then as the internationally famous comedy star of musicals such as* Les P'tites Michu *(General des Ifs, right).*

mon, the Maiden and the Little Militaire (Corporal Zoug-Zoug and, most famously, the Heathen Chinee), *Paris, or the Apple of Discord* (Pollux), *Lurline, or the Knight of the Naiad* (Wavelet) *Robin Hood* (Baron Front de Boeuf), *Oxygen* (Franz), *Mephisto, or the Four Sensations* (Aescalaphus), *Robinson Crusoe* (Man Friday) and *Piff Paff* (Cherub).

When Lydia returned to Britain in 1877, Edouin, his wife, Alice Atherton, their young children, and a number of other ex-members of the Thompson troupe joined up first with Samuel Colville's Folly Company and, the following season, with E E Rice's Surprise Party, two of the most substantial of the companies purveying the roughshod kind of low farce and extravaganza with songs billed as "farce comedy." Amongst the shows in which they played were Willie Gill's versions of *Babes in the Wood* (Tommy, Clown and interpolating his ballet-dancer routine), and *Robinson Crusoe* (Man Friday), *Evangeline* (Le Blanc), the comical extravaganzas *Horrors, or the Maharadjah of Zogobad* (Hamsetjee Bumsetjee) and *Revels* (Callapat) and the burlesques *Hiawatha (and Minnehaha)* (William Penn Brown) and *The Corsair* (Syng Smaul).

In 1880 he formed his own company, Willie Edouin's Sparks, which included both his wife and his sister, Julia, among its personnel and which toured a similar repertoire of farcical and burlesque pieces on the circuits he had trodden with Rice. Amongst these pieces were *Dreams, or Fun in a Photograph Gallery* (1880, John Antonio Binks with Julia as Kitty/Mrs Chillington and Alice as Ruby), in which he also had a hand in the writing, Byron's *Aladdin* (Widow Twankey), *Babes in the Wood* (Tommy), Joseph Bradford's specially written *Ripples* (Napoleon Bonaparte Wax, Grand Opera House, New Orleans 6 November 1881) and the young Charles Hoyt's *A Bunch of Keys* (Park Theatre, Newark, NJ 13 December 1882, Littleton Snaggs). In 1883 he took his company to Britain, and ventured a season at London's Avenue Theatre. His very low-brow entertainments did not suit the West End, but they proved effective enough in the provinces for Edouin and his wife, both of whom had scored personal successes even with the London critics, to decide to remain in Britain.

Edouin continued to tour his own company, with himself and his wife at its head, venturing into town occasionally with either a comedy or a musical piece or occasionally a composite program. In 1884 they had a splendid success with the burlesque *The Babes,* a descendant of their old American touring piece rewritten by Harry Paulton and composed by W C Levey, the musical director at Drury Lane; in 1885 they introduced a little piece called *The Japs;* and in 1886 they produced a burlesque, *Oliver Grumble* (Harry), and the musical comedy drama *Blackberries* (Uncle Jim), but they struck their biggest success with Mark Melford's comedy *Turned Up*—a classic of farcical comedy which they played 159 times at the Comedy Theatre and toured for many years thereafter.

On the strength of this success, Edouin took on the management of the West End's little Royalty Theatre and in the next 10 years, moving from one lesser London theatre to another (Novelty, Strand, Opera Comique, Comedy), devoted his efforts largely to the straight theatre, turning up one other fine comedy hit in *Our Flat* (1889) but also losing his shirt and his wife's on more than one occasion. Apart from Harry Paulton's only occasionally musical *Niobe* (1892), his musical productions had little success: a burlesque *Airey Annie* (on *Ariane*) in which he played Harvey Neville Lomax to his wife's Airey Annie, had a brief life at the Strand in 1888; *Les 28 Jours de Clairette,* anglicized for his wife to play the title role, lasted a month; *Jaunty Jane Shore* (1894), which he directed for Mackay Robertson, again starring Miss Atherton, made six weeks at the Strand; and another farcical Orientalism, *Quong Hi* (1895, Qwong Hi), built around Edouin's famous impersonation of the ''heathen Chinee,'' proved just too insubstantial for London. He had little more success when he abandoned producing and instead directed and starred with his daughter, May, in the early musical comedy *All Abroad* (1896) at the Court Theatre and in the racing musical *Newmarket* (1896) for Alexander Loftus.

Edouin's career took a decisive turn upwards when Henry Lowenfeld offered him the role, turned down late in the day by Arthur Roberts, of the doll-maker, Hilarius, in the London edition of Audran's *La Poupée* (1897). The show turned out a major hit and Edouin himself was ''discovered'' at the age of 51. He followed up in Lowenfeld's next production, Clérice's *The Royal Star* (1898, Macready Valybow), and in a burlesque, *Great Caesar,* and then took on what would be his most successful role of all, the star comic part of Anthony Tweedlepunch in *Florodora* (1899). He triumphed in the part of the machinating old phrenologist in both Britain and America, setting himself up as a major star of modern musical comedy of a decidedly more upmarket kind than previously on both sides of the Atlantic.

He appeared for *Florodora* producer Tom B Davis in his next show, *The Silver Slipper* (1901, Samuel Twanks) and visited South Africa with his own company (1902), before moving across to the management of George Edwardes, for whom his first creation was the memorable ''Piggy'' Hoggenheimer, the Yankee millionaire (''Rude? I'm not rude, I'm rich'') in *The Girl from Kays* (1902) and to Frank Curzon first for *Amorelle* (1903) and then to invest *Sergeant Brue* (1904), one of librettist Owen Hall's happiest creations, with stage life.

During this period Edouin also directed several touring musicals including *Black and White* (1898) for Loftus and *Bébé* (1901), but he stayed clear of the cares of management, and instead continued his now furiously booming and top-line performing career in the West End productions of *Les P'tites Michu* (1905, General des Ifs), *The Blue Moon* (1905, Moolraj) and *The Little Cherub* (1906, Earl of Sanctobury). He made his last starring appearance on the musical stage in Boston, where he was top-billed in De Koven and Stange's *The Snow Man* (1907, Professor Maximilian Hooker) before taking a turn round the variety theatres of Britain and America in sketches to cash in on his fame in what were to be the last years of his life.

His elder daughter **May EDOUIN** [May Alice BRYER] (b London, 18 February 1875; d September 1944) won America-wide celebrity before her third birthday as the subject of an angelic photo entitled ''Angela'' which sold more than 20,000 copies. She played in Colville's company as a small child—notably as Jenny Wren in *Babes in the Wood* when barely able to walk—appeared in leading juvenile roles alongside her mother in *A Trip to Chinatown* (1894, Willie Grow) and her father in the revival of *All Abroad* (1896), *Newmarket* (1896), and on Broadway as Angela in *Florodora* (1900), and without him in Fred Harris's short-lived production of *Man About Town,* as Trixie Triplet in the touring company of *Little Miss Nobody* (1899), and in her father's mounting of the musical drama *Wildflower* (1900, Mrs Lane/Josephine). She subsequently worked largely in vaudeville (*All in the Family,* 1901, etc). A second daughter, who worked as **Daisy Atherton** (b London, 13 September 1876; d New York, 18 December 1961), also had a career as a performer.

Of the other members of the original Edouin troupe, it was sister Rose who had the best career. She established herself in Melbourne, ahead of all the other Edouins, as a favorite player in burlesque (Morgiana in *Forty Thieves,* etc), and later had a long career as a trouping actress, partially under her married name of Mrs George B Lewis. She was sometime proprietor of the English Theatre in China, went reciting in South Africa, and appeared in London in later life on the musical stage in the revival of *The Dairymaids* (1915) and on tour in the short-lived *The Light Blues* (1915). She also authored a musical comedy, *A Spree in Paris, and What Happened* (mus: George Encyl Lewis) mounted first in Australia and later at Belfast's Theatre Royal (25 November 1907).

1878 **The Babes in the Wood, or Who Killed Cock Robin?**

(later *Blooming Babes of Macassar Hall*) (comp & arr Henry Sator/ad from Byron's *Babes in the Wood* w Willie Gill) Globe Theater, Boston 14 January; Grand Opera House 28 January; Park Theater, New York 24 December

1880 **Dreams, or Fun in a Photograph Gallery** (W A Rostetter, Woolson Morse, E E Rice, Harry Braham, et al/Dexter Smith, Nat Childs, John J McNally, F T Robinson, et al/w Childs) Park Theater, Boston 23 August; Bijou Theater, New York 30 August

EDWARDES, Felix (b London, ?1870; d London, 6 February 1954).

An actor in Britain, then from 1903 an actor and stage director in America, Edwardes worked largely with touring companies and in stock, winning his most notable credits as a director with the traveling companies of Lily Langtry and Maxine Elliott until he was engaged by Grossmith and Laurillard to direct the American comedian Raymond Hitchcock in the London musical *Mr Manhattan* (1916). He subsequently staged *Kissing Time* and *Baby Bunting* for the same partnership, and *The Cousin from Nowhere* at the Prince's, then began a fruitful association with the Astaires with his staging of the London version of *Stop Flirting* (1923). That association with Fred Astaire continued through *Lady, Be Good!, Funny Face* and *Gay Divorce.*

In 1925 he directed the London production of *Rose Marie* at the Theatre Royal, Drury Lane and, thereafter, staged the Drury Lane productions of *Show Boat, The New Moon, The Three Musketeers, The Land of Smiles* and *The Song of the Drum,* as well as mounting *Lady Luck* for the opening of the Carlton Theatre, *Frederica* at the Palace, *The Dubarry* at His Majesty's, Grossmith's production of *Tell Me More!* at the Winter Garden and Friml's *Luana* which closed out of town. He retired from the theatre in 1934.

EDWARDES, George [EDWARDS, George Joseph (Pius Nono)] (b Clee, Great Grimsby, 8 October 1855; d London, 4 October 1915). One of the most important producers of musical plays in the history of the genre, Edwardes, by his activities at the end of the 19th and in the early 20th century, set styles and standards in the musical theatre throughout the world.

Plain ''George Edwards'' seems to have begun his life in the theatre working for Eliot Galer at the brand new Royal Opera House in Leicester in 1877. However, he moved soon after to London to work for his cousin, the Dublin theatre manager, Michael Gunn. He was subsequently appointed treasurer at the Opera Comique and then acting manager at the Savoy Theatre under Gunn's friend and partner Richard D'Oyly Carte and he worked at those houses during the original productions of several of the Gilbert and Sullivan musicals. In 1885 (now having acquired the ''e'' in his Edwardes) he moved from the Savoy to the Gaiety Theatre, where the theatre's founder, John Hollingshead, who had established the Gaiety over its 17 years of existence as one of London's foremost light musical theatres, was preparing his retirement. Together, the two produced the burlesque *Little Jack Sheppard,* before Hollingshead stepped down, leaving Edwardes to take over the running of the theatre.

Hollingshead left behind not only a burgeoning new tradition in musical shows—the new burlesque with its lively comic scenes and original songs—but also a group of stars, headed by Nellie Farren and Fred Leslie, who would, under Edwardes's guidance, bring the genre to a point where it became, for a number of years, the principal light musical entertainment of the world. *Little Jack Sheppard* was followed by *Monte Cristo Jr, Miss Esmeralda, Frankenstein, Faust Up-to-Date, Ruy Blas and the Blasé Roué, Carmen Up-to-Data, Joan of Arc* and *Cinder-Ellen Up Too Late,* as Edwardes spread his activities and influence beyond the Gaiety Theatre with national and international tours which took in Broadway, the Continent and Australia and, eventually, other London theatres.

During this period he also made a fill-in foray into the field of comic opera with the production of the B C Stephenson/Alfred Cellier *Dorothy,* but he sold off the show soon after its production to the theatre accountant H J Leslie under whose management it became the longest-running London musical of the 19th century. It was one of very few errors of judgment on Edwardes's part in a long career as a producer and theatre manager.

The new burlesque developed in such a way that eventually its title held very little relevance to its subject matter and content and, soon, with Fred Leslie dead and Nellie Farren too ill to work, all such pretence was given up. Instead, Edwardes produced a new kind of piece which contained all the song, dance and comedy elements of the new burlesque but was, rather than an extravaganza costume piece, a topical comedy entertainment of light and bright song and dance played in modern dress. *In Town* and *A Gaiety Girl* were the earliest of what came to be known as ''musical comedies'' and, in the next decade, Edwardes produced a whole series of like pieces including *The Shop Girl, My Girl, A Runaway Girl, The Circus Girl, The Messenger Boy* and *The Toreador,* principally at the Gaiety Theatre, a series which became one half of the staple diet of both London's and the world's musical theatre.

The other half of that diet also stemmed from Edwardes's management. In 1893 he built and opened Daly's Theatre, in partnership with the American impresario Augustin Daly, and, from 1895, he commissioned and produced a series of musicals for that theatre which were very different in character to those at the froth-weight and frivolous Gaiety. The Daly's Theatre musicals, beginning with *An Artist's Model* and continuing through such pieces as *The Geisha, A Greek Slave, San Toy* and *A Country Girl,* were much more substantial both in their writing and in their music than their Gaiety fellows and, in the hands of such artists as Marie Tempest, Hayden Coffin, Huntley Wright, Letty Lind and Rutland Barrington, they provided first-class fare for theatregoers who preferred a more substantially comic-opera kind of entertainment.

Edwardes continued to run both the Gaiety and Daly's Theatres into the 20th century and finally enlarged his permanent empire to three by the purchase of the lease of the Adelphi Theatre. During all this time, he presided over the development of English musical comedy and held the tiller of the genre during the eventual fusion of the Gaiety and Daly's style of shows into the more vertebrate musical comedies of Edwardian times—*The Spring Chicken, The Quaker Girl, The Girl from Kays, The Duchess of Dantzic, Kitty Grey* and *The Girls of Gottenberg.*

Ever watchful for a change in public taste, he encouraged the extra-light musicals of Paul Rubens (*Three Little Maids, Lady Madcap*), tried a dip into a quickly discontinued revival of burlesque with *The New Aladdin* and, with particular success, imported the best of the Continental pieces of the turn of the century years, scoring huge successes with Messager's *Véronique* and *Les P'tites Michu,* Lehár's *Die lustige Witwe* (*The Merry Widow*), and *Der Graf von Luxemburg* (*The Count of Luxembourg*), Leo Fall's *Die Dollarprinzessin* (*The Dollar Princess*), Fall's *Die geschiedene Frau* (*The Girl in the Train*) and Victor Jacobi's *Leányvásár* (*The Marriage Market*). He had forward plans involving both original and imported musicals for each of the three major theatres under his management when, in 1914, his final illness forced him to hand active control over to his lieutenants. Few of those plans came to fruition without him.

After his death, the empire he had created was soon broken up as the postwar musical theatre underwent profound alterations in style which Edwardes, had he lived, might well have taken under his control in the same way that he had done with the variations of public taste through his 30 years as the most important figure in the international musical theatre. Although his co-executor Robert Evett temporarily saved Daly's Theatre with the production of *The Maid of the Mountains* (mounted under the banner "George Edwardes presents . . ."), none of his theatres was ever again to know a period of prosperity comparable to that which he had given it.

Edwardes was used as the "inspiration for" the hero of a 1948 film called *Gaiety George* in which "he" was

Plate 112. **George Edwardes.** *For many years the principal purveyor of musical theatre to the world.*

portrayed by Richard Greene, better known as television's Robin Hood. The conventional plot of the film had virtually nothing in common with its alleged "inspiration."

Edwardes was married in 1885 to **Julia GWYNNE** [Julia Lavinia PUTNEY] (b Islington, 13 November 1856; d 10 July 1934), a chorister and small-part player with the Savoy and other comic opera companies.

Biography: Bloom, U: *Curtain Call for the Guv'nor* (Hutchinson, London, 1954)

EDWARDES, Paula (b Boston, 29 September 1878). Buxom Broadway soubrette whose career went awry soon after she reached the top.

"Petite and droll" Miss Edwardes made her first Broadway appearances at the admitted age of 13 in Harrigan's *Squatter Sovereignty* and in a minor role and as understudy to the soubrette in Thomas Q Seabrooke's Boston musical *Tabasco* (1894). She subsequently appeared in another Seabrooke show, *The Island of Champagne,* and in Hoyt's *A Black Sheep* (in which once again a failing principal enabled her to go on for the leading role) on the road before taking a slightly more sizeable role in the American version of Varney's *La Falote* at the Casino Theater (1897, Mariolle).

Her next role at the Casino was a tiny one in *A Dangerous Maid* (1899), but she finally came to the front as the broadly common Mamie Clancy (''Coney Island'') in *The Belle of New York.* She repeated her impersonation of Ameri-cockney Mamie in the show's enormously successful London run to such effect that on returning home she was cast in comic roles in a series of British musicals, beginning on Broadway with the Connie Ediss role of Carmenita from Hackney in *A Runaway Girl* and continuing on the road in *The Circus Girl* (Lucille), *San Toy* (Dudley) and *The Geisha* (Molly). She played in *An Arabian Girl and the Forty Thieves* (1899), *Mamselle 'Awkins* (1900, Honorah Hawkins, until replaced by the manager's wife) and *A Royal Rogue* with Jefferson de Angelis and returned to Broadway in *The Show Girl* (1902, Lady Betty Pringle) and as circus-rider Jelly Canvas in the ''nautico-musical extravaganza'' *The Defender* (1902), before winning top-billing in the title role of *Winsome Winnie* in 1903 (Winnie Walker). She had a second Broadway star role in *The Princess Beggar* (1907, Princess Elaine) but soon after she retired without explanation from the stage.

She was briefly seen in vaudeville in 1910 and in 1923 unsuccessfully attempted a comeback in revue. Three years later she was found kneeling in the middle of a New York street, praying in the pouring rain, and was removed into psychiatric care.

EDWARDS, [George] Julian (b Manchester, England, 11 December 1855; d Yonkers, NY, 5 September 1910). Prolific comic opera composer whose works proved much more ephemeral than the lighter musical theatre music of his time.

The son of a Scottish auctioneer-bookseller-tailor-etc, the young Edwards studied at Edinburgh University and began his musical theatre career as a teenager, working as musical director at Birmingham's and Liverpool's Star Music Hall, and regularly as pianist-cum-musical director to the little comic operetta company run by his sister, Fanny. It was for this company that he wrote and composed his first stage works, a series of short operettas which Fanny played on the road and in occasional fringe London venues between 1873 and 1877. One, *Dorothy,* was later played as an afterpiece to *HMS Pinafore* on D'Oyly Carte's first tour.

Edwards toured as chorus master and assistant conductor with van Biene's Opera Company (1880–81) and as musical director/pianist with the little Alice Barth operetta company (*The Chalet, Widows Bewitched,* etc) before taking a pause in his conducting activities to pursue serious musical studies. He composed his first short opera, *Corinna,* in 1880, followed by a four-act opera, *Victorian, the Spanish Student,* which was published by Joseph Williams and produced at the Theatre Royal, Sheffield (6 April 1883) and at Covent Garden (19 January 1884), winning one critic's nomination as ''the worst specimen of English opera we have seen for many years.'' He took up a baton again as a conductor with the Sidney Leslie Opera Company and the Carl Rosa Opera Company, but ultimately he returned to the musical theatre, where he was to make the bulk of his career, at first in Britain and later in America.

In 1887 Edwards toured Britain as musical director for Horace Lingard's production of *Pepita* (*La Princesse des Canaries*), but his career got the upward impetus it had failed to find in Britain when he left his home country for America. In 1888 he crossed the Atlantic to work for J C Duff, for whom he conducted the American production of Harry Paulton's *Paola* (1889) and a series of Gilbert and Sullivan revivals. He was in between times musical director for the quickly vanished *Dovetta* (1889), A M Palmer's American production of *The Red Hussar* (1890) with Marie Tempest and, thereafter, made himself a good career as a conductor of musicals, a career which soon became paired with a parallel one as a theatre composer.

Edwards's first score for the musical theatre in 15 years, and his first ever full-length piece for the musical-comedy stage, was *Jupiter,* produced in Washington, DC, in 1892 with Digby Bell and his wife, Laura Joyce Bell, starring under the ''Digby Bell Comic Opera Company'' banner in Harry B Smith's melange of ancient Greek fooleries. In spite of his penchant for rather correct comic opera writing—something which would throughout his career bring him some appreciative nods from the papers, but also a lack of either outstanding song successes or general popularity—the music of *Jupiter* did not win particular critical notice. Edwards's score was, however, diluted by interpolations ranging from minstrel songs to ''Annie Rooney.'' *Jupiter* visited Broadway later in the year for 72 performances.

After an attempt at something a little more effortfully artistic with an operatic version of Henrik Hertz's *King René's Daughter* (the same piece tackled by Tchaikovsky in his *Iolanta*), Edwards teamed for the first time with another English expatriate, Stanislaus Stange, a playwright and lyricist who was to become his chief collaborator over the next decade, and returned definitively to lighter music. Their first work together, *Friend Fritz,* a play with some songs for vocalist-turned-actress Marion Manola, was another based on a work previously used by another composer. Mascagni's version of Erckmann-Chatrian's novel as *L'amico Fritz* would remain rather more interesting than that produced by the ex-British pair. They did, however, have considerably more success with the neatly old-fashioned comic opera *Madeleine,* starring Camille

D'Arville in its title role as the maiden whose magic kisses bring a greybeard back down to his loveable twenties. After a summer run in Boston, *Madeleine* ran through 10 weeks in New York, toured and was given a number of subsequent productions, especially as a thoroughly revivable vehicle for the popular Miss D'Arville.

The pair subsequently collaborated on *The Goddess of Truth,* a version of the Pygmalion legend produced with Lillian Russell in the title role, and on an Irish light opera for F C Whitney with *Brian Boru* for hero; revamped Audran's *La Petite Fronde* as a vehicle for the star trio of Miss Russell, Jefferson de Angelis and Della Fox; and supplied de Angelis with a touring vehicle, *The Jolly Musketeer,* for his comic opera company—in each case with respectable rather than exciting results. Edwards had a more lucrative success when he teamed with Kirk La Shelle, the former business manager of the Bostonians now turned producer, on a piece called *Princess Chic.* Although the show had a short Broadway life, it toured for two years.

In 1902 Stange and Edwards produced their two most successful pieces. The first was a rehash of Garrick's *The Country Girl* musicalized as *Dolly Varden* and played by Lulu Glaser on Broadway. Greeted with great enthusiasm by the lovers of comic opera (''a prodigious hit . . . real comic opera''), it had a fine touring life in America and was even given a London season—the only time one of Edwards's works was transported back to his home country. The other, generally agreed to be their best work, found these specialists of the formula old-style comic opera tackling a surprisingly verismo setting: *When Johnny Comes Marching Home* was a dramatic tale of the American Civil War with no big-name star and no low comedy. It was seen twice on Broadway, toured extensively around the country and the hero's song, ''My Own United States,'' which at one stage was mooted as a candidate for a national anthem for the United States of America, was the nearest that Edwards came to turning out a hit song.

The pair had sufficient reputation for the great contralto Ernestine Schumann-Heinck to make a venture into comic opera in their *Love's Lottery,* but, although Edwards subsequently composed the music for F C Whitney's production of Stange's version of *The School for Wives* (1905), they combined on only one more musical theatre piece thereafter, another rather thee-and-thou comic opera called *The Belle of London Town* in which Camille D'Arville and Orville Harrold toured for the Shuberts in 1907–8.

In the meanwhile, Edwards had had a slightly unlikely success in collaboration with songwriter-cum-producer Alfred Aarons. Their *His Honor the Mayor,* jollied up into a girls-and-songs show by producer Whitney, ran through the country for several seasons. Thereafter, without ever switching from his unshakeably proper musical style, Edwards had several more tries at this end of the market, the most liked of which was the Shuberts' Sam Bernard vehicle *The Girl and the Wizard,* which played for 87 performances on Broadway prior to touring. On this occasion Edwards's score was permeated with numbers by Jerome Kern, Louis Hirsch, Edward Madden, director Ned Wayburn and other representatives of the up-and-coming generation of Broadway musicals. His musical conscience, however, was probably somewhat salved by the production of his one-act ''grand opera'' *The Patriot* at the Fifth Avenue vaudeville house in 1908 (30 November), of his cantata *The Mermaid* (Carnegie Hall 22 April 1907) and of his oratorio, *Lazarus,* at a Metropolitan Opera House Sunday concert in 1910.

Edwards remained a respected and well-liked member of the Broadway establishment throughout his career, his musicianship praised by critics and his scores regularly presented by top managements over a period of nearly 20 years. Yet his style of composition was already old-fashioned when he began writing for the Broadway stage, and, lacking the essential gaiety and versatility of a Victor Herbert, he never reached that composer's level or popularity.

Edwards was married to the German vocalist Philippine Siedle (b Woolwich, c1850) whose brother was co-librettist for his *The Gay Musician.*

His sister, contralto vocalist **Fanny EDWARDS** [Frances Wright EDWARDS] (b Burnley, 5 October 1843; d Yonkers, NY, 28 August 1908) was, so the publicity said, originally a Yorkshire millworker. The story went that traveling entertainer Harry Clifton (''Paddle Your Own Canoe'') heard her sing whilst staying in digs with her mother, had her trained, and subsequently she toured with him in his entertainment up till his death in 1872 (15 July). Although she passed as Mrs Clifton, and bore Harry a daughter, the fact of there being a previous and continuing Mrs Clifton prevented the liaison being regularized. It did not, however, prevent Fanny calling herself Mrs Clifton. In fact, Fanny Edwards, ''contralto of the Manchester, Newcastle and provincial concerts, and late of Mark's and Julian Adams's concerts,'' had been appearing as a vocalist in good provincial company since her mid-teens, well before joining Clifton in 1866. After his death she spent a number of years running her own concert party/drawing-room entertainment (latterly Miss Fanny Edwards' Entertainment and Comic Opera Company), with performers such as Michael Dwyer, Arthur Rousbey, Ethel Pierson and Redfern Hollins featured, and she subsequently enjoyed a good career in comic opera. She toured as Lady Sangazure (alongside

Dwyer and Rousbey) in 1878, was the first touring Little Buttercup in Britain and later took the same role in the Comedy Opera Company's rebel *HMS Pinafore* (1879) in London. She toured in contralto roles for Carte (Dame Hannah in *Ruddigore,* 1887, etc), appeared at the Alhambra as the Duchess in *La Fille du tambour-major* (1880), created the part of Savillia dei Franchi in George Fox's operatic *The Corsican Brothers* (1888) and, after removing to America in 1889, appeared there under her brother's baton as Margarine in the American production of *Paola* (1889), the Duchess of Plaza Toro in *The Gondoliers* (Chicago, 1890), with John Duff's company as Ruth in *The Pirates of Penzance* (1890), The Fairy Queen in *Iolanthe* (1890) and Lady Jane in *Patience* (1890), and as Mrs Magpie in *The Red Hussar* (1890) and Mrs Partlett in *The Sorcerer* (1892).

A second singing Edwards sister, Hannah (ka **Annie KINNAIRD**, b Burnley, 6 October 1851; d Yonkers, 16 July 1910), was the soprano of Fanny's little company and the wife of the well-known Yorkshire tenor **[Jacob] Redfe[a]rn HOLLINS** (b Sheffield, 22 January 1842), the creator of the role of Geoffrey Wilder in *Dorothy.* They were the parents of three Broadway musical comedy performers: **[Alice] Hilda HOLLINS** (b Shepherd's Bush, London 1873) (*Jupiter, La Mascotte, The Tar and the Tartar, Africa, Madeleine, Dorothy, Jack and the Beanstalk, Piff! Paff! Pouff!, The Belle of London Town,* Artea in *Adonis,* etc), **Maud [Fanny] HOLLINS** (b Newington, Edinburgh 1871) (*Jupiter, Patience, The Tar and the Tartar, Madeleine, Dorothy, Jack and the Beanstalk,* Yvette in *The Jolly Musketeer,* Cocodilla in *The Monks of Malabar* 1900, etc) and **Mabel [Haydee M] HOLLINS** (b London, 25 December 1884) (Molly in *The Geisha,* Nora Melon in *Piff! Paff! Pouff!*, Daisy in *His Honor the Mayor,* Dorothy Congress in *The Little Cherub,* Minna in *The Girls of Gottenburg,* etc), wife to Broadway librettist **William LE BARON** (b Elgin, Ill, 16 February 1883; d Santa Monica, 9 February 1958).

1872 **Cornarino's Mistake** (Edwards) 1 act Public Rooms, Uxbridge 17 September

1874 **A Camp Adventure** (J R Anderson) 1 act Institute, Swindon 14 March

1874 **Love's Test** (Edwards) Victoria Hall, Norwich 4 September

1875 **May and December** (Edwards) 1 act Assembly Rooms, Tunbridge Wells 16 March

1876 **The Marquis de St Valéry** (Edwards) 1 act Reading Town Hall 20 January

1877 **Dorothy** (Edwards) Colchester 13 January, Ladbroke Hall, London 24 September

1877 **Buckingham** (Edwards) Town Hall, Northampton 28 December

1892 **Jupiter, or The Cobbler and the King** (Harry B Smith) Palmer's Theater 2 May

1893 **Friend Fritz** (Stanislaus Stange) Herrmann's Theater 26 January

1893 **King René's Daughter** 1 act Herrmann's Theater 22 November

1894 **Madeleine, or The Magic Kiss** (ex- *Baron Grim*) (Stange) Tremont Theater, Boston 30 July; Bijou Theater, New York 25 February 1895

1896 **The Goddess of Truth** (Stange) Abbey's Theater 26 February

1896 **Brian Boru** (Stange) Broadway Theater 19 October

1897 **The Wedding Day** (*La Petite Fronde*) (Stange) Casino Theater 8 April

1898 **The Jolly Musketeer** (Stange) Broadway Theater 14 November

1900 **Princess Chic** (Kirk La Shelle) Casino Theater 12 February

1901 **Dolly Varden** (Stange) Princess Theater, Toronto 23 September; Herald Square Theater 27 January 1902

1901 **Gringoire the Street Singer** (Willard Holcomb) 1 act Brooklyn; Keith's Union Square 20 January 1902; Oxford Music Hall, London 30 June 1902

1902 **When Johnny Comes Marching Home** (Stange) Opera House, Detroit 29 September; New York Theater 16 December

1904 **Love's Lottery** (Stange) Broadway Theater 3 October

1905 **The Pink Hussars** (later *His Honor the Mayor*) (w Alfred Aarons/Charles J Campbell, Ralph McGay Skinner) Chicago Opera House 23 October; New York Theater 28 May 1906

1906 **The Girl and the Governor** (S M Brenner) National Theater, Washington, DC 9 October; Manhattan Theater 4 February 1907

1907 **The Belle of London Town** (Stange) Lincoln Square Theater 28 January

1908 **The Gay Musician** (Edward Siedle, Campbell) Wallack's Theater 18 May

1908 **The Patriot** (Stange) 1 act Keith's Theater, Providence, RI 14 September; Fifth Avenue Theater 30 November

1909 **The Motor Girl** (Campbell, Skinner) Lyric Theater 15 June

1909 **The Girl and the Wizard** (Robert B Smith/J Hartley Manners) Casino Theater 27 September

1909 **[Miss] Molly May** (Walter Browne) New Haven, 8 December; Colonial Theater, Boston 13 December; Hackett Theater, New York 8 April 1910

1910 **The Aero Girl** revised *The Motor Girl* Collingwood Opera House, Poughkeepsie 13 October

1910 **Two Men and a Girl** revised *The Motor Girl* Broadway Theater, Brooklyn 11 November

EGGERTH, Marta [EGGERT, Márta] (b Budapest, 17 April 1912). International Operette prima donna of stage and screen, often in partnership with her husband, tenor Jan Kiepura.

Márta Eggert began her career in her native Budapest, playing juvenile roles at the Magyar Királyi Operaház (1924) and at the Magyar Színház in the French musical *Mannequins* (1926). She appeared in Stockholm in revue, and was then seen at the Fővárosi Operettszínház in further juvenile parts including Annuska in *Az utolsó Verebély lány* (1928), and in Egon Kemény's *Kikelet utca 3.* She was still in her teens when she succeeded Adele Kern in the title role of *Das Veilchen vom Montmartre* in Vienna (1930). She also starred in Ziehrer's *Die verliebte Eskadron* (1930, Ilka Barady) and, later, in Komjáti's *Ein Liebestraum* (1933, Carla) at the Theater an der Wien in the early stages of a career which—interspersed with frequent performances on film (*Ein Lied, ein Küss, ein Mädel,* Steffi Pirzinger in the Lehár/Billy Wilder *Es war einmal ein Walzer* 1932, *Kaiserwalzer* 1932, *Der Zarewitsch* 1933, *Die Blume von Hawaii* 1933, *Mein Herz ruft nach dir,* as Gräfin Esterházy in *Leise flehen meine Lieder* 1934, *Die Csárdásfürstin* 1934, *Casta diva* 1935, as Christine Holm in *Das Hofkonzert* 1936, *Wo die Lerche singt* 1936, *Das Schloss in* Flandern 1936, *Zauber der Bohème* 1937, *Immer wenn ich glücklich bin* 1938, etc)—spread through the world from Hamburg to Broadway, London and Paris.

She was seen in New York as Minnie Sorensen in the musical *Higher and Higher* (1940), opposite her husband in revivals of *The Merry Widow* at Majestic Theater (1943) and the City Center (1944), and again in a romantic Chopin pastiche, *Polonaise* (1945, Mariska). She appeared as Sylva Varescu in a souped-up *Princesse Czardas* in Paris (Théâtre de Paris, 1950), and also repeated her ''widow'' on several occasions in five different languages (London, 1955, New York, 1957, etc), as well as contributing further to both Continental (*Addio Mimi* 1947, *Das Land des Lächelns* 1952, Verena Illing in *Frühling in Berlin* 1957) and American musical film (*For Me and my Gal* 1942, *Presenting Lily Mars* 1943, *La Valse Brillante* 1949).

In 1982 she appeared alongside Diana Rigg's Colette in the role of Sido in *Colette,* and she subsequently appeared in a production of *Follies* and in 1992, at 80 years of age, was seen guesting at Vienna's Volksoper in the Robert Stolz compilation show *Servus Du.*

EICHBERG, Julius (b Düsseldorf, 13 June 1824; d Boston, 18 January 1893).

German-born, Würzburg- and Brussels-educated, Eichberg taught at the Geneva conservatoire before emigrating to America in 1856. In 1859 he settled in Boston where he worked as a conductor, as musical director of the Boston Museum through seven seasons, and later founded and ran both the local conservatory and his own violin school. During his time at the Museum he composed four musical theatre pieces in the style of the earlier years of the Continental 19th century. His *The Doctor of Alcantara* was the most successful and important of early American comic operas, being produced in Britain and Australia and toured in America for a number of years, whilst his *The Rose of Tyrol* and *A Night in Rome* joined *The Doctor of Alcantara* and *The Two Cadis* (whose projected Broadway debut failed to take place when the management went bust on opening night 2 July 1866) in the touring repertoire of Caroline Richings's pioneering English opera company alongside such offerings as *Lucia di Lammermoor* and Balfe's *The Enchantress, Satanella* and *The Rose of Castille.* Miss Richings was still playing *The Rose of Tyrol* in the mid-1870s.

Eichberg latterly worked as director of music for the schools of Boston and also authored a number of musical teaching works, both on the violin and on music in general, and performed as a concert violinist and chamber musician.

1862 **The Doctor of Alcantara** (Benjamin E Woolf) Boston Museum 7 April; Théâtre Français, New York 28 May 1866

1863 **The Rose of Tyrol** (Woolf) Boston Museum 6 April

1864 **A Night in Rome** Boston Museum 26 November; Théâtre Français, New York 25 June 1866

1866 **The Two Cadis** Boston Museum ?5 March

EINÖDSHOFER, Julius (b Vienna, 10 February 1863; d Berlin, 17 October 1930).

Einödshofer studied in Vienna and worked as a theatre conductor in the Austrian provinces before taking a post as conductor and house composer at the Scala Theater, Berlin, in 1892. He subsequently worked in the same capacity at the Centraltheater and at the Thalia-Theater, at each of which he provided the scores for a series of musical comedies of the late 1890s and the early 1900s. Between 1906 and 1910 he was the conductor of the Kurorchester in Heringdorf and, from 1911 to 1921, at Berlin's Admiralspalast, where he composed the music for that theatre's celebrated spectacular ballets, and in wartime contributed such pieces as ''Die Welt kann ohne mich wohl sein, doch ohne Deutschland nie!'' (ly: Otto Emanuel Enskat) and ''Was hat ein Deutsches Mädchen gern'' (ly: K Schneider) to the nation's musical good. In 1921 he retired from the theatre and became a conductor for radio, and he died in 1930 after a heart attack suffered whilst he was on the air.

Although Einödshofer supplied the Berlin stage with large amounts of revue and dance music for more than 20 years, little of his work was heard further afield. One song, ''Mr Mosenstein,'' was, however, interpolated into George Edwardes's London musical *The Girl from Kays,* and he got a couple of Broadway showings—one in 1899 when he was credited with an interpolation into the Casino's *La Belle Hélène,* another 17 years later in the Hippodrome spectacular *The Big Show,* when an ice ballet *The Merry Doll* announced as ''direct from the Admiralspalast'' sported his name (along with that of Raymond Hubbell, so it can't have been that direct) as composer.

1884 **14 Tage im Arrest** (Friedrich Rotter) 1 act Fürsttheater, Vienna 28 June

1884 **Ein Invalide von Aspern** (Wilhelm Ernst) 1 act Fürsttheater, Vienna 18 August

1889 **Die Spiritisten** (Emil Weissenturm) Stadttheater, Innsbruck April

1893 **Berliner Vollblut** (Jean Kren) Centraltheater 31 August

1894 **Ein gesunder Junge** (Kren) Centraltheater 6 March

1894 **Der neue Kurs** (Kren, Leopold Ely) Centraltheater

1894 **O, diese Berliner** (Julius Freund) Centraltheater 2 September

1895 **Unsere Rentiers** (Freund, Wilhelm Mannstädt) Centraltheater 16 February

1895 **Eine tolle Nacht** (Freund, Mannstädt) Centraltheater 4 September

1896 **1000 Jahre** (Ferdinand Maierfeld) Jantschtheater, Vienna 2 April

1896 **Der Mandarin [von Tsing-ling-ling]** (Freund) Metropoltheater August

1896 **Eine wilde Sache** (Freund, Mannstädt) Centraltheater 20 September

1897 **Ein fideler Abend** (Freund, Mannstädt) Centraltheater 7 February

1897 **Berliner Fahrten** (Freund, Mannstädt) Centraltheater 4 September

1898 **Die Tugendfalle** (Freund, Mannstädt) Centraltheater 20 January

1898 **Das Paradies der Frauen** (*Le Royaume des femmes*) German version by Freund w new music w Bertram Sänger (Metropoltheater)

1898 **Sterzl in Berlin** (Freund, Mannstädt) Theater an der Wien, Vienna 2 April

1899 **Die verkehrte Welt** (*Le Royaume des femmes*) add music for German version by Freund (Metropoltheater)

1901 **Ein tolles Geschaft** (Schönfeld/Kren) Thalia-Theater 7 September

1901 **Die Badepuppe** (Schönfeld/Kren) Thalia-Theater 26 November

1902 **Seine kleine** (Schönfeld/Kren, Ely) Thalia-Theater 18 January

1902 **Die bösen Mädchen** (Schönfeld/Kren, Ely) Thalia-Theater 23 December

1903 **Der Kamelienonkel** (w Fritz Reichmann/Leo Leipziger) Thalia-Theater 6 February

1903 **Der Posaunenengel** (w Max Schmidt/Schönfeld/Kren) Thalia-Theater 24 March

1903 **Der reicheste Berliner** (w Schmidt/Schönfeld/Kren) Belle-Alliance Theater 23 December

1904 **Götterweiber** (Kurt Kraatz, Wilhelm Jacoby) Belle-Alliance Theater 4 February

1904 **Freut euch des Lebens** (Schönfeld/Jacoby, R Stein ad Kren) Belle-Alliance Theater 8 April

1904 **Kam'rad Lehmann** (w Julius Stern/Schönfeld/Kren, Ely) Belle-Alliance Theater 7 May

1904 **Der Weiberkönig** (Schönfeld/Kren, Ely) Thalia-Theater 15 September

1904 **Rossbach** (Leo Walther Stein) Stadttheater, Bromberg 16 December

1904 **Der grosse Stern** (Schönfeld/Kren) Thalia-Theater 23 December

1909 **Tohuwabohu** (Heinz Gordon) Apollotheater 1 October

1911 **Liebesbarometer** (Max Reichert) 1 act Apollotheater 1 March

1915 **Mamas Liebling** (Ely) Rose-Theater 14 August

1915 **Aus der Jugendzeit** (Ely) Walhalla-Theater 4 October

1922 **Die Frau ohne Mann** (Erich Kaiser) Residenztheater, Dresden 6 February

1927 **Ja, ihr Mädels müsst dran glauben** (Carl Bretschneider) Theater in der Lutzowstrasse 9 July

EISEMANN, Mihály (b Bács, Paripás, Hungary, 19 June 1898; d Budapest, 25 February 1966). One of the most successful Hungarian musical theatre composers of the years between the wars.

Eisemann studied law in Budapest before attending the Zeneakadémia and orientating his career towards music. Whilst working as a pianist in a coffee-house, he made his first ventures into popular songwriting in team with lyricist Imre Harmath (''Szeret-e még? csak ennyit mondjon!'') and, in 1929, he produced his first theatre score, for the revusical comedy *Miss Amerika,* mounted with great success at the Fővárosi Operettszínház with Teri Fejes, Erzsi Péchy and Gyula Kabos starred and a musical part made up of blues, fox-trots and tangos. The following year, *Alvinci huszárok* (''Van aki bevallja''), produced at the Király Színház with Juci Lábass, Rózsi Bársony, Oszkár Dénes, Árpád Latabár and Dezső Kertész in the lead rôles, confirmed that success.

Eisemann contributed to the music for the same theatre's musical version of the Broadway play *The Poor Nut* (*Amerikai lányok* 7 February 1931), whose principal score was credited to an unidentifiable (and fictitious?) transatlantic team of Cowan, C I May and Albert Gumble, before a third collaboration with librettist László Szilágyi, author of his first two hits, brought him his greatest success of all. *Zsákbamacska,* produced at the Pesti Színház with the rising Marika Rökk starred, ran for more than 250 performances in Budapest and was subsequently played in Vienna as *Katz im Sack* (Die Komödie, 1933) and in London as *Happy Weekend* (ad Dion Titheradge, Arthur Stanley 30 May 1934), under the management of Claude B Yearsley and Percival Mackey, with Hungarians Magda Kun and Steve Geray starred.

His two following works also traveled. *Egy csók és más semmi,* originally produced in Budapest with Hanna

Honthy featured, was played as *Ein Kuss—und sonst gar nichts* at Berlin's Theater am Kurfürstendamm (6 October 1932) with Friedl Schuster starring, in France as *Rien qu'un baiser* and at Vienna's Scala Theater (14 March 1934) with Rita Georg, whilst *Vadvirág* (ad Fritz Löhner-Beda) was adapted into German and played by Rökk under the title *Der Sterne von Manege*. The former was filmed, and later revived at the Fővárosi Operettszínház in 1946 (22 June), whilst the latter, after an original run at the Andrássy-uti Színház and the Magyar Színház (24 May 1934), also returned in 1946 for a new run at the Markus Park Színház.

A cirkusz csillaga (1934) had a excellent first run of 168 performances in Budapest with Rökk starred, whilst *Én és a kisöcsém*, first produced in the same year with Bársony at the top of the bill, was another Eisemann musical deemed worthy of revival, with the same star, in the postwar years (15 May 1948). *Ezüstmenyasszony*, produced at the Royal Színház with Sári Fedák as prima donna, and *Meseáruház*, first mounted at the Vígszínház with Bársony and Ella Gombaszögi featured, were also successes. In 1940 no fewer than five new Eisemann operetts were seen in Budapest, beginning with the jazz-operett *Handa-Banda* (a revised version of a piece mounted two years earlier in Szeged), including pieces written with both Szilágyi and Zsolt Harsányi, and ending, 10 months after the first premiere, with another piece by the same author, Gyula Halász, *Fiatalság-bolondság*, staged with considerable success at the Fővárosi Operettszínház.

Eisemann continued to write shows and popular songs through the 1940s, having perhaps his best theatrical successes of that period with *Fekete Péter*—a piece with a score still rich in such rhythms as fox-trots and rumbas—which was played 143 times at the Vígszínház with György Dénes in its title role, and the fairytale operett *Ő felsége a mama*, before *Ő vagy Ő?* produced at the Fővárosi Operettszínház, with Hanna Honthy, Kálmán Latabár and Andor Ajtay starred, brought nearly 20 years of almost unbroken representation on the Budapest stage to an end. Thereafter, Eisemann was heard from only occasionally, but he contributed his last score to the musical theatre as late as 1963, more than three decades after his first hit.

His works, however, have survived strongly in the local repertoire and the 1990s have seen revivals of *Én és a kisöcsém* (József Attila Színház 1 October 1994, Kecskemét 4 December 1996, Győr 21 September 1996), *Handa banda* (Józsefvárosi Színház 8 October 1994), *XIVik René* (Szolnok 19 November 1993), *Én és a kisöcsém* (József Attila Színház 1 October 1994, Kecskemét 4 December 1996, Győr 21 September 1996), *Fiatalság-bolondság* (Ódry Színpad 4 February 1993, Vidám Színpad 4 June 1993, Miskolc 23 January 1998), *Fekete Péter* (Székesfehérvár 5 July 1996, Vígszínház 11 October 1997) and *Hyppolit, a lakáj* (Veszprém 17 December 1993, Nyíregyháza 30 September 1995, Ruttkai Éva Színház 25 April 1996, Sopron 14 March 1997, Székesfehérvár 20 October 1997).

Eisemann was also active as a composer for the cinema, and his film scores included *Hippolyt a lakáj, Lebegő szűz, Szerelemmel vádollak, Vadrózsa* and *A miniszter barátja*. The film *Hippolyt a lakáj* was subsequently twice remade for the theatre with less (1965) or more (1984) music.

1929 **Miss Amerika** (László Szilágyi) Fővárosi Operettszínház 12 January

1930 **Alvinci huszárok** (Szilágyi) Király Színház 9 April

1932 **Zsákbamacska** (Szilágyi) Pesti Színház 3 November

1933 **Egy csók és más semmi** (István Békeffy/Imre Halász) Magyar Színház 12 May

1934 **Vadvirág** (Imre Harmath/Ernő Andai) Andrássy-uti Színház 24 March

1934 **A cirkusz csillaga** (w Károly Komjáthy/I Békeffy/László Bus Fekete) Vígszínház 22 June

1934 **Ma éjjel szabad vagyok** (Andor Szenes/János Vaszary) Andrássy-uti Színház 25 October

1934 **En és a kisöcsém** (Szilágyi) Fővárosi Operettszínház 21 December

1935 **Ezüstmenyasszony** (Szilágyi) Royal Színház 20 December

1936 **Meseáruház** (Szilágyi) Vígszínház/Fővárosi Operettszínház 11 April

1937 **Egy vidám éjszaka** (János Vaszary) Magyar Színház 15 May

1937 **Gólyaszanatórium** (Szilágyi, Dezső Kellér) Markus Park Színház 25 June

1937 **Macskazene** (Gyula Halász, Károly Kristóf) Szeged 18 December

1938 **A hölgy hozzám tartozik** (Pierre Veber ad István Békeffy, Adorján Stella) Andrássy Színház 21 January

1938 **Kávé habbal** (Harmath/Pál Barabás) Royal Színház 30 November

1940 **Handa-Banda** revised *Macskazene* Fővárosi Operettszínház 26 January

1940 **Tokaji aszu** (Szilágyi) Magyar Színház 15 March

1940 **Angóramacska** (Szilágyi) Vígszínház 26 April

1940 **XIV-ik René** (Zsolt Harsányi, István Zágon) Vígszínház 14 September

1940 **Fiatalság-bolondság** (G Halász) Fővárosi Operettszínház 25 October

1942 **Leány a talpán** (G Molnár) Royal Színház 28 March

1943 **Egy boldog pesti nyár** (w Denes Buday, Szabolcs Fényes/ Szilágyi, Attila Orbók) Fővárosi Operettszínház 14 April

1943 **Fekete Péter** (Gyula Somogyi) Vígszínház 4 June

1944 **Mesebeszéd** (Béla Mátrai Betegh/Somogyi) Vígszínház 28 September

1944 **Őfelsége a mama** (Gábor Vaszary) Magyar Színház 29 April

1946 **Szabotál a gólya** (revised *Gólyaszanatórium*) Művesz Színház 11 May

1947 **Ő vagy Ő?** (Zágon, Vaszary) Fővárosi Operettszínház 27 September

1958 **Bástyasátány 77** (László Dalos/Géza Baróti) Lujza Blaha Színház 11 April

1959 **A princesszin** (Ferenc Felkai) Győr 6 November

1962 **Nőgyűlölő** (Sándor Balázs/László Sólyom) Szolnők 2 February

1963 **Annabál** (Baróti) Miskolc 23 December

1964 **Fel a kezekkel** revised *Leány a talpán* (László Tabi/János Erdődy) Pécs 18 November

1965 **Hyppolit a lakáj** (Zágon István) Kis Szinpad 10 December

1984 **Hyppolit a lakáj** (arr István Orosz/Zágon István ad Katalin Vajda, Anikó Vajda) Hild Udvár 14 June

AZ ELEVEN ÖRDÖG Comic opera in 3 acts by Antal Deréki taken from *Le Vicomte de Letorrières* by Jean-François Bayard and Philippe Dumanoir. Music by József Konti. Budai Színkör, Budapest, 8 August 1884.

One of the most successful of 19th-century Hungarian operetts, *Az eleven ördög* (the living devil) was based on Bayard and Dumanoir's highly popular play *Le Vicomte de Letorrières,* the subject for a number of comic operas and musical plays throughout Europe.

"The living devil" of the title is the young and penniless Vicomte de Letorrières (Emilia Pajor). Although he has not been spared by the fates who control financial fortune, another kind of fortune has been granted him—the Vicomte has enormous charm, a charm that operates on both women and men alike. One day it seems that his days of pauperdom are at an end—he has received a fine inheritance. But it is not that easy. There is another claimant, the baron Tibulle de Hugéon (Aurél Follinusz). The Vicomte sets out to beat his rival to the jackpot and events rise to a duel in which our hero is wounded. But Letorrières turns the wound to his advantage—his recovery is spent in the house of the Prince Soubise (Jenő Balassa), and the Princess (Amalia Ebergényiné) soon falls under the spell of the young man. Soubise is the head of the court which is to decide the way of the will, and it is not surprising that Letorrières ends the evening triumphant.

Az eleven ördög was a hit on its production at the Budai Színkör and it played 50 performances in the repertoire there during its first 12 months (50th: 7 August 1885) before moving into the Népszínház (16 December 1885) with Lujza Blaha starred as Letorrières alongside Szilágyi (Hugéon), Szathmári (Soubise) and Ebergényiné repeating her original role, and with Vidor Kassai (Pomponiusz), József Németh (Desperrières), Zsofi Csatay (Veronika) and Célia Margó (Marianne) in support. Once again it was a considerable hit; it played 54 times and was revived there 19 February 1897, with Klára Küry as the Vicomte, and again on 31 March 1900 when Margit Ámon took up the title role alongside Imre Szirmai (Hugéon), Vince Horváth (Soubise) and Siposné (the Princess).

ELISABETH Musical in 2 acts by Michael Kunze. Music by Sylvester Levay. Theater an der Wien, 3 September 1992.

Some characters have been taken over and over again to be the subject of musical plays, often—one thinks of Cyrano de Bergerac as an example—with repeated failure. Others, in spite of being just as frequently called to the stage, seem to court success there. The Empress Elisabeth of Austria, already the subject of the well-liked Fritz Kreisler Operette *Sissi* (1932) and of the French variant *Sissi, futur impératrice* (1959), seems to be one. Her most recent appearance on the musical stage, as the heroine of the *Elisabeth* produced in Vienna in 1992, was a record-breaking one. The show became quite simply the most successful musical to come out of central Europe since *Im weissen Rössl* more than half a century earlier.

The piece begins in the realms of the dead, where Elisabeth's assassin, Lucheni (Ethan Freeman) is trying to justfy his crime. Elisabeth (Pia Douwes), he says, courted death throughout her life. And it is, indeed, Death (Uwe Kröger) who becomes the heroine's leading man for the remainder of the evening, an evening in which Elisabeth struggles to be a wife and an empress, to overcome her domineering mother-in-law (Else Ludwig), to manage her problematic relationship with her husband, the Emperor Franz Josef (Victor Gernot), and later restlessly to escape from Vienna's court are depicted. Death takes her son Rudolf (Andreas Bieber) to him before, at the evening's end, with the Hapsburg Empire in ruins, he carries off Elisabeth.

Levay's score, "a mixture of rock, pop, jazz and classic," flipped from one mode to the other, the rockiest moments falling to the lot of Death and of Lucheni, who ushered the story along, in various guises, in the same cynical manner as Che in *Evita.* The show's principal number, however, fell to Elisabeth: the driving declaration "Ich gehör nur mir," which returned several times during the course of the night and ultimately served as the evening's Schlussgesang ("Der Schleier fällt"). Death reveled in "Der Letzten Tanz" and Rudolf had his moment in the appealing "Wenn ich dein Spiegel war," but the score's other most attractive moments came in duet—Elisabeth and Franz-Josef's final "Boote in der Nacht" and the simple, strident two-tenor piece for Death and

Rudolf, "Die Schatten werden länger"—and in an eerie and but briefly heard Mayerling waltz.

Elisabeth played 1,278 performances at the Theater an der Wien between its premiere and April 1998, whilst at the same time going out to productions in Japan (8 November 1966) where it was played by the all-female Takarazuka company, in Hungary (ad Sziámi Péter Müller) with a cast headed by Mónika Sáfár (Sissy), Tamás Mester (Death) and Sándor Sasvári (Franz Josef), in Germany, Holland (with Pia Douwes repeating her original role) and in Scandinavia (Musiktheater Värmland, Karlstad 30 September 1999).

Hungary: Szeged 18 August 1996, Budapest Operett Színház ?5 October

Recordings: original cast (Polydor), live recording original production (Polydor), Japanese cast, Hungarian cast (Polydor)

ELLE EST À VOUS Opérette in 3 acts by André Barde. Music by Maurice Yvain. Théâtre des Nouveautés, Paris, 22 January 1929.

One of Yvain's longest-running modern musical comedies, *Elle est à vous* was presented under the management of Benoît-Léon Deutsch at the Nouveautés. It had an 11-month run in Paris, but for some reason it failed either to endure into revivals in the manner of such pieces as *Ta bouche, Pas sur la bouche* or *Là-haut,* or to travel as others of its contemporaries did.

A cast headed by Gabrielle Ristori ("Son Doudou"), Eliane de Creus ("Jeune fille," "Dans une guinguette"), Urban ("Elle est à vous") and Pierre Darmant ("Honolulu," w Mlle de Creus), was topped by the comedian Milton who made a nationwide hit out of the nonsensical, slangy "Pouet-Pouet" and joined Suzanne Dehelly in the brightly suggestive duet "En auto."

Plate 113. **Az eleven ördög.** *Buxom little Klára Küry was the "living devil" of the famous Hungarian operett's title, but the Vicomte de Letorrières was a devil only with the women.*

ELLINGER, Desirée [ELLINGER, Dorothy Sophie] (b Manchester, 7 October 1893; d London, 30 April 1951).

Born in Britain and educated in Brussels and Paris, Miss Ellinger led a theatrical career of nearly 20 years which was even more international than her early years. She first appeared in opera, playing with the Beecham Opera Company as Nedda (*Pagliacci*) at 21 and, in the years that followed, was seen as Butterfly, Marguerite, Susanna, Blondchen and Micaëla with the same company. She made her first appearances in the light musical theatre when she played Clairette, to Amy Augarde's Lange, in a 1919 revival of *La Fille de Madame Angot,* as Sylvia in the light opera *Sylvia's Lovers* (1919), and in revue at the London Hippodrome.

She subsequently toured in a third-rate piece called *The Early Girl* (1923) and as Sylva Varescu in *Die Csárdásfürstin* (1924) and appeared in the starring roles of the short-lived Spanish musical *The First Kiss* (1924, Mariposa) and the even briefer Rudolf Friml *Sometime* (1925, Enid Vaughan) in London. The last failure had its sunny side, however, for she was hurried from a subsequent engagement in Boston to New York to succeed Mary Ellis in the title role of the same composer's *Rose Marie.* She won considerable publicity from the fact that this dash was bravely accomplished in an open-cockpit biplane. She remained in America to star in a third Friml piece, *The Wild Rose* (1926, Princess Elise), in Romberg's *Cherry Blossoms* (1927, O Yuki San), and in *Kiss Me* (1927, Doris Durant Dodo), adding three more to her impressive collection of lead roles in flop shows.

Things looked up, however, when she changed country again and appeared as Julie in the Paris production of *Show Boat* (*Mississippi*), while the spectacular *Silver Wings* (1930, Inez) at London's Dominion Theatre gave her what would be her only satisfactory West End run. Her last appearances on the musical stage were in another large-scale failure, *Eldorado* (1930, Elvira), as Orestes in

Plate 114. **Desirée Ellinger** *starred in plenty of flops; London's* El Dorado *was one of them.*

C B Cochran's extravagant, stellar production of a vandalized *La Belle Hélène* (*Helen!*) in 1932, and as Heart's Desire in the short-lived 1935 revival of *The Rose of Persia.*

ELLIOTT, Madge [ELLIOTT, Leah Madeleine] (b Kensington, London, 12 May 1896; d New York, 8 August 1955). Cool, tall, dancing ingenue who partnered Cyril Ritchard in series of musicals in Britain and Australia.

Brought up in Australia, Miss Elliott appeared there first as a chorus dancer and later a principal dancer in such musicals as *High Jinks, Tonight's the Night* (Mimi), *So Long, Letty, Canary Cottage, You're in Love, Oh, Lady! Lady!!,* then moved through supporting roles to progressively larger ones in *A Night Out* (Victorine), *Yes, Uncle!* (Nichette), *The Girl in the Taxi* (Jacqueline), *Going Up, Kissing Time, The Cabaret Girl* (Flick Morgan), *Whirled into Happiness* (Delphine de Lavallière) and *Mary* (Madeleine).

In 1925 she went to Britain, and she and her Australian dance partner (and later husband), Cyril Ritchard, appeared together in the revue *Bubbly* and in the earliest London cabaret, the *Midnight Follies* at the Metropole Hotel, before being cast by Laddie Cliff in the musical comedy *Lady Luck* (1927, Patience) at the Carlton. The elegant dancing act performed by this tall, graceful pair was a considerable success and they were thereafter built into leading dance-and-song roles as the romantic hero and heroine of the Cliff musicals *So This Is Love* (1928, Pamela Stuart), *Love Lies* (1929, Valerie St Clair), *The Love Race* (1930, Mary Dale) and *The Millionaire Kid* (1931, Gloria Devenish).

Returning to Australia, they performed there in another Cliff musical *Blue Roses* (Susan Winslow), in *Hold My Hand, Our Miss Gibbs, The Quaker Girl, Roberta* (Stephanie), *Gay Divorce* (Mimi, with the Astaire-Luce dances), the inexhaustible *High Jinks* and the Australian musical *Blue Mountain Melody* (1934) before making a second trip to Britain.

Many of their subsequent appearances were in revue or in light comedy, but in 1943 Miss Elliott appeared at His Majesty's Theatre in the title role of *The Merry Widow,* with Ritchard as Danilo, and in 1945 the two paired at the head of a production of *Tonight at 8.30* in Australia.

ELLIS, Mary [ELSAS, Mary] (b New York, 15 June 1900). Star soprano and actress who introduced a handful of important musical leads on Broadway and in London.

Miss Ellis began her career as an 18-year-old operatic singer at the Metropolitan Opera House where she appeared in the first performances of Puccini's triptych, playing a young nun in *Suor Angelica,* in Albert Wolff's *The Blue Bird* as the boy Myltyl, and as Siebel, Lauretta, the tsarevitch and Gianetta (*L'Elisir d'Amore*) alongside such artists as Chaliapine, Caruso, de Luca, Jeritza and Farrar. After three years she left the operatic world to venture into the straight theatre, but a role in which she had to perform a Victor Herbert song brought her to the notice of Arthur Hammerstein and, in 1924, she was hired to create the title role of the Oscar Hammerstein/Rudolf Friml *Rose Marie* (''Indian Love Call'').

She left the cast of the show after a year to return to the dramatic theatre and for nearly 10 years she sang no more, until C B Cochran hired her to play the role of the prima donna Frieda Hatzfeld in the London production of *Music in the Air* (1933). Film commitments almost led her to have to turn down her next London singing role, but Ivor Novello was willing to wait for her availability, and so she returned to London in 1935 to create the star part of Militza Hájos in *Glamorous Night* (''Glamorous Night,'' ''Fold Your Wings''), the first of Novello's series of Drury Lane musicals. In 1939 she returned again for the best of that series, *The Dancing Years* (''I Can Give You the Starlight,'' ''Waltz of My Heart,'' ''My Dearest Dear''), and in 1943 a third time for the less successful *Arc de Triomphe,* but, in between, she occupied herself in comedy, drama and film.

She subsequently added television to these areas of credit, and played in only one further musical, Noël Coward's adaptation of Lady Windermere's Fan as *After the Ball* (1954). Coward wrote the role of Mrs Erlynne with Miss Ellis in mind, but the Miss Ellis he had in mind was the star of *The Dancing Years.* Fifteen years on she was no longer vocally equipped for its demands and *After the Ball* was not a success.

She also appeared on musical film in *All the King's Horses* (1935), *Fatal Lady* (1936) and *Paris in Spring* (1936).

Autobiography: *Those Dancing Years* (John Murray, London, 1982)

ELLIS, Vivian [John Herman] (b London, 29 October 1903; d London, 19 June 1996).

The grandson of pianist and composer Julia Woolf, whose comic opera *Carina* had been mounted in the West End in 1888, Ellis also started his musical career studying classical piano. He began composing songs whilst in his mid-teens, and contributed to a number of revues (*The Curate's Egg, Yoicks!, The Looking Glass*), before scoring his first notable success with the basic score for the revue *By the Way.* He wrote the songs for the revues *Palladium Pleasures* and *Will o'the Whispers,* and contributed interpolated numbers to such other West End revues as *Still Dancing, Cochran's Revue of 1926, Blue Skies, Clowns in Clover* and *Charlot's Revue of 1928,* to the imported musicals *Mercenary Mary, Just a Kiss, Kid Boots,* the remake of Oscar Straus's *Riquette* as *My Son John, The Girl Friend* and *A Yankee at the Court of King Arthur,* and the British-made *Merely Molly,* but his earliest full-scale musicals were not mounted in London, but on the touring circuits.

It was one of these—however, Julian Wylie's production of *Mr Cinders* (''Spread a Little Happiness,'' ''On the Amazon'')—which gave him his biggest success to date when a London transfer topped five hundred nights at the London Hippodrome and the Adelphi Theatre. The show ultimately proved itself one of the classics of its period. Thereafter, Ellis kept up a heavy schedule of writing for the West End, both for revue (contributions to *The House That Jack Built, Cochran's Revue of 1930, Folly to Be Wise, Over the Page, Please!, The Town Talks, Floodlight*) and, more particularly, for musical comedy. In three seasons he wrote much of the score for the Sophie Tucker vehicle *Follow a Star* (''If Your Kisses Can't Hold the Man You Love''), for the short-lived *Little Tommy Tucker,* the Drury Lane military spy epic *The Song of the Drum,* the Gaiety musical *Blue Roses,* Jack Buchanan and Elsie Randolph's *Stand Up and Sing,* and the musical version of *The Brass Bottle, Out of the Bottle,* often tied in with the fashionably (if rarely fashionable) American composers whom London managers of the period seemed unwilling to do wholly without—Ted Shapiro, Arthur Schwartz, Oscar Levant, Phil Charig. However, it was when he was left to supply the entire score for another touring piece, *Jack and Jill,* that Ellis scored another musical comedy hit. Whilst his much-admired revue *Streamline,* with its one-act parody of Gilbert and Sullivan, *Perseverance,* played at the Palace, the retitled *Jill Darling* gave the composer a second simultaneous success at the Saville Theatre (''I'm on a See-Saw'').

Success came again when he was teamed with a hydra of imported writers for the Bobby Howes-Cicely Courtneidge show *Hide and Seek,* with the Hippodrome naval piece *The Fleet's Lit Up* and the Gaiety Theatre comedy show *Running Riot* and, most lengthily, with another piece for Miss Courtneidge, *Under Your Hat,* which gave the composer his second five hundred–performance-plus run in the West End.

When Ellis returned to the theatre after the Second World War, he teamed again with his *Streamline* collaborator, writer A P Herbert, and the lightweight dancing shows of the previous decades gave place to a some more romantic works. The first of these, *Big Ben,* suffered from an inept libretto, but the second, *Bless the Bride,* turned out to be Ellis's most successful work of all. A pretty period comic operetta full of memorable melodies (''Ma Belle Marguerite,'' ''A Table for Two,'' ''I Was Never Kissed Before,'' ''This Is My Lovely Day,'' etc) it hit the West End around the same time as the London productions of *Oklahoma!* and *Annie Get Your Gun* and held its place, alongside those two blockbusting successes, at the head of London's musical hits until Cochran, in a curious piece of managerial miscalculation, took it off to mount Ellis and Herbert's next collaboration, an oddly Ruritanian piece called *Tough at the Top.* It did not succeed.

Ellis composed a merry mock-medieval score for a musical version of J B Fagan's hit play *And So to Bed,* and collaborated one more time with Herbert on a musical version of the author's novel *The Water Gipsies,* both with some degree of success (particularly from the musical portion) before taking his distance from the musical stage. His last new show, an adaptation of Wilde's *The Importance of Being Earnest,* originally intended for a West End staging by C B Cochran but subsequently put aside, was given showings later at America's Bucks County Playhouse, at Australia's Independent Theatre and, in England, at Coventry.

Ellis supplied the music and/or songs for several British films, including Jack Hulbert and Cicely Courtneidge's *Jack's the Boy* (''The Flies Crawled Up the Window''), the original *The Water Gipsies, Falling for You* and *Public Nuisance Number 1.*

Throughout his career, in the face of important transatlantic influences, Ellis maintained an elegant light musical style of some class which, if it did not produce as many obvious hit numbers as were achieved by some other writers, nevertheless established him as the most important and most appreciable composer of the British musical stage in the musical comedy years between the wars before he sealed his career with *Bless the Bride* in the late 1940s.

A compilation show based on Ellis's works (*Spread a Little Happiness,* ad Sheridan Morley) was produced at London's King's Head Theatre Club (14 January 1992) and later given a West End season (Whitehall Theatre 29 June 1992).

His name is an attached to an Award given annually in London to encourage new musical-theatre writing.

1927 **The Grass Widow** (William Helmore/Lauri Wylie) Empire Theatre, Bristol 8 August

1927 **The Other Girl** (Helmore, Collie Knox/Wylie) Empire Theatre, Bristol 17 October

1927 **Peg o' Mine** (w Phil Charig, et al/Desmond Carter/Fred Jackson) Empire Theatre, Sunderland 31 October

1928 **Mr Cinders** (w Richard Myers/Greatrex Newman, Clifford Grey) Opera House, Blackpool 25 September; Adelphi Theatre 11 February 1929

1930 **Follow a Star** (w others/Douglas Furber, Dion Titheradge) Winter Garden Theatre 17 September

1930 **Little Tommy Tucker** (Carter, Caswell Garth, R P Weston, Bert Lee) Daly's Theatre 19 November

1931 **The Song of the Drum** (w Herman Finck/Carter, Fred Thompson, Guy Bolton) Theatre Royal, Drury Lane 9 January

1931 **Blue Roses** (Carter, Garth) Gaiety Theatre 20 January

1931 **Stand Up and Sing** (w Charig/Furber, Jack Buchanan) London Hippodrome 5 March

1932 **Out of the Bottle** (ex- *If It Happened to You*) (w Oscar Levant/Grey, Thompson) London Hippodrome 11 June

1934 **Jill Darling** (ex- *Jack and Jill*) (Carter, Marriott Edgar) Saville Theatre 19 December

1936 **Going Places** (Bolton, Thompson) Savoy Theatre 8 October

1937 **Hide and Seek** (w Sam Lerner, Al Goodhart, Al Hoffman/ Bolton, Thompson, Furber) London Hippodrome 14 October

1938 **The Fleet's Lit Up** (Bolton, Thompson, Lee) London Hippodrome 17 August

1938 **Running Riot** (Furber, Bolton, Firth Shephard) Gaiety Theatre 31 August

1938 **Under Your Hat** (Archie Menzies, Arthur Macrae, Jack Hulbert) Palace Theatre 24 November

1946 **Big Ben** (A P Herbert) Adelphi Theatre 17 July

1947 **Bless the Bride** (Herbert) Adelphi Theatre 26 April

1949 **Tough at the Top** (Herbert) Adelphi Theatre 15 July

1951 **And So to Bed** (J B Fagan) New Theatre 17 October

1955 **The Water Gipsies** (Herbert) Winter Garden Theatre 31 August

1957 **Half in Earnest** (Ellis) Bucks County Playhouse, New Hope, Pa 17 June

Autobiography: *I'm on a See-saw* (Michael Joseph, London, 1953)

ELLISON, Sydney [GREENLEAF, George William] (b Westminster, London, 27 July 1867; d London, 21 December 1930). Director and choreographer who found fame with his staging of *Florodora.*

Originally a performer, Ellison appeared in the West End as a replacement in *An Artist's Model* (1895, t/o

Maddox) and as the original George Grimston in *The Geisha* (1896), but he quickly found his métier as a director and choreographer when he restaged George Edwardes's production of *An Artist's Model* for its Broadway season (1895). He subsequently mounted *L'Amour mouillé* (1899) for Tom Davis, and had a major success when he directed and choreographed the same producer's original production of *Florodora* (1899), creating the famous "Tell Me, Pretty Maiden" double sextet routine which was sensationally reproduced in America, France (by Ellison, 1903), the colonies and everywhere the show went. He followed this up with another personal triumph when his Champagne Dance from *The Silver Slipper* scored an enormous Broadway success inside another decidedly successful show.

Ellison's services, thereafter, were much in demand by managers and he staged a long list of musicals over the next decade including *My Lady Molly* (1902), *The Medal and the Maid* (1903) for Davis, *The Orchid* (1903) and *The Spring Chicken* (1905) at the Gaiety Theatre, *The Gay Lord Vergy* (1905), *See See* (1906), *Two Naughty Boys* (1907), *Nelly Neil* (1907), *King of Cadonia* (1908), *The Belle of Brittany* (1908), *A Persian Princess* (1909) and *The Mountaineers* (1909), working for virtually all the top London managements. He visited America to stage *He Came from Milwaukee* (1910) and *The Girl and the Kaiser* (1911, *Die Förster-Christl*) for the Shuberts, *My Best Girl* (1912) for Henry Harris and *The Lilac Domino* (1914) for Andreas Dippel and, after spending much of the war in the army, continued to work through the later 1910s, mounting *Flora* for André Charlot in 1918, and the highly successful London musical, *Kissing Time,* in 1919. Soon after, however, victim of a stroke and a cab accident, he slipped from view and fell upon hard times. In his last years he lived in one room, worked as a walk-on, and, in spite of a benefit mounted for him in 1925, ended in the workhouse where his last illness claimed him.

It was said that Ellison "revolutionized the whole style of musical comedy chorus work by putting action and special rhythm into it" and, even if the word "revolutionized" carries things altogether too far, there is little doubt that his dance-based work, as displayed to such effect in *Florodora,* marked another stage on the way from the static and elegantly strolling choruses of previous decades to a more active kind of musical comedy staging.

Ellison was married in 1900, during the run of *Florodora,* to the show's ingenue, Kate Cutler.

ELSIE, Lily [COTTON, Elsie] (b Wortley, 8 April ?1886; d London, 16 December 1962). Lovely young vocalist who shot to stardom as Britain's "Merry Widow."

A child of mysterious origins (she was rumored, when fame came, to have been the illegitimate daughter

Plate 115. **Sydney Ellison.** *The man who invented "Tell Me, Pretty Maiden."*

of an aristocrat by a Midlands wardrobe mistress), Lily Elsie was brought up as the daughter of theatre-manager William Cotton and worked as a juvenile performer in pantomime and comedy and in variety as "Little Elsie." She made her first appearances in musical comedy touring, at 16, first in *The Silver Slipper* and then in *Three Little Maids* and in *Madame Sherry* (1904, Barbara). She was first seen in London when, at 17, she took over the soprano role of Princess Soo-Soo in *A Chinese Honeymoon* at the old Strand Theatre. Thereafter she worked exclusively for George Edwardes, rising swiftly and surely up the playbill. She succeeded to Delia Mason's soubrette role of Gwenny Holden in *Lady Madcap,* toured as Lady Patricia in *The Cingalee,* took a tiny role in *Les P'tites Michu* (1905, Madame du Tertre) and teamed up with Zena Dare and Gabrielle Ray as Willie Edouin's daughters in *The Little Cherub* (1906, Lady Agnes Congress), until the family was reduced to just two in a rewrite and she was moved on to appear in a supporting role in the same management's *See See* instead (1906, Humming Bird).

Owing to the unavailability of Gertie Millar, she created the title role in *The New Aladdin* (1906, Lally) at the Gaiety, but she was removed when Miss Millar was ready to come back to the theatre. Edwardes more than made it up to the young singer, however, when he cast her in a much more suitable role as the heroine of *The Merry Widow* (1907), a role and a show which made her into a major star. She followed up in the starring roles of *The Dollar Princess* (1909, Alice), *A Waltz Dream* (1911, Franzi) and *The Count of Luxembourg* (1911, Angèle Didier), as the passion for the Viennese Operette reached its peak in London, before retiring to marriage in 1911.

She returned to the musical stage in *Pamela* (1917, Pamela) and once more in *The Blue Train* (1927, Eileen Mayne), during various downs in her up-and-down married life, but she was unable to find again the success of her five years as Edwardes's Daly's Theatre star.

ELSSLER, Fanny *see* DIE TÄNZERIN FANNY ELSSLER

THE EMERALD ISLE, or The Caves of Carrig-Cleena Comic opera in 2 acts by Basil Hood. Music by Arthur Sullivan and Edward German. Savoy Theatre, London, 27 April 1901.

Arthur Sullivan's last work, *The Emerald Isle,* was written in collaboration with the generally accepted successor of W S Gilbert, Basil Hood, with whom the composer had already worked on the successful *The Rose of Persia.* However, the piece was left uncompleted at Sullivan's death, and Carte asked Edward German, who had until that time never written for the comic opera stage, to undertake the task of filling out Sullivan's sketches and composing the missing parts of the music. Before the production got to the stage, Carte, too, had died and *The Emerald Isle* was mounted by his widow, Helen, as a virtual postscript to the heyday of the Carte regime and the Savoy Theatre.

Hood's libretto was not as good as his previous one. The Lord Lieutenant of Ireland (Jones Hewson) is anglicizing the Irish, sending out elocutionists, including one Professor Bunn (Walter Passmore), to take the begorrahs out of the local speech. Would-be patriot Terence O'Brien (Robert Evett) already speaks English, for he has been brought up in London, where he has—o, incongruity!—fallen in love with Rosie Pippin (Isabel Jay), who is none other than the Lord Lieutenant's daughter. Terence hides out in the reputedly haunted caves of Carrig-Cleena, and soubrette Molly (Louie Pounds) impersonates the fairy of the place to keep away the superstitious British soldiers who would capture him. Henry Lytton played Pat Murphy, the hereditary blind fiddler, Rosina Brandram was the wife of the Lord Lieutenant, to whom she spoke only in blank verse, and Robert Rous the family chaplain, Dr Fiddle, D D, each of whom had their moments as the plot wound its way towards the union of Rosie and Terence.

The show's songs were often (and, undoubtedly, intentionally) reminiscent of the earlier Gilbert and Sullivan works, but none the worse for that, as Passmore sang about the clichés of on- and off-stage Irishness in "The Popular Type of Pat," and the Lord Lieutenant delivered his curriculum vitae in song ("At an Early Stage of Life") and joined his wife and chaplain in a expository piece reminiscent of the introduction of the Plaza Toroi in *The Gondoliers.* Bunn pattered through a traditional comic song ("Oh, the Age in Which We're Living") and Terence got romantic over his first meeting with Rosie ("'Twas in Hyde Park Beside the Row") in suitable strains.

The Emerald Isle ran for 205 performances at the Savoy, during which time William Greet took over control of the theatre and the company. At the end of the London run, he sent the piece on tour, whilst Jefferson de Angelis (also Bunn) and R H Burnside put together a production for Broadway in which John Dudley (Terence), Kate Condon (Molly), Josephine Knapp (Rosie), Charles Dungan (Lord Lieutenant) and Bernard Sullivan (Pat) joined the producer/star for 50 performances in New York and more on the road. The show was subsequently played in Australia, where J C Williamson's production featured George Lauri (Bunn), Florence Young (Rosie), Reginald Roberts (Terence), Carrie Moore (Molly) and Harold Thorley (Lieutenant), and on other English-language stages, but it eventually found its place rather as a concert piece with choral societies, than as a revivable comic opera.

USA: Herald Square Theater 1 September 1902; Australia: Her Majesty's Theatre, Melbourne 17 March 1903

Recording: complete (Pearl)

EMMET, J[oseph] K[line] (b St Louis, Mo, 13 March 1841; d Cornwall, NY, 15 June 1891). Celebrated star of the "Fritz" series of comico-weepie-melodramas with songs which delighted America, in particular, for a generation.

After beginnings as a snare-drummer with Freebrothuser's Minstrels and Bellringers, 22-year-old Emmett appeared as a singer, under the name of "Joe Dutten, the World's Greatest Warbler," at his hometown's old Bowery Theater. His subsequently decided to follow the fashion and go "Dutch" and in 1867 he became "Joe Granfrau, the Great German Warbler—just over." He soon returned both to his own name and to the minstrel world, appearing with Morris and Wilson's Minstrels in St Louis and in 1868 he made his first New York appearance with Bryant's Minstrels, singing his Dutch songs ("Schneider Don't You Want to Buy a Dog?," "The Deutscher Girl That Winked at Me," etc) and performing a clog dance.

In 1869 Emmet moved into the theatre, and straight away made his fame in the character of the broken-

Englished, curly-headed Fritz in the sentimental comedy-melodrama *[The Adventures of] Fritz, Our Cousin German* (1869). As Fritz pursued the search for his long-lost sister, battled the villainous Colonel Crafton and conducted his courtship of pretty Dutch Katarina, there were numerous opportunities for him to pause, unhitch the guitar from his back, and deliver a song. One of these songs, a Lullaby written and composed by the actor himself, became one of the most loved show songs of its time.

Emmet played Fritz for the rest of his life, the original play being switched about, expanded and altered with alternative or additional scenes, songs or musical specialities on the harmonica (five variations on ''Home, Sweet Home'') or the fiddle, as it was taken round and round America by its star. In 1872 he took it as far afield as London's Adelphi Theatre in a ''London version,'' a couple of years later he traveled his show, with considerable success, to Australia, and in 1878 he played it again on Broadway in a ''new'' version. He also tried a couple of other pieces on the same lines before his American audiences—*Carl the Fiddler* (1871), H J Byron's *Max, the Merry Swiss Boy* (1873)—and introduced Australians to *Jan, the New German, or The Swiss Avalanche* (1875) and Byron's *Phil the Foundling* (1875), but without the same success. He inevitably returned to *Fritz, Our Cousin German,* before switching to a series of soi-disant sequels, beginning with the most durable (the original apart), *Fritz in Ireland* (1879), which allowed German-accented Emmet to sing some Irish songs and, of course, a lullaby, and continuing with *Fritz Among the Gipsies* (1882), in which he introduced another song, ''Sweet Violets,'' which would become a long-lived standard, *Fritz the Bohemian* (1883) and *Fritz in a Madhouse* (1889).

Hugely popular wherever he went, Emmet was the most successful of the many purveyors of the unsophisticated ''sensation-and-songs'' pieces which for many years proved such enormous favorites in the provincial cities and villages of America, Britain and the English-speaking colonies, and he and his character and material became the prototypes for many subsequent performers and plays in the same vein.

His son, J K Emmet jr, later took the the touring circuits and the halls in his father's famous part (*Fritz in Clover,* etc) without comparable joy.

EMNEY, Fred[erick Charles] (b Islington, London, 5 March 1865; d New Malden, 7 January 1917). Character actor on the British musical and straight stages.

A nephew of the great comedian Arthur Williams, Emney originally worked as a commercial clerk in an accountant's office, but at 20 he was hired for a Gaiety Theatre road company, and made his first professional stage appearances in the burlesque *The Forty Thieves* (1885, Cassim) and such extravaganzas as *Ariel* and *Aladdin.* He toured in drama and farce (including comedian Harry Monkhouse's musical comedy *Larks*) and he made his first London musical appearance in the Jubilee curtain-raiser *Jubilation* before going on tour in uncle Williams's famous role of Lurcher in *Dorothy* for three seasons. Thereafter, he mixed much musical with his comedy work, both in the West End—Jacques d'Arc in *Joan of Arc* (t/o 1891), *Blue-Eyed Susan* (Raker, 1892, t/o from Williams as Doggrass), *The Baroness* (1892, Bruno), *Jaunty Jane Shore* (1894, Grist, tour as Matthew Shore), Baron Fontenay in *All Abroad* (1895), Mr Dingley in *The Yashmak* (1897), *Great Caesar,* (1899, Cicero), *Madame Sherry* (1903, Joseph), *Les Merveilleuses* (1906, Tournesol), *See See* (1906, Hoang), *The Antelope* (1908, Joe Derrick)—and on the road (*My Sweetheart,* Duvet in *Captain Thérèse, Fun on the Bristol, A Gaiety Girl, La Mascotte, Madame Favart,* Mr Wapshott in *Belinda* (1896), Rev Amos Basingstoke in *The Gay Grisette* (1898), *The Telephone Girl,* Chambertin in *Regina B.A.* (1897), *The Girl from Kays, Véronique,* etc). His best new roles on the London musical stage were the burglar, Posh Jenkins, in *Lady Madcap* (1904), Nervy Nat in *The Gay Gordons* (1907) and the blackmailing sleeping car attendant, Cornelius Scrop, in *The Girl in the Train* (1910). Emney died as the result of an on-stage accident at the London Opera House, where he was appearing as Baroness de Bounce in the Christmas pantomime of *Cinderella.*

His son, who also worked as **Fred[erick Patrick Round] EMNEY** (b Woolton, Liverpool, 12 February 1900; d Bognor Regis, 25 December 1980), began a career on the stage as a teenager and toured in musicals in Britain prior to going to America, where he remained throughout the 1920s. On returning, he appeared in *Mr Whittington* (1934) and *The Flying Trapeze* (1935) and, with his obese figure, flourishing jowls and eyeglass as a trademark, soon became established as a favorite character in musical comedy, starring in a famous team with Leslie Henson and Richard Hearne in a series of Gaiety Theatre productions (*Seeing Stars, Swing Along, Going Greek, Running Riot*). He supported Jack Buchanan in *It's Time to Dance,* and appeared top-billed at the Saville in 1945 in *Big Boy,* a musical tailored to his own considerable measure. He had a big success as the ''baby'' in *Blue for a Boy* and collaborated on the writing of a second musical vehicle for himself, *Happy as a King* (1954). It proved, like his previous solo star effort, less than a success.

Emney appeared in the films of the stage musicals *Hold My Hand* (1938, Lord Milchester), *Yes, Madam?* (1939, Sir Charles Drake-Drake), *The Lilac Domino* (1940, Baron de Gonda) and *Oliver!* (1968) and of the de-musicalized *Lock Up Your Daughters* (1969) and, in his seventies, toured as Erronius in *A Funny Thing Happened on the Way to the Forum.*

His sister, Joan Fred Emney (b London 12 February 1898), also appeared on the musical stage, notably as Mabel in the London production of *The Pajama Game.*

Biography: Fairlie, G: *The Fred Emney Story* (Hutchinson, London, 1960)

THE ENCHANTRESS Comic opera in 3 acts by Fred de Grésac and Harry B Smith. Lyrics by Harry B Smith. Music by Victor Herbert. New York Theater, New York, 19 October 1911.

Victor Herbert's *The Enchantress,* produced by Joseph Gaites in a spectacular staging, with a cast of one hundred, was played for only 72 New York performances in the Broadway season of 1911–12, but, even though it was not picked up for overseas productions, its career in the theatre was extended well beyond that by a long and profitable life—mostly in the hands of original star Kitty Gordon—on the American touring circuits.

Madame Fred de Grésac and Harry Smith's libretto used a familiar plot in the love-and-power genre, here set in the Ruritanian principality of Zergovia. The ambitious minister Ozir (Arthur Forrest) has his eyes on the throne of Prince Ivan (Hal Forde) and he determines to make use of the law forbidding a monarch to wed a commoner, to gain his ends. When the Prince is about to succeed to his throne, and needs to take a bride, Ozir convinces the seductive singer Vivien Savary (Kitty Gordon) to enchant the boy into a marriage. However, although she succeeds, she also falls in love with Ivan, and turns against Ozir. When it eventuates that Vivien is actually a little bit (sufficiently) royal, the happy ending is assured.

The tale of *The Enchantress* was illustrated by a shapely and attractive score entirely from the pen of Herbert, which profited greatly from not being disfigured by the unsuitable interpolations which were so liberally practiced on imported shows. Herbert, not writing here for a Fritzi Scheff, tactfully kept his leger lines under control and the fine-voiced Miss Gordon was only required to encompass an A in her principal solo and in her duo with the King, "One Word from You," in which the lyrics (altogether better throughout than in many shows of the era) still showed traces of the libretto's original "unhappy" ending, in which unroyal Vivien had renounced her King for his own good.

The heroine's entrance song, "To the Land of My Own Romance," turned out to be the most appreciated item in the score, but otherwise the best numbers went to the supporting characters. There were comic songs for Vivien's Aunt Mamout (Hattie Arnold) and the head of the secret service (Ralph Riggs), and Nelly McCoy sang a little novelty number tracing the history of a melody ("That Pretty Little Song") as it went from its original composition around the world and ended up—oh, horror—being arranged into unrecognizableness by ragtime writers. However, it was Louise Bliss as a plump Princess insisting "I Want to Be a Prima Donna" ("I want to be a peachy, screechy cantatrice . . ."), giving as reference the fact that she is at least the same size as Tetrazzini, who had the comic gem of the evening. "To the Land of My Own Romance" got itself interpolated into a Broadway revival of *Sweethearts* in 1947, but it is "I Want to Be a Prima Donna," rediscovered in recent years by sopranos and brought back to the concert and auditions stages, and even to record, which has proven the most enduring portion of the show.

The title *The Enchantress* had been previously used for a successful opera in three acts by Alfred Bunn, taken from a text by J H Vernoy de Saint-Georges, set to music by Michael Balfe, and introduced at the Theatre Royal, Drury Lane, 14 May 1845, prior to productions in America and Australia. It was for many years played on the American circuits as part of the repertoire of the Caroline Richings company.

UK: Ladbroke Hall (copyright performance) 9 October 1911

EN CHEMYSE Opérette-bouffe in 3 acts by Albert Willemetz and Cami. Music by Raoul Moretti. Théâtre des Bouffes-Parisiens, Paris, 7 March 1924.

The first stage musical by the newly popular songwriter, Raoul Moretti, *En chemyse* burlesqued the well-known story of the Burghers of Calais. *Phi-Phi* star Alice Cocéa, back in period costume as the heroine of the piece, gave several extralight songs including "Isoline, va dans la cuisine," whilst Dranem, dressed up in a medieval coat of mail in the chief comic role of Lahirette, told the tale of "La girl et le homard."

The piece aroused the ire of those who considered that the good burghers of Calais, though centuries dead and already the subject of several comic operas, should not be made fun of, but the merry burlesque with its dance-based score stayed on the bill for nearly three months, and set its composer on the road to more, and more successful, works.

ENCORE CINQUANTE CENTIMES Opérette in 3 acts by André Barde. Music by Henri Christiné and Maurice Yvain. Théâtre des Nouveautés, Paris, 17 September 1931.

Over a decade into the era of new-style French musical comedy, and in spite of the rise of a number of successful composers, the two who had started it all still remained at the top of the tree. For *Encore cinquante centimes,* producer Benoît-Leon Deutsch had the bright idea of bringing Christiné and Yvain together to collaborate on a score to a text by André Barde who was, with Willemetz, the most successful author of the genre.

The most popular musical comedian of the time, Dranem, starred as Hercule Boulot, a penniless circus strongman whisked off to the Balkan republic of Rouffionie to help the Queen, whose husband (José Sergy) prefers chasing butterflies, to continue the dynasty and thus save the country from the hands of the horrid Republican Prime Minister, Rapescu (Edmond Carlus). Gabrielle Ristori (Queen Stasia), soubrette Suzanne Dehelly (Boulot's girlfriend, Pirouette) and Edith Méra (Héléna Tubasek, a Rouffionian agent) provided the pulchritude and the singing voices for a delightful series of musical numbers, of which Dranem contributed ''Avec les femmes,'' ''Je reviendrais demain matin'' and ''Essayez donc'' as well as the lively Parade duo ''Encore cinquante centimes'' and ''L'amour est un plaisir vraiment doux'' with Pirouette. The King had a little piece explaining ''J'aime les papillons'' which led naturally into a butterfly dance, and the Queen sang passionately of ''Le Sang de mes aïeux,'' which was eventually stirred up by a little ''Bonheur caché'' with the handsome Brancomir (André Dupin), allowing Pirouette to reclaim her man unsullied (''Quand on n'a qu'un homme'').

The combination of fun, tunes and top names proved a winning one, and the piece had a fine Paris run prior to touring and a production in Budapest (ad Jenő Heltai) under the title ''the kiss doctor.''

Hungary: Magyar Színház *A csodadoktor* 12 May 1934

ENDLICH ALLEIN Operette in 3 acts by A M Willner and Robert Bodanzky. Music by Franz Lehár. Theater an der Wien, Vienna, 30 January 1914.

An attractive Lehár score, which included a sung-through second act and which occasionally prefigured the style, if not the tone, of his later and more heftily romantic works, *Endlich allein* was set to a book which sent Dolly Doverland, a kookie American heiress (Mizzi Günther), mountain-climbing with a guide (Hubert Marischka) who turns out to be the amorous Baron Frank Hansen in disguise. The Theater an der Wien's top light-comedy team of Ernst Tautenhayn (Graf Willibald Splenningen) and Luise Kartousch (Tilly), as the offspring of the Graf Maximilian Splenningen (Paul Guttmann) and the Gräfin Konstanze Dachau (Mizzi Schütz) respectively, provided a different weight of romance and the soubret music in parallel to the lyrical lovemaking.

Endlich allein did well enough through 115 performances at the Theater an der Wien, and a handful more at the Raimundtheater, to win a number of productions in areas where Germanic stage shows were not being wartimely boycotted, without ever becoming a real favorite. An American version (ad Edgar Smith, Joseph W Herbert), produced by the Shubert brothers, with John Charles Thomas as the Baron romancing Marguerite Namara, squeezed some additional numbers by the show's conductor Gaetano Merola, plus Silvio Hein and Benjamin Hapgood Burt's ''Some Little Bug is Going to Find You,'' into Lehár's rich score, and was compensated with a fine Broadway run of 180 performances. Zsolt Harsányi's Hungarian adaptation was performed at the Király Színház with rather less success.

The show was later revised and reproduced with considerably more success under the title of its principal waltz song, *Schön ist die Welt* (3 December 1930).

Hungary: Király Színház *Végre egyedül* 20 February 1915; USA: Shubert Theater *Alone at Last* 19 October 1915

ENGEL, Alexander (b Turocz-Neczpal, Hungary, 10 April 1868; d Vienna, 17 November 1940).

Hungarian-born journalist (sometime editor of the *Neuer Wiener Journal* and theatre correspondent for Berlin's *Klein Journal*), theatre critic, author and playwright, Engel had his first musical work, *Rhodope,* with a score by Hugo Felix, played at the Carltheater and Theater des Westens (23 June 1900) without notable success. That success came, however, when he formed a writing team with Julius Horst and, although their initial musical piece, *Der Schätzmeister,* had only a disappointing 34-performance run at the Carltheater prior to an Hungarian production (*A Becsüs*), they turned out a series of often long-running comedies—several of which included some musical content—for the Raimundtheater (the highly successful *Die blaue Maus, Seine kleine Freundin,* etc), the Bürgertheater (*Glück bei Frauen, Einheirat*), and for the Munich and Berlin stages, whilst each simultaneously pursuing other collaborations. Engel paired at various times with such other successful authors as August Neidhart, Carl Lindau, Victor Léon, Leo Stein, Alfred Grünwald and Ralph Benatzky. He did not, however, have a success with his original libretti equivalent to that made with his plays, and although pieces such as Eysler's *Der junge Papa,* Benatzky's *Adieu Mimi* and *Pipsi* and Richard Fall's *Die Puppenbaronessen* did well enough, he did not find a musical hit to come up to the success of *Die blaue Maus.*

Die blaue Maus (Raimundtheater 15 February 1908) was set to music in Austria by Ludwig Grüber, and again in America, where the libretto was manufactured under the title *The Little Blue Devil* (Central Theater 3 November 1919) by Harold Atteridge from Clyde Fitch's local adaptation of the play, and the songs provided by Harry Carroll, whilst Horst and Engel's hit play *Glück bei Frauen* became *Pariser Luft* in the hands of Louis Taufstein and Martin Knopf (Luisen-Theater, Königsberg 22 June

1912) and their *Der Schrei nach dem Kind* (Theater in der Josefstadt 7 May 1914) was used as the basis for the libretto to the Lehár/Jenbach Operette *Cloclo* (1924). In Hungary, unspecified Engel works were used as the bases for several musicals: *Rózsanyilás idején* (w Ernest Gettke) was presented as a musical comedy at the Budai Színkör (13 September 1902), as was *Marci* (w Horst), adapted by Adolf Mérei and set to music by Alfréd Márkus (Budai Színkör 17 June 1916). *Toeff-Toeff* (Königliches Hoftheater, Berlin 6 February 1901 w Léon), adapted in a version by Zsolt Harsányi, was musicalized as *Őzvegy kisasszony* by Adorján Ötvős (1 September 1916), a further unnamed Engel and Horst play, which seems to have been their 1903 *Der g'rade Michl,* served as the basis for the operett *Rézi* (Izsó Barna/Jenő Faragó, Árpád Abonyi Népszínház 16 September 1904) and America's Earl Carroll availed himself of an unspecified Engel and Stobitzer original when writing *The Love Mill* (1917).

1900 **Rhodope** (Hugo Felix) Carltheater 1 February

1904 **Der Schätzmeister** (Carl Michael Ziehrer/w Julius Horst) Carltheater 10 December

1906 **Der blaue Klub** (Karl Kappeller/w Horst) Theater am Gärtnerplatz, Munich 24 November

1909 **Der Rodelbaron** (Fritz Fürst/w Horst) 2 scenes Apollotheater 1 January

1909 **Der junge Papa** (Edmund Eysler/w August Neidhart) 1 act Apollotheater 3 February

1909 **Der Ehemännerzug** (Kappeller/w Carl Lindau) Stadttheater, Nuremberg 14 November

1910 **Miss Exzentrik** (Heinrich Reinhardt/w Armin Friedmann) 1 act Apollotheater 31 October

1911 **Der Liftboy** (Otto Weber) 1 act Hölle 1 March

1912 **Der Lockvogel** (Leo Ascher/w Horst) Walhalla-Theater, Wiesbaden 11 January

1913 **Die Bretteldiva** (Josef Snaga/w Rudolf Lothar) Stadttheater, Magdeburg 21 February

1913 **Die blaue Maus** (Ludwig Grüber/w Horst) Graben Kino 11 November

1917 **Die Puppenbaronessen** (Richard Fall/w Fritz Grünbaum) Apollotheater 1 September

1918 **Die tanzende Maske** (w Ralph Benatzky) Apollotheater 1 December

1921 **Die ewige Braut** (Hugo Hirsch) Volkstheater, Munich 2 March

1921 **Pipsi** (Benatzky/w Horst) Wiener Bürgertheater 30 December

1926 **Adieu Mimi** (Benatzky/w Horst) Johann Strauss-Theater 9 June

ENGLÄNDER, Ludwig (b Vienna, 20 October 1851; d Far Rockaway, NY, 13 September 1914). Austrian-American composer who provided functional rather than memorable scores for a generation of Broadway shows.

Born in Vienna, Engländer left home in his late twenties and proceeded first to Paris and then, in 1882, to America. He became conductor at New York's German-language Thalia Theater, under Gustav Amberg's management, and his operetta *Der Prinz Gemahl,* written to a Viennese text by Julius Hopp and the Bohrmann-Riegen partnership, was staged there the following year. Played originally in German, both in and outside New York, it was later given in English (Baltimore Academy of Music 28 November 1883) by the doggedly touring Wilbur Opera Company under the title *The Prince Consort.*

His second composition, *1776,* allegedly written to a text by the brother of composer Karl Goldmark (''though the libretto has been claimed by another''), was produced at the same theatre, briefly, early in 1884 with no less a star than Marie Geistinger and with the German Hans Junker playing a Red Indian. Less successful than the first, this, too, was ultimately seen in English, but not until more than a decade later when it was reworked under the title *A Daughter of the Revolution.* A third Operette to a German-language text, *Madelaine,* was produced in Hamburg.

Englander (having abandoned his umlaut en route) subsequently became conductor at New York's Casino Theater but, after supplying George Lederer with much of the score for the successful revue, *The Passing Show* (1894), he gave up the conducting side of his work to concentrate on composing.

Over 20 years of subsequent writing he provided a steady stream of music for Broadway shows, both book musicals and revues (*A Round of Pleasure,* etc), mostly as basic scores into which the comic artists and other stars of the day could interpolate individual numbers written by various popular songsmiths. In spite of providing music for stars of the popularity of Jefferson de Angelis, Francis Wilson, Sam Bernard, Eddie Foy, Blanche Ring, Fritzi Scheff, Marie Cahill, Anna Held and many others such, he did not ever succeed in composing a genuine hit show, although several of his pieces had reasonable touring lives.

His most successful efforts were *The Little Corporal* (1898), played by Francis Wilson in America and subsequently produced in Vienna, and three further collaborations with *Little Corporal* author Harry B Smith—*The Rounders* (adapted from the Continental hit *Les Fêtards*), *The Strollers* (taken from another successful Continental piece, *Die Landstreicher*) and, most particularly, *The Casino Girl,* not adapted from anything but modeled closely on the Gaiety Theatre shows, which played both New York and London for respectable runs and was even briefly seen, in Hungarian, in Budapest.

Engländer's longest Broadway runs came with *Miss Innocence,* in which Florenz Ziegfeld's magnificent production, built around Anna Held in the title role, helped keep the show alight for 176 performances, and the 1899 spectacular extravaganza *The Man in the Moon* for which he contributed only part of the music (with Kerker and De Koven) and which again owed its run to its production values rather than its content.

In 1910 Engländer returned to Vienna where (with his umlaut back on) he succeeded, over the next few years, in having a couple of short pieces and one full-length Operette produced. *Vielliebchen* was a little before its time. Although its brisk score was as waltz- and march-orientated as most European pieces, it apparently seemed disagreeably American to much of a town that had treated *The Belle of New York* as an attractive novelty but which was not yet tuned to transatlantic rhythms. *Vielliebchen* nevertheless succeeded in earning other productions in Europe following its brief Viennese run.

1883 **Der Prinz Gemahl** (*The Prince Consort*) (Julius Hopp, Bohrmann-Riegen) Thalia Theater 11 April; Wallack's Theater 4 June

1884 **1776** (aka *Adjutant James*) (Leo Goldmark) Thalia Theater 26 February

1884 **The Seven Ravens** part new score for American version by G P Lathrop, Niblo's Gardens 18 August

1888 **Madelaine** (aka *Die Rose der Champagne*) (Karl Hauser) Carl-Schultze Theater, Hamburg 26 June

1893 **The Woman-King** revised score to Rudolf Aronson's *The Rainmaker of Syria* Miner's Newark Theater, Newark, NJ 20 November

1895 **The Twentieth Century Girl** (Sydney Rosenfeld) Bijou Theater 25 January

1895 **A Daughter of the Revolution** revised *1776* (J Cheever Goodwin) Broadway Theater 27 May

1896 **The Caliph** (H B Smith) Broadway Theater 3 September

1896 **Half a King** (*Le Roi de carreau*) English version by H B Smith w new score Knickerbocker Theater 14 September

1897 **Gayest Manhattan** (H B Smith) Koster and Bial's Music Hall 22 March

1898 **The Little Corporal** (H B Smith) Broadway Theater 19 September

1899 **In Gay Paree** (Grant Stewart/ad Clay Greene) Casino Theater 20 March

1899 **The Man in the Moon** (w Gustave Kerker, Reginald De Koven/Stange, Louis Harrison) New York Theater 24 April

1899 **The Rounders** (*Les Fêtards*) American version by H B Smith with new score Casino Theater 12 July

1900 **The Casino Girl** (H B Smith) Casino Theater 19 March

1900 **The Cadet Girl** (*Les Demoiselles de Saint-Cyriens*) American version by H B Smith, Goodwin w partial new score Herald Square Theater 25 July

1900 **The Monks of Malabar** (Goodwin) Knickerbocker Theater 14 September

1900 **The Belle of Bohemia** (H B Smith) Casino Theater 24 September

1901 **The Strollers** (*Die Landstreicher*) English version by H B Smith w new score Knickerbocker Theater 24 June

1901 **The New Yorkers** (Glen MacDonough/George V Hobart) Herald Square Theater 7 October

1902 **The Wild Rose** (H B Smith/Hobart) Knickerbocker Theater 5 May

1902 **Sally in Our Alley** (Hobart) Broadway Theater 29 August

1903 **The Jewel of Asia** (Frederick Ranken/H B Smith) Criterion Theater 16 February

1903 **The Office Boy** (*Le Jockey malgré lui*) English version by H B Smith w new score Victoria Theater 2 November

1904 **A Madcap Princess** (H B Smith) Knickerbocker Theater 5 September

1904 **The Two Roses** (Stanislaus Stange) Broadway Theater 21 November

1905 **The White Cat** (ad H B Smith) New Amsterdam Theater 2 November

1906 **The Rich Mr Hoggenheimer** (ad H B Smith) Wallack's Theater 22 October

1908 **Miss Innocence** (H B Smith) New York Theater 30 November

1911 **Vielliebchen** (Rudolf Österreicher, Carl Lindau) Venedig in Wien, Vienna 5 May

1912 **Kitty's Ehemänner** (Emil Kolberg, Fritz Lunzer) 1 act Hölle, Vienna 1 November

1914 **Madame Moselle** (aka *Hotel Eva*) (ad Edward A Paulton) Shubert Theater 23 May

1914 **Seebaddrummel** (Schubert) 1 act Zirkus Schumann, Vienna 31 October

AN ENGLISH DAISY Musical comedy in 2 acts by Seymour Hicks. Music by Walter Slaughter. Royal County Theatre, Kingston, 11 August 1902.

Written for London, *An English Daisy* was eventually staged on the provincial circuits. Several love affairs, a disguised heiress, a couple of American low comics (Thomas E Murray, Will Spray), a marriage ceremony in a lion's cage and an unexceptional set of songs made up a show which introduced 15-year-old Zena Dare in the title role in her first adult show. A second tour followed, but *An English Daisy* did not make it to London. In the then-current craze for British product, however, the show was taken up for Broadway by the recently ''divorced'' (from his partner of 30 years, Joe Weber) Lew Fields. Rewritten by Edgar Smith, much remusicked by expatriate Austrian composer Alfred Müller-Norden and others, and with Christie Macdonald, Templar Saxe, Charles Bigelow and Truly Shattuck heading the cast, it lasted 41 performances, winning notoriety only as one of the few British shows to have played Broadway without having reached London, and for introducing the first Broadway songs by a young composer named Jerome D Kern.

USA: Casino Theater 18 January 1904

L'ENLÈVEMENT DE LA TOLEDAD Opérette in 3 acts by Fabrice Carré. Music by Edmond Audran. Théâtre des Bouffes-Parisiens, Paris, 17 October 1894.

A welcome production for the Bouffes-Parisiens, where things had been going so poorly that bankruptcy seemed nigh, *L'Enlèvement de la Toledad* also once again gave Audran the kind of success that had, after so many years of major hits, for several seasons been avoiding him.

The La Toledad who was carried off in Fabrice Carré's libretto is a Spanish song-and-dancer (Juliette Simon-Girard) and her "enlèvement" is not all that it might seem. The stockbroking Gaston (Charles Lamy) has romanced her and whisked her away from her extravagant mother, La Maracona (Rosine Maurel), her lover Antonio (Félix Huguenet), and a successful theatrical season solely so that the theatre where she is playing will go broke, revenging him for a lost bet. Amorous and financial fortunes yo-yo up and down until the right pairings are (re-)established and the stock market has come good.

Audran's score was all that a vehicle should be. The star set things rolling with a habañera ("Je suis la Toledad"), had a letter song with Gaston's letter of intent ("Mes intentions, ma belle"), joined her "captor" in a duo de l'enlèvement ("Un enlèvement c'est étonnant") and in what became a celebrated duo, the third act "Y'avait un arrêt à Dijon" with Antonio, with whom she had previously shared a duo espagnole in the second act. The soubrets of the evening had the best of the rest: Poulet (Barral) declaring his affiliations in a Chanson Naturaliste ("Le Verbe haut"), and then renouncing naturalism for symbolism before the end of the evening ("Je n'suis plus naturaliste"), whilst the Toledad's fellow actress, Mélie Cruchet (Mlle Burty), had her Couplets de la divette ("Je chant' d'un air embêté") and Germaine Gallois, in the role of the sculptural Baronne Trippmann had her moment with the couplets "Faut être gentil."

The show comfortably passed the one hundred–performance mark in a successful first Paris run of more than three solid months, and it was revived at the Théâtre des Menus-Plaisirs in 1896 before becoming an interminable touring vehicle for the prima donna Jenny Syril in the 1920s.

La Toledad also traveled widely, although without making any indelible marks. A German-language version (ad Victor Léon, Heinrich von Waldberg) was played in Vienna with Frln Virag as the Toledad, Viktoria Pohl-Meiser as Maracona and Karl Pfann as Tardivet, and later in Hamburg and Berlin, with Franz Tewele, Schultz, Frln Delma and Frau Ferenczy as a slightly overaged Toledad heading José Ferenczy's Hamburg troupe, and in Prague. An Hungarian version (ad Béla J Fái, Emil Makai) mounted at the Népszínház with Klára Küry in the title role played 17 times, an Italian version was played in Venice (11 May 1903), while an English version (ad Augustus Moore), produced in Britain at Windsor with Georgina Delmar and Roland Cunningham starring and the aged queen of the opéra-bouffe era, Emily Soldene, in the splendid role of La Maracona, was given a brief tour. A potted version of the show was subsequently brought in to London's Palace Music Hall, only to be closed down by the law for playing a non-theatre venue.

Austria: Theater in der Josefstadt *Toledad* 10 October 1896; Germany: Carl-Schultze Theater, Hamburg 3 April 1897, Lessing-Theater, Berlin 17 April 1897; Hungary: Népszínház *Toledad* 24 May 1899; UK: Theatre Royal, Windsor 2 April 1903

ENLEVEZ-MOI!.. Opérette in 3 acts by Raoul Praxy and Henri Hallais. Lyrics by Pierre Varenne and Max Eddy. Music by Gaston Gabaroche. Comédie Caumartin, Paris, 4 October 1930.

Enlevez-moi!.. was produced first at the Comédie Caumartin, under the management of Robert Gallois, with Eliane de Creus starring as Simone, the wife of the prefect of Issoudun, who diverts innocent young René Dargelle (Gabaroche) from his mineralogic studies for the space of three acts. Jean Devalde played best friend Edgard Renaud, whose second thoughts over seducing the hitherto virtuous Simone in the privacy of his Parisian garçonniere are the cause of the helpful René, deputized to cancel their culpable rendezvous, getting into his "troubles." Mary Richard was Edgard's interfering old nurse, Joséphine, Suzanne Préville was everything that the name of Lulu suggested, and Réda Caire was the exotic Prince Agka. The cast of 12 also included a dog.

Gabaroche's feather-light musical ("Ce n'est qu'un petit moment," "J'hésite," "Chagrin d'amour," Rondeau de Province, "Je n'os'rais plus fair' ça!") was transferred to the Théâtre des Nouveautés where, with Jacqueline Francell, Christiane Dor, André Dupuis and the show's original director, Paul Villé, in its lead roles and Réda Caire repeating as the Prince Agka, it completed a run of almost a year. It was later revived at the Folies-Wagram (13 January 1935) and again at the Théâtre Daunou (1947) as well as having a busy provincial life, proving itself in the process the most successful of Gabaroche's musical comedies.

A 1932 film version featured Mlle Francell alongside Roger Tréville, Arletty and Félix Oudart.

Film: 1932

ENRICO '61 Commedia musicale in 2 acts by Pietro Garinei and Sandro Giovannini. Music by Renato Rascel. Teatro Sistina, Rome, 23 February 1961.

A "spettacolo patriottico" produced on the occasion of the centenary of the unification of Italy, giving star/composer/co-producer Rascel the opportunity to skip through the history of the past century with the help of a selection of hats, co-stars Clelia Matania and Gianrico Tedeschi, and what were apparently the first theatrical travelators seen in Italy. Following a Milan premiere, the show had a fine Rome run and two seasons of touring. The orchestrations of *Enrico '61* were by Ennio Morricone, soon to be known as Italy's most popular film composer.

Taken to Britain, where Garinei and Giovannini had earlier had a success with *When in Rome* (*Buona notte, Bettina*), and played there in an English version by Myers and Cass, it lasted but 86 West End performances.

UK: Piccadilly Theatre 3 July 1963; Germany: Staatsoperette, Dresden 20 October 1966

Recording: complete (RCA)

EPHRAIM, Lee (b Hopkinsville, Ky, 7 July 1877; d London, 26 September 1953). West End producer of many imported shows, and a series of successful new wartime musicals.

American Ephraim moved to Britain in 1909 and worked for a time as a theatrical agent, and then, between 1918 and 1926, in the office of producer Daniel Meyer (*The Street Singer, Rose Marie, Betty in Mayfair,* etc). In 1926 he set up as a producing management on his own behalf and had his first success with the London version of *Sunny* mounted at the London Hippodrome the same year. In the late 1920s he also produced or co-produced the British productions of Broadway's *The Desert Song* (w Alfred Butt) and *Funny Face* as well as the less successful *Peggy-Ann* and *The Five o'Clock Girl* (w R H Gillespie), and initiated in London several new musicals with an American bent (*Blue Eyes* with a score by Kern, *Lady Mary* with music by Hungarian Albert Szirmai and Phil Charig).

In the 1930s he produced a version of the French musical *Toi c'est moi* as *The Gay Deceivers* with Charlotte Greenwood starred, the Robert Stolz *Venus in Seide* which did not reach town, and other losers in *Rio Rita, Nina Rosa,* Rogers and Hart's *Heads Up* and *On Your Toes,* and the custom-made *Here's How* with George Robey, but he had markedly more success with the comical *Hide and Seek* (w Moss's Empires), which presented Cicely Courtneidge and Bobby Howes together for the first and only time. He subsequently co-produced Miss Courtneidge's long-running vehicles *Under Your Hat, Full Swing* (w Tom Arnold), *Something in the Air* (w Arnold) and *Under the Counter* (w Emile Littler, Arnold).

He later produced several more original pieces including the Ann Ziegler-Webster Booth piece *Sweet Yesterday* (1945), the flop *The Nightingale* (1947) and the successful romantic musical *Carissima* (1949), alongside a continued touring schedule amongst which was included a stage version of the film musical *Waltz Time.*

ÉPOUSE-LA! Opérette in 3 acts by Pierre Veber. Music by Henri Hirschmann. Théâtre Fémina, Paris, 15 February 1923.

The high-living André Montrachet (Aimé Simon-Girard) and his cousin Nicolette (Germaine Webb) marry each other in order to please their rich aunt, Mme de Monbissac (Lyse Berty), but things go poorly and their respective replacement partners—Roger la Chambotte (M George) and the much-divorced Marcelline (Hélène Beryll)—persuade them to divorce. However, the young lady of purchasable favors, Mlle Florise de Mézidon (Mlle Davia, equipped with a saucy argot-laden number, "J'ai les pieds en Valenciennes"), who is hired to go through the motions as a professional co-respondent, does her job so curiously that the spouses end up happily reunited.

Veber's lively text and lyrics—which included a particularly jolly number for André, relating how his friend Philibert was encouraged to "Va vit' rue Thérèse," where you can have "tout ça pour cinq cents francs," in order to get himself caught in flagrante delicto and divorced—paired happily with Hirschmann's dance-rhythmic music. The 10-handed piece won a good run in André Gailhard's Paris production, a run which was followed by a tour in which Mlle Davia repeated the personal success she had won, in a role which appeared only in the very last part of the play, alongside Lina Berny and Bartholomez.

ERDÉLYI, Mihály (b Szeged, 28 May 1895; d Budapest, 27 January 1979).

Actor, director, librettist and composer for the musical stage, the musically self-taught Erdélyi began his theatrical career, as a performer and writer, after wartime service in the navy. His earliest ventures in the musical theatre were as a librettist, and he supplied the texts for four original musical plays for Budapest's Budai Színkör before, from 1933, writing both text and music for his later pieces. From 1934 he became administrator of the Erzsebétvárosi Színház, the Józsefvárosi Színház and the Kisfaludy Színház—a group known as "a kültelki színházi" or suburban theatres—and, at the first-named, mounted a series of summertime productions of his own musicals, a number of them with top musical-comedy star Hanna Honthy featured, and often with some considerable successes.

1922 **Hazudik a muzsikaszó** (Ferenc Neumann) Budai Színkör 9 June

1923 **Mintha álom volna** (Izsó Barna/Ernő Kulinyi) Budai Színkör 1 September

1929 **Mit susog a fehér akác?** (Mihály Szántó) Budai Színkör 18 May

1930 **Lehullott a rezgőnyárfa** (Szántó) Budai Színkör 17 May

1931 **Tahi Tóth Veronika** Bethlen-téri Színház 25 September

1932 **Csókos Regiment** Bethlen-téri Színház 24 September

1933 **Fehérvári huszárok** Budai Színkör 15 August

1934 **Szabad a csók** Városi Színház 17 February

1934 **A Dorozsmai szélmalom** Budai Színkör 5 September

1939 **Zimberi Zombori szép asszony** Erzsebétvárosi Színház 22 June

1940 **Sárgarigófészek** Erzsebétvárosi Színház 20 June

1941 **Becskereki menyecske** Erzsebétvárosi Színház 21 June

1943 **A két Kapitány** Erzsebétvárosi Színház 12 June

1944 **Cserebogár, sárga cserebogár** Erzsebétvárosi Színház 23 June

ERKEL, Elek (b Pest, 2 November 1843; d Pest, 10 June 1893).

The son of Ferenc Erkel (1810–1893), the composer of the celebrated Hungarian operas *Bánk Bán, Hunyadi László* and *István Király,* Elek Erkel was principal conductor at the Népszínház from 1875, and, from 1884, at the Budapest Operaház. During his time at the Népszínház he composed the scores for two successful operetts and supplied incidental music for many plays and spectaculars including Csepregi's enormously successful *A sárga csikó* (1877) and *A piros bugyellaris* and Sándor Lukácsy's *A vereshajú* (1877). He later provided the score for a musical version of Szigligeti's *Az udvari bolond,* produced under the title *A kassai diák* with Lujza Blaha starred.

1880 **Székely Katalin** (Sándor Lukácsy) Népszínház 16 January

1883 **Tempefői** (Jenő Rákosi) Népszínház 16 November

1890 **A kassai diák** (Ede Szigligeti ad Pál Vidor) Népszínház 15 November

ERLANGER, A[braham] L[incoln] (b Buffalo, NY, 4 May 1860; d New York, 7 March 1930). Long-powerful and successful American theatre-owner and producer.

After early employment as an usher at the Academy of Music in Cleveland and later as a theatre box-office manager in the same city, Abe Erlanger went into management as a producer of touring melodrama. During this period he had his own bit of melodrama when he shot the husband of his leading lady and paramour, Louise Balfe, in a confrontation in Philadelphia.

In 1888 he joined forces with lawyer Marc Klaw and, together, the pair became influential theatrical agents under the banner of the Klaw and Erlanger Exchange (1890, "they have over two hundred of the best one-night stands in the country on their books"). They also continued their producing activities and, in 1895, they joined with some of the principal theatrical producers of the time to form the Theatrical Syndicate, an organization which aimed to put the haphazard booking practices of the country's very large and necessarily far-flung theatrical circuits into some kind of profitable (to them) order. With Erlanger effectively at its head, the Syndicate, or Trust, as it became known, quickly succeeded in its aims, taking over theatres throughout the country with a speed and efficacity which soon led to those who were less speedy and efficient, less large, or did not wish to do business with such an organization crying out loudly about restrictive practices. Like other men in successful and powerful positions, Erlanger got bad press and became disliked by those less successful than he, the legend of his toughness being given no relief by his suaver partner, Klaw, who like to let it be believed that he was the good-hearted gentleman of the pair whilst his physically unattractive and less well-spoken partner was the forceful bully.

As producers, Klaw and Erlanger mounted a long list of musicals over a period of 23 years and, after the dissolution of their partnership, Erlanger continued alone, remaining on the Broadway musical theatre scene for a further eight years. Their early shows included such original comic operas as Sousa's *The Bride Elect* and De Koven's *Foxy Quiller,* but they concentrated largely on the lower-brow side of the musical stage, sponsoring the Rogers Brothers series of musicals, as a challenge to non-Syndicate members Weber and Fields, pieces like *In Newport,* with former Weber and Fields's stars featured, the vaudevillesque *The Ham Tree* with McIntyre and Heath, an attempt at reviving Emmet's long-popular Fritz shows with *Fritz in Tammany Hall* for Joseph Cawthorn, the fairy-tale pieces *Sleeping Beauty, Mr Bluebeard, Mother Goose, The Pearl and the Pumpkin* and Americanized versions of Drury Lane's pantomimes *Humpty Dumpty* and *The White Cat.*

In 1906 they had a considerable success with George M Cohan's *Forty-Five Minutes from Broadway,* a second with Richard Carle's version of the London musical *The Spring Chicken* and a flop with Sousa's *The Free Lance.* In 1908 they mounted Victor Herbert's spectacular cartoon musical *Little Nemo,* and in 1911 they had their biggest success of all when they teamed up with composer Ivan Caryll, who gave them successively *The Pink Lady, Oh! Oh! Delphine, The Little Café, Papa's Darling* and *The Girl Behind the Gun.*

They ventured into the continental Operette on the tidal wave of hopeful grabbing which followed the success of *The Merry Widow,* and thus brought botched versions of Lehár's *The Count of Luxembourg* and *Eva* and Kálmán's *Zsuzsi kisasszony* (*Miss Springtime*) and *Die Csárdásfürstin* (*The Riviera Girl*) to Broadway. Amongst their last productions together were Louis Hirsch's delightful *The Rainbow Girl* and Victor Herbert's disappointing *The Velvet Lady.*

On his own, Erlanger mounted Vincent Youmans's *Two Little Girls in Blue,* the Ed Wynn show *The Perfect*

Fool and a made-over version of Kálmán's *Die Bajadere* played in America as *The Yankee Princess.* He also imported the London revue *By the Way,* and had a fine success with Eddie Dowling's blithe little tale of *Honeymoon Lane* (1926). His last production of a book musical, *Happy Go Lucky* (1926), was, however, a flop.

As well as his stream of musical shows, Erlanger also produced a number of plays, and he took a financial interest—often larger, sometimes smaller—in a good number of productions which did not bear his name as official producer or co-producer. The original *Ziegfeld Follies* was produced largely on Erlanger capital, and a number of celebrated Broadway producers of his era—from Nixon and Zimmerman to Ziegfeld and Dillingham—owed a good deal of their ability to continue to produce their shows through good times and, more often, bad ones, to the bad-mouthed baron of Broadway. With their acceptance of his investment, of course, came an obligation for these producers to account to Erlanger, who thus knew precisely what was going on in the accounts departments and the box offices of most of the town's most important musical theatres. Although the Syndicate outlived its use, and was eventually split up and replaced by other equally and, eventually, more powerful controlling interests, Erlanger remained active and important in the Broadway theatre almost up to his death.

ERMINIE Comic opera in 3 acts by Harry Paulton "and Claxson Bellamy" based on *L'Auberge des Adrets* by Benjamin Antier, Saint-Amand and Paulyanthe. Music by Edward Jakobowski. Comedy Theatre, London, 9 November 1885.

The melodrama *L'Auberge des Adrets,* produced at Paris's Ambigu-Comique in 1823, featured Frédéric Lemaître in the role of its thieving hero, Robert Macaire. However, to the authors' fury, Lemaître and his partner Firmin played their parts as the caddish exploiter and his scruffy sidekick, Bertrand, not for drama but for comedy, and the result (later fictionally depicted on film in the celebrated *Les Enfants du Paradis*) was a major success which resulted in a sequel, *Robert Macaire,* being produced by Lemaître and co-author Antier (obviously reconciled once the money came pouring in) in 1834. The character of the popular comic thief, subsequently immortalized in the cartoons of Daumier, was thus developed from what was intended to be that of a melodrama villain.

A pantomime, *Robert and Bertrand, or The Two Fugitives,* was produced at Drury Lane in 1945 and by P T Barnum's company at New York's Winter Garden Theater in 1865, and a burnt-cork version was given at the Fifth Avenue Opera Theater in 1866 by the Griffith and Christy Minstrels. A British ballet version *Robert Macaire or the Exploits of a Gentleman at Large* was produced at the Adelphi as early as 1835, a further pantomime was played in America by James Maffit and Bartholomew in the 1850s, a burlesque, written by H J Byron and subtitled *The Roadside Inn Turned Innside Out,* was staged at London's Royal Globe Theatre in 1870 (16 April), and another as *Les Deux Voleurs, or a pretty pair of purloiners* at Blackpool's Grand Theatre in July 1884. In 1885, however, author-actor Harry Paulton and, apparently, his young son, Edward (uncredited), put together a full-scale comic opera version of the piece, under the title *Erminie,* as a vehicle for the elder Paulton in the principal comic role of Jacques Strop.

The dashing Macaire (Frank Wyatt) and his foolish sidekick, Strop (Paulton), have escaped from prison and robbed a traveler of his clothes and papers. The unfortunate traveler is the Vicomte de Brissac (Horace Bolini), son of an old friend of the Marquis de Pontvert (Fred Mervin), and he is on his way to that nobleman's home to be given in marriage to his daughter, Erminie de Pontvert (Florence St John). Macaire and Strop—here called Ravannes and Cadeau—opportunistically take on the identities of Brissac and his imaginary noble friend, "the Baron," and head for the Château Pontvert, plotting to steal the jewels of the fine company gathered together to celebrate the betrothal. The evening's ball produces much comedy, as Strop bewitches the elderly Princesse de Gramponeur (Mary Ann Victor) with his comicalities and argot, a touch of melodrama as the real Vicomte, arriving late on the scene and promptly imprisoned as an impostor, attempts to prove his identity, and romance as Erminie plots to elope with her father's secretary, Eugène Marcel (Henry Bracy) before the betrothal can take place. Robbery, impersonations and elopement are all exposed when a strategically placed suit of armor is shifted, and the dodderingly wandering Chevalier de Brabazon (Percy Compton) shocks the old Princesse to screams by accidentally invading her bedroom in the dark of night, causing the whole house to turn out at the vital moment. A happy ending is tied up when the real Vicomte turns out to be the childhood sweetheart of Eugène's sister, Cérise (Violet Melnotte).

Edward Jakobowski's score was an attractive light comic opera one, featuring, notably, two romantic numbers for Erminie—the Dream Song ("At Midnight on my Pillow Lying") and the Lullaby ("Dear Mother, in Dreams I see Her")—and one fine, despairing one for Eugène ("Darkest the Hour"), a military moment for the Marquis ("A Soldier's Life"), and comical pieces for the thieves ("Downy Jailbirds of a Feather" together, and Cadeau's topical "What the Dicky Birds Say") alongside some well-made ensemble music.

Erminie was produced by the young Violet Melnotte and brought from its provincial tryout (an unusual thing

Plate 116. **Erminie.** *Sketched on the cover of the show's sheet music. Francis Wilson (left) and W S Daboll made the roles and the show even more famous in America.*

in those days) to her base at London's Comedy Theatre. There it proved a distinct success through a run of 154 performances before being taken on the road for an enormous first tour of no less than 65 weeks in the British provinces. A second company followed, after a brief return season in the West End, and thereafter *Erminie* remained on the British touring schedules almost nonstop for five years. However, if the show was a tidy and enduring success in Britain, in America it proved a sensation. Rudolf Aronson purchased the piece from agent Frank Sanger (who had bought it for Nat Goodwin but—in spite of a bigger offer from E E Rice—sold it to the ''uptown'' house when the comedian left his management) and mounted it at the Casino Theater, with Paulton directing Pauline Hall as Erminie, William S Daboll and Francis Wilson as the pair of thieves, and Jennie Weathersby in the plum role of the old Princesse. If critical reaction was pleased but unextravagant (''it possesses the advantage of having a comprehensible story and a certain amount of character[;] . . . the dialogue is flowing and not larded with crack-jaw puns . . . but it lacks wit and repartee. The music is tuneful but reminiscent [and] there are no salient points. Compared with Offenbach, Lecocq, Solomon, Sullivan or even Genée or Strauss, Jakobowski must be considered a journeyman not a master'') the public reaction was startling. The beautiful Miss Hall made a major hit and her Lullaby, which had been politely noticed in Britain, became a major song hit in America (so there was a ''salient point'' after all!); Wilson was boosted to stardom in the made-for-the-author comic role which—after being carefully coached to success by Paulton—he later embellished with some even lower comedy than originally catered for; and even the scenery proved a hit, the second-act ballroom scene, painted by Henry Hoyt in different shades of pink, being considered the last thing in sophistication.

Aronson ran the show for 150 nights before, still unaware of what had hit him, he took it off to Boston and took in Lord Lonsdale's company with Offenbach's *La Créole* (*The Commodore*) and *Kenilworth.* When that season was blasted out of town by scandalmongering and other non-theatrical problems, he quickly brought his hit show back to the Casino where it promptly settled in to run for 10 further months (362 performances). He attempted to leaven what—given his past experience at the Casino—seemed like an unimaginable run with versions of two fine Parisian hits, *Jeanne, Jeannette et Jeanneton* (*The Marquis*) and *La Petite Mademoiselle,* but after these were done he each time brought the inexhaustible *Erminie* back again to hold the Casino boards for four months more, closing it almost exactly two years after its first performance. At the end of this chopped-about run Aronson announced a total run of 1,256 performances (774 at the Casino and 482 out-of-town in the breaks) which seems a little hard to justify. Still, even with a more conservative calculation of 648 Broadway performances during its curious, carved-up career, *Erminie* became the greatest theatrical phenomenon of its time.

Like the music of all foreign musicals, the published score of *Erminie* was considered non-copyright in America, and since the old *Auberge des Adrets* tale was equally "free," pirate versions of the show sprung up quickly outside New York. Aronson tried to challenge a phony *Erminie* in which Jakobowski's music had been pinned to a Strop-and-Macaire book by Fred Dixon for production at the Chicago Casino, but the court ruled that he could stop the pirates only from using his title. So the rest of America got *Macaire, Robert Macaire, or The Two Thieves, The Baron, The Two Vagabonds* and various other fake and semi-fake copycat pieces until the real *Erminie* came along. After that, as in every like case before and since, the fakes quickly showed up as no hopers. The burlesquers, too, got into the action and Lew Dockstader came out with an *Our Minnie* which didn't shirk at helping itself to the "free" music either.

As in Britain, *Erminie* went profitably and long on the road in America, and it returned to Broadway twice in 1889, in 1893, 1897, 1898 (for a limited season which refused to be limited), 1899, 1903 (in a heavily revamped form which allowed Jessie Bartlett Davis to sing "Promise Me" and Francis Wilson and Madge Lessing to burlesque modern dance duos in a number from *The Monks of Malabar*), 1915 and, finally, in a major revival with Wilson still in his favorite role teamed with De Wolf Hopper, Irene Williams (Erminie) and with Jennie Weathersby, who, like Wilson, had taken part in many of the revivals and tours, still playing the Princesse. This Lawrence J Anhalt production, with a libretto adapted by Marc Connolly, played 104 performances at the Park Theater (3 January 1921).

The English-speaking theatre world followed en masse where Britain and America so enthusiastically led. *Erminie* was played in Canada and in both South Africa and South America by the Edgar Perkins Co (with Alice Aynsley Cook as the Princesse), whilst Australia saw the Savoy Theatre stars Leonora Braham as Erminie and Alice Barnett as the Princesse alongside Howard Vernon (Ravannes), William Elton (Cadeau) and Jack Leumane (Eugène). The piece was also played in Amsterdam in 1889 (6 September), and the following year appeared in a German translation at Vienna's Carltheater (ad Victor Léon, Heinz von Waldberg). Producer Karl Blasel paired with Karl Tuschl as Jack and Bob, as Macaire and Strop had once again become, Frln Jules was Erminie and Wilhelm Knaack took the small role of the innkeeper, in a version which was, for some reason, resituated in England with the Marquis de Pontvert becoming Lord Losberne. The shift did no good, for Vienna's *Erminy* flopped in just a handful of performances. The managers of Paris, never very interested in the product of the British stage, produced their own musical version of "their" Robert Macaire tale by Charles Esquier and W Salabert as *Robert Macaire et Cie* at the Théâtre des Mathurins in March 1901. Two years later, in the wake of the Parisian success of *The Belle of New York,* producer Aronson—now very much out of it all—arranged for Paul Gavault to adapt the book of *Erminie* into French, and announced a production. Like all Aronson's latter-day projects it failed to come to fruition.

The *Auberge des Adrets* characters surfaced several more times in the musical theatre after the triumph of *Erminie.* George Fox's comic opera *Macaire* came out in 1887 (Crystal Palace 20 September) with the composer/author himself starred as Macaire, whilst Ivor Novello composed the score to a piece called *The Golden Moth* (lib: Fred Thompson, P G Wodehouse, Adelphi Theatre 5 October 1921) which had a respectable 281-performance London run with Robert Michaelis and Bill Berry playing what were now called Pierre Caravan and Dipper Tigg. In France, a second local *Robert Macaire* (Marc Berthomieu/Guillot de Saix) was produced 18 November 1933 at the Grand Théâtre du Havre and Belgium weighed in with a *Robert Macaire et Bertrand* (Siroux/R de Man, J Nossent) at Brussels's Théâtre du Bois-Sacré in 1916. None, of course, came within coo-ee of *Erminie's* huge success.

Many years after the event, Harry Paulton related the reasoning behind the strange credits on the most successful comic opera in American stage history. "Bellamy was a young fellow in the mercantile business who wrote songs and was continually bothering me to collaborate with him in an opera. To satisfy him, I gave him an outline and started him at a piece intending to fix it up for production when it was done. At that time I was constantly beset, like all writers for the stage, by musicians anxious to write music to my words. One of them was Jakobowski. To set him at rest I turned him over to the Bellamy opera. I had the music for *Erminie* written by Florian Pascal. When time came for Violet Melnotte to produce a new opera at the Comedy Theatre, several were laid before her, among them both *Erminie* and the Bellamy opera. Her decision was a peculiar one. She wanted the *Erminie* libretto and the Jakobowski music. Jakobowski jumped at the chance and Pascal didn't demur, but Bellamy threatened litigation and various things unless his name were attached to whatever libretto was fitted to Jakobowski's music. Fearing Miss Melnotte might be annoyed into declining both pieces, we agreed although it was an injustice to me and to my son who had a good share in the authorship of *Erminie.* The lyrics had to be rewritten to suit the other music, and *Erminie* happens to be a chance combination of words and music not originally intended.''

Erminie, as it made the stage, then, and as it made its remarkable success, showed nothing more clearly than the acumen of Miss Violet Melnotte. Paulton, alas, showed no such acumen. Shortly before the end of the original American run he sold his 50 percent interest in the piece to Willie Edouin for £1,000. That interest was to be worth many, many times more than that.

USA: Casino Theater 10 May 1886; Australia: Princess Theatre, Melbourne 26 December 1887; Austria: Carltheater 7 November 1890

ERROL, Leon [SIMMS, Leonce Errol] (b Sydney, Australia, 3 July 1881; d Hollywood, Calif, 12 October 1951). Broadway comedy star who also worked as a director and choreographer.

Errol studied in his Australian youth for a medical career, supporting himself through his studies by appearing as a red-nose comic singer to such effect that he abandoned his Hippocratic prospects for theatrical ones. He appeared in Sydney in circus, in the Rignold stock company, in musical theatre and in variety, prior to shifting to America in his late teens. There, he made his way from San Francisco to Chicago, working as a comic, a director, an eccentric dancer, a stock actor, and even penning a couple of musical farces which were staged on the touring circuits. It was whilst he was appearing in one of these, *The Lilies,* that he came to notice of Abe Erlanger. Not long after that, he was working on Broadway in no less a show than the *Ziegfeld Follies of 1911.*

Although he amassed a list of revue credits in both America and Britain over the next decade, Errol made only one book musical appearance in New York, in Ziegfeld's souped-up revival of *A Trip to Chinatown, A Winsome Widow* (1912, Ben Gay), before he made himself into a Broadway musical comedy star in the principal comedy role of the down-and-out Continental ex-monarch ''Connie'' in another Ziegfeld show, *Sally* (1920). His subsequent musical comedy vehicles—*Louie the 14th* (1925, Louie Ketchup), *Yours Truly* (1927, Truly) and *Fioretta* (1929, Julio Pepoli)—were not in the same class, and in later years he worked largely in comedy and musical comedy films, including screen versions of a Bernauer and Österreicher play and German-language film (*Her Majesty Love,* 1931, Baron von Schwarzdorf) with his *Sally* co-star Marilyn[n] Miller and, without Miller, *Higher and Higher* (1943, Drake).

Errol also worked throughout as a director and choreographer, notably on several editions of the *Ziegfeld Follies,* the *Hitchy Koo* revues and, in the area of the book musical, on the 1918 *Look Who's Here, Lassie* (choreographer), Friml's musical comedy *The Blue Kitten* (1922) and the London musical *The Kiss Call* (1919).

ER UND SEINE SCHWESTER Posse mit Gesang in 4 acts by Bernhard Buchbinder. Music by Rudolf Raimann. Theater in der Josefstadt, Vienna, 11 April 1902.

The postman Gustav Flenz (Alexander Girardi) has only one desire in life, that his little sister Lotti (Hansi Niese) shall become a great singing star. Lotti starts off with a job as a supporting player in the local Possen-Theater but then, one day, her big chance comes. House diva Anna Mehler throws a tantrum and refuses to play the lead role in a new work. Lotti is given the part. On opening night, however, the miffed diva bribes the conductor to vanish just before Lotti's big number. There she stands, the orchestra is silent, and the villainess and her baronial admirer laugh triumphantly in their box. But Gustav leaps from his seat in the auditorium, bounds into the pit, tells the audience what has happened and then himself conducts the orchestra and Lotti to triumph. In the final act, he has to resign himself to losing his little sister to the amorous author of the show she has made into a hit.

The show's third act was the production of the ''Volksstück mit Gesang'' *Graf und Näherin,* the show within the show, and it presented the then original feature of using the audience in the theatre as the audience in the story. The program (like others since) also included the ''program within a program.''

The combination of Girardi and Niese, with a lively piece, was irresistible and *Er und seine Schwester* proved a magnificent hit for the Josefstadter Theater, being played 80 times in its initial season, and brought back frequently all around Austria. In 1915 it was given in Vienna again, at the Johann-Strauss Theater, with Fritz Werner and Mimi Marlow featured. A German version (ad Kren and Schönfeld, mus: Julius Einödshofer, Max Schmidt) was produced in Berlin months after the Vienna premiere, with local stars Guido Thielscher and Gerda Walde in the top roles, and an Hungarian version (ad Kornél Sziklai, Jenő Faragó, and entitled, more precisely, ''the postman and his sister'') similarly proved a major success. After its first run at the Magyar Színház, it was brought back to the Városi Színház in 1925 (13 June).

Leon Waschner's Stock company produced the piece in German at Milwaukee's Pabst Theater with considerable success, leading to several restagings, but New York's German theatres do not seem to have picked up on the show.

Hungary: Magyar Színház *A postás fíu és a huga* 6 June 1902; Germany: Thalia Theater August 1902; USA: Pabst Theater, Milwaukee 3 January 1903

ESPINOSA, Edouard [Henry] (b London, 2 February 1872; d Worthing, 22 March 1950). British choreographer who provided the dances for such hits as *Chu Chin Chow* and *The Maid of the Mountains* in a career of more than 20 years in the musical theatre.

The son of the internationally celebrated dancer, ballet-master and choreographer **Léon [Moïse] ESPINOSA** (b Portugal, 6 June 1829; d Wandsworth, London, 1 June 1903), and his ballet-mistress/teacher wife, Matilda Espinosa, Edouard Espinosa originally appeared as a dancer in Paris, London and New York, before, from 1896, beginning a career as a choreographer in the musical theatre with the dances for the musical comedy *Monte Carlo.* He later claimed improbably that this was "the very first production of dance ensembles with set figures and formation effects ever done in musical comedy," but reviewers of the time noted no innovation and merely nodded towards the "pretty and lively dances."

Whilst still, occasionally, appearing on the stage (*Hotel Topsy Turvy, A Good Time,* etc), he choreographed the touring productions of *The New Barmaid, The New Mephisto, Billy, Orlando Dando,* Marie Lloyd's *The ABC* and *The Southern Belle* as well as many pantomimes and plays (a number for Beerbohm Tree), and later claimed to have set, altogether, some 180 (or, variously, 300) shows. Amongst the musical shows which he choreographed or co-choreographed for the British stage were *A Good Time, Great Caesar,* the revue *Pot Pourri, The Land of Nod, Castles in Spain, Amasis* (1906), *Lady Tatters* (1907), *The Mousmé, Bonita* (1911), *The Pearl Girl* (1913), *The Laughing Husband* (1913), *Mam'selle Tralala* (1914), *The Light Blues, My Lady Frayle, Tonight's the Night* (1915), *Chu Chin Chow, Young England, The Maid of the Mountains, Oh, Caesar!* (1916), *A Night Out* (1920), *Cairo* (1921, replacing the dances done for New York by Fokine), *The Rebel Maid, The Little Girl in Red* (1921), *The Last Waltz, The Little Duchess* (1922), *Catherine* (1923), *Our Nell* (1924), *The Good Old Days* (1925), *Riki Tiki* (1926) and *Kong* (1931). He also visited Australia, where he directed and choreographed several productions in 1918 and 1919 (*My Lady Frayle,* etc).

Espinosa was, for a period, ballet master at Covent Garden, wrote a number of books on dance and also founded a school of dance in London which continues its activities today.

Autobiography: *And Then He Danced* (Sampson, Low, Marston, London, 1946)

ESSEX, David [COOK, David Albert] (b London, 23 July 1947). Bright-eyed teeny-pop idol who, in a well-maintained career of some 30 years, appeared in several stage musicals.

After early ventures into pop music and into repertory theatre acting, during which he was seen in several provincial musical productions, Essex came to the musical-theatre fore when he appeared in the London production of the musical *Godspell* (1971). He subsequently consolidated that success on film and as a pop vocalist ("Gonna Make You a Star," "Hold Me Close," etc), returning to the musical stage, in 1978, to create the role of Che in *Evita* ("O What a Circus," etc). In 1985 he wrote, composed and appeared as Fletcher Christian to the Captain Bligh of Frank Finlay in a musical based on *The Mutiny on the Bounty,* the 494-performance run of which was accounted due to the singer's great personal popularity rather than the merits of the show. The song "Fallen Angels," used in the show, reached the upper regions of the pop charts attached to a video portraying highwaymen rather than mutineers.

1985 **Mutiny** Piccadilly Theatre 11 July

Biography: Tremlett, G: *The David Essex Story* (Futura, London, 1974)

ESTRELLA Comic opera in 3 acts by Walter Parke. Music by Luscombe Searelle. Prince's Theatre, Manchester, 15 May 1883; Gaiety Theatre, London, 24 May 1883.

Estrella was the most slimly successful of the not-very-successful works of New Zealand's most internationally played musical theatre composer. Parke's libretto mixed quasi-tragic and comic in a tale of a Venetian lady trying against lecherous odds to remain true to her lost husband. Under the impetus of its energetic composer, the piece was produced at Manchester with an excellent cast, given a hopeful showcasing at a Gaiety matinée, and then opportunistically hurried into the Folies-Dramatiques, at a loss after Strauss's *Prinz Methusalem* had folded suddenly. It ran there for 36 performances.

A New York production got a sour reaction and was burnt out of its theatre after three nights, but when *Estrella* was introduced to Australia, with its Broadway and West End tag attached, it proved, much thanks to an extended comedy turn by Philip Day as a loopy Doge, a definite success. Australia and South Africa (under Searelle's management) both saw *Estrella* again over the years that followed, and it was reproduced in 1884 in a fairly unconfident production by America's Wilbur Opera Company ("Estrella is trashy enough without forgetting lines and slaughtering music"), with much of Searelle's score replaced by selections from *Das Spitzentuch der Königin, The Sorcerer, The Prince Consort* and other shows. Richard Stahl did the botching, A W F McCollin played the Doge, and Cleveland, Ohio seemed to like the result. It was taken on tour in the Wilburs repertoire. A less "improved" version resurfaced at San Francisco's Tivoli Theater (musical director: L Searelle) as late as 1892.

USA: Standard Theatre 11 December 1883; Australia: Theatre Royal, Sydney 27 September 1884

THE ETERNAL WALTZ Satirical operetta in 1 act by Austen Hurgon. Music by Leo Fall. London Hippodrome, 22 December 1911.

This 50-minute, two-scene operetta, in which an actor-manager pursues the overworked composer Feo Lahl for a waltz for his theatre, and eventually finds both it and the lovely Lulu in a cabaret, was put together by director/author Austen Hurgon to make up part of a variety bill at the London Hippodrome. It was built around melodies which Leo Fall, hugely popular in England following the productions of *The Dollar Princess, The Merry Peasant* and *The Girl in the Train,* provided from his trunk to make up a five-number score from which the title waltz, sung by Lulu, became a wide-selling hit and was recorded by original star, Clara Evelyn. A considerable success, the show encouraged the Hippodrome to continue to follow the operetta-in-variety-houses trend, long used in similar Continental houses, with one-act operettas commissioned from Richard Fall and Emmerich Kálmán—and other London theatres followed where it led.

In France *La Valse Éternelle* (ad Paul Ardot) was played as part of the program at the Folies-Bergère, with Jane Marnac performing the waltz, and the show was introduced to America on the opening bill at Broadway's new Palace Theater and later at Chicago's Palace Music Hall (14 October 1914).

France: Folies-Bergère *La Valse Eternelle* 31 August 1912; USA: Palace Theater 24 March 1913

L'ÉTOILE Opéra-bouffe in 3 acts by Eugène Leterrier and Albert Vanloo. Music by Emmanuel Chabrier. Théâtre des Bouffes-Parisiens, Paris, 28 November 1877.

The established stage authors Vanloo and Leterrier, struck by the musical talents of the young Chabrier, confided their libretto for *L'Étoile* to the as yet untried composer. The result was a classy opéra-bouffe score of much charm and more than a little musical complexity, which was accepted for production by Charles Comte at the Bouffes-Parisiens with some slight misgivings and by his orchestra with horror. What the composer saw as the simplest possible style of orchestration was, to players used to chipping out the uncomplicated and mostly unvarying form of musical accompaniment used in most musical shows, strewn with finger-tricking difficulties.

On his 40th birthday, King Ouf of the 36 realms (Daubray) is required to make a political marriage to the Princess Laoula of Mataquin (Berthe Stuart). The Princess is, all unawares, being brought to his headquarters by the extravagantly secretive ambassador Hérisson de Porc-épic (Alfred Jolly), his wife Aloès (Mlle Luch), and extremely private secretary, Tapioca (Jannin). Another part of the birthday celebrations is supposed to be a nice public execution, and Ouf, short of a victim, is relieved when he finally manages to get an insult from the penniless peddler, Lazuli (Paola Marié), which qualifies the boy for a friendly bit of torture and a public impaling. But it is not to be. The royal astrologer, Siroco (Scipion), discovers that Lazuli's fate is linked to that of the King. One day after the boy's death, the King will also die, followed (thanks to a crafty clause in the King's will) at fifteen minutes' distance by Siroco himself. And so, for the next two acts, Ouf goes to extravagant lengths to keep the love-struck Lazuli—ready to defy all dangers for the sake of the Princess—happy and safe from danger. When it seems the boy has drowned, the King and his astrologer prepare for the worst, but he turns up alive and then threatens to kill himself if Laoula cannot be his. Ouf exhaustedly gives up the girl rather than the ghost.

The score mixed solos and some particularly lovely ensembles happily, with Lazuli's romance ''O petite étoile'' (a version of which had been one of the pieces which had originally attracted the librettists to their composer) being one of the most appealing moments, alongside a pretty Kissing Quartet (''Quand on veut ranimer sa belle''), the sparkling trio in which Aloès and Laoula tickle the sleeping Lazuli with straws (''Il faut le chatouiller'') and the comical duo between the King and the astrologer, getting drunk on ''Chartreuse verte'' at the thought of imminent death.

Comte's production of *L'Étoile* did not win a wholehearted reception. It was played 48 times and then put aside. However, Berlin's Friedrich-Wilhelmstädtisches Theater picked the show up, and an Hungarian version (ad Jenő Rákosi) was played four times at Budapest's Népszínház. In spite of this unpromising start, *L'Étoile* did not, however, stop there. At least the libretto did not, for, over the years that followed, the show suffered more at the hands of rewriters and improvers than practically any other work of class. But it was the book they liked, and the music they attacked or, more often, simply threw out.

American J Cheever Goodwin, a repeated ''borrower'' of Continental libretti, turned out a version of *L'Étoile* called *The Merry Monarch* with more music by Woolson Morse than by ''composer Emile Chabie [*sic*] who has suggested himself the alterations to the score.'' It was produced at New York's Broadway Theater (18 August 1890) with a cast headed by Marie Jansen as Lazuli and Francis Wilson as the King Anso IV (and-so-forth, get it?) performing such ditties as ''The Omniscient

Ostrich,'' ''Love Will Find the Way,'' the topical ''I Draw the Line at That'' and ''When I Was a Child of Three'' to orchestrations by J P Sousa. It played a set New York run to 4 October, served Wilson as a road vehicle for the season—more and more of Chabrier's music being replaced by interpolated ditties gathered from hither and yon on the way—and was subsequently produced in goodness knows what precise state by J C Williamson's comic opera company in Australia (Princess Theatre, Melbourne 26 December 1891), where Charles Ryley (a male Lazuli), William Elton (Anso IV) and Florence Young (Lillita) topped the bill. In Hungary a similar process later took place, and the Budapest Népszínház hosted an *Uff Király* (21 May 1887) in which Vanloo and Leterrier's libretto was reset musically by Béla Hegyi and Szidor Bátor. Ilka Pálmay headed the cast of a production which succeeded very much better than the original piece had done when produced at the same theatre, a decade earlier.

In England, Alexander Henderson hosted Reece and Farnie's *Stars and Garters* at London's Folly Theatre with Lydia Thompson as Lazuli, Lionel Brough as King Jingo XIX, Harry Paulton as Zadkiel (Siroco) and Annie Poole as Laoula and ''new music selected from the most popular sources'' of which Chabrier was apparently not one, whilst 20 years later *The Lucky Star* with ''new English dialogue by C H E Brookfield, lyrics by Adrian Ross and Aubrey Hopwood, the whole revised and assembled by Helen Lenoir (Mrs D'Oyly Carte) with new music by Ivan Caryll'' was played for 143 performances at the Savoy Theatre (7 January 1899). This piece, in its turn, was translated into Hungarian (ad Emil Makai, Adolf Mérei) and Budapest,which had already had the real *A csillag,* plus the remusicked *Uff Király,* now had its third *Étoile* variant with *A szerencse csillag* (Magyar Színház 1 October 1901).

The original *L'Étoile* reappeared only rarely thereafter—a 1909 production at Berlin's Komische Oper with Mary Hagen, Kreuder and Susanne Bachrich was a noteworthy revival—but in 1941 it was taken into the repertoire of the Paris Opéra-Comique (10 April) in a production which featured Fanély Revoil (Lazuli) and René Hérent (Ouf) in the lead roles, and which was brought back in 1946. In 1984 a slightly altered version was mounted at Lyon with Colette Alliot-Lugaz and Georges Gauthier featured, and this production was subsequently played at the Opéra-Comique with Mlle Alliot-Lugaz paired with Michel Sénéchal. This exposure, and the major recording which followed it, gave *L'Étoile* a life to more than the small band of connoisseurs who had previously prized it as a forgotten gem, and in 1991 Britain finally got the ''real'' *L'Étoile* (ad Jeremy Sams) when the piece was produced by Opera North with a cast headed by Pamela Helen Stephen (Lazuli), Anthony Mee (Ouf), Kate Flowers (Aloès) and Mary Hegarty (Laoula).

Plate 117. **Eva.** *Pipsi Paquerette (Luise Kartousch) gets her meal ticket for the holidays in the person of Dagobert Millefleurs (Ernst Tautenhayn).*

With the opérette and opéra-bouffe repertoire having now become largely the province of subsidized opera houses rather than the commercial stage, *L'Étoile* and its musicianly score (with the recognizably musicianly name of Chabrier attached to it) have probably attracted more attention in their second century than they ever did in their first.

Germany: Friedrich-Wilhelmstädtisches Theater, Berlin *Sein Stern* 4 October 1878, Komische Oper *Lazuli* 4 February 1909; Hungary: Népszínház *A csillag* 29 November 1878; UK: Grand Theatre, Leeds 17 September 1991

Recordings: complete Lyon cast recording 1984 (EMI), complete (MRF)

Video: TV (Polygram) Opéra de Lyon 1986

EVA (Das Fabriksmädel) Operette in 3 acts by A M Willner and Robert Bodanzky. Music by Franz Lehár. Theater an der Wien, Vienna, 24 November 1911.

Without ever being one of Lehár's most popular or enduring works, *Eva* nevertheless had a more than satisfactory career. It had a fine initial run of 226 performances at the Theater an der Wien—broken only by the summer recess and by a two-week guest season played at the Raimundtheater (26 March 1912) with Ida Russka and Ludwig Herold starred—and won itself several productions further afield in the years after its first showing.

Eva (Mizzi Günther) is a little foundling factory girl, brought up by the foreman, Larousse (Fritz Albin) and the folk who are now her fellow workers, but carrying within her a far-off memory of a lovely, bejeweled and richly gowned mother. When the new owner of the factory, man-about-Paris Octave Flaubert (Louis Treumann), takes a fancy to her, and lures her into the company of his fast-living friends from the big city, the factory folk come to the rescue. But Eva has taken a taste for the high life, and she runs off to Paris where her fresh beauty soon attracts the attention of the rich, lecherous and powerful. Octave arrives with a proposal of marriage, in time to rescue her from the demi-mondaine fate which she now realizes was her ''rich'' mother's. Luise Kartousch played Pipsi Paquerette, a vendeuse from the men's underwear department of Printemps, who wins herself a holiday meal-ticket each year by publicly flinging herself into the protection of a gentleman and begging him to save her from a brutal husband, and Kartousch's partner of always, Ernst Tautenhayn, was Dagobert Millefleurs, a friend of Octave, who is Pipsi's target for the year.

Amongst the romantic pieces of the music, Eva's tale of ''Das Fabrikskind'' (''Im heimlichen Dämmer der silbernen Ampel'') with her reminiscence of the past (''So war meine Mutter, so möchte ich sein''), and the waltzing duo with Octave, ''War' es auch nichts als ein Traum vom Glück,'' were the most substantial, but the lighter moments of the score prevailed most strongly. Dagobert's besotted plea to ''Pipsi, holde Pipsi'' was the show's stand-out number, alongside the march duo (Pipsi/Octave) in praise of ''Die Geister von Montmartre,'' Octave's march tune in a similar vein (''O du Pariser Pflaster''), Pipsi's comical encouragements to her man to face up to his purse-closing papa (''Ziehe hin zu deinem Vater'') and her jolly praises of the demimonde (''Wenn die Pariserin spazieren geht'').

Eva was played in Budapest (ad Andor Gábor) with Sári Fedák starred in the title role, whilst Klaw and Erlanger's Broadway production (ad Glen MacDonough) featured Sallie Fisher alongside Walter Percival (Octave), Alma Francis (Pipsi) and Walter Lawrence (Dagobert) through an unloved 24 performances which nevertheless established ''the waltz from *Eva* ''(''War' es auch nichts'') as a popular favorite. Maurice Ordonneau and Jean Bénédict's French version was played in Belgium (Théâtre de l'Alhambra 4 December 1912) with Germaine Huber and Charles Casella starring, but when the show was mounted by Mme Rasimi in Paris, more than a decade later, with Maguy Warna (Eva), Fernand Francell (Henri Nogent, ex- Octave) and Robert Hasti (Balzar, ex- Dagobert) featured, a different version, adapted by Lucien Meyrargue, was played. None did well enough to encourage a repeat.

The piece was put on film silently in 1918, and at more length and with sound in 1936. Adele Sandrock was Eva on this occasion and Hans Moser featured.

Germany: Neues Operettentheater 23 December 1911; Hungary: Király Színház 12 October 1912; USA: New Amsterdam Theater 30 December 1912; France: Théâtre Ba-ta-clan 13 December 1924

Films: Alfred Deesy 1918 (silent), Johannes Riemann 1936

Recordings: selection (Philips), selection in Spanish (Montilla), selections in Italian (EDM, Fonit Cetra), selection in German (Capriccio), etc

EVANGELINE, or The Belle of Acadia Burlesque [later Extravaganza] in 3 acts by J Cheever Goodwin. Music by Edward E Rice [''assisted by John J Braham'']. Niblo's Garden, New York, 27 July 1874.

A burlesque of Longfellow's poem of the same name, the extravaganza *Evangeline* followed the trials and tribulations of its heroine (Ione Burke) and her beloved Gabriel (Connie Thompson) following their eviction from their sweetly peaceful native village by the beastly British. The burlesque version allowed the heroine to travel to and through some of the more exotic parts of the world, including darkest Africa and the wildish West, which had not been on the itinerary of her prototype, but which were helpfully and theatrically colorful. On the way she met some creatures whom Longfellow had not quite imagined either—a dancing heifer (a blatant pinch from Lydia Thompson's dancing donkey in *Forty Thieves*), an amorous whale and, above all, the silent but eloquent and ubiquitous Lone Fisherman—whose performances became favorite highlights of the piece. In keeping with the piece's burlesque nature, the chief low-comedy role of Catherine was played in travesty by Louis Mestayer. A future star in W H Crane was the original Leblanc, W B Cahill of Lydia Thompson blondes fame was amongst the supporting cast, and the Lone Fisherman was created by pantomimist J W Thoman.

Rice's bulging score included numbers of every shape and size. Ballads and sentimental songs were prominent (''Thinking, Love, of Thee,'' the jaunty ''Sweet Evangeline,'' the waltz ''He says I Must Go,'' ''Sweet the Song of the Birds,'' ''Come Back to the Heart that Is Thine,'' ''Where art thou now my beloved?,'' The Kissing Song, ''Go Not Happy Day,'' the heroine's ''Wouldst Know the Way?,'' etc) alongside the comical ''I Lofe you,'' the martial ''A Hundred Years Ago,'' the tale of ''Sammy Smug,'' a bathing trio, a soldiers' chorus, a dance for the heifer and even a chorus which nodded its recognition to ''Longfellow.''

The piece was apparently given some kind of a trial run in Rice's hometown of Cambridge, Mass, in 1873, and the young songwriter previewed some of his songs in concert and amongst his clubland cronies in Boston, but *Evangeline* got its official premiere in New York as played by the Niblo's stock company, in a semi-vanity production in which the company were paid by the authors. Dully directed, it was dismissed after 16 performances ''to fair audiences'' in favor of a spectacular drama. However, Rice persisted, and the following season he dipped into his pocket again and organized a revised, revamped and richly decorated version of his show at Boston's Globe Theatre (5 July 1875), directed by Lydia Thompson's former chief comic Harry Beckett, with the young English contralto Laura Joyce (Evangeline), Ella Morant (Gabriel) and the well-known pantomimist James Maffit in a built up (by him) but still wholly mimed role as the Fisherman. It played four weeks and closed. The following summer, however, R M Field took the production up and played it—''considerably cut and pruned, with a number of changes which are decided improvements,'' with ''several new bits of music,'' with Lillian Conway (Evangeline) and ex-Lydia Thompson blonde, Eliza Weathersby (Gabriel) featured, and with ''three acts, twelve sets, quite a number of tableaux, several original sensations, situations and effects''—as a summer show at the Boston Museum (15 July 1876). The show was kept ''fresh'' with new songs, actors and variety-runs being popped weekly into its loose fabric, and this time it ran for five weeks after which Rice sent it touring. Annis Montague (later to be an Australian operatic institution) and Kitty Blanchard headed the cast. The road proved friendly to the picturesque remake with its patriotic trimmings (''the first American opéra-bouffe,'' ''the marching of the Centennial Fusileers to the song 'A Hundred Years Ago''')—and in the summer of 1877 the still-touring piece took itself a second turn in the metropolis (Daly's Theater 4 June). It found sufficient friends to stay for a good part of the not-so-fussy summer. The following summer it was again played at the Boston Museum, with Laura Joyce now teamed with Alice Harrison, and bit by persistent bit *Evangeline* made itself into a familiar favorite, with certain artists such as Maffitt and low comedian George K Fortescue (Catherine) making themselves synonomous with their roles as the burlesque toured tirelessly through the seasons and paid several further, brief visits to New York. It was played a fortnight at the Standard Theater (5 January 1880) and again at Niblo's Garden shortly after, and as *The New Evangeline* (ad J J McNally) for two weeks at Haverley's 14th Street Theater (30 August 1880) (''it is called new because some fresh jokes have replaced those that drooped with age and probably a dozen pieces of original music by Mr Rice are added''), at Niblo's again (3 January 1887) and again at the Star Theater (March 1889). It did, however, finally have a genuine Broadway run when, by now a reliable old friend, it was staged at the 14th Street Theater (7 October 1885), with Fay Templeton as Gabriel, for a run of 201 performances.

The show's touring life took it as far afield as Britain, where M B Leavitt's ''Rentz-Santley Company'' production appeared at Liverpool, with Nellie Larkelle starred as Gabriel. It did not appeal. Dubbing the evening a ''wet blanket'' one critic went on: ''Mere feminine beauty and symmetry can never prove a satisfactory substitute for wit and humour, and as a result *Evangeline* must be vetoed as not coming within the pale of legitimate stage literature.'' A few weeks later Leeds opined ''it has neither beginning or ending, as far as we could judge, and the entire performance was utterly beneath criticism.'' *Evangeline* did not progress to London. A number of years later, however, it turned up in Australia, played alongside *The Corsair* in the repertoire of one of Rice's own companies. Buxom local Fannie Liddiard (Gabriel) and American teenager Virginia Earle (Evangeline) were featured, and a boxing match between Jack, the fighting kangaroo, and the Lone Fisherman introduced as local color. It then proceeded on to Tasmania and to South Africa but, although it covered plenty of ground, *Evangeline*'s real and long-lived success was found wholly in America.

In 1896 the piece was produced at Manhattan Beach (June) and subsequently visited Broadway one more time (Garden Theater 1 October), with Theresa Vaughn as Evangeline, Fred Solomon as Le Blanc, Fortescue again as Catherine and Henry E Dixey as the Lone Fisherman, and in 1901 a major revival was mounted back in Boston (Columbia Theater 14 September) by spectacle merchant David Henderson with Rosemary Gloss (Gabriel) and Frances Burkhardt (Evangeline) featured. It too subsequently went on the road.

A staged cantata by the same name, also based on Longfellow's poem, was composed by Virginia Gabriel and played in London in 1870, whilst an unsuccessful musical version of James Laver's novel *Nymph Errant* (George Posford, Harry Jacobson/Eric Maschwitz/Romney Brent), produced with Frances Day in its title role at London's Cambridge Theatre (14 March 1946), also took the same title. In Belgium, *Evangeline* was a ''légende canadienne'' by Louis de Gramont and André Alexandre, with music by Xavier Leroux, produced at the Théâtre de la Monnaie in Brussels, 28 December 1895.

UK: Court Theatre, Liverpool 11 June 1883; Australia: Opera House, Melbourne 27 April 1891

EVERARD, Miss [WOOLLAMS, Harriette Emily] (b Marylebone, London, 12 March 1844; d London, 22 February 1882). Favorite burlesque and comic opera contralto who created Gilbert and Sullivan's Little Buttercup.

Miss Everard (as she was always plainly billed, although she began life as Miss Woollams, before becoming first Mrs Parry and then, at 35, Mrs Beswick) first appeared on stage at the Theatre Royal, Exeter at the age of 16, and at 20 was to be found touring with her husband, comedian William Parry, in the operetta company of Eliot Galer and Fanny Reeves (*Blonde and Brunette, The Haunted Mill,* etc). However, she soon made it to London where, during her late teens and twenties, she played at the Marylebone, Greenwich's New Theatre (1864, Leicester in *Kenilworth,* Sybil in *Jack the Giant Killer, Ixion*), the Princess's, the Olympic (1865, Prince Pecki in *Princess Primrose, Barbe-bleue,* etc), in drama at the Victoria (1867, *Raymond and Agnes, Tricks of the Turf*), in a bit of everything at the Queen's (1868–69, Mrs Pellett in *Dearer Than Life,* Mrs Corney in *Oliver Twist,* Mrs Subtle in *Paul Pry* &c, Mrs Spriggins in *Ici on parle français,* Countess Wintersen in *The Stranger—stranger than ever,* Lady Greymarebetterhausen in *The Gnome King),* at the Royal Alfred (1869, Dame Margery in *Ploughman Turned Lord,* etc), the Royalty and the St James's Theatres (1869–71, Catherine in *Le Mariage aux lanternes,* Krosascanbe in *La Belle Sauvage, To Oblige Benson, Bombastes Furioso*) and at the Theatre Royal, Drury Lane. She appeared in all types of entertainments, playing roles such as Stratonice in Bulwer-Lytton's *The Last Days of Pompeii* on the one hand and the tart governess Krosascanbe to Mrs John Wood's *La Belle Sauvage* or the grotesque Distaffina in *Bobastes Furioso* on the other, and having particular success in burlesque where her rich contralto and buxom form (*The Era* called it "her singular appearance and excellent voice") led to her being given breeches parts and heavy-lady and character roles from a young age.

She had an early connection with opéra-bouffe when she played Queen Greymare (otherwise Clémentine) in the English-language premiere of Offenbach's *Barbe-bleue* at the Olympic in 1866, and with W S Gilbert when she appeared as the Marchioness of Birkenfelt in his early burlesque, *La Vivandière* (1868). She also appeared as Omphale in the Covent Garden spectacular *Babil and Bijou* (1872), at the Princess's Theatre in James Albery's extravaganza *The Will of Wise King Kino* (1873), and at the Philharmonic as the dragonistic Aurore in London's English-language premiere of *Giroflé-Girofla* (1874) and Javotte in *La Fille de Madame Angot* (1875), and played Mrs Rip in the burlesque *Young Rip van Winkle* (1876) alongside Nellie Farren and E W Royce at the Gaiety.

In 1877 she joined D'Oyly Carte's company at the Opera Comique to appear as Mrs Partlett in the original production of *The Sorcerer.* She had her most memorable success when she created the role of Little Buttercup in *HMS Pinafore* the following year, but a bad stage accident during the rehearsals of *The Pirates of Penzance* prevented her from opening as London's Ruth and, although she eventually recovered sufficiently to succeed Emily Cross in the role during the run, she was herself replaced by Alice Barnett, who was then given the equivalent part of Lady Jane in *Patience.* Although she did appear on the stage subsequently, playing Aunt Priscilla in the short-lived *Lola* (1881), she had not, in fact, recovered from her accident and she died shortly after her last show closed.

Miss Everard's Woollams brothers, Walter (d 11 April 1924) and Percy, also had careers on the sometimes musical stage under the name of Everard.

EVETT, Robert [Percy N] (b King's Norton, Worcs, 16 October 1871; d Beachampton, North Bucks, 15 January 1949). Star tenor of the earliest years of the 20th century who later had a successful run as a producer.

A former choirboy, Evett joined one of D'Oyly Carte's touring companies at the age of 19 (Sandford in *The Vicar of Bray,* 1892, Oswald in *Haddon Hall,* 1893, Hilarion, t/o Dramaleigh 1894, Vasquez in *The Chieftain* 1895, Ernest in *Grand Duke* 1896, Max in *His* Majesty 1897, etc), and was subsequently promoted to the Savoy Theatre company where he succeeded Charles Kenningham in the role of Marco in a revival of *The Gondoliers* (1898) and appeared as Alexis in the same year's revival of *The Sorcerer.* He remained at the Savoy, appearing in Gilbert and Sullivan revivals and creating lead tenor roles in *The Rose of Persia* (1899, Yussuf), *The Emerald Isle* (1901, Terence O'Brien), *Merrie England* (1902, Walter Raleigh, "The English Rose"), *Ib and Little Christina* (Ib) and *A Princess of Kensington* (1903, Lt Brook Green) until the end of the Carte family's regime. When William Greet took over the Savoy and its company, he remained with him to appear in the musical comedies *The Earl and the Girl* (1903, Hon Crewe Boodle), *Little Hans Andersen* (1903, Prince with the Magic Pipe) and *The Talk of the Town* (1905, Duke of Topford).

In 1905 he joined George Edwardes to star at Daly's Theatre as Gaston in *Les P'tites Michu,* Dorlis in *Les Merveilleuses* (1906) and Camille in the original London *Merry Widow* (1907), following up as Niki in *A Waltz Dream* (1908), Karel in *The Girl in the Train* (1910, *Die geschiedene Frau*) and Frank Falconer in Kálmán's *Autumn Manoeuvres* (1912). He had established himself as London's premier operetta tenor, before spending 18 months in the United States where he appeared both on the variety stage and in the musical theatre in Fall's *The Doll Girl* (1913, Tiborius) and, partnered with José Collins, in Renyi's *Suzi* (1914, Stephan).

After the death of Edwardes, with whom he had entertained a strong personal friendship, he returned to

Daly's Theatre to help Edwardes's daughter run the now beleaguered theatre. Appointed as managing director of George Edwardes (Daly's Theatre) Ltd, he mounted *The Happy Day* there in 1916 and was responsible for the production in 1917 of *The Maid of the Mountains* which—with his *Suzi* partner José Collins as a memorable star—restored the theatre's and the firm's fortunes. He followed up with other successful vehicles for Miss Collins (*A Southern Maid, Sybil*) but when James A White, the chairman of the Daly's board, bought the theatre and began to take a hand in the artistic direction, Evett and Miss Collins moved on. They became based at the Gaiety where Evett produced Lehár's *Der letzte Walzer,* then a Tchaikovsky pasticcio which allowed his star to appear as *Catherine* (the Great), followed by an *Our Nell* in which she played Nell Gwynne, each with diminishing results. The complete failure of one last Collins vehicle, Lehár's *Frasquita* (1925), ended his career as a producer.

1922 **The Last Waltz** (*Der letzte Walzer*) English version w Reginald Arkell (Gaiety Theatre)

EVITA Musical in 2 acts by Tim Rice. Music by Andrew Lloyd Webber. Prince Edward Theatre, London, 21 June 1978.

To follow up their initial hit *Jesus Christ Superstar,* the team of Tim Rice (author) and Andrew Lloyd Webber (composer) found themselves another, on the surface, highly unlikely subject for a piece of modern musical theatre. Once again their show was in the way of a musical biography, and once again their central figure was one from a field in which most people kowtowed to the ''proper'' way of thinking, as purveyed by the Sunday newspapers: for in the earnestly liberal atmosphere of the flaky 1970s, before the days when it was anything that dealt with a person's race that was the fashionable quiver-maker to the Sunday-reader, if anything was more touchy than religion, it was politics. Touchy, that is, if not treated in an earnestly liberal fashion, and extremely touchy when it came to Madame Eva Peron, wife of former Argentine president Juan Peron, and the much-vilified (by the foreign press) popular heroine of that country's people.

However, the writers of *Evita* looked beyond the politics of the subject, to the people involved, and most particularly to the character and tale of Eva. Madame Peron's rise from country girl to the status of goddess of the poor, her vengeful treatment of the right-wing establishment which had long denied her everything she had finally won, and her death from cancer at what seemed like the height of her glory were the stuff of operatic drama. Later, as *Evita* went on to enormous worldwide success, some Sunday papers (and even some weekday ones) flailed furiously at Rice for his ''glorification'' of

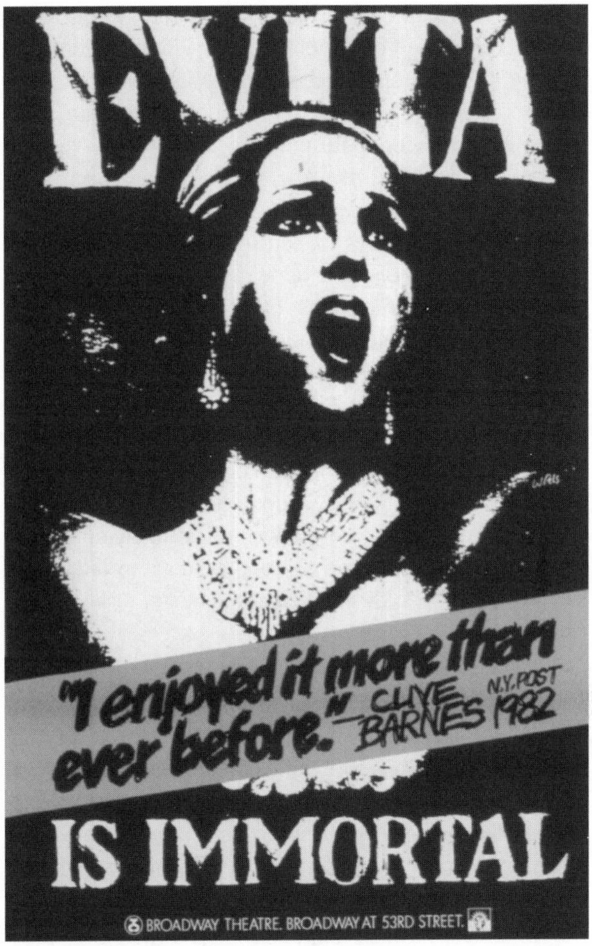

Plate 118. **Evita**

this woman whom they had always painted as an unmitigated monster, and of whom many people's perception was now forever altered. But, much as some might have wished it otherwise, *Evita* was not a show about politics, any more than the slightly satirical musical comedies of the 1930s Broadway stage had been: like them, it was about personalities, but unlike them it did not use those personalities to produce humor but, for the large part, to produce a musical drama.

Eva Duarte (Elaine Paige) is still a teenager when she clamps on to an unbuttoned tango singer, Agustin Magaldi (Mark Ryan), visiting her home town, and uses him as a means to get out of the country and up to Buenos Aires. Magaldi is soon dropped and, whilst building a fairly desultory career as an actress in the capital, Eva soon begins to get to know the influential and the famous, in particular the rising politician Juan Peron (Joss Ackland). Determinedly removing Peron's 16-year-old mistress (Siobhan McCarthy) from his bed, Eva moves in and, before long, she is pushing and persuading her lover towards taking over the supreme power in the country.

Eva Peron is still only in her mid-twenties when Peron becomes President of Argentina. But whilst pleading his cause with the people of the country she has also established herself in their hearts through her enthusiastic promises of something for nothing. The myth of ''Saint'' Eva Peron continues to grow, as she works to promote herself, her husband and the cockeyed kind of democracy she apparently believes in, setting up a charitable Foundation which is more charitable to those who get from it than to those—largely her old ''establishment'' enemies—who are virtually forced to contribute. Growing to believe in her own myth, she finally insists on recognition, on the post of Vice President, not realizing that there are still barriers against her ambitions. However, the more pragmatic Peron does not have to face her with a ''no,'' for her last illness is upon her. When Eva Peron died the people of Argentina were distraught, for like so many who have survived as popular icons to later ages, she did not grow old: she died at the height of her young powers.

This tale was told in a series of linked musical scenes and, through the episodes of its telling, the character of Eva was faced up to another, imaginary character, a sneering, jeering narrator and commentator called Che (David Essex), who represented generally the helpless opposition to Eva Peron more than he represented that other mythicized media icon, the teenagers' wall-poster of a decade who called himself Che Guevara.

Like *Jesus Christ Superstar, Evita* was first presented to the public as a two-record album, in 1976. Julie Covington (Eva) and Colm Wilkinson (Che) headed the cast on a recording which, in retrospect, showed up the key to the presentation of the show: when the protagonists are equally matched, the drama of the piece is at its best, when (as in many later productions) one or the other of the pair is the stronger performer, the excitement is dimmed. The recording produced a surprise. Eva's monologue, ''Don't Cry for Me, Argentina,'' spoken to the public after Peron's election victory, as performed by Miss Covington, shot to the top spot on the British hit parade. It was closely followed by the plaintive little ballad of the deposed mistress, ''Another Suitcase in Another Hall,'' performed on the disc by folksinger Barbara Dickson. It was many years since a musical theatre score had performed in such a way, and unprecedented in the case of the score of an unproduced musical. But the buzz around the theatre circles of the time was that *Evita* was unproduceable: what was on the record could not make up a viable stage show.

However *Superstar* producer Bob Stigwood went ahead with a stage production, the biggest hoo-ha in memory in theatrical London was staged over the selection of the girl to play Eva and, when *Evita* opened at the previously unloved Prince Edward (ex- Casino) Theatre in London's Soho in June 1978, director Hal Prince and choreographer Larry Fuller proved that not only was the show stageable, it was triumphantly so.

Highlights of the night, apart from the two already well-known songs, included the carousel of lovers parading choreographically through Eva's door as she delivered ''Good Night and Thank You,'' the grim musical chairs played through the Generals' ''Dice Are Rolling,'' Eva's approaches to Peron in ''I'd Be Surprisingly Good for You,'' as a pair of tango dancers danced mutely in the background, and the thrilling first-act closure with the people massed together by flare-light to hail a ''New Argentina.'' Essex scored with his mockery of Eva's death in ''O What a Circus'' (soon to follow the two previous hits to the charts, in his version) and of her life in ''High Flying, Adored,'' Eva excitingly declared herself ''Rainbow High'' (reaching improbable notes in chest register in the process) as she prepared to set off on what should have been her international confirmation in the ''Rainbow Tour'' and the two fenced acidly through the Waltz for Eva and Che.

Evita was one of the greatest musical theatre hits ever seen in London. By the time it closed, it had played 2,900 performances in the West End, a record second only to that set up by *Jesus Christ Superstar,* gobbled up half a dozen Evas, and had been seen all around the world. America's production came first, beginning in Los Angeles and opening on Broadway little more than a year into the London run. In preparation for Broadway, the production (which had won some peeved criticism in London and Manchester theatre columns for not blackening the central character they disapproved of unambiguously) was repainted in more primary colors. Eva (Patti LuPone) was made harsher, harder and less attractive, Che (Mandy Patinkin) was set up to be more entertaining. It didn't make the slightest difference. Those journalists brought up on wall-posters shrieked louder than they had or would over the most extreme violent or sexual performances on stage at what they perceived as a challenge to their perception of Eva Peron (''one of the most sinister, morally disgusting entertainments to appear on the Broadway stage in many years . . .''), whilst, as in London, a public who mostly didn't even know where Argentina was filled the Broadway Theater for nearly four years and 1,568 performances. Theatre professionals also showed their approval: *Evita* walked off with seven Tony Awards at the end of its first season.

There was little more protest as *Evita*—now copper-bottomed as one of the musical theatre's all-time hits—made its way round the world, although the piece was banned in Argentina. Australia's production featured Jennifer Murphy (until she gave out and had to be replaced, ultimately by Miss LuPone) and John O'May through its production in producer Stigwood's home town of Adelaide and some six months in Melbourne, prior to a run in Sydney (Her Majesty's Theatre, 14 February 1981) and then performances around the rest of the country. Spain followed suit with the first foreign-language production (ad Ignacio Artime, Jaime Azpilicueta) at Madrid's Teatro Monumental with Paloma San Basilio and Paxti Andion in the lead roles, and the Theater an der Wien mounted the first German-language adaptation (ad Michael Kunze) with Isabel Wiecken and Alexander Goebel top-billed. Mexico, South Africa, Japan, New Zealand, Brazil and Hungary (ad Tibor Miklós) all followed. In France, in spite of rumors being regularly floated as to a French-language production, the only version that was seen was an under-par European touring mounting sent out from America, which improbably billed Hal Prince's name very large as director.

Over more than a decade, regular paragraphs announcing a screen *Evita* appeared in the trade (and gutter) press. Faye Dunaway, Liza Minnelli, Meryl Streep and Madonna were amongst the less unlikely names at various times promoted in stories about a forthcoming film. It had, in fact, been talked about so much that it seemed unlikely that it would ever happen, but in 1996 the filmed version of *Evita* made it to the screen. Madonna proved to have all the necessary looks and talents for the much discussed lead role (she also upset the whole balance of the affair by nicking the mistress's song) and although some of the other casting was less felicitous, and the people-centered tale was dissipated by a director with a fetish for rumbling tanks, the screen *Evita* included some most effective moments. It also included a rather pale and out-of-character new song for the star, ''You Must Love Me,'' which was awarded the year's Academy Award.

Mr Guevara later got a musical all of his own when a piece called *Ernesto Che Guevara—The Musical* (what else?) was brought out in Italy in 1999.

USA: Broadway Theater 25 September 1979; Australia: Her Majesty's Theatre, Melbourne 2 August 1980; Hungary: Margitszigeti Vörösmarty Színpad 14 August 1980; Austria: Theater an der Wien 20 January 1981; Germany: Theater des Westens, Berlin 10 September 1982; France: Palais de Congrès (Eng) 20 December 1989

Film: Cinergi/Stigwood 1996

Recordings: concept album (MCA), original cast (MCA), Broadway cast (MCA), Australian cast (MCA), Spanish cast (Epic), Austrian cast (Jupiter), Mexican cast (Peerless), South African cast (Gallo), Japanese cast (Trio), New Zealand cast (Stetson), Brazilian cast (Somlivree), Hungarian cast (Favorit), Korean cast (DRG), Dutch cast (CNR/Endemol), Japanese revival cast 1997 (Pony Canyon), film soundtrack (Warner Brothers), etc

Literature: Rice, T, Lloyd Webber, A: *Evita—the Legend of Eva Peron 1919–1952* (Elm Tree Books, London, 1978), Parker, A: *The Making of Evita* (Collins, London, 1996)

EVVA, Lajos (b Fegyvernek, 17 August 1851; d Budapest, 12 October 1912). Theatre director, adapter and lyricist.

Evva took over the management of the Népszínház, Budapest's most important producing house for musical theatre, from its initial manager, Jenő Rákosi, at the age of 30 (15 October 1881), and directed its fortunes for 16 years before going on to be director of the Magyar Színház (11 June 1898 sq).

During his years at the Népszínház, which were initiated by a production of the French spectacular *L'Arbre de Noël,* he produced many highly successful pieces including Hungarian versions of *Le Jour et la nuit, Les Contes d'Hoffmann,* his new adaptation of *Orphée aux enfers, Lili, Der Bettelstudent, Rip van Winkle, Les Pilules du Diable, Der Zigeunerbaron, The Mikado, Mam'zelle Nitouche* and *Der Vogelhändler* and, most notably, the most important early Hungarian operetts—Konti's *Az eleven ördög* (1884), *Királyfogás* (1886), *A suhanc* (1888) and *A citerás* (1894), and dramaturg György Verő's *A szultán* (1892) and *A Virágcsata* (1894), as well as works by Béla Hegyi, Szidor Bátor, Jenő Sztojanovits, Béla Szabados, Elek Erkel, Dezső Megyeri, Aladár Váradi, Miklós Forrai and others.

Having made a major hit with his first operettic adaptation for Rákosi and the Népszínház, Suppé's *Boccaccio,* Evva continued to turn out a heavy schedule of adaptations both before and during (especially the earlier years of) his direction of the theatre. Many of these were done in collaboration, notably with Rákosi and with the even more prolific Béla J Fái who often provided the textual adaptations whilst Evva worked on the lyrics.

1879 **Boccaccio** Hungarian version (Népszínház)

1879 **Favartné** (*Madame Favart*) Hungarian version w Fái (Népszínház)

1880 **A pipacs** (*Coquelicot*) Hungarian version (Népszínház)

1880 **Fatinitza** Hungarian version w Jenő Rákosi (Népszínház)

1880 **A kecskepásztor márkiné** (*Les Voltigeurs de la 32ème*) Hungarian version w Ferenc Nemes (Népszínház)

1880 **A szép perzsalány** (*La Jolie Persane*) Hungarian version (Népszínház)

1880 **A kétnejü gróf** (*Der Graf von Gleichen*) Hungarian version w Rákosi (Népszínház)

1880 **A Franciák Milánóban** (*La Fille du tambour-major*) Hungarian version w Fái (Népszínház)

1881 **Dragonyosok** (*Les Dragons de Villars*) Hungarian version w Rákosi (Népszínház)

1881 **Tiszturak a zárdában** (*Les Mousquetaires au couvent*) Hungarian version w Fái (Népszínház)

1881 **Apajune, a vízitündér** (*Apajune der Wassermann*) Hungarian version w Rákosi (Népszínház)

1881 **Az ácslegények gazdasszonykája** (*La Mère des compagnons*) Hungarian version w Fái (Népszínház)

1881 **A szélkakas** (*La Girouette*) Hungarian version w Fái (Népszínház)

1881 **Olivette lakodalma** (*Les Noces d'Olivette*) Hungarian version (Népszínház)

1881 **A Királykisasszony bábui** (*Les Poupées de l'Infante*) Hungarian version (Népszínház)

1882 **Nap és hold** (*Le Jour et la nuit*) Hungarian version w Fái (Népszínház)

1882 **A furcsa háboru** (*Der lustige Krieg*) Hungarian version w Fái (Népszínház)

1882 **Viola-Ibolya** (*Giroflé-Girofla*) Hungarian version w Fái (Népszínház)

1882 **Orpheus a pokolban** (*Orphée aux enfers*) Hungarian version (Népszínház)

1882 **A denevér** (*Die Fledermaus*) Hungarian version (Népszínház)

1882 **Lili** Hungarian version w Fái (Népszínház)

1882 **A kertészleány** (*Le Coeur et la main*) Hungarian version w Fái (Népszínház)

1883 **A koldusdiák** (*Der Bettelstudent*) Hungarian version w Fái (Népszínház)

1883 **A gyürü** (*Gillette de Narbonne*) Hungarian version w ''Imre Ukki'' (Népszínház)

1883 **A hercegasszony** (*Madame l'Archiduc*) Hungarian version w Fái (Népszínház)

1883 **Az Afrikautázo** (*Die Afrikareise*) Hungarian version w Rákosi (Népszínház)

1883 **Kanári hercegnő** (*La Princesse des Canaries*) Hungarian version w Fái (Népszínház)

1883 **Rip** (*Rip van Winkle*) Hungarian version w Fái (Népszínház)

1884 **Kék Féri** (*François les bas-bleus*) Hungarian version w Fái (Népszínház)

1884 **Gasparone** Hungarian version w Árpád Berczik (Népszínház)

1884 **A hercegnő** (*La Princesse*) Hungarian version (Népszínház)

1884 **A gerolsteini nagyhercegnő** (*La Grande-Duchesse de Gérolstein*) Hungarian version w Fái (Népszínház)

1885 **Az ébren álmódo** (*La Dormeuse éveillée*) Hungarian version w Fái (Népszínház)

1886 **A bearni leány** (*La Béarnaise*) Hungarian version w Fái (Népszínház)

1887 **A komédias hercegnő** (*Nell Gwynne*) Hungarian version w Fái (Népszínház)

1887 **Nebántsvirág** (*Mam'zelle Nitouche*) Hungarian version w Viktor Rákosi (Népszínház)

1887 **Fejő lány, vagy költőimádás** (*Patience*) Hungarian version w Fái (Népszínház)

1888 **Szedtevette nagysám** (*Mam'selle Crénom*) Hungarian version w Fái (Népszínház)

1889 **A gárdista** (*The Yeomen of the Guard*) Hungarian version w Ukki (Népszínház)

1890 **Szinitanoda** (*Un lycée de jeunes filles*) Hungarian version w V Rákosi (Népszínház)

1891 **A tékozló fiu** (*Le Fils prodigue*) Hungarian version w Ukki (Népszínház)

1891 **Miss Heliett** (*Miss Helyett*) Hungarian version w V Rákosi (Népszínház)

1891 **A tollkirály** (*Isoline*) Hungarian version w Fái (Népszínház)

1895 **A királyné dragonyosa** (*Le Dragon de la reine*) Hungarian version w V Rákosi (Népszínház)

EXPRESSO BONGO Musical in 2 acts taken from a story by Wolf Mankowitz. Book by Wolf Mankowitz and Julian More. Lyrics by Julian More. Music by David Heneker and Monty Norman. Saville Theatre, London, 23 April 1958.

One of the most interesting musical plays to come out of the British theatre in the 1950s, the stark and seedy *Expresso Bongo* was an adaptation of a newspaper novella written by Academy Award-winning screenplay author, Wolf Mankowitz, which was itself imaginatively based on the career of Britain's first rock-and-roll star, Tommy Steele.

Herbert Rudge (James Kenney) is discovered by agent Johnnie (Paul Scofield) playing bongo drums in a Soho coffee bar. Renamed ''Bongo'' and fitted out with a loud, rhythmic song called ''Expresso Party,'' the boy rises quickly to the top, attracts the young and the hangers-òn, and, having established his youth/sex/violence image, is then manipulated into widening his appeal to the mums and dads with a sob-stuff number dedicated to his mother. But, under the influence of the sex-bent actress Dixie Collins (Hy Hazell), Bongo begins to slip away from the agent who made him a star. He starts to become unreliable and, before Johnnie knows what is happening, the boy has deserted him for a fashionable agent. The big time is as far away as ever for Johnnie, but he will keep on trying.

Millicent Martin was the little Soho stripper, Maisie, with dreams of a singing career, Charles Gray was Captain Mavors, the classy, shoddy club manager whose character was indubitably based on the real-life Major Donald Neville-Willing, Meier Tzelniker was Mayer, the pop record producer who only likes opera, and Aubrey Morris was ''Kakky'' Katz, the down-on-his-luck ex-film producer running around Soho trying to set up just one more deal. The supporting cast included such rising performers as Susan Hampshire, Victor Spinetti, Barry Cryer, Trevor Griffiths, Anna Sharkey and Jill Gascoine as well as dancer Anne Donaghue—the future Mrs Tommy Steele.

The songs illustrated the story splendidly, with Johnnie rejoicing initially that ''I've Never Had It So Good'' and later regretting that he has fallen off ''The Gravy Train,'' Dixie musing frightenedly over the ravages of ''Time'' and revusically singing with a classy pal of how ''We Bought It,'' Bongo pounding out the acid parodies of rock-and-roll music, and little Maisie chirping out her ballads as a little ray of light in all the grey shadows.

Oscar Lewenstein and Neil Crawford's production of *Expresso Bongo* ran for 316 performances at the Saville Theatre before being toured and then made into a film with the young Cliff Richard playing the role of Bongo to the Johnnie of Laurence Harvey, the Dixie of Yolande Donlan and the Maisie of Sylvia Syms. Most of the music was omitted, although Richard performed the mother-loving "The Shrine on the Second Floor" alongside a new number, "A Voice in the Wilderness," which made it to the charts. In 1964 the show was performed in Hungary (ad Sándor Kosnár, Peter Tardos).

The first and easily the most accomplished of the low-life musicals which became for a while fashionable in the London theatre, *Expresso Bongo* encouraged other, mostly less skillful, writers into an area which proved, in the end, only spasmodically fertile.

Hungary: Fővárosi Operettszínház 18 September 1964

Film: 1959

Recordings: original cast (Nixa), film songs (Columbia, EP)

EYSLER, Edmund [EISLER, Edmund S] (b Vienna, 12 March 1874; d Vienna, 4 October 1949). One of the most melodiously Viennese composers of his era, with a long list of successful shows to his credit.

Born in Vienna, the son of an erratically solvent and only occasionally rich Jewish businessman, the young Eysler did sufficiently badly at his lessons to be allowed to follow the example of his schoolfriend and contemporary, Leo Fall, and pursue musical studies instead. After his years at the Vienna Conservatoire were successfully completed, he was for some while unable to find himself any more lucrative employ than as a piano teacher but, at the same time, he made his first attempts at composing for the stage. A ballet, *Schlaraffenland,* was rejected by the Hofoperntheater, where Mahler ruled, as being too expensive to stage, and Eysler turned instead to Operette, setting a libretto by Ignaz Schnitzer, the author of *Der Zigeunerbaron* and a friend of a friend. *Der Schelm von Bergen,* which had been turned down by Johann Strauss as being too similar in key areas to *The Mikado,* became *Der Hexenspiegel* in the 26-year-old Eysler's version. It evoked enough enthusiasm in the old librettist for him to sponsor Eysler sufficiently for him to quit piano teaching and take a small house at Grinzing where he might work on his composition and orchestration, and in publisher Josef Weinberger to earn the young man a helpful advance. Eysler had an income from his work, but had still had nothing produced.

Weinberger's efforts to convince producers to stage *Der Hexenspiegel* did not succeed. Mahler preferred to stick with Lortzing, the Prague theatre was unwilling to venture with an untried composer, and Leipzig simply didn't get round to it. Since Eysler's benefactors were unable to support him indefinitely, the composer found employment with Gabor Steiner at the adventurous summer theatre Venedig in Wien where, as a number-three house composer, he supplied some dance music for Ivan Caryll's *Die Reise nach Cuba* and some individual numbers for the cabaret-concerts played by members of the company. One of these was the young Frln Massari [*sic*], later to find fame as Fritzi Massary.

When the summer theatre season finished, Eysler moved on to Steiner's winter house, Danzers Orpheum, and there, later in the year, he had his first stage works, a one-act Operette, *Das Gastmahl des Lucullus,* and a two-scene pantomime, adapted from the French by Lindau and Louis Gundlach under the title *Das Frauenduell,* produced as sections of a five-part program. The composer was still "Edmund S Eisler," but the deliberately less common "Eysler" would soon follow.

Weinberger, however, had not forgotten the young composer and he sent Eysler another text, an Operette by Zeller's librettist, Moritz West, in which he suggested the young man could reuse the lighter portions of the unplayed *Hexenspiegel* score. What became *Bruder Straubinger* was a text conceived to feature Alexander Girardi, the greatest star of the Viennese musical theatre and the original *Vogelhändler* of Zeller and West's famous Operette. As a result, in 1903, Eysler's first produced full-length piece was mounted at no less a venue than the Theater an der Wien with the great Girardi starring in its title role. It proved an enormous success, its waltz song "Küssen ist keine Sünd" became the hit of the period, and Eysler was at last launched on what was to be an exceptionally busy and regularly successful career.

In the years that followed, he became one of the most popular and prolific composers of Viennese light theatre music, as he turned out a veritable shower of mostly successful shows. *Pufferl* was another successful venture with Girardi, and one which provided the artist with a second hit song, the Kirschenlied, and when after 60 performances Girardi broke his long relationship with the Theater an der Wien, he took his new favorite composer with him to the opposition Carltheater. There, together, they had two further fine successes with *Die Schützenliesel,* in which Girardi introduced his famous "Mutterllied," and with the more substantial *Künstlerblut.*

After *Künstlerblut,* star and composer went different ways, but success continued for Eysler with a little one-acter, *Vera Violetta,* produced at the Apollotheater, before he met his first comparative reverses. *Das Glücksschweinchen,* with Fritzi Massary starring, had only a short summer run at Venedig in Wien and a Budapest appearance as *A szerencsemalac* (Budai Színkör 1 May 1909), and a modern-dress Viennese piece, *Johann der Zweite,* produced at the Carltheater was also a 28-

performance disappointment. However, both pieces did altogether better when produced in Germany, and Eysler's music, shorn of Stein and Lindau's libretti, was heard in America (where the composer had been represented as early as 1905 by a waltz interpolated into Broadway's *The Rollicking Girl*) when impresario Henry Savage bought up the rights to both to top up what he saw as the undersized score of *Künstlerblut* and fabricated two musicals from the three. *The Love Cure* (ex-mostly-*Künstlerblut*) loudly touted by Savage as the legitimate successor to his production of *The Merry Widow* played five weeks on Broadway then toured with rather more success. The piece announced as *Forgetmenot* apparently didn't make it to the stage. However, a version of *Johann der Zweite* did ultimately appear, under the management of Weber and Fields. Adapted by Harry B Smith and E Ray Goetz as *The June Bride* (Majestic Theater, Boston 23 September 1912) it stopped short of Broadway.

After this temporary lull, a second very fine series of Viennese Eysler successes was quickly under way. Oskar Fronz, director of the Wiener Bürgertheater, decided to leap on the lucrative Operette bandwagon and began his new policy with the production of Eysler's latest piece, *Der unsterbliche Lump.* It was followed by *Der Frauenfresser, Der lachende Ehemann* and *Ein Tag im Paradies,* all substantial successes, which between them filled Fronz's theatre for some four years, up to the outbreak of war. Eysler simultaneously turned out one last vehicle for Girardi, *Das Zirkuskind,* and also contributed to the programs at the variety and Operette house the Apollotheater (which had introduced *Vera Violetta*), scoring notably with the little *Der Natursanger,* played 106 times in 1911–12.

It was at the Apollotheater, in fact, that was produced the most successful of the steady supply of cheerfully tuneful and mostly alt-Wienerische Operetten and musical comedies which the composer turned out through the war years. *Hanni geht tanzen* outdid, statistically at least, all of the run of successful pieces with which Eysler steadily supplied the Bürgertheater, equaled the greatest successes of his Girardi days, and was exported to fine effect. It was followed by another piece in a similar vein, *Graf Toni,* which happily confirmed that success, whilst *Die—oder keine* ran for more than 125 performances at the Bürgertheater, *Wenn zwei sich lieben* notched up 110 nights at the Theater an der Wien and *Warum geht's denn jetzt?* went through 102 performances at the Bundestheater and the Bürgertheater.

When the fashion for the more modern, foreign dance rhythms caught on in the 1920s Eysler was unable or unwilling to take them up. Although he ventured a charleston amongst the traditional rhythms in the two-month run of the 1926 Bürgertheater piece *Das Land der Liebe,* he largely stuck to what he knew and did best, and what the Viennese public seemed never to tire of hearing from him: flowing Viennese melody.

It was not only Vienna, either, that wanted this mode of music. If America had fabricated its own Eysler shows, Italy preferred to purchase one ready-made and, when Fronz demurred over Eysler's new piece *Die schöne Mama,* there was a willing taker in Rome's Teatro Nazionale. Thus *Die schöne Mama* was produced as *La bella mammina* before, its credentials proven, being re-imported to Vienna and the Bürgertheater to play under its original title for 111 performances.

In 1927 Eysler scored his most substantial success since *Bruder Straubinger* when he composed perhaps his most dazzling and melodious ''old Vienna'' score for the ''old Vienna'' story of *Die gold'ne Meisterin.* Staged at the Theater an der Wien, *Die gold'ne Meisterin* was played more than two hundred times in its first run and produced several popular songs in the prewar style.

Eysler continued to compose into the 1930s, scoring another fair success at the Bürgertheater with *Ihr erster Ball* in 1929 (76 performances), but he was forced into hiding during the 1939–45 war and, unable to work or to have his Operetten played, he saw the prosperity he had achieved frittered away. When the war was over, he was once again able to compose and to conduct freely and, in his seventies, now regarded as the grand old man from the good old days, he saw his shows return to Viennese stages.

Eysler's works, an extremely large proportion of which were both popular and financial successes, won lively audiences, particularly in the Vienna of 1900–1920. Most were played at that time in Germany and at least 17 were seen in Hungary, whilst several were exported further. *Der lachende Ehemann* reached London as *The Laughing Husband* and *The Girl Who Didn't, Vera Violetta* was played at Paris's Olympia, and, after *The Love Cure,* Broadway hosted Americanized versions of *Vera Violetta, Der Frauenfresser* (*The Woman Haters*), *Der lachende Ehemann* (*The Laughing Husband*), *Ein Tag im Paradies* (*The Blue Paradise*), with Sigmund Romberg interpolations and considerable success, *Wenn zwei sich lieben* (*Lieutenant Gus*) and an Italian version of *Pufferl* called *Amor di Principi,* played by a visiting company from Palermo. Apart from *La Bella mammina* and *Amor di Principi,* Italy also staged a number of further Eysler works including a version of *Wenn zwei sich lieben* under the title *Julicka* (Luna Palace, Rome, 1922).

1901 **Das Gastmahl des Lucullus** (Carl Lindau, A Paulus) 1 act Danzers Orpheum 23 November

1903 **Bruder Straubinger** (Moritz West, Ignaz Schnitzer) Theater an der Wien 20 February

1905 **Pufferl** (Schnitzer, Sigmund Schlesinger) Theater an der Wien 10 February

1905 **Die Schützenliesel** (Leo Stein, Lindau) Carltheater 7 October

1906 **Phryne** (Fritz Grünbaum, Robert Bodanzky) 1 act Hölle 6 October

1906 **Künstlerblut** (Stein, Lindau) Carltheater 20 October

1907 **Vera Violetta** (Stein) 1 act Apollotheater 30 November

1908 **Ein Tag auf dem Mars** (Ottokar Tann-Bergler, Alfred Deutsch-German) 1 act Wiener Colosseum 17 January

1908 **Das Glücksschweinchen** (Stein, Lindau) Venedig in Wien 26 June

1908 **Johann der Zweite** (Stein, Lindau) Carltheater 3 October

1909 **Der junge Papa** (Alexander Engel, August Neidhart) 1 act Apollotheater 3 February

1910 **Lumpus und Pumpus** (Stein) 1 act Apollotheater 21 January

1910 **Der unsterbliche Lump** (Felix Dörmann) Wiener Bürgertheater 15 October

1911 **Das Zirkuskind** (Bodanzky, Friedrich Thelen) Raimundtheater 18 February

1911 **Der Natursänger** (Stein, Jenbach) 1 act Apollotheater 22 December

1911 **Der Frauenfresser** (Stein, Lindau) Wiener Bürgertheater 23 December

1913 **Der lachende Ehemann** (Julius Brammer, Alfred Grünwald) Wiener Bürgertheater 19 March

1913 **Ein Tag im Paradies** (Stein, Bela Jenbach) Wiener Bürgertheater 23 December

1914 **Komm, deutscher Brüder** (Lindau, Neidhart) Raimundtheater 4 October

1914 **Der Kriegsberichterstatter** (w others/Rudolf Österreicher, Willy Sterk) Apollotheater 9 October

1914 **Frühling am Rhein** (Lindau, Fritz Löhner-Beda) Wiener Bürgertheater 10 October

1914 **Der Durchgang der Venus** (Willner, Österreicher) Apollotheater 28 November

1915 **Die—oder keine** (Stein, Jenbach) Wiener Bürgertheater 9 October

1915 **Wenn zwei sich lieben** (Willner, Bodanzky) Theater an der Wien 29 October

1915 **Das Zimmer der Pompadour** (Oskar Friedmann, Ludwig Herzer) 1 act Hölle 1 December

1916 **Warum geht's denn jetzt?** (Jacobson, Bodanzky) Bundestheater 5 July

1916 **Hanni geht tanzen** (Bodanzky) Apollotheater 7 November

1916 **Der berühmte Gabriel** (Ludwig Hirschfeld, Rudolf G Eger) Wiener Bürgertheater 8 November

1917 **Graf Toni** (Österreicher) Apollotheater 2 March

1917 **Der Aushilfsgatte** (O Friedmann, Herzer) Apollotheater 7 November

1918 **Leute von heute** (w Robert Stolz, Arthur Werau/Fritz Lunzer, Arthur Rebner) Bundestheater 22 June

1918 **Der dunkle Schatz** (Herzer, O Friedmann) Wiener Bürgertheater 14 November

1919 **Der fidele Geiger** (Louis Taufstein, Hans Herling) Wiener Bürgertheater 17 January

1920 **Rund um die Bühne** (Armin Friedmann, Gustav Beer) Apollotheater 1 March

1920 **Der König heiratet** (Beer, Ernst Marischka) 1 act Künstlerbühne April

1920 **Wer hat's gemacht** (Willy Sterk) 1 act Variété Reclame 1 October

1921 **Die schöne Mama** (*La bella Mammina*) (Heinrich von Waldberg, Bruno Hardt-Warden) Teatro Nazionale, Rome 9 April; Wiener Bürgertheater 17 September

1921 **Die fromme Helene** (Arnold Golz, Emil Golz) Komödienhaus 22 December

1922 **Die Parliamentskathi** (Robert Blum, Alois Ulreich) Komödienhaus 15 April

1922 **Fräulein Sopherl, die schöne vom Markt** (Josco Schubert) Lustspieltheater 19 May

1922 **Schummel macht alles** (Karl Marfeld-Neumann) Komödienhaus 1 July

1923 **Drei auf einmal** (O Friedmann) Komödienhaus 29 March

1923 **Der ledige Schwiegersohn** (A Golz, E Golz) Wiener Bürgertheater 20 April

1923 **Lumpenlieschen** (Else Tauber) Carltheater 21 May

1923 **Vierzehn Tage (im) Arrest** (Horst, Österreicher) Raimundtheater 16 June

1926 **Das Land der Liebe** (''Habakuk,'' ie, Gustav Tintner, Herling) Wiener Bürgertheater 27 August

1927 **Die gold'ne Meisterin** (Brammer, Grünwald) Theater an der Wien 13 September

1929 **Ihr erster Ball** (Herling, Tintner) Wiener Bürgertheater 21 November

1930 **Das Strumpfband der Pompadour** (Lunzer, Emil von Meissner) Stadttheater, Augsburg 16 March

1930 **Durchlaucht Mizzi** (Lunzer, Beer) Neues Wiener Schauspielhaus 23 December

1931 **Die schlimme Paulette** (Stephan Walter, Karl Lustig-Prean) Stadttheater, Augsburg 1 March

1932 **Zwei alte Wiener** (Hans Borutzky, von Meissner) Neues Wiener Operetten-Theater 12 February

1932 **Die Rakete** (Fred Rhoden, Eduard Rogati) Stadttheater, Innsbrück 23 December

1932 **Donauliebchen** (Brammer, Emil Marboth) Wiener Bürgertheater 25 December

1934 **Das ist der erste Liebe(lei)** (Beer, Hans Kottow) Volksoper 23 December

1947 **Wiener Musik** (Herz, Kosta) Wiener Bürgertheater 22 December

Biographies: Ewald, K: *Edmund Eysler: ein Musikus aus Wien* (Vienna, 1934), Prosl, R M: *Edmund Eysler* (Verlag Karl Kuhne, Vienna, 1947)

EYTON, Frank (b London, 30 August 1894; d London, 11 November 1962).

City man turned lyricist and occasional playwright/librettist (*She Shall Have Music, Runaway Love, Happy Birthday*), Eyton formed an effective partnership with pianist/composer Billy Mayerl which produced the musical part of such successful shows as *Sporting Love, Twenty to One* and *Over She Goes,* and, later, with Noel Gay for the shows which followed *Me and My Girl* at the Victoria Palace.

He also wrote material for revue, additional lyrics for the shows *Love Lies* (1929), *Darling I Love You* (1929), *Silver Wings* (1930), *The One Girl* (1933), *The Flying Trapeze* (1935), *La-di-da-di-da* (1943) and *Six Pairs of Shoes* (1944), the words to Mischa Spoliansky's popular title song for the film *Tell Me Tonight,* and paired with Noel Gay on the songs for the film *Sailors Three* (''All Over the Place'').

1928 **So Long, Letty!** (later *Oh! Letty*) (Billy Mayerl/Austin Melford, later w Stanley Lupino) Theatre Royal, Birmingham 22 October

1929 **Change Over** revised *Oh, Letty!* (S Lupino) Hippodrome, Portsmouth 8 April

1930 **Nippy** (Mayerl/Melford, Arthur Wimperis) Prince Edward Theatre 30 October

1931 **The Millionaire Kid** (Mayerl/Noel Scott) Gaiety Theatre 20 May

1933 **Nice Goings On** (Arthur Schwartz/Douglas Furber) Strand Theatre 13 September

1934 **Sporting Love** (Mayerl/w Carter/Stanley Lupino) Gaiety Theatre 31 March

1934 **She Shall Have Music** (Christopher Fry, Monte Crick/ Ronald Frankau)

1935 **Twenty to One** (Mayerl/L Arthur Rose) London Coliseum 12 November

1936 **Over She Goes** (Mayerl/w Carter/S Lupino) Saville Theatre 23 September

1937 **Crazy Days** (Mayerl/w Carter/S Lupino) Shaftesbury Theatre 14 September

1939 **Runaway Love** (Mayerl/w B Lupino) Saville 3 November

1940 **Present Arms** (Noel Gay/Fred Thompson) Prince of Wales Theatre 13 May

1940 **Happy Birthday** (Mayerl/w B Lupino, Arthur Rigby) Manchester 9 September

1941 **Lady Behave** (Edward Horan/S Lupino) His Majesty's Theatre 24 July

1942 **Kiki** (Mayerl/Martin Henry) Leeds 30 March

1942 **Susie** revised *Jack o' Diamonds* (Gay/w Clifford Grey/H F Maltby) Oxford 13 June

1942 **Wild Rose** revised *Sally* new lyrics (Prince's Theatre)

1943 **The Love Racket** (Gay/w others/Lupino) Victoria Palace 21 October

1944 **Meet Me Victoria** (Gay/Lupino Lane, Lauri Wylie) Victoria Palace 8 April

1944 **Ring Time** (Gay/Stanley Brightman, Melford) Glasgow 28 August

1946 **Sweetheart Mine** (Gay/Wylie, Lane) Victoria Palace 1 August

1948 **Bob's Your Uncle** (Gay, Melford) Saville Theatre 5 May

1949 **Roundabout** (ex- *Hat in the Air*) (Horan, Melford, Ken Attiwill) Saville Theatre 4 August

F

FABRAY, Nanette [FABARES, Ruby Bernadette Nanette Theresa] (b San Diego, Calif, 27 October 1920). Laughing-cheeked musical comedy juvenile of the Broadway 1940s.

Miss Fabray appeared in vaudeville and in the *Our Gang* films as a child, and made her first Broadway musical appearance at 17 in the revue *Meet the People* as Nanette Fabares (''Hurdy Gurdy Verdi''). A minor role the following year in Cole Porter's *Let's Face It* (1941, Jean Blanchard) was followed by a takeover of a larger one, Constance Moore's featured juvenile part of Antiope, in *By Jupiter* (1943), and roles in two short-lived pieces, the 45-performance *My Dear Public* (1943, Jean) and as the ''demoiselle en loterie'' Sally Madison in *Jackpot* (1944), before she succeeded Celeste Holm in the title role of *Bloomer Girl* (1945).

She created the lead in *High Button Shoes* (1947, Sara Longstreet), introducing with Jack McCauley ''Papa, Won't You Dance with Me?'' and ''I Still Get Jealous'' and the following season starred in with Ray Middleton in *Love Life* (1948, Susan Cooper), Alan Jay Lerner's examination of 150 years of marriage, to Kurt Weill music (''Green-up Time'') and a Tony Award. She played opposite Georges Guétary as a fourth successive period heroine in *Arms in the Girl* (1950, Jo Kirkland) and starred as the wandering French orphan of *Make a Wish* (1951, Janette) both for rather shorter runs than the previous two shows had garnered, before going to Hollywood to feature in the film *The Band Wagon* with Fred Astaire and Jack Buchanan.

She subsequently had a considerable television success, and appeared only once more in a Broadway musical, as the wife of the President of the United States (Robert Ryan) in the Irving Berlin musical *Mr President* (1962, Nell Henderson). She continued intermittently thereafter to appear in regional musical productions (Margo Channing in *Applause,* Ruth Sherwood in *Wonderful Town, Follies,* etc) and reappeared off-Broadway in a senior role in a play in 1997.

FADE OUT—FADE IN Musical comedy in 2 acts by Adolph Green and Betty Comden. Music by Jule Styne. Mark Hellinger Theater, New York, 26 May 1964.

A musical comedy set in the Hollywood of the 1930s, *Fade Out—Fade In* 100 percent top-billed comedienne Carol Burnett, who had blundered hilariously onto the musical stage as the heroine of *Once Upon a Mattress* five years previously, as a klutzy movieland chorine accidentally cast in a starring role by an overwieldy studio. In the best cinematic tradition, the unlikely movie becomes a hit and the new star can galumph off into the sunset with the boss's helpful nephew (Dick Patterson).

Jack Cassidy featured as plastic film star Byron Prong (a name as happily in the best burlesque tradition as that of Miss Burnett's character, Hope Springfield), whilst characters like studio boss Lionel Z Governor (Lou Jacobi) with his plethora of despised nephews, Dora Dailey (Virginia Payne), Helga Sixtrees, Myra May Melrose, Custer Corkley, Gloria Currie (Tina Louise) and Viennese psychiatrist Dr Traurig (Rube Singer), all lived up to the expectations aroused by their names.

Miss Burnett wondered musically at how she, ''The Usher from the Mezzanine,'' had made it to stardom, mused on the profit of a pretty name change to ''Lila Tremaine'' and imitated Shirley Temple to Tiger Haynes's version of Bojangles Robinson (''You Mustn't Be Discouraged''), whilst Jacobi pursued the ravishing Miss Louise through a nightmare ballet (''L Z in Quest of his Youth''), haunted by Hope.

The show closed down after 199 performances when Miss Burnett, discontented with a role which did not fulfill its paper promises, fell ill. The show's book was revamped, two replacement songs supplied for the star, and the piece remounted (15 February 1965), but it closed definitively after another 72 performances.

An Australian production mounted on the Tivoli circuit with Sheila Smith, John Stratton and H F Green featured was not a success.

Australia: Tivoli, Sydney 20 February 1965

Recording: original cast (ABC-Paramount)

FAIN, Sammy [FEINBERG, Samuel] (b New York, 17 June 1902; d Los Angeles, 6 December 1989). Celebrated songwriter, particularly for film, whose stage career was less productive.

A striving songwriter from a young age, Fain found his first success when he paired with lyricist Irving Kahal to produce a series of popular songs, beginning with the 1927 "Let a Smile Be Your Umbrella" and including such numbers as "I Left My Sugar Standing in the Rain," "Wedding Bells are Breaking Up That Old Gang of Mine," "You Brought a New Kind of Love" as sung by Maurice Chevalier in the film *The Big Pond* (1930), "When I Take My Sugar to Tea," "Sitting on a Back Yard Fence," "By a Waterfall" (delivered by Dick Powell and a good deal of pulchritude in *Footlight Parade*), "A Sunbonnet Blue" and "I'll Be Seeing You," mostly for movie musicals, over a period of some 15 years. After Kahal's death in 1942 Fain continued in the film world with other partners, supplying whole or part-scores and/or title songs for such movies as *Calamity Jane* (1953), *Love Is a Many Splendored Thing* (1955, Academy Award), *April Love* (1957) and *A Certain Smile* (1958), as well as ringing up a further series of popular songs ("Dear Hearts and Gentle People," "I Can Dream, Can't I?," "Home is Where the Heart Is," etc).

During his early Hollywood years, Fain also contributed one score to the musical stage, for the Shuberts' musicalization of their play hit *Up Pops the Devil* as *Everybody's Welcome* (1931). The musical was not a success and its one song hit was not Fain's, but Herman Hupfeld's interpolated "As Time Goes By." Fain himself supplied individual songs to a number of theatre revues and musicals (*Right This Way, Hellzapoppin, Blackbirds of 1939, George White's Scandals of 1939, Boys and Girls Together, Sons o' Fun, Ziegfeld Follies*) and, although his stage work was less considerable than his film work, he subsequently wrote, over two decades, full scores for five further Broadway shows and one, Dennis King's attempt at actor-management with *She Had To Say "Yes,"* which didn't get that far.

Toplitzky of Notre Dame, a fantasy piece about an angel who comes to earth to help a football team, and *Flahooley,* another fantasy which involved a genie, the bass-to-soprano voice of Yma Sumac (equipped with three interpolated wordless songs by Moïses Vivanco) and the more normal one of Barbara Cook, were failures and though the cheerfully unsophisticated *Ankles Aweigh* lasted 176 performances at the Mark Hellinger Theater, it could not be accounted a hit. East failed to meet West in good *Geisha* fashion for just 12 performances in *Christine, Something More!* survived 15 showings and none of the five shows left songs which won the popularity of Fain's film music.

In 1962 he supplemented Victor Young's film score for *Around the World in 80 Days* to make it into a full-scale stage musical for the St Louis Muny and, subsequently, the Jones Beach Marine Theatre, and a stage adaptation of his *Calamity Jane* ("Black Hills of Dakota," "Secret Love") was produced at the Muny in 1961 with Edie Adams in the title role, and subsequently played in Britain with Barbara Windsor (briefly) and then Susan Jane Tanner starred.

1931 **Everybody's Welcome** (ex- *Kissable Girl*) (Harold Atteridge) Shubert Theater 13 October

1940 **She Had To Say "Yes"** (Al Dubin/Bob Henly, Richard Pinkham) Forrest Theater, Philadelphia 30 December

1946 **Toplitzky of Notre Dame** (George Marion jr, Jack Barnett) Century Theater 26 December

1951 **Flahooley** (E Y Harburg/Fred Saidy) Broadhurst Theater 14 May

1952 **Jollyanna** (revised *Flahooley* w William Friml) Curran Theater, San Francisco 11 August

1955 **Ankles Aweigh** (Dan Shapiro/Guy Bolton, Eddie Davis) Mark Hellinger Theater 18 April

1960 **Christine** (Paul Francis Webster/Pearl Buck, Charles Peck) 46th Street Theater 28 April

1961 **Calamity Jane** (Webster ad Charles K Freeman/James O'Hanlon) Municipal Opera, St Louis 12 June

1962 **Around the World in 80 Days** (w Victor Young/Harold Adamson/Sig Herzig) Municipal Opera, St Louis 11 June

1964 **Something More!** (Marilyn Bergman, Alan Bergman/Nate Monaster) Eugene O'Neill Theater 10 November

FAIRBROTHER, Sydney [PARSELLE, Emilie Sidney] (aka Emilie EBSWORTH) (b London, 31 July 1873; d London, 10 January 1941). Prominent character actress in British straight and musical theatre.

Daughter of John Parselle, actor and sometime stage manager at the Strand Theatre, a granddaughter of the famous comic singer Sam Cowell, and a member of a many-tentacled and -talented theatre family, Miss Fairbrother played in the straight theatre for the first 25 years of her career before creating a series of musical-comedy character roles for Seymour Hicks between 1905 and 1907. She scored a personal success in her first musical show, playing Evelyn Snipe and singing "The Nice Young Man (who whistled down the lane)" in *The Talk of the Town* (1905) and followed up memorably as the smitten landlady, Mrs Goodge, in *The Beauty of Bath* and as the roustabout, Charlotte Siddons, in *The Gay Gordons.* She then returned to comedy and to the music halls, playing a scena with Fred Emney, but came back to the musical theatre in 1916 when she was cast as Ali Baba's shrewish wife, Mahbubah, in *Chu Chin Chow,* a part which she created, played for the three and a half years of the show's record-breaking run at His Majesty's Theatre and made her own.

She subsequently made further musical appearances as another shrewish wife, opposite Jack Buchanan in *Battling Butler* (1922, Mrs Butler), briefly in the disastrous *All for Joy* (1932, Countess of Axminster) and the touring *Let's Pretend* (1934, Mrs Ford), then as the busybody Adela Teetle in *Nice Goings On* (1934) and as Mrs Flower in *Lucky Break* (1935), both alongside Leslie Henson, and as Miss Schnapps in the Alhambra spectacle *Tulip Time* (1935). Although her musical theatre appearances were comparatively few in an extremely busy stage and film career of 50 years, her characterful performances of often harshly spinsterish ladies were highly praised and prized. Her portrayal of Mahbubah was captured on film in the 1934 movie version of *Chu Chin Chow.*

Autobiography: *Through an Old Stage Door* (Müller, London, 1939)

FALKA *see* LE DROIT D'AÎNESSE

FALL, Leo[pold] (b Olmütz, 2 February 1873; d Vienna, 16 September 1925). Arguably the most distinguished and, in any case, one of the most successful composers of the 20th-century Viennese Operette stage.

Leo Fall was born in what was, at that stage, part of the Austro-Hungarian Empire, the son of musician and military bandmaster **Moritz FALL** (1840–1922), himself the composer of several Operetten (*Prinz Bummler, Mirolan, Robin Hood,* the 1-act *Das Modell* mounted by the Berlin Theater Unter den Linden in 1892, *Leuchtkäfer,* produced at Magdeburg's Wilhelm-Theater in 1899) and theatre music for numerous Possen and other musical plays (*Berliner Raubthiere* 1895, *Berliner Spezialitaten* Theater des Westens 1898, etc).

A fresh posting for his father meant that the boy was brought up in Lemberg and there, from an early age, he was given a sound musical education, one which prepared him, by the age of 14, to complete his studies at the Vienna Conservatoire. His first professional work was as a violinist in a military orchestra, but he soon returned home to work with his father, who was now retired and running a coffee-house orchestra in Berlin, and doing a little of the composing his earlier duties had limited. Fall supplemented this work by giving music lessons, as he had during his Vienna student days, until at the age of 21 he won his first theatre job as a junior conductor at Berlin's Centraltheater. He quickly rose to improved positions at the Belle-Alliance-Theater and at Hamburg's Centralhallen-Theater where, at the age of 23, he was engaged as principal conductor. At Hamburg, he composed his first original music for the stage in the form of incidental music and songs for the Lokalposse *Lustige Blätter,* and the musical accompaniment to a Zeitbild by the prolific playwright and librettist Georg Okonkowski.

After two seasons in Hamburg he returned to Berlin, where he held successive conducting posts at the Centraltheater and the Metropoltheater before taking what seems to have been a decided step downwards to become musical director in a cabaret, the Intimes-Theater. There, alongside his principal duties, he provided songs and, on one occasion, a comic opera, *Paroli,* for house production. The piece was successful enough to warrant publication, with its soprano "Nachtigallenlied" and the tenor "Soldatenlied" picked out as singles. During this period, Fall worked on writing a grand opera, but his ambitions in operatic directions were kneecapped when the resultant *Irrlicht,* written with the librettist of *Paroli* and produced at Mannheim in 1905, turned out to be a failure.

Fall had, however, started working in a different direction even prior to *Irrlicht*'s stage premiere, and, shortly afterwards, he succeeded in placing his first Operette with no less a house than the Theater an der Wien. *Der Rebell* (1905) gave him his second resounding failure within a year. His first operettic success was, however, not too long in coming. *Der fidele Bauer,* produced less than two years later at Mannheim, was an enormous success and just a few months after its premiere—and before it had yet made its appearance in Vienna—his next piece, *Die Dollarprinzessin,* was produced at the Theater an der Wien. It roundly confirmed Fall's new reputation as one of the rising stars of the European Operette, alongside Lehár, currently basking in the incomparable success of *Die lustige Witwe,* Oscar Straus, who had arrived hot on his heels with *Ein Walzertraum,* and *Bruder Straubinger*'s Edmund Eysler.

On the wings of the post–*lustige Witwe* craze for Viennese Operette, *Die Dollarprinzessin* was soon on its way to splendid successes in Britain and in America and Fall was quickly established as an international favorite. That favoritism was vastly increased by his next work, *Die geschiedene Frau.* A splendid success at the Vienna Carltheater, this lively, tuneful "French" musical comedy also traveled the world in various tongues (*La Divorcée, The Girl in the Train, Az elvált asszony,* etc) and it repeated its German and Austrian success almost wherever it went.

Of his following Operetten, *Das Puppenmädel* and *Die schöne Risette* had fine successes in Vienna and central Europe without winning comparable fame overseas, and *Die Sirene,* produced in America as *The Siren,* and the one-act *Brüderlein fein,* which was played on the music halls in Britain and elsewhere, only confirmed the esteem in which their composer was held, but the next piece to win him a major international success was nothing more than a rewrite of the originally ill-fated *Der Rebell.* Its rearranged score was matched up with a fresh libretto and fresh lyrics, and the new show staged under the title *Der liebe Augustin.* One of those relyricked songs, the waltz ''Und der Himmel hängt voller Geigen,'' proved to be one of the most popular amongst all Fall's Operette melodies, and the show itself (played in Britain, notably, with great success as *Princess Caprice*) perhaps his most delightfully melodious and lighthearted to date.

Fall's popularity in Britain was such that he was commissioned to write an original piece for the well-paying London Hippodrome, but his activity on the home front was too great to leave him time, and the little *The Eternal Waltz* was put together from his leftovers. It was to be the last Fall musical to be seen in Britain for some time, as the coming of the war brought down the shutters on Germanic shows on the London stage, and writers such as Fall and Jean Gilbert, for whom London had been a superb showplace for the international market, found themselves at the end of a very lucrative half-dozen years as the darlings of the world's musical theatre.

If Fall's outlets, thus, shrank, his output did not and, between 1913 and 1916, he wrote and saw staged in Berlin and Vienna a half-dozen further full-scale Operetten which, if they had, owing to circumstances, lesser international careers than the prewar works, nevertheless included two of his musically most outstanding shows—the brilliant *Die Kaiserin* (*Fürstenliebe*), which he claimed later as his own favorite amongst his works, and the swirlingly romantic and extremely long-running *Die Rose von Stambul* with its ultimate star tenor role and its ringing star tenor music.

After the First World War, he had two works produced at Dresden, one of which, *Der goldene Vogel,* he described as an opera, and he continued a regular more than one-per-year supply of splendid scores to the Berlin theatre. Both *Die spanische Nachtigall* and *Die Strassensängerin* (with its third-act jazz band) played some 140 performances in Berlin, but none of this series of shows won the same enormous success as *Die Rose von Stambul* had done until his 1922 offering, a deliciously comical piece written around the fictional amours of *Madame Pompadour,* was produced at the Berliner Theater. *Madame Pompadour* brought him once again not only European attention, but the kind of international response he had first won 15 years earlier. London welcomed the composer back with rabid enthusiasm and *Madame Pompadour* went round the world, engraving herself into the permanent repertoire at home and into international popularity for many years.

Regarded by many as Fall's most complete work, it is a piece which is as far from the deliciously frisky, up-to-date *Die Dollarprinzessin* or the winningly rural *Der fidele Bauer* as Lehár's *Das Land des Lächelns* is from his early *Die lustige Witwe.* Unlike the later Lehár works, however, the pieces of Fall's maturer period—and most specifically the two most enduring shows of that period, *Die Rose von Stambul* and *Madame Pompadour*—contain a substantial and genuine comic element in both their music and text. Happily placed alongside their richly romantic musical part, in classic proportions, this contrasting element helps give these shows a very different feeling and flavor to the willfully darkened tones of the pieces with which Lehár would, a few years later, take the Operette into more pretentious areas.

What Fall, some of whose own best work had been tempered by writing for a singular star in the person of prima donna Fritzi Massary, would have made of the Tauberesque fashion in musical theatre in the late 1920s and early 1930s would, on the evidence of *Die Rose von Stambul* alone, have been worth hearing, but the composer did not live that long. After just one more stage work, *Der süsse Kavalier,* produced in Vienna in 1923, he fell ill, and in 1925 he died of cancer at the age of 52. A posthumous *Jugend im Mai* was produced in Dresden the following year and in 1929 the Theater an der Wien, which had staged Fall's first Operette, staged his last—a compilation made from 16 pieces of music which the composer had left behind him, attached to a libretto by the experienced Willner and Reichert and played as *Rosen aus Florida.*

The years since his death have not treated Fall as kindly as they should have. *Madame Pompadour* and *Die Rose von Stambul* have held a place in the standard repertoire in Germany and Austria, but scarcely with the kind of prominence allotted to other, contemporary composers' works, and whilst *Die Dollarprinzessin, Der liebe Augustin* and *Der fidele Bauer* loiter on the fringe of that repertoire, *Die geschiedene Frau,* such an enormous hit in the wars prior to the Great War, and *Die Kaiserin* seem wholly forgotten. Perhaps through lack of an interested party to plug his works to producers of the second half of the 20th century in the style which has so profited other writers, the man who was, in the opinion of many, the most outstanding Operette composer of his period has ended up deeply in the shadow of Lehár, Straus and Kálmán, and unknown to the modern public at large.

1896 **Lustige Blätter** (Franz Fuchs) Centralhallen-Theater, Hamburg 25 July

1897 **1842 (Der grosse Brand in Hamburg)** (Georg Okonkowski) Centralhallen-Theater, Hamburg 1 August

1899 **Der Brandstifter** (Okonkowski) Ostendtheather, Berlin 1 January

1900 **Die Jagd nach dem Glück** (Carl Weiss) Carl Weiss Theater, Berlin 30 January

1901 **'ne feine Nummer** (w Victor Holländer/Julius Freund) Metropoltheater, Berlin 26 December

1902 **Paroli** (*Frau Denise*) (Ludwig Fernand) 1 act Intimes-Theater 4 October

1905 **Der Rebell** (Rudolf Bernauer, Ernst Welisch) Theater an der Wien 29 November

1906 **Der Fuss** (Bernauer) 1 act Centraltheater, Chemnitz 18 September

1907 **Der fidele Bauer** (Victor Léon) Hoftheater, Mannheim 27 July

1907 **Die Dollarprinzessin** (A M Willner, Fritz Grünbaum) Theater an der Wien 2 November

1908 **Die geschiedene Frau** (Léon) Carltheater 23 December

1908 **Brüderlein fein** (H E Falschholz) Bernhard-Rose-Theater, Berlin 31 December

1909 **Die Schrei nach der Ohrfeige**

1909 **Brüderlein fein** (Julius Wilhelm) 1 act Hölle 1 December

1910 **Das Puppenmädel** (Willner, Leo Stein) Carltheater 4 November

1910 **Die schöne Risette** (Willner, Robert Bodanzky) Theater an der Wien 19 November

1911 **Die Sirene** (Willner, Stein) Johann Strauss-Theater 5 January

1911 **The Eternal Waltz** (Austen Hurgon) 1 act London Hippodrome 22 December

1912 **Der liebe Augustin** revised *Der Rebell* Neues Theater, Berlin 3 February

1913 **Die Studentengräfin** (Léon) Theater am Nollendorfplatz, Berlin 18 January

1913 **Der Nachtschnellzug** (Léon, Stein) Johann Strauss-Theater 20 December

1914 **Jung England** (Bernauer, Welisch) Montis Operetten-Theater, Berlin 14 February

1915 **Der künstliche Mensch** (Willner, Rudolf Österreicher) Theater des Westens, Berlin 2 October

1915 **Die Kaiserin** (aka *Fürstenliebe*) (Julius Brammer, Alfred Grünwald) Metropoltheater, Berlin 16 October

1916 **Tantalus im Dachstuberl** 1 act Stadttheater, Würzburg 26 March

1916 **Seemansliebchen** (w Franz Ferdinand Warnke/Karl Hermann, Max Berger) Walhalla-Theater, Berlin 4 September

1916 **Die Rose von Stambul** (Brammer, Grünwald) Theater an der Wien 2 December

1920 **Frau Ministerpräsident** revised *Jung England* Residenztheater, Dresden 3 February

1920 **Der goldene Vogel** (Wilhelm, Paul Frank) Staatsoper, Dresden 21 May

1920 **Die spanische Nachtigall** (Schanzer, Welisch) Berliner Theater, Berlin 18 November

1921 **Die Strassensängerin** (August Neidhart, Lo Portem) Metropoltheater, Berlin 24 September

1921 **Der heilige Ambrosius** (Willner, Arthur Rebner) 1 act Deutsches Künstlertheater, Berlin 3 November

1922 **Madame Pompadour** (Schanzer, Welisch) Berliner Theater, Berlin 9 September

1923 **Der süsse Kavalier** (Schanzer, Welisch) Apollotheater 11 December

1926 **Jugend im Mai** (Schanzer, Welisch) Zentraltheater, Dresden 22 October; Städtische Oper, Berlin 1927

1929 **Rosen aus Florida** (arr Erich Wolfgang Korngold/Willner, Heinz Reichert) Theater an der Wien 22 February

1935 **Der junge Herr René** revised *Der süsse Kavalier* (ad Michael Krasznay-Krausz/ad Welisch)

Fall's brother **Richard FALL** (b Senitsch, 3 April 1882; d Auschwitz, 1943) had a regular if unspectacular career in the wake of Leo's dazzling one. He worked as a conductor, notably at Vienna's Apollotheater, and was the composer of a number of Operetten and revues, principally for Viennese theatres, of which *Der Weltenbummler,* also staged in Budapest (as *Világjáro* ad Zsolt Harsányi) and in Germany; *Das Damenparadies,* given in Hungary as *Borbäla Kisasszony;* and *Die Puppenbaronessen* were the most successful.

1909 **Goldreifchen** (Paul Wertheimer, Mia Ewers) 1 act Johann Strauss-Theater 11 December

1911 **Das Damenparadies** (Julius Brammer, Alfred Grünwald) 1 act Wiener Colosseum 1 November

1912 **Der Wiener Fratz** (Ernst Klein) 1 act Hölle 1 January

1912 **Arms and the Girl** (Austen Hurgon) London Hippodrome 29 April

1913 **Leute vom Stand** (Robert Bodanzky, Fritz Grünbaum) 1 act Hölle 1 March

1915 **Der Weltenbummler** (Fritz Löhner-Beda, Carl Lindau) Montis Operetten-Theater, Berlin 18 November

1917 **Die Dame von Welt** (Löhner-Beda, Hans Kottow) Apollotheater 31 January

1917 **Die Puppenbaronessen** (Alexander Engel, Grünbaum) Apollotheater 1 September

1920 **Grossstadtmärchen** (Bruno Hardt-Warden, Erwin Weill) Carltheater 10 January

1921 **Im Alpenhotel** (Julius Horst, Ernst Wengraf) 1 act Apollotheater 6 August

1922 **Der geizige Verschwender** (Richard Kessler, Arthur Rebner) Deutsches Künstlertheater 24 February

1927 **Die Glocken von Paris** (Paul Knepler, Ignaz M Welleminsky) Carltheater 14 October

Biography: Zimmerli, W: *Leo Fall* (Zürich, 1957)

LA FALOTE Opérette in 3 acts by Maurice Ordonneau and Armand Liorat. Music by Louis Varney. Théâtre des Folies-Dramatiques, Paris, 17 April 1896.

The libretto of *La Falote,* one of the most successful of Louis Varney's works of the 1890s, mixed a series of particularly saucy and amusing episodes with a touch of the (apparently) supernatural. The Baronne du Hoguette (Armande Cassive) masqueraded as an apparition known as "La Falote" to escape the discovery of her infidelities by her husband (Paul Hittemans) in a piece which was textually rather like a cross between *Les Cloches de Corneville* and *La Dame blanche,* but decidedly none the worse for that.

The naughty Baronne has the habit of meeting her boyfriend up amongst the gothic pillars of Mont-St-

Michel, and she encourages the legend of the blue-cloaked ghost known as La Falote to keep the inquisitive away from her trysting place. However, her husband has become fascinated by the spectre and has, indeed, begun a serious scientific research into this phenomenon. His discoveries will, he is convinced, secure his fame. When, after many farcical incidents, he finally realizes the truth, he prefers to let his wife have her fling with the pretty Captain Mirasol (Baron fils) rather than compromise the scientific standing his work has won him.

The young Jean Périer starred as the youthful fisherman Pierre, and made a hit with the show's most attractive number, the Chanson Bretonne, with Suzanne Elven as his country Thérèse, deeply involved, like him, in the multiple comical convolutions in the tale. Jane Evans (Mme Pigeon) was the heavy lady—Thérèse's aunt—who tries to alienate Pierre from her niece by pretending that ''La Falote'' wants him for a bridegroom, and Mlle Dulaurens played the little maid who stirs up the plot by revealing the truth to the Baron.

The piece ran for a superb 190 performances in its initial run at the Folies-Dramatiques. It was similarly well received in Budapest (ad Emil Makai, Béla J Fái, as ''the blue girl'') with Klára Küry starring, but an American production (ad J Cheever Goodwin) mounted by J C Duff with a cast headed by Julius Steger, W J Le Moyne, Guy Standing, Yvonne de Tréville, May Norton and Georgia Powers was a quick Broadway failure (16 performances) in a period where the fashion for French opérette had largely passed from the American stage.

USA: Casino Theater 1 March 1897; Hungary: Népszínház *A kék asszony* 3 April 1897

FALSETTOS *see* MARCH OF THE FALSETTOS

FAME Musical in 2 acts by Jose Fernandez. Lyrics by Jacques Levy. Music by Steve Margoshes. Coconut Grove Playhouse, 21 October 1988.

A musical based on the 1980 Alan Parker film set in a high school for performing arts, and on the hugely popular television series, starring Debbie Allen, taken therefrom, the stage *Fame* did not sport the film version's Michael Gore score (''Red Light,'' ''I Sing the Body electric''), with its number-one hit title song (Academy Award), but a fresh set of numbers to set to a libretto which did not utilize the widely familiar characters of the television series, but simply the situation and the idea behind it.

In *A Chorus Line* fashion—if without that show's delicacy—it used the young trainee performers (''a barely post-pubescent ensemble of showbiz stereotypes'') of its slim story line in a series of character songs, wannabe songs and dance routines in the modern mode and at the modern level of volume, until, again like its famous predecessor, the big moment arrives and success (graduation, in this case) or failure is decreed for each character.

Originally produced at Miami's Coconut Grove Playhouse without attracting much positive attention, *Fame* went on to be seen in Philadelphia, but progressed no further until it was mounted with considerable success in Stockholm (China Teatr 22 January 1993). Karl Dyall (Tyrone), Petra Nielsen (Carmen) and Blossom Tainton (Mabel) were amongst the cast. The piece was subsequently produced in London with Scandanavian choreographer Lars Bethke repeating his task. Sonia Swaby in the role of foodie Mabel, alarmed at the thought of growing up the world's fattest dancer, delivered a devastating ''Think of Meryl Streep'' (Mabel's Prayer) and, in spite of tutting notices and incredulous word-of-mouth, the show ran for 18 months in the West End, and toured lengthily, making two returns to London for festive seasons (Prince of Wales Theatre 15 October 1998). Subsequently, whilst intelligently avoiding Broadway, this unambitious entertainment has gone on to touring productions in Europe, Canada, South America, Australia and America.

UK: Cambridge Theatre 27 June 1995; Germany: Schiller Theater Berlin 1 March 1997; France: Folies-Bergère 1998; Australia: Star City Casino, Sydney 29 July 1999

Recordings: London cast (Polydor), European tour cast (Polydor), US tour cast (DRG), Hispanic cast (*Fama*) (Polygram), Swedish cast (Polydor), Venezuelan cast (Rodven)

LA FAMILLE TROUILLAT Opérette in 3 acts by Hector Crémieux and Ernest Blum. Music by Léon Vasseur. Théâtre de la Renaissance, Paris, 10 September 1874.

Léon Vasseur, struggling to follow up the enormous success of *La Timbale d'argent,* had little luck with *La Famille Trouillat,* a sprightly period piece produced with a certain amount of pre-publicity and some weighty resources. In spite of a cast headed by the splendid Vauthier, and with the novelty casting of the actor Paulin Ménier and the bulky, salacious café-concert star Thérésa, it was a failure, yet it was subsequently played both in Vienna and London. Vienna's production starred Gallmeyer and Schweighofer. The English version, ''assembled'' by Alfred Maltby and Richard Mansell, added music by Grevé and others to Vasseur's score, but in spite of an equally top-flight cast (Frank Celli, Harry Paulton, Furneaux Cook, Kate Munroe, Mme Amadi, Maria Davis), what they called *La Belle Normande* ran just six weeks.

The ''family'' of Crémieux and Blum's lively, saucy story was the Norman peasant family of little Pervenche Trouillat (Mlle Noémie). Headed by sister Mariotte (Thérésa) and her husband (Ménier) they all descend rageously on Paris to winkle out the culpable fellow who had his wicked way with their Pervenche during a storm at Honfleur. Their search is complicated by a comical chap called Bobinet (Vauthier) who tries to set the one thousand–volt Mariotte onto his landlord, Cactus, but it eventuates that the "culprit" in the affair was not the elder Cactus but rather his attractive nephew, Anatole. And that naughty little Pervenche had cried "rape" only to trick her family into helping her trace her lost beloved.

The musical part of the evening gave Vauthier his share of melodies, and one song to the ingenue, but the centerpiece of the score was the group of four numbers written to feature the evening's main attraction, Thérésa, a group topped by her Norman-patriotic number explaining "C'est les Normands, m'a dit ma mère, c'est les Normands qu'ont conquis l'Angleterre."

Austria: Strampfertheater *Die Familie Trouillat* 29 January 1875; UK: Globe Theatre *La Belle Normande* 26 January 1881

FANFAN LA TULIPE Opérette in 3 acts by Paul Ferrier and Jules Prével. Music by Louis Varney. Théâtre des Folies-Dramatiques, Paris, 21 October 1882.

The character of the womanizing soldier *Fanfan la Tulipe,* familiar on stage and in song since his first appearance as the hero of an 1819 popular song, was woven into an operettic intrigue by the librettists of Varney's earliest hit *Les Mousquetaires au couvent* (1880). Their book—to which Prével, as usual, was known to have contributed a "very slight share"—was made up of a good deal of amorous goings-on during which our hero is followed to his camp by no less than three adoring females each in soldierly disguise. When the timid soldier Michel (Simon-Max) believes Fanfan (Max Bouvet) has been tampering with his Pimprenelle (Juliette Simon-Girard) he challenges him to a duel, and the two men are arrested. But our hero escapes, and using the *David Garrick* technique of behaving appallingly to the girl so that she will go back to her real lover, rids himself of all these women and heads off to win a war or two. The final tableau of the evening—including "nearly two hundred people, a military band and six horses (real live horses)"—represented the French victory over the English at Fontenoy and the review of the victorious troops by the Maréchale de Saxe.

Varney used the familiar old "Fanfan la Tulipe" refrain, which Émile Debraux had originally culled from street minstrelsy, as the main motif of his attractive and eminently theatrical score and the piece won sufficient public approval to run for one hundred performances in its initial season, before heading on to Brussels where with Marchetti, Gardin and Jeanne Andrée featured it scored once again. It also gave rise to an interesting and unprecedented lawsuit when the stage director, Haymé, sued to have his name added to the authors' credits, claiming he had largely rewritten the piece in rehearsal. A shocked court non-suited him, aghast at the preposterous idea that a mere functionary like a metteur-en-scène should, by right, have a continuing interest in an author's work.

It was revived at the Château d'Eau in 1889, in a spectacularized version which altered the action from the days of Louis XV to the time of the first republic and featured its hero as a member of Pichegru's hussars at the capture of the icebound Dutch fleet. Lamy, Badiali, Minne, Mlles Chassaing and Balanqué featured, but not as strongly as a troupe of cossack horesemen who executed a downstage charge to within inches of the footlights. The show was brought back again at the Gaîté-Lyrique in 1904 (14 September) with Mme Simon-Girard in her original role and Lucien Noël as Fanfan. In 1911 it was seen briefly in New York played by an Italian operetta company in Italian.

In 1892 the Grand Théâtre at Bordeaux mounted another *Fanfan la Tulipe* (Charles Haring/Ernest Laroche) whilst yet another opérette under the same title (Jacques Debronckart/René Wheeler, Henri Jeanson), this one based on the successful 1952 film screenplay on which its authors had collaborated, was produced at the Opéra de Nantes (24 December) in 1979. A German-language *Fanfan la Tulipe* (Thomas Bürkholz/Klaus Eidam) was produced at the Rathen Freilichtbühne in 1991 (11 May).

USA: Irving Place Theater (It) 19 June 1911

Recording: 1991 German musical (Monopol)

FANNY Musical in 2 acts by S N Behrman and Joshua Logan based on the plays of Marcel Pagnol. Music and lyrics by Harold Rome. Majestic Theater, New York, 4 November 1954.

The libretto of *Fanny* was a melted-down version of the famous trio of Marseillais plays of Marcel Pagnol (*Marius, Fanny, César*), which had already been memorably adapted into a trilogy of Alexander Korda films by their author in the early 1930s. Here the atmospheric, life-paced plays were compressed into a hurried three-into-one skeleton, the text scampering blandly through the tale of Marseillaise Fanny (Florence Henderson), who weds the kindly, ageing Panisse (Walter Slezak) when she is left alone and pregnant by Marius (William Tabbert), the son of the café owner César (Ezio Pinza), who has been unable to resist the call of the sea.

With *South Pacific* director Joshua Logan at its helm and two of that show's leading players (Pinza, Tabbert) in starring roles, *Fanny* was written and presented as a Rodgers-and-Hammerstein-style romantic musical, and, in spite of the fact that the adaptation and its brightly straightforward scoreful of songs wiped out virtually all of the character and depth of the original plays and films, the show as written proved a popular piece of Broadway entertainment, running for 888 performances in David Merrick and Logan's production at the Majestic Theater between 1954 and 1957.

Pinza, cast in the role forever connected with the great French actor Raimu, sang ''Love Is a Very Light Thing'' and ''Why Be Afraid to Dance?'' whilst Tabbert had his best moments in the show's title-song and ''Restless Heart,'' but, in the inevitable comparison with *South Pacific,* they were shallowly served. Whilst Lawrence Tibbett succeeded Pinza on Broadway, a London production was staged with vocalist Ian Wallace (César) and Kevin Scott (Marius) starring alongside the comic actor Robert Morley (Panisse), making an unprecedented appearance on the musical stage. It was poorly received, but was propped up for a run of 333 perfomances by the Theatre Royal, Drury Lane, which had no replacement offering to hand. A belated Australian production, mounted at the Marian Street Theatre in 1979, limited its life to Sydney. The show has been subsequently played outside New York, a recent revival—featuring George S Irving and Jose Ferrer—being played at the Paper Mill Playhouse, New Jersey, in 1990.

A film made subsequent to the appearance of the show on Broadway ignored the musical score and instead gave just a similarly simplified version of the original stories.

UK: Theatre Royal, Drury Lane 15 November 1956; Australia: Marian Street Theatre, Sydney 8 June 1979

Recording: original cast (RCA)

FANTANA Musical comedy in 3 acts by Robert B Smith and Sam S Shubert. Lyrics by Robert B Smith. Music by Raymond Hubbell. Garrick Theater, Chicago, 9 October 1904. Lyric Theater, New York, 14 January 1905.

Sam Shubert's production of *Fantana* with ''the Jefferson de Angelis Opera Company'' came to New York from a remarkable 14-week Chicago season and proved itself a fine and typical example of the cheerful and colorful comic opera fare that the most enjoyable American writers had been turning out over the previous decade. The libretto had its principal comedian (de Angelis) cast as valet to the father (Hubert Wilke) of the heroine (Adele Ritchie), who is sent sailing out in disguise from Monterey, Calif, into hot Japanese water as a decoy duck for a condemned politician. Some jaunty, if reminiscent, numbers included a solid dose of waltz rhythms and had ''geisha'' and ''Asia'' rhymed yet again—but, less predictably, also ''vile'' and ''canaille'' . . . from the lips of a comic opera Jap. There were a couple of topical pieces for de Angelis (''What Would Mrs Grundy Say?,'' ''That's Art''), and the song list also featured such predictable titles as ''A Truculent Governor, I'' for the Japanese potentate, ''Laughing Little Almond Eyes'' for the heroine's baritone (Frank Rushworth), ''The Girl at the Helm'' and ''A Lesson in Etiquette'' for Wilke and the music-hally ''My Word'' for English comedienne Katie Barry as a cockney maid very like the one she had played in Shubert's hit of a little earlier, *A Chinese Honeymoon.* There was also half a duet (''The Secret'') attached to the role of ''Elsie, a schoolmate of Fanny's'' played by the very young Julia Sanderson. There was, however, no music attached to the supporting role played by one Douglas Fairbanks.

Well made, and well run in before it was shown on the New York stage, where an up-to-date dance number (''Can-Can versus Cakewalk''), a bit more local color (''In My Riksha of Bamboo'') and the already popular ''Tammany'' (Gus Edwards/Vincent Bryan) were added to the score for good measure, *Fantana* had an excellent Broadway run of 322 performances, proving one of the most effective American-bred pieces of its time. A 1906 production announced for London's Waldorf Theatre did not eventuate, but following its Broadway run *Fantana* moved swiftly back to Chicago and the Garrick Theater at the top of the first of what were to be several good tours of America.

THE FANTASTICKS Musical in 2 acts by Tom Jones suggested by the play *Les Romanesques* by Edmond Rostand. Music by Harvey Schmidt. Sullivan Street Playhouse, New York, 3 May 1960.

A statistical phenomenon in the musical theatre, *The Fantasticks* has, at the time of writing, recently completed its 40th consecutive year at New York's 150-seater Sullivan Street Playhouse (16,000 performances to 18 December 1998).

The Fantasticks (the title comes from George Fleming's original English translation) is a reduction of Rostand's successful play, *Les Romanesques,* and it follows the growing up of the boy Matt (Kenneth Nelson) and the girl Luisa (Rita Gardener). Brought together by the plotting of their fond fathers (William Larsen, Hugh Thomas), who pretend to wish to keep them apart, they find that they have to be disabused of their romantic notions by the harsh realities of the world before they can finally and happily come together. Jerry Orbach appeared as El Gallo, compere and tempter in turn, who won the best musical moment of the gentle, winning score in the ruefully recalling song ''Try to Remember,'' which opens the show. The song became a hit-parade success for Gladys Knight and a longtime cabaret favorite, whilst the girl's youthful ''Much More'' and ''Soon It's Gonna Rain'' also proved take-out successes in their time.

A small-scale musical, making a virtue of being presented with simplicity on a bare stage with rudimentary properties and a cast of nine, it was originally presented in an even more compact, one-act, version by Mildred Dunnock's Summer Theater at Barnard College in 1959 with a cast including the 21-year-old Susan Watson. Expanded and reproduced in New York, under the management of Lore Noto, with a cast which included author Jones, performing under the nom de théâtre of Bruce in the role of henchman Henry, it proved, after a discreet beginning, to be wholly to the taste of the 1960s.

While the original production began its three-decade run in the tiny venue which it life-savingly never abandoned for a larger one and the possibility of larger grosses, overseas productions proliferated. Played in a Shaftesbury Avenue theatre in London, it found the fate of virtually all off-Broadway pieces there and folded in just 44 performances, but in Britain, as in many other countries, its reduced demands in casting and staging made it for some years a favorite with smaller provincial houses and groups. In 1990 it received a London summertime revival from the company at the Regent's Park Open Air Theatre, with Roy Hudd at the head of the cast.

An NBC television version, mounted in 1964 (18 October), whilst the stage show ran on, featured Susan Watson and John Davidson as the youngsters, Bert Lahr and Stanley Holloway as the fathers, and Ricardo Montalban as El Gallo. A 1995 film version with Joel Grey and Brad Sullivan as the warring parents remains unreleased.

Both by its sentiments and by its staging and style, *The Fantasticks* remains a very 1960s musical, but one which has successfully carried those 1960s feelings through the 1970s and the 1980s and out the other end with as much durability as, and with more gentle grace than, such a piece as *Hair.*

UK: Apollo Theatre 7 September 1961; Australia: Russell Street Theatre, Melbourne 30 October 1962; Austria: Neues Theater am Kärtnertor *Die Romanticks* 1 December 1965; Germany: Ulmer Theater *Die Romantiker* 30 December 1966; France: 1966–67 season; Hungary: Fővárosi Operettszínház *Fantasztikus!* 28 January 1972

Recordings: original cast (MGM), Mexican cast (Columbia), French cast (Polydor), Japanese cast (RCA), etc

Literature: Farber, D, Viagas, R: *The Amazing Story of the Fantasticks* (Citadel Press, New York, 1991)

Plate 119. **The Fantasticks**

FARADAY, Philip Michael (b Islington, London, 1 January 1875; d London, 6 February 1944). Composer turned producer who had some fine London success with Continental Operette productions.

After an adventurous life, which apparently involved periods as a rating expert, a musician, an auctioneer and a surveyor—as well as the production of a full-scale musical comedy *The Ogre and the Witch* (Myddelton Hall 21 December 1897, lib: Alec Rabone) produced by the amateur Parkhurst Dramatic Club with its young composer and his sister heavily featured—jeweler's son Philip Faraday came to thoroughly professional theatrical notice with the fine score for the very comic opera *Amasis* (''Little Princess, Look Up''), the surprise success of London's 1906 season and a piece which led to him and his witty partner, Frederick Fenn, being rather hastily hailed as a new Gilbert and Sullivan. The pair later wrote a curtain-raiser for the Savoy Theatre, but Faraday's only other substantial stage score, for an indifferent piece called *The Islander,* produced in 1910, did less well. In that same year, however, he entered management and he had a considerable success with his first venture, a collaboration with the American producer F C Whitney on the London version of Straus's *The Chocolate Soldier* (*Der tapfere Soldat*). The production ran five hundred performances at the Lyric Theatre, of which Faraday subsequently became the lessee, and was long and profitably toured thereafter.

An adaptation of *Die Fledermaus* produced as *Nightbirds* had only a fair run, but a third Continental musical, *The Girl in the Taxi* (*Die keusche Susanne*), gave Faraday a second long-running and interminably touring success. His subsequent productions of Oscar Straus's *Love and*

Laughter, Eysler's *The Laughing Husband* (*Der lachende Ehemann*), and Gilbert's *Mam'selle Tralala* (*Fräulein Tralala*) had indifferent runs before his importation of German-language musicals stopped in the face of wartime sentiments and an August 1914 bankruptcy. After the war he took the Duke of York's Theatre and again began producing, but in his remaining four years of unhighlighted activity the only musical piece which he included among his productions was the children's show, *Teddy Tail* (1920).

1906 **Amasis** (Frederick Fenn) New Theatre 9 August

1908 **A Welsh Sunset** (Fenn) 1 act Savoy Theatre 15 July

1910 **The Islander** (Major Frank Marshall) Apollo Theatre 23 April

FARAGÓ, Jenő (b Budapest, 6 April 1872; d Budapest, 28 March 1940).

At first a journalist on several Budapest papers, Faragó subsequently became a librettist and lyricist for, and a prolific translator of, operettas and musical comedies. Amongst his earliest efforts were Hungarian versions of Luard Selby's little Savoy Theatre curtain-raiser *Weather or No* and of Adolphe Ferron's indifferent *Das Krokodil,* but there were a good number of more significant pieces amongst the many which he adapted first for the Magyar Színház, then for the Népszínház and, after that theatre's eclipse, for a variety of other houses. His list included works from Britain (the Gaiety Theatre hit *The Circus Girl,* the record-breaking *A Chinese Honeymoon*), Vienna (Heuberger's *Der Opernball,* Fall's *Die Dollarprinzessin,* Eysler's *Bruder Straubinger*), Berlin (Paul Lincke's *Lysistrata,* Kollo's *Drei alte Schachteln*), Paris (Terrasse's *M de la Palisse*) and even a pair from New York in Harry Archer's well-traveled *Little Jessie James,* here known by the name of its hit song as *I Love You!,* and Gustave Luders's *The Sho-Gun.*

Although these translations made up a large part of his theatre work, Faragó also provided libretti and/or lyrics for a variegated number of original pieces, mostly with a musical content. His early works included Hungarian libretti made from French pieces ranging from musical farce to a Jules Verne spectacular, a successful operett on *Casanova* with his habitual partner, composer Izsó Barna, and another, *Katinka grofnő,* with Iván Hűvös, and his later works varied from the rising revue genre to the fashionable biographical musical (*Fanny Elssler, Chopin,* etc). However, in spite of his regular presence on the Budapest stage, few of his pieces were played outside Hungary. The exceptions were Komjáti's *A kóristalány,* produced in Vienna as *Lily vom Chor,* and Offenbach and Chopin pasticcio-biographies on *Dreimäderlhaus* lines which were exported both to Vienna and to Broadway.

1897 **Derül-Borul** (*Weather or No*) 1 act Hungarian version (Magyar Színház)

1898 **Háromláb kapitány** (Albert Kövessy) Budai Színkör 14 July

1899 **A krokodilus** (*Das Krokodil*) Hungarian version (Magyar Színház)

1899 **Az operabál** (*Der Opernball*) Hungarian version (Magyar Színház)

1899 **Vasúti baleset** (Lajos Donáth) Magyar Színház 31 May

1900 **A szerelem óvodája** (Károly Stephanides/w József Hevesi) Magyar Színház 7 June

1901 **Lotty ezredesei** (Rudyard Stone ad w Adolf Mérei) Magyar Színház 17 January

1901 **Budapest szépe** (Izsó Barna/w Géza Markus) Budai Színkőr 20 July

1901 **Czirkusz-élet** (*The Circus Girl*) Hungarian version (Népszínház)

1901 **Mézeshetek** (Barna/Ede Sas) Népszínház 13 April

1901 **Teréz kapitány** (*Le Capitaine Thérèse*) Hungarian version w Béla J Fái (Népszínház)

1902 **Kin-Fu,vagy egy kinai ember kalandjai** (Barna/w Markus) Népszínház 31 May

1902 **Casanova** (Barna) Népszínház 11 October

1903 **Trouville gyöngye** (*Die Dame aus Trouville*) Hungarian version (Magyar Színház)

1903 **Khinai mézeshetek** (*A Chinese Honeymoon*) Hungarian version (Népszínház)

1903 **Makrancos hölgyek** (*Lysistrata*) Hungarian version w Ferenc Molnár (Király Színház)

1903 **Hektor kisasszony** (*Die Karlsschülerin*) Hungarian version (Népszínház)

1903 **Vándorlegény** (*Bruder Straubinger*) Hungarian version (Népszínház)

1904 **Katinka grófnő** (Iván Hűvös) Népszínház 29 January

1904 **A hét Schlesinger** (w Matyás Feld) Városligeti Nyári Színház 23 June

1904 **Rézi** (Barna/Árpád Abonyi) Népszínház 16 September

1904 **A löcsei fehér asszony** (Barna) Népszínház 27 October

1905 **7777** (*Der Fremdenführer*) Hungarian version w Dezső Balint (Népszínház)

1906 **A Sogun** (*The Sho-Gun*) Hungarian version (Király Színház)

1906 **Mimi hercegnő** (*Messalinette / Die Ringstrassen-Prinzessin*) Hungarian version (Magyar Színház)

1907 **Az erényes nagykövet** (*Monsieur de la Palisse*) Hungarian version (Népszínház)

1908 **A dollárkirálynő** (*Die Dollarprinzessin*) Hungarian version (Király Színház)

1908 **Ezeregy éj** (*Tausend und eine Nacht*) Hungarian version (Népszínház-Vigopera)

1910 **Dudakisasszony** (*Miss Dudelsack*) Hungarian version (Városligeti Színkör)

1910 **Édes öregem** (*Brüderlein fein*) 1 act Hungarian version (Uránia Színház)

1911 **A lengyel menyecske** (*Polnische Wirtschaft*) Hungarian version (Városligeti Színkör)

1912 **A papa csatába megy** (Barna) Ferenczy kabaré 30 October

1913 **A csodavászon** (Barna) Népopera 12 December

1915 **Kávéházi Konrád** (Barna/Soma Guthi) Budai Színkör 30 July

1914 **Szervusz, Pest!** (Feld) Budapesti Színház 1 July

1918 **A kóristalány** (Károly Komjáti) Városi Színház 18 January

1918 **Pitypalaty kisasszony** (Béla Zerkovitz) Royal Orfeum 1 June

1918 **Páratlan menyecske** (Zerkovitz) Royal Orfeum 1 October

1918 **A kis szeleburdi** (*Die tolle Komtess*) Hungarian version (Városi Színház)

1918 **A táncos grófnő** (*Hanni geht tanzen*) Hungarian version (Budai Színkör)

1918 **A Marcsa katonája** (*Der Soldat der Marie*) Hungarian version (Városi Színház)

1919 **Százszorszép** (Zerkovitz) Városi Színház 28 November

1920 **Offenbach** (Offenbach arr Mihály Nádor) Király Színház 24 November

1920 **Három a vénlány** (*Drei alte Schachteln*) Hungarian version (Budapesti Színház)

1922 **Három a tánc** (Komjáti/w István Szomaházy) Király Színház 20 May

1923 **Fanny Elssler** (Nádor) Király Színház 20 September

1924 **I Love You!** (*Little Jessie James*) Hungarian version (Lujza Blaha Színház)

1925 **A császárnő aprodja** (Ákos Buttykay/Imre Harmath) Király Színház 24 March

1925 **A feleségem babája** (*Der Hampelmann*) Hungarian version (Lujza Blaha Színház)

1925 **A kis huncut** (*Die kleine Sünderin*) Hungarian version (Városi Színház)

1926 **Chopin** (István Bertha) Király Színház 4 December

1930 **A három muskétás** (*Die drei Musketiere*) Hungarian version (Városi Színház)

1932 **Régi orfeum** (Lajos Lajtai/w István Békeffy) Fővárosi Operettszínház 12 March

FARKAS, Ferenc (b Nagykanizsa, 15 December 1905).

The son of an army officer, Farkas studied music first in his home region, from 1927 in Budapest and then, from 1929 to 1931, in Rome where he counted Respighi amongst his teachers at the Academia di Santa Cecilia. His earliest compositions were orchestral pieces, one of which, a "Divertimento," was awarded the Ferenc Liszt Prize in 1933. His first venture into the dramatic world was as a composer and conductor of film scores for Sacha Films in Vienna and for Nordisk Films in Copenhagen and, in the theatre, with incidental music for the dramatic *És Pippa táncol, Timon of Athens* and *Madách—az ember tragédiájá.*

Farkas was for a number of years a teacher at the Budapest Zeneakadémia and in 1941 took up a post at the conservatoire in Kolozsvár where, two years later, he was appointed principal. He subsequently spent a period as chorus master at the Budapest Opera and returned to teaching at the Zeneakadémia, whilst producing occasional compositions including art songs, dance suites, and a comic opera, *Der Wunderschrank.*

His first attempt at a musical comedy, *Csinom Palkó,* originated on the radio in 1949, where it attracted sufficient interest to be revised for a stage production in 1951 with great success. It was subsequently played in Germany as *Heisse Herzen in Ungarn,* as well as in several Russian cities and it has survived to many revivals. Amongst a varied list of compositions, including ballets, religious music, piano, instrumental and orchestral music, songs and film scores, he wrote several other dramatic pieces for radio (*Zeng az erdő, Májusi fenyő, Vidróczki,* etc) and also for the theatre, of which *Vők iskolája* (played in German as *Der Paradies der Schwiegersöhne*) was the most successful.

1938 **Bethlehembe** (Béla Paulini) 1 act Fővárosi Operettszínház 21 May

1940 **Afülemüle** (Árpád Szabados) Nemzeti Színház 9 April

1942 **A bűvös szekrény** (*Der Wunderschrank*) (Gyula Kunszery) Magyar Királyi Operaház 22 April

1951 **Csinom Palkó** (András Dékány) Erkel Színház 22 February

1955 **Zeng az erdő** (Géza Baróti/Dékány) Miskolc 4 November

1958 **Vők iskolája** (Rezső Török, Ernő Innocent Vincze) Fővárosi Operettszínház 31 May

1964 **Vidróczki** (Innocent Vincze) Szeged 30 July

1970 **Piroschka** (H Hartung, K H Gutheim) Kaiserslautern 31 March

1971 **A Noszty fiu esete Tóth Marival** (Dezső Mészöly/Kálmán Mikszáth) Fővárosi Operettszínház 12 November

1991 **Egy úr Velencéből** (Sándor Márai) Magyar Királyi Operaház 4 July

FARKAS, Imre (b Debrecen, 1 May 1879; d Budapest, 25 March 1976).

Popular poet, novelist and composer, and sometime official of the Hungarian ministry of defence, Farkas supplied the text for Jenő Hubay's opera *Lavotta szerelme* (1906) and, later, for Buttykay's *Hamupipőke,* but he principally wrote and composed his works alone. He scored a long-lived success with his first piece, the musical student tale *Iglói diákok,* and an even better one with the musical comedy *Túl a nagy Kriválon* (1918), played for over 150 performances in two years at the Budai Színkör and at many other theatres thereafter. His *A királyne rózsája,* mounted at the Király Színház in 1926 also had an initial run of over one hundred nights and *Debrecenbe kéne menni!* (1920), *A kis kadett* (1921) and *A nótás kapitány* (1924) all won revivals following their original productions.

1905 **Jeannette** 1 act Népszínház 27 April

1907 **Iglói diákok** Kolozsvár 7 October; Budai Színkör 11 September 1909

1909 **Szentgalleni kaland** Kaposvár 23 October

1910 **Narancsvirág** Uránia Színház 24 November

1912 **Hamupipőke** (Ákos Buttykay/w Károly Bakonyi) Magyar Királyi Operaház 26 October

1918 **Túl a nagy Kriván on** Budai Színkör 23 July

1920 **Pünkösdi rózsa** (w István Brody) Revü Színház 3 January

1920 **Debrecenbe kéne menni!** (later *A cseregyerek*) Budai Színkör 6 August

1920 **Rózsika lelkem** Budai Színkör 11 August

1921 **A kis kadett** Budai Színkör 9 August

1924 **A nótás kapitány** Fővárosi Operettszínház 10 October

1925 **Májusi muzsika** (w Zsolt Harsányi) Renaissance Színház 2 May

1926 **A királyné rózsája** Király Színház 12 February

1927 **Repülj, fecském** Király Színház 5 March

1928 **A Gyurkovics fiúk** Városi Színház 7 April

1929 **Szupécsárdás** Városi Színház 28 February

1929 **Kaszárnya áristom** Andrássy-uti Színház 8 October

1930 **Poldi** Király Színház 13 September

1931 **Hajnali csók** Városi Színház 4 May

1932 **Nyitott áblak** (Károly Nóti) Fővárosi Operettszínház 6 February

1932 **Amit a lányok akarnak** Király Színház 22 December

FARKOA, Maurice (b Smyrna, 23 April 1863; d New York, 21 March 1916). Dark and slickly handsome light baritone, a "professional foreigner" and matinée idol even into the days of his plumpness.

Born in Smyrna of Franco-English parentage, Farkoa went to Britain in 1892 and made his first appearance in the London theatre as part of a duet act with Alfred Nilsson Fysher, interpolated into the flexible structure of *Morocco Bound* at the Shaftesbury Theatre (1893). He subsequently headed for the concert platform, but in 1895 he was engaged by George Edwardes for a solo spot as a bohemian artist in *An Artist's Model* (Carbonnet). He proved popular enough to be given a fresh number, the Laughing Song, with which he made a great hit and also several gramophone records, the first of which, made in 1896, would seem to be the first example of an "original cast recording."

Sporting a white[ned?] forelock in his dark hair, and a parade of exotic clothes and jewelry, Farkoa followed up in a series of romantic roles for George Edwardes: a French vicomte celebrating "Wine, Women and Song" in *The Circus Girl* (1896, Vicomte Gaston), as the jeune premier (Paul Blanchard, a French student) in *Topsy Turvy Hotel* (1899), paired with Edna May as the Baron de Trègue (called Sir John Binfield until the very un-English Farkoa was cast) in *Kitty Grey* (1902) with friend Fysher as Pontbichet, the romancing Monsieur de l'Orme, a written-to-measure role, in *Three Little Maids* (1903), as yet another Frenchman (with French versions of the hit songs "Sammy" and "Bedelia" and a major hit in "I Like You in Velvet") in *Lady Madcap* (1904, Comte St Hubert), as a womanizing Indian Rajah in *The Little Cherub* (1906, Rajah of Talcutta, "The Supper Girl") and as a romantic Chinaman in *See See* (1906, Yen).

By now over 40 and looking distinctly more corseted, but still apparently a Liberace-like matinée lady's delight, he visited America (where he had made a first venture in 1904 with *Three Little Maids*) in 1906 to appear for Joe Weber in Victor Herbert's *The Dream City* (Henri d'Absinthe) and as a burlesque Lohengrin in *The Magic Knight,* and then returned to Britain to take over the specially expanded role of the amorous Dutch bandmaster in *Miss Hook of Holland* (1907, van Vuyt). He followed up as a Niçois café owner in *My Mimosa Maid* (1908, Émile Gerard) and appeared in Lehár's *Mitislaw der moderne* (1909) at the Hippodrome but then retired to the stout safety of the concert stage. He emerged again to appear as Gábor Szabo in *The Nightbirds* (1911) and repeated that role on Broadway (*The Merry Countess*), where he also played a small role in George Grossmith's production of *Tonight's the Night* (1914, Pedro). He returned to appear alongside Fysher, now running the fashionable Chez Fysher night-clubs in Paris and in New York's 45th Street, in his cabaret mondaine and was playing in *Montmartre à Minuit* at the Winter Garden when he died suddenly.

His obituary described him as "a clever singer of chansonettes, the full artistic effect of which was perhaps marred to some tastes by a rather ogling and effeminate manner; a remark that also applies to his dapper and fixedly smiling musical comedy lovers—always with a Whistlerian white curl in his black hair."

FARNIE, H[enry] B[rougham] (b Burntisland, Fife, 8 April 1836; d Paris, 21 September 1889). Adapter, "borrower" and librettist who through some two decades authored, arranged, pasted together and directed an amazingly large number of major London musical successes.

Scots-born Farnie—allegedly (but unprovenly) a distant connection of Lord Brougham, and named in function of that—was educated at St Andrews University and destined for a career as a schoolmaster. However, he found his way first into journalism, as a sub-editor on the *Edinburgh Courant,* and then south from his home in Cupar to London, where he became the editor of a small journal put out by Cramer, the music publisher, called

The Orchestra. During the early days of his period of employment with Cramer he began writing lyrics and before long penned his first works for the theatre.

His first staged work was the one-act opera *The Sleeping Queen* (1864), with music by no less a composer than the aged Michael Balfe, and the young author continued in the best company when he followed up with *The Bride of Song* for Sir Julius Benedict. He was working on a piece with Vincent Wallace, the third of the trio of outstanding contemporary English romantic opera writers, at the time of the composer's death. He also translated Gounod's opera *La Reine de Saba* and his "sacred drama" *Tobias* for British production, but had his biggest early success away from the stage, with the words for Arditi's hugely popular song "The Stirrup Cup," one of the three hundred or so like pieces which he lyricked for the nation's drawing-room pianos during this period.

Farnie moved on to other journalistic jobs as editor of *The Paris Times* and then of his own short-lived magazine *Sock and Buskin,* whilst keeping warm his contacts with Cramer, who would prove as useful to him over the coming years as he to them. He also spent some time in 1868–69 in New York, and it was there that he had his introduction to the lightest part of the musical theatre when he supplied his first burlesques to the newly opened (and soon closed) theatre at Tammany Hall, to Horace Lingard at the Theatre Comique, and to Lydia Thompson's English burlesque company. The vast success of the Thompson company and their productions (even though the texts which gave the company the opportunity to shine were dutifully slammed by the press) launched him as an author of stage musical plays. He made his first move on to the British stage the following year, stepping in to replace Dion Boucicault as the translator of Hervé's *Le Petit Faust* for its London production of 1870, and thereafter he worked almost nonstop in the musical theatre for nearly 20 hit-filled years.

His first attempt at West End burlesque, a variant of the Jack Sheppard tale called *The Idle Prentice,* was produced at the Strand Theatre later in 1870 and became highly popular, whilst one of two entertainments written for Benjamin Webster's theatres for the 1870–71 Christmas season, the burlesque *Little Gil Blas,* was acclaimed by the press for "less puns and rhymes and more humour" than was usual, and within months of his first appearance on a West End playbill Farnie was established as a busy musical-theatre author. Another seasonal piece, a spectacular called *Superba* produced at the Alhambra was an exercise in skirting round the laws forbidding stage plays in music halls. It got on, but it was soon banned.

Farnie had his landmark success, adjoined to liberal praise for his adaptation and for his lively stage direction, with the English version of Offenbach's *Geneviève de Brabant* staged at the Philharmonic Theatre, Islington, in 1871. The Farnie remake of *Geneviève de Brabant* became the musical theatre super-hit of its era, and it established its (re)creator alongside Burnand, Byron and Gilbert at the very head of the town supply of burlesque and comic opera writers and directors.

He adapted several other opéras-bouffes for the British stage and, in spite of the concurrence of several other anglicizations of the work, had a further enormous success with his version of *La Fille de Madame Angot* as he spread his success through all areas of the musical theatre. He provided many of the burlesques with which Lydia Thompson and her team of "blondes" dazzled America and amused London (*Robinson Crusoe, Bluebeard, Oxygen, Piff-Paff, Stars and Garters,* etc) and, above all, he created and mounted a novel series of pasticcio pieces for the Swanborough family at the Strand Theatre, pieces which were neither burlesque nor comic opera, but a combination of plot and dialogue patched together from one or more French comedies and illustrated with songs and dances from the most popular music-hall and musical-theatre sources. Veritable musical comedies. *Nemesis* (based on Alfred *Duru's Les Deux Noces de M Boisjoli*) and *Loo and the Party Who Took Miss* (from Chivot and Duru's vaudeville *Le Carnaval d'un merle blanc* but replacing most of Lecocq's music with melodies by Serpette, Offenbach and Hervé) were long-running musical comedy successes which were brought back several times for repeat seasons. His *Eldorado* (1874), which was part of the same series, was a reasonably straight musical adaptation of the famous farce *La Cagnotte.*

Farnie's penchant for do-it-yourself French musicals got him a pasting in print from an angry Lecocq when he put his name to "a new Lecocq opéra-bouffe" called *The Black Prince,* fabricated from his usual mixture of French sources (mostly *Le Voyage en Chine* in this case) and, in any case, from music that was not all Lecocq's, but he continued cheerfully and mostly successfully to turn out these bric-a-brac entertainments and, at the same time, to consort with the best and most popular of musical-theatre musicians. He wrote the libretto for Offenbach's original British opéra-comique *Whittington,* worked with Alfred Cellier on an adaptation of Moncrieff's *Rochester* which in his hands became the story of *Nell Gwynne,* and he turned out English versions of the most recent hits of the Continental musical stage for Alexander Henderson. Planquette's *Les Cloches de Corneville,* in the English version made by Farnie and Robert Reece, caused a record-breaking sensation on British stages, and the pair's subsequent versions of Audran's *Olivette* and *La Mascotte* and Suppé's *Boccaccio* also went on to huge successes around the world.

In 1882 Farnie combined with Planquette on a comic opera, *Rip van Winkle.* This piece—one of its librettist's few apparently original texts—proved to be one of the most outstanding products of the English musical stage of its era. It went on to international success and remained in the repertoire of French musical houses for a century. This success encouraged him to continue such trans-Channel collaborations, and he followed up by presenting Planquette with his old *Nell Gwynne* libretto for a fresh score, and, in collaboration with the composer, he later metamorphosed two of Planquette's more than satisfactory but hardly major hit Parisian shows, *Surcouf* and *Les Voltigeurs de la 32ème,* into enormous English successes as *Paul Jones* and *The Old Guard.* He did the same good turn for Francis Chassaigne's unsuccessful *Le Droit d'aînesse,* anglicizing it into an international hit as *Falka,* and he also paired with Edmond Audran, whose *La Mascotte* he had put into English with such notable success, to write the comic opera *Indiana* for the London and New York stages.

Throughout, Farnie also worked widely as a stage director, staging—in the wake of *Geneviève de Brabant*—a number of his own pieces, and also such opéra-bouffe revivals as the overblown *Chilpéric* with which George Edwardes and his partners opened the new Empire Theatre in 1884.

Paul Jones, in 1889, turned out to be the last big hit for the theatrical cobbler who had managed to make himself one of the most successful authors and directors of burlesque, opéra-bouffe and opéra-comique (as tastes progressively changed) in the English-speaking world. Long a sufferer from diabetes, he died in 1889, leaving an outline for the new New York Casino Theater musical, *The Brazilian* (mus: Chassaigne) to be completed by other hands.

One newspaper summed up the snobbish attitude the press had long taken to the man whom F C Burnand (who had sued him for plagiarism) described irritatedly as "a burly swaggerer": "most probably his like will not be seen again . . . the best interests of the stage compel the admission that it can advantageously be spared." Praised for his early works, Farnie had soon been sneered at for his theatrical borrowings ("he went to the Parisian stage for his material and to others for his translations"), and then, when the papers postulated the dying decadence of burlesque, the highly typical Farnie had become their favorite target of scorn. When the critics—many of them adapters and stage writers themselves—got tired of the French opéra-bouffe they had originally welcomed so enthusiastically, Farnie got the blame for watering down the libretti which they hypocritically called "indecent" in the original French, but nevertheless hurried across the channel to witness. But, if Henry Farnie was personally disliked, critically loathed (and jealoused) and, indubitably, a journeyman as a writer, he nevertheless had a rarely fallible theatrical skill both in writing and staging musical plays, a "nose" which made him and so many of his works enormously popular with the world's English-speaking public for more than 20 years . . . which was much more of a career than any of his critics could claim. Or anyone else in the English-language musical theatre of the era.

1864 **The Bride of Song** (Julius Benedict) Hanover Square Rooms 23 May; Covent Garden Theatre 3 December

1864 **The Sleeping Queen** (Michael Balfe) 1 act Gallery of Illustration 1 September

1864 **Punchinello** (William Charles Levey) 1 act Her Majesty's Theatre 28 December

1869 **The Page's Revel, or A Summer Night's Bivouac** (pasticcio) Tammany, New York 4 January

1869 **Robinson Crusoe** (pasticcio) Tammany, New York 21 January

1869 **Pluto, or The Young Lady Who Charmed the Rocks** adaptation of Byron's *Orpheus and Eurydice* (pasticcio arr David Braham) Theatre Comique 1 February

1869 **The Forty Thieves, or Striking Oil in Family Jars** (pasticcio) Niblo's Garden, New York 1 February

1869 **Sin[d]bad, the Sailor or The Ungenial Genii and the Cabin Boy** (pasticcio) Niblo's Garden, New York 29 May

1869 **The Rose of Auvergne** (*La Rose de Saint-Flour*) English version (Gaiety Theatre)

1870 **Little Faust** (*Le Petit Faust*) English version (Lyceum)

1870 **The Idle Prentice, or High, Low, Jack and his Little Game** (pasticcio, arr Frank Musgrave) Strand Theatre 10 September

1870 **Little Gil Blas and How He Played the Spanish D(j)euce** (pasticcio arr Musgrave) Princess's Theatre 24 December

1870 **The Mistletoe Bough, or Lord Lovel, Lady Nancy and the Milk White Steed** (pasticcio arr Musgrave) Adelphi Theatre 26 December

1870 **Breaking the Spell** (*Le Violoneux*) English version (Lyceum)

1871 **Vesta** (pasticcio arr Musgrave) St James's Theatre 9 February

1871 **Les Deux Aveugles** English version (Gaiety Theatre)

1871 **Blue Beard, or The Mormon, the Maiden and the Little Militaire** (pasticcio) Wallack's Theater, New York 16 August

1871 **The Crimson Scarf** (*La Tartane*) English version (Alhambra Theatre)

1871 **Geneviève de Brabant** English version (Philharmonic Theatre)

1872 **Forty Winks** (*Une nuit blanche*) English version (Haymarket Theatre)

1872 **L'Oeil crevé, or The Merry Toxophilites** English version (Opera Comique)

1872 **Leo and Lotos** (various) Niblo's Gardens, New York 30 November

1873 **La Fille de Madame Angot** English "Gaiety" version (Gaiety Theatre)

1873 **The Bohemians** (*Le Roman comique*) Opera Comique 24 February

1873 **Fleur de Lys** (*La Cour du Roi Pétaud*) English version (Philharmonic Theatre)

1873 **Nemesis, or Not Wisely But Too Well** (pasticcio) Strand Theatre 17 April

1874 **Eldorado** (pasticcio arr Fitzgerald) Strand Theatre 19 February

1874 **Loo and the Party Who Took Miss** (pasticcio arr Fitzgerald) Strand Theatre 28 September

1874 **The Black Prince** (pasticcio) St James's Theatre 24 October

1874 **Whittington** (Jacques Offenbach) Alhambra Theatre 26 December

1875 **Intimidad, or The Lost Regalia** (pasticcio arr Henry Reed) Strand Theatre 8 April

1875 **Antarctica, or The Pole and the Traces** (pasticcio arr Reed) Strand Theatre 26 December

1876 **Piff-Paff, or The Magic Armoury** (*Le Grand Duc de Matapa*) (later *The Golden Butterfly*) English version w pasticcio score Criterion Theatre 31 January

1876 **Madame l'Archiduc** English version (Opera Comique)

1876 **Nell Gwynne** (Alfred Cellier) Prince's Theatre, Manchester 17 October

1876 **[The Very Latest Edition of] Robinson Crusoe** (pasticcio) Prince's Theatre, Manchester 9 October; Folly Theatre, London 11 November

1877 **Oxygen** (pasticcio arr Fitzgerald/w Robert Reece) Folly Theatre 31 March

1877 **Sea Nymphs** (*Les Ondines au champagne*) English version (Folly Theatre)

1877 **Up the River, or The Strict Kew-Tea** (Hervé) 1 act Folly Theatre 15 September

1877 **La Créole** English version w Reece (Folly Theatre)

1877 **Champagne, or A Question of Phiz** (pasticcio arr H Reed/w Reece) Strand 29 September

1877 **Shooting Stars** (*L'Oeil crevé*) new English version (Folly Theatre)

1877 **Wildfire** (pasticcio/w Reece) Alhambra Theatre 24 December

1878 **Les Cloches de Corneville** English version w Reece (Folly Theatre)

1878 **Madcap** (*La Chaste Susanne*) (pasticcio arr A J Levey/ w Reece) Royalty Theatre 7 February

1878 **My New Maid** (Lecocq) 1 act St George's Hall 22 June

1878 **Stars and Garters** (*L'Étoile*) (pasticcio ad w Reece) Folly Theatre 21 September

1879 **Madame Favart** English version (Strand Theatre)

1879 **Rothomago, or The Magic Watch** (Edward Solomon, Procida Bucalossi, Gaston Serpette, Georges Jacobi/ad) Alhambra Theatre 22 December

1880 **The Barber of Bath** (*Apothécaire et perruquier*) 1 act English version (Olympic Theatre)

1880 **Les Mousquetaires au couvent** English version (Globe Theatre)

1880 **Olivette** (*Les Noces d'Olivette*) English version (Strand Theatre)

1880 **La Fille du Tambour-Major** English version (Alhambra Theatre)

1881 **La Boulangère** (*La Boulangère a des écus*) English version (Globe Theatre)

1881 **La Mascotte** English version w Reece (Comedy Theatre)

1882 **Manola, or Blonde and Brunette** (*Le Jour et la nuit*) English version (Fifth Avenue Theater, New York)

1882 **Boccaccio** English version w Reece (Comedy Theatre)

1882 **Rip van Winkle** (Robert Planquette) Comedy Theatre 14 October

1882 **Frolique** 1 act (pasticcio/w Henry J Byron) Strand Theatre 18 November

1883 **La Vie** altered English version of *La Vie parisienne* (Avenue Theatre)

1883 **Falka** (*Le Droit d'aînesse*) English version (Comedy Theatre)

1884 **Nell Gwynne** (Planquette) Avenue Theatre 7 February

1884 **The Grand Mogol** English version (Comedy Theatre)

1884 **Chilpéric** new English version (Empire Theatre)

1885 **Kenilworth** (pasticcio arr Michael Connelley/w Reece) Avenue Theatre 19 December

1886 **Lurline** (pasticcio arr Connelley/w Reece) Avenue Theatre 24 April

1886 **The Commodore** revised English version of *La Créole* (Avenue Theatre)

1886 **Glamour** revised *Piff Paff* w Alfred Murray, mus: William M Hutchinson Theatre Royal, Edinburgh 30 August

1886 **Indiana** (Edmond Audran) Avenue Theatre 11 October

1886 **Robinson Crusoe** (John Crook/w Reece) Avenue Theatre 23 December

1887 **The Old Guard** revised English version of *Les Voltigeurs de la 32ème* (Avenue Theatre)

1889 **La Prima Donna** (Tito Mattei/w Murray) Avenue Theatre 16 October

1889 **Paul Jones** revised English version of *Surcouf* (Prince of Wales Theatre)

1893 **The Rehearsal** 1 act Koster & Bial's Music Hall, New York 13 February

FARREN, Nellie [FARREN, Ellen] (b ?Brighton, ?16 April 1848; d London, 28 April 1904). Celebrated soubrette and burlesque "boy," for a generation the most beloved actress on the British musical stage.

The daughter of actor Henry Farren (b c1828; d St Louis, 8 January 1860) and a member of a large theatrical family of some considerable celebrity, "Nellie" Farren was put on the stage by her father for the first time at Exeter at the age of 5 as the Genie of the Ring in *Aladdin* (12 December 1853). Bankrupted by his management of

Plate 120. **Nellie Farren** *and Fred Leslie: The most famous team of the British 19th-century musical stage, here dressed up to perform "Ma's Advice" in* Ruy Blas and the Blasé Roué.

Brighton's Theatre Royal, Henry walked out on his family soon after and disappeared to the other side of the Atlantic never to return. Nellie worked irregularly as child vocalist and actress, and she made her first appearance on the London stage, at 14, as the Fairy Queen in Morton Price and Catherine Lucette's Sadlers Wells pantomime of 1862, *The Rose of Blarney, or Dannymanoranyotherman,* before joining the company at the transpontine Victoria Theatre, playing small parts in the traditionally blood 'n' thunder dramas played there (Begum in *Nana Sahib, The Chimes, He's Not Dead Yet, Kiddle-a-wink* ["after she has learned to be a little less demonstrative she will be an acquisition]," *The Outcasts, Found at Sea, Eleanor's Victory,* creating Ninetta in Stirling Coyne's *The Woman in Red* with Mme Celeste, *Troubled Waters, The Colleen Bawn,* etc), in ballet (Girondello in *Volante*), farce (*T'was I*), extravaganza (*The Adventures of Cheek and Plant, or the Sauce of the Nile)* and pantomime (Hymen in *Giselle and the Phantom Night Dancers*), for 10 months under the management of Fred Frampton and Fred Fenton. She then moved on to Horace Wigan's Olympic Theatre, where she spent two years (November 1864–65) performing in every kind of entertainment from Shakespeare (Clown in *Twelfth Night,* etc) and modern drama (*The Hidden,* Sam Willoughby in *The Ticket of Leave Man, The Whiteboy, The Hidden Hand,* etc *)* to comedy (*My Wife's Bonnet, London Assurance*) and to the burlesques which were one of the specialities of the house. She played supporting boy's roles in *Cupid and Psyche* (1864, Bacchus) and in the first British production of Offenbach's *Barbe-bleue* (*Bluebeard Re-paired,* Robert, ie, Oscar) there before taking over the leading boys from the departing Patti Josephs and appearing in the title roles of the burlesques *Glaucus* and *Prince Camaralzaman,* as Zimple Zimon in *Princess Primrose* (1866), as Faust in *Dr Faust and the* — (1866–67), as Alectryon in Burnand's *Olympic Games* (1867) and as Paris to the *Belle Hélène* of Theresa Furtado (1868).

In mid-1868 she appeared at Henrietta Hodson's Queen's Theatre in the burlesque *Fowl Play* (Nancy Rouse), by which time she had established herself to such effect that when John Hollingshead gathered together his company for the opening of the new Gaiety Theatre in December 1868, he hired Nellie Farren to be his principal burlesque boy. The 20-year-old actress appeared on the first-night bill in the title role of W S Gilbert's burlesque *Robert the Devil* and in the play *On the Cards,* and thus set in motion a 20-year association with the Gaiety Theatre, with Hollingshead and his successor as manager, George Edwardes, which made her the most beloved performer of her time, and which ended only with her retirement from the stage. Although she toured in Britain and overseas, always under the aegis of the Gaiety, she otherwise appeared very rarely away from that theatre except when Hollingshead's company visited another house, or on the rare occasion when she was loaned out, as she was on one occasion to the Olympic to play the part of Giselle in Byron's burlesque of the ballet.

In the early years of the Gaiety the actress often appeared in more than one item on the two- or three-part bills but, if she sported skirts for the plays, when burlesque came on she became a boy: Christopher in *Columbus,* Henry Plantaganet in *Wat Tyler MP* and so on. With the coming of opéra-bouffe and Hollingshead's determination to make the Gaiety the main musical theatre of London, she found a little more variety in her musical roles, appearing as Régina in *La Princesse de Trébizonde,* Ganymede in *Ganymede and Galatea* (*Die schöne Galathee*), James Gilter in *The Great Metropolis* (ie, *MM Dunanan*) and as the comical Eglantine in *The Island of Bachelors* (*Les Cent Vierges*) as well as playing Lubin in Dibdin's *The Quaker* and Distaffina in *Bombastes*

Furioso as a contrast to a continuing run of burlesque boys (Mercury in *Thespis,* Ganem in *Ali Baba à la Mode,* Leporello in *Don Giovanni in Venice,* Lord Monteagle in *Guy Fawkes*) and the title role in the Gaiety's first original musical, *Aladdin II* (1870) in which she was paired, as so often at this time, with Johnnie Toole at the head of the bill.

In 1876, with Toole moving on to other areas, Hollingshead teamed Nellie with E W Royce, W H Denny and his wife Alice Burville, and Harriet Everard in a *Young Rip van Winkle,* but—abandoning both soprano and contralto vocalists—he finally settled for his star team on Farren, Royce, Edward Terry and Kate Vaughan. He introduced this foursome in H J Byron's burlesque of the opera *Maritana, Little Don Caesar de Bazan* (1876), with Nellie in the inevitable breeches in the title role. Both the burlesque and the new teaming proved an instant and huge success. The new Gaiety formula only increased the theatre's popularity and in the next 10 years Nellie and her partners triumphed in one burlesque after another—*The Bohemian G'yurl and the Unapproachable Pole* (1877, Thaddeus), *Our Babes in the* Wood (1877, as Polly with Toole returning in place of Terry as Tommy), *Little Doctor Faust* (1877, Faust, with her husband appearing as Old Faust), *Il Sonnambulo* (1878, Alessio), *Young Fra Diavolo* (1878, Fra Diavolo), *The Lady of Lyons Married and Settled* (1878, Pauline), *Pretty Esmeralda* (1879, Captain Phoebus), *Handsome Hernani* (1879, Hernani), *Robbing Roy* (1879, Francis Osbaldistone), *Gulliver* (1879, Gulliver), *Young Rip van Winkle* revival (1880), *Trovatore or Larks with a Libretto* (1880, Manrico), and latterly with sometime one, or more, of the team absent *The Corsican Brothers and Co Ltd* (1880, M de Château-Renard), the famous *The Forty Thieves* (1880, Ganem), *Whittington and His Cat* 1881, Dick Whittington), *Aladdin* (1881, Aladdin), *Little Robin Hood* (1882, Robert Fitzooth), *Valentine and Orson* (1882, Valentine), *Ariel* (1883, Ariel, wearing electric lights in her hair), *Bluebeard or the Hazard of the Dye* (1883, Baron Abomélique de Barbe Bleue), *Galatea or Pygmalion Re-versed* (1883, Galatea), *Camaralzaman* (1884, Camaralzaman), *Our Helen* (1884, Helen), *Called There and Back* (1884, Gilbert), *Very Little Hamlet* (1884, Hamlet), and *Mazeppa, or Bound to Win* (1885, Casimir).

During the same years there were many other opportunities beyond burlesque. Nellie's roles ranged from Sam Weller in *Bardell v Pickwick* to Judic's star role in the vaudeville-operette *Niniche,* and from the title role of the play *La Cigale* to Angelina in Lecocq's *Le Grand Casimir,* and even when a piece was less successful than it might have been, the nimble, peaked-faced little star was always adored by the public and barely criticized by the press unless it be, perhaps, for the scantiness of a costume.

With the end of Hollingshead's tenure and the coming of George Edwardes to the Gaiety, began the third era of Gaiety burlesque, the full-length "new burlesque." Once again the star team changed, and once again the constant element was Nellie Farren. For the first of the genuine series of new burlesques she appeared as *Little Jack Sheppard* (1885) to the Jonathan Wild of the newest Gaiety star, Fred Leslie, and, if anything, the combination proved the theatre's most outstanding and potent yet. Fred and Nellie immediately became the biggest thing in the London musical theatre, and they remained so through *Monte Cristo Jr* (1886, Edmond Dantès), *Frankenstein* (1887, Frankenstein) and *Ruy Blas and the Blasé Roué* (1889, Ruy Blas), playing long London seasons, and touring Britain, America and Australia with their pieces whilst Edwardes's second team held the fort at the Gaiety with further popular burlesques which, though hugely successful, could not ever have quite the same hold on the public's heart as the Farren/Leslie pieces.

Ruy Blas, however, turned out to be Nellie Farren's last appearance at the Gaiety. She had long suffered from an arthritic complaint which was not cured by the Australian air, as had been hoped. She opened the newest burlesque, *Cinder-Ellen Up Too Late,* in Melbourne, but when she got back to London, was unable to play there in the show that had been especially named for her.

In the 15 years of her retirement she made a brief and unfortunate essay into management at the Opera Comique but, in spite of repeated rumors, did not return to the stage.

Nellie Farren married **Robert SOUTAR** (b London, c1829; d London, 28 September 1908), a journalist turned actor (Marquis in *Hit and Miss,* etc), in 1867, during her time at the Olympic and he moved with her to the Gaiety Theatre at the house's inception. Although he at first still appeared on the stage, and also turned his hand regularly to authorship and to producing, it was as Hollingshead's stage director that Soutar long held an important place at the Gaiety and in the British theatre. He left the Gaiety in 1885, having already left Nellie some years earlier.

Their younger son **[Joseph] Farren Soutar** (b Greenwich, 17 February 1870; d Cookham, 23 January 1962) was a successful juvenile leading man on the musical stage; whilst Nellie's cousin, **William Farren** (b c1825; d Siena, 25 September 1908), also a highly successful actor, was the first to play the Jupiter of Offenbach's *Orphée aux enfers* in Britain (*Orpheus in the Haymarket,* Her Majesty's, 1865).

Biography: Hilton, G W: *Nellie Farren* (Sir Arthur Sullivan Society, London, 1997)

FARSANGI LAKODALOM Comic opera in 3 acts by Ernő Vajda. Music by Ede Poldini. Magyar Királyi Operaház, Budapest, 16 February 1924.

''Wedding at Carnival Time'' was the most significant lighter work of the Hungarian opera composer Poldini (b Pest, 13 June 1869; d Vevey, 28 June 1957) whose other credits included operatic versions of Hans Andersen's *The Princess and the Swineherd* (*Csavargó és királyleány*) and of Cinderella (*Hamupipőke*).

Country Peter and his wife (''a nemzetes nagyasszony'') are preparing for a big wedding feast, for today their daughter Zsuzsika is to wed Jonas Bükky. But Zsuzsika isn't awfully keen on the idea, and doesn't mind at all when a raging snowstorm stops the bridegroom and the guests from arriving. But other folk do arrive, begging shelter from the storm, among them a Countess (''a grófné''), the guardsman Zoltán, and the student Kálmán. Over the six days that the storm rages, the Countess and Zoltán begin a romance. Zsuzsika's worried mother also sees love blossoming between her daughter and Kálmán and she tries to get the other pair to break it up, but her efforts are in vain, and when the bridegroom's mother finally arrives to embarrasedly explain that her son got snowed-up with a young lady and doesn't now wish to marry Zsuzsika, there are gusts of relief breathed all round.

The piece was written to be sung through, with its juvenile lady being a mezzo-soprano, rather than the usual soprano, and the soprano music entrusted to the role of the mother. Kálmán was cast as a tenor, with the Countess and Zoltán singing in the baritone/mezzo range.

Farsangi lakodalom was a major success in Hungary, being acclaimed as the greatest local comic opera hit in decades, and it was subsequently played on German-speaking stages, in Göteburg, Oslo, and at London's then floundering Gaiety Theatre (ad M D Calvocoressi) where Henri M Taunay and William Foss's production of *Love Adrift* ran for 21 performances with a cast headed by Eva Sternroyd as Suzy and Eva van der Osten as the mother and with a young vocalist called Cavan O'Connor in a tiny role. It played its 50th Hungarian performance on 27 May 1926, its 75th on 20 September 1929, and was revived at Budapest's Erkel Színház in 1958.

Germany: Staatsoper, Dresden *Hochzeit im Fasching* 24 October 1925; Austria: Hofoper *Hochzeit im Fasching* 22 February 1926; UK: Gaiety Theatre *Love Adrift* 6 October 1926

Recording: complete (Hungaraton)

DIE FASCHINGSFEE Operette in 3 acts by A M Willner and Rudolf Österreicher. Music by Emmerich Kálmán. Johann Strauss-Theater, Vienna, 21 September 1917.

Kálmán's score for the operett *Zsuzsi kisasszony* (''little Miss Susi''), first heard at the Vígszínház in Budapest on 27 February 1915 attached to a libretto by Ferenc Martos and Miksa Bródy, went thereafter through a curious series of transformations which resulted in its turning up back in Budapest, four years and several versions later, as the accompaniment to another Operette entitled *A Farsang tündére* (''the carnival fairy''). After playing more than 50 performances in Budapest, *Zsuzsi kisasszony* was exported by Abe Erlanger, adapted by P G Wodehouse and Guy Bolton, peppered with some additional songs by the then ubiquitous Jerome Kern, and mounted as *Miss Springtime* (New Amsterdam Theater 25 September 1916) for a fine 230 performances' worth of Broadway success and a goodly American road life. For some reason, however, the show went no further. But the score, or much of it, did. The following year, Kálmán's *Die Faschingsfee* was produced in Vienna, and there, attached to a different story by Österreicher and Willner, was a goodly amount of the *Zsuzsi kisasszony* music.

When her car breaks down, the young, widowed, re-engaged Countess Alexandra Maria (Mizzi Günther) takes refuge in a Munich artists' café, and there she meets the painter Viktor Ronai (Karl Bachmann) who is celebrating having secured a 30,000-mark contract for a fresco. Viktor comes to duel-threats with the roving-handed Count Lothar Mereditt (Emil Guttmann) over this assumed chorus girl, without knowing that his rival is also his patron, and when all is done he finds that he has lost his commission. Alexandra secretly assures that the artist gets the money he would have made, and Viktor duly opens his new studio. But soon the truth comes out, and the proud and piqued Viktor burns the painting he had made of Alexandra as the ''carnival fairy'' rather than sell it at vast price to her future husband, the elderly Herzog Ottokar von Grevlingen (Max Ralf-Ostermann). Before the night is out, of course, von Grevlingen has seen that it will be wiser to let his bride-to-never-be follow her heart and her artist rather than her duty. Max Brod took the chief comic role of fellow-painter Andreas Lubitschek.

The favorite moments of the score included Alexandra's march song ''Was sonst verboten'' which had previously done duty as a duet, ''Légy az ici, pici párocskám'' in *Zsuzsi kisasszony,* Viktor's waltz-rhythmed ''Neulich sah ich eine'' (formerly ''Csillag száll az égen''), and the duo between Alexandra and the buffo Hubert (Oskar Sabo) ''Sonnenglut lag auf den Feldern'' which had been, first time round, the popular ''Jaj Zsuzsikám'' and whose lyric still made reference to a Susi. The original show's ''Suzter Nóta'' became a trio (''Falsch wär wie die Klapperschlänge''), ''Romeo és Julia'' was turned into a light-comedy duo for Hubert and the soubrette Lori (Mizzi Delorm) which instead made reference to ''Loreley, schöne Zaubermaid,'' and ''Előre hát az angyalát'' was remade as a march song for Viktor and Lubitschek (''Heut' flieg' ich aus'').

Erich Müller's production of *Die Faschingsfee* had a fine wartime run in Vienna but, although it was popular and published, both musically and textually, in its ''original'' Viennese form, somewhere along the line the show underwent major changes to its score. In the opening act, Alexandra's entrance song ''Wenn mir der zufall Champagner kredenzt,'' another relic of the Hungarian show, was dropped in favor of a new ''Punkt neun—da fuhr mein Kavalier,'' her duo with Hubert was replaced by one for Lori and Hubert, the big first-act duet with Viktor exchanged for another (''Seh'n sich zwei nur einmal'') and a comic trio added to make up an act in which only the opening, part of the finale and Ronai and Lubitschek's duo of the original score was retained. The second act suffered the same drastic rewriting, with Viktor getting a new waltz song, and a new duet (''Küss mich still''). ''Was sonst verboten,'' Hubert and Lori's little duo about the Loreley and bits of the finale were all that remained. It was, curiously, not even a case of getting rid of all the *Zsuzsi* music—most of what remained was from the old show—but it was seemingly the new-style *Faschingsfee* which made its way back to Hungary as *A Farsang tündére* (ad Andor Gábor). Needless to say, ''Was sonst verboten'' and its fellow melodies were recognized, but otherwise *A Farsang tündére* had come a long and wandering way from *Zsuzsi kisasszony.*

A 1931 film version featured Viktor de Kowa and Anny Ahlers.

Germany: Metropoltheater, Berlin 14 September 1918; Hungary: Király Színház *A farsang tündere* 3 October 1919

Film: 1931

Recording: complete (WDR/Laser Light)

FATINITZA Operette in 3 acts by F Zell and Richard Genée based on the libretto to *La Circassienne* by Eugène Scribe. Music by Franz von Suppé. Carltheater, Vienna, 5 January 1876.

Suppé had been writing theatre music ranging from songs for Singspiele, burlesque, farce and spectaculars to short and medium-sized Operetten for the various Viennese theatres in which he had been engaged for 25 years before he was encouraged, in the wake of Strauss's success with *Die Fledermaus,* to compose a full-length Operette of his own. He was supplied with a well-dosed comic-romantic libretto by Richard Genée (author of the libretto to *Die Fledermaus*) and ''F Zell'' (Camillo Walzel), a libretto which was adapted, like Strauss's success, from a French original, although one very different in tone: a Scribe script which had previously been set with an Auber score as *La Circassienne.*

The young lieutenant Wladimir Samoiloff (Antonie Link) has disguised himself as a girl to escape the vigilance of the fire-breathing General Kantschukoff (Wilhelm Knaack) and thus court his niece, Lydia (Hermine Meyerhoff) but, unluckily, Kantschukoff develops a passion for the disguised ''Fatinitza.'' Even more unluckily, Wladimir is dolled up in his disguise when the Turks invade the Russian camp, and they carry off both ''girls,'' Lydia and ''Fatinitza'' to the harem of Izzet Pascha (Josef Matras). The Russians, led by the marauding journalist Julian van Golz (Karl Blasel), are obliged to head for Isaktscha to get them back. The rescue accomplished, ''Fatinitza'' disappears by simply turning back into Wladimir, but Lydia is taken home by her uncle to be wed to an elderly Prince. Finally, the General agrees to cede his niece to Wladimir if the boy can produce the lusted-after Fatinitza. Nothing could be easier, and all ends happily. For the young lovers, anyway.

The role of Fatinitza/Wladimir provided a splendid semi-travesty role for a leading lady—in this case Antonie Link, who also fulfilled breeches duty in her time as Strauss's *Prinz Methusalem* and Suppé's subsequent *Boccaccio*—whilst top comedians Knaack, Blasel and Matras were given plenty of comical opportunities in their roles as General, journalist and Pasha, and the colorful Turkish settings of the second act contributed an additional visual attraction. The biggest attraction, however, was the splendid score which Suppé provided for the occasion. It produced two sizeable hits—the driving march ensemble ''Vörwarts mit frischem Mut,'' which became one of the most popular songs of its time (so popular, indeed, that the ear-bashed Commander-in-Chief at Königsberg banned his regimental bands from playing it!), and the Pascha's comical ''Ein bissel auffrischen''—but it also held many other delights, from Wladimir's longing ''Sie, die ich darf nie nennen'' with its infectious waltz refrain, and the two-soprano duo ''Mein Herz, es zagt'' to some lovely choruses and another particularly successful ensemble, the tinkling ''Silberglöckchen rufen helle.''

The immediate success of *Fatinitza* thoroughly rivaled that of *Die Fledermaus.* Thirty straight nights through the month of January were followed by a further eight in February, the 50th performance was passed on 20 July, the 60th on 28 August, and by the end of 1879 the Carltheater had played the show a remarkable 122 times, latterly with Regina Klein in the star role. The original production remained several seasons in the Carltheater repertoire, and the piece was reproduced there in 1892 with Anna von Bocskay and Knaack, in 1899 with Ludmilla Gaston starred and Louis Treumann as Izzet Pasha, in 1905, 1906, and in 1907 with Gabriele Mödl, Blasel and Richard Waldemar. In 1909 it was played at the Raimundtheater with Lotte Klein, Marthe Winternitz-Dorda and Gross in the leading roles, and in 1912 it got a further showing at the Johann Strauss-Theater, establishing itself through repeated performances as a classic of its kind.

Within months of its first appearance, the show had been put into production in Hungary, Czechoslovakia, the Netherlands, Sweden and in Germany, in each case with outstanding success and as a prelude to a number of revivals. Budapest's first production was mounted by Andor Gerőffy and the Fatinitza was his wife, playing alongside the Lydia of Etel Roth, but four years later the Népszínház mounted their version of the show (ad Jenő Rákosi, Lajos Evva) with Abonyiné (Wladimir), Elek Solymossy (Kantschukoff), Emilia Sziklai (Lydia) and János Kápolnai (Julian). It proved good for an initial 20 nights and a revival (29 November 1882).

In London, H S Leigh's English version was staged at the vast Alhambra Theatre with Jessie Greville, Adelaide Newton and Pattie Laverne all taking turns at the lead role in an undercast and under-successful three-month run, whilst in America, after an initial 1878 mounting in San Francisco (ad Percy Wilson) with Mathilde Cottrelly making her English-singing debut as Wladimir alongside another German, Max Freeman, Harry Gates (Julian) and Marie Prescott (Lydia), there were almost simultaneous English- and German-language versions produced in New York in 1879. Boston followed up swiftly with its version (ad Sylvester Baxter, J B Bradford) with Adelaide Phillips starred (2 June), and the show soon got up speed. In the next 12 months, no less than five different productions of *Fatinitza* visited Broadway, the two most substantial of which featured Cottrelly and the Boston Ideal Opera Company's Mme Phillips as their heroes. *Fatinitza* went on to become a standard item in the American Operette repertoire, repeated time and again in productions from one side of the country to the other, and one canny company even invented a musequel, *The Pasha,* fabricated by revamping Suppé's later success, *Die Afrikareise,* and changing the names of the characters to those of *Fatinitza.* The original show was seen in New York as late as 1904 (28 December, ad Harry B Smith) when Fritzi Scheff appeared in the central role of a Charles Dillingham revival.

A French version (ad Félix Coveliers) was produced at Brussels's Fantaisies-Parisiennes (28 December 1878) with enormous success, but when the Belgian manager Eugène Humbert arranged to bring his hit show to Paris's Théâtre des Nouveautés, trouble struck. Mme Scribe took out a court order to stop this unauthorized remake of her husband's piece being staged in Paris. Humbert, however, found a way round the problem. Since Scribe's text had itself been an adaptation, drawn from Louvet's novel *Faublas,* he simply ordered a new text drawn from *Faublas* to be written around Suppé's score. Mlle Preziosi (the Brussels Fatinitza), Jeanne Nadaud (Lydia, replacing Blanche Roosevelt, dropped in rehearsal because of her villainous French accent which meant another lawsuit), Ernest Vois (Moulinot, ie, Julian), Paul Ginet (Tschatchichef) and Pradeau (Makouli, a slave merchant) headed 60 spectacular and spectacularly successful performances of Alfred Delacour and Victor Wilder's recognizable but distinctly different *Fatinitza* at Brasseur's Théâtre des Nouveautés. Marguerite Ugalde took a turn three seasons later at the now-famous star role.

Australia saw its first *Fatinitza* in 1881, with Eva Davenport starred alongside Miss E A Lambert (Lydia), C H Templeton (Kantschukoff) and Howard Vernon (Julian), and Belgium, Italy, Switzerland, Argentina, Poland and Mexico all staged versions of *Fatinitza,* which was even translated into and staged in Croatian and Estonian.

In spite of the huge vogue it enjoyed in the years after its production, the show faded from the repertoire as newer products of the blossoming Austrian Operette stage appeared and, when it reappeared in Munich in 1950, it was in one of those "revised" versions so dear to German houses, German publishers and German percentage-takers. And today, whilst second-rate pieces by the handful of buzz-name 19th century writers win intermittent revivals, *Fatinitza*—internationally one of the most successful Operetten of the 19th century—is no longer played.

Hungary: Budai Színkör 26 May 1876; Germany: Friedrich-Wilhelmstädtisches Theater 16 September 1876; UK: Alhambra Theatre 20 June 1878; France: Théâtre des Nouveautés 15 March 1879; USA: California Theater, San Francisco 21 October 1878, Germania Theater (Ger) 14 April 1879, 5th Avenue Theater (Eng) 22 April 1879; Australia: Novelty Theatre, Melbourne 19 March 1881

Recording: selection (Amiga, EP)

FAUST UP-TO-DATE Burlesque in 2 acts by George R Sims and Henry Pettitt. Music by W Meyer Lutz. Gaiety Theatre, London, 30 October 1888.

The overwhelmingly popular "new burlesque" had been safely initiated at George Edwardes's Gaiety Theatre by *Little Jack Sheppard* (1885) and *Monte Cristo Jr* (1886), but *Miss Esmeralda* (1887) which had not benefited from the presence of the Fred Leslie/Nellie Farren star tandem and *Frankenstein* (1887), which had, had been a little less well received. All was set to rights, however, by *Faust Up-to-Date,* a burlesque of Gounod's opera, which scored as well or better than any of its predecessors—and that without the benefit of the drawing-power of Leslie and Farren.

Edwin J Lonnen, the new Gaiety star comic, was Mephistopheles, declaring "I Shall 'Ave 'Em" on the one hand and swinging into an Irish ballad (''Enniscorthy'') on the other, Fanny Robina (Faust) burlesqued the opera's ''Salut, demeure chaste et pure'' and showed her principal-boy legs to advantage, and ''the queen of comic opera,'' Florence St John, switched from straight ballad (''The Dawn of Love'') to comedy adroitly, displaying, at the same time, one of the best soprano voices in town.

The story, which maintained versions of most of the plot elements and major situations of the opera, mixed prose with the old-fashioned burlesque rhyming couplets and plenty of topical and social references, amongst which Sims—the author of some strong pamphlets on social issues—was not afraid to include some that were urgent and unpleasant, and also left space for an acrobatic dance duel, much low comedy and a pas de quatre danced in frilly low-cut blouses, blue skirts and black silk stockings. That dance turned out to be the hit of the show, and Meyer Lutz's music for it, ''the Pas de Quatre from *Faust Up-to-Date,*'' became a long-lived favorite, being still published in the 1950s as ''the famous barn dance.''

The show's other legacy was to the language. Sims took his title from the commercial expression ''your account up to date,'' and from that time on, helped by a popular song from the show, ''Up to Date,'' the phrase assumed a new meaning—''the latest thing''—which has lasted through to the present day.

The show ran for a fine 180 nights at the Gaiety, took in seasons at Islington and the Globe and returned for another month of performances before going on the road in what was to be the first of many tours over the next decade. Lonnen headed a Gaiety company to America in 1889–90 and another to Australia in 1892, and in that same year the Gaiety welcomed a summer season of its old hit with the rising Teddy Payne as Mephistopheles. Germany, too, got a glimpse of the show when Kate Santley took a company to the Continent, playing Marguerite, alongside the Faust of Addie Conyers, to the central Europeans in English, but the idea of foreigners burlesqueing Goethe (even though they'd done it themselves) didn't appeal to the German press. No one, however, took too much notice of the German press, and *Faust Up-to-Date* confirmed itself, even in Berlin, as one of the most popular of all the Gaiety burlesques.

Apart from the operas by Gounod, Meyerbeer, Boito and Spohr, there have been numerous other musical shows based on the Faust legend, including, most notably, Hervé's durable *Le Petit Faust* (1869). There were many English-language burlesques on both the subject in general and the Gounod opera in particular, but the first, by J Halford (*Faust and Marguerite* Strand Theatre 17 July 1854), was a parody of the Princess's Theatre drama *Faust and Marguerite,* and Halford used it to impersonate the Princess's star Charles Kean. Twelve years later it was revised and re-presented at the Olympic, with Nellie Farren as Faust and George Vincent imitating Phelps rather than Kean. Meyer Lutz and Henri Drayton also precursed Gounod with their operatic *Mephistopheles, or Faust and Marguerite* presented at the Surrey in 1855 (26 May) and later (1886) given a showing at a Gaiety matinée with a Savoyard cast including Richard Temple, Marion Hood and Durward Lely.

F C Burnand turned out the first of four works on the subject with *Alonzo the Brave, or Faust and the Fair Imogene* (1857, USA: *Little Faust*), followed by a *Faust and Marguerite* (St James's Theatre 1864 with Charles Mathews as Mephistopheles), a *Very Little Faust* (Charing Cross, 1869) and a *Faust and Loose, or Brocken Vows* (Toole's Theatre, 1886 with Toole as Mephistoolpheles). William M Akhurst concocted an Australian ''nigger-minstrel'' piece, *Faust MD, or The Doctor, the Damsel, the Demon and the Dragoon* (1865); a Britannia Theatre *Faust* of 1867 subtitled itself *or Marguerite's Mangle;* and H J Byron's *Little Doctor Faust,* described as ''the Gaiety not the Goethe version'' (1877). gave Nellie Farren another turn as Faust. And still they came. *Faust in Forty Minutes* (1885), Byron McGuinness's *Mephisto* (1886, Royalty), B L Farjeon's *Dr Faustus* (1886), and the latter-day *Faust on Toast* (1921, Gaiety Theatre with Jack Buchanan as Faust) all got a showing in London, whilst the Alcazar's *Faust et Marguerite* (1867) and Claude Terrasse's one-act *Faust en ménage* (Théâtre de la Potinière, 1924) represented the tale in France. Several 18th- and 19th-century German-language pieces also burlesqued the tale, with J Sixtus and Julius Hopp's *(Fäustling und) Margarethl* (aka *Mefeles*), first produced at the Theater an der Wien, proving the most substantial. An earlier burlesque under the same title, with text by Guigno and music by the elder Adolf Müller, had been produced at the same house in 1862 (6 October), on the heels of the first German showing of Gounod's opera. The Carltheater joined the burlesqueing of the opera, known in German as *Margarethe,* with a little one-person burlesque of that title in 1867 (6 July), and it too was played at the Theater an der Wien.

The British musical play *My Lady Frayle* turned the sexes around and made its Faust the Lady Frayle of the title, whilst the most successful of postwar Faust variants—this time with a hero who sells his soul not for a girl but for an entire baseball team—has been Broadway's *Damn Yankees.* The most recent *Faust* musical also hails from America: Randy Newman's *Faust* (La Jolla Playhouse 19 September 1995) in which the Devil (David Garrison) and the Lord (Ken Page) took part in the temptations of one Henry Faust (Kurt Deutsch). A German-language piece credited to Messrs Mosa and

Merta, with the schoolboy-naughty title of *Bastard,* was produced at a Faust-Symposium in 1994 (7 September), and the apparently endless stream of Faustian musicals continued in 1997 with an *UR-Faust* (Achim Gieseler) at Essen (Junges Theater 1 March 1997) and a *Faust und Fisto* at Karlsruhe.

USA: Broadway Theater 11 December 1889; Germany: Concordia-Palast Theater June 1891; Australia: Opera House, Melbourne 14 May 1892

Recording: Randy Newman version (Reprise)

LA FAUVETTE DU TEMPLE Opéra-comique in 3 acts by Paul Burani and Eugène Humbert. Music by André Messager. Théâtre des Folies-Dramatiques, Paris, 17 November 1885.

In order to find the money to save her lover, Pierre (Jourdan), from being drafted, Thérèse, "the nightingale of Le Temple" (Juliette Simon-Girard), agrees to become the pupil of the eccentric but wealthy singing teacher Saint-Angénor (Gobin). Pierre jealously refuses the musician's money and goes off to war in Algeria and, when Thérèse follows him, accompanied by Angénor and by her friend Zélie (Mlle Vialda), she falls into the clutches of an amorous sheik (Chauvrau). Pierre, and Zélie's little boyfriend Joseph (Simon-Max), are also captured, and only after two acts of comical incidents is everyone rescued in time for a happy and heroic ending.

Messager's first full-scale piece for the theatre, *La Fauvette du Temple* was commissioned from the young composer by Gautier of the Théâtre des Folies-Dramatiques following the success there of Firmin Bernicat's *François les bas-bleus,* which Messager had completed following the composer's death. The new piece was all that might have been hoped for, a combination of a fine and funny libretto—full of the colorful military moments and music which were so popular at the time—and a charming and lively score. The little comedian's Chanson de la Casquette ("As-tu vu la casquette, la casquette au pèr' Bugeaud?"), the baritone's patriotic "Je suis soldat," and the extravagant Angénor's delighted Chanson de la Musique Militaire displayed the different sides of soldierly song, while the prima donna showed off her vocal credentials to her basso captor prettily in the Chanson des blés and joined him, in suitable disguise, to pretend that they are camel-drovers (Duo des chameliers) in a score which included variations on the most of the popular kinds of numbers of the time.

Gautier's production of *La Fauvette du Temple* won a splendid Parisian success, a first run of 130 performances, and started Messager on what would be a memorable career in the musical theatre. The piece was subsequently played at Marseille's Théâtre des Variétés and throughout France and it was revived at the Folies-Dramatiques in 1890 with Jeanne Thibault starring and again, at the same house, in 1898. It was played at the Théâtre de la Gaîté-Lyrique in 1914 with Jane Marnac in the title role, Lucien Noël as Pierre and Henri Defreyn as Joseph and was also seen at the Empire Théâtre in 1921 with Mlle Frémont starred.

The show also got a number of English-language productions. An American adaptation (ad Aaron Hoffman) was staged at San Francisco's Tivoli Theatre in 1889, with Louise Manfred (Thérèse) and Henry Norman (Sheik) featured, another (ad Benjamin Woolf, R M Field) at the Boston Museum the following year (14 July 1890) with Henri Laurent as Saint-Angénor and Maude Williams in the title role, and a third (ad Alfred Rae, L Fontaine), organized by Messager's publishers, Enoch, was toured in Britain by Horace Lingard in 1891. W H Rawlins (St Angénor), Miss Emmott Herbert (Thérèse), Victor Stevens (Abriral) and Harry Child (Pierre) introduced the piece to Britain for a solid life on the tour circuits, and it was showcased for a week at London's Royalty Theatre, on the heels of the well-praised British production of the composer's *La Basoche.*

USA: Tivoli Theater, San Francisco *The Nightingale* 11 February 1889; UK: Lyceum, Edinburgh *Fauvette* 18 May 1891, Royalty Theatre 16 November 1891

FAVART, Edmée [Zélie] (b Paris, 23 November 1886; d Marseille, 28 October 1941). Prima donna of the Paris opérette, opéra-comique and musical comedy stage.

The daughter of the baritone Edmond Favart and of the opéra-bouffe prima donna Zélie Weil, Mlle Favart made her first stage appearance as a child, singing at the Casino Saint-Martin—then run by her post-career parents. She had her first significant role on the Paris stage at the Théâtre des Variétés, under the management of Fernand Samuel, when she appeared in the 1904 revival of Lecocq's *Le Petit Duc* playing the little Duchess to the little Duke of Jeanne Saulier. In 1907 she joined the company at the Brussels Théâtre des Nouveautés where she created the title role of the opérette *Betty* and appeared in the Belgian premiere of Cuvillier's *Son p'tit frère,* and then returned to Paris to play at the Boîte à Fursy. She came to the fore in Paris when she played the ingenue role of Daisy in the Scala production of *Princesse Dollar* (1911), featured in a revival of *Paris, ou le bon juge* (1911), Redstone's *Mik 1er* (1911) and the following year confirmed herself amongst the stars of the prewar opérette with her performances as Clairette to the Lange of Germaine Gallois (*La Fille de Madame Angot*) and as Stella in *La Fille du tambour-major* at the Théâtre de la Gaîté. She had a further success as Omphale in a revival of Terrasse's *Les Travaux d'Hercule* and paired with Marthe Chenal to repeat her *Fille de Madame Angot* role when that piece was given a special performance at the Opéra-Comique.

In spite of the fact that her excellent light soprano was an adjunct to a personality of charm and a fine actress's projection, rather than being an operatic instrument, she spent some time at the Opéra-Comique (1915 sq) where she appeared as Mignon, Mimi, Manon, Micaëla, Cherubino, Despina, Colette in *La Basoche,* Suzel in *Le Juif polonais,* Véronique and Rose Friquet and created the role of Catherine in Charles Levadé's *La Rotisserie de la Reine Pédauque* (1920) and *La Charmante Rosalie.*

In the early 1920s she appeared in revivals of *Véronique, Madame l'Archiduc* (Marietta) and *Le Petit Duc* (this time as the Duc to Mlle Roncey's Duchesse) at the new Théâtre Mogador, and in *Paris, ou le bon juge* (1922, Glycère) at the Théâtre Michel, made her debut in the non-musical theatre, and created the ingenue roles of Suzanne in Messager's semi-successful *La Petite Fonctionnaire* (1921) and of Charlotte in Madame Louis Urgel's *Monsieur Dumollet* (1922), before taking up the role of her career as Reynoldo Hahn's *Ciboulete* (1923). In a part which had been conceived for her by the composer, as the adorable country lass who becomes a prima donna and wins herself a nobleman (Henri Defreyn, also her partner in *La Petite Fonctionnaire*) in the best old-fashioned opérette style, she introduced the winsome "Dans ma charrette," "Comme frère et soeur," "Moi, je m'appelle Ciboulette," "C'est sa banlieu" and the Chanson de route and scored a memorable success.

She subsequently starred in José Padilla's *Pépète* (1924, Monique), in Josef Szulc's successful musical comedies *Quand on est trois* (1925, Claude) and *Mannequins* (1925, Micheline) at the little Théâtre des Capucines, paired in both these last with her other *Ciboulette* co-star Jean Périer, in Marcel Lattès's *Le Diable à Paris* (1927) alongside Dranem and Raimu, in Cuvillier's *Boulard et ses filles* (1929) and in the title role of the Châtelet's opérette à grand spectacle, *Sidonie Panache* (1930–31). As late as 1933 she was seen as Bettina in a revival of *La Mascotte,* but she retired to being Mme Paul Gazagne in 1935 and thereafter ventured only the odd broadcast.

Biography: *Les Grands Acteurs du siècle: Edmée Favart et l'opérette* (Paris, 1925)

FEDÁK, Sári (b Beregszász, 26 September 1880; d Budapest, 5 May 1955).

The most celebrated star of the Hungarian musical theatre in the first decades of the 20th century, Sári Fedák had an outstanding career in both the musical and non-musical theatre, and created the starring roles in several of the most important original Hungarian operetts of her time.

Plate 121a. **Sári Fedák.** *Budapest's greatest musical-theatre star of the early 20th century, creating the title role in* János vitéz.

She was just 17 when she was cast in the soubrette role of Molly in the first Hungarian performances of *A gésák* (*The Geisha*) at the Magyar Színház, and, after the huge success of that production, she went on to appear in several other imported musical shows (Théa in *A bibliás asszony, Toledad, San Toy,* etc) before, in 1902, she created the travesty title role in Jenő Huszka's hit musical *Bob herceg* (Prince Bob). The following year she created the title role in Huszka's next success, *Aranyvirág,* and in 1904 that of Pongrác Kacsoh's *János vitéz* (John the hero), the glorious folk-tale operett which would go on to become Hungary's most popular and admired native piece.

She subsequently appeared in a revival of another major Hungarian work, Verő's *A szultán,* and in the premieres of his *Leányka* (1906), of the Károly Czobor/ Ferenc Rajna *Rab Mátyás* (1906), of Jacobi's *Az istenhegyi székely leány* (1907, Lóna-Szendile) and *Jánoska* (1909), as well as in the starring roles of classic pieces such as *Gerolsteini nagyhercegnő* (*La Grande-*

Plate 121b. **Sári Fedák** *as Szibill, alongside Ernö Király.*

Duchesse), *A víg özvegy* (*Die lustige Witwe*) and *Cigányszerelem* (*Zigeunerliebe,* Ilona). In 1911 she created another durable role as Bessy in Victor Jacobi's internationally successful *Leányvásár,* before going on to play the title role in the Hungarian production of Lehár's *Eva* (1912), to star in Kollo and Bredschneider's *A Mozikirály* (*Filmzauber,* 1913) and as Sári in *Cigányprimás* (Der *Zigeunerprimas*) and to create two further important roles, as the richly romantic masquerading diva of Jacobi's *Szibill* (1914, Szibill) and as the soubrette of Szirmai's *Mágnás Miska* (1916, Marcsa).

Fedák spread her success abroad when she appeared at Berlin's Deutsches Theater in a version of Verő's *Kleopatra* (*Die Bettelgräfin,* 1908), at the Deutsches Landestheater in Prague, in Vienna with the Király Színház company (1913) in *János vitéz, Leányvásár, Eva* and *Cigányprimás,* and again in 1920 as Rosi in *Der Pusztakavalier* (*Mágnás Miska*), as well as visiting in America in Szirmai's *Mézeskalács* (Manhattan Opera House 5 October 1924) and to play the title role of the play *Antonia,* one of her greatest hometown successes. She continued, at the same time, to hold her place at the head of her profession at home, with starring appearances in such pieces as *A bajadér, Pompadour* (1923) and Oscar Straus's *Teresina* (1925). Latterly, however, she included more non-musical roles in her schedule (Gárdonyi's *Fehér Anna,* Molnár's *Farsang,* etc) and, although she still appeared in such musical pieces as the 1929 *Pista néni* and the Magyar Színház's 1942 *Vén diófa,* much of the latter part of her career was devoted to the straight stage.

Fedák was married briefly to the playwright Ferenc Molnár, but the golden couple of the Hungarian theatre went through a scandal-showered divorce in 1925 after some three lively and limelit years together.

DER FELDPREDIGER Operette in 3 acts by Hugo Wittmann and Alois Wohlmuth based on the story *Der seltsame Brautgemach* by Friedrich Schilling. Music by Carl Millöcker. Theater an der Wien, Vienna, 31 October 1884.

The tale of *Der Feldprediger* is set in 1812–13 in the little Prussian border-town of Trautenfeld, a key point on the fighting retreat path of the Napoléonic army from Russia. The "field-chaplain" of the title is Hellwig (Josef Joseffy), sent secretly to this potential hot-spot to stir up insurrection, and quartered in the house of the patriotically pliable alderman Heidekrug (Carl Adolf Friese). Hellwig quickly falls in love with Heidekrug's daughter Minna (Ottilie Collin), who has been disguised by her father as an old crone to escape unwelcome attentions from the marauding military. The town changes hands between Russians and French, and Hellwig escapes detection by diverting suspicion on to Heidekrug before he and his merry men bring in the Black Hussar regiment to free the town from the various invaders. Hellwig's winning of Minna was paralleled by his friend Kühnwald's (Graselli) conquest of Minna's similarly disguised sister, Rosette (Rosa Streitmann), Therese Schäfer played Heidekrug's housekeeper, Barbara, and Alexander Girardi joined the comedy as the alderman's subordinate, Piffkow, who confusedly mistakes the rehearsing of the actor, Bliemchen (Alexander Guttmann), for enemy action.

Megastar Girardi, of course, topped the musical part of the show with his obligatory third-act waltz song, "Nur ein Traum," but although the comic characters were particularly well provided for—notably Heidekrug, with his self-descriptory "Ein Diplomat," his lively "Ich witt're Blut" and a jolly trio, trying to persuade his daughters that ugliness is not the "Grösstes Unglück" in the world—there were plenty of lyrical moments as well. Minna, with her Act III solo "Ich aber fühle' and a pretty, bright duo with her Hellwig ("Endlich wieder eine

Stunde'') had the more obviously vocal lines, whilst sister Rosette (''And're Mädchen mögen schmachten'') took the soubrettier area. All three joined in another successful ensemble with Kühnwald (''Zög're nicht mein Volk erwach''), and Hellwig had his main moment in a hussar song.

Der Feldprediger did not repeat the success of Millöcker's *Der Bettelstudent* in Vienna, but it did fairly well. It ran through November and into December, was brought back in 1886, with Siegmund Stelzer (Heidekrug) and Carl Lindau (Bliemchen) alongside the other original stars, and reached its 50th performance on 1 April 1887. It was subsequently seen in Budapest, Berlin, Prague, Warsaw and in Madrid (as *El alcade di Strassberg*), Prague and Amsterdam, but it had its only really significant success in America.

The piece was initially played in New York, and with considerable success, in German at the Thalia Theater with Max Lube (Heidekrug), Emma Seebold (Minna), Eduard Elsbach (Hellwig), Ferdinand Schütz (Piffkow), Bernhard Rank (Bliemchen), Conrad Junker (Kühnwald) and Franziska Raberg (Rosette) in the leading roles, but just three days after this German-language premiere, John McCaull opened his English production (ad Sydney Rosenfeld), at Wallack's Theater under the more swashbuckling title of *The Black Hussar.* Mark Smith was Friedrich von Helbert, Edwin Hoff looked after the tenor music as his pal Hans von Waldemann, and their girls were played by Lilly Post (Minna) and Marie Jansen (Rosette). De Wolf Hopper played papa Theophil Hackenback, Mathilde Cottrelly took Schäfer's role and Digby Bell the Girardi part. This time the piece was a genuine tin-plated hit, with Hopper, Bell and Mme Cottrelly's topical trio, ''Read the Answer in the Stars,'' becoming one of the song hits of the season and a good number of other seasons beyond. *The Black Hussar* played 104 straight performances at Wallack's and, when it closed, its hit song was retained as part of the music for the following show, *Die Näherin.* It was seen on Broadway again at the Star Theater as soon as December, and the following season, while being played with great success all around America, it was brought back for a further run at Wallack's (7 May). *The Black Hussar* stayed in McCaull's repertoire until the end of his producing days, and was a feature of comic-opera seasons throughout the country for many years. In California, the show was played as *The Grenadier* (Tivoli 1 December 1890).

In Germany, the piece found a renewed audience when its ''patriotic'' subject—duly adapted to the circumstances—made it a suitable candidate for first-wartime revival, and Vienna, too, saw *Der Feldprediger* afresh when it was revived at the Raimundtheater in 1914 (December 4) and again in 1915 with Otto Langer (Hellwig), Rosa Mittermardi (Minna), Anton Matscheg (Heidekrug), Franz Glawatsch (Piffkow) and Paula Zulka (Rosette) featured. The Second World War saw it surface again, in a version by Rudolf Kattnigg and Hans Rainer, now entitled *Husarenstreiche* (1941, Nuremberg), before, its ''patriotic'' purpose served, it drifted from the repertoire.

Two numbers from the show's score survived longer, however, finding their remade way into the Mackeben/Millöcker pasticcio score to the longer-surviving *The Dubarry.*

Hungary: *A tábori lelkész* 20 December 1884; Germany: Walhalla Theater 10 January 1885; USA: Thalia Theater 1 May 1885, Wallack's Theater *The Black Hussar* 4 May 1885

FELIX, Hugo [Victor] (b Vienna, 19 November 1871; d Hollywood, 25 August 1934). Austrian composer of musicals for four countries.

The musician who called himself ''Felix'' graduated from Vienna University with a Doctorate in Science, but then eschewed a scientific career in favor of one in music. His first Operette, *Die Kätzchen,* was staged in Lemberg when he was but 18 years old, and had sufficient success for it to be introduced to Vienna two seasons later in a production at the Carltheater (8 performances). He had two further pieces produced in Vienna, one of which, *Rhodope,* on which he also collaborated on the libretto, was also played by José Ferenczy's company at Berlin's Theater des Westens (23 June 1900) and Lessing-Theater after its 31 performances in Vienna. He extended his libretto-writing by adapting the highly successful British musical *San Toy* for the German-language stage, but in 1902 he made good as a composer when his *Madame Sherry,* premiered in Berlin, scored him a major hit.

After the singular success of *Madame Sherry* in Europe, Felix went to Britain (where it had, notoriously, not been successful) and was commissioned by George Edwardes to compose the score for his homemade European musical play *Les Merveilleuses,* to a text by Victorien Sardou, anglicized by Basil Hood. The piece was well reviewed, but did only fair business at Daly's Theatre (196 performances), in comparison with the extended runs which had become the norm there under Edwardes's management, and a production at Paris's Théâtre des Variétés also had only limited success. Felix's next attempt at a musical for London, written on the French musical comedy / *Madame Sherry* lines, was an unsuccessful adaptation of the celebrated vaudeville *Le Cabinet Piperlin* called *The Antelope* (22 performances) and his only subsequent contributions to the musical stage during his London years seem to have been the supply of the pretty ''Or Thereabouts'' as an interpolated number for Gertie Millar in *The Quaker Girl,* ''Der Umberrufen Guards'' (w Leslie Stiles) sung by Robert Nainby and May de Souza in the revised *The New Aladdin,* and a share in the score of the latter-day old-style musical comedy *The Pearl Girl,* produced with some success by Robert Courtneidge (254 performances).

Since *Madame Sherry* had been Americanized to the extent of dropping Felix's entire score for its Broadway production, the composer was first represented on Broadway by a musical version of Paul Gavault's *La Petite Chocolatière,* produced in Chicago under the title which had been given to the play in London, *Tantalising Tommy.* It was a 31-performance failure in New York, but Felix, now fixed in America, did better with *Pom-Pom,* a remake of the Hungarian operett *Csibészkirály* as a vehicle for Mitzi Hájos, *Lassie,* a version of Catherine Chisholm Cushing's play *Kitty McKay* which won enormous critical and out-of town plaudits but found the New York public diffident, and the Chicago-born *The Sweetheart Shop* which, although it had only a brief Broadway life, was a decided success on the road.

A second collaboration with Mrs Cushing produced *Marjolaine,* a musical version of Louis N Parker's popular play *Pomander Walk,* which ran 136 performances at the Broadhurst Theater and found willing American audiences, but which failed when later produced at London's Gaiety Theatre, but his last works—the music and songs to Russell Janney's comedy-with-songs version of *Don Quixote* and musical versions of the famous play *Peg o' My Heart* and of Margaret Mayo's *Polly of the Circus,* each adapted by their original author—were less appreciated.

In his last days Felix went to Hollywood to find work as an orchestrator and conductor, but it was said that in the seven months of his stay, up to his death, he earned but $15.

1890 **Die Kätzchen** (Albert Klischnegg, Ernst Niedl) Lemberg 23 January; Carltheater, Vienna 19 January 1892

1894 **Husarenblut** (Ignaz Schnitzer) Theater an der Wien 10 March

1898 **Sein Bébé** (Eugène Labiche ad H Paul) 1 act Carltheater 15 January

1900 **Rhodope** (w Alexander Engel) Carltheater 1 February

1900 **San Toy** German version (Carltheater)

1902 **Madame Sherry** (w Benno Jacobson) Centraltheater, Berlin 1 November

1906 **Les Merveilleuses** (aka *The Lady Dandies*) (Victorien Sardou, Basil Hood) Daly's Theatre, London 27 October

1908 **The Antelope** (Adrian Ross) Waldorf Theatre, London 28 November

1912 **Tantalizing Tommy** (Michael Morton, Ross) Criterion Theater, New York 1 October

1913 **The Pearl Girl** (w Howard Talbot/Hood) Shaftesbury Theatre, London 25 September

1916 **Pom-Pom** (Anne Caldwell) Cohan Theater, New York 28 February

1920 **Lassie** (Catherine Cushing) Nora Bayes Theater, New York 6 April

1920 **The Sweetheart Shop** (Caldwell) Knickerbocker Theater, New York 31 August

1922 **Marjolaine** (Cushing) Broadhurst Theater, New York 24 January

1923 **Sancho Panza** (Cervantes ad Sydney Howard, Melchior Lengyel) Hudson Theater, New York 26 November

1924 **Peg o' My Dreams** (Caldwell/J Hartley Manners) Jolson Theater, New York 5 May

1924 **Polly of the Circus** (Margaret Mayo) Alcazar, San Francisco 20 October

LA FEMME À PAPA Vaudeville in 3 acts by Alfred Hennequin and Albert Millaud. Music by Hervé. Théâtre des Variétés, Paris, 3 December 1879.

La Femme à papa marked the beginning of a second great period of success for ''the crazy composer,'' Hervé, who, since his brilliant opéra-bouffe successes with *Chilpéric, Le Petit Faust* and their ilk, had been rather overshadowed by the less outrageous and less frivolous opérettes and opéras-comiques of Lecocq and his kind, whose styles he had tried to follow with narrowing results. The freely comical vaudeville style suited him much better, and his contribution to this bright-hearted comedy with songs did much to ensure its success.

Anna Judic starred as pretty Belgian Anna who is intended by the sober, 30-year-old, butterfly-fancying Aristide (José Dupuis), at the outset of things, to be his ''papa's wife.'' Aristide is anxious to marry off papa, the widowed, 60-year-old Baron Florestan de la Boucanière (also Dupuis) to stop his embarrassing gadabout of a parent running around town and getting involved with the likes of the flibberty-gibbet Coralie (Augustine Leriche), before Aristide himself gets tidily married to the daughter of his illustrious zoology professor. By the time the quiproquos of the evening are done, it is, of course, Aristide who ends up in the arms of Anna. Baron completed the star team in the role of Professor Baudin-Bridet. The ''scandalous'' highlight of the piece was a scene where Anna, ignorant of the powers of alcohol, gets herself drunk.

Judic scored a bit song hit with the tipsy couplets of the Chanson du Colonel (''Tambour, clairon, musique en tête'') with its tale of a regiment quartered in a convent and its suggestive ''Ta ra ta, ta ra ta ta ta, Ra fla fla fla'' refrain, and she compounded her triumph with ''Le Champagne,'' ''La Pensionnaire,'' the rondeau ''Les Parisiennes'' and ''Les Inséparables,'' leaving little in the way of songs—after her seven solos and three duos with Dupuis in the final act—for the rest of the cast.

La Femme à papa played at the Variétés for four solid months and, after allowing space for some of the other pieces of the house's repertoire to be played, it returned for several months more, passing its 200th Parisian night before giving way to more made-for-Judic vaudevilles including Hervé's most successful pieces, *Lili* and *Mam'zelle Nitouche.* In spite of the huge success of its successors, it was by no means shelved thereafter. Judic kept *La Femme à papa* prominently in her repertoire for many years, repeating it in Paris in 1885, in 1895 with Dupuis and Baron both repeating their original roles, and in 1898, and on tour throughout the world, notably at Vienna's Theater an der Wien (20 November 1883) and at Broadway's Wallack's Theater and Star Theater.

La Femme à papa was later given another Paris showing, at the Théâtre de la Gaîté, with Jeanne Pierny starring, and was played on international tour with other pieces of the Judic repertoire by the same artist (Theater an der Wien, 1900 etc). In 1909 it was revived at Paris's Trianon-Lyrique (15 November).

A German-language version was mounted—after some difficulties with the local censor—at the Vienna Carltheater, with Hervé's score replaced by new music by Brandl and with Rosa Streitmann (Anna), Tewele (Aristide/Florestan), Wilhelm Knaack (Bodin-Bridet) and Karl Blasel (the butler, Tob) featured. It did not have a notable success (29th performance 4 October 1881), but it was this Brandlized version that was subsequently played in Germany. Hungary, on the other hand retained the original music for *A papa felesége* (ad Aurél Follinusz). In America, however, the show suffered an even stranger fate. The 1899 Anna Held vehicle *Papa's Wife,* although taking the title of this work, actually mixed together elements of its plot with bits of *Mam'zelle Nitouche* and replaced Hervé's music with some Reginald De Koven/Harry B Smith songs. The following year, Vienna tried a similar trick. Frln Worm appeared alongside Josef Joseffy, Carl Streitmann, Ferdinand Pagin and Giampietro in *Die Stiefmama,* a version of *La Femme à papa* (re)written by Ludwig Held with music by Leo Held (Theater an der Wien 20 February 1900) which ran nine performances. England got rid of the music too, but did not replace it and the show originally produced at Brighton as *The Mulberry Bush* (19 June 1882 ad James Albery) and by Charles Wyndham at London's Criterion Theatre as *Little Miss Muffet* (2 September 1882) was played as a non-musical comedy. Beerbohm Tree was the son, Herbert Standing the father, Kate Rorke the heroine, and soon-to-be musical producer Violet Melnotte featured in a small role.

Austria: Carltheater *Papas Frau* 20 March 1880; Germany: Carl-Schultze Theater, Hamburg *Papas Frau* 5 March 1881; Hungary: Népszínház *A papa felesége* 12 January 1895; USA: Wallack's Theater (Fr) 6 October 1885

THE FENCING MASTER Comic [romantic] opera in 3 acts by Harry B Smith. Music by Reginald De Koven. Star Theater, Buffalo, 26 September 1892; Casino Theater, New York, 14 November 1892.

One of Smith and De Koven's most successful successors to their biggest hit, *Robin Hood, The Fencing Master* had a run of 120 Broadway performances with Marie Tempest starring in breeches (most of the time) as Francesca, the daughter of a maître d'armes who has been brought up thinking she is a boy. She suspects that perhaps she isn't when she falls in love with the deposed Fortunio, Duke of Milan (Hubert Wilke), but alas the non-Duke is devoted to a court lady, Countess Filippa (Grace Golden), whose hand has just been bartered to a rich Venetian to boost the income of the usurper, Galeazzo Visconti (Charles Hopper). The heroine scuppers her beloved's attempt to elope and is challenged to a duel, and then, amongst the fetes and masked meetings of Venetian tradition, things to do with gender begin to come to light, as the tale rolls on towards its predictable ending. The fencing master of the title was played by William Broderick, whilst Jerome Sykes provided the laughs as Visconti's comical astrologer, Pasquino, and Louise Pemberton-Hincks appeared as the Marchesa Goldoni, altogether too taken with the charms of the ''son'' of the fencing master.

J M Hill's production of *The Fencing Master* toured happily, was brought back to Broadway for a brief reshowing in December 1893, and was subsequently played widely in comic opera seasons throughout America.

FÉNYES, Szabolcs (b Nagyvárad, 30 April 1912; d Budapest, 12 October 1986). Composer, theatre administrator and perhaps the most important and prolific single contributor to the Hungarian musical stage of the mid-twentieth century.

Fényes studied at the Liszt Academy of Music in Budapest and began his career as a theatrical composer at the age of 19, scoring a major hit with his score for the operett *Maya* before his 20th birthday. *Maya* went on from its original production at Budapest's Fővárosi Operettszínház to be played in Vienna and throughout Europe, and Fényes also moved on, to Berlin, where he spent the next three years writing (as Peter Fényes) for the cinematic company UFA. This was the beginning of a screen career which ultimately totaled scores for more than a hundred films.

Both during his years in Germany and after his return to Hungary, Fényes continued to turn out a regular supply of superior popular songs and a steady list of scores for the musical stage. If none of his many subsequent musicals and operetts scored the same international success as *Maya,* he did, however, have hometown hits with such pieces as *Vén diófa* (1942), *Rigó Jancsi* (1947), *Szombat délutan* (1954), *Dunaparti randevú* (1957), *A csók* (1968) and *A kutya, akit Bozzi úrnak hívnak* (1976, subsequently played in Germany as *Der Hund, der Herr Bozzi hiess*).

In 1942 he took over the management of the Fővárosi Operettszínház which he left in 1949 to run the Vidam Színpad, returning to the Operettszínház in 1957 for a further period until 1960.

Der Hund was seen at Heilbronn in 1994, and *Rigo Jancsi* was revived at the Pécsi Nemzeti Színház in 1997.

1931 **A hárem** (Imre Harmath/Ernő Vajda) Fővárosi Operettszínház 24 April

1931 **Maya** (Harmath) Fővárosi Operettszínház 10 December

1932 **Manolita** (Harmath) Fővárosi Operettszínház 24 September

1933 **Csipetke** (Rezső Török) Fővárosi Operettszínház 25 November

1934 **Music Hall** (w Támás Bródy/Harmath/Charles Méré) Fővárosi Operettszínház 13 October

1935 **Mimi** (Harmath/Ivan Törs, Endre Solt) Royal Színház 13 February

1936 **Sok hühó Emmiért** (Harmath/Károly Aszlányi) Kamara Színház 24 October

1939 **Pusztai szerenád** (István Békeffy/László Szilágyi) Fővárosi Operettszínház 29 September

1940 **Az ördög nem alszik** (Gábor Vaszary) Magyar Színház 14 September

1942 **Vén diófa** (Szilágyi) Magyar Színház 26 March

1943 **Egy boldog pesti nyár** (w Mihály Eisemann, Dénes Buday/Szilágyi, Attila Orbok) Fővárosi Operettszínház 14 April

1943 **A királynő csókja** (Attila Orbók) Fővárosi Operettszínház 20 December

1947 **Rigó Jancsi** (Békeffy) Fővárosi Operettszínház 9 May

1954 **Szombat délután** (Békeffy/Dezső Kellér) Fővárosi Vígszínház 19 February

1954 **Két szerelem** (Elemer Boros) Fővárosi Operettszínház 18 June

1955 **Szerencsés flótás** (Békeffy) Fővárosi Kis Színpad 23 March

1957 **Dunaparti randevú** (A Szantó/Milály Szécsen) Szolnőki Szigligeti Színház 8 October

1958 **Majd a papa** (István Kállai) Fővárosi Kis Színpad 11 January

1958 **Ibusz kisasszony** (József Nádasi) Pecsi Színház 19 December

1962 **Légy szives Jeromos** (György Moldova) Petofi Színház 28 September

1962 **Csacsifogat** (Imre Kertész) Déryné Színház 18 October

1963 **Cyrano házassága** (Kertész) József Attila Színház 9 November

1964 **Csintalan csillagok** (Rudolf Halász/Mátyás Czizmarek) Fővárosi Operettszínház 14 May

1967 **Lulu** (Iván Szenes/Michel André) József Attila Színház 20 May

1968 **A csók** (Szenes/Lajos Dóczy) Pesti Színház 29 March

1968 **Csészealj-szerenád** (Szenes/Lajos K Nagy) Györi Kisfaludy Színház 15 May

1971 **Mit vesztett el kisasszony?** (Békeffy, Iván Szenes) Fővárosi Operettszínház 26 February

1972 **Részeg éjszaka** (Gábor Görgey/Béla Gádor) Vidám Színpad 20 October

1972 **Tizenkét lakáskulcs** (Halász) Kaposvár 27 October

1976 **A kutya akit Bozzi úrnak hívnak** (Békeffy) Fővárosi Operettszínház 27 February

1979 **Florentin kalap** (Szenes/Labiche ad) Fővárosi Operettszínház 30 March

1983 **Szerdán tavasz lesz** (Péter Bacsó) Fővárosi Operettszínház 26 March

1984 **Uraim, csak egymás után** (Yves Mirande, André Mouëzy-Éon ad Adorján Stella) Városmajori Színpad 28 June

1985 **A kikapós patikárius** (*Ferdinand le noceur*) (Szenes/Léon Gandillot ad Jenő Heltai) Székesfehérvári Nyári Színház 24 June

1990 **A nagymama** (György G Kardos/Gergely Csiky ad) Fővárosi Operettszínház 21 September

Biography: Sugar, R; *Ugye, hogy nem felejtesz el?* (Ifjusági Lap-és Könyvkiadó, Budapest, 1987)

FERENCZY, José (d Buenos Aires, July 1908).

At one time the leading tenor of the Court Theater at Weimar, Ferenczy subsequently took over the management of the Carl-Schultze Theater in Hamburg. He stayed at Hamburg for some ten years, touring his company in the off-season as far afield as America (1893–94, *Der Vogelhändler, Lachende Erben,* etc; 1895–96, *Der Obersteiger, Das Modell,* etc) before moving on to Carlsbad and then to Berlin, where he took over the running of the Centraltheater (1 September 1898). His productions of the record-breaking *Die Geisha* (1897), *Die Puppe* (1899) and *Madame Sherry* (1902), in particular, made him one of the most successful musical-theatre producers in Germany in the turn of the century years. Weinberger's *Lachende Erben* (1893), German versions of *L'Enlèvement de la Toledad* (1897) and *A Chinese Honeymoon* (*Chinesiche Flitterwochen,* 1903), *Das süsse Mädel* (1901) and Heuberger's *Die kleine Excellenz* were amongst his other productions. However, ill health handicapped his later efforts, and after the good times came the bad ones. Ferenczy gave up the Centraltheater but he mounted productions at several other Berlin houses (Lehár's *Der Klavierstimmer* 1903, *Der Sonnenvogel, Zur indische Witwe,* etc), and in 1903–4 he toured his company once more to America (*Die Puppe, Die Geisha, Das süsse Mädel*). In 1907, however, he went bankrupt. The following year he took a troupe out to South America, and they were playing in Buenos Aires when the producer died.

FERNANDEL [CONTANDIN, Fernand Joseph Désiré] (b Marseille, 8 May 1903; d Paris, 26 February 1971).

Celebrated long-faced, toothy comedian of the French stage, music hall and cinema who appeared on the musical comedy stage in four shows during a star career of some 40 years: as the gormless hero of Louis Verneuil's 1935 *Le Rosier de Mme Husson,* in the star role of the made-to-measure military opérette *Ignace* (1936, revival 1947), at Marseille in the 1940 Vincent Scotto piece, *Hugues* (written, like *Ignace,* by his brother-in-law, Jean Manse), and again in the Théâtre du Châtelet's *Le Chasseur d'images* in 1947. Amongst his many screen credits, he appeared in the role of Célestin in a cinematic version of *Mam'zelle Nitouche.*

Biographies: Castans, R: *Fernandel m'a raconté* (La Table Ronde, Paris, 1976), Lorcey, J: *Fernandel* (PAC, Paris, 1981), Lorcey, J: *Fernandel: Le Livre d'Or* (Ramsey, Paris, 1990)

FERRIER, Paul [Raoul Michel Marie] (b Montpellier, 29 March 1843; d Nouan-le-Fuzelier, Loir-et-Cher, 11 September 1920).

Paul Ferrier threw in his career as a Montpellierain lawyer for a much more grateful one as a prolific and successful playwright and librettist which ended with his becoming honorary president of the French Société des auteurs.

His first piece, *La Revanche d'Iris,* was played at the Comédie-Française in 1868, and he thereafter turned out a long series of plays including the musical comedy *La Chaste Suzanne* (1877), *La Vie de Bohème* (1898) and *La Troisième Lune* (1904, w Fred de Grésac) to good effect. In 1877 he made his first full-scale contribution to the musical theatre with the libretto to Gaston Serpette's *La Petite Muette* at the Bouffes-Parisiens, and he followed this with two collaborations with Offenbach (*Maître Péronilla, La Marocaine*) for the same theatre. Neither of these rang any bells, but his fourth piece for Bouffes director Louis Cantin hit the mark in no uncertain way: *Les Mousquetaires au couvent* (1880), the first major work of the young composer Louis Varney, scored a huge hit. Several other extremely fruitful collaborations with Varney followed (*Fanfan la Tulipe, Babolin, Les Petits Mousquetaires, Miss Robinson*), but Ferrier's other enduring musical theatre hit came in a different area of the musical theatre, in a collaboration with Victor Roger on the vaudeville *Joséphine vendue par ses soeurs,* an hilarious modern retelling—with the sexes reversed—of the biblical Joseph legend. Like *Les Mousquetaires,* it became part of the standard repertoire in France and won many overseas productions.

Roger, Varney and Serpette remained Ferrier's principal musical collaborators through the most important part of his career, but he also collaborated with André Messager, Franco Leoni, Gabriel Pierné and others on works for the Opéra-Comique, co-authored several féeries including the Châtelet's *Les Mille et une nuits* (1881 w Adolphe d'Ennery), *Coco fêlé* (1885), *Le Petit Chaperon rouge* (1900), the particularly spectacular *Le Trésor des Radjahs* (w d'Ennery, 1894), the remarkedly sexy spectacular musical fairy pieces *Le Carnet du Diable* and *Le Carillon* and the widely played latest revision of the 1833 favorite *Le Royaume des femmes.* He also supplied the libretti for several operas, notably Bemberg's *Elaine* (1892) for Nellie Melba, Xavier Leroux's *Theodora* (1907), Le Borne's *La Catalane* (1907) and Franco Leoni's *La Tsigane* (1910).

Latterly Ferrier became involved in adapting and translating and he was responsible for revamping Hervé's *Chilpéric* for a major Paris revival in 1895 and also for the French versions of such diverse pieces as *Die Fledermaus* and *The Quaker Girl.* His most significant success in this field was, however, in the operatic world where he supplied the standard French versions of Puccini's *La Bohème* (the libretto of which had been in any case partly taken from his play *La Vie de Bohème*), *Tosca, Madama Butterfly, Suor Angelica* and *Gianni Schicchi* as well as new French texts for *Die Zauberflöte, Don Giovanni* and *The Marriage of Figaro* for the Paris Opéra.

He was also, for a period, involved with Debruyère in the management of the Théâtre de la Gaîté.

Several of Ferrier's plays were used as the bases for later musical comedies, notably the ''comédie melée d'ariettes'' *La Chaste Suzanne* which in London, shorn of its Paul Lacome and Bariller songs, became Kate Santley's pasticcio entertainment *Madcap,* and *La Troisième Lune* (w Fred de Grésac), which was used as the basis for George Edwardes's English musical *See See* (1906). His libretto for *Babolin* was reset in America (with J Cheever Goodwin taking the whole credit for it) as *The Devil's Deputy,* with a score by Edward Jakobowski (1894).

1877 **La Chaste Suzanne** (Paul Lacome, Jules Bariller) Théâtre du Palais-Royal 4 July

1877 **La Petite Muette** (Gaston Serpette) Théâtre des Bouffes-Parisiens 3 October

1878 **Maître Péronilla** (Jacques Offenbach/w Charles Nuitter, Offenbach) Théâtre des Bouffes-Parisiens 13 March

1879 **La Marocaine** (Offenbach/w Ludovic Halévy) Théâtre des Bouffes-Parisiens 13 January

1880 **Les Mousquetaires au couvent** (Louis Varney/w Jules Prével) Théâtre des Bouffes-Parisiens 16 March

1881 **Les Mille et une nuits** (uncredited/w Adolphe d'Ennery) Théâtre du Châtelet 12 December

1882 **Fanfan la Tulipe** (Varney/w Prével) Théâtre des Folies-Dramatiques 21 October

1884 **Babolin** (Varney/w Prével) Théâtre des Nouveautés 19 March

1884 **La Nuit aux soufflets** (Hervé/w d'Ennery) Théâtre des Nouveautés 18 September

1885 **La Vie mondaine** (Lecocq/w Émile de Najac) Théâtre des Nouveautés 13 February

1885 **Les Petits Mousquetaires** (Varney/w Prével) Folies-Dramatiques 5 March

1885 **Coco-fêlé** (uncredited/w Paul Burani, E Floury fils) Théâtre du Châtelet 26 September

1886 **Joséphine vendue par ses soeurs** (Victor Roger/w Fabrice Carré) Théâtre des Bouffes-Parisiens 20 March

1887 **Dix jours aux Pyrénées** (Varney) Théâtre de la Gaîté 22 November

1887 **Nos bons jurés** (Marius Boullard/w Fabrice Carré) Théâtre des Variétés 5 December

1888 **Le Valet de coeur** (Raoul Pugno/w Charles Clairville) Théâtre des Bouffes-Parisiens 19 April

1888 **Les Premières Armes de Louis XV** revised *Les Beignets du Roi* (Théâtre des Menus-Plaisirs)

1889 **La Vénus d'Arles** (Varney/w Liorat) Théâtre des Nouveautés 30 January

1889 **Riquet à la houppe** (Varney/w C Clairville) Théâtre des Folies-Dramatiques 20 April

1890 **Cendrillonnette** (Roger, Serpette) Théâtre des Bouffes-Parisiens 24 January

1890 **Le Fétiche** (Roger/w C Clairville) Théâtre des Menus-Plaisirs 13 March

1890 **Samsonnet** (Roger) Théâtre des Nouveautés 26 November

1890 **La Fée aux chèvres** (Varney/w Albert Vanloo) Théâtre de la Gaîté 18 December

1891 **Le Coq** (Roger/w Ernest Depré) Théâtre des Menus-Plaisirs 30 October

1891 **Mademoiselle Asmodée** (Roger, Lacome/w C Clairville) Théâtre de la Renaissance 23 November

1892 **Mé-na-ka** (Serpette) 1 act Théâtre des Nouveautés 2 May

1892 **Miss Robinson** (Varney) Théâtre des Folies-Dramatiques 17 December

1893 **La Prétentaine** (Vasseur/w R Bénédite) Nouveau-Théâtre 10 October

1895 **Chilpéric** revised version w Hervé (Théâtre des Variétés)

1895 **La Dot de Brigitte** (Roger, Serpette/w Antony Mars) Théâtre des Bouffes-Parisiens 6 May

1895 **Le Carnet du diable** (Serpette/w Ernest Blum) Théâtre des Variétés 23 October

1895 **Le Capitole** (Serpette/w C Clairville) Théâtre des Nouveautés 5 December

1896 **Le Royaume des femmes** (Serpette/w Blum) Eldorado 24 February

1896 **Le Chevalier d'Harmental** (Messager) Opéra-Comique 5 May

1896 **Le Carillon** (Serpette/w Blum) Théâtre des Variétés 7 November

1897 **La Peur du gendarme** (Jules Darien/w Henri Bocage) Théâtre des Bouffes-Parisiens 21 February

1898 **La Revanche de Galathée** (Edmond Diet) 1 act Théâtre Bodinière 20 April

1900 **Le Portrait magique** (Domergue) 1 act Parisiana 28 May

1900 **Mariage princier** (Ernest Gillet) Théâtre de la Renaissance 17 August

1900 **Le Petit Chaperon rouge** (Marius Baggers/w Blum, Pierre Decourcelle) Théâtre du Châtelet 22 December

1901 **La Fille du Tabarin** (Gabriel Pierné/w Victorien Sardou) Opéra-Comique 20 February

1901 **Le Tout Petit Chaperon rouge** (Diet) 1 act Charleville 14 December

1902 **Ordre de l'empereur** (Justin Clérice) Théâtre des Bouffes-Parisiens 4 March

1902 **Madame la Présidente** (Diet/w Auguste Germain) Casino, Enghien-les-Bains 13 June; Théâtre des Bouffes-Parisiens 4 September 1902

1904 **La Fille de Roland** (Henri Rabaud) Opéra-Comique 16 March

1904 **Le Voyage de la mariée** (Diet, Clérice/w Ordonneau) Galeries Saint-Hubert, Brussels 9 December

1904 **La Chauve-souris** (*Die Fledermaus*) French version (Théâtre des Variétés)

1905 **La Petite Bohème** (Henri Hirschmann) Théâtre des Variétés 19 January

1907 **La Feuille de vigne** (Hirschmann) Théâtre du Moulin-Rouge 24 February

1908 **Oeil de gazelle** (Clérice) Opéra, Monte Carlo February

1910 **Rhodope** (Louis Ganne/w Paul de Choudens) Monte Carlo 13 December

1910 **Noël** (Frédéric d'Erlanger/w Jeanne Ferrier) Opéra-Comique 28 December

1911 **La Danseuse de Tanagra** (Hirschmann/w Felicien Champsaur) Opéra, Nice 10 February

1911 **Le Voile de bonheur** (Charles Pons) 1 act Opéra-Comique 26 April

1912 **La Petite Quaker** (*The Quaker Girl*) French version w Charles Quinel (L'Olympia)

1913 **Les Merveilleuses** French version (Théâtre des Variétés)

1914 **Miousic** (Lecocq, Messager, Hahn, Redstone, Hirschmann, Xavier Leroux, Camille Erlanger, Cuvillier, Paul Vidal, Paul Letombe) L'Olympia 21 March

LES FÊTARDS Opérette in 3 acts by Antony Mars and Maurice Hennequin. Music by Victor Roger. Théâtre du Palais-Royal, Paris, 28 October 1897.

Les Fêtards, a vastly comical piece said, semi-privately, to be based on a real-life tale of courtesan-dancer Cléo de Mérode and a certain royal personage, was produced by MM Mussay and Boyer at the height of the fashion for the most sophisticated form of vaudeville or comedy with songs, and it saw a return by musical theatre to Paris's home of classy comedy, the Palais-Royal. A top-notch Parisian cast including Jeanne Cheirel, Charles Lamy and the greatest character lady of them all, Marie Desclauzas, played Mars and Hennequin's delightful musical comedy tale of a dancing girl who teaches a modest Marquise how to use woman's arts to woo back a straying husband, through a highly successful initial run of 74 performances.

The pious, provincial Marquise Edith de Chatellerault (Mlle Cheirel), who has brought her millions from

America and wed her title (Gaston Dubosc), heads horrifiedly for Paris when she discovers her Marquis's tendency to duplicity and dancing girls and there, angry, troubled and at first incognito, she befriends Théa (Mlle Sidley), the dancer whom he is, so far unsuccessfully, chasing. As a lesson in how to handle a man, Théa makes Edith listen from behind a screen as her own husband tries to win something more than a kiss from the dancer. Edith, determining to win back her husband by following Théa's example, is surprised in the dressing room by the lubricious King Ernest III of Illyria (Raimond), who has come to pay court to the famous Théa. With—at first, anyway—the dancer's connivance, Edith remains ''Théa'' to the enraptured King for a night of partying and, by various stratagems, manages both to keep her husband and the dancer apart and at the same time chastely misdirect the royal clutches on to the King's old flame, the now buxom wardrobe-mistress Mme Maréchal (Desclauzas), in the dark. After a third act of the liveliest of quiproquos, the Marquise has well and truly had her revenge on her almost-strayed spouse, the Marquis finds he has a rather different kind of wife, and the King realizes the ''night of bliss'' he has been singing about since the end of the last act was spent not with a young dancer but with the aging but expert duenna.

The piece gave rise to some exceptionally fine roles—the royal roué savoring, in Victor Roger's lively song, the delights in store from ''La p'tit' Théa,'' the tight-laced Marquise turned coquette, with her transformation song (''Si le révérend me voyait''), her vengeful ''Vous verrez, mon cher'' and her troubled duet with Théa (''C'est par la coquetterie''), the sprightly dancer, the archetypal and omnipresent silly-ass Frenchman, Duc Jéhan de Beaugeancy (Charles Lamy), the would-be marquis-of-the-world, and the show-stealing character lady, Madame Maréchal. In the part of the weighty duenna, once little ''Zozo'' and the plaything of the pre-throned king, Desclauzas had, for the second time in her remarkable career, the role of a lifetime, with the pick of the comic songs—her advice to the coryphées of the Opéra to get into ''du bon trois pour cent'' while they have the chance and their lovers the money, her chase after the King (''Je n'avais pas de parapluie'') and her apologetic apostrophe to her late husband (''Grégoire, Grégoire'') for her naughty doings.

Following its Paris success, *Les Fêtards* was played in Austria and Germany as *Wie man Männer fesselt* (''how to tie up men,'' ad Otto Eisenschitz) and in Hungary as *A bibliás asszony* (''the bible girl'') with Roger's amusingly apt and tongue-in-cheek original score attached, but in English-speaking countries, producers preferred to provide their own music. George Edwardes called upon Lionel Monckton and Howard Talbot to write the score for the piece he had already successfully staged as a straight comedy, and which he called *Kitty Grey* (Apollo Theatre 7 September 1901) through a long and international career, whilst in America, George Lederer commissioned music from Ludwig Englander to illustrate a more low-comedy version of the libretto called *The Rounders* (Casino Theater 12 July 1899). Thomas Q Seabrooke was Maginnis Pasha, an Irish Turk instead of a King of Illyria, Phyllis Rankin played Théa, Mabelle Gilman was Priscilla and Dan Daly turned the dude role into the Duke of Paty de Clam. The piece was an indubitable hit through 131 performances and a return season (with Joseph Herbert replacing as the Duke and Madge Lessing as Priscilla) of 35 nights the following year (25 June 1900). German-speaking New Yorkers had, however, the opportunity to hear the original score when Annie Dirkens, Georgine Neuendorff, Willy Thaller and Jo Hegyi played Eisenschitz's version at the Irving Place Theater in 1906.

That version had already scored a hit in Europe, the sensational initial season of 150 consecutive and 210 total performances at the Vienna Theater in der Josefstadt with Annie Dirkens (Edith), Adele Moraw (Théa), Karl Tuschl (Fürst Niki), Gustav Maran (Beaugency), Karl Pfann (Baron) and the little character actress Viktoria Pohl-Meiser (Mme Maréchal) being followed by a tour which included a guest season at the Munich Theater am Gärtnerplatz, and productions at Berlin's Thalia-Theater, where Frln Dirkens teamed with Wellhof and Frln Kramm, and at Hamburg's Carl-Schultze Theater (16 September 1900). The piece's mode was even strong enough to provoke the Munich Volkstheater to come out with a Rudolf Kneisl comedy defensively entitled *Wie man Weiber fesselt.* In Hungary (ad Jenő Heltai) ''the bible girl'' with Klára Küry, Gábi Bárdi and Terus Boján, later supplanted by the young Sári Fedák as Théa, was seen for a fine 59 performances at the Népszínház in its first run, prior to widespread productions.

Hungary: Népszínház *A bibliás asszony* 4 November 1898; Austria: Theater in der Josefstadt *Wie man Männer fesselt* 28 October 1898; Germany: Thalia-Theater *Wie man Männer fesselt* 11 May 1900; USA: Irving Place Theater *Wie man Männer fesselt* 27 December 1906

FEUER, Cy (b New York, 15 January 1911). Broadway producer of a number of major hits in the 1950s and 1960s.

Trained at the Juilliard School of Music, Feuer worked as a trumpeter in orchestras and bands, and as a musical director, before joining Republic Pictures in 1938 for a four-year stint as a film composer. He subsequently became head of the music department there (1945–47). In 1948, in partnership with Ernest Martin, he produced the Frank Loesser musical *Where's Charley?,* and the pair followed up with Loesser's next and most successful show, *Guys and Dolls* (1950) and a series of other musicals which included a high percentage rate of successes: Cole Porter's *Can-Can* (1953), the Broadway version of the London hit *The Boy Friend* (1954), Porter's *Silk Stockings* (1955), *Whoop-Up* (1958), Loesser's *How to Succeed in Business without Really Trying* (1961), the brilliant burlesque *Little Me* (1962), *Skyscraper* (1965), a musicalized *Hobson's Choice* called *Walking Happy* (1966), and *The Act* (1977). They also produced the highly successful film version of the musical *Cabaret* and the less successful screen *A Chorus Line*.

Feuer also directed *Silk Stockings, Whoop-Up, Little Me, Skyscraper, Walking Happy,* and *I Remember Mama,* and was credited with a contribution to the libretto of *Whoop-Up*.

Between 1975 and 1980 Feuer and Martin were co-managers of the Los Angeles and San Francisco Light Opera Association and in 1989 Feuer became President of the League of American Theatres.

His son, Jed Feuer, composed the score for the off-Broadway musical *Eating Raoul* (Boyd Graham/Paul Bartel) .

[DAS] FEUERWERK Musical comedy in 3 acts by Erik Charell and Jürg Amstein based on the comedy *De sächzigscht Giburtstag* by Emil Sautter and the musical play *Der schwarze Hecht* by Amstein. Lyrics by Jürg Amstein and Robert Gilbert. Music by Paul Burkhard. Bayerische Staatsoperette, Munich, 16 May 1950.

Amstein and Burkhard's musical adaptation of Sautter's locally colored Swiss play was originally produced in a small-scale version at the Zürich Schauspielhaus in 1939, and it was revived there in a revised version in 1948. This revival resulted in the show coming to the attention of the director Erik Charell, many years earlier the stager of the glitziest and grandest musical theatre spectacles in Berlin, who saw in its circus connection the possibilities for expansion into something like his London *The Flying Trapeze* of 1935. As a result, *Der schwarze Hecht* became *Feuerwerk,* Charell's name joined Amstein's in the credits, and the revised piece was produced by the Bayerische Staatsoperette in Munich in 1950.

On the occasion of Albert Oberholzer's 60th birthday his family gather together from far and wide. Frau Oberholzer and daughter Anna greet papa's four respectable brothers and sister, whilst the cook, Kati, prepares the birthday supper. But then the black sheep of the family turns up: brother Alexander, now a circus manager called Obolski (Gustav Knuth), and his circus-artiste wife, Iduna (Rita Wottawa). Anna, enchanted by Iduna and the visions of a colorful and extraordinary life she represents, determines to go off and join the circus, and things begin to boil up. Her parents are aghast; her boyfriend, the little gardener Robert, furious; the cook gives notice because no one is eating her food; a hen-pecked husband rebels; and Obolksi and Iduna are loudly accused of bringing discontent into a well-ordered house, before the party breaks up. The family depart, and Anna puts aside her momentarily stirred-up dreams and settles for the safe gentility of her home, the not terribly satisfactory Robert, and Kati's dinner. The second act of this version contained a long, tacked-in ''dream'' circus scenario in which all the actors took part, filling the show out into a full and highly colored Charellish evening.

Burkhard's score produced several pretty pieces, notably Iduna's ''Ich hab' ein kleines süsses Pony,'' but it was her description of her father, the clown, which proved to be the hit of the evening—''O mein Papa war eine wunderbare Clown.'' It was that number, as purveyed to popularity on disc variously by Eddie Calvert, Eddie Fisher, Lys Assia and Connie Francis, which helped to spread the show further afield. Vienna's Theater in der Josefstadt welcomed 57 performances, Suzy Delair (Iduna), Jacqueline Cadet and Jean Bretonnière headed the cast of a Simone Volterra production (ad Jean Boyer, Pierre Destailles) at Paris's Théâtre Marigny, Britain's Bristol Old Vic presented *Oh, My Papa!* (ad Elizabeth Montagu) with sufficient success for it to be taken to London, with Rachel Roberts (Iduna) and Laurie Payne (Obolski) featured, for a brief run, and a film version, directed by Charell, was made by Sacha-Films and Kurt Hoffmann, with Lili Palmer (Iduna), Karl Schönböck (Obolski), Romy Schneider (Anna) and Claus Biederstädt (Robert) heading the cast.

In 1983 *Feuerwerk* was reproduced at Vienna's Volksoper with Helga Papouschek (Iduna), Kurt Heumer (Obolski) and Elisabeth Kales (Anna), and it continues to win regional productions, both in its original (*Der schwarze Hecht* Stadttheater St Gallen 30 December 1992, etc) and its inflated forms.

Austria: Theater in der Josefstadt 15 May 1952; France: Théâtre Marigny *Feu d'artifice* 1952; UK: Bristol Old Vic *Oh, My Papa!* 2 April, Garrick Theatre, London 17 July 1957

Recordings: selections (Ariola-Eurodisc, Philips), selection in English (Parlophone EP)

FEYDEAU, Georges [Léon Jules Marie] (b Paris, 8 December 1862; d Paris, 5 June 1921).

The famous French author of farce and comedy dipped into the musical theatre early in his career with an opérette written in collaboration with Gaston Serpette. It was a two-week failure, and it was another 15 years and many of his best plays later before he tried another full-length musical show. The second piece ran just two performances longer than the first. Thereafter his only musical theatre venture was with a musical spectacular, *L'Âge d'or,* for the Théâtre des Variétés, but several of his plays proved to be the material for altogether more successful musical comedies.

The most famous, *L' Hôtel du Libre-Échange* (w Desvallières), was the source of the successful 1920 London musical *A Night Out* (Willie Redstone/Clifford Grey/ George Grossmith, Arthur Miller) and the less fortunate American version of that adaptation played under the same title (w Vincent Youmans/Irving Caesar). A second American adaptation, *Hotel Passionato* (Philip Springer/ Joan Javits/Jerome J Schwartz, 1965), also failed.

La Dame de Chez Maxim (1899) became the successful *Das Mädel von Montmartre* with a score by Henri Berény, which was later played in America as *The Girl from Montmartre* (1912), as well as *La dama di Montmartre* (mus: Ermete Liberati, 1920) in Italy and *Dama od Maxima* (Ryszard Sielicki/Antoni Marianowicz) in Romania (1967), whilst *La Duchesse des Folies-Bergère* became *Die Nachtprinzessin,* described as a musical vaudeville, with a score by Carl Weinberger (Hamburg, 4 April 1914), and *Un fil à la patte* was musicalized by Robert Winterberg as *Der letzte Kuss* (Komödienhaus, 1925). Most recently, Feydeau's *Le Système Ribadier* (w M Hennequin) was set to music for France (Vincennes, 25 November 1994, Michel Frantz/J Pelebrat).

1887 **La Lycéenne** (Gaston Serpette) Théâtre des Nouveautés 23 December

1890 **Mademoiselle Nounou** (w Maurice Desvallières) 1 act Brussels 25 April

1902 **Le Billet de Joséphine** (Alfred Kaiser/w Joseph Méry) Théâtre de la Gaîté 23 February

1905 **L'Âge d'or** (Louis Varney/w Desvallières) Théâtre des Variétés 1 May

Biographies: Lorcey, J: *Georges Feydeau* (La Table Ronde, Paris, 1972), Pronko, L: *Georges Feydeau* (Ungar, New York, 1975), Gidel, H: *Feydeau* (Flammarion, Paris, 1991), etc

FIDDLER ON THE ROOF Musical in 2 acts by Joseph Stein based on the stories of Sholom Aleichem. Lyrics by Sheldon Harnick. Music by Jerry Bock. Imperial Theater, New York, 22 September 1964.

The stories of the Russian-American humorist Sholom Aleichem (né Solomon Rabinowitz, 1859–1916), which had been used several years previously as the basis for a play by Arnold Perl called *Tevya and His Daughters* (Carnegie Hall Playhouse, New York 16 September 1957), were reused to create the libretto for the most successful Broadway musical play of the 1960s. Mr Perl was given a footnoted ''by special permission of . . .'' attached to an asterisk following ''based on Sholom Aleichem's stories.''

Fiddler on the Roof told a tale of the breaking-down of established, traditional ways of life—in this case, Russian Jewish traditional life—in the early 20th century, partly under the pressure of changes from the inside, where the younger generation prove no longer willing to bend their individual will to the laws of their fathers, and partly under the pressure of the jealousy, greed and hatred of people outside the community. The first crack in the hard-working, unexpansive life of Anatevka's village milkman Tevye (Zero Mostel), his wife Golde (Maria Karnilova) and their daughters comes when, in accordance with tradition, Tevye has the matchmaker Yente (Beatrice Arthur) make an advantageous match for his eldest daughter Tzeitel (Joanna Merlin), with the widowed butcher Lazar Wolf (Michael Granger). Tzeitel has, unfortunately, had time to fall in love with the poor tailor Motel (Austin Pendleton), and her soft-hearted father has to go to great and shaming lengths to break off the promised match. The second daughter, Hodel (Julia Migenes), falls under the charms of the jingoistic ''student,'' Perchik (Bert Convy), who ends up in a labor camp, whilst little Chava (Tanya Everett) goes furthest of all and chooses as her bridegroom the Christian, Fyedka. And while the bewildered Tevye's world is breaking down around him, the pogroms arrive to finish off the community of Anatevka. Tevye and the remaining members of his family set off to America, taking their battered traditions with them.

Bock and Harnick's musical illustration of the tale was of a rare warmth. The gently lilting ''Sunrise, Sunset,'' Motel's explosion of joy in ''Miracle of Miracles,'' Tevye's sudden and unexpected question to his wife after 25 years of an arranged marriage, ''Do You Love Me?,'' Perchik and Hodel's ''Now I Have Everything'' and Hodel's ballad as she leaves to follow him, ''Far from the Home I Love,'' were feeling moments. There were colorful ones too—the butcher and the milkman raising a tipsy paean ''To Life,'' the celebration of ''Tradition,'' the three eldest daughters taking sudden three-part-harmonized fright at the realization that ''Matchmaker, Matchmaker'' might not bring them what they want in a husband, and Tevye's stand-up spot, apostrophizing God as to what would be the harm ''If I Were a Rich Man?'' There was a sufficiency of Jewish and local coloring in the score to be apt without being obtrusively ethnic, and only rarely did this most atypical of Broadway shows reach into the out-front or the showy in its music or in its staging. The principal dance routine, in a musical play set in a time and place in history where women may not dance in public, was director/choreographer Jerome Robbins's memorable version of the all-male bottle dance.

Harold Prince's production of *Fiddler on the Roof* won a clutch of Tony Awards, including that for Best Musical, and broke the Broadway long-run record for a musical play by remaining 3,242 performances at the Imperial Theater, where it used up a half-dozen Tevyes including Herschel Bernardi and singing star Jan Peerce. The first replacement, Luther Adler, headed out the initial American touring company, which traveled for more than two years. *Fiddler on the Roof* returned to Broadway in 1976 (Winter Garden Theater 28 December), with Mostel repeating his original role alongside Thelma Lee (Golde) for 167 performances, and again in 1990–91 when a touring production with Topol starred pitched camp at the Gershwin Theater (18 October 1990) for seven months.

Israeli actor Topol was the first British Tevye in Harold Prince and Richard Pilbrow's production at London's Her Majesty's Theatre. Miriam Karlin (Golde), Rosemary Nicols (Tzeitel), Jonathan Lynn (Motel), Cynthia Grenville (Yente), Paul Whitsun-Jones (Wolf), Linda Gardner (Hodel) and Caryl Little (Chava) were the initial supporting cast, and once again the show proved to be a major hit, playing through 2,030 London performances during which Alfie Bass and Lex Goudsmit were also seen as Tevye, and Avis Bunnage and Hy Hazell as Golde. Topol subsequently starred in the 1971 film version of the show, with Norma Crane (Golde), Molly Picon (Yente), Rosalind Harris (Tzeitel) and Leonard Frey (Motel), and he continued thereafter to appear regularly as Tevye, notably in a revival at London's Apollo Victoria Theatre in 1983 (28 June), again on Broadway in 1990, and yet again at the London Palladium in 1994 (28 June).

Australia's *Fiddler on the Roof,* featuring Hayes Gordon and Brigid Lenihan, played 11 months in Sydney and Melbourne (Her Majesty's Theatre 28 October 1967) and the show established itself as a perennial favorite there as well, eventually finding itself a home as a regular money-maker in the repertoire of the Australian Opera in the 1990s.

Fiddler on the Roof was one of the very few English-language musical plays of its period to make a significant and enduring mark in Europe. The first German-language version (ad Rolf Merz) was produced by Werner Schmid in Hamburg, under the title *Anatevka,* with Shmuel Rodensky as Tevye and Lilly Towska as Golde, and the show was subsequently seen in Düsseldorf and in Berlin before being mounted at Vienna's Theater an der Wien. Oddly, the credits now read ''musical based on the tale 'Tevye, the Milkman' by Sholem Aleichem with permission of Arnold Perl''—just one tale and no asterisk. Yossi Yadin was Vienna's Tevye and Lya Dulizkaya, who had already played Golde some six hundred times opposite Bomba J Zur in the hugely successful Israeli production, was Golde. The Vienna season of 232 performances was the most substantial among those achieved by any of the series of imported musicals staged at the Theater an der Wien in the later 1960s and early 1970s, and the German-language version (later played also as *Der Fiedler auf dem Dach*) maintained its position at the top of the heap throughout the following decades. It was most recently revived at the Theater an der Wien (31 January 1997) with Karl Merkatz as Tevye.

Helsinki, Copenhagen, Tokyo and Amsterdam were others amongst the earliest cities to mount productions of the show and in 1972 even Paris, disinterested for decades in the produce of the overseas musical theatre, mounted *Un violon sur le toit* (ad Robert Manuel, Maurice Vidalin) with Yvan Rebroff as a richly basso Tevye and Maria Murano as Golde. In Hungary, *Hegedüs a háztetőn* (ad György Dénes, István Reményi Gyenes) was produced at the Fővárosi Operettszínház in 1973, and it remains in the repertoire in Hungary to this day, having been given a major revival at the Madách Színház as recently as 1996 (28 September).

Performed incessantly around the world, *Fiddler on the Roof* is firmly fixed in the international repertoire as one of the outstanding, most frequently and widely played musicals of its or any other era. Which goes to prove that—in turn-of-the-century times where glitz and hydraulics, soap-opera and cartoon-dimensioned characters and action dominate the musical theatre—a warm and characterful musical play, unextravagant and unexaggerated in sentiment, staging and song, has more public appeal than the glitz merchants would seem to recognize. And they don't come any warmer and more characterful than *Fiddler on the Roof.*

Aleichem was included in the credits of another American musical—an adaptation of his *Hard to Be a Jew* illustrated with songs by Itzak Perlow (lyrics) and Sholom Secunda (music), produced at New York's Eden Theater 28 November 1973—but Moscow's Jewish Theatre beat both pieces to the punch. Their musical comedy *200,000* (''adapted from Sholom Aleichem'') was on the stage already in the 1920s.

UK: Her Majesty's Theatre 16 February 1967; Australia: Her Majesty's Theatre, Sydney 16 June 1967; Germany: Operettenhaus, Hamburg *Anatevka* 1 February 1968; Austria: Theater an der Wien *Anatevka* 15 February 1969; France: Théâtre Marigny *Un violon sur le toit* 1972; Hungary: Fővárosi Operettszínház *Hegedüs a háztetőn* 9 February 1973

Film: United Artists 1971

Recordings: original cast (RCA), London cast (CBS), German/Hamburg cast (Decca), Austrian cast (Preiser), French cast (CBS), South African Cast (RCA), Israel casts in Yiddish and Hebrew (Columbia), Japanese cast (Toho, 2 records), Mexican cast (Capitol), Hungarian cast (Qualiton), Argentine cast (PAR), Norwegian cast (Nordisc), Dutch cast (RCA), Danish cast (Decca), Icelandic cast (SG EP), Austrian cast 1997 (Reverso), Netherlands cast 1998 (Endemol), film soundtrack (United Artists), Czech cast (ASA), etc

DER FIDELE BAUER Operette in a prologue and 2 acts by Victor Léon. Music by Leo Fall. Hoftheater, Mannheim, 27 July 1907; Theater an der Wien, Vienna, 1 June 1908.

In spite of being written to a text by Victor Léon, recently the co-author of the blockbusting *Die lustige Witwe,* the Operette with which the young Leo Fall first made his name was not initially produced in Vienna or in Berlin, but at the Hoftheater in Mannheim. The success of the first staging of *Der fidele Bauer* was, however, indubitable, and the show racked up an enormous number of productions throughout the provinces of Germany in the years that followed. Keller's survey of musical-theatre performances in Germany during the first 20 years of the 20th century rates it statistically an all-time sixth behind *Die Fledermaus, Die lustige Witwe, Das Dreimäderlhaus, Die Geisha* and *Der Zigeunerbaron.* However, in spite of this rush of popularity, it was nearly 12 months after the Mannheim premiere before the show was given its first production in the Austrian capital—which had by then seen Fall thoroughly launched with the production of *Die Dollarprinzessin*—and more than 4 months more before Berlin saw its first production of *Der fidele Bauer.*

Matthäus Scheichelroither (Louis Treumann) is a peasant farmer, firmly and happily fixed in his old-fashioned ways and with ambition only that his son, Stefan (Adolf Lussmann), should have all the advantages in life. Eight years at a good school in Linz are followed by 11 years more study until Stefan becomes a doctor. But when he pays a quick visit home, it is embarrassedly to tell his father and his sister, Annamirl (Gusti Stagl), that he is to be wed to Friederike von Grunow (Nelly Ridon), the daughter of a Privy Councillor. It would not be comfortable for his peasant family to attend the wedding. So the Scheichelroithers stay home. But when neighbor Lindoberer (Max Pallenberg) takes Matthäus and Annamirl to Vienna six months later, the meeting of the town and country families finally takes place and, thanks to Matthäus's ingenuous sincerity and the genuine goodness of Friederike and her family, the ending is a happy one. Parallel to the main tale ran the little love story of Annamirl and Lindoberer's son, Vincenz (Hugo Machiau).

Fall's musical score was full of winning melodies, from the swinging Bauernmarsch ("Ich bin nix wie a Bauer") to the gentle thankfulness of Matthäus's waltz "Jeder tragt sein Pinkerl," Stefan's more forwardly waltzing "O frag' mich nicht, mein süsser Schatz," a jolly trio for Matthäus, Lindoberer and Annamirl "Wir waren unser drei" and a winning little folksy number ("Heinerle, Heinerle hab' kein Geld") for an incidental girl called Red Lisi (Grete Freund), explaining to her little son (Klara Meissel) that she cannot afford to buy him presents from the village fair.

Der fidele Bauer was played 54 times under Karczag and Wallner at the Theater an der Wien, before and after the summer break of 1908, and it then moved on to the Raimundtheater (9 October) with Franz Gross as Matthäus and Grete Petrovits as Annamirl, for additional performances in 1908, 1909 (including a season at the Carltheater from 9 November) and again in 1910, with Ernst Tautenhayn taking the show's title role alongside the Lindoberer of Franz Glawatsch. In Vienna, however, the show did not win the same degree of popularity as *Die Dollarprinzessin.* It nevertheless returned several times to the Raimundtheater, being seen there in 1914, in 1920 and again as recently as 1979. A new production was mounted at the Vienna Volksoper in 1997 (13 September) with Peter Minich in the title role.

In Berlin (Theater des Westens 23 October 1908), the show scored heavily, racing to its hundredth performance on 15 September 1909, ending up with a score of 234, and engraving itself thereafter into the list of the time's biggest successes.

An Hungarian version (ad Ferenc Révesz, Emil Tábori) and an English adaptation (ad Cosmo Hamilton) were produced the year following the Vienna premiere. The London version featured one-time *Gondoliers* star Courtice Pounds as Matthäus, Julius Walther (Stefan), Marie West (Frieda) and former top-billed stars Florence St John and Arthur Williams in the small roles of Red Lisi and Zopf, and it also included additional numbers by one Theodore Holland. After a poor start, its book was revised by Hamilton, but the production still managed only 71 performances.

Although Henry Savage advertised that he would produce *A Sturdy Peasant* in the wake of *The Merry Widow,* and Werba and Luescher announced *The Jolly Peasant* for 1911 (before going bust), and both George Marion (1911) and David Bispham (1913) were variously reported as being "in rehearsal" to play Matthäus, Broadway did not ever see *Der fidele Bauer* in English. It was produced in New York only by Gustav Amberg at the German-speaking Garden Theater with Konrad Dreher (Matthäus), Lotte Engel (Annamirl) and Hansen (Vincent). Philadelphia had already enjoyed it in the original language more than a year earlier, and Dreher also played it in Chicago (1911). The Vienna Volksoper also played the piece in New York in repertoire during a tour in 1997.

Paris, likewise, did not take the piece up and the first French-language performances (ad Gustave Jonghbeys) were seen at Brussels's Théâtre Molière with Michel Dufour starred as Matthäus alongside Germaine Huber (Annamirl), Duncan (Stefan), Mlle Armel (Frida) and George (Lindoberer).

A 1951 film entitled *Der fidele Bauer* had a conventionalized screenplay by Rudolf Österreicher and Hubert and Georg Marischka in which Matthias's son Heinerle became not a doctor but a pianist, and paired off not with a middle-class German but with an American called Vivian Harrison. The music was ''arranged'' by Bruno Uher. Paul Hörbiger played the merry peasant, with Erich Auer as his son, Marianne Wischmann as the American and Elisabeth Karlan as sister Resi. Annamirl (Helly Servi) was someone else's daughter, but still romanced Vincenz (Franz Marischka), son of Lindoberer (Heinrich Gretler). An earlier screen version, made on the cusp of silent and sound films, was made without dialogue, but with an accompanying music track. A pre-Hollywooden Szőke (''Cuddles'') Szakall was the fidele Bauer.

Hungary: Fővárosi Nyari Színház *A kedélyes paraszt* 25 June 1909; UK: Strand Theatre *The Merry Peasant* 23 October 1909; Belgium: Théâtre Molière, Brussels *Le Joyeux Paysan* 20 October 1910; USA: German Theater, Philadelphia February 1910, Garden Theater (Ger) 22 February 1911

Films: Franz Seitz 1927, Donau-Berna/International films/Georg Marischka 1951

Recordings: selection (part-record) (Philips, EMI Columbia, Polydor), etc

FIELD, Ron[ald] (b New York, ?1934; d New York, 6 February 1989). Broadway choreographer and director.

Field worked as a child performer (*Lady in the Dark*) and a dancer (*Seventeen, Kismet, The Boy Friend*) in the theatre, but largely in television, before coming into evidence as the choreographer for the 1962 off-Broadway revival of *Anything Goes* and the St Louis Muny's Stephen Foster musical *I Dream of Jeannie* (1963, also lead dancer). His subsequent major choreography credits in a career which his biographical note claimed curiously included ''over 14 Broadway musicals'' were the original productions of *Cabaret* (Tony Award), *Zorba, Applause* (also director, Tony Awards) and the 1971 revival of *On the Town* (also director). His subsequent work, largely away from Broadway, included the musical staging of part of the Opening Ceremony for the Los Angeles Olympic Games, and the dances for a British revival of *Kiss Me, Kate* (1987). His last Broadway credit was on the short-lived *Rags* (1987).

FIELDING, Harold [Lewis] (b Woking, 4 December 1916).

Originally a child prodigy violinist who appeared on touring programs with Luisa Tetrazzini, then later an orchestral and concert promoter, Harold Fielding made his first London theatrical venture, in collaboration with C B Cochran, in the world of ballet. He entered the musical theatre with a spectacular staging of Rodgers and Hammerstein's television musical *Cinderella* at the London Coliseum in 1958 and followed that profitable production with the less successful *Aladdin* of Cole Porter and with London productions of the *Billy Barnes Revue, The Music Man* (1961) and *Sail Away* (1962) before launching his first original musical, the highly successful *Half a Sixpence* (1963).

Fielding subsequently produced a number of plays and revues (*Round Leicester Square, Hullaballoo, Let My People Come, Swann and Topping*) and ran Fielding's Music Hall at the Prince Charles Theatre for several years, but he concentrated largely on the musical theatre. There he scored further successes with the very long-running *Charlie Girl* (1965), the London versions of *Sweet Charity* (1967) and *Mame* (1969), the Wright and Forrest remake of *Walzer aus Wien* as *The Great Waltz* (1970) mounted at the Theatre Royal, Drury Lane, a revival of *Show Boat* (1971) which gave that show its longest-ever run, Cy Coleman's Broadway hit *I Love My Wife,* a revised version of Harry Rigby's revised *Irene,* and stage versions of the Frank Loesser *Hans Andersen* (1974) and the classic film *Singin' in the Rain* (1983), both featuring *Half a Sixpence* star, Tommy Steele. Each of these last two pieces returned for a second London season as did his highly successful production of the circus musical, *Barnum,* with Michael Crawford in its leading role.

A fine revival of *Charlie Girl* did less well, and joined the Houdini musical *Man of Magic* (1966), a London production of *You're a Good Man, Charlie Brown,* the Percy French tale *Phil, the Fluter* (1969), a musical version of the famous *Gone with the Wind* (1972) which lost more in America than it made in London, the tiny Hollywood tale of *The Biograph Girl,* the unfortunate Italian *Beyond the Rainbow* (*Aggiungi un posto a tavola*), and a dazzling London version of the burlesque operetta *On the Twentieth Century* in the debit column.

The successive failures of the expensive extravaganza *Ziegfeld* (1988) and the Petula Clark musical *Someone Like You* (1990) drove the man widely considered as the cleverest London showman of two generations from the production arena in which he had co-produced with both the aged Cochran and the young Cameron Mackintosh (*My Fair Lady* revival) but, largely, had supplied 30 years of entertainment which, if often sniffed at as ''popular'' by critics, had proven to be just that with the public.

THE FIELD OF THE CLOTH OF GOLD Burlesque by William Brough. Music composed and arranged by Frank Musgrave. Strand Theatre, London, 11 April 1868.

The most successful of the very long list of pasticcio burlesques produced by the Swanborough family at the Strand Theatre, *The Field of the Cloth of Gold* was an extravaganza based on an episode of British History—the meeting of Britain's King Henry VIII and France's François I and their courts at Ardres, near Guisnes (31 May

1520). Each monarch trying to outshine the other in splendor, their retainers were put to vast expense to caparison themselves and their followers, and it was said that many a rich man was that day ruined for life by the vain expense to which he was put. Into this unparalleled oportunity for stage spectacle, author Brough dropped a few plot elements from G P R James's popular historical novel *Darnley.* Thus, in between the stage pictures of the arrival of the British fleet at Calais, King Henry's tent, a tournament, and the Field of the Cloth of Gold itself, burlesque star Lydia Thompson as Earl Darnley got to romance the Lady Constance de Grey (Ada Swanborough), and challenge King Hal (Charles Fenton, also scenery) to tourney, to the accompaniment of much song and dance, and "some of the best puns to have been heard in the theatre." H J Turner played Queen Katherine in travesty, Fanny Hughes was Ann Boleyn (still, at this stage, but a maid of honor), Elise Holt was a leggy French noble, Tom Thorne was the villainous Guy the Cripple and David James the French King.

The score, in the manner of the time, was arranged from popular tunes and Ada Swanborough's parody of Vance's well-known "Walking in the Zoo" proved one of the evening's pop song highlights.

Produced as the theatre's annual Easter extravaganza, *The Field of the Cloth of Gold* ended up playing right through from one Easter to the next (298 performances) before going out on to the road and to the colonies with equal vigor. It was revived at the Strand in 1870 (June 20) with Elise Holt now playing Darnley and introducing the latest American novelty, "Shoo fly," and again in 1874 (2 July) with Angelina Claude (Darnley), Marius (François), Harry Cox (Henry) and Edward Terry (Guy), and Turner still playing the Queen. George Sims provided new lyrics, and John Fitzgerald arranged new music including popular songs and pieces of *Geneviève de Brabant, Chilpéric* and *La Fille de Madame Angot.* It returned again as a stopgap in 1877 (24 February) with Lottie Venne as Darnley and yet again in 1889 for a Christmas season at the Avenue Theatre (24 December) equipped with "new and popular music arranged by John Crook." Minnie Byron was Darnley and Albert Chevalier played the French king, equipped with the number "C'est chic." As late as 1901, when the old style of burlesque had been many years dead and buried, a new production of *The Field of the Cloth of Gold* (ad Fred Flexmore) was mounted at Kingston's Royal County Theatre (30 September).

Lydia Thompson did not take *The Field of the Cloth of Gold* with her in her repertoire when she left, to go to America, after the show's 104th night, but it crossed the Atlantic briskly in any case. The Worrell sisters produced what they claimed was Brough's show "rewritten by Charles Webb" at the New York Theatre in opposition to Lydia's performances at Wood's Museum. Sophie Worrell was Darnley, Jennie played Suffolk and did a clog dance, and the gendarmes' duo from *Geneviève de Brabant* was eased into the plot. When Lydia Thompson quit Wood's Museum for Niblo's, the management of Wood's brought in Mr and Mrs Florence with the same show "localised by Florence" (1 February 1869), with new music by Howard Glover and with the Florences top-billed as François and Constance and Rose Massey as Darnley. A few weeks later, when the Worrells hit Chicago's McVickers Theatre, they found that the opposition Crosby's Opera House had opened 48 hours earlier with a much more splendid production of *The Field of the Cloth of Gold* with the young Alice Oates as Darnley. The features, apart from "the tourney, the prize fight, the meeting of the kings and the bandit scene" included renditions of "The Pretty Girl That Winked at Me" and a burlesque of "Pretty Little Dark-Eyed Nell," a guitar solo, imitations, a pas de deux, "the Niagara Leap by the Leon Brothers, and Mlle Tournour on the trapeze." The production wiped out the Worrells and stayed on the boards for a remarkable 16 weeks, and Mrs Oates kept it in her repertoire for several years. In the years that followed, many a company of burlesquers touted *The Field of the Cloth of Gold* in its baggage round and round America.

USA: New York Theater 4 January 1869

FIELDS, Dorothy (b Allenhurst, NJ, 15 July 1901; d New York, 28 March 1974). Highly successful Broadway and Hollywood lyricist who also co-authored the libretti for several long-running musicals.

The daughter of Lew Fields, and the sister of Herbert Fields and Joseph Fields, Dorothy Fields was still in her early twenties when she formed a songwriting partnership with composer Jimmy McHugh which bore its first fruits with songs for the Cotton Club in 1927. The pair had their first hits with "I Can't Give You Anything But Love," "Diga, Diga, Doo" and "Doin' the New Low-Down" as performed in the hit revue *Blackbirds of 1928,* for which Miss Fields was also credited with the "book," and they followed up with the songs for what was virtually a Fields family show—Herbert wrote the text, and Lew produced and starred in the not unsuccessful *Hello Daddy*—and for *Blackbirds* producer Lew Leslie's less successful *International Revue* (1930, "On the Sunny Side of the Street," "Exactly Like You"). They also interpolated a successful number into *The Vanderbilt Revue* ("Blue Again").

In the 1930s Fields and McHugh abandoned the theatre and turned, instead, to supplying songs for a long list of Hollywood films, including *Love in the Rough* ("Go

Home and Tell Your Mother''), *Cuban Love Song, Singin' the Blues* (''It's the Darndest Thing,'' ''Singin' the Blues''), *Dinner at Eight* (''Don't Blame Me,'' ''Dinner at Eight''), *Have a Heart* (''Lost in a Fog''), and *Every Night at Eight* (''I'm in the Mood for Love,'' ''I Feel a Song Comin' On''). Miss Fields also collaborated with Jerome Kern on ''Lovely to Look At'' and a revised version of ''I Won't Dance'' for the film of *Roberta* (1935), and the partnership with Kern was pursued in such pieces as the Lily Pons film *I Dream Too Much, Swing Time* (''A Fine Romance,'' ''Pick Yourself Up,'' ''Waltz in Swing Time,'' ''The Way You Look Tonight'' [Academy Award]) and *The Joy of Living.* Amongst her other projects, Miss Fields provided the lyrics to Fritz Kreisler's melody for ''Stars in my Eyes'' in the Grace Moore film *The King Steps Out.*

In 1939 she worked on her first Broadway show for nearly a decade when she supplied the lyrics for the revusical *Stars in Your Eyes* (mus: Arthur Schwartz), but since her return to the book musical was on a Cole Porter musical, her contribution was not to the songwords but to the libretto, on which she collaborated with brother Herbert. *Let's Face It, Something for the Boys* and *Mexican Hayride* gave the lyricist three long-running successes as a librettist, and she added a fourth when she returned to lyric-writing for Sigmund Romberg's *Up in Central Park* (''Close as Pages in a Book''). When the Fieldses, brother and sister, combined with another songwriter in Irving Berlin on *Annie Get Your Gun,* Dorothy again returned to the post of co-librettist, and on this occasion won not only a long run but also her most enduring show hit.

She supplied lyrics and part-book for the 1950 *Arms and the Girl,* and the lyrics to Arthur Schwartz's attractive, if only moderately successful, pair of shows *A Tree Grows in Brooklyn* (''He Had Refinement'') and *By the Beautiful Sea* (''I'd Rather Wake Up By Myself,'' also co-librettist), and again for the music-hall murder musical *Redhead,* but found her greatest success as a Broadway lyricist when she combined with composer Cy Coleman on the score for *Sweet Charity* (1966, ''Big Spender,'' ''If My Friends Could See Me Now,'' ''The Rhythm of Life,'' ''There's Gotta Be Something Better Than This,'' ''Where Am I Going?'').

She contributed a score to only one further Broadway musical, Coleman's *Seesaw,* shortly before her death, turning out ''Nobody Does It Like Me,'' ''Welcome to Holiday Inn'' and the extravagantly youthful ''It's Not Where You Start (it's where you finish)'' to add to the long list of successful songs produced in a career of some 45 years in the theatre and film.

Her other credits include a television musical version of her brother Joseph's *Junior Miss* with music by Burton Lane (CBS 20 December 1957, lib: Joseph Stein, Will Glickman).

1928 **Hello Daddy** (Jimmy McHugh/Herbert Fields) Fields' Theater 26 December

1931 **Singin' the Blues** (McHugh/J P McGowan) Liberty Theater 16 September

1939 **Stars in Your Eyes** (Arthur Schwartz/J P McEvoy) Majestic Theater 9 February

1941 **Let's Face It** (Cole Porter/w H Fields) Imperial Theater 29 October

1943 **Something for the Boys** (Porter/w H Fields) Alvin Theater 7 January

1944 **Mexican Hayride** (Porter/w H Fields) Winter Garden Theater 28 January

1945 **Up in Central Park** (Sigmund Romberg/w H Fields) Century Theater 27 January

1946 **Annie Get Your Gun** (Irving Berlin/w H Fields) Imperial Theater 16 May

1950 **Arms and the Girl** (Morton Gould/w H Fields, Rouben Mamoulian) 46th Street Theater 2 February

1951 **A Tree Grows in Brooklyn** (Arthur Schwartz/Betty Smith, George Abbott) Alvin Theater 19 April

1954 **By the Beautiful Sea** (Schwartz/w H Fields) Majestic Theater 8 April

1959 **Redhead** (Albert Hague/w H Fields, Sidney Sheldon, David Shaw) 46th Street Theater 5 February

1966 **Sweet Charity** (Cy Coleman/Neil Simon) Palace Theater 29 January

1973 **Seesaw** (Coleman/Michael Stewart, Michael Bennett) Uris Theater 18 March

Biography: Winer, D G: *On the Sunny Side of the Street: The Life and Times of Dorothy Fields* (Schirmer, New York, 1997)

FIELDS, Herbert (b New York, 26 July 1897; d New York, 24 March 1958).

The son of Lew Fields, and brother of Dorothy Fields and Joseph Fields, Herbert Fields made his earliest forays into the musical theatre in college and amateur theatricals alongside the young Richard Rodgers and Lorenz Hart, variously directing, choreographing and writing as the occasion demanded. He collaborated with his two friends on a flop play, *The Melody Man,* produced by his father, and had his first successes alongside them with his contribution to the revue *The Garrick Gaieties* and the libretto for their first book musical, *Dearest Enemy* (1925).

The trio had further successes with *The Girl Friend,* and with adaptations of the favorite old play *Tillie's Nightmare* as *Peggy-Ann* and of Mark Twain's *A Connecticut Yankee (in King Arthur's Court),* but Fields had an even bigger success when he stepped outside the team to adapt the play *Shore Leave* as the libretto for the Vincent Youmans musical *Hit the Deck.* Later musicals with Rodgers and Hart—*Present Arms,* the adaptation of

Charles Pitts's *The Son of the Grand Eunuch* as the short-lived *Chee-Chee,* and the filmland burlesque *America's Sweetheart*—had less success than their earlier shows, and the songwriters and librettist went their separate ways.

Fields began an association with Cole Porter on the musical *Fifty Million Frenchmen,* and the pair continued with a series of long-running shows from *Dubarry Was a Lady* and *Panama Hattie,* both written with Buddy De Sylva, through *Let's Face It, Something for the Boys* and *Mexican Hayride* in which Fields was joined as co-librettist by his sister, Dorothy, with whom all his future stage musicals were written. Of these, *Up in Central Park* found a fine Broadway run, and *By the Beautiful Sea* and the posthumous *Redhead* some success, but it was the Fields's collaboration with Irving Berlin on the biomusical of sharp-shooting Annie Oakley, *Annie Get Your Gun,* which gave Herbert his biggest and most memorable hit.

1925 **Dearest Enemy** (Richard Rodgers/Lorenz Hart) Knickerbocker Theater 18 September

1926 **The Girl Friend** (Rodgers/Hart) Vanderbilt Theater 17 March

1926 **Peggy-Ann** (Rodgers/Hart) Vanderbilt Theater 27 December

1927 **Hit the Deck** (Vincent Youmans/Clifford Grey, Leo Robin) Belsaco Theater 25 April

1927 **A Connecticut Yankee** (Rodgers/Hart) Vanderbilt Theater 3 November

1928 **Present Arms** (Rodgers/Hart) Mansfield Theater 26 April

1928 **Chee-Chee** (Rodgers/Hart) Mansfield Theater 25 September

1928 **Hello Daddy** (Jimmy McHugh/Dorothy Fields) Fields' Theater 26 December

1929 **Fifty Million Frenchmen** (Cole Porter) Lyric Theater 27 November

1930 **The New Yorkers** (Porter) Broadway Theater 8 December

1931 **America's Sweetheart** (Rodgers/Hart) Broadhurst Theater 10 February

1933 **Pardon My English** (George Gershwin/Ira Gershwin) Majestic Theater 20 January

1939 **Dubarry Was a Lady** (Porter/w B G De Sylva) 46th Street Theater 6 December

1940 **Panama Hattie** (Porter/w De Sylva) 46th Street Theater 30 October

1941 **Let's Face It** (Cole Porter/w D Fields) Imperial Theater 29 October

1943 **Something for the Boys** (Porter/w D Fields) Alvin Theater 7 January

1944 **Mexican Hayride** (Porter/w D Fields) Winter Garden Theater 28 January

1945 **Up in Central Park** (Sigmund Romberg/w D Fields) Century Theater 27 January

1946 **Annie Get Your Gun** (Irving Berlin/w D Fields) Imperial Theater 16 May

1950 **Arms and the Girl** (Morton Gould/w D Fields, Rouben Mamoulian) 46th Street Theater 2 February

1954 **By the Beautiful Sea** (Schwartz/D Fields/w D Fields) Majestic Theater 8 April

1959 **Redhead** (Albert Hague/w D Fields, Sidney Sheldon, David Shaw) 46th Street Theater 5 February

FIELDS, Joseph [Albert] (b New York, 21 February 1895; d Beverly Hills, Calif, 3 March 1966).

Son of Lew Fields, brother of Herbert Fields and Dorothy Fields, and the co-author of the hit plays *My Sister Eileen* and *Junior Miss* (w Jerome Chodorov), Joseph Fields also worked with considerable success as a librettist in the musical theatre. He collaborated on the musical adaptation of Anita Loos's celebrated novel *Gentlemen Prefer Blondes* (1949) with its original author, on the adaptation of Chin Y Lee's novel as the Rodgers and Hammerstein musical *Flower Drum Song* (1958) with Hammerstein, and on *The Girl in Pink Tights,* a piece which used a fictitious version of the staging of the 19th-century extravaganza *The Black Crook* as its backdrop, and the adaptation of *My Sister Eileen* as *Wonderful Town,* both with Chodorov. *Junior Miss* was also musicalized, by his sister Dorothy and Burton Lane, for CBS-TV (20 December 1957).

1949 **Gentlemen Prefer Blondes** (Jule Styne/Leo Robin/w Anita Loos) Ziegfeld Theater 8 December

1953 **Wonderful Town** (Leonard Bernstein/Betty Comden, Adolph Green/w Jerome Chodorov) Winter Garden Theater 25 February

1954 **The Girl in Pink Tights** (Sigmund Romberg/Robin/w Chodorov) Mark Hellinger Theater 5 March

1958 **Flower Drum Song** (Richard Rodgers/Oscar Hammerstein II/w Hammerstein) St James Theater 1 December 1958

FIELDS, Lew [SCHANFIELD, Lewis Maurice] (b New York, 1 January 1867; d Beverly Hills, Calif, 20 July 1941). Variety and burlesque comedian who made his fame as half of the team of Weber and Fields before going on to a solo career as a producer of, and comedy star in, musicals.

Fields made his first stage appearances at the age of 10 in a dialect comedy double-act with another youngster, Joseph Weber, in minor variety theatres, and the pair continued to tour their act through the United States over the next 20 years, at first under other managements and, from 1885, with a company of their own. Fields, taller and slimmer, and Weber, shorter and stockier (and padded to emphasize the difference), both gaudily suited, derbied and whiskered, traded warm and heavily ''Dutch''-accented banter of a homely and broadly comical kind, and established themselves as considerable favorites.

In 1896 they took over the Imperial Music Hall at 29th Street and Broadway and renamed it Weber and

Fields' Broadway Music Hall, and there they produced and starred in a series of variety-cum-burlesque productions which have become remembered as the most famous of their kind in the American musical theatre. Their first program (5 September 1896) included a travesty of David Belasco's civil war drama *The Heart of Maryland* (*The Art of Maryland*), and their first big burlesque success was *The Geezer* (October 1896), a burlesque of Sidney Jones's musical play *The Geisha,* which had opened a month earlier at Daly's Theatre. The piece was written by Joseph Herbert and composed by John Stromberg, who was to be the team's resident composer for a number of years. Other recognizable-to-ostensible burlesques of popular shows followed—*Under the Red Globe* (of the Cardinal Richelieu drama *Under the Red Robe*), *The Glad Hand, or Secret Servants* (William Gillette's *Secret Service*), *Pousse Café, or The Worst Born* (*La Poupée* and Belasco's *The First-Born,* etc), *The Con-Curers* (Paul Potter's *The Conquerors*), *Cyranose de Bric-a-Brac* (*Cyrano de Bergerac*), etc, etc—but each found its mixture of low and parodic comedy in more than just its admitted target, taking potshots at all of Broadway and anything else of a topical nature in a lively, colorful and girlie-filled entertainment.

The pair made an early effort at what was less genuine burlesque and more a semi-plotless topical musical comedy with *Mister New York, Esquire* (1897) but, after a couple of years, they developed what proved to be their most popular formula with a series of what were basically variety musicals: a fairly irregular plot outline filled with comic scenes, songs, specialities and topicalities and usually with a sizeable piece of up-to-date specific burlesque introduced. *Hurly Burly* (1898), *Helter Skelter* (1899), *Whirl-I-gig* (1899), *Fiddle-dee-dee* (1900), *Hoity-Toity* (1901), *Twirly Whirly* (1902) and *Whoop-dee-Doo* (1903) presented such artists as Sam Bernard, Lillian Russell, Fay Templeton, De Wolf Hopper, David Warfield and Bessie Clayton alongside the star comedy pair, equipped with songs including "Dinah," "Ma Blushin' Rosie" and "Come "Down Ma Evenin' Star," and burlesques within the burlesques in *Zaza, Barbara Fidgety, The Girl from Martin's, Sapolio, The Other Way, Quo Vass Iss?, Arizona, Exhibit II, Madame du Hurry, The Curl and the Judge, The Man from Mars, Catherine, The College Widower, The Squawman's Girl of the Golden West* and others of the ilk.

The Weber and Fields shows were enormously popular with a large section of the public but, after nearly 30 years together, Weber and Fields finally fell out over Weber's role in one of their burlesques and, after the run of *Whoop-dee-Doo,* Fields seceded from the partnership.

He combined with his longtime dramaturg, Edgar Smith, to produce one of the English musical comedies which were the rage of Broadway but he unfortunately chose one which had failed even to make London: *An English Daisy* (1904) was not a success. He then went into a producing partnership with Fred Hamlin and Julian Mitchell, and opened Fields' Theater, beginning his tenancy there with the successful production by "Field's Stock Company" of Victor Herbert's *It Happened in Nordland* (1904). He himself took the principal comic role of Hubert alongside Marie Cahill. Although Fields' Theater and Fields' Stock Company were short-lived ventures, he produced and appeared in several other musicals and burlesques, starring most notably as Henry Schniff in a rewritten-to-measure version of the Willie Edouin comedy role which paired him with the buxom London Gaiety comedienne Connie Ediss in the British musical *The Girl Behind the Counter* (Herald Square, 1907 w S & L Shubert). He also played in his productions of *About Town/The Great Decide* (1905), *Old Dutch* (1909 w S & L Shubert, Ludwig Streusand), *The Summer Widowers* (1910, Otto Ott) and *The Henpecks* (1911, Henry Peck) while at the same time turning out a full schedule of other pieces in which he did not appear, mostly of home-bred musical comedies—the revue *The Mimic World* (1908 w S & L Shubert), *The Midnight Sons* (1908), Victor Herbert's tuneful *The Rose of Algeria* (1909), *The Jolly Bachelors* (1910) *The Prince of Bohemia* (1910), *The Yankee Girl* (1910), Marie Dressler's best vehicle *Tillie's Nightmare* (1910), *The Never Homes* (1911), *The Wife Hunters* (1911)—these totaling more than a dozen shows in the four years 1908–12.

In 1912 he again joined up temporarily with Joe Weber, and they appeared together in *Hokey Pokey* and *Roly Poly* and produced the unconsummated *The June Bride* (*Johann der Zweite*) before separating once more. During this period the pair also achieved what seems to have been a famous first. They had the entire production of *Hokey Pokey* recorded on film, during a performance at Rochester, NJ (2 April 1915), thus producing what would seem to be the first full-length film of a stage musical.

Fields continued both to produce (*Hanky Panky, The Sun Dodgers, Suzi,* etc) and also to perform, appearing as Jan van Haan in his production of *All Aboard* (1913), in a revival of *The Girl Behind the Counter,* rechristened *Step This Way* (1916, Henry Schniff) and in the non-singing star comic role of Augustus Tripp in his 1918 production (w the Shuberts) of *A Lonely Romeo,* but his attentions were now more orientated towards production. Having staged the first more-or-less Rodgers and Hart musical, *Poor Little Ritz Girl,* in 1920, he picked up on the subsequent musicals on which they collaborated with his librettist son, Herbert, and produced *The Girl Friend* (1926), their updated *Tillie's Nightmare, Peggy-Ann*

(1926), *A Connecticut Yankee* (1927), *Present Arms* (1928) and *Chee-Chee* (1928). His most successful latter-day production, however, was another of son Herbert's collaborations, this time with Vincent Youmans, *Hit the Deck* (1927).

Fields had to drop out of the production of *Wild Rose* (1924) two days before opening, through illness, and he made only one further stage musical appearance in New York thereafter, in *Hello Daddy* (1929), the suitably named show written by his children, Herbert and Dorothy, with a score by Jimmy McHugh. He ultimately also retired from production following a two-week revue flop (*The Vanderbilt Revue*) in 1930 having spent more than half a century as a performer and 40 years as a manager. However, he was later seen recreating some of his famous routines on film: performing the barbershop duo routine which had helped Vernon Castle make lift-off in *The Story of Vernon and Irene Castle* and pairing with Weber in their old act in a movie purporting to tell the life story of *Lillian Russell.*

Biographies: Isman, F: *Weber and Fields* (Boni & Liveright, New York, 1924), Fields A, Fields, L: *From the Bowery to Broadway* (OUP, New York, 1993)

FIELDS, W C [DUKINFIELD, William Claude] (b Philadelphia, 9 April 1879; d Pasadena, Calif, 25 December 1946).

Originally a juggler in vaudeville, Fields made an isolated appearance on the Broadway musical stage in his twenties, as the juggling detective Sherlock Baffles in the McIntyre and Heath variety musical *The Ham Tree* (1905, ''A New Way to Play Tennis''). Thereafter his fame was made in a half dozen editions of *The Ziegfeld Follies* (1915–21), but he appeared again in a musical, and with great success, as the expansively comical Professor Eustace McGargle in the 1923 show *Poppy,* before going on to the second portion of his memorable career in films. The third of his decidedly widely spaced Broadway musical performances took place in 1930 when he played the role of Q Q Quayle in *Ballyhoo,* a show set up to feature his talents but which instead sent its producer, Arthur Hammerstein, bankrupt.

At Owing Mills, Maryland, in 1971 Fields was made the subject of a musical unblushingly called *W. C.* (Al Carmines/Milton Sperling, Sam Locke) in which he was portrayed by Mickey Rooney, and he also put in an appearance in the British musical comedy *A Saint She Ain't* (1999), where he was impersonated by comedian Barry Cryer.

Autobiography: Fields, R (ed): *W C Fields by Himself: His Intended Autobiography* (Cassell, 1950; Prentice Hall, Englewood Cliffs, NJ, 1972); Biographies: Taylor, R L: *W C Fields, His Follies and Fortunes* (Doubleday, New York, 1949), Louvish, S: *The Man on the Flying Trapeze* (Faber, London, 1997)

FIFTY MILLION FRENCHMEN Musical comedy in 2 acts by Herbert Fields. Music and lyrics by Cole Porter. Lyric Theater, New York, 27 November 1929.

Songwriter Cole Porter and librettist Herbert Fields came together for what was to be the first of seven almost always successful shows on this revusically constructed piece with its reminiscences of such old British musicals as *A Runaway Girl* or *After the Girl* and their Cook's Tours of picturesque places.

The girl in this case is Looloo (Genevieve Tobin), the daughter of socially overambitious Emmitt Carroll (Thurston Hall) and his wife (Bernice Mershon). Mama and Papa have destined their daughter to be the Grand Duchess of the Grand Duke Ivan Ivanovitch (Mannart Kippen), but one fine day in Paris the wealthy playboy Peter Forbes (William Gaxton) falls flamboyantly in love with her. He bets his pal Michael (Jack Thompson) that he can win Looloo away from her Duke without disclosing his own attractive financial situation and, like his predecessors of *La Vie parisienne* and *Der Fremdenführer,* he takes on the role of a tourist guide in order to do so.

The revusical outline suited Porter's revusical style of song splendidly, and two pieces which would become Porter favorites found a home in *Fifty Million Frenchmen*: Looloo and Peter's mutual admission that ''You Do Something to Me'' and Michael's duet with the soubrette Betty Compton, in the role of Joyce Wheeler, asserting ''You've Got That Thing.'' Evelyn Hoey introduced ''Find Me a Primitive Man'' and ''I'm Unlucky at Gambling'' in the role of May de Vere, Helen Broderick, as Violet Hildegarde, delivered ''The Tale of an Oyster'' (until it was cut) and ''Where Would You Get Your Coat?,'' and there were only two songs which had Paree [*sic*] in the title.

Fifty Million Frenchmen had a muted reception, but it soon grew into a popular success on Broadway and ultimately had a run of 254 performances. It met with no such favor, however, in Britain. Produced at Glasgow, with Frances Day starred as Looloo, it fizzled out on the road, and never made it to London.

A 1931 Warner film entitled *Fifty Million Frenchmen,* used Gaxton and Miss Broderick and the show's format, as well as Olsen and Johnson, but not the songs, whilst, conversely, a short 1934 Vitaphone film called *Paree, Paree* [*sic, sic*] featuring Dorothy Stone and Bob Hope used both portions of *Fifty Million Frenchmen*'s music (four songs) and its tale.

UK: King's Theatre, Glasgow 1 September 1931

Recordings: selection (New World), studio cast (New World)

LA FILLE DE FANCHON LA VIELLEUSE Opéra-comique in 4 acts by Armand Liorat, William Busnach and Albert Fonteny. Music by Louis Varney. Théâtre des Folies-Dramatiques, Paris, 3 November 1891.

It seems that the famous street-singer Fanchon has left her orphaned daughter Javotte nothing but her viol as a legacy, but the truth is that her fortune has been gambled away by the Chevalier de Saint-Florent (Lacroix) to whom she entrusted its safekeeping and delivery. Before the wretch succeeds in gambling it back, the action has largely concerned the farcical events surrounding the attempts of the notary Bellavoine (Gobin) to seduce Javotte (Mlle Thuillier-Leloir), those of his wife Hermine (Zélo Duran) to consummate an affair with the flautist Zéphyrin (Guyon fils), and those of Javotte's country sweetheart, Jacquot (Larbaudière), to secure his bride.

A patent attempt, in its title, to repeat the success of *La Fille de Madame Angot,* it was not in the same class or in the same style as Lecocq's great work, although Varney's pretty score, featuring the old song of ''Fanchon la vielleuse'' as a sop to the title, helped the undoubtedly merry piece thorugh its well-received 110 Parisian performances. Even though it did not establish itself in the revivable repertoire, *La Fille de Fanchon la vielleuse* nevertheless got a number of foreign-language showings. A German-language production (ad uncredited) was mounted by Alexandrine von Schönerer at Vienna's Theater an der Wien with Ilka Pálmay as Javotte, Girardi as Zephirin, Ferdinand Pagin as Jacquot and Josef Joseffy as St Florent, without success (7 performances), and again at Dresden, but an Hungarian adaptation (ad Béla J Fái, Ferenc Rajna) played a good 37 performances at the Budapest Népszínház and was well enough regarded to be given a revival in 1902 (26 September). An American edition, *Fanchon's Daughter,* was announced by T Henry French in 1892, but was canceled in favor of W S Gilbert's *The Mountebanks.*

Hungary: Népszínház *Fanchon asszony leánya* 14 October 1892; Austria: Theater an der Wien *Fanchons Leyer* 15 October 1892; Germany: Residenztheater, Dresden *Fanchons Leier* 5 November 1892

LA FILLE DE MADAME ANGOT Opéra-comique in 3 acts by Clairville, Paul Siraudin and Victor Koning. Music by Charles Lecocq. Théâtre des Fantaisies-Parisiennes, Brussels, 4 December 1872.

Along with Planquette's *Les Cloches de Corneville, La Fille de Madame Angot* was the most successful product of the French-language musical stage in the postwar decades of the 19th century. Even such pieces as *HMS Pinafore* and *Die Fledermaus,* vastly successful though they were in their original languages, did not have the enormous international careers of Lecocq's opéra-comique, which swept the theatre world from one side to every other with unmitigated triumph for many, many years before settling into a permanent and prominent place at the head of the all-time French musical theatre repertoire.

In fact, *La Fille de Madame Angot* had its first showing not in France, but in Brussels, under the management of the producer, Eugène Humbert, who had mounted Lecocq and Clairville's previous work, *Les Cent Vierges.* The story goes (one of them, anyway) that the success of *Les Cent Vierges* led wheeler-dealing Victor Koning to thinking that another original work might do equally as well in Brussels. He proposed the idea to the playwright Paul Siraudin, who came up with the thought that there might be a libretto in the series of *Madame Angot* plays, written by the dramatist Maillot, which had found such success at the turn of the 19th century. Playwright Clairville was called in to put Koning's notion and Siraudin's idea (which may, or may not, have included dipping into Dumas's 1853 historical novel, *Ange Pitou,* for a hero) into libretto form, Lecocq to set the resultant piece to music, and Humbert was only too pleased to take in a new piece by the writers who had given him his earlier hit. Koning and Siraudin—neither of whom had written a word of the text—both kept their names on the bill as co-authors and, naturally, in the share-out of the royalties.

Another version of the birth of *La Fille de Madame Angot* gives the ideas all to Humbert who is supposed to have seen Clairville, Siraudin and Koning's *Revue en ville,* approached them to do an opéra-bouffe *Roméo et Juliette* for the Alcazar and, when they found that that didn't work, proposed instead a piece with a Directoire setting. If the piece were light in character he intended to give it to Lecocq to set, if heavier then to Litolff. But it was still Clairville who wrote it (with all the lyrics molded, vaudeville fashion, to exisiting tunes), Siraudin who put up ideas, and Koning who did the business.

Take your pick.

Clairette (Pauline Luigini) is the orphaned daughter of the famous fishwife Madame Angot, whose gallivanting with the Grand Turk has gone down in legend. She has been brought up, with all the advantages their money can buy, by the market-folk of Les Halles and her multiple ''parents'' are happy that she should wed the adoring, gentle little wig-maker Pomponnet (Alfred Jolly). But Clairette has other thoughts. She has been enraptured by the dashing political poet Ange Pitou (Mario Widmer), and so, rather than be wed to Pomponnet, she gets herself arrested, on what should have been her wedding day, for singing one of Pitou's dangerous songs in public. She is freed by the influence of a former schoolmate, the actress Mademoiselle Lange (Marie Desclauzas), who has risen to power as the mistress of Barras, a member of the ruling Directoire. Lange, however, is secretly part of a conspiracy to overthrow the feeble and corrupt new oligarchic government of the country.

Trouble arrives with a vengeance when Lange and Pitou meet and strike instant sparks. Clairette is not slow to recognize the signs, and she sets a trap for the pair, luring each to a rendezvous at the Bal du Calypso with a forged letter. When the actress and the poet openly express their feelings amongst the hedgerows of the Calypso, Clairette is waiting, with her ever-protective ''family'' at her back. But Mademoiselle Angot does not need protecting: it quickly becomes clear that she is no little cowering beastie, but the hard-tongued, strong-backed daughter of her famous mother. The two women go for each other, and when it is all over Clairette hands the faithless Pitou over to her friend and rival. She will wed the good and true Pomponnet, but given the strain of her mother that is so evident in her, one cannot fear that she will never see Ange Pitou again.

Chambéry played the financier Larivaudière, Mlle Lange's second string lover, Ernotte was the snooping policeman, Louchard, Mme Delorme played Amaranthe, the most vocal of the heroine's deputy mothers, and Touzé played the stand-out cameo role of the conspiring ''incroyable'' Trénitz, effete and foolish in his dress and speech, but a veritable icy hero under danger.

The score of the show was a nonstop run of winning numbers, beginning in the first act with Clairette's sweetly grateful romance ''Je vous dois tout,'' Amaranthe's lusty description of the late Madame Angot (Légende de la mère Angot: ''Marchande de marée''), Pitou's lilting admission that although ''Certainement, j'aimais Clairette'' other attentions do not leave him indifferent, and the plot-worthy anti-governmental song (''Jadis les rois, race proscrite''). Lange's cleverly delayed appearance, at the top of the second act, was made all the more effective by her dazzling and difficult first number, ''Les Soldats d'Augereau sont des hommes,'' in which she counts on the masculine weakness of the Directoire's forces in her organization of a grand ball as a cover for a conspirators' meeting. From there, Pomponnet's featherweight ''Elle est tellement innocente,'' the happy duo of the old schoolfriends (''Jours fortunés de notre enfance'') and the first meeting of Lange and Pitou (''Voyons, Monsieur, raisonnons politique'') led up to the highlight and climax of the act, the whispered Conspirators' Chorus—soon to be world-famous—and the whirling waltz (''Tournez, Tournez'') in which Lange leads her conspirator-guests into their cover-up dance as the government troops approach.

Unlike many contemporary third acts, that of *La Fille de Madame Angot* did not fritter away into a brisk pairing-off of its participants, and the musical part of the last portion of piece was equally as strong as its text. Larivaudière and Pomponnet, in the dark alleyways at the Calypso, joined in the Duo des deux forts, and Pitou and Lange shared a Letter duet (''Cher ennemi que je devrais haïr''), on the way to the other famous moment of the night's music and drama, the blazing Quarreling Duet (''C'est donc toi, Madam' Barras'') in which Clairette and Lange face up to each other at the show's dénouement, bringing the final act, like the preceding one, to a particularly effective musical and dramatic peak.

La Fille de Madame Angot was a huge hit in Brussels. *Les Cent Vierges* was put quite in the shade by the new piece and Marie Desclauzas, in the role of Lange, made a veritable triumph. Koning soon had a Paris transfer underway, and Louis Cantin mounted the show at the Folies-Dramatiques less than three months after its Belgian premiere whilst the original production continued on towards its 400th and 500th nights in Brussels. Paola Marié was cast as Clairette for Paris, alongside former daredevil circus-rider Mendasti (Pitou), Luco (Larivaudière), Mme Toudouze (Amaranthe), Philippe Dupin (Pomponnet) and Legrain (Louchard) and, at Lecocq's insistence, Marie Desclauzas was brought from Brussels to recreate her role of Lange.

In spite of some undercasting (Luce had been cast for Pitou, but died while the show was in preparation), some sloppy staging and a fire in some paper draperies on opening night, the Brussels triumph was repeated in Paris and *La Fille de Madame Angot* became a sensation, with the Quarreling Duet and the Conspirators' Chorus immediately proving themselves the hit songs of the time. The show ran through 411 performances, until April 1874, on its first run, setting a Parisian record as the first show in stage history to have run an entire year without a break, and topping a profit of an unheard of 800,000 francs. It was brought back following the summer recess in the same September, and remained in the repertoire at the Folies-Dramatiques continuously through the years that followed, passing its 800th performance on 17 May 1883. Juliette Simon was amongst those who took over the role of Clairette (the first year had used seven of them), Simon-Max took his turn as Pomponnet, and Vois (Ange Pitou) and Mlle Daltona (Lange) were among the other pensionnaires of the Folies-Dramatiques to take a turn at the now famous roles.

Parisian revivals thereafter were legion. An 1888 Eden Théâtre production put Anna Judic and Jeanne Granier together as the two rivals (10 February); in 1889, at the Variétés, Garnier teamed with Marcelle Lender; and a revival at the Gaîté paired Juliette Simon-Girard's Clairette with the Lange of Yvonne Kerlord for 200 nights (1901). Germaine Gallois and Edmée Favart played another 106 performances (1912) at the same house before the Opéra-Comique's Marguerite Carré and first Raymonde Delaunois (1920) and then Jenny Syril (1921) gave their versions of the star roles. In 1918 the piece was produced at the Opéra-Comique, first for a single performance with Mlle Favart and Marthe Chénal, and then as a full-scale repertoire piece (19 June 1919) with Mlle Favart paired with Mme Merentié and Edmond Tirmont as Pitou. It was brought back there in 1953 with Maria Murano and Colette Riedinger, and again in 1969 with Michèle Herbé and Christiane Darbell, and it made its most recent Parisian appearance in 1984 at the Théâtre Musical de Paris.

Although Cantin reaped the rewards of the Paris season, Humbert did not let go of his hit. In May he took the original cast, with Jeanne d'Albert replacing the departed Desclauzas, to London, and these first French performances (''a success of the most unqualified character . . . exactly what opéra-bouffe should be'') were followed some four months later by the first English-language version. Henry Byron's adaptation, produced at the Philharmonic Theatre, added the Alcazar Dancers in a ''Nuit de Carnival'' as a speciality in the third act, and popped in a song by musical director George Richardson (''Can This Be Love?'') who had also reorchestrated Lecocq's score. With Julia Mathews (Lange) and Selina Dolaro (Clairette) starred, the show ran no less than 235 performances at its suburban house, as other theatres moved quickly to produce their own versions. The copyright laws of the time allowed protection only to the Philharmonic's English version and not to the French original: anyone could mount a *Fille de Madame Angot* on the British stage with impunity, and they did.

The Gaiety was the first West End house to enter the ranks, six weeks after Islington's premiere, taking in Emily Soldene's company with an H B Farnie version, which fattened up the role of Lange for Soldene by having her appear in disguise as a street-singer in the first act. Soldene was again Lange to Pattie Laverne's Clairette at the Opera Comique before the year was done (26 December) for three and a half months and a quick reprise. That one was no sooner done that the Globe Theatre took up a five-week season of another *Angot* (ad H F Du Terreaux) with Cornélie d'Anka as Lange, so that London had two versions of the show running concurrently for seven months.

Productions of the show flooded Britain's provincial theatres, and they also continued to bombard London: the Philharmonic, Gaiety, Criterion (Humbert's troupe), Opera Comique, Royalty (ad Frank Desprez in a dramatically reshaped star-vehicle version for Dolaro), Alexandra and the Holborn Amphitheatre all played the show in 1875, the Opera Comique took it in again in 1876 and in 1878 d'Anka and Dolaro starred in a production at the Alhambra which introduced a sabot divertissement, the French grotesques Les Quatre Bossus, the Gardes Françaises in a grand military ballet, a children's ''Dresden China minuet'' and ''illuminated cascades of real water'' into the final act. The Theatre Royal, Drury Lane, took in productions in 1880 and again in 1919 (ad Dion Clayton Calthrop, G Marsden), the Criterion Theatre staged another in 1893 and the Coronet hosted a revival in 1901 (11 February) before the show's West End life was done.

Like London, New York saw its first *Angot* in French, with Marie Aimée starring as Clairette opposite Rosina Stani in 1873 and opposite Leontyne Minelly in 1874, and it spent most of its life—rather less outstanding here than in France and England, partly because of the system—being played by repertoire companies rather than in a continuous run. Alice Oates's company introduced the first English performances soon after, Soldene sang Lange as part of her New York season of 1874–75, Lydia Thompson helped herself to the score for the musical part of her burlesque *Mephisto* (1874), Paola Marié repeated her Paris performance to the Lange of Mme Angèle in 1879, Louise Théo played the piece in her repertoire, and it was part and parcel of the touring baggage of every touring opéra-bouffe and -comique company of the era. The Casino Theater mounted a production in 1890 with Marie Halton as Clairette and Camille D'Arville as Lange, with Henry Hallam (Ange Pitou) and Fred Solomon (Larivaudière) and ''a new Ballet des Fariniers written especially for this production by M Lecocq,'' which was the nearest the show got to having a straight Broadway run.

Yet another English-language *Fille de Madame Angot* was seen when the piece was given its first Australian performances. This one was the work of Fred Lyster, brother to producer W S Lyster, and known for taking large liberties with operatic scripts. Clara Thompson (Clairette), Jennie Winston (Lange), Armes Beaumont (Pitou) and Henry Bracy (Pomponnet) were starred in this production, the first of many, usually in the London adaptations, which followed in the repertoires of virtually every opéra-bouffe company which appeared in Sydney and Melbourne over the years that followed. Amongst these were included the much-traveled Soldene, with Rose Stella as her Clairette, and Emilie Melville who cast herself in the other of the two lead roles, and who took the show on to India and the South Pacific. Luscombe Searelle exported the piece to South Africa, where it was played with his wife, Blanche Fenton, as Clairette.

La Fille de Madame Angot has been seen as recently as 1989 in America, played by the Ohio Light Opera as *Clairette* (ad James Stuart), but Britain's revived D'Oyly Carte Opera Company jibbed at a remounting when its publicity director objected of the internationally most famous musical play of the 19th century ''no-one has ever heard of it.''

Ernst Dohm's German version was produced at Berlin's Friedrich-Wilhelmstädtisches Theater, and achieved ''one of the longest runs known [for] some time'' topping

100, then 150 nights and going on for more, whilst a different German adaptation by Anton Langer was mounted by Franz Jauner at the Vienna Carltheater a few weeks later. Hermine Meyerhoff (Clairette) and Antonie Link (Lange) starred alongside Wilhelm Knaack (Larivaudière), Franz Eppich (Ange Pitou), Küstner (Pomponnet), Karl Blasel (Trénitz) and Therese Schäfer (Amaranthe) and the show scored up 55 almost en suite performances. The 100th was passed on 13 August 1874, the 150th on 28 July 1875, and the 181st and last under Jauner's management on 19 May 1878 with Carl Streitmann playing Pomponnet. The show continued for a few performances more in repertoire under Franz Tewele's management and later got a couple of short showings at the Theater an der Wien in 1886 (13 April) and in 1901 with Ottilie Fellwock (Lange), Turk Rohn/Frln Genscher (Clairette) and Blasel in his original role (10 performances), but it did not attract the later revivals its fine original run might have presaged.

Hungary's version (ad Pál Tarnay) also proved a hit when produced at the Népszínház with Lujza Blaha (as Soldosné) in the role of Clairette, Karolin Daray as Lange, János Kápolnai as Ange Pitou and Elek Solymossy as Larivaudière, after its first performances had been seen at Kolozsvár with Ilka Medgyaszay and Zoltanné starred. A first run of 48 performances was followed by revivals in 1887 and 1897, a production at the Magyar Királyi Operaház (1887) and another at the Magyar Színház in 1900 with Ilona Szoyer featured as Clairette. The piece was also adapted into Russian, Spanish, Italian, Swedish, Turkish, Polish, Danish and Czech and a Russian-language production from the Moscow Art Theatre was seen in both Berlin and in New York in 1925. The Portuguese, however, instead of just lifting the libretto, as was the usual habit of their Spanish neighbours, turned out a *Le Fils de Madame Angot* (Angelo Frodoni) at the Theatro del Prince Royal in Lisbon (5 May 1875).

The show set loose a very flood of *Angot* parodies and spin-offs of all kinds on the Parisian stage. Armand Jallais authored a short vaudeville *Madame Angot et ses demoiselles* produced at the Folies-Marigny (19 June 1873) and Adolphe Joly provided another, *Madame Angot ou la Poissarde parvenue,* for the Ba-ta-clan (8 November 1873). A one-act opérette *Le Fils de Madame Angot* by Dorfeuil using Lecocq's music, was produced at the Gaîté-Montparnasse (25 September 1873), and *L'Héritage de Madame Angot* by Jules de Rieux and Villemer, with a Chassaigne score, at the Eldorado (24 October 1873), whilst Blondeau and Monréal went deeper and displayed *La Nuit de noces de la fille Angot* on the same stage (29 November 1873). The Funambules mounted a pantomime *La Mère Angot* by Hippolyte Demanet, the Alhambra christened its new-year revue *Pas bégueule la Mère Angot* (30 December 1873), and Clairville and Lecocq combined on a follow-up to their own piece with a saynète *La Résurrection de la Mère Angot* for the Folies-Dramatiques (24 February 1874). An Alfred Aubert vaudeville, *L'Héritage de la fille de Madame Angot,* was played at the Théâtre Sérafin (25 March 1875), a pantomime *Le Fils Angot* appeared at the Scala (9 July 1876), a vaudeville *Le Fils de Mme Angot* at the Menus-Plaisirs in 1892 (26 November) and a *L'arrière-petite-fille de Madame Angot* by André Mauprey even turned up at the Théâtre des Folies-Dramatiques as late as 29 November 1912. Naples got a piece about *Il padre di fglia di madama Angot* (1881), and Vienna, too, had its *Angot* parody when F Zell and Karl Pleininger combined on an *Angot und der blauen Donau* for the Strampfertheater in 1874 (13 November). "It is an imitation rather than a parody," sniffed a Viennese reviewer. So, undoubtedly, were a number of the others.

In the last half-century, productions of *La Fille de Madame Angot* have become fewer and, outside France, where it remains one of the staples of the classic repertoire, the show has not maintained the popularity which it won in the decades immediately following its production. With the movement of the operettic repertoire into the opera houses of the 1980s and 1990s, *La Fille de Madame Angot,* with its exceptionally strong dramatic, yet sophisticatedly comic, libretto and challenging star roles, would have seemed a natural candidate for opera-house revivals, but the tendency up to date has been for such houses to stick to the frothier part of the repertoire and a handful of not always worthy shows by "posh musicians" and "big names."

A version of the show was filmed by Jean-Bernard Derosne in 1935 with André Baugé as Ange Pitou alongside Danielle Brégis (Lange) and Moniquella (Clairette). Arletty was amongst the supporting cast.

France: Théâtre des Folies-Dramatiques 21 February 1873; UK: St James's Theatre (Fr) 17 May 1873, Philharmonic Theatre, Islington (Eng) 4 October 1873; USA: Broadway Theater (Fr) 25 August 1873, Olympic Theater *Madame Angot's Child* 29 September 1873; Germany: Friedrich-Wilhelmstädtisches Theater *Angot, die Tochter der Halle* 20 November 1873; Austria: Carltheater *Angot, die Tochter der Halle* 2 January 1874; Hungary: Kolozsvár 23 March 1875, Népszínház *Angot asszony leánya* 2 December 1875; Australia: Opera House, Melbourne 24 September 1874

Film: Jean-Bernard Derosne 1935

Recordings: complete (EMI-Pathé, Decca), selections (EMI-Pathé, Philips, etc), selection in Italian (Fonit Cetra), etc

LA FILLE DU TAMBOUR-MAJOR Opéra-comique in 3 acts by Henri Chivot and Alfred Duru. Music by Jacques Offenbach. Théâtre des Folies-Dramatiques, Paris, 13 December 1879.

One of the outstanding works of Offenbach's late period, *La Fille du tambour-major,* like the previous year's *Madame Favart,* proved that the Empire's favorite composer could turn out opéra-comique in the style of the postwar Lecocq pieces with a potency as great as that with which he could illustrate the most extravagantly bubbling of burlesques.

The drum major's daughter of the title is Stella (Juliette Simon-Girard) who, at the beginning of the evening, is the stepdaughter of the exceptionally noble Italian Duc della Volta (Édouard Maugé). When the French invade northern Italy to "liberate" the area from the Austrian empire, Stella's convent boarding school is in the path of the advancing troops and she, locked in the linen room as a punishment, is left behind when the nuns and pupils flee. This means that she comes face to face with the dashing Lieutenant Robert (Lepers) whose gallant attentions to her go down badly with the jealous vivandière Claudine (Noëmie Vernon). The Duc is anxious to marry Stella off to the unattractive and somewhat perverse Marquis Ernesto Bambini (Bartel), but the French are on the move and his ducal palace is invaded by the billet-seeking regiment, whose drum major Monthabor (Luco) discovers that his long-lost ex-wife is now the Duchess della Volta (Caroline Girard, mother of the prima donna). And Stella, thus, is his equally long-lost daughter. Wartime quiproquos mix with amorous ones (with disguises included) as the action winds up to its height, but all is brought to a happy ending when the main body of the French army arrives to shock the Duc into a sudden change of loyalties, and Stella into the arms of Robert.

The score of the show was in Offenbach's most tuneful mode, shot through with a delicious vein of sophisticated comedy which was a long way from the burlesque frivolities of earlier days. Stella's defiant song about the "Petit Français" was delightful enough to put off any comparison with Clairette's rebellious song from the all-influencing *La Fille de Madame Angot,* whilst Claudine's braying song to her military donkey ("Ce n'est pas un âne ordinaire"), the Duchess's affectations of an aristocratic headache ("J'ai ma migraine"), the lovesick song of the little tailor-turned-soldier Griolet (Simon-Max), devotedly sewing a uniform for Claudine ("Un tailleur amoureux"), and the ensemble in which the officers claim their billet at the Palazzo della Volta ("Un billet de logement") were thoroughly winning musical-comic moments in a score that glittered happily from beginning to end.

La Fille du tambour-major was produced by Blandin at the Folies-Dramatiques and won a splendid success. It played all through the winter and spring, up to the summer recess and held its place at the opening of the new season, playing for more than a month more and passing its 200th performance almost on the day of Offenbach's death. It was removed just short of its 250th night, but was remounted in 1884 (10 March) with Mme Simon-Girard, Simon-Max and Mlle Vernon in their original roles alongside Péricaud (Monthabor), Mme Claudia (Duchess) and Bartel, now promoted to the role of the Duc (46 performances). The show was revived at the Gaîté in 1889, with Mme Simon-Girard and Simon-Max repeating alongside Vauthier, Alexandre, Mesmacker and Marie Gélabert as Claudine and with a series of grandiose tacked-in ballets (to music from *Orphée aux enfers*) upping the visual content. The entry of the French into Milan in the final act was turned into a chauvinistic spectacle of the most crowd-pleasing kind. The piece returned again in 1891, in 1907 with Juliette Méaly playing Stella, and in 1917 with Edmée Favart starred, whilst the Théâtre du Château d'Eau played a season in 1901 with Mme Simon-Girard in her original role more than 20 years on. In 1920 Jenny Syril starred as the drum major's daughter in yet another revival at the Gaîté-Lyrique, which featured Lucien Fugère as Monthabor (7 October) and Roberte Jan headed the cast of a 1945 revival at the same house, as *La Fille du tambour-major* established itself firmly in the basic repertoire of the French opéra-comique.

The show also won lively appreciation outside France, though by no means in all areas and languages, making up for the lack of the one showy central role of a *Madame Favart,* with its potential for grand and glorious scenic and military display. In Belgium it proved quite simply a record-breaker. Mounted at the Galeries Saint-Hubert in Brussels, it totted up a run of no less than 174 almost consecutive nights, with a skip to Antwerp for ten more, a total never before known in that then musical-theatre-wise city.

Maximilian Steiner staged the first German version (ad Julius Hopp), subtitled *Die Franzözen in Holland,* at the Theater an der Wien. For reasons of state, the locality of the action was shifted to the Netherlands, and Utrecht and Breda took the place of Novara and Milan, with the action being set back a handful of years in historical consequence. Marie Geistinger starred as Stella, alongside Carl Adolf Friese as one Van Hokenbroing (ex- Duc della Volta) and Lori Hild as his wife, Steiner as Robert, Ausim as Monthabor and Girardi as the little tailor. The change of nationality did no one any good and *Die Tochter des Tambour-Major* lasted only seven nights. In London, however, where the show opened just nine days later, the result was very different. H B Farnie's "grand spectacular opera" adaptation for the vast Alhambra stage maintained the original setting, but added a military band and extra chorus for the "grand entry of the French Army" which concluded the show. Constance Loseby was Stella, with Fred Leslie and Fanny Edwards as the ducal pair, Fred Mervin as the drum major, and Fannie Leslie played Griolet in travesty to the Claudine of Edith Blande. The piece ran a magnificent 10 months at the Alhambra, passing its 200th performance on 6 December and ending after 212 nights only to be remounted soon after at the Connaught Theatre with Amy Grundy, Miss Edwards, Jennie Lee (Griolet), W H Woodfield and Aynsley Cook featured, for several weeks' more performances on the London stage.

La Fille du tambour-major reached New York first in French, with Paola Marié playing Stella alongside Mary Albert (Claudine), Mezières and Mme Delorme as the Duc and Duchesse, Tauffenberger (Griolet), Duplan (Monthabor) and Nigri (Robert). Just a few weeks later an English version followed, mounted under the management of M B Leavitt, with Selina Dolaro in the title role, James A Meade as Monthabor and former burlesque boy Alma Stanley, now graduated to the senior role of the Duchess. Nearly a decade later, the show was reprised at the Casino Theater in a new version (ad Max Freeman, Edgar Smith) under the title *The Drum Major.* Pauline Hall (Stella), Marie Halton (Claudine), James T Powers (Griolet) and Edwin Stevens (Monthabor) featured in a strong cast, but the new version proved to have only two months' life in it.

In Hungary, the title became the subtitle in Lajos Evva and Béla J Fái's tale of ''the French in Milan'' for a disappointing 20 nights, and, as in so many other cases, it was Farnie's successful English translation which gave the show its other major success. Neophyte Australian producer George Musgrove mounted *La Fille du tambour-major* as his maiden venture at Melbourne's Prince of Wales Theatre just 12 months after the Paris premiere and eight from the first performance of the Farnie version. Pattie Laverne, the Alhambra's Fred Mervin and tenor Albert R Brennir came from London to play Stella, Monthabor and Robert alongside an imported ''front line'' of girls and a local cast of 150 singers and extras in which the young Nellie Stewart made a particular success when she succeeded Jessie Grey in the role of Griolet. The show, staged with the utmost care and unusual splendor by London's Johnnie Wallace (famous in Australia for his direction of the Emily Soldene shows), proved the biggest hit the city had known. The production played for 18 weeks, creating a long-run record for Melbourne which would hold until *Florodora* arrived on the scene two decades later, and it continued on to spread its success throughout Australia. The show was later taken into the repertoire of J C Williamson's Royal Comic Opera Company and played in 1887 with Colbourne Baber in its title role, as *La Fille du tambour-major* became established as a revivable prospect in a way that it had previously done only in France.

The show has survived through the century since its debut, however, almost only in the French language. During the Boer War the oldtime producer Richard Mansell put out a version, *The Drum Major* (1 October 1900, ad Fred Bowyer, W E Sprange), which updated the piece to the present and set it in the context of the current war. John Ironfield, as played by Savoy veteran Richard Temple, battled the Boers, and Marie Elba was his long-lost Elsie. The show's last West End performances were in a French repertoire season at the Shaftesbury Theatre in 1908, and rare have been the performances since that time in any other tongue but the original.

Austria: Theater an der Wien *Die Tochter des Tambour-Major* 10 April 1880; UK: Alhambra Theatre 19 April 1880; USA: Standard Theater (Fr) 13 September 1880, 14th Street Theater (Eng) 4 October 1880; Hungary: Népszínház *A Franciák Milanoban (Az ezreddobos leánya)* 17 December 1880; Australia: Prince of Wales Theatre, Melbourne 27 December 1880; Germany: Aachen 12 February 1881, Walhalla Theater, Berlin 11 September 1883

Recordings: selection (EMI-Pathé), etc

LA FILLEULE DU ROI Opérette in 3 acts by Eugène Cormon and Raimond Deslandes. Music by Adolphe Vogel. Théâtre des Fantaisies-Parisiennes, Brussels, 10 April 1875.

Eugène Humbert, so successful with the works of the young Lecocq, gave opportunities to several other theatrically inexperienced composers at his Brussels theatre. Adolphe Vogel, who had studied for a career in serious music, written an opera (*Le Siège de Leyde,* 1847), a ''drame lyrique'' (*La Moissoneuse,* 1853), had a one-act operette, *Rompons!* (1857), produced by Offenbach at the Bouffes-Parisiens and another at the Folies-Marigny (*Gredin de Pigoche,* 1866), supplied him with *La Filleule du Roi.* With a cast containing many veterans of the Lecocq successes, designs by Grévin, and a groundswell of goodwill left over from Humbert's previous triumphs it did good business in Brussels.

The show's book told the tale of the overly unbuttoned Captain Phoebus de Pibrac (Georges Pagès) who throws over Loïsa, a girl he had seduced to wed another, Henriette Camescas (Jane May), who is supposed to be the ''god-daughter'' of King Henry IV, and, as a result, he is made to suffer the complicated and disguised revenge of the first one's sister, Marion (Pauline Luigini) . . . whom he ends the piece marrying. Paul Ginet and Mme Delorme played Henriette's parents, Alfred Jolly had a comical part as the Captain's servant, Jacquin, and Ernotte, the creator of Trénitz in *La Fille de Madame Angot,* had a small character part.

The text was a rather old-fashioned one which, paired with the not-so-young Vogel's similarly made music, did not appeal to audiences either in London, where Humbert presented it following its Brussels season, nor in Paris where it played only 11 performances with Mme Peschard singing the role of Phoebus in travesty opposite Mlle Luigini, nor in its German version at Vienna's Carltheater.

UK: Criterion Theatre 7 June 1875; France: Théâtre de la Renaissance 23 October 1875; Austria: Carltheater *Das Patenkind des Königs* 15 September 1877

FILMZAUBER Posse mit Gesang in 3 acts by Rudolf Bernauer and Rudolf Schanzer. Music by Walter Kollo and Willy Bredschneider. Berliner Theater, Berlin, 19 October 1912.

The first of Walter Kollo's series of original musical comedies written with Bernauer and Schanzer, and staged with great success at the Berliner Theater, *Filmzauber* used as its subject-matter the world of the newly popular cinema. The heroine of the piece, Franzi von Pappenheim, runs away from her upper-class home, disguised as a boy, to work in the cinematic firm run by Antonius Lichtenstadt and Quasta Pilsen. In the face of necessity, the disguise comes off, she takes the star role in a film, and, in the final reel, pairs off with Antonius. The ingenue Lina Hammerschmidt and the personable Max Rademacher made up the evening's second pair to the accompaniment of much song and dance. The show's attitude to the (silent) film world was displayed by its over-the-top depiction of the aptly named Italian film actress Maria Gesticulata and its comical scena of the filming of a meant-to-be dramatic Napoléonic movie (mus: Bredschneider), with Antonius playing Napoléon and Quasta and Franzi featured, a scena which was ultimately broken in upon by the heroine's furious father, hot on the trail of his disobedient child.

From the lively bundle of up-to-date numbers that made up the show's score (''Kind, ich schlafe so schlecht,'' ''Haben wir uns nicht schon mal kennengelernt,'' ''Machen wir zusammen eine Firma auf'') it was Kollo's Lindenmarsch (''Unter'n Linden promenier' ich immer gern vorbei'') which scored the biggest hit both in and out of the theatre.

Filmzauber ran for the best part of a year at the Berliner Theater, and this success led to productions throughout the world in 1913. George Edwardes took it up for London and, rechristened *The Girl on the Film* (ad James Tanner, Adrian Ross) in order to point it up as a successor to *The Girl in the Train* (*Die geschiedene Frau*) and *The Girl in the Taxi* (*Die keusche Susanne*), it was produced during his final illness by J A E Malone, with a cast headed by Connie Ediss (Euphemia Knox of the Vioscope film company), Emmy Wehlen (Winifred, otherwise Freddy), Madeleine Seymour (Linda) and George Grossmith (Max Daly). Albert Szirmai was now credited as co-composer, and was, indeed, responsible for more than half the show's music, including the evening's principal waltz, ''Won't You Come and Waltz with Me?,'' alongside further additional numbers by Paul Rubens and Philip Braham. ''Unter'n Linden'' survived, but it became a song in praise of Bond Street.

The Girl on the Film had an eight-month run (232 performances) in the West End, was sent out in two tours, and then exported to Broadway with most of its London principals for an eight-week run under the management of the Shuberts. There, as in Berlin and in London, it was closely followed on to the boards by Jean Gilbert's *Die Kino-Königin* (*The Cinema Star, The Queen of the Movies*) which outpointed it in each case. But *The Girl on the Film* stayed on the road in Britain through 1914 and again, in spite of wartime anti-German feelings, in 1915, and it also made its first appearance, in the London Szirmai-ed version, on the Australian stage, at Christmas 1914. Dorothy Brunton was Winifred, C H Workman played Max, Alfred Frith the General and Marie Eaton the Italian lady through not very impressive seasons in Sydney and Melbourne (Her Majesty's Theatre 3 July 1915) which were easily bested by *The Cinema Star* shortly after. The score now included, amongst other items, Jerome Kern's ''You're Here and I'm Here,'' and not very much Kollo seemed to remain.

Die Kino-Königin also won out in Vienna, where *Filmzauber* was seen at Josef Jarno's Theater in der Josefstadt for only three weeks in a Viennese-localized version by Max Baer (but without the Szirmai music), and Budapest alone reversed the decision. Produced there in a version (ad Zsolt Harsányi) of the London version, with local lad Szirmai given the chief composing credit, and with Sári Fedák (Franzi) and Márton Rátkai (Antonius) starred, *A mozikirály* (''the movie king'') fairly outpointed *A mozitünder* (''the film fairy'') which arrived a year later at the Nepopera.

UK: Gaiety Theatre *The Girl on the Film* 5 April 1913; Austria: Theater in der Josefstadt 15 April 1913; Hungary: Király Színház *A mozikirály* 20 September 1913; USA: 44th Street Theater *The Girl on the Film* 29 December 1913; Australia: Her Majesty's Theatre, Sydney *The Girl on the Film* 19 December 1914

FINALY, Karolin[e] (b Pest, ?5 July 1852). ''The prettiest of Viennese soubrettes'' of the 1870s.

Pretty, little Karoline Finaly came to Friedrich Strampfer's Theater an der Wien at the age of 16 (or 21, depending on which of her very diverse given birthdates is correct) and made her first appearance there in the little role of the lady-in-waiting, Olga, in *Die Grossherzogin von Gerolstein.* She rose quickly through the ranks, playing the soubrette part of Brigitte in *Genovefa von Brabant* (1868) and the title role in Lecocq's *Theeblüthe* (*Fleur de thé,* 1869), appearing as Irma in Millöcker's *Drei Paar*

Schuhe (1871) and later the same year as Mephisto in *Dr Faust Junior* and as Fragoletto to the Fiorella of Marie Geistinger in Offenbach's *Les Brigands* (1871).

In 1875 she created the role of Emilie in Johann Strauss's *Cagliostro in Wien* and won the particular approval of the composer who subsequently had her play the part of Pulcinella in the first performances of his 1877 piece *Prinz Methusalem* at the Carltheater to where she had previously gone to play in *Prinz Conti* (Friquette), the title role in the Viennese premiere of *Graziella* (*La Petite Mariée*) and Toinon in *Margot die reiche Bäckerin* (*La Boulangère a des écus*). She visited Berlin during the 1875–76 season, played the dual title role of *Giroflé-Girofla* at the Carltheater in 1876, and made an essay into the operatic as Gounod's Juliette (*Roméo et Juliette,* 1879) before creating the leading soprano roles in two of Millöcker's most important works, *Apajune der Wassermann* (1880, Natalitzka) and *Der Bettelstudent* (1882, Laura), and introducing the Vienna versions of Bettina in *La Mascotte* (*Der Glücksengel*) and of Simonne in *Die Musketiere in Damenstift* (*Les Mousquetaires au couvent*).

Strauss created the brilliant soprano music of the role of the heroine Violetta in his 1881 *Der lustige Krieg* for Finaly, and she subsequently took the prima donna roles of Manola in *Tag und Nacht* (*Le Jour et la nuit*), Praskovia in *Le Docteur Ox,* Teresina in *Der kleine Prinz* (1882) and of Titania Fanfani in the premiere of Suppé's *Die Afrikareise* (1883). She also appeared in the title role of *Boccaccio,* and, when the swiftly revised *Eine Nacht in Venedig* was brought to Vienna after its dubious Berlin premiere, she was given the principal soprano role of the fishermaid Annina. It was the last role she would play, for in December of 1883 she announced her marriage, retired from the stage, and disappeared from my (and, it seems, everyone else's) ken.

FINCK, Herman [VAN DER VINCK, Hermann] (b London, 4 November 1872; d London, 21 April 1939). London conductor and composer for the musical theatre, revue and variety stages.

The son of an Amsterdam-born violinist who called himself Louis von der Finck, Finck began playing in his father's theatre orchestra at the Princess's Theatre at the age of 14. He subsequently played at Drury Lane, the Empire and the Comedy (deputy md) and then joined the orchestra of London's Palace Theatre, on the house's conversion from opera house to variety theatre. He progressed from his initial place at the keyboards to rank-and-file and then first violin, to deputy and, finally, in replacement of Alfred Plumpton, conductor of the theatre's orchestra. He maintained that position through the Palace's varying metamorphoses as a theatre and a music hall until 1919, before moving on to the Queen's Theatre and then, in 1922, to the newly reconstructed Theatre Royal, Drury Lane, now run by former Palace Theatre supremo Alfred Butt. He remained in charge of the Lane's orchestra for the eight years of Butt's control.

Finck studied orchestration with Edward Solomon and, although he is credited with an interpolated number in the burlesque *King Kodak* as early as 1894 and another in the musical comedy *The Yashmak* (1897), his early work as a composer consisted largely of incidental and dance music for John Tiller's shows, for the Palace Theatre variety programs, and for such sketches and musical playlets as a music-hall sketch for Cora Stuart (1894), Amy Augarde's impersonation of *La Carmencita, À la Carte* for Gaby Deslys, and *Paris Frissons* for Régine Flory. In 1907 his name appeared on the bill of Vienna's Apollotheater as the composer of *Tag und Nacht (in ein Amerikanisches Knaben und Mädchenpensionat),* an evidently saucy four-scene "vaudeville" mounted by Tiller at the fledgling Austrian variety house. Amongst the individual pieces which he wrote and published at this time, the waltz "In the Shadows" (1911) became a very long-lived favorite.

With the coming of revue, Finck provided a flood of songs and scores for the revue productions at the Palace, notably for *The Passing Show* ("I'll Make a Man of You," "Gilbert the Filbert," later used in *The Girl from Utah* in America), *Bric à Brac, Airs and Graces* ("Toy Town," "Whisper to Me" w Lionel Monckton) and *Hullo! America,* as well as for similar productions at other theatres (*By Jingo if We Do, Round the Map, Its All Wrong, The Curate's Egg, Brighter London, The Little Revue, Leap Year, Better Days,* etc). He also ventured into musical plays, contributing songs to *Bill Adams* (1903), *Winnie Brooke Widow* (1904), *Carminetta* (1917), *Flora* (1918) and Broadway's *Queen o' Hearts* (1922), collaborating with Howard Talbot on the score for the interesting *My Lady Frayle* (1915, "Just One Hour") and the flop *The Light Blues* (1915), composing all the music for Martin Henry's touring musicals *The Love Flower* (1920) and *Kiki* (1921) and providing part of the score of the gentle *Merely Molly* and Drury Lane's picturesquely heroic *The Song of the Drum.*

At the Palace, he conducted the production of *Pamela* (1917), during an attempt to turn the revue house to musical comedy, and at Drury Lane he was musical director not only for his own *The Song of the Drum* but for the memorable series of American musicals of the 1920s—*Rose Marie, The Desert Song, The New Moon, Show Boat* and *The Three Musketeers.* He also conducted these shows for gramophone recordings. As late as 1935 he took the baton for a revival of *Merrie England* at the Prince's Theatre.

1897 **The Cruise of the Saucy Puss** (Arthur M Binstead) sketch Empire Theatre 21 June

1900 **In Gay Paree** (J Hickory Wood, John Tiller) Palace of Varieties, Manchester 31 December

1905 **Moonshine** (Eustace Baynes) 4 scenes Palace Theatre 26 December

1906 **In Sunny Spain, or The Troubles of a Tourist** (George R Sims, Charles Fletcher) 3 scenes Winter Gardens, Blackpool 9 July

1907 **La Carmencita** (Louis Cohen) sketch Palace Theatre 13 May

1908 **Charles, His Friend** (w Harold Samuel) sketch Palace Theatre (pre-August)

1910 **The Billposter** (Herman Finck/w Herbert Sergent) sketch, Palace Theatre 31 October

1912 **O-Mi-Iy** (w Frank E Tours/Seymour Hicks) 1 act London Hippodrome 25 March

1913 **What a Game** (arr/Michael Morton) sketch Palace Theatre 31 May

1913 **À la Carte** (Dion Clayton Calthrop) 1 act Palace Theatre 1 September

1913 **Palace Frissons** (M Tharp/L E Berman) 1 act Palace Theatre 9 December

1914 **The Slush Girl** (Arthur Wimperis) 1 act Palace Theatre 14 September

1915 **The Swiss Maid** (John Tiller) 1 act Hippodrome, Balham 9 March

1915 **The Light Blues** (w Howard Talbot/Adrian Ross/Mark Ambient, Jack Hulbert) Birmingham 13 September; Shaftesbury Theatre 14 September 1916

1915 **Vivien** (later *My Lady Frayle*) (w Talbot/Arthur Wimperis/Max Pemberton) Prince of Wales Theatre, Birmingham 27 December; Shaftesbury Theatre as *My Lady Frayle* 1 March 1916

1920 **The Love Flower** (Adrian Ross, James Heard/Robert Marshall) Theatre Royal, Brighton 8 March

1921 **Kiki** (Reginald Arkell/José G Levy ad Martin Henry) Palace Theatre, Ramsgate 7 March

1926 **Merely Molly** (w Joseph Meyer/Harry Graham/J Hastings Turner) Adelphi Theatre 22 September

1931 **The Song of the Drum** (w Vivian Ellis/Desmond Carter/Fred Thompson, Guy Bolton) Theatre Royal, Drury Lane 9 January

Other titles credited: *The Sin of St Hulda* (1896), *A Doubtful Prospect* (1900), *Hiawatha* (1905), *The Belle of Andalucia* (1908), *Amsterdam* (1909), *The Comforters* (1913)

Autobiography: *My Melodious Memories* (Hutchinson, London, 1937)

FINGS AIN'T WOT THEY USED T'BE Musical in 2 acts by Frank Norman. Music and lyrics by Lionel Bart. Theatre Royal, Stratford East, London, 17 February 1959. Revised version, 22 December 1959. Garrick Theatre, London, 11 February 1960.

The first original musical piece of the many which came from the Theatre Workshop, headquartered at Stratford East's Theatre Royal in the 1950s and 1960s, *Fings Ain't Wot They Used t'Be* was an attempt at an *Irma la Douce*–ish piece about life in London's Soho district. The piece had, however, none of the French musical's shapeliness or subtle comedy, but simply threw together a bunch of conventional characters including a copper (bent, of course), some whores (hearts of gold, naturally), an interior decorator (limp-wristed, needless to say) and an ex-gangman turned café-keeper and his live-in lady, who climaxed the few not-very-events of the evening by getting married, the whole topped with a set of bright and bristling songs. If the book of *Fings* was a giant step backward after the recent *Expresso Bongo,* Lionel Bart's 10 songs were, on the other hand, a lively lot. It was the title song which proved the winner, but the cheery ''G'night Dearie'' taken over from an earlier Bart piece, *Wally Pone,* and the langorous ''Layin' Abaht'' made up for the occasional dip into banality with such as ''The Student Ponce.''

The show was successful enough to attract attention from producers Oscar Lewenstein and Donald Albery and, having been given a tightening and a larger musical content (''The Ceiling's Comin' Dahn,'' ''Where Do Little Birds Go?,'' etc) it was given a second season at Stratford, then, boosted by Max Bygraves's hoisting of the title song to number five on the charts (with nicer words), into the West End. Glynn Edwards, Miriam Karlin, Toni Palmer, Barbara Windsor, James Booth and George Sewell were amongst a cast which imbued the strangely amateurish-sounding piece and its primary-colored characters with boundless energy through 897 performances in London, before *Fings* went on to several provincial productions.

Recordings: original cast (Decca), etc

FINIAN'S RAINBOW Musical in 2 acts by E Y Harburg and Fred Saidy. Lyrics by Harburg. Music by Burton Lane. 46th Street Theater, New York, 10 January 1947.

A tale of Americo-Irish whimsy with some political points to play with was the basis of *Finian's Rainbow,* which ran to a 725-performance success in Lee Sabinson and William R Katzell's 1947 Broadway production.

Finian McLonergan (Albert Sharpe) and his daughter Sharon (Ella Logan) arrive in America from Glocca Morra with a crock of gold, apparently stolen from the little people of Ireland, which the old man hopes to plant in the ground near Fort Knox on the principle that, if the American government's money multiplies there, so will his. They are pursued by a leprechaun called Og (David Wayne), determined to regain his people's gold. In Rainbow Valley, Missitucky, they meet up with a band of sharecroppers, engaged in fighting for their land against a nasty politician called Billboard Rawkins (the name was an open reference to two American politicians of the time who were regarded as culpably ultra-conservative). Rawkins (Robert Pitkin) is made to see the error of his horrid ways when the magic of the leprechaun gold turns him black, and he has temporarily to feel the feelings of a different group of people. Whilst the big, bad lawmaker is being transformed into a good little liberal, Sharon is smiling at a handsome sharecropper, Woody Mahoney (Donald Richards), and Og romancing his mute, dancing sister, Susan (Anita Alvarez).

The songs from *Finian's Rainbow* included several which had a wider life than the show itself: Sharon and Will's ''Old Devil Moon,'' ''Look to the Rainbow'' and ''If This isn't Love,'' the heroine's pretty ''How Are Things in Glocca Morra?'' and the leprechaun's jaunty ''When I'm Not Near the Girl I Love'' all becoming favorites.

Ten months into its Broadway run, *Finian's Rainbow* was mounted in London under the management of Emile Littler with Beryl Seton (Sharon), Patrick J Kelly (Finian), Alfie Bass (Og), Frank Royde (Rawkins) and Alan Gilbert (Woody Mahoney) in the principal roles. It failed in 55 performances. There was no better luck for an Elizabethan Trust/Garnet Carroll Australian production with Bobby Howes (Og), Sheila Bradley (Sharon) and Bruce Barry (Will) which flopped out in six weeks in Melbourne and—a rare thing—did not then even bother to face Sydney, whilst an American revival, brought to Broadway from the City Center under the management of Robert Fryer and Lawrence Carr (46th Street Theater 23 May 1960) and featuring Jeannie Carson as Sharon did less well again, folding in 12 performances. A film version, made in 1968, kept virtually all the score but reallotted some of it to allow Fred Astaire (Finian) to share in the singing with Petula Clark (Sharon), Tommy Steele (Og) and Don Francks (Will).

UK: Palace Theatre, London 21 October 1947; Australia: Princess Theatre, Melbourne 17 December 1964; Germany: Kaiserlautern 28 September 1975

Film: Warner Brothers-Seven Arts Inc 1968

Recordings: original cast (Columbia), revival cast (RCA Victor), film soundtrack (Warner Bros), etc

FINN, William [Alan] (b Boston, Mass, 28 February 1952).

Author-composer of the trio of small-scale off-Broadway musicals based on the emotional and sexual life of their central character, Marvin. After being developed at Playwrights Horizons and presented singly over a period of almost two decades to increasing, and in some quarters very enthusiastic, interest, two of the three were ultimately brought together to make up a Broadway show entitled *Falsettos. Falsettos* took Tony Awards for its music and libretto in the no-contest that was the 1991–92 season.

Finn worked on several other projects which have not found the same following, nor the same success. The 1983 *America Kicks Up Its Heels* did not progress from its tryout, the dance musical *Dangerous Games* played 4 performances on Broadway, the 1930s depression piece, *Romance in Hard Times,* 6 performances at New York Shakespeare Festival, and the slightly autobiographical *A New Brain* played for 116 performances in the summer of 1998.

1979 **In Trousers** Playwrights Horizons 21 February; Promenade Theater 26 March 1985

1981 **March of the Falsettos** Playwrights Horizons Studio 1 April; Main Stage 20 May; Chelsea Westside Arts Theater 13 October

1983 **America Kicks Up Its Heels** (Charles Rubin) Playwrights Horizons 3 March

1989 **Dangerous Games** (Astor Piazzolla/Graciela Daniele, Jim Lewis) Nederlander Theater 19 October

1989 **Romance in Hard Times** Public Theater 28 December

1990 **Falsettoland** Playwrights Horizons 28 June; Lucille Lortel Theater 14 September

1992 **Falsettos** revised *March of the Falsettos* and *Falsettoland* (w James Lapine) John Golden Theater 29 April

1998 **A New Brain** (w Lapine) Lincoln Center Theater 18 June

FIORELLO! Musical in 2 acts by Jerome Weidman and George Abbott. Lyrics by Sheldon Harnick. Music by Jerry Bock. Broadhurst Theater, New York, 23 November 1959.

Fiorello! was a mildly hagiographic biomusical of politician Fiorello Henry La Guardia (1882–1947), a former member of the American House of Representatives (1917–21, 1923–33) and mayor of New York between 1934 and 1945. Jerome Weidman and George Abbott's libretto did not attempt to cover the whole of their subject's life, but concentrated, in flashback, on his rise from successful lawyer to Republican congressman, via a wartime interlude and a misguided marriage, and then, following an interval-time-skip of a decade, to his two campaigns for the mayordom of New York, the first unsuccessful and the second, which, although we don't see it, we know will be as successful as the second marriage.

The young lawyer Fiorello La Guardia (Tom Bosley) volunteers to stand on the apparently hopeless Republican ticket against the corrupt politicians of Tammany Hall. He is seen courting a labor group—and particularly the strike leader, Thea (Ellen Hanley), who is later to become his wife—who are being harassed by a corrupt policeman (Mark Dawson), then wooing the immigrant population, in their own pre-American languages, and, to general surprise, he wins the election. As a congressman, he supports mobilization and goes off in uniform himself to win the Great War at the end of the first act. The second act begins with his defeat in the mayoral race against the sitting candidate, Jimmy Walker. His efforts, in the time-honored style, to show the popular mayor up as corrupt have failed. However, the administration finally has its scandal and, as the show ends, the widowed Fiorello is preparing to try again, with his faithful longtime secretary and wife-to-be, Marie (Patricia Wilson), at his side. Pat Stanley played factory-worker Dora who falls for and marries the Tammany Hall-tied policeman, Howard da Silva was Ben Marino, New York Republican leader, and Nathaniel Frey played Morris Cohen, the hero's law office manager.

The score by Bock, who at this time had one success (*Mr Wonderful*) and one flop (*The Body Beautiful*) to his Broadway credit, and Harnick, his collaborator on the second show, added some happy humor to a tale which, with its whiter-than-white hero battling shiningly against a world where everyone else in authority is dishonest and dirty, could otherwise have become a simplistic modern fairy tale. The number which stood out was a piece in which Ben Marino and his cohorts joyously detailed the uses of ''The Little Tin Box'' in dishonest politics. The same group had another lively piece, a polka, in which to sing about ''Politics and Poker,'' whilst right at the top of the show a trio of Fiorello's employees took any sanctimoniousness out of the tale with a tongue-in-cheek hymn to being ''On the Side of the Angels.'' Romance was served by the waltzing '''Til Tomorrow'' (Thea and chorus) and ''When Did I Fall in Love?'' (Fiorello/Thea), the soubrette element by Dora's admission that ''I Love a Cop,'' and by the Walker campaign song, ''Gentleman Jimmy,'' as performed by musical-comedy actress Mitzi (Eileen Rodgers) and her chorines.

Harold Prince and Robert E Griffith's production of *Fiorello!* tied for the year's Tony Award with *The Sound of Music,* followed the example set by another politically flavored musical, *Of Thee I Sing,* in being awarded a Pulitzer Prize, and had a fine 795-performance run on Broadway, with the previously little-known Bosley making a great personal hit. A London mounting was sponsored by Donald Albery in 1962, with Derek Smith featured as Fiorello alongside Marion Grimaldi (Thea), Nicolette Roeg (Marie), Patricia Michael (Mitzi) and Peter Reeves (Ben), but the piece did not prove to have the same attractions for Britain as for Broadway and lasted only 56 performances.

La Guardia was seen again on the musical stage in the short-lived *Annie 2* (Kennedy Center, Washington, DC 4 January 1990) when he was portrayed by Michael Cone.

The ''villain'' of *Fiorello!,* Mayor James Walker, got his own show in 1969 (*Jimmy* Winter Garden Theater 23 October) but did not manage to challenge La Guardia's record (84 performances) and another, more recent New York mayor got a musical doing-over when *Mayor,* a cabaret musical based on the autobiography of mayor Edward Koch (Charles Strouse/Warren Leigh), was played at New York's Top of the Gate (13 May 1985). Another mayor, John Lindsay, actually took to the boards as a performer, but the New York mayors still have a long way to go to catch up with the most famous musical mayor of all: London's Sir Richard Whittington.

UK: Piccadilly Theatre 8 October 1962

Recording: original cast (Capitol)

THE FIREFLY Musical comedy in 3 acts by Otto Harbach. Music by Rudolf Friml. Lyric Theater, New York, 2 December 1912.

Little street-singing Nina (Emma Trentini) escapes from a cruel master by disguising herself as a cabin-boy on the Bermuda-going yacht of wealthy socialite Mrs van Dare (Katherine Stewart). Professor Franz (Henry Vogel) thinks he has found a wonderful choirboy but, if he is disappointed when the truth of Nina's sex comes out, Mrs van Dare's intended son-in-law Jack Travers (Craig Campbell) is not. After some Caribbean high-jinks, including a false accusation and a misdirected letter, and the passing of a little time, the jilted Geraldine van Dare (Audrey Maple) gets a more suitable husband in the comfortable ''uncle'' John Thurston (Melville Stewart) and little Nina—now a famous prima donna—becomes Mrs Jack. Geraldine's maid, Suzette (Ruby Norton), and Thurston's valet, Pietro (Sammy Lee), provided the soubret song-and-dance moments and Mrs van Dare's fussy confidential secretary, Jenkins (Roy Atwell), added to the comic moments.

The Firefly was put together by producer Oscar Hammerstein as a vehicle for the former opera singer Trentini, following her great success as the heroine of his *Naughty Marietta.* Harbach cannily cast the tiny star in another role where she had the opportunity to dress up as a boy, but since Victor Herbert refused to work with the temperamental and too often unprofessional vocalist a second time, Rudolf Friml was given the opportunity to compose the score. He duly supplied his star with a new hit song in the quasi-Neapolitan ''Giannina Mia,'' the delightfully tripping ''Love Is Like a Firefly'' and the showy aria ''Kiss Me and 'Tis Day'' to deliver in her metamorphosis as a third-act prima donna. The score, however, produced a second and even more durable standard in a different vein, the gentle waltz song ''Sympathy,'' introduced by Melville Stewart, offering Geraldine a not disinterested shoulder to whimper on, as well as several other highly attractive pieces: Papa Franz's sweet "Beautiful Ship from Toyland," the richly swimming "In Sapphire Seas" and the lovely lighthearted ensemble "When a Maid Comes Knocking at Your Heart."

The show ran for 120 performances at New York's Lyric Theater before taking to the road and was thereafter the subject of productions throughout America, whilst its two favorite songs got a wide recording and broadcast coverage. It did not, however, travel much abroad and the only major foreign production was one mounted in Australia under the aegis of J C Williamson Ltd. René Maxwell starred as Nina, alongside Edith Drayson (Geraldine), George Gee (Jenkins), Ralph Errolle (Jack), Claude Flemming (Uncle John) and Ethel Morrison (Mrs Vandare) in a version which seemed to sport some unfamiliar numbers—Hugh Steyne as Pietro, for example, performed a Weston and Lee piece entitled "The Bolshevik"—through a fine two-and-a-half months in Sydney and a disappointing month in Melbourne (Her Majesty's Theatre 29 September 1921).

A 1937 MGM film of the same title shared little with the stage show beyond a selection of its music. Jeanette MacDonald sang "Giannina Mia" and Allan Jones made a hit with a new piece, "The Donkey Serenade," concocted by Wright and Forrest from an old Friml melody, "Chansonette," as illustration to a wholly different story.

In 1942 a putative revival of *The Firefly* ended up being a show with little in common with its original. Irving Actman, Leopold Spitany and composer Jean Schwartz contributed to what was ultimately called *Full Steam Ahead,* featured topical Nazis in its libretto and got no further than Philadelphia (25 December). Things were put more sanely back on the rails by a 1943 revival by Edwin Lester's Los Angeles Civic Light Opera, with Francia White starring, a cast including Al Shean (Franz), Dorothy Stone (Suzette), Odette Myrtil (Mrs van Dare) and a third-act appearance by Friml himself ("The Composer Plays"). It slipped a four-handed version of "The Donkey Serenade" and three new Friml numbers ("A Composite Picture of Love," "You're Gorgeous," "I Give My Heart Away") into a revised book (ad Erna Lazarus, W Houston Branch) whilst cutting several principal pieces of the original score ("Beautiful Ship from Toyland," "Tommy Atkins," "Call Me Uncle," "Kiss Me and 'Tis Day," etc). It stayed in the west.

Australia: Her Majesty's Theatre, Sydney 30 April 1921

Recordings: selection (RCA), selection (part-record) (World Records), etc

FIRTH, Elizabeth (b Phillipsburg, NJ, 11 April 1884).

Miss Firth left her native America for Britain while in her late teens and was promptly engaged there by George Edwardes, for whom she first appeared in *The Duchess of Dantzic,* playing the role of one of Napoléon's sisters and covering Evie Greene in the title role, both in London (1903) and New York (1905). She played in George Grossmith's revue *Venus 1906* at the Empire, took over the role of Agathe in Edwardes's production of *Véronique* (1906) and appeared in supporting parts in his *Les P'tites Michu* and *Les Merveilleuses* (1906, Liane) before being chosen to create the role of Nathalie (ie, Valencienne) in the first English production of *The Merry Widow* (1907).

She later starred opposite Ellaline Terriss in *The Dashing Little Duke* (1909) and returned to Edwardes's management to play the vampy Olga in *The Dollar Princess* (1910), before going back to America where she appeared as Clarisse (a role very close in nature to that of Valencienne in *Die lustige Witwe*) in Leo Fall's *The Siren* (1911). She then returned to England, but does not seem again to have taken to the stage, ending her short but impressive career at the age of 27.

FISCHER, Betty (b Vienna, 12 October 1887; d Vienna, 19 January 1969).

Betty Fischer became the musical-theatre darling of the Austrian capital in the years during and following the First World War, creating starring roles in a vast list of often memorable Operetten, and spending 13 years as prima donna at the Theater an der Wien, where she made up a celebrated star team with Hubert Marischka, Luise Kartousch and Ernst Tautenhayn.

After early work in variety and in Operette, 23-year-old Frln Fischer joined Wilhelm Karczag's company at the Raimundtheater and, over three seasons, played leading roles in such pieces as *Wiener Blut* (Fransizka Cagliari), *Giroflé-Girofla* (Giroflé/Girofla) *Die Dollarprinzessin* (Olga), *Casimirs Himmelfahrt* (Rudy) and *Die keusche Barbara* (Barbara) whilst creating the roles of Prinzessin Marie in Leo Ascher's highly successful *Hoheit tanzt Walzer* (1912), Komtesse Irene in *Die liebe Unschuld* (1912), Bessie Phelps-Butt-Johnston in Berény's *Mein Mäderl* (1913), Mitzi Hipsinger in Ziehrer's *Der Husarengeneral* (1913) and the actress, Therese Krones, in the successful Strauss père pasticcio *Die tolle Therese* (1913).

In 1914 she moved up to Karczag's flagship company at the Theater an der Wien and made her first starring appearance there in the patriotically remade version of Kálmán's *Az obsitos, Gold gab ich für Eisen* (Marlene). She followed up by creating the roles of Edith Lloyd in *Die schöne Schwedin* (1915), Dina in Eysler's *Wenn zwei sich lieben* (1915), Julja Lella in Nedbal's *Die Winzerbraut* (1916), Kondja Gül in the triumphant and long-running *Die Rose von Stambul* (1916), Kitty Höfer in *Der Sterngucker* (1916), Vilma Garamy in the Vienna version

Plate 122. **Betty Fischer.** *Longtime prima donna of the Theater an der Wien and the creator of many famous Viennese roles.*

of *Wo die Lerche singt* (1918), Blanka von Lossin in *Die blaue Mazur* (1920), Vera Lisaweta in Vienna's *Der letzte Walzer* (1921), the title role of *Frasquita* (1922), Lea—the prototype of *Das Land des Lächelns's* Lisa—in *Die gelbe Jacke* (1923), the title role in *Gräfin Mariza* (1924), Gladys Harrison in *Der Milliardensouper* (1925), Nadja Nadjakowska in the hugely successful *Der Orlow* (1925), Princess Fedora in *Die Zirkusprinzessin* (1926), Helena in *Die Königin* (1927) and the vocally wide-ranging Margarete in Eysler's *Die gold'ne Meisterin* (1927). She also appeared as Hortense in the 1915 revival of *Der Opernball,* played alongside Marischka as *Die lustige Witwe,* as Sáffi to the Barinkay of Richard Tauber in *Der Zigeunerbaron* (1921) and in the 1923 revival of *Eine Nacht in Venedig.*

In 1928 she moved to the Johann Strauss-Theater to play the title role of Miss Evelyne Bliss in Granichstaedten's Operette *Die Milliardärin,* and thereafter made a long series of guest appearances at houses both in Vienna and outside, creating the part of the Countess Olga Baranskaia in *Walzer aus Wien* at the Stadttheater in 1930 and returning to the Theater an der Wien in 1931 in that part, as Yvonne Duprès in *Der Bauerngeneral* and in the title role of *Viktoria und ihr Husar.*

Although the principal part of her career, as a metropolitan prima donna, was now past its peak, she continued to appear on the musical stage whilst pursuing a second career as a teacher at the Vienna Conservatoire, appearing at the Raimundtheater in character roles over half a century after she had first starred there as a young leading lady.

FITYFIRITTY Operett in 3 acts by Rudolf Halász. Music by Dénes Buday. Fővárosi Operettszínház, Budapest, 8 March 1941.

One of the most popular of the list of operetts composed by Dénes Buday, the wartime *Fityfiritty* was written to a text by the neophyte Halász whose previous work had been largely as a lyricist for popular songs.

Fityfiritty was the nickname of the little shopgirl heroine of the piece (Manyi Kiss), but the star role was that of her best friend, Mária Patkay (Hanna Honthy), once a shopgirl like her, but now a rich and famous singing star. Maria's heart, however, is still in the shop—more specifically with the shop's director (György Solthy)—and it is her little friend who smooths the obstacles between stage and shop in time for a happy ending. Kálmán Latabár, Ella Gombaszögi and Lajos Hajmássy took the other principal roles.

Buday's score featured the popular dance rhythms of the recent decades—fox-trot, tango, English waltz—and turned out a song hit in the fox-trot ''Szép hely, jó hely Teherán, de ott is teher ám a feleség'' (''A lovely, happy place is Teheran, but there as well as here a wife's a burden'').

Following its successful original run at the Fővárosi Operettszínház, the show was revived there in 1946 (21 April, book now credited to Rudolf Halász and Dezső Kellér).

THE 5 O'CLOCK GIRL Fairy tale in modern clothes in 2 acts by Guy Bolton and Fred Thompson. Music by Bert Kalmar and Harry Ruby. 44th Street Theater, New York, 10 October 1927.

Alongside the French play *The 5 o'Clock Man* (which became *A Kiss in a Taxi* in Clifford Grey's American version and, subsequently, the musical *Sunny Days*) in the 1927–28 Broadway season there was also presented *The 5 o'Clock Girl.* Patricia Brown (Mary Eaton) is worthy of this title because 5 o'clock is the time when she, a working girl in a cleaners' shop, talks on the telephone to a young man who is clearly both attractive and attracted. Since this is a fairy tale in modern clothes, Gerald Brooks (Oscar Shaw) also turns out to be rich and social. In order not to lose him, Patricia pretends that she, too, is rich and social, and when she goes out to meet him, she dresses up in clothes borrowed from her shop. However, although the deception is inevitably unmasked, a happy Cinderella-style ending is finally arrived at thanks to some helpful interference from comical friend Susie Snow (Pert Kelton), who is striking simultaneous sparks with Brooks' valet Hudgins (Louis John Bartels), who is also pretending to be something wealthier and more social than he is.

Although the show included less dancing than was generally fashionable at the time, Kalmar and Ruby's score was in the usual dancing mode, with ''Thinking of You,'' Patricia and Gerald's duo ''Up in the Clouds,'' ''Who Did? You Did!'' and Gerald's ''Happy-go-lucky'' proving the favorites.

Philip Goodman's production of *The 5 o'Clock Girl* played 280 performances on Broadway, and the show was taken up by R H Gillespie and Lee Ephraim to be staged at the London Hippodrome 18 months later. A fiddled-with version, which took in such additional numbers as ''Happy Little Bluebird,'' featured Jean Colin and Ernest Truex in the principal roles, with Hermione Baddeley and George Grossmith providing the comedy song-and-dance, and Richard Murdoch and Ursula Jeans amongst the supporting cast. It played a rather disappointing three months (122 performances) before going out to do a little better in the provinces. An Australian production, with Alfred Frith (''and his million-dollar face'') top-billed as Hudgins, Helen Paterson as Patricia, William Valentine as Gerald and a swatch of interpolated songs, had fair runs in Melbourne (8 weeks) and in Sydney (Her Majesty's Theatre 10 August 1929, 7 weeks).

A 1979 revival of a revised version, which supplemented a half-dozen of the original show's songs with rather more Kalmar and Ruby numbers from other sources, was mounted at Connecticut's Goodspeed Opera House (19 June) and it was brought back for a second season the following year. The production was then taken to Broadway (Helen Hayes Theater 28 January 1981) but lasted there for only 14 performances.

UK: London Hippodrome 21 March 1929; Australia: Theatre Royal, Melbourne 18 May 1929

Plate 123. **Fityfiritty**

FLAHERTY, Stephen (b Pittsburgh, Pa, 18 September 1960). Composer of the scores for two successful musicals of the 1990s.

Teamed from early on with lyricist Lynn Ahrens, Flaherty had his first musical produced at Playwrights Horizons in 1988. *Lucky Stiff,* a merry piece of musical comedy with some lively songs did not win itself a run, but subsequently went on to be seen in other small venues, including productions in Britain and Europe.

The partners won more notice with the Caribbean tale *Once on This Island,* with its warmly West Indian–flavored music and pretty tale, and yet more with the score to the doctored Doctorow musical *Ragtime.*

Flaherty's other assignments include the incidental music to the 1997 play *Proposals,* the score to the animated film *Anastasia* and orchestral works derived from both the *Ragtime* and *Anastasia* scores.

1988 **Lucky Stiff** (Lynn Ahrens) Playwrights Horizons 25 April

1990 **Once on This Island** (Ahrens) Playwrights Horizons, New York 6 May; Booth Theater 18 October

1993 **My Favorite Year** (Ahrens/Joseph Dougherty) Lincoln Center 10 December

1996 **Ragtime** (Ahrens/Terrence McNally) Ford Center, Toronto 8 December; Ford Center, New York January 1998

2000 **Seussical** (Ahrens/w Ahrens) Colonial Theater, Boston 27 August; Richard Rodgers Theater 30 November

DIE FLEDERMAUS Comic Operette in 3 acts by [Carl Haffner and] Richard Genée based on *Le Réveillon* by Henri Meilhac and Ludovic Halévy. Lyrics by Richard Genée. Music by Johann Strauss. Theater an der Wien, Vienna, 5 April 1874.

The greatest theatrical success of composer Johann Strauss, and the most internationally enduring of all 19th-

Plate 124. **Die Fledermaus.** *After a night out gallivanting, Governor Frank is not up to dealing with the drunken jailer Frosch. Carl Adolf Friese and Schreiber in Vienna's original production.*

century Viennese Operetten—the second fact indubitably owing something to the first—*Die Fledermaus* has come to represent the "golden age" of the Austrian musical stage to the modern world, much in the same way that *Die lustige Witwe* has come to represent the "silver age" of the early 20th-century Viennese theatre in the general consciousness.

Like *Die lustige Witwe, Die Fledermaus* had a libretto based on a French comedy by Henri Meilhac, this time written in conjunction with his habitual partner, Ludovic Halévy, and said to be taken, in its turn, from a German original, *Das Gefängnis* by Roderich Benedix. *Le Réveillon* had been produced for the first time at Paris's Palais-Royal just 18 months prior to the appearance of the Operette, with MM Geoffroy and Mme Reynold appearing as Gabriel and Fanny Gaillardin, from Pincornet-les-Boeufs, and Hyacinthe, the comedian with the famous nose, as Alfred, the chef d'orchestra of the Prince Yermontoff (played in travesty by Georgette Olivier). Alfred tracks his ex-beloved, Fanny, to her provincial home and persists in serenading her with a violin fantasy from *La Favorita* whilst awaiting her husband's condemnation to prison for insulting a garde-champêtre, before getting closer. Pellerin was Duparquet, the friend whom Gaillardin once stranded after a masked ball, still ridiculously dressed in a bluebird costume, and who now persuades him to postpone prison for a night out at the Prince's pavilion in the company of some pretty actresses from Paris. He is, in reality, plotting his revenge. Lhéritier played the prison governor, Tourillon, off in an aristocratic disguise to the same party.

Following the Palais-Royal production, Maximilian Steiner, co-director of the Theater an der Wien, ordered a German translation from the veteran playwright Carl Haffner. He did not judge the result worth producing, but subsequently he—or music publisher Gustave Lewy—had the idea of making a musical libretto from the piece instead, and he handed Haffner's version over to house-composer and adapter Richard Genée. Genée was apparently no more fond of Haffner's version than Steiner, and he later asserted that nothing of that first adaptation remained in the final text of *Die Fledermaus.* However, so as not to offend the old playwright (who died in 1876), he agreed that his name should remain on the playbills. The libretto of *Die Fledermaus* contained one major alteration to the text of *Le Réveillon* (which, in other places, in spite of Genée's assertion, it followed virtually line for line)—it introduced two major female roles into a play which had been an almost wholly masculine affair. An Operette, and certainly one written for a theatre whose co-director was none other than the great Marie Geistinger, could not manage without its prima donna and its soubrette. *Le Réveillon*'s Fanny and her maid are not seen again after the first act. The gamboling of Gaillardin at the ball, and the little episode of the chiming watch, were in the play directed on to one farmer's girl/actress, Métella, whilst the centerpiece of the third act is a long and highly comical scene between the imprisoned Alfred and Gaillardin, who comes there disguised as a lawyer in order to get to see the man who has been arrested in a compromising situation with his wife.

Die Fledermaus's Viennese Rosalinde (Marie Geistinger) is wooed by an Alfred who is a throbbing vocalist rather than a chef d'orchestre but who, like his predecessor, is bundled off to prison in place of her legitimate husband, Gabriel Eisenstein (Jani Szíka). When Eisenstein turns up at the ball chez Prince Orlofsky (Irma Nittinger), he is enchanted not only by the actress Olga—who is his own maid, Adele (Karoline Charles-Hirsch), in disguise—but by a mysterious Hungarian countess who woos his watch from him. The countess is Rosalinde. After their merry evening, Eisenstein and Frank, the prison governor (Carl Adolf Friese), end up facing each other at the jail with their night's disguises torn away, and the confrontation with the "false" Eisenstein takes place, before Rosalinde puts the cap on things by producing the watch she wooed from her husband, and Falke (Ferdinand Lebrecht) reveals that the whole thing has been a setup. As in the play, the final act opened with a low-comedy scena for a tipsy jailer.

If the libretto replaced many of the subtleties and comicalities of the play with more conventional and well-used elements, it did, nevertheless, produce two fine—if not particularly original—leading lady's roles, as well as many a chance for music. Strauss, to whom the libretto was given for setting, took fine and full advantage of them. Geistinger was well-served, with a showpiece csárdás (''Klänge der Heimat'') in which to prove her Hungarianness, and paired with Eisenstein in a delicious sung version of the watch-scene (''Dieser Anstand, so manierlich''), whilst the soubrette had two showy coloratura pieces, a mocking laughing song (''Mein Herr Marquis'') reproving the disguised Eisenstein for mistaking her for a ladies' maid, and a tacked-in ariette à tiroirs (''Spiel' ich die Unschuld vom Lande''), allowing Adele to show off her range as she demonstrates her suitability for a stage career. The bored Orlofsky summoned his guests to enjoy themselves in a loping mezzo-soprano ''Ich lade gern mir Gäste ein.'' The men were less showily served, although Falke led a swaying hymn to brotherly love in ''Brüderlein und Schwesterlein'' and Alfred indulged in some operatic extravagances as well as an intimate supper-table duet with the almost errant wife (''Trinke, liebchen, trinke schnell''). Orlofsky's party also provided the opportunity for a display of dancing.

Many myths have grown up around the show and its original success or non-success, particularly in Vienna. The truth is that *Die Fledermaus* was well—if not extravagantly—received, and, like virtually all Strauss's pieces, good, bad and indifferent, was quickly taken up to be mounted in other Austrian, German and German-language houses where his name was a sure draw. In Vienna, it was played 45 times in repertoire before the summer break, and was brought back again in 1875 and in 1876, reaching its 100th performance on 17 October 1876 with Frlns Meinhardt (Rosalinde) and Steinherr (Adele) featured alongside Szíka, Alexander Girardi (Falke) and Felix Schweighofer (Frank). Thereafter it remained fairly steadily in the repertoire at the Theater an der Wien, good for a regular number of performances in most years, reaching its 200th performance on 15 May 1888 and the 300th on 9 December 1899. If the original run, within the repertoire system, had been less stunning than the show's later reputation might have suggested, and indeed far from the record compiled by such pieces as *Die schöne Helena* at the same house, its initial showing was above average and its (not unbroken) longevity in the repertoire exceptional. Carl Streitmann, Phila Wolff and Gerda Walde featured in a new production in 1905 (1 April), and the piece was seen at other theatres including the Hofoper, at the Volksoper for the first time in 1907, the Raimundtheater in 1908, the Johann Strauss-Theater in 1911 and the Bürgertheater in 1916, making up part of the repertoire of any self-respecting Operette theater in Vienna in the same way that it did in the provinces. Amongst the memorable Viennese *Fledermaus* productions of later years was one at the Staatsoper in 1960 which featured Hilde Güden (Rosalinde), Rita Streich (Adele) and Eberhard Wächter (Eisenstein).

In Berlin, the show was produced at the Friedrich-Wilhelmstädtisches Theater with a singular success which allegedly gave a boost to its reputation back in Vienna. The 200th performance was passed within two years of the first, and *Die Fledermaus* went on to become the most popular Operette of the 19th century on German stages. Budapest also saw its first performance of the show in German, as did New York when the Stadt Theater mounted the piece just seven months after the Viennese premiere with Lina Mayr (Rosalinde), Ferdinand Schütz (Eisenstein), Schönwolff (Frank) and Antonie Heynold (Adele), but neither city proved in much haste to provide a vernacular version. It was eight years before the Hungarian capital saw an Hungarian-language production, and, although the piece got regular showings in New York's German theatres—including an 1881 season with Geistinger starred in her original role alongside Mathilde Cottrelly (Adele) and Max Schnelle (Eisenstein)—it was over a decade before New Yorkers got *Die Fledermaus* in an English translation.

The first English-language version was mounted on the vast stage of London's Alhambra Theatre (ad Hamilton Aidé) as a Christmas entertainment for the 1876–77 season with a cast headed by Cora Cabella, Kate Munroe, Adelaide Newton, Guillaume Loredan, Edmund Rosenthal and J H Jarvis. It ran for a sufficient season of some four months, and encouraged the theatre to try Strauss's earlier *Indigo* the following Christmas, but—although a performance of the original version was given at the Royalty Theatre in January 1895 by a touring German company—it was more than 30 years after this before another English *Fledermaus* was seen in the city. The following October, Australia was given its first glimpse of the show, under the aegis of Martin Simonsen's company (and billed, with typical local mendacity, as having been played 500 nights at the Alhambra) at Sydney's Queen's Theatre. Fannie Simonsen was Rosalind and Henry Bracy Eisenstein with Minna Fischer (Adele), Maud Walton (Orlofsky), Henry Hod[g]son (Frank) and G Johnson (Falke) in support. The company left town after 10 days.

Boston (which had already seen versions of *Le Réveillon* as *The Christmas Supper* [ad Fred Williams, George A Ernst, 24 March 1873], and *On Bail* ad W S

Gilbert) got America's first English-language *Fledermaus,* under the clever title *The Lark,* in March 1880. The piece had been reset in America by adaptors Nat Childs and F S Harris, and since the Boston management were aggrieved over the idea of composer Strauss wishing actually to be paid for the use of his orchestrations, local md John Braham stuck his own under the published melody lines of the 17 pieces of Strauss used for the occasion. J B Mason and Rose Temple played Harold and Lillian Allison, who were Boston's equivalent of the Eisensteins, and Alice Carle was Bessie Dooling, ie, Adele. This version was later seen at San Francisco's Tivoli Opera House (July 1880). New York's first English *Die Fledermaus* (ad Sydney Rosenfeld, "if Mr Rosenfeld cannot turn out better work than this he should retire from the field") was mounted by John McCaull at the Casino Theater, after a Philadelphia run-in, some five years further down the line, with Mme Cottrelly now playing her Adele in English alongside Rosalba Beecher (Rosalinde), Mark Smith (Eisenstein) and De Wolf Hopper (Frank), It was voted "a mild failure" but, after the split between McCaull and the Casino management, it was repeated later the same season at Wallack's Theater (14 September 1886) before, as in England, going on the shelf for several decades.

Hungary's first vernacular *Denevér* was mounted not in Budapest but at Kolozsvár with Sarolta Krecsányi and Béla Szombathelyi featured. It was played at Szeged the following year, and only in 1882 did a version (ad Lajos Evva) arrive in Budapest. Aranka Hegyi was the first Budapest Rosalinde with Mariska Komáromi (Ghita, ex-Adele), Elek Solymossy (Bussola), Vidor Kassai (Fujo), Pál Vidor (Crapotti) and János Kápolnai (Ritenuto, ex-Alfred) in the other major roles. It played 54 times and was revived in 1891 (24 January) and 1907 (22 October) before going on to productions at the Népopera (1912, 1915), the Városi Színház (1926) and other houses as, in line with the rest of the world, it worked its way up past more immediately popular pieces into its present-day place at the peak of popularity. It was most recently seen in Budapest at the Erkel Színház in 1992 (31 December) in an adaptation by Agnes Romhányi and in 1997 (20 December) in a version by Sándor Fischer.

Italy, Sweden, Russia, the Netherlands and Switzerland all took in *Die Fledermaus* in the first years after its debut, but it was France which took the longest time to catch up with the show, and, according to one variation of the story, not without reason. In those slaphappy copyright days, nobody in Vienna, apparently, had bothered to ask Meilhac and Halévy for permission to make a musical out of their play. So producer Victor Koning called on authors Alfred Delecour and Victor Wilder who had, to Strauss's satisfaction, heavily rewritten the libretto of *Indigo* for France, and ordered a brand new script to be written around some portions of Strauss's score. The story they used was a well-worn one, featuring a womanizing Prince, wed by necessity and by procuration, who goes out gallivanting with some bohémiennes on the day of his marriage. His bride-to-be gets herself into gypsy gear, seeks him out, and tames him. If the story was familiar, the score was less so. Many favorite pages of *Die Fledermaus* were missing. There was no csárdás, no Orlofsky's song, no Audition couplets and the bits that remained, often uncomfortably tacked one to another, were topped up with Lorenza Feliciana's valse brilliante "O süsses Wörtchen" (pasted onto a *Fledermaus* melody) and "Zigeunerkind wie glänzt dein Haar" ("Pourquoi pleurer") from *Cagliostro in Wien* and some other spare and written-for-the-occasion Strauss music. *La Tzigane,* with Zulma Bouffar as Princess Arabelle, the baritone Ismaël (who garnered both the "Brüderlein" and "Trincke liebchen" melodies as solos) as the naughty Prince, and Berthelier, Urbain and Léa d'Asco featured, was equipped with one of the most luxurious stagings Koning's theatre had ever provided. However, although the show emerged as an uncomfortable paste-up job, with Strauss himself on hand to win masses of journalistic space, it nevertheless managed 63-plus performances before Koning replaced it with the premiere of *Le Petit Duc. La Tzigane* was only seen again when a German version of it (ad Hans Weigel, additional music Max Schönherr) was for some reason mounted at Graz in 1985 (16 November).

It was 1904 before a regular *La Chauve-Souris* (ad Paul Ferrier) was seen in Paris. Fernand Samuel's production at the Variétés featured Albert Brasseur and Max Dearly as Gaillardin and Tourillon (since the action was reset in France, the names from *Le Réveillon* had been resurrected for this pair), with Cécile Thévenet (Caroline, ex- Rosalinde), Jane Saulier (Arlette, ex- Adele) and Ève Lavallière as Orlofsky. It was played 56 times. However, late though this production may have been, it was still too soon. The lawsuits flew, and the heirs of not Meilhac or Halévy but of Victor Wilder were awarded 50 percent of the royalties on *La Chauve-Souris* and 3,000 francs in damages by the Tribunal de la Seine. On the grounds of his authorship of *La Tzigane!*

Die Fledermaus was still, even in the early days of 20th century, far from the all-obscuring international favorite it was to become, but it was a regular part of the repertoire in, in particular, German-speaking countries where it had been integrated into the repertoire of such houses as the Berlin Opera (8 May 1899). In 1905 it was produced at New York's Metropolitan Opera in German with Marcella Sembrich and Andreas Dippel featured, and in 1910 (4 July) a new English version (ad Armand

Kalisch) starring Carrie Tubb, Joseph O'Mara and Frederick Ranalow was played by Thomas Beecham's company at London's Her Majesty's Theatre in the pro-Viennese atmosphere engendered by *The Merry Widow* and its successors. The following year, yet another anglicized *Fledermaus* (ad Gladys Unger, Arthur Anderson) was produced at London's Lyric Theatre under the title *Nightbirds* with C H Workman and Constance Drever, Paris's *Veuve joyeuse,* starred for 138 performances. This version was picked up for Broadway and played, as *The Merry Countess* (20 August 1912, Casino Theater), with José Collins, Claude Flemming, Maurice Farkoa and one of the Dolly Sisters as Adele (the girls interpolated their turn into the proceedings) and with the addition to Strauss's score of Arthur Gutman and Joseph H McKeon's "Must We Say Goodbye?" and a duo for a couple of prison warders made out of the "Blue Danube."

Another round of productions was set off by Max Reinhardt's typically big and typically botched Berlin production of 1929 (Deutsches Theater 8 June). Hermann Thimig, Maria Rajdl, Adele Kern and Oscar Karlweis as a non-travesty Orlofsky were featured in a lavishly staged version which purported to have gone back to *Le Réveillon* for its text (ad Karl Rössler, Marcellus Schiffer) . . . but which nevertheless did not leave Rosalinde and Adèle at home for the second and third acts! The version's vanities included some additional lyrics by Schiffer glorifying Reinhardt, whilst Strauss's music had been "improved" by E W Korngold. The Paris Théâtre Pigalle (5 October 1929 ad Nino) played Reinhardt's version with Lotte Schöne, Jarmila Novotna, Dorville and Roger Tréville featured, whilst the Shuberts had Fanny Todd Mitchell do a version, which claimed with equal lack of veracity to be a version of *Le Réveillon* and which, as *A Wonderful Night* (31 October 1929), played 125 Broadway performances with, of course, its leading ladies well and truly intact.

London's Royal Opera House gave a faithful *Fledermaus* in 1930 (14 May) with Willi Wörle, Lotte Lehmann, Gerhard Hüsch and Elisabeth Schumann, whilst another American version (ad Alan Child, Robert A Simon) arrived in 1933 (14 October) with Peggy Wood (Rosalinde), Helen Ford (Adele) and John Hazzard as Frosch, to add a further 115 performances to *Die Fledermaus*'s bitty Broadway record, before the Reinhardt/Korngold version turned up, on the wings of the war, for its Broadway season under the title *Rosalinda* (44th Street Theater 28 October 1942). Dorothy Sarnoff took the title role, whilst Karlweis repeated his Berlin Orlofsky and Korngold conducted "his" music, and *Rosalinda*—if scarcely *Die Fledermaus*— proved a perfect piece of good-old-days, richly produced wartime entertainment through 521 performances. London promptly followed up, and Tom Arnold and Bernard Delfont presented *Gay Rosalinda* (ad Austin Melford, Rudolf Bernauer, Sam Heppner 8 March 1945) at the Palace Theatre with Cyril Ritchard and Ruth Naylor featured and Richard Tauber conducting. The success was repeated for 413 London performances.

Since this late and unexpected burst of commercial theatre success for more or less botched versions of *Die Fledermaus,* the show has largely retreated—in normally less tampered-with shape—into the opera houses of those countries which do not sport repertoire Operette companies. Covent Garden, the Metropolitan (ad Howard Dietz, then ad Betty Comden, Adolph Green), the Berlin and Vienna Opera Houses, and the Paris Opera have all hosted the show, and divas of the ilk of Joan Sutherland and Kiri te Kanawa have played Rosalinde. Some of the lightness and gaiety which was the chief attraction of the commercial version has unavoidably been lost in this rehousing of what is basically a musical-comedy piece but, whilst Suppé, Millöcker and Zeller are forgotten, the waltz king's most popular work has become in the process regarded as the one "safe" 19th-century Viennese Operette for the world's 20th-century operatic houses. Even in bitterly butchered shapes. Thus, more than a century after its premiere, *Die Fledermaus* is going more strongly than ever, with an international production rate that only the favorite works of Offenbach and Gilbert and Sullivan's *The Mikado* among 19th-century works can come near.

Versions of *Die Fledermaus* have been put on film on a number of occasions in the German language—in 1931 by Carl Lamac with Anny Ondra, Georg Alexander and Ivan Petrovitch, by Paul Verhoven in 1937 with Lidia Baarova and Hans Söhnker, by Géza von Bolvary in 1945 with Marte Harell, Willy Frisch and Johannes Heesters, and in 1962 by Géza von Cziffra with Peter Alexander, Marianne Koch and Marika Rökk. Powell and Pressburger were reponsible for an English-language version (*Oh, Rosalinda!*) released in 1955 in which Michael Redgrave was paired with Anneliese Rothenberger. The 1931 edition had a French equivalent in which Ms Ondra teamed with Marcelle Denya, Mauricet and Géo Bury. A silent version, with accompanying music, was put out in 1923 in which Lya de Putti and Harry Liedtke featured. In the days of television and video recordings such operatic names as Gundula Janowitz (1972), Joan Sutherland (Australian Opera 1982, Royal Opera 1990), Kiri te Kanawa and Herman Prey (Royal Opera, 1983) and Ms te Kanawa again (Metropolitan Opera, 1986) have attempted the cross-over into Operette.

An attempt at a musequel to *Die Fledermaus* was put out by Leon Treptow (text) and K A Raida (music) at Berlin's Viktoria Theater in 1882 (8 April) under the title *Prinz Orlofsky.* In fact, it was not a genuine sequel, telling a wholly conventional and oft-used comic-opera tale and simply tacking the names of the characters of Genée's Operette on to its characters. Prince Orlofsky pretends he is married and a father to win financial favors from an elderly uncle. The uncle turns up, is gotten drunk for an act of revelry, Adele poses as Mrs Orlofsky and at the end, of course, becomes her for real. Frosch had become the Prince's butler, Alfred got himself a country lass who had a showy role in the second act, and Frank, Eisenstein and Falke put in appearances. Rosalinde had the good sense to stay at home this time.

Germany: Friedrich-Wilhelmstädtisches Theater 8 July 1874; USA: Stadt Theater (Ger) 21 November 1874, Boston Museum *The Lark* March 1880, Casino Theater (Eng) 16 March 1885; UK: Alhambra Theatre 18 December 1876; Australia: Queen's Theatre, Sydney 17 October 1877; Hungary: (Ger) 14 November 1874; Kolozsvár *Denevér* 19 October 1877, Népszínház, Budapest 25 August 1882; France: Théâtre de la Renaissance *La Tzigane* 30 October 1877, Théâtre des Variétés *La Chauve-Souris* 22 April 1904

Films: Max Mack 1923, Pathé 1931 (Ger and Fr), 1937 (Ger), 1945 (Ger), 1955 *Oh, Rosalinda!* (Eng), etc

Recordings: complete (Decca, EMI, RCA, Deutsche Grammophon, HMV, Eurodicsc, Teldec, Teletheater etc), complete in French (Polydor), complete in Hungarian (Qualiton), complete in Russian (MK), complete in English (CBS), complete in Spanish (Montilla), etc

FLERS, P-L [PUYOL, Léon Pierre Édouard] (b Paris, 27 April 1865; d Antibes, 8 September 1932).

The "author" of more revues, plays, libretti and other diverse theatre texts than would seem possible, thanks to a very efficient team of ghostwriters and some celebrated collaborators, Flers was, nevertheless, most famed as a producer of revues, often with a British tinge, mounted at the Folies-Bergère (the annual *Le Revue des Folies-Bergère*), the Alcazar, the Moulin-Rouge, Les Ambassadeurs, La Cigale and other such houses, but also in more legitimate theatre venues.

Flers is credited with having contributed to the texts of a number of pieces which straddled the line between the revue or variety show, in which he was most active, and the book musical, but also to several regular musical plays, both in translation and, occasionally, original. If an early collaboration with Audran was a straight-out flop, the musical comedy *Shakespeare!*, written with Paul Gavault to a score by Serpette, was both a clever piece of farce writing and reasonably successful, whilst the revusical *Messalinette, ou le tour du demi-monde en 80 nuits* was exported with success to both Vienna (*Die Ringstrassen-Prinzessin,* ad Carl Lindau, Leopold Krenn, 10 February 1905, Danzers Orpheum) and to Budapest (*Mimi hercegnő* ad Jenő Faragó, 11 May 1906, Magyar Színház) before being revived at the Moulin-Rouge in 1909. He adapted another variety-house spectacle, the German *Lysistrata,* to the French stage, but also reorganized Ivan Caryll's *The Earl and the Girl* for Parisian consumption (adding the "Shimmy Shake" to the evening's entertainment) and, in later years, he authored the text for Josef Szulc's successful musical comedy *Le Petit Choc.*

Flers ran the Moulin-Rouge through 1903, and during that time introduced there the American musical comedy *The Belle of New York,* which he had seen in Vienna, in a girlie-spectacular staging and with an enormous success. This prompted him to follow up with another opérette, written this time by himself. For *Voluptata* he assembled a cast including Anna Tariol-Baugé, Sulbac, Arlette Dorgère and Carlos Avril, and reputedly introduced ragtime dance to Paris as part of the show's choreography.

He worked on several occasions in London, staging parts of *The Passing Show* and also of the Gaiety Theatre musical play *The Beauty Spot,* in which Parisian revue star Régine Flory was starred, and for which he also took a co-librettist's and/or "based on" credit.

1896 **La Reine des reines** (Edmond Audran) Eldorado 14 October

1898 **Fémina** (Rodolphe Berger) 1 act La Cigale 6 May

1898 **Un flagrant délit** (Georges Charton) 1 act Versailles 20 March; La Roulotte 11 November

1899 **Ohé! Venus** (Monteux-Brissac/w Gavault) Lyon; La Cigale 24 February

1899 **Shakespeare!** (Gaston Serpette/w Paul Gavault) Théâtre des Bouffes-Parisiens 23 November

1900 **Les Petits Croisés** (?/w Gavault) La Cigale 24 January

1901 **Paris Froufrous** Folies-Marigny 3 May

1902 **Messalinette, ou le tour du demi-monde en 80 nuits** (Berger) Concert de la Scala 19 February

1903 **Cabriole** (Laurent Halet/w Alévy) 1 act Parisiana 13 January

1904 **Voluptata** (Paul Marcelles/w ?Charles Clairville) Moulin-Rouge 20 January

1904 **Lysistrata** French version (Moulin-Rouge)

1905 **Coco barmaid** Scala 2 February

1906 **Ah! Moumounte!** (Eugène Héros) La Cigale 22 March

1907 **Madame Barbe-bleue** (Georges Arnould) La Cigale 18 January

1908 **Geneviève de Brabant** revised version (Théâtre des Variétés)

1908 **La Course à l'amour** (Héros, Ondet/w André Matieux) La Cigale 17 April

1910 **Le Circuit du Leste** (Héros) Scala 16 September

1917 **The Beauty Spot** (James W Tate/Clifford Harris, Valentine/w Arthur Anderson) Gaiety Theatre, London 22 December

1919 **Hello!! Charley** (*The Earl and the Girl*) French version (Théâtre Apollo)

1921 **Les Bijoux indiscrètes** (Leo Daniderff) Théâtre Marjol 15 September

1923 **Le Petit Choc** (Joseph Szulc) Théâtre Daunou 25 May

Other title attributed: *Ma bonne cousine* (1903)

FLERS, Robert de [DE LA MOTTE-ANGO, Marie Joseph Louis Camille Robert, Marquis] (b Pont l'Evêque, Calvados, 25 November 1872; d Vittel, 30 July 1927).

One of the most highly regarded French writers of light comedy in the first part of the 20th century, the Marquis de Flers collaborated for 14 years with Gaston de Caillavet on a long series of plays and musical comedies. The former included such pieces as *La Montansier* (1904), *L'Ange du foyer* (1905), *Miquette et sa mère* (1906), *L'Amour veille* (1907), *Le Roi* (1908), *L'Âne de Buridan* (1909), *Primerose* (1911) and *La Belle Aventure* (1913), whilst the latter, mostly attached to scores by Claude Terrasse, included the young composer's two major successes, the opéras-bouffes *Le Sire de Vergy* and *M de la Palisse.*

Amongst their other musical collaborations, the pair also turned out noteworthy French-language versions of Lehár's two biggest French successes, *La Veuve joyeuse* and *Le Comte de Luxembourg,* and provided the libretti for André Messager's successful opéra-comique *Fortunio* and his "légende lyrique," *Béatrice* (Monte Carlo 21 March 1914).

After the death of de Caillavet, in 1915, de Flers paired up with another successful comic writer, Francis de Croisset, and together they compiled the pretty, genteel text for Reynaldo Hahn's consciously old-fashioned opérette *Ciboulette,* the most enduring of de Flers's original works for the musical theatre.

His plays subsequently proved popular as the bases for other people's musicals. Leo Fall's successful Operette *Das Puppenmädel* was based on de Flers and de Caillavet's *Miquette et sa mère;* the libretto written by Carlo Lombardo and Renato Simoni for the Italian operetta *Primarosa* (1926) was taken from their *Primerose; Le Roi* (1908), which had already been illustrated with some music by Emmanuel Arène on its original production, was made into a full-scale musical comedy by Ralph Benatzky under the title *Majestät-privat* (Theater an der Wien 18 December 1937); and *La Belle Aventure* (1914) became the source for the musical *In der Johannisnacht* (Jean Gilbert/Robert Gilbert, Thalia Theater, Hamburg 1 July 1926).

Long an influential theatrical columnist and literary director for the *Figaro,* a force in the field of organizing the laws and enforcement of copyright and other author's benefits, sometime president and "Président d'honneur" of the Société des Auteurs, and the author of a number of books, de Flers nevertheless won his greatest renown and respect through his writings for the stage.

1901 **Les Travaux d'Hercule** (Claude Terrasse/w Gaston de Caillavet) Théâtre des Bouffes-Parisiens 7 March

1902 **Chonchette** (Terrasse/w de Caillavet) 1 act Théâtre des Capucines 11 April

1903 **Le Sire de Vergy** (Terrasse/w de Caillavet) Théâtre des Variétés 16 April

1904 **M de la Palisse** (Terrasse/w de Caillavet) Théâtre des Variétés 2 November

1906 **Paris, ou le bon juge** (Terrasse/w de Caillavet) Théâtre des Capucines 18 March

1907 **Fortunio** (André Messager/w de Caillavet) Opéra-Comique 5 June

1909 **La Veuve joyeuse** (*Die lustige Witwe*) French version w de Caillavet (Théâtre Apollo)

1912 **Le Comte de Luxembourg** (*Der Graf von Luxemburg*) French version w de Caillavet (Théâtre Apollo)

1923 **Ciboulette** (Reynaldo Hahn/w Francis de Croisset) Théâtre des Variétés 7 April

1927 **Le Diable à Paris** (Marcel Lattès/w de Croisset) Théâtre Marigny 27 November

FLETCHER, Percy E[astman] (b Derby, 12 December 1879; d Windsor, 10 September 1932).

Musical director at a series of West End theatres from 1906 onwards, Fletcher made his first composing contribution to the musical stage with part of the score for the little "conventional tragical musical absurdity," *An Exile from Home,* played as a forepiece to *The Shulamite* in 1906.

He joined Beerbohm Tree at His Majesty's Theatre in 1915 and remained there to act as the conductor of the long run of *Chu Chin Chow.* He composed the score for Oscar Asche's successor to *Chu Chin Chow,* the spectacular eastern piece *Mecca,* produced in New York and then, with its title altered to *Cairo* under pressure from an Islamic element, in London (where he was also conductor).

His light orchestral works won him his principal recognition as a composer, but he also composed and conducted a further, short-lived musical, the olde Englishe spectacular *The Good Old Days,* produced by Asche at the Gaiety Theatre with disastrous results.

1906 **An Exile from Home** (w R Hess/William Watson) 1 act Savoy Theatre 12 June

1920 **Mecca** (aka *Cairo*) (Asche) Century Theater, New York 4 October

1925 **The Good Old Days** (Asche) Gaiety Theatre 27 October

FLEUR DE THÉ Opéra-bouffe in 3 acts by Alfred Duru and Henri Chivot. Music by Charles Lecocq. Théâtre de l'Athénée, Paris, 11 April 1868.

When the rehearsal pianist of the Théâtre de l'Athénée showed signs of promise as a composer with his two-act *L'amour et son carquois,* the theatre director, William Busnach, gave him a Chivot and Duru libretto to set. The young Charles Lecocq's score to *Fleur de thé* proved one of its most attractive attributes, and the piece turned out to be by far the happiest of those ever mounted by Busnach at his unsteady little theatre.

Fleur de thé (Lucie Cabel), the daughter of the Chinese mandarin Tien-Tien (Désiré), has broken the oriental law by leaving her home to look out into the world. Her father and her future husband, Ka-o-lin (Léonce), set off in pursuit of the runaway girl who takes refuge in an inn, and is hidden by the ship's cook Pinsonnet (Sytter) in his room. When the cantinière Césarine (Mlle Lovato/Irma Marié), the cook's wife, jealously bundles her out, the little Chinese maiden is captured and condemned, by another local law, to be instantly wed to the man to whom she first spoke in her flight. When it turns out that China doesn't count previous foreign marriages and that it is her husband who is nominated, Césarine takes things in hand. She disguises herself as Fleur de thé, gets rewed to her husband, and spends the wedding night with him, but when Tien-Tien discovers that his "married" daughter has spent the night alone he is furious at this lack of marital respect and is preparing to take horrid revenge when Ka-o-lin leads on the marines. In a happy ending, everyone ends up drinking Césarine's stock of cliquot.

Lecocq's score mixed the romantic-comic and the lively with some pieces which were clearly in line of descent from the zanier moments of *Ba-ta-clan.* The role of Césarine, if not the title role, was certainly the best and most musically substantial one. She began with a Chanson de la Cantinière, continued in the second act with an anti-man ariette ("En tous pays l'homme est un être"), joined with Pinsonnet in the duo and couplets de l'alcôve, in which he tries to convince her that nothing happened during his rewedding night whilst she, who had taken the bride's place, knows he is lying, and ended with the jolly Ronde du cliquot. Pinsonnet spent his tenor tones on two solos, whilst the broader comicalities, such as the Chinoiserie "Je fourre mon nez partout," or Ka-o-lin's dubious explanation of how his calm oriental temperament prevents him getting sexually over-excited, were the province of the two Chinamen.

Played at the Athénée up to the summer break, the show was brought back in the new season, and soon began to make its way both around the country and beyond its confines. Perhaps not surprisingly, given its sulphurous content, *Fleur de thé* suffered somewhat in its overseas productions. In England, the Gaiety Theatre took the libretto and decorated its caponized remnants, under the title *Malala* (8 April 1871), with music from the fashionable Offenbach canon instead of that by the unknown Lecocq. The French-speaking part of the population were able to see the piece as it was written later that same year as given by a visiting French company, headed by Grenier and Luce, at the Lyceum, but the regular English version (ad Andrew Baildon), first produced in Newcastle by Norman Kirby's touring Metropolitan Opéra-bouffe Company with Carlotta Zerbini (Césarine), J A Shaw (Ka-o-lin), Edith Percy (Fleur de thé), Norman Kirby (Chang Wang) and W G Bedford (Pinsonnet) in its leading roles, finally made it to town (ad J H Jarvis) four years later—after Lecocq had been made famous by *La Fille de Madame Angot*—with a cast headed by Alice Burville and Bessie Sudlow, was another watered-down affair which was even then considered to be too indelicate for polite consumption. Spain didn't worry about the indelicacy. It, like the Gaiety, took the libretto and left behind the music: the *Fior di rosa* produced in Barcelona in 1877 had a score by Galleani.

America, in spite of also getting a successful taste of the original show from Jacob Grau's troupe with Mlle Rizarelli (Fleur de thé) and Marie Desclauzas (Césarine) at its head, and also from Marie Aimée and her company, similarly put out a botched version under the tellingly burlesque title of *The Pearl of Pekin, or The Tar Outwitted by His Wife.* Charles Alfred Byrne laid claim to the libretto, and the remnants of Lecocq's score was heavily adulterated with Gustave Kerker tunelets. Thus remade for general consumption, it was produced on Broadway by E E Rice and Henry Dixey billed as the "sumptuous production of C A Byrne's Chinese comic opera," with Louis Harrison (Tyfoo), Irene Verona (Finette) and Joseph Herbert starred for 67 performances (Bijou Theater 19 March 1888), found considerable popular success on the American touring circuits, and went on to pay several further brief visits to Broadway in the years that followed.

The first German adaptation (ad Ernst Dohm) was seen in Berlin, and in Vienna F Zell's German version was given a fine Theater an der Wien cast with Karoline Finaly (Theeblütchen), Matthias Rott (Wau-wau), Carl Adolf Friese (Fi-Fi), Albin Swoboda (Pinsonnet) and Fräulein Fischer (Cäsarine) sharing the spotlight with an entr'acte of "chinesescher Feuer und Waffenspiele" and Auguste Maywood's Chinese ballet (music by Adolf Müller) for 17 performances. Hungary, Russia, South America and, most notably, Scandinavia also welcomed Lecocq's opéra-bouffe, it being maintained in the repertoire in Sweden (*Theblomma*) past the turn of the century, long after Lecocq's later works had displaced it elsewhere.

At the turn of the century, when *A Chinese Honeymoon* became the first musical ever to run one thousand consecutive performances on the London stage, more than one commentator remarked on the similarity of its plot to the 30-year-old French piece, and one even referred to George Dance's libretto as an adaptation of Chivot and Duru's work. They were, perhaps, not wholly without justification, even if the plot element concerned was only one of several in the English piece, and the characters were wholly (if not nationally) different.

Fleur de thé returned to the Paris stage, first at the Théâtre des Variétés (June 1869) with Lise Tautin and Gourdon featured, and subsequently (17 January 1880) at the Bouffes-Parisiens, where Mme Grivot (Césarine), Mlle Burton (Fleur de thé), Paul Hittemans (Tien-Tien) and Léonce, back in his original role, led the cast of the by-then-famous composer's early work through 35 performances.

Germany: Friedrich-Wilhelmstädtisches Theater 13 January 1869; Austria: Theater an der Wien *Theeblüthe* 10 February 1869; USA: Theatre Français (Fr) 1 February 1869; UK: Lyceum Theatre (Fr) 12 June 1871, Tyne Theatre, Newcastle-upon-Tyne (Eng) *Fleur de thé, or The Rose of Canton* 15 March 1875, Criterion Theatre, London 9 October 1875; Hungary: Budai Színkör *Bájvirág* 13 April 1877

FLORA, THE RED MENACE Musical in 2 acts by George Abbott and Robert Russell based on the novel *Love is Just Around the Corner* by Lester Atwell. Lyrics by Fred Ebb. Music by John Kander. Alvin Theater, New York, May 11 1965.

Flora, the Red Menace was an unsuccessful 1965 musical (87 performances) which has become fondly remembered in retrospect as having assembled a group of Broadway's most admired talents. Amongst the proven folk were producer Harold Prince and veteran director-cum-co-author George Abbott; amongst those on their way up were songwriters John Kander and Fred Ebb and leading lady Liza Minnelli, better known at that stage as Judy Garland's teenaged daughter than for her own talents.

Fresh out of art school, Flora Mezaros (Miss Minnelli) gets a job at a department store and a fascination with a stuttering artist called Harry Toukarian (Bob Dishy) who is, himself, into communism and sex. Flora tries the communism, turns down the sex, but then surprises Harry in the company of the more willing Comrade Charlotte (Cathryn Damon). Comrade Charlotte plants the *Daily Worker* in Flora's locker and she gets the sack but, although Harry clears her and she is reinstated, Flora firmly puts both him and communism behind her as she gets down to beginning her adult life. Dortha Duckworth and James Cresson played a pair of striving performers, and Mary Louise Wilson was the equally, if differently, striving Comrade Ada.

Flora's song ''A Quiet Thing'' proved the favorite number from the show's score, a score which was supplemented with four new or old-new numbers when a considerably revised, small-scale version of *Flora, the Red Menace* was produced at the Vineyard Theater in 1987 (6 December) with Veanne Cox and Peter Frechette featured. The libretto (ad David Thompson) was given a major facelift, replacing the original innocence with a 1980s ''sophistication,'' the characters largely altered and the point of the piece changed to suit the fashions of the time. An English production of this version was played at Cambridge and at the Orange Tree Theater in 1994 and 1995, and a German one at a Hamburg dinner theatre in 1994.

UK: Arts Theatre, Cambridge 29 June 1992, Orange Tree Theatre 1 December 1994; Germany: Hotel Steigenburger, Hamburg *Flora der rote Gefahr* 1 February 1994

Recordings: original cast (RCA Victor), revival cast 1987 (TER)

FLORESTAN 1er, PRINCE DE MONACO Opérette in 3 acts by Sacha Guitry. Lyrics by Albert Willemetz. Music by Werner Richard Heymann. Théâtre des Variétés, Paris, 8 December 1933.

An opérette allegedly put together by Guitry around the theme of an article discovered in the *Figaro* which described how the historical Prince Florestan of Monaco (1785–1856), during youthful years passed in Paris following the deposition of his father in the French Revolution, became an actor, playing at 19 the role of the King of Prussia. The music for the work was composed by Heymann, best known for his score to the film *Der Kongress tanzt* (1931). With Henri Garat (then, very quickly, René Lestelly), in the role of the actor-prince, encouraging everyone to ''Amusez-vous, foutez-vous d'tout,'' serenading ''Margot,'' and insisting ''Je l'aime, je l'adore'' and ''C'est si charmant,'' the grossly oversized Pauley as the extravagant and adorable actor Rosambeau singing ''Ah! si j'avais été ténor'' and Jacqueline Francell (Mesange) and Genevieve Vix (La Duchesse) at the head of the feminine team, the piece had a fine Paris run under the management of Max Maurey.

FLORODORA Musical comedy in 2 acts by Owen Hall. Lyrics by Ernest Boyd-Jones and Paul Rubens. Music by Leslie Stuart. Additional songs by Paul Rubens. Lyric Theatre, London, 11 November 1899.

The story goes that actor-agent Ben Nathan and businessman Walter Weill formed a syndicate with the intention of producing a musical comedy. In something of a coup, they signed up Leslie Stuart, the highly successful songwriter, to provide the score and, somewhere along the way, got into cahoots with Tom B Davis, the newly successful producer of *Little Miss Nobody,* who put up half of the finance for the venture, became the show's nominal producer, and provided the services of a younger songwriter, the rising Paul Rubens. History does not re-

Plate 125. **Florodora.** *One of the greatest hits of its era, wherever it went. Australia's production featured George Lauri as the charlatan Tweedlepunch, with the famous double-sextet here as popular as it had been everywhere else.*

late who booked "Owen Hall," the most skillful librettist of the era, for the book, but since Hall was perpetually bankrupt and wrote for cash down and no royalties, he was not, in spite of his track record, difficult to hire.

Hall's story was set in the picturesque Philippine Islands where millionaire Cyrus W Gilfain (Charles E Stevens) manufactures the profitable "Florodora" perfume and simultaneously courts the lovely Dolores (Evie Greene), although she is but a working girl on his land. Dolores, however, loves the overseer Frank Abercoed (Melville Stewart) whom Gilfain has earmarked for his daughter, Angela (Kate Cutler) who, in her turn, fancies Captain Arthur Donegal (Edgar Stevens). Gilfain's love is tactical, however, for Dolores is the rightful heir to the whole place, and he knows it. A wandering phrenologist, Tweedlepunch (Willie Edouin), is suborned by the plotting Gilfain to pair off the islanders "suitably," but Abercoed rebels at the imposition of an instant and unwanted marriage and he leaves the Pacific to head back to his impoverished Welsh seat. Unfortunately for him, Gilfain has just bought his family castle as a British base for "Florodora" and is busy settling in. However a little bit of ghostly masquerading scares the villain out of his wits and into both a confession and a happy ending.

It was scarcely the most original or well-constructed plot, but it had the merit of being malleable and, in rehearsal, it needed to be. Hall discovered that Ada Reeve was out of a job, having been effectively dropped from George Edwardes's *San Toy* at Daly's, and he offered to write her into *Florodora.* Ada became Lady Holyrood, the latest in Hall's line of brisk, modern society women, so effectively begun by Lottie Venne as Lady Virginia Forrest in *A Gaiety Girl,* and she was woven into the fabric, if scarcely the plot, of the piece.

Some of the songs for *Florodora* were a touch unusual. Stuart wrote many of his melodies rather differently from his contemporaries—with long, almost wandering lines—and his skill at the coon song meant that, alongside more English tones, a whiff of burnt cork sometimes intruded. He forebore to put a blatant coon number into his Philippine Island musical, but turned out several more suitable songs which were winningly attractive—Angela's lovely long-limbed solo about "The Fellow Who Might," Dolores's ballad "The Silver Star of Love" and Abercoed's baritone hymn to "The Shade of the Palm." Others were swingingly so, notably Donegal's assertion that "I Want to Be a Military Man," whilst the late-in-the-day additions for Miss Reeve, written largely by Rubens, were in the sort-of-schoolboy-saucy vein he favored and which she delivered so well. "Tact" and "I've an Inkling" both scored hits. However, the big hit of the show was not a solo but an ensemble. "Are There Any More at Home Like You?" was, so latter-day rumor says, intended initially to have been a duet, but for some reason director/choreographer Sidney Ellison decided to make it up into a double sextet. The Big Six of his front line of chorus girls were paired with six chorus men, elegantly dressed and choreographed into a gently promenading routine to perform the number which quickly became not only the hit of the evening but—now better known by its first line, "Tell Me, Pretty Maiden"—the most famous single show number of its kind since the celebrated pas de quatre from *Faust Up-to-Date.*

Florodora caused a sensation, and a huge £6,000 in advance bookings were taken in the days after the premiere. In the end, it ran for 17 months and 455 performances at the Lyric Theatre. When the show was secure as a hit, Davis was able to get such artists as W Louis Bradfield, Florence St John and Decima Moore to take over, whilst Ben Nathan, the initiator of the whole thing, allowed himself on occasions to go on both in the sextet and as Tweedlepunch. The cast changes brought with them new material, and the score of *Florodora* was constantly updated. None of the replacement songs, however, found the vogue of the original ones.

With the production of *Florodora* Tom Davis won himself a famous first in musical-theatre history. In what seems to be the first example of musical-comedy merchandising in history, he had a "Florodora" perfume manufactured and sold in the auditorium.

John C Fisher, John W Dunne and Thomas Ryley produced *Florodora* on Broadway with Edouin repeating his London role in the company of his daughter May (Angela), Edna Wallace Hopper (Lady Holyrood), Sydney Deane (Abercoed), Fannie Johnstone (Dolores) and R E Graham (Cyrus). London chorus-boy Harry B Burcher restaged the famous routine, and the production was greeted with an even bigger success than the original had been, with the sextet girls becoming the celebrities of the day. The show ran 379 performances at the Casino Theater, transferred to the New York Theater for a further 122, and reopened the Monday after closing there in another production, with no less than 250 cast members, at the Winter Garden Theater (27 January 1902) for another 48 nights. By the time the show left Broadway it had totaled 549 unbroken performances. It had also provoked many an imitator and burlesque—Burcher himself staged a "Tell Me, Dusky Maiden" and a "Flora, I Am Your Adorer" for Broadway's *Sleeping Beauty and the Beast* (1901)—and also more than its quota of scandals and Broadway lawsuits. In one of these latter, a gent called Jacob Eppinger who had "loaned" the producers $5,000 claimed he was an investor and sued for a share of the profits, whilst the producers countered that he'd been repaid with interest and was not an investor. But whilst the lawsuits ran on, and both Britain and America welcomed the first of the *Florodora* tours which would continue for many decades to come, the piece continued its way round the world.

In Australia George Lauri (Tweedlepunch), Grace Palotta (Lady Holyrood), Carrie Moore (Dolores), Wallace Brownlow (Abercoed), Charles Kenningham (Donegal, with interpolations), and Maud Chetwynd (Angela) headed the cast of J C Williamson's production to a record-breaking run of 106 performances in Melbourne as *Florodora* became as ingrained in the repertoire there as it was on the other side of the world. Mabel Nelson and Frank Danby headed the South African production to similar triumph, Budapest's Magyar Színház produced a version in Hungarian (ad Adolf Mérei, Dezső Bálint), and in 1903 *Florodora* was mounted at the Théâtre des Bouffes-Parisiens in Paris (ad Adrien Vély, F A Schwab), under the direction of Ellison, with Paulette Darty playing Dolores alongside Piccaluga as Abercoed, Simon-Max as Plum-Quick (Tweedlepunch), Edmond Roze (Gilfain) and Mlle Dziri (Lady Holyrood). Leslie Stuart had this time to suffer the interpolation of a cakewalk performed by one Mlle Nanon to "The Honeysuckle and the Bee." In May 1907 an Italian version was mounted in Milan.

Florodora returned to New York's Broadway Theater on 27 March 1905 with "new sets and costumes" and announced as having been "revised by Frank Pixley," for four weeks, and again in 1920 (Century Theater) when J J Shubert mounted a major revival with the script this time updated by Harry B Smith, the score tricked out with some Stuart numbers from his subsequent successes, a cast headed by Eleanor Painter (Dolores), Christie MacDonald (Lady Holyrood), George Hassell (Tweedlepunch) and Walter Woolf (Abercoed) and a lavish production, and won a 150-performance run. In London, too, there were revivals, in 1915 and in 1932, but the show's life in Britain continued largely in the provinces. The last touch of *Florodora* to be heard in London, nearly 90 years after its opening, was in the extravaganza *Ziegfeld* which included "The Fellow Who Might" in its score.

Officially, there was no film made of *Florodora.* However, in 1925 an Australian movie called *Painted Daughters* and boasting "a cast of 100 native Australians" confided in its advertising that it was "based on *Florodora* "and Hollywood's 1930 *The Florodora Girl* included a performance of "Tell Me, Pretty Maiden" alongside filmland's own contribution to the song content: "Pass the Beer and Pretzels" and "My Kind of Man."

USA: Casino Theater 12 November 1900; Australia: Her Majesty's Theatre, Melbourne 15 December 1900; Hungary: Magyar Színház 5 December 1901; France: Théâtre des Bouffes-Parisiens 27 January 1903; Germany: Stadttheater, Leipzig 21 November 1903

Recording: archive compilation of original cast recordings (Opal)

FLORY, Régine [ARTAZ, Marie Louise] (b Marseille, 24 July 1894; d London, 7 June 1926). Dancer turned vocalist and actress who won a feverish following on both sides of the English channel.

Mlle Flory first appeared in Paris in revue at the Théâtre des Capucines. She played the role of Chiquette in the metropolitan production of the Marseille musical *La Reine s'amuse* (1913) as a teenager, but made her fame in revue in Paris (Fémina, La Cigale, etc) and then in London where she featured in *Paris Frissons, The Passing Show, By Jingo, if We Do . . .* and *Vanity Fair,* and in the revusical musical play *The Beauty Spot,* dancing the Haschisch Dance with Jan Oyra.

Alfred Butt, who had presented her in London, built and opened the Théâtre Mogador in Paris in 1919 and starred her there in *Hullo Paris,* a revue built on the model of the London successes *Hullo Ragtime* and *Hullo Tango.* The show failed and Butt abandoned both the venue and the star. The febrile and highly sexual performer, something of a "special taste" with that part of the public which championed her, starred in several further revues, and also created leading roles in two highly successful musical comedies, Szulc's *Le Petit Choc* (1923, Féfé Mimosa) and Yvain's *Pas sur la bouche* (1925, Gilberte Valandray) before, after one attempt at drowning herself in the Seine, she terminally turned a gun on herself in Butt's office at the Theatre Royal, Drury Lane.

FLOSSIE Opérette in 3 acts by Marcel Gerbidon. Lyrics by Charles L Pothier. Music by Joseph Szulc. Théâtre des Bouffes-Parisiens, Paris, 9 May 1929.

A successful example of the lightest kind of French 1920s musical comedy, *Flossie* had a book in which the daughters of an English minister and a Swiss pastor swap places and thus find themselves marriage partners. The show featured Jacqueline Francell as the English Flossie ("Je m'appelle Flossie," "Le Chemin de mon coeur"), Mireille as her Swiss equivalent and René Koval in the chief comic role of the Reverend Good-Bye ("Paris"). The show gave producers Quinson and Willemetz a good run both at the Bouffes-Parisiens and as a touring proposition and it still appears occasionally in the French provinces today.

An unsuccessful piece under the same title (Armand Robi/Ralph Murphy) was produced on Broadway in 1924 (Lyric Theater 3 June).

FLOTTE BURSCHE Operette in 1 act by Josef Braun. Music by Franz von Suppé. Theater am Franz-Josefs-Kai, Vienna, 18 April 1863.

One of the most successful of Suppé's early, short Operetten on the French model, *Flotte Bursche* was written whilst the musician was working as musical director and house composer at Karl Treumann's adventurous little Theater am Franz-Josefs-Kai. It proved, both on Treumann's initial production and later, to be one of the most popular of all early Viennese Operetten.

The jolly fellows of the title were the students Brand and Frinke (Anna Grobecker) and the comical Fleck (Treumann) who set out to swindle the miserly pawnbroker Hieronymus Geier out of the 500 thalers he is illegally withholding from poor Anton. Brand dresses up as an Italian painter and offers the pawnbroker an old picture. When two Englishmen—the disguised Frinke and Fleck—go into ecstasies over it and offer to buy it for 1,000 thalers, Geier hurriedly buys the worthless canvas for 700. Anton now has enough cash to wed his Lieschen and there is a bit over for jollity.

The score of the show consisted of an overture (as in so many cases with Suppé, the piece which has survived the best) and nine numbers. Frinke opened proceedings with his ''Aus den Federn auf ihr Hechte,'' Fleck delivered a long comic tenor piece as an entrance song and Brand introduced an Italian-style arietta with florid passages, whilst the student song ''Gaudeamus igitur'' was introduced into a first act-quartet and served again as the Schlussgesang to the show. The disguised English pair had the evening's best fun, indulging in a cod-English duettino which gabbled ''Bless my dear, how the sun is shining, what's o'clock, at four jam dining, English Lord, English Word, English dog, English fog, Oh Cheer old England cheer.''

Flotte Bursche was played 31 times in the less than two months between its production and the destruction by fire of the Kai-Theater, and when Treumann took up at the Carltheater two months later, Suppé's Operette was played on the opening bill (19 August 1863). It remained a regular part of the repertoire, with Wilhelm Knaack (Geier) Hermine Meyerhoff (Lieschen), Josef Matras (Fleck), Grobecker (Frinke) and Rosa Streitmann (Brand) amongst the casts which gave the piece a good dozen showings in 1869, 11 in 1870, 8 in 1871, 3 in 1872, 8 in 1873 and a handful more each year through the 1870s, whilst also putting in isolated appearances at other Vienna houses (Theater an der Wien 28 October 1863, etc).

Flotte Bursche was picked up in other central European and Scandinavian countries, notably in Germany, and in Hungary where it was played first in German and then in Hungarian (ad Endre Latabár). It was seen at the Budai Színkör in both languages in 1867 and taken into the repertoire at the Népszínház in 1877. The show returned periodically to the Viennese stage in the 20th century, being seen at the Carltheater in 1903 in a double bill with Offenbach's *Salon Pitzelberger* and again in 1911, at the Theater an der Wien in 1914 paired with *Leichte Kavallerie,* and at the Redoutensaal in 1931 (26 December).

Although translated into several other European languages, the show did not apparently get seen in either France or Britain and the only performances played in New York were in the German theatres, the first being in 1867 with the dwarves Jean Petit (Geier), Jean Piccolo (Fleck) and Józsi Kiss (Anton) cast alongside full-sized women as Brand, Fricke and Lieschen. Later performances were more conventional. Robert Tagg's German opera company toured the piece in tandem with *Zehn Mädchen* in 1881, and in 1891 an English-language version did make it to the stage outside New York when *Jolly Students* was mounted by Rudolf Aronson's touring Casino Theater company in Philadelphia with Pauline L'Allemand and Jeff de Angelis at the head of the cast. Suppé's little show shared a bill with *Cavalleria Rusticana.* It was later toured in the repertoire of the New England Opera Company (1899).

Hungary: (Ger) July 1863, Budai Színkör *A pajkos diákok* 15 May 1867; Germany: Friedrich-Wilhelmstädtisches Theater 3 December 1863; USA: Stadttheater (Ger) 25 October 1867, Broad Street Theater, Philadelphia *Jolly Students* 2 November 1891

FLOWER DRUM SONG Musical in 2 acts by Oscar Hammerstein II and Joseph Fields based on the novel by C Y Lee. Lyrics by Oscar Hammerstein II. Music by Richard Rodgers. St James Theater, New York, 1 December 1958.

Although successful on both the American and British stage, and the source of one distinctly popular song and of a Hollywood film, Rodgers and Hammerstein's musical *Flower Drum Song* has never attained the same classic status in the public or professional mind as their, admittedly very much more successful, *The Sound of Music, South Pacific, The King and I, Oklahoma!* and *Carousel.*

Librettist Joseph Fields winkled out *Flower Drum Song,* C Y Lee's novel about the generation gap in the Chinese-American community, purchased the dramatic rights, and presented it to the songwriters as a possible basis for a musical. The authors themselves produced the resultant piece with song-and-dance man Gene Kelly taking on the task of directing. The story of the show, with its arranged marriage theme and its hundred-times used veiled wedding trick, had more than a little flavor of the turn-of-the-century comic opera, but *Flower Drum Song* was set firmly in the present and the tone of the piece was almost wholly a romantic, rather than a comic, one.

San Francisco bar-owner Sammy Fong (Larry Blyden) has been betrothed to Mei Li (Miyoshi Umeki), who has been sent from China for the marriage, but his tastes run rather to the nightclub stripper, Linda Low (Pat Suzuki). Determined to free himself from his obligations to Mei Li's family, Sammy sets himself to find a replacement bridegroom for her, and he chooses Wang Ta (Ed Kenney), the son of the wholly traditional Wang Chi Yang (Keye Luke), who is more or less engaged to Linda. Sammy arranges for the elder Wang and his sister-in-law Madame Liang (Juanita Hall) to see Linda at work, and the damage is done. By the time that Linda and Sammy have got themselves engaged, and Wang Ta has switched his preference to Mei Li, it is too late: the elders of the community have decided that Sammy must honor his contract. The wedding goes ahead but, of course, when Sammy lifts his bride's veil he finds not Mei Li but Linda, who, in the best tradition of *The Sultan of Mocha, The Geisha* or *A Chinese Honeymoon,* has taken her place.

The score to the show included some attractive numbers—the gentle ''A Hundred Million Miracles,'' Wang Ta's ballad ''You Are Beautiful,'' addressed not to either girl but explaining to his aunt what he would say when the occasion arises, and the sad ''Love, Look Away'' of the shoulder-to-cry-on Helen (Arabella Hong), but it was a more upbeat piece, Linda's bouncing declaration that ''I Enjoy Being a Girl,'' which proved to be the most enduring piece outside the show. It made its way into cabaret and variety acts around the world, and for many years became the favorite musical-comedy audition song for actresses attempting to cover vocal limitations with a wash of ''personality.''

Broadway's production of *Flower Drum Song* was played 600 times, and the authors (Williamson Music Ltd) also sponsored London's version in which Tim Herbert (Sammy), Kevin Scott (Wang Ta), Yau Shan Tung (Mei Li) and Yama Saki (Linda) featured for a good run of 464 performances, but in spite of this the show apparently went no further in its stage form. Wider viewing was left to the cinema. At the time of writing, a rewritten version (ad David Henry Hwang), however, was mooted for production at Los Angeles's Ahmanson Theater in April 2001.

In 1961 a film version was made, in which Miss Umeki and Miss Hall repeated their original roles alongside Nancy Kwan (Linda, dubbed by B J Baker) and James Shigeta. ''Love, Look Away'' was dubbed by the young singer Marilyn Horne.

UK: Palace Theatre, London 24 March 1960

Film: Universal 1961

Recordings: original cast (Columbia), London cast (HMV), film soundtrack (Decca), etc

FLUP..! Opérette in 3 acts by Gaston Dumestre. Music by Joseph Szulc. Théâtre de l'Alhambra, Brussels, 19 December 1913.

The Belgian production of *Flup..!,* staged under the management of Paul Clerget, introduced the Polish-born composer Szulc to the musical theatre where, in the years after the war, he was to have a prominent Parisian career. At this time, however, he was sufficiently ill-known as to be billed in the Alhambra's program as Joseph Szule. Although the show's title had the ring of a postwar musical comedy to it, the curious word was, in fact, the name of the comic sub-hero of the piece, one Antonin Flup, a part created in Brussels by the young, rising (and very fourth-billed) André Urban.

Set amongst the colonial British on the island of Ceylon, with a suffragette heroine (Germaine Huber) and an amorous French aristocrat (Charles Casella) as hero, the show followed the comical events that occur when a French railway porter (Urban) is—in the place of the aristocrat—put in charge of the social affairs of the colony of Kandy, whilst the real Duke works his way, incognito, around to marriage with the staunchly feminist Maud. Camus appeared as Lord Archibald, the Governor of Kandy, Hélène Gérard was Edith Smithson, the vice president of the London suffragette movement, and Mme Lepers played Mrs Flatwell, a suffragette with intentions towards what she does not suspect is a phony ''Duke.''

The willfully topical text was paired with a score which also introduced the first feelings of the new age. The predominant waltz and march rhythms—Maud sang waltzes when being a woman, and marches when being a suffragette—were varied by such ''coming'' dances as the tango (which was, nevertheless, followed immediately by a more conventional ''ballet Hindoue'').

When *Flup..!* finally made its way to Paris and Mme Rasimi's Théâtre Ba-ta-clan after the First World War, the title role was taken by top comedian Dranem, starred alongside Henri Defreyn (Duc de Florigny) and Maguy Warna (Maud Archibald), and supported by Saulieu (Archibald), Anne Martens (Edith) and Mary Théry (Mme Flatwell). The show scored a fine success, and was both toured and later twice revived in Paris.

Some of Szulc's music for *Flup..!* was pirated by Carlo Lombardo for the patchwork pilfered score of the successful Italian musical *Madama di Tebe.*

France: Théâtre des Célestins, Lyon 1917, Théâtre Ba-ta-clan, Paris 18 March 1920

FÖLDES, Imre (b Kaposvár, 15 September 1881; d Budapest, 30 April 1958).

Internationally successful Hungarian playwright (*A császár katonái, Hivatalnok urak, Hallo!, Vörös szegfű,* the hugely successful *Grün Lili,* etc), Földes ventured rarely into the musical field, yet in those rare ventures produced the texts for three widely played operetts. Ákos Buttykay's *Az ezüst sirály* was produced in Germany and Austria as *Liebesrausch* and was also apparently (though I cannot trace this) seen in America, whilst Paul Ábrahám's two most popular Operetten, *Viktória* (*Viktoria and Her Hussar*) and *Die Blume von Hawaii,* both of which he authored, won productions throughout the world and remain in the European repertoire up to this day.

1905 **Két Hippolit** (Iván Hüvös) Népszínház 13 January

1920 **Az ezüst sirály** (Ákos Buttykay) Városi Színház 6 February

1922 **Olivia hercegnő** (Buttykay/Miksa Bródy) Fővárosi Operettszínház 23 December

1925 **Die blonde Sphinx** (Max Niederberger/ad Gustav Beer) Bürgertheater, Vienna 27 March

1930 **Viktória** (Pal Ábrahám/Imre Harmath) Király Színház 21 February

1931 **Die Blume von Hawaii** (Ábrahám/Harmath/w Grünwald, Löhner-Beda) Neues Theater, Leipzig 24 July

1946 **Fekete liliom** (Egon Kemény/w Károly Nóti) Fővárosi Operettszínház 20 December

FOLLIES Broadway legend in 2 acts by James Goldman. Music and lyrics by Stephen Sondheim. Winter Garden Theater, New York, 4 April 1971.

Built on somewhat the same kind of framework as Sondheim's successful *Company, Follies* similarly brought together a group of people for an occasion and then proceeded to peer into their lives. However, if *Company*'s people were a group of reasonably common-or-garden, middle-ageing New Yorkers with mostly normal-sized neuroses and personalities, those of *Follies* were anything but.

The occasion which brings the *Follies* folk together is, not unsuitably, a destruction. The theatre in which they performed as members of Weissman's Follies in their younger days is being pulled down, and Mr Weissman is giving it a wake to which several decades of the now aging or, indeed, positively aged artistes are invited. Many of them flit briefly through the party and across the stage, their characters encapsulated in a song or a few lines, and the main focus falls on two of the less elderly ex-chorines, former best friends Sally (Dorothy Collins) and Phyllis (Alexis Smith), who married their stage-door Johnnies and went different ways. Sally and Buddy (Gene Nelson) have a comfortable, unhappy small-town existence, whilst Phyllis and her successful businessman husband Ben (John McMartin) have an equally dissatisfied brittle-plastic, New York-stylish life. Both women—for it is the women who are the real center of attention—are, under dissimilar façades, wallowing in more neuroses and discontent than could be justified by the worst misfortune.

The entertainment moves, first, into a flashback, showing the foursome in their young days, and introducing a whiff of the infidelity which is apparently responsible for a half-ton of the neuroses, and then into a stylized *Follies*-style series of routines in which their emotions are expressed in the exaggerated showbizzy tones of everything from torch song and soft-shoe to low vaudeville comedy. When the four have finished having a wonderful, theatrical time mildly torturing themselves and each other with accusations of infidelities and insufficiencies ancient and modern, the party comes to an end and they head home to carry on their miserable lives.

The score of *Follies* produced a number of attractive and successful songs, written in the wide range of theatrical styles covered by its characters. Sally's powerful, self-lacerating number from the *Follies* sequence, ''Losing My Mind,'' went on to become a torch singer's favorite, whilst the crackling, comical musical biography of the faded film actress Carlotta Campion (Yvonne de Carlo), ''I'm Still Here,'' became the century's anthem for all Carlotta's real-life equivalents and wannabes, and a cabaret standard. The vacuously satirical squeakings of an elderly ''Broadway Baby'' (Ethel Shutta) also took the same trip, but like the over-the-top torch song, normally sung straight instead of tongue-in-cheek. However, in the show itself, some of the less larger-than-life pieces showed up more effectively than the take-out tunes—the dainty performance of an aging team of song-and-dance sweethearts (''Rain on the Roof''), the voice of the old Viennese soprano blending touchingly with the sounds of her young self in ''One More Kiss,'' the cheerfully gutsy sound of an old featured artist leading a half-remembered dance routine (''Who's That Woman?'') or the still-tenor tones of the front-man Roscoe, announcing his ''Beautiful Girls'' once more, were contrasted with some fresher singing from the four young folk (''Waiting for the Girls Upstairs,'' ''You're Gonna Love Tomorrow,'' ''Love Will See Us Through''), and with the bitter self-searching of the four principals, which was given an almost comical face in Buddy's Blues (''I've got those God-why-don't-you-love-me-oh-you-do-I'll-see-you-later-blues . . .'') or a taunting, sarcastic one in Phyllis's self-centred spiking of her husband, ''Could I Leave You?''

Harold Prince's original production of *Follies* played 522 performances on Broadway without somehow registering in public or professional eyes as a success and, although the songs won Sondheim a Tony Award in a season where *Two Gentlemen of Verona* topped the Best Musical category, even the songs took their time to take off as favorites. They were materially helped, particularly outside America, by their exposure in the compilation revue *Side by Side by Sondheim;* Julia McKenzie's pianissimo ''Broadway Baby'' and Millicent Martin's

Plate 126. **Follies**

husky ''I'm Still Here'' were responsible for making the numbers popular in Britain. The show itself won a boost from a highly cast concert performance at New York's Avery Fisher Hall in 1985.

Finally, carried on the increasing wave of Sondheimania in British theatre circles, *Follies* was produced in Britain in 1985, 14 years after its Broadway premiere, at Manchester's Wythenshawe Forum with Josephine Blake, Kevin Colson and Mary Miller in its lead roles. It was subsequently given a London showing under the management of Cameron Mackintosh. The show was revised for this occasion, and several numbers replaced, mostly to good effect. Julia McKenzie (Sally), Diana Rigg (Phyllis), Daniel Massey (Ben) and David Healy (Buddy) played the four central characters whilst such popular British performers of yesteryear as soprano Adele Leigh and duo vocalists Pearl Carr and Teddy Johnson supported alongside London's original *Annie Get Your Gun* star, Dolores Gray. The production ran, like the first, for 522 performances without, once again, wholly convincing, and rumors of a return to Broadway had no tomorrow. However, *Follies* did not vanish. It has, in the turn-of-the-century years, become a revivable prospect with those folk who like to drag their favorites of yesteryear up on the stage to do one last time and now not-so-well (or even plain dreadfully) what they once did very well indeed.

A German version (ad Michael Kunze) was produced in 1991 with Fritz Hille (Ben), Heinz Rennhack (Buddy), Australian Gaye MacFarlane (Sally), Daniela Ziegler (Phyllis), a list of well-known names in the supporting roles which included Renate Holm (Heidi), Eartha Kitt (Carlotta) and Brigitte Mira (Hattie), and with the role of Stella turned into two people—Ella and Stella—to feature the Kessler twins. It played 87 nights in Berlin. In 1998 New Jersey's Paper Mill Playhouse produced a revival featuring Donna McKechnie (Sally), Tony Roberts (Buddy), Dee Hoty (Phyllis), Martin Vidnovic (Ben), and Ann Miller (Carlotta), and a return to Broadway was mooted for April 2001 with a cast headed by Blythe Danner, Gregory Harrison, Judith Ivey and Treat Williams, and with Polly Bergen, Marge Champion, Betty Garrett, Joan Roberts, Donald Saddler and Carol Woods amongst the featured old (and not so very old) favorites.

UK: Forum, Wythenshawe, Manchester 30 April 1985; Shaftesbury Theatre (revised version) 21 July 1987; Germany: Theater des Westens 27 September 1991

Recordings: original cast (Capitol), concert 1985 (RCA), London cast 1987 (First Night), Paper Mill Playhouse (TVT)

FOLLOW A STAR Musical comedy in 2 acts by Douglas Furber and Dion Titheradge. Music by Vivian Ellis. Additional songs by Jack Yellen and Ted Shapiro. Winter Garden, London, 17 September 1930.

A made-to-measure vehicle for cabaret singer Sophie Tucker, here cast in a minimal plot as a cabaret singer. Miss Tucker interpolated songs old and new into Ellis's score, but did best with his ''If Your Kisses Can't Hold the Man You Love (then your tears won't bring him back).'' With its star proving less ''red-hot'' than might have been hoped, the show ran out 118 performances, dying on its feet when Miss Tucker left and the lead role was revamped for comedienne Maisie Gay.

Recording: selection (part-record) (AJA)

FOLLOW THAT GIRL Musical in 2 acts by Julian Slade and Dorothy Reynolds, based on their revue *Christmas in King Street.* Music by Julian Slade. Vaudeville Theatre, London, 17 March 1960.

Following their great success with *Salad Days* and another, lesser, with *Free as Air,* Slade and Reynolds revamped the Bristol Old Vic revue which had been their first collaboration as a musical. In a plot which neatly spoofed Victorian musical comedy, Victoria (Susan Hampshire) was pursued round the sights of London by worried parents and suitors, an amorous policeman (Peter Gilmore) and a collection of interested Londoners, to the accompaniment of some of Slade's best songs, including a lilting title number and an hilarious duo for two of Victoria's suitors who, thinking that she is not just missing but dead, try to find excuses to avoid being forced into unattractive mourning black (''Life Must Go On''). However, in spite of its merry attractions, the show had but a six months West End run (211 performances), and did not follow *Salad Days* to international stages.

Recording: original cast (HMV)

FOLLOW THE GIRLS Musical comedy in 2 acts by Guy Bolton, Eddie Davis and Fred Thompson. Lyrics by Dan Shapiro and Milton Pascal. Music by Philip Charig. Century Theater, New York, 8 April 1944.

Bolton and Thompson, who had been responsible in the 1910s and thereafter for a number of tightly constructed farcical libretti for the musical comedy stage, here turned out a sprawling piece of wartime foolery as the basis for a musical which was not far distant from being a variety show, and which, with a little help from the war, scored them one of their longest-running successes.

Follow the Girls featured nightclub vocalist Gertrude Niesen, at the head of a large line of scantily clad chorines, as Bubbles La Marr from burlesque, and comedian Jackie Gleason as Goofy Gale, who has to imitate one of the said chorines to follow her into action when she takes over the running of the soldiers' Spotlight Canteen in Great Neck, Long Island. Ballerina Irina Baronova featured in there somewhere as Anna Viskinova, and the score was topped by Miss Niesen's suggestive ''I Wanna Get Married.'' The logically titled ''Today Will Be Yesterday Tomorrow,'' ''Your Perf,'' ''I'm Gonna Hang My Hat,'' ''Twelve O'Clock and All Is Well'' and an encouraging title song were amongst the other musical moments of the evening.

Given the boost which wartime always seems to give to comfortably old-fashioned and picturesque entertainments, *Follow the Girls* played for no less than 882 performances at the Century and the 44th Street (12 June 1944) Theaters, and compounded its hometown success by going on, almost simultaneously, to both Australia and to London, when the helpful war was over. It turned out to be a hit all over again at London's His Majesty's Theatre with Arthur Askey heading the comedy, Evelyn Dall the nightclub glamor and Wendy Toye playing a person called Betty Deleaninnion in place of Baronova's more Russian dancer through 572 performances, and it had an agreeable run of almost four months in Sydney and nearly three in Melbourne (Her Majesty's Theatre 15 February 1947) with Don Nicol and Lois Green heading the cast.

Australia: Theatre Royal, Sydney 12 October 1946; UK: His Majesty's Theatre 25 October 1946

FOLLOW THRU Musical slice of country club life in 2 acts by Laurence Schwab and B G De Sylva. Lyrics by B G De Sylva and Lew Brown. Music by Ray Henderson. 46th Street Theater, New York, 9 January 1929.

De Sylva, Brown and Henderson, having mounted successful musical shows with footballing and boxing themes, switched to golf as the sporting element in their next musical, *Follow Thru,* and repeated that success all over again.

Lora Moore (Irene Delroy) and Ruth van Horn (Madeleine Cameron) are both in the running for the ladies' golf championship of the Bound Brook Country Club, and also for the affections of top golfer Jerry Downs (John Barker). Since Lora has and holds the latter she is, by musical comedy law, also quite, quite certain also to win the former. The light comedy folk were the demure Jack Martin (Jack Haley) and the very much less than demure Angie Howard (Zelma O'Neal).

The songs for *Follow Thru* included one which would become a standard, as Miss O'Neal (who had already made a hit with the team's ''Varsity Drag'' in *Good News*) joined with Haley in the naively cute ''Button Up Your Overcoat.'' Barker sang romantically of ''My Lucky Star'' and joined his girl to query ''You Wouldn't Fool Me, Would You?,'' Miss Cameron gave out with the title song and assured of the hero that ''He's a Man's Man,'' and Miss O'Neal insisted ''I Want to Be Bad.''

Schwab and Mandel's production of *Follow Thru*—well in the most modern style (''gymnastic dancing, agreeable songs, funny lines and the pace that kills everyone except musical comedy folk . . . a frenzied, sufficiently original carnival'')—gave them a splendid Broadway run of 403 performances and, as the show continued its run, Firth Shephard and Leslie Henson took up the piece for a London presentation at the large Dominion Theatre. Henson himself took the role created by Haley, giving it a rather different comic aspect, and paired himself with the American comedienne Ada May, whilst the personable Bernard Clifton played the male part of the prize sought by Ivy Tresmand and Elsie Randolph. However, in spite of the popularity of De Sylva, Brown and Henderson's songs in Britain, their shows—even with a star name like Henson attached to them—could never get off the ground there. *Follow Thru* (grammatically revamped as *Follow Through*) did a little better than *Good News* had done, a little less well than *Hold Everything!* and, in the end, lasted only 148 performances. It proved even more disappointing in Australia where Gus Bluett appeared in the lead comedy role alongside Molly Fisher (Lora), Madge Aubrey, Cecil Kellaway, Robert Purdie and Michael Cole, folding in five weeks at Melbourne's Theatre Royal.

A film version of the show was produced in Hollywood in 1930 in which Haley and Miss O'Neal repeated their original roles alongside Nancy Carroll and Charles ''Buddy'' Rogers.

UK: Dominion Theatre *Follow Through* 3 October 1929; Australia: Theatre Royal, Melbourne *Follow Through* 8 February 1930

Film: Paramount 1930

LES FORAINS Opérette in 3 acts by Maxime Boucheron and Antony Mars. Music by Louis Varney. Théâtre des Bouffes-Parisiens, Paris, 9 February 1894.

A musical play about sideshow folk, *Les Forains* centered on the family of the famous wrestler Toulouse (Bartel) whose daughter and star attraction, the strong-woman Olympia (Juliette Simon-Girard), is wed to the lion-tamer, Jules César (Charles Lamy). Unfortunately, between the civil ceremony and the wedding night, Olympia discovers that Jules César's lions are actually as tame as lambs and she goes right off him. Then the amateur strong-man Paul Vaubert (Félix Huguenet) declares his love, and proves it by defeating Toulouse for the first time ever—the qualification for an ideal man his daughter had given up hope of finding. Olympia runs away with Paul and his friends Gaillac (Leriche) and Valpurgis (Dupré) and they tour Europe for two months as an act—with Olympia, of course, keeping Paul at a correct distance—before they meet up on the road with Toulouse's troupe. Jules César turns on his strong-woman wife and wallops her . . . and she decides to come home. Mariette Sully was Olympia's unstrong sister, Clorinde, in love with Paul throughout (and, of course, getting him in the end), and Rosine Maurel featured as a comical fortuneteller. The play, which gave a number of opportunities for wrestling matches, weight lifting, acrobatics and other feats, was decorated by a slim Varney score, largely for the benefit of the two girls.

Eugène Larcher's production of *Les Forains* played for 73 performances at the Bouffes-Parisiens, and the show was adjudged to share with *L'Enlevèment de la Toledad* the honors of the year's musical stage in Paris. It was featured in that year's Monte Carlo season, played through the provinces and, although it did not ultimately prove particularly enduring, it nevertheless got a good first-time-round coverage throughout Europe. Berlin's Theater Unter den Linden produced a version by Louis Herrmann and Julius Freund later the same year, as *Der Gaukler,* with Frln Kramm as the heroine, and Karl Blasel mounted another version (ad Theodor Taube) at the Vienna Carltheater, with Julie Kopácsi-Karczag starring as Olympia ''the muscle-Venus'' and himself as Toulouse, for 28 performances. The Budapest Népszínház followed three seasons later with an Hungarian version (ad Emil Makai) which was played 10 times.

Germany: Theater Unter den Linden *Die Gaukler* 10 November 1894; Austria: Carltheater *Olympia (die Muskelvenus)* 2 March 1895; Hungary: Népszínház *Komediások* 30 September 1898

FORD, Helen [née BARNETT, Helen Isabel] (b Troy, NY, 6 June 1894; d Glendale, Calif, 19 January 1982).

First seen on Broadway as a replacement in the 1919 production of *Sometime,* pretty, little Mrs Ford followed up in ingenue roles in several Broadway musicals, appearing as Toinette Fontaine in *Always You* (1920, ex-*Joan of Ark-ansaw*), as Natalie Blythe in *The Sweetheart Shop* (1920), and as Marjorie Leeds in *For Goodness' Sake* (1922). She stuck with the slow-growing *A Man of Affairs* as it turned into *Love and Kisses* and, finally, into a success as *The Gingham Girl* (1922, Mary Thompson), took the title role in the less-than-successful *Helen of Troy, New York* (who was not, apart from Mrs Ford's presence, in any way a descendant of *Joan of Ark-ansaw*), and was Hope Franklin in another indifferent piece, *No Other Girl.* Patience was in evidence again when she stuck with another slow-moving project and reaped the reward of a fine run and a hit song (''Here in My Arms'') as Betsy Burke, the heroine of Rodgers and Hart's *Dearest Enemy* (1925), produced by her husband, George Ford. She followed up with two other starring roles in Rodgers and Hart shows: the title roles of *Peggy-Ann* (1926) and of the short-lived *Chee-Chee* (1928).

She returned to Broadway to appear as Adele in the version of *Die Fledermaus* known as *Champagne Sec* in 1933, but an underpowered attempt to launch an English-language version of Guitry's *Mariette,* with Mrs Ford in the lead, in 1937, failed to make it to town. She made one last Broadway musical appearance in the failed *Great Lady* in 1938.

FORD, Nancy (b New York, 1 October 1935).

The composer of several off-Broadway musicals, in a collaboration with author Gretchen Cryer which had begun in University days, Ford had a first success with *The Last Sweet Days of Isaac* and major one with the long-running *I'm Getting My Act Together and Taking It on the Road* (1978). During the run of the show, she succeeded to the show's central role. She also supplied music to the revues *Hang on to the Good Times* (1985) and *Cut the Ribbons* (1992).

Cryer and Ford have also appeared performing their own material and on record.

1967 **Now Is the Time for All Good Men** (aka *Grass Roots*) (Gretchen Cryer) Theater de Lys 26 September

1970 **The Last Sweet Days of Isaac** (Cryer) Eastside Playhouse 26 January

1973 **Shelter** (Cryer) John Golden Theater 6 February

1978 **I'm Getting My Act Together and Taking It on the Road** (Cryer) Public Theater 14 June; Circle in the Square 16 December

1986 **Eleanor** (*Don't Frighten the Horses*) (Cryer) The Extension, Williamstown, Mass 15 August

FOR GOODNESS' SAKE Musical comedy in 2 acts by Frederick Jackson. Music by William Daly and Paul Lannin. Lyric Theater, New York, 20 February 1922.

The production of the musical comedy *For Goodness' Sake* was an occasion where a show made up of very limited material was turned into a singular success by the performance it was given. Frederick Jackson's story turned on one of those overly suspicious wives who, thinking her husband unfaithful, decides on a fling of her own. He fakes suicide in response, and so it continues up to a reconciliatory final curtain, the wanderings of the plot accompanied by some functional songs, including two by the Gershwin brothers. Comedian John E Hazzard (Perry Reynolds) and Marjorie Gateson (Vivian Reynolds) as the husband and wife of the affair had to give best to the young second leads—the dance team of Fred and Adele Astaire (as Teddy Lawrence and Susan Hayden) who, with the aid of some lively Teddy Royce choreography, won the plaudits for 103 performances.

The next year, producer Alex Aarons whisked the show—now more provocatively retitled *Stop Flirting,* but with Perry Renolds (Jack Melford) and Vivian Marsden (Marjorie Gordon) now listed only as ''fiancés'' instead of being married—and his light-footed stars off to London. There, he allied himself with London producers George Grossmith and J A E Malone, and theatre-manager Alfred Butt to put *Stop Flirting* on in the West End. The show's score of eight numbers, two openings and two finales was tactfully lifted by the insertion of an additional ''additional number by George Gershwin,'' ''Stairway to Paradise'' (ex- of *George White's Scandals of 1922*), and Aarons and the Astaires repeated their American success in a broken run of 224 performances in three separate London theatres (Shaftesbury Theatre, Queens Theatre 28 July, Strand Theatre 22 October). A revival, mounted the following year (28 March 1924) added another 194 performances to the show's career and Florence Bayfield and Gerald Seymour then deputized for the Astaires in a touring version of a show which its stars had well and truly established. *Stop Flirting* could still be seen on the English provincial stage in 1926 when *For Goodness' Sake* had long disappeared in America.

UK: Shaftesbury Theatre *Stop Flirting* 30 May 1923

FORREST, George [CHICHESTER, George Forrest jr] (b Brooklyn, NY, 31 July 1915; d Miami, Fla, 10 October 1999).

Forrest began a career-long partnership with fellow musician and lyricist Robert Wright whilst the two were still in their teens. In 1936 they were employed on the music staff at MGM studios, writing and/or adapting music and lyrics for a series of films which included cinema adaptations of *Maytime* (1937), *The Firefly* (1937), *Sweethearts* (1938), *Balalaika* (1939) and *I Married an Angel* (1942). They scored a standard with the song ''The Donkey Serenade,'' created from a Friml instrumental melody for *The Firefly,* and collaborated with Herbert Stothart on ''Ride, Cossack, Ride'' (*Balalaika*) and on several new numbers for *I Married an Angel.* The song ''It's a Blue World,'' as sung by Tony Martin in *Music in My Heart,* won them one of their three Academy Award nominations.

The team's earliest theatre work consisted of similar rewrites and additions for revivals of musical shows of the past, but also included two original pieces produced at the Hollywood Playhouse in the early 1940s. Their first major musical credit came, however, with the production of *Song of Norway,* a *Dreimäderlhaus*-type treatment of the life and works of Norwegian composer Edvard Grieg, mounted by Edwin Lester in California. With a score, including "Freddy and His Fiddle" and "Strange Music," fabricated by Wright and Forrest from a range of Grieg melodies, *Song of Norway* went east to find success on Broadway and subsequently around the world.

An original musical, *Spring in Brazil,* produced the following year with Milton Berle starring, did not catch on, but another Lester production, *Gypsy Lady,* a musical remolding of Victor Herbert's lyrical scores for *The Fortune Teller* and *The Serenade,* was sufficiently well thought of to be taken both to New York and to London (as *Romany Love*).

The partners wrote the lyrics to Villa Lobos's score for *Magdalena,* a show which aroused considerable interest but ultimately failed, and Johann Strauss was given the *Dreimäderlhaus* treatment in *The Great Waltz,* before Wright and Forrest brought out their greatest success: an adaptation of the music of Borodin as an accompaniment to Eddie Knoblock's Oriental comedy classic *Kismet* ("The Olive Tree," "Stranger in Paradise," "And This is My Beloved," "Not Since Nineveh," "Baubles, Bangles and Beads"). Following long runs on Broadway (Tony Award) and in London, *Kismet* established itself as one of the all-time classics of the American operetta stage.

Wright and Forrest's subsequent musicals did not find the same success. They tackled Molière with *The Carefree Heart,* Vicki Baum's famous novel and film *Grand Hotel* in *At the Grand,* and the French play *Kean,* each with original scores, before turning to further musical collages, one based on the works of Rachmaninov, as the musical illustration to a version of the Anastasia story, another on Saint-Saëns as the musical part of the story of *Dumas and Son.* However, *The Great Waltz,* a second attempt at the Strauss story, based on the Viennese success *Walzer aus Wien,* proved altogether more successful than the first and resulted both in a long-running London production and a new 1972 film version.

Another second-time-round production gave the partnership one further satisfaction, at least from a financial point of view. Their *At the Grand* was revised and remounted in 1989, under the title *Grand Hotel,* but alterations and interpolations made by the producers on the road rendered the show a rather different piece by the time it reached New York. In spite of poor notices, it glitzed itself into a good run, nearly half a century after its originators' first success on Broadway.

1940 **Thank You, Columbus** (w Robert Wright) Hollywood Playhouse 15 November

1941 **Fun for the Money** (w Wright) Hollywood Playhouse August

1944 **Song of Norway** (Edvard Grieg ad w Wright/Milton Lazarus) Imperial Theater 21 August

1945 **Spring in Brazil** (w Wright/Philip Rapp) Shubert Theater, Boston 1 October

1946 **Gypsy Lady** (Victor Herbert ad w Wright/Henry Myers) Century Theater 17 September

1948 **Magdalena** (Villa Lobos/w Wright/Frederick Hazlitt Brennan, Homer Curran) Ziegfeld Theater 20 September

1949 **The Great Waltz** (*Walzer aus Wien*) new English adaptation w Wright (Curran Theater, San Francisco)

1953 **Kismet** (Borodin ad w Wright/Charles Lederer, Luther Davis) Ziegfeld Theater 3 December

1957 **The Carefree Heart** (aka *The Love Doctor*) (w Wright) Cass Theater, Detroit 30 September

1958 **At the Grand** (w Wright/Luther Davis) Philharmonic Theater, Los Angeles 7 July

1961 **Kean** (w Wright/Peter Stone) Broadway Theater 2 November

1965 **The Great Waltz** (*Walzer aus Wien*) new adaptation w Wright, Jerome Chodorov, Moss Hart, Lazarus San Francisco 14 September

1965 **Anya** (Rachmaninov ad w Wright/George Abbott, Guy Bolton) Ziegfeld Theater 29 November

1967 **Dumas and Son** (Camille Saint-Saens ad w Wright/ Chodorov) Dorothy Chandler Pavilion, Los Angeles 1 August

1972 **A Song for Cyrano** (w Wright/Jose Ferrer) Pocono Playhouse, Pa 4 September

1978 **Timbuktu!** revised *Kismet* ad Luther Davis Mark Hellinger Theater 1 March

1989 **Grand Hotel** revised *At the Grand* (w Maury Yeston/ Davis) Martin Beck Theater 12 November

DIE FÖRSTER-CHRISTL Operette in 3 acts by Bernhard Buchbinder. Music by Georg Jarno. Theater in der Josefstadt, Vienna, 17 December 1907.

Jarno's most popular Operette was set to a libretto which was one of those allegedly based on a true event, but it was no less thoroughly and conventionally operettic for all that.

Christl (Hansi Niese), a forester's daughter, travels from her home in the Hungarian borderlands to Vienna to beg the Kaiser, Josef II (Robert Valberg), to intercede on behalf of her lover, Franz Földessy (Kurt von Lessen), the steward to the Sternfeld estates, who has been exposed as an army deserter who killed his vicious lieutenant. When feelings of love spring up between the Kaiser and the country girl, he pushes them dutifully aside and Christl goes home to her soldier. The other principal characters were the Graf Sternfeld (Louis Ralph/

Alexander Beer) and his sister, the Komtesse Josefine (Betty Myra/Isa Károly), Christl's comical suitor, Imperial tailor Peter Walperl (Max Pallenberg/Franz Stenger), the gypsy girl Minka (Käthe Krem/Hansi Reichsberg), and the courtly grande dame Baronesse Agathe von Othegraven (Viktoria Pohl-Meiser).

The show was produced in Vienna with Niese, the wife of the composer's brother Josef (himself the manager of the Theater in der Josefstadt), and the city's most popular soubrette, starring and it was an enormous success. Christl's entrance number, "Die Christl aus dem Wiener-Wald," her detailing of how she will approach the Emperor ("Herr Kaiser, Herr Kaiser"), the waltz song "Gebt mir die Geigen der ganzen Welt," the lusty Hungarian-flavored ensemble "Steht ein Mädel auf der Puszta" and Josefine and Minka's duo Zieguner-Marsch ("Heissa, Heissa, ihr Mädel seid bereit") were the musical highlights of an evening which, just occasionally, recalled the very special folksy simplicity of *Der Vogelhändler,* here given a dash of Hungarian spice. The role of the Kaiser was a non-singing one.

In spite of being produced in the same year as *Ein Walzertraum* and *Die Dollarprinzessin, Die Förster-Christl* ran for an excellent 62 nights at the Josefstadter Theater before being transferred to Jarno's Lustspiel Theater to carry on its run. It passed its 100th performance there in May 1908. Continually played in and out of Vienna thereafter, the show was taken in to the repertoire at the Johann Strauss-Theater on 22 December 1912 with Otto Storm and Mimi Marlow in the star roles, and given further performances there with Eugene Jensen and Lisl Kurt during the run of *Der Zigeunerprimás* (1912–13), in 1914 with Fritz Schönhof and Else Adler, and again with Frln Marlow. It remained steadily in the theatre's repertoire until 1925, passing its 700th performance on 2 February 1924 with Raoul Aslan and Maria Escher featured. It was revived again in Vienna in 1945.

Die Förster-Christl became one of the most popular Viennese shows of its particularly fertile decade. Its Viennese triumph was repeated in Germany, where a run at the Berliner Theater was prelude to a vast number of provincial productions (the show rates eighth on Keller's German list of silver-age musicals, edging out *Die Csárdásfürstin, Die Rose von Stambul* and *Polenblut*) and a revival at the Centraltheater in 1923 (2 April), and in Hungary. *Az Erdészleány* (ad Adolf Mérei, Ferenc Révész, Bertalan Országh), produced in Budapest in June 1909, passed its 100th night on 16 April 1910, was seen throughout the country and returned to town in 1927 (Városi Színház 16 April 1927) with Irén Zilahy and Jenő Törzs featured, and again in 1936 at the Király Színház (2 January).

Although the show's life was largely confined to central Europe, it did cross the Atlantic, winning Broadway productions both in German, with Lucie Engelke and Thomas Burgarth featured, at the Irving Place Theater, and, soon after, in English (ad Leonard Liebling). Lulu Glaser starred as "the girl" and Julius McVicker as "the Kaiser" in *The Girl and the Kaiser,* but both had to give star billing over to Harry Conor as the comical Peter Wenzel in the Shubert brothers' production. Thomas Richards was Franz, the Baroness von Graven was played by Flavia Arcaro and Victor and Blanche Hyde contributed a "Whirlwind Hungarian Dance" to a version which seems, otherwise, to have been remarkably (for a Shubert production) close to the original. The show played for eight weeks on Broadway, and toured usefully.

Several film versions of *Die Förster-Christl* have been made, the first a silent one, and the two most recent both by Carlton films. The first sound version featured Hannerl Matz (Christl) and Karl Schönböck (Kaiser) in a recognizable version of the tale with the music adapted by Robert Gilbert and Bruno Uher; another starred Irene Eisinger as Christl alongside Paul Richter, Oscar Karlweis and Adele Sandrock. The most recent film version starred Sabine Sinjen and Peter Weck, was musically adapted by Franz Grothe, and included interpolations by Robert Gilbert and Ronald Binge.

Germany: Berliner Theater 28 February 1908; Hungary: Városligeti Színkör *Az Erdészleány* 20 June 1909, *Die Förster-Christl* (Ger) June 1912; USA: Irving Place Theatre (Ger) 13 January 1910, Herald Square Theater *The Girl and the Kaiser* 22 November 1910

Films: 1926 (silent), Friedrich Zelnick 1931, Artur Maria Rabenalt 1952, Fraz-Josef Gottlieb 1962

Recording: selection (part-record) (Eurodisc)

FOR THE LOVE OF MIKE Play with tunes in 3 acts, adapted from the play of the same title by H F Maltby, by Clifford Grey. Lyrics by Clifford Grey and Sonny Miller. Additional lyrics by Valentine. Music by Jack Waller and Joseph Tunbridge. Saville Theatre, London, 8 October 1931.

The first of the successful series of musical comedies—by and large, more comedy than musical—produced by Jack Waller at the Saville Theatre with Bobby Howes as their comical star, *For the Love of Mike* had been originally written by playwright H F Maltby as a vehicle for Tom Walls. Turned down by him, it was picked up by Waller, decorated with a handful of songs, and turned out to be a 239-performance West End hit with a long subsequent touring life.

Love-struck little Bob (Bobby Howes) sets out to rob the safe at the home of nasty Mr Miller (Alfred Drayton) to retrieve the power of attorney which Miller has tricked his ward, "Mike" (Peggy Cartwright), into signing. He is caught in the act by Paton (Arthur Riscoe), Miller's private detective, who turns out to be an old school chum, and the two fake a robbery to cover the incident. Syd Walker featured as the havoc-wreaking PC Wildgoose, Wylie Watson was the local clergyman, and the lanky, aristocratic Viola Tree warbled her way through a discouragement to ''Walk with Me'' as Mrs Miller. The song hit of the evening, however, fell to Howes and Miss Cartwright as they duetted through one of Waller and Tunbridge's most enduring little songs, ''Got a Date With an Angel.''

For the Love of Mike was an unusual piece for its time, putting the accent firmly on the comedy part of the entertainment rather than on the currently top-rated dancing element, or on spectacle, or even on a full-sized score. Its success proved that there was a distinct audience for musical comedy worthy of the name, and Waller followed the thus proven recipe for a number of years. But this first show proved the most enduring of the group, and was still to be seen on the British touring circuits 20 years after its premiere.

In 1932 a film version was made with Howes, Riscoe, Watson and Miss Tree repeating their original roles alongside Constance Shotter (Mike) and Jimmy Godden (Miller).

Film: BIP 1932

THE FORTUNE TELLER Comic opera in 3 acts by Harry B Smith. Music by Victor Herbert. Wallack's Theater, New York, 26 September 1898.

When the ambitious young soprano of the famed Bostonians company, Alice Nielsen, decided to break away from the group and start up a comic opera company in opposition, she and her producer Frank Perley launched their project with a piece commissioned from Bostonians' chief suppliers, Harry B Smith and Victor Herbert.

The Fortune Teller of the show's title was the gypsy maiden Musette (Miss Nielsen), whose amazing resemblance to the wealthy and social but long-lost Irma (also Miss Nielsen) provided what plot there was to the piece, and also enabled the canny manageress to play the two largest roles in the show. Irma, with a little help from Musette, manages to avoid wedding the unprepossessing Polish pianist Count Berezowski (Joseph W Herbert) in favor of the handsome baritone hussar Ladislas (Frank Rushworth), whilst Musette, once everything is satisfactorily explained, pairs off with her jealous gypsy Sándor (Eugene Cowles). Joseph Cawthorn joined Herbert at the head of the comedy in the role of Musette's father; Richard Golden played the ballet-master of the company where Irma, before becoming un-long-lost, is a dancing girl; whilst Marguerite Sylva, as the actress Pompon, picked up the crumbs of the feminine music and also the heroine's hussar brother, Fedor (whom Irma, for a while, impersonates to ensure her safety from the Pole).

Four of the evening's eight solo songs (in a 16-piece score) fell to the prima donna. She began with the schoolgirlish ''Always Do As People Say You Should'' (Irma), switched to csárdás-rhythm for the more tempestuous praises of ''Romany Life'' (Musette), waxed Irish, Spanish, Chinese, French and finally indulged in a coon song in the sequence ''Serenades of All Nations'' whilst still in the character of the gypsy girl, then shifted back to more conventional waltz-time to finish off her multicolored evening. Ladislas sang in praise of ''Hungaria's Hussars'' and joined Pompon in the waltz duo ''Only in the Play,'' but it was Cowles who scored the biggest hit of the evening—and of his career—with his basso rendition of the ''Gypsy Love Song'' (''Slumber on, my little gypsy sweetheart'').

Built to travel, *The Fortune Teller* did not compile a long Broadway run. Following its Toronto baptism (14 September) and a week in Buffalo, it played just five weeks in New York before Miss Nielsen moved on to her next date, but there was no doubt as to its success, and its manageress-star kept the show on the road in repertoire even when she had a newer piece to play. In 1901, when she joined the rush of American companies to Britain in the wake of the success of *The Belle of New York,* it was *The Fortune Teller* which Nielsen chose to present, with Cowles (who now had an extra song, ''I Sing in Praise of the Sword''), Cawthorn, Herbert and Rushworth all in their original roles and Viola Gillette as Pompon. If notices for the piece were mixed, Miss Nielsen and, in particular, Cowles were much liked and the show stayed at London's Shaftesbury Theatre for 88 performances.

In 1903 *The Fortune Teller* was seen in Australia when George Musgrove, formerly of the Shaftesbury Theatre, mounted it with Madame Slapoffski (née Lillian Williams) in the title role alongside W R Shirley (Berezowski), Lemprière Pringle (Sándor) and May Beatty (Pompon) at the Sydney Theatre Royal, the Princess, Melbourne (28 February 1903) and the Theatre Royal, Adelaide (2 May 1903).

The Fortune Teller returned briefly to Broadway when it was remounted by the Shuberts in their series of revivals of classic pieces at the Jolson Theater in 1929 (4 November). Much later, a heavily adapted version, with bits of the score combined with some music from Herbert's earlier *The Serenade,* was produced on the West Coast as *Gypsy Lady* and subsequently seen, without success, in New York (Century Theater 17 September 1946) and, under the title *Romany Love* (His Majesty's Theatre 7 March 1947), in London.

Bits of the score (though not the lyrics) also turned up in a 1934 Warner Brothers film based on the show in which Anita Campillo played the heroine's double role.

UK: Shaftesbury Theatre 9 April 1901; Australia: Theatre Royal, Sydney 17 January 1903 Film: Warner Brothers 1934

FORTY-FIVE MINUTES FROM BROADWAY Musical play in 3 acts by George M Cohan. Great Southern Theater, Columbus, Ohio, 25 September 1905, New Amsterdam Theater, New York, 1 January 1906.

After thoroughly establishing the vigorously here-and-now musical comedy style which would be his for more than two decades with his written-composed-directed-and-starred-in *Little Johnny Jones* (1904), George M Cohan followed up with a second nationwide hit in *Forty-Five Minutes from Broadway.* As in the earlier piece, he was author, composer and director, but he—still touring with *Little Johnny Jones*—left the leading male role this time to Victor Moore, and the star billing to Fay Templeton.

The title of the show (a switch from the originally announced *The Maid and the Millionaire*) referred to its location—the events of the tale took place in the country-bumpkin town of New Rochelle, situated just 45 minutes away from the heart of Manhattan, where the late Mr Castleton had lived. Though defunct, Mr Castleton is still important in the story for, like so many plays, musical and straight, of the previous half-century, *Forty-Five Minutes from Broadway* had a plot which centered on a will. Since Mr Castleton's will cannot be found, his money goes to his nephew, Tom Bennett (Donald Brian), who is quickly pursued by the money-grubbing Mrs David Dean (Julia Ralph) and her unmarried daughter, the "footlight favorite" Flora Dora Dean (Lois Ewell). However, when the will does turn up it eventuates that the beneficiary is not Tom but the old man's devoted servant girl, Mary Jane Jenkins (Miss Templeton). But such riches deter the girl's sweetheart, Tom's secretary Kid Burns (Moore), and Mary prefers to tear up the will and leave the money to Tom rather than lose her chap.

The handful of musical numbers which were inserted into the tale included the cheery title song, Tom's "I Want To Be a Popular Millionaire," Mary's "So Long, Mary," a male-voice chorus of four "Gentlemen of the Press" and three reporters, and the piece which would be one of its writer's most enduring, "Mary's a Grand Old Name." Initially, these were supplemented by "Retiring from the Stage" and "Stand Up and Fight Like Hell" (sung by Charles Prince as James Blake and voted "out of place and very vulgar"), but these both swiftly disappeared, leaving the settled five-song quota of the evening to be complemented by as much music again written by musical director Fred Solomon, whose orchestra supplied "Reminiscences of the South," the descriptive fantasia "Going to School" and a Spanish Dance in between the acts.

Klaw and Erlanger's production was first mounted in Columbus, moved on to Chicago and it took in a Broadway season of 90 performances before continuing on its way round the lucrative touring circuits with Miss Templeton and Moore holding on to their parts through into 1907. In 1912 Cohan and his partner Sam Harris revived the show and, with Cohan now playing Moore's role, it dropped into New York for 36 further performances at the Cohan Theater (14 March). In the early 1920s Charles Ray starred in a First National film version which advertised that "It has knocked the 'o's out of gloom" and in 1959 *Forty-Five Minutes from Broadway* was given a potted showing on NBC-TV (15 March). Tammy Grimes starred as Mary alongside Russell Nype and Larry Blyden.

Film: First National 1921

Recording: TV cast (AEI)

42ND STREET Musical in 2 acts by Michael Stewart and Mark Bramble based on the screenplay of the same name and the novel by Bradford Ropes. Lyrics by Al Dubin. Music by Harry Warren. Winter Garden Theater, New York, 25 August 1980.

A stage musical version of the 1933 musical film which became the great classic of its genre: the tale of the insignificant chorus girl who deputizes for an ailing star and wins herself stardom. Impossibly innocent Ruby Keeler and pumpkin-pie Dick Powell incarnated the singing and dancing youngsters who tap-danced and sang their way to stardom and sweetheartdom, Bebe Daniels was the displaced star, whilst Warner Baxter ground out the immortal line about going out there a youngster but coming back a star, in the role of the director of the show-within-a-film.

Peggy Sawyer (Wanda Richert) from Allentown, NJ, gets a last-minute job as a chorus girl in the Broadway show *Pretty Lady* and catches the eye of juvenile lead Billy Lawler (Lee Roy Reams). Producer Julian Marsh (Jerry Orbach) has financed his show by casting the professional but no-longer-juvenile Dorothy Brock (Tammy Grimes) in the ingenue role and thus winning backing from her sugar daddy, Abner Dillon (Don Crabtree), but Dorothy insists on meeting up with her old boyfriend, Pat Denning (James Congdon), and Julian has to get some friendly gangsters to keep Pat out of the way, to protect his investment and his show. *Pretty Lady* makes it safely to its tryout opening, but during the first performance Dorothy falls and breaks her ankle. The chorus persuade Marsh to give Peggy the chance to take over, and she triumphs, whilst Dorothy, discovering she prefers love to stardom, weds her Pat. Carole Cook and Joe Bova played Maggie and Bert, the comical authors of *Pretty Lady,* whilst Karen Prunczik headed the remaining chorines as soubrette Anytime Annie.

The score of the show included several numbers taken from the film of *42nd Street* (''42nd Street,'' ''Young and Healthy,'' ''You're Getting to Be a Habit with Me,'' ''Shuffle Off to Buffalo'') but also a selection of songs from other Al Dubin and/or Harry Warren films, notably the *Gold Diggers* series (''Lullaby of Broadway,'' ''We're in the Money''), *Dames* (''Dames''), *Go into Your Dance* (''About a Quarter to Nine'') and *The Singing Marine* (''I Know Now''). The title song was used as the basis for an opening ensemble tap routine on which the curtain rose very gradually to display the mass of frenetically auditioning feet, and later for a dramatic dance scena, whilst ''Dames'' served for a costume parade, and ''We're in the Money'' for another large-scale tap number with Billy featured as soloist.

David Merrick's production of *42nd Street* had a dramatic opening night when the death of director/choreographer Gower Champion was announced at the final curtain, and it went on from there to win the season's Tony Award as best musical and to run for 3,486 performances in some eight and a half years, following a shift to the Majestic Theater (30 March 1981). Merrick also sponsored a London edition, produced at the Theatre Royal, Drury Lane, with James Laurenson (Marsh), Clare Leach (Peggy), Michael Howe (Billy) and Georgia Brown (Dorothy) featured in its original cast, which also achieved a highly successful run of four and a half years (1,823 performances) followed by a tour and return season at the large Dominion Theatre (27 February 1991).

The show toured both in America and in Britain, and was given a successful Australian production under the management of Helen Montagu, with Barry Quin (Marsh), Leonie Page (Peggy), Nancye Hayes (Dorothy) and Toni Lamond (Maggie) in the leading roles. This production was announced for a tour to East Berlin, but the plan was abandoned when East Germany ceased to be, prior to the trip. Germany, however, did get *42nd Street* when an American touring company with Michael Dantuono (Marsh) and Elizabeth Allen (Dorothy) top-billed and Miss Prunczik in her original role played an extremely out-front English-language version there, in Austria and France. The Australian version contented itself with a second round of Australia.

At the time of writing, a restaging of the show was announced for a fresh whirl through Broadway (Ford Center 30 April 2001).

UK: Theatre Royal, Drury Lane 8 August 1984; Australia: Her Majesty's Theatre, Sydney 2 June 1989; Austria: Theater an der Wien (Eng) 27 June 1990; France: Théâtre du Châtelet (Eng) 6 November 1990; Germany: Deutsches Theater, Munich (Eng) 3 May 1991

Recordings: original cast (RCA), Australian cast (RCA)

FOSSE, Bob [FOSSE, Robert Louis] (b Chicago, 23 June 1927; d Washington, DC, 23 September 1987). Choreographer-director of several major Broadway hits of the 1960s and 1970s.

Fosse began his performing life as a young teenager in vaudeville and burlesque before dancing in touring revues (*Call Me Mister, Make Mine Manhattan*) and on Broadway in *Dance Me a Song* (1950). He subsequently appeared in several films, notably in the screen version of *Kiss Me, Kate* (1953, Hortensio, co-choreographer) and as Frank in the musical film of *My Sister Eileen* (1955).

His first Broadway choreographic credit was on *The Pajama Game* (1954) in which his routines to ''Steam Heat'' and ''Hernando's Hideaway'' won him a Tony Award and established him presto at the forefront of his profession. In *The Pajama Game*'s follow-up, *Damn Yankees* (1955), he staged ''Who's Got the Pain?'' and ''Whatever Lola Wants'' and won a second consecutive Tony Award, and he subsequently shared the choreographic work of *Bells Are Ringing* with Jerome Robbins before making his debut as a director in the musicalized *Anna Christie, New Girl in Town,* featuring, as had *Damn Yankees,* a dancing leading lady in Gwen Verdon. He was again director and choreographer to Miss Verdon in the music-hall murder musical *Redhead,* which won him a third Tony citation for its dances.

Fosse made a return to the stage to appear as Joey in two productions of *Pal Joey* at the City Center, but thereafter stayed strictly beyond the footlights, staging a virtually unbroken run of successful and often outstanding shows for the Broadway stage. He choreographed *How to Succeed in Business without Really Trying* (Broadway and London), co-directed and choreographed the swingingly funny burlesque *Little Me* (1962, Tony Award choreography, ''Rich Kids' Rag''), the conceived-and-made-for-Verdon *Sweet Charity* (''Big Spender,'' ''The Rhythm of Life,'' Tony Award choreography) and the whimsical 1960s-flavored *Pippin* (''Magic to Do'') which at last won him a first Tony Award as a director as well as his sixth as a choreographer (Broadway and London). In 1975 he directed, choreographed and co-wrote the adaptation of Maurine Dallas Watkins's *Chicago* as a ''vaudeville musical'' in which Miss Verdon and Chita Rivera showed off his infallibly stylish dance numbers through a long and successful run.

The break in all this success came with the production of Frank Loesser's 1965 *Pleasures and Palaces* which failed to make it to Broadway, but he had a final Broadway success when he put together the dance revue

Plate 127. **Bob Fosse** *in rehearsal.*

Dancin' (1978). The 1986 pasticcio show, *Big Deal,* for which he took writer's, director's and choreographer's credits was a 70-performance failure, but nevertheless brought him yet another Tony Award for choreography.

Amongst an array of television and cinema credits Fosse repeated his *Pajama Game* and *Damn Yankees* (also mambo dancer) assignments in the filmed versions of the stage shows, and he both directed and choreographed the film version of *Sweet Charity* with Shirley MacLaine in the title role and that of *Cabaret* (Academy Award) with Liza Minnelli and Joel Grey. In 1979 he also turned out a rather masochistic autobiographical movie called *All That Jazz* which won what comment it evoked over a scene showing open-heart surgery. Fosse himself was played by Roy Scheider.

In 1999 (14 January) a compilation show of his work entitled *Fosse: A Celebration in Song and Dance,* with the names of Richard Maltby jr, Ann Reinking and Chet Walker attached to it and overseen by Fosse's third wife, his oft-times collaborator, Gwen Verdon, was produced at the Broadhurst Theater and in a season which, once again, could not produce a new book musical worthy of honors, it was awarded a Tony as ''best musical.''

1975 **Chicago** (John Kander/Fred Ebb/w Ebb) 46th Street Theater 3 June

1986 **Big Deal** (pasticcio) Broadway Theater 10 April

Biographies: Boyd Grubb, K: *Razzle Dazzle: The Life and Work of Bob Fosse* (St Martin's Press, New York, 1989), Gottfried, M: *All His Jazz* (Bantam, New York, 1990), Beddow, M: *Bob Fosse's Broadway* (Heinemann, New York, 1996)

THE FOUR MUSKETEERS Comedy musical in 2 acts by Michael Pertwee. Lyrics by Herbert Kretzmer. Music by Laurie Johnson. Theatre Royal, Drury Lane, London, 5 December 1967.

An attempt to follow up popular vocalist and comedian Harry Secombe's success as *Pickwick* cast him, with less adroitness, as a burlesque version of Dumas's musketeer D'Artagnan. Producer Bernard Delfont, director Peter Coe, and designer Sean Kenny repeated their assignments of the earlier show in a travesty tale which had Secombe as a bumbling bumpkin of a hero, achieving his heroics all unawares, and his fellow musketeers (Jeremy Lloyd, Glyn Owen, John Junkin) as a bunch of louts. They duly went off in search of missing diamonds of the Queen of France (Sheena Marshe), but not to Britain, and duly brought them back. Comedian Kenneth Connor was the King, Elizabeth Larner took over the role of Milady at the last minute, and Stephanie Voss was the beloved Constance Bonacieux.

With no "If I Ruled the World" coming from its score, the show tottered suicidally through no fewer than 462 performances on its vast, rumbling sets before folding severely in the red. But the statistics just show that it ran 462 performances.

Recording: original cast (Philips)

FOX, Della [May] (b St Louis, Mo, 13 October 1871; d New York, 16 June 1913).

Tiny soubrette who became a star as the partner of De Wolf Hopper, and helped set the fashion for bobbed hair in the 1890s.

Daughter of a St Louis photographer, Miss Fox worked first as a juvenile actress, appearing as the midshipmite in *HMS Pinafore* at seven and later in local productions of such pieces as *Chispa, A Celebrated Case* and *Editha's Burglar* and in farce comedy (Jem in *Combustion,* 1885, etc). In her teens, she took employment as a very young leading lady at St Louis' Park Garden summer season (1886), led another local summer season of musical theatre at Uhrig's Cave, and took to the road as leading lassie with the touring Bennett and Moulton comic opera company (*The Bohemian Girl, Fra Diavolo,* etc). She made her big breakthrough when she joined Hans Conried's troupe and appeared on Broadway as the soubrette, Yvonne, in Adolf Müller's *The King's Fool* (*Der Hofnarr,* 1890). The petite performer was then hired to partner the extremely tall De Wolf Hopper in his Comic Opera Company's production of Kerker's *Castles in the Air* (1890, Blanche) and she shot to stardom when she featured, again alongside Hopper, in the travesty role of another American comic opera, *Wang* (1891, Prince Mataya). She teamed with the comedian yet again, with less happy results, in a revival of *The Lady and the Tiger* (1892, Hilaria) and *Panjandrum* (1893, Paquita), but moved on before his next big hit, *El Capitan,* to take top billing herself in the title role of *The Little Trooper* (*Les 28 Jours de Clairette,* 1894, Clairette Duval), with Jefferson de Angelis in William Furst's *Fleur de lis* (ex- *Pervenche,* 1895, Fleur de Lis), and in 1897 in the lead role of the Julian Edwards/Audran *The Wedding Day* (semi-*La Petite Fronde,* Rose-Marie) alongside de Angelis and Lillian Russell.

Her next role was in a rather different style of piece: a low-brow musical comedy called *The Little Host* (1898, Margery Dazzle) which proved both less suitable and less successful, but Miss Fox then retired to marriage, peritonitis and a nervous breakdown ("she has been taken to Wave Crest Sanatorium, Astoria. Physicians certified that her mind has been wrecked by drugs"). She emerged again a few years later with the money of her husband, jeweler "Diamond John" Levy, backing her and the Shuberts to star in a dual role as a brother and sister in an Americanized version of the highly successful French musical *Toto* produced at the Princess's Theater as *The West Point Cadet* (1904). A weak adaptation, it folded quickly, taking Miss Fox's career and her husband's business with it. Thereafter she largely limited her performances to the vaudeville stage, where she was boasted (like several other folk) as being the variety theatre's highest-paid performer, until her early death "of indigestion" at the age of 41.

FOY, Eddie [FITZGERALD, Edwin] (b New York, 9 March 1854; d Kansas City, 16 February 1928). Star little-fellow comedian of the Broadway musical stage and of vaudeville.

Foy had a career of nearly 20 years in the less upmarket backwaters of the variety and minstrel circuits, in stock theatres and touring farce comedies, changing his style of employment from juveniles and heavies to comedy (Barry & Fay's Co, "English—a detective of course" in Kelly & Mason's *The Tigers* 1885, with Carrie Swain in *Jack-in-the-Box* 1886, William Smith in Kate Castleton's *Crazy Patch* 1886–87, Julius Snitz in Sophie Worrell's *Over the Garden Wall* 1886–87, etc) before making his first substantial appearances in the musical theatre. In his mid-thirties he was "discovered" by producer David Henderson, while working in a West Side music hall, and cast in the comic leads of the Chicago extravaganzas *The Crystal Slipper* (1888, Yossemite), *Bluebeard Jr* (1889, O'Mahdi Benzini), *Sinbad* (1891, Fresco, and later the Cannibal King as well) and *Ali Baba* (1892, Cassim). This series of highly successful money-no-object spectaculars made Foy into a top comedy name. In 1894 he left Henderson to go out on his own as a self-producing star. He made a long-running success out of his American Travesty Company's spectacular extravaganza *Off the Earth* (1894–97, Chester) and, supported by Marie Cahill and Marie Dressler, took the fairy-tale line with *Little Robinson Crusoe* (1895, Daredevil Willie) but he ultimately ended up renouncing the perils of producership and going to work for Klaw and Erlanger in revue.

Foy was first introduced to Broadway musical-comedy audiences at the Herald Square Theater in 1898 when he appeared alongside Miss Dressler as Lebeau in Charles Frohman's production of Victor Roger's *Hotel Topsy-Turvy* (*L'Auberge du Tohu-bohu*). He followed up in the burlesque extravaganza *The Arabian Girl and the Forty Thieves* (1899, Cassim d'Artagnan) and, more significantly, in the featured comedy role of Kamfer in the Knickerbocker Theater production of another made-over show, *The Strollers* (*Die Landstreicher,* 1901). He compounded his popularity at the Knickerbocker in *The Wild Rose* (1902, Paracelsus Noodle) and the Drury Lane spectacular *Mr Bluebeard* (1903, Sister Ann), starred at the Casino Theater in *Piff! Paff! Pouf!* (1904, Peter Pouffle), and spent several years in New York and on the road in the Shuberts' productions of two highly successful British musical comedies— *The Earl and the Girl* and *The Orchid.* In *The Earl and the Girl* he played the part of Jim Cheese (created by Savoy comic Walter Passmore), the little dog-trainer who imitates an earl through an evening of swapped identities, while in *The Orchid* he played a remake of Teddy Payne's classic little-chappie role of Meakin, here rechristened Artie Choke, chasing the flower of the title around a series of lively situations and songs.

He alternated theatre and variety engagements in the following half-dozen years, appearing at Brighton Beach's Music Hall as a burlesque Hamlet (''in red tights and a brown tunic'') to such good effect that he had a musical comedy written around the act and took it back to Broadway, starring as Joey Wheeze in *Mr Hamlet of Broadway* (1908). He appeared in New York again in the revue *Up and Down Broadway* (1910, Momus) and in the revusical spectacular *Over the River* (1912, Madison Parke), but then abandoned the musical theatre to go touring with his children in the act ''Eddie Foy and the Seven Little Foys,'' and to appear on the motion picture stage (*A Favorite Fool,* etc).

The ''Eddie Foy Kiddies'' appeared in the 1909 season in the touring musical *The Girl Question.*

One of the ''Seven Little Foys'' was **Eddie FOY jr** [Edwin FITZGERALD] (b New Rochelle, 4 February 1905; d Woodland Hills, Calif, 15 July 1983) who moved from variety to the musical stage in his mid-twenties. He appeared on Broadway in *Show Girl, Ripples, Smiles, At Home Abroad, All the King's Horses* and *Orchids Preferred,* and in London in the very brief *Royal Exchange* (1935), but his most notable creation as a juvenile was the salesman-turned-dancer, Alexander Sheridan, in *The Cat and the Fiddle* (1931). Towards the end of the Second World War, and after some 10 years in which his musical appearances had all been away from New York (Bunny in *Hit the Deck,* the Jule Styne road-folder *Glad to See You,* etc) he returned to Broadway to pair with Michael O'Shea in the Montgomery and Stone comedy roles of *The Red Mill* (1945). He toured as Harrison Floy in *High Button Shoes* (1948), and in 1954, after another lengthy absence from Broadway, returned to create the part of the time-and-motion-study expert, Hines, in *The Pajama Game* (''I'll Never Be Jealous Again''), a role he repeated in the subsequent film version (1957). Later stage roles in *Rumple* (1957, Rumple) and *Donnybrook!* (1961, Mikeen Flynn) did not find the same level, and he was dropped from the flop *Royal Flush* in rehearsals before it became, without him, an even more thorough flop.

He appeared in the film versions of *Yokel Boy* (1942, Joe Ruddy) and *Bells Are Ringing* (1960, J Otto Prantz), alongside Texas Guinan in the 1929 *Queen of the Nightclubs,* impersonated his father in the films *Lillian Russell* (1940), *Yankee Doodle Dandy* (1942), *Wilson* (1944) and *Bowery to Broadway* (1944) and narrated the tale of *The Seven Little Foys* (1955) in which Bob Hope played the role of Eddie Foy sr.

Autobiography: (w Harlow, A F) *Clowning through Life* (E P Dutton & Co, New York, 1928)

FRA DIAVOLO, or L'Hôtellerie de Terracine Opéra-comique in 3 acts by Eugène Scribe. Music by Daniel Auber. Opéra-Comique, Paris, 28 January 1830.

One of the most successful works of the opéra-comique tradition of the mid-19th-century French theatre, Scribe and Auber's *Fra Diavolo,* though by no means the first work to introduce the comic-opera bandit to the stage, was largely influential in popularizing him through a vast number of works throughout the world.

Scribe's libretto followed the vicious bandit chief, Fra Diavolo, as, disguised as a Marquis, he tracks the runaway-married English couple, Lord and Lady Cokbourg, to the inn at Terracina, intending to rob them of their jewels and money. He is thwarted by the efforts of the young brigadier of carabiniers, Lorenzo, who desperately decimates the bandit band on the day his sweetheart, Zerline, is to be wed to another, and by the clumsiness of his newest recruit. If the story had its dramatic moments, it also had many comical ones, with the English pair played for comedy, and the midnight comings and goings of the brigands in the hotel's bedrooms bordering on pure farce.

The first English-language performance (ad Charles Shannon, mus ad A Lee), at Drury Lane in 1831, featured Eliza Vestris in the title role.

Hugely popular throughout the world, *Fra Diavolo* indubitably inspired the burlesque of *Les Brigands,* as well as Burnand's comical bandits in *The Contrabandista* and W S Gilbert's teams of thieves in *Princess Toto, The Pirates of Penzance* and *The Mountebanks,* but it also prompted some more direct burlesques including Henry J Byron's early work *Fra Diavolo, or Beauty and the Brigands* (Strand Theatre 5 April 1858), which featured

Louisa Swanborough as its hero and Charles Young as Beppo, and the same author's Gaiety Theatre *Young Fra Diavolo* (17 November 1878) in Britain, and Meisl and Drechsler's *Fra Diavolo, das Gasthaus auf der Strasse* produced at Vienna's Theater in der Leopoldstadt (24 November 1830) just weeks after that city's first glimpse of Auber's work.

A silent three-reeler starring Billy Quirk introduced *Fra Diavolo* to the screen in 1912; several attempts to film the opera with accompanying music were made; and, as late as 1933, Hollywood turned out a piece entitled *Fra Diavolo* (*The Devil's Brother*), featuring the knockabout team Laurel and Hardy in a tale now only distantly related to Scribe's.

Germany: 16 July 1830; Austria: Graz 9 April 1830, Hofoperntheater 18 September 1830; Hungary: 23 October 1830; UK: Theater Royal, Drury Lane *The Devil's Brother* 1 February 1831; USA: (Fr) 17 October 1831, Park Theater (Eng) 20 June 1833; Australia: Royal Victoria Theatre, Hobart 3 October 1842

Films: Solax (silent) 1912, Bosia 1924, Mario Bonnard 1930, etc

Recordings: complete in French (EMI), complete in German (Urania), etc

FRAGONARD Opérette in 3 acts by André Rivoire and Romain Coolus. Music by Gabriel Pierné. Théâtre de la Monnaie, Brussels, 1933.

A rare venture by the composer Pierné into the light musical theatre, *Fragonard* was greeted by the connoisseurs of the classy and refined variety of musical theatre with delight, but its production at the Paris Théâtre de la Porte-Saint-Martin under Maurice Lehmann failed to provoke more than indifference from the general public, and the show closed in 57 performances.

Marie-Anne Fragonard (Louisette Rousseau) is a patient ninny who puts up with her husband's infidelities on the excuse that he is an artist. She is a little jealous only of his model, the dancer La Guimard (Jane Marnac). In an attempt to distract him from this woman, she brings her young sister Marguerite (Simone Lencret) to town, but the distraction succeeds only too well and Fragonard (André Baugé) finds himself caught up amongst the three women until Marguerite finds a more suitable lover. Edmond Castel had the principal comic role as Soubise.

Lehmann subsequently produced *Fragonard* at the Opéra-Comique (21 February 1946) with Jacques Jansen as Fragonard, Fanély Revoil as La Guimard, Lucienne Jourfier as Marguerite and Duvaleix as Soubise for 18 performances, and the piece was also later seen in the composer's native Metz.

La Guimard got an Operette all to herself in 1929 when the Aussig Stadttheater produced *Madeleine Guimard* (11 April, Carl Prohaska/Lily Braun).

France: Théâtre de la Porte-Saint-Martin 17 October 1934

FRANCK, Alphonse (b Strasbourg, 11 October 1863; d Paris, 11 February 1932). Parisian producer whose fine career included France's blockbusting *Veuve joyeuse.*

Originally a journalist, secretary at the Théâtre du Vaudeville and the Théâtre du Gymnase, and an occasional author of revues in collaboration with no less a writer than Gaston de Caillavet, Franck moved into management when he became the director, first, of Paris's little Théâtre des Capucines and then of the Théâtre du Gymnase. An excellent manager, he confirmed the latter house's reputation for top-class performances of drama, comedy and vaudeville and was sufficiently successful there to branch out further by taking on the management of the Théâtre Apollo. There he changed genre, and with the most amazing results.

On 28 April 1909 he produced at his new theatre a version, written by his old collaborator Gaston de Caillavet and Caillavet's now partner, Robert de Flers, of a successful Viennese Operette based on Henri Meilhac's comedy *L'Attaché d'ambassade.* It was Franz Lehár's *La Veuve joyeuse* / *Die lustige Witwe,* the biggest musical theatre success Paris had seen in years. Eighty-five successive performances each took an amazing equivalent of £250 per night before Franck was obliged to close his theatre for repairs. Even the break in the run did no harm in a city used to such things. At the reopening in September the public flocked back and, in a Paris where the musical theatre had been wallowing in a considerable doldrum, Franck and the Apollo were suddenly launched as the most important producer of, and house for opérette in the city. He followed up with another splendid, if necessarily lesser, success with *Rêve de valse* (*Ein Walzertraum*), and scored again with Ganne's delightful *Hans le joueur de flûte,* produced earlier at Monte-Carlo, but Leoncavallo's *Malbrouk s'en va t'en guerre* was a failure and Franck hastened to bring back *La Veuve joyeuse.*

His 1911 productions included another Viennese success, Fall's *Die geschiedene Frau* (*La Divorcée*), as well as Terrasse's *Les Transatlantiques,* a revival of Offenbach's *Madame Favart,* and Hirschmann's *Les Petites Étoiles,* and 1912 found two other Viennese works, *Le Comte de Luxembourg* (*Der Graf von Luxemburg*) and *Le Soldat de chocolat* (*Der tapfere Soldat*), the mainstays of his program, alongside revivals of *Les Saltimbanques, Les Cloches de Corneville* and the infallible *La Veuve joyeuse. La Veuve* had to be called on the following year again, for although another triumphant import, Jean Gilbert's *La Chaste Susanne* (*Die keusche Susanne*), played over a 100 performances, a revival of *Monsieur de la Palisse* held up for two months plus, and one of *La Mascotte* a little less, the two new French works Franck loyally included in his program—Lattès's *La Jeunesse dorée* and Ganne's *Cocorico*—lasted but 17 and 28 performances respectively, and Franck had to tighten his belt.

Latterly, things had not been going as well as they might at the Gymnase as well, and in 1913 Franck found himself obliged to take in there as a partner the ubiquitous Gustave Quinson, whose tentacles were spreading round a dozen Parisian houses in a manoeuvre which would make him the most powerful individual in the Paris theatre. At the Apollo, Franck tried one final new piece, Xavier Leroux's pretty *La Fille de Figaro,* and when that went under after 40 performances, he was obliged to throw in his hand. On 15 April 1914 he handed over the theatre to one M Maillart. Instead of two theatres, he now had half of one. Opérette made an unaccustomed appearance at the Gymnase when Franck and Quinson produced *La Petite Dactylo* with Yvonne Printemps in the title role, but Franck had soon had enough of partnership and Quinson and, determined to be his own master again, struck out with a new theatre, the smaller Théâtre Édouard VII.

The new house was opened in November 1916 with a Rip revue, and Franck then entered on a policy of "petite opérette" with a revival of Cuvillier's *Son p'tit frère,* followed by a successful new piece, *La Folle Nuit,* composed by Marcel Pollet and a less successful one, *La Petite Bonne d'Abraham.* After one more disastrous attempt at opérette with a fortnight's run of a piece by the young Tiarko Richepin and Albert Willemetz, *Rapatipatoum* (1919), he renounced musicals and thereafter devoted his theatre to comedy, and especially the comedies of Sacha Guitry, full-time. The nearest he came thereafter to opérette at the Édouard VII was the production of Guitry's plays-with-song-for-Yvonne, the vehicles for Mme Guitry, otherwise Yvonne Printemps, who was the star of her husband's delicious *L'Amour masqué* (1923, music by Messager), *Mozart* (1925, music by Hahn), *Jean de la Fontaine* (1927, music from Lully) and *Mariette* (1928, music by Oscar Straus).

In 1924 Franck again spread himself when he opened the little Théâtre de l'Étoile on the corner of the Champs-Élysées and the rue Balzac. Guitry's *L'Accroche-coeur* and *La Revue de printemps* (w Willemetz) and the personal attractions of Mlle Printemps kept the theatre going briefly, but subsequent pieces, including the opérette *Pouche,* of which Franck was himself the adaptor, did insufficiently well to keep the new theatre afloat. Franck sold it and it was soon transformed into the ateliers of the couturiere Maggy Rouff.

In 1929 he also gave up the Théâtre Édouard VII and put the end to a career in theatrical management which had had three periods of great prominence and prosperity, one in the musical theatre and two in the non-musical, but which had also known the inevitable ration of hefty lows.

1925 **Pouche** (Henri Hirschmann/René Peter, Henri Falk ad) Théâtre de l'Étoile 18 February

FRANÇOIS LES BAS-BLEUS Opéra-comique in 3 acts by Ernest Dubreuil, Paul Burani and Eugène Humbert. Music by Firmin Bernicat. Additional music by André Messager. Théâtre des Folies-Dramatiques, Paris, 8 November 1883.

The young composer Firmin Bernicat strove for many years for success in the theatre, and he finally achieved it when his opéra-comique *François les bas-bleus* (named for Paul Meurice's 1863 drama) was produced in Paris in 1883. But, by the time the show opened, its composer was dead, and *François les bas-bleus,* instead of launching the career of Bernicat, launched that of the younger musician who had completed the score: André Messager. In fact, the original collaborators on this highly popular show fared sadly, for Dubreuil, the young librettist of *François les bas-bleus,* died soon after (April 1886), in a Paris madhouse, aged just 26.

François (Bouvet), the public scribe, and the little street-singer Fanchon (Jeanne Andrée) are heading cosily towards marriage when the Comtesse de la Savonnière (Mme d'Harville) recognizes the girl as her long-lost niece, the daughter of the Marquis de Pontcornet (Montrouge). Whilst the new Mlle de Pontcornet turns down her father's proposed suitor, de Lansac (Dekernel), and her aunt turns warm glances on François, the young scribe writes out the newest attempt of the would-be-songwriter Pontcornet. However, he makes some changes on the way, and the conservative sentiments of the Marquis's lyrics are altered to ones of a liberality which earns both the men temporary popular support, social disgrace, and a trip to the Bastille. The 14th of July 1789 comes in time to get them released, and heading towards a happy ending.

Quite what part of the winning score of *François les bas-bleus* is to be attributed to which composer is, of course, only to be guessed, although it has been claimed (by a biographer of Messager) that Messager was responsible for a full half of the music, as well as the entire orchestration. A biographer of Bernicat might have different figures. In any case, the score as a whole contributed much to the success of the show. The strong baritone role of François was well served, setting off the evening, after the traditional warm-up chorus and number by a minor character, with a ronde calling his profession ("C'est François les bas-bleus"), which was soon to become popular, duetting sweetly with his Fanchon as he attempts to teach her her letters ("Avec soin formez chaque lettre"), soaring out his sabotaged version of the Chanson Politique ("Peuple français, la politique"), sadly realizing that he is no match for a rich and noble Fanchon ("Il faut bannir tout espérance"/"Espérance en d'heureux jours") and finally soliloquizing desperately over his lost love ("À toi, j'avais donné ma vie"), before the fall of the Bastille puts all right.

Fanchon's "La complainte du petit matelot," the song of her childhood which leads to her origins being recognized, gave the ingenue her best moment, whilst the lovesick Countess had some fine and funny moments, describing her own charms to François in a rondo ("J'ai de la figure") or cautiously impersonating a coffee-seller ("Un barbon près de sa belle") on Bastille day. The funny moments of the Marquis came largely in the tale.

François les bas-bleus was a veritable hit at a theatre where the management was undergoing a difficult time, and on the morning following its triumphant opening the three librettists sent a crown of gilt laurel leaves to Bernicat's mother in Lyon, to be laid on the young musician's grave. The show was played 143 times in its first run, a run which was succeeded by others in 1887, 1895, 1896, 1900, 1908 and in 1916 as the piece established itself as a solid item in the opérette repertoire, just a touch below the most successful and famous.

The show was quickly transported to other countries and languages, with an Hungarian production (ad Lajos Evva, Béla J Fái) opening just days after the Paris season closed (10 performances), and with New York getting its first glimpse of the show later in the same year, under the title *Fanchon,* when Maurice Grau included it in his season at Wallack's Theater, with Louise Théo as Fanchon, Francis Gaillard as François, Mme Delorme (Countess) and Mezières (Pontcornet). An English version called *Fantine* (ad Benjamin Woolf, Roswell Martin Field) which included additional music apparently written by Woolf had, however, already been produced at the Boston Museum earlier in the same year with Madeleine Lucette as the heroine and John Howson as Pontcornet. It was greeted with such considerable success that it was revived there for further seasons twice within the next two years. *François* was played by various touring and repertoire companies throughout America in the years that followed, and two further versions were seen in New York: in 1888 the Boston Ideal Company brought their *François* to Broadway under the title of *Victor, the Bluestocking* (ad Oscar Weil) with Henry Clay Barnabee featured as the Marquis and Zélie de Lussan as Fanchette, and in 1890 Lotta gave her version under the title *Fanchette* at Brooklyn's Amphion Academy (18 September). Since this was the title of the version produced at Liverpool's Royal Court Theatre (18 January 1894) by Britain's Carl Rosa company, who credited it to Weil, it seems as if it may have been identical with *Victor the Bluestocking.* Lotta later switched and called her version *Ina.* The Victor, in the Carl Rosa, mounting was star tenor Barton McGuckin, the Fanchette Zélie de Lussan, with the veteran opéra-bouffe stars basso Aynley Cook (Gruyer) and Mme Amadi (Célestine) in support.

Yet another English version, done by Justin McCarthy MP (which may have accounted for its title, *François, the Radical*), was prepared for Kate Santley who produced it at her Royalty Theatre in London, herself playing Fanchon alongside Deane Brand (François), Henry Ashley (Pontcornet) and Lizzie Mulholland (Countess). After three weeks it was withdrawn, allegedly for rewrites on the book, and did not reappear, but Miss Santley seems to have lifted a goodly helping of its music for her own comic opera, *Vetah,* with which she later played several tours.

One of these English versions (probably Woolf's) was presented in Australia by Luscombe Searelle and Charles Harding as part of an 1886 season at Sydney's New Opera House. Gracie Plaisted, in what was now the title role of *Fantine,* paired with Harding's François for 10 nights. A number of years later, a German version (ad Karl Saar) which again switched the title to the heroine (from *Der Volks-sänger* to *Die Strassensängerin*), was produced in Berlin, with Fr Grimm-Einödshofer, Steiner and Steinberger featured, but it was only in France that the show won real popularity.

Hungary: Népszínház *Kék Feri* 14 March 1884; UK: Royalty Theatre *François the Radical* 4 April 1885; USA: Boston Museum (Eng) *Fantine* 14 July 1884, Wallack's Theater (Fr) *Fanchon* 29 September 1884, Fifth Avenue Theater *Victor the Bluestocking* 6 February 1888; Australia: New Opera House, Sydney *Fantine* 1 May 1886; Germany: Friedrich-Wilhelmstädtisches Theater *Der Volks-sänger* (*Die Strassensängerin*) 1 September 1894

Recording: complete (Gaîté-Lyrique)

FRASER, Agnes [FRASER-SMITH, Agnes Fraser Elder] (b Springfield, Scotland, 8 November 1877; d London, 22 July 1968).

Miss Fraser began her career singing in D'Oyly Carte's touring companies and graduated to the Savoy Theatre company in 1899. Her first role there was in *The Rose of Persia,* where she succeeded Isabel Jay in the supporting part of Blush-of-the-Morning when Jay herself replaced the show's quickly departed original star, Ellen Beach Yaw. She appeared as Isabel, Lady Ella and Celia in Gilbert and Sullivan revivals, and as Kathleen in *The Emerald Isle* (1901), occasionally replacing Miss Jay in leading roles before, in 1902, taking over definitively as the Savoy company's last prima donna. In that capacity she starred in the roles of Bessie Throckmorton in *Merrie England* ("She Had a Letter from Her Love," "Who Shall Say That Love Is Cruel") and Kenna in *A Princess of Kensington* (1903). After the break-up of the Savoy outfit, she starred with her husband, Savoy comic Walter Passmore, in the musical comedies *The Earl and the Girl* (1903, Elphin Haye) and *The Talk of the Town* (1905, Ellaline Lewin), in the ingenue role of Robert Courtneidge's highly successful *The Dairymaids* (1906, Winifred) and in the Christmas show *Little Hans Ander-*

sen (1903, The Princess Who Married the Sailor). She later appeared with Passmore in musical playlets in variety houses (*Sweet William, Queer Fish*) before retiring from the stage.

Her daughter, **Nancy FRASER** [Agnes Fraser Elder PASSMORE], also had a career as a vocalist and appeared in her mother's role in *Merrie England* in a 1934 revival at the Prince's Theatre, and as Renée in the 1932 West End revival of *The Duchess of Dantzic.*

Her brother, **Alec FRASER** [SMITH] (b Cupar, 16 February 1884; d London, 20 June 1956), also had a considerable career as a vocalist in the musical theatre, playing in London in *A Princess of Kensington* (1903, Oberon), *The Earl and the Girl* (1903, Hugh Wallender), *Little Hans Andersen* (1903, The Prince Who Was Wrecked), *The Dairymaids* (1906, t/o Fred Leverton), *Havana* (1908, t/o Diego de la Concha), *Our Miss Gibbs* (1909, chorus), *The Girl in the Train* (1910, van Lieje), *The Dollar Princess* (1911, t/o Earl of Quorn), *A Waltz Dream* (1911, Montschi), *The Count of Luxembourg* (1911, de Trésac), *The Girl in the Taxi* (1912, René), *Are You There?* (1913, Gordon Grey), *The Only Girl* (1915, John Martin), *The Belle of New York* (revival 1919, Harry), *Cleopatra* (1925, Silvius), *Betty in Mayfair* (1926, t/o Barnaby Haddon), *The Girl from Cook's* (1927, Henri de Beaupret), as the Red Shadow in a revival of *The Desert Song* (1930), *Clancarty* (1933, Lord Spencer) and also in revue and plays. He also appeared in the provinces in *The Belle of New York* (1900, Harry), *The Blue Moon* (1906), *Mamselle Kiki* (1924, Victor), for several years as the Red Shadow, in *The Rebel Princess* (1931, Prince René), and in *The Lady of the Rose* (1932, Belovar).

A sister, **Mary FRASER** [SMITH] also appeared on the musical stage, and was married to star comedian Huntley Wright.

FRASER-SIMSON, Harold [SIMSON, Harold Fraser] (b London, 15 August 1872; d Inverness, 19 January 1944). The musician of *The Maid of the Mountains.*

The son of a London merchant and educated at Charterhouse and King's College, Fraser-Simson was at first involved in the world of commercial shipping, successfully operating, from an office in Mincing Lane, as a ship-owner. His first appearance in the musical theatre was with the score for the colorful, if old-fashioned, comic opera *Bonita,* for which he organized a West End production, directed by no less a luminary than Granville Barker, in 1911. *Bonita* lasted only 42 performances, but its music was sufficiently well received for its composer to be offered, five years later, the opportunity of composing the score for Robert Evett's Daly's Theatre musical, *The Maid of the Mountains.*

The enormous success of this show, and of his individual songs (''Farewell,'' ''Love Will Find a Way,'' ''Husbands and Wives''), set Fraser-Simson firmly in place as one of the most touted show composers of the time, and he subsequently supplied the scores for Evett for two other vehicles for *Maid of the Mountains* star José Collins, *A Southern Maid* and *Our Peg.* The first of these followed *The Maid of the Mountains* into Daly's and had another remarkable success; the second, frozen out of Evett's London theatre by the long-running success of the other two, played only in the provinces and was later adapted into *Our Nell* (the original heroine, Peg Woffington, being replaced by Nell Gwynne for presumably commercial reasons) and played at the Gaiety.

The touring musical *Missy Jo,* a vehicle for comic W H Berry called *Head Over Heels,* and the remade *Our Nell* had only limited lives, but Fraser-Simson scored another fine success when he teamed again with Frederick Lonsdale on the romantic artists-in-Montmartre musical, *The Street Singer,* which ran nearly a year at the Lyric Theatre and toured widely thereafter.

The pretty *Betty in Mayfair* did prettily at the Adelphi the following year, but Fraser-Simson's most enduring stage work apart from *The Maid of the Mountains* was his last, a sprightly and loveable musical setting of Kenneth Grahame's *Toad of Toad Hall* as dramatized for juvenile audiences by A A Milne. This piece became a British Christmas annual and its success prompted the compilation in 1970 of a *Winnie the Pooh,* put together from Milne's book and Fraser-Simson's settings of the Pooh lyrics as the song-cycle *The Hums of Pooh* (''Christopher Robin Is Saying His Prayers,'' ''They're Changing Guard at Buckingham Palace''). *Winnie the Pooh* also proved, for many years, a regular children's festive season favorite.

1911 **Bonita** (Wadham Peacock) Queen's Theatre 22 September

1916 **The Maid of the Mountains** (Harry Graham/Frederick Lonsdale) Prince's Theatre, Manchester 23 December; Daly's Theatre 10 February 1917

1917 **A Southern Maid** (Dion Clayton Calthrop, Graham/Harry Miller) Prince's Theatre, Manchester 24 December; Daly's Theatre 15 May 1920

1919 **Our Peg** (Graham/Edward Knoblock) Prince's Theatre, Manchester 24 December

1921 **Missy Jo** (Graham/James Clive) Folkestone 4 July

1923 **Head Over Heels** (Adrian Ross, Graham/Seymour Hicks) Adelphi Theatre 8 September

1924 **Our Nell** (revised *Our Peg*) (w Ivor Novello/Louis N Parker, Reginald Arkell) Gaiety Theatre 16 April

1924 **The Street Singer** (Percy Greenbank/Lonsdale) Lyric Theatre 27 June

1925 **Betty in Mayfair** (Graham/J Hastings Turner) Adelphi Theatre 11 November

1929 **Toad of Toad Hall** (A A Milne) Liverpool Repertory Theatre 17 December; Lyric Theatre 17 December 1930

1970 **Winnie the Pooh** (ad Julian Slade/Milne) Phoenix Theatre 17 December

FRASQUITA Operette in 3 acts by A M Willner and Heinz Reichert based on *La Femme et le pantin* by Pierre Louÿs. Music by Franz Lehár. Theater an der Wien, Vienna, 12 May 1922.

For some reason, librettists Willner and Reichert, in setting up their heroine for Lehár's newest Operette, elected to make her not a central-European gypsy, of the kind their Hungarian composer had already proven himself expert at musicking, but a Spanish gypsy, in the Carmen mold, involved with a group of Frenchmen in modern-day Barcelona.

Armand Mirbeau (Hubert Marischka) has been summoned to Barcelona to meet up with his uncle Aristide Girot (Emil Guttmann) and the cousin, Dolly (Henny Hilmar), whom he hasn't seen for nearly 20 years, and whom he is now scheduled to marry. Once in Barcelona, however, he falls under the charms of the gypsy, Frasquita (Betty Fischer). She, scornfully determined only to lead him on and make a fool of him, ultimately finds herself falling in love, in her turn, and she follows Armand to Paris. There a happy ending is lying in wait. Dolly pairs off with best friend Hippolyt (Hans Thimig).

Lehár's score produced one hit number in Armand's rapturous "Hab' ein blaues Himmelbett," but it was the heroine of the piece who garnered the largest share of the score, her role including the sensuous waltz "Wüsst ich, wer morgen mein Liebster ist," the introductory "Fragst mich, was Liebe ist?" and the waltz duet with Armand "Weisst du nicht, was ein Herz voller Sehnsucht begehrt." The lighter numbers were largely the province of Dolly and Hippolyt, whose shimmy and polka strains contrasted in traditional fashion with the more romantic musical moments.

Wilhelm Karczag's Vienna production of *Frasquita* had a good run of over six months and, with some extra performances in the months that followed, totaled 195 performances before it was replaced on the schedules. During that time a number of cast changes took place, with Harry Bauer, Karl Meister and Richard Tauber taking over, in turn, from Marischka, and Anny Fields, Else Kochhann and Marthe Serak replacing Fischer.

Soon after the Vienna closure, the show was mounted at the Berlin Thalia-Theater, and then in Britain (ad Fred de Grésac, Reginald Arkell) where Robert Evett took it up as a natural vehicle for gypsyish-lady specialist José Collins. Mounted in the provinces, with Miss Collins paired with Robert Michaelis and Edmund Gwenn as Hippolyt, it had an unsteady start and when it reached London, four months later, with Michaelis replaced by Thorpe Bates, it flopped briskly in 36 performances.

If the piece's fate in Britain was a downbeat one, it was nevertheless destined to fall even further in America. The operatic singer Geraldine Farrar, the Metropolitan Opera's Carmen and a favorite star of the silent movies, was signed to make her light musical stage debut as Frasquita at an unheard of salary of $6,000 a week. After two managements had withdrawn from the project, Miss Farrar finally opened at Hartford, Connecticut, in a version called *The (Romany) Love Spell,* which was sponsored by her own manager, C J Foley, and the music publishers, the Dreyfus brothers, prefatory to an immediate opening at Broadway's Shubert Theater. Miss Farrar played just one performance before announcing that she was not happy with the music and closing the production. A second attempt to get the piece away took place in Los Angeles where *The Love Call* was played for a season (1925–26) with the lovely vocalist Grace La Rue starred, but it too failed to make its way to Broadway.

In spite of these failures, Australia's J C Williamson Ltd also mounted a *Frasquita,* with Marie Burke cast in the title role alongside Herbert Browne (Armand), H Barrett-Lennard (Hippolyt) and Marie Eaton (Luisa). They did not succeed in reversing the thumbs-down given to the other English-language productions.

Budapest saw a version of the show at the Városi Színház (ad Zsolt Harsányi) with the operatic tenor József Gábor as Armand, whilst a French version mounted at Le Havre (ad Max Eddy, Jean Marietti) with Fanély Revoil as Frasquita continued the show's unhappy record by failing to progress further. Two years later, however, a version of the show did make it to Paris when another famous singer tackled Frasquita, in an adaptation labeled "opéra-comique." Conchita Supervia was no happier in Lehár's music than Farrar had been, and the production at the Opéra-Comique, with Louis Arnoult, Annie Gueldy and René Herent supporting, was considered something of an aberration.

In 1935 Carl Lamac produced an updated film version of the show with Jarmila Novotna and Hans-Heinz Bollmann starred and some additional Lehár music introduced.

An Hungarian version of the Louÿs/Pierre Frondaie stage adaptation of *La Femme et le pantin,* with accompanying music by Károly Stephanides, was produced at the Budapest Vígszínház (ad Jenő Heltai) 27 April 1918 under the title *Az asszony és a bábu* (36 performances).

Germany: Thalia-Theater, Berlin 1 February 1924; UK: Lyceum, Edinburgh 24 December 1924, Prince's Theatre, London 23 April 1925; Hungary: Városi Színház *Fraskita* 3 March 1925; USA: Parsons' Theater, Hartford *The (Romany) Love Spell* 24 November 1925; Australia: Her Majesty's Theatre, Sydney 16 April 1927; France: Théâtre du Havre, Le Havre October 1931, Opéra-Comique, Paris 5 May 1933

Film: Atlantis-Film 1935

Recordings: Supervia recording (Pacific, etc), selection (Capriccio), selections in French (Decca, Véga), selection in Italian (EDM), etc

EINE FRAU, DIE WEISS, WAS SIE WILL Musical comedy in 5 scenes by Alfred Grünwald based on *Le Fauteuil* by Louis Verneuil. Music by Oscar Straus. Metropoltheater, Berlin, 1 September 1932.

Oscar Straus's last great pre-Nazi-era hit marked the return to the musical stage of Berlin's favorite musical star, Fritzi Massary, who had avoided the Operette stage since her unhappy experience with a jazzed-up version of *Die lustige Witwe,* and who now tackled a prima-donna part which was no glamorous heroine, but a ''mother'' role.

The revue-star Manon Cavallini (Fritzi Massary) had an illegitimate daughter in her young days, and that child, Lucy (Ellen Schwanneke), has been brought up by her father, ignorant of her mother's identity, until she has reached the age of indiscretion, and has fallen in love. However, the young man with whom she is so taken has developed a crush on an actress, and that actress is none other than Manon. The girl decides to go and speak to her rival, to ask her to renounce the boy, and the older woman agrees to do so. Finally and inevitably the truth of the two women's relationship comes out.

Straus's score for *Eine Frau* treated its aging prima donna gently. There were no wide-ranging vocal lines. But the composer brought forth one number which would become a worldwide hit: Manon's gentle, worldly wise little piece ''Jede Frau hat irgendeine Sehnsucht'' (''Every Woman Thinks She Wants to Wander''). She also chatted to reporters (''Was so die Gesellschaft''), as she led up to the evening's title song (''I am a woman who knows what she wants . . .''), delivered a number about Ninon de l'Enclos (''Ninon, Ninon'') and took part in various duos and scenes.

The show was well received in the Berlin production mounted by the Rotter brothers—''Grünwald has treated an age-old theme with just the right modern veneer of sophistication'' one critic wrote—and Massary's return to the musical stage was a decided success. It was also her last appearance on the Berlin stage, for soon after she—like Grünwald and Straus, and like the Rotter brothers, hounded to death by the Nazis—joined the exodus from Germany.

After the Berlin run, Massary and Frln Schwanneke headed a company at Vienna's Scala Theater for a season (15 September–26 October 1933), by which time the show had already made its debut in Budapest, played in Hungarian (ad Tamás Emőd, István Békeffy) for 32 performances at the Vígszínház, and in London where C B Cochran's punningly titled *Mother of Pearl* (ad A P Herbert) had a good run of 181 performances. Alice Delysia played Josephine Pavani, memorably singing ''Every Woman Thinks She Wants to Wander,'' Sepha Treble was daughter Pearl and Frederick Ranalow her father, here turned into Richard Moon, MP in a version which resituated the story in England and filled it with Lords and lieutenants. Delysia repeated her great personal success when she appeared in *Mother of Pearl* under Frank Thring's management in Australia the following year alongside Phyllis Baker as Pearl, Frank Harvey (Moon), Robert Coote (Sterling) and Cecil Scott, playing the musical in repertoire with the play *Her Past.*

In 1954 a revised version of the show (ad Leonard Steckel) was played at Vienna's Theater in der Josefstadt (23 February, 43 performances) under the title *Manon,* and in 1959 the film star Zarah Leander appeared at the Raimundtheater in a new production under the direction of Karl Farkas.

The piece was first filmed in 1934 with Lil Dagover in the central role. An Arthur Maria Rabenalt film under the title *Eine Frau, die weiss, was sie will* was produced in 1958, starring Lilli Palmer both as revue-star Angela Cavallini and her granddaughter, teacher Julia Klöhn, in a routine showbiz tale which had nothing to do with the original, but which was attached to some of Straus's music.

Hungary: Vígszínház *Egy asszony, aki tudja, mit akar* 23 December 1932; UK: Gaiety Theatre *Mother of Pearl* 27 January 1933; Austria: Scala-Theater 9 September 1933; Australia: Princess Theatre, Melbourne *Mother of Pearl* 14 July 1934

Films: Viktor Janson 1934, Bavaria Film 1958

DER FRAUENFRESSER Operette in 3 acts by Leo Stein and Carl Lindau. Music by Edmund Eysler. Wiener Bürgertheater, Vienna, 23 December 1911.

The libretto of *Der Frauenfresser* (''the woman hater''), the second of the series of highly successful musical plays composed by Eysler for Oscar Fronz's Wiener Bürgertheater, was submitted to the composer by Leo Stein along with the text of another Operette. Always more at home with a wholly Austrian subject, Eysler elected to set *Der Frauenfresser,* leaving the more highly colored *Polenblut* to make the reputation of Oskar Nedbal.

As the result of an ancestor's will, the Schloss Aichegg, left jointly to two parts of the family, is inhabited half by Major Hubertus von Murner (Fritz Werner) and half by Frau Natalie von Roffan (Viktoria Pohl-Meiser) and her daughter, the principal living room being divided down the middle. Hubertus, who was betrayed in his youth by his fiancée, Mary Wilton (Erna Fiebinger), has become a woman-hater and has founded a misogynists' club into which he is trying to induct his nephew,

Camillo (Marcel Noë). The boy, however, is more interested in Tilly von Roffan (Emmy Petko) than misogyny. The widowed Mary, still in love with the fiancé of her young days, arrives on the scene to buy up the von Roffans' half of the castle and, after two acts of quiproquos and decidedly unmisogynistic behaviour by Hubertus, who at one stage even sets his sights on Tilly, the pair come happily together for the final curtain.

Eysler's score was based largely on waltz music, with Hubertus's first-act song ''Sie hiess Marie,'' the popular ''Junge Mädchen tanzen gern'' from the first-act finale, and the second act's ''Das war Gott Amors blauer Bogen'' proving the choice numbers, alongside a polka duet for Tilly and Hubertus (''Kommen Sie, kommen Sie Polka tanzen'') and a jaunty quartet in which life is compared to racing—you need a little luck in both (''Ja im Leben, wie im Rennen braucht man Glück''). The musically light final act was topped by a brisk trio and dance for Mary, Tilly and Camillo (''Kinder, lasst den Kopf nicht hängen'').

Der Frauenfresser gave the Bürgertheater its biggest hit to date. It passed its 100th performance on 1 April 1912, before Karl Streitmann took over as Hubertus, then shared the bill with a stage version of the Passion Play until the end of the season (159 performances). When the theatre resumed, *Der Frauenfresser* was reopened with Hans Fürst starred, before Werner returned to his original role as the show ran on to its 200th night (11 October). It closed its main run after 270 performances (20 December), but remained in the theatre's repertoire for two further seasons as Fronz went on to mount newer Eysler musicals with equal profit. It was seen again at the Bürgertheater in 1920, then at the Johann Strauss-Theater in 1925 with Madame Pohl-Meiser repeating alongside Fritz Imhoff as Hubertus (13 August–3 September). It was produced in Vienna once more in 1946 but, like the rest of this popular series, was effectively wiped out of the repertoire by time, aided by the wartime embargo on Eysler's music.

A Budapest production (ad Adolf Mérei) was mounted at the Budapesti Színház in 1912, and later the same year Miksa Preger's company from Berlin played the piece in German during its season at the Vígszínház, whilst a Broadway production (ad George Hobart, and with only one non-Eysler number added to the musical part) was staged the Astor Theater under the management of A H Woods a few months later. Hobart altered the plot so that Major von Essenburg (Walter Lawrence) was again jilted by Marie (Sallie Fisher) in the final act, but Camillo (Joseph Santley) was allowed to keep his Tilly (Dolly Castles), now upgraded to being the daughter of a Baroness (Mrs Stuart Robson). Eysler's score won delighted praise (''lovely music,'' ''a delightful score . . . fresh, insinuating, soothing or inspiring as the mood of the action demands'') and the book and staging were both well-liked (''a cleanly amusing story, dancing that is not mere acrobatics''), but *The Woman Haters [Club]* was a quick failure in four weeks and 32 performances on Broadway. ''There are no big features in the pieces and it is consequently difficult to advertise,'' mused one critic who had liked it; ''the quiet and steady charm which pervades the entire performance cannot easily be crystallized into billboard phrases.'' When it was sent on the American road the show was given a more conventional title: *The Pretty Little Widow.*

Hungary: Budapesti Színház *Az asszonyfaló* 15 May 1912, Vígszínház *Der Frauenfresser* 22 May 1912; Germany: Theater des Westens 9 February 1913; USA: Astor Theater *The Woman Haters* 7 October 1912

DIE FRAU IM HERMELIN Operette in 3 acts by Rudolf Schanzer and Ernst Welisch. Music by Jean Gilbert. Theater des Westens, Berlin, 23 August 1919.

If Jean Gilbert's most memorable successes came with his scores to those sparkling prewar and wartime musical comedies of which *Die keusche Susanne* was the most internationally successful example, he subsequently proved his ability also to write the score for pieces in the fashionable postwar romantic-costume-musical line. The most successful of these was *Die Frau im Hermelin,* which profited from the eventual loosening in anti-German feelings in the lucrative English and allied markets to run up a series of long-running productions around the world, making the piece, statistically at least, possibly Gilbert's most internationally successful work of all.

The ''woman in ermine'' is a ghost, said to appear in time of danger at the Beltrami castle near Verona. During the Russian invasion of 1810, Mariana Beltrami, the wife of the Italian Count Adrien Beltrami, sees her, and the danger soon follows. The enemy Colonel Paltitsch imposes himself, with the support of his regiment, on the Beltrami household and before long is tempted to impose himself, equally, on the lady of the household. Count Adrien, who has been forced into disguise as a servant in his own home, reveals himself to stop the seduction and is sentenced to be shot as a spy. Mariana can buy his life with her favors, as apparently the ghostly lady in ermine did in the past in a similar situation. Events, however, ultimately come to a happy and unbloody ending. The comical moments fell to Suitangi, an itinerant silhoutte artist who stands in as the Count whilst the Count is being a servant; the visiting ballet dancer Sophie Lavalle; and Baron Kajetan Sprotti-Sprotti.

The most popular moments of Gilbert's score were, on the romantic side, the Adrien/Mariana waltz duet, ''Liebchen, du mein reizendes Liebchen,'' and the seductive waltz duo between Mariana and Paltitsch, ''Man sagt doch nicht gleich, 'nein,''' which reappeared throughout the show as the relationship between the two grew variously hotter and colder, and, on the more lighthearted side, the lively trio ''Nur an die Alten muss man sich halten'' (Sophie/Suitangi/Sprotti), Suitangi's waltz number about ''Meine Silhouetten'' and the polka invitation to ''Tanz mit mir den Holubiak'' (apparently a kind of cossack dance).

Die Frau im Hermelin played at the Theater des Westens, under the management of Messrs Beese and Bieber, through 310 performances before going on to further successes further afield. Budapest was the quickest of the other main centers to take the show up, and *A hermelines nő* (ad Sándor Hevesi) was produced at the Vígszínház (31 performances) soon after the end of the Berlin run, and prior to its mounting in Vienna where Margit Suchy (Mariana), Harry Peyer (Adrien), Louis Treumann (Paltitsch), Luise Kartousch (Sophie), Ernst Tautenhayn (Suitangi) and Karl Tuschl (Sprotti) featured. The piece played at the Theater an der Wien through the three months till the end of the spring season, with Christl Mardayn later replacing Suchy in the star role, and it returned again in the autumn for a further seven weeks to bring its total run to 141 performances in Vienna.

In London, *The Lady of the Rose* (ad Frederick Lonsdale, Harry Graham) was presented by James White at Daly's Theatre, billed as a ''George Edwardes production'' in spite of the fact that the great producer had been some years dead. Phyllis Dare (Mariana), Roy Royston (Adrien), Harry Welchman (Colonel Belovar), Huntley Wright (Suitangi) and Ivy Tresmand (Sophie) led the cast, the score was supplemented with a Leslie Stuart number called ''Catch a Butterfly While You Can'' for Miss Tresmand, and the production proved a major hit, playing for 514 performances in the West End before going on the road and into the colonies, notably to Australia. There, after a tryout in Brisbane, it was produced in Melbourne with Edith Drayson starred alongside Howett Worster and Leslie Holland and later in Sydney (Theatre Royal 9 May 1925) with Gladys Moncrieff teamed with Claude Flemming and John Ralston. The show was brought back briefly to London and Daly's Theatre in 1929 with Marjery Wyn playing alongside Welchman and Wright.

Another English adaptation of the libretto (ad Cyrus Wood) was made for Broadway, although Harry Graham's London lyrics were again used for such of the original songs as remained. This time the beastly Colonel—still called Belovar, and played by Walter Woolf—actually got the girl (Wilda Bennett) in the end, for Count Adrien (Harry Fender) turned out to be not her husband, but . . . wait for it . . . her brother! Gilbert's score was given the usual Shubert treatment, being decorated (not to say submerged) by additional material by Sigmund Romberg (''When Hearts Are Young,'' etc) and by the latest addition to the Shubert botching team, Al Goodman. The resultant show ran for 232 performances.

In spite of its successes, *Die Frau im Hermelin* did not become part of the revivable repertoire, and the best of its reputation remained in England. However, the piece's story was used as the basis for a 1927 Hollywood film in which Corinne Griffith, Francis X Bushman and Einar Hansen took the star roles, and again for a 1930 First National-Pathé musical movie starring Vivienne Segal, Lupino Lane, Allen Prior, Walter Pidgeon, Claude Flemming and Myrna Loy. Here Gilbert's score was replaced by numbers by Al Dubin, Al Bryan and Ed Ward, Schanzer and Welisch's title by the curious *Bride of the Regiment* (all of them?) and even much of their plot by Hollywooden film-flam. The Australians retitled the movie *The Lady of the Rose,* and a 1948 Hollywood remake went further back to source and called itself *That Lady in Ermine.* It didn't get much closer to the original story, however, and Friedrich Holländer and Leo Robin's musical moments included Betty Grable cooing ''Oooh, What I'll Do to That Wild Hungarian.''

Hungary: Vígszínház *A hermelines nő* 1 July 1920; Austria: Theater an der Wien 29 April 1921; UK: Daly's Theatre *The Lady of the Rose* 21 February 1922; USA: Ambassador Theater *The Lady in Ermine* 2 October 1922; Australia: Brisbane *The Lady of the Rose* 9 August 1924, Her Majesty's Theatre, Melbourne 20 September 1924

Film: First National *The Lady in Ermine* 1927

DAS FRAULEIN VOM AMT Operette in 3 acts by Ernst Arnold and Georg Okonkowski. Music by Jean Gilbert. Theater des Westens, Berlin, 13 November 1915.

Rich Uncle Felix Förster plans to wed his nephew to the daughter of his business partner, unaware that young Robert has already got himself married to Marie, the little ''lady from the office.'' When Uncle Felix himself develops an unseen passion for Agathe Blutenhain, the author of a novel he has read, he is disappointed to find out that ''Agathe'' is actually one Eduard Hazelhun and there is little left to do but allow himself to be prettily consoled by his new niece-in-law.

Although not one of Gilbert's biggest hits, the show was a wartime success in Germany, playing 178 nights at the Theater des Westens, and was also produced in both Vienna and in Budapest (ad Zsolt Harsányi).

Austria: Wiener Stadttheater 1 February 1916; Hungary: Vígszínház *Ő Terez!* 18 August 1917

FRAU LUNA Burlesk-phantastich Austattungs-Operette in 1 act (4 scenes) by Heinrich Bolten-Bäckers. Music by Paul Linke. Apollotheater, Berlin, 1 May 1899.

Frau Luna was a little revusical spectacular (burlesque-fantasy-spectacular-Operette) written to fill the needs and a part of the bill of the popular Berlin variety house, the Apollotheater, where Emil Waldmann had earlier had a fine success with Bolten-Bäckers and Lincke's earlier little songs-sex-and-scenery piece, *Venus auf Erden.*

The tale of the show took the inventor Fritz Steppke (Robert Steidl) up to the moon in his homemade balloon, accompanied by his friends Lämmermeier (Arnold Rieck) and Pannecke, and their landlady, Frau Iduna Pusebach (Emmy Krochert). There they meet the moon-factotum, Theophil (Harry Bender), who turns out to be a fellow with whom Frau Pusebach once had a little adventure when he popped down to earth during an eclipse, and the intergalactic Prinz Sternschnuppe (Siegmund Lieban), come thence in his space-automobile for one of his periodic proposals to the lady-in-the-moon, Frau Luna (Willy Walden). Frau Luna takes a violent fancy to Steppke, but the mortal man resists all temptations, remains true to his earthbound Marie, and gratefully accepts the offer from Theophil to ferry the little group back to earth. Frau Luna will become the bride of Sternschnuppe, whilst Theophil gets the space-car as a thank-you present for his happy interference.

The song hits of the show were the waltz ''Schlösser, die im Monde liegen'' and Frau Luna's soprano march number ''Lasst den Kopf nicht hängen,'' whilst Frau Pusebach scored in the comical reminiscence of her affair in the dark, ''O Theophil,'' and Sternschnuppe had his moment in ''Frohe munt're Lieder'' in a score which ranged from a jolly Automobile-quartet (''Des Menschen Forschungsstreben zeigt'') to a grand ballet staged in Frau Luna's magic garden.

Frau Luna was a big success in Berlin, where its favorite songs became enormously popular, and the Apollo management continued with the policy of including Lincke/Bolten-Bäckers Operetten, always written with the house's large scenic and dance possibilities in mind, in their programs for a number of years. *Frau Luna,* however, remained the most successful of the series. The Berlin company played the piece as part of their repertoire in a season at Vienna's Danzers Orpheum in 1903 with Lucie Medlon as Luna, Felix Müller as Steppke and Helene Voss as Frau Pusebach, Budapest's Royal Orfeum was opened in 1902 with *Luna asszony* (followed up by the Apollo's other pieces, *Nakiri* and *Vénusz a földön*), and the show found a Parisian production at L'Olympia in 1904 when the Isola brothers attempted to follow the Apollotheater formula and include Operette in their variety programs. Fabrice Lemon and Maurice de Marsan's six-scene version featured Lucien Noël (Karl), Louise Blot (Mme La Lune), Vilbert (Théophile), Yette Bertholy (Mlle Pusebach) and Colas (Prince Soleil), and the piece shared the program with a magician, some comic acrobats, jugglers, trained animals and ''jeux athlétiques.''

It was 1911 before London got a glimpse of *Castles in the Air* (ad Mrs Cayley Robinson, Adrian Ross) when it was produced at the unfashionable Scala Theatre, paired not this time with variety acts but with a lecture on and demonstration of the new Kinemacolour process. What audiences there preferred were films of ''Our Farmyard Friends'' and ''Picturesque North Wales'' to Sybil Lonsdale, St John Hamund, Sybil Tancredi and Lincke's music, and the Operette was quickly dropped from the program.

A new, full-length version of *Frau Luna* was subsequently put together and remounted at the Apollotheater in 1922, the original tale being expanded with more scene-changes (11 scenes) and with some songs taken from other Lincke works. The most successful of these was the the march ''Das macht die Berliner Luft'' previously heard in the composer's *Berliner Luft,* a revue which also contributed the duet ''Schenck mir doch ein kleines bisschen Liebe'' to the new score. Frau Luna's ''Von Sternen umgeben'' was borrowed from the role of Venus in *Venus auf Erden.* Yet another new version was produced at the Stadttheater, Döbeln in 1929, and more remade versions of the piece were seen in Berlin in 1935, at the Admiralspalast in 1936, at the Metropoltheater in 1957 and, again, at the same house in recent years. It was written over once more (ad Kay and Lore Lorentz, mus ad Jürgen Knieper) for a production at Nuremberg in 1972. In 1965 (16 September) and 1981 (2 October) revivals were mounted at the Theater des Westens, and in 1990 the Metropoltheater company took their version of what has become accepted as the ''most Berlinish of all Berlin Operetten'' beyond the confines of the city and, now past its 100th birthday, various versions of the show are still solidly anchored in the repertoire of its home country.

A film *Frau Luna* (scr: Ernst Marischka) was produced in Germany with 1941 with Irene von Meyerndorff, Lizzi Waldmüller, Karl Schönböck, Paul Kemp and Georg Alexander featured. It dealt rather with romantic doings that take place alongside a production of the show than the show itself.

Hungary: Royal Orfeum *Luna asszony* 17 March 1902; Austria: Danzers Orpheum 18 February 1903; France: Olympia-Théâtre *Madame la Lune* 6 May 1904; UK: Scala Theatre *Castles in the Air* 11 April 1911

Film: Theo Lingen 1941

Recordings: selections (Polydor, EMI, Tele Funken, Baccarola), revised version (RCA)

FRAZEE, Harry H[erbert] (b Peoria, Ill, 29 June 1880; d New York, 4 June 1929).

Frazee worked in the theatre from the age of 16, first as an usher, then as an accountant, as road advance agent with the *Uncle Josh Spruceby* company (1900) and, from the age of 22, regularly as a producer. His first productions, plays and musical comedies, were confined to Chicago and the touring circuits (*The Girl Question, The Girl at the Helm, Knight for a Day, The Time, the Place and the Girl, The Isle of Spice* w Thomas Hanks, *The Yankee Regent,* etc) where he was ''associated in numerous enterprises'' with John Cort, but it was his co-production of a heavily revamped and wholly remusicked version of the Continental hit *Madame Sherry* (1910 w George Lederer, A H Woods) that gave him his first major success.

Thereafter, although such further musical ventures as *Jumping Jupiter* (1910) with Richard Carle, *The Happiest Night of His Life* (1911) with Victor Moore, *The Ladies' Lion* (1911) by and with Jeff de Angelis (all w Lederer), *Modest Susanne* (1912 w Woods), Victor Herbert's *The Madcap Duchess* (1913) and *Iole* (1913) were mostly less successful, he did quite well with an adaptation of Hoyt's *A Contented Woman* re-musically mounted as *Ladies First* (1912, 164 Broadway performances) and generally prospered, as he invested in theatre building in both Chicago (Cort Theater) and New York (Longacre Theater). He subsequently acquired the New York Lyric Theater and Wallack's Theater which he renamed the Frazee. At the same time he kept up a very high profile in the sporting world as owner of the Boston Red Sox.

Frazee continued producing plays until, in 1923, he outdid even his *Madame Sherry* success when he commissioned and produced the musical *No, No, Nanette,* a piece based on a play he had mounted earlier in his career. Staged first in Detroit, then in Chicago, London and ultimately on Broadway, *No, No, Nanette* was one of the greatest musical-theatre hits of its time. An attempt to repeat with another musical made from one of his play successes, a musical version of *Nothing But the Truth* called *Yes, Yes, Yvette,* was a failure, but the earlier show was still earning its producer plenty of money when he died a few years later, aged 48.

FREEAR, Louie [FREEAR, Louisa] (b Lambeth, London, 26 November 1871; d London, 20 March 1939). Tiny, munchkinnish low-comedy performer who became the rage of the London stage for several years at the turn of the century.

The daughter and sister of professional vocalists, Louie Freear began her stage career as a child, appearing (as a boy) with the Moore and Burgess Minstrels, in pantomime (AD 1882 in *Bluebeard Down Brown,* 1881, etc), and with a touring juvenile comic opera company as well as in music hall and as a member of a midget minstrel company. At 21 she went seriously, if temporarily, legit when Ben Greet hired her to play such roles as Puck in *A Midsummer Night's Dream* and Mopsa in *A Winter's Tale* in his Shakespearean repertoire. However, she next appeared in George Dance's musical comedy *Buttercup and Daisy* (1895, Liza Ellen) and, as a result of the success of her comic performance, the author wrote a made-to-measure role for her, as the low comedy cockney slavey, Ruth, into his musical *The Gay Parisienne* when, after several years on the road, it was produced in the West End.

Little Miss Freear became an overnight star with her rendition of Ruth's ''Sister Mary Jane's Top Note,'' but her new status did little good when she was tacked into the London production of the American musical *Lost, Stolen or Strayed* (aka *A Day in Paris*) in a vain attempt to save an unpromising production. She went to America for the starrily cast musical extravaganza *The Man in the Moon* (1899, Liza Ellen again) and, on returning home, appeared again as Puck, this time with Tree at His Majesty's, before going on the road with her own company, in a boy's role.

She returned to London in 1901 to play a specially enlarged version of the role of Fi-fi, the low-comedy cockney waitress, in the London production of Dance's *A Chinese Honeymoon* and, as she had in *The Gay Parisienne,* she caused a sensation with her music-hally songs ''I Want to Be a Lidy'' and ''The Twiddley Bits.'' After two years of the record-breaking run of *A Chinese Honeymoon* she left the still-running show to cash in on her zooming reputation in the lucrative music halls, but, as the momentary fashion for low-comedy munchkins oozed away, she found herself with fewer opportunities and the latter part of her career was limited to variety and to the occasional reprise of her most famous roles.

FREE AS AIR Musical play in 2 acts by Julian Slade and Dorothy Reynolds. Music by Julian Slade. Grand Theatre, Leeds, 8 April 1957; Savoy Theatre, London, 6 June 1957.

The successor to the enormously successful *Salad Days* retained something of the naive charm of that piece but, being built for a London house rather than as a repertory-theatre end-of-term entertainment, it was made in a slightly more substantial form, with a plot, an orchestral accompaniment, a considerably larger cast, and a chorus.

Set on an island in the Channel Islands, *Free as Air* told the tale of the lovely and wealthy Geraldine (Gillian Lewis) who escapes both the nosy press and a pressing suitor and finds her way to the quiet island of Terhou. There she finds both peace and the handsome local Albert Postumous (John Trevor), whilst the pushy Jack (Gerald Harper) and the gushing newspaperwoman Ivy Crush

(Josephine Tewson), who are ready to launch a ''development programme'' on the island, are routed. Patricia Bredin was the island's little soprano Molly, co-author Miss Reynolds the booming Miss Catamole, and Michael Aldridge played the Lord of the island.

The songs were gently suitable, with the loping philosophy of the islanders, ''Let the Grass Grow Under Your Feet,'' contrasting with inane Jack's tales of his past conquests ''Her Mummy Doesn't Like Me Any More'' and the semi-surprised love song for the formidable Miss Catamole and the gentle little Mr Potter (Howard Goorney), ''We're Holding Hands,'' proving the pick.

Free as Air's 417 performances in London thoroughly confirmed the authors' success with *Salad Days,* and also the fact that there was a place in the theatre for simplicity and charm alongside the increasingly loud, brash and over-amplified brand of musical show. The piece had a successful provincial life and was subsequently played, on the heels of *Salad Days,* in Australia and in other English-speaking regions as well as in the Netherlands.

Australia: Princess Theatre, Melbourne 11 October 1958

Recordings: original cast (Oriole), Dutch cast (Philips)

FREEDLEY, Vinton (b Philadelphia, 5 November 1891; d New York, 5 June 1969). Actor turned highly successful producer of Broadway musicals through 20 years of hits.

Freedley began in the theatre as a performer and appeared during his young career as the juvenile heroes of *Miss Millions* (1919, Jack Honeydew), Victor Herbert's ill-fated *Oui, Madame* (1920, Richard Ogden) and Percy Wenrich's road-folding *Maid to Love* (1920), with the Astaires in *For Goodness' Sake* (1922, Jefferson Dangerfield) and in the short-lived Carlo and Sanders musical *Elsie* (1923, Harry Hammond).

He went into partnership with *Oui, Madame* and *For Goodness' Sake*'s producer, Alex Aarons, in the same year and, after initiating their new firm with the play *The New Poor,* the pair embarked on a 10-year string of musical-comedy productions which included seven George Gershwin musicals: *Lady, Be Good!* (1924), which featured Freedley's former stage partners, the Astaires, *Tip-Toes* (1925), *Oh, Kay!* (1926), *Funny Face* (1927), *Treasure Girl* (1928), *Girl Crazy* (1930) and *Pardon My English* (1933), as well as Rodgers and Hart's *Spring Is Here* and *Heads Up!* (both 1929), *Here's Howe* (1928), De Sylva, Brown and Henderson's *Hold Everything!* (1928), and the ''melodrama with music'' *Singin' the Blues* which they quickly hived off to the show's cast to run as a cooperative following an unimpressive opening.

The partnership with Aarons was ended in 1933, and Freedley then continued as a solo producer, beginning auspiciously with the Broadway staging of Cole Porter's *Anything Goes* (1934) which featured *Girl Crazy*'s Ethel Merman in its starring role. He produced three further Porter musicals in the next seven years—*Red, Hot and Blue!* (1936), *Leave It to Me!* (1938) and *Let's Face It* (1941)—as well as the Vernon Duke *Cabin in the Sky* (1940), but his later musical pieces did not find the same success. *Jackpot* (1945) and *Great to Be Alive!* (1950 w Anderson Lawler, Russell Markert) were Broadway failures, whilst *Dancing in the Streets* (1943) did not get even that far.

Freedley made one appearance as a director of a Broadway musical with a souped-up *HMS Pinafore* called *Memphis Bound* which failed in 1945.

DER FREMDENFÜHRER Operette in a prologue and 3 acts by Leopold Krenn and Carl Lindau. Music by Carl Michael Ziehrer. Theater an der Wien, Vienna, 11 October 1902.

The Baron Niki Schlipp (Edmund Löwe) makes a bet with his fellow club-members that he can actually earn his living for a fortnight. He gets a job quickly, for on his way round the Ringstrasse he meets his old girlfriend, Anna Weisskopf (Lina Abarbanell), who is now a prima donna and calling herself Bianca Testa. She suggests that the apparently down-on-his-luck Niki act as a guide for her father (Siegmund Natzler), who is coming to Vienna for the wedding of her sister, Hedwig (Dora Keplinger), to the forester Hanns (Karl Meister). By the time Weisskopf's visit is done, the old man has discovered that his once-disowned daughter is rich and famous and, indeed, his own employer, whilst Niki has both won his bet and the hand and heart of Anna-Bianca. Alexander Girardi and Mila Theren provided the soubret moments as the military bandsman Ratz and his sweetheart Gabriele, maid to Bianca.

Ziehrer's score to *Der Fremdenführer* included some locally flavored pieces in the composer's best manner, with Bianca's entry waltz, ''Töne, Liedchen, töne durch die Nacht,'' Niki's waltz song in praise of Vienna, ''O Wien, mein liebes Wien,'' and the pretty duo for Hanns and Hedwig, ''Braucht es denn Samt und Seide,'' proving amongst the favorites. There were a pair of jolly numbers for Ratz, and the novelties included a yodeling duo for two bored aristocratic gentlemen and a Hannakischer dance.

Der Fremdenführer did not prove a particular success at the Theater an der Wien. It played its 40th performance on 19 November, and was replaced two days later by Lehár's maiden Operette, *Wiener Frauen,* being given just a handful of intermittent matinée performances thereafter. However, after decades of oblivion the piece was cannily remounted as a wartime good-old-days piece dur-

Plate 128. **Vinton Freedley.** *The producer (left) poses with choreographer George Hale, songwriter Cole Porter and some* Red, Hot and Blue! *chorines.*

ing the second war. Adapted by Walter Hauttmann (book) and Erik Jaksch (music), it was produced by Willy Seidl at the Raimundtheater with a cast including aging stars Mizzi Günther, Luise Kartousch, Fritz Imhoff and Richard Waldemar alongside Toni Niessner (Ratz), Maya Mayska (Bianca Testina) and Alfred Hulgert (Nikolaus), a program decorated with swastikas and air-raid warnings, and considerable success. It was brought back for a further production in 1961, and in 1978 was remodeled yet again, with additional Ziehrer numbers added, for a production at the Volksoper (22 October). Alois Aichorn, Erich Kuchar, Rudolf Wasserlof, Gisela Ehrensperger and Helga Papouschek were amongst the initial cast.

It it took quite a while, and a war, to make a success out of *Der Fremdenführer* in Austria, and it did not manage the same resurrection elsewhere. It had only a fair life in Germany and in Hungary where, under the curious title of *7777* (ad Dezső Balint, Jenő Faragó), it was played 10 times at the Népszínház.

Germany: ?1903; Hungary: Népszínház *7777* 15 April 1905

THE FRENCH MAID Musical comedy in 2 acts by Basil Hood. Music by Walter Slaughter. Theatre Royal, Bath, 4 April 1896; Terry's Theatre, London, 24 April 1897.

Touring manager Milton Bode, who had trouped Hood and Slaughter's *Gentleman Joe* through Britain with great success, mounted a new piece by the same authors at Bath, in 1896, for a 9-week tour. The 9 were followed by a further 19, and the attractions of *The French Maid* proved so potent that the strictly provincial Bode was able to sell off the rights for a London production of the piece the following year. Whilst Bode's tours continued, W H Griffiths mounted *The French Maid* at the unfashionable Terry's Theatre with Kate Cutler cast in the title role alongside several ex-D'Oyly Carte players, and he scored a splendid success. *The French Maid* played a

Plate 129. **Der Fremdenführer.** *Gisela Ehrensperger as Maria in the Vienna Volksoper's latest revival.*

remarkable 480 London performances in its number-two venue.

Hood's plot was (for him) amazingly insubstantial, dealing almost entirely with the caprices and love affairs of Suzette (Andrée Corday/Kate Cutler), who is courted by the gendarme, Paul Lecuire (Arthur Watts/Herbert Standing), the waiter Charles Brown (Windham Guise/Murray King) and, more intermittently, by both Brown's twin brother Jack (Joseph Wilson) and the visiting Maharajah of Punkapore (Percy Percival). Alongside the soubrette, there was also an ingenue, Dorothy Travers (Louie Pounds), paired off, eventually, with the tenor, Lt Harry Fife (Spenser Kelly/Richard Green), and a couple of comical elders—Admiral Sir Hercules Hawser (H O Clarey) and his Lady (Caroline Ewell/Kate Talby). Instead of plot, however, Hood supplied nifty dialogue and some delightful and well-above-average lyrics for songs angled in the same popular line as those for *Gentleman Joe.*

Jack sang of "The Jolly British Sailor" and related the music-hally tale "I've 'er Portrait Next My 'eart" in which his life was saved from a bullet by the thickness of the packet of his various sweethearts' photos in his breast pocket, Hawser declared in Gilbertian style "I'm an Admiral," Charles advised "Do Not Jump at Your Conclusions," Harry got patriotic about "Britannia's Sons" and Suzette had a selection of bright pieces to be delivered brightly, but it was a duet for the twin brothers (The Twin Duet) which turned out to be the song hit of the piece.

As *The French Maid* settled in for a very long career in the British provinces and colonies, a career which almost equaled the phenomenal records of such pieces as *The Lady Slavey, The New Barmaid* and *The Gay Parisienne* (all of which it had outpointed in London), it also found success in all corners of the English-speaking theatre world. On Broadway, where Marguerite Sylva featured in the title role with Charles A Bigelow and Hallen Mostyn as the twins, E E Rice's production ran through 175 performances before going on the road. It was brought back for a three-week repeat the following season (Herald Square Theater 12 September 1898), continuing a merry life around the country for several seasons. In Australia, too, the piece proved highly successful. After Ada Willoughby and Carrie Moore had each given Australians their Suzette, the addition to the cast of London variety and musical-comedy star Ada Reeve gave Williamson and Musgrove's production the kind of a boost that helped to establish *The French Maid* as one of the most popular entertainments of the time.

Australia: Her Majesty's Theatre, Sydney 4 September 1897; USA: Herald Square Theater 27 September 1897

Plate 130. *Comedian H O Clarey as Admiral Sir Hercules Hawser in the original production of the long-running* **The French Maid.**

FRESNAY, Pierre [LAUDENBACH, Pierre] (b Paris, 4 April 1897; d Paris, 9 January 1975). Non-singing star of several musical shows.

Fresnay joined the Comédie-Française direct from drama school and spent the first 10 years of his career (minus wartime service) playing classic and modern roles at the "grande maison" before buying his release at the age of 29. He found a plethora of leading juvenile parts and classic roles from Cyrano de Bergerac to Don Juan awaiting him in the commercial theatre, amongst which were his memorable stage and film portrayal of the wandering Marius in the Pagnol trilogy *Marius, Fanny* and *César.* His introduction to the musical theatre came about through his liaison à la ville with the actress and vocalist Yvonne Printemps, opposite whom he starred, at her insistence, in London and New York in *Conversation Piece* (1934, as Paul replacing Noël Coward), in London in *O Mistress Mine* (1936, Max) and in the French stage (1937) and film (1938) versions of *Les Trois Valses,* versions specially adapted from the German original to allow Fresnay to play a non-singing role. On film, again without singing, he portrayed Offenbach to Mlle Printemps's version of Hortense Schneider (*Valse de Paris*).

FREUND, Julius (b Breslau, 8 December 1862; d Partenkirchen, 6 January 1914). Revue and musical-comedy author at the turn of the German century.

An actor from the age of 19, Freund worked at the Vienna Burgtheater and then in various theatres in Berlin. He subsequently turned to writing and, after an early attempt at opera (*Margitta* w R Bunge, mus: Erich Meyer-Hellmund, Magdeburg 5 December 1889, *Spielmannsglück* mus: L R Herrmann), in 1895 joined Richard Schultz at the Centraltheater in the post of dramaturg. There, in collaboration with Wilhelm Mannstädt and composer Julius Einödshofer, he turned out text and lyrics for a series of musical comedies, including the extremely successful *Eine tolle Nacht,* before moving on, when Schulz shifted theatres, to a similar post at the newly renovated Metropoltheater.

At the Metropoltheater he supplied the texts and lyrics for a long and steady line of topical Berlin revues, written in collaboration with house composers Viktor Holländer (*Neuestes! Allerneustes!* 1903, *Ein tolles Jahr* 1904, *Auf ins Metropol* 1905, *Der Teufel lacht dazu!* 1906, *Das muss man seh'n* 1907, *Hurrah! Wir leben noch!* 1910, *Die Nacht in Berlin* 1911) and Paul Lincke (*Donnerwetter tadellos!* 1908, *Halloh! die grosse Revue* 1909), several of which were later mounted in other centers in suitably localized versions (*Das gündige Wien, Münchner Luft,* etc). He also contributed texts for a number of spectacular musical plays, both adapted from the French and original, of which *Die verkehrte Welt* and *'ne feine Nummer,* with its cast of two hundred, were subsequently played in Viennese versions (ad Krenn, Lindau) at the Venedig in Wien summer theatre and the Theater an der Wien.

He later worked with both the American composer Gustave Kerker, in his attempt to turn out an Operette for the Continental stage, and with the indefatigable Rudolf Nelson on both Operette and revue, and his final works before his death, again for the Metropoltheater, were a rewrite of the highly successful Okonkowski/Jean Gilbert musical *Die elfte Muse* for its Berlin production as *Die Kino-Königin,* and an original piece with a score by Gilbert, the spectacular *Die Reise um die Erde in 40 Tagen.*

1894 **O, diese Berliner** (Julius Einödshofer) Centraltheater 2 September

1895 **Unsere Rentiers** (Einödshofer/w Mannstädt) Centraltheater 16 February

1895 **Eine tolle Nacht** (Einödshofer/w Mannstädt) Centraltheater 4 September

1896 **Eine wilde Sache** (Einödshofer/w Mannstädt) Centraltheater 20 September

1896 **Der Gaukler** (*Les Forains*) German version w Louis Herrmann (Theater Unter den Linden)

1896 **Der Mandarin (von Tsing-ling-ling)** (Einödshofer) Metropoltheater August

1897 **Ein fideler Abend** (Einödshofer/w Mannstädt) Centraltheater 7 February

1897 **Berliner Fahrten** (Einödshofer/w Mannstädt) Centraltheater 4 September

1897 **Die Geisha** German version w C M Röhr (Lessing-Theater)

1898 **Die Tugendfalle** (Einödshofer/ad w Mannstädt) Centraltheater 20 January

1898 **Sterzl in Berlin** (Einödshofer/w Mannstädt) Theater an der Wien, Vienna 2 April

1898 **Das Paradies der Frauen** (*Le Royaume des femmes*) German version with new music by Einödshofer and Bertram Sänger (Metropoltheater)

1898 **Die kleine Michus** (*Les P'tites Michu*) German version w Heinrich Bolten-Bäckers (Metropoltheater)

1899 **Die verkehrte Welt** (*Le Royaume des femmes*) German version w add music by Einödshofer (Metropoltheater)

1899 **Mandanika** (Gustav Lazarus) Elberfeld 21 February

1900 **Der Zauberer von Nil** (*The Wizard of the Nile*) German version (Metropoltheater)

1901 **Schön war's doch** (Viktor Holländer) Metropoltheater 24 August

1901 **Diogenes** (Bogumil Zepler) 1 act Centraltheater 8 October

1901 **'ne feine Nummer** (Holländer, Leo Fall) Metropoltheater 26 December

1902 **Berlin beibt Berlin** (Erik Meyer Helmund) Metropoltheater 17 August

1902 **Die zwölf Frauen des Japhet** (*Les douze femmes de Japhet*) German version with new music by Holländer Metropoltheater 29 November

1903 **Durchlaucht Radieschen** (Holländer) Metropoltheater 31 October

1904 **Die Herren von Maxim** (Holländer/ad) Metropoltheater 29 October

1905 **Die oberen Zehntausend** (Gustave Kerker) Metropoltheater 24 April

1905 **In Lebensgefahr** (Kerker) Walhalla-Theater 1 November

1911 **Hoheit amüsiert sich** (Rudolf Nelson) Metropoltheater 29 April

1912 **Schwindelmeier & Cie** (*The Arcadians*) German version with new music by Nelson Metropoltheater 27 April

1913 **Die Kino-Königin** revised *Die elfte Muse* w Georg Okonkowski Metropoltheater 8 March

1913 **Die Reise um die Erde in 40 Tagen** (Jean Gilbert) Metropoltheater 13 September

FRIEDERIKE Singspiel in 3 acts by Ludwig Herzer and Fritz Löhner-Beda. Music by Franz Lehár. Metropoltheater, Berlin, 4 October 1928.

Having musicalized the fictional love lives of the composer Paganini and the tsarevich of Russia, Lehár took a step to an area rather closer to home in his next Operette. Hard behind the Berlin production of what purported to be a tale about *Casanova,* his librettists picked the celebrated poet Goethe as the next victim for their romantic imaginings. It was a choice which would allow German program-writers of later years to fill page after irrelevant page with learned pieces on the real life of the poet, but at the time (in spite of the fact that Berlin's Kammerspiele had mounted a burlesque called *Goethe* 1 May 1910) the choice was regarded as a rather daring and even slightly unsavory one. In spite of the fact that the show was a made-for-Tauber one, the authors stopped short of calling their piece *Goethe* or even *Johann Wolfgang!* and, this time, it was *Friederike,* the little Alsacian maiden who was the other half of the love story, who became the title.

Friederike (Käthe Dorsch), the daughter of the rector of the village of Sesenheim, is the youthful sweetheart of the would-be poet Goethe (Richard Tauber), who is, for the moment, a medical student. When he wins an appointment as Court Poet to the Grand-Duchy of Saxe-Weimar, he believes that he is at last in a position to get married, but the Duke, because of past experiences, is insistent that he will hire only a bachelor. Goethe decides to refuse the post, but Friederike, knowing how important it is that he should accept, pointedly flirts with his friend Lenz (Curt Wespermann) and, thinking that his love is rejected, Goethe duly goes off to Weimar. Eight years later, passing through Sesenheim, the now-famous poet learns the truth.

The authors called their piece a Singspiel, and displayed a rustic simplicity in the flavor of their libretto which justified that title. The score, too, was made to that measure and, echoing a libretto where passions did not rise and fall in the dramatically doomed fashion of the two earlier pieces, there was a pleasing simplicity to be found in a score altogether less drivingly romantic in tone than was now usual for the composer, from the poet's reciting of his poem ''Sah ein Knab' ein Röslein steh'n,'' the jolly Ländler of Lenz and Salomea (Hilde Wörner), ''Elsässer Kind,'' Lenz's little song to his ''Lämmchen brav'' and Friederike's gently heart-broken ''Warum hast du mich wachgeküsst,'' to the ringing hit song of the piece, Goethe's love song ''O Mädchen, mein Mädchen,'' written to size for Tauber, and destined to become one of Lehár's most enduring sentimental tenor numbers.

In spite of the fact that Tauber's physique had nothing of the romantic to it, and that Dorsch, in the twilight of her musical-theatre career prior to a second stardom as an actress, was some 20 years older than her character and rather lacking in singing voice, the two artists did a great deal to help the Rotter brothers' production of *Friederike* to a considerable success at the Metropoltheater and then at the Theater des Westens (262 performances). He supplied the vocal values, reaching memorable heights in the hit song, while she gave the promise of what was to come in the straight theatre with an equally memorable acting performance. The piece, itself, was also largely liked, and one important Berlin critic crowed delightedly ''at last an Operette that can be listened to without mental ear-muffs on.''

The following year *Friederike* was played in Vienna, with Hans-Heinz Bollmann and Lea Seidl (later Josef Buresch, Betty Werner) starred. Again it scored a success, passing its 200th performance on 4 September 1929, before closing a week later. It returned after the run of Gilbert's *Hotel Stadt-Lemberg* for another two weeks and was given further performances in repertoire in 1930. In that same year, the show was seen widely in the rest of Europe, being mounted in Paris (ad André Rivoire) with René Gebert and Louise Dhamarys starred, in London (ad Adrian Ross, Harry S Pepper) where Lea Seidl was paired with the celebrated opera tenor Joseph Hislop for a rather disappointing 110-performance run under the management of Laddie Cliff, and in Hungary where Andor Szenes's version, starring Tibor Szentmihályi and Hanna Honthy, proved again a success.

America waited until 1937 before welcoming a different English version (ad Edward Eliscu), produced by the Shuberts with Dennis King and Helen Gleason in the starring roles. As in England, however, the now thoroughly well-known hit song proved not to be enough to ensure success for the unshowy piece, and the production lasted only a fair 12 weeks on Broadway.

Käthe Dorsch subsequently played her role opposite Alfred Piccaver at the Volksoper, and *Friederike* was seen again in Vienna in 1945, but the piece did not establish itself as an Operette regular in the same way that the most deeply, colorfully romantic of Lehár's later works did.

A film version was produced by Fritz Friedmann-Friedrich in 1932 in which Bollmann repeated the role he had played in Vienna alongside Mady Christians.

Austria: Johann Strauss-Theater 15 February 1929; France: Théâtre de la Gaîté-Lyrique *Frédérique* 17 January 1930; UK: Palace Theatre *Frederica* 9 September 1930; Hungary: Király Színház *Friderika* 31 October 1930; USA: Imperial Theater *Frederika* 4 February 1937

Film: Fritz Friedmann-Friedrich 1932

Recordings: complete (EMI/HMV), selections (Eurodisc, Telefunken, Philips, Electrola, Decca, etc), selections in Italian (EDM)

FRIESE, Carl Adolf (b Bamberg, 21 October 1831; d Vienna, 24 January 1900). The creator of a long list of important comedy roles in classic Viennese Operette.

The son of an actor/theatre director and a singer, Friese went on the stage at 12 in children's roles. He became a chorus dancer, then a pantomime comedy-dancer in Pest, before first making his mark as a straight comedian in Temesvár. In 1852 the young comedian played at Vienna's Theater in der Josefstadt, and he subsequently appeared at various theatres around Austria and Hungary before becoming a member of the companies at the Vienna Carltheater (1860) and at the Theater an der Wien under Friedrich Strampfer (1863) and subsequently Steiner and Geistinger. Friese was, along with Karl Blasel and Matthias Rott, Albin Swoboda and Marie Geistinger, an important part of the comic backbone of this famous troupe during the years when it introduced the new repertoire of French opéras-bouffes to Vienna, alongside a regular run of native Possen and the earliest important examples of the Viennese Operette.

In the Strampfer years he appeared in Offenbach's *Die schöne Helena* (1865, Agamemnon), *Blaubart* (1866, Oscar), *Die Schäfer* (1866, Beautendon) and *Geneviève von Brabant* (1868, Golo), in Bazin's *Die Reise nach China* (1866, Bonneteau), in *Prinzessin Hirschkuh* (1866, Pelikan), *Theeblüthe* (1869, Fi-Fi) and as the theatre director in *Die falsche Carlotta Patti* (1866, Ullmann). Under Steiner and Geistinger he carried on in the same vein, playing in *Die Grossherzogin von Gerolstein* (1870, Baron Puck) and scoring his biggest hit to date in the 1871 version of *Drei Paar Schuhe* (Julius von Nachtfalter, singing the hit song ''Bei Tag bin ich hektisch, bei Nacht werd' ich elektrisch''). He played in more Offenbach as the Caissier in *Die Banditen* (1871), Marinoni in *Fantasio* (1872), Polycarp in *Die Theaterprinzessin* (1872), Bibel in *Die Wilderer* (1873), Alfonso in *Madame Herzog* (1875) and King Vlan IV in *Der Reise in den Mond* (1876), and created lead comedy roles in the first of Strauss's works: *Indigo* (1871, Romadour), *Carneval in Rom* (1873, Graf Falconi), *Die Fledermaus* (1874, the prison governor, Frank) and *Cagliostro in Wien* (1875, Cagliostro) as well as in Millöcker's *Abenteur in Wien* (1873, Hummel), Jonas's *Die Japanesin* (1874, Kamakuro) and Zeller's *Joconde* (1876, Laird Dunstan Meredith), before briefly leaving the company.

He guested at the Theater an der Wien in 1877 to create the role of the Marquis de Marsillac in *Nanon* and again for Millöcker's *Das verwunschene Schloss* (1878, Graf von Geiersberg) and Offenbach's *Der Brasilianer* (1879, Von Bloomberg) before again joining the resident company, under Maximilian Steiner, in 1880 for another long list of roles in pieces such as *Die hübsche Perserin* (1880, Salamalek), *Apajune der Wassermann* (1880, Fürst Prutschesko), *Die Näherin* (1880, Julius von Sombár), *Die Tochter des Tambour-Major* (1880, Van Hokenbroing, ie, Duc della Volta), *Der Bettelstudent* (1880, Bogumil) and Delibes's *Ein Schotte* (1880, Ducornet). He was Lorenzo XVII in the original Vienna production of *La Mascotte* (1881), Calabazas in Lecocq's *Tag und Nacht* (1882), Chaoura in Offenbach's *Doktor Ox* (1882), Gigonnet in Millöcker's *Ein süsses Kind* (1882) and Bompain in *Lili* (1882), and also appeared as Balthasar Groot in *Der lustige Krieg* and in several other repertoire roles created originally by Felix Schweighofer.

In 1883–84 he went to America with Geistinger, playing principal comedy roles in plays, musical comedies (*Der Zigeuner, Das tägliche Brot, Die Kindsfrau*) and Operetten (Ollendorf, Vicomte in *Lili,* etc), but he soon returned once more to the Theater an der Wien where he created a further series of often important comic roles including Heidekrug in *Der Feldprediger,* Carnero in *Der Zigeunerbaron,* Derrick in the Viennese *Rip* (1885), Dauberval in *Zwillinge,* Philip of Navarre in *Der Hofnarr* (1886) and Graf Varoldi in Brandl's *Der liebe Augustin* (1887), whilst also appearing as Casimir in *Prinzessin von Trapezunt* and in such of his old roles as Frank in *Fledermaus.*

A second American season under the management of Gustav Amberg (Zsupán, Don Onofrio in *Don Cesar, Nachtfalter,* Nasoni in a remade version of *Gasparone,* Rumpelmeier in *Hundert Jungfrauen,* etc), was followed by an engagement at the Carltheater under Franz Steiner, where, between 1887–89, he was seen as Josef Grauperl in *Die Dreizehn,* Captain Gordon in *Der Glücksritter,* Josef Lanner in the Genrebild on the composer's life and music, Don Onofrio, Doctor Track in *Die Jagd nach dem Glück,* Sergeant Meryll in *Capitän Wilson,* Don Riassa in *Farinelli* and Petrovic in Ziehrer's *Ein Deutschmeister.* He also directed many of that theatre's productions during this period, including *Tulipatan, Rikiki, Der Glücksritter, Der Sänger von Palermo, Der Freibuter (Surcouf), Die Jagd nach dem Glück, Ein Deutschmeister* and *Colombine.*

In 1889 he made a third voyage to America, this time accompanied by his son, with the company that opened the new Amberg Theatre in New York. They played *Farinelli* (Pancho), *Der Viceadmiral, Die sieben Schwaben* (Allgauerle), *Die Novize* (Severin Holberg), *Ihr Corporal, Boccaccio, Der Zigeunerbaron, Die Afrikareise, Der lustige Krieg,* Hopp's *Morilla* and much of the Carltheater repertoire, in many of which pieces Friese limited himself to directing and left the lead comedy to his son. When he finally returned to Vienna, however, he found that time had moved on and that, after 50 years on the stage, he was apparently forgotten and out-of-date. He took to the touring circuits until, in 1894, he was engaged as director and chief comic at the Theater in der Josefstadt where he had made his first Vienna appearance, 40 years earlier. It was there that he made his final stage appearances (including Bernard in the French musical comedy *Tata-Toto*) in 1895.

Plate 131. **Trixie Friganza** *and the beauties of the American cities in* The Prince of Pilsen.

An outstanding comic singer, Friese also won himself first-rate laurels as a straight actor, appearing alongside Raimund in the original production of *Der Verschwender* as a young man, and ultimately developing into the best elderly comedy actor-singer of the Vienna musical theatre. In his young days, he also authored several burlesques including *Liebesqualen eines Tanzmeisters* and *Bei der Gaslanterne, oder Einer vom 57 Infanterieregiment* (mus: Johann Baptiste Klerr).

A daughter, **Dora Friese,** and two sons, **Bruno Friese** and **Carl FRIESE jr** (b 1856; d Dresden May 1912), who followed their father on to the Operette stage appeared with him in his American trips. Several other children also went on the stage.

FRIGANZA, Trixie [O'CALLAHAN, Delia] (b Grenola, Kans, 29 November 1870; d Flintridge, Calif, 27 February 1955). Buxom soubrette who successfully carried her musical comedy career through to attractive middle-aged roles and to comedy.

Trixie Friganza began a career in the musical theatre at the age of 19 playing in an Americanized version of Lecocq's *Fleur de thé* (*The Pearl of Pekin*) and toured in *A Trip to Chinatown* (1890, Mrs Guyer) before first appearing in New York in supporting roles in Henry Dixey's Gilbert and Sullivan company (Celia, Lady Saphir), in comic opera (Ganymede in *Jupiter,* 1892), and in opérette (Angelo in *La Mascotte, The Little Trooper, Fleur de lis, La Poupée,* La Paloma in *The Rounders* 1900). In 1895 she toured with *Our Uncle Dudley* and spent the summer soubretting at the Lyceum, Atlanta in comic opera.

In 1900 she won her first notices when she appeared at the Casino Theatre as Mrs Muggins in *The Belle of Bohemia* and with Frank Perley's Comedians in *The Chaperons.* She played Nurse Chloe in *The Belle of Bohemia* in London the following year, toured Europe with the Casino Company in *The Belle of New York* and *The Casino Girl* and took part in the unfortunate reopening of London's Adelphi Theatre with *The Whirl of the Town* before returning home to take up her first major role, touring as the blackmailing Julie Bon-Bon in the American version of Ivan Caryll's *The Gay Parisienne* (*The Girl from Paris*). As her success grew, so too did her embonpoint, but her popularity on the road, where she was known as ''good value,'' proved solid as she took Marie Cahill's *Sally in Our Alley* and the umpteenth company of *A Trip to Chinatown* to the country, appeared regularly in vaudeville, and featured in George Lederer's Broadway burlesque season in *The Darling of the Gallery Gods* (1903, Whoa-San).

She created the role of Omee-Omi in *The Sho-Gun* (1904) in Chicago, and, while Georgia Caine took the part when the show went to Broadway, she went on to play the distinctly superior role of the devastating widow, Mrs Madison Crocker, in *The Prince of Pilsen* (1904) both around America and then in London. She appeared in Chicago's *The Three Graces* (1906, Grace Caryll), *The Girl from Yama, Twiddle-Twaddle* (1906, Mrs van Shaik) and *His Honor the Mayor* and had a genuine Broadway star success when she appeared in Connie Ediss's big-lady role of Caroline Vokins in the American production of *The Orchid* (1907). She confirmed that success the following year in George M Cohan's *The American Idea* (1908, Mrs William Waxtapper), before returning to Chicago for *The Sweetest Girl in Paris* (1910, Mrs Ned Radcliffe), a vehicle she then toured—still, at 40, billed as ''the girl with the baby face''—for several seasons.

Her later career was mostly in vaudeville, but she played in Will Hough's *Lonesome Lassies* (1915) in variety houses and on Broadway in revue on several occasions (*The Passing Show of 1912, Ned Waynburn's Town Topics*), and as late as 1929 in *Murray Anderson's Almanac* as well as on the cinema stage. She made her final New York musical-comedy appearance in *Canary Cottage* (1916, Blanche Moss), imported from the West Coast to Broadway in 1917, although she continued to appear in interstate productions for a number of years before chronic arthritis confined her to a bed for much of the last 15 years of her life.

FRIML, [Charles] Rudolf (b Prague, 8 December 1879; d Hollywood, Calif, 12 November 1972). Leading Broadway composer of romantic musical plays during the 1910s and 1920s.

The Prague-born Friml studied music in his native city from a young age, and made his early career principally as a pianist, touring the world for several years as accompanist to the violinist Jan Kubelik. He had what seems to be an isolated credit as a composer for the theatre when he wrote the music for August Berger's Tanz-Idyll *Auf Japan,* mounted at the Dresden Hoftheater in 1903 (7 June). In 1904 he settled in America where he made a career as a pianist (''wonderful technique and undoubted ability, but [he has a] tendency to appear brilliant at the expense of the music and [is] in danger of breaking the keys'') and also as a composer of light instrumental and vocal music, winning the opportunity to write his first stage musical score when Victor Herbert refused to work for a second time with the ill-behaved *Naughty Marietta* prima donna, Emma Trentini. The score for Arthur Hammerstein's production of *The Firefly* (1912) was allotted to Friml, and songs such as ''Giannina Mia,'' ''Sympathy'' and ''When a Maid Comes Knocking at Your Heart,'' widely heard in that successful show and then outside it, immediately established his reputation. The worldwide hit of the musical farce *High Jinks* (1913) gave the newcomer a second successive triumph and, if the Shuberts' production of *The Ballet Girl*—mounted for Trentini in Albany with its score attributed to Friml—turned into *The Peasant Girl,* with a score more akin to its original (Nedbal's *Polenblut*), on the road to Broadway, the slighted composer was revenged when the star walked out for lust of him and closed the show. His affair with Trentini led to a divorce from his wife of half-a-dozen years, during the proceedings of which it was revealed that the rising composer's royalties ran to ''at times $50,000.''

That figure certainly didn't shrink in the near future, for the 1915 *Katinka* followed *High Jinks* to the corners of the English-speaking theatre world, and Arthur Hammerstein got a healthy 176 Broadway performances and an Australian sale out of *You're in Love. Kitty Darlin,* a musical version of *Sweet Kitty Bellairs* written to suit another singing star, Alice Nielsen, who had been most recently singing in opera, did less well, but *Glorianna,* Catherine Chisholm Cushing's adaptation of her own *Widow by Proxy,* which gave another fine soprano, Eleanor Painter only 96 performances in New York, went onto a good touring life as taken around America by Fritzi Scheff. Friml had further good Broadway runs with the musical plays *Sometime* (1918), in which comedian Ed Wynn was the biggest draw, and *The Little Whopper* (1919, 224 performances), without producing any music or individual numbers which attracted particular attention, but of a series of further such pieces—musical versions of Mary Roberts Rinehart and Avery Hopwood's *Seven Days* as *Tumble In* (128 performances) and Charlotte Thompson's play *In Search of a Sinner* as *June Love* (50 performances), the tale of *Cinders* (31 performances) and *Bibi of the Boulevards,* which failed to reach New York—only *The Blue Kitten,* a remake of the famous French farce *Le Chasseur de Chez Maxim* (140 performances), made any kind of impression.

When Friml switched from supplying tunes for comedy musicals back to the frankly operettic style he had employed so successfully in his pieces for Trentini, his luck changed from the just all right to the extravagantly splendid. His *Rose Marie* (1924, ''Rose Marie,'' ''The Indian Love Call'') became one of the great American international operetta hits not only of its time but of all time, whilst the swashbuckling saga of *The Vagabond King* (1925, ''Only a Rose,'' ''Song of the Vagabonds'') gave him a second major success with a romantic musical and score.

A semi-Ruritanian piece, *The Wild Rose* (61 performances), and a musical version of the play *The Squaw Man* as *The White Eagle* (48 performances) were failures, and a South Seas tale called *Luana* failed in both America and Britain, but Friml swashbuckled to the front again with another genuine romantic piece in the form of a musical version of *The Three Musketeers* (''Ma Belle''). By this time, however, the composer was headquartered in Hollywood. With lyric musicals no longer the vogue, his last Broadway show, *Music Hath Charms* (1934), developed from what was originally intended to be a botched version of *Eine Nacht in Venedig* for another operatic star, Maria Jeritza, was a failure and he abandoned the theatre to do his remaining work, including film versions of *Rose Marie* (three between 1928 and 1954), *The Vagabond King* (1930 and 1956) and *The Firefly* (1937) for the screen.

Friml was at his best in the lyrical, Continental operetta style which he managed to wrap attractively around libretti as diverse as the comedic *Katinka* and the period drama *The Vagabond King* and of which he was one of the most successful exponents in a period where the world's musical theatres were largely dominated by dance-and-comedy musicals and songwriters' shows.

1912 **The Firefly** (Otto Harbach) Lyric Theater 2 December

1913 **High Jinks** (Harbach/Leo Ditrichstein) Lyric Theater 10 December

1914 **The Ballet Girl** (*Polenblut*) Albany, NY 12 November (later *The Peasant Girl* with Nedbal's music restored)

1915 **Katinka** (Harbach) 44th Street Theater 23 December

1917 **You're in Love** (Edward Clark/Harbach) Casino Theater 6 February

1917 **Kitty Darlin'** (Harbach, P G Wodehouse) Casino Theater 7 November

1918 **Sometime** (Rida Johnson Young) Shubert Theater 4 October

1918 **Glorianna** (Catherine Chisholm Cushing) Liberty Theater 28 October

1919 **Tumble In** (Harbach) Selwyn Theater 24 March

1919 **The Little Whopper** (Bide Dudley/Harbach) Casino Theater 13 October

1921 **June Love** (Brian Hooker/W H Post, Harbach) Knickerbocker Theater 25 April

1922 **The Blue Kitten** (Harbach, William Cary Duncan) Selwyn Theater 13 January

1922 **Bibi of the Boulevards** (Cushing) Majestic Theater, Providence 12 February

1923 **Cinders** (Clark) Dresden Theater 3 April

1924 **Rose Marie** (w Herbert Stothart/Harbach, Oscar Hammerstein II) Imperial Theater 2 September

1925 **The Vagabond King** (Hooker, Post) Casino Theater 21 September

1926 **The Wild Rose** (Harbach, Hammerstein) Martin Beck Theater 20 October

Plate 132. **Rudolf Friml**

1927 **The White Eagle** (Hooker, Post) Casino Theater 26 December

1928 **The Three Musketeers** (Wodehouse, Clifford Grey/William A McGuire) Lyric Theater 13 March

1930 **Luana** (Howard Emmett Rogers/J Keirn Brennan) Hammerstein Theater 17 September

1934 **Annina** (aka *Music Hath Charms*) (Rowland Leigh, John Schubert, G Rosener) Majestic Theater 29 December

[The Adventures of] FRITZ, OUR COUSIN GERMAN Musical play in 4 (later 3) acts by Charles Gayler. Music by various hands. Buffalo, NY, 22 November 1869; Wallack's Theater, New York, 11 July 1870.

The most successful of all the comedy-melodramas with songs and dances which were popular provincial and occasionally metropolitan fare in America, Britain and in the English-speaking colonies in the second half of the 19th century, *Fritz, Our Cousin German,* was a vehicle for performer J K Emmet, which allowed its star to run the gamut from extravagant sentimentality to dashing bravado and to broad comedy, whilst pausing regularly to deliver a song, a dance or an instrumental or speciality item.

Emmet starred as the heavily accented Fritz, from Germany, who goes to the United States of America to look for his long-lost sister and the inheritance which their late father left in her charge. On his way, he falls in love with another passenger, Katrina (Georgia Langley), and she proves to be his Achilles heel, for the villainous Colonel Crafton (Charles Fisher), who has adopted Fritz's sister for all kinds of horrid motives, now kidnaps the boy's beloved. Fritz manages to rescue his sister and wed Katrina, but Crafton is not yet done. When the Fritzes have a baby, he whisks Little Fritz away, and the whole chase starts all over again.

The musical content of the show varied during its long life, but in an 1872 playbill it was announced that the third and final scene of Act II would comprise "Fritz's Entertainment" including "Dat's vat's de matter mit Jacob," "Bologna Sausage Boy," "Christine Nilsson Strauss," "Sauer Kraut Receipt with Banjo," "Kaiser, Don't You Want to Buy a Dog?," "Schneider How You Vas?," "Seven Up," "Dat Toy Harmonic" upon which Mr J K Emmet plays Five distinct variations on "Home, Sweet Home," "The Brothers' Lullaby," "Shonnie Vas a Nice Young Man" and "Sauer Kraut is Bully." It was, however, none of these German funnies which was the hit of the evening, but a gentle little lullaby, written by Emmet, and introduced into the piece as the key to recognition between Fritz and his sister. "Emmet's Lullaby" became one of the favorite songs of its era.

When *Fritz* was originally produced, in 1869, Emmet toured it as a star, to stock companies who provided him with a supporting cast that changed with each week and each town, but as the piece proved itself a winner he began to troupe his own company. Emmet played Fritz for the rest of his life, the original play being switched about, expanded and altered with alternative or additional scenes, songs or musical specialities on the harmonica, as it was taken round and round America and as far afield as London's Adelphi Theatre in a "London version" (1872) and Melbourne's Theatre Royal (1874) and Opera House (18 March 1876), where the show broke every record with a run of 65 successive nights and a return later the same year. It was also played on Broadway in a "new" version (1878). Emmet tried a couple of other pieces on the same lines without success—*Carl the Fiddler* (1871), *Max, the Merry Swiss Boy* (1873) and even *Jan, the New German*—before switching to a series of soi-disant sequels, beginning with the most durable (the original apart), *Fritz in Ireland, or The Bellringer of the Rhineand the Love of the Shamrock* (Grand Opera House, Cincinatti 13 October 1879), which allowed Emmet to sing some Irish songs and, of course, a lullaby, and continuing with *Fritz Among the Gipsies* (Olympic Theater, St Louis 11 September 1882), which had him searching this time for a lost brother and introducing another song, "Sweet Violets," which would become a standard, *Fritz the Bohemian* (Academy of Music, Buffalo 5 November 1883), *The Strange Marriage of Fritz, or The Love of an Irish Girl* (Leland Opera House, Albany 15 September 1884) and *[Uncle Joe, or] Fritz in a Madhouse* (14th Street Theater 22 April 1889).

When Emmet had passed by, *Fritz*—or versions of it which used the famous title, if not quite its text—was often taken up by other performers, and the American smaller circuits and the Pacific and colonial theatres saw such actors as Charles Verner, Tom Buckley or, eventually, Emmet's own son (*Fritz in Ireland, Fritz in Prosperity, Fritz in Love, Fritz in Clover,* etc), give their versions of Fritz. The younger Emmet and his wife, Lottie Gilson, later toured a potted *Fritz in a Madhouse* through the vaudeville circuits under the title *Collie's Dilemma* (1900). The cheery hero's last Broadway appearance came in 1905, when Joseph Cawthorn starred in a new Fritz show, *Fritz in Tammany Hall* (Herald Square Theater 16 October).

UK: Adelphi Theatre 7 December 1872; Australia: Theatre Royal, Melbourne 12 December 1874

FROHMAN, Charles (b Sandusky, Ohio, 17 June 1860; d *Lusitania* at sea, 7 May 1915). Successful and popular producer of the turn-of-the-century decades who shared his activities freely between London and New York.

The son of tobacco merchant and enthusiastic first-nighter, Henry Frohman (b Darmstadt, 1827; d New York, 18 October 1899), the young Frohman began his working life in New York as a clerk in the offices of *New York Tribune,* and later of the *Daily Graphic,* before moving into the theatre as a member of the box office staff at Hooley's Theater in Brooklyn. He progressed to the hectic job of advance manager for a number of touring shows, notably Haverley's Minstrels, with which he toured as far afield as Britain, before joining his two brothers, Daniel and Gustave, as assistant managers at Steele MacKaye's Madison Square Theater, New York, organizing the road companies of MacKaye's productions.

He dabbled as a dramatic agent and then as a touring manager before attempting his first New York production, in 1886, with the farce-comedy *A Toy Pistol,* and he had his first success when he picked up the Boston production of Bronson Howard's *Shenandoah* and produced it at New York's Star Theater in 1889 with huge profit. Thereafter, his producing interests, often tied in with those of Al Hayman and/or Messrs Klaw and Erlanger in what became pejoratively known by competitors as "the syndicate," grew flourishingly, at first with New York and nationwide play productions and tours, run to a standard of efficiency and quality which some circuits had not too often seen, and (after an 1891 venture with David Belasco on *Miss Helyett*) from 1895 with musicals.

Early on, Frohman developed close links with the London theatre and virtually all of his Broadway musical productions in the first dozen years of his musical theatre career were imports from London, at that time the thriving center of musical-comedy production. With Hayman, he hosted a Broadway season and American tour by George Edwardes's London company, playing the earliest Gaiety ''musical comedy'' shows, *The Shop Girl* (1895) and *In Town* (1897), and the Daly's Theatre *An Artist's Model* (1895), as well as mounting Edwardes's production of W S Gilbert's *His Excellency* (1895) with a virtually all-English cast, the London hit *Little Miss Nobody* (1898) which folded pre-Broadway, and the English version of *L'Auberge du Tohu-bohu* (1898), before taking the opposite tack and exporting *The Girl from Up There,* an attempt to give the new star Edna May a follow-on to her West End hit in *The Belle of New York,* from New York (1901) to London. It had a limited run, but Frohman, who had been increasing his British production schedule over the previous 18 months, then set up office in England and tried his hand as a producer there.

His first musical-theatre ventures on British soil, a collaboration with George Edwardes on *Kitty Grey,* and a production with Seymour Hicks and his wife, Ellaline Terriss, of the seasonal favorite, *Alice in Wonderland* (1900), were notable successes. Frohman and Hicks then teamed the following Christmas on a different kind of children's Christmas musical play, and *Bluebell in Fairyland* turned out to be the most successful of its kind ever produced in England, with an appeal much wider than the simply juvenile. The tie-up with the Hicks family proved in the years that followed to be even more profitable for their new producer.

Over the next four years, whilst continuing his alliance with Edwardes with joint productions of *Three Little Maids* (London and Broadway), *The Girl from Kays* (USA), *The School Girl* (UK, USA solo) and *The Little Cherub* (USA), he also exported Frederick Mouillot's production of *My Lady Molly* to Broadway (but killed it by quirky casting) and took a major tumble with what should have been a good thing, the London mounting of Hugo Felix's German musical *Madame Sherry.* At the same time, however, he saw the Hicks connection build into a major success with *The Cherry Girl* (1903), the long-running *The Catch of the Season* (1904 and Broadway 1905), a revival of *Bluebell* (1905), *The Beauty of Bath* (1906), the less successful *My Darling* (1907), *The Gay Gordons* (1908) and *The Dashing Little Duke* (1909), whilst his parallel roster of plays produced, amongst other successes, the initial performances of J M Barrie's *Peter Pan.* The profits of *The Catch of the Season* allowed Frohman to construct what he obligingly called the Hicks Theatre (nowadays the Globe) on London's Shaftesbury Avenue, where he installed his coining stars for the first time with the transfer of *The Beauty of Bath.*

He also continued to look after another lucrative star in Edna May, and starred her in the London production of *The Belle of Mayfair,* a musical commissioned from Leslie Stuart, the triumphant composer of *Florodora.* When Miss May walked out because the competition from the show-stealing Camille Clifford threatened her status, Frohman stuck by his star (whilst the money-men Stefano and Agostino Gatti stood by producers' rights to produce and by Miss Clifford) and had another show, *Nelly Neil,* written for Edna (1907). It flopped and she got married and retired.

During all this period of English and exported-English activity, Frohman produced just one almost home-bred musical as part of his continuing heavy Broadway production schedule. The so-so fate of *The Rollicking Girl* (1905, a readaptation of the old German Posse *Heisses Blut,* already seen on Broadway in German and English versions) did not tempt him to try very often in the future. His New York productions remained resolutely and almost exclusively British, although, in a busy schedule, he later commissioned a musequel to the London piece *The Girl from Kays* for Sam Bernard from American writers (*The Rich Mr Hoggenheimer,* 1906) and in 1908 produced his first wholly native piece since *The Girl from Up There,* the cartoon musical *Fluffy Ruffles,* a vehicle for his *Rollicking Girl* and *Little Cherub* star, Hattie Williams. On one occasion he even produced a virtually British musical—a Cosmo Hamilton adaptation of the French play *La Soeur* with music by London's Paul Rubens and Frank Tours called *The Hoyden* (1907)—which had not been played in Britain, as a vehicle for Elsie Janis.

His last British productions—*The Hon'ble Phil* (1908), a collaboration with Edwardes on *A Waltz Dream* (1908, *Ein Walzertraum*) and *The Dashing Little Duke* (1909)—also did indifferently, and his only further London venture, the management of an import of Klaw and Erlanger's production of *The Pink Lady,* though a decided public favorite, proved to have its sums badly done and made a loss on full houses. After a decade straddling the Atlantic, his musical-comedy activity from 1909 was wholly Broadway-based.

Robert Courtneidge's productions of *The Dairymaids* (1907) and *The Arcadians* (1910) and Frank Curzon's *Miss Hook of Holland* (1907) swelled the list of Frohman imports from England alongside a steady stream of Edwardes product—*The Girls of Gottenberg*

(1908), *Kitty Grey* (1909), *Our Miss Gibbs* (1910), *The Sunshine Girl* (1913), *The Girl from Utah* (1914)—and with, or rather behind, Edwardes, Frohman made the switch to Viennese Operette at the moment when the massive swing in popularity away from the English musicals and towards the music of Austria occurred. In fact, he made his switch a little late and missed out on *The Merry Widow,* which Edwardes had turned into an English-language hit, but he brought Broadway its London/ Edwardes successor, *The Dollar Princess* (*Die Dollarprinzessin,* 1909), *The Marriage Market* (*Leányvásár,* 1913), which Edwardes had staged at Daly's Theatre with such success, and Eysler's *Der lachende Ehemann* (*The Laughing Husband*), and he also tried a few Continental pieces which had not come by way of Britain: Leo Fall's *Die Sirene* (*The Siren,* 1911), Berény's *Das Mädel von Montmartre* (*The Girl from Montmartre,* 1912) and Fall's *Das Puppenmädel* (*The Doll Girl,* 1913), which he had botched, Broadway-fashion, and which did not succeed as the others had done.

Alongside this very full schedule of musical productions, Frohman continued to lead an equally busy life as a producer of plays, plays which, like his musicals, were very often imported. But the overseas contact proved his undoing for, at 54 years of age and still at the height of his career in the theatre after 20 years of vast activity, he took the *Lusitania* from New York to Britain in the first year of the First World War, and was drowned when the ship was torpedoed by the Germans.

In 1916 his top musical stars, Julia Sanderson, Joseph Cawthorn and Donald Brian starred, as he had planned, in the Hungarian musical *Sybil* under the billhead "Charles Frohman presents," a billhead which, like London's "George Edwardes presents," lasted a little longer than was credible or, perhaps, tasteful following the deaths of the two friends and collaborators. But it meant that—like Edwardes with *The Maid of the Mountains*—Charles Frohman "presented" one of his most delightful successes posthumously.

Biography: Frohman, D, Marcosson, I: *Charles Frohman, Manager and Man* (Harper, New York, 1916)

FRÜHJAHRSPARADE Operette in 2 acts and 9 scenes by Hugo Wiener based on the screenplay by Ernst Marischka. Music by Robert Stolz. Volksoper, Vienna, 25 March 1964.

Géza von Bolvary's 1934 film *Frühjahrsparade,* featuring Paul Hörbiger, Franziska Gaal, Theo Lingen, Wolf-Albach Retty and Adele Sandrock, plus a lighthearted Viennesey score by Robert Stolz, was such a success in Europe that, in 1940, Universal Pictures decided to make a Hollywood version. *Spring Parade* starred Deanna Durbin, and the hit waltz, "Singend, klingend ruft dich das Glück," was metamorphosed into "Waltzing, waltzing, high in the clouds" (Academy Award nomination). A second German film version, with Romy Schneider, Hörbiger, Magda Schneider and Walter Breuer starred, and a screenplay credited to Marischka and "Gustav Holm" was produced under the title *Ein Deutschmeister* (French: *Mam'zelle Cri-cri*) in 1955 and, a decade later, a combination of the two films, reorganized and enlarged to make up a stage musical, was mounted at the Vienna Volksoper. It held a place in their repertoire for a decade thereafter.

Little Hungarian Marika (Guggi Löwinger), new in Vienna and seeking her way to her aunt's bakery, gets a helping hand from a handsome military bandsman and composer called Willi Sedlmeier (Erich Kuchar). Willi is hoping that the successful singer Hansi Grüber (Mimi Coertse) will introduce his new song, but when he gets tangled up in the love affair between Hansi and the aristocratic Gustl (Peter Minich), nephew of the Court Chamberlain, he finds that "undue influence" has got his song banned. Marika uses her bakery connections, gets the music baked in one of the Emperor's (Fred Liewehr) favorite breakfast rolls, and the result is that Willi's "Frühjahrsparade" march becomes a royal regular and everyone lives happily ever after.

Alongside Marika's well-known waltz, and the march tune which is the be-all of the plot ("Frühjahrsparad' ist heut'"), the score of the show also took in the lovely "Im Frühling, im Mondschein, in Grinzing in Wien" from *Ein Deutschmeister* as a number for Hansi and a selection of numbers gathered from Stolz's song successes.

Frühjahrsparade continued to find performances over the years that followed its Vienna premiere. A French adaptation (ad Marc-Cab, André Hornez) was mounted in Bordeaux in 1973 with Cathy Albert (Marika), Caroline Dumas (Hansi), Bernard Sinclair (Franz, ex- Willi) and Christian Borel (Fritz, ex- Gustl), an Italian version (*Parata di primavera*) was premiered in 1992 at Trieste's Teatro Verdi (27 June), and in 1995 the show was mounted at Berlin's Metropoltheater.

France: Grand Théâtre, Bordeaux *Parade de Printemps* 26 October 1973; Germany: Opernhaus, Leipzig 17 April 1994, Metropoltheater, Berlin 18 May 1995

Films: Hunnia-Universal 1934, Universal 1940 *Spring Parade* (Eng), Erma 1955 *Ein Deutschmeister*

Recordings: selection (Eurodisc), selection in French (SPI)

FRÜHLINGSLUFT Operette in 3 acts by Carl Lindau and Julius Wilhelm based on the play *Coquin de printemps* by Adolphe Jaime and Georges Duval. Music taken from the works of Josef Strauss arranged by Ernst Reiterer. Venedig in Wien, Vienna, 9 May 1903.

Frühlingsluft ("spring air") was a version of the celebrated Parisian farce which also did duty for the libretti of the highly successful Gaiety Theatre musical comedy *The Spring Chicken.* The Viennese version—the first off the blocks—did not let the average down.

Wilhelm and Lindau's text reset the play's action in Vienna and in the present. The lawyer Gustave Landtmann, a model of virtue two thirds of the year, gets annually frisky when spring approaches, and this year his eye falls on the Baroness Ida von Croisé whose husband he is supposed to be representing in their divorce. He attempts to rendezvous with her in the gardens at Blumenau whilst and where his equally frisky father-in-law, Knicklebein, is having a jolly time with the local young folk, headed by the clerk Hildebrandt and the maidservant Hanni. Mother-in-law Apollonia, wife Emilie, and Landtmann's client the Baron follow in pursuit, but all ultimately ends, after a lot of frisking and no fait accompli, in reunions all round, and Landtmann goes back to model living until next spring.

First produced by Gabor Steiner at his summer theatre in the Prater, *Frühlingsluft* was an immediate success. It played right through till the end of September (129 performances) and was promptly transferred to Steiner's winter house, Danzers Orpheum, to continue its run. It returned to the Prater for the summer of 1904, and was played in both houses in repertoire until 1907. It later appeared at the Theater an der Wien in 1912 (26 December), at the Bürgertheater in 1920, and at the Carltheater in 1926 (16 February) with Gustave Werner starred, and was produced with considerable popularity in Germany. A revised version, done over by Bruno Hardt-Warden (text) and August Pepöck (music) was produced at the Bürgertheater in 1944. An Hungarian version (ad Adolf Mérei) was mounted as *Tavasz* (''spring'') at the Magyar Színház in 1903 and revived at the Revü Színház in 1919 (6 September), and the Király Színház hosted the German-language original in 1928 when the Miksa Preger/Alfred Piccaver company played it there in their repertoire.

The show does not seem to have been produced in English, perhaps hampered by the huge success of the not-very-subsequent *The Spring Chicken,* but New York's German-language theatre mounted it in 1905 with Lina Abarbanell making her American debut as Hanni and Curt Weber as Gustave for a fine season of 40 successive nights, and it was reprised under the title of *Spring Zephyrs* at Chicago's German-language theatre as late as 1911.

Reiterer later made up a second score, for the Operette *Frauenherz, oder die kleine Milliardarin* (lib: Carl Lindau), from Josef Strauss's music. Without equaling the popularity of *Frühlingsluft,* it was given performances in Austria (Danzers Orpheum 29 September 1905), Germany and Hungary (*A milliardos kisasszony*). He also put together a piece called *Gräfin Pepi* from Johann Strauss's *Simplicius* and *Blindekuh* scores (Venedig in Wien 5 July 1902).

Germany: 1903; Hungary: Magyar Színház *Tavasz* 6 October 1903; USA: Irving Place Theater (Ger) 5 October 1905

FRYER, Robert (b Washington, DC, 18 November 1920; d Los Angeles, 28 May 2000).

At first an assistant producer in theatre and television, then a casting director, Fryer moved into the production arena in partnership with George Abbott on *A Tree Grows in Brooklyn* (1951), an attractive and almost successful piece with Shirley Booth in its starring role. He had a fine success with his second production, Leonard Bernstein's *Wonderful Town* (1953, Tony Award), and then joined forces with Lawrence Carr with whom he produced a second Shirley Booth piece, *By the Beautiful Sea* (1954), the unsuccessful *Shangri-La* (1956), the Tony-winning mystery musical *Redhead* (1959) and the unsuccessful *Saratoga* (1959) and *Hot Spot* (1963). The partners shared the producing credit on *Sweet Charity* (1966 w Sylvia and Joseph Harris) and the same team combined to mount *Mame* (1966), the musical version of *Auntie Mame,* which Fryer had already produced as a play.

In 1975, after almost a decade away from the musical theatre, Fryer produced another hit in *Chicago,* followed by a share in the Broadway mountings of the splendid *On the Twentieth Century* (1978 as Producers' Circle), *Sweeney Todd* (1979, Tony Award), and the unsuccessful *A Doll's Life* (1982) in a career largely now orientated towards the non-musical theatre.

He subsequently became artistic director of Los Angeles's Ahmanson Theater.

FUGÈRE, Paul (b Paris, 25 January 1851; d Paris, 1 March 1920).

Paul Fugère made his earliest appearances as a light comedian and tenor in vaudeville and opérette, appearing in his twenties, thirties and earlier forties in roles such as Carlo in *La Sorrentine* (1877) at the Bouffes-Parisiens, Prince Moutonnet in *Les Pommes d'or* at the Menus-Plaisirs (1883), Grénicheux in *Les Cloches de Corneville,* Ichabod in *Rip!,* Fructueux in *Le Troisième Hussards,* Lamidou in *La Fée aux chèvres,* Edgard Jolicock in *Le Pays de l'or,* the comical peasant Nicolas in *Le Talisman,* Flagéolet in *Surcouf,* Cocolati in *Panurge,* the juvenile leading man Michel in *Mam'zelle Quat' Sous,* the comical Cabrion in *Les Mystères de* Paris (1887), or the buffoonish Maillochon in *Les Bicyclists en voyage* (1893). His most important creation of this period was the role of the novice, Lancelot, in Audran's *La Poupée* (1896), but the management judging that he was playing this the-

Plate 133. **Paul Fugère** *matured from light-comedy tenor into weighty character-man. Brother* **Lucien Fugère** *went from the café concert to the Opéra-Comique.*

oretically juvenile-lead role for its comedy to the detriment of its tenorizing—just as he had with the part of Mignapour in a recent revival of *Le Grand Mogol*—he was replaced soon after the opening.

Thereafter, with an ever-thickening waistline, Fugère moved on to the comic roles of the repertoire—Larivaudière, the Abbé Bridaine, Don Boléro, Nick Vedder, King Laurent—whilst creating a series of new roles in such pieces as *Le Maréchal Chaudron* (1898, Pigeonnet), *Les Soeurs Gaudichard* (1899, Boniface), *Capitaine Thérèse* (1901, Duvet), the spectacular *Monsieur Polichenelle* (1904, Pickwick), *La Petite Bohème* (1905, Barbemuche), *L'Age d'or* (1905, Louis XV), and *Les Filles Jackson et Cie* (1905, Janicot).

His elder brother, the baritone **Lucien FUGÈRE** (b Paris, 22 July 1848; d Paris, 15 January 1935), emerged from the cafés-concerts (''Sambre et Meuse'') to play in opérette at the Bouffes-Parisiens in the 1870s (*La Branche cassée, La Boîte au lait,* Le Comte in *Madame l'Archiduc, Le Moulin du Vert-Galant,* Saint-Chamas in *La Créole,* Parfait in *M Landry,* etc). In 1877 he joined the company at the Opéra-Comique and there built a famous career which included the premieres of a handful of works by composers better known in the world of opérette—Lecocq's *Plutus* (1886, Plutus), Chabrier's *Le Roi malgré lui* (1887, Duc de Fritelli), Messager's *La Basoche* (1890, a famous portrayal of the comical Duc de Longueville), *Le Chevalier d'Harmental* (1896, Buvat) and *Fortunio* (1907, Maître André), Terrasse's *Le Mariage de Télémaque* (1910, Ulysses), Pessard's *Les Folies amoureuses* (1891, Albert), Chaumet's *La Petite Maison* (1903, Pichon) and Missa's *Muguette* (1903, Klotz)—as well as Saint-Saëns's *Phryne* (1893, Dicéphile), the title role in *Le Bonhomme Jadis* and de Beauval in *La Fille de Tabarin.* He also appeared at the Salle Favart as Père Mathieu in *Le Violoneux* and Jean in *Les Noces de Jeannette* and more operatically as Papageno, Don Pasquale, Leporello and Schaunard. Late in life, he was seen back on the opérette stage, playing Monthabor in a revival of *La Fille du tambour-major* at the Gaîté-Lyrique in 1920.

Biography: Duhamel, R: *Lucien Fugère: chanteur scénique français* (Bernard Grasset, Paris, 1929)

FULLER, Loïe [FULLER, Marie Louise] (b nr Chicago, Ill, 15 or 22 January 1862; d Paris, 2 January 1928). Variety and stage performer who made herself a star with a novelty dance act.

The daughter of Reuben Fuller, a minstrel musician, ''Loie'' was put on the stage from childhood and toured through her teens and early twenties in a variety of theatre and non-theatre shows ranging from temperance lectures (1875) to the "Felix A Vincent Dramatic Co" in Ohio (1878), to Buffalo Bill's show (1882–83) and farce comedy with Murray and Murphy and to a "starring tour" in a play she had written herself (*Larks*), before making her first appearances on the New York stage as a takeover in *The Bridal Trap* (1886) and in the comedy with songs *Humbug* (1886, Nettie, "the fatal gifts of grace and beauty are not hers"). She appeared for a Broadway season alongside Nat Goodwin in the title role of *Little Jack Sheppard,* created in London by Nellie Farren, in a slightly musicalized version of Mark Medford's English farce *Turned Up* (1886), a revival of the on-wheels show *The Skating Rink* (1887, Phoebe) and in the farce-comedy *Big Pony, or the Gentlemanly Savage* (1887, Marie), and then moved on to the realm of musical spectacular to play in the Chicago extravaganza *The Arabian Nights* (1887, Aladdin, "she lacks snap") and in a musical version of Rider Haggard's *She* (1887, Ustane) at Niblo's Garden. She also appeared as Serpolette in *Les Cloches de Corneville* at the over-named Grand Opera House ("sprightly and amusing though not endowed with any too much voice"), at St Louis as Josephine in *HMS Pinafore,* and created the title role of the Missouri comic opera *Florette* (1888) alongside Will Rising and William H Hamilton.

Miss Fuller then began her travels. She went first to the West Indies and then to England, where she presented herself at London's Globe Theatre in a comedy, *Caprice.* It failed badly, and, lowering her sights, she accepted a job as understudy to Letty Lind at the Gaiety Theatre. She played in the musical curtain-raisers traditionally given to the stars' understudies (*His Last Chance, The Woman in Pink*), deputized on occasion for Miss Lind, and repeated her Jack Sheppard at the suburban Elephant and Castle Theatre but, unwilling to wait for promotion under Edwardes's management, she instead struck out as a variety act with a cleverly produced version of Miss Lind's celebrated skirt dance. Whereas Miss Lind had relied for success solely on her graceful dancing and her expertly pretty manipulation of the vast folds of her skirt, "La Loïe Fuller" added a further element: light projections which were played on to the moving dress to make, most notably, an effect of fluttering butterfly wings.

This novelty act caught on with a vengeance and Paris, London and New York all welcomed Miss Fuller as a dancing star. Her act was interpolated into several loose-limbed shows both on Broadway—*Quack MD* (1892), *Uncle Célestin* (1892), *A Trip to Chinatown* (1892)—and in London, where she appeared in *In Town* (1892) and later, simultaneously, in *Morocco Bound* (1893), where her financial demands (50 percent of the gross over £138) made her a bit of a burden on the production budget. *Morocco Bound* replaced her with Letty Lind, and Miss Fuller went on to do her act as a booster for the failing *King Kodak* (1894). She appeared as an isolated act in Broadway's *Panjandrum* (1894) and London's *Little Miss Nobody* (1898), but by and large conducted the remainder of her career in music halls and variety houses as performer in and promoter of dance-related speciality productions. Although she was agreed to be not even the best performer in her own narrow field (a certain Mlle Diana of the Paris music halls apparently took the palm) her habile use of publicity ensured that Miss Fuller remained the best-known both to her contemporaries and to posterity.

In 1920 she put a performance "written by Queen Marie of Romania" on to film under the title *Le lys de la vie.*

A sister, Ida, equally unendowed with looks, and equally hardy, followed her sibling's style and appeared in lit draperies under such banners as "Ida Fuller's High Class Vaudevilles" with (very) limited success.

Autobiographies: *Quinze ans de ma vie* (Paris, 1908), *Fifteen Years of a Dancer's Life* (Herbert Jenkins, London, 1913); Biographies: Brandstetter, G, Ochaim, B M: *Loïe Fuller* (Rombach, Freiburg im Breisgau, 1990), Ewing, M, Current, R N: *Loie Fuller: Goddess of Light* (Northeastern UP, Boston, 1997)

FULL SWING Musical comedy in 2 acts by Archie Menzies, Arthur Macrae and Jack Hulbert. Music by George Posford and Harry Parr Davies. Additional songs by Max Kester, Robert Probst, Harold Purcell and Kenneth Leslie-Smith. Additional lyrics by Davy Burnaby, Barbara Gordon and Basil Thomas. Palace Theatre, London, 16 April 1942.

A British wartime musical, concocted to follow the success scored by Cicely Courtneidge and Jack Hulbert in *Under Your Hat, Full Swing* followed the earlier piece extremely thoroughly by casting the two stars in the same characters—Kay Porter and Jack Millet—and setting them off on another secret mission, replete with disguises, on behalf of the British War Office. Once again, the luscious foreign spy, Carole Markoff (now played by Nora Swinburne), appeared as part of the opposition.

The stars appeared as able seamen, as a pair of Hampstead aesthetes called Dr and Mrs Patmore ("Lovely to Be Loose"), and Courtneidge gave an impersonation of a gross and grotesque secretary to parallel her frightful maid in the first show. She also had the most successful song, a little sentimental George Posford/Harold Purcell piece about "The Wedding of the Gingerbread Boy and Girl." Most of the music, however, went to Gabrielle Brune as someone called Sally ("Mamma, Buy Me That," "Follow My Dancing Feet," "Cleo from Rio," etc).

Full Swing, without coming up to its predecessor as a piece, proved happy wartime entertainment and played 468 times at the Palace before the team replaced it with more of the same.

FUNNY FACE Musical comedy in 2 acts by Fred Thompson and Paul Gerard Smith. Lyrics by Ira Gershwin. Music by George Gershwin. Alvin Theater, New York, 22 November 1927.

Aarons and Freedley's production opened at the Shubert Theater in Philadelphia on 11 October 1927 in a version by Thompson and drama critic-cum-humorist Robert Benchley under the title *Smarty.* It didn't work, and by the time that it reached their Alvin Theater on Broadway, after four weeks in Philadelphia and another in Wilmington, it had undergone some severe changes. It was, in fact, ''an almost entirely new show and score.'' A bundle of songs, one of which was the later famous ''How Long Has This Been Going On?'' had been dropped (and replaced by five new ones), and comedian Victor Moore and juvenile leading man Allen Kearns had been brought in to stiffen up the cast. Known play-doctor Paul Gerard Smith had replaced Benchley on the bill, and the show was now called *Funny Face,* after one of its songs.

Thompson had fallen back on one of the musical theatre's most over-used plots as the basis for his book—the stolen jewels syndrome, an item which hadn't been precisely new when Owen Hall had used it for *A Gaiety Girl* before the turn of the century. Jimmy Reeve (Fred Astaire) has locked up the jewels belonging to his ward, June Wynne (Gertrude MacDonald), in his safe along with the diary to which another of his wards, Frankie Wynne (Adele Astaire), has confided some rather exaggerated thoughts. Frankie wants her book back, so she gets her boyfriend, aviator Peter Thurston (Allen Kearns), to help her burgle the safe. But, at the same time, there are some real thieves on the prowl. Since they were played by William Kent (Dugsie Gibbs) and Victor Moore (Herbert), there were more comical complications and disguises involved than there was menace, as the story and its characters followed the jewels—which had been mistakenly taken from the safe by Peter—to the final curtain. Betty Compton played Jimmy's third ward, Dora, who paired off with Dugsie.

The songs for *Funny Face* included two which became firm favorites: Frankie and Peter's duet '''S Wonderful'' and the oft-reprised title-song, first sung by Jimmy to Frankie. The juvenile pair had another winner in their ''He Loves and She Loves,'' whilst Jimmy wooed June with ''My One and Only'' and donned evening dress to lead a line of top-hatted chaps and frilly frocked chorines in ''High Hat.'' The more conventional comedy was represented by Kent's send-up of psychiatry in ''Tell the Doc'' and by a burlesque of the manners of the characters of Sinclair Lewis's *Babbit* in ''The Babbit and the Bromide'' (Jimmy/Frankie).

Funny Face did not turn out to have quite the pull that *Lady, Be Good!,* the first Aarons/Freedley/Gershwins/Thompson/Astaires collaboration, three years earlier, had had, but it did almost as well as the producers' previous year's Gershwin production, the rather less textually conventional *Oh, Kay!* It played a healthy 244 performances at the Alvin Theater, and soon after its producers shipped it off to London where, in conjunction with Alfred Butt and Lee Ephraim, they reproduced the show at the Prince's Theatre, with the Astaires now supported by Leslie Hendon (Dugsie), Sydney Howard (Herbert), Bernard Clifton (Peter) and Eileen Hatton (June). The Astaires proved as popular as they had been on their two previous visits to London with *Stop Flirting* and *Lady, Be Good!,* and the piece was played 263 times at the Prince's and later at the Winter Garden Theatre. In Australia, however, without its magnetic stars, *Funny Face* proved a flop. Ernest Rolls's production, with Janette Gilmore, Jim Gerald and Charley Sylber featured, played a season at Sydney's St James Theatre but did not go on to Melbourne, and it was five years before a brief season of *Funny Face,* mounted by the young producer Garnet Carroll, gave that city a three-week glimpse of the show (Apollo Theatre 26 September 1936).

Funny Face was revived at Connecticut's Goodspeed Opera House in 1981 (17 June) and in 1983 a ''new Gershwin musical'' was produced, using the title of *Funny Face*'s ''My One and Only'' as its title and 5 numbers from the 13 which made up the show's original score as part of its musical pasticcio. It did away with the never-very-wonderful book, but replaced it with one which was not much less conventional. However, *My One and Only,* mounted, like its predecessor, largely as a song-and-dance show, had a fine 767-performance run on Broadway with Tommy Tune and Twiggy starred and it was subsequently toured, with Sandy Duncan and Lucie Arnaz taking turns in its feminine lead role.

A 1957 Paramount film entitled *Funny Face* starred Audrey Hepburn and Fred Astaire who, along with four songs (supplemented by three others by Roger Edens and Leonard Gershe and one from *Oh, Kay!*), was the only element it had in common with the stage show.

UK: Prince's Theatre 8 November 1928; Australia: St James Theatre, Sydney 23 May 1931

Recordings: London cast (World Record Club), original cast reconstruction (Smithsonian)

FUNNY GIRL Musical in 2 acts by Isobel Lennart based on incidents in the life of Fanny Brice. Lyrics by

Bob Merrill. Music by Jule Styne. Winter Garden Theater, New York, 26 March 1964.

A romanticized bit-of-a-biomusical of the famous revue comedienne Fanny Brice, produced by the star's son-in-law, *Funny Girl* focused very largely on the performer's relationship with the shady but charming Nick Arnstein to whom she was, for a period, married. The first act followed Fanny (Barbra Streisand) through her early attempts to get into the theatre, and through her discovery of both her comic talent and of Arnstein (Sydney Chaplin), who turns up every so often in her life but always leaves as suddenly as he arrives. She rises to a job in the *Ziegfeld Follies,* to stardom and, with determination, to a romance with Arnstein which ends in marriage. When his interminable financial castles in the air come tumbling down, Fanny, earning star wages in the theatre, is able to pay the bills, but that is not enough for the man. He shrugs off a safe job she sets up for him to go for another big flashy gamble, and this time he ends up in prison. Fanny has waited for him to come out to take up their life together but when, in the final scene, he arrives in her dressing room, it is to say goodbye. Kay Medford played Fanny's mother, Danny Meehan was Eddie, her first and faithful coach, and Jean Stapleton featured as the neighboring Mrs Strakosh.

The accompanying songs threw up two pieces which proved particularly popular outside the show. Miss Streisand made a worldwide hit out of the reaching ballad ''People,'' which posited that ''people who need people are the luckiest people in the world,'' whilst her driving double-curtain number (it closed both acts) ''Don't Rain on My Parade,'' a piece of blind, bulldogging optimism, was long popular as a cabaret and concert item. There were plenty of other, less extractable, pieces which made their effect in the show: the practical point-of-view of her mother and Mrs Strakosh which queries ''If a Girl Isn't Pretty'' what is she going to do in show business, Fanny's first flush of optimism in ''I'm the Greatest Star,'' the proud ''Who Taught Her Everything She Knows?'' of Eddie and Mrs Brice, and the delightfully comic-romantic supper table scene ''You Are Woman, I Am Man.'' All these winning musical moments came in the first act, but the less musically weighted second part also included Fanny's ''Sadie, Sadie'' in which she revels in being a married lady, as well as the final reprise of ''Don't Rain on My Parade.''

The biggest armament in the success of *Funny Girl* was, undoubtedly, its star. Barbra Streisand's funny, touching and superbly sung performance as Fanny Brice was one of the performances of an epoch and, although she left the show well before the end of its 1,348-performance Broadway run, *Funny Girl* had, by then, become thoroughly established. Whilst Mimi Hines took

Plate 134. **Funny Girl.** *Barbra Streisand as Fanny Brice.*

over on Broadway and Marilyn Michaels headed out a touring company, Miss Streisand repeated her performance in London alongside Miss Medford and Michael Craig as Nick. However, Bernard Delfont and Arthur Lewis's production folded after 112 performances when it was confirmed that the star was pregnant. In 1968 she took up the role of Fanny once more, in a film version which used seven of the show's numbers, topped up by such period numbers as ''Mon Homme,'' ''Second-Hand Rose'' and ''I'd Rather Be Blue.'' The film, which featured Omar Sharif as Nick and Miss Medford in her original stage role, was a success, and ''Second-Hand Rose'' became a hit all over again.

J C Williamson Ltd mounted a production of *Funny Girl* in Australia, with Jill Perryman starred as Fanny alongside Bruce Barry and Evie Hayes, which followed a fine Sydney season with four months in Melbourne in 1966, and the show has been subsequently regularly produced in regional theatres in English-speaking countries. One of America's latter day *Funny Girl*s was film nymphet Pia Zadora.

The first German-language production (ad Heidi Zerning) was mounted at Coburg in 1992 with Carol Lentner as Fanny and the piece was subsequently seen at Berlin's Metropoltheater with Christina-Agnes Weiske in the starring part.

Plate 135. **A Funny Thing Happened on the Way to the Forum.** *''Everybody Ought to Have a Maid'' is the opinion of the gentlemen of ancient Rome.*

UK: Prince of Wales Theatre 13 April 1966; Australia: Her Majesty's Theatre, Sydney 6 March 1966; Germany: Landestheater, Coburg 22 November 1992, Metropoltheater 19 May 1994; Austria: Stadttheater, Baden bei Wien 18 January 1997

Film: Columbia 1968

Recordings: original cast (Capitol), film soundtrack (Columbia)

A FUNNY THING HAPPENED ON THE WAY TO THE FORUM Musical comedy in 2 acts by Burt Shevelove and Larry Gelbart based on the works of Plautus. Music and lyrics by Stephen Sondheim. Alvin Theater, New York, 8 May 1962.

A musical comedy more than worthy of that description, *A Funny Thing Happened on the Way to the Forum* was constructed from the standard characters and situations which were used, used and reused to make up the classic Roman comedies of the Plautian-Terentian age. As in the works of Plautus, the most important character is the wily slave or ''servus,'' whose preoccupations in life are money and that elusive dream of freedom. Several of the other characters in the piece were christened by the names of their Latin types—the senex (old man), domina (mistress of the house), the miles gloriosus (the boastful soldier, also a Plautus play)—other names, like Erronius and Hysterium, spoke for themselves (which was just as well, for hysterium in Latin means the womb)—as did those of the leading juveniles, Hero and Philia, for all that they were Greek rather than Latin.

Pseudolus (Zero Mostel) and Hysterium (Jack Gilford) are slaves in the household of the frisky Senex (David Burns), his stringent wife Domina (Ruth Kobart), and his pubescent son Hero (Brian Davies). Hero falls in love with the maiden Philia (Preshy Marker), whom he has glimpsed at the window of the neighboring courtesan-keeper, Marcus Lycus (John Carradine), and, during his parents' absence, he bribes Pseudolus to help him win her. Unfortunately: (1) Philia has already been sold to the Miles Gloriosus (Ron Holgate) and (2) Senex arrives home unexpectedly. Pseudolus ends up trying to get the young lovers away together whilst simultaneously preparing a recondite passion-potion for the randy Senex, who thinks he has an assignation with a virgin, and staving off the pressing demands of the soldier that he produce his bought-and-paid-for merchandise. When things are at their most farcically complex, a splendidly Plautian denouement intervenes: Philia and the Miles Gloriosus are discovered to be the children of neighbor Erronius (Raymond Wallburn), stolen in childhood by pirates. So Hero gets his virgin and Pseudolus his reward—freedom.

Gelbart and Shevelove's tight, farcical libretto was illustrated by some equally funny songs: the opening assertion that, although the troupe performs tragedy on other occasions, it will be "Comedy Tonight," the old men's drooling routine "Everybody Ought to Have a Maid," Philia's admission that she has no talent except to be "Lovely," Hysterium's unconvinced and unconvincing declaration that "I'm Calm," the father and son's comical sizing-up of each other's sexual potential in "Impossible," and some ringing burlesque bass-baritone music ("Bring Me My Bride," Funeral Sequence) for the soldier which was as fine and funny as anything of its kind in musical theatre.

Harold Prince's production of *A Funny Thing* was the winner of both the 1963 Tony Award for Best Musical and a 964-performance run on Broadway, and a London mounting, which Prince co-sponsored with designer Tony Walton and Richard Pilbrow, ran almost as long. Frankie Howerd was London's Pseudolus, teamed with former Crazy Gang member "Monsewer" Eddie Gray (Senex), *Carry On* filmstar Kenneth Connor (Hysterium), famous farceur Robertson Hare (Erronius), Jon Pertwee (Lycus) and Leon Greene (Miles), and the deftly cast production played 762 performances before the show went on to become a durable favorite in provincial houses.

Paris saw *Sur le chemin du forum* (the joke of the title didn't work in French) at the Palais-Royal in 1964, J C Williamson Ltd mounted a production in Australia also in 1964, with a cast headed by another famous musical comedy veteran, Clifford Mollison, and several German language versions have been produced under such titles as *Ein verrückter Tag auf dem Forum, Die Spinner die Romer, Zustände wie in alten Rom.* Evidently the title joke doesn't work in German either. In 1966 United Artists and Richard Lester produced a film version. Mostel repeated his stage role alongside Phil Silvers, for whom the part of Pseudolus had been originally intended, in the role of Lycus. Gilford was again Hysterium, Michael Hordern played Senex, Buster Keaton was a memorable Erronius and the juvenile pair were played by Michael Crawford and Annette André. Only five musical numbers were used.

In 1972 Silvers finally got to play the role he had been scheduled to have, when David Black mounted a revival of a slightly revised version of the show at the Lunt-Fontanne Theater (30 March, 156 performances) and, whilst the show continued a life as a solid part of the standard revivable repertoire, a Chichester Festival Theatre revival was taken to London in 1986 (14 November). Howerd repeated as a now rather aged Pseudolus alongside Ronnie Stevens (Hysterium), Patrick Cargill (Senex) and Fred Evans (Lycus) through 51 performances of an unstylish reproduction of much of the original staging.

There was nothing aged, however, about Broadway's 1996 revival of the piece (St James Theater 18 April). Nathan Lane's lively young Pseudolus teamed with Lewis J Stadlen (Senex), Mark Linn-Baker (Hysterium), Ernie Sabella (Lycus) and Cris Groenedaal (Miles) to make *Forum* a hit all over again. However, when Lane moved on to other successes with the show still steaming along happily, the producers resorted to gimmicky "star" casting and—in a gesture that killed much of the show's intelligent parody—replaced him with film actress Whoopi Goldberg. The revival totaled 715 performances.

In the wake of this revival, a fresh production (ad Frank Thannhäuser) was mounted at Berlin's Theater des Westens with Ilja Richter as Pseudolus, as *A Funny Thing Happened on the Way to the Forum* continues on, 40 years later, as popular and effective as it was in its very first performances.

The works of Plautus, specifically the *Miles gloriosus,* had previously been used as the basis for the German musical play *Der Weiberheld* (Erika Wilde, Magdeburg 15 September 1956).

UK: Strand Theatre 3 October 1963; France: Théâtre du Palais-Royal *Sur le chemin du forum* 1964; Australia: Theatre Royal, Sydney 18 July 1964; Germany: Theater im Reichskabarett *Ein verrückter Tag auf dem Forum* 22 February 1972, Theater des Westens *Zustände wie in alten Rom* 16 March 1997; Austria: Graumann Theater *Die Spinner die Romer* 17 June 1992

Film: United Artists 1966

Recordings: original cast (Capitol), London cast (HMV), film soundtrack (United Artists), Mexican cast, New York revival cast (EMI)

FUN ON THE BRISTOL, or A Night on the Sound [or A Night at Sea] Musical comedy oddity in 3 acts by George Fawcett Rowe (uncredited). Newport, RI, 26 January 1880; 14th Street Theater, New York, 9 August 1880.

One of the internationally most popular pieces of its kind, this American-bred "musical comedy oddity" with

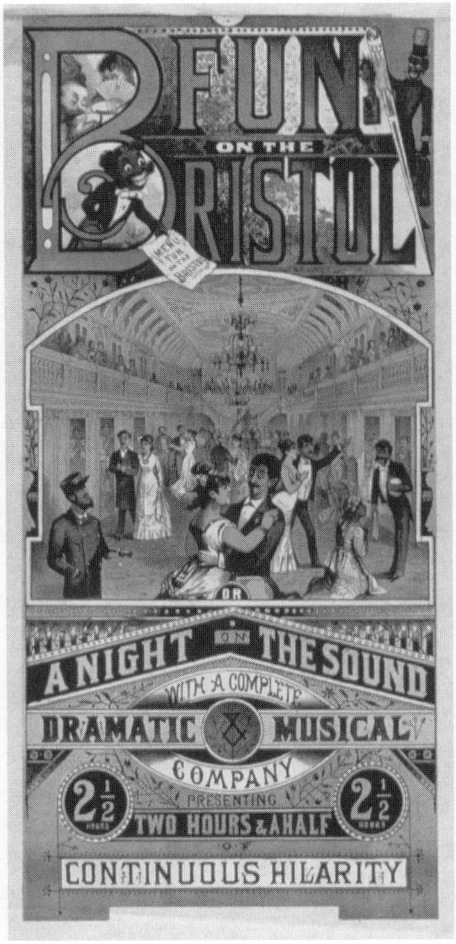

Plate 136. **Fun on the Bristol.** *The Widow O'Brien on the road.*

its mixture of low comedy, pantomime, variety acts and concert ("the music is culled from *The Royal Middy, Boccaccio, Madame Favart, Cups and Saucers,* etc") had an indifferent start to life, and it was played for only two weeks in the sophisticated purlieus of New York in its first season. But it got up steam as it trouped the roads of America and soon made itself so popular that copycat productions (*Fun on the Pacific, Fun on the Brussels*) were soon to be seen following it round the country. *Fun on the Bristol* not only toured America thereafter for years, it went even further and was successfully played in English-language theatres throughout the world, mostly and most effectively with its instigator, the actor John F Sheridan, starred famously in the dame role of the Widow O'Brien.

Such plot as there was to the piece was that of the Widow O'Brien's search for a replacement husband. The other characters of the imbroglio included the unscrupulous singing master, Count Menaggio, who is after Bridget's money, her two daughters, Nora and Dora, by her deceased mate, and the black maid, Bella Thompson. The title came from the fact that (imitating the concurrent *The Tourists in a Pullman Palace Car* which went through a similar routine on board a train) the characters were all dumped aboard the steamer *Bristol* for the course of the evening. The story was merely "a peg on which to hang a variety programme—comic songs, nigger sketches, grotesque dances, stump speeches, operatic selections, burlesque marches, a guitar solo, etc" and its music was of the movable kind, ranging as it did from a selection from Gounod's *Faust* to "O, Dem Golden Slippers."

The piece was produced by Henry C Jarrett (once of Jarrett and Palmer and *Black Crook* fame) and the original cast featured William Courtleigh, Mark Smith, Frank Tannehill, Myron Calice, Henry Saville, Agnes Hallock, Marion Fiske and Alicia Jourdain alongside the overwhelmingly starred Sheridan.

Once it was established at home ("over a thousand performances in America and Canada," the bills boasted mendaciously), the show was transported to Britain. Edward Rice paid Jarrett $3,000 for a one-third share in the speculation and it was as "Jarrett and Rice's American Comedy Company" that Sheridan, Carrie Daniels (Dora), Lulu Evans (Nora) and Tannehill in his original role opened at Manchester. They took the provinces by storm with their merry, un-English entertainment, moved swiftly to the West End and held up there for a season of over three months, before returning to the touring circuits. Sheridan became a bankable star and his show a durable feature of the number-two (and occasionally number-one) English circuits. Typically, Jarrett never paid Rice a cent on his investment, and was dragged to court for the umpteenth time in his career by his irritated "partner."

Sheridan subsequently took "his" piece to Australia, then back to America and wherever he went others took up the role of the Widow in ever changing "versions" of his show when he moved on ("Mr Richard Hicks, the only REAL Irishman who has attempted to play the part . . . the only REFINED representative of the Widow O'Brien in this country," etc). In 1887 he reasserted himself in the role in Britain when he presented and starred alongside Edith Vane in a fresh London season of the show at the Gaiety (5 September) and the Opera Comique, but he then took himself and his show back to Australia (1889) and it was there his later days were largely spent. He carried his favorite character on into a second show, *Bridget O'Brien Esq* (aka *Mrs O'Brien Esq*) in which he played in Australia and America (Bijou Theater 31 October 1892), but the original Widow O'Brien show remained the most popular standby for its creator up to his death.

In America, *Fun on the Bristol* continued to get showings even after Sheridan's final departure for Australia, and it was seen under a variety of titles (*The Widow O'Brien,* etc) in musical comedy seasons through into the new century.

UK: Theatre Royal, Manchester 15 May 1882, Olympic Theatre 7 August 1882; Australia: Gaiety Theatre, Sydney 16 March 1884

FURBER, Douglas [SULTAN, Lewin Michael] (b London, 13 May 1885; d London, 19 February 1961). Ubiquitous lyricist for nearly 30 years of British shows.

Furber made his earliest steps in the theatre as a writer for and performer in revues, the first of which was the 1917 piece *150* in which he supplied the words to Australian songwriter Archie Emmett Adams's tunes and played the show's 24 performances at the Ambassadors' Theatre. Things looked up soon after, when he made his first venture into musical comedy with the lyrics for two successful C B Cochran French imports, the opéra-bouffe *Carminetta* and the slightly-less-saucy-than-before *Afgar,* and he had equally good fortune with his first original musical, Emmett Adams's touring piece *Pretty Peggy* (1919), which Cochran subsequently brought into the West End in the following year. His version of *Afgar* got a Broadway showing, *Pretty Peggy* was exported to Australia (New Princess Theatre, Melbourne 6 October 1923), and their author's career was well and truly launched.

He continued his performance career in revue, notably under the management of André Charlot, for whom he played both in London (*A to Z*) and on Broadway (*The Charlot Revue of 1926,* his last stage appearance) and also played in musical comedy on the West End stage, taking supporting roles in the Jack Buchanan productions of *Battling Butler* (1922, Ted Spink) and *Boodle* (1924, Dixon), before giving up performing to concentrate on a solid 20-year career as a lyricist and occasional librettist for London musicals and revues.

His first West End successes were with the series of musicals produced by and for Jack Buchanan, a series with which he was associated from its beginning with *Battling Butler* through the ex-German *Toni* (co-adaptation and lyrics), *Boodle* and its three biggest successes, *That's a Good Girl* (librettist, co-lyricist), *Stand Up and Sing* (lyricist, co-librettist) and *Mr Whittington,* up to the Ralph Benatzky pasticcio *The Flying Trapeze,* and the final *It's Time to Dance,* 17 years after the first.

In the late 1920s and 1930s most of London's principal musical producers had use for Furber's services at one stage or another: for Clayton and Waller he did some additional material for *Virginia* and co-wrote the book and all the the lyrics for *Silver Wings;* for Jack Hulbert he contributed lyrics and, with Dion Titheradge, the book for the Sophie Tucker vehicle *Follow a Star;* for Firth Shephard and Leslie Henson the English book and most of the lyrics for the ex-German *Nice Goings On,* an English rewrite of Broadway's *Little Jessie James* as *Lucky Break,* a bit of the book of their Gaiety shows *Swing Along, Going Greek* and *Running Riot,* and most of Shephard's *Wild Oats* and *Sitting Pretty;* and for Lee Ephraim part of the book of the Cicely Courtneidge/Bobby Howes *Hide and Seek.* His most singular success, however came with the songwords for his only musical for Lupino Lane, *Me and My Girl,* which produced, beyond its title song, the celebrated "Lambeth Walk."

On the revue side he contributed more or less material to the Vaudeville Theatre's *Yes* and the Little Theatre's *The Little Revue Starts at 9* (1923), *Charlot's Revue* (1924), the successful Adelphi piece *The House That Jack Built* (1929, co-book, additional lyrics), the brief *Let's Raise the Curtain* (book only), the Savoy Theatre's unmemorable *And On We Go* (1937) and, following the war, giving a larger preference to revue over the musical-comedy stage for the meanwhile, George Black's triumphant London Hippodrome piece *Black Velvet* (1939), Shephard's long-running *Shephard's Pie* (1939), *Up and Doing* (1940) and *Fun and Games* (1941), the Coliseum's *It's Foolish But It's Fun,* the Prince's Theatre *The Magic Carpet* and Leslie Henson's Winter Garden *The Gaieties* (1945).

For his final work he returned to the musical theatre to provide much of the book and all of the lyrics for Fred Emney, whom he had so happily suited in Shephard's shows, in his star vehicle *Big Boy.*

Furber also made lesser contributions to *Fifinella* (1919, "addditional witticisms by"), *Now and Then, A Southern Maid, The Cabaret Girl* and *Soldier Boy* (*Az obsitos*), supplied additional lyrics for the revival of *The Maid of the Mountains* and lyricked such popular songs as Emmett Adams's "The Bells of Saint-Mary's" and "God Send You Back to Me."

He also wrote screenplays for both British and American films, including the screen versions of *The Maid of the Mountains* (1932 w Lupino Lane) and *That's a Good Girl* (1933).

1917 **Carminetta** English lyrics (Prince of Wales Theatre)

1919 **Afgar** English lyrics (London Pavilion)

1919 **Sons of the Sea** (H Sullivan Brooke/w J Peterman) 1 act Shoreditch Empire

1919 **Pretty Peggy** (Archie Emmett Adams/Charles Austin, Arthur Rose) Empire, Kilburn 25 August

1921 **Gabrielle** (G H Clutsam, Archibald Joyce/w Helen Williams, Bertrand Davis, et al) Glasgow 26 December

1922 **Battling Butler** (Phil Braham/Stanley Brightman, Austin Melford) New Oxford Theatre 8 December

1923 **The Cousin from Nowhere** (*Der Vetter aus Dingsda*) English version (Prince's Theatre)

1923 **Toni** (*Der Fürst von Pappenheim*) (Hugo Hirsch/w Harry Graham) Theatre Royal, Hanley 6 August; Shaftesbury Theatre 12 May 1924

1924 **Boodle** (Braham, Max Darewski/Sydney Blow, Douglas Hoare) Prince of Wales Theatre, Birmingham 26 December; Empire Theatre 10 March 1925

1925 **The Bamboula** (Albert Szirmai, Harry Rosenthal/w Irving Caesar/Guy Bolton, Harry M Vernon) His Majesty's Theatre 24 March

1925 **Cloclo** English lyrics w Graham (Shaftesbury Theatre)

1927 **Up with the Lark** (Braham/w Hartley Carrick) Adelphi Theatre 25 August

1928 **That's a Good Girl** (Phil Charig, Joseph Meyer/w Ira Gershwin, Desmond Carter) London Hippodrome 5 June

1928 **Virginia** (Jack Waller, Joseph Tunbridge/w Herbert Clayton, R P Weston, Bert Lee) Palace Theatre 24 October

1928 **Lucky Girl** (Charig/w Weston, Lee) Shaftesbury Theatre 14 November

1930 **Silver Wings** (Waller, Tunbridge/w Dion Titheradge) Dominion Theatre 14 February

1930 **Follow a Star** (Vivian Ellis/w Titheradge) Winter Garden Theatre 17 September

1931 **Stand Up and Sing** (Charig, Ellis/w Titheradge) London Hippodrome 5 March

1933 **Nice Goings On** (Arthur Schwartz/w Frank Eyton) Strand Theatre 13 September

1933 **Mr Whittington** (John Green, Tunbridge, Waller/w Clifford Grey, Greatrex Newman) Alahambra, Glasgow 30 November; London Hippodrome 1 February 1934

1934 **Lucky Break** (*Little Jessie James*) revised version Strand Theatre 2 October

1935 **The Flying Trapeze** (Ralph Benatzky, Mabel Wayne/w Desmond Carter, Frank Eyton/Hans Müller ad) English version Alhambra Theatre 4 May

1936 **Swing Along** (Martin Broones/Graham John/w Bolton, Fred Thompson) Gaiety Theatre 2 September

1937 **Going Greek** (Sam Lerner, Al Goodhart, Al Hoffman/w Bolton, Thompson) Gaiety Theatre 16 September

1937 **Hide and Seek** (Ellis, Lerner, Goodhart, Hoffman/w Bolton, Thompson) London Hippodrome 14 October

1937 **Me and My Girl** (Noel Gay/w Rose) Victoria Palace 16 December

1938 **Wild Oats** (Gay/w Firth Shephard) Prince's Theatre 13 April

1938 **Running Riot** (Ellis, w Bolton, Shephard) Gaiety Theatre 31 August

1939 **Sitting Pretty** (Manning Sherwin) Prince's Theatre 17 August

1943 **It's Time to Dance** (Kenneth Leslie-Smith, et al/w Rose) Winter Garden Theatre 22 July

1945 **Big Boy** (Carroll Gibbons/w Fred Emney, Max Kester) Saville Theatre 12 September

FURST, William W[allace] (b Baltimore, 25 March 1852; d Freeport, NY, 11 June 1917).

Conductor at Ford's Theatre in his native Baltimore, Furst saw his maiden stage work, a topical piece about the invention of the electric light, produced there in 1879 with a top-notch cast inclduing Caroline Richings, Edwin Hoff, Joseph Greenfelder and Pierre Bernard. He went on to work as musical director of Charles Ford's Comic Opera Co (1882), and later for a number of years of San Francisco's Tivoli Theater, for which he composed a version of Rider Haggard's *She*—which played a splendid 51 nights there before, in a rewritten version by William Gillette, making its way east—and an operatic version of Sardou's *Theodora.* Furst toured as musical director of E E Rice's Surprise Party (1890), worked as conductor at New York's Star Theater, for some nine years as head of music at the Empire Theater (1893–1902) for Frohman, and then from 1902 as general musical director with David Belasco, supplying incidental music, and songs when required, for the plays on each house's bill. Amongst these were included *The Darling of the Gods,* J M Barrie's *The Little Minister* with Maude Adams starred, William Gillette's famous *Sherlock Holmes,* Mrs Leslie Carter's *Adrea,* the oriental spectacle *The Yellow Jacket,* and Thomas Broadhurst's disastrous play version of Longfellow's *Evangeline* (1913). He also composed the scores for a number of stage musicals, the most successful of which was the long-touring Thomas Q Seabrooke extravaganza *The Isle of Champagne.* His other works included a vehicle for Lillian Russell (*Princess Nicotine*), revue for the Casino (*The Merry World*), and new scores for *Les 28 Jours de Clairette* as a starring piece for Della Fox (*The Little Trooper*), and for the less successful French opérettes *Pervenche* and *La Gardeuse d'oies.*

Furst was married to musical comedy actress Mamie Taylor, and subsequently to singer Lotta Nicol.

1879 **Electric Light** (William B Hazelton, Edward Spencer) Ford's Theater, Baltimore 25 August

1887 **She** (comp & arr/R C White, James O Barrows) Tivoli Opera House, San Francisco 4 July (subsequently rewritten by William Gillette, 1888)

1889 **Theodora** (Fritz La Fontaine) Tivoli Opera House, San Francisco 14 September

1890 **R.I.P., or Many a Slip Twixt the Cup and the Lip** (William Gill) Columbia Theater, Chicago 23 July

1892 **The Isle of Champagne** (Charles Alfred Byrne, Louis Harrison) Star Theater, Buffalo 16 May; Fifth Avenue Theater 5 December

1893 **The Honeymooners** (C M S McLellan) Columbia Theater, Boston 23 October

1893 **Princess Nicotine** (Byrne, Harrison) Casino Theater 5 December

1894 **The Little Trooper** (*Les 28 Jours de Clairette*), new score for American version by Clay Greene (Casino Theater)

1895 **Fleur de lis** (*Pervenche*) (ad J Cheever Goodwin) Palmer's Theater 29 August

1897 **A Normandy Wedding** (aka *Papa Gougou*) (*La Gardeuse* *d'oies*) new score for American version by Goodwin, Byrne (Opera House, Detroit, revised version Herald Square Theater 21 February 1898)

DAS FÜRSTENKIND Operette in a Vorspiel and 2 acts by Victor Léon adapted from *Le Roi des monatgnes* by Edmond About. Music by Franz Lehár. Johann Strauss-Theater, Vienna, 7 October 1909.

The Athenian Count of Parnes is not simply the Count of Parnes, he is Hadschi Stavros (Louis Treumann), a kind of Greek Robin Hood, sought by the police and, in particular, by the commissioner Perikles (Max Brod). The confident American commandant Bill Harris (Erich Deutsch-Haupt) bets Perikles that he will capture Stavros in 10 days, little realising that the bandit is the Count and the father of his beloved Photini (Grete Freund). In the pursuit of his calling, Stavros kidnaps the comical botanist Dr Hippolyte Clérinay (Carlo Böhm), and the English tourists Mrs Gwendolyne Barley (Marie Gribl) and her daughter Mary-Ann (Mizzi Günther), with whom he falls in love. His band also overwhelms Bill and his sailors, but, preoccupied by Mary-Ann, he lets the tables be turned: he is captured by the American and thus wins him his bet. However, Perikles is balked of his prey, for when Bill realizes that the Count and the bandit are the same person, he lets him go. And so he can happily wed his Photini without her ever learning about her father's double life.

Lehár's score for his bandit musical was made up largely of ensemble music, with Stavros's 9/8 Pallikarenlied (''Lange Jahre, bange Jahre'') and Mary-Ann's entrance number, beginning with a mountain echo section before segueing into the waltz ''Kindchen sei hübsch brav,'' being the principal solos of the piece alongside a Robber March, a pair of duets for the two stars (''Ich diene so gerne den Damen,'' ''Jung und alt'') and another for the juveniles (''Papa, ich bin verliebt'').

With the famous *Die lustige Witwe* pair of Treumann and Günther leading the cast, Leopold Müller's production of *Das Fürstenkind* brought, not unsurprisingly, a first real hit to the recently opened Johann Strauss-Theater. It passed its 100th performance on 15 January 1910 and its 200th on 28 April before closing the next night, and it was subsequently seen for a few performances at the Theater an der Wien (30 September 1911) with the leading pair supported by Betty Fischer (Photini) and Ludwig Herold (Bill), and again in 1914. In 1920 the piece was brought back at the Apollotheater (17 November) with Treumann in his original role.

Das Fürstenkind was rather overshadowed by the huge success of Lehár's *Der Graf von Luxemburg,* produced just a month later, and although the show was duly produced in most main theatre centres it was the composer's other piece which attracted the success. Andor Gábor's Hungarian *Hercegkisasszony* was produced at the Magyar Királyi Operaház, a French version (ad Maurice Ordonneau, Jean Bénédict) was staged at Brussels's Théâtre Molière (21 December 1913) as *Le Roi des montagnes* with Guillot (Stavros), Alice Favier (Mary-Ann), Eva Retty (Photini) and Nandès (Bill) and was subsequently played in the repertoire at Paris's Trianon-Lyrique the following year, whilst Henry Savage mounted a weakly adapted version (ad Carolyn Wells) which, rather than taking the more fun title of *The Brigand and the Banker* adopted for Tom Taylor's English version of About's play, or the masculine (and originally announced) *The King of the Mountains,* was for some reason entitled *The Maids of Athens.* Only Photini and her old nurse (scarcely a ''maid''!) of the cast-list are Greek—the other ladies in the play are all English! The Broadway cast was headed by Elbert Fretwell, Albert Pellaton, Cecil Cunningham and Leila Hughes, and the production was scuttled after 22 performances. London made do with just *The Count of Luxembourg.*

In 1932 a revised version of *Das Fürstenkind* entitled *Der Fürst der Berge* was produced as Berlin's Theater am Nollendorfplatz (23 September).

Hungary: Magyar Királyi Operaház *Hercegkisasszony* 20 December 1910; Germany: Gross-Berlin Theater 27 December 1912; France: Trianon-Lyrique *Le Roi des montagnes* 18 February 1914; USA: New Amsterdam Theater *The Maids of Athens* 18 March 1914

Recording: selection (Roscoe)

FURTH, George (b Chicago, 14 December 1932). At first an actor on the straight and musical (*Hot Spot,* 1963) stages, and in cinema, Furth made a highly successful entry into the musical theatre as an author with the text for the 1970 musical *Company* (Tony Award). He subsequently returned to the area twice more, providing the libretto to the Liza Minnelli vehicle *The Act* and adapting Moss Hart and George S Kaufman's play *Merrily We Roll Along* as a musical.

1970 **Company** (Stephen Sondheim) Alvin Theater 26 April

1977 **The Act** (John Kander/Fred Ebb) Majestic Theater 29 October

1981 **Merrily We Roll Along** (Sondheim) Alvin Theater 16 November

G

GABAROCHE, [Charles] Gaston (b Bordeaux, 29 September 1884; d Marseille, 28 August 1961).

A popular singer and songwriter (''C'était une petite blonde,'' ''Le Regret,'' ''La Femme à la rose,'' ''Les Beaux Dimanches de printemps,'' etc), Gabaroche had a long and varied career as a performer (La Lune Rousse, Les Deux Ânes, La Pie-qui-chante, etc), which included a considerable amount of work in revue and in musical comedy, starring in both Paris and/or the provinces in such successful musical-theatre pieces as *Pouche, Madame, Qu'en dit l'abbé,* his own *Enlevez-moi!..* and *Deux fois deux, Mademoiselle Star, Plume au vent* and *Au pays du soleil.*

In 1923 he contributed to the score of the highly successful musical comedy *Je t'veux* and, through the 1920s and 1930s, continued to write songs for the extremely light and small-scale musical comedies typical of the era. His most considerable success came with Robert Gallois's production of the 1929 *Enlevez-moi!..,* a piece which was subsequently revived (1935) and filmed.

In 1919 he combined with Saint-Granier to build and, briefly, operate the Théâtre de la Potinière where they produced several revues (*Danseront-ils, Vas-y-voir,* etc) and other entertainments written by themselves.

1920 **Je t'adore** (Saint-Granier) 1 act Théâtre de la Potinière 1 December

1923 **Je t'veux** (w Fred Pearly, René Mercier, Albert Valsien/Battaille-Henri/Wilned, Marcel Grandjean) Théâtre Marigny 12 February

1924 **Mon vieux** (w Pearly, Josef Szulc, Raoul Moretti, Pierre Chagnon, Albert Chantrier, Laurent Halet/André Birabeau, Battaille-Henri) Théâtre de la Potinière 18 December

1927 **Ketty Boxeur** (Pierre Varenne/Luc Mourier) Théâtre de la Potinière 1 June

1929 **Gaston** (Fernand Beissier, Louis Hennevé) Comédie Caumarti

1930 **Enlevez-moi!..** (Varenne, Max Eddy/Raoul Praxy, Henri Hallais) Comédie Caumartin 4 October

1932 **Deux fois deux** (Eddy/Praxy) Théâtre Daunou 28 January

1932 **Azor** (w Pearly, Chagnon/Eddy/Praxy) Théâtre des Bouffes-Parisiens 16 September

1936 **Faites ça pour moi** (Eddy/Praxy) Théâtre Antoine 25 January

1938 **J'hésite** (w Pearly/Praxy) Théâtre Antoine 16 February

A GAIETY GIRL Musical comedy in 2 acts by Owen Hall. Lyrics by Harry Greenbank. Music by Sidney Jones. Prince of Wales Theatre, London, 14 October 1893.

George Edwardes had tentatively heralded a move away from the ''new burlesque'' and into something a little bit more like a modern musical play with his production of the up-to-date tale of London and backstage life *In Town* (1892). With *A Gaiety Girl* he took a further step towards a vertebrate comedy with songs and dances in a piece which, similarly, mixed society and theatre folk to the advantage of the latter. The story goes that lawyer-turned-journalist Jimmy Davis met Edwardes on a train and remarked unfavorably on the libretto of *In Town,* declaring he could do better. Edwardes told him to do so. The result was a text with a minimal plot line about a stolen comb, which relied for what action it had on the marital maneuverings of a group of social and theatrical characters. It was, however, written in a satirical, snappy and occasionally risqué style and with grateful roles for the cast which Edwardes engaged: popular comedy actress Lottie Venne as the handsome widow, Lady Virginia Forrest; comics Eric Lewis and Harry Monkhouse as a judge and a clergyman respectively, both getting the worst of the librettist's satire; statuesque baritone Hayden Coffin as hero; French soubrette Juliette Nesville as a French maid; tall and beautiful Maud Hobson as the wrongly accused actress (it was the French maid who did it); and the Savoy Theatre's original *Gondoliers* Casilda, Decima Moore, as ingenue.

Sidney Jones, whom Edwardes had remarked as a new talent, was commissioned to write the score. He turned out a number of songs to Harry Greenbank's lyrics which actually had something to do with the show's story, but won his biggest single song success with Coffin's straightforward ballad ''Sunshine Above.'' Coffin, however, in a way that characterized his career, interpolated a song he had heard in another show, Henry Hamilton's *Captain Fritz,* and it was that number, the patriotic "Tommy Atkins," which became the hit of the show.

Edwardes had a last-minute rush to get Hall's text past the censor, but succeeded, although he was later obliged to alter the character of the clergyman after a complaint to the Lord Chamberlain, apparently from an over-touchy but influential Archbishop. The audiences took with a will to Hall's wicked wit, Jones's lively music and Edwardes's top production values and cast, and *A Gaiety Girl* was an immediate and much-discussed success. It ran 11 months at the Prince of Wales Theatre after which Edwardes shifted it to the new Daly's Theatre, following the definitive departure of Augustin Daly's drama company. It settled in there for another three months (413 performances in all), thus setting the scene for the famous Daly's series of musicals which would follow. It also, more than either *In Town* or *Morocco Bound,* which had preceded it, set the style and tone for the species of musical comedy in which George Edwardes subsequently dealt at the Gaiety Theatre and elsewhere, and which swept the English-speaking world, in particular, as the most popular form of musical theatre entertainment in the last part of the 19th century.

Davis, under his pseudonym of "Owen Hall," went on to have a remarkable career in the musical theatre, as did the short-lived Greenbank and, most especially, the third *Gaiety Girl* neophyte, Sidney Jones, who was to become resident composer to Daly's Theatre at the top of a memorable career.

Edwardes toured a British company with *A Gaiety Girl* to America and Australia (the tale of this tour is told in the little book *Round the World with A Gaiety Girl*) with a cast headed by Maud Hobson, Harry Monkhouse, Leedham Bantock, Charles Ryley, W Louis Bradfield and Decima Moore, playing a season on Broadway, where the show was later reproduced with a largely American cast (Daly's Theater 7 May 1895, 31 performances), and throughout both countries, and in 1899 he staged a London revival to fill in the gap created by Greenbank's death and the late delivery of a new Daly's show (5 June, 58 performances). Miss Venne repeated her original role alongside Rutland Barrington, H Scott Russell, Huntley Wright, Hilda Moody and Aileen d'Orme but, in spite of the insertion of even more of the updatings to which it had been subjected ever since opening, it did not have the same effect as it had had the first time round. Caught in the shadow of its more developed Daly's successors, it was nevertheless compared fondly and favorably by the press with more recent "musical comedies."

The show also got a production in Germany where *Ein fideles Corps* (ad Jean Kren, Eduard Jacobson) was mounted at the Adolf-Ernst Theater with London danseuse Rose Bachelor featured alongside Herrn Guido Thielscher, Weiss, Haskerl, Klein and the Fräuleins Seemann, Fischer and Frühling.

USA: Daly's Theater 18 September 1894; Germany: Adolf-Ernst Theater *Ein fideles Corps* 25 December 1894; Australia: Princess Theatre, Melbourne 13 April 1895

Literature: Bantock, G, Aflalo, F G: *Round the World with A Gaiety Girl* (John McQueen, London, 1896)

GALLAGHER, Helen (b Brooklyn, NY, 19 July 1926). Lively dance-and-song girl who led a fuller and more variegated career in her years in the American musical theatre than almost any other.

Miss Gallagher made her first Broadway appearance as a takeover in the revue *The Seven Lively Arts* (1944) and, after an early career as a chorus dancer (*Mr Strauss Goes to Boston, Billion Dollar Baby, Brigadoon*) progressed to featured roles in *High Button Shoes* (1947, Nancy), the revue *Touch and Go* (New York and London) and *Make a Wish* (1951, Poupette), and the dance-and-comedy role of Gladys Bumps in the 1952 revival of *Pal Joey* (Tony Award).

She subsequently took the title role in the 1953 musical *Hazel Flagg,* appeared regionally as Annie Oakley and Miss Adelaide, and as Sharon in *Finian's Rainbow* at the City Center, and replaced Carol Haney as Gladys in Broadway's *The Pajama Game* (1955). She returned to the City Center to play Meg Brockie in a revival of *Brigadoon* and Ado Annie in *Oklahoma!,* played the three Broadway performances of *Portofino* (1958, Kitty) and again went interstate to play Lola (*Damn Yankees*) and Nellie Forbush and to create the role of Daisy Dean in *Molly Darling* at the St Louis Muny before taking up her most memorable Broadway role as Nickie ("Big Spender") in *Sweet Charity* (1966). She succeeded Gwen Verdon in the title role of that piece, toured with the show, and then returned to Broadway to replace Jane Connell as Agnes Gooch in *Mame* (1968).

Another short-lived flop, *Cry for Us All* (1970, Bessie Legg), preceded a major success in the role of Lucille Early ("You Can Dance with Any Girl," "Where Has My Hubby Gone Blues") in the 1971 revival of *No, No, Nanette,* a performance which won her a second Tony Award as best supporting actress.

She subsequently appeared off-Broadway in the cabaret musical *Tickles by Tucholsky,* played Arisone in a musical version of *Le Misanthrope* produced at the New York Shakespeare Festival (1977), Maggie Simpson in the short-lived *A Broadway Musical* (1978), succeeded Ann Miller in the burlesque show *Sugar Babies* (1981), played off-Broadway in *I Can't Keep Running in Place* (1981), as *Tallulah* (1983) and played a one-woman show, *Tallulah Tonight,* at off-Broadway's American Place Theater (1988), whilst simultaneously keeping in the eye of that public which watches daytime television as Maeve Ryan in the soap *Ryan's Hope.*

GALLMEYER, Josefine [TOMASELLI, Josefina] (b Leipzig, 27 February 1838; d Vienna, 2 February 1884). ''Die fesche Pepi''—''Jolly Josie''—one of the most popular and famous stars of the Viennese musical stage of her time, best remembered today for the now fictionalized-up tales of her battles with fellow star, Marie Geistinger.

The daughter of theatre folk, ''Pepi'' Gallmeyer began her career on the stage at 15, playing in Brünn, Budapest and Hermannstadt, making an early Viennese appearance alongside Nestroy at the Theater in der Josefstadt, and working between 1860 and 1862 at Temesvár. When Temesvár manager Friedrich Strampfer moved to Vienna to take over the running of the Theater an der Wien, Gallmeyer was engaged to go there as soubrette, and she remained at that theatre for three years starring in such Possen as *Der Goldonkel* and *Eine gezogene Kanone* until the success of Marie Geistinger led to a well-publicized rivalry and, eventually, to Gallmeyer's departure. She appeared in Berlin in Geistinger's role of Boulotte (1867, *Barbe-bleue*) and on returning to Vienna joined the company at the opposition Carltheater. There she came into her own, soon challenging for the position of the biggest popular singing star in town as she featured in such roles as Vienna's original Gabrielle in *Pariser Leben,* Catherine in *Toto* and Régina in *Die Prinzessin von Trapezunt.*

In 1874 she joined Julius Rosen in the direction of the Strampfertheater, where she appeared, amongst other roles, as Ophelia to Felix Schweighofer's *Hammlet* in Julius Hopp's burlesque of Shakespeare, and alongside the same comedian in a local version of *Die Familie Trouillat* (1875). The venture turned out a financial disaster, however, and she returned first to the Carltheater (*Vindobona,* Lucrezia in *Graziella/La Petite Mariée*) and then, for several years, to the Theater an der Wien to star in a series of Possen including *Die Landpomeranze, Ihr Corporal, Plausch net Pepi, Die Trutzige, Die Böhmin* and *Die Gypsfigur,* whilst also creating the role of Regerl, alongside Girardi, in Millöcker's successful Operette *Das verwunschene Schloss* (1878) and introducing the Viennese versions of the title role of *La Mascotte* (*Der Glücksengel*) and Angelina in *Der grosse Casimir.*

In 1882 she played in *Herzblättchen* at the Carltheater before following the example so successfully set by her old rival, Geistinger, and taking a tour to America. She appeared at New York's Thalia Theater with a repertoire of her most successful pieces and a supporting company including such stars as Tewele and Knaack and, in a season dogged by absences through illness, she was seen in *Der Goldonkel, Ihr Corporal, Die Näherin* and *Die Prinzessin von Trapezunt* as well as a selection of comedies. The illness soon proved not be a tactical one but stomach cancer and, not long after her return home in May 1883, she died. It was reported that 100,000 people followed her funeral procession to Vienna's Protestant cemetery.

Plate 137. **Helen Gallagher** *as the heroine of the St Louis Muny's production,* Molly Darling. *Her partner is Richard Tone.*

In 1905 a Volksstück, *Josefine Gallmeyer,* was produced at the Vienna Lustspieltheater (26 September) and in 1921 a Singspiel of the same title, written and composed by Paul Knepler, was mounted by Oskar Fronz at the Wiener Bürgertheater with Rosy Werginz playing the role of Pepi.

Biography: Waldstein, M: *Erinnerungen an Josefine Gallmeyer* (R Jacobsthal, Berlin, 1885)

GALLOIS, Germaine [GALLAIS, Jeanne] (b Paris, 28 February 1869).

Originally employed in the dressmaking business, Mlle Gallois made her first appearance on the stage as a slave girl in *Adam et Ève* at the Nouveautés and played in revue at the Menus-Plaisirs and at the Renaissance in *Isoline* (1888), before disappearing from the stage for several years for ''personal reasons.'' On her return, however, she quickly began to rise through the ranks. She played in *Madame l'Archiduc* at the Menus-Plaisirs, *Les Pilules du Diable* at the Châtelet, in two plays at the Ambigu, and then took up the role of Métella in Fernand Samuel's revival of *La Vie parisienne* at the Variétés. After further ventures into spectacular opéra-bouffe (Fantasia in *Le Voyage dans la lune,* 1892, etc), revue (Rose d'Espignolles in *Voyage dans Paris,* 1891) and drama at the Porte-Saint-Martin, where she appeared as Madame de Pompadour in *Latude,* the Empress Marie-Louise in *Napoléon* (with a Méhul song) and as other such regal beauties, she returned to the musical stage for a long series of fine roles in *L'Enlèvement de la Toledad* (1894, Baronne Trippmann), *La Duchesse de Ferrare* (1895, Angèle), *La Saint-Valentin* (1895, Maud), *La Dot de Brigitte* (1895, Hortense), *Monsieur Lohengrin* (1896, Cécile), *Ninette* (1896, Ninon de l'Enclos), *L'Oeil crevé* revival (Fleur de Noblesse), *Le Pompier de service* (1897, Fabienne), *Les Petites Barnett* (1898, Suzannah) and *La Mascotte* revival (1901, Bettina) at the Gaîté as well as a continuing ration of revue.

She kept up a regular presence in all areas of the theatre in the early years of the 20th century, acting as a commère in revue and being seen in such opérettes as Lincke's *Lysistrata* (1904, Lysistrata) at the Moulin-Rouge, *Les Dragons de l'imperatrice* (1905, Lucrèce), *Paris, ou le bon juge* (1906, Vénus), as Mlle Lange in *La Fille de Madame Angot* at the Variétés and the Théâtre de la Gaîté and as Isoline and Briscotte in the 1908 revival of *Geneviève de Brabant.* She moved on to slightly more senior parts (*Miousic* 1920, *Amour de Princesse* 1923, Madame Cocardier in *J'adore ça* 1925, Madame d'Épinay in *Mozart* 1925, *Monsieur Dumollet,* etc) in the later years of a full and fine career on the Parisian stage.

Mlle Gallois was equipped not only with a fine voice and notable acting charms, but also with a figure which was the marvel of Parisian womanhood. This figure, however, was not acquired without effort. She wore an amazing corset to give her a fashionable shape in spite of being, without its help, ''blonde avec une tête de poupée, un front bombé, des yeux étincelants, une bouche éblouissante . . . une exquise chanteuse d'opérette . . . la plus belle de toutes les belles artistes des Variétés à la grand epoque.''

Mlle Gallois was married to the comedian Guy of the Variétés.

GANDOLFO Opérette in 1 act by Henri Chivot and Albert Duru. Music by Charles Lecocq. Théâtre des Bouffes-Parisiens, Paris, 16 January 1869.

An early and successful short piece by composer Lecocq and his equally up-and-coming librettists, *Gandolfo* was an old-fashioned little tale borrowed from Boccaccio and decked out with some charming music. The Gandolfo (May) of the title is a jealous old legal man with a young wife, Angela (Mlle Boulanger). Angela is rather taken by the young musician Stenio (Mlle Joly) who sings under her window, and altogether less by the pushy Captain Sabino Sabrinardi (Arnould) who pursues his suit by letter, but it is the latter who is enterprising enough to be delivered to her room in a crate in search of a kiss. When Gandolfo finally finds his wife with the musician in her room, she pretends he is being pursued by Sabrinardi and needs legal help, but the tables are turned when Sabrinardi discovers that old Gandolfo is the mysterious person who has been having an affair with his wife. The errant husband can only engage Stenio as his wife's music teacher, invite everyone to supper and promise never to be jealous again.

The score featured a little serenade for the musician (''Nina, ma bien aimée'), a trilly ariette for Angela (''L'homme est fort''), a bullocking bit for the Captain (''C'est moi qui suis l'invincible''), a quartet leading into a drinking song (''C'est le vin qui fait que soudain'') and a finale.

First introduced at the Théâtre des Bouffes-Parisiens, *Gandolfo* was revived at the tiny Salle Taitbout in 1875 and was also played in several European houses in both French and in German. However, the only English-language performances seem to have been those given in two vastly contrasting sets of circumstances—in England at Drury Lane, as curtain-raiser to a production of *A Winter's Tale,* with Messrs Lascelles and Howard, Agnes Lyndhurst and Miss Lonsdale featured, and in America by an all-women's company under the management of leg-show merchant M B Leavitt (ad Marius de Lazare) with Marie Sanger, Amy Ames, Tiny Vining, May Stembler and Marie Mülle featured, on a double bill with *An Adamless Eden.*

Austria: Strampfertheater 28 December 1872; UK: Theatre Royal, Drury Lane *Angela, or a Woman's Wit* 28 September 1878; USA: Comedy Theater 18 December 1884

GANNE, [Gustave] Louis (b Buxières-les-Mines, 5 April 1862; d Paris, 13 July 1923). French conductor and composer whose limited output of stage works included two pieces which have survived into the modern repertoire.

The young Louis Ganne made his earliest theatre venture as a composer of ballet music, and his *Les*

Sources du Nil was mounted at the Folies-Bergère when he was but 20 years old. In the years that followed he composed other such pieces for the Folies-Bergère and the Casino de Paris (*Volapuk, Au Japon, Le Réveil d'une Parisienne, L'Abeille et la fleur,* etc) as well as songs, drawing-room and dance music and marches. He won particular success with the march ''Le Père la Victoire''—a piece based on a theme from *Volapuk,* and the ''Marche Lorraine.'' At the same time he worked as a conductor at the Parisian Bals de l'Opéra and in several spa towns, and made his first steps as a composer of vaudeville (*Tout Paris*) and of opérette.

Ganne found an enduring success with the circus musical *Les Saltimbanques* (1899), which became a great favorite in the French provinces following its initial Paris run, and in 1906, having installed himself since the previous season at Monaco at the head of a little orchestra of what he described as ''soloists'' for the ''Concerts Louis Ganne,'' he had his second successful opérette presented at the local Opéra. *Hans, le joueur de flûte,* artistically a much more satisfying piece than the tuppence-colored *Saltimbanques,* went on from its Monégasque premiere to productions round the world.

Hans, le joueur de flûte did not lead, however, to further successes. An ancient Egyptian comic opera *Rhodope,* also produced in Monaco, did not provoke the same interest, playing some 40 first-run Parisian performances when it eventually found a home at the Théâtre des Variétés, and the composer's last major produced piece, *Cocorico,* composed to a rather palely routine libretto about an old monarch with a young wife and the need to produce an heir, was seen only 28 times at the Théâtre Apollo in 1913.

Amongst Ganne's other theatre credits were a little opérette *Phryne,* first produced at the Royan Casino at later at the Olympia with Cléo de Merode and Louise Willy starred; the completion of the score for the late Robert Planquette's last work, *Le Paradis de Mahomet*; the incidental music (w Olivier Métra) for Catulle Mendès' 1906 play, *Glatigny*; and a continuing supply of dance music (*Cythère, Les Arles,* etc). An opérette, *La Belle de Paris,* with a pasticcio score made up from Ganne's works, was mounted in Paris in 1921 for a run of 110 performances.

Ganne got a rare Broadway hearing when his ''pantomime ballet'' scena *Au Japon* (given, for some reason in Italian as *Nel Giappone*) was featured in the revue *The Revue of Revues* (Winter Garden 27 September 1911) with Albertina Rasch in its principal role.

1891 **Tout Paris** (Georges Duval) Théâtre du Châtelet 16 June

1892 **Rabelais** (Oscar Méténier, Dubut de la Forêt) Nouveau Théâtre (Casino de Paris) 25 October

1893 **Les Colles des femmes** (Henri Kéroul, Adolphe Jaime) Théâtre des Menus-Plaisirs 29 September

1899 **Les Saltimbanques** (Maurice Ordonneau) Théâtre de la Gaîté 30 December

1902 **Miss Bouton d'or** (Michel Carré) Olympia 14 October

1904 **Phryne** (Auguste Germain) Casino, Royan; Olympia September

1906 **Hans, le joueur de flûte** (Maurice Vaucaire, Georges Mitchell) Monte Carlo 14 April; Théâtre Apollo 31 May 1910

1910 **Rhodope** (Paul Ferrier, Paul de Choudens) Monte Carlo 13 December; Théâtre des Variétés, Paris 24 December 1914

1913 **Cocorico** (Georges Duval, Maurice Soulié, P Jailly) Théâtre Apollo 29 November

1916 **L'Archiduc des Folies-Bergère** (Lucien Boyer, Fernand Rouvray) 7 October

1921 **La Belle de Paris** (pasticcio/Boyer, Rouvray) Théâtre Apollo 22 October

GARINEI, Pietro (b Trieste, 25 February 1919). Italy's godfather of postwar musical theatre.

Pharmacist Garinei went into partnership with journalist **[Ales]Sandro GIOVANNINI** (b Rome, 10 July 1915; d Rome, 26 April 1977) in 1944 to produce a revue, *Cantachiaro,* at Rome's Teatro Quattro Fontane, and the pair continued their collaboration thereafter through more than 30 years, becoming Italy's foremost producers of musical theatre and co-writing and staging a number of original musical shows which found their way into productions beyond Italy.

Their earliest productions were in the field of revue, with stars such as Anna Magnani, Renato Rascel, Wanda Osiris and Enrico Viarisio topping the bills, before they moved on to more vertebrate stage shows and to the cinema. After a handful of pieces described as ''favola musicale'' (*Alvaro, piuttosto corsaro*; *Tobia, la candida spia*—a piece inspired by *The Third Man*) or ''avventura musicale'' (the *Amphytrion* musical *Giove in doppiopetto*), they co-wrote and produced such book-pieces as *La Granduchessa e i camerieri* (a new musical version of Savoir's *La Grande-Duchesse et le garçon d'étage*) and the footballing *La padrona di raggio di luna* with Broadway's Robert Alda starred, moving into unashamed musical comedy with their version of the Rainier-Grace Kelly romance *Carlo, non farlo*; the *Naked Truth* piece *Buona notte, Bettina*; *Un paio d'ali*; *L'adorabile Guilio*; the Aristophanean *Un Trapezio per Lisistrata*; the movieland *Un Mandarino per Teo*; *Rinaldo in campo,* which prided itself on having Italy's first musical hero-who-dies; *Enrico '61*; the old-Rome tale of *Rugantino*; *Il Giorno della tartaruga*; *Ciao, Rudy,* which featured Marcello Mastroianni as Valentino; *Viola, violino e viola d'amore*; *Angeli in bandiera*; *Alleluia, brava gente*; the internationally successful *Aggiungi un posto a tavola*; the revusical *Felicibumta*; and *Anche i bancari hanno un' anima.*

After Giovannini's death, Garinei continued to produce and direct under their banner, adding *Accendiamo la lampada* (his own last credit as author), *Bravo!, Amore miei, Pardon, Monsieur Molière* and others to their long list of productions. The Sistina is still open, in the year 2000, purveying a mixture of homemade and imported musicals.

The producers were credited with the whole or part of the libretti and lyrics for most of their shows, but their most internationally successful song, "Arrivederci, Roma" (mus: Rascel) was a single. "Domani è sempre domenica" (from *Un paio d'ali*) gave them another sizeable hit.

Buona notte, Bettina gave the producer-authors a first international success, being played in London as *When in Rome* (298 performances), in Spain as *Buenas noches Bettina,* in Budapest (*Tigris a garázsban,* ie, "a tiger in the garage"), Germany (*Gute Nacht Bettina*), South America, Czechoslovakia and Poland; *Un paio d'ali* was seen in Russia, Germany (*Ein Sonntag in Rom*) and Hungary (*Romai Vasarnáp*); *Rinaldo in campo* as *Rinaldo Rinaldini* also in Germany and in Belgrade; *Enrico '61* in Germany and London; *Rugantino* in its original Italian in New York; and *Il giorno della tartaruga* in France (*Le Jour de la tortue*) and Germany (*Amore mio*). *Alleluia, brave gente* became *Halleluja, brave Leute* in Germany, but it was the mixture of low comedy and religion of *Aggiungi un posto a tavola* which—under a rainbow of titles—traveled the most widely of all his pieces since *Buona notte, Bettina,* being produced throughout Europe and South America.

1953 **Alvaro, piuttosto corsaro** (Gorni Kramer/w Sandro Giovannini) Teatro Sistina 25 December

1954 **Giove in doppiopetto** (Kramer/w Giovannini) Teatro Lirico, Milan 27 September

1954 **Tobia, la candida spia** (Kramer/w Giovannini) Teatro Sistina 30 December

1955 **La Granduchessa e i camerieri** (Kramer/w Giovannini) Teatro Lirico, Milan 24 September

1955 **La Padrona di raggio di luna** (Kramer/w Giovannini) Teatro Alfieri 10 December

1956 **Carlo non farlo** (Kramer/ w Giovannini) Teatro Sistina 21 September

1956 **Buona notte, Bettina** (Kramer/w Giovannini) Teatro Lirico, Milan 14 November

1957 **L'adorabile Giulio** (Kramer/w Giovannini) Teatro Sistina

1957 **Un paio d'ali** (Kramer/w Giovannini) Teatro Lirico, Milan 18 September

1959 **Un Trapezio per Lisistrata** (Kramer/w Giovannini) Teatro Sistina 18 December

1960 **Un Mandarino per Teo** (Kramer/w Giovannini) Teatro Sistina 11 October

1961 **Enrico '61** (Renato Rascel/w Giovannini) Teatro Sistina 23 February

1961 **Rinaldo in campo** (Domenico Modugno/w Giovannini) Turin 13 September

1963 **Rugantino** (Armando Trovaioli/w Massimo Franciosa, Festa Campanile) Teatro Sistina 15 December

1965 **Il Giorno della tartaruga** (Rascel/w Gigi Magni, Franciosa, Giovannini) Teatro Sistina 24 October

1966 **Ciao, Rudy** (Trovaioli/w Magni, Giovannini) Teatro Sistina 7 January

1967 **Viola, violino, e viola d'amore** (Bruno Canfora/w Magni, Giovannini) Teatro Sistina 16 September

1969 **Angeli in bandiera** (Canfora/w Iaia Fiastri, Giovannini) Teatro Sistina 24 October

1970 **Alleluia, brava gente** (Rascel, Modugno/w Fiastri, Giovannini) Teatro Sistina 23 December

1974 **Aggiungi un posto a tavola** (Trovaioli/w Fiastri, Giovannini) Teatro Sistina 8 December

1979 **Accendiamo la lampada** (Trovaioli/w Fiastri) Teatro Sistina 30 December

Biography: Garinei, L, Giovannini, M: *Garinei e Giovannini presentano* (Rizzoli, Milan, 1985)

GARRICK, [Reginald] John [aka DANDY, Reginald] (b Brighton, 31 August 1902; d San Francisco, 22 October 1966). Pudgily pretty leading man of stage and screen.

Reginald Garrick made his first stage appearances in variety under his mother's maiden surname, and he retained that name through his first London appearances (*Come In, Vogues of 1924)* and for a period spent in Australia where, in his mid-twenties, he made himself a name as a favorite leading man in musicals (Jim Kenyon in *Rose Marie,* Torelli in *Princess Charming,* etc).

In the late 1920s he moved on to the American West Coast, and played there in similar roles in the musical theatre (*The Desert Song, The Geisha, Katja the Dancer, Princess Charming, The Wishing Well,* etc) before leaving the stage for the newly speaking screen (1929), where he played alongside Norma Terris in *Married in Hollywood.* Under Hollywood's influence he stopped being Dandy and became the roundly rolling-off-the-theatrical-tongue "John Garrick."

John Garrick came down off the screen to star with Queenie Smith in the Broadway musical *A Little Racketeer* in 1932 (Dick Barrison) and in *Face the Music* (1933, Pat Mason), before returning to Britain. There, amongst a bevy of film roles, he took the juvenile lead in the 1933 British film of *Chu Chin Chow,* the 1934 celluloid *The Lily of Killarney* and *Street Song* (1935), and also appeared on the London stage in *Wild Violets* (1932, Paul Hoffman), *Give Me a Ring* (1933, Cliff Reed), *The Laughing Cavalier* (1937, Franz Hals) and *Maritza* (1938, Bela Török). He subsequently returned to America, the screen (*The Great Victor Herbert,* 1939) and, at a still young age, a life outside the theatre and studio.

His wife, American soprano **Harriet Bennett,** starred opposite him as Australia's Rose Marie, and in the down-under production of *Lilac Time.*

GASPARONE Operette in 3 acts by F Zell and Richard Genée. Music by Carl Millöcker. Theater an der Wien, Vienna, 26 January 1884.

Millöcker's brigands-and-smugglers musical, produced little more than a year after his phenomenal success with *Der Bettelstudent,* did not come anywhere near challenging the popularity of his most famous piece, but it did well enough first time round, and proved to be made of sufficiently solid stuff to last rather better than some of his other equally or more popular pieces from around the same period. A century on, whilst shows like *Das verwunschene Schloss, Der Viceadmiral* and *Der Feldprediger,* and even the later and much more successful *Der arme Jonathan,* have vanished from the repertoire, various versions of *Gasparone* find their way regularly to the stage in the Operette houses of Europe.

The famous bandit Gasparone is rumored to be abroad in 1820s Sicily and the Mayor of Syracuse, Baboleno Nasoni (Felix Schweighofer), has his men out hunting him. They are unuscсessful . . . because he isn't there. It is the innkeeper Benozzo (Alexander Girardi) who has started the rumors in order to distract the law's attention from his family's smuggling activities. Benozzo's tricks are, however, discovered by Count Erminio (Josef Joseffy) and, in exchange for his silence, the smugglers agree to stage an attack on the coach of the rich, beautiful and widowed Countess Carlotta della Santa Croce (Maria Theresia Massa), so that Erminio can stage a dramatic rescue and impress the lady.

The trick works, but Nasoni is furious, as he had planned to wed the Countess to his son, Sindulfo (Alexander Guttmann), and he quickly offers to help her win a lucrative lawsuit in which she is involved in exchange for the alliance. Since he knows the case is already won, he is taking no risk. But, just when the betrothal has been fixed, Gasparone strikes. Sindulfo is kidnapped and held for ransom and all the Countess's money stolen. Panic reigns, martial law is declared, and Nasoni backpedals out of the betrothal to the now penniless noblewoman, leaving Carlotta free to turn to Erminio who can return to her the money of which he, temporarily disguised as "Gasparone," had robbed her, whilst Sindulfo was tied up amongst the contraband in Benozzo's inn.

Millöcker's music included some delightful numbers, ranging from Erminio's dashing denial of banditry ("O, dass ich doch der Räuber wär'") and Carlotta's soprano description of the attack on her coach ("Ein höchst romantisch Abenteuer") to Benozzo's comical "Stockfinster war die Nacht' and his obligatory Girardi-waltz song "Er soll dein Herr sein!" It was, however, the tarantella of the first-act finale, "Anzoletto sang "komm, mia bella!" sung by Benozzo's wife Sora (Rosa Streitmann), which proved the most popular piece of all Millöcker's score.

Plate 138. **Gasparone.** *Fun and games as the soubrets (Franz Supper, Rhonda Ann Ingle) take their turn at the stage (Landestheater, Salzburg, 1987).*

Gasparone played solidly for a month (30th performance, 24 February) at the Theater an der Wien, but its run was interrupted by a short French season and a revival of *Donna Juanita* and, by the time producer Steiner gave up the theatre at the end of April, it was still short of its 50th night. It was brought back in 1892 with Joseffy again starring, and was given odd performances in repertoire between 1898 and 1901, but without establishing itself as a particular favorite. However, it held on. In 1915 the Volksoper mounted a production (21 April) and in 1933 a revised version written by Paul Knepler with the music rearranged by Ernst Steffan, which had been introduced the previous year at Berlin's Theater am Nollendorfplatz, was mounted at the same house. This revision introduced the waltz "Dunkelrote Rosen," plucked from the score of Millöcker's *Der Viceadmiral* (where it had been the trio "Geh'n wir in den Garten, atmen Blumenduft"), for the character who had once been Erminio, but who was now "The Stranger," otherwise the Governor of the area—and thus Nasoni's superior—in a good old comic-opera disguise. It was this role which benefited most largely from the unimpressively conventional rewrite, particularly in that ''Dunkelrote Rosen'' became not only the hit number of the show but a hit that went beyond the show to become a regular recital item.

Further revisions to the revisions followed. In 1980 (3 March) a new production of a *Gasparone* was mounted at the Volksoper whilst Berlin's Metropoltheater saw another version two years later, and regional theatres in Austria and Germany continued to rewrite and produce their own remakes of the show, most of which, in spite of the definite appeal of ''Dunkelrote Rosen'' (now confirmed in its place in all versions), were distinctly less imaginative and less fun than the original.

Gasparone quickly followed its Vienna premiere with productions in Germany—where it proved much more immediately popular than in Austria, following its Dresden premiere by running swiftly through to 200 performances at Berlin's Friedrich-Wilhelmstädtisches Theater—in Prague (23 March 1884), and in Budapest (ad Árpád Berczik, Lajos Evva), where the Népszínház production, with a cast headed by Aranka Hegyi, Ilka Pálmay, Pál Vidor and Elek Solymossy, played a good 36 nights. It also made its way to the German theatre of New York, where it was mounted with Max Lube (Nasoni), Bertha Kirchner (Carlotta), Emmy Meffert (Cora), Ferdinand Schütz (Benozzo) and Eduard Elsbach (Erminio) for a fortnight. The very same night John Duff presented the show in English, with a ''weak'' cast—featuring Richard Mansfield (Nasoni, interpolating an old monologue), Harry Hilliard (Erminio), Emma Seebold (Carlotta), Mae St John (Sora) and Alfred Klein (Benozzo)—but ''beautifully staged'' and with sufficient success for it to be given a further showing the following season. The German theatre also repeated the piece, first in its original form and then in what seems to have been the first of its interminable rewritten versions. *Die Banditen* (Thalia-Theater, Berlin 4 January 1887) starred Carl Adolf Friese as Nasoni, but its reception did not encourage Gustav Amberg to persevere with it, and when he played *Gasparone* again in 1892 he returned to the original version.

Although many other European cities mounted the piece during the 1880s and early 1890s, neither France nor Britain took up *Gasparone* and its career, both pre- and, in particular, post-''Dunkelrote Rosen'' has been very largely in its original language. A film *Gasparone* made by George Jacoby in 1937, with Johannes Heesters and Marika Rökk featured, was even less faithful to the original than the various stage remakes. Waltraud Haas and Gerd Riedmann featured in a 1963 television version.

Germany: Residenztheater, Dresden 13 April 1884, Friedrich-Wilhelmstädtisches Theater, Berlin 26 September 1884; Hungary: Népszínház 25 April 1884; USA: Standard Theater (Eng) 21 February 1885, Thalia-Theater (Ger) 21 February 1885

Films: Georg Jacoby 1937, TV Film ARD 1963

Recordings: complete (1932 version) (EMI), selection (1932 version) (RCA), etc

GAVAULT, Paul [Armand Marcel] (b Algiers, 1 September 1865; d Paris, 25 December 1951). Comic playwright and revue writer who scored musical-theatre hits at both first- and secondhand.

A law graduate and sometime barrister, Gavault began his literary career at twenty-one whilst journalisting on the staff of *Le National* and subsequently worked on a long list of other papers (*Petite République, Voltaire,* as theatre editor of *Le Soir, Le Gaulois,* etc) whilst taking his first steps in the theatre. From the production of his first piece, the revue *Tout à la scène* (w Victor de Cottens) at the Théâtre Moderne in 1892, he had 20 years of success as a stage author, producing a highly successful line of comedies and vaudevilles, often, at first, in tandem with de Cottens, then with Georges Berr and a variety of other partners. He also collaborated on a long list of revues and on the libretti for several opérettes and musical comedies which found some success in their Parisian productions and were also occasionally produced abroad. These latter included the four opérettes on which he collaborated with composer Louis Varney: *Le Papa de Francine* (1896), subsequently produced in Britain as *A Lucky Girl* (1898) and in Austria as *Lolas Cousin* (1898); *Les Demoiselles de Saint-Cyriens* (*Diákkisasszonyok* Budapest, 1898, *The Cadet Girl* New York, 1900); Les Pettes Barnett (*A Barnett-lanyok* Budapest, 1899); and *Le Pompier de service* (*A tűzolto* Budapest, 1899). Later in life he also became a theatrical administrator, spending periods at the head successively of the Nouvel-Ambigu, the Odéon (1914–21) and the Théâtre de la Porte-Saint-Martin before retiring from the theatre world.

Several of Gavault's plays were used as the bases for musical comedies during the period when established French vaudevilles and comedies were widely used as sources for libretti. In Britain, the musical comedy *The Girl for the Boy* (Duke of York's Theatre 23 September 1919) was based on his *La Petite Chocolatière* (1909) and the Ivan Caryll musical *The Kiss Call* (Gaiety Theatre 8 October 1919) on *Un Coup de téléphone* (1912, w Georges Berr), whilst the long-running *Theodore and Co* (Gaiety Theatre 19 September 1916) was taken from *Théodore et Cie,* a play to which his name was sometimes appended alongside those of Paul Armont and Nicolas Nancey. The American *Tantalizing Tommy* (1912), the German *Bezauberndes Fräulein* (1933) and the Italian *La piccola cioccolataia* also used *La Petite Chocolatière* as their starting point. Lajos Lajtai's Hungarian operett, *Az ártatlan özvegy* (the innocent widow) (Városi Színház 25 December 1925), was based on Gavault's play, *Mademoiselle Josette, ma femme* (1906 w Robert Charvay) and

Düsseldorf's 1912 musical *Eine kitzliche Geschichte* (Hugo Hirsch/Rudolf Schanzer, 31 October) was a version of the Gavault/Ordonneau *Une affaire scandaleuse.* The libretto for Gavault's 1902 opérette *Le Jockey malgré lui* was reused as the text for the American musical comedy *The Office Boy* (Victoria Theater 2 November 1903) with the names of Harry B Smith and composer Ludwig Englander attached to it, in much the same way that *Les Demoiselles de Saint-Cyriens* had been earlier stripped of half its score and transformed into *The Cadet Girl.*

1896 **Napoléon malgré lui** (mus: uncredited/w Victor de Cottens) 1 act Fourmi 3 April

1896 **Le Papa de Francine** (Louis Varney/w Victor de Cottens) Théâtre Cluny 5 November

1897 **Le Pompier de service** (Varney/w de Cottens) Théâtre des Variétés 18 February

1898 **Les Demoiselles de Saint-Cyriens** (Varney/w de Cottens) Théâtre Cluny 28 January

1898 **Les Petites Barnett** (Varney) Théâtre des Variétés 8 November

1899 **Ohé Venus** (Monteux-Brissac/w P-L Flers) Lyon; La Cigale 24 February

1899 **Shakespeare!** (Gaston Serpette/w Flers) Théâtre des Bouffes-Parisiens 23 November

1900 **Les Petits Croisés** (w Flers) La Cigale 24 January

1902 **Le Jockey malgré lui** (Victor Roger/w Maurice Ordonneau) Théâtre des Bouffes-Parisiens 4 December

1903 **La Belle de New-York** (*The Belle of New York*) French version (Moulin-Rouge)

1905 **Les Poupées de M Dupont** (Charles Lecocq) 1 act Théâtre des Variétés 26 May

GAXTON, William [GAXIOLA, Arturo Antonio] (b San Francisco, 2 December 1890; d New York, 12 February 1963).

Gaxton made a start in show business as a teenager in vaudeville, and won his first Broadway appearance in *The Music Box Revue* in 1922. After several years working out of town, including musical-comedy assignments touring in the title role of *All for You, John Henry* (1925), in *Betty Lee* (1925, Wallingford Speed), and in the flop *Miss Happiness* (1926, Steve Colwell), he played his first Broadway leading roles as the heroes of Rodgers and Hart's *A Connecticut Yankee* (1927, Martin, "My Heart Stood Still," "Thou Swell") and of Cole Porter's *Fifty Million Frenchmen* (1929, Peter Forbes, "You Do Something to Me"). However, his combination of leading-man good looks and edgy comic style got their best showcase when he was cast as John Wintergreen, President of the United States, in Gershwin's *Of Thee I Sing* (1931, "Of Thee I Sing, Baby").

Of Thee I Sing paired him for the first time with comedian Victor Moore, there cast as the opaque Vice President Throttlebottom. Moore's style, as the muddled and hard-done-by little fellow, contrasted well with Gaxton's dashing, forward comic persona, and they were paired again at the top of the bill for *Let 'em Eat Cake* (1933), the sequel to *Of Thee I Sing,* and, most famously, in *Anything Goes* (1934) where Gaxton created the role of Billy Crocker ("You're the Top," "All Through the Night"), opposite Ethel Merman, whilst Moore appeared as Public Enemy Number Thirteen.

Gaxton went on to star as Leopold in the Broadway version of *White Horse Inn* (1936) and joined up with Moore again for *Leave It to Me!* (1938, Buck Thomas), *Louisiana Purchase* (1940, Jim Taylor), and two less successful ventures, *Hollywood Pinafore* (1945, Dick Live-Eye) and, finally, *Nellie Bly* (1946, Frank Jordan), but he was still to be seen on the musical stage as late as 1961 and 1962, when he appeared at Jones Beach, NY, in the Hawaiian musical *Paradise Island.*

He appeared on the screen in the movie versions of *Fifty Million Frenchmen* and *Best Foot Forward.*

GAY, John (b Barnstaple, September 1685; d London, 4 December 1732).

The young Gay worked as domestic steward to the Duchess of Monmouth and as secretary to the Earl of Clarendon, and during this time he made his first attempts at writing, including several pieces for the stage. For many years he hovered on the edge of court circles, making himself agreeable and useful and awaiting the comfortable position he was sure must come his way but, when, in 1727, the offer of an ushership to one of the royal princesses was made, he was disappointed and refused the post.

His disappointment was short-lived, however, for the following year Rich staged his ballad opera *The Beggar's Opera* at the theatre at Lincoln's Inn Fields, and Gay's name and fortune were made. He wrote a sequel to *The Beggar's Opera,* under the title *Polly,* but the disfavor with which he was now regarded in high places resulted in its being banned. When it finally was staged, it was clear that he had been done a favor, for the second piece was a pale imitation of the first and could very well have harmed the booming success of his one and only hit.

His opera *Acis and Galatea* (mus: Händel) was produced at the Little Haymarket Theatre 28 May 1732) and an operatic *Achilles* (1735) was mounted after his death.

Gay's *Achilles in Petticoats* was subsequently adapted as a comic opera, with music by Thomas Arne (Covent Garden 16 December 1773), but it was *The Beggar's Opera* which, of his works, was subsequently the most tampered with by other hands. The Viennese *Der Liebling von London,* the 1928 German musical *Die Dreigroschenoper* and Broadway's *The Beggar's Holiday*

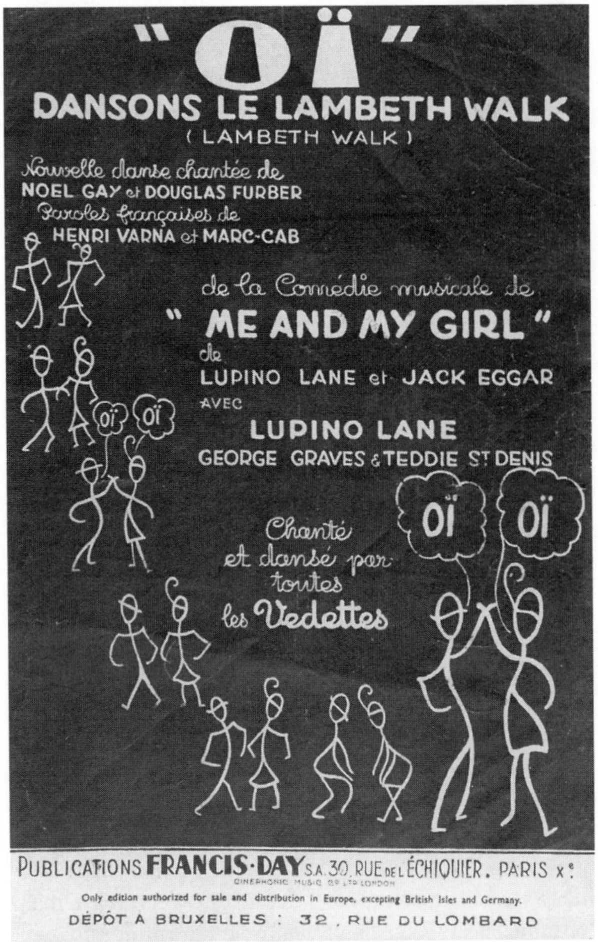

Plate 139. **Noel Gay's** *most famous number went round the world—but its composer got pretty poor billing.*

(Broadway Theater 26 December 1946) are amongst the pieces founded on the text of Gay's most famous and enduring work.

1728 **The Beggar's Opera** (pasticcio arr J C Pepusch) Lincoln's Inn Fields Theatre 29 January

1777 **Polly** (pasticcio arr Pepusch and Arnold/as George Colman) Little Haymarket Theatre 19 June

Biographies: Melville, L: *The Life and Letters of John Gay* (Folcroft, Philadelphia, 1921), Erving, W H: *John Gay: Favorite of the Wits* (Durham, NC, 1940), Spack, P A M: *John Gay* (Twayne, New York, 1965), Nokes, D: *John Gay—a profession of friendship—a critical biography* (OUP, 1995)

GAY, Noel [ARMITAGE, Reginald Moxon] (b Wakefield, Yorks, 15 July 1898; d London, 4 March 1954). British songwriter who provided scores for a number of shows in the 1930s and 1940s.

A cathedral choirboy at 12, assistant organist at the Chapel Royal, St James's, and musical director at Saint Anne's church, Soho, at 18, Armitage followed a musical training at the Royal College of Music and Cambridge destining him for a career in church music. At the age of 25, however, he switched direction and within a few years the songs of "Noel Gay" were being played in revues in London (*Stop Press, The Charlot Show of 1926, Clowns in Clover*) and in the provinces (*Merry Mexico, Jumbles,* etc). He composed the song "Tondeleyo" for the film *White Cargo* (1929), but it was "The King's Horses," performed by Cicely Courtneidge in the revue *Folly to Be Wise* (w Harry Graham), which gave him his first significant song hit.

In 1931 Gay contributed to his first book musical when he teamed with Stanley Lupino and lyricist Desmond Carter on the Gaiety musical comedy *Hold My Hand.* In the next four years, whilst turning out regular amounts of music for the blossoming sound-film industry, notably for Jack Hulbert and/or Cicely Courtneidge ("There's Something About a Soldier," "Who's Been Polishing the Sun," etc), as well as individual numbers for the popular-song market ("I Took My Harp to a Party" for Gracie Fields, "Round the Marble Arch," etc), he also wrote the songs for several similar musical plays. It was with his songs for Arthur Rose's vehicle for another member of the Lupino family, the acrobatic little singing comedian Lupino Lane, that he finally hit the bull's eye. Following a fine initial run at the Victoria Palace at the edge of the war, *Me and My Girl* (1937) became a perennial Lupino family production both in the provinces and in regular London return seasons and its favorite songs, "The Lambeth Walk" and "Me and My Girl," became perhaps the best-known of Gay's many popular songs.

Several further vehicles for Lane and the cheeky cockney character he favored followed (*La-di-da-di-da,* revised *Twenty to One, Meet Me Victoria, Sweetheart Mine*), along with songs for a number of other musical comedies, for the Crazy Gang shows at the London Palladium (*Swing Is in the Air, These Foolish Things, The Little Dog Laughed*) and their return in 1947 to the Victoria Palace (*Together Again*), as well as for a number of further revues. Many of these shows had long and successful London runs as Gay's total of song successes mounted ("Leaning on a Lamp-post," "Run, Rabbit, Run," "Only a Glass of Champagne," "Hey Little Hen"). His final London show, *Bob's Your Uncle,* produced in 1948, had to it a marked air of the prewar shows to which the composer had so happily contributed, but it nevertheless proved a distinct hit, seeing out on a high note the fashion for low-comedy musical texts with light, catchy and simple songs attached.

Gay founded his own music-publishing company in 1938, and in 1984 the company, under the management of his son, Richard Armitage, staged a revised version of

Me and My Girl. This version proved enormously successful and went on to give Gay the kind of international exposure he had not achieved in his lifetime. The firm subsequently produced several other, unsuccessful musical plays, and in 1992 mounted a pasticcio musical, *Radio Times* (Abi Grant, Queen's Theatre 15 October), based on Gay's catalogue.

1931 **Hold My Hand** (Desmond Carter/Stanley Lupino) Gaiety Theatre 23 December
1933 **That's a Pretty Thing** (ex- *Paste*) (Carter/Lupino) Daly's Theatre 22 November
1935 **Jack o' Diamonds** (H F Maltby, Clifford Grey) Gaiety Theatre 25 February
1935 **Love Laughs—!** (ex- *Leave It to Love*) (Grey, Greatrex Newman) London Hippodrome 25 June
1937 **Me and My Girl** (L Arthur Rose, Douglas Furber) Victoria Palace 16 December
1938 **Wild Oats** (Furber) Prince's Theatre 13 April
1940 **Present Arms** (Frank Eyton/Fred Thompson, Bert Lee) Prince of Wales Theatre 13 May
1942 **Susie** revised *Jack o' Diamonds* New Theatre, Oxford 13 June
1943 **La-di-da-di-da** revised *That's a Pretty Thing* (Lupino) Victoria Palace 30 March
1943 **The Love Racket** (Eyton, Barbara Gordon, Basil Thomas, Leslie Gibbs/Lupino) Victoria Palace 21 October
1944 **Meet Me Victoria** (Eyton/Lupino Lane, Lauri Wylie) Victoria Palace 8 April
1944 **Ring Time** revised *Battling Butler* with new score (Eyton/Stanley Brightman, Austin Melford) Glasgow 28 August
1946 **Sweetheart Mine** (Eyton/Lane, Wylie) Victoria Palace 1 August
1948 **Bob's Your Uncle** (Eyton/Melford) Saville Theatre 5 May

GAY DIVORCE Musical comedy in 2 acts by Dwight Taylor based on the play *An Adorable Adventure* by J Hartley Manners. Music and lyrics by Cole Porter. Ethel Barrymore Theater, New York, 29 November 1932.

Fred Astaire appeared in only one further stage musical following the retirement of his sister, Adele, to marriage, and *Gay Divorce* paired him with the attractive Clare Luce on a rather different footing than that of the previous partnership. The Astaire pair's greatest musicals had never matched them as a romantic couple—they had been brother and sister, guardian and ward—but this time Astaire's character was at last able to ''get'' the leading lady.

Miss Luce played a certain Mrs Mimi Pratt, who is decidedly anxious to rid herself of Mr Pratt (Roland Bottomley). To this purpose, she hires herself a professional co-respondent, Tonetti (Erik Rhodes), with whom to go through the motions of infidelty, but the young novelist Guy Holden (Astaire), who has fallen in love with Mimi, substitutes himself for the paid separator, and performs so convincingly that Mimi, her divorce gaily achieved, finds she is ready to go straight back into marriage again.

Plate 140. **Gay Divorce.** *Fred Astaire and Clare Luce dance ''Night and Day.''*

The score used several songs (''Mister and Missus Fitch,'' ''I've Got You on My Mind,'' ''I Still Love the Red, White and Blue'') which Porter had intended for a non-starter of a musical called *Stardust,* but the song hit of the evening was the insinuating ''Night and Day'' as sung by the star, and danced by him with Miss Luce.

Astaire played seven months in Dwight Deere Wiman and Tom Weatherly's production of *Gay Divorce,* which shifted to the Shubert Theater a few weeks after its opening, and it was Joseph Santley who saw out the Broadway run of 248 performances in the role of Holden, before taking the show on tour.

As had been successfully done with the other Astaire shows from *For Goodness' Sake* (*Stop Flirting*) through *Lady, Be Good!* and *Funny Face, Gay Divorce* was exported to London soon after the end of its Broadway run, with Astaire, Miss Luce, Rhodes and the English Eric Blore repeating their Broadway roles. It was gussied up with three extra songs (''I Love Only You,'' ''Never Say No,'' ''Waiters v Waitresses'') and Luella Gear's Broadway paean to the star-spangled banner was replaced by ''Where Would You Get Your Coat?,'' previously heard on Broadway in the musical *Fifty Million Frenchmen,* which had folded on the British road prior to London. Lee Ephraim's London production ran for 180 performances, during which time the show was given its Australian premiere. With Astaire occupied in England, Billy Milton and Mona Potts took on the lead roles, dancing to Edward Royce's original choreography, for six weeks in Melbourne and Sydney (Theatre Royal 28 July 1934) apiece.

The show was revived in 1960 at the Cherry Lane Theater (3 April, 25 performances).

A soi-disant 1934 film version, starring Astaire alongside Ginger Rogers, Betty Grable and Edward Everett Horton, altered the title (to *The Gay Divorcée*) and retained only "Night and Day" from Porter's score, replacing the remainder of the music with songs by Mack Gordon and Harry Revel ("Don't Let It Bother You," "Let's K-nock K-nees") and by Con Conrad and Herb Magidson ("A Needle in a Haystack" and "The Continental"). The last-named song won an Academy Award.

This film version, however, itself became the basis for an Hungarian stage musical entitled *Vidám válás* ("gay divorce") written by Iván Bradányi and Márton Karinthy and with a score credited to Gershwin, Youmans and Porter. It was produced at Budapest's Karinthy Színház on 29 October 1991 with József Bozsó (Guy) and Krisztina Simonyi (Mimi) featured.

UK: Palace Theatre 2 November 1933; Australia: King's Theatre, Melbourne 23 December 1933

Film: RKO *The Gay Divorcée* 1934

THE GAY GRISETTE Musical farce in 2 acts by George Dance. Music by Carl Kiefert. Theatre Royal, Bradford, 1 August 1898.

Written specifically for a Provincial Managers' Syndicate, to provide a musical show to fill their stages, *The Gay Grisette* was sent on tour under the management of the young Robert Courtneidge. Put together by George Dance, who had a particular flair for writing for out-of-town audiences, the piece ran through the register of comic situations as a colonel's niece disguised as a grisette galloped through Europe, and through situations amorous and awkward, to the accompaniment of a series of songs in all the most popular styles of the moment. The West End's favorite orchestrator, Carl Kiefert, this time supplied the tunes as well as the accompaniments.

Claire Romaine, daughter of composer Teddy Solomon, was the original Babette, but she gave way to a stream of successors as *The Gay Grisette* ran through several years of popularity on the touring and colonial circuits. Australia's *Gay Grisette* was mounted under the management of Clarke & Meynell, with Florence Imeson as Babette, and the piece was also seen in South Africa. It was announced for an American production under the management of Adolphus H Chamberlyn—first in 1900 with May Yohe, then for Boston's Columbia Theater, then with Mabelle Gilman starred—but didn't, seemingly, make it to the stage before the producer's death a few years later.

Australia: Theatre Royal, Melbourne 4 February 1911

THE GAY PARISIENNE Musical comedy in 2 acts by George Dance based on his play *The Barmaid.* Music by Ernest Vousden. Theatre Royal, Northampton, 1 October 1894.

The huge provincial success of *The Lady Slavey* encouraged its author, George Dance, to try another piece in the same vein—made to suit the tastes of provincial audiences rather than those of the more sophisticated West End theatregoer. With an unerring hand, he remixed some of the melodramatic elements which had long been the joy of touring plays, musical and unmusical, with some classic English comedy elements, and instead of the story of the naughty, blackmailing barmaid Minnie Dewdrop, created by Louise Appleby at Manchester's Comedy Theatre three years earlier (31 August 1891), he came up with the tale of the conniving Mlle Julie Bon-Bon (Nellie Murray). Like Minnie, Julie has tricked country Canon Honeycombe (J T MacMillan) into signing a document promising her marriage, and she now turns up to sue for enough breach-of-promise cash to set her and her real boyfriend, Adolphe, up for a comfortable life. But Julie mistakes her target, and it is Amos Dingle (Alfred Fisher) who ends up in court being prosecuted for marriage-avoidance by Tom Everleigh (Richard Temple jr), the fiancé of Miss Nora Honeycombe (Amy Thornton). Julie charms a verdict from the judge, but Tom comes to the rescue with some dirt on Adolphe and, as poor Honeycombe flees through a series of colorful situations and some pretty Swiss scenery, his son-in-law-to-be so manages affairs that Julie is forced finally to back down.

Accompanied by a set of songs partly written and partly arranged by musical director Vousden, the lively, comical *The Gay Parisienne* proved a major provincial hit. William Greet's touring companies completed three tours, and were joined on the road by Wallace Erskine's number-two-towns company before Horace Sedger took up the show for a London production. Dance did over the libretto, introducing a new character, the little maid Ruth, in order to feature his latest discovery, tiny, cockney Louie Freear; Ivan Caryll was hired to write a new score; and *The Gay Parisienne* moved into the little Duke of York's Theatre with Ada Reeve starred as Julie and Lionel Rignold as Honeycombe. It ran there for a fine 369 performances. Miss Freear caused a sensation with her song about "Sister Mary Jane's Top Note," W H Denny as the judge described himself happily as one of the "Battersea Butterfly Shooters," Ada Reeve sang "I'm All the Way from Gay Paree" and interpolated the American coon song "Sambo," and the show's new shape and score were promptly taken up by Greet's touring company as they moved into their third, fourth and fifth years on the road. There were many more, for *The Gay Parisienne,* like *The Lady Slavey,* became a feature of the road schedules through two decades, with Greet, Erskine and Rudolph Kloss's number-three-towns companies all touring simultaneously for a remarkable number of seasons.

The London version of the show was taken up by E E Rice and, revised and rechristened *The Girl from Paris,* mounted on Broadway, with Clara Lipman (Julie), Charles A Bigelow (Honeycombe) and Josephine Hall (Ruth) in the main roles. Again, it proved a real hit, running for 266 performances, breaking for the summer and then returning for 33 nights more before going on to a touring career which almost challenged the amazing longevity of its British one. In 1898 (Wallack's Theater 17 January) Rice even brought the show back for further Broadway month with Georgia Caine as Julie.

Ada Reeve introduced Julie Bon-Bon to Australian audiences in 1897 (popping in ''Susie-oo'' instead of ''Sambo'' and scoring another hit) in Williamson and Musgrove's production, played it for a season in repertoire with *The French Maid,* and took it round again in 1898. The other English-speaking venues followed suit, and all the time the British provinces and the American circuits welcomed returns and repeats, season after season, from *The Gay Parisienne.*

USA: Herald Square Theater *The Girl from Paris* 8 December 1896; Australia: Her Majesty's Theatre, Sydney 31 July 1897

GAY'S THE WORD Musical play in 2 acts by Ivor Novello. Lyrics by Alan Melville. Saville Theatre, London, 16 February 1951.

Cicely Courtneidge and author/composer Ivor Novello had both become firmly set into ''series''—successful runs of pieces all of a like kind—with the comedienne scoring in her versatile light comedy with bits of music, and he turning out lush and large-scale romantic operettas. Apparently, when the actress went to see the writer about a job for a friend, he jokingly(?) said he'd thought her visit might have been to ask him to compose her next show. He not only composed it, but also replaced the originally intended book-writer as well.

Miss Courtneidge starred as Gay Daventry, an actress with an out-of-town flop on her hands, who sets up a drama school in her house in Folkestone. It turns out that smugglers have been using it as an entrepôt while she's been touring, but Gay is more than a match for the miscreants, and before the evening is over she has handed them all over to justice and also has placed all her pupils on the professional stage in a nice, new show.

Gay's the Word had its tongue firmly in its cheek, especially when lyricist Alan Melville was let loose, and Miss Courtneidge ended up with the most comical score of all her time on the stage as she lauded ''Vitality'' as a recipe for success, explained what it means when ''Bees Are Buzzin',''chortled her way through ''Gaiety Glad,'' mused over the prospects of her hopeless show in ''It's Bound To Be Right on the Night'' before coming to the conclusion that it, of course, won't be, and gave her all in the role of the turkey's Ruritanian Queen, warbling semi-voicelessly about ''Guards on Parade'' in a burlesque of Novello's own kind of musical. Lizbeth Webb played the show's ingenue alongside Courtneidge's regular (off- and on-stage) leading man, Thorley Walters.

A book which was little more than a series of set pieces nevertheless provided endless opportunities for its star and *Gay's the Word* remained in London for 504 performances before going into the country.

Recording: selection (part-record) (WRC)

THE GEISHA, a story of a tea house Japanese musical play in 2 acts by Owen Hall. Lyrics by Harry Greenbank. Music by Sidney Jones. Additional songs by Lionel Monckton and James Philp. Daly's Theatre, London, 25 April 1896.

The most successful of the series of important musical plays produced by George Edwardes at Daly's Theatre around the turn of the century, *The Geisha* not only proved to be one of the best-loved and most enduring of all 19th-century British musicals on its home territory, but also made its mark in a remarkable way beyond the English-speaking theatre world. It spread itself further abroad, and with more success, than any other previous English-language piece, not excepting the works of Gilbert and Sullivan, had done, becoming one of the most popular shows in central Europe (Keller's statistical survey of 1921 rates it behind only *Die Fledermaus, Die lustige Witwe* and *Das Dreimäderlhaus*) and remaining in the repertoire there until quite recently.

British tar Reginald Fairfax (Hayden Coffin), on duty in the East, spends some time in the company of the geisha O Mimosa San (Marie Tempest), at the Teahouse of Ten Thousand Joys, run by the comical little Chinaman Wun-Hi (Huntley Wright). His worried fiancée Molly Seamore (Letty Lind) gets dressed up as a Japanese girl to see if she appeals to Reggie that way, but unfortunately she is trapped as a Jap when the local overlord Marquis Imari (Harry Monkhouse), determined to have Mimosa for himself, orders Wun-Hi's establishment sold up. The wealthy Lady Constance Wynne (Maud Hobson) rescues Mimosa from his clutches in the subsequent auction, but the Marquis happily buys lot two instead—the disguised Molly. To prevent this wedding from taking place, Mimosa disguises herself as a fortune teller and predicts dire unhappiness for the superstitious Marquis in a life with an unloving wife and, when she is sent to bewitch Molly into a loving frame of mind, she instead uses the opportunity to substitute the teahouse's eager little French interpreter, Juliette (Juliette Nesville), under the marquisal bridal canopy.

Sidney Jones's score was full of winning numbers, with the soprano role of Mimosa being equipped with a superb pair of waltz songs—one describing the less attractive side of ''A Geisha's Life'' and the other, in her fortune-teller's disguise, singing of ''Love, Love''—as well as the rueful tale of what happened to ''The Amorous Goldfish'' and a Kissing Duet with Fairfax. The other characters were also well served, with the high spots ranging from the comical antics of Wun-Hi in the enduring ''Chin-chin-chinaman'' to Fairfax's baritone ballad, ''Star of My Soul,'' Molly's Japanese song ''Chon-kina,'' her anthropomorphic tale of ''The Interfering Parrot,'' and some delightful ensembles, including a first-act finale which gave the tenor playing Katana, Mimosa's real Japanese beloved, his one chance to burst into song. Lionel Monckton supplied several additional numbers, scoring a hit with the baritone sea-song ''Jack's the Boy'' and also with the soubrette's ''The Toy Monkey,'' whilst James Philp wrote the music to an interpolated piece called ''The Jewel of Asia'' with which Marie Tempest scored a great success.

The Geisha was a resounding London hit, running for 760 performances at Daly's Theatre whilst the piece began to spread itself around, first, the British provinces and then the world. Edwardes had the first tour on the road within four months of the premiere, with Geraldine Ulmar, John Coates, Marie Studholme and Huntley Wright's brother Bert featured, and Mouillot and Morrell simultaneously started out their number-two-towns company with Minnie Leverentz starred. A month later, Broadway got its first *Geisha* when Augustin Daly mounted the show at his theatre with Dorothy Morton (Mimosa), Van Rensselaer Wheeler (Fairfax), Violet Lloyd (Molly) and William Samson (Wun-Hi) and with a dancer called Isadora Duncan amongst the chorus. Daly's repertoire schedule meant that the piece did not play a straight run, but *The Geisha* popped in and out of his theatre during the last months of 1896 and 1897, playing 194 Broadway performances (later with Nancy McIntosh as Mimosa and James T Powers as Wun-Hi) during that time, and becoming a great favorite. Such a favorite, indeed, that it won the honor of being the only musical to be granted a full-scale burlesque by the Weber and Fields team. Joseph Herbert's *The Geezer* (October 1896) was one of the jolly house's first and biggest burlesque hits. *The Geisha* was seen thereafter in every corner of America, and notably at the musical-theatre Mecca of the West Coast, San Francisco's Tivoli Opera House, where it ran up an unprecedented series of performances and was voted ''more successful and attractive than any other piece produced at this house during the past ten years.''

In May of 1897 the Lessing-Theater, Berlin, hosted José Ferenczy's production of *Die Geisha, eine japanische Theehausgeschichte* (ad C M Röhr, Julius Freund). The piece became a vast success in Berlin and, before long, around the whole of Germany. Ferenczy's production, with the tiny Viennese singer Mia Werber starred as Mimosa and Emil Sondermann as Wun-Hi, became a musical must in the capital city (''enthusiasm has seldom reached such a pitch in the Berlin theatre'') and, as in America, the local burlesquers leapt in to give the show the compliment of a *Geisha Parodie* (H Buffe, Alexanderplatz-Theater 6 June 1897). Regularly revived thereafter *The Geisha* had its 1,000th Berlin performance in 1905, and Ferenczy also toured it through Russia and the American continent.

Vienna picked up the Berlin version of the show, and *Die Geisha* was mounted at the Carltheater later in the same year with Frln Golz (Mimosa), Betty Stojan (Molly) and Sigmund Natzler (Wun-Hi) starred. As in America, it was not allowed a straight run, but alternated with a program showing ''The American Biograph'' and other Operetten of the theatre's repertoire. It was, however, seen 28 times before the end of 1897 and was continued in the repertoire the following year with the peripatetic American soubrette Marie Halton featured as Mimosa, as it headed towards its 100th Viennese night (8 March 1900). *Die Geisha* was held seven years in the Carltheater repertoire, during which time Mizzi Günther played Mimosa and Louis Treumann took over as Wun-Hi, produced there again in 1912, and yet again in a new production in 1920 with Grete Seidlitz and Ernst Arnold (9 December, 175th night 31 December), as other Viennese and provincial houses took the show up and found it one of the most loved of all their presentations. *The Geisha*'s German version ultimately proved as popular as and even more enduring than its English one, and the show was seen in Vienna again as recently as 1954 (Raimundtheater) and 1973 (Raimundtheater), with a new adaptation (ad Hans Herbert Pudor, Hermann Wetzlar) being mounted at Bremerhaven in 1956 (6 October).

There was a similar kind of success for the Hungarian version of the show (ad Béla J Fái, Emil Makai), first seen at the Magyar Színház with Gizella Vlád playing Mimosa, Kornél Sziklai (Wuncsi) and Sári Fedák (Molly), which ran up its first one hundred performances by 31 January 1899. Amongst the subsequent Budapest revivals was one at the Király Színház (12 April 1912) in which Fedák took the star role (the ''title role'' had been cleverly designed at the beginning to apply to either

Miss Tempest or Miss Lind) alongside Márton Rátkai and Lilly Berky, and another at the Fővárosi Operettszínház in 1926 (11 February).

The first French production of *La Geisha* (ad Charles Clairville, Antony Mars, Jacques Le Maire), with Jeanne Petit as Mimosa and Guyon fils as Mac-Chou-Li (ex-Wun-Hi), was a short-lived one, but the ubiquitous success of the show encouraged a second try and it was revived at the Moulin-Rouge, recently host to a spectacular if butchered version of *The Belle of New York,* 14 July 1906, with Jeanne Petit starring alongside Morton, Alberthal and Spinelly. It was acclaimed "a masterpiece of its kind" and "an ideal Parisian evening" (!) and was played through the summer. A Gabriel Trarieux/Georges Bravard mounting followed in 1920 at the Gaîté-Lyrique with Opéra-Comique diva Marguerite Carré (Mimosa), Max Dearly (Imari) and Denise Grey (Zoe, ie, Molly). However, in spite of this three-part Parisian life, *La Geisha* never found the enormous success of *Die Geisha, A gésák* or *The Geisha.*

The show was produced throughout Europe, with notable success in Holland, Italy and in Spain, but with some problems in Russia, where it was given in a rather impromptu and approximate version. Ferenczy toured his Berlin version widely, including a long trip to South America, whilst J C Williamson and George Musgrove introduced Australia to *The Geisha,* and the Scandinavian countries produced adaptations in their various tongues. And, all this time, companies purveying the English-language *Geisha* flooded the touring circuits in Britain before the show returned to London in 1906 (18 June), when Edwardes produced a stop-gap mounting with May de Souza (Mimosa), Mariette Sully (Juliette), George Graves (Imari), Marie Studholme (Molly) and a third Wright brother, Fred Wright jr as Wun-Hi (60 performances).

The Shuberts mounted a 52-performance season of *The Geisha* in 1913 (27 March, 44th Street Theater) with Alice Zeppili, Lina Abarbanell and James T Powers featured, and several American companies mounted versions with Japanese prima donnas: in 1919 Tamaki Miura starred in a San Francisco production and in 1931 the Civic Light Opera played a season with Hizi Koyke as Mimosa. The show was actually seen on Broadway for the last time shortly after this . . . given by a touring marionette troupe in Italian! In the same year J Bannister Howard's season of old favorites at London's Daly's Theatre included 48 performances of *The Geisha,* and there was a barely professional production at the Garrick Theatre in 1934 (24 April, 39 performances). However, whilst the piece continued in the Continental repertoire in the postwar years, British light-opera companies preferred to play adaptations of imported works and *The Geisha* finally dropped from the English-language lists.

Plate 141. *Vienna's queen of opera-bouffe,* **Marie Geistinger,** *as the page, Drogan, in* Genovefa von Brabant.

USA: Daly's Theater 9 September 1896; Germany: Lessing-Theater *Die Geisha* 1 May 1897; Hungary: Magyar Színház *A gésák* 16 October 1897; Austria: Carltheater *Die Geisha* 16 Octoberr 1897; France: Théâtre de l'Athenée-Comique *La Geisha* 8 March 1898; Australia: Princess Theatre, Melbourne 17 December 1898

Recordings: studio cast (Hyperion), selections in German (Decca, Urania, etc), selections in Italian (Fonit-Cetra, EDM)

GEISTINGER, Marie [GEISTINGER, Maria Charlotte Cäcilia] (b Graz, 26 July 1836; d Klagenfurt, 30 September 1903). Vienna's queen of the 19th-century opéra-bouffe stage.

Born in Graz to theatrical parents, Geistinger first went on the stage as a child and had an early exposure in Vienna when, at 16, she appeared in the title role of the Posse *Die falsche Pepita* (Theater in der Josefstadt, 1852). She did not follow up this success in Vienna but instead, over the next dozen years, moved on to Berlin, Hamburg, Riga and Berlin again, appearing mainly in juvenile light-comedy roles in plays, including many with song and dance elements. She returned to Vienna in 1865 at the bidding of Friedrich Strampfer, director of the Theatre an der Wien, to introduce the title role of Offenbach's *Die schöne Helena* (*La Belle Hélène*) to Viennese audiences. This show and this role established her as a musical-theatre star, and she followed up as Offenbach's Boulotte (*Blaubart,* 1866), Coscoletto (*Coscoletto,* 1866), La Sincère (*Die Schäfer,* ie, *Les Bergers* 1866), *Die Grossherzogin von Gérolstein* (1867) and Drogan (*Genovefa von Brabant*), as Emma in Julius Hopp's *Die Donauweibchen* (1866) and in a whole list of smilar roles under Strampfer's direction, before herself taking over the part-direction of the theatre in tandem with his successor, Maximilian Steiner.

She appeared at the Theater an der Wien in a wide variety of roles in both plays and musical plays (Leni in Alois Berla's *Drei Paar Schuhe,* Anna Birkmeier in *Der Pfarrer von Kirchfeld,* etc), and made another personal hit in an Operette—this time an Austrian one—when she starred as Fantasca in Johann Strauss's early piece, *Indigo und die vierzig Räuber* (1871). Continually varying plays and Operetten, she was seen in the Viennese productions of Offenbach's *Le Corsair noir* (1872), *Die Theaterprinzessin* (1872, *La Diva,* Susi Apfelwein) and *Fantasio* (1872, Fantasio), starred as Leokadia Blumenau in Millöcker's *Abenteuer in Wien* (1873), in Offenbach's *Die Wilderer* (*Les Braconniers,* Ginetta) and *Madame l'Archiduc* (Marietta), and as Wosana in Jonas's *Die Japanesin* (1874). She rejoined Strauss for *Carneval in Rom* (1873, Marie) and again, in 1874, to create the role of Rosalinde in *Die Fledermaus,* introducing "Dieser Anstand" with Jani Szíka, and the famous csárdás "Klänge der Heimat," and yet again as the first Lorenza Feliciani in *Cagliostro in Wien* (1875).

In spite of her considerable successes, the tenuous financial climate in Vienna following the stock-market crash of 1875 found Geistinger in a parlous monetary state and, although she continued at the Theater an der Wien, playing in such pieces as Offenbach's *Les Brigands* (1875, Fiorella) and a version of *La Créole* (1876, Antoinette), she was finally obliged to give up her part of the management of the theatre.

After more than a decade as Vienna's reigning queen of musical theatre, she moved on to profit from the high fees available from guest performances and to take up dramatic roles at the Stadttheater. She then proceeded to Leipzig, where she once again mixed drama, comedy and Operette during a stay of more than two years, returning to Vienna and the Theater an der Wien in 1879 to introduce her first successful new role for a number of years as the German version of Offenbach's *Madame Favart.* She also played in the "scene aus den Österreichischen Alpen mit National-Gesängen," *Das Versprechen hinter'm Herd,* and in 1880 was seen as Lotti in *Die Näherin* and as Stella, the heroine of Offenbach's *Die Tochter des Tambour-Major.*

Gustav Amberg, the proprietor of one of New York's flourishing German-language theatres, now proposed her a long and lucrative American engagement and, in 1881, the 44-year-old star crossed the Atlantic and made her debut at Amberg's Thalia Theater (5 January 1881) as Offenbach's *Grande-Duchesse,* to the sort of reception she had had in Vienna 20 years earlier ("she plays it as high comedy rather than rollicking bouffe"; "she is quieter than Aimée and touches the double entendres so that they are funny without being coarse"; "she sinks her personality in each character . . . a great artist"). Geistinger extended her American stay over more than three years, playing across the whole country and appearing regularly in New York as Madame Favart, Boccaccio, Boulotte, Rosalinde, Fatinitza, Leni in *Drei Paar Schuhe,* the schöne Galathee and the schöne Helena, in *Carneval in Rom, Die Näherin, Der Seekadett, Madame Angots Tochter* and a whole range of other musical pieces, whilst also taking a turn in such dramatic roles as Camille, Therese Krones, Elizabeth I in *Graf Essex* and Donna Diana in an ever-whirling repertoire.

After two seasons she moved to the rival Germania Theater and the Thalia promptly imported her celebrated Vienna rival Josefine Gallmeyer as competition. However, Gallmeyer was mortally ill and soon returned to Europe whilst Geistinger continued to reign over the New York German theatre in a repertoire including such pieces as *Capitän Nicol* (ie, *I Carbonari*), *Durchgegangende Weiber,* Lecocq's *Trompette* (ie, *La Petite Mademoiselle,* Countess Cameroni), *Pariser Leben* (Gabrielle), *Leichte Kavallerie, Donna Juanita, Der Bettelstudent* (Symon), Gallmeyer's vehicle *Das verwunschene Schloss* (Regerl), Herve's *Lili* (Lili), *Sieben Mädchen und kein Mann* (Suppé's Operette with a reduced number of maidens), *Die Afrikareise* (Titania), *Apajune der Wassermann* (Natalitza) and Hennequin's *Die Kindsfrau* with a score now credited to Millöcker, along with those already played in her earlier seasons. She also appeared in an original American-German Lokalposse, *1776* (1884, Marion), composed by the young Ludwig Engländer.

Back in Europe she appeared at Vienna's Carltheater and in other theatres around Austria and Germany, scoring a particular success in the title role of *Therese Krones,* and otherwise appearing still in the famous roles of her earlier years, in such standard repertoire pieces as *Die schöne Galathee, Boccaccio* and *Der Bettelstudent* and, bit by bit, in marginally less central parts more suited to her age. She retired in 1889, but was forced by money problems to return in 1891 for a second American season, in 1896 for a third, and one last time in 1899 just before finally ending her memorable career at the age of 64.

In more recent times, Geistinger was musically portrayed on the stage by Elfie Mayerhofer as the heroine of the Operette *Die Walzerkönigin* (Ludwig Schmidseder/Aldo Pinelli, Hubert Marischka, Wiener Bürgertheater 1948) and on the screen in Willy Forst's *Operette,* by Maria Holst. In the biomusical made on the life of Gallmeyer, however, the old rivalry was continued: although Treumann, Matras, Offenbach and Anna Grobecker were portrayed as characters in the piece, Geistinger was left out.

Biography: Pirchan, E: *Marie Geistinger* (Verlag Wilhelm Frick, Vienna, 1947)

GÉLABERT, Marie (''Conchita'') (b Madrid, 1857; d Paris, 1922).

The young Marie Gélabert was freshly out of the Paris Conservatoire when she was chosen to play a third of the title role in *Jeanne, Jeannette et Jeanneton* (1876) at the Folies-Dramatiques alongside Mme Prelly and Berthe Stuart and, when the last-named singer was unable to fulfill the role allotted to her in the following year's *Les Cloches de Corneville* (1877), Gélabert, who had been on the point of giving up the theatre for married life, was given the creation of the part of Germaine. If the equally young Juliette Girard, in the showier role of Serpolette, won the more attention, Mlle Gélabert, who introduced the celebrated Chanson des Cloches, the Chanson des ''oui'' et ''non'' and ''Ne parlez pas de mon courage,'' was nevertheless—after two star roles in two outstandingly successful musicals—thoroughly launched as a Parisian opérette star.

She appeared in a third hit at the Folies-Dramatiques, playing the ingenue, Suzanne, to the *Madame Favart* of Girard, and then moved to the Renaissance where she appeared in the travesty role of the Prince in Lecocq's *La Jolie Persane* (1879), and to the Nouveautés for the vaudeville *La Beauté du Diable* (1880), in which she decorated her debut as a comedienne with some specially written songs by Coedès. She appeared at the Théâtre de la Porte-Saint-Martin in 1882 as Siebel in a revival of *Le Petit Faust* and scored a huge success with one of the Spanish songs which had long since landed her with the life-long nickname of ''Conchita,'' before going on to new roles in Planquette's *Les Voltigeurs de la 32ème* (1882, Béatrix), Audran's *Gillette de Narbonne* (1882, Rosita), *Les Pommes d'or* (1883, Princess Églantine), *La Dormeuse éveillée* (1883, Diane) and *Le Grand Mogol* (1884, Bengaline), alongside repeats of, in particular, her Germaine and Suzanne.

She was later seen creating roles in such pieces as *Le Dragon de la reine* (1888, Rose), *Le Voyage de Suzette* (1890, Paquita), *La Fée aux chèvres* (1890, Jacotte) and *Le Pays d'or* (1892, Flora Michon), and appearing as Claudine in *La Fille du tambour-major* (1889), etc, in a fine career, without again finding a part which reached the heights of the great roles of her earliest years.

GELBART, Larry [Simon] (b Chicago, 25 February 1923).

Primarily a writer for film and for television, in which areas he created the enormously successful television comedy series *M*A*S*H* and authored the screenplay for *Tootsie* (1982), Gelbart has worked only very infrequently for the theatre (*Sly Fox, Jump, Mastergate*) and for the musical stage. However, two of those infrequent musical ventures produced, at more than a quarter of a century's distance, two of the cleverest comical libretti of the postwar musical stage—the classical burlesque *A Funny Thing Happened on the Way to the Forum* (1962, Tony Award) and his parody of Hollywood's gumshoe detective films, *City of Angels* (1989, Tony Award).

1961 **The Conquering Hero** (Mark Charlap/Norman Gimbel) ANTA Theater 16 January

1962 **A Funny Thing Happened on the Way to the Forum** (Stephen Sondheim/w Burt Shevelove) Alvin Theater 8 May

1989 **City of Angels** (Cy Coleman/David Zippel) Virginia Theater 11 December

DIE GELBE JACKE *see* DAS LAND DES LÄCHELNS

GELD, Gary (b Paterson, NJ, 18 October 1935).

In a 1960s songwriting partnership with lyricist Peter Udell, Geld composed a series of hit songs, including ''Ain't Gonna Wash for a Week,'' ''Hurting Each Other,'' ''Ginny Come Lately,'' and ''Sealed with a Kiss,'' before making his debut as a Broadway composer with the score for the successful musical *Purlie* (''I Got Love,'' ''Walk Him Up the Stairs,'' ''The Bigger They Are, the Harder They Fall,'' ''Purlie''). An even bigger success came with the adaptation to the musical stage of the screenplay *Shenandoah,* for which Geld switched from the negro-toned music of his previous work to a country style which he had used with success in his earlier songwriting. *Shenandoah* mixed some richly baritone soliloquies (''I've Heard It All Before,'' etc) with such numbers as the country duo ''We Make a Beautiful Pair,'' the affecting ''The Only Home I Know'' and the rip-roaring ''Next to Lovin' (I like fightin')'' in an effective and popular combination which helped the piece to a long Broadway run.

A third attempt at a musical, with a 1978 adaptation of the Thomas Wolfe novel and its subsequent play *Look Homeward, Angel* was not a success (5 performances).

1970 **Purlie** (Peter Udell/Ossie Davis, Philip Rose, Udell) Broadway Theater 15 March

1975 **Shenandoah** (Udell/James Lee Barrett, Rose, Udell) Alvin Theater 7 January

1978 **Angel** (ex- *Look Homeward, Angel*) (Udell/Ketti Frings, Rose, Udell) Minskoff Theater 10 May

GENÉE, [Franz Friedrich] Richard (b Danzig, 7 February 1823; d Baden bei Wien, 15 June 1895). The most effective librettist and lyricist of the classic Viennese theatre, the musically trained Genée also scored a major success with his most important works as a composer for the Operette stage.

Born in Danzig, where his actor father was at the time engaged at the Stadttheater, Genée was brought up in Berlin and, after initially going through the earliest stages of medical studies, he turned to music as a career. In 1847 he became a conductor at the Danzig Stadttheater, by then run by his father, and he subsequently held engagements at Reval, Riga, Cologne, Aachen and Düsseldorf before returning to Danzig, where his first compositions, the burlesque Operette *Polyphem oder Ein Abenteuer auf Martinique* and the comic opera *Der Geiger von Tirol,* written to a libretto by his brother Rudolf, were staged. This latter piece went on to other productions, including one at Broadway's Thalia Theater (6 December 1884).

After his father's death, Genée left Danzig and held further conducting posts, initially at Mainz, where he provided the music for several short pieces, saw *Der Geiger von Tirol* revived (14 February 1859), and composed a two-act romantic comic opera for which he had himself written the text; then at Schwerin, where his Operette *Der Musikfeind* was produced, with sufficient success for it to be subsequently seen in Berlin and in Vienna; then at Amsterdam; and, between 1863–68, at the Landestheater in Prague. Whilst working in Prague, his composing and writing output included a two-act opera, *Am Runenstein* (1868), on which he collaborated with von Flotow, and an Operette, *Der schwarze Prinz. Der schwarze Prinz* was subsequently taken up for production by Maximilian Steiner at the Theater an der Wien (1 February 1867), and the following year Genée was taken on to the music staff at that same theatre. He was to remain an employee at the Theatre an der Wien for 10 years, until his success as an author finally allowed him to devote himself full time to writing.

Although the Theater an der Wien staged another of his short Operetten soon after his arrival, and he was called upon for such occasional music as the incidental score for the theatre's production of Sardou's *Vaterland* (*La Patrie*), Genée soon found himself heavily involved, beyond his musical duties, in another side of the theatre's business. With the huge vogue for French opéra-bouffe beginning to sweep Vienna, authors were needed to translate, adapt or largely rewrite the libretti and lyrics of these works for German-language audiences. Genée, who had written the texts for nearly all his own pieces, found himself promoted to adaptor-in-chief for the Theater an der Wien, at first alongside, and then overtaking, the equally versatile Julius Hopp. Over the next five years and more he turned out not very faithful, but highly stage-worthy, versions of the works of the librettists of Offenbach, Hervé, Lecocq and Jonas, as well as German-language versions of such pieces as von Flotow's *L'Ombre* and *Zilda* and Massé's *Galathée.*

Genée was amongst those who persuaded (somewhat) and then helped (considerably) dance-music composer Johann Strauss to write for the theatre in general and the Theater an der Wien in particular, and he returned to the writing of new libretti and lyrics when he supplied the texts for Strauss's *Die Fledermaus* and *Cagliostro in Wien.* On the second of these he worked with Camillo Walzel ("F Zell"), with whom he had recently formed a writing and adapting partnership. It was a partnership which would subsequently be responsible for the books and lyrics of a large proportion of the most important Viennese Operetten of the 1870s and 1880s: Suppé's *Fatinitza, Boccaccio* and *Donna Juanita*; Millöcker's *Apajune der Wassermann, Der Bettelstudent* and *Gasparone*; and Strauss's *Der lustige Krieg, Eine Nacht in Venedig* and *Das Spitzentuch der Königin*—most, but not all, adapted from French originals.

Genée's own musical knowledge contributed greatly to his value as, in particular, a lyricist but, whilst aiding the composers with whom he worked, he also continued to write theatre music himself and he had significant success with his own earliest Operette scores for the Theater an der Wien. *Der Seekadett* and *Nanon* both went on from their Viennese debuts to became major international successes.

After his retirement from the staff of the Theater an der Wien in 1879, Genée moved out of the city of Vienna and settled in Pressbaum where, in a villa overflowing with all kinds of animals from the more usual dogs and cats to birds, rabbits, monkeys and even a small bear, he continued his collaboration with Walzel by post. The division of their labor left much of the plot and dialogue to Walzel and the bulk of the lyric-writing to Genée, but such a division was by no means automatic and, on occasions, Genée worked alone on libretti. When Genée was involved in a project as composer, his collaborator took full credit for the text.

When the best years of Suppé, Millöcker and Strauss were past, Genée, sometimes with Zell and sometimes without, provided texts for several of the younger generation of composers, notably for Alfons Czibulka's pair of exportable successes, *Pfingsten in Florenz* and *Der Glücksritter,* but by and large these found much less success. Genée also composed several further Operetten of his own. None of these attained anything like the success of his two principal works, although *Nisida* won itself a Broadway production in a botched Augustin Daly version under the title *Zanina, or the Rover of Cambaye* and other productions in San Francisco, Prague and several German cities; *Der letzte Mohikaner* was seen at Berlin's Friedrich-Wilhelmstädtisches Theater, in Prague and in many provincial houses; *Die Dreizehn* also appeared at the Friedrich-Wilhelmstadtiches Theater (10 February 1888); and *Rosina,* a musical version of the famous farce *Un Chapeau de paille d'Italie* for which he wrote text and music, was played in Hungary and Germany after its Vienna showing.

Amongst Genée's other projects were an opera, *Die Fornariner,* mounted in Munich in October 1879, an adaptation of Scribe and St-George's *La Reine d'un jour* as the text for Ignaz Brüll's opera *Königin Mariette* (w Zell, Munich 16 June 1883), the scenario for a ballet *Viola,* based on Shakespeare's *Twelfth Night* and produced at the Hamburg Stadttheater (16 March 1893, mus: A Arensen), and the libretti for Flotow's *Die Musikanten* (Hannover, 1887) and Tomaschek's opera *Die Teufelsbrücke* (1892, w Julius Riegen).

A pastiche Operette, *Veilchenredoute* (Wiener Stadttheater 27 January 1942), by Hans Adler and Carl Cerne, was put together posthumously from Genée's music.

His brother **Rudolf GENÉE** (b Berlin, 12 December 1824; d Berlin, 19 January 1914), with whom he wrote *Der Geiger von Tirol,* wrote several other pieces for the musical stage including the one-act musical play *Der Kapellmeister,* set with Mozart music (Krolls Theater, Berlin 13 March 1896). He also wrote on theatrical and literary history.

His sister **Ottilie GENÉE** (b Berlin, 1830; d Berlin, 17 November 1911) was a successful performer in straight and musical theatre on both sides of the Atlantic, running the German theatre in San Francisco for nearly 20 years.

1856 **Polyphem, oder ein Abenteuer auf Martinique** (w Trautmann) 1 act Stadttheater, Danzig 20 September

1857 **Der Geiger von Tirol** (Rudolf Genée) Stadttheater, Danzig March

1858 **Benjamin, der seinen Vater sucht** (Theodore Hauptner/Ernst Dohm) 1 act Carltheater 17 July

1860 **Ein Trauerspiel** 1 act Mainz; Friedrich-Wilhelmstädtisches Theater, Berlin 22 June 1862

1861 **Ein Narrentraum** Mainz

1862 **Der Musikfeind** 1 act Grossherzogliches Hoftheater, Schwerin 8 February

1862 **Der Generalprobe** 1 act Friedrich-Wilhelmstädtisches Theater December

1862 **Die Herren von der Livree** (Eduard Jacobson) 1 act Berlin

1863 **Die Talismänner** (Ludwig Ullinger) Mainz March

1864 **Rosita** Mainz 1 January

1864 **Der Zopfabschneider** 1 act Schwerin 25 May

186? **Die Prinzessin von Kannibalen, oder Narrheit und Fotografie** 1 act

186? **Don Trabuco di Trabucillos** 1 act

1866 **Der schwarze Prinz** (Kotzebue ad) Landestheater, Prague 14 June

1869 **Der Däumling** (*Le Petit Poucet*) German version (Theater an der Wien)

1869 **Perichole, die Strassensängerin** (*La Périchole*) German version (Theater an der Wien)

1869 **Der Schrecken des Krieges** (*Les Horreurs de la guerre*) German version (Theater an der Wien)

1869 **Schwefeles der Höllenagent** 1 act Theater an der Wien 24 November

1870 **Ein Konzertprobe** 1 act Vaudevilletheater 19 March

1870 **Der Hexensabbath** 1 act Theater an der Wien 4 May

1870 **Der schöne Ritter Dunois** (*Le Beau Dunois*) German version (Theater an der Wien)

1870 **Die Banditen** (*Les Brigands*) German version (Theater an der Wien)

1870 **Doktor Faust Jr** (*Le Petit Faust*) German version (Theater an der Wien)

1872 **Fantasio** German version w Eduard Mäutner (Theater an der Wien)

1872 **Der schwarze Korsar** (*Le Corsair noir*) German version (Theater an der Wien)

1872 **Die Theaterprinzessin** (*La Diva*) German version w F Zell (Theater an der Wien)

1873 **Die Wilderer** (*Les Braconniers*) German version w Zell (Theater an der Wien)

1873 **Heloise und Abälard** German version (Theater an der Wien)

1874 **Die Japanesin** German version w Zell (Theater an der Wien)

1874 **Die Fledermaus** (Strauss/w Karl Haffner) Theater an der Wien 5 April

1875 **Cagliostro in Wien** (Strauss/w Zell) Theater an der Wien 27 February

1875 **Kleopatra** (w Carl Michael Ziehrer/Josef Steinher) Komische Oper 13 November

1876 **Fatinitza** (Suppé/w Zell) Carltheater 5 January

1876 **Luftschlösser** (Wilhelm Mannstädt, A Weller ad Karl Costa) Theater an der Wien 11 July

1876 **Fliegende Blätter** (arr/Costa) Theater an der Wien 1 August

1876 **Der Seekadett** (Zell) Theater an der Wien 24 October

1877 **Die Porträt-Dame, oder Die Profezeiungen des Quiribi** (Max Wolf/w Zell) Theater an der Wien 1 March

1877 **Nanon, die Wirthin vom "goldenen Lamm"** (Zell) Theater an der Wien 10 March

1877 **Im Wunderland der Pyramiden** (Zell) Komische Oper 25 December

1878 **Die letzten Mohikaner** (Zell) Theater am Gärtnerplatz, Munich 29 September; Theater an der Wien 4 January 1879

1878 **Niniche** German version w replacement score by Brandl (Carltheater)

1879 **Boccaccio** (Suppé/w Zell) Carltheater 1 February

1879 **Gräfin Dubarry** (Millöcker/w Zell) Theater an der Wien 31 October

1880 **Donna Juanita** (Suppé/w Zell) Carltheater 21 February

1880 **Die hübsche Perserin** (*La Jolie Persane*) German version w Zell (Theater an der Wien)

1880 **Das Spitzentuch der Königin** (Strauss/w Bohrmann-Riegen) Theater an der Wien 1 October

1880 **Nisida** (Zell, Moritz West) Carltheater 9 October

1880 **Papas Frau** (*La Femme a Papa*) German version with replacement score by Brandl (Carltheater)

1880 **Die drei Langhälse** (Josef Brandl/w Emil Pohl) Carltheater 11 December

1880 **Apajune der Wassermann** (Millöcker/w Zell) Theater an der Wien 18 December

1881 **Der Gascogner** (Suppé/w Zell) Carltheater 22 March

1881 **Die Jungfrau von Belleville** (Millöcker/w Zell) Theater an der Wien 29 October

1881 **Der lustige Krieg** (Strauss/w Zell) Theater an der Wien 25 November

1881 **Rosina** (Eugène Labiche ad) Carltheater 25 December

1882 **Der Bettelstudent** (Millöcker/w Zell) Theater an der Wien 6 December

1883 **Tag und Nacht** (*Le Jour et la nuit*) German version (Theater an der Wien)

1883 **Die Afrikareise** (Suppé/w West) Theater an der Wien 17 March

1883 **Eine Nacht in Venedig** (Strauss/w Zell) Friedrich-Wilhelmstädtisches Theater, Berlin, 3 October

1884 **Gasparone** (Millöcker/w Zell) Theater an der Wien 26 January

1884 **Der Marquis von Rivoli** (Louis Roth/w Benjamin Schier) Theater an der Wien 13 April

1884 **Pfingsten in Florenz** (Alfons Czibulka/w Julius Riegen) Theater an der Wien 20 December

1885 **Eine gemachte Frau** (E Jacobson) Residenztheater, Dresden 6 January

1885 **Zwillinge** (w L Roth/w Zell) Theater an der Wien 14 February

1885 **Der Jagdjunker [der Kaiserin]** (Alfons Czibulka/w Genée) Walhalla Theater, Berlin 3 December; revised version Carltheater 20 March 1886

1886 **Der Nachtwandler** (L Roth/w Zell) Friedrich-Wilhelmstädtisches Theater, Berlin 25 September

1886 **Die Piraten** (Scribe ad w Zell) Walhalla-Theater, Berlin 8 October

1886 **Der Viceadmiral** (Millöcker/w Zell) Theater an der Wien 9 October

1887 **Rikiki** (Josef Hellmesberger/w Mannstädt) Carltheater 28 September

1887 **Die Dreizehn** (Scribe ad w Zell) Carltheater 14 November

1887 **Der Glücksritter** (Czibulka/w Mannstädt, Bruno Zappert) Carltheater 22 December

1888 **Der Freibuter** (*Surcouf*) German version w Zappert (Carltheater)

1888 **Der Mikado** German version w Zell (Theater an der Wien)

1888 **Die Jagd nach dem Glück** (Suppé/w Zappert) Carltheater 27 October

1888 **Ein Deutschmeister** (Ziehrer/w Zappert) Carltheater 30 November

1889 **Die indische Witwe** (Gustav Geiringer/w Zell) 1 act Theater an der Wien 9 February

1889 **Capitän Fracassa** (Rudolf Dellinger/w Zell) Theater an der Wien 21 September

1889 **Page Fritz** (Max von Weinzierl, Alfred Strasser/w Alexander Landesberg) Deutsches Theater, Prague 24 November; Friedrich-Wilhelmstädtisches Theater, Berlin July 1891

1889 **Die Piraten** (*The Pirates of Penzance*) German version (Theater an der Wien)

1889 **Der Königsgardist** (*The Yeomen of the Guard*) German version w Zell (Krolls Theater, Berlin)

1889 **Polnische Wirtschaft** (Hermann Zumpe/w West) Carl-Schultze Theater, Hamburg; Friedrich-Wilhelmstädtisches Theater, Berlin 26 November 1891

1890 **Die Gondoliere** (*The Gondoliers*) German version w Zell (Theater an der Wien)

1890 **Mam'zelle Nitouche** German version (Theater an der Wien)

1891 **Die Basoche** (*La Basoche*) German version (Friedrich-Wilhelmstädtisches Theater, Berlin)

1891 **Madame Bonbon** (*Madame Boniface*) German version w Heinrich Thalboth (Theater an der Wien)

1891 **Miss Helyett** German version (Wallner Theater, Berlin)

1892 **Fanchon's Leyer** (*La Fille de Fanchon la vielleuse*) German version (Theater an der Wien)

1892 **Mädchenschule** (*Un lycée de jeunes filles*) German version and additional music (Thomas-Theater, Berlin)

1892 **Rotkäppchen** (*La Roussotte*) German version w new score Thomas-Theater, Berlin 6 February

1892 **Signora Vendetta** (Hermann Hirschel) Wiesbaden 14 June

1892 **Der Millionen-Onkel** (Adolf Müller jr/w Zell) Theater an der Wien 5 November

1892 **Der Freiwillige** (Friedrich Sonkup/w Costa) Prague 27 December

1893 **Die wachsame Schildwache** (Rudolf Genée) 1 act Philharmonia, Berlin 28 February

1893 **Der Taugenichts** (*A suhanc*) German version (Theater Unter den Linden, Berlin)

1893 **Das Mädchen von Mirano** (Alexander Neumann/w Zell) Carltheater 6 April

1893 **Freund Felix** (w L Herrmann) Friedrich-Wilhelmstädtisches Theater, Berlin 14 October

1894 **Mam'sell Cerevis** (*Mam'zelle Carabin*) German version w Robert Pohl (Theater am Gärtnerplatz, Munich)

1894 **Die Königin von Gamara** (Neumann/w Leo Stein) Carltheater 27 October

1895 **Engelsherz** (Raoul Mader/w Hugo Regel) Carltheater 12 January

1895 **Die Welsenbraut** (Alfred Zamara/w Max Tull) Stadttheater, Hamburg 20 March

1895 **The Chieftain** (German version) (Theater am Gärtnerplatz, Munich)

GENEVIÈVE DE BRABANT Opéra-bouffe in 3 acts by Hector Crémieux and Étienne Tréfeu. Music by Jacques Offenbach. Original version in 2 acts by Tréfeu. Théâtre des Bouffes-Parisiens, Paris, 19 November 1859; revised version Théâtre des Menus-Plaisirs, Paris, 26 December 1867.

Of the great opéras-bouffes of Offenbach's early years, the one which has suffered the most inexplicable eclipse in the 20th century is *Geneviève de Brabant.* Whilst *Orphée aux enfers* and *La Belle Hélène* still hold the top of the market in musical and opera houses round the world, *La Grande-Duchesse* and the not-so-bouffe *La Périchole* surface from time to time, and marginally more imaginative houses are occasionally tempted into a *Barbe-bleue,* a *Pont des soupirs* or a *Les Brigands,* Tréfeu's hilarious burlesque of the medieval age has followed the other most celebrated medieval parody of the era, *Chilpéric,* into obscurity.

Geneviève de Brabant was the heroine of a favorite tale from the *Legenda Aurea* (''The Golden Legend''), a collection of saints' lives compiled in the 13th century by the Italian monk Jacobus de Voragine, which had won particular popularity in variant versions in Germany (by Ludwig Tieck) and in France, where it had appeared in a burlesque form (''complainte bouffe'') on the stage of the Palais-Royal as recently as 1851 (15 March). The wife of Count Palatine Sigfried of Brabant, in the days of Charles Martel, Geneviève was accused of infidelity and chased into the Ardennes forest where she gave birth to a son. The babe was suckled by a white doe before the Count discovered the accusations to be false and brought wife and son home.

Tréfeu stayed close to the old tale, but told it with burlesque humour rather than saintly drama. His Geneviève (Mlle Maréchal) is the victim of Duke Sifroy (Léonce)'s bosom buddy, Golo (Désiré), who has systematically distracted Sifroy from his conjugal sex life with the hope that he, Golo, will, in the absence of a legitimate heir, become the next Duke of Brabant. The pretty little pastry cook, Drogan (Lise Tautin), bakes a virility pie for the Duke which puts a fathering flicker into his eye, and Golo has to move swiftly to put Sifroy off his stride. He counters the danger by accusing Drogan of dilly-dallying with Geneviève. Then, just to complicate

Plate 142a. **Geneviève de Brabant.** *A French artist's impressions of two scenes from the original production of the show.*

matters, Sifroy is dragged crossly off to the crusades by Charles Martel (Guyot), and, since best buddy has had his ear the last, he goes off repudiating Geneviève and leaving Golo as regent. The abandoned heroine takes refuge from the lubricious villain in the forest. There she meets a crazy jack-in-the-box hermit and has a generally comico-melodramatic time, whilst her husband—who has got no closer to Palestine than Asnières—is holed up with Martel and his mates, having a very convivial time with a rough and tough lady called Isoline. However, he gets home in time to checkmate Golo, rescue the blameless Geneviève, and hand over the termagent Isoline to her long-lost husband, who is none other than the horrified Golo.

In the very first version of *Geneviève,* as produced in 1859, the part which would become Drogan in the later rewrites was a multiple role, with Mlle Tautin appearing as Mathieu, as Gracioso (a page), as Isoline and also as

Plate 142b. **Geneviève de Brabant.** *An English poster showing the main attractions of the hugely successful British version—the duo of the gens d'armes and the bulging charms of Miss Emily Soldene.*

''le chevalier noir'' and ''la bohémienne'' in the many disguises the plot involved. Another role, that of ''le jeune Arthur,'' played by Bonnet, was also due for a quick extinction, as *Geneviève* was altered and made over into its definitive version.

Offenbach's score was a delicious mixture of the broadly burlesque and the charming. Amongst the happiest bits of burlesque were what became Drogan's rondo du pâté (''Salut! Noble assemblée''), vaunting his potent pie; Sifroy's nonsensical crowing Couplets de la poule; and Charles Martel's arrival to a merry bolero (''J'arrive armé de pied en cap''), whilst pieces such as the superb three-soprano Trio de la main et de la barbe and Drogan's serenade to Geneviève (''En passant sous la fenêtre'') supplied the beauty, and the swingeing march finale which saw the Carolan army depart for Palestine, the booming climax. In the original layout, Mlle Tautin also indulged in a Chanson de la bohémienne, a hymn to Geneviève and a Rondo des jeux, and Bonnet had a ''fable de l'enfant.'' There was, as yet, no gens d'armes duo for, in this early version, the two comical law enforcers had not yet been tacked into the action.

The 1859 *Geneviève de Brabant* did not have the same huge and instant success that *Orphée aux enfers* had done, and after 50 performances the composer-producer took the show off and replaced it with a hasty pasticcio revue. In spite of this, foreign producers were still interested and the first to move was the ever-ready Karl Treumann in Vienna. Treumann mounted an uncredited adaptation (possibly his own) at his Theater am Franz-Josefs-Kai under the title *Die schöne Magellone.* He himself played Sifroy (now called Siegfried), Therese Schäfer was his wife, Magellone, Anton Ascher the villainous Ulfo and Herr Grois played Charles Martel, whilst Fr Majeranowska played Isoline who, in this version, was still also the page, Grazioso, the gypsy girl and the black knight. Knaack appeared as ''little Arthur'' and Hopp was Narcziss, the court poet. *Die schöne Magellone*'s popularity was limited, but it nevertheless went on to be played in Berlin and in Prague in German, and in Hungary in Hungarian (ad Endre Latabár) with Véla Szilágyi, József Kovacs, Jenő Toth, Rosa Víg, János Parthenyi and Gyula Virágh featured in the Budai Népszínház's original production.

If the beginning had been only mildly promising, however, things soon looked up. In 1867 Offenbach, Tréfeu and Hector Crémieux put together a new, enlargened and slightly less extravagantly burlesque three-act/nine-scene version of *Geneviève de Brabant* which was mounted by Gaspari at the new Théâtre des Menus-Plaisirs (25 December). Most of the original score was maintained, but there were some additions made, including the veritable double act for two goonish gens d'armes (''Protéger le repos des villes'') which would become the show's long-range hit, whilst the Asnières scene was expanded to include a yodeling tyrolienne and a dance divertissement. Zulma Bouffar took the now star role of Drogan with Mme Baudier as Geneviève, Gourdon as Sifroy, Daniel Bac as Golo, and Ginet and Gabel in the low comedy roles of sergent Grabuge and fusilier Pitou. Once again, the piece was only a fair success in Paris, but this time the rest of the world took a little more notice, and this time (and in more or less this form) *Geneviève de Brabant* became an international hit.

The ''new'' *Geneviève* was given a rather more faithful German-language rendering under Strampfer at Vienna's Theater an der Wien (ad Julius Hopp) soon after the end of the Paris season. Albin Swoboda (Siegfried), Lori Hild (Genovefa), Jani Szíka (Martell), Carl Adolf Friese (Golo), Marie Geistinger (Drogan) and Blasel and Rott as the gens d'armes headed a starry cast, and there was a spectacular ballet, ''Die drei Lebensalter,'' interpolated into the sixth of the seven scenes in which the high jinks at Asnières was replaced by an ''Altdeutscher Narrenabend.'' It was played 12 times. Conversely, *Geneviève*'s American production was a notable success. Joseph Grau's newly imported French opéra-bouffe company introduced the piece at the Théâtre Français with Rose Bell starring as Drogan, Marie Desclauzas as Geneviève and Bourgoin and Gabel as the gens d'armes. They were so successful that H L Bateman's previously all-conquering opéra-bouffe company, headed by Lucille Tostée, found its audiences at Pike's Opera House sadly depleted, and the canny Bateman, having reaped the rewards of introducing *La Grande-Duchesse* and the can-can to America, swiftly sold out his interests. *Geneviève* proved to be the backbone of the new company's repertoire (*L'Oeil crevé, Fleur de thé, La Vie parisienne, La Grande-Duchesse, Chilpéric, M Choufleuri*) and it was played more than one hundred times during their season, provoking the burlesquers of Kelly and Leon's Minstrels to mount a *Gin-ne-veve de Graw,* with Leon impersonating Rose Bell, at their famous minstrel house (2 January 1869), and Dan Bryant to come out with the felicitously titled *Geneviève de Bryant.*

The Broadway success, however, was nothing to that which the piece won in Britain. Music-hall manager Charles Morton and wealthy bookmaker, Charles Head, had gone into businesss producing opéra-bouffe at the old Philharmonic Music Hall in suburban Islington, and Morton allied himself with rising star Emily Soldene and adapter/director H B Farnie to produce Farnie's version of *Geneviève de Brabant.* With Soldene as Drogan, Selina Dolaro (Geneviève), John Rouse (Sifroy), Henry Lewens (Golo) and Edward Marshall and Felix Bury as the gens d'armes, Farnie's production of *Geneviève* caused the kind of sensation that *Orphée* had done in Paris (but not in London) and that only *Chilpéric* of French pieces had even approached in England. The English adaptation of the "very amusing but very indelicate" piece was lauded to the skies; the gens d'armes duo (in Farnie's famous translation "We're public guardians, bold yet wa-a-ry"), the Serenade, and the Balcony duo became the hits of the era; and Soldene and Dolaro the idolized heroines of the London stage, as the piece played on at its out-of-the-mainstream theatre for a remarkable first limited season of 175 performances, before heading off round the country.

Henry Hersee hurried out another version of the show for Liverpool, and others (Edward Adams, John Grantham, etc) followed suit, but it was the Farnie version which was the hit. It returned to the Philharmonic after its tour for a second run which allowed it to total an amazing 307 London nights by 30 March 1873. The following year it was back again, for a season at the Opera Comique (18 April) with Soldene, Rouse, Marshall and Bury all still in their original roles, and, after the buxom Emily had given her version to New York—the city's first English-language performances of the show, and its first sighting of genuine opéra-bouffe in English—it was mounted there again in 1876 (20 March) with the star still featured in her favorite role. In 1878 (23 January), the Philharmonic brought their big hit back, with Alice May as Drogan, but Soldene reclaimed her own when she starred in a glamorous production at the Alhambra later the same year (16 September) alongside Lewens, Thomas Aynsley Cook and Constance Loseby, and again, one last time, at the Royalty Theatre in 1881—a whole decade after she had first squeezed into the tights of the plump little page. Soldene played Drogan for the last times in San Francisco in 1890 and in Sydney in 1892, and her most famous number, the Balcony duet, at galas and benefits till the end of her life.

Australia followed Britain's example, and a localized version of Farnie's *Geneviève de Brabant* was mounted there by W S Lyster (ad Garnet Walch) in 1873. Alice May (Drogan), Armes Beaumont (Sifroy) and Carrie Emmanuel (Geneviève) featured in a version which played fast and loose with both text and music, but which was undeniably successful through 15 performances. Following the Melbourne season, the show was due to be seen in Sydney, but the traditional pantomime period was nigh. Willie Gill at the Queen's solved the problem of the latest hit by simply interpolating half of *Geneviève*'s music into his homemade pantomime, but the Royal Victoria Theatre's B N Jones went further and presented what was basically *Geneviève* as a putative pantomime, equipped with a harlequinade, under the title *Geneviève de Brabant, or Harlequin King of the Bakers, or Four-and-Twenty Baker Boys Baked in a Pie, When the Pie Was Opened*... (26 December 1873). Miss May repeated her Drogan alongside Henry Hallam (Sifroy), Sam Poole (Golo) and Miss Lambert (Geneviève) through a fine 24 nights. Australia later saw Soldene's Drogan, for *Geneviève de Brabant* was one of the prime pieces in the prima donna's repertoire when she visited Australia and New Zealand, equipped with the usual exaggerated publicity of the era ("as performed by her over 500 consecutive nights at the Philharmonic, London") and one of her original gens d'armes, Edward Marshall. Edward Farley (Cocorico, ie, Sifroy), the lanky J H Jarvis (Golo) and Rose Stella (Geneviève) took the other main roles.

Whilst *Geneviève* had been going on to become the rage of Britain, back in France Offenbach and Tréfeu had had another go at proving to Parisians that they should be making it an equal success there (Théâtre de la Gaîté 25 February 1875). Adolphe Jaime joined the rewriting team on this occasion, and the piece was expanded with a goodly dose of the kind of spectacle that had served Offenbach productions well on earlier occasions. The 14 scenes and tableaux now included "a divertissement of nurses and babies" in Act I, a fourth-act visit to an enchanted fairy garden where a pageant of the heroes and heroines of poetry and drama was displayed before the genius of the place, and a huge parade that was included to allow the use of a vast and expensive array of armor which the composer-producer had had made for his disastrous production of Sardou's *La Haine.* A special role, Briscotte, was written in to allow the appearance (with songs, some new Offenbach, some from her repertoire) of the celebrated heroine of the cafés-concerts, Mlle Thérésa, alongside whom Mme Matz-Ferrare played Drogan, Christian was Golo, Mlle Perret Geneviève, and Scipion and Gabel were the gens d'armes. The production inspired a ''folie-vaudeville'' *Geneviève de Brébant* at the Théâtre Déjazet (Grangé, Buguet, Bernard, plus some of Offenbach's music, 18 March) but it proved to be far too luxurious ever to break even and, although it ran more than 100 nights, it broke the bank. However, if Offenbach had failed thrice to make a success out of his witty and tuneful work, Fernand Samuel proved at the last that it could be done. In 1908 he mounted a version of the last version of *Geneviève de Brabant* for 58 nights at the Variétés with Jeanne Saulier (Drogan), Max Dearly (Golo), Guy (Sifroy), André Simon (Martell) and Geneviève Vix (Geneviève). The merits of the piece were, at last, agreed on by French audiences, but in the three-quarters of a century since, Paris has not again seen *Geneviève de Brabant.*

In habitual style, the Spanish borrowed Tréfeu's libretto and attached a fresh score to it for a *Genoveva de Brabante* produced in Madrid in 1868.

Austria: Theater am Franz-Josefs-Kai *Die schöne Magellone* 3 April 1861, Theater an der Wien *Genovefa von Brabant* 9 May 1868; Germany: Friedrich-Wilhelmstädtisches Theater 1 July 1861; Hungary: Budai Népszínház *Genoveva* 11 May 1864; USA: Théâtre Français 22 October 1868, Lyceum Theater (Eng) 2 November 1874; UK: Philharmonic Theatre, Islington 11 November 1871; Australia: Prince of Wales Theatre, Melbourne 11 September 1873

Recordings: complete (Bourg), selection (Golden Age of Opera)

GENNARO, Peter (b Metairie, La, 23 November 1919; d Oxford, Conn, 28 September 2000).

Peter Gennaro danced in a number of Broadway musicals, including *Make Mine Manhattan, Kiss Me, Kate, Guys and Dolls, By the Beautiful Sea* and *The Pajama Game* and had a featured role as Carl, dancing ''Mu-cha-cha'' in *Bells Are Ringing* (1956).

His first choreographic assignment for Broadway was on the 1955 *Seventh Heaven,* and in 1957 he assisted Jerome Robbins on the celebrated dances for *West Side Story* before going on to choreograph *Fiorello!* (1959), *The Unsinkable Molly Brown* (1960 and film), *Mr President* (1962), *Bajour* (1964), *Jimmy* (1969), the 1973 version of *Irene,* the long-running *Annie, Carmelina, One Night Stand* and the 1982 *Little Me* revival for Broadway and to provide the original part of the dance content for the London stage version of *Singin' in the Rain.* He later repeated that assignment in a different show based on the same source on the road in America. In 1989 he choreographed a Broadway revival of *The Threepenny Opera.*

GENSLER, Lewis E (b New York, 4 December 1891; d New York, 10 January 1978).

In a decade as a Broadway composer, Gensler was responsible for all or part of a half-dozen musical comedy scores, which included one hit and one near-miss. A Nora Bayes vehicle, *Queen o' Hearts,* was a 39-performance flop, *Be Yourself,* a curiously uneven piece on which George S Kaufman, Marc Connelly and Ira Gershwin also worked, lasted 93 nights, and Gensler contributed the song ''Keep Smiling at Trouble'' to Al Jolson's *Big Boy* (1925), before his musical version of *Captain Jinks* arrived in town with a dazzling pre-Broadway run to its credit. Under the circumstances, its 21 weeks in New York were considered a disappointment. However, the following season Gensler finally hit the target when *Queen High,* which had had almost as promising a tryout, not only won a fine Broadway run and a couple of overseas productions but also brought its composer his biggest-ever song hit with ''Cross Your Heart.''

Ups-a-Daisy, with a libretto just a little too similar to that of *Going Up,* had no song similar to ''Cross Your Heart'' and a much shorter life, whilst *The Gang's All Here* lasted only three weeks. Gensler made his last Broadway venture with the revue *Ballyhoo* of 1932 (also co-director) before moving on to Hollywood in 1933. There he operated as a composer, a writer and as a producer (*The Big Broadcast of 1937, Artists and Models*), turning out a series of songs of which ''Love Is Just Around the Corner'' (w Leo Robin), sung by Bing Crosby in *Here Is My Heart,* was amongst the most successful.

Gensler also ventured as a producer on Broadway, joining with Morris Green to mount the successful 1930 show *Fine and Dandy,* with Joe Cook starred, and his own *The Gang's All Here* later the same season. This was apparently followed by a piece called *Hot and Bothered* which didn't make it to Broadway, and may not have, in spite of being announced, even made it to the stage. Another musical, *Melody in Spring,* also credited to him, seems to have gone the same way, leaving no trace.

He put in one posthumous reappearance when his ''Love Is Just Around the Corner'' resurfaced in 1986 as part of the score of the Broadway musical *Big Deal.*

1922 **Queen o' Hearts** (w Dudley Wilkinson/Oscar Hammerstein II/Hammerstein, Frank Mandel) Cohan Theater 10 October

1924 **Be Yourself** (w Milton Schwarzwald/Ira Gershwin/Marc Connelly, George S Kaufman) Harris Theater 3 September

1925 **Captain Jinks** (w Stephen Jones/B G De Sylva/Laurence Schwab) Martin Beck Theater 8 September

1926 **Queen High** (De Sylva/Schwab) Ambassador Theater 8 September

1928 **Ups-a-Daisy** (Clifford Grey, Robert A Simon) Shubert Theater 8 October

1931 **The Gang's All Here** (w Owen Murphy/Simon/Hammerstein, Russel Crouse, Morrie Ryskind) Imperial Theater 18 February

GENTLEMAN JOE Musical farce in 2 acts by Basil Hood. Music by Walter Slaughter. Prince of Wales Theatre, London, 2 March 1895.

Gentleman Joe was written to provide comedian Arthur Roberts, the original top-biller of *In Town* and of many burlesques, with a star role in a reasonably legitimate musical comedy. Legitimacy was ensured by selecting the promising Basil Hood, not yet acclaimed as the successor to Gilbert, as book and lyric writer, and Hood succeeded in coming up with a character and a plot which provided the undisciplined Roberts with the finest role of his career.

Gentleman Joe, a cockney cabbie, goes courting housemaid Emma while her mistress, Mrs Ralli Carr, a society "woman who arranges things," is away. He finds himself mistaken for the poor but titled Irishman whom Mrs Carr is angling to separate from one of her poor but pretty clients (who requires a rich husband) and attach to a rich American (who requires a titled husband). Many complications emerge, first in London and then on the beach to where everyone repairs in Act II, before Joe and his Emma can, like everyone else, get safely together.

Joe was a splendid creation, and since the plot was one which allowed the popular Roberts his head with his usual and intermittently even original ad-libbing, disguises and grimacing, without destroying the run of things, the star was able to make a great hit with the character and with his songs, "In My 'Ansom," "Gentleman Joe" and anything else he liked to ease into the minstrel show featured in the beach section of the show ("new scene . . . 'The Bathing Incident' tonight"; "Arthur Roberts' new song . . . 5 recalls nightly"). The most successful of these interpolations was the smutty "She Wanted Something to Play With," the most substantial a whole burlesque scene on the currently successful *Trilby.*

Kitty Loftus (Emma) had a hit with "The Magic of His Eye," Aida Jenoure (Mrs Carr) stopped the show with her description of how she earns "A Little Commission," and Kate Cutler and William Philp had the prettiest of Walter Slaughter's songs in the roles of the Irish peer and his girl, but the big success of the score was a raucous piece for the extremely spirited American performer Sadie Jerome, playing a title-seeking, transatlantic heiress, declaring "Lalage Potts, That's Me." The song made a temporary star of Miss Jerome who was promptly hired for the next Roberts show but sacked when the world finally realized that she couldn't sing and couldn't act and endless energy and a blossoming bust line only went so far.

Gentleman Joe had 391 London performances, was sent out in no less than four touring companies in 1896 with Frank Danby, Edwin Brett, Harry Roxbury and Fred Lyne all giving their Joes to the various corners of Britain, and it cleaned up over many years on the British and colonial circuits. In America, however, it ran into trouble. First of all, the exiled English writer Paul Potter (the same Potter who would make his fortune with *Trilby*) ripped off several numbers, the designs and much of Roberts's stage business for a farce comedy called *A Stag Party* and then two rival *Gentleman Joe*s turned up on Broadway. Lawsuits flew, in the finest American theatrical tradition, and, in the storm, not only was the pirate sunk but also the legitimate *Joe.* Rudolf Aronson and James T Powers's production (Bijou Theater 30 January 1896) played 48 performances, whilst M B Curtis, with the law put on to him by the more powerful Aronson, had to hide away on his own first night (Newark 25 December, Fifth Avenue Theater 6 January) and let the director play the lead role; his *Gentleman Joe* came off after 10 nights. Both gentlemen, of course, claimed to have the rights direct from Lowenfeld. The truth of it seems to be that Lowenfeld had sold to Curtis, but then felt inclined to take the classier offer when it came along behind, and looked around for a get-out. He found one, but he killed his show.

Australia saw W Louis Bradfield as Joe, whilst London's production ran on: the touring Gaiety Theatre company played some performances of this non-George Edwardes production amongst their *Gaiety Girls* and *Shop Girls* later in 1895, another Edwardes rep company introduced *Gentleman Joe* to South Africa around the same time, and the show, while it did not penetrate the non-English-speaking markets, made its way, usually with unbounded success, to most corners of the world where there was an Anglophone audience.

Australia: Lyceum, Sydney 24 August 1895; USA: Miner's Fifth Avenue Theater 6 January 1896

GENTLEMEN PREFER BLONDES Musical in 2 acts by Anita Loos and Joseph Fields based on Anita Loos's book of the same title. Lyrics by Leo Robin. Music by Jule Styne. Ziegfeld Theater, New York, 8 December 1949.

Anita Loos's comic novella *Gentlemen Prefer Blondes,* with its memorable blonde money-box of a heroine, Lorelei Lee, was made into a stage play by its author with (apparently very) little help from her husband, John Emerson, in 1926 (Times Square Theater 28 September), and was filmed in 1928 before going on to be made up into a stage musical in 1949.

Lorelei Lee (Carol Channing) from Little Rock, Arkansas, is nicely looked after by Gus Esmond (Jack McCauley), the heir to a button-manufacturing fortune, who supplies her with the diamonds necessary to a girl's well-being. Business means Gus has to stay behind when they should have sailed for Europe together, so Lorelei sets off with just her good friend, a Follies girl called Dorothy Shaw (Yvonne Adair), who has curious ideas about love being more important than diamonds, as chaperone. On the voyage, Lorelei persuades one Sir Francis Beekman (Rex Evans) to sponsor her purchase of a diamond tiara, and in Paris she whizzes round the shops with fitness freak Josephus Gage (George S Irving), the wealthy owner of the patent to the new zip-fastener. When button-man Gus turns up, the zip-fastener in Lorelei's new dress causes a breach between them, but, by the time an act full of incidental entertainments has passed, Lorelei has not only rewon over her most reliable gentleman, but also conquered his enormously wealthy father. Zip-fasteners and buttons amalgamate, and Lorelei weds her Gus. As for Dorothy, she overcomes her curious ideas long enough to pair off with vastly wealthy Henry Spofford (Eric Brotherson). Alice Pearce played Henry's mother, converted from a careful life to hedonism under Lorelei's spell, Howard Morris and Mort Marshall were a pair of four-faced Parisian lawyers, and Anita Alvarez was a running joke of a permanently practicing dancer.

The score to *Gentlemen Prefer Blondes* was topped by two numbers for its heroine which became favorites: ''Diamonds Are a Girl's Best Friend'' and ''A Little Girl from Little Rock,'' but the rest of the cast were less well served, best-friend Dorothy finding her merriest moment in ''I Love What I'm Doing (when I'm doing it for love).''

Carol Channing's bordering-on-the-burlesque portrayal of the blonder-than-a-bombshell Lorelei proved the high spot of Herman Levin and Oliver Smith's production which ran for 740 performances on Broadway before going right on back west to be made into a Hollywood film with Marilyn Monroe and Jane Russell as its Lorelei and its Dorothy. Only the star's two top songs and ''Bye Bye Baby'' were retained from the score, being supplemented by a pair of additional songs by Hoagy Carmichael and Harold Adamson.

In spite of its genuine success in America, *Gentlemen Prefer Blondes* moved very slowly abroad. It was 13 years after its premiere before the show was produced in London, with Dora Bryan starred as Lorelei and Anne Hart as Dorothy, for a run of 223 performances, and Europe passed until a German *Blondinen bevorzugt* (ad Gabrielle Peter, Beate Rygiert-Schmidt, music arr by Volker M Plangg) was mounted in Pforzheim in 1988.

Broadway, however, did get a second and even a third helping. A revised *Gentlemen Prefer Blondes,* with Miss Channing repeating a version of her original role which had her looking back, 25 years on, was produced by Guber and Gross at the Civic Center, Oklahoma City under the title *Lorelei* (26 February 1973, billed as a ''world première''). Comden, Green and Styne wrote a number of additional and replacement songs to the revised book by Kenny Solms and Gail Parent, several of which went by the board before the show reached Broadway, nearly a year later (27 January 1974 Palace Theater), for a run of 320 performances. The original version was returned to in 1995 when a Goodspeed Opera House mounting was brought to the Lyceum Theater (10 April) with K T Sullivan (Lorelei) and Karen Prucznik (Dorothy) featured. It went its way after just 24 showings. However, London too got a second showing when the Open Air Theatre, Regent's Park, mounted a revival in their 1998 repertoire season (21 July) with Debby Bishop, Sara Crowe and Clive Rowe amongst the cast.

Lorelei Lee, it has to be recorded, was and is a very close relative indeed of C M S McLellan's *Glittering Gloria,* who had made her way to the London (without music) and American (musical) stages more than half a century before her. Adele Ritchie was Gloria Grant, Lorelei's prototype, at Daly's Theatre (15 February 1904, mus: Bernard Rolt), good friend Dorothy (even the name was the same) was played by Phyllis Rankin, and the diamond-giving gentleman was played by Cyril Scott. But Lorelei didn't nod her recognition to Gloria anymore than Gloria did to what looked very much as if it might in any case have been a French original.

UK: Prince's Theatre 20 August 1962; Germany: Stadttheater, Pforzheim *Blondinen bevorzugt* 31 December 1988

Film: Twentieth Century Fox 1953

Recordings: original cast (Columbia), London cast (HMV) *Lorelei* (MGM), 1995 US revival cast (DRG), film soundtrack (DRG)

GEORGE M! Musical in 2 acts by Michael Stewart and John & Fran Pascal. Music and lyrics taken from the works of George M Cohan. Palace Theater, New York, 10 April 1968.

A biomusical put together around the songs of George M Cohan, *George M!* allowed Joel Grey, in the character of the actor-author-composer, Jerry Dodge (father Jerry Cohan), Betty Ann Grove (mother Nellie Cohan), Bernadette Peters (sister Josie Cohan), Jamie Donnelly (wife Ethel Levey), Jacqueline Alloway (Fay Templeton) and the rest of the cast to run through such Cohan hits as ''Mary,'' ''Forty-Five Minutes from

Broadway," "Give My Regards to Broadway," "I'm a Yankee Doodle Dandy," "Nellie Kelly, I Love You," "Harrigan," "Over There" and many more, to the accompaniment of a gently slanted version of his life story.

David Black, Konrad Matthaei and Lorin E Price produced *George M!* for a 435-performance run on Broadway; it was subsequently televised, with Grey repeating his stage role, in 1970, and stayed around long enough to be mounted as a Las Vegas spectacular in 1993.

A two-handed Hungarian musical Cohan-compilation by Gábor Marton and Attila Galambos entitled *A Broadway harangja,* produced at Budapest's Komédium Színház in 1994 (26 March), featured Tamás Dunai as Cohan.

Recording: original cast (Columbia)

LES GÉORGIENNES Opéra-bouffe in 3 acts by Jules Moinaux. Music by Jacques Offenbach. Théâtre des Bouffes-Parisiens, Paris, 16 March 1864.

The men of Djégani, Georgia, like a peaceful family life and they are not fond of fighting. However, the women of the town are furious and humiliated when 150 of their menfolk get beaten by default by only 32 of the enemy and so, with the perfumer's wife, Feroza (Delphine Ugalde), at their head, they take up arms to revenge and defend their city. The Pasha of the opposing forces, Rhododendron (Pradeau), is caught inside the city, whence he has come to prospect for his harem, and is swept up in the affair. When the two-faced Boboli (Léonce) lets it out that the men have never actually been to war, and their wounds are all sham, Feroza has them all thrown into prison, but each woman helps her own man to escape and they next appear disguised as gypsies, apparently ready to help Rhododendron in his plan to carry off a supply of harem material. However, the Pasha's disguise has been seen through, and in the end the men and women of Djégani join happily together to celebrate his capture. Zulma Bouffar played Nani, the wife of Poterno (Jean-Paul), and Désiré was the perfumer Jol-Hiddin, both of them partaking largely of the action.

The music of *Les Géorgiennes* featured some strong and showy pieces for Feroza on the normally masculine subjects of war and wine (Chanson de la treille, Chanson à boire, Chant de guerre), and some gentler but equally soprano pieces for Nani ("Ah! vraiment c'est charmant," "Sous cet uniforme modeste"), whilst the comic moments included two songs for the Pasha—one relating the tale of his depleted harem ("Je suis ce Pasha") and another a "rataplan" piece in his second-act disguise as drummer to the female army ("Attention, tapons ferme")—and a duo with Boboli discussing the relative merits of impaling or hanging as a form of execution. There was also plenty of martial ensemble music, varied by a fake gypsy chorus for the disguised men in the final act.

In spite of the fact that the leading lady was replaced shortly before opening, *Les Géorgiennes,* with its galaxy of tightly uniformed ladies and its glittering score, was an indubitable hit. It played for more than one hundred performances for its composer-producer at the Bouffes-Parisiennes, and was soon seen throughout Europe. Karl Treumann staged his adaptation of *Die schönen Weiber von Georgien* at the Carltheater, with Frau Friedrich-Materna (Feroza), Franz Eppich (Rhododendron), Josef Matras (Paterno), Fräulein von Edelsberg (Nani) and Therese Schäfer (Zaida) featured, and the piece scored a considerable success, holding its place in the repertoire for more than six years. The German version was also played in Budapest where an Hungarian adaptation was subsequently mounted at the Budai Népszínház with Laura Istvánti, Sarolta Krecsanyi, Vizvari and Vidor Kassai in the leading roles. However, the piece's list of productions was rather cut short by the arrival, just months later, of the all-conquering *La Belle Hélène,* and thus it was 1871 before New York saw *Les Géorgiennes,* and when it did, it was in French. That performance was played by Mlle Aimée's company with the star as Feroza supported by Constant Gausins (Rhododenron), Paul Hittemans (Boboli), Elise Persini (Nani) and Legros (Jol-Hiddin), not to mention a full-sized elephant on which the star rode on to the stage. The show was later seen at the Germania in German (25 December 1873), with Frln Rindoli (Feroza), Merten (Rhododendron), Antonie Heynold (Nani) and Schutz (Boboli)—though apparently no elephant.

An English version (ad C J S Wilson) was produced in London in 1875 with Rose Bell (Feroza), Carlotta Zerbini (Nani) and Richard Temple (Rhododendron) featured, for a month's run, and what seems to have been another English remake was shown at San Francisco's Tivoli Theater in 1885 with Helen Dingeon playing Feroza, alongside Kate Marchi and H W Frilman. The German version later turned up at the Theater an der Wien in 1877 (18 November) for just two performances, but *Les Géorgiennes,* in spite of its successful original run, did not establish itself in the preferred Offenbach repertoire.

Austria: Carltheater *Die schönen Weiber von Georgien* 5 October 1864; Germany: Friederich-Wilhelmstädtisches Theater *Die schönen Weiber von Georgien* December 1864; Hungary: Budai Színkör *Die schönen Weiber von Georgien* (Ger) 15 July 1865, Budai Népszínház *A georgai nők* 14 February 1865; USA: Grand Opera House (Fr) 6 March 1871, Tivoli Opera House, San Francisco *The Georgians* 10 August 1885; UK: Philharmonic Theatre, Islington 2 October 1875

GERMAN, Edward (Sir) [JONES, German Edward] (b Whitchurch, 17 February 1862; d London, 11 November 1936). Orchestral composer who succeeded Sullivan as the purveyor of comic opera to the Savoy Theatre, but who disappeared from the musical theatre without fulfilling his potential.

A self-taught violinist and conductor, German attended the Royal Academy from the age of 18 and earned himself some spare cash by playing the violin in theatre orchestras. In 1888 he became musical director at the Globe Theatre, and he made his first notable contribution to the stage with an incidental score for their *Richard III* with Richard Mansfield (1889).

Amongst the more substantial compositions of his early years, the young composer numbered orchestral pieces, symphonies and songs, amongst which was a considerable amount of music for both concert and theatrical stages. The theatre works included dance music for Henry Irving's production of *Henry VIII,* and incidental music for Beerbohm Tree's 1893 production of Henry Arthur Jones's *The Tempter* (Haymarket Theatre), the Forbes Robertson/Mrs Patrick Campbell *Romeo and Juliet* at the Lyceum (1895) and George Alexander's St James's Theatre *As You Like It* (1898). His dances for Anthony Hope and Edward Rose's 1900 comedy *English Nell* at the Prince of Wales Theatre won particular success and, like the *Henry VIII* dances, were subsequently made up into an orchestral suite.

When Sir Arthur Sullivan died, with his new Savoy Theatre comic opera *The Emerald Isle* incomplete, it was expected that either Savoy musical director François Cellier or Ernest Ford, both of whom had strong connections with the D'Oyly Carte regime and had previously written music for the Savoy, would be asked to finish the work. In fact, it was German, who had no experience as a composer of comic opera, who was commissioned by Mrs D'Oyly Carte to bring *The Emerald Isle* to completion. He proved a wise choice, for he won praise for his taste and tact in turning out a Sullivan score which was neither pastiche nor sturdily two-parted and *The Emerald Isle* gave the Savoy a good, if not outstanding, success.

German subsequently teamed with Basil Hood—touted as the "new Gilbert" to German's "new Sullivan"—on two further comic operas, the highly successful *Merrie England* (1902) ("The Yeomen of England," "She Had a Letter from Her Love," "The English Rose," "Who Shall Say That Love Is Cruel?") and the charming *A Princess of Kensington* (1903), produced for the Savoy company by William Greet who had, in the meanwhile, purchased the D'Oyly Carte interests. In spite of a fair run and a score which included the perennially popular "Four Jolly Sailormen," *A Princess of Kensington* did not balance the books, and Greet gave up producing the quality English light and/or comic operas with which he had determined to continue the Savoy tradition and turned to the much more financially solid modern musical comedy. As for German, he returned, seemingly without any regret, to orchestral and concert vocal writing.

In 1907 he came back to the theatre with a commission to compose the score for another period light opera, a version of Henry Fielding's *Tom Jones* produced by Robert Courtneidge on the occasion of the Fielding bicentenary. *Tom Jones* turned out to be an expertly made piece, and its score an ideal combination of strongly made music, period flavor and tunefulness ("For Tonight," "The Green Ribbon," "West Country Lad," "Dream o'Day Jill"). The show remains, almost a century later, a classic of the otherwise fairly limited English light opera repertoire.

Sadly, German returned only once more to the musical theatre, to collaborate with W S Gilbert on a musical adaptation of his 1873 play *The Wicked World* as *Fallen Fairies* (1909). However, Gilbert's fairies were sadly out-of-date, and the show failed utterly. Thereafter the composer withdrew from the theatre and, by and large, from composing in general.

A thorough and conservative musician, German excelled at illustrating historical subjects with a form of light operatic music which, although it was perhaps broadly uncommercial, proved both immensely singable and thoroughly durable.

1901 **The Emerald Isle, or The Caves of Carric-Cleena** (w Arthur Sullivan/Basil Hood) Savoy Theatre 27 April

1901 **The Rival Poets** (W H Scott) 1 act St George's Hall (1886, by amateurs)

1902 **Merrie England** (Hood) Savoy Theatre 2 April

1903 **A Princess of Kensington** (Hood) Savoy Theatre 22 January

1907 **Tom Jones** (Charles H Taylor/Alexander M Thompson, Robert Courtneidge) Apollo Theatre 17 April

1909 **Fallen Fairies** (W S Gilbert) Savoy Theatre 15 December

Biographies: Scott, W: *Edward German* (Cecil Palmer, London, 1932), Rees, B: *A Musical Peacemaker* (Kensal Press, Bucks, 1988)

GERRARD, Gene [SULLIVAN, Eugene Morris] (b London, 31 August 1892; d Sidmouth, Devon, 1 June 1971).

Gerrard worked first as a comic singer in variety and came to the musical theatre, by way of revue, after the First World War. He took supporting roles in *The Officers' Mess* (1918, t/o), and *His Little Widows* (1919, Jack Grayson) and, after spells in variety and in Australia, he played his first important musical-comedy role in the West End when he was given the lead comic part of Leander in *Katja, the Dancer* (1925) at the Gaiety Theatre. This led to his being cast in the choice comic role of Bennie in the London production of *The Desert Song* (1927) at the Theatre Royal, Drury Lane, and top-billed in the musical comedy *Lucky Girl* (1928, Hudson Greener). He returned to Drury Lane for *The New Moon* (1929, Alexander) and a revival of *Rose Marie* (1929, Herman).

His subsequent musical roles in such pieces as *Little Tommy Tucker* (1930, Bill Coverdale) and *The Gay Hussar* (1933, Nicolai) were not in the same class as those in the three imported classics, and his last parts, in *Take It Easy* (1937, Danny Waring) and *The Silver Patrol* (1940, Albert Stamp), were little short of disastrous. His later stage appearances were in pantomime and the occasional comedy.

Gerrard worked, in tandem with his performing, as a director, and shared the directing credit on the film of *Little Tommy Tucker* (1931). He was also the director of the original production of *Me and My Girl,* although his name had disappeared from the bills, and Lupino Lane took the credit, when the show finally opened in town.

He also appeared in the screen version of *Lucky Girl.*

GERSHWIN, George [GERSHVIN, Jacob] (b New York, 26 September 1898; d Hollywood, Calif, 11 July 1937). Versatile composer of everything from songs and dances to opéra-bouffe and folk opera for the Broadway stage.

After a schooling which included limited conventional musical studies, the young George Gershwin went straight to work as a pianist and song-plugger in the musical publishing firm of Jerome H Remick. During this time, he began composing songs and in 1916 he had his first piece published. This comedy number, ''When You Want 'em You Can't Get 'em,'' written to a lyric by Murray Roth, and performed by Sophie Tucker, ultimately appeared on the musical theatre stage more than 70 years later when it was used as part of the score for the London extravaganza *Ziegfeld.*

The young pianist-songwriter worked as a rehearsal pianist, and as an accompanist to Nora Bayes for the musical *Ladies First,* before being taken on by Max Dreyfus at Harms (a step up from the not-negligible Remicks) as a regularly-waged composer. This arrangement resulted in his having several songs interpolated into the scores of such contemporary stage shows as the British *Good Morning, Judge* (*The Boy*) and the German *The Lady in Red* (*Die Dame in Rot*) and being given the chance to write the score for the revue *Half Past Eight.* The revue folded on the road, but Harms did not have long to wait for better results. In 1919 the young songwriter scored a major song hit with ''Swanee'' (ly: Irving Caesar) and was also given the opportunity to write a full set of songs for a Broadway book show.

Plate 143. **George Gershwin** *goes Groucho for a night out with Evelyn Laye.*

Whilst Al Jolson introduced ''Swanee'' and ''Dixie Rose'' into *Sinbad,* Alex Aarons's production of *La La Lucille,* music by George Gershwin, opened in Atlantic City. However, the young composer didn't make much impression on the local critic, who devoted most of his review to the physical production and merely commented ''the musical decorations are by George Gershwin.'' *La La Lucille* made its way to Broadway's Henry Miller Theater where it lasted a fair 104 performances. Over the next few years, however, the book musical did not prove a profitable field for Gershwin. Whilst he had a happy time supplying songs to revue—most notably the *George White's Scandals* series (''Stairway to Paradise,'' ''Somebody Loves Me'')—*A Dangerous Maid,* a musicalized version of Charles Bell's comedy *The Dislocated Honeymoon,* folded without making it to Broadway, a one-act tragic jazz opera, *Blue Monday,* was cut from the *George White's Scandals of 1922* after opening night, and *Our Nell,* a piece of burlesque melodrama with songs, died in five unpatronized weeks. And of the book shows into which he interpolated songs, few did better. *Dere Mabel,* composed by a Boston businessman's daughter but advertised to have additional numbers by Irving Berlin, instead had one by Gershwin for its short life in Baltimore and Boston, Hugo Felix's *The Sweetheart Shop* did much better on the road than in town, and

''Someone'' contributed less to the success of Aarons's *For Goodness' Sake* than the young song and dance pair, the Astaires. Irene Bordoni took in Gershwin songs for the multi-source scores of her Continental plays *The French Doll* and *Little Miss Bluebeard,* both of which did better than Romberg's *The Dancing Girl* to which Gershwin again contributed a single song.

It was not until 1924, the same year that his jazz-band concerto ''Rhapsody in Blue'' brought him international celebrity, that the composer achieved success with stage scores in both London and in New York. In London, where he had already contributed more or less of the songs to several revues beginning with *Mayfair and Montmartre* (on which the remainder of the music was done by Maurice Yvain—much more Montmartre than Gershwin was Mayfair), and continuing with *The Rainbow* (principal composer) and *The Punch Bowl* (one of many), he was commissioned to compose the score for George Grossmith and Pat Malone's Winter Garden show, *Primrose.* Gershwin mixed some of his already-written songs with some others written for the occasion and scored his best musical theatre run to date when his ''Wait a Bit, Susie'' and ''Boy Wanted'' (rescued from *A Dangerous Maid*) were heard in London for a fine run of 255 performances, before *Primrose* crossed the world to represent him in Australia.

That total was soon topped by a first Broadway hit. A fairish January to April showing by Frank Mandel's production *Sweet Little Devil* (120 performances) was succeeded by Alex Aarons's new show for Adele and Fred Astaire, who had served him so well in *For Goodness' Sake.* In *Lady, Be Good!* they also served George Gershwin well, as he did them: the show was a 330-performance Broadway hit, and launched ''Oh Lady, Be Good!'' and ''Fascinating Rhythm'' as individual favorites.

Thereafter, whilst Gershwin continued to compose and perform instrumental music (Concerto in F, *An American in Paris*), he turned out a series of scores for Broadway which included many successes and produced many popular songs. An undercast production of *Tell Me More!* managed only a round 100 performances on a Broadway struck by a heat wave, but the Winter Garden Theatre team in London got 262 performances from it and its ''Kickin' the Clouds Away,'' whilst the wide-eyed tale of a little girl called *Tip-Toes* (''Sweet and Low Down,'' ''That Certain Feeling'') played 192 times on Broadway and 182 at the London Winter Garden. Just two nights after the New York opening of the *Tip-Toes,* the lavishly-staged ''romantic opera'' *Song of the Flame* followed. London didn't want this one, but Broadway listened to its Russian passions and Gershwin's title song for a fine 219 performances.

With *Oh, Kay!* (primitively titled *Cheerio!*), Gershwin left the Russian passions and returned to Aarons and Freedley and to what had become his most familiar and best-loved musical style. ''Someone to Watch Over Me,'' ''Maybe,'' ''Clap Yo' Hands'' and ''Do, Do, Do'' contributed effectively to a show which again had fine runs in New York (256 performances) and London (214 performances) and established itself—no small thanks to a brisker than usual comedy libretto—as arguably Gershwin's best light musical comedy.

Gershwin came together again with Aarons and Freedley and the Astaires in *Funny Face* (''Funny Face,'' '''S Wonderful,'' ''He Loves and She Loves'') for 244 performances on Broadway and 263 in London, but, in the meantime, he had suffered his first out-of-town closure since *A Dangerous Maid* with a would-be political satire penned by George S Kaufman. *Strike Up the Band* and its title number went on ice, however, and a few years later the show was given a rewrite and a New York showing of 191 performances. Another piece away from the Aarons and Freedley management was another venture into the romantic, and again in collaboration. Ziegfeld's Marilyn(n) Miller vehicle, *Rosalie,* was more successful in so far as the length of its run was concerned (335 performances), and with his ''Oh Gee! Oh Joy!'' Gershwin provided a bit of the snap which characterized his best works to contrast with Romberg's more romantic moments.

The 1920s ended on a less favorable turn when *Treasure Girl* turned out a 68-performance flop and Ziegfeld's *Show Girl* (''Liza,'' An American in Paris ballet) made its way through an indifferent 111 nights, but the revised *Strike Up the Band* did better, and the Aarons/Freedley production of *Girl Crazy* (''I Got Rhythm,'' ''Embraceable You,'' ''Bidin' My Time'') brought its composer back to Broadway success (272 performances). Broadway success was something which Gershwin had tasted regularly over the past half-dozen years, and which he was to find in even more appreciable doses in the years to come, but the end of the Grossmith era at the London Winter Garden and the departure of the Astaires for other spheres marked the end of the composer's London showings. From now on, his new musicals got productions only at home.

London would, in any case, perhaps not quite have known what to do with Kaufman and Ryskind's political burlesque, *Of Thee I Sing,* a zany tale of an everyday American President and Vice-President which Gershwin set with music of a twinkling burlesque humor which little in either his serious work or his dance-and-song shows had presaged. The authors of *Of Thee I Sing* won a Pulitzer Prize, Sam Harris's production played 441 Broadway nights (Gershwin's longest-ever run) and the piece made itself a special place in the history and repertoire of America's musical theatre. The barely extractable pieces of the musical score, such as the title song (''Of Thee I Sing, Baby''), ''Who Cares?'' and ''Love Is Sweeping the Country,'' gave evidence of a differently and delightfully fun-flavored Gershwin.

An effort to repeat the success of *Of Thee I Sing* with a musequel, *Let 'em Eat Cake,* failed, as did a final musical with Aarons and Freedley (*Pardon My English,* 46 performances), before Gershwin's ''American Folk Opera'' *Porgy and Bess* (1935), a stunning amalgam of contemporary popular and serious musical and textual styles, was brought to Broadway. Once again, the composer came up with another facet of his composing talent, and *Porgy and Bess* and its songs (''It Ain't Necessarily So,'' ''Bess, You Is My Woman Now,'' ''I Got Plenty of Nothin',' ''Summertime,'' ''My Man's Gone Now,'' etc) gave him yet another niche in the classic register.

Gershwin died less than two years after the premiere of *Porgy and Bess* without composing another score for the musical stage. His final work had been for Hollywood, where he returned to the popular songwriting style which had characterized his musical comedies of the 1920s with the songs for *Shall We Dance?* (''Let's Call the Whole Thing Off,'' ''Shall We Dance,'' ''They Can't Take That Away from Me''), *A Damsel in Distress* (''Nice Work, If You Can Get It'') and the posthumous *The Goldwyn Follies.*

The three shows which stand highest as a monument to Gershwin's talents—*Oh, Kay!, Of Thee I Sing* and *Porgy and Bess*—are three pieces in vastly different tones: the bright, light flippancy of the first, the blithely boisterous burlesque of the second, and the strong drama of the third gave him musical opportunities of widely disparate types, and the composer encompassed all three with an enduring success which speaks volumes for his musical versatility. Yet it was the popular songwriting style of his earliest successes to which he most naturally seemed to gravitate, and the character of that style gave to his more ambitious writing melodic, rhythmic and structural qualities which helped win wide popular acceptance for pieces ranging from ''Rhapsody in Blue'' to *Porgy and Bess.*

George Gershwin died young, and he won the ''future'' that so many artists of all kinds who shared his fate have won. He became a show-business icon. Over the years, he has been written and rewritten about, analyzed and over-analyzed, appraised, praised and over-praised in a way that virtually no other writer for the American musical stage has been, and often to the exclusion of contemporaries and other songwriters of considerable talents. Yet although the name of Gershwin has become a deeply fashionable one, few of his stage musicals remain in the theatre repertoire. *Porgy and Bess* has found a home in the world's opera houses, *Oh, Kay!* and *Lady, Be Good!* have been given modest revivals, and very occasionally *Of Thee I Sing* wins a hometown production. Pasticcio shows distantly related to *Funny Face* (*My One and Only*) and *Girl Crazy* (*Crazy for You*) have cashed in on the heavily promoted Gershwin fashion in America where aficionados have—more and more—won rehearings (if not restagings) for such scores as *Primrose* and *Strike Up the Band,* and the in-and-out-of-copyright composer's estate have sponsored recordings of his lesser works. Like Strauss in Vienna or Offenbach in France, the name of Gershwin is considered ''OK'' whilst Youmans, Hirsch, Friml, Archer, Romberg and others are largely brushed aside as part of a lightweight disposable tradition. It is a curious phenomenon and one that, in the end, does its icon no favors.

1919 **La La Lucille** (Arthur J Jackson, B G De Sylva/Frederick Jackson) Henry Miller Theater 26 April

1921 **A Dangerous Maid** (Ira Gershwin/Charles W Bell) Apollo Theater, Atlantic City 21 March

1922 **Blue Monday** (later *135th Street*) (De Sylva) 1 act in George White's Scandals Globe Theater 28 August

1922 **Our Nell** (w William Daly/Brian Hooker, A E Thomas) Bayes Theater 4 December

1924 **Sweet Little Devil** (ex- *A Perfect Lady*) (De Sylva/ Laurence Schwab, Frank Mandel) Astor Theater 21 January

1924 **Primrose** (Desmond Carter, I Gershwin/George Grossmith, Guy Bolton) Winter Garden Theatre, London 11 September

1924 **Lady, Be Good!** (I Gershwin/Fred Thompson, Bolton) Liberty Theater 1 December

1925 **Tell Me More!** (ex- *My Fair Lady*) (I Gershwin, De Sylva/ Thompson, William K Wells) Gaiety Theater 13 April

1925 **Tip-Toes** (I Gershwin/Thompson, Bolton) Liberty Theater 28 December

1925 **Song of the Flame** (w Herbert Stothart/Oscar Hammerstein II, Otto Harbach) 44th Street Theater 30 December

1926 **Oh, Kay!** (I Gershwin, Howard Dietz/Bolton, P G Wodehouse) Imperial Theater 8 November

1927 **Strike Up the Band** (I Gershwin/George S Kaufman) Broadway Theater, Long Branch, NJ 29 August; Shubert Theater, Philadelphia 5 September

1927 **Funny Face** (ex- *Smarty*) (I Gershwin/Thompson, Paul Gerard Smith) Alvin Theater 22 November

1928 **Rosalie** (w Sigmund Romberg/I Gershwin, Wodehouse/ Bolton, William Anthony McGuire) New Amsterdam Theater 10 January

1928 **Treasure Girl** (I Gershwin/Thompson, Vincent Lawrence) Alvin Theater 8 November

1929 **Show Girl** (I Gershwin, Gus Kahn/McGuire, J P McEvoy) Ziegfeld Theater 2 July

1930 **Strike Up the Band** revised version by Morrie Ryskind Times Square Theater 14 January

1930 **Girl Crazy** (I Gershwin/Bolton, Jack McGowan) Alvin Theater 14 October

1931 **Of Thee I Sing** (I Gershwin, Kaufman, Ryskind) Music Box Theater 26 December

1933 **Pardon My English** (I Gershwin/Herbert Fields) Majestic Theater 20 January

1933 **Let 'em Eat Cake** (I Gershwin, Kaufman, Ryskind) Imperial Theater 21 October

1935 **Porgy and Bess** (I Gershwin, DuBose Heyward/Heyward) Alvin Theater 10 October

Biographies, etc: Goldberg, I, Garson, E: *George Gershwin: A Study in American Music* (Simon & Schuster, New York, 1931), Ewen, D: *George Gershwin: His Journey to Greatness* (Prentice Hall, New Jersey, 1956), Armitage, M: *George Gershwin: Man and Legend* (Duell Sloane, New York, 1958), Payne, R: *Gershwin* (Pyramid, New York, 1960), Jablonski, E: *George Gershwin* (Doubleday, New York, 1962), Kimball, R, Simon, A: *The Gershwins* (Athenaeum, New York, 1973), Schwartz, C: *Gershwin: His Life and Music* (Bobbs-Merrill, Indianapolis, 1973), Kendall, A: *George Gershwin* (London, 1987), Rosenberg, D: *Fascinating Rhythm* (Dutton, New York, 1991), Peyser, J: *The Memory of All That* (Simon & Schuster, New York, 1993), Greenberg, R: *George Gershwin, Twentieth Century Composer* (Phaidon, New York, 1998), etc

GERSHWIN, Ira [GERSHOVITZ, Israel] (b New York, 6 December 1896; d Los Angeles, 17 August 1983).

Ira Gershwin began writing lyrics whilst at college, and combined with his brother, George, in his first theatrical ventures: a song interpolated into Nora Bayes's *Ladies First* and the words to the songs for the quickly interred *A Dangerous Maid,* some of which would be later exhumed for the score of the London musical *Primrose* in 1924.

His first success, however, came not with his brother but, under the pseudonym of "Arthur Francis," as the lyricist for the successful *Two Little Girls in Blue* produced by George's *La La Lucille* producer Alex Aarons but composed by Vincent Youmans and Paul Lannin. He subsequently provided some additional lyrics for Kaufman and Connelly's *Be Yourself* but, following the production of *Primrose,* again joined up with brother George for the series of 1920s musical comedies which, topped with the two memorable Gershwin brothers pieces of the last days of George's career, *Of Thee I Sing* (Pulitzer Prize) and *Porgy and Bess,* made up the heart of their careers.

Ira, who had rarely worked with another composer during these years—some lyrics for Phil Charig ("Sunny Disposish") and Joseph Meyer for songs used in London's *That's a Good Girl* and the Harold Arlen revue *Life Begins at 8.40* being amongst the few theatre occasions—worked on only three stage musicals after George's premature death, although film brought him such further song successes as "The Man That Got Away" (*A Star Is Born*) and "Long Ago and Far Away" (*Cover Girl*). The first of those three shows, *Lady in the Dark,* brought him both kudos and success, but a second collaboration with composer Kurt Weill on *The Firebrand of Florence* brought neither, and another flop, *Park Avenue,* saw out the end of the 25-year Broadway career of Gershwin-the-words on an atypical downbeat.

A collection of his lyrics, accompanied by commentary and anecdotes, was published as *Lyrics on Several Occasions* (Knopf, New York, 1959 and Elm Tree, England, 1977).

1921 **A Dangerous Maid** (George Gershwin/Charles W Bell) Apollo Theater, Atlantic City 21 March

1921 **Two Little Girls in Blue** (Vincent Youmans, Paul Lannin/ Frederick Jackson) George M Cohan Theater 3 May

1924 **Be Yourself** (Lewis Gensler, Milton Schwarzwald/George S Kaufman, Marc Connelly) Sam H Harris Theater 3 September

1924 **Primrose** (G Gershwin/w Desmond Carter/George Grossmith, Guy Bolton) Winter Garden Theatre, London 11 September

1924 **Lady, Be Good!** (G Gershwin/Fred Thompson, Bolton) Liberty Theater 1 December

1925 **Tell Me More!** (ex- *My Fair Lady*) (G Gershwin/w De Sylva/Thompson, William K Wells) Gaiety Theater 13 April

1925 **Tip-Toes** (G Gershwin/Thompson, Bolton) Liberty Theater 28 December

1926 **Oh, Kay!** (G Gershwin/w Howard Dietz/Bolton, P G Wodehouse) Imperial Theater 8 November

1927 **Strike Up the Band** (G Gershwin/Kaufman) Broadway Theater, Long Branch, NJ 29 August; Shubert Theater, Philadelphia 5 September

1927 **Funny Face** (ex- *Smarty*) (G Gershwin/Thompson, Paul Gerard Smith) Alvin Theater 22 November

1928 **Rosalie** (G Gershwin, Sigmund Romberg/w Wodehouse/ Bolton, William Anthony McGuire) New Amsterdam Theater 10 January

1928 **That's a Good Girl** (Phil Charig, Joseph Meyer/w Douglas Furber, Carter/Furber) London Hippodrome 5 June

1928 **Treasure Girl** (G Gershwin/Thompson, Vincent Lawrence) Alvin Theater 8 November

1929 **Show Girl** (G Gershwin/w Gus Kahn/McGuire, J P McEvoy) Ziegfeld Theater 2 July

1930 **Strike Up the Band** revised version by Morrie Ryskind, Times Square Theater 14 January

1930 **Girl Crazy** (G Gershwin/Bolton, Jack McGowan) Alvin Theater 14 October

1931 **Of Thee I Sing** (G Gershwin/Kaufman, Ryskind) Music Box Theater 26 December

1933 **Pardon My English** (G Gershwin/Herbert Fields) Majestic Theater 20 January

1933 **Let 'em Eat Cake** (G Gershwin/Kaufman, Ryskind) Imperial Theater 21 October

1935 **Porgy and Bess** (G Gershwin/w DuBose Heyward/ Heyward) Alvin Theater 10 October

1941 **Lady in the Dark** (Kurt Weill/Moss Hart) Alvin Theater 23 January

1945 **The Firebrand of Florence** (Weill/w Edwin Justus Mayer) Alvin Theater 22 March

1946 **Park Avenue** (Arthur Schwartz/Nunnally Johnson, Kaufman) Shubert Theater 4 November

Biography: Furia, P: *Ira Gershwin: The Art of the Lyricist* (OUP, New York, 1997); *see also* GERSHWIN, GEORGE

DIE GESCHIEDENE FRAU Operette in 3 acts by Victor Léon. Music by Leo Fall. Carltheater, Vienna, 23 December 1908.

Victor Léon's particularly sparky libretto for *Die geschiedene Frau* ("the divorced woman") told a tale of marital mistrust in which Jana van Lysseweghe (Mizzi Zwerenz), the lady of the title, hastily divorces her much-loved husband Karel (Hubert Marischka), after an unsatisfactorily explained episode involving him with a free-loving young actress called Gonda van der Loo (Annie Dirkens) in a railway sleeper. Shades of *Trial by Jury* hover as, after many social and railroad complications, including more than a touch of blackmail and sexual misbehaviour, the dazzling Miss van der Loo is paired off with the divorce court judge, Lucas van Deesteldonck (Richard Waldemar), whilst the foolish, loving couple who should never have been divorced are remarried. Karl Blasel was Pieter te Bakkenskijl, Jana's father and the head of the Wagons-Lits company, whilst Max Rohr (Willem Krouwevliet) and Mizzi Jesel (Martje) played a simple and happily married Dutch couple, devoted to the central pair.

Leo Fall's score was in his happiest and brightest style and supplied the star soubrette, in the role of the sexy actress, with a splendid series of songs and duos, highlighted by the waltzes "O Schlafcoupé, O Schlafcoupé" in which she describes the pleasures of rail travel in a sleeper berth, and the lilting "Gonda, liebe kleine Gonda," the duo in which the unjustly divorced husband attempts to do the right thing by his blithe co-respondent by dutifully offering to marry her. Karl and Jana shared two attractive duets, a waltz in which they sing together about the time-honored encounter between a masked husband and wife ("Kind, du kannst tanzen wie meine Frau") and the second which brings the show to a soaringly reconciled curtain ("Du, ach du bist wieder mein"). The humorous musical moments included a comical burlesque funeral march for the blackmailing sleeping-car attendant, Scrop (Josef König), and a heavily accented quintet featuring the Krouwevliets ("O Echestand, O Echestand, wie schön bist du"), and the dancing ones a display of the "Roger de Coverley," a novelty dance display by Gonda to the strains of the marching "Ich und du und Müllers Kuh" and a comical one, in tandem with Scrop, to "Man steigt nach!"

The Carltheater production of *Die geschiedene Frau* was a first-rate hit. With the billing of the two big female stars solved by simply placing their names in a cross formation, it played at the managerless theatre through 126 nights to the end of the season, then returned after the summer to run up its total to 227 nights under the management of newly installed Sigmund Eibenschütz. By the end of 1909 that total read 256 performances and the show continued to be played in repertoire at the Carltheater until 1915. Berlin followed suit, and *Die geschiedene Frau* installed itself for no less than 371 performances at the Theater des Westens turning itself in the process into one of the most popular musical comedies of its time, throughout Germany and Austria.

That popularity was confirmed almost everywhere else that the piece was played. Hungary, as usual, was first off the mark, with a Király Színház production starring Vilma Medgyaszay as *Elvált asszony* ("the divorced girl," ad Andor Gábor), Ilka Pálmay as Gonda, Ernő Király as Karel and Mihály Papp as Scrop. A fine success, it played its 100th night on 26 December 1916, and continued to be revived in Hungary for decades thereafter. England's Adrian Ross dropped the element of "divorce" from the title and instead turned the focus on to the little marriage-breaker who was the real star of the show, calling the piece *The Girl in the Train.* George Edwardes cast Phyllis Dare as Gonda, with Robert Evett (Karel), Clara Evelyn (Jana) and a set of top comedians—Huntley Wright (Judge), Fred Emney (Scrop) and Rutland Barrington (father, now called Lucas van Tromp)—and added one Theo Wendt number to the score to allow Wright and Barrington to vocally justify their billing. The result was a 340-performance West End triumph which was followed by years of touring through Britain and productions throughout the English-language theatre world.

One of these was in America, where Charles Dillingham had the piece readapted, under—give or take a preposition—the London title, by Harry B Smith, with songs by Clare Kummer and Carter de Haven added, and played by a cast headed by Vera Michelena and Melville Stewart. It proved to be the only major production of the piece which flopped (40 performances). Australia, on the other hand, set in motion a production headed by London's Sybil Arundale (Jana) and Talleur Andrews (Karel), and locals Florence Young (Gonda), W S Percy (Judge), Jack Cannot (Scrop) and Victor Prince (Lucas) with a run of nearly two months in Sydney before *The Girl in the Train* (London version) moved on round the country.

Paris welcomed *La Divorcée* (ad Maurice Vaucaire) to Alphonse Franck's Théâtre Apollo, where Jane Marnac starred as Gonda alongside Henry Defreyn (Karl) and Jane Alba (Jana) with Colombey as Vandenparaboum (father) and Tréville as Van Plottledam (Judge) for a successful run, which earned the show a long provincial life and a reprise in 1924 at the Ba-ta-clan in which Odette Darthys played Gonda.

As the stage versions of *Die geschiedene Frau* ran long and often through European theatres, two films were made, the first by Victor Janson in 1926 with Mady Christians featured as a silent Gonda, and the second in 1953 with Marika Rökk starred alongside Johannes Heesters and Hans Nielsen.

Hungary: Király Színház *Elvált asszony* 12 March 1909; Germany: Theater des Westens 2 October 1909; UK: Vaudeville Theatre *The Girl in the Train* 4 June 1910; USA: Globe Theater *The Girl in the Train* 3 October 1910; France: Théâtre Apollo *La Divorcée* 18 February 1911; Australia: Criterion Theatre, Sydney *The Girl in the Train* 4 December 1911

Films: Viktor Janson 1926, Georg Jacoby 1953

Recording: Ariola Eurodisc (EP)

GEST, Morris (b Vilna, Russia, 17 January 1881; d New York, 16 May 1942). Broadway producer who had successes with both intimate musicals and with the most extravagant and sometimes titillating of spectaculars.

Gest left Russia as a child to settle in America and he spent his early life in Boston where he made his first forays into the theatre at the age of 19. He subsequently became a ticket tout in New York, married (1909) Reina, the daughter of David Belasco, and was hired by William Hammerstein to go to Europe and scout for talent. Whilst doing so, he began to fraternize with the competition as represented by F Ray Comstock and in 1905 the two went into partnership. Over the next 23 years they produced both plays and musicals (for a while in a threesome with another Belasco son-in-law, William Elliott), often on a large scale and often with a fondness for the slightly scandalous. Amongst their productions were included the famous Oscar Asche musical spectaculars *Chu Chin Chow* (1917) and *Mecca* (1920), with its celebrated orgy scene, as well as the London pantomime *Hop o' my Thumb* (1913 w William Brady), the period's other major London success *The Maid of the Mountains* (1918), the homegrown *The Beauty Spot* (1909), *Sweet Kitty Bellairs* (1917) and *The Rose of China* (1919), and—on the titillating side—the lavish and scantily dressed *Aphrodite* (1919), and the fairly cleaned-up C B Cochran version of Cuvillier's opérette *Afgar* (1920).

At the other end of the spectrum, Gest was involved with the production and, more particularly, the touring of such modern musical comedies as *Oh, Boy!, Leave It to Jane, Oh, Lady! Lady!!, Oh, My Dear!,* the unfortunate *Zip Goes a Million,* and *Sitting Pretty.* Comstock and Gest's other productions included a number with a Russian or Continental affiliation, notably such events as the Russian ballet, seasons with Duse and the Moscow Art Theatre 1923), the fashionable Russian revue *La Chauve-Souris* (1922 and again 1931), Ibsen in Italian (1923), Max Reinhardt's vast production of *The Miracle* (1924) and the German Passion Plays (1929).

At various times Gest took charge of both the little La Salle Theater, Chicago, and the large Manhattan Opera House and Century Theater in New York as well as the Harmanus-Bleeker Hall in Albany and the Von Quiller in Schenectady. After the end of his association with Comstock, he continued to produce, with less éclat, joining the Shuberts to produce an unsuccessful version of Robert Katscher's Revue-Operette *Wonder Bar* for Al Jolson as one of his last projects.

GET A LOAD OF THIS A surprise musical by James Hadley Chase. Additional dialogue by Arthur Macrae. Music and lyrics by Manning Sherwin and Val Guest. Additional numbers by Arthur Young, Michael Carr and Jack Popplewell, Al Lewis, Larry Stock and Vincent Rose. London Hippodrome, 19 November 1941.

Largely a variety show, disguised as a book musical, *Get a Load of This* was hung together on a gangstery story, by *No Orchids for Miss Blandish* mystery-writer James Hadley Chase, which was usefully set in a night club. Whilst the acts flowed on to the stage of the London Hippodrome (rebuilt to reach out into the audience like a cabaret floor), in a palpable imitation of the Continental hit *Die Wunder-Bar,* the plot continued very much in the background. Vic Oliver, as the compère of the night club, and his stooge Jack Allan ran a show in which vocalist Celia Lipton featured alongside the musical clowns, the Cairoli Brothers, dancers Jeanne Ravel and Jean Barnes and a series of other acts through 698 performances.

In Australia, the show was played on the Tivoli circuit, normally reserved for variety shows, and billed as a twice-daily melodrama-revue. Jenny Howard, Arundel Nixon, Thelma Grigg, George and Joy Nichols, Teddie Scanlon and Eddie Gordon were top-lined alongside the Musical Macs and the juggling act the three Ciscos. After two-and-a-half months of *Get a Load of This* in Melbourne and a further month in Sydney, the Tivolis returned to playing unadorned variety.

Australia: Tivoli, Melbourne 7 May 1945

GIGI Musical in 2 acts by Alan Jay Lerner based on the novel by Colette and the screenplay of its film version. Music by Frederick Loewe. Uris Theater, New York, 13 November 1973.

A 1973 attempt to revamp the score and story of the Academy Award-winning MGM musical film *Gigi* (1958) with its champagne-bucketful of hit songs ("Gigi," The Night They Invented Champagne," "I Remember It Well,'' ''I'm Glad I'm Not Young Anymore,'' ''Thank Heaven for Little Girls,'' ''It's a Bore,'' ''She Is Not Thinking of Me'') as a full-Broadway-sized stage musical hit trouble early on. Having shed its Gigi (lusty British performer Terese Stevens) pre–New York, it then came to grief on its arrival in town (103 performances) with Karin Wolfe replacing. Alfred Drake played Maurice Chevalier (with one of four new musical pieces), otherwise the crusty Uncle Honoré—a non-Colette and balance-destroying invention of the author of the screenplay—Agnes Moorehead and Maria Karnilova were the heroine's Aunt and Grandmother respectively, whilst Daniel Massey (Gaston) serenaded ''Gigi.'' The enormous success of *My Fair Lady* on German-speaking stages encouraged productions of *Gigi* in Berlin and Vienna, and Robert Gilbert's German-language version won some success at the Theater des Westens (134 performances), and the Theater an der Wien (221 performances), where the inspired casting of veteran star Johannes Heesters (Honoré) alongside the ravishing Christiane Rücker (Gigi) helped to produce the most successful stage *Gigi* to date. As a result, *Gigi* is still occasionally to be seen on central European stages to this day (Stadttheater, Baden bei Wien 1998, w Peter Minich as Chevalier, Volksoper 28 May 1999).

Another attempt to bring *Gigi* to the theatrical big time was mounted, under Lerner's instigation, in London a dozen years after the Broadway attempt. It retained the mostly unprepossessing new musical material invented for the Broadway version, but brought the show back down to something nearer to the more intimate and manageable proportions of the original play, with a cast of 17 and an orchestra of 10. With stars Jean-Pierre Aumont (who made ''Little Girls'' sound perfectly filthy), Beryl Reid (grandmother), Sîan Phillips (aunt) and Amanda Waring (Gigi) all sadly short on singing ability, an agreeable adaptation was given little chance of success (242 performances).

Austria: Theater an der Wien 24 October 1974; Germany: Theater des Westens 23 September 1976; UK: Lyric Theatre 17 September 1985

Recordings: original film soundtrack (MGM), French version (Columbia), Spanish version (MGM), original Broadway cast (RCA), German cast (Fair Play), London cast (Safari)

GILBERT, Jean [WINTERFELD, Max] (b Hamburg, 11 February 1879; d Buenos Aires, 20 December 1942). One of the most successful composers for the German musical stage, Gilbert won a brief but enormous worldwide vogue which was interrupted by the First World War.

Winterfeld-Gilbert studied music from an early age in Kiel, Sonderhausen, Weimar and Berlin and became a theatre conductor at the Stadttheater in Bremerhaven at the age of 18. He moved on from there to Hamburg's important Carl-Schultze Theater and then, in 1900, to the Centralhallen-Theater where his first stage work as a composer, a French vaudeville-opérette based on a Paul de Kock comedy and entitled *Das Jungfernstift,* was produced in 1901, under his newly acquired and fashionably foreign-sounding pseudonym of Gilbert (pronounce Zjilbair). The show had sufficient success for it to remain in the provincial lists for a decade and more and it was later seen briefly in America's German-language theatre (Irving Place Theater 23 January 1911). Gilbert worked at the Berlin Apollotheater for two seasons, and had his next two theatre works staged in Hamburg, but he lost his musical director's position in a change of management at the Centralhallen-Theater, and his career regressed as, for some six years, he found conducting engagements only in lesser and provincial venues and even with a circus, and no outlet for his writings. In this time he placed just one work, the short *Onkel Casimir* at Düsseldorf, and for that he abandoned his posh pseudonym and returned to being plain Max Winterfeld.

The turning point came with the production of his hugely successful musical comedy *Polnische Wirtschaft* at Cottbus in December 1909, a success which was followed just two months later by an even more successful musical version of the French play *Fils à Papa,* produced as *Die keusche Susanne* at Magdeburg in February 1910. The former of this famous pair ran up a vast first series in Berlin whilst the second proved a major hit not only in Germany but, most notably, in France (*La Chaste Susanne*), Britain (*The Girl in the Taxi*) and Spain (*La casta Suzanna*), and its favorite songs became the hits of the period.

This double triumph swiftly earned Gilbert a return to Berlin and a post at the Thalia-Theater where, replacing Viktor Holländer and Max Schmidt as the purveyor of musical scores to Kren and Schönfeld's texts, he produced a veritable gusher of musical comedies over the next few years, ranging himself alongside Walter Kollo as the most prolific and popular German theatre composer of the era. His output, between 1910 and 1914, included such grand and exportable successes as the revamped metropolitan *Polnische Wirtschaft, Autoliebchen* (''Ja, das haben die Mädel so gern''), *Puppchen* (''Puppchen, du bist mein Augenstern''), *Die Kino-Königin* (''In der Nacht'') and *Die Tangoprinzessin.* Vienna, Budapest (*Az ártatlan Zsusi, Lengyel menyecske, Az autó tündére, A mozitünder, Buksi*), Paris (*La Chaste Susanne*) and New York (*Modest Suzanne, The Queen of the Movies, A Modern Eve*) all welcomed his works and, following the enormous British success of *The Girl in the Taxi,* Gilbert became the most sought-after composer in Britain. His *Autoliebchen* (*The Joy Ride Lady*), *Fräulein Tralala*

(*Mam'zelle Tralala, Oh! Be Careful*) and *Die Kino-Königin* (*The Cinema Star*) were all produced in London's West End in a period of little over three months, but Gilbert's London career was cut short by the war. *Die Kino-Königin* was forced out of town at the height of what looked like being a hugely successful run, and George Edwardes, who had purchased the English-language rights to *Puppchen* and *Die Tango-Prinzessin,* as well as hiring Gilbert to write the original score for a new musical for the Adelphi Theatre, was obliged to abandon all German-flavored plans.

Although his most promising overseas outlet was now closed, Gilbert continued to produce regular and mostly successful musical comedies for the German, Austrian and Hungarian stages—*Die Dose seiner Majestät* (*Jojó három vőlegenye* in Budapest), *Die Fräulein vom Amt* (*Ő, Teréz!*), *Arizonda, Die Fahrt ins Glück* (*Az aranyfácán*), *Das Vagabundenmädel* (*A csavargolány*), *Blondinchen,* the little *Eheurlaub*—throughout the First World War, along with scores of songs for some morale-manufacturing patriotic musicals. Then, in 1919, he essayed a slightly more substantial score with the romantic *Die Frau im Hermelin,* and the result was his biggest international success since *Die keusche Susanne,* with London in particular feting Gilbert's return to its stages by welcoming Phyllis Dare as *The Lady of the Rose* to Daly's Theatre for more than 500 performances. This was a total reached by only two other West End musicals in the years following the War and prior to the arrival of the fashion for American musicals. One of the two was Vienna's *Lilac Time,* the other was Gilbert's own most wide-flung success *Katja, die Tänzerin* which, produced in Vienna, followed up its German-language success by triumphing through Europe and from London (Daly's Theatre, 501 performances) to Australia.

Das Weib im Purpur (played in Hungary as *A biborruhas asszony*), *Die kleine Sünderin* ("In Berlin an der Ecke von der Kaiserallee," *A kis huncut* in Budapest) and the small-scale *Dorine und der Zufall,* which was played for nearly 200 nights at the Theater am Zoo, then at the Artushof-Theater, in Vienna and in Budapest (*Dorine és a véletlen*), were all produced with success in 1922–23. *Geliebte seiner Hoheit* was played at the Theater am Nollendorfplatz with Fritzi Massary and in Hungary as *A nagy nő,* and the Schiller Theater happily hosted *Annemarie* ("Durch Berlin fliesst immer noch die Spree!") before Gilbert, who had sponsored tours of his own works for narly a decade, began to expand his interests in the business side of the theatre.

He formed a firm to set up an ambitious international musical theatre circuit, but his grandiose projects failed and left him in a financially parlous state. He attempted to recoup his losses by writing for the cinema and also by allowing all sorts of depredations to be practiced on his works overseas. His name appeared as composer of what was virtually a new musical availing itself of some of his *Das Weib im Purpur* score, and staged by the Shuberts on Broadway as *The Red Robe,* and again on a London piece made up of a libretto apparently borrowed from his 1924 *Zwei um Eine,* some Vernon Duke songs and some of the score of his reasonably successful *Uschi,* which had already been played in Budapest (*Csak egy kislány*), all mixed together under the title *Yvonne* (280 performances). He also came up with one last new success in *Hotel Stadt Lemberg* (1929), which reached Broadway as *Marching By* and Budapest under its original title. However, his best moments as a composer were now past, both at home and in the almost always supportive British theatre where his last representations were sad ones: Edward Laurillard's production of *Lovely Lady* (1932) lasted 3 performances, and a mish-mash called *The Girl from Cook's* was unhappily served up at the Gaiety Theatre in 1927 for 34 performances.

In 1933, under the threat of Nazi rule, Gilbert left Germany and went successively to Vienna, where his *Die Dame mit dem Regenbogen* was produced for 72 performances at the Theater an der Wien, and then, with his career effectively ended, to Paris, London, Barcelona and Madrid before finally emigrating in 1939 to Buenos Aires, where he promoted the fourth film of his enduring *Die keusche Susanne* prior to his death in 1942.

1901 **Das Jungfernstift** (*Comtesse Marie*) (Ernest Quinot ad Max von Ritterfeld) Centralhallen-Theater, Hamburg 8 February

1903 **Der Prinzregent** (Hans Forsten) Carl-Schultze Theater, Hamburg 12 September

1903 **Jou-Jou** (Hans Buchholz) Centralhallen-Theater, Hamburg 23 October

1908 **Onkel Casimir** (as Max Winterfeld/Heinz Gorden) 1 act Apollotheater, Düsseldorf 1 November

1909 **Polnische Wirtschaft** (Alfred Schönfeld/Kurt Kraatz, Georg Okonkowski) Stadttheater, Cottbus 26 December; Thalia-Theater, Berlin 6 August 1910

1910 **Die keusche Susanne** (Schönfeld/Okonkowski) Wilhelm-Theater, Magdeburg 26 February; Neues Operetten-Theater, Berlin 6 August 1911

1910 **Die lieben Ottos** (Schönfeld/Jean Kren) Thalia-Theater 30 April

1911 **Die moderne Eva** (Schönfeld/Okonowski) Neues Operettentheater 11 November

1912 **Autoliebchen** (Schönfeld/Kren) Thalia-Theater 16 March

1912 **So bummeln wir** (Gustav Kadelburg) Theater Gross-Berlin 21 November

1912 **Die elfte Muse** (Okonkowski) Operettentheater, Hamburg 22 November

1912 **Puppchen** (Schönfeld/Kren, Kraatz) Thalia-Theater 19 December

1913 **Die Kino-Konigin** revised *Die elfte Muse* ad Julius Freund Metropoltheater 8 March

1913 **Die Reise um die Erde in vierzig Tagen** (Julius Freund) Metropoltheater 13 September

1913 **Die Tangoprinzessin** (Kren, Kraatz) Thalia-Theater 4 October

1913 **Fräulein Tralala** (Leo Leipziger/Okonkowski) Neues Luisen-Theater, Königsberg 15 November

1914 **Die Sünde der Lulatsch** (Hugo Doblin) Centraltheater, Chemnitz 15 March

1914 **Wenn der Frühling kommt!** (Schönfeld/Kren, Okonkowski) Thalia-Theater 28 March

1914 **Kam'rad Männe** (Schönfeld/Kren, Okonowski) Thalia-Theater 3 August

1914 **Woran wir denken** (Franz Arnold, Walter Turszinksy) Metropoltheater 25 December

1915 **Drei Paar Schuhe** (Schönfeld/Carl Görlitz ad Kren) Thalia-Theater 10 September

1915 **Jung muss man sein** (Leipziger/Erich Urban) Komische Oper 27 August

1915 **Das Fräulein vom Amt** (Okonowski, Ernst Arnold) Theater des Westens 13 November

1915 **Der tapfere Ulan** (Karl Herrmann) Komische Oper 20 November

1916 **Arizonda** (Felix Dörmann) Apollotheater, Vienna 1 February

1916 **Blondinchen** (Schönfeld/Jean Kren, Kurt Kraatz) Thalia-Theater 4 March

1916 **Die Fahrt ins Glück** (F Arnold, Ernst Bach) Theater des Westens 2 September

1916 **Das Vagabundenmädel** (Schönfeld/Kren, Buchbinder) Thalia-Theater 2 December

1917 **Die Dose seiner Majestät** (Leo Walther Stein, Rudolf Presber) Komische Oper 7 March

1917 **Der verliebte Herzog** (aka *Der verliebte Prinz*) (Okonkowski, Hans Bachwitz) Theater des Westens 1 September

1918 **Der ersten Liebe goldene Zeit** (Leo Kastner) Zentraltheater, Dresden 8 March; Theater des Westens 20 June 1920

1918 **Eheurlaub** (Julius Horst, Bachwitz) Liebich-Theater, Breslau 1 August; Apollotheater, Vienna 1 May 1919

1919 **Zur wilden Hummel** (Kren, Eduard Ritter) Thalia-Theater 19 March

1919 **Die Schönste von allen** (Okonkowski) Centraltheater 22 March

1919 **Die Frau im Hermelin** (Rudolf Schanzer, Ernst Welisch) Theater des Westens 23 August

1920 **Der Geiger von Lugano** (Schanzer, Welisch) Wallner Theater 25 September

1921 **Onkel Muz** (Bruno Decker, Robert Pohl) Apollotheater, Halle am Saale 2 April

1921 **Die Braut des Lucullus** (Schanzer, Welisch) Theater des Westens 26 August

1921 **Prinzessin Olala** (Schanzer, Rudolf Bernauer) Berliner Theater 17 September

1922 **Dorine und der Zufall** (Grünbaum, Wilhelm Sterk) Neues Theater am Zoo 15 September

1922 **Die kleine Sünderin** (Hans Hellmut Zerlett, Willy Prager) Wallner-Theater 1 October

1923 **Katja, die Tänzerin** (Leopold Jacobson, Rudolf Österreicher) Johann Strauss-Theater, Vienna 5 January

1923 **Das Weib im Purpur** (Jacobson, Österreicher) Wiener Stadttheater, Vienna 21 December

1923 **Der Gauklerkönig** (Presber, L W Stein, Zerlett)

1924 **Zwei um Eine** (Jacobson)

1924 **Geliebte seiner Hoheit** (Bernauer, Österreicher) Theater am Nollendorfplatz, Berlin 30 September

1925 **Uschi** (Leon Kastner, Alfred Möller) Carl-Schultze Theater, Hamburg 24 January; Theater in der Kommandantenstrasse, Berlin March

1925 **Annemarie** (Robert Gilbert/Okonkowski, Martin Zickel) Schiller-Theater 2 July

1925 **Das Spiel um die Liebe** (Schanzer, Welisch) Theater des Westens 19 December

1925 **Lebenskünstler** Zentraltheater, Dresden 25 December

1926 **Lene, Lotte, Liese, Josefinens Tochter** (w R Gilbert/Okonkowski) Thalia-Theater 14 January

1926 **Yvonne** pastiche of *Uschi,* et al (w Vernon Duke/lib credited to Percy Greenbank) Daly's Theatre, London 22 May

1926 **In der Johannisnacht** (R Gilbert) Thalia Theater, Hamburg 1 July

1927 **The Girl from Cook's** (w Raymond Hubbell/R H Burnside, Greatrex Newman) Gaiety Theatre, London 1 November

1928 **Eine Nacht in Kairo** (Bruno Hardt-Warden, Jacobson) Centraltheater, Dresden 22 December

1928 **The Red Robe** revised *Das Weib im Purpur* (H B Smith) Shubert Theater, New York 25 December

1929 **Hotel Stadt Lemberg** (Ernst Neubach) Deutsches Schauspielhaus, Hamburg 1 July

1930 **Das Mädel am Steuer** (Schanzer, Welisch) Komische Oper 17 September

1932 **Lovely Lady** (Zerlett, R Gilbert ad Arthur Wimperis) Phoenix Theatre, London 25 February

1933 **Die Dame mit dem Regenbogen** (Julius Brammer, Gustav Beer) Theater an der Wien 25 August

Literature: Schönfeld, A: *Jean Gilbert-Album* (Globus Verlag, Berlin)

GILBERT, Olive [Sarah] (b Lampeter, Carmarthen, 22 November 1898; d Hove, 19 February 1981). British contralto who became an institution in the musicals of Ivor Novello.

After a sizeable career in opera, mostly with the Carl Rosa touring company, Miss Gilbert appeared on the light musical stage for the first time in Ivor Novello's *Glamorous Night* (1935), playing the role of an opera singer. However, the stocky, middle-aged contralto eventually replaced Elisabeth Welch in the larger role of the seductively toned stowaway (''Shanty Town''). Novello provided her with increasingly important and staunchly suitable roles in each of his subsequent shows—Madame

Simonetti in *Careless Rapture,* Queen Manuelita in *Crest of the Wave,* the booming singing teacher Cäcilie Kurt in *The Dancing Years* (''Fold Your Wings''), Agnes Sorel in the opera-within-a-musical in *Arc de Triomphe* (which she doubled with her role in *The Dancing Years* with the aid of a quick mid-evening switch of theatres), perhaps the most grateful of all, the jolly Ernestine/Mrs Bridport in *Perchance to Dream* (''Highwayman Love,'' ''We'll Gather Lilacs''), and, finally, the heroine's confidante, Countess Lemainken in *King's Rhapsody* (''Fly Home, Little Heart'').

Between repeating her Novello roles on tour, on film and abroad, she later appeared as Sister Margaretta in London's *The Sound of Music* (1961) for five-and-a-half years, and as The Housekeeper in the London production of *Man of La Mancha* (1968). Her final appearance was, largely billed, in a number-three touring production of *King's Rhapsody.*

Novello's fondness for and fidelity to Miss Gilbert meant that she is largely responsible for the existence of a contralto repertoire in the post-Gilbert and Sullivan musical theatre in Britain.

GILBERT, Robert [WINTERFELD, David Robert] (aka Rudolph BERTRAM, Karl BUDA) (b Berlin, 29 September 1899; d Minusio, 20 March 1978).

The son of Jean Gilbert, Robert Gilbert led an eclectic early career doubling playwriting and composing, providing lyrics for his father's *Annemarie,* sharing the composing of the score of *Lene, Lotte, Liese, Josefinens Tochter* with him, and adapting de Flers, de Caillavet and Rey's *La Belle Aventure* as the libretto for his musical play *In der Johannisnacht.* He also ventured book, music and lyrics for the 1928 *Aeffchen* and composed the whole music for Zerlett's *Leichte Isabell* and the Deutsches Künstlertheater's *Prosit, Gipsy* (''he has inherited as little talent as is usual''), but found a first genuine success when he supplied the lyrics and one delightfully jaunty song (''Was kann der Sigismund dafür'') for the Ralph Benatzky musical *Im weissen Rössl.*

After the Second World War, he collaborated on the reorganization of *Der schwarze Hecht* into the successful *Feuerwerk,* and remade some of his father's early successes, but, most successfully, he became the principal adaptor of American musicals for the German-speaking stage, with the local versions of *My Fair Lady* and *Hello, Dolly!* amongst his credits.

His contribution to the musical film included the lyrics to Werner Heymann's music for the spectacular *Der Kongress tanzt* (1931, ''Just Once for All Time,'' etc), subsequently adapted to the stage, and *Die Drei von der Tankstelle* (1930), which was, nearly 70 years on, turned into two stage musicals (Metropol, Vienna 6 November 1998; Altona Theater, Hamburg 9 January 1999).

- 1924 **Die vertagte Nacht** (Walter Kollo/Franz Arnold, Ernst Bach) Stadttheater, Mainz 11 November
- 1925 **Annemarie** (Jean Gilbert/Georg Okonkowski, Martin Zickel) Schiller-Theater 2 July
- 1926 **Lene, Lotte, Liese, Josefinens Tochter** (w J Gilbert/Okonkowski) Thalia-Theater 14 January
- 1926 **In der Johannisnacht** (J Gilbert) Thalia-Theater, Hamburg 1 July
- 1926 **Leichte Isabell** (Hans Hellmut Zerlett) Schiller-Theater 1 July
- 1927 **Pit-Pit** (Zerlett) Centraltheater, Dresden 19 February
- 1928 **Aeffchen** Centraltheater, Dresden 23 March
- 1928 **Die Männer von Manon** (Walter Goetze/w August Neidhart) Kleines Haus, Düsseldorf 30 September
- 1929 **Prosit, Gipsy** (Neidhart, Henry Gilbert) Deutsches Künstlertheater, Berlin 19 April
- 1930 **Im weissen Rössl** (Ralph Benatzky/Hans Müller) Grosses Schauspielhaus 8 November
- 1932 **Lovely Lady** (Gilbert/w Zerlett ad Arthur Wimperis) Phoenix Theatre, London 25 February
- 1933 **Zwei Herzen im Dreivierteltakt** (aka *Der verlorene Walzer*) (Robert Stolz/Paul Knepler, Ignaz M Welleminsky) Stadttheater, Zürich 30 September
- 1934 **Grüezi** (aka *Servus, Servus, Himmelblaue Träume*) (Stolz/''Georg Burkhard'') Stadttheater, Zürich 3 November
- 1936 **Rise and Shine** (aka *Darling You*) original German lyrics (Theatre Royal, Drury Lane, London)
- 1936 **Gloria und der Clown** (Stolz/w Julius Horst) Stadttheater, Aussig 31 December
- 1937 **Herzen im Schnee** (Benatzky/w H Gilbert, Armin Robinson) Volksoper 8 September
- 1937 **Die Reise um die Erde in 80 Minuten** (Robert Stolz/w Hugo Wiener, H Gilbert) Volksoper 22 December
- 1947 **Drei von der Donau** (Stolz/Johann Nestroy ad w Rudolf Österreicher) Wiener Stadttheater 24 September
- 1950 **Ihr erster Walzer** (Oscar Straus/w Paul Knepler, Robinson) Theater am Gärtnerplatz, Munich 31 March
- 1950 **Feuerwerk** (Paul Burkhard/Erik Charell, Jürg Amstein) revised *Der schwarze Hecht* Bayerische Staatsoper, Munich 16 May
- 1953 **Mädi** revised lyrics (Stadttheater, Zürich)
- 1953 **Strammer Junge angekommen** (Bach, Arnold ad) Theater am Besenbinderhof, Hamburg 1 May
- 1953 **Der Blumentopf** Renaissance-Theater 10 September
- 1954 **Kiki vom Montmartre** (Werner Richard Heymann/André Picard ad E F Brücklmeier, Janne Furch) Würtembergisches Staatstheater, Stuttgart 30 June
- 1955 **Signorina** (Stolz/w Per Schwenzen) Städtische Bühnen, Nürnberg-Furth 23 April
- 1956 **Der kleine Schwindel in Paris** (Stolz/Rudolf Weys) Theater in der Josefstadt, Vienna 25 December
- 1957 **Hopsa** revised version (Burkhard/w Robinson/Paul Baudisch, Robinson) Wiesbaden 12 October
- 1959 **Kitty und die Weltkonferenz** (aka *Die kleine und die grosse Welt*) (Stolz/Kurt Nachmann, Peter Preses) Theater in der Josefstadt, Vienna 4 February

1959 **Das Blaue von Himmel** (Friedrich Holländer/w Schwenzen) Städtische Bühnen, Nürnberg-Fürth 14 November

1961 **Die Kino-Königin** revised version (Opernhaus, Nürnberg-Furth)

1961 **My Fair Lady** German version (Theater des Westens)

1962 **Lili** (*Carnival*) German version (Stadttheater, Zürich)

1962 **Trauminsel** revised *Signorina* (Bregenz)

1962 **Die Dame mit der Brille** (Burkhard/w Karl Suter) Schauspielhaus, Zürich 31 December

1963 **Annie, schiess los!** (*Annie Get Your Gun*) German version (Theater des Westens)

1965 **Can-Can** German lyrics w Kurt Feltz (Kleinen Haus, Staatstheater, Stuttgart)

1965 **Wie man was wird im Leben, ohne sich anzustrengen** (*How to Succeed in Business without Really Trying*) German version w Gerhard Bronner (Theater an der Wien)

1966 **Hallo, Dolly!** (*Hello, Dolly!*) German version (Schauspielhaus, Düsseldorf)

1967 **Wie lernt man Liebe** (Mischa Spoliansky/ad) Bayerisches Staatsoper, Munich 5 March

1967 **Charleys Tante** (Ralph Maria Siegel/w Max Colpet) Deutsches Theater, Munich 9 March

1968 **Der Mann von la Mancha** (*Man of La Mancha*) German version (Theater an der Wien)

1969 **Hochzeit am Bodensee** revised *Grüezi* (Bregenz)

1969 **Illya Darling** German version (Schauspielhaus, Düsseldorf)

1970 **Canterbury Tales** German version (Theater am Goetheplatz, Bremen)

1970 **Cabaret** German version (Theater an der Wien)

1970 **Mame** German version (Nuremberg)

1971 **Sorbas** (*Zorba*) German version w Bronner (Theater an der Wien)

1972 **Karusell** (*Carousel*) German version (Volksoper)

1972 **Godspell** German lyrics (Hamburg)

1973 **Oklahoma!** German version (Münster)

1974 **Pippin** German version (Theater an der Wien)

1980 **Brigadoon** German version (Staatstheater, Karlsruhe)

Other works credited include *Der geliebte Dieb* (Victor Reinshagen/Ludwig Herzer) and *Tanz um Daisy* (Reinshagen)

GILBERT, W[illiam] S[chwenk] (Sir) (b London, 18 November 1836; d Harrow Weald, 29 May 1911). The most talented librettist and lyricist for—and, as one half of the show-writing tandem Gilbert and Sullivan, the modern flagbearer of—the 19th-century English-language theatre.

Originally destined for a legal career, Gilbert swiftly abandoned the law to take up writing. The most effective of his earliest work, mostly published in humorous magazines such as *Fun,* was in the form of comic verses, and some of these, written under the pseudonym of "Bab," brought him particular renown. They were subsequently collected into book form in 1869 under the title *The Bab Ballads.*

Plate 144. **W S Gilbert**

Gilbert began writing for the theatre in his twenties, making his debut with the short play, *Hush a Bye,* produced by the eccentric W H C Nation at Astley's Theatre, but he won his first real success in the realm of burlesque. His *Dulcamara* (1866), a burlesque of Donizetti's *L'Elisir d'amore, La Vivandière* (1867) which took the same composer's *La Fille du régiment* as its basis, a *Bohemian Girl* parody called *The Merry Zingara,* the Gaiety Theatre's opening burlesque of Meyerbeer's *Robert the Devil* (1868), a *Norma* burlesque called *The Pretty Druidess* (1869) and *The Princess* (1870), a burlesque based not, for once, on an opera but on Tennyson's poem of the same title, all won notice as particularly intelligently made and classy examples of an often ill-treated genre.

By the time he abandoned the pasticcio burlesque, Gilbert had already begun to branch out in different areas. In 1869 he had considerable success with some short comic operettas written for the German Reeds' Gallery of Illustration, and the following year he scored a hit with the play *The Palace of Truth.* This was followed by other plays equally as successful, mostly based on whimsical or supernatural notions, and including *Pygmalion and Galatea* (1871) and *The Wicked World* (1873), a piece which—under the pseudonym of "F Latour Tomline"—he also used as the basis for a burlesque *The Happy Land. The Happy Land* won him a different kind of notice—it was stopped in mid-performance by a detective and banned by the Lord Chamberlain, allegedly for including in its staged version 18 pages of interpolations not in the approved script, but in reality for its ridiculing of government and the representation of Mr Gladstone on the parody stage.

On the musical-comedy front, his *No Cards, Ages Ago, Our Island Home, A Sensation Novel* and *Happy Arcadia* all proved highly popular at the little "drawing room entertainment" purveyed by the Reed family and their friends, and, while they prospered, Gilbert made his first venture with a full-length musical play: a piece based on the theatrically popular theory of metempsychosis, *The Gentleman in Black,* set to music by his preferred collaborator Frederic Clay. *The Gentleman in Black,* which held the seeds of many of the topsy-turvy ideas that Gilbert would later use repeatedly in his more famous works, played for only 26 performances, but another, shorter piece in a similar vein, *Creatures of Impulse,* won a number of further productions, both with and without its Randegger score.

Gilbert returned to the area of burlesque and extravaganza when he was commissioned to write a Christmas entertainment for the Gaiety Theatre. On this occasion, he was paired with the white hope of the light musical theatre, the young composer Arthur Sullivan, and their joint effort, a jolly festive "grotesque opera" called *Thespis* served the Gaiety's purposes more than adequately.

The author and composer were paired again when they produced a one-act curtain-raiser, *Trial by Jury,* for Selina Dolaro's *La Périchole* company, but when the actress-manager Kate Santley commissioned a full-length comic opera from Gilbert, it was to his old collaborator of the Gallery of Illustration and *The Gentleman in Black,* Freddie Clay, that he turned for music. In spite of the special wit of some of its text and the charm of its score, the production of *Princess Toto,* dogged by backstage problems, was only a half-success.

The author's next commission came from the former company manager of the Selina Dolaro company, Richard D'Oyly Carte, and he reconstituted the Gilbert/Sullivan partnership for the occasion. The resulting piece, *The Sorcerer,* set in motion the phenomenon which would become "the Savoy operas." The success of the witty and whimsical English version of the opéra-bouffe form in which Gilbert excelled, and of which *The Sorcerer* was his best example to date, was confirmed with wild international success by its successor, *HMS Pinafore,* as manager Carte, author Gilbert and composer Sullivan set forth on a decade of work together which was to become one of the wonders of the theatrical world. Together, they produced, first for the old Opera Comique and then for the Savoy Theatre built by D'Oyly Carte to house his productions, *The Pirates of Penzance, Patience, Iolanthe, Princess Ida* (a remake of *The Princess*), *The Mikado, Ruddigore, The Yeomen of the Guard* and *The Gondoliers,* each of which followed its London run by an international career of greater or, just occasionally, lesser dimensions.

After *The Gondoliers,* the tensions which had grown up among the trio resulted in Gilbert breaking with the other two members of the team. He continued, however, to write for the musical stage and combined, with only some success, with Alfred Cellier on *The Mountebanks* and with very little with George Grossmith on a musical version of his old adaptation of *Un Chapeau de paille d'Italie* under the title *Haste to the Wedding,* before the breach at the Savoy was pasted over. He rejoined Sullivan—who had been no more successful away from him—for two final pieces, *Utopia (Limited)* and *The Grand Duke.* Neither reached the level of the earlier Savoy pieces, and, after the comparative failure of *The Grand Duke,* the collaboration was put to rest.

Gilbert subsequently wrote a libretto and lyrics worthy of his heyer-days for the comic opera *His Excellency* (1894), set to music by Osmond Carr; the play *The Fairies' Dilemma* (1904); and an unsuccessful musical adaptation of his *The Wicked World* composed by Edward German under the title *Fallen Fairies,* but he was unable to find a producer for his last musical in a world which had moved well away from the style of Victorian comic opera in which he had made his name.

In later years, Gilbert's 1877 comedy *Engaged* was set several times to music by other hands. In 1925 a version by Brian Hooker, set with a pasticcio score, was produced at New York's 52nd Street Theater (18 June), and in 1962 Britain's Theatre Royal, Windsor put out a version which decorated Gilbert's play with a pasticcio of melodies taken from the just-out-of-copyright Gilbert and Sullivan comic operas. *The Wicked World,* already auto-disemboweled for *The Happy Land,* was again burlesqued by Owen Marlowe's Comedy Company at Hooley's Theatre, Brooklyn in 1874 (5 January) in a version by local writer William C Hudson, and a localized version of *The Happy Land* was played by Tony Pastor as *[H B S] Venus* in May 1879 and again in June 1882. *The Wedding March* (*Un Chapeau de paille d'Italie*) was also remusicalized, at Chicago's Bush Temple in June 1906. This "americanised version," which "Mr Gilbert wouldn't have owned if he had been here and recognized it," featured "a row of girls in short dresses[,] . . . a waltz song about a local amusement resort . . . and such ditties as 'I Was Just Making Believe' and 'One Boy in the World for Me.'"

1866 **Dulcamara, or The Little Duck and the Great Quack** (pasticcio arr van Hamme) St James's Theatre 29 December

1867 **La Vivandière, or True to the Corps** (pasticcio arr Ferdinand Wallerstein) St James's Hall, Liverpool 15 June; Queen's Theatre, London 22 January 1868

1868 **The Merry Zingara, or The Tipsy Gipsy and the Pipsy Wipsy** (pasticcio) Royalty Theatre 21 March

1868 **Robert the Devil, or The Nun, the Dun and the Son of a Gun** (pasticcio arr Kettenus) Gaiety Theatre 21 December

1869 **The Pretty Druidess, or The Mother, the Maid and the Mistletoe Bough** (pasticcio) Charing Cross Theatre 19 June

1869 **No Cards** (Thomas German Reed) 1 act Gallery of Illustration 29 March

1869 **Ages Ago** (Frederic Clay) 1 act Gallery of Illustration 22 November

1870 **The Princess** (pasticcio arr John Winterbottom) Olympic Theatre 8 January

1870 **The Gentleman in Black** (Clay) Charing Cross Theatre 26 May

1870 **Our Island Home** (German Reed) 1 act Gallery of Illustration 20 June

1871 **A Sensation(al) Novel** (German Reed) 1 act Gallery of Illustration 30 January

1871 **Creatures of Impulse** (Alberto Randegger) Court Theatre 15 April

1871 **Thespis, or The Gods Grown Old** (Arthur Sullivan) Gaiety Theatre 26 December

1872 **Happy Arcadia** (Clay) Gallery of Illustration 28 October

1873 **The Happy Land** (pasticcio arr A E Bartle/w Gilbert a'Beckett) Court Theatre 3 March

1874 **Topseyturveydom** (Alfred Cellier) Criterion Theatre 21 March

1875 **Trial by Jury** (Sullivan) 1 act Royalty Theatre 25 March

1875 **Eyes and No Eyes, or The Art of Seeing** (German Reed) 1 act St George's Hall 5 July

1876 **Princess Toto** (Clay) Theatre Royal, Nottingham 26 June; Strand Theatre, London 2 October

1877 **The Sorcerer** (Sullivan) Opera Comique 17 November

1878 **HMS Pinafore** (Sullivan) Opera Comique 25 May

1879 **The Pirates of Penzance** (Sullivan) Fifth Avenue Theatre, New York 31 December

1881 **Patience** (Sullivan) Opera Comique 23 April

1882 **Iolanthe** (Sullivan) Savoy Theatre 25 November

1884 **Princess Ida** (Sullivan) Savoy Theatre 5 January

1885 **The Mikado** (Sullivan) Savoy Theatre 14 March

1887 **Ruddigore** (Sullivan) Savoy Theatre 22 January

1888 **The Yeomen of the Guard** (Sullivan) Savoy Theatre 3 October

1889 **The Brigands** *(Les Brigands)* English version (Casino Theater, New York)

1889 **The Gondoliers** (Sullivan) Savoy Theatre 7 December

1892 **The Mountebanks** (Cellier) Lyric Theatre 4 January

1892 **Haste to the Wedding** (George Grossmith) Criterion Theatre 27 July

1893 **Utopia (Limited)** (Sullivan) Savoy Theatre 7 October

1894 **His Excellency** (F Osmond Carr) Lyric Theatre 27 October

1896 **The Grand Duke** (Sullivan) Savoy Theatre 7 March

1909 **Fallen Fairies** (Edward German) Savoy Theatre 15 December

Biographies: Browne, E: *W S Gilbert* (John Lane, London, 1907), Dark, S, Grey, R: *William Schwenk Gilbert: His Life and Letters* (Methuen, London, 1923), Pearson, H: *Gilbert: His Life and Strife* (Methuen, London, 1957), Sutton, M: *W S Gilbert* (Twayne, Boston, 1975), Cox-Ife, W: *W S Gilbert: Stage Director* (Dobson, London, 1977), Stedman, J: *W S Gilbert: A Classic Victorian and His Theatre* (OUP, New York, 1996), etc

GILFORD, Jack [GELLMAN, Jacob] (b New York, 25 July 1908; d New York, 4 June 1990). Little comic actor whose few Broadway musical appearances included several memorable new shows and roles.

Originally a vaudeville performer, Gilford appeared on Broadway in revue and, after an appearance at the Metropolitan Opera House as Frosch in *Die Fledermaus,* had his first modern musical-comedy role as the mute, browbeaten King Sextimus in *Once Upon a Mattress* (1959), miming his way unforgettably through a ''Man to Man Talk'' about the bees and the birds with his son. His damp-eyed, put-upon kind of comedy got an even more extensive showing when he created the role of the fall-guy Roman slave Hysterium in *A Funny Thing Happened on the Way to the Forum* (1962, ''I'm Calm''), and he had further fine roles as the original Herr Schultz in *Cabaret* (1966, ''Meeskite'') and as the only slightly wayward publisher, Jimmy Smith, in the 1971 revival of *No, No, Nanette* (1971). In 1985 he appeared in London in the E Y Harburg compilation show *Look to the Rainbow.*

Gilford also appeared regularly in films, repeating his *Funny Thing* role for the show's movie version.

Biography: Mostel, K, Gilford, M: *170 Years of Show Business* (Random House, New York, 1978)

GILL, William B[ain] (b Trinity Bay, Newfoundland, Canada, 10 May 1842; d West Farms, NY). Australia's most successful ever international manufacturer of musical plays.

The grandson of Sir William and Lady Isabella Bain of Granton, Edinburgh, Scotland and the son of an apparently peripatetic London surgeon, author-comedian Willie Gill was (under circumstances not yet explained) actually born in a remote area of what was to become a part of Canada. He was, however, apparently brought up in Melbourne, Australia. It was there, in any case, that he began—paragraphed as ''an Australian comedian''—what was to be a variegated and highly successful career in the theatre.

He related in later life that he had supported Charles Kean during the actor's 1863–64 tour of Australia, that he had appeared at the Melbourne Princess's with Fawcett Rowe, and that he had spent some time playing at the goldfields theatre in Ballarat, but the first occasion on which I have actually spotted his name in active print, alongside that of his mother, is in a list of a company made up largely of the Edouin family which went to play in Shanghai and Hong Kong in the winter of 1864.

He turns up in 1866 cast alongside his mother for the part of Mercury in Australia's original production of the burlesque *Ixion* at Melbourne's Princess's Theatre and again, in 1867, as stage director for Messrs Coker and Nish at the Melbourne Theatre of Varieties, where he directed and starred in such pieces as his personalized adaptation of the London burlesque *Grin Bushes* (''Madame Celeste Gill as Miami''), and in a version of Byron's burlesque *Lucy de Lammermoor.* Later that year he is billed at the Haymarket in the same city, playing Captain Crosstree in the burlesque *Black-Eyed Susan,* and early the next he appeared as Bermudas in *Under the Gaslight* at the renamed Duke of Edinburgh's Theatre (''a gentleman who although only on the stage a few years now ranks amongst the foremost in his profession''; ''Mr Gill's serio-comic characters often awake in me recollections of the past when Robson was in his prime at the Olympic'').

In 1868 he is seen at Melbourne's Theatre Royal, starring in the title role of *Rip van Winkle,* and in mid-1869 he turns up again in India, now principal comedian with the former Rose Edouin (Mrs G B Lewis). The following year he returned to India to take over the management of Mr Sultana's Theatre Royal, Calcutta, bringing a company and a repertoire of comedies, dramas and burlesques from Australia. He didn't stay in Asia too long, however, for he resurfaces, in 1871, at the Sydney School of Arts in an ''original musical entertainment'' called *Laughing Faces* (''rapid changes—marvellous transformations—witty songs—grotesque dances—and faithful representation of eccentric characters'') in tandem with his recently acquired wife, the former Eleanor Smith [nee Wardock SHINTON] (b Adelaide, 3 April 1848), daughter of the well-known actor Henry S DEERING [Henry William SHINTON] (b England, c1816; d Ballarat, 21 April 1856), and then again as manager, stage director, sometime author and star at the Royal Victoria Theatre in Sydney in 1872–73. His appearances there included another Captain Crosstree in a remade version of Burnand's famous burlesque *Black-Eyed Susan* (here subtitled ''*or All-in-the-Breakdowns*''), and the title role of a ''localized and adapted'' (by him w S H Banks) version of the London pantomime of *The Yellow Dwarf,* for which he supplied songs (''What Will It Go the Ton?,'' etc) for his own use.

Gill then took over the city's Queen's Theatre, starring himself and his wife in a series of dramatic and comic roles from Rip van Winkle to Shallabullah (*Belphegor*) and Jack Gong (*The Green Bushes*), the dramas supported by smaller comic and musical pieces, some of his own making. The season's program also included his pantomime *The Man in the Moon* (1873, Prince of Larrikins), burlesques such as *The Orange Tree and the Humble Bee* (1873) and his own *Mephistophiles DDD,* and his comedy-drama *Ups and Downs.*

Soon after this, Gill crossed the ocean to the American West Coast and in 1874 he could be spotted managing John Piper's stock theatre in Virginia City, Nevada. In 1875 he spent some time ''playing comedy'' in Salt Lake City, and in 1876 he showed up purveying journalism to the *Clipper* theatrical newspaper. In 1877 he was, for a while, stage manager at MacDaniels Variety Theatre in Cheyenne, and ''Rose and Willie Gill, the English and Australian dramatic, musical and burlesque sketch artists''—advertising ''all their specialities are original . . . the largest repertoire of any artists travelling''—were seen purveying ''musical burlettas'' in variety houses around the Amercian goldfields circuits. However, after some three years slogging around minor houses, things finally looked up for them. In late 1877 the pair were playing their act at Newark, NJ, at the time when ''Uncle'' Samuel Colville was setting up his new Folly Company, a company featuring many of the members of Lydia Thompson's famous and recently disbanded troupe, notably old friend Willie Edouin. Thanks to Edouin, Gill was engaged as stage manager for, and an actor in the new company, playing along with his wife (now billed as ''Eleanor Deering'') in the kind of burlesque, extravaganza and farce comedy which had been Lydia's speciality.

His name first appeared under a title in America when he adapted H J Byron's English burlesque *Babes in the Wood,* in which he appeared as the super-melodramatic ''The Very Bad Man'' and as Pantaloon in a seasonally affixed harlequinade, as a burlesque extravaganza for the Colville company's maiden season. It was to gain him many years of endlessly touring royalties. He rearranged Lydia Thompson's *Oxygen* for the same company and thereafter continued a career as an author of farce-comedies, extravaganzas, melodramatic musical comedies, star-vehicles and other parti-colored entertainments which, although roughly written and often little more than a basis on which artists and producers could embroider at will, proved to have a singular place in the less sophisticated theatres of the time.

He moved from the Colville company to rejoin Edouin in E E Rice's Surprise Party for whom he supplied the extravaganza *Horrors* (1879) an ''ingenious combination of bad puns, popular music and a trite nursery tale from the Orient'' which proved enormously to the taste of the company's provincial audiences and remained, along with this company's reproduction of Gill's *Babes in the Wood,* long a feature of Rice's repertoire. Colville added to his productions of *Babes, Robinson Crusoe* and *Oxygen* Gill's re-readaptation of H J Byron's *Cinderella,* played eventually under the title *The Magic Slipper.*

Later the same year he wrote, directed and played in (as Benjamin Franklin Cobb to his wife's Mrs Cobb) the five-handed "nightmare" extravaganza *Our Goblins,* which he toured under the banner of W C Mitchell's Pleasure Party. *Our Goblins* proved as popular as his earlier pieces. A one-week summer stop on Broadway stretched to a full month as "the greatest hit of the season," and it was played for several years on the American touring circuits as well as getting a showing in the British provinces (Circus Pavilion, Leamington 18 September 1882). He subsequently provided Mitchell with the musical comedy *A Gay Time at Whymple's,* in which he appeared as the pageboy, Geranium, and his wife as Mrs Arabella Whymple, and appeared on Broadway in support of Henry Dixey in a one-act burlesque of Henry Irving entitled *Distinguished Foreigners* (25 January 1884).

His vast list of long-traveling pieces did him and his purse proud, but Gill also managed to hit the jackpot with a success of much more substantial proportions not just once, but twice during his career. The first was in America, where he collaborated with Rice on the writing of the burlesque *Adonis* (1884), a Broadway record-breaker and one of the most popular homemade musical pieces of its era, and the other very largely in Britain, where the American actress Minnie Palmer became an institution as she trouped his Dutch-accented variety-musical-weepie *My Sweetheart* around the provinces, into London, back into the provinces and at considerable length through the colonies.

Whilst continuing to work as an actor (alongside Paul Arthur in his own *Two Bad Men* 1884–85, as Flute in *Bottom's Dream* 1885 w Nat Goodwin, etc), he turned out a regular run of more-or-less musical plays (often in collaboration with George H Jessop). These included *In Paradise* for John T Raymond (Albany, NY 9 January 1883), *An Old Stager* (Baltimore 1 March 1883), *Fact, or His Little Hatchet* for Mr and Mrs W J Florence (Walnut Theater, Philadelphia 24 September 1883; toured in duplicate in Britain for a number of years as *Muddles*), *Stolen Money* (1884)—in which Gill himself played—*Mam'selle* for opéra-bouffe star Marie Aimée (it outlived its star on the touring circuits by 20 years), the hugely successful *Old Jed Prouty* for Richard Golden and *Chestnuts* (1885) for Richard Golden and his wife Dora Wiley. To the Extravaganza circuits he contributed a musical piece based on the nursery rhyme "Tom the Piper's Son" called *Arcadia* (1886, The Piper)—which was damned by the critics but still being toured, by Corinne, through good dates seven years later—and also supplied *Hendrik Hudson* for Fay Templeton. He provided Tony Hart with a pair of farce-comedy vehicles (*Buttons, A Toy Pistol*) following the comedian's split with his author-partner Harrigan, and turned out another of the kind for the comedy duo of George Richards and Eugene Canfield (*My Boys,* 1897); a colorful "pantomime-burlesque-vaudeville" called (*The*) *Spider and* (*the*) *Fly* which held the road for half a dozen seasons; a musequel to their highly successful *The Nabobs* (Norristown, Pa 30 August 1890) for May Ten Broeck and John E Henshaw; a musical comedy that "fits her perfectly" for Annie Pixley as *Miss Blythe of Duluth* (1892); a "rollickingly funny Irish play of considerable merit" in *The Rising Generation* (1893), toured for several seasons by Billy Barry; and—for ready money—he even took on the thankless task of remaking Jeff Leerburger's book to the hopeless *Penny Ante, or The Last of the Fairies* (14th Street Theater 9 June 1884) for composer Fred Eustis.

Willie Gill's name was, in these years, to be found on bills from one end of America to the other and, if the critics frequently execrated his writing (whilst always praising his comic acting), his frequent success proved that his stage plays were if nothing else deftly made to suit their stars and American small-town taste, and many of them, like his early extravaganzas, spent years and years on the touring circuits.

Gill kept on compiling his loose-limbed combinations of musical potpourri, low comedy and ingenuous and/or melodramatic sentiment and even bringing them to the cities, when their time was long since past, and some of his later works got short shrift. However, he kept going, and well into the 1890s he was still around to supply the text for, and—in a still-continuing parallel career as a performer—take to the stage in, another vehicle for Minnie Palmer, *The School Girl* (1895, Professor Gainsbury), to supply Odell Williams with the slightly musical play *The Alderman* (14th Street Theater 24 May 1897) and the vaudeville sketch *The Judge* (1897) and more in the same mold.

Willie was still churning out plays, from his home in West Farms, NY, after the turn of the century—*The King's Highway* for Roland Reed and a romantic comedy *The Loves of David Garrick* in 1900, a little operetta for the vaudeville houses, and the play *The Honest Blacksmith* for boxer Fitzsimmons and his contortionist wife in 1901. In 1902 Frank L Perley announced that he would produce Willie's *The Merry Marquis* (mus: David Dorée), in 1903 he was paragraphed as the co-author (w Fitzhugh) of a piece called *The Little Outcast* and the writer of *Estella, the Outcast* for Millie Blanchard, and in 1904 his name appeared as author of the ''comedy melodrama'' with songs *Mrs Mac, the Mayor,* a vehicle for vast old-timer George W Monroe (''a much better play than he has had recently'')—but these apparently did not make ends meet, for in these later years he was obliged to take employment as an ''Inspector of Highways'' in the Bronx.

However, he apparently kept his pen active into his grey age if, that is, he was the William Gill who supplied book and lyrics to the music of one James H Stauring for an amateur production called *P.G.F. (Pretty Good Fun)* at Schenectady's van Curler Opera House as late as 16 February 1912.

1867 **The Grin Bushes** (pasticcio) readapted version of Byron's burlesque Varieties, Melbourne 11 May

1873 **Mephistophiles DDD, or Faust and His Fair Marguerite** (pasticcio) Queen's Theatre, Sydney 6 April

1877 **The Babes in the Wood, or Who Killed Cock Robin?** (later *Blooming Babes of Macassar Hall*) (comp & arr Henry Sator/ad from Byron's *Babes in the Wood* w Willie Edouin) Eagle Theater 24 December

1878 **Oxygen, or Gas in a Burlesque Metre** rearranged version of H B Farnie and Robert Reece's burlesque Boston Theater 8 June

1878 **Our New Cinderella** (pasticcio arr William Withers/ adaptation of H J Byron's *Cinderella*) Hooley's Theater, Chicago 17 August

1878 **Horrors, or the Maharajah of Zogobad** (pasticcio/w Willie Edouin) Opera House, Milwaukee 10 October; Haverley's Theater, Chicago 14 October; Union Square Theater, New York 28 May 1879

1879 **The Magic Slipper** revised version of *Our Cinderella* Haverley's Theater 25 August

1879 **Our Goblins, or Fun on the Rhine [in Germany]** 1 act (comp & arr George Loesch) Olympic Theater, Chicago 16 November; enlarged version Beloit, Wis 24 November; Haverley's Theater, New York 14 June 1880

1881 **Our Goblins at Home, or Society in a Nutshell** (pasticcio) Academy of Music, Reading, Pa 14 February

1881 **Billy Taylor** American version (Gaiety Theatre, Boston)

1881 **My Sweetheart** (various) Shattuck's Opera House, Hornellsville, NY 27 August; Gaiety Theater, Boston 12 September; Haverly's 14th Street Theater 14 September 1882

1882 **A Gay Time at Whymple's** Leland Opera House, Albany 7 January

1884 **Adonis** (E E Rice) Hooley's Theater, Chicago 6 July; Bijou Theater, New York 4 September

1884 **Mam'zelle, or The Little Milliner** (various/w George H Jessop) Sampson's Opera House, Kingston, NY 11 September; Fifth Avenue Theater, New York 15 December

1884 **A Bottle of Ink** (Rice, et al/w Jessop) Bijou Theater, Boston 3 November; Comedy Theater, New York 6 January 1885

1884 **Two Bad Men** (pasticcio) Yonkers, NY 9 December

1885 **Oxygen** new version with mus arr John J Braham, Gustave Kerker (Bijou Theater, Boston)

1885 **A Modern Venus** (revised *Penny Ante, or the Last of the Fairies*) (Fred J Eustis) Bigelow's Garden, Worcester, Mass 22 June; Oakland Gardsen, Boston 6 July

1885 **Buttons** (pasticcio) Howard Opera House, Burlington, Vt, 17 August

1885 **Bluff** (pasticcio/w Jessop) McVicker's Theater, Chicago, 23 August

1885 **Mugwumps** (ex- *Chestnuts,* revised *A Bottle of Ink*) (pasticcio) New Britain, Conn 2 November

1885 **Capers** (revised *Fun in a Boarding School*) Standard Theatre, London 23 November

1886 **Aphrodite Still in the Ring** (uncredited/w Jessop) Library Hall, Pittsburgh 25 January

1886 **Oxygen** new version with mus arr John J Braham, Gustave Kerker (Bijou Theater, Boston)

1886 **A Toy Pistol** (revised *A Bottle of Ink*) Comedy Theater 20 February

1886 **Arcadia** (pasticcio arr John J Braham) Bijou Theater, Boston, 5 April; Bijou Theater 26 April

1889 **A Royal Tramp** (Charles Puerner) Allbaugh's Lyceum, Baltimore 22 January

1889 **Old Jed Prouty** (w Richard Golden) Opera House, Bangor, Maine 22 April; Union Square Theater 13 May

1889 **The Seven Ages** (Rice, Braham/w Rice) Standard Theater 7 October

1889 **Spider and Fly** (Fred W Zaulig/w Fraser) Taylor Opera House, Trenton, NJ 20 September; Theatre Comique, Harlem 14 October

1890 **Rip, or Many a Slip Twixt the Cup and the Lip** (William Furst) Columbia Theater, Chicago 23 July

1890 **Hendrik Hudson, or The Discovery of Columbus** (arr Watty Hydes, Fred Perkins/w Robert Fraser) 14th Street Theater 18 August

1892 **Miss Blythe of Duluth** (Harry Braham) Lyceum Theater, New London, Conn 26 September; Tremont Theater, Boston 3 October; Grand Opera House 26 December

1893 **The Rising Generation** (Emil O Wolff) Schenectady 23 August; Park Theater 11 September

1893 **The Nabobs ''fin de siècle''** (various) Dover, NH 3 October

1895 **A Fatted Calf** (various) H R Jacobs Theater, Newark 15 April; Amphion Theater, Brooklyn 31 August

1895 **The School Girl** (Albert Maurice, et al/ George Manchester Cohen ad) Grand Theatre, Cardiff 21 September; Bijou Theater, New York 30 December

1897 **My Boys** (revised *The Fatted Calf*) (various) Lyceum Theater, Elizabeth, NJ 21 August; Manhattan Theater, New York 6 December

1901 **In a Japanese Garden** (A Baldwin Sloane) 1 act Casino Theater 3 May

1904 **Mrs Mac, the Mayor** (Albert von Tilzer) Metropolis Theater 14 November

GILLE, Philippe [Emmanuel François] (b Paris, 10 December 1831; d Paris, 19 March 1901).

Playwright, art critic, author, journalist and librettist, Philippe Gille worked as an ''expéditionnaire'' at the

Préfecture de la Seine in his twenties, but found more congenial and theatrical employ in 1861 when he became secretary to the Théâtre Lyrique and a regular contributor to Paris newspapers. This latter career culminated in his taking charge of the famous *Figaro* courrier de theatre, or theatre gossip, rubrique from 1869, under the nom de plume of ''Masque de fer.''

From his mid-twenties, when he made his entry into the musical theatre with the text for Bizet's *La Prêtresse,* Gille also became a regular supplier of texts for Offenbach's Théâtre des Bouffes-Parisiens, several of his pieces being set by the manager himself, and a number of others by Léo Delibes. If the full-length works on which he worked with Offenbach (*Les Bergers, Docteur Ox*) were not amongst the composer's happiest pieces, he had better fortune in his collaboration with Delibes, co-authoring the whimsical fairytale text for his *La Cour du Roi Pétaud,* and in his one produced work with Lecocq, the adaptation of Victorien Sardou's *Les Prés Saint-Gervais* as a light opera. A second Lecocq piece (1879, w d'Ennery), *La Femme aux deux coeurs,* failed to make it to the stage. However, even his most enduring texts for the light musical stage, the French adaptation of H B Farnie's London musical *Rip van Winkle* and the little one-act piece *Les Charbonniers,* were outshone by his accomplishments in the sphere of grand opera—the libretti for Massenet's *Manon* (w Henri Meilhac) and for Delibes' *Lakmé* and *Jean de Nivelle* (w Edmond Gondinet).

Gille also wrote a number of non-musical theatre pieces, collaborating with Eugène Labiche on *Les 30 Millions de Gladiateur* and *Garanti dix ans,* and penned many volumes of poetry, literary criticism and humorous writing.

His *Cent mille francs et ma fille* (w Jaime fils, Théâtre Déjazet 11 April 1868), adapted by Dorn and with music composed by Ludwig Gothov-Grüneke replacing the original accompaniment provided by Costé, was played at Vienna's Theater in der Josefstadt as *100,000 Gulden und meine Tochter* (18 January 1879).

Gille also authored a biography of Offenbach under the pen name ''Argus.''

1857 **Vent du Soir, ou l'horrible festin** (Jacques Offenbach) 1 act Théâtre des Bouffes-Parisiens 16 May

1860 **Monsieur de Bonne-Étoile** (Léo Delibes[/w Adolphe Jaime]) 1 act Théâtre des Bouffes-Parisiens 4 February

1860 **Les Valets de Gascogne** (Alfred Dufresne) 1 act Théâtre Lyrique 2 June

1860 **Maître Palma** (Mlle Rivay/w Eugène Furpille) 1 act Théâtre Lyrique 17 June

1860 **L'Hôtel de la [Rue de la] Poste** (Dufresne) 1 act Théâtre des Bouffes-Parisiens 15 November

1861 **Les Deux Cadis** (Théodore Imbert/w Furpille) 1 act Théâtre Lyrique 8 March

1861 **La Fille d'Egypte** (J Beer/w Jules Barbier) Théâtre Lyrqiue 28 April

1864 **Le Serpent à plumes** (Delibes/w Cham) 1 act Théâtre des Bouffes-Parisiens 16 December

1865 **Le Boeuf Apis** (Delibes/w Furpille) Théâtre des Bouffes-Parisiens 15 April

1865 **Les Bergers** (Offenbach/w Hector Crémieux) Théâtre des Bouffes-Parisiens 11 December

1866 **Tabarin duelliste** (Léon Pillaud/w Furpille) 1 act Théâtre des Bouffes-Parisiens 13 April

1866 **Le Sacripant** (Jules Duprato) Fantaisies-Parisiennes 24 September

1868 **Les Horreurs de la Guerre** (Jules Costé) Cercle des Mirlitons/Théâtre de l'Athenée 9 December

1869 **L'Écossais de Chatou** (Delibes/w Jaime) Théâtre des Bouffes-Parisiens 16 January

1869 **La Cour du Roi Pétaud** (Delibes/w Jaime) Théâtre des Variétés 24 April

1871 **La Tour du chien vert** (Duprato) Théâtre des Folies-Dramatiques 21 December

1874 **Cent Mille Francs et Ma Fille** (Costé/w Jaime) Théâtre des Menus-Plaisirs 27 April

1874 **Les Prés Saint-Gervais** (Charles Lecocq/w Victorien Sardou) Théâtre des Variétés 14 November

1876 **Pierrette et Jacquot** (Offenbach/w Jules Noriac) Théâtre des Bouffes-Parisiens 13 October

1877 **Le Docteur Ox** (Offenbach/w Arnold Mortier) Théâtre des Variétés 26 January

1877 **Les Charbonniers** (Costé) 1 act Théâtre des Variétés 4 April

1884 **Rip!** (*Rip van Winkle*) French version w Meilhac (Théâtre des Folies-Dramatiques)

GILLETTE DE NARBONNE Opéra-comique in 3 acts by Henri Chivot and Alfred Duru founded on *La Femme courageuse* by Boccaccio and on Shakespeare's *All's Well That Ends Well.* Music by Edmond Audran. Théâtre des Bouffes-Parisiens, Paris, 11 November 1882.

Produced by Bouffes-Parisiens director Louis Cantin on the heels of the huge success of Audran's *La Mascotte, Gillette de Narbonne* gave him and his theatre yet another substantial success. The libretto, set in those medieval times which had encouraged Hervé's opéra-bouffe extravagances, was comic rather than burlesque, with its story of pretty Gillette (Mlle Montbazon) who takes advantage of a favor from the King (Riga) to be granted her childhood sweetheart's hand in marriage. His masculine vanity piqued at this ''ladies' choice,'' her Roger (Louis Morlet) goes off to war and there asserts his bruised manhood in the dark with Rosita (Marie Gélabert), the young wife of his foolish companion, Griffardin (Édouard Maugé). When he gets home from the wars and finds Gillette has given birth he is piqued all over again, but then she produces the ring that he gave his paramour in the dark and the thwarted Roger at least knows that, although he may have been fooled, at least he is the father of his own son.

Audran's score gave its leading players plenty of opportunities, with Gillette being equipped with a waltzing Chanson provençale, a little 3/8 "Quand on atteint un certain âge" and a reminiscing duo with Roger ("Rappelez-vous nos promenades") in the first act, the "Chanson du Sergeant Briquet" in her wartime disguise as her own brother, and the duo wooing the ring from Roger ("A votre doigt que vois-je donc") in the second, and a charming ariette ("On m'avait dans un cage") and her final scenes of triumph in the third. Roger had no less than four numbers, and Rosita supplied the soubrette moments with her first-act ronde ("Claudine dans notre village"), the Couplets du Turlututu and a little lullaby (Couplets du Dodo). The light, high tenor music fell to the role of Gillette's unfavored suitor, Prince Olivier (Charles Lamy).

Without quite attaining the huge vogue of *La Mascotte, Gillette* ran into the new year and right up to the summer recess, eight solid months of performances, giving Cantin another splendid success to add to those of *Les Mousquetaires au couvent* and *La Mascotte,* both premiered in the two previous years. The show was not taken up again at the Bouffes, which was well supplied with new pieces and old hits, but it was liberally played in the provinces and it got a fresh Paris showing at the Folies-Dramatiques in 1890, with Zélo Duran starred, and another as late as 1935, with Fanély Revoil and André Baugé in the principal roles.

In the meanwhile it had also been produced in most of the major European centers including Geneva, Brussels and Zagreb as well as the more regular ones: Budapest (ad Imre Ukki, Lajos Evva as *A gyürü,* ie, "the ring"); London, where Kate Santley, her production and the show (ad H Savile Clarke) were condemned as morally quite beyond the pale but still failed to run more than a few weeks; Vienna for 25 nights at the Theater an der Wien with Adolfine Ziemaier (Gillette), Rosa Streitmann (Rosita), Josef Joseffy (Robert) and Karl Blasel (Griffardin), in a season dominated by the production of Strauss's *Der Zigeunerbaron*; and Berlin. It was also seen in Clarke's adaptation in San Francisco, with Hattie Moore and Harry Gates starred, and a hacked-about version called *La Belle Coquette* was played for some time in the touring repertoire of the young Fay Templeton's company, but in New York it was performed only in German with Madame Ziemaier again taking the title role alongside Selma Kronold (Rosita), Kemlitz (Roger) and Rank (Griffardin).

Hungary: Népszínház *A gyürü* 10 March 1883; UK: Royalty Theatre *Gilette* 19 November 1883; Germany: Walhalla Theater 24 October 1884; Austria: Theater an der Wien 27 March 1885; USA: Standard Theater, Chicago *La Belle Coquette* 3 January 1884, Tivoli Theater, San Francisco *Gillette* 7 July 1884, Terrace Garden, New York (Ger) 23 May 1887

Recording: complete (Gaîté-Lyrique)

GILMAN, Mabelle (b San Francisco, 16 June 1881). Broadway leading lady of the turn of the century.

Whilst still at high school in San Francisco, Mabelle Gilman made her first venture into the professional theatre, as the in-the-wings singing voice of the actress Edith Crane who was playing the part of Trilby in the hit show of the moment. She soon moved east, appeared in the chorus at Daly's Theatre, New York, and at 16 played a small role in the Broadway production of *The Geisha* (1896, O Kinkoto San). Mixing classic plays and musical theatre, as a member of Daly's house company, she understudied Dorothy Morton and Violet Lloyd in the two star parts of *The Geisha* (1897), then succeeded to the soubrette roles of his productions of *The Circus Girl* (1897, Lucille) and *The Geisha* (1898, Molly) and played the equivalent role in *A Runaway Girl* (1898, Alice). She appeared at the Casino Theater in 1899 as the other woman in *In Gay Paree* (Louisette Gireaud) and in the famous *Les Fêtards* role of the demure wife in Ludwig Englander's *The Rounders* (1899, Priscilla), and then created the title role in *The Casino Girl* (1900, Laura Lee) which was exported to London following its New York run in the least unsuccessful of the transatlantic attempts to repeat the success of *The Belle of New York.*

Back home, she played in the variety musicals *The King's Carnival* (1901) and *The Hall of Fame* (1902), and starred as the heroine of A Baldwin Sloane's pretty *The Mocking Bird* (1902, Yvette Millet) before taking over Lulu Glaser's role in *Dolly Varden* (1903, Dolly) for the London season of that piece. She remained in London to take the title role in the 28 performances of Serpette's last musical *Amorelle* (1904, Amorelle) and then, in 1907, retired to a married life as Mrs William Ellis Corey, wife of the President of the Steel Trust (for a while), and to a chateau in France (for rather longer).

GIRARDI, Alexander (b Graz, 5 December 1850; d Vienna, 20 April 1918).

The single greatest star of the heyday of the Viennese Operette stage, Girardi and his light comic, light-tenor performances provided the much-loved heart to a generation of Operetten, from the earlier days of Johann Strauss and Carl Millöcker to well into the 20th century.

After teenage years spent working in his father's metalwork and locksmith business, the young Girardi made his first appearance on the professional stage in 1869 at the Kurtheater in Rohitsch-Sauerbrunn. Engagements at Krems, Karlsbad, Ischl and Salzburg followed. The last of these proved the most fortunate for the young actor, for his performance there was seen by the playwright O F Berg, who was instrumental in his being engaged, at the age of 20, as a general juvenile at the Vienna Strampfertheater. There, he played often small supporting roles alongside the theatre's stars Pepi Gallmeyer and Felix Schweighofer, appearing in a series of Possen and Schwänke and finally getting himself noticed in the role of a comical butler in the Posse *Nur zwei Gläschen.*

When Schweighofer moved on to the Theater an der Wien, Girardi got given a few of the more substantial comedy roles that would have been the older actor's but then, in 1874, Girardi too made the move to the Theater an der Wien. He made his debut there in June of the year, appearing in three of the eight scenes of O F Berg and Carl Millöcker's revusical *Errinerung an bessere Zeiten* as, in turn, Hungerl, Hilarion and the shoemaker Morgenstern. He subsequently appeared in Berg's *Der barmherziger Bruder* and as the baritonic Falke in *Die Fledermaus,* then still a newish item in the theatre's repertoire, and he did well enough to be given his first major creation the following February, appearing alongside Geistinger, Friese, Szíka and Karoline Finaly, as the comical servant Blasoni in Johann Strauss's *Cagliostro in Wien.*

He appeared during 1875–76 as Menelaos in *Die schöne Helena,* Jockel in Léon Vasseur's *Die Perle der Wäscherinnen* (*La Blanchisseuse de Berg-op-Zoom*), First Notary in *La Créole,* Mister Bob Cadwallader in Zeller's *Joconde,* Mikroskop in Offenbach's *Der Reise in den Mond* (*Le Voyage dans la lune*) and Pirkholzer in the Posse *Luftschlösser,* created the second comedy role of Don Domingos in *Der Seekadett* (the principal comedy role was the province of Schweighofer) and played Truck in *König Carotte,* with Schweighofer in the title role.

In 1877 he appeared in Max Wolf's *Der Porträt-Dame* (Hofmarschall Graf von Loos), created the juvenile light-comedy role of Hector de Marsillac in Genée's *Nanon,* played Grévin in *Der galante Vicomte* and Nicolas in Offenbach's *Der Jahrmarkt von Saint-Laurent,* and was given notable billing for the first time when he played Ali Baba in *Königin Indigo,* the revamped version of Strauss's first Operette which was played for just 15 performances. This line of secondary and young comic roles continued into 1878, but that year brought him rather more considerable chance, for he was cast first as the sweetly gormless peasant boy Andredl, opposite no less a star than Gallmeyer, in Millöcker's *Das verwunschene Schloss,* and then in the staunchly tenorial part of the cowardly Jean Grénicheux in the Viennese premiere of *Die Glocken von Corneville.* His status in the company was still such, however, that it was Gallmeyer, soprano Bertha Olma and comic Carl Adolf Friese who got the billing in the Millöcker piece and, even though Schweighofer was cast in the main character role of the miser, Hermine Meyerhoff and Sofie König, as the two heroines—who were put above the title in Planquette's blockbuster, Strauss's *Blindekuh* (Johann) and Genée's *Der letzte Mohikaner* (Hans Graupe)—did not give him

Plate 145. **Alexander Girardi.** *The biggest star the Viennese musical theatre ever knew as the apparently devout Celestin in Mam'zelle Nitouche.*

similar chances. 1879–80, however, saw him cast opposite Marie Geistinger as Charles Favart in Offenbach's *Madame Favart,* a substantial baritone singing role with plenty of comedy but, nevertheless, more than a touch of the romantic about it; as the hairdresser Leonard in Millöcker's *Gräfin Dubarry*; as Brududur in the Viennese version of Lecocq's La Jolie Persane; Stefan Hoch in *Die Näherin*; the little tailor, Griolet in *Die Tochter des Tambour-Majors*; Benjamin in Adam's *Die Nürnberger Puppe*; Don Sancho d'Avellaneda in Strauss's *Das Spitzentuch der Königin*; and Marcu, yet another young peasant, in *Apajune der Wassermann.*

It was 1881, however, which was the year that would finally make Girardi into a star. It was not the splendid roles with which he opened the year which wrought this subtle transformation—Pippo to the Bettina of Karoline Finaly in *Der Glücksengel* (*La Mascotte*) with its and their celebrated Gobbling Duet, the overwhelming lead role of the swingeingly baritonic musketeer Brissac in

Les Mousquetaires au couvent or Godibert in Millöcker's *Die Jungfrau von Belleville*—but the last production of the year, Johann Strauss's *Der lustige Krieg.* Cast in the supporting comedy role of the Marchese Sebastiani—Schweighofer again had the best of the fun—Girardi, who had now become used to something rather better, was irked to find that Strauss had not even given him a solo number. He stamped his foot (something he was quite good at), threatened to walk out, and he got his number. Sebastiani was still not the best role he had had, but the tacked-in waltz song "Nur für Natur," in spite of being only loosely linked to the plot, caused a sensation. And on the crest of that sensation, Alexander Girardi became a star.

He was, however, a member of the Theater an der Wien company and not every show—particularly the many imported ones—threw up a role and a song which would put the new star in evidence, so Girardi was obliged to mix the great roles which he now held in the repertoire with some less grateful ones. Thus, while *Der lustige Krieg, Apajune* and *Les Cloches de Corneville* continued in repertoire, he played a mixture of fine and less fine new parts in Lecocq's *Tag und Nacht* (Don Brasiero), Millöcker's *Ein süsses Kind* (Medard), Offenbach's *Doktor Ox* (Ygèn), *Lili* (Antonin Plinchard) and Müller's *Der kleine Prinz* (Antonio Hasenlauf) before the end of the year brought him a fresh triumph. The newest piece was Millöcker's *Der Bettelstudent,* and Girardi starred in the title role as Symon, the poor student sent by a rejected suitor to woo proud Laura. He launched into waltz-time again in "Ich knüpfte manche zarte Bande" and "Ich hab' kein Geld," two splendid, thoroughly tenor pieces, apparently more in the romantic and patriotic vein than the comical, and he and his songs caught the public fancy with the same enormous success that the Operette did.

In a year full of *Bettelstudent* performances, Girardi was also seen briefly in Lacome's *Der schöne Nikolaus* (Criquet) and with more success as the explorer Miradello in Suppé's merry *Die Afrikareise* and as Caramello in the "improved" Viennese production of *Eine Nacht in Venedig* ("Lagunen-Walzer"). The year 1884 saw him introduce *Gasparone* (Benozzo), *Donna Juanita* (Diego Manrique), Louis Roth's *Der Marquis von Rivoli* (Breton), *Der Feldprediger* (Piffkow) and *Pfingsten in Florenz* (Fra Bombardo), 1885 brought *Zwillinge* (Adonis Duprat), new productions of *Der lustige Krieg* and *Nanon* and, finally, Strauss's *Der Zigeunerbaron,* which brought with it another first-rate role for Girardi, no longer playing a hero but cast as the low-comic pig-farmer Kálmán Zsupán ("Ja, das Schreiben und das Lesen").

The series of new shows and new roles continued, although now Girardi was in a position where he no longer had to appear in virtually every piece of the repertoire, and he was able to render up some of those parts of which he was less fond to other performers. In 1886, whilst *Der Zigeunerbaron* played out its first run, he created the role of the Rigolettoish jester Carillon in *Der Hofnarr,* in 1887 he took the title roles in Brandl's *Der liebe Augustin* and Strauss's *Simplicius* and that of the comical Spätzle in Millöcker's *Die sieben Schwaben,* but the next couple of years produced little in the way of new roles. *Der Schlösserkönig* (Charles), Dellinger's *Kapitän Fracassa* (Fracassa) and Hellmesberger's *Das Orakel* (Dioskuros) rang no bells. In 1890, however, the wind changed. Millöcker's *Der arme Jonathan* supplied Girardi with one of his best recent roles as the poor servant become suddenly and uncomfortably rich, and the Vienna production of *Mam'zelle Nitouche* gave him another splendid comic role as the naughty music master, Célestin.

The year 1891 brought a further triumph with the production of Zeller's *Der Vogelhändler.* In the title role of Adam, the country bird-seller, Girardi was given the most winning set of songs he had yet had: the lilting entrance song with its "flix, flux, flax Florian!" refrain, the wonderful waltz "Schenkt man sich Rosen in Tirol" and its partner "Wie mein Ahnl zwanzig Jahr," and the sad little song of homesickness "Kom' ih iazt wieder ham," which all went to make up a role full of panache, comedy and sympathy. Whilst *Der Vogelhändler* formed the backbone of the theatre's season, Girardi also appeared in the burlesque *Krawalleria musicana* (Duriduri Salamucci), Brandl's remusicked *Die Kosakin* (Casimir) and in a distinctly minor role as Puycardas, the bullfighter, in *Miss Helyett.* In 1892–93 he introduced *Das Sonntagskind* (Tristan Florival), *Fanchon's Leyer* (Zephirin), *Der Millionen-Onkel* (Mihail Cakov), *Der Bajazzo* (Quadrillo), *Fürstin Ninetta* (Kassim Pacha) and *Der Schwiegerpapa* (Baptiste Maillot) without finding any new role to equal his best.

At the end of the year he played a revival of *Das verwunschene Schloss* with Therese Biedermann as partner, and things looked up when Zeller's *Der Obersteiger* was produced, giving him the best role and the best song ("Sei nicht bös") that he had had since *Der Vogelhändler,* as the rather anti-heroic mine-foreman Martin. *Husarenblut* (Streicher-Pepi), Strauss's *Jabuka* (Joschko), Millöcker's *Der Probekuss* (Hans Pfeifli), Dellinger's *Die Chansonette* (Antonio Mazzuchetti), Strauss's *Waldmeister* (Erasmus Müller), Müller's *General Gogo* (Dagobert Fragonard), Josef Bayer's *Mister Menelaus* (Septimus Wisbottle) and *Der Wunderknabe* (Kajetan Tween), which followed, did not, however, give him anything more than ephemeral roles.

Now, after more than 20 years at the Theater an der Wien, Girardi decided to move on. He went first to the other principal Vienna Operette house, the Carltheater, where he played during 1896 in a musical version of Meilhac and Halévy's *La Cigale* called *Bum-Bum* (Brandemayer), and then to the Deutsches Volkstheater where he put aside musical theatre to appear in Shakespeare, Raimund (notably his famous portrayal of Valentin in *Der Verschwender*), Molière and as Leopold in the play *Im weissen Rössl.* In 1899 he returned to the musical stage. He guested at the Hofoper as Frosch in *Die Fledermaus,* starred with Marie Halton in the new Operette *Adam und Eva* at the Carltheater and appeared in shows at the Raimundtheater and the Theater in der Josefstadt before, in 1902, he returned to the scene of his great triumphs and signed up once again with the Theater an der Wien, beginning his new contract by reappearing in one of his most famous old roles, Zsupán in *Der Zigeunerbaron,* and as Frosch.

His first new roles were that of little corporal Ratz in *Der Fremdenführer*; Willibald Brandl in *Wiener Frauen,* the maiden work of the young Franz Lehár; and Josef Flins in *Der Lebemann,* but February of 1903 brought him another item to add to his list of great creations when he took on the title role of the first work of another young composer, Edmund Eysler, in *Bruder Straubinger* and scored another huge song hit with the part of the old-young soldier and the waltz ''Küssen ist keine Sund.'' The short or medium runs of *Die beiden Don Juans* (*Mam'zelle Quat' Sous,* Michel Borniche), *Der Herr Professor* (as Dr Roderich Benarius, who opium-dreams himself to adventures in the ruins of Pompeii), *Der neue Bürgermeister* (Jan Pieters), *Der Generalkonsul* (Peter Dingl), *Das Garnisonsmädel* (Hektor Trumpus) and Lehár's *Die Juxheirat* (Philly Kapps) were capped by a second Eysler/Girardi success with the title role of *Pufferl* (1905, Kirschenlied)—a success which meant that Girardi went out from the Theater an der Wien on a high note. For the star had struck up a personal animosity against the theatre's director, ex-actor Karl Wallner, who had refused to let Girardi run the show the way he wanted, and he had determined that he would go elsewhere.

As he had the first time, he added as much pepper to his departure as possible by choosing the rival Carltheater as his new home. But Girardi ensured that the man who had done so much to make his last two big hits was also part of the exodus from the Theater an der Wien, and Edmund Eysler was on hand to compose the score for the star's opening attraction at the Carltheater. *Die Schützenliesel* (1905, Blasius, Mutterl-Lied) proved as big a hit as its two predecessors, and a fourth Eysler piece, *Künstlerblut* (1906, Franz Torelli), which followed it scored again, with Girardi playing a role which for the first time—at fifty-six years of age—made him (to his wife's loudly expressed indignation) an aging if not quite elderly man. In between these two Carltheater hits, Girardi took a quick trip to the Theater in der Josefstadt to star with Hansi Niese in a lucrative Posse, *Der Schusterbub.*

Raoul Mader's *Der selige Vincenz* (1907, Baron Vincenz von Rosenheim zu Schleifstein) was less successful, and Girardi once again moved on, this time to Berlin and the Thalia-Theater where he appeared for Jean Kren and Alfred Schönfeld in the hit Posse *Immer oben auf!* He scored a great hit with the Ackerlied from Suppé's *Dichter und Bauer* and with the famous Fiakerlied, and he remained in Berlin to perform two of his most celebrated play roles: *Der Verschwender* and Schuster Weigl in *Mein Leopold.*

Now 40 years into his career in the theatre, Girardi was still at the top of the tree, and he was billed large when he returned to the management of Karczag and Wallner at the Raimundtheater between 1909–11 playing a repertoire which mixed his best plays with his equally famous portrayals of Zsupán, Bruder Straubinger, Franz Torelli and Célestin. The once-despised Wallner directed him in some of the four new musicals he would create at the Raimundtheater: the Strauss-remake *Reiche Mädchen* (1909, Michael Karinger), *Das Glücksmädel* (1910, Andreas Lindhuber), Oscar Straus's *Mein junger Herr* (1910, Florian) and Eysler's *Das Zirkuskind* (1911, Friedl Möller). Each did well enough, but none proved memorable.

However, one final great musical starring vehicle still awaited Girardi. In October 1912, after having run through more than two hundred performances as the star of Paul Ottenheimer's *Heimliche Liebe* (1911, Der Profoss) at the Johann Strauss-Theater, he appeared at the same house as the old violinist, Pali Rácz, in Kálmán's latest Operette, *Der Zigeunerprimás,* singing ''Mein alte Stradivari'' and scoring a memorable success. He appeared thereafter in *Der arme Millionär* (1913, Fridolin Stoss), *Der Nachtschnellzug* (1913, Rittmeister von Winkler) and *Das dumme Herz* (1914, Florian Strobl), and played Frosch *in Die Fledermaus,* Straubinger, Josef Drechsler in *Brüderlein fein* and *Mein Leopold* all at the same house. He subsequently created *Mein Annerl* (1916–17, Dominik Domaier) and repeated his Zsupán at the Raimundtheater, and he was still performing right up to his last days, appearing at the Burgtheater two months before his death.

Girardi died in 1918, having achieved the most outstanding career of any artist in the history of the Viennese musical theatre. Today there is a street named after him in his home town of Graz, and the Girardigasse in Vienna runs near the Theater an der Wien where so much of his fame was garnered.

Unlike his female counterparts, Girardi did not get a bio-Operette named after him, but he did appear on the screen—in person in some silent Operette films, and as a character in Willy Forst's *Operette* where he was impersonated by Paul Hörbiger.

Biographies: Nowak, K F: *Girardi* (Concordia, Berlin, 1908), Girardi, A M: *Das Shicksal setzt den Hobel an* (Viehweg Verlag, Braunschweig, 1942), Wutzky, Anna Charlotte: *Girardi* (Wilhelm Frick Verlag, Vienna, 1943), etc

THE GIRL BEHIND THE COUNTER Farcical musical play in 2 acts by Leedham Bantock and Arthur Anderson. Lyrics by Arthur Anderson. Additional lyrics by Percy Greenbank. Music by Howard Talbot. Additional music by Augustus Barratt and J St A Johnson. Wyndham's Theatre, London, 21 April 1906.

Using the regular motifs of the musical of the period—a shopgirl heroine who is actually a rich lady, a barrel-chested baritone hero and a plot hinging on a theft and including a lot of amorous combinations—producer Frank Curzon's team concocted with skill and taste a ''dainty and diverting'' model of the genre. With Hayden Coffin singing ''In the Land Where the Best Man Wins,'' and Isabel Jay declaring ''I Mean to Marry a Man'' with a capital M, it only remained for these two favorite singing stars to get through two acts to be paired off. The second act was set at a costume ball and gave comedians George Grossmith (dude), Horace Mills (little) and J P McArdle (heavy and low), soubrette Coralie Blythe and comedienne Marie Dainton, as a French girl, the chance to do speciality numbers.

After fine notices, *The Girl Behind the Counter* inexplicably failed to go beyond 141 performances in London, but a Broadway version—which accentuated the low-comedy element by writing up roles for Lew Fields and the Gaiety's Connie Ediss as Mr and Mrs Henry Schniff, rearranged the plot to give the heroine a red-blooded American instead of an English Lord as her second-act reward, and interpolated songs including Paul Lincke's Glühwürmchen Idyll from *Lysistrata*—did much better (232 performances and a 1916 revival as *Step This Way,* Shubert Theater 29 May).

Rupert Clarke and Clyde Meynell took *The Girl Behind the Counter* to Australia, where Ruth Lincoln and Harold Thorley headed the romance and Edwin Brett, Essie Perrin and Tom Payne the fun for seasons in Melbourne and Sydney (Criterion Theatre 27 December 1909).

USA: Herald Square Theater 1 October 1907; Australia: Theatre Royal, Melbourne 17 April 1909

GIRL CRAZY Musical comedy in 2 acts by Guy Bolton and Jack McGowan. Lyrics by Ira Gershwin. Music by George Gershwin. Alvin Theater, New York, 14 October 1930.

The sixth of the series of Gershwin musicals produced by Alexander A Aarons and Vinton Freedley, *Girl Crazy* followed behind the unfortunate *Treasure Girl* and, statistically speaking, succeeded better on Broadway than any of their previous collaborations excepting *Lady, Be Good!,* notching up an initial metropolitan run of 272 performances.

Its tale told of a gallivanting young New Yorker called Danny Churchill (Allen Kearns), exiled from the bright lights, bosoms and booze of the big city by his worried, wealthy father. Undeterred, Danny turns Custerville, Arizona, into an outback replica of wine, women and song-land and finally finds true love with postmistress Molly Gray (Ginger Rogers). The show's comedy star, Willie Howard (a late replacement for Bert Lahr, originally slated) was cast as Jewish taxi driver Gieber Goldfarb, who drives the hero to his exile and remains in Custerville with him to become town sheriff; William Kent was the town saloon keeper, Slick Fothergill; and Ethel Merman, in the role of his daughter, was the principal representative of the wine, women and song.

This jolly, traditional musical comedy story was illustrated by a lively score which yielded some memorable moments. The teenaged Miss Rogers had the more winsome musical numbers with the puzzled and unself-pitying ''But Not for Me'' and the gliding melody of ''Embraceable You'' (plucked by Gershwin from the score of an aborted musical for Ziegfeld), as well as the comical ''(When it's) Cactus Time in Arizona,'' and Miss Merman had the lusty ones with an ''I Got Rhythm'' which lived up to its title, the tale of ''Sam and Delilah'' and a rather different kind of lament in ''Boy! What Love Has Done to Me!'' One of the highlights of the score, however was a rarer masculine moment: a male-voice quartet harmonizing their way winningly through the loping ''Bidin' my Time.''

Girl Crazy has won itself a special place in the historical hearts of a generation of Broadway students, partly because of its fine musical score, but largely because it gave the dazzlingly truncheon-voiced Ethel Merman her first Broadway opportunity. Without Miss Merman, and in spite of ''I Got Rhythm'' and ''Embraceable You,'' however, the show did not travel beyond America, although elements of it went into the makings of three different film musicals. RKO produced a movie under the same title in 1932 which retained the plot line but only three of the show's songs, and MGM followed up in 1943 with a Mickey Rooney/Judy Garland vehicle which was, not unsurprisingly, unable to follow the plot but which used, instead, seven of the musical's songs plus ''Fascinating Rhythm'' from *Lady, Be Good!* A 1965 MGM film, produced as *Where the Boys Meet the Girls,* used neither the story nor much of the score (four numbers, supplemented by a half-dozen interpolations, one written by cast member Liberace).

A remake of *Girl Crazy,* done much on the same lines as the *Funny Face / My One and Only* remake of some years earlier, under the title *Crazy for You* (ad Ken Ludwig) was produced in America in 1992 (Shubert Theater 19 February) with Harry Groener and Jodi Benson featured. A Broadway starved of light entertainment welcomed it ravenously and it quickly galloped past *Girl Crazy*'s original total, picking up a Tony Award as best musical of the utterly arid 1991–92 season before going on to give some sweetly nostalgic—if amazingly conventional—enjoyment to theatregoers further afield. Broadway's edition of *Crazy for You* ran up 1,622 performances, London's more than two years, but Australia proved immune to frilly pink frocks and old-time dancing and (yet again) to even a reconstituted Gershwin show. Budapest saw the new-old show under the title *Bolondulok érted* at the Fővárosi Operettszínház in 1995 (11 August), the rest of Europe was given an English-language touring production, and nobody probably realized how much more they would have enjoyed an untampered-with, honest-to-goodness revival of *Girl Crazy.*

Germany: Pfalztheater, Kaiserslautern 19 February 1977

Films: RKO 1932, MGM 1943, MGM 1965 *Where the Boys Meet the Girls*

Recordings: complete (Electra), selection (Columbia), *Crazy For You* original cast (EMI-Angel), *Crazy for You* London cast (First Night)

THE GIRL FRIEND Musical comedy in 2 acts by Herbert Fields. Lyrics by Lorenz Hart. Music by Richard Rodgers. Vanderbilt Theater, New York, 17 March 1926.

The Girl Friend, Rodgers and Hart's follow-up to their successful debut with the period piece *Dearest Enemy,* was a show much more in the contemporary idiom. Herbert Fields's book centered around the efforts of little Leonard Silver (Sammy White) to win a bicycle race and his sweetheart Mollie (Eva Puck) in the face both of crooked gamblers, who try to nobble him, and of the hoity charms of Wynn Spencer (Evelyn Cavanaugh), whilst the show's score was in the light, bright and dance-based mood of the 1920s. White and Miss Puck danced the charleston and sang the show's two most successful pieces, the lively dance number "The Girl Friend" and the sweetly balladic "The Blue Room." Although Lew Fields's production of *The Girl Friend* started slowly, business gradually improved, and in the end, the show remained on the Broadway boards for a highly respectable 301 performances prior to going on the road.

The Girl Friend went on to appear in London, in 1927, by which time the West End had already appreciatively tasted Rodgers and Hart's work in the made-for-London *Lido Lady,* the revue *One Dam Thing After Another* and the rather less-than-successful *Peggy-Ann.* However, the piece as seen in London differed very largely from that played on Broadway, and it could almost have been said to be sailing under false colors. Producers Jack Waller and Herbert Clayton purchased two 1926 Broadway musicals, *The Girl Friend* and *Kitty's Kisses* (Con Conrad/Gus Kahn/Otto Harbach, Philip Bartholomae), and they made one out of the two. They jettisoned Fields's bicycling libretto and replaced it with the decidedly better farcical high jinks in a hotel suite which were the basis of *Kitty's Kisses,* done over by Bert Lee and Bob Weston. They added the plum songs ("The Girl Friend," "The Blue Room") and title of *The Girl Friend* along with "Mountain Greenery" and "What's the Use of Talking?" from Rodgers and Hart's *Garrick Gaieties,* one number by local Vivian Ellis ("We Must Discover the Girl"), and a chunk of Tchaikovsky for the leading lady to dance to, to the remaining ensembles and solos of the *Kitty's Kisses* score, and produced the result at the Palace Theatre with Roy Royston (Robert), Louise Browne (Kitty), Clifford Mollison (Dennison), George Gee (Jerry) and Emma Haig (Jennie) featured to a delighted reception and a run of precisely a year (401 performances). The "new" *Girl Friend* (which was altogether more *Kitty's Kisses* than *Girl Friend*) subsequently had a fine provincial career in Britain and was produced in both Australia, with Annie Croft and her husband Reginald Sharland starred as Kitty and Robert, and in Budapest, hot on the heels of London's season.

A version of the London *The Girl Friend,* retaining the basic *Kitty's Kisses* libretto and with a score similarly made up from *Girl Friend, Kitty's Kisses* and other material, was produced at Colchester, England in 1987 as "Rodgers and Hart's *The Girl Friend.*" Which, of course, it was very far from being.

UK: Palace Theatre 8 September 1927; Australia: Her Majesty's Theatre, Sydney 30 December 1927; Hungary: Király Színház *Puszipajtás* 21 September 1928

Recordings: Colchester cast recording (UK version) (TER), selection (US version) (Fontana)

THE GIRL FROM KAYS Musical play in 3 acts by Owen Hall [based on *La Mariée recalcitrante* by Léon Gandillot]. Lyrics by Adrian Ross and Claude Aveling. Music by Ivan Caryll and Cecil Cook. Additional numbers by Lionel Monckton, Howard Talbot, Paul Rubens, Bernard Rolt, Edward Jones, Meyer Lutz, Kitty Ashmead, Charles H Taylor and A D Cammeyer. Apollo Theatre, London, 15 November 1902.

The Girl from Kays began its life amongst some publicity, thanks to a curious lawsuit from the Regent Street firm of Jay's Ltd who objected to the piece's pre-production title, *The Girl from Jay's,* and injuncted George Edwardes to prevent him sullying their good name with a musical comedy. There was further bother when the names allotted to the chorus girls—each named prettily after a bishopric—aroused a storm in churchy circles. Again the producer didn't fight, he simply changed the offending words slightly and no one was fooled—merely made to look foolish. Another, much later, lawsuit was a claim for royalties from the French author, Gandillot, whose play (Théâtre Déjazet 1 October 1897) had allegedly been used—without credit—as a basis for the script, and who had been palmed off with a £50 one-off payment when he had protested. There was a good bit more reason behind that one.

In spite of all this unaccustomed (for Britain) musical-comedy legal action, *The Girl from Kays* turned out to be a model Edwardian musical comedy. Its basic story concerned the woes of freshly wed Norah (Kate Cutler) who sees her brand new husband (W Louis Bradfield) getting a congratulatory kiss from the shopgirl Winnie (Ethel Irving), who has delivered her new hat, and floods away with her family for two acts of damp indignation and making up. Those two acts were decorated with the best of musical-theatre comedy, song and dance. The comedy was in the hands of Willie Edouin who created a memorable character as ''Piggy'' Hoggenheimer, an American millionaire with social pretensions (the character had been a rich Brazilian, and a bit part, in Gandillot's play). For once, however, the audience, used to mocking these exaggerated Yankee dollar characters, laughed with and not at the brash, eager, kindly ''Mr Hoggenheimer of Park Lane'' (''Rude? I'm not rude, I'm rich'') who became the show's favorite character and one of its greatest assets. The song and dance was shared amongst Miss Cutler, who delivered a delightful sobbing waltz ''Papa!'' as she watered her parent's shoulder after her wedding night betrayal; Letty Lind and America's Ella Snyder as a pair of shopgirls (the Howard Talbot coon song, ''Smiling Sambo''); Bradfield (''I Don't Care'' and a charming duo with his bride, ''Semi-Detached''); and Aubrey Fitzgerald in the dude role.

However, in spite of all its attractions, *The Girl from Kays* put up a warning sign in the Edwardes establishment. Economics were changing. Although it played happily for over a year at the Apollo and Comedy Theatres (432 performances), its lavish production led it to end its London life in the red, to the vast tune of £20,000. The piece recouped later when it proved a fine touring prospect, but production economics were now far from those of a few years earlier where a half-dozen weeks' run had served to recoup the prettiest of shows.

The Girl from Kays also scored a major success on Broadway where the popular comedian Sam Bernard took up Edouin's role for a run of more than two hundred performances at the Herald Square Theater. Having made the hit of his career as ''Piggy,'' Bernard returned regularly for further doses of Hoggenheimer, appearing on Broadway in 1906 in a revised version of *The Girl from Kays* called *The Rich Mr Hoggenheimer* (Savoy Theater, Atlantic City 17 September) and again in 1914 in a rather clumsy second remake under the title of *The Belle of Bond Street.* This version was subsequently played by its star in Britain where it had but a brief run. In 1927 Bernard starred in a fourth Hoggenheimer musical, *Piggy,* for 11 Broadway weeks, up until shortly before his death.

Australia had the treat of seeing rather a different kind of ''Piggy,'' when the endearing star comedian G P Huntley headed an exported production from Britain for a repertoire season in Australia under the Gaiety Theatre/J C Williamson banner. Delia Mason (Norah), Madge Crichton (Winnie) and Maurice Farkoa supported the comedian through three weeks of performances before the company switched to *Kitty Grey* and *Three Little Maids.*

USA: Herald Square Theater 2 November 1903; Australia: Princess Theatre, Melbourne 4 June 1904

THE GIRL FROM UTAH Musical play in 2 acts by James T Tanner. Dialogue by James T Tanner and Paul Rubens. Lyrics by Adrian Ross, Percy Greenbank and Paul Rubens. Music by Sidney Jones and Paul Rubens. Adelphi Theatre, London, 18 October 1913.

With the production of *The Girl from Utah,* George Edwardes replaced the Lionel Monckton/Gertie Millar combination which had served him so well at the Adelphi Theatre since his takeover of that house's fortunes. Instead, he mounted a piece of which the text had all the attributes of an old Gaiety musical, plus some music by his more substantial Daly's Theatre composer Sidney Jones, contrasted with the lightest of Paul Rubens, and introduced a new star in America's Ina Claire, who had made a great success in Miss Millar's *Quaker Girl* role on Broadway.

Mormons had recently become the fashionable villains of the British theatre, in succession to wicked Uncles, Marquises and Puritans, and Tanner's book had little Una Trance (Ina Claire) fleeing to Britain from her home in Utah to avoid a Mormon marriage with a gruesome fellow of her father's choice (only the villain was different, the plot remained as conventional as could be). Joseph Coyne, Phyllis Dare, Edmund Payne and Gracie Leigh were amongst the Adelphi Theatre friends who helped to rescue the breathless Una, after which everyone repaired to the Arts Ball for some costumes, half of the show's songs and a rather perfunctory ending.

Payne, as the little ham-and-beef-shop man, Trimmit, had a role full of disguises and comical action and a cheery number about ''The Bottom of Brixton Hill,'' whilst Gracie Leigh played Irish and Coyne gave another lazily suave variant of the light-comedy-hero performance his successes as Danilo and Tony Chute (*Quaker Girl*) had cast him in forever, but it was Miss Claire, in a role which was little more than the classic ingenue, who won the public's biggest cheers.

The Girl from Utah's fair-to-mediocre run of 195 performances in London showed that the fashion for its type of entertainment was waning very noticeably, but the show was nevertheless taken profitably on the road and also won itself a number of foreign performances. In New York, Julia Sanderson, Donald Brian and Joseph Cawthorn starred in an Americanized version with not only the inevitable Kern songs added to the London score (''Land of 'Let's Pretend,''' ''Alice in Wonderland,'' ''Same Sort of Girl''), but also such proven British pieces as ''Gilbert the Filbert'' (Finck/Wimperis) which had been introduced in London's 1914 *The Passing Show*. However, this time one of the pasted-in Jerome Kern songs (in a show in which pasting was the easiest thing in the world) was the wistful ''They Didn't Believe Me'' (ly: Herbert Reynolds) and ''the botchings of a decade of Kern/Frohman British musicals could be forgiven in one wonderful song.''

In spite of this choice morsel in the score, and in spite of the undoubted success of the show, *The Girl from Utah* was played only 120 times on Broadway. Times were changing there, too, and the interest of the moment was rather for anything Viennese than for what looked like just another old-fashioned British musical comedy. Nevertheless, the piece toured healthily (growing interpolations all the way), returning to Broadway the following year, and Frohman had announced plans to take the company to Paris's Théâtre du Vaudeville when the war intervened and all European plans were abandoned.

The show did however get a Budapest showing (ad Frigyes Karinthy, Árpád Tóth, István Zágon) in what was basically its unbotched version. ''Brixton'' even remained in the lyrics, but it was joined, in Zágon's version of the songwords, by ''Budapest.'' However the mood of the times was evident in the fact that Australia, like Budapest always a happy host to whatever was most interesting in the musical theatre at this time, did not bother with *The Girl from Utah*. It did, however, take ''They Didn't Believe Me'' and interpolated it into the highly popular Californian musical *So Long, Letty* instead. As for Britain, it popped the song into an even bigger hit—the classic musical comedy *Tonight's the Night*.

USA: Knickerbocker Theater 24 August 1914; Hungary: Király Színház *Az Utahi Leány* 18 September 1920

THE GIRL IN THE TAXI *see* DIE KEUSCHE SUSANNE

THE GIRL IN THE TRAIN *see* DIE GESCHIEDENE FRAU

THE GIRL ON THE FILM *see* FILMZAUBER

THE GIRLS OF GOTTENBERG Musical play in 2 acts by George Grossmith and L E Berman. Lyrics by Adrian Ross and Basil Hood. Music by Ivan Caryll and Lionel Monckton. Gaiety Theatre, London, 15 May 1907.

The book for *The Girls of Gottenberg* was said to have been based on a real-life and recent incident—a scandalous episode in which a German cobbler from Kopenick had masqueraded as a high-up official and got away with it for longer than was credible. In fact, for all that, when all was said and done, the show's libretto was a fairly conventional piece, with the usual kind of disguises and romances set, this time, in a pretty Prussian setting which allowed lots of uniforms to be paraded across the Gaiety stage.

Max Moddelkopf (Edmund Payne), barber and valet to Prince Otto of Saxe-Hildesheim (George Grossmith), commander of the Blue Hussars, takes the place of an envoy sent to order the rival Red Hussars to the town of Gottenberg and switches the man's orders so that it is his employer's regiment which gets the posting. There is, you see, a ladies' university in Gottenberg. Otto, however, ends up romancing Elsa (May de Sousa), the apparent daughter of the half-blind local innkeeper (Arthur Hatherton), who—guess what—turns out to be the very aristocrat he was supposed to wed anyway, out playing at peasants in the best operettic style. The principal female role, however, was reserved for the theatre's star, Gertie Millar, whose Mitzi paired with Payne's Max, as the little fellow kept up his pretence of importance and caused havoc in Gottenberg with his curious commands.

The songs were not the best bunch to have come from the Gaiety, but Lionel Monckton's ''Two Little Sausages,'' Grossmith's rendering (to his own lyrics and Monckton's tune) of ''Otto of Roses,'' Miss Millar's description of ''Berlin on the Spree'' and some Wagnerian parody in ''Rheingold'' all proved popular.

After the flop of *The New Aladdin, The Girls of Gottenberg* brought success back to the Gaiety Theatre through a fine run of 303 performances, and the show duly set off round the world. South Africa was one of the first to grab the latest Gaiety hit, and its mounting, along with J C Williamson's Australian production with George Lauri and Fanny Dango starred, and Maurice Bandmann's oriental touring edition were all under way by the time Edwardes sent out the first British provincial company with Miss Millar at its head.

New York followed the next year, when Charles Frohman mounted his version of the show at the Knickerbocker Theater with Miss Millar supported by a star team from London headed by James Blakeley (Max) and Lionel Mackinder (Otto). The show ran 103 performances. Several years later, whilst *Girls of Gottenberg* touring companies continued their way around Britain and the colonies, a French version (ad Maurice de Marsan, Gabriel Timmory) was played at the Paris Moulin-Rouge with Marise Fairy and Jane Marnac featured.

Australia: Her Majesty's Theatre, Melbourne 26 October 1907; USA: Knickerbocker Theater 2 September 1908; France: Théâtre du Moulin-Rouge *Les Jolies Filles de Gottenberg* 17 October 1912

GIROFLÉ-GIROFLA Opéra-bouffe in 3 acts by Albert Vanloo and Eugène Leterrier. Music by Charles Lecocq. Théâtre des Fantaisies-Parisiennes, Brussels, 21 March 1874.

The immense success of *La Fille de Madame Angot* established Charles Lecocq as the new hero of the French musical theatre and his next work was impatiently awaited. It came, like the earlier piece, from the Brussels theatre run by Eugène Humbert, and was written to a Vanloo/Leterrier libretto which was fairly firmly in the line of the comically absurd tradition of the opéra-bouffe, used by Lecocq in *Les Cent Vierges,* rather than in the more legitimate theatrical vein of *La Fille de Madame Angot.*

Don Boléro (Alfred Jolly), Governor of a Spanish seaside province, has arranged advantageous marriages for his twin daughters (both Pauline Luigini)—one to Marasquin (Mario Widmer), the son of a banker to whom he is indebted, the other to his belligerent Moorish neighbor, Mourzouk (Paul Ginet). When one sister is carried off by pirates on what should have been the double wedding day, the other has to act for two—with all the blushes and bother that involves—until Boléro and his wife, Aurore (Félicie Delorme), can manage to get the other missing virgin back from the pirates. They don't manage until after the wedding night has passed, so there was bother and blushes aplenty.

The delightfully extravagant and farcical libretto for *Giroflé-Girofla* (a title used 16 years earlier for a Crisafulli and Devicque Théâtre du Gymnase drama) was allied to a score in Lecocq's most lighthearted and lyrical style, which gave splendid opportunities to its leading players. The dual role of Giroflé and Girofla—mostly Giroflé, for Girofla gets captured fairly early on, and doesn't reappear until the denouement—included parallel waltz couplets for the two sisters (''Père adoré,'' ''Petit Papa'') with an orchestral break which allowed the actress to exit, change the pink bow on her frock for a blue one, and re-enter in her new character, and a brilliant drinking song (''Le Punch scintille''), whilst the comic tenor Marasquin, the banker's son, scored with the naively threatening ''Mon père est un très gros banquier,'' and there were major comic roles for both the frantic parents and for the marauding and baritonic Moor, roaring lubriciously for his bride.

The concerted music of the show was particularly successful, with critics and public both approving especially the first-act sextet and finale, the quintet ''Matamoros, grand capitaine,'' and a humorous pirates' chorus which prefigured Gilbert and Sullivan's ''With Catlike Tread'' (*The Pirates of Penzance*) in contrasting loud singing with secretive words, as the burlesque pirates stalk their feminine prey.

A triumph in Brussels (80 performances), *Giroflé-Girofla* was still at the height of its popularity when Humbert decided to take the production to London. It met with a delighted response there and was only closed after a nine-week run to permit the Philharmonic Theatre, which had been the launching pad for the huge English success of *La Fille de Madame Angot,* to produce an English-language version (ad Clement O'Neil, Campbell Clarke). Julia Mathews starred alongside E M Garden (Boléro), Harriette Everard (Aurore), Walter Fisher (Maraschino) and Edmund Rosenthal (Mourzouk) in a 14-week run and a quick revival. Before the year was out, the piece had also been seen both in Paris—with Madame Alphonsine triumphing in the role of Aurore and the young Jeanne Granier scoring her first big success in the title role through a run of 170 performances—and in Berlin.

Hermine Meyerhoff was the double heroine, alongside Karl Blasel (Boléro), Therese Schäfer (Aurore), Albin Swoboda (Marasquin) and Ausim (Mourzouk), in a successful Vienna production (63 performances in 1875, 17 in 1876 with Karoline Finaly), whilst in New York, with Coralie Geoffroy starring, the usual opéra-bouffe routine of nightly or weekly changes in the repertoire was abandoned to allow *Giroflé-Girofla* to run consecutively for 50 nights at the Park Theatre. Mlle Geoffroy's French version—which had actually been preempted by an English-language adaptation (ad J Cheever Goodwin, Harris) played by Alice Oates and John Howson in Boston—was followed by a German one starring Lina Mayr and several English editions, including one with Julia Mathews. America's queen of opéra-bouffe, Marie Aimée, also appeared in her production of the show (Wade's Opera House, San Francisco 26 July 1876) and, for some time, four or five companies were to be found simultaneously playing *Giroflé-Girofla,* in and out of Broadway, in a selection of languages. It returned there in 1893 (ad Matt C Woodward) with Lillian Russell in the lead role and William T Carleton (Mourzouk) and Hayden Coffin (Marasquin) as the two husbands, in 1905 with Fritzi Scheff starred (Broadway Theater 31 January) and one last time at the Jolson Theater as late as 1926 (22 November).

In Australia the piece proved equally popular. First introduced by W S Lyster's company with Clara Thompson as the twins, her husband Henry Bracy as Boléro, Mrs J H Fox (Aurore), Edward Farley (Mourzouk) and Jennie Winston as a travesty Maraschino, it scored a big success and was seen regularly in the repertoires of opéra-bouffe companies for many years thereafter. Emily Soldene opened the new Adelaide Theatre Royal in 1878 playing the twins in her production of *Giroflé-Girofla.*

Curiously, the usually quick-off-the-mark Hungarian stage seems to have taken eight years to mount *Viola-Ibolya* (ad Lajos Evva, Béla J Fái) and, when it did, in the wake of Lecocq's many later successes, it did not catch on. Elsewhere, however, the piece established itself firmly in the opéra-bouffe repertoire and it was regularly and widely played as long as the vogue for that kind of piece lasted. From the 1890s, however, its revivals became rarer, and its poor (not to say negligible) place in the modern repertoire does not reflect its popularity in the years immediately following its first production, nor its value in comparison with some pieces which are still regularly played.

UK: Opera Comique (Fr) 6 June 1874, Philharmonic Theatre, Islington (Eng) 3 October 1874; France: Théâtre de la Renaissance 11 November 1874; Germany: Friedrich-Wilhelmstädtisches Theater 22 December 1874; Austria: Carltheater 2 January 1875; USA: Boston Museum (Eng) 7 December 1874, Park Theater, New York (Fr) 4 February 1875, Robinson Hall (Eng) 19 May 1875; Australia: Prince of Wales Opera House, Melbourne 22 May 1875; Hungary: Népszínház *Viola-Ibolya* 22 March 1882

Recordings: complete (Gaîté-Lyrique), complete in German (Urania), complete in Russian (Melodiya)

LA GIROUETTE Opérette in 3 acts by Henri Bocage and Émile Hémery. Music by Auguste Coedès. Théâtre des Fantaisies-Parisiennes, Paris, 3 March 1880.

The most widely played of Coedès's opérettes, *La Girouette*—apparently composed in just a few days to meet the production deadline—was played for 90 performances at the Fantaisies-Parisiennes, under the management of Debruyère, with sufficient appeal for the show to be taken up for a number of overseas productions.

The comical King Pépin de Birmenstorf (Denizot) has a daughter, Frédérique (Maria Thève), who, for reasons of state, is to wed Eustache de Tolède (Jannin). She prefers one Hildebert de Brindès (Villars). After the regulation amount of disguises and mistaken identities, she has her way, whilst the genuine Eustache (as opposed to a phony one) is paired off with the evening's phony Frédérique (as opposed to the genuine one)—otherwise the unaristocratic Suzanne (Mme Devaure). The other comic moments fell to the evening's third pair, Captain Colardo (Bellot) and Pélagie (Mme Tassilly).

Following its Paris run, *La Girouette* was taken up by Budapest's Népszínház (ad Lajos Evva, Béla J Fái), by San Francisco's Bush Street Theatre (ad Oscar Weil), where Emilie Melville starred as Eustache to the Frederica of Lily Post, and by Broadway's Augustin Daly, who mounted the show (ad Fred Williams, Robert Stoepel) at his New York base with a cast from his number two company headed by William Gilbert (Pépin), May Fielding (Frédérique), Sgr Montegriffo and Harry MacDonough as the real and the false Eustaches, and Francesca Guthrie as Suzanne. Broadway's version did well enough, playing 44 times prior to its being taken briefly and markedly unsuccessfully into the repertoire of the famous Bostonians touring company.

Paris saw the show for a second time when Debruyère revived it in 1885 at the Théâtre de la Gaîté, and Britain several years later when it was produced for the touring circuits in a Robert Reece version starring Giulia Warwick, Durward Lely, Charles Wibrow and Robert Courtneidge. A trial matinée at the Avenue Theatre did not, however, convince the management to take it to the West End.

USA: Bush Street Theater, San Francisco *The Weathercock* 26 July 1880, Daly's Theater *The Weathercock* 13 April 1882; Hungary: Népszínház *A szélkakas* 5 May 1881; UK: Theatre Royal, Portsmouth 25 March 1889, Avenue Theatre 24 April 1889

GIUDITTA Musical play in 5 scenes by Paul Knepler and Fritz Löhner-[Beda]. Music by Franz Lehár. Staatsoper, Vienna, 20 January 1934.

Giuditta was the last of the series of darkly colored romantic Operetten (this one purposely titled "musikalische Komödie") composed by Lehár in the late 1920s and early 1930s and created by the star tenor, Richard Tauber. It made its first appearance, after some shocked in-house resistance from those who felt an Operette unsuitable for Vienna's famous opera theatre, on the stage of the Staatsoper, where Tauber was counted on as an enormous box-office draw.

Tauber played Octavio, an army Captain who ultimately abandons his career and his well-being for the charms of the tempestuous wife of a Mediterranean artisan, and Lehár supplied him with a violently high-pitched and showy entrance ("Freunde, das Leben ist lebenswert") and some passionate arias ("Schönste der Frau'n," "Du bist meine Sonne") to follow. However, the bonbons of the score of *Giuditta* fell to the vamping lady of the title role, created by soprano Jarmila Novotna. In the first scene she describes her frustrated longing to

Plate 146. **Giuditta.** *"Meine Lippen sie küssen so heiss"—Josephine Cook as Giuditta at the Landestheater, Coburg.*

sink "In einem Meer von Liebe," in the third she weeps out her passionate frenzy at failing to make Octavio desert the army to stay with her ("In die Stirne fällt die Locke") and in the fourth, now a night-club performer with rich men in her bed, she hymns her own sexuality in the popular waltz song "Meine Lippen sie küssen so heiss."

There was some light relief to the dark main story in the parallel affair of the fruit-seller Pierrino (Erich Zimmermann) and his girlfriend Anita (Margit Bokor), and some greener comedy in the nightclub sequences, but basically *Giuditta* was an Operette of dreadful and destructive passions, set with some of the darkest and most thickly orchestrated of Lehár's music.

The original production was not well received, but it played 42 times during the season in which it was introduced. The following year, after only a few performances had been played, came the Anschluss—Tauber left town and *Giuditta* was played no more in Vienna. It received little attention overseas. It was produced in Budapest shortly after its introduction in Vienna, and the Théâtre de la Monnaie, Brussels, staged a production (ad André Mauprey) the following season with Kate Walter-Lippert and José Janson in the leading roles. Janson also featured in the first French performance, at Toulouse in 1936, opposite Mme Chauny-Lasson, but *Giuditta,* in spite of a handful of provincial productions, did not play Paris, nor London, nor New York. However the piece got a late English-language and American premiere at the Ohio Light Opera in 1994.

In 1970 a German television version was made with Rudolf Schock and Teresa Stratas featured.

In spite of its poor track record, however, the piece survives. It has subsequently twice been given major recordings, its principal numbers have been frequently performed by vocalists attempting crossovers between opera and Operette and, in an age which prizes the heaviest and most sentimental/dramatic end of the repertoire, it has received several stage productions, notably at the Vienna Volksoper in 1993 (24 February). However, it has never become popular in the way that Lehár's lighter works or *Das Land des Lächelns,* the most successful of his romantic pieces, have done.

Hungary: Magyar Királyi Operaház 8 April 1934; France: Théâtre du Capitole, Toulouse March 1936; USA: Ohio Light Opera 1994

TV film: 1970

Recordings: complete (EMI, Decca), selections (Eurodisc, EMI Electrola, etc), selection in Hungarian (Qualiton)

GIVE ME A RING Musical in 2 acts by Guy Bolton, R P Weston and Bert Lee. Lyrics by Graham John. Music by Martin Broones. London Hippodrome, 22 June 1933.

Moss' Empires Ltd's theatre division, headed by the budding impresario George Black, put together *Give Me a Ring* with a lavish hand and with a showman's taste for the big and the fashionable name. From the world of variety, Black took the famous Scots comic Will Fyffe and the comedy duo Flanagan and Allen; from musical comedy; the country's top ingenue, Evelyn Laye; from Hollywood, composer Martin Broones, along with two Britons who had made themselves a name in American shows and films—baritone John Garrick and the formidable Bertha Belmore—and the American soubrette Gina Malo. The band of Debroy Somers was topped by the harmonizing band-singers the Carlyle Cousins, a Big Ten of dancers was hired to front the Hippodrome girls, Norman Hartnell signed to dress the leading ladies, and Hungarian actor-singer Ernest Verebes was brought in to give a romantic Continental air to the role of the hero.

The stars were cast as employees in a hotel, Miss Laye being the telephone operator, Peggy (thus the double-meaning title), Fyffe a steward, Allen a telephone engineer and Flanagan his assistant. Verebes was Jack, the assistant manager, Miss Belmore the staff supervisor and Miss Malo the manageress of the dress shop. Garrick played a guest, radio star Cliff Reed, momentarily distracting Peggy from true-love Jack, amongst the comedy turns and numbers which were the raison d'être of a show which was little more than a virtual variety bill. "A Couple of Fools in Love" (Verebes/Miss Laye) proved the most catchy number of an agreeable if ephemeral score.

Give Me a Ring played 239 performances in London, and Black kept up the quality throughout. Miss Laye was succeeded by Adele Dixon and then Binnie Hale, Fyffe was replaced by none other than 64-year-old Huntley Wright, and Verebes by the young John Mills. At the end of the London season, the piece went on the road, with Flanagan and Allen top-billed, playing the Moss' Empires houses on a schedule of once- or, sometimes, twice-nightly.